S0-AEY-652

Welcome to Norton Literature Online, outstanding resources for students of literature

search literature sites

Enter search terms below to search all of **Norton's Literature** sites:

Search **SEARCHING TIPS**

English Literature
Visit the site
Learn More

American Literature
Visit the site
Learn More

World Literature
Visit the site
Learn More

Introduction to Literature
Visit the site
Learn More

Introduction to Literature
Visit the site
Learn More

Poetry
Visit the site
Learn More

general resources

- writing about literature
- glossary of literary terms
- elements of literature review quiz
- timelines
- maps
- music
- history
- author portrait gallery
- citation guidelines
- norton scholar's prize
- norton literature in the news
- norton poets online
- the favorite poem project

NORTON LITERATURE ONLINE

w w n o r t o n . c o m / l i t e r a t u r e

Visit this exciting gateway to the outstanding online literature resources available from Norton.

Detach your registration card. On the front of the card you will find a registration code. This code offers free access to the site for twelve months. Once you register, you can change your password however you wish.

If the registration card has been removed from your textbook, visit wwnorton.com/literature for instructions regarding site access.

HOW TO ACCESS THIS WEB SITE:

STEP 1: Go to wwnorton.com/literature.

STEP 2: Click on "Access Norton Literature Online."

STEP 3: Click on "First-Time User? Register Here."

STEP 4: Fill out all fields and click "Submit." Your password is set instantly (and a confirmation will be emailed to you).

STEP 5: Click "Enter the Site." Wait for the Web site to load.

You're in!

Registration is good for 12 months from activation.

REGISTRATION CODE ➡

OGYD-EWQV

A SHAKESPEAREAN GENEALOGY

This chart reflects Shakespeare's history plays and is thus not historically accurate. Many descendants of Henry II and Edward III are omitted. On occasion, Shakespeare combined or simply invented historical figures. These deviations from fact are explained in the notes.

In the chart, the names of Kings and Queens are printed in capitals, and the dates of their reigns are printed in bold. The names of characters appearing in the plays are underlined.

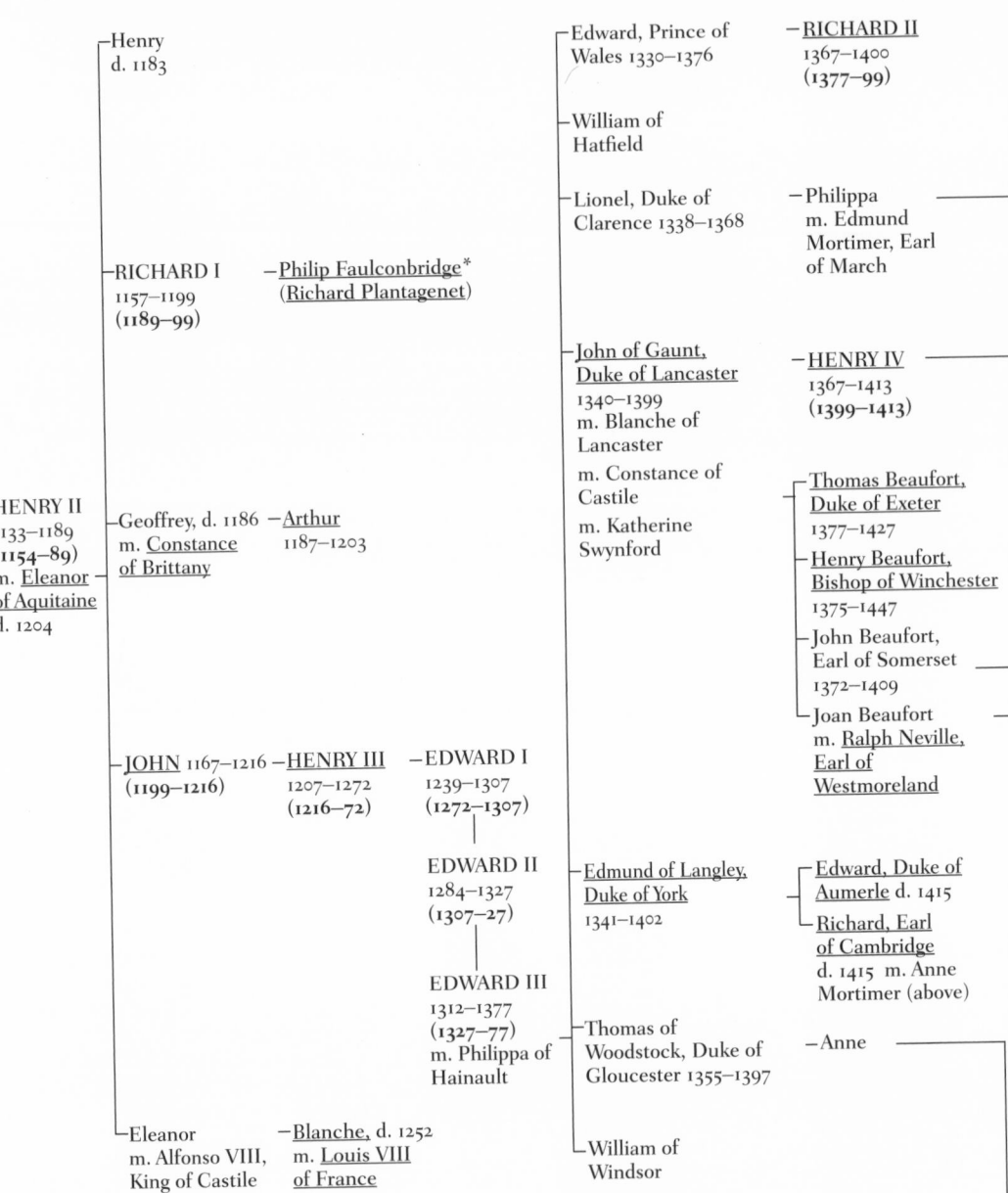

*Philip Faulconbridge, the bastard son of Richard I, had no historical existence. Such a character appears in the play *The Life and Death of King John* and is referred to in passing in Holinshed's *Chronicles*.

† In the character of Edmund Mortimer, Shakespeare combines two historical figures. The Edmund Mortimer who married Catrin, daughter of Owain Glyndŵr, was the grandson of Lionel, Duke of Clarence, and the younger brother of Roger, Earl of March. He died in 1409. Shakespeare combines him with his nephew, the Edmund Mortimer recognized by Richard II as his heir (d. 1424). This second Edmund was the brother of Anne Mortimer and the uncle of Richard Plantagenet.

‡ The character of the Duke of Somerset combines Henry Beaufort with his younger brother Edmund (d. 1471), who succeeded him as Duke.

Elizabeth Mortimer
("Kate")
m. Henry Percy
("Hotspur")
1364–1403

Henry, Earl of
Northumberland
1394–1455

EDWARD IV
1442–1483 (1461–83)
m. Elizabeth
Woodville d. 1492

EDWARD V
1470–1483 (1483)

Richard, Duke
of York 1472–1483

Elizabeth of York
1465–1503
m. HENRY VII
(below)

Edmund, Earl of
Rutland 1443–1460

George, Duke of
Clarence 1449–1478
m. Isabel Neville
(below)

Edmund Mortimer†

Anne Mortimer
m. Richard, Earl of
Cambridge (below)

Richard Plantagenet,
Duke of York
1411–1460
m. Cicely Neville
(below)

RICHARD III
1452–1485 (1483–85)
m. Anne Neville
(below)

Edward, Prince of Wales

HENRY V 1387–1422
(1413–22)
m. Catherine
1401–1437

HENRY VI 1421–1471
(1422–61)
m. Margaret of Anjou
d. 1482

Edward, Prince of
Wales 1453–1471
m. Anne Neville
(below)

Arthur
m. Catherine of
Aragon (below)

Thomas, Duke of
Clarence d. 1421

Margaret
m. James IV
of Scotland

James V
of Scotland

John of Lancaster,
Duke of Bedford
1389–1435

Mary, Queen of
Scots

Humphrey, Duke of
Gloucester 1391–1447
m. Eleanor Cobham
d. 1454

JAMES I
1566–1625
(1603–25)

John Beaufort, Duke
of Somerset
1403–1444

Margaret Beaufort
m. Edmund Tudor,
Earl of Richmond

HENRY VII 1457–1509
(1485–1509)
m. Elizabeth of York
(above)

HENRY VIII
1491–1547
(1509–47)
m. Catherine of
Aragon

MARY I 1516–1558
(1553–58)
m. Philip of Spain

Edmund Beaufort,
Duke of Somerset
1406–1455

Henry Beaufort,
Duke of Somerset
1436–1464‡

m. Anne Boleyn

ELIZABETH I
1533–1603
(1558–1603)

Isabel Neville
d. 1476
m. George, Duke
of Clarence
(above)

m. Jane Seymour

EDWARD VI
1537–1553
(1547–53)

Richard Neville,
Earl of Salisbury
1400–1460

Richard Neville,
Earl of Warwick
1428–1471

m. Anne of Cleves

John Neville,
Marquess of
Montague d. 1471

Anne Neville
d. 1485
m. Edward, Prince
of Wales (above)
m. RICHARD III
(above)

m. Katherine Howard

m. Katherine Parr

Cicely Neville
m. Richard
Plantagenet,
Duke of York (above)

Mary
m. Charles Brandon

Frances

Jane Grey
1537–1554

Humphrey, Duke of
Buckingham
1402–1460

Humphrey Stafford
d. 1455

Henry, Duke of
Buckingham
1454?–1483

Edward, Duke of
Buckingham
1478–1521

1377–1625

RICHARD II, 1377–99 RICHARD was the eldest son of EDWARD THE BLACK PRINCE, himself the eldest son of KING EDWARD III, who ruled England from 1327 to 1377. When the BLACK PRINCE died in battle in France in 1376, RICHARD became the legitimate heir to the throne. He ruled from EDWARD's death in 1377 until he was deposed in 1399 by HENRY BOLINGBROKE, the eldest son of JOHN OF GAUNT, DUKE OF LANCASTER. Because he was the fourth son of EDWARD III, GAUNT and his Lancastrian descendants had weaker hereditary claims to the throne than did RICHARD. When deposed, RICHARD had no children to succeed him, but he recognized EDMUND MORTIMER, FIFTH EARL OF MARCH, as his heir presumptive. This MORTIMER was descended from LIONEL, DUKE OF CLARENCE, the third son of EDWARD III, and therefore also had stronger hereditary claims to the throne than did BOLINGBROKE. SHAKESPEARE combined this MORTIMER with his uncle EDMUND MORTIMER, who married OWAIN GLYNDŴR'S DAUGHTER.

HENRY IV, 1399–1413 HENRY BOLINGBROKE, eldest son of JOHN OF GAUNT, seized the throne from RICHARD II in 1399. When HENRY died in 1413, he was succeeded by his eldest son, PRINCE HAL, who became HENRY V.

HENRY V, 1413–22 HENRY V became king in 1413 and reigned until his death in 1422. He was succeeded by his son, HENRY VI.

HENRY VI, 1422–61 HENRY VI was less than one year old when he succeeded his father, HENRY V. In the young king's minority, his uncle HUMPHREY, DUKE OF GLOUCESTER, was named Lord Protector, and the kingdom was ruled by an aristocratic council. HENRY VI assumed personal authority in 1437. He was deposed in 1461 by his third cousin, who was crowned EDWARD IV. HENRY was murdered in 1471.

EDWARD IV, 1461–83 EDWARD, the eldest son of RICHARD, DUKE OF YORK, seized the throne from HENRY VI in 1461. His Yorkist claim to the throne derived from his grandmother, ANNE MORTIMER, who was descended from LIONEL, third son of EDWARD III, and was sister to that EDMUND MORTIMER recognized by RICHARD II as his heir presumptive; EDWARD IV's grandfather, RICHARD, EARL OF CAMBRIDGE, was the son of EDMUND OF LANGLEY, fifth son of EDWARD III. EDWARD IV reigned until his death in 1483. His heir was his eldest son (EDWARD), but the throne was usurped by his brother RICHARD, DUKE OF GLOUCESTER.

RICHARD III, 1483–85 RICHARD III was the youngeer brother of EDWARD IV. After the death of EDWARD IV in 1483, RICHARD prevented the coronation of EDWARD V with a claim of illegitimacy and succeeded to the throne himself. EDWARD and his younger brother, RICHARD, DUKE OF YORK, were murdered in the Tower of London. RICHARD III was killed at the Battle of Bosworth Field in 1485, and the kingdom fell to the victor, HENRY TUDOR, EARL OF RICHMOND.

HENRY VII, 1485–1509 HENRY TUDOR seized the throne from RICHARD III in 1485. He was descended from JOHN OF GAUNT by JOHN's third marriage, with CATHERINE SWYNFORD. He married ELIZABETH, daughter of EDWARD IV, uniting the houses of Lancaster and York. He died in 1509 and was succeeded by his son, HENRY VIII.

HENRY VIII, 1509–47 HENRY was the second son of HENRY VII. His older brother, ARTHUR, died in 1502. HENRY VIII's first wife was CATHERINE OF ARAGON, who bore his daughter MARY. His second wife, ANNE BOLEYN, was the mother of ELIZABETH. His third wife, JANE SEYMOUR, bore him a son, who succeeded to the throne as EDWARD VI after HENRY VIII died in 1547.

EDWARD VI, 1547–53 EDWARD VI was nine years old when he became king. From 1547 to 1549, the realm was governed by a Lord Protector, the DUKE OF SOMERSET; power then passed to JOHN DUDLEY, DUKE OF NORTHUMBERLAND. When EDWARD VI died in 1553, NORTHUMBERLAND attempted unsuccessfully to prevent the succession of MARY TUDOR by installing as queen his daughter-in-law, LADY JANE GREY, a great-granddaughter of HENRY VII.

MARY I, 1553–58 MARY, daughter of HENRY VIII and his first wife, CATHERINE OF ARAGON, came to the throne in 1553. She married KING PHILIP OF SPAIN but died childless. She was succeeded by her half sister, ELIZABETH.

ELIZABETH I, 1558–1603 ELIZABETH, the daughter of HENRY VIII and his second wife, ANNE BOLEYN, became queen after the death of her half sister, MARY, in 1558. She ruled until her death in 1603. She was succeeded by her cousin JAMES.

JAMES I, 1603–1625 JAMES VI OF SCOTLAND became JAMES I OF ENGLAND in 1603. His claim to the throne of England derived from his great-grandmother, MARGARET TUDOR, a daughter of HENRY VII who married JAMES IV OF SCOTLAND. JAMES ruled England and Scotland until his death in 1625; he was succeeded by his son, CHARLES I.

THE NORTON
SHAKESPEARE

BASED ON THE OXFORD EDITION

SECOND EDITION

ESSENTIAL PLAYS • THE SONNETS

The original Oxford Text on which this
edition is based was prepared by

Stanley Wells
Gary Taylor
General Editors

John Jowett
William Montgomery

The Norton Shakespeare, Second Edition, is based on *William Shakespeare: The Complete Works*,
Second Edition, and is published by arrangement with Oxford University Press,
with additional material from W. W. Norton & Company, Inc.

THE NORTON SHAKESPEARE

Based on the Oxford Edition

SECOND EDITION

ESSENTIAL PLAYS • THE SONNETS

Stephen Greenblatt, *General Editor*
HARVARD UNIVERSITY

Walter Cohen
CORNELL UNIVERSITY

Jean E. Howard
COLUMBIA UNIVERSITY

Katharine Eisaman Maus
UNIVERSITY OF VIRGINIA

With an Essay on the Shakespearean stage
by Andrew Gurr

W · W · NORTON & COMPANY · NEW YORK · LONDON

W. W. Norton & Company has been independent since its founding in 1923, when William Warder Norton and Mary D. Herter Norton first published lectures delivered at the People's Institute, the adult education division of New York City's Cooper Union. The Nortons soon expanded their program beyond the Institute, publishing books by celebrated academics from America and abroad. By mid-century, the two major pillars of Norton's publishing program—trade books and college texts—were firmly established. In the 1950s, the Norton family transferred control of the company to its employees, and today—with a staff of four hundred and a comparable number of trade, college, and professional titles published each year—W. W. Norton & Company stands as the largest and oldest publishing house owned wholly by its employees.

Editor: Julia Reidhead
Manuscript editor: Carol Flechner
Electronic media editor: Eileen Connell
Editorial assistants: Rivka Genesen, Carly Fraser
Production managers: Diane O'Connor, Eric Pier-Hocking
Photo research: Rivka Genesen, Carly Fraser
Interior design: Antonina Krass
Managing editor, College: Marian Johnson

Composition by Binghamton Valley Composition
Manufacturing by R. R. Donnelley
ISBN: 978-0-393-93313-0

W. W. Norton & Company, Inc., 500 Fifth Avenue, New York, NY 10110
wwnorton.com

W. W. Norton & Company Ltd., Castle House, 75/76 Wells Street, London W1T 3QT

1 2 3 4 5 6 7 8 9 0

Contents

GENERAL INTRODUCTION   1

Stephen Greenblatt

Comedies   101

Histories   577

Tragedies   911

Romances   1497

The Sonnets   1659

Appendices   1725

TIMELINE   1780

Illustrations

Preface

The Norton Shakespeare: Essential Plays/The Sonnets offers the core of the great play-wright and poet's creative achievement. We have brought together, in a compact and portable paperback, twenty of the plays that are most often read and produced. The selection includes key works in each of the genres in which Shakespeare distinguished himself: seven comedies, seven tragedies, four English history plays, and two romances. These represent slightly more than half of the plays in the surviving canon, and, though inevitably there are omissions that will pain any lover of Shakespeare, the works assembled here will enable readers to grasp the unfolding of the playwright's astonishing gifts and his imaginative vision. We also include Shakespeare's sonnets, the most celebrated sequence of love poems in the English language. Altogether, a magnificent feast.

Shakespeare's principal medium, the drama, was thoroughly collaborative, and it involved as well continual efforts at revision and renewal. It seems appropriate, then, that this edition is itself the result of sustained collaboration and revision. The text on which the *Norton Shakespeare* is based was published in both modern-spelling and original-spelling versions by Oxford University Press in 1986. Under the general editorship of Stanley Wells and Gary Taylor, the Oxford text was a thorough rethinking of the entire body of Shakespeare's works, the most influential and innovative revision of the traditional canon in centuries. When many classroom instructors expressed a need for pedagogical apparatus oriented toward students, Norton negotiated with Oxford to assemble an editorial team of its own to prepare the necessary teaching materials around the existing Oxford text.

To what extent is this the *Norton Shakespeare* and to what extent the Oxford text? Introductions (the General Introduction, the genre introductions, and those to individual plays and poems), footnotes, glosses, bibliographies, genealogies, annals, maps, documents, and illustrations have all been the responsibility of the Norton team. Likewise, Norton commissioned Andrew Gurr's much-admired essay on the London theater in Shakespeare's time.

The textual notes and variants derive for the most part from the work of the Oxford team, especially as represented in *William Shakespeare: A Textual Companion* (Oxford University Press, 1987), a remarkably comprehensive explanation of editorial decisions that is herewith strongly recommended to instructors as a valuable companion to this volume. With the consent of the Oxford editors, a small number of textual changes have been made by the Norton team, in the interest of the classroom: we wished to make fully and clearly available the scholarly innovation and freshness of the Oxford text, while at the same time making certain that this was a superbly useful teaching text. The following notes summarize all of these changes, which are also indicated in appropriate play introductions, footnotes, or textual notes:

1. The complete *Norton Shakespeare* follows the Oxford editors in printing, on facing pages, the two substantive versions of Shakespeare's great tragedy, *The History of King Lear* and *The Tragedy of King Lear*. For the convenience of readers who want to encounter the text on which innumerable performances of the play have been based and on which a huge body of literary criticism has been written, that edition also includes a conflated version of *King Lear,* that is, a version of the play, edited by Barbara K. Lewalski of Harvard University, that incorporates the maximum number of lines from both of the early texts. *The Norton Shakespeare: Essential Plays/The Sonnets*, for reasons of length, prints only this conflated version, along with a sampling, on facing

pages, of the two distinct early texts. Readers who are fascinated by the subtle differences between these texts, differences that may reflect rewriting by Shakespeare, are urged to consult the complete edition.

2. Among several other plays, *Hamlet*, like *King Lear*, also first appeared in distinct versions. We provide in this edition a convenient selection of parallel passages that will enable teachers to convey some of the complex, often enigmatic issues, at once stylistic and conceptual, raised by the different texts of the play. We have also indicated, through indention, a distinctive typeface, and different numbering, those lines that appear only in the Second Quarto (Q2) of *Hamlet* and not in the Folio.

3. For reasons understood by every Shakespearean (and rehearsed at some length in this volume), the Oxford editors chose to restore the name "Sir John Oldcastle" to the character much better known as Falstaff in *1 Henry IV*. (They made comparable changes in the names of the characters known as Bardolph and Peto.) But for reasons understood by everyone who has presented this play to undergraduates or sampled the centuries of enthusiastic criticism, the Norton editors, with the Oxford editors' gracious agreement, have for this classroom edition opted for the familiar name "Falstaff" (and those of his boon companions), properly noting the change and its significance in the play's introduction.

4. The Oxford editors chose not to differentiate between those stage directions that appeared in the early editions up to and including the Folio and those added by subsequent editors. Instead, in *A Textual Companion* they include separate lists of the original stage directions. These lists are not readily available to readers of the Norton text, whose editors opted instead to bracket all stage directions that derive from editions published after the Folio. Readers can thus easily see which stage directions derive from texts that may bear at least some relationship to performances in Shakespeare's time, if not to Shakespeare's own authorship. The Norton policy is more fully explained in the General Introduction.

The collaboration with Oxford was obviously essential to the creation of the *Norton Shakespeare*. But in preparing the Second Edition on which this concise edition is based and making it something fresh and engaging, the critically important collaboration was with the thousands of people who used the book. Many of these, teachers and students alike, generously offered helpful suggestions along with praise. Guided by their responses, as well as by recent developments in Shakespeare scholarship, we determined to look afresh at every detail and to make a wide range of changes. The General Introduction and the individual play introductions have been substantially revised, in some cases wholly rewritten, to make them clearer and more accessible. Textual notes throughout have been updated in response to new findings, and there are hundreds of new and fine-tuned notes and glosses, designed to make this edition an even better tool for learning and pleasure. The General Bibliography has been reorganized and extensively updated, with 7 new sections and over 350 new entries. The Selected Bibliographies, too, have been updated as well as newly annotated. A new introduction provides an illuminating guide to the array of maps, three of them archival and three new, showing places important to Shakespeare's plays. The genealogies have been revised, as has been the text/contexts timeline. New annotated film lists, including over 50 films, now follow the play introductions. Instructors who emphasize films in their courses may wish to assign *Shakespeare and Film: A Norton Guide*, by Samuel Crowl, available packaged with the *Norton Shakespeare*.

The *Norton Shakespeare: Essential Plays/The Sonnets* is accompanied by the extensive online resources of Norton Literature Online (wwnorton.com/literature). Students who activate the free password in each new copy of the book gain access to an array of general resources, among them a glossary of literary terms, advice on writing about literature and using MLA documentation style, an author portrait gallery, more than 100 maps, and over 90 minutes of recorded readings and musical selections, including 80 songs by Shakespeare. With their passwords, students also gain access to a site specifically developed to support the *Norton Shakespeare* (wwnorton.com/shakespeare). Based on content prepared by Mark Rose, University of California, Santa Barbara, this Web site invites students to explore six of the most widely taught plays—*The Merchant of Venice, 1 Henry IV, Hamlet, Othello, King Lear,* and *The Tempest*—through different contextual lenses. For each of these plays, the site provides materials on the elements of theater, sources, stage history, and critical receptions, as well as the complete Oxford text. Audio clips and stills from classic productions, etchings, photographs, and costume-design illustrations help students appreciate performance aspects of the plays. The student Web site also includes the redesigned "Shakespearean Chronicle, 1558–1616," an illustrated timeline that interweaves three kinds of chronologies illuminating Shakespeare's life and times. A password-protected section of the site also includes the complete texts of *The Book of Sir Thomas More* and *The Reign of King Edward the Third,* prepared by the editors of the *Oxford Shakespeare.*

The creation of this edition has drawn heavily on the resources, experience, and skill of its remarkable publisher, the independent, employee-owned company W. W. Norton. Our principal guide has been our brilliant editor, Julia Reidhead, whose calm intelligence, common sense, and steady focus have been essential in enabling us to reach our goal. With this Second Edition, we were blessed with the characteristically thoughtful oversight of Marian Johnson, managing editor, college department; scrupulous manuscript editing by Carol Flechner; and the assistance of an extraordinary group of Norton staffers: editorial assistants Rivka Genesen and Carly Fraser, who, among many other things, coordinated the art program; production managers Diane O'Connor and Eric Pier-Hocking; designer Antonina Krass; editor of the *Norton Shakespeare* Web site Eileen Connell; and proofreaders Paula Noonan, Ann Warren, and Barbara Necol.

The *Norton Shakespeare* editors have, in addition, had the valuable—indeed, indispensable—support of a host of undergraduate and graduate research assistants, colleagues, friends, and family. Even a partial listing of those to whom we owe our heartfelt thanks is very long, but we are all fortunate enough to live in congenial and supportive environments, and the edition has been part of our lives for a long time. We owe special thanks for sustained dedication and learning to our principal assistants: Tiffany Alkan, Lianne Habinek, and Emily Peterson. Particular thanks are due to Noah Heringman for his work on the texts assembled in the documents section and for the prefatory notes and comments on those texts; to Philip Schwyzer for preparing the genealogies and the glossary, and for conceiving and preparing the (now online) "Shakespearean Chronicle"; and to Holger Schott Syme for reconceiving and extensively updating the General Bibliography. In addition, we are deeply grateful to Ezra Feldman, Francesca Mari, Douglas McQueen-Thomson, Jeffrey Patterson, and Benjamin Woodring. All of these companions, and many more besides, have helped us find in this long collective enterprise what the "Dedicatorie Epistle" to the First Folio promises to its readers: delight. We make the same promise to the readers of our edition and invite them to continue the great Shakespearean collaboration.

STEPHEN GREENBLATT
WALTER COHEN
JEAN E. HOWARD
KATHARINE EISAMAN MAUS

Acknowledgments

Among our many critics, advisers, and friends, the following were of special help in providing critiques for particular plays or of the project as a whole: Janet Adelman (University of California, Berkeley), Joel Altman (University of California, Berkeley), Rebecca Bach (University of Alabama at Birmingham), John Baxter (Dalhousie University), Edward I. Berry (University of Victoria), Timothy Billings (Middlebury College), Bruce Boehrer (Florida State University), Barbara Bono (University at Buffalo, SUNY), Gordon M. Braden (University of Virginia), Douglas Brooks (Texas A&M University), Stephen Buhler (University of Nebraska—Lincoln), Richard Burt (University of Florida), Joseph F. Ceccio (University of Akron), Julie Crawford (Columbia University), Christy Desmet (University of Georgia), Heather Dubrow (University of Wisconsin—Madison), Laurie Ellinghausen (University of Missouri—Kansas City), Chris Fitter (Rutgers, State University of New Jersey), Susan Fraiman (University of Virginia), Daniel Gil (University of Oregon), Miriam Gilbert (University of Iowa), Suzanne Gossett (Loyola University), Elizabeth Hanson (Queen's University), Jim Harner (Texas A&M University), Jonathan Gil Harris (George Washington University), Don Hedrick (Kansas State University), Roze Hentschell (Colorado State University), Clifford Huffman (Stony Brook University, SUNY), John Huntington (University of Illinois at Chicago), Sujata Iyengar (University of Georgia), Kimberly Johnson (Brigham Young University), Coppélia Kahn (Brown University), Sean Keilen (University of Pennsylvania), Theodore B. Leinwand (University of Maryland), Zachary Lesser (University of Pennsylvania), Naomi Liebler (Montclair State University), Joyce MacDonald (University of Kentucky), Leah Marcus (Vanderbilt University), Mark Matheson (University of Utah), Robert Matz (George Mason University), Kristen McDermott (Central Michigan University), Ted McGee (University of Waterloo), Scott McMillin (late of Cornell University), Gordon McMullan (King's College London), John Moore (Pennsylvania State University), Carol Neely (University of Illinois at Urbana-Champaign), Lori Newcomb (University of Illinois at Urbana-Champaign), Karen Newman (New York University), Hillary Nunn (University of Akron), Thomas G. Olsen (SUNY at New Paltz), Jim O'Rourke (Florida State University), Paul Parrish (Texas A&M University), Michael Payne (Bucknell University), Rebecca J. Perederin (University of Virginia), Curtis Perry (Arizona State University), Susan Phillips (Northwestern University), Tanya Pollard (Brooklyn College, CUNY), Kristen Poole (University of Delaware), Arnold Preussner (Truman State University), Phyllis Rackin (University of Pennsylvania), Peter L. Rudnytsky (University of Florida), Benjamin Saunders (University of Oregon), Barbara Sebek (Colorado State University), Tracey Sedinger (University of Northern Colorado), Jyotsna Singh (Michigan State University), Andrew Stott (University at Buffalo, SUNY), Garrett Sullivan (Pennsylvania State University), Ramie Targoff (Brandeis University), Henry Turner (University of Wisconsin—Madison), Martine van Elk (California State University, Long Beach), William N. West (University of Colorado at Boulder), Linda Woodbridge (Pennsylvania State University), Lingui Yang (Texas A&M University).

General Introduction

by

STEPHEN GREENBLATT

"He was not of an age, but for all time!"

The celebration of Shakespeare's genius, eloquently initiated by his friend and rival Ben Jonson, has over the centuries become an institutionalized rite of civility. The person who does not love Shakespeare has made, the rite implies, an incomplete adjustment not simply to a particular culture—English culture of the late sixteenth and early seventeenth centuries—but to "culture" as a whole, the dense network of constraints and entitlements, dreams and practices that links us to nature. Indeed, so absolute is Shakespeare's achievement that he has himself come to seem like great creating nature: the common bond of humankind, the principle of hope, the symbol of the imagination's power to transcend time-bound beliefs and assumptions, peculiar historical circumstances, and specific artistic conventions.

The near-worship that Shakespeare inspires is one of the salient facts about his art. But we must at the same time acknowledge that this art is the product of peculiar historical circumstances and specific conventions, four centuries distant from our own. The acknowledgment is important because Shakespeare the working dramatist did not typically lay claim to the transcendent, visionary truths attributed to him by his most fervent admirers; his characters more modestly say, in the words of the magician Prospero, that their project was "to please" (*The Tempest*, Epilogue, line 13). The starting point, and perhaps the ending point as well, in any encounter with Shakespeare is simply to enjoy him, to savor his imaginative richness, to take pleasure in his infinite delight in language.

"If then you do not like him," Shakespeare's first editors wrote in 1623, "surely you are in some manifest danger not to understand him." Over the years, accommodations have been devised to make liking Shakespeare easier for everyone. When the stage sank to melodrama and light opera, Shakespeare—in suitably revised texts—was there. When the populace had a craving for hippodrama, plays performed entirely on horseback, *Hamlet* was dutifully rewritten and mounted. When audiences went mad for realism, live frogs croaked in productions of *A Midsummer Night's Dream*. When the stage was stripped bare and given over to stark exhibitions of sadistic cruelty, Shakespeare was our contemporary. And when the theater itself had lost some of its cultural centrality, Shakespeare moved effortlessly to Hollywood and the soundstages of the BBC.

This virtually universal appeal is one of the most astonishing features of the Shakespeare phenomenon: plays that were performed before glittering courts thrive in junior-high-school auditoriums; enemies set on destroying one another laugh at the same jokes and weep at the same catastrophes; some of the richest and most complex English verse ever written migrates with spectacular success into German and Italian, Hindi, Swahili, and Japanese. Is there a single, stable, continuous object that underlies all of these migrations and metamorphoses? Certainly not. The global diffusion and long life of Shakespeare's works depend on their extraordinary malleability, their protean capacity to elude definition and escape secure possession. At the same time, they are not without identifiable shared features: across centuries and continents, family resemblances link many of the wildly diverse manifestations of plays such as *Romeo and Juliet, Hamlet,* and *Twelfth Night*. And if there is no clear limit or end point, there is a reasonably clear beginning: the

1

England of the late sixteenth and early seventeenth centuries, when the plays and poems collected in this volume made their first appearance.

An art virtually without end or limit but with an identifiable, localized, historical origin: Shakespeare's achievement defies the facile opposition between transcendent and time-bound. It is not necessary to choose between an account of Shakespeare as the scion of a particular culture and an account of him as a universal genius who created works that continually renew themselves across national and generational boundaries. On the contrary: crucial clues to understanding his art's remarkable power to soar beyond its originary time and place lie in the very soil from which that art sprang.

Shakespeare's World

Life and Death

Life expectancy at birth in early modern England was exceedingly low by our standards: under thirty years old, compared with over seventy today. Infant mortality rates were extraordinarily high, and it is estimated that in the poorer parishes of London only about half the children survived to the age of fifteen, while the children of aristocrats fared only a little better. In such circumstances, some parents must have developed a certain detachment—one of Shakespeare's contemporaries writes of losing "some three or four children"—but there are many expressions of intense grief, so that we cannot assume that the frequency of death hardened people to loss or made it routine.

Still, the spectacle of death, along with that other great threshold experience, birth, must have been far more familiar to Shakespeare and his contemporaries than to ourselves. There was no equivalent in early modern England to our hospitals, and most births and deaths occurred at home. Physical means for the alleviation of pain and suffering were extremely limited—alcohol might dull the terror, but it was hardly an effective anesthetic—and medical treatment was generally both expensive and worthless, more likely to intensify suffering than to lead to a cure. This was a world without a concept of antiseptics, with little actual understanding of disease, with few effective ways of treating earaches or venereal disease, let alone the more terrible instances of what Shakespeare calls "the thousand natural shocks that flesh is heir to."

The worst of these shocks was the bubonic plague, which repeatedly ravaged England, and particularly English towns, until the third quarter of the seventeenth century. The plague was terrifyingly sudden in its onset, rapid in its spread, and almost invariably lethal. Physicians were helpless in the face of the epidemic, though they prescribed amulets,

Bill recording plague deaths in London, 1609.

preservatives, and sweet-smelling substances (on the theory that the plague was carried by noxious vapors). In the plague-ridden year of 1564, the year of Shakespeare's birth, some 254 people died in Stratford-upon-Avon, out of a total population of 800. The year before, some 20,000 Londoners are thought to have died; in 1593, almost 15,000; in 1603, 36,000, or over a sixth of the city's inhabitants. The social effects of these horrible visitations were severe: looting, violence, and despair, along with an intensification of the age's perennial poverty, unemployment, and food shortages. The London plague regulations of 1583, reissued with modifications in later epidemics, ordered that the infected and their households be locked in their homes for a month; that the streets be kept clean; that vagrants be expelled; and that funerals and plays be restricted or banned entirely.

The plague, then, had a direct and immediate impact on Shakespeare's own profession. City officials kept records of the weekly number of plague deaths; when these surpassed a certain number, the theaters were peremptorily closed. The basic idea was not only to prevent contagion but also to avoid making an angry God still angrier with the spectacle of idleness. While restricting public assemblies may in fact have slowed the epidemic, other public policies in times of plague, such as killing the cats and dogs, may have made matters worse (since the disease, as we now know, was spread not by these animals but by the fleas that bred on the black rats that infested the poorer neighborhoods). Moreover, the playing companies, driven out of London by the closing of the theaters, may have carried plague to the provincial towns.

Even in good times, when the plague was dormant and the weather favorable for farming, the food supply in England was precarious. A few successive bad harvests, such as occurred in the mid-1590s, could cause serious hardship, even starvation. Not surprisingly, the poor bore the brunt of the burden: inflation, low wages, and rent increases left large numbers of people with very little cushion against disaster. Further, at its best, the diet of most people seems to have been seriously deficient. The lower classes then, as throughout most of history, subsisted on one or two foodstuffs, usually low in protein. The upper classes disdained green vegetables and milk and gorged themselves on meat. Illnesses that we now trace to vitamin deficiencies were rampant. Some, but not much, relief from pain was provided by the beer that Elizabethans, including children, drank almost incessantly. (Home brewing aside, enough beer was sold in England for every man, woman, and child to have consumed 40 gallons a year.)

Wealth

Despite rampant disease, the population of England in Shakespeare's lifetime was steadily growing, from approximately 3,060,000 in 1564 to 4,060,000 in 1600 and 4,510,000 in 1616. Though the death rate was more than twice what it is in England today, the birthrate was almost three times the current figure. London's population in particular soared, from 60,000 in 1520 to 120,000 in 1550, 200,000 in 1600, and 375,000 half a century later, making it the largest and fastest-growing city not only in England but in all of Europe. Every year in the first half of the seventeenth century, about 10,000 people migrated to London from other parts of England—wages in London tended to be around 50 percent higher than in the rest of the country—and it is estimated that one in eight English people lived in London at some point in their lives. The economic viability of Shakespeare's profession was closely linked to this extraordinary demographic boom: between 1567 and 1642, a theater historian has calculated, the London playhouses were paid close to 50 million visits.

As these visits to the theater indicate, in the capital city and elsewhere a substantial number of English men and women, despite hardships that were never very distant, had money to spend. After the disorder and dynastic wars of the fifteenth century, England in the sixteenth and early seventeenth centuries was for the most part a nation at peace, and with peace came a measure of enterprise and prosperity: the landowning classes busied themselves building great houses, planting orchards and hop gardens, draining marshlands, bringing untilled "wastes" under cultivation. The artisans and laborers who actually accomplished these tasks, although they were generally paid very little, often managed to accumulate something, as did the small freeholding farmers, the yeomen, who are repeatedly celebrated in the period as the backbone of English national independence and well-being. William Harrison's *Description of England* (1577) lovingly itemizes the yeoman's precious possessions: "fair garnish of pewter on his cupboard, with so much more odd vessel going about the house, three or four featherbeds, so many coverlets and carpets of tapestry, a silver salt[cellar], a bowl for wine (if not a whole nest) and a dozen of spoons." There are comparable accounts of the hard-earned acquisitions of the city dwellers—masters and apprentices in small workshops, shipbuilders, wool merchants, clothmakers, chandlers, tradesmen, shopkeepers, along with lawyers, apothecaries, schoolteachers, scriveners, and the like—whose pennies from time to time enriched the coffers of the players.

The chief source of England's wealth in the sixteenth century was its textile industry, an industry that depended on a steady supply of wool. In *The Winter's Tale*, Shakespeare provides a warm, richly comic portrayal of a rural sheepshearing festival, but the increasingly intensive production of wool had in reality its grim side. When a character in Thomas More's *Utopia* (1516) complains that "the sheep are eating the people," he is referring to the practice of enclosure: throughout the sixteenth and early seventeenth centuries, many acres of croplands once farmed in common by rural communities were enclosed with fences by wealthy landowners and turned into pasturage. The ensuing misery, displacement, and food shortages led to repeated riots, some of them violent and bloody, along with a series of government proclamations, but the process of enclosure was not reversed.

The economic stakes were high, and not only for the domestic market. In 1565, woolen cloth alone made up more than three-fourths of England's exports. (The remainder consisted mostly of other textiles and raw wool, with some trade in lead, tin, grain, and skins.) The Company of Merchant Adventurers carried cloth to distant ports on the Baltic and Mediterranean, establishing links with Russia and Morocco (each took about 2 percent of London's cloth in 1597–98). English lead and tin, as well as fabrics, were sold in Tuscany and Turkey, and merchants found a market for Newcastle coal on the island of Malta. In the latter half of the century, London, which handled more than 85 percent of all exports, regularly shipped abroad more than 100,000 woolen cloths a year at a value of at least £750,000. This figure does not include the increasingly important and profitable trade in so-called New Draperies, including textiles that went by such exotic names as bombazines, calamancoes, damazellas, damizes, mockadoes, and virgenatoes. When the Earl of Kent in *King Lear* insults Oswald as a "filthy worsted-stocking knave" (2.2.14–15) or when the aristocratic Biron in *Love's Labour's Lost* declares that he will give up "taffeta phrases, silken terms precise, / Three-piled hyperboles" and woo henceforth "in russet yeas, and honest kersey noes" (5.2.406–07, 413), Shakespeare is assuming that a substantial portion of his audience will be alert to the social significance of fabric.

There is amusing confirmation of this alertness from an unexpected source: the report of a visit made to the Fortune playhouse in London in 1614 by a foreigner, Father Orazio Busino, the chaplain of the Venetian embassy. Father Busino neglected to mention the name of the play he saw, but like many foreigners, he was powerfully struck by the presence of gorgeously dressed women in the audience. In Venice, there was a special gallery for courtesans, but socially respectable women would not have been permitted to attend plays, as they could in England. In London, not only could middle- and upper-class women go to the theater, but they could also wear masks and mingle freely with male spectators and women of ill repute. The bemused cleric was uncertain about the ambiguous social situation in which he found himself:

> These theatres are frequented by a number of respectable and handsome ladies, who come freely and seat themselves among the men without the slightest hesitation. On the evening in question his Excellency and the Secretary were pleased to play me a trick by placing me amongst a bevy of young women. Scarcely was I seated ere a very

elegant dame, but in a mask, came and placed herself beside me. . . . She asked me for my address both in French and English; and, on my turning a deaf ear, she determined to honour me by showing me some fine diamonds on her fingers, repeatedly taking off not fewer than three gloves, which were worn one over the other. . . . This lady's bodice was of yellow satin richly embroidered, her petticoat of gold tissue with stripes, her robe of red velvet with a raised pile, lined with yellow muslin with broad stripes of pure gold. She wore an apron of point lace of various patterns: her head-tire was highly perfumed, and the collar of white satin beneath the delicately-wrought ruff struck me as extremely pretty.

Father Busino may have turned a deaf ear on this "elegant dame" but not a blind eye: his description of her dress is worthy of a fashion designer and conveys something of the virtual clothes cult that prevailed in England in the late sixteenth and early seventeenth centuries, a cult whose major shrine, outside the royal court, was the theater.

Imports, Patents, and Monopolies

England produced some luxury goods, but the clothing on the backs of the most fashionable theatergoers was likely to have come from abroad. By the late sixteenth century, the English were importing substantial quantities of silks, satins, velvets, embroidery, gold and silver lace, and other costly items to satisfy the extravagant tastes of the elite and of those who aspired to dress like the elite. The government tried to put a check on the sartorial ambitions of the upwardly mobile by passing sumptuary laws—that is, laws restricting to the ranks of the aristocracy the right to wear certain of the most precious fabrics. But the very existence of these laws, in practice almost impossible to enforce, only reveals the scope and significance of the perceived problem.

Sumptuary laws were in part a conservative attempt to protect the existing social order from upstarts. Social mobility was not widely viewed as a positive virtue, and moralists repeatedly urged people to stay in their place. Conspicuous consumption that was tolerated, even admired, in the aristocratic elite was denounced as sinful and monstrous in less exalted social circles. English authorities were also deeply concerned throughout the period about the effects of a taste for luxury goods on the balance of trade. One of the principal English imports was wine: the "sherris" whose virtues Falstaff extols in 2 Henry IV came from Xeres in Spain; the malmsey in which poor Clarence is drowned in Richard III was probably made in Greece or in the Canary Islands (from whence came Sir Toby Belch's "cup of canary" in Twelfth Night); and the "flagon of rhenish" that Yorick in Hamlet had once poured on the Gravedigger's head came from the Rhine region of Germany. Other imports included canvas, linen, fish, olive oil, sugar, molasses, dates, oranges and lemons, figs, raisins, almonds, capers, indigo, ostrich feathers, and that increasingly popular drug from the New World, tobacco.

Joint-stock companies were established to import goods for the burgeoning English market. The Merchant Venturers of the city of Bristol (established in 1552) handled great shipments of Spanish sack, the light, dry wine that largely displaced the vintages of Bordeaux and Burgundy when trade with France was disrupted by war. The Muscovy Company (established in 1555) traded English cloth and manufactured goods for Russian furs, oil, and beeswax. The Venice Company and the Turkey Company—uniting in 1593 to form the wealthy Levant Company—brought silk and spices home from Aleppo and carpets from Istanbul. The East India Company (founded in 1600), with its agent at Bantam in Java, brought pepper, cloves, nutmeg, and other spices from east Asia, along with indigo, cotton textiles, sugar, and saltpeter from India. English privateers "imported" American products, especially sugar, fish, and hides, in huge quantities, along with more precious cargoes. In 1592, a privateering expedition principally funded by Sir Walter Ralegh captured a huge Portuguese carrack (sailing ship), the Madre de Dios, in the Azores and brought it back to Dartmouth. The ship, the largest that had ever entered any English port, held 536 tons of pepper, cloves, cinnamon, cochineal, mace, civet, musk, ambergris,

Cannoneer. From *Edward Webbe, . . . His Travailes* (1590).

and nutmeg, as well as jewels, gold, ebony, carpets, and silks. Before order could be established, the English seamen began to pillage this immensely rich prize, and witnesses said they could smell the spices on all the streets around the harbor. Such piratical expeditions were rarely officially sanctioned by the state, but the queen had in fact privately invested £1,800, for which she received about £80,000.

In the years of war with Spain, 1586–1604, the goods captured by the privateers annually amounted to 10 to 15 percent of the total value of England's imports. But organized theft alone could not solve England's balance-of-trade problems. Statesmen were particularly worried that the nation's natural wealth was slipping away in exchange for unnecessary things. In his *Discourse of the Commonweal* (1549), the prominent humanist Sir Thomas Smith exclaims against the importation of such trifles as mirrors, paper, laces, gloves, pins, inkhorns, tennis balls, puppets, and playing cards. And more than a century later, the same fear that England was trading its riches for trifles and wasting away in idleness was expressed by the Bristol merchant John Cary. The solution, Cary argues in "An Essay on the State of England in Relation to Its Trade" (1695), is to expand productive domestic employment. "People are or may be the Wealth of a Nation," he writes, "yet it must be where you find Employment for them, else they are a Burden to it, as the Idle Drone is maintained by the Industry of the laborious Bee, so are all those who live by their Dependence on others, as Players, Ale-House Keepers, Common Fiddlers, and such like, but more particularly Beggars, who never set themselves to work."

Stage players, all too typically associated here with vagabonds and other idle drones, could have replied in their defense that they not only labored in their vocation but also exported their skills abroad: English acting companies routinely traveled overseas and performed as far away as Bohemia. But their labor was not regarded as a productive contribution to the national wealth, and plays were in truth no solution to the trade imbalances that worried authorities.

The government attempted to stem the flow of gold overseas by establishing a patent system initially designed to encourage skilled foreigners to settle in England by granting them exclusive rights to produce particular wares by a patented method. Patents were granted for such things as the making of hard white soap (1561), ovens and furnaces (1563), window glass (1567), sailcloths (1574), drinking glasses (1574), sulphur, brimstone, and oil (1577), armor and horse harness (1587), starch (1588), white writing paper made from rags (1589), aqua vitae and vinegar (1594), playing cards (1598), and mathematical instruments (1598).

Although their ostensible purpose was to increase the wealth of England, encourage technical innovation, and provide employment for the poor, the effect of patents was often the enrichment of a few and the hounding of poor competitors by wealthy monopolists, a group that soon extended well beyond foreign-born entrepreneurs to the favorites of the monarch who vied for the huge profits to be made. "If I had a monopoly out" on folly, the Fool in *King Lear* protests, glancing at the "lords and great men" around him, "they would have part on't." The passage appears only in the quarto version of the play (*History of King Lear* 4.135–36); it may have been cut for political reasons from the Folio. For the issue of monopolies provoked bitter criticism and parliamentary debate for decades. In 1601, Elizabeth was prevailed upon to revoke a number of the most hated monopolies, including aqua vitae and vinegar, bottles, brushes, fish livers, the coarse sailcloth known as poldavis and mildernix, pots, salt, and starch. The whole system was revoked during the reign of James I by an act of Parliament.

Haves and Have-Nots

When in the 1560s Elizabeth's ambassador to France, the humanist Sir Thomas Smith, wrote a description of England, he saw the commonwealth as divided into four sorts of people: "gentlemen, citizens, yeomen artificers, and laborers." At the forefront of the class of gentlemen was the monarch, followed by a very small group of nobles—dukes, marquesses, earls, viscounts, and barons—who either inherited their exalted titles, as the eldest male heirs of their families, or were granted them by the monarch. Under Elizabeth, this aristocratic peerage numbered between 50 and 60 individuals; James's promotions increased the number to nearer 130. Strictly speaking, Smith notes, the younger sons of the nobility were only entitled to be called "esquires," but in common speech they were also called "lords."

Below this tiny cadre of aristocrats in the social hierarchy of gentry were the knights, a title of honor conferred by the monarch, and below them were the "simple gentlemen." Who was a gentleman? According to Smith, "whoever studieth the laws of the realm, who studieth in the universities, who professeth liberal sciences, and to be short, who can live idly and without manual labor, and will bear the port, charge and countenance of a gentleman, he shall be called master . . . and shall be taken for a gentleman." To "live idly and without manual labor": where in Spain, for example, the crucial mark of a gentleman was "blood," in England it was "idleness," in the sense of sufficient income to afford an education and to maintain a social position without having to work with one's hands.

For Smith, the class of gentlemen was far and away the most important in the kingdom. Below were two groups that had at least some social standing and claim to authority: the citizens, or burgesses, those who held positions of importance and responsibility in their cities, and yeomen, farmers with land and a measure of economic independence. At the bottom of the social order was what Smith calls "the fourth sort of men which do not rule." The great mass of ordinary people have, Smith writes, "no voice nor authority in our commonwealth, and no account is made of them but only to be ruled." Still, even they can bear some responsibility, he notes, since they serve on juries and are named to such positions as churchwarden and constable.

In everyday practice, as modern social historians have observed, the English tended to divide the population not into four distinct classes but into two: a very small empowered group—the "richer" or "wiser" or "better" sort—and all the rest who were without much social standing or power, the "poorer" or "ruder" or "meaner" sort. References to the "middle sort of people" remain relatively rare until after Shakespeare's lifetime; these people are absorbed into the rulers or the ruled, depending on speaker and context.

The source of wealth for most of the ruling class, and the essential measure of social status, was landownership, and changes to the social structure in the sixteenth and seventeenth centuries were largely driven by the land market. The property that passed into private hands as the Tudors and early Stuarts sold off confiscated monastic estates and then their own crown lands for ready cash amounted to nearly a quarter of all the land in England. At the same time, the buying and selling of private estates was on the rise throughout the period. Land was bought up not only by established landowners seeking to enlarge their estates but by successful merchants, manufacturers, and urban professionals; even if the taint of vulgar moneymaking lingered around such figures, their heirs would be taken for true gentlemen. The rate of turnover in landownership was great; in many counties, well over half the gentle families in 1640 had appeared since the end of the fifteenth century. The class that Smith called "simple gentlemen" was expanding rapidly: in the fifteenth century, they had held no more than a quarter of the land in the country; but by the later seventeenth century, they controlled almost half. Over the same period, the land held by the great aristocratic magnates held steady at 15 to 20 percent of the total.

Riot and Disorder

London was a violent place in the first half of Shakespeare's career. There were thirty-five riots in the city in the years 1581–1602, twelve of them in the volatile month of June 1595. These included protests against the deeply unpopular lord mayor Sir John Spencer, attempts to release prisoners, anti-alien riots, and incidents of "popular market regulation." There is an unforgettable depiction of a popular uprising in *Coriolanus*, along with many other glimpses in Shakespeare's works, including John Cade's grotesque rebellion in *The First Part of the Contention* (*2 Henry VI*), the plebeian violence in *Julius Caesar,* and Laertes' "riotous head" in *Hamlet*.

The London rioters were mostly drawn from the large mass of poor and discontented apprentices who typically chose as their scapegoats foreigners, prostitutes, and gentlemen's servingmen. Theaters were very often the site of the social confrontations that sparked disorder. For two days running in June 1584, disputes between apprentices and gentlemen triggered riots outside the Curtain Theatre involving up to a thousand participants. On one occasion, a gentleman was said to have exclaimed that "the apprentice was but a rascal, and some there were little better than rogues that took upon them the name of gentlemen, and said the prentices were but the scum of the world." These occasions culminated in attacks by the apprentices on London's law schools, the Inns of Court.

The most notorious and predictable incidents of disorder came on Shrove Tuesday (the Tuesday before the beginning of Lent), a traditional day of misrule when apprentices ran riot. Shrove Tuesday disturbances involved attacks by mobs of young men on the brothels of the South Bank, in the vicinity of the Globe and other public theaters. The city authorities took precautions to keep these disturbances from getting completely out of control but evidently did not regard them as serious threats to public order.

Of much greater concern throughout the Tudor and early Stuart years were the frequent incidents of rural rioting against the enclosure of commons and wasteland by local landlords (and, in the royal forests, by the crown). This form of popular protest was at its height during Shakespeare's career: in the years 1590–1610, the frequency of anti-enclosure rioting doubled from what it had been earlier in Elizabeth's reign.

Although they often became violent, anti-enclosure riots were usually directed not against individuals but against property. Villagers—sometimes several hundred, often

fewer than a dozen—gathered to tear down newly planted hedges. The event often took place in a carnival atmosphere, with songs and drinking, that did not prevent the participants from acting with a good deal of political canniness and forethought. Especially in the Jacobean period, it was common for participants to establish a common fund for legal defense before commencing their assault on the hedges. Women were frequently involved, and on a number of occasions wives alone participated in the destruction of the enclosure, since there was a widespread, though erroneous, belief that married women acting without the knowledge of their husbands were immune from prosecution. In fact, the powerful Court of Star Chamber consistently ruled that both the wives and their husbands should be punished.

Peddler. From Jost Amman, *The Book of Trades* (1568).

Although Stratford was never the scene of serious rioting, enclosure controversies there turned violent more than once in Shakespeare's lifetime. In January 1601, Shakespeare's friend Richard Quiney and others leveled the hedges of Sir Edward Greville, lord of Stratford manor. Quiney was elected bailiff of Stratford in September of that year but did not live to enjoy the office for long. He died from a blow to the head struck by one of Greville's men in a tavern brawl. Greville, responsible for the administration of justice, neglected to punish the murderer.

There was further violence in January 1615, when William Combe's men threw to the ground two local aldermen who were filling in a ditch by which Combe was enclosing common fields near Stratford. The task of filling in the offending ditch was completed the next day by the women and children of Stratford. Combe's enclosure scheme was eventually stopped in the courts. Although he owned land whose value would have been affected by this controversy, Shakespeare took no active role in it, since he had previously come to a private settlement with the enclosers insuring him against personal loss.

Most incidents of rural rioting were small, localized affairs, and with good reason: when confined to the village community, riot was a misdemeanor; when it spread outward to include multiple communities, it became treason, punishable by death. The greatest of the anti-enclosure riots, those in which hundreds of individuals from a large area participated, commonly took place on the eve of full-scale regional rebellions. The largest of these disturbances, Kett's Rebellion, involved some 16,000 peasants, artisans, and townspeople who rose up in 1549 under the leadership of a Norfolk tanner and landowner, Robert Kett, to protest economic exploitation. The agrarian revolts in Shakespeare's lifetime were on a much smaller scale. In the abortive Oxfordshire Rebellion of 1596, a carpenter named Bartholomew Steere attempted to organize a rising against enclosing gentlemen. The optimistic Steere promised his followers that "it was but a month's work to overrun England" and informed them "that the commons long since in Spain did rise and kill all gentlemen . . . and since that time have lived merrily there." Steere expected several hundred men to join him on Enslow Hill on November 21, 1596, for the start of the rising; no more than twenty showed up. They were captured, imprisoned, and tortured. Several were executed, but Steere apparently cheated the hangman by dying in prison.

Rebellions, most often triggered by hunger and oppression, continued into the reign of James I. The Midland Revolt of 1607, which may be reflected in *Coriolanus*, consisted of a string of agrarian risings in the counties of Northamptonshire, Warwickshire, and Leicestershire, involving assemblies of up to 5,000 rebels in various places. The best known of their leaders was John Reynolds, called "Captain Powch" because of the pouch he wore, whose magical contents were supposed to defend the rebels from harm. (According to the chronicler Edmund Howes, when Reynolds was captured and the pouch opened, it contained "only a piece of green cheese.") The rebels, who were called by themselves and others both "Levelers" and "Diggers," insisted that they had no quarrel with the king but only sought an end to injurious enclosures. But Robert Wilkinson, who preached a sermon against the leaders at their trial, credited them with the intention to "level all states as they leveled banks and ditches." Most of the rebels got off relatively lightly, but, along with other ringleaders, Captain Powch was executed.

The Legal Status of Women

Even though England was ruled for over forty years by a powerful woman, the great majority of women in the kingdom had very restricted social, economic, and legal standing. To be sure, a tiny number of influential aristocratic women, such as the formidable Countess of Shrewsbury, Bess of Hardwick, wielded considerable power. But, these rare exceptions aside, women were denied any rightful claim to institutional authority or personal autonomy. When Sir Thomas Smith thinks of how he should describe his country's social order, he declares that "we do reject women, as those whom nature hath made to keep home and to nourish their family and children, and not to meddle with matters abroad, nor to bear office in a city or commonwealth."

Then, with a kind of glance over his shoulder, he makes an exception of those few for whom "the blood is respected, not the age nor the sex": for example, the queen.

English women were not under the full range of crushing constraints that afflicted women in some countries in Europe. Foreign visitors were struck by their relative freedom, as shown, for example, by the fact that respectable women could venture unchaperoned into the streets and attend the theater. Single women, whether widowed or unmarried, could, if they were of full age, inherit and administer land, make a will, sign a contract, possess property, sue and be sued, without a male guardian or proxy. But married women had no such rights under the common law.

Early modern writings about women and the family constantly return to a political model of domination and submission, in which the father justly rules over wife and children as the monarch rules over the state. This conception of a woman's role conveniently ignores the fact that a *majority* of the adult women at any time in Shakespeare's England were not married. They were either widows or spinsters (a term that was not yet pejorative), and thus for the most part managing their own affairs. Even within marriage, women typically had more control over certain spheres than moralizing writers on the family cared to admit. For example, village wives oversaw the production of eggs, cheese, and beer, and sold these goods in the market. As seamstresses, pawnbrokers, secondhand clothing dealers, peddlers, and the like—activities not controlled by the all-male guilds—women managed to acquire some economic power of their own, and, of course, they participated as well in the unregulated, black-market economy of the age and in the underworld of thievery and prostitution.

Women were not in practice as bereft of property as, according to English common law, they should have been. Demographic studies indicate that the inheritance system called primogeniture, the orderly transmission of property from father to eldest male heir, was more often an unfulfilled wish than a reality. Some 40 percent of marriages failed to produce a son, and in such circumstances fathers often left their land to their daughters, rather than to brothers, nephews, or male cousins. In many families, the father died before his male heir was old enough to inherit property, leaving the land, at least temporarily, in the hands of the mother. And while they were less likely than their brothers to inherit land ("real property"), daughters normally inherited a substantial share of their father's personal property (cash and movables).

In fact, the legal restrictions upon women, though severe in Shakespeare's time, actually worsened in subsequent decades. The English common law, the system of law based on court decisions rather than on codified written laws, was significantly less egalitarian in its approach to wives and daughters than were alternative legal codes (manorial, civil, and ecclesiastical) still in place in the late sixteenth century. The eventual triumph of common law stripped women of many traditional rights, slowly driving them out of economically productive trades and businesses.

Limited though it was, the economic freedom of Elizabethan and Jacobean women far exceeded their political and social freedom—the opportunity to receive a grammar-school or university education, to hold office in church or state, to have a voice in public debates, or even simply to speak their mind fully and openly in ordinary conversation. Women who asserted their views too vigorously risked being perceived as shrewish and labeled "scolds." Both urban and rural communities had a horror of scolds. In the Elizabethan period, such women came to be regarded as a threat to public order, to be dealt with by the local authorities. The preferred methods of correction included public humiliation—of the sort Katherine endures in *The Taming of the Shrew*—and such physical abuse as slapping, bridling, and soaking by means of a contraption called the "cucking stool" (or "ducking stool"). This latter punishment originated in the Middle Ages, but its use spread in the sixteenth century, when it became almost exclusively a punishment for women. From 1560 onward, cucking stools were built or renovated in many English provincial towns; between 1560 and 1600, the contraptions were installed by rivers or ponds in Norwich, Bridport, Shrewsbury, Kingston-upon-Thames, Marlborough, Devizes, Clitheroe, Thornbury, and Great Yarmouth.

Such punishment was usually intensified by a procession through the town to the sound of "rough music," the banging together of pots and pans. The same cruel festivity accompanied the "carting" or "riding" of those accused of being whores. In some parts of the country, villagers also took the law into their own hands, publicly shaming women who married men much younger than themselves or who beat or otherwise domineered over their husbands. One characteristic form of these charivaris, or rituals of shaming, was known in the West Country as the Skimmington Ride. Villagers would rouse the offending couple from bed with rough music and stage a raucous pageant in which a man, holding a distaff, would ride backward on a donkey, while his "wife" (another man dressed as a woman) struck him with a ladle. In these cases, the collective ridicule and indignation was evidently directed at least as much at the henpecked husband as at his transgressive wife.

Women and Print

Books published for a female audience surged in popularity in the late sixteenth century, reflecting an increase in female literacy. (It is striking how many of Shakespeare's women are shown reading.) This increase is probably linked to a Protestant longing for direct access to the Scriptures, and the new books marketed specifically for women included devotional manuals and works of religious instruction. But there were also practical guides to such subjects as female education (for example, Giovanni Bruto's *Necessarie, Fit, and Convenient Education of a Young Gentlewoman*, 1598), midwifery (James Guillemeau's *Child-birth; or, The Happy Delivery of Women*, 1612), needlework (Federico di Vinciolo's *New and Singular Patternes and Workes of Linnen*, 1591), cooking (Thomas Dawson's *The Good Husewifes Jewell*, 1587), gardening (Pierre Erondelle's *The French Garden for English Ladyes and Gentlewomen to Walke In*, 1605), and married life (Patrick Hannay's *A Happy Husband; or, Directions for a Maide to Choose Her Mate*, 1619). As the authors' names suggest, many of these works were translations, and almost all were written by men.

Starting in the 1570s, writers and their publishers increasingly addressed works of recreational literature (romance, fiction, and poetry) partially or even exclusively to women. Some books, such as Robert Greene's *Mamillia, a Mirrour or Looking-Glasse for the Ladies of Englande* (1583), directly specified in the title their desired audience. Others, such as Sir Philip Sidney's influential and popular romance *Arcadia* (1590–93), solicited female readership in their dedicatory epistles. The ranks of Sidney's followers eventually included his own niece, Mary Wroth, whose romance *Urania* was published in 1621.

In the literature of Shakespeare's time, women readers were not only wooed but also frequently railed at, in a continuation of a popular polemical genre that had long inspired heated charges and countercharges. Both sides in the polemic generally agreed that it was the duty of women to be chaste, dutiful, shamefast, and silent; the argument was whether women fulfilled or fell short of this proper role. Ironically, then, a modern reader is more likely to find inspiring accounts of courageous women not in the books written in defense of female virtue but in attacks on those who refused to be silent and obedient.

The most famous English skirmish in this controversy took place in a rash of pamphlets at the end of Shakespeare's life. Joseph Swetnam's crude *Araignment of Lewd, Idle, Froward, and Unconstant Women* (1615) provoked three fierce responses attributed to women: Rachel Speght's *A Mouzell [Muzzle] for Melastomus*, Ester Sowernam's *Ester Hath Hang'd Haman*, and Constantia Munda's *Worming of a Mad Dogge*, all 1617. There was also an anonymous play, *Swetnam, the Woman-hater, Arraigned by Women* (1618), in which Swetnam, depicted as a braggart and a lecher, is put on trial by women and made to recant his misogynistic lies.

Prior to the Swetnam controversy, only one English woman, "Jane Anger," had published a defense of women (*Jane Anger, Her Protection for Women*, 1589). Learned women writers in the sixteenth century tended not to become involved in public debate but rather to undertake a project to which it was difficult for even obdurately chauvinistic

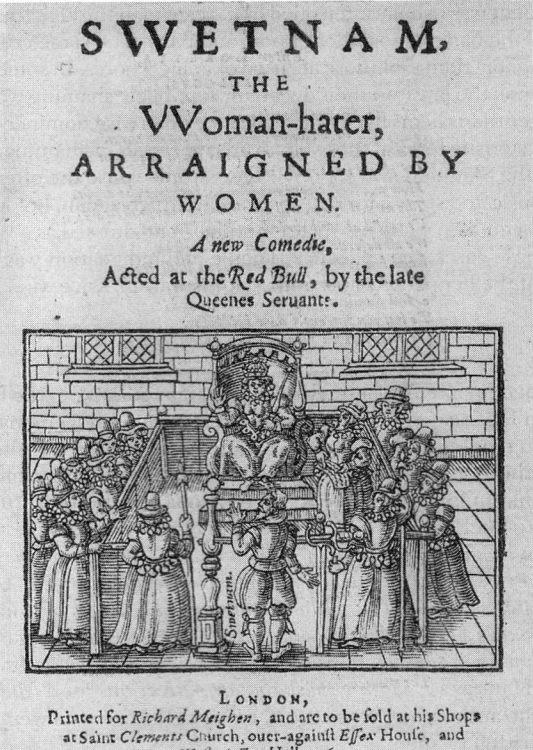

SWETNAM,

THE

VVoman-hater,

ARRAIGNED BY

WOMEN.

A new Comedie,

Acted at the *Red Bull*, by the late
Queenes Seruants.

LONDON,
Printed for *Richard Meighen*, and are to be sold at his Shops
at Saint *Clements* Church, ouer-against *Essex* House, and
at *Westminster* Hall. 1 6 2 0.

Title page of *Swetnam, the Woman-hater, Arraigned by Women* (1620), a play written in response to Joseph Swetnam's *The Araignment of Lewd, Idle, Froward and Unconstant Women* (1615); the woodcut depicts the trial of Swetnam in Act 4.

males to object: the translation of devotional literature into English. Thomas More's daughter Margaret More Roper translated Erasmus (*A Devout Treatise upon the Pater Noster*, 1524); Francis Bacon's mother, Anne Cooke Bacon, translated Bishop John Jewel (*An Apologie or Answere in Defence of the Churche of Englande*, 1564); Anne Locke Prowse, a friend of John Knox, translated the *Sermons of John Calvin* in 1560; and Mary Sidney, Countess of Pembroke, completed the metrical version of the Psalms that her brother Sir Philip Sidney had begun. Elizabeth Tudor (the future queen) herself translated, at the age of eleven, Marguerite de Navarre's *Miroir de l'âme pécheresse* (*The Glass of the Sinful Soul*, 1544). The translation was dedicated to her stepmother, Catherine Parr, herself the author of a frequently reprinted book of prayers.

There was in the sixteenth and early seventeenth centuries a social stigma attached to print. Far from celebrating publication, authors, and particularly female authors, often apologized for exposing themselves to the public gaze. Nonetheless, a number of women ventured beyond pious translations circulated in manuscript. Some, including Elizabeth Tyrwhitt, Anne Dowriche, Isabella Whitney, Mary Sidney, and Aemilia Lanyer, composed and published their own poems. Aemilia Lanyer's *Salve Deus Rex Judaeorum*, published in 1611, is a poem in praise of virtuous women, from Eve and the Virgin Mary to her noble patron, the Countess of Cumberland. "A Description of Cookeham," appended to the poem, may be the first English-country-house poem.

The first Tudor woman to translate a play was the learned Jane Lumley, who composed an English version of Euripides' *Iphigenia at Aulis* (c. 1550). The first known original play in English by a woman was by Elizabeth Cary, Viscountess Falkland, whose *Tragedie of Mariam, the Faire Queene of Jewry* was published in 1613. This remarkable play, which was not intended to be performed, includes speeches in defense of women's equality, though the most powerful of these is spoken by the villainous Salome, who schemes to divorce her husband and marry her lover. Cary, who bore eleven children, herself had a deeply troubled marriage, which effectively came to an end in 1625, when, defying her husband's staunchly Protestant family, she openly converted to Catholicism. Her biography was written by one of her four daughters, all of whom became nuns.

Henry VIII and the English Reformation

There had long been serious ideological and institutional tensions in the religious life of England, but officially, at least, England in the early sixteenth century had a single religion, Catholicism, whose acknowledged head was the pope in Rome. In 1517, drawing upon long-standing currents of dissent, Martin Luther, an Augustinian monk and professor of theology at the University of Wittenberg, challenged the authority of the pope and attacked several key doctrines of the Catholic Church. According to Luther, the Church, with its elaborate hierarchical structure centered in Rome, its rich monasteries and convents, and its enormous political influence, had become hopelessly corrupt, a conspiracy of venal priests who manipulated popular superstitions to enrich themselves and amass worldly power. Luther began by vehemently attacking the sale of indulgences—certificates promising the remission of punishments to be suffered in the afterlife by souls sent to purgatory to expiate their sins. These indulgences were a fraud, he argued; purgatory itself had no foundation in the Bible, which in his view was the only legitimate source of religious truth. Christians would be saved not by scrupulously following the ritual practices fostered by the Catholic Church—observing fast days, reciting the ancient Latin prayers, endowing chantries to say prayers for the dead, and so on—but by faith and faith alone.

This challenge, which came to be known as the Reformation, spread and gathered force, especially in northern Europe, where major leaders like the Swiss pastor Huldrych Zwingli and the French theologian John Calvin established institutional structures and elaborated various and sometimes conflicting doctrinal principles. Calvin, whose thought came to be particularly influential in England, emphasized the obligation of governments to implement God's will in the world. He advanced too the doctrine of predestination, by which, as he put it, "God adopts some to hope of life and sentences others to eternal death." God's "secret election" of the saved made Calvin uncomfortable, but his study of the Scriptures had led him to conclude that "only a small number, out of an incalculable multitude, should obtain salvation." It might seem that such a conclusion would lead to passivity or even despair, but for Calvin predestination was a mystery bound up with faith, confidence, and an active engagement in the fashioning of a Christian community.

The Reformation had a direct and powerful impact on those territories, especially in northern Europe, where it gained control. Monasteries were sacked, their possessions seized by princes or sold off to the highest bidder; the monks and nuns, expelled from their cloisters, were encouraged to break their vows of chastity and find spouses, as Luther and his wife, a former nun, had done. In the great cathedrals and in hundreds of smaller churches and chapels, the elaborate altarpieces, bejeweled crucifixes, crystal reliquaries holding the bones of saints, and venerated statues and paintings were attacked as "idols" and often defaced or destroyed. Protestant congregations continued, for the most part, to celebrate the most sacred Christian ritual, the Eucharist, or Lord's Supper, but they did so in a profoundly different spirit from that of the Catholic Church—more as commemoration than as miracle—and they now prayed not in the ancient liturgical Latin but in the vernacular.

"The Pope as Antichrist riding the Beast of the Apocalypse." From *Fierie Tryall of God's Saints* (1611; author unknown).

The Reformation was at first vigorously resisted in England. Indeed, with the support of his ardently Catholic chancellor, Thomas More, Henry VIII personally wrote (or at least lent his name to) a vehement, often scatological attack on Luther's character and views, an attack for which the pope granted him the honorific title "Defender of the Faith." Protestant writings, including translations of the Scriptures into English, were seized by officials of the church and state and burned. Protestants who made their views known were persecuted, driven to flee the country, or arrested, put on trial, and burned at the stake. But the situation changed drastically and decisively when in 1527 Henry decided to seek a divorce from his first wife, Catherine of Aragon, in order to marry Anne Boleyn.

Catherine had given birth to six children, but since only a daughter, Mary, survived infancy, Henry did not have the son he craved. Then as now, the Catholic Church did not ordinarily grant divorce, but Henry's lawyers argued on technical grounds that the marriage was invalid (and, therefore, by extension, that Mary was illegitimate and hence unable to inherit the throne). Matters of this kind were far less doctrinal than diplomatic: Catherine, the daughter of Ferdinand of Aragon and Isabella of Castile, had powerful allies in Rome, and the pope ruled against Henry's petition for a divorce. A series of momentous events followed, as England lurched away from the Church of Rome. In 1531, Henry charged the entire clergy of England with having usurped royal authority in the administration of canon law (the ecclesiastical law that governed faith, discipline, and morals, including such matters as divorce). Under extreme pressure, including the threat of mass confiscations and imprisonment, the Convocation of the English Clergy begged for pardon, made a donation to the royal coffers of over £100,000, and admitted that the king was "supreme head of the English Church and clergy" (modified by the rider "as far as the law of Christ allows"). On May 15 of the next year, the convocation submitted to the demand that the king be the final arbiter of canon law; on the next day, Thomas More resigned his post.

In 1533, Henry's marriage to Catherine was officially declared null and void, and on June 1 Anne Boleyn was crowned queen (a coronation Shakespeare depicts in his late play *All Is True*). The king was promptly excommunicated by the pope, Clement VII. In the following year, the parliamentary Act of Succession confirmed the effects of the divorce and required an oath from all adult male subjects confirming the new dynastic settlement. Thomas More and John Fisher, Bishop of Rochester, were among the small number who refused. The Act of Supremacy, passed later in the year, formally declared the king to be "Supreme Head of the Church in England" and again required an oath to this effect. In 1535 and 1536, further acts made it treasonous to refuse the oath of royal supremacy or, as More had tried to do, to remain silent. The first victims were three Carthusian monks who rejected the oath—"How could the king, a layman," said one of them, "be Head of the Church of England?"—and in May 1535, they were duly hanged, drawn, and quartered. A few weeks later, Fisher and More were convicted and beheaded. Between 1536 and 1539, the monasteries were suppressed and their vast wealth seized by the crown.

Royal defiance of the authority of Rome was a key element in the Reformation but did not by itself constitute the establishment of Protestantism in England. On the contrary, in the same year that Fisher and More were martyred for their adherence to Roman Catholicism, twenty-five Protestants, members of a sect known as Anabaptists, were burned for heresy on a single day. Through most of his reign, Henry remained an equal-opportunity persecutor, ruthless to Catholics loyal to Rome and hostile to some of those who espoused Reformation ideas, though many of these ideas gradually established themselves on English soil.

Even when Henry was eager to do so, it proved impossible to eradicate Protestantism, as it would later prove impossible for his successors to eradicate Catholicism. In large part this tenacity arose from the passionate, often suicidal heroism of men and women who felt that their souls' salvation depended on the precise character of their Christianity. It arose, too, from a mid-fifteenth-century technological innovation that made it almost impossible to suppress unwelcome ideas: the printing press. Early Protestants quickly grasped that with a few clandestine presses they could defy the Catholic authorities and flood the country with their texts. "How many printing presses there be in the world," wrote the Protestant polemicist John Foxe, "so many blockhouses there be against the high castle" of the pope in Rome, "so that either the pope must abolish knowledge and printing or printing at length will root him out." By the century's end, it was the Catholics who were using the clandestine press to propagate their beliefs in the face of Protestant persecution.

The greatest insurrection of the Tudor age was not over food, taxation, or land but over religion. On Sunday, October 1, 1536, stirred up by their vicar, the traditionalist parishioners of Louth in Lincolnshire, in the north of England, rose up in defiance of the ecclesiastical visitation sent to enforce royal supremacy. The rapidly spreading rebellion, which became known as the Pilgrimage of Grace, was led by the lawyer Robert Aske. The city of Lincoln fell to the rebels on October 6, and though it was soon retaken by royal forces, the rebels seized cities and fortifications throughout Yorkshire, Durham, Northumberland, Cumberland, Westmoreland, and northern Lancashire. Carlisle, Newcastle, and a few castles were all that were left to the king in the north. The Pilgrims soon numbered 40,000, led by some of the region's leading noblemen. The Duke of Norfolk, representing the crown, was forced to negotiate a truce, with a promise to support the rebels' demands that the king restore the monasteries, shore up the regional economy, suppress heresy, and dismiss his evil advisers.

The Pilgrims kept the peace for the rest of 1536, on the naive assumption that their demands would be met. But Henry moved suddenly early in 1537 to impose order and capture the ringleaders; 130 people, including lords, knights, heads of religious houses, and, of course, Robert Aske, were executed.

In 1549, two years after the death of Henry VIII, the west and the north of England were the sites of further unsuccessful risings for the restoration of Catholicism. The Western Rising is striking for its blend of Catholic universalism and intense regionalism among people who did not yet regard themselves as English. One of the rebels' articles, protesting against the imposition of the English Bible and religious service, declares, "We the Cornish men (whereof certain of us understand no English) utterly refuse this new English." The rebels besieged but failed to take the city of Exeter. As with almost all Tudor rebellions, the number of those executed in the aftermath of the failed rising was far greater than those killed in actual hostilities.

Henry VIII's Children: Edward, Mary, and Elizabeth

Upon Henry's death in 1547, his ten-year-old son, Edward VI, came to the throne, with his maternal uncle Edward Seymour named as Lord Protector and Duke of Somerset. Both Edward and his uncle were staunch Protestants, and reformers hastened to transform the English Church accordingly. During Edward's reign, Archbishop Thomas Cranmer formulated the forty-two articles of religion that became the core of Anglican orthodoxy and wrote the first Book of Common Prayer, which was officially adopted in 1549 as the basis of English worship services.

Somerset fell from power in 1549 and was replaced as Lord Protector by John Dudley, later Duke of Northumberland. When Edward fell seriously ill, probably of tuberculosis, Northumberland persuaded him to sign a will depriving his half sisters, Mary (the daughter of Catherine of Aragon) and Elizabeth (the daughter of Anne Boleyn), of their claim to royal succession. The Lord Protector was scheming to have his daughter-in-law, the Protestant Lady Jane Grey, a granddaughter of Henry VII, ascend to the throne. But when Edward died in 1553, Mary marshaled support, quickly secured the crown from Lady Jane (who had been titular queen for nine days), and had Lady Jane executed, along with her husband and Northumberland.

Queen Mary immediately took steps to return her kingdom to Roman Catholicism. Even though she was unable to get Parliament to agree to restore church lands seized under Henry VIII, she restored the Catholic Mass, once again affirmed the authority of the pope, and put down a rebellion that sought to depose her. Seconded by her ardently Catholic husband, Philip II, King of Spain, she initiated a series of religious persecutions that earned her (from her enemies) the name "Bloody Mary." Hundreds of Protestants took refuge abroad in cities such as Calvin's Geneva; almost three hundred less fortunate Protestants were condemned as heretics and burned at the stake.

The Family of Henry VIII: An Allegory of the Tudor Succession. By Lucas de Heere (c. 1572). Henry, in the middle, is flanked by Mary to his right, and Edward and Elizabeth to his left.

Mary died childless in 1558, and her younger half sister Elizabeth became queen. Elizabeth's succession had been by no means assured. For if Protestants regarded Henry VIII's marriage to Catherine as invalid and hence deemed Mary illegitimate, so Catholics regarded his marriage to Anne Boleyn as invalid and deemed Elizabeth illegitimate. Henry VIII himself seemed to support both views, since only three years after divorcing Catherine, he beheaded Anne Boleyn on charges of treason and adultery, and urged Parliament to invalidate the marriage. Moreover, though during her sister's reign Elizabeth outwardly complied with the official Catholic religious observance, Mary and her advisers were deeply suspicious, and the young princess's life was in grave danger. Poised and circumspect, Elizabeth warily evaded the traps that were set for her. As she ascended the throne, her actions were scrutinized for some indication of the country's future course. During her coronation procession, when a girl in an allegorical pageant presented her with a Bible in English translation—banned under Mary's reign—Elizabeth kissed the book, held it up reverently, and laid it to her breast; when the abbot and monks of Westminster Abbey came to greet her in broad daylight with candles (a symbol of Catholic devotion) in their hands, she briskly dismissed them with the telling words "Away with those torches! we can see well enough." England had returned to the Reformation.

Many English men and women, of all classes, remained loyal to the old Catholic faith, but English authorities under Elizabeth moved steadily, if cautiously, toward ensuring at least an outward conformity to the official Protestant settlement. Recusants, those who refused to attend regular Sunday services in their parish churches, were fined heavily. Anyone who wished to receive a university degree, to be ordained as a priest in the Church of England, or to be named as an officer of the state had to swear an oath to the royal supremacy. Commissioners were sent throughout the land to confirm that religious services were following the officially approved liturgy and to investigate any reported backsliding into Catholic practice or, alternatively, any attempts to introduce more radical reforms than the queen and her bishops had chosen to embrace. For the Protestant exiles who streamed back were eager not only to undo the damage Mary had done but to carry the Reformation much further. They sought to dismantle the church hierarchy, to purge the calendar of folk customs deemed pagan and the church service of ritual practices deemed superstitious, to dress the clergy in simple garb, and, at the extreme edge, to smash "idolatrous" statues, crucifixes, and altarpieces. Throughout her long reign, however, Elizabeth herself remained cautiously conservative and determined to hold in check what she regarded as the religious zealotry of Catholics, on the one side, and Puritans, on the other.

Shakespeare's plays tap into the ongoing confessional tensions: "Sometimes," Maria in *Twelfth Night* says of the sober, festivity-hating steward Malvolio, "he is a kind of puritan" (2.3.125). But they tend to avoid the risks of direct engagement: "The dev'l a puritan that he is, or anything constantly," Maria adds a moment later, "but a time-pleaser, an affectioned ass" (2.3.131–32). *The Winter's Tale* features a statue that comes to life—exactly the kind of magical image that Protestant polemicists excoriated as Catholic superstition and idolatry—but the play is set in pre-Christian world of the Delphic oracle. And as if this careful distancing might not be enough, the play's ruler goes out of his way to pronounce the wonder legitimate: "If this be magic, let it be an art / Lawful as eating" (5.3.110–11).

In the space of a single lifetime, England had gone officially from Roman Catholicism, to Catholicism under the supreme headship of the English king, to a guarded Protestantism, to a more radical Protestantism, to a renewed and aggressive Roman Catholicism, and finally to Protestantism again. Each of these shifts was accompanied by danger, persecution, and death. It was enough to make some people wary. Or skeptical. Or extremely agile.

The English Bible

Luther had undertaken a fundamental critique of the Catholic Church's sacramental system, a critique founded on the twin principles of salvation by faith alone (*sola fide*) and the absolute primacy of the Bible (*sola scriptura*). *Sola fide* contrasted faith with "works," by which was meant primarily the whole elaborate system of rituals sanctified, conducted, or directed by the priests. Protestants proposed to modify or reinterpret many of these rituals or, as with the rituals associated with purgatory, to abolish them altogether. *Sola scriptura* required direct lay access to the Bible, which meant in practice the widespread availability of vernacular translations. The Roman Catholic Church had not always and everywhere opposed such translations, but it generally preferred that the populace encounter the Scriptures through the interpretations of the priests, trained to read the Latin translation known as the Vulgate. In times of great conflict, this preference for clerical mediation hardened into outright prohibition of vernacular translation and into persecution and book burning.

Zealous Protestants set out, in the teeth of fierce opposition, to put the Bible into the hands of the laity. A remarkable translation of the New Testament, by an English Lutheran named William Tyndale, was printed on the Continent and smuggled into England in 1525; Tyndale's translation of the Pentateuch, the first five books of the Hebrew Bible, followed in 1530. Many copies of these translations were seized and burned, as was the translator himself, but the printing press made it extremely difficult for authorities to eradicate books for which there was a passionate demand. The English Bible was a force that could not be suppressed, and it became, in its various forms, the single most important book of the sixteenth century.

Tyndale's translation was completed by an associate, Miles Coverdale, whose rendering of the Psalms proved to be particularly influential. Their joint labor was the basis for the Great Bible (1539), the first authorized version of the Bible in English, a copy of which was ordered to be placed in every church in the kingdom. With the accession of Edward VI, many editions of the Bible followed, but the process was sharply reversed when Mary came to the throne in 1553. Along with people condemned as heretics, English Bibles were burned in great bonfires.

Marian persecution was indirectly responsible for what would become the most popular as well as most scholarly English Bible, the translation known as the Geneva Bible, prepared, with extensive, learned, and often fiercely polemical marginal notes, by English exiles in Calvin's Geneva and widely diffused in England after Elizabeth came to the throne. In addition, Elizabethan church authorities ordered a careful revision of the Great Bible, and this version, known as the Bishops' Bible, was the one read in the churches. The success of the Geneva Bible in particular prompted those Elizabethan Catholics who now in turn found themselves in exile to bring out a vernacular translation of their own in order to counter the Protestant readings and glosses. This Catholic translation, known as the Rheims Bible, may have been known to Shakespeare, but he seems to have been far better acquainted with the Geneva Bible, and he would also have repeatedly heard the Bishops' Bible read aloud. Scholars have identified over three hundred references to the Bible in Shakespeare's work; in one version or another, the Scriptures had a powerful impact on his imagination.

A Female Monarch in a Male World

In the last year of Mary's reign, 1558, the Scottish Calvinist minister John Knox thundered against what he called "the monstrous regiment of women." When the Protestant Elizabeth came to the throne the following year, Knox and his religious brethren were less inclined to denounce female rulers, but in England as elsewhere in Europe there remained a widespread conviction that women were unsuited to wield power over men. Many men seem to have regarded the capacity for rational thought as exclusively male; women, they assumed, were led only by their passions. While gentlemen mastered the arts of rhetoric and warfare, gentlewomen were expected to display the virtues of silence and good housekeeping. Among upper-class males, the will to dominate others was acceptable and, indeed, admired; the same will in women was condemned as a grotesque and dangerous aberration.

One of the Armada portraits (c. 1588). Note Elizabeth's hand on the globe.

Apologists for the queen countered these prejudices by appealing to historical precedent and legal theory. History offered inspiring examples of just female rulers, notably Deborah, the biblical prophetess who judged Israel. In the legal sphere, crown lawyers advanced the theory of "the king's two bodies." As England's crowned head, Elizabeth's person was mystically divided between her mortal "body natural" and the immortal "body politic." While the queen's natural body was inevitably subject to the failings of human flesh, the body politic was timeless and perfect. In political terms, therefore, Elizabeth's sex was a matter of no consequence, a thing indifferent.

Elizabeth, who had received a fine humanist education and an extended, dangerous lesson in the art of survival, made it immediately clear that she intended to rule in more than name only. She assembled a group of trustworthy advisers, foremost among them William Cecil (later named Lord Burghley, also known as Burleigh), but she insisted on making many of the crucial decisions herself. Like many Renaissance monarchs, Elizabeth was drawn to the idea of royal absolutism, the theory that ultimate power was properly concentrated in her person and, indeed, that God had appointed her to be His deputy in the kingdom. Opposition to her rule, in this view, was not only a political act but also a kind of impiety, a blasphemous grudging against the will of God. Apologists for absolutism contended that God commands obedience even to manifestly wicked rulers whom He has sent to punish the sinfulness of humankind. Such arguments were routinely made in speeches and political tracts and from the pulpits of churches, where they were incorporated into the *First* and *Second Book of Homilies*, which clergymen were required to read out to their congregations.

In reality, Elizabeth's power was not absolute. The government had a network of spies, informers, and agents provocateurs, but it lacked a standing army, a national police force, an efficient system of communication, and an extensive bureaucracy. Above all, the queen had limited financial resources and needed to turn periodically to an independent and often recalcitrant Parliament, which by long tradition had the sole right to levy taxes and to grant subsidies. Members of the House of Commons were elected from their boroughs, not appointed by the monarch, and although the queen had considerable influence over their decisions, she could by no means dictate policy. Under these constraints, Elizabeth ruled through a combination of adroit political maneuvering and imperious command, all the while enhancing her authority in the eyes of both court and country by means of an extraordinary cult of love.

"We all loved her," Elizabeth's godson Sir John Harington wrote, with just a touch of irony, a few years after the queen's death, "for she said she loved us." Ambassadors, courtiers, and parliamentarians all submitted to Elizabeth's cult of love, in which the queen's gender was transformed from a potential liability into a significant asset. Those who approached her generally did so on their knees and were expected to address her with extravagant compliments fashioned from the period's most passionate love poetry; she in turn spoke, when it suited her to do so, in the language of love poetry. The court moved in an atmosphere of romance, with music, dancing, plays, and the elaborate, fancy-dress entertainments called masques. The queen adorned herself in gorgeous clothes and rich jewels. When she went on one of her summer "progresses," ceremonial journeys through her land, she looked like an exotic, sacred image in a religious cult of love, and her noble hosts virtually bankrupted themselves to lavish upon her the costliest pleasures. England's leading artists, such as the poet Edmund Spenser and the painter Nicholas Hilliard, enlisted themselves in the celebration of Elizabeth's mystery, likening her to the goddesses and queens of mythology: Diana, Astraea, Gloriana. Her cult drew its power from cultural discourses that ranged from the secular (her courtiers could pine for her as a cruel Petrarchan mistress) to the sacred (the veneration that under Catholicism had been due to the Virgin Mary could now be directed toward England's semidivine queen).

There was a sober, even grim, aspect to these poetical fantasies: Elizabeth was brilliant at playing one dangerous faction off another, now turning her gracious smiles on one favorite, now honoring his hated rival, now suddenly looking elsewhere and raising an obscure upstart to royal favor. And when she was disobeyed or when she felt that her prerogatives had been challenged, she was capable of an anger that, as Harington put it, "left no doubtings whose daughter she was." Thus, when Sir Walter Ralegh, one of the queen's glittering favorites, married without her knowledge or consent, he found himself promptly imprisoned in the Tower of London. And when the Protestant polemicist John Stubbs ventured to publish a pamphlet stridently denouncing the queen's proposed marriage to the French Catholic Duke of Alençon, Stubbs and his publisher were arrested and had their right hands chopped off. (After receiving the blow, the now prudent Stubbs lifted his hat with his remaining hand and cried, "God save the Queen!")

The queen's marriage negotiations were a particularly fraught issue. When she came to the throne at twenty-five years old, speculation about a suitable match, already widespread, intensified and remained for decades at a fever pitch, for the stakes were high. If Elizabeth died childless, the Tudor line would come to an end. The nearest heir was her cousin Mary, Queen of Scots, a Catholic whose claim was supported by France and by the papacy, and whose penchant for sexual and political intrigue confirmed the worst fears of English Protestants. The obvious way to avert the nightmare was for Elizabeth to marry and produce an heir, and the pressure upon her to do so was intense.

More than the royal succession hinged on the question of the queen's marriage; Elizabeth's perceived eligibility was a vital factor in the complex machinations of international diplomacy. A dynastic marriage between the Queen of England and a foreign ruler would forge an alliance powerful enough to alter the balance of power in Europe. The English court hosted a steady stream of ambassadors from kings and princes eager to win the hand of the royal maiden, and Elizabeth, who prided herself on speaking fluent French and Italian (and on reading Latin and Greek), played her romantic part with exemplary skill, sighing and spinning the negotiations out for months and even years.

Most probably, she never meant to marry any of her numerous foreign (and domestic) suitors. Such a decisive act would have meant the end of her independence, as well as the end of the marriage game by which she played one power off against another. One day she would seem to be on the verge of accepting a proposal; the next, she would vow never to forsake her virginity. "She is a Princess," the French ambassador remarked, "who can act any part she pleases."

The Kingdom in Danger

Beset by Catholic and Protestant extremists, Elizabeth contrived to forge a moderate compromise that enabled her realm to avert the massacres and civil wars that poisoned France and other countries on the Continent. But menace was never far off, and there were constant fears of conspiracy, rebellion, and assassination. Many of the fears swirled around Mary, Queen of Scots, who had been driven from her own kingdom in 1568 by a powerful faction of rebellious nobles and had taken refuge in England. Her presence, under a kind of house arrest, was the source of intense anxiety and helped generate continual rumors of plots. Some of these plots were real enough, others imaginary, still others traps set in motion by the secret agents of the government's intelligence service under the direction of Sir Francis Walsingham. The situation worsened greatly after the St. Bartholomew's Day Massacre of Protestants (Huguenots) in France (August 24, 1572), after Spanish imperial armies invaded the Netherlands in order to stamp out Protestant rebels, and after the assassination there of Europe's other major Protestant leader, William of Orange (1584).

The queen's life seemed to be in even greater danger after Pope Gregory XIII's proclamation in 1580 that the assassination of the great heretic Elizabeth (who had been excommunicated a decade before) would not constitute a mortal sin. The immediate effect of the proclamation was to make existence more difficult for English Catholics, most of whom were loyal to the queen but who fell under grave suspicion. Suspicion was intensified by the clandestine presence of English Jesuits, trained at seminaries abroad and smuggled back into England to serve the Roman Catholic cause. When Elizabeth's spymaster Walsingham unearthed an assassination plot in the correspondence between the Queen of Scots and the Catholic Anthony Babington, the wretched Mary's fate was sealed. After vacillating, a very reluctant Elizabeth signed the death warrant in February 1587, and her cousin was beheaded.

The long-anticipated military confrontation with Catholic Spain was now unavoidable. Elizabeth learned that Philip II, her former brother-in-law and onetime suitor, was preparing to send an enormous fleet against her island realm. It was to sail to the Netherlands, where a Spanish army would be waiting to embark and invade England. Barring its way was England's small fleet of well-armed and highly maneuverable fighting vessels, backed up by ships from the merchant navy. The Invincible Armada reached English waters in July 1588, only to be routed in one of the most famous and decisive naval battles in European history. Then, in what many viewed as an act of God on behalf of Protestant England, the Spanish fleet was dispersed and all but destroyed by violent storms.

As England braced itself to withstand the invasion that never came, Elizabeth appeared in person to review a detachment of soldiers assembled at Tilbury. Dressed in a white gown and a silver breastplate, she declared that though some among her councillors had urged her not to appear before a large crowd of armed men, she would never fail to trust the loyalty of her faithful and loving subjects. Nor did she fear the Spanish armies. "I know I have the body of a weak and feeble woman," Elizabeth declared, "but I have the heart and stomach of a king, and of England too." In this celebrated speech, Elizabeth displayed many of her most memorable qualities: her self-consciously histrionic command of grand public occasion, her subtle blending of magniloquent rhetoric and the language of love, her strategic appropriation of traditionally masculine qualities, and her great personal courage. "We princes," she once remarked, "are set on stages in the sight and view of all the world."

The English and Otherness

Shakespeare's London had a large population of resident aliens, mainly artisans and merchants and their families, from Portugal, Italy, Spain, Germany, and, above all, France and the Netherlands. Many of these people were Protestant refugees, and they were accorded some legal and economic protection by the government. But they were not always welcome by the local populace. Throughout the sixteenth century, London was the site of repeated demonstrations and, on occasion, bloody riots against the communities of foreign artisans, who were accused of taking jobs away from Englishmen. There was widespread hostility as well toward the Welsh, the Scots, and especially the Irish, whom the English had for centuries been struggling unsuccessfully to subdue. The kings of England claimed to be rulers of Ireland, but in reality they effectively controlled only a small area known as the Pale, extending north from Dublin. The great majority of the Irish people remained stubbornly Catholic and, despite endlessly reiterated English repression, burning of villages, destruction of crops, and massacres, incorrigibly independent.

Shakespeare's *Henry V* (1598–99) seems to invite the audience to celebrate the conjoined heroism of English, Welsh, Scots, and Irish soldiers all fighting together as a "band of brothers" against the French. But such a way of imagining the national community must be set against the tensions and conflicting interests that often set these brothers at each other's throats. As Shakespeare's King Henry realizes, a feared or hated foreign enemy helps at least to mask these tensions, and, indeed, in the face of the Spanish Armada, even the bitter gulf between Catholic and Protestant Englishmen seemed to narrow significantly. But the patriotic alliance was only temporary.

Another way of partially masking the sharp differences in language, belief, and custom among the peoples of the British Isles was to group these people together in contrast to the Jews. Medieval England's Jewish population, the recurrent object of persecution, extortion, and massacre, had been officially expelled by King Edward I in 1290, but Elizabethan England harbored a tiny number of Jews or Jewish converts to

A Jewish man poisoning a well. From Pierre Boaistuau, *Certaine Secrete Wonders of Nature* (1569).

Christianity who were treated with suspicion and hostility. One of these was Elizabeth's own physician, Roderigo Lopez, who was tried in 1594 for an alleged plot to poison the queen. Convicted and condemned to the hideous execution reserved for traitors, Lopez went to his death, in the words of the Elizabethan historian William Camden, "affirming that he loved the Queen as well as he loved Jesus Christ; which coming from a man of the Jewish profession moved no small laughter in the standers-by." It is difficult to gauge the meaning here of the phrase "the Jewish profession," used to describe a man who never, as far as we know, professed Judaism, just as it is difficult to gauge the meaning of the crowd's cruel laughter.

Elizabethans appear to have been fascinated by Jews and Judaism but uncertain whether the terms referred to a people, a foreign nation, a set of strange practices, a living faith, a defunct religion, a villainous conspiracy, or a messianic inheritance. Protestant Reformers brooded deeply on the Hebraic origins of Christianity; government officials ordered the arrest of those "suspected to be Jews"; villagers paid pennies to itinerant fortune-tellers who claimed to be descended from Abraham or masters of cabalistic mysteries; and London playgoers, perhaps including some who laughed at Lopez on the scaffold, enjoyed the spectacle of the downfall of the wicked Barabas in Christopher Marlowe's *Jew of Malta* (c. 1592) and the forced conversion of Shylock in Shakespeare's *Merchant of Venice* (1596–97). Few if any of Shakespeare's contemporaries would have encountered on English soil Jews who openly practiced their religion, though England probably harbored a small number of so-called Marranos, Spanish or Portuguese Jews who had officially converted to Christianity but secretly continued to observe Jewish practices. Jews were not officially permitted to resettle in England until the middle of the seventeenth century, and even then their legal status was ambiguous.

Shakespeare's England also had a small African population whose skin color was the subject of pseudoscientific speculation and theological debate. Some Elizabethans believed that Africans' blackness resulted from the climate of the regions in which they lived, where, as one traveler put it, they were "so scorched and vexed with the heat of the sun, that in many places they curse it when it riseth." Others held that blackness was a curse inherited from their forefather Chus, the son of Ham, who had, according to Genesis, wickedly exposed the nakedness of the drunken Noah. George Best, a proponent of this theory of inherited skin color, reported that "I myself have seen an Ethiopian as black as coal brought into England, who taking a fair English woman to wife, begat a son in all respects as black as the father was, although England were his native country, and an English woman his mother: whereby it seemeth this blackness proceedeth rather of some natural infection of that man."

As the word "infection" suggests, Elizabethans frequently regarded blackness as a physical defect, though the blacks who lived in England and Scotland throughout the sixteenth century were also treated as exotic curiosities. At his marriage to Anne of Denmark, James I entertained his bride and her family by commanding four naked black youths to dance before him in the snow. (The youths died of exposure shortly afterward.) In 1594, in the festivities celebrating the baptism of James's son, a "Black-Moor" entered pulling an elaborately decorated chariot that was, in the original plan, supposed to be drawn in by a lion. There was a black trumpeter in the courts of Henry VII and Henry VIII, while Elizabeth had at least two black servants, one an entertainer and the other a page. Africans became increasingly popular as servants in aristocratic and gentle households in the last decades of the sixteenth century.

Man with head beneath his shoulders. From a Spanish edition of Sir John Mandeville's *Travels*. See *Othello* 1.3.144–45: "and men whose heads / Do grow beneath their shoulders." Such men were occasionally reported by medieval travelers to the East.

An Indian dance. From Thomas Hariot, *A Briefe and True Report of the New Found Land of Virginia* (1590 ed.).

Some of these Africans were almost certainly slaves, though the legal status of slavery in England was ambiguous. In Cartwright's case (1569), the court ruled "that England was too Pure an Air for Slaves to breathe in," but there is evidence that black slaves were owned in Elizabethan and Jacobean England. Moreover, by the mid-sixteenth century, the English had become involved in the profitable trade that carried African slaves to the New World. In 1562, John Hawkins embarked on his first slaving voyage, transporting some three hundred blacks from the Guinea coast to Hispaniola, where they were sold for £10,000. Elizabeth is reported to have said of this venture that it was "detestable, and would call down the Vengeance of Heaven upon the Undertakers." Nevertheless, she invested in Hawkins's subsequent voyages and loaned him ships.

English men and women of the sixteenth century experienced an unprecedented increase in knowledge of the world beyond their island, for a number of reasons. Religious persecution compelled both Catholics and Protestants to live abroad; wealthy gentlemen (and, in at least a few cases, ladies) traveled in France and Italy to view the famous cultural monuments; merchants published accounts of distant lands such as Turkey, Morocco, and Russia; and military and trading ventures took English ships to still more distant shores. In 1496, a Venetian tradesman living in Bristol, John Cabot, was granted a license by Henry VII to sail on a voyage of exploration; with his son Sebastian, he discovered Newfoundland and Nova Scotia. Remarkable feats of seamanship and reconnaissance soon followed: on his ship the *Golden Hind,* Sir Francis Drake circumnavigated the globe in 1579 and laid claim to California on behalf of the queen; a few years later, a ship commanded by Thomas Cavendish also completed a circumnavigation. Sir Martin Frobisher explored bleak Baffin Island in search of a Northwest Passage to the Orient; Sir John Davis explored the west coast of Greenland and discovered the Falkland Islands off the coast of Argentina; Sir Walter Ralegh ventured up the Orinoco Delta, in what is now Venezuela, in search of the mythical land of El Dorado. Accounts of these and other exploits were collected by a clergyman and promoter of empire, Richard Hakluyt, and published as *The Principal Navigations* (1589; expanded edition 1599).

"To seek new worlds for gold, for praise, for glory," as Ralegh characterized such enterprises, was not for the faint of heart: Drake, Cavendish, Frobisher, and Hawkins all died at sea, as did huge numbers of those who sailed under their command. Elizabethans sensible enough to stay at home could do more than read written accounts of their fellow countrymen's far-reaching voyages. Expeditions brought back native plants (including, most famously, tobacco), animals, cultural artifacts, and, on occasion, samples of the native peoples themselves, most often seized against their will. There were exhibitions in London of a kidnapped Eskimo with his kayak and of Virginians with their canoes. Most of these miserable captives, violently uprooted and vulnerable to European diseases, quickly perished, but even in death they were evidently valuable property: when the English will not give one small coin "to relieve a lame beggar," one of the characters in *The Tempest* wryly remarks, "they will lay out ten to see a dead Indian" (2.2.30–31).

Perhaps most nations learn to define what they are by defining what they are not. This negative self-definition is, in any case, what Elizabethans seemed constantly to be doing, in travel books, sermons, political speeches, civic pageants, public exhibitions, and theatrical spectacles of otherness. The extraordinary variety of these exercises (which include public executions and urban riots, as well as more benign forms of curiosity) suggests that the boundaries of national identity were by no means clear and unequivocal. Even peoples whom English writers routinely, viciously stigmatize as irreducibly alien— Italians, Indians, Turks, and Jews—have a surprising instability in the Elizabethan imagination and may appear for brief, intense moments as powerful models to be admired and emulated before they resume their place as emblems of despised otherness.

James I and the Union of the Crowns

Though under great pressure to do so, the aging Elizabeth steadfastly refused to name her successor. It became increasingly apparent, however, that it would be James Stuart, the son of Mary, Queen of Scots, and by the time Elizabeth's health began to fail, several of her principal advisers, including her chief minister, Robert Cecil, had been for several years in secret correspondence with him in Edinburgh. Crowned King James VI of Scotland in 1567 when he was but one year old, Mary's son had been raised as a Protestant by his powerful guardians, and in 1589 he married a Protestant princess, Anne of Denmark. When Elizabeth died on March 24, 1603, English officials reported that on her deathbed the queen had named James to succeed her.

Upon his accession, James—now styled James VI of Scotland and James I of England—made plain his intention to unite his two kingdoms. As he told Parliament in 1604, "What God hath conjoined then, let no man separate. I am the husband, and all of the whole isle is my lawful wife; I am the head and it is my body; I am the shepherd and it is my flock." But the flock was less perfectly united than James optimistically envisioned: English and Scottish were sharply distinct identities, as were Welsh and Cornish and other peoples who were incorporated, with varying degrees of willingness, into the realm.

Fearing that to change the name of the kingdom would invalidate all laws and institutions established under the name of England, a fear that was partly real and partly a cover for anti-Scots prejudice, Parliament balked at James's desire to be called "King of

Funeral procession of Queen Elizabeth. From a watercolor sketch by an unknown artist (1603).

Great Britain" and resisted the unionist legislation that would have made Great Britain a legal reality. Although the English initially rejoiced at the peaceful transition from Elizabeth to her successor, there was a rising tide of resentment against James's advancement of Scots friends and his creation of new knighthoods. Lower down the social ladder, English and Scots occasionally clashed violently on the streets: in July 1603, James issued a proclamation against Scottish "insolencies," and in April 1604, he ordered the arrest of "swaggerers" waylaying Scots in London. The ensuing years did not bring the amity and docile obedience for which James hoped, and, though the navy now flew the Union Jack, combining the Scottish cross of St. Andrew and the English cross of St. George, the unification of the kingdoms remained throughout his reign an unfulfilled ambition.

Unfulfilled as well were James's lifelong dreams of ruling as an absolute monarch. Crown lawyers throughout Europe had long argued that a King, by virtue of his power to make law, must necessarily be above law. But in England, sovereignty was identified not with the King alone or with the people alone but with the "King in Parliament." Against his absolutist ambitions, James faced the crucial power to raise taxes that was vested not in the monarch but in the elected members of the Parliament. He faced as well a theory of republicanism that traced it roots back to ancient Rome and that prided itself on its steadfast and, if necessary, violent resistance to tyranny. Shakespeare's fascination with monarchy is apparent throughout his work, but in his Roman plays in particular, as well as in his long poem *The Rape of Lucrece*, he manifests an intense imaginative interest in the idea of a republic.

The Jacobean Court

With James as with Elizabeth, the royal court was the center of diplomacy, ambition, intrigue, and an intense jockeying for social position. As always in monarchies, proximity to the king's person was a central mark of favor, so that access to the royal bedchamber was one of the highest aims of the powerful, scheming lords who followed James from his sprawling London palace at Whitehall to the hunting lodges and country estates to which he loved to retreat. A coveted office, in the Jacobean as in the Tudor court, was the Groom of the Stool, the person who supervised the disposal of the king's wastes. The officeholder was close to the king at one of his most exposed and vulnerable moments, and enjoyed the further privilege of sleeping on a pallet at the foot of the royal bed and putting on the royal undershirt. Another, slightly less privileged official, the Gentleman of the Robes, dressed the king in his doublet and outer garments.

The royal lifestyle was increasingly expensive. Unlike Elizabeth, James had to maintain separate households for his queen and for the heir apparent, Prince Henry. (Upon Henry's death at the age of eighteen in 1612, his younger brother, Prince Charles, became heir, eventually succeeding his father in 1625.) James was also extremely generous to his friends, amassing his own huge debts in the course of paying off theirs. As early as 1605, he told his principal adviser that "it is a horror to me to think of the height of my place, the greatness of my debts, and the smallness of my means." This smallness notwithstanding, James continued to lavish gifts upon handsome favorites such as the Earl of Somerset, Robert Carr, and the Duke of Buckingham, George Villiers.

The attachment James formed for these favorites was highly romantic. "God so love me," the king wrote to Buckingham, "as I desire only to live in the world for your sake, and that I had rather live banished in any part of the earth with you than live a sorrowful widow's life without you." Such sentiments, not surprisingly, gave rise to widespread rumors of homosexual activities at court. The rumors are certainly plausible, even though the surviving evidence of same-sex relationships, at court or elsewhere, is extremely difficult to interpret. A statute of 1533 made "the detestable and abominable vice of buggery committed with mankind or beast" a felony punishable by death. (English law declined to recognize or criminalize lesbian acts.) The effect of the draconian laws against buggery and sodomy seems to have been to reduce actual prosecutions to the barest minimum: for the next hundred years, there are no known cases of trials resulting in a death sentence for homosexual activity alone. If the legal record is, therefore, unreliable as an index of the extent of homosexual relations, the literary record (including, most famously, the majority of Shakespeare's sonnets) is equally opaque. Any poetic avowal of male-male love may simply be a formal expression of affection based on classical models, or, alternatively, it may be an expression of passionate physical and spiritual love. The interpretive difficulty is compounded by the absence in the period of any clear reference to a homosexual "identity," even though there are many references to same-sex acts and feelings. What is clear is that male friendships at the court of James and elsewhere were suffused with a potential eroticism, at once delightful and threatening, that subsequent periods policed more anxiously.

In addition to the extravagant expenditures on his favorites, James was also the patron of ever more

James I. By John De Critz the Elder (c. 1606).

Two Young Men. By Crispin van den Broeck (c. 1590).

elaborate feasts and masques. Shakespeare's work provides a small glimpse of these in *The Tempest*, with its exotic banquet and its "majestic vision" of mythological goddesses and dancing nymphs and reapers. The actual Jacobean court masques, designed by the great architect, painter, and engineer Inigo Jones, were spectacular, fantastic, technically ingenious, and staggeringly costly celebrations of regal magnificence. With their exquisite costumes and their elegant blend of music, dancing, and poetry, the masques, generally performed by the noble lords and ladies of the court, were deliberately ephemeral exercises in conspicuous expenditure and consumption: by tradition, at the end of the performance, the private audience would rush forward and tear to pieces the gorgeous scenery. And although masques were enormously sophisticated entertainments, often on rather esoteric allegorical themes, they could on occasion collapse into grotesque excess. In a letter of 1606, Sir John Harington describes a masque in honor of the visiting Danish king in which the participants, no doubt toasting their royal majesties, had had too much to drink. A lady playing the part of the Queen of Sheba attempted to present precious gifts, "but, forgetting the steps arising to the canopy, overset her caskets into his Danish Majesty's lap. . . . His Majesty then got up and would dance with the Queen of Sheba; but he fell down and humbled himself before her, and was carried to an inner chamber and laid on a bed." Meanwhile, Harington writes, the masque continued with a pageant of Faith, Hope, and Charity, but Charity could barely keep her balance, while Hope and Faith "were both sick and spewing in the lower hall." This was, we can hope, not a typical occasion.

While the English seem initially to have welcomed James's free-spending ways as a change from the relative parsimoniousness of Queen Elizabeth, they were dismayed by its consequences. Elizabeth had died owing £400,000. In 1608, the royal debt had risen to £1,400,000 and was increasing by £140,000 a year. The money to pay off this debt, or at least to keep it under control, was raised by various means. These included customs farming (leasing the right to collect customs duties to private individuals); the highly unpopular impositions (duties on the import of nonnecessities, such as spices, silks, and currants); the sale of crown lands; the sale of baronetcies; and appeals to an increasingly grudging and recalcitrant Parliament. In 1614, Parliament demanded an end to impositions before it would relieve the king and was angrily dissolved without completing its business.

James's Religious Policy and the Persecution of Witches

Before his accession to the English throne, the king had made known his view of Puritans, the general name for a variety of Protestant sects that were agitating for a radical reform of the Church, the overthrow of its conservative hierarchy of bishops, and the rejection of a large number of traditional rituals and practices. In a book he wrote, *Basilikon Doron* (1599), James denounced "brainsick and heady preachers" who were prepared "to let King, people, law and all be trod underfoot." Yet he was not entirely unwilling to consider religious reforms. In religion, as in foreign policy, he was above all concerned to maintain peace.

On his way south to claim the throne of England in 1603, James was presented with the Millenary Petition (signed by 1,000 ministers), which urged him as "our physician" to heal the disease of lingering "popish" ceremonies. He responded by calling a conference on the ceremonies of the Church of England, which duly took place at Hampton Court Palace in January 1604. The delegates who spoke for reform were moderates, and there was little in the outcome to satisfy Puritans. Nevertheless, while the Church of England continued to cling to such remnants of the Catholic past as wedding rings, square caps, bishops, and Christmas, the conference did produce some reform in the area of ecclesiastical discipline. It also authorized a new English translation of the Bible, known as the King James Bible, which was printed in 1611, too late to have been extensively used by Shakespeare. Along with Shakespeare's works, the King James Bible has probably had the profoundest influence on the subsequent history of English literature.

Having arranged this compromise, James saw his main task as ensuring conformity. He promulgated the 1604 Canons (the first definitive code of canon law since the Reformation), which required all ministers to subscribe to three articles. The first affirmed royal supremacy; the second confirmed that there was nothing in the Book of Common Prayer "contrary to the Word of God" and required ministers to use only the authorized

The "swimming" of a suspected witch (1615).

services; the third asserted that the central tenets of the Church of England were "agreeable to the Word of God." There were strong objections to the second and third articles from those of Puritan leanings inside and outside the House of Commons. In the end, many ministers refused to conform or subscribe to the articles, but only about 90 of them, or 1 percent of the clergy, were deprived of their livings. In its theology and composition, the Church of England was little changed from what it had been under Elizabeth. In hindsight, what is most striking are the ominous signs of growing religious divisions that would by the 1640s burst forth in civil war and the execution of James's son Charles.

James seems to have taken seriously the official claims to the sacredness of kingship, and he certainly took seriously his own theories of religion and politics, which he had printed for the edification of his people. He was convinced that Satan, perpetually warring against God and His representatives on earth, was continually plotting against him. James thought, moreover, that he possessed special insight into Satan's wicked agents, the witches, and in 1597, while King of Scotland, he published his *Daemonology*, a learned exposition of their malign threat to his godly rule. Hundreds of witches, he believed, were involved in a 1590 conspiracy to kill him by raising storms at sea when he was sailing home from Denmark with his new bride.

In the 1590s, Scotland embarked on a virulent witch craze of the kind that had since the fifteenth century repeatedly afflicted France, Switzerland, and Germany, where many thousands of women (and a much smaller number of men) were caught in a nightmarish web of wild accusations. Tortured into lurid confessions of infant cannibalism, night flying, and sexual intercourse with the devil at huge, orgiastic "witches' Sabbaths," the victims had little chance to defend themselves and were routinely burned at the stake.

In England, too, there were witchcraft prosecutions, but on a much smaller scale and with significant differences in the nature of the accusations and the judicial procedures. Witch trials began in England in the 1540s; statutes against witchcraft were enacted in 1542, 1563, and 1604. English law did not allow judicial torture, stipulated lesser punishments in cases of "white magic," and mandated jury trials. Juries acquitted more than half of the defendants in witchcraft trials; in Essex, where the judicial records are particularly extensive, some 24 percent of those accused were executed, while the remainder of those convicted were pilloried and imprisoned or sentenced and reprieved. The accused were generally charged with *maleficium,* an evil deed—usually harming neighbors, causing destructive storms, or killing farm animals—but not with worshipping Satan.

After 1603, when James came to the English throne, he somewhat moderated his enthusiasm for the judicial murder of witches, for the most part defenseless, poor women resented by their neighbors. Although he did nothing to mitigate the ferocity of the ongoing witch hunts in his native Scotland, he did not try to institute Scottish-style persecutions and trials in his new realm. This relative waning of persecutorial eagerness principally reflects the differences between England and Scotland, but it may also bespeak some small, nascent skepticism on James's part about the quality of evidence brought against the accused and about the reliability of the "confessions" extracted from them. It is sobering to reflect that plays like Shakespeare's *Macbeth* (1606), Thomas Middleton's *Witch* (before 1616), and Thomas Dekker, John Ford, and William Rowley's *Witch of Edmonton* (1621) seem to be less the allies of skepticism than the exploiters of fear.

The Playing Field

Cosmic Spectacles

The first permanent, freestanding public theaters in England date only from Shakespeare's own lifetime: a London playhouse, the Red Lion, is mentioned in 1567, and James Burbage's playhouse, The Theatre, was built in 1576. (The innovative use of these new stages, crucial to a full understanding of Shakespeare's achievement, is, in this volume, the subject of a separate essay by the theater historian Andrew Gurr, pages 79–99.) But it is misleading to identify English drama exclusively with these spe-cially constructed playhouses, for in fact there was a rich and vital theatrical tradition in England stretching back for centuries. Many towns in late medieval England were the sites of annual festivals that mounted elaborate cycles of plays depicting the great biblical stories, from the creation of the world to Christ's Passion and its miraculous aftermath. Most of these plays have been lost, but the surviving cycles, such as those from York, are magnificent and complex works of art. They are sometimes called "mys-tery plays," either because they were performed by the guilds of various crafts (known as "mysteries") or, more likely, because they represented the mysteries of the faith. The cycles were most often performed on the annual feast day instituted in the early four-teenth century in honor of the Corpus Christi, the sacrament of the Lord's Supper, which is perhaps the greatest of these religious mysteries.

The Feast of Corpus Christi, celebrated on the Thursday following Trinity Sunday, helped give the play cycles their extraordinary cultural resonance, but it also con-tributed to their downfall. For along with the specifically liturgical plays traditionally performed by religious confraternities and the "saints' plays," which depicted miracu-lous events in the lives of individual holy men and women, the mystery cycles were closely identified with the Catholic Church. Protestant authorities in the sixteenth cen-tury, eager to eradicate all remnants of popular Catholic piety, moved to suppress the annual procession of the Host, with its gorgeous banners, pageant carts, and cycle of visionary plays. In 1548, the Feast of Corpus Christi was abolished. Towns that con-tinued to perform the mysteries were under increasing pressure to abandon them. It is sometimes said that the cycles were already dying out from neglect, but recent research has shown that many towns and their guilds were extremely reluctant to give them up. Desperate offers to strip away any traces of Catholic doctrine and to submit the play scripts to the authorities for their approval met with unbending opposition from the government. In 1576, the courts gave York permission to perform its cycle but only if

> in the said play no pageant be used or set forth wherein the Majesty of God the Father, God the Son, or God the Holy Ghost or the administration of either the Sacraments of baptism or of the Lord's Supper be counterfeited or represented, or anything played which tend to the maintenance of superstition and idolatry or which be contrary to the laws of God . . . or of the realm.

Such "permission" was tantamount to an outright ban. The local officials in the city of Norwich, proud of their St. George and the Dragon play, asked if they could at least parade the dragon costume through the streets, but even this modest request was refused. It is likely that as a young man Shakespeare had seen some of these plays: when Hamlet says of a noisy, strutting theatrical performance that it "out-Herods Herod," he is alluding to the famously bombastic role of Herod of Jewry in the mystery plays. But by the century's end, the cycles were no longer performed.

Early English theater was by no means restricted to these civic and religious festi-vals. Payments to professional and amateur performers appear in early records of towns and aristocratic households, although the terms—"ministralli," "histriones," "mimi," "lusores," and so forth—are not used with great consistency and make it difficult to dis-tinguish among minstrels, jugglers, stage players, and other entertainers. Performers acted in town halls and the halls of guilds and aristocratic mansions, on scaffolds erected in town squares and marketplaces, on pageant wagons in the streets, and in inn yards. By the fifteenth century and probably earlier, there were organized companies of players traveling under noble patronage. Such companies earned a living providing amusement, while enhancing the prestige of the patron.

A description of a provincial performance in the late sixteenth century, written by one R. Willis, provides a glimpse of what seems to have been the usual procedure:

> In the City of Gloucester the manner is (as I think it is in other like corporations) that when the Players of Interludes come to town, they first attend the Mayor to

Panorama of London, showing two theaters, both round and both flying flags: a flying flag indicated that a performance was in progress. The Globe is in the foreground, and the Beargarden or Hope is to the left.

inform him what nobleman's servant they are, and so to get licence for their public playing; and if the Mayor like the Actors, or would show respect to their Lord and Master, he appoints them to play their first play before himself and the Aldermen and common Council of the City and that is called the Mayor's play, where everyone that will come in without money, the Mayor giving the players a reward as he thinks fit to show respect unto them.

In addition to their take from this "first play," the players would almost certainly have supplemented their income by performing in halls and inn yards, where they could pass the hat after the performance or even on some occasions charge an admission fee. It was no doubt a precarious existence.

The "Interludes" mentioned in Willis's description of the Gloucester performances are likely plays that were, in effect, staged dialogues on religious, moral, and political themes. Such works could, like the mysteries, be associated with Catholicism, but they were also used in the sixteenth century to convey polemical Protestant messages, and they reached outside the religious sphere to address secular concerns as well. Henry Medwall's *Fulgens and Lucrece* (c. 1490–1501), for example, pits a wealthy but dissolute nobleman against a virtuous public servant of humble origins, while John Heywood's *Play of the Weather* (c. 1525–33) stages a debate among social rivals, including a gentleman, a merchant, a forest ranger, and two millers. The structure of such plays reflects the training in argumentation that students received in Tudor schools and, in particular, the sustained practice in examining all sides of a difficult question. Some of Shakespeare's amazing ability to look at critical issues from multiple perspectives may be traced back to this practice and the dramatic interludes it helped to inspire.

Another major form of theater that flourished in England in the fifteenth century and continued on into the sixteenth was the morality play. Like the mysteries, moralities addressed questions of the ultimate fate of the soul. They did so, however, not by rehearsing scriptural stories but by dramatizing allegories of spiritual struggle. Typically, a person named Human or Mankind or Youth is faced with a choice between a pious life in the company of such associates as Mercy, Discretion, and Good Deeds and a dissolute life among riotous companions like Lust or Mischief. Plays like *Mankind* (c. 1465–70) and *Everyman* (c. 1495) show how powerful these unpromising-sounding dramas could be, in part because of the extraordinary comic vitality of the evil character, or Vice, and in part because of the poignancy and terror of an individual's encounter with death. Shakespeare clearly grasped this power. The hunchbacked Duke of Gloucester in *Richard III* gleefully likens himself to "the formal Vice, Iniquity." And when Othello wavers between Desdemona and Iago (himself a Vice figure), his anguished dilemma echoes the fateful choice repeatedly faced by the troubled, vulnerable protagonists of the moralities.

If such plays sound a bit like sermons, it is because they were. Clerics and actors shared some of the same rhetorical skills. It would be misleading to regard churchgoing and playgoing as comparable entertainments, but in attacking the stage, ministers often seemed to regard the professional players as dangerous rivals. The players themselves were generally too discreet to rise to the challenge; it would have been foolhardy to present the theater as the Church's direct competitor. Yet in its moral intensity and its command of impassioned language, the stage frequently emulates and outdoes the pulpit.

Music and Dance

Playacting took its place alongside other forms of public expression and entertainment as well. Perhaps the most important, from the perspective of the theater, were music and dance, since these were directly and repeatedly incorporated into plays. Many plays, comedies and tragedies alike, include occasions that call upon the characters to dance: hence Beatrice and Benedick join the other masked guests at the dance in *Much Ado About Nothing;* in *Twelfth Night,* the befuddled Sir Andrew, at the instigation of the drunken Sir Toby Belch, displays his skill, such as it is, in capering; Romeo and Juliet first see each other at the Capulet ball; the witches dance in a ring around the hideous caldron and perform an "antic round" to cheer Macbeth's spirits; and, in one of Shakespeare's strangest and most wonderful scenes, the drunken Antony in *Antony and Cleopatra* joins hands with Caesar, Enobarbus, Pompey, and others to dance "the Egyptian Bacchanals."

Moreover, virtually all plays in the period, including Shakespeare's, apparently ended with a dance. Brushing off the theatrical gore and changing their expressions from woe to pleasure, the actors in plays like *Hamlet* and *King Lear* would presumably have received the audience's applause and then bid for a second round of applause by performing a stately pavane or a lively jig. Indeed, jigs, with their comical leaping dance steps often accompanied by scurrilous ballads, became so popular that they drew not only large crowds but also official disapproval. A court order of 1612 complained about the "cutpurses and other lewd and ill-disposed persons" who flocked to the theater at the end of every play to be entertained by "lewd jigs, songs, and dances." The players were warned to suppress these disreputable entertainments on pain of imprisonment.

The displays of dancing onstage clearly reflected a widespread popular interest in dancing outside the walls of the playhouse as well. Renaissance intellectuals conjured up visions of the universe as a great cosmic dance, poets figured relations between men and women in terms of popular dance steps, stern moralists denounced dancing as an incitement to filthy lewdness, and, perhaps as significant, men of all classes evidently spent a great deal of time worrying about how shapely their legs looked in tights and how gracefully they could leap. Shakespeare assumes that his audience will be quite familiar with a variety of dances. "For hear me, Hero," Beatrice tells her friend, "wooing, wedding, and repenting is as a Scotch jig, a measure, and a cinquepace" (2.1.60–61). Her speech dwells on the comparison a bit, teasing out its implications, but it still does not make much sense if you do not already know something about the dances and perhaps occasionally venture to perform them yourself.

Closely linked to dancing and even more central to the stage was music, both instrumental and vocal. In the early sixteenth century, the Reformation had been disastrous for sacred music: many church organs were destroyed, choir schools were closed, the glorious polyphonal liturgies sung in the monasteries were suppressed. But by the latter part of the century, new perspectives were reinvigorating English music. Latin Masses were reset in English, and tunes were written for newly translated, metrical psalms. More important for the theater, styles of secular music were developed that emphasized music's link to humanist eloquence, its ability to heighten and to rival rhetorically powerful texts.

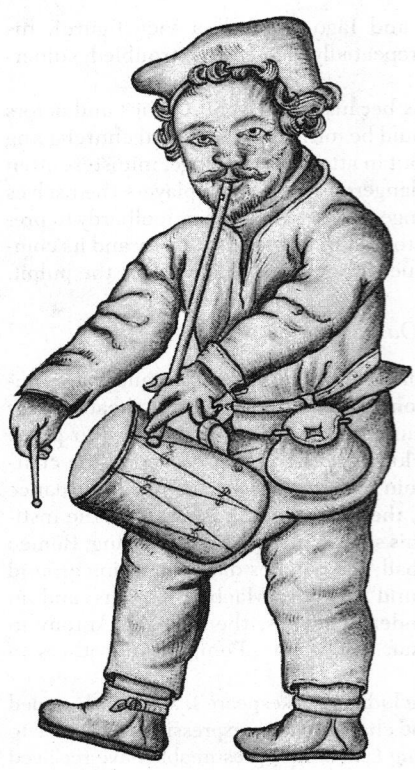

Richard Tarlton. Tarlton was the lead comedian of the Queen's Company from 1583, the year of its founding, until 1588, when he died.

This link is particularly evident in vocal music, at which Elizabethan composers excelled. Renowned composers William Byrd, Thomas Morley, John Dowland, and others wrote a rich profusion of madrigals (part songs for two to eight voices unaccompanied) and ayres (songs for solo voice, generally accompanied by the lute). These works, along with hymns, popular ballads, rounds, catches, and other forms of song, enjoyed immense popularity, not only in the royal court, where musical skill was regarded as an important accomplishment, and in aristocratic households, where professional musicians were employed as entertainers, but also in less exalted social circles. In his *Plaine and Easie Introduction to Practicall Musicke* (1597), Morley tells a story of social humiliation at a failure to perform that suggests that a well-educated Elizabethan was expected to be able to sing at sight. Even if this is an exaggeration in the interest of book sales, there is evidence of impressively widespread musical literacy, reflected in a splendid array of music for the lute, viol, recorder, harp, and virginal, as well as the marvelous vocal music.

Whether it is the aristocratic Orsino luxuriating in the dying fall of an exquisite melody or bully Bottom craving "the tongs and the bones," Shakespeare's characters frequently call for music. They also repeatedly give voice to the age's conviction that there was a deep relation between musical harmony and the harmonies of the well-ordered individual and state. "The man that hath no music in himself," warns Lorenzo in *The Merchant of Venice*, "nor is not moved with concord of sweet sounds, / Is fit for treasons, stratagems, and spoils" (5.1.82–84). This conviction, in turn, reflects a still deeper link between musical harmony and the divinely created harmony of the cosmos. When Ulysses, in *Troilus and Cressida*, wishes to convey the image of universal chaos, he speaks of the untuning of a string (1.3.109).

The playing companies must have regularly employed trained musicians, and many actors (like the actor who in playing Pandarus in *Troilus and Cressida* is supposed to accompany himself on the lute) must have possessed musical skill. Unfortunately, we possess the original settings for very few of Shakespeare's songs, possibly because many of them may have been set to popular tunes of the time that everyone knew and no one bothered to write down.

Alternative Entertainments

Plays, music, and dancing were by no means the only shows in town. There were jousts, tournaments, royal entries, religious processions, pageants in honor of newly installed civic officials or ambassadors arriving from abroad; wedding masques, court masques, and costumed entertainments known as "disguisings" or "mummings"; juggling acts, fortune-tellers, exhibitions of swordsmanship, mountebanks, folk healers, storytellers, magic shows; bearbaiting, bullbaiting, cockfighting, and other blood sports; folk festivals such as Maying, the Feast of Fools, Carnival, and Whitsun Ales. For several years, Elizabethan Londoners were delighted by a trained animal—Banks's Horse—that could, it was thought, do arithmetic and answer questions. And there was always the grim but compelling spectacle of public shaming, mutilation, and execution.

Most English towns had stocks and whipping posts. Drunks, fraudulent merchants, adulterers, and quarrelers could be placed in carts or mounted backward on asses and paraded through the streets for crowds to jeer and throw refuse at. Women accused of being scolds could be publicly muzzled by an iron device called a "brank" or tied to a cucking stool and dunked in the river. Convicted criminals could have their ears cut off, their noses slit, their foreheads branded. Public beheadings (generally reserved for the elite) and hangings were common. In the worst cases, felons were sentenced to be "hanged by the neck, and being alive cut down, and your privy members to be cut off, and your bowels to be taken out of your belly and there burned, you being alive."

Shakespeare occasionally takes note of these alternative entertainments: at the end of *Macbeth,* for example, with his enemies closing in on him, the doomed tyrant declares, "They have tied me to a stake. I cannot fly,/But bear-like I must fight the course" (5.7.1–2). The audience is reminded then that it is witnessing the human equivalent of a popular spectacle—a bear chained to a stake and attacked by fierce dogs—that they could have paid to watch at an arena near the Globe. And when, a few moments later, Macduff enters carrying Macbeth's head, the audience is seeing the theatrical equivalent of the execution of criminals and traitors that they could have also watched in the flesh, as it were, nearby. In a different key, the audiences who paid to see *A Midsummer Night's Dream* or *The Winter's Tale* got to enjoy the comic spectacle of a Maying and a Whitsun Pastoral, while the spectators of *The Tempest* could gawk at what the Folio list of characters calls a "salvage and deformed slave" and to enjoy an aristocratic magician's wedding masque in honor of his daughter.

An Elizabethan hanging.

The Enemies of the Stage

In 1624, a touring company of players arrived in Norwich and requested permission to perform. Permission was denied, but the municipal authorities, "in regard of the honorable respect which this City beareth to the right honorable the Lord Chamberlain," gave the players 20 shillings to get out of town. Throughout the sixteenth and early seventeenth centuries, there are many similar records of civic officials prohibiting performances and then, to appease a powerful patron, paying the actors to take their skills elsewhere. As early as the 1570s, there is evidence that the London authorities, while mindful of the players' influential protectors, were energetically trying to drive the theater out of the city.

Why should what we now regard as one of the undisputed glories of the age have aroused so much hostility? One answer, curiously enough, is traffic: plays drew large audiences—the public theaters could accommodate thousands—and residents objected to the crowds, the noise, and the crush of carriages. Other, more serious concerns were public health and crime. It was thought that numerous diseases, including the dreaded bubonic plague, were spread by noxious odors, and the packed playhouses were obvious breeding grounds for infection. (Patrons often tried to protect themselves by sniffing nosegays or stuffing cloves into their nostrils.) The large crowds drew pickpockets and other scoundrels. On one memorable afternoon, a pickpocket was caught in the act and tied for the duration of the play to one of the posts that held up the canopy above the stage.

Syphilis victim in a tub. Frontispiece to the play *Cornelianum Dolium* (1638), possibly authored by Thomas Randolph. The tub inscription translates as "I sit on the throne of love, I suffer in the tub," and the banner as "Farewell O sexual pleasures and lusts."

The theater was, moreover, a well-known haunt of prostitutes and, it was alleged, a place where innocent maids were seduced and respectable matrons corrupted. It was darkly rumored that "chambers and secret places" adjoined the theater galleries, and in any case, taverns, disreputable inns, and whorehouses were close at hand.

There were other charges as well. Plays were performed in the afternoon and, therefore, drew people, especially the young, away from their work. They were schools of idleness, luring apprentices from their trades, law students from their studies, housewives from their kitchens, and potentially pious souls from the sober meditations to which they might otherwise devote themselves. Wasting their time and money on disreputable shows, citizens exposed themselves to sexual provocation and outright political sedition. Even when the content of plays was morally exemplary—and, of course, few plays were so gratifyingly high-minded—the theater itself, in the eyes of most mayors and aldermen, was inherently disorderly.

The attack on the stage by civic officials was echoed and intensified by many of the age's moralists and religious leaders, especially those associated with Puritanism. While English Protestants earlier in the sixteenth century had attempted to counter the Catholic mystery cycles and saints' plays by mounting their own doctrinally correct dramas, by the century's end a fairly widespread consensus, even among those mildly sympathetic toward the theater, held that the stage and the pulpit were in tension with one another. After 1591, a ban on Sunday performances was strictly enforced, and in 1606, Parliament passed an act imposing a fine of £10 on any person who shall "in any stage-play, interlude, show, May-game, or pageant, jestingly or profanely speak or use the holy name of God, or of Christ Jesus, or of the Holy Ghost, or of the Trinity (which are not to be spoken but with fear and reverence)." If changes in the printed texts are a reliable indication, the players seem to have complied at least to some degree with the ruling. The Folio (1623) text of *Richard III*, for example, omits the Quarto's (1597) four uses of "zounds" (for "God's wounds"), along with a mention of "Christ's dear blood shed for our grievous sins"; "God's my judge" in *The Merchant of Venice* becomes "well I know"; "By Jesu" in *Henry V* becomes a very proper "I say"; and in all the plays, "God" from time to time metamorphoses to "Jove."

But for some of the theater's more extreme critics, these modest expurgations were tiny bandages on a gaping wound. In his huge book *Histriomastix* (1633), William Prynne regurgitates half a century of frenzied attacks on the "sinful, heathenish, lewd, ungodly Spectacles." In the eyes of Prynne and his fellow antitheatricalists, stage plays were part of a demonic tangle of obscene practices proliferating like a cancer in the body of society. It is "manifest to all men's judgments," he writes, that

> effeminate mixed dancing, dicing, stage-plays, lascivious pictures, wanton fashions, face-painting, health-drinking, long hair, love-locks, periwigs, women's curling, powdering and cutting of their hair, bonfires, New-year's gifts, May-games, amorous pastorals, lascivious effeminate music, excessive laughter, luxurious disorderly Christmas-keeping, mummeries . . . [are] wicked, unchristian pastimes.

Given the anxious emphasis on effeminacy, it is not surprising that denunciations of this kind obsessively focused on the use of boy actors to play the female parts. The enemies of the stage charged that theatrical transvestism excited illicit sexual desires, both heterosexual and homosexual.

Since cross-dressing violated a biblical prohibition (Deuteronomy 22:5), religious antitheatricalists attacked it as wicked regardless of its erotic charge; indeed, they often seemed to consider any act of impersonation as inherently wicked. In their view, the theater itself was Satan's domain. Thus a Cambridge scholar, John Greene, reports the sad fate of "a Christian woman" who went to the theater to see a play: "She entered in well and sound, but she returned and came forth possessed of the devil. Whereupon certain godly brethren demanded Satan how he durst be so bold, as to enter into her a Christian. Whereto he answered, that *he found her in his own house,* and therefore took possession of her as his own" (italic in original). When the "godly brethren" came to power in the mid-seventeenth century, with the overthrow of Charles I, they saw to it that the playhouses, temporarily shut down in 1642 at the onset of the Civil War, remained closed. The theater did not resume until the restoration of the monarchy in 1660.

Faced with enemies among civic officials and religious leaders, Elizabethan and Jacobean playing companies relied on the protection of their powerful patrons. As the liveried servants of aristocrats or of the monarch, the players could refute the charge that they were mere vagabonds, and they claimed, as a convenient legal fiction, that their public performances were necessary rehearsals in anticipation of those occasions when they would be called upon to entertain their noble masters. But harassment by the mayor and aldermen continued unabated, and the players were forced to build their theaters outside the immediate jurisdiction of the city authorities, either in the suburbs or in the areas known as the "liberties." A liberty was a piece of land within the City of London itself that was not directly subject to the authority of the lord mayor. The most significant of these from the point of view of the theater was the area near St. Paul's Cathedral called "the Blackfriars," where, until the dissolution of the monasteries in 1538, there had been a

Dominican monastery. It was here that in 1608 Shakespeare's company, then called the King's Men, built the indoor playhouse in which they performed during the winter months, reserving the open-air Globe in the suburb of Southwark for their summer performances.

Censorship and Regulation

In addition to those authorities who campaigned to shut down the theater, there were others whose task was to oversee, regulate, and censor it. Given the outright hostility of the former, the latter may have seemed to the London players equivocal allies rather than enemies. After all, plays that passed the censor were at least licensed to be performed and hence conceded to have some limited legitimacy. In April 1559, at the very start of her reign, Queen Elizabeth drafted a proposal that for the first time envisaged a system for the prior review and regulation of plays throughout her kingdom:

> The Queen's Majesty doth straightly forbid all manner interludes to be played either openly or privately, except the same be notified beforehand, and licensed within any city or town corporate, by the mayor or other chief officers of the same, and within any shire, by such as shall be lieutenants for the Queen's Majesty in the same shire, or by two of the Justices of Peace inhabiting within that part of the shire where any shall be played. . . . And for instruction to every of the said officers, her Majesty doth likewise charge every of them, as they will answer: that they permit none to be played wherein either matters of religion or of the governance of the estate of the commonweal shall be handled or treated upon, but by men of authority, learning and wisdom, nor to be handled before any audience, but of grave and discreet persons.

This proposal, which may not have been formally enacted, makes an important distinction between those who are entitled to address sensitive issues of religion and politics—authors "of authority, learning and wisdom" addressing audiences "of grave and discreet persons"—and those who are forbidden to do so.

The London public theater, with its playwrights who were the sons of glovers, shoemakers, and bricklayers and its audiences in which the privileged classes mingled with rowdy apprentices, masked women, and servants, was clearly not a place to which the government wished to grant freedom of expression. In 1581, the Master of the Revels, an official in the lord chamberlain's department whose role had hitherto been to provide entertainment at court, was given an expanded commission. Sir Edmund Tilney, the functionary who held the office, was authorized

> to warn, command, and appoint in all places within this our Realm of England, as well within franchises and liberties as without, all and every player or players with their playmakers, either belonging to any nobleman or otherwise . . . to appear before him with all such plays, tragedies, comedies, or shows as they shall in readiness or mean to set forth, and them to recite before our said Servant or his sufficient deputy, whom we ordain, appoint, and authorize by these presents of all such shows, plays, players, and playmakers, together with their playing places, to order and reform, authorize and put down, as shall be thought meet or unmeet unto himself or his said deputy in that behalf.

What emerged from this commission was in effect a national system of regulation and censorship. One of its consequences was to restrict virtually all licensed theater to the handful of authorized London-based playing companies. These companies would have to submit their plays for official scrutiny, but in return they received implicit, and on occasion explicit, protection against the continued fierce opposition of the local authorities. Plays reviewed and allowed by the Master of the Revels had been deemed fit to be performed before the monarch; how could mere aldermen legitimately claim that such plays should be banned as seditious?

The key question, of course, is how carefully the Master of the Revels scrutinized the plays brought before him either to hear or, more often from the 1590s onward, to peruse. What was Tilney, who served in the office until his death in 1610, or his successor, Sir George Buc, who served from 1610 to 1621, looking for? What did they insist be cut before they would release what was known as the "allowed copy," the only version licensed for performance? Unfortunately, the office books of the Master of the Revels in Shakespeare's time have been lost; what survives is a handful of scripts on which Tilney, Buc, and their assistants jotted their instructions. These suggest that the readings were rather painstaking, with careful attention paid to possible religious, political, and diplomatic repercussions. References, directly or strongly implied, to any living Christian prince or any important English nobleman, gentleman, or government official were particularly sensitive and likely to be struck. Renaissance political life was highly personalized; people in power were exceptionally alert to insult and zealously patrolled the boundaries of their prestige and reputation.

Moreover, the censors knew that audiences and readers were quite adept at applying theatrical representations distanced in time and space to their own world. At a time of riots against resident foreigners, Tilney read *Sir Thomas More*, a play in which Shakespeare probably had a hand, and instructed the players to cut scenes that, even though they were set in 1517, might have had an uncomfortable contemporary resonance. "Leave out the insurrection wholly," Tilney's note reads, "and the cause thereof and begin with Sir Thomas More at the Mayor's sessions, with a report afterwards of his good service done being sheriff of London upon a mutiny against the Lombards only by a short report and not otherwise at your own perils. E. Tilney." Of course, as Tilney knew perfectly well, most plays succeed precisely by mirroring, if only obliquely, their own times, but this particular reflection evidently seemed to him too dangerous or provocative.

The topical significance of a play depends in large measure on the particular moment in which it is performed and on certain features of the performance—for example, a striking resemblance between one of the characters and a well-known public figure—that the script itself will not necessarily disclose to us at this great distance or even to the censor at the time. Hence the Master of the Revels noted angrily of one play performed in 1632 that "there were diverse personated so naturally, both of lords and others of the court, that I took it ill." Hence, too, a play that was deemed allowable when it was first written and performed could return, like a nightmare, to haunt a different place and time. The most famous instance of such a return involves Shakespeare, for on the day before the Earl of Essex's attempted coup against Queen Elizabeth in 1601, someone paid the Lord Chamberlain's Men (the name of Shakespeare's company at the time) 40 shillings to revive their old play about the deposition and murder of Richard II. "I am Richard II," the queen declared. "Know ye not that?" However distressed she was by this performance, the queen significantly did not take out her wrath on the players: neither the playwright nor his company was punished, nor was the Master of the Revels criticized for allowing the play in the first place. It was Essex and several of his key supporters who lost their heads.

Evidence suggests that the Master of the Revels often regarded himself not as the strict censor of the theater but as its friendly guardian, charged with averting catastrophes. He was a bureaucrat concerned less with subversive ideas per se than with potential trouble. That is, there is no record of a dramatist being called to account for his heterodox beliefs; rather, plays were censored if they risked offending influential people, including important foreign allies, or if they threatened to cause public disorder by exacerbating religious or other controversies. The distinction is not a stable one, but it helps to explain the intellectual boldness, power, and freedom of a censored theater in a society in which the perceived enemies of the state were treated mercilessly. Shakespeare could have Lear articulate a searing indictment of social injustice—

> Robes and furred gowns hide all. Plate sin with gold,
> And the strong lance of justice hurtless breaks;
> Arm it in rags, a pygmy's straw does pierce it.
>
> (4.5.155–57)

—and evidently neither the Master of the Revels nor the courtiers in their robes and furred gowns protested. But when the Spanish ambassador complained about Thomas Middleton's anti-Spanish allegory *A Game at Chess,* performed at the Globe in 1624, the whole theater was shut down, the players were arrested, and the king professed to be furious at his official for licensing the play in the first place and allowing it to be performed for nine consecutive days.

In addition to the system for the licensing of plays for performance, there was also a system for the licensing of plays for publication. At the start of Shakespeare's career, such press licensing was the responsibility of the Court of High Commission, headed by the Archbishop of Canterbury and the Bishop of London. Their deputies, a panel of junior clerics, were supposed to review the manuscripts, granting licenses to those worthy of publication and rejecting any they deemed "heretical, seditious, or unseemly for Christian ears." Without a license, the Stationers' Company, the guild of the book trade, was not supposed to register a manuscript for publication. In practice, as various complaints and attempts to close loopholes attest, some playbooks were printed without a license. In 1607, the system was significantly revised when Sir George Buc began to license plays for the press. When Buc succeeded to the post of Master of the Revels in 1610, the powers to license plays for the stage and the page were vested in one man.

Theatrical Innovations

The theater continued to flourish under this system of regulation after Shakespeare's death; by the 1630s, as many as five playhouses were operating daily in London. When the theater reemerged after the eighteen-year hiatus imposed by Puritan rule, it quickly resumed its cultural importance, but not without a number of significant changes. Major innovations in staging resulted principally from Continental influences on the English artists who accompanied the court of Charles II into exile in France, where they supplied it with masques and other theatrical entertainments.

The institutional conditions and business practices of the two companies chartered by Charles after the Restoration in 1660 also differed from those of Shakespeare's theater. In place of the more collective practice of Shakespeare's company, the Restoration theaters were controlled by celebrated actor-managers who not only assigned themselves starring roles, in both comedy and tragedy, but also assumed sole responsibility for many business decisions, including the setting of their colleagues' salaries. At the same time, the power of the actor-manager, great as it was, was limited by the new importance of outside capital. No longer was the theater, with all of its properties from script to costumes, owned by the "sharers"—that is, by those actors who held shares in the joint-stock company. Instead, entrepreneurs would raise capital for increasingly fantastic sets and stage machinery that could cost as much as £3,000, an astronomical sum, for a single production. This investment, in turn, not only influenced the kinds of new plays written for the theater but helped to transform old plays that were revived, including Shakespeare's.

In his diary entry for August 24, 1661, Samuel Pepys notes that he has been "to the Opera, and there saw Hamlet, Prince of Denmark, done with scenes very well, but above all, Betterton did the prince's part beyond imagination." This is Thomas Betterton's first review, as it were, and it is typical of the enthusiasm he would inspire throughout his fifty-year career on the London stage. Pepys's brief and scattered remarks on the plays he voraciously attended in the 1660s are precious because they are among the few records from the period of concrete and immediate responses to theatrical performances. Modern readers might miss the significance of Pepys's phrase "done with scenes": this production of *Hamlet* was only the third play to use the movable sets first introduced to England by its producer, William Davenant. The central historical fact that makes the productions of this period so exciting is that public theater had been banned altogether for eighteen years until the Restoration of Charles II.

A brief discussion of theatrical developments in the Restoration period will enable us at least to glance longingly at a vast subject that lies outside the scope of this introduction: the rich performance history that extends from Shakespeare's time to our own, involving tens of thousands of productions and adaptations for theater, opera, Broadway musicals, and, of course, films. The scale of this history is vast in space as well as time: as early as 1607, there is a record of a *Hamlet* performed on board an English ship, HMS *Dragon,* off the coast of Sierra Leone, and troupes of English actors performed in the late sixteenth and early seventeenth centuries as far afield as Poland and Bohemia.

William Davenant, who claimed to be Shakespeare's bastard son, had become an expert on stage scenery while producing masques at the court of Charles I, and when the theaters reopened, he set to work on converting an indoor tennis court into a new kind of theater. He designed a broad open platform like that of the Elizabethan stage, but he replaced the relatively shallow space for "discoveries" (tableaux set up in an opening at the center of the stage, revealed by drawing back a curtain) and the "tiring-house" (the players' dressing room) behind this space with one expanded interior, framed by a proscenium arch, in which scenes could be displayed. These elaborately painted scenes could be moved on and off, using grooves on the floor. The perspectival effect for a spectator of one central painted panel with two "wings" on either side was that of three sides of a room. This effect anticipated that of the familiar "picture frame" stage, developed fully in the nineteenth century, and began a subtle shift in theater away from the elaborate verbal descriptions that are so central to Shakespeare and toward the evocative visual poetry of the set designer's art.

Another convention of Shakespeare's stage, the use of boy actors for female roles, gave way to the more complete illusion of women playing women's parts. The king issued a decree in 1662 forcefully permitting, if not requiring, the use of actresses. The royal decree is couched in the language of social and moral reform: the introduction of actresses will require the "reformation" of scurrilous and profane passages in plays, and this, in turn, will help forestall some of the objections that shut the theaters down in 1642. In reality, male theater audiences, composed of a narrower range of courtiers and aristocrats than in Shakespeare's time, met this intended reform with the assumption that the new actresses were fair game sexually; most actresses (with the partial exception of those who married male members of their troupes) were regarded as, or actually became, whores. But despite the social stigma and the fact that their salaries were predictably lower than those of their male counterparts, the stage saw some formidable female stars by the 1680s.

The first recorded appearance of an actress was that of a Desdemona in December 1660. Betterton's Ophelia in 1661 was Mary Saunderson (c. 1637–1712), who became Mrs. Betterton a year later. The most famous Ophelia of the period was Susanna Mountfort, who appeared in that role for the first time at the age of fifteen in 1705. The performance by Mountfort that became legendary occurred in 1720, after a disappointment in love, or so it was said, had driven her mad. Hearing that *Hamlet* was being performed, Mountfort escaped from her keepers and reached the theater, where she concealed herself until the scene in which Ophelia enters in her state of insanity. At this point, Mountfort rushed onto the stage and, in the words of a contemporary, "was in truth Ophelia herself, to the amazement of the performers and the astonishment of the audience."

That the character Ophelia became increasingly and decisively identified with the mad scene owes something to this occurrence, but it is also a consequence of the text used for Restoration performances of *Hamlet.* Having received the performance rights to a good number of Shakespeare's plays, Davenant altered them for the stage in the 1660s, and many of these acting versions remained in use for generations. In the case of *Hamlet,* neither Davenant nor his successors did what they so often did with other plays by Shakespeare—that is, alter the plot radically and interpolate other material. But many of the lines were cut or "improved." The cuts included most of Ophelia's sane speeches, such as her spirited retort to Laertes' moralizing; what remained made her part almost entirely an emblem of "female love melancholy."

Thomas Betterton (1635–1710), the prototype of the actor-manager, who would be the dominant figure in Shakespeare interpretation and in the theater generally through

The Spanish Tragedie:
OR,
Hieronimo is mad againe.

Containing the lamentable end of *Don Horatio*, and
Belimperia; with the pittifull death of *Hieronimo*.

Newly corrected, amended, and enlarged with new
Additions of the *Painters* part, and others, as
it hath of late been diuers times acted.

LONDON,
Printed by W. White, for I. White and T. Langley,
and are to be fold at their Shop ouer againft the
Sarazens head without New-gate. 1615.

Title page of Thomas Kyd's *Spanish Tragedie*
(1615). The first known edition dates from 1592.

the nineteenth century, made Hamlet his premier role. A contemporary who saw his last performance in the part (at the age of seventy-four, a rather old Prince of Denmark) wrote that to *read* Shakespeare's play was to encounter "dry, incoherent, & broken sentences," but that to see Betterton was to "prove" that the play was written "correctly." Spectators especially admired his reaction to the Ghost's appearance in the Queen's bedchamber: "his Countenance . . . thro' the violent and sudden Emotions of Amazement and Horror, turn[ed] instantly on the Sight of his fathers Spirit, as pale as his Neckcloath, when every Article of his Body seem's affected with a Tremor inexpressible." A piece of stage business in this scene, Betterton's upsetting his chair on the Ghost's entrance, became so thoroughly identified with the part that later productions were censured if the actor left it out. This business could very well have been handed down from Richard Burbage, the star of Shakespeare's original production, for Davenant, who had coached Betterton in the role, had known the performances of Joseph Taylor, who had succeeded Burbage in it. It is strangely gratifying to notice that Hamlets on stage and screen still occasionally upset their chairs.

Shakespeare's Life and Art

Playwrights, even hugely successful playwrights, were not ordinarily the objects of popular curiosity in early modern England, and few personal documents survive from Shakespeare's life of the kind that usually give the biographies of artists their appeal: no diary, no letters, private or public, no accounts of his childhood, almost no contemporary gossip, no scandals. Shakespeare's exact contemporary, the great playwright Christopher Marlowe, lived a mere twenty-nine years—he was murdered in 1593—but he left behind tantalizing glimpses of himself in police documents, the memos of high-ranking government officials, and detailed denunciations by sinister double agents. Ben Jonson recorded his opinions and his reading in a remarkable published notebook, *Timber; or, Discoveries Made upon Men and Matter,* and he also shared his views of the world (including some criticisms of his fellow playwright Shakespeare) with a Scottish poet, William Drummond of Hawthornden, who had the wit to jot them down for posterity. From Shakespeare, there is nothing comparable, not even a book with his name scribbled on the cover and a few marginal notes such as we have for Jonson, let alone working notebooks.

Yet Elizabethan England was a record-keeping society, and centuries of archival labor have turned up a substantial number of traces of its greatest playwright and his family. By themselves the traces would have relatively little interest, but in the light of Shakespeare's plays and poems, they have come to seem like precious relics and manage to achieve a considerable resonance.

Shakespeare's Family

William Shakespeare's grandfather Richard farmed land by the village of Snitterfield, near the small, pleasant market town of Stratford-upon-Avon, about 96 miles northwest of London. The playwright's father, John, moved in the mid-sixteenth century to Stratford, where he became a successful glover, landowner, moneylender, and dealer in wool and other agricultural goods. In or about 1557, he married Mary Arden, the daughter of a prosperous and well-connected farmer from the same area, Robert Arden of Wilmcote.

John Shakespeare was evidently highly esteemed by his fellow townspeople, for he held a series of important posts in local government. In 1556, he was appointed ale taster, an office reserved for "able persons and discreet," in 1558 was sworn in as a constable, and in 1561 was elected as one of the town's fourteen burgesses. As burgess, John served as one of the two chamberlains, responsible for administering borough property and revenues. In 1567, he was elected bailiff, Stratford's highest elective office and the equivalent of mayor. Although John Shakespeare signed all official documents with a cross or other sign, it is likely, but not certain, that he knew how to read and write. Mary, who also signed documents only with her mark, is less likely to have been literate.

According to the parish registers, which recorded baptisms and burials, the Shakespeares had eight children, four daughters and four sons, beginning with a daughter Joan born in 1558. A second daughter, Margaret, was born in December 1562 and died a few months later. William Shakespeare ("Gulielmus, filius Johannes Shakespeare"), their first son, was baptized on April 26, 1564. Since there was usually a few days' lapse between birth and baptism, it is conventional to celebrate Shakespeare's birthday on April 23, which happens to coincide with the feast of St. George, England's patron saint, and with the day of Shakespeare's death fifty-two years later.

William Shakespeare had three younger brothers, Gilbert, Richard, and Edmund, and two younger sisters, Joan and Anne. (It was often the custom to recycle a name, so the firstborn Joan must have died before the birth in 1569 of another daughter

"Southeast Prospect of Stratford-upon-Avon, 1746." From *The Gentleman's Magazine* (December 1792).

christened Joan, the only one of the girls to survive childhood.) Gilbert, who died in his forty-fifth year in 1612, is described in legal records as a Stratford haberdasher; Edmund followed William to London and became a professional actor, but evidently of no particular repute. He was only twenty-eight when he died in 1607 and was given an expensive funeral, perhaps paid for by his successful older brother.

At the high point of his public career, John Shakespeare, the father of this substantial family, applied to the Herald's College for a coat of arms, which would have marked his (and his family's) elevation from the ranks of substantial middle-class citizenry to that of the gentry. But the application went nowhere, for soon after he initiated what would have been a costly petitioning process, John apparently fell on hard times. The decline must have begun when William was still living at home, a boy of twelve or thirteen. From 1576 onward, John Shakespeare stopped attending council meetings. He became caught up in costly lawsuits, started mortgaging his land, and incurred substantial debts. In 1586, he was finally replaced on the council; in 1592, he was one of nine Stratford men listed as absenting themselves from church out of fear of being arrested for debt.

The reason for the reversal in John Shakespeare's fortunes is unknown. Some have speculated that it may have stemmed from adherence to Catholicism, since those who remained loyal to the old faith were subject to increasingly vigorous and costly discrimination. But if John Shakespeare was a Catholic, as seems quite possible, it would not necessarily explain his decline, since other Catholics (and Puritans) in Elizabethan Stratford and elsewhere managed to hold on to their offices. In any case, his fall from prosperity and local power, whatever its cause, was not absolute. In 1601, the last year of his life, his name was included among those qualified to speak on behalf of Stratford's rights. And he was by that time entitled to bear a coat of arms, for in 1596, some twenty years after the application to the Herald's office had been initiated, it was successfully renewed. There is no record of who paid for the bureaucratic procedures that made the grant possible, but it is likely to have been John's oldest son William, by that time a highly successful London playwright.

Education

Stratford was a small provincial town, but it had long been the site of an excellent free school, originally established by the Church in the thirteenth century. The main purpose of such schools in the Middle Ages had been to train prospective clerics; since many aristocrats could neither read nor write, literacy by itself conferred no special distinction and was not routinely viewed as desirable. But the situation began to change markedly in the sixteenth century. Protestantism placed a far greater emphasis upon lay literacy: for the sake of salvation, it was crucially important to be intimately acquainted with the Holy Book, and printing made that book readily available. Schools became less strictly bound up with training for the Church and more linked to the general acquisition of "literature," in the sense both of literacy and of cultural knowledge. In keeping with this new emphasis on reading and with humanist educational reform, the school was reorganized during the reign of Edward VI (1547–53). School records from the period have not survived, but it is almost certain that William Shakespeare attended the King's New School, as it was renamed in Edward's honor.

Scholars have painstakingly reconstructed the curriculum of schools of this kind and have even turned up the names and rather impressive credentials of the schoolmasters who taught there when Shakespeare was a student. (Shakespeare's principal teacher was Thomas Jenkins, an Oxford graduate, who received £20 a year and a rent-free house.) A child's education in Elizabethan England began at age four or five with two years at what was called the "petty school," attached to the main grammar school. The little scholars carried a "hornbook," a sheet of paper or parchment framed in wood and covered, for protection, with a transparent layer of horn. On the paper was written

The Cholmondeley sisters, c. 1600–10. This striking image brings to mind Shakespeare's fascination with twinship, both identical (notably in *The Comedy of Errors*) and fraternal (in *Twelfth Night*).

the alphabet and the Lord's Prayer, which were reproduced as well in the slightly more advanced *ABC with the Catechism,* a combination primer and rudimentary religious guide.

After students demonstrated some ability to read, the boys could go on, at about age seven, to the grammar school. Shakespeare's images of the experience are not particularly cheerful. In his famous account of the Seven Ages of Man, Jaques in *As You Like It* describes

> the whining schoolboy with his satchel
> And shining morning face, creeping like snail
> Unwillingly to school.
>
> (2.7.144–46)

The schoolboy would have crept quite early: the day began at 6:00 A.M. in summer and 7:00 A.M. in winter and continued until 5:00 P.M., with very few breaks or holidays.

At the core of the curriculum was the study of Latin, the mastery of which was in effect a prolonged male puberty rite involving much discipline and pain as well as pleasure. A late sixteenth-century Dutchman (whose name fittingly was Batty) proposed that God had created the human buttocks so that they could be severely beaten without risking permanent injury. Such thoughts dominated the pedagogy of the age, so that even an able young scholar, as we might imagine Shakespeare to have been, could scarcely have escaped recurrent flogging.

Shakespeare evidently reaped some rewards for the miseries he probably endured: his works are laced with echoes of many of the great Latin texts taught in grammar schools. One of his earliest comedies, *The Comedy of Errors,* is a brilliant variation on a theme by the Roman playwright Plautus, whom Elizabethan schoolchildren often performed as well as read; and one of his earliest tragedies, *Titus Andronicus,* is heavily indebted to Seneca. These are among the most visible of the classical influences that are often more subtly and pervasively interfused in Shakespeare's works. He seems to have had a particular fondness for *Aesop's Fables,* Apuleius's *Golden Ass,* and above all Ovid's *Metamorphoses.* His learned contemporary Ben Jonson remarked that Shakespeare had "small Latin and less Greek," but from this distance what is striking is not the limits of Shakespeare's learning but rather the unpretentious ease, intelligence, and gusto with which he draws upon what he must have first encountered as laborious study.

Traces of a Life

In November 1582, William Shakespeare, at the age of eighteen, married twenty-six-year-old Anne Hathaway, who came from the village of Shottery, near Stratford. Their first daughter, Susanna, was baptized six months later. This circumstance, along with the fact that Anne was eight years Will's senior, has given rise to a mountain of speculation, all the more lurid precisely because there is no further evidence. Shakespeare depicts in several plays situations in which marriage is precipitated by a pregnancy, but he also registers, in *Measure for Measure* (1.2.125ff.), the Elizabethan belief that a "true contract" of marriage could be legitimately made and then consummated simply by the mutual vows of the couple in the presence of witnesses.

On February 2, 1585, the twins Hamnet and Judith Shakespeare were baptized in Stratford. Hamnet died at the age of eleven, when his father was already living for much of the year in London as a successful playwright. These are Shakespeare's only known children, although the playwright and impresario William Davenant in the mid-seventeenth century claimed to be his bastard son. Since people did not ordinarily advertise their illegitimacy, the claim, though impossible to verify, at least suggests the unusual strength of the Shakespeare's posthumous reputation.

William Shakespeare's father, John, died in 1601; his mother died seven years later. They would have had the satisfaction of witnessing their eldest son's prosperity, and not only from a distance, for in 1597 William purchased New Place, the second largest house in Stratford. In 1607, the playwright's daughter Susanna married a successful and well-known physician, John Hall. The next year, the Halls had a daughter, Elizabeth, Shakespeare's first grandchild. In 1616, the year of Shakespeare's death, his daughter Judith married a vintner, Thomas Quiney, with whom she had three children. Shakespeare's widow, Anne, died in 1623, at the age of sixty-seven. His first-born, Susanna, died at the age of sixty-six in 1649, the year that King Charles I was beheaded by the parliamentary army. Judith lived through Cromwell's Protectorate and on to the Restoration of the monarchy; she died in February 1662, at the age of seventy-seven. By the end of the century, the line of Shakespeare's direct heirs was extinct.

Patient digging in the archives has turned up other traces of Shakespeare's life as a family man and a man of means: assessments, small fines, real-estate deeds, minor actions in court to collect debts. In addition to his fine Stratford house and a large garden and cottage facing it, Shakespeare bought substantial parcels of land in the vicinity. When in *The Tempest* the wedding celebration conjures up a vision of "barns and garners never empty," Shakespeare could have been glancing at what the legal documents record as his own "tithes of corn, grain, blade, and hay" in the fields near Stratford. At some point after 1610, Shakespeare seems to have begun to shift his attention from the London stage to his Stratford properties, although the term "retirement" implies a more decisive and definitive break than appears to have been the case. By 1613, when the Globe Theatre burned down during a performance of *All Is True* (*Henry VIII*), Shakespeare was probably residing for the most part in Stratford, but he retained his financial interest in the rebuilt playhouse and probably continued to have some links to his theatrical colleagues. Still, by this point, his career as a playwright was substantially over. Legal documents from his last years show his main concern to be the protection of his real-estate interests in Stratford.

Half a century after Shakespeare's death, a Stratford vicar and physician, John Ward, noted in his diary that Shakespeare and his fellow poets Michael Drayton and Ben Jonson "had a merry meeting, and it seems drank too hard, for Shakespeare died of a fever there contracted." It is not inconceivable that Shakespeare's last illness was somehow linked, if only coincidentally, to the festivities on the occasion of the wedding in February 1616 of his daughter Judith (who was still alive when Ward made his diary entry). In any case, on March 25, 1616, Shakespeare revised his will, and on April 23 he died. Two days later, he was buried in the chancel of Holy Trinity Church beneath a stone bearing an epitaph he is said to have devised:

> Good friend for Jesus' sake forbear,
> To dig the dust enclosed here:
> Blest be the man that spares these stones,
> And curst be he that moves my bones.

The verses are hardly among Shakespeare's finest, but they seem to have been effective: though bones were routinely dug up to make room for others—a fate imagined with unforgettable intensity in the graveyard scene in *Hamlet*—his own remains were undisturbed. Like other vestiges of sixteenth- and early seventeenth-century Stratford, Shakespeare's grave has for centuries been the object of a tourist industry that borders on a religious cult.

Shakespeare's will has been examined with an intensity befitting this cult; every provision and formulaic phrase, no matter how minor or conventional, has borne a heavy weight of interpretation, none more so than the bequest to his wife, Anne, of only "my second-best bed." Scholars have pointed out that Anne would in any case have been provided for by custom and that the terms are not necessarily a deliberate slight, but the absence of the customary words "my loving wife" or "my well-beloved wife" is difficult to ignore.

Portrait of the Playwright as Young Provincial

The great problem with the surviving traces of Shakespeare's life is not that they are few but that they are dull. Christopher Marlowe was a double or triple agent, accused of brawling, sodomy, and atheism. Ben Jonson, who somehow clambered up from bricklayer's apprentice to classical scholar, served in the army in Flanders, killed a fellow actor in a duel, converted to Catholicism in prison in 1598, and returned to the Church of England in 1610. Provincial real-estate investments and the second-best bed cannot compete with such adventurous lives. Indeed, the relative ordinariness of Shakespeare's social background and life has contributed to a persistent current of speculation that the glover's son from Stratford-upon-Avon was not in fact the author of the plays attributed to him.

The anti-Stratfordians, as those who deny Shakespeare's authorship are sometimes called, almost always propose as the real author someone who came from a higher social class and received a more prestigious education. Francis Bacon, the Earl of Oxford, the Earl of Southampton, even Queen Elizabeth, have been advanced, among many others, as glamorous candidates for the role of clandestine playwright. Several famous people, including Mark Twain and Sigmund Freud, have espoused these theories, though very few scholars have joined them. Since Shakespeare was quite well-known in his own time as the author of the plays that bear his name, there would need to have been an extraordinary conspiracy to conceal the identity of the real master who (the theory goes) disdained to appear in the vulgarity of print or on the public stage. Like many conspiracy theories, the extreme implausibility of this one only seems to increase the fervent conviction of its advocates.

To the charge that a middle-class author from a small town could not have imagined the lives of kings and nobles, one can respond by citing the exceptional qualities that Ben Jonson praised in Shakespeare: "excellent *Phantsie*; brave notions, and gentle expressions." Even in ordinary mortals, the human imagination is a strange faculty; in Shakespeare, it seems to have been uncannily powerful, working its mysterious, transforming effects on everything it touched. His imagination was intensely engaged by what he found in books. He seems throughout his life to have been an intense, voracious reader, and it is fascinating to witness his creative encounters with Raphael Holinshed's *Chronicles of England, Scotlande, and Irelande*, Plutarch's *Lives of the Noble Grecians and Romans*, Ovid's *Metamorphoses*, Montaigne's *Essays*, and the Bible, to name only some of his favorite books. But books were clearly not the only objects of Shakespeare's attention; like most artists, he drew upon the whole range of his life experiences.

To integrate some of the probable circumstances of Shakespeare's early years with the particular shape of the theatrical imagination associated with his name, let us indulge briefly in the biographical daydreams that modern scholarship is supposed to have rendered forever obsolete. The vignettes that follow are conjectural, but they may suggest ways in which his life as we know it found its way into his art.

1. THE GOWN OF OFFICE

Shakespeare was a very young boy—not quite four years old—when the Stratford council elected his father, John, to a year's term as bailiff (the equivalent of mayor). The office, the town's highest, was attended with considerable ceremony. The bailiff and his deputy were entitled to appear in public in furred gowns, attended by leather-clad sergeants bearing maces before them. On Rogation Days (three days of prayer for the harvest, before Ascension Day), they would solemnly pace out the parish boundaries, and they would similarly walk in processions on market and fair days. On Sundays, the sergeants would accompany the bailiff to church, where he would sit with his wife in a front pew, and he would have a comparable seat of honor at sermons in the Guild Chapel.

Public deference was a matter of law as well as custom: any inhabitant who spoke disrespectfully to the bailiff or other town officer was subject to the penalty of three days and three nights in the stocks. Newcomers who sought employment—notably including traveling players who hoped to stage performances—were obliged to obtain the bailiff's permission. In the year that John Shakespeare held office, two such professional playing companies arrived in Stratford. They must have proceeded to the bailiff's house on Henley Street and presented the letters of recommendation, with wax seals, that showed that they were not vagabonds. They would have spoken with more than ordinary deference, since it was the bailiff who would decide whether they would be sent packing or—as was the case—allowed to post their bills announcing the performances. The first of these performances was usually free to all comers. The bailiff would have been expected to attend, for it was his privilege to determine the level of the reward to be paid out of the city coffers; he would, presumably, have been given one of the best seats in the guildhall, where a special stage had been erected. It is impossible to know whether John Shakespeare took his family to these plays, but his little boy would certainly have been aware of what was happening.

On a precocious child (or even, for that matter, on an ordinary child), the effect of his father's office and the elaborate rituals that attended it would be at least threefold. First, the ceremony would convey irresistibly the power of clothes (the gown of office) and of symbols (the mace) to transform identity as if by magic. Second, it would invest the father with immense power, distinction, and importance, awakening what we may call a lifelong dream of high station. And third, pulling slightly against this dream, it would provoke an odd feeling that the father's clothes do not fit, a perception that the office is not the same as the man, and an intimate, firsthand knowledge that when the robes are put off, their wearer is inevitably glimpsed in a far different, less exalted light.

2. PROGRESSES AND ELECTIONS

This second biographical fantasy, slightly less plausible than the first but still quite likely, involves a somewhat older child witnessing two characteristic forms of Elizabethan political ceremony, both of which were well known in the provinces. Queen Elizabeth was fond of going on what were known as "progresses," triumphant ceremonial journeys around her kingdom. Let us imagine that the young Shakespeare—say, in 1574, when he was ten years old—went with his kinsfolk or friends to Warwick, some 8 miles distant, to witness a progress. He would thus have participated as a spectator in an elaborate celebration of charismatic power: the courtiers in their gorgeous clothes, the nervous local officials bedecked in velvets and silks, and at the center, carried in a special litter like a painted idol, the bejeweled queen. Let us imagine further that in addition to being struck by the overwhelming force of this charisma, the boy was struck, too, by the way this force depended paradoxically on a sense that the queen was after all quite human. Elizabeth was in fact fond of calling attention to this peculiar tension between near-divinization and human ordinariness. For example, on this occasion at Warwick (and what follows really happened), after the trembling Recorder, presumably a local civil official of high standing, had made his official welcoming speech, Elizabeth offered her hand to him to be kissed: "Come hither, little Recorder," she said. "It was told me that you would be afraid to look upon me or to speak boldly; but you were not so afraid of me as I was of you; and I now thank you for putting me in mind of my duty." Of course, the charm of this royal "confession" of nervousness depends on its manifest implausibility: it is, in effect, a theatrical performance of humility by someone with immense confidence in her own histrionic power.

A royal progress was not the only form of spectacular political activity that Shakespeare might well have seen in the 1570s; it is still more likely that he would have witnessed parliamentary elections, particularly since his father was qualified to vote. In 1571, 1572, 1575, and 1578, there were shire elections conducted in nearby Warwick, elections that would certainly have attracted well over a thousand voters. These were often memorable events: large crowds came together; there was usually heavy drinking and carnivalesque festivity; and, at the same time, there was enacted, in a very different register from that of the monarchy, a ritual of empowerment. The people, those entitled to vote by virtue of meeting the property and residence requirements, chose their own representatives by giving their votes—their voices—to candidates for office. Here, legislative sovereignty was conferred not by God but by the consent of the community, a consent marked by shouts and applause.

Recent cultural historians have been so fascinated by the evident links between the spectacles of the absolutist monarchy and the theater that they have largely ignored the significance of this alternative public arena, one that generated intense excitement throughout the country. A child who was a spectator at a parliamentary election in the 1570s might well have found the occasion enormously compelling. It is striking, in any case, how often the adult Shakespeare returns to scenes of acclamation and mass consent, and striking, too, how much the theater depends on the soliciting of popular voices.

3. EXORCISMS

A third and final fantasy is even more speculative than the second and involves a controversial claim, which has long been hotly debated— that Shakespeare either was a secret Catholic or was at least raised in a Roman Catholic household in a time of official suspicion and persecution of recusancy. A late seventeenth-century Anglican clergyman, Richard Davies, jotted down in some notes on Shakespeare that "he died a papist." In a modern biographical study, E. A. J. Honigmann convincingly linked several of the schoolmasters who taught in Stratford at the time that Shakespeare would have been a pupil to a network of Catholic families in Lancashire with whom one "William Shakeshafte," possibly a young schoolmaster or player, was connected in the late 1570s or early 1580s.

Exorcism: Nicole Aubry in the cathedral at Laon, 1566.

Catholics in Elizabethan England were not free to practice their religion—any more than Protestants, in Catholic countries, were free to practice theirs—and the beleaguered faithful, beset with spies, came together only at great risk to confess and receive Communion from clandestine priests. Under the circumstances, although a substantial portion of the population may have retained a residual inward loyalty to the traditional faith, the vast majority fell away from outward Catholic practice. After all, the churches, great and small, were now the places of Protestant worship; the innumerable local saints' shrines and pilgrimage sites had been systematically destroyed; the monasteries and convents had been abolished, their property bestowed on royal favorites or sold at bargain prices to local magnates. Seeking a spectacular way to demonstrate the enduring spiritual power and authenticity of the Roman Church, the embattled Counter-Reformers turned to an ancient ritual: exorcism. Devils who possessed the souls of troubled men and women had once been exorcised in public, but now the healing rite had to be conducted in secret, in a barn in a remote village, perhaps, or in the attic of the secluded house of a Catholic loyalist. The danger for those who presided was enormous—brutal interrogation, torture, and an unspeakably horrible execution was the usual fate of the missionary priests who were caught—but the vivid demonstration of the Church's triumph over evil was sufficiently compelling to warrant the risk. For despite the lynx-eyed alertness of the Protestant authorities, Catholics staged a surprising number of clandestine exorcisms, many of which drew substantial crowds.

Accepting for the moment that William Shakespeare was raised in the recusant faith of his father and mother, let us imagine that one day in the early 1580s the young man attended an exorcism of which he had learned through the secret network of the faithful. Here, based on an eyewitness account of such an occasion recently transcribed by Gerard Kilroy, is what he is likely to have seen. At the center of a large room, emptied of other furniture in order to accommodate the many observers, stood a bed. A young woman sat on the bed, and a priest, in clerical vestments, stood over her, preaching a sermon. As he spoke, the woman began to writhe and scream. At first the screams, uttered by a deep voice that could not have been the woman's although it came from her mouth, were not intelligible. Gradually, the bystanders began to make out some of the words, blasphemous oaths—"God's wounds! God's nails!"—followed by menaces, spoken as if by a rabid Protestant: "Popish priests, popish priests, to prison with them and hang them, hang them, hang them." The exorcist held up the Eucharist over the writhing woman, and the screams intensified. "Who are you?" he demanded. "I am Modu," the voice replied. "Depart, Modu!" shouted the priest, bringing the consecrated wafer closer to the demoniac. When that did not succeed in driving the devil out, the priest advanced a chafing dish of fire and brimstone, provoking more shouting and cursing, and then displayed a painting of the Blessed Virgin. "I will not behold or see her," screamed the demonic voice.

The longer the scene continued, the more there was confirmation of the contested tenets of the Catholic faith. The devil admitted that the Virgin Mary was a particularly efficacious intercessor, that purgatory existed, that the wafer, consecrated by the priest, actually was the body and blood of Christ. The devil also revealed that all Protestants were his followers. Finally, under the irresistible force of spiritual compulsion, he agreed to depart forever from the body of the possessed. The departure was difficult: again and again the tormented young woman gaped, as if her mouth were being torn open. She screamed in pain, rose up only to be cast down violently by invisible hands, cried out that she was being drowned, and called upon Jesus and his mother to save her. Only when a sacred relic was placed directly on her flesh did the devil finally leave her.

There is no way to know if William Shakespeare actually witnessed such a scene, but if he did, he would have carried away several indelible impressions: an awareness that strange, alien voices may speak from within ordinary, familiar bodies; an intimation of the immense, cosmic forces that may impinge upon human life; a belief in the possibility of making contact with these forces and compelling them to speak. These are, after all, the foundation stones of great tragedy.

Many years later, Shakespeare brooded about demonic possession when he was writing his greatest tragedy about the presence of evil in the world, *King Lear*. "This is the foul fiend Flibbertigibbet," shouts the madman, Poor Tom; "The Prince of Darkness is a gentleman. Modo he's called, and Mahu" (3.4.103, 127–28). But Poor Tom in that play is faking it; he is actually the noble Edgar, who has disguised himself as a madman in order to escape persecution. Did Shakespeare as a teenager already think that the whole compelling event, in all of its metaphysical weirdness, was a powerful theatrical fraud, a piece of pious propaganda? Perhaps. But if so, he also clearly understood that evil exists, that persecution is real, and that illusion has an irresistible force.

These imaginary portraits of the playwright as a young provincial introduce us to several of the root conditions of the Elizabethan theater. Biographical fantasies, though entirely speculative and playful, are useful in part because some people have found it difficult to conceive how Shakespeare, with his provincial roots and his restricted range of experience, could have so rapidly and completely mastered the central imaginative themes of his times. Moreover, it is sometimes difficult to grasp how seeming abstractions such as market society, monarchical state, and theological doctrine were actually experienced directly by peculiar, distinct individuals. Shakespeare's plays were social and collective events, but they also bore the stamp of a particular artist, one endowed with a remarkable capacity to craft lifelike illusions (what Jonson called "excellent *Phantsie*"), a daring willingness to articulate an original vision ("brave notions"), and a loving command, at once precise and generous, of language ("gentle expressions"). These plays are stitched together from shared cultural experiences, inherited dramatic devices, and the pungent vernacular of the day, but we should not lose sight of the extent to which they articulate an intensely personal vision, a bold shaping of the available materials. Four centuries of feverish biographical speculation, much of it foolish, bears witness to a basic intuition: the richness of these plays, their inexhaustible openness, is the consequence not only of the auspicious collective conditions of the culture but also of someone's exceptional skill, inventiveness, and courage at taking those conditions and making of them something rich and strange.

The Theater of the Nation

What precisely are the collective conditions highlighted by these vignettes? First, the growth of Stratford-upon-Avon, the bustling market town of which John Shakespeare was bailiff, is a small version of a momentous sixteenth-century development that made Shakespeare's career possible: the making of an urban "public." That development obviously depended on adequate numbers; the period experienced a rapid and still unexplained growth in population. With it came an expansion and elaboration of market relations: markets became less periodic, more continuous, and more abstract—centered, that is, not on the familiar materiality of goods but on the liquidity of capital and goods. In practical terms, this meant that it was possible to conceive of the theater not only as festive entertainment for special events—lord mayor's pageants, visiting princes, seasonal festivals, and the like—but as a permanent, year-round business venture. The venture relied on ticket sales—it was an innovation of this period to have money advanced in the expectation of pleasure rather than offered to servants afterward as a reward—and counted on habitual playgoing with a concomitant demand for new plays from competing theater companies: "But that's all one, our play is done," sings Feste at the end of *Twelfth Night* and adds a glance toward the next afternoon's proceeds: "And we'll strive to please you every day" (5.1.394–95).

Second, the royal progress is an instance of what the anthropologist Clifford Geertz has called the Theater State, a state that manifests its power and meaning in exemplary public performances. Professional companies of players, like the one Shakespeare belonged to, understood well that they existed in relation to this Theater State and would, if they were fortunate, be called upon to serve it. Unlike Ben Jonson, Shakespeare did not, as far as we know, write royal entertainments on commission, but his plays were frequently performed before Queen Elizabeth and then before King James and Queen Anne, along with their courtiers and privileged guests. There are many fascinating glimpses of these performances, including a letter from Walter Cope to Robert Cecil, early in James's reign. "Burbage is come," Cope writes, referring to the leading actor of Shakespeare's company, "and says there is no new play that the queen hath not seen, but they have revived an old one, called *Love's Labours Lost,* which for wit and mirth he says will please her exceedingly. And this is appointed to be played tomorrow night at my Lord of Southampton's." Not only would such theatrical performances have given great pleasure—evidently, the queen had already exhausted the company's new offerings—but they conferred prestige upon those who commanded them and those in whose honor they were mounted.

Monarchical power in the period was deeply allied to spectacular manifestations of the ruler's glory and disciplinary authority. The symbology of power depended on regal magnificence, reward, punishment, and pardon, all of which were heavily theatricalized. Indeed, the conspicuous public display does not simply serve the interests of power; on many occasions in the period, power seemed to exist in order to make pageantry possible, as if the nation's identity were only fully realized in theatrical performance. It would be easy to exaggerate this perception: the subjects of Queen Elizabeth and King James were acutely aware of the distinction between shadow and substance. But they were fascinated by the political magic through which shadows could be taken for substantial realities, and the ruling elite was largely complicit in the formation and celebration of a charismatic absolutism. At the same time, the claims of the monarch who professes herself or himself to be not the representative of the nation but its embodiment were set against the counterclaims of the House of Commons. And this institution, too, as we have glimpsed, had its own theatrical rituals, centered on the crowd whose shouts of approval, in heavily stage-managed elections, chose the individuals who would stand for the polity and participate in deliberations held in a hall whose resemblance to a theater did not escape contemporary notice.

Third, illicit exorcism points both to the theatricality of much religious ritual in the late Middle Ages and the Renaissance and to the heightened possibility of secularization. English Protestant authorities banned the medieval mystery plays, along with pilgrimages and other rituals associated with holy shrines and sacred images, but playing companies could satisfy at least some of the popular longings and appropriate aspects of the social energy no longer allowed a theological outlet. That is, official attacks on certain Catholic practices made it more possible for the public theater to appropriate and exploit their allure. Hence, for example, the plays that celebrated the solemn miracle of the Catholic Mass were banned, along with the most elaborate church vestments, but in *The Winter's Tale* Dion can speak in awe of what he witnessed at Apollo's temple:

> I shall report,
> For most it caught me, the celestial habits—
> Methinks I so should term them—and the reverence
> Of the grave wearers. O, the sacrifice—
> How ceremonious, solemn, and unearthly
> It was i'th' off'ring!
>
> (3.1.3–8)

And at the play's end, the statue of the innocent mother breathes, comes to life, and embraces her child.

The theater in Shakespeare's time, then, is intimately bound up with all three crucial cultural formations: the market society, the theater state, and the Church. But it is important to note that the institution is not *identified* with any of them. The theater may be a market phenomenon, but it is repeatedly and bitterly attacked as the enemy of diligent, sober, productive economic activity. Civic authorities generally regarded the theater as a pestilential nuisance, a parasite on the body of the commonwealth, a temptation to students, apprentices, housewives, even respectable merchants to leave their serious business and lapse into idleness and waste. That waste, it might be argued, could be partially recuperated if it went for the glorification of a guild or the entertainment of an important dignitary, but the only group regularly profiting from the theater were the players and their disreputable associates.

For his part, Shakespeare made a handsome profit from the commodification of theatrical entertainment, but he seems never to have written "city comedy"—plays set in London and more or less explicitly concerned with market relations—and his characters express deep reservations about the power of money and commerce: "That smooth-faced gentleman, tickling commodity," Philip the Bastard observes in *King John,* "wins of all, / Of kings, of beggars, old men, young men, maids" (2.1.574, 570–71). We could argue that the smooth-faced gentleman is none other than Shakespeare himself, for his drama famously mingles kings and clowns, princesses and panderers. But the mingling is set against a romantic current of social conservatism: in *Twelfth Night,* the aristocratic heiress Olivia falls in love with someone who appears far beneath her in wealth and social station, but it is revealed that he (and his sister Viola) are of noble blood; in *The Winter's Tale,* Leontes' daughter Perdita is raised as a shepherdess, but her noble nature shines through her humble upbringing, and she marries the Prince of Bohemia; the strange island maiden with whom Ferdinand, son of the King of Naples, falls madly in love in *The Tempest* turns out to be the daughter of the rightful Duke of Milan. Shakespeare pushes against this conservative logic in *All's Well That Ends Well,* but the noble young Bertram violently resists the unequal match thrust upon him by the King, and the play's mood is notoriously uneasy.

Similarly, Shakespeare's theater may have been patronized and protected by the monarchy—after 1603, his company received a royal patent and was known as the King's Men—but it was by no means identical in its interests or its ethos. To be sure, *Richard III* and *Macbeth* incorporate aspects of royal propaganda, but given the realities of censorship, Shakespeare's plays, and the period's drama as a whole, are surprisingly independent and complex in their political vision. There is, in any case, a certain inherent tension between kings and player kings: Elizabeth and James may both have likened themselves to actors onstage, but they were loath to admit their dependence on the applause and money, freely given or freely withheld, of the audience. The charismatic monarch insists that the sacredness of authority resides in the body of the ruler, not in a costume that may be worn and then discarded by an actor. Kings are not *representations* of power—or do not admit that they are—but claim to be the thing itself. The government institution that was actually based on the idea of representation, Parliament, had theatrical elements, as we have seen, but it significantly excluded any audience from its deliberations. And Shakespeare's oblique portraits of parliamentary representatives, the tribunes Sicinius Velutus and Junius Brutus in *Coriolanus,* are anything but flattering.

Finally, the theater drew significant energy from the liturgy and rituals of the late medieval Church, but as Shakespeare's contemporaries widely remarked, the playhouse and the Church were scarcely natural allies. Not only did the theater represent a potential competitor to worship services, and not only did ministers rail against prostitution and other vices associated with playgoing, but theatrical representation itself, even when ostensibly pious, seemed to many to empty out whatever it presented, turning substance into mere show. The theater could and did use the period's deep currents of religious feeling, but it had to do so carefully and with an awareness of conflicting interests.

Shakespeare Comes to London

How did Shakespeare decide to turn his prodigious talents to the stage? When did he make his way to London? How did he get his start? To these and similar questions we have a mountain of speculation but no secure answers. There is not a single surviving record of Shakespeare's existence from 1585, when his twins were baptized in Stratford church, until 1592, when a rival London playwright made an envious remark about him. In the late seventeenth century, the delightfully eccentric collector of gossip John Aubrey was informed that prior to moving to London the young Shakespeare had been a schoolteacher in the country. Aubrey also recorded a story that Shakespeare had been a rather unusual apprentice butcher: "When he killed a calf, he would do it in a high style, and make a speech."

These and other legends, including one that has Shakespeare whipped for poaching game, fill the void until the unmistakable reference in Robert Greene's *Groats-Worth of Witte, Bought with a Million of Repentance* (1592). An inspired hack writer with a university education, a penchant for self-dramatization, a taste for wild living, and a strong streak of resentment, Greene, in his early thirties, was dying in poverty when he penned his last farewell, piously urging his fellow dramatists Christopher Marlowe, Thomas Nashe, and George Peele to abandon the wicked stage before they were brought low, as he had been, by a new arrival: "For there is an upstart crow, beautified with our feathers, that with his 'Tiger's heart wrapped in player's hide' supposes he is as well able to bombast out a blank verse as the best of you, and, being an absolute *Johannes Factotum*, is in his own conceit the only Shake-scene in a country." If "Shake-scene" is not enough to identify the object of his attack, Greene parodies a line from Shakespeare's early play *Richard Duke of York* (3 *Henry VI*): "O tiger's heart wrapped in a woman's hide!" (1.4.138). Greene is accusing Shakespeare of being an upstart, a plagiarist, an egomaniacal jack-of-all-trades—and, above all perhaps, a popular success.

By 1592, then, Shakespeare had already arrived on the highly competitive London theatrical scene. He was successful enough to be attacked by Greene and, a few months later, defended by Henry Chettle, another hack writer who had seen Greene's manuscript through the press (or, some scholars speculate, had written the attack himself and passed it off as the dying Greene's). Chettle expresses his regret that he did not suppress Greene's diatribe and spare Shakespeare "because myself have seen his demeanor no less civil than he excellent in the quality he professes." Besides, Chettle adds, "divers of worship have reported his uprightness of dealing, which argues his honesty and his facetious [polished] grace in writing that approves his art." "Divers of worship": not only was Shakespeare established as an accomplished writer and actor, but he evidently had aroused the attention and the approbation of several socially prominent people. In Elizabethan England, aristocratic patronage, with the money, protection, and prestige it alone could provide, was probably a professional writer's most important asset.

This patronage, or at least Shakespeare's quest for it, is most visible in the dedications in 1593 and 1594 of his narrative poems *Venus and Adonis* and *The Rape of Lucrece* to the young nobleman Henry Wriothesley, Earl of Southampton. It may be glimpsed as well, perhaps, in the sonnets, with their extraordinary adoration of the fair youth, though the identity of that youth has never been determined. What return Shakespeare got for his exquisite offerings is likewise unknown. We do know that among wits and gallants, the narrative poems won Shakespeare a fine reputation as an immensely stylish and accomplished poet. An amateur play performed at Cambridge University at the end of the sixteenth century, *The Return from Parnassus*, makes fun of this vogue, as a foolish character effusively declares, "I'll worship sweet Mr. Shakespeare, and to honour him will lay his *Venus and Adonis* under my pillow." Many readers at the time may have done so: the poem went through sixteen editions before 1640, more than any other work by Shakespeare.

Patronage was crucially important not only for individual artists but also for the actors, playwrights, and investors who pooled their resources to form professional theater companies. The public playhouses had enemies, especially among civic and religious authorities, who wished greatly to curb performances or to ban them altogether. An act of 1572 included players among those classified as vagabonds, threatening them, therefore, with the horrible punishments meted out to those regarded as economic parasites. The players' escape route was to be nominally enrolled as the servants of high-ranking noblemen. The legal fiction was that their public performances were a kind of rehearsal for the command performances before the patron or the monarch.

When Shakespeare came to London, presumably in the late 1580s, there were more than a dozen of these companies operating under the patronage of various aristocrats.

We do not know for which of these companies, several of which had toured in Stratford, he originally worked, nor whether he began, as legend has it, as a prompter's assistant and then graduated to acting and playwriting. Shakespeare is listed among the actors in Ben Jonson's *Every Man in His Humour* (performed in 1598) and *Sejanus* (performed in 1603), but we do not know for certain what roles he played, nor are there records of any of his other performances. Tradition has it that he played Adam in *As You Like It* and the Ghost in *Hamlet,* but he was clearly not one of the leading actors of the day.

By the 1590s, the number of playing companies in London had been considerably reduced, in part through competition and in part through legislative restriction. (In 1572, knights and gentry lost the privilege of patronizing a troupe of actors; in 1598, justices of the peace lost the power to authorize performances.) By the early years of the seventeenth century, there were usually only three companies competing against one another in any season, along with two children's companies, which were often successful at drawing audiences away from the public playhouses. Shakespeare may initially have been associated with the Earl of Leicester's company or with the company of Ferdinando Stanley, Lord Strange; both groups included actors with whom Shakespeare was later linked. Or he may have belonged to the Earl of Pembroke's Men, since there is evidence that they performed *The Taming of a Shrew* and a version of *Richard Duke of York (3 Henry VI)*. At any event, by 1594, Shakespeare was a member of the Lord Chamberlain's Men, for his name, along with those of Will Kemp (or Kempe) and Richard Burbage, appears on a record of those "servants to the Lord Chamberlain" paid for performance at the royal palace at Greenwich on December 26 and 28. Shakespeare stayed with this company, which during the reign of King James received royal patronage and became the King's Men, for the rest of his career.

Many playwrights in Shakespeare's time worked freelance, moving from company to company as opportunities arose, collaborating on projects, adding scenes to old plays, scrambling from one enterprise to another. But certain playwrights, among them the most successful, wrote for a single company, often agreeing contractually to give that company exclusive rights to their theatrical works. Shakespeare seems to have followed such a pattern. For the Lord Chamberlain's Men, he wrote an average of two plays per year. His company initially performed in The Theatre, a playhouse built in 1576 by an entrepreneurial carpenter, James Burbage, the father of the actor Richard, who was to perform many of

Edward Alleyn (1566–1626). Artist unknown. Alleyn was the great tragic actor of the Lord Admiral's Men (the principal rival to Shakespeare's company). He was famous especially for playing the great Marlovian heroes.

Shakespeare's greatest roles. When in 1597 their lease on this playhouse expired, the Lord Chamberlain's Men passed through a difficult and legally perilous time, but they formed a joint-stock company, raising sufficient capital to lease a site and put up a splendid new playhouse in the suburb of Southwark, on the south bank of the Thames. This playhouse, the Globe, opened in 1599. Shakespeare is listed in the legal agreement as one of the principal investors; and when the company began to use Blackfriars as their indoor playhouse around 1609, he was a major shareholder in that theater as well. The Lord Chamberlain's Men, later the King's Men, dominated the theater scene, and the shares were quite valuable. Then as now, the theater was an extremely risky enterprise—most of those who wrote plays and performed in them made pathetically little money—but Shakespeare was a notable exception. The fine house in Stratford and the coat of arms he succeeded in acquiring were among the fruits of his multiple mastery, as actor, playwright, and investor in the London stage.

The Shakespearean Trajectory

Even though Shakespeare's England was in many ways a record-keeping society, no reliable record survives that details the performances, year by year, in the London theaters. Every play had to be licensed by a government official, the Master of the Revels, but the records kept by the relevant officials from 1579 to 1621, Sir Edmund Tilney and Sir George Buc, have not survived. A major theatrical entrepreneur, Philip Henslowe, kept a careful account of his expenditures, including what he paid for the scripts he commissioned, but unfortunately Henslowe's main business was with the Rose and the Fortune theaters and not with the playhouses at which Shakespeare's company performed. A comparable ledger must have been kept by the shareholders of the Lord Chamberlain's Men, but it has not survived. Shakespeare himself apparently did not undertake to preserve for posterity the sum of his writings, let alone to clarify the chronology of his works or specify which plays he wrote alone and which with collaborators.

The principal source for Shakespeare's works is the 1623 Folio volume of *Mr. William Shakespeares Comedies, Histories, & Tragedies*. Most scholars believe that the editors were careful to include only those plays for which they knew Shakespeare to be the main author. Their edition does not, however, include any of Shakespeare's nondramatic poems, and it omits two plays in which Shakespeare is now thought to have had a significant hand, *Pericles, Prince of Tyre* and *The Two Noble Kinsmen*, along with his probable contribution to the multiauthored *Sir Thomas More*. (A number of other plays were attributed to Shakespeare, both before and after his death, but scholars have not generally accepted any of these into the established canon.) Moreover, the Folio edition does not print the plays in chronological order, nor does it attempt to establish a chronology. We do not know how much time would normally have elapsed between the writing of a play and its first performance, nor with

Title page of Thomas Heywood's *If You Know Not Me, You Know No Body; or, The Troubles of Queene Elizabeth* (1632 ed.).

a few exceptions, do we know with any certainty the month or even the year of the first performance of any of Shakespeare's plays. The quarto editions of those plays that were published during Shakespeare's lifetime obviously establish a date by which we know a given play had been written, but they give us little more than an end point, because there was likely to be a substantial though indeterminate gap between the first performance of a play and its publication.

With enormous patience and ingenuity, however, scholars have gradually assembled a considerable archive of evidence, both external and internal, for dating the composition of the plays. Besides actual publication, the external evidence includes explicit reference to a play, a record of its performance, or (as in the case of Greene's attack on the "upstart crow") the quoting of a line, though all of these can be maddeningly ambiguous. The most important single piece of external evidence appears in 1598 in *Palladis Tamia*, a long book of jumbled reflections by Francis Meres that includes a survey of the contemporary literary scene. Meres finds that "the sweet, witty soul of Ovid lives in mellifluous and honey-tongued Shakespeare, witness his *Venus and Adonis*, his *Lucrece*, his sugered Sonnets among his private friends, etc." Meres goes on to list Shakespeare's accomplishments as a playwright as well:

> As Plautus and Seneca are accounted the best for Comedy and Tragedy among the Latins: so Shakespeare among the English is the most excellent in both kinds for the stage; for Comedy, witness his *Gentlemen of Verona*, his *Errors*, his *Love labors lost*, his *Love labours won*, his *Midsummers night dream*, & his *Merchant of Venice*: for Tragedy his *Richard the 2*, *Richard the 3*, *Henry the 4*, *King John*, *Titus Andronicus* and his *Romeo and Juliet*.

Meres thus provides a date by which twelve of Shakespeare's plays had definitely appeared (including one, *Love's Labour's Won*, that appears to have been lost or that we know by a different title). Unfortunately, Meres provides no clues about the order of appearance of these plays, and there are no other comparable lists.

Faced with the limitations of the external evidence, scholars have turned to a bewildering array of internal evidence, ranging from datable sources and topical allusions on the one hand to evolving stylistic features (ratio of verse to prose, percentage of rhyme to blank verse, colloquialisms, use of extended similes, and the like) on the other. Thus, for example, a cluster of plays with a high percentage of rhymed verse may follow closely upon Shakespeare's writing of the rhymed poems *Venus and Adonis* and *The Rape of Lucrece* and, therefore, be datable to 1594–95. Similarly, vocabulary overlap probably indicates proximity in composition, so if four or five plays share relatively "rare" vocabulary, it is likely that they were written in roughly the same period. Again, there seems to be a pattern in Shakespeare's use of colloquialisms, with a steady increase from *As You Like It* (1599–1600) to *Coriolanus* (1608), followed in the late romances by a retreat from the colloquial.

More sophisticated computer analysis should provide further guidance in the future, even though the precise order of the plays, still very much in dispute, is never likely to be settled to universal satisfaction. Still, certain broad patterns are now widely accepted. These patterns can be readily grasped in the *Norton Shakespeare*, which presents the plays in the chronological order proposed by the Oxford editors.

Shakespeare began his career, probably in the early 1590s, by writing both comedies and history plays. The attack by Greene suggests that he made his mark with the series of theatrically vital but rather crude plays based on the foreign and domestic broils that erupted during the unhappy reign of the Lancastrian Henry VI. Modern readers and audiences are more likely to find the first sustained evidence of unusual power in *Richard III* (c. 1592), a play that combines a brilliantly conceived central character, a dazzling command of histrionic rhetoric, and an overarching moral vision of English history.

At virtually the same time that he was setting his stamp on the genre of the history play, Shakespeare was writing his first—or first surviving—comedies. Here, there are even fewer signs than in the histories of an apprenticeship: *The Comedy of Errors*, one of his early efforts in this genre, already displays a rare command of the resources of comedy: mistaken identity, madcap confusion, and the threat of disaster, giving way in the end to reconciliation, recovery, and love. Shakespeare's other comedies from the early 1590s, *The Taming of the Shrew, The Two Gentlemen of Verona,* and *Love's Labour's Lost,* are no less remarkable for their sophisticated variations on familiar comic themes, their inexhaustible rhetorical inventiveness, and their poignant intimation, in the midst of festive celebration, of loss.

Successful as are these early histories and comedies, and indicative of an extraordinary theatrical talent, Shakespeare's achievement in the later 1590s would still have been all but impossible to foresee. Starting with *A Midsummer Night's Dream* (c. 1595), Shakespeare wrote an unprecedented series of romantic comedies—*The Merchant of Venice, The Merry Wives of Windsor, Much Ado About Nothing, As You Like It,* and *Twelfth Night* (c. 1602)—whose poetic richness and emotional complexity remain unmatched. In the same period, he wrote a sequence of profoundly searching and ambitious history plays—*Richard II, 1* and *2 Henry IV,* and *Henry V*—which together explore the death throes of feudal England and the birth of the modern nation-state ruled by a charismatic monarch. Both the comedies and histories of this period are marked by their capaciousness, their ability to absorb characters who press up against the outermost boundaries of the genre: the comedy *Merchant of Venice* somehow contains the figure, at once nightmarish and poignant, of Shylock, while the *Henry IV* plays, with their somber vision of crisis in the family and the state, bring to the stage one of England's greatest comic characters, Falstaff.

If in the mid to late 1590s Shakespeare reached the summit of his art in two major genres, he also manifested a lively interest in a third. As early as 1593, he wrote the crudely violent tragedy *Titus Andronicus,* the first of several plays on themes from Roman history, and a year or two later, in *Richard II,* he created in the protagonist a figure who achieves by the play's close the stature of a tragic hero. In the same year that Shakespeare wrote the wonderfully farcical "Pyramus and Thisbe" scene in *A Midsummer Night's Dream,* he probably also wrote the deeply tragic realization of the same story in *Romeo and Juliet.* But once again, the lyric anguish of *Romeo and Juliet* and the tormented self-revelation of *Richard II,* extraordinary as they are, could not have led anyone to predict the next phase of Shakespeare's career, the great tragic dramas that poured forth in the early years of the seventeenth century: *Hamlet, Othello, King Lear, Macbeth, Antony and Cleopatra,* and *Coriolanus.* These plays, written from 1601 to 1607, seem to mark a major shift in sensibility, an existential and metaphysical darkening that many readers think must have originated in a deep personal anguish, perhaps caused by the death of Shakespeare's father, John, in 1601.

Whatever the truth of these speculations—and we have no direct, personal testimony either to support or to undermine them—there appears to have occurred in the same period a shift as well in Shakespeare's comic sensibility. The comedies written between 1601 and 1604, *Troilus and Cressida, All's Well That Ends Well,* and *Measure for Measure,* are sufficiently different from the earlier comedies—more biting in tone, more uneasy with comic conventions, more ruthlessly questioning of the values of the characters and the resolutions of the plots—to have led many twentieth-century scholars to classify them as "problem plays" or "dark comedies." This category has recently begun to fall out of favor, since Shakespeare criticism is perfectly happy to demonstrate that *all* of the plays are "problem plays." But there is another group of plays, among the last Shakespeare wrote, that continue to constitute a distinct category. *Pericles, Cymbeline, The Winter's Tale,* and *The Tempest,* written between 1608 and 1611, when the playwright had developed a remarkably fluid, dreamlike sense of plot and a poetic style that could veer, apparently effortlessly, from the tortured to the ineffably sweet, are known as the "romances." These plays share an interest in the moral and emotional life less of the adolescents who dominate the earlier comedies than of their parents. The romances are deeply concerned with patterns of loss and recovery, suffering and redemption, despair and renewal. They have seemed to many critics to constitute a deliberate conclusion to a career that began in histories and comedies and passed through the dark and tormented tragedies.

One effect of the practice of printing Shakespeare's plays in a reconstructed chronological order, as this edition does, is to produce a kind of authorial plot, a progress from youthful exuberance and a heroic grappling with history, through psychological anguish and radical doubt, to a mature serenity built upon an understanding of loss. The ordering of Shakespeare's "complete works" in this way reconstitutes the figure of the author as the beloved hero of his own, lived romance. There are numerous reasons to treat this romance with considerable skepticism: the precise order of the plays remains in dispute, the obsessions of the earliest plays crisscross with those of the last, the drama is a collaborative art form, and the relation between authorial consciousness and theatrical representation is murky. Yet a longing to identify Shakespeare's personal trajectory, to chart his psychic and spiritual as well as professional progress, is all but irresistible.

The Fetishism of Dress

Whatever the personal resonance of Shakespeare's own life, his art is deeply enmeshed in the collective hopes, fears, and fantasies of his time. For example, throughout his plays, Shakespeare draws heavily upon his culture's investment in costume, symbols of authority, visible signs of status—the fetishism of dress he must have witnessed from early childhood. Disguise in his drama is often assumed to be incredibly effective: when Henry V borrows a cloak, when Portia dresses in a jurist's robes, when Viola puts on a young man's suit, it is as if each has become unrecognizable, as if identity resided in clothing. At the end of *Twelfth Night,* even though Viola's true identity has been disclosed, Orsino continues to call her Cesario; he will do so, he says, until she resumes her maid's garments, for only then will she be transformed into a woman:

> Cesario, come—
> For so you shall be while you are a man;
> But when in other habits you are seen,
> Orsino's mistress, and his fancy's queen.
> (5.1.372–75)

The pinnacle of this fetishism of costume is the royal crown, for whose identity-conferring power men are willing to die, but the principle is everywhere from the filthy blanket that transforms Edgar into Poor Tom to the coxcomb that is the badge of the licensed fool. Antonio, wishing to express his utter contempt, spits on Shylocks' "Jewish gaberdine," as if the clothing were the essence of the man; Kent, pouring insults on the loathsome Oswald, calls him a "filthy worsted-stocking knave"; and innocent Innogen, learning that her husband has ordered her murder, thinks of herself as an expensive cast-off dress, destined to be ripped at the seams:

> Poor I am stale, a garment out of fashion,
> And for I am richer than to hang by th' walls
> I must be ripped. To pieces with me!
> (*Cymbeline* 3.4.50–52)

What can be said, thought, felt, in this culture seems deeply dependent on the clothes one wears—clothes that one is, in effect, *permitted* or *compelled* to wear, since there is little freedom in dress. Shakespearean drama occasionally represents something like such freedom: after all, Viola in *Twelfth Night* chooses to put off her "maiden weeds," as does Rosalind, who declares, "We'll have a swashing and a martial outside" (*As You Like It* 1.3.114). But these choices are characteristically made under the pressure of desperate circumstances, here shipwreck and exile. Part of the charm of Shakespeare's heroines is their ability to transform distress into an opportunity for self-fashioning, but the plays often suggest that there is less autonomy than meets the eye. What looks like an escape from cultural determinism may be only a deeper form of constraint. We may take, as an allegorical emblem of this constraint, the transformation of the beggar Christopher Sly into a nobleman in the playful Induction to *The Taming of the Shrew*. The transformation seems to suggest that you are free to make of yourself whatever you choose to be—the play begins with the drunken Sly indignantly claiming the dignity of his pedigree ("Look in the Chronicles" [Induction 1.3–4])—but in fact he is only the subject of the mischievous lord's experiment, designed to demonstrate the interwovenness of clothing and identity. "What think you," the lord asks his huntsman,

> if he were conveyed to bed,
> Wrapped in sweet clothes, rings put upon his fingers,
> A most delicious banquet by his bed,
> And brave attendants near him when he wakes—
> Would not the beggar then forget himself?

To which the huntsman replies, in words that underscore the powerlessness of the drunken beggar, "Believe me, lord, I think he cannot choose" (Induction 1.33–38).

Petruccio's taming of Katherine is similarly constructed around an imposition of identity, an imposition closely bound up with the right to wear certain articles of clothing. When the haberdasher arrives with a fashionable lady's hat, Petruccio refuses it over his wife's vehement objections: "This doth fit the time, / And gentlewomen wear such caps as these." "When you are gentle," Petruccio replies, "you shall have one, too, / And not till then" (4.3.69–72). At the play's close, Petruccio demonstrates his authority by commanding his tamed wife to throw down her cap: "Off with that bauble, throw it underfoot" (5.2.126). Here as elsewhere in Shakespeare, acts of robing and disrobing are intensely charged, a charge that culminates in the trappings of monarchy. When Richard II, in a scene that was probably censored from the stage as well as the printed text during the reign of Elizabeth, is divested of his crown and scepter, he experiences the loss as the eradication of his name, the symbolic melting away of his identity:

> Alack the heavy day,
> That I have worn so many winters out
> And know not now what name to call myself!
> O, that I were a mockery king of snow,
> Standing before the sun of Bolingbroke
> To melt myself away in water-drops!
>
> (4.1.247–52)

When Lear tears off his regal "lendings" in order to reduce himself to the nakedness of the Bedlam beggar, he is expressing not only his radical loss of social identity but the breakdown of his psychic order as well, expressing, therefore, his reduction to the condition of the "poor bare forked animal" that is the primal condition of undifferentiated existence. And when Cleopatra determines to kill herself in order to escape public humiliation in Rome, she magnificently affirms her essential being by arraying herself as she had once done to encounter Antony:

> Show me, my women, like a queen. Go fetch
> My best attires. I am again for Cydnus
> To meet Mark Antony.
>
> (5.2.223–25)

Such scenes are a remarkable intensification of the everyday symbolic practice of Renaissance English culture, its characteristically deep and knowing commitment to illusion: "I know perfectly well that the woman in her crown and jewels and gorgeous gown is an aging, irascible, and fallible mortal—she herself virtually admits as much—yet I profess that she is the Virgin Queen, timelessly beautiful, wise, and just." Shakespeare understood how close this willed illusion was to the spirit of the theater, to the actors' ability to work on what the chorus in *Henry V* calls the "imaginary forces" of the audience. But there is throughout Shakespeare's works a counterintuition that, while it does not exactly overturn this illusion, renders it poignant, vulnerable, fraught. The "masculine usurp'd attire" that is donned by Viola, Rosalind, Portia, Jessica, and other Shakespeare heroines alters what they can say and do, reveals important aspects of their character, and changes their destiny, but it is, all the same, not theirs and not all of who they are. They have, the plays insist, natures that are neither transformed nor altogether concealed by their dress: "Pray God defend me," exclaims the frightened Viola. "A little thing would make me tell them how much I lack of a man" (*Twelfth Night* 3.4.268–69).

The Paradoxes of Identity

The gap between costume and identity is not simply a matter of what women supposedly lack; virtually all of Shakespeare's major characters, men and women, convey the sense of both a *self-division* and an *inward expansion*. The belief in a complex inward realm beyond costumes and status is a striking inversion of the clothes cult: we know perfectly well that the characters have no inner lives apart from what we see on the stage, and yet we believe that they continue to exist when we do not see them, that they exist apart from their represented words and actions, that they have hidden dimensions. How is this conviction aroused and sustained? In part, it is the effect of what the characters themselves say: "My grief lies all within," Richard II tells Bolingbroke,

> And these external manner of laments
> Are merely shadows to the unseen grief
> That swells with silence in the tortured soul.
> (4.1.285–88)

Similarly, Hamlet, dismissing the significance of his outward garments, declares, "I have that within which passeth show— / These but the trappings and the suits of woe" (1.2.85–86). And the distinction between inward and outward is reinforced throughout this play and elsewhere by an unprecedented use of the aside and the soliloquy.

The soliloquy is a continual reminder in Shakespeare that the inner life is by no means transparent to one's surrounding world. Prince Hal seems open and easy with his mates in Eastcheap, but he has a hidden reservoir of disgust:

> I know you all, and will a while uphold
> The unyoked humour of your idleness.
> Yet herein will I imitate the sun,
> Who doth permit the base contagious clouds
> To smother up his beauty from the world,
> That when he please again to be himself,
> Being wanted he may be more wondered at
> By breaking through the foul and ugly mists
> Of vapours that did seem to strangle him.
> (*1 Henry IV* 1.2.173–81)

"When he please again to be himself": the line implies that identity is a matter of free choice—you decide how much of yourself you wish to disclose—but Shakespeare employs other devices that suggest more elusive and intractable layers of inwardness. There is a peculiar, recurrent lack of fit between costume and character, in fools as in princes, that is not simply a matter of disguise and disclosure. If Hal's true identity is partially "smothered" in the tavern, it is not completely revealed either in his soldier's armor or in his royal robes, nor do his asides reach the bedrock of unimpeachable self-understanding.

Identity in Shakespeare repeatedly slips away from the characters themselves, as it does from Richard II after the deposition scene and from Lear after he has given away his land and from Macbeth after he has gained the crown. The slippage does not mean that they retreat into silence; rather, they embark on an experimental, difficult fashioning of themselves and the world, most often through role-playing. "I cannot do it," says the deposed and imprisoned Richard II. "Yet I'll hammer it out" (5.5.5). This could serve as the motto for many Shakespearean characters: Viola becomes Cesario, Rosalind calls herself Ganymede, Kent becomes Caius, Edgar presents himself as Poor Tom, Hamlet plays the madman that he has partly become, Hal pretends that he is his father and a highwayman and Hotspur and even himself. Even in comedy, these ventures into alternate identities are rarely matters of choice; in tragedy, they are always undertaken under pressure and compulsion. And often enough it is not a matter of role-playing at all, but of a drastic transformation whose extreme emblem is the harrowing madness of Lear and of Leontes.

There is a moment in *Richard II* in which the deposed King asks for a mirror and then, after musing on his reflection, throws it to the ground. The shattering of the glass serves to remind us not only of the fragility of identity in Shakespeare but of its characteristic appearance in fragmentary mirror images. The plays continually generate alternative reflections, identities that intersect with, underscore, echo, or otherwise set off that of the principal character. Hence, Desdemona and Iago are not only important figures in Othello's world, they also seem to embody partially realized aspects of himself; Falstaff and Hotspur play a comparable role in relation to Prince Hal, Fortinbras and Horatio in relation to Hamlet, Gloucester and the Fool in relation to Lear, and so forth. In many of these plays, the complementary and contrasting characters figure in subplots, subtly interwoven with the play's main plot and illuminating its concerns. The note so conspicuously sounded by Fortinbras at the close of *Hamlet*—what the hero might have been, "had he been put on"—is heard repeatedly in Shakespeare and contributes to the overwhelming intensity, poignancy, and complexity of the characters. This is a world in which outward appearance is everything and nothing, in which individuation is at once sharply etched and continually blurred, in which the victims of fate are haunted by the ghosts of the possible, in which everything is simultaneously as it must be and as it need not have been.

Are these antinomies signs of a struggle between contradictory and irreconcilable perspectives in Shakespeare? In certain plays—notably, *Measure for Measure, All's Well That Ends Well, Coriolanus*, and *Troilus and Cressida*—the tension seems both high and entirely unresolved. But Shakespearean contradictions are more often reminiscent of the capacious spirit of Montaigne, who refused any systematic order that would betray his sense of reality. Thus, individual characters are immensely important in Shakespeare—he is justly celebrated for his unmatched skill in the invention of particular dramatic identities, marked with distinct speech patterns, manifested in social status, and confirmed by costume and gesture—but the principle of individuation is not the rock on which his theatrical art is founded. After the masks are stripped away, the pretenses exposed, the claims of the ego shattered, there is a mysterious remainder; as the shamed but irrepressible Paroles declares in *All's Well That Ends Well*, "Simply the thing I am / Shall make me live" (4.3.310–11). Again and again, the audience is made to sense a deeper energy, a source of power that at once discharges itself in individual characters and seems to sweep right through them.

The Poet of Nature

In *The Birth of Tragedy*, Nietzsche called a comparable source of energy that he found in Greek tragedy "Dionysos." But the god's name, conjuring up Bacchic frenzy, does not seem appropriate to Shakespeare. In the late seventeenth and eighteenth centuries, it was more plausibly called Nature: "The world must be peopled," says the delightful Benedick in *Much Ado About Nothing* (2.3.213–14), and there are frequent invocations elsewhere of the happy, generative power that brings couples together—

> Jack shall have Jill,
> Naught shall go ill,
> the man shall have his mare again, and all shall be well.
> (*A Midsummer Night's Dream* 3.3.45–47)

—and the melancholy, destructive power that brings all living things to the grave: "Golden lads and girls all must, / As chimney-sweepers, come to dust" (*Cymbeline* 4.2.263–64).

But the celebration of Shakespeare as a poet of nature—often coupled with an inane celebration of his supposedly "natural" (that is, untutored) genius—has its distinct limitations. For Shakespearean art brilliantly interrogates the "natural," refusing to take for granted precisely what the celebrants think is most secure. His comedies are endlessly inventive in showing that love is not simply natural: the playful hint of bestiality in the line quoted above, "the man shall have his mare again" (from a play in which the Queen of the Fairies falls in love with an ass-headed laborer), lightly unsettles the boundaries between the natural and the perverse. These boundaries are called into question throughout Shakespeare's work, from the cross-dressing and erotic crosscurrents that deliciously complicate the lives of the characters in *Twelfth Night* and *As You Like It* to the terrifying violence that wells up from the heart of the family in *King Lear* or from the sweet intimacy of sexual desire in *Othello*. Even the boundary between life and death is not secure, as the ghosts in *Julius Caesar, Hamlet,* and *Macbeth* attest, while the principle of natural death (given its most eloquent articulation by old Hamlet's murderer, Claudius!) is repeatedly tainted and disrupted.

Disrupted, too, is the idea of order that constantly makes its claim, most insistently in the history plays. Scholars have observed the presence in Shakespeare's works of the so-called Tudor myth—the ideological justification of the ruling dynasty as a restoration of national order after a cycle of tragic violence. The violence, Tudor apologists claimed, was divine punishment unleashed after the deposition of the anointed king, Richard II, for God will not tolerate violations of the sanctified order. Traces of this propaganda certainly exist in the histories—Shakespeare may, for all we know, have personally subscribed to its premises—but a closer scrutiny of his plays has disclosed so many ironic reservations and qualifications and subversions as to call into question any straightforward adherence to a political line. The plays manifest a profound fascination with the monarchy and with the ambitions of the aristocracy, but the fascination is never simply endorsement. There is always at least the hint of a slippage between the great figures, whether admirable or monstrous, who stand at the pinnacle of authority and the vast, miscellaneous mass of soldiers, scriveners, ostlers, poets, whores, gardeners, thieves, weavers, shepherds, country gentlemen, sturdy beggars, and the like who make up the commonwealth. And the idea of order, though eloquently articulated (most memorably by Ulysses in *Troilus and Cressida*), is always shadowed by a relentless spirit of irony.

The Play of Language

If neither the individual nor nature nor order will serve, can we find a single comprehensive name for the underlying force in Shakespeare's work? Certainly not. The work is too protean and capacious. But much of the energy that surges through this astonishing body of plays and poems is closely linked to the power of language. Shakespeare was the supreme product of a rhetorical culture, a culture steeped in the arts of persuasion and verbal expressiveness. In 1512, the great Dutch humanist Erasmus published a work called *De copia verborum* that taught its readers how to cultivate "copiousness," verbal richness, in discourse. (Erasmus obligingly provides, as a sample, a list of 144 different ways of saying "Thank you for your letter.") Recommended modes of variation include putting the subject of an argument into fictional form, as well as the use of synonym, substitution, paraphrase, metaphor, metonymy, synecdoche, hyperbole, diminution, and a host of other figures of speech. To change emotional tone, he suggests trying *ironia, interrogatio, admiratio, dubitatio, abominatio*—the possibilities seem infinite.

In Renaissance England, certain syntactic forms or patterns of words known as "figures" (also called "schemes") were shaped and repeated in order to confer beauty or heighten expressive power. Figures were usually known by their Greek and Latin names, though in an Elizabethan rhetorical manual, *The Arte of English Poesie,* George Puttenham made a valiant if short-lived attempt to give them English equivalents, such as "*Hyperbole,* or the Overreacher," "*Ironia,* or the Dry Mock," and "*Ploce,* or the Doubler." Those who received a grammar-school education throughout Europe at almost any point between the Roman Empire and the eighteenth century probably knew by heart the names of up to one hundred such figures, just as they knew by heart their multiplication tables. According to one scholar's count, Shakespeare knew and made use of about two hundred.

As certain grotesquely inflated Renaissance texts attest, lessons from *De copia verborum* and similar rhetorical guides could encourage mere prolixity and verbal self-display. But even though he shared his culture's delight in rhetorical complexity, Shakespeare always understood how to swoop from baroque sophistication to breathtaking simplicity. Moreover, he grasped early in his career how to use figures of speech, tone, and rhythm not only to provide emphasis and elegant variety but also to articulate the inner lives of his characters. Take, for example, these lines from *Othello,* where, as scholars have noted, Shakespeare deftly combines four common rhetorical figures—*anaphora, parison, isocolon,* and *epistrophe*—to depict with painful vividness Othello's psychological torment:

> By the world,
> I think my wife be honest, and think she is not.
> I think that thou art just, and think thou art not.
> I'll have some proof.
>
> (3.3.388–91)

Anaphora is simply the repetition of a word at the beginning of a sequence of sentences or clauses ("I/I"). *Parison* is the correspondence of word to word within adjacent sentences or clauses, either by direct repetition ("think/think") or by the matching of noun with noun, verb with verb ("wife/thou"; "be/art"). *Isocolon* gives exactly the same length to corresponding clauses ("and think she is not/and think thou art not"), and *epistrophe* is the mirror image of *anaphora* in that it is the repetition of a word at the end of a sequence of sentences or clauses ("not/not"). Do we need to know the Greek names for these figures in order to grasp the effectiveness of Othello's lines? Of course not. But Shakespeare and his contemporaries, convinced that rhetoric provided the most natural and powerful means by which feelings could be conveyed to readers and listeners, were trained in an analytical language that helped at once to promote and to account for this effectiveness. In his 1593 edition of *The Garden of Eloquence,* Henry Peacham remarks that *epistrophe* "serveth to leave a word of importance in the end of a sentence, that it may the longer hold the sound in the mind of the hearer," and in *Directions for Speech and Style* (c. 1599), John Hoskins notes that *anaphora* "beats upon one thing to cause the quicker feeling in the audience."

Shakespeare also shared with his contemporaries a keen understanding of the ways that rhetorical devices could be used not only to express powerful feelings but to hide them: after all, the artist who created Othello also created Iago, Richard III, and Lady Macbeth. He could deftly skewer the rhetorical affectations of Polonius in *Hamlet* or the pedant Holophernes in *Love's Labour's Lost.* He could deploy stylistic variations to mark the boundaries not of different individuals but of different social realms; in *A Midsummer Night's Dream,* for example, the blank verse of Duke Theseus is played off against the rhymed couplets of the well-born young lovers, and both in turn contrast with the prose spoken by the artisans. At the same time that he thus marks boundaries between both individuals and groups, Shakespeare shows a remarkable ability to establish unifying patterns of imagery that knit together the diverse strands of his plot and suggest subtle links among characters who may be scarcely aware of how much they share with one another.

One of the hidden links in Shakespeare's own works is the frequent use he makes of a somewhat unusual rhetorical figure called *hendiadys*. An example from the Roman poet Virgil is the phrase *pateris libamus et auro*, "we drink from cups and gold" (*Georgics* 2.192). Rather than serving as an adjective or a dependent noun, as in "golden cups" or "cups of gold," the word "gold" serves as a substantive joined to another substantive, "cups," by a conjunction, "and." Shakespeare uses the figure over three hundred times in all, and since it does not appear in ancient or medieval lists of tropes and schemes and is treated only briefly by English rhetoricians, he may have come upon it directly in Virgil. *Hendiadys* literally means "one through two," though Shakespeare's versions often make us quickly, perhaps only subliminally, aware of the complexity of what ordinarily passes for straightforward perceptions. When Othello, in his suicide speech, invokes the memory of "a malignant and a turbaned Turk," the figure of speech at once associates enmity with cultural difference and keeps them slightly apart. And when Macbeth speaks of his "strange and self-abuse," the *hendiadys* seems briefly to hold both "strange" and "self" up for scrutiny. It would be foolish to make too much of any single feature in Shakespeare's varied and diverse creative achievement, and yet this curious rhetorical scheme has something of the quality of a fingerprint.

But all of his immense rhetorical gifts, though rich, beautiful, and supremely useful, do not adequately convey Shakespeare's relation to language, which is less strictly functional than a total immersion in the arts of persuasion may imply. An Erasmian admiration for copiousness cannot fully explain Shakespeare's astonishing vocabulary of some 25,000 words. (His closest rival among the great English poets of the period was John Milton, with about 12,000 words, and most major writers, let alone ordinary people, have much smaller vocabularies.) This immense word hoard, it is worth noting, was not the result of scanning a dictionary; in the late sixteenth century, there were no English dictionaries of the kind to which we are now accustomed. Shakespeare seems to have absorbed new words from virtually every discursive realm he ever encountered, and he experimented boldly and tirelessly with them. These experiments were facilitated by the very fact that dictionaries as we know them did not exist and by a flexibility in grammar, orthography, and diction that the more orderly, regularized English of the later seventeenth and eighteenth centuries suppressed.

Owing in part to the number of dialects in London, pronunciation was variable, and there were many opportunities for phonetic association between words: the words "bear," "barn," "bier," "bourne," "born," and "barne" could all sound like one another. Homonyms were given greater scope by the fact that the same word could be spelled so many different ways—Christopher Marlowe's name appears in the records as Marlowe, Marloe, Marlen, Marlyne, Merlin, Marley, Marlye, Morley, and Morle—and by the fact that a word's grammatical function could easily shift, from noun to verb, verb to adjective, and so forth. Since grammar and punctuation did not insist on relations of coordination and subordination, loose, nonsyntactic sentences were common, and etymologies were used to forge surprising or playful relations between distant words.

It would seem inherently risky for a popular playwright to employ a vocabulary so far in excess of what most mortals could possibly possess, but Shakespeare evidently counted on his audience's linguistic curiosity and adventurousness, just as he counted on its general and broad-based rhetorical competence. He was also usually careful to provide a context that in effect explained or translated his more arcane terms. For example, when Macbeth reflects with horror on his murderous hands, he shudderingly imagines that even the sea could not wash away the blood; on the contrary, his blood-stained hand, he says, "will rather / The multitudinous seas incarnadine." The meaning of the unfamiliar word "incarnadine" is explained by the next line: "Making the green one red" (2.2.59–61).

What is most striking is not the abstruseness or novelty of Shakespeare's language but its extraordinary vitality, a quality that the playwright seemed to pursue with a kind of passionate recklessness. Perhaps Samuel Johnson was looking in the right direction when he complained that the "quibble," or pun, was "the fatal Cleopatra for which

[Shakespeare] lost the world, and was content to lose it." For the power that continually discharges itself throughout the plays, at once constituting and unsettling everything it touches, is the polymorphous power of language, language that seems both costume and that which lies beneath the costume, personal identity and that which challenges the merely personal, nature and that which enables us to name nature and thereby distance ourselves from it.

Shakespeare's language has an overpowering exuberance and generosity that often resembles the experience of love. Consider, for example, Oberon's description in *A Midsummer Night's Dream* of the moment when he saw Cupid shoot his arrow at the fair vestal: "Thou rememb'rest," he asks Puck,

> Since once I sat upon a promontory
> And heard a mermaid on a dolphin's back
> Uttering such dulcet and harmonious breath
> That the rude sea grew civil at her song
> And certain stars shot madly from their spheres
> To hear the sea-maid's music?
>
> (2.1.148–54)

Here, Oberon's composition of place, lightly alluding to a classical emblem, is infused with a fantastically lush verbal brilliance. This brilliance, the result of masterful alliterative and rhythmical technique, seems gratuitous—that is, it does not advance the plot, but rather exhibits a capacity for display and self-delight that extends from the fairies to the playwright who has created them. The rich music of Oberon's words imitates the "dulcet and harmonious breath" he is intent on recalling, breath that has, in his account, an oddly contradictory effect: it is at once a principle of order, so that the rude sea is becalmed like a lower-class mob made civil by a skilled orator, and a principle of disorder, so that celestial bodies in their fixed spheres are thrown into mad confusion. And this contradictory effect, so intimately bound up with an inexplicable, supererogatory, and intensely erotic verbal magic, is a key to *A Midsummer Night's Dream,* with its exquisite blend of confusion and discipline, lunacy and hierarchical ceremony.

The fairies in this comedy seem to embody a pervasive sense found throughout Shakespeare's work that there is something uncanny about language, something that is not quite human, at least in the conventional and circumscribed sense of the human that dominates waking experience. In the comedies, this intuition is alarming but ultimately benign: Oberon and his followers trip through the great house at the play's close, blessing the bridebeds and warding off the nightmares that lurk in marriage and parenthood. But there is in Shakespeare an alternative, darker vision of the uncanniness of language, a vision also embodied in creatures that test the limits of the human—not the fairies of *A Midsummer Night's Dream* but the weird sisters of *Macbeth.* When in the tragedy's opening scene the witches chant "Fair is foul, and foul is fair" (1.1.10), they unsettle through the simplest and most radical act of linguistic equation (x is y) the fundamental antinomies through which a moral order is established. And when Macbeth appears onstage a few minutes later, his first words unconsciously echo what we have just heard from the witches' mouths: "So foul and fair a day I have not seen" (1.3.36). What is the meaning of this linguistic "unconscious"? On the face of things, Macbeth presumably means only that the day of fair victory is also a day of foul weather, but the fact that he echoes the witches (something that we hear but that he cannot know) intimates an occult link between them, even before their direct encounter. It is difficult, perhaps impossible, to specify exactly what this link signifies—generations of emboldened critics have tried without notable success—but we can at least affirm that its secret lair is in the play's language, like a half-buried pun whose full articulation will entail the murder of Duncan, the ravaging of his kingdom, and Macbeth's own destruction.

Macbeth is haunted by half-buried puns, equivocations, and ambiguous grammatical constructions known as amphibologies. They manifest themselves most obviously in the words of the witches, from the opening exchanges to the fraudulent assurances that deceive Macbeth at the close, but they are also present in his most intimate and private reflections, as in his tortured broodings about his proposed act of treason:

> If it were done when 'tis done, then 'twere well
> It were done quickly. If th'assassination
> Could trammel up the consequence, and catch
> With his surcease success: that but this blow
> Might be the be-all and the end-all, here,
> But here upon this bank and shoal of time,
> We'd jump the life to come.
>
> (1.7.1–7)

The dream is to reach a secure and decisive end, to catch as in a net (hence "trammel up") all of the slippery, unforeseen, and uncontrollable consequences of regicide, to hobble time as one might hobble a horse (another sense of "trammel up"), to stop the flow ("success") of events, to be, as Macbeth later puts it, "settled." But Macbeth's words themselves slip away from the closure he seeks; they slide into one another, trip over themselves, twist and double back and swerve into precisely the sickening uncertainties their speaker most wishes to avoid. And if we sense a barely discernible note of comedy in Macbeth's tortured language, a discordant playing with the senses of the word "done" and the hint of a childish tongue twister in the phrase "catch / With his surcease success," we are in touch with a dark pleasure to which Shakespeare was all his life addicted.

Look again at the couplet from *Cymbeline*: "Golden lads and girls all must, / As chimney-sweepers, come to dust."

The playwright who insinuated a pun into the solemn dirge is the same playwright whose tragic heroine in *Antony and Cleopatra*, pulling the bleeding body of her dying lover into the pyramid, says, "Our strength is all gone into heaviness" (4.16.34). He is the playwright whose Juliet, finding herself alone on the stage, says, "My dismal scene I needs must act alone" (*Romeo and Juliet* 4.3.19), and the playwright who can follow the long, wrenching periodic sentence that Othello speaks, just before he stabs himself, with the remark "O bloody period!" (5.2.366). The point is not merely the presence of puns in the midst of tragedy (as there are stabs of pain in the midst of Shakespearean comedy); it is rather the streak of wildness that they so deliberately disclose, the sublimely indecorous linguistic energy of which Shakespeare was at once the towering master and the most obedient, worshipful servant.

The Dream of the Master Text

Shakespeare and the Printed Book

Ben Jonson's famous tribute to Shakespeare—"He was not of an age, but for all time!"—comes in one of the dedicatory poems to the 1623 First Folio of *Mr. William Shakespeares Comedies, Histories, & Tragedies.* This large, handsome volume, the first collection of Shakespeare's plays, was not, as far as we know, the product of the playwright's own design. We do not even know if he would have approved of the Folio's division of each play into five acts or its organization of the plays into three loose generic categories. Several of the plays grouped among the histories—*Richard Duke of York* (3 *Henry VI*), *Richard II,* and *Richard III*—had been printed separately during Shakespeare's lifetime as tragedies; one of the most famous of his tragedies had appeared as *The History of King Lear.* The Folio editors evidently decided to group together as "histories" only those plays which dealt with English history after the Norman Conquest; hence, *King Lear,* set in ancient Britain, appears with the "tragedies," and so, too, despite its happy ending, does *Cymbeline, King of Britain.* One play, *Troilus and Cressida,* was printed first as a "history," then printed in a second version with a preface that describes it as a "comedy," and then printed in the Folio as a "tragedy." As a fitting

Sixteenth-century printing shop. Engraving by Jan van der Straet. From *Nova Reperta* (1580).

emblem of the confusion, *Troilus and Cressida* does not appear in the Folio title page: apparently included only at the last minute, it was placed, unpaginated, after the last of the histories and the first of the tragedies. Modern readers, who remain perplexed by its genre, may take some consolation from the fact that for Shakespeare and his contemporaries generic boundaries were not hard and fast.

Published seven years after the playwright's death, the Folio was printed by the London printers William and Isaac Jaggard, who were joined in this expensive venture by Edward Blount, John Smethwicke, and William Aspley. It was edited by two of Shakespeare's old friends and fellow actors, John Heminges and Henry Condell, who claimed to be using "True Originall Copies" in the author's own hand. (None of these copies has survived, or, more cautiously, none has to date been found.) Eighteen plays included in the First Folio had already appeared individually in print in the small-format and relatively inexpensive texts called "Quartos" (or, in one case, the still smaller format called "Octavo"); to these, Heminges and Condell added eighteen others never before published: *All's Well That Ends Well, Antony and Cleopatra, As You Like It, The Comedy of Errors, Coriolanus, Cymbeline, All Is True (Henry VIII), Julius Caesar, King John, Macbeth, Measure for Measure, The Taming of the Shrew, The Tempest, Timon of Athens, Twelfth Night, The Two Gentlemen of Verona, The Winter's Tale,* and *1 Henry VI.** None of the

*This sketch simplifies several complex questions such as the status of the 1594 Quarto called *The Taming of a Shrew,* sufficiently distinct from the similarly titled Folio text as to constitute for many editors a different play.

plays included in the Folio has dropped out of the generally accepted canon of Shakespeare's works, and only two plays not included in the volume (*Pericles* and *The Two Noble Kinsmen*) have been allowed to join this select company, along with the nondramatic poems. Of the latter, *Venus and Adonis* (1593) and *The Rape of Lucrece* (1594) first appeared during Shakespeare's lifetime in Quartos with dedications from the author to the Earl of Southampton. *Shakespeare's Sonnets* (1609) were apparently printed without his authorization, as were his poems in a collection called *The Passionate Pilgrim* (1599).

Over the centuries, there have been many attempts to discover and authenticate additional works partly or entirely written by Shakespeare. An interesting case has been made for sections of a history play entitled *King Edward the Third* and for some small traces in the eighteenth-century tragicomedy *The Double Falsehood*, allegedly based on a manuscript of the lost Shakespearean play *Cardenio*. The *Norton Shakespeare* includes a poem, "Shall I die?" whose original inclusion in the 1988 *Oxford Shakespeare* provoked vigorous debate and much skepticism. Still more skepticism greeted the attribution to Shakespeare of a long poem called "A Funeral Elegy," printed in an appendix to *The Norton Shakespeare*'s first edition and now dropped in the wake of widespread consensus that the attribution was false. In the future, other claimants will no doubt come forward, but, with the very few additions already noted, the Folio will always remain the foundation of Shakespeare's dramatic canon.

The plays were the property of the theatrical company in which Shakespeare was a shareholder. It was not normally in the interest of such companies to have their scripts circulating in print, at least while the plays were actively in repertory: players evidently feared competition from rival companies and thought that reading might dampen playgoing. Plays were generally sold only when the theaters were temporarily closed by plague, or when the company was in need of capital (four of Shakespeare's plays were published in 1600, presumably to raise money to pay the debts incurred in building the new Globe), or when a play had grown too old to revive profitably. There is no evidence that Shakespeare himself disagreed with this professional caution, no sign that he wished to see his plays in print. Unlike Ben Jonson, who took the radical step of rewriting his own plays for publication in the 1616 folio of his *Works*, Shakespeare evidently was not interested in constituting his plays as a canon. If in the sonnets he imagines his verse achieving a symbolic immortality, this dream apparently did not extend to his plays, at least through the medium of print.

Moreover, there is no evidence that Shakespeare had an interest in asserting authorial rights over his scripts or that he or any other working English playwright had a public "standing," legal or otherwise, from which to do so. (Jonson was ridiculed for his presumption.) There is no indication whatever that he could, for example, veto changes in his scripts or block interpolated scenes or withdraw a play from production if a particular interpretation, addition, or revision did not please him. To be sure, in his advice to the players, Hamlet urges that those who play the clowns "speak no more than is set down for them," but—apart from the question of whether the Prince speaks for the playwright—the play within the play in *Hamlet* is precisely an instance of a script altered to suit a particular occasion. It seems likely that Shakespeare would have routinely accepted the possibility of such alterations. Moreover, he would of necessity have routinely accepted the possibility, and in certain cases the virtual inevitability, of cuts in order to stage his plays in the two to two and one-half hours that was the normal performing time. There is an imaginative generosity in many of Shakespeare's scripts, as if he were deliberately offering his fellow actors more than they could use on any one occasion and, hence, giving them abundant materials with which to reconceive and revivify each play again and again as they or their audiences liked it. The Elizabethan theater, like most theater in our own time, was a collaborative enterprise, and the collaboration almost certainly extended to decisions about selection, trimming, shifts of emphasis, and minor or major revision.

For many years, it was thought that Shakespeare himself did little or no revising. Some recent editors—above all the editors of the *Oxford Shakespeare*, whose texts the

Norton presents—have argued persuasively that there are many signs of authorial revision, even wholesale rewriting. But there is no sign that Shakespeare sought through such revision to bring each of his plays to its "perfect," "final" form. On the contrary, many of the revisions seem to indicate that the scripts remained open texts, that the playwright and his company expected to add, cut, and rewrite as the occasion demanded.

Ralph Waldo Emerson once compared Shakespeare and his contemporary Francis Bacon in terms of the relative "finish" of their work. All of Bacon's work, wrote Emerson, "lies along the ground, a vast unfinished city." Each of Shakespeare's dramas, by contrast, "is perfect, hath an immortal integrity. To make Bacon's work complete, he must live to the end of the world." Recent scholarship suggests that Shakespeare was more like Bacon than Emerson thought. Neither the Folio nor the quarto texts of Shakespeare's plays bear the seal of final authorial intention, the mark of decisive closure that has served, at least ideally, as the guarantee of textual authenticity. We want to believe, as we read the text, "This is the play as Shakespeare himself wanted it read," but there is no license for such a reassuring sentiment. To be "not of an age, but for all time" means in Shakespeare's case not that the plays have achieved a static perfection, but that they are creatively, inexhaustibly unfinished.

That we have been so eager to link certain admired scripts to a single known playwright is closely related to changes in the status of artists in the Renaissance, changes that led to a heightened interest in the hand of the individual creator. Like medieval painting, medieval drama gives us few clues as to the particular individuals who fashioned the objects we admire. We know something about the places in which these objects were made, the circumstances that enabled their creation, the spaces in which they were placed, but relatively little about the particular artists themselves. It is easy to imagine a wealthy patron or a civic authority in the late Middle Ages commissioning a play on a particular subject (appropriate, for example, to a seasonal ritual, a religious observance, or a political festivity) and specifying the date, place, and length of the performance, the number of actors, even the costumes to be used, but it is more difficult to imagine him specifying a particular playwright and still less insisting that the entire play be written by this dramatist alone. Only with the Renaissance do we find a growing insistence on the name of the maker, the signature that heightens the value and even the meaning of the work by implying that it is the emanation of a single, distinct shaping consciousness.

In the case of Renaissance painting, we know that this signature does not necessarily mean that every stroke was made by the master. Some of the work, possibly the greater part of it, may have been done by assistants, with only the faces and a few finishing touches from the hand of the illustrious artist to whom the work is confidently attributed. As the skill of individual masters became more explicitly valued, contracts began to specify how much was to come from the brush of the principal painter. Consider, for example, the Italian painter Luca Signorelli's contract of 1499 for frescoes in Orvieto Cathedral:

> The said master Luca is bound and promises to paint [1] all the figures to be done on the said vault, and [2] especially the faces and all the parts of the figures from the middle of each figure upwards, and [3] that no painting should be done on it without Luca himself being present. . . . And it is agreed [4] that all the mixing of colours should be done by the said master Luca himself.

Such a contract at once reflects a serious cash interest in the characteristic achievement of a particular artist and a conviction that this achievement is compatible with the presence of other hands, provided those hands are subordinate, in the finished work. For paintings on a smaller scale, it was more possible to commission an exclusive performance. Thus, the contract for a small altarpiece by Signorelli's great teacher, Piero della Francesca, specifies that "no painter may put his hand to the brush other than Piero himself."

There is no record of any comparable concern for exclusivity in the English theater. Unfortunately, the contracts that Shakespeare and his fellow dramatists almost certainly signed have not, with one significant exception, survived. But plays written for the professional theater are by their nature an even more explicitly collective art form than paintings; they depend for their full realization on the collaboration of others, and that collaboration may well extend to the fashioning of the script. It seems that some authors may simply have been responsible for providing plots that others then dramatized; still others were hired to "mend" old plays or to supply prologues, epilogues, or songs. A particular playwright's name came to be attached to a certain identifiable style—a characteristic set of plot devices, a marked rhetorical range, a tonality of character—but this name may refer in effect more to a certain product associated with a particular playing company than to the individual artist who may or may not have written most of the script. The one contract whose details do survive, that entered into by Richard Brome and the actors and owners of the Salisbury Court Theatre in 1635, does not stipulate that Brome's plays must be written by him alone or even that he must be responsible for a certain specifiable proportion of each script. Rather, it specifies that the playwright "should not nor would write any play or any part of a play to any other players or playhouse, but apply all his study and endeavors therein for the benefit of the said company of the said playhouse." The Salisbury Court players want rights to everything Brome writes for the stage; the issue is not that the plays associated with his name be exclusively *his* but rather that he be exclusively *theirs*.

Recent textual scholarship, then, has been moving steadily away from a conception of Shakespeare's plays as direct, unmediated emanations from the mind of the author and toward a conception of them as working scripts, composed and continually reshaped as part of a collaborative commercial enterprise in competition with other, similar enterprises. One consequence has been the progressive weakening of the idea of the solitary, inspired genius, in the sense fashioned by Romanticism and figured splendidly in the statue of Shakespeare in the public gardens in Germany's Weimar, the city of Goethe and Schiller: the poet, with his sensitive, expressive face and high domed forehead sitting alone and brooding, a skull at his feet, a long-stemmed rose in his crotch. In place of this projection of German Romanticism, we have now a playwright and sometime actor who is also (to his considerable financial advantage) a major shareholder in the company—the Lord Chamberlain's Men, later the King's Men—to which he loyally supplies for most of his career an average of two plays per year.

These developments are salutary insofar as they direct attention to the actual conditions in which the textual traces that the Folio calls Shakespeare's "Comedies, Histories, & Tragedies" came to be produced, reproduced, consumed, revised, and transmitted to future generations. They highlight elements that Shakespeare shared with his contemporaries, and they insistently remind us that we are encountering scripts written primarily for the stage and not for the study. They make us more attentive to such matters as business cycles, plague rolls, the cost of costumes, government censorship, and urban topography and less concerned with the elusive and enigmatic details of the poet's biography—his supposed youthful escapades and erotic yearnings and psychological crises.

All well and good. But the fact remains that in 1623, seven years after the playwright's death, Heminges and Condell thought they could sell copies of their expensive collection of Shakespeare's plays—"What euer you do," they urge their readers, "buy"— by insisting that their texts were "as he conceiued them." This means that potential readers in the early seventeenth century were already interested in Shakespeare's "conceits"—his "wit," his imagination, and his creative power—and were willing to assign a high value to the products of his particular, identifiable skill, one distinguishable from that of his company and of his rival playwrights. After all, Jonson's tribute praises Shakespeare not as the playwright of the incomparable King's Men but as the equal of Aeschylus, Sophocles, and Euripides. And if we now see Shakespeare's dramaturgy in the context of his contemporaries and of a collective artistic practice, readers continue to have little difficulty recognizing that most of the plays attached to his name tower over those of his rivals.

From Foul to Fair: The Making of the Printed Play

What exactly is a printed play by Shakespeare? Is it like a novel or a poem? Is it like the libretto or the score of an opera? Is it the trace of an absent event? Is it the blueprint of an imaginary structure that will never be completed? Is it a record of what transpired in the mind of a man long dead? We might say cautiously that it is a mechanically reproduced version of what Shakespeare wrote, but unfortunately, with the possible (and disputed) exception of a small fragment from a collaboratively written play called *Sir Thomas More,* virtually nothing Shakespeare actually wrote in his own hand survives. We might propose that it is a printed version of the script that an Elizabethan actor would have held in his hands during rehearsals, but here, too, no such script of a Shakespeare play survives; and besides, Elizabethan actors were evidently not given the whole play to read. To reduce the expense of copying and the risk of unauthorized reproduction, each actor received only his own part, along with the cue lines. (Shakespeare uses this fact to delicious comic effect in *A Midsummer Night's Dream* 3.1.80–88.) Nonetheless, the play certainly existed as a whole, either in the author's original manuscript or in the copy prepared for the government censor or for the company's prompter or stage manager, so we might imagine the text we hold in our hands as a printed copy of one of these manuscripts. But since no contemporary manuscript survives of any of Shakespeare's plays, we cannot verify this hypothesis. And even if we could, we would not have resolved the question of the precise relation of the printed text either to the playwright's imagination or to the theatrical performance by the company to which he belonged.

All of Shakespeare's plays must have begun their textual careers in the form of "foul papers," drafts presumably covered with revisions, crossings-out, and general "blotting." To be sure, Heminges and Condell remark that so great was the playwright's facility that they "have scarce received from him a blot in his papers." This was, however, a routine and conventional compliment in the period. The same claim, made for the playwright John Fletcher in an edition published in 1647, is clearly contradicted by the survival of Fletcher's far-from-unblotted manuscripts. It is safe to assume that, since Shakespeare was human, his manuscripts contained their share of second and third thoughts scribbled in the margins and between the lines. Once complete, this authorial draft would usually have to be written out again, either by the playwright or by a professional scribe employed by the theater company, as "fair copy."

In the hands of the theater company, the fair copy (or sometimes, it seems, the foul papers themselves) would be annotated and transformed into "the book of the play" or the "playbook" (what we would now call a "promptbook"). Shakespeare's authorial draft presumably contained a certain number of stage directions, though these may have been sketchy and inconsistent. The promptbook clarified these and added others, noted theatrical properties and sound effects, and on occasion cut the full text to meet the necessities of performance. The promptbook was presented to the Master of the Revels for licensing, and it incorporated any changes upon which the master insisted. As the editors of the *Oxford Shakespeare* put it, the difference between foul papers and promptbook is the difference between "the text in an as yet individual, private form" and "a socialized text."

But the fact remains that for Shakespeare's plays, we have neither foul papers nor fair copies nor promptbooks. We have only the earliest printed editions of these texts in numerous individual quartos and in the First Folio. (Quartos are so called because each sheet of paper was folded twice, making four leaves or eight pages front and back; folio sheets were folded once, making two leaves or four pages front and back.) From clues embedded in these "substantive" texts—substantive because (with the exception of *The Two Noble Kinsmen*) they date from Shakespeare's own lifetime or from the collected works edited by his associates using, or claiming to use, his own manuscripts—editors attempt to reconstruct each play's journey from manuscript to print. Different plays took very different journeys.

Of the thirty-six plays included in the First Folio, eighteen had previously appeared in quarto editions, some of these in more than one printing. Generations of editors have distinguished between "good Quartos," presumably prepared from the author's own draft or from a scribal transcript of the play (fair copy), and "bad Quartos." The latter category, first formulated as such by A. W. Pollard in 1909, includes, by widespread but not universal agreement, the 1594 version of *The First Part of the Contention (2 Henry VI)*, the 1595 *Richard Duke of York (3 Henry VI)*, the 1597 *Richard the Third*, the 1597 *Romeo and Juliet*, the 1600 *Henry the Fifth*, the 1602 *Merry Wives of Windsor*, the 1603 *Hamlet*, and *Pericles* (1609). Some editors also regard the 1591 *Troublesome Reign of King John*, the 1594 *Taming of a Shrew*, and the 1608 *King Lear* as bad Quartos, but others have strenuously argued that these are distinct rather than faulty texts, and the whole concept of the bad Quarto has come under increasingly critical scrutiny. The criteria for distinguishing between "good" and "bad" texts are imprecise, and the evaluative terms seem to raise as many questions as they answer. Nevertheless, the striking mistakes, omissions, repetitions, and anomalies in a number of the Quartos require some explanation beyond the ordinary fallibility of scribes and printers.

The explanation most often proposed for suspect Quartos is that they are the products of "memorial reconstruction." The hypothesis, first advanced in 1910 by W. W. Greg, is that a series of features found in what seem to be particularly flawed texts may be traced to the derivation of the copy from the memory of one or more of the actors. Elizabethan actors, Greg observed, often found themselves away from the London theaters—for example, on tour in the provinces during plague periods—and may not on those occasions have had access to the promptbooks they would ordinarily have used. In such circumstances, those in the company who remembered a play may have written down or dictated the text, as best they could, perhaps adapting it for provincial performance. Moreover, unscrupulous actors may have sold such texts to enterprising printers eager to turn a quick profit.

Memorially reconstructed texts tend to be much shorter than those prepared from foul papers or fair copy; they frequently paraphrase or garble lines, drop or misplace speeches and whole scenes, and on occasion fill in the gaps with scraps from other plays. In several cases, scholars think they can detect which roles the rogue actors played, since these parts (and the scenes in which they appear) are reproduced with greater accuracy than the rest of the play. Typically, these roles are minor ones, since the leading parts would be played by actors with a greater stake in the overall financial interest of the company and, hence, less inclination to violate its policy. Thus, for example, editors speculate that the bad Quarto of *Hamlet* (Q1) was provided by the actor playing Marcellus (and doubling as Lucianus). What is often impossible to determine is whether particular differences between a bad Quarto and a good Quarto or Folio text result from the actor's faulty memory or from changes introduced in performance, possibly with the playwright's own consent, or from both. Shakespearean bad Quartos ceased to appear after 1609, perhaps as a result of greater scrutiny by the Master of the Revels, who after 1606 was responsible for licensing plays for publication as well as performance.

The syndicate that prepared the Folio had access to the manuscripts of the King's Men. In addition to the previously published editions of eighteen plays, they made use of scribal transcripts (fair copies), promptbooks, and (more rarely) foul papers. The indefatigable labors of generations of bibliographers, antiquaries, and textual scholars have recovered an extraordinary fund of information about the personnel, finances, organizational structure, and material practices of Elizabethan and Jacobean printing houses, including the names and idiosyncrasies of particular compositors who calculated the page length, set the type, and printed the sheets of the Folio. This impressive scholarship has for the most part intensified respect for the seriousness with which the Folio was prepared and printed, and where the Folio is defective, it has provided plausible readings from the Quartos or proposed emendations to approximate what Shakespeare is likely to have written. But it has not succeeded, despite all its heroic efforts, in transforming the Folio, or any other text, into an unobstructed, clear window into Shakespeare's mind.

The dream of the master text is a dream of transparency. The words on the page should ideally give the reader unmediated access to the astonishing forge of imaginative power that was the mind of the dramatist. Those words welled up from the genius of the great artist, and if the world were not an imperfect place, they would have been set down exactly as he conceived them and transmitted to each of us as a precious inheritance. Such is the vision—at its core closely related to the preservation of the holy text in the great scriptural religions—that has driven many of the great editors who have for centuries produced successive editions of Shakespeare's works. The vision was not yet fully formed in the First Folio, for Heminges and Condell still felt obliged to apologize to their noble patrons for dedicating to them a collection of mere "trifles." But by the eighteenth century, there were no longer any ritual apologies for Shakespeare; instead, there was a growing recognition not only of the supreme artistic importance of his works but also of the uncertain, conflicting, and in some cases corrupt state of the surviving texts. Every conceivable step, it was thought, must be undertaken to correct mistakes, strip away corruptions, return the texts to their pure and unsullied form, and make this form perfectly accessible to readers.

Paradoxically, this feverishly renewed, demanding, and passionate editorial project has produced the very opposite of the transparency that was the dream of the master text. The careful weighing of alternative readings, the production of a textual apparatus, the writing of notes and glosses, the modernizing and regularizing of spelling and punctuation, the insertion of scene divisions, the complex calculation of the process of textual transmission from foul papers to print, the equally complex calculation of the effects that censorship, government regulation, and, above all, theatrical performance had on the surviving documents all make inescapably apparent the fact that we do not have and never will have any direct, unmediated access to Shakespeare's imagination. Every Shakespeare text, from the first that was published to the most recent, has been edited: it has come into print by means of a tangled social process and inevitably exists at some remove from the author.

Heminges and Condell, who knew the author and had access to at least some of his manuscripts, lament the fact that Shakespeare did not live "to have set forth and overseen his own writings." And even had he done so—or, alternatively, even if a cache of his manuscripts were discovered in a Warwickshire attic tomorrow—all of the editorial problems would not be solved, nor would all of the levels of mediation be swept away. Certainly, the entire textual landscape would change. But the written word has strange powers: it seems to hold on to something of the very life of the person who has written it, but it also seems to pry that life loose from the writer, exposing it to vagaries of history and chance independent of those to which the writer was personally subject. Moreover, with the passing of centuries, the language itself and the whole frame of reference within which language and symbols are understood have decisively changed. The most learned modern scholar still lives at a huge experiential remove from Shakespeare's world and, even holding a precious copy of the First Folio in hand, cannot escape having to read across a vast chasm of time what is, after all, an edited text. The rest of us cannot so much as indulge in the fantasy of direct access: our eyes inevitably wander to the glosses and the explanatory notes.

The Oxford Shakespeare

The shattering of the dream of the master text is no cause for despair, nor should it lead us to throw our hands up and declare that one text is as good as another. What it does is to encourage the reader to be actively interested in the editorial principles that underlie the particular edition that he or she is using. It is said that the great artist Brueghel once told a nosy connoisseur who had come to his studio, "Keep your nose out of my paintings; the smell of the paint will poison you." In the case of Shakespeare, it is increasingly important to bring one's nose close to the page, as it were, and sniff the ink. More precisely, it is important to understand the rationale for the choices that the editors have made.

The text of the *Norton Shakespeare* is, with very few changes, that published by the Oxford University Press in 1988 and, in a second edition, in 2005. The *Oxford Shakespeare* was the extraordinary achievement of a team of editors, Stanley Wells, Gary Taylor, John Jowett, and William Montgomery, with Wells and Taylor serving as the general editors. The Oxford editors approached their task with a clear understanding that, as we have seen, all previous texts have been mediated by agents other than Shakespeare; however, they regard this mediation not as a melancholy obstacle intervening between the reader and the "true" Shakespearean text but rather as a constitutive element of this text. The art of the playwright is thoroughly dependent on the craft of go-betweens.

Shakespeare's plays were not written to be circulated in manuscript or printed form among readers. They were written to be performed by the players and, as the preface to the Quarto *Troilus and Cressida* indelicately puts it, "clapper-clawed with the palms of the vulgar." The public was, thus, never meant to be in a direct relationship with the author but in a "triangular relationship" in which the players gave voice and gesture to the author's words. As we have seen, Shakespeare was the master of the unfinished, the perpetually open. And even if we narrow our gaze and try to find only what Shakespeare himself might have regarded as a textual resting point, a place to stop and go on to another play, we have, the Oxford editors point out, a complex task. For whatever Shakespeare wrote was meant from the start to be supplemented by an invisible "paratext" consisting of words spoken by Shakespeare to the actors and by the actors to each other concerning emphasis, stage business, tone, pacing, possible cuts, and so forth. To the extent that this paratext was ever written down, it was recorded in the promptbook. Therefore, in contrast to standard editorial practice, the Oxford editors prefer, when there is a choice, copy based on the promptbook to copy based on the author's own draft. They choose the text immersed in history—that is, in the theatrical embodiment for which it was intended by its author—over the text unstained by the messy, collaborative demands of the playhouse. The closest we can get to Shakespeare's "final" version of a play—understanding that for him as for us there is no true "finality" in a theatrical text—is the latest version of that play performed by his company during his professional life—that is, during the time in which he could still oversee and participate in any cuts and revisions.

This choice does not mean that the Oxford editors are turning away from the very idea of Shakespeare as author. On the contrary, Wells and Taylor are deeply committed to establishing a text that comes as close as possible to the plays as Shakespeare wrote them, but they are profoundly attentive to the fact that he wrote them as a member of a company of players, a company in which he was a shareholder and an actor as well as a writer. "Writing" for the theater, at least for Shakespeare, is not simply a matter of setting words to paper and letting the pages drift away; it is a social process as well as an individual act. The Oxford editors acknowledge that some aspects of this social process may have been frustrating to Shakespeare: he may, for example, have been forced on occasion to cut lines and even whole scenes to which he was attached, or his fellow players may have insisted that they could not successfully perform what he had written, compelling him to make changes he did not welcome. But compromise and collaboration are part of what it means to be in the theater, and Wells and Taylor return again and again to the recognition that Shakespeare was, supremely, a man of the theater.

Is there a tension between the Oxford editors' preference for the performed, fully socialized text and their continued commitment to recovering the text as Shakespeare himself intended it? Yes. The tension is most visible in their determination to strip away textual changes arising from circumstances, such as government censorship, over which Shakespeare had no control. ("We have, wherever possible," they write, put "profanities back in Shakespeare's mouth.") It can be glimpsed as well in the editors' belief, almost a leap of faith, that there was little revision of Shakespeare's plays in his company's revivals between the time of his death and the publication of the Folio. But the tension is mainly a creative one, for it forces them (and, therefore, us) to attend to the playwright's unique imaginative power as well as his social and historical entanglements.

The Oxford editors took a radical stance on a second major issue: the question of authorial revision. Previous editors had generally accepted the fact that Shakespeare practiced revision within individual manuscripts—that is, while he was still in the act of writing a particular play—but they generally rejected the notion that he undertook substantial revisions from one version of a play to another (and, hence, from one manuscript to another). Wells and Taylor point out that six major works (*Hamlet, Othello, 2 Henry IV, King Lear, Richard II,* and *Troilus and Cressida*) survive in two independent substantive sources, both apparently authoritative, with hundreds of significant variant readings. Previous editors have generally sought to deny authority to one edition or another ("faced with two sheep," the Oxford editors observe wryly, "it is all too easy to insist that one *must* be a goat") or have conflated the two versions into a single text in an attempt to reconstruct the ideal, definitive, complete, and perfect version that they imagine Shakespeare must have reached for each of his plays. But if one doubts that Shakespeare ever conceived of his plays as closed, finished entities, if one recalls that he wrote them for the living repertory of the commercial playing company to which he belonged, then the whole concept of the single, authoritative text of each play loses its force. In a startling departure from the editorial tradition, the *Oxford Shakespeare* printed two distinct versions of *King Lear*, quarto and Folio, and the editors glanced longingly at the impractical but alluring possibility of including two texts of *Hamlet, Othello,* and *Troilus.*

The *Oxford Shakespeare* was published in both old-spelling and modern-spelling editions. The former, the first of its kind ever published, raised some reviewers' eyebrows because the project, a critical edition rather than a facsimile, required the modern editors to invent plausible Elizabethan spellings for their emendations and to add stage directions. The modern-spelling edition, which is the basis for Norton's text, is noteworthy for taking the principles of modernization further than they had generally been taken. Gone are such words as "murther," "mushrump," "vild," and "porpentine," which confer on many modern-spelling editions a certain cozy, Olde-English quaintness; Oxford replaces them with "murder," "mushroom," "vile," and "porcupine."

The inclusion of two texts of *King Lear* aroused considerable controversy when the *Oxford Shakespeare* first appeared, although by now the arguments for doing so have received widespread, though not unanimous, scholarly support. Other features remain controversial: "Ancients" Pistol and Iago have been modernized to "Ensigns"; *Henry VIII* has reverted to its performance title *All Is True*; demonic spirits in *Macbeth* sing lyrics written by Thomas Middleton. The white-hot intensity of the debates triggered by the *Oxford Shakespeare*'s editorial choices casts an interesting light on the place of Shakespeare not only in the culture at large but in the psyches of millions of individuals: any alteration, however minor, in a deeply familiar and beloved text, even an alteration based on thoughtful and highly plausible scholarly principles, arouses genuine anxiety. The anxiety in this case was intensified not only by the boldness of certain crucial emendations but also by the fact that the editors' explanations, arguments, and justifications for all their decisions were printed in a separate, massive volume, *William Shakespeare: A Textual Companion.* This formidable, dense volume is an astonishing monument to the seriousness, scholarly rigor, and immense labor of the Oxford editors. Anyone who is interested in pursuing why Shakespeare's words appear as they do in the current edition, anyone who wishes insight into the editors' detailed reasons for making the thousands of decisions required by a project of this kind, should consult the *Textual Companion.*

The Norton Shakespeare

The primary task that the editors of the *Norton Shakespeare* set themselves was to present the modern-spelling Oxford *Complete Works* in a way that would make the text more accessible to modern readers. The *Oxford Shakespeare* prints little more than the text itself: along with one-page introductions to the individual works, it contains a short general introduction, a list of contemporary allusions to Shakespeare, and a brief glossary. But while it is possible to enjoy a Shakespeare play on stage or screen without any assistance beyond the actors' own art, many readers at least since the eighteenth century have found it far more difficult to understand and to savor the texts without some more substantial commentary.

In addition to writing introductions, textual notes, and brief bibliographies for each of the works, the Norton editors provide glosses and footnotes designed to facilitate comprehension. Such is the staggering richness of Shakespeare's language that it is tempting to gloss everything. But there is a law of diminishing returns: too much explanatory whispering at the margins makes it difficult to enjoy what the reader has come for in the first place. Our general policy is to gloss only those words that cannot be found in an ordinary dictionary or whose meanings have altered out of recognition. The glosses attempt to be simple and straightforward, giving multiple meanings for words only when the meanings are essential for making sense of the passages in which they appear. We try not to gloss the same word over and over—it becomes distracting to be told three times on a single page that "an" means "if"—but we also assume that the reader does not have a perfect memory, so after an interval we will gloss the same word again.

Marginal glosses generally refer to a single word or a short phrase. The footnotes paraphrase longer units or provide other kinds of information, such as complex plays on words, significant allusions, textual cruxes, historical and cultural contexts. Here, too, however, we have tried to check the impulse to annotate so heavily that the reader is distracted from the pleasure of the text, and we have avoided notes that provide interpretation, as distinct from information.

Following the works, the Norton editors have provided lists of textual variants. These are variants from the control text only—that is, they do not record all of the variants in all of the substantive texts, nor do they record all of the myriad shifts of meaning that may arise from modernization of spelling and repunctuation. Readers who wish to pursue these interesting, if complex, topics are encouraged to consult the *Textual Companion*, along with the old-spelling *Oxford Shakespeare*, the Norton facsimile of the First Folio, and the quarto facsimiles published by the University of California Press. The *Norton Shakespeare* does provide a convenient list for each play of the different ways the same characters are designated in the speech prefixes in the substantive texts. These variants (for example, Lady Capulet in *Romeo and Juliet* is called, variously, "Lady, "Mother," "Wife," "Old Woman," etc.) often cast an interesting light on the ways a particular character is conceived. Variants as they appear in this edition, as well as their line numbers, are printed in boldface; each is followed by the corresponding reading in the control text, and sometimes the source from which the variant is taken. Further information on readings in substantive texts is given in brackets.

Stage directions pose a complex set of problems for the editors of a one-volume Shakespeare. The printing conventions for the stage directions in sixteenth- and seventeenth-century plays were different from those of our own time. Often all of the entrances for a particular scene are grouped together at the beginning, even though some of the characters clearly do not enter until later; placement in any case seems at times haphazard or simply incorrect. There are moments when the stage directions seem to provide stunning insight into the staging of the plays in Shakespeare's time, other moments when they are absent or misleading. It is difficult to gauge how much the stage directions in the substantive editions reflect Shakespeare's own words or at least decisions. It would seem that he was often relatively careless about them, understanding perhaps that these decisions in any precise sense would be the first to be made and unmade by different productions.

The Oxford editors, like virtually all modern editors, necessarily altered and supplemented the stage directions in their control texts. They decided to mark certain of the stage directions with a special sign to indicate a dubious action or placement, but they did not distinguish between the stage directions that came from the substantive texts and those added in later texts, from the seventeenth century to the present. They referred readers instead to the *Textual Companion,* which provides lists of the exact wording of the stage directions in the substantive texts.

The editors of the *Norton Shakespeare* share a sense of the limitations of the early stage directions and share as well some skepticism about how many of these should be attributed even indirectly to Shakespeare. Hence, we do not routinely differentiate between quarto and Folio stage directions; we do so only when we think it is a significant point. But there is, it seems to us, a real interest in knowing which stage directions come from those editions of the plays published up to the 1623 Folio (and including *The Two Noble Kinsmen,* published shortly thereafter) and which were added when the editors were no longer in contact with Shakespeare's presence or his manuscripts. Therefore, we have placed brackets around all stage directions that were added after the First Folio. Unbracketed stage directions, then, all derive from editions up through the Folio.

The *Norton Shakespeare* has made several other significant departures from the Oxford text. The Oxford editors note that when *1 Henry IV* was first performed, probably in 1596, the character we know as Sir John Falstaff was called Sir John Oldcastle. But in the wake of protests from Oldcastle's descendants, one of whom, William Brooke, tenth Baron Cobham, was Elizabeth I's lord chamberlain, Shakespeare changed the name to "Falstaff" (and probably for similar reasons changed the names of Falstaff's companions, Russell and Harvey, to "Bardolph" and "Peto"). Consistent with their decision not to honor changes that Shakespeare was *compelled* to make by censorship or other forms of pressure, the Oxford editors changed the names back to their initial form. But this decision is a problem for several reasons. It draws perhaps too sharp a distinction between those things that Shakespeare did under social pressure and those he did of his own accord. More seriously, it pulls against the principle of a text that represents the latest performance version of a play during Shakespeare's lifetime: after all, even the earliest quarto title page advertises "the humorous conceits of Sir John Falstaff." And, of course, it asks the reader to ignore completely and radically centuries of response—elaboration, fascination, and love—all focused passionately on Sir John Falstaff. The response is not a modern phenomenon: it began with Shakespeare, who developed the character as Sir John Falstaff in *2 Henry IV* and *The Merry Wives of Windsor.* Norton thus restores the more familiar names.

Another major departure from the Oxford text is Norton's printing of the so-called Additional Passages, especially in *Hamlet.* Consistent with their decision not to conflate quarto and Folio texts, the Oxford editors adhere to their control text for *Hamlet,* the Folio, and print those passages that appear only in the Second Quarto in an appendix at the end of the play. As explained at length in the Textual Note to the play, the Norton editors decided not to follow this course, but instead chose a different way of demarcating the quarto and Folio texts (inserting the quarto passages, indented, in the body of the text), one that makes it easier to see how the quarto passages functioned in a version of the play that Shakespeare also authored.

The *Norton Shakespeare* follows Oxford in printing separate quarto and Folio texts of *King Lear,* to which we have added a conflated version of the play so that readers will have the opportunity to assess for themselves the effects of the traditional editorial practice. Moreover, we have departed from Oxford in printing the quarto and Folio texts of the plays on facing pages, so that their differences can be readily weighed. In the hundreds of changes, some trivial and other momentous, it is possible to glimpse, across what Prospero calls "the dark backward and abysm of time," a thrilling sight: Shakespeare at work.

The Shakespearean Stage
by
ANDREW GURR

Publication by Performance

The curt exchange between the sentries in the first six lines of *Hamlet* tells us that it is very late at night (" 'Tis now struck twelve") and that " 'tis bitter cold." This opening was staged originally at the Globe in London in broad daylight, at 2 o'clock probably on a hot summer's afternoon. The words required the audience, half of them standing on three sides of the stage platform and all of them as visible to one another as the players were, to imagine themselves watching a scene quite the opposite of what they could see and feel around them. The original mode of staging for a Shakespearean play was utterly different from the cinematic realism we are used to now, where the screen gives us close-ups on a simulacrum of reality, an even more privileged view of the actors' facial twitches than we get in ordinary life. Eloquence then was in words, not facial expressions.

The playgoers of Shakespeare's time knew the plays in forms at which we can only now guess. It is a severe loss. Shakespeare's own primary concept of his plays was as stories "personated" onstage, not as words on a page. He himself never bothered to get his playscripts into print, and more than half of them were not published until seven years after his death, in the First Folio of his plays published as a memorial to him in 1623. His fellow playwright Francis Beaumont called the printing of plays "a second publication"; the first was their showing onstage. Print recorded a set of scripts, written for the original players to teach them what they should speak in the ensemble of the play in production. The only technology then available to record the performances was the written word. If video recordings had existed at that time, our understanding of Shakespeare would be vastly different from what it is today.

Since the texts were composed only to be a record of the words the players were to memorize, we now have to infer how the plays were originally staged largely by guess-work. Shakespeare was himself a player and shareholder in his acting company, and he expected to be present at rehearsals. Consequently, the stage directions in his scripts are distinctly skimpy compared with some of those provided by his fellow playwrights. He was cursory even in noting entrances and exits, let alone how he expected his company to stage the more complex spectacles, such as heaving Antony up to Cleopatra on her monument. There are sometimes hints in the stage directions and more frequently in the words used to describe some of the actions, and knowing what the design of the theater was like is a help as well. Knowing more about how Shakespeare expected his plays to be staged can transform how we think about them. But gaining such knowledge is no easy matter. One of the few certainties is that Shakespeare's plays in modern performance are even more different from the originals than modern printed editions are from the first much-thumbed manuscripts.

The Shakespearean Mindset

The general mindset of the original playgoers, the patterns of thinking and expectation that Tudor culture imposed on Shakespeare's audiences, is not really difficult to identify.

It is less easy, though, to pin it down in the sort of detail that tells us what the original concept of staging the plays would have been like. We know that all the original playgoers paid for the privilege of attending the plays and committed themselves willingly to suspend their disbelief in what they were to see. They knew as we do that they were paying to be entertained by fictions. Beyond that, we need reminding today that going to open-air performances in daylight in Shakespeare's time meant being constantly aware that one was in a theater, a place designed to offer illusions. On the one hand, this consciousness of oneself and where one was meant that the players had to do more to hold attention than is needed now, when audiences have nothing but the stage to look at and armchairs to sit in. On the other hand, it made everyone more receptive to extratheatrical tricks, such as Hamlet's reference to "this distracted globe," or Polonius's claim in the same play to have taken the part of Julius Caesar at the university and been killed by Brutus. The regular playgoers at the Globe who recognized Polonius as the man who had played Caesar in Shakespeare's play of the year before, and who recognized Hamlet as the man who had played Brutus, would laugh at this theatrical in-joke. But two scenes later, when Hamlet kills Polonius, they would think of it again, in a different light.

Features of the original mindset such as these are readily identifiable. For others, though, we need to look further, into the design of the theaters and into the staging traditions that they housed and that Shakespeare exploited. Invisibility has a part to play in *A Midsummer Night's Dream* that we can easily underrate, for instance. Invisibility onstage is a theatrical in-joke, an obvious privileging of the audience, which is allowed to see what the characters onstage can't. The impresario Philip Henslowe's inventory of costumes used at the Rose theater in 1597, which lists "a robe for to go invisible," indicates a fictional device that openly expects the willing suspension of the audience's disbelief. In *A Midsummer Night's Dream*, the ostensible invisibility of all the visible fairies emphasizes the theatricality of the whole presentation while pandering to the audience's self-indulgent superiority, the feeling that it knows what is going on better than any character, whether he be Bottom or even Duke Theseus. That prepares us for the mockery of stage realism we get later, in the mechanicals' play in Act 5, and even for the doubt we as willing audience might feel over Theseus's own skepticism about the dangers of imagination that he voices in his speech at the beginning of Act 5.

More to the point, though, it throws into question our readiness to be an audience, since we have ourselves been indulging in just the games of suspending disbelief that the play staged by the mechanicals enters into so unsuccessfully. When Theseus disputes with Hippolyta about the credibility of the lovers' story, he voices the very skepticism—about the lover, the lunatic, and the poet—that any sensible realist in the audience would have been feeling for most of the previous three acts in the forest. The play starts and ends at the court in broad daylight, while the scenes of midsummer madness take place at night in a forest. At the early amphitheaters, all the plays were staged in broad daylight, between 2 and 5 o'clock in the afternoon, and without any persuasive scenery: the two stage posts served as trees onstage. So the play, moving as it does from daylight realism to nocturnal fantasy and back again, with a last challenge to credulity in the mechanicals' burlesque of how to stage a play, has already thoroughly challenged the willing suspension of the viewers' disbelief. *A Midsummer Night's Dream* is a play about nocturnal dreams and fictions that are accepted as truths in broad daylight. It was only a small extension of this game to have the women's parts played by boys, as well as plots in which the girls dressed as boys, to the point where in *As You Like It* Rosalind was played by a boy playing a girl pretending to be a boy playing a girl.

The Shakespeare plays were written for a new and unique kind of playhouse, the Elizabethan amphitheater, which had a distinctive design quite different from modern theaters. Elizabethans knew what the standard features in their theaters stood for, and Shakespeare drew on that knowledge for the staging of his plays. The physical features of the playhouses were a potent element in the ways that the plays were designed for the Elizabethan mindset. When Richard III, the archdeceiver and playactor, appears "aloft between two Bishops" to claim the crown in *Richard III* 3.7, his placing on the stage balcony literally above the crowd on the stage would, even without the accompanying priests, have signified his ironic claim to a social and moral superiority that ought to have matched his elevation. When Richard II comes down from the wall of Flint Castle to the "base court" in *Richard II* 3.3, Elizabethans would have seen his descent as a withdrawal from power and status. These theaters were still new when Shakespeare started to write for them, and their novelty meant that the plays were written more tightly to fit their specific design than the plays of later years, when theatergoing had become a more routine social activity and different kinds of theater were available.

London Playgoing and the Law

This heightened sense of theatricality, or "metatheater," in Shakespearean audiences was far from the only difference in their mindset from that of all modern audiences. Regular playgoing in London only started in the 1570s, and through Shakespeare's earlier years it was always a perilous and precarious activity. The Lord Mayor of London and the mayors of most of England's larger towns hated playgoing and tried to suppress it whenever and wherever it appeared. Playgoing was exciting not only because it was new but because it was dangerous. The hostility of so many authorities to plays meant that they were seen almost automatically as subversive of authority. Paradoxically, the first London companies were only able to establish themselves in London through the active support of Queen Elizabeth and her Privy Council, which tried hard, in the face of constant complaints from the Lord Mayor, to ensure that the best companies would be on hand every Christmas to entertain the Queen's leisure hours. Popular support for playgoing depended on royal protection for the leading companies.

London was by far the largest city in England. Within a few years of Shakespeare's death, it became the largest in Europe. It was generally an orderly place to live, especially in the city itself. Even in the suburbs, where the poorer people had to live, there were not many of the riots and other disorders that preachers always associated with the brothels, animal-baiting arenas, and playhouses clustering there. The reputation that the playhouses gained for promoting riots was not well justified. Any crowd of people was seen by the authorities as a potential riot, and playhouses regularly drew some of the largest crowds that London had yet seen. The city's government was not designed to control large crowds of people. There was no paid police force, and the Lord Mayor was held responsible by the Privy Council, the Queen's governing committee, for any disorders that did occur. So the city authorities found that playgoing challenged their control over their people.

The rapid growth of London did not help the situation. Officially, the city was governed by the Lord Mayor and his council. But he had authority only inside the city, and London now spread through a large suburban area in the adjacent counties of Middlesex to the north and Surrey across the river to the south. Because the court and the national government were housed in London, the Privy Council often intervened in city affairs in its own interests, as well as when orders were needed that covered broader zones than the city itself. The periodic outbreaks of bubonic plague were one clear instance of such a need, because the plague took no notice of parish or city boundaries. The intrusion of the professional companies to play in London provided another. In the early years, they were chronic travelers, and London was simply one of many stopovers. But the Queen enjoyed seeing plays at Christmas, and her council accordingly supported the best companies so that they could perform for her. It protected the playing companies against the hatred of successive Lord Mayors, except when a national emergency such as a plague epidemic erupted. The Privy Council took control then by ordering the 126 parishes in and around London to list all deaths from plague separately from ordinary deaths. Each Thursday, the parish totals were added together. When the total number of deaths from plague in these lists rose above 30 in any one week, the Privy Council closed all places of public assembly. This meant especially the playhouses, which created by far the largest gatherings. When the theaters were closed, the playing companies had to revert to their traditional practice of going on tour to play in the towns through the country, provided that the news of plague did not precede them.

Plague was not the only reason for the government to lay its controlling hand on the companies. From the time the post was inaugurated in 1578, the Master of the Revels controlled all playing. He was executive officer to the Lord Chamberlain, the Privy Council officer responsible for the annual season of royal entertainment and thus, by extension, for the professional playing companies. The Master of the Revels licensed each company and censored its plays. He was expected to cut out any references to religion or affairs of state, and he tried to prevent other offenses by banning the depiction of any living person onstage. After 1594, he issued licenses to the approved London playhouses, too. Later still, the printing of any playbook was allowed only if he gave authority for it. The companies had to accept this tight control because the government was its only protector against the hostile municipal authorities, who included not only the Lord Mayor of London but also the mayors of most of the major towns in the country.

Most mayors had the commercial interest of keeping local employees at work to justify their hostility to playgoing. But across the country, the hostility went much deeper. A large proportion of the population disliked the very idea of playacting. Their reasons, ostensibly religious, were that for actors to pretend to be characters they were unlike in life was a deception and that for boys to dress as women was contrary to what the Bible said. Somewhere beneath this was a more basic fear of pretense and deceit, of people not acting honestly. It put actors into the same category as con men, cheats, and thieves. That was probably one reason why companies of boys acting men's parts were thought rather more tolerable than men pretending to be other kinds of men. The deception involved in boys playing men was more transparent than when men played characters other than themselves. There was also a strong Puritan suspicion about shows of any kind, which looked too much like the Catholic ceremonial that the new Church of England had renounced. Playgoing found much better favor on the Catholic side of English society than on the Puritan side. Different preachers took different positions over the new phenomenon of playgoing. But few would speak in its favor, and most of them openly disapproved of it. Playgoing was an idle pastime, and the devil finds work for idle hands.

In the 1590s, when *Romeo and Juliet* and Shakespeare's histories and early comedies were exciting audiences, only two playhouses and two companies were officially approved by the Queen's Privy Council for the entertainment of London's citizens. The other main forms of paid entertainment were bear- and bullbaiting, which were much harder on the performers than was playing and so could be staged less frequently. The hostility to plays meant that the right to perform was confined to only a few of the most outstanding companies. These few companies were in competition with one another, and this led to a rapid growth in the quality of their offerings. But playacting was always a marginal activity. Paying to enter a specially built theater in order to see professional companies perform plays was still a new phenomenon, and it still met with great opposition from the London authorities. The open-air theaters like the Globe were built out in the suburbs. London as a city had no centrally located playhouses until after the civil war and the restoration of the monarchy, in 1661. And even playing in the city's suburbs, where they were free from the Lord Mayor's control, the companies had to work under the control of the Privy Council. All the great amphitheaters were built either in Middlesex or in Surrey. At the height of their success, in the years after Shakespeare's death, the Privy Council never licensed more than four or five playhouses in London.

Playgoing in London was viewed even by the playgoers as an idle occupation. The largest numbers who went to the Globe were apprentices and artisans taking time off from work, often surreptitiously, and law students from the Inns of Court doing the same. These fugitives were linked with the wealthier kind of idler, "gallants" or rich gentlemen and other men of property, along with soldiers and sailors on leave from the wars, people visiting London from the country on business or pleasure (usually both), and above all the women of London. Women were not expected to be literate, but one did not need to be able to read and write to enjoy hearing and seeing a play. A respectable woman had to make sure she was escorted by a man. He might be a husband or a friend, or her page if she was rich, or her husband's apprentice if she was a middle-class citizen. She might have a mask on, part of standard women's wear outdoors to protect the face against the weather and to assert modesty—and perhaps anonymity. Market women (applewives and fishwives) went to plays in groups. Whores were expected to be there looking for business, especially from the gallants, but they usually had male escorts, too.

The social range of playgoers at the two playhouses approved for use in 1594 was almost complete, stretching from the aristocracy to the poorest workmen and boys. Many people disapproved of plays, but at peak times up to 25,000 a week flocked to see the variety of plays being offered. Prices for playgoing remained much the same throughout the decades up to 1642, when the parliamentary government that was fighting the King closed all the theaters for eighteen years. Until then, one could get standing room at an amphitheater for 1 penny (¹⁄₂₄₀th of a modern pound, roughly 1 cent),

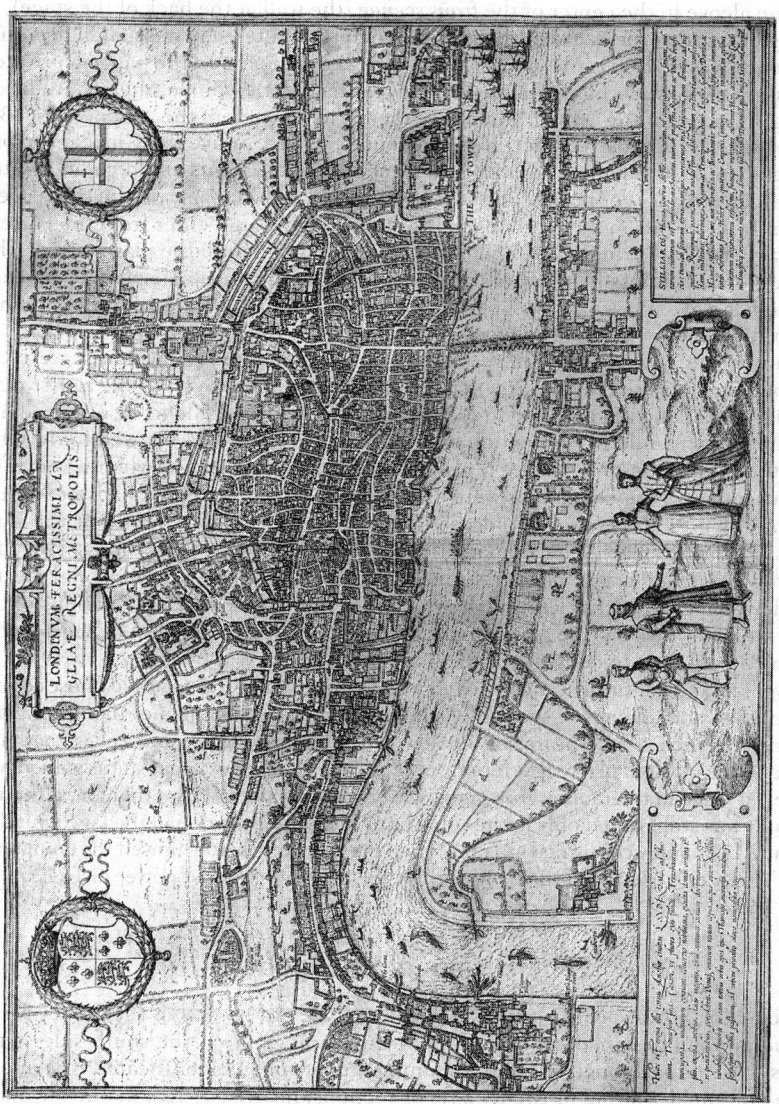

The city of London and its suburbs in 1572.

or a seat on a bench in the roofed galleries for twopence. A seat in a lord's room cost sixpence, which was not much less than a day's wage for a skilled artisan in 1600. The smaller roofed theaters that opened in 1599 were much more expensive. They were called "private" theaters to distinguish them from the "public" open-air amphitheaters, although the claim to privacy was mainly a convenient fiction to escape the controls imposed on the "public" theaters. At the Blackfriars hall theater, sixpence only gained you a seat in the topmost gallery, while a seat in the pit near the stage cost three times that amount and a seat in a box five times, or half a skilled worker's weekly wage.

It was not only the plays and players that were the sights at the playhouses. The richest lords and gallants went to be seen as much as they went to see. At the Globe, the costliest rooms were positioned alongside the balcony "above," over the stage. They were called "lords' rooms," and the playgoers who chose to sit there had a limited view of what went on beneath them. They saw no "discoveries," for instance, such as Portia's three caskets in *The Merchant of Venice*, which were uncovered underneath them inside the alcove in the center of the *frons scenae* (the wall at the back of the stage), or anything other than the backs of the players when they entered. But as audience, they were themselves highly visible, and that was what they paid for. In the hall, or "private," playhouses, with much higher admission prices than at the Globe, there were boxes flanking the stage for the gentry, which gave them a better view of the "discoveries." But at these "select" (because costlier) hall playhouses, where, unlike the Globe, everyone had a seat, some of the most colorful and exhibitionistic gallants could go one better. Up to fifteen gallants could pay for a stool to sit and watch the play on the stage itself, sitting in front of the boxes that flanked the stage. Each would enter from the players' dressing room (the "tiring-house") with his stool in hand before the play started. This gave them the best possible view of the play and easily the most conspicuous place in the audience's eye. Playgoing was a public occasion in which the visibility of audience members allowed them to play almost as large a part as the players.

Through the 1590s, the only permanent and custom-made playhouses were the large open-air theaters. Paying sixpence for a ferry across the river, as the richer playgoers did, or walking across London Bridge to the Rose or the Globe, or else trudging north through the mud of Shoreditch and Finsbury Fields or Clerkenwell to the Theatre or the Fortune in order to see a play, did not have great appeal when it was raining. Consequently, the companies were always trying to secure roofed halls nearer the city center. Up to 1594, they could use city inns, especially in winter, but the Lord Mayor's hostility to playing never made them reliable places for performing. Two constant problems troubled the players throughout these first years of professional theater in London: the city officials' chronic hatred of plays and the periodic visitations of the plague, which always led the government to close the theaters as soon as the number of plague deaths rose to dangerously high levels.

Playgoing was not firmly established in London until the Privy Council chose to protect it in 1594 and to approve specific playhouses for the two companies that it officially sanctioned. By then, Shakespeare had already made his mark. He became a player, a shareholder, and the resident playwright for one of these two companies. That status gained him a privileged place in the rapidly growing new world of playgoing. From then on, although his theater was still located only in the suburbs of the city, his work had the law behind it. That status was amply confirmed in 1603, when the new King made himself the company's patron. The King's Men held their status until the King himself lost power in 1642.

The Design of the Globe

The Globe was Shakespeare's principal playhouse. He put up part of the money for its construction and designed his best plays for it. It was built on the south side of the Thames in 1599, fashioned out of the framing timbers of an older theater. Essentially, it was a polygonal scaffold of twenty bays or sections, nearly 100 feet in outside diameter, making a circle of three levels of galleries that rose to more than 30 feet high, with wooden bench seating and cushions for those who could afford them. This surrounded an open "yard," into which the stage projected.

The yard was over 70 feet in diameter. Nearly half the audience stood on their feet to watch the play from inside this yard, closest to the stage platform. The stage extended out nearly to the middle of the yard, so the actors could stand in the center of the crowd. The uncertain privilege of having standing room in the open air around the stage platform could be bought with the minimal price for admission, 1 penny (about a cent). It had the advantage of proximity to the stage and the players; its disadvantage was keeping you on your feet for the two or three hours of the play, as well as leaving you subject to the weather. If you wanted a seat, or if it rained and you wanted shelter, you paid twice as much to sit in the three ranks of roofed galleries that circled behind the crowd standing in the yard. With some squeezing, the theater could hold over 3,000 people. It was an open-air theater because that gave it a larger capacity than a roofed hall. The drawback of its being open to the weather was more than outweighed by the gain in daylight that shone on stage and spectators alike.

The stage was a great square platform as much as 40 feet wide. It had over it a canopied roof, or "heavens," to protect the players and their expensive costumes from rain. This canopy was held up by two pillars rising through the stage. The stage platform was about 5 feet high and without any protective rails, so that the eyes of the audience in the yard were at the level of the players' feet. At the back of the stage, a wall—the *frons scenae*—stretched across the front of the players' tiring-house, the attiring or dressing room. It had a door on each flank and a wider curtained space in the center, which was used for major entrances and occasionally for set-piece scenes. Above these entry doors was a gallery or balcony, most of which was partitioned into rooms for the wealthiest spectators. A central room "above" was sometimes used in staging: for example, as Juliet's balcony, as the place for Richard III to stand between the bish-

The second Globe, from Wenceslaus Hollar's engraving of the "Long View" of London (1647). The two captions saying "The Globe" and "Beere bayting h." were accidentally transposed in the original. The Globe is the round structure in the center of the picture.

A photograph of the interior framework of the "new" Globe, on the south bank of the Thames in London, showing the general dimensions of the yard and the surrounding galleries.

ops, as the wall of Flint Castle in *Richard II*, and as the wall over the city gates of Harfleur in *Henry V*. After 1608, when Shakespeare's company acquired the Blackfriars consort of musicians, this central gallery room was turned into a curtained-off music room that could double as an "above" when required. Fewer than half of Shakespeare's plays need an "above."

The Original Staging Techniques

Shakespearean staging was emblematic. The "heavens" that covered the stage was the colorful feature from which gods descended to the earth of the stage platform. When Jupiter made his appearance in *Cymbeline*, in clouds of "sulphurous breath" provided by fireworks, he was mounted on an eagle being lowered through a trapdoor in the heavens. The other trapdoor, set in the stage platform itself, symbolized the opposite, a gateway to hell. The large stage trap was the place where the Gravedigger came to work at the beginning of Act 5 of *Hamlet*. It was the cell where Malvolio was imprisoned in *Twelfth Night*. The Shakespearean mindset accepted such conventions automatically.

Shakespeare inherited from Marlowe a tradition of using the stage trap as the dreaded hell's mouth. Barabbas plunges into it in *The Jew of Malta*, and the demons drag the screaming Faustus down it at the end of *Dr. Faustus*. Hell was not a fiction taken lightly by Elizabethans. Edward Alleyn, by far the most famous player of Faustus in the 1590s, wore a cross on his breast while he played the part, as insurance—just in case the fiction turned serious. Tracking the Elizabethan mindset about the stage trapdoor can give us a few warnings of what we might overlook when we come fresh to the plays today.

In the original staging of *Hamlet* at the Globe, the stage trap had two functions. Besides serving as Ophelia's grave, it was the distinctive entry point, not used by any other character, for the Ghost in Act 1. When he tells his son that he is "for the day confined to fast in fires," the first audiences would have already taken the point that he

The Globe as reconstructed in Southwark near the original site in London.

had come up from the underworld. His voice comes from under the stage, telling the soldiers to swear the oath of secrecy that Hamlet lays upon them. The connection between that original entry by the Ghost through the trap and the trap's later use for Ophelia is one we might easily miss. At the start of Act 5, the macabre discussion between the Gravediggers about whether she committed suicide and is, therefore, con-

The *frons scenae* of the new Globe.

A gesture using the language of hats, as shown by the man attending the brothers Browne.

signed to hell gets its sharpest edge from the association of the trap, here the grave being dug for her, with the Ghost's purgatorial fires. More to the point, though, Hamlet, as he eavesdrops on the curtailed burial ceremony, makes the same connection when he discovers that it is the body of Ophelia being so neglectfully interred. He remembers the other apparition that came up through the trap and springs forward in a grotesque parody of the Ghost, crying, "This is I, Hamlet the Dane!" It is a melodramatic claim to be acting a new role, that of his father the dead King. The first audiences would have remembered the ghost of dead King Hamlet using the stage trap at this point more readily than we do now. Hamlet's private knowledge of the Ghost and the trapdoor sets him, as so often happens in the play, at odds with his audience. Consequently, centuries of editors, like the characters onstage, have misread this claim as a declaration that young Hamlet ought to be King.

Since his own name is Hamlet, and since he alone could have made the connection between the Ghost and the trapdoor, he was all too likely to be misunderstood. In the next scene, Osric certainly shows that he understands Hamlet's graveside claim that he is his father's ghost to be a claim that he should now be King of Denmark. That explains why Osric insists on keeping his hat in his hand when he comes to invite Hamlet to duel with Laertes. With equals, an Elizabethan gentleman would doff his hat in greeting and then put it back on. Only in the presence of your master, or as a courtier in the presence of the King, did you keep it in your hand. Osric is trying tactfully to acknowledge what he thinks is Hamlet's lunatic claim to be King. He missed the private connection that Hamlet had made with the trapdoor and his father's ghost. Tudor body language, with its wordless gestures and signals that defined human relations, was an aspect of social life so widely understood that it needed no stage direction. The language of hats was a part of the Shakespearean mindset that we now have to register in footnotes.

Other signifiers are necessarily more elusive. We might take heart from the range of the comments made in *Much Ado About Nothing* 4.1 when Hero is accused and is seen to go red. Each of the viewers—Claudio, Leonato, and Friar Francis—gives a different reading (or "noting") of her blush. Different mindsets lead to visual indicators being read in different ways. Each reading tells as much about the observer as about the thing observed. We might add that since the blush is commented on so extensively, Shakespeare must have been concerned to save the boy playing Hero from the necessity of holding his breath long enough to produce the right visual effect.

Costume was a vital element in the plays, a mute and instant signifier of the scene. If a character entered carrying a candle and dressed in a gown with a nightcap on his head, he had evidently just been roused from bed. Characters who entered wearing cloaks and riding boots and possibly holding a whip had just ended a long journey. York,

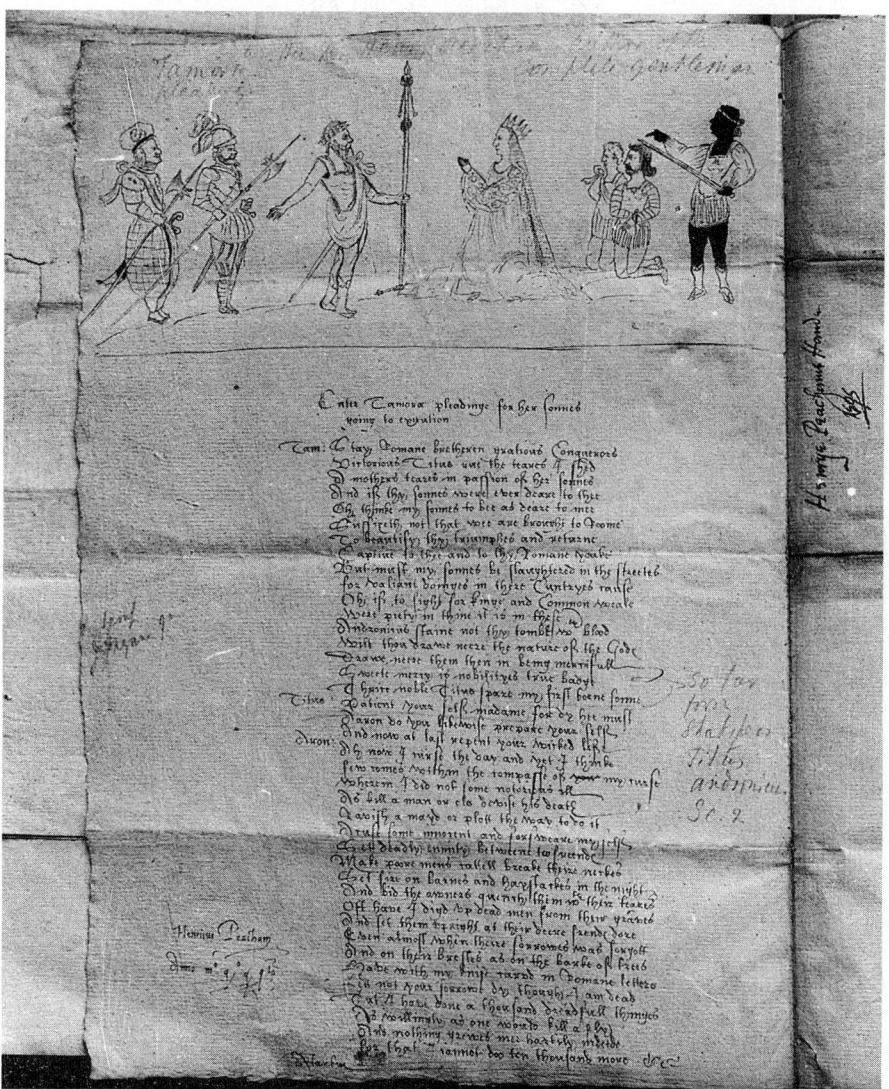

A sketch by Henry Peacham of an early staging of *Titus Andronicus* by Shakespeare's company (1595). Note the attempt at a Roman costume for Titus but not for his soldiers, who carry Tudor halberds, and note Aaron's makeup and wig.

entering in *Richard II* with a gorget (a metal neck plate, the "signs of war about his agèd neck" [2.2.74]), was preparing for battle. Even the women's wigs that the boys wore could be used to indicate the wearer's state of mind. Hair worn loose and unbound meant madness, whether in *Hamlet*'s Ophelia or *Troilus*'s Cassandra.

Comparable audience expectations could be roused by other visual features. Characters with faces blackened and wigs of curly black wool were recognized as Moors,

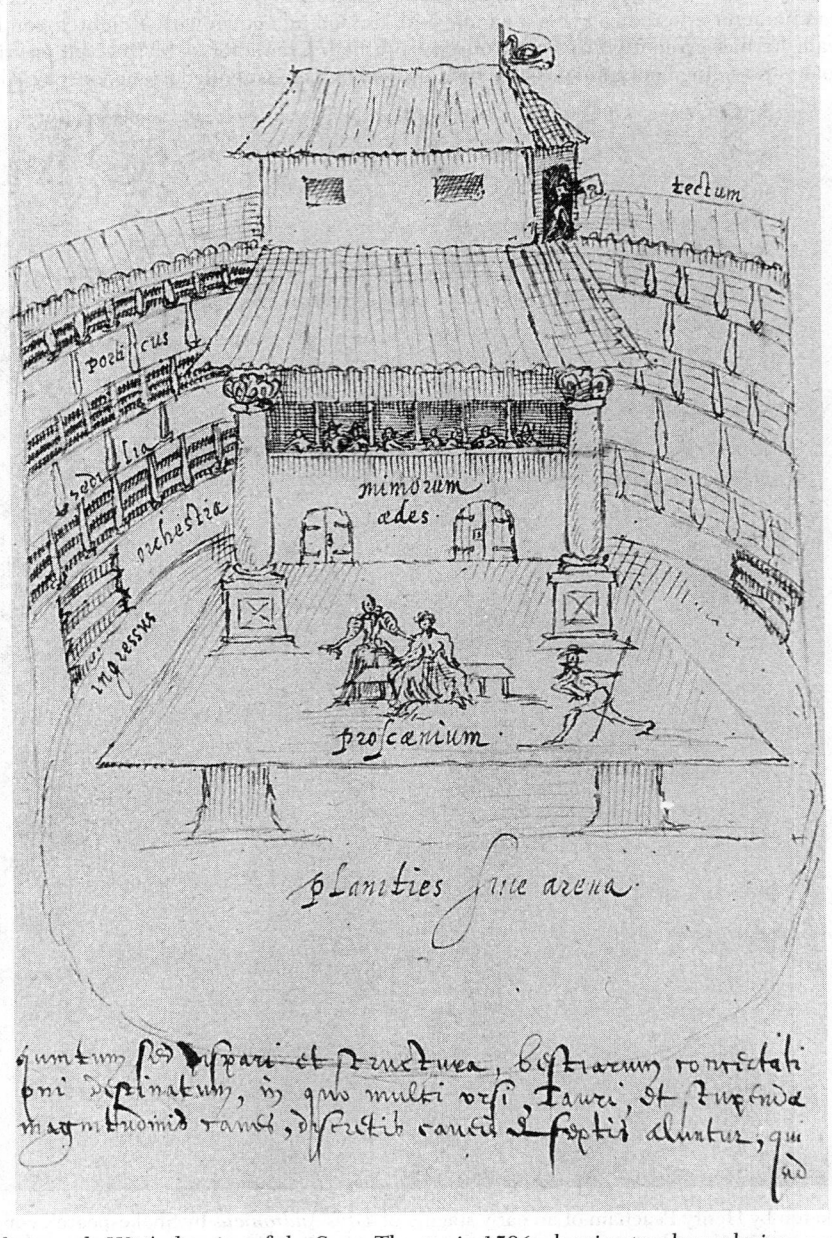

Johannes de Witt's drawing of the Swan Theatre in 1596, showing two boys playing women greeted by a chamberlain.

alien and dangerous non-Christians. Aaron the Moor in *Titus Andronicus* and the Prince of Morocco in *The Merchant of Venice* acquire that character as soon as they come in view. Othello, by Iago's report and by his own first appearance, takes on the same stereotype. By contrast, Iago is dressed like a simple and honest soldier. Only in the course of Act 1 does it become apparent that it is Othello who is the honest soldier, Iago the un-Christian alien. The play neatly reverses the visual stereotypes of Elizabethan staging. Twentieth-century playgoers miss most of these signals and the ways that the original players used them to show the discrepancy between outward appearance and inner person. As King Lear said, robes and furred gowns hide all.

For *The Merchant of Venice*, Shylock wore his "Jewish gabardine" and may also have put on a false nose, as Alleyn was said to have done for the title role in *The Jew of Malta*. Other national characteristics were noted by features of dress, such as the Irish "strait strossers" (tight trousers) that Macmorris would have worn in *Henry V*. The dress of the women in the plays, who were usually played by boys with unbroken voices, was always a special expense. The records kept by Philip Henslowe, owner of the Rose playhouse and impresario for the rival company to Shakespeare's, show that he paid the author less for the script of *A Woman Killed with Kindness* than he paid the costumer for the heroine's gown.

Women's clothing and the decorums and signals that women's costume contained were very different from those of men and men's clothing. Men frequently used their hats, doffing them to signal friendship and holding them in their hands while speaking to anyone in authority over them. Women's hats were fixed to their heads and were rarely if ever taken off in public. The forms and the language of women's clothes reflected the silent modesty and the quiet voices that men thought proper for women. Women had other devices to signal with, including handkerchiefs, fans, and face masks, and the boys playing the women's parts in the theaters exploited such accessories to the full. A lady out of doors commonly wore a mask to protect her complexion. When Othello is quizzing Emilia in 4.2 about his wife's behavior while she spoke to Cassio, he asks Emilia, who should have been chaperoning her mistress, whether Desdemona had not sent her away "to fetch her fan, her gloves, her mask, nor nothing?" There is little doubt that the boys would have routinely worn masks when they played gentlewomen onstage, and not just at the masked balls in *Romeo and Juliet*, *Love's Labour's Lost*, and *Much Ado About Nothing*.

Other features of the original staging stemmed from the actor–audience relationship, which differs radically in daylight, when both parties can see one another, from what we are used to in modern, darkened, theaters. An eavesdropping scene onstage, for instance, works rather on the same basis as the "invisible" fairies in *A Midsummer Night's Dream*, where the audience agrees to share the pretense. At the Globe, it also entailed adopting the eavesdropper's perspective. In *Much Ado*, the two games of eavesdropping played on Benedick and Beatrice are chiefly done around the two stage posts. In these scenes, the posts that held up the stage cover, or "heavens," near what we now think of as the front of the stage were round, like the whole auditorium, and their function was to allow things to be seen equally by all of the audience, wherever people might be standing or sitting. Members of the audience, sitting in the surrounding galleries or standing around the stage itself at the Globe or its predecessors, had the two tall painted pillars in their sight all the time, wherever they were in the playhouse. And since the audience was in a complete circle all around the stage, if the stage posts were used for concealment there was always a large proportion of the audience who could see the player trying to hide behind a post. It was a three-dimensional game in which the audience might find itself behind any of the game players, victims or eavesdroppers, complicit in either role.

The first of *Much Ado*'s eavesdropping scenes, 2.3, starts as usual in Shakespeare with a verbal indication of the locality. Benedick tells his boy, "Bring it hither to me in the orchard." So we don't need stage trees to tell us where we are supposed to be. He later hides "in the arbour" to listen to what Don Pedro and the others have set for him; this means concealing himself behind a stage post, closer to the audience than the playactors who are talking about him. Don Pedro asks, "See you where Benedick hath hid himself?" a self-contradiction that confirms the game. When it is Beatrice's turn in her arbor scene, 3.1, she slips into a "bower" behind "this alley," which again signals a retreat behind the prominent stage post. These games are played with both of the eavesdroppers hiding behind the post at the stage edge, while the others do their talking at center stage between the two posts.

Such games of eavesdropping, using the same bits of the stage structure, make a strong visual contrast with all that goes on at what we two-dimensional thinkers, used to the pictorial staging of the cinema, call the "back" of the stage, or upstage—where, for instance, the Friar starts the broken-off wedding and where Claudio and Don Pedro later figure at Leonato's monument. These events are more distant from the audience, less obviously comic and intimate. The close proximity of players to audience in such activities as eavesdropping strongly influenced the audience's feeling of kinship with the different groupings of players.

A multitude of other staging differences can be identified. Quite apart from the fact that the language idioms were more familiar to the playgoers at the original Globe than they are now, all playgoers in 1600, many of them illiterate, were practiced listeners. The speed of speech, even in blank verse, was markedly higher then than the recitation of Shakespeare is today. The original performances of *Hamlet*, if the Folio version reflects what was usually acted, would have run for not much more than two and a half hours (the time quoted by Ben Jonson for a play as long as *Hamlet*), compared with the more than four hours that the full Folio or 1605 quarto text with at least one intermission would take today. Quicker speaking, quicker stage action, no intermissions, and the audience's ability to grasp the language more quickly meant that the plays galloped along. The story, not the verse, carried the thrust of the action. Occasional set speeches, like Hamlet's soliloquies or Gaunt's "sceptred isle" speech in *Richard II*, would be heard, familiar as they already were to many in the audience, like a solo aria in a modern opera. In theory if not in practice, the business of hearing, as "audience" (from the Latin *audire*, "to hear"), was more important than the business of seeing, as "spectators" (from the Latin *spectare*, "to see"). The visual aspects of acting, like scenic staging, are inherently two-dimensional and do not work well when the audience completely surrounds the actors. Most of Shakespeare's fellow writers, notably Jonson, understandably set a higher priority on the audience's hearing their verse than on their seeing what the players did with the lines. The poets wanted listeners, although the players did try to cater to the viewers. Yet for all the games with magic tricks and devils spouting fireworks that were part of the Shakespearean staging tradition, spectacle was a limited resource on the scene-free Elizabethan stage. Shakespeare in this was a poet more than a player. Even in his last and most richly staged plays—*Cymbeline*, *The Winter's Tale*, and *The Tempest*—he made notably less use of such "spectacles" than did his contemporaries.

One piece of internal evidence about the original staging is Hamlet's advice to the visiting players. In 3.2, before they stage the *Mousetrap* play that he has rewritten for them, he lectures them on what a noble student of the theater then considered to be good acting. He objects first to overacting and second to the clown who ad libs with his own jokes and does not keep to the script. How far this may have been Shakespeare's own view it is impossible to say. Hamlet is an amateur lecturing professionals about how they should do their job. His views are what we would expect an amateur playwright with a liking for plays that are "caviar to the general" to hold. His objections to the clown are noteworthy, because once the original performances ended, the clown would conclude the afternoon's entertainment with a comic song-and-dance jig. Thomas Platter, a young German-speaking Swiss student, went to the Globe in 1599 to see *Julius Caesar*. He reported back home that

> on 21 September after lunch I and my party crossed the river, and there in the playhouse with the thatched roof witnessed an excellent performance of the tragedy of the first emperor Julius Caesar with a cast of about fifteen people. When the play

The hall screen in the Middle Temple Hall, built in 1574. Shakespeare's company staged *Twelfth Night* in this hall in February 1602.

was over they danced marvellously and gracefully together as their custom is, two dressed as men and two as women.[1]

The script for one jig survives, probably played by Will Kemp, who was the Shakespeare company clown until he left just before *Hamlet* came to the Globe. Its story is a bawdy knockabout tale of different men trying to seduce a shopkeeper's wife in rhyming couplets, hiding in a chest from her husband, and beating one another up. There is nothing to say what the audience reaction to such a jig might have been after they had seen a performance of *Julius Caesar* or *Hamlet*. It is possible that the Globe players stopped offering that kind of coda when they acquired the clown who played Feste in *Twelfth Night* in 1601. The song with which Feste ends that play might have become an alternative form of closure, replacing the traditional bawdy jig.

Vigorous and rapid staging was inevitable when the half of the audience closest to the stage had to stand throughout the performance. Shakespeare's plays were distinctive among the other plays of the time for their reliance on verbal sparkle over scenes of battle and physical movement, but even the soliloquies raced along. There was little occasion for long pauses and emoting. Dumb shows, like the players' prelude to the *Mousetrap* play in *Hamlet,* were the nearest that the players came to silent acting. There were no intermissions—apples, nuts, and drink were peddled in the auditorium throughout the performance—and the only "comfort stations" were, for the men, the nearest blank wall; for the women, whatever convenient pots or bottles they might be carrying under their long skirts.

Nor were there any pauses to change scenes. There was no static scenery apart from an emblematic candle to signify a night scene, a bed "thrust out" onto the stage, or the canopied chair of state on which the ruler or judge sat for court scenes. Usually any

1. *Thomas Platter's Travels in England* (1599), rendered into English from the German, and with introductory matter by Clare Williams (London: Cape, 1937), p. 166.

special locality would be signaled in the first words of a new scene, but unlocalized scenes were routine. Each scene ended when all the characters left the stage and another set entered. No act breaks appear in the plays before *The Tempest*. *Henry V* marked each act with a Chorus, but even he entered on the heels of the characters from the previous scene. Blue-coated stagehands were a visibly invisible presence onstage. They would draw back the central hangings on the *frons scenae* for a discovery scene, carry on the chair of state on its dais for courtroom scenes, or push out the bed with Desdemona on it for the last act of *Othello*. They served the stage like the house servants with whom the nobility peopled every room in their great houses, silent machines ready to spring into action when needed.

There has been a great deal of speculation about the tiring-house front at the rear of the stage platform: did it look more like an indoor set or an outdoor one, like the hall screen of a great house or palace or like a housefront exterior? In fact, it could easily be either. The upper level of the *frons*, the balconied "above," might equally represent a musicians' gallery, like those in the main hall of a great house, or a city wall under which the central discovery space served as the city gates, as it did for York in *Richard Duke of York* (3 *Henry VI*) 4.8, or *Henry V*'s Harfleur (3.3.78). The "above" could equally be an indoor gallery or an outdoor balcony. The appearance of the stage was everything and nothing, depending on what the play required. Players and playwrights expected the audience members to use their imagination, as they had to with the opening lines of *Hamlet*, or, as the Prologue to *Henry V* put it, to "piece out our imperfections with your thoughts."

Shakespeare's Companies and Their Playhouses

Shakespeare's plays were written for a variety of staging conditions. Until 1594, when he joined a new company under the patronage of the Lord Chamberlain, the Queen's officer responsible for licensing playing companies, poets had written their plays for any kind of playhouse. The Queen's Men, the largest and best company of the 1580s, is on record as playing at the Bell, the Bel Savage, and the Bull inns inside the city, and at the Theatre and the Curtain playhouses in the suburbs. Early in 1594, it completed this sweep of all the available London venues by playing at the Rose. But in that year, the system of playing changed. The Lord Mayor had always objected to players using the city's inns, and in May 1594 he succeeded in securing the Lord Chamberlain's agreement to a total ban. From then on, only the specially built playhouses in the suburbs were available for plays.

The Queen's Men had been set up in 1583, drawn from all the then-existing major companies with the best players. This larger and favored group at first monopolized playing in London. But it was in decline by the early 1590s, and the shortage of companies to perform for the Queen at Christmas led the Lord Chamberlain and his son-in-law, the Lord Admiral, to set up two new companies in its place as a duopoly in May 1594. Shakespeare became a "sharer," or partner, in one of these companies. As part of the same new establishment, his company, the Lord Chamberlain's Men, was allocated the Theatre to perform in, while its partner company in the duopoly, the Lord Admiral's Men, was assigned to the Rose. This was the first time any playing company secured a playhouse officially authorized for its use alone.

The Theatre, originally built in 1576 by James Burbage, father of the leading player of the Lord Chamberlain's company, was in Shoreditch, a suburb to the north of the city. The Rose, built in 1587 by Philip Henslowe, father-in-law of the Lord Admiral's leading player, Edward Alleyn, was in the suburb of Southwark, on the south bank of the Thames. Henslowe's business papers, his accounts, some lists of costumes and other resources, and his "diary," a day-by-day listing of each day's takings and the plays that brought the money in, have survived for the period from 1592 until well into the next decade. Together they provide an invaluable record of how one of the two major companies of the later 1590s, the only rival to Shakespeare's company, operated through these years.[2] Some of Shakespeare's earlier plays, written before he joined the Lord Chamberlain's Men, including 1 Henry VI and Titus Andronicus, were performed at the Rose. After May 1594, the new company acquired all of his early plays; every Shakespeare play through the next three years was written for the Theatre. Its familiarity supplied one sort of resource to the playwright. But the repertory system laid heavy demands on the company.

Henslowe's papers give a remarkable record of the company repertory for these years. Each afternoon, the same team of fifteen or so players would stage a different play. With only two companies operating in London, the demand was for constant change. No play at the Rose was staged more than four or five times in any month, and it was normal to stage a different play on each of the six afternoons of each week that they performed. A new play would be introduced roughly every three weeks—after three weeks of transcribing and learning the new parts; preparing the promptbook, costumes, and properties; and rehearsing in the mornings—while each afternoon, whichever of the established plays had been advertised around town on the playbills would be put on. The leading players had to memorize on average as many as eight hundred lines for each afternoon. Richard Burbage, who played the first Hamlet in 1601, probably had to play Richard III, Orlando in As You Like It, and Hamlet on successive afternoons while at the same time learning the part of Duke Orsino and rehearsing the new Twelfth Night—and still holding at least a dozen other parts in his head for the rest of the month's program. In the evenings, he might be called on to take the company to perform a different play at court or at a nobleman's house in the Strand. The best companies made a lot of money, but not without constant effort.

The companies were formed rather like guilds, controlled by their leading "sharers." Each senior player shared the company's profits and losses equally with his fellows. Most of the plays have seven or eight major speaking parts for the men, plus two for the boys playing the women. A normal London company had eight or ten sharers, who collectively chose the repertory of plays to be performed, bought the playbooks from the poets, and put up the money for the main company resource of playbooks and costumes (not to mention the wagon and horses for touring when plague forced the London theaters to close). Shakespeare made most of his fortune from his "share," first in his company and later in its two playhouses.

As a playhouse landlord, Henslowe took half of the takings from the galleries each afternoon for his rent, while the players shared all the yard takings and the other half of the gallery money. From their takings, the sharers paid hired hands to take the walk-on parts and to work as stagehands, musicians, bookkeeper or prompter, and "gatherers" at the different entry gates. The leading players also kept the boys who played the women's parts, housing and feeding them as "apprentices" in an imitation of the London livery companies and trades, which ran apprenticeships to train boys to become skilled artisans, or "journeymen." City apprenticeships ran for seven years from the age of seventeen, but the boy players began much younger, because unbroken voices were needed. They graduated to become adult players at an age when the city apprentices were only beginning their training. Most of the "extras," apart from the playing boys, would be left in London whenever the company had to go on tour.

Because the professional companies of the kind that Shakespeare joined all started as traveling groups rather than as companies settled at a single playhouse in London, the years up to 1594 yielded plays that could be staged anywhere. The company might be summoned to play at court, at private houses, or at the halls of the Inns of Court as readily as at inns or innyards or the custom-built theaters themselves. They traveled the country with their plays, using the great halls of country houses, or town guildhalls and local inns, wherever the town they visited allowed them. Consequently, the plays could not demand elaborate resources for staging. In this highly mobile tradition of traveling

2. See Henslowe's Diary, ed. R. A. Foakes (Cambridge, Eng.: Cambridge University Press, 1961).

companies, they were written in the expectation of the same basic but minimal features being available at each venue. Besides the stage platform itself, the basic features appear to have been two entry doors, usually a trap in the stage floor, a pair of stage pillars, sometimes a discovery space, and very occasionally a heavens with descent machinery. Apart from these fixtures, properties such as chairs and a table, a canopied throne on a dais, and sometimes a bed were also in regular use, though in a pinch these could be as mobile as the players themselves. The only essential traveling properties were players, playbooks, and costumes.

Once the two authorized companies settled permanently at the Theatre and the Rose in 1594, they slowly lost some of this mobility. The demands of versatility and readiness to make rapid changes now had to be switched from the venues to the plays themselves. A traveling company needed very few plays, since the locations and audiences were always changing. When the venues became fixed, it was the plays that had to keep changing. The Henslowe papers record that the Lord Admiral's Men staged an amazingly varied repertory of plays at the Rose. Shakespeare's company must have been equally versatile. The practice of giving popular plays long runs did not begin until the 1630s, by which time the number of London playhouses had grown to as many as five, all offering their plays each afternoon. Shakespeare's company in London had only the one peer from 1594 until 1600; and only two from then until 1608, aside from the once-weekly plays by the two boy companies, the "little eyases" mentioned in *Hamlet*, that started with the new century.

From May 1594 to April 1597 at the Theatre, in addition to all his earlier plays that he brought to his new company, Shakespeare gave them possibly *Romeo and Juliet* and *King John*, and certainly *Richard II, A Midsummer Night's Dream, 1 Henry IV,* and *The Merchant of Venice*. But then they ran into deep trouble, because they lost the Theatre. In April 1597, its original twenty-one-year lease expired, and the landlord, who disliked plays, refused to let them renew it. Anticipating this, the company's impresario, James Burbage, had built a new theater for them, a roofed place in the Blackfriars near St. Paul's Cathedral. The Blackfriars precinct was a "liberty," free from the Lord Mayor's jurisdiction. But the plan proved a disaster. The rich residents of Blackfriars objected, and the Privy Council stopped the theater from opening. From April 1597, Shakespeare's company had to rent the Curtain, an old neighbor of their now-silent Theatre, and it was there that the next four of Shakespeare's plays—*2 Henry IV, Much Ado About Nothing, The Merry Wives of Windsor,* and probably *Henry V*—were first staged.

In December 1598, losing hope of a new lease for the old Theatre, the Burbage sons had it pulled down and quietly transported its massive framing timbers across the Thames to make the scaffold for the Globe on the river's south bank, near the Rose. Most of their capital was sunk irretrievably into the Blackfriars theater, and they could afford only half the cost of rebuilding. So they raised money as best they could. Some of the company's more popular playbooks were sold to printers, including *Romeo and Juliet, Richard III, Richard II,* and *1 Henry IV*. More to the point, the Burbage brothers raised capital for the building by cutting in five of the leading players, including Shakespeare, and asking them to put up the other half of its cost. The Globe, its skeleton taken from the old Theatre, thus became the first playhouse to be owned by its players, and, within the limits set by the old frame, the first one built to their own design.

For this theater, one-eighth of which he personally owned, Shakespeare wrote his greatest plays: *Julius Caesar, As You Like It, Hamlet, Twelfth Night, Othello, All's Well That Ends Well, Measure for Measure, King Lear, Macbeth, Pericles, Antony and Cleopatra, Coriolanus, Cymbeline, The Winter's Tale,* and most likely *Troilus and Cressida* and *Timon of Athens*. As the first playhouse to be owned by the players who expected to use it, its fittings must have satisfied all the basic needs of Shakespearean staging. At one time or another, the company staged every one of Shakespeare's plays there.

In 1600, a company consisting entirely of boys started using the Blackfriars playhouse that Richard Burbage's father had tried to open four years before. Companies of boy players had a higher social status than the adult professionals, and, playing only in halls, they commanded a more affluent clientele. The boys performed only once a week, and the relative infrequency of their crowds, plus their skills as trained singers (they were choir-school children turned to making money for their choirmasters), proved less offensive to the local residents than a noisy adult company with its drums and trumpets. Leasing the Blackfriars to the boy company made a minor profit for the Burbages, who took the rent for eight years.

In the longer run, though, this arrangement provided a different means for the Burbage–Shakespeare company to advance its career. The boys' eight years of playing in their rented hall playhouse eventually made it possible for the company of adult players to renew Burbage's old plan of 1596. Shakespeare's company had been made the King's Men when James came to the throne in 1603, and their new patron gave them a status that made it impossible for the residents of Blackfriars to prevent them from implementing the original plan. During a lengthy closure of all the theaters because of a plague epidemic in 1608, the boys' manager surrendered his lease of the hall playhouse to the Burbages. They then took possession for their own company of the playhouse that their father had built for them twelve years before. They divided the new playhouse property among the leading players as they had done in 1599 with the Globe.

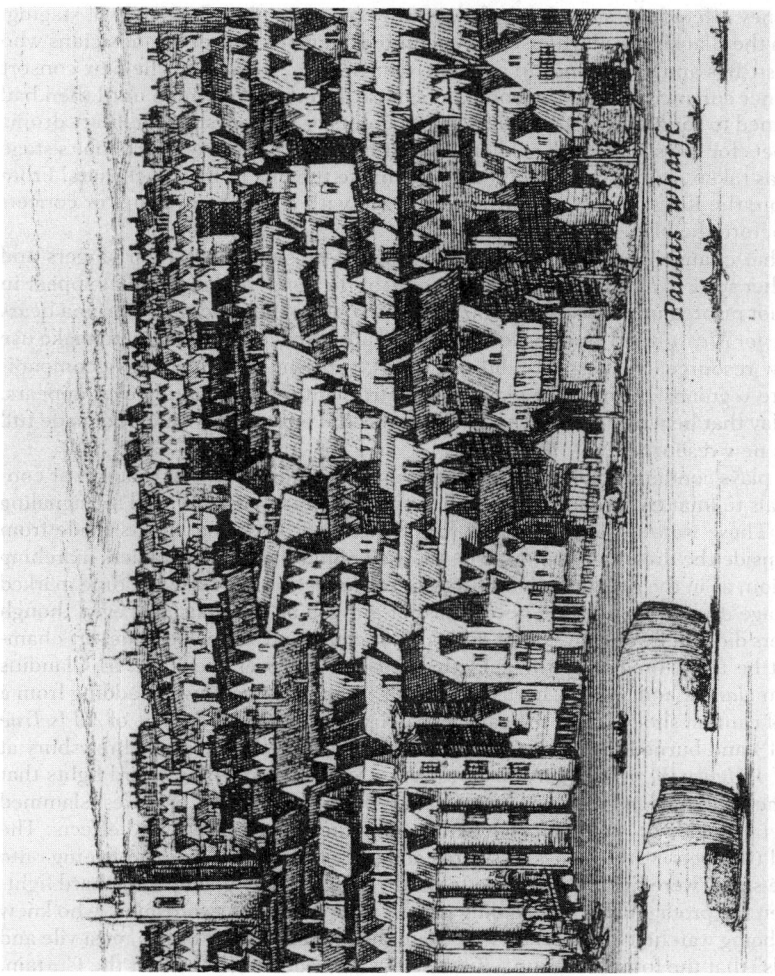

A section from Wenceslaus Hollar's "Long View" of London, printed in 1644. Drawn from a standpoint on the tower of the church that is now Southwark Cathedral, Hollar's view shows the roof of the great hall in which the Blackfriars playhouse was built. It can be seen as the long angled roof with two central chimneys, below and to the east of St. Bride's Church.

They were the King's Men, the leading company in the country, and their status after ten years of playing at the Globe was matched by their wealth. By the time theaters reopened late in 1609, the company had established a new system of playing.

The King's Men now had two playhouses, a large open amphitheater and a much smaller roofed hall. Instead of selling or renting one out and using the other for themselves, they decided to use both in turn, for half of each year. It was a reversion to the old system with the city inns, where through the summer they played in the large open yards and in the winter played at inns with big indoor rooms. This time, though, the company owned both playhouses. Their affluence and their high status are signaled by the fact that they chose to keep one of their playhouses idle while they used the other, despite there now being a shortage of playhouses in London. That affluence was needed in 1613, when the Globe burned down at a performance of *All Is True (Henry VIII)* and the company chose the much more expensive option of rebuilding it instead of reverting to the Blackfriars for both winter and summer. That decision, in its way, was the ultimate gesture of affection for their original playhouse. It was a costly gesture, but it meant that the Globe continued in use by the company until all the theaters were closed down by Parliament in 1642.

In 1609, when they reopened after the closure for plague, Shakespeare's company had made several changes in their procedures. The restart was at the Blackfriars, and although they offered the same kind of plays, they began to alter their style of staging. Along with the Blackfriars playhouse, they acquired a famous consort of musicians who played on strings and woodwinds in a music room set over the stage. The new consort was a distinct enhancement of the company's musical resources, which until then had been confined to song, the occasional use of recorders or hautboys, and military drums and trumpets for the scenes with soldiery. In 1608, a central room on the Globe's stage balcony was taken over to serve as a music room like the one at the Blackfriars. From this time on, the King's Men's performances began with a lengthy overture or concert of music before the play.

With that change, the plays themselves now had music to back their singers and provide other sorts of atmospheric effects. Some of the songs and music that appear in the plays not printed until the First Folio of 1623, such as the song that Mariana hears in *Measure for Measure* 4.1, may have been added after Shakespeare's time to make use of this new resource. Shakespeare did use songs, sometimes with string accompaniment, quite regularly in the early plays, but instrumental music hardly ever appears. The last play that he wrote alone, *The Tempest,* was the only one in which he made full use of this new resource.

All the plays containing soldiers and battles used the military drums that in war conveyed signals to infantry formations, as well as the trumpets that were used for signaling to cavalry. These were usually employed for offstage noises, sound effects made from "within" (inside the dressing room or tiring-house behind the stage). Soldiers marching in procession, as in the dead march at the close of *Hamlet,* would have the time marked by an onstage drum. Shakespeare never calls for guns to be fired onstage, even though other writers did, but he did have other noises at his command. A small cannon or "chamber" might be used, fired from the gable-fronted heavens over the stage, as Claudius demands in *Hamlet* and as the Chorus to Act 3 of *Henry V* notes. It was wadding from a ceremonial cannon shot that set the gallery thatch alight at a performance of *All Is True* in July 1613 and burned the Globe to the ground. Stage battles such as Shrewsbury at the end of *1 Henry IV,* written for the Theatre, were accompanied by sword fights that were not the duels of *Hamlet*'s finale but exchanges with broadswords or "foxes" slammed against metal shields or "targets." That action guaranteed emphatic sound effects. The drums and trumpets, with clashes of swords and a great deal of to-ing and fro-ing onto and off the stage, were highlighted in between the shouted dialogue by some hard fighting between the protagonists. The leading players were practiced swordsmen, who knew they were being watched by experts. These were the scenes of "four or five most vile and ragged foils" that the fourth Chorus self-consciously derided in *Henry V* at the Curtain.

The second great reason for noise in the amphitheaters was to mark storm and tempest. Stagehands used the kind of device that Jonson mocked in the Prologue to *Every Man in His Humour,* written for its 1616 publication. His play, wrote Jonson, was free from choruses that wafted you over the seas, "nor rolled bullet heard / To say, it thunders; nor tempestuous drum / Rumbles, to tell you when the storm doth come." For centuries, lead balls rolling down a tin trough were a standard way of making thunder noises in English theaters. The tempest in Act 3 of *King Lear* is heralded several times in the text before a stage direction, "Storm and tempest" (Folio 2.2.450), tells us that it has at last arrived. In 2.2, Cornwall notes its coming twice (Folio 2.2.452, 473). Kent comments on the "Foul weather" in his first line in Act 3, prefaced by the entry stage direction for Act 3, "Storm still," which is repeated for 3.2. Such stage directions appear in both texts (Q has "Storm" for the equivalent Scenes 8, 9, and also at 11, F's 3.4, where F omits any further reference to these noises). These explicit signals indicate that the stagehands provided offstage noises, for all that Lear himself outstorms them with his violent speeches in 3.2.

The main question about the storm scenes in *King Lear* is this: with such consistent emphasis on storm in the language, what was the design behind the stage directions? In the centuries that *Lear* has been restaged, the tempest has been made to roar offstage in a wide variety of ways, often with so much effect that, in the face of complaints that the storm noises made it difficult for the audience to hear the words, some modern productions reduced the storm to solely visual effects, or even left Lear's own raging language to express it unsupported. But the two stage directions indicate that in the original performances the "storm in nature" was not left to Lear himself to convey. The two "Storm still" directions in the Folio suggest a constant rumbling, not the intermittent crashes that might allow Lear to conduct a dialogue with the occasional outbursts of storm noises, as some modern productions have done.

Shakespeare left regrettably few stage directions to indicate the special tricks or properties that he wanted. Curtained beds are called for in *Othello* 5.2 and *Cymbeline* 2.2, and there is the specification "Stocks brought out" in *King Lear* 2.2.132. Small and portable things like papers were a much more common device, from the letters in *The Two Gentlemen of Verona* 1.2.46, 1.3.44, and 2.1.95 to Lear's map at 1.1.35. Across the whole thirty-eight plays, though, there are very few such directions. Shakespeare's economy in preparing his scripts is a major impediment to the modern reader. He hardly ever bothered to note the standard physical gestures, such as kneeling or doffing a hat, and did little more to specify any special effects. Nonetheless, it is important not to imagine elaborate devices or actions where the text does not call for them. On the whole, the demands Shakespeare made of his fellows for staging his plays appear to have been remarkably modest. Since he was a company shareholder, his parsimony may have had a simple commercial motive. Stage properties cost the company money, and one had to be confident of a new play's popularity before investing much in its staging.

There may have been other reasons for avoiding extravagant staging spectacles. Shakespeare made little use of the discovery space until the last plays, for instance, for reasons that we can only guess at. The few definite discoveries in the plays include Portia's caskets in *The Merchant of Venice,* Falstaff sleeping off his sack in *1 Henry IV* 2.5.482, the body of Polonius in *Hamlet,* Hermione's statue in *The Winter's Tale* 5.3.20, and the lovers in *The Tempest* 5.1.173, who are found when discovered to be playing chess. The audience's shock when Hermione moves and comes out of the discovery space onto the main stage is rare in Shakespeare: in every other play, whether comedy or tragedy, the audience knows far more than the characters onstage about what is going on. Shakespeare matched this late innovation in *The Winter's Tale* with his last play, *The Tempest.* After the preliminary and soothing concert by the resident Blackfriars musicians, it opens with a storm at sea so realistic that it includes that peculiarly distinctive stage direction "Enter Mariners, wet" (1.1.46). That startling piece of stage realism turns out straightaway to be not real at all but a piece of stage magic.

COMEDIES

Shakespearean Comedy

by

KATHARINE EISAMAN MAUS

SLY   Is not a comonty
A Christmas gambol, or a tumbling trick?
BARTHOLOMEW   No, . . . it is a kind of history.
—*The Taming of the Shrew* Induction 2.132–135

When, after Shakespeare's death, his colleagues in his theater company, the King's Men, collected and printed his works in the First Folio, they organized them into three groups: comedies, tragedies, and histories. Since the late nineteenth century, several plays written late in Shakespeare's career—*Pericles, The Winter's Tale, Cymbeline,* and *The Tempest*—have been relegated (as they are in the *Norton Shakespeare*) to a separate group, the romances. With the romances subtracted, Shakespeare's comic output comes to twelve plays, plus *Troilus and Cressida* and the coauthored *Two Noble Kinsman,* which are sometimes classified as comedies and sometimes as tragedies.

Writing about 350 B.C.E., the Greek philosopher Aristotle speculated that comedy had originated in the *phallaka,* ribald songs that accompanied a fertility rite in which young men paraded a large model of an erect penis through a village to celebrate a bountiful grape harvest. The procession of youths who sang these songs was called a *komos,* from which the word *comedy* is perhaps derived. At this historical remove, it is impossible to recover exactly how "phallic songs" might have detached from their original performance circumstances and developed into staged drama. Yet many modern critics as well as Aristotle have remarked upon comedy's association with ancient myths of seasonal rebirth and renewal, and with festivities in which sexuality and fertility are celebrated, inhibitions loosened, bodily pleasures indulged, bounds of decorum overturned. Shakespeare's England was familiar neither with grape harvests nor with the *phallaka,* but it shared similar traditions with other European agrarian societies. May Day on May 1 and Midsummer Night at the summer solstice celebrated the effects of the burgeoning spring and fertile summer for plants, animals, and people. In late summer and fall, "harvest home" festivities marked the end of the arduous toil required to gather the year's crop in an age before mechanized farm equipment. The period between Christmas Eve and Epiphany, or Twelfth Night, was a time of revelry sometimes presided over by a "lord of misrule," who issued topsy-turvy edicts and encouraged playful role-playing and overindulgence in food and drink. Carnival—less elaborate in England than in southern Europe but still a period of feasting, mirth, and masquerade—took place just before Lent, the season of abstinence and penance, when the previous year's food supply was dwindling but the new year's crop was not yet available.

By the 1590s, rapid urbanization had begun to detach some English people, especially the Londoners who attended Shakespeare's theater, from the rhythms of planting and harvest that governed life in the countryside. Moreover, some Protestant reformers objected to all "holidays of indulgence" because of their pagan or Catholic origin. Yet the traditional holidays were still celebrated, and perhaps controversy sharpened Shakespeare's interest in them. Several of his comedies—*A Midsummer Night's*

An ancient Greek phallic procession. This drawing was made from a vase painting.

Dream, Twelfth Night, and *The Merry Wives of Windsor*—make overt references to such holidays or incorporate some of their rituals into the action. The dialogue between Spring and Winter in *Love's Labour's Lost* and many of the songs in *As You Like It* and *Twelfth Night* evoke the seasonal round which all these festivals commemorate and honor.

In addition, medieval and Renaissance England was home to a rich indigenous tradition of clowning, which flourished during holiday seasons but which was not necessarily tied to special occasions. Many medieval morality plays—dramas in which a religious or moral dilemma is allegorically represented—feature boisterously anarchic "Vices" or devil characters who comment irreverently on the action while sowing playful mayhem onstage. Wealthy men sometimes employed professional fools in their household, whose function was to amuse their employers with ridiculous banter. Although some written parts for Vice characters have survived, neither the "Vice" nor the professional fool necessarily tied his performance to a script. He was like a modern jazz performer, improvising ingeniously, rather than like a classical musician who aims to render a beautiful intepretation of a fully notated score. In *Twelfth Night,* the heroine Viola remarks upon the agile intelligence that the professional clown's spur-of-the-moment preposterousness requires:

> He must observe their mood on whom he jests,
> The quality of persons, and the time,
> And, like the haggard [hunting hawk], check at every feather
> That comes before his eye. This is a practice
> As full of labour as a wise man's art.
>
> (3.1.55–59)

Laborious, and perilous, too. The fool could not be funny if he refrained from obscene, satirical, or disrespectful remarks, and he was, therefore, permitted some liberty of speech. Still, his uninhibited, irreverent commentary risked offending those more powerful than himself. In Shakespeare's plays, every professional fool is threatened at some point with a whipping for having presumptuously overstepped his bounds. "The more pity that fools may not speak wisely what wise men do foolishly," remarks one of these fools, Touchstone, in *As You Like It* (1.2.72–73).

Once the public theaters opened in London in the 1570s, the stage became a place where professional clowns could entertain larger and more diverse audiences: Will Kempe, one of the members of Shakespeare's theater company in the 1590s, was famous for his witty jests and pranks both onstage and off. In *Hamlet,* Hamlet's advice to the acting company who visits him in Elsinore suggests both the scene-stealing appeal of improvisatory clowning and its potential to deform a carefully crafted play with random interpolations:

Will Kemp, the clown in Shakespeare's company, during the 1590s. From the title page of *Kempes Nine Daies Wonder* . . . (1600).

> And let those that play your clowns speak no more than is set down for them; for there be of them that will themselves laugh to set on some quantity of barren spectators to laugh too, though in the mean time some necessary question of the play be then to be considered. That's villainous, and shows a most pitiful ambition in the fool that uses it.
>
> (3.2.34–40)

Yet scripted comedies retain some of the clown's typical focus upon what the fool Feste, in *Twelfth Night*, calls "present mirth" (2.3.44)—an emphasis on enjoyment in the here and now regardless of context or consequences.

In scripted drama, the word *comedy* can refer to anything from a short entertaining scene or improvisation to a whole play. Renaissance playwrights did not necessarily maintain strict demarcations between genres—they were prone to "mingling kings and clowns," as Shakespeare's contemporary Philip Sidney noted disapprovingly in *The Defence of Poesie*. Shakespeare's tragedies and history plays often contain comic episodes or subplots. In fact, Falstaff, arguably Shakespeare's greatest comic character, makes his most memorable appearances in the history plays, *1 Henry IV and 2 Henry IV*; in *Macbeth*, a drunken Porter staggers onstage to make obscene jokes immediately after Macbeth, offstage, has murdered Duncan; in *King Lear*, the Fool provides moments of extremely dark humor that blur the distinction between the tragic and the comically absurd.

Yet by Shakespeare's time, comedy, considered as a distinctive kind of play, was more than merely a series of jokes and funny sketches or a collection of festive customs. As Bartholomew informs the uncouth Christopher Sly in *The Taming of the Shrew*, a comedy "is a kind of history" (Induction 2.135)—that is, it has a plot. In the Renaissance, the most widely influential comic patterns were derived from the classical Roman dramatists Plautus and Terence, who were read in Latin, and sometimes performed or declaimed, in grammar schools of the kind Shakespeare attended as a boy in Stratford. Plautus and Terence had, in turn, appropriated plots and characters from Greek predecessors, most of whose works have since been lost. Their kind of drama is often called New Comedy to distinguish it from Old Comedy, an earlier Greek form that had satirized well-known living people and commented on current events.

Although, of course, individual New Comedies vary, they tend to follow a predictable pattern. A youth is in love with an apparently unsuitable maiden—often a slave girl. Various stock characters help or hinder his love: the "heavy father" or uncle, who prohibits the union and sometimes lusts after the maiden himself; the ingenious slave, who plots on the youth's behalf while remarking self-delightedly upon his own tricky skill; the stupid slave, who misconstrues the speech and action of other characters; the braggart soldier home from war, who exaggerates his exploits in battle but turns out to be a ridiculous coward. Sometimes the true identities of various characters are unclear, either because they have suffered some mishap that has obscured their family history or because they are in disguise. In the course of the play, one or both of the lovers find themselves in peril—"the course of true love never did run smooth" (1.1.134), as Shakespeare's Lysander remarks in *A Midsummer Night's Dream*—yet in the end nobody dies. Ultimately, confusions are sorted out and family members reunited and reconciled; often the maiden turns out to be freeborn and, therefore, marriage material. The couple may then be ushered to wedded bliss.

New Comedy registers the surprising triumph of the apparently weak over the apparently powerful: of youth over age, of love over property, of wit over authority, of pleasure-seekers over prudent calculators. At the same time, the end of the play channels the characters' unruly energies into a form that seems ultimately to reinforce rather than challenge the status quo. The tricky slave may hoodwink his masters, but he does not flee his household or agitate for the abolition of servitude. The lovers, though they flout their parents' authority, enter into marriage and prepare to become parents themselves in their turn. New Comedy implies that rebelliousness marks a phase of life; it is not a precursor to revolutionary social change. Human beings follow a predictable cycle just as the seasons do, with one life stage succeeding another in due course and the younger generation replacing the old.

Plautus's and Terence's plays were a treasure trove for later writers. The plots were easy to recycle because they were generalized rather than tied to particular people and to current events, as Old Comedy had been. New Comedy represents human eccentricities as perennial; absurd behavior apparently takes much the same form in ancient Greece or Rome as it does in Italy in the 1400s or in England in the 1590s. Moreover, New Comedy was well adapted to societies in which, like Shakespeare's England, censorship and slander laws prohibited the lampooning of powerful individuals and most public discussion of contemporary political affairs. The romance novella, adapting and recombining New Comic plot devices, flourished all over Renaissance Europe; Shakespeare knew versions from Italy, Spain, and France as well as, more immediately, romances written in the late sixteenth-century by such English writers as Thomas Lodge, Robert Greene, and Barnabe Riche. When, following age-old precedent, Shakespeare appropriates his plots from others, he sometimes adapts plot formulas directly from the classical originals and sometimes relies upon one of their mediated forms. In *The Comedy of Errors*, he goes straight to a classical source, Plautus's *Menaechmi*, but follows more recent renditions of New Comic devices for the plots of *The Two Gentlemen of Verona, The Merry Wives of Windsor, As You Like It, Twelfth Night, Much Ado About Nothing, Measure for Measure*, and *All's Well That Ends Well*.

The "marriage plot" of New Comedy is absolutely fundamental to Shakespeare's comic drama: most of his comedies involve multiple courtships and weddings. Sometimes, indeed, Shakespeare alters the expected formula, as in *Love's Labour's Lost*, in which the women defer the weddings for at least a year, or in *Measure for Measure*, in which most of the concluding marriages are apparently loveless ones. Yet in these cases, the familiarity of the pattern

A woodcut from a 1493 edition of Terence, showing a performance of *The Eunuch*.

means that characters as well as audiences register these changes as troubling departures from the norm. "Our wooing doth not end like an old play," complains Biron in *Love's Labour's Lost*. "Jack hath not Jill" (5.2.851–52). Many of Shakespeare's comedies also feature situations drawn from New Comic tradition: characters in disguise, separated family members reunited at the end of the play, smart-mouthed servant characters turning the tables on their masters, and (in *The Merry Wives of Windsor* and *All's Well That Ends Well*) cowardly braggart soldiers.

Aristotle and the Latin literary theorist Horace had maintained that comedy typically dealt with people worse, both in merit and in social class, than the audience, whereas tragedy dealt with people better than the audience. Following these authorities, some Renaissance critics likewise argued that comedy teaches spectators good behavior by holding bad behavior up to ridicule. This way of thinking about comic characters, which predicates the spectator's pleasure upon contempt, is inadequate to Shakespearean comedy. Many of Shakespeare's comic characters are empathetic, articulate, and self-aware. Moreover, and significantly in Shakespeare's hierarchy-conscious world, the central protagonists of his comedies are often of high rank. While classical New Comedies typically feature urban characters of the middling sort, the Renaissance romances derived from them move up the social scale so that the main characters are often kings and dukes, princesses and countesses. While Shakespeare's plays have plenty of lower-status characters in supporting roles, the marriage plots tend to retain this upscale orientation. In *Love's Labour's Lost*, a king and his nobles square off against a princess and her ladies; in *As You Like It*, the daughters of two dukes fall in love with noblemen brothers; *The Two Gentlemen of Verona*, *Twelfth Night*, *A Midsummer Night's Dream*, *Measure for Measure*, and *All's Well That Ends Well* all involve characters of high degree in the marriage plot. Countess Olivia, in *Twelfth Night*, suggests how indelible the markers of status were imagined to be. Olivia falls in love with a woman, Viola, disguised as a man, who is employed as a servant. When Olivia asks after her beloved's parentage, Viola replies that it is "above my fortunes. . . . I am a gentleman" (1.5.248–49). After Viola departs, Olivia soliloquizes:

> 'I am a gentleman.' I'll be sworn thou art.
> Thy tongue, thy face, thy limbs, actions, and spirit
> Do give thee five-fold blazon.
>
> (1.5.261–63)

Although unable to discern Viola's true sex, Olivia has no trouble at all accurately assessing Viola's class origins, which her behavior seems to set forth for all to view, as a gentleman's coat of arms, or "blazon," reveals his identity and family background. Even less exalted heroes and heroines, such as Katherine and Petruccio in *The Taming of the Shrew*, or the Antipholus twins in *The Comedy of Errors*, or the Page and Ford families in *The Merry Wives of Windsor*, live above the social line, critical in Shakespeare's time, that separated the landowning, professional, servant-employing classes from the vast majority who earned their living through manual toil.

Nonetheless, the emphasis in comedy tends to be on traits that all human beings share, not on those that elevate one person over another. Shakespeare's comedies tend not to focus upon the fate of a magnificent titular hero, as the tragedies do, but to feature a large collection of protagonists. Often, the different characters participate in several interlocking plots, a technique that originated in classical theater and was much elaborated in the middle ages and Renaissance. *The Two Gentlemen of Verona* follows the initially diverging but eventually reconnecting adventures of Valentine and of his faithless friend, Proteus. *The Taming of the Shrew* deals not only with Kate and Petruccio, but with Bianca and Lucentio, and Hortensio and the Widow; and this entire action is prefaced by a framing story about a practical joke on a drunken tinker, Christopher Sly. *Much Ado About Nothing* pairs the courtship of Claudio and Hero with the courtship of Beatrice and Benedick. *The Merry Wives of Windsor* combines Falstaff's attempt to seduce two middle-aged wives with a competition among several other men for the nubile daughter of one of the wives. *A Midsummer Night's Dream* attends to the wedding of Duke Theseus and Hippolyta, to the marital quarrels of Oberon and Titania, to the mishaps of four Athenian lovers lost in the woods, and to the attempts of a group of artisans to rehearse a play for the Duke's wedding.

The multiplot action encourages the audience to take a wide view, to make comparisons among various characters who often are doing more or less the same thing—for instance, falling in love—in different ways. No single story, no single individual, has a monopoly on the stage nor, implicitly, a monopoly on the truth, Often, the collisions among the various plotlines are surprising and funny: *The Comedy of Errors* is a tissue of such unlikely interpenetrations, as bewildered characters find themselves hijacked again and again into the wrong story. Not until the entire cast is assembled at the end of the play can the multiple farcical misunderstandings be sorted out. In most of Shakespeare's comedies the multiplot structure helps to foreground the importance of "hap," or fortune, in the outcome of the plot as apparently independent causal sequences intersect and react upon one another. In *A Midsummer Night's Dream,* the chance encounter of the fairies Oberon and Puck with the Athenian lovers in the woods proves unexpectedly fateful for the lovers. In *As You Like It,* an inexplicable twist of fate brings Orlando, roaming far from home, to the same forest to which his beloved Rosalind has fled, and then later brings Orlando's older brother to the same forest, where Orlando can happen upon him just in the nick of time to save him from being eaten by a lioness. In *Twelfth Night,* the lovesick Olivia, seeking to marry a man who is actually a woman in disguise, stumbles instead upon her beloved's identical twin brother, a shipwreck survivor who has just arrived in town that morning. For the audience, the pleasure of such plots depends upon an interplay between the completely predictable "happy ending" and the unforeseen, wildly fortuitous means by which the characters arrive there.

In the crowded comic world, the aggressively self-actualizing individual who tries to carve out his own destiny tends to make himself ridiculous. By contrast, those who surrender themselves to circumstances often benefit from the workings of accident or providence. *Twelfth Night* rewards Viola, the lucky survivor of a shipwreck who waits for time to untangle her dilemmas, but humiliates the unctuous steward Malvolio, who strives assiduously to better his social standing. Moreover, in a world in which rules of probability seem not to hold, laughably foolish characters often prove weirdly discerning: Bottom in *A Midsummer Night's Dream,* Lance in *The Two Gentlemen of Verona,* Dogberry in *Much Ado About Nothing,* Pompey in *Measure for Measure.* Another important source of insight is the professional fool with his honed expertise as an improviser of absurdity: *As You Like It'*s Touchstone, *Twelfth Night'*s Feste, or *All's Well'*s Lavatch. These characters' crackpot misprisions and sly puns, bringing unrelated words and meanings into unanticipated conjunctions, are the verbal equivalents of the multilayered plot structure, in which apparently incompatible elements collide in productive chance encounters.

In an influential analysis, the critic Northrop Frye claimed that the comic world typically includes many characters and plots because comedy, as a genre, concerns itself with the renewal of an entire community, a renewal for which the concluding marriages are a kind of metaphor. As a practical matter, in order to perpetuate themselves, societies need their adult, fertile members to procreate—or, as Benedick comments in *Much Ado About Nothing,* "the world must be peopled" (2.3.213–14). The marriage of two people thus serves a social purpose beyond their individual gratification, as Shakespeare frequently reminds us by including some reference at the end of the play to the newlyweds' prospective children. Interestingly, the two genres with which Shakespeare is deeply involved as a young dramatist for a large swathe of the mid to late 1590s—chronicle history and comedy—both concern themselves with the construction of a community but consider the problem from different, even complementary, angles. While the history play is concerned with matters of state, with the fate of nations, and with a struggle for political power, comedy is concerned with domestic life and with the relations among family members and neighbors. Thus, features that seem marginal or supplemental in the history plays become central in the comedies, and vice versa. In the history plays, wars typically determine the outcome of events, so valor in battle is highly prized; in *2 Henry IV*, Prince Harry must renounce his association with the fat, pleasure-loving, admittedly cowardly Falstaff and embrace his own heroic destiny. In comedy, however, war is pushed to the margins. In *As You Like It*, the bad duke musters an army to defeat the good duke but, offstage, happens to meet a holy man who converts him to a hermit's life so that the threat of force simply evaporates. Moreover, bravery in battle is no longer a proxy for merit in other areas of life. As *Much Ado About Nothing* opens, a group of men are

Falstaff and Mistress Quickly, detail of the frontispiece to *The Wits; or, Sport upon Sport* (1662), a collection of short dramatic pieces, one of which featured Falstaff and his exploits.

returning from a military campaign: the soldier most remarked upon, who "hath borne himself beyond the promise of his age, doing in the figure of a lamb the feats of a lion" (1.1.11–12) is Claudio, whose ferocious misogyny eventually brings the play close to tragedy. In *All's Well That Ends Well*, Bertram likewise wins high honors on the battlefield but treats both his wife and his would-be lover shamefully.

One effect of this refocusing of perspective is that women, typically excluded from politics but central to domestic life, become likewise central to Shakespearean comedy. Whereas the young women in classical New Comedies tend to be fairly pallid—in some plays, the "love interest" does not even appear onstage—Shakespeare's comic women are highly realized and distinctive. He has a special partiality for vocal, opinionated heroines, who are dramatically much more compelling than the demure females held up for admiration by most Renaissance conduct books. In one of Shakespeare's first plays, *The Taming of the Shrew*, Kate, the "shrew" or overbearing woman of the title, puts up furious resistance to her marriage to the eccentric Petruccio, before finally testifying to her "taming" in a long public speech of flamboyantly abject submission that makes her once again the center of attention. In later plays, a clever woman—a softened, better-socialized version of the "shrew"—typically stage-manages some of the crucial action of the play. Beatrice, in *Much Ado About Nothing*, interrupts her raillery with Benedick to facilitate the rehabilitation of her cousin, who has been falsely accused of unchastity. In *As You Like It*, the talkative, quirky Rosalind presides over much of the action in male disguise, finally ushering in the marriage god Hymen to officiate at the weddings with which the play concludes. In *Twelfth Night*, the "fair shrew" Maria devises an elaborate practical joke on the killjoy Malvolio. In *Merchant of Venice*, Portia disguises herself as a young male lawyer and saves the life of her new husband's best friend in a stunning courtroom reversal. In *All's Well That Ends Well*, Helena is even more enterprising, first curing the King of a deadly malady and then following her caddish husband from France to Italy and arranging to get pregnant by him without his knowledge.

Despite their high-spiritedness, their frankness about their desires, their volubility, and, in some cases, their willingness to don transvestite disguise—all traits associated with promiscuity in Renaissance treatises about women—the premarital virginity of

OR,
The Man-Woman:
Being a Medicine to cure the Coltish Disease of
the Staggers in the Masculine-Feminines
of our Times.

Exprest in a briefe Declamation.

Non omnes possumus omnes.

Mistris, will you be trim'd or truss'd?

London printed for I. T. and are to be sold at Christ Church gate. 1620.

The title page of *Hic Mulier; or, The Man-Woman* (1620), a pamphlet denouncing the "unnatural" practice of women wearing men's clothing and adopting masculine styles (the women in this image are at a men's barber). *Hic Mulier* was answered by *Haec-Vir; or, The Womanish-Man* (also 1620).

Shakespeare's comic heroines is a nonnegotiable requirement, both for the men that love them and, apparently, for Shakespeare himself. The social value of chastity is suggested in *Measure for Measure* 5.1.170–77, when the Duke enumerates the categories of respectable women: they may be "maids" (that is, virgins) or "wives" or "widows." The only other category is "punk," or prostitute. Not surprisingly, then, Portia in *The Merchant of Venice* declares that if a husband does not claim her by passing the casket test devised by her father, she will live "chaste as Diana" (1.3.89–90), the goddess of virginity—taking a lover outside of marriage does not seem to occur to her as an option. In *A Midsummer Night's Dream*, when the eloping lovers Hermia and Lysander find themselves lost in the wood by night, Hermia insists that they sleep at some distance from one another: "Such separation as may well be said / Becomes a virtuous bachelor and a maid" (2.2.64–65). As a "virtuous bachelor," Lysander respects her scruples, but when the fairy Robin Goodfellow comes upon the sleeping couple, he misconstrues the situation: "Pretty soul, she durst not lie / Near this lack-love, this kill-courtesy" (2.2.282–83). Fairies, the play suggests, live by different rules of sexual conduct than mortals do. In other plays, the standards for servant women and for minor characters are considerably more relaxed than they are for the genteel heroines. In *Much Ado About Nothing*, when Hero is imagined to have talked out of the window at night with a man, her fiancé and father agree that she has so shamed herself that she might as well die. Yet her maid Margaret, for whom Hero was mistaken, apparently escapes without rebuke when the confusion becomes known. Similarly, Jaquenetta, the wench in *Love's Labour's Lost*, turns out to be pregnant by one of her two suitors at the end of the play; her evident consent to premarital intimacy contrasts with the behavior of the princess and her ladies-in-waiting, who engage their lovers in elegant mockery but at the same time carefully preserve their "maiden honour, yet as pure / As the unsullied lily" (5.2.351–52).

The wit of Shakespeare's heroines, then, is not simply anarchic or subversive: it coexists with implicit constraints upon their conduct. In Renaissance England, women's political and legal rights were severely restricted; yet Shakespeare's women, although often more intelligent and resourceful than the men with whom they are paired, only rarely chafe openly against their subordination or argue for a reconfiguration of gender roles. There are two different reasons for their acquiescence. One is that the comedies generally represent the restrictions upon women's freedom as easy to evade. In *The Merry Wives of Windsor,* Mistress Ford and Mistress Page, the merry wives of the title, will be ruined socially if their husbands discover that they are entertaining a man who is paying court to them. Twice, one of the husbands bursts in with a posse of neighbors to investigate their supposed adulterous scheming. Yet instead of being intimidated by this show of male authority or inveighing against the double standard for sexual behavior, the wives deliberately place themselves in risky situations, taking enormous pleasure in their narrow escapes and easily making fools of both the jealous husband and the would-be lover. In other comedies, faced with some restriction or impediment, women simply pass themselves off as men. In *As You Like It,* for instance, Celia and Rosalind know that two women traveling alone will be vulnerable to robbery and rape; so Rosalind disguises herself as a "youth," and they arrive at their destination safely. In *The Merchant of Venice,* Portia likewise disguises herself as a young man in order to gain access to the male preserve of the courtroom. In both cases, male disguise allows the heroine to combine her superior intelligence with the social privileges accorded to men.

Yet if the constraints of gender seem simple for a clever woman to renegotiate, they also, in many plays, do not seem especially onerous to those who must live within them. Shakespeare's heroines are not chaste because chastity needs to be imposed forcibly upon them, but because they accept their culture's notion of admirable conduct and take pride in their physical "purity." Moreover, many of Shakespeare's comic heroines associate erotic feeling with a happy acceptance of inferiority to the beloved man. In *A Midsummer Night's Dream,* Helena, desperate for Demetrius's affection, is especially abject:

> I am your spaniel, and, Demetrius,
> The more you beat me I will fawn on you.
> Use me but as your spaniel: spurn me, strike me,
> Neglect me, lose me; only give me leave,
> Unworthy as I am, to follow you.
> (2.1.203–07)

Other women in Shakespeare's comedy possess more self-respect, but even Portia in *The Merchant of Venice,* who (disguised as a youthful lawyer) will shortly take masterful charge of a Venetian courtroom, professes to consider herself, in comparison to her intended husband, Bassanio, "an unlessoned girl, unschooled, unpractisèd" (3.2.159):

> Happiest of all is that her gentle spirit
> Commits herself to yours to be directed
> As from her lord, her governor, her king.
> (3.2.163–65)

A married woman in Shakespeare's time could not own property in her own name: her estate was normally, upon marriage, at her husband's disposal. Portia alludes to this rule, called *couverture,* as her speech continues:

> But now I was the lord
> Of this fair mansion, master of my servants,
> Queen o'er myself; and even now, but now,
> This house, these servants, and this same myself
> Are yours, my lord's.
> (3.2.167–71)

Portia is both cleverer and much wealthier than her intended; but instead of seeing the obligation to defer to her new husband as a degradation of her status, Portia embraces it, as if a willingness to relinquish her authority were an intrinsic part of her experience of love.

Shakespeare's comic heroines, then, triumph not in spite of, but because of, the restrictions placed upon them: in other words, they find constraint enabling. This paradox has generated a certain amount of disagreement among Shakespeare's critics. Some see him as a protofeminist because of the way his heroines challenge gender norms by donning transvestite disguises, devising "bed tricks," or distinguishing themselves in the male professions of law or medicine. Other critics emphasize the conservatism of the heroine's goal, marriage to a husband whom she accepts as her "lord." In fact, the heroine's preeminence in comedy seems of a piece with the almost magical conferral of power upon the ordinarily powerless that is an intrinsic aspect of the comic pattern. Often, her successes seem inexplicable by ordinary means: in *As You Like It,* Rosalind describes herself as a magician's disciple; and in *All's Well That Ends Well,* though "miracles are past" (2.3.1)—that is, the remarkable events described in the Bible no longer occur—Helen's cure of the king is called "the rarest argument of wonder that hath shot out in our latter times" (2.3.6–7).

In classical New Comedy, as I have already mentioned, an older authority figure, usually a father, refuses to permit the marriage of the young lovers, thus creating an obstacle that the action of the play has to overcome. Shakespeare sometimes uses this convention: in *A Midsummer Night's Dream,* Hermia flees Athens with her lover, Lysander, because her father, Egeus, backed by law, is trying to force her to marry Demetrius. In *The Merchant of Venice,* the Jewish Jessica must elope with Lorenzo, a Christian her father would never countenance. In *The Merry Wives of Windsor,* Anne and Fenton outwit both her parents, who have other matches for her in mind. Yet often in Shakespearean comedy, the young lovers woo without the interference, or even with the positive assistance, of parents and other older authority figures. In *The Two Gentlemen of Verona, Love's Labour's Lost,* and *Twelfth Night,* parents are elsewhere or dead. In *As You Like It,* Rosalind's father does not recognize her because she is in disguise, and he has nothing to do with her marriage plans. In *The Merchant of Venice,* Bassanio's father is apparently deceased; and while Portia's late father has devised an apparently arbitrary test for her suitors, it ends up selecting the man with whom she is already in love. In *Much Ado About Nothing,* Claudio asks his commanding officer, as his surrogate father, to help him arrange a marriage with Hero, whose father is likewise accommodating; in the same play, friends and relatives intervene to "undertake one of Hercules' labours, which is to bring Signor Benedick and the Lady Beatrice into a mountain of affection th'one with th'other" (2.1.317–19). In *All's Well That Ends Well,* the older generation is more enthusiastic about the union of the poor physician's daughter Helen and the aristocrat Bertram than are the young people themselves, generously dismissing the class difference between husband and wife, and ignoring property considerations as well.

By minimizing, in many plays, the importance of parental prohibition, Shakespeare focuses attention instead on the way that the young lovers create their own roadblocks to marriage. In their jubilant multiple weddings, the comedies generally celebrate the delights of heterosexual love, and Shakespeare seems to take as axiomatic that this celebration pleases the audience as well. Such titles as *Twelfth Night, or What You Will* and *As You Like It* suggest that Shakespeare sees his comedies as pleasurably gratifying his audience's wishful fantasies. The epilogues of several comedies invite the audience to share in the concluding festivities. In *A Midsummer Night's Dream,* after the lovers troop off to bed—to beget healthy children, we are told—Robin Goodfellow asks the audience to "give me your hands" (Epilogue.15): he both requests applause for the actor's performance and suggests that the world of the play and the world of the audience is continuous, and that the spectators of the play are part of the happy community of the comic conclusion. In *As You Like It,* even more explicitly, Rosalind's epilogue makes the connection between the comedy's onstage flirtations and a charged sexual atmosphere among the play's spectators: "I charge you, O women, for the love you bear to men, to like as much of this play as please you. And I charge you, O men, for the love you bear to women—as I perceive by your simpering none of you hates them—that between you and the women the play may please" (10–14).

Yet Shakespeare tempers this affirmative view of heterosexual attraction and gratification with some attention to inherently contradictory or recalcitrant aspects of sexuality. In fact, over the course of his career as a comic dramatist he seems to grow more pessimistic, so that in his last two comedies, *Measure for Measure* and *All's Well That Ends Well,* love's difficulties and disappointments come close to overwhelming its rewards. As we have seen, sexual congress is a social necessity—a community cannot survive unless its members procreate. Nonetheless, sexual passion figures, in Shakespearean comedy as in most Renaissance love poetry, as profoundly resistant to social control: a highly subjective, even solipsistic or isolating, experience.

> The lunatic, the lover, and the poet
> Are of imagination all compact.
> (*Midsummer Night's Dream* 5.1.7–8)

Again and again, Shakespeare stresses that, in love, there is no accounting for taste: beauty lies in the eye of the beholder, and socially mandated standards of beauty mean little to individual beholders. In *Love's Labour's Lost,* Biron's male friends tease him unmercifully for loving a "black," or dark-complexioned, woman, because the ideal female beauty in Shakespeare's day was fair-haired and white-skinned; but Biron staunchly defends his preference. In *Much Ado About Nothing,* when Claudio enthuses about Hero, "the sweetest lady that ever I looked on," Benedick replies that "I can see yet without spectacles, and I see no such matter" (1.1.151–54). In *A Midsummer Night's Dream,* Helena, unrequitedly in love with Demetrius, compares herself to Hermia, the woman Demetrius does love:

> Through Athens I am thought as fair as she.
> But what of that? Demetrius thinks not so.
> ....
> Love looks not with the eyes, but with the mind,
> And therefore is winged Cupid painted blind.
> (1.2.227–28, 233–34)

Yet at the same time as the lover's experience seems unshared by others, it also seems to come from outside the self, an alien invader. "What's this? What's this?" (2.2.167), asks the shocked Angelo in *Measure for Measure,* surprised by his sudden overpowering desire for Isabella. Both Biron, in *Love's Labour's Lost,* and Benedick, in *Much Ado About Nothing,* ridicule the follies of lovers until, unexpectedly, they fall in love themselves: "What? I love, I sue, I seek a wife?" (4.1.174), Biron asks himself incredulously. In *A Midsummer Night's Dream,* the fairies interfere with attachments between the human lovers by treating the humans' eyes with juice squeezed from a flower obtained by supernatural means from the other side of the globe. Yet ordinary sexual passion, generated from "within" the lover, apparently operates exactly the same way as the exotic flower juice operating from "without." In fact, Demetrius, one of the lovers, must remain permanently under the influence of the fairies' flower juice in order for the final pairing off to proceed.

How can this mysterious, giddy impulse be subjected to discipline? In particular, how can it be harnessed to what the Queen in *Love's Labour's Lost* calls the "world-without-end bargain" (5.2.771) of marriage, a bond that could not, in Shakespeare's time, be dissolved by divorce? "Tell me how long you would have her after you have possessed her?" the disguised Rosalind commands her lover, Orlando, who answers: "For ever and a day." "Say a day without the ever," Rosalind advises him (4.1.121–24). Shakespeare's plays are full of jokes about the brief half-life of erotic attraction, a desire that seems immense but will disappear as soon as its sexual goal is achieved. In *Much Ado About Nothing*, Balthasar sings:

> Sigh no more, ladies, sigh no more.
>   Men were deceivers ever,
> One foot in sea, and one on shore,
>   To one thing constant never.
> ....
> The fraud of men was ever so
>   Since summer first was leafy.
>   (2.3.56–59, 66–67)

Elsewhere, women are said to betray men, their infidelities imposing the shame of the "cuckold's horn" upon their husbands. In *Much Ado About Nothing*, Benedick worries that if he marries, he will inevitably "hang my bugle in an invisible baldric" (1.1.198) or horn belt; in *As You Like It*, the Duke's men, coming home from hunting the deer, sing a song that ends in a jolly insult to the listener and his presumed lineage:

> Take thou no scorn to wear the horn;
> It was a crest ere thou wast born.
> Thy father's father wore it,
> And thy father bore it.
>   (4.2.14–17)

It is not surprising, then, that Shakespeare's comedies should be much concerned with the problem of constancy and with the making and breaking of vows, since a vow is essentially an assurance about the future. As the weaker parties to the love transaction, women are especially likely to insist upon the importance of the vow, since they have more to lose if it is breached. In *The Merchant of Venice*, as we have seen, Portia subjects herself and her estate to her new husband, Bassanio, but she does so conditionally:

> This house, these servants, and this same myself
> Are yours, my lord's. I give them with this ring,
> Which when you part from, lose, or give away,
> Let it presage the ruin of your love.
>   (3.2.170–73)

In the event, Bassanio does give away the ring. In *The Two Gentlemen of Verona* and in *A Midsummer Night's Dream*, likewise some of the men, despite their professed ardor, do not remain faithful to the women they have courted. And in *Love's Labour's Lost*, the women warily impose a year's waiting period on the men in an attempt to test their dependability. If love is often instantly kindled, it must be perpetuated by promises, and the dependability of those promises rests upon the trustworthiness of the persons who make them.

Shakespeare's comedies thus hold in suspension two apparently disparate views of love: one highly idealized and idealizing, the other subjecting the idealism to critique and mockery. Shakespeare was certainly not the first to take a double view of "lover's follies": they had long generated much of the humor in New Comic plot situations. In many classical and Renaissance New Comedies, the enthusiastic young lover is laughably wholehearted and naive, the subject of his friends' sardonic commentary. Shakespeare often complicates this simple paradigm. Many of his most appealing characters deal with the complexities of sexual love neither by repudiating love nor by abandoning their capacity for critical detachment. Rather they fall in love but simultaneously remain entirely cognizant of their own absurdity; in other words, they combine the role of lover and love's critic. Biron in *Love's Labour's Lost* and Benedick in *Much Ado About Nothing* both play this double game, and in *As You Like It* Rosalind, in her disguise as "Ganymede," regales her lover, Orlando, with what she represents as sage advice. "Men have died from time to time, and worms have eaten

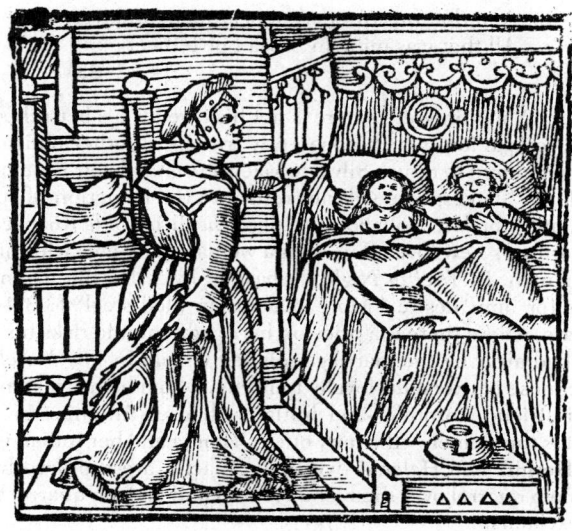

King Solomon *in flagrante delicto*, reproduced from *The Deceyte of Women* (1558?) by permission of The Huntington Library, San Marino, California.

them, but not for love," she assures him briskly in *As You Like It* 4.1.91–92; "men are April when they woo, December when they wed. Maids are May when they are maids, but the sky changes when they are wives" (lines 124–27). Yet after Orlando departs, Rosalind tells her cousin Celia: "O coz, coz, coz, my pretty little coz, that thou didst know how many fathom deep I am in love" (lines 175–76). Viola, in *Twelfth Night*, performs the same trick of detachment with less humor and more pathos, recounting her own story of apparently unrequited love to her beloved, Duke Orsino, as a story about her sister:

> ORSINO   And what's her history?
> VIOLA A blank, my lord. She never told her love,
>   But let concealment, like a worm i'th' bud,
>   Feed on her damask cheek. She pined in thought,
>   And with a green and yellow melancholy
>   She sat like patience on a monument,
>   Smiling at grief.
>
>   (2.4.108–14)

Whether this oblique utterance counts as "telling" her love is, of course, an open question, as uncertain, or "blank," as Viola perceives her own future to be. The self-aware lover, alert to the excesses of passionate sexual attachment but at the same time fully immersed in them, is a natural ally of the clown, with his professional expertise in ironic participation. Thus in *As You Like It*, the fool Touchstone throws in his lot with Rosalind and Celia, and Viola comments appreciatively upon Feste's skill in *Twelfth Night*.

If one problem for lovers is a temporal one—how to make a fleeting, if powerful, impulse the basis of a permanent relationship—another is how to reconcile the heterosexual, potentially procreative liaison with other kinds of relationship. While, compared to other comic dramatists, Shakespeare tends to play down generational strife, he again and again shows the emotional demands of heterosexual pairing in conflict with powerful same-sex loyalties. In the early *Two Gentlemen of Verona*, best friends Valentine and Proteus fall in love with the same woman: Proteus betrays his friend in an attempt to get Silvia for himself, and then Valentine (without consulting Silvia) cedes her to Proteus:

> And that my love may appear plain and free
> All that was mine in Silvia I give thee.
> (5.4.82–83)

The "love" to which Valentine refers here is not his love for his betrothed but his devotion to his male companion, which apparently trumps all other obligations. Another turn of the plot is required to return Silvia to Valentine and to pair Proteus with his original girlfriend, Julia. Shakespeare will not return to the depiction of so bald a rivalry between friends until the late, collaborative play *The Two Noble Kinsmen,* but in many other comedies a man's new love affair with a woman competes with his prior attachment to another man. In *Twelfth Night,* Sebastian owes his life to Antonio, a noble pirate who feels for him "desire / More sharp than filèd steel" (3.3.4–5). Following Sebastian to Illyria, where there is a price on his head, Antonio risks his life only to see Sebastian snatched away by the marriage-minded Olivia. In *The Merchant of Venice,* Bassanio must choose between his loyalty to Portia, whom he has just married, and his obligation to his friend Antonio—and initially chooses Antonio. In *A Midsummer Night's Dream,* it is the women—the fairy queen Titania and her Indian votress, and the mortal women Hermia and Helena—whose intimacies are ruptured by heterosexual passion. As the men quarrel over them and Hermia and Helena quarrel between themselves, Helena exclaims:

> O, is all quite forgot?
> All schooldays' friendship, childhood innocence?
> We, Hermia, like two artificial gods
> Have with our needles created both one flower,
> Both on one sampler, sitting on one cushion,
> Both warbling of one song, both in one key,
> As if our hands, our sides, voices, and minds
> Had been incorporate. So we grew together,
> Like to a double cherry: seeming parted,
> But yet a union in partition.
> (3.2.202–11)

Here, as in the other plays, Shakespeare leaves unspecified whether the emotional closeness between two persons of the same sex is ever physically consummated. But like marriage, female friendship as Helena describes it mysteriously makes one out of two: the word "incorporate," for instance, derives from a Latin word meaning "made into a single body." The implication is that whether or not such relationships are ever homosexually expressed, their intensity rivals that of heterosexual love.

Nonetheless, the potentially procreative marriages with which the comedy ends cannot occur if the characters sort permanently with persons of their own sex. Often, therefore, as here, idyllic moments of same-sex love are imagined retrospectively, as something already lost. At other times, same-sex attachment must be renounced. Thus, in *Much Ado About Nothing,* Beatrice requires her lover, Benedick, to challenge his friend, Claudio, to a duel for having slandered her cousin, Hero. Benedick initially recoils but then relents to her demand, a sign that his primary allegiance has shifted from his comrades-in-arms to the woman whom he will marry at the end of the play. In *The Merchant of Venice,* Portia forgives her husband, Bassanio, for having given away his wedding ring only after Bassanio's close friend Antonio pledges, essentially, that he will no longer claim priority in Bassanio's affections. In *A Midsummer Night's Dream,* the fairy queen Titania at first retains her Indian votress's child out of a sense of loyalty to the dead votress but ends up tamely relinquishing the child to her husband, Oberon.

Nonetheless, because Shakespeare portrays same-sex friendship as so rewarding and significant, some sense of loss as well as gain lingers over the happiness of the comic conclusion. Moreover some characters cannot—or refuse to be—included in the marital finale. Thus, in *Twelfth Night,* as so many of the main characters form heterosexual couples, the valiant Antonio is left isolated, an isolation the directors of some productions have emphasized by having him exit separately at the end of the play. In *As You Like It,* the "melancholy" Jaques simply declines to participate in the wedding revelry: "So, to your pleasures; / I am for other than for dancing measures" (5.4.181–82). Such characters make vivid the fact that not everybody is "the marrying kind" and that the inclusiveness of the comic conclusion has its limits.

Also left out of the comic conclusion or only shakily reintegrated are characters who might be considered scapegoats. The word *scapegoat* originates in an ancient ceremony in which a community ritually cleansed itself by delegating the responsibility for all its sins to a single person or animal—a goat in Israel, a slave or foreigner in ancient Greece—who was then punished and expelled. In modern parlance, a scapegoat is someone unfairly blamed as an individual for faults or crimes that are actually committed by a group. In many of his plays, Shakespeare manifests keen interest in the psychological mechanism by which people project their faults onto others and the way uniting against a despised "outsider" can help a community cohere more tightly. Thus, in *The Merchant of Venice,* the Christians revile the Jew Shylock, whose bald pursuit of self-interest and refusal to mix financial arrangements with friendship lay bare unwelcome truths about their own handling of money. Likewise the prim Malvolio, in *Twelfth Night,* is treated as a madman for having dared to imagine for himself the social advancement through marriage that the glamorous twins Sebastian and Viola actually achieve. The residents of Windsor humiliate Falstaff, in *The Merry Wives of Windsor,* for thinking that he can trade sex for money, even while Anne's parents plan to marry her off to one of her wealthy suitors rather than to the man she loves. Don John, the scheming bastard in *Much Ado About Nothing,* embodies the possibility of extramarital sexual activity, the prospect of which triggers so much of the suspicion and pain in the play. In all these cases, the scapegoat is indeed guilty, sometimes murderously so. Yet the community's investment in punishing him seems excessive in a way that exposes its own hypocrisy or blindness to its own motives.

In a few of the comedies, the scapegoat character remains completely beyond the pale at the end of the play: in *Much Ado About Nothing,* the Duke cheerfully anticipates devising "brave tortures" for his bastard brother Don John the day after the weddings. More often, there is some attempt at reconciliation, an effort to encircle the offender and keep him within the community after all. In *The Merry Wives of Windsor,* Falstaff is tormented but then invited to a feast; and in *All's Well That Ends Well,* the pretentious unscrupulous Paroles is first exposed as a liar and a coward, and then given a small pension. The attempt at reconciliation may seem profoundly hurtful, as when Shylock is given his life with the proviso that he convert to Christianity, a form of "mercy" that seems merely to substitute psychological for physical violence. Or the conciliatory gesture may be rejected: in *Twelfth Night,* despite Olivia's attempts to make peace, Malvolio storms off with a vow to "be revenged on the whole pack of you" (5.1.365).

Yet despite these darker notes, forgiveness and charity remain critically important in Shakespearean comedy. And since, as we have seen, the obstacles to happy love are so often self-imposed, not only the scapegoat characters are in need of it. A good deal of pain in the plays is the result of immature or unworthy young men behaving badly: Proteus in *The Two Gentlemen of Verona,* Demetrius in *A Midsummer Night's Dream,* Oliver in *As You Like It,* Bassanio in *The Merchant of Venice,* Claudio in *Much Ado About Nothing,* Angelo in *Measure for Measure,* Bertram in *All's Well That Ends Well.* All these characters, with greater or lesser motive and with more or less serious consequences, violate the bonds of relationship and must be forgiven at the end of the play. At times, indeed, they seem to get off too lightly—their efforts at repentance unconvincing, the pardons they are extended unmerited, and the women with whom they are matched too good for them. In Shakespeare's hands, however, comedy is not merely a genre that celebrates youth, abundance, and fertility, but one that represents for us, as we like it, the heartwarming possibility of getting more than we deserve.

SELECTED BIBLIOGRAPHY

Bamber, Linda. *Comic Women, Tragic Men: A Study of Gender and Genre in Shakespeare*. Stanford: Stanford University Press, 1982.

Barber, C. L. *Shakespeare's Festive Comedy: A Study of Dramatic Form and Its Relation to Social Custom*. Princeton: Princeton University Press, 1959.

Bradbrook, Muriel C. *The Growth and Structure of Elizabethan Comedy*. London: Chatto & Windus, 1955.

Frye, Northrop. *A Natural Perspective: The Development of Shakespearean Comedy and Romance*. New York: Columbia University Press, 1965.

———. *Anatomy of Criticism: Four Essays*. Princeton: Princeton University Press, 1957.

Miola, Robert S. *Shakespeare and Classical Comedy: The Influence of Plautus and Terence*. Oxford: Clarendon, 1994.

Wheeler, Richard. *Shakespeare's Development and the Problem Comedies: Turn and Counter-Turn*. Berkeley: University of California Press, 1981.

The Taming of the Shrew

One of Shakespeare's first comedies—probably written in 1592 or earlier—*The Taming of the Shrew* is also one of his most controversial, focusing as it does on the battle between the sexes and on the process by which a strong-willed woman is made to submit to the control of her husband. In actuality, the play is more complex than such a bald description indicates. An early example of Shakespeare's extraordinary theatrical craftsmanship, it consists of two interwoven plots and a frame tale. This complex structure allows for contrasts and parallels in the development of the play's main themes, complicating how the audience thinks about the drama's examination of the relationship between the sexes and the possibility that people can change their social identities either as a result of choice or of coercion. Perhaps not surprisingly, the play has elicited wildly varying reactions from generations of readers, audiences, and theater practitioners.

In the frame story, a poor tinker, Christopher Sly, is made to believe that he is a nobleman with servants, a wife, fine food, and even erotic artwork at his command. This hoax, shown in the play's first two scenes (called Inductions), is engineered by a real Lord who has found Sly drunk and asleep outside a tavern. The Lord's trick leads to many jokes at Sly's expense. While the tinker likes playing the part of a nobleman, he doesn't do it very well. His language, especially, betrays him. For example, Sly doesn't know how to address a lady, anxiously inquiring of his servants what to call his elegant spouse and settling on the absurd title "Madam wife." The hilarity of this scene is compounded by the fact that Sly's "wife" is really the Lord's page, Bartholomew, dressed up to impersonate a woman. Sly thus mistakes the sex of the person he would take to bed. He is also ignorant of the tastes and customs of the nobility, asking for cheap ale when he should call for sack, the sweet wine favored by gentlemen.

While these blunders make Sly an object of humor, he is also the figure for whose viewing pleasure the main play's two central plots unroll. As a temporary lord, Sly has a troupe of actors to entertain him. At least until he falls asleep, Sly watches them enact a comedy about courtship and marriage in which the primary plot involves a strong-willed woman, Katherine Minola, who is "tamed" by a fortune-seeking suitor named Petruccio. In the other plot, Kate's seemingly demure sister, Bianca, is pursued by three adoring suitors and eventually elopes with one of them without her father's knowledge or consent. All three actions are united by themes of disguise and transformation. Snatched from the mud and given the clothes and the privileges of a lord, Sly is temporarily translated from one social class and identity to another, even though his behavior and the snickers of his "attendants" repeatedly remind the audience that he is not *really* a nobleman. In their pursuit of Bianca, several of her suitors also don disguises. One, Hortensio, poses as a teacher of music and mathematics; another, Lucentio, pretends to be Cambio, a language instructor; meanwhile, Lucentio's servant, Tranio, assumes his master's identity and in that disguise poses as yet another of Bianca's many admirers. Love makes men willing to transform themselves, although in this plot these changes are volitional and reversible. When the disguised gentlemen tire of acting as scholars-for-hire, they simply reclaim their houses, fortunes, and social positions and demote their servants.

In the main plot, more subtle questions of disguise arise. Petruccio, to teach Katherine that she must obey him, acts the part of "shrew tamer," a role in which he appears at his own wedding in outlandish and ragged clothes and, during a sojourn at his country house, turns the world on its head by denying Kate sleep, food, and any exercise of her own will. But if his servant Grumio is to be believed, this may not simply be a one-time disguise. Hearing of his master's plan to wed the rich and shrewish Katherine, Grumio says:

> O' my word, an she knew him as well as I do she would think scolding would do little good upon him. She may perhaps call him half a score knaves or so. Why, that's nothing; an he begin once he'll rail in his rope-tricks. I'll tell you what, sir, an she stand him but a little he will throw a figure in her face and so disfigure her with it that she shall have no more eyes to see withal than a cat. You know him not, sir.
>
> (1.2.104–10)

Grumio's words raise doubts about Petruccio's "real" nature. Is he temporarily adopting the role of a shrew tamer and verbal bully, or is that his customary mode of being or a role that he has previously adopted in dealing with servants and other social inferiors? And as Petruccio attempts to transform Kate from shrew to obedient spouse, new questions arise: is he forcing her to deform her nature or helping her experiment with a role that might bring out untapped aspects of her personality or lead to greater control of her social environment? Is there, in fact, anything like a "real self," or is personhood a succession of social roles adopted because of coercion, social expectations, material circumstances, or the drive for social mastery?

The multiple instances of disguise and transformation in the three plots certainly invite reflection on the sources of and possibilities for change both in people's behavior and in their social circumstances. From the play one might, for example, conclude that lords and gentlemen can play with their social roles with more success and less risk than can tinkers. Sly's transformation is thrust upon him; but his lack of wealth and education would in any case make it impossible for him to "pass" as nobility without the complicity of the Lord who found him asleep outside the tavern. His transformation is precarious, a mere dream from which he will have to awaken, no matter how much he might want to live on in his new circumstances. But for Lucentio, his role as a Latin master is nothing *but* a temporary stratagem, a part that his education allows him to play to perfection but that his social rank permits him to cast aside when he has won his bride. Similarly, the social fact of gender sets different limits on possible presentations and transformations of self. Petruccio's outrageous behavior—striking his servants and starving his wife—makes him admired by other men. Hortensio, for example, one of Bianca's suitors who eventually marries a wealthy widow, decides to model himself after Petruccio and to take lessons from him on how to tame a wife. But what is deemed to be Kate's outrageous behavior—striking a sister and defying a father and would-be husband—elicits only scorn and condemnation. Like class, gender limits one's permissible or possible range of action and the transformations of self one can effect. Unless she is willing to endure severe privation and penalties, Kate can only undergo one kind of transformation—toward greater docility and subservience to her husband. In such circumstances, it is difficult to determine—as many critics wish to do—whether Katherine finds her "real" self through her encounters with Petruccio. Like many characters in the play, she can only improvise a self in relation to the social constraints and possibilities available to her, and the constraints operating upon a tinker or a woman are very different from those affecting a university-educated gentleman or a lord.

The social hierarchies that shape the possibilities for personal transformations are, in the Sly frame tale, given a peculiarly English inflection. The Sly episodes refer repeatedly to the Warwickshire countryside that was Shakespeare's own birthplace. Sly mentions Greet, an actual village near Stratford, and Burton Heath (possibly Barton-on-the-Heath, another village close to Stratford), and the men enumerated as his tavern companions—Stephen Sly, John Naps, Peter Turf, and Henry Pimpernel—for the most part have homely English names. Moreover, the contrast between Sly and the Lord who carries him to his house mirrors the gap in sixteenth-century rural England between poor laborers, barely making a living at a succession of marginal jobs, and wealthy landowners. As arable and common land was fenced in or enclosed to increase the opportunities for grazing sheep, many landowners made huge profits, wool being one of England's most important exports. But enclosures, a number of which occurred in the Stratford region, also caused hardship for small tenant farmers forced off the enclosed land and, in some cases, driven into vagrancy.

Sly, simply called "Beggar" in the speech prefixes in the First Folio, is a poor man with a checkered employment history. He describes himself as "old Sly's son of Burton Heath, by birth a pedlar, by education a cardmaker, by transmutation a bearherd, and now by present profession a tinker" (Induction 2.17–19). A cardmaker makes the metal combs used to prepare wool for spinning; thus Sly has had some tangential involvement with the wool industry, although he seems primarily to have led an itinerant life mending pots, selling cheap goods from a pedlar's pack, and running up whatever tab he could at the local tavern. The Induction reveals the enormous gap in wealth and education separating this man from the leisured aristocrats who pick him up on the way home from hunting and use him for their evening's sport. The trick they play upon him is a fantastic one, but the details of the Lord's privilege and Sly's drunken poverty are evoked with vivid realism. For such a man as Sly, what hope is there of becoming a Lord?

By contrast, Bianca and her suitors exist in an Italian setting at many removes from Sly's English-countryside milieu. The events in this story line are drawn directly from George Gascoigne's *Supposes* (1566), itself an adaption of a work by Ariosto, *I Suppositi*, which employs the disguised identities, clever servants, and gullible fathers found in classical comedy. Wealth is also a crucial factor in this plot, for despite his speeches about the necessity for suitors to gain his daughters' love, Baptista is willing to give them to their wealthiest wooers. The suitors' money comes mostly from trade. Bianca's suitors testify to the number of ships they have at sea and to the luxury goods and property they have acquired through their ventures. In this world of prosperous urban merchants, Baptista can indulge his daughters with some training in the arts and languages, but he still expects to control their marriage choices. Kate he delivers to the frankly fortune-hunting Petruccio, but he ultimately has less luck with his supposedly compliant daughter, Bianca, whose name, meaning "white," implies her virtue and purity. Bianca not only elopes, but, in the play's final banquet scene, she refuses to come when her new husband summons her, suggesting that her earlier docility may have been a calculated pose. If her sister is gradually tamed, Bianca ultimately reveals her own considerable capacity to play the shrew, her education and social position having given her the wherewithal to manipulate the courtship process to her own advantage.

It is against this backdrop that the particular features of the main plot become apparent. The relationship between Kate and Petruccio has long been regarded as the play's most riveting story line. In fact, in the eighteenth century, the famous actor David Garrick produced a shortened version of the play simply called *Catharine and Petruchio,* which cut the Bianca plot and held the stage for nearly one hundred years. The interest in Kate and Petruccio is understandable, for Shakespeare created for them a story of taming at once enjoyable and deeply troubling. Though set in Italy, this plot line feels English, connected in subterranean ways to the world of Christopher Sly. For one thing, Petruccio is not just a creature of the city; he has a farmhouse that serves as this play's "green world," or place of transformations. Moreover, Petruccio is distinguished in many ways from the other Italian suitors. He has, for example, a sullen and quarrelsome servant, Grumio, in every respect the antithesis of the clever attendants, Tranio and Biondello, who help Lucentio win Bianca and, in fact, seem to do most of their master's thinking and plotting for him. This may be a kind of affectionate joke made at the expense of English domestic servants, who, despite their crude ways, at least aren't shown as mastering their masters. Moreover, while Hortensio, Gremio, and Lucentio woo Bianca with song and poetry, Petruccio woos Kate by contradicting her every word and taming her, like a hawk, by making her go hungry and sleepless. The language of

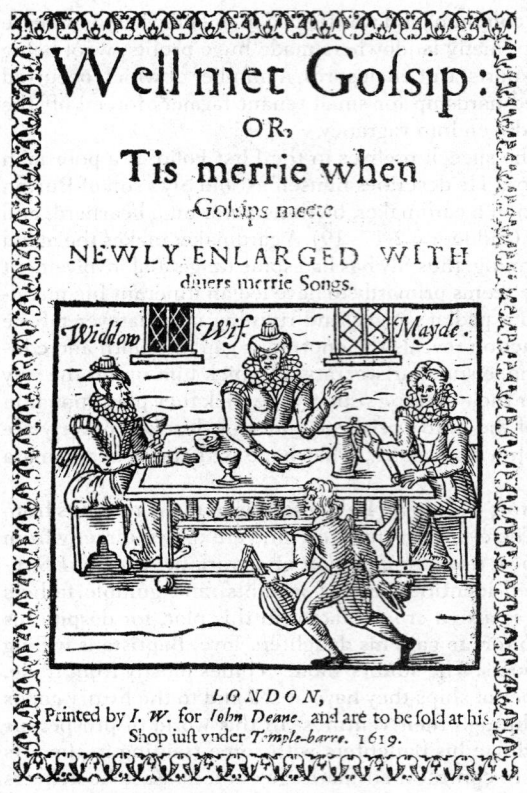

Well met Goßip:
OR,
Tis merrie when
Goßips meete

NEWLY ENLARGED WITH
diuers merrie Songs.

Widdow *Wif* *Mayde.*

LONDON,
Printed by *I. W.* for *Iohn Deane.* and are to be fold at his
Shop iuft vnder *Temple-barre.* 1619.

"Gadding." Title page of Samuel Rowlands, *Tis Merrie When Gossips Meete* (1619).

blood sport permeates both the Induction and the Petruccio scenes. The Lord who picks up Sly has just returned from hunting and speaks knowledgeably about the abilities of each of his hounds; Petruccio repeatedly compares the taming of a wife to the transformation of a wild hawk into a docile hunting falcon, aligning wife taming with other manly English sports.

Finally, of course, the source for the Petruccio-Kate plot is not an Italian comedy, as in the Bianca-Lucentio plot, but a folk story about taming a difficult wife, variants of which circulated throughout northern Europe in Shakespeare's day, including the vicious English ballad entitled "A Merry Jest of a Shrewd and Curst Wife Lapped in Morel's Skin for Her Good Behavior." In this ballad, a strong-willed wife is beaten bloody by her husband and then wrapped inside the salted skin of a dead horse named Morel. This mode of taming is more physically brutal than that employed by Petruccio, but both the play and the ballad assume that a husband can use extreme means to curb the will of a forward wife.

Despite his Italian name, then, Petruccio is in many ways an Englishman; and the play implicitly suggests that unlike his Italian counterpart, the true Englishman defines his manhood through the firm and, if necessary, cruel mastery of wife and servant. By contrast, the less assertive Lucentio takes direction from his servant, supplicates his betrothed on bended knee, and ends up with a wife he cannot master. Petruccio's bluff manliness constituted one of the period's privileged versions of English masculinity. In some respects he resembles the English military hero Talbot in *1 Henry VI*, a history play that Shakespeare had a hand in writing probably sometime not long after he composed *The Taming of the Shrew*. Petruccio also anticipates Shakespeare's portrait of England's great warrior king Henry V, the protagonist in a series of history plays that Shakespeare penned in the second half of the 1590s. Outspoken, commanding in battle or brawl, and adept at the blunt rhetorical and physical mastery of women, each of these male heroes in his own way helped define what distinguished a proper Englishman from what was French, Italian, or simply foreign.

This subtle Englishing of Kate and Petruccio may have heightened the original audience's interest in and even identification with them, as the play implicitly pits virile English wooing and wedding against the sophisticated ineffectiveness of Italian practices. Men and women, however, may not have been equally drawn to what they witnessed. In the wake of the modern women's movement, certainly, the very idea of "taming" a woman and curbing her tongue have seemed offensive to many readers and viewers. In *Taming of the Shrew*, language is a vehicle for domination. Sly cannot effectively play

Cucking stool, used to discipline scolds, shrews, and witches. From T. N. Brushfield, *Chester Archaeological and Historic Society Journal* (1855–62).

a lord because he has not mastered the language of the elite. Kate can be eloquent, but because of her gender her verbal independence is read by her father and suitors as a sign of shrewishness. In part, Petruccio tames Kate's tart tongue by aggressive use of his own. A clear sign that he has succeeded occurs in 4.6, when, at her husband's behest, Kate calls the sun the moon and an old man a budding virgin. Her words at this point no longer express her own perceptions but her husband's blatantly willful reading of reality. In the play's last scene, she also makes a lengthy speech about a wife's duty to obey her husband that conforms to the patriarchal ideology of the day and her husband's wishes but is disturbingly far from her earlier expression of women's right to independent speech and thought. Some directors have found this curbing of the female tongue and will so intolerable that they have made production choices that downplay the extent of Kate's submission to Petruccio or that mitigate the linguistic coercion and physical cruelty that are part of his taming methods. For example, in many productions, Kate delivers her last speech about wifely duty while signaling, by winks and gestures, that she does not really believe it, or the director omits the lines in which Kate offers to put her hand beneath her husband's foot as a token of submission. Such choices signal a desire to "save" Shakespeare from accusations that his play celebrates a crude form of male dominance.

Even in Shakespeare's own day, it is not clear that everyone, including men, would have found Petruccio's behavior entirely laudable. The proper relationship between husband and wife was a matter of discussion and debate. Many Protestant preachers enjoined husbands to use no violence against their wives and to treat them as spiritual equals and domestic helpmeets. They lauded marriage not merely as an economic arrangement but as a union demanding mutual affection and respect from both parties. At the same time, few disputed that in the last analysis husbands were masters of their wives and that the household was "a little commonwealth," a realm in which the husband's supremacy over wife and children mirrored the supremacy of the monarch over his subjects. Disorder in the domestic realm was treated as a serious matter, intimating the possibility of a breakdown of order and hierarchy in the culture at large.

Strong-willed women were particularly apt to be labeled as disorderly in early modern towns and villages, even if their "crimes" involved nothing more than talkativeness.

Husband dominator. From a German playing card by Peter Flötner (1520).

A shrew, in fact, was commonly defined as a woman with a wagging tongue who, partly because of her garrulousness, was not properly submissive to her husband. The ideal wife, by contrast, was chaste, silent, and obedient. The talkativeness that could mark a woman as a shrew could also be interpreted as a sign of her sexual promiscuity, on the theory that one kind of looseness leads to another. Women deemed unruly were subject to various kinds of punishment. These could include being "cucked"—ducked into water on a "cucking stool"—or being fitted with a scold's bridle, a torturous harness that fitted around a woman's head with a metal bit that went into her mouth and prevented her from speaking and sometimes caused her to gag and her mouth to bleed or her teeth to be knocked loose. The husbands of disorderly and aggressive women could also be punished for failure to control their wives. Charivaris, or "rough ridings," were shaming rituals in which neighbors came to the house of a disorderly woman and made her or her husband ride backward through the town on a horse while bystanders shouted and played cacophonous music. This signaled that the world had been turned upside down and rendered inharmonious by her disorderliness and his inability to control his wife.

In *The Taming of the Shrew*, no man is submitted to a "rough riding" even though at the end of the play both Lucentio and Hortensio seem to have lost control of their wives. Instead, all the attention focuses on the taming of Kate and on the strategies employed by Petruccio to make her compliant with his will. On the eighteenth- and nineteenth-century stage, Petruccio often carried a whip, symbol of his power to control his wife and servants with physical force. Whether or not he *literally* carries a whip, Petruccio employs coercion—verbal, psychological, and physical—to control his wife, subjecting her to public humiliation and private deprivation in order to teach her proper submissiveness to the authority of her husband. In so doing, he reinforces the hierarchical principle upon which the entire Elizabethan social order was premised, warning not only unruly men but also servants and beggars that, except in jest, they cannot usurp the places of their masters. But is this account of *The Taming of the Shrew* adequate? Is the play as fiercely repressive as some critics assume? It is precisely on this point that readers, critics, and actors differ.

Some critics, for example, emphasize how Shakespeare mitigates the violence of many versions of the folktale on which the main plot is modeled. Kate is not, for example, beaten and wrapped in a salted horsehide, nor does Petruccio force her to sleep with him before their return to Padua. In his farmhouse, he keeps her awake by disordering the bed and talking at her, but only after their return to the relative safety and familiarity of her father's house does he speak of his intention to "bed" her. In short, sexual conquest does not seem to be part of his taming practices. Perhaps more importantly, many actors, audiences, and critics have seen in Kate and Petruccio's relationship an attractive mutuality and vitality they find difficult to reconcile with the idea that the play is simply a lesson in how to subordinate a woman. For example, when Petruccio first woos Kate in 2.1, the two of them engage in a verbal sparring match dazzling in its complexity and speed. Puns and insults fly back and forth, with Kate giving as good as she gets. The following exchange is typical:

> PETRUCCIO   Come, come, you wasp, i'faith you are too angry.
> KATHERINE   If I be waspish, best beware my sting.
> PETRUCCIO   My remedy is then to pluck it out.
> KATHERINE   Ay, if the fool could find it where it lies.
> PETRUCCIO   Who knows not where a wasp does wear his sting?
> In his tail.
> KATHERINE   In his tongue.
> PETRUCCIO   Whose tongue?
> KATHERINE   Yours, if you talk of tales, and so farewell.
> PETRUCCIO   What, with my tongue in your tail? Nay, come again,
> Good Kate, I am a gentleman.
> KATHERINE   That I'll try.
> *She strikes him*
> PETRUCCIO   I swear I'll cuff you if you strike again.
>
>   (2.1.207–16)

This is a beautifully orchestrated encounter, with Kate and Petruccio trading rapid-fire, one-line insults and deftly topping one another's puns. Their exchange has erotic intensity. These two are taking one another's measure, listening intently, struggling for advantage. Petruccio is not above talking dirty, and Katherine is not above making physical contact, albeit with a blow and not a caress. This is light years away from the vapid wooing of Lucentio and Bianca, hiding behind the screen of school Latin. On the stage, something vital and alive goes on between Katherine and Petruccio, and they have often been compared with Shakespeare's other witty couples, such as Benedick and Beatrice in *Much Ado About Nothing,* iconoclasts who seem more real and finally better and more equally matched than the more conventional couples with whom they are contrasted. Many critics, in fact, have argued that the real love story of the play belongs to Kate and Petruccio, and that his taming of her is merely a way of showing her the advantages of outwardly conforming to society's expectations so that she can have the husband, the home, and the social approval she surely must crave. Many argue that it is Kate's spirit that attracts Petruccio and that her spirit is never broken, just redirected, as in the final scene when Kate takes out her aggressions not against her husband but against the other wives, whom she lectures on their marriage duties.

The debate about how to interpret *The Taming of the Shrew* will surely continue. In performance, directors and actors sometimes emphasize the drama's playful and farcical elements, sometimes its dark, violent, and repressive potential. Critics and readers remain similarly divided as to what they see in this tale of woman tamed. Most agree, however, that *The Taming of the Shrew* deals with issues that deserve the thoughtful and sometimes heated critical debate the play has engendered. For example, while Kate's taming does not involve the kinds of physical brutality in the "Merry Jest" ballad, it is nonetheless true that in Petruccio's farmhouse Kate is deprived of sleep, food, and the protection of family and female companionship—techniques akin to modern methods of torture and brainwashing. As Kate says, she is "starved for meat, giddy for lack of sleep, / With oaths kept waking and with brawling fed" (4.3.9–10). This is horrifying, even if the horror is mitigated by the laughter-inducing techniques of knockabout farce. Grumio makes the audience laugh as he tantalizes Kate with one kind of food and then another, while ultimately withholding them all, but this does not erase the fact that Kate is hungry and that her hunger is used to starve her into complying with Petruccio's wishes. There is similar cruelty lurking behind the trick played on Sly in the Induction. The beggar is tantalized with the prospect of riches he can never retain. *The Taming of the Shrew* makes a joke out of the enormous gap between the poverty of a tinker and the privilege of a lord, comedy from the physical and psychic trials that lie in wait for a strong-willed woman.

It is perhaps appropriate to conclude by focusing again on the role of Sly. As he watches the play the actors perform for him, he at first makes comments on the action, but these stop after the first act, and he presumably falls asleep on stage. In another contemporary play, however, called *The Taming of a Shrew*, Sly makes interjections throughout, including a brief speech in which he vows to go home and tame his own wife, having learned from Petruccio how it is done. Scholars disagree about the relationship of *The Taming of the Shrew* and *The Taming of a Shrew*: they dispute which came first and whether Shakespeare had a hand in both (for a fuller discussion, see the Textual Note). Among the many differences between the two texts, however, is Sly's continuing stage prominence right to the end of *The Taming of a Shrew* and his final assertion that

> I'll to my
> Wife presently and tame her too,
> An if she anger me.
> (Additional Passages E.19–21)

No one knows for certain if Shakespeare wrote these lines or why they don't appear in *The Taming of the Shrew*. Like almost everything else connected to this play, they are subject to various interpretations. Perhaps because they are put in Sly's mouth they are discredited, taken as another example of the reductiveness of his responses to the pastimes of the cultural elite—in this case, to the play staged in the Lord's house by the traveling players. Maybe *only* a tinker would take this as the "message" of the play. On the other hand, perhaps Sly's response to what he has just watched indicates why this vital and attractive play seems to many readers to traffic in dangerous matters and to be easily used to justify the crudest kinds of male tyranny. It is a little disconcerting that *even* a downtrodden tinker can find comfort in the thought that while he is neither a lord nor a gentleman, he shares with them the same right to tame his wife "an if she anger me." Impoverished and ridiculed, Sly nonetheless feels entitled by virtue of his gender to dominate his spouse, perhaps thereby compensating for his powerlessness in other areas. In short, there is always something lower than a beggar—a beggar's wife. The play published in the First Folio omits Sly's speech, but in our day *The Taming of the Shrew* nonetheless remains, along with *The Merchant of Venice*, one of Shakespeare's most controversial plays: a spur to thought and to debate, a reminder of the serious matters that often lie at the heart of Shakespeare's "festive" comedies.

JEAN E. HOWARD

TEXTUAL NOTE

The Taming of the Shrew was first printed in the 1623 First Folio (F), the control text for this edition. Certain features of the text indicate that it was set from Shakespeare's "foul papers," or perhaps a scribal copy of them, rather than from a theatrical promptbook. Stage directions, exits, and entrances are not handled with the precision customary for a text that would have been used as the basis for an actual performance.

The greatest mystery surrounding the text is its relationship to another play, *The Taming of a Shrew*, entered in the Stationers' Register on May 2, 1594, and published the same year. This play bears many resemblances to Shakespeare's, and for years scholars have debated which preceded the other or whether, in fact, they both derived from a common original, now lost. Many editors have assumed that Shakespeare's play was the source for *The Taming of a Shrew*, though the subplots, in particular, differ substantially; and an interesting argument has been advanced by Leah Marcus that *A Shrew* is earlier than *The Shrew*, that it is at least partly by Shakespeare, and that, in her view, it inscribes an older version of patriarchy than that evident in *The Shrew*. Whatever one decides about order of composition, it is significant that *A Shrew* contains a number of passages involving Christopher Sly not found in *The Shrew*, passages in which Sly continues to comment on the play he watches and finally wakes from his "dream" announcing his intention to go home and tame his own wife. No one knows why these passages appear in one play and not the other. One possibility is that they were written by Shakespeare but for some reason deleted by him or by someone else from the manuscript that served as the basis for the Folio edition of the play, or were added by him at a date later than the composition of that manuscript. For their intrinsic interest, and because of their possible Shakespearean origin, these materials concerning Sly are printed at the end of this edition of *The Shrew* as Additional Passages.

The Oxford editors believe, on balance, that *A Shrew* imitates and is later than *The Shrew*, and this assumption affects their dating of Shakespeare's play, which would have to have been written before 1594, when *A Shrew* was published and designated as belonging to Pembroke's Men, a company that went bankrupt in 1593 and so must have had the play in their repertoire before that time. In addition, a stage direction in *A Shrew* refers to "Simon," who has been plausibly identified as Simon Jewell, an actor who was buried on August 21, 1592. This circumstantial evidence, along with stylistic features that mark the play as an early example of Shakespeare's art, suggests a date of composition of 1592 or earlier.

The Folio text of *The Taming of the Shrew* bears some marks of confusion or incomplete revision in the subplot, particularly in the handling of the character of Hortensio. Shakespeare may have decided rather late to make him one of Bianca's wooers. He is, for example, not included in the "bidding" for Bianca in which Tranio (disguised as Lucentio) and Gremio engage in 2.1. Other anomalies regarding his part are mentioned in the notes to this text, but in performance these issues seldom bother audiences.

In two instances, the present edition marks new scenes where most contemporary editions do not. The first is 3.3, which follows Petruccio's arrival in disheveled dress for his wedding. During this prenuptial scene, Lucentio has no speaking part, and there is no requirement that he be onstage. Consequently, the Oxford editors mark a new scene, 3.3, after everyone exits to attend the wedding and Lucentio comes onstage speaking with Tranio about Bianca before Gremio returns at 3.3.21 to describe the offstage wedding. Another new scene is marked after 4.4—that is, after the episode in which the Pedant, posing as Lucentio's father, meets Baptista and negotiates the marriage of Bianca and Lucentio. This edition makes a separate scene of the ensuing conversation between Biondello and Lucentio in which Biondello explains how Lucentio can elope with Bianca. This change is justified both because the stage has just been cleared before Lucentio's and Biondello's entry and also because there is plausibly a time gap between the two events. In addition, 4.4 shows signs of revision on Shakespeare's part, including indecision about whether or not to include Lucentio in that scene. Making Lucentio and Biondello's conversation a separate scene clarifies the different foci of the two episodes: the first concentrating on Tranio and the Pedant's tricking of Baptista, the second on Biondello's plans for Lucentio to elope.

SELECTED BIBLIOGRAPHY

Aspinall, Dana E., ed. *The Taming of the Shrew: Critical Essays*. New York: Routledge, 2002. A broad selection of twentieth-century critical essays about the play plus reviews of notable film, television, and stage versions.

Boose, Lynda. "Scolding Brides and Bridling Scolds: Taming the Woman's Unruly Member." *Shakespeare Quarterly* 42 (1991): 179–213. Draws on the research of nineteenth-century scholars to recover the early modern punishments, including iron gags and ducking stools, used against women accused of being shrews or scolds.

Haring-Smith, Tori. *From Farce to Metadrama: A Stage History of "The Taming of the Shrew," 1594–1983*. Westport, Conn.: Greenwood Press, 1985. A comprehensive stage history of the play and of some major adaptations from the late 1590s to the early 1980s.

Huston, J. Dennis. "Enter the Hero: The Power of Play in *The Taming of the Shrew*." *Shakespeare's Comedies of Play*. New York: Columbia University Press, 1981. 58–93. Argues that Shakespeare playfully experiments with comic form in *The Taming of the Shrew* and creates a hero, Petruccio, who teaches Kate how to play with social roles in order to gain control over her environment.

Korda, Natasha. "Household Kates: Domesticating Commodities in *The Taming of the Shrew*." *Shakespeare's Domestic Economies: Gender and Property in Early Modern England*. Philadelphia: University of Pennsylvania Press, 2002. 52–75. Explores the play as part of an historical shift that made women managers of domestic property and suggests that in taming Kate, Petruccio educates her about the proper management and consumption of household goods.

Marcus, Leah. "The Shakespearean Editor as Shrew-Tamer." *English Literary Renaissance* 22 (1992): 177–200. Examines and queries the historical process by which *The Taming of a Shrew* came to be regarded, not as a source for Shakespeare's *The Taming of the Shrew*, but as a debased derivative of it.

Newman, Karen. "Renaissance Family Politics and Shakespeare's *Taming of the Shrew*." *Fashioning Femininity and English Renaissance Drama*. Chicago: University of Chicago Press, 1991. 33–50. Argues that Kate's linguistic freedom constitutes her main threat to male authority and that that freedom is never completely curtailed.

Orlin, Lena Cowen. "The Performance of Things in *The Taming of the Shrew*." *Yearbook of English Studies* 23 (1993): 167–88. Notes the abundance of objects, especially household objects, in *The Taming of the Shrew* and analyzes their functions.

Smith, Amy L. "Performing Marriage with a Difference: Wooing, Wedding, and Bedding in *The Taming of the Shrew*." *Comparative Drama* 36 (2002): 289–320. Uses Judith Butler's theories of performativity to argue that within Kate and Petruccio's self-conscious performance of courtship and marriage lies the potential for a critical reworking of gender norms, rather than outright submission to or resistance of them.

Walker, Kim. "Wrangling Pedantry: Education in *The Taming of the Shrew*." *Shakespeare Matters: History, Teaching, Performance*. Ed. Lloyd Davis. Newark: University of Delaware Press, 2003. 191–208. Examines the importance of women's education in the play and in several adaptations of it and suggests that humanist education plays a role in Bianca's transformation into a shrew.

FILMS

The Taming of the Shrew. 1929. Dir. Samuel Taylor. USA. 63 min. One of the first "talkies," this black-and-white film, starring Douglas Fairbanks as Petruccio and Mary Pickford as Katherine, ends with Pickford's famous "wink" at the conclusion of her speech of submission.

Kiss Me Kate. 1953. Dir. George Sidney. USA. 109 min. Film version of the Cole Porter musical starring Howard Keel and Kathryn Grayson in which a group of actors is shown performing Shakespeare's play, the events of which mirror their own circumstances. Songs include "Brush Up Your Shakespeare" and "Where Is the Life That Late I Led?"

The Taming of the Shrew. 1967. Dir. Franco Zeffirelli. Italy/USA. 122 min. Broad-comedy performance starring the real-life couple of Elizabeth Taylor and Richard Burton as Katherine and Petruccio.

The Taming of the Shrew. 1980. Dir. Jonathan Miller. UK. 127 min. Intelligent BBC-TV version starring John Cleese as Petruccio and Sarah Badel as Katherine with sets modeled on Vermeer interiors.

10 Things I Hate About You. 1999. Dir. Gil Juner. USA. 97 min. Loose adaptation of Shakespeare's plot in which Julia Stiles plays a headstrong character, Kat Stratford, who comes to an accommodation with bad boy Heath Ledger as Patrick Verona.

The Taming of the Shrew

THE PERSONS OF THE PLAY

In the Induction

CHRISTOPHER SLY, beggar and tinker
A HOSTESS
A LORD
BARTHOLOMEW, his page
HUNTSMEN
SERVANTS
PLAYERS

In the play-within-the-play

BAPTISTA Minola, a gentleman of Padua
KATHERINE, his elder daughter
BIANCA, his younger daughter
PETRUCCIO, a gentleman of Verona, suitor of Katherine
GRUMIO⎫ his servants
CURTIS ⎭
GREMIO, a rich old man of Padua, suitor of Bianca
HORTENSIO, another suitor, who disguises himself as Licio, a
    teacher
LUCENTIO, from Pisa, who disguises himself as Cambio, a
    teacher
TRANIO⎫ his servants
BIONDELLO⎭
VINCENTIO, Lucentio's father
A PEDANT (schoolmaster), from Mantua
A WIDOW
A TAILOR
A HABERDASHER
An OFFICER
SERVINGMEN, including NATHANIEL, PHILIP, JOSEPH, and PETER
Other servants of Baptista and Petruccio

Induction 1

Enter CHRISTOPHER SLY *[the] beggar, and [the]*
    HOSTESS

SLY   I'll feeze you,° in faith.   *fix you; beat you*
HOSTESS   A pair of stocks,[1] you rogue.
SLY   You're a baggage.° The Slys are no rogues. Look in the   *whore*
    Chronicles[2]—we came in with Richard Conqueror,[3] therefore
5   *paucas palabras*,[4] let the world slide.° Sessa![5]   *go by*

Induction 1 Location: In front of a country tavern.
1. A threat to have him put in the stocks (an instrument of public punishment consisting of two wooden planks with semicircles carved into them; the criminal sat with his or her feet clamped between the planks).
2. Histories, especially histories of England such as

Raphael Holinshed's *Chronicles of England, Scotland, and Ireland* (2nd ed., 1587).
3. A blunder for "William the Conqueror," who took the English throne in 1066.
4. Misquoting *pocas palabras*, Spanish for "few words," a phrase from Thomas Kyd's *Spanish Tragedy* (c. 1587).
5. Probably equivalent to "Be quiet."

HOSTESS   You will not pay for the glasses you have burst?

SLY   No, not a denier. Go by, Saint Jeronimy![6] Go to thy cold
bed and warm thee.

HOSTESS   I know my remedy, I must go fetch the headborough.°   *constable*

[*Exit*]

10 SLY   Third or fourth or fifth borough, I'll answer him by law. I'll
not budge an inch, boy.[7] Let him come, and kindly.°   *and welcome! (ironic)*

[*He*] *falls asleep.*

Wind horns.° Enter a LORD *from hunting, with his train*   *Horns sound*

LORD   Huntsman, I charge thee, tender well° my hounds.   *care well for*

Breathe Merriman[8]—the poor cur is embossed°—   *exhausted*

And couple Clowder with the deep-mouthed brach.[9]

15   Saw'st thou not, boy, how Silver made it good

At the hedge corner, in the coldest fault?[1]

I would not lose the dog for twenty pound.

FIRST HUNTSMAN   Why, Belman is as good as he, my lord.

He cried upon it at the merest loss,[2]

20   And twice today picked out the dullest scent.

Trust me, I take him for the better dog.

LORD   Thou art a fool. If Echo were as fleet

I would esteem him worth a dozen such.

But sup° them well, and look unto them all.   *feed*

25   Tomorrow I intend to hunt again.

FIRST HUNTSMAN   I will, my lord.

LORD [*seeing* SLY]   What's here? One dead, or drunk? See, doth he breathe?

SECOND HUNTSMAN   He breathes, my lord. Were he not warmed with ale

This were a bed but cold to sleep so soundly.

30 LORD   O monstrous beast! How like a swine he lies.

Grim death, how foul and loathsome is thine image.[3]

Sirs, I will practise° on this drunken man.   *play a trick on*

What think you: if he were conveyed to bed,

Wrapped in sweet° clothes, rings put upon his fingers,   *scented*

35   A most delicious banquet by his bed,

And brave° attendants near him when he wakes—   *finely dressed*

Would not the beggar then forget himself?

FIRST HUNTSMAN   Believe me, lord, I think he cannot choose.°   *do otherwise*

SECOND HUNTSMAN   It would seem strange unto him when he waked.

40 LORD   Even as a flatt'ring° dream or worthless fancy.   *pleasing*

Then take him up, and manage well the jest.

Carry him gently to my fairest chamber,

And hang it round with all my wanton pictures.°   *erotic artworks*

Balm° his foul head in warm distillèd waters,   *Anoint*

45   And burn sweet wood to make the lodging sweet.[4]

---

6. Misquoting a popular line—"Hieronimo, beware! go by, go by!"—from Kyd's *Spanish Tragedy* and confusing Hieronimo, Kyd's hero, with Saint Jerome. *denier*: French coin of little value.
7. Term of abuse applicable to either sex.
8. Give Merriman time to recover his breath.
9. And put Clowder on a leash with the female hound

("brach") who bays deeply.
1. When the scent was faintest.
2. When the scent had been completely lost.
3. Your likeness (invoking the common comparison between sleep and death).
4. Aromatic woods like juniper were often burned to make a room smell fragrant.

Procure me music ready when he wakes
To make a dulcet° and a heavenly sound,   *melodious*
And if he chance to speak be ready straight,°   *at once*
And with a low submissive reverence°   *deep bow*
50 Say 'What is it your honour will command?'
Let one attend him with a silver basin
Full of rose-water and bestrewed with flowers;
Another bear the ewer,° the third a diaper,°   *water jug / towel*
And say 'Will't please your lordship cool your hands?'
55 Someone be ready with a costly suit,
And ask him what apparel he will wear.
Another tell him of his hounds and horse,
And that his lady mourns at his disease.
Persuade him that he hath been lunatic,
60 And when he says he is,° say that he dreams,   *is indeed mad*
For he is nothing but a mighty lord.
This do, and do it kindly,° gentle sirs.   *naturally; fittingly*
It will be pastime passing° excellent,   *exceedingly*
If it be husbanded with modesty.°   *prudently managed*
65 FIRST HUNTSMAN   My lord, I warrant you we will play our part
As he shall think by our true diligence
He is no less than what we say he is.
LORD   Take him up gently, and to bed with him;
And each one to his office° when he wakes.   *assigned role*

[SERVINGMEN *carry* SLY *out*]

Trumpets sound

70 Sirrah,[5] go see what trumpet 'tis that sounds.

[*Exit a* SERVINGMAN]

Belike° some noble gentleman that means,   *Perhaps*
Travelling some journey, to repose him here.

Enter [a] SERVINGMAN

How now? Who is it?
SERVINGMAN   An't° please your honour, players   *If it*
That offer service to your lordship.

Enter PLAYERS

75 LORD   Bid them come near. Now fellows, you are welcome.
PLAYERS   We thank your honour.
LORD   Do you intend to stay with me tonight?
A PLAYER   So please your lordship to accept our duty.°   *services; respect*
LORD   With all my heart. This fellow I remember
80 Since once he played a farmer's eldest son.
'Twas where you wooed the gentlewoman so well.
I have forgot your name, but sure that part
Was aptly fitted° and naturally performed.   *well suited (to you)*
ANOTHER PLAYER   I think 'twas Soto[6] that your honour means.
85 LORD   'Tis very true. Thou didst it excellent.
Well, you are come to me in happy time,°   *at the right time*
The rather for° I have some sport in hand   *Especially since*
Wherein your cunning° can assist me much.   *skill*

---

5. A form of address to social inferiors.
6. Possibly a reference to a character of this name in John Fletcher's *Women Pleased*. Since that play was first acted around 1620, the reference must be a late addition to Shakespeare's text or else refer to a character in an earlier play, now lost.

There is a lord will hear you play tonight;
90 But I am doubtful of your modesties°   *self-control*
Lest, over-eyeing of° his odd behaviour—   *noticing; staring at*
For yet his honour never heard a play—
You break into some merry passion,°   *fit of laughter*
And so offend him; for I tell you, sirs,
95 If you should smile he grows impatient.
A PLAYER   Fear not, my lord, we can contain ourselves
Were he the veriest antic° in the world.   *most eccentric fellow*
LORD [*to a* SERVINGMAN]   Go, sirrah, take them to the buttery[7]
And give them friendly welcome every one.
100 Let them want° nothing that my house affords.   *lack*

Exit one with the PLAYERS

[*To a* SERVINGMAN] Sirrah, go you to Barthol'mew, my page,
And see him dressed in all suits° like a lady.   *in every detail*
That done, conduct him to the drunkard's chamber
And call him 'madam', do him obeisance.°   *pay him respects*
105 Tell him° from me, as he will win my love,   *(Bartholomew, the page)*
He bear himself with honourable° action   *becoming*
Such as he hath observed in noble ladies
Unto their lords by them accomplished.°   *performed*
Such duty to the drunkard let him do
110 With soft low tongue° and lowly courtesy,   *voice*
And say 'What is't your honour will command
Wherein your lady and your humble wife
May show her duty and make known her love?'
And then with kind embracements, tempting kisses,
115 And with declining head into his bosom[8]
Bid him shed tears, as being overjoyed
To see her noble lord restored to health,
Who for this seven years hath esteemèd him°   *thought himself to be*
No better than a poor and loathsome beggar.
120 And if the boy have not a woman's gift
To rain a shower of commanded° tears,   *produced on demand*
An onion will do well for such a shift,°   *purpose*
Which, in a napkin being close conveyed,°   *secretly carried*
Shall in despite[9] enforce a watery eye.
125 See this dispatched with all the haste thou canst.
Anon° I'll give thee more instructions.   *Soon*

Exit a SERVINGMAN

I know the boy will well usurp° the grace,   *assume*
Voice, gait, and action of a gentlewoman.
I long to hear him call the drunkard husband,
130 And how my men will stay themselves from laughter
When they do homage to this simple peasant.
I'll in to counsel them. Haply° my presence   *Perhaps*
May well abate the over-merry spleen[1]
Which otherwise would grow into extremes.   [*Exeunt*]

---

7. Pantry, often used to store liquor as well as food.
8. And with his head bowing down into his chest.
9. In spite of an inability to cry.

1. May well lessen the impulse to laugh. Emotional
outbursts, including laughter, were thought to originate
in the spleen.

Induction 2

Enter aloft[1] *[SLY,] the drunkard, with attendants, some*
with apparel, basin, and ewer, and other appurte-
nances; and LORD

SLY For God's sake, a pot of small ale!°   *weak, cheap ale*

FIRST SERVINGMAN Will't please your lordship drink a cup of
sack?°   *costly imported wine*

SECOND SERVINGMAN Will't please your honour taste of these
conserves?°   *candied fruits*

THIRD SERVINGMAN What raiment will your honour wear today?

5 SLY I am Christophero Sly. Call not me 'honour' nor 'lordship'.
I ne'er drank sack in my life, and if you give me any conserves,
give me conserves of beef.° Ne'er ask me what raiment I'll   *salted beef*
wear, for I have no more doublets° than backs, no more stock-   *jackets*
ings than legs, nor no more shoes than feet—nay, sometime
10 more feet than shoes, or such shoes as my toes look through
the over-leather.

LORD Heaven cease this idle humour[2] in your honour.
O that a mighty man of such descent,
Of such possessions and so high esteem,
15 Should be infusèd with so foul a spirit.

SLY What, would you make me mad? Am not I Christopher
Sly—old Sly's son of Burton Heath,[3] by birth a pedlar, by
education a cardmaker,[4] by transmutation a bearherd,° and   *keeper of a tame bear*
now by present profession a tinker?° Ask Marian Hacket, the   *pot mender*
20 fat alewife[5] of Wincot, if she know me not. If she say I am
not fourteen pence on the score[6] for sheer° ale, score me up *for nothing but*
for the lying'st knave in Christendom. What, I am not
bestraught;° here's—   *crazy*

THIRD SERVINGMAN O, this it is that makes your lady mourn.

25 SECOND SERVINGMAN O, this is it that makes your servants droop.

LORD Hence comes it that your kindred shuns your house,
As beaten hence by your strange lunacy.
O noble lord, bethink thee of thy birth.
Call home thy ancient° thoughts from banishment,   *former*
30 And banish hence these abject lowly dreams.
Look how thy servants do attend on thee,
Each in his office, ready at thy beck.°   *command*
Wilt thou have music?   *Music*
            Hark, Apollo[7] plays,
And twenty cagèd nightingales do sing.
35 Or wilt thou sleep? We'll have thee to a couch
Softer and sweeter than the lustful bed

Induction 2 Location: A bedroom in the Lord's house.
1. Upon the gallery above the stage. Whether this long
and complex scene was in fact performed "aloft" is open
to question. At a later point (1.1.242–47), F has Sly
commenting from above on the play presented by the
traveling actors who arrive in Induction 1. If Induction 2
is played on the main stage, Sly must at some point
ascend to the gallery, or he must observe the entire play
from the side of the main stage.
2. Heaven put an end to this foolish fantasy. According
to Renaissance medical theory, humors, or bodily fluids,

determined one's disposition.
3. Possibly Barton-on-the-Heath, a village not far from
Stratford-upon-Avon.
4. Maker of metal combs used to prepare wool for
spinning.
5. Female proprietor of a tavern. Wincot is a small vil-
lage near Stratford; individuals named Hacket were liv-
ing there in 1591.
6. In debt. Accounts were originally kept by notching, or
"scoring," a stick, later by making marks on a wall or door.
7. Greek god of music, who played the lyre.

On purpose trimmed up for Semiramis.[8]
Say thou wilt walk, we will bestrew the ground.
Or wilt thou ride, thy horses shall be trapped,°   *fitted with adornments*
40   Their harness studded all with gold and pearl.
Dost thou love hawking? Thou hast hawks will soar
Above the morning lark. Or wilt thou hunt,
Thy hounds shall make the welkin° answer them   *sky*
And fetch shrill echoes from the hollow earth.
45   FIRST SERVINGMAN   Say thou wilt course,° thy greyhounds are as swift   *hunt hares*
As breathèd° stags, ay, fleeter than the roe.[9]   *well-exercised*
SECOND SERVINGMAN   Dost thou love pictures?[1] We will fetch thee straight
Adonis[2] painted by a running brook,
And Cytherea all in sedges° hid,   *water rushes*
50   Which seem to move and wanton° with her breath   *play amorously*
Even as the waving sedges play wi'th' wind.
LORD   We'll show thee Io[3] as she was a maid,
And how she was beguilèd and surprised,
As lively° painted as the deed was done.   *realistically*
55   THIRD SERVINGMAN   Or Daphne[4] roaming through a thorny wood,
Scratching her legs that one shall swear she bleeds,
And at that sight shall sad Apollo weep,
So workmanly° the blood and tears are drawn.   *skillfully*
LORD   Thou art a lord, and nothing but a lord.
60   Thou hast a lady far more beautiful
Than any woman in this waning age.[5]
FIRST SERVINGMAN   And till the tears that she hath shed for thee
Like envious° floods o'errun her lovely face   *spiteful*
She was the fairest creature in the world;
65   And yet° she is inferior to none.   *still*
SLY   Am I a lord, and have I such a lady?
Or do I dream? Or have I dreamed till now?
I do not sleep. I see, I hear, I speak.
I smell sweet savours,° and I feel soft things.   *odors*
70   Upon my life, I am a lord indeed,
And not a tinker, nor Christopher Sly.
Well, bring our lady hither to our sight,
And once again a pot o'th' smallest° ale.   *weakest*
SECOND SERVINGMAN   Will't please your mightiness to wash your hands?
75   O, how we joy to see your wit restored!
O that once more you knew but what you are!
These fifteen years you have been in a dream,
Or when you waked, so waked as if you slept.
SLY   These fifteen years—by my fay,° a goodly nap.   *faith*
80   But did I never speak of° all that time?   *during*

---

8. Legendary Queen of Assyria, known for her great beauty and many sexual adventures.
9. Small deer proverbial for its swiftness.
1. Probably the "wanton pictures" referred to earlier (Induction 1.43). As described in the following lines, they are conventional erotic scenes, mostly derived from Ovid's *Metamorphoses*.
2. In classical mythology, a beautiful boy whom Aphrodite (Cytherea) loved. This scene shows Aphrodite

spying on Adonis while he bathes in the brook.
3. Raped by Zeus, who concealed himself in a cloud or thick mist, she was then turned into a cow by Hera.
4. A nymph who was turned into a laurel tree as she fled from Apollo.
5. Alluding to the popular belief that the world had steadily degenerated from the perfection of paradise or the classical Golden Age.

FIRST SERVINGMAN   O yes, my lord, but very idle words,
   For though you lay here in this goodly chamber
   Yet would you say ye were beaten out of door,
   And rail upon the hostess of the house,°   *tavern*
85   And say you would present° her at the leet°   *accuse / local court*
   Because she brought stone jugs and no sealed quarts.[6]
   Sometimes you would call out for Cicely Hacket.
SLY   Ay, the woman's maid of the house.
THIRD SERVINGMAN   Why, sir, you know no house, nor no such maid,
90   Nor no such men as you have reckoned up,
   As Stephen Sly, and old John Naps of Greet,[7]
   And Peter Turf, and Henry Pimpernel,
   And twenty more such names and men as these,
   Which never were, nor no man ever saw.
95 SLY   Now Lord be thankèd for my good amends.°   *recovery*
ALL   Amen.
SLY   I thank thee. Thou shalt not lose by it.
     Enter [BARTHOLOMEW *the Page, as*] *Lady, with attendants*
BARTHOLOMEW   How fares my noble lord?
SLY   Marry,[8] I fare° well,   *get on; feed*
   For here is cheer° enough. Where is my wife?   *food*
100 BARTHOLOMEW   Here, noble lord. What is thy will with her?
SLY   Are you my wife, and will not call me husband?
   My men should call me lord. I am your goodman.[9]
BARTHOLOMEW   My husband and my lord, my lord and husband;
   I am your wife in all obedience.
105 SLY   I know it well. [*To the* LORD] What must I call her?
LORD   Madam.
SLY   Al'ce Madam or Joan Madam?[1]
LORD   Madam, and nothing else. So lords call ladies.
SLY   Madam wife, they say that I have dreamed,
   And slept above some fifteen year or more.
110 BARTHOLOMEW   Ay, and the time seems thirty unto me,
   Being all this time abandoned° from your bed.   *banned*
SLY   'Tis much. Servants, leave me and her alone.
     [*Exeunt* LORD *and attendants*][2]
   Madam, undress you and come now to bed.
BARTHOLOMEW   Thrice-noble lord, let me entreat of you
115   To pardon me yet for a night or two,
   Or if not so, until the sun be set,
   For your physicians have expressly charged,
   In peril to incur[3] your former malady,
   That I should yet absent me from your bed.
120   I hope this reason stands for my excuse.
SLY   Ay, it stands[4] so that I may hardly tarry° so long. But I would   *delay*

---

6. She served from unmarked stone jugs rather than from the officially measured and stamped ("sealed") quarts.
7. Greet is a small village not far from Stratford. The names may be those of Stratford citizens.
8. Mild oath, derived from the Virgin Mary's name.
9. Husband: a term normally not used by lords.
1. Misusing the usual title for a noblewoman. "Alice"

and "Joan" are names rarely associated with the upper classes in Elizabethan texts.
2. F has no stage direction here, but those attending on Sly probably obey his command and leave the stage. It is unclear, however, whether the Lord leaves the stage with the other attendants at this point.
3. *In peril to incur:* Because of the risk of bringing on.
4. Punning on "stand" as meaning "to have an erection."

be loath to fall into my dreams again. I will therefore tarry in
despite of the flesh and the blood.

Enter A MESSENGER

MESSENGER   Your honour's players, hearing your amendment,
125 Are come to play a pleasant comedy,
For so your doctors hold it very meet,°   suitable
Seeing too much sadness hath congealed your blood,
And melancholy is the nurse of frenzy.[5]
Therefore they thought it good you hear a play
130 And frame your mind to mirth and merriment,
Which bars° a thousand harms and lengthens life.   prevents

SLY   Marry, I will let them play it. Is not a comonty°   (for "comedy")
A Christmas gambol, or a tumbling trick?

BARTHOLOMEW   No, my good lord, it is more pleasing stuff.

SLY   What, household stuff?°   furnishings; events

135 BARTHOLOMEW   It is a kind of history.°   story

SLY   Well, we'll see't. Come, madam wife, sit by my side
And let the world slip. We shall ne'er be younger.

[BARTHOLOMEW *sits*]

1.1

Flourish.° Enter LUCENTIO *and his man,* TRANIO   Fanfare of trumpets

LUCENTIO   Tranio, since for° the great desire I had   because of
To see fair Padua, nursery of arts,[1]
I am arrived fore° fruitful Lombardy,   before
The pleasant garden of great Italy,
5   And by my father's love and leave am armed
With his good will and thy good company,
My trusty servant, well approved° in all,   reliable
Here let us breathe,° and haply institute   pause; rest
A course of learning and ingenious° studies.   liberal; intellectual
10   Pisa, renownèd for grave citizens,
Gave me my being, and my father first°—   before me
A merchant of great traffic° through the world,   business
Vincentio, come of the Bentivolii.[2]
Vincentio's son, brought up in Florence,
15   It shall become° to serve° all hopes conceived[3]   befit / fulfill
To deck° his fortune with his virtuous deeds.   adorn
And therefore, Tranio, for the time I study,
Virtue and that part of philosophy
Will I apply° that treats of happiness   pursue; study
20   By virtue specially to be achieved.
Tell me thy mind, for I have Pisa left
And am to Padua come as he that leaves
A shallow plash° to plunge him in the deep,   pool
And with satiety seeks to quench his thirst.

25   TRANIO   *Mi perdonate,°* gentle master mine.   Pardon me
I am in all affected° as yourself,   inclined
Glad that you thus continue your resolve

---

5. According to Renaissance humoral theory, excessive
sadness could cause thickening of the blood and thus
delirium, or "frenzy." nurse: nourisher.
1.1 Location: A street in Padua.
1. A center for learning ("arts"). Padua's famous univer-

sity attracted many English students in Shakespeare's
time.
2. Descended from the Bentivolii (perhaps a reference
to the famous Bentivoglio family of Bologna).
3. That is, by relatives and friends.

To suck the sweets of sweet philosophy.
Only, good master, while we do admire
30   This virtue and this moral discipline,
Let's be no stoics nor no stocks,[4] I pray,
Or so devote to Aristotle's checks[5]
As Ovid be an outcast quite abjured.[6]
Balk logic° with acquaintance that you have,   *Bandy words*
35   And practise rhetoric in your common talk.
Music and poesy use to quicken° you;   *revive; animate*
The mathematics and the metaphysics,
Fall to them as you find your stomach° serves you.   *appetite*
No profit grows where is no pleasure ta'en.
40   In brief, sir, study what you most affect.°   *like*
LUCENTIO   Gramercies,° Tranio, well dost thou advise.   *Thank you*
If, Biondello, thou wert come ashore,[7]
We could at once put us in readiness
And take a lodging fit to entertain
45   Such friends as time in Padua shall beget.
But stay a while, what company is this?
TRANIO   Master, some show to welcome us to town.
        Enter BAPTISTA *with his two daughters,* KATHERINE
        and BIANCA; GREMIO, *a pantaloon,*[8] HORTENSIO, *suitor*
        to Bianca. LUCENTIO, [and] TRANIO *stand by*
BAPTISTA   Gentlemen, importune me no farther,
For how I firmly am resolved you know:
50   That is, not to bestow° my youngest daughter   *give in marriage*
Before I have a husband for the elder.
If either of you both love Katherina,
Because I know you well and love you well
Leave shall you have to court her at your pleasure.
55   GREMIO   To cart her[9] rather. She's too rough for me.
There, there, Hortensio. Will you° any wife?   *Do you want*
KATHERINE [*to* BAPTISTA]   I pray you, sir, is it your will
To make a stale of me amongst these mates?[1]
HORTENSIO   'Mates', maid? How mean you that? No mates° for you   *husbands*
60   Unless you were of gentler, milder mould.°   *nature*
KATHERINE   I'faith, sir, you shall never need to fear.
Iwis it is not half-way to her heart,[2]
But if it were, doubt not her care should be
To comb your noddle° with a three-legged stool,   *hit your head*
65   And paint° your face, and use you like a fool.   *(with blood)*
HORTENSIO   From all such devils, good Lord deliver us.
GREMIO   And me too, good Lord.
TRANIO [*aside to* LUCENTIO]   Husht, master, here's some good
        pastime toward.°   *in view*

4. Wooden posts devoid of feeling. Punning on "stoics," the Greek philosophers who advocated both indifference to pleasure or pain and patient endurance.
5. Restraints. Aristotle defined virtue as a mean, the avoiding of excess (or deficiency).
6. *As . . . abjured:* That Ovid be renounced. Ovid was a Roman poet whose erotic writings were popular in the Renaissance. (His *Ars Amatoria* is mentioned by Lucentio at 4.2.8.)
7. Padua, an inland city, did not have a port. Shake-speare's knowledge of Italian geography seems to have been shaky.
8. Foolish old man: a stock character from the Italian commedia dell'arte whose usual role was to hinder young lovers.
9. To carry her though the street in, or tied to, a cart. This was a common punishment for disorderly women.
1. To make me a laughingstock or a prostitute or a decoy (for Bianca) among these crude fellows.
2. Certainly, marriage does not even half interest her. (Kate speaks of herself in the third person here.)

That wench is stark mad or wonderful froward.°   *incredibly willful*
70   LUCENTIO [*aside to* TRANIO]   But in the other's silence do I see
    Maid's mild behaviour and sobriety.
    Peace, Tranio.
    TRANIO [*aside to* LUCENTIO]   Well said, master. Mum, and gaze your fill.
    BAPTISTA   Gentlemen, that I may soon make good
75   What I have said—Bianca, get you in.
    And let it not displease thee, good Bianca,
    For I will love thee ne'er the less, my girl.
    KATHERINE   A pretty peat!° It is best   *pet; spoiled child*
    Put finger in the eye,° an° she knew why.   *(to weep) / if*
80   BIANCA   Sister, content you° in my discontent.   *satisfy yourself*
    [*To* BAPTISTA] Sir, to your pleasure° humbly I subscribe.°   *will / submit*
    My books and instruments shall be my company,
    On them to look and practise by myself.
    LUCENTIO [*aside to* TRANIO]   Hark, Tranio, thou mayst hear
      Minerva[3] speak.
85   HORTENSIO   Signor Baptista, will you be so strange?°   *unnatural; cruel*
    Sorry am I that our good will effects°   *causes*
    Bianca's grief.
    GREMIO   Why will you mew° her up,   *confine (like a falcon)*
    Signor Baptista, for° this fiend of hell,   *because of*
    And make her bear the penance° of her tongue?   *punishment*
90   BAPTISTA   Gentlemen, content ye. I am resolved.
    Go in, Bianca.   [*Exit* BIANCA]
    And for I know she taketh most delight
    In music, instruments, and poetry,
    Schoolmasters will I keep within my house
95   Fit to instruct her youth. If you, Hortensio,
    Or, Signor Gremio, you know any such,
    Prefer° them hither; for to cunning° men   *Recommend / skillful*
    I will be very kind, and liberal
    To mine own children in good bringing up.
100   And so farewell. Katherina, you may stay,
    For I have more to commune with Bianca.   *Exit*
    KATHERINE   Why, and I trust I may go too, may I not? What,
    shall I be appointed hours, as though belike I knew not what
    to take and what to leave? Ha!   *Exit*
105   GREMIO   You may go to the devil's dam.[4] Your gifts are so good
    here's none will hold° you. Their love[5] is not so great, Horten-   *tolerate*
    sio, but we may blow our nails° together and fast it fairly out.[6]   *wait patiently*
    Our cake's dough on both sides.[7] Farewell. Yet for the love I
    bear my sweet Bianca, if I can by any means light on a fit man
110   to teach her that wherein she delights, I will wish° him to her   *recommend*
    father.
    HORTENSIO   So will I, Signor Gremio. But a word, I pray.
    Though the nature of our quarrel yet never brooked parle,°   *permitted discussion*
    know now, upon advice,° it toucheth° us both—that we may   *reflection / concerns*
115   yet again have access to our fair mistress and be happy rivals
    in Bianca's love—to labour and effect one thing specially.

---

3. Roman goddess of wisdom.   5. Love of them (that is, of women).
4. The devil's mother, imagined as the stereotypical   6. And abstain as best we can.
shrew and said to be worse than the devil himself.   7. Proverbial expression of failure.

GREMIO   What's that, I pray?

HORTENSIO   Marry, sir, to get a husband for her sister.

GREMIO   A husband?—a devil!

120 HORTENSIO   I say a husband.

GREMIO   I say a devil. Think'st thou, Hortensio, though her
father be very rich, any man is so very° a fool to be married to   *completely*
hell?

HORTENSIO   Tush, Gremio. Though it pass° your patience and   *exceeds*
125   mine to endure her loud alarums,° why, man, there be good   *calls to arms; scoldings*
fellows in the world, an a man could light on them, would take
her with all faults, and money enough.

GREMIO   I cannot tell, but I had as lief° take her dowry with this   *would as willingly*
condition: to be whipped at the high cross[8] every morning.

130 HORTENSIO   Faith, as you say, there's small choice in rotten
apples. But come, since this bar in law° makes us friends, it   *legal obstacle*
shall be so far forth friendly maintained[9] till by helping Bap-
tista's eldest daughter to a husband we set his youngest free for
a husband, and then have to't° afresh. Sweet Bianca! Happy   *begin the fight*
135   man be his dole.[1] He that runs fastest gets the ring.[2] How say
you, Signor Gremio?

GREMIO   I am agreed, and would I had given him the best horse
in Padua to begin his wooing that would thoroughly woo her,
wed her, and bed her, and rid the house of her. Come on.

Exeunt [HORTENSIO *and* GREMIO]. *Manent*°   *Remain*
TRANIO *and* LUCENTIO

140 TRANIO   I pray, sir, tell me: is it possible
That love should of a sudden take such hold?

LUCENTIO   O Tranio, till I found it to be true
I never thought it possible or likely.
But see, while idly I stood looking on
145   I found the effect of love in idleness,[3]
And now in plainness do confess to thee,
That art to me as secret° and as dear   *intimate*
As Anna[4] to the Queen of Carthage was,
Tranio, I burn, I pine, I perish, Tranio,
150   If I achieve not this young modest girl.
Counsel me, Tranio, for I know thou canst.
Assist me, Tranio, for I know thou wilt.

TRANIO   Master, it is no time to chide you now.
Affection is not rated° from the heart.   *driven out by scolding*
155   If love have touched you, naught remains but so—
Redime te captum quam queas minimo.[5]

LUCENTIO   Gramercies,° lad. Go forward, this contents.   *Thanks*
The rest will comfort, for thy counsel's sound.

TRANIO   Master, you looked so longly° on the maid   *persistently*
160   Perhaps you marked not what's the pith° of all.   *main point*

---

8. Cross set on a pedestal in the town center, the nor-
mal site for punishment in an English village.
9. *it . . . maintained*: we'll pursue the matter as
friends.
1. May the winner's fate be that of a happy man.
2. A proverb alluding to the ring that riders in a joust-
ing match try to catch on their lances. Also punning on
"ring" as referring to both "wedding ring" and female
genitalia.
3. Punning on a flower known as "love-in-idleness,"

whose juice was thought to induce love. (See *A Mid-
summer Night's Dream* 2.1.166–68.)
4. Sister to Dido, Queen of Carthage. In both Virgil's
Aeneid and Christopher Marlowe's *Dido, Queen of
Carthage* (1594), Dido tells Anna of her secret love for
Aeneas.
5. Latin: Ransom yourself from captivity at the lowest
possible price. A phrase from Terence, quoted as it
appears in Lily's Latin grammar, a standard Elizabethan
school text.

LUCENTIO   O yes, I saw sweet beauty in her face,
   Such as the daughter of Agenor[6] had,
   That made great Jove to humble him to her hand
   When with his knees he kissed the Cretan strand.
165 TRANIO   Saw you no more? Marked you not how her sister
   Began to scold and raise up such a storm
   That mortal ears might hardly endure the din?
   LUCENTIO   Tranio, I saw her coral lips to move,
   And with her breath she did perfume the air.
170   Sacred and sweet was all I saw in her.
   TRANIO [*aside*]   Nay, then 'tis time to stir him from his trance.
   [*To* LUCENTIO] I pray, awake, sir. If you love the maid,
   Bend thoughts and wits to achieve her. Thus it stands:
   Her elder sister is so curst° and shrewd°   *quarrelsome / shrewish*
175 That till the father rid his hands of her,
   Master, your love must live a maid at home,
   And therefore has he closely mewed her up
   Because° she will not be annoyed with° suitors.   *So that / troubled with*
   LUCENTIO   Ah, Tranio, what a cruel father's he!
180 But art thou not advised° he took some care   *aware*
   To get her cunning schoolmasters to instruct her?
   TRANIO   Ay, marry am I, sir, and now 'tis plotted.
   LUCENTIO   I have it, Tranio.
   TRANIO   Master, for° my hand,   *by*
   Both our inventions° meet and jump° in one.   *schemes / agree*
   LUCENTIO   Tell me thine first.
185 TRANIO   You will be schoolmaster
   And undertake the teaching of the maid.
   That's your device.°   *plan*
   LUCENTIO   It is. May it be done?
   TRANIO   Not possible; for who shall bear your part,
   And be in Padua here Vincentio's son,
190 Keep house, and ply his book,° welcome his friends,   *study*
   Visit his countrymen, and banquet them?
   LUCENTIO   *Basta,*° content thee, for I have it full.°   *Enough / fully planned*
   We have not yet been seen in any house,
   Nor can we be distinguished by our faces
195 For man or master. Then it follows thus:
   Thou shalt be master, Tranio, in my stead;
   Keep house, and port,° and servants, as I should.   *social position*
   I will some other be, some Florentine,
   Some Neapolitan, or meaner° man of Pisa.   *poorer*
200 'Tis hatched, and shall be so. Tranio, at once
   Uncase° thee. Take my coloured hat and cloak.[7]   *Undress*
   When Biondello comes he waits on thee,
   But I will charm° him first to keep his tongue.   *persuade; use magic on*
   TRANIO   So had you need.
          [*They exchange clothes*][8]
205 In brief, sir, sith° it your pleasure is,   *since*

6. Europa. Jove transformed himself into a bull and carried her across the sea to Crete to rape her.
7. The outfit of an Elizabethan gentleman. Servants usually wore uniforms, like the "blue coats" of Petruccio's servants (4.1.74).
8. F does not indicate at what point in this exchange

Lucentio and Tranio trade clothes; perhaps they begin during Lucentio's previous speech. This exchange of clothes, emphasizing the ease with which social identity is shifted, is an important visual enactment of one of the play's main preoccupations.

And I am tied to be obedient—
For so your father charged me at our parting,
'Be serviceable° to my son,' quoth he,   *diligent in service*
Although I think 'twas in another sense—
210   I am content to be Lucentio
Because so well I love Lucentio.
LUCENTIO   Tranio, be so, because Lucentio loves,
And let me be a slave t'achieve that maid
Whose sudden sight hath thralled° my wounded⁹ eye.   *enslaved*
       Enter BIONDELLO
215   Here comes the rogue. Sirrah, where have you been?
BIONDELLO   Where have *I* been? Nay, how now, where are *you?*
Master, has my fellow Tranio stolen your clothes, or you
stolen his, or both? Pray, what's the news?
LUCENTIO   Sirrah, come hither. 'Tis no time to jest,
220   And therefore frame your manners to the time.
Your fellow Tranio here, to save my life
Puts my apparel and my count'nance on,
And I for my escape have put on his,
For in a quarrel since I came ashore
225   I killed a man, and fear I was descried.°   *observed*
Wait you on him, I charge you, as becomes,°   *is fitting*
While I make way from hence to save my life.
You understand me?
BIONDELLO   I sir? Ne'er a whit.°   *Not at all*
LUCENTIO   And not a jot of Tranio in your mouth.
230   Tranio is changed into Lucentio.
BIONDELLO   The better for him. Would I were so too.
TRANIO   So could I, faith, boy, to have the next wish after—
That Lucentio indeed had Baptista's youngest daughter.
But sirrah, not for my sake but your master's I advise
235   You use your manners discreetly in all kind of companies.
When I am alone, why then I am Tranio,
But in all places else your master, Lucentio.
LUCENTIO   Tranio, let's go.
One thing more rests° that thyself execute°—   *remains / must do*
240   To make one among these wooers. If thou ask me why,
Sufficeth my reasons are both good and weighty.   *Exeunt*
       The presenters[1] *above speak*
FIRST SERVINGMAN   My lord, you nod. You do not mind° the play.   *pay attention to*
SLY   Yes, by Saint Anne[2] do I. A good matter, surely. Comes
there any more of it?
245   BARTHOLOMEW   My lord, 'tis but begun.
SLY   'Tis a very excellent piece of work, madam lady. Would
'twere done.
       They sit and mark°   *observe*

1.2

Enter PETRUCCIO *and his man,* GRUMIO
PETRUCCIO   Verona, for a while I take my leave
To see my friends in Padua; but of all

---

9. Wounded by Cupid's arrow.
1. Figures who introduce and comment on the action
of a play for the audience.

2. A common oath. St. Anne was the mother of the Virgin Mary and the patron saint of married women.
1.2 Location: In front of Hortensio's house in Padua.

My best-belovèd and approvèd friend
Hortensio, and I trow° this is his house.   *believe*
5   Here, sirrah Grumio, knock, I say.

GRUMIO   Knock, sir? Whom should I knock? Is there any man
has rebused[1] your worship?

PETRUCCIO   Villain, I say, knock me here[2] soundly.

GRUMIO   Knock you here, sir? Why, sir, what am I, sir, that I
10   should knock you here, sir?

PETRUCCIO   Villain, I say, knock me at this gate,
And rap me well or I'll knock your knave's pate.

GRUMIO   My master is grown quarrelsome. I should knock you first,
And then I know after who comes by the worst.[3]

15   PETRUCCIO   Will it not be?
Faith, sirrah, an° you'll not knock, I'll ring it.[4]   *if*
I'll try how you can sol-fa° and sing it.   *sing a scale*

He wrings him by the ears. [GRUMIO *kneels*][5]

GRUMIO   Help, masters, help! My master is mad.

PETRUCCIO   Now knock when I bid you, sirrah villain.

Enter HORTENSIO

20   HORTENSIO   How now, what's the matter? My old friend Grumio
and my good friend Petruccio? How do you all at Verona?

PETRUCCIO   Signor Hortensio, come you to part the fray?
Con tutto il cuore ben trovato,[6] may I say.

HORTENSIO   *Alla nostra casa ben venuto, molto onorato signor*
25   *mio Petruccio.*[7]

Rise, Grumio, rise. We will compound° this quarrel.   *settle*
[GRUMIO *rises*]

GRUMIO   Nay, 'tis no matter, sir, what he 'leges° in Latin. If this   *alleges*
be not a lawful cause for me to leave his service—look you, sir:
he bid me knock him and rap him soundly, sir. Well, was it fit
30   for a servant to use his master so, being perhaps, for aught
I see, two-and-thirty, a pip out?[8]
Whom would to God I had well knocked at first,
Then had not Grumio come by the worst.

PETRUCCIO   A senseless villain. Good Hortensio,
35   I bade the rascal knock upon your gate,
And could not get him for my heart to do it.

GRUMIO   Knock at the gate? O heavens, spake you not these
words plain? 'Sirrah, knock me here, rap me here, knock me
well, and knock me soundly'? And come you now with
40   knocking at the gate?

PETRUCCIO   Sirrah, be gone, or talk not, I advise you.

HORTENSIO   Petruccio, patience. I am Grumio's pledge.°   *guarantor*
Why this' a heavy chance[9] 'twixt him and you,

---

1. Grumio regularly blunders and puns. Here he means "abused" or "rebuked," or perhaps both.
2. Knock here for me: a conventional usage that Grumio misunderstands or pretends to understand as "strike me." *Villain*: low-born man (often a contemptuous term of address).
3. *I should . . . worst*: You want me to give the first blow, but then I know I'd have the worse of it.
4. I'll ring the bell; with a pun on "wring."
5. While F gives no stage direction indicating that Grumio kneels at this point, at line 26 Hortensio orders him to "rise." This may mean that he has been

brought to his knees when Petruccio wrings his ears at line 17.
6. With all my heart, welcome (Italian).
7. Welcome to our house, my most honored Signor Petruccio.
8. Drunk; a bit crazy. Probably alluding to the card game one-and-thirty, in which the aim is to accumulate exactly thirty-one points. To collect thirty-two means the player has overshot or been excessive. A "pip" is a spot on a card; hence "a pip out" means "off by one."
9. *Why . . . chance*: This is a sad occurrence.

Your ancient,° trusty, pleasant servant Grumio.   *long-standing*
45 And tell me now, sweet friend, what happy gale
Blows you to Padua here from old Verona?
PETRUCCIO   Such wind as scatters young men through the world
To seek their fortunes farther than at home,
Where small experience grows. But in a few,°   *in short*
50 Signor Hortensio, thus it stands with me:
Antonio, my father, is deceased,
And I have thrust myself into this maze[1]
Happily to wive and thrive as best I may.
Crowns° in my purse I have, and goods at home,   *Five-shilling coins*
55 And so am come abroad to see the world.
HORTENSIO   Petruccio, shall I then come roundly° to thee   *speak plainly*
And wish thee to a shrewd, ill-favoured wife?
Thou'dst thank me but a little for my counsel,
And yet I'll promise thee she shall be rich,
60 And very rich. But thou'rt too much my friend,
And I'll not wish thee to her.
PETRUCCIO   Signor Hortensio, 'twixt such friends as we
Few words suffice; and therefore, if thou know
One rich enough to be Petruccio's wife—
65 As wealth is burden° of my wooing dance—   *refrain; chief theme*
Be she as foul° as was Florentius' love,[2]   *ugly*
As old as Sibyl,[3] and as curst and shrewd
As Socrates' Xanthippe[4] or a worse,
She moves° me not—or not° removes at least°   *annoys / nor / at all*
70 Affection's edge° in me, were she as rough   *intensity*
As are the swelling Adriatic seas.
I come to wive it wealthily in Padua;
If wealthily, then happily in Padua.
GRUMIO [*to* HORTENSIO]   Nay, look you, sir, he tells you flatly
75 what his mind is. Why, give him gold enough and marry him
to a puppet or an aglet-baby,[5] or an old trot° with ne'er a tooth *hag*
in her head, though she have as many diseases as two-and-fifty
horses. Why, nothing comes amiss so money comes withal.°   *with it*
HORTENSIO   Petruccio, since we are stepped thus far in,
80 I will continue that° I broached in jest.   *what*
I can, Petruccio, help thee to a wife
With wealth enough, and young and beauteous,
Brought up as best becomes a gentlewoman.
Her only fault—and that is faults enough—
85 Is that she is intolerable curst,°   *shrewish*
And shrewd and froward° so beyond all measure   *willful*
That, were my state° far worser than it is,   *fortune*
I would not wed her for a mine of gold.
PETRUCCIO   Hortensio, peace. Thou know'st not gold's effect.
90 Tell me her father's name and 'tis enough,

---

1. This uncertain world; this unpredictable business of
"wiving and thriving."
2. Florent, the knight in John Gower's *Confessio Aman-
tis*, who had to marry the ugly old woman who had
saved his life by answering a riddle he had been com-
manded to solve. On their wedding night, as a reward
for his compliance, she became young and beautiful.

A version of this story also appears in Chaucer's *Wife of
Bath's Tale*.
3. The Cumaean Sibyl, a prophetess in classical
mythology, had immortality without eternal youth.
4. The philosopher's notoriously shrewish wife.
5. Small figure used as a tag or ornament on dresses,
laces, and other goods.

For I will board[6] her though she chide as loud
As thunder when the clouds in autumn crack.

HORTENSIO Her father is Baptista Minola,
An affable and courteous gentleman.

95 Her name is Katherina Minola,
Renowned in Padua for her scolding tongue.

PETRUCCIO I know her father, though I know not her,
And he knew my deceasèd father well.
I will not sleep, Hortensio, till I see her,
100 And therefore let me be thus bold with you
To give you over° at this first encounter, *leave you*
Unless you will accompany me thither.

GRUMIO I pray you, sir, let him go while the humour° lasts. *mood*
O' my word, an she knew him as well as I do she would think
105 scolding would do little good upon him. She may perhaps call
him half a score knaves or so. Why, that's nothing; an he begin
once he'll rail in his rope-tricks.[7] I'll tell you what, sir, an she
stand° him but a little he will throw a figure[8] in her face and *withstand; arouse*
so disfigure her with it that she shall have no more eyes to see
110 withal than a cat. You know him not, sir.

HORTENSIO Tarry, Petruccio, I must go with thee,
For in Baptista's keep° my treasure is. *custody; stronghold*
He hath the jewel of my life in hold,
His youngest daughter, beautiful Bianca,
115 And her withholds from me and other more,° *others besides*
Suitors to her and rivals in my love,
Supposing it a thing impossible,
For those defects I have before rehearsed,
That ever Katherina will be wooed.
120 Therefore this order hath Baptista ta'en:
That none shall have access unto Bianca
Till Katherine the curst have got a husband.

GRUMIO Katherine the curst—
A title for a maid of all titles the worst.

125 HORTENSIO Now shall my friend Petruccio do me grace,° *a favor*
And offer me disguised in sober robes
To old Baptista as a schoolmaster
Well seen° in music, to instruct Bianca, *skilled*
That so I may by this device at least
130 Have leave and leisure to make love to her,
And unsuspected court her by herself.

Enter GREMIO [*with a paper,*][9] *and* LUCENTIO *disguised*
[*as a schoolmaster*]

GRUMIO Here's no knavery.[1] See, to beguile the old folks, how
the young folks lay their heads together. Master, master, look
about you. Who goes there, ha?

135 HORTENSIO Peace, Grumio, it is the rival of my love.
Petruccio, stand by a while.

---

6. Woo aggressively; go aboard, as in a sea battle; have sexual intercourse with.
7. An obscure phrase: "rope-tricks" may refer to rhetorical or sexual feats. Grumio's point seems to be that when Petruccio "rails," he will be more aggressive than Katherine.
8. A figure of speech.
9. Presumably Lucentio's list of books for Bianca's studies.
1. Spoken sarcastically; perhaps referring to the plotting of Petruccio and Hortensio rather than to that of Gremio and Lucentio, whom Grumio may not yet have seen.

GRUMIO   A proper stripling,° and an amorous!   *handsome youth (ironic)*
    [PETRUCCIO, HORTENSIO, *and* GRUMIO *stand aside*]
GREMIO [*to* LUCENTIO]   O, very well—I have perused the note.°   *listing of books*
    Hark you, sir, I'll have them° very fairly bound—   *(the books)*
140   All books of love, see that at any hand°—   *in any case*
    And see you read no other lectures to her.
    You understand me. Over and beside
    Signor Baptista's liberality,
    I'll mend° it with a largess.° Take your paper, too,   *increase / gift*
145   And let me have them very well perfumed,
    For she is sweeter than perfume itself
    To whom they go to. What will you read to her?
LUCENTIO   Whate'er I read to her, I'll plead for you
    As for my patron, stand you so assured,
150   As firmly as yourself were still in place°—   *always present*
    Yea, and perhaps with more successful words
    Than you, unless you were a scholar, sir.
GREMIO   O this learning, what a thing it is!
GRUMIO [*aside*]   O this woodcock,² what an ass it is!
155 PETRUCCIO   Peace, sirrah.
HORTENSIO   Grumio, mum. [*Coming forward*] God save you, Signor Gremio.
GREMIO   And you are well met, Signor Hortensio.
    Trow° you whither I am going?   *Know*
    To Baptista Minola.
160   I promised to enquire carefully
    About a schoolmaster for the fair Bianca,
    And by good fortune I have lighted well
    On this young man, for learning and behaviour
    Fit for her turn,° well read in poetry   *use*
165   And other books—good ones, I warrant ye.
HORTENSIO   'Tis well, and I have met a gentleman
    Hath promised me to help me to another,
    A fine musician, to instruct our mistress.
    So shall I no whit be behind in duty
170   To fair Bianca, so beloved of me.
GREMIO   Beloved of me, and that my deeds shall prove.
GRUMIO [*aside*]   And that his bags° shall prove.   *money bags*
HORTENSIO   Gremio, 'tis now no time to vent° our love.   *express*
    Listen to me, and if you speak me fair°   *courteously*
175   I'll tell you news indifferent° good for either.   *equally*
    Here is a gentleman whom by chance I met,
    Upon agreement from us to his liking°   *If we accept his terms*
    Will undertake to woo curst Katherine,
    Yea, and to marry her, if her dowry please.
180 GREMIO   So said, so done, is well.
    Hortensio, have you told him all her faults?
PETRUCCIO   I know she is an irksome brawling scold.
    If that be all, masters, I hear no harm.
GREMIO   No, sayst me so, friend? What countryman?
185 PETRUCCIO   Born in Verona, old Antonio's son.
    My father dead, his fortune lives for me,°   *is mine*

2. Wild bird easily caught and so thought to be stupid.

And I do hope good days and long to see.
GREMIO   O sir, such a life with such a wife were strange.
    But if you have a stomach, to't, a'° God's name.   *in*
190   You shall have me assisting you in all.
    But will you woo this wildcat?
PETRUCCIO   Will I live!
GRUMIO   Will he woo her? Ay, or I'll hang her.
PETRUCCIO   Why came I hither but to that intent?
    Think you a little din can daunt mine ears?
195   Have I not in my time heard lions roar?
    Have I not heard the sea, puffed up with winds,
    Rage like an angry boar chafèd with sweat?
    Have I not heard great ordnance° in the field,   *cannon*
    And heaven's artillery thunder in the skies?
200   Have I not in a pitchèd battle heard
    Loud 'larums,° neighing steeds, and trumpets' clang?   *calls to arms*
    And do you tell me of a woman's tongue,
    That gives not half so great a blow° to hear   *loud noise*
    As will a chestnut in a farmer's fire?
205   Tush, tush—fear° boys with bugs.°   *frighten / bogeymen*
GRUMIO   For he fears none.
GREMIO   Hortensio, hark.
    This gentleman is happily° arrived,   *fortunately*
    My mind presumes, for his own good and ours.
210   HORTENSIO   I promised we would be contributors,
    And bear his charge° of wooing, whatsoe'er.   *expense*
GREMIO   And so we will, provided that he win her.
GRUMIO   I would I were as sure of a good dinner.
       Enter TRANIO, *brave,° [as Lucentio,] and* BIONDELLO *richly dressed*
TRANIO   Gentlemen, God save you. If I may be bold, tell me, I
215   beseech you, which is the readiest way to the house of Signor
    Baptista Minola?
BIONDELLO   He that has the two fair daughters—is't he you
    mean?
TRANIO   Even he, Biondello.
220   GREMIO   Hark you, sir, you mean not her to—
TRANIO   Perhaps him and her, sir. What have you to do?[3]
PETRUCCIO   Not her that chides, sir, at any hand, I pray.
TRANIO   I love no chiders, sir. Biondello, let's away.
LUCENTIO [*aside*]   Well begun, Tranio.
HORTENSIO   Sir, a word ere you go.
225   Are you a suitor to the maid you talk of—yea or no?
TRANIO   And if I be, sir, is it any offence?
GREMIO   No, if without more words you will get you hence.
TRANIO   Why, sir, I pray, are not the streets as free
    For me as for you?
GREMIO   But so is not she.
230   TRANIO   For what reason, I beseech you?
GREMIO   For this reason, if you'll know—
    That she's the choice° love of Signor Gremio.   *chosen; excellent*
HORTENSIO   That she's the chosen of Signor Hortensio.
TRANIO   Softly, my masters. If you be gentlemen,

---

3. What business is it of yours?

235 Do me this right,° hear me with patience.   *justice*
Baptista is a noble gentleman
To whom my father is not all unknown,
And were his daughter fairer than she is
She may more suitors have, and me for one.
240 Fair Leda's daughter⁴ had a thousand wooers;
Then well one more may fair Bianca have,
And so she shall. Lucentio shall make one,
Though Paris came,⁵ in hope to speed° alone.   *succeed*
GREMIO   What, this gentleman will out-talk us all!
245 LUCENTIO   Sir, give him head, I know he'll prove a jade.°   *worn-out horse*
PETRUCCIO   Hortensio, to what end are all these words?
HORTENSIO   Sir, let me be so bold as ask you,
Did you yet ever see Baptista's daughter?
TRANIO   No, sir, but hear I do that he hath two,
250 The one as famous for a scolding tongue
As is the other for beauteous modesty.
PETRUCCIO   Sir, sir, the first's for me. Let her go by.
GREMIO   Yea, leave that labour to great Hercules,
And let it be more than Alcides' twelve.⁶
255 PETRUCCIO   Sir, understand you this of me in sooth,°   *truth*
The youngest daughter whom you hearken° for   *lie in wait; yearn*
Her father keeps from all access of suitors,
And will not promise her to any man
Until the elder sister first be wed.
260 The younger then is free, and not before.
TRANIO   If it be so, sir, that you are the man
Must stead° us all, and me amongst the rest,   *help*
And if you break the ice and do this feat,
Achieve° the elder, set the younger free   *Win*
265 For our access, whose hap shall be° to have her   *he who is lucky enough*
Will not so graceless be to be ingrate.
HORTENSIO   Sir, you say well, and well you do conceive;°   *understand*
And since you do profess to be a suitor
You must, as we do, gratify° this gentleman,   *reward*
270 To whom we all rest generally beholden.
TRANIO   Sir, I shall not be slack. In sign whereof,
Please ye we may contrive° this afternoon,   *pass, spend (time)*
And quaff carouses° to our mistress' health,   *toasts*
And do as adversaries do in law—
275 Strive mightily, but eat and drink as friends.
GRUMIO *and* BIONDELLO   O excellent motion!° Fellows, let's be gone.   *proposal*
HORTENSIO   The motion's good indeed, and be it so.
Petruccio, I shall be your *ben venuto*.°   *Exeunt*   *welcome (your host)*

2.1
Enter KATHERINE *and* BIANCA [*her hands bound*]
BIANCA   Good sister, wrong me not, nor wrong yourself
To make a bondmaid and a slave of me.

4. Helen of Troy. In Marlowe's *Doctor Faustus*, her face
is said to have "launched a thousand ships."
5. Even if Paris (who stole Helen of Troy from her hus-
band) were to come.
6. Hercules, the hero of classical mythology who suc-
cessfully performed twelve seemingly impossible tasks
("labours"), was also called Alcides (descendant of
Alcaeus).
2.1 Location: Baptista's house in Padua.

That I disdain, but for these other goods,°   *possessions*
Unbind my hands, I'll pull them off myself,
5 Yea, all my raiment to my petticoat,
Or what you will command me will I do,
So well I know my duty to my elders.

KATHERINE   Of all thy suitors here I charge thee tell
Whom thou lov'st best. See thou dissemble not.

10 BIANCA   Believe me, sister, of all the men alive
I never yet beheld that special face
Which I could fancy more than any other.

KATHERINE   Minion,° thou liest. Is't not Hortensio?   *Hussy*

BIANCA   If you affect° him, sister, here I swear   *love*
15 I'll plead for you myself but you shall have him.

KATHERINE   O then, belike you fancy riches more.
You will have Gremio to keep you fair.

BIANCA   Is it for him you do envy me so?
Nay, then, you jest, and now I well perceive
20 You have but jested with me all this while.
I prithee, sister Kate, untie my hands.

KATHERINE   If that be jest, then all the rest was so. *Strikes her*
    Enter BAPTISTA

BAPTISTA   Why, how now, dame, whence grows this insolence?
Bianca, stand aside.— Poor girl, she weeps.—
25 Go ply thy needle, meddle not with her.
[*To* KATHERINE] For shame, thou hilding° of a devilish spirit,   *worthless creature*
Why dost thou wrong her that did ne'er wrong thee?
When did she cross thee with a bitter word?

KATHERINE   Her silence flouts° me, and I'll be revenged.   *mocks*
    [*She*] *flies after* BIANCA

30 BAPTISTA   What, in my sight? Bianca, get thee in. *Exit* [BIANCA]

KATHERINE   What, will you not suffer me?° Nay, now I see   *let me have my way*
She is your treasure, she must have a husband.
I must dance barefoot on her wedding day,[1]
And for your love to her lead apes in hell.[2]
35 Talk not to me. I will go sit and weep
Till I can find occasion of revenge.   [*Exit*]

BAPTISTA   Was ever gentleman thus grieved as I?
But who comes here?
    Enter GREMIO, LUCENTIO [*as a schoolmaster*] *in the*
    habit of a mean man,° PETRUCCIO *with* [HORTENSIO *as*   *man of low social rank*
    a musician,] TRANIO [*as Lucentio*], *with* [BIONDELLO]
    his boy bearing a lute and books

GREMIO   Good morrow, neighbour Baptista.

40 BAPTISTA   Good morrow, neighbour Gremio. God save you,
gentlemen.

PETRUCCIO   And you, good sir. Pray, have you not a daughter
Called Katherina, fair and virtuous?

BAPTISTA   I have a daughter, sir, called Katherina.

45 GREMIO   You are too blunt. Go to it orderly.°   *properly*

PETRUCCIO   You wrong me, Signor Gremio. Give me leave.
[*To* BAPTISTA] I am a gentleman of Verona, sir,

---

1. Proverbially expected of older unmarried sisters.   2. *lead apes in hell:* the proverbial destiny of unmarried
women.

That hearing of her beauty and her wit,
Her affability and bashful modesty,
50 Her wondrous qualities and mild behaviour,
Am bold to show myself a forward° guest   *eager*
Within your house to make mine eye the witness
Of that report which I so oft have heard,
And for an entrance to my entertainment³
55 I do present you with a man of mine [*presenting* HORTENSIO]
Cunning in music and the mathematics
To instruct her fully in those sciences,
Whereof I know she is not ignorant.
Accept of him, or else you do me wrong.
60 His name is Licio, born in Mantua.
BAPTISTA   You're welcome, sir, and he for your good sake.
But for my daughter, Katherine, this I know:
She is not for your turn,° the more my grief.   *will not suit you*
PETRUCCIO   I see you do not mean to part with her,
65 Or else you like not of my company.
BAPTISTA   Mistake me not, I speak but as I find.°   *as the facts stand*
Whence are you, sir? What may I call your name?
PETRUCCIO   Petruccio is my name, Antonio's son,
A man well known throughout all Italy.
70 BAPTISTA   I know him well.⁴ You are welcome for his sake.
GREMIO   Saving° your tale, Petruccio, I pray   *With all respect to*
Let us that are poor petitioners speak too.
Baccare,° you are marvellous forward.   *Stand back (mock Latin)*
PETRUCCIO   O pardon me, Signor Gremio, I would fain be doing.⁵
75 GREMIO   I doubt it not, sir. But you will curse your wooing.
[*To* BAPTISTA] Neighbour, this is a gift⁶ very grateful,° I am sure   *pleasing*
of it. To express the like kindness, myself, that have been more
kindly beholden to you than any, freely give unto you this
young scholar [*presenting* LUCENTIO] that hath been long
80 studying at Rheims,⁷ as cunning in Greek, Latin, and other
languages as the other in music and mathematics. His name
is Cambio.⁸ Pray accept his service.
BAPTISTA   A thousand thanks, Signor Gremio. Welcome, good
Cambio. [*To* TRANIO] But, gentle sir, methinks you walk like a
85 stranger. May I be so bold to know the cause of your coming?
TRANIO   Pardon me, sir, the boldness is mine own
That, being a stranger in this city here,
Do make myself a suitor to your daughter,
Unto Bianca, fair and virtuous.
90 Nor is your firm resolve unknown to me
In the preferment of the eldest sister.
This liberty is all that I request:
That upon knowledge of my parentage
I may have welcome 'mongst the rest that woo,
95 And free access and favour as the rest.
And toward the education of your daughters

---

3. And as an entrance fee for my reception ("enter-
tainment") as a suitor.
4. Probably, I know him by reputation.
5. I am eager to get on with it (with a pun on "doing"
as meaning "have sexual intercourse").
6. That is, Petruccio's gift of Hortensio/Licio.
7. French city famous for its university.
8. Italian for "exchange"

I here bestow a simple instrument,
And this small packet of Greek and Latin books.
If you accept them, then their worth is great.
100 BAPTISTA Lucentio is your name⁹—of whence, I pray?
TRANIO Of Pisa, sir, son to Vincentio.
BAPTISTA A mighty man of Pisa. By report
I know him well. You are very welcome, sir.
[*To* HORTENSIO] Take you the lute, [*to* LUCENTIO] and you the
set of books.
105 You shall go see your pupils presently.°   *immediately*
Holla, within!
      Enter a Servant
          Sirrah, lead these gentlemen
To my daughters, and tell them both
These are their tutors. Bid them use them well.
      [*Exit Servant with* LUCENTIO *and* HORTENSIO,
                  BIONDELLO *following*]
[*To* PETRUCCIO] We will go walk a little in the orchard,°   *garden*
110 And then to dinner. You are passing° welcome—   *extremely*
And so I pray you all to think yourselves.
PETRUCCIO Signor Baptista, my business asketh haste,
And every day I cannot come to woo.
You knew my father well, and in him me,
115 Left solely heir to all his lands and goods,
Which I have bettered rather than decreased.
Then tell me, if I get your daughter's love,
What dowry shall I have with her to wife?
BAPTISTA After my death the one half of my lands,
120 And in possession° twenty thousand crowns.   *immediately*
PETRUCCIO And for that dowry I'll assure her of
Her widowhood,¹ be it that she survive me,
In all my lands and leases whatsoever.
Let specialties° be therefore drawn between us,   *explicit contracts*
125 That covenants may be kept on either hand.
BAPTISTA Ay, when the special thing is well obtained—
That is her love, for that is all in all.
PETRUCCIO Why, that is nothing, for I tell you, father,
I am as peremptory as she proud-minded,
130 And where two raging fires meet together
They do consume the thing that feeds their fury.
Though little fire grows great with little wind,
Yet extreme gusts will blow out fire and all.²
So I to her, and so she yields to me,
135 For I am rough, and woo not like a babe.
BAPTISTA Well mayst thou woo, and happy be thy speed.°   *fortune*
But be thou armed for some unhappy words.
PETRUCCIO Ay, to the proof,³ as mountains are for winds,
That shakes not though they blow perpetually.
      Enter HORTENSIO *with his head broke*
140 BAPTISTA How now, my friend, why dost thou look so pale?

---

9. How Baptista knows this is unclear. He may read the name in one of the schoolbooks.
1. Widow's share of the estate.
2. Implying that those who have opposed Katherine so far have been too weak ("little wind") and that he will subdue her with his "extreme gusts."
3. In impenetrable armor. Proof armor was tested for its strength.

HORTENSIO   For fear, I promise you, if I look pale.

BAPTISTA   What, will my daughter prove a good musician?

HORTENSIO   I think she'll sooner prove a soldier.
    Iron may hold with° her, but never lutes.   withstand

145 BAPTISTA   Why then, thou canst not break° her to the lute?   train

HORTENSIO   Why no, for she hath broke the lute to me.
    I did but tell her she mistook her frets,[4]
    And bowed° her hand to teach her fingering,   bent
    When, with a most impatient devilish spirit,

150   'Frets,[5] call you these?' quoth she, 'I'll fume° with them,'   be in a rage
    And with that word she struck me on the head,
    And through the instrument my pate made way,
    And there I stood amazèd for a while,
    As on a pillory,[6] looking through the lute,

155   While she did call me rascal, fiddler,
    And twangling jack,° with twenty such vile terms,   knave
    As° had she studied to misuse me so.   As if

PETRUCCIO   Now, by the world, it is a lusty° wench!   lively
    I love her ten times more than e'er I did.

160   O, how I long to have some chat with her!

BAPTISTA [to HORTENSIO]   Well, go with me, and be not so
        discomfited.
    Proceed in practice° with my younger daughter.   Continue your lessons
    She's apt to learn, and thankful for good turns.
    Signor Petruccio, will you go with us,

165   Or shall I send my daughter Kate to you?

PETRUCCIO   I pray you, do.   Exeunt. Manet° PETRUCCIO   Remains
                I'll attend° her here,   await
    And woo her with some spirit when she comes.
    Say that she rail, why then I'll tell her plain
    She sings as sweetly as a nightingale.

170   Say that she frown, I'll say she looks as clear
    As morning roses newly washed with dew.
    Say she be mute and will not speak a word,
    Then I'll commend her volubility,
    And say she uttereth piercing° eloquence.   moving

175   If she do bid me pack,° I'll give her thanks   go away
    As though she bid me stay by her a week.
    If she deny to wed, I'll crave° the day   beg to know
    When I shall ask the banns,[7] and when be marrièd.
    But here she comes, and now, Petruccio, speak.

        Enter KATHERINE

180   Good morrow, Kate, for that's your name, I hear.

KATHERINE   Well have you heard, but something° hard of hearing.   somewhat
    They call me Katherine that do talk of me.

PETRUCCIO   You lie, in faith, for you are called plain Kate,
    And bonny Kate, and sometimes Kate the curst,

185   But Kate, the prettiest Kate in Christendom,

---

4. Placed her fingers upon the wrong bars ("frets") on the lute's fingerboard.
5. Kate plays on "frets" as also meaning "annoyances" or "vexations."
6. An instrument of public punishment in which the offender's head and hands were fastened in wooden clamps.
7. Have the banns read. Banns were required announcements in church of a forthcoming wedding.

Kate of Kate Hall,[8] my super-dainty Kate—
For dainties are all cates,[9] and therefore 'Kate'—
Take this of me, Kate of my consolation:
Hearing thy mildness praised in every town,
190   Thy virtues spoke of, and thy beauty sounded[1]—   *Indeed*
Yet not so deeply as to thee belongs—
Myself am moved to woo thee for my wife.

KATHERINE   Moved? In good time.° Let him that moved you hither
Re-move you hence. I knew you at the first
You were a movable.[2]

195 PETRUCCIO   Why, what's a movable?

KATHERINE   A joint-stool.[3]

PETRUCCIO   Thou hast hit it. Come, sit on me.

KATHERINE   Asses are made to bear,° and so are you.   *carry loads*

PETRUCCIO   Women are made to bear,[4] and so are you.

KATHERINE   No such jade° as you, if me you mean.   *worn-out horse*

200 PETRUCCIO   Alas, good Kate, I will not burden[5] thee,
For knowing° thee to be but young and light.[6]   *Because I know*

KATHERINE   Too light° for such a swain° as you to catch,   *quick / bumpkin*
And yet as heavy as my weight should be.[7]

PETRUCCIO   Should be?—should buzz.[8]

KATHERINE   Well ta'en, and like a buzzard.[9]

205 PETRUCCIO   O slow-winged turtle,° shall a buzzard take thee?   *turtledove*

KATHERINE   Ay, for a turtle, as he takes a buzzard.[1]

PETRUCCIO   Come, come, you wasp, i'faith you are too angry.

KATHERINE   If I be waspish, best beware my sting.

PETRUCCIO   My remedy is then to pluck it out.

210 KATHERINE   Ay, if the fool could find it where it lies.

PETRUCCIO   Who knows not where a wasp does wear his sting?
In his tail.

KATHERINE   In his tongue.

PETRUCCIO   Whose tongue?

KATHERINE   Yours, if you talk of tales,° and so farewell.   *gossip; genitals*

PETRUCCIO   What, with my tongue in your tail? Nay, come again,
Good Kate, I am a gentleman.

215 KATHERINE   That I'll try.°   *test*

    She strikes him

PETRUCCIO   I swear I'll cuff you if you strike again.

KATHERINE   So may you lose your arms.[2]
If you strike me you are no gentleman,
And if no gentleman, why then, no arms.

---

8. Either an obscure allusion or an ironic reference to Kate's home as a place famous because she lives there.

9. For delicacies ("dainties") are called "cates."

1. Proclaimed; tested for depth.

2. Piece of furniture; changeable person.

3. Wooden stool made by a joiner.

4. Bear children; bear the weight of a lover.

5. Lie on you in sexual intercourse; make you pregnant; make accusations against you; accompany you with a musical refrain, or "burden."

6. Not heavy; wanton; lacking a musical accompaniment.

7. She is claiming social prominence ("weight") and refusing the implication that she is wanton ("light") or like a coin that has been clipped so that it is lighter than it should be.

8. Punning on "be" and "bee," Petruccio suggests Kate should make a buzzing sound.

9. A hawk that cannot be trained to "take," or capture, prey; a fool.

1. Obscure line probably meaning that if a fool ("buzzard") mistakes me for a faithful love ("turtledove"), he'll be making as big a mistake as the turtledove makes when it captures a buzzing insect (another meaning of "buzzard").

2. Lose your claim to a coat of arms (sign of noble status); loosen your grip on me.

220	PETRUCCIO	A herald,° Kate? O, put me in thy books.³	*An authority on heraldry*
	KATHERINE	What is your crest⁴—a coxcomb?⁵	
	PETRUCCIO	A combless cock,⁶ so Kate will be my hen.	
	KATHERINE	No cock of mine. You crow too like a craven.°	*cock that won't fight*
	PETRUCCIO	Nay, come, Kate, come. You must not look so sour.	
225	KATHERINE	It is my fashion when I see a crab.°	*crab apple; sour person*
	PETRUCCIO	Why, here's no crab, and therefore look not sour.	
	KATHERINE	There is, there is.	
	PETRUCCIO	Then show it me.	
	KATHERINE	Had I a glass° I would.	*mirror*
	PETRUCCIO	What, you mean my face?	
230	KATHERINE	Well aimed,° of such a young one.	*A good guess*
	PETRUCCIO	Now, by Saint George,° I am too young for you.	*England's patron saint*
	KATHERINE	Yet you are withered.	
	PETRUCCIO	'Tis with cares.	
	KATHERINE	I care not.	
	PETRUCCIO	Nay, hear you, Kate. In sooth, you scape° not so.	*escape*
	KATHERINE	I chafe° you if I tarry. Let me go.	*annoy; inflame*
235	PETRUCCIO	No, not a whit. I find you passing gentle.	

> 'Twas told me you were rough, and coy,° and sullen,   *disdainful*
> And now I find report a very liar,
> For thou art pleasant, gamesome,° passing° courteous,   *playful / very*
> But slow in speech, yet sweet as springtime flowers.
> 240 Thou canst not frown. Thou canst not look askance,°   *scornfully*
> Nor bite the lip, as angry wenches will,
> Nor hast thou pleasure to be cross in talk,
> But thou with mildness entertain'st thy wooers,
> With gentle conference,° soft, and affable.   *conversation*
> 245 Why does the world report that Kate doth limp?
> O sland'rous world! Kate like the hazel twig
> Is straight and slender, and as brown in hue
> As hazelnuts, and sweeter than the kernels.
> O let me see thee walk. Thou dost not halt.°   *limp*

| 250 | KATHERINE | Go, fool, and whom thou keep'st command.⁷ | |
| | PETRUCCIO | Did ever Dian⁸ so become a grove | |

> As Kate this chamber with her princely gait?
> O, be thou Dian, and let her be Kate,
> And then let Kate be chaste and Dian sportful.°   *playful; amorous*

255	KATHERINE	Where did you study all this goodly speech?	
	PETRUCCIO	It is extempore, from my mother-wit.°	*native intelligence*
	KATHERINE	A witty mother, witless else° her son.	*otherwise*
	PETRUCCIO	Am I not wise?	
	KATHERINE	Yes, keep you warm.⁹	
	PETRUCCIO	Marry, so I mean, sweet Katherine, in thy bed.	
260		And therefore setting all this chat aside,	

> Thus in plain terms: your father hath consented
> That you shall be my wife, your dowry 'greed on,

---

3. Heralds kept books listing gentlemen and their coats of arms.
4. Image on a coat of arms; a fleshy ridge or comb on a rooster's head.
5. Court fool's cap (resembling a cock's comb or crest).
6. A cock with its comb cut down (and thought, there-

fore, to be gentle), with a pun on "cock" as "penis."
7. And command your servants (not me).
8. Goddess of the hunt and of chastity.
9. Alluding to the proverbial phrase "enough wit to keep oneself warm," implying that the person has few brains.

And will you, nill you,° I will marry you.   *if you will or not*
Now, Kate, I am a husband for your turn,°   *needs*
265 For by this light, whereby I see thy beauty—
Thy beauty that doth make me like thee well—
Thou must be married to no man but me,
        Enter BAPTISTA, GREMIO, [*and*] TRANIO [*as Lucentio*]
For I am he am born to tame you, Kate,
And bring you from a wild Kate° to a Kate   *(punning on "wildcat")*
270 Conformable° as other household Kates.   *Submissive*
Here comes your father. Never make denial.
I must and will have Katherine to my wife.
BAPTISTA   Now, Signor Petruccio, how speed you with my daughter?
PETRUCCIO   How but well, sir, how but well?
275 It were impossible I should speed amiss.
BAPTISTA   Why, how now, daughter Katherine—in your dumps?°   *dejected*
KATHERINE   Call you me daughter? Now I promise you
You have showed a tender fatherly regard,
To wish me wed to one half-lunatic,
280 A madcap ruffian and a swearing Jack,
That thinks with oaths to face the matter out.°   *get his way brazenly*
PETRUCCIO   Father, 'tis thus: yourself and all the world
That talked of her have talked amiss of her.
If she be curst, it is for policy,°   *part of a scheme*
285 For she's not froward,° but modest as the dove.   *willful*
She is not hot, but temperate as the morn.
For patience she will prove a second Grissel,[1]
And Roman Lucrece[2] for her chastity.
And to conclude, we have 'greed so well together
290 That upon Sunday is the wedding day.
KATHERINE   I'll see thee hanged on Sunday first.
GREMIO   Hark, Petruccio, she says she'll see thee hanged first.
TRANIO   Is this your speeding?° Nay then, goodnight our part.[3]   *progress*
PETRUCCIO   Be patient, gentlemen. I choose her for myself.
295 If she and I be pleased, what's that to you?
'Tis bargained 'twixt us twain, being alone,
That she shall still be curst in company.
I tell you, 'tis incredible to believe
How much she loves me. O, the kindest Kate!
300 She hung about my neck, and kiss on kiss
She vied° so fast, protesting oath on oath,   *went me one better*
That in a twink° she won me to her love.   *instant*
O, you are novices. 'Tis a world° to see   *worth a world*
How tame, when men and women are alone,
305 A meacock° wretch can make the curstest shrew.   *timid*
Give me thy hand, Kate. I will unto Venice,
To buy apparel 'gainst° the wedding day.   *in preparation for*
Provide the feast, father, and bid the guests.
I will be sure my Katherine shall be fine.°   *richly dressed*
310 BAPTISTA   I know not what to say, but give me your hands.
God send you joy, Petruccio! 'Tis a match.

1. Griselda, proverbial for "wifely patience." Chaucer's *Clerk's Tale* offers one version of her story.
2. In Roman legend, a married woman who killed herself after being raped by Tarquin. Shakespeare's *Rape of Lucrece* recounts the story.
3. Good-bye to our chances (of gaining Bianca).

GREMIO *and* TRANIO Amen, say we. We will be witnesses.

PETRUCCIO Father, and wife, and gentlemen, adieu.

I will to Venice. Sunday comes apace.

315 We will have rings, and things, and fine array;

And kiss me, Kate. We will be married o' Sunday.

> *Exeunt* PETRUCCIO *and* KATHERINE [*severally*]°   *separately*

GREMIO Was ever match clapped up° so suddenly?   *settled*

BAPTISTA Faith, gentlemen, now I play a merchant's part,

And venture madly on a desperate mart.°   *risky bargain*

320 TRANIO 'Twas a commodity lay fretting by you.[4]

'Twill bring you gain, or perish on the seas.

BAPTISTA The gain I seek is quiet in the match.

GREMIO No doubt but he hath got a quiet catch.

But now, Baptista, to your younger daughter.

325 Now is the day we long have looked for.

I am your neighbour, and was suitor first.

TRANIO And I am one that love Bianca more

Than words can witness, or your thoughts can guess.

GREMIO Youngling, thou canst not love so dear° as I.   *deeply; expensively*

TRANIO Greybeard, thy love doth freeze.

330 GREMIO   But thine doth fry.

Skipper,° stand back. 'Tis age that nourisheth.   *Irresponsible youth*

TRANIO But youth in ladies' eyes that flourisheth.

BAPTISTA Content you, gentlemen. I will compound° this strife.   *settle*

'Tis deeds must win the prize, and he of both°   *whichever of you*

335 That can assure my daughter greatest dower

Shall have my Bianca's love.

Say, Signor Gremio, what can you assure her?

GREMIO First, as you know, my house within the city

Is richly furnishèd with plate and gold,

340 Basins and ewers to lave° her dainty hands;   *wash*

My hangings all of Tyrian[5] tapestry.

In ivory coffers I have stuffed my crowns,°   *coins*

In cypress chests my arras counterpoints,°   *tapestry bedcovers*

Costly apparel, tents° and canopies,   *bed curtains*

345 Fine linen, Turkey cushions bossed° with pearl,   *embossed*

Valance° of Venice gold in needlework,   *Fringe on bed drapery*

Pewter, and brass, and all things that belongs

To house or housekeeping. Then at my farm

I have a hundred milch-kine° to the pail,   *dairy cows*

350 Six score fat oxen standing in my stalls,

And all things answerable to° this portion.   *on the same scale as*

Myself am struck° in years, I must confess,   *advanced*

And if I die tomorrow this is hers,

If whilst I live she will be only mine.

355 TRANIO That 'only' came well in. Sir, list to me.

I am my father's heir and only son.

If I may have your daughter to my wife

I'll leave her houses three or four as good,

Within rich Pisa walls, as any one

360 Old Signor Gremio has in Padua,

---

4. It (that is, Katherine) was a piece of merchandise deteriorating in value or a sexually available woman fretting with irritation while in your possession.

5. Crimson or purple. (The Mediterranean city of Tyre was famous for dye of this color.)

Besides two thousand ducats by the year
Of fruitful land,[6] all which shall be her jointure.°   *marriage settlement*
What, have I pinched° you, Signor Gremio?   *distressed*

GREMIO   Two thousand ducats by the year of land—
365   My land amounts not to so much in all.
That she shall have; besides, an argosy°   *a merchant ship*
That now is lying in Marseilles road.°   *harbor*
What, have I choked you with an argosy?

TRANIO   Gremio, 'tis known my father hath no less
370   Than three great argosies, besides two galliasses°   *large cargo ships*
And twelve tight° galleys. These I will assure her,   *watertight*
And twice as much whate'er thou off 'rest next.

GREMIO   Nay, I have offered all. I have no more,
And she can have no more than all I have.
375   If you like me, she shall have me and mine.

TRANIO   Why then, the maid is mine from all the world.
By your firm promise Gremio is out-vied.°   *outbid*

BAPTISTA   I must confess your offer is the best,
And let° your father make her the assurance,   *provided*
380   She is your own. Else, you must pardon me,
If you should die before him, where's her dower?

TRANIO   That's but a cavil. He is old, I young.

GREMIO   And may not young men die as well as old?

BAPTISTA   Well, gentlemen,
385   I am thus resolved. On Sunday next, you know,
My daughter Katherine is to be married.
[*To* TRANIO] Now, on the Sunday following shall Bianca
Be bride to you, if you make this assurance;
If not, to Signor Gremio.
390   And so I take my leave, and thank you both.

GREMIO   Adieu, good neighbour.   *Exit* [BAPTISTA]
Now I fear thee not.
Sirrah, young gamester, your father were a fool
To give thee all, and in his waning age
Set foot under thy table.[7] Tut, a toy!°   *nonsense*
395   An old Italian fox is not so kind, my boy.   *Exit*

TRANIO   A vengeance on your crafty withered hide!
Yet I have faced it with a card of ten.[8]
'Tis in my head to do my master good.
I see no reason° but supposed Lucentio   *possible action*
400   Must get° a father called supposed Vincentio—   *beget; obtain*
And that's a wonder; fathers commonly
Do get their children, but in this case of wooing
A child shall get a sire, if I fail not of my cunning.   *Exit*

3.1

Enter LUCENTIO [*with books, as Cambio*], HORTENSIO
[*with a lute, as Licio*], *and* BIANCA

LUCENTIO   Fiddler, forbear. You grow too forward, sir.
Have you so soon forgot the entertainment

---

6. *Besides . . . land:* As well as fertile land that brings in an income of 2,000 ducats (Venetian gold coins) each year.
7. Become your dependent.

8. I have bluffed and won with a card of little value (a ten spot).
3.1 Location: Baptista's house in Padua.

Her sister Katherine welcomed you withal?°   *with*
HORTENSIO   But, wrangling pedant, this Bianca is,
5   The patroness of heavenly harmony.
Then give me leave to have prerogative,°   *precedence*
And when in music we have spent an hour
Your lecture° shall have leisure for as much.   *lesson*
LUCENTIO   Preposterous[1] ass, that never read so far
10   To know the cause why music was ordained!
Was it not to refresh the mind of man
After his studies or his usual pain?°   *labor*
Then give me leave to read philosophy,
And while I pause, serve in° your harmony.   *serve up (contemptuous)*
15   HORTENSIO   Sirrah, I will not bear these braves° of thine.   *insults*
BIANCA   Why, gentlemen, you do me double wrong
To strive for that which resteth in my choice.
I am no breeching[2] scholar in the schools.
I'll not be tied to hours nor 'pointed times,
20   But learn my lessons as I please myself;
And to cut off all strife, here sit we down.
[*To* HORTENSIO] Take you your instrument, play you the whiles.°   *in the meantime*
His lecture will be done ere you have tuned.
HORTENSIO   You'll leave his lecture when I am in tune?[3]
25   LUCENTIO   That will be never. Tune your instrument.
[HORTENSIO *tunes his lute.* LUCENTIO *opens a book*]
BIANCA   Where left we last?
LUCENTIO   Here, madam.
[*Reads*]   'Hic ibat Simois, hic est Sigeia tellus,
            Hic steterat Priami regia celsa senis.[4]
30   BIANCA   Construct them.°   — *Translate the lines*
LUCENTIO   'Hic ibat', as I told you before—'Simois', I am
Lucentio—'hic est', son unto Vincentio of Pisa—'Sigeia tellus',
disguised thus to get your love—'hic steterat', and that Lucen-
tio that comes a-wooing—'Priami', is my man Tranio—'regia',
35   bearing my port°—'celsa senis', that we might beguile the old   *taking my social position*
pantaloon.°   *foolish old man*
HORTENSIO   Madam, my instrument's in tune.
BIANCA   Let's hear. [HORTENSIO *plays*] O fie, the treble jars.°   *is discordant*
LUCENTIO   Spit in the hole,[5] man, and tune again.
[HORTENSIO *tunes his lute again*]
40   BIANCA   Now let me see if I can construe it. 'Hic ibat Simois',
I know you not—'hic est Sigeia tellus', I trust you not—
'hic steterat Priami', take heed he hear us not—'regia', presume
not—'celsa senis', despair not.
HORTENSIO   Madam, 'tis now in tune.
LUCENTIO   All but the bass.
45   HORTENSIO   The bass is right, 'tis the base knave that jars.
[*Aside*] How fiery and forward our pedant is!

---

1. Literally, putting last what should come first; revers-
ing the natural order of things.
2. Youthful (in breeches); liable to be whipped
(breeched).
3. When my lute is in the proper pitch. Lucentio
responds with a pun on "in tune" as meaning "in har-
mony" with Bianca.

4. Latin lines from Penelope's letter to her husband
Ulysses in Ovid's *Heroides:* "Here flowed the Simois;
here is the Sigeian land; here stood old Priam's lofty
palace."
5. Moisten the lute's peg hole (to aid tuning). Lucen-
tio speaks contemptuously and may not be giving seri-
ous advice.

Now, for my life, the knave doth court my love.
Pedascule,° I'll watch you better yet.   *Little pedant*
BIANCA [*to* LUCENTIO]   In time I may believe; yet, I mistrust.
50   LUCENTIO   Mistrust it not, for sure Aeacides[6]
    Was Ajax, called so from his grandfather.
    BIANCA   I must believe my master, else, I promise you,
    I should be arguing still upon that doubt.
    But let it rest. Now Licio, to you.
55   Good master, take it not unkindly, pray,
    That I have been thus pleasant with you both.
    HORTENSIO [*to* LUCENTIO]   You may go walk and give me leave°   *allow me leisure*
        awhile.
    My lessons make no music in three parts.°   *for three voices*
    LUCENTIO   Are you so formal,° sir? Well, I must wait.   *precise*
60   [*Aside*] And watch withal, for but° I be deceived   *unless*
    Our fine musician groweth amorous.
    HORTENSIO   Madam, before you touch the instrument
    To learn the order of my fingering,
    I must begin with rudiments of art,
65   To teach you gamut[7] in a briefer sort,°   *quicker way*
    More pleasant, pithy, and effectual
    Than hath been taught by any of my trade;
    And there it is in writing, fairly drawn.
        [*He gives a paper*]
    BIANCA   Why, I am past my gamut long ago.
70   HORTENSIO   Yet read the gamut of Hortensio.
    BIANCA [*reads*]
        '*Gam-ut* I am, the ground° of all accord,   *lowest note; basis*
        A—re—to plead Hortensio's passion.
        B—mi—Bianca, take him for thy lord,
           C—fa, ut—that loves with all affection.
75   D—sol, re—one clef, two notes[8] have I,
        E—la, mi—show pity, or I die.'
    Call you this gamut? Tut, I like it not.
    Old fashions please me best. I am not so nice°   *capricious*
    To change true rules for odd inventions.
        Enter a MESSENGER
80   MESSENGER   Mistress, your father prays you leave your books
    And help to dress your sister's chamber up.
    You know tomorrow is the wedding day.
    BIANCA   Farewell, sweet masters both. I must be gone.
    LUCENTIO   Faith, mistress, then I have no cause to stay.
        [*Exeunt* BIANCA, MESSENGER, *and* LUCENTIO]
85   HORTENSIO   But I have cause to pry into this pedant.
    Methinks he looks as though he were in love.
    Yet if thy thoughts, Bianca, be so humble°   *low*
    To cast thy wand'ring eyes on every stale,°   *bait; lure*
    Seize thee that list.[9] If once I find thee ranging,°   *unfaithful*
90   Hortensio will be quit with thee by changing.[1]   *Exit*

---

6. Aeacides, or Ajax, was named after his grandfather   8. Referring perhaps to his one love and two identities.
Aeacus. Lucentio pretends to continue the lesson.   9. Let anyone who wants you take you.
7. A musical scale, named after its lowest note,   1. Will get even with you or get rid of you by finding
"gamma-ut."   another love.

3.2

Enter BAPTISTA, GREMIO, TRANIO [AS LUCENTIO],
KATHERINE, BIANCA, AND OTHERS, ATTENDANTS[1]

BAPTISTA [*to* TRANIO] Signor Lucentio, this is the 'pointed day
That Katherine and Petruccio should be married,
And yet we hear not of our son-in-law.
What will be said, what mockery will it be,
5 To want° the bridegroom when the priest attends   *lack*
To speak the ceremonial rites of marriage?
What says Lucentio to this shame of ours?
KATHERINE No shame but mine. I must forsooth be forced
To give my hand opposed against my heart
10 Unto a mad-brain rudesby° full of spleen,[2]   *unmannerly fellow*
Who wooed in haste and means to wed at leisure.
I told you, I, he was a frantic° fool,   *mad*
Hiding his bitter jests in blunt behaviour,
And to be noted for a merry man
15 He'll woo a thousand, 'point the day of marriage,
Make friends, invite them, and proclaim the banns,
Yet never means to wed where he hath wooed.
Now must the world point at poor Katherine
And say 'Lo, there is mad Petruccio's wife,
20 If it would please him come and marry her.'
TRANIO Patience, good Katherine, and Baptista, too.
Upon my life, Petruccio means but well.
Whatever fortune stays° him from his word,   *incident keeps*
Though he be blunt, I know him passing wise;
25 Though he be merry, yet withal he's honest.[3]
KATHERINE Would Katherine had never seen him, though.
                                                                    Exit weeping
BAPTISTA Go, girl. I cannot blame thee now to weep.
For such an injury would vex a very saint,
Much more a shrew of thy impatient humour.
       Enter BIONDELLO
30 BIONDELLO Master, master, news—old news, and such news as
you never heard of.
BAPTISTA Is it new and old too? How may that be?
BIONDELLO Why, is it not news to hear of Petruccio's coming?
BAPTISTA Is he come?
35 BIONDELLO Why, no, sir.
BAPTISTA What then?
BIONDELLO He is coming.
BAPTISTA When will he be here?
BIONDELLO When he stands where I am and sees you there.
40 TRANIO But say, what to thine old news?
BIONDELLO Why, Petruccio is coming in a new hat and an old
jerkin,° a pair of old breeches thrice-turned,[4] a pair of boots   *jacket*

3.2 Location: In front of Baptista's house.
1. Many editors include Lucentio, disguised as Cambio, among the characters who enter at this point, though he speaks no lines in the events leading up to and including Petruccio's arrival for his wedding. The Oxford editors feel that Lucentio only comes onstage when all the characters who enter at 3.2 leave to attend Katherine and Petruccio's wedding (3.2.116–20). They then mark a new scene, 3.3, when Lucentio enters with Tranio.

2. Caprice; impulsiveness. Contemporary medical theorists claimed that high and low spirits originated in the spleen.
3. Some critics find Tranio's familiarity with Petruccio improbable. Possibly these lines were originally meant to be spoken by Hortensio.
4. Turned inside out three times (to make them last longer).

that have been candle-cases,[5] one buckled, another laced, an
old rusty sword ta'en out of the town armoury with a broken
hilt, and chapeless,[6] with two broken points,[7] his horse hipped,°   *lame in the hips*
with an old mothy saddle and stirrups of no kindred,° besides,   *unmatched*
possessed with the glanders[8] and like to mose in the chine,[9]
troubled with the lampass,[1] infected with the fashions,° full   *farcins (small tumors)*
of windgalls,[2] sped with spavins,[3] rayed with the yellows,°   *disfigured by jaundice*
past cure of the fives,[4] stark spoiled with the staggers,[5] be-
gnawn with the bots,[6] weighed in the back° and shoulder-   *swaybacked*
shotten,[7] near-legged before[8] and with a half-cheeked° bit and   *improperly attached*
a headstall[9] of sheep's leather which, being restrained° to   *tightened*
keep him from stumbling, hath been often burst and now
repaired with knots, one girth° six times pieced,° and a woman's   *saddle strap / mended*
crupper of velour[1] which hath two letters for her name fairly set
down in studs, and here and there pieced with packthread.°   *twine*

BAPTISTA   Who comes with him?

BIONDELLO   O sir, his lackey, for all the world caparisoned° like   *outfitted*
the horse, with a linen stock° on one leg and a kersey boot-   *stocking*
hose[2] on the other, gartered with a red and blue list;° an old   *strip of cloth*
hat, and the humour of forty fancies pricked in't for a
feather[3]—a monster, a very monster in apparel, and not like a
Christian footboy or a gentleman's lackey.

TRANIO   'Tis some odd humour pricks° him to this fashion;   *incites, urges*
  Yet oftentimes he goes but mean-apparelled.

BAPTISTA   I am glad he's come, howsoe'er he comes.

BIONDELLO   Why, sir, he comes not.

BAPTISTA   Didst thou not say he comes?

BIONDELLO   Who? That Petruccio came?

BAPTISTA   Ay, that Petruccio came.

BIONDELLO   No, sir. I say his horse comes with him on his back.

BAPTISTA   Why, that's all one.°   *the same thing*

BIONDELLO   Nay, by Saint Jamy,
          I hold° you a penny,   *bet*
          A horse and a man
          Is more than one,
          And yet not many.

Enter PETRUCCIO *and* GRUMIO[*fantastically dressed*]

PETRUCCIO   Come, where be these gallants? Who's at home?

BAPTISTA   You are welcome, sir.

PETRUCCIO   And yet I come not well.

BAPTISTA   And yet you halt° not.   *limp*

---

5. In other words, discarded and used to store old can-
dle ends.
6. Without the metal tip that protects the sword's
point.
7. With two laces that don't hold up his hose; with two
points (instead of one) on his broken sword.
8. The first in a catalogue of horse diseases, most of
which are described in Gervase Markham's *Discourse of
Horsemanship* (1593). The glanders caused swellings
and nasal discharge.
9. Obscure phrase, probably meaning the horse was
apt to suffer discharge from the nostrils, indicating the
last stage of glanders.
1. A disease characterized by swellings in the mouth.
2. Soft tumors usually appearing on the fetlock, so

called because they were thought to contain air.
3. Rendered useless by swelling of the leg joints.
4. Swelling of glands below the ears.
5. A disease causing loss of balance.
6. Eaten by intestinal worms.
7. With sprained shoulders.
8. With knock-kneed forelegs.
9. The part of the bridle that fits around the horse's
head. Sheepskin would be inferior to the animal skins
normally used.
1. *crupper*: strap that passes under a horse's tail to keep
the saddle straight, *velour*: velvet.
2. A coarse wool stocking.
3. Possibly an absurdly fanciful decoration attached to
the hat instead of a feather.

TRANIO   Not so well apparelled as I wish you were.
PETRUCCIO   Were it not better I should rush in thus—
85 But where is Kate? Where is my lovely bride?
How does my father? Gentles,[4] methinks you frown.
And wherefore gaze this goodly company
As if they saw some wondrous monument,
Some comet or unusual prodigy?
90 BAPTISTA   Why, sir, you know this is your wedding day.
First were we sad, fearing you would not come;
Now sadder that you come so unprovided.°   °unprepared
Fie, doff this habit,° shame to your estate,°   °outfit / social place
An eyesore to our solemn festival.
95 TRANIO   And tell us what occasion of import
Hath all so long detained you from your wife
And sent you hither so unlike yourself?
PETRUCCIO   Tedious it were to tell, and harsh to hear.
Sufficeth I am come to keep my word,
100 Though in some part enforcèd to digress,°   °deviate from my plan
Which at more leisure I will so excuse
As you shall well be satisfied withal.
But where is Kate? I stay too long from her.
The morning wears, 'tis time we were at church.
105 TRANIO   See not your bride in these unreverent° robes.   °disrespectful
Go to my chamber, put on clothes of mine.
PETRUCCIO   Not I, believe me. Thus I'll visit her.
BAPTISTA   But thus, I trust, you will not marry her.
PETRUCCIO   Good sooth,° even thus. Therefore ha' done with words.   °Yes indeed
110 To me she's married, not unto my clothes.
Could I repair what she will wear° in me   °wear out (in sex)
As I can change these poor accoutrements,
'Twere well for Kate and better for myself.
But what a fool am I to chat with you
115 When I should bid good morrow to my bride,
And seal the title with a lovely° kiss!   Exit [with GRUMIO]   °loving
TRANIO   He hath some meaning in his mad attire.
We will persuade him, be it possible,
To put on better ere he go to church.   [Exit with GREMIO]
120 BAPTISTA   I'll after him, and see the event° of this.   Exeunt   °outcome

3.3
[Enter LUCENTIO as Cambio, and TRANIO as Lucentio]
TRANIO   But, sir, to love concerneth us to add[1]
Her father's liking, which to bring to pass,
As I before imparted to your worship,
I am to get a man—whate'er he be
5 It skills° not much, we'll fit him to our turn—   °matters
And he shall be Vincentio of Pisa,
And make assurance here in Padua
Of greater sums than I have promisèd.

4. The polite term of address to men and women of the gentry.
3.3 Location: Scene continues.

1. To the love between Bianca and Lucentio it is necessary for us to add.

So shall you quietly enjoy your hope,°   *what you hope for*
10 And marry sweet Bianca with consent.
    LUCENTIO   Were it not that my fellow schoolmaster
    Doth watch Bianca's steps so narrowly,
    'Twere good, methinks, to steal our marriage,°   *elope*
    Which once performed, let all the world say no,
15 I'll keep mine own, despite of all the world.
    TRANIO   That by degrees we mean to look into,
    And watch our vantage° in this business.   *opportunity*
    We'll overreach the greybeard Gremio,
    The narrow-prying° father Minola,   *overly suspicious*
20 The quaint° musician, amorous Licio,   *skillful; crafty*
    All for my master's sake, Lucentio.
            Enter GREMIO
    Signor Gremio, came you from the church?
    GREMIO   As willingly as e'er I came from school.
    TRANIO   And is the bride and bridegroom coming home?
25 GREMIO   A bridegroom, say you? 'Tis a groom° indeed—   *crude, lower-class man*
    A grumbling groom, and that the girl shall find.
    TRANIO   Curster° than she? Why, 'tis impossible.   *More cantankerous*
    GREMIO   Why, he's a devil, a devil, a very fiend.
    TRANIO   Why, she's a devil, a devil, the devil's dam.²   *mother*
30 GREMIO   Tut, she's a lamb, a dove, a fool to him.²
    I'll tell you, Sir Lucentio: when the priest
    Should ask if Katherine should be his wife,
    'Ay, by Gog's woun's,'³ quoth he, and swore so loud
    That all amazed the priest let fall the book,
35 And as he stooped again to take it up
    This mad-brained bridegroom took° him such a cuff   *gave*
    That down fell priest, and book, and book, and priest.
    'Now take them up,' quoth he, 'if any list.'°   *choose*
    TRANIO   What said the vicar when he rose again?
40 GREMIO   Trembled and shook, forwhy° he° stamped and swore   *because / (Petruccio)*
    As if the vicar meant to cozen⁴ him.
    But after many ceremonies done
    He calls for wine. 'A health,' quoth he, as if
    He had been aboard,° carousing to his mates   *(a ship)*
45 After a storm; quaffed off the muscatel⁵
    And threw the sops all in the sexton's face,
    Having no other reason
    But that his beard grew thin and hungerly°   *sparsely; as if hungry*
    And seemed to ask him sops as he was drinking.
50 This done, he took the bride about the neck
    And kissed her lips with such a clamorous smack
    That at the parting all the church did echo,
    And I seeing this came thence for very shame,
    And after me, I know, the rout° is coming.   *crowd*
55 Such a mad marriage never was before.
            Music plays
    Hark, hark, I hear the minstrels play.

---

2. A good-natured innocent compared with him.
3. By God's (Christ's) wounds (a common oath).
4. Cheat (by not performing a legally binding ceremony).

5. Wine with small cakes, or "sops," soaked in it, traditionally drunk by the newly married couple and their guests.

Enter PETRUCCIO, KATHERINE, BIANCA, HORTENSIO
[*as Licio*], BAPTISTA, [GRUMIO, *and others*, attendants]

PETRUCCIO   Gentlemen and friends, I thank you for your pains.
  I know you think to dine with me today,
  And have prepared great store of wedding cheer.°   *food and drink*
60 But so it is my haste doth call me hence,
  And therefore here I mean to take my leave.
BAPTISTA   Is't possible you will away tonight?
PETRUCCIO   I must away today, before night come.
  Make° it no wonder. If you knew my business,   *Consider*
65 You would entreat me rather go than stay.
  And, honest° company, I thank you all   *worthy*
  That have beheld me give away myself
  To this most patient, sweet, and virtuous wife.
  Dine with my father, drink a health to me,
70 For I must hence; and farewell to you all.
TRANIO   Let us entreat you stay till after dinner.
PETRUCCIO   It may not be.
GREMIO   Let me entreat you.
PETRUCCIO   It cannot be.
KATHERINE   Let me entreat you.
PETRUCCIO   I am content.
KATHERINE   Are you content to stay?
75 PETRUCCIO   I am content you shall entreat me stay,
  But yet not stay, entreat me how you can.
KATHERINE   Now, if you love me, stay.
PETRUCCIO   Grumio, my horse.
GRUMIO   Ay, sir, they be ready. The oats have eaten the horses.[6]
KATHERINE   Nay, then, do what thou canst, I will not go today,
80 No, nor tomorrow—not till I please myself.
  The door is open, sir, there lies your way.
  You may be jogging whiles your boots are green.[7]
  For me, I'll not be gone till I please myself.
  'Tis like you'll prove a jolly,° surly groom,   *an arrogant*
85 That take it on you at the first so roundly.[8]
PETRUCCIO   O Kate, content thee. Prithee, be not angry.
KATHERINE   I will be angry. What hast thou to do?[9]
  Father, be quiet. He shall stay° my leisure.   *await*
GREMIO   Ay, marry, sir. Now it begins to work.
90 KATHERINE   Gentlemen, forward to the bridal dinner.
  I see a woman may be made a fool
  If she had not a spirit to resist.
PETRUCCIO   They shall go forward, Kate, at thy command.
  Obey the bride, you that attend on her.
95 Go to the feast, revel and domineer,°   *feast sumptuously*
  Carouse full measure to her maidenhead.
  Be mad and merry, or go hang yourselves.
  But for my bonny Kate, she must with me.
  Nay, look not big,° nor stamp, nor stare, nor fret.   *defiant*

---

6. Either Grumio gets it the wrong way around, or he
is joking about the great quantity of oats the horses
have eaten.
7. You can be off now while your boots are new

("green"). Proverbial expression for getting an early
start or getting rid of an unwelcome guest.
8. That takes charge at the outset so outspokenly.
9. What business is it of yours?

100   I will be master of what is mine own.
She is my goods, my chattels. She is my house,
My household-stuff, my field, my barn,
My horse, my ox, my ass, my anything,
And here she stands, touch her whoever dare.[1]
105   I'll bring mine action on° the proudest he   *attack; sue (in court)*
That stops my way in Padua. Grumio,
Draw forth thy weapon, we are beset with thieves.
Rescue thy mistress if thou be a man.
Fear not, sweet wench. They shall not touch thee, Kate.
110   I'll buckler° thee against a million.   *shield*

           Exeunt PETRUCCIO, KATHERINE [*and* GRUMIO]

BAPTISTA   Nay, let them go—a couple of quiet ones!
GREMIO   Went they not quickly I should die with laughing.
TRANIO   Of all mad matches never was the like.
LUCENTIO   Mistress, what's your opinion of your sister?
115 BIANCA   That being mad herself she's madly mated.
GREMIO   I warrant him, Petruccio is Kated.[2]
BAPTISTA   Neighbours and friends, though bride and bridegroom wants° *are missing*
For to supply° the places at the table,   *To fill*
You know there wants no junkets° at the feast.   *sweetmeats*
120 Lucentio, you shall supply the bridegroom's place,
And let Bianca take her sister's room.
TRANIO   Shall sweet Bianca practise how to bride it?
BAPTISTA   She shall, Lucentio. Come, gentlemen, let's go.
                          Exeunt

4.1

    Enter GRUMIO

GRUMIO   Fie, fie on all tired jades,° on all mad masters, and all *worn-out horses*
foul° ways. Was ever man so beaten? Was ever man so rayed?° *muddy / dirtied*
Was ever man so weary? I am sent before to make a fire, and
they are coming after to warm them. Now were not I a little
5 pot and soon hot,[1] my very lips might freeze to my teeth, my
tongue to the roof of my mouth, my heart in my belly ere
I should come by a fire to thaw me. But I with blowing the fire
shall warm myself, for considering the weather, a taller[2] man
than I will take cold. Holla! Hoa, Curtis!

    Enter CURTIS

10 CURTIS   Who is that calls so coldly?
GRUMIO   A piece of ice. If thou doubt it, thou mayst slide from
my shoulder to my heel with no greater a run but my head and
my neck. A fire, good Curtis!
CURTIS   Is my master and his wife coming, Grumio?
15 GRUMIO   O ay, Curtis, ay, and therefore fire, fire! Cast on no
water.[3]
CURTIS   Is she so hot a shrew as she's reported?

---

1. Petruccio warns others to leave Kate alone. In cataloguing the ways she is one of his possessions, he alludes to the Tenth Commandment, which forbids coveting a neighbor's wife or property.
2. Mated with a "Kate"; afflicted with Kate (imagined as a disease).
4.1 Location: Petruccio's country house.

1. Proverbial for a small person who quickly becomes angry.
2. Punning on "taller" as meaning "sturdier."
3. Alluding to the popular song "Scotland's Burning," in which the words "Fire, fire" are followed by "Cast on water, cast on water."

GRUMIO She was, good Curtis, before this frost; but thou
know'st, winter tames man, woman, and beast, for it hath
20 tamed my old master, and my new mistress, and myself, fel-
low Curtis.

CURTIS Away, you three-inch° fool. I am no beast.   *short*

GRUMIO Am I but three inches? Why, thy horn[4] is a foot, and
so long am I, at the least. But wilt thou make a fire, or shall I
25 complain on thee to our mistress, whose hand—she being
now at hand—thou shalt soon feel to thy cold comfort, for
being slow in thy hot office.°   *fire-making duties*

CURTIS I prithee, good Grumio, tell me—how goes the world?

GRUMIO A cold world, Curtis, in every office but thine. And
30 therefore fire, do thy duty, and have thy duty,° for my master   *take your reward*
and mistress are almost frozen to death.

CURTIS There's fire ready, and therefore, good Grumio, the
news.

GRUMIO Why, 'Jack boy, ho boy!',[5] and as much news as wilt thou.

35 CURTIS Come, you are so full of cony-catching.[6]

GRUMIO Why, therefore fire, for I have caught extreme cold.
Where's the cook? Is supper ready, the house trimmed, rushes
strewed,[7] cobwebs swept, the servingmen in their new fustian,°   *coarse cloth*
the white stockings, and every officer° his wedding garment   *servant*
40 on? Be the Jacks fair within, the Jills fair without,[8] the carpets°   *table coverings*
laid, and everything in order?

CURTIS All ready, and therefore, I pray thee, news.

GRUMIO First, know my horse is tired, my master and mistress
fallen out.

45 CURTIS How?

GRUMIO Out of their saddles into the dirt, and thereby hangs a
tale.

CURTIS Let's ha't, good Grumio.

GRUMIO Lend thine ear.

50 CURTIS Here.

GRUMIO [cuffing him] There.

CURTIS This 'tis to feel a tale, not to hear a tale.

GRUMIO And therefore 'tis called a sensible tale,[9] and this cuff
was but to knock at your ear and beseech listening. Now I
55 begin. Inprimis,° we came down a foul° hill, my master riding   *First / muddy*
behind my mistress.

CURTIS Both of° one horse?   *on*

GRUMIO What's that to thee?

CURTIS Why, a horse.

60 GRUMIO Tell thou the tale. But hadst thou not crossed° me   *interrupted*
thou shouldst have heard how her horse fell and she under
her horse; thou shouldst have heard in how miry a place, how
she was bemoiled,° how he left her with the horse upon her,   *covered with mud*
how he beat me because her horse stumbled, how she waded
65 through the dirt to pluck him off me, how he swore, how she
prayed that never prayed before, how I cried, how the horses
ran away, how her bridle was burst, how I lost my crupper,

---

4. The proverbial sign of a cuckold; an erect penis.
Grumio implies that he is "long" enough to cuckold
Curtis.
5. A line from another popular song.
6. Trickery, with a play on the "catches," or songs, of

which Grumio is fond. A cony is a rabbit.
7. Scattered on the floor.
8. Jacks and Jills were manservants and maidservants;
also leather drinking vessels and metal drinking vessels.
9. Reasonable; capable of being felt.

with many things of worthy memory which now shall die in
oblivion, and thou return unexperienced° to thy grave.   *ignorant; unknowing*
70   CURTIS   By this reckoning he is more shrew than she.
    GRUMIO   Ay, and that thou and the proudest of you all shall find
when he comes home. But what° talk I of this? Call forth   *why*
Nathaniel, Joseph, Nicholas, Philip, Walter, Sugarsop, and
the rest. Let their heads be sleekly combed, their blue coats[1]
75   brushed, and their garters of an indifferent° knit. Let them   *ordinary; a matching*
curtsy with their left legs and not presume to touch a hair of
my master's horse-tail till they kiss their hands.[2] Are they all
ready?
    CURTIS   They are.
80   GRUMIO   Call them forth.
    CURTIS [*calling*]   Do you hear, ho? You must meet my master to
countenance[3] my mistress.
    GRUMIO   Why, she hath a face of her own.
    CURTIS   Who knows not that?
85   GRUMIO   Thou, it seems, that calls for company to countenance
her.
    CURTIS   I call them forth to credit[4] her.
          Enter four or five servingmen
    GRUMIO   Why, she comes to borrow nothing of them.
    NATHANIEL   Welcome home, Grumio!
90   PHILIP   How now, Grumio?
    JOSEPH   What, Grumio?
    NICHOLAS   Fellow Grumio!
    NATHANIEL   How now, old lad!
    GRUMIO   Welcome you, how now you, what you, fellow you, and
95   thus much for greeting. Now, my spruce° companions, is all   *smartly dressed*
ready and all things neat?
    NATHANIEL   All things is ready. How near is our master?
    GRUMIO   E'en at hand, alighted by this, and therefore be not—
Cock's° passion, silence! I hear my master.   *God's (a common oath)*
          Enter PETRUCCIO *and* KATHERINE
100   PETRUCCIO   Where be these knaves? What, no man at door
To hold my stirrup nor to take my horse?
Where is Nathaniel, Gregory, Philip?
    ALL SERVANTS   Here, here sir, here sir.
    PETRUCCIO   Here sir, here sir, here sir, here sir!
105   You logger-headed° and unpolished grooms,   *stupid*
What! No attendance! No regard! No duty!
Where is the foolish knave I sent before?
    GRUMIO   Here, sir, as foolish as I was before.
    PETRUCCIO   You peasant swain,° you whoreson,° malthorse   *farm laborer / bastard*
110   drudge,[5]
Did I not bid thee meet me in the park[6]
And bring along these rascal knaves with thee?
    GRUMIO   Nathaniel's coat, sir, was not fully made,
And Gabriel's pumps° were all unpinked° i'th' heel.   *shoes / not ornamented*
There was no link[7] to colour Peter's hat,

1. The usual servant uniform.
2. A greeting signifying inordinate submissiveness.
3. Greet, pay respects to; with a pun in the next line on
"countenance" as meaning "face."
4. Honor, with pun in next line on "credit" as meaning
"offer financial assistance."

5. Stupid, menial worker. The slow, heavy malt horse
was used to grind malt by turning a treadmill.
6. A piece of ground comprising woodland and pasture
attached to a country house and used for recreation.
7. Torch, the smoke of which was used to blacken shoes.

115 And Walter's dagger was not come from sheathing.°   *having a sheath fixed*
There were none fine but Adam, Ralph, and Gregory.
The rest were ragged, old, and beggarly.
Yet as they are, here are they come to meet you.
PETRUCCIO   Go, rascals, go and fetch my supper in.

                                               Exeunt servants

120 [*Sings*]   'Where is the life that late I led?
             Where are those—'[8]
Sit down, Kate, and welcome. Soud, soud, soud, soud.[9]
        Enter servants with supper
Why, when, I say?—Nay, good sweet Kate, be merry.—
Off with my boots, you rogues, you villains. When?
125 [*Sings*]   'It was the friar of orders gray,
            As he forth walkèd on his way.'[1]
Out, you rogue, you pluck my foot awry.
[*Kicking a servant*] Take that, and mend the plucking of the other.
Be merry, Kate. [*Calling*] Some water, here. What, hoa!
        Enter one with water
130 Where's my spaniel Troilus? Sirrah, get you hence,
And bid my cousin Ferdinand come hither—
One, Kate, that you must kiss and be acquainted with.
[*Calling*] Where are my slippers? Shall I have some water?
Come, Kate, and wash, and welcome heartily.
        [*A servant drops water*]
135 You whoreson villain, will you let it fall?
KATHERINE   Patience, I pray you, 'twas a fault unwilling.
PETRUCCIO   A whoreson, beetle-headed,° flap-eared knave.   *thick-headed*
Come, Kate, sit down, I know you have a stomach.°   *an appetite; temper*
Will you give thanks, sweet Kate, or else shall I?
What's this—mutton?
FIRST SERVINGMAN   Ay.
PETRUCCIO   Who brought it?
140 PETER   I.
PETRUCCIO   'Tis burnt, and so is all the meat.
What dogs are these? Where is the rascal cook?
How durst you villains bring it from the dresser°   *cook; sideboard*
And serve it thus to me that love it not?
145 There, [*throwing food*] take it to you, trenchers,° cups, and all,   *plates*
You heedless jolt-heads° and unmannered slaves.   *careless blockheads*
What, do you grumble? I'll be with you straight.
        [*He chases the servants away*]
KATHERINE   I pray you, husband, be not so disquiet.
The meat was well, if you were so contented.
150 PETRUCCIO   I tell thee, Kate, 'twas burnt and dried away,
And I expressly am forbid to touch it,
For it engenders choler,[2] planteth anger,
And better 'twere that both of us did fast,
Since of ourselves° ourselves are choleric,   *by our natures*
155 Than feed it with such overroasted flesh.

---

8. Probably a fragment of a ballad, now lost, lamenting a newlywed's loss of freedom.
9. An expression of impatience.
1. Another fragment of a lost song, perhaps one of the many songs about a friar's seduction of a nun.
2. It causes anger. An excess of the choleric humor was believed to provoke anger.

Be patient, tomorrow't shall be mended,
And for this night we'll fast for company.°   *together*
Come, I will bring thee to thy bridal chamber.   *Exeunt*

Enter servants severally

NATHANIEL   Peter, didst ever see the like?

160   PETER   He kills her in her own humour.[3]

Enter CURTIS, *a servant*

GRUMIO   Where is he?

CURTIS   In her chamber,
Making a sermon of continency° to her,   *on self-control*
And rails, and swears, and rates,° that she, poor soul,   *scolds*

165   Knows not which way to stand, to look, to speak,
And sits as one new risen from a dream.
Away, away, for he is coming hither.   [*Exeunt*]

Enter PETRUCCIO

PETRUCCIO   Thus have I politicly° begun my reign,   *cunningly*
And 'tis my hope to end successfully.

170   My falcon[4] now is sharp° and passing° empty,   *hungry / extremely*
And till she stoop[5] she must not be full-gorged,°   *fully fed*
For then she never looks upon her lure.°   *falconer's bait*
Another way I have to man my haggard,°   *tame my female hawk*
To make her come and know her keeper's call—

175   That is, to watch her° as we watch these kites°   *keep her awake / hawks*
That bate and beat,[6] and will not be obedient.
She ate no meat today, nor none shall eat.
Last night she slept not, nor tonight she shall not.
As with the meat, some undeservèd fault

180   I'll find about the making of the bed,
And here I'll fling the pillow, there the bolster,
This way the coverlet, another way the sheets,
Ay, and amid this hurly I intend°   *will pretend*
That all is done in reverent care of her,

185   And in conclusion she shall watch° all night,   *stay awake*
And if she chance to nod I'll rail and brawl
And with the clamour keep her still awake.
This is a way to kill a wife with kindness,
And thus I'll curb her mad and headstrong humour.

190   He that knows better how to tame a shrew,
Now let him speak. 'Tis charity to show.°   *Exit*   (*his methods*)

4.2

Enter TRANIO [*as Lucentio,*] *and* HORTENSIO [*as Licio*]

TRANIO   Is't possible, friend Licio, that Mistress Bianca
Doth fancy any other but Lucentio?
I tell you, sir, she bears me fair in hand.°   *leads me on*

HORTENSIO   Sir, to satisfy you in what I have said,

5   Stand by, and mark the manner of his teaching.
[*They stand aside.*]

Enter BIANCA [*and* LUCENTIO *as Cambio*]

LUCENTIO   Now, mistress, profit you in what you read?

BIANCA   What, master, read you? First resolve° me that.   *answer*

---

3. He subdues her choleric humor by outdoing her in bad temper.
4. In what follows, Petruccio likens his methods of disciplining Katherine to the training of a wild hawk.
5. Fly to the bait; submit to my authority.
6. That flutter and flap their wings (instead of settling on the falconer's fist).
4.2 Location: Padua, in front of Baptista's house.

LUCENTIO   I read that I profess,° *The Art to Love.*[1]   *what I practice*
BIANCA   And may you prove, sir, master of your art.
10   LUCENTIO   While you, sweet dear, prove mistress of my heart.
     [*They stand aside*]
HORTENSIO   Quick proceeders,[2] marry! Now tell me, I pray,
     You that durst swear that your mistress Bianca
     Loved none in the world so well as Lucentio.
TRANIO   O despiteful° love, unconstant womankind!   *cruel*
15   I tell thee, Licio, this is wonderful.°   *astonishing*
HORTENSIO   Mistake no more, I am not Licio,
     Nor a musician as I seem to be,
     But one that scorn to live in this disguise
     For such a one° as leaves a gentleman   *(Bianca)*
20   And makes a god of such a cullion.°   *base fellow*
     Know, sir, that I am called Hortensio.
TRANIO   Signor Hortensio, I have often heard
     Of your entire° affection to Bianca,   *sincere*
     And since mine eyes are witness of her lightness°   *sexual infidelity*
25   I will with you, if you be so contented,
     Forswear Bianca and her love for ever.
HORTENSIO   See how they kiss and court. Signor Lucentio,
     Here is my hand, and here I firmly vow
     Never to woo her more, but do forswear her
30   As one unworthy all the former favours
     That I have fondly° flattered her withal.   *foolishly*
TRANIO   And here I take the like unfeignèd oath
     Never to marry with her, though she would entreat.
     Fie on her, see how beastly° she doth court him!   *lewdly*
35   HORTENSIO   Would all the world but he had quite forsworn.[3]
     For me, that I may surely keep mine oath
     I will be married to a wealthy widow
     Ere three days pass, which hath as long loved me
     As I have loved this proud disdainful haggard.°   *intractable woman; hawk*
40   And so farewell, Signor Lucentio.
     Kindness in women, not their beauteous looks,
     Shall win my love; and so I take my leave,
     In resolution as I swore before.   [*Exit*]
TRANIO   Mistress Bianca, bless you with such grace
45   As 'longeth° to a lover's blessèd case.°   *belongs / state*
     Nay, I have ta'en you napping, gentle love,
     And have forsworn you with Hortensio.
BIANCA   Tranio, you jest. But have you both forsworn me?
TRANIO   Mistress, we have.
LUCENTIO   Then we are rid of Licio.
50   TRANIO   I'faith, he'll have a lusty° widow now,   *lively; lustful*
     That shall be wooed and wedded in a day.
BIANCA   God give him joy.
TRANIO   Ay, and he'll tame her.
BIANCA   He says so, Tranio.
55   TRANIO   Faith, he is gone unto the taming-school.

---

1. Ovid's *Ars Amatoria*, in which the poet calls himself the "Professor of Love" and treats erotic love as a science.
2. Taking up the allusion to a university degree implicit in Bianca's "master of your art," Hortensio puns on

"proceeding" from a bachelor's to a master's degree.
3. I wish that everyone but Cambio had given her over (so that she will be left an old maid as she deserves; Hortensio apparently assumes that Bianca would never marry a poor musician).

BIANCA   The taming-school—what, is there such a place?

TRANIO   Ay, mistress, and Petruccio is the master,
That teacheth tricks eleven-and-twenty long[4]
To tame a shrew and charm her chattering tongue.[5]

Enter BIONDELLO

60 BIONDELLO   O, master, master, I have watched so long
That I am dog-weary, but at last I spied
An ancient angel[6] coming down the hill
Will serve the turn.

TRANIO   What is he, Biondello?

BIONDELLO   Master, a marcantant[7] or a pedant,°   *schoolmaster*
65 I know not what, but formal in apparel,
In gait and countenance surely like a father.

LUCENTIO   And what of him, Tranio?

TRANIO   If he be credulous and trust my tale,
I'll make him glad to seem° Vincentio   *pretend to be*
70 And give assurance to Baptista Minola
As if he were the right Vincentio.
Take in your love, and then let me alone.

[*Exeunt* LUCENTIO *and* BIANCA]

Enter a PEDANT[8]

PEDANT   God save you, sir.

TRANIO   And you, sir. You are welcome.
Travel you farre on, or are you at the farthest?

75 PEDANT   Sir, at the farthest for a week or two,
But then up farther and as far as Rome,
And so to Tripoli,[9] if God lend me life.

TRANIO   What countryman, I pray?

PEDANT   Of Mantua.

TRANIO   Of Mantua, sir? Marry, God forbid,
80 And come to Padua careless of your life!

PEDANT   My life, sir? How, I pray? For that goes hard.°   *is difficult to deal with*

TRANIO   'Tis death for anyone in Mantua
To come to Padua. Know you not the cause?
Your ships are stayed° at Venice, and the Duke,   *detained*
85 For private quarrel 'twixt your Duke and him,
Hath published and proclaimed it openly.
'Tis marvel, but that you are but newly come,
You might have heard it else proclaimed about.[1]

PEDANT   Alas, sir, it is worse for me than so,°   *my plight is even worse*
90 For I have bills for money by exchange[2]
From Florence, and must here deliver them.

TRANIO   Well, sir, to do you courtesy
This will I do, and this I will advise you.
First tell me, have you ever been at Pisa?

95 PEDANT   Ay, sir, in Pisa have I often been,

---

4. Who teaches tricks that are exactly appropriate or of just the right number. An allusion to the card game one-and-thirty, in which the object is to accumulate exactly thirty-one points. See note to 1.2.31.
5. Tranio's apparent knowledge of Hortensio's plans is puzzling and may be an indication that some text has been lost.
6. Worthy old man. Punning on "angel" as meaning both "valuable gold coin" and "divine messenger." The coin had a picture of the archangel Michael on it.

7. Biondello's version of *mercatante*, the Italian word for "merchant."
8. Because this character is said (at line 90) to have "bills for money," some editors have designated him a "merchant" like the corresponding character in George Gascoigne's comedy *Supposes* (1566).
9. The north African trading center or the city in Syria.
1. *but that . . . about*: if you hadn't just arrived, you would have heard it announced everywhere.
2. Promissory notes that the bearer could exchange for cash.

Pisa renownèd for grave citizens.

TRANIO Among them know you one Vincentio?

PEDANT I know him not, but I have heard of him,
A merchant of incomparable wealth.

100 TRANIO He is my father, sir, and sooth to say,
In count'nance somewhat doth resemble you.

BIONDELLO [aside] As much as an apple doth an oyster, and all
one.°   but no matter

TRANIO To save your life in this extremity

105 This favour will I do you for his sake,
And think it not the worst of all your fortunes
That you are like to Sir Vincentio.
His name and credit° shall you undertake,°   social status / assume
And in my house you shall be friendly lodged.

110 Look that you take upon you° as you should.   act your part
You understand me, sir? So shall you stay
Till you have done your business in the city.
If this be courtesy, sir, accept of it.

PEDANT O sir, I do, and will repute° you ever   consider

115 The patron of my life and liberty.

TRANIO Then go with me to make the matter good.
This, by the way, I let you understand—
My father is here looked for every day
To pass assurance° of a dower in marriage   convey legal guarantee

120 'Twixt me and one Baptista's daughter here.
In all these circumstances I'll instruct you.
Go with me to clothe you as becomes you.   *Exeunt*

4.3

Enter KATHERINE *and* GRUMIO

GRUMIO No, no, forsooth. I dare not, for my life.

KATHERINE The more my wrong, the more his spite appears.[1]
What, did he marry me to famish me?
Beggars that come unto my father's door

5 Upon entreaty have a present° alms,   immediate
If not, elsewhere they meet with charity.
But I, who never knew how to entreat,
Nor never needed that I should entreat,
Am starved for meat, giddy for lack of sleep,

10 With oaths kept waking and with brawling fed,
And that which spites° me more than all these wants,   vexes
He does it under name of perfect love,
As who should say° if I should sleep or eat   As if to say
'Twere deadly sickness, or else present° death.   instant

15 I prithee, go and get me some repast.
I care not what, so it be wholesome food.

GRUMIO What say you to a neat's foot?°   ox foot or calf's foot

KATHERINE 'Tis passing good. I prithee, let me have it.

GRUMIO I fear it is too choleric° a meat.   conducive to anger

20 How say you to a fat tripe finely broiled?

KATHERINE I like it well. Good Grumio, fetch it me.

GRUMIO I cannot tell, I fear 'tis choleric.

4.3 Location: Petruccio's country house.
1. The more injustice I suffer, the more he seems to want me to suffer.

What say you to a piece of beef, and mustard?

KATHERINE   A dish that I do love to feed upon.

25   GRUMIO   Ay, but the mustard is too hot a little.

KATHERINE   Why then, the beef, and let the mustard rest.

GRUMIO   Nay, then I will not. You shall have the mustard,
Or else you get no beef of Grumio.

KATHERINE   Then both, or one, or anything thou wilt.

30   GRUMIO   Why then, the mustard without the beef.

KATHERINE   Go, get thee gone, thou false, deluding slave,
    Beats him
That feed'st me with the very name° of meat.   *only the name*
Sorrow on thee and all the pack of you,
That triumph thus upon my misery.
35   Go, get thee gone, I say.

    Enter PETRUCCIO *and* HORTENSIO, *with meat*

PETRUCCIO   How fares my Kate? What, sweeting,° all amort?°   *sweetheart / dejected*

HORTENSIO   Mistress, what cheer?

KATHERINE   Faith, as cold as can be.

PETRUCCIO   Pluck up thy spirits, look cheerfully upon me.
Here, love, thou seest how diligent I am
40   To dress° thy meat myself and bring it thee.   *prepare*
I am sure, sweet Kate, this kindness merits thanks.
What, not a word? Nay then, thou lov'st it not,
And all my pains is sorted to no proof.°   *are to no purpose*
Here, take away this dish.

KATHERINE   I pray you, let it stand.

45   PETRUCCIO   The poorest service is repaid with thanks,
And so shall mine before you touch the meat.

KATHERINE   I thank you, sir.

HORTENSIO   Signor Petruccio, fie, you are to blame.
Come, Mistress Kate, I'll bear you company.

50   PETRUCCIO [*aside*]   Eat it up all, Hortensio, if thou lov'st me.
[*To* KATHERINE] Much good do it unto thy gentle heart.
Kate, eat apace; and now, my honey love,
Will we return unto thy father's house,
And revel it as bravely as the best,
55   With silken coats, and caps, and golden rings,
With ruffs, and cuffs, and farthingales,[2] and things,
With scarves, and fans, and double change of bravery,°   *finery*
With amber bracelets, beads, and all this knavery.°   *tricks of dress*
What, hast thou dined? The tailor stays thy leisure,
60   To deck thy body with his ruffling° treasure.   *ornate (with ruffles)*

    Enter TAILOR [*with a gown*]

Come, tailor, let us see these ornaments.
Lay forth the gown.

    Enter HABERDASHER [*with a cap*]

                What news with you, sir?

HABERDASHER   Here is the cap your worship did bespeak.

PETRUCCIO   Why, this was moulded on a porringer°—   *porridge bowl*
65   A velvet dish.[3] Fie, fie, 'tis lewd and filthy.
Why, 'tis a cockle° or a walnut-shell,   *mollusk shell*

---

2. *ruffs*: fashionable high collars made of starched linen or lace. *cuffs*: bands, often made of lace, sewn onto sleeves for ornament. *farthingales*: hooped petticoats.

3. It's merely a dish made of velvet. Velvet caps were often associated with prostitutes.

A knack,° a toy, a trick,° a baby's cap.   *knickknack / trifle*
Away with it! Come, let me have a bigger.
KATHERINE I'll have no bigger. This doth fit the time,°   *suit current fashion*
70   And gentlewomen wear such caps as these.
PETRUCCIO When you are gentle you shall have one, too,
And not till then.
HORTENSIO [*aside*] That will not be in haste.
KATHERINE Why, sir, I trust I may have leave to speak,
And speak I will. I am no child, no babe.
75   Your betters have endured me say my mind,
And if you cannot, best you stop your ears.
My tongue will tell the anger of my heart,
Or else my heart concealing it will break,
And rather than it shall I will be free
80   Even to the uttermost as I please in words.
PETRUCCIO Why, thou sayst true. It is a paltry cap,
A custard-coffin,⁴ a bauble, a silken pie.
I love thee well in that thou lik'st it not.
KATHERINE Love me or love me not, I like the cap
85   And it I will have, or I will have none.   [*Exit* HABERDASHER]
PETRUCCIO Thy gown? Why, ay. Come, tailor, let us see't.
O mercy, God, what masquing stuff⁵ is here?
What's this—a sleeve? 'Tis like a demi-cannon.°   *large cannon*
What, up and down carved like an apple-tart?⁶
90   Here's snip, and nip, and cut, and slish and slash,
Like to a scissor in a barber's shop.
Why, what i'° devil's name, tailor, call'st thou this?   *in the*
HORTENSIO [*aside*] I see she's like° to have nor cap nor gown.   *likely*
TAILOR You bid me make it orderly and well,
95   According to the fashion and the time.
PETRUCCIO Marry, and did,° but if you be remembered   *Indeed I did*
I did not bid you mar it to the time.
Go hop me⁷ over every kennel° home,   *gutter*
For you shall hop without my custom,° sir.   *patronage; business*
100   I'll none of it. Hence, make your best of it.
KATHERINE I never saw a better fashioned gown,
More quaint,° more pleasing, nor more commendable.   *elegant*
Belike° you mean to make a puppet of me.   *It seems*
PETRUCCIO Why true, he means to make a puppet of thee.
105 TAILOR She says your worship means to make a puppet of her.
PETRUCCIO O monstrous arrogance! Thou liest, thou thread,
    thou thimble,
Thou yard, three-quarters, half-yard, quarter, nail,⁸
Thou flea, thou nit,° thou winter-cricket, thou.   *egg of a louse*
Braved° in mine own house with° a skein of thread!   *Defied; adorned / by*
110 Away, thou rag, thou quantity,° thou remnant,   *fragment*
Or I shall so bemete° thee with thy yard°   *measure; beat / ruler*
As thou shalt think on prating⁹ whilst thou liv'st.
I tell thee, I, that thou hast marred her gown.

4. Pastry crust around a custard or open pie (perhaps with a pun on "costard," slang for "head").
5. Extravagant clothing suitable for theatrical masques.
6. With slits like the top of an apple pie. The gown's sleeves may have been designed so as to reveal fabric of another color underneath.
7. You can go hopping.
8. Measure of cloth, a sixteenth of a yard; Petruccio is literally belittling the tailor. "Yard" is slang for "penis."
9. You will think twice before you talk idly, with a pun on "prat" as slang for "beat on the buttocks."

TAILOR   Your worship is deceived. The gown is made
115   Just as my master had direction.
   Grumio gave order how it should be done.
GRUMIO   I gave him no order, I gave him the stuff.°   *material*
TAILOR   But how did you desire it should be made?
GRUMIO   Marry, sir, with needle and thread.
120   TAILOR   But did you not request to have it cut?
GRUMIO   Thou hast faced° many things.   *trimmed; defied*
TAILOR   I have.
GRUMIO   Face not me. Thou hast braved° many men. Brave°   *dressed finely / Defy*
   not me. I will neither be faced nor braved. I say unto thee
125   I bid thy master cut out the gown, but I did not bid him cut it
   to pieces. *Ergo°* thou liest.   *Therefore*
TAILOR   [*showing a paper*]   Why, here is the note of the fashion,
   to testify.
PETRUCCIO   Read it.
130   GRUMIO   The note lies in's throat if he° say I said so.   *it*
TAILOR   [*reads*]   'Imprimis,° a loose-bodied gown.'[1]   *First*
GRUMIO   Master, if ever I said loose-bodied gown, sew me in the
   skirts of it and beat me to death with a bottom° of brown   *spool*
   thread. I said a gown.
135   PETRUCCIO   Proceed.
TAILOR   [*reads*]   'With a small compassed° cape.'   *flared*
GRUMIO   I confess the cape.
TAILOR   [*reads*]   'With a trunk° sleeve.'   *wide*
GRUMIO   I confess two sleeves.
140   TAILOR   [*reads*]   'The sleeves curiously° cut.'   *carefully; elaborately*
PETRUCCIO   Ay, there's the villany.
GRUMIO   Error i'th' bill,° sir, error i'th' bill. I commanded the   *order (for the dress)*
   sleeves should be cut out and sewed up again, and that I'll
   prove upon thee though thy little finger be armed in a thimble.
145   TAILOR   This is true that I say. An° I had thee in place where,°   *If / in a suitable place*
   thou shouldst know it.
GRUMIO   I am for thee straight. Take thou the bill,[2] give me thy
   mete-yard,° and spare not me.   *yardstick*
HORTENSIO   Godamercy, Grumio, then he shall have no odds.°   *advantage*
150   PETRUCCIO   Well, sir, in brief, the gown is not for me.
GRUMIO   You are i'th' right, sir. 'Tis for my mistress.
PETRUCCIO   [*to the* TAILOR]   Go, take it up unto° thy master's use.   *take it away for*
GRUMIO   [*to the* TAILOR]   Villain, not for thy life. Take up my
   mistress' gown for thy master's use!°   *sexual purposes*
155   PETRUCCIO   Why, sir, what's your conceit° in that?   *meaning*
GRUMIO   O, sir, the conceit is deeper than you think for. 'Take
   up my mistress' gown to his master's use'—O fie, fie, fie!
PETRUCCIO   [*aside*]   Hortensio, say thou wilt see the tailor paid.
   [*To the* TAILOR] Go, take it hence. Be gone, and say no more.
HORTENSIO   [*aside to the* TAILOR]   Tailor, I'll pay thee for thy
160   gown tomorrow.
   Take no unkindness of his hasty words.
   Away, I say. Commend me to thy master.   *Exit* TAILOR
PETRUCCIO   Well, come, my Kate. We will unto your father's
   Even in these honest, mean habiliments.

---

1. A loose-fitting dress. In the next line, Grumio takes this   2. Grumio puns on "bill" as also meaning a "weapon" or
to mean a dress suitable for a wanton, or loose, woman.   "halberd," a staff with a blade attached.

165   Our purses shall be proud, our garments poor,
      For 'tis the mind that makes the body rich,
      And as the sun breaks through the darkest clouds,
      So honour peereth° in the meanest habit.   *can be seen*
      What, is the jay more precious than the lark
170   Because his feathers are more beautiful?
      Or is the adder better than the eel
      Because his painted skin contents the eye?
      O no, good Kate, neither art thou the worse
      For this poor furniture° and mean array.   *clothing; attire*
175   If thou account'st it shame, lay it on me,°   *blame me*
      And therefore frolic; we will hence forthwith
      To feast and sport us° at thy father's house.   *amuse ourselves*
      Go call my men, and let us straight to him,
      And bring our horses unto Long Lane end.
180   There will we mount, and thither walk on foot.
      Let's see, I think 'tis now some seven o'clock,
      And well we may come there by dinner-time.°   *about noon*
    KATHERINE   I dare assure you, sir, 'tis almost two,
      And 'twill be supper-time° ere you come there.   *about 6 P.M.*
185   PETRUCCIO   It shall be seven ere I go to horse.
      Look what I speak, or do, or think to do,
      You are still crossing° it. Sirs, let't alone.   *contradicting*
      I will not go today, and ere I do
      It shall be what o'clock I say it is.
190   HORTENSIO [*aside*]   Why, so this gallant will command the sun.

                                                [*Exeunt*]

4.4

Enter TRANIO [*as Lucentio,*] *and the* PEDANT *dressed*
like Vincentio, booted and bare-headed[1]

    TRANIO   Sir, this is the house. Please it you that I call?
    PEDANT   Ay, what else. And but[2] I be deceived,
      Signor Baptista may remember me
      Near twenty years ago in Genoa—
5   TRANIO   Where we were lodgers at the Pegasus.[3]—
      'Tis well, and hold your own° in any case   *keep to your role*
      With such austerity as 'longeth° to a father.   *belongs*

         Enter BIONDELLO

    PEDANT   I warrant you. But sir, here comes your boy.
      'Twere good he were schooled.
10   TRANIO   Fear you not him. Sirrah Biondello,
      Now do your duty throughly,° I advise you.   *thoroughly*
      Imagine 'twere the right Vincentio.
    BIONDELLO   Tut, fear not me.
    TRANIO   But hast thou done thy errand to Baptista?
15   BIONDELLO   I told him that your father was at Venice
      And that you looked for him this day in Padua.

4.4 Location: Padua. In front of Baptista's house.
1. In F, the Pedant is mistakenly given a second entry
at line 18, where he is described as "booted and bare-
headed," indicating that he is dressed for travel but has
taken off his hat, perhaps in deference to Baptista,
whom he is about to meet. The present stage direction
conflates F's two stage directions regarding the Pedant's
entrance.
2. Unless (the Pedant is rehearsing his speech to
Baptista).
3. Common name for an inn (marked by a sign of the
flying horse of classical mythology).

TRANIO [*giving money*] Thou'rt a tall° fellow. Hold thee° that   *worthy / Take*
      to° drink.   *for*

     Here comes Baptista. Set your countenance, sir.

          Enter BAPTISTA, *and* LUCENTIO [*as Cambio*]

TRANIO   Signor Baptista, you are happily met.

20   [*To the* PEDANT] Sir, this is the gentleman I told you of.
     I pray you stand good father to me now.
     Give me Bianca for my patrimony.

PEDANT   Soft,° son. [*To* BAPTISTA] Sir, by your leave, having   *Just a moment*
      come to Padua
     To gather in some debts, my son Lucentio

25   Made me acquainted with a weighty cause
     Of love between your daughter and himself,
     And for the good report I hear of you,
     And for the love he beareth to your daughter,
     And she to him, to stay him° not too long   *keep him waiting*

30   I am content in a good father's care[4]
     To have him matched, and if you please to like
     No worse than I, upon some agreement
     Me shall you find ready and willing
     With one consent to have her so bestowed,

35   For curious° I cannot be with you,   *overly particular*
     Signor Baptista, of whom I hear so well.

BAPTISTA   Sir, pardon me in what I have to say.
     Your plainness and your shortness please me well.
     Right true it is your son Lucentio here

40   Doth love my daughter, and she loveth him,
     Or both dissemble deeply their affections.
     And therefore if you say no more than this,
     That like a father you will deal with him
     And pass° my daughter a sufficient dower,   *grant*

45   The match is made, and all is done.
     Your son shall have my daughter with consent.

TRANIO   I thank you, sir. Where then do you know best
     We be affied,° and such assurance ta'en   *betrothed*
     As shall with either part's agreement stand?[5]

50 BAPTISTA   Not in my house, Lucentio, for you know
     Pitchers have ears,[6] and I have many servants.
     Besides, old Gremio is heark'ning still,°   *always listening*
     And happily° we might be interrupted.   *perhaps*

TRANIO   Then at my lodging, an it like you.°   *if it please you*

55   There doth my father lie,° and there this night   *lodge*
     We'll pass° the business privately and well.   *settle*
     Send for your daughter by your servant here.
     My boy shall fetch the scrivener° presently.   *scribe; notary*
     The worst is this, that at so slender warning

60   You are like to have a thin and slender pittance.°   *scanty meal*

BAPTISTA   It likes me well. Cambio, hie° you home   *hurry*
     And bid Bianca make her ready straight,
     And if you will, tell what hath happened—
     Lucentio's father is arrived in Padua—

---

4. Content with the care that should be shown by a   6. Proverbial for "Someone may be eavesdropping."
good father.   The handles of a pitcher are its "ears."
5. As shall confirm the agreements of both parties.

65 And how she's like to be Lucentio's wife.   [*Exit* LUCENTIO][7]
BIONDELLO   I pray the gods she may with all my heart.
TRANIO   Dally not with the gods, but get thee gone.
        Exit [BIONDELLO][8]
    Signor Baptista, shall I lead the way?
    Welcome. One mess° is like to be your cheer.°   *dish / entertainment*
70 Come, sir, we will better it in Pisa.
BAPTISTA   I follow you.   *Exeunt*

4.5

Enter LUCENTIO *and* BIONDELLO
BIONDELLO   Cambio.
LUCENTIO   What sayst thou, Biondello?
BIONDELLO   You saw my master wink and laugh upon you?
LUCENTIO   Biondello, what of that?
5 BIONDELLO   Faith, nothing, but he's left me here behind to
    expound the meaning or moral of his signs and tokens.
LUCENTIO   I pray thee, moralize° them.   *interpret*
BIONDELLO   Then thus: Baptista is safe, talking with the deceiv-
    ing father of a deceitful son.
10 LUCENTIO   And what of him?
BIONDELLO   His daughter is to be brought by you to the supper.
LUCENTIO   And then?
BIONDELLO   The old priest at Saint Luke's church is at your
    command at all hours.
15 LUCENTIO   And what of all this?
BIONDELLO   I cannot tell, except they are busied about a coun-
    terfeit assurance.° Take you assurance[1] of her *cum privilegio*   *betrothal agreement*
    ad imprimendum solum[2]—to th' church take the priest, clerk,
    and some sufficient honest witnesses.
20 If this be not that you look for, I have no more to say,
    But bid Bianca farewell for ever and a day.
LUCENTIO   Hear'st thou, Biondello?
BIONDELLO   I cannot tarry, I knew a wench married in an after-
    noon as she went to the garden for parsley to stuff a rabbit,
25 and so may you, sir, and so adieu, sir. My master hath
    appointed me to go to Saint Luke's to bid the priest be ready
    t'attend against° you come with your appendix.[3]   *Exit*   *by the time*
LUCENTIO   I may and will, if she be so contented.
    She will be pleased, then wherefore should I doubt?
30 Hap what hap may, I'll roundly go about her.[4]
    It shall go hard° if Cambio go without her.   *Exit*[5]   *be unfortunate*

---

7. F does not mark an exit for Lucentio/Cambio here, but it makes sense that he would follow Baptista's order. If Lucentio exits here and Biondello at line 66 as in F, or at line 67 as in this text, then their reentry a few lines later can mark a new scene (see Textual Note). Some editors assume Biondello and perhaps Lucentio never leave the stage since Biondello says (at 4.5.5–6) that he has been left behind by Tranio to explain things to Lucentio. In that case, no scene break would be introduced after Baptista exits.
8. F here has a mysterious stage direction: "Enter Peter." Some editors have argued that this is the name of an actor inadvertently introduced into the stage directions. Others assume it is the name of one of Lucentio's servants, who enters to tell the disguised Tranio and Baptista that their meal is ready; this possibility is not

entirely satisfactory, especially since Baptista and Tranio still have to *proceed* to Lucentio's house for their meal. Perhaps something has been lost or garbled in this portion of the scene.
4.5 Location: Scene continues.
1. Make yourself sure.
2. With the exclusive right to print (a Latin phrase used by printers on the title pages of their books). Biondello urges Lucentio to confirm his "exclusive right" to Bianca and may be punning on "print" as meaning "to father a child."
3. Appendage (the bride).
4. Come what may, I'll pursue her eagerly.
5. At the corresponding point in *A Shrew*, Sly, still on-stage, comments on the action. See Additional Passages B.

4.6

Enter PETRUCCIO, KATHERINE, HORTENSIO *[and servants]*

PETRUCCIO   Come on, i' God's name. Once more toward our father's.
Good Lord, how bright and goodly shines the moon!

KATHERINE   The moon?—the sun. It is not moonlight now.

PETRUCCIO   I say it is the moon that shines so bright.

5 KATHERINE   I know it is the sun that shines so bright.

PETRUCCIO   Now, by my mother's son—and that's myself—
It shall be moon, or star, or what I list°   please
Or ere° I journey to your father's house.   Before
Go on, and fetch our horses back again.

10 Evermore crossed° and crossed, nothing but crossed.   contradicted

HORTENSIO [TO KATHERINE]   Say as he says or we shall never go.

KATHERINE   Forward, I pray, since we have come so far,
And be it moon or sun or what you please,
And if you please to call it a rush-candle[1]

15 Henceforth I vow it shall be so for me.

PETRUCCIO   I say it is the moon.

KATHERINE   I know it is the moon.

PETRUCCIO   Nay then you lie, it is the blessèd sun.

KATHERINE   Then God be blessed, it is the blessèd sun,

20 But sun it is not when you say it is not,
And the moon changes even as your mind.[2]
What you will have it named, even that it is,
And so it shall be still for Katherine.

HORTENSIO   Petruccio, go thy ways.° The field is won.   do as you wish

25 PETRUCCIO   Well, forward, forward. Thus the bowl should run,
And not unluckily against the bias.[3]
But soft, company is coming here.

Enter [old] VINCENTIO

[*To* VINCENTIO] Good morrow, gentle mistress, where away?
Tell me, sweet Kate, and tell me truly too,

30 Hast thou beheld a fresher gentlewoman,
Such war of white and red within her cheeks?
What stars do spangle heaven with such beauty
As those two eyes become that heavenly face?
Fair lovely maid, once more good day to thee.

35 Sweet Kate, embrace her for her beauty's sake.

HORTENSIO   A° will make the man mad to make the woman of   He
him.°   call him a woman

KATHERINE   Young budding virgin, fair, and fresh, and sweet,
Whither away, or where is thy abode?

40 Happy the parents of so fair a child,
Happier the man whom° favourable stars   to whom
Allots thee for his lovely bedfellow.

PETRUCCIO   Why, how now, Kate, I hope thou art not mad.
This is a man, old, wrinkled, faded, withered,

45 And not a maiden as thou sayst he is.

KATHERINE   Pardon, old father, my mistaking eyes

4.6 Location: A road somewhere between Petruccio's
house and Padua.
1. Candle made from rush dripped in grease, thus giv-
ing poor light.
2. Implying that Petruccio is mad as well as fickle.

Lunatics and women were imagined to be governed by
the moon.
3. A metaphor from the game of bowls in which the
ball, or bowl, was weighted so that it ran along a "bias,"
or curving path.

That have been so bedazzled with the sun
That everything I look on seemeth green.°   *youthful*
Now I perceive thou art a reverend father.
50   Pardon, I pray thee, for my mad mistaking.
PETRUCCIO   Do, good old grandsire, and withal° make known   *in addition*
Which way thou travell'st. If along with us,
We shall be joyful of thy company.
VINCENTIO   Fair sir, and you, my merry mistress,
55   That with your strange encounter° much amazed me,   *greeting*
My name is called Vincentio, my dwelling Pisa,
And bound I am to Padua, there to visit
A son of mine which long I have not seen.
PETRUCCIO   What is his name?
VINCENTIO   Lucentio, gentle sir.
60   PETRUCCIO   Happily met, the happier for thy son.
And now by law as well as reverend age
I may entitle thee my loving father.
The sister to my wife, this gentlewoman,
Thy son by this hath married.[4] Wonder not,
65   Nor be not grieved. She is of good esteem,
Her dowry wealthy, and of worthy birth,
Beside, so qualified° as may beseem   *with such qualities*
The spouse of any noble gentleman.
Let me embrace with old Vincentio,
70   And wander we to see thy honest son,
Who will of thy arrival be full joyous.
      [*He embraces* VINCENTIO]
VINCENTIO   But is this true, or is it else your pleasure
Like pleasant travellers to break a jest°   *crack a joke*
Upon the company you overtake?
75   HORTENSIO   I do assure thee, father, so it is.
PETRUCCIO   Come, go along, and see the truth hereof,
For our first merriment hath made thee jealous.°   *suspicious*
              Exeunt [*all but* HORTENSIO]
HORTENSIO   Well, Petruccio, this has put me in heart.
Have to my widow, and if she be froward,°   *difficult*
80   Then hast thou taught Hortensio to be untoward.°   *Exit*   *unmannerly*

5.1

Enter BIONDELLO, LUCENTIO, *and* BIANCA. GREMIO
    is out before°   *Gremio enters first*
BIONDELLO   Softly and swiftly, sir, for the priest is ready.
LUCENTIO   I fly, Biondello; but they may chance to need thee at
   home, therefore leave us.
BIONDELLO   Nay, faith, I'll see the church a' your back[1] and then
5   come back to my master's as soon as I can.
          Exeunt [LUCENTIO, BIANCA, *and* BIONDELLO][2]
GREMIO   I marvel Cambio comes not all this while.

---

4. By now has married. It is unclear how Petruccio and
Hortensio know this, especially since Hortensio has
heard "Lucentio" (Tranio) forswear Bianca (in 4.2).
The inconsistency may suggest textual alteration in the
role of Hortensio.
5.1 Location: Padua, in front of Lucentio's house.
1. At your back. Probably, I'll see the church as you

leave it after the wedding.
2. In F, Lucentio and Bianca exit first (after line 3)
and Biondello presumably follows after line 5, though
no exit is explicitly marked for him. Gremio, onstage
before this trio, apparently does not see them stealing
away to the church.

Enter PETRUCCIO, KATHERINE, VINCENTIO, GRUMIO,
with attendants

PETRUCCIO   Sir, here's the door. This is Lucentio's house.
  My father's bears° more toward the market-place.   *lies*
  Thither must I, and here I leave you, sir.

10 VINCENTIO   You shall not choose but drink before you go.
  I think I shall command your welcome here,
  And by all likelihood some cheer is toward.°   *food is being prepared*
      [*He*] *knocks*

GREMIO   They're busy within. You were best knock louder.
      [VINCENTIO *knocks again. The*] PEDANT *looks out*
      of the window

PEDANT   What's he that knocks as he would beat down the gate?

15 VINCENTIO   Is Signor Lucentio within, sir?

PEDANT   He's within, sir, but not to be spoken withal.

VINCENTIO   What if a man bring him a hundred pound or two
  to make merry withal?

PEDANT   Keep your hundred pounds to yourself. He shall need
20   none so long as I live.

PETRUCCIO [*to* VINCENTIO]   Nay, I told you your son was well
  beloved in Padua. [*To the* PEDANT] Do you hear, sir, to leave
  frivolous circumstances,° I pray you tell Signor Lucentio that   *matters*
  his father is come from Pisa and is here at the door to speak
25   with him.

PEDANT   Thou liest. His father is come from Padua and here
  looking out at the window.

VINCENTIO   Art thou his father?

PEDANT   Ay, sir, so his mother says, if I may believe her.

30 PETRUCCIO [*to* VINCENTIO]   Why, how now, gentleman? Why,
  this is flat knavery, to take upon you another man's name.

PEDANT   Lay hands on the villain. I believe a° means to cozen°   *he / cheat*
  somebody in this city under my countenance.°   *name; person*

      Enter BIONDELLO

BIONDELLO [*aside*]   I have seen them in the church together,
35   God send 'em good shipping.° But who is here? Mine old mas-   *fair sailing*
  ter, Vincentio—now we are undone and brought to nothing.

VINCENTIO [*to* BIONDELLO]   Come hither, crackhemp.[3]

BIONDELLO   I hope I may choose, sir.

VINCENTIO   Come hither, you rogue. What, have you forgot me?

40 BIONDELLO   Forgot you? No, sir, I could not forget you, for
  I never saw you before in all my life.

VINCENTIO   What, you notorious villain, didst thou never see
  thy master's father, Vincentio?

BIONDELLO   What, my old worshipful old master? Yes, marry,
45   sir, see where he looks out of the window.

VINCENTIO   Is't so indeed?

      He beats BIONDELLO

BIONDELLO   Help, help, help! Here's a madman will murder me.
                                                        [*Exit*]

PEDANT   Help, son! Help, Signor Baptista!   [*Exit above*]

PETRUCCIO   Prithee, Kate, let's stand aside and see the end of
50   this controversy.
      [*They stand aside.*]

3. Rogue (deserving to stretch the hangman's hemp rope).

Enter PEDANT *with servants,* BAPTISTA, TRANIO [*as Lucentio*]

TRANIO [*to* VINCENTIO]   Sir, what are you that offer° to beat my   *presume*
    servant?

VINCENTIO   What am I, sir? Nay, what are you, sir? O immortal
    gods, O fine villain, a silken doublet, a velvet hose, a scarlet
55   cloak, and a copintank° hat—O, I am undone, I am undone!   *high-crowned*
    While I play the good husband at home, my son and my ser-
    vant spend all at the university.

TRANIO   How now, what's the matter?

BAPTISTA   What, is the man lunatic?

60 TRANIO   Sir, you seem a sober, ancient gentleman by your habit,
    but your words show you a madman. Why sir, what 'cerns° it   *concerns*
    you if I wear pearl and gold? I thank my good father, I am able
    to maintain it.

VINCENTIO   Thy father! O villain, he is a sailmaker in Bergamo.[4]

65 BAPTISTA   You mistake, sir, you mistake, sir. Pray what do you
    think is his name?

VINCENTIO   His name? As if I knew not his name—I have
    brought him up ever since he was three years old, and his
    name is Tranio.

70 PEDANT   Away, away, mad ass. His name is Lucentio, and he is
    mine only son, and heir to the lands of me, Signor Vincentio.

VINCENTIO   Lucentio? O, he hath murdered his master! Lay
    hold on him, I charge you, in the Duke's name. O my son, my
    son! Tell me, thou villain, where is my son Lucentio?

75 TRANIO   Call forth an officer.
      [*Enter an* OFFICER]
    Carry this mad knave to the jail. Father Baptista, I charge you
    see that he be forthcoming.°   *available when needed*

VINCENTIO   Carry me to the jail?

GREMIO   Stay, officer, he shall not go to prison.

80 BAPTISTA   Talk not, Signor Gremio. I say he shall go to prison.

GREMIO   Take heed, Signor Baptista, lest you be cony-catched°   *duped*
    in this business. I dare swear this is the right Vincentio.

PEDANT   Swear if thou dar'st.

GREMIO   Nay, I dare not swear it.

85 TRANIO   Then thou wert best say that I am not Lucentio.

GREMIO   Yes, I know thee to be Signor Lucentio.

BAPTISTA   Away with the dotard. To the jail with him.
    Enter BIONDELLO, LUCENTIO, *and* BIANCA

VINCENTIO   Thus strangers may be haled° and abused. O mon-   *dragged about*
    strous villain!

90 BIONDELLO   O, we are spoiled and—yonder he is. Deny him,
    forswear him, or else we are all undone.
    Exeunt BIONDELLO, TRANIO, *and* PEDANT, *as fast as may be*

LUCENTIO [*to* VINCENTIO]   Pardon, sweet father.
      [*He*] *kneels*

VINCENTIO   Lives my sweet son?

BIANCA [*to* BAPTISTA]   Pardon, dear father.

95 BAPTISTA   How hast thou offended? Where is Lucentio?

LUCENTIO   Here's Lucentio, right son to the right Vincentio,
    That have by marriage made thy daughter mine,

---

4. An Italian town associated with Harlequin, the witty, resourceful servant of the Italian commedia dell'arte.

While counterfeit supposes[5] bleared thine eyne.°   *deceived your eyes*
GREMIO   Here's packing° with a witness,[6] to deceive us all.   *plotting*
100 VINCENTIO   Where is that damnèd villain Tranio,
That faced and braved° me in this matter so?   *defied*
BAPTISTA   Why, tell me, is not this my Cambio?
BIANCA   Cambio is changed into Lucentio.
LUCENTIO   Love wrought these miracles. Bianca's love
105 Made me exchange my state° with Tranio   *social position*
While he did bear my countenance in the town,
And happily I have arrived at the last
Unto the wishèd haven of my bliss.
What Tranio did, myself enforced him to.
110 Then pardon him, sweet father, for my sake.
VINCENTIO   I'll slit the villain's nose that would have sent me to
the jail.
BAPTISTA   But do you hear, sir, have you married my daughter
without asking my good will?
115 VINCENTIO   Fear not, Baptista. We will content you. Go to, but
I will in to be revenged for this villainy.   *Exit*
BAPTISTA   And I to sound the depth° of this knavery.   *Exit*   *discover the extent*
LUCENTIO   Look not pale, Bianca. Thy father will not frown.
          Exeunt [LUCENTIO *and* BIANCA]
GREMIO   My cake is dough,[7] but I'll in among the rest, Out of
120 hope of all° but my share of the feast.   [*Exit*]   *With hope of nothing*
KATHERINE [*coming forward*]   Husband, let's follow to see the
end of this ado.
PETRUCCIO   First kiss me, Kate, and we will.
KATHERINE   What, in the midst of the street?
125 PETRUCCIO   What, art thou ashamed of me?
KATHERINE   No, sir, God forbid; but ashamed to kiss.
PETRUCCIO   Why then, let's home again. Come sirrah, let's away.
KATHERINE   Nay, I will give thee a kiss. Now pray thee love, stay.
    [*They kiss*]
PETRUCCIO   Is not this well? Come, my sweet Kate.
130 Better once than never, for never too late.[8]   *Exeunt*

5.2

Enter BAPTISTA, VINCENTIO, GREMIO, *the* PEDANT,
LUCENTIO *and* BIANCA, [PETRUCCIO, KATHERINE,
and HORTENSIO,] TRANIO, BIONDELLO, GRUMIO, *and*
[*the*] WIDOW, *the servingmen with* TRANIO *bringing
in a banquet*[1]

LUCENTIO   At last, though long,° our jarring notes agree,   *after a long time*
And time it is when raging war is done
To smile at scapes° and perils overblown.   *escapes*
My fair Bianca, bid my father welcome,
While I with selfsame kindness welcome thine.
5 Brother Petruccio, sister Katherina,
And thou, Hortensio, with thy loving widow,
Feast with the best, and welcome to my house.

---

5. False ideas. Possibly an illusion to Gascoigne's *Supposes* (1566), which was Shakespeare's main source for the Bianca and Lucentio plot.
6. With clear evidence; without any doubt.
7. Proverbial expression for a failed project.

8. Two proverbs combined: "Better late than never" and "It is never too late to mend."
5.2 Location: Lucentio's house in Padua.
1. Light meal of fruit, sweetmeats, and wine following the main meal.

My banquet is to close our stomachs up

10   After our great good cheer.° Pray you, sit down,   *feast; happiness*

For now we sit to chat as well as eat.

    [*They sit*]

PETRUCCIO   Nothing but sit, and sit, and eat, and eat.

BAPTISTA   Padua affords this kindness, son Petruccio.

PETRUCCIO   Padua affords nothing but what is kind.

15   HORTENSIO   For both our sakes I would that word were true.

PETRUCCIO   Now, for my life, Hortensio fears² his widow.

WIDOW   Then never trust me if I be afeard.°   *afraid*

PETRUCCIO   You are very sensible, and yet you miss my sense.

    I mean Hortensio is afeard of you.

20   WIDOW   He that is giddy thinks the world turns round.³

PETRUCCIO   Roundly° replied.   *Boldly*

KATHERINE   Mistress, how mean you that?

WIDOW   Thus I conceive by him.⁴

PETRUCCIO   Conceives° by me! How likes Hortensio that?   *Becomes pregnant*

25   HORTENSIO   My widow says thus she conceives her tale.⁵

PETRUCCIO   Very well mended. Kiss him for that, good widow.

KATHERINE   'He that is giddy thinks the world turns round'—

    I pray you tell me what you meant by that.

WIDOW   Your husband, being troubled with a shrew,

30   Measures my husband's sorrow by his woe.

    And now you know my meaning.

KATHERINE   A very mean meaning.

WIDOW   Right, I mean you.

KATHERINE   And I am mean indeed respecting you.⁶

PETRUCCIO   To her, Kate!

35   HORTENSIO   To her, widow!

PETRUCCIO   A hundred marks⁷ my Kate does put her down.°   *defeat her*

HORTENSIO   That's my office.⁸

PETRUCCIO   Spoke like an officer!⁹ Ha' to thee,° lad.   *Here's to you*

    [*He*] *drinks to* HORTENSIO

BAPTISTA   How likes Gremio these quick-witted folks?

40   GREMIO   Believe me, sir, they butt together¹ well.

BIANCA   Head and butt? An hasty-witted body

    Would say your head and butt were head and horn.²

VINCENTIO   Ay, mistress bride, hath that awakened you?

BIANCA   Ay, but not frighted me, therefore I'll sleep again.

45   PETRUCCIO   Nay, that you shall not. Since you have begun,

    Have at° you for a better jest or two.   *I shall come at*

BIANCA   Am I your bird? I mean to shift my bush,³

    And then pursue me as you draw your bow.

    You are welcome all.

    Exit BIANCA [*with* KATHERINE *and the* WIDOW]

---

2. Is afraid of. The widow takes it to mean "frightens."
3. That is, people judge everything by their own experience, implying that Petruccio is afraid of his wife.
4. Thus I understand him.
5. Thus she understands or intends her remark, with a pun on "tail" as meaning "genitalia."
6. I am moderate (like the mathematical "mean") compared with you; I demean myself in dealing with you.
7. A substantial wager, since 1 mark was equivalent to 13 shillings and 4 pence, or two-thirds of a pound. An unskilled laborer might earn £6 to £8 in a year.

8. That's my job, with a pun on "put her down" as meaning "force or lay her down in sexual intercourse."
9. Like one who knows his duty.
1. They thrust their heads or horns together, with a pun on "butt" as meaning "buttocks."
2. Would say your butting head was a cuckold's horned head.
3. Alluding to the Elizabethan sport of shooting sitting birds with a bow and arrow. There may also be a bawdy pun on "bush" as meaning "pubic area" and the target of Petruccio's (phallic) arrow.

50 PETRUCCIO   She hath prevented° me here, Signor Tranio.   *stopped; anticipated*
        This bird you aimed at, though you hit her not.
        Therefore a health to all that shot and missed.
    TRANIO   O sir, Lucentio slipped° me like his greyhound,   *unleashed*
        Which runs himself and catches for his master.
55 PETRUCCIO   A good swift° simile, but something currish.°   *witty/base; doglike*
    TRANIO   'Tis well, sir, that you hunted for yourself.
        'Tis thought your deer does hold you at a bay.⁴
    BAPTISTA   O, O, Petruccio, Tranio hits you now.
    LUCENTIO   I thank thee for that gird,° good Tranio.   *taunt*
60 HORTENSIO   Confess, confess, hath he not hit you here?
    PETRUCCIO   A° has a little galled° me, I confess,   *He/wounded*
        And as the jest did glance away from me,
        'Tis ten to one it maimed you two outright.
    BAPTISTA   Now in good sadness,° son Petruccio,   *in all seriousness*
65   I think thou hast the veriest shrew of all.
    PETRUCCIO   Well, I say no.—And therefore, Sir Assurance,
        Let's each one send unto° his wife,   *summon*
        And he whose wife is most obedient
        To come at first when he doth send for her
70   Shall win the wager which we will propose.
    HORTENSIO   Content.° What's the wager?   *Agreed*
    LUCENTIO   Twenty crowns.°   *coin worth 5 shillings*
    PETRUCCIO   Twenty crowns!
        I'll venture so much of° my hawk or hound,   *on*
75   But twenty times so much upon my wife.
    LUCENTIO   A hundred, then.
    HORTENSIO   Content.
    PETRUCCIO   A match,° 'tis done.   *Agreed*
    HORTENSIO   Who shall begin?
80 LUCENTIO   That will I.
        Go, Biondello, bid your mistress come to me.
    BIONDELLO   I go.   *Exit*
    BAPTISTA   Son, I'll be your half Bianca comes.⁵
    LUCENTIO   I'll have no halves, I'll bear it all myself.
            Enter BIONDELLO
        How now, what news?
85 BIONDELLO   Sir, my mistress sends you word
        That she is busy and she cannot come.
    PETRUCCIO   How? She's busy and she cannot come?
        Is that an answer?
    GREMIO   Ay, and a kind one, too.
        Pray God, sir, your wife send you not a worse.
    PETRUCCIO   I hope, better.
90 HORTENSIO   Sirrah Biondello,
        Go and entreat my wife to come to me forthwith.
            Exit BIONDELLO
    PETRUCCIO   O ho, 'entreat' her—nay, then she must needs come.
    HORTENSIO   I am afraid, sir, do what you can,
            Enter BIONDELLO
        Yours will not be entreated. Now, where's my wife?

---

4. Your deer turns on you and holds you at a distance.
Punning on "deer" and "dear."
5. I'll put up half the stake (and therefore collect half
of any winnings) in wagering that Bianca will come
first.

95   BIONDELLO   She says you have some goodly jest in hand.
     She will not come. She bids you come to her.
    PETRUCCIO   Worse and worse! She will not come—O vile,
     Intolerable, not to be endured!
     Sirrah Grumio, go to your mistress.
100   Say I command her come to me.   *Exit* [GRUMIO]
    HORTENSIO   I know her answer.
    PETRUCCIO   What?
    HORTENSIO   She will not.
    PETRUCCIO   The fouler fortune mine, and there an end.[6]

        Enter KATHERINE

    BAPTISTA   Now by my halidom,° here comes Katherina.   *by all I hold sacred*
    KATHERINE [*to* PETRUCCIO]   What is your will, sir, that you send
     for me?
105   PETRUCCIO   Where is your sister and Hortensio's wife?
    KATHERINE   They sit conferring by the parlour fire.
    PETRUCCIO   Go, fetch them hither. If they deny° to come,   *refuse*
     Swinge me them soundly forth[7] unto their husbands.
     Away, I say, and bring them hither straight.   [*Exit* KATHERINE]
110 LUCENTIO   Here is a wonder, if you talk of wonders.
    HORTENSIO   And so it is. I wonder what it bodes.
    PETRUCCIO   Marry, peace it bodes, and love, and quiet life;
     An aweful° rule and right supremacy,   *inspiring awe*
     And, to be short, what not° that's sweet and happy.   *everything*
115 BAPTISTA   Now fair befall thee, good Petruccio,
     The wager thou hast won, and I will add
     Unto their losses twenty thousand crowns,
     Another dowry to another daughter,
     For she is changed as she had never been.[8]
120 PETRUCCIO   Nay, I will win my wager better yet,
     And show more sign of her obedience,
     Her new-built virtue and obedience.

        Enter KATHERINE, BIANCA, *and* [*the*] WIDOW

     See where she comes, and brings your froward° wives   *willful*
     As prisoners to her womanly persuasion.
125   Katherine, that cap of yours becomes you not.
     Off with that bauble, throw it underfoot.

        [KATHERINE *throws down her cap*]

    WIDOW   Lord, let me never have a cause to sigh
     Till I be brought to such a silly pass.
    BIANCA   Fie, what a foolish duty call you this?
130 LUCENTIO   I would your duty were as foolish, too.
     The wisdom of your duty, fair Bianca,
     Hath cost me a hundred crowns since supper-time.
    BIANCA   The more fool you for laying° on my duty.   *gambling*
    PETRUCCIO   Katherine, I charge thee tell these headstrong women
135   What duty they do owe their lords and husbands.
    WIDOW   Come, come, you're mocking. We will have no telling.
    PETRUCCIO   Come on, I say, and first begin with her.
    WIDOW   She shall not.

---

6. Worse luck for me (if you're right), and that's that.
7. Beat them soundly for me, and bring them out.

8. As if she had never existed before; as if she had never been what she was before (a shrew).

PETRUCCIO   I say she shall: and first begin with her.
140   KATHERINE   Fie, fie, unknit that threat'ning, unkind brow,
    And dart not scornful glances from those eyes
    To wound thy lord, thy king, thy governor.
    It blots° thy beauty as frosts do bite the meads,°   *disfigures / meadows*
    Confounds thy fame° as whirlwinds shake fair buds,   *Ruins your reputation*
145   And in no sense is meet° or amiable.   *fitting*
    A woman moved° is like a fountain troubled,   *angry*
    Muddy, ill-seeming,° thick, bereft of beauty,   *ugly*
    And while it is so, none so dry or thirsty
    Will deign to sip or touch one drop of it.
150   Thy husband is thy lord, thy life, thy keeper,
    Thy head, thy sovereign, one that cares for thee,
    And for thy maintenance commits his body
    To painful labour both by sea and land,
    To watch the night in storms, the day in cold,
155   Whilst thou liest warm at home, secure and safe,
    And craves no other tribute at thy hands
    But love, fair looks, and true obedience,
    Too little payment for so great a debt.
    Such duty as the subject owes the prince,
160   Even such a woman oweth to her husband,
    And when she is froward, peevish,° sullen, sour,   *obstinate*
    And not obedient to his honest will,
    What is she but a foul contending rebel,
    And graceless traitor to her loving lord?
165   I am ashamed that women are so simple°   *foolish*
    To offer war where they should kneel for peace,
    Or seek for rule, supremacy, and sway
    When they are bound to serve, love, and obey.
    Why are our bodies soft, and weak, and smooth,
170   Unapt to° toil and trouble in the world,   *Unfitted for*
    But that our soft conditions° and our hearts   *dispositions*
    Should well agree with our external parts?
    Come, come, you froward and unable worms,°   *weak creatures*
    My mind hath been as big° as one of yours,   *proud*
175   My heart° as great, my reason haply more,   *spirit*
    To bandy word for word and frown for frown;
    But now I see our lances are but straws,
    Our strength as weak,° our weakness past compare,   *(as straws)*
    That seeming to be most which we indeed least are.
180   Then vail your stomachs, for it is no boot,⁹
    And place your hands below your husband's foot,
    In token of which duty, if he please,
    My hand is ready, may it do him ease.°   *give him comfort*
PETRUCCIO   Why, there's a wench! Come on, and kiss me, Kate.
    [*They kiss*]
185   LUCENTIO   Well, go thy ways, old lad, for thou shalt ha't.¹
    VINCENTIO   'Tis a good hearing° when children are toward.²   *thing to hear*
    LUCENTIO   But a harsh hearing when women are froward.
    PETRUCCIO   Come, Kate, we'll to bed.

---

9. Then lower your pride, for it is of no profit.   2. Obedient (the opposite of "froward," line 187).
1. You shall have the prize.

We three are married, but you two are sped.°   *defeated*
190   'Twas I won the wager, though [*to* LUCENTIO] you hit the white,³
And being a winner,° God give you good night.   *since I am a winner*
                    Exit PETRUCCIO [*with* KATHERINE]
HORTENSIO   Now go thy ways, thou hast tamed a curst shrew.
LUCENTIO   'Tis a wonder, by your leave, she will be tamed so.
                                        [*Exeunt*]⁴

Additional Passages

The Taming of a Shrew, printed in 1594 and believed to derive from Shakespeare's play as performed, contains episodes continuing and rounding off the Christopher Sly framework that may echo passages written by Shakespeare but not printed in the Folio. They are given below.

A. The following exchange occurs at a point for which there is no exact equivalent in Shakespeare's play. It could come before 2.1. The "two fine gentlewomen" to whom Sly refers in line 8 would thus be Katherine and Bianca. The "fool" of the first line is Sander, the counterpart of Grumio. "Sim" is short for Simon, the name of the Lord with whom Sly converses.

         Then SLY *speaks*
SLY   Sim, when will the fool come again?
LORD   He'll come again, my lord, anon.
SLY   Gi's° some more drink here. Zounds,¹ where's the tapster?°   *Give us / tavern keeper*
   Here, Sim, eat some of these things.
5   LORD   So I do, my lord.
SLY   Here, Sim, I drink to thee.
LORD   My lord, here comes the players again.
SLY   O brave, here's two fine gentlewomen.

B. This passage comes between 4.5 and 4.6. If it originates with Shakespeare, it implies that Grumio accompanies Petruccio at the beginning of 4.6. Ferando is the name of Petruccio's counterpart in *A Shrew*.

SLY   Sim, must they be married now?
LORD   Ay, my lord.
         Enter FERANDO *and* KATE *and* SANDER
SLY   Look, Sim, the fool is come again now.

C. Sly interrupts the action of the play-within-the-play. This could be inserted at 5.1.92 of Shakespeare's play, when Biondello, Tranio, and the Pedant all run away from the angry Vincentio. In *A Shrew*, the Duke (Vincentio's counterpart) has threatened to send to prison the people (Phylotus and Valeria) who have impersonated him and his son.

         PHYLOTUS *and* VALERIA *runs away*.
         Then SLY *speaks*
SLY   I say we'll have no sending to prison.
LORD   My lord, this is but the play. They're but in jest.
SLY   I tell thee, Sim, we'll have no sending to prison, that's flat.°   *final*

3. Hit the target (with a pun on "Bianca," which means "white" in Italian).
4. In *A Shrew*, the Christopher Sly story concludes the play. See Additional Passages E.
1. By God's wounds (a strong oath).

Why, Sim, am not I Don Christo Vary? Therefore I say they
5   shall not go to prison.
LORD   No more they shall not, my lord. They be run away.
SLY   Are they run away, Sim? That's well. Then gi's some more
    drink, and let them play again.
LORD   Here, my lord.
        SLY   *drinks and then falls asleep*

D. Sly is carried off. This could be placed between 5.1 and 5.2 in Shakespeare's play.

                                 Exeunt omnes°   *They all exit*
        SLY *sleeps*
LORD   Who's within there? Come hither, sirs, my lord's
    Asleep again. Go take him easily° up   *gently*
    And put him in his own apparel again,
    And lay him in the place where we did find him
5   Just underneath the alehouse side below.
    But see you wake him not in any case.
BOY   It shall be done, my lord. Come help to bear him hence.
                                              Exit

E. *The Taming of a Shrew* ends with the following episode.

        Then enter two bearing of SLY *in his own apparel again*
        and leaves him where they found him and then goes out.
        Then enter the TAPSTER
TAPSTER   Now that the darksome night is overpast
    And dawning day appears in crystal sky,
    Now must I haste abroad. But soft, who's this?
    What, Sly! O wondrous, hath he lain here all night?
5   I'll wake him. I think he's starved[1] by this,°   *this time*
    But° that his belly was so stuffed with ale.   *Except*
    What ho, Sly, awake, for shame!
SLY   Sim, gi's some more wine. What, 's all the players gone?
    Am not I a lord?
10   TAPSTER   A lord with a murrain![2] Come, art thou drunken still?
SLY   Who's this? Tapster? O Lord, sirrah, I have had
    The bravest° dream tonight that ever thou   *finest*
    Heardest in all thy life.
TAPSTER   Ay, marry, but you had best get you home,
15   For your wife will course° you for dreaming here tonight.   *trounce*
SLY   Will she? I know now how to tame a shrew.
    I dreamt upon it all this night till now,
    And thou hast waked me out of the best dream
    That ever I had in my life. But I'll to my
20   Wife presently and tame her too,
    An if° she anger me.   *An if = If*
TAPSTER   Nay, Tarry, Sly, for I'll go home with thee
    And hear the rest that thou hast dreamt tonight.
                                 Exeunt omnes

---

1. He'd have died from cold.
2. Pestilence or plague. "With a murrain" was often used as an oath or expression of anger. The tapster probably means "A plague on that" (Sly's dream of being a lord).

A Midsummer Night's Dream

Imagine an aristocratic wedding in a grand English country house. Imagine that after the solemnities and the wedding supper, the newlyweds and their distinguished guests—including the most distinguished guest of all, Queen Elizabeth I—are treated to a private entertainment, a play written especially for them. Imagine that the play is Shakespeare's *A Midsummer Night's Dream,* a comedy that culminates not only in three marriages but in a play, *Pyramus and Thisbe,* performed for the newlyweds with delicious incompetence by well-meaning, hopelessly bumbling artisans. Their inept performance amuses the happy couples and helps to "wear away this long age of three hours," as the amorously impatient Duke Theseus puts it, "between our after-supper and bedtime" (5.1.33–34). At the end of the play within the play, the stage brides and grooms exit to consummate their marriages—"Sweet friends, to bed"—and so, too, amid the blessings and sly jokes of their guests, the real newlyweds retire to bed.

Scholars have told and retold this story of the aristocratic wedding for which Shakespeare wrote his most enchanting comedy until it has come to seem like an established truth, one of the few things we actually know about the composition of the plays. But while the story is both charming and plausible, there is not a shred of actual evidence that *A Midsummer Night's Dream* was ever performed at, let alone written expressly for, such a wedding. What we do know is that this play was performed on the London stage: the title page of the First Quarto says that it "hath been sundry times publikely acted" by the Lord Chamberlain's Men and that it was written by William Shakespeare.

The precise date that *A Midsummer Night's Dream* was written and first performed is unknown; the Elizabethan writer Francis Meres mentions it admiringly in 1598, and certain of its stylistic features have led many scholars to place it around 1594–96, the probable period of the comparably lyrical *Romeo and Juliet* and *Richard II*. Attempts to find more precise coordinates by locating an allusion to a particular Royal Progress in Oberon's lines about the "fair vestal thronèd by the west" (2.1.158) or to a particular wet season in Titania's lines about the miserable weather (2.1.88ff.) have been defeated by the frequency of both Queen Elizabeth's travels and English rainstorms.

What accounts, then, for all the speculation about the wedding ceremony, complete with royal attendance? In part, the answer lies in the comedy's thematic focus on love consummated in marriage. The final ritual blessing of the bride beds—the fairies' version of a traditional Catholic practice deemed superstitious by zealous Protestants— can be seen as the culmination of the elaborate festivities, including song, music, dancing, and plays, that often accompanied upper-class Elizabethan marriages. In part, imagining a specific historical occasion helps to highlight an uncertainty, at once pleasurable and disturbing, about the borderline between reality and illusion: as in a hall of mirrors, the real-life newlyweds whiling away the hours before bedtime by watching a play would see onstage other newlyweds whiling away the hours before bedtime by watching a play.

But, as four centuries of readers and playgoers have found, you do not need to see *A Midsummer Night's Dream* on your wedding day, nor do you need to be an aristocrat, to savor its delights. There have, to be sure, been a few dissenters: the diarist Samuel Pepys wrote after seeing a production in 1662 that "it is the most insipid ridiculous play that ever I saw in my life," although he took note of "some good dancing and some handsome women." Most audiences have been vastly more enthusiastic. The play has inspired a succession of musical adaptations and settings, along with famously lavish productions. By the nineteenth century, Shakespeare's bare stage had given way to

Cupid and his victims. From Gilles Corrozet, *Hecatomgraphie* (1540).

gorgeous sets, with twinkling lights, fairies rising on midnight mushrooms, the moon shining over the Acropolis, and live rabbits hopping across carpets of flowers. Film is, of course, well suited to such fantasies, as a series of famous motion pictures have shown, but *A Midsummer Night's Dream* has proved equally at home in the simplest of settings. Generations of schoolchildren have romped through cardboard forests, while in Peter Brook's influential 1970 production for the Royal Shakespeare Company the actors performed (often on trapeze) in a three-sided, brightly lit, bare white box.

Working its magic on the imagination, Shakespeare's visionary poetic drama appeals to an unusually broad spectrum of spectators. The play may induce fantasies of aristocratic or private pleasure, but it does so with the resources of the public stage. If it mocks working-class artisans (skilled craftsmen who are simply called "the rabble" in one quarto stage direction), it also laughs at well-born young lovers. Its language reflects an unusually high incidence of the tropes familiar to those who had received rhetorical and literary training, but you do not have to learn the Greek names for these tropes—*anaphora, isocolon, epizeuxis,* and the like—to enjoy their effects. Take, for example, the exchange between Lysander and Hermia in the wake of Egeus's attempt to block their betrothal:

> LYSANDER The course of true love never did run smooth,
> But either it was different in blood—
> HERMIA O cross!—too high to be enthralled to low.
> LYSANDER Or else misgrafted in respect of years—
> HERMIA O spite!—too old to be engaged to young.
> LYSANDER Or merit stood upon the choice of friends—
> HERMIA O hell!—to choose love by another's eyes.
> (1.1.134–40)

The alternation of single lines, called *stichomythia,* is a scheme that Shakespeare borrowed from the Roman playwright Seneca and used in different ways in many of his plays. The effect here is to convey the lovers' mutual anguish, tinging it slightly perhaps with a gently ironic distance that evaporates in the poignant lament that follows (lines 141–49). The rhetorical devices, along with the subtle modulations from blank verse to rhymed couplets to boisterous comic prose, are so deftly handled that their pleasures are accessible to the learned and unlearned alike. This breadth also reflects the very wide range of cultural materials that the playwright has cunningly woven together, from the classical heritage of the educated elite to popular ballads and folk customs, from refined and sophisticated entertainments to the coarser delights of farce.

The exquisite lyricism of much of the play, the celebration of aristocratic pastimes such as the hunt, and a vision of courtly glamour conjure up an upper-class milieu. There is no single literary source for Shakespeare's depiction of this world, or indeed for the play as a whole, but he is indebted for the legendary Theseus and Hippolyta to Thomas North's translation (1579) of Plutarch's *Lives of the Noble Grecians and Romanes,* and still more to Chaucer's *Knight's Tale.* The *Dream* repeatedly echoes Chaucer's references to observing "the rite of May," a folk custom still current in Elizabethan England and quite possibly known to Shakespeare personally. To the dismay of Puritans, who regarded the celebration as a lascivious remnant of paganism, young men and women of all classes would go out into the woods and fields to welcome the

Pyramus and Thisbe. From George Wither, *A Collection of Emblemes* (1635).

May with singing and dancing. Shakespeare's title associates this custom with another occasion for festive release: Midsummer Eve (June 23), when the solstice was marked not only by holiday license but by tales of fairy spells and temporary madness.

Some Elizabethan aristocrats kept theatrical troupes as liveried servants, along with young pages who could sing and perform, and powerful magnates, both secular and religious, often had plays, masquerades, and elaborate shows staged in their houses. From this milieu, Shakespeare derives a vision of what we can call the revels of power, performances designed to entertain, gratify, and reflect the values of those at the top. From this milieu too Shakespeare absorbs a sense of social hierarchy: a distinction between Duke Theseus, at once imperious and genteel, and Egeus, wealthy but distinctly lower in rank and harping on what is his by law, along with a more marked distinction between these characters and the artisans, loyal members of the lower orders, regarded by their social superiors with condescending indulgence.

The artisans—or "rude mechanicals," as they are called—enable Shakespeare to introduce wonderful swoops into earthy prose, snatches of jigs, a comical taste for the grotesque, a glimpse of a world that usually resides beyond the horizon of courtly vision. The lovers at the pinnacle of the play's society do not know the names and trades of the "hard-handed men that work in Athens here" (5.1.72) who have come to offer them entertainment, but we the audience do, and we even know something of their hopes and dreams. As with the Pageant of the Nine Worthies in *Love's Labour's Lost,* we are invited at once to join in the mockery of the inept performers and to distance ourselves from the mockers. That is, the audience of *A Midsummer Night's Dream* is not simply mirrored in the play's upper classes: the real audience is given a broader perspective, a more capacious understanding than anyone onstage.

This understanding is signaled not only in our ability to take in both the courtly and popular dimensions of the play, but also in our ability to see what escapes both aristocrats and artisans: the world of the fairies. But what are the fairies? From what social milieu do they spring? It is tempting to reply that they are denizens of the country—that is, characters drawn from the semipagan folklore of rural England. This is at least partially true: Reginald Scot, who wrote a brilliant attack on witchcraft persecutions (*The Discoverie of Witchcraft*, 1584), suggests that Robin Goodfellow, the mischievous spirit also called a Puck, was once feared by villagers, but was now widely recognized to be a figure of mere "illusion and knaverie." Yet intensive scholarly research over several generations has suggested that Shakespeare's fairies are quite unlike those his audience might have credited, half-credited, or—as Scot hoped—discredited.

The fairies of Elizabethan popular belief were often threatening and dangerous, while those of *A Midsummer Night's Dream* are generally benevolent. The former steal human infants, perhaps to sacrifice them to the devil, while the latter, even when they quarrel over the possession of a young boy, do so to bestow love and favor upon him; the former leave deformed, emaciated children in place of those they have stolen, while the latter trip nimbly through the palace blessing the bride beds and warding off deformities. Shakespeare's fairies have some of the menacing associations of "real" fairies—Puck speaks of shrouds and gaping graves, while the quarrel between Oberon and Titania has disrupted the seasons and damaged the crops, as wicked spirits were said to do. But the fairies we see are, as Oberon says, "spirits of another sort." Oberon and Titania (whose names Shakespeare took from the French romance *Huon of Bordeaux* and from Ovid, respectively) repeatedly demonstrate their good will toward mortals, though they have very little good will toward each other. The fairy king and queen are distressed at the unintended consequences of their quarrel, and each is involved, with romantic generosity, in the happiness of Theseus and Hippolyta. This generosity extends beyond the immediate range of their interests: in the midst of plotting to humiliate Titania, Oberon attempts to intervene on behalf of the spurned Helena, and though this intervention proves, through Puck's mistake, to lead to hopeless confusion, the fairies make amends.

Indeed, if Puck takes mischievous delight in the discord he has helped to sow among the four young lovers—"Lord, what fools these mortals be!" (3.2.115)—he is not the originator of that discord, and he is the indispensable agent for setting things right. In his role as both mischief-maker and matchmaker, Puck resembles the crafty slave in comedies by the Latin playwrights Plautus and Terence, a stock character who sometimes seems to enjoy and contribute to the plot's tangles but who manages in the end to remove the obstacles that stand in the way of the young lovers.

This resemblance brings us to yet another of the cultural elements that Shakespeare cunningly interweaves in the plot of *A Midsummer Night's Dream*. From the classical literary tradition, which he must have first encountered in grammar school, Shakespeare derives the ancient Greek setting, the story of Pyramus and Thisbe as told in Ovid's *Metamorphoses,* the comic transformation of a man into an ass as told in Apuleius's *Golden Ass,* and, above all, the basic plot device of young lovers contriving to escape the rigid will of a stern father. This device was one of the staples of the New Comedy of ancient Greece and was a mainstay as well in Roman comedy. The literary convention corresponds to certain aspects of actual life in Shakespeare's England, where lawsuits provide records of parents trying to compel children to marry against their will. But the historical problem of marital consent has a complex relation to its artistic representation. Not only does the play exaggerate the actual punitive power of the father—Egeus threatens his disobedient daughter with death (to which Theseus offers, as a grim alternative, the nunnery)—but it also exaggerates the release from this power by staging the giddy possibility of a marriage based entirely on love and desire rather than parental will.

In *A Midsummer Night's Dream,* this release, a highly implausible dream for any Elizabethan member of the middle or upper classes, is brought about by a further plot device: the escape from the court or city to the "green world" of the forest. This the-atrical structure is not characteristic of the New Comedy, but it somewhat resembles the Saturnalian rhythms of the Old Comedy of Aristophanes, with its festive release from the discipline and sobriety of everyday life, and, still more perhaps, it reflects cer-tain English folk customs, such as Maying. When Theseus comes upon the four exhausted lovers asleep in the woods, he thinks that "they rose up early to observe / The rite of May" (4.1.129–30).

But, of course, Theseus is wrong. The lovers were not out a-Maying, but had spent the night stumbling through the woods in a confused state of fear, anger, and desire. When it enters the charmed, moonlit space of *A Midsummer Night's Dream*, "the rite of May," along with the other rituals and representations Shakespeare stitched together in creating his play, is transformed; to use Peter Quince's term for the metamorphosed Bottom, the rites and rituals are "translated." Folk customs, the revels of power, the classical tradition as taught in schools, all are displaced from their points of origin, their enabling institutions and assumptions, and brought into a new space, the space of the Shakespearean stage.

This "translation" has, in every case, the odd effect of simultaneous elevation and enervation, celebration and parody. Thus the minor Ovidian tale of Pyramus and Thisbe is greatly elaborated but also travestied; the popular realm is at once lovingly repre-sented and mercilessly ridiculed; the revels of power are reproduced but also ironically distanced.

Some of the play's most wonderful moments spring from the zany conjunction of distinct and even opposed theatrical modes (a conjunction characteristically parodied in the oxymoronic title of the artisans' play, "A tedious brief scene of young Pyramus / And his love Thisbe: very tragical mirth" [5.1.56–57]). Thus, for example, exquisite love poetry and low comedy meet in the wonderful moment in which the queen of fairies awakens to become enraptured at the sight of the most flatulently absurd of the mechanicals, Bottom. Bottom has been transformed with perfect appropriateness into an ass, yet it is he who is granted the play's most exquisite vision of delight and who articulates, in a comically confused burlesque of St. Paul (1 Corinthians 2:9), the deep-est sense of wonder: "The eye of man hath not heard, the ear of man hath not seen, man's hand is not able to taste, his tongue to conceive, nor his heart to report what my dream was" (4.1.204–07).

It would be asinine, the play suggests, to try to expound this dream, but we can at least suggest that, whatever its meaning, its existence is closely linked to the nature of

A fairy hill. From Olaus Magnus, *Historia de Gentibus Septentrionalibus* (1555).

the theater itself. Puck suggests as much when he proposes in the Epilogue that the audience imagine that it has all along been slumbering: the play it has seen has been a collective hallucination. The play, then, is a dream about watching a play about dreams. Fittingly, the comedy devotes much of its last act to a parody of a theatrical performance, as if its most enduring concern were not the fate of the lovers but the possibility of performing plays. The entire last act of *A Midsummer Night's Dream* is unnecessary in terms of the plot: by Oberon's intervention and Theseus's fiat, the plot complications have all been resolved at the end of Act 4. Knots that had seemed almost impossible to untangle—Theseus had declared in Act 1 that he was powerless to overturn the ancient privilege of Athens invoked by Egeus—suddenly dissolve. The absurdly easy resolution of an apparently hopeless dilemma characterizes not only the lovers' legal but also their emotional condition, a blend of mad confusion and geometric logic that is settled, apparently permanently, with the aid of the fairies' magical love juice.

But this diagrammatic settling of affairs sits uncomfortably with all that the lovers have experienced in the woods. Both critics and directors have given different weight to this experience. Some treat the lovers as mindless comic puppets, jerked by the playwright's invisible strings, while others take more seriously the darkness that shadows their words and actions. This darkness includes emotional violence and masochism, the betrayal of friendship, the radical fickleness of desire. It extends to the play's sexual politics. Under the strain of the night's adventures, the friendship between Hermia and Helena begins to crack apart, while Lysander and Demetrius become bitter rivals. Although they are eventually reconciled, it is as if the heterosexual couplings can only be formed by painfully sundering the intimate same-sex bonds that preceded them. Shakespeare had begun to reflect on this problem as early as *The Two Gentlemen of Verona*, possibly his first play, and throughout his career he returned to it repeatedly, including in what is possibly his last play, *The Two Noble Kinsmen*. For the most part, the broken friendships are repaired, but, as with Antonio and Sebastian in *Twelfth Night* and Leontes and Polixenes in *The Winter's Tale*, there is usually a lingering sense of loss, from which even the sunnier *Midsummer Night's Dream* is not completely exempt.

In another very early play, *The Taming of the Shrew*, Shakespeare had also begun his lifelong reflection on the struggle between men and women, a struggle frequently focused on the male desire to dominate and subdue the female. In *A Midsummer Night's Dream*, tension flares in the case of the fairies into open conflict over the Indian boy, the locus of Oberon's assertion of patriarchal power and Titania's claim to independence. In the human world of the play, this tension is less immediately apparent, but in the first scene Theseus alludes to his military conquest of the Amazon queen Hippolyta, and there are other brief glimpses of cruelty, indifference, and rage. Those who see *A Midsummer Night's Dream* as lighthearted entertainment must somehow laugh off this darkness; those who wish to emphasize the play's more troubling and discordant notes must somehow neutralize the comic register in which such notes are sounded. For example, the brutal insults hurled at Hermia by the young man who had loved her and with whom she has eloped might well seem extremely painful, but the fantastic language in which these insults are expressed—

> Get you gone, you dwarf,
> You *minimus* of hind'ring knot-grass made,
> You bead, you acorn
>
> (3.2.329–31)

—distances audiences from the pain and generates laughter.

Audiences for most productions tend to oscillate between engagement and detachment. In the young lovers' choices and sufferings, we encounter a situation where the final outcome doesn't matter greatly to us but matters greatly to them. And while we see the characters from a distance—although Hermia and Helena are distinct enough, even attentive readers occasionally find it difficult to remember which is Lysander and which Demetrius—we also experience at least glancingly *their* sense of how important the difference is, how unbearable to be matched against one's consent, how painfully difficult to make a match that corresponds to one's desires.

Desires in *A Midsummer Night's Dream* are intense, irrational, and alarmingly mobile. This mobility, the speed with which desire can be detached from one object and attached to a different object, does not diminish the exigency of the passion, for the lovers are convinced at every moment that their choices are irrefutably rational and irresistibly compelling. But there is no security in these choices, and the play is repeatedly haunted by a fear of abandonment. The emblem, as well as agent, of a dangerously mobile desire is the fairies' love juice. No human being in the play experiences a purely abstract, objectless desire; when you desire, you desire *someone*. But the love juice is the distilled essence of erotic mobility itself, and it is appropriately in the power of the fairies. For the fairies seem to embody the principle of what we might call polytropic desire—that is, desire that can instantaneously alight on any object, including an ass-headed man, and that can with equal instantaneousness swerve away from that object and on to another. Oberon and Titania have, we learn, long histories of amorous adventures; they are aware of each other's wayward passions; and, endowed with an extraordinary, eroticizing rhetoric, they move endlessly through the spiced, moonlit night.

If there is a link between the fairies and the erotic, there is a still more powerful link between the fairies and the imagination. Theseus makes the connection explicit when he rejects the stories that the lovers have told him: "I never may believe / These antique fables, nor these fairy toys." In a famous speech (5.1.2–22), he accounts for such fables and toys as products of the imagination. The speech reflects Theseus's misplaced confidence in his own sense of waking reality, a reality that does not include fairies. Yet paradoxically, in dismissively categorizing the lunatic, the lover, and the poet as "of imagination all compact," he manages to articulate insights that the play seems to uphold. Those in the grip of a powerful imagination may be loosed from the moorings of reason and nature, and they may inhabit a world of wish fulfillment and its converse, nightmare. But the poet whose imagination "bodies forth / The forms of things unknown" (5.1.14–15) has created *A Midsummer Night's Dream*, giving his fantasies—including the fantasy called "Theseus"—"a local habitation and a name." Finally, it is the imagination that enables giddy, restless, changeable mortals to attach their desires to a particular person.

For Theseus, the imagination is the agent of delusion—and there is much in the play that would seem to support this conclusion. But his account is not complete without Hippolyta's insistence that the story the four young lovers tell seems to have something that goes beyond delusion. Their minds, she observes, have been "transfigured" together, and this shared transfiguration bears witness to "something of great constancy; / But howsoever, strange and admirable" (5.1.26–27). It is as if we were all to wake up one morning and discover we had had the same dream.

And, of course, *we* in the audience have, as Puck's epilogue suggests, had just this experience: the experience of the theater. In the theater, we confront a living representation of the complex relation between transfiguration and delusion, a relation explored with fantastic, anxious literalness in the artisans' performance of *Pyramus and Thisbe*. In reassuring the ladies that the lion is only Snug the Joiner, that nothing is what it claims to be, the players simultaneously burlesque the stage and call attention to the basic elements from which any performance is made: rudimentary scenery, artisans, language, imagination, desire.

There is precious little evidence, to be sure, of either imagination or desire in the artisans' performance of *Pyramus and Thisbe*. Their absence is part of the comical awfulness of the play within the play, the reason in effect that it does not become the Shakespearean tragedy it so strikingly resembles, *Romeo and Juliet*. And yet, as Theseus says, "The best in this kind are but shadows, and the worst are no worse if imagination amend them." "It must be your imagination, then," Hippolyta points out, "and not theirs" (5.1.208–10). But that is true of performances far greater than that of which the artisans are capable. If we are to see fairies onstage in *A Midsummer Night's Dream*, and not simply flesh-and-blood actors (probably boy actors in Shakespeare's theater), it must be our imagination that makes amends. So too if we are to believe in the lovers' desire and sympathize with their predicament, it must be *our* desire that animates their words.

Such, at least, is the vision of the theater suggested by the play that Bottom and company offer to the newlyweds. There is nothing really out there, their performance implies, except what the audience graciously consents to dream. Yet in the closing moments of the play, when the fairies emerge from the woods and venture into Theseus's mansion to bless the bride beds, a quite different vision of theater is suggested, one in which the dreams and desires that we have are determined by forces over which we have no control, forces that only a playwright's love juice can make visible under an imaginary moon.

STEPHEN GREENBLATT

TEXTUAL NOTE

A Midsummer Night's Dream was entered in the Stationers' Register on October 8, 1600, and printed that same year in quarto:

> A Midsommer nights dreame. As it hath beene sundry times pub*lickely acted, by the Right honourable,* the Lord Chamberlaine his *seruants. Written by William Shakespeare.* Imprinted at London, for *Thomas Fisher,* and are to be soulde at his shoppe, at the Signe of the White Hart, in *Fleetestreete.* 1600.

This quarto (Q1) was evidently prepared from a manuscript in Shakespeare's hand. A second quarto (Q2), printed in 1619 (though falsely dated 1600), corrects some errors in Q1, but it also introduces new errors. This second quarto was used as the basis for the 1623 First Folio text of the play (F), though the Folio editors also had recourse to a theatrical manuscript, probably a promptbook in the possession of Shakespeare's company, the King's Men. Evidence for this manuscript includes a Folio stage direction before 5.1.126: "Tawyer with a Trumpet before them." "Tawyer" presumably refers to William Tawyer, a musician employed by the King's Men.

From this theatrical manuscript evidently derived several alterations in stage directions and in speech prefixes, the most notable of which is the substitution in Act 5 of Egeus for Philostrate as the master of ceremonies. The substitution may simply be a mistake: in an early performance, the same actor may have played the parts of both Egeus and Philostrate, and this doubling may have led to an error in the speech prefix. But it is also possible that the play was revised in order to integrate the disgruntled Egeus more fully into the festive conclusion.

Act and scene divisions all derive from F; there are none in the quarto text. Traditionally, Act 3, Scene 2 continues to the end of the act, but since the stage is apparently cleared at 3.2.413, this edition marks a break (perhaps indicating a gap in time and place) by dividing the scene in two and designating a third scene. In F, at the end of Act 3 there is a stage direction, "They sleepe all the Act," which indicates that the four lovers remain asleep onstage during the interval customary between acts and that the action that resumes in the next act is understood to be continuous.

On the basis of mislined verses in 5.1.1–84, scholars have conjectured that Shakespeare may have revised Theseus's speech as originally conceived and added lines in the margin of his copy. Since these revisions may give us a glimpse of Shakespeare's process of composition, this book appends a reconstruction of what would have been the original speech.

The control text for this edition of *A Midsummer Night's Dream* is Q1 (1600). But in keeping with the Oxford editors' principle of basing their text on the most theatrical early version of each play—that is, the version closest to the play as performed by Shakespeare's company during the playwright's own lifetime—changes in speech prefixes and other substantive variants have been adopted from F.

SELECTED BIBLIOGRAPHY

Barber, C. L. "May Games and Metamorphoses on a Midsummer's Night." *Shakespeare's Festive Comedy: A Study of Dramatic Form and Its Relation to Social Custom*. Princeton: Princeton University Press, 1959. 119–62. *A Midsummer Night's Dream* combines folk customs, Ovidian fancy, and Elizabethan pageantry to produce a clarifying release of imagination.

Bate, Jonathan. *Shakespeare and Ovid*. New York: Oxford University Press, 1993. *A Midsummer Night's Dream* indirectly dramatizes Ovid, gathering themes of myth, metamorphosis, and love into a mixed mode typical of sixteenth-century mythography.

Briggs, K. M. *The Anatomy of Puck: An Examination of Fairy Beliefs Among Shakespeare's Contemporaries and Successors*. London: Routledge and Kegan Paul, 1959. A survey of early modern notions about fairies, especially in English literary tradition, describing also the influence of Shakespeare's innovations.

Dash, Irene G. *Women's Worlds in Shakespeare's Plays*. London: Associated University Presses, 1997. Looks at *A Midsummer Night's Dream* in performance, arguing that traditional staging practices have tended reductively to simplify Shakespeare's women.

Girard, René. "Myth and Ritual in Shakespeare: *A Midsummer Night's Dream*." *Textual Strategies: Perspectives in Post-Structuralist Criticism*. Ed. Josué V. Harari. Ithaca, N.Y.: Cornell University Press, 1979. 189–212. This play presents a genetic theory of myth, charting a collective mental transformation.

Loomba, Ania. "The Great Indian Vanishing Trick—Colonialism, Property, and the Family in *A Midsummer Night's Dream*." *A Feminist Companion to Shakespeare*. Ed. Dympna Callaghan. Malden, Mass.: Blackwell, 2000. 163–87. Argues that the Indian boy represents the shaping dialectic between non-European practices and Western domestic ideology.

Montrose, Louis. *The Purpose of Playing: Shakespeare and the Cultural Politics of the Elizabethan Theatre*. Chicago: University of Chicago Press, 1996. Examines the play's relationship to Elizabethan ideology through discourses of gender, physiology, social rank, and royal iconography.

Traub, Valerie. *The Renaissance of Lesbianism in Early Modern England*. Cambridge: Cambridge University Press, 2002. Observes how renovated classical idioms and new scientific knowledge made female-female desire intelligible in the Renaissance.

Williams, Gary Jay. *Our Moonlight Revels: "A Midsummer Night's Dream" in the Theatre*. Iowa City: University of Iowa Press, 1997. The major stage, film, and opera adaptations, understood in relation to the cultures that produced them.

Young, David P. *Something of Great Constancy: The Art of "A Midsummer Night's Dream."* New Haven: Yale University Press, 1966. Extensive, variegated study covering sources, structure, performance, and contexts.

FILMS

A Midsummer Night's Dream. 1935. Dir. William Dieterle and Max Reinhardt. USA. 133 min. Sumptuous production, with balletic fairies, a serpentine Hippolyta, an elaborate Mendelssohn score, and Mickey Rooney as Puck.

A Midsummer Night's Dream. 1968. Dir. Peter Hall. UK. 124 min. Noted for its mini-skirted sensuality, body paint, and extremely gnarled and muddy forest. With Diana Rigg and Helen Mirren.

A Midsummer Night's Dream. 1996. Dir. Adrian Noble. UK. 105 min. Theseus and Hippolyta double as Oberon and Titania, with a frame device of a boy dreaming the play. Starring Lindsay Duncan and Alex Jennings.

A Midsummer Night's Dream. 1999. Dir. Michael Hoffman. USA. 116 min. In Victorian costume against the Tuscan backdrop, this dreamy and erotic version amplifies Bottom's role. With Kevin Kline and Michelle Pfeiffer.

A Midsummer Night's Dream

THE PERSONS OF THE PLAY

THESEUS, Duke of Athens
HIPPOLYTA, Queen of the Amazons, betrothed to Theseus
PHILOSTRATE, Master of the Revels to Theseus
EGEUS, father of Hermia
HERMIA, daughter of Egeus, in love with Lysander
LYSANDER, loved by Hermia
DEMETRIUS, suitor to Hermia
HELENA, in love with Demetrius
OBERON, King of Fairies
TITANIA, Queen of Fairies
ROBIN GOODFELLOW, a puck
PEASEBLOSSOM
COBWEB
MOTE } fairies
MUSTARDSEED
Peter QUINCE, a carpenter
Nick BOTTOM, a weaver
Francis FLUTE, a bellows-mender
Tom SNOUT, a tinker
SNUG, a joiner
Robin STARVELING, a tailor
Attendant lords and fairies

1.1

Enter THESEUS, HIPPOLYTA, [*and* PHILOSTRATE,] *with others*

THESEUS   Now, fair Hippolyta, our nuptial hour
　　Draws on apace. Four happy days bring in
　　Another moon—but O, methinks how slow
　　This old moon wanes! She lingers° my desires   *delays fulfillment of*
5　　Like to a stepdame° or a dowager   *stepmother*
　　Long withering out a young man's revenue.[1]
HIPPOLYTA   Four days will quickly steep° themselves in night,   *plunge*
　　Four nights will quickly dream away the time;
　　And then the moon, like to a silver bow
10　　New bent in heaven, shall behold the night
　　Of our solemnities.
THESEUS　　　　　　Go, Philostrate,
　　Stir up the Athenian youth to merriments.
　　Awake the pert and nimble spirit of mirth.
　　Turn melancholy forth to funerals—
15　　The pale companion is not for our pomp. [*Exit* PHILOSTRATE]
　　Hippolyta, I wooed thee with my sword,
　　And won thy love doing thee injuries.[2]

1.1 Location: Theseus's palace in Athens.
1. *a dowager . . . revenue*: a widow using up the inher-
itance that will go to her husband's (young) heir on her

death.
2. Theseus captured Hippolyta in his military conquest
of the Amazons.

But I will wed thee in another key—
With pomp, with triumph,° and with revelling.   *public festivity*

    Enter EGEUS[3] *and his daughter* HERMIA, *and* LYSANDER
    and DEMETRIUS

20 EGEUS   Happy be Theseus, our renownèd Duke.

    THESEUS   Thanks, good Egeus. What's the news with thee?

    EGEUS   Full of vexation come I, with complaint
    Against my child, my daughter Hermia.—
    Stand forth Demetrius.—My noble lord,
25 This man hath my consent to marry her.—
    Stand forth Lysander.—And, my gracious Duke,
    This hath bewitched the bosom of my child.
    Thou, thou, Lysander, thou hast given her rhymes,
    And interchanged love tokens with my child.
30 Thou hast by moonlight at her window sung
    With feigning[4] voice verses of feigning love,
    And stol'n the impression of her fantasy[5]
    With bracelets of thy hair, rings, gauds,° conceits,°   *trinkets / clever gifts*
    Knacks,° trifles, nosegays,° sweetmeats—messengers   *Knickknacks / bouquets*
35 Of strong prevailment° in unhardened youth.   *persuasiveness*
    With cunning hast thou filched my daughter's heart,
    Turned her obedience which is due to me
    To stubborn harshness. And, my gracious Duke,
    Be it so° she will not here before your grace   *If*
40 Consent to marry with Demetrius,
    I beg the ancient privilege of Athens:
    As she is mine, I may dispose of her,
    Which shall be either to this gentleman
    Or to her death, according to our law
45 Immediately° provided in that case.   *Expressly*

    THESEUS   What say you, Hermia? Be advised, fair maid.
    To you your father should be as a god,
    One that composed° your beauties, yea, and one   *fashioned*
    To whom you are but as a form in wax,
50 By him imprinted,[6] and within his power
    To leave° the figure or disfigure° it.   *maintain / destroy*
    Demetrius is a worthy gentleman.

    HERMIA   So is Lysander.

    THESEUS   In himself he is,
    But in this kind,° wanting your father's voice,[7]   *respect*
55 The other must be held the worthier.

    HERMIA   I would my father looked but with my eyes.

    THESEUS   Rather your eyes must with his judgement look.

    HERMIA   I do entreat your grace to pardon me.
    I know not by what power I am made bold,
60 Nor how it may concern° my modesty   *befit*
    In such a presence here to plead my thoughts,
    But I beseech your grace that I may know
    The worst that may befall me in this case
    If I refuse to wed Demetrius.

---

3. Pronounced "Ege-us," accented on the second syllable.
4. A triple pun: desiring; feigning; soft (in music).
5. stol'n . . . fantasy: by craftily impressing your image on her imagination, like a seal in wax, you have stolen her love.
6. you are . . . imprinted: you are a wax impression of his seal.
7. Lacking your father's consent or vote.

65	THESEUS Either to die the death,° or to abjure	*be executed*
	For ever the society of men.	
	Therefore, fair Hermia, question your desires.	
	Know° of your youth, examine well your blood,°	*Inquire / passions*
	Whether, if you yield not to your father's choice,	
70	You can endure the livery° of a nun,⁸	*habit*
	For aye° to be in shady cloister mewed,°	*ever / caged in*
	To live a barren sister all your life,	
	Chanting faint hymns to the cold fruitless moon.⁹	
	Thrice blessèd they that master so their blood	
75	To undergo such maiden pilgrimage;°	*life as a virgin*
	But earthlier happy is the rose distilled¹	
	Than that which, withering on the virgin thorn,	
	Grows, lives, and dies in single blessedness.°	*celibate*
	HERMIA So will I grow, so live, so die, my lord,	
80	Ere I will yield my virgin patent² up	
	Unto his lordship whose unwishèd yoke	
	My soul consents not to give sovereignty.	
	THESEUS Take time to pause, and by the next new moon—	
	The sealing day betwixt my love and me	
85	For everlasting bond of fellowship—	
	Upon that day either prepare to die	
	For disobedience to your father's will,	
	Or else to wed Demetrius, as he would,	
	Or on Diana's altar to protest°	*vow*
90	For aye austerity and single life.	
	DEMETRIUS Relent, sweet Hermia; and, Lysander, yield	
	Thy crazèd title° to my certain right.	*unsound claim*
	LYSANDER You have her father's love, Demetrius;	
	Let me have Hermia's. Do you marry him.	
95	EGEUS Scornful Lysander! True, he hath my love;	
	And what is mine my love shall render him,	
	And she is mine, and all my right of her	
	I do estate° unto Demetrius.	*settle; bestow*
	LYSANDER [*to* THESEUS] I am, my lord, as well derived° as he,	*descended*
100	As well possessed.° My love is more than his,	*endowed with wealth*
	My fortunes every way as fairly ranked,	
	If not with vantage,° as Demetrius;	*superiority*
	And—which is more than all these boasts can be—	
	I am beloved of beauteous Hermia.	
105	Why should not I then prosecute° my right?	*pursue*
	Demetrius—I'll avouch it to his head°—	*face*
	Made love to Nedar's daughter, Helena,	
	And won her soul, and she, sweet lady, dotes,	
	Devoutly dotes, dotes in idolatry	
110	Upon this spotted and inconstant³ man.	
	THESEUS I must confess that I have heard so much,	
	And with Demetrius thought to have spoke thereof;	
	But, being over-full of self affairs,°	*my own concerns*
	My mind did lose it. But, Demetrius, come;	
115	And come, Egeus. You shall go with me.	

8. Orders of nuns were established in the Christian Middle Ages, but Elizabethans used the term as well for women devoted to a religious life in classical antiquity.
9. The emblem of Diana, goddess of chastity.

1. Made use of (roses were distilled to make perfumes). *earthlier happy:* happier on earth.
2. My right to remain a virgin.
3. *spotted and inconstant:* stained with fickleness.

I have some private schooling° for you both.   *advice*
For you, fair Hermia, look you arm° yourself   *prepare*
To fit your fancies° to your father's will,   *desires*
Or else the law of Athens yields you up—
120 Which by no means we may extenuate°—   *mitigate*
To death or to a vow of single life.
Come, my Hippolyta; what cheer, my love?—
Demetrius and Egeus, go along.
I must employ you in some business
125 Against° our nuptial, and confer with you   *In preparation for*
Of something nearly that⁴ concerns yourselves.
EGEUS With duty and desire we follow you.

      Exeunt. Manent° LYSANDER *and* HERMIA   *Remain*

LYSANDER How now, my love? Why is your cheek so pale?
How chance the roses there do fade so fast?
130 HERMIA Belike° for want of rain, which I could well   *Probably*
Beteem° them from the tempest of my eyes.   *Afford; grant*
LYSANDER Ay me, for aught that I could ever read,
Could ever hear by tale or history,
The course of true love never did run smooth,
135 But either it was different in blood°—   *hereditary rank*
HERMIA O cross!°—too high to be enthralled to low.   *vexation*
LYSANDER Or else misgrafted° in respect of years—   *badly matched*
HERMIA O spite!—too old to be engaged to young.
LYSANDER Or merit stood° upon the choice of friends°—   *rested / kin*
140 HERMIA O hell!—to choose love by another's eyes.
LYSANDER Or if there were a sympathy° in choice,   *an agreement*
War, death, or sickness did lay siege to it,
Making it momentany° as a sound,   *momentary*
Swift as a shadow, short as any dream,
145 Brief as the lightning in the collied° night,   *coal-black*
That, in a spleen,° unfolds° both heaven and earth, *swift impulse / reveals*
And, ere a man hath power to say 'Behold!',
The jaws of darkness do devour it up.
So quick⁵ bright things come to confusion.
150 HERMIA If then true lovers have been ever° crossed,   *always*
It stands as an edict in destiny.
Then let us teach our trial patience,⁶
Because it is a customary cross,
As due to love as thoughts, and dreams, and sighs,
155 Wishes, and tears, poor fancy's° followers.   *love's*
LYSANDER A good persuasion.° Therefore hear me, Hermia. *principle; doctrine*
I have a widow aunt, a dowager
Of great revenue, and she hath no child,
And she respects° me as her only son.   *regards*
160 From Athens is her house remote seven leagues.
There, gentle Hermia, may I marry thee,
And to that place the sharp Athenian law
Cannot pursue us. If thou lov'st me then,
Steal forth thy father's house tomorrow night,
165 And in the wood, a league without° the town,   *outside*
Where I did meet thee once with Helena

---

4. *nearly that:* that closely.   6. Let us teach ourselves to be patient in this trial.
5. Quickly (adverb); vital, lively (adjective).

To do observance to a morn of May,°   *celebrate May Day*
There will I stay for thee.
HERMIA   My good Lysander,
I swear to thee by Cupid's strongest bow,
170   By his best arrow with the golden head,⁷
By the simplicity° of Venus' doves,⁸   *innocence*
By that which knitteth souls and prospers loves,
And by that fire which burned the Carthage queen
When the false Trojan under sail was seen;⁹
175   By all the vows that ever men have broke—
In number more than ever women spoke—
In that same place thou hast appointed me
Tomorrow truly will I meet with thee.
LYSANDER   Keep promise, love. Look, here comes Helena.
      Enter HELENA
180   HERMIA   God speed, fair¹ Helena. Whither away?
HELENA   Call you me fair? That 'fair' again unsay.
Demetrius loves your fair—O happy fair!°   *fortunate beauty*
Your eyes are lodestars,° and your tongue's sweet air°   *guiding stars / melody*
More tuneable° than lark to shepherd's ear   *tuneful*
185   When wheat is green, when hawthorn buds appear.
Sickness is catching. O, were favour° so!   *looks; charms*
Your words I catch, fair Hermia; ere I go,
My ear should catch your voice, my eye your eye,
My tongue should catch your tongue's sweet melody.
190   Were the world mine, Demetrius being bated,°   *excepted*
The rest I'd give to be to you translated.°   *transformed*
O, teach me how you look, and with what art
You sway the motion° of Demetrius' heart.   *desire*
HERMIA   I frown upon him, yet he loves me still.
195   HELENA   O that your frowns would teach my smiles such skill!
HERMIA   I give him curses, yet he gives me love.
HELENA   O that my prayers could such affection move!
HERMIA   The more I hate, the more he follows me.
HELENA   The more I love, the more he hateth me.
200   HERMIA   His folly, Helen, is no fault of mine.
HELENA   None but your beauty; would that fault were mine!
HERMIA   Take comfort. He no more shall see my face.
Lysander and myself will fly this place.
Before the time I did Lysander see
205   Seemed Athens as a paradise to me.
O then, what graces in my love do dwell,
That he hath turned a heaven unto a hell?
LYSANDER   Helen, to you our minds we will unfold.
Tomorrow night, when Phoebe° doth behold   *Diana (the moon)*
210   Her silver visage in the wat'ry glass,
Decking with liquid pearl the bladed grass—
A time that lovers' sleights doth still° conceal—   *always*
Through Athens' gates have we devised to steal.
HERMIA   And in the wood where often you and I
215   Upon faint° primrose beds were wont° to lie,   *pale / accustomed*

---

7. Cupid's sharp golden arrow was said to create love; his blunt lead arrow caused dislike.
8. Said to draw Venus's chariot.
9. *fire . . . seen*: Dido, Queen of Carthage, burned herself on a funeral pyre when her lover, Aeneas, sailed away.
1. The dialogue plays on the meanings "blonde," "beautiful," "beauty." Helena is presumably fair-haired and Hermia (called a "raven" at 2.2.120) a brunette.

Emptying our bosoms of their counsel sweet,
There my Lysander and myself shall meet,
And thence from Athens turn away our eyes
To seek new friends and stranger companies.°   *the company of strangers*
220 Farewell, sweet playfellow. Pray thou for us,
And good luck grant thee thy Demetrius.—
Keep word, Lysander. We must starve our sight
From lovers' food till morrow deep midnight.
LYSANDER   I will, my Hermia.   *Exit* HERMIA
               Helena, adieu.
225 As you on him, Demetrius dote on you.   *Exit*
HELENA   How happy some o'er other some² can be!
Through Athens I am thought as fair as she.
But what of that? Demetrius thinks not so.
He will not know what all but he do know.
230 And as he errs, doting on Hermia's eyes,
So I, admiring of his qualities.
Things base and vile, holding no quantity,°   *shape; proportion*
Love can transpose to form and dignity.
Love looks not with the eyes, but with the mind,³
235 And therefore is winged Cupid painted blind.
Nor hath love's mind of any judgement taste;°   *any trace of judgment*
Wings and no eyes figure° unheedy haste.   *symbolize*
And therefore is love said to be a child
Because in choice he is so oft beguiled.
240 As waggish° boys in game° themselves forswear,   *playful / sport; play*
So the boy Love is perjured everywhere.
For ere Demetrius looked on Hermia's eyne°   *eyes*
He hailed down oaths that he was only mine,
And when this hail some heat from Hermia felt,
245 So he dissolved,° and showers of oaths did melt.   *broke faith; melted*
I will go tell him of fair Hermia's flight.
Then to the wood will he tomorrow night
Pursue her, and for this intelligence°   *information*
If I have thanks it is a dear expense.⁴
250 But herein mean I to enrich my pain,
To have his sight thither and back again.   *Exit*

1.2

Enter QUINCE *the carpenter, and* SNUG *the joiner, and*
BOTTOM *the weaver, and* FLUTE *the bellows-mender, and*
SNOUT *the tinker, and* STARVELING *the tailor*¹
QUINCE   Is all our company here?
BOTTOM   You were best to call them generally,² man by man,
    according to the scrip.°   *script; list*
QUINCE   Here is the scroll of every man's name which is thought

---

2. *o'er other some:* in comparison with others.
3. Love is promoted not by the evidence of the senses, but by the fancies of the mind.
4. Costly (because of the betrayal of secrecy and because it leads Demetrius to Hermia); or welcome (because the potential return is Demetrius's love regained).
1.2 Location: Somewhere in the city of Athens.
1. The artisans' names recall their occupations. Quince's name is probably derived from "quoins," wooden wedges used by carpenters who made buildings

such as houses and theaters. The name "Snug" evokes well-finished wooden furniture made by joiners. A bottom was the piece of wood on which thread was wound; Bottom's name also connotes "ass" and "lowest point." As Flute's name suggests, domestic bellows whistle through holes when needing repair. Snout's name may refer to the spouts of the kettles he repairs, or to his nose. Tailors, as Starveling's name recalls, were proverbially thin.
2. Bottom's error for "individually" (he frequently mistakes words in this manner).

5   fit through all Athens to play in our interlude° before the Duke   *brief play*
    and the Duchess on his wedding day at night.

  BOTTOM   First, good Peter Quince, say what the play treats on;
    then read the names of the actors; and so grow to a point.³

  QUINCE   Marry,° our play is *The Most Lamentable Comedy and*   *By the Virgin Mary*
10   *Most Cruel Death of Pyramus and Thisbe.*⁴

  BOTTOM   A very good piece of work, I assure you, and a merry.
    Now, good Peter Quince, call forth your actors by the scroll.
    Masters, spread yourselves.

  QUINCE   Answer as I call you. Nick Bottom, the weaver?

15   BOTTOM   Ready. Name what part I am for, and proceed.

  QUINCE   You, Nick Bottom, are set down for Pyramus.

  BOTTOM   What is Pyramus? A lover or a tyrant?

  QUINCE   A lover, that kills himself most gallant for love.

  BOTTOM   That will ask some tears in the true performing of it. If
20   I do it, let the audience look to their eyes. I will move stones.
    I will condole,° in some measure. To the rest.—Yet my chief   *lament; arouse pity*
    humour° is for a tyrant. I could play 'erc'les⁵ rarely,° or a part   *inclination / excellently*
    to tear a cat° in, to make all split.°   *rant / go to pieces*

                      The raging rocks
25   And shivering shocks
                  Shall break the locks
                    Of prison gates,
                  And Phibus' car⁶
                  Shall shine from far
30   And make and mar
                    The foolish Fates.

    This was lofty. Now name the rest of the players.—This is
    'erc'les' vein, a tyrant's vein. A lover is more condoling.

  QUINCE   Francis Flute, the bellows-mender?

35   FLUTE   Here, Peter Quince.

  QUINCE   Flute, you must take Thisbe on you.

  FLUTE   What is Thisbe? A wand'ring knight?°   *knight-errant*

  QUINCE   It is the lady that Pyramus must love.

  FLUTE   Nay, faith, let not me play a woman.⁷ I have a beard
40   coming.

  QUINCE   That's all one.° You shall play it in a mask,⁸ and you   *irrelevant*
    may speak as small° as you will.   *high-pitched; shrill*

  BOTTOM   An° I may hide my face, let me play Thisbe too. I'll   *If*
    speak in a monstrous° little voice: 'Thisne, Thisne!'⁹—'Ah   *exceptionally*
45   Pyramus, my lover dear, thy Thisbe dear and lady dear.'

  QUINCE   No, no, you must play Pyramus; and Flute, you Thisbe.

  BOTTOM   Well, proceed.

  QUINCE   Robin Starveling, the tailor?

  STARVELING   Here, Peter Quince.

50   QUINCE   Robin Starveling, you must play Thisbe's mother. Tom
    Snout, the tinker?

  SNOUT   Here, Peter Quince.

  QUINCE   You, Pyramus' father; myself, Thisbe's father. Snug the

---

3. *grow to a point*: draw to a conclusion.
4. Parodying titles such as that of Thomas Preston's
*Cambyses: A Lamentable Tragedy Mixed Full of Pleasant
Mirth* . . . (c. 1570).
5. Hercules (a stock ranting role in early plays).
6. The chariot of Phoebus Apollo, the sun god (the odd
spelling may represent Bottom's pronunciation).

7. On the Elizabethan stage, women's parts were
played by boys and young men.
8. Elizabethan ladies regularly wore masks for
anonymity and to protect their complexions.
9. Probably intended as a pet name for Thisbe; or it
may mean "in this manner."

joiner, you the lion's part; and I hope here is a play fitted.°   *(well) cast*

55   SNUG   Have you the lion's part written? Pray you, if it be, give it
me; for I am slow of study.

QUINCE   You may do it extempore, for it is nothing but roaring.

BOTTOM   Let me play the lion too. I will roar that I will do any
man's heart good to hear me. I will roar that I will make the
60   Duke say 'Let him roar again; let him roar again'.

QUINCE   An you should do it too terribly you would fright the
Duchess and the ladies that they would shriek, and that were
enough to hang us all.

ALL THE REST   That would hang us, every mother's son.

65   BOTTOM   I grant you, friends, if you should fright the ladies out
of their wits they would have no more discretion but to hang us,
but I will aggravate° my voice so that I will roar you as gently   *(for "moderate")*
as any sucking dove.[1] I will roar you an 'twere° any nightingale.   *as though it were*

QUINCE   You can play no part but Pyramus; for Pyramus is a
70   sweet-faced man; a proper° man as one shall see in a summer's   *handsome*
day; a most lovely, gentlemanlike man. Therefore you must
needs play Pyramus.

BOTTOM   Well, I will undertake it. What beard were I best to
play it in?

75   QUINCE   Why, what you will.

BOTTOM   I will discharge° it in either your straw-colour beard,   *perform*
your orange-tawny[2] beard, your purple-in-grain° beard, or your   *very deep red*
French-crown-colour° beard, your perfect yellow.   *gold-coin-colored*

QUINCE   Some of your French crowns have no hair at all,[3] and
80   then you will play bare faced.° But masters, here are your   *beardless; undisguised*
parts,[4] and I am to entreat you, request you, and desire you to
con° them by tomorrow night, and meet me in the palace wood   *memorize*
a mile without the town by moonlight. There will we rehearse;
for if we meet in the city we shall be dogged with company,
85   and our devices° known. In the meantime I will draw a bill°   *plans / list*
of properties such as our play wants. I pray you fail me not.

BOTTOM   We will meet, and there we may rehearse most
obscenely[5] and courageously. Take pains; be perfect.[6] Adieu.

QUINCE   At the Duke's oak we meet.

90   BOTTOM   Enough. Hold, or cut bowstrings.[7]   *Exeunt*

2.1

Enter a FAIRY *at one door and* ROBIN GOODFELLOW [*a*
puck][1] *at another*

ROBIN   How now, spirit, whither wander you?

FAIRY   Over hill, over dale,
    Thorough° bush, thorough brier,   *Through*
  Over park, over pale,°   *enclosure; fence*
5   Thorough flood, thorough fire:
  I do wander everywhere

---

1. Bottom confuses "sitting dove" and "sucking lamb."
2. Dark yellow, a recognized name for the dye. (Bottom the weaver shows his professional knowledge.)
3. Referring to the baldness caused by venereal disease ("the French disease").
4. Literally; an Elizabethan actor was generally given only his own lines and cues.
5. A comic blunder, possibly for "out of sight" (from the scene or from being seen).
6. Letter perfect in learning your parts.
7. *Hold, or cut bowstrings* (from archery): Keep your word, or be disgraced (?).
2.1 Location: A wood near Athens.
1. A puck is a devil or an imp; in Elizabethan folklore, Robin Goodfellow (also known as Puck) was a mischievous spirit who would do housework if well treated.

Swifter than the moonës sphere,[2]
And I serve the Fairy Queen
To dew her orbs[3] upon the green.
10   The cowslips tall her pensioners° be.   *royal bodyguards*
In their gold coats spots you see;
Those be rubies, fairy favours;°   *gifts*
In those freckles live their savours.°   *scent*
I must go seek some dewdrops here,
15   And hang a pearl in every cowslip's ear.
Farewell, thou lob° of spirits; I'll be gone.   *country bumpkin*
Our Queen and all her elves come here anon.
ROBIN   The King doth keep his revels here tonight.
Take heed the Queen come not within his sight,
20   For Oberon is passing fell and wroth[4]
Because that she, as her attendant, hath
A lovely boy stol'n from an Indian king.
She never had so sweet a changeling;[5]
And jealous Oberon would have the child
25   Knight of his train, to trace° the forests wild.   *range*
But she perforce° withholds the lovèd boy,   *forcibly*
Crowns him with flowers, and makes him all her joy.
And now they never meet in grove, or green,
By fountain° clear, or spangled starlight sheen,°   *spring / shining starlight*
30   But they do square,° that all their elves for fear   *quarrel*
Creep into acorn cups, and hide them there.
FAIRY   Either I mistake your shape and making° quite   *form*
Or else you are that shrewd° and knavish sprite   *mischievous*
Called Robin Goodfellow. Are not you he
35   That frights the maidens of the villag'ry,°   *villages*
Skim milk, and sometimes labour in the quern,°   *hand mill*
And bootless° make the breathless housewife churn,   *in vain*
And sometime° make the drink to bear no barm°—   *at times / froth on ale*
Mislead night wanderers, laughing at their harm?
40   Those that 'hobgoblin' call you, and 'sweet puck',
You do their work, and they shall have good luck.
Are not you he?
ROBIN   Thou speak'st aright;
I am that merry wanderer of the night.
I jest to Oberon, and make him smile
45   When I a fat and bean-fed horse beguile,°   *trick*
Neighing in likeness of a filly foal;
And sometime lurk I in a gossip's° bowl   *an old woman's*
In very likeness of a roasted crab,[6]
And when she drinks, against her lips I bob,
50   And on her withered dewlap° pour the ale.   *loose skin on neck*
The wisest aunt° telling the saddest° tale   *old woman / most serious*
Sometime for three-foot stool mistaketh me;
Then slip I from her bum. Down topples she,
And 'tailor' cries,[7] and falls into a cough,
55   And then the whole choir° hold their hips, and laugh,   *company*

---

2. Each planet, including the moon, was thought to be fixed in a transparent hollow globe revolving round the earth. *moonës*: the obsolete genitive of "moon."
3. Sprinkle her fairy rings (circles of dark grass).
4. *passing fell and wroth*: exceedingly fierce and angry.
5. Usually a child left by fairies in exchange for one stolen, but here the stolen child.
6. Crab apple ("lamb's wool," a winter drink, was made with roasted apples and warm ale).
7. Possibly the old woman cries this because she ends up cross-legged on the floor as tailors sat to work or because she falls on her "tail."

And waxen° in their mirth, and sneeze, and swear   *increase*
A merrier hour was never wasted there.—
    Enter [OBERON] *King of Fairies at one door, with his*
    train, and [TITANIA] *Queen at another, with hers*
But make room, fairy: here comes Oberon.
FAIRY And here my mistress. Would that he were gone.

60 OBERON Ill met by moonlight, proud Titania.
TITANIA What, jealous Oberon?—Fairies, skip hence.
    I have forsworn his bed and company.
OBERON Tarry, rash wanton.° Am not I thy lord?   *impetuous creature*
TITANIA Then I must be thy lady; but I know

65   When thou hast stol'n away from fairyland
    And in the shape of Corin[8] sat all day,
    Playing on pipes of corn, and versing love[9]
    To amorous Phillida. Why art thou here
    Come from the farthest step° of India,   *limit*

70   But that, forsooth, the bouncing° Amazon,   *vigorous*
    Your buskined° mistress and your warrior love,   *wearing hunting boots*
    To Theseus must be wedded, and you come
    To give their bed joy and prosperity?
OBERON How canst thou thus for shame, Titania,

75   Glance at my credit° with Hippolyta,   *Question my good name*
    Knowing I know thy love to Theseus?
    Didst not thou lead him through the glimmering night
    From Perigouna whom he ravishèd,
    And make him with fair Aegles[1] break his faith,

80   With Ariadne and Antiopa?[2]
TITANIA These are the forgeries of jealousy,
    And never since the middle summer's spring°   *beginning of midsummer*
    Met we on hill, in dale, forest, or mead,
    By pavèd fountain or by rushy[3] brook,

85   Or in° the beachèd margin° of the sea   *on / shore*
    To dance our ringlets° to the whistling wind,   *circular dances*
    But with thy brawls thou hast disturbed our sport.
    Therefore the winds, piping to us in vain,
    As in revenge have sucked up from the sea

90   Contagious fogs which, falling in the land,
    Hath every pelting° river made so proud   *paltry*
    That they have overborne their continents.°   *banks*
    The ox hath therefore stretched his yoke in vain,
    The ploughman lost his sweat, and the green corn°   *grain*

95   Hath rotted ere his youth attained a beard.
    The fold stands empty in the drownèd field,
    And crows are fatted with the murrain° flock.   *dead of disease*
    The nine men's morris[4] is filled up with mud,
    And the quaint mazes in the wanton green[5]

100   For lack of tread are undistinguishable.

---

8. Corin and Phillida are typical names for a shepherd and shepherdess in pastoral poetry.
9. Making or reciting love poetry. *pipes of corn:* musical instruments made of oat stalks.
1. Perigouna and Aegles were previous mistresses of Theseus (taken from Plutarch's *Life of Theseus*).
2. Taken from Plutarch; some writers used "Antiopa" as an alternative name for the Amazonian queen Theseus married, although here it seems to refer to a different

woman. Ariadne helped Theseus kill the Minotaur and escape from his labyrinth on Crete; she fled with Theseus, but he deserted her on Naxos.
3. Fringed with reeds. *pavèd:* pebbled.
4. The playing area for this outdoor game (traditionally, a board game played with nine pebbles or pegs) was cut in turf.
5. Luxuriant grass. *quaint mazes:* intricate arrangements of paths (kept visible by use).

The human mortals want° their winter cheer.[6]   *lack*
No night is now with hymn or carol blessed.
Therefore[7] the moon, the governess of floods,
Pale in her anger washes° all the air,   *moistens; wets*
105 That rheumatic[8] diseases do abound;
And thorough this distemperature° we see   *bad weather; disturbance*
The seasons alter: hoary-headed frosts
Fall in the fresh lap of the crimson rose,
And on old Hiems'° thin and icy crown   *winter's*
110 An odorous chaplet° of sweet summer buds   *wreath*
Is, as in mock'ry, set. The spring, the summer,
The childing° autumn, angry winter change   *fruitful*
Their wonted liveries,[9] and the mazèd° world   *bewildered*
By their increase° now knows not which is which; *crop yield*
115 And this same progeny of evils comes
From our debate,° from our dissension.   *quarrel*
We are their parents and original.°   *origin*
OBERON Do you amend it, then. It lies in you.
Why should Titania cross her Oberon?
120 I do but beg a little changeling boy
To be my henchman.°   *page of honor*
TITANIA   Set your heart at rest.[1]
The fairyland buys not the child of me.
His mother was a vot'ress[2] of my order,
And in the spicèd Indian air by night
125 Full often hath she gossiped by my side,
And sat with me on Neptune's yellow sands,
Marking th'embarkèd traders° on the flood,° *merchant ships / tide*
When we have laughed to see the sails conceive
And grow big-bellied with the wanton° wind,   *playful; amorous*
130 Which she with pretty and with swimming[3] gait
Following,° her womb then rich with my young squire, *Copying*
Would imitate, and sail upon the land
To fetch me trifles, and return again
As from a voyage, rich with merchandise.
135 But she, being mortal, of that boy did die;
And for her sake do I rear up her boy;
And for her sake I will not part with him.
OBERON How long within this wood intend you stay?
TITANIA Perchance till after Theseus' wedding day.
140 If you will patiently dance in our round,
And see our moonlight revels, go with us.
If not, shun me, and I will spare° your haunts.   *avoid*
OBERON Give me that boy and I will go with thee.
TITANIA Not for thy fairy kingdom.—Fairies, away.
145 We shall chide° downright if I longer stay.   *quarrel*
     Exeunt [TITANIA *and her train*]
OBERON Well, go thy way. Thou shalt not from° this grove *go from*
Till I torment thee for this injury.°—   *insult*
My gentle puck, come hither. Thou rememb'rest

6. Winter cheer would include the hymns and carols of
the Yuletide. But Q, F reading: here.
7. As in lines 88 and 93 above, referring to the con-
sequences of their quarrel.
8. Characterized by rheum: colds, coughs, etc.

9. Customary clothing.
1. Proverbial expression for "Abandon that idea."
2. Woman who has taken a vow to serve (often religious).
3. As though gliding through the waves.

Since° once I sat upon a promontory   *When*

150   And heard a mermaid on a dolphin's back

Uttering such dulcet° and harmonious breath°   *sweet / voice; song*

That the rude° sea grew civil at her song   *rough*

And certain stars shot madly from their spheres°   *orbits*

To hear the sea-maid's music?

ROBIN   I remember.

155   **OBERON**   That very time I saw, but thou couldst not,

Flying between the cold moon and the earth

Cupid, all armed. A certain aim he took

At a fair vestal thronèd by the west,[4]

And loosed his love-shaft° smartly from his bow   *golden arrow*

160   As° it should pierce a hundred thousand hearts.   *As though*

But I might° see young Cupid's fiery shaft   *could*

Quenched in the chaste beams of the wat'ry moon,

And the imperial vot'ress passèd on,

In maiden meditation, fancy-free.°   *free of love thoughts*

165   Yet marked I where the bolt° of Cupid fell.   *arrow*

It fell upon a little western flower—

Before, milk-white; now, purple with love's wound—

And maidens call it love-in-idleness.[5]

Fetch me that flower; the herb I showed thee once.

170   The juice of it on sleeping eyelids laid

Will make or° man or woman madly dote   *either*

Upon the next live creature that it sees.

Fetch me this herb, and be thou here again

Ere the leviathan[6] can swim a league.

175   **ROBIN**   I'll put a girdle° round about the earth   *circle*

In forty minutes.   *Exit*

OBERON   Having once this juice

I'll watch Titania when she is asleep,

And drop the liquor° of it in her eyes.   *juice*

The next thing then she waking looks upon—

180   Be it on lion, bear, or wolf, or bull,

On meddling monkey, or on busy ape—

She shall pursue it with the soul of love.

And ere I take this charm from off her sight—

As I can take it with another herb—

185   I'll make her render up her page to me.

But who comes here? I am invisible,

And I will overhear their conference.

          Enter DEMETRIUS, HELENA *following him*

DEMETRIUS   I love thee not, therefore pursue me not.

Where is Lysander, and fair Hermia?

190   The one I'll slay, the other slayeth me.

Thou told'st me they were stol'n unto this wood,

And here am I, and wood° within this wood   *insane*

Because I cannot meet my Hermia.

Hence, get thee gone, and follow me no more.

195   **HELENA**   You draw me, you hard-hearted adamant,[7]

---

4. To the west of India; in England. *vestal:* virgin (a compliment to Queen Elizabeth, the Virgin Queen, and possibly an allusion to a specific entertainment in her honor, such as the water pageant at Elvetham in 1591).
5. Pansy. (Classical legend describes how the mulberry turned purple with Pyramus's blood and the hyacinth with Hyacinthus's, but does not mention the pansy.)
6. Biblical sea monster, identified with the whale.
7. Very hard stone supposed to have magnetic properties. *draw me:* the magnetic power of attraction.

But yet you draw not iron; for my heart
Is true as steel.[8] Leave you° your power to draw,   *Relinquish*
And I shall have no power to follow you.
DEMETRIUS   Do I entice you? Do I speak you fair?[9]
200   Or rather do I not in plainest truth
Tell you I do not nor I cannot love you?
HELENA   And even for that do I love you the more.
I am your spaniel, and, Demetrius,
The more you beat me I will fawn on you.
205   Use me but as your spaniel: spurn me, strike me,
Neglect me, lose me; only give me leave,
Unworthy as I am, to follow you.
What worser place can I beg in your love—
And yet a place of high respect with me—
210   Than to be usèd as you use your dog?
DEMETRIUS   Tempt not too much the hatred of my spirit;
For I am sick when I do look on thee.
HELENA   And I am sick when I look not on you.
DEMETRIUS   You do impeach° your modesty too much,   *call into question*
215   To leave the city and commit yourself
Into the hands of one that loves you not;
To trust the opportunity of night,
And the ill counsel of a desert° place,   *deserted*
With the rich worth of your virginity.
220 HELENA   Your virtue is my privilege,° for that°   *protection / because*
It is not night when I do see your face;
Therefore I think I am not in the night,
Nor doth this wood lack worlds of company;
For you in my respect° are all the world.   *As far as I am concerned*
225   Then how can it be said I am alone,
When all the world is here to look on me?
DEMETRIUS   I'll run from thee, and hide me in the brakes,°   *thickets*
And leave thee to the mercy of wild beasts.
HELENA   The wildest hath not such a heart as you.
230   Run when you will. The story shall be changed:
Apollo flies, and Daphne holds the chase.[1]
The dove pursues the griffin,[2] the mild hind°   *doe*
Makes speed to catch the tiger: bootless° speed,   *useless*
When cowardice pursues, and valour flies.
235 DEMETRIUS   I will not stay thy questions.[3] Let me go;
Or if thou follow me, do not believe
But I shall do thee mischief in the wood.
HELENA   Ay, in the temple, in the town, the field,
You do me mischief. Fie, Demetrius,
240   Your wrongs do set a scandal on my sex.[4]
We cannot fight for love as men may do;
We should be wooed, and were not made to woo.
I'll follow thee, and make a heaven of hell,
To die upon the hand I love so well.

---

8. Hermia contrasts the base metal iron with steel, which holds its temper.
9. Do I speak kindly to you?
1. A reversal of the traditional myth in which the nymph Daphne, flying from Apollo, was transformed into a laurel tree to escape him.

2. Fabulous monster with a lion's body and an eagle's head and wings.
3. I will not wait here any longer to hear you talk.
4. Your injustice to me causes me to behave in a way that disgraces my sex (by wooing him rather than being wooed).

Exit [DEMETRIUS, HELENA *following him*]

245 OBERON   Fare thee well, nymph. Ere he do leave this grove
　　　Thou shalt fly him, and he shall seek thy love.
　　　Enter [ROBIN GOODFELLOW *the*] *puck*
　　　Hast thou the flower there? Welcome, wanderer.

ROBIN   Ay, there it is.

OBERON　　　　　　　　　I pray thee give it me.
　　　I know a bank where the wild thyme blows,
250　Where oxlips⁵ and the nodding violet grows,
　　　Quite overcanopied with luscious woodbine,°   *honeysuckle*
　　　With sweet musk-roses,⁶ and with eglantine.°   *sweetbrier, a type of rose*
　　　There sleeps Titania sometime of the night,
　　　Lulled in these flowers with dances and delight;
255　And there the snake throws° her enamelled skin,   *throws off ; casts*
　　　Weed° wide enough to wrap a fairy in;   *Garment*
　　　And with the juice of this I'll streak° her eyes,   *anoint*
　　　And make her full of hateful fantasies.
　　　Take thou some of it, and seek through this grove.
260　A sweet Athenian lady is in love
　　　With a disdainful youth. Anoint his eyes;
　　　But do it when the next thing he espies
　　　May be the lady. Thou shalt know the man
　　　By the Athenian garments he hath on.
265　Effect it with some care, that he may prove
　　　More fond° on her than she upon her love;   *doting*
　　　And look thou meet me ere the first cock crow.⁷

ROBIN   Fear not, my lord. Your servant shall do so.

　　　　　　　　　　　　　　　Exeunt [*severally*]°   *separately*

2.2

Enter TITANIA, *Queen of Fairies, with her train*

TITANIA   Come, now a roundel° and a fairy song,   *circular dance*
　　　Then for the third part of a minute¹ hence:
　　　Some to kill cankers° in the musk-rose buds,   *caterpillars*
　　　Some war with reremice° for their leathern wings   *bats*
5　　To make my small elves coats, and some keep back
　　　The clamorous owl, that nightly hoots and wonders
　　　At our quaint° spirits. Sing me now asleep;   *dainty*
　　　Then to your offices, and let me rest.
　　　[*She lies down.*] FAIRIES *sing*

FIRST FAIRY　　　You spotted snakes with double° tongue,   *forked*
10　　　　　　　Thorny hedgehogs, be not seen;
　　　　　　　Newts and blindworms,² do no wrong;
　　　　　　　Come not near our Fairy Queen.

CHORUS [*dancing*]   Philomel³ with melody,
　　　　　　　Sing in our sweet lullaby;
15　　　　　　　Lulla, lulla, lullaby; lulla, lulla, lullaby.
　　　　　　　Never harm
　　　　　　　Nor spell nor charm

---

5. Hybrid between primrose and cowslip.
6. Large rambling white roses.
7. Some spirits were thought unable to bear daylight (compare *Hamlet* 1.1.28–36).
2.2 Location: The wood.
1. The fairies are quick enough to do their tasks in

twenty seconds.
2. Newts (water lizards) and blindworms were thought to be poisonous, as were spiders (line 20).
3. Philomel, the nightingale (in classical mythology, a woman who, raped by her sister's husband, was transformed into a bird).

Come our lovely lady nigh.
So good night, with lullaby.

20 FIRST FAIRY Weaving spiders, come not here;
Hence, you long-legged spinners, hence;
Beetles black, approach not near;
Worm nor snail do no offence.

CHORUS [*dancing*] Philomel with melody,
25 Sing in our sweet lullaby;
Lulla, lulla, lullaby; lulla, lulla, lullaby.
Never harm
Nor spell nor charm
Come our lovely lady nigh.
30 So good night, with lullaby.

[TITANIA] *sleeps*

SECOND FAIRY Hence, away. Now all is well.
One aloof° stand sentinel.   *at a distance*

[*Exeunt all but* TITANIA *and the sentinel*]
Enter OBERON. [*He drops the juice on Titania's eyelids*]

OBERON What thou seest when thou dost wake,
Do it for thy true love take;
35 Love and languish for his sake.
Be it ounce,° or cat, or bear,   *lynx*
Pard,° or boar with bristled hair,   *Leopard*
In thy eye that shall appear
When thou wak'st, it is thy dear.
40 Wake when some vile thing is near.   [*Exit*]

Enter LYSANDER *and* HERMIA

LYSANDER Fair love, you faint with wand'ring in the wood,
And, to speak truth, I have forgot our way.
We'll rest us, Hermia, if you think it good,
And tarry for the comfort of the day.
45 HERMIA Be it so, Lysander. Find you out a bed;
For I upon this bank will rest my head.

[*She lies down*]

LYSANDER One turf shall serve as pillow for us both;
One heart, one bed; two bosoms, and one troth.°   *pledged faith*
HERMIA Nay, good Lysander; for my sake, my dear,
50 Lie further off yet; do not lie so near.
LYSANDER O, take the sense,° sweet, of my innocence!   *true meaning*
Love takes the meaning in love's conference[4]—
I mean that my heart unto yours is knit,
So that but one heart we can make of it.
55 Two bosoms interchainèd with an oath;
So, then, two bosoms and a single troth.
Then by your side no bed-room me deny;
For lying so, Hermia, I do not lie.[5]
HERMIA Lysander riddles very prettily.
60 Now much beshrew[6] my manners and my pride
If Hermia meant to say Lysander lied.
But, gentle friend, for love and courtesy,
Lie further off, in humane° modesty.   *courteous*

---

4. Love enables lovers truly to understand one another.   6. Curse (used in a mild sense).
5. Deceive; punning on "lie down."

Such separation as may well be said
65 Becomes a virtuous bachelor and a maid,
So far be distant; and good night, sweet friend.
Thy love ne'er alter till thy sweet life end.

LYSANDER Amen, amen, to that fair prayer say I;
And then end life when I end loyalty.
70 Here is my bed; sleep give thee all his rest.
    [*He lies down*]
HERMIA With half that wish the wisher's eyes be pressed.[7]
    They sleep [apart.]
    *Enter [*ROBIN GOODFELLOW *the] puck*

ROBIN Through the forest have I gone,
But Athenian found I none
On whose eyes I might approve°   *test*
75 This flower's force in stirring love.
Night and silence. Who is here?
Weeds of Athens he doth wear.
This is he my master said
Despisèd the Athenian maid—
80 And here the maiden, sleeping sound
On the dank and dirty ground.
Pretty soul, she durst not lie
Near this lack-love, this kill-courtesy.
Churl,° upon thy eyes I throw   *Rude fellow*
85 All the power this charm doth owe.°   *own*
    [*He drops the juice on Lysander's eyelids*]
When thou wak'st, let love forbid
Sleep his seat on thy eyelid.[8]
So, awake when I am gone.
For I must now to Oberon.   *Exit*
    Enter DEMETRIUS *and* HELENA, *running*
90 HELENA Stay, though thou kill me, sweet Demetrius.
DEMETRIUS I charge thee hence, and do not haunt me thus.
HELENA O, wilt thou darkling° leave me? Do not so.   *in darkness*
DEMETRIUS Stay, on thy peril;[9] I alone will go.   *Exit*
HELENA O, I am out of breath in this fond° chase.   *foolish*
95 The more my prayer, the lesser is my grace.°   *reward*
Happy is Hermia, wheresoe'er she lies;
For she hath blessèd and attractive° eyes.   *magnetic*
How came her eyes so bright? Not with salt tears—
If so, my eyes are oft'ner washed than hers.
100 No, no; I am as ugly as a bear,
For beasts that meet me run away for fear.
Therefore no marvel though Demetrius
Do, as° a monster, fly my presence thus.   *as if I were*
What wicked and dissembling glass of mine
105 Made me compare° with Hermia's sphery eyne!°   *compete / starry eyes*
But who is here? Lysander, on the ground?
Dead, or asleep? I see no blood, no wound.
Lysander, if you live, good sir, awake.
LYSANDER [*awaking*] And run through fire I will for thy sweet sake.
110 Transparent[1] Helena, nature shows art°   *skill; magic power*

---

7. May sleep's rest be shared between us. *pressed:*   9. Stay here or risk peril (if you follow me).
closed in sleep.   1. Radiant; capable of being seen through.
8. *forbid . . . eyelid:* prevent you from sleeping.

That through thy bosom makes me see thy heart.
Where is Demetrius? O, how fit a word
Is that vile name to perish on my sword!
HELENA Do not say so, Lysander; say not so.
115   What though he love your Hermia? Lord, what though?
Yet Hermia still loves you; then be content.
LYSANDER Content with Hermia? No, I do repent
The tedious minutes I with her have spent.
Not Hermia but Helena I love.
120   Who will not change a raven for a dove?
The will of man is by his reason swayed,[2]
And reason says you are the worthier maid.
Things growing are not ripe until their season,
So I, being young, till now ripe not to reason.
125   And, touching now the point of human skill,[3]
Reason becomes the marshal[4] to my will,
And leads me to your eyes, where I o'erlook°   look over; read
Love's stories written in love's richest book.
HELENA Wherefore was I to this keen° mockery born?   sharp
130   When at your hands did I deserve this scorn?
Is't not enough, is't not enough, young man,
That I did never—no, nor never can—
Deserve a sweet look from Demetrius' eye,
But you must flout my insufficiency?[5]
135   Good troth,° you do me wrong; good sooth,° you do,   Truly / indeed
In such disdainful manner me to woo.
But fare you well. Perforce I must confess
I thought you lord of more true gentleness.°   courtesy; breeding
O, that a lady of one man refused
140   Should of ° another therefore be abused!   Exit   by
LYSANDER She sees not Hermia. Hermia, sleep thou there,
And never mayst thou come Lysander near;
For as a surfeit of the sweetest things
The deepest loathing to the stomach brings,
145   Or as the heresies that men do leave
Are hated most of those they did deceive,[6]
So thou, my surfeit and my heresy,
Of all be hated, but the most of me;
And all my powers, address° your love and might   direct; apply
150   To honour Helen, and to be her knight.   Exit
HERMIA [awaking] Help me, Lysander, help me! Do thy best
To pluck this crawling serpent from my breast!
Ay me, for pity. What a dream was here?
Lysander, look how I do quake with fear.
155   Methought a serpent ate my heart away,
And you sat smiling at his cruel prey.°   act of preying
Lysander—what, removed? Lysander, lord—
What, out of hearing, gone? No sound, no word?
Alack, where are you? Speak an if ° you hear,   an if = if
160   Speak, of ° all loves. I swoon almost with fear.   for the sake of

---

2. Renaissance psychology considered the will (that is, the passions) to be in constant conflict with, and ideally subject to, the faculty of reason.
3. Reaching (only) now the highest point of human judgment.
4. Officer who led guests to their appointed places.
5. *flout my insufficiency:* mock my shortcomings by pretending they are wonderful qualities.
6. *as the heresies . . . deceive:* as men most hate the false opinions they once held.

No? Then I well perceive you are not nigh.
Either death or you I'll find immediately.   *Exit*

3.1

Enter the clowns:° [QUINCE, SNUG, BOTTOM, FLUTE,   *rustics*
SNOUT, *and* STARVELING]

BOTTOM   Are we all met?

QUINCE   Pat,° pat; and here's a marvellous convenient place for   *On the dot*
our rehearsal. This green plot shall be our stage, this hawthorn
brake° our tiring-house,° and we will do it in action as we will   *thicket / dressing room*
5   do it before the Duke.

BOTTOM   Peter Quince?

QUINCE   What sayst thou, bully° Bottom?   *good fellow; jolly*

BOTTOM   There are things in this comedy of Pyramus and
Thisbe that will never please. First, Pyramus must draw a sword
10   to kill himself, which the ladies cannot abide. How answer you
that?

SNOUT   By'r la'kin,[1] a parlous° fear.   *perilous*

STARVELING   I believe we must leave the killing out, when all is
done.[2]

15   BOTTOM   Not a whit. I have a device to make all well. Write me
a prologue, and let the prologue seem to say we will do no
harm with our swords, and that Pyramus is not killed indeed;
and for the more better assurance, tell them that I, Pyramus,
am not Pyramus, but Bottom the weaver. This will put them
20   out of fear.

QUINCE   Well, we will have such a prologue; and it shall be writ-
ten in eight and six.[3]

BOTTOM   No, make it two more: let it be written in eight and
eight.

25   SNOUT   Will not the ladies be afeard of the lion?

STARVELING   I fear it, I promise you.

BOTTOM   Masters, you ought to consider with yourself, to bring
in—God shield us—a lion among ladies is a most dreadful
thing;[4] for there is not a more fearful° wild fowl than your lion   *frightening*
30   living, and we ought to look to't.

SNOUT   Therefore another prologue must tell he is not a lion.

BOTTOM   Nay, you must name his name, and half his face must
be seen through the lion's neck, and he himself must speak
through, saying thus or to the same defect:° 'ladies', or 'fair   *(for "effect")*
35   ladies, I would wish you' or 'I would request you' or 'I would
entreat you not to fear, not to tremble. My life for yours.[5] If you
think I come hither as a lion, it were pity of ° my life. No, I am   *a threat to*
no such thing. I am a man, as other men are'—and there,
indeed, let him name his name, and tell them plainly he is
40   Snug the joiner.

QUINCE   Well, it shall be so; but there is two hard things: that is,
to bring the moonlight into a chamber—for you know Pyramus
and Thisbe meet by moonlight.

3.1 Location: Remains the same, although F intro-
duces an act break.
1. By our ladykin (Virgin Mary): a mild oath.
2. When all is said and done.
3. Alternate lines of eight and six syllables (a common
ballad measure).

4. In 1594, at a feast in honor of the christening of
King James's son, a tame lion that was supposed to draw
a chariot was replaced by a black African in order to
avoid frightening the audience.
5. I pledge my life to defend yours.

SNOUT[6] Doth the moon shine that night we play our play?

45 BOTTOM A calendar, a calendar—look in the almanac, find out
moonshine, find out moonshine.

Enter [ROBIN GOODFELLOW[7] *the*] *puck* [*invisible*]

QUINCE [*with a book*][8] Yes, it doth shine that night.

BOTTOM Why, then may you leave a casement of the great
chamber window where we play open, and the moon may
50 shine in at the casement.

QUINCE Ay, or else one must come in with a bush of thorns and
a lantern and say he comes to disfigure,[9] or to present,° the   *represent*
person of Moonshine. Then there is another thing: we must
have a wall in the great chamber; for Pyramus and Thisbe, says
55 the story, did talk through the chink of a wall.

SNOUT You can never bring in a wall. What say you, Bottom?

BOTTOM Some man or other must present Wall; and let him
have some plaster, or some loam, or some rough-cast[1] about
him, to signify 'wall'; and let him hold his fingers thus, and
60 through that cranny shall Pyramus and Thisbe whisper.

QUINCE If that may be, then all is well. Come, sit down every
mother's son, and rehearse your parts. Pyramus, you begin.
When you have spoken your speech, enter into that brake; and
so everyone according to his cue.

65 ROBIN [*aside*] What hempen homespuns[2] have we swagg'ring
here
So near the cradle of the Fairy Queen?
What, a play toward?° I'll be an auditor—   *in preparation*
An actor, too, perhaps, if I see cause.

QUINCE Speak, Pyramus. Thisbe, stand forth.

70 BOTTOM [*as Pyramus*] Thisbe, the flowers of odious° savours   *(for "odorous")*
sweet.

QUINCE Odours, odours.

BOTTOM [*as Pyramus*] Odours savours sweet.
So hath thy breath, my dearest Thisbe dear.
But hark, a voice. Stay thou but here a while,
75 And by and by I will to thee appear.   *Exit*

ROBIN[3] [*aside*] A stranger Pyramus than e'er played here. [*Exit*]

FLUTE Must I speak now?

QUINCE Ay, marry must you. For you must understand he goes
but to see a noise that he heard, and is to come again.

80 FLUTE [*as Thisbe*] Most radiant Pyramus, most lily-white of hue,
Of colour like the red rose on triumphant brier,
Most bristly juvenile,° and eke° most lovely Jew,[4]   *lively youth / also*
As true as truest horse that yet would never tire:
I'll meet thee, Pyramus, at Ninny's° tomb.   *fool's*

85 QUINCE Ninus'[5] tomb, man!—Why, you must not speak that
yet. That you answer to Pyramus. You speak all your part at

---

6. Or Snug: Q2, F abbreviate as "Sn."
7. Robin's entrance here (in F only) is also noted (in both F and Q) at line 65.
8. The book, perhaps comically supplied by Robin, is an editorial conjecture.
9. Blunder for "figure," represent. *bush of thorns:* bundle of thornbush kindling (like the lantern, a traditional accessory of the man in the moon).
1. Mixture of lime and gravel used to plaster outside walls.

2. Peasants, country bumpkins, dressed in coarse homespun fabric made from hemp.
3. Q gives this line to Quince.
4. Not often considered "lovely" by Elizabethan Christians; usually a term of abuse (here echoing the first syllable of "juvenile").
5. Mythical founder of Nineveh, whose wife, Semiramis, was believed to have founded Babylon, the setting for the story of Pyramus and Thisbe.

once, cues and all.—Pyramus, enter: your cue is past; it is
'never tire'.

FLUTE   O.

90   [*As Thisbe*] As true as truest horse that yet would never tire.
      [*Enter* ROBIN *leading* BOTTOM *with the ass-head*]

BOTTOM [*as Pyramus*]   If I were fair,° Thisbe, I were° only thine.   handsome / would be

QUINCE   O monstrous! O strange! We are haunted. Pray, mas-
      ters; fly, masters: help!   *The clowns all exeunt*

ROBIN   I'll follow you, I'll lead you about a round,°   in circles
95   Through bog, through bush, through brake, through brier.
      Sometime a horse I'll be, sometime a hound,
      A hog, a headless bear, sometime a fire,°   will-o'-the-wisp
      And neigh, and bark, and grunt, and roar, and burn,
      Like horse, hound, hog, bear, fire, at every turn.   *Exit*
      Enter [BOTTOM[6] *again,*] *with the ass-head*

100   BOTTOM   Why do they run away? This is a knavery of them to
      make me afeard.
            Enter SNOUT

SNOUT   O Bottom, thou art changed. What do I see on thee?

BOTTOM   What do you see? You see an ass-head of your own,[7]
      do you?   [*Exit* SNOUT]
            Enter QUINCE

105   QUINCE   Bless thee, Bottom, bless thee. Thou art translated.°   transformed
                                                                  Exit

BOTTOM   I see their knavery. This is to make an ass of me, to
      fright me, if they could; but I will not stir from this place, do
      what they can. I will walk up and down here, and I will sing,
      that they shall hear I am not afraid.

110   [*Sings*]   The ousel cock° so black of hue,   male blackbird
                      With orange-tawny bill;
                  The throstle° with his note so true,   song thrush
                  The wren with little quill.°   reed pipe

TITANIA [*awaking*]   What angel wakes me from my flow'ry bed?

115   BOTTOM [*sings*]   The finch, the sparrow, and the lark,
                      The plainsong[8] cuckoo grey,
                  Whose note full many a man doth mark,
                      And dares not answer 'Nay'[9]—
      for indeed, who would set his wit to° so foolish a bird? Who   pay heed to
120   would give a bird the lie,[1] though he cry 'Cuckoo' never so?°   ever so much

TITANIA   I pray thee, gentle mortal, sing again.
      Mine ear is much enamoured of thy note;
      So is mine eye enthrallèd to thy shape;
      And thy fair virtue's force[2] perforce doth move me
125   On the first view to say, to swear, I love thee.

BOTTOM   Methinks, mistress, you should have little reason for
      that. And yet, to say the truth, reason and love keep little com-
      pany together nowadays—the more the pity that some honest
      neighbours will not make them friends. Nay, I can gleek° upon   make jokes
130   occasion.

TITANIA   Thou art as wise as thou art beautiful.

6. He might have remained onstage when the others
left. Entrance noted in F only.
7. You see a figment of your own asinine imagination.
8. A melody sung without adornment; the repeated

"cuckoo" (associated with cuckoldry).
9. Deny (that he is a cuckold).
1. Who would call a bird a liar.
2. Your patience; power of your good qualities.

BOTTOM Not so, neither; but if I had wit enough to get out of
this wood, I have enough to serve mine own turn.°   *purpose*

TITANIA Out of this wood do not desire to go.

135   Thou shalt remain here, whether thou wilt or no.
I am a spirit of no common rate:°   *rank*
The summer still° doth tend upon my state;³   *always; continually*
And I do love thee. Therefore go with me.
I'll give thee fairies to attend on thee,

140   And they shall fetch thee jewels from the deep,
And sing while thou on pressèd flowers dost sleep;
And I will purge thy mortal grossness° so   *fleshly being*
That thou shalt like an airy spirit go.
Peaseblossom, Cobweb, Mote, and Mustardseed!

     Enter four fairies: PEASEBLOSSOM, COBWEB, MOTE,⁴ *and*
     MUSTARDSEED

A FAIRY Ready.

ANOTHER   And I.

ANOTHER   And I.

ANOTHER   And I.

145 ALL FOUR   Where shall we go?

TITANIA Be kind and courteous to this gentleman.
Hop in his walks, and gambol in his eyes.
Feed him with apricots and dewberries,
With purple grapes, green figs, and mulberries;

150   The honeybags steal from the humble-bees,°   *bumblebees*
And for night tapers crop their waxen thighs
And light them at the fiery glow-worms' eyes
To have° my love to bed, and to arise;   *lead*
And pluck the wings from painted butterflies

155   To fan the moonbeams from his sleeping eyes.
Nod to him, elves, and do him courtesies.

A FAIRY Hail, mortal.

ANOTHER Hail.

ANOTHER Hail.

160 ANOTHER Hail.

BOTTOM I cry your worships mercy,⁵ heartily.—I beseech your
worship's name.

COBWEB Cobweb.

BOTTOM I shall desire you of more acquaintance, good Master

165   Cobweb. If I cut my finger,⁶ I shall make bold with you.—Your
name, honest gentleman?

PEASEBLOSSOM Peaseblossom.

BOTTOM I pray you commend me to Mistress Squash, your
mother, and to Master Peascod,⁷ your father. Good Master

170   Peaseblossom, I shall desire you of more acquaintance, too.—
Your name, I beseech you, sir?

MUSTARDSEED Mustardseed.

BOTTOM Good Master Mustardseed, I know your patience⁸ well.
That same cowardly giantlike ox-beef⁹ hath devoured many a

175   gentleman of your house. I promise you your kindred hath

---

3. Serves me, as part of my royal retinue.
4. Speck. "Mote" and "moth" were pronounced alike.
5. I beg pardon of your honors.
6. Cobwebs were used to stop bleeding.

7. Ripe pea pod (called "your father" because it suggests "codpiece"). *Squash*: unripe pea pod.
8. What you have suffered with fortitude.
9. Because beef is often eaten with mustard.

made my eyes water ere now. I desire you of more acquain-
tance, good Master Mustardseed.

TITANIA [*to the fairies*]   Come, wait upon him, lead him to my bower.
   The moon, methinks, looks with a wat'ry eye,
180 And when she weeps, weeps every little flower,[1]
   Lamenting some enforcèd° chastity.   *violated; involuntary*
   Tie up my love's tongue;[2] bring him silently.   *Exeunt*

3.2

Enter [OBERON,] *King of Fairies*
OBERON   I wonder if Titania be awaked,
   Then what it was that next came in her eye,
   Which she must dote on in extremity.
      Enter [ROBIN GOODFELLOW *the*] *puck*
   Here comes my messenger. How now, mad spirit?
5   What nightrule° now about this haunted grove?   *night revels; sports*
ROBIN   My mistress with a monster is in love.
   Near to her close° and consecrated bower   *private*
   While she was in her dull° and sleeping hour   *drowsy*
   A crew of patches,° rude mechanicals°   *fools / rough workmen*
10 That work for bread upon Athenian stalls,°   *market stands*
   Were met together to rehearse a play
   Intended for great Theseus' nuptial day.
   The shallowest thickskin of that barren sort,°   *witless lot*
   Who Pyramus presented,° in their sport   *acted*
15 Forsook his scene° and entered in a brake,   *stage*
   When I did him at this advantage take.
   An ass's nole° I fixèd on his head.   *noddle; head*
   Anon his Thisbe must be answerèd,
   And forth my mimic° comes. When they him spy— *burlesque actor*
20 As wild geese that the creeping fowler° eye,   *hunter of birds*
   Or russet-pated choughs, many in sort,[1]
   Rising and cawing at the gun's report,
   Sever° themselves and madly sweep the sky—   *Scatter*
   So, at his sight, away his fellows fly,
25 And at our stamp[2] here o'er and o'er one falls.
   He° 'Murder' cries, and help from Athens calls.   *One (workman)*
   Their sense thus weak, lost with their fears thus strong,
   Made senseless things begin to do them wrong.
   For briers and thorns at their apparel snatch;
30 Some sleeves, some hats—from yielders all things catch.[3]
   I led them on in this distracted fear,
   And left sweet Pyramus translated there;
   When in that moment, so it came to pass,
   Titania waked and straightway loved an ass.
35 OBERON   This falls out better than I could devise.
   But hast thou yet latched° the Athenian's eyes   *anointed*
   With the love juice, as I did bid thee do?
ROBIN   I took him sleeping; that is finished, too;
   And the Athenian woman by his side,

---

1. Dew was thought to originate on the moon.
2. Bottom is perhaps making involuntary asinine noises.
3.2 Location: The wood.
1. Together, in a flock. *russet-pated choughs*: gray-

headed jackdaws.
2. Editors have wondered how a fairy's presumably
tiny foot could cause the human to fall.
3. Everything robs the timid.

40   That° when he waked of force° she must be eyed.   *So that / necessity*
                 Enter DEMETRIUS *and* HERMIA
       OBERON   Stand close. This is the same Athenian.
       ROBIN   This is the woman, but not this the man.
                 [They stand apart]
       DEMETRIUS   O, why rebuke you him that loves you so?
       Lay breath so bitter on your bitter foe.
45   HERMIA   Now I but chide, but I should use thee worse;
       For thou, I fear, hast given me cause to curse.
       If thou hast slain Lysander in his sleep,
       Being o'er shoes° in blood, plunge in the deep,   *Having waded so far*
       And kill me too.
50   The sun was not so true unto the day
       As he to me. Would he have stolen away
       From sleeping Hermia? I'll believe as soon
       This whole° earth may be bored, and that the moon   *solid*
       May through the centre creep, and so displease
55   Her brother's noontide with th'Antipodes.[4]
       It cannot be but thou hast murdered him.
       So should a murderer look—so dead,° so grim.   *deathly pale*
       DEMETRIUS   So should the murdered look, and so should I,
       Pierced through the heart with your stern cruelty.
60   Yet you, the murderer, look as bright, as clear
       As yonder Venus in her glimmering sphere.°   *orbit*
       HERMIA   What's this to my Lysander? Where is he?
       Ah, good Demetrius, wilt thou give him me?
       DEMETRIUS   I had rather give his carcass to my hounds.
65   HERMIA   Out, dog; out, cur. Thou driv'st me past the bounds
       Of maiden's patience. Hast thou slain him then?
       Henceforth be never numbered among men.
       O, once tell true; tell true, even for my sake.
       Durst thou have looked upon him being awake,
70   And hast thou killed him sleeping? O brave touch!°   *noble stroke*
       Could not a worm,° an adder do so much?—   *serpent*
       An adder did it, for with doubler[5] tongue
       Than thine, thou serpent, never adder stung.
       DEMETRIUS   You spend your passion on a misprised mood.° *in misconceived anger*
75   I am not guilty of Lysander's blood,
       Nor is he dead, for aught that I can tell.
       HERMIA   I pray thee, tell me then that he is well.
       DEMETRIUS   And if I could, what should I get therefor?°   *for that*
       HERMIA   A privilege never to see me more;
80   And from thy hated presence part I so.
       See me no more, whether he be dead or no.   *Exit*
       DEMETRIUS   There is no following her in this fierce vein.
       Here therefore for a while I will remain.
       So sorrow's heaviness[6] doth heavier grow
85   For debt that bankrupt sleep doth sorrow owe,[7]
       Which now in some slight measure it will pay,

---

4. *that . . . Antipodes:* that the moon could creep
through a hole bored through the earth's center and
emerge on the other side, the Antipodes, displeasing
the inhabitants by displacing the noontime sun with the
darkness of night. (Apollo, the sun god, was the brother
of Diana, the moon goddess.)

5. More forked (of the adder); more duplicitous (of
Demetrius).
6. Sadness (punning on "heavy": drowsy).
7. *For . . . owe:* Because of the sleeplessness sorrow
causes.

If for his tender here I make some stay.[8]
      [He lies] down [and sleeps]
OBERON [*to* ROBIN]   What hast thou done? Thou hast mistaken quite,
  And laid the love juice on some true love's sight.
90   Of thy misprision° must perforce ensue   *mistake*
  Some true love turned, and not a false turned true.
ROBIN   Then fate o'errules, that, one man holding troth,°   *faith*
  A million fail, confounding oath on oath.[9]
OBERON   About the wood go swifter than the wind,
95   And Helena of Athens look° thou find.   *be sure*
  All fancy-sick° she is, and pale of cheer°   *lovesick / face*
  With sighs of love that costs the fresh blood dear.[1]
  By some illusion see thou bring her here.
  I'll charm his eyes against° she do appear.   *in readiness for when*
100 ROBIN   I go, I go—look how I go,
  Swifter than arrow from the Tartar's bow.[2]   *Exit*
OBERON   Flower of this purple dye,
              Hit with Cupid's archery,
              Sink in apple° of his eye.   *pupil*
     [He drops the juice on Demetrius' eyelids]
105   When his love he doth espy,
              Let her shine as gloriously
              As the Venus of the sky.
              When thou wak'st, if she be by,
              Beg of her for remedy.
      Enter [ROBIN GOODFELLOW *the*] *puck*
110 ROBIN   Captain of our fairy band,
              Helena is here at hand,
              And the youth mistook by me,
              Pleading for a lover's fee.°   *reward*
              Shall we their fond° pageant see?   *foolish*
115   Lord, what fools these mortals be!
OBERON   Stand aside. The noise they make
              Will cause Demetrius to awake.
ROBIN   Then will two at once woo one.
              That must needs be sport alone;°   *unique*
120   And those things do best please me
              That befall prepost'rously.°   *ass backward*
     [They stand apart.]
     Enter HELENA, LYSANDER *[following her]*
LYSANDER   Why should you think that I should woo in scorn?
  Scorn and derision never come in tears.
  Look when I vow, I weep; and vows so born,
125   In their nativity all truth appears.[3]
  How can these things in me seem scorn to you,
  Bearing the badge of faith[4] to prove them true?
HELENA   You do advance° your cunning more and more,   *increase; display*
  When truth kills truth[5]—O devilish holy fray!
130 These vows are Hermia's. Will you give her o'er?

---

8. *Which . . . stay:* I will rest here awhile to give sleep
the opportunity to pay off some of its debt to sorrow.
9. Among the millions of faithless men, the one true
man's oath has been subverted by fate.
1. Sighs were thought to cause loss of blood.
2. Tartars, a dark-skinned, supposedly savage people in
Asia Minor, were famed for their archery.
3. *Look . . . appears:* The fact that I am weeping
authenticates my vow's sincerity.
4. Insignia, such as worn on a servant's livery (here, his
tears).
5. When one vow nullifies another.

Weigh oath with oath, and you will nothing weigh.[6]
Your vows to her and me put in two scales
Will even weigh, and both as light as tales.°   *lies; fiction*
LYSANDER   I had no judgement when to her I swore.
135 HELENA   Nor none, in my mind, now you give her o'er.
LYSANDER   Demetrius loves her, and he loves not you.
HELENA[7]   [   ]
DEMETRIUS [*awaking*]   O Helen, goddess, nymph, perfect, divine!
To what, my love, shall I compare thine eyne?
140 Crystal is muddy. O, how ripe in show°   *appearance*
Thy lips, those kissing cherries, tempting grow!
That pure congealèd white—high Taurus'[8] snow,
Fanned with the eastern wind—turns to a crow[9]
When thou hold'st up thy hand. O, let me kiss
145 This princess of pure white, this seal° of bliss!   *pledge*
HELENA   O spite! O hell! I see you all are bent
To set against me for your merriment.
If you were civil, and knew courtesy,
You would not do me thus much injury.
150 Can you not hate me—as I know you do—
But you must join in souls to mock me too?
If you were men, as men you are in show,
You would not use a gentle° lady so,   *well-born; mild*
To vow and swear and superpraise my parts°   *overpraise my qualities*
155 When I am sure you hate me with your hearts.
You both are rivals and love Hermia,
And now both rivals to mock Helena.
A trim° exploit, a manly enterprise—   *fine*
To conjure tears up in a poor maid's eyes
160 With your derision. None of noble sort°   *rank; nature*
Would so offend a virgin, and extort°   *torture*
A poor soul's patience, all to make you sport.
LYSANDER   You are unkind, Demetrius. Be not so.
For you love Hermia; this you know I know.
165 And here with all good will, with all my heart,
In Hermia's love I yield you up my part;
And yours of Helena to me bequeath,
Whom I do love, and will do till my death.
HELENA   Never did mockers waste more idle breath.
170 DEMETRIUS   Lysander, keep thy Hermia. I will none.[1]
If e'er I loved her, all that love is gone.
My heart to her but as guestwise° sojourned   *as a guest*
And now to Helen is it home returned,
There to remain.
LYSANDER   Helen, it is not so.
175 DEMETRIUS   Disparage not the faith thou dost not know,
Lest to thy peril thou aby it dear.°   *pay for it dearly*
            Enter HERMIA
Look where thy love comes; yonder is thy dear.
HERMIA   Dark night, that from the eye his° function takes,   *its*
The ear more quick of apprehension makes.

---

6. *you . . . weigh:* you will find that neither oath has
any substance; you, Lysander, will be found to have no
substance.
7. Helena's retort, awakening Demetrius, may have

been inadvertently omitted by the Q and F texts.
8. Range of high mountains in Asia Minor.
9. *turns to a crow:* appears black by contrast.
1. I will have nothing to do with her.

180   Wherein it doth impair the seeing sense,
       It pays the hearing double recompense.
       Thou art not by mine eye, Lysander, found;
       Mine ear, I thank it, brought me to thy sound.
       But why unkindly didst thou leave me so?
185 LYSANDER   Why should he stay whom love doth press to go?
    HERMIA   What love could press Lysander from my side?
    LYSANDER   Lysander's love, that would not let him bide:
       Fair Helena, who more engilds the night
       Than all yon fiery O's and eyes of light.[2]
190   Why seek'st thou me? Could not this make thee know
       The hate I bare thee made me leave thee so?
    HERMIA   You speak not as you think. It cannot be.
    HELENA [aside]   Lo, she is one of this confederacy.
       Now I perceive they have conjoined all three
195   To fashion this false sport in spite of° me.—   ° to spite
       Injurious Hermia, most ungrateful maid,
       Have you conspired, have you with these contrived
       To bait[3] me with this foul derision?
       Is all the counsel° that we two have shared—   ° confidences
200   The sisters' vows, the hours that we have spent
       When we have chid the hasty-footed time
       For parting us—O, is all quite forgot?
       All schooldays' friendship, childhood innocence?
       We, Hermia, like two artificial gods
205   Have with our needles created both one flower,
       Both on one sampler, sitting on one cushion,
       Both warbling of one song, both in one key,
       As if our hands, our sides, voices, and minds
       Had been incorporate.° So we grew together,   ° of one body
210   Like to a double cherry: seeming parted,
       But yet an union in partition,
       Two lovely berries moulded on one stem.
       So, with two seeming bodies but one heart,
       Two of the first[4]—like coats in heraldry,
215   Due but to one and crownèd with one crest.
       And will you rend our ancient love asunder,
       To join with men in scorning your poor friend?
       It is not friendly, 'tis not maidenly.
       Our sex as well as I may chide you for it,
220   Though I alone do feel the injury.
    HERMIA   I am amazèd at your passionate words.
       I scorn you not. It seems that you scorn me.
    HELENA   Have you not set Lysander, as in scorn,
       To follow me, and praise my eyes and face?
225   And made your other love, Demetrius—
       Who even but now° did spurn me with his foot—   ° just now
       To call me goddess, nymph, divine, and rare,
       Precious, celestial? Wherefore speaks he this
       To her he hates? And wherefore doth Lysander
230   Deny your love so rich within his soul,

2. Stars (punning on the vowels and on lovers' exclam-
atory "oh"s and "ay"s). An "o" was a spangle.
3. To torment (as Elizabethans set dogs to bait a bear).
4. A technical phrase in heraldry, referring to the first

quartering in a coat of arms, which may be repeated.
The friends then have two bodies but a single, over-
arching identity.

And tender° me, forsooth, affection,   *offer*
But by your setting on, by your consent?
What though I be not so in grace° as you,   *favor*
So hung upon with love, so fortunate,
235 But miserable most, to love unloved—
This you should pity rather than despise.

HERMIA   I understand not what you mean by this.

HELENA   Ay, do. Persever, counterfeit sad° looks,   *serious*
Make mouths upon° me when I turn my back,   *Make faces at*
240 Wink each at other, hold the sweet jest up.°   *keep up the joke*
This sport well carried shall be chronicled.
If you have any pity, grace, or manners,
You would not make me such an argument.°   *a subject of merriment*
But fare ye well. 'Tis partly my own fault,
245 Which death or absence soon shall remedy.

LYSANDER   Stay, gentle Helena, hear my excuse,
My love, my life, my soul, fair Helena.

HELENA   O excellent!

HERMIA [*to* LYSANDER]   Sweet, do not scorn her so.

DEMETRIUS [*to* LYSANDER]   If she cannot entreat I can compel.[5]
250 LYSANDER   Thou canst compel no more than she entreat.
Thy threats have no more strength than her weak prayers.—
Helen, I love thee; by my life I do.
I swear by that which I will lose for thee
To prove him false that says I love thee not.

255 DEMETRIUS [*to* HELENA]   I say I love thee more than he can do.

LYSANDER   If thou say so, withdraw,[6] and prove it too.

DEMETRIUS   Quick, come.

HERMIA   Lysander, whereto tends all this?
[*She takes him by the arm*]

LYSANDER   Away, you Ethiope.[7]

DEMETRIUS   No, no, sir, yield.°   *(to Hermia)*
Seem to break loose, take on as° you would follow,   *pretend*
260 But yet come not. You are a tame man; go.

LYSANDER [*to* HERMIA]   Hang off,° thou cat, thou burr; vile thing, let loose,   *Let go*
Or I will shake thee from me like a serpent.

HERMIA   Why are you grown so rude? What change is this,
Sweet love?

LYSANDER   Thy love? Out, tawny Tartar, out;
265 Out, loathèd med'cine;[8] O hated potion, hence.

HERMIA   Do you not jest?

HELENA   Yes, sooth,° and so do you.   *truly*

LYSANDER   Demetrius, I will keep my word with thee.

DEMETRIUS   I would I had your bond, for I perceive
A weak bond[9] holds you. I'll not trust your word.

270 LYSANDER   What, should I hurt her, strike her, kill her dead?
Although I hate her, I'll not harm her so.

HERMIA   What, can you do me greater harm than hate?
Hate me—wherefore? O me, what news,° my love?   *what has happened*
Am not I Hermia? Are not you Lysander?

---

5. If Hermia cannot entreat you to stop, I can make you do it.
6. Come with me ("step outside").
7. Allusion to Hermia's dark hair and complexion. Elizabethans generally regarded light complexions as more beautiful than dark and often stigmatized dark-skinned peoples (such as Ethiopians or Tartars) as ugly.
8. Any drug (including poison).
9. Hermia's weak grasp (with a pun on "bond": oath, in the previous line).

275 I am as fair now as I was erewhile.°   *a while ago*
Since night you loved me, yet since night you left me.
Why then, you left me—O, the gods forbid—
In earnest, shall I say?

LYSANDER   Ay, by my life,
And never did desire to see thee more.

280 Therefore be out of hope, of question, doubt.
Be certain, nothing truer; 'tis no jest
That I do hate thee and love Helena.

HERMIA [*to* HELENA]   O me, you juggler,° you canker blossom,[1]   *trickster*
You thief of love—what, have you come by night
And stol'n my love's heart from him?

285 HELENA   Fine, i'faith.
Have you no modesty, no maiden shame,
No touch of bashfulness? What, will you tear
Impatient answers from my gentle tongue?
Fie, fie, you counterfeit, you puppet,[2] you!

290 HERMIA   Puppet? Why, so! Ay, that way goes the game.
Now I perceive that she hath made compare
Between our statures; she hath urged her height,
And with her personage, her tall personage,
Her height, forsooth, she hath prevailed with him—

295 And are you grown so high in his esteem
Because I am so dwarfish and so low?
How low am I, thou painted maypole?[3] Speak,
How low am I? I am not yet so low
But that my nails can reach unto thine eyes.

HELENA [*to* DEMETRIUS *and* LYSANDER]   I pray you, though you
300   mock me, gentlemen,
Let her not hurt me. I was never curst.°   *quarrelsome*
I have no gift at all in shrewishness.
I am a right° maid for my cowardice.   *proper*
Let her not strike me. You perhaps may think

305 Because she is something° lower than myself   *somewhat*
That I can match her—

HERMIA   Lower? Hark again.

HELENA   Good Hermia, do not be so bitter with me.
I evermore did love you, Hermia,
Did ever keep your counsels, never wronged you—

310 Save that in love unto Demetrius
I told him of your stealth° unto this wood.   *stealing away*
He followed you; for love I followed him.
But he hath chid me hence, and threatened me
To strike me, spurn me, nay, to kill me too.

315 And now, so° you will let me quiet go,   *if only*
To Athens will I bear my folly back,
And follow you no further. Let me go.
You see how simple and how fond° I am.   *foolish*

HERMIA   Why, get you gone. Who is't that hinders you?

320 HELENA   A foolish heart that I leave here behind.

HERMIA   What, with Lysander?

---

1. Worm that devours blossoms (of love).   3. Proverbial for someone tall and skinny. *painted*:
2. Fraudulent imitation; but Hermia interprets "pup-   insulting allusion to the use of cosmetics.
pet" as a reference to her height.

HELENA   With Demetrius.
LYSANDER   Be not afraid; she shall not harm thee, Helena.
DEMETRIUS   No, sir, she shall not, though you take her part.
HELENA   O, when she is angry she is keen° and shrewd.°   *sharp / shrewish*
325   She was a vixen when she went to school,
          And though she be but little, she is fierce.
HERMIA   Little again? Nothing but 'low' and 'little'?—
          Why will you suffer her to flout me thus?
          Let me come to her.
LYSANDER   Get you gone, you dwarf,
330   You *minimus* of hind'ring knot-grass[4] made,
          You bead, you acorn.
DEMETRIUS   You are too officious
          In her behalf that scorns your services.
          Let her alone. Speak not of Helena.
          Take not her part. For if thou dost intend
335   Never so little° show of love to her,   *Even the smallest*
          Thou shalt aby° it.   *pay for*
LYSANDER   Now she holds me not.
          Now follow, if thou dar'st, to try whose right,
          Of thine or mine, is most in Helena.
DEMETRIUS   Follow? Nay, I'll go with thee, cheek by jowl.[5]
                     Exeunt LYSANDER *and* DEMETRIUS
340 HERMIA   You, mistress, all this coil° is long° of you.   *turmoil / because*
          Nay, go not back.
HELENA   I will not trust you, I,
          Nor longer stay in your curst company.
          Your hands than mine are quicker for a fray;°   *fight*
          My legs are longer, though, to run away.   [*Exit*]
345 HERMIA   I am amazed, and know not what to say.   *Exit*
          OBERON *and* ROBIN [*come forward*]
OBERON   This is thy negligence. Still° thou mistak'st,   *Always*
          Or else commit'st thy knaveries wilfully.
ROBIN   Believe me, king of shadows,° I mistook.   *fairy spirits*
          Did not you tell me I should know the man
350   By the Athenian garments he had on?—
          And so far° blameless proves my enterprise   *to this extent*
          That I have 'nointed an Athenian's eyes;
          And so far am I glad it so did sort°   *turn out*
          As° this their jangling° I esteem a sport.   *Since / bickering*
355 OBERON   Thou seest these lovers seek a place to fight.
          Hie° therefore, Robin, overcast the night;   *Hurry*
          The starry welkin° cover thou anon   *sky*
          With drooping fog as black as Acheron,°   *river of hell*
          And lead these testy rivals so astray
360   As° one come not within another's way.   *So that*
          Like to Lysander sometime frame thy tongue,
          Then stir Demetrius up with bitter wrong;°   *insults*
          And sometime rail thou like Demetrius,
          And from each other look thou lead them thus
365   Till o'er their brows death-counterfeiting sleep

___

4. Creeping binding weed (its sap was thought to stunt   5. Proverbial for "side by side."
human growth). *minimus:* diminutive thing (Latin).

With leaden legs and batty° wings doth creep.   *batlike*
Then crush this herb into Lysander's eye—
Whose liquor hath this virtuous° property,   *potent*
To take from thence all error with his might,
370   And make his eyeballs roll with wonted° sight.   *normal*
When they next wake, all this derision
Shall seem a dream and fruitless° vision,   *inconsequential*
And back to Athens shall the lovers wend°   *go*
With league° whose date° till death shall never end.   *covenant / duration*
375   Whiles I in this affair do thee employ,
I'll to my queen and beg her Indian boy;
And then I will her charmèd° eye release   *enchanted*
From monster's view, and all things shall be peace.
ROBIN   My fairy lord, this must be done with haste,
380   For night's swift dragons[6] cut the clouds full fast,
And yonder shines Aurora's harbinger,[7]
At whose approach ghosts, wand'ring here and there,
Troop home to churchyards; damnèd spirits all
That in cross-ways and floods[8] have burial
385   Already to their wormy beds are gone,
For fear lest day should look their shames upon.
They wilfully themselves exiled from light,
And must for aye° consort with black-browed night.   *forever*
OBERON   But we are spirits of another sort.
390   I with the morning's love[9] have oftmade sport,
And like a forester[1] the groves may tread
Even till the eastern gate, all fiery red,
Opening on Neptune° with fair blessèd beams   *the sea*
Turns into yellow gold his salt° green streams.   *salty*
395   But notwithstanding, haste, make no delay;
We may effect this business yet ere day.   [*Exit*]
ROBIN   Up and down, up and down,
I will lead them up and down.
I am feared in field and town.
400   Goblin,° lead them up and down.   (*Puck himself*)
Here comes one.
            Enter LYSANDER
LYSANDER   Where art thou, proud Demetrius? Speak thou now.
ROBIN [*shifting place*][2]   Here, villain, drawn° and ready. Where   *with sword drawn*
    art thou?
LYSANDER   I will be with thee straight.°   *immediately*
ROBIN [*shifting place*]   Follow me then
To plainer° ground.   [*Exit* LYSANDER][3]   *clearer*
            Enter DEMETRIUS
405   DEMETRIUS [*shifting place*]   Lysander, speak again.
Thou runaway, thou coward, art thou fled?
Speak! In some bush? Where dost thou hide thy head?

---

6. Imagined as drawing the chariots of the goddess of
night.
7. Herald of the goddess of dawn; the morning star.
8. In which the drowned were "buried," without Chris-
tian sacrament. *cross-ways:* crossroads (where suicides
were buried, also without Christian sacrament). Robin
is differentiating here between two types of spirits: those
who wandered from their churchyard graves and those
who have no proper resting place. These two types, both

ghosts of former humans, are differentiated in turn
from the fairy spirits by Oberon in the ensuing lines.
9. The love of Aurora, goddess of dawn (or Cephalus,
a brave hunter, Aurora's lover).
1. Keeper of a royal forest or private park.
2. In F, this direction is placed in the margin in the
middle of this episode. (In what follows, Robin pre-
sumably mimics the voices of Demetrius and Lysander.)
3. He might instead wander about the stage.

ROBIN [*shifting place*]   Thou coward, art thou bragging to the stars,
    Telling the bushes that thou look'st for wars,
410   And wilt not come? Come, recreant;° come, thou child,   *coward; wretch*
    I'll whip thee with a rod. He is defiled
    That draws a sword on thee.[4]
DEMETRIUS [*shifting place*]   Yea, art thou there?
ROBIN [*shifting place*]   Follow my voice; we'll try° no manhood here.   *test*
Exeunt

3.3

[*Enter* LYSANDER]

LYSANDER   He goes before me, and still dares me on;
    When I come where he calls, then he is gone.
    The villain is much lighter heeled than I;
    I followed fast, but faster he did fly,
5   That° fallen am I in dark uneven way,   *With the result that*
    And here will rest me.
        [*He lies*] *down*
                Come, thou gentle day;
    For if but once thou show me thy grey light,
    I'll find Demetrius, and revenge this spite.   [*He sleeps*]
      Enter ROBIN [GOODFELLOW] *and* DEMETRIUS
ROBIN [*shifting place*]   Ho, ho, ho, coward, why com'st thou not?
10 DEMETRIUS   Abide° me if thou dar'st, for well I wot°   *Wait for / know*
    Thou runn'st before me, shifting every place,
    And dar'st not stand nor look me in the face.
    Where art thou now?
ROBIN [*shifting place*]   Come hither, I am here.
DEMETRIUS   Nay, then thou mock'st me. Thou shalt buy° this   *pay for*
    dear°   *dearly*
15   If ever I thy face by daylight see.
    Now go thy way. Faintness constraineth me
    To measure out my length on this cold bed.
        [*He lies down*]
    By day's approach look to be visited.   [*He sleeps*]
      Enter HELENA
HELENA   O weary night, O long and tedious night,
20   Abate° thy hours; shine comforts from the east   *Shorten*
    That I may back to Athens by daylight
        From these that my poor company detest;
    And sleep, that sometimes shuts up sorrow's eye,
    Steal me a while from mine own company.
      [*She lies down and sleeps*]
25 ROBIN   Yet but three? Come one more,
    Two of both kinds makes up four.
      Enter HERMIA
    Here she comes, curst° and sad.   *angry*
    Cupid is a knavish lad
    Thus to make poor females mad.
30 HERMIA   Never so weary, never so in woe,
    Bedabbled° with the dew, and torn with briers,   *Sprinkled*
    I can no further crawl, no further go.
    My legs can keep no pace with my desires.

---

4. I.e., it would be a disgrace to treat you as an honor-   3.3 Location: Scene continues.
able opponent.

Here will I rest me till the break of day.
[*She lies down*]
35   Heavens shield Lysander, if they mean a fray.
[*She sleeps*]
ROBIN   On the ground sleep sound.
I'll apply to your eye,
Gentle lover, remedy.
[*He drops the juice on Lysander's eyelids*]
When thou wak'st thou tak'st
40   True delight in the sight
Of thy former lady's eye,
And the country proverb known,
That 'every man should take his own',
In your waking shall be shown.
45   Jack shall have Jill,
Naught shall go ill,
the man shall have his mare again, and all shall be well. [*Exit*]

4.1

Enter [TITANIA,] *Queen of Fairies, and* [BOTTOM *the*]
clown [*with the ass-head*], *and fairies:* [PEASEBLOSSOM,
COBWEB, MOTE, *and* MUSTARDSEED]

TITANIA [*to* BOTTOM]   Come, sit thee down upon this flow'ry bed,
While I thy amiable° cheeks do coy,°   *lovable / caress*
And stick musk-roses in thy sleek smooth head,
And kiss thy fair large ears, my gentle joy.
5   BOTTOM   Where's Peaseblossom?
PEASEBLOSSOM   Ready.
BOTTOM   Scratch my head, Peaseblossom. Where's Monsieur
Cobweb?
COBWEB   Ready.
10   BOTTOM   Monsieur Cobweb, good monsieur, get you your
weapons in your hand and kill me a red-hipped humble-bee
on the top of a thistle; and, good monsieur, bring me the hon-
eybag. Do not fret yourself too much in the action, monsieur;
and, good monsieur, have a care the honeybag break not. I
15   would be loath to have you overflowen with° a honeybag, signor.   *submerged by*
[*Exit* COBWEB]
Where's Monsieur Mustardseed?
MUSTARDSEED   Ready.
BOTTOM   Give me your neaf,° Monsieur Mustardseed. Pray you,   *fist*
leave your courtesy,[1] good monsieur.
20   MUSTARDSEED   What's your will?
BOTTOM   Nothing, good monsieur, but to help Cavaliery[2] Pease-
blossom[3] to scratch. I must to the barber's, monsieur, for
methinks I am marvellous hairy about the face; and I am such
a tender ass, if my hair do but tickle me I must scratch.
25   TITANIA   What, wilt thou hear some music, my sweet love?
BOTTOM   I have a reasonable good ear in music. Let's have the
tongs and the bones.[4]

4.1 Location: The wood. The original text has no act
break here. F has the four lovers sleep through the
action onstage.
1. *leave your courtesy:* stop bowing, or do not stand
bareheaded.

2. Blunder for "Cavalier," perhaps influenced by the
Italian term *cavaliere.*
3. The early texts have "Cobweb" (Shakespeare's or the
printer's error).
4. Triangle and clappers (rustic musical instruments).

Rural music[5]

TITANIA   Or say, sweet love, what thou desir'st to eat.

BOTTOM   Truly, a peck of provender.° I could munch your good   *fodder*
30   dry oats. Methinks I have a great desire to a bottle° of hay. Good   *bundle*
hay, sweet hay, hath no fellow.°   *equal*

TITANIA   I have a venturous fairy that shall seek
The squirrel's hoard, and fetch thee off new nuts.

BOTTOM   I had rather have a handful or two of dried peas. But I
35   pray you, let none of your people stir me. I have an exposition
of° sleep come upon me.   *disposition to*

TITANIA   Sleep thou, and I will wind thee in my arms.
Fairies, be gone, and be all ways° away.   [*Exeunt* fairies]   *in every direction*
So° doth the woodbine[6] the sweet honeysuckle   *Thus*
40   Gently entwist; the female ivy so
Enrings the barky fingers of the elm.
O how I love thee, how I dote on thee!
          [*They sleep.*]
          Enter ROBIN GOODFELLOW [*the puck*] *and* OBERON[7]
          [*King of Fairies, meeting*]

OBERON   Welcome, good Robin. Seest thou this sweet sight?
Her dotage now I do begin to pity,
45   For meeting her of late behind the wood,
Seeking sweet favours° for this hateful fool,   *love tokens*
I did upbraid her and fall out with her,
For she his hairy temples then had rounded
With coronet of fresh and fragrant flowers,
50   And that same dew which sometime° on the buds   *formerly*
Was wont° to swell like round and orient[8] pearls   *accustomed*
Stood now within the pretty flow'rets' eyes,
Like tears that did their own disgrace bewail.
When I had at my pleasure taunted her,
55   And she in mild terms begged my patience,
I then did ask of her her changeling child,
Which straight she gave me, and her fairy sent
To bear him to my bower in fairyland.
And now I have the boy, I will undo
60   This hateful imperfection of her eyes.
And, gentle puck, take this transformèd scalp
From off the head of this Athenian swain,
That he, awaking when the other° do,   *others*
May all to Athens back again repair,
65   And think no more of this night's accidents
But as the fierce vexation of a dream.
But first I will release the Fairy Queen.
          [*He drops the juice on Titania's eyelids*]
Be as thou wast wont to be,
See as thou wast wont to see.
70   Dian's bud o'er Cupid's flower[9]
Hath such force and blessèd power.

---

5. Probably background music, which continues during the following dialogue, rather than a separate musical interlude. The direction only occurs in F.
6. Here, "woodbine" cannot mean "honeysuckle," as it did at 2.1.251, and thus must refer to a different plant.
7. In Q, he enters earlier, unseen, with Titania and her train.

8. Lustrous (the best pearls were from the Far East).
9. "Dian's bud," the herb of 2.1.184 and 3.2.367, is perhaps *Agnus castus,* or chaste tree: said to preserve chastity and hence the antidote to "Cupid's flower," or the love-in-idleness of 2.1.166 etc.

Now, my Titania, wake you, my sweet queen.
TITANIA [*awaking*]   My Oberon, what visions have I seen!
Methought I was enamoured of an ass.
OBERON   There lies your love.
75   TITANIA   How came these things to pass?
O, how mine eyes do loathe his visage now!
OBERON   Silence a while.—Robin, take off this head.—
Titania, music call, and strike more dead
Than common sleep of all these[1] the sense.
80   TITANIA   Music, ho—music such as charmeth sleep.
        Still° music   Soft
ROBIN [*taking the ass-head off* BOTTOM]   Now when thou wak'st
with thine own fool's eyes peep.
OBERON   Sound music.
        [*The music changes*]
                    Come, my queen, take hands with me,
And rock the ground whereon these sleepers be.
        [OBERON *and* TITANIA *dance*]
Now thou and I are new in amity,
85   And will tomorrow midnight solemnly
Dance in Duke Theseus' house, triumphantly,
And bless it to all fair prosperity.
There shall the pairs of faithful lovers be
Wedded with Theseus, all in jollity.
90   ROBIN   Fairy King, attend and mark.
I do hear the morning lark.
OBERON   Then, my queen, in silence sad
Trip we after nightës[2] shade.
We the globe can compass° soon,   orbit
95   Swifter than the wand'ring moon.
TITANIA   Come, my lord, and in our flight
Tell me how it came this night
That I sleeping here was found
With these mortals on the ground.
                    Exeunt [OBERON, TITANIA, *and*
                        ROBIN. *The*] *sleepers lie still*
                Wind horns [*within*]. *Enter* THESEUS [*with*] EGEUS, HIP-
                POLYTA, *and all his train*
100   THESEUS   Go, one of you, find out the forester,
For now our observation[3] is performed;
And since we have the vanguard° of the day,   earliest part
My love shall hear the music of my hounds.
Uncouple[4] in the western valley; let them go.
105   Dispatch, I say, and find the forester.   [*Exit one*]
We will, fair Queen, up to the mountain's top,
And mark the musical confusion
Of hounds and echo in conjunction.
HIPPOLYTA   I was with Hercules and Cadmus[5] once
110   When in a wood of Crete they bayed° the bear   brought to bay
With hounds of Sparta.[6] Never did I hear

---

1. The lovers and Bottom.
2. The obsolete genitive inflection.
3. "Observance to a morn of May," as at 1.1.167.
4. Release (the dogs, leashed in pairs).

5. Mythical founder of Thebes. (No source for the anecdote is known.)
6. Famous in antiquity as hunting dogs.

Such gallant chiding;° for besides the groves, *barking*
The skies, the fountains, every region near
Seemed all one mutual cry. I never heard
115 So musical a discord, such sweet thunder.
THESEUS   My hounds are bred out of the Spartan kind,
So flewed,[7] so sanded;° and their heads are hung *sandy-colored*
With ears that sweep away the morning dew,
Crook-kneed, and dewlapped[8] like Thessalian bulls,
120 Slow in pursuit, but matched in mouth like bells,
Each under each.[9] A cry more tuneable[1]
Was never holla'd to nor cheered with horn
In Crete, in Sparta, nor in Thessaly.
Judge when you hear. But soft:° what nymphs are these? *stop; look*
125 EGEUS   My lord, this is my daughter here asleep,
And this Lysander; this Demetrius is;
This Helena, old Nedar's Helena.
I wonder of their being here together.
THESEUS   No doubt they rose up early to observe
130 The rite of May, and, hearing our intent,
Came here in grace of our solemnity.° *ceremony*
But speak, Egeus: is not this the day
That Hermia should give answer of her choice?
EGEUS   It is, my lord.
135 THESEUS   Go bid the huntsmen wake them with their horns.

                                          [*Exit one*]
        Shout within: wind horns. [*The lovers*] *all start up*
Good morrow, friends. Saint Valentine[2] is past.
Begin these wood-birds but to couple now?
LYSANDER   Pardon, my lord.
            [*The lovers kneel*]
THESEUS   I pray you all stand up.
            [*The lovers stand*]
[*To* DEMETRIUS *and* LYSANDER] I know you two are rival enemies.
140 How comes this gentle concord in the world,
That hatred is so far from jealousy° *suspicion*
To sleep by hate, and fear no enmity?
LYSANDER   My lord, I shall reply amazèdly,° *confusedly*
Half sleep, half waking. But as yet, I swear,
145 I cannot truly say how I came here,
But as I think—for truly would I speak,
And, now I do bethink me, so it is—
I came with Hermia hither. Our intent
Was to be gone from Athens where° we might, *wherever*
150 Without° the peril of the Athenian law— *Outside*
EGEUS [*to* THESEUS]   Enough, enough, my lord, you have enough.
I beg the law, the law upon his head.—
They would have stol'n away, they would, Demetrius,
Thereby to have defeated° you and me— *defrauded*
155 You of your wife, and me of my consent,
Of my consent that she should be your wife.
DEMETRIUS [*to* THESEUS]   My lord, fair Helen told me of their stealth,

---

7. Flews were large hanging, fleshy chaps.
8. With hanging folds of skin under the neck (compare 2.1.50).
9. *matched . . . each*: harmoniously matched in the

pitch of their barking, like a set of bells.
1. A pack of hounds more well tuned.
2. Birds were said to choose their mates on Valentine's Day.

Of this their purpose hither to this wood,
And I in fury hither followed them,
160 Fair Helena in fancy° following me.   *love*
But, my good lord, I wot not by what power—
But by some power it is—my love to Hermia,
Melted as the snow, seems to me now
As the remembrance of an idle gaud°   *a worthless trinket*
165 Which in my childhood I did dote upon,
And all the faith, the virtue of my heart,
The object and the pleasure of mine eye
Is only Helena. To her, my lord,
Was I betrothed ere I saw Hermia.
170 But like in sickness[3] did I loathe this food;
But, as in health come to my natural taste,
Now I do wish it, love it, long for it,
And will for evermore be true to it.

THESEUS   Fair lovers, you are fortunately met.
175 Of this discourse we more will hear anon.—
Egeus, I will overbear your will,
For in the temple by and by with us
These couples shall eternally be knit.—
And, for° the morning now is something° worn,   *since / somewhat*
180 Our purposed hunting shall be set aside.
Away with us to Athens. Three and three,
We'll hold a feast in great solemnity.
Come, Hippolyta.

Exit Duke [THESEUS *with* HIPPOLYTA, EGEUS,
and all his train]

DEMETRIUS   These things seem small and undistinguishable,
185 Like far-off mountains turnèd into clouds.
HERMIA   Methinks I see these things with parted° eye,   *improperly focused*
When everything seems double.
HELENA   So methinks,
And I have found Demetrius like a jewel,
Mine own and not mine own.[4]
DEMETRIUS   It seems to me
190 That yet we sleep, we dream. Do not you think
The Duke was here and bid us follow him?
HERMIA   Yea, and my father.
HELENA   And Hippolyta.
LYSANDER   And he did bid us follow to the temple.
DEMETRIUS   Why then, we are awake. Let's follow him,
195 And by the way let us recount our dreams.   *Exeunt lovers*
            BOTTOM *wakes*

BOTTOM   When my cue comes, call me, and I will answer. My
next is 'most fair Pyramus'. Heigh-ho.° Peter Quince? Flute the   *(Perhaps a yawn)*
bellows-mender? Snout the tinker? Starveling? God's my life!°   *Good Lord*
Stolen hence, and left me asleep?—I have had a most rare
200 vision. I have had a dream past the wit of man to say what
dream it was. Man is but an ass if he go about° t'expound this   *try*
dream. Methought I was—there is no man can tell what.
Methought I was, and methought I had—but man is but a

---

3. Only as a person does when ill or nauseated.
4. Mine on the principle of "finders keepers," but once someone else's.

patched fool[5] if he will offer° to say what methought I had. The   *venture*
205 eye of man hath not heard, the ear of man hath not seen, man's
hand is not able to taste, his tongue to conceive, nor his heart
to report[6] what my dream was. I will get Peter Quince to write
a ballad of this dream. It shall be called 'Bottom's Dream',
because it hath no bottom,[7] and I will sing it in the latter end
210 of a play, before the Duke. Peradventure,° to take it the more   *Perhaps*
gracious, I shall sing it at her° death.   *Exit*   *(Thisbe's?)*

4.2

Enter QUINCE, FLUTE, SNOUT, *and* STARVELING

QUINCE   Have you sent to Bottom's house? Is he come home
yet?
STARVELING   He cannot be heard of. Out of doubt° he is trans-   *Doubtless*
ported.[1]
5 FLUTE   If he come not, then the play is marred. It goes not for-
ward. Doth it?
QUINCE   It is not possible. You have not a man in all Athens able
to discharge° Pyramus but he.   *perform*
FLUTE   No, he hath simply the best wit° of any handicraft-man   *intellect*
10 in Athens.
QUINCE   Yea, and the best person,° too; and he is a very para-   *looks*
mour for a sweet voice.
FLUTE   You must say 'paragon'. A paramour is, God bless us, a
thing of naught.°   *something wicked*
Enter SNUG *the joiner*
15 SNUG   Masters, the Duke is coming from the temple, and there
is two or three lords and ladies more married. If our sport° had   *entertainment*
gone forward we had all been made men.[2]
FLUTE   O sweet bully Bottom! Thus hath he lost sixpence a day[3]
during his life. He could not have scaped sixpence a day. An°   *If*
20 the Duke had not given him sixpence a day for playing Pyra-
mus, I'll be hanged. He would have deserved it. Sixpence a
day in Pyramus, or nothing.
Enter BOTTOM
BOTTOM   Where are these lads? Where are these hearts?°   *mates*
QUINCE   Bottom! O most courageous[4] day! O most happy hour!
25 BOTTOM   Masters, I am to discourse wonders; but ask me not
what. For if I tell you, I am no true Athenian. I will tell you
everything right as it fell out.
QUINCE   Let us hear, sweet Bottom.
BOTTOM   Not a word of° me. All that I will tell you is that the   *out of*
30 Duke hath dined. Get your apparel together, good strings° to   *(to attach the beards)*
your beards, new ribbons to your pumps. Meet presently° at the   *immediately*
palace; every man look o'er his part. For the short and the long
is, our play is preferred.° In any case let Thisbe have clean   *recommended*
linen, and let not him that plays the lion pare his nails, for they
35 shall hang out for the lion's claws. And, most dear actors, eat
no onions nor garlic, for we are to utter sweet breath, and I do

---

5. Jester in a patchwork or motley costume.
6. *The eye . . . report*: burlesque of Scripture: "The eye
hath not seen, and the ear hath not heard, neither have
entered into the heart of man" those things that God
has prepared (1 Corinthians 2:9–10 [Bishops' Bible]).
7. Because it is unfathomable, has no substance (foun-
dation).

4.2 Location: Athens.
1. Carried away (by the fairies); transformed.
2. *we . . . men*: our fortunes would have been made.
3. As a royal pension, considerably more than the aver-
age daily wage of an Elizabethan workman.
4. Blunder for "brave," meaning "splendid."

not doubt but to hear them say it is a sweet comedy. No more
words. Away, go, away!   *Exeunt*

5.1

Enter THESEUS, HIPPOLYTA, EGEUS,[1] *and [attendant]
lords*

HIPPOLYTA   'Tis strange, my Theseus, that° these lovers speak of.   *that which*
THESEUS   More strange than true. I never may believe
   These antique[2] fables, nor these fairy toys.°   *trifles*
   Lovers and madmen have such seething brains,
5 Such shaping fantasies,° that apprehend°   *imaginations / conceive*
   More than cool reason ever comprehends.
   The lunatic, the lover, and the poet
   Are of imagination all compact.°   *composed*
   One sees more devils than vast hell can hold:
10 That is the madman. The lover, all as frantic,
   Sees Helen's beauty in a brow of Egypt.[3]
   The poet's eye, in a fine frenzy rolling,
   Doth glance from heaven to earth, from earth to heaven,
   And as imagination bodies forth
15 The forms of things unknown, the poet's pen
   Turns them to shapes, and gives to airy nothing
   A local habitation and a name.
   Such tricks hath strong imagination
   That if it would but apprehend some joy
20 It comprehends some bringer° of that joy;   *source*
   Or in the night, imagining some fear,°   *object to be feared*
   How easy is a bush supposed a bear!
HIPPOLYTA   But all the story of the night told over,
   And all their minds transfigured so together,
25 More witnesseth than fancy's images,[4]
   And grows to something of great constancy;°   *consistency*
   But howsoever,° strange and admirable.°   *in any case / wondrous*
           Enter lovers: LYSANDER, DEMETRIUS, HERMIA, *and*
           HELENA
THESEUS   Here come the lovers, full of joy and mirth.
   Joy, gentle friends—joy and fresh days of love
   Accompany your hearts.
30 LYSANDER   More than to us
   Wait in your royal walks, your board, your bed.[5]
THESEUS   Come now, what masques, what dances shall we have
   To wear away this long age of three hours
   Between our after-supper and bed-time?
35 Where is our usual manager of mirth?
   What revels are in hand? Is there no play
   To ease the anguish of a torturing hour?
   Call Egeus.
EGEUS   Here, mighty Theseus.
THESEUS   Say, what abridgement[6] have you for this evening?

5.1 Location: Athens. Theseus's palace.
1. Q does not call for Egeus, but gives all his speeches
to Philostrate (the character briefly addressed in 1.1).
F's substitution of Egeus here may be a mistake (the
possible result of the same actor playing both parts in
an early performance) or an attempt to incorporate the
angry father into the festive close.

2. Ancient; strange, grotesque (as in "antic").
3. In a gypsy's face. *Helen:* Helen of Troy.
4. *More . . . images:* Testifies to something more than
mere figments of the imagination.
5. *More . . . bed:* May even more joy and love attend
your daily lives.
6. Pastime, something to make the evening seem shorter.

40 What masque, what music? How shall we beguile
The lazy time if not with some delight?
EGEUS   There is a brief° how many sports are ripe.   *short list*
Make choice of which your highness will see first.
LYSANDER[7] [*reads*] 'The battle with the centaurs,[8] to be sung
45 By an Athenian eunuch to the harp.'
THESEUS   We'll none of that. That have I told my love
In glory of my kinsman Hercules.[9]
LYSANDER [*reads*] 'The riot of the tipsy bacchanals
Tearing the Thracian singer in their rage.'[1]
50 THESEUS   That is an old device,° and it was played   *show*
When I from Thebes came last a conqueror.
LYSANDER [*reads*] 'The thrice-three muses mourning for the death
Of learning, late deceased in beggary.'[2]
THESEUS   That is some satire, keen and critical,
55 Not sorting with° a nuptial ceremony.   *befitting*
LYSANDER [*reads*] 'A tedious brief scene of young Pyramus
And his love Thisbe: very tragical mirth.'
THESEUS   'Merry' *and* 'tragical'? 'Tedious' *and* 'brief'?—
That is, hot ice and wondrous strange black[3] snow.
60 How shall we find the concord of this discord?
EGEUS   A play there is, my lord, some ten words long,
Which is as 'brief' as I have known a play;
But by ten words, my lord, it is too long,
Which makes it 'tedious'; for in all the play
65 There is not one word apt, one player fitted.°   *appropriately cast*
And 'tragical', my noble lord, it is,
For Pyramus therein doth kill himself;
Which when I saw rehearsed, I must confess,
Made mine eyes water; but more merry tears
70 The passion of loud laughter never shed.
THESEUS   What are they that do play it?
EGEUS   Hard-handed men that work in Athens here,
Which never laboured in their minds till now,
And now have toiled° their unbreathed° memories   *taxed / unexercised*
75 With this same play against° your nuptial.   *in preparation for*
THESEUS   And we will hear it.
EGEUS   No, my noble lord,
It is not for you. I have heard it over,
And it is nothing, nothing in the world,
Unless you can find sport in their intents
80 Extremely stretched,° and conned° with cruel pain   *strained / memorized*
To do you service.
THESEUS   I will hear that play;
For never anything can be amiss
When simpleness and duty tender it.
Go, bring them in; and take your places, ladies. [*Exit* EGEUS]

7. In Q, Theseus both reads the list and comments on it himself.
8. Probably the battle that occurred when the Centaurs tried to carry off the bride of Theseus's friend Pirithous.
9. According to Plutarch, Hercules and Theseus were cousins.
1. The murder of the poet Orpheus by drunken women, devotees of Dionysus.

2. Possibly a topical reference: Robert Greene, Christopher Marlowe, and Thomas Kyd, university wits who began writing for the stage in the 1580s, all died in desperate circumstances in 1592–94. But satiric laments on the poverty of scholars and poets were commonplace.
3. "Black" is an editorial conjecture. Q and F omit a word that would make "snow" an oxymoron comparable to "hot ice."

85 HIPPOLYTA   I love not to see wretchedness o'ercharged,[4]
And duty in his service° perishing.   *its attempt to serve*
THESEUS   Why, gentle sweet, you shall see no such thing.
HIPPOLYTA   He says they can do nothing in this kind.°   *kind of thing*
THESEUS   The kinder we, to give them thanks for nothing.
90 Our sport shall be to take what they mistake,
And what poor duty cannot do,
Noble respect° takes it in might, not merit.[5]   *consideration*
Where I have come, great clerks° have purposèd   *scholars*
To greet me with premeditated welcomes,
95 Where I have seen them shiver and look pale,
Make periods in the midst of sentences,
Throttle their practised accent[6] in their fears,
And in conclusion dumbly have broke off,
Not paying me a welcome. Trust me, sweet,
100 Out of this silence yet I picked a welcome,
And in the modesty of fearful° duty   *frightened*
I read as much as from the rattling tongue
Of saucy and audacious eloquence.
Love, therefore, and tongue-tied simplicity
105 In least speak most, to my capacity.°   *in my judgment*
          [*Enter* EGEUS]
EGEUS   So please your grace, the Prologue is addressed.[7]
THESEUS   Let him approach.
          Flourish trumpets. Enter [QUINCE *as*] *the Prologue*
QUINCE [*as Prologue*]   If we offend, it is with our good will.
That you should think: we come not to offend
110 But with good will. To show our simple skill,
That is the true beginning of our end.
Consider then we come but in despite.
We do not come as minding° to content you,   *intending*
Our true intent is. All for your delight
115 We are not here. That you should here repent you
The actors are at hand, and by their show
You shall know all that you are like to know.[8]
THESEUS   This fellow doth not stand upon points.[9]
LYSANDER   He hath rid his prologue like a rough° colt: he knows   *an unbroken*
120 not the stop.[1] A good moral, my lord: it is not enough to speak,
but to speak true.
HIPPOLYTA   Indeed, he hath played on this prologue like a child
on a recorder[2]—a sound, but not in government.°   *control*
THESEUS   His speech was like a tangled chain—nothing°   *not at all*
125 impaired, but all disordered. Who is next?
          Enter with a trumpeter before them [BOTTOM *as*] *Pyra-*
          mus, [FLUTE *as*] *Thisbe,* [SNOUT *as*] *Wall,* [STARVELING
          as] *Moonshine, and* [SNUG *as*] *Lion* [*for the dumb*
          show][3]

---

4. Overburdened. *wretchedness:* incompetence or weakness; poor people.
5. *in . . . merit:* with respect to the giver's capacity, not the merit of the performance.
6. Rehearsed eloquence; usual manner of speaking.
7. The speaker of the Prologue is ready.
8. The humor of Quince's speech rests in its mispunctuation; repunctuated, it becomes a typical courteous address.

9. Bother about niceties; heed punctuation marks.
1. How to rein the colt to a stop; punctuation mark.
2. A woodwind instrument resembling a flute.
3. Elizabethan plays were often prefaced by a "dumb show" in which the actors silently mimed the main action, occasionally to the accompaniment (as here) of a narrator. The artisans may enact the story as Quince tells it, merely adopt symbolic attitudes, or introduce themselves.

QUINCE [*as Prologue*] Gentles, perchance you wonder at this show,
    But wonder on, till truth make all things plain.
This man is Pyramus, if you would know;
This beauteous lady Thisbe is, certain.
130 This man with lime and roughcast doth present
    Wall, that vile wall which did these lovers sunder;
And through Wall's chink, poor souls, they are content
    To whisper; at the which let no man wonder.
This man, with lantern, dog, and bush of thorn,
135   Presenteth Moonshine. For if you will know,
By moonshine did these lovers think no scorn°   *(it) no disgrace*
    To meet at Ninus' tomb, there, there to woo.
This grizzly beast, which 'Lion' hight° by name,   *is called*
    The trusty Thisbe coming first by night
140 Did scare away, or rather did affright;
And as she fled, her mantle she did fall,°   *drop*
    Which Lion vile with bloody mouth did stain.
Anon comes Pyramus, sweet youth and tall,°   *brave*
    And finds his trusty Thisbe's mantle slain;
145 Whereat with blade—with bloody, blameful blade—
    He bravely broached° his boiling bloody breast;   *stabbed*
And Thisbe, tarrying in mulberry shade,
    His dagger drew and died. For all the rest,
Let Lion, Moonshine, Wall, and lovers twain
150 At large° discourse, while here they do remain.   *length*
               *Exeunt all [the clowns] but [*SNOUT *as] Wall*
THESEUS   I wonder if the lion be to speak.
DEMETRIUS No wonder, my lord—one lion may when many
asses do.
SNOUT [*as Wall*]   In this same interlude° it doth befall   *play*
155 That I, one Snout by name, present a wall;
And such a wall as I would have you think
That had in it a crannied hole or chink,
Through which the lovers Pyramus and Thisbe
Did whisper often, very secretly.
160 This loam, this roughcast, and this stone doth show
That I am that same wall; the truth is so.
And this the cranny is, right and sinister,[4]
Through which the fearful lovers are to whisper.
THESEUS   Would you desire lime and hair to speak better?
165 DEMETRIUS It is the wittiest partition[5] that ever I heard dis-
course, my lord.
             *Enter [*BOTTOM *as] Pyramus*
THESEUS   Pyramus draws near the wall. Silence.
BOTTOM [*as Pyramus*]   O grim-looked° night, O night with hue   *grim-looking*
       so black,
    O night which ever art when day is not;
170 O night, O night, alack, alack, alack,
    I fear my Thisbe's promise is forgot.
And thou, O wall, O sweet O lovely wall,
    That stand'st between her father's ground and mine,
Thou wall, O wall, O sweet and lovely wall,

---

4. Left; running horizontally. Or on the one side (Pyramus's) and the other (Thisbe's).   5. Wall; formal term for part of an oration.

175 Show me thy chink, to blink through with mine eyne.
  [*Wall shows his chink*]
Thanks, courteous wall. Jove shield thee well for this.
But what see I? No Thisbe do I see.
O wicked wall, through whom I see no bliss,
Cursed be thy stones[6] for thus deceiving me.

180 THESEUS The wall methinks, being sensible,° should curse   *capable of feeling*
again.°   *back*

BOTTOM [*to* THESEUS] No, in truth, sir, he should not. 'Deceiv-
ing me' is Thisbe's cue. She is to enter now, and I am to spy
her through the wall. You shall see, it will fall pat° as I told you.   *precisely*
  Enter [FLUTE *as*] *Thisbe*

185 Yonder she comes.

FLUTE [*as Thisbe*] O wall, full often hast thou heard my moans
 For parting my fair Pyramus and me.
My cherry lips have often kissed thy stones,
 Thy stones with lime and hair knit up in thee.

190 BOTTOM [*as Pyramus*] I see a voice. Now will I to the chink
 To spy an° I can hear my Thisbe's face.   *if*
Thisbe?

FLUTE [*as Thisbe*] My love—thou art my love, I think.

BOTTOM [*as Pyramus*] Think what thou wilt, I am thy lover's
 grace°   *gracious lover*
And like Lemander[7] am I trusty still.

195 FLUTE [*as Thisbe*] And I like Helen,[8] till the fates me kill.

BOTTOM [*as Pyramus*] Not Shaphalus to Procrus[9] was so true.

FLUTE [*as Thisbe*] As Shaphalus to Procrus, I to you.

BOTTOM [*as Pyramus*] O kiss me through the hole of this vile wall.

FLUTE [*as Thisbe*] I kiss the wall's hole, not your lips at all.

BOTTOM [*as Pyramus*] Wilt thou at Ninny's tomb meet me
200 straightway?

FLUTE [*as Thisbe*] Tide° life, tide death, I come without delay.   *Betide; come*
    [*Exeunt* BOTTOM *and* FLUTE *severally*]

SNOUT [*as Wall*] Thus have I, Wall, my part dischargèd so;
And being done, thus Wall away doth go.   *Exit*

THESEUS Now is the wall down between the two neighbours.

205 DEMETRIUS No remedy, my lord, when walls are so wilful to°   *as to*
hear without warning.[1]

HIPPOLYTA This is the silliest stuff that ever I heard.

THESEUS The best in this kind are but shadows,[2] and the worst
are no worse if imagination amend them.

210 HIPPOLYTA It must be your imagination, then, and not theirs.

THESEUS If we imagine no worse of them than they of them-
selves, they may pass for excellent men. Here come two noble
beasts in: a man and a lion.
  Enter [SNUG *as*] *Lion,* [*and* STARVELING *as*] *Moonshine*
  [*with a lantern, thorn bush, and dog*]

SNUG [*as Lion*] You, ladies, you whose gentle hearts do fear

---

6. Punning on "testicles."
7. Blunder for "Leander," who drowned while swim-
ming across the Hellespont to meet his lover, Hero.
8. Helen of Troy was notoriously untrustworthy; a
blunder for "Hero."
9. Blunder for "Cephalus" and "Procris." Procris was in

fact seduced by her husband in disguise as another
man; he later accidentally killed her.
1. Informing the parents. *hear:* proverbially, "walls
have ears."
2. Mere likenesses without substance. *kind:* profession
(that is, actors)

215 The smallest monstrous mouse that creeps on floor,
May now perchance both quake and tremble here
  When lion rough in wildest rage doth roar.
Then know that I as Snug the joiner am
A lion fell,[3] nor else no lion's dam.
220 For if I should as Lion come in strife
Into this place, 'twere pity on my life.
THESEUS A very gentle beast, and of a good conscience.
DEMETRIUS The very best at a beast, my lord, that e'er I saw.
LYSANDER This lion is a very fox[4] for his valour.
225 THESEUS True, and a goose[5] for his discretion.
DEMETRIUS Not so, my lord, for his valour cannot carry his dis-
cretion, and the fox carries the goose.
THESEUS His discretion, I am sure, cannot carry his valour, for
the goose carries not the fox. It is well. Leave it to his discretion,
230 and let us listen to the moon.
STARVELING [as Moonshine] This lantern doth the hornèd°   *crescent*
  moon present.
DEMETRIUS He should have worn the horns on his head.[6]
THESEUS He is no crescent,° and his horns are invisible within   *waxing moon*
the circumference.
235 STARVELING [as Moonshine] This lantern doth the hornèd moon present.
  Myself the man i'th' moon do seem to be.
THESEUS This is the greatest error of all the rest—the man
should be put into the lantern. How is it else the man i'th'
moon?
240 DEMETRIUS He dares not come there for° the candle; for you see   *for fear of*
it is already in snuff.[7]
HIPPOLYTA I am aweary of this moon. Would he would change.
THESEUS It appears by his small light of discretion that he is in
the wane; but yet in courtesy, in all reason, we must stay the
245 time.
LYSANDER Proceed, Moon.
STARVELING All that I have to say is to tell you that the lantern
is the moon, I the man i'th' moon, this thorn bush my thorn
bush, and this dog my dog.
250 DEMETRIUS Why, all these should be in the lantern, for all these
are in the moon. But silence; here comes Thisbe.
  Enter [FLUTE *as*] *Thisbe*
FLUTE [as Thisbe] This is old Ninny's tomb. Where is my love?
SNUG [as Lion] O.
  Lion roars. Thisbe [drops her mantle and] runs off
DEMETRIUS Well roared, Lion.
255 THESEUS Well run, Thisbe.
HIPPOLYTA Well shone, Moon.—Truly, the moon shines with a
good grace.
  [*Lion worries Thisbe's mantle*]
THESEUS Well moused,[8] Lion.
DEMETRIUS And then came Pyramus.
  Enter [BOTTOM *as*] *Pyramus*
260 LYSANDER And so the lion vanished.   [*Exit Lion*]

---

3. Fierce; or skin (punning on the costume to which
Snug reassuringly calls attention).
4. Symbolic of low cunning, rather than courage.
5. Symbolic of foolishness.

6. The symbol of a cuckold.
7. In need of snuffing; angry.
8. The mantle is like a mouse in the mouth of a cat.

BOTTOM [as Pyramus]   Sweet moon, I thank thee for thy sunny beams.
　　I thank thee, moon, for shining now so bright;
　For by thy gracious, golden, glittering gleams
　　I trust to take of truest Thisbe sight.
265　　　　But stay, O spite!
　　　　But mark, poor knight,
　　What dreadful dole° is here?　　　　　　　　　　　　　*grief*
　　　　　Eyes, do you see?
　　　　　How can it be?
270　　O dainty duck, O dear!
　　　　Thy mantle good,
　　　　What, stained with blood?
　　Approach, ye furies fell.
　　　　O fates,[9] come, come,
275　　　　Cut thread and thrum,[1]
　　Quail,° crush, conclude, and quell.°　　　　　*Overpower / kill*
THESEUS　This passion—and[2] the death of a dear friend—would
　go near to make a man look sad.
HIPPOLYTA　Beshrew my heart, but I pity the man.
280 BOTTOM [as Pyramus]　O wherefore, nature, didst thou lions frame,
　　Since lion vile hath here deflowered[3] my dear?—
　Which is—no, no, which *was*—the fairest dame
　　That lived, that loved, that liked, that looked, with cheer.
　　　Come tears, confound;
285　　　Out sword, and wound
　　The pap° of Pyramus.　　　　　　　　　　　　　　　*breast*
　　　　Ay, that left pap,
　　　Where heart doth hop.
　　Thus die I: thus, thus, thus.
　　　　[*He stabs himself*]
290　　Now am I dead,
　　　Now am I fled,
　　My soul is in the sky.
　　　Tongue, lose thy light;
　　　Moon, take thy flight.　　　　　　　　[*Exit Moonshine*]
295　　Now die, die, die, die, die.　　　　　　　　[*He dies*]
DEMETRIUS　No die but an ace for him; for he is but one.[4]
LYSANDER　Less than an ace, man; for he is dead; he is nothing.
THESEUS　With the help of a surgeon he might yet recover and
　prove an ass.
300 HIPPOLYTA　How chance Moonshine is gone before Thisbe
　comes back and finds her lover.
THESEUS　She will find him by starlight.
　　　　Enter [FLUTE *as*] *Thisbe*
　Here she comes, and her passion° ends the play.　　　*passionate speech*
HIPPOLYTA　Methinks she should not use a long one for such a
305　Pyramus. I hope she will be brief.
DEMETRIUS　A mote° will turn the balance which Pyramus,　　*speck*

---

9. The three Fates in Greek mythology spun and cut the thread of a person's life.
1. A technical term from Bottom's occupation: the tufted end of a weaver's warp, or set of yarns placed lengthwise in a loom when the woven fabric is cut.
2. Only if combined with. *passion*: suffering; extravagant speech.
3. Ruined (but commonly suggesting "deprived of her virginity"); his error for "devoured."
4. Pun on "die" as one of a pair of dice. *one*: the ace, or lowest throw.

which[5] Thisbe, is the better—he for a man, God warrant us;
she for a woman, God bless us.

LYSANDER   She hath spied him already with those sweet eyes.

310 DEMETRIUS   And thus she means, videlicet:[6]

FLUTE [as Thisbe]   Asleep, my love?
    What, dead, my dove?
    O Pyramus, arise.
      Speak, speak. Quite dumb?
315   Dead, dead? A tomb
    Must cover thy sweet eyes.
      These lily lips,
      This cherry nose,
    These yellow cowslip cheeks
320   Are gone, are gone.
      Lovers, make moan.
    His eyes were green as leeks.
      O sisters three,°   *the Fates*
      Come, come to me
325   With hands as pale as milk.
      Lay them in gore,
      Since you have shore°   *shorn*
    With shears his thread of silk.
      Tongue, not a word.
330   Come, trusty sword,
    Come, blade, my breast imbrue.°   *stain with blood*
      [She stabs herself]
      And farewell friends,
      Thus Thisbe ends.
    Adieu, adieu, adieu.   [She dies]

335 THESEUS   Moonshine and Lion are left to bury the dead.

DEMETRIUS   Ay, and Wall too.

BOTTOM[7]   No, I assure you, the wall is down that parted their
fathers. Will it please you to see the epilogue or to hear a berga-
mask dance[8] between two of our company?

340 THESEUS   No epilogue, I pray you; for your play needs no excuse.
Never excuse; for when the players are all dead there need
none to be blamed. Marry, if he that writ it had played Pyramus
and hanged himself in Thisbe's garter it would have been a
fine tragedy; and so it is, truly, and very notably discharged. But
345 come, your bergamask. Let your epilogue alone.
    [BOTTOM and FLUTE[9] dance a bergamask, then exeunt]
The iron tongue of midnight hath told° twelve.   *counted; tolled*
Lovers, to bed; 'tis almost fairy time.
I fear we shall outsleep the coming morn
As much as we this night have overwatched.°   *stayed awake too late*
350 This palpable-gross° play hath well beguiled   *palpably crude*
The heavy° gait of night. Sweet friends, to bed.   *drowsy; slow*
A fortnight hold we this solemnity
In nightly revels and new jollity.   *Exeunt*

---

5. *which . . . which:* whether . . . or.
6. As follows. *means:* moans; lodges a formal legal complaint.
7. Spoken by Snug, the Lion, in Q.

8. A dance named after Bergamo, in Italy (commonly ridiculed for its rusticity).
9. The only "two of our company" onstage at the end of the play.

5.2

Enter Puck [ROBIN GOODFELLOW, with a broom]

ROBIN   Now the hungry lion roars,
    And the wolf behowls the moon,
  whilst the heavy° ploughman snores,   *weary*
    All with weary task fordone.°   *"done in"; exhausted*
5   Now the wasted brands° do glow   *burned-out logs*
    Whilst the screech-owl, screeching loud,
  Puts the wretch that lies in woe
    In remembrance of a shroud.
  Now it is the time of night
10   That the graves, all gaping wide,
  Every one lets forth his sprite[1]
    In the churchway paths to glide;
  And we fairies that do run
    By the triple Hecate's[2] team
15   From the presence of the sun,
    Following darkness like a dream,
  Now are frolic.° Not a mouse   *merry*
  Shall disturb this hallowed house.
  I am sent with broom[3] before
20   To sweep the dust behind° the door.   *from behind*

Enter [OBERON and TITANIA,] King and Queen of
Fairies, with all their train

OBERON   Through the house give glimmering light.
    By the dead and drowsy fire
  Every elf and fairy sprite
    Hop as light as bird from brier,
25   And this ditty after me
  Sing, and dance it trippingly.

TITANIA   First rehearse your song by rote,
  To each word a warbling note.
  Hand in hand with fairy grace
30   Will we sing and bless this place.

The song.[4] [The fairies dance]

OBERON   Now until the break of day
  Through this house each fairy stray.
  To the best bride bed will we,[5]
  Which by us shall blessèd be,
35   And the issue there create°   *created; conceived*
  Ever shall be fortunate.
  So shall all the couples three
  Ever true in loving be,
  And the blots of nature's hand
40   Shall not in their issue stand.
  Never mole, harelip, nor scar,
  Nor mark prodigious° such as are   *ominous birthmark*
  Despisèd in nativity
  Shall upon their children be.

5.2 Location: Theseus's palace.
1. Each grave lets forth its ghost.
2. Hecate was goddess of the moon and night, and had three realms: heaven (as Cynthia), earth (as Diana), and hell (as Proserpine).
3. One of his traditional emblems; he helped good housekeepers and punished lazy ones.
4. F does not assign lines 31–52 to Oberon. They are indented and printed in italics as "The Song."
5. Oberon and Titania will bless the bed of Theseus and Hippolyta.

45   With this field-dew consecrate[6]
       Every fairy take his gait°   *way*
       And each several° chamber bless   *separate*
       Through this palace with sweet peace;
       And the owner of it blessed
50   Ever shall in safety rest.
       Trip away, make no stay,
       Meet me all by break of day.
                           Exeunt [*all but* ROBIN]

                    Epilogue
ROBIN   If we shadows have offended,
           Think but this, and all is mended:
           That you have but slumbered here,
           While these visions did appear;
5   And this weak and idle theme,
           No more yielding but° a dream,   *than*
           Gentles, do not reprehend.
           If you pardon, we will mend.
           And as I am an honest puck,
10   If we have unearnèd luck
           Now to 'scape the serpent's tongue,[1]
           We will make amends ere long,
           Else the puck a liar call.
           So, good night unto you all.
15   Give me your hands,° if we be friends,   *applause*
           And Robin shall restore amends.

                 Additional Passage

An unusual quantity and kind of mislineation in Q1 has persuaded most scholars that
the text at the beginning of 5.1 was revised, with new material written in the margins.
The Oxford editors here offer a reconstruction of the passage as originally drafted, which
can be compared with 5.1.1–86 of the edited text.

                     5.1
           Enter THESEUS, HIPPOLYTA, *and* PHILOSTRATE
HIPPOLYTA   'Tis strange, my Theseus, that these lovers speak of.
THESEUS   More strange than true. I never may believe
           These antique fables, nor these fairy toys.
           Lovers and mad men have such seething brains.
5   One sees more devils than vast hell can hold:
           That is the madman. The lover, all as frantic,
           Sees Helen's beauty in a brow of Egypt.
           Such tricks hath strong imagination
           That if it would but apprehend some joy
10   It comprehends some bringer of that joy;
           Or in the night, imagining some fear,
           How easy is a bush supposed a bear!
HIPPOLYTA   But all the story of the night told over,
           And all their minds transfigured so together,

---

6. Consecrated, blessed. Playfully alludes to traditional   **Epilogue**
Catholic custom of blessing the bride bed with holy   1. Hissing from the audience.
water.

15   More witnesseth than fancy's images,
        And grows to something of great constancy;
        But howsoever, strange and admirable.
            Enter the lovers: LYSANDER, DEMETRIUS, HERMIA, *and*
            HELENA
        THESEUS   Here come the lovers, full of joy and mirth.
        Come now, what masques, what dances shall we have
20   To ease the anguish of a torturing hour?
        Call Philostrate.
        PHILOSTRATE   Here mighty Theseus.
        THESEUS   Say, what abridgement have you for this evening?
        What masque, what music? How shall we beguile
        The lazy time if not with some delight?
25   PHILOSTRATE   There is a brief how many sports are ripe.
        Make choice of which your highness will see first.
        THESEUS   'The battle with the centaurs to be sung
        By an Athenian eunuch to the harp.'
        We'll none of that. That have I told my love
30   In glory of my kinsman Hercules.
        'The riot of the tipsy Bacchanals
        Tearing the Thracian singer in their rage.'
        That is an old device, and it was played
        When I from Thebes came last a conquerer.
35   'The thrice-three Muses mourning for the death
        Of learning, late deceased in beggary.'
        That is some satire, keen and critical,
        Not sorting with a nuptial ceremony.
        'A tedious brief scene of young Pyramus
40   And his love Thisby.' 'Tedious' *and* 'brief'?
        PHILOSTRATE   A play there is, my lord, some ten words long,
        Which is as 'brief' as I have known a play;
        But by ten words, my lord, it is too long,
        Which makes it 'tedious'; for in all the play
45   There is not one word apt, one player fitted.
        THESEUS   What are they that do play it?
        PHILOSTRATE   Hard-handed men that work in Athens here,
        Which never laboured in their minds till now,
        And now have toiled their unbreathed memories
50   With this same play against your nuptial.
        THESEUS   Go, bring them in; and take your places, ladies.
                                                Exit PHILOSTRATE
        HIPPOLYTA   I love not to see wretchedness o'ercharged
        And duty in his service perishing.

The Merchant of Venice

Jew. Jew. Jew. The word echoes through *The Merchant of Venice*. The play has generated controversy for centuries. Is it anti-Semitic? Does it criticize anti-Semitism? Does it merely represent anti-Semitism without either endorsement or condemnation? Are the Christians right to call Shylock, the Jewish moneylender, a "devil," an "inexorable dog"; or is he merely the understandably resentful victim of their bigotry? Does Portia, Shylock's antagonist in the courtroom, exemplify the best in womanly virtue, or is she a manipulative virago? These questions about character suggest others that might be phrased more generally. What are the obligations of majority cultures to minorities in their midst? Do universally shared human characteristics outweigh racial and religious differences, or are such differences decisive?

Perhaps these issues seem more pressing nowadays than they did for Shakespeare. He could hardly could have predicted Nazi genocide or other modern forms of "ethnic cleansing." Nor could he have foreseen the opportunities and problems faced by multiracial societies centuries after his death. Nevertheless, by Shakespeare's time, the legacy of Jew hating in western Europe was already long and bitter. Depictions of fiendish Jews were routine in medieval and Renaissance drama; the villainous protagonist of Christopher Marlowe's *Jew of Malta,* a popular success in the early 1590s, was only the latest precedent. In 1594, shortly before Shakespeare wrote *The Merchant of Venice,* an outpouring of anti-Semitic outrage was triggered by the case of Roderigo Lopez, a Portuguese Jewish convert to Christianity accused of attempting to murder Queen Elizabeth.

Of course, the existence of anti-Semitism in sixteenth-century England says little about Shakespeare's own attitudes. He could have written *The Merchant of Venice* either to capitalize on or to criticize the prejudices of his society. Interestingly, Shakespeare had probably never encountered practicing Jews, since they had been forcibly expelled from England in the Middle Ages. And England was not alone in its intolerance. In 1492, Spain banished all non-Christians. Christians fought among themselves as well: during the sixteenth century, northern Europe saw decades of bloody conflict between Catholics and Protestants, while much of southern Europe was in the grip of the Inquisition. The impulse behind these persecutions was the conviction that a stable society required a shared belief system. A community based on consensus can indeed be impressively cohesive. Its homogeneity, however, makes it impatient of those who do not share its assumptions. Moreover, by the 1590s, when Shakespeare wrote *The Merchant of Venice,* bloody religious conflict all over Europe was making such consensus seem increasingly elusive—something obtainable, if at all, only at appalling human cost.

Possibly Venice seemed to Shakespeare to offer an alternative social prototype. Although it had no natural resources to speak of, it was the richest city in Renaissance Europe, located where the products of Asia could most conveniently be exchanged with those of western Europe. As a town of traders, Venice was full of foreigners: Turks, Jews, Arabs, Africans, Christians of various nationalities and denominations. By sixteenth-century standards, the city was unusually tolerant of diversity. This relative toleration was intimately linked with the city's wealth: its legal guarantees of fair treatment for all were designed to keep its markets running smoothly. Antonio tells Solanio:

> The Duke cannot deny the course of law,
> For the commodity that strangers have

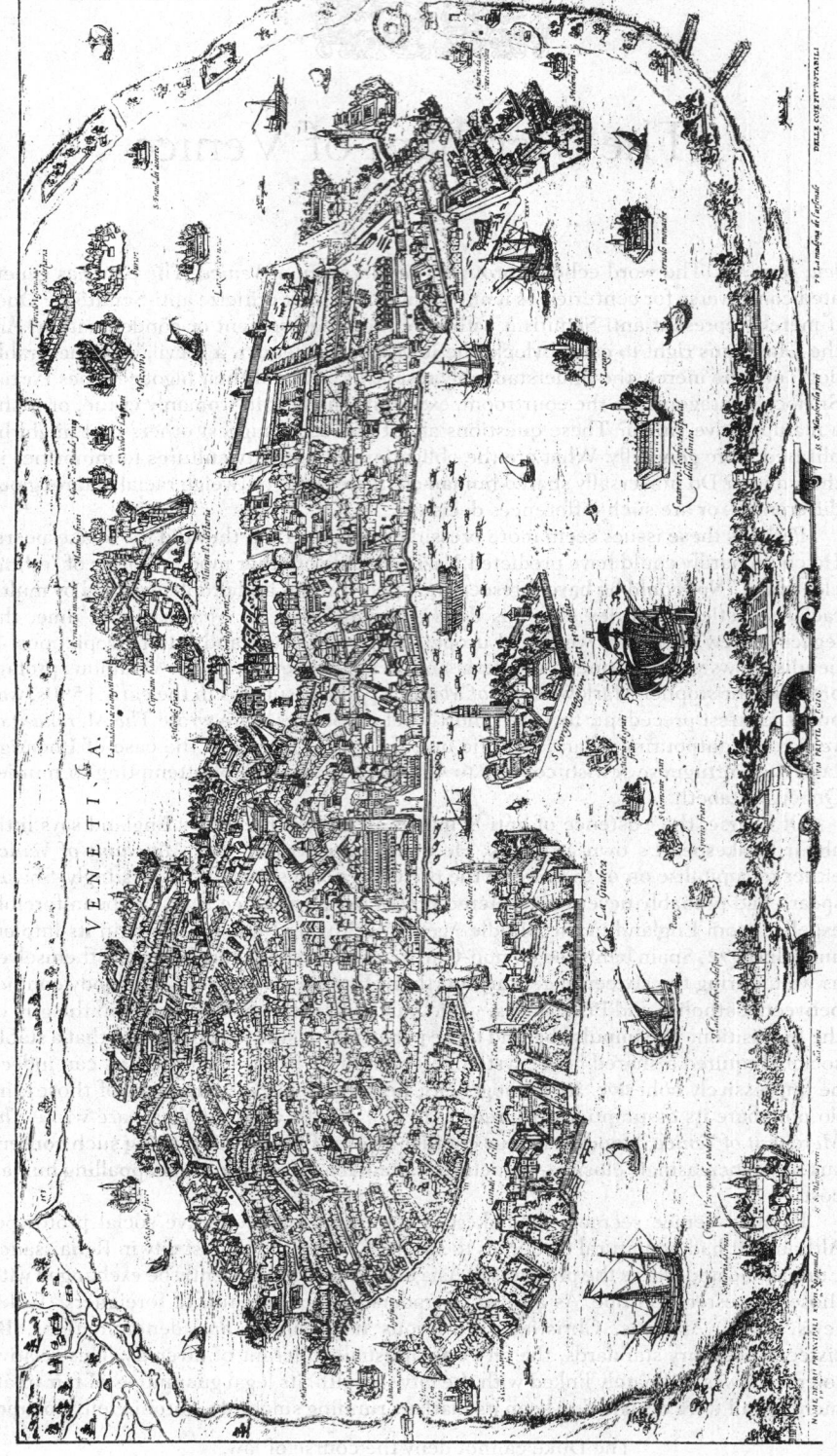

Prospect of Venice. From George Braun and Franz Hogenberg, *Civitates Orbis Terrarum* (1593).

> With us in Venice, if it be denied,
> Will much impeach the justice of the state,
> Since that the trade and profit of the city
> Consisteth of all nations.
>
> (3.3.26–31)

Shakespeare stresses, even exaggerates, this evenhanded cosmopolitanism. Historically, for instance, Venetian Jews were confined to a ghetto, gated and locked at night, but Shakespeare either did not know this fact or chose to ignore it. Venice thus provided Shakespeare with an example—perhaps the only example in sixteenth-century Europe—of a place where people with little in common culturally might coexist peacefully solely because it was materially expedient to do so. The laws of the marketplace seemed to have little to do with religion or nationality.

In *The Merchant of Venice,* Shakespeare juxtaposes social relations based on similarity with social relations based on economic self-interest. The Christian gentlemen who populate the opening scenes comprise a community with a common value system. Acutely aware of what they have in common, these individuals are openhanded to others in their group. When Bassanio asks Antonio for a loan, Antonio rushes to supply him even though he does not have the money at hand. When Graziano asks a favor of Bassanio, Bassanio grants it before he even hears what it is. Later in the play, when Portia finds out that Antonio's life is forfeit because of 3,000 ducats, she instantly offers to pay twelve times that sum to redeem him. Not entirely surprisingly, Bassanio is an amiable spendthrift whose plan to recoup his monetary losses involves considerable risk:

> In my schooldays, when I had lost one shaft,
> I shot his fellow of the selfsame flight
> The selfsame way, with more advisèd watch,
> To find the other forth; and by adventuring both,
> I oft found both.
>
> (1.1.140–44)

"Oft" is not "always." Sometimes, presumably, Bassanio lost both arrows. His temperamental similarity to his friend Antonio, the merchant-adventurer, is an optimism about gambling at long odds.

Such prodigal panache is undeniably attractive, especially in comedy, where generic conventions typically ensure that characters beat long odds. It generates, moreover, some of the most gorgeous poetry of the play, a language of risky munificence, in which phenomenal wealth is accumulated only to be splendidly dispersed. Salerio, for instance, describes a shipwreck as a beautiful squandering of luxury goods:

> dangerous rocks,
> Which, touching but my gentle vessel's side,
> Would scatter all her spices on the stream,
> Enrobe the roaring waters with my silks.
>
> (1.1.31–34)

Likewise, Portia tells Bassanio:

> for myself alone
> I would not be ambitious in my wish
> To wish myself much better, yet for you
> I would be trebled twenty times myself,
> A thousand times more fair, ten thousand times more rich,
> That only to stand high in your account
> I might in virtues, beauties, livings, friends,
> Exceed account.
>
> (3.2.150–57)

Unfortunately, it soon becomes obvious that the Christians' generosity, grace, and self-assurance have a disconcerting racist tinge. The magnanimous, depressive Antonio proudly acknowledges kicking and spitting on Shylock. The charming Portia rejoices in the failure of her black suitor to choose the correct casket: "Let all of his complexion choose me so" (2.7.79). These people find it hard to deal with those different from themselves: their society is based as much on the exclusion of the alien as on the inclusion of the similar. The moral ambiguity of the Christians' outlook is captured in their fondness for the loaded word "kind," which in Renaissance English meant not only "compassionate" but "similar," or "akin." People act benevolently toward those who are of the same *kind* as themselves.

Shylock's relation to the Venetian Christians exemplifies a different social mechanism. Unable to trust to love and generosity, Shylock relies instead on contractually enforceable promises and networks of mutual material need. Shylock's emphasis on purely economic factors means that he does not think about money the way Antonio and Bassanio do. He tends not to spend but to conserve, not to expand but to defend, not to seek risk but to minimize it. When he imagines disaster, he envisions not a spectacular swirl of silk and spices, but a sordid scenario of thievery and nibbling rats.

Although Shylock identifies strongly with his "sacred nation," his "tribe," and although he apparently relies on fellow Jews like Tubal, the play gives little sense of Jewish community. The play represents Shylock as an isolated figure, shunned by his daughter, abandoned by his servant. His calculating, loveless existence seems to result from the way he manages his property. Or perhaps isolation has made him cautious and selfish. Shylock has little motive to be generous with the Christians who despise him, and every reason to believe that he cannot depend on others to rescue him from misfortune.

The psychological and social contrasts between the Christians and Shylock reflect both class and religious differences. The Christians' magnificent improvidence is, in Shakespeare's time, a distinctively aristocratic trait. A true gentleman refuses to be too obviously concerned with monetary expenditure, especially where friends are concerned. He also feels socially obliged to display himself properly. Bassanio spends huge sums of borrowed money equipping himself for his trip to Belmont, even though all he technically need do is arrive alone and select the correct casket. Coming to Portia unattended or in shabby clothes is unthinkable even though (or perhaps because) "all the wealth I had," as Bassanio freely admits, "ran in my veins" (3.2.253–54). By contrast Shylock, despite his evident wealth, is obviously no gentleman. He locks up his possessions, regrets how much his servant eats, fumes over the money he spends searching for his missing daughter.

"Jews." From Jost Amman, *The Panoplia* (1568).

At the same time, the opposition between the Christians and Shylock seems rooted in religious disparities. Judaism in the play is presented not in its actual complexity but as a sixteenth-century Christian like Shakespeare would have construed it, as a set of dramatically vivid contrasts with Christian norms. The law of Moses, as set down in Deuteronomy and Leviticus, specifies numerous aspects of the observant Jew's life—what to eat and wear, how to worship, how to conduct business, how to punish crimes. The Mosaic code places a high value upon justice and emphasizes the importance of adhering to the letter of the law. Shylock's Judaism reveals itself not merely in his distinctive dress and his avoidance of pork, but in his trust of literal meanings, his respect for observable facts, his expectation that contracts will be rigorously enforced.

The typical Christian outlook is different. Christians obtain divine approval not by wearing certain garments, avoiding particular foods, or circumcising their boys, but by believing in Christ's power to save them. The central virtues in this religious system are not justice and scrupulous compliance with the law but charity, mercy, and a willingness to believe what seems incredible. In the terms Shakespeare provides in *The Merchant of Venice*, the Christian demeanor is entrepreneurial, even reckless, the spiritual equivalent of what Antonio does with his ships or Bassanio does with the money he borrows from his friend. "Give up everything you have and follow me," Jesus tells his would-

Young man in Venice. From Cesare Vecellio, *De gli habiti antichi et moderni* (1590).

be follower, advice echoed in the inscription on the lead casket: "Who chooseth me must give and hazard all he hath." Like the word "kind," the similarly complex word "gentle" is used repeatedly in the play to describe this distinctive set of traits: the word simultaneously refers to considerate behavior, to aristocratic family background, and to "gentile," or Christian, religious convictions.

The differences between Christian and Jew become starkly apparent over the issue of usury. Antonio thinks he ought to lend money to friends as an act of charity, properly performed as freely as God Himself dispenses grace. "For when did friendship take / A breed for barren metal of his friend?" (1.3.128–29). The charging of interest seems improperly to generate money from money alone: wealth loses its purely instrumental quality and acquires an uncanny capacity to "breed," or reproduce, like a live organism. Usury, blurring the distinction between the domain of the spirit and the merely material realm, threatens to collapse friendship, a spiritual relationship, into a mere economic transaction.

Shylock, by contrast, refuses to distinguish between human relations and money relations. His "pound of flesh" proposal, baldly insisting that flesh is convertible to ducats, demands that the Christians violate their own taboo against confusing categories of spirit and matter, flesh and money, live and dead. Thus Bassanio initially finds the bargain absolutely unacceptable. At the same time, the very existence of the taboo encourages the Christians to accept Shylock's characterization of the contract as a "merry sport": they simply cannot believe he is serious. Antonio mistakenly binds himself under the gross but entirely typical misapprehension that Shylock has mysteriously become "kind."

As the play proceeds, it modifies somewhat these initially vivid contrasts between Christian and Jew. Shylock pretends that he thinks of people in purely material, economic terms; but he becomes a moving character precisely at those moments when he admits another kind of value. After Jessica's flight, Solanio claims that Shylock has been seen running through the streets crying, "O, my ducats! O, my daughter! . . . My ducats and my daughter!" (2.8.15ff.). It is impossible to know how accurate this rumor might be: the equation of ducats and daughter is exactly what Christians expect of Shylock. But when Shylock finally appears onstage, he says nothing of the kind. When Tubal tells him that Jessica has exchanged a turquoise ring for a monkey, Shylock replies: "Out upon her! Thou torturest me, Tubal. It was my turquoise. I had it of Leah when I was a bachelor. I would not have given it for a wilderness of monkeys" (3.1.100–02). Insisting upon the sentimental value of the turquoise ring, Shylock seems directly to deny the convertibility of human into monetary relations. His grief over his daughter's defection, and her insensitivity to his relation with her dead mother, exceeds his financial loss. Likewise in the courtroom, Shylock is remarkable not for his calculating prudence but for his refusal to be swayed by monetary appeals. There is something in the quality of his oppression that he refuses to convert into a payoff.

The Christians are also more complicated than they profess to be. Although human values, in their view, transcend marketplace values, and they are commanded to love not only neighbors but even enemies, only some persons elicit a humane response. Others are disregarded or treated as nonhuman. When Salerio and Solanio ridicule Shylock, he protests: "Hath not a Jew eyes? Hath not a Jew hands, organs, dimensions, senses, affections, passions; fed with the same food, hurt with the same weapons, subject to the same diseases, healed by the same means, warmed and cooled by the same winter and summer as a Christian is?" (3.1.49–54). Shylock asserts that a common human experience of embodiment ought to override considerations of religious or racial difference. These lines are among the most memorable in the play, but the argument does not follow from the position Shylock has taken earlier. Rather, it is effective because it exposes Christian hypocrisy. Similarly, in the trial scene, Shylock points out that the Christian practice of slavery plainly sets a monetary value upon human beings. The Christians' creed mandates universal love, but they fail to behave in accord with their precepts.

These inconsistencies haunt the play's friendships and marriages. Marriage is a hybrid social relation: obviously associated with love and with the reproduction of living organisms, it is simultaneously a property relation, involving the economic alliance of individuals and families. Bassanio's courtship of Portia is doubly motivated: he loves her, and he needs her money. The language of his attraction, even at its most generous and disinterested, is full of the metaphors of commerce and exchange. And although Antonio protests against thinking of friendship as an economic transaction, it is not difficult to construe his generosity as an attempt to buy Bassanio's love. So although the Christians attempt to differentiate spiritual values from economic ones, those values continually turn out to be intimately intertwined.

The casket test directly confronts this problem. The failures of Morocco and Aragon demonstrate that it is possible to find a plausible reason for choosing any one of the three caskets. But when Bassanio makes his choice, we see how the test works: it can be solved only by one who views its puzzles from the correct point of view. Bassanio must abstract from his particular relation with Portia to a general distinction between "ornament" and "truth":

> Look on beauty
> And you shall see 'tis purchased by the weight,
> Which therein works a miracle in nature,
> Making them lightest that wear most of it.
> (3.2.88–91)

Surely Bassanio does not believe that because Portia is lovely, she must be unchaste. Instead, his upbringing as a Christian gentleman has acquainted him with a particular frame of mind that prefers invisible over visible things, spirit over body, metaphor over literal meaning. The same cultural background makes him willing to take chances: to "hazard all he hath" on the unprepossessing lead casket. Because every suitor gets the same chance, the casket test seems to be fair; in fact, it is rather like those "objective" intelligence tests that, in subtle or not-so-subtle ways, reward the belief systems of dominant groups while stigmatizing outsiders. In this case, the person best fitted to be Portia's husband is one who, by Christian standards, knows the limitations and right use of wealth. This knowledge enables him to value characteristics in his wife—virtue, intelligence, and beauty—that make her precious in more than monetary ways.

One of the surprises of the casket test is that it takes place at all. Portia's obedience to her dead father's apparently irrational plans for her is remarkable in comedy, for comic heroines more often, like Jessica, defy their fathers than conscientiously follow their orders. Perhaps Portia could be seen as synthesizing the best of Jewish and Christian characteristics; obeying the letter of a wise Father's law, even while cultivating the spiritual virtues of love and generosity. Perhaps, then, Jewish and Christian outlooks are not *necessarily* in conflict (any more than there is a necessary conflict in being, as Portia is, both rich and beautiful). Certainly Portia's respect for the letter of the law, combined with her willingness to go beyond that letter, makes her the only character who can effectively confront Shylock in the trial scene.

When she disguises herself as a young lawyer, Portia becomes one of many Shakespearean comic heroines to assume male attire. The power that she achieves by her transvestism signals an interesting development in Shakespeare's treatment of the relations between men and women. Earlier plays often differentiate sharply between the sexes: between the male political domain and the female domestic domain in *Richard II*, between the male street and the female bedchamber in *Romeo and Juliet*. In *The Merchant of Venice* and the comedies Shakespeare wrote immediately thereafter, women seem to possess a new liberty of action. Their freedom coincides with another new development in Shakespearean comedy, the presence of a scapegoat character—someone like Shylock, who cannot be assimilated into the comic society at the end of the play. Perhaps when the most serious social threats seem to be posed by outsiders, there is more freedom for women within the "in" group: the crucial bifurcation is no longer between male and female but between "us" and "them."

Portia's legal strategy is complex, and thus the trial has several stages. At first, she both offers and recommends generosity:

> Therefore, Jew,
> Though justice be thy plea, consider this:
> That in the course of justice none of us
> Should see salvation. We do pray for mercy,
> And that same prayer doth teach us all to render
> The deeds of mercy.
> (4.1.192–97)

Not surprisingly, Shylock is deaf to this eloquence. Portia's argument is based on the distinctively Christian premise that salvation is an undeserved gift. She derives her authority from the Lord's Prayer: "forgive us our trespasses as we forgive those who trespass against us." But Shylock doesn't accept, or even perhaps know the existence of, a prayer that supposedly "teaches us all." Portia's plea for tolerance and compassion might seem to rest on universal premises, but in fact Portia's "we" who "pray for mercy" neatly excludes the Jew.

The judgment upon Shylock at the end of the trial has disturbed many critics and audiences. After the Christians win the case—not only saving Antonio's life but also keeping the 3,000 ducats Shylock had lent Bassanio—Portia seems to take exactly the revenge she has up to now deplored. Her legal ground is provided by a previously unmentioned law against any alien who plots the death of a Venetian citizen. The law in which Shylock trusted, because it seemed to provide a refuge from prejudice, turns out to have prejudice inscribed within it from the start. In this respect, it resembles the casket test—everybody seems to get the same chance, but in fact the test blatantly favors the insider.

Portia and the Duke apparently regard the dismissal of Shylock as merciful; his *life* is preserved, although half or all of his mere money is taken away. Portia's sentence forces Shylock to behave as a Christian citizen and father should: to worship in a Christian church, to grant money to his daughter, to recognize the difference between spiritual and economic well-being. Eschewing lethal force, the Duke demands that Shylock acquiesce in his punishment: "I am content," he says at last. But what else can he say? The coercive inclusion of Shylock in the Christian community seems all the more violent because it professes to renounce coercion, dropping "as the gentle rain from heaven." If designating people outcasts is bad, compelling them to participate in a society they find intolerable may be even worse.

The Merchant of Venice thus hovers on the edge of tragedy. Shylock's ferocious negativity is poised against, and arguably elicited by, the Christians' hypocritical refusal to admit the way their spiritual lives depend on material prosperity. The presence of the scapegoated Jew lays bare the mechanisms by which Venetian society works. Shylock can be reviled and dismissed, but the possibilities that he represents do not simply vanish when he flees the courtroom. Thus the moral disquiet the play raises among directors, readers, and audiences: Christian and Jewish perspectives seem mutually invalidating, and both finally inadequate.

Shakespeare suggests the stubbornness of the problems broached by the play in the way he structures the last act. Most Shakespeare comedies return to the city or the court at the end, or at least look forward to that return; but in *The Merchant of Venice*, the play ends at Belmont, the nostalgically depicted, magically copious "green world." It is as if the formal demand for comic closure conflicts with Shakespeare's awareness that no neat resolution of Venice's problems is forthcoming.

Indeed, some muted version of those problems pursues the Christians even to Portia's estate. The act begins with the banter between the newlyweds Jessica and Lorenzo, who have stayed behind at Belmont in Portia's absence. It is a bit ominous that all the love stories they recall are unhappy ones. Still, the couple's affectionate banter makes the scene a welcome change from what has immediately preceded it. Showing Jessica and Lorenzo in married bliss minutes after the brutal expulsion of Shylock seems an attempt to confine the punitive energies of the play to the usurer alone. The scene offers an alternative vision of interaction between racial groups, one that involves love rather than hatred. Jessica's marriage to a Christian has exempted her from Shylock's fate. Of course, this is a vision not of mutual tolerance but of assimilation: majority cultures do not need to exterminate people unlike themselves if they can merely exterminate their differences. Lorenzo describes to his wife the "music of the spheres"—a perfect heavenly harmony made inaudible by the corruption of this life. Perhaps, analogously, the Christians' failure lies not in the nature of their ideals, but in the imperfect realization of those ideals in the everyday world. The inevitable dissonance between the mundane and the ideal world does not necessarily, however, simply drain the ideal of its meaning.

The moral dilemmas posed by high but perhaps unrealizable ideals come under scrutiny yet again in the ring tricks with which the play ends. After Antonio's trial, Portia-as-Balthazar asks Bassanio for his wedding ring as payment for legal services. This request poses Bassanio a harder problem than Shylock had. Bassanio can imagine breaking a written contract, but not denying the request of an ally to whom he's indebted. By giving the ring to Balthazar, Bassanio demonstrates both that his loyalty to Antonio still outweighs his allegiance to Portia and that he has trouble governing his generous impulses. Portia's trick teaches Bassanio and Antonio that the marital relationship involves unique responsibilities and that those responsibilities impose a limit on munificence.

Again and again in *The Merchant of Venice* oppositions between potentially tragic alternatives miraculously dissolve—between being rich and being virtuous, marrying for money and marrying for love, following paternal orders and making one's own choice, enforcing the letter of the law and enforcing its spirit, remaining faithful to one's wife and loving one's male friend. Balthazar turns out to have been Portia, Bassanio has given his ring to its original owner, and all seems to be well. But by setting the play's last act in a magical world of trust and abundance, Shakespeare stresses the artifice involved in his resolution. Even as this beautiful, troubling play comes to a close, it pointedly emphasizes the distance between the final act's charmed fictional world and the intransigent real one.

KATHARINE EISAMAN MAUS

TEXTUAL NOTE

The textual history of *The Merchant of Venice* is not as complicated as that of some other Shakespeare plays. Two quarto editions exist, both dated 1600 on the title page. One, printed "by I. R. for Thomas Heys," is now called Q1; nineteen copies of this text have survived. Another Quarto (Q2), printed "by I. Roberts," is a falsely dated text actually produced in 1619 by William Jaggard (the same man who printed the First Folio four years later). Yet another version of *The Merchant of Venice* appears in the 1623 First Folio (F).

Q1 seems to have been prepared either directly from Shakespeare's own manuscript or from an accurate transcript of that manuscript. Internal evidence indicates that both Q2 and F were based on copies of Q1. F has some additions, chiefly stage directions, which suggests that a text marked up for stage production was likely to have been consulted at some point in preparing this text. Q1 is not divided into acts or scenes; F adds act divisions. Scene divisions were not added until the eighteenth century.

Q1, therefore, with the exception of some stage directions, is the most reliable authority for a modern text of *The Merchant of Venice*. The Oxford text follows Q1 closely, adopting from F and later editors the traditional divisions into acts and scenes, and accepting many of the Folio stage directions as representing the performance practice of Shakespeare's company.

The title *The Jew of Venice* does not appear in any printed text of the play. It was used, however, when the play was entered on the Stationers' Register in 1598. Since the theatrical company, not a bookseller, was responsible for the entry, the Oxford editors believe that members of Shakespeare's company considered *The Jew of Venice* an acceptable alternative title.

SELECTED BIBLIOGRAPHY

Barber, C. L. "The Merchants and the Jew of Venice: Wealth's Communion and an Intruder." *Shakespeare's Festive Comedy: A Study of Dramatic Form and Its Relation to Social Custom.* Princeton: Princeton University Press, 1959. The Christian's opulent festivity challenged by Shylock's fiercely reductive attitude toward money.

Burckhardt, Sigurd. "*The Merchant of Venice*: The Gentle Bond." *Shakespearean Meanings.* Princeton: Princeton University Press, 1968. 206–89. The importance of various kinds of bonds in *The Merchant of Venice*.

Cohen, Walter. "*The Merchant of Venice* and the Possibilities of Historical Criticism." *English Literary History* 49 (1982): 765–89. The play's theatrical artifice as reflecting economic conflicts in early modern Europe.

Danson, Lawrence. *The Harmonies of "The Merchant of Venice."* New Haven: Yale University Press, 1978. Describes the play's conflicts in detail, and argues for their satisfactory resolution.

Engle, Lars. "Money and Moral Luck in *The Merchant of Venice*." *Shakespearean Pragmatism: Market of His Time.* Chicago: University of Chicago Press, 1993. 77–106. Emotional and financial balance sheets, and their ethical consequences: *The Merchant of Venice* read through the lens of late twentieth-century ethical philosophy.

Gross, Kenneth. *Shylock Is Shakespeare*. Chicago: University of Chicago Press, 2006. Shakespeare's personal connection to Shylock.

Lewalski, Barbara. "Biblical Allusion and Allegory in *The Merchant of Venice*." *Shakespeare Quarterly* 13 (1962): 327–43. Shakespeare's use of biblical typology.

Lupton, Julia Reinhard. "Merchants of Venice, Circles of Citizenship." *Citizen-Saints: Shakespeare and Political Theology*. Chicago: University of Chicago Press, 2005. 75–101. Judaism and citizenship in early modern Venice.

Newman, Karen. "Portia's Ring: Unruly Women and the Structure of Exchange in *The Merchant of Venice*." *Shakespeare Quarterly* 38 (1987): 19–33. Portia, as gift-giver, occupies a position of power usually coded as masculine.

Shapiro, James. *Shakespeare and the Jews*. New York: Columbia University Press, 1996. Anti-Semitism in Shakespeare's time.

Shell, Marc. "'The Wether and the Ewe': Verbal Usury in *The Merchant of Venice*." *Kenyon Review* 1.4 (1979): 65–92. A close analysis of exchange and redemption in *Merchant of Venice*, focusing particularly on Shylock's story of Laban and Jacob.

Wilson, Luke. "Drama and Marine Insurance in Shakespeare's London." *The Law in Shakespeare*. Ed. Constance Jordan and Karen Cunningham. London: Palgrave Macmillan, 2007. 127–42.

FILMS

The Merchant of Venice. 1973. Dir. John Sichel. UK. 131 min. Laurence Olivier as Shylock.

The Merchant of Venice. 1980. Dir. Jack Gold. UK. 157 min. Textually faithful but stilted. Gemma Jones is a chilly, calculating Portia.

The Merchant of Venice. 2001. Dir. Trevor Nunn. UK. 141 min. A film version of an acclaimed Royal National Theatre production, set in Europe between the world wars. Vividly acted, with many interesting directorial choices. Henry Goodman's Shylock is especially memorable.

The Merchant of Venice. 2004. Dir. Michael Radford. UK. 131 min. Al Pacino as Shylock, Lynn Collins as Portia. Sumptuous period costumes and sets. This production emphasizes the disquieting aspects of the play, not only the Venetians' anti-Semitism but the struggle between Portia and Antonio over Bassanio's allegiance.

The Comical History of the Merchant of Venice, or Otherwise Called the Jew of Venice

THE PERSONS OF THE PLAY

ANTONIO, a merchant of Venice
BASSANIO, his friend and Portia's suitor
LEONARDO, Bassanio's servant
LORENZO ⎤
GRAZIANO ⎟
SALERIO ⎬ friends of Antonio and Bassanio
SOLANIO ⎦
SHYLOCK, a Jew
JESSICA, his daughter
TUBAL, a Jew
LANCELOT, a clown, first Shylock's servant and then Bassanio's
GOBBO, his father
PORTIA, an heiress
NERISSA, her waiting-gentlewoman
BALTHASAR ⎤
STEFANO ⎦ } Portia's servants
Prince of MOROCCO ⎤
Prince of ARAGON ⎦ } Portia's suitors
DUKE of Venice
Magnificoes of Venice
A jailer, attendants, and servants

1.1

Enter ANTONIO, SALERIO, *and* SOLANIO

ANTONIO In sooth,° I know not why I am so sad.   *truth*
It wearies me, you say it wearies you,
But how I caught it, found it, or came by it,
What stuff 'tis made of, whereof it is born,
5 I am to learn;°   *have yet to discover*
And such a want-wit° sadness makes of me   *dullard*
That I have much ado to know myself.
SALERIO Your mind is tossing on the ocean,
There where your argosies° with portly° sail,   *merchant ships / stately*
10 Like signors° and rich burghers on the flood—   *lords*
Or as it were the pageants¹ of the sea—
Do overpeer° the petty traffickers   *tower over*
That curtsy² to them, do them reverence,
As they fly by them with their woven wings.

1.1 Location: Venice.
1. Movable stages used by itinerant actors or in parades.
2. By bobbing on the waves or by lowering their flags in salute.

SOLANIO [*to* ANTONIO]   Believe me, sir, had I such venture°   *a risky undertaking*
15   forth
    The better part of my affections would
    Be with my hopes abroad. I should be still°   *always*
    Plucking the grass to know where sits the wind,
    Peering in maps for ports and piers and roads,°   *open harbors*
20   And every object that might make me fear
    Misfortune to my ventures out of doubt
    Would make me sad.
SALERIO   My wind cooling my broth
    Would blow me to an ague° when I thought   *make me shiver*
    What harm a wind too great might do at sea.
25   I should not see the sandy hour-glass run
    But I should think of shallows and of flats,°   *shoals*
    And see my wealthy Andrew,[3] decks in sand,
    Vailing her hightop° lower than her ribs   *Lowering her topmast*
    To kiss her burial.° Should I go to church   *burial place*
30   And see the holy edifice of stone
    And not bethink me straight° of dangerous rocks   *immediately think*
    Which, touching but my gentle vessel's side,
    Would scatter all her spices on the stream,
    Enrobe the roaring waters with my silks,
35   And, in a word, but even now° worth this,°   *moments ago / so much*
    And now worth nothing? Shall I have the thought
    To think on this, and shall I lack the thought
    That such a thing bechanced° would make me sad?   *having occurred*
    But tell not me. I know Antonio
40   Is sad to think upon his merchandise.
ANTONIO   Believe me, no. I thank my fortune for it,
    My ventures are not in one bottom° trusted,   *ship*
    Nor to one place;° nor is my whole estate   *destination*
    Upon the fortune of this present year.
45   Therefore my merchandise makes me not sad.
SOLANIO   Why then, you are in love.
ANTONIO   Fie, fie.
SOLANIO   Not in love neither? Then let us say you are sad
    Because you are not merry, and 'twere as easy
    For you to laugh, and leap, and say you are merry
50   Because you are not sad. Now, by two-headed Janus,[4]
    Nature hath framed strange fellows in her time:
    Some that will evermore peep through their eyes[5]
    And laugh like parrots° at a bagpiper,[6]   *(screeching loudly)*
    And other of such vinegar aspect°   *sour looks*
55   That they'll not show their teeth in way of smile
    Though Nestor[7] swear the jest be laughable.
          Enter BASSANIO, LORENZO, *and* GRAZIANO
    Here comes Bassanio, your most noble kinsman,
    Graziano, and Lorenzo. Fare ye well.
    We leave you now with better company.
60 SALERIO   I would have stayed till I had made you merry
    If worthier friends had not prevented me.

3. Name of a Spanish galleon captured by the English   5. Eyes almost shut by violent laughter.
at Cádiz in 1596.   6. Whose music was considered woeful.
4. Roman god with faces looking both forward and   7. Sober, elderly Greek hero in *The Iliad.*
backward.

ANTONIO   Your worth is very dear in my regard.
I take it your own business calls on you,
And you embrace th'occasion to depart.
65 SALERIO   Good morrow, my good lords.
BASSANIO   Good signors both, when shall we laugh?° Say, when?   *make merry together*
You grow exceeding strange.° Must it be so?   *reserved*
SALERIO   We'll make our leisures to attend on° yours.   *suit*

Exeunt SALERIO *and* SOLANIO

LORENZO   My lord Bassanio, since you have found Antonio,
70 We two will leave you; but at dinner-time
I pray you have in mind where we must meet.
BASSANIO   I will not fail you.
GRAZIANO   You look not well, Signor Antonio.
You have too much respect upon the world.°   *anxiety about business*
75 They lose it that do buy it with much care.
Believe me, you are marvellously changed.
ANTONIO   I hold the world but as the world, Graziano—
A stage where every man must play a part,
And mine a sad one.
GRAZIANO   Let me play the fool.
80 With mirth and laughter let old[8] wrinkles come,
And let my liver[9] rather heat with wine
Than my heart cool with mortifying[1] groans.
Why should a man whose blood is warm within
Sit like his grandsire cut in alabaster,[2]
85 Sleep when he wakes, and creep into the jaundice[3]
By being peevish? I tell thee what, Antonio—
I love thee, and 'tis my love that speaks—
There are a sort of men whose visages
Do cream and mantle[4] like a standing° pond,   *stagnant*
90 And do a wilful stillness entertain
With purpose to be dressed in an opinion°   *a reputation*
Of wisdom, gravity, profound conceit,°   *judgment*
As who should say 'I am Sir Oracle,
And when I ope my lips, let no dog bark.'
95 O my Antonio, I do know of these
That therefore only are reputed wise
For saying nothing, when I am very sure,
If they should speak, would almost damn those ears
Which, hearing them, would call their brothers fools.[5]
100 I'll tell thee more of this another time.
But fish not with this melancholy bait
For this fool gudgeon,° this opinion.—   *tiny, easily caught fish*
Come, good Lorenzo.—Fare ye well a while.
I'll end my exhortation after dinner.
LORENZO [*to* ANTONIO *and* BASSANIO]   Well, we will leave you
105   then till dinner-time.
I must be one of these same dumb° wise men,   *mute*
For Graziano never lets me speak.

8. Accompanying old age; abundant.
9. The liver was considered the seat of passion.
1. Deadly (groans were believed to drain blood from the heart).
2. Stone from which tomb effigies were carved.
3. Thought to result from too much yellow bile, a bodily substance associated with irritability.
4. *cream and mantle:* grow a scum; that is, assume a fixed countenance.
5. *would . . . fools:* alluding to Matthew 5:22: "And whosoever shall say to his brother . . . , fool, shall be in danger of hell fire."

GRAZIANO   Well, keep me company but two years more
Thou shalt not know the sound of thine own tongue.

110 ANTONIO   Fare you well. I'll grow a talker for this gear.[6]

GRAZIANO   Thanks, i'faith, for silence is only commendable
In a neat's° tongue dried and a maid not vendible.[7]   *an ox's*

Exeunt [GRAZIANO *and* LORENZO]

ANTONIO   Yet is that anything now?

BASSANIO   Graziano speaks an infinite deal of nothing, more
115 than any man in all Venice. His reasons° are as two grains of   *sensible remarks*
wheat hid in two bushels of chaff: you shall seek all day ere
you find them, and when you have them they are not worth
the search.

ANTONIO   Well, tell me now what lady is the same
120 To whom you swore a secret pilgrimage,
That you today promised to tell me of.

BASSANIO   'Tis not unknown to you, Antonio,
How much I have disabled mine estate
By something showing a more swelling port°   *extravagant lifestyle*
125 Than my faint means would grant continuance,°   *allow to continue*
Nor do I now make moan to be abridged°   *reduced*
From such a noble rate;° but my chief care   *style*
Is to come fairly off from the great debts
Wherein my time, something too prodigal,
130 Hath left me gaged.° To you, Antonio,   *pledged*
I owe the most in money and in love,
And from your love I have a warranty°   *sanction*
To unburden all my plots and purposes
How to get clear of all the debts I owe.

135 ANTONIO   I pray you, good Bassanio, let me know it,
And if it stand as you yourself still do,
Within the eye of honour, be assured
My purse, my person, my extremest means
Lie all unlocked to your occasions.°   *requirements*

140 BASSANIO   In my schooldays, when I had lost one shaft,
I shot his° fellow of the selfsame flight°   *its / size and weight*
The selfsame way, with more advisèd° watch,   *careful*
To find the other forth; and by adventuring° both,   *hazarding*
I oft found both. I urge this childhood proof
145 Because what follows is pure innocence.
I owe you much, and, like a wilful youth,
That which I owe is lost; but if you please
To shoot another arrow that self° way   *same*
Which you did shoot the first, I do not doubt,
150 As I will watch the aim, or° to find both   *either*
Or bring your latter hazard° back again,   *risk*
And thankfully rest debtor for the first.

ANTONIO   You know me well, and herein spend but° time   *only lose*
To wind about my love with circumstance;°   *circumlocution*
155 And out of doubt you do me now more wrong
In making question of my uttermost[8]
Than if you had made waste of all I have.
Then do but say to me what I should do

---

6. *for this gear:* as a result of your talk.   8. In doubting that I would do my utmost to help you.
7. Sellable—that is, marriageable.

That in your knowledge may by me be done,
160 And I am pressed unto° it. Therefore speak.   *obliged to do*
BASSANIO   In Belmont is a lady richly left,°   *left a fortune*
And she is fair, and, fairer than that word,
Of wondrous virtues. Sometimes° from her eyes   *At times*
I did receive fair speechless messages.
165 Her name is Portia, nothing undervalued
To° Cato's daughter, Brutus' Portia;[1]
Nor is the wide world ignorant of her worth,
For the four winds blow in from every coast
Renownèd suitors, and her sunny locks
170 Hang on her temples like a golden fleece,
Which makes her seat of Belmont Colchis' strand,[2]
And many Jasons come in quest of her.
O my Antonio, had I but the means
To hold a rival place with one of them,
175 I have a mind presages me such thrift°   *prosperity*
That I should questionless be fortunate.
ANTONIO   Thou know'st that all my fortunes are at sea,
Neither have I money nor commodity°   *goods*
To raise a present sum. Therefore go forth—
180 Try what my credit can in Venice do;
That shall be racked° even to the uttermost   *stretched*
To furnish thee to Belmont, to fair Portia.
Go presently enquire, and so will I,
Where money is; and I no question make
185 To have it of my trust or for my sake.[3]   *Exeunt [severally]*°   *separately*

1.2

Enter PORTIA *with her waiting-woman,* NERISSA
PORTIA   By my troth,° Nerissa, my little body is aweary of this   *faith*
    great world.
NERISSA   You would be,[1] sweet madam, if your miseries were in
    the same abundance as your good fortunes are; and yet, for
5   aught I see, they are as sick that surfeit with too much as they
    that starve with nothing. It is no mean° happiness, therefore,   *slight*
    to be seated in the mean.° Superfluity comes sooner by° white   *middle / sooner gets*
    hairs, but competency° lives longer.   *moderate estate*
PORTIA   Good sentences,° and well pronounced.   *aphorisms*
10 NERISSA   They would be better if well followed.
PORTIA   If to do were as easy as to know what were good to do,
    chapels had been churches, and poor men's cottages princes'
    palaces. It is a good divine° that follows his own instructions.   *clergyman*
    I can easier teach twenty what were good to be done than to
15   be one of the twenty to follow mine own teaching. The brain
    may devise laws for the blood,° but a hot temper[2] leaps o'er a   *passion*
    cold decree. Such a hare is madness, the youth, to skip o'er
    the meshes° of good counsel, the cripple.[3] But this reasoning   *snares*
    is not in the fashion° to choose me a husband. O me, the word   *of a kind*

---

9. *nothing . . . / To:* no less worthy than.
1. Roman matron famous for heroic fidelity to her hus-
band; a character in *Julius Caesar.*
2. Coast of Colchis, where in classical mythology Jason
won the Golden Fleece.
3. *of . . . sake:* because of my creditworthiness or as a

personal favor.
1.2 Location: Belmont.
1. You would have reason to be weary.
2. An impetuous disposition.
3. Because wisdom is imagined as elderly.

20 'choose'! I may neither choose who I would nor refuse who I
dislike; so is the will° of a living daughter curbed by the will°   *wish / testament*
of a dead father. Is it not hard, Nerissa, that I cannot choose
one nor refuse none?

NERISSA   Your father was ever virtuous, and holy men at their
25   death have good inspirations; therefore the lottery that he
hath devised in these three chests of gold, silver, and lead,
whereof who chooses his meaning chooses you, will no doubt
never be chosen by any rightly but one who you shall rightly
love. But what warmth is there in your affection towards any
30   of these princely suitors that are already come?

PORTIA   I pray thee overname them, and as thou namest them
I will describe them; and according to my description, level°   *guess*
at my affection.

NERISSA   First there is the Neapolitan prince.

35 PORTIA   Ay, that's a colt⁴ indeed, for he doth nothing but talk of
his horse, and he makes it a great appropriation° to his own   *augmentation*
good parts° that he can shoe him himself. I am much afeard   *own abilities*
my lady his mother played false with a smith.

NERISSA   Then is there the County Palatine.⁵

40 PORTIA   He doth nothing but frown, as who should say 'An° you   *If*
will not have me, choose'.° He hears merry tales and smiles   *do as you wish*
not. I fear he will prove the weeping philosopher⁶ when he
grows old, being so full of unmannerly° sadness in his youth.   *immoderate*
I had rather be married to a death's-head with a bone in his
45   mouth than to either of these. God defend me from these two!

NERISSA   How say you by the French lord, Monsieur le Bon?

PORTIA   God made him, and therefore let him pass for a man. In
truth, I know it is a sin to be a mocker, but he—why, he hath
a horse better than the Neapolitan's, a better bad habit of
50   frowning than the Count Palatine. He is every man in no man.
If a throstle° sing, he falls straight° a-cap'ring. He will fence   *thrush / immediately*
with his own shadow. If I should marry him, I should marry
twenty husbands. If he would despise me, I would forgive him,
for if he love me to madness, I shall never requite him.

55 NERISSA   What say you then to Falconbridge, the young baron
of England?

PORTIA   You know I say nothing to him, for he understands not
me, nor I him. He hath neither Latin, French, nor Italian, and
you will come into the court and swear that I have a poor pen-
60   nyworth in the English. He is a proper° man's picture, but   *handsome*
alas, who can converse with a dumb show?° How oddly he is   *pantomime*
suited! I think he bought his doublet° in Italy, his round hose⁷   *upper garment*
in France, his bonnet° in Germany, and his behaviour every-   *hat*
where.

65 NERISSA   What think you of the Scottish lord, his neighbour?

PORTIA   That he hath a neighbourly charity in him, for he bor-
rowed a box of the ear of the Englishman and swore he would
pay him again when he was able. I think the Frenchman
became his surety, and sealed under for another.⁸

---

4. Foolish young man. Neapolitans were excellent
horsemen.
5. Count possessing royal powers.
6. Heracleitus, a melancholy Greek philosopher.
7. Puffed breeches.

8. The Frenchman vouched for the Scot's payment (of
a box on the ear) and promised to add another himself
(referring to France's frequent promises to help the
Scots against the English).

70 NERISSA How like you the young German, the Duke of Saxony's
nephew?

PORTIA Very vilely in the morning when he is sober, and most
vilely in the afternoon when he is drunk. When he is best he
is a little worse than a man, and when he is worst he is little
75 better than a beast. An the worst fall that ever fell, I hope I
shall make shift° to go without him.   *manage*

NERISSA If he should offer° to choose, and choose the right   *endeavor*
casket, you should refuse to perform your father's will if you
should refuse to accept him.

80 PORTIA Therefore, for fear of the worst, I pray thee set a deep
glass of Rhenish wine° on the contrary casket; for if the devil   *white German wine*
be within and that temptation without, I know he will choose
it. I will do anything, Nerissa, ere I will be married to a sponge.

NERISSA You need not fear, lady, the having any of these lords.
85 They have acquainted me with their determinations, which is
indeed to return to their home and to trouble you with no
more suit unless you may be won by some other sort° than   *way*
your father's imposition° depending on the caskets.   *conditions*

PORTIA If I live to be as old as Sibylla⁹ I will die as chaste as
90 Diana unless I be obtained by the manner of my father's will.
I am glad this parcel of wooers are so reasonable, for there is
not one among them but I dote on his very absence; and I pray
God grant them a fair departure.

NERISSA Do you not remember, lady, in your father's time, a
95 Venetian, a scholar and a soldier, that came hither in company
of the Marquis of Montferrat?

PORTIA Yes, yes, it was Bassanio—as I think, so was he called.

NERISSA True, madam. He of all the men that ever my foolish
eyes looked upon was the best deserving a fair lady.

100 PORTIA I remember him well, and I remember him worthy of
thy praise.

Enter a SERVINGMAN

How now, what news?

SERVINGMAN The four strangers seek for you, madam, to take
their leave, and there is a forerunner come from a fifth, the
105 Prince of Morocco, who brings word the Prince his master
will be here tonight.

PORTIA If I could bid the fifth welcome with so good heart as I
can bid the other four farewell, I should be glad of his
approach. If he have the condition° of a saint and the complex-   *character*
110 ion of a devil,¹ I had rather he should shrive me° than wive me. *absolve me of my sins*
Come, Nerissa. [*To the* SERVINGMAN] Sirrah, go before.
Whiles we shut the gate upon one wooer,
Another knocks at the door.   *Exeunt*

1.3

Enter BASSANIO *with* SHYLOCK *the Jew*

SHYLOCK Three thousand ducats.¹ Well.

BASSANIO Ay, sir, for three months.

SHYLOCK For three months. Well.

9. In classical mythology, the Cumaean Sibyl asked
Apollo for as many years of life as the grains of sand she
held in her hand; she forgot to ask for eternal youth.

1. Devils were imagined as black.
1.3 Location: Street in Venice.
1. Gold coins. The sum is very large.

BASSANIO   For the which, as I told you, Antonio shall be bound.°   *contractually responsible*

5   SHYLOCK   Antonio shall become bound. Well.

BASSANIO   May you stead° me? Will you pleasure me? Shall I   *accommodate*
know your answer?

SHYLOCK   Three thousand ducats for three months, and Antonio
bound.

10   BASSANIO   Your answer to that.

SHYLOCK   Antonio is a good man.

BASSANIO   Have you heard any imputation to the contrary?

SHYLOCK   Ho, no, no, no, no! My meaning in saying he is a good
man is to have you understand me that he is sufficient.° Yet   *of adequate wealth*
15   his means are in supposition.° He hath an argosy bound to   *doubt*
Tripolis, another to the Indies. I understand moreover upon
the Rialto[2] he hath a third at Mexico, a fourth for England,
and other ventures he hath squandered abroad. But ships are
but boards, sailors but men. There be land rats and water rats,
20   water thieves and land thieves—I mean pirates—and then
there is the peril of waters, winds, and rocks. The man is,
notwithstanding, sufficient. Three thousand ducats. I think I
may take his bond.

BASSANIO   Be assured you may.

25   SHYLOCK   I will be assured[3] I may, and that I may be assured,
I will bethink me. May I speak with Antonio?

BASSANIO   If it please you to dine with us.

SHYLOCK   Yes, to smell pork, to eat of the habitation which your
prophet the Nazarite[4] conjured the devil into! I will buy with
30   you, sell with you, talk with you, walk with you, and so fol-
lowing, but I will not eat with you, drink with you, nor pray
with you.

　　　　Enter ANTONIO

[*To* ANTONIO] What news on the Rialto? [*To* BASSANIO] Who is
he comes here?

35   BASSANIO   This is Signor Antonio.

　　　　[BASSANIO *and* ANTONIO *speak silently to one another*]

SHYLOCK [*aside*]   How like a fawning publican[5] he looks.
I hate him for he is a Christian;
But more, for that in low simplicity[6]
He lends out money gratis,° and brings down   *free*
40   The rate of usance° here with us in Venice.   *interest*
If I can catch him once upon the hip[7]
I will feed fat the ancient grudge I bear him.
He hates our sacred nation,° and he rails,   *(the Jews)*
Even there where merchants most do congregate,
45   On me, my bargains, and my well-won thrift°—   *profit*
Which he calls interest. Cursèd be my tribe
If I forgive him.

BASSANIO   Shylock, do you hear?

SHYLOCK   I am debating of my present store,°   *supply of money*
And by the near guess of my memory

2. Merchants' exchange in Venice.
3. Sure (but Shylock uses the word to mean "given financial guarantees").
4. Jesus, who cast devils into a herd of swine.
5. Tax collector; he robs me, but now, like the publican
in Luke 18:10–14 who prays to Jesus for mercy, tries to ingratiate himself because he wants a favor.
6. In meek honesty; in base folly.
7. *upon the hip*: at a disadvantage (wrestling terminology).

50 I cannot instantly raise up the gross°   *total*
  Of full three thousand ducats. What of that?
  Tubal, a wealthy Hebrew of my tribe,
  Will furnish me. But soft°—how many months   *wait*
  Do you desire? [*To* ANTONIO] Rest you fair, good signor.
55 Your worship was the last man in our mouths.[8]
ANTONIO   Shylock, albeit I neither lend nor borrow
  By taking nor by giving of excess,
  Yet to supply the ripe° wants of my friend   *urgent*
  I'll break a custom. [*To* BASSANIO] Is he yet possessed°   *informed*
60 How much ye would?
SHYLOCK   Ay, ay, three thousand ducats.
ANTONIO   And for three months.
SHYLOCK   I had forgot—three months. [*To* BASSANIO] You told me so.—
  Well then, your bond; and let me see—but hear you,
65 Methoughts you said you neither lend nor borrow
  Upon advantage.°   *interest*
ANTONIO   I do never use it.
SHYLOCK   When Jacob grazed his uncle Laban's sheep—
  This Jacob from our holy Abram was,
  As his wise mother wrought in his behalf,
70 The third possessor; ay, he was the third[9]—
ANTONIO   And what of him? Did he take interest?
SHYLOCK   No, not take interest, not, as you would say,
  Directly int'rest. Mark what Jacob did:
  When Laban and himself were compromised°   *agreed*
75 That all the eanlings° which were streaked and pied°   *lambs / spotted*
  Should fall as Jacob's hire, the ewes, being rank,°   *in heat*
  In end of autumn turnèd to the rams,
  And when the work of generation° was   *mating*
  Between these woolly breeders in the act,
80 The skilful shepherd peeled me certain wands,[1]
  And in the doing of the deed of kind°   *nature*
  He stuck them up before the fulsome ewes
  Who, then conceiving, did in eaning° time   *lambing*
  Fall° parti-coloured lambs; and those were Jacob's.   *Deliver*
85 This was a way to thrive; and he was blest;
  And thrift is blessing, if men steal it not.
ANTONIO   This was a venture, sir, that Jacob served for[2]—
  A thing not in his power to bring to pass,
  But swayed and fashioned by the hand of heaven.
90 Was this inserted to make interest good,[3]
  Or is your gold and silver ewes and rams?
SHYLOCK   I cannot tell. I make it breed as fast.
  But note me, signor—
ANTONIO   Mark you this, Bassanio?
  The devil can cite Scripture for his purpose.
95 An evil soul producing holy witness
  Is like a villain with a smiling cheek,

8. We were just mentioning you.
9. After Abraham and Isaac; his mother, Rebecca, helped him cheat his brother Esau of his birthright. The story of Laban's sheep is told in Genesis 30:25–43.

1. Stripped part of the bark off some sticks ("me" is colloquial).
2. This was a speculative enterprise on which Jacob staked his wages as a servant.
3. Was this brought up to defend taking interest.

A goodly apple rotten at the heart.
O, what a goodly outside falsehood hath!

SHYLOCK   Three thousand ducats. 'Tis a good round sum.
100   Three months from twelve—then let me see the rate.
ANTONIO   Well, Shylock, shall we be beholden to you?
SHYLOCK   Signor Antonio, many a time and oft
   In the Rialto you have rated° me   berated
   About my moneys and my usances.
105   Still° have I borne it with a patient shrug,   Always
   For suff 'rance is the badge[4] of all our tribe.
   You call me misbeliever, cut-throat, dog,
   And spit upon my Jewish gaberdine,°   long coat
   And all for use of that which is mine own.
110   Well then, it now appears you need my help.
   Go to, then. You come to me, and you say
   'Shylock, we would have moneys'—you say so,
   You, that did void your rheum° upon my beard,   spit
   And foot me as you spurn° a stranger cur   contemptuously kick
115   Over your threshold. Moneys is your suit.
   What should I say to you? Should I not say
   'Hath a dog money? Is it possible
   A cur can lend three thousand ducats?' Or
   Shall I bend low, and in a bondman's° key,   slave's
120   With bated breath and whisp'ring humbleness
   Say this: 'Fair sir, you spat on me on Wednesday last;
   You spurned me such a day; another time
   You called me dog; and for these courtesies
   I'll lend you thus much moneys'?
125 ANTONIO   I am as like to call thee so again,
   To spit on thee again, to spurn thee too.
   If thou wilt lend this money, lend it not
   As to thy friends; for when did friendship take
   A breed[5] for barren metal of his friend?
130   But lend it rather to thine enemy,
   Who if he break,° thou mayst with better face   fail to repay
   Exact the penalty.
SHYLOCK   Why, look you, how you storm!
   I would be friends with you, and have your love,
   Forget the shames that you have stained me with,
135   Supply your present wants, and take no doit°   small coin
   Of usance for my moneys; and you'll not hear me.
   This is kind[6] I offer.
BASSANIO   This were° kindness.   would be
SHYLOCK   This kindness will I show.
140   Go with me to a notary, seal me there
   Your single bond,[7] and, in a merry sport,
   If you repay me not on such a day,
   In such a place, such sum or sums as are
   Expressed in the condition, let the forfeit°   penalty
145   Be nominated for an equal° pound   Be stipulated as an exact

---

4. For enduring insult is the characteristic.
5. Offspring (interest); alluding to an ancient argument that it was unnatural to use money to "breed," or make, more money.

6. Benevolent; natural (but perhaps with the covert suggestion "in kind").
7. Bond signed by the debtor alone (Antonio) without additional guarantors.

Of your fair flesh to be cut off and taken
In what part of your body pleaseth me.
ANTONIO   Content, in faith. I'll seal to such a bond,
And say there is much kindness in the Jew.
150   BASSANIO   You shall not seal to such a bond for me.
I'll rather dwell in my necessity.°   *remain in need*
ANTONIO   Why, fear not, man; I will not forfeit it.
Within these two months—that's a month before
This bond expires—I do expect return
155   Of thrice three times the value of this bond.
SHYLOCK   O father Abram, what these Christians are,
Whose own hard dealings teaches them suspect
The thoughts of others! [*To* BASSANIO] Pray you tell me this:
If he should break his day, what should I gain
160   By the exaction of the forfeiture?
A pound of man's flesh taken from a man
Is not so estimable,° profitable neither,   *valuable*
As flesh of muttons, beeves, or goats. I say,
To buy his favour I extend this friendship.
165   If he will take it, so. If not, adieu,
And, for my love, I pray you wrong me not.
ANTONIO   Yes, Shylock, I will seal unto this bond.
SHYLOCK   Then meet me forthwith at the notary's.
Give him direction for this merry bond,
170   And I will go and purse the ducats straight,
See to my house—left in the fearful° guard   *doubtful*
Of an unthrifty knave—and presently
I'll be with you.
ANTONIO   Hie thee,° gentle Jew.   *Exit* [SHYLOCK]   *Hurry*
The Hebrew will turn Christian; he grows kind.
175   BASSANIO   I like not fair terms and a villain's mind.
ANTONIO   Come on. In this there can be no dismay.
My ships come home a month before the day.   *Exeunt*

2.1

[*Flourish of cornets.*] *Enter* [*the Prince of*] MOROCCO,
a tawny Moor all in white, and three or four followers
accordingly,[1] *with* PORTIA, NERISSA, *and their train*
MOROCCO [*to* PORTIA]   Mislike me not for my complexion,
The shadowed livery° of the burnished sun,   *servant's uniform*
To whom I am a neighbour and near bred.°   *close kin*
Bring me the fairest creature northward born,
5   Where Phoebus'° fire scarce thaws the icicles,   *the sun god*
And let us make incision for your love
To prove whose blood is reddest,[2] his or mine.
I tell thee, lady, this aspect° of mine   *countenance*
Hath feared° the valiant. By my love I swear,   *frightened*
10   The best regarded virgins of our clime
Have loved it too. I would not change this hue
Except to steal your thoughts, my gentle queen.
PORTIA   In terms of choice I am not solely led
By nice direction° of a maiden's eyes.   *fastidious guidance*

2.1 Location: Belmont.   2. Red blood was considered a sign of valor.
1. Of similar complexion and dress.

15   Besides, the lott'ry of my destiny
    Bars me the right of voluntary choosing.
    But if my father had not scanted° me,   *limited*
    And hedged° me by his wit° to yield myself   *restricted / wisdom*
    His wife who wins me by that means I told you,
20   Yourself, renownèd Prince, then stood as fair³
    As any comer I have looked on yet
    For my affection.
MOROCCO   Even for that I thank you.
    Therefore I pray you lead me to the caskets
    To try my fortune. By this scimitar,
25   That slew the Sophy° and a Persian prince   *Shah of Persia*
    That won three fields of Sultan Suleiman,°   *Turkish ruler*
    I would o'erstare the sternest eyes that look,
    Outbrave the heart most daring on the earth,
    Pluck the young sucking cubs from the she-bear,
30   Yea, mock the lion when a° roars for prey,   *he*
    To win the lady. But alas the while,
    If Hercules and Lichas° play at dice   *Hercules' servant*
    Which is the better man, the greater throw
    May turn by fortune from the weaker hand.
35   So is Alcides° beaten by his rage,⁴   *Hercules*
    And so may I, blind Fortune leading me,
    Miss that which one unworthier may attain,
    And die with grieving.
PORTIA   You must take your chance,
    And either not attempt to choose at all,
40   Or swear before you choose, if you choose wrong
    Never to speak to lady afterward
    In way of marriage. Therefore be advised.°   *careful*
MOROCCO   Nor will not. Come, bring me unto my chance.
PORTIA   First, forward to the temple. After dinner
    Your hazard shall be made.
45 MOROCCO   Good fortune then,
    To make me blest or cursèd'st among men.
                [Flourish of] cornets. Exeunt

2.2

Enter [LANCELOT] *the clown*

LANCELOT   Certainly my conscience will serve° me to run from   *allow*
this Jew my master. The fiend is at mine elbow and tempts me,
saying to me 'Gobbo, Lancelot Gobbo, good Lancelot,' or
'good Gobbo,' or 'good Lancelot Gobbo—use your legs, take the
5 start,° run away.' My conscience says 'No, take heed, honest   *begone*
Lancelot, take heed, honest Gobbo,' or, as aforesaid, 'honest
Lancelot Gobbo—do not run, scorn running with thy heels.'° *indignantly (with pun)*
Well, the most courageous fiend bids me pack. '*Via!*'° says the   *Away*
fiend; 'Away!' says the fiend. 'For the heavens, rouse up a brave
10 mind,' says the fiend, 'and run.' Well, my conscience hanging
about the neck of my heart says very wisely to me, 'My honest
friend Lancelot'—being an honest man's son, or rather an hon-
est woman's son, for indeed my father did something smack,

---

3. Seemed as attractive; stood as good a chance.   **2.2** Location: Venice.
4. Often amended to "page."

something grow to; he had a kind of taste[1]—well, my con-
15 science says, 'Lancelot, budge not'; 'Budge!' says the fiend;
'Budge not', says my conscience. 'Conscience,' say I, 'you
counsel well'; 'Fiend,' say I, 'you counsel well.' To be ruled by
my conscience I should stay with the Jew my master who, God
bless the mark,[2] is a kind of devil; and to run away from the
20 Jew I should be ruled by the fiend who, saving your reverence,
is the devil himself. Certainly the Jew is the very devil incar-
nation;° and in my conscience, my conscience is but a kind of   *(for "incarnate")*
hard conscience to offer to counsel me to stay with the Jew.
The fiend gives the more friendly counsel. I will run, fiend.
25 My heels are at your commandment. I will run.
        Enter old GOBBO, [*blind,*] *with a basket*
    GOBBO   Master young man, you, I pray you, which is the way to
        Master Jew's?
    LANCELOT [*aside*]   O heavens, this is my true-begotten father
        who, being more than sand-blind—high-gravel-blind[3]—
30   knows me not. I will try confusions[4] with him.
    GOBBO   Master young gentleman, I pray you which is the way
        to Master Jew's?
    LANCELOT   Turn up on your right hand at the next turning, but
        at the next turning of all on your left, marry at the very next
35   turning, turn of no hand but turn down indirectly to the Jew's
        house.
    GOBBO   By God's sonties,° 'twill be a hard way to hit. Can you   *saints*
        tell me whether one Lancelot that dwells with him dwell with
        him or no?
40 LANCELOT   Talk you of young Master[5] Lancelot? [*Aside*]   Mark
        me now, now will I raise the waters.[6] [*To* GOBBO]   Talk you of
        young Master Lancelot?
    GOBBO   No master, sir, but a poor man's son. His father, though
        I say't, is an honest exceeding poor man, and, God be thanked,
45   well to live.[7]
    LANCELOT   Well, let his father be what a° will, we talk of young   *he*
        Master Lancelot.
    GOBBO   Your worship's friend, and Lancelot, sir.
    LANCELOT   But I pray you, *ergo*° old man, *ergo* I beseech you,   *therefore*
50   talk you of young Master Lancelot?
    GOBBO   Of Lancelot, an't° please your mastership.   *if it*
    LANCELOT   *Ergo* Master Lancelot. Talk not of Master Lancelot,
        father,[8] for the young gentleman, according to fates and destin-
        ies and such odd sayings—the sisters three° and such branches   *the Fates*
55   of learning—is indeed deceased; or, as you would say in plain
        terms, gone to heaven.
    GOBBO   Marry, God forbid! The boy was the very staff of my age,
        my very prop.
    LANCELOT [*aside*]   Do I look like a cudgel or a hovel-post,° a   *shed post*
60   staff or a prop? [*To* GOBBO] Do you know me, father?

1. *my father . . . taste:* that is, my father was licentious.   4. Lancelot's version of "try conclusions" (experiment).
2. Conventional apology before a rude remark, like   5. "Master" was only applied to gentlemen's sons.
"saving your reverence."   6. Start something; bring on tears.
3. Lancelot's coinage for a degree of blindness between   7. Well-to-do (contradicts the previous line).
sand-blind (partly blind) and stone-blind.   8. Customary address to an old man.

GOBBO   Alack the day, I know you not, young gentleman. But I
pray you tell me, is my boy—God rest his soul—alive or dead?

LANCELOT   Do you not know me, father?

GOBBO   Alack, sir, I am sand-blind. I know you not.

65   LANCELOT   Nay, indeed, if you had your eyes you might fail of
the knowing me. It is a wise father that knows his own child.[9]
Well, old man, I will tell you news of your son. [*Kneeling*]
Give me your blessing. Truth will come to light; murder can-
not be hid long—a man's son may, but in the end truth will

70   out.

GOBBO   Pray you, sir, stand up. I am sure you are not Lancelot,
my boy.

LANCELOT   Pray you, let's have no more fooling about it, but give
me your blessing. I am Lancelot, your boy that was, your son

75   that is, your child that shall be.

GOBBO   I cannot think you are my son.

LANCELOT   I know not what I shall think of that, but I am
Lancelot the Jew's man, and I am sure Margery your wife is
my mother.

80   GOBBO   Her name is Margery indeed. I'll be sworn, if thou be
Lancelot thou art mine own flesh and blood.
[*He feels Lancelot's head*]
Lord worshipped might he be, what a beard hast thou got![1]
Thou hast got more hair on thy chin than Dobbin my fill-
horse° has on his tail.   cart horse

85   LANCELOT   It should seem then that Dobbin's tail grows back-
ward.[2] I am sure he had more hair of his tail than I have of my
face when I last saw him.

GOBBO   Lord, how art thou changed! How dost thou and thy
master agree?° I have brought him a present. How 'gree you   get along

90   now?

LANCELOT   Well, well; but for mine own part, as I have set up
my rest[3] to run away, so I will not rest till I have run some
ground. My master's a very Jew.[4] Give him a present?—give
him a halter!° I am famished in his service. You may tell° every   noose / count

95   finger I have with my ribs. Father, I am glad you are come.
Give me° your present to one Master Bassanio, who indeed   Give
gives rare new liveries.° If I serve not him, I will run as far as   servants' uniforms
God has any ground.
Enter BASSANIO *with* [LEONARDO *and*] *follower*[s]
O rare fortune! Here comes the man. To him, father, for I am

100   a Jew if I serve the Jew any longer.

BASSANIO   [*to one of his men*]   You may do so, but let it be so
hasted° that supper be ready at the farthest° by five of the   hurried / latest
clock. See these letters delivered, put the liveries to making,
and desire° Graziano to come anon° to my lodging. [*Exit one*]   tell / at once

105   LANCELOT   [*to* GOBBO]   To him, father.

GOBBO   [*to* BASSANIO]   God bless your worship.

BASSANIO   Gramercy.° Wouldst thou aught° with me?   Many thanks / anything

GOBBO   Here's my son, sir, a poor boy—

---

9. Transposing the proverb "A wise child knows his
own father."
1. Gobbo mistakes Lancelot's hair for a beard.
2. Gets shorter; grows from the wrong end.

3. As I have definitely determined (phrase in the card
game primero meaning "risk everything").
4. Cruel, grasping person; Hebrew. *a very:* an absolute.

LANCELOT [*to* BASSANIO]   Not a poor boy, sir, but the rich Jew's
110   man that would, sir, as my father shall specify.
GOBBO [*to* BASSANIO]   He hath a great infection,° sir, as one   (for "affection"; wish)
          would say, to serve—
LANCELOT   Indeed, the short and the long is, I serve the Jew,
          and have a desire as my father shall specify.
115   GOBBO [*to* BASSANIO]   His master and he, saving your worship's
          reverence, are scarce cater-cousins.°   close friends
LANCELOT [*to* BASSANIO]   To be brief, the very truth is that the
          Jew, having done me wrong, doth cause me, as my father—
          being, I hope, an old man—shall frutify° unto you.   (for "certify")
120   GOBBO [*to* BASSANIO]   I have here a dish of doves that I would
          bestow upon your worship, and my suit is—
LANCELOT [*to* BASSANIO]   In very brief, the suit is impertinent°   (for "pertinent")
          to myself, as your worship shall know by this honest old man;
          and though I say it, though old man, yet, poor man, my father.
125   BASSANIO   One speak for both. What would you?
LANCELOT   Serve you, sir.
GOBBO [*to* BASSANIO]   That is the very defect° of the matter, sir.   (for "effect")
BASSANIO [*to* LANCELOT]   I know thee well. Thou hast obtained
          thy suit.
130   Shylock thy master spoke with me this day,
          And hath preferred thee, if it be preferment⁵
          To leave a rich Jew's service to become
          The follower of so poor a gentleman.
LANCELOT   The old proverb⁶ is very well parted between my
135   master Shylock and you, sir: you have the grace of God, sir,
          and he hath enough.
BASSANIO   Thou speak'st it well. [*To* GOBBO]   Go, father, with thy son.
          [*To* LANCELOT]   Take leave of thy old master and enquire
          My lodging out. [*To one of his men*]   Give him a livery
140   More guarded° than his fellows'. See it done.   decorated
LANCELOT [*to* GOBBO]   Father, in. I cannot get a service, no, I
          have ne'er a tongue in my head—well!
              [*He looks at his palm*]
          If any man in Italy have a fairer table⁷ which doth offer to swear
          upon a book,⁸ I shall have good fortune. Go to, here's a simple°   unremarkable (ironic)
145   line of life, here's a small trifle of wives—alas, fifteen wives is
          nothing. Eleven widows and nine maids is a simple coming-in⁹
          for one man, and then to scape drowning thrice, and to be in
          peril of my life with the edge of a featherbed¹—here are simple
          scapes. Well, if Fortune be a woman, she's a good wench for
150   this gear.° Father, come. I'll take my leave of the Jew in the   matter
          twinkling.   *Exit* [*with old* GOBBO]
BASSANIO   I pray thee, good Leonardo, think on this.
          These things being bought and orderly bestowed,°   stowed on ship
          Return in haste, for I do feast tonight
155   My best-esteemed acquaintance. Hie thee. Go.
LEONARDO   My best endeavours shall be done herein.
              [*He begins to leave.*] *Enter* GRAZIANO

5. And has recommended you, if it be advancement.   8. To tell the truth (referring to the practice of taking
6. "The grace of God is gear enough."   an oath with the palm on the Bible).
7. Palm (Lancelot reads the lines of his palm to predict   9. A scanty income; an easy sexual entrance.
the future).   1. Alluding to a sexual adventure.

GRAZIANO [*to* LEONARDO] Where's your master?

LEONARDO   Yonder, sir, he walks.

                                                                    Exit

GRAZIANO Signor Bassanio.

BASSANIO   Graziano.

GRAZIANO I have a suit to you.

BASSANIO   You have obtained it.

160 GRAZIANO You must not deny me. I must go with you to Belmont.

BASSANIO Why then, you must. But hear thee, Graziano,
    Thou art too wild, too rude and bold of voice—
    Parts° that become thee happily enough,   Attributes
    And in such eyes as ours appear not faults;
165 But where thou art not known, why, there they show
    Something too liberal.° Pray thee, take pain   unrestrained
    To allay with some cold drops of modesty
    Thy skipping spirit, lest through thy wild behaviour
    I be misconstered° in the place I go to,   misconstrued
    And lose my hopes.
170 GRAZIANO   Signor Bassanio, hear me.
    If I do not put on a sober habit,°   behavior; clothing
    Talk with respect, and swear but now and then,
    Wear prayer books in my pocket, look demurely—
    Nay more, while grace is saying hood mine eyes
175 Thus with my hat,² and sigh, and say 'Amen',
    Use all the observance of civility,
    Like one well studied in a sad ostent°   solemn appearance
    To please his grandam,° never trust me more.°   grandmother / again

BASSANIO Well, we shall see your bearing.

180 GRAZIANO Nay, but I bar tonight. You shall not gauge me
    By what we do tonight.

BASSANIO   No, that were pity.
    I would entreat you rather to put on
    Your boldest suit of mirth, for we have friends
    That purpose merriment. But fare you well.
185 I have some business.

GRAZIANO And I must to Lorenzo and the rest.
    But we will visit you at supper-time.   *Exeunt* [*severally*]

2.3

Enter JESSICA *and* [LANCELOT] *the clown*

JESSICA I am sorry thou wilt leave my father so.
    Our house is hell, and thou, a merry devil,
    Didst rob it of some taste of tediousness.
    But fare thee well. There is a ducat for thee.
5   And, Lancelot, soon at supper shalt thou see
    Lorenzo, who is thy new master's guest.
    Give him this letter, do it secretly;
    And so farewell. I would not have my father
    See me in talk with thee.
10 LANCELOT Adieu. Tears exhibit° my tongue, most beautiful   (for "inhibit")
    pagan; most sweet Jew; if a Christian do not play the knave and
    get thee, I am much deceived. But adieu. These foolish drops
    do something drown my manly spirit. Adieu.

2. Hats were worn at meals but taken off for grace.   2.3 Location: Shylock's house in Venice.

JESSICA Farewell, good Lancelot.   *Exit* [LANCELOT]
15   Alack, what heinous sin is it in me
To be ashamed to be my father's child!
But though I am a daughter to his blood,
I am not to his manners.° O Lorenzo,   behavior
If thou keep promise I shall end this strife,
20   Become a Christian and thy loving wife.   *Exit*

2.4
Enter GRAZIANO, LORENZO, SALERIO, *and* SOLANIO
LORENZO Nay, we will slink away in° supper-time,   during
Disguise us at my lodging, and return
All in an hour.
GRAZIANO We have not made good preparation.
5   SALERIO We have not spoke as yet of ° torchbearers.   not yet arranged for
SOLANIO 'Tis vile, unless it may be quaintly ordered,°   cleverly managed
And better in my mind not undertook.
LORENZO 'Tis now but four o'clock. We have two hours
To furnish us.
Enter LANCELOT *with a letter*
Friend Lancelot, what's the news?
10   LANCELOT [*presenting the letter*] An° it shall please you to break   If
up° this, it shall seem to signify.   open
LORENZO [*taking the letter*] I know the hand. In faith, 'tis a fair
hand,
And whiter than the paper it writ on
Is the fair hand that writ.
GRAZIANO   Love-news, in faith.
15   LANCELOT [*to* LORENZO] By your leave, sir.
LORENZO Whither goest thou?
LANCELOT Marry, sir, to bid my old master the Jew to sup tonight
with my new master the Christian.
LORENZO Hold,° here, take this. [*Giving money*] Tell gentle Jessica   Wait
20   I will not fail her. Speak it privately.
Go.   *Exit* [LANCELOT *the*] *clown*
Gentlemen,
Will you prepare you for this masque tonight?
I am provided of a torchbearer.
SALERIO Ay, marry, I'll be gone about it straight.°   immediately
SOLANIO And so will I.
25   LORENZO   Meet me and Graziano
At Graziano's lodging some hour hence.
SALERIO 'Tis good we do so.   *Exit* [*with* SOLANIO]
GRAZIANO Was not that letter from fair Jessica?
LORENZO I must needs tell thee all. She hath directed
30   How I shall take her from her father's house,
What gold and jewels she is furnished with,
What page's suit she hath in readiness.
If e'er the Jew her father come to heaven
It will be for his gentle daughter's sake;
35   And never dare misfortune cross her foot
Unless she° do it under this excuse: (*misfortune*)

That she° is issue° to a faithless Jew.   *(Jessica) / offspring*
Come, go with me. Peruse this as thou goest.
[*He gives* GRAZIANO *the letter*]
Fair Jessica shall be my torchbearer.   *Exeunt*

2.5

Enter [SHYLOCK *the*] *Jew and his man that was,*°   *former servant*
[LANCELOT] *the clown*

SHYLOCK   Well, thou shalt see, thy eyes shall be thy judge,
The difference of old Shylock and Bassanio.
[*Calling*] What, Jessica! [*To* LANCELOT] Thou shalt not gormandize°   *overeat*
As thou hast done with me. [*Calling*] What, Jessica!
5   [*To* LANCELOT] And sleep and snore and rend apparel out.°   *wear out clothes*
[*Calling*] Why, Jessica, I say!
LANCELOT [*calling*]   Why, Jessica!
SHYLOCK   Who bids thee call? I do not bid thee call.
LANCELOT   Your worship was wont to tell me I could do nothing
without bidding.
Enter JESSICA
10   JESSICA [*to* SHYLOCK]   Call you? What is your will?
SHYLOCK   I am bid forth to supper, Jessica.
There are my keys. But wherefore° should I go?   *why*
I am not bid for love. They flatter me,
But yet I'll go in hate, to feed upon
15   The prodigal Christian. Jessica, my girl,
Look to my house. I am right loath° to go.   *very unwilling*
There is some ill a-brewing towards my rest,
For I did dream of money-bags tonight.°   *last night*
LANCELOT   I beseech you, sir, go. My young master doth expect
20   your reproach.°   *(for "approach")*
SHYLOCK   So do I his.
LANCELOT   And they have conspired together. I will not say you
shall see a masque, but if you do, then it was not for nothing
that my nose fell a-bleeding on Black Monday° last at six   *Easter Monday*
25   o'clock i'th' morning, falling out that year on Ash Wednesday
was four year in th'afternoon.[1]
SHYLOCK   What, are there masques? Hear you me, Jessica,
Lock up my doors; and when you hear the drum
And the vile squealing of the wry-necked[2] fife,
30   Clamber not you up to the casements then,
Nor thrust your head into the public street
To gaze on Christian fools with varnished° faces,   *painted; masked*
But stop my house's ears—I mean my casements.
Let not the sound of shallow fopp'ry° enter   *frivolity*
35   My sober house. By Jacob's staff[3] I swear
I have no mind of feasting forth° tonight.   *away from home*
But I will go. [*To* LANCELOT] Go you before me, sirrah.
Say I will come.
LANCELOT   I will go before, sir.
[*Aside to* JESSICA]
Mistress, look out at window for all this.[4]

2.5 Location: Outside Shylock's house.
1. Lancelot mocks Shylock's superstition.
2. Fifes were played with the head turned sideways.

3. See Genesis 32:10 and Hebrews 11:21.
4. *for all this*: despite Shylock's instructions.

40   There will come a Christian by
    Will be worth a Jewës eye.   *[Exit]*
    SHYLOCK [*to* JESSICA] What says that fool of Hagar's offspring,⁵ ha?
    JESSICA   His words were 'Farewell, mistress'; nothing else.
    SHYLOCK   The patch° is kind enough, but a huge feeder,   *fool*
45   Snail-slow in profit,° and he sleeps by day   *proficiency*
    More than the wildcat. Drones hive not with me;
    Therefore I part with him, and part with him
    To one that I would have him help to waste
    His borrowed purse. Well, Jessica, go in.
50   Perhaps I will return immediately.
    Do as I bid you. Shut doors after you.
    Fast bind, fast find⁶—
    A proverb never stale in thrifty mind.   *Exit [at one door]*
    JESSICA   Farewell; and if my fortune be not crossed,
55   I have a father, you a daughter lost.   *Exit [at another door]*

2.6

Enter the masquers, GRAZIANO *and* SALERIO *[with torchbearers]*

    GRAZIANO   This is the penthouse¹ under which Lorenzo
    Desired us to make stand.
    SALERIO   His hour is almost past.
    GRAZIANO   And it is marvel he outdwells his hour,
    For lovers ever run before the clock.
5   SALERIO   O, ten times faster Venus' pigeons² fly
    To seal love's bonds new made than they are wont
    To keep obligèd° faith unforfeited.°   *pledged / unbroken*
    GRAZIANO   That ever holds.° Who riseth from a feast   *remains true*
    With that keen appetite that he sits down?
10   Where is the horse that doth untread° again   *retrace*
    His tedious measures with the unbated fire
    That he did pace them first? All things that are
    Are with more spirit chasèd than enjoyed.
    How like a younker or a prodigal³
15   The scarfèd barque° puts from her native bay,   *streamer-bedecked ship*
    Hugged and embracèd by the strumpet wind!
    How like the prodigal doth she return,
    With over-weathered ribs° and raggèd sails,   *weatherbeaten timbers*
    Lean, rent,° and beggared by the strumpet wind!   *torn*
    Enter LORENZO *[with a torch]*
20   SALERIO   Here comes Lorenzo. More of this hereafter.
    LORENZO   Sweet friends, your patience for my long abode.°   *delay*
    Not I but my affairs have made you wait.
    When you shall please to play the thieves for wives
    I'll watch° as long for you therein. Approach.   *wait*
25   Here dwells my father° Jew. [*Calling*] Ho, who's within?   *father-in-law*
    [*Enter*] JESSICA *above [in boy's apparel]*
    JESSICA   Who are you? Tell me for more certainty,

---

5. That despicable gentile. Hagar, Abraham's gentile servant, bore him a son, Ishmael; she and her child were cast out after the birth of Abraham's legitimate son, Isaac.
6. Something firmly secured will remain fastened.

2.6 Location: Scene continues.
1. Projecting roof of an upper story.
2. Doves that drew the love goddess's chariot.
3. See Luke 15:11–31. *younker:* fashionable youth; junior seaman.

Albeit I'll swear that I do know your tongue.

LORENZO Lorenzo, and thy love.

JESSICA Lorenzo, certain, and my love indeed,

30 For who love I so much? And now who knows
But you, Lorenzo, whether I am yours?

LORENZO Heaven and thy thoughts are witness that thou art.

JESSICA Here, catch this casket. It is worth the pains.
I am glad 'tis night, you do not look on me,

35 For I am much ashamed of my exchange;°   change of clothes
But love is blind, and lovers cannot see
The pretty° follies that themselves commit;   ingenious
For if they could, Cupid himself would blush
To see me thus transformèd to a boy.

40 LORENZO Descend, for you must be my torchbearer.

JESSICA What, must I hold a candle to my shames?
They in themselves, good sooth,° are too too light.°   in truth / clear; wanton
Why, 'tis an office of discovery,⁴ love,
And I should be obscured.

LORENZO   So are you, sweet,

45 Even in the lovely garnish° of a boy.   dress
But come at once,
For the close° night doth play the runaway,°   secret / steals away
And we are stayed° for at Bassanio's feast.   waited

JESSICA I will make fast the doors, and gild myself

50 With some more ducats, and be with you straight.

[Exit above]

GRAZIANO Now, by my hood, a gentile, and no Jew.

LORENZO Beshrew° me but I love her heartily,   Evil befall
For she is wise, if I can judge of her;
And fair she is, if that mine eyes be true;

55 And true she is, as she hath proved herself;
And therefore like herself, wise, fair, and true,
Shall she be placèd in my constant soul.

Enter JESSICA [below]

What, art thou come? On, gentlemen, away.
Our masquing mates by this time for us stay.

Exit [with JESSICA and SALERIO]

Enter ANTONIO

ANTONIO Who's there?

60 GRAZIANO   Signor Antonio?

ANTONIO Fie, fie, Graziano, where are all the rest?
'Tis nine o'clock. Our friends all stay for you.
No masque tonight. The wind is come about.
Bassanio presently° will go aboard.   immediately

65 I have sent twenty out to seek for you.

GRAZIANO I am glad on't. I desire no more delight
Than to be under sail and gone tonight.   Exeunt

2.7

[Flourish of cornets.] Enter PORTIA with MOROCCO and
both their trains

PORTIA Go, draw aside the curtains, and discover°   reveal
The several caskets to this noble prince.

---

4. (Torchbearing) is a task of disclosure.   2.7 Location: Belmont.

[*The curtains are drawn aside, revealing three caskets*]
[*To* MOROCCO]   Now make your choice.
MOROCCO   This first of gold, who° this inscription bears: which
5   'Who chooseth me shall gain what many men desire.'
       The second silver, which this promise carries:
       'Who chooseth me shall get as much as he deserves.'
       This third dull lead, with warning all as blunt:[1]
       'Who chooseth me must give and hazard all he hath.'
10   How shall I know if I do choose the right?
PORTIA   The one of them contains my picture, Prince.
       If you choose that, then I am yours withal.°   with it
MOROCCO   Some god direct my judgement! Let me see.
       I will survey th'inscriptions back again.
15   What says this leaden casket?
       'Who chooseth me must give and hazard all he hath.'
       Must give, for what? For lead? Hazard for lead?
       This casket threatens. Men that hazard all
       Do it in hope of fair advantages.
20   A golden mind stoops not to shows of dross.°   rubbish
       I'll then nor° give nor hazard aught for lead.   neither
       What says the silver with her virgin hue?
       'Who chooseth me shall get as much as he deserves.'
       'As much as he deserves': pause there, Morocco,
25   And weigh thy value with an even° hand.   impartial
       If thou beest rated by thy estimation
       Thou dost deserve enough, and yet 'enough'
       May not extend so far as to the lady.
       And yet to be afeard of my deserving
30   Were but a weak disabling° of myself.   disparagement
       As much as I deserve—why, that's the lady!
       I do in birth deserve her, and in fortunes,
       In graces, and in qualities of breeding;
       But more than these, in love I do deserve.
35   What if I strayed no farther, but chose here?
       Let's see once more this saying graved in gold:
       'Who chooseth me shall gain what many men desire.'
       Why, that's the lady! All the world desires her.
       From the four corners of the earth they come
40   To kiss this shrine, this mortal breathing saint.
       The Hyrcanian deserts[2] and the vasty° wilds   vast
       Of wide Arabia are as throughfares° now   main roads
       For princes to come view fair Portia.
       The watery kingdom, whose ambitious head°   (of a storm)
45   Spits in the face of heaven, is no bar
       To stop the foreign spirits, but they come
       As o'er a brook to see fair Portia.
       One of these three contains her heavenly picture.
       Is't like° that lead contains her? 'Twere damnation   probable
50   To think so base a thought. It° were too gross   (lead)
       To rib her cerecloth[3] in the obscure grave.
       Or shall I think in silver she's immured,°   enclosed
       Being ten times undervalued to tried° gold?   purified

---

1. Plainly spoken; not sharp (with play on "dull lead").   3. To enclose her shroud (normally covered with a
2. Wild region south of the Caspian Sea.   layer of lead).

O sinful thought! Never so rich a gem
55 Was set in worse than gold. They have in England
A coin that bears the figure of an angel[4]
Stamped in gold, but that's insculped° upon;   *engraved*
But here an angel in a golden bed
Lies all within. Deliver me the key.
60 Here do I choose, and thrive I as I may.
        [*He is given a key*]
PORTIA There, take it, Prince; and if my form° lie there,   *image*
Then I am yours.
        [MOROCCO *opens the golden casket*]
MOROCCO   O hell! What have we here?
A carrion death,° within whose empty eye   *A skull*
There is a written scroll. I'll read the writing.
65 'All that glisters is not gold;
Often have you heard that told.
Many a man his life hath sold
But my outside[5] to behold.
Gilded tombs do worms infold.°   *enclose*
70 Had you been as wise as bold,
Young in limbs, in judgement old,
Your answer had not been enscrolled.
Fare you well; your suit is cold.'
Cold indeed, and labour lost.
75 Then farewell heat, and welcome frost.
Portia, adieu. I have too grieved a heart
To take a tedious leave. Thus losers part.
        Exit [*with his train*]. *Flourish* [*of*] *cornets*
PORTIA A gentle riddance. Draw the curtains, go.
Let all of his complexion choose me so.
        [*The curtains are drawn.*] *Exeunt*

2.8

Enter SALERIO *and* SOLANIO
SALERIO Why, man, I saw Bassanio under sail.
With him is Graziano gone along,
And in their ship I am sure Lorenzo is not.
SOLANIO The villain Jew with outcries raised° the Duke,   *roused*
5 Who went with him to search Bassanio's ship.
SALERIO He came too late. The ship was under sail.
But there the Duke was given to understand
That in a gondola were seen together
Lorenzo and his amorous Jessica.
10 Besides, Antonio certified the Duke
They were not with Bassanio in his ship.
SOLANIO I never heard a passion° so confused,   *an outburst*
So strange, outrageous, and so variable
As the dog Jew did utter in the streets.
15 'My daughter! O, my ducats! O, my daughter!
Fled with a Christian! O, my Christian ducats!
Justice! The law! My ducats and my daughter!
A sealèd bag, two sealèd bags of ducats,

---

4. The gold coin called angel had the figure of St.   5. Gold; face that once covered the skull.
Michael on its face.   2.8 Location: Venice.

Of double ducats, stol'n from me by my daughter!

20 And jewels, two stones, two rich and precious stones,[1]
Stol'n by my daughter! Justice! Find the girl!
She hath the stones upon her, and the ducats!'

SALERIO Why, all the boys in Venice follow him,
Crying, 'His stones, his daughter, and his ducats!'

25 SOLANIO Let good Antonio look he keep his day,°   *repay his debt on time*
Or he shall pay for this.

SALERIO   Marry, well remembered.
I reasoned° with a Frenchman yesterday,   *conversed*
Who told me in the narrow seas° that part   *(English Channel)*
The French and English there miscarrièd°   *wrecked*

30 A vessel of our country, richly fraught.°   *laden*
I thought upon Antonio when he told me,
And wished in silence that it were not his.

SOLANIO You were best to tell Antonio what you hear—
Yet do not suddenly, for it may grieve him.

35 SALERIO A kinder gentleman treads not the earth.
I saw Bassanio and Antonio part.
Bassanio told him he would make some speed
Of his return. He answered, 'Do not so.
Slubber° not business for my sake, Bassanio,   *Hastily perform*

40 But stay the very riping of the time;
And for the Jew's bond which he hath of me,
Let it not enter in your mind° of love.   *interrupt your thoughts*
Be merry, and employ your chiefest thoughts
To courtship and such fair ostents° of love   *displays*

45 As shall conveniently° become you there.'   *properly*
And even there, his eye being big with tears,
Turning his face, he put his hand behind him
And, with affection wondrous sensible,°   *obvious; heartfelt*
He wrung Bassanio's hand; and so they parted.

50 SOLANIO I think he only loves the world for him.
I pray thee let us go and find him out,
And quicken his embracèd heaviness[2]
With some delight or other.

SALERIO   Do we so.   *Exeunt*

2.9

Enter NERISSA *and a servitor*

NERISSA Quick, quick, I pray thee, draw the curtain straight.°   *immediately*
The Prince of Aragon hath ta'en his oath,
And comes to his election presently.°   *his choice at once*
[*The servitor draws aside the curtain, revealing the three
caskets. Flourish of cornets.*] *Enter* ARAGON, *his train,
and* PORTIA

PORTIA Behold, there stand the caskets, noble Prince.

5 If you choose that wherein I am contained,
Straight shall our nuptial rites be solemnized.
But if you fail, without more speech, my lord,
You must be gone from hence immediately.

---

1. With the suggestion "testicles," taken up by the
mocking boys in line 24.

2. And lighten the grief he embraces.
2.9 Location: Belmont.

ARAGON   I am enjoined by oath to observe three things:
10   First, never to unfold to anyone
        Which casket 'twas I chose. Next, if I fail
        Of the right casket, never in my life
        To woo a maid in way of marriage.
        Lastly, if I do fail in fortune of my choice,
15   Immediately to leave you and be gone.
PORTIA   To these injunctions everyone doth swear
        That comes to hazard° for my worthless self.   gamble
ARAGON   And so have I addressed° me. Fortune now   prepared
        To my heart's hope! Gold, silver, and base lead.
        [He reads the leaden casket]
20   'Who chooseth me must give and hazard all he hath.'
        You shall look fairer ere I give or hazard.
        What says the golden chest? Ha, let me see.
        'Who chooseth me shall gain what many men desire.'
        'What many men desire'—that 'many' may be meant
25   By° the fool multitude, that choose by show,   For
        Not learning more than the fond° eye doth teach,   foolish
        Which pries not to th'interior but, like the martlet,°   swallow
        Builds in the weather° on the outward wall   open air
        Even in the force and road of casualty.°   mishap
30   I will not choose what many men desire,
        Because I will not jump° with common spirits   agree
        And rank me with the barbarous multitudes.
        Why then, to thee, thou silver treasure-house.
        Tell me once more what title thou dost bear.
35   'Who chooseth me shall get as much as he deserves'—
        And well said too, for who shall go about
        To cozen° fortune, and be honourable   cheat
        Without the stamp° of merit? Let none presume   official seal
        To wear an undeservèd dignity.
40   O, that estates, degrees,° and offices   social ranks
        Were not derived° corruptly, and that clear honour   gained
        Were purchased° by the merit of the wearer!   acquired
        How many then should cover that stand bare,[1]
        How many be commanded that command?
45   How much low peasantry would then be gleaned°   separated
        From the true seed of honour, and how much honour
        Picked from the chaff and ruin of the times
        To be new varnished?° Well; but to my choice.   regain its luster
        'Who chooseth me shall get as much as he deserves.'
50   I will assume° desert. Give me a key for this,   claim
        And instantly unlock my fortunes here.
        [He is given a key, and opens the silver casket]
PORTIA   Too long a pause for that which you find there.
ARAGON   What's here? The portrait of a blinking idiot
        Presenting me a schedule.° I will read it.   document
55   How much unlike art thou to Portia!
        How much unlike my hopes and my deservings!
        'Who chooseth me shall have as much as he deserves.'

1. Should wear hats who now stand bareheaded (before their social superiors).

Did I deserve no more than a fool's head?
Is that my prize? Are my deserts no better?
60 PORTIA   To offend and judge are distinct offices,[2]
And of opposèd natures.
ARAGON   What is here?
[*He reads the schedule*]
'The fire seven times tried° this;   *purified*
Seven times tried that judgement is
That did never choose amiss.
65 Some there be that shadows kiss;[3]
Such have but a shadow's bliss.
There be fools alive, iwis,°   *in truth*
Silvered[4] o'er; and so was this.
Take what wife you will to bed,
70 I° will ever be your head.   (*the blinking idiot*)
So be gone; you are sped.'°   *finished*
Still more fool I shall appear
By the time I linger here.
With one fool's head I came to woo,
75 But I go away with two.
Sweet, adieu. I'll keep my oath
Patiently to bear my wroth.°   *grief*
[*Flourish of cornets. Exit with his train*]
PORTIA   Thus hath the candle singed the moth.
O, these deliberate° fools! When they do choose   *careful*
80 They have the wisdom by their wit to lose.
NERISSA   The ancient saying is no heresy:
Hanging and wiving goes by destiny.
PORTIA   Come, draw the curtain, Nerissa.
[NERISSA *draws the curtain*]
Enter MESSENGER
MESSENGER   Where is my lady?
PORTIA   Here. What would my lord?
85 MESSENGER   Madam, there is alighted at your gate
A young Venetian, one that comes before
To signify th'approaching of his lord,
From whom he bringeth sensible regreets,°   *tangible greetings*
To wit, besides commends and courteous breath,
90 Gifts of rich value. Yet° I have not seen   *Until now*
So likely° an ambassador of love.   *suitable*
A day in April never came so sweet
To show how costly° summer was at hand   *lavish*
As this fore-spurrer comes before his lord.
95 PORTIA   No more, I pray thee, I am half afeard
Thou wilt say anon° he is some kin to thee,   *soon*
Thou spend'st such high-day[5] wit in praising him.
Come, come, Nerissa, for I long to see
Quick Cupid's post° that comes so mannerly.   *messenger*
100 NERISSA   Bassanio, Lord Love,° if thy will it be!   *Exeunt*   *Cupid*

---

2. To err and to judge are different functions.
3. Like Narcissus in classical mythology, a youth who
fell in love with his own reflection.

4. Silver-haired (thus apparently wise).
5. Holiday (fit for special occasions).

3.1

Enter SOLANIO *and* SALERIO

SOLANIO   Now, what news on the Rialto?

SALERIO   Why, yet it lives there unchecked[1] that Antonio hath
a ship of rich lading wrecked on the narrow seas—the Good-
wins[2] I think they call the place—a very dangerous flat, and
5   fatal, where the carcasses of many a tall ship lie buried, as they
say, if my gossip Report° be an honest woman of her word.   *Dame Rumor*

SOLANIO   I would she were as lying a gossip in that as ever
knapped° ginger or made her neighbours believe she wept for   *nibbled*
the death of a third husband. But it is true, without any slips
10   of prolixity° or crossing the plain highway of talk, that the   *any wordy lies*
good Antonio, the honest Antonio—O that I had a title good
enough to keep his name company—

SALERIO   Come, the full stop.°   *period*

SOLANIO   Ha, what sayst thou? Why, the end is he hath lost a
15   ship.

SALERIO   I would it might prove the end of his losses.

SOLANIO   Let me say amen betimes, lest the devil cross° my   *thwart*
prayer—

Enter SHYLOCK

for here he comes in the likeness of a Jew. How now, Shylock,
20   what news among the merchants?

SHYLOCK   You knew, none so well, none so well as you, of my
daughter's flight.

SALERIO   That's certain. I for my part knew the tailor that made
the wings[3] she flew withal.

25   SOLANIO   And Shylock for his own part knew the bird was
fledge,° and then it is the complexion° of them all to leave the   *feathered / disposition*
dam.°   *mother (here, parent)*

SHYLOCK   She is damned for it.

SALERIO   That's certain, if the devil may be her judge.

30   SHYLOCK   My own flesh and blood to rebel![4]

SOLANIO   Out upon it, old carrion, rebels it at these years?

SHYLOCK   I say my daughter is my flesh and my blood.

SALERIO   There is more difference between thy flesh and hers
than between jet° and ivory; more between your bloods than   *black mineral*
35   there is between red wine and Rhenish.° But tell us, do you   *white wine*
hear whether Antonio have had any loss at sea or no?

SHYLOCK   There I have another bad match.° A bankrupt, a   *bad deal*
prodigal, who dare scarce show his head on the Rialto; a beg-
gar, that was used to come so smug upon the mart. Let him look
40   to his bond. He was wont to call me usurer: let him look to his
bond. He was wont to lend money for a° Christian courtesy: let   *out of*
him look to his bond.

SALERIO   Why, I am sure if he forfeit thou wilt not take his
flesh. What's that good for?

45   SHYLOCK   To bait fish withal.° If it will feed nothing else it will   *with*
feed my revenge. He hath disgraced me, and hindered me half
a million; laughed at my losses, mocked at my gains, scorned

3.1   Location: Venice.
1. It circulates there without denial.
2. Goodwin Sands, where the Thames joins the sea.
"Goodwin" means "friend."

3. Playing on "wing," a decorative flap on the upper
sleeve.
4. Shylock means "my own offspring"; Solanio pretends
he means "carnal appetite."

my nation, thwarted my bargains, cooled my friends, heated
mine enemies, and what's his reason?—I am a Jew. Hath not a
50 Jew eyes? Hath not a Jew hands, organs, dimensions,° senses,   *bodily form*
affections, passions; fed with the same food, hurt with the
same weapons, subject to the same diseases, healed by the
same means, warmed and cooled by the same winter and
summer as a Christian is? If you prick us do we not bleed? If
55 you tickle us do we not laugh? If you poison us do we not die?
And if you wrong us shall we not revenge? If we are like you
in the rest, we will resemble you in that. If a Jew wrong a
Christian, what is his° humility? Revenge. If a Christian   *(the Christian's)*
wrong a Jew, what should his sufferance° be by Christian   *patience*
60 example? Why, revenge. The villainy you teach me I will exe-
cute, and it shall go hard but I will better the instruction.
　　　Enter a MAN *from Antonio*
MAN [*to* SOLANIO *and* SALERIO]   Gentlemen, my master Antonio
is at his house and desires to speak with you both.
SALERIO　We have been up and down to seek him.
　　　Enter TUBAL
65 SOLANIO　Here comes another of the tribe. A third cannot be
matched° unless the devil himself turn Jew.   *found to match*
　　　Exeunt [SOLANIO *and* SALERIO, *with Antonio's* MAN]
SHYLOCK　How now, Tubal? What news from Genoa? Hast thou
found my daughter?
TUBAL　I often came where I did hear of her, but cannot find
70 her.
SHYLOCK　Why, there, there, there, there. A diamond gone cost
me two thousand ducats in Frankfurt.⁵ The curse never fell
upon our nation till now—I never felt it till now. Two thousand
ducats in that and other precious, precious jewels. I would my
75 daughter were dead at my foot and the jewels in her ear! Would
she were hearsed° at my foot and the ducats in her coffin! No   *coffined*
news of them? Why, so. And I know not what's spent in the
search. Why thou, loss upon loss: the thief gone with so
much, and so much to find the thief, and no satisfaction, no
80 revenge, nor no ill luck stirring but what lights o' my shoulders,
no sighs but o' my breathing, no tears but o' my shedding.
TUBAL　Yes, other men have ill luck too. Antonio, as I heard in
Genoa—
SHYLOCK　What, what, what? Ill luck, ill luck?
85 TUBAL　Hath an argosy cast away coming from Tripolis.
SHYLOCK　I thank God, I thank God! Is it true, is it true?
TUBAL　I spoke with some of the sailors that escaped the wreck.
SHYLOCK　I thank thee, good Tubal. Good news, good news! Ha,
ha—heard in Genoa?
90 TUBAL　Your daughter spent in Genoa, as I heard, one night
fourscore ducats.
SHYLOCK　Thou stick'st a dagger in me. I shall never see my gold
again. Fourscore ducats at a sitting? Fourscore ducats?
TUBAL　There came divers of Antonio's creditors in my company
95 to Venice that swear he cannot choose but break.°   *go bankrupt*
SHYLOCK　I am very glad of it. I'll plague him, I'll torture him.
I am glad of it.

5. Site of a jewel market.

TUBAL   One of them showed me a ring that he had of your
        daughter for a monkey.

100 SHYLOCK   Out upon her! Thou torturest me, Tubal. It was my
        turquoise. I had it of Leah when I was a bachelor. I would not
        have given it for a wilderness of monkeys.

TUBAL   But Antonio is certainly undone.

SHYLOCK   Nay, that's true, that's very true. Go, Tubal, fee° me   hire
105   an officer. Bespeak him a fortnight before. I will have the heart
        of him if he forfeit, for were he out of Venice I can make what
        merchandise° I will. Go, Tubal, and meet me at our synagogue.   drive what bargains
        Go, good Tubal; at our synagogue, Tubal.

                                        Exeunt [*severally*]

                            3.2

Enter BASSANIO, PORTIA, NERISSA, GRAZIANO, *and all
their trains.* [*The curtains are drawn aside, revealing the
three caskets*]

PORTIA [*to* BASSANIO]   I pray you tarry. Pause a day or two
        Before you hazard, for in choosing° wrong   if you choose
        I lose your company. Therefore forbear a while.
        There's something tells me—but it is not love—
5   I would not lose you; and you know yourself
        Hate counsels not in such a quality.°   way
        But lest you should not understand me well—
        And yet a maiden hath no tongue but thought—
        I would detain you here some month or two
10   Before you venture for me. I could teach you
        How to choose right, but then I am forsworn.
        So° will I never be; so may you miss me.¹   (forsworn)
        But if you do, you'll make me wish a sin,
        That I had been forsworn. Beshrew your eyes,
15   They have o'erlooked° me and divided me.   bewitched
        One half of me is yours, the other half yours—
        Mine own, I would say, but if mine, then yours,
        And so all yours. O, these naughty° times   evil
        Puts bars between the owners and their rights;
20   And so, though yours, not yours. Prove it so,
        Let fortune go to hell for it, not I.²
        I speak too long, but 'tis to piece° the time,   extend
        To eke° it, and to draw it out in length   augment
        To stay° you from election.°   delay/choosing
BASSANIO   Let me choose,
25   For as I am, I live upon the rack.³
PORTIA   Upon the rack, Bassanio? Then confess
        What treason there is mingled with your love.
BASSANIO   None but that ugly treason of mistrust°   uncertainty
        Which makes me fear° th'enjoying of my love.   doubt
30   There may as well be amity and life
        'Tween snow and fire as treason and my love.
PORTIA   Ay, but I fear you speak upon the rack,
        Where men enforcèd do speak anything.

3.2 Location: Belmont.   fault, not mine (for breaking my oath).
1. Fail to attain me.   3. Instrument of torture used on traitors.
2. *Prove . . . I:* If it turns out thus, let it be fortune's

BASSANIO   Promise me life and I'll confess the truth.

PORTIA   Well then, confess and live.

35   BASSANIO   'Confess and love'
Had been the very sum of my confession.
O happy torment, when my torturer
Doth teach me answers for deliverance!°   *release*
But let me to my fortune and the caskets.

40   PORTIA   Away then. I am locked in one of them.
If you do love me, you will find me out.
Nerissa and the rest, stand all aloof.
Let music sound while he doth make his choice.
Then if he lose he makes a swanlike end,[4]

45   Fading in music. That the comparison
May stand more proper, my eye shall be the stream
And wat'ry deathbed for him. He may win,
And what is music then? Then music is
Even as the flourish° when true subjects bow   *fanfare*

50   To a new-crownèd monarch. Such it is
As are those dulcet sounds in break of day
That creep into the dreaming bridegroom's ear
And summon him to marriage.[5] Now he goes,
With no less presence° but with much more love   *dignity*

55   Than young Alcides when he did redeem
The virgin tribute paid by howling Troy
To the sea-monster.[6] I stand for sacrifice.
The rest aloof are the Dardanian° wives,   *Trojan*
With blearèd° visages come forth to view   *weepy*

60   The issue° of th'exploit. Go, Hercules.   *outcome*
Live thou,° I live. With much much more dismay   *If you live*
I view the fight than thou that mak'st the fray.

Here music. A song the whilst BASSANIO comments on
the caskets to himself

[ONE FROM PORTIA'S TRAIN]
                Tell me where is fancy° bred,   *love; infatuation*
                Or° in the heart, or in the head?   *Whether*

65   How begot, how nourishèd?

[ALL]   Reply, reply.

[ONE FROM PORTIA'S TRAIN]
                It is engendered in the eyes,[7]
                With gazing fed; and fancy dies
                In the cradle[8] where it lies.

70   Let us all ring fancy's knell.
                I'll begin it: ding, dong, bell.

ALL   Ding, dong, bell.

BASSANIO [*aside*]   So may the outward shows be least themselves.[9]
The world is still° deceived with ornament.   *continually*

75   In law, what plea so tainted and corrupt
But, being seasoned with a gracious voice,
Obscures the show of evil? In religion,

---

4. The swan was thought to sing only once, just before
its death.
5. It was customary to play music under a bridegroom's
window on the morning of his wedding.
6. Alcides (Hercules) saved the Trojan princess He-
sione when she was to be sacrificed to a sea monster,
not because he loved her but to win two horses her
father offered as a reward.
7. Love was imagined to enter through the eyes.
8. In infancy, in the eyes (?)
9. Least express the truth.

What damnèd error but some sober brow
Will bless it and approve° it with a text,   prove
80   Hiding the grossness with fair ornament?
There is no vice so simple° but assumes   unalloyed; stupid
Some mark of virtue on his° outward parts.   its
How many cowards whose hearts are all as false
As stairs of sand, wear yet upon their chins
85   The beards of Hercules and frowning Mars,
Who, inward searched,° have livers white as milk?[1]   examined
And these assume but valour's excrement[2]
To render them redoubted.° Look on beauty   feared
And you shall see 'tis purchased by the weight,°   (like cosmetics)
90   Which therein works a miracle in nature,
Making them lightest° that wear most of it.   most licentious
So are those crispèd,° snaky, golden locks   curled
Which makes such wanton gambols with the wind
Upon supposèd fairness,° often known   beauty
95   To be the dowry° of a second head,   endowment (in a wig)
The skull that bred them in the sepulchre.
Thus ornament is but the guilèd° shore   beguiling
To a most dangerous sea, the beauteous scarf
Veiling an Indian° beauty; in a word,   a swarthy (pejorative)
100 The seeming truth which cunning times put on
To entrap the wisest. [Aloud] Therefore, thou gaudy gold,
Hard food for Midas,[3] I will none of thee.
[To the silver casket] Nor none of thee, thou pale and com-
mon drudge°   laborer (in coins)
'Tween man and man. But thou, thou meagre lead,
105 Which rather threaten'st than dost promise aught,
Thy paleness moves me more than eloquence,
And here choose I. Joy be the consequence!
PORTIA [aside]   How all the other passions fleet to air,
As° doubtful thoughts, and rash-embraced despair,   Such as
110 And shudd'ring fear, and green-eyed jealousy.
O love, be moderate! Allay thy ecstasy.
In measure rain thy joy; scant° this excess.[4]   lessen
I feel too much thy blessing: make it less,
For fear I surfeit.
[BASSANIO opens the leaden casket]
BASSANIO   What find I here?
115 Fair Portia's counterfeit.° What demi-god[5]   likeness
Hath come so near creation? Move these eyes?
Or whether, riding on the balls of mine,°   my eyes
Seem they in motion? Here are severed lips
Parted with sugar breath. So sweet a bar
120 Should sunder such sweet friends. Here in her hairs
The painter plays the spider, and hath woven
A golden mesh t'untrap° the hearts of men   entrap (phonetic?)
Faster than gnats in cobwebs. But her eyes—
How could he see to do them? Having made one,

---

1. Lily-livered (the liver was considered the seat of
courage).
2. External attribute; hair (the beard).
3. Everything King Midas touched, including his food,
turned to gold.
4. Synonym for "interest" or "usury."
5. Supernaturally gifted painter.

125   Methinks it should have power to steal both his
        And leave itself unfurnished.° Yet look how far   *unaccompanied*
        The substance of my praise doth wrong this shadow°   *portrait*
        In underprizing° it, so far this shadow   *understating*
        Doth limp behind the substance.° Here's the scroll,   *real thing (Portia)*
130   The continent° and summary of my fortune.   *container*
           'You that choose not by the view
           Chance as fair° and choose as true.   *Gamble as luckily*
           Since this fortune falls to you,
           Be content, and seek no new.
135   If you be well pleased with this,
           And hold your fortune for your bliss,
           Turn you where your lady is,
           And claim her with a loving kiss.'
        A gentle scroll. Fair lady, by your leave,
140   I come by note to give[6] and to receive,
        Like one of two contending in a prize,°   *contest*
        That thinks he hath done well in people's eyes,
        Hearing applause and universal shout,
        Giddy in spirit, still gazing in a doubt
145   Whether those peals of praise be his° or no.   *for him*
        So, thrice-fair lady, stand I even so,
        As doubtful whether what I see be true
        Until confirmed, signed, ratified by you.
       PORTIA   You see me, Lord Bassanio, where I stand,
150   Such as I am. Though for myself alone
        I would not be ambitious in my wish
        To wish myself much better, yet for you
        I would be trebled twenty times myself,
        A thousand times more fair, ten thousand times more rich,
155   That only to stand high in your account°   *estimation*
        I might in virtues, beauties, livings,° friends,   *possessions*
        Exceed account. But the full sum of me
        Is sum of something which, to term in gross,°   *to describe fully*
        Is an unlessoned girl, unschooled, unpractisèd,
160   Happy° in this, she is not yet so old   *Fortunate*
        But she may learn; happier than this,
        She is not bred so dull but she can learn;
        Happiest of all is that her gentle spirit
        Commits itself to yours to be directed
165   As from her lord, her governor, her king.
        Myself and what is mine to you and yours
        Is now converted.° But° now I was the lord   *transferred / Just*
        Of this fair mansion, master of my servants,
        Queen o'er myself; and even now, but now,
170   This house, these servants, and this same myself
        Are yours, my lord's. I give them with this ring,
        Which when you part from, lose, or give away,
        Let it presage the ruin of your love,
        And be my vantage to exclaim on you.[7]
175   BASSANIO   Madam, you have bereft me of all words.
        Only my blood speaks to you in my veins,

---

6. I come by written authorization to give a kiss; to give   7. And be my opportunity to reproach you.
myself.

And there is such confusion in my powers°   *faculties*
As after some oration fairly spoke
By a belovèd prince there doth appear
180 Among the buzzing pleasèd multitude,
Where every something being blent° together   *blended*
Turns to a wild° of nothing save of joy,   *chaos*
Expressed and not expressed. But when this ring
Parts from this finger, then parts life from hence.
185 O, then be bold to say° Bassanio's dead.   *say confidently*
NERISSA My lord and lady, it is now our time
 That have stood by and seen our wishes prosper
 To cry 'Good joy, good joy, my lord and lady!'
GRAZIANO My lord Bassanio, and my gentle lady,
190 I wish you all the joy that you can wish,
 For I am sure you can wish none from me.[8]
 And when your honours mean to solemnize
 The bargain of your faith, I do beseech you
 Even at that time I may be married too.
195 BASSANIO With all my heart, so° thou canst get a wife. *if*
GRAZIANO I thank your lordship, you have got me one.
 My eyes, my lord, can look as swift as yours.
 You saw the mistress, I beheld the maid.
 You loved, I loved; for intermission°   *delay*
200 No more pertains to me, my lord, than you.
 Your fortune stood upon the caskets there,
 And so did mine too, as the matter falls;
 For wooing here until I sweat again,°   *repeatedly*
 And swearing till my very roof° was dry   *(of his mouth)*
205 With oaths of love, at last—if promise[9] last—
 I got a promise of this fair one here
 To have her love, provided that your fortune
 Achieved her mistress.
PORTIA   Is this true, Nerissa?
NERISSA Madam, it is, so you stand pleased withal.
210 BASSANIO And do you, Graziano, mean good faith?
GRAZIANO Yes, faith, my lord.
BASSANIO Our feast shall be much honoured in your marriage.
GRAZIANO [*to* NERISSA] We'll play° with them the first boy for a *wager*
 thousand ducats.
215 NERISSA What, and stake down?[1]
GRAZIANO No, we shall ne'er win at that sport and stake down.
   Enter LORENZO, JESSICA, *and* SALERIO, *a messenger from*
   Venice
 But who comes here? Lorenzo and his infidel!
 What, and my old Venetian friend Salerio!
BASSANIO Lorenzo and Salerio, welcome hither,
220 If that the youth of my new int'rest° here   *position*
 Have power° to bid you welcome. [*To* PORTIA] By your leave, *Gives me the right*
 I bid my very° friends and countrymen,   *true*
 Sweet Portia, welcome.
PORTIA So do I, my lord. They are entirely welcome.
225 LORENZO I thank your honour. For my part, my lord,

8. You do not need my good wishes.
9. Nerissa's, to wed Graziano.

1. Put the money down now (Graziano follows with a bawdy joke on "flaccid penis").

My purpose was not to have seen you here,
But meeting with Salerio by the way
He did entreat me past all saying nay
To come with him along.

230 SALERIO   I did, my lord,
And I have reason for it. Signor Antonio
Commends him° to you.   *Sends greeting*
          [*He gives* BASSANIO *a letter*]
BASSANIO   Ere I ope his letter
I pray you tell me how my good friend doth.
SALERIO   Not sick, my lord, unless it be in mind;
Nor well, unless in mind. His letter there
235 Will show you his estate.°   *situation*
          [BASSANIO] *opens the letter [and reads]*
GRAZIANO   Nerissa, [*indicating* JESSICA] cheer yon stranger. Bid
          her welcome.
Your hand, Salerio. What's the news from Venice?
How doth that royal° merchant good Antonio?   *princely*
I know he will be glad of our success.
240 We are the Jasons; we have won the fleece.
SALERIO   I would you had won the fleece° that he hath lost.   *(punning on "fleets")*
PORTIA   There are some shrewd° contents in yon same paper   *evil*
That steals the colour from Bassanio's cheek.
Some dear friend dead, else nothing in the world
245 Could turn° so much the constitution   *change*
Of any constant° man. What, worse and worse?   *resolute*
With leave, Bassanio, I am half yourself,
And I must freely have the half of anything
That this same paper brings you.
BASSANIO   O sweet Portia,
250 Here are a few of the unpleasant'st words
That ever blotted paper. Gentle lady,
When I did first impart my love to you
I freely told you all the wealth I had
Ran in my veins: I was a gentleman;
255 And then I told you true; and yet, dear lady,
Rating myself at nothing, you shall see
How much I was a braggart. When I told you
My state° was nothing, I should then have told you   *wealth*
That I was worse than nothing, for indeed
260 I have engaged° myself to a dear friend,   *pledged*
Engaged my friend to his mere° enemy,   *utter*
To feed my means. Here is a letter, lady,
The paper° as the body of my friend,   *(ripped open)*
And every word in it a gaping wound
265 Issuing life-blood. But is it true, Salerio?
Hath all his ventures failed? What, not one hit?°   *success*
From Tripolis, from Mexico, and England,
From Lisbon, Barbary, and India,
And not one vessel scape the dreadful touch
Of merchant-marring rocks?
270 SALERIO   Not one, my lord.
Besides, it should appear that if he had
The present° money to discharge° the Jew   *ready/pay*
He° would not take it. Never did I know   *(Shylock)*

A creature that did bear the shape of man

275 So keen° and greedy to confound° a man.   *eager / destroy*

He plies the Duke at morning and at night,

And doth impeach the freedom of the state[2]

If they deny him justice. Twenty merchants,

The Duke himself, and the magnificoes°   *Venetian magnates*

280 Of greatest port,° have all persuaded° with him,   *dignity / argued*

But none can drive him from the envious° plea   *malicious*

Of forfeiture, of justice, and his bond.

JESSICA   When I was with him I have heard him swear

To Tubal and to Cush, his countrymen,

285 That he would rather have Antonio's flesh

Than twenty times the value of the sum

That he did owe him; and I know, my lord,

If law, authority, and power deny not,

It will go hard with poor Antonio.

290 PORTIA [*to* BASSANIO]   Is it your dear friend that is thus in trouble?

BASSANIO   The dearest friend to me, the kindest man,

The best-conditioned° and unwearied spirit   *best-natured*

In doing courtesies, and one in whom

The ancient Roman honour more appears

295 Than any that draws breath in Italy.

PORTIA   What sum owes he the Jew?

BASSANIO   For me, three thousand ducats.

PORTIA   What, no more?

Pay him six thousand and deface° the bond.   *destroy*

Double six thousand, and then treble that,

300 Before a friend of this description

Shall lose a hair thorough Bassanio's fault.

First go with me to church and call me wife,

And then away to Venice to your friend;

For never shall you lie by Portia's side

305 With an unquiet soul. You shall have gold

To pay the petty debt twenty times over.

When it is paid, bring your true friend along.

My maid Nerissa and myself meantime

Will live as maids and widows. Come, away,

310 For you shall hence upon your wedding day.

Bid your friends welcome, show a merry cheer.°   *countenance*

Since you are dear° bought, I will love you dear.°   *expensively / dearly*

But let me hear the letter of your friend.

BASSANIO [*reads*]   'Sweet Bassanio, my ships have all miscarried,

315 my creditors grow cruel, my estate is very low, my bond to the

Jew is forfeit, and since in paying it, it is impossible I should

live, all debts are cleared between you and I if I might but see

you at my death. Notwithstanding, use your pleasure.° If your   *follow your wishes*

love do not persuade you to come, let not my letter.'

320 PORTIA   O, love! Dispatch all business, and be gone.

BASSANIO   Since I have your good leave to go away

I will make haste, but till I come again

No bed shall e'er be guilty of my stay

Nor rest be interposer 'twixt us twain.   *Exeunt*

---

2. Accuse the state of not preserving commercial liberty.

3.3

Enter [SHYLOCK] *the Jew,* SOLANIO, ANTONIO, *and the*
  jailer

SHYLOCK   Jailer, look to him. Tell not me of mercy.
  This is the fool that lent out money gratis.
  Jailer, look to him.

ANTONIO   Hear me yet, good Shylock.

SHYLOCK   I'll have my bond. Speak not against my bond.
5 I have sworn an oath that I will have my bond.
  Thou called'st me dog before thou hadst a cause,
  But since I am a dog, beware my fangs.
  The Duke shall grant me justice. I do wonder,
  Thou naughty° jailer, that thou art so fond°   *wicked/foolish*
10 To come abroad° with him at his request.   *outside*

ANTONIO   I pray thee hear me speak.

SHYLOCK   I'll have my bond. I will not hear thee speak.
  I'll have my bond, and therefore speak no more.
  I'll not be made a soft and dull-eyed° fool   *gullible*
15 To shake the head, relent, and sigh, and yield
  To Christian intercessors. Follow not.
  I'll have no speaking. I will have my bond.   *Exit*

SOLANIO   It is the most impenetrable cur
  That ever kept° with men.   *lived*

ANTONIO   Let him alone.
20 I'll follow him no more with bootless° prayers.   *fruitless*
  He seeks my life. His reason well I know:
  I oft delivered° from his forfeitures   *saved*
  Many that have at times made moan to me.
  Therefore he hates me.

SOLANIO   I am sure the Duke
25 Will never grant this forfeiture to hold.

ANTONIO   The Duke cannot deny° the course of law,   *prevent*
  For the commodity that strangers[1] have
  With us in Venice, if it be denied,
  Will much impeach the justice of the state,
30 Since that the trade and profit of the city
  Consisteth of all nations. Therefore go.
  These griefs and losses have so bated° me   *diminished*
  That I shall hardly spare a pound of flesh
  Tomorrow to my bloody creditor.
35 Well, jailer, on. Pray God Bassanio come
  To see me pay his debt, and then I care not.   *Exeunt*

3.4

Enter PORTIA, NERISSA, LORENZO, JESSICA, *and*
  [BALTHASAR,] *a man of Portia's*

LORENZO [*to* PORTIA]   Madam, although I speak it in your presence,
  You have a noble and a true conceit°   *conception*
  Of godlike amity, which appears most strongly
  In bearing thus the absence of your lord.
5 But if you knew to whom you show this honour,

3.3 Location: Street in Venice.
1. For the trading privileges that foreigners (including
Jews).

3.4 Location: Belmont.

How true a gentleman you send relief,
How dear a lover° of my lord your husband,   *friend*
I know you would be prouder of the work
Than customary bounty can enforce you.[1]

10 PORTIA   I never did repent for doing good,
Nor shall not now; for in companions
That do converse and waste° the time together,   *spend (not pejorative)*
Whose souls do bear an equal yoke of love,
There must be needs a like proportion
15 Of lineaments, of manners, and of spirit,
Which makes me think that this Antonio,
Being the bosom lover of my lord,
Must needs be like my lord. If it be so,
How little is the cost I have bestowed
20 In purchasing the semblance of my soul[2]
From out the state of hellish cruelty.
This comes too near the praising of myself,
Therefore no more of it. Hear other things:
Lorenzo, I commit into your hands
25 The husbandry° and manage of my house   *care*
Until my lord's return. For mine own part,
I have toward heaven breathed a secret vow
To live in prayer and contemplation,
Only attended by Nerissa here,
30 Until her husband and my lord's return.
There is a monastery two miles off,
And there we will abide. I do desire you
Not to deny this imposition,°   *decline this charge*
The which my love and some necessity
Now lays upon you.
35 LORENZO   Madam, with all my heart,
I shall obey you in all fair commands.
PORTIA   My people do already know my mind,
And will acknowledge you and Jessica
In place of Lord Bassanio and myself.
40 So fare you well till we shall meet again.
LORENZO   Fair thoughts and happy hours attend on you!
JESSICA   I wish your ladyship all heart's content.
PORTIA   I thank you for your wish, and am well pleased
To wish it back on you. Fare you well, Jessica.
               Exeunt [LORENZO *and* JESSICA]
45 Now, Balthasar,
As I have ever found thee honest-true,
So let me find thee still. Take this same letter,
And use thou all th'endeavour of a man
In speed to Padua. See thou render this
50 Into my cousin's hands, Doctor Bellario,
And look what notes and garments he doth give thee,
Bring them, I pray thee, with imagined° speed   *all imaginable*
Unto the traject,° to the common° ferry   *ferry / public*
Which trades° to Venice. Waste no time in words,   *goes back and forth*
55 But get thee gone. I shall be there before thee.
BALTHASAR   Madam, I go with all convenient° speed.   [*Exit*]   *due*

---

1. Than ordinary generosity permits you.   2. In redeeming the likeness of my Bassanio (Antonio).

PORTIA   Come on, Nerissa. I have work in hand
    That you yet know not of. We'll see our husbands
    Before they think of us.
NERISSA   Shall they see us?
60   PORTIA   They shall, Nerissa, but in such a habit°   *garb*
    That they shall think we are accomplishèd°   *equipped*
    With that we lack.° I'll hold thee any wager,   *(i.e., penises)*
    When we are both accoutered like young men
    I'll prove the prettier fellow of the two,
65   And wear my dagger with the braver grace,
    And speak between the change of man and boy
    With a reed° voice, and turn two mincing steps   *piping*
    Into a manly stride, and speak of frays
    Like a fine bragging youth, and tell quaint° lies   *elaborate*
70   How honourable ladies sought my love,
    Which I denying, they fell sick and died.
    I could not do withal.° Then I'll repent,   *help it*
    And wish for all that that I had not killed them;
    And twenty of these puny lies I'll tell,
75   That men shall swear I have discontinued° school   *been out of*
    Above° a twelvemonth. I have within my mind   *At least*
    A thousand raw tricks of these bragging Jacks°   *fellows*
    Which I will practise.
NERISSA   Why, shall we turn to³ men?
80   PORTIA   Fie, what a question's that
    If thou wert near a lewd interpreter!
    But come, I'll tell thee all my whole device°   *plan*
    When I am in my coach, which stays for us
    At the park gate; and therefore haste away,
85   For we must measure twenty miles today.   *Exeunt*

3.5

Enter [LANCELOT] the clown, and JESSICA

LANCELOT   Yes, truly; for look you, the sins of the father are to
    be laid upon the children, therefore I promise you I fear° you.   *fear for*
    I was always plain with you, and so now I speak my agitation°   *(for "cogitation")*
    of the matter, therefore be o' good cheer, for truly I think you
5   are damned. There is but one hope in it that can do you any
    good, and that is but a kind of bastard hope, neither.
JESSICA   And what hope is that, I pray thee?
LANCELOT   Marry, you may partly hope that your father got you
    not, that you are not the Jew's daughter.
10   JESSICA   That were a kind of bastard hope indeed. So the sins
    of my mother should be visited upon me.
LANCELOT   Truly then, I fear you are damned both by father and
    mother. Thus, when I shun Scylla your father, I fall into
    Charybdis your mother.¹ Well, you are gone° both ways.   *doomed*
15   JESSICA   I shall be saved by my husband.² He hath made me a
    Christian.
LANCELOT   Truly, the more to blame he! We were Christians

---

3. Turn into (with bawdy suggestion).
3.5 Location: Portia's garden in Belmont.
1. Scylla was a mythological sea monster, Charybdis a
whirlpool in the Strait of Messina. Mariners had to avoid

both, a proverbially difficult task.
2. "The unbelieving wife is sanctified by the husband"
(1 Corinthians 7:14).

enough before, e'en as many as could well live one by another.[3]
This making of Christians will raise the price of hogs. If we
20   grow all to be pork-eaters we shall not shortly have a rasher° on   bacon strip
the coals for money.°   any price

Enter LORENZO

JESSICA   I'll tell my husband, Lancelot, what you say. Here he
comes.

LORENZO   I shall grow jealous of you shortly, Lancelot, if you
25   thus get my wife into corners.

JESSICA   Nay, you need not fear us, Lorenzo. Lancelot and I are
out.° He tells me flatly there's no mercy for me in heaven   quarreling
because I am a Jew's daughter, and he says you are no good
member of the commonwealth, for in converting Jews to Chris-
30   tians you raise the price of pork.

LORENZO [*to* LANCELOT]   I shall answer° that better to the com-   explain
monwealth than you can the getting up of the Negro's belly.
The Moor[4] is with child by you, Lancelot.

LANCELOT   It is much that the Moor should be more than rea-
35   son,[5] but if she be less than an honest° woman, she is indeed   a chaste
more than I took her for.

LORENZO   How every fool can play upon the word! I think the
best grace of wit will shortly turn into silence, and discourse
grow commendable in none only but parrots. Go in, sirrah, bid
40   them prepare for dinner.

LANCELOT   That is done, sir. They have all stomachs.°   appetites

LORENZO   Goodly Lord, what a wit-snapper are you! Then bid
them prepare dinner.

LANCELOT   That is done too, sir; only 'cover'[6] is the word.

45   LORENZO   Will you cover then, sir?

LANCELOT   Not so, sir, neither. I know my duty.

LORENZO   Yet more quarrelling with occasion![7] Wilt thou show
the whole wealth of thy wit in an instant? I pray thee under-
stand a plain man in his plain meaning. Go to thy fellows; bid
50   them cover the table, serve in the meat, and we will come in
to dinner.

LANCELOT   For the table,° sir, it shall be served in. For the meat,   meal
sir, it shall be covered.[8] For your coming in to dinner, sir, why,
let it be as humours and conceits° shall govern.   *Exit*   whims and notions

55   LORENZO   O dear discretion, how his words are suited![9]
The fool hath planted in his memory
An army of good words, and I do know
A many fools that stand in better place,
Garnished° like him, that for a tricksy word   Provided (with words)
60   Defy the matter.° How cheer'st thou,[1] Jessica?   Refuse to talk sense
And now, good sweet, say thy opinion:
How dost thou like the Lord Bassanio's wife?

JESSICA   Past all expressing. It is very meet°   proper
The Lord Bassanio live an upright life,
65   For, having such a blessing in his lady,

---

3. *well . . . another:* reside next door to one another;
earn a living off one another.
4. Apparently an African woman of Portia's household.
5. Should be bigger than is reasonable (punning on
"more/ Moor").
6. Set the table; but Lancelot puns on "cover" as mean-
ing "put on the hat."

7. Playing on words whenever possible.
8. Served in covered dishes (playfully or unconsciously
reversing Lorenzo's instructions).
9. Adapted to the occasion. *dear discretion:* precious
discrimination (ironic).
1. How are you.

He finds the joys of heaven here on earth,
And if on earth he do not merit it,
In reason he should never come to heaven.
Why, if two gods should play some heavenly match
70 And on the wager lay two earthly women,
And Portia one, there must be something else
Pawned° with the other; for the poor rude world   *Wagered*
Hath not her fellow.
LORENZO   Even such a husband
Hast thou of me as she is for a wife.
75 JESSICA   Nay, but ask my opinion too of that!
LORENZO   I will anon.° First let us go to dinner.   *soon*
JESSICA   Nay, let me praise you while I have a stomach.°   *an appetite; desire*
LORENZO   No, pray thee, let it serve for table-talk.
Then, howsome'er° thou speak'st, 'mong other things   *however*
I shall digest° it.   *ingest; analyze*
80 JESSICA   Well, I'll set you forth.[2]   *Exeunt*

4.1

Enter the DUKE, *the magnificoes,* ANTONIO, BASSANIO,
GRAZIANO, *and* [SALERIO]

DUKE   What, is Antonio here?
ANTONIO   Ready, so please your grace.
DUKE   I am sorry for thee. Thou art come to answer
A stony adversary, an inhuman wretch
Uncapable of pity, void and empty
From any dram° of mercy.   *trace*
5 ANTONIO   I have heard
Your grace hath ta'en great pains to qualify°   *alleviate*
His rigorous course, but since he stands obdurate,
And that no lawful means can carry me
Out of his envy's° reach, I do oppose   *malice's*
10 My patience to his fury, and am armed°   *prepared*
To suffer with a quietness of spirit
The very tyranny° and rage of his.   *cruelty*
DUKE   Go one, and call the Jew into the court.
SALERIO   He is ready at the door. He comes, my lord.
Enter SHYLOCK
15 DUKE   Make room, and let him stand before our° face.   *(the royal "we")*
Shylock, the world thinks—and I think so too—
That thou but lead'st this fashion° of thy malice   *sustain the pretense*
To the last hour of act,° and then 'tis thought   *brink of performance*
Thou'lt show thy mercy and remorse° more strange   *compassion / extraordinary*
20 Than is thy strange apparent cruelty,
And where thou now exacts the penalty—
Which is a pound of this poor merchant's flesh—
Thou wilt not only loose° the forfeiture,   *waive*
But, touched with human gentleness and love,
25 Forgive a moiety° of the principal,   *part*
Glancing an eye of pity on his losses,
That have of late so huddled° on his back   *piled*
Enough to press a royal merchant down

---

2. I'll serve you up (like a dinner); I'll extol you.   **4.1** Location: The Venetian court.

And pluck commiseration of his state

30 From brassy° bosoms and rough hearts of flint,   *unfeeling*

From stubborn Turks and Tartars never trained

To offices° of tender courtesy.   *acts*

We all expect a gentle answer, Jew.

SHYLOCK   I have possessed° your grace of what I purpose,   *informed*

35 And by our holy Sabbath have I sworn

To have the due and forfeit of my bond.

If you deny it, let the danger° light   *damage*

Upon your charter and your city's freedom.

You'll ask me why I rather choose to have

40 A weight of carrion flesh than to receive

Three thousand ducats. I'll not answer that,

But say it is my humour.° Is it answered?   *caprice*

What if my house be troubled with a rat,

And I be pleased to give ten thousand ducats

45 To have it baned?° What, are you answered yet?   *poisoned*

Some men there are love not a gaping pig,[1]

Some that are mad if they behold a cat,

And others when the bagpipe sings i'th' nose

Cannot contain their urine; for affection,°   *impulse*

50 Mistress of passion, sways it to the mood

Of what it likes or loathes. Now for your answer:

As there is no firm reason to be rendered

Why he° cannot abide a gaping pig,   *one man*

Why he° a harmless necessary cat,   *another*

55 Why he° a woollen bagpipe, but of force°   *yet another / necessarily*

Must yield to such inevitable shame

As to offend himself being offended,

So can I give no reason, nor I will not,

More than a lodged° hate and a certain loathing   *settled*

60 I bear Antonio, that I follow thus

A losing° suit against him. Are you answered?   *An unprofitable*

BASSANIO   This is no answer, thou unfeeling man,

To excuse the current of thy cruelty.

SHYLOCK   I am not bound to please thee with my answers.

65 BASSANIO   Do all men kill the things they do not love?

SHYLOCK   Hates any man the thing he would not kill?

BASSANIO   Every offence is not a hate at first.

SHYLOCK   What, wouldst thou have a serpent sting thee twice?

ANTONIO   I pray you think you question° with the Jew.   *dispute*

70 You may as well go stand upon the beach

And bid the main flood bate his° usual height;   *high tide reduce its*

You may as well use question with the wolf

Why he hath made the ewe bleat for the lamb;

You may as well forbid the mountain pines

75 To wag their high tops and to make no noise

When they are fretten° with the gusts of heaven,   *fretted; agitated*

You may as well do anything most hard

As seek to soften that—than which what's harder?—

His Jewish heart. Therefore, I do beseech you,

80 Make no more offers, use no farther means,

---

1. Roasted pig with its mouth propped open.

But with all brief and plain conveniency°   *suitability*
Let me have judgement and the Jew his will.
BASSANIO [*to* SHYLOCK]   For thy three thousand ducats here is six.
SHYLOCK   If every ducat in six thousand ducats
85   Were in six parts, and every part a ducat,
I would not draw° them. I would have my bond.   *take*
DUKE   How shalt thou hope for mercy, rend'ring none?
SHYLOCK   What judgement shall I dread, doing no wrong?
You have among you many a purchased slave
90   Which, like your asses and your dogs and mules,
You use in abject and in slavish parts°   *roles*
Because you bought them. Shall I say to you
'Let them be free, marry them to your heirs.
Why sweat they under burdens? Let their beds
95   Be made as soft as yours, and let their palates
Be seasoned with such viands.'° You will answer   *food*
'The slaves are ours.' So do I answer you.
The pound of flesh which I demand of him
Is dearly bought. 'Tis mine, and I will have it.
100   If you deny me, fie upon your law:
There is no force in the decrees of Venice.
I stand for judgement. Answer: shall I have it?
DUKE   Upon° my power I may dismiss this court   *In accordance with*
Unless Bellario, a learnèd doctor
105   Whom I have sent for to determine° this,   *resolve*
Come here today.
SALERIO   My lord, here stays without°   *waits outside*
A messenger with letters from the doctor,
New come from Padua.
DUKE   Bring us the letters. Call the messenger.   [*Exit* SALERIO]
110 BASSANIO   Good cheer, Antonio. What, man, courage yet!
The Jew shall have my flesh, blood, bones, and all
Ere thou shalt lose for me one drop of blood.
ANTONIO   I am a tainted wether° of the flock,   *castrated ram*
Meetest for death.° The weakest kind of fruit   *Most fit for slaughter*
115   Drops earliest to the ground; and so let me.
You cannot better be employed, Bassanio,
Than to live still and write mine epitaph.
        Enter [SALERIO, *with*] NERISSA [*apparelled as a judge's
        clerk*]
DUKE   Came you from Padua, from Bellario?
NERISSA   From both, my lord. Bellario greets your grace.
        [*She gives a letter to the* DUKE.
        SHYLOCK *whets his knife on his shoe*]
120 BASSANIO [*to* SHYLOCK]   Why dost thou whet thy knife so earnestly?
SHYLOCK   To cut the forfeit from that bankrupt there.
GRAZIANO   Not on thy sole but on thy soul, harsh Jew,
Thou mak'st thy knife keen. But no metal can,
No, not the hangman's° axe, bear° half the keenness   *executioner's / have*
125   Of thy sharp envy.° Can no prayers pierce thee?   *malice*
SHYLOCK   No, none that thou hast wit enough to make.
GRAZIANO   O, be thou damned, inexorable dog,
And for thy life° let justice be accused!   *for allowing you to live*
Thou almost mak'st me waver in my faith

130 To hold opinion with Pythagoras[2]
That souls of animals infuse themselves
Into the trunks of men. Thy currish spirit
Governed a wolf who, hanged for human slaughter,[3]
Even from the gallows did his fell soul fleet,°   *his cruel soul flit*
135 And, whilst thou lay'st in thy unhallowed dam,
Infused itself in thee; for thy desires
Are wolvish, bloody, starved, and ravenous.
SHYLOCK   Till thou canst rail the seal from off my bond
Thou but offend'st° thy lungs to speak so loud.   *hurt*
140 Repair thy wit, good youth, or it will fall
To cureless° ruin. I stand here for law.   *incurable*
DUKE   This letter from Bellario doth commend
A young and learnèd doctor to our court.
Where is he?
NERISSA   He attendeth here hard by
145 To know your answer, whether you'll admit him.
DUKE   With all my heart. Some three or four of you
Go give him courteous conduct° to this place.   *escort*
              [*Exeunt three or four*]
Meantime the court shall hear Bellario's letter.
[*Reads*] 'Your grace shall understand that at the receipt of your
150 letter I am very sick, but in the instant that your messenger
came, in loving visitation was with me a young doctor of Rome;
his name is Balthasar. I acquainted him with the cause in con-
troversy between the Jew and Antonio, the merchant. We
turned o'er many books together. He is furnished with my opin-
155 ion which, bettered with his own learning—the greatness
whereof I cannot enough commend—comes with him at my
importunity to fill up° your grace's request in my stead. I   *answer*
beseech you let his lack of years be no impediment to let him
lack° a reverend estimation, for I never knew so young a body   *keep him from having*
160 with so old a head. I leave him to your gracious acceptance,
whose trial shall better publish his commendation.'[4]
      Enter [*three or four with*] PORTIA [*as Balthasar*].
You hear the learn'd Bellario, what he writes;
And here, I take it, is the doctor come.
[*To* PORTIA   Give me your hand. Come you from old Bellario?
PORTIA   I did, my lord.
165 DUKE   You are welcome. Take your place.
Are you acquainted with the difference°   *dispute*
That holds this present question[5] in the court?
PORTIA   I am informèd throughly° of the cause.°   *thoroughly / case*
Which is the merchant here, and which the Jew?
170 DUKE   Antonio and old Shylock, both stand forth.
       [ANTONIO *and* SHYLOCK *stand forth*]
PORTIA   Is your name Shylock?
SHYLOCK   Shylock is my name.
PORTIA   Of a strange nature is the suit you follow,
Yet in such rule° that the Venetian law   *order*

2. Greek philosopher who believed in the transmigra-
tion of souls.
3. In Elizabethan times, animals were tried and hanged
for wrongdoing; possibly an allusion to the 1594 execu-
tion of the Jewish physician Lopez (Latin *lupus*, "wolf").
4. Whose performance ("trial") shall better make
known his worth.
5. That is now being tried.

Cannot impugn you as you do proceed.

175 [*To* ANTONIO] You stand within his danger,° do you not?   *power to harm*

ANTONIO Ay, so he says.

PORTIA   Do you confess the bond?

ANTONIO I do.

PORTIA   Then must the Jew be merciful.

SHYLOCK On what compulsion must I? Tell me that.

PORTIA The quality of mercy is not strained.°   *compelled*

180 It droppeth as the gentle rain from heaven
Upon the place beneath. It is twice blest:
It blesseth him that gives, and him that takes.
'Tis mightiest in the mightiest. It becomes
The thronèd monarch better than his crown.

185 His sceptre shows the force of temporal power,
The attribute to° awe and majesty,   *of*
Wherein doth sit the dread and fear of kings;
But mercy is above this sceptred sway.
It is enthronèd in the hearts of kings;

190 It is an attribute to God himself,
And earthly power doth then show likest° God's   *most like*
When mercy seasons° justice. Therefore, Jew,   *moderates*
Though justice be thy plea, consider this:
That in the course of justice none of us

195 Should see salvation. We do pray for mercy,
And that same prayer° doth teach us all to render   *(the Lord's Prayer)*
The deeds of mercy. I have spoke thus much
To mitigate the justice of thy plea,°   *your demand for justice*
Which if thou follow, this strict court of Venice

200 Must needs give sentence 'gainst the merchant there.

SHYLOCK My deeds upon my head![6] I crave the law,
The penalty and forfeit of my bond.

PORTIA Is he not able to discharge the money?

BASSANIO Yes, here I tender it for him in the court,

205 Yea, twice the sum. If that will not suffice
I will be bound to pay it ten times o'er
On forfeit of my hands, my head, my heart.
If this will not suffice, it must appear
That malice bears down° truth. And, I beseech you,   *overwhelms*

210 Wrest once° the law to your authority.   *For once twist*
To do a great right, do a little wrong,
And curb this cruel devil of his will.

PORTIA It must be not. There is no power in Venice
Can alter a decree establishèd.

215 'Twill be recorded for a precedent,
And many an error by the same example
Will rush into the state. It cannot be.

SHYLOCK A Daniel come to judgement, yea, a Daniel![7]
O wise young judge, how I do honour thee!

220 PORTIA I pray you let me look upon the bond.

SHYLOCK Here 'tis, most reverend doctor, here it is.

PORTIA Shylock, there's thrice thy money offered thee.

---

6. The Jewish crowd at Jesus' trial cried, "His blood be on us, and on our children" (Matthew 27:25).
7. In the Apocrypha, the youth Daniel judges the case of Susanna, accused of inchastity by the Elders; he rescues her and convicts them.

SHYLOCK An oath, an oath! I have an oath in heaven.
Shall I lay perjury upon my soul?
No, not for Venice.

225 PORTIA   Why, this bond is forfeit,
And lawfully by this the Jew may claim
A pound of flesh, to be by him cut off
Nearest the merchant's heart. [*To* SHYLOCK] Be merciful.
Take thrice thy money. Bid me tear the bond.

230 SHYLOCK When it is paid according to the tenor.°   condition
It doth appear you are a worthy judge.
You know the law. Your exposition
Hath been most sound. I charge you, by the law
Whereof you are a well-deserving pillar,
235 Proceed to judgement. By my soul I swear
There is no power in the tongue of man
To alter me. I stay° here on my bond.   insist

ANTONIO Most heartily I do beseech the court
To give the judgement.

PORTIA   Why, then thus it is:
240 You must prepare your bosom for his knife—

SHYLOCK O noble judge, O excellent young man!

PORTIA For the intent and purpose of the law
Hath full relation to[8] the penalty
Which here appeareth due upon the bond.

245 SHYLOCK 'Tis very true. O wise and upright judge!
How much more elder art thou than thy looks!

PORTIA [*to* ANTONIO] Therefore lay bare your bosom.

SHYLOCK   Ay, his breast.
So says the bond, doth it not, noble judge?
'Nearest his heart'—those are the very words.

250 PORTIA It is so. Are there balance° here to weigh the flesh?   scales

SHYLOCK I have them ready.

PORTIA Have by some surgeon, Shylock, on your charge°   expense
To stop his wounds, lest he do bleed to death.

SHYLOCK Is it so nominated in the bond?

255 PORTIA It is not so expressed, but what of that?
'Twere good you do so much for charity.

SHYLOCK I cannot find it. 'Tis not in the bond.

PORTIA [*to* ANTONIO] You, merchant, have you anything to say?

ANTONIO But little. I am armed and well prepared.
260 Give me your hand, Bassanio; fare you well.
Grieve not that I am fall'n to this for you,
For herein Fortune shows herself more kind
Than is her custom; it is still her use°   commonly her habit
To let the wretched man outlive his wealth
265 To view with hollow eye and wrinkled brow
An age of poverty, from which ling'ring penance
Of such misery doth she cut me off.
Commend me to your honourable wife.
Tell her the process° of Antonio's end.   tale
270 Say how I loved you. Speak me fair° in death,   well of me
And when the tale is told, bid her be judge
Whether Bassanio had not once a love.

8. Is entirely in agreement with.

Repent but you° that you shall lose your friend,   *Sorrow only*

And he repents not that he pays your debt;

275 For if the Jew do cut but deep enough,

I'll pay it instantly, with all my heart.

BASSANIO Antonio, I am married to a wife

Which is as dear to me as life itself,

But life itself, my wife, and all the world

280 Are not with me esteemed above thy life.

I would lose all, ay, sacrifice them all

Here to this devil, to deliver you.

PORTIA [*aside*] Your wife would give you little thanks for that

If she were by to hear you make the offer.

285 GRAZIANO I have a wife who, I protest, I love.

I would she were in heaven so she could

Entreat some power to change this currish Jew.

NERISSA [*aside*] 'Tis well you offer it behind her back;

The wish would make else an unquiet house.

290 SHYLOCK [*aside*] These be the Christian husbands. I have a daughter.

Would any of the stock of Barabbas⁹

Had been her husband rather than a Christian.

[*Aloud*] We trifle° time. I pray thee pursue° sentence.   *waste / proceed with*

PORTIA A pound of that same merchant's flesh is thine.

295 The court awards it, and the law doth give it.

SHYLOCK Most rightful judge!

PORTIA And you must cut this flesh from off his breast.

The law allows it, and the court awards it.

SHYLOCK Most learnèd judge! A sentence: [*to* ANTONIO] come, prepare.

300 PORTIA Tarry a little. There is something else.

This bond doth give thee here no jot of blood.

The words expressly are 'a pound of flesh'.

Take then thy bond. Take thou thy pound of flesh.

But in the cutting it, if thou dost shed

305 One drop of Christian blood, thy lands and goods

Are by the laws of Venice confiscate

Unto the state of Venice.

GRAZIANO   O upright judge!

Mark, Jew! O learnèd judge!

SHYLOCK Is that the law?

310 PORTIA Thyself shalt see the act;

For as thou urgest justice, be assured

Thou shalt have justice more than thou desir'st.

GRAZIANO O learnèd judge! Mark, Jew! O learnèd judge!

SHYLOCK I take this offer, then. Pay the bond thrice,

And let the Christian go.

315 BASSANIO   Here is the money.

PORTIA Soft,° the Jew shall have all justice. Soft, no haste.   *Not so fast*

He shall have nothing but the penalty.

GRAZIANO O Jew, an upright judge, a learnèd judge!

PORTIA [*to* SHYLOCK] Therefore prepare thee to cut off the flesh.

320 Shed thou no blood, nor cut thou less nor more

But just° a pound of flesh. If thou tak'st more   *exactly*

Or less than a just pound, be it but so much

---

9. Thief whom the Jews asked Pilate to set free instead of Jesus (Mark 15:6–15).

As makes it light or heavy in the substance°   *weight*
Or the division° of the twentieth part   *fraction*
325   Of one poor scruple°—nay, if the scale do turn   *tiny weight*
But in the estimation° of a hair,   *amount*
Thou diest, and all thy goods are confiscate.
GRAZIANO   A second Daniel, a Daniel, Jew!
Now, infidel, I have you on the hip.[1]
330   PORTIA   Why doth the Jew pause? Take thy forfeiture.
SHYLOCK   Give me my principal, and let me go.
BASSANIO   I have it ready for thee. Here it is.
PORTIA   He hath refused it in the open court.
He shall have merely justice and his bond.
335   GRAZIANO   A Daniel, still say I, a second Daniel!
I thank thee, Jew, for teaching me that word.
SHYLOCK   Shall I not have barely° my principal?   *even*
PORTIA   Thou shalt have nothing but the forfeiture
To be so taken at thy peril, Jew.
340   SHYLOCK   Why then, the devil give him good of it.
I'll stay no longer question.[2]
PORTIA   Tarry, Jew.
The law hath yet another hold on you.
It is enacted in the laws of Venice,
If it be proved against an alien
345   That by direct or indirect attempts
He seek the life of any citizen,
The party 'gainst the which he doth contrive°   *plot*
Shall seize one half his goods; the other half
Comes to the privy coffer° of the state,   *private treasury*
350   And the offender's life lies in° the mercy   *at*
Of the Duke only, 'gainst all other voice—
In which predicament I say thou stand'st,
For it appears by manifest proceeding
That indirectly, and directly too,
355   Thou hast contrived against the very life
Of the defendant, and thou hast incurred
The danger° formerly by me rehearsed.°   *penalty / described*
Down, therefore, and beg mercy of the Duke.
GRAZIANO [*to* SHYLOCK]   Beg that thou mayst have leave to hang thyself—
360   And yet, thy wealth being forfeit to the state,
Thou hast not left the value of a cord.
Therefore thou must be hanged at the state's charge.°   *expense*
DUKE [*to* SHYLOCK]   That thou shalt see the difference of our spirit,
I pardon thee thy life before thou ask it.
365   For half thy wealth, it is Antonio's.
The other half comes to the general state,
Which humbleness may drive° unto a fine.   *reduce*
PORTIA   Ay, for the state, not for Antonio.[3]
SHYLOCK   Nay, take my life and all, pardon not that.
370   You take my house when you do take the prop
That doth sustain my house; you take my life
When you do take the means whereby I live.[4]

---

1. At a disadvantage (see 1.3.41).
2. I'll press my case no further.
3. With respect to the state's half, not Antonio's.

4. "He that taketh away his neighbor's living, slayeth him" (Ecclesiasticus 34:22).

PORTIA   What mercy can you render him, Antonio?

GRAZIANO   A halter,° gratis. Nothing else, for God's sake.   *hangman's noose*

375 ANTONIO   So please my lord the Duke and all the court
To quit the fine for one half of his goods,
I am content, so he will let me have
The other half in use,⁵ to render it
Upon his death unto the gentleman
380 That lately stole his daughter.
Two things provided more: that for this favour
He presently° become a Christian;   *immediately*
The other, that he do record a gift
Here in the court of all he dies possessed
385 Unto his son, Lorenzo, and his daughter.

DUKE   He shall do this, or else I do recant°   *withdraw*
The pardon that I late pronouncèd here.

PORTIA   Art thou contented, Jew? What dost thou say?

SHYLOCK   I am content.

390 PORTIA [*to* NERISSA]   Clerk, draw a deed of gift.

SHYLOCK   I pray you give me leave to go from hence.
I am not well. Send the deed after me,
And I will sign it.

DUKE   Get thee gone, but do it.

GRAZIANO [*to* SHYLOCK]   In christ'ning shalt thou have two godfathers.
395 Had I been judge thou shouldst have had ten more,°   *(to constitute a jury)*
To bring thee to the gallows, not the font.   *Exit* [SHYLOCK]

DUKE [*to* PORTIA]   Sir, I entreat you home with me to dinner.

PORTIA   I humbly do desire your grace of pardon.
I must away this night toward Padua,
400 And it is meet° I presently set forth.   *proper*

DUKE   I am sorry that your leisure serves you not.°   *you haven't the time*
Antonio, gratify° this gentleman,   *reward*
For in my mind you are much bound to him.

Exit DUKE *and his train*

BASSANIO [*to* PORTIA]   Most worthy gentleman, I and my friend
405 Have by your wisdom been this day acquitted
Of grievous penalties, in lieu whereof
Three thousand ducats due unto the Jew
We freely cope° your courteous pains withal.   *repay*

ANTONIO   And stand indebted over and above
410 In love and service to you evermore.

PORTIA   He is well paid that is well satisfied,
And I, delivering you, am satisfied,
And therein do account myself well paid.
My mind was never yet more mercenary.
415 I pray you know me when we meet again.
I wish you well; and so I take my leave.

BASSANIO   Dear sir, of force° I must attempt you further.   *necessity*
Take some remembrance of us as a tribute,
Not as fee. Grant me two things, I pray you:
420 Not to deny me, and to pardon me.°   *excuse my urging*

---

5. Antonio's conditions are unclear, because "quit" in line 376 (requite) could mean "pardon" or "make him pay," and "in use" (line 378) could mean either "in trust" or "for my own purposes." But the arrangements for Shylock's property later in the scene suggest that Antonio succeeds in getting Shylock's penalty reduced: Shylock retains half of his wealth, and Antonio holds the other half in trust for Jessica and Lorenzo until Shylock dies, at which point they inherit the whole estate.

PORTIA   You press me far, and therefore I will yield.
[*To* ANTONIO] Give me your gloves. I'll wear them for your sake.
[*To* BASSANIO] And for your love I'll take this ring from you.
Do not draw back your hand. I'll take no more,
425   And you in love shall not deny me this.
BASSANIO   This ring, good sir? Alas, it is a trifle.
I will not shame myself to give you this.
PORTIA   I will have nothing else, but only this;
And now, methinks, I have a mind to it.
430   BASSANIO   There's more depends on this° than on the value.   *involved here*
The dearest ring in Venice will I give you,
And find it out by proclamation.
Only for this, I pray you pardon me.
PORTIA   I see, sir, you are liberal in offers.
435   You taught me first to beg, and now methinks
You teach me how a beggar should be answered.
BASSANIO   Good sir, this ring was given me by my wife,
And when she put it on she made me vow
That I should neither sell, nor give, nor lose it.
440   PORTIA   That 'scuse serves many men to save their gifts.
An if° your wife be not a madwoman,   *An if = If*
And know how well I have deserved this ring,
She would not hold out enemy for ever
For giving it to me. Well, peace be with you.
                                   Exeunt [PORTIA *and* NERISSA]
445   ANTONIO   My lord Bassanio, let him have the ring.
Let his deservings and my love withal
Be valued 'gainst your wife's commandëment.
BASSANIO   Go, Graziano, run and overtake him.
Give him the ring, and bring him, if thou canst,
450   Unto Antonio's house. Away, make haste.   *Exit* GRAZIANO
Come, you and I will thither presently,
And in the morning early will we both
Fly toward Belmont. Come, Antonio.   *Exeunt*

4.2

Enter PORTIA *and* NERISSA [*still disguised*]

PORTIA   Enquire the Jew's house out, give him this deed,[1]
And let him sign it. We'll away tonight,
And be a day before our husbands home.
This deed will be well welcome to Lorenzo.
        Enter GRAZIANO
5   GRAZIANO   Fair sir, you are well o'erta'en.
My lord Bassanio upon more advice°   *further thought*
Hath sent you here this ring, and doth entreat
Your company at dinner.
PORTIA   That cannot be.
His ring I do accept most thankfully,
10   And so I pray you tell him. Furthermore,
I pray you show my youth old Shylock's house.
GRAZIANO   That will I do.
NERISSA   Sir, I would speak with you.
[*Aside to* PORTIA] I'll see if I can get my husband's ring

4.2 Location: Street in Venice.   1. Mentioned in 4.1.390.

Which I did make him swear to keep for ever.

15 PORTIA [*aside to* NERISSA]   Thou mayst; I warrant we shall have

old° swearing   *lots of*

That they did give the rings away to men.

But we'll outface them, and outswear them too.

Away, make haste. Thou know'st where I will tarry.

[*Exit at one door*]

NERISSA [*to* GRAZIANO]   Come, good sir, will you show me to this house?

Exeunt [*at another door*]

5.1

Enter LORENZO *and* JESSICA

LORENZO   The moon shines bright. In such a night as this,

When the sweet wind did gently kiss the trees

And they did make no noise—in such a night

Troilus, methinks, mounted the Trojan walls,

5   And sighed his soul toward the Grecian tents

Where Cressid lay that night.[1]

JESSICA   In such a night

Did Thisbe fearfully o'ertrip the dew

And saw the lion's shadow ere himself,

And ran dismayed away.[2]

LORENZO   In such a night

10   Stood Dido with a willow in her hand

Upon the wild sea banks, and waft her love

To come again to Carthage.[3]

JESSICA   In such a night

Medea gatherèd the enchanted herbs

That did renew old Aeson.[4]

LORENZO   In such a night

15   Did Jessica steal° from the wealthy Jew,   *escape; rob*

And with an unthrift° love did run from Venice   *a spendthrift*

As far as Belmont.

JESSICA   In such a night

Did young Lorenzo swear he loved her well,

Stealing her soul with many vows of faith,

And ne'er a true one.

20   LORENZO   In such a night

Did pretty Jessica, like a little shrew,

Slander her love, and he forgave it her.

JESSICA   I would outnight you, did nobody come.

But hark, I hear the footing° of a man.   *footsteps*

Enter [STEFANO,] *a messenger*

25   LORENZO   Who comes so fast in silence of the night?

STEFANO   A friend.

LORENZO   A friend—what friend? Your name, I pray you, friend?

STEFANO   Stefano is my name, and I bring word

5.1 Location: Belmont.

1. Troilus was a Trojan Prince whose lover, Cressida, forsook him for the Greek Diomedes after she was sent from Troy to the Greek camp. See *Troilus and Cressida*.

2. Thisbe, going at night to meet her lover, Pyramus, was frightened by a lion and fled. Pyramus, assuming she was dead, killed himself; when she found his body, Thisbe committed suicide too. The story is dramatized

by "the rude mechanicals" in *A Midsummer Night's Dream*.

3. Dido, Queen of Carthage, was abandoned by her lover, the Trojan hero Aeneas. *willow*: emblem of forsaken love. *waft*: waved to.

4. Medea was a sorceress who loved Jason and helped him win the Golden Fleece; she magically restored Aeson, Jason's father, to youth.

My mistress will before the break of day
30 Be here at Belmont. She doth stray about
By holy crosses,° where she kneels and prays   *roadside shrines*
For happy wedlock hours.
LORENZO   Who comes with her?
STEFANO   None but a holy hermit and her maid.
I pray you, is my master yet returned?
35 LORENZO   He is not, nor we have not heard from him.
But go we in, I pray thee, Jessica,
And ceremoniously let us prepare
Some welcome for the mistress of the house.
                Enter [LANCELOT] *the clown*
LANCELOT [*calling*]   Sola, sola! Wo, ha, ho! Sola, sola!⁵
40 LORENZO   Who calls?
LANCELOT [*calling*]   Sola!—Did you see Master Lorenzo? [*Call-
ing*] Master Lorenzo! Sola, sola!
LORENZO   Leave hollering, man: here.
LANCELOT [*calling*]   Sola!—Where, where?
45 LORENZO   Here.
LANCELOT   Tell him there's a post° come from my master with his   *messenger*
horn full of good news. My master will be here ere morning.
                                                    [*Exit*]
LORENZO [*to* JESSICA]   Sweet soul, let's in, and there expect°   *await*
their coming.
And yet no matter. Why should we go in?
50 My friend Stefano, signify,° I pray you,   *announce*
Within the house your mistress is at hand,
And bring your music forth into the air.   *Exit* STEFANO
How sweet the moonlight sleeps upon this bank!
Here will we sit, and let the sounds of music
55 Creep in our ears. Soft stillness and the night
Become the touches⁶ of sweet harmony.
Sit, Jessica.
                [*They sit*]
                Look how the floor of heaven
Is thick inlaid with patens° of bright gold.   *disks*
There's not the smallest orb which thou behold'st
60 But in his motion like an angel sings,
Still° choiring to the young-eyed⁷ cherubins.   *Continually*
Such harmony⁸ is in immortal souls,
But whilst this muddy vesture of decay°   *this mortal body*
Doth grossly close it° in, we cannot hear it.°   *(the soul) / (the music)*
                [*Enter Musicians*]
65 [*To the Musicians*] Come, ho, and wake Diana⁹ with a hymn.
With sweetest touches pierce your mistress'° ear,   *(Portia's)*
And draw her home with music.
                [*The Musicians*] *play*
JESSICA   I am never merry when I hear sweet music.
LORENZO   The reason is your spirits are attentive,
70 For do but note a wild and wanton herd
Or race° of youthful and unhandled colts,   *group*

---

5. Imitating a messenger's horn.
6. Suit the notes (literally, the fingering of a stringed instrument).
7. Keen-sighted.
8. The music of the spheres.
9. Goddess of the moon and of chastity.

Fetching mad bounds, bellowing and neighing loud,
Which is the hot condition of their blood,
If they but hear perchance a trumpet sound,
75 Or any air of music touch their ears,
You shall perceive them make a mutual° stand,   *simultaneous*
Their savage eyes turned to a modest gaze
By the sweet power of music. Therefore the poet[1]
Did feign that Orpheus drew° trees, stones, and floods,   *allured*
80 Since naught so stockish,° hard, and full of rage   *stolid*
But music for the time doth change his nature.
The man that hath no music in himself,
Nor is not moved with concord of sweet sounds,
Is fit for treasons, stratagems,° and spoils.°   *plots / plunder*
85 The motions of his spirit are dull as night,
And his affections° dark as Erebus.°   *inclinations / hell*
Let no such man be trusted. Mark the music.
　　　　　Enter PORTIA *and* NERISSA [*as themselves*]
PORTIA　That light we see is burning in my hall.
How far that little candle throws his beams—
90 So shines a good deed in a naughty° world.   *an evil*
NERISSA　When the moon shone we did not see the candle.
PORTIA　So doth the greater glory dim the less.
A substitute° shines brightly as a king   *deputy*
Until a king be by, and then his state
95 Empties itself as doth an inland brook
Into the main of waters.° Music, hark.   *the ocean*
NERISSA　It is your music, madam, of the house.
PORTIA　Nothing is good, I see, without respect.°   *reference to context*
Methinks it sounds much sweeter than by day.
100 NERISSA　Silence bestows that virtue on it, madam.
PORTIA　The crow doth sing as sweetly as the lark
When neither is attended,[2] and I think
The nightingale, if she should sing by day,
When every goose is cackling, would be thought
105 No better a musician than the wren.
How many things by season seasoned are[3]
To their right praise and true perfection!
　　　　　[*She sees* LORENZO *and* JESSICA]
Peace, ho!
　　　　　[*Music ceases*]
　　　　　The moon sleeps with Endymion,[4]
And would not be awaked.
LORENZO [*rising*]　　　　　That is the voice,
110 Or I am much deceived, of Portia.
PORTIA　He knows me as the blind man knows the cuckoo—
By the bad voice.
LORENZO　　　　　Dear lady, welcome home.
PORTIA　We have been praying for our husbands' welfare,
Which speed° we hope the better for our words.   *Who prosper*
Are they returned?
115 LORENZO　　　　　Madam, they are not yet,

---

1. Ovid, in *Metamorphoses* 10, tells the story of Orpheus,
a legendary musician.
2. Is listened to; is accompanied.

3. *by season . . . are:* by proper time are adapted.
4. In classical mythology, a shepherd beloved of the
moon goddess, who caused him to sleep forever.

But there is come a messenger before
To signify their coming.
PORTIA   Go in, Nerissa.
  Give order to my servants that they take
  No note at all of our being absent hence;
120 Nor you, Lorenzo; Jessica, nor you.
         A tucket° sounds   *trumpet flourish*
LORENZO   Your husband is at hand. I hear his trumpet.
  We are no tell-tales, madam. Fear you not.
PORTIA   This night, methinks, is but the daylight sick.
  It looks a little paler. 'Tis a day
125 Such as the day is when the sun is hid.
        Enter BASSANIO, ANTONIO, GRAZIANO, *and their follow-*
        ers. [GRAZIANO *and* NERISSA *speak silently to one*
        another]
BASSANIO   We should hold day with the Antipodes
  If you would walk in absence of the sun.[5]
PORTIA   Let me give light, but let me not be light;°   *unfaithful*
  For a light wife doth make a heavy° husband,   *sad*
130 And never be Bassanio so for me.
  But God sort° all. You are welcome home, my lord.   *decide*
BASSANIO   I thank you, madam. Give welcome to my friend.
  This is the man, this is Antonio,
  To whom I am so infinitely bound.
135 PORTIA   You should in all° sense be much bound to him,   *every*
  For as I hear he was much bound for you.
ANTONIO   No more than I am well acquitted° of.   *freed*
PORTIA   Sir, you are very welcome to our house.
  It must appear in other ways than words,
140 Therefore I scant this breathing courtesy.[6]
GRAZIANO [*to* NERISSA]   By yonder moon I swear you do me wrong.
  In faith, I gave it to the judge's clerk.
  Would he were gelt° that had it for my part,   *gelded; castrated*
  Since you do take it, love, so much at heart.
145 PORTIA   A quarrel, ho, already! What's the matter?
GRAZIANO   About a hoop of gold, a paltry ring
  That she did give me, whose posy° was   *motto*
  For all the world like cutlers' poetry
  Upon a knife—'Love me and leave me not'.
150 NERISSA   What talk you of the posy or the value?
  You swore to me when I did give it you
  That you would wear it till your hour of death,
  And that it should lie with you in your grave.
  Though not for me, yet for your vehement oaths
155 You should have been respective° and have kept it.   *careful*
  Gave it a judge's clerk?—no, God's my judge,
  The clerk will ne'er wear hair on's face that had it.
GRAZIANO   He will an if he live to be a man.
NERISSA   Ay, if a woman live to be a man.
160 GRAZIANO   Now by this hand, I gave it to a youth,
  A kind of boy, a little scrubbèd° boy   *stunted*

5. *We . . . sun:* We would share daylight with the
other side of the world (Antipodes) if you habitually
walked when the sun was gone (implying "such is your
radiance").
6. I make brief this verbal welcome.

No higher than thyself, the judge's clerk,
A prating° boy that begged it as a fee.   *chattering*
I could not for my heart deny it him.

165 PORTIA You were to blame, I must be plain with you,
To part so slightly with your wife's first gift,
A thing stuck on with oaths upon your finger,
And so riveted with faith unto your flesh.
I gave my love a ring, and made him swear
170 Never to part with it; and here he stands.
I dare be sworn for him he would not leave° it,   *part with*
Nor pluck it from his finger for the wealth
That the world masters.° Now, in faith, Graziano,   *possesses*
You give your wife too unkind a cause of grief.
175 An 'twere to me, I should be mad at it.

BASSANIO [*aside*] Why, I were best to cut my left hand off
And swear I lost the ring defending it.

GRAZIANO [*to* PORTIA] My lord Bassanio gave his ring away
Unto the judge that begged it, and indeed
180 Deserved it, too, and then the boy his clerk,
That took some pains in writing, he begged mine,
And neither man nor master would take aught
But the two rings.

PORTIA [*to* BASSANIO] What ring gave you, my lord?
Not that, I hope, which you received of me.

185 BASSANIO If I could add a lie unto a fault
I would deny it; but you see my finger
Hath not the ring upon it. It is gone.

PORTIA Even so void is your false heart of truth.
By heaven, I will ne'er come in your bed
Until I see the ring.

190 NERISSA [*to* GRAZIANO] Nor I in yours
Till I again see mine.

BASSANIO   Sweet Portia,
If you did know to whom I gave the ring,
If you did know for whom I gave the ring,
And would conceive for what I gave the ring,
195 And how unwillingly I left the ring
When naught would be accepted but the ring,
You would abate the strength of your displeasure.

PORTIA If you had known the virtue° of the ring,   *power*
Or half her worthiness that gave the ring,
200 Or your own honour to contain° the ring,   *retain*
You would not then have parted with the ring.
What man is there so much unreasonable,
If you had pleased to have defended it
With any terms of zeal, wanted° the modesty°   *would lack / moderation*
205 To urge° the thing held as a ceremony?°   *insist on / sacred symbol*
Nerissa teaches me what to believe.
I'll die for't but some woman had the ring.

BASSANIO No, by my honour, madam, by my soul,
No woman had it, but a civil doctor°   *doctor of civil law*
210 Which did refuse three thousand ducats of me,
And begged the ring, the which I did deny him,
And suffered° him to go displeased away,   *permitted*
Even he that had held up the very life

Of my dear friend. What should I say, sweet lady?
215 I was enforced to send it after him.
I was beset with shame and courtesy.
My honour would not let ingratitude
So much besmear it. Pardon me, good lady,
For by these blessèd candles of the night,
220 Had you been there I think you would have begged
The ring of me to give the worthy doctor.
PORTIA   Let not that doctor e'er come near my house.
Since he hath got the jewel that I loved,
And that which you did swear to keep for me,
225 I will become as liberal° as you.   *generous; licentious*
I'll not deny him anything I have,
No, not my body nor my husband's bed.
Know° him I shall, I am well sure of it.   *(with sexual suggestion)*
Lie not a night from home. Watch me like Argus.[7]
230 If you do not, if I be left alone,
Now by mine honour, which is yet mine own,
I'll have that doctor for my bedfellow.
NERISSA [*to* GRAZIANO]   And I his clerk, therefore be well advised
How you do leave me to mine own protection.
235 GRAZIANO   Well, do you so. Let not me take him then,
For if I do, I'll mar the young clerk's pen.°   *(with sexual suggestion)*
ANTONIO   I am th'unhappy subject of these quarrels.
PORTIA   Sir, grieve not you. You are welcome notwithstanding.
BASSANIO   Portia, forgive me this enforcèd wrong,
240 And in the hearing of these many friends
I swear to thee, even by thine own fair eyes,
Wherein I see myself—
PORTIA   Mark you but that?
In both my eyes he doubly sees himself,
In each eye one. Swear by your double° self,   *twofold; deceitful*
And there's an oath of credit.[8]
245 BASSANIO   Nay, but hear me.
Pardon this fault, and by my soul I swear
I never more will break an oath with thee.
ANTONIO [*to* PORTIA]   I once did lend my body for his wealth
Which, but for him that had your husband's ring,
250 Had quite miscarried. I dare be bound again,
My soul upon the forfeit, that your lord
Will never more break faith advisedly.°   *intentionally*
PORTIA   Then you shall be his surety.° Give him this,   *guarantor of a loan*
And bid him keep it better than the other.
255 ANTONIO   Here, Lord Bassanio, swear to keep this ring.
BASSANIO   By heaven, it is the same I gave the doctor!
PORTIA   I had it of him. Pardon me, Bassanio,
For by this ring, the doctor lay with me.
NERISSA   And pardon me, my gentle Graziano,
260 For that same scrubbèd boy, the doctor's clerk,
In lieu of° this last night did lie with me.   *In exchange for*
GRAZIANO   Why, this is like the mending of highways
In summer where the ways are fair enough![9]

7. Mythical many-eyed monster.   9. *where . . . enough:* when repair is not required.
8. An oath to be believed (ironic).

What, are we cuckolds ere we have deserved it?

265 PORTIA   Speak not so grossly. You are all amazed.°   *confused*
    Here is a letter. Read it at your leisure.
    It comes from Padua, from Bellario.
    There you shall find that Portia was the doctor,
    Nerissa there her clerk. Lorenzo here
270   Shall witness I set forth as soon as you,
    And even but now returned. I have not yet
    Entered my house. Antonio, you are welcome,
    And I have better news in store for you
    Than you expect. Unseal this letter soon.
275   There you shall find three of your argosies
    Are richly come to harbour suddenly.
    You shall not know by what strange accident
    I chancèd on this letter.

ANTONIO   I am dumb!°   *dumbstruck*

BASSANIO [*to* PORTIA]   Were you the doctor and I knew you not?

280 GRAZIANO [*to* NERISSA]   Were you the clerk that is to make me cuckold?

NERISSA   Ay, but the clerk that never means to do it
    Unless he live until he be a man.

BASSANIO [*to* PORTIA]   Sweet doctor, you shall be my bedfellow.
    When I am absent, then lie with my wife.

285 ANTONIO [*to* PORTIA]   Sweet lady, you have given me life and
      living,°   *possessions*
    For here I read for certain that my ships
    Are safely come to road.°   *harbor*

PORTIA   How now, Lorenzo?
    My clerk hath some good comforts, too, for you.

NERISSA   Ay, and I'll give them him without a fee.
290   There do I give to you and Jessica
    From the rich Jew a special deed of gift,
    After his death, of all he dies possessed of.

LORENZO   Fair ladies, you drop manna in the way
    Of starvèd people.

PORTIA   It is almost morning,
295   And yet I am sure you are not satisfied
    Of these events at full. Let us go in,
    And charge us there upon inter'gatories,[1]
    And we will answer all things faithfully.

GRAZIANO   Let it be so. The first inter'gatory
300   That my Nerissa shall be sworn on is
    Whether till the next night she had rather stay,
    Or go to bed now, being two hours to day.
    But were the day come, I should wish it dark
    Till I were couching° with the doctor's clerk.   *lying*
305   Well, while I live I'll fear no other thing
    So sore as keeping safe Nerissa's ring.°   *Exeunt*   (*with sexual suggestion*)

---

1. And question us under oath.

Much Ado About Nothing

Much Ado About Nothing, first published in 1600 and probably written in 1598, weaves together two stories: the benevolent luring of Beatrice and Benedick into mutual declarations of love and the villainous luring of Claudio into the mistaken belief that Hero is unchaste. For the former plot, there seems to be no specific source, though Shakespeare would have encountered stories of scorners of love who fall in love (including Chaucer's *Troilus and Criseyde*). For the story of the virtuous lady falsely accused, sources abound, including Ludovico Ariosto's wonderful version in Canto V of *Orlando Furioso* (1516, translated into English by Sir John Harington in 1591) and Matteo Bandello's twenty-second *Novella* (1554, translated into French by François de Belleforest in 1574). Shakespeare probably knew these and other versions, both dramatic and non-dramatic, among them a tragic retelling by Edmund Spenser in Book II of *The Faerie Queene* (1590). By deftly intertwining the two plots, *Much Ado About Nothing* mingles lightheartedness with a certain haunting sadness.

This sadness is a recurrent note in Shakespeare's earlier comedies: *The Comedy of Errors* opens with a condemned man's lament, *The Merchant of Venice* is darkened by Antonio's melancholy and Shylock's bitter rage, and *Love's Labour's Lost* (which features in Biron and Rosaline a pair of sparring lovers who strikingly anticipate Benedick and Beatrice) ends with a death. In several later comedies, most notably *Measure for Measure*, the darkness is so intensified as to make the term "comedy" seem a problem. But in *Much Ado About Nothing*, Shakespeare creates a balance of laughter, longing, and pain that he equals only in two other great romantic comedies from the same period, *As You Like It* and *Twelfth Night, or What You Will*. The titles of all three plays convey an impression of easy, festive wit, a magical effortlessness that is in fact the product of an extraordinary discipline and skill.

This cunning use of effort to produce the effect of effortlessness can be understood in the light of Baldassare Castiglione's famous courtesy manual *The Book of the Courtier* (1528). Castiglione's remarkable book, published in an English translation in 1561, depicts a witty and sophisticated group of men and women who, in several extended conversations, discuss the qualities that must be possessed by the ideal courtier. The courtier, as they envisage him, must be equally adept at making war and at making love. He must be able to assist the Prince and to dance elegantly, to grasp the subtleties of diplomacy and to sing in a pleasant, unaffected voice, to engage in philosophical speculation and to tell amusing after-dinner stories. In similar fashion, court ladies must be at once modest and spirited, chaste and slyly knowing, unspoiled and elegant. These are, in less idealized and rarefied form, the social roles that Benedick and Beatrice are called upon to play. They are roles that demand exceptionally versatile actors.

Such courtly performances, Castiglione's conversationalists acknowledge, risk seeming stilted and artificial; will be successful only if they appear entirely spontaneous and natural. However carefully they prepare their parts, courtiers should hide all signs of study and rehearsal. To achieve grace, they must practice what Castiglione calls *sprezzatura*, a cultivated nonchalance. *Sprezzatura* is a technique for the manipulation of appearance, for masking the hard work that underlies successful performances. This masking is an open secret: others know that you are masking, but they must keep this knowledge suspended in the belief that it is a breach of decorum to acknowledge their own knowledge.

The society of *The Book of the Courtier* lives with other open secrets. Dark forces lie just outside the charmed circle of delightful lords and ladies: war, arbitrary power, the high risk of betrayal and double-dealing, the commodification of women, the grinding labor to which the great mass of human beings are condemned. The courtier's artful refusal to acknowledge any of these forces could be a mode of escapism, but Castiglione is alert to reality's harsh demands. For him, fashioning the self is a means not of withdrawing from a treacherous world, but of operating successfully within it.

Like Castiglione's *Courtier, Much Ado About Nothing* (whose title suggests the playwright's own mastery of *sprezzatura*) is pervasively concerned with social performance that seems at once spontaneous and calculated. Beatrice and Benedick, at the play's center, are both exquisitely self-conscious, but their self-consciousness takes the paradoxical form of a jaunty indifference to conventional niceties, an almost reckless exuberance that masks a heightened sensitivity to the social currents in which they swim.

By contrast, Don John, the bastard brother, characterizes himself from the start as a radically antisocial creature: "I had rather be a canker in a hedge than a rose in his grace, and it better fits my blood to be disdained of all than to fashion a carriage to rob love from any" (1.3.21–23). These are the sentiments of the outsider, one who, like the bastard Edmund in *King Lear,* is not properly part of the family and kinship network, and they are sufficient, in this play, to account for Don John's relentless, curiously disinterested villainy. He is a man who refuses to "fashion a carriage"—to observe the appropriate code of manners—and this refusal is itself a sign of rebellion. For manners are the lived texture of social life in *Much Ado*, not in the sense of a compulsory set of rules but rather in the sense of an evolving awareness of mutual obligation and interconnectedness.

There is, to be sure, something like compulsion in the obligations and pressures within which the men and women of *Much Ado* live, but the play frustrates any attempt to strip away the fabric of graciousness, apparent choice, and pretended spontaneity with which the compulsions are dressed. An exchange in the comedy's opening moments exemplifies the perfect balance between obligation and will that governs the play's vision of social life. Leonato, the Governor of Messina, is informed by letter of the imminent arrival of Don Pedro of Aragon. Entertainment must be provided at once, and Don Pedro's first words call attention to the pressure of compulsory courtesy: "Good Signor Leonato, are you come to meet your trouble? The fashion of the world is to avoid cost, and you encounter it." It is obviously the fashion of the world to apologize in just this way for imposition, and such an apology calls for an equally conventional denial that any trouble is involved. Leonato duly produces such a denial, a particularly gracious and well-turned one: "Never came trouble to my house in the likeness of your grace; for trouble being gone, comfort should remain, but when you depart from me, sorrow abides and happiness takes his leave." Don Pedro responds to this exquisite compliment with an elegantly modified renewal of his first words and then a polite turn toward Leonato's daughter, Hero: "You embrace your charge too willingly. I think this is your daughter" (1.1.77–85).

In a strict calculation of power politics, these words are meaningless: they posture emptily above the "real" social exchange, which involves the obligation of the civilian authority toward the military authority (as it happens, a foreign military) at the close of a successful campaign. But such a view neglects the importance of graceful social performance, performance whose ease signals the elite status of the speakers and tacitly acknowledges the possibility of failure or refusal. With a ceremonial greeting such as this, the possibility may seem merely theoretical, but in fact it comes to hover over the entire play (whose main plot is in effect formally initiated by Don Pedro's polite notice of Leonato's daughter). By the fifth act, after Don Pedro's officer Claudio has publicly humiliated and repudiated his intended bride, all courtesy has withered away, and only bitterness and recrimination exist between the gracious host and his princely guest.

Dogberry's zany sleuthing resolves the crisis, but the crucial point is that there is nothing absolute and automatic about the code of manners. Social rituals are vulnerable to disruption and misunderstanding, and this vulnerability underscores the importance of consciously keeping up appearances, patrolling social perimeters, and fabricating civility.

In Castiglione's world, there is a high premium placed on the concealment of the labor expended in this fabrication, but Shakespeare's comedy gives us glimpses in the frequent references to the support staff and attentiveness involved in entertainment: "Where is my cousin, your son? Hath he provided this music?" (1.2.1–2); "Being entertained for a perfumer, as I was smoking a musty room . . ." (1.3.46–47); "The revellers are entering, brother. Make good room" (2.1.70). Social labor is still more visible in the diverse kinds of discourse in which the characters participate or to which they refer: greeting, entertainment, embassy, formal letter, conjuration, courtship, epigraph, sonneteering, gossip, legal deposition, aggressive wit, formal denunciation, ritualized apology.

Each of these forms of speech requires a display of skill and hence confers a measure of the honor or shame to which the characters of *Much Ado About Nothing* are intensely attuned. Honor and shame are particularly social emotions, the emotions of those who exist in a world of watching and being watched. "Nothing" in Shakespeare's time was pronounced "noting": this is a play obsessed with characters noting other characters. Hence the special force of *masking*, where the serious business of watching is playfully disrupted by disguise, and hence too the crucial significance of those scenes in which Beatrice and Benedick think they are noting others and are in reality being noted (and tricked). Sensitivity to the possibility of being shamed—which includes being laughed at, rejected, insulted, dishonored, humiliated, and so forth—is never very far from the characters of *Much Ado*. It extends from Leonato, who thinks that death is the fairest cover for his daughter's public humiliation, to Benedick, whose intellectual and sexual endurance is ridiculed by Beatrice when he ducks out of their first exchange with "a jade's trick" (1.1.118), to Dogberry, who longs to be writ down an ass. At its core is intense male anxiety about female infidelity, manifested in the constant nervous jokes about cuckoldry and played on viciously by Don John. "If I see anything tonight why I should not marry her, tomorrow," Claudio tells Don John, "in the congregation where I should wed, there will I shame her." Don Pedro promises to join with his friend "to disgrace her" (3.2.103–07).

Honor and shame, as the play develops them, are closely bound up with linguistic performance. Language is society's way of being intimately present in the individual; the characters may adjust to that social presence, may like Beatrice and Benedick playfully resist it, may like Dogberry distort it unintentionally, but the shared codes of language are more powerful than any individual.

Close attention to the language of *Much Ado About Nothing* begins with the observation that the comedy is written largely, though not entirely, in prose, a medium far more familiar to modern audiences than the blank verse that dominates many of Shakespeare's plays. This prose, however, is of a kind to which we are no longer accustomed. Modern prose tends by design to be rather plain and colorless; Elizabethan prose is often playful, rhetorically inventive, and richly metaphorical. *Much Ado About Nothing* at once plays elaborate prose games and pokes fun at them, as when Benedick complains that lovesick Claudio "was wont to speak plain and to the purpose, like an honest man and a soldier, and now is he turned orthography. His words are a very fantastical banquet, just so many strange dishes" (2.3.16–19). Shakespeare was certainly capable of writing what we would regard as clear, uncluttered prose: "I learn in this letter that Don Pedro of Aragon comes this night to Messina" (1.1.1–2). But he could also produce astonishing rhetorical effects:

> She told me—not thinking I had been myself—that I was the Prince's jester, that I was duller than a great thaw, huddling jest upon jest with such impossible conveyance upon me that I stood like a man at a mark, with a whole army shooting at me. She speaks poniards, and every word stabs. If her breath were as terrible as her terminations, there were no living near her, she would infect to the North Star. I would not marry her though she were endowed with all that Adam had left him before he transgressed. She would have made Hercules have turned spit, yea, and have cleft his club to make the fire, too. (2.1.212–21)

A night watchman. From Thomas Dekker, *The Belman of London* (1608).

The wonderful improvisational piling up of images, each at once subtly linked to the preceding one and yet swerving in a new direction, captures the movement of Benedick's mind: the rush of genuine anger and hurt feelings mingled with the impulse to turn his pain into a comically misogynistic performance to entertain Don Pedro (a performance that, ironically, confirms the charge—that he is the Prince's jester—that originally stung him).

Linguistic performance is the social equivalent of the performance in warfare that is both alluded to and conspicuously excluded from the play's action. Language is violence, and language is the alternative to violence: the play entertains both hypotheses and plays them off against each other. "There is a kind of merry war betwixt Signor Benedick and her," says Leonato of his niece. "They never meet but there's a skirmish of wit between them" (1.1.49–51). If words are the agents of civility, they are also dangerous weapons: "Thy slander hath gone through and through her heart, / And she lies buried with her ancestors"; "God knows, I loved my niece, / And she is dead, slandered to death by villains" (5.1.68–69, 87–88). What we glimpse in the symbolic murder of Hero is not only the maligning power of slander, but also the aggressive potential of even polite or playful speech. The "merry war" between Beatrice and Benedick leaves scars.

The more one attends to the language of *Much Ado About Nothing*, the more it seems saturated with violence. In the lighthearted opening scene alone, there are almost constant comic references to war, plague, betrayal, heresy, burning at the stake, blinding, hanging, spying, poisoning. To be sure, the horrors are not themselves realized dramatically in the play; they are present as mere jokes. Nonetheless, they are present, recalled again and again by the constant threat of disaster, by symbolic death, by public shaming. Even in the tidal rush of the comic resolution, amid the marriages, the music, and the dance, Benedick's final words, indeed the final words of the play, deliberately call attention to the violence that the language has continually, if obliquely, registered. Informed of Don John's capture, Benedick declares, "Think not on him till tomorrow, I'll devise thee brave punishments for him. Strike up, pipers." *Dance* (5.4.121–22).

Viewed in the light of the close, with its conspicuous deferral of torture, but only until tomorrow, the play does not simply transform human misery and violence into wit, but rather addresses itself to the ways in which society manages to endure, to reproduce, to avoid immersion in its own destructive element, to dance. It does so by conscious and unconscious deferral, by the manipulation of appearances, by the deployment of illusions that are known by at least some of its members (the worst and the best) to be illusions.

Illusions are tricks and deceptions, but they are also the social fictions men and women live by. Claudio and Hero exist in the play almost entirely in and as such fictions: their emotions seem less something they possess inwardly than something constructed for them out of the appropriate conventions and rituals. A more complex manifestation in the play of the primacy of illusion is the relation between Beatrice and Benedick. The plot to trick the celebrated skirmishers into marriage originates with Don Pedro, who promises, if Leonato, Hero, and Claudio cooperate with him, to "fash-

Lovers sparring with torches. From George Wither, *A Collection of Emblemes* (1635).

ion" the match. The key to his success is his ability to mobilize the social code of shame and honor to which Beatrice and Benedick are bound and to use this code as a means to discipline—to shape into a plot that will culminate in marriage—the powerful chafing between them. For both Beatrice and Benedick, the force that pushes them toward declarations of love and hence toward marriage vows is as much hearing themselves criticized by their friends as hearing that the other is desperately in love. "Can this be true?" asks Beatrice, her ears burning. "Stand I condemned for pride and scorn so much?" (3.1.108–09). "I hear how I am censured," Benedick declares, resolving that he "must not seem proud" (2.3.199–200, 202–03).

The conspiratorial fabrication of appearances so as to manipulate the code of shame and honor has the odd effect of establishing a link between the socially approved practices of Don Pedro and the wicked practices of Don John, his bastard brother. Shakespeare seems to go out of his way to call attention to this link: moments after Don Pedro undertakes to "fashion" the affection between Beatrice and Benedick, the villainous Borachio declares that he "will so fashion the matter that Hero shall be absent" and hence can be impersonated by Margaret. In effect, the play's term for the social system in which all the characters—evil as well as virtuous—are involved is "fashion." Shakespeare deftly uses the term both as noun and verb—that is, both to designate the images (including the fashionable costumes) that elicit emotions and to describe the process that shapes these images.

Fashion is closely related not only to image but also to verbal style, which in the aesthetics of the period was regarded as a kind of dress. "The body of your discourse," laughs Benedick, "is sometimes guarded with fragments, and the guards are but slightly basted on neither" (1.1.232–34). The pervasiveness of fashion allows the possibility of drastic deception, but it is also society's redemptive principle. The movement of the play is not so much the unmasking of fraud to reveal the true, virtuous essence within as rather the refashioning, after a dangerous illusion, of the proper image and the appropriate words: "Sweet Hero," cries Claudio after his eyes have been opened to the deception, "now thy image doth appear / In the rare semblance that I loved it first" (5.1.235–36).

The fashioning with which the play is concerned complicates any simple opposition between authentic inner feelings and social norms. This is, after all, a plot that features a wooing by masked proxy instead of direct wooing, a theatrical ritual of remorse instead of remorse, a declaration of love based upon a set of illusions and motivated by the fear of shame. Near the play's close, we see Benedick struggling to compose the required sonnet to Beatrice—an entirely conventional exercise performed to fulfill the theatrical role in which he has been cast ("myself in love"). And in the final moments, when the deception is revealed, it is this exercise, rather than any feelings of the heart, that confirms the match. "I'll be sworn upon't that he loves her," declares Claudio:

> For here's a paper written in his hand,
> A halting sonnet of his own pure brain,
> Fashioned to Beatrice.

When a similar sonnet by Beatrice is produced, Benedick cries, "A miracle! Here's our own hands against our hearts" (5.4.85–88, 91).

Many readers of the play, and most performers, have tried to reverse this formulation: Beatrice and Benedick's conversations may be hostile, the interpretation goes, but in their hearts they are, and have long been, deeply in love. Beatrice seems to refer to an earlier time when she had given her heart to Benedick and had evidently been disappointed: "once before he won it of me, with false dice" (2.1.243–44). If they do not declare their love, it is because they are too defensive or, alternatively, too wise to play society's conventional game. In a world of pervasive conventionality and social control, one clever way to insist upon some spontaneity and hence to achieve some authenticity is to quarrel. Perhaps. But what if we do not dismiss their own words? What if we take the conspiracy against them seriously? Beatrice and Benedick would in that case not "love" each other from the start; it would not at all be clear that they love each other, entirely independent of social manipulation, at the close. They are, at least to some extent, tricked into marriage; without the pressure that moves them to professions of love, they would have remained unmarried. Beatrice and Benedick constantly tantalize us with the possibility of an identity quite different from that of Claudio and Hero, an identity deliberately fashioned to resist the constant pressure of society. But that pressure finally prevails. Marriage is a social conspiracy.

If such a view seems ultimately too unsentimental to be tenable in a romantic comedy, it nonetheless makes possible the brilliant scene in which Benedick asks what he can do to prove his love for Beatrice, and Beatrice replies, "Kill Claudio" (4.1.287). Similarly, it helps to account for the laughter provoked by the disillusioned exchange very near the play's close: "Do not you love me?" "Why no, no more than reason" (5.4.74). In both cases, where we might expect tender words, we get the opposite. If we feel nonetheless that romantic love triumphs in the end, we do so in effect because we—audience and readers—participate in the conspiracy to gull the pair into marriage by insisting that they love each other more than reason. In doing so, we confer upon the general restoration of civility at the play's close something more deeply pleasurable.

Benedick and Beatrice have rational arguments, grounded in the gender politics of their world, for remaining single. Benedick knows that a married man must put his honor at risk by entrusting it to a woman, while Beatrice knows that a married woman must put her integrity at risk by submitting herself to a man: "Would it not grieve a woman to be overmastered with a piece of valiant dust?" (2.1.51–52). Even when they are manipulated into declaring their love, they cannot settle into the language of conventional courtship: "Thou and I are too wise," Benedick tells Beatrice, "to woo peaceably" (5.2.61). Their union at the close is a triumph of folly over the "wisdom" of the

A man trapped in the yoke of matrimony. From Henry Peacham. *Minerva Britanna* (1612).

single life, a triumph that recalls Erasmus's *Praise of Folly,* where love is said to be possible only because men and women are induced to put aside their reason and plunge into saving foolishness. Why should they do so? The answer is that it is better to live in illusion than in social isolation and that, as Benedick says, "the world must be peopled" (2.3.213–14).

In most productions of the play, audiences are made to feel that submission to the discipline of love and marriage—"taming my wild heart" (3.1.113), as Beatrice so wonderfully puts it—is a magnificent release of love and energy. Shakespeare had already experimented with comparable themes in *The Taming of the Shrew,* but Petruchio's conquest of Kate seems, at least for many modern viewers, too brutal to accept without a lingering sense of constriction and loss. What keeps the conclusion of *Much Ado About Nothing* from appearing brittle or bitter is a sense that the triumph of illusion is life-affirming, a sense that the friction between Beatrice and Benedick can be turned into mutual pleasure.

If the Claudio/Hero plot and the Beatrice/Benedick plot are two ways in which Shakespeare's comedy shows the saving necessity of illusion, there is a third manifestation: the illusion that evil manifests itself as Don John—that is, in a supremely incompetent and finally impotent form—and that, although it fools clear-eyed and sophisticated observers like Don Pedro, it may be exposed by a bumbling idiot like Dogberry. Some years later, Shakespeare returned to a ruthlessly disillusioned version of the same story, the lover tricked into believing that his beloved has been unfaithful, and called it not *Much Ado About Nothing* but *Othello.*

STEPHEN GREENBLATT

TEXTUAL NOTE

"Much adoe about Nothing . . . *Written by William Shakespeare*" was first published in 1600, in a quarto (Q) printed by Valentine Simmes (or Sims) for Andrew Wise and William Aspley. This is the only version of the play that appeared during Shakespeare's lifetime. The title page states that the play "hath been sundrie times publikely acted by the right honourable, the Lord Chamberlaine his seruants."

Much Ado About Nothing is listed in a Stationers' Register entry of August 4, 1600, along with *As You Like It, Henry V,* and Ben Jonson's *Every Man in His Humour.* All are marked "to be staied"—that is, not published without further permission. It is generally thought that the Lord Chamberlain's Men were attempting to ensure that they would be paid for any printing of these popular plays and that the release of *Much Ado About Nothing* later that same year indicates that the company had resolved whatever dispute had led them to stay publication.

Most scholars, including the Oxford editors, believe that the 1600 Quarto of *Much Ado About Nothing* was set from Shakespeare's "foul papers"—that is, his own manuscript of the play. Evidence includes the omission of several entrances and exits, certain loose ends in the dialogue, and the presence of "ghost" characters. For example, Q's stage directions at the beginning of Acts 1 and 2 list Leonato's wife, Innogen, but Innogen neither speaks nor is spoken to in the course of the play. Evidently she is the ghostly trace of an idea that the playwright abandoned.

Q's speech prefixes are inconsistent, another characteristic feature of foul papers, and in 4.2 they preserve the names of the actors Shakespeare had in mind for two of the comic parts: Will Kemp for Dogberry and Richard Cowley for Verges. Since Kemp left the Lord Chamberlain's Men in 1599, scholars think the play must have been first performed before the date of his departure. And since Francis Meres does not include *Much Ado About Nothing* in a list of Shakespeare's plays he compiled in September 1598 (unless that is what he meant by the play he calls *Loue Labours wonne*), scholars think it probable that the play was first performed after that date. Therefore the likeliest date of the first performance is the winter of 1598–99.

The First Folio (1623) text of the play (F) was based on Q. There are no act or scene divisions in Q; F indicates only act divisions (with the exception of 1.1).

SELECTED BIBLIOGRAPHY

Barish, Jonas A. "Pattern and Purpose in the Prose of *Much Ado About Nothing*." *Rice University Studies* 60.2 (Spring 1974): 19–30. Variations in the play's mannered rhetorical scheme offer insights into its characters and situations.

Berger, Harry, Jr. "Against the Sink-a-Pace: Sexual and Family Politics in *Much Ado About Nothing*." *Shakespeare Quarterly* 33 (1982): 302–13. Characterizes Messina's gender conventions in terms of virtue, constancy, reputation, deception, and fashion.

Berry, Ralph. *Shakespeare's Comedies: Explorations in Form.* Princeton: Princeton University Press, 1972. 154–74. Focusing on the difficult reconciliation of sensory experience and judgment, *Much Ado About Nothing* explores the limits of knowledge.

Cook, Carol. "'The Sign and Semblance of Her Honor': Reading Gender Difference in *Much Ado About Nothing*." *PMLA* 101.2 (1986): 186–202. The play presents the polysemous threat of woman in a world where men are the manipulators and interpreters of signs.

Everett, Barbara. "*Much Ado About Nothing*: The Unsociable Comedy." *English Comedy.* Ed. Michael Cordner, Peter Holland, and John Kerrigan. New York: Cambridge University Press, 1994. 68–84. Shakespeare's realistic portrait of love in society typically mixes its comic nothings with serious concerns.

Gay, Penny. "*Much Ado About Nothing*: A Kind of Merry War." *As She Likes It: Shakespeare's Unruly Women.* London: Routledge, 1994. 143–77. Performance history since the 1950s, spotlighting representations of Beatrice and Benedick.

Howard, Jean. "Renaissance Antitheatricality and the Politics of Gender and Rank in *Much Ado About Nothing*." *Shakespeare Reproduced: The Text in History and Ideology.* Ed. Jean E. Howard and Marion F. O'Connor. New York: Methuen, 1987. 163–87. *Much Ado About Nothing* supports Elizabethan ideology, condemning marginal social groups through accusations of illegitimate theatrical practice.

Moisan, Thomas. "Deforming Sources: Literary Antecedants and Their Traces in *Much Ado About Nothing*." *Shakespeare Studies* 31 (2003): 165–83. The play's furtive and ambivalent relationship to its sources reflects its depiction of character, politics, power, and representation.

Myhill, Nova. "Spectatorship in/of *Much Ado About Nothing.*" *Studies in English Literature* 39.2 (1999): 291–311. Considers how *Much Ado About Nothing*'s unreliable "notings" challenge the theater audience's assumptions of omniscience and invulnerability.

Salingar, Leo. "Borachio's Indiscretion: Some Noting about Much Ado." *The Italian World of English Renaissance Drama: Cultural Exchange and Intertextuality.* Ed. Michele Marrapodi. London: Associated University Presses, 1998. 225–38. *Much Ado About Nothing* as a bittersweet masquerade of social ambiguity and false communications.

Traugott, John. "Creating a Rational Rinaldo: A Study in the Mixture of the Genres of Comedy and Romance in *Much Ado About Nothing.*" *Genre* 15 (1982): 157–81. Shows how comedy and romance contaminate and purify each other, one becoming ennobled and the other cured of cruelty.

FILM

Much Ado About Nothing. 1993. Dir. Kenneth Branagh. UK/USA. 111 min. Festive romp set in sunny, country-house Italy. With Kenneth Branagh and Emma Thompson.

Much Ado About Nothing

THE PERSONS OF THE PLAY

DON PEDRO, Prince of Aragon
BENEDICK, of Padua
CLAUDIO, of Florence } lords, companions of Don Pedro
BALTHASAR, attendant on Don Pedro, a singer
DON JOHN, the bastard brother of Don Pedro
BORACHIO
CONRAD } followers of Don John
LEONATO, governor of Messina
HERO, his daughter
BEATRICE, an orphan, his niece
ANTONIO, an old man, brother of Leonato
MARGARET
URSULA } waiting-gentlewomen attendant on Hero
FRIAR FRANCIS
DOGBERRY, the Constable in charge of the Watch
VERGES, the Headborough, Dogberry's partner
A SEXTON
WATCHMEN
A BOY, serving Benedick
Attendants and messengers

1.1

Enter LEONATO, *governor of Messina,* HERO *his
daughter, and* BEATRICE *his niece, with a*
MESSENGER

LEONATO°   I learn in this letter that Don Pedro of Aragon comes
this night to Messina.

MESSENGER   He is very near by this. He was not three leagues off
when I left him.

5   LEONATO   How many gentlemen have you lost in this action?°   campaign

MESSENGER   But few of any sort,° and none of name.°   rank / distinction

LEONATO   A victory is twice itself when the achiever brings home
full numbers. I find here that Don Pedro hath bestowed much
honour on a young Florentine called Claudio.

10   MESSENGER   Much deserved on his part, and equally remem-
bered° by Don Pedro. He hath borne himself beyond the prom-   rewarded
ise of his age, doing in the figure of a lamb the feats of a lion.
He hath indeed better bettered° expectation than you must   exceeded
expect of me to tell you how.

15   LEONATO   He hath an uncle here in Messina will be very much
glad of it.

MESSENGER   I have already delivered him letters, and there
appears much joy in him—even so much that joy could not
show itself modest° enough without a badge° of bitterness.°   moderate / show / grief

---

1.1 Location: Messina (a city in Sicily). Before the house of Leonato.

322

20 LEONATO Did he break out into tears?

MESSENGER In great measure.

LEONATO A kind° overflow of kindness,° there are no faces truer   *natural / tenderness*
than those that are so washed. How much better is it to weep
at joy than to joy at weeping!

25 BEATRICE I pray you, is Signor Montanto¹ returned from the
wars, or no?

MESSENGER I know none of that name, lady. There was none
such in the army, of any sort.

LEONATO What is he that you ask for, niece?

30 HERO My cousin means Signor Benedick of Padua.²

MESSENGER O, he's returned, and as pleasant° as ever he was.   *entertaining*

BEATRICE He set up his bills° here in Messina, and challenged   *public notices*
Cupid at the flight;³ and my uncle's fool,° reading the chal-   *jester*
lenge, subscribed for Cupid and challenged him at the bird-
35 bolt.⁴ I pray you, how many hath he killed and eaten in these
wars? But how many hath he killed? For indeed I promised to
eat all of his killing.

LEONATO Faith, niece, you tax° Signor Benedick too much. But   *abuse*
he'll be meet° with you, I doubt it not.   *even*

40 MESSENGER He hath done good service, lady, in these wars.

BEATRICE You had musty victual, and he hath holp° to eat it. He   *helped*
is a very valiant trencherman,° he hath an excellent stomach.   *eater*

MESSENGER And a good soldier too, lady.

BEATRICE And a good soldier° to a lady, but what is he to a lord?   *servant; lady-killer*

45 MESSENGER A lord to a lord, a man to a man, stuffed° with all   *well furnished*
honourable virtues.

BEATRICE It is so, indeed. He is no less than a stuffed man.° But   *mannequin*
for the stuffing—well, we are all mortal.⁵

LEONATO You must not, sir, mistake my niece. There is a kind
50 of merry war betwixt Signor Benedick and her. They never
meet but there's a skirmish of wit between them.

BEATRICE Alas, he gets nothing by that. In our last conflict four
of his five wits⁶ went halting° off, and now is the whole man   *limping*
governed with one, so that if he have wit enough to keep him-
55 self warm,⁷ let him bear it for a difference⁸ between himself
and his horse, for it is all the wealth that he hath left to be
known a reasonable creature. Who is his companion now? He
hath every month a new sworn brother.

MESSENGER Is't possible?

60 BEATRICE Very easily possible. He wears his faith° but as the   *loyalty*
fashion of his hat, it ever changes with the next block.⁹

MESSENGER I see, lady, the gentleman is not in your books.°   *favor*

BEATRICE No. An° he were, I would burn my study. But I pray   *If*
you, who is his companion? Is there no young squarer° now   *boisterous quarreler*
65 that will make a voyage with him to the devil?

MESSENGER He is most in the company of the right noble
Claudio.

---

1. In fencing, a montanto is an upright blow or thrust.
2. A city in northern Italy.
3. To an archery match. (He claimed to surpass Cupid
at arousing love.)
4. To a contest using bird bolts, or blunt, short-range
arrows allowed to fools and children (and thus appro-
priate to young Cupid). *subscribed for*: took up the
challenge on behalf of.

5. But as for what he is made of (his "stuffing"), he is
probably as faulty as the rest of us.
6. *five wits*: mental faculties (memory, imagination,
judgment, fantasy, and common sense).
7. If he have minimal common sense.
8. Let him display the fact in his coat of arms in order
to distinguish himself.
9. Newest mold for a hat; fashion.

BEATRICE   O Lord, he will hang upon him like a disease. He is
    sooner caught than the pestilence,° and the taker° runs pres-   *plague / victim*
70   ently° mad. God help the noble Claudio. If he have caught the   *immediately*
    Benedick, it will cost him a thousand pound ere a° be cured.   *he*

MESSENGER   I will hold friends[1] with you, lady.

BEATRICE   Do, good friend.

LEONATO   You will never run mad,[2] niece.

75 BEATRICE   No, not till a hot January.

MESSENGER   Don Pedro is approached.

        Enter DON PEDRO, CLAUDIO, BENEDICK, BALTHASAR, *and*
        [DON] JOHN *the bastard*

DON PEDRO   Good Signor Leonato, are you come to meet your
    trouble? The fashion° of the world is to avoid cost, and you   *custom*
    encounter° it.   *go to meet*

80 LEONATO   Never came trouble to my house in the likeness of
    your grace; for trouble being gone, comfort should remain, but
    when you depart from me, sorrow abides and happiness takes
    his leave.

DON PEDRO   You embrace your charge° too willingly. I think this   *duty*
85 is your daughter.

LEONATO   Her mother hath many times told me so.

BENEDICK   Were you in doubt, sir, that you asked her?

LEONATO   Signor Benedick, no, for then were you a child.

DON PEDRO   You have it full,[3] Benedick. We may guess by this
90 what you are, being a man. Truly, the lady fathers herself.[4] Be
    happy, lady, for you are like an honourable father.

BENEDICK   If Signor Leonato be her father, she would not have
    his head;[5] on her shoulders for all Messina, as like him as she
    is.

95 BEATRICE[6]   I wonder that you will still° be talking, Signor Bene-   *always*
    dick. Nobody marks you.

BENEDICK   What, my dear Lady Disdain! Are you yet living?

BEATRICE   Is it possible disdain should die while she hath such
    meet° food to feed it as Signor Benedick? Courtesy itself must   *suitable*
100 convert° to disdain if you come in her presence.   *turn*

BENEDICK   Then is courtesy a turncoat. But it is certain I am
    loved of° all ladies, only you excepted. And I would I could   *by*
    find in my heart that I had not a hard heart, for truly I love
    none.

105 BEATRICE   A dear happiness to women. They would else have
    been troubled with a pernicious suitor. I thank God and my
    cold blood I am of your humour° for that. I had rather hear my   *disposition*
    dog bark at a crow than a man swear he loves me.

BENEDICK   God keep your ladyship still in that mind. So some
110 gentleman or other shall scape a predestinate° scratched face.   *escape an inevitable*

BEATRICE   Scratching could not make it worse an 'twere such a
    face as yours were.

BENEDICK   Well, you are a rare parrot-teacher.[7]

BEATRICE   A bird of my tongue is better than a beast of yours.[8]

---

1. I will stay on good terms (so as not to provoke your sarcasm).
2. "Catch the Benedick."
3. Your sarcasm is fully repaid.
4. She shows by her looks who her father is.
5. The head of an old man.

6. During Beatrice and Benedick's conversation, Don Pedro talks with Leonato (see line 119).
7. Chatterer (repetitive, like one who teaches a parrot to speak).
8. A bird with my powers of speech is better than a dumb beast who, like you, has none.

115 BENEDICK   I would my horse had the speed of your tongue,
and so good a continuer.⁹ But keep your way,° i' God's name. I   *carry on*
have done.

BEATRICE   You always end with a jade's trick.¹ I know you of old.

DON PEDRO   That is the sum of all, Leonato. Signor Claudio and
120   Signor Benedick, my dear friend Leonato hath invited you all.
I tell him we shall stay here at the least a month, and he heart-
ily prays some occasion may detain us longer. I dare swear he
is no hypocrite, but prays from his heart.

LEONATO   If you swear, my lord, you shall not be forsworn. [*To*
125   DON JOHN] Let me bid you welcome, my lord. Being° recon-   *Since you are*
ciled to the Prince your brother, I owe you all duty.

DON JOHN   I thank you. I am not of many words, but I thank you.

LEONATO [*to* DON PEDRO]   Please it your grace lead on?

DON PEDRO   Your hand, Leonato. We will go together.²

Exeunt. Manent° BENEDICK *and* CLAUDIO   *Remain*

130   CLAUDIO   Benedick, didst thou note the daughter of Signor Leo-
nato?

BENEDICK   I noted her not,³ but I looked on her.

CLAUDIO   Is she not a modest young lady?

BENEDICK   Do you question me as an honest man should do, for
135   my simple true judgement, or would you have me speak after
my custom, as being a professed tyrant° to their sex?   *pitiless critic*

CLAUDIO   No, I pray thee speak in sober judgement.

BENEDICK   Why, i'faith, methinks she's too low° for a high   *short*
praise, too brown for a fair praise, and too little for a great
140   praise. Only this commendation I can afford her, that were she
other than she is she were unhandsome, and being no other
but as she is, I do not like her.

CLAUDIO   Thou thinkest I am in sport.° I pray thee tell me truly   *jest*
how thou likest her.

145   BENEDICK   Would you buy her, that you enquire after her?

CLAUDIO   Can the world buy such a jewel?

BENEDICK   Yea, and a case to put it into. But speak you this with
a sad° brow, or do you play the flouting jack, to tell us Cupid   *serious*
is a good hare-finder and Vulcan a rare carpenter?⁴ Come, in
150   what key shall a man take° you to go° in the song?   *understand / join*

CLAUDIO   In mine eye she is the sweetest lady that ever I looked
on.

BENEDICK   I can see yet without spectacles, and I see no such
matter. There's her cousin, an she were not possessed with a
155   fury, exceeds her as much in beauty as the first of May doth the
last of December. But I hope you have no intent to turn hus-
band, have you?

CLAUDIO   I would scarce trust myself though I had sworn the
contrary, if Hero would be my wife.

160   BENEDICK   Is't come to this? In faith, hath not the world one
man but he will wear his cap with suspicion?⁵ Shall I never see

---

9. And had your staying power ("continuer," in horse-
manship, means "stayer").
1. A trick worthy of a badly trained horse (here, drop-
ping out of a race).
2. We will walk out hand in hand (and thus avoid tak-
ing precedence).
3. I paid her no special attention.
4. *play . . . carpenter:* spout praises contrary to fact and

intended satirically. Blind Cupid is poorly suited to the
sharp-sighted sport of hunting hares, while Vulcan, the
god of fire, was an excellent ("rare") blacksmith, not a
carpenter. *flouting jack:* mocking rogue.
5. *but . . . suspicion:* who will not be suspected of wear-
ing his cap in order to hide a cuckold's horns (conven-
tional sign of a wife's infidelity).

a bachelor of three-score again? Go to,° i'faith, an thou wilt   *Go on*
needs thrust thy neck into a yoke, wear the print of it, and sigh
away Sundays.[6] Look, Don Pedro is returned to seek you.

    Enter DON PEDRO

165 DON PEDRO   What secret hath held you here that you followed
not to Leonato's?

BENEDICK   I would your grace would constrain me to tell.

DON PEDRO   I charge thee on thy allegiance.

BENEDICK   You hear, Count Claudio? I can be secret as a dumb
170 man, I would have you think so. But on my allegiance, mark
you this, on my allegiance! He is in love. With who? Now that
is your grace's part. Mark how short his answer is: with Hero,
Leonato's short daughter.

CLAUDIO   If this were so, so were it uttered.[7]

175 BENEDICK   Like the old tale, my lord—it is not so, nor 'twas not
so, but indeed, God forbid it should be so.[8]

CLAUDIO   If my passion change not shortly, God forbid it should
be otherwise.

DON PEDRO   Amen, if you love her, for the lady is very well
180 worthy.

CLAUDIO   You speak this to fetch me in,° my lord.   *to trick me*

DON PEDRO   By my troth, I speak my thought.

CLAUDIO   And in faith, my lord, I spoke mine.

BENEDICK   And by my two faiths and troths,[9] my lord, I spoke
185 mine.

CLAUDIO   That I love her, I feel.

DON PEDRO   That she is worthy, I know.

BENEDICK   That I neither feel how she should be loved nor know
how she should be worthy is the opinion that fire cannot melt
190 out of me. I will die in it at the stake.

DON PEDRO   Thou wast ever an obstinate heretic in the despite°   *contempt*
of beauty.

CLAUDIO   And never could maintain his part° but in the force of   *argument*
his will.[1]

195 BENEDICK   That a woman conceived me, I thank her. That she
brought me up, I likewise give her most humble thanks. But
that I will have a recheat winded in my forehead, or hang my
bugle in an invisible baldric,[2] all women shall pardon me.
Because I will not do them the wrong to mistrust any,[3] I will
200 do myself the right to trust none. And the fine° is—for the   *conclusion*
which I may go the finer[4]—I will live a bachelor.

DON PEDRO   I shall see thee ere I die look pale with love.

BENEDICK   With anger, with sickness, or with hunger, my lord;
not with love. Prove° that ever I lose more blood with love than   *If you prove*
205 I will get again with drinking,[5] pick out mine eyes with a bal-

---

6. *thrust . . . Sundays:* take on the burdens and tedium
of marriage, when you might be enjoying yourself as a
bachelor.
7. *so . . . uttered:* this is how Benedick would tell it.
8. In an English fairy tale (a variant on the Bluebeard
story), a man suspected by his bride-to-be of having
killed his former wives denies his guilt with the refrain
Benedick quotes.
9. His loyalty to both Don Pedro and Claudio, and jok-
ingly, his duplicity.
1. But through prideful obstinacy rather than reason.
2. *But . . . baldric:* But that I should wear a cuckold's

horns. A recheat was a call sounded ("winded") on a
horn to recall the hounds. A baldric was a belt to hold
a horn ("bugle"); it was invisible, a sign of the cuckold's
ignorance.
3. Because I do not wish to wrong women by suspect-
ing any of infidelity.
4. I may dress better (because he will have more money
to spare).
5. *lose . . . drinking:* alluding to the belief that sighing
like a lover caused the blood to evaporate, and drinking
wine renewed it.

lad-maker's[6] pen and hang me up at the door of a brothel house
for the sign of blind Cupid.[7]

DON PEDRO Well, if ever thou dost fall from this faith thou wilt
prove a notable argument.°   *subject of talk*

210 BENEDICK If I do, hang me in a bottle like a cat, and shoot at
me,[8] and he that hits me, let him be clapped on the shoulder
and called Adam.[9]

DON PEDRO Well, as time shall try.° 'In time the savage bull doth   *prove*
bear the yoke.'[1]

215 BENEDICK The savage bull may, but if ever the sensible° Bene-   *rational*
dick bear it, pluck off the bull's horns and set them in my fore-
head, and let me be vilely painted, and in such great letters as
they write 'Here is good horse to hire' let them signify under
my sign 'Here you may see Benedick, the married man'.

220 CLAUDIO If this should ever happen thou wouldst be horn-mad.[2]

DON PEDRO Nay, if Cupid have not spent all his quiver in Ven-
ice[3] thou wilt quake for this shortly.

BENEDICK I look for an earthquake[4] too, then.

DON PEDRO Well, you will temporize with the hours.[5] In the
225 mean time, good Signor Benedick, repair° to Leonato's, com-   *go*
mend me to him, and tell him I will not fail him at supper, for
indeed he hath made great preparation.

BENEDICK I have almost matter° enough in me for such an   *intelligence*
embassage.° And so I commit you—   *errand*

230 CLAUDIO To the tuition[6] of God, from my house if I had it—

DON PEDRO The sixth of July,
Your loving friend,
Benedick.

BENEDICK Nay, mock not, mock not. The body of your dis-
course is sometime guarded with fragments,[7] and the guards
are but slightly basted on[8] neither. Ere you flout° old ends° any   *mock / clichés*
235 further, examine your conscience. And so I leave you.   *Exit*

CLAUDIO My liege, your highness now may do me good.

DON PEDRO My love is thine to teach. Teach it but how
And thou shalt see how apt it is to learn
Any hard lesson that may do thee good.

240 CLAUDIO Hath Leonato any son, my lord?

DON PEDRO No child but Hero. She's his only heir.
Dost thou affect° her, Claudio?   *love*

CLAUDIO   O my lord,
When you went onward on this ended action°   *campaign*
I looked upon her with a soldier's eye,
245 That liked, but had a rougher task in hand
Than to drive liking to the name of love.
But now I am returned, and that° war-thoughts   *now that*

---

6. Popular love poet or satirist.
7. A painted sign, such as might hang before a brothel.
8. *hang . . . me:* cats in baskets ("bottles") were com-
mon Elizabethan targets for recreational archery.
9. Perhaps Adam Bell, a celebrated archer.
1. Proverbial; here, apparently a variation on a line
from Thomas Kyd's *Spanish Tragedy* (c. 1587): "In time
the savage bull sustains the yoke" (2.1.3).
2. Furious, raving like a wild beast (referring to the
rage of a cuckolded husband).
3. Venice was famous in Shakespeare's time for its beau-
tiful courtesans. *spent all his quiver:* used all his arrows.

4. An earthquake would be as unlikely as my quaking
with love.
5. You will soften as time passes; with perhaps a bawdy
pun on "hours," "whores" (pronounced similarly).
6. Protection (Claudio and Don Pedro parody a con-
ventional formula for ending a letter).
7. *The body . . . fragments:* The substance (also pun-
ning on the dressmaker's "bodice") of what you say is
sometimes ornamented ("guarded") with odds and ends
("fragments") such as you are mocking me for using.
8. And the decorative phrases are barely relevant.

Have left their places vacant, in their rooms
Come thronging soft and delicate desires,
250   All prompting me how fair young Hero is,
Saying I liked her ere I went to wars.

DON PEDRO   Thou wilt be like a lover presently,
And tire the hearer with a book of words.°   *lover's set speeches*
If thou dost love fair Hero, cherish it,
255   And I will break° with her, and with her father,   *speak*
And thou shalt have her. Was't not to this end
That thou began'st to twist° so fine a story?   *spin*

CLAUDIO   How sweetly you do minister to love,
That know love's grief by his complexion!°   *by its appearance*
260   But lest my liking might too sudden seem
I would have salved° it with a longer treatise.   *smoothed*

DON PEDRO   What need the bridge much broader than the flood?°   *river*
The fairest grant is the necessity.[9]
Look what° will serve is fit. 'Tis once:° thou lovest,   *Whatever / In brief*
265   And I will fit thee with the remedy.
I know we shall have revelling° tonight.   *festivity; masked ball*
I will assume thy part° in some disguise,   *role*
And tell fair Hero I am Claudio.
And in her bosom I'll unclasp my heart[1]
270   And take her hearing prisoner with the force
And strong encounter° of my amorous tale.   *assault*
Then after to her father will I break,
And the conclusion is, she shall be thine.
In practice let us put it presently.°   *Exeunt*   *at once*

1.2

Enter LEONATO *and* [ANTONIO,] *an old man brother to
Leonato,* [*severally*]°   *separately*

LEONATO   How now, brother, where is my cousin,° your son?   *kinsman (nephew)*
Hath he provided this music?

ANTONIO   He is very busy about it. But brother, I can tell you
strange news that you yet dreamt not of.

5   LEONATO   Are they good?

ANTONIO   As the event stamps them.[1] But they have a good
cover, they show well outward. The Prince and Count Clau-
dio, walking in a thick-pleached[2] alley in mine orchard,° were   *garden*
thus much overheard by a man of mine: the Prince discovered°   *revealed*
10   to Claudio that he loved my niece, your daughter, and meant
to acknowledge it this night in a dance, and if he found her
accordant° he meant to take the present time by the top[3] and   *consenting*
instantly break° with you of it.   *speak*

LEONATO   Hath the fellow any wit° that told you this?   *intelligence*
15   ANTONIO   A good sharp fellow. I will send for him, and question
him yourself.

LEONATO   No, no. We will hold it as a dream till it appear° itself.   *manifest*
But I will acquaint my daughter withal,° that she may be the   *with it*

---

9. The best gift is something that is truly needed.
1. And I will privately reveal to her my feelings (as if
I were you).
1.2 Location: Leonato's house.
1. As good as the outcome ("event") proves ("stamps")

them. The image is of news bound in a book with a
handsome cover.
2. Enclosed by trees with intertwining boughs.
3. He meant to seize the opportunity. (Time is prover-
bially bald except for the "top," or forelock.)

better prepared for an answer if peradventure° this be true. Go
20 you and tell her of it.
    [*Enter Attendants*]⁴
Cousins, you know what you have to do. O, I cry you mercy,⁵
friend. Go you with me and I will use your skill.—Good
cousin, have a care this busy time.   *Exeunt*

by chance

1.3

    Enter [DON] JOHN *the bastard and* CONRAD, *his com-
panion*

CONRAD   What the goodyear, my lord, why are you thus out of
measure¹ sad?
DON JOHN   There is no measure in the occasion that breeds it,
therefore the sadness is without limit.
5 CONRAD   You should hear reason.
DON JOHN   And when I have heard it, what blessing brings it?
CONRAD   If not a present° remedy, at least a patient sufferance.   *an immediate*
DON JOHN   I wonder that thou—being, as thou sayst thou art,
born under Saturn²—goest about to apply a moral medicine to
10 a mortifying mischief.° I cannot hide what I am. I must be sad *a deadly sickness*
when I have cause, and smile at no man's jests; eat when I have
stomach,° and wait for no man's leisure; sleep when I am   *appetite*
drowsy, and tend on° no man's business; laugh when I am   *attend to*
merry, and claw° no man in his humour.°   *flatter / mood*
15 CONRAD   Yea, but you must not make the full show of this till
you may do it without controlment.° You have of late stood *restraint*
out° against your brother, and he hath ta'en you newly into his *rebelled*
grace,° where it is impossible you should take true root but by *favor*
the fair weather that you make yourself. It is needful that you
20 frame the season for your own harvest.
DON JOHN   I had rather be a canker° in a hedge than a rose³ in *wild rose; weed*
his grace, and it better fits my blood° to be disdained of all than *disposition*
to fashion° a carriage° to rob love from any. In this, though I *affect; feign / behavior*
cannot be said to be a flattering honest man, it must not be
25 denied but I am a plain-dealing villain. I am trusted with a
muzzle, and enfranchised with a clog.⁴ Therefore I have
decreed° not to sing in my cage. If I had my mouth I would *determined*
bite. If I had my liberty I would do my liking. In the mean
time, let me be that I am, and seek not to alter me.
30 CONRAD   Can you make no use of your discontent?
DON JOHN   I make all use of it, for I use it only. Who comes
here?
    Enter BORACHIO⁵
What news, Borachio?
BORACHIO   I came yonder from a great supper. The Prince your

---

4. The attendants are evidently engaged in prepara-
tions for the reveling (2.1). "Cousins" (line 21) may be
dependents in Leonato's household.
5. I beg your pardon (perhaps because he has not ini-
tially recognized one of the attendants, or because he
has bumped into him). Leonato's reference to "skill"
suggests that he might be talking to a musician.
1.3 Location: Leonato's house.
1. *What the goodyear:* unexplained exclamation. *out of
measure:* disproportionately.

2. Born when Saturn was in the ascendant (therefore
"saturnine," melancholy).
3. Cultivated rose.
4. I am trusted by being muzzled (in other words, not
trusted at all), and given my freedom with a clog (a
heavy block of wood attached to an animal or man as a
restraint).
5. The name, from the Spanish for "wine bottle," was
used for drunkards.

35 brother is royally entertained by Leonato, and I can give you
intelligence of an intended marriage.

DON JOHN   Will it serve for any model° to build mischief on?   *ground plan*
What is he for a fool⁶ that betroths himself to unquietness?

BORACHIO   Marry,⁷ it is your brother's right hand.

40 DON JOHN   Who, the most exquisite Claudio?

BORACHIO   Even he.

DON JOHN   A proper squire.⁸ And who, and who? Which way
looks he?

BORACHIO   Marry, on Hero, the daughter and heir of Leonato.

45 DON JOHN   A very forward March chick.⁹ How came you to this?

BORACHIO   Being entertained for a perfumer,¹ as I was smoking°   *perfuming*
a musty room comes me the Prince and Claudio hand in hand,
in sad° conference. I whipped me behind the arras,° and there   *serious / wall hanging*
heard it agreed upon that the Prince should woo Hero for him-
50 self and, having obtained her, give her to Count Claudio.

DON JOHN   Come, come, let us thither. This may prove food to
my displeasure.° That young start-up° hath all the glory of my   *hatred / upstart*
overthrow. If I can cross² him any way I bless myself every way.
You are both sure,° and will assist me?   *reliable*

55 CONRAD   To the death, my lord.

DON JOHN   Let us to the great supper. Their cheer is the greater
that° I am subdued. Would the cook were o' my mind.³ Shall   *since*
we go prove° what's to be done?   *find out*

BORACHIO   We'll wait° upon your lordship.   *Exeunt*   *attend*

2.1

Enter LEONATO, [ANTONIO] *his brother,* HERO *his daugh-*
ter, BEATRICE *his niece[,* MARGARET, *and* URSULA]

LEONATO   Was not Count John here at supper?

ANTONIO   I saw him not.

BEATRICE   How tartly° that gentleman looks. I never can see him   *sour*
but I am heartburned¹ an hour after.

5 HERO   He is of a very melancholy disposition.

BEATRICE   He were° an excellent man that were made just in the   *would be*
midway between him and Benedick. The one is too like an
image° and says nothing, and the other too like my lady's eldest   *a statue*
son,² evermore tattling.°   *chattering*

10 LEONATO   Then half Signor Benedick's tongue in Count John's
mouth, and half Count John's melancholy in Signor Benedick's
face—

BEATRICE   With a good leg and a good foot, uncle, and money
enough in his purse—such a man would win any woman in
15 the world, if a° could get her good will.   *he*

LEONATO   By my troth, niece, thou wilt never get thee a husband
if thou be so shrewd° of thy tongue.   *shrewish*

ANTONIO   In faith, she's too curst.°   *sharp-tongued*

BEATRICE   Too curst is more³ than curst. I shall lessen God's

---

6. What kind of fool is he.
7. By the Virgin Mary (a mild oath).
8. A fine young lover (ironic).
9. Precocious youngster, like a bird hatched early in the season.
1. Being hired to burn sweet herbs (to mask unpleasant domestic odors).

2. Thwart (punning on "make the sign of the cross").
3. *o' my mind:* inclined to poison the food.
2.1 Location: Leonato's house.
1. I suffer from heartburn, caused by Don John's tart looks.
2. That is, a spoiled child.
3. By one, punning on "too/two."

20 sending that way, for it is said God sends a curst cow short
horns,[4] but to a cow too curst he sends none.

LEONATO So, by being too curst, God will send you no horns.

BEATRICE Just,° if he send me no husband,[5] for the which bless-   *Just so*
ing I am at him upon my knees every morning and evening.

25 Lord, I could not endure a husband with a beard on his face. I
had rather lie in the woollen.[6]

LEONATO You may light on a husband that hath no beard.

BEATRICE What should I do with him—dress him in my apparel
and make him my waiting gentlewoman? He that hath a beard

30 is more than a youth, and he that hath no beard is less than a
man; and he that is more than a youth is not for me, and he
that is less than a man, I am not for him. Therefore I will even
take sixpence in earnest of the bearherd and lead his apes into
hell.[7]

35 LEONATO Well then, go you into hell?

BEATRICE No, but° to the gate, and there will the devil meet me   *only*
like an old cuckold with horns on his head, and say, 'Get you
to heaven, Beatrice, get you to heaven. Here's no place for you
maids.' So deliver I up my apes and away to Saint Peter fore

40 the heavens.[8] He shows me where the bachelors[9] sit, and there
live we as merry as the day is long.

ANTONIO [*to* HERO] Well, niece, I trust you will be ruled by your
father.

BEATRICE Yes, faith, it is my cousin's duty to make curtsy and

45 say, 'Father, as it please you.' But yet for all that, cousin, let
him be a handsome fellow, or else make another curtsy and
say, 'Father, as it please me.'

LEONATO Well, niece, I hope to see you one day fitted with a
husband.

50 BEATRICE Not till God make men of some other mettle° than   *substance*
earth. Would it not grieve a woman to be overmastered with° a   *by*
piece of valiant dust?—to make an account of her life to a clod
of wayward marl?° No, uncle, I'll none. Adam's sons are my   *clay*
brethren, and truly I hold it a sin to match in my kindred.[1]

55 LEONATO [*to* HERO] Daughter, remember what I told you. If the
Prince do solicit you in that kind,[2] you know your answer.

BEATRICE The fault will be in the music, cousin, if you be not
wooed in good time. If the Prince be too important,° tell him   *importunate*
there is measure[3] in everything, and so dance out the answer.

60 For hear me, Hero, wooing, wedding, and repenting is as a
Scotch jig, a measure, and a cinquepace.[4] The first suit° is hot   *courtship*
and hasty, like a Scotch jig—and full as fantastical; the wed-
ding mannerly° modest, as a measure, full of state and   *graciously*
ancientry.° And then comes repentance, and with his bad legs   *old-fashioned decorum*

---

4. Proverbial: God makes sure that the vicious ("curst")
have little power to do harm.
5. That is, if God sent her a husband, she would cuck-
old him.
6. Sleep between rough blankets (without sheets).
7. *take . . . hell*: take advance payment from the bear
keeper (who trained bears for the popular sport of bear-
baiting and who usually had charge of other animals);
leading apes into hell was the proverbial fate of old
maids.

8. Peter is gatekeeper of heaven. Q prints "Peter: for
the heavens"; it is possible that Beatrice means "as far
as heaven is concerned."
9. Unwed men or women.
1. *to . . . kindred*: to marry incestuously.
2. *in that kind*: that is, to marry him.
3. Moderation (punning on the name of a slow, stately
dance [line 63] and continuing the link between danc-
ing and wooing "in good time" [line 58]).
4. A lively five-step dance.

65   falls into the cinquepace faster and faster till he sink into his
    grave.

LEONATO   Cousin, you apprehend passing° shrewdly.   *understand more than*

BEATRICE   I have a good eye, uncle. I can see a church by day-
    light.[5]

70 LEONATO   The revellers are entering, brother. Make good room.

    *Enter [*DON*] PEDRO [the] Prince,* CLAUDIO, BENEDICK,
    and BALTHASAR, DON JOHN, *[and* BORACHIO, *as] Mask-
    ers, with a drum*

DON PEDRO *[to* HERO*]*   Lady, will you walk a bout with your
    friend?[6]

HERO   So you walk softly, and look sweetly, and say nothing, I
    am yours for the walk; and especially when I walk away.

75 DON PEDRO   With me in your company?

HERO   I may say so when I please.

DON PEDRO   And when please you to say so?

HERO   When I like your favour;° for God defend the lute should   *face*
    be like the case.[7]

80 DON PEDRO   My visor° is Philemon's roof. Within the house is   *mask*
    Jove.[8]

HERO   Why, then, your visor should be thatched.[9]

DON PEDRO   Speak low if
    you speak love.
    [They move aside]

BALTHASAR *[to* MARGARET*]*   Well, I would you did like me.

MARGARET   So would not I, for your own sake, for I have many
85   ill° qualities.   *bad*

BALTHASAR   Which is one?

MARGARET   I say my prayers aloud.

BALTHASAR   I love you the better—the hearers may cry amen.

MARGARET   God match me with a good dancer.

90 BALTHASAR   Amen.

MARGARET   And God keep him out of my sight when the dance
    is done. Answer, clerk.[1]

BALTHASAR   No more words. The clerk is answered.
    [They move aside]

URSULA *[to* ANTONIO*]*   I know you well enough, you are Signor
95   Antonio.

ANTONIO   At a word,° I am not.   *In short*

URSULA   I know you by the waggling of your head.

ANTONIO   To tell you true, I counterfeit him.

URSULA   You could never do him so ill-well[2] unless you were the
100   very man. Here's his dry hand up and down.[3] You are he, you
    are he.

ANTONIO   At a word, I am not.

URSULA   Come, come, do you think I do not know you by your

---

5. That is, see what's in front of me.
6. Often used to mean "lover." *walk a bout*: take a turn
(apparently a term in dancing).
7. God forbid your face should be as unappealing as
your mask.
8. The peasant Philemon and his wife, Baucis, enter-
tained Jove, disguised, in their humble cottage (Ovid,
Metamorphoses 8). This and the following line are in
"fourteeners," a verse form old-fashioned in Shake-

speare's time but used by Arthur Golding in his 1567
translation of the *Metamorphoses*.
9. According to Golding, Philemon's roof was
"thatched all with straw"; Hero means that the mask
should be fitted with false hair or beard.
1. That is, say "Amen" again. The parish clerk led the
responses in church services.
2. *do him so ill-well*: mime his imperfections so ably.
3. His wrinkled hand exactly.

105 excellent wit? Can virtue° hide itself ? Go to, mum,° you are *excellence / be quiet*
he. Graces will appear, and there's an end.⁴

　　　[*They move aside*]

BEATRICE [*to* BENEDICK]　　Will you not tell me who told you so?

BENEDICK　　No, you shall pardon me.

BEATRICE　　Nor will you not tell me who you are?

BENEDICK　　Not now.

110 BEATRICE　　That I was disdainful, and that I had my good wit out
of the Hundred Merry Tales⁵—well, this was Signor Benedick
that said so.

BENEDICK　　What's he?

BEATRICE　　I am sure you know him well enough.

115 BENEDICK　　Not I, believe me.

BEATRICE　　Did he never make you laugh?

BENEDICK　　I pray you, what is he?

BEATRICE　　Why, he is the Prince's jester, a very dull fool. Only
his° gift is in devising impossible° slanders. None but libertines　*His only / unbelievable*
120 delight in him, and the commendation is not in his wit but in
his villainy,° for he both pleases men and angers them, and　*rudeness*
then they laugh at him, and beat him. I am sure he is in the
fleet.° I would he had boarded me.⁶　*company (of dancers)*

BENEDICK　　When I know the gentleman, I'll tell him what you
125 say.

BEATRICE　　Do, do. He'll but break a comparison⁷ or two on me,
which peradventure° not marked, or not laughed at, strikes him　*perhaps*
into melancholy, and then there's a partridge wing saved, for
the fool will eat no supper that night.

　　　Music

130 We must follow the leaders.°　*leaders in the dance*

BENEDICK　　In every good thing.

BEATRICE　　Nay, if they lead to any ill I will leave them at the
next turning.

　　　Dance. Exeunt [*all but* DON JOHN, BORACHIO, *and*
　　　CLAUDIO]

DON JOHN [*aside to* BORACHIO]　　Sure my brother is amorous on
135 Hero, and hath withdrawn her father to break with him about
it. The ladies follow her, and but one visor° remains.　*(man wearing a) mask*

BORACHIO [*aside to* DON JOHN]　　And that is Claudio. I know him
by his bearing.

DON JOHN　　Are not you Signor Benedick?

140 CLAUDIO　　You know me well. I am he.

DON JOHN　　Signor, you are very near my brother in his love.° He　*favor*
is enamoured on Hero. I pray you dissuade him from her. She
is no equal for his birth. You may do the part of an honest man
in it.

145 CLAUDIO　　How know you he loves her?

DON JOHN　　I heard him swear his affection.

BORACHIO　　So did I, too, and he swore he would marry her
tonight.

DON JOHN　　Come, let us to the banquet.°　*after-dinner sweets*

　　　Exeunt. Manet° CLAUDIO　*Remains*

---

4. And that is all there is to be said.
5. A famously bad joke-book, first published in 1526.
6. Assaulted me like a ship.

7. He'll only try out, or "crack," a satirical comparison
(as one "breaks" a lance).

150	CLAUDIO Thus answer I in name of Benedick,	
	But hear these ill news with the ears of Claudio.	
	'Tis certain° so, the Prince woos for himself.	*certainly*
	Friendship is constant in all other things	
	Save in the office° and affairs of love.	*business*
155	Therefore all° hearts in love use their own tongues.	*let all*
	Let every eye negotiate for itself,	
	And trust no agent; for beauty is a witch	
	Against whose charms faith° melteth into blood.°	*loyalty / passion*
	This is an accident of hourly proof,[8]	
160	Which I mistrusted° not. Farewell, therefore, Hero.	*suspected*

Enter BENEDICK

BENEDICK   Count Claudio?

CLAUDIO   Yea, the same.

BENEDICK   Come, will you go with me?

CLAUDIO   Whither?

165	BENEDICK Even to the next willow,[9] about your own business,	
	County.° What fashion will you wear the garland° of ? About	*Count / (of willow)*
	your neck, like an usurer's chain?[1] Or under your arm, like a	
	lieutenant's scarf?[2] You must wear it one° way, for the Prince	*some*
	hath got your Hero.	
170	CLAUDIO I wish him joy of her.	
	BENEDICK Why, that's spoken like an honest drover;° so they sell	*cattle dealer*
	bullocks. But did you think the Prince would have served you	
	thus?	
	CLAUDIO I pray you leave me.	
175	BENEDICK Ho, now you strike like the blind man—'twas the boy	
	that stole your meat, and you'll beat the post.[3]	
	CLAUDIO If it° will not be, I'll leave you. *Exit*	*(your departure)*
	BENEDICK Alas, poor hurt fowl, now will he creep into sedges.[4]	
	But that my Lady Beatrice should know me, and not know me!	
180	The Prince's fool! Ha, it may be I go under that title because I	
	am merry. Yea, but so I am apt to do myself wrong. I am not so	
	reputed. It is the base, though bitter, disposition of Beatrice	
	that puts the world into her person, and so gives me out.[5] Well,	
	I'll be revenged as I may.	

Enter [DON PEDRO *the*] *Prince*

185	DON PEDRO Now, signor, where's the Count? Did you see him?	
	BENEDICK Troth, my lord, I have played the part of Lady Fame.°	*Lady Rumor*
	I found him here as melancholy as a lodge in a warren.[6] I told	
	him—and I think I told him true—that your grace had got the	
	good will of this young lady, and I offered him my company to	
190	a willow tree, either to make him a garland, as being forsaken,	
	or to bind him up a rod,° as being worthy to be whipped.	*bundle of sticks*
	DON PEDRO To be whipped—what's his fault?	
	BENEDICK The flat° transgression of a schoolboy who, being	*stupid*
	overjoyed with finding a bird's nest, shows it his companion,	
195	and he steals it.	

8. This is an occurrence demonstrated every hour, common event.
9. Symbol of unrequited love.
1. A gold chain worn by a moneylender.
2. A sash across the chest.
3. Probably alluding to a folktale, which existed in various forms, of a boy who robbed and played a trick on his blind master. *post:* pillar (with play on Benedick as

the "post," or messenger, who bears bad news).
4. *creep into sedges:* hide to nurse his wounds, as an injured bird crawls into the tall grass along a riverbank.
5. It is Beatrice's low but sarcastic disposition that makes her believe the whole world is of her opinion and represents me accordingly.
6. As a burrow in a rabbit warren. (The rabbit was a traditional symbol of melancholy.)

DON PEDRO   Wilt thou make a trust a transgression? The transgression is in the stealer.

BENEDICK   Yet it had not been amiss the rod had been made, and the garland too, for the garland he might have worn himself, and the rod he might have bestowed on you, who, as I take it, have stolen his bird's nest.

DON PEDRO   I will but teach them° to sing, and restore them to the owner.   *(the chicks)*

BENEDICK   If their singing answer your saying, by my faith you say honestly.[7]

DON PEDRO   The Lady Beatrice hath a quarrel to° you. The gentleman that danced with her told her she is much wronged by you.   *with*

BENEDICK   O, she misused° me past the endurance of a block.   *abused*
An oak but with one green leaf on it[8] would have answered her. My very visor began to assume life and scold with her. She told me—not thinking I had been myself—that I was the Prince's jester, that I was duller than a great thaw,[9] huddling jest upon jest with such impossible conveyance° upon me that   *speed*
I stood like a man at a mark,° with a whole army shooting at   *target*
me. She speaks poniards,° and every word stabs. If her breath   *daggers*
were as terrible as her terminations,° there were no living near   *expressions*
her, she would infect to the North Star.[1] I would not marry her though she were endowed with all that Adam had left him before he transgressed. She would have made Hercules have turned spit, yea, and have cleft his club to make the fire, too.[2] Come, talk not of her. You shall find her the infernal Ate° in   *goddess of discord*
good apparel. I would to God some scholar would conjure[3] her, for certainly, while she is here a man may live as quiet in hell as in a sanctuary, and people sin upon purpose because they would go thither, so indeed all disquiet, horror, and perturbation follows° her.   *attends upon*

Enter CLAUDIO *and* BEATRICE, [*and*] LEONATO [*with*]
HERO

DON PEDRO   Look, here she comes.

BENEDICK   Will your grace command me any service to the world's end? I will go on the slightest errand now to the Antipodes that you can devise to send me on. I will fetch you a toothpicker° now from the furthest inch of Asia, bring you the length   *toothpick*
of Prester John's foot, fetch you a hair off the Great Cham's beard, do you any embassage to the pigmies,[4] rather than hold three words' conference with this harpy.[5] You have no employment for me?

DON PEDRO   None but to desire your good company.

BENEDICK   O God, sir, here's a dish I love not. I cannot endure my Lady Tongue.   *Exit*

---

7. If they sing as you say they will—if you have wooed Hero for Claudio—then you are talking honorably.
8. An oak with barely any life remaining in it.
9. When the muddy roads kept everyone at home.
1. Thought to be the remotest star.
2. The Amazon Omphale made Hercules wear her clothes and spin; Benedick imagines an even greater humiliation and more menial duty—turning the spit.
3. Conjure the evil spirits out of, or supernaturally

consign to hell. *scholar:* learned person (who could speak Latin, the language of exorcism).
4. *Prester John's . . . pigmies:* all distant, fantastic figures. In legend, Prester John ruled in Ethiopia, while the Great Cham (Kublai Khan) reigned in Mongolia, and a race of dwarfs was said to inhabit the mountains of India.
5. Mythical creature with the face and body of a woman and the wings and claws of a bird of prey.

240 DON PEDRO   Come, lady, come, you have lost the heart of Signor
      Benedick.
    BEATRICE   Indeed, my lord, he lent it me a while, and I gave   *interest*
      him use° for it, a double heart for his single one. Marry, once
      before he won it of ° me, with false dice. Therefore your grace   *from*
245   may well say I have lost it.
    DON PEDRO   You have put him down, lady, you have put him
      down.[6]
    BEATRICE   So I would not he should do me, my lord, lest I
      should prove the mother of fools. I have brought Count Clau-
250   dio, whom you sent me to seek.
    DON PEDRO   Why, how now, Count, wherefore are you sad?
    CLAUDIO   Not sad, my lord.
    DON PEDRO   How then? Sick?
    CLAUDIO   Neither, my lord.
255 BEATRICE   The Count is neither sad, nor sick, nor merry, nor
      well, but civil° count, civil[7] as an orange, and something° of   *serious / somewhat*
      that jealous complexion.[8]
    DON PEDRO   I'faith, lady, I think your blazon° to be true, though *formal description*
      I'll be sworn, if he be so, his conceit° is false. Here, Claudio, I   *imagined idea*
260   have wooed in thy name, and fair Hero is won. I have broke°   *spoken*
      with her father and his good will obtained. Name the day of
      marriage, and God give thee joy.
    LEONATO   Count, take of me my daughter, and with her my for-
      tunes. His grace hath made the match, and all grace say amen
265   to it.[9]
    BEATRICE   Speak, Count, 'tis your cue.
    CLAUDIO   Silence is the perfectest herald of joy. I were but little
      happy if I could say how much. [*To* HERO] Lady, as you are
      mine, I am yours. I give away myself for you, and dote upon
270   the exchange.
    BEATRICE [*to* HERO]   Speak, cousin. Or, if you cannot, stop his
      mouth with a kiss, and let not him speak, neither.
    DON PEDRO   In faith, lady, you have a merry heart.
    BEATRICE   Yea, my lord, I thank it. Poor fool, it keeps on the
275   windy° side of care.—My cousin tells him in his ear that he is   *windward; safe*
      in her heart.
    CLAUDIO   And so she doth, cousin.
    BEATRICE   Good Lord, for alliance![1] Thus goes everyone to the
      world but I, and I am sunburnt.[2] I may sit in a corner and cry
280   'Heigh-ho for a husband'.[3]
    DON PEDRO   Lady Beatrice, I will get you one.
    BEATRICE   I would rather have one of your father's getting.° Hath *begetting*
      your grace ne'er a° brother like you? Your father got excellent   *no*
      husbands if a maid could come by them.
285 DON PEDRO   Will you have me, lady?
    BEATRICE   No, my lord, unless I might have another for working

---

6. Humiliated him. (Beatrice, in reply, puns on the
physical sense.)
7. Punning on "Seville," famous for its bitter oranges.
8. Yellow (the traditional color of jealousy).
9. And may God, the source of all grace, confirm it.
1. Kinship through marriage. (Claudio has just

addressed Beatrice as one of the family.)
2. Unattractive, and therefore unlikely to marry.
(Suntans, like dark complexions, were unfashionable.)
goes . . . to the world: gets married.
3. Title of a ballad; probably a catchphrase in Shake-
speare's time.

days. Your grace is too costly to wear every day. But I beseech
your grace, pardon me. I was born to speak all mirth and no
matter.°   *substance*

290 DON PEDRO   Your silence most offends me, and to be merry best
becomes you; for out o' question, you were born in a merry
hour.

BEATRICE   No, sure, my lord, my mother cried. But then there
was a star danced, and under that was I born. [*To* HERO *and*
295   CLAUDIO] Cousins, God give you joy.

LEONATO   Niece, will you look to those things I told you of?

BEATRICE   I cry you mercy,° uncle. [*To* DON PEDRO] By your
grace's pardon.   *Exit* BEATRICE   *I beg your pardon*

DON PEDRO   By my troth, a pleasant-spirited lady.

300 LEONATO   There's little of the melancholy element in her, my
lord. She is never sad° but when she sleeps, and not ever° sad   *serious / not always*
then; for I have heard my daughter say she hath often dreamt
of unhappiness and waked herself with laughing.

DON PEDRO   She cannot endure to hear tell of a husband.

305 LEONATO   O, by no means. She mocks all her wooers out of suit.°   *wooing (her)*

DON PEDRO   She were an excellent wife for Benedick.

LEONATO   O Lord, my lord, if they were but a week married they
would talk themselves mad.

DON PEDRO   County Claudio, when mean you to go to church?

310 CLAUDIO   Tomorrow, my lord. Time goes on crutches till love
have all his rites.

LEONATO   Not till Monday, my dear son, which is hence a just
sevennight, and a time too brief, too, to have all things answer°   *match*
my mind.°   *wishes*

315 DON PEDRO   Come, you shake the head at so long a breathing,°   *an interval*
but I warrant° thee, Claudio, the time shall not go dully by us.   *assure*
I will in the interim undertake one of Hercules' labours, which
is to bring Signor Benedick and the Lady Beatrice into a moun-
tain of affection th'one with th'other. I would fain° have it a   *gladly*
320 match, and I doubt not but to fashion it, if you three will but
minister such assistance as I shall give you direction.

LEONATO   My lord, I am for you, though it cost me ten nights'
watchings.°   *staying awake*

CLAUDIO   And I, my lord.

325 DON PEDRO   And you too, gentle Hero?

HERO   I will do any modest office,° my lord, to help my cousin   *task*
to a good husband.

DON PEDRO   And Benedick is not the unhopefullest° husband   *least promising*
that I know. Thus far can I praise him: he is of a noble strain,°   *descent*
330 of approved° valour and confirmed honesty.° I will teach you   *proven / honor*
how to humour your cousin that she shall fall in love with
Benedick, and I, with your two helps, will so practise on°   *so trick*
Benedick that, in despite of his quick wit and his queasy stom-
ach,° he shall fall in love with Beatrice. If we can do this,   *qualms (about love)*
335 Cupid is no longer an archer; his glory shall be ours, for we are
the only love-gods. Go in with me, and I will tell you my drift.°   *scheme*
                                                   Exeunt

2.2

Enter [DON] JOHN *and* BORACHIO

DON JOHN It is so. The Count Claudio shall marry the daughter
of Leonato.

BORACHIO Yea, my lord, but I can cross° it.   *thwart*

DON JOHN Any bar, any cross, any impediment will be medi-
5 cinable° to me. I am sick in displeasure to him, and whatsoever   *medicinal*
comes athwart his affection ranges evenly with mine.[1] How
canst thou cross this marriage?

BORACHIO Not honestly, my lord, but so covertly that no dishon-
esty shall appear in me.

10 DON JOHN Show me briefly how.

BORACHIO I think I told your lordship a year since how much
I am in the favour of Margaret, the waiting gentlewoman to
Hero.

DON JOHN I remember.

15 BORACHIO I can at any unseasonable instant of the night
appoint° her to look out at her lady's chamber window.   *arrange with*

DON JOHN What life is in that to be the death of this marriage?

BORACHIO The poison of that lies in you to temper.° Go you to   *concoct*
the Prince your brother. Spare not to tell him that he hath
20 wronged his honour in marrying the renowned Claudio—
whose estimation° do you mightily hold up°—to a contami-   *reputation / esteem*
nated stale,° such a one as Hero.   *prostitute*

DON JOHN What proof shall I make of that?

BORACHIO Proof enough to misuse° the Prince, to vex° Claudio,   *deceive / torment*
25 to undo Hero, and kill Leonato. Look you for any other issue?°   *result*

DON JOHN Only to despite° them I will endeavour anything.   *Merely to spite*

BORACHIO Go then. Find me a meet hour to draw Don Pedro
and the Count Claudio alone. Tell them that you know that
Hero loves me. Intend° a kind of zeal both to the Prince and   *Pretend*
30 Claudio as in° love of your brother's honour who hath made   *as if for*
this match, and his friend's reputation who is thus like to be
cozened with the semblance of a maid,[2] that you have discov-
ered thus. They will scarcely believe this without trial. Offer
them instances, which shall bear no less likelihood than to see
35 me at her chamber window, hear me call Margaret Hero, hear
Margaret term me Claudio.[3] And bring them to see this the
very night before the intended wedding, for in the mean time
I will so fashion the matter that Hero shall be absent, and there
shall appear such seeming truth of Hero's disloyalty that jeal-
40 ousy shall be called assurance,[4] and all the preparation° over-   *wedding preparation*
thrown.

DON JOHN Grow this° to what adverse issue it can, I will put it   *Let this lead*
in practice. Be cunning in the working this,° and thy fee is a   *of this*
thousand ducats.°   *gold coins*

45 BORACHIO Be you constant in the accusation, and my cunning
shall not shame me.

DON JOHN I will presently go learn their day of marriage.

Exeunt

2.2 Location: Leonato's house.
1. And whatever frustrates his wishes conforms with
mine.
2. To be cheated with the mere appearance of a virgin.

3. Most editors assume an error here and emend to
"Borachio."
4. That suspicion shall be called certainty.

2.3

Enter BENEDICK

BENEDICK Boy!

[*Enter* BOY]

BOY Signor?

BENEDICK In my chamber window lies a book. Bring it hither to
me in the orchard.

5   BOY I am here already,[1] sir.

BENEDICK I know that, but I would have thee hence and here
again.   *Exit* [BOY]
I do much wonder that one man, seeing how much another
man is a fool when he dedicates his behaviours to love, will,
10   after he hath laughed at such shallow follies in others, become
the argument° of his own scorn by falling in love. And such a   subject
man is Claudio. I have known when there was no music with
him but the drum and the fife, and now had he rather hear the
tabor and the pipe.[2] I have known when he would have walked
15   ten mile afoot to see a good armour, and now will he lie ten
nights awake carving° the fashion of a new doublet.° He was   designing / jacket
wont° to speak plain and to the purpose, like an honest man   accustomed
and a soldier, and now is he turned orthography.[3] His words
are a very fantastical° banquet, just so many strange dishes. May   poetic
20   I be so converted, and see° with these eyes? I cannot tell. I   still see
think not. I will not be sworn but love may transform me to an
oyster, but I'll take my oath on it, till he have made an oyster
of me he shall never make me such a fool. One woman is fair,
yet I am well. Another is wise, yet I am well. Another virtuous,
25   yet I am well. But till all graces be in one woman, one woman
shall not come in my grace.° Rich she shall be, that's certain.   favor
Wise, or I'll none.[4] Virtuous, or I'll never cheapen° her. Fair,   bargain for
or I'll never look on her. Mild, or come not near me. Noble, or
not I for an angel.[5] Of good discourse, an excellent musician,
30   and her hair shall be of what colour it please God. Ha! The
Prince and Monsieur Love. I will hide me in the arbour.

[*He hides.*]

Enter [DON PEDRO *the*] *Prince,* LEONATO, *and* CLAUDIO[6]

DON PEDRO Come, shall we hear this music?

CLAUDIO Yea, my good lord. How still the evening is,
As° hushed on purpose to grace harmony.   As if

35   DON PEDRO [*aside*] See you where Benedick hath hid himself?

CLAUDIO [*aside*] O, very well, my lord. The music ended,
We'll fit the hid-fox with a pennyworth.[7]

Enter BALTHASAR *with music*

DON PEDRO Come, Balthasar, we'll hear that song again.

BALTHASAR O good my lord, tax° not so bad a voice   task
40   To slander music any more than once.

DON PEDRO It is the witness still° of excellency   the mark always

---

2.3 Location: Leonato's garden.
1. That is, it's as good as done. (Benedick takes him lit-
erally.)
2. The drum and fife were used by the military; the
tabor (a small drum) and pipe were used in social fes-
tivities.
3. Become overelaborate in his speech.
4. Or I'll have none (of her).
5. Not I, though she be an angel (punning on coins: an

angel was worth 10 shillings, and a noble 6 shillings 8
pence).
6. Q's stage direction includes "Music," which seems
premature as the singer, Balthasar, enters at line 38.
7. We'll give our sly eavesdropper more than he bar-
gained for. *hid-fox:* apparently refers to the game of
hide-and-seek (compare *Hamlet* 4.2.28: "Hide, fox, and
all after").

To put a strange face on[8] his own perfection.
I pray thee sing, and let me woo° no more.   *cajole*

BALTHASAR Because you talk of wooing[9] I will sing,
45   Since many a wooer doth commence his suit
To her he thinks not worthy, yet he woos,
Yet will he swear he loves.

DON PEDRO   Nay pray thee, come;
Or if thou wilt hold longer argument,
Do it in notes.°   *music*

BALTHASAR   Note this before my notes:
50   There's not a note of mine that's worth the noting.

DON PEDRO Why, these are very crotchets[1] that he speaks—
Note notes, forsooth, and nothing![2]

        [*The accompaniment begins*]

BENEDICK Now, divine air! Now is his soul ravished. Is it not
strange that sheep's guts[3] should hale° souls out of men's bod-   *drag*
55   ies? Well, a horn[4] for my money, when all's done.

BALTHASAR [*sings*]
            Sigh no more, ladies, sigh no more.
                Men were deceivers ever,
            One foot in sea, and one on shore,
                To one thing constant never.
60   Then sigh not so, but let them go,
                And be you blithe and bonny,°   *beautiful*
            Converting all your sounds of woe
                Into hey nonny, nonny.

            Sing no more ditties, sing no more
65   Of dumps[5] so dull and heavy.
            The fraud of men was ever so
                Since summer first was leafy.
            Then sigh not so, but let them go,
                And be you blithe and bonny,
70   Converting all your sounds of woe
                Into hey nonny, nonny.

DON PEDRO By my troth, a good song.
BALTHASAR And an ill singer, my lord.
DON PEDRO Ha, no, no, faith. Thou singest well enough for a
75   shift.°   *to make do*

BENEDICK [*aside*] An° he had been a dog that should have   *If*
howled thus, they would have hanged him; and I pray God his
bad voice bode no mischief. I had as lief° have heard the night-   *as gladly*
raven,° come what plague could have come after it.   *bird of ill omen*

80 DON PEDRO Yea, marry,[6] dost thou hear, Balthasar? I pray thee
get us some excellent music, for tomorrow night we would
have it at the Lady Hero's chamber window.

---

8. *To put . . . on:* Not to admit.
9. Because you put it in terms of wooing (and so are
likely to continue to flatter me insincerely).
1. Whimsies; quarter notes (in music).
2. *Note . . . nothing:* Get on with your singing, and
nothing else. ("Nothing" and "noting" sounded the
same in Elizabethan pronunciation. Compare the same

play on words in the title.)
3. Used to string musical instruments.
4. Military or hunting horn.
5. Melancholy tunes or moods.
6. A mild oath. (Don Pedro is continuing the speech
interrupted by Benedick's aside.)

BALTHASAR The best I can, my lord.   *Exit*

DON PEDRO Do so. Farewell. Come hither, Leonato. What was
85   it you told me of today, that your niece Beatrice was in love
      with Signor Benedick?

CLAUDIO [*aside*] O, ay, stalk on, stalk on. The fowl sits.[7]—I did
      never think that lady would have loved any man.

LEONATO No, nor I neither. But most wonderful° that she   *astounding*
90   should so dote on Signor Benedick, whom she hath in all out-
      ward behaviours seemed ever to abhor.

BENEDICK [*aside*] Is't possible? Sits the wind in that corner?

LEONATO By my troth, my lord, I cannot tell what to think of it.
      But that she loves him with an enraged° affection, it is past the   *a frenzied*
95   infinite° of thought.   *furthest bounds*

DON PEDRO Maybe she doth but counterfeit.

CLAUDIO Faith, like° enough.   *likely*

LEONATO O God! Counterfeit? There was never counterfeit of
      passion came so near the life of passion as she discovers° it.   *exhibits*
100 DON PEDRO Why, what effects of passion shows she?

CLAUDIO [*aside*] Bait the hook well. This fish will bite.

LEONATO What effects, my lord? She will sit you[8]—you heard
      my daughter tell you how.

CLAUDIO She did indeed.
105 DON PEDRO How, how, I pray you? You amaze me. I would have
      thought her spirit had been invincible against all assaults of
      affection.

LEONATO I would have sworn it had, my lord, especially against
      Benedick.
110 BENEDICK [*aside*] I should think this a gull,° but that the white-   *trick*
      bearded fellow speaks it. Knavery cannot, sure, hide himself in
      such reverence.

CLAUDIO [*aside*] He hath ta'en th'infection. Hold° it up.   *Keep*

DON PEDRO Hath she made her affection known to Benedick?
115 LEONATO No, and swears she never will. That's her torment.

CLAUDIO 'Tis true, indeed, so your daughter says. 'Shall I,' says
      she, 'that have so oft encountered him with scorn, write to him
      that I love him?'

LEONATO This says she now when she is beginning to write to
120 him, for she'll be up twenty times a night, and there will she sit
      in her smock° till she have writ a sheet of paper. My daughter   *slip*
      tells us all.

CLAUDIO Now you talk of a sheet of paper, I remember a pretty
      jest your daughter told us of.
125 LEONATO O, when she had writ it and was reading it over, she
      found Benedick and Beatrice between the sheet.

CLAUDIO That.

LEONATO O, she tore the letter into a thousand halfpence,°   *small pieces*
      railed at herself that she should be so immodest to write to one
130 that she knew would flout° her. 'I measure him,' says she, 'by   *jeer at*
      my own spirit, for I should flout him if he writ to me, yea,
      though I love him I should.'

CLAUDIO Then down upon her knees she falls, weeps, sobs,
      beats her heart, tears her hair, prays, curses, 'O sweet Benedick,
135 God give me patience.'

---

7. *stalk . . . sits:* go on quietly. Our prey has alighted.   8. She will sit down (i.e., weak with lovesickness).

LEONATO   She doth indeed, my daughter says so, and the ecstasy° *passion*
hath so much overborne her that my daughter is sometime
afeard she will do a desperate outrage° to herself. It is very true. *injury*

DON PEDRO   It were good that Benedick knew of it by some
140 other, if she will not discover° it. *reveal*

CLAUDIO   To what end? He would make but a sport of it and
torment the poor lady worse.

DON PEDRO   An he should, it were an alms° to hang him. She's *a charitable deed*
an excellent sweet lady, and, out of all suspicion,° she is vir- *doubt*
145 tuous.

CLAUDIO   And she is exceeding wise.

DON PEDRO   In everything but in loving Benedick.

LEONATO   O my lord, wisdom and blood° combating in so tender *passion*
a body, we have ten proofs to one that blood hath the victory. I
150 am sorry for her, as I have just cause, being her uncle and her
guardian.

DON PEDRO   I would she had bestowed this dotage° on me. I *infatuation*
would have doffed⁹ all other respects° and made her half *considerations*
myself. I pray you tell Benedick of it, and hear what a° will say. *he*
155 LEONATO   Were it good, think you?

CLAUDIO   Hero thinks surely she will die, for she says she will die
if he love her not, and she will die ere she make her love
known, and she will die if he woo her, rather than she will
bate° one breath of her accustomed crossness.° *abate / contrariness*
160 DON PEDRO   She doth well. If she should make tender° of her *make an offer*
love 'tis very possible he'll scorn it, for the man, as you know
all, hath a contemptible° spirit. *contemptuous*

CLAUDIO   He is a very proper° man. *handsome*

DON PEDRO   He hath indeed a good outward happiness.[1]
165 CLAUDIO   Before God; and in my mind, very wise.

DON PEDRO   He doth indeed show some sparks that are like wit.

CLAUDIO   And I take him to be valiant.

DON PEDRO   As Hector,[2] I assure you, and in the managing of
quarrels you may say he is wise, for either he avoids them with
170 great discretion or undertakes them with a most Christianlike
fear.

LEONATO   If he do fear God, a must necessarily keep peace. If
he break the peace, he ought to enter into a quarrel with fear
and trembling.

175 DON PEDRO   And so will he do, for the man doth fear God, how-
soever it seems not in him by some large° jests he will make. *broad*
Well, I am sorry for your niece. Shall we go seek Benedick and
tell him of her love?

CLAUDIO   Never tell him, my lord. Let her wear it out with good
180 counsel.° *advice*

LEONATO   Nay, that's impossible. She may wear her heart out
first.

DON PEDRO   Well, we will hear further of it by° your daughter. *from*
Let it cool the while. I love Benedick well, and I could wish he
185 would modestly examine himself to see how much he is unwor-
thy so good a lady.

---

9. Set aside or cast off.   2. The noblest and bravest Trojan warrior.
1. He is well endowed with looks and bearing.

LEONATO   My lord, will you walk? Dinner is ready.

CLAUDIO [*aside*]   If he do not dote on her upon this, I will never
trust my expectation.°   *predictions*

190   DON PEDRO [*aside*]   Let there be the same net spread for her,
and that must your daughter and her gentlewomen carry.° The   *manage*
sport will be when they hold one an opinion of another's dot-
age, and no such matter.³ That's the scene that I would see,
which will be merely a dumb show.⁴ Let us send her to call

195   him in to dinner.

Exeunt [DON PEDRO, CLAUDIO, *and* LEONATO]

BENEDICK [*coming forward*]   This can be no trick. The confer-
ence was sadly borne.° They have the truth of this from Hero.   *seriously conducted*
They seem to pity the lady. It seems her affections have their
full bent.⁵ Love me! Why, it must be requited. I hear how I am

200   censured. They say I will bear myself proudly if I perceive the
love come from her. They say too that she will rather die than
give any sign of affection. I did never think to marry. I must not
seem proud. Happy are they that hear their detractions and can
put them to mending.° They say the lady is fair. 'Tis a truth, I   *amending*

205   can bear them witness. And virtuous—'tis so, I cannot reprove°   *contradict*
it. And wise, but for loving me. By my troth, it is no addition to
her wit⁶—nor no great argument of her folly, for I will be horri-
bly in love with her. I may chance have some odd quirks° and   *quips*
remnants of wit broken on° me because I have railed so long   *cracked against*

210   against marriage; but doth not the appetite alter? A man loves
the meat in his youth that he cannot endure in his age. Shall
quips and sentences° and these paper bullets of the brain awe   *epigrams*
a man from the career° of his humour?° No. The world must   *swift course / liking*
be peopled. When I said I would die a bachelor, I did not think

215   I should live till I were married. Here comes Beatrice.

Enter BEATRICE

By this day, she's a fair lady. I do spy some marks of love in her.

BEATRICE   Against my will I am sent to bid you come in to
dinner.

BENEDICK   Fair Beatrice, I thank you for your pains.

220   BEATRICE   I took no more pains for those thanks than you take
pains to thank me. If it had been painful I would not have
come.

BENEDICK   You take pleasure, then, in the message?

BEATRICE   Yea, just so much as you may take upon a knife's

225   point and choke a daw withal.° You have no stomach,° signor?   *jackdaw with / appetite*
Fare you well.   *Exit*

BENEDICK   Ha! 'Against my will I am sent to bid you come in to
dinner.' There's a double meaning in that. 'I took no more
pains for those thanks than you took pains to thank me.' That's

230   as much as to say 'Any pains that I take for you is as easy as
thanks.'—If I do not take pity of her I am a villain. If I do not
love her I am a Jew.⁷ I will go get her picture.⁸   *Exit*

---

3. *when . . . matter*: when each believes that the other
is madly in love, without any basis in fact.
4. A pantomime (because words for once will fail
them).
5. Are stretched to the limit (like a bent bow).

6. No additional proof of her intelligence.
7. That is, lacking in Christian charity (an anti-Semitic
stereotype).
8. *get her picture*: have her portrait painted (for a love
locket) or sketch it himself.

3.1

Enter HERO *and two gentlewomen,* MARGARET *and*
    URSULA

HERO   Good Margaret, run thee to the parlour.
There shalt thou find my cousin Beatrice
Proposing° with the Prince and Claudio.   *Talking*
Whisper her ear, and tell her I and Ursula
5   Walk in the orchard, and our whole discourse
Is all of her. Say that thou overheard'st us,
And bid her steal into the pleachèd¹ bower
Where honeysuckles, ripened by the sun,
Forbid the sun to enter—like favourites
10   Made proud by princes, that advance their pride
Against that power that bred it.² There will she hide her
To listen° our propose.° This is thy office.   *hear / conversation*
Bear thee well in it, and leave us alone.
MARGARET   I'll make her come, I warrant you, presently. *[Exit]*
15 HERO   Now, Ursula, when Beatrice doth come,
As we do trace° this alley up and down   *pace*
Our talk must only be of Benedick.
When I do name him, let it be thy part
To praise him more than ever man did merit.
20 My talk to thee must be how Benedick
Is sick in love with Beatrice. Of this matter
Is little Cupid's crafty arrow made,
That only wounds by hearsay.³
    Enter BEATRICE
                        Now begin,
For look where Beatrice like a lapwing⁴ runs
25 Close by the ground to hear our conference.
URSULA   The pleasant'st angling is to see the fish
Cut with her golden oars the silver stream
And greedily devour the treacherous bait.
So angle we for Beatrice, who even now
30 Is couchèd° in the woodbine coverture.⁵   *hidden*
Fear you not my part of the dialogue.
HERO   Then go we near her, that her ear lose nothing
Of the false-sweet bait that we lay for it.—
    [They approach Beatrice's hiding-place]
No, truly, Ursula, she is too disdainful.
35 I know her spirits are as coy° and wild   *disdainful; shy*
As haggards° of the rock.   *wild female hawks*
URSULA   But are you sure
That Benedick loves Beatrice so entirely?
HERO   So says the Prince and my new trothèd lord.
URSULA   And did they bid you tell her of it, madam?
40 HERO   They did entreat me to acquaint her of it,
But I persuaded them, if they loved Benedick,
To wish him wrestle with affection
And never to let Beatrice know of it.
URSULA   Why did you so? Doth not the gentleman

3.1 Location: Leonato's garden.
1. Screened by intertwining branches.
2. *that advance . . . it:* who presumptuously oppose the power that created them.

3. Wounds by rumor or gossip.
4. A peewit, a bird that scuttles along the ground.
5. In the honeysuckle arbor.

45 Deserve as full° as fortunate a bed   *fully*
  As ever Beatrice shall couch upon?
  HERO O god of love! I know he doth deserve
  As much as may be yielded to a man.
  But nature never framed a woman's heart
50 Of prouder stuff than that of Beatrice.
  Disdain and scorn ride sparkling in her eyes,
  Misprising° what they look on, and her wit   *Despising*
  Values itself so highly that to her
  All matter else seems° weak. She cannot love,   *other matters seem*
55 Nor take no shape nor project of affection,⁶
  She is so self-endearèd.
  URSULA   Sure, I think so.
  And therefore certainly it were not good
  She knew his love, lest she'll make sport at it.
  HERO Why, you speak truth. I never yet saw man,
60 How° wise, how noble, young, how rarely° featured,   *However / finely*
  But she would spell him backward.⁷ If fair-faced,
  She would swear the gentleman should be her sister.
  If black,° why nature, drawing of an antic,°   *dark / a buffoon*
  Made a foul blot.° If tall, a lance ill headed;   *error*
65 If low, an agate⁸ very vilely cut;
  If speaking, why, a vane blown with all winds;
  If silent, why, a block movèd with° none.   *by*
  So turns she every man the wrong side out,
  And never gives to truth and virtue that
70 Which simpleness° and merit purchaseth.°   *integrity / deserve*
  URSULA Sure, sure, such carping is not commendable.
  HERO No, not to be so odd and from all fashions⁹
  As Beatrice is cannot be commendable.
  But who dare tell her so? If I should speak
75 She would mock me into air, O, she would laugh me
  Out of myself, press me to death¹ with wit.
  Therefore let Benedick, like covered fire,
  Consume away in sighs,² waste inwardly.
  It were a better death than die with mocks,
80 Which is as bad as die with tickling.
  URSULA Yet tell her of it, hear what she will say.
  HERO No. Rather I will go to Benedick
  And counsel him to fight against his passion.
  And truly, I'll devise some honest° slanders   *harmless*
85 To stain my cousin with. One doth not know
  How much an ill word may empoison liking.
  URSULA O, do not do your cousin such a wrong.
  She cannot be so much without true judgement,
  Having so swift and excellent a wit
90 As she is prized° to have, as to refuse   *esteemed*
  So rare a gentleman as Signor Benedick.

---

6. *Nor take . . . affection:* Nor form the image or even the concept of love.
7. She would speak of his virtues as faults.
8. Tiny figures were carved in agates and used as seals or in rings.
9. *from all fashions:* contrary to normal behavior.

1. Crushing weights were loaded upon accused criminals who refused to enter a plea; Hero suggests that she will be silenced with mockery and then mocked for her silence.
2. Each sigh was said to draw a drop of blood from the heart.

HERO He is the only man of Italy,
　　Always excepted my dear Claudio.
URSULA I pray you be not angry with me, madam,
95　Speaking my fancy. Signor Benedick,
　　For shape, for bearing, argument,[3] and valour
　　Goes foremost in report through Italy.
HERO Indeed, he hath an excellent good name.
URSULA His excellence did earn it ere he had it.
100　When are you married, madam?
HERO Why, every day, tomorrow.[4] Come, go in.
　　I'll show thee some attires and have thy counsel
　　Which is the best to furnish me tomorrow.
URSULA [aside] She's limed,[5] I warrant you. We have caught
105　her, madam.
HERO [aside] If it prove so, then loving goes by haps.°　　　　chance
　　Some Cupid kills with arrows, some with traps.
　　　　　　　　　　Exeunt [HERO and URSULA]
BEATRICE [coming forward] What fire is in mine ears?[6] Can this be true?
　　Stand I condemned for pride and scorn so much?
110　Contempt, farewell; and maiden pride, adieu.
　　No glory lives behind the back of such.[7]
　　And, Benedick, love on. I will requite thee,
　　Taming my wild heart to thy loving hand.[8]
　　If thou dost love, my kindness shall incite thee
115　To bind our loves up in a holy band.
　　For others say thou dost deserve, and I
　　Believe it better than reportingly.°　　　Exit　　than as mere rumor

3.2

*Enter [DON PEDRO the] Prince, CLAUDIO, BENEDICK,
and LEONATO*

DON PEDRO I do but stay till your marriage be consummate, and
　　then go I toward Aragon.
CLAUDIO I'll bring° you thither, my lord, if you'll vouchsafe° me.　　accompany / allow
DON PEDRO Nay, that would be as great a soil in the new gloss
5　of your marriage as to show a child his new coat and forbid
　　him to wear it. I will only be bold with° Benedick for his com-　　only ask
　　pany, for from the crown of his head to the sole of his foot he
　　is all mirth. He hath twice or thrice cut Cupid's bow-string,
　　and the little hangman° dare not shoot at him. He hath a heart　　rogue; executioner
10　as sound as a bell, and his tongue is the clapper, for what his
　　heart thinks his tongue speaks.
BENEDICK Gallants, I am not as I have been.
LEONATO So say I. Methinks you are sadder.°　　more serious
CLAUDIO I hope he be in love.
15　DON PEDRO Hang him, truant! There's no true drop of blood
　　in him to be truly touched with love. If he be sad, he wants°　　lacks
　　money.

---

3. Intellect and rhetorical skill.
4. From tomorrow on, I shall be a married woman
every day.
5. Snared with birdlime, a glue spread on branches to
catch birds.
6. Proverbially, if others were talking about you else-
where, your ears would burn.
7. No one praises such people behind their backs.
8. In falconry, the bird is tamed by the hand of the fal-
coner.
3.2 Location: Leonato's house.

BENEDICK   I have the toothache.[1]

DON PEDRO   Draw° it.   *Extract*

20   BENEDICK   Hang it.

CLAUDIO   You must hang it first and draw it afterwards.[2]

DON PEDRO   What? Sigh for the toothache?

LEONATO   Where is but a humour[3] or a worm.

BENEDICK   Well, everyone can master a grief but he that has it.

25   CLAUDIO   Yet say I he is in love.

DON PEDRO   There is no appearance of fancy° in him, unless it   *love*
    be a fancy that he hath to strange disguises, as to be a Dutch-
    man today, a Frenchman tomorrow, or in the shape of two
    countries at once, as a German from the waist downward, all
30   slops,° and a Spaniard from the hip upward, no doublet.[4]   *baggy breeches*
    Unless he have a fancy to this foolery, as it appears he hath, he
    is no fool for fancy, as you would have it appear he is.

CLAUDIO   If he be not in love with some woman there is no
    believing old° signs. A° brushes his hat o' mornings, what should   *time-honored / He*
35   that bode?

DON PEDRO   Hath any man seen him at the barber's?

CLAUDIO   No, but the barber's man hath been seen with him,
    and the old ornament of his cheek hath already stuffed ten-
    nis balls.[5]

40   LEONATO   Indeed, he looks younger than he did by the loss of a
    beard.

DON PEDRO   Nay, a rubs himself with civet.° Can you smell him   *perfume*
    out[6] by that?

CLAUDIO   That's as much as to say the sweet youth's in love.

45   DON PEDRO   The greatest note of it is his melancholy.

CLAUDIO   And when was he wont to wash[7] his face?

DON PEDRO   Yea, or to paint himself?—for the which I hear what
    they say of him.

CLAUDIO   Nay, but his jesting spirit, which is now crept into a
50   lute-string, and now governed by stops.[8]

DON PEDRO   Indeed, that tells a heavy tale for him. Conclude,
    conclude, he is in love.

CLAUDIO   Nay, but I know who loves him.

DON PEDRO   That would I know, too. I warrant, one that knows
55   him not.

CLAUDIO   Yes, and his ill conditions,° and in despite of all, dies   *qualities*
    for him.

DON PEDRO   She shall be buried with her face upwards.[9]

BENEDICK   Yet is this no charm for the toothache. Old signor,
60   walk aside with me. I have studied eight or nine wise words to
    speak to you which these hobby-horses° must not hear.   *clowns*

                  [*Exeunt* BENEDICK *and* LEONATO]

DON PEDRO   For° my life, to break° with him about Beatrice.   *Upon / speak*

---

1. Toothaches supposedly plagued lovers.
2. *hang it*: a mild expletive (like "darn it"). Claudio plays on the notion of hanging criminals, who were then cut down and "drawn" (disemboweled).
3. Poisonous fluid in the body (which, along with worms, was thought to be the cause of toothache).
4. His doublet is covered with a Spanish cloak.
5. Benedick has shaved off his beard. Tennis balls were stuffed with hair.
6. Detect his secret (with play on literal "smell").

7. When was he accustomed to use cosmetics on (com-pare "paint" in following line).
8. Frets on a lute's fingerboard; restraints. (Lutes were associated with lovers' serenades.)
9. That is, in Benedick's arms, where she will die (Eliza-bethan slang for "orgasm") in the act of love; perhaps a joking reversal of the idea that as one responsible for her own fate, she should be buried, like a suicide, with her face downward.

CLAUDIO 'Tis even so. Hero and Margaret¹ have by this° played   *now*
their parts with Beatrice, and then the two bears will not bite
65 one another when they meet.

Enter [DON] JOHN *the bastard*

DON JOHN My lord, and brother, God save you.
DON PEDRO Good-e'en,° brother.   *Good evening*
DON JOHN If your leisure served I would speak with you.
DON PEDRO In private?
70 DON JOHN If it please you. Yet Count Claudio may hear, for
what I would speak of concerns him.
DON PEDRO What's the matter?
DON JOHN [*to* CLAUDIO] Means your lordship to be married
tomorrow?
75 DON PEDRO You know he does.
DON JOHN I know not that when he knows what I know.
CLAUDIO If there be any impediment, I pray you discover° it.   *reveal*
DON JOHN You may think I love you not. Let that appear here-
after, and aim better at° me by that I now will manifest. For my   *think better of*
80 brother, I think he holds you well° and in dearness° of heart   *in high respect / affection*
hath holp° to effect your ensuing marriage—surely suit ill   *helped*
spent, and labour ill bestowed.
DON PEDRO Why, what's the matter?
DON JOHN I came hither to tell you, and, circumstances short-
85 ened°—for she has been too long a-talking of²—the lady is   *put simply*
disloyal.°   *unfaithful*
CLAUDIO Who, Hero?
DON JOHN Even she. Leonato's Hero, your Hero, every man's
Hero.
90 CLAUDIO Disloyal?
DON JOHN The word is too good to paint out° her wickedness. I   *fully describe*
could say she were worse. Think you of a worse title, and I will
fit her to it. Wonder not till further warrant.° Go but with me   *evidence*
tonight, you shall see her chamber window entered, even the
95 night before her wedding day. If you love her then, tomorrow
wed her. But it would better fit your honour to change your
mind.
CLAUDIO May this be so?
DON PEDRO I will not think it.
100 DON JOHN If you dare not trust that you see, confess not that you
know.³ If you will follow me I will show you enough, and when
you have seen more and heard more, proceed accordingly.
CLAUDIO If I see anything tonight why I should not marry her,
tomorrow, in the congregation where I should wed, there will
105 I shame her.
DON PEDRO And as I wooed for thee to obtain her, I will join
with thee to disgrace her.
DON JOHN I will disparage her no farther till you are my wit-
nesses. Bear it coldly° but till midnight, and let the issue show   *calmly*
110 itself.
DON PEDRO O day untowardly turned!°   *miserably changed*
CLAUDIO O mischief strangely thwarting!

1. Ursula and Hero played the trick on Beatrice with   3. If you won't risk seeing for yourself, don't claim to
help from Margaret.   know.
2. For we have already talked about her too much.

DON JOHN   O plague right well prevented!—So will you say
when you have seen the sequel.   *Exeunt*

3.3

Enter DOGBERRY *and his compartner* [VERGES], *with the*
WATCH[1]

DOGBERRY   Are you good men and true?

VERGES   Yea, or else it were pity but they should suffer salvation,[2]
body and soul.

DOGBERRY   Nay, that were a punishment too good for them if

5   they should have any allegiance° in them, being chosen for the   *(for "disloyalty")*
Prince's watch.

VERGES   Well, give them their charge,° neighbour Dogberry.   *instructions*

DOGBERRY   First, who think you the most desertless° man to be   *(for "deserving")*
constable?[3]

10   SECOND WATCHMAN   Hugh Oatcake, sir, or George Seacoal, for
they can write and read.

DOGBERRY   Come hither, neighbour Seacoal, God hath blest
you with a good name.[4] To be a well-favoured° man is the gift   *good-looking*
of fortune, but to write and read comes by nature.

15   FIRST WATCHMAN   Both which, Master Constable—

DOGBERRY   You have. I knew it would be your answer. Well, for
your favour,° sir, why, give God thanks, and make no boast of   *looks*
it. And for your writing and reading, let that appear when there
is no need of such vanity. You are thought here to be the most

20   senseless° and fit man for the constable of the watch, therefore   *(for "sensible")*
bear you the lantern. This is your charge: you shall compre-
hend all vagrom[5] men. You are to bid any man stand,° in the   *stop*
Prince's name.

FIRST WATCHMAN   How if a will not stand?

25   DOGBERRY   Why then take no note of him, but let him go, and
presently° call the rest of the watch together, and thank God   *immediately*
you are rid of a knave.

VERGES   If he will not stand when he is bidden he is none of the
Prince's subjects.

30   DOGBERRY   True, and they are to meddle with none but the
Prince's subjects.—You shall also make no noise in the streets,
for for the watch to babble and to talk is most tolerable° and   *(for "intolerable")*
not to be endured.

A WATCHMAN   We will rather sleep than talk. We know what

35   belongs° to a watch.   *is appropriate*

DOGBERRY   Why, you speak like an ancient° and most quiet   *experienced*
watchman, for I cannot see how sleeping should offend. Only
have a care that your bills[6] be not stolen. Well, you are to call
at all the alehouses and bid those that are drunk get them to

40   bed.

A WATCHMAN   How if they will not?

DOGBERRY   Why then, let them alone till they are sober. If they

---

3.3 Location: A street.
1. Watchmen who patrolled the streets, proclaiming the
hour and performing police duties. "Verges" probably
alludes to a "verge," or wand of office, carried by officials.
2. For "damnation." (Verges and Dogberry repeatedly
say the opposite of what they mean.)
3. The leader of the Watch. (Dogberry himself is the

parish constable.) Q's speech prefixes are confusing in
this scene, making it difficult to identify the leader of
the Watch; some of them have been rearranged.
4. Sea coal from Newcastle was known for its high
quality (thus the "good name").
5. For "vagrant." *comprehend:* for "apprehend."
6. Weapons (long shafts with blades or ax heads).

make you not then the better answer, you may say they are not
the men you took them for.

45   A WATCHMAN   Well, sir.

DOGBERRY   If you meet a thief you may suspect him, by virtue of
your office, to be no true° man; and for such kind of men, the   *honest*
less you meddle or make° with them why, the more is° for your   *have to do / better it is*
honesty.

50   A WATCHMAN   If we know him to be a thief, shall we not lay
hands on him?

DOGBERRY   Truly, by your office you may, but I think they that
touch pitch will be defiled.[7] The most peaceable way for you if
you do take a thief is to let him show himself what he is, and
55   steal out of your company.

VERGES   You have been always called a merciful man, partner.

DOGBERRY   Truly, I would not hang a dog by my will, much
more° a man who hath any honesty in him.   *(for "less")*

VERGES   If you hear a child cry in the night you must call to the
60   nurse and bid her still° it.   *calm*

A WATCHMAN   How if the nurse be asleep and will not hear us?

DOGBERRY   Why then, depart in peace and let the child wake
her with crying, for the ewe that will not hear her lamb when
it baes will never answer a calf° when he bleats.   *blockhead*

65   VERGES   'Tis very true.

DOGBERRY   This is the end of the charge. You, constable, are to
present° the Prince's own person.[8] If you meet the Prince in the   *represent*
night you may stay° him.   *stop*

VERGES   Nay, by'r Lady, that I think a cannot.

70   DOGBERRY   Five shillings to one on't with any man that knows
the statutes he may stay him. Marry, not without° the Prince   *unless*
be willing, for indeed the watch ought to offend no man, and
it is an offence to stay a man against his will.

VERGES   By'r Lady, I think it be so.

75   DOGBERRY   Ha ha ha! Well, masters, good night. An there be
any matter of weight chances,° call up me. Keep your fellows'   *that occurs*
counsels, and your own, and good night. Come, neighbour.

FIRST WATCHMAN   Well, masters, we hear our charge. Let us go
sit here upon the church bench till two, and then all to bed.

80   DOGBERRY   One word more, honest neighbours. I pray you
watch about Signor Leonato's door, for the wedding being
there tomorrow, there is a great coil° tonight. Adieu. Be vigi-   *to-do, bustle*
tant,° I beseech you.   *(for "vigilant")*

          Exeunt [DOGBERRY *and* VERGES. *The* WATCH *sit*]

          Enter BORACHIO *and* CONRAD

BORACHIO   What, Conrad!

85   FIRST WATCHMAN [*aside*]   Peace; stir not.

BORACHIO   Conrad, I say.

CONRAD   Here, man, I am at thy elbow.

BORACHIO   Mass,° an my elbow itched,[9] I thought there would a   *By the mass*
scab[1] follow.

---

7. A proverbial saying, derived from the Apocryphal
book of Ecclesiasticus (13:1).
8. Dogberry presents a parodic version of the notion
that the monarch's authority was in theory separable
from his person (others could represent that authority

when he was physically absent).
9. Proverbially, itching elbows alerted you against
shady company.
1. Contemptible person; punning on a literal "scab."

90   CONRAD   I will owe thee an answer for that. And now, forward
with thy tale.

    BORACHIO   Stand thee close, then, under this penthouse,° for it   *overhanging structure*
drizzles rain, and I will, like a true drunkard, utter[2] all to thee.

    A WATCHMAN [*aside*]   Some treason, masters. Yet stand close.°   *keep hidden*

95   BORACHIO   Therefore, know I have earned of Don John a thou-
sand ducats.

    CONRAD   Is it possible that any villainy should be so dear?°   *valuable*

    BORACHIO   Thou shouldst rather ask if it were possible any vil-
lainy should be so rich. For when rich villains have need of

100   poor ones, poor ones may make what price they will.

    CONRAD   I wonder at it.

    BORACHIO   That shows thou art unconfirmed.° Thou knowest   *inexperienced*
that the fashion of a doublet, or a hat, or a cloak is nothing to[3]
a man.

105   CONRAD   Yes, it is apparel.

    BORACHIO   I mean the fashion.

    CONRAD   Yes, the fashion is the fashion.

    BORACHIO   Tush, I may as well say the fool's the fool. But seest
thou not what a deformed° thief[4] this fashion is?   *deforming*

110   A WATCHMAN [*aside*]   I know that Deformed. A° has been a vile   *He*
thief this seven year. A goes up and down° like a gentleman. I   *struts here and there*
remember his name.

    BORACHIO   Didst thou not hear somebody?

    CONRAD   No, 'twas the vane on the house.

115   BORACHIO   Seest thou not, I say, what a deformed thief this fash-
ion is, how giddily a turns about all the hot-bloods° between   *dandies*
fourteen and five-and-thirty, sometimes fashioning them like
Pharaoh's soldiers in the reechy° painting,[5] sometime like god   *grimy*
Bel's[6] priests in the old church window, sometime like the

120   shaven Hercules[7] in the smirched, worm-eaten tapestry, where
his codpiece[8] seems as massy as his club?

    CONRAD   All this I see, and I see that the fashion wears out more
apparel than the man.[9] But art not thou thyself giddy with the
fashion, too, that thou hast shifted[1] out of thy tale into telling

125   me of the fashion?

    BORACHIO   Not so, neither. But know that I have tonight wooed
Margaret, the Lady Hero's gentlewoman, by the name of Hero.
She leans me° out at her mistress' chamber window, bids me a   *leans*
thousand times good night—I tell this tale vilely, I should first

130   tell thee how the Prince, Claudio, and my master, planted and
placed and possessed[2] by my master, Don John, saw afar off in
the orchard this amiable° encounter.   *loving*

    CONRAD   And thought they Margaret was Hero?

    BORACHIO   Two of them did, the Prince and Claudio, but the

135   devil my master knew she was Margaret, and partly by his oaths,

---

2. The drunken Borachio, whose name means "drunk-ard," alludes to the Latin tag *in vino veritas*.
3. Tells us nothing about (but Conrad takes him to mean "means nothing to").
4. Used here to mean "rogue"—but also that keeping up with fashion robs men of their money.
5. Perhaps refers to a painting of the fleeing Israelites pursued by Pharaoh's army.
6. Bel (Baal) was a Babylonian god who had seventy priests. His story, told in the biblical Apocrypha, is

sometimes depicted in stained-glass windows.
7. Probably referring to the story of Omphale (compare 2.1.220), or perhaps confusing Hercules with Samson.
8. Pouch, often stuffed and ornamented, worn over a man's breeches, covering the genitals.
9. *fashion . . . man*: fashions change before clothes wear out.
1. Punning on "changed clothes."
2. Informed; but, perhaps also, controlled (as by the devil).

which first possessed them, partly by the dark night, which did
deceive them, but chiefly by my villainy, which did confirm
any slander that Don John had made, away went Claudio
enraged, swore he would meet her as he was appointed next
140 morning at the temple,° and there, before the whole congrega-   church
tion, shame her with what he saw o'ernight, and send her home
again without a husband.

FIRST WATCHMAN [*coming forward*] We charge you in the
Prince's name. Stand.

145 A WATCHMAN Call up the right[3] Master Constable. We have here
recovered the most dangerous piece of lechery[4] that ever was
known in the commonwealth.

FIRST WATCHMAN And one Deformed is one of them. I know
him—a wears a lock.[5]

150 CONRAD Masters, masters!

A WATCHMAN You'll be made bring Deformed forth, I warrant
you.

CONRAD Masters—

A WATCHMAN Never speak. We charge you. Let us obey° you to   (for "compel")
155 go with us.

BORACHIO [*to* CONRAD] We are like to prove a goodly° commod-   fine (ironic)
ity, being taken up of these men's bills.[6]

CONRAD A commodity in question,[7] I warrant you. Come, we'll
obey you.   *Exeunt*

3.4

Enter HERO, MARGARET, *and* URSULA

HERO Good Ursula, wake my cousin Beatrice, and desire her to
rise.

URSULA I will, lady.

HERO And bid her come hither.

5 URSULA Well.°   [*Exit*]   Very well

MARGARET Troth, I think your other rebato° were better.   stiffly wired ruff

HERO No, pray thee, good Meg, I'll wear this.

MARGARET By my troth, 's° not so good, and I warrant° your   it's / am sure
cousin will say so.

10 HERO My cousin's a fool, and thou art another: I'll wear none
but this.

MARGARET I like the new tire° within excellently, if the hair were   headdress with wig
a thought browner. And your gown's a most rare fashion, i'faith.
I saw the Duchess of Milan's gown that they praise so.

15 HERO O, that exceeds,° they say.   surpasses all

MARGARET By my troth, 's but a night-gown° in respect of yours—   dressing gown
cloth o' gold, and cuts, and laced with silver, set with pearls,
down sleeves, side sleeves, and skirts round underborne with a
bluish tinsel.[1] But for a fine, quaint,° graceful, and excellent   elegant
20 fashion, yours is worth ten on't.

3. Respectfully, as in "right worshipful."
4. For "treachery." *recovered*: for "discovered."
5. A "lovelock," or curl of hair, worn by courtiers.
6. *being . . . bills*: a multiple pun: after we have been
hoisted on their halberds (weapons); been arrested on
their warrants; been obtained on credit ("taken up") in
exchange for their bonds ("bills").
7. Of doubtful value; about to be judicially interrogated.

3.4 Location: Leonato's house.
1. *cloth . . . tinsel*: made of silk or woolen cloth inter-
woven with gold thread, with ornamental slashes
("cuts") showing the fabric beneath, and decorated
with silver embroidery or lace and with pearls; with fit-
ted ("down") sleeves and another pair that hung open
from the shoulder; trimmed at the hem or fully lined
("underborne") with another kind of metallic fabric.

HERO   God give me joy to wear it, for my heart is exceeding
heavy.

MARGARET   'Twill be heavier soon by the weight of a man.

HERO   Fie upon thee, art not ashamed?

25   MARGARET   Of what, lady? Of speaking honourably? Is not mar-
riage honourable in° a beggar? Is not your lord honourable   *even in*
without marriage? I think you would have me say 'saving your
reverence,[2] a husband'. An° bad thinking do not wrest° true   *If / pervert*
speaking, I'll offend nobody. Is there any harm in 'the heavier
30   for a husband'? None, I think, an it be the right husband and
the right wife—otherwise 'tis light° and not heavy. Ask my Lady   *licentious*
Beatrice else. Here she comes.

            Enter BEATRICE

HERO   Good morrow, coz.

BEATRICE   Good morrow, sweet Hero.

35   HERO   Why, how now? Do you speak in the sick tune?

BEATRICE   I am out of all other tune, methinks.

MARGARET   Clap 's° into 'Light o' love'. That goes without a bur-   *Let us shift*
den.[3] Do you sing it, and I'll dance it.

BEATRICE   Ye light o' love with your heels.[4] Then if your hus-
40   band have stables enough, you'll see he shall lack no barns.[5]

MARGARET   O illegitimate construction![6] I scorn that with my
heels.[7]

BEATRICE   [*to* HERO]   'Tis almost five o'clock, cousin. 'Tis time
you were ready. By my troth, I am exceeding ill. Heigh-ho!

45   MARGARET   For a hawk, a horse,[8] or a husband?

BEATRICE   For the letter that begins them all—h.[9]

MARGARET   Well, an you be not turned Turk,[1] there's no more
sailing by the star.[2]

BEATRICE   What means the fool, trow?°   *I wonder*

50   MARGARET   Nothing, I. But God send everyone their heart's
desire.

HERO   These gloves the Count sent me, they are an excellent
perfume.[3]

BEATRICE   I am stuffed,[4] cousin. I cannot smell.

55   MARGARET   A maid, and stuffed! There's goodly catching of cold.

BEATRICE   O, God help me, God help. How long have you
professed apprehension?°   *claimed to be witty*

MARGARET   Ever since you left it. Doth not my wit become me
rarely?°   *excellently*

60   BEATRICE   It is not seen enough. You should wear it in your cap.[5]
By my troth, I am sick.

MARGARET   Get you some of this distilled *carduus benedictus,*[6]
and lay it to your heart. It is the only thing for a qualm.°   *sudden faintness*

HERO   There thou prickest her with a thistle.

2. A polite expression of apology (as if "husband" were
an offensive term).
3. Bass part (for a man's voice), with play on heavy
"weight of a man." "Light o' Love" was a popular tune.
4. Ye . . . *heels:* Your dancing toys with love ("light-
heeled" was slang for "promiscuous").
5. Punning on "bairns," children.
6. A multiple pun: forced interpretation; making of
bastards; illegal building (of stables and barns).
7. I kick that away (reject it).
8. Responding to Beatrice's ostentatious sigh as a
hunting cry.

9. Punningly: "ache" was pronounced in the same way.
1. If you have not reneged (on your vows against mar-
riage). "To turn Turk" is, in the Christian proverb, to
become a renegade (by going over to the enemy, the
Muslim Turks).
2. No more navigating by the polestar. (No truths can
be trusted from now on.)
3. Perfumed gloves were fashionable.
4. In the nose; Margaret follows with an obscene pun.
5. Like the coxcomb of a professional fool.
6. Holy thistle, or blessed thistle (a medicinal herb
good for the heart).

65 BEATRICE   Benedictus—why Benedictus? You have some moral[7] in this Benedictus.

MARGARET   Moral? No, by my troth, I have no moral meaning. I meant plain holy-thistle. You may think perchance° that I think *perhaps* you are in love. Nay, by'r Lady, I am not such a fool to think

70 what I list,° nor I list not to think what I can, nor indeed I *please* cannot think, if I would think my heart out of thinking, that you are in love, or that you will be in love, or that you can be in love. Yet Benedick was such another,[8] and now is he become a man. He swore he would never marry, and yet now in despite of his heart he eats his meat without grudging.[9] And how you

75 may be converted I know not, but methinks you look with your eyes, as other women do.

BEATRICE   What pace is this that thy tongue keeps?

MARGARET   Not a false gallop.[1]

Enter URSULA

80 URSULA [*to* HERO]   Madam, withdraw. The Prince, the Count, Signor Benedick, Don John, and all the gallants of the town are come to fetch you to church.

HERO   Help to dress me, good coz, good Meg, good Ursula.

Exeunt

3.5

Enter LEONATO, *and* [DOGBERRY] *the constable, and* [VERGES] *the headborough°*   *local constable*

LEONATO   What would you with me, honest neighbour?

DOGBERRY   Marry, sir, I would have some confidence° with you *(for "conference")* that decerns° you nearly.   *(for "concerns")*

LEONATO   Brief° I pray you, for you see it is a busy time with me.   *Be brief*

5 DOGBERRY   Marry, this it is, sir.

VERGES   Yes, in truth it is, sir.

LEONATO   What is it, my good friends?

DOGBERRY   Goodman° Verges, sir, speaks a little off the mat-   *(commoner's title)* ter°—an old man, sir, and his wits are not so blunt° as, God   *subject / (for "sharp")*

10 help, I would desire they were. But in faith, honest as the skin between his brows.

VERGES   Yes, I thank God, I am as honest as any man living that is an old man and no honester than I.

DOGBERRY   Comparisons are odorous.° Palabras,[1] neighbour   *(for "odious")*

15 Verges.

LEONATO   Neighbours, you are tedious.[2]

DOGBERRY   It pleases your worship to say so, but we are the poor Duke's° officers. But truly, for mine own part, if I were as   *the Duke's poor* tedious as a king I could find in my heart to bestow it all of

20 your worship.

LEONATO   All thy tediousness on me, ah?

DOGBERRY   Yea, an 'twere a thousand pound more than 'tis, for I hear as good exclamation[3] on your worship as of any man in the city, and though I be but a poor man, I am glad to hear it.

25 VERGES   And so am I.

7. Hidden meaning (with ensuing pun on "no moral" as "immoral").
8. Benedick was once an enemy of love.
9. Nonetheless, he has a perfectly good appetite.
1. Not a canter. (I am not speaking at a false pace.)
3.5 Location: Leonato's house.

1. Be brief (from a Spanish expression, *pocas palabras*: "few words").
2. Dogberry takes it to mean "rich."
3. Properly, "accusation"; but Dogberry probably intends "acclamation."

LEONATO   I would fain° know what you have to say.   *gladly*

VERGES   Marry, sir, our watch tonight, excepting your worship's
presence,[4] ha' ta'en a couple of as arrant knaves as any in Mes-
sina.

30   DOGBERRY   A good old man, sir. He will be talking. As they say,
when the age is in, the wit is out.[5] God help us, it is a world to
see.[6] Well said, i'faith, neighbour Verges. Well, God's a good
man. An° two men ride of a horse, one must ride behind. An   *If*
honest soul, i'faith, sir, by my troth he is, as ever broke bread.[7]

35   But, God is to be worshipped, all men are not alike, alas, good
neighbour.

LEONATO   Indeed, neighbour, he comes too short of you.

DOGBERRY   Gifts that God gives!

LEONATO   I must leave you.

40   DOGBERRY   One word, sir. Our watch, sir, have indeed compre-
hended two auspicious[8] persons, and we would have them this
morning examined before your worship.

LEONATO   Take their examination yourself, and bring it me. I am
now in great haste, as it may appear unto you.

45   DOGBERRY   It shall be suffigance.°   *(for "sufficient")*

LEONATO   Drink some wine ere you go. Fare you well.

[*Enter a* MESSENGER]

MESSENGER   My lord, they stay° for you to give your daughter to   *wait*
her husband.

LEONATO   I'll wait upon them, I am ready.

[*Exeunt* LEONATO *and* MESSENGER]

50   DOGBERRY   Go, good partner, go get you to Francis Seacoal,[9]
bid him bring his pen and inkhorn to the jail. We are now to
examination° these men.   *(for "examine")*

VERGES   And we must do it wisely.

DOGBERRY   We will spare for no wit, I warrant you. Here's that°   *that which*

55   shall drive some of them to a non-com.[1] Only get the learned
writer to set down our excommunication,° and meet me at the   *(for "examination")*
jail.   *Exeunt*

4.1

Enter [DON PEDRO *the*] *Prince,* [DON JOHN *the*] *bastard,*
LEONATO, FRIAR [FRANCIS], CLAUDIO, BENEDICK,
HERO, *and* BEATRICE

LEONATO   Come, Friar Francis, be brief. Only to the plain form
of marriage, and you shall recount their particular duties
afterwards.

FRIAR [*to* CLAUDIO]   You come hither, my lord, to marry this
5   lady?

CLAUDIO   No.

LEONATO   To be married to her. Friar, you come to marry her.

FRIAR [*to* HERO]   Lady, you come hither to be married to this
count?

---

4. For "respecting your worship's presence": an apology
for speaking what might displease.
5. Dogberry's version of the proverb "When the wine is
in, the wit is out."
6. Dogberry seems to mean "a strange world"; the
expression normally meant "wonderful to behold."
7. Dogberry strings together three proverbial sentences,

all of which are remembered correctly but irrelevantly.
8. For "suspicious." *comprehended*: for "apprehended."
9. Refers to the Sexton in 4.2, not the George Seacoal
of the Watch in 3.3.
1. For "nonplus" (bewilderment); perhaps confused by
Dogberry with *non compos mentis* (insane).
4.1 Location: A church.

10   HERO   I do.
     FRIAR   If either of you know any inward° impediment why you   secret
        should not be conjoined, I charge you on your souls to utter it.
     CLAUDIO   Know you any, Hero?
     HERO   None, my lord.
15   FRIAR   Know you any, Count?
     LEONATO   I dare make his answer—none.
     CLAUDIO   O, what men dare do! What men may do! What men
        daily do, not knowing what they do!
     BENEDICK   How now! Interjections? Why then, some be of
20   laughing, as 'ah, ha, he!'[1]
     CLAUDIO   Stand thee by, Friar. Father, by your leave,
        Will you with free and unconstrainèd soul
        Give me this maid, your daughter?
     LEONATO   As freely, son, as God did give her me.
25   CLAUDIO   And what have I to give you back whose worth
        May counterpoise° this rich and precious gift?   equal
     DON PEDRO   Nothing, unless you render her again.
     CLAUDIO   Sweet Prince, you learn° me noble thankfulness.   teach
        There, Leonato, take her back again.
30   Give not this rotten orange to your friend.
        She's but the sign° and semblance of her honour.   mere appearance
        Behold how like a maid she blushes here!
        O, what authority and show of truth
        Can cunning sin cover itself withal!
35   Comes not that blood° as modest evidence   blush
        To witness° simple virtue? Would you not swear,   testify to
        All you that see her, that she were a maid,
        By these exterior shows? But she is none.
        She knows the heat of a luxurious° bed.   lustful
40   Her blush is guiltiness, not modesty.
     LEONATO   What do you mean, my lord?
     CLAUDIO   Not to be married,
        Not to knit my soul to an approvèd° wanton.   a proven
     LEONATO   Dear my lord, if you in your own proof°   testing (of her)
        Have vanquished the resistance of her youth
45   And made defeat of her virginity—
     CLAUDIO   I know what you would say. If I have known her,
        You will say she did embrace me as a husband,
        And so extenuate the forehand sin.[2]
        No, Leonato,
50   I never tempted her with word too large,°   immodest
        But as a brother to his sister showed
        Bashful sincerity and comely love.
     HERO   And seemed I ever otherwise to you?
     CLAUDIO   Out on thee,[3] seeming! I will write against it.
55   You seem to me as Dian in her orb,[4]
        As chaste as is the bud ere it be blown.°   blossom
        But you are more intemperate in your blood°   passion

---

1. Benedick alludes to a passage in William Lily's Latin
grammar, used in all Elizabethan schools: "Some [inter-
jections] are of laughing; as Ha ha he" (1567 edition).
2. And so sin only in anticipation of marriage.

3. A curse; "thee" could refer to Hero or "seeming"
(putting on a false show).
4. Diana (Roman goddess of chastity and of the moon)
in her orbit, or sphere of activity.

Than Venus or those pampered animals
That rage in savage sensuality.

60 HERO   Is my lord well that he doth speak so wide?°   *wildly*
LEONATO   Sweet Prince, why speak not you?
DON PEDRO   What should I speak?
   I stand dishonoured, that have gone about°   *have tried*
   To link my dear friend to a common stale.°   *prostitute*
LEONATO   Are these things spoken, or do I but dream?
65 DON JOHN   Sir, they are spoken, and these things are true.
BENEDICK   This looks not like a nuptial.
HERO   'True'! O God!
CLAUDIO   Leonato, stand I here?
   Is this the Prince? Is this the Prince's brother?
70   Is this face Hero's? Are our eyes our own?
LEONATO   All this is so. But what of this, my lord?
CLAUDIO   Let me but move° one question to your daughter,   *put*
   And by that fatherly and kindly° power   *natural*
   That you have in her, bid her answer truly.
75 LEONATO [*to* HERO]   I charge thee do so, as thou art my child.
HERO   O God defend me, how am I beset!
   What kind of catechizing⁵ call you this?
CLAUDIO   To make you answer truly to your name.⁶
HERO   Is it not Hero? Who can blot that name
   With any just reproach?
80 CLAUDIO   Marry, that can Hero.
   Hero itself⁷ can blot out Hero's virtue.
   What man was he talked with you yesternight
   Out at your window betwixt twelve and one?
   Now if you are a maid, answer to this.
85 HERO   I talked with no man at that hour, my lord.
DON PEDRO   Why, then are you no maiden. Leonato,
   I am sorry you must hear. Upon mine honour,
   Myself, my brother, and this grievèd° Count   *wronged*
   Did see her, hear her, at that hour last night
90   Talk with a ruffian at her chamber window,
   Who hath indeed, most like a liberal° villain,   *loose-tongued*
   Confessed the vile encounters they have had
   A thousand times in secret.
DON JOHN   Fie, fie, they are
   Not to be named, my lord, not to be spoke of.
95   There is not chastity enough in language
   Without offence to utter them. Thus, pretty lady,
   I am sorry for thy much misgovernment.°   *ample misconduct*
CLAUDIO   O Hero! What a Hero hadst thou been
   If half thy outward graces had been placed
100   About thy thoughts and counsels of thy heart!
   But fare thee well, most foul, most fair, farewell
   Thou pure impiety and impious purity.
   For° thee I'll lock up all the gates of love,   *Because of*
   And on my eyelids shall conjecture° hang   *suspicion*

---

5. A catechism was a set of formal questions and   called.
answers used to teach church doctrine.   7. The name (or reputation) of Hero.
6. To make you admit that you are what you have been

105   To turn all beauty into thoughts of harm,
       And never shall it more be gracious.°   *attractive*
LEONATO   Hath no man's dagger here a point for me?
       [HERO *falls to the ground*]
BEATRICE   Why, how now, cousin, wherefore sink you down?
DON JOHN   Come. Let us go. These things come thus to light
110   Smother her spirits° up.   *vital forces*
                  [*Exeunt* DON PEDRO, DON JOHN, *and* CLAUDIO]
BENEDICK   How doth the lady?
BEATRICE   Dead, I think. Help, uncle.
       Hero, why Hero! Uncle, Signor Benedick, Friar—
LEONATO   O fate, take not away thy heavy hand.
       Death is the fairest cover for her shame
       That may be wished for.
115   BEATRICE   How now, cousin Hero?
FRIAR   [*to* HERO]   Have comfort, lady.
LEONATO   [*to* HERO]   Dost thou look up?
FRIAR   Yea, wherefore should she not?
LEONATO   Wherefore? Why, doth not every earthly thing
120   Cry shame upon her? Could she here deny
       The story that is printed in her blood?°   *blush*
       Do not live, Hero, do not ope thine eyes,
       For did I think thou wouldst not quickly die,
       Thought I thy spirits were stronger than thy shames,
125   Myself would on the rearward° of reproaches   *in the wake*
       Strike at thy life. Grieved I I had but one?
       Chid I for that at frugal nature's frame?°   *plan*
       O one too much by thee! Why had I one?
       Why ever wast thou lovely in my eyes?
130   Why had I not with charitable hand
       Took up a beggar's issue at my gates,
       Who smirchèd thus° and mired with infamy,   *(as you are)*
       I might have said 'No part of it is mine,
       This shame derives itself from unknown loins.'
135   But mine, and mine I loved, and mine I praised,
       And mine that I was proud on,° mine so much   *of*
       That I myself was to myself not mine,[8]
       Valuing of her—why she, O she is fallen
       Into a pit of ink, that the wide sea
140   Hath drops too few to wash her clean again,
       And salt too little which may season[9] give
       To her foul tainted flesh.
BENEDICK   Sir, sir, be patient.
       For my part, I am so attired in wonder
       I know not what to say.
145   BEATRICE   O, on my soul, my cousin is belied.°   *slandered*
BENEDICK   Lady, were you her bedfellow last night?
BEATRICE   No, truly not, although until last night
       I have this twelvemonth been her bedfellow.
LEONATO   Confirmed, confirmed. O, that is stronger made
150   Which was before° barred up with ribs of iron.   *already*
       Would the two princes lie? And Claudio lie,

---

8. That I cared nothing for myself in comparison.   9. Give renewal. (Salt is a preservative for meat.)

Who loved her so that, speaking of her foulness,
Washed it with tears? Hence from her, let her die.
FRIAR   Hear me a little,
155 For I have only been silent so long
And given way unto this course of fortune[1]
By noting of the lady.[2] I have marked
A thousand blushing apparitions
To start into her face, a thousand innocent shames
160 In angel whiteness beat away those blushes,
And in her eye there hath appeared a fire
To burn the errors° that these princes hold   (like heretics)
Against her maiden truth. Call me a fool,
Trust not my reading nor my observations,
165 Which with experimental seal doth warrant
The tenor of my book.[3] Trust not my age,
My reverence, calling, nor divinity,
If this sweet lady lie not guiltless here
Under some biting error.
LEONATO   Friar, it cannot be.
170 Thou seest that all the grace that she hath left
Is that she will not add to her damnation
A sin of perjury. She not denies it.
Why seek'st thou then to cover with excuse
That which appears in proper° nakedness?   true
175 FRIAR [to HERO]   Lady, what man is he you are accused of?
HERO   They know that do accuse me. I know none.
If I know more of any man alive
Than that which maiden modesty doth warrant,
Let all my sins lack mercy. O my father,
180 Prove you that any man with me conversed
At hours unmeet,° or that I yesternight   improper
Maintained the change° of words with any creature,   exchange
Refuse° me, hate me, torture me to death.   Disown
FRIAR   There is some strange misprision° in the princes.   misunderstanding
185 BENEDICK   Two of them have the very bent of° honour,   are wholly devoted to
And if their wisdoms be misled in this
The practice° of it lives in John the bastard,   trickery
Whose spirits toil in frame of° villainies.   in plotting
LEONATO   I know not. If they speak but truth of her
190 These hands shall tear her. If they wrong her honour
The proudest of them shall well hear of it.
Time hath not yet so dried this blood of mine,
Nor age so eat up my invention,°   cleverness
Nor fortune made such havoc of my means,°   wealth
195 Nor my bad life reft me so much of friends,
But they shall find awaked in such a kind°   manner
Both strength of limb and policy° of mind,   cunning
Ability in means, and choice of friends,
To quit me of[4] them throughly.°   thoroughly
FRIAR   Pause awhile,

---

1. Q erroneously sets the beginning of the speech in
cramped prose; some words seem to have been lost in
the compression.
2. By . . . lady: So I could observe, or because I was
observing, Hero.

3. Which . . . book: Which guarantees, with the con-
firmation of experience, the truth of the conclusions I
have drawn from my study.
4. To be avenged upon.

200   And let my counsel sway you in this case.
    Your daughter here the princes left for dead,
    Let her a while be secretly kept in,
    And publish° it that she is dead indeed.   *announce*
    Maintain a mourning ostentation,°   *formal display*
205   And on your family's old monument°   *burial vault*
    Hang mournful epitaphs, and do all rites
    That appertain unto a burial.
    LEONATO   What shall become of this? What will this do?
    FRIAR   Marry, this, well carried,° shall on her behalf   *managed*
210   Change slander to remorse.° That is some good.   *pity*
    But not for that dream I on this strange course,
    But on° this travail look for greater birth.[5]   *from*
    She—dying, as it must be so maintained,
    Upon the instant that she was accused—
215   Shall be lamented, pitied, and excused
    Of° every hearer. For it so falls out   *By*
    That what we have, we prize not to the worth°   *full value*
    Whiles we enjoy it, but, being lacked and lost,
    Why then we rack[6] the value, then we find
220   The virtue that possession would not show us
    Whiles it was ours. So will it fare with Claudio.
    When he shall hear she died upon° his words,   *as a result of*
    Th'idea° of her life shall sweetly creep   *The image*
    Into his study of imagination,°   *reverie*
225   And every lovely organ° of her life   *aspect*
    Shall come apparelled in more precious habit,
    More moving-delicate, and full of life,
    Into the eye and prospect° of his soul   *vision*
    Than when she lived indeed. Then shall he mourn,
230   If ever love had interest in his liver,[7]
    And wish he had not so accusèd her,
    No, though he thought his accusation true.
    Let this be so, and doubt not but success°   *what follows*
    Will fashion the event° in better shape   *result*
235   Than I can lay it down in likelihood.
    But if all aim but this be levelled false,[8]
    The supposition of the lady's death
    Will quench the wonder of her infamy.
    And if it sort° not well, you may conceal her,   *turn out*
240   As best befits her wounded reputation,
    In some reclusive° and religious life,   *cloistered*
    Out of all eyes, tongues, minds, and injuries.°   *calumny*
    BENEDICK   Signor Leonato, let the Friar advise you.
    And though you know my inwardness° and love   *intimacy*
245   Is very much unto the Prince and Claudio,
    Yet, by mine honour, I will deal in this
    As secretly and justly as your soul
    Should with your body.
    LEONATO   Being that I flow in° grief,   *Since I am flooded by*
250   The smallest twine may lead me.

---

5. Look for a more important consequence (with pun on "travail" as "labor pains" as well as "effort").
6. Stretch (as on a rack, an instrument of torture).
7. Thought of as the seat of passions, including love.
8. But if we miss our aim in all but this.

FRIAR 'Tis well consented. Presently away,
For to strange sores strangely they strain the cure.[9]
[*To* HERO] Come, lady, die to live. This wedding day
Perhaps is but prolonged.° Have patience, and endure.   *postponed*

Exeunt [all but BEATRICE *and* BENEDICK]

255 BENEDICK Lady Beatrice, have you wept all this while?
BEATRICE Yea, and I will weep a while longer.
BENEDICK I will not desire that.
BEATRICE You have no reason, I do it freely.
BENEDICK Surely I do believe your fair cousin is wronged.
260 BEATRICE Ah, how much might the man deserve of me that
would right her!
BENEDICK Is there any way to show such friendship?
BEATRICE A very even° way, but no such friend.   *clear*
BENEDICK May a man do it?
265 BEATRICE It is a man's office, but not yours.
BENEDICK I do love nothing in the world so well as you. Is not
that strange?
BEATRICE As strange as the thing I know not. It were as possible
for me to say I loved nothing so well as you, but believe me
270 not, and yet I lie not. I confess nothing nor I deny nothing. I
am sorry for my cousin.
BENEDICK By my sword, Beatrice, thou lovest me.
BEATRICE Do not swear and eat it.[1]
BENEDICK I will swear by it that you love me, and I will make
275 him eat it that says I love not you.
BEATRICE Will you not eat your word?
BENEDICK With no sauce that can be devised to it. I protest° I   *affirm*
love thee.
BEATRICE Why then, God forgive me.
280 BENEDICK What offence, sweet Beatrice?
BEATRICE You have stayed me in a happy hour.[2] I was about to
protest I loved you.
BENEDICK And do it with all thy heart.
BEATRICE I love you with so much of my heart that none is left
285 to protest.
BENEDICK Come, bid me do anything for thee.
BEATRICE Kill Claudio.
BENEDICK Ha! Not for the wide world.
BEATRICE You kill me to deny° it. Farewell.   *by refusing*
290 BENEDICK Tarry, sweet Beatrice.
BEATRICE I am gone though I am here. There is no love in
you.—Nay, I pray you, let me go.
BENEDICK Beatrice.
BEATRICE In faith, I will go.
295 BENEDICK We'll be friends first.
BEATRICE You dare easier be friends with me than fight with
mine enemy.
BENEDICK Is Claudio thine enemy?
BEATRICE Is a not approved in the height[3] a villain, that hath
300 slandered, scorned, dishonoured my kinswoman? O that I were

---

9. Compare the proverb "A desperate disease must
have a desperate cure."
1. Eat your words, go back on your oath. Benedick takes
it to mean his sword (as does F: "swear by it and eat it").
2. You have stopped me at a fortunate moment.
3. Is he not proved in the highest degree.

a man! What, bear her in hand[4] until they come to take hands, and then with public accusation, uncovered° slander, unmit- igated rancour—O God that I were a man! I would eat his heart in the market place.   *barefaced*

305 BENEDICK   Hear me, Beatrice.

BEATRICE   Talk with a man out at a window—a proper saying!°   *a likely story*

BENEDICK   Nay, but Beatrice.

BEATRICE   Sweet Hero, she is wronged, she is slandered, she is undone.

310 BENEDICK   Beat—

BEATRICE   Princes and counties! Surely a princely testimony, a goodly count,[5] Count Comfit,° a sweet gallant, surely. O that I were a man for his sake! Or that I had any friend would be a man for my sake! But manhood is melted into courtesies,   *Sugarplum*

315 valour into compliment, and men are only turned into tongue, and trim° ones, too. He is now as valiant as Hercules that° only tells a lie and swears it. I cannot be a man with° wishing, there- fore I will die a woman with grieving.   *fine (ironic) / who*   *by*

BENEDICK   Tarry, good Beatrice. By this hand, I love thee.

320 BEATRICE   Use it for my love some other way than swearing by it.

BENEDICK   Think you in your soul the Count Claudio hath wronged Hero?

BEATRICE   Yea, as sure as I have a thought or a soul.

325 BENEDICK   Enough, I am engaged,° I will challenge him. I will kiss your hand, and so I leave you. By this hand, Claudio shall render me a dear account.° As you hear of me, so think of me. Go comfort your cousin. I must say she is dead. And so, farewell.   [*Exeunt*]   *pledged*   *pay me dearly*

4.2

*Enter [*DOGBERRY *and* VERGES] *the constables, and the Town Clerk [the* SEXTON], *in gowns,*[1] [*and the* WATCH, *with*] BORACHIO [*and* CONRAD]

DOGBERRY   Is our whole dissembly° appeared?   *(for "assembly")*

VERGES   O, a stool and a cushion for the Sexton.

SEXTON [*sits*]   Which be the malefactors?[2]

DOGBERRY   Marry, that am I, and my partner.

5 VERGES   Nay, that's certain, we have the exhibition° to examine.   *(for "commission")*

SEXTON   But which are the offenders that are to be examined? Let them come before Master Constable.

DOGBERRY   Yea, marry, let them come before me. What is your name, friend?

10 BORACHIO   Borachio.

DOGBERRY [*to the* SEXTON]   Pray write down 'Borachio'.[*To* CON- RAD] Yours, sirrah?[3]

CONRAD   I am a gentleman, sir, and my name is Conrad.

DOGBERRY   Write down 'Master Gentleman Conrad'.—Masters,

15 do you serve God?

---

4. *bear her in hand:* lead her on with false hopes.
5. Story, tale (with plays on "count" as a legal indict- ment and as Claudio's title).
4.2 Location: A prison or hearing room in Messina.
1. Constables wore black gowns. The Sexton is pre- sumably Francis Seacoal (3.5.50). Q's direction calls him the town clerk, an office more appropriate to his

function in the scene than sexton, with which, however, it seems often to have been combined.
2. Dogberry seems to mistake "malefactors" for "fac- tors," or agents.
3. Contemptuous, since "sirrah" is used to address inferiors, provoking Conrad's claim to be a gentleman.

CONRAD *and* BORACHIO   Yea, sir, we hope.

DOGBERRY   Write down that they hope they serve God. And
write 'God' first, for God defend° but God should go before[4]   *forbid*
such villains. Masters, it is proved already that you are little
20   better than false knaves, and it will go near to be thought so
shortly. How answer you for yourselves?

CONRAD   Marry, sir, we say we are none.

DOGBERRY   A marvellous witty° fellow, I assure you, but I will go   *clever*
about with° him. Come you hither, sirrah. A word in your ear,   *will outwit*
25   sir. I say to you it is thought you are false knaves.

BORACHIO   Sir, I say to you we are none.

DOGBERRY   Well, stand aside. Fore God, they are both in a tale.°   *telling the same story*
Have you writ down that they are none?

SEXTON   Master Constable, you go not the way to examine. You
30   must call forth the watch that are their accusers.

DOGBERRY   Yea, marry, that's the eftest° way. Let the watch come   *(for "aptest")*
forth. Masters, I charge you in the Prince's name accuse these
men.

FIRST WATCHMAN   This man said, sir, that Don John, the Prince's
35   brother, was a villain.

DOGBERRY   Write down Prince John a villain. Why, this is flat
perjury,[5] to call a prince's brother villain.

BORACHIO   Master Constable.

DOGBERRY   Pray thee, fellow, peace. I do not like thy look, I
40   promise thee.

SEXTON   What heard you him say else?

SECOND WATCHMAN   Marry, that he had received a thousand
ducats of Don John for accusing the Lady Hero wrongfully.

DOGBERRY   Flat burglary, as ever was committed.

45   VERGES   Yea, by mass,[6] that it is.

SEXTON   What else, fellow?

FIRST WATCHMAN   And that Count Claudio did mean upon° his   *with*
words to disgrace Hero before the whole assembly, and not
marry her.

50   DOGBERRY   O villain! Thou wilt be condemned into everlasting
redemption° for this.   *(for "damnation")*

SEXTON   What else?

WATCH   This is all.

SEXTON   And this is more, masters, than you can deny. Prince
55   John is this morning secretly stolen away. Hero was in this man-
ner accused, in this very manner refused, and upon the grief of
this suddenly died. Master Constable, let these men be bound
and brought to Leonato's. I will go before and show him their
examination.   [*Exit*]

60   DOGBERRY   Come, let them be opinioned.°   *(for "pinioned")*

VERGES   Let them be, in the hands—

CONRAD   Off, coxcomb![7]

DOGBERRY   God's° my life, where's the Sexton? Let him write   *God save*
down the Prince's officer coxcomb. Come, bind them. Thou
65   naughty varlet!°   *wicked knave*

CONRAD   Away, you are an ass, you are an ass.

---

4. (Punningly) take precedence over.
5. Perhaps a mistake for "treason" or "slander."
6. "By the mass," a common oath.

7. This is an emendation of a corrupt passage, given in
Q as part of the previous speech. These words could be
spoken by Borachio.

DOGBERRY   Dost thou not suspect° my place? Dost thou not sus-   *(for "respect")*
pect my years? O that he were here to write me down an ass!
But masters, remember that I am an ass. Though it be not
70   written down, yet forget not that I am an ass. No, thou villain,
thou art full of piety,° as shall be proved upon thee by good   *(for "impiety")*
witness. I am a wise fellow, and which is more, an officer, and
which is more, a householder, and which is more, as pretty a
piece of flesh⁸ as any is in Messina, and one that knows the
75   law, go to, and a rich fellow enough, go to, and a fellow that
hath had losses,⁹ and one that hath two gowns, and everything
handsome about him. Bring him away. O that I had been writ
down an ass!   *Exeunt*

5.1

Enter LEONATO *and* [ANTONIO] *his brother*

ANTONIO   If you go on thus, you will kill yourself,
And 'tis not wisdom thus to second° grief   *assist*
Against yourself.

LEONATO   I pray thee cease thy counsel,
Which falls into mine ears as profitless
5   As water in a sieve. Give not me counsel,
Nor let no comforter delight mine ear
But such a one whose wrongs do suit° with mine.   *match*
Bring me a father that so loved his child,
Whose joy of° her is overwhelmed like mine,   *in*
10   And bid him speak of patience.
Measure his woe the length and breadth of mine,
And let it answer every strain° for strain,   *strong feeling*
As thus for thus, and such a grief for such,
In every lineament, branch, shape, and form.
15   If such a one will smile and stroke his beard,
Bid sorrow wag,° cry 'hem'¹ when he should groan,   *be off*
Patch° grief with proverbs, make misfortune drunk°   *Mend / insensible*
With candle-wasters,² bring him yet to me,
And I of him will gather patience.
20   But there is no such man, for, brother, men
Can counsel and speak comfort to that grief
Which they themselves not feel, but tasting it
Their counsel turns to passion, which before
Would give preceptial° medicine to rage,   *precepts as*
25   Fetter strong madness in a silken thread,
Charm ache with air° and agony with words.   *breath*
No, no, 'tis all men's office° to speak patience   *business*
To those that wring° under the load of sorrow,   *writhe*
But no man's virtue nor sufficiency°   *ability*
30   To be so moral° when he shall endure   *moralizing*
The like himself. Therefore give me no counsel.
My griefs cry louder than advertisement.°   *advice*

ANTONIO   Therein do men from children nothing differ.

LEONATO   I pray thee peace, I will be flesh and blood,
35   For there was never yet philosopher

---

8. *as pretty . . . flesh:* as fine (or gallant) a mortal man.
9. *hath had losses:* was once richer.
5.1 Location: Near Leonato's house.

1. Clear his throat (as if about to make a speech).
2. Philosophers, burners of midnight oil (and their works).

That could endure the toothache patiently,
However they have writ the style of gods,
And made a pish at chance and sufferance.[3]

ANTONIO   Yet bend° not all the harm upon yourself.   *direct*
40   Make those that do offend you suffer, too.

LEONATO   There thou speak'st reason, nay I will do so.
My soul doth tell me Hero is belied,
And that shall Claudio know, so shall the Prince,
And all of them that thus dishonour her.

              Enter [DON PEDRO *the*] *Prince and* CLAUDIO

45 ANTONIO   Here comes the Prince and Claudio hastily.

DON PEDRO   Good e'en,° good e'en.   *evening*

CLAUDIO   Good day to both of you.

LEONATO   Hear you, my lords?

DON PEDRO   We have some haste, Leonato.

LEONATO   Some haste, my lord! Well, fare you well, my lord.
Are you so hasty now? Well, all is one.°   *no matter*

50 DON PEDRO   Nay, do not quarrel with us, good old man.

ANTONIO   If he could right himself with quarrelling,
Some of us° would lie low.   *(Don Pedro and Claudio)*

CLAUDIO   Who wrongs him?

LEONATO   Marry, thou dost wrong me, thou dissembler, thou.[4]
Nay, never lay thy hand upon thy sword,
I fear thee not.

55 CLAUDIO   Marry, beshrew° my hand   *curse*
If it should give your age such cause of fear.
In faith, my hand meant nothing to[5] my sword.

LEONATO   Tush, tush, man, never fleer° and jest at me.   *sneer; mock*
I speak not like a dotard nor a fool,
60 As under privilege of age to brag
What I have done being young, or what would do
Were I not old. Know Claudio to thy head,°   *face*
Thou hast so wronged mine innocent child and me
That I am forced to lay my reverence by
65 And with grey hairs and bruise of many days
Do challenge thee to trial of a man.°   *of manhood*
I say thou hast belied mine innocent child.
Thy slander hath gone through and through her heart,
And she lies buried with her ancestors,
70 O, in a tomb where never scandal slept
Save this of hers, framed° by thy villainy.   *created*

CLAUDIO   My villainy?

LEONATO   Thine, Claudio, thine I say.

DON PEDRO   You say not right, old man.

LEONATO   My lord, my lord,
I'll prove it on his body if he dare,
75 Despite his nice fence[6] and his active practice,
His May of youth and bloom of lustihood.°   *virility*

CLAUDIO   Away, I will not have to do with you.

LEONATO   Canst thou so doff me?° Thou hast killed my child. *brush me off*
If thou kill'st me, boy, thou shalt kill a man.

---

3. *writ . . . sufferance:* written as if they transcended human passion, and expressed themselves scornfully about (said "pish" to) bad luck and suffering.

4. "Thou" is used contemptuously here.
5. My hand had no designs upon.
6. His nimble fencing (said contemptuously).

80 ANTONIO   He shall kill two of us, and men indeed.
　　　But that's no matter, let him kill one first.
　　　Win me and wear me.[7] Let him answer me.°　　　　　　　*(in a duel)*
　　　Come follow me boy, come sir boy, come follow me,
　　　Sir boy, I'll whip you from your foining fence.[8]
85　　Nay, as I am a gentleman, I will.
　　LEONATO   Brother.
　　ANTONIO   Content yourself.° God knows, I loved my niece,　　*Don't interfere*
　　　And she is dead, slandered to death by villains
　　　That dare as well answer a man indeed
90　　As I dare take a serpent by the tongue.
　　　Boys, apes,° braggarts, jacks,° milksops!　　　　　　*fools / knaves*
　　LEONATO   Brother Antony—
　　ANTONIO   Hold you content. What, man, I know them, yea
　　　And what they weigh, even to the utmost scruple.°　　　*¼4 ounce*
95　　Scambling, outfacing, fashion-monging boys,[9]
　　　That lie, and cog,° and flout,° deprave,° and slander,　*cheat / mock / defame*
　　　Go anticly,° and show an outward hideousness,[1]　*outlandishly dressed*
　　　And speak off half a dozen dangerous words,
　　　How they might hurt their enemies, if they durst,
100　　And this is all.
　　LEONATO   But brother Antony—
　　ANTONIO   Come, 'tis no matter,
　　　Do not you meddle, let me deal in this.
　　DON PEDRO   Gentlemen both, we will not wake° your patience.　　*test*
105　　My heart is sorry for your daughter's death,
　　　But on my honour she was charged with nothing
　　　But what was true and very full of proof.
　　LEONATO   My lord, my lord—
　　DON PEDRO   　　　　　　　I will not hear you.
　　LEONATO   No? Come brother, away. I will be heard.
110　ANTONIO   And shall, or some of us will smart for it.
　　　　　　　　Exeunt [LEONATO *and* ANTONIO]
　　　　　Enter BENEDICK
　　DON PEDRO   See, see, here comes the man we went to seek.
　　CLAUDIO   Now signor, what news?
　　BENEDICK   [*to* DON PEDRO]   Good day, my lord.
　　DON PEDRO   Welcome, signor. You are almost come to part
115　　almost a fray.
　　CLAUDIO   We had liked to have had° our two noses snapped off　*We nearly had*
　　　with° two old men without teeth.　　　　　　　　　　　*by*
　　DON PEDRO   Leonato and his brother. What thinkest thou? Had
　　　we fought, I doubt° we should have been too young for them.　*suspect*
120　BENEDICK   In a false quarrel there is no true valour. I came to
　　　seek you both.
　　CLAUDIO   We have been up and down to seek thee, for we are
　　　high-proof° melancholy and would fain have it beaten away.　*to a high degree*
　　　Wilt thou use thy wit?
125　BENEDICK   It is in my scabbard. Shall I draw it?
　　DON PEDRO   Dost thou wear thy wit by thy side?

7. A form of challenge: let him beat me and only then boast of it.
8. Thrusting position in fencing (Antonio probably means that he will compel Claudio to close with him in the duel, or that he will literally take a whip to him).
9. *Scambling . . . boys:* Quarrelsome, insolent, faddish boys.
1. A fearsome exterior.

CLAUDIO   Never any did so, though very many have been beside
their wit.° I will bid thee draw as we do the minstrels,[2] draw to   *out of their minds*
pleasure us.

130   DON PEDRO   As I am an honest man he looks pale. Art thou sick,
or angry?

CLAUDIO   What, courage, man. What though care killed a cat,
thou hast mettle° enough in thee to kill care.   *spirit; courage*

BENEDICK   Sir, I shall meet your wit in the career° an you   *at full gallop*
135   charge° it against me. I pray you choose another subject.   *aim*

CLAUDIO   Nay then, give him another staff.° This last was broke   *lance*
cross.[3]

DON PEDRO   By this light, he changes° more and more. I think   *changes color*
he be angry indeed.

140   CLAUDIO   If he be, he knows how to turn his girdle.[4]

BENEDICK   [*aside to* CLAUDIO]   Shall I speak a word in your ear?

CLAUDIO   God bless° me from a challenge.   *protect*

BENEDICK   You are a villain. I jest not. I will make it good how
you dare, with what° you dare, and when you dare. Do me   *whatever weapon*
145   right,[5] or I will protest° your cowardice. You have killed a sweet   *proclaim*
lady, and her death shall fall heavy on you. Let me hear from
you.

CLAUDIO   Well, I will meet you, so I may have good cheer.

DON PEDRO   What, a feast, a feast?

150   CLAUDIO   I'faith, I thank him, he hath bid me to a calf's head
and a capon, the which if I do not carve most curiously,° say   *daintily*
my knife's naught.° Shall I not find a woodcock[6] too?   *useless*

BENEDICK   Sir, your wit ambles[7] well, it goes easily.

DON PEDRO   I'll tell thee how Beatrice praised thy wit the other
155   day. I said thou hadst a fine wit. 'True,' said she, 'a fine little
one.' 'No,' said I, 'a great wit.' 'Right,' says she, 'a great gross
one.' 'Nay,' said I, 'a good wit.' 'Just,' said she, 'it hurts nobody.'
'Nay,' said I, 'the gentleman is wise.' 'Certain,' said she, 'a wise
gentleman.'[8] 'Nay,' said I, 'he hath the tongues.'° 'That I   *knows several languages*
160   believe,' said she, 'for he swore a thing to me on Monday night
which he forswore on Tuesday morning. There's a double
tongue, there's two tongues.' Thus did she an hour together
trans-shape° thy particular virtues, yet at last she concluded   *distort*
with a sigh thou wast the properest° man in Italy.   *handsomest*

165   CLAUDIO   For the which she wept heartily and said she cared
not.

DON PEDRO   Yea, that she did. But yet for all that, an if° she did   *an if = if*
not hate him deadly she would love him dearly. The old man's
daughter told us all.

170   CLAUDIO   All, all. And moreover, God saw him when he was hid
in the garden.[9]

DON PEDRO   But when shall we set the savage bull's horns on the
sensible Benedick's head?

---

2. *draw . . . minstrels:* draw a sword, the way a minstrel
is bidden to draw a bow across his musical instrument.
3. Was snapped in the middle, like a badly handled
lance. (Claudio is mocking Benedick's attempt at wit.)
4. A colloquialism of uncertain derivation, possibly
meaning "let him get on with it" or "that's his problem."
5. Give me satisfaction.
6. The calf's head, capon, and woodcock were varieties

of food that also symbolize stupidity.
7. Moves slowly (in other words, it does not gallop as a
quick wit would).
8. A phrase often used ironically to mean "an old fool."
9. Allusion to Genesis 3:8 (Adam attempting to hide
from God in the Garden of Eden); contains a half-
hidden reference to the trick played on Benedick in the
garden.

CLAUDIO Yea, and text underneath, 'Here dwells Benedick the
175 married man'.[1]

BENEDICK Fare you well, boy, you know my mind. I will leave
you now to your gossip-like° humour. You break° jests as brag-   *old-womanish / crack*
garts do their blades[2] which, God be thanked, hurt not. [*To*
DON PEDRO] My lord, for your many courtesies I thank you.
180 I must discontinue your company. Your brother the bastard is
fled from Messina. You have among you killed a sweet and
innocent lady. For my lord Lackbeard there, he and I shall
meet, and till then, peace be with him.   *Exit*

DON PEDRO He is in earnest.
185 CLAUDIO In most profound earnest, and, I'll warrant you, for the
love of Beatrice.

DON PEDRO And hath challenged thee.

CLAUDIO Most sincerely.

DON PEDRO What a pretty thing man is when he goes in his
190 doublet and hose and leaves off his wit![3]

> *Enter* [DOGBERRY *and* VERGES] *the constables,* [*the*
> WATCH,] CONRAD, *and* BORACHIO

CLAUDIO He is then a giant to an ape. But then is an ape a
doctor to such a man.[4]

DON PEDRO But soft you,° let me be. Pluck up,° my heart, and   *wait / Collect yourself*
be sad. Did he not say my brother was fled?
195 DOGBERRY Come you sir, if justice cannot tame you, she shall
ne'er weigh more reasons[5] in her balance.° Nay, an you be a   *scales*
cursing hypocrite once,° you must be looked to.   *even once*

DON PEDRO How now, two of my brother's men bound? Bora-
chio one.
200 CLAUDIO Hearken after° their offence, my lord.   *Inquire into*

DON PEDRO Officers, what offence have these men done?

DOGBERRY Marry, sir, they have committed false report, more-
over they have spoken untruths, secondarily they are slanders,° *(for "slanderers")*
sixth and lastly they have belied a lady, thirdly they have veri-
205 fied° unjust things, and to conclude, they are lying knaves.   *affirmed as true*

DON PEDRO First I ask thee what they have done, thirdly I ask
thee what's their offence, sixth and lastly why they are commit-
ted,° and to conclude, what you lay to their charge.   *held on arrest*

CLAUDIO Rightly reasoned, and in his own division.° And by my   *logical organization*
210 troth there's one meaning well suited.[6]

DON PEDRO [*to* CONRAD *and* BORACHIO] Who have you of-
fended, masters, that you are thus bound to your answer?[7] This
learned constable is too cunning to be understood. What's your
offence?
215 BORACHIO Sweet Prince, let me go no farther to mine answer.° *trial; account*
Do you hear me, and let this Count kill me. I have deceived
even your very eyes. What your wisdoms could not discover,
these shallow fools have brought to light, who in the night over-
heard me confessing to this man how Don John your brother

1. Claudio and Don Pedro recall that Benedick joked
that if he ever fell in love, his friends could set horns in
his forehead, have his picture painted, and title it
"Benedick, the married man" (1.1.215–19).
2. Braggarts secretly dent their swords to make it
appear that they have been dealing fierce blows.
3. When he puts on fine clothes but forgets to wear his
brain.

4. Such a man is much bigger than an ape, but an ape
is a learned man ("doctor") compared with him.
5. Legal cases. Also, "reason" was pronounced like
"raisin," producing a comic image here.
6. Dressed in several different costumes (with play on
legal "suit").
7. Required to respond (punning on "bound over for
trial" and "bound with ropes").

220   incensed° me to slander the Lady Hero, how you were brought   *incited*
into the orchard and saw me court Margaret in Hero's gar-
ments, how you disgraced her when you should marry her. My
villainy they have upon record, which I had rather seal° with   *confirm; end*
my death than repeat over to my shame. The lady is dead upon
225   mine and my master's false accusation, and briefly, I desire
nothing but the reward of a villain.

DON PEDRO [*to* CLAUDIO]   Runs not this speech like iron through
your blood?

CLAUDIO   I have drunk poison whiles he uttered it.

230   DON PEDRO [*to* BORACHIO]   But did my brother set thee on to
this?

BORACHIO   Yea, and paid me richly for the practice° of it.   *execution*

DON PEDRO   He is composed and framed° of treachery,   *made up*
And fled he is upon this villainy.

235   CLAUDIO   Sweet Hero, now thy image doth appear
In the rare semblance° that I loved it first.   *likeness*

DOGBERRY   Come, bring away the plaintiffs.° By this time our   *(for "defendants")*
Sexton hath reformed° Signor Leonato of the matter. And mas-   *(for "informed")*
ters, do not forget to specify, when time and place shall serve,
240   that I am an ass.

VERGES   Here, here comes Master Signor Leonato, and the Sex-
ton, too.
Enter LEONATO, [ANTONIO *his*] *brother, and the* SEXTON

LEONATO   Which is the villain? Let me see his eyes,
That when I note another man like him
245   I may avoid him. Which of these is he?

BORACHIO   If you would know your wronger, look on me.

LEONATO   Art thou the slave that with thy breath hast killed
Mine innocent child?

BORACHIO   Yea, even I alone.

LEONATO   No, not so, villain, thou beliest thyself.
250   Here stand a pair of honourable men.°   *men of rank*
A third is fled that had a hand in it.
I thank you, Princes, for my daughter's death.
Record it with your high and worthy deeds.
'Twas bravely done, if you bethink you of it.

255   CLAUDIO   I know not how to pray your patience,
Yet I must speak. Choose your revenge yourself,
Impose° me to what penance your invention   *Subject*
Can lay upon my sin. Yet sinned I not
But in mistaking.

DON PEDRO   By my soul, nor I,
260   And yet to satisfy this good old man
I would bend under any heavy weight
That he'll enjoin me to.

LEONATO   I cannot bid you bid my daughter live—
That were impossible—but I pray you both
265   Possess° the people in Messina here   *Inform*
How innocent she died, and if your love
Can labour aught in sad invention,[8]
Hang her an epitaph upon her tomb
And sing it to her bones, sing it tonight.

---

8. Can create any fruit from your sad imagination.

270   Tomorrow morning come you to my house,
       And since you could not be my son-in-law,
       Be yet my nephew. My brother hath a daughter,
       Almost the copy of my child that's dead,
       And she alone is heir to both of us.⁹
275   Give her the right you should have giv'n her cousin,
       And so dies my revenge.
       CLAUDIO   O noble sir!
       Your overkindness doth wring tears from me.
       I do embrace your offer; and dispose
       For henceforth° of poor Claudio.   *For the future*
280   LEONATO   Tomorrow then I will expect your coming.
       Tonight I take my leave. This naughty° man   *evil*
       Shall face to face be brought to Margaret,
       Who I believe was packed° in all this wrong,   *confederate*
       Hired to it by your brother.
       BORACHIO   No, by my soul, she was not,
285   Nor knew not what she did when she spoke to me,
       But always hath been just and virtuous
       In anything that I do know by° her.   *of*
       DOGBERRY [*to* LEONATO]   Moreover, sir, which indeed is not
       under white and black, this plaintiff¹ here, the offender, did
290   call me ass. I beseech you let it be remembered in his punish-
       ment. And also the watch heard them talk of one Deformed.
       They say he wears a key in his ear and a lock hanging by it,²
       and borrows money in God's name, the which he hath used°   *done habitually*
       so long and never paid that now men grow hard-hearted and
295   will lend nothing for God's sake.³ Pray you examine him upon
       that point.
       LEONATO   I thank thee for thy care and honest pains.
       DOGBERRY   Your worship speaks like a most thankful and rever-
       end youth, and I praise God for you.
300   LEONATO [*giving him money*]   There's for thy pains.
       DOGBERRY   God save the foundation.⁴
       LEONATO   Go. I discharge thee of thy prisoner, and I thank thee.
       DOGBERRY   I leave an arrant knave with your worship, which I
       beseech your worship to correct yourself,⁵ for the example of
305   others. God keep your worship, I wish your worship well. God
       restore you to health. I humbly give you leave to depart, and
       if a merry meeting may be wished, God prohibit° it. Come,   *(for "permit")*
       neighbour.   *Exeunt* [DOGBERRY *and* VERGES]
       LEONATO   Until tomorrow morning, lords, farewell.
310   ANTONIO   Farewell, my lords. We look for you tomorrow.
       DON PEDRO   We will not fail.
       CLAUDIO   Tonight I'll mourn with Hero.
       LEONATO [*to the* WATCH] Bring you these fellows on.—We'll talk
           with Margaret
       How her acquaintance grew with this lewd° fellow.   *Exeunt*   *worthless*

---

9. Shakespeare (or Leonato) has apparently forgotten
Antonio's son mentioned at 1.2.1.
1. For "defendant." *under white and black:* in writing.
2. Dogberry's garbled recollection of the lovelock men-
tioned at 3.3.149.
3. "In God's name" and "for God's sake" were phrases

used by beggars.
4. A conventional response to alms from a charitable
foundation.
5. Dogberry wishes Leonato himself to punish ("cor-
rect") Borachio but accidentally says that Leonato
should be punished.

5.2

Enter BENEDICK *and* MARGARET

BENEDICK   Pray thee, sweet Mistress Margaret, deserve well at
my hands by helping me to the speech of Beatrice.

MARGARET   Will you then write me a sonnet in praise of my
beauty?

5 BENEDICK   In so high a style, Margaret, that no man living shall
come over[1] it, for in most comely truth, thou deservest it.

MARGARET   To have no man come over me—why, shall I always
keep below stairs?[2]

BENEDICK   Thy wit is as quick as the greyhound's mouth, it
10 catches.

MARGARET   And yours as blunt as the fencer's foils,[3] which hit
but hurt not.

BENEDICK   A most manly wit, Margaret, it will not hurt a
woman. And so I pray thee call Beatrice. I give thee the buck-
15 lers.[4]

MARGARET   Give us the swords. We have bucklers of our own.

BENEDICK   If you use them, Margaret, you must put in the pikes
with a vice°—and they are dangerous weapons for maids.   screw

MARGARET   Well, I will call Beatrice to you, who I think hath
20 legs.   *Exit*

BENEDICK   And therefore will come.[5]
        [*Sings*]   The god love
                    That sits above,
                    And knows me, and knows me,
25   How pitiful I deserve—[6]
I mean in singing; but in loving, Leander the good swimmer,
Troilus the first employer of panders,[7] and a whole book full
of these quondam carpet-mongers[8] whose names yet run
smoothly in the even road of a blank verse, why they were never
30 so truly turned over and over° as my poor self in love. Marry, I   head over heels
cannot show it in rhyme. I have tried. I can find out no rhyme
to 'lady' but 'baby', an innocent° rhyme; for 'scorn' 'horn', a   a childish
hard[9] rhyme; for 'school' 'fool', a babbling rhyme. Very omi-
nous endings. No, I was not born under a rhyming planet,[1] nor
35 I cannot woo in festival terms.°   in fancy rhetoric
        Enter BEATRICE
Sweet Beatrice, wouldst thou come when I called thee?

BEATRICE   Yea, signor, and depart when you bid me.

BENEDICK   O, stay but till then.

BEATRICE   'Then' is spoken. Fare you well now. And yet ere I go,

---

5.2 Location: Near Leonato's house or in his garden.
1. Surpass; climb over (punning on "stile": stairs over
a fence). Margaret humorously takes "come over" in a
sexual sense.
2. In the servants' quarters (and therefore never as a
"mistress").
3. Practice rapiers, capped at the tip.
4. Benedick offers to surrender by giving up the buck-
lers: shields with spikes ("pikes") in the center. Mar-
garet bawdily interprets this as the female sexual organ.
5. A popular question and answer of the time was
"How came you hither?" "On my legs."
6. How greatly I deserve pity (but Benedick takes it as

"How pitifully small my deserts are"). These four lines
are the beginning of a popular sentimental ballad.
7. Troilus, loving Cressida, employed her uncle Pan-
darus as go-between. Leander swam the Hellespont
nightly to be with his love, Hero.
8. Knights of long ago ("quondam") who avoided mili-
tary service and spent their time in ladies' carpeted
boudoirs.
9. Disagreeable, because horns were associated with
cuckoldry.
1. At a time when the stars would influence me to
become a poet.

40   let me go with that° I came for, which is with knowing what   *what*
    hath passed between you and Claudio.

BENEDICK   Only foul words, and thereupon I will kiss thee.

BEATRICE   Foul words is but foul wind, and foul wind is but foul
    breath, and foul breath is noisome,° therefore I will depart   *nauseating*
45   unkissed.

BENEDICK   Thou hast frighted the word out of his° right sense,°   *its / meaning; wits*
    so forcible is thy wit. But I must tell thee plainly, Claudio
    undergoes° my challenge, and either I must shortly hear from   *is subject to*
    him or I will subscribe° him a coward. And I pray thee now tell   *proclaim*
50   me, for which of my bad parts didst thou first fall in love with
    me?

BEATRICE   For them all together, which maintain so politic° a   *cunningly governed*
    state of evil that they will not admit any good part to intermin-
    gle with them. But for which of my good parts did you first
55   suffer° love for me?   *feel*

BENEDICK   Suffer love—a good epithet.° I do suffer° love indeed,   *expression / suffer from*
    for I love thee against my will.

BEATRICE   In spite of your heart, I think. Alas, poor heart. If you
    spite it for my sake I will spite it for yours, for I will never love
60   that which my friend hates.

BENEDICK   Thou and I are too wise to woo peaceably.

BEATRICE   It appears not in this confession.[2] There's not one
    wise man among twenty that will praise himself.

BENEDICK   An old, an old instance,° Beatrice, that lived in the   *proverb*
65   time of good neighbours.[3] If a man do not erect in this age his
    own tomb ere he dies, he shall live no longer in monument°   *remembrance*
    than the bell rings and the widow weeps.

BEATRICE   And how long is that, think you?

BENEDICK   Question[4]—why, an hour in clamour° and a quarter   *ringing*
70   in rheum.° Therefore is it most expedient for the wise, if Don   *tears*
    Worm—his conscience[5]—find no impediment to the contrary,
    to be the trumpet of his own virtues, as I am to myself. So
    much for praising myself who, I myself will bear witness, is
    praiseworthy. And now tell me, how doth your cousin?

75 BEATRICE   Very ill.

BENEDICK   And how do you?

BEATRICE   Very ill too.

BENEDICK   Serve God, love me, and mend.° There will I leave   *recover*
    you too, for here comes one in haste.

Enter URSULA

80 URSULA   Madam, you must come to your uncle. Yonder's old
    coil° at home. It is proved my lady Hero hath been falsely   *great disturbance*
    accused, the Prince and Claudio mightily abused,° and Don   *deceived*
    John is the author of all, who is fled and gone. Will you come
    presently?

85 BEATRICE   Will you go hear this news, signor?

BENEDICK   I will live in thy heart, die[6] in thy lap, and be buried
    in thy eyes. And moreover, I will go with thee to thy uncle's.

Exeunt

---

2. Since it is not wise to claim to be wise.
3. In the good old days, when neighbors praised each
other.
4. That is the question.

5. Facetious way of referring to the proverbial gnawing
"worm of conscience."
6. With the common Elizabethan connotation of
orgasm.

5.3

Enter CLAUDIO, [DON PEDRO *the*] *Prince, and three or*
four with tapers][1] *all in black*

CLAUDIO   Is this the monument of Leonato?

A LORD   It is, my lord.

CLAUDIO[2]   [*reading from a scroll*]

> Done to death by slanderous tongues
> Was the Hero that here lies.

5

> Death in guerdon° of her wrongs   recompense
> Gives her fame which never dies.
> So the life that died with° shame   from
> Lives in death with glorious fame.

[He hangs the] epitaph [on the tomb]

> Hang thou there upon the tomb,

10

> Praising her when I am dumb.

Now music sound, and sing your solemn hymn.

Song

> Pardon, goddess of the night,[3]
> Those that slew thy virgin knight,[4]
> For the which with songs of woe

15

> Round about her tomb they go.
> Midnight, assist our moan,
> Help us to sigh and groan,
> > Heavily, heavily.
> Graves yawn, and yield your dead

20

> Till death be utterèd,°   fully lamented
> > Heavily, heavily.

CLAUDIO   Now, unto thy bones good night.
    Yearly will I do this rite.

DON PEDRO   Good morrow, masters, put your torches out.

25

    The wolves have preyed,[5] and look, the gentle day
    Before the wheels of Phoebus[6] round about
        Dapples the drowsy east with spots of grey.
    Thanks to you all, and leave us. Fare you well.

CLAUDIO   Good morrow, masters. Each his several° way.   separate

30

DON PEDRO   Come, let us hence, and put on other weeds,°   garments
    And then to Leonato's we will go.

CLAUDIO   And Hymen now with luckier issue speed 's[7]
    Than this° for whom we rendered up this woe.   *Exeunt*   this woman

5.4

Enter LEONATO, [ANTONIO,] BENEDICK, BEATRICE, MAR-
GARET, URSULA, FRIAR [FRANCIS], *and* HERO

FRIAR   Did I not tell you she was innocent?

LEONATO   So are the Prince and Claudio who accused her
    Upon° the error that you heard debated.   Because of

5.3 Location: A churchyard.
1. Candles or torches carried in token of penitence.
2. In Q, the poem is headed "Epitaph" and is not
ascribed to a particular speaker.
3. Diana, Roman goddess of the moon and patroness
of virgins.

4. Hero (imagined as a knight, or follower, of Diana).
5. Have finished preying (for the night has passed).
6. The sun god's chariot wheels.
7. And may Hymen (Greek god of marriage) grant us
more favorable results.
5.4 Location: Leonato's house.

But Margaret was in some fault for this,
5 Although against her will° as it appears   *unintentionally*
In the true course of all the question.°   *investigation*

ANTONIO   Well, I am glad that all things sorts° so well.   *turn out*

BENEDICK   And so am I, being else by faith° enforced   *my pledge*
To call young Claudio to a reckoning for it.

10 LEONATO   Well, daughter, and you gentlewomen all,
Withdraw into a chamber by yourselves,
And when I send for you come hither masked.

Exeunt [BEATRICE, HERO, MARGARET, *and* URSULA]

The Prince and Claudio promised by this hour
To visit me. You know your office,° brother,   *task*
15 You must be father to your brother's daughter,
And give her to young Claudio.

ANTONIO   Which I will do with confirmed° countenance.   *serious*

BENEDICK   Friar, I must entreat your pains, I think.

FRIAR   To do what, signor?

20 BENEDICK   To bind me or undo° me, one of them.   *ruin; unbind*
Signor Leonato, truth it is, good signor,
Your niece regards me with an eye of favour.

LEONATO   That eye my daughter lent her, 'tis most true.

BENEDICK   And I do with an eye of love requite her.

25 LEONATO   The sight whereof I think you had from me,
From Claudio and the Prince. But what's your will?

BENEDICK   Your answer, sir, is enigmatical.
But for my will, my will is° your good will   *is that*
May stand with ours this day to be conjoined
30 In the state of honourable marriage,
In which, good Friar, I shall desire your help.

LEONATO   My heart is with your liking.

FRIAR   And my help.
Here comes the Prince and Claudio.

Enter [DON PEDRO *the*] *Prince and* CLAUDIO *with attendants*

DON PEDRO   Good morrow to this fair assembly.

35 LEONATO   Good morrow, Prince. Good morrow, Claudio.
We here attend you. Are you yet° determined   *still*
Today to marry with my brother's daughter?

CLAUDIO   I'll hold my mind,° were she an Ethiope.[1]   *intention*

LEONATO   Call her forth, brother, here's the Friar ready.

[*Exit* ANTONIO]

40 DON PEDRO   Good morrow, Benedick. Why, what's the matter
That you have such a February face,
So full of frost, of storm and cloudiness?

CLAUDIO   I think he thinks upon the savage bull.[2]
Tush, fear not, man, we'll tip thy horns with gold,
45 And all Europa° shall rejoice at thee   *Europe*
As once Europa did at lusty Jove
When he would play the noble beast in love.[3]

BENEDICK   Bull Jove, sir, had an amiable° low,   *amorous*
And some such strange bull leapt your father's cow

---

1. In other words, black and therefore, according to the Elizabethan racist stereotype, ugly.
2. Continuing the teasing of 5.1.172.

3. In Greek mythology, Jove took the form of a bull to carry off the princess Europa, with whom he was in love.

50 And got a calf° in that same noble feat   *begot a blockhead*
Much like to you, for you have just his bleat.
   Enter [ANTONIO *with*] HERO, BEATRICE, MARGARET, *and*
   URSULA [*masked*]
CLAUDIO For this I owe you.⁴ Here comes other reck'nings.°   *accounts to settle*
Which is the lady I must seize upon?
ANTONIO This same is she, and I do give you her.
55 CLAUDIO Why then, she's mine. Sweet, let me see your face.
LEONATO No, that you shall not till you take her hand
Before this Friar and swear to marry her.
CLAUDIO [*to* HERO] Give me your hand before this holy friar.
I am your husband if you like of me.°   *like me*
60 HERO [*unmasking*] And when I lived I was your other wife;
And when you loved, you were my other husband.
CLAUDIO Another Hero!
HERO   Nothing certainer.
One Hero died defiled,° but I do live,   *slandered*
And surely as I live, I am a maid.
65 DON PEDRO The former Hero, Hero that is dead!
LEONATO She died, my lord, but whiles her slander lived.
FRIAR All this amazement can I qualify°   *lessen*
When after that the holy rites are ended
I'll tell you largely° of fair Hero's death.   *in full*
70 Meantime, let wonder° seem familiar,°   *marvels / commonplace*
And to the chapel let us presently.
BENEDICK Soft and fair,° Friar, which is Beatrice?   *Wait a minute*
BEATRICE [*unmasking*] I answer to that name, what is your will?
BENEDICK Do not you love me?
BEATRICE   Why no, no more than reason.
75 BENEDICK Why then, your uncle and the Prince and Claudio
Have been deceived. They swore you did.
BEATRICE Do not you love me?
BENEDICK   Troth no, no more than reason.
BEATRICE Why then, my cousin, Margaret, and Ursula
Are much deceived, for they did swear you did.
80 BENEDICK They swore that you were almost sick for me.
BEATRICE They swore that you were wellnigh dead for me.
BENEDICK 'Tis no such matter. Then you do not love me?
BEATRICE No, truly, but in friendly recompense.
LEONATO Come, cousin, I am sure you love the gentleman.
85 CLAUDIO And I'll be sworn upon't that he loves her,
For here's a paper written in his hand,
A halting sonnet of his own pure brain,
Fashioned° to Beatrice.   *Addressed*
HERO   And here's another,
Writ in my cousin's hand, stol'n from her pocket,
90 Containing her affection unto Benedick.
BENEDICK A miracle! Here's our own hands against our hearts.⁵
Come, I will have thee, but by this light, I take thee for pity.
BEATRICE I would not deny you, but by this good day, I yield
upon great persuasion, and partly to save your life, for I was
95 told you were in a consumption.°   *wasting away ill*

---

4. I will pay you back later (for the insults).   indifference we claim to feel in our hearts (or proves
5. Our own handwritten testimony contradicts the our hearts to be guilty of loving).

BENEDICK [*kissing her*]   Peace, I will stop your mouth.

DON PEDRO   How dost thou, Benedick the married man?

BENEDICK   I'll tell thee what, Prince: a college of wit-crackers
cannot flout° me out of my humour. Dost thou think I care for   *jeer*

100   a satire or an epigram? No, if a man will be beaten with brains,
a° shall wear nothing handsome about him.⁶ In brief, since I   *he*
do purpose° to marry, I will think nothing to any purpose that   *intend*
the world can say against it, and therefore never flout at me for
what I have said against it. For man is a giddy thing, and this is

105   my conclusion. For thy part, Claudio, I did think to have
beaten thee, but in that thou art like° to be my kinsman, live   *likely*
unbruised, and love my cousin.

CLAUDIO   I had well hoped thou wouldst have denied Beatrice,
that I might have cudgelled thee out of thy single life to make

110   thee a double dealer,° which out of question thou wilt be, if   *married man; adulterer*
my cousin do not look exceeding narrowly° to thee.   *closely*

BENEDICK   Come, come, we are friends, let's have a dance ere
we are married, that we may lighten our own hearts and our
wives' heels.

115 LEONATO   We'll have dancing afterward.

BENEDICK   First, of my word. Therefore play, music. [*To* DON
PEDRO] Prince, thou art sad, get thee a wife, get thee a wife.
There is no staff more reverend than one tipped with horn.⁷

     Enter MESSENGER

MESSENGER   My lord, your brother John is ta'en in flight,

120   And brought with armèd men back to Messina.

BENEDICK   Think not on him till tomorrow, I'll devise thee
brave° punishments for him. Strike up, pipers.   *fine*

     Dance [*and exeunt*]

---

6. No, if a man is easily injured by ridicule, he will
never even dare to dress well (since that would provoke

attention).
7. A final allusion to the cuckold's horns.

As You Like It

Much of *As You Like It* takes place in a forest, where characters in flight from treachery at court and injustice in the family take refuge. The play thus participates in the rich tradition of Renaissance pastoral literature in which the rustic world of forest and field offers an alternative to and a sanctuary from the urban or courtly milieu to which it is contrasted. The pastoral mode had its origins in ancient Greece, where the poet Theocritus used rural settings and rustic shepherds to explore the sorrows of love and the harsh injustices of daily life. The Roman poet Virgil expanded this tradition, elaborating in particular the opposition between city and country life that in the Renaissance was often transmuted into an opposition between court and country. In England, many of Shakespeare's contemporaries worked in pastoral forms, particularly Edmund Spenser, whose *Shepheardes Calendar* (1579) was modeled on Virgil's *Eclogues,* and Sir Philip Sidney, whose vast prose romance *The Countess of Pembrokes Arcadia* was first published in revised form in 1590.

As a literary mode, pastoral can take many forms. There can be pastoral lyrics, dialogues, prose romances, and dramas. Certain topics and situations, however, are common features of many kinds of pastoral. Often, for example, exiles from urban or courtly life temporarily take up residence in the country where they live and converse with shepherds, often disguising *themselves* as shepherds before an eventual return to the life from which they had fled. In their rural retreat, they hold singing contests and discuss the relative merits of country and court life, whether nature is improved or spoiled by art, and whether "gentleness" (meaning both "nobility" and "a virtuous nature") is a condition one can achieve or to which one must be born.

Fundamental to pastoral debates is a concern about the relationship of what is "natural" to what is "artificial," that is, about whether what human beings have made—cities, gardens, or systems of social hierarchy—is preferable to the simplicity and lack of artifice supposedly found in rural settings and communities. This preoccupation makes pastoral particularly suited to social criticism. Pastoral figures often dissect the evils of various ways of life—the cruelty of hard-hearted mistresses, the greed of landlords, the deceit of courtiers, and the venality of the clergy. But while pastoral frequently celebrates simplicity, it does so in a highly artful manner, drawing on conventions that have been part of the Western literary tradition for at least two thousand years. Pastoral is therefore not so much a spontaneous expression of "natural" simplicity as the artful imitation of such simplicity by characters exiled from more sophisticated realms who for a time assume the guise of shepherds and play an elaborate game of "Let's pretend." Hence the many disguises found in pastoral, where courtiers pose as rustic shepherds, men as women, women as men, and dukes as forest outlaws. To minds of a stolidly serious cast, pastoral can appear to be a silly, escapist genre. To those less dismissive of the world of "Let's pretend," it offers an opportunity to see more clearly—and perhaps then to change—the world in which one ordinarily lives by entering for a time the playful, meditative, and artificial realm of imaginary shepherds.

In *As You Like It,* Shakespeare gave himself over to the pleasures and the seriousness of pastoral without seeming to find them antithetical. In the main action, a good ruler, Duke Senior, has been ousted from his throne by a usurping younger brother, Duke Frederick. The banished Duke takes refuge in the Forest of Ardenne, where he lives like Robin Hood with a band of loyal followers. When his daughter, Rosalind, companion to Frederick's daughter, Celia, is likewise banished, she disguises herself as a

First page of the *Gest of Robin Hood*, one of the most important sixteenth-century renditions of the Robin Hood legend.

young man named Ganymede and also journeys to Ardenne. Celia, posing as a lowborn woman named Aliena, goes with her, as does Touchstone the clown. A second line of action concerns two other brothers: Orlando, the youngest son, and Oliver, the oldest son of Sir Rowland de Bois. The inheritor of his father's estate, Oliver treats Orlando cruelly, denying him the education befitting a gentleman. In danger both from Duke Frederick and from his brother, Orlando also flees to the forest, accompanied by Adam, his dead father's eighty-year-old servant. By Act 2, all of these refugees from court life find themselves in a natural world, which, in spite of its considerable hardships, they prefer to the treachery of court. Ardenne is not Edenic. There are lions and snakes in this pastoral retreat and real shepherds like Corin who speak matter-of-factly about the hard and dirty labor that tending real sheep entails. But in Ardenne, there is also room for courtship games, for brotherly kindness, and for music. In fact, this play contains more songs than any other Shakespearean drama. In their song-filled green world, the characters hunt deer, tend sheep, and converse endlessly about love, exile, and the relative merits of court and country. Eventually, their chief troubles resolved, most return to court, leaving the forest once more to its native inhabitants and to those few courtiers who permanently embrace it.

The broad outlines of this story are taken from Thomas Lodge's enormously popular prose romance *Rosalynde,* written in 1586–87 and published in 1590, although Shakespeare changes many details and points of emphasis. In Lodge, for example, the Duke Senior and Duke Frederick characters are not brothers, but in both the ducal and the Orlando-Oliver plots, Shakespeare makes the enmity of brothers the principal sign of the corruption of "civilized" life. In Lodge, moreover, the father in the Orlando-Oliver plot does not follow the English custom of primogeniture, by which all property is settled on the oldest son; instead, he divides his property among his male offspring according to their merits. By having Oliver inherit almost everything, Shakespeare evokes an English social practice that caused great hardship to many younger brothers. The court women are handled differently as well by Shakespeare: he reduces the Celia character's centrality and instead emphasizes Rosalind and her love affair with Orlando. Shakespeare also tempers the violence of Lodge's resolution and adds to his cast of characters. In *Rosalynde*, the exiled Duke defeats the usurper in battle, but Shakespeare's Frederick has a religious conversion and voluntarily relinquishes the dukedom. Oliver Martext, William, Audrey, Touchstone the clown, and Jaques the melancholy satirist are all Shakespeare's creations. Jaques, in particular, adds a touch of caustic salt and Touchstone a dash of earthy realism to the play's exploration of competing value systems.

In fact, *As You Like It* is poised carefully on the razor's edge separating fantasy from harsh reality. Shakespeare's use of place is a case in point. Lodge's romance is set in the Forest of Ardenne, an ancient woodland comprising part of what is now France, Belgium, and Luxembourg. Shakespeare also uses a French setting, and this edition emphasizes that fact by giving the French spelling, "Ardenne," to the forest. But in the First Folio (1623), this woodland is called the Forest of Arden, an anglicized spelling that also happens to be the name of an English forest near Shakespeare's birthplace in Warwickshire. This fortuitous overlapping of French and English place-names is indicative of the play's double vision. Overtly set in a fantastical foreign kingdom, *As You Like It* nonetheless alludes to places (such as the Forest of Arden) people (such as Robin Hood), and practices (such as primogeniture) native to Shakespeare's own England. Through the distancing artifice of pastoral, the play deals with problems close to home.

Lodge's prose romance is not the only source for *As You Like It*. The play also draws upon *The Tale of Gamelyn*, a violent Middle English narrative in which a younger brother seeks revenge upon an older brother who mistreats him, and which explicitly evokes the name of Robin Hood, the popular English hero whose deeds were celebrated in countless ballads and stories. In the opening scene of *As You Like It*, Charles the wrestler reports that the banished Duke is "already in the forest of Ardenne, and a many merry men with him; and there they live like the old Robin Hood of England. They say many young gentlemen flock to him every day, and fleet the time carelessly, as they did in the golden world" (1.1.99–103). Shakespeare could count on his audience to know the story of Robin Hood, and its evocation carried certain associations. The legendary figure and his band of men stood not only for the community and brotherhood characteristic of the Golden Age and absent in modern life, but also for resistance to tyranny. The great forests of England were the King's own preserves. To kill the deer in those forests was a crime against the monarch. Yet Robin Hood lived in the forest, dined on the King's deer, and opposed King John's unjust reign. In the 1590s, many of those resisting the enclosure of farmland for sheep grazing took refuge in forest areas, and poaching the King's deer had long been one way the poor defied the law to feed themselves when food was short, as it often was because of bad food harvests in the late 1590s.

As You Like It only obliquely alludes to this immediate social context, but Act 1 depicts a world of injustice and social disorder that both motivates the flight to Ardenne and evokes the tradition of opposition to injustice associated with Robin Hood. Orlando's situation speaks to the peculiarly English plight of younger brothers who, under the system of primogeniture, inherited little from their fathers and were often at the mercy of elder siblings. Oliver is a nightmare version of an eldest son: he deprives Orlando of a gentleman's education, connives with the Duke's professional wrestler to have his brother injured, and throws his father's old servant, Adam, out of the house. His cruelty is echoed by the tyranny of Duke Frederick. The play's opening thus clearly underscores the existence of inhumanity and tyrannical willfulness in the court and in the household of old Sir Rowland's eldest son. Less clear is whether this corruption stems from human institutions, particularly the system of primogeniture, or from the "naturally" evil natures of Frederick and Oliver. The play does not answer this or other thorny questions directly. In fact, it seems organized to provoke thought rather than urge conclusions, and the ending does not so much lay out a plan for social reform as indulge the fantasy that all desires, however contradictory, can be fulfilled through marriage and the renewal of brotherly affection. The play's most sustained examination of human folly focuses on the behavior of those who succumb to Cupid's arrows. There are many lovers in Ardenne, and for almost none does the course of love run smooth. Lovesickness was a recognized malady in early modern culture, a condition that so disordered those who endured it that it could cause paleness, sighing, tears, fainting, melancholy, palpitations, and a host of other symptoms. The play represents all lovers as slightly mad and approaches their tribulations with a mixture of sympathy, detached amusement, and analytical curiosity. In part, Shakespeare draws on the critical capacities of pastoral to explore the causes of lovers' unhappiness and to probe the surprisingly complex issue of what is natural in matters of love and sexual desire. In this regard, the play takes little for granted—neither the stability of gender difference nor the naturalness of heterosexuality nor the invariant nature of being in love.

Rosalind and Orlando are the play's most prominent lovers, and through their courtship the play begins its exploration of the problems of loving well. Orlando, for example, loves by the book—that is, in imitation of the conventions employed by the fourteenth-century Italian poet Petrarch, whose love poems to a woman named Laura established one of the paradigmatic love rhetorics of Renaissance culture. Conventionally, the Petrarchan lover worships and idealizes a woman who is inaccessible to him, either because of her rank or because of her cold heart. He burns with passion; he wastes from despair; she does not respond. Orlando, rushing through the forest pinning bad love poems on trees, is a sendup of a Petrarchan lover. Touchstone makes fun of his verses; Rosalind, dressed as a man but pretending to be "Rosalind" in order to cure Orlando of his lovesickness, delights in showing how exaggerated and unrealistic are the Petrarchan lover's claims for the perfection of his mistress and the vastness of his suffering. As she caustically says to him, when he protests that he will die for his passion: "Men have died from time to time, and worms have eaten them, but not for love" (4.1.91–92). She is equally hard on the idealization of women, insisting that real women can be fickle and bad-tempered as easily as they can be goddesses. One way to interpret Orlando and Rosalind's interactions is to see her slowly educating him in a more realistic and egalitarian approach to the relationship of man to woman than that offered by the Petrarchan tradition. Yet the self-mockery, realism, and genuine regard for the other that come to characterize their relationship are hardly in themselves natural behaviors, but ones in which Orlando must be tutored.

Rosalind and Orlando, however, are not the only lovers in the forest. There is also the mooning shepherd, Silvius, who believes no one has ever loved with his intensity, and his proud mistress, Phoebe, who thinks much too well of her own limited charms and throws herself quite inappropriately into the part of the disdainful Petrarchan mistress. As Rosalind informs her: "I must tell you friendly in your ear, / Sell when you can. You are not for all markets" (3.5.60–61). Even Touchstone, ever ready to puncture the romantic ravings of Orlando and Rosalind, Silvius and Phoebe, cannot escape love's call. Functioning as the clown figure often does, to provide a detached commentary on the action around him, Touchstone is nonetheless a participant as well as an observer. His "love" is about as natural—in the sense of urgently physical—and as far removed from Petrarchan idealizations as can be imagined. His intended, Audrey, does not know what "poetical" means, and Touchstone laments that she has such a rudimentary command of language that she often cannot understand what he says to her. And yet, as he confides to Jaques, "As the ox hath his bow, sir, the horse his curb, and the falcon her bells, so man hath his desires" (3.3.65–66)—that is, as each creature has some restraint placed on his movement, so a man's sexual desires constrain him to accommodate himself to a woman, even one like Audrey, and to the marriage yoke. If Orlando and Silvius live too much in the thrall of poetic idealizations, Touchstone and Audrey starkly reveal what love looks like when it is reduced to a matter of pure desire, and all artfulness, all poetry, and all sweet amorous delay are eschewed.

The figure who instigates much of the play's talk about love is Rosalind, one of Shakespeare's liveliest heroines. Her attractiveness stems partly from the fact that she is at once an observer and critic of others and herself a full participant in the whirligig of love. In this, she resembles Touchstone and differs from the melancholy Jaques, who persistently catalogs the follies of others but holds back from full participation in the life around him. (Fittingly, Jaques remains in the forest at the end of the play, when most of the others return to their lives outside the pastoral retreat.) Rosalind is at the center of nearly everything that happens in As You Like It, and the complexity of her role is enhanced by the fact that for much of four acts she dresses like a man and successfully passes for one. In the 1590s, Shakespeare wrote a number of other comedies (Two Gentlemen of Verona, The Merchant of Venice, Twelfth Night) in which women dress as men to protect themselves from danger, to pursue a lover, or temporarily to acquire the prerogatives of the socially dominant gender. Rosalind's is arguably the most complicated of these cases of cross-dressing because she not only passes as a man, but while in her male disguise plays the role of Rosalind in her forest encounters with Orlando. A woman disguised as a man thus makes her own identity into a fiction she performs!

Rosalind's complex cross-dressing has many consequences. For one thing, it makes problematic how natural are the gender distinctions that supposedly separate man from woman. In a literal sense, clothes here make the man—or woman. A doublet and hose and a swaggering demeanor effectively create the illusion of masculinity, and Rosalind uses her disguise to try on the privileges of the supposedly superior sex. Far from a passive object of Petrarchan adoration, she takes charge of her escape from Frederick's court and her encounters with Orlando in the forest. Typically, Renaissance women remained under the control of their fathers and mothers until marriage bequeathed them to the care of a husband. Rosalind's special circumstances—a father banished, an uncle who wants her gone from court—put her in an unusual situation. Her decision to cross-dress further sets her apart. Mobile, loquacious, and bossy, Rosalind confutes the idea that women are by nature passive, silent, and in need of masculine supervision. At the same time, she exhibits certain stereotypically "female" behavior: to Celia she confesses how much she is in love with Orlando, and when he is wounded, she faints when she sees his blood on a cloth. Perhaps the point is that the figure of the cross-dressed Rosalind keeps open the question of what a woman (or a man) "really" is.

To the question of how men and women differ, Renaissance anatomical theory gave some answers dissimilar to those we now take for granted. According to Galen, an ancient Greek anatomist whose work on the body was widely influential in the early modern period, men and woman had the same anatomical structures; women were simply less perfect than men, there having been less heat present when they were conceived. This meant, among other things, that women's genitalia were just like a man's—with the vagina and ovaries corresponding to the penis and scrotum—except that they had not been pushed outside the body as a man's had been. Because by this account male-female difference was less grounded in ideas of absolute bodily difference than is typical today, much emphasis was placed on behavioral differences and on distinctions of dress. Preachers enjoined women to be chaste, silent, and obedient, and forbade them to wear the clothes of the opposite sex. In such a context, female cross-dressing, however playfully undertaken, always threatened to expose the artifice of gender distinctions by showing how easily one sex could assume the clothes and ape the behavior of the other.

The particularities of Rosalind's disguise, moreover, complicate her representation

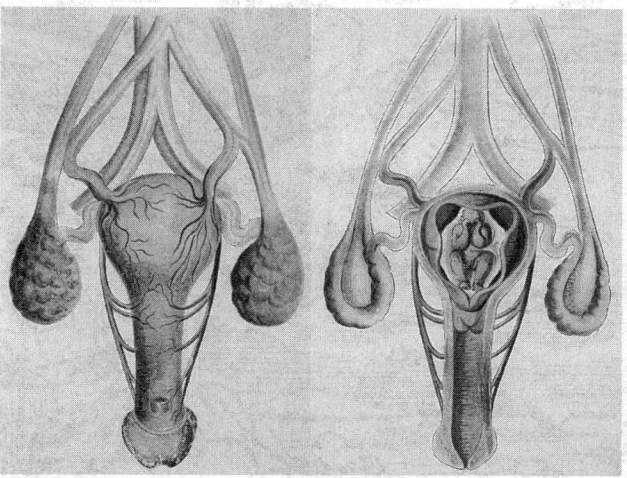

Typical sixteenth-century anatomy-book illustration of the female organs of generation. *Left:* the vagina and uterus are almost indistinguishable from the male penis and scrotum. *Right:* they have been cut open to reveal a tiny fetus in the uterus. From Fritz Weindler, *Geschichte der Gynäkologisch-anatomischen Abbildung* (1908). (Originally appeared in George Bartisch, *Kunstbuch*, 1575.)

even further. In disguise, Rosalind calls herself Ganymede, a name that had long-standing and unmistakable associations with homoerotic love. In Greek mythology, Ganymede was a beautiful boy whom Jove desired and whom he seized and carried to Mount Olympus to be cupbearer to the gods. A number of early modern paintings, woodcuts, and engravings depict the moment when Jove, in the form of an eagle, sweeps the boy away from earth and into the heavens. In Shakespeare's day, the word "Ganymede" commonly signified a young boy who was the lover of another (usually older) man. Shakespeare could hardly have been unaware of these associations when he had Rosalind choose this name as her alias. Consequently, when the cross-dressed heroine commands Orlando to woo his "Rosalind," he woos a figure who is dressed like a man and who bears a name signifying his status as a homoerotic love object. In performance, what the audience *sees* is one "man" flirting with another, even while the audience *knows* that one of these "men" is a woman. Provocatively, Shakespeare uses Orlando and Rosalind's encounters to overlay a story of male-female desire with traces of another tale of a man's love for a boy.

Long before *As You Like It* was penned, pastoral had been used to depict the beauty of both male friendship and homoerotic love. Edmund Spenser, in the January Eclogue of *The Shepheardes Calender*, describes the passion of Hobbinol for Colin Cloute, who in turn loves an unresponsive woman named Rosalind. Commenting on this passage, E. K., the anonymous annotator of *The Shepheardes Calender*, drew on classical precedent to defend pederastic love (love of an older man for a younger boy) as less dangerous than gynerastic love (love of man for woman). Since women were generally considered men's intellectual and moral inferiors, love for a woman was—so the argument went—less likely to be a rational passion than was love for a boy or a man. In the 1580s, Richard Barnfield wrote a pastoral work called *The Affectionate Shepherd*, in which the male speaker celebrates his love for a beautiful young man named Ganymede.

Ganymede being abducted by Jupiter in the form of an eagle. Woodcut by Virgil Solis. From *Metamorphosis Ovidii . . .* (1563).

Shakespeare is therefore not unique in introducing a Ganymede figure into the pastoral landscape, though he does so with a difference. In *As You Like It,* Ganymede is a disguise, a persona assumed and eventually discarded by Rosalind. As with much else in this play, Shakespeare thus has things at least two ways at once. For several acts, Orlando seems to pursue in one person both a boy and a woman, but in the final scene Rosalind reassumes her female clothes and Ganymede disappears, thus ending the play with an emphasis on the culmination of male-female love in marriage. But even this is not quite the whole story. On the Renaissance stage, women's parts were played by boy actors. In the Epilogue, which she speaks, Rosalind calls attention to this fact, making it clear that if Orlando has finally won his Rosalind, the two players who enact this union are a young boy and a man.

In *As You Like It,* the erotic possibilities never seem to stop. The friendship between Rosalind and Celia, for example, is remarkably close. Charles the wrestler says, "Never two ladies loved as they do" (1.1.97). Celia readily gives up her father, her fortune, and her position at the court to follow Rosalind to Ardenne, where the two women in effect set up household together. Although they are yoked in love like Juno's swans, from the beginning Celia is afraid that Rosalind does not love her as much as she loves Rosalind (1.2.6–11). Quite quickly, Rosalind's primary interest does become her pursuit of Orlando. Yet in the midst of her love games with him, Rosalind also dallies with the ambitious and amorous Phoebe, who has taken the disguised Rosalind for a man. Overtly, Rosalind scorns Phoebe and directs her to love Silvius, but she also takes care to tell Phoebe where she lives (3.5.75–76) and encourages her attentions even as she denies them. As with other relationships in the play, it is not altogether clear whom Phoebe really desires: is it the man she thinks she sees or the woman beneath? Though the play eventually deposits Rosalind, Celia, and Phoebe all within Hymen's circle, it does so only after raising the possibility of other erotic conjunctions, including woman's love for woman.

In part, *As You Like It* can play so freely with various erotic possibilities because in the early modern period people were not assumed, as they often are today, to have a fixed sexual identity, to *be,* that is, a lesbian or a heterosexual. Often, one could engage in a range of sexual practices without contradiction. Depending on life stage and social circumstance, a man might have sex with a dependent man, such as a servant, and with a woman, such as his wife. The point is that performing a specific sexual act did not presume—or guarantee—a particular sexual identity. And yet Shakespeare's comedy, like many others, also acknowledges the social weight that the early modern period placed on marriage, the institution through which political alliances were forged, property passed, and lineage established. *As You Like It* both celebrates and pokes fun at the social inevitability of marriage by having Hymen, god of marriage, appear onstage in the last act to preside over a veritable spate of betrothals—four, to be exact. As Jaques suggests (5.4.35–36), it is indeed as if the beasts were proceeding, two by two, into Noah's ark.

Besides yoking individual man to individual woman, marriage in this play also helps to resolve seemingly intractable social problems. For example, Orlando's situation as younger brother is miraculously ameliorated through his marriage to Rosalind. As her husband, he becomes Duke Senior's heir, thus achieving a fortune equal to his gentle nature. Again, the play has things two ways at once. Duke Senior is restored to his dukedom, which confirms the prerogatives of older brothers, but Orlando does not have to suffer permanently the disadvantages of being a younger son. Primogeniture is simultaneously affirmed and circumvented. Moreover, when Oliver reforms, that reformation is sealed by his marriage to Celia, an indication that he now takes part in the communal life of his culture without the willful displays of indifference and selfishness that marked his earlier behavior.

Yet as this comedy celebrates marriage, it also registers a certain resistance to it and persistently maps alternative routings of desire. Rosalind registers that resistance when she complains of how avidly men court women before marriage and how indifferently they treat them afterward: "Men are April when they woo, December when they wed" (4.1.124–25). Marriage, she implies, can dull a man's desire and lessen a woman's emotional power over him. It also, of course, made women legally subject to their husbands. When Rosalind doffs her man's disguise to become a wife, she relinquishes many kinds of freedom. But the play also records *men's* resistance to marriage, partly through its many cuckold jokes. These jokes acknowledge that marriage may not fully circumscribe or satisfy a woman's sexual desires, that a man's control of his wife's sexuality may be more fiction than fact, leaving him vulnerable to public mockery. As the Duke's men sing as they bring home a slaughtered deer:

> Take thou no scorn to wear the horn;
> It was a crest ere thou wast born.
> Thy father's father wore it,
> And thy father bore it.
> (4.2.14–17)

The song transforms cuckold anxiety into entertainment, but it cannot erase that anxiety.

Consider, as well, the strange moment when Orlando comes across his brother Oliver lying asleep under an old oak. As Oliver sleeps, a female snake approaches his open mouth, threatening his life. Though the snake is frightened off, it is immediately replaced in this fantastic, dreamlike scenario by a hungry female lion with whom Orlando fights in order to save his brother's life (4.3.97–131). Twice, danger is represented in female form, and the reconciliation of the two brothers occurs only when Orlando spills his blood to beat back these threats. In *As You Like It*, as marriage is both desired and feared, so the feminine is represented as both an attraction and a source of danger.

In pastoral, little is immune from critique; the world men and women have made is an imperfect world. Yet the remarkable thing about *As You Like It* is that critique does not cancel affirmation. The play anatomizes court life and exposes its treachery, but many leave Ardenne to journey back to the court when Frederick has repented and the benevolent Duke Senior has returned to power. The play likewise dissects the problems of marriage, yet many marry at the end. Pastoral has a utopian as well as a critical dimension. The green world of shepherds holds traces of the simplicity of a lost Golden Age, and a sojourn in that world can prompt transformations in the everyday world to which the sojourners return. *As You Like It* is to a remarkable degree open to the infinite malleability of human beings and their social practices. A duke can become a forest outlaw and embrace the change; a tyrannical usurper can be touched by the words of a holy man, relinquish his power, and retire from the world. What men and women have marred, they may also mend.

It is with the heroine, however, that *As You Like It* offers its richest dramatization of a figure who plays endlessly with the limits and possibilities of her circumstances. This is true even in the Epilogue, when Rosalind, now in woman's clothing, steps forward to address the audience and solicit their applause. The persona of Ganymede cast aside, the heroine appears as the woman she "really is." But it is precisely at this moment of closure that she breaks the dramatic frame to remind the audience of *another* reality: that "she" is played by a "he." Dressed like a woman but declaring she is not, this unpredictable figure, this he/she, continues to the end to defy the fixed identities and the exclusionary choices of the everyday world, offering instead a world of multiple possibilities and transformable identities, a world as perhaps we might come to like it.

JEAN E. HOWARD

TEXTUAL NOTE

As You Like It was probably written between 1598 and 1600. It was entered in the Stationers' Register on August 4, 1600, but no edition followed this entry. Francis Meres, one of Shakespeare's contemporaries, in September of 1598 published a list of the Shakespeare plays known to him. It did not include *As You Like It,* suggesting that the play was performed sometime after that date but prior to its entry in the Stationers' Register. Two topical references suggest 1599 as the likely time of composition. At one point, Jaques, the play's cynical satirist, opines, "All the world's a stage" (2.7.138), perhaps an allusion to the motto *Totus mundus agit histrionem* (All the world plays the actor), of the Globe Theater, to which Shakespeare's company moved in the summer of 1599. Elsewhere, Touchstone, the play's clown, refers to the time "since the little wit that fools have was silenced" (1.2.74–75), a possible reference to the banning and burning of satirical books in June of 1599 by order of the Bishop of London.

The play was first published in the First Folio of 1623 (F) either from a promptbook or, less probably, from a literary transcript of either the promptbook or Shakespeare's foul papers. The present edition follows the act and scene divisions of F.

SELECTED BIBLIOGRAPHY

Colie, Rosalie L. "Perspectives on Pastoral: Romance, Comic and Tragic." *Shakespeare's Living Art*. Princeton: Princeton University Press, 1974. 243–83. Analyzes the many pastoral conventions found in *As You Like It* and how they contribute to the play's perspectivism—that is, its juxtaposition of competing viewpoints.

Crane, Mary. "Theatrical Practice and the Ideologies of Status in *As You Like It.*" *Shakespeare's Brain: Reading with Cognitive Theory*. Princeton: Princeton University Press, 2001. 67–93. Examines how, through its emphasis on words like *villain* and *clown, As You Like It* explores possibilities for upward and downward mobility in the world of the play and in the social world at large, including the theatrical community of which Shakespeare was a part.

Elam, Keir. "As They Did in the Golden World: Romantic Rapture and Semantic Rupture in *As You Like It.*" *Reading the Renaissance: Culture, Poetics, and Drama*. Ed. Jonathan Hart. New York: Garland, 1996. 163–76. Focuses on the way Shakespeare rewrites pastoral in *As You Like It* to banish nostalgia and linguistic earnestness in favor of the magical, forward-looking affirmations of romance.

Erickson, Peter. "Sexual Politics and Social Structure in *As You Like It.*" *Patriarchal Structures in Shakespeare's Drama*. Berkeley: University of California Press, 1985. 15–38. Argues that the play advocates a benevolent patriarchy that ultimately subordinates women to men while allowing men to assume nurturing functions.

Howard, Jean E. "Power and Eros: Crossdressing in Dramatic Representation and Theatrical Practice." *The Stage and Social Struggle in Early Modern England*. London: Routledge, 1994. 93–128. Examines cross-dressing as a convention through which *As You Like It* and other comedies explore the politics of early modern gender relations and the fluidity of sexual desire.

Marshall, Cynthia. "The Doubled Jaques and Constructions of Negation in *As You Like It.*" *Shakespeare Quarterly* 49 (1998): 375–92. Argues that in *As You Like It* the repression of melancholia, registered as a trace in the figure of Jaques, allows for the release of the high spirits and verbal fireworks proper to comedy.

Montrose, Louis. " 'The Place of a Brother' in *As You Like It*: Social Process and Comic Form." *Shakespeare Quarterly* 32 (1981): 28–54. Argues that in *As You Like It* the process of comedy repairs the negative consequences of primogeniture for younger sons as Orlando finds a surrogate father in Duke Senior and a fortune through marriage.

Neely, Carol Thomas. "Destabilizing Lovesickness, Gender, and Sexuality: *Twelfth Night* and *As You Like It.*" *Distracted Subjects: Madness and Gender in Shakespeare and Early Modern Culture*. Ithaca, N.Y.: Cornell University Press, 2004. 99–135. Details the increasingly strong link between lovesickness and women in the Renaissance and compares its representation in *Twelfth Night* and *As You Like It*.

Traub, Valerie. "The Homoerotics of Shakespearean Comedy." *Desire and Anxiety: Circulations of Sexuality in Shakespearean Drama*. London: Routledge, 1992. 117–44. Explores the role of the boy actor in the production and circulation of homoerotic desire and argues that *As You Like It* playfully refuses the binary distinction between the heteroerotic and the homoerotic.

Wilson, Richard. "Like the Old Robin Hood: *As You Like It* and the Enclosure Riots." *Will Power: Essays on Shakespearean Authority*. London: Harvester Wheatsheaf, 1993. 63–82. Connects *As You Like It* to the social disturbances and food shortages of the 1590s but argues that the play pulls back from lodging a radical critique of social injustice.

FILMS

As You Like It. 1936. Dir. Paul Czinner. UK. 96 min. This black-and-white film features Laurence Olivier, in his first Shakespeare performance on film, as the dashing but moody Orlando with Elisabeth Bergner as an insipid Rosalind. Charming woodland scenes in a significantly cut production.

As You Like It. 1978. Dir. Basil Coleman. UK. 150 min. Traditional BBC-TV production with lively performances by Helen Mirren as Rosalind, Angharad Rees as Celia, and Victoria Plucknett as Phoebe. Playing Jaques, Richard Pasco brings poignant understatement to the famous "seven ages of man" speech.

As You Like It. 2006. Dir. Kenneth Branagh. UK. 127min. In this gorgeous production, the action is relocated from medieval France to nineteenth-century Japan. With Bryce Dallas Howard (Rosalind), David Oyelowo (Orlando), Rowola Garai (Celia), Brian Blessed (Duke Senior and Duke Frederick), and Alfred Molina (Touchstone).

As You Like It

1.1

Enter ORLANDO *and* ADAM

ORLANDO As I remember, Adam, it was upon this fashion bequeathed me by will but poor° a thousand crowns,[1] and, as thou sayst, charged° my brother on his blessing[2] to breed me well—and there begins my sadness. My brother Jaques he keeps at school,° and report speaks goldenly of his profit. For my part, he keeps me rustically at home—or, to speak more properly, stays° me here at home unkept;° for call you that keeping for a gentleman of my birth, that differs not from the stalling of an ox? His horses are bred better, for besides that they are fair with° their feeding, they are taught their manège,[3] and to that end riders dearly° hired. But I, his brother, gain nothing under him but growth, for the which his animals on his dunghills are as much bound to him as I. Besides this nothing that he so plentifully gives me, the something that nature gave me his countenance° seems to take from me. He lets me feed with his hinds,° bars me[4] the place of a brother, and as much as in him lies, mines my gentility with my education.[5]

only
he (my father) charged

university

detains / uncared for

handsome because of
expensively

conduct
farmworkers

5

10

15

1.1 Location: The orchard of Oliver's house, in the vicinity of Duke Frederick's court in France.
1. Equivalent to about 250 English pounds. Orlando's inheritance is worth twice as much as Adam's life savings (see 2.3.39).

2. On pain of losing his blessing.
3. Paces and actions of a trained horse.
4. Excludes me from.
5. Undermines my gentility by my (poor) education.

This is it, Adam, that grieves me; and the spirit of my father,
which I think is within me, begins to mutiny against this servi-
tude. I will no longer endure it, though yet I know no wise
remedy how to avoid it.

     Enter OLIVER

ADAM   Yonder comes my master, your brother.

ORLANDO   Go apart, Adam, and thou shalt hear how he will
shake me up.°   *insult me*

     [ADAM *stands aside*]

OLIVER   Now, sir, what make you° here?   *are you doing*

ORLANDO   Nothing. I am not taught to make anything.

OLIVER   What mar you then, sir?

ORLANDO   Marry,[6] sir, I am helping you to mar that which God
made, a poor unworthy brother of yours, with idleness.

OLIVER   Marry, sir, be better employed, and be nought° awhile.   *get lost*

ORLANDO   Shall I keep your hogs, and eat husks with them?
What prodigal portion have I spent, that I should come to such
penury?[7]

OLIVER   Know you where you are, sir?

ORLANDO   O sir, very well; here in your orchard.

OLIVER   Know you before whom, sir?

ORLANDO   Ay, better than him I am before knows me. I know
you are my eldest brother, and in the gentle condition of blood
you should so know me.[8] The courtesy of nations[9] allows you
my better, in that you are the first-born; but the same tradition
takes not away my blood, were there twenty brothers betwixt
us. I have as much of my father in me as you, albeit I confess
your coming before me is nearer to his reverence.[1]

OLIVER   [*assailing him*]   What, boy!

ORLANDO   [*seizing him by the throat*]   Come, come, elder
brother, you are too young° in this.   *inexperienced*

OLIVER   Wilt thou lay hands on me, villain?°   *lowborn man; scoundrel*

ORLANDO   I am no villein.° I am the youngest son of Sir Rowland   *serf (pun on "villain")*
de Bois. He was my father, and he is thrice a villain that says
such a father begot villeins. Wert thou not my brother, I would
not take this hand from thy throat till this other had pulled out
thy tongue for saying so. Thou hast railed on° thyself.   *abused*

ADAM   [*coming forward*]   Sweet masters, be patient. For your
father's remembrance, be at accord.

OLIVER   [*to* ORLANDO]   Let me go, I say.

ORLANDO   I will not till I please. You shall hear me. My father
charged you in his will to give me good education. You have
trained me like a peasant, obscuring and hiding from me all
gentleman-like qualities.° The spirit of my father grows strong   *accomplishments*
in me, and I will no longer endure it. Therefore allow me such
exercises° as may become a gentleman, or give me the poor   *pursuits*
allottery° my father left me by testament. With that I will go   *portion*
buy my fortunes.

OLIVER   And what wilt thou do—beg when that is spent? Well,

---

6. An oath, derived from the name of the Virgin Mary.
7. Alluding to the biblical parable of the prodigal son (Luke 15:11–32), who after squandering his share of his father's fortune envied the swine he tended and wished to eat their fodder.
8. And because of the noble blood that we share, you

should acknowledge me as a brother.
9. Customs of civil society. Referring to the English system of primogeniture, which allowed for the transmission of all property to the eldest son.
1. Your being older than I makes you more worthy of the respect that he commanded.

65   sir, get you in. I will not long be troubled with you. You shall
        have some part of your will. I pray you, leave me.
        ORLANDO   I will no further offend you than becomes me for my
        good.
        OLIVER [*to* ADAM]   Get you with him, you old dog.
70   ADAM   Is 'old dog' my reward? Most true, I have lost my teeth in
        your service. God be with my old master, he would not have
        spoke such a word.   *Exeunt* ORLANDO [*and*] ADAM
        OLIVER   Is it even so? Begin you to grow upon me?² I will physic°   *give medicine to*
        your rankness,³ and yet give no thousand crowns neither.
75   Holla, Denis!
                Enter DENIS
        DENIS   Calls your worship?
        OLIVER   Was not Charles, the Duke's wrestler, here to speak with
        me?
        DENIS   So please you, he is here at the door, and importunes
80   access to you.
        OLIVER   Call him in.   [*Exit* DENIS]
        'Twill be a good way. And tomorrow the wrestling is.
                Enter CHARLES
        CHARLES   Good morrow to your worship.
        OLIVER   Good Monsieur Charles—what's the new news at the
85   new court?
        CHARLES   There's no news at the court, sir, but the old news: that
        is, the old Duke is banished by his younger brother, the new
        Duke, and three or four loving lords have put themselves into
        voluntary exile with him, whose lands and revenues enrich the
90   new Duke; therefore he gives them good leave° to wander.   *full permission*
        OLIVER   Can you tell if Rosalind, the Duke's daughter, be ban-
        ished with her father?
        CHARLES   O no; for the Duke's daughter her cousin so loves her,
        being ever from their cradles bred° together, that she would   *brought up*
95   have followed her exile, or have died to stay behind her. She is
        at the court, and no less beloved of her uncle than his own
        daughter; and never two ladies loved as they do.
        OLIVER   Where will the old Duke live?
        CHARLES   They say he is already in the forest of Ardenne,⁴ and a
100   many merry men with him; and there they live like the old
        Robin Hood⁵ of England. They say many young gentlemen
        flock to him every day, and fleet° the time carelessly,° as they   *pass* / *without worries*
        did in the golden world.⁶
        OLIVER   What, you wrestle tomorrow before the new Duke?
105   CHARLES   Marry do I, sir, and I came to acquaint you with a
        matter. I am given, sir, secretly to understand that your younger
        brother, Orlando, hath a disposition to come in disguised
        against me to try a fall.° Tomorrow, sir, I wrestle for my credit,°   *bout* / *reputation*
        and he that escapes me without some broken limb, shall acquit
110   him well. Your brother is but young and tender, and for your
        love I would be loath to foil° him, as I must for my own honour   *defeat*

---

2. To grow so big you crowd upon me.
3. Overgrown vegetation; diseased blood.
4. The name of an ancient forest encompassing parts
of France, Belgium, and Luxembourg. F uses the angli-
cized spelling "Arden," evoking the English forest of
Arden near Shakespeare's birthplace in Warwickshire.
5. A legendary English outlaw, associated with

Nottingham's Sherwood Forest, who robbed from the
rich and gave his plunder to the poor.
6. Alluding to the classical myth of an earlier world of
perpetual spring, abundance, and ease from which
humankind had degenerated (Ovid, *Metamorphoses* 1).
This golden world was often identified with a pastoral life.

if he come in. Therefore out of my love to you I came hither
to acquaint you withal,° that either you might stay° him from   *with this / keep*
his intendment,° or brook° such disgrace well as he shall run   *intent / endure*
115 into, in that it is a thing of his own search,° and altogether   *seeking*
against my will.

OLIVER   Charles, I thank thee for thy love to me, which thou
shalt find I will most kindly requite. I had myself notice of my
brother's purpose herein, and have by underhand° means   *subtle*
120 laboured to dissuade him from it; but he is resolute. I'll tell
thee, Charles, it is the stubbornest young fellow of France, full
of ambition, an envious emulator of every man's good parts,° a   *qualities*
secret and villainous contriver against me his natural brother.
Therefore use thy discretion. I had as lief° thou didst break his   *willingly*
125 neck as his finger. And thou wert best look to't; for if thou dost
him any slight disgrace, or if he do not mightily grace° himself   *win credit for*
on thee, he will practise° against thee by poison, entrap thee by   *plot*
some treacherous device, and never leave thee till he hath ta'en
thy life by some indirect means or other. For I assure thee—
130 and almost with tears I speak it—there is not one so young and
so villainous this day living. I speak but brotherly[7] of him, but
should I anatomize° him to thee as he is, I must blush and   *dissect; fully open*
weep, and thou must look pale and wonder.

CHARLES   I am heartily glad I came hither to you. If he come
135 tomorrow I'll give him his payment. If ever he go alone° again,   *walk without aid*
I'll never wrestle for prize more. And so God keep your wor-
ship.

OLIVER   Farewell, good Charles.   *Exit* [CHARLES]
Now will I stir this gamester.° I hope I shall see an end of him,   *(Orlando)*
140 for my soul—yet I know not why—hates nothing more than
he. Yet he's gentle;° never schooled, and yet learned; full of   *of noble character*
noble device;° of all sorts enchantingly beloved;[8] and, indeed,   *purposes*
so much in the heart of the world, and especially of my own
people, who best know him, that I am altogether misprized.°   *despised*
145 But it shall not be so long. This wrestler shall clear all.° Noth-   *fix everything*
ing remains but that I kindle° the boy thither,° which now I'll   *urge / (to the court)*
go about.   *Exit*

1.2

Enter ROSALIND *and* CELIA

CELIA   I pray thee Rosalind, sweet my coz,° be merry.   *cousin*

ROSALIND   Dear Celia, I show more mirth than I am mistress of;
and would you yet I were merrier? Unless you could teach me
to forget a banished father you must not learn° me how to   *teach*
5 remember any extraordinary pleasure.

CELIA   Herein I see thou lovest me not with the full weight that
I love thee. If my uncle, thy banished father, had banished thy
uncle, the Duke my father, so° thou hadst been still with me I   *provided*
could have taught my love to take thy father for mine. So
10 wouldst thou, if the truth of thy love to me were so righteously
tempered° as mine is to thee.   *properly constituted*

ROSALIND   Well, I will forget the condition of my estate° to   *circumstances*
rejoice in yours.

7. In a manner proper to a brother.   1.2 Location: The grounds of Duke Frederick's court.
8. Beloved of all ranks as if by enchantment.

CELIA   You know my father hath no child but I, nor none is like
15   to have. And truly, when he dies thou shalt be his heir; for what
he hath taken away from thy father perforce,° I will render thee   *by force*
again in affection. By mine honour I will, and when I break
that oath, let me turn monster. Therefore, my sweet Rose, my
dear Rose, be merry.
20 ROSALIND   From henceforth I will, coz, and devise sports.° Let   *entertainments*
me see, what think you of falling in love?
CELIA   Marry, I prithee do, to make sport withal;° but love no   *to provide amusement*
man in good earnest, nor no further in sport neither than with
safety of a pure blush thou mayst in honour come off again.[1]
25 ROSALIND   What shall be our sport, then?
CELIA   Let us sit and mock the good housewife Fortune[2] from
her wheel, that her gifts may henceforth be bestowed equally.
ROSALIND   I would we could do so, for her benefits are mightily
misplaced; and the bountiful blind woman° doth most mistake   *(Fortune)*
30   in her gifts to women.
CELIA   'Tis true; for those that she makes fair she scarce makes
honest,° and those that she makes honest she makes very ill-   *chaste*
favouredly.°   *ugly*
ROSALIND   Nay, now thou goest from Fortune's office° to   *function*
35   Nature's. Fortune reigns in° gifts of the world, not in the linea-   *presides over*
ments of nature.°   *one's natural features*
          Enter [TOUCHSTONE[3] *the*] *clown*
CELIA   No. When Nature hath made a fair creature, may she not
by Fortune fall into the fire? Though Nature hath given us wit
to flout at Fortune, hath not Fortune sent in this fool to cut off
40   the argument?
ROSALIND   Indeed, there is Fortune too hard for Nature, when
Fortune makes Nature's natural° the cutter-off of Nature's wit.   *fool*
CELIA   Peradventure° this is not Fortune's work, neither, but   *Perhaps*
Nature's, who perceiveth our natural wits too dull to reason of
45   such goddesses, and hath sent this natural for our whetstone;°   *stone to sharpen tools*
for always the dullness of the fool is the whetstone of the wits.
How now, wit: whither wander you?[4]
TOUCHSTONE   Mistress, you must come away to your father.
CELIA   Were you made the messenger?
50 TOUCHSTONE   No, by mine honour, but I was bid to come for
you.
ROSALIND   Where learned you that oath, fool?
TOUCHSTONE   Of a certain knight that swore 'by his honour' they
were good pancakes, and swore 'by his honour' the mustard
55   was naught.° Now I'll stand to it° the pancakes were naught and   *worthless / affirm*
the mustard was good, and yet was not the knight forsworn.°   *perjured*
CELIA   How prove you that in the great heap of your knowledge?
ROSALIND   Ay, marry, now unmuzzle your wisdom.
TOUCHSTONE   Stand you both forth now. Stroke your chins, and
60   swear by your beards that I am a knave.
CELIA   By our beards—if we had them—thou art.

1. Than, with the protection afforded by your inno-
cence ("pure blush"), you may honorably escape
("come off again").
2. Referring to the blind goddess of classical mythology
who directed human destiny with the movements of her
wheel, here likened to the mistress of a household with
a spinning wheel.
3. A touchstone was a black mineral used to test the
purity of gold and silver. Touchstone, the fool, tests the
wit of those he encounters.
4. Alluding to the catchphrase "wandering wits."

TOUCHSTONE   By my knavery—if I had it—then I were; but if
you swear by that that is not, you are not forsworn. No more
was this knight, swearing by his honour, for he never had any;
65   or if he had, he had sworn it away before ever he saw those
pancakes or that mustard.

CELIA   Prithee, who is't that thou meanest?

TOUCHSTONE   One that old Frederick, your father, loves.

CELIA[5]   My father's love is enough to honour him. Enough,
70   speak no more of him; you'll be whipped for taxation° one of   *slander*
these days.

TOUCHSTONE   The more pity that fools may not speak wisely
what wise men do foolishly.

CELIA   By my troth, thou sayst true; for since the little wit that
75   fools have was silenced,[6] the little foolery that wise men have
makes a great show. Here comes Monsieur Le Beau.

        Enter LE BEAU

ROSALIND   With his mouth full of news.

CELIA   Which he will put on° us as pigeons feed their young.   *force upon*

ROSALIND   Then shall we be news-crammed.[7]

80   CELIA   All the better: we shall be the more marketable. *Bonjour,*°   *Good day*
Monsieur Le Beau, what's the news?

LE BEAU   Fair princess, you have lost much good sport.

CELIA   Sport? Of what colour?°   *kind*

LE BEAU   What colour, madam? How shall I answer you?

85   ROSALIND   As wit and fortune will.°   *desire*

TOUCHSTONE   Or as the destinies decrees.

CELIA   Well said. That was laid on with a trowel.[8]

TOUCHSTONE   Nay, if I keep not my rank[9]—

ROSALIND   Thou losest thy old smell.

90   LE BEAU   You amaze° me, ladies. I would have told you of good   *confuse*
wrestling, which you have lost the sight of.

ROSALIND   Yet tell us the manner of the wrestling.

LE BEAU   I will tell you the beginning, and if it please your lady-
ships you may see the end, for the best is yet to do,° and here,   *to come*
95   where you are, they are coming to perform it.

CELIA   Well, the beginning that is dead and buried.

LE BEAU   There comes an old man and his three sons—

CELIA   I could match this beginning with an old tale.[1]

LE BEAU   Three proper° young men, of excellent growth and   *handsome*
100   presence.

ROSALIND   With bills° on their necks: 'Be it known unto all men   *proclamations*
by these presents'[2]—

LE BEAU   The eldest of the three wrestled with Charles, the
Duke's wrestler, which Charles in a moment threw him, and
105   broke three of his ribs, that there is little hope of life in him.
So he served the second, and so the third. Yonder they lie, the

5. F attributes this speech to Rosalind, but most editors
assign it to Celia on the grounds that she asked the
question to which Touchstone has just responded. It is
unlikely that Rosalind would insert herself here or insist
on the preeminence of her father's love over Frederick's.
6. This is a possible allusion to the Bishop of London's
order for the burning of satirical books in June 1599.
7. Forced to digest news, with a pun on "mews" as
meaning the cages in which pigeons were kept before
being fattened, or "crammed," for the table.

8. Bluntly; excessively. With a reference to a builder's
heavy application of mortar.
9. My status (as a jester). Rosalind then puns on the
meaning of "rank" as "foul smelling."
1. *Old tale*: Celia suggests that the motif of a father and
his three sons is the starting point for many familiar
folktales.
2. That is, by these legal documents. A legal phrase
that appears at the start of formal documents, with a
pun on "presence."

poor old man their father making such pitiful dole° over them   *mourning*
that all the beholders take his part with weeping.

ROSALIND Alas!

110 TOUCHSTONE But what is the sport, monsieur, that the ladies
have lost?

LE BEAU Why, this that I speak of.

TOUCHSTONE Thus men may grow wiser every day. It is the first
time that ever I heard breaking of ribs was sport for ladies.

115 CELIA Or I, I promise thee.

ROSALIND But is there any else° longs to see this broken music³ *anyone else who*
in his sides? Is there yet another dotes upon rib-breaking? Shall
we see this wrestling, cousin?

LE BEAU You must if you stay here, for here is the place
120 appointed for the wrestling, and they are ready to perform it.

CELIA Yonder sure they are coming. Let us now stay and see it.

  *Flourish.*⁴ *Enter* DUKE [FREDERICK], *Lords*, ORLANDO,
  CHARLES, *and attendants*

DUKE FREDERICK Come on. Since the youth will not be
entreated,° his own peril on his forwardness.⁵   *persuaded (to desist)*

ROSALIND Is yonder the man?

125 LE BEAU Even he, madam.

CELIA Alas, he is too young. Yet he looks successfully.° *as if he would do well*

DUKE FREDERICK How now, daughter and cousin;⁶ are you
crept hither to see the wrestling?

ROSALIND Ay, my liege, so please you give us leave.

130 DUKE FREDERICK You will take little delight in it, I can tell you,
there is such odds° in the man. In pity of the challenger's youth *superiority*
I would fain° dissuade him, but he will not be entreated. Speak *willingly*
to him, ladies; see if you can move him.

CELIA Call him hither, good Monsieur Le Beau.

135 DUKE FREDERICK Do so. I'll not be by.

  [*He stands aside*]

LE BEAU [*to* ORLANDO] Monsieur the challenger, the Princess
calls for you.

ORLANDO I attend them with all respect and duty.

ROSALIND Young man, have you challenged Charles the wres-
140 tler?

ORLANDO No, fair Princess. He is the general challenger; I come
but in as others do, to try with him the strength of my youth.

CELIA Young gentleman, your spirits are too bold for your years.
You have seen cruel proof of this man's strength. If you saw
145 yourself with your eyes, or knew yourself with your judgement,⁷
the fear° of your adventure would counsel you to a more equal *danger*
enterprise. We pray you for your own sake to embrace your
own safety and give over this attempt.

ROSALIND Do, young sir. Your reputation shall not therefore be
150 misprized.° We will make it our suit to the Duke that the wres- *undervalued*
tling might not go forward.

ORLANDO I beseech you, punish me not with your hard
thoughts,° wherein I confess me much guilty to deny so fair *displeasure*

---

3. Literally, a musical composition for a variety of
instruments; here referring to the labored breathing
caused by the broken ribs.
4. The sounding of horns or trumpets to signal the
arrival of an important person.

5. *his own . . . forwardness:* let the danger he encoun-
ters be blamed on his own rashness.
6. *cousin:* a term used to signify many kinship relations.
7. If you used your discernment and judgment upon
yourself.

and excellent ladies anything. But let your fair eyes and gentle
wishes go with me to my trial, wherein if I be foiled,° there is
but one shamed that was never gracious,° if killed, but one
dead that is willing to be so. I shall do my friends no wrong, for
I have none to lament me; the world no injury, for in it I have
nothing. Only in the world I fill up a place which may be better
supplied when I have made it empty.

ROSALIND The little strength that I have, I would it were with
you.

CELIA And mine, to eke out hers.

ROSALIND Fare you well. Pray heaven I be deceived in you.

CELIA Your heart's desires be with you.

CHARLES Come, where is this young gallant that is so desirous
to lie with his mother earth?⁸

ORLANDO Ready, sir; but his will° hath in it a more modest
working.°

DUKE FREDERICK You shall try but one fall.

CHARLES No, I warrant your grace you shall not entreat him to
a second that have so mightily persuaded him from a first.

ORLANDO You mean to mock me after; you should not have
mocked me before. But come your ways.°

ROSALIND [to ORLANDO] Now Hercules be thy speed,⁹ young
man!

CELIA I would I were invisible, to catch the strong fellow by the
leg.

[CHARLES and ORLANDO] wrestle

ROSALIND O excellent young man!

CELIA If I had a thunderbolt in mine eye, I can tell who should
down.

[ORLANDO throws CHARLES.] Shout

DUKE FREDERICK No more, no more.

ORLANDO   Yes, I beseech your grace.
I am not yet well breathed.°

DUKE FREDERICK How dost thou, Charles?

LE BEAU He cannot speak, my lord.

DUKE FREDERICK Bear him away.

[Attendants carry CHARLES off]
What is thy name, young man?

ORLANDO Orlando, my liege, the youngest son of Sir Rowland
de Bois.

DUKE FREDERICK I would thou hadst been son to some man else.
The world esteemed thy father honourable,
But I did find him still° mine enemy.
Thou shouldst have better pleased me with this deed
Hadst thou descended from another house.
But fare thee well, thou art a gallant youth.
I would thou hadst told me of another father.

Exeunt DUKE [FREDERICK, LE BEAU, TOUCHSTONE,¹
Lords, and attendants]

CELIA [to ROSALIND] Were I my father, coz, would I do this?

___

8. To fall to the ground. Echoing biblical descriptions of the body's return to earth at death and punning on "lie with" as slang for "have sexual relations with."
9. May Hercules bring you luck. Alluding to a mythological wrestling match in which Hercules, whose name was synonymous with physical strength, vanquished Antaeus.
1. Although F does not indicate an exit for Touchstone, many editors assume that he leaves the stage with the Duke's party and does not reappear until 2.4.

ORLANDO I am more proud to be Sir Rowland's son,
His youngest son, and would not change that calling°   *title*
200 To be adopted heir to Frederick.
ROSALIND My father loved Sir Rowland as his soul,
And all the world was of my father's mind.
Had I before known this young man his son
I should have given him tears unto° entreaties   *as well as*
Ere he should thus have ventured.
205 CELIA   Gentle° cousin,   *Noble; kind*
Let us go thank him, and encourage him.
My father's rough and envious° disposition   *spiteful*
Sticks° me at heart.—Sir, you have well deserved.   *Stabs*
If you do keep your promises in love
210 But justly,° as you have exceeded all promise,   *to the same degree*
Your mistress shall be happy.
ROSALIND [*giving him a chain from her neck*] Gentleman,
Wear this for me—one out of suits° with fortune,   *favor*
That could° give more but that her hand lacks means.   *would*
Shall we go, coz?
CELIA   Ay. Fare you well, fair gentleman.
  [ROSALIND *and* CELIA *turn to go*]
215 ORLANDO [*aside*] Can I not say 'I thank you'? My better parts
Are all thrown down, and that which here stands up
Is but a quintain,² a mere lifeless block.
ROSALIND [*to* CELIA] He calls us back. My pride fell with my fortunes,
I'll ask him what he would.—Did you call, sir?
220 Sir, you have wrestled well, and overthrown
More than your enemies.
CELIA Will you go, coz?
ROSALIND Have with you.° [*To* ORLANDO] Fare you well.   *I'll go with you*
    Exeunt [ROSALIND *and* CELIA]³
ORLANDO What passion hangs these weights upon my tongue?
225 I cannot speak to her, yet she urged conference.°   *conversation*
   Enter LE BEAU
O poor Orlando! Thou art overthrown.
Or° Charles or something weaker masters thee.   *Either*
LE BEAU Good sir, I do in friendship counsel you
To leave this place. Albeit you have deserved
230 High commendation, true applause, and love,
Yet such is now the Duke's condition°   *state of mind*
That he misconsters° all that you have done.   *misconstrues*
The Duke is humorous.⁴ What he is indeed
More suits you to conceive than I to speak of.
235 ORLANDO I thank you, sir. And pray you tell me this,
Which of the two was daughter of the Duke
That here was at the wrestling?
LE BEAU Neither his daughter, if we judge by manners—
But yet indeed the shorter⁵ is his daughter.

---

2. A wooden post used as a target in jousts and other aristocratic sports. Orlando suggests that his reason and speech (his "better parts") have been "thrown down," or defeated, in his encounter with Rosalind, leaving him standing speechless, like a post.
3. F marks only a single exit for Rosalind here, but Celia almost certainly accompanies her offstage.
4. Moody. The term derives from Renaissance medical theory, which held that good mental and physical health depended on the proper balance of four bodily fluids, or humors.
5. F reads "taller," but see 1.3.109, where Rosalind declares that she is "more than common tall" and will therefore disguise herself as a man. Shakespeare may not have been consistent in determining who was to be the taller woman.

240 The other is daughter to the banished Duke,
And here detained by her usurping uncle
To keep his daughter company, whose loves
Are dearer than the natural bond of sisters.
But I can tell you that of late this Duke
245 Hath ta'en displeasure 'gainst his gentle niece,
Grounded upon no other argument°   *reason*
But that the people praise her for her virtues
And pity her for her good father's sake.
And, on my life, his malice 'gainst the lady
250 Will suddenly break forth. Sir, fare you well.
Hereafter, in a better world than this,
I shall desire more love and knowledge of you.
ORLANDO I rest much bounden° to you. Fare you well.   *obliged*
                              [*Exit* LE BEAU]
Thus must I from the smoke into the smother,[6]
255 From tyrant Duke unto a tyrant brother.—
But heavenly Rosalind!   *Exit*

1.3

Enter CELIA *and* ROSALIND

CELIA Why cousin, why Rosalind—Cupid have mercy,[1] not a
    word?
ROSALIND Not one to throw at a dog.
CELIA No, thy words are too precious to be cast away upon curs.
5   Throw some of them at me. Come, lame me with reasons.[2]
ROSALIND Then there were two cousins laid up, when the one
    should be lamed with reasons and the other mad without any.
CELIA But is all this for your father?
ROSALIND No, some of it is for my child's father.[3] O how full of
10   briers is this working-day world!
CELIA They are but burs, cousin, thrown upon thee in holiday
    foolery. If we walk not in the trodden paths our very petticoats
    will catch them.
ROSALIND I could shake them off my coat. These burs are in my
15   heart.
CELIA Hem[4] them away.
ROSALIND I would try, if I could cry 'hem' and have him.
CELIA Come, come, wrestle with thy affections.
ROSALIND O, they take the part of a better wrestler than myself.
20 CELIA O, a good wish upon you!° You will try in time, in despite   *good luck to you*
    of a fall.[5] But turning these jests out of service,° let us talk in   *dismissing these jokes*
    good earnest. Is it possible on such a sudden you should fall
    into so strong a liking with old Sir Rowland's youngest son?
ROSALIND The Duke my father loved his father dearly.
25 CELIA Doth it therefore ensue that you should love his son
    dearly? By this kind of chase° I should hate him, for my father   *logic*
    hated his father dearly; yet I hate not Orlando.
ROSALIND No, faith, hate him not, for my sake.

---

6. Out of the frying pan into the fire. *smother:* thick,
suffocating smoke.
1.3 Location: Duke Frederick's court.
1. May Cupid (god of love) be compassionate.
2. Throw so many reasons (for your silence) at me that
if they were stones, I would be made lame.

3. That is, for one who will be father to my child.
4. Cough, with a pun on "bur" (line 14) as meaning
"something that sticks in your throat."
5. You are destined to wrestle with him eventually even
though it will cause you to fall, with a pun on "fall" as
"lapse from chastity."

CELIA   Why should I not? Doth he not deserve well?

Enter DUKE [FREDERICK], *with Lords*

30 ROSALIND   Let me love him for that, and do you love him
because I do. Look, here comes the Duke.

CELIA   With his eyes full of anger.

DUKE FREDERICK [*to* ROSALIND]   Mistress, dispatch you with your safest haste,[6]
And get you from our court.

35 ROSALIND   Me, uncle?

DUKE FREDERICK   You, cousin.
Within these ten days if that thou beest found
So near our public court as twenty miles,
Thou diest for it.

ROSALIND   I do beseech your grace
40 Let me the knowledge of my fault bear with me.
If with myself I hold intelligence,°   I communicate
Or have acquaintance with mine own desires,
If that I do not dream, or be not frantic°—   insane
As I do trust I am not—then, dear uncle,
45 Never so much as in a thought unborn
Did I offend your highness.

DUKE FREDERICK   Thus do all traitors.
If their purgation° did consist in words   exoneration
They are as innocent as grace itself.
Let it suffice thee that I trust thee not.

50 ROSALIND   Yet your mistrust cannot make me a traitor.
Tell me whereon the likelihood depends?

DUKE FREDERICK   Thou art thy father's daughter—there's enough.

ROSALIND   So was I when your highness took his dukedom;
So was I when your highness banished him.
55 Treason is not inherited, my lord,
Or if we did derive it from our friends,°   relatives
What's that to me? My father was no traitor.
Then, good my liege, mistake me not so much
To think my poverty is treacherous.

60 CELIA   Dear sovereign, hear me speak.

DUKE FREDERICK   Ay, Celia, we stayed° her for your sake,   detained
Else had she with her father ranged° along.   roamed

CELIA   I did not then entreat to have her stay.
It was your pleasure, and your own remorse.°   pity; sense of guilt
65 I was too young that time to value her,
But now I know her. If she be a traitor,
Why, so am I. We still° have slept together,   always
Rose at an instant,° learned, played, eat together,   at the same moment
And wheresoe'er we went, like Juno's swans
70 Still we went coupled and inseparable.[7]

DUKE FREDERICK   She is too subtle° for thee, and her smoothness,   cunning
Her very silence, and her patience
Speak to the people, and they pity her.
Thou art a fool. She robs thee of thy name,°   reputation
75 And thou wilt show more bright and seem more virtuous
When she is gone. Then open not thy lips.

6. Leave quickly, which is your best safety.
7. That is, yoked together inseparably like the swans
that draw the chariot of Juno (queen of the gods).

According to Ovid, swans were associated with Venus
(goddess of love), not with Juno.

Firm and irrevocable is my doom°   *judgment*
Which I have passed upon her. She is banished.
CELIA   Pronounce that sentence then on me, my liege.
80   I cannot live out of her company.
DUKE FREDERICK   You are a fool.—You, niece, provide yourself.°   *make preparation*
If you outstay the time, upon mine honour
And in the greatness of my word,[8] you die.

                    Exit DUKE [FREDERICK, *with Lords*]

CELIA   O my poor Rosalind, whither wilt thou go?
85   Wilt thou change° fathers? I will give thee mine.   *exchange*
I charge thee, be not thou grieved than I am.
ROSALIND   I have more cause.
CELIA   Thou hast not, cousin.
Prithee, be cheerful. Know'st thou not the Duke
Hath banished me, his daughter?
ROSALIND   That he hath not.
90 CELIA   No, hath not? Rosalind, lack'st thou then the love
Which teacheth thee that thou and I am one?
Shall we be sundered? Shall we part, sweet girl?
No. Let my father seek another heir.
Therefore devise with me how we may fly,
95   Whither to go, and what to bear with us,
And do not seek to take your change upon you,[9]
To bear your griefs yourself, and leave me out.
For by this heaven, now at our sorrows pale,
Say what thou canst, I'll go along with thee.
100 ROSALIND   Why, whither shall we go?
CELIA   To seek my uncle in the forest of Ardenne.
ROSALIND   Alas, what danger will it be to us,
Maids as we are, to travel forth so far!
Beauty provoketh thieves sooner than gold.
105 CELIA   I'll put myself in poor and mean° attire,   *lowly*
And with a kind of umber[1] smirch my face.
The like do you, so shall we pass along
And never stir° assailants.   *provoke*
ROSALIND   Were it not better,
Because that I am more than common tall,
110   That I did suit° me all points° like a man,   *dress / ways*
A gallant curtal-axe° upon my thigh,   *short sword*
A boar-spear[2] in my hand, and in my heart,
Lie there what hidden woman's fear there will.
We'll have a swashing° and a martial outside,   *swaggering*
115   As many other mannish cowards have,
That do outface it with their semblances.[3]
CELIA   What shall I call thee when thou art a man?
ROSALIND   I'll have no worse a name than Jove's own page,
And therefore look you call me Ganymede.[4]
120   But what will you be called?

8. And in accordance with the power of my decree as Duke.
9. To bear alone the burden of your change of fortunes.
1. Brown pigment. By rubbing it on their faces, Rosalind and Celia take on the dark or sunburned complexion that in Elizabethan society marked the low social status of those who labored outside. Ladies wore masks to keep their complexions white.

2. A long-bladed spear used to impale boar.
3. Who brazenly defy the world with the mere appearance of bravery.
4. The name of a beautiful young man who, according to classical mythology, was so beloved by Jove (king of the gods) that Jove carried him off to heaven and made him his cupbearer. Also a slang term for a young man who sold his sexual services to or was kept by an older man.

CELIA Something that hath a reference to my state.
No longer Celia, but Aliena.°   *"the estranged one"*
ROSALIND But cousin, what if we essayed° to steal   *tried*
The clownish fool out of your father's court.
125   Would he not be a comfort to our travel?
CELIA He'll go along o'er the wide world with me.
Leave me alone to woo him. Let's away,
And get our jewels and our wealth together,
Devise the fittest time and safest way
130   To hide us from pursuit that will be made
After my flight. Now go we in content,
To liberty, and not to banishment.   *Exeunt*

2.1

Enter DUKE SENIOR, AMIENS,[1] *and two or three* LORDS
like° foresters   *dressed as*
DUKE SENIOR Now, my co-mates and brothers in exile,
Hath not old custom° made this life more sweet   *long acquaintance*
Than that of painted pomp?° Are not these woods   *artificial splendor*
More free from peril than the envious court?
5   Here feel we not the penalty of Adam,[2]
The seasons' difference,° as° the icy fang   *change / such as*
And churlish° chiding of the winter's wind,   *rough*
Which when it bites and blows upon my body
Even till I shrink with cold, I smile, and say
10   'This is no flattery. These are counsellors
That feelingly° persuade me what I am.'   *through my senses*
Sweet are the uses° of adversity   *benefits*
Which, like the toad, ugly and venomous,
Wears yet a precious jewel in his head;[3]
15   And this our life, exempt from public haunt,°   *free from crowds*
Finds tongues in trees, books in the running brooks,
Sermons in stones, and good in everything.
AMIENS I would not change it. Happy is your grace
That can translate the stubbornness of fortune
20   Into so quiet and so sweet a style.
DUKE SENIOR Come, shall we go and kill us venison?
And yet it irks me the poor dappled fools,°   *innocent creatures*
Being native burghers° of this desert° city,   *citizens / unpeopled*
Should in their own confines with forkèd heads°   *two-pronged arrows*
Have their round haunches gored.
25 FIRST LORD   Indeed, my lord,
The melancholy Jaques[4] grieves at that,
And in that kind° swears you do more usurp   *vein*
Than doth your brother that hath banished you.
Today my lord of Amiens and myself
30   Did steal behind him as he lay along°   *stretched out*
Under an oak, whose antic° root peeps out   *old; oddly shaped*
Upon the brook that brawls° along this wood,   *loudly flows*

2.1 Location: The Forest of Ardenne.
1. The name of a town in northern France with which
this character is perhaps associated.
2. In Genesis 3, Adam's punishment for disobeying God
involved expulsion from Eden and the laying of a curse
upon the earth. This was frequently interpreted as the
end of the temperate climate associated with paradise.

3. The toad was popularly believed to be poisonous and
to have in its head a jewel, the toadstone.
4. Jaques's name, usually pronounced with two sylla-
bles, puns on "jakes," the word for "privy" (toilet). He is
a stock figure of the melancholic man prone to solitude
and black thoughts because of an excess of black bile,
one of the four humors.

To the which place a poor sequestered° stag   *cut off from the herd*
That from the hunter's aim had ta'en a hurt
35   Did come to languish. And indeed, my lord,
The wretched animal heaved forth such groans
That their discharge did stretch his leathern coat
Almost to bursting, and the big round tears
Coursed° one another down his innocent nose   *Pursued*
40   In piteous chase. And thus the hairy fool,
Much markèd of° the melancholy Jaques,   *observed by*
Stood on th'extremest verge° of the swift brook,   *farthest edge*
Augmenting it with tears.
DUKE SENIOR   But what said Jaques?
Did he not moralize° this spectacle?   *draw a moral from*
45   FIRST LORD   O yes, into a thousand similes.
First, for his weeping into the needless° stream;   *needing no more water*
'Poor deer,' quoth he, 'thou mak'st a testament
As worldlings do, giving thy sum of more°   *your supplement*
To that which had too much.' Then being there alone,
50   Left and abandoned of° his velvet friend,[5]   *by*
'Tis right,' quoth he, 'thus misery doth part°   *separate from*
The flux° of company.' Anon a careless[6] herd   *flow*
Full of the pasture° jumps along by him   *Full from grazing*
And never stays to greet him. 'Ay,' quoth Jaques,
55   'Sweep on, you fat and greasy citizens,
'Tis just the fashion. Wherefore should you look
Upon that poor and broken bankrupt there?'
Thus most invectively he pierceth through
The body of the country, city, court,
60   Yea, and of this our life, swearing that we
Are mere usurpers, tyrants, and what's worse,°   *whatever is worse*
To fright the animals and to kill them up°   *off*
In their assigned and native dwelling place.
DUKE SENIOR   And did you leave him in this contemplation?
65   SECOND LORD   We did, my lord, weeping and commenting
Upon the sobbing deer.
DUKE SENIOR   Show me the place.
I love to cope° him in these sullen fits,   *contend with*
For then he's full of matter.°   *material for thought; pus*
FIRST LORD   I'll bring you to him straight.°   *immediately*
                                                        Exeunt

2.2

Enter DUKE [FREDERICK], *with* LORDS

DUKE FREDERICK   Can it be possible that no man saw them?
It cannot be. Some villains of my court
Are of consent and sufferance in this.[1]
FIRST LORD   I cannot hear of any that did see her.
5   The ladies her attendants of her chamber
Saw her abed, and in the morning early
They found the bed untreasured of their mistress.
SECOND LORD   My lord, the roynish° clown at whom so oft   *vulgar*

---

5. Smooth-coated companion. Alluding both to the   6. Just then a carefree.
velvet covering the male deer's antlers and to an expen-   2.2 Location: Duke Frederick's court.
sive fabric worn by the prosperous.   1. Have agreed to and tolerated this.

Your grace was wont° to laugh is also missing.   *accustomed*
10 Hisperia, the Princess' gentlewoman,
Confesses that she secretly o'erheard
Your daughter and her cousin much commend
The parts° and graces of the wrestler   *qualities*
That did but lately foil the sinewy Charles,
15 And she believes wherever they are gone
That youth is surely in their company.
DUKE FREDERICK Send to his brother;° fetch that gallant hither. *(Oliver)*
If he° be absent, bring his brother to me,   *(Orlando)*
I'll make him find him. Do this suddenly,
20 And let not search and inquisition quail°   *fail*
To bring again° these foolish runaways.   *Exeunt [severally]*°   *back / separately*

2.3
Enter ORLANDO *and* ADAM *[meeting]*
ORLANDO Who's there?
ADAM What, my young master, O my gentle master,
O my sweet master, O you memory
Of old Sir Rowland, why, what make you° here!   *what are you doing*
5 Why are you virtuous? Why do people love you?
And wherefore° are you gentle, strong, and valiant?   *why*
Why would you be so fond° to overcome   *foolish*
The bonny prizer° of the humorous° Duke?   *robust champion / moody*
Your praise is come too swiftly home before you.
10 Know you not, master, to some kind of men
Their graces° serve them but as enemies?   *virtues*
No more° do yours. Your virtues, gentle master,   *No better*
Are sanctified and holy traitors to you.
O, what a world is this, when what is comely
15 Envenoms° him that bears it!   *Poisons*
ORLANDO Why, what's the matter?
ADAM O, unhappy youth,
Come not within these doors. Within this roof
The enemy of all your graces lives,
20 Your brother—no, no brother—yet the son—
Yet not the son, I will not call him son—
Of him I was about to call his father,
Hath heard your praises, and this night he means
To burn the lodging where you use° to lie,   *are accustomed*
25 And you within it. If he fail of that,
He will have other means to cut you off.
I overheard him and his practices.°   *plots*
This is no place,° this house is but a butchery.°   *home / slaughterhouse*
Abhor it, fear it, do not enter it.
30 ORLANDO Why, whither, Adam, wouldst thou have me go?
ADAM No matter whither, so you come not here.
ORLANDO What, wouldst thou have me go and beg my food,
Or with a base and boisterous° sword enforce   *violent*
A thievish living on the common road?
35 This I must do, or know not what to do.
Yet this I will not do, do how I can.

2.3 Location: Oliver's house.

I rather will subject me to the malice
Of a diverted blood[1] and bloody° brother. *murderous*

ADAM But do not so. I have five hundred crowns,[2]
40 The thrifty hire I saved[3] under your father,
Which I did store to be my foster-nurse[4]
When service should in my old limbs lie lame,° *be lamely performed*
And unregarded age in corners thrown.° *be thrown*
Take that, and he that doth the ravens feed,
45 Yea providently caters for the sparrow,[5]
Be comfort to my age. Here is the gold.
All this I give you. Let me be your servant.
Though I look old, yet I am strong and lusty,° *robust*
For in my youth I never did apply
50 Hot and rebellious° liquors in my blood, *unhealthful*
Nor did not with unbashful forehead° woo *bold countenance*
The means of weakness and debility.
Therefore my age is as a lusty winter,
Frosty but kindly.° Let me go with you, *pleasant; natural*
55 I'll do the service of a younger man
In all your business and necessities.

ORLANDO O good old man, how well in thee appears
The constant° service of the antique world, *faithful*
When service sweat° for duty, not for meed!° *labored / reward*
60 Thou art not for the fashion of these times,
Where none will sweat but for promotion,
And having that do choke their service up° *cease service*
Even with the having. It is not so with thee.
But, poor old man, thou prun'st a rotten tree,
65 That cannot so much as a blossom yield
In lieu of° all thy pains and husbandry.° *return for / gardening*
But come thy ways. We'll go along together,
And ere we have thy youthful wages spent,
We'll light upon some settled low content.° *humble contentment*
70 ADAM Master, go on, and I will follow thee
To the last gasp with truth and loyalty.
From seventeen years till now almost fourscore
Here lived I, but now live here no more.
At seventeen years, many their fortunes seek,
75 But at fourscore, it is too late a week.° *a time*
Yet fortune cannot recompense me better
Than to die well, and not my master's debtor. *Exeunt*

2.4

Enter ROSALIND [*in man's clothes*] *for*° *Ganymede;* *as*
CELIA *for Aliena,* [*a shepherdess;*] *and* TOUCHSTONE
[*the*] *clown*

ROSALIND O Jupiter,[1] how weary are my spirits!
TOUCHSTONE I care not for my spirits, if my legs were not weary.
ROSALIND I could find in my heart to disgrace my man's apparel

---

1. Of a kinship diverted from its natural course.
2. Approximately 125 English pounds.
3. The wages I thriftily saved.
4. Caretaker. A foster nurse was a woman hired to breast-feed and care for other people's children.
5. Alluding to various biblical passages (especially

Luke 12:6 and 22–24 and Psalm 147:9) that characterize God as the caretaker of all creatures.
2.4 Location: The remainder of Act 2 takes place in the Forest of Ardenne.
1. Another name for Jove, king of the gods in classical mythology and Ganymede's master.

and to cry like a woman. But I must comfort the weaker vessel,°   *woman*

5   as doublet and hose² ought to show itself courageous to petti-
coat; therefore, courage, good Aliena!

CELIA   I pray you, bear with me. I cannot go no further.

TOUCHSTONE   For my part, I had rather bear with you than bear
you. Yet I should bear no cross³ if I did bear you, for I think

10   you have no money in your purse.

ROSALIND   Well, this is the forest of Ardenne.

TOUCHSTONE   Ay, now am I in Ardenne; the more fool I. When
I was at home I was in a better place; but travellers must be
content.

        Enter CORIN *and* SILVIUS

15 ROSALIND   Ay, be so, good Touchstone. Look you, who comes
here—a young man and an old in solemn talk.

CORIN [*to* SILVIUS]   That is the way to make her scorn you still.

SILVIUS   O Corin, that thou knew'st how I do love her!

CORIN   I partly guess; for I have loved ere now.

20 SILVIUS   No, Corin, being old thou canst not guess,
Though in thy youth thou wast as true a lover
As ever sighed upon a midnight pillow.
But if thy love were ever like to mine—
As sure I think did never man love so—

25   How many actions most ridiculous
Hast thou been drawn to by thy fantasy?°   *imagination*

CORIN   Into a thousand that I have forgotten.

SILVIUS   O, thou didst then never love so heartily.
If thou rememberest not the slightest folly

30   That ever love did make thee run into,
Thou hast not loved.
Or if thou hast not sat as I do now,
Wearing° thy hearer in thy mistress' praise,   *Wearying*
Thou hast not loved.

35   Or if thou hast not broke from company
Abruptly, as my passion now makes me,
Thou hast not loved.
O, Phoebe, Phoebe, Phoebe!   *Exit*

ROSALIND   Alas, poor shepherd, searching of° thy wound,   *probing*

40   I have by hard adventure° found mine own.   *unlucky chance*

TOUCHSTONE   And I mine. I remember when I was in love I
broke my sword upon a stone and bid him take that for coming
a-night to Jane Smile,⁴ and I remember the kissing of her bat-
let,⁵ and the cow's dugs° that her pretty chapped hands had   *udder*

45   milked; and I remember the wooing of a peascod instead of
her, from whom I took two cods, and giving her them again,
said with weeping tears, 'Wear these for my sake.'⁶ We that are
true lovers run into strange capers. But as all is mortal in
nature, so is all nature in love mortal in folly.⁷

---

2. That is, as manhood (signified by male attire, close-fitting jacket and breeches).
3. Trouble; money, specifically Elizabethan coins stamped with the image of a cross.
4. *I broke . . . Smile:* I struck a stone as though it were a rival to me in my nocturnal visits to Jane Smile.
5. A wooden bat for beating clothes while washing them.

6. *wooing . . . sake':* referring to English country courtship rituals in which a pea pod ("peascod") and its husks ("cods") were considered lucky gifts. "Peascod" and "cods" were also slang terms for "male genitalia," suggesting the implicit sexual import of these gifts.
7. So all lovers show their humanity in their foolishness.

50 ROSALIND   Thou speak'st wiser than thou art ware° of.   *aware*
   TOUCHSTONE   Nay, I shall ne'er be ware° of mine own wit till I   *wary*
      break my shins against it.
   ROSALIND   Jove, Jove, this shepherd's passion
      Is much upon my fashion.°   *of my sort*
55 TOUCHSTONE   And mine, but it grows something° stale with me.   *somewhat*
   CELIA   I pray you, one of you question yon man
      If he for gold will give us any food.
      I faint almost to death.
   TOUCHSTONE   [*to* CORIN]   Holla, you clown!°   *peasant; yokel*
60 ROSALIND   Peace, fool, he's not thy kinsman.
   CORIN   Who calls?
   TOUCHSTONE   Your betters, sir.
   CORIN   Else are they very wretched.
   ROSALIND   [*to* TOUCHSTONE]   Peace, I say. [*To* CORIN]   Good
      even° to you, friend.   *evening*
65 CORIN   And to you, gentle sir, and to you all.
   ROSALIND   I prithee, shepherd, if that love or gold
      Can in this desert place buy entertainment,°   *accommodation*
      Bring us where we may rest ourselves, and feed.
      Here's a young maid with travel much oppressed,
      And faints for succour.°   *for lack of aid (food)*
70 CORIN   Fair sir, I pity her,
      And wish, for her sake more than for mine own,
      My fortunes were more able to relieve her.
      But I am shepherd to another man,
      And do not shear the fleeces that I graze.
75   My master is of churlish° disposition,   *miserly*
      And little recks° to find the way to heaven   *thinks*
      By doing deeds of hospitality.
      Besides, his cot,° his flocks, and bounds of feed°   *cottage / grazing rights*
      Are now on sale, and at our sheepcote° now   *cottage*
80   By reason of his absence there is nothing
      That you will feed on. But what is, come see,
      And in my voice[8] most welcome shall you be.
   ROSALIND   What° is he that shall buy his flock and pasture?   *Who*
   CORIN   That young swain that you saw here but erewhile,°   *just now*
85   That little cares for buying anything.
   ROSALIND   I pray thee, if it stand with honesty,
      Buy thou the cottage, pasture, and the flock,
      And thou shalt have to pay° for it of us.   *the money to pay*
   CELIA   And we will mend° thy wages. I like this place,   *improve*
90   And willingly could waste° my time in it.   *spend*
   CORIN   Assuredly the thing is to be sold.
      Go with me. If you like upon report
      The soil, the profit, and this kind of life,
      I will your very faithful feeder° be,   *servant*
95   And buy it with your gold right suddenly.   *Exeunt*

8. And insofar as my authority stretches.

2.5

Enter AMIENS, JAQUES, *and other* [*Lords dressed as foresters*]

AMIENS [*sings*]¹   Under the greenwood tree
        Who loves to lie with me,
        And turn° his merry note   *tune*
        Unto the sweet bird's throat,°   *voice*
5   Come hither, come hither, come hither.
          Here shall he see
           No enemy
        But winter and rough weather.

JAQUES   More, more, I prithee, more.

10 AMIENS   It will make you melancholy, Monsieur Jaques.

JAQUES   I thank it. More, I prithee, more. I can suck melancholy
    out of a song as a weasel sucks eggs. More, I prithee, more.

AMIENS   My voice is ragged,° I know I cannot please you.   *harsh*

JAQUES   I do not desire you to please me, I do desire you to sing.

15   Come, more; another stanza. Call you 'em stanzas?²

AMIENS   What you will, Monsieur Jaques.

JAQUES   Nay, I care not for their names,³ they owe me nothing.
    Will you sing?

AMIENS   More at your request than to please myself.

20 JAQUES   Well then, if ever I thank any man, I'll thank you. But
    that° they call compliment is like th'encounter of two dog-   *what*
    apes,° and when a man thanks me heartily methinks I have   *dog-faced baboons*
    given him a penny and he renders me the beggarly thanks.⁴
    Come, sing; and you that will not, hold your tongues.

25 AMIENS   Well, I'll end the song.—Sirs, cover the while.⁵
    [*Lords prepare food and drink*]
    The Duke will drink under this tree. [*To* JAQUES] He hath been
    all this day to look° you.   *searching for*

JAQUES   And I have been all this day to avoid him. He is too
    disputable° for my company. I think of as many matters as he,   *argumentative*
30   but I give heaven thanks, and make no boast of them. Come,
    warble, come.

ALL [*sing*]⁶   Who doth ambition shun,
        And loves to live i'th' sun,
        Seeking the food he eats
35   And pleased with what he gets,
    Come hither, come hither, come hither.
          Here shall he see
           No enemy
        But winter and rough weather.

40 JAQUES   I'll give you a verse to this note° that I made yesterday in   *tune*
    despite of my invention.⁷

AMIENS   And I'll sing it.

JAQUES   Thus it goes:
        If it do come to pass
45   That any man turn ass,

2.5

1. F does not indicate who sings this song. Traditionally it has been assigned to Amiens, whose part may have been played by Robert Armin, a clown who joined Shakespeare's company in 1599 and who was known for his fine singing voice.
2. A relatively new, and Italianate, word at the time of the play's composition.

3. Punning on the legal sense of "names" as "signatures of borrowers."
4. Excessive thanks, like that given by a beggar.
5. Set the table in the meantime.
6. F's direction before this song reads: "Song. Altogether here."
7. Even though I have little power of creativity.

Leaving his wealth and ease
A stubborn will to please,
Ducdame,[8] ducdame, ducdame.
Here shall he see
50   Gross fools as he,
An if° he will come to me.   *If only*

AMIENS   What's that 'ducdame'?

JAQUES   'Tis a Greek[9] invocation to call fools into a circle. I'll go
sleep if I can. If I cannot, I'll rail against all the firstborn of
55   Egypt.[1]

AMIENS   And I'll go seek the Duke; his banquet[2] is prepared.

Exeunt

2.6

Enter ORLANDO *and* ADAM

ADAM   Dear master, I can go no further. O, I die for food. Here
lie I down and measure out my grave. Farewell, kind master.

ORLANDO   Why, how now, Adam? No greater heart in thee? Live
a little, comfort° a little, cheer thyself a little. If this uncouth°   *be comforted / wild*
5   forest yield anything savage I will either be food for it or bring it
for food to thee. Thy conceit° is nearer death than thy powers.   *imagination*
For my sake be comfortable. Hold death awhile at the arm's
end. I will here be with thee presently,° and if I bring thee not   *soon*
something to eat, I will give thee leave to die. But if thou diest
10   before I come, thou art a mocker of my labour. Well said. Thou
lookest cheerly,° and I'll be with thee quickly. Yet thou liest in   *cheerfully*
the bleak air. Come, I will bear thee to some shelter, and thou
shalt not die for lack of a dinner if there live anything in this
desert.° Cheerly, good Adam.   [ORLANDO *carries* ADAM *off*]   *uninhabited place*

2.7

Enter DUKE SENIOR *and* LORD[S] *like° outlaws*   *dressed as*

DUKE SENIOR   I think he be transformed into a beast,
For I can nowhere find him like° a man.   *in the shape of*

FIRST LORD   My lord, he is but even now gone hence.
Here was he merry, hearing of a song.

5   DUKE SENIOR   If he, compact of jars,° grow musical   *made up of discords*
We shall have shortly discord in the spheres.[1]
Go seek him. Tell him I would speak with him.

Enter JAQUES

FIRST LORD   He saves my labour by his own approach.

DUKE SENIOR   Why, how now, monsieur, what a life is this,
10   That your poor friends must woo your company!
What, you look merrily.

JAQUES   A fool, a fool, I met a fool i'th' forest,
A motley fool[2]—a miserable world!—
As I do live by food, I met a fool,

---

8. A word of unknown meaning. Possibly a variation on a Welsh phrase meaning "Come hither" or on a Gypsy phrase meaning "I foretell."
9. "Greek" was used to signify anything unintelligible.
1. According to Exodus 11 and 12, the Hebrew God caused the deaths of all firstborn Egyptian children after Pharaoh would not let the Israelites leave his country. Jaques may be vowing to denounce all firstborn sons, which would include Duke Senior.

2. A light meal of sweetmeats and wine.
2.7
1. Alluding to the Pythagorean belief that the earth was the center of eight concentric spheres whose movements created a heavenly harmony (the music of the spheres) inaudible to humans.
2. Someone wearing "motley," the multicolored costume conventionally associated with fools and jesters.

15 Who laid him down and basked him in the sun,
    And railed on Lady Fortune in good terms,
    In good set° terms, and yet a motley fool.   *outspoken; rhetorical*
    'Good morrow, fool,' quoth I. 'No, sir,' quoth he,
    'Call me not fool till heaven hath sent me fortune.'³
20 And then he drew a dial⁴ from his poke,°   *pocket; pouch*
    And looking on it with lack-lustre eye
    Says very wisely 'It is ten o'clock.'
    'Thus we may see', quoth he, 'how the world wags.°   *moves on*
    'Tis but an hour ago since it was nine,
25 And after one hour more 'twill be eleven.
    And so from hour to hour we ripe and ripe,
    And then from hour to hour we rot and rot;
    And thereby hangs a tale.'⁵ When I did hear
    The motley fool thus moral on the time
30 My lungs began to crow like chanticleer,°   *a rooster*
    That fools should be so deep°-contemplative,   *profoundly*
    And I did laugh sans° intermission   *without*
    An hour by his dial. O noble fool,
    A worthy fool—motley's the only wear.°   *garb worth wearing*
35 DUKE SENIOR   What fool is this?
    JAQUES   O worthy fool!—One that hath been a courtier,
    And says 'If ladies be but young and fair
    They have the gift to know it.' And in his brain,
    Which is as dry⁶ as the remainder° biscuit   *last*
40 After a voyage, he hath strange places° crammed   *sites; commonplaces*
    With observation, the which he vents
    In mangled forms. O that I were a fool,
    I am ambitious for a motley coat.
    DUKE SENIOR   Thou shalt have one.
    JAQUES   It is my only suit,°   *request; costume*
45 Provided that you weed your better judgements
    Of all opinion that grows rank° in them   *wild*
    That I am wise. I must have liberty
    Withal, as large a charter° as the wind,   *license*
    To blow on whom I please, for so fools have;
50 And they that are most gallèd° with my folly,   *vexed*
    They most must laugh. And why, sir, must they so?
    The why is plain as way to parish church:
    He that a fool doth very wisely hit
    Doth very foolishly, although he smart,
55 Seem aught but senseless of the bob.° If not,   *unaware of the taunt*
    The wise man's folly is anatomized°   *dissected; laid open*
    Even by the squandering glances° of the fool.   *random hits*
    Invest me in my motley. Give me leave
    To speak my mind, and I will through and through
60 Cleanse the foul body of th'infected world,
    If they will patiently receive my medicine.
    DUKE SENIOR   Fie on thee, I can tell what thou wouldst do.

3. Referring to the proverbial notion that fortune favored fools.
4. Probably a portable sundial about the size of a napkin ring.
5. *Tis . . . tale*: the puns and sexual wordplay in these lines suggest a story of male sexual activity leading to debility: "hour" puns on "whore" (they were pronounced similarly); "ripe" means "to come of age sexually"; "rot" puns on "rut," which means "to have sex in an animal-like state of excitement"; and "tale" puns on "tail," slang for "penis." "And thereby hangs a tale" was an Elizabethan commonplace.
6. According to Renaissance medical theory, dry brains signified slow wits and strong memories.

JAQUES   What, for a counter,[7] would I do but good?

DUKE SENIOR   Most mischievous foul sin, in chiding sin;

65   For thou thyself hast been a libertine,
     As sensual as the brutish sting° itself,   *lust*
     And all th'embossèd sores and headed evils[8]
     That thou with licence of free foot° hast caught   *travel*
     Wouldst thou disgorge° into the general world.   *vomit*

70   JAQUES   Why, who cries out on pride°   *extravagance*
     That can therein tax° any private party?   *blame*
     Doth it not flow as hugely as the sea,
     Till that the weary very means° do ebb?   *source itself*
     What woman in the city do I name

75   When that I say the city-woman bears
     The cost° of princes on unworthy shoulders?   *costly attire*
     Who can come in and say that I mean her
     When such a one as she, such is her neighbour?
     Or what is he of basest function,°   *lowliest social status*

80   That says his bravery° is not on° my cost,   *fine attire / at*
     Thinking that I mean him, but therein suits
     His folly to the mettle° of my speech?   *spirit*
     There then, how then, what then, let me see wherein
     My tongue hath wronged him. If it do him right,°   *describe him justly*

85   Then he hath wronged himself. If he be free,°   *virtuous*
     Why then my taxing° like a wild goose flies,   *reproof*
     Unclaimed of any man. But who comes here?

     Enter ORLANDO [*with sword drawn*]

ORLANDO   Forbear, and eat no more!

JAQUES   Why, I have eat° none yet.   *eaten*

ORLANDO   Nor shalt not till necessity be served.

90   JAQUES   Of what kind° should this cock come of?   *lineage; stock*

DUKE SENIOR   Art thou thus boldened, man, by thy distress?
     Or else a rude despiser of good manners,
     That in civility thou seem'st so empty?

ORLANDO   You touched my vein° at first. The thorny point   *assessed my condition*

95   Of bare distress hath ta'en from me the show
     Of smooth civility. Yet am I inland bred,[9]
     And know some nurture. But forbear, I say.
     He dies that touches any of this fruit
     Till I and my affairs are answerèd.°   *satisfied*

100 JAQUES   An° you will not be answered with reason, I must die.   *If*

DUKE SENIOR   What would you have? Your gentleness° shall   *gentility; kindness*
        force
     More than your force move us to gentleness.

ORLANDO   I almost die for food; and let me have it.

DUKE SENIOR   Sit down and feed, and welcome to our table.

105 ORLANDO   Speak you so gently? Pardon me, I pray you.
     I thought that all things had been savage here,
     And therefore put I on the countenance
     Of stern commandment. But whate'er you are
     That in this desert inaccessible,

110   Under the shade of melancholy boughs,

---

7. In return for a coin of no value (normally used for reckoning sums).
8. Swollen sores and boils that have come to a head. Both were symptoms of venereal disease.

9. Brought up in a civilized way—that is, raised in the country's interior regions rather than near its supposedly savage borders.

Lose and neglect the creeping hours of time,
If ever you have looked on better days,
If ever been where bells have knolled° to church,   *summoned*
If ever sat at any good man's feast,
115   If ever from your eyelids wiped a tear,
And know what 'tis to pity, and be pitied,
Let gentleness my strong enforcement be,[1]
In the which hope I blush, and hide my sword.
DUKE SENIOR   True is it that we have seen better days,
120   And have with holy bell been knolled to church,
And sat at good men's feasts, and wiped our eyes
Of drops that sacred pity hath engendered.
And therefore sit you down in gentleness,
And take upon command° what help we have   *at your will*
125   That to your wanting may be ministered.
ORLANDO   Then but forbear your food a little while
Whiles, like a doe, I go to find my fawn
And give it food. There is an old poor man
Who after me hath many a weary step
130   Limped in pure love. Till he be first sufficed,°   *satisfied*
Oppressed with two weak° evils, age and hunger,   *enfeebling*
I will not touch a bit.
DUKE SENIOR   Go find him out,
And we will nothing waste° till you return.   *consume*
ORLANDO   I thank ye; and be blessed for your good comfort!
                                                                    [*Exit*]
135   DUKE SENIOR   Thou seest we are not all alone unhappy.
This wide and universal theatre
Presents more woeful pageants° than the scene   *spectacles*
Wherein we play in.
JAQUES   All the world's a stage,
And all the men and women merely players.
140   They have their exits and their entrances,
And one man in his time plays many parts,
His acts being seven ages. At first the infant,
Mewling° and puking in the nurse's arms.   *Crying*
Then the whining schoolboy with his satchel
145   And shining morning face, creeping like snail
Unwillingly to school. And then the lover,
Sighing like furnace,[2] with a woeful ballad
Made to his mistress' eyebrow. Then, a soldier,
Full of strange oaths, and bearded like the pard,[3]
150   Jealous in honour,[4] sudden, and quick in quarrel,
Seeking the bubble reputation
Even in the cannon's mouth. And then the justice,
In fair round belly with good capon[5] lined,°   *filled; stuffed*
With eyes severe and beard of formal cut,
155   Full of wise saws° and modern° instances;   *sayings / trite*
And so he plays his part. The sixth age shifts

1. Let natural kindness or gentility be what compels your compassion.
2. Emitting sighs as a furnace emits smoke.
3. Leopard. The soldier's bristling mustache is being compared to the leopard's whiskers.
4. Vigilant in matters of honor.
5. A cock, castrated and fattened as a delicacy (proverbially, a bribe for magistrates).

Into the lean and slippered pantaloon,[6]
With spectacles on nose and pouch on side,
His youthful hose, well saved, a world too wide
160 For his shrunk shank,° and his big, manly voice,   *calf*
Turning again toward childish treble, pipes
And whistles in his° sound. Last scene of all,   *its*
That ends this strange, eventful history,
Is second childishness and mere° oblivion,   *complete*
165 Sans° teeth, sans eyes, sans taste, sans everything.   *Without*
            Enter ORLANDO *[bearing]* ADAM
DUKE SENIOR   Welcome. Set down your venerable burden
    And let him feed.
ORLANDO   I thank you most for him.
ADAM   So had you need;
170 I scarce can speak to thank you for myself.
DUKE SENIOR   Welcome. Fall to. I will not trouble you
    As yet to question you about your fortunes.
    Give us some music, and, good cousin, sing.
AMIENS *[sings]*[7]   Blow, blow, thou winter wind,
175   Thou art not so unkind
                            As man's ingratitude.
                    Thy tooth is not so keen,
                    Because thou art not seen,
                            Although thy breath be rude.°   *rough*
180   Hey-ho, sing hey-ho, unto the green holly.[8]
            Most friendship is feigning, most loving, mere folly.
                    Then hey-ho, the holly;
                    This life is most jolly.

                    Freeze, freeze, thou bitter sky,
185   That dost not bite so nigh°   *closely*
                            As benefits forgot.
                    Though thou the waters warp,°   *cause to contract; freeze*
                    Thy sting is not so sharp
                    As friend remembered not.
190   Hey-ho, sing hey-ho, unto the green holly.
            Most friendship is feigning, most loving, mere folly.
                    Then hey-ho, the holly;
                    This life is most jolly.
DUKE SENIOR *[to* ORLANDO*]*   If that you were the good Sir Rowland's son,
195   As you have whispered faithfully you were,
    And as mine eye doth his effigies° witness   *likeness*
    Most truly limned° and living in your face,   *portrayed*
    Be truly welcome hither. I am the Duke
    That loved your father. The residue of your fortune,
200   Go to my cave and tell me. *[To* ADAM*]* Good old man,
    Thou art right welcome, as thy master is.—
    [To LORDS*]* Support him by the arm. *[To* ORLANDO*]* Give me your hand,
    And let me all your fortunes understand.   *Exeunt*

---

6. A foolish old man named after a figure in *commedia*   usually assigned to Amiens.
dell'arte, Italian popular comedy.   8. The evergreen associated with English holiday festivi-
7. Again, F does not indicate who sings this song. It is   ties.

3.1

Enter DUKE [FREDERICK], *Lords, and* OLIVER

DUKE FREDERICK   Not see him since? Sir, sir, that cannot be.
But were I not the better part made° mercy,   *composed of*
I should not seek an absent argument°   *subject*
Of my revenge, thou present. But look to it:
5   Find out thy brother wheresoe'er he is.
Seek him with candle.° Bring him, dead or living,   *diligently*
Within this twelvemonth, or turn° thou no more   *return*
To seek a living in our territory.
Thy lands, and all things that thou dost call thine
10 Worth seizure, do we seize into our hands
Till thou canst quit° thee by thy brother's mouth   *acquit*
Of what we think against thee.
OLIVER   O that your highness knew my heart in this.
I never loved my brother in my life.
DUKE FREDERICK   More villain thou. [*To Lords*] Well, push
15   him out of doors,
And let my officers of such a nature°   *whose job it is*
Make an extent° upon his house and lands.   *a writ of seizure*
Do this expediently,° and turn° him going. *Exeunt* [*severally*]   *quickly / set*

3.2

Enter ORLANDO [*with a paper*]

ORLANDO   Hang there, my verse, in witness of my love;
And thou thrice-crownèd queen of night,[1] survey
With thy chaste eye, from thy pale sphere above,
Thy huntress' name° that my full life doth sway.°   *(Rosalind) / rule*
5   O Rosalind, these trees shall be my books,
And in their barks my thoughts I'll character°   *inscribe*
That every eye which in this forest looks
Shall see thy virtue witnessed everywhere.
Run, run, Orlando; carve on every tree
10 The fair, the chaste, and unexpressive° she.   *Exit*[2]   *inexpressible*

Enter CORIN *and* [TOUCHSTONE *the*] *clown*

CORIN   And how like you this shepherd's life, Master Touchstone?
TOUCHSTONE   Truly, shepherd, in respect of° itself, it is a good   *with regard to*
life; but in respect that it is a shepherd's life, it is naught.° In   *worthless*
respect that it is solitary, I like it very well; but in respect that it
15 is private, it is a very vile life. Now in respect it is in the fields,
it pleaseth me well; but in respect it is not in the court, it is
tedious. As it is a spare° life, look you, it fits my humour° well;   *frugal / temperament*
but as there is no more plenty in it, it goes much against my
stomach.° Hast any philosophy in thee, shepherd?   *inclination*
20 CORIN   No more but that I know the more one sickens, the worse
at ease he is, and that he that wants° money, means, and con-   *lacks*
tent is without three good friends; that the property of rain is to

---

3.1   Location: Duke Frederick's court.
3.2   Location: The remaining scenes of the play take place in the Forest of Ardenne.
1.   The goddess who ruled on earth as Diana, patron of chastity and of the hunt; in the heavens as Cynthia, Phoebe, or Luna, goddess of the moon; and in the underworld as Hecate.

2.   Orlando's appearance at lines 1–10 is self-contained and could form a separate scene. However, the ensuing conversation between Corin and Touchstone appears to take place on the same spot where Orlando has just stood, making the action continuous. This edition, like F, makes Orlando's lines part of the longer scene involving Corin, Touchstone, and eventually Rosalind and others.

wet, and fire to burn; that good pasture makes fat sheep; and
that a great cause of the night is lack of the sun; that he that
25 hath learned no wit by nature nor art may complain° of good   *lament his lack*
breeding or comes of a very dull kindred.

TOUCHSTONE   Such a one is a natural philosopher.[3] Wast ever in
court, shepherd?

CORIN   No, truly.

30 TOUCHSTONE   Then thou art damned.

CORIN   Nay, I hope.

TOUCHSTONE   Truly thou art damned, like an ill-roasted egg, all
on one side.

CORIN   For not being at court? Your reason?

35 TOUCHSTONE   Why, if thou never wast at court thou never sawest
good manners.° If thou never sawest good manners, then thy   *etiquette; morals*
manners must be wicked, and wickedness is sin, and sin is dam-
nation. Thou art in a parlous° state, shepherd.   *perilous*

CORIN   Not a whit, Touchstone. Those that are good manners at
40 the court are as ridiculous in the country as the behaviour of
the country is most mockable at the court. You told me you
salute not at the court but° you kiss your hands. That courtesy   *unless*
would be uncleanly if courtiers were shepherds.

TOUCHSTONE   Instance,° briefly; come, instance.   *An example*

45 CORIN   Why, we are still° handling our ewes, and their fells,° you   *constantly / skins*
know, are greasy.

TOUCHSTONE   Why, do not your courtier's hands sweat? And is
not the grease of a mutton as wholesome as the sweat of a man?
Shallow, shallow. A better instance, I say. Come.

50 CORIN   Besides, our hands are hard.

TOUCHSTONE   Your lips will feel them the sooner. Shallow again.
A more sounder instance. Come.

CORIN   And they are often tarred over with the surgery of our
sheep;[4] and would you have us kiss tar? The courtier's hands
55 are perfumed with civet.[5]

TOUCHSTONE   Most shallow, man. Thou worms' meat in respect
of° a good piece of flesh indeed, learn of the wise, and per-   *in comparison with*
pend:° civet is of a baser birth than tar, the very uncleanly flux° *consider / discharge*
of a cat. Mend° the instance, shepherd.   *Improve*

60 CORIN   You have too courtly a wit for me. I'll rest.

TOUCHSTONE   Wilt thou rest damned? God help thee, shallow
man. God make incision in thee, thou art raw.[6]

CORIN   Sir, I am a true labourer. I earn that° I eat, get° that I   *what / make*
wear; owe no man hate, envy no man's happiness; glad of other
65 men's good, content with my harm;° and the greatest of my   *misfortune*
pride is to see my ewes graze and my lambs suck.

TOUCHSTONE   That is another simple° sin in you, to bring the   *simpleminded*
ewes and the rams together, and to offer° to get your living by   *undertake*
the copulation of cattle; to be bawd to a bell-wether,[7] and to
70 betray a she-lamb of a twelve-month to a crooked-pated old

---

3. A born philosopher; a philosopher who studies nat-
ural phenomena; a fool.
4. Referring to the practice of treating sheep wounds
with tar.
5. A musk-scented substance obtained from the anal
glands of certain cats.

6. Make a cut to let blood (and thus cure you of your
"raw"ness, or inexperience); make a cut to score you, as
raw meat was scored in preparation for cooking.
7. The leading sheep of a flock, who usually wore a
bell.

cuckoldly ram,[8] out of all reasonable match. If thou beest not
damned for this, the devil himself will have no shepherds.[9] I
cannot see else how thou shouldst scape.

CORIN   Here comes young Master Ganymede, my new mistress's
75   brother.

Enter ROSALIND [*as Ganymede*]

ROSALIND [*reads*]   'From the east to western Ind°   *Indies*
        No jewel is like Rosalind.
        Her worth being mounted on the wind
        Through all the world bears Rosalind.
80   All the pictures fairest lined°   *drawn*
        Are but black to° Rosalind.   *compared to*
        Let no face be kept in mind
        But the fair of Rosalind.'

TOUCHSTONE   I'll rhyme you so eight years together, dinners, and
85   suppers, and sleeping-hours excepted. It is the right butter-
        women's rank to market.[1]

ROSALIND   Out, fool.

TOUCHSTONE   For a taste:
        If a hart° do lack a hind,°   *male deer / female deer*
90   Let him seek out Rosalind.
        If the cat will after kind,°   *act naturally; mate*
        So, be sure, will Rosalind.
        Wintered garments must be lined,[2]
        So must slender Rosalind.
95   They that reap must sheaf and bind,
        Then to cart[3] with Rosalind.
        'Sweetest nut hath sourest rind',
        Such a nut is Rosalind.
        He that sweetest rose will find
100   Must find love's prick,° and Rosalind.   *thorn; penis*
        This is the very false gallop of verses.° Why do you infect your-   *way verses canter on*
        self with them?

ROSALIND   Peace, you dull fool, I found them on a tree.

TOUCHSTONE   Truly, the tree yields bad fruit.

105 ROSALIND   I'll graft it with you,° and then I shall graft it with a   *(punning on "yew")*
        medlar;[4] then it will be the earliest fruit i'th' country, for you'll
        be rotten ere you be half-ripe, and that's the right° virtue of the   *true*
        medlar.

TOUCHSTONE   You have said; but whether wisely or no, let the
110   forest judge.

Enter CELIA [*as Aliena*], *with a writing*

ROSALIND   Peace, here comes my sister, reading. Stand aside.

CELIA [*reads*]   'Why should this a desert be?
        For it is unpeopled? No.
        Tongues I'll hang on every tree,
115   That shall civil° sayings show.   *civilized*

8. Cuckolds, men whose wives were sexually unfaith-
ful, supposedly wore horns to signify their shame. The
ram may *make* cuckolds—that is, be lecherous.
crooked-pated: with crooked horns.
9. It will be because the devil refuses to admit shep-
herds into hell.
1. *It . . . market:* The rhymes are truly like a stream of
dairywomen going to market at the same time. Such
women were proverbially talkative.

2. Clothes worn in winter must be stuffed with mate-
rial, with a pun on "lined" as meaning "mated," used
especially of female animals.
3. A cart on which harvests were transported to the
market; a cart on which women accused of prostitution
or other forms of disorderly conduct were transported
and exposed to public abuse.
4. A tree whose fruit was not ripe until it was so soft as
to be rotten, with a pun on "meddler," one who meddles.

Some, how brief the life of man
   Runs his erring° pilgrimage,   *wandering*
That the stretching of a span
   Buckles in his sum of age.⁵
120   Some of violated vows
   'Twixt the souls of friend and friend.
But upon the fairest boughs,
   Or at every sentence end,
Will I 'Rosalinda' write,
125   Teaching all that read to know
The quintessence of every sprite°   *spirit; soul*
   Heaven would in little show.⁶
Therefore heaven nature charged
   That one body should be filled
130   With all graces wide-enlarged.⁷
   Nature presently° distilled   *at once*
Helen's cheek, but not her heart,⁸
   Cleopatra's⁹ majesty,
Atalanta's better part,¹
135   Sad Lucretia's modesty.²
Thus Rosalind of many parts
   By heavenly synod° was devised   *assembly*
Of many faces, eyes, and hearts
   To have the touches° dearest prized.   *traits*
140   Heaven would that she these gifts should have
And I to live and die her slave.'

ROSALIND O most gentle Jupiter! What tedious homily of love
have you wearied your parishioners withal, and never cried
'Have patience, good people.'

145 CELIA How now, back, friends. Shepherd, go off a little. Go with
him, sirrah.

TOUCHSTONE Come, shepherd, let us make an honourable
retreat, though not with bag and baggage, yet with scrip and
scrippage.³   *Exit* [*with* CORIN]

150 CELIA Didst thou hear these verses?

ROSALIND O yes, I heard them all, and more, too, for some of
them had in them more feet° than the verses would bear. *metrical units*

CELIA That's no matter; the feet might bear° the verses. *carry*

ROSALIND Ay, but the feet were lame, and could not bear them-
155 selves without° the verse, and therefore stood lamely in the *out of*
verse.

CELIA But didst thou hear without wondering how thy name
should be° hanged and carved upon these trees? *came to be*

---

5. *the stretching . . . age:* the width of an open hand (a "span") encompasses an entire lifetime. A comparison derived from verses appearing in Elizabethan prayer books.
6. Which heaven would portray in miniature, or through one individual (Rosalind).
7. Graces that otherwise have been widely distributed.
8. The features, but not the false heart, of Helen of Troy. Supposedly Helen's abduction by Paris from her husband, Menelaus, was the event that precipitated the Trojan War. In some accounts, Helen is blamed for her abduction and so could be said to have a false heart.
9. Queen of Egypt and the tragic heroine of Shake-

speare's *Antony and Cleopatra.*
1. In Greek myth, Atalanta was a fleet-footed and chaste hunter who challenged her suitors to a race. She was only defeated when one of them dropped three golden apples, which she stopped to pick up. The reference here is possibly to her beauty or her speed, rather than her greed.
2. Lucretia killed herself to save her honor after being raped by Tarquin (a story told by Shakespeare in *The Rape of Lucrece*).
3. Though not with the belongings retained by an army in retreat, yet with a shepherd's pouch and its contents.

ROSALIND   I was seven of the nine days out of the wonder[4] before
160   you came; for look here what I found on a palm-tree; [*showing*
CELIA *the verses*] I was never so berhymed since Pythagoras'
time that I was an Irish rat,[5] which I can hardly remember.

CELIA   Trow you° who hath done this?   *Can you imagine*

ROSALIND   Is it a man?

165   CELIA   And a chain that you once wore about his neck. Change
you colour?

ROSALIND   I prithee, who?

CELIA   O Lord, Lord, it is a hard matter for friends to meet. But
mountains may be removed with° earthquakes, and so   *moved by*
170   encounter.

ROSALIND   Nay, but who is it?

CELIA   Is it possible?

ROSALIND   Nay, I prithee now with most petitionary vehemence,
tell me who it is.

175   CELIA   O wonderful, wonderful, and most wonderful-wonderful,
and yet again wonderful, and after that out of all whooping![6]

ROSALIND   Good my complexion![7] Dost thou think, though I am
caparisoned° like a man, I have a doublet and hose in my dispo-   *dressed*
sition? One inch of delay more is a South Sea of discovery.[8] I
180   prithee tell me who is it quickly, and speak apace.° I would   *at once*
thou couldst stammer, that thou mightst pour this concealed
man out of thy mouth as wine comes out of a narrow-mouthed
bottle—either too much at once, or none at all. I prithee, take
the cork out of thy mouth, that I may drink thy tidings.

185   CELIA   So you may put a man in your belly.°   *stomach; womb*

ROSALIND   Is he of God's making? What manner of man? Is his
head worth a hat? Or his chin worth a beard?

CELIA   Nay, he hath but a little beard.

ROSALIND   Why, God will send more, if the man will be thank-
190   ful. Let me stay° the growth of his beard, if thou delay me not   *wait for*
the knowledge of his chin.

CELIA   It is young Orlando, that tripped up the wrestler's heels
and your heart both in an instant.

ROSALIND   Nay, but the devil take mocking. Speak sad brow and
195   true maid.[9]

CELIA   I'faith, coz, 'tis he.

ROSALIND   Orlando?

CELIA   Orlando.

ROSALIND   Alas the day, what shall I do with my doublet and
200   hose! What did he when thou sawest him? What said he? How
looked he? Wherein went he?° What makes he here? Did he   *What was he wearing*
ask for me? Where remains he? How parted he with thee? And
when shalt thou see him again? Answer me in one word.

CELIA   You must borrow me Gargantua's[1] mouth first, 'tis a word

---

4. Referring to the proverbial "nine days' wonder," a
novelty that caused amazement.
5. I was never so overwhelmed with rhyme since the
days of the ancient Greeks, when I was an Irish rat.
Alluding to Pythagoras's doctrine of the transmigration
of souls and to the popular belief in England that Irish
bards were capable of rhyming rats to death.
6. After that, beyond what all shouts of astonishment
can express.
7. An expression of impatience. "Complexion" means

"temperament," believed to be caused by the particular
mixture of the four humors in one's body. Her meaning
seems to be: Pay attention to my womanly temperament
(which is impatient)!
8. More delay will seem as infinite as a voyage of dis-
covery to the South Seas.
9. Speak seriously and as a virtuous woman or on your
honor as a virgin.
1. A voracious giant famous in French folklore and
from the writings of Rabelais.

205 too great for any mouth of this age's size. To say ay and no to
these particulars is more than to answer in a catechism.[2]

ROSALIND But doth he know that I am in this forest, and in
man's apparel? Looks he as freshly as he did the day he wres-
tled?

210 CELIA It is as easy to count atomies° as to resolve the proposi- *specks (of dust)*
tions° of a lover; but take a taste of my finding him, and relish *answer the questions*
it with good observance.[3] I found him under a tree, like a
dropped acorn—

ROSALIND It may well be called Jove's tree[4] when it drops forth
215 such fruit.

CELIA Give me audience, good madam.

ROSALIND Proceed.

CELIA There lay he, stretched along like a wounded knight—

ROSALIND Though it be pity to see such a sight, it well becomes
220 the ground.

CELIA Cry 'holla'° to thy tongue, I prithee: it curvets° unseason- *hold / leaps about*
ably.—He was furnished° like a hunter— *dressed*

ROSALIND O ominous—he comes to kill my heart.

CELIA I would sing my song without a burden;° thou bringest *refrain*
225 me out of tune.

ROSALIND Do you not know I am a woman? When I think, I
must speak.—Sweet, say on.

Enter ORLANDO *and* JAQUES

CELIA You bring me out.° Soft, comes he not here? *make me lose the tune*

ROSALIND 'Tis he. Slink by, and note him.

230 [ROSALIND *and* CELIA *stand aside*]

JAQUES [*to* ORLANDO] I thank you for your company, but, good
faith, I had as lief° have been myself alone. *as willingly*

ORLANDO And so had I. But yet for fashion' sake, I thank you too
for your society.

JAQUES God b'wi'you;° let's meet as little as we can. *Good-bye*

235 ORLANDO I do desire we may be better strangers.

JAQUES I pray you mar no more trees with writing love-songs in
their barks.

ORLANDO I pray you mar no more of my verses with reading
them ill-favouredly.° *unsympathetically*

240 JAQUES Rosalind is your love's name?

ORLANDO Yes, just.

JAQUES I do not like her name.

ORLANDO There was no thought of pleasing you when she was
christened.

245 JAQUES What stature is she of?

ORLANDO Just as high as my heart.

JAQUES You are full of pretty answers. Have you not been
acquainted with goldsmiths' wives, and conned them out of
rings?[5]

250 ORLANDO Not so; but I answer you right painted cloth,[6] from
whence you have studied your questions.

2. A summary, in question-and-answer form, of basic
tenets of religious doctrine. In Shakespeare's time, all
members of the Church of England learned to recite
such a catechism.
3. And enhance its flavor by paying careful attention.
4. The oak was traditionally viewed as sacred to Jove, the
god of thunder, and was said therefore to be often struck
by lightning.
5. Romantic verses were often inscribed on rings sold
in shops managed by the wives of goldsmiths; with a
pun on "rings" as a slang term for "vaginas."
6. I answer you in the style of the pithy sayings issuing
from the mouths of figures in painted wall hangings (a
popular and inexpensive form of interior decoration).

JAQUES You have a nimble wit; I think 'twas made of Atalanta's
  heels.[7] Will you sit down with me, and we two will rail against
  our mistress the world, and all our misery?

255 ORLANDO I will chide no breather° in the world but myself,   *person*
  against whom I know most faults.

JAQUES The worst fault you have is to be in love.

ORLANDO 'Tis a fault I will not change for your best virtue. I am
  weary of you.

260 JAQUES By my troth, I was seeking for a fool when I found you.

ORLANDO He is drowned in the brook. Look but in, and you
  shall see him.

JAQUES There I shall see mine own figure.

ORLANDO Which I take to be either a fool or a cipher.[8]

265 JAQUES I'll tarry no longer with you. Farewell, good Signor
  Love.

ORLANDO I am glad of your departure. Adieu, good Monsieur
  Melancholy.   [*Exit* JAQUES][9]

ROSALIND [*to* CELIA] I will speak to him like a saucy lackey, and
270 under that habit° play the knave with him. [*To* ORLANDO] Do   *guise; disguise*
  you hear, forester?

ORLANDO Very well. What would you?

ROSALIND I pray you, what is't o'clock?

ORLANDO You should ask me what time o' day. There's no clock
275 in the forest.

ROSALIND Then there is no true lover in the forest, else sighing
  every minute and groaning every hour would detect° the lazy   *reveal*
  foot of time as well as a clock.

ORLANDO And why not the swift foot of time? Had not that been
280 as proper?

ROSALIND By no means, sir. Time travels in divers paces with
  divers persons. I'll tell you who time ambles withal,° who time   *with*
  trots withal, who time gallops withal, and who he stands still
  withal.

285 ORLANDO I prithee, who doth he trot withal?

ROSALIND Marry, he trots hard° with a young maid between the   *uncomfortably*
  contract of her marriage and the day it is solemnized. If the
  interim be but a se'nnight,° time's pace is so hard that it seems   *week*
  the length of seven year.

290 ORLANDO Who ambles time withal?

ROSALIND With a priest that lacks Latin, and a rich man that
  hath not the gout; for the one sleeps easily because he cannot
  study, and the other lives merrily because he feels no pain, the
  one lacking the burden of lean and wasteful° learning, the   *weakening*
295 other knowing no burden of heavy tedious penury.° These time   *poverty*
  ambles withal.

ORLANDO Who doth he gallop withal?

ROSALIND With a thief to the gallows; for though he go as softly°   *slowly*
  as foot can fall, he thinks himself too soon there.

300 ORLANDO Who stays it still withal?

---

7. See note to 3.2.134.
8. A zero; punning on "figure" (line 263) as meaning "numeral."
9. Editors usually give Jaques an exit here, although none is indicated in F. It would not be out of character,

however, for Jaques to remain onstage in the background during Orlando and Rosalind's exchange (as he does during Touchstone's courting of Audrey in 3.3) and to exit with them at the end of the scene.

ROSALIND   With lawyers in the vacation; for they sleep between
term[1] and term, and then they perceive not how time moves.

ORLANDO   Where dwell you, pretty youth?

ROSALIND   With this shepherdess, my sister, here in the skirts° of   *edges*
305   the forest, like fringe upon a petticoat.

ORLANDO   Are you native of this place?

ROSALIND   As the coney° that you see dwell where she is kin-   *rabbit*
dled.°   *born*

ORLANDO   Your accent is something finer than you could pur-
310   chase° in so removed° a dwelling.   *acquire / remote*

ROSALIND   I have been told so of many; but indeed an old reli-
gious uncle of mine taught me to speak, who was in his youth
an inland man; one that knew courtship° too well, for there he   *court life; wooing*
fell in love. I have heard him read many lectures against it, and
315   I thank God I am not a woman, to be touched with so many
giddy offences as he hath generally taxed their whole sex
withal.

ORLANDO   Can you remember any of the principal evils that he
laid to the charge of women?

320   ROSALIND   There were none principal; they were all like one
another as halfpence are, every one fault seeming monstrous
till his fellow-fault came to match it.

ORLANDO   I prithee, recount some of them.

ROSALIND   No. I will not cast away my physic but° on those that   *my medicine except*
325   are sick. There is a man haunts the forest that abuses our young
plants with carving Rosalind on their barks; hangs odes upon
hawthorns and elegies on brambles; all, forsooth, deifying the
name of Rosalind. If I could meet that fancy-monger,° I would   *dealer in love*
give him some good counsel, for he seems to have the quotid-
330   ian[2] of love upon him.

ORLANDO   I am he that is so love-shaked. I pray you, tell me your
remedy.

ROSALIND   There is none of my uncle's marks upon you. He
taught me how to know a man in love, in which cage of rushes[3]
335   I am sure you are not prisoner.

ORLANDO   What were his marks?

ROSALIND   A lean cheek, which you have not; a blue eye[4] and
sunken, which you have not; an unquestionable° spirit, which   *a taciturn*
you have not; a beard neglected, which you have not—but I
340   pardon you for that, for simply your having in beard° is a   *such beard as you have*
younger brother's revenue.[5] Then your hose should be ungar-
tered, your bonnet unbanded,° your sleeve unbuttoned, your   *lacking a band*
shoe untied, and everything about you demonstrating a careless
desolation. But you are no such man. You are rather point-
345   device° in your accoutrements, as loving yourself than seeming   *extremely precise*
the lover of any other.

ORLANDO   Fair youth, I would I could make thee believe I love.

ROSALIND   Me believe it? You may as soon make her that you love
believe it, which I warrant she is apter to do than to confess
350   she does. That is one of the points in the which women still°   *always*

1. *terms:* limited periods of time in which the courts   4. An eye ringed with dark circles (suggesting insom-
were in session and when lawyers were therefore busy.   nia).
Vacation came between terms.   5. Younger brothers traditionally received small inher-
2. Daily recurring fever said to be a sign of love.   itances, here suggesting that Orlando's beard is likewise
3. A prison easy to escape from.   thin or small.

give the lie to their consciences. But in good sooth,° are you   *truth*
he that hangs the verses on the trees wherein Rosalind is so
admired?

ORLANDO   I swear to thee, youth, by the white hand of Rosalind,
355   I am that he, that unfortunate he.

ROSALIND   But are you so much in love as your rhymes speak?

ORLANDO   Neither rhyme nor reason can express how much.

ROSALIND   Love is merely a madness, and I tell you, deserves as
well a dark house and a whip as madmen do;[6] and the rea-
360   son why they° are not so punished and cured is that the lunacy   *(lovers)*
is so ordinary that the whippers are in love too. Yet I profess
curing it by counsel.

ORLANDO   Did you ever cure any so?

ROSALIND   Yes, one; and in this manner. He was to imagine me
365   his love, his mistress; and I set him every day to woo me. At
which time would I, being but a moonish° youth, grieve, be   *changeable*
effeminate,[7] changeable, longing and liking, proud, fantasti-
cal,° apish,° shallow, inconstant, full of tears, full of smiles; for   *capricious / affected*
every passion something, and for no passion truly anything, as
370   boys and women are for the most part cattle of this colour—
would now like him, now loathe him; then entertain him,°   *treat him kindly*
then forswear him; now weep for him, then spit at him, that I
drave° my suitor from his mad humour of love to a living   *drove*
humour° of madness, which was to forswear the full stream of   *an actual condition*
375   the world and to live in a nook merely monastic.° And thus I   *as a hermit*
cured him, and this way will I take upon me to wash your liver[8]
as clean as a sound sheep's heart, that there shall not be one
spot of love in't.

ORLANDO   I would not be cured, youth.

380   ROSALIND   I would cure you if you would but call me Rosalind
and come every day to my cot,° and woo me.   *cottage*

ORLANDO   Now by the faith of my love, I will. Tell me where it
is.

ROSALIND   Go with me to it, and I'll show it you. And by the way
385   you shall tell me where in the forest you live. Will you go?

ORLANDO   With all my heart, good youth.

ROSALIND   Nay, you must call me Rosalind.—Come, sister. Will
you go?   *Exeunt*

3.3

Enter [TOUCHSTONE *the*] *clown and* AUDREY, [*followed
by*] JAQUES

TOUCHSTONE   Come apace, good Audrey. I will fetch up your
goats, Audrey. And how, Audrey, am I the man yet? Doth my
simple feature° content you?   *appearance*

AUDREY   Your features, Lord warrant° us—what features?   *defend*

5   TOUCHSTONE   I am here with thee and thy goats as the most
capricious° poet honest Ovid was among the Goths.[1]   *witty; lascivious*

---

6. Confinement in a dark room and whipping, common
treatments for insanity, were believed to rid the insane
of the devils that possessed them.
7. Like a woman; sensual or self-indulgent; a term
often used to deride men perceived as excessive in their
sexual interest in women.

8. In Renaissance medical theory, the seat of the pas-
sions.
3.3
1. Punning on "goats / Goths," which were similarly
pronounced, and referring to the Roman poet's exile
among the Goths.

JAQUES [*aside*]   O knowledge ill-inhabited; worse than Jove in a
thatched house.[2]

TOUCHSTONE   When a man's verses cannot be understood, nor a
man's good wit seconded with° the forward child, understand- — *supported by*
ing, it strikes a man more dead than a great reckoning° in a — *tavern bill*
little room.[3] Truly, I would the gods had made thee poetical.

AUDREY   I do not know what 'poetical' is. Is it honest in deed
and word? Is it a true thing?

TOUCHSTONE   No, truly; for the truest poetry is the most
feigning,° and lovers are given to poetry; and what they swear — *imaginative; false*
in poetry it may be said, as lovers, they do feign.

AUDREY   Do you wish, then, that the gods had made me poetical?

TOUCHSTONE   I do, truly; for thou swearest to me thou art hon-
est.° Now if thou wert a poet, I might have some hope thou — *chaste*
didst feign.

AUDREY   Would you not have me honest?

TOUCHSTONE   No, truly, unless thou wert hard-favoured;° for — *ugly*
honesty coupled to beauty is to have honey a sauce to sugar.

JAQUES [*aside*]   A material° fool. — *full of matter or sense*

AUDREY   Well, I am not fair, and therefore I pray the gods make
me honest.

TOUCHSTONE   Truly, and to cast away honesty upon a foul slut
were to put good meat into an unclean dish.

AUDREY   I am not a slut, though I thank the gods I am foul.[4]

TOUCHSTONE   Well, praised be the gods for thy foulness. Slut-
tishness may come hereafter. But be it as it may be, I will marry
thee; and to that end I have been with Sir Oliver Martext, the
vicar of the next village, who hath promised to meet me in this
place of the forest, and to couple us.

JAQUES [*aside*]   I would fain° see this meeting. — *gladly*

AUDREY   Well, the gods give us joy.

TOUCHSTONE   Amen.—A man may, if he were of a fearful heart,
stagger° in this attempt; for here we have no temple but the — *hesitate*
wood, no assembly but horn-beasts.[5] But what though? Cour-
age. As horns are odious, they are necessary. It is said many a
man knows no end of his goods.[6] Right: many a man has good
horns, and knows no end of them. Well, that is the dowry of
his wife, 'tis none of his own getting.[7] Horns? Even so. Poor
men alone? No, no; the noblest deer hath them as huge as the
rascal.° Is the single man therefore blessed? No. As a walled — *young or lean deer*
town is more worthier than a village, so is the forehead of a
married man more honourable than the bare brow of a bache-
lor. And by how much defence° is better than no skill, by so — *skill in self-defense*
much is a horn more precious than to want.° — *to lack (one)*

Enter SIR OLIVER MARTEXT

Here comes Sir Oliver.—Sir Oliver Martext, you are well met.
Will you dispatch us here under this tree, or shall we go with
you to your chapel?

2. In *Metamorphoses* 8, Ovid tells how the king of the
gods was given shelter for a time in the humble
dwelling of Philemon and Baucis.
3. These lines have been taken to refer to the death in
1593 of Christopher Marlowe, a contemporary play-
wright, in a quarrel in a tavern over a bill.
4. Ugly. Audrey apparently takes "foul" as a term of
praise.

5. Horned beasts such as deer, goats, and the like that
inhabited the forest, with an allusion to the horns of the
cuckolded husband.
6. A proverbial expression suggesting a man so wealthy
he can't count all his money.
7. *'tis . . . getting:* he is not responsible for the horns;
he is not responsible for conceiving his children (since
his wife has been sexually unfaithful).

SIR OLIVER MARTEXT   Is there none here to give the woman?

55   TOUCHSTONE   I will not take her on gift of any man.

SIR OLIVER MARTEXT   Truly she must be given, or the marriage is not lawful.

JAQUES   [*coming forward*]   Proceed, proceed. I'll give her.

TOUCHSTONE   Good even, good Monsieur What-ye-call't. How
60   do you, sir? You are very well met. God'ield you for your last
company.[8] I am very glad to see you. Even a toy° in hand here,   *trifling matter*
sir.

[JAQUES *removes his hat*]
Nay, pray be covered.°   *replace your hat*

JAQUES   Will you be married, motley?

65   TOUCHSTONE   As the ox hath his bow,° sir, the horse his curb,[9]   *yoke*
and the falcon her bells,[1] so man hath his desires; and as
pigeons bill,° so wedlock would be nibbling.   *rub bill to bill*

JAQUES   And will you, being a man of your breeding, be married
under a bush, like a beggar? Get you to church, and have a
70   good priest that can tell you what marriage is. This fellow will
but join you together as they join wainscot;° then one of you   *wood paneling*
will prove a shrunk panel and, like green timber, warp,° warp.   *go wrong; shrink*

TOUCHSTONE   I am not in the mind but° I were better to be mar-   *not sure but that*
ried of° him than of another, for he is not like to marry me   *by*
75   well, and not being well married, it will be a good excuse for
me hereafter to leave my wife.

JAQUES   Go thou with me, and let me counsel thee.

TOUCHSTONE   Come, sweet Audrey.
We must be married,° or we must live in bawdry.°   *(properly wed) / in sin*
80   Farewell, good Master Oliver. Not
          O, sweet Oliver,
          O, brave Oliver,
          Leave me not behind thee[2]
but
85   Wind° away,   *Go*
          Begone, I say,
I will not to wedding with thee.

SIR OLIVER MARTEXT   [*aside*]   'Tis no matter. Ne'er a fantastical
knave of them all shall flout me out of my calling.

                                                                      Exeunt

3.4

Enter ROSALIND [*as Ganymede*] *and* CELIA [*as Aliena*]

ROSALIND   Never talk to me. I will weep.

CELIA   Do, I prithee, but yet have the grace to consider that tears
do not become a man.

ROSALIND   But have I not cause to weep?

5   CELIA   As good cause as one would desire; therefore weep.

ROSALIND   His very hair is of the dissembling colour.[1]

CELIA   Something° browner than Judas's. Marry, his kisses are   *Somewhat*
Judas's own children.

ROSALIND   I'faith, his hair is of a good colour.

---

8. God yield you (a salutation meaning "May God
reward you") for your recent companionship.
9. A bit placed in the horse's mouth to control its
movements.
1. Bells attached to a falcon's legs before releasing it for

the hunt so that it might be easily reclaimed afterward.
2. Lines from a popular Elizabethan ballad.
3.4
1. Alluding to the tradition that Judas, the disciple who
betrayed Jesus, had red hair.

10 CELIA   An excellent colour. Your chestnut was ever the only
     colour.
   ROSALIND   And his kissing is as full of sanctity as the touch of
     holy bread.[2]
   CELIA   He hath bought a pair of cast° lips of Diana.[3] A nun of   *cast-off; sculpted*
15   winter's sisterhood° kisses not more religiously. The very ice of   *devoted to coldness*
     chastity is in them.
   ROSALIND   But why did he swear he would come this morning,
     and comes not?
   CELIA   Nay, certainly, there is no truth in him.
20 ROSALIND   Do you think so?
   CELIA   Yes. I think he is not a pick-purse, nor a horse-stealer; but
     for his verity° in love, I do think him as concave° as a covered   *truthfulness / hollow*
     goblet, or a worm-eaten nut.
   ROSALIND   Not true in love?
25 CELIA   Yes, when he is in. But I think he is not in.
   ROSALIND   You have heard him swear downright he was.
   CELIA   'Was' is not 'is'. Besides, the oath of a lover is no stronger
     than the word of a tapster. They are both the confirmer of false
     reckonings. He attends° here in the forest on the Duke your   *waits*
30   father.
   ROSALIND   I met the Duke yesterday, and had much question°   *conversation*
     with him. He asked me of what parentage I was. I told him, of
     as good as he, so he laughed and let me go. But what talk we
     of fathers when there is such a man as Orlando?
35 CELIA   O that's a brave° man. He writes brave verses, speaks   *splendid*
     brave words, swears brave oaths, and breaks them bravely, quite
     traverse,[4] athwart the heart of his lover, as a puny° tilter that   *an unskilled*
     spurs his horse but° on one side breaks his staff, like a noble   *only*
     goose.° But all's brave that youth mounts, and folly guides.   *fool*
40   Who comes here?
          Enter CORIN
   CORIN   Mistress and master, you have oft enquired
     After the shepherd that complained of love
     Who you saw sitting by me on the turf,
     Praising the proud disdainful shepherdess
     That was his mistress.
45 CELIA   Well, and what of him?
   CORIN   If you will see a pageant truly played
     Between the pale complexion of true love
     And the red glow of scorn and proud disdain,[5]
     Go hence a little, and I shall conduct you,
     If you will mark° it.   *observe*
50 ROSALIND [*to* CELIA]   O come, let us remove.
     The sight of lovers feedeth those in love.
     [*To* CORIN] Bring us to this sight, and you shall say
     I'll prove a busy actor in their play.   *Exeunt*

---

2. Referring to bread blessed after the Eucharist dur-
ing Christian religious services and distributed to those
who did not take Communion.
3. The goddess of chastity. See note to 3.2.2.
4. Crossways. A term from jousting used to designate

the dishonorable practice of breaking one's lance
across, rather than directly against, an opponent's
shield.
5. Referring to the paleness of Silvius, the true lover,
and the red cheeks of the disdainful Phoebe.

3.5

Enter SILVIUS *and* PHOEBE

SILVIUS   Sweet Phoebe, do not scorn me, do not, Phoebe.
Say that you love me not, but say not so
In bitterness. The common executioner,
Whose heart th'accustomed sight of death makes hard,

5   Falls not° the axe upon the humbled neck   *Does not let fall*
But first begs° pardon. Will you sterner be   *Without first begging*
Than he that dies and lives by bloody drops?

Enter ROSALIND [*as Ganymede*], CELIA [*as Aliena*], *and*
CORIN [*and stand aside*]

PHOEBE [*to* SILVIUS]   I would not be thy executioner.
I fly thee for I would not injure thee.

10   Thou tell'st me there is murder in mine eye.
'Tis pretty, sure, and very probable
That eyes, that are the frail'st and softest things,
Who shut their coward gates on atomies,°   *dust motes*
Should be called tyrants, butchers, murderers.

15   Now I do frown on thee with all my heart,
And if mine eyes can wound, now let them kill thee.
Now counterfeit to swoon, why now fall down;
Or if thou canst not, O, for shame, for shame,
Lie not, to say mine eyes are murderers.

20   Now show the wound mine eye hath made in thee.
Scratch thee but with a pin, and there remains
Some scar of it. Lean upon a rush,
The cicatrice and capable impressure[1]
Thy palm some moment keeps. But now mine eyes,

25   Which I have darted at thee, hurt thee not;
Nor I am sure there is no force in eyes
That can do hurt.

SILVIUS   O dear Phoebe,
If ever—as that ever may be near—

30   You meet in some fresh cheek the power of fancy,°   *love*
Then shall you know the wounds invisible
That love's keen arrows make.

PHOEBE   But till that time
Come not thou near me. And when that time comes,
Afflict me with thy mocks, pity me not,

35   As till that time I shall not pity thee.

ROSALIND [*coming forward*]   And why, I pray you? Who might
be your mother,
That you insult, exult, and all at once,°   *all in one breath*
Over the wretched? What though you have no beauty—
As, by my faith, I see no more in you

40   Than without candle may go dark to bed[2]—
Must you be therefore proud and pitiless?
Why, what means this? Why do you look on me?
I see no more in you than in the ordinary°   *common run*
Of nature's sale-work.°—'Od's my little life,[3]   *ready-made goods*

45   I think she means to tangle° my eyes, too.   *entrap*
No, faith, proud mistress, hope not after it.

3.5
1. The scarlike mark and the impression that the skin
receives.

2. *I see . . . bed:* I see you have not enough beauty to
light your way to bed without a candle.
3. An abbreviated version of the oath "God save my life."

'Tis not your inky brows, your black silk hair,
Your bugle° eyeballs, nor your cheek of cream,   *like black glass beads*
That can entame my spirits to your worship.°   *the worship of you*
50 [*To* SILVIUS] You, foolish shepherd, wherefore do you follow her
Like foggy south,° puffing with wind and rain?⁴   *south wind*
You are a thousand times a properer° man   *more attractive*
Than she a woman. 'Tis such fools as you
That makes the world full of ill-favoured° children.   *ugly*
55 'Tis not her glass° but you that flatters her,   *mirror*
And out of you° she sees herself more proper   *from you (as mirror)*
Than any of her lineaments can show her.
[*To* PHOEBE] But, mistress, know yourself; down on your knees
And thank heaven, fasting, for a good man's love;
60 For I must tell you friendly in your ear,
Sell when you can. You are not for all markets.
Cry the man mercy,° love him, take his offer;   *Beg his pardon*
Foul is most foul, being foul to be a scoffer.⁵—
So, take her to thee, shepherd. Fare you well.
65 PHOEBE   Sweet youth, I pray you chide a year together.°   *without interruption*
I had rather hear you chide than this man woo.
ROSALIND [*to* PHOEBE]   He's fallen in love with your foulness, [*to*
SILVIUS] and she'll fall in love with my anger. If it be so, as fast
as she answers thee with frowning looks, I'll sauce° her   *sharply rebuke*
70 with bitter words.
[*To* PHOEBE] Why look you so upon me?
PHOEBE   For no ill will I bear you.
ROSALIND   I pray you do not fall in love with me,
For I am falser than vows made in wine.°   *when drinking*
75 Besides, I like you not. If you will know my house,
'Tis at the tuft of olives,° here hard by.   *olive trees*
[*To* CELIA] Will you go, sister? [*To* SILVIUS] Shepherd, ply her
    hard.°—   *assail her vigorously*
Come, sister. [*To* PHOEBE] Shepherdess, look on him better,
And be not proud. Though all the world could see,
80 None could be so abused in sight as he.—
Come, to our flock.   *Exeunt* [ROSALIND, CELIA, *and* CORIN]⁶
PHOEBE [*aside*]   Dead shepherd,⁷ now I find thy saw of might:°   *your saying powerful*
'Who ever loved that loved not at first sight?'
SILVIUS   Sweet Phoebe—
PHOEBE   Ha, what sayst thou, Silvius?
85 SILVIUS   Sweet Phoebe, pity me.
PHOEBE   Why, I am sorry for thee, gentle Silvius.
SILVIUS   Wherever sorrow is, relief would be.
If you do sorrow at my grief in love,
By giving love your sorrow and my grief
90 Were both extermined.°   *Would both be ended*
PHOEBE   Thou hast my love, is not that neighbourly?⁸
SILVIUS   I would have you.
PHOEBE   Why, that were covetousness.⁹

---

4. That is, with sighs and tears.
5. The ugly seem most ugly when they are abusive.
6. F marks a single exit for Rosalind here, but it is unlikely that Celia and Corin remain.
7. Referring to Christopher Marlowe, poet and playwright who died in 1593. Line 83 is taken from his poem *Hero and Leander*.

8. With a reference to Romans 13:9: "Thou shalt love thy neighbour as thyself."
9. With a reference to Exodus 20:17: "Thou shalt not covet thy neighbour's house, thou shalt not covet thy neighbour's wife, nor his manservant, nor his maid servant, nor his ox, nor his ass, nor any thing that is thy neighbour's."

Silvius, the time was that I hated thee;
And yet it is not° that I bear thee love.   *it has not yet happened*
95   But since that thou canst talk of love so well,
Thy company, which erst° was irksome to me,   *formerly*
I will endure; and I'll employ thee, too.
But do not look for further recompense
Than thine own gladness that thou art employed.
100 SILVIUS   So holy and so perfect is my love,
And I in such a poverty of grace,¹
That I shall think it a most plenteous crop
To glean the broken ears° after the man   *(of corn)*
That the main harvest reaps. Loose now and then
105 A scattered° smile, and that I'll live upon.   *stray*
PHOEBE   Know'st thou the youth that spoke to me erewhile?
SILVIUS   Not very well, but I have met him oft,
And he hath bought the cottage and the bounds°   *pastures*
That the old Carlot once was master of.
110 PHOEBE   Think not I love him, though I ask for him.
'Tis but a peevish boy. Yet he talks well.
But what care I for words? Yet words do well
When he that speaks them pleases those that hear.
It is a pretty youth—not very pretty—
115 But sure he's proud; and yet his pride becomes him.
He'll make a proper° man. The best thing in him   *handsome*
Is his complexion; and faster than his tongue
Did make offence, his eye did heal it up.
He is not very tall; yet for his years he's tall.
120 His leg is but so-so; and yet 'tis well.
There was a pretty redness in his lip,
A little riper and more lusty-red
Than that mixed in his cheek. 'Twas just the difference
Betwixt the constant red and mingled damask.²
125 There be some women, Silvius, had they marked him
In parcels° as I did, would have gone near   *Item by item*
To fall in love with him; but for my part,
I love him not, nor hate him not. And yet
Have I more cause to hate him than to love him,
130 For what had he to do to chide at me?
He said mine eyes were black, and my hair black,
And now I am remembered, scorned at me.
I marvel why I answered not again.
But that's all one. Omittance is no quittance.³
135 I'll write to him a very taunting letter,
And thou shalt bear it. Wilt thou, Silvius?
SILVIUS   Phoebe, with all my heart.
PHOEBE   I'll write it straight.°   *immediately*
The matter's in my head and in my heart.
I will be bitter with him, and passing° short.   *extremely*
140 Go with me, Silvius.   *Exeunt*

---

1. And I so lacking in (your) favor.
2. *constant . . . damask:* uniform red and a mixture of red and white characteristic of certain kinds of roses.
3. A proverbial expression meaning that a debt is not canceled simply because one fails ("omits") to exact it.

4.1

Enter ROSALIND [*as Ganymede*], CELIA [*as Aliena*], *and*
JAQUES

JAQUES I prithee, pretty youth, let me be better acquainted with
thee.

ROSALIND They say you are a melancholy fellow.

JAQUES I am so. I do love it better than laughing.

5 ROSALIND Those that are in extremity of either are abominable
fellows, and betray themselves to every modern censure worse
than drunkards.

JAQUES Why, 'tis good to be sad° and say nothing.   *serious*

ROSALIND Why then, 'tis good to be a post.

10 JAQUES I have neither the scholar's melancholy, which is emula-
tion,° nor the musician's, which is fantastical,° nor the court-   *envy / overly fanciful*
ier's, which is proud, nor the soldier's, which is ambitious, nor
the lawyer's, which is politic, nor the lady's, which is nice,° nor   *fastidious*
the lover's, which is all these; but it is a melancholy of mine
15 own, compounded of many simples,° extracted from many   *ingredients*
objects,° and indeed the sundry contemplation of my travels,[1]   *sights*
in° which my often° rumination wraps me in a most humor-   *upon / frequent*
ous° sadness.   *moody*

ROSALIND A traveller! By my faith, you have great reason to be
20 sad. I fear you have sold your own lands to see other men's.
Then to have seen much and to have nothing is to have rich
eyes and poor hands.

JAQUES Yes, I have gained my experience.

Enter ORLANDO

ROSALIND And your experience makes you sad. I had rather have
25 a fool to make me merry than experience to make me sad—
and to travel for it too!

ORLANDO Good day and happiness, dear Rosalind.

JAQUES Nay then, God b'wi'you an° you talk in blank verse.   *if*

ROSALIND Farewell, Monsieur Traveller. Look you lisp,[2] and
30 wear strange° suits; disable° all the benefits of your own coun-   *foreign / disparage*
try; be out of love with your nativity,° and almost chide God for   *birthplace*
making you that countenance you are, or I will scarce think
you have swam in a gondola.[3]   [*Exit* JAQUES][4]
Why, how now, Orlando? Where have you been all this while?
35 You a lover? An you serve me such another trick, never come
in my sight more.

ORLANDO My fair Rosalind, I come within an hour of my
promise.

ROSALIND Break an hour's promise in love! He that will divide a
40 minute into a thousand parts and break but a part of the thou-
sand part of a minute in the affairs of love, it may be said of
him that Cupid hath clapped him o'th' shoulder, but I'll war-
rant him heartwhole.[5]

ORLANDO Pardon me, dear Rosalind.

4.1

1. The various thoughts arising during my travels, with
a pun on "travails," meaning "labors."
2. Speak with an affected (foreign) accent.
3. Ridden in a gondola—that is, seen Venice, a popu-
lar destination for English travelers.

4. F marks no exit for Jaques here, but he and Rosalind
have formally parted, and Jaques enters with a new
group of characters at the beginning of 4.2.
5. Cupid has tapped him (as in an arrest) or wounded
him (with his arrow), but I'll guarantee he left his heart
intact.

45	ROSALIND Nay, an you be so tardy, come no more in my sight. I had as lief be wooed of a snail.
	ORLANDO Of a snail?
	ROSALIND Ay, of a snail; for though he comes slowly, he carries his house on his head—a better jointure,° I think, than you
50	make a woman. Besides, he brings his destiny with him.
	ORLANDO What's that?
	ROSALIND Why, horns, which such as you are fain to be beholden to your wives for.[6] But he comes armed in his fortune,[7] and prevents the slander of his wife.
55	ORLANDO Virtue is no hornmaker, and my Rosalind is virtuous.
	ROSALIND And I am your Rosalind.
	CELIA It pleases him to call you so; but he hath a Rosalind of a better leer° than you.
	ROSALIND Come, woo me, woo me, for now I am in a holiday
60	humour, and like enough to consent. What would you say to me now an I were your very, very Rosalind?
	ORLANDO I would kiss before I spoke.
	ROSALIND Nay, you were better speak first, and when you were gravelled° for lack of matter you might take occasion to kiss.
65	Very good orators, when they are out,° they will spit; and for lovers, lacking—God warr'nt° us— matter, the cleanliest shift° is to kiss.
	ORLANDO How if the kiss be denied?
	ROSALIND Then she puts you to entreaty, and there begins new
70	matter.
	ORLANDO Who could be out, being before his beloved mistress?
	ROSALIND Marry, that should you if I were your mistress, or I should think my honesty ranker than my wit.[8]
	ORLANDO What, of my suit?[9]
75	ROSALIND Not out of your apparel, and yet out of your suit. Am not I your Rosalind?
	ORLANDO I take some joy to say you are because I would be talking of her.
	ROSALIND Well, in her person I say I will not have you.
80	ORLANDO Then in mine own person I die.
	ROSALIND No, faith; die by attorney.° The poor world is almost six thousand years old,[1] and in all this time there was not any man died in his own person, videlicet,° in a love-cause. Troilus[2] had his brains dashed out with a Grecian club, yet he did
85	what he could to die before, and he is one of the patterns of love. Leander,[3] he would have lived many a fair year though Hero had turned nun if it had not been for a hot midsummer night, for, good youth, he went but forth to wash him in the Hellespont and, being taken with the cramp, was drowned; and
90	the foolish chroniclers of that age found° it was Hero of Sestos. But these are all lies. Men have died from time to time, and worms have eaten them, but not for love.

Glosses (right margin):
- *marriage settlement* (line 49)
- *more attractive* (line 57)
- *at a loss* (line 64)
- *speechless* (line 65)
- *defend / cleverest device* (line 66)
- *proxy* (line 81)
- *namely* (line 83)
- *claimed* (line 90)

6. An allusion to the cuckold's horns.
7. Equipped with the insignia of his destined future.
8. I would think my chastity was fouler than my intelligence; with a pun on "out" (lines 65, 71) as meaning "not permitted sexual entrance."
9. My petition. Orlando asks if he will be at a loss for words ("out") in furthering his courtship ("suit"). Ros-

alind puns on "suit" as meaning "clothing."
1. Elizabethan divines generally dated the world's creation somewhere around 4000 B.C.E.
2. The forsaken Trojan lover of Cressida, killed by the Greek warrior Achilles.
3. In Greek mythology, the lover of Hero; he swam the Hellespont nightly to visit her and was drowned.

ORLANDO   I would not have my right° Rosalind of this mind, for   *true*
I protest her frown might kill me.

95   ROSALIND   By this hand, it will not kill a fly. But come, now I
will be your Rosalind in a more coming-on° disposition; and   *agreeable*
ask me what you will, I will grant it.

ORLANDO   Then love me, Rosalind.

ROSALIND   Yes, faith, will I, Fridays and Saturdays and all.

100   ORLANDO   And wilt thou have me?

ROSALIND   Ay, and twenty such.

ORLANDO   What sayst thou?

ROSALIND   Are you not good?

ORLANDO   I hope so.

105   ROSALIND   Why then, can one desire too much of a good thing?
[*To* CELIA] Come, sister, you shall be the priest and marry us.—
Give me your hand, Orlando.—What do you say, sister?

ORLANDO [*to* CELIA]   Pray thee, marry us.

CELIA   I cannot say the words.

110   ROSALIND   You must begin, 'Will you, Orlando'—

CELIA   Go to.[4] Will you, Orlando, have to wife this Rosalind?

ORLANDO   I will.

ROSALIND   Ay, but when?

ORLANDO   Why now, as fast as she can marry us.

115   ROSALIND   Then you must say, 'I take thee, Rosalind, for wife.'

ORLANDO   I take thee, Rosalind, for wife.

ROSALIND   I might ask you for your commission;° but I do take   *authority*
thee, Orlando, for my husband. There's a girl goes before° the   *who anticipates*
priest; and certainly a woman's thought runs before her actions.

120   ORLANDO   So do all thoughts; they are winged.

ROSALIND   Now tell me how long you would have her after you
have possessed her?

ORLANDO   For ever and a day.

ROSALIND   Say a day without the ever. No, no, Orlando; men are

125   April when they woo, December when they wed. Maids are
May when they are maids, but the sky changes when they are
wives. I will be more jealous of thee than a Barbary cock-
pigeon[5] over his hen, more clamorous than a parrot against°   *in expectation of*
rain, more new-fangled° than an ape, more giddy in my desires   *in love with novelty*

130   than a monkey. I will weep for nothing, like Diana in the foun-
tain,[6] and I will do that when you are disposed to be merry. I
will laugh like a hyena, and that when thou art inclined to
sleep.

ORLANDO   But will my Rosalind do so?

135   ROSALIND   By my life, she will do as I do.

ORLANDO   O, but she is wise.

ROSALIND   Or else she could not have the wit to do this. The
wiser, the waywarder. Make° the doors upon a woman's wit,   *Close*
and it will out at the casement. Shut that, and 'twill out at the

140   key-hole. Stop that, 'twill fly with the smoke out at the
chimney.

---

4. An expression of mild impatience.
5. An ornamental bird, traditionally an emblem of jealousy. It was introduced into Europe from Asia by Turks, whom Elizabethans associated with North Africa's Barbary Coast. Turkish husbands were imag-
ined by the English to be excessively vigilant about the sexual fidelity of their wives.
6. Referring to the figures of the goddess Diana used as centerpieces for ornamental fountains in London and elsewhere.

ORLANDO   A man that had a wife with such a wit, he might say
'Wit, whither wilt?'[7]

ROSALIND   Nay, you might keep that check° for it till you met   *rebuke*
145   your wife's wit going to your neighbour's bed.

ORLANDO   And what wit could wit have to excuse that?

ROSALIND   Marry, to say she came to seek you there. You shall
never take her without her answer unless you take her without
her tongue. O, that woman that cannot make her fault her
150   husband's occasion,[8] let her never nurse her child herself, for
she will breed it like a fool.

ORLANDO   For these two hours, Rosalind, I will leave thee.

ROSALIND   Alas, dear love, I cannot lack thee two hours.

ORLANDO   I must attend the Duke at dinner. By two o'clock I
155   will be with thee again.

ROSALIND   Ay, go your ways, go your ways. I knew what you
would prove;° my friends told me as much, and I thought no   *turn out to be*
less. That flattering tongue of yours won me. 'Tis but one cast
away,° and so, come, death! Two o'clock is your hour?   *one lover jilted*
160   ORLANDO   Ay, sweet Rosalind.

ROSALIND   By my troth, and in good earnest, and so God mend
me, and by all pretty oaths that are not dangerous, if you break
one jot of your promise or come one minute behind your hour,
I will think you the most pathetical° break-promise, and the   *pathetic*
165   most hollow lover, and the most unworthy of her you call Rosa-
lind that may be chosen out of the gross° band of the unfaith-   *entire*
ful. Therefore beware my censure, and keep your promise.

ORLANDO   With no less religion° than if thou wert indeed my   *faith*
Rosalind. So, adieu.

170   ROSALIND   Well, Time is the old justice that examines all such
offenders; and let Time try.° Adieu.   *Exit* [ORLANDO]   *determine*

CELIA   You have simply misused° our sex in your love-prate. We   *completely slandered*
must have your doublet and hose plucked over your head, and
show the world what the bird hath done to her own nest.

175   ROSALIND   O coz, coz, coz, my pretty little coz, that thou didst
know how many fathom deep I am in love. But it cannot be
sounded. My affection hath an unknown bottom, like the Bay
of Portugal.

CELIA   Or rather bottomless, that° as fast as you pour affection   *so that*
180   in, it runs out.

ROSALIND   No, that same wicked bastard of Venus,[9] that was
begot of thought, conceived of spleen,° and born of madness,   *caprice*
that blind rascally boy that abuses° everyone's eyes because his   *deceives*
own are out, let him be judge how deep I am in love. I'll tell
185   thee, Aliena, I cannot be out of the sight of Orlando. I'll go
find a shadow° and sigh till he come.   *shady place*

CELIA   And I'll sleep.   *Exeunt*

7. Wit, where would you go? A catchphrase addressed
to one who talks too much.
8. Who cannot make her error a means of putting her
husband in the wrong.
9. Cupid, the son of Venus by her lover Mercury, not by
her husband, Vulcan.

4.2

Enter JAQUES *and* LORDS [*dressed as*] *foresters*[1]

JAQUES   Which is he that killed the deer?

FIRST LORD   Sir, it was I.

JAQUES [*to the others*]   Let's present him to the Duke like a
Roman conqueror. And it would do well to set the deer's horns
5   upon his head for a branch° of victory. Have you no song, for-   *wreath*
ester, for this purpose?

SECOND LORD   Yes, sir.

JAQUES   Sing it. 'Tis no matter how it be in tune, so it make
noise enough.

10   LORDS [*sing*][2]   What shall he have that killed the deer?
　　　　　　His leather skin and horns to wear.
　　　　　　Then sing him home; the rest shall bear°   *carry; sing*
　　　　　　This burden.°   *(the deer); refrain*
　　　　　　Take thou no scorn° to wear the horn;   *Do not disdain*
15　　　　　　It was a crest[3] ere thou wast born.
　　　　　　　　Thy father's father wore it,
　　　　　　　　And thy father bore it.
　　　　　　The horn, the horn, the lusty horn
　　　　　　Is not a thing to laugh to scorn.   *Exeunt*

4.3

Enter ROSALIND [*as Ganymede*] *and* CELIA [*as Aliena*]

ROSALIND   How say you now? Is it not past two o'clock? And
here much Orlando.

CELIA   I warrant you, with pure love and troubled brain he hath
ta'en his bow and arrows and is gone forth to sleep.

Enter SILVIUS

5   Look who comes here.

SILVIUS [*to* ROSALIND]   My errand is to you, fair youth.
My gentle Phoebe did bid me give you this.

[*He offers* ROSALIND *a letter, which she takes and reads*]

I know not the contents, but as I guess
By the stern brow and waspish action
10   Which she did use as she was writing of it,
It bears an angry tenor. Pardon me;
I am but as a guiltless messenger.

ROSALIND   Patience herself would startle at this letter,
And play the swaggerer. Bear this, bear all.
15   She says I am not fair, that I lack manners;
She calls me proud, and that she could not love me
Were man as rare as Phoenix.[1] 'Od's° my will,   *God's*
Her love is not the hare that I do hunt.
Why writes she so to me? Well, shepherd, well,
20   This is a letter of your own device.

SILVIUS   No, I protest; I know not the contents.
Phoebe did write it.

ROSALIND　　　　　　Come, come, you are a fool,

4.2
1. F's stage direction—"Enter Jaques and Lords,
Foresters"—leaves ambiguous whether Jaques and the
lords are dressed as foresters or are accompanied by
them.
2. F does not assign this song to anyone. The stage

direction reads: "Music, Song."
3. Coat of arms; head ornament.
4.3
1. A legendary bird of Arabia, supposedly unique,
which lived five hundred years, died in flames, and was
reborn from its own ashes.

And turned° into the extremity of love.   *brought*
I saw her hand. She has a leathern hand,
25   A free-stone° coloured hand. I verily did think   *yellow-brown limestone*
That her old gloves were on; but 'twas her hands.
She has a housewife's hand—but that's no matter.
I say she never did invent this letter.
This is a man's invention, and his hand.
30   SILVIUS   Sure, it is hers.
ROSALIND   Why, 'tis a boisterous and a cruel style,
A style for challengers. Why, she defies me,
Like Turk to Christian.[2] Women's gentle brain
Could not drop forth such giant-rude invention,
35   Such Ethiop[3] words, blacker in their effect
Than in their countenance. Will you hear the letter?
SILVIUS   So please you, for I never heard it yet,
Yet heard too much of Phoebe's cruelty.
ROSALIND   She Phoebes me.[4] Mark how the tyrant writes:
40   *Read*[s]   'Art thou god to shepherd turned,
That a maiden's heart hath burned?'
Can a woman rail thus?
SILVIUS   Call you this railing?
ROSALIND *read*[s]   'Why, thy godhead laid apart,°   *set aside*
45   Warr'st thou with a woman's heart?'
Did you ever hear such railing?
'Whiles the eye of man did woo me
That could do no vengeance° to me.'—   *harm*
Meaning me a beast.
50   'If the scorn of your bright eyne°   *eyes*
Have power to raise such love in mine,
Alack, in me what strange effect
Would they work in mild aspect?°   *if they looked kindly*
Whiles you chid me I did love;
55   How then might your prayers move?
He that brings this love to thee
Little knows this love in me,
And by him seal up thy mind[5]
Whether that thy youth and kind°   *nature*
60   Will the faithful offer take
Of me, and all that I can make,°   *offer you*
Or else by him my love deny,
And then I'll study how to die.'
SILVIUS   Call you this chiding?
65   CELIA   Alas, poor shepherd.
ROSALIND   Do you pity him? No, he deserves no pity. [*To* SIL-
VIUS] Wilt thou love such a woman? What, to make thee an
instrument,[6] and play false strains upon thee?—not to be
endured. Well, go your way to her—for I see love hath made
70   thee a tame snake—and say this to her: that if she love me, I

---

2. Alluding to medieval plays in which Turks and Christians appeared as bitter enemies or to a common Elizabethan perception of the Turk as an enemy to the Christian countries of western Europe.
3. Ethiopian. In Elizabethan racial discourse, the term signified blackness and evil.

4. Addresses me as Phoebe would—that is, in a disdainful manner.
5. And by means of him (Silvius), send your thoughts to me (in a letter).
6. Tool; musical instrument.

charge her to love thee. If she will not, I will never have her
unless thou entreat for her. If you be a true lover, hence, and
not a word; for here comes more company.   *Exit* SILVIUS
          Enter OLIVER

OLIVER   Good morrow, fair ones. Pray you, if you know,
75   Where in the purlieus° of this forest stands   outskirts
      A sheepcote fenced about with olive trees?
CELIA   West of this place, down in the neighbour bottom.°   next valley
      The rank of osiers° by the murmuring stream   row of willows
      Left on your right hand brings you to the place.
80   But at this hour the house doth keep itself.
      There's none within.
OLIVER   If that an eye may profit by a tongue,
      Then should I know you by description.
      Such garments, and such years. 'The boy is fair,
85   Of female favour,° and bestows° himself   appearance / behaves
      Like a ripe° sister. The woman low°   mature / short
      And browner than her brother.' Are not you
      The owner of the house I did enquire for?
CELIA   It is no boast, being asked, to say we are.
90 OLIVER   Orlando doth commend him to you both,
      And to that youth he calls his Rosalind
      He sends this bloody napkin.° Are you he?   handkerchief
ROSALIND   I am. What must we understand by this?
OLIVER   Some of my shame, if you will know of me
95   What man I am, and how, and why, and where
      This handkerchief was stained.
CELIA   I pray you tell it.
OLIVER   When last the young Orlando parted from you,
      He left a promise to return again
      Within an hour, and pacing through the forest,
100   Chewing the food of sweet and bitter fancy,
      Lo what befell. He threw his eye aside,
      And mark what object° did present itself.   what a spectacle
      Under an old oak, whose boughs were mossed with age
      And high top bald with dry antiquity,
105   A wretched, ragged man, o'ergrown with hair,
      Lay sleeping on his back. About his neck
      A green and gilded snake had wreathed itself,
      Who with her head, nimble in threats, approached
      The opening of his mouth. But suddenly
110   Seeing Orlando, it unlinked° itself,   uncoiled
      And with indented° glides did slip away   undulating
      Into a bush, under which bush's shade
      A lioness, with udders all drawn dry,[7]
      Lay couching, head on ground, with catlike watch
115   When that° the sleeping man should stir. For 'tis   In readiness for when
      The royal disposition of that beast
      To prey on nothing that doth seem as dead.
      This seen, Orlando did approach the man
      And found it was his brother, his elder brother.
120 CELIA   O, I have heard him speak of that same brother,
      And he did render him the most unnatural

---

7. Having been nursed dry, the lion would be ferociously hungry.

That lived amongst men.
OLIVER   And well he might so do,
For well I know he was unnatural.
ROSALIND   But to Orlando. Did he leave him there,
125   Food to the sucked and hungry lioness?
OLIVER   Twice did he turn his back, and purposed so.
But kindness, nobler ever than revenge,
And nature, stronger than his just occasion,°   *fair opportunity*
Made him give battle to the lioness,
130   Who quickly fell before him; in which hurtling°   *conflict*
From miserable slumber I awaked.
CELIA   Are you his brother?
ROSALIND   Was't you he rescued?
CELIA   Was't you that did so oft contrive° to kill him?   *plot*
OLIVER   'Twas I, but 'tis not I. I do not shame
135   To tell you what I was, since my conversion
So sweetly tastes, being the thing I am.
ROSALIND   But for° the bloody napkin?   *What about*
OLIVER   By and by.
When from the first to last betwixt us two
Tears our recountments° had most kindly bathed—   *narratives*
140   As how I came into that desert place—
I' brief, he led me to the gentle Duke,
Who gave me fresh array, and entertainment,°   *hospitality*
Committing me unto my brother's love,
Who led me instantly unto his cave,
145   There stripped himself, and here upon his arm
The lioness had torn some flesh away,
Which all this while had bled. And now he fainted,
And cried in fainting upon Rosalind.
Brief, I recovered° him, bound up his wound,   *revived*
150   And after some small space, being strong at heart,
He sent me hither, stranger as I am,
To tell this story, that you might excuse
His broken promise, and to give this napkin,
Dyed in his blood, unto the shepherd youth
155   That he in sport doth call his Rosalind.
                              [ROSALIND *faints*]
CELIA   Why, how now, Ganymede, sweet Ganymede!
OLIVER   Many will swoon when they do look on blood.
CELIA   There is more in it. Cousin Ganymede!
OLIVER   Look, he recovers.
160   ROSALIND   I would I were at home.
CELIA   We'll lead you thither.
[*To* OLIVER] I pray you, will you take him by the arm?
OLIVER   Be of good cheer, youth. You a man? You lack a man's
heart.
165   ROSALIND   I do so, I confess it. Ah, sirrah, a body would think
this was well counterfeited. I pray you, tell your brother how
well I counterfeited. Heigh-ho!
OLIVER   This was not counterfeit. There is too great testimony in
your complexion that it was a passion of earnest.°   *a genuine fit*
170   ROSALIND   Counterfeit, I assure you.
OLIVER   Well then, take a good heart, and counterfeit to be a
man.

ROSALIND   So I do; but, i'faith, I should have been a woman by
right.

175   CELIA   Come, you look paler and paler. Pray you, draw home-
wards. Good sir, go with us.

OLIVER   That will I, for I must bear answer back
How you excuse my brother, Rosalind.

ROSALIND   I shall devise something. But I pray you commend
180   my counterfeiting to him. Will you go?   *Exeunt*

5.1

Enter [TOUCHSTONE *the*] *clown and* AUDREY

TOUCHSTONE   We shall find a time, Audrey. Patience, gentle
Audrey.

AUDREY   Faith, the priest was good enough, for all the old gen-
tleman's° saying.   *(Jaques's)*

5   TOUCHSTONE   A most wicked Sir Oliver, Audrey, a most vile
Martext. But, Audrey, there is a youth here in the forest lays
claim to you.

AUDREY   Ay, I know who 'tis. He hath no interest in me° in the   *no right to me*
world. Here comes the man you mean.

Enter WILLIAM

10   TOUCHSTONE   It is meat and drink to me to see a clown.° By my   *peasant; yokel*
troth, we that have good wits have much to answer for. We
shall be flouting; we cannot hold.°   *refrain*

WILLIAM   Good ev'n, Audrey.

AUDREY   God ye° good ev'n, William.   *God give you*

15   WILLIAM [*to* TOUCHSTONE]   And good ev'n to you, sir.

TOUCHSTONE   Good ev'n, gentle friend. Cover thy head,[1] cover
thy head. Nay, prithee, be covered. How old are you, friend?

WILLIAM   Five-and-twenty, sir.

TOUCHSTONE   A ripe age. Is thy name William?

20   WILLIAM   William, sir.

TOUCHSTONE   A fair name. Wast born i'th' forest here?

WILLIAM   Ay, sir, I thank God.

TOUCHSTONE   Thank God—a good answer. Art rich?

WILLIAM   Faith, sir, so-so.

25   TOUCHSTONE   So-so is good, very good, very excellent good. And
yet it is not, it is but so-so. Art thou wise?

WILLIAM   Ay, sir, I have a pretty wit.

TOUCHSTONE   Why, thou sayst well. I do now remember a say-
ing: 'The fool doth think he is wise, but the wise man knows
30   himself to be a fool.' The heathen philosopher, when he had a
desire to eat a grape, would open his lips when he put it into
his mouth, meaning thereby that grapes were made to eat, and
lips to open.[2] You do love this maid?

WILLIAM   I do, sir.

35   TOUCHSTONE   Give me your hand. Art thou learned?

WILLIAM   No, sir.

TOUCHSTONE   Then learn this of me: to have is to have. For it is
a figure in rhetoric° that drink, being poured out of a cup into   *rhetorical commonplace*
a glass, by filling the one doth empty the other. For all your

---

5.1
1. Evidently William has taken off his hat in a gesture
of deference.

2. Touchstone's speech may be a response to William's
gaping mouth.

40 writers do consent that *ipse* is he.³ Now you are not *ipse*, for I
am he.

WILLIAM Which he, sir?

TOUCHSTONE He, sir, that must marry this woman. Therefore,
you clown, abandon—which is in the vulgar, leave—the soci-
45 ety—which in the boorish is company—of this female—which
in the common is woman; which together is, abandon the soci-
ety of this female, or, clown, thou perishest; or, to thy better
understanding, diest; or, to wit, I kill thee, make thee away,
translate thy life into death, thy liberty into bondage. I will deal
50 in poison with thee, or in bastinado,° or in steel. I will bandy   beating with a club
with thee in faction, I will o'errun thee with policy.⁴ I will kill
thee a hundred and fifty ways. Therefore tremble, and depart.

AUDREY Do, good William.

WILLIAM God rest you merry, sir.   *Exit*

        Enter CORIN
55 CORIN Our master and mistress seeks you. Come, away, away.

TOUCHSTONE Trip, Audrey, trip, Audrey. [*To* CORIN] I attend, I
attend.   *Exeunt*

5.2

            Enter ORLANDO *and* OLIVER

ORLANDO Is't possible that on so little acquaintance you should
like her? That but seeing, you should love her? And loving,
woo? And wooing, she should grant? And will you persevere to
enjoy her?

5 OLIVER Neither call the giddiness° of it in question, the poverty   foolish haste
of her, the small acquaintance, my sudden wooing, nor her
sudden consenting; but say with me, 'I love Aliena'; say with
her, that she loves me; consent with both that we may enjoy
each other. It shall be to your good, for my father's house and
10 all the revenue that was old Sir Rowland's will I estate° upon   settle
you, and here live and die a shepherd.

            Enter ROSALIND [*as Ganymede*]

ORLANDO You have my consent. Let your wedding be tomorrow.
Thither will I invite the Duke and all's contented followers. Go
you, and prepare Aliena; for look you, here comes my Rosalind.

15 ROSALIND God save you, brother.

OLIVER And you, fair sister.   [*Exit*]

ROSALIND O, my dear Orlando, how it grieves me to see thee
wear thy heart in a scarf.°   sling

ORLANDO It is my arm.

20 ROSALIND I thought thy heart had been wounded with the claws
of a lion.

ORLANDO Wounded it is, but with the eyes of a lady.

ROSALIND Did your brother tell you how I counterfeited to
swoon when he showed me your handkerchief?

25 ORLANDO Ay, and greater wonders than that.

ROSALIND O, I know where you are. Nay, 'tis true. There was
never anything so sudden but the fight of two rams, and Cae-

---

3. For all authorities agree that *ipse* is translated as "he
himself." The Latin word was proverbially applied to
successful lovers.

4. I will contend ("bandy") with you in argument, I will
overrun you with craftiness.
5.2

sar's thrasonical° brag of 'I came, saw, and overcame',[1] for your   *boastful*
brother and my sister no sooner met but they looked; no sooner
30   looked but they loved; no sooner loved but they sighed; no
sooner sighed but they asked one another the reason; no sooner
knew the reason but they sought the remedy; and in these
degrees have they made a pair° of stairs to marriage, which they   *flight*
will climb incontinent,° or else be incontinent[2] before mar-   *hastily*
35   riage. They are in the very wrath of love,° and they will together.   *heat of passion*
Clubs cannot part them.

ORLANDO   They shall be married tomorrow, and I will bid the
Duke to the nuptial. But O, how bitter a thing it is to look into
happiness through another man's eyes. By so much the more
40   shall I tomorrow be at the height of heart-heaviness by how
much I shall think my brother happy in having what he wishes
for.

ROSALIND   Why, then, tomorrow I cannot serve your turn[3] for
Rosalind?

45   ORLANDO   I can live no longer by thinking.

ROSALIND   I will weary you then no longer with idle talking.
Know of me then—for now I speak to some purpose—that I
know you are a gentleman of good conceit.° I speak not this   *understanding*
that you should bear a good opinion of my knowledge, inso-
50   much° I say I know you are; neither do I labour for a greater   *inasmuch as*
esteem than may in some little measure draw a belief from you
to do yourself good,[4] and not to grace me. Believe then, if you
please, that I can do strange things. I have since I was three
year old conversed° with a magician, most profound in his art,   *associated*
55   and yet not damnable.[5] If you do love Rosalind so near the
heart as your gesture° cries it out, when your brother marries   *behavior*
Aliena shall you marry her. I know into what straits of fortune
she is driven, and it is not impossible to me, if it appear not
inconvenient to you, to set her before your eyes tomorrow,
60   human as she is, and without any danger.

ORLANDO   Speakest thou in sober meanings?

ROSALIND   By my life, I do, which I tender° dearly, though I say   *value*
I am a magician. Therefore put you in your best array, bid°   *invite*
your friends: for if you will be married tomorrow, you shall;
65   and to Rosalind if you will.

Enter SILVIUS *and* PHOEBE

Look, here comes a lover of mine and a lover of hers.

PHOEBE [*to* ROSALIND]   Youth, you have done me much ungentleness,°   *discourtesy*
To show the letter that I writ to you.

ROSALIND   I care not if I have. It is my study
70   To seem despiteful° and ungentle to you.   *contemptuous*
You are there followed by a faithful shepherd.
Look upon him; love him. He worships you.

PHOEBE [*to* SILVIUS]   Good shepherd, tell this youth what 'tis to love.

SILVIUS   It is to be all made of sighs and tears,
75   And so am I for Phoebe.

---

1. Caesar's well-known announcement of military vic-
tory, quoted as it appears in Thomas North's translation
of Plutarch's *Lives* (1579).
2. Be sexually unrestrained.
3. Substitute for Rosalind; satisfy you sexually in Ros-
alind's place.

4. *neither . . . good:* nor am I attempting to enhance my
reputation more than is necessary to persuade you to do
yourself some good.
5. That is, not meriting execution for heresy. Eliza-
bethan statutes made certain forms of witchcraft and
black magic punishable by death.

PHOEBE   And I for Ganymede.

ORLANDO   And I for Rosalind.

ROSALIND   And I for no woman.

SILVIUS   It is to be all made of faith and service,

80   And so am I for Phoebe.

PHOEBE   And I for Ganymede.

ORLANDO   And I for Rosalind.

ROSALIND   And I for no woman.

SILVIUS   It is to be all made of fantasy,

85   All made of passion, and all made of wishes,

All adoration, duty, and observance,°   *devotion*

All humbleness, all patience and impatience,

All purity, all trial, all obedience,

And so am I for Phoebe.

90   PHOEBE   And so am I for Ganymede.

ORLANDO   And so am I for Rosalind.

ROSALIND   And so am I for no woman.

PHOEBE [*to* ROSALIND]   If this be so, why blame you me to love
you?

95   SILVIUS [*to* PHOEBE]   If this be so, why blame you me to love
you?

ORLANDO   If this be so, why blame you me to love you?

ROSALIND   Why do you speak too, 'Why blame you me to love
you?'

100   ORLANDO   To her that is not here nor doth not hear.

ROSALIND   Pray you, no more of this, 'tis like the howling of Irish
wolves against the moon.⁶   [*To* SILVIUS] I will help you if I can.
[*To* PHOEBE] I would love you if I could.—Tomorrow meet
me all together. [*To* PHOEBE] I will marry you if ever I

105   marry woman, and I'll be married tomorrow. [*To* ORLANDO] I
will satisfy you if ever I satisfy man, and you shall be married
tomorrow. [*To* SILVIUS] I will content you if what pleases you
contents you, and you shall be married tomorrow. [*To*
ORLANDO] As you love Rosalind, meet. [*To* SILVIUS] As you

110   love Phoebe, meet. And as I love no woman, I'll meet. So fare
you well. I have left you commands.

SILVIUS   I'll not fail, if I live.

PHOEBE   Nor I.

ORLANDO   Nor I.   *Exeunt* [*severally*]

5.3

Enter [TOUCHSTONE *the*] *clown and* AUDREY

TOUCHSTONE   Tomorrow is the joyful day, Audrey, tomorrow
will we be married.

AUDREY   I do desire it with all my heart; and I hope it is no
dishonest° desire to desire to be a woman of the world.° Here   *unchaste / married*

5   come two of the banished Duke's pages.

Enter two PAGES

FIRST PAGE   Well met, honest gentleman.

TOUCHSTONE   By my troth, well met. Come, sit, sit, and a song.

---

6. That is, it is barbaric. The howling of wolves at the
moon was a proverbial way of referring to an irrational or
futile course of action. Irish wolves might be perceived as
especially disorderly, for Ireland's abundance of wolves
was for many Elizabethan writers a mark of that coun-
try's lack of civility.
5.3

SECOND PAGE   We are for you.° Sit i'th' middle.   *That suits us*

FIRST PAGE   Shall we clap into't roundly, without hawking¹, or

10 spitting, or saying we are hoarse, which are the only° prologues   *proper*

to a bad voice?

SECOND PAGE   I'faith, i'faith, and both in a tune,° like two gipsies   *in unison*

on a horse.

BOTH PAGES [*sing*]²   It was a lover and his lass,

15   With a hey, and a ho, and a hey-nonny-no,

That o'er the green cornfield° did pass   *field of wheat*

In spring-time, the only pretty ring-time,°   *time for weddings*

When birds do sing, hey ding-a-ding ding,

Sweet lovers love the spring.

20   Between the acres of the rye,

With a hey, and a ho, and a hey-nonny-no,

These pretty country folks would lie,

In spring-time, the only pretty ring-time,

When birds do sing, hey ding-a-ding ding,

25   Sweet lovers love the spring.

This carol they began that hour,

With a hey, and a ho, and a hey-nonny-no,

How that a life was but a flower,

In spring-time, the only pretty ring-time,

30   When birds do sing, hey ding-a-ding ding,

Sweet lovers love the spring.

And therefore take° the present time,   *seize*

With a hey, and a ho, and a hey-nonny-no,

For love is crownèd with the prime,°   *spring; perfection*

35   In spring time, the only pretty ring-time,

When birds do sing, hey ding-a-ding ding,

Sweet lovers love the spring.

TOUCHSTONE   Truly, young gentlemen, though there was no

great matter° in the ditty, yet the note³ was very untunable.   *sense*

40 FIRST PAGE   You are deceived, sir, we kept time, we lost not our

time.

TOUCHSTONE   By my troth, yes, I count it but time lost to hear

such a foolish song. God b'wi'you, and God mend your voices.

Come, Audrey.   *Exeunt* [*severally*]

5.4

Enter DUKE SENIOR, AMIENS, JAQUES, ORLANDO, OLIVER,
[*and*] CELIA [*as Aliena*]

DUKE SENIOR   Dost thou believe, Orlando, that the boy

Can do all this that he hath promisèd?

ORLANDO   I sometimes do believe, and sometimes do not,

As those that fear they hope,¹ and know they fear.

Enter ROSALIND [*as Ganymede*], [*with*] SILVIUS *and*
PHOEBE

1. Shall we begin energetically and at once, without
clearing our throats?
2. F does not include this speech prefix, simply the
world "song." This is one of the few Shakespeare songs
for which contemporary music survives. It is set for a

single voice with lute accompaniment in Thomas Mor-
ley's *First Booke of Ayres* (1600).
3. Yet the music was disagreeable.
5.4
1. Fear that their hope will not be fulfilled.

5   ROSALIND Patience once more, whiles our compact is urged.°   *declared*
      [*To the* DUKE] You say if I bring in your Rosalind
      You will bestow her on Orlando here?
      DUKE SENIOR That would I, had I° kingdoms to give with her.   *even if I had*
      ROSALIND [*to* ORLANDO] And you say you will have her when I
         bring her?
10   ORLANDO That would I, were I of all kingdoms king.
      ROSALIND [*to* PHOEBE] You say you'll marry me if I be willing?
      PHOEBE That will I, should I die the hour after.
      ROSALIND But if you do refuse to marry me
      You'll give yourself to this most faithful shepherd?
15   PHOEBE So is the bargain.
      ROSALIND [*to* SILVIUS] You say that you'll have Phoebe if she will.
      SILVIUS Though to have her and death were both one thing.
      ROSALIND I have promised to make all this matter even.°   *smooth*
      Keep you your word, O Duke, to give your daughter.
20   You yours, Orlando, to receive his daughter.
      Keep your word, Phoebe, that you'll marry me,
      Or else refusing me to wed this shepherd.
      Keep your word, Silvius, that you'll marry her
      If she refuse me; and from hence I go
25   To make these doubts all even. *Exeunt* ROSALIND *and* CELIA
      DUKE SENIOR I do remember in this shepherd boy
      Some lively° touches of my daughter's favour.°   *vivid / appearance*
      ORLANDO My lord, the first time that I ever saw him,
      Methought he was a brother to your daughter.
30   But, my good lord, this boy is forest-born,
      And hath been tutored in the rudiments
      Of many desperate° studies by his uncle,   *dangerous*
      Whom he reports to be a great magician
      Obscurèd in the circle of this forest.²
           Enter [TOUCHSTONE *the*] *clown and* AUDREY
35   JAQUES There is sure another flood toward,° and these couples   *at hand*
      are coming to the ark.³ Here comes a pair of very strange
      beasts, which in all tongues are called fools.
      TOUCHSTONE Salutation and greeting to you all.
      JAQUES [*to the* DUKE] Good my lord, bid him welcome. This is
40   the motley-minded° gentleman that I have so often met in the   *foolish-brained*
      forest. He hath been a courtier, he swears.
      TOUCHSTONE If any man doubt that, let him put me to my pur-
      gation.⁴ I have trod a measure,° I have flattered a lady, I have   *danced*
      been politic with my friend, smooth with mine enemy, I have
45   undone° three tailors, I have had four quarrels, and like to have   *made bankrupt*
      fought° one.   *came close to fighting*
      JAQUES And how was that ta'en up?°   *settled*
      TOUCHSTONE Faith, we met, and found the quarrel was upon
      the seventh cause.
50   JAQUES How, seventh cause?—Good my lord, like this fellow.
      DUKE SENIOR I like him very well.
      TOUCHSTONE God'ield you, sir, I desire you of the like. I press

---

2. Concealed within the boundaries of this forest. Per-
haps a reference to the magic circle within which magi-
cians were supposed to be able to practice their art safely.
3. Alluding to a biblical account in Genesis 7:2 in
which pairs of male and female animals shelter on
Noah's ark to escape the flood that covers the earth.
4. Let me be put to trial to clear myself (of the charge
of lying).

in here, sir, amongst the rest of the country copulatives,[5] to
swear, and to forswear, according as marriage binds and blood
breaks.° A poor virgin, sir, an ill-favoured thing, sir, but mine   *passion rebels*
own. A poor humour° of mine, sir, to take that that no man else   *whim*
will. Rich honesty° dwells like a miser, sir, in a poor house, as   *chastity*
your pearl in your foul oyster.

DUKE SENIOR   By my faith, he is very swift and sententious.°   *witty and wise*

TOUCHSTONE   According to the fool's bolt,[6] sir, and such dulcet
diseases.°   *sweet afflictions*

JAQUES   But for the seventh cause. How did you find the quar-
rel on the seventh cause?

TOUCHSTONE   Upon a lie seven times removed.—Bear your body
more seeming,° Audrey.—As thus, sir: I did dislike[7] the cut of   *becomingly*
a certain courtier's beard. He sent me word if I said his beard
was not cut well, he was in the mind it was. This is called the
Retort Courteous. If I sent him word again it was not well cut,
he would send me word he cut it to please himself. This is
called the Quip Modest. If again it was not well cut, he disa-
bled° my judgement. This is called the Reply Churlish. If again   *disparaged*
it was not well cut, he would answer I spake not true. This is
called the Reproof Valiant. If again it was not well cut, he
would say I lie. This is called the Countercheck° Quarrelsome.   *rebuff*
And so to the Lie Circumstantial,° and the Lie Direct.   *indirect*

JAQUES   And how oft did you say his beard was not well cut?

TOUCHSTONE   I durst go no further than the Lie Circumstantial,
nor he durst not give me the Lie Direct; and so we measured
swords,[8] and parted.

JAQUES   Can you nominate° in order now the degrees of the lie?   *name*

TOUCHSTONE   O sir, we quarrel in print, by the book,[9] as you
have books for good manners.[1] I will name you the degrees.
The first, the Retort Courteous; the second, the Quip Modest;
the third, the Reply Churlish; the fourth, the Reproof Valiant;
the fifth, the Countercheck Quarrelsome; the sixth, the Lie
with Circumstance; the seventh, the Lie Direct. All these you
may avoid but the Lie Direct; and you may avoid that, too, with
an 'if'. I knew when seven justices could not take up° a quarrel,   *settle*
but when the parties were met themselves, one of them
thought but of an 'if', as 'If you said so, then I said so', and they
shook hands and swore brothers.° Your 'if' is the only peace   *became sworn brothers*
maker; much virtue in 'if'.

JAQUES [*to the* DUKE]   Is not this a rare fellow, my lord? He's as
good at anything, and yet a fool.

DUKE SENIOR   He uses his folly like a stalking-horse,[2] and under
the presentation° of that he shoots his wit.   *appearance*

       Still° music. Enter HYMEN[3] [*with*] ROSALIND *and* CELIA   *Soft*
       [*as themselves*]

HYMEN   Then is there mirth in heaven

---

5. People about to copulate.
6. And his wittiness quickly disappears. Alluding to the
proverb "A fool's bolt (or arrow) is soon shot."
7. Show my dislike of.
8. Checked that our swords were of the same length
(as was usual prior to a duel).
9. According to the rules as set down in books on the
etiquette of dueling. Touchstone's speech exposes the
absurd aspects of the elaborate codes of behavior set

forth in such books.
1. Elizabethan England witnessed an outpouring of
courtesy literature aimed at both social aspirants and
established courtiers.
2. A real or imitation horse used as a means of camou-
flage in hunting.
3. The god of marriage in classical mythology, conven-
tionally depicted as a young man who carried a veil and
a bridal torch.

When earthly things made even°   *set right*
Atone° together.   *Are at one; unite*
100   Good Duke, receive thy daughter;
Hymen from heaven brought her,
Yea, brought her hither,
That thou mightst join her hand with his
Whose heart within his bosom is.
105   ROSALIND [*to the* DUKE]   To you I give myself, for I am yours.
[*To* ORLANDO] To you I give myself, for I am yours.
DUKE SENIOR   If there be truth in sight, you are my daughter.
ORLANDO   If there be truth in sight, you are my Rosalind.
PHOEBE   If sight and shape be true,
110   Why then, my love adieu!
ROSALIND [*to the* DUKE]   I'll have no father if you be not he.
[*To* ORLANDO]   I'll have no husband if you be not he,
[*To* PHOEBE]   Nor ne'er wed woman if you be not she.
HYMEN   Peace, ho, I bar° confusion.   *forbid*
115   'Tis I must make conclusion
Of these most strange events.
Here's eight that must take hands
To join in Hymen's bands,°   *bonds of marriage*
If truth holds true contents.[4]
[*To* ORLANDO *and* ROSALIND]
120   You and you no cross° shall part.   *adversity*
[*To* OLIVER *and* CELIA]
You and you are heart in heart.
[*To* PHOEBE]
You to his love must accord,°   *consent*
Or have a woman to° your lord.   *as*
[*To* TOUCHSTONE *and* AUDREY]
You and you are sure together°   *tightly bound*
125   As the winter to foul weather.—
Whiles a wedlock hymn we sing,
Feed° yourselves with questioning,   *Satisfy*
That reason wonder may diminish
How thus we met, and these things finish.

                            Song
130   Wedding is great Juno's° crown,   *goddess of marriage*
O blessèd bond of board and bed.
'Tis Hymen peoples every town.
High° wedlock then be honourèd.   *Solemn*
Honour, high honour and renown
135   To Hymen, god of every town.
DUKE SENIOR [*to* CELIA]   O my dear niece, welcome thou art to me,
Even daughter; welcome in no less degree.[5]
PHOEBE [*to* SILVIUS]   I will not eat my word. Now thou art mine,
Thy faith my fancy° to thee doth combine.   *love*
            Enter [JAQUES DE BOIS, *the*] *second brother*
140   JAQUES DE BOIS   Let me have audience for a word or two.
I am the second son of old Sir Rowland,

---

4. If truth is true; if truth please you.   5. You are no less welcome than a daughter.

That bring these tidings to this fair assembly.
Duke Frederick, hearing how that every day
Men of great worth resorted to this forest,
145   Addressed a mighty power,° which were on foot,   army
In his own conduct,° purposely to take   Under his command
His brother here, and put him to the sword.
And to the skirts° of this wild wood he came   outskirts
Where, meeting with an old religious man,
150   After some question° with him was converted   conversation
Both from his enterprise and from the world,
His crown bequeathing to his banished brother,
And all their lands restored to them again
That were with him exiled. This to be true
I do engage° my life.   pledge
155   DUKE SENIOR   Welcome, young man.
Thou offer'st fairly° to thy brothers' wedding: You bring fine gifts
To one° his lands withheld, and to the other°   (Oliver) / (Orlando)
A land itself at large,[6] a potent° dukedom.   powerful
First, in this forest let us do° those ends   accomplish
160   That here were well begun, and well begot.°   conceived
And after, every° of this happy number   every one
That have endured shrewd° days and nights with us   evil
Shall share the good of our returnèd fortune
According to the measure of their states.°   ranks
165   Meantime, forget this new-fallen° dignity   newly acquired
And fall into our rustic revelry.
Play, music, and you brides and bridegrooms all,
With measure heaped in joy to th' measures fall.[7]
JAQUES   Sir, by your patience.° [To JAQUES DE BOIS] If I heard   with your permission
       you rightly
170   The Duke hath put on a religious life
And thrown into neglect the pompous° court.   ceremonious
JAQUES DE BOIS   He hath.
JAQUES   To him will I. Out of these convertites°   converts
There is much matter to be heard and learned.
[To the DUKE]
175   You to your former honour I bequeath;
Your patience and your virtue well deserves it.
[To ORLANDO]
You to a love that your true faith doth merit;
[To OLIVER]
You to your land, and love, and great allies;°   relatives
[To SILVIUS]
You to a long and well-deservèd bed;
[To TOUCHSTONE]
180   And you to wrangling, for thy loving voyage
Is but for two months victualled.°—So, to your pleasures;   supplied with food
I am for other than for dancing measures.
DUKE SENIOR   Stay, Jaques, stay.
JAQUES   To see no pastime, I. What you would have°   like (from me)
185   I'll stay to know at your abandoned cave.   Exit

---

6. An entire country. As Rosalind's husband, Orlando
is heir to the dukedom returned to Duke Senior.

7. With a measure of overflowing joy, begin your
dances ("measures").

DUKE SENIOR   Proceed, proceed. We'll so begin these rites
  As we do trust they'll end, in true delights.
    [*They dance; then*] *exeunt* [*all but* ROSALIND][8]

[Epilogue]

ROSALIND [*to the audience*]   It is not the fashion to see the lady
the epilogue;[1] but it is no more unhandsome than to see the
lord the prologue. If it be true that good wine needs no bush,[2]
'tis true that a good play needs no epilogue. Yet to good wine
5 they do use good bushes, and good plays prove the better by
the help of good epilogues. What a case° am I in then, that am
neither a good epilogue nor cannot insinuate° with you in the
behalf of a good play! I am not furnished like a beggar, there-
fore to beg will not become me. My way is to conjure° you;
10 and I'll begin with the women. I charge you, O women, for the
love you bear to men, to like as much of this play as please you.
And I charge you, O men, for the love you bear to women—as
I perceive by your simpering none of you hates them—that
between you and the women the play° may please. If I were a
15 woman[3] I would kiss as many of you as had beards that pleased
me, complexions that liked° me, and breaths that I defied° not.
And I am sure, as many as have good beards, or good faces, or
sweet breaths will for my kind offer, when I make curtsy, bid
me farewell.°   *Exit*

plight; costume
ingratiate myself

charge; bewitch

drama; love play

pleased / disdained

(with applause)

8. F indicates only a single exit for Duke Senior, but
most editors assume that Rosalind remains alone
onstage to deliver the Epilogue.
Epilogue
1. In the vast majority of Elizabethan plays, the Epi-
logue is spoken by a male character.

2. Advertisement. A proverb derived from the practice
of hanging a branch of ivy in tavern windows to indicate
that wine was for sale.
3. A pointed reference to the fact that women's roles in
the Elizabethan theater were played by boys.

Twelfth Night

Shakespeare's contemporary Thomas Coryat wrote that he witnessed something quite remarkable when he went to the theater in Venice: "I saw women act, a thing that I never saw before." That an Englishman had to travel abroad to see women actors for the first time is not surprising. All the great women's roles in Elizabethan and Jacobean plays were written to be performed by trained adolescent boys, and boys played the female parts as well in all grammar school and university productions. But what struck Coryat in Venice was neither the gratifying naturalness of finally seeing women play women's parts nor the comparative inadequacy of English boy actors. Rather, he was impressed that the women actors managed to hold their own in representing the female sex: "They performed it," he writes, "with as good a grace, as ever I saw any masculine Actor."

Recent scholars have observed that there were in fact occasions in which audiences in England could have seen women performing: troupes from abroad, including women actors, occasionally toured England, and English women performed in the theatrical spectacles known as masques and in other entertainments. But in England, women did not perform on the public stage (the word "actress" had not yet entered the English language), and the remarks of Coryat and others suggest that their absence was rarely if ever lamented. The boy actors were evidently extraordinarily skillful, and the audiences were sufficiently immersed in the conventions both of theater and of social life in general to accept gesture, makeup, and above all dress as a convincing representation of femininity.

Twelfth Night, or What You Will, written for Shakespeare's all-male company, plays brilliantly with these conventions. The comedy depends on an actor's ability to transform himself, through costume, voice, and gesture, into a young noblewoman, Viola, who transforms herself, through costume, voice, and gesture, into a young man, Cesario. The play's delicious complications follow from the emotional crosscurrents that Viola's transformation engenders. Shipwrecked on a strange coast and bereft of her twin brother, the disguised Viola finds a place in the service of the powerful Duke Orsino, with whom she promptly falls in love. Orsino is in love with Lady Olivia, a wealthy aristocrat whose household includes, among its servants and dependents, a steward or house manager, a waiting-gentlewoman, a professional entertainer, and a down-at-the-heels, perpetually drunken uncle. When Orsino sends Cesario to help him woo the proud Olivia, Olivia not only rejects the Duke's suit but falls in love with his messenger. Discomfited to learn that she is the object of Olivia's love, Viola reflects on the plot's impassioned triangle:

> My master loves her dearly,
> And I, poor monster, fond as much on him,
> And she, mistaken, seems to dote on me.
> What will become of this?
>
> (2.2.31–34)

"Poor monster": in *Twelfth Night,* clothes do not simply reveal or disguise identity; they partly constitute identity—or so Viola playfully imagines—making her a strange, hybrid creature. To be sure, she understands perfectly well the narrow biological definition of her sex (though in the characteristically male-centered language of Shakespeare's culture, she phrases that definition in terms of what she "lacks" [3.4.269]). Yet there is something almost magical in this play about costume, so that even at the close, when identities have been sorted out and the couples happily matched, Orsino cannot bring himself to call his bride-to-be by her rightful name or to address her as a woman:

> Cesario, come—
> For so you shall be while you are a man;
> But when in other habits you are seen,
> Orsino's mistress, and his fancy's queen.
> (5.1.372–75)

It would have been simple for Shakespeare to devise a concluding scene in which Viola appears in women's "habits," but he goes out of his way to leave her in men's clothes and hence to disrupt with a delicate comic touch the return to the "normal." The transforming power of costume unsettles fixed categories of gender and social class, and allows characters to explore emotional territory that a culture officially hostile to same-sex desire and cross-class marriage would ordinarily have ruled out of bounds. In *Twelfth Night,* conventional expectations repeatedly give way to a different way of perceiving the world.

Shakespeare wrote *Twelfth Night* around 1601. He had already written such comedies as *A Midsummer Night's Dream, Much Ado About Nothing,* and *As You Like It,* with their playful, subtly ironic investigations of the ways in which heterosexual couples are produced out of the murkier crosscurrents of male and female friendships; as interesting, perhaps, he had probably just recently completed *Hamlet,* with its unprecedented exploration of mourning, betrayal, antic humor, and tragic isolation. *Twelfth Night* would prove to be, in the view of many critics, both the most perfect and in some sense the last of the great festive comedies. Shakespeare returned to comedy later in his career, but always with more insistent overtones of bitterness, loss, and grief. There are dark notes in *Twelfth Night* as well: Olivia is in mourning for her brother, Viola thinks that her brother, too, is dead, Antonio believes that he has been betrayed by the man he loves, Orsino threatens to kill Cesario. Desire is repeatedly linked to frustration and loss. But these notes are swept up in the current of sweet music that pervades the play, and the characters are all drawn into a giddy, carnivalesque dance of illusion, disguise, folly, and clowning.

The play's subtitle, *What You Will,* underscores the celebratory spirit associated with Twelfth Night, the Feast of the Epiphany (January 6), which in Elizabethan England marked the culminating night of the traditional Christmas revels. On Twelfth Night 1601, the queen's guest of honor was a twenty-eight-year-old Italian nobleman, Don Virginio Orsino, Duke of Bracciano. Orsino wrote to his wife that he was entertained that night with "a mingled comedy, with pieces of music and dances." Since the company that performed was the Lord Chamberlain's Men—Shakespeare's company—it has been argued that the comedy was *Twelfth Night,* but there is no scholarly consensus on this hypothesis. The title, in any case, would for Shakespeare's contemporaries have conjured up a whole series of time-honored festivities associated with the midwinter season. A rigidly hierarchical social order that ordinarily demanded deference, sobriety, and strict obedience to authority temporarily gave way to raucous rituals of inversion: young boys were crowned for a day as bishops and carried through the streets in mock religious processions; abstemiousness was toppled by bouts of heavy drinking and feasting; the spirit of parody, folly, and misrule reigned briefly in places normally reserved for stern-faced moralists and sober judges.

The fact that these festivities were associated with Christian holidays—the Epiphany marked the visit of the Three Kings to Bethlehem to worship the Christ child—did not altogether obscure the continuities with pagan winter rituals such as the Roman Saturnalia, with its comparably explosive release from everyday discipline into a disorderly realm of belly laughter and belly cheer. Puritans emphasized these continuities in launching a fierce attack on the Elizabethan festive calendar and its whole ethos, just as they attacked the theater for what they saw as its links with paganism, idleness, and sexual license. Elizabethan and Jacobean authorities in the church and the state had their own concerns about idleness and subversion, but they generally protected and patronized both festive ritual and theater on the grounds that these provided a valuable release from tensions that might otherwise prove dangerous. Sobriety, piety, and discipline were no doubt admirable virtues, but most human beings were not saints. "Dost thou think because thou art virtuous," the drunken Sir Toby asks the censorious steward Malvolio, "there shall be no more cakes and ale?" (2.3.103–04).

Fittingly, the earliest firm record of a performance of *Twelfth Night,* as noted in the diary of John Manningham, was "at our feast" in the Middle Temple (one of London's law schools) in February 1602. Manningham wrote observantly that the play was "much like the *Comedy of Errors,* or *Menaechmi* in Plautus, but most like and near to that in Italian called *Inganni."* That is, *Twelfth Night* resembles Shakespeare's own earlier play on identical twins (along with that play's Roman source) and still more resembles a series of sixteenth-century Italian comedies built around the intertwining themes of love, fraud *(inganno),* and mistaken identity. Several of these comedies feature the plot device of a female twin who takes service as a page with the man she loves. Closest of these to Shakespeare's comedy is *Gl'Ingannati* (The Deceived), written for performance at Carnival time in Siena in 1531 and translated into French in 1543. It seems likely that Shakespeare knew this play or one that derived from it, and may have picked up several details in addition to the overall plot line. But the tone of *Gl'Ingannati,* with its bawdy jokes about nuns and old men, its sly, sardonic servants, and its farcical intrigues, is far from *Twelfth Night'*s mingled melancholy and delight, its bittersweet play of divided and contradictory desires. Tellingly, in the Italian comedy, the heroine is all along plotting to win the love of the man she serves; she has disguised herself in order to dissuade him from wooing elsewhere. Viola's predicament—her attempt to serve Orsino even at the cost of her own deepest longings—represents a wholly different emotional register.

That predicament is not Shakespeare's invention; he found it, with many other elements of his plot, in an English story, Barnabe Riche's tale "Apollonius and Silla" in *Riche His Farewell to Militarie Profession* (1581), which was in turn based on French and Italian sources. Riche is too addicted to moralizing to explore his heroine's character with much subtlety, but he does underscore how painful it is for her to hide her feelings while acting as go-between, and hence he anticipates, if only woodenly, the mood that Shakespeare exquisitely captures in Viola's lines about one who "sat like patience on a monument, / Smiling at grief" (2.4.113–14). There is less precedent, in Riche or in any of the known sources, for the aspect of *Twelfth Night* that Manningham

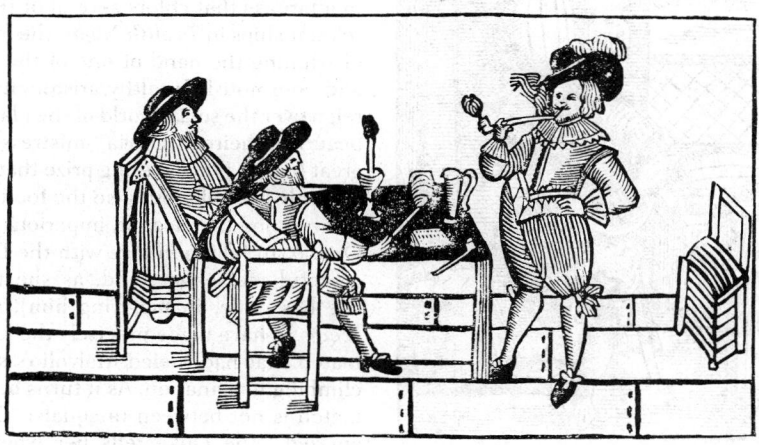

Gentlemen drinking and smoking. From Phillip Stubbes, *The Anatomie of Abuses* (1583).

found particularly memorable and that has continued to delight audiences: the gulling of Malvolio.

Malvolio (*mal volio,* "ill will") is explicitly linked to those among Shakespeare's contemporaries most hostile to the theater and to such holidays as Twelfth Night: "Sometimes," says Lady Olivia's waiting-gentlewoman Maria, "he is a kind of puritan" (2.3.125). When we first see Malvolio, he is harshly critical of Feste the clown, who is attempting to win back Olivia's favor. "Unless you laugh and minister occasion to him," Malvolio sourly observes, "he is gagged" (1.5.74–75). Though ungenerous, the observation is canny, for comedy does seem to depend on a collaborative spirit from which Malvolio conspicuously excludes himself. He is a man without friends. More dangerously, he is a man in a socially dependent position with a gift for acquiring enemies, as he does when he tries to silence the noisy revelry of that classic carnivalesque threesome a drunkard, a blockhead, and a professional fool: Olivia's uncle Sir Toby, his boon companion Sir Andrew Aguecheek, and Feste.

Olivia remarks to Malvolio that he is "sick of self-love" (1.5.77), and it is this narcissism that his enemies exploit to undo him. When Malvolio finds Maria's forged letter, he is in the midst of a deliciously self-gratifying fantasy that he has married Olivia, a fantasy less of erotic bliss than of social domination. The dream of rising above his station fuels his credulous eagerness to interpret the letter according to his fondest wishes and to comply with its absurd suggestions for his festive dress and demeanor. This compliance, by making it seem to Olivia that he has gone mad, renders Malvolio vulnerable to a further humiliation. In a parody of the age's brutal "therapy" for insanity, he is clapped into a dark room and subjected to a mock exorcism. Finally, he suffers what is perhaps the cruelest punishment for someone who dreams that greatness will be thrust upon him: he is simply forgotten. When in the play's final moments he is released, Malvolio is in no mood to join in the general air of communal wonder and rejoicing. More alone than ever, he introduces into the comedy's resolution an extraordinary note of vindictive bitterness: "I'll be revenged on the whole pack of you!" (5.1.365). Shakespeare does not hide the cruelty of the treatment to which Malvolio has been subjected—"He hath been most notoriously abused" (5.1.366), says Olivia—nor does he shrink from showing the audience other disagreeable qualities in Sir Toby and his companions. But while the close of the comedy seems to embrace these failings in a tolerant, bemused, aristocratic recognition of human folly, it can find no place for Malvolio's blend of puritanism and social climbing.

Lutenist. By Jost Amman.

Malvolio is scapegoated for indulging in a fantasy that colors several of the key relationships in *Twelfth Night:* the fantasy of winning the hand of one of the noble and enormously wealthy aristocrats who reign over the social world of the play. The beautiful heiress Olivia, mistress of a great house, is a glittering prize that lures not only Malvolio but also the foolish Sir Andrew and the elegant, imperious Duke Orsino. In falling in love with the Duke's graceful messenger (and, as she thinks she has done, in marrying him), Olivia seems to have made precisely the kind of match that had fueled Malvolio's social-climbing imagination. As it turns out, the match is not between unequals: "Be not amazed," the Duke tells her when she realizes that she has married someone she scarcely knows. "Right noble is his blood" (5.1.257). The social order, then, has not been overturned: as in a carnival, when the disguises are removed, the revelers resume their "proper," socially and sexually approved positions.

Yet there is something decidedly improper about the perverse erotic excitement that the play discovers in disguise, displacement, indirection, and deferral and something irreducibly strange about the marriages with which *Twelfth Night* ends. Sir Toby has married Maria as a reward for devising the plot against Malvolio. Olivia has entered into a "contract of eternal bond of love" (5.1.152) with someone whose actual identity is only revealed to her after the marriage ceremony. (In Riche's version of the story, she is pregnant and her marriage saves her from social disgrace, but Shakespeare omits this plot twist, thereby raising the tone but heightening the irrationality of the finale.) The strangeness of the bond between virtual strangers is matched by the strangeness of Orsino's instantaneous decision to marry Cesario—as soon as "he" can become Viola by changing into women's clothes. Only a few minutes earlier, in a fit of jealous rage at Olivia's love for Cesario, Orsino had threatened to kill "the lamb that I do love" (5.1.126); now he will wed that lamb.

The sudden transformation is prepared for in part by Orsino's passionate insistence that he loves the boy he intends to kill and in part by the earlier signs of intimacy between them: "I have," he tells Cesario, "unclasped / To thee the book even of my secret soul" (1.4.12–13). But this intimacy has been formed around Orsino's grand passion for Olivia, a passion that is reiterated through virtually the entire play. The revelation at the play's climax—"One face, one voice, one habit, and two persons" (5.1.208)—forces a realignment of all the relationships. With Sebastian married to Olivia, Viola becomes Olivia's "sister" (or, as we would say, sister-in-law); and by marrying Viola, Orsino likewise makes Olivia his "sweet sister" (5.1.371). Orsino then will continue in a sense to "love" Olivia but only through the bond of kinship formed by the linked twins: a strangely appropriate fate for someone who tried to woo by proxy!

That this solution does not seem entirely zany—that it seems a fit ending for a romantic comedy—depends on several key features in *Twelfth Night*'s emotional landscape. It is significant that Orsino's love for Olivia, though poetically intense, is detached from any direct personal encounter. Not only does her vow of a seven-year seclusion compel Orsino to delegate his passion to a messenger, this passion seems largely self-regarding and self-indulgent. His famous opening lines on the paradoxes of love—its close intertwining of fulfillment and decline, stealing and giving, freshness and decay—revolve around the contemplation less of the lady than of his own solitary, self-gratifying imagination: "So full of shapes is fancy / That it alone is high fantastical" (1.1.14–15). The play does not ridicule Orsino's aristocratic reveries, although they seem at moments like elegant versions of what is cruelly mocked in Malvolio, but it does invite the audience to treat them with a certain ironic detachment.

Orsino's love seems to circle all too readily back upon himself: he is fascinated by his role as melancholy lover. That self-absorption is not the only shape of passion is made clear by several contrasting figures of whom the most selfless is the sea captain Antonio, consumed with desire for his friend Sebastian. In a play full of coy allusions to same-sex desire, Antonio's "willing love" (3.3.11) is the most explicit representation of passion as absolute devotion, a willingness to sacrifice everything in the service of the beloved. The mistaken belief that this devotion has been callously betrayed is one of the play's most poignant moments, a moment perhaps only partially redeemed by the manifest relief and joy with which the newly wed Sebastian greets his friend in the last act.

Intense, intimate bonding between men is a recurrent theme in Shakespeare's culture. (A comparable interest in female friendship is reflected in the love between Hermia and Helena in *A Midsummer Night's Dream* and Rosalind and Celia in *As You Like It*.) Shakespeare explores the pleasures and perils of male friendship in such plays as *The Two Gentlemen of Verona*, *The Merchant of Venice*, and *Much Ado About Nothing* and, most famously, in the sonnets to the fair young man whom he calls "the master-mistress of my passion" (sonnet 20). Orsino expresses doubt that a woman can love with an intensity equal to a man's:

> There is no woman's sides
> Can bide the beating of so strong a passion
> As love doth give my heart; no woman's heart
> So big, to hold so much. They lack retention.
> (2.4.91–94)

It is perhaps this belief (which the play proves to be utterly wrong) that conditions the only authentic emotional bond that we see Orsino forge, the bond with his devoted young servant Cesario. In conversation with Cesario, the haughty Duke manages for a few moments at least to escape from his languid self-absorption and express interest in someone else's thoughts and feelings: "What dost thou know?"; "And what's her history?"; "But died thy sister of her love, my boy?" (2.4.103, 108, 118). These simple questions, modest in themselves, are sufficiently distinct from Orsino's usual manner of speech to signal both a curiosity and a responsiveness that he does not manifest with anyone else. Part of the quirky delight of the play's resolution is to give to the union between Orsino and Viola something of the intimacy that had only seemed possible between men.

This resolution depends principally on the remarkable qualities of the play's central character, Viola. Like Antonio, Viola is prepared to sacrifice herself for her beloved: "And I most jocund, apt, and willingly," she tells Orsino, "to do you rest a thousand deaths would die" (5.1.128–29). But where Antonio experiences passion as tragic compulsion—he speaks of Sebastian's beauty as "witchcraft" drawing him into danger—Viola's spirit, as her word "jocund" suggests, is extraordinarily resilient. No sooner does she sadly observe that her brother must have perished in the shipwreck than she remarks, "Perchance he is not drowned" (1.2.4); no sooner does she find herself isolated and unprotected than she determines to serve Lady Olivia, and then, learning that this route is blocked, she at once resolves to disguise herself as a man and serve Orsino instead. Here and throughout the play, Viola seems to draw on an inward principle of hope. That principle, along with an improvisational boldness, an eloquent tongue, and a keen wit, enables her to keep afloat in an increasingly mad swirl of misunderstandings and cross-purposes.

Those misunderstandings, of course, are largely her creation in the sense that they mainly derive from a disguise that confounds the distinction between male and female. "They shall yet belie thy happy years / That say thou art a man," Orsino says to Cesario (1.4.29–30). The description that follows seems to imagine that boys begin almost as girls and only subsequently become males:

> Diana's lip
> Is not more smooth and rubious; thy small pipe
> Is as the maiden's organ, shrill and sound,
> And all is semblative a woman's part.
> (1.4.30–33)

This perception of ambiguity, rooted in early modern ideas about sexuality and gender, is one of the elements that enabled a boy actor in this period convincingly to mime "a woman's part." According to an ancient anatomical tradition, still highly influential in Shakespeare's time, sexual difference is not absolute: males and females share a single physiological structure whose differentiation only occurs over time. Such a theory implies a prolonged period of indistinction upon which *Twelfth Night* continually plays, and that helps to account for the emotional tangle that the cross-dressed Viola inspires.

Having, in her role as intermediary, aroused Olivia's love, Viola does not see how to disabuse the enamored Countess without abandoning the disguise. For all her lively resolution, she is passive in the face of the complexities she has engendered, counting on time and chance to sort out what she cannot: "O time, thou must untangle this, not

I. / It is too hard a knot for me t'untie" (2.2.38–39). Perhaps this passivity, or more accurately this trust in time, is a form of wisdom in a world where everything seems topsy-turvy. If so, it is a wisdom that links Viola to the fool Feste, who exults at the play's close in what he calls "the whirligig of time" (5.1.364).

Feste does not have a major part in the comedy's plot, but he shares with Viola a place at its imaginative center. A few years before the creation of *Twelfth Night,* the famous, boisterous clown Will Kempe quit Shakespeare's company in a huff and was replaced by Robert Armin, a comic actor of unusual sensitivity and subtlety. In paying handsome tribute to Feste's intelligence, Viola seems to acknowledge Armin's special gift: "This fellow is wise enough to play the fool, / And to do that well craves a kind of wit" (3.1.53–54). His wit often takes the form of a perverse literalism that slyly calls attention to the play's repeated confounding of such simple binaries as male and female, outside and inside, role and reality. The paradox of the wise fool, celebrated by Erasmus in his famous *Praise of Folly* (1509), is one that fascinated Shakespeare, who returned to it in plays as diverse as *As You Like It* and *King Lear.* In *Twelfth Night,* Feste is irresponsible, vulnerable, and dependent, but he also understands, as he teasingly shows Olivia, that it is foolish to bewail forever a loss that cannot be recovered. And he understands that it is important to take such pleasures as life offers and not to wait: "In delay there lies no plenty," he sings. "Then come kiss me, sweet and twenty. / Youth's a stuff will not endure" (2.3.46–48). There is in this wonderful song, as in all of his jests, a current of sadness. Feste knows, as the refrain of the last of his songs puts it, that "the rain it raineth every day" (5.1.379). His counsel is for "present mirth" and "present laughter" (2.3.44). This is, of course, the advice of a fool. But do the Malvolios of the world have anything wiser to suggest?

STEPHEN GREENBLATT

TEXTUAL NOTE

The text of *Twelfth Night* is mercifully straightforward: the play first appeared in the 1623 First Folio (F), and the text is unusually clean, including careful act and scene divisions. Contemporary or near-contemporary musical settings survive for several of the songs in the play. For example, "O mistress mine" (2.3.35ff.) appears in three early versions, including Thomas Morley's *First Book of Consort Lessons* (1599). "Hold thy peace" (2.3.59) appears in a manuscript book of rounds collected by Thomas Lant (1580), as well as a version printed in 1609. The well-known setting for Feste's epilogue, "When that I was and a little tiny boy" (5.1.376), was first printed in Joseph Vernon's 1772 volume *The New Songs in the Pantomime of the Witches: The Celebrated Epilogue in the Comedy of Twelfth Night . . . Sung by Mr. Vernon at Vaux Hall, Composed by J. Vernon.* It is not entirely clear whether this setting was composed by Vernon (as the title page seems to suggest) or arranged from a traditional tune.

SELECTED BIBLIOGRAPHY

Auden, W. H. "Music in Shakespeare." *The Dyer's Hand, and Other Essays.* New York: Random House, 1948. Analyzing songs from the plays, Auden reflects on music as a social exercise, dramatic convention, and supernatural signifier.

Bloom, Harold, ed. *William Shakespeare's "Twelfth Night."* Modern Critical Interpretation series. New York: Chelsea House, 1987. Essays written since the 1960s, treating the representation of character, music, class ideology, gender, and role-playing.

Booth, Stephen. "*Twelfth Night* 1.1: The Audience as Malvolio." *Shakespeare's "Rough Magic": Essays in Honor of C. L. Barber.* Ed. Peter Erickson and Coppélia Kahn.

Newark: University of Delaware Press, 1985. 149–67. An otherwise nonsensical play makes sense only when audiences ignore the textual evidence in favor of contextual probability.

Callaghan, Dympna. "'And all is semblative a woman's part': Body Politics and *Twelfth Night*." *Shakespeare Without Women: Representing Gender and Race on the Renaissance Stage.* New York: Routledge, 2000. 26–48. The misogynistic ridicule of Olivia's genitals in the Malvolio letter is an assertion of male control over the female body.

Gay, Penny. "*Twelfth Night*: Desire and Its Discontents." *As She Likes It: Shakespeare's Unruly Women.* London: Routledge, 1994. 17–47. Describes key postwar English stage productions.

Greenblatt, Stephen. "Fiction and Friction." *Shakespearean Negotiations: The Circulation of Social Energy in Renaissance England.* Berkeley: University of California Press, 1988. 66–93. In light of contemporary anatomical theories, relates sexual chafing to verbal sparring and the generation of identity.

Hollander, John. "*Twelfth Night* and the Morality of Indulgence." *Sewanee Review* 67 (1959): 220–38. In *Twelfth Night*'s intense moral vision, the surfeit of appetite through indulgence leads to the rebirth of the unencumbered self.

Neely, Carol Thomas. *Distracted Subjects: Madness and Gender in Shakespeare and Early Modern Culture.* Ithaca: Cornell University Press, 2004. *Twelfth Night*'s displaced erotic choices cohere with changing medical discourse about pathological female lovesickness.

Orgel, Stephen. *Impersonations: The Performance of Gender in Shakespeare's England.* Cambridge, Mass.: Cambridge University Press, 1996. Approaches paradoxes in English playacting practice through contemporary notions of gender construction and sexual desire.

Wells, Stanley, ed. "*Twelfth Night*": *Critical Essays.* New York: Garland, 1986. Twenty essays from the nineteenth century onward, treating mainly formal and structural aspects and early twentieth-century productions.

FILM

Twelfth Night. 1996. Dir. Trevor Nunn. UK. 134 min. Romantic Celtic coastlines combine with a poignant musical score, a stuffy Malvolio, and a gravely wise Feste. With Ben Kingsley, Helena Bonham Carter, and Nigel Hawthorne.

Twelfth Night, or What You Will

THE PERSONS OF THE PLAY

ORSINO, Duke of Illyria
VALENTINE ⎫
CURIO ⎬ attending on Orsino
FIRST OFFICER
SECOND OFFICER
VIOLA, a lady, later disguised as Cesario
A CAPTAIN
SEBASTIAN, her twin brother
ANTONIO, another sea-captain
OLIVIA, a Countess
MARIA, her waiting-gentlewoman
SIR TOBY Belch, Olivia's kinsman
SIR ANDREW Aguecheek, companion of Sir Toby
MALVOLIO, Olivia's steward
FABIAN, a member of Olivia's household
FESTE the clown, her jester
A PRIEST
A SERVANT of Olivia
Musicians, sailors, lords, attendants

1.1

Music. Enter ORSINO *Duke of Illyria,* CURIO, *and other lords*

ORSINO If music be the food of love, play on,
Give me excess of it that, surfeiting,
The appetite may sicken and so die.
That strain again, it had a dying fall.°   cadence
5   O, it came o'er my ear like the sweet sound
That breathes upon a bank of violets,
Stealing and giving odour. Enough, no more,
'Tis not so sweet now as it was before.
      [*Music ceases*]
O spirit of love, how quick and fresh° art thou   *lively and eager*
10   That, notwithstanding thy capacity
Receiveth as the sea,° naught enters there,   *Receives without limit*
Of what validity° and pitch° so e'er,   *value / height; excellence*
But falls into abatement° and low price   *lesser value*
Even in a minute! So full of shapes is fancy°   *love; desire*
15   That it alone is high fantastical.°   *uniquely imaginative*
CURIO Will you go hunt, my lord?
ORSINO   What, Curio?
CURIO   The hart.
ORSINO Why so I do, the noblest that I have.[1]
O, when mine eyes did see Olivia first
Methought she purged the air of pestilence;[2]

1.1 Location: Illyria, Greek and Roman name for the
eastern Adriatic coast; probably not suggesting a real
country to Shakespeare's audience.

1. Orsino plays on "hart/heart."
2. Plague and other illnesses were thought to be caused
by bad air.

20 That instant was I turned into a hart,
And my desires, like fell° and cruel hounds,   *savage*
E'er since pursue me.[3]
Enter VALENTINE
How now, what news from her?
VALENTINE   So please my lord, I might not be admitted,
But from her handmaid do return this answer:
25 The element itself till seven years' heat[4]
Shall not behold her face at ample° view,   *full*
But like a cloistress° she will veilèd walk   *nun*
And water once a day her chamber round
With eye-offending brine°—all this to season   *stinging tears*
30 A brother's dead love,[5] which she would keep fresh
And lasting in her sad remembrance.
ORSINO   O, she that hath a heart of that fine° frame   *exquisitely made*
To pay this debt of love but to a brother,
How will she love when the rich golden shaft[6]
35 Hath killed the flock of all affections else°   *other emotions*
That live in her—when liver, brain, and heart,[7]
These sovereign thrones, are all supplied, and filled
Her sweet perfections[8] with one self° king!   *one and the same*
Away before me to sweet beds of flowers.
40 Love-thoughts lie rich when canopied with bowers.
Exeunt

1.2

Enter VIOLA, *a* CAPTAIN, *and sailors*
VIOLA[1]   What country, friends, is this?
CAPTAIN   This is Illyria, lady.
VIOLA   And what should I do in Illyria?
My brother, he is in Elysium.[2]
Perchance° he is not drowned. What think you sailors?   *Perhaps*
5 CAPTAIN   It is perchance° that you yourself were saved.   *by chance*
VIOLA   O my poor brother!—and so perchance may he be.
CAPTAIN   True, madam, and to comfort you with chance,[3]
Assure yourself, after our ship did split,
When you and those poor number savèd with you
10 Hung on our driving boat,[4] I saw your brother,
Most provident in peril, bind himself—
Courage and hope both teaching him the practice—
To a strong mast that lived° upon the sea,   *remained afloat*
Where, like Arion[5] on the dolphin's back,
15 I saw him hold acquaintance with the waves
So long as I could see.
VIOLA [*giving money*]   For saying so, there's gold.

3. Alluding to the classical legend of Actaeon, who was
turned into a stag and hunted by his own hounds for
having seen Artemis naked.
4. The sky itself / for seven hot summers.
5. *all . . . love:* all this to preserve (by the salt of the
tears) the love of a dead brother.
6. Of Cupid's golden-tipped arrow, which caused desire.
7. In Elizabethan psychology, these were the seats of
passion, intellect, and feeling.
8. *and filled . . . perfections:* and all her flawless qualities

are governed by.
1.2 Location: The coast of Illyria.
1. Viola is not named in the dialogue until 5.1.237.
2. The heaven of classical mythology.
3. With what may have happened.
4. The ship's boat. *driving:* being driven by the wind.
5. A legendary Greek musician who, in order to save
himself from being murdered on a voyage, jumped over-
board and was carried to land by a dolphin.

Mine own escape unfoldeth to° my hope,   *encourages*
Whereto thy speech serves for authority,°   *support*
The like of him.[6] Know'st thou this country?
20 CAPTAIN   Ay, madam, well, for I was bred and born
Not three hours' travel from this very place.
VIOLA   Who governs here?
CAPTAIN   A noble duke, in nature
As in name.
VIOLA   What is his name?
CAPTAIN   Orsino.
VIOLA   Orsino. I have heard my father name him.
25   He was a bachelor then.
CAPTAIN   And so is now, or was so very late,°   *lately*
For but a month ago I went from hence,
And then 'twas fresh in murmur°—as, you know,   *newly rumored*
What great ones do the less will prattle of—
30 That he did seek the love of fair Olivia.
VIOLA   What's she?
CAPTAIN   A virtuous maid, the daughter of a count
That died some twelvemonth since, then leaving her
In the protection of his son, her brother,
35 Who shortly also died, for whose dear love,
They say, she hath abjured the sight
And company of men.
VIOLA   O that I served that lady,
And might not be delivered° to the world   *revealed*
Till I had made mine own occasion mellow,°   *ripe (to be revealed)*
What my estate° is.   *social rank*
40 CAPTAIN   That were hard to compass,°   *achieve*
Because she will admit no kind of suit,°   *petition*
No, not the Duke's.
VIOLA   There is a fair behaviour[7] in thee, captain,
And though that nature with a beauteous wall
45 Doth oft close in pollution, yet of thee
I will believe thou hast a mind that suits
With this thy fair and outward character.[8]
I pray thee—and I'll pay thee bounteously—
Conceal me what I am, and be my aid
50 For such disguise as haply shall become
The form of my intent.[9] I'll serve this duke.
Thou shalt present me as an eunuch[1] to him.
It may be worth thy pains, for I can sing,
And speak to him in many sorts of music
55 That will allow° me very worth his service.   *prove*
What else may hap, to time I will commit.
Only shape thou thy silence to my wit.°   *imagination; plan*
CAPTAIN   Be you his eunuch, and your mute[2] I'll be.
When my tongue blabs, then let mine eyes not see.
60 VIOLA   I thank thee. Lead me on.   *Exeunt*

---

6. That he too has survived.
7. Outward appearance; conduct.
8. Appearance (suggesting moral qualities).
9. *as . . . intent*: that perhaps may be fitting to my purpose. *form*: shape.
1. Castrati (hence, "eunuchs") were prized as male sopranos; the disguise would have explained Viola's

feminine voice. Viola (or perhaps Shakespeare) seems to have changed plans: she presents herself instead as a young page.
2. In Turkish harems, eunuchs served as guards and were assisted by "mutes" (usually servants whose tongues had been cut out).

1.3

Enter SIR TOBY [*Belch*] *and* MARIA

SIR TOBY   What a plague means my niece to take the death of
her brother thus? I am sure care's an enemy to life.

MARIA   By my troth, Sir Toby, you must come in earlier o' nights.
Your cousin,[1] my lady, takes great exceptions to your ill hours.

5   SIR TOBY   Why, let her except, before excepted.[2]

MARIA   Ay, but you must confine yourself within the modest°   moderate
limits of order.

SIR TOBY   Confine? I'll confine myself no finer[3] than I am. These
clothes are good enough to drink in, and so be these boots too;

10   an° they be not, let them hang themselves in their own straps.   if

MARIA   That quaffing and drinking will undo you. I heard my
lady talk of it yesterday, and of a foolish knight that you brought
in one night here to be her wooer.

SIR TOBY   Who, Sir Andrew Aguecheek?

15   MARIA   Ay, he.

SIR TOBY   He's as tall a man as any's[4] in Illyria.

MARIA   What's that to th' purpose?

SIR TOBY   Why, he has three thousand ducats a year.

MARIA   Ay, but he'll have but a year in all these ducats.[5] He's a

20   very° fool, and a prodigal.   an absolute

SIR TOBY   Fie that you'll say so! He plays o'th' viol-de-gamboys,[6]
and speaks three or four languages word for word without
book,° and hath all the good gifts of nature.   from memory

MARIA   He hath indeed, almost natural,[7] for besides that he's a

25   fool, he's a great quarreller, and but that he hath the gift° of a   talent; present
coward to allay the gust° he hath in quarrelling, 'tis thought   gusto
among the prudent he would quickly have the gift of a grave.

SIR TOBY   By this hand, they are scoundrels and substractors[8] that
say so of him. Who are they?

30   MARIA   They that add, moreover, he's drunk nightly in your
company.

SIR TOBY   With drinking healths to my niece. I'll drink to her as
long as there is a passage in my throat and drink in Illyria. He's
a coward and a coistrel° that will not drink to my niece till his   horse groom; lout

35   brains turn o'th' toe, like a parish top. What wench, *Castiliano,*
vulgo,[9] for here comes Sir Andrew Agueface.

Enter SIR ANDREW [*Aguecheek*]

SIR ANDREW   Sir Toby Belch! How now, Sir Toby Belch?

SIR TOBY   Sweet Sir Andrew.

SIR ANDREW [*to* MARIA]   Bless you, fair shrew.[1]

40   MARIA   And you too, sir.

SIR TOBY   Accost, Sir Andrew, accost.[2]

SIR ANDREW   What's that?

1.3 Location: The Countess Olivia's house.
1. Term used generally of kinsfolk.
2. Playing on the legal jargon *exceptis excipiendis,* "with
the previously stated exceptions." Sir Toby refuses to take
Olivia's displeasure seriously.
3. Suggesting both "a refined manner of dress" and
"narrowly" (referring to his girth).
4. Any (man who) is. *tall:* brave; worthy. (Maria takes it
in the modern sense of height.)
5. He'll spend his fortune in a year.
6. A facetious corruption of "viola da gamba," a bass viol
held between the knees.

7. Idiots and fools were called "naturals."
8. Corruption of "detractors." (In reply, Maria puns on
"substract" as "subtract.")
9. Variously interpreted, but may mean "Speak of the
devil," since Castilians were considered devilish, and
vulgo refers to the common tongue (?). *parish top:* par-
ishes kept large tops that were spun by whipping them,
for the parishioners' amusement and exercise.
1. Andrew possibly confuses "shrew" (ill-tempered
woman) with "mouse," an endearment.
2. Address (her); originally a naval term meaning "go
alongside; greet."

SIR TOBY   My niece's chambermaid.[3]

SIR ANDREW   Good Mistress Accost, I desire better acquaintance.

45   MARIA   My name is Mary, sir.

SIR ANDREW   Good Mistress Mary Accost.

SIR TOBY   You mistake, knight. 'Accost' is front° her, board her,   *confront*
woo her, assail[4] her.

SIR ANDREW   By my troth, I would not undertake[5] her in this
50   company.° Is that the meaning of 'accost'?   *the audience*

MARIA   Fare you well, gentlemen.

SIR TOBY   An thou let part so,[6] Sir Andrew, would thou mightst
never draw sword again.

SIR ANDREW   An you part so, mistress, I would I might never draw
55   sword again. Fair lady, do you think you have fools in hand?°   *to deal with*

MARIA   Sir, I have not you by th' hand.

SIR ANDREW   Marry, but you shall have, and here's my hand.

MARIA [*taking his hand*]   Now sir, thought is free.[7] I pray you,
bring your hand to th' buttery-bar,[8] and let it drink.

60   SIR ANDREW   Wherefore, sweetheart? What's your metaphor?

MARIA   It's dry,[9] sir.

SIR ANDREW   Why, I think so. I am not such an ass but I can
keep my hand dry.[1] But what's your jest?

MARIA   A dry jest,[2] sir.

65   SIR ANDREW   Are you full of them?

MARIA   Ay, sir, I have them at my fingers' ends.[3] Marry, now I let
go your hand I am barren.°   *Exit*   *empty of jokes*

SIR TOBY   O knight, thou lackest a cup of canary.[4] When did I
see thee so put down?[5]

70   SIR ANDREW   Never in your life, I think, unless you see canary
put me down. Methinks sometimes I have no more wit than a
Christian° or an ordinary man has; but I am a great eater of   *an average man*
beef,[6] and I believe that does harm to my wit.

SIR TOBY   No question.

75   SIR ANDREW   An I thought that, I'd forswear it. I'll ride home
tomorrow, Sir Toby.

SIR TOBY   *Pourquoi,*° my dear knight?   *Why*

SIR ANDREW   What is 'Pourquoi'? Do, or not do? I would I had
bestowed that time in the tongues[7] that I have in fencing, danc-
80   ing, and bear-baiting. O, had I but followed the arts!

SIR TOBY   Then hadst thou had an excellent head of hair.

SIR ANDREW   Why, would that have mended° my hair?   *improved*

SIR TOBY   Past question, for thou seest it will not curl by nature.[8]

SIR ANDREW   But it becomes me well enough, does't not?

85   SIR TOBY   Excellent, it hangs like flax on a distaff,[9] and I hope to
see a housewife[1] take thee between her legs and spin it off.[2]

---

3. Lady-in-waiting; not a menial servant, but a gentle-
woman in attendance on a great lady.
4. *board:* speak to; tackle. *assail:* greet (also nautical).
5. Take her on (with sexual implication).
6. If you let her go without protest or without bidding
her farewell.
7. The customary retort to "Do you think I am a fool?"
8. Ledge on the half door to a buttery or a wine cellar
on which drinks were served.
9. Thirsty; but also thought to be a sign of impotence.
1. Alluding to the proverb "Even fools have enough wit
to come in out of the rain."
2. A stupid joke (referring to Andrew's stupidity); an
ironic quip; a joke about dryness.

3. Always ready; or "by th' hand" (line 56).
4. A sweet wine, like sherry, originally from the Canary
Islands.
5. Defeated in repartee; "put down" with drink.
6. Contemporary medicine held that beef dulled the
intellect.
7. Foreign languages; Toby takes him to mean "curling
tongs."
8. To contrast with Andrew's "arts" (line 80).
9. In spinning, flax would hang in long, thin, yellowish
strings on the "distaff," a pole held between the knees.
1. Housewives spun flax; the pronunciation, "huswife,"
also suggests the meaning "prostitute."
2. Make him bald (as a result of venereal disease).

SIR ANDREW   Faith, I'll home tomorrow, Sir Toby. Your niece
will not be seen, or if she be, it's four to one she'll none of me.
The Count himself here hard by woos her.

90 SIR TOBY   She'll none o'th' Count. She'll not match above her
degree,° neither in estate,[3] years, nor wit, I have heard her   *social rank*
swear't. Tut, there's life in't,[4] man.

SIR ANDREW   I'll stay a month longer. I am a fellow o'th' strangest
mind i'th' world. I delight in masques and revels sometimes
95 altogether.

SIR TOBY   Art thou good at these kickshawses,[5] knight?

SIR ANDREW   As any man in Illyria, whatsoever he be, under the
degree of my betters; and yet I will not compare with an old
man.[6]

100 SIR TOBY   What is thy excellence in a galliard,[7] knight?

SIR ANDREW   Faith, I can cut a caper.[8]

SIR TOBY   And I can cut the mutton to't.

SIR ANDREW   And I think I have the back-trick[9] simply as strong
as any man in Illyria.

105 SIR TOBY   Wherefore are these things hid? Wherefore have these
gifts a curtain[1] before 'em? Are they like to take dust, like Mis-
tress Mall's[2] picture? Why dost thou not go to church in a gal-
liard, and come home in a coranto?[3] My very walk should be a
jig. I would not so much as make water but in a cinquepace.[4]
110 What dost thou mean? Is it a world to hide virtues in? I did
think by the excellent constitution of thy leg it was formed
under the star of a galliard.[5]

SIR ANDREW   Ay, 'tis strong, and it does indifferent° well in a   *moderately*
divers-coloured stock.° Shall we set about some revels?   *stocking*

115 SIR TOBY   What shall we do else—were we not born under
Taurus?[6]

SIR ANDREW   Taurus? That's sides and heart.

SIR TOBY   No, sir, it is legs and thighs: let me see thee caper.
[SIR ANDREW *capers*]
Ha, higher! Ha ha, excellent.   *Exeunt*

1.4

Enter VALENTINE, *and* VIOLA [*as Cesario*] *in man's attire*

VALENTINE   If the Duke continue these favours towards you,
Cesario, you are like to be much advanced. He hath known
you but three days, and already you are no stranger.

VIOLA   You either fear his humour° or my negligence, that you   *moodiness*
5 call in question the continuance of his love. Is he inconstant,
sir, in his favours?

VALENTINE   No, believe me.
Enter DUKE, CURIO, *and attendants*

---

3. Status; possession.
4. Proverbial: "While there's life, there's hope."
5. Trifles; trivialities (from the French *quelque chose*).
6. Expert (perhaps a backhanded compliment).
7. A lively, complex dance, including the caper.
8. Leap. (Toby puns on the pickled flower buds used in
a sauce of mutton.)
9. Probably a dance movement, a kick of the foot behind
the body (also suggesting sexual prowess, with later ref-
erence to "mutton" as "prostitute").

1. Used to protect paintings from dust.
2. Like "Moll[y]," "Mall" was a nickname for "Mary."
3. An even more rapid dance than the galliard.
4. Galliard, or, more properly, the steps joining the fig-
ures of the dance; punning on "sink," as in "sewer."
5. Astrological influences favorable to dancing.
6. The astrological sign of the bull was usually thought
to govern the neck and throat (appropriate to heavy
drinkers).
1.4 Location: Orsino's palace.

VIOLA   I thank you. Here comes the Count.

ORSINO   Who saw Cesario, ho?

10 VIOLA   On your attendance,° my lord, here. *Waiting at your service*

ORSINO [*to* CURIO *and attendants*]   Stand you a while aloof.° [*To* *aside*
   VIOLA] Cesario,
Thou know'st no less but all.° I have unclasped *than everything*
To thee the book even of my secret soul.
Therefore, good youth, address thy gait° unto her, *go*
15 Be not denied access, stand at her doors,
And tell them there thy fixèd foot shall grow° *take root*
Till thou have audience.

VIOLA   Sure, my noble lord,
If she be so abandoned to her sorrow
As it is spoke, she never will admit me.

20 ORSINO   Be clamorous, and leap all civil bounds,[1]
Rather than make unprofited° return. *unsuccessful*

VIOLA   Say I do speak with her, my lord, what then?

ORSINO   O then unfold the passion of my love,
Surprise[2] her with discourse of my dear° faith. *heartfelt*
25 It shall become thee well to act my woes—
She will attend it better in thy youth
Than in a nuncio's° of more grave aspect.° *messenger's / appearance*

VIOLA   I think not so, my lord.

ORSINO   Dear lad, believe it;
For they shall yet belie thy happy years
30 That say thou art a man. Diana's lip
Is not more smooth and rubious;° thy small pipe° *ruby red / voice*
Is as the maiden's organ, shrill and sound,[3]
And all is semblative° a woman's part. *like*
I know thy constellation[4] is right apt
35 For this affair. [*To* CURIO *and attendants*] Some four or five attend him.
All if you will, for I myself am best
When least in company. [*To* VIOLA] Prosper well in this
And thou shalt live as freely as thy lord,
To call his fortunes thine.

VIOLA   I'll do my best
40 To woo your lady—[*aside*] yet a barful strife[5]—
Whoe'er I woo, myself would be his wife. *Exeunt*

1.5

Enter MARIA, *and* [FESTE,[1] *the*] *clown*

MARIA   Nay, either tell me where thou hast been or I will not
open my lips so wide as a bristle may enter in° way of thy *by*
excuse. My lady will hang thee for thy absence.

FESTE   Let her hang me. He that is well hanged in this world
5 needs to fear no colours.[2]

MARIA   Make that good.° *Explain that*

FESTE   He shall see none to fear.

---

1. All constraints of polite behavior.
2. Capture by unexpected attack (of military origin).
3. High-pitched and uncracked.
4. Nature and abilities (as supposedly determined by the stars).

5. An undertaking full of impediments.
1.5 Location: Olivia's house.
1. The name is used only once, at 2.4.11.
2. Proverbial for "fear nothing." *colours:* worldly deceptions, with a pun on "collars" as "hangman's noose."

MARIA   A good lenten[3] answer. I can tell thee where that saying
was born, of 'I fear no colours'.

10 FESTE   Where, good Mistress Mary?

MARIA   In the wars,[4] and that may you be bold to say in your
foolery.

FESTE   Well, God give them wisdom that have it; and those that
are fools, let them use their talents.[5]

15 MARIA   Yet you will be hanged for being so long absent, or to be
turned away[6]—is not that as good as a hanging to you?

FESTE   Many a good hanging prevents a bad marriage;[7] and for
turning away, let summer bear it out.°   *make it endurable*

MARIA   You are resolute then?

20 FESTE   Not so neither, but I am resolved on two points.°   *matters; laces*

MARIA   That if one break, the other will hold; or if both break,
your gaskins° fall.   *wide breeches*

FESTE   Apt, in good faith, very apt. Well, go thy way. If Sir Toby
would leave drinking thou wert as witty a piece of Eve's flesh[8]

25 as any in Illyria.

MARIA   Peace, you rogue, no more o' that. Here comes my lady.
Make your excuse wisely, you were best.°   [*Exit*]   *you had better*

Enter Lady OLIVIA, *with* MALVOLIO° [*and attendants*]   *"ill will"*

FESTE [*aside*]   Wit,[9] an't° be thy will, put me into good fooling!   *if it*
Those wits that think they have thee do very oft prove fools,

30 and I that am sure I lack thee may pass for a wise man. For
what says Quinapalus?[1]—'Better a witty fool than a foolish wit.'
[*To* OLIVIA] God bless thee, lady.

OLIVIA [*to attendants*]   Take the fool away.

FESTE   Do you not hear, fellows? Take away the lady.

35 OLIVIA   Go to, you're a dry[2] fool. I'll no more of you. Besides,
you grow dishonest.°   *unreliable*

FESTE   Two faults, madonna,° that drink and good counsel will   *my lady*
amend, for give the dry fool drink, then is the fool not dry; bid
the dishonest man mend° himself : if he mend, he is no longer   *reform*

40 dishonest; if he cannot, let the botcher° mend him. Anything   *tailor; cobbler*
that's mended is but patched. Virtue that transgresses is but
patched with sin, and sin that amends is but patched with vir-
tue. If that this simple syllogism will serve, so. If it will not, what
remedy? As there is no true cuckold but calamity, so beauty's a

45 flower.[3] The lady bade take away the fool, therefore I say again,
take her away.

OLIVIA   Sir, I bade them take away you.

FESTE   Misprision[4] in the highest degree! Lady, '*Cucullus non
facit monachum*'[5]—that's as much to say as I wear not motley[6]

50 in my brain. Good madonna, give me leave to prove you a fool.

---

3. Thin or meager (like Lenten fare).
4. *In the wars:* "colours" in line 9 refers to military flags.
5. Alluding to the parable of the talents, Matthew 25.
The comic implication is that a fool should strive to
increase his measure of folly. Since "fool" and "fowl" had
similar pronunciations, there may also be a play on
"talents/talons."
6. Dismissed; also, perhaps, turned off or hanged.
7. *Many . . . marriage:* Proverbial. *hanging:* execution;
sexual prowess.
8. Woman. Feste may imply both that Maria and Toby
would make a good match and that Maria is as witty as

Toby is sober.
9. Intelligence, which is often contrasted with will.
1. Feste frequently invents his own authorities.
2. Dull, but Feste interprets as "thirsty." *Go to:* an
expression of impatience.
3. *As . . . flower:* In taking her vow (1.2.36–37), Olivia
has wedded herself to calamity but must be unfaithful,
or let pass her moment of beauty.
4. Misapprehension; wrongful arrest.
5. The cowl does not make the monk (a Latin proverb).
6. The multicolored costume of a fool.

OLIVIA Can you do it?

FESTE Dexterously,° good madonna.   *Dexterously*

OLIVIA Make your proof.

FESTE I must catechize[7] you for it, madonna. Good my mouse

55 of virtue,° answer me.   *My good virtuous mouse*

OLIVIA Well, sir, for want of other idleness° I'll bide° your proof.   *pastime / await*

FESTE Good madonna, why mournest thou?

OLIVIA Good fool, for my brother's death.

FESTE I think his soul is in hell, madonna.

60 OLIVIA I know his soul is in heaven, fool.

FESTE The more fool, madonna, to mourn for your brother's
soul, being in heaven. Take away the fool, gentlemen.

OLIVIA What think you of this fool, Malvolio? Doth he not
mend?[8]

65 MALVOLIO Yes, and shall do till the pangs of death shake him.
Infirmity,° that decays the wise, doth ever make the better fool.[9]   *(Old) age*

FESTE God send you, sir, a speedy infirmity for the better
increasing your folly. Sir Toby will be sworn that I am no fox,
but he will not pass his word for twopence that you are no fool.

70 OLIVIA How say you to that, Malvolio?

MALVOLIO I marvel your ladyship takes delight in such a barren
rascal. I saw him put down° the other day with an ordinary fool   *defeated in repartee*
that has no more brain than a stone. Look you now, he's out of
his guard° already. Unless you laugh and minister occasion[1] to   *defenseless*

75 him, he is gagged. I protest I take these wise men that crow so
at these set° kind of fools no better than the fools' zanies.°   *artificial / "straight men"*

OLIVIA O, you are sick of self-love, Malvolio, and taste with a
distempered[2] appetite. To be generous, guiltless, and of free°   *magnanimous*
disposition is to take those things for birdbolts[3] that you deem

80 cannon bullets. There is no slander in an allowed fool, though
he do nothing but rail; nor no railing in a known discreet man,
though he do nothing but reprove.

FESTE Now Mercury indue thee with leasing,[4] for thou speakest
well of fools.

Enter MARIA

85 MARIA Madam, there is at the gate a young gentleman much
desires to speak with you.

OLIVIA From the Count Orsino, is it?

MARIA I know not, madam. 'Tis a fair young man, and well
attended.

90 OLIVIA Who of my people hold him in delay?

MARIA Sir Toby, madam, your kinsman.

OLIVIA Fetch him off, I pray you, he speaks nothing but mad-
man.° Fie on him. Go you, Malvolio. If it be a suit from the   *madman's talk*
Count, I am sick, or not at home—what you will to dismiss it.

Exit MALVOLIO

95 Now you see, sir, how your fooling grows old,° and people dis-   *stale*
like it.

FESTE Thou hast spoke for us, madonna, as if thy eldest son

---

7. Question (as in catechism, which tests the ortho-
doxy of belief).
8. Improve, but Malvolio takes "mend" to mean "grow
more foolish."
9. Make the fool more foolish.

1. And give opportunity.
2. An unbalanced; a sick.
3. Blunt arrows for shooting birds.
4. May Mercury, the god of deception, endow you with
the talent of tactful lying.

should be a fool, whose skull Jove cram with brains, for—here
he comes—

Enter SIR TOBY

100   one of thy kin has a most weak *pia mater.*[5]

OLIVIA   By mine honour, half-drunk. What is he at the gate,
cousin?°   *kinsman*

SIR TOBY   A gentleman.

OLIVIA   A gentleman? What gentleman?

105   SIR TOBY   'Tis a gentleman here. [*He belches*] A plague o' these
pickle herring! [*To* FESTE] How now, sot?°   *fool; drunkard*

FESTE   Good Sir Toby.

OLIVIA   Cousin, cousin, how have you come so early by this
lethargy?

110   SIR TOBY   Lechery? I defy lechery. There's one° at the gate.   *someone*

OLIVIA   Ay, marry, what is he?

SIR TOBY   Let him be the devil an° he will, I care not. Give me   *if*
faith,[6] say I. Well, it's all one.°   *Exit*   *it doesn't matter*

OLIVIA   What's a drunken man like, fool?

115   FESTE   Like a drowned man, a fool, and a madman—one
draught above heat[7] makes him a fool, the second mads him,
and a third drowns him.

OLIVIA   Go thou and seek the coroner, and let him sit o'° my   *hold an inquest for*
coz,° for he's in the third degree of drink, he's drowned. Go   *cousin; uncle*
120   look after him.

FESTE   He is but mad yet, madonna, and the fool shall look to
the madman.   [*Exit*]

Enter MALVOLIO

MALVOLIO   Madam, yon young fellow swears he will speak with
you. I told him you were sick—he takes on him to understand
125   so much, and therefore° comes to speak with you. I told him   *for that very reason*
you were asleep—he seems to have a foreknowledge of that
too, and therefore comes to speak with you. What is to be said
to him, lady? He's fortified against any denial.

OLIVIA   Tell him he shall not speak with me.

130   MALVOLIO   He's been told so, and he says he'll stand at your door
like a sheriff's post,[8] and be the supporter to a bench, but he'll
speak with you.

OLIVIA   What kind o' man is he?

MALVOLIO   Why, of mankind.°   *like any other*

135   OLIVIA   What manner of man?

MALVOLIO   Of very ill manner: he'll speak with you, will you or
no.

OLIVIA   Of what personage° and years is he?   *appearance*

MALVOLIO   Not yet old enough for a man, nor young enough for
140   a boy; as a squash[9] is before 'tis a peascod, or a codling° when   *an unripe apple*
'tis almost an apple. 'Tis with him in standing water° between   *at the turn of the tide*
boy and man. He is very well-favoured,° and he speaks very   *handsome*
shrewishly.° One would think his mother's milk were scarce   *sharply*
out of him.

145   OLIVIA   Let him approach. Call in my gentlewoman.

MALVOLIO   Gentlewoman, my lady calls.   *Exit*

---

5. Brain; or literally, the membrane enclosing it.
6. To defy the devil by faith alone.
7. One drink ("draught")/beyond the quantity necessary
to warm him.

8. A decorative post set before a sheriff's door, as a sign
of authority.
9. An undeveloped pea pod.

Enter MARIA

OLIVIA Give me my veil. Come, throw it o'er my face.
We'll once more hear Orsino's embassy.

Enter VIOLA [*as Cesario*]

VIOLA The honourable lady of the house, which is she?

150 OLIVIA Speak to me, I shall answer for her. Your will.

VIOLA Most radiant, exquisite, and unmatchable beauty.—I pray
you, tell me if this be the lady of the house, for I never saw
her. I would be loath to cast away° my speech, for besides that   *waste*
it is excellently well penned, I have taken great pains to
155 con° it. Good beauties, let me sustain° no scorn; I am very   *memorize / suffer*
'countable,° even to the least sinister usage.[1]   *sensitive*

OLIVIA Whence came you, sir?

VIOLA I can say little more than I have studied,[2] and that ques-
tion's out of my part. Good gentle one, give me modest° assur-   *adequate*
160 ance if you be the lady of the house, that I may proceed in my
speech.

OLIVIA Are you a comedian?°   *an actor*

VIOLA No, my profound heart;[3] and yet—by the very fangs of
malice I swear—I am not that I play. Are you the lady of the
165 house?

OLIVIA If I do not usurp[4] myself, I am.

VIOLA Most certain if you are she you do usurp yourself, for what
is yours to bestow is not yours to reserve. But this is from my
commission.° I will on with my speech in your praise, and then   *beyond my instructions*
170 show you the heart of my message.

OLIVIA Come to what is important in't, I forgive you° the praise.   *excuse you from*

VIOLA Alas, I took great pains to study it, and 'tis poetical.

OLIVIA It is the more like to be feigned, I pray you keep it in. I
heard you were saucy° at my gates, and allowed your approach   *impertinent*
175 rather to wonder at you than to hear you. If you be not mad,°   *utterly mad*
be gone. If you have reason,° be brief. 'Tis not that time of   *any sanity*
moon with me to make one in so skipping a dialogue.[5]

MARIA Will you hoist sail, sir? Here lies your way.

VIOLA No, good swabber, I am to hull[6] here a little longer.
180 [*To* OLIVIA] Some mollification for your giant,[7] sweet lady. Tell
me your mind, I am a messenger.[8]

OLIVIA Sure, you have some hideous matter to deliver when the
courtesy° of it is so fearful. Speak your office.°   *introduction / business*

VIOLA It alone concerns your ear. I bring no overture° of war,   *declaration*
185 no taxation of homage.[9] I hold the olive[1] in my hand. My words
are as full of peace as matter.°   *meaning*

OLIVIA Yet you began rudely. What are you? What would you?

VIOLA The rudeness that hath appeared in me have I learned
from my entertainment.° What I am and what I would are as   *reception*
190 secret as maidenhead;° to your ears, divinity; to any others',   *virginity*
profanation.

1. To the slightest discourteous treatment.
2. Learned by heart (a theatrical term).
3. My most wise lady; upon my soul.
4. Counterfeit; misappropriate.
5. *'Tis . . . dialogue:* I am not lunatic enough to take part in so flighty a conversation. (Lunacy was thought to be influenced by the phases of the moon.)
6. To lie unanchored with lowered sails. *swabber:* a cleaner of boat decks.
7. Mythical giants guarded ladies; here, also mocking Maria's diminutive size. *Some . . . for:* Please pacify.
8. From Orsino; Olivia pretends she understands her to mean a king's messenger, or a messenger-at-arms, employed on important state affairs.
9. Demand for dues paid to a superior.
1. Olive branch (as a symbol of peace).

OLIVIA [*to* MARIA *and attendants*]   Give us the place alone, we
will hear this divinity.°   [*Exeunt* MARIA *and attendants*]   *religious discourse*
Now sir, what is your text?[2]

195 VIOLA   Most sweet lady—

OLIVIA   A comfortable° doctrine, and much may be said of it.   *comforting*
Where lies your text?

VIOLA   In Orsino's bosom.

OLIVIA   In his bosom? In what chapter of his bosom?

200 VIOLA   To answer by the method,° in the first of his heart.   *in the same style*

OLIVIA   O, I have read it. It is heresy. Have you no more to say?

VIOLA   Good madam, let me see your face.

OLIVIA   Have you any commission from your lord to negotiate
with my face? You are now out of° your text. But we will draw   *straying from*

205 the curtain and show you the picture.
[*She unveils*]
Look you, sir, such a one I was this present.[3] Is't not well done?

VIOLA   Excellently done, if God did all.[4]

OLIVIA   'Tis in grain,° sir, 'twill endure wind and weather.   *The dye is fast*

VIOLA   'Tis beauty truly blent,[5] whose red and white

210 Nature's own sweet and cunning° hand laid on.   *skillful*
Lady, you are the cruell'st she° alive   *woman*
If you will lead these graces to the grave
And leave the world no copy.[6]

OLIVIA   O sir, I will not be so hard-hearted. I will give out divers

215 schedules° of my beauty. It shall be inventoried and every parti-   *various inventories*
cle and utensil labelled[7] to my will, as, *item*, two lips, indiffer-
ent° red; *item*, two grey eyes, with lids[8] to them; *item*, one neck,   *moderate*
one chin, and so forth. Were you sent hither to praise° me?   *appraise; flatter*

VIOLA   I see you what you are, you are too proud,

220 But if° you were the devil, you are fair.   *Even if*
My lord and master loves you. O, such love
Could be but recompensed though[9] you were crowned
The nonpareil of beauty.°   *An unequaled beauty*

OLIVIA   How does he love me?

VIOLA   With adorations, fertile° tears,   *ever-flowing*

225 With groans that thunder love, with sighs of fire.

OLIVIA   Your lord does know my mind, I cannot love him.
Yet I suppose him virtuous, know him noble,
Of great estate, of fresh and stainless youth,
In voices well divulged,° free,° learned, and valiant,   *spoken of / generous*

230 And in dimension and the shape of nature[1]
A gracious person; but yet I cannot love him.
He might have took his answer long ago.

VIOLA   If I did love you in° my master's flame,°   *with / passion*
With such a suff'ring, such a deadly° life,   *deathlike*

235 In your denial I would find no sense,
I would not understand it.

---

2. Quotation (as a theme of a sermon, in keeping with "divinity," "doctrine," "heresy," etc.).
3. Portraits usually gave the year of painting. "This present" was a term used to date letters.
4. If it is natural (without the use of cosmetics).
5. Blended, or mixed (of paints). Shakespeare uses the same metaphor in sonnet 20, lines 1–2, and Viola's next lines recall sonnet 11, lines 13–14. As Cesario, Viola is playing with established conventions of poetic courtship.

6. Viola means "child"; Olivia takes her to mean "list" or "inventory."
7. Every single part and article added as a codicil (parodying the legal language of a last will and testament).
8. Eyelids, but also punning on "pot lids" (punning on "utensil" as a household implement).
9. *Could . . . though*: Would have to be requited even if.
1. *dimension . . . shape of nature*: the two terms are synonymous, meaning "bodily form."

OLIVIA   Why, what would you?

VIOLA   Make me a willow² cabin at your gate

And call upon my soul° within the house,   *(Olivia)*

Write loyal cantons of contemnèd° love,   *songs of rejected*

240   And sing them loud even in the dead of night;

Halloo³ your name to the reverberate° hills,   *echoing*

And make the babbling gossip of the air⁴

Cry out 'Olivia!' O, you should not rest

Between the elements of air and earth

245   But you should pity me.

OLIVIA   You might do much.

What is your parentage?

VIOLA   Above my fortunes, yet my state° is well.   *social status*

I am a gentleman.

OLIVIA   Get you to your lord.

250   I cannot love him. Let him send no more,

Unless, perchance, you come to me again

To tell me how he takes it. Fare you well.

I thank you for your pains. [*Offering a purse*] Spend this for me.

VIOLA   I am no fee'd post,° lady. Keep your purse.   *hired messenger*

255   My master, not myself, lacks recompense.

Love make his heart of flint that you shall love,⁵

And let your fervour, like my master's, be

Placed in contempt. Farewell, fair cruelty.   *Exit*

OLIVIA   'What is your parentage?'

260   'Above my fortunes, yet my state is well.

I am a gentleman.' I'll be sworn thou art.

Thy tongue, thy face, thy limbs, actions, and spirit

Do give thee five-fold blazon.⁶ Not too fast. Soft,° soft—   *Wait*

Unless the master were the man.⁷ How now?

265   Even so quickly may one catch the plague?

Methinks I feel this youth's perfections

With an invisible and subtle stealth

To creep in at mine eyes. Well, let it be.

What ho, Malvolio.

        Enter MALVOLIO

MALVOLIO   Here, madam, at your service.

270   OLIVIA   Run after that same peevish messenger

The County's° man. He left this ring behind him,   *Count's*

Would I° or not. Tell him I'll none of it.   *Whether I wished it*

Desire him not to flatter with° his lord,   *encourage*

Nor hold him up with hopes. I am not for him.

275   If that the youth will come this way tomorrow,

I'll give him reasons for't. Hie thee,° Malvolio.   *Hurry*

MALVOLIO   Madam, I will.   *Exit* [*at one door*]

OLIVIA   I do I know not what, and fear to find

Mine eye too great a flatterer for my mind.⁸

---

2. Traditional symbol of rejected love.
3. Shout; or perhaps "hallow," as in "bless."
4. For the love of Narcissus, the nymph Echo wasted away to a mere voice, only able to repeat whatever she heard spoken.
5. *Love . . . love:* May love make the heart of the man you

love as hard as flint.
6. Formal description of a gentleman's coat of arms.
7. If Orsino were Cesario (*man:* servant).
8. My eye (through which love has entered my heart) has seduced my reason.

280 Fate, show thy force. Ourselves we do not owe.° _own_
What is decreed must be; and be this so.

[_Exit at another door_]

2.1

Enter ANTONIO _and_ SEBASTIAN

ANTONIO Will you stay no longer, nor will° you not that I go _wish_
with you?

SEBASTIAN By your patience, no. My stars shine darkly over me.
The malignancy of my fate[1] might perhaps distemper° yours, _infect_
5 therefore I shall crave of you your leave that I may bear my
evils alone. It were a bad recompense for your love to lay any
of them on you.

ANTONIO Let me yet know of you whither you are bound.

SEBASTIAN No, sooth,° sir. My determinate° voyage is mere _truly / destined_
10 extravagancy.° But I perceive in you so excellent a touch of _idle wandering_
modesty° that you will not extort from me what I am willing to _politeness_
keep in. Therefore it charges me in manners[2] the rather to
express° myself. You must know of me then, Antonio, my name _reveal_
is Sebastian, which I called Roderigo. My father was that Sebas-
15 tian of Messaline[3] whom I know you have heard of. He left
behind him myself and a sister, both born in an° hour. If the _within the same_
heavens had been pleased, would we had so ended. But you,
sir, altered that, for some hour before you took me from the
breach° of the sea was my sister drowned. _surf_

20 ANTONIO Alas the day!

SEBASTIAN A lady, sir, though it was said she much resembled
me, was yet of many accounted beautiful. But though I could
not with such estimable° wonder over-far believe that, yet _appreciative_
thus far I will boldly publish° her: she bore a mind that _proclaim_
25 envy° could not but call fair. She is drowned already, sir, with _malice_
salt water, though I seem to drown her remembrance again
with more.

ANTONIO Pardon me, sir, your bad entertainment.[4]

SEBASTIAN O good Antonio, forgive me your trouble.

30 ANTONIO If you will not murder me[5] for my love, let me be your
servant.

SEBASTIAN If you will not undo what you have done—that is,
kill him whom you have recovered°—desire it not. Fare ye well _rescued_
at once. My bosom is full of kindness,° and I am yet° so near _tender emotion / still_
35 the manners of my mother[6] that upon the least occasion more
mine eyes will tell tales of me.° I am bound to the Count _betray my feelings_
Orsino's court. Farewell.   _Exit_

ANTONIO The gentleness° of all the gods go with thee! _favor_
I have many enemies in Orsino's court,
40 Else would I very shortly see thee there.
But come what may, I do adore thee so
That danger shall seem sport, and I will go.   _Exit_

2.1 Location: Near the coast of Illyria.
1. Evil influence of the stars; "malignancy" also signifies
a deadly disease.
2. Therefore courtesy requires.

3. Possibly Messina, Sicily.
4. Your poor reception; your inhospitality.
5. Murder him by insisting that they part.
6. So near woman's readiness to weep.

2.2

Enter VIOLA *as Cesario, and* MALVOLIO, *at several° doors*   separate

MALVOLIO   Were not you ev'n° now with the Countess Olivia?   just

VIOLA   Even now, sir, on° a moderate pace, I have since arrived   at
  but hither.°   come only this far

MALVOLIO [*offering a ring*]   She returns this ring to you, sir.

5   You might have saved me my pains to have taken° it away your-   by taking
  self. She adds, moreover, that you should put your lord into a
  desperate assurance° she will none of him. And one thing   hopeless certainty
  more: that you be never so hardy° to come again in his affairs,   bold
  unless it be to report your lord's taking of this.[1] Receive it so.

10   VIOLA   She took the ring of me.[2] I'll none of it.

MALVOLIO   Come, sir, you peevishly threw it to her, and her will
  is it should be so returned.
    [*He throws the ring down*]
  If it be worth stooping for, there it lies, in your eye;° if not, be   sight
  it his that finds it.   *Exit*

15   VIOLA [*picking up the ring*]   I left no ring with her. What means this lady?
  Fortune forbid my outside° have not charmed her.   appearance
  She made good view of° me, indeed so much   looked carefully at
  That straight methought her eyes had lost° her tongue,   made her lose
  For she did speak in starts, distractedly.

20   She loves me, sure. The cunning of her passion
  Invites me in° this churlish messenger.   by means of
  None of my lord's ring! Why, he sent her none.
  I am the man.[3] If it be so—as 'tis—
  Poor lady, she were better love a dream!

25   Disguise, I see thou art a wickedness
  Wherein the pregnant enemy[4] does much.
  How easy is it for the proper false[5]
  In women's waxen hearts to set their forms![6]
  Alas, our frailty is the cause, not we,

30   For such as we are made of, such we be.[7]
  How will this fadge?° My master loves her dearly,   turn out
  And I, poor monster,[8] fond° as much on him,   dote
  And she, mistaken, seems to dote on me.
  What will become of this? As I am man,

35   My state is desperate° for my master's love.   hopeless
  As I am woman, now, alas the day,
  What thriftless° sighs shall poor Olivia breathe!   unprofitable
  O time, thou must untangle this, not I.
  It is too hard a knot for me t'untie.   [*Exit*]

2.3

Enter SIR TOBY *and* SIR ANDREW

SIR TOBY   Approach, Sir Andrew. Not to be abed after midnight
  is to be up betimes,° and *diliculo surgere*,[1] thou knowest.   early

---

2.2 Location: Between Olivia's house and Orsino's
palace.
1. Reception of this rejection.
2. Viola pretends to believe Olivia's story. *of:* from.
3. The man with whom she has fallen in love.
4. The devil, who is always quick and ready (to deceive).
5. Handsome, but deceitful (men).

6. *In . . . forms:* To impress their images on women's
affections (as a seal stamps its image in wax).
7. For being made of frail flesh, we are frail.
8. Since she is both man and woman.
2.3 Location: Olivia's house.
1. Part of a Latin proverb, meaning "to rise at dawn (is
most healthy)."

SIR ANDREW   Nay, by my troth,° I know not; but I know to be up
late is to be up late.   *faith*

5   SIR TOBY   A false conclusion. I hate it as an unfilled can.° To be   *tankard*
up after midnight and to go to bed then is early; so that to go
to bed after midnight is to go to bed betimes. Does not our lives
consist of the four elements?²

SIR ANDREW   Faith, so they say, but I think it rather consists of
10 eating and drinking.

SIR TOBY   Thou'rt a scholar; let us therefore eat and drink. Mar-
ian, I say, a stoup° of wine.   *two-pint tankard*

Enter [FESTE, the] clown

SIR ANDREW   Here comes the fool, i'faith.

FESTE   How now, my hearts. Did you never see the picture of
15 'we three'?³

SIR TOBY   Welcome, ass. Now let's have a catch.⁴

SIR ANDREW   By my troth, the fool has an excellent breast.° I had   *singing voice*
rather than forty shillings I had such a leg,° and so sweet a   *(for dancing)*
breath to sing, as the fool has. In sooth, thou wast in very gra-
20 cious fooling last night, when thou spokest of Pigrogromitus, of
the Vapians passing the equinoctial of Queubus.⁵ 'Twas very
good, i'faith. I sent thee sixpence for thy leman.° Hadst it?   *sweetheart*

FESTE   I did impeticos thy gratility;⁶ for Malvolio's nose is no
whipstock. My lady has a white hand, and the Myrmidons are
25 no bottle-ale houses.⁷

SIR ANDREW   Excellent! Why, this is the best fooling, when all is
done. Now a song.

SIR TOBY   *[to FESTE]*   Come on, there is sixpence for you. Let's
have a song.

30 SIR ANDREW   *[to FESTE]*   There's a testril⁸ of me, too. If one knight
give a—⁹

FESTE   Would you have a love-song, or a song of good life?

SIR TOBY   A love song, a love-song.

SIR ANDREW   Ay, ay. I care not for good life.

FESTE   *(sings)*

35   O mistress mine, where are you roaming?
            O stay and hear, your true love's coming,
                That can sing both high and low.
            Trip° no further, pretty sweeting.   *Go*
            Journeys end in lovers meeting,
40   Every wise man's son doth know.¹

SIR ANDREW   Excellent good, i'faith.

SIR TOBY   Good, good.

FESTE   What is love? 'Tis not hereafter,
            Present mirth hath present laughter.
45   What's to come is still° unsure.   *always*
            In delay there lies no plenty,

2. The four elements, thought to make up all matter, were earth, air, fire, and water.
3. A trick picture portraying two fools' or asses' heads, the third being the viewer.
4. Round: a simple song for several voices.
5. *Pigrogromitus . . . Queubus:* Feste's mock learning. *equinoctial:* equator of the astronomical heavens.
6. Comic jargon for "impocket (or impetticoat) your gratuity."
7. *for . . . houses:* perhaps it is the sheer inscrutability of Feste's foolery that so impresses Sir Andrew (line 26).

whipstock: handle of a whip. *bottle-ale houses:* cheap taverns.
8. Sir Andrew's version of "tester" (sixpence).
9. In F, "give a" appears at the end of a justified line; an omission is possible.
1. *O mistress . . . know:* the words are not certainly Shakespeare's; they fit the tune of an instrumental piece printed in Thomas Morley's *First Book of Consort Lessons* (1599). *wise man's son:* wise men were thought to have foolish sons.

Then come kiss me, sweet and twenty.° *twenty times sweet*
Youth's a stuff will not endure.

SIR ANDREW A mellifluous voice, as I am true knight.

50 SIR TOBY A contagious breath.[2]

SIR ANDREW Very sweet and contagious, i'faith.

SIR TOBY To hear by the nose, it is dulcet in contagion.[3] But
shall we make the welkin° dance indeed? Shall we rouse the *sky*
night-owl in a catch that will draw three souls out of one
55 weaver?[4] Shall we do that?

SIR ANDREW An° you love me, let's do't. I am dog° at a catch. *If / clever*

FESTE By'r Lady, sir, and some dogs will catch well.

SIR ANDREW Most certain. Let our catch be 'Thou knave'.

FESTE 'Hold thy peace, thou knave',[5] knight. I shall be con-
60 strained in't to call thee knave, knight.

SIR ANDREW 'Tis not the first time I have constrained one to call
me knave. Begin, fool. It begins 'Hold thy peace'.

FESTE I shall never begin if I hold my peace.

SIR ANDREW Good, i'faith. Come, begin.

[They sing the] catch.
Enter MARIA

65 MARIA What a caterwauling do you keep here! If my lady have
not called up her steward Malvolio and bid him turn you out
of doors, never trust me.

SIR TOBY My lady's a Cathayan,[6] we are politicians,° Malvolio's *schemers*
a Peg-o'-Ramsey,[7] and 'Three merry men be we'. Am not I con-
70 sanguineous?[8] Am I not of her blood? Tilly-vally°—'lady'! *Fiddlesticks*
'There dwelt a man in Babylon, lady, lady.'[9]

FESTE Beshrew° me, the knight's in admirable fooling. *Curse*

SIR ANDREW Ay, he does well enough if he be disposed, and so
do I, too. He does it with a better grace, but I do it more
75 natural.[1]

SIR TOBY 'O' the twelfth day of December'[2]—

MARIA For the love o' God, peace.

Enter MALVOLIO

MALVOLIO My masters, are you mad? Or what are you? Have
you no wit,° manners, nor honesty,° but to gabble like tinkers *sense / decency*
80 at this time of night? Do ye make an alehouse of my lady's
house, that ye squeak out your coziers' catches without any
mitigation or remorse[3] of voice? Is there no respect of place,
persons, nor time in you?

SIR TOBY We did keep time, sir, in our catches. Sneck up!° *Go hang yourself*

85 MALVOLIO Sir Toby, I must be round° with you. My lady bade *plainspoken*
me tell you that though she harbours you as her kinsman she's
nothing allied to your disorders. If you can separate yourself
and your misdemeanours you are welcome to the house. If not,

---

2. Catchy voice; with a play on "disease-causing air."
3. If one could hear through the nose, the sound would be sweetly ("dulcet") infectious.
4. Weavers were traditionally addicted to psalm singing, so to move them with popular catches would be a great triumph. Music was said to be able to draw the soul from the body.
5. The words of the catch are "Hold thy peace, I prithee hold thy peace, thou knave" (see Textual Note). Each singer repeatedly calls the others knaves and tells them to stop singing.
6. Chinese; but also ethnocentric slang for "trickster" or

"cheat."
7. Name of a dance and popular song; here, used contemptuously.
8. A blood relative of Olivia's. 'Three . . . we': a refrain from a popular song.
9. The opening and refrain of a popular song called "Constant Susanna."
1. Effortlessly; but unconsciously playing on "fool" or "idiot."
2. Snatch of a ballad; or possibly a drunken version of "twelfth day of Christmas"—that is, Twelfth Night.
3. Without any abating or softening.

an it would please you to take leave of her she is very willing to
90 bid you farewell.
SIR TOBY 'Farewell, dear heart, since I must needs be gone.'⁴
MARIA Nay, good Sir Toby.
FESTE 'His eyes do show his days are almost done.'
MALVOLIO Is't even so?
95 SIR TOBY 'But I will never die.'
FESTE 'Sir Toby, there you lie.'
MALVOLIO This is much credit to you.
SIR TOBY 'Shall I bid him go?'
FESTE 'What an if° you do?'   an if = if
100 SIR TOBY 'Shall I bid him go, and spare not?'
FESTE 'O no, no, no, no, you dare not.'
SIR TOBY Out o' tune, sir, ye lie. [To MALVOLIO] Art any more
than a steward? Dost thou think because thou art virtuous there
shall be no more cakes and ale?⁵
105 FESTE Yes, by Saint Anne, and ginger⁶ shall be hot i'th' mouth,
too.
SIR TOBY Thou'rt i'th' right. [To MALVOLIO] Go, sir, rub your
chain with crumbs.⁷ [To MARIA] A stoup of wine, Maria.
MALVOLIO Mistress Mary, if you prized my lady's favour at any-
110 thing more than contempt you would not give means° for this   drink
uncivil rule.° She shall know of it, by this hand.   Exit⁸   behavior
MARIA Go shake your ears.°   (like an ass)
SIR ANDREW 'Twere as good a deed as to drink when a man's a-
hungry to challenge him the field° and then to break promise   to a duel
115 with him, and make a fool of him.
SIR TOBY Do't, knight. I'll write thee a challenge, or I'll deliver
thy indignation to him by word of mouth.
MARIA Sweet Sir Toby, be patient for tonight. Since the youth
of the Count's was today with my lady she is much out of quiet.
120 For Monsieur Malvolio, let me alone with him. If I do not gull
him into a nayword⁹ and make him a common recreation,° do   sport; jest
not think I have wit enough to lie straight in my bed. I know I
can do it.
SIR TOBY Possess° us, possess us, tell us something of him.   Inform
125 MARIA Marry, sir, sometimes he is a kind of puritan.¹
SIR ANDREW O, if I thought that I'd beat him like a dog.
SIR TOBY What, for being a puritan? Thy exquisite° reason, dear   ingenious
knight.
SIR ANDREW I have no exquisite reason for't, but I have reason
130 good enough.
MARIA The dev'l a puritan that he is, or anything constantly but
a time-pleaser,° an affectioned° ass that cons state without book   boot licker / affected
and utters it by great swathes;² the best persuaded of himself,³
so crammed, as he thinks, with excellencies, that it is his

---

4. Part of another song that Sir Toby and Feste adapt for
the occasion.
5. *cakes and ale*: traditionally associated with church
festivals, and therefore disliked by Puritans.
6. Used to spice ale. *Saint Anne*: mother of the Virgin;
the oath would be offensive to Puritans who attacked her
cult.
7. Clean your steward's chain; mind your own business.
8. Feste plays no further part in this scene, and he seems
not to be present by line 153. This is the suggested exit

for him.
9. If I do not trick ("gull") him into a byword (for
"dupe").
1. Could mean "morally strict and censorious," as well as
"a follower of the Puritan religious faith."
2. *cons . . . swathes*: memorizes dignified and high-flown
language and utters it in great sweeps (like hay falling
under a scythe).
3. Having the highest opinion of himself.

135 grounds of faith° that all that look on him love him; and on   *his creed*
      that vice in him will my revenge find notable cause to work.
   SIR TOBY   What wilt thou do?
   MARIA   I will drop in his way some obscure epistles of love,
      wherein by the colour of his beard, the shape of his leg, the
140   manner of his gait, the expressure° of his eye, forehead, and   *expression*
      complexion, he shall find himself most feelingly personated.° I   *represented*
      can write very like my lady your niece; on a forgotten° matter   *bygone*
      we can hardly make distinction of our hands.°   *handwriting*
   SIR TOBY   Excellent, I smell a device.
145 SIR ANDREW   I have't in my nose too.
   SIR TOBY   He shall think by the letters that thou wilt drop that
      they come from my niece, and that she's in love with him.
   MARIA   My purpose is indeed a horse of that colour.
   SIR ANDREW   And your horse now would make him an ass.
150 MARIA   Ass° I doubt not.   *(punning on "as")*
   SIR ANDREW   O, 'twill be admirable.
   MARIA   Sport royal, I warrant you. I know my physic° will work   *medicine*
      with him. I will plant you two—and let the fool make a third—
      where he shall find the letter. Observe his construction° of it.   *interpretation*
155 For this night, to bed, and dream on the event.° Farewell.   *outcome*
                                              Exit
   SIR TOBY   Good night, Penthesilea.[4]
   SIR ANDREW   Before me,[5] she's a good wench.
   SIR TOBY   She's a beagle true bred, and one that adores me. What
      o' that?
160 SIR ANDREW   I was adored once, too.
   SIR TOBY   Let's to bed, knight. Thou hadst need send for more
      money.
   SIR ANDREW   If I cannot recover° your niece, I am a foul way   *win*
      out.°   *out of money*
165 SIR TOBY   Send for money, knight. If thou hast her not i'th' end,
      call me cut.[6]
   SIR ANDREW   If I do not, never trust me, take it how you will.
   SIR TOBY   Come, come, I'll go burn some sack,[7] 'tis too late to
      go to bed now. Come knight, come knight.   *Exeunt*

2.4

Enter Duke, VIOLA [*as Cesario*], CURIO, *and others*
   ORSINO   Give me some music. Now good morrow,° friends.   *morning*
      Now good Cesario, but° that piece of song,   *just*
      That old and antic° song we heard last night.   *quaint*
      Methought it did relieve my passion° much,   *suffering*
5   More than light airs and recollected° terms   *studied; artificial*
      Of these most brisk and giddy-pacèd times.
      Come, but one verse.
   CURIO   He is not here, so please your lordship, that should sing
      it.
10 ORSINO   Who was it?

---

4. Queen of the Amazons (a joke about Maria's small size).
5. On my soul (a mild oath).
6. A dock-tailed horse; also, slang for "gelding" or for "female genitals."
7. I'll go warm and spice some Spanish wine.
2.4 Location: Orsino's palace.

CURIO Feste the jester, my lord, a fool that the lady Olivia's
　　　father took much delight in. He is about the house.
ORSINO Seek him out, and play the tune the while.

　　　　　　　　　　　　　　　　　　　　　　　　[*Exit* CURIO]
　　　Music plays
　　　[*To* VIOLA] Come hither, boy. If ever thou shalt love,
15　　In the sweet pangs of it remember me;
　　　For such as I am, all true lovers are,
　　　Unstaid° and skittish in all motions° else　　　　　*Unstable / emotions*
　　　Save in the constant image of the creature
　　　That is beloved. How dost thou like this tune?
20　VIOLA It gives a very echo to the seat
　　　Where love is throned.[1]
ORSINO　　　　　　　　Thou dost speak masterly.°　　　*expertly*
　　　My life upon't, young though thou art thine eye
　　　Hath stayed upon some favour° that it loves.　　　*face*
　　　Hath it not, boy?
VIOLA　　　　　　　　A little, by your favour.°　　　*leave; face*
ORSINO What kind of woman is't?
25　VIOLA　　　　　　　　Of your complexion.
ORSINO She is not worth thee then. What years, i'faith?
VIOLA About your years, my lord.
ORSINO Too old, by heaven. Let still° the woman take　*always*
　　　An elder than herself. So wears° she to him;　　*adapts*
30　So sways she level[2] in her husband's heart.
　　　For, boy, however we do praise ourselves,
　　　Our fancies° are more giddy and unfirm,　　　　*affections*
　　　More longing, wavering, sooner lost and worn,°　*exhausted*
　　　Than women's are.
VIOLA　　　　　　　　I think° it well, my lord.　　　*believe*
35　ORSINO Then let thy love be younger than thyself,
　　　Or thy affection cannot hold the bent;[3]
　　　For women are as roses, whose fair flower
　　　Being once displayed,° doth fall that very hour.　*opened*
VIOLA And so they are. Alas that they are so:
40　To die even° when they to perfection grow.　　　*just*
　　　　　Enter CURIO *and* [FESTE, *the*] *clown*
ORSINO [*to* FESTE] O fellow, come, the song we had last night.
　　　Mark it, Cesario, it is old and plain.
　　　The spinsters,° and the knitters in the sun,　　*spinners*
　　　And the free° maids that weave their thread with bones,[4]　*carefree*
45　Do use to chant it. It is silly sooth,°　　　　　　*simple truth*
　　　And dallies with° the innocence of love,　　　　*lingers lovingly on*
　　　Like the old° age.　　　　　　　　　　　　　*golden*
FESTE Are you ready, sir?
ORSINO I prithee, sing.
　　　　　Music
50　FESTE [*sings*] Come away,° come away death,　　*Come hither*
　　　　　　　And in sad cypress[5] let me be laid.
　　　　　　　Fie away, fie away breath,
　　　　　　　I am slain by a fair cruel maid.

1. *It . . . throned:* It reflects back to the heart.
2. So does she balance influence and affection.
3. Cannot remain at full stretch (like the tautness of a
bowstring).
4. Spools made from bone on which lace (called "bone
lace") was woven.
5. Cypress-wood coffin. Like yews, cypresses were
emblematic of mourning.

My shroud of white, stuck all with yew,°   *yew sprigs*
55   O prepare it.
My part of death no one so true
     Did share it.[6]
Not a flower, not a flower sweet

     On my black coffin let there be strewn.
60   Not a friend, not a friend greet
        My poor corpse, where my bones shall be thrown.
A thousand thousand sighs to save,
     Lay me O where
Sad true lover never find my grave,
65   To weep there.

ORSINO [*giving money*]   There's for thy pains.

FESTE   No pains, sir. I take pleasure in singing, sir.

ORSINO   I'll pay thy pleasure then.

FESTE   Truly, sir, and pleasure will be paid,° one time or   *paid for*
70   another.

ORSINO   Give me now leave° to leave° thee.   *permission / dismiss*

FESTE   Now the melancholy god[7] protect thee, and the tailor
make thy doublet of changeable taffeta,[8] for thy mind is a very
opal.[9] I would have men of such constancy put to sea, that their
75   business might be everything, and their intent° everywhere, for   *destination*
that's it that always makes a good voyage of nothing.[1] Farewell.
                                           Exit

ORSINO   Let all the rest give place:°   [*Exeunt* CURIO *and others*]   *withdraw*
                    Once more, Cesario,
Get thee to yon same sovereign cruelty.
Tell her my love, more noble than the world,
80 Prizes not quantity of dirty lands.
The parts° that fortune hath bestowed upon her   *possessions*
Tell her I hold as giddily[2] as fortune;
But 'tis that miracle and queen of gems
That nature pranks° her in attracts my soul.   *adorns*

85 VIOLA   But if she cannot love you, sir?

ORSINO   I cannot be so answered.

VIOLA   Sooth,° but you must.   *In truth*
Say that some lady, as perhaps there is,
Hath for your love as great a pang of heart
As you have for Olivia. You cannot love her.
90 You tell her so. Must she not then be answered?

ORSINO   There is no woman's sides
Can bide° the beating of so strong a passion   *withstand*
As love doth give my heart; no woman's heart
So big, to hold so much. They lack retention.°   *constancy*
95 Alas, their love may be called appetite,
No motion of the liver, but the palate,[3]
That suffer surfeit, cloyment,° and revolt.°   *satiety / revulsion*
But mine is all as hungry as the sea,

---

6. *My part . . . it:* No one has died so true to love as I.
7. Saturn (thought to control the melancholic).
8. Shot silk, whose color changes with the angle of vision. *doublet:* close-fitting jacket.
9. An iridescent gemstone that changes color depending on the angle from which it is seen.
1. *that's . . . nothing:* this fickle lack of direction can make a voyage in the notoriously changeful sea carefree and consonant with one's desires.
2. Lightly (fortune being fickle).
3. *appetite . . . palate:* appetite, like the palate, is easily sated, and thus lacks the emotional depth and complexity of real love, whose seat is the liver. *motion:* impulse.

And can digest as much. Make no compare
100 Between that love a woman can bear me
And that I owe° Olivia.   *have for*
VIOLA   Ay, but I know—
ORSINO   What dost thou know?
VIOLA   Too well what love women to men may owe.
105 In faith, they are as true of heart as we.
My father had a daughter loved a man
As it might be, perhaps, were I a woman
I should your lordship.
ORSINO   And what's her history?
VIOLA   A blank, my lord. She never told her love,
110 But let concealment, like a worm i'th' bud,
Feed on her damask⁴ cheek. She pined in thought,
And with a green and yellow° melancholy   *pale and sallow*
She sat like patience on a monument,⁵
Smiling at grief. Was not this love indeed?
115 We men may say more, swear more, but indeed
Our shows are more than will;⁶ for still° we prove   *always*
Much in our vows, but little in our love.
ORSINO   But died thy sister of her love, my boy?
VIOLA   I am all the daughters of my father's house,
120 And all the brothers too; and yet I know not.
Sir, shall I to this lady?
ORSINO   Ay, that's the theme,
To her in haste. Give her this jewel. Say
My love can give no place, bide no denay.⁷ *Exeunt [severally]*

2.5

Enter SIR TOBY, SIR ANDREW, *and* FABIAN
SIR TOBY   Come thy ways,° Signor Fabian.   *Come along*
FABIAN   Nay, I'll come. If I lose a scruple° of this sport let me be   *miss a scrap*
boiled to death with melancholy.¹
SIR TOBY   Wouldst thou not be glad to have the niggardly rascally
5   sheep-biter² come by some notable shame?
FABIAN   I would exult, man. You know he brought me out o'
favour with my lady about a bear-baiting³ here.
SIR TOBY   To anger him we'll have the bear again, and we will
fool° him black and blue, shall we not, Sir Andrew?   *mock*
10   SIR ANDREW   An° we do not, it is pity of our lives.   *If*
Enter MARIA [*with a letter*]
SIR TOBY   Here comes the little villain. How now, my metal of
India?⁴
MARIA   Get ye all three into the box-tree.° Malvolio's coming   *hedge of boxwood*
down this walk. He has been yonder i' the sun practising behav-
15   iour to his own shadow this half-hour. Observe him, for the
love of mockery, for I know this letter will make a contempla-
tive° idiot of him. Close,° in the name of jesting!   *vacuous / Keep close; hide*

---

4. Pink and white, like a damask rose.
5. A memorial statue symbolizing patience.
6. Our displays of love are greater than our actual feelings.
7. My love cannot be bated, nor tolerate refusal.
2.5 Location: Olivia's garden.

1. Melancholy was a cold humor; "boiled" puns on "bile," the surplus of which produced melancholy.
2. Literally, a dog that attacks sheep; here, a malicious sneak.
3. Puritans disapproved of blood sports like bearbaiting.
4. A woman worth her weight in gold.

[*The men hide.* MARIA *places the letter*]
Lie thou there, for here comes the trout that must be caught
with tickling.[5] *Exit*

Enter MALVOLIO

20 MALVOLIO 'Tis but fortune, all is fortune. Maria once told me
she° did affect° me, and I have heard herself come thus near,   *(Olivia) / care for*
that should she fancy° it should be one of my complexion.   *fall in love*
Besides, she uses me with a more exalted respect than anyone
else that follows her. What should I think on't?

25 SIR TOBY Here's an overweening rogue.

FABIAN O, peace! Contemplation makes a rare turkeycock[6] of
him—how he jets° under his advanced° plumes!   *struts / raised*

SIR ANDREW 'Slight,[7] I could so beat the rogue.

SIR TOBY Peace, I say.

30 MALVOLIO To be Count Malvolio!

SIR TOBY Ah, rogue.

SIR ANDREW Pistol him, pistol him.

SIR TOBY Peace, peace.

MALVOLIO There is example° for't: the Lady of the Strachey mar-   *precedent*
35 ried the yeoman of the wardrobe.[8]

SIR ANDREW Fie on him, Jezebel.[9]

FABIAN O peace, now he's deeply in. Look how imagination
blows him.°   *puffs him up*

MALVOLIO Having been three months married to her, sitting in
40 my state°—   *chair of state*

SIR TOBY O for a stone-bow[1] to hit him in the eye!

MALVOLIO Calling my officers° about me, in my branched[2] vel-   *household attendants*
vet gown, having come from a day-bed° where I have left Olivia   *couch*
sleeping—

45 SIR TOBY Fire and brimstone!

FABIAN O peace, peace.

MALVOLIO And then to have the humour of state[3] and—after a
demure travel of regard,[4] telling them I know my place, as I
would they should do theirs—to ask for my kinsman Toby.

50 SIR TOBY Bolts and shackles!

FABIAN O peace, peace, peace, now, now.

MALVOLIO Seven of my people with an obedient start make° out   *go*
for him. I frown the while, and perchance wind up my watch,
or play with my—[*touching his chain*][5] some rich jewel. Toby
55 approaches; curtsies° there to me.   *bows*

SIR TOBY Shall this fellow live?

FABIAN Though our silence be drawn from us with cars,[6] yet
peace.

MALVOLIO I extend my hand to him thus, quenching my famil-
60 iar smile with an austere regard of control—

SIR TOBY And does not Toby take° you a blow o' the lips, then?   *give*

---

5. Flattery; trout can be caught by stroking them under
the gills.
6. Proverbially proud; they display their feathers like
peacocks.
7. By God's light (an oath).
8. Perhaps an allusion to a noblewoman who had mar-
ried her manservant, but there is no certain identifica-
tion. *yeoman of the wardrobe:* keeper of clothes and linen.
9. Biblical allusion to the proud wife of Ahab, King of
Israel.

1. Catapult, or crossbow for stones.
2. Embroidered with branch patterns.
3. To adopt the grand air of exalted greatness.
4. After casting my eyes gravely about the room.
5. Malvolio momentarily forgets that he will have aban-
doned his steward's chain; watches were an expensive
luxury at this time.
6. A prisoner might be tied to two carts or chariots
("cars") and pulled by horses in opposite directions to
extort information.

MALVOLIO   Saying 'Cousin Toby, my fortunes, having cast me
on your niece, give me this prerogative of speech'—
SIR TOBY   What, what!
65 MALVOLIO   'You must amend your drunkenness.'
SIR TOBY   Out, scab.
FABIAN   Nay, patience, or we break the sinews of our plot.
MALVOLIO   'Besides, you waste the treasure of your time with a
foolish knight'—
70 SIR ANDREW   That's me, I warrant you.
MALVOLIO   'One Sir Andrew.'
SIR ANDREW   I knew 'twas I, for many do call me fool.
MALVOLIO [*seeing the letter*]   What employment° have we here?   business
FABIAN   Now is the woodcock near the gin.[7]
75 SIR TOBY   O peace, and the spirit of humours intimate[8] reading
aloud to him.
MALVOLIO [*taking up the letter*]   By my life, this is my lady's
hand. These be her very c's, her u's, and her t's,[9] and thus
makes she her great P's. It is in contempt of° question her   beyond
80 hand.
SIR ANDREW   Her c's, her u's, and her t's? Why that?
MALVOLIO [*reads*]   'To the unknown beloved, this, and my good
wishes.' Her very phrases! [*Opening the letter*] By your leave,
wax[1]—soft,° and the impressure her Lucrece,[2] with which she   wait
85 uses to seal° —'tis my lady. To whom should this be?   habitually seals
FABIAN   This wins him, liver and all.
MALVOLIO   'Jove knows I love,
                            But who?
                    Lips do not move,
90   No man must know.'
'No man must know.' What follows? The numbers altered.°   meter changed
'No man must know.' If this should be thee, Malvolio?
SIR TOBY   Marry, hang thee, brock.[3]
MALVOLIO   'I may command where I adore,
95   But silence like a Lucrece knife
                With bloodless stroke my heart doth gore.
                M.O.A.I. doth sway my life.'
FABIAN   A fustian° riddle.   bombastic
SIR TOBY   Excellent wench, say I.
100 MALVOLIO   'M.O.A.I. doth sway my life.' Nay, but first let me
see, let me see, let me see.
FABIAN   What dish o' poison has she dressed° him!   prepared
SIR TOBY   And with what wing the staniel checks at it![4]
MALVOLIO   'I may command where I adore.' Why, she may com-
105 mand me. I serve her, she is my lady. Why, this is evident to
any formal capacity.° There is no obstruction in this. And the   normal intelligence
end—what should that alphabetical position° portend? If I   arrangement
could make that resemble something in me. Softly—'M.O.A.I.'
SIR TOBY   O ay,[5] make up that, he is now at a cold scent.

---

7. Snare. *woodcock:* a proverbially foolish bird.
8. And may a capricious impulse suggest.
9. Malvolio unwittingly spells out "cut," slang for "female genitals"; the meaning is compounded by "great P's." In fact, these letters do not appear on the outside of the letter.

1. *By . . . wax:* addressed to the sealing wax.
2. The figure of Lucrece, Roman model of chastity, is the device ("impressure") imprinted on the seal.
3. Badger (proverbially stinking).
4. And with what alacrity the sparrow hawk goes after it.
5. *O, ay:* playing on "O.I."

110 FABIAN Sowter will cry upon't for all this, though it be as rank
as a fox.[6]
MALVOLIO 'M.' Malvolio—'M'—why, that begins my name.
FABIAN Did not I say he would work it out? The cur is excellent
at faults.[7]
115 MALVOLIO 'M.' But then there is no consonancy in the sequel.[8]
That suffers under probation.[9] 'A' should follow, but 'O' does.
FABIAN And 'O'[1] shall end, I hope.
SIR TOBY Ay, or I'll cudgel him, and make him cry 'O!'
MALVOLIO And then 'I' comes behind.
120 FABIAN Ay, an you had any eye behind you you might see more
detraction° at your heels than fortunes before you. *defamation*
MALVOLIO 'M.O.A.I.' This simulation° is not as the former; and *disguise; riddle*
yet to crush° this a little, it would bow° to me, for every one of *force / yield; point*
these letters are in my name. Soft, here follows prose: 'If this
125 fall into thy hand, revolve.° In my stars° I am above thee, but *consider / fortunes*
be not afraid of greatness. Some are born great, some achieve
greatness, and some have greatness thrust upon 'em. Thy fates
open their hands,° let thy blood and spirit embrace them, and *bestow gifts*
to inure° thyself to what thou art like° to be, cast thy humble *accustom / likely*
130 slough,[2] and appear fresh. Be opposite° with a kinsman, surly *contrary*
with servants. Let thy tongue tang arguments of state;[3] put thy-
self into the trick of singularity.° She thus advises thee that sighs *cultivate eccentricity*
for thee. Remember who commended thy yellow stockings,
and wished to see thee ever cross-gartered.[4] I say remember, go
135 to,[5] thou art made if thou desirest to be so; if not, let me see
thee a steward still, the fellow of servants, and not worthy to
touch Fortune's fingers. Farewell. She that would alter ser-
vices[6] with thee,
                              The Fortunate-Unhappy.'
140 Daylight and champaign discovers[7] not more. This is open.° I *clear*
will be proud, I will read politic° authors, I will baffle[8] Sir *political*
Toby, I will wash off gross acquaintance, I will be point-device
the very man.[9] I do not now fool myself, to let imagination
jade° me; for every reason excites to this, that my lady loves me. *trick*
145 She did commend my yellow stockings of late, she did praise
my leg, being cross-gartered, and in this she manifests herself
to my love, and with a kind of injunction drives me to these
habits° of her liking. I thank my stars, I am happy. I will be *clothes*
strange,° stout,° in yellow stockings, and cross-gartered, even *aloof / proud*
150 with the swiftness of putting on. Jove and my stars be praised.
Here is yet a postscript. 'Thou canst not choose but know who
I am. If thou entertainest° my love, let it appear in thy smiling, *accept*
thy smiles become thee well. Therefore in my presence still° *constantly*
smile, dear my sweet, I prithee.' Jove, I thank thee. I will smile,
155 I will do everything that thou wilt have me.   *Exit*

6. "Sowter" (the name of a hound), having lost the scent,
will start to bay loudly as he picks up the new, rank (stink-
ing) smell of the fox. *though:* as though.
7. At picking up a scent after it is momentarily lost. A
"fault" is a "cold scent" (line 109).
8. There is no consistency in what follows.
9. That weakens upon being put to the test.
1. As in the hangman's noose; the last letter of Malvolio's
name; or "O" as a lamentation.
2. A snake's old skin, which peels away.
3. Let your tongue ring out arguments of statecraft or

politics.
4. An antiquated way of adjusting a garter—going once
below the knee, crossing behind it, and knotting above
the knee at the side.
5. An emphatic expression, like "I tell you."
6. Change places (of servant and mistress or master).
7. *champaign discovers:* open countryside reveals.
8. Term used to describe the formal unmaking of a
knight; hence, "disgrace."
9. I will be in every detail the identical man (described
in the letter).

[SIR TOBY, SIR ANDREW, *and* FABIAN *come from hiding*]

FABIAN I will not give my part of this sport for a pension of
   thousands to be paid from the Sophy.°   *Shah of Persia*

SIR TOBY I could marry this wench for this device.

SIR ANDREW So could I, too.

160 SIR TOBY And ask no other dowry with her but such another jest.

          Enter MARIA

SIR ANDREW Nor I neither.

FABIAN Here comes my noble gull-catcher.°   *trickster*

SIR TOBY [*to* MARIA] Wilt thou set thy foot o' my neck?

SIR ANDREW [*to* MARIA] Or o' mine either?

165 SIR TOBY [*to* MARIA] Shall I play my freedom at tray-trip,[1] and
   become thy bondslave?

SIR ANDREW [*to* MARIA] I'faith, or I either?

SIR TOBY [*to* MARIA] Why, thou hast put him in such a dream
   that when the image of it leaves him, he must run mad.

170 MARIA Nay, but say true, does it work upon him?

SIR TOBY Like aqua vitae° with a midwife.   *spirits; liquor*

MARIA If you will then see the fruits of the sport, mark his first
   approach before my lady. He will come to her in yellow stock-
   ings, and 'tis a colour she abhors, and cross-gartered, a fashion
175 she detests; and he will smile upon her, which will now be so
   unsuitable to her disposition, being addicted to a melancholy
   as she is, that it cannot but turn him into a notable contempt.[2]
   If you will see it, follow me.

SIR TOBY To the gates of Tartar,° thou most excellent devil of   *hell*
180 wit.

SIR ANDREW I'll make one,° too.   *Exeunt*   *go along*

3.1

Enter VIOLA [*as Cesario*] *and* [FESTE, *the*] *clown* [*with
   pipe and tabor*][1]

VIOLA Save° thee, friend, and thy music. Dost thou live by thy   *God save*
   tabor?

FESTE No, sir, I live by° the church.   *near*

VIOLA Art thou a churchman?

5 FESTE No such matter, sir. I do live by[2] the church for I do live
   at my house, and my house doth stand by the church.

VIOLA So thou mayst say the king lies by[3] a beggar if a beggar
   dwell near him, or the church stands° by thy tabor if thy tabor   *is maintained*
   stand by the church.

10 FESTE You have said, sir. To see this age!—A sentence° is but a   *saying*
   cheverel° glove to a good wit, how quickly the wrong side may   *kidskin*
   be turned outward.

VIOLA Nay, that's certain. They that dally nicely° with words   *play subtly*
   may quickly make them wanton.[4]

15 FESTE I would therefore my sister had had no name, sir.

VIOLA Why, man?

FESTE Why, sir, her name's a word, and to dally with that word

---

1. A game of dice in which the winner throws a three
("tray" is from the Spanish *tres*). *play:* wager.
2. A notorious object of contempt.
3.1 Location: Olivia's garden.
1. The dialogue demands only a tabor, but jesters com-

monly played a pipe with one hand while tapping a tabor
(small drum, hanging from the neck) with the other.
2. I do earn my keep with.
3. Lives near; punning on "goes to bed with."
4. Equivocal; Feste puns on the sense "unchaste."

might make my sister wanton. But indeed, words are very ras-
cals since bonds disgraced them.[5]
20 VIOLA　Thy reason, man?
FESTE　Troth, sir, I can yield you none without words, and words
are grown so false I am loath to prove reason with them.
VIOLA　I warrant thou art a merry fellow, and carest for nothing.
FESTE　Not so, sir, I do care for something; but in my con-
25 science, sir, I do not care for you. If that be to care for nothing,
sir, I would it would make you invisible.
VIOLA　Art not thou the Lady Olivia's fool?
FESTE　No indeed, sir, the Lady Olivia has no folly, she will keep
no fool, sir, till she be married, and fools are as like husbands
30 as pilchards[6] are to herrings—the husband's the bigger. I am
indeed not her fool, but her corrupter of words.
VIOLA　I saw thee late° at the Count Orsino's.　　　　　　　°*lately*
FESTE　Foolery, sir, does walk about the orb[7] like the sun, it
shines everywhere. I would be sorry, sir, but the fool should be
35 as oft with your master as with my mistress.[8] I think I saw your
wisdom[9] there.
VIOLA　Nay, an thou pass upon[1] me, I'll no more with thee. [*Giv-
ing money*] Hold, there's expenses for thee.
FESTE　Now Jove in his next commodity° of hair send thee a　　°*shipment*
40 beard.
VIOLA　By my troth I'll tell thee, I am almost sick for one,[2]
though I would not have it grow on *my* chin. Is thy lady within?
FESTE　Would not a pair of these have bred,[3] sir?
VIOLA　Yes, being kept together and put to use.[4]
45 FESTE　I would play Lord Pandarus[5] of Phrygia, sir, to bring a
Cressida to this Troilus.
VIOLA [*giving money*]　I understand you, sir, 'tis well begged.
FESTE　The matter I hope is not great, sir; begging but a beg-
gar—Cressida was a beggar.[6] My lady is within, sir. I will con-
50 ster° to them whence you come. Who you are and what you　　°*explain*
would are out of my welkin—I might say 'element', but the
word is over-worn.[7]　　　　　　　　　　　　　　　　　　*Exit*
VIOLA　This fellow is wise enough to play the fool,
And to do that well craves a kind of wit.°　　　　　　　　°*intelligence*
55 He must observe their mood on whom he jests,
The quality of persons, and the time,
And, like the haggard, check at every feather
That comes before his eye.[8] This is a practice°　　　　　　°*skill*
As full of labour as a wise man's art,
60 For folly that he wisely shows is fit,[9]

5. Since legal contracts replaced a man's word of honor.
("Bonds" plays on "sworn statements" and "fetters," beto-
kening criminality.)
6. Small fish similar to herring.
7. World; the sun was still believed to circle the earth.
8. I, Feste, should visit master and mistress alike;
Orsino should be called "fool" as often as Olivia.
9. *your wisdom:* a mocking title for Cesario.
1. If you express an opinion of; if you joke about.
2. Almost eager for a beard; almost pining for a man
(Orsino).
3. Would not a pair of coins such as these have multi-
plied (with possible pun on "be enough to buy bread").

4. *put to use:* invested to produce interest.
5. Go-between, or "pander," since Feste needs a "mate"
for his coin(s). Shakespeare dramatizes the story in
Troilus and Cressida.
6. In asking for the "mate" to his Troilus coin, Feste
draws on a version of the story of Troilus and Cressida in
which Cressida became a beggar.
7. "Welkin" (sky or air) is synonymous with one meaning
of "element," used in what Feste regards as the overworn
phrase "out of my element."
8. *And . . . eye:* As a wild hawk ("haggard") must be sen-
sitive to its prey's disposition.
9. For folly that he skillfully displays is proper.

But wise men, folly-fall'n, quite taint[1] their wit.

Enter SIR TOBY *and* [SIR] ANDREW

SIR TOBY   Save you, gentleman.

VIOLA   And you, sir.

SIR ANDREW   *Dieu vous garde,*[2] *monsieur.*

65   VIOLA   *Et vous aussi, votre serviteur.*[3]

SIR ANDREW   I hope, sir, you are, and I am yours.

SIR TOBY   Will you encounter[4] the house? My niece is desirous
you should enter if your trade be to her.

VIOLA   I am bound to° your niece, sir: I mean she is the list° of   *for / destination*
70   my voyage.

SIR TOBY   Taste° your legs, sir, put them to motion.   *Try*

VIOLA   My legs do better understand° me, sir, than I understand   *stand under*
what you mean by bidding me taste my legs.

SIR TOBY   I mean to go, sir, to enter.

75   VIOLA   I will answer you with gait and entrance.

Enter OLIVIA, *and* [MARIA, *her*] *gentlewoman*

But we are prevented.° [*To* OLIVIA] Most excellent accom-   *anticipated*
plished lady, the heavens rain odours on you.

SIR ANDREW [*to* SIR TOBY]   That youth's a rare° courtier; 'rain   *an excellent*
odours'—well.°   *well put*

80   VIOLA   My matter hath no voice,° lady, but to your own most   *must not be spoken*
pregnant° and vouchsafed° ear.   *receptive / proffered*

SIR ANDREW [*to* SIR TOBY]   'Odours', 'pregnant', and 'vouch-
safed'—I'll get 'em all three all ready.[5]

OLIVIA   Let the garden door be shut, and leave me to my
85   hearing.   [*Exeunt* SIR TOBY, SIR ANDREW, *and* MARIA]
Give me your hand, sir.

VIOLA   My duty, madam, and most humble service.

OLIVIA   What is your name?

VIOLA   Cesario is your servant's name, fair princess.

90   OLIVIA   My servant, sir? 'Twas never merry world[6]
Since lowly feigning° was called compliment.   *pretended humility*
You're servant to the Count Orsino, youth.

VIOLA   And he is yours, and his must needs be yours.
Your servant's servant is *your* servant, madam.

95   OLIVIA   For° him, I think not on him. For his thoughts,   *As for*
Would they were blanks rather than filled with me.

VIOLA   Madam, I come to whet your gentle thoughts
On his behalf.

OLIVIA   O by your leave,[7] I pray you.
I bade you never speak again of him;
100   But would you undertake another suit,
I had rather hear you to solicit that
Than music from the spheres.[8]

VIOLA   Dear lady—

OLIVIA   Give me leave, beseech you. I did send,
After the last enchantment you did here,
105   A ring in chase of you. So did I abuse°   *deceive; dishonor*

---

1. Discredit; spoil. *folly-fall'n:* fallen into folly.
2. God protect you (French).
3. And you also, (I am) your servant. (Sir Andrew's awk-ward reply demonstrates that his French is limited.)
4. Pedantry for "enter" (Toby mocks Viola's courtly lan-guage).

5. *I'll . . . ready:* to commit to memory for later use.
6. *'Twas . . . world:* the proverbial "Things have never been the same."
7. Permit me to interrupt (polite expression).
8. Exquisite music thought to be made by the planets as they moved, but inaudible to mortal ears.

Myself, my servant, and I fear me you.°   *and, as I fear, you*
Under your hard construction[9] must I sit,
To force° that on you in a shameful cunning   *For forcing*
Which you knew none of yours. What might you think?
110   Have you not set mine honour at the stake
And baited it with all th'unmuzzled thoughts[1]
That tyrannous heart can think? To one of your receiving°   *perception*
Enough is shown. A cypress,[2] not a bosom,
Hides my heart. So let me hear you speak.
  VIOLA   I pity you.
115   OLIVIA   That's a degree to° love.   *toward*
  VIOLA   No, not a grece,° for 'tis a vulgar proof°   *step / common experience*
That very oft we pity enemies.
  OLIVIA   Why then, methinks 'tis time to smile again.[3]
O world, how apt° the poor are to be proud!   *ready*
120   If one should be a prey, how much the better
To fall before the lion than the wolf![4]
        Clock strikes
The clock upbraids me with the waste of time.
Be not afraid, good youth, I will not have you;
And yet when wit and youth is come to harvest
125   Your wife is like to reap a proper° man.   *handsome; worthy*
There lies your way, due west.
  VIOLA   Then westward ho![5]
Grace and good disposition° attend your ladyship.   *peace of mind*
You'll nothing, madam, to my lord by me?
  OLIVIA   Stay. I prithee tell me what thou[6] think'st of me.
130   VIOLA   That you do think you are not what you are.[7]
  OLIVIA   If I think so, I think the same of you.[8]
  VIOLA   Then think you right, I am not what I am.
  OLIVIA   I would you were as I would have you be.
  VIOLA   Would it be better, madam, than I am?
135   I wish it might, for now I am your fool.[9]
  OLIVIA [*aside*]   O, what a deal of scorn looks beautiful
In the contempt and anger of his lip!
A murd'rous guilt shows not itself more soon
Than love that would seem hid. Love's night is noon.[1]
140   [*To* VIOLA] Cesario, by the roses of the spring,
By maidhood, honour, truth, and everything,
I love thee so that, maugre° all thy pride,   *despite*
Nor° wit nor reason can my passion hide.   *Neither*
Do not extort thy reasons from this clause,[2]
145   For that° I woo, thou therefore hast no cause.   *That because*
But rather reason thus with reason fetter:[3]
Love sought is good, but given unsought, is better.

---

9. Your unfavorable interpretation (of my behavior).
1. set . . . thoughts: as bears that were tied up at the stake and baited with dogs.
2. Veil of transparent silken gauze; the cypress tree was also emblematic of mourning.
3. Time to discard love's melancholy.
4. If . . . wolf: If I had to fall prey to love, it would have been better to succumb to the noble Orsino than to the hardhearted Cesario.
5. Thames watermen's cry to attract passengers for the court at Westminster from London.
6. Olivia changes from "you" to the familiar "thou."

7. That you think you are in love with a man, but you are mistaken.
8. Olivia may think that Cesario has suggested that she is mad; or she may imply that she thinks that Cesario, despite his subordinate position, is noble.
9. You have made a fool of me.
1. Love, though attempting secrecy, still shines out as bright as day.
2. Do not take the position that just because I woo you, you are under no obligation to reciprocate.
3. But instead constrain your reasoning with this argument.

VIOLA   By innocence I swear, and by my youth,
I have one heart, one bosom, and one truth,
150 And that no woman has, nor never none
Shall mistress be of it save I alone.
And so adieu, good madam. Never more
Will I my master's tears to you deplore.°   *lament*
OLIVIA   Yet come again, for thou perhaps mayst move
155 That heart which now abhors, to like his love.

                    Exeunt [severally]

3.2

Enter SIR TOBY, SIR ANDREW, *and* FABIAN

SIR ANDREW   No, faith, I'll not stay a jot longer.
SIR TOBY   Thy reason, dear venom,° give thy reason.   *venomous one*
FABIAN   You must needs yield your reason, Sir Andrew.
SIR ANDREW   Marry, I saw your niece do more favours to the
5 Count's servingman than ever she bestowed upon me. I saw't
i'th' orchard.°   *garden*
SIR TOBY   Did she see thee the while, old boy? Tell me that.
SIR ANDREW   As plain as I see you now.
FABIAN   This was a great argument° of love in her toward you.   *proof*
10 SIR ANDREW   'Slight,° will you make an ass o' me?   *By God's light*
FABIAN   I will prove it legitimate, sir, upon the oaths of judge-
ment and reason.
SIR TOBY   And they have been grand-jurymen[1] since before
Noah was a sailor.
15 FABIAN   She did show favour to the youth in your sight only to
exasperate you, to awake your dormouse° valour, to put fire in   *meek; timid*
your heart and brimstone in your liver. You should then have
accosted her, and with some excellent jests, fire-new from the
mint,° you should have banged the youth into dumbness. This   *newly minted*
20 was looked for at your hand, and this was balked.° The double   *neglected*
gilt[2] of this opportunity you let time wash off, and you are now
sailed into the north of my lady's opinion,[3] where you will hang
like an icicle on a Dutchman's[4] beard unless you do redeem it
by some laudable attempt either of valour or policy.°   *cunning*
25 SIR ANDREW   An't° be any way, it must be with valour, for policy   *If it*
I hate. I had as lief° be a Brownist as a politician.[5]   *as soon*
SIR TOBY   Why then, build me thy fortunes upon the basis of
valour. Challenge me° the Count's youth to fight with him,   *for me*
hurt him in eleven places. My niece shall take note of it; and
30 assure thyself, there is no love-broker in the world can more
prevail in man's commendation with woman than report of
valour.
FABIAN   There is no way but this, Sir Andrew.
SIR ANDREW   Will either of you bear me a challenge to him?
35 SIR TOBY   Go, write it in a martial hand, be curst° and brief. It is   *sharp*
no matter how witty so it be eloquent and full of invention.°   *imagination; untruth*

3.2 Location: Olivia's house.
1. Grand jurymen were supposed to be good judges of evidence.
2. Twice gilded, and as such, Sir Andrew's "golden opportunity" to prove both love and valor.
3. Into Olivia's cold disfavor.
4. Perhaps an allusion to navigator Willem Barents, who led an expedition to the Arctic in 1596–97.
5. Schemer. A Brownist was a member of the Puritan sect founded in 1581 by Robert Browne.

Taunt him with the licence of ink.[6] If thou 'thou'st'[7] him some
thrice, it shall not be amiss, and as many lies° as will lie in thy   *accusations of lying*
sheet of paper, although the sheet were big enough for the bed
40 of Ware,[8] in England, set 'em down, go about it. Let there be
gall[9] enough in thy ink; though thou write with a goose-pen,[1]
no matter. About it.
SIR ANDREW   Where shall I find you?
SIR TOBY   We'll call thee at the cubiculo.° Go.   *little chamber*

Exit SIR ANDREW

45 FABIAN   This is a dear manikin° to you, Sir Toby.   *puppet*
SIR TOBY   I have been dear° to him, lad, some two thousand   *costly*
strong or so.
FABIAN   We shall have a rare letter from him; but you'll not
deliver't.
50 SIR TOBY   Never trust me then; and by all means stir on the youth
to an answer. I think oxen and wain-ropes[2] cannot hale° them   *drag*
together. For Andrew, if he were opened and you find so much
blood in his liver[3] as will clog° the foot of a flea, I'll eat the rest   *weigh down*
of th'anatomy.°   *cadaver*
55 FABIAN   And his opposite,° the youth, bears in his visage no great   *adversary*
presage of cruelty.

Enter MARIA

SIR TOBY   Look where the youngest wren of nine[4] comes.
MARIA   If you desire the spleen,° and will laugh yourselves into   *a laughing fit*
stitches, follow me. Yon gull° Malvolio is turned heathen, a   *fool*
60 very renegado,[5] for there is no Christian that means to be saved
by believing rightly can ever believe such impossible passages
of grossness.[6] He's in yellow stockings.
SIR TOBY   And cross-gartered?
MARIA   Most villainously,° like a pedant° that keeps a school i'th'   *abominably / teacher*
65 church.[7] I have dogged him like his murderer. He does obey
every point of the letter that I dropped to betray him. He does
smile his face into more lines than is in the new map with the
augmentation of the Indies.[8] You have not seen such a thing as
'tis. I can hardly forbear hurling things at him. I know my lady
70 will strike him. If she do, he'll smile, and take't for a great
favour.
SIR TOBY   Come bring us, bring us where he is.   *Exeunt*

3.3

Enter SEBASTIAN *and* ANTONIO

SEBASTIAN   I would not by my will have troubled you,
But since you make your pleasure of your pains
I will no further chide you.
ANTONIO   I could not stay behind you. My desire,

6. *licence of ink:* freedom taken in writing, but not risked in conversation.
7. Call him "thou" (an insult to a stranger).
8. Famous Elizabethan bedstead, nearly eleven feet square, now in the Victoria and Albert Museum, London.
9. Oak gall, an ingredient in ink; bitterness or rancor.
1. Quill made of a goose feather. (The goose was proverbially cowardly and foolish.)
2. Wagon ropes pulled by oxen.
3. Supposed to be the source of blood, which engendered courage.

4. The smallest of small birds; the smallest wren in a family of nine.
5. Renegade (Spanish); a Christian converted to Islam.
6. Such patent absurdities (in the letter).
7. Because no schoolroom is available in a small rustic community.
8. Possibly refers to a map published in 1599 showing the East Indies more fully than in earlier maps and crisscrossed by many rhumb lines.
3.3 Location: A street scene.

5 More sharp than filèd steel, did spur me forth,
And not all° love to see you—though so much   *only*
As might have drawn one to a longer voyage—
But jealousy° what might befall your travel,   *apprehension*
Being skilless in° these parts, which to a stranger,   *unfamiliar to*
10 Unguided and unfriended, often prove
Rough and unhospitable. My willing love
The rather° by these arguments of fear   *more willingly*
Set forth in your pursuit.

SEBASTIAN   My kind Antonio,
I can no other answer make but thanks,
15 And thanks; and ever oft° good turns   *very often*
Are shuffled off° with such uncurrent[1] pay.   *shrugged off*
But were my worth as is my conscience° firm,   *sense of indebtedness*
You should find better dealing. What's to do?
Shall we go see the relics° of this town?   *sights*
20 ANTONIO   Tomorrow, sir. Best first go see your lodging.

SEBASTIAN   I am not weary, and 'tis long to night.
I pray you let us satisfy our eyes
With the memorials and the things of fame
That do renown this city.

ANTONIO   Would you'd pardon me.
25 I do not without danger walk these streets.
Once in a sea-fight 'gainst the Count his° galleys   *(the Count's)*
I did some service, of such note indeed
That were I ta'en° here it would scarce be answered.[2]   *captured*

SEBASTIAN   Belike° you slew great number of his people.   *Perhaps*
30 ANTONIO   Th'offence is not of such a bloody nature,
Albeit the quality° of the time and quarrel   *circumstances*
Might well have given us bloody argument.°   *cause for bloodshed*
It might have since been answered in repaying
What we took from them, which for traffic's° sake   *trade's*
35 Most of our city did. Only myself stood out,
For which if I be latchèd° in this place   *caught*
I shall pay dear.

SEBASTIAN   Do not then walk too open.

ANTONIO   It doth not fit me. Hold, sir, here's my purse.
In the south suburbs at the Elephant°   *name of an inn*
40 Is best to lodge. I will bespeak our diet°   *order our meals*
Whiles you beguile° the time and feed your knowledge   *pass*
With viewing of the town. There shall you have me.

SEBASTIAN   Why I your purse?

ANTONIO   Haply° your eye shall light upon some toy°   *Perhaps / trifle*
45 You have desire to purchase; and your store°   *resources*
I think is not for idle markets,[3] sir.

SEBASTIAN   I'll be your purse-bearer, and leave you
For an hour.

ANTONIO   To th' Elephant.

SEBASTIAN   I do remember.
Exeunt [severally]

---

1. Out of currency; worthless.
2. It would be difficult for me to make reparation (and   thus my life would be in danger).
3. Not large enough to spend on luxuries.

3.4

Enter OLIVIA *and* MARIA

OLIVIA [*aside*] I have sent after him, he says he'll come.
How shall I feast him? What bestow of° him?   *on*
For youth is bought more oft than begged or borrowed.[1]
I speak too loud.

5   [*To* MARIA] Where's Malvolio? He is sad° and civil,°   *sober / respectful*
And suits well for a servant with my fortunes.
Where is Malvolio?

MARIA   He's coming, madam, but in very strange manner. He is
sure possessed,° madam.   *(by the devil); insane*

10 OLIVIA   Why, what's the matter? Does he rave?

MARIA   No, madam, he does nothing but smile. Your ladyship
were best to have some guard about you if he come, for sure
the man is tainted in's wits.

OLIVIA   Go call him hither.   [*Exit* MARIA]
                                  I am as mad as he,

15 If sad and merry madness equal be.

Enter MALVOLIO [*cross-gartered and wearing yellow
stockings, with* MARIA]

How now, Malvolio?

MALVOLIO   Sweet lady, ho, ho!

OLIVIA   Smil'st thou? I sent for thee upon a sad occasion.°   *about a serious matter*

MALVOLIO   Sad, lady? I could be sad. This does make some

20 obstruction in the blood, this cross-gartering, but what of that?
If it please the eye of one, it is with me as the very true sonnet°   *song*
is, 'Please one, and please all'.[2]

OLIVIA   Why, how dost thou, man? What is the matter with thee?

MALVOLIO   Not black in my mind, though yellow[3] in my legs. It

25 did come to his hands, and commands shall be executed. I
think we do know the sweet roman hand.°   *italic calligraphy*

OLIVIA   Wilt thou go to bed,[4] Malvolio?

MALVOLIO [*kissing his hand*] To bed? 'Ay, sweetheart, and I'll
come to thee.'[5]

30 OLIVIA   God comfort thee. Why dost thou smile so, and kiss thy
hand so oft?

MARIA   How do you, Malvolio?

MALVOLIO   At your request?—yes, nightingales answer daws.[6]

MARIA   Why appear you with this ridiculous boldness before my

35 lady?

MALVOLIO   'Be not afraid of greatness'—'twas well writ.

OLIVIA   What meanest thou by that, Malvolio?

MALVOLIO   'Some are born great'—

OLIVIA   Ha?

40 MALVOLIO   'Some achieve greatness'—

OLIVIA   What sayst thou?

MALVOLIO   'And some have greatness thrust upon them.'

OLIVIA   Heaven restore thee.

3.4 Location: The garden of Olivia's house.
1. "Better to buy than to beg or borrow" was proverbial.
2. If I please one, I please all I care to please (words of a popular bawdy ballad).
3. Black and yellow biles indicated choleric and melancholic dispositions, respectively. "Black and yellow" was

the name of a popular song; to "wear yellow hose" was to be jealous.
4. In order to cure his madness with sleep.
5. A line from a popular song.
6. Shall I deign to reply to you? Yes, since even the nightingale sings in response to the crowing of the jackdaw.

MALVOLIO 'Remember who commended thy yellow
45   stockings'—
OLIVIA 'Thy yellow stockings'?
MALVOLIO 'And wished to see thee cross-gartered.'
OLIVIA 'Cross-gartered'?
MALVOLIO 'Go to, thou art made, if thou desirest to be so.'
50 OLIVIA Am I made?
MALVOLIO 'If not, let me see thee a servant still.'
OLIVIA Why, this is very midsummer madness.
            Enter a SERVANT
SERVANT Madam, the young gentleman of the Count Orsino's
        is returned. I could hardly entreat him back. He attends your
55   ladyship's pleasure.
OLIVIA I'll come to him.   [*Exit* SERVANT]
        Good Maria, let this fellow be looked to. Where's my cousin
        Toby? Let some of my people have a special care of him, I
        would not have him miscarry° for the half of my dowry.   come to harm
            Exeunt [OLIVIA *and* MARIA, *severally*]
60 MALVOLIO O ho, do you come near° me now? No worse man   appreciate
        than Sir Toby to look to me. This concurs directly with the
        letter, she sends him on purpose, that I may appear stubborn to
        him, for she incites me to that in the letter. 'Cast thy humble
        slough,' says she, 'be opposite with a kinsman, surly with ser-
65   vants, let thy tongue tang arguments of state, put thyself into
        the trick of singularity', and consequently° sets down the man-   subsequently
        ner how, as a sad face, a reverend carriage, a slow tongue, in
        the habit of some sir of note,° and so forth. I have limed[7] her,   gentleman
        but it is Jove's doing, and Jove make me thankful. And when
70   she went away now, 'let this fellow be looked to'. Fellow![8]—not
        'Malvolio', nor after my degree, but 'fellow'. Why, everything
        adheres together that no dram of a scruple, no scruple of a
        scruple,[9] no obstacle, no incredulous or unsafe circumstance—
        what can be said?—nothing that can be can come between me
75   and the full prospect of my hopes. Well, Jove, not I, is the doer
        of this, and he is to be thanked.
            Enter [SIR] TOBY, FABIAN, *and* MARIA
SIR TOBY Which way is he, in the name of sanctity? If all the
        devils of hell be drawn in little,[1] and Legion[2] himself possessed
        him, yet I'll speak to him.
80 FABIAN Here he is, here he is. [*To* MALVOLIO] How is't with you,
        sir? How is't with you, man?
MALVOLIO Go off, I discard you. Let me enjoy my private.° Go   privacy
        off.
MARIA Lo, how hollow° the fiend speaks within him. Did not I   resonantly
85   tell you? Sir Toby, my lady prays you to have a care of him.
MALVOLIO Aha, does she so?
SIR TOBY Go to, go to. Peace, peace, we must deal gently with
        him. Let me alone.° How do you, Malvolio? How is't with you?   Leave him to me

---

7. Birds were caught by smearing sticky birdlime on branches.
8. Malvolio takes the word to mean "companion."
9. *no dram . . . scruple:* both phrases mean "no scrap of a doubt." *dram:* one-eighth of a fluid ounce. *scruple:* one-third of a dram.
1. Be contracted into a small space (punning on

"painted in miniature").
2. Alluding to a scene of exorcism in Mark 5:8–9: "For he [Jesus] said unto him, Come out of the man, thou unclean spirit. And he asked him, What is thy name? And he answered saying, My name is Legion: for we are many."

What, man, defy the devil. Consider, he's an enemy to man-
90   kind.

MALVOLIO   Do you know what you say?

MARIA   La° you, an you speak ill of the devil, how he takes it at   *Look*
heart. Pray God he be not bewitched.

FABIAN   Carry his water to th' wise woman.[3]

95   MARIA   Marry, and it shall be done tomorrow morning, if I live.
My lady would not lose him for more than I'll say.

MALVOLIO   How now, mistress?

MARIA   O Lord!

SIR TOBY   Prithee hold thy peace, this is not the way. Do you not
100   see you move° him? Let me alone with him.   *anger*

FABIAN   No way but gentleness, gently, gently. The fiend is
rough,° and will not be roughly used.   *violent*

SIR TOBY   Why how now, my bawcock?[4] How dost thou, chuck?

MALVOLIO   Sir!

105   SIR TOBY   Ay, biddy,° come with me. What man, 'tis not for grav-   *hen*
ity° to play at cherry-pit[5] with Satan. Hang him, foul collier.[6]   *for a man of dignity*

MARIA   Get him to say his prayers. Good Sir Toby, get him to
pray.

MALVOLIO   My prayers, minx?°   *impertinent girl*

110   MARIA   No, I warrant you, he will not hear of godliness.

MALVOLIO   Go hang yourselves, all. You are idle° shallow things,   *foolish*
I am not of your element.° You shall know more hereafter.   *social sphere*
                                                                                              Exit

SIR TOBY   Is't possible?

FABIAN   If this were played upon a stage, now, I could condemn
115   it as an improbable fiction.

SIR TOBY   His very genius° hath taken the infection of the   *spirit*
device,° man.   *trick*

MARIA   Nay, pursue him now, lest the device take air and taint.[7]

FABIAN   Why, we shall make him mad indeed.

120   MARIA   The house will be the quieter.

SIR TOBY   Come, we'll have him in a dark room and bound.[8] My
niece is already in the belief that he's mad. We may carry it
thus° for our pleasure and his penance till our very pastime,   *continue the pretense*
tired out of breath, prompt us to have mercy on him, at which
125   time we will bring the device to the bar[9] and crown thee for a
finder of madmen.[1] But see, but see.
                Enter SIR ANDREW [*with a paper*]

FABIAN   More matter for a May morning.[2]

SIR ANDREW   Here's the challenge, read it. I warrant there's vine-
gar and pepper in't.

130   FABIAN   Is't so saucy?

SIR ANDREW   Ay—is't? I warrant him. Do but read.

SIR TOBY   Give me.
    [*Reads*] 'Youth, whatsoever thou art, thou art but a scurvy
    fellow.'

---

3. *water:* urine (for medical diagnosis). *wise woman:* local
healer, "good witch."
4. Fine fellow (from the French *beau coq,* "fine bird").
5. A children's game in which cherrystones were thrown
into a hole.
6. Dirty coal man (the devil was supposed to be black).
7. Spoil (like leftover food) by exposure to air; become

known (and thus ruined).
8. Customary treatments for madness.
9. Into the open court (to be judged).
1. *finder of madmen:* one of a jury "finding," or declaring,
a man to be mad.
2. More pastime fit for a holiday.

135   FABIAN   Good, and valiant.

SIR TOBY   'Wonder not, nor admire° not in thy mind why I do   *marvel*
call thee so, for I will show thee no reason for't.'

FABIAN   A good note, that keeps you from the blow of the law.[3]

SIR TOBY   'Thou comest to the Lady Olivia, and in my sight she
140   uses thee kindly; but thou liest in thy throat,° that is not the   *deeply*
matter I challenge thee for.'

FABIAN   Very brief, and to exceeding good sense [*aside*] -less.[4]

SIR TOBY   'I will waylay thee going home, where if it be thy
chance to kill me'—

145   FABIAN   Good.

SIR TOBY   'Thou killest me like a rogue and a villain.'

FABIAN   Still you keep o'th' windy side[5] of the law—good.

SIR TOBY   'Fare thee well, and God have mercy upon one of our
souls. He may have mercy upon mine, but my hope is better,[6]
150   and so look to thyself.
Thy friend as thou usest him, and thy sworn enemy,
                           Andrew Aguecheek.'
If this letter move° him not, his legs cannot. I'll give't him.   *provoke*

MARIA   You may have very fit occasion for't. He is now in some
155   commerce° with my lady, and will by and by depart.   *conversation*

SIR TOBY   Go, Sir Andrew. Scout me° for him at the corner of   *Look out*
the orchard like a bum-baily.[7] So soon as ever thou seest him,
draw, and as thou drawest, swear horrible, for it comes to pass
oft that a terrible oath, with a swaggering accent sharply
160   twanged off, gives manhood more approbation° than ever   *credit*
proof° itself would have earned him. Away.   *trial*

SIR ANDREW   Nay, let me alone for swearing.[8]   *Exit*

SIR TOBY   Now will not I deliver his letter, for the behaviour of
the young gentleman gives him out to be of good capacity° and   *ability*
165   breeding. His employment between his lord and my niece
confirms no less. Therefore this letter, being so excellently
ignorant, will breed no terror in the youth. He will find it
comes from a clodpoll.° But, sir, I will deliver his challenge by   *blockhead*
word of mouth, set upon Aguecheek a notable report of valour,
170   and drive the gentleman—as I know his youth will aptly receive
it[9]—into a most hideous opinion of his rage, skill, fury, and
impetuosity. This will so fright them both that they will kill one
another by the look, like cockatrices.[1]

        Enter OLIVIA, *and* VIOLA [*as Cesario*]

FABIAN   Here he comes with your niece. Give them way° till he   *Stand aside*
175   take leave, and presently after him.

SIR TOBY   I will meditate the while upon some horrid message
for a challenge.   [*Exeunt* SIR TOBY, FABIAN, *and* MARIA]

OLIVIA   I have said too much unto a heart of stone,
And laid mine honour too unchary° out.   *carelessly*
180   There's something in me that reproves my fault,
But such a headstrong potent fault it is
That it but mocks reproof.

---

3. That protects you from a charge of a breach of peace.
4. F's "sence-lesse" appears to use the hyphen to signal an aside.
5. To windward (and therefore safe, not exposed to the law's blasts).
6. *my hope is better:* Andrew means he expects to survive, but he ineptly implies that he expects to be damned.

7. Petty sheriff's officer employed to arrest debtors.
8. Have no doubts as to my swearing ability.
9. As I know his inexperience will readily believe the report.
1. Basilisks; mythical creatures supposed to kill at a glance.

VIOLA   With the same 'haviour
That your passion bears[2] goes on my master's griefs.
OLIVIA [*giving a jewel*]   Here, wear this jewel[3] for me, 'tis my picture—
185   Refuse it not, it hath no tongue to vex you—
And I beseech you come again tomorrow.
What shall you ask of me that I'll deny,
That honour, saved, may upon asking give?[4]
VIOLA   Nothing but this: your true love for my master.
190 OLIVIA   How with mine honour may I give him that
Which I have given to you?
VIOLA   I will acquit you.[5]
OLIVIA   Well, come again tomorrow. Fare thee well.
A fiend like thee might bear my soul to hell.   *Exit*
          Enter [SIR] TOBY *and* FABIAN
SIR TOBY   Gentleman, God save thee.
195 VIOLA   And you, sir.
SIR TOBY   That defence thou hast, betake thee to't. Of what
nature the wrongs are thou hast done him, I know not, but thy
intercepter, full of despite,° bloody as the hunter, attends° thee   *defiance / awaits*
at the orchard end. Dismount thy tuck,[6] be yare° in thy prepara-   *prompt*
200   tion, for thy assailant is quick, skilful, and deadly.
VIOLA   You mistake, sir, I am sure no man hath any quarrel to
me. My remembrance° is very free and clear from any image   *memory*
of offence done to any man.
SIR TOBY   You'll find it otherwise, I assure you. Therefore, if you
205   hold your life at any price, betake you to your guard, for your
opposite° hath in him what youth, strength, skill, and wrath can   *opponent*
furnish man withal.
VIOLA   I pray you, sir, what is he?
SIR TOBY   He is knight dubbed with unhatched[7] rapier and on
210   carpet consideration,[8] but he is a devil in private brawl. Souls
and bodies hath he divorced three, and his incensement at this
moment is so implacable that satisfaction can be none but by
pangs of death and sepulchre. Hob nob[9] is his word,° give't or   *motto*
take't.
215 VIOLA   I will return again into the house and desire some con-
duct° of the lady. I am no fighter. I have heard of some kind of   *escort*
men that put quarrels purposely on others, to taste° their   *test*
valour. Belike this is a man of that quirk.
SIR TOBY   Sir, no. His indignation derives itself out of a very com-
220   petent° injury, therefore get you on, and give him his desire.   *sufficient*
Back you shall not to the house unless you undertake that° with   *(a duel)*
me which with as much safety you might answer him. There-
fore on, or strip your sword stark naked, for meddle° you must,   *engage in a duel*
that's certain, or forswear to wear iron about you.[1]
225 VIOLA   This is as uncivil as strange. I beseech you do me this
courteous office, as to know of° the knight what my offence   *ascertain from*
to him is. It is something of my negligence, nothing of my
purpose.

---

2. *'haviour . . . bears*: behavior that characterizes your lovesickness.
3. Jeweled ornament, here a brooch or a locket with Olivia's picture.
4. That honor may grant without compromising itself.
5. I will release you from your promise.

6. Draw your rapier.
7. Unhacked, or undented; never used in battle.
8. A "carpet knight" obtained his title through connections at court rather than valor on the battlefield.
9. Have or have not ("all or nothing").
1. Or forfeit your right to wear a sword.

SIR TOBY   I will do so. Signor Fabian, stay you by this gentleman
230 till my return.   *Exit*
VIOLA   Pray you, sir, do you know of this matter?
FABIAN   I know the knight is incensed against you even to a mor-
       tal arbitrement,° but nothing of the circumstance more.   *deadly duel*
VIOLA   I beseech you, what manner of man is he?
235 FABIAN   Nothing of that wonderful promise to read him by his
       form² as you are like to find him in the proof of his valour. He
       is indeed, sir, the most skilful, bloody, and fatal opposite that
       you could possibly have found in any part of Illyria. Will you°   *If you will*
       walk towards him, I will make your peace with him if I can.
240 VIOLA   I shall be much bound to you for't. I am one that had
       rather go with Sir Priest³ than Sir Knight—I care not who
       knows so much of my mettle.°   *Exeunt*   *disposition*
              Enter [SIR] TOBY *and* [SIR] ANDREW
SIR TOBY   Why, man, he's a very devil, I have not seen such a
       virago.⁴ I had a pass° with him, rapier, scabbard, and all, and   *fencing bout*
245 he gives me the stuck-in⁵ with such a mortal motion that it is
       inevitable, and on the answer,° he pays you as surely as your   *return hit*
       feet hits the ground they step on. They say he has been fencer
       to the Sophy.°   *Shah of Persia*
SIR ANDREW   Pox on't, I'll not meddle with him.
250 SIR TOBY   Ay, but he will not now be pacified, Fabian can scarce
       hold him yonder.
SIR ANDREW   Plague on't, an° I thought he had been valiant and   *if*
       so cunning in fence I'd have seen him damned ere I'd have
       challenged him. Let him let the matter slip and I'll give him
255 my horse, grey Capulet.
SIR TOBY   I'll make the motion.° Stand here, make a good show   *offer*
       on't—this shall end without the perdition of souls.°   *loss of lives*
       [*Aside*] Marry, I'll ride your horse as well as I ride you.
              Enter FABIAN, *and* VIOLA [*as Cesario*]
       [*Aside to* FABIAN] I have his horse to take up° the quarrel, I have   *settle*
260 persuaded him the youth's a devil.
FABIAN [*aside to* SIR TOBY]   He is as horribly conceited⁶ of him,
       and pants and looks pale as if a bear were at his heels.
SIR TOBY [*to* VIOLA]   There's no remedy, sir, he will fight with
       you for's oath' sake. Marry, he hath better bethought him of his
265 quarrel, and he finds that now scarce to be worth talking of.
       Therefore draw for the supportance of his vow, he protests he
       will not hurt you.
VIOLA [*aside*]   Pray God defend me. A little thing would make
       me tell them how much I lack of a man.
270 FABIAN [*to* SIR ANDREW]   Give ground if you see him furious.
SIR TOBY   Come, Sir Andrew, there's no remedy, the gentleman
       will for his honour's sake have one bout with you, he cannot
       by the duello° avoid it, but he has promised me, as he is a   *code of dueling*
       gentleman and a soldier, he will not hurt you. Come on, to't.
275 SIR ANDREW   Pray God he keep his oath.
              Enter ANTONIO

2. *Nothing . . . form:* From his outward appearance,
you cannot perceive him to be as remarkable.
3. Priests were often addressed as "sir."
4. Woman warrior (suggesting great ferocity with a
feminine appearance).
5. Thrust (from the Italian *stoccata*).
6. He has as terrifying an idea.

VIOLA   I do assure you 'tis against my will.
        [SIR ANDREW *and* VIOLA *draw their swords*]
ANTONIO [*drawing his sword, to* SIR ANDREW]   Put up your sword.
  If this young gentleman
  Have done offence, I take the fault on me.
  If you offend him, I for him defy you.
280   SIR TOBY   You, sir? Why, what are you?
ANTONIO   One, sir, that for his love dares yet do more
  Than you have heard him brag to you he will.
SIR TOBY [*drawing his sword*]   Nay, if you be an undertaker,[7] I
  am for you.
        Enter OFFICERS
285   FABIAN   O, good Sir Toby, hold. Here come the officers.
SIR TOBY [*to* ANTONIO]   I'll be with you anon.
VIOLA [*to* SIR ANDREW]   Pray, sir, put your sword up if you please.
SIR ANDREW   Marry will I, sir, and for that° I promised you I'll be   *as for that*
  as good as my word. He will bear you easily, and reins well.
        [SIR ANDREW *and* VIOLA *put up their swords*]
290   FIRST OFFICER   This is the man, do thy office.
SECOND OFFICER   Antonio, I arrest thee at the suit of Count
  Orsino.
ANTONIO   You do mistake me, sir.
FIRST OFFICER   No, sir, no jot. I know your favour° well,   *face*
295   Though now you have no seacap on your head.
  [*To* SECOND OFFICER] Take him away, he knows I know him well.
ANTONIO   I must obey. [*To* VIOLA] This comes with seeking you.
  But there's no remedy, I shall answer° it.   *answer for*
  What will you do now my necessity
300   Makes me to ask you for my purse? It grieves me
  Much more for what I cannot do for you
  Than what befalls myself. You stand amazed,
  But be of comfort.
SECOND OFFICER   Come, sir, away.
ANTONIO [*to* VIOLA]   I must entreat of you some of that money.
305   VIOLA   What money, sir?
  For the fair kindness you have showed me here,
  And part° being prompted by your present trouble,   *in part*
  Out of my lean and low ability
  I'll lend you something. My having is not much.
310   I'll make division of my present° with you.   *ready money*
  Hold, [*offering money*] there's half my coffer.
ANTONIO   Will you deny me now?
  Is't possible that my deserts to you
  Can lack persuasion?[8] Do not tempt my misery,
  Lest that it make me so unsound° a man   *morally weak*
315   As to upbraid you with those kindnesses
  That I have done for you.
VIOLA   I know of none,
  Nor know I you by voice, or any feature.
  I hate ingratitude more in a man
  Than lying, vainness, babbling drunkenness,

7. One who would take upon himself a task (here, a challenge).

8. *Is't . . . persuasion:* Is it possible my past kindness can fail to persuade you?

320 Or any taint of vice whose strong corruption
Inhabits our frail blood.
ANTONIO   O heavens themselves!
SECOND OFFICER   Come, sir, I pray you go.
ANTONIO   Let me speak a little. This youth that you see here
I snatched one half out of the jaws of death,
325 Relieved him with such sanctity° of love,   *great devotion*
And to his image,⁹ which methought did promise
Most venerable worth,¹ did I devotion.
FIRST OFFICER   What's that to us? The time goes by, away.
ANTONIO   But O, how vile an idol proves this god!
330 Thou hast, Sebastian, done good feature° shame.   *physical beauty*
In nature there's no blemish but the mind.
None can be called deformed but the unkind.
Virtue is beauty, but the beauteous evil
Are empty trunks o'er-flourished² by the devil.
335 FIRST OFFICER   The man grows mad, away with him. Come, come, sir.
ANTONIO   Lead me on.   *Exit [with* OFFICERS]
VIOLA [*aside*]   Methinks his words do from such passion fly
That he believes himself. So do not I.³
Prove true, imagination, O prove true,
340 That I, dear brother, be now ta'en for you!
SIR TOBY   Come hither, knight. Come hither, Fabian. We'll
whisper o'er a couplet or two of most sage saws.°   *sayings; maxims*
[*They stand aside*]
VIOLA   He named Sebastian. I my brother know
Yet living in my glass.° Even such and so   *mirror*
345 In favour° was my brother, and he went   *appearance*
Still° in this fashion, colour, ornament,   *Always*
For him I imitate. O, if it prove,
Tempests are kind, and salt waves fresh in love!   *Exit*
SIR TOBY [*to* SIR ANDREW]   A very dishonest,° paltry boy, and   *dishonorable*
350 more a coward than a hare. His dishonesty appears in leaving
his friend here in necessity, and denying him; and for his cow-
ardship, ask Fabian.
FABIAN   A coward, a most devout coward, religious in it.
SIR ANDREW   'Slid,° I'll after him again, and beat him.   *By God's eyelid*
355 SIR TOBY   Do, cuff him soundly, but never draw thy sword.
SIR ANDREW   An I do not—   [*Exit*]
FABIAN   Come, let's see the event.°   *outcome*
SIR TOBY   I dare lay any money 'twill be nothing yet.°   *Exeunt*   *after all*

4.1

Enter SEBASTIAN *and* [FESTE, *the*] *clown*

FESTE   Will you° make me believe that I am not sent for you?   *Are you trying to*
SEBASTIAN   Go to, go to, thou art a foolish fellow,
Let me be clear° of thee.   *rid*
FESTE   Well held out,° i'faith! No, I do not know you, nor I am   *kept up*
5 not sent to you by my lady to bid you come speak with her, nor

---

9. Appearance (with a play on "religious icon").
1. *did . . . worth*: was worthy of veneration.
2. Chests decorated with carving or painting; beautified bodies.

3. *So do not I*: I do not entirely believe the passionate hope (for my brother's rescue) that is arising in me.
4.1 Location: Near Olivia's house.

your name is not Master Cesario, nor this is not my nose, nei-
ther. Nothing that is so, is so.

SEBASTIAN   I prithee vent° thy folly somewhere else,   *utter; excrete*
Thou know'st not me.

10 FESTE   Vent my folly! He has heard that word of some great
man, and now applies it to a fool. Vent my folly—I am afraid
this great lubber° the world will prove a cockney.° I prithee   *lout / sissy*
now ungird thy strangeness,¹ and tell me what I shall 'vent' to
my lady? Shall I 'vent' to her that thou art coming?

15 SEBASTIAN   I prithee, foolish Greek,° depart from me.   *buffoon*
There's money for thee. If you tarry longer
I shall give worse payment.

FESTE   By my troth, thou hast an open hand. These wise men
that give fools money get themselves a good report,° after four-   *reputation*
20 teen years' purchase.²

        Enter [SIR] ANDREW, [SIR] TOBY, *and* FABIAN

SIR ANDREW [*to* SEBASTIAN]   Now, sir, have I met you again?
[*Striking him*] There's for you.

SEBASTIAN [*striking* SIR ANDREW *with his dagger*]   Why, there's
        for thee, and there, and there.
Are all the people mad?

25 SIR TOBY [*to* SEBASTIAN, *holding him back*]   Hold, sir, or I'll throw
your dagger o'er the house.

FESTE   This will I tell my lady straight,° I would not be in some   *straightaway*
of your coats for twopence.   [*Exit*]

SIR TOBY   Come on, sir, hold.

30 SIR ANDREW   Nay, let him alone, I'll go another way to work with
him. I'll have an action of battery° against him if there be any   *a lawsuit for assault*
law in Illyria. Though I struck him first, yet it's no matter for
that.

SEBASTIAN   Let go thy hand.

35 SIR TOBY   Come, sir, I will not let you go. Come, my young sol-
dier, put up your iron. You are well fleshed.³ Come on.

SEBASTIAN [*freeing himself*]   I will be free from thee. What wouldst thou now?
If thou dar'st tempt me further, draw thy sword.

SIR TOBY   What, what? Nay then, I must have an ounce or two
40 of this malapert° blood from you.   *impudent*

        [SIR TOBY *and* SEBASTIAN *draw their swords.*]
        Enter OLIVIA

OLIVIA   Hold, Toby, on thy life I charge thee hold.

SIR TOBY   Madam.

OLIVIA   Will it be ever thus? Ungracious wretch,
Fit for the mountains and the barbarous caves,
45 Where manners ne'er were preached—out of my sight!
Be not offended, dear Cesario.
[*To* SIR TOBY] Rudesby,° be gone.   *Ruffian*

        [*Exeunt* SIR TOBY, SIR ANDREW, *and* FABIAN]
                                I prithee, gentle friend,
Let thy fair wisdom, not thy passion sway
In this uncivil and unjust extent°   *assault*

---

1. *I . . . strangeness*: Stop pretending not to know me.
(Feste mocks Sebastian's affected language.)
2. *after . . . purchase*: at a high price. The purchase price
of land was normally twelve times its annual rent.
3. Experienced in combat. Hunting hounds were said to
be "fleshed" after being fed part of their first kill.

50   Against thy peace. Go with me to my house,
        And hear thou there how many fruitless pranks
        This ruffian hath botched up,° that thou thereby   clumsily contrived
        Mayst smile at this. Thou shalt not choose but go.
        Do not deny. Beshrew° his soul for me,   Curse
55   He started one poor heart of mine in thee.⁴
        SEBASTIAN   What relish° is in this? How runs the stream?   task; meaning
        Or° I am mad, or else this is a dream.   Either
        Let fancy° still my sense in Lethe⁵ steep.   imagination
        If it be thus to dream, still let me sleep.
60   OLIVIA   Nay, come, I prithee, would thou'dst be ruled by me.
        SEBASTIAN   Madam, I will.
        OLIVIA   O, say so, and so be.   *Exeunt*

                              4.2
        Enter MARIA [*carrying a gown and false beard, and*
            FESTE, *the*] *clown*
        MARIA   Nay, I prithee put on this gown and this beard, make
            him believe thou art Sir Topas¹ the curate. Do it quickly. I'll
            call Sir Toby the whilst.°   *Exit*   in the meantime
        FESTE   Well, I'll put it on, and I will dissemble² myself in't, and
5   I would I were the first that ever dissembled in such a gown.
                    [*He disguises himself*]
            I am not tall enough to become the function well,³ nor lean
            enough to be thought a good student,° but to be said° 'an hon-   (of divinity) / reputed
            est man and a good housekeeper'° goes as fairly as⁴ to say 'a   host
            careful man and a great scholar'. The competitors° enter.   associates
                    Enter [SIR] TOBY [*and* MARIA]
10   SIR TOBY   Jove bless thee, Master Parson.
        FESTE   *Bonos dies,*⁵ Sir Toby, for, as the old hermit of Prague,⁶
            that never saw pen and ink, very wittily° said to a niece of King   intelligently
            Gorboduc,° 'That that is, is.' So I, being Master Parson, am   legendary British king
            Master Parson; for what is 'that' but 'that', and 'is' but 'is'?
15   SIR TOBY   To him, Sir Topas.
        FESTE   What ho, I say, peace in this prison.
        SIR TOBY   The knave counterfeits well—a good knave.
                    MALVOLIO *within*
        MALVOLIO   Who calls there?
        FESTE   Sir Topas the curate, who comes to visit Malvolio the
20   lunatic.
        MALVOLIO   Sir Topas, Sir Topas, good Sir Topas, go to my lady.
        FESTE   Out, hyperbolical fiend,⁷ how vexest thou this man! Talk-
            est thou nothing but of ladies?
        SIR TOBY   Well said, Master Parson.
25   MALVOLIO   Sir Topas, never was man thus wronged. Good Sir

---

4. He . . . thee: By attacking Sebastian, Sir Toby fright-
ened Olivia, who has exchanged hearts with Sebastian.
started: an allusion to hunting, creating a pun on "hart /
heart."
5. The mythical river of oblivion.
4.2 Location: Olivia's house, where Malvolio will be
found (offstage) "in a dark room and bound" (3.4.121).
1. The comical hero of Chaucer's *Rime of Sir Topas*.
Also alluding to the mineral topaz, which was thought to

have special curative qualities for insanity.
2. Disguise; with subsequent play on "lie."
3. Grace the priestly office. *tall*: stout, rather than of
great height.
4. *goes as fairly as*: sounds as well as.
5. Good day (false Latin).
6. Probably an invented authority.
7. Feste treats Malvolio as a man possessed by vehement
("hyperbolical") evil spirits.

Topas, do not think I am mad. They have laid me here in
hideous darkness.

FESTE Fie, thou dishonest Satan—I call thee by the most mod-
est° terms, for I am one of those gentle ones that will use the   *mildest*
30 devil himself with courtesy. Sayst thou that house° is dark?   *room*

MALVOLIO As hell, Sir Topas.

FESTE Why, it hath bay windows transparent as barricadoes, and
the clerestories[8] toward the south-north are as lustrous as
ebony,[9] and yet complainest thou of obstruction?

35 MALVOLIO I am not mad, Sir Topas; I say to you this house is
dark.

FESTE Madman, thou errest. I say there is no darkness but igno-
rance, in which thou art more puzzled than the Egyptians in
their fog.[1]

40 MALVOLIO I say this house is as dark as ignorance, though igno-
rance were as dark as hell; and I say there was never man thus
abused. I am no more mad than you are. Make the trial of it in
any constant question.°   *logical discussion*

FESTE What is the opinion of Pythagoras[2] concerning wildfowl?

45 MALVOLIO That the soul of our grandam might haply° inhabit a   *perhaps*
bird.

FESTE What thinkest thou of his opinion?

MALVOLIO I think nobly of the soul, and no way approve his
opinion.

50 FESTE Fare thee well. Remain thou still in darkness. Thou shalt
hold th'opinion of Pythagoras ere I will allow of thy wits,° and   *certify your sanity*
fear to kill a woodcock[3] lest thou dispossess the soul of thy gran-
dam. Fare thee well.

MALVOLIO Sir Topas, Sir Topas!

55 SIR TOBY My most exquisite Sir Topas.

FESTE Nay, I am for all waters.[4]

MARIA Thou mightst have done this without thy beard and
gown, he sees thee not.

SIR TOBY [*to* FESTE] To him in thine own voice, and bring me
60 word how thou findest him. I would we were well rid of this
knavery. If he may be conveniently delivered, I would he were,
for I am now so far in offence with my niece that I cannot
pursue with any safety this sport to the upshot. [*To* MARIA]
Come by and by to my chamber.   *Exit* [*with* MARIA]

65 FESTE [*sings*][5] 'Hey Robin, jolly Robin,
                     Tell me how thy lady does.'

MALVOLIO Fool!

FESTE   'My lady is unkind, pardie.'[6]

MALVOLIO Fool!

70 FESTE   'Alas, why is she so?'

MALVOLIO Fool, I say!

FESTE   'She loves another.'
Who calls, ha?

---

8. Upper windows, usually in a church or great hall. *bar-*
ricadoes: barricades (subsequent paradoxes are equiva-
lent to "as clear as mud").
9. A dense and naturally dull black wood.
1. One of the plagues of Egypt was a "black darkness"
lasting for three days (Exodus 10:21–23).
2. An ancient Greek philosopher who held that the same

soul could successively inhabit different creatures.
3. A traditionally stupid bird.
4. I am able to turn my hand to anything.
5. Feste's song, which makes Malvolio aware of his pres-
ence, is traditional. There is a version by Sir Thomas
Wyatt.
6. A corruption of the French *pardieu,* "by God."

MALVOLIO   Good fool, as ever thou wilt deserve well at my hand,
75   help me to a candle and pen, ink, and paper. As I am a gentle-
man, I will live to be thankful to thee for't.

FESTE   Master Malvolio?

MALVOLIO   Ay, good fool.

FESTE   Alas, sir, how fell you besides° your five wits?[7]   out of

80   MALVOLIO   Fool, there was never man so notoriously° abused. I   outrageously
am as well in my wits, fool, as thou art.

FESTE   But as well? Then you are mad indeed, if you be no bet-
ter in your wits than a fool.

MALVOLIO   They have here propertied me,[8] keep me in darkness,
85   send ministers to me, asses, and do all they can to face me[9] out
of my wits.

FESTE   Advise you° what you say, the minister is here.   Be careful
[As Sir Topas] Malvolio, Malvolio, thy wits the heavens restore.
Endeavour thyself to sleep, and leave thy vain bibble-babble.

90   MALVOLIO   Sir Topas.

FESTE [as Sir Topas]   Maintain no words with him, good fellow.
[As himself] Who I, sir? Not I, sir. God b'wi' you,° good Sir   God be with you
Topas. [As Sir Topas] Marry, amen. [As himself] I will, sir, I
will.

95   MALVOLIO   Fool, fool, fool, I say.

FESTE   Alas, sir, be patient. What say you, sir? I am shent° for   scolded
speaking to you.

MALVOLIO   Good fool, help me to some light and some paper. I
tell thee I am as well in my wits as any man in Illyria.

100   FESTE   Well-a-day° that you were, sir.   Alas

MALVOLIO   By this hand, I am. Good fool, some ink, paper, and
light, and convey what I will set down to my lady. It shall advan-
tage thee more than ever the bearing of letter did.

FESTE   I will help you to't. But tell me true, are you not mad
105   indeed, or do you but counterfeit?

MALVOLIO   Believe me, I am not, I tell thee true.

FESTE   Nay, I'll ne'er believe a madman till I see his brains. I
will fetch you light, and paper, and ink.

MALVOLIO   Fool, I'll requite it in the highest degree. I prithee,
110   be gone.

FESTE   I am gone, sir,
                And anon, sir,
                    I'll be with you again,
                In a trice,
115   Like to the old Vice,[1]
                    Your need to sustain,
                Who with dagger of lath
                In his rage and his wrath
                    Cries 'Aha,' to the devil,
120   Like a mad lad,
                'Pare thy nails, dad,
                    Adieu, goodman[2] devil.'   Exit

---

7. Usually regarded as common sense, fantasy, memory,
judgment, and imagination.
8. Treated me as a piece of property.
9. face me: brazenly construe me as.

1. A stock comic figure in the old morality plays; the Vice
often carried a wooden dagger.
2. Yeoman; a title given to one not of gentle birth, hence
a parting insult to Malvolio.

4.3

Enter SEBASTIAN

SEBASTIAN   This is the air, that is the glorious sun.
This pearl she gave me, I do feel't and see't,
And though 'tis wonder that enwraps me thus,
Yet 'tis not madness. Where's Antonio then?
5   I could not find him at the Elephant,
Yet there he was,° and there I found this credit,°   had been / report
That he did range the town to seek me out.
His counsel now might do me golden service,
For though my soul disputes well with my sense[1]
10   That this may be some error but no madness,
Yet doth this accident and flood of fortune
So far exceed all instance,° all discourse,°   precedent / reasoning
That I am ready to distrust mine eyes
And wrangle with my reason that persuades me
15   To any other trust° but that I am mad,   belief
Or else the lady's mad. Yet if 'twere so
She could not sway° her house, command her followers,   rule
Take and give back affairs and their dispatch[2]
With such a smooth, discreet, and stable bearing
20   As I perceive she does. There's something in't
That is deceivable.° But here the lady comes.   deceptive

Enter OLIVIA *and* PRIEST

OLIVIA   Blame not this haste of mine. If you mean well
Now go with me, and with this holy man,
Into the chantry by.° There before him,   nearby chapel
25   And underneath that consecrated roof,
Plight me the full assurance of your faith,[3]
That my most jealous° and too doubtful soul   anxious
May live at peace. He shall conceal it
Whiles° you are willing it shall come to note,   Until
30   What° time we will our celebration keep   At which
According to my birth.° What do you say?   rank

SEBASTIAN   I'll follow this good man, and go with you,
And having sworn truth, ever will be true.

OLIVIA   Then lead the way, good father, and heavens so shine
35   That they may fairly note° this act of mine.   *Exeunt*   look favorably upon

5.1

Enter [FESTE, *the*] *clown and* FABIAN

FABIAN   Now, as thou lovest me, let me see his letter.
FESTE   Good Master Fabian, grant me another request.
FABIAN   Anything.
FESTE   Do not desire to see this letter.
5   FABIAN   This is to give a dog, and in recompense desire my dog
again.[1]

Enter Duke, VIOLA [*as Cesario*], CURIO, *and lords*

ORSINO   Belong you to the Lady Olivia, friends?

4.3 Location: Near Olivia's house.
1. For though my reason and my sense both concur.
2. Undertake business, and ensure that it is carried out.
3. Enter into the solemn contract of betrothal.
5.1 Location: Before Olivia's house.

1. Perhaps a reference to an anecdote, recorded in John Manningham's diary, in which Queen Elizabeth requested a dog, and the donor, when granted a wish in return, asked for the dog back.

FESTE Ay, sir, we are some of her trappings.°   *ornaments*

ORSINO I know thee well. How dost thou, my good fellow?

10 FESTE Truly, sir, the better for my foes and the worse for my
friends.

ORSINO Just the contrary—the better for thy friends.

FESTE No, sir, the worse.

ORSINO How can that be?

15 FESTE Marry, sir, they praise me, and make an ass of me. Now
my foes tell me plainly I am an ass, so that by my foes, sir, I
profit in the knowledge of myself, and by my friends I am
abused;° so that, conclusions to be as kisses, if your four nega-   *deceived*
tives make your two affirmatives,² why then the worse for my

20 friends and the better for my foes.

ORSINO Why, this is excellent.

FESTE By my troth, sir, no, though it please you to be one of my
friends.

ORSINO [*giving money*] Thou shalt not be the worse for me.

25 There's gold.

FESTE But° that it would be double-dealing,³ sir, I would you   *Except for the fact*
could make it another.

ORSINO O, you give me ill counsel.

FESTE Put your grace in your pocket,⁴ sir, for this once, and let

30 your flesh and blood obey it.⁵

ORSINO Well, I will be so much a sinner to° be a double-dealer.   *as to*
[*Giving money*] There's another.

FESTE *Primo, secundo, tertio*⁶ is a good play,° and the old saying   *game*
is 'The third pays for all'.⁷ The triplex,° sir, is a good tripping   *triple time in music*

35 measure, or the bells of Saint Bennet,⁸ sir, may put you in
mind—'one, two, three'.

ORSINO You can fool no more money out of me at this throw.°   *throw of the dice*
If you will let your lady know I am here to speak with her, and
bring her along with you, it may awake my bounty further.

40 FESTE Marry, sir, lullaby to your bounty till I come again. I go,
sir, but I would not have you to think that my desire of having
is the sin of covetousness. But as you say, sir, let your bounty
take a nap, I will awake it anon.   *Exit*

Enter ANTONIO *and* OFFICERS

VIOLA Here comes the man, sir, that did rescue me.

45 ORSINO That face of his I do remember well,
Yet when I saw it last it was besmeared
As black as Vulcan⁹ in the smoke of war.
A baubling° vessel was he captain of,   *trifling*
For shallow draught and bulk unprizable,¹

50 With which such scatheful° grapple did he make   *destructive*
With the most noble bottom° of our fleet   *ship*

---

2. *conclusions . . affirmatives:* as in grammar, a double
negative can make an affirmative (and therefore four neg-
atives can make two affirmatives); so when a coy girl is
asked for a kiss, her four refusals can be construed as
"yes, yes."
3. A duplicity; a double donation.
4. Set aside (pocket up) your virtue; also (with a play on
the customary form of address for a duke, "your grace"),
reach into your pocket and grace me with another coin.
5. Let your normal human instincts (as opposed to

grace) follow the "ill counsel" (line 28).
6. First, second, third (Latin); perhaps an allusion to a
dice throw or a child's game.
7. Third time lucky (proverbial).
8. A London church, across the Thames from the Globe,
was known as St. Bennet Hithe.
9. Blacksmith of the Roman gods.
1. Of no value because of its small size. *draught:* water
displaced by a vessel.

That very envy° and the tongue of loss°   *even enmity / the losers*
Cried fame and honour on him. What's the matter?

FIRST OFFICER   Orsino, this is that Antonio
55   That took the Phoenix and her freight from Candy,[2]
And this is he that did the *Tiger* board
When your young nephew Titus lost his leg.
Here in the streets, desperate of shame and state,[3]
In private brabble° did we apprehend him.   *brawl*

60   VIOLA   He did me kindness, sir, drew on my side,[4]
But in conclusion put strange speech upon° me.   *spoke strangely to*
I know not what 'twas but distraction.°   *if not insanity*

ORSINO [*to* ANTONIO]   Notable° pirate, thou salt-water thief,   *Notorious*
What foolish boldness brought thee to their mercies
65   Whom thou in terms so bloody and so dear°   *dire*
Hast made thine enemies?

ANTONIO   Orsino, noble sir,
Be pleased that I shake off these names you give me.
Antonio never yet was thief or pirate,
Though, I confess, on base° and ground enough   *foundation*
70   Orsino's enemy. A witchcraft drew me hither.
That most ingrateful boy there by your side
From the rude sea's enraged and foamy mouth
Did I redeem. A wreck past hope he was.
His life I gave him, and did thereto add
75   My love without retention° or restraint,   *reservation*
All his in dedication. For his sake
Did I expose myself, pure° for his love,   *only*
Into the danger of this adverse° town,   *hostile*
Drew to defend him when he was beset,
80   Where being apprehended, his false cunning—
Not meaning to partake with me in danger—
Taught him to face me out of his acquaintance,[5]
And grew a twenty years' removèd thing
While one would wink,[6] denied me mine own purse,
85   Which I had recommended° to his use   *consigned*
Not half an hour before.

VIOLA   How can this be?

ORSINO   When came he to this town?

ANTONIO   Today, my lord, and for three months before,
90   No int'rim, not a minute's vacancy,°   *interval*
Both day and night did we keep company.

                    Enter OLIVIA *and attendants*

ORSINO   Here comes the Countess. Now heaven walks on earth.
But for thee, fellow—fellow, thy words are madness.
Three months this youth hath tended upon me.
95   But more of that anon. Take him aside.

OLIVIA   What would my lord, but that he may not have,[7]
Wherein Olivia may seem serviceable?
Cesario, you do not keep promise with me.

VIOLA   Madam—

---

2. Candia, capital of Crete.
3. *desperate . . . state*: recklessly oblivious of the danger
to his honor and his position (as a free man and public
enemy).
4. Drew his sword in my defense.

5. To brazenly deny my acquaintance.
6. *And . . . wink*: In the wink of an eye, pretended we had
been estranged for twenty years.
7. Except that which he may not have (my love).

100 ORSINO Gracious Olivia—
OLIVIA What do you say, Cesario? Good my lord—
VIOLA My lord would speak, my duty hushes me.
OLIVIA If it be aught° to the old tune, my lord,   *anything*
It is as fat and fulsome° to mine ear   *gross and offensive*
105 As howling after music.
ORSINO Still so cruel?
OLIVIA Still so constant, lord.
ORSINO What, to perverseness? You uncivil lady,
To whose ingrate and unauspicious° altars   *unfavorable*
110 My soul the faithfull'st off 'rings hath breathed out
That e'er devotion tendered—what shall I do?
OLIVIA Even what it please my lord that shall become° him.   *be fitting for*
ORSINO Why should I not, had I the heart to do it,
Like to th' Egyptian thief, at point of death
115 Kill what I love⁸—a savage jealousy
That sometime savours nobly.° But hear me this: *of nobility*
Since you to non-regardance° cast my faith,   *oblivion*
And that I partly know the instrument
That screws° me from my true place in your favour,   *wrenches*
120 Live you the marble-breasted tyrant still.
But this your minion,° whom I know you love,   *darling*
And whom, by heaven I swear, I tender° dearly,   *regard*
Him will I tear out of that cruel eye
Where he sits crownèd in his master's spite.⁹
125 [*To* VIOLA] Come, boy, with me. My thoughts are ripe in mischief.
I'll sacrifice the lamb that I do love
To spite a raven's heart within a dove.
VIOLA And I most jocund,° apt,° and willingly   *cheerfully / ready*
To do you rest a thousand deaths would die.
OLIVIA Where goes Cesario?
130 VIOLA   After him I love
More than I love these eyes, more than my life,
More by all mores¹ than e'er I shall love wife.
If I do feign, you witnesses above,
Punish my life for tainting of my love.
135 OLIVIA Ay me detested, how am I beguiled!
VIOLA Who does beguile you? Who does do you wrong?
OLIVIA Hast thou forgot thyself? Is it so long?
Call forth the holy father.   [*Exit an attendant*]
ORSINO [*to* VIOLA]   Come, away.
OLIVIA Whither, my lord? Cesario, husband, stay.
ORSINO Husband?
140 OLIVIA   Ay, husband. Can he that deny?
ORSINO [*to* VIOLA] Her husband, sirrah?²
VIOLA   No, my lord, not I.
OLIVIA Alas, it is the baseness of thy fear
That makes thee strangle thy propriety.³
Fear not, Cesario, take thy fortunes up,

---

8. In Heliodorus of Emesa's *Ethiopica*, a Greek prose
romance translated into English in 1569 and popular in
Shakespeare's day, the Egyptian robber chief Thyamis
tries to kill his captive Chariclea, whom he loves, when he
is in danger from a rival band.

9. To the mortification of his master.
1. More beyond all comparison.
2. Contemptuous form of address to an inferior.
3. That makes you deny your identity (as my husband).

145 Be that thou know'st thou art, and then thou art
As great as that° thou fear'st.   *him whom*
       Enter PRIEST
                    O welcome, father.
Father, I charge thee by thy reverence
Here to unfold—though lately we intended
To keep in darkness what occasion° now   *necessity*
150 Reveals before 'tis ripe—what thou dost know
Hath newly passed between this youth and me.
PRIEST   A contract of eternal bond of love,
Confirmed by mutual joinder° of your hands,   *joining*
Attested by the holy close° of lips,   *meeting*
155 Strengthened by interchangement of your rings,
And all the ceremony of this compact
Sealed in my function,[4] by my testimony;
Since when, my watch hath told me, toward my grave
I have travelled but two hours.
160 ORSINO [*to* VIOLA]   O thou dissembling cub, what wilt thou be
When time hath sowed a grizzle on thy case?[5]
Or will not else thy craft° so quickly grow   *craftiness*
That thine own trip shall be thine overthrow?[6]
Farewell, and take her, but direct thy feet
165 Where thou and I henceforth may never meet.
VIOLA   My lord, I do protest.
OLIVIA   O, do not swear!
Hold little° faith, though thou hast too much fear.   *Preserve some*
       Enter SIR ANDREW
SIR ANDREW   For the love of God, a surgeon—send one pres-
ently° to Sir Toby.   *immediately*
170 OLIVIA   What's the matter?
SIR ANDREW   He's broke° my head across, and has given Sir Toby   *cut*
a bloody coxcomb,[7] too. For the love of God, your help! I had
rather than forty pound I were at home.
OLIVIA   Who has done this, Sir Andrew?
175 SIR ANDREW   The Count's gentleman, one Cesario. We took him
for a coward, but he's the very devil incardinate.[8]
ORSINO   My gentleman, Cesario?
SIR ANDREW   'Od's lifelings,° here he is. [*To* VIOLA] You broke   *By God's little lives*
my head for nothing, and that that I did I was set on to do't by
180 Sir Toby.
VIOLA   Why do you speak to me? I never hurt you.
You drew your sword upon me without cause,
But I bespake you fair,[9] and hurt you not.
       Enter [SIR] TOBY *and* [FESTE, *the*] *clown*
SIR ANDREW   If a bloody coxcomb be a hurt you have hurt me. I
185 think you set nothing by° a bloody coxcomb. Here comes Sir   *think nothing of*
Toby, halting.° You shall hear more; but if ° he had not been   *limping / if only*
in drink he would have tickled° you othergates° than he did.   *chastised / in other ways*
ORSINO [*to* SIR TOBY]   How now, gentleman? How is't with you?

4. Ratified by priestly authority.
5. A gray hair ("grizzle") on your hide (sustaining the metaphor of "cub").
6. That your attempt to trip someone else will be the cause of your downfall.
7. Head; also, a fool's cap, which resembles the crest of a cock.
8. Sir Andrew's blunder for "incarnate" (in the flesh).
9. But I spoke courteously to you.

SIR TOBY That's all one,° he's hurt me, and there's th'end on't.   *No matter*

190 [*To* FESTE] Sot,° didst see Dick Surgeon, sot?   *Fool; drunkard*

FESTE O, he's drunk, Sir Toby, an hour agone. His eyes were
    set[1] at eight i'th' morning.

SIR TOBY Then he's a rogue, and a passy-measures pavan.[2] I hate
    a drunken rogue.

195 OLIVIA Away with him! Who hath made this havoc with them?

SIR ANDREW I'll help you, Sir Toby, because we'll be dressed[3]
    together.

SIR TOBY Will *you* help—an ass-head, and a coxcomb,° and a   *fool*
    knave; a thin-faced knave, a gull?°   *dupe*

200 OLIVIA Get him to bed, and let his hurt be looked to.

    [*Exeunt* SIR TOBY, SIR ANDREW, FESTE, *and* FABIAN]

    Enter SEBASTIAN

SEBASTIAN [*to* OLIVIA] I am sorry, madam, I have hurt your kinsman,
    But had it been the brother of my blood
    I must have done no less with wit and safety.[4]
    You throw a strange regard upon me,° and by that   *regard me strangely*

205 I do perceive it hath offended you.
    Pardon me, sweet one, even for the vows
    We made each other but so late ago.

ORSINO One face, one voice, one habit, and two persons,
    A natural perspective,[5] that is and is not.

210 SEBASTIAN Antonio! O, my dear Antonio,
    How have the hours racked and tortured me
    Since I have lost thee!

ANTONIO Sebastian are you?

SEBASTIAN Fear'st thou° that, Antonio?   *Do you doubt*

215 ANTONIO How have you made division of yourself ?
    An apple cleft in two is not more twin
    Than these two creatures. Which is Sebastian?

OLIVIA Most wonderful!°   *full of wonder*

SEBASTIAN [*seeing* VIOLA] Do I stand there? I never had a brother,

220 Nor can there be that deity° in my nature   *divine power*
    Of here and everywhere.° I had a sister,   *Of omnipresence*
    Whom the blind waves and surges have devoured.
    Of charity,° what kin are you to me?   *Please*
    What countryman? What name? What parentage?

225 VIOLA Of Messaline. Sebastian was my father.
    Such a Sebastian was my brother, too.
    So went he suited° to his watery tomb.   *in appearance; clad*
    If spirits can assume both form and suit
    You come to fright us.

SEBASTIAN   A spirit I am indeed,

230 But am in that dimension grossly clad
    Which from the womb I did participate.[6]
    Were you a woman, as the rest goes even,°   *the rest suggests*
    I should my tears let fall upon your cheek
    And say 'Thrice welcome, drownèd Viola.'

235 VIOLA My father had a mole upon his brow.

---

1. Closed (as the sun sets).
2. A variety of the slow dance known as "pavane" (from the Italian *passamezzo pavana*). Sir Toby may think its swaying movements suggest drunkenness.
3. We'll have our wounds dressed.

4. With any sense of my welfare.
5. An optical illusion produced by nature (rather than by a mirror).
6. *But . . . participate:* I am clad, like all mortals, in the flesh in which I was born.

SEBASTIAN   And so had mine.

VIOLA   And died that day when Viola from her birth
Had numbered thirteen years.

SEBASTIAN   O, that record is lively[7] in my soul.
240   He finishèd indeed his mortal act
That day that made my sister thirteen years.

VIOLA   If nothing lets° to make us happy both   hinders
But this my masculine usurped attire,
Do not embrace me till each circumstance
245   Of place, time, fortune do cohere and jump°   agree
That I am Viola, which to confirm
I'll bring you to a captain in this town
Where lie my maiden weeds,° by whose gentle help   clothes
I was preserved to serve this noble count.
250   All the occurrence of my fortune since
Hath been between this lady and this lord.

SEBASTIAN [to OLIVIA]   So comes it, lady, you have been mistook.
But nature to her bias drew in that.[8]
You would have been contracted° to a maid,   betrothed
255   Nor are you therein, by my life, deceived.
You are betrothed both to a maid and man.[9]

ORSINO [to OLIVIA]   Be not amazed. Right noble is his blood.
If this be so, as yet the glass seems true,[1]
I shall have share in this most happy wreck.
260   [To VIOLA] Boy, thou hast said to me a thousand times
Thou never shouldst love woman like to me.

VIOLA   And all those sayings will I overswear,°   swear again
And all those swearings keep as true in soul
As doth that orbèd continent[2] the fire
That severs day from night.

265   ORSINO   Give me thy hand,
And let me see thee in thy woman's weeds.

VIOLA   The captain that did bring me first on shore
Hath my maid's garments. He upon some action°   legal charge
Is now in durance,° at Malvolio's suit,   prison
270   A gentleman and follower of my lady's.

OLIVIA   He shall enlarge° him. Fetch Malvolio hither—   release
And yet, alas, now I remember me,
They say, poor gentleman, he's much distraught.

Enter [FESTE, *the*] *clown with a letter, and* FABIAN

A most extracting° frenzy of mine own   distracting
275   From my remembrance clearly banished his.
How does he, sirrah?

FESTE   Truly, madam, he holds Beelzebub at the stave's end[3] as
well as a man in his case may do. He's here writ a letter to you.
I should have given't you today morning. But as a madman's
280   epistles are no gospels,[4] so it skills° not much when they are   matters
delivered.

OLIVIA   Open't and read it.

---

7. The memory of that is vivid.
8. But nature followed her inclination. (The image is from the game of bowls, which uses a ball with an off-centered weight that causes it to curve away from a straight course.)
9. *maid and man:* a man who is a virgin.
1. *the glass seems true:* the "natural perspective" (line

209) continues to seem real.
2. Referring to either the sun or the sphere within which the sun was thought to be fixed.
3. He holds the devil (who threatens to possess him) at a distance (proverbial).
4. Gospel truths. *epistles:* letters (playing on the sense of apostolic accounts of Christ in the New Testament).

FESTE   Look then to be well edified when the fool delivers° the   *speaks the words of*
madman. [*Reads*] 'By the Lord, madam'—
285 OLIVIA   How now, art thou mad?
FESTE   No, madam, I do but read madness. An your ladyship
will have it as it ought to be you must allow *vox*.[5]
OLIVIA   Prithee, read i'thy right wits.
FESTE   So I do, madonna, but to read his right wits[6] is to read
290 thus. Therefore perpend,° my princess, and give ear.   *pay attention*
OLIVIA [*to* FABIAN]   Read it you, sirrah.
          [FESTE *gives the letter to* FABIAN]
FABIAN (*reads*)   'By the Lord, madam, you wrong me, and the
world shall know it. Though you have put me into darkness
and given your drunken cousin rule over me, yet have I the
295 benefit of my senses as well as your ladyship. I have your own
letter that induced me to the semblance I put on, with the
which I doubt not but to do myself much right or you much
shame. Think of me as you please. I leave my duty a little
unthought of, and speak out of my injury.[7]
300   The madly-used Malvolio.
OLIVIA   Did he write this?
FESTE   Ay, madam.
ORSINO   This savours not much of distraction.°   *insanity*
OLIVIA   See him delivered,° Fabian, bring him hither.   *released*
305 My lord, so please you—these things further thought on—
To think me as well a sister as a wife,[8]
One day shall crown th'alliance[9] on't, so please you,
Here at my house and at my proper cost.°   *own expense*
ORSINO   Madam, I am most apt° t'embrace your offer.   *ready*
310 [*To* VIOLA] Your master quits° you, and for your service done him   *releases*
So much against the mettle° of your sex,   *disposition*
So far beneath your soft and tender breeding,
And since you called me master for so long,
Here is my hand. You shall from this time be
Your master's mistress.
315 OLIVIA [*to* VIOLA]   A sister, you are she.
          Enter MALVOLIO
ORSINO   Is this the madman?
OLIVIA   Ay, my lord, this same.
How now, Malvolio?
MALVOLIO   Madam, you have done me wrong,
Notorious wrong.
OLIVIA   Have I, Malvolio? No.
MALVOLIO [*showing a letter*]   Lady, you have. Pray you peruse that letter.
320 You must not now deny it is your hand.°   *handwriting*
Write from° it if you can, in hand or phrase,   *differently from*
Or say 'tis not your seal, not your invention.°   *composition*
You can say none of this. Well, grant it then,
And tell me in the modesty of honour[1]
325 Why you have given me such clear lights° of favour,   *signs*

---

5. The appropriate voice (Latin).
6. To accurately represent his mental state.
7. I neglect the formality I owe you as your servant and
speak as an injured person.
8. To think as well of me as a sister-in-law as you would

have thought of me as a wife.
9. The impending double-marriage ceremony.
1. Tell me with the propriety that becomes a noble-
woman.

Bade me come smiling and cross-gartered to you,
To put on yellow stockings, and to frown
Upon Sir Toby and the lighter° people,   *lesser*
And acting° this in an obedient hope,   *Upon doing*
330 Why have you suffered me to be imprisoned,
Kept in a dark house, visited by the priest,
And made the most notorious geck° and gull   *fool*
That e'er invention° played on? Tell me why?   *trickery*
OLIVIA Alas, Malvolio, this is not my writing,
335 Though I confess much like the character,°   *handwriting*
But out of question, 'tis Maria's hand.
And now I do bethink me, it was she
First told me thou wast mad; then cam'st° in smiling,   *you came*
And in such forms which here were presupposed°   *previously suggested*
340 Upon thee in the letter. Prithee be content;
This practice hath most shrewdly passed² upon thee,
But when we know the grounds and authors of it
Thou shalt be both the plaintiff and the judge
Of thine own cause.
FABIAN   Good madam, hear me speak,
345 And let no quarrel nor no brawl to come
Taint the condition of this present hour,
Which I have wondered° at. In hope it shall not,   *marveled*
Most freely I confess myself and Toby
Set this device against Malvolio here
350 Upon° some stubborn and uncourteous parts°   *Because / behavior*
We had conceived against him.³ Maria writ
The letter, at Sir Toby's great importance,°   *importunity*
In recompense whereof he hath married her.
How with a sportful malice it was followed°   *followed through*
355 May rather pluck on° laughter than revenge   *incite*
If that the injuries be justly weighed
That have on both sides passed.
OLIVIA [*to* MALVOLIO]   Alas, poor fool, how have they baffled° thee!   *disgraced*
FESTE Why, 'Some are born great, some achieve greatness, and
360 some have greatness thrown upon them.' I was one, sir, in this
interlude,° one Sir Topas, sir; but that's all one. 'By the Lord,   *comedy*
fool, I am not mad'—but do you remember, 'Madam, why
laugh you at such a barren rascal, an you smile not, he's
gagged'—and thus the whirligig° of time brings in his revenges.   *spinning top*
365 MALVOLIO I'll be revenged on the whole pack of you.   [*Exit*]
OLIVIA He hath been most notoriously abused.
ORSINO Pursue him, and entreat him to a peace.
He hath not told us of the captain yet.   [*Exit one or more*]
When that is known, and golden time convents,°   *summons; is convenient*
370 A solemn combination shall be made
Of our dear souls. Meantime, sweet sister,
We will not part from hence.°   *(Olivia's house)*
Cesario, come—
For so you shall be while you are a man;
But when in other habits you are seen,
375 Orsino's mistress, and his fancy's° queen.   *love's; imagination's*
                        Exeunt [*all but* FESTE]

---

2. This trick has most mischievously played.   3. *We . . . him:* To which we took exception.

FESTE (*sings*)   When that I was and a little tiny boy,
                        With hey, ho, the wind and the rain,
                    A foolish thing was but a toy,
                        For the rain it raineth every day.

380   But when I came to man's estate,
                        With hey, ho, the wind and the rain,
                    'Gainst knaves and thieves men shut their gate,
                        For the rain it raineth every day.

                    But when I came, alas, to wive,
385   With hey, ho, the wind and the rain,
                    By swaggering° could I never thrive,   *bullying*
                        For the rain it raineth every day.

                    But when I came unto my beds,
                        With hey, ho, the wind and the rain,
390   With tosspots° still had drunken heads,   *drunkards*
                        For the rain it raineth every day.

                    A great while ago the world begun,
                        With hey, ho, the wind and the rain,
                    But that's all one, our play is done,
395   And we'll strive to please you every day.   *Exit*

Measure for Measure

A young man is in grave trouble with the law, and his beautiful sister goes to the magistrate to plead for mercy. The magistrate offers to remit the penalty if the sister will sleep with him. It is an old story in more ways than one. Shakespeare knew several sixteenth-century versions: the Italian Giovanbattista Giraldi Cinthio produced both prose and dramatic renderings, and in 1578 the English playwright George Whetstone published *Promos and Cassandra,* the most important source for *Measure for Measure.* Shakespeare took the title of his play from Jesus' Sermon on the Mount: "Judge not, that ye be not judged. For with what judgment ye judge, ye shall be judged: and with what measure ye mete, it shall be measured to you again" (Matthew 7:1–2). Jesus' advice combines threat with promise: a prudent fear of heavenly retaliation persuades believers not to pass judgment themselves, while at the same time, an apparent abdication of equity is folded into an overall scheme of just compensation. As we shall see, the passage in all its complexity complements the intricacies of Shakespeare's treatment of the ancient tale.

   Measure for Measure was performed in 1604 at a pivotal moment in Shakespeare's career. The play is the last in a long series of comedies that explore complex issues of sex, marriage, and personal identity. Its tone, themes, and methods of characterization, however, veer close to tragedy, the genre that largely, though not exclusively, preoccupied Shakespeare in the years immediately following. Many critics, therefore, classify *Measure for Measure* as a "problem" comedy. The designation attests both to the difficult moral issues that the play confronts and to the boldness with which it stretches—some would say shatters—the normal limits of comic form.

   The play's distinctiveness becomes evident almost immediately. In Act 1, Scene 2, Claudio and his pregnant lover, Juliet, appear in the custody of the Provost, being led away to prison. Their crime is premarital sex; the penalty, for Claudio at least, is death. The seriousness of their situation is not in itself unusual: "The course of true love never did run smooth," Lysander remarks in *A Midsummer Night's Dream,* and if it did, it would hardly make an engrossing dramatic subject. Nonetheless, Claudio's initial description of his plight is quite remarkable:

> LUCIO   Why, how now, Claudio? Whence comes this restraint?
> CLAUDIO   From too much liberty, my Lucio, liberty.
>   As surfeit is the father of much fast,
>   So every scope, by the immoderate use,
>   Turns to restraint. Our natures do pursue,
>   Like rats that raven down their proper bane,
>   A thirsty evil; and when we drink, we die.
>
> (1.2.104–10)

Claudio likens his passion for his beloved to a rat's craving for poison: compulsive, irrational, and self-destructive. Excessive indulgence, or "surfeit," inevitably brings regret and punishment in its train. Claudio sounds as if he is describing the most arrant kind of lust, although, as he will subsequently explain, he is actually "precontracted" to Juliet, bound by a promise of marriage that many in Renaissance England saw as providing conjugal privileges. (Shakespeare himself may have subscribed to this view, since his wife gave birth to their daughter five months after their wedding. More pertinently, the Duke, in his guise as a friar, affirms that the precontract sanctions Mariana's intimacy with Angelo later in the play.) Interestingly, however, neither Claudio nor Juliet is inclined to argue that their devotion to one another mitigates their guilt. Instead, they admit that they have committed "fornication," a severely condemnatory term that conflates all kinds of sex outside of marriage under the same rubric, recognizing no difference between long-term relationships and sheerest promiscuity.

As the play continues, it becomes clear that Claudio's imagery of suicidal animalism, havoc, and pollution is not merely the consequence of his immediate agitation, but expresses a profound assumption of the society in which he lives. For his sister, Isabella, sexual intercourse is "what I abhor to name" (3.1.100); the Duke deplores Pompey's "filthy vice" and Juliet's "most offenseful act"; the wise Escalus acknowledges Claudio's "error" even as he attempts to alleviate his punishment. Few doubt that human sexuality is an essentially sordid matter, a sign of degradation rather than a means of creativity or love. Occasional glimpses of an alternative vision—Lucio's brief, radiant analogy between Juliet's pregnancy and agricultural fertility, for instance—by their very rarity reinforce the prevailing pessimism.

Such austere views of human sexuality have ancient roots. When the Duke calls Vienna's sex laws "needful bits and curbs to headstrong weeds" (1.3.20), he recalls an image from Plato, who compared the desiring part of the soul to a useful but refractory horse, which the rational part of the soul needs to keep strictly bridled and under firm control. When Isabella refers to erotic desire as a "natural guiltiness" (2.2.142), she draws upon a traditional Christian connection between sexuality and original sin, the disobedience committed by Adam and Eve in the Garden of Eden and passed on to all their offspring as a kind of intrinsic pollution.

To say that a view is traditional, however, is not to say that it is inevitable. What makes sexuality so troublesome in this particular play? In Shakespeare's earlier, more optimistic comedies, the prospect of heterosexual consummation usually seems automatically to entail marriage, so that the weddings with which the plays conclude seem to follow spontaneously from the eroticism that fuels the plot. By marrying and establishing a family, the young couples simultaneously satisfy their mutual yearning for one another, and their community's demand for clear kinship structures and for orderly means of transferring property to "legitimate" members of a new generation. In *Measure for Measure,* however, the link between heterosexual desire and marriage seems to have snapped. Claudio and Juliet defer their wedding day; Angelo abandons Mariana; Lucio refuses to support his child or marry its mother. Prostitution flourishes. Rampant promiscuity makes syphilis a familiar ailment and a standard topic for nervous jokes.

Once carnal desire comes unhinged from the institution of marriage, it begins to seem subversive of personal and civic order. And if one believes, rightly or wrongly, that one's sexuality is intrinsically antisocial and depraved, then complete sexual renunciation might seem the wisest course. In *Measure for Measure,* the morally ambitious characters—the Duke, Angelo, and Isabella—initially assume that their virtue is tied up with, perhaps even identical with, their chastity. "Believe not that the dribbling dart of love / Can pierce a complete bosom," the Duke boasts to the Friar (1.3.2–3). Angelo attempts to

Charioteer with two galloping horses. From Geffrey Whitney, *A Choice of Emblemes* (1586).

protect his reputation for austerity even as he hopelessly compromises his scruples in secret. Isabella believes that sleeping with Angelo will defile her forever, even if she does so in order to save her brother's life.

The value of celibacy is endorsed by characters who do not themselves aspire to such high standards of conduct. Lucio is a libertine, but he believes that Isabella's intention to enter a nunnery renders her "a thing enskied and sainted" (1.4.33). Likewise, Pompey admits that his life as a pimp "does stink in some sort, sir" (3.1.283). A few of those who cannot be chaste themselves are, like Claudio, capable of moments of shame or self-loathing; others, like Lucio, shruggingly accept their lack of saintliness. The Vienna of *Measure for Measure* is full of people unlikely to be enlisted for projects of social or spiritual improvement: the moronic Elbow, the impenitent Pompey, the unregenerate Mistress Overdone, the "gravel-hearted" Barnardine, the heedless First and Second Gentlemen, the gullible Froth. These people are part of the commonwealth, subject to the law, and willy-nilly part, too, of a Catholic church that aspires—unlike some of the Protestant sects of Shakespeare's time—to include the entire community. Should the laws of this community reflect its stringent ideals or the actual behavior of most of its members? Throughout the play, those who aspire to belong to a principled moral elite deplore the weaknesses of the reprobate. At the same time, because the rascals in *Measure for Measure* are so vividly memorable, the play also suggests that moral "failure" is often at least as humanly compelling as moral excellence is—at least moral excellence defined in the narrow, self-denying terms that prevail in Vienna.

For the intransigent majority unable or unwilling to control the horses of lust, the "needful bits and curbs" of which the Duke speaks impose an external system of repression. Such a system would not have been unfamiliar to Shakespeare's original audience. Courts administered by the Church of England prosecuted many sexual infractions: among them fathering or giving birth to a bastard, committing adultery or bigamy, deserting a spouse, reneging on a wedding engagement, or groundlessly accusing others of such transgressions. Convicted individuals could be fined, whipped, displayed in the marketplace, or made to announce their sins in church. (Thus Claudio and Juliet are paraded about the streets of Vienna before being taken to prison, to humiliate them and to serve as an example for others.) Repeat offenders were excommunicated, or cast out of the church.

Underlying such proceedings was the assumption, as in *Measure for Measure,* that morality could and should be legislated; that the sexual conduct of individuals was the business of the entire community. Indeed, in the early seventeenth century, when Shakespeare was writing *Measure for Measure,* an increasingly powerful group of Puritans, or "precisians," argued that the church courts' punishments were far too mild. Threats of disgrace and excommunication failed to deter the most egregious offenders, who had no reputation to lose and were unlikely to fret at their exclusion from church. Moreover, shaming punishments worked less well in the increasingly busy, heterogeneous neighborhoods of Jacobean London than they had in the smaller rural communities for which they had originally been designed.

In *Measure for Measure,* the repeated characterization of Angelo as "precise" associates him with the rigorists of Shakespeare's time; and since Viennese justice treats Claudio more strictly than it does professionals in the sex trade, the question of what constitutes adequate severity is certainly at issue. Perhaps, then, the play comprises Shakespeare's reflection on an issue of contemporary concern: what would happen if, as some argued, sexual misconduct could be punished with death? At the same time, Shakespeare carefully distinguishes the world of his play from seventeenth-century England, most obviously by making Vienna a Catholic city peopled with the nuns and friars who had been eliminated from Protestant England over half a century earlier. For despite obvious connections between *Measure for Measure* and some of the issues of its own day, Shakespeare's play hardly constitutes a clear policy recommendation. He is more deeply attentive to general issues about the often-vexed relationship between civic life and human passion, and between religious commitment and the conduct of secular affairs. What happens to individuals and a community when sexuality is viewed as transgressive, when it becomes the subject of public discipline? Is it possible or advisable to regulate sexual behavior through the courts? How do religious convictions affect the experience of sexual desire? These concerns resonate in an era like our own, characterized by a lack of consensus in religion and in sexual mores, by widespread transformations in the institution of marriage, and by debates over the extent to which the state ought to monitor the sexual behavior of citizens.

In *Measure for Measure*, Angelo's disastrous career suggests one possible effect of strict sexual self-denial: that the habits of restraint can themselves provoke sexual excitement. Rigid and self-righteous, Angelo seems not to have experienced the violence of desire until Isabella's first visit on behalf of her brother awakens his appetite:

> What's this? What's this? Is this her fault or mine?
> The tempter or the tempted, who sins most, ha?
> Not she; nor doth she tempt; but it is I
> That, lying by the violet in the sun,
> Do, as the carrion does, not as the flower,
> Corrupt with virtuous season.
>
> (2.2.167–72)

Like Claudio, Angelo thinks of passion in terms of death and decay, but the resemblance between the two men ends there. Angelo imagines himself as tainted meat rotting all the

Jost Amman, Poor Clare nun, from *Cleri totius Romanae ecclesiae subjecti* (1585).

faster under the very sun that gives life to innocent, lovely things. What ought to improve Angelo—his keen appreciation for the presence of virtue—makes him worse.

Angelo is sexually aroused by prohibition. Mariana loves him, and his relationship with her breaches no social norms; he discards her. Isabella is ostentatiously pristine, and her nun's habit marks her as taboo; he finds her irresistible. In order to extract pleasure from the encounter, however, Angelo must force himself to remain aware of the principles he attempts so flagrantly to violate. If he rationalized his behavior or blamed it on Isabella, he would lose the nearly sensual luxury of self-hatred. Therefore, the lucidity with which Angelo analyzes his own motives leads not to penitence but to an increasing moral recklessness. His inclination to categorize all sexual conduct as transgressive actually makes his offense easier to commit. Propositioning Isabella in their second meeting together, he tells her: "I have begun, / And now I give my sensual race the rein" (2.4.159–60). Angelo explains why he cannot govern himself with the same image the Duke used to underscore the necessity of control. Once embarked on the "sensual race," he imagines, there is no alternative to utter abandon.

For Isabella, however, sleeping with Angelo is out of the question. Some modern critics have found her defiance heroic, others chilling or selfish. Doubtless in Shakespeare's time, she elicited a similarly mixed response. Shakespeare alters his source story considerably to expand Isabella's role and specify its implications more exactly. In Whetstone's *Promos and Cassandra*, the sister has no plans to enter a convent, and she eventually goes to bed with the deputy in order to save her brother's life. For Isabella, by contrast, virginity is a principled choice, not an accident of youth. The vow of lifelong, religiously dedicated chastity she plans to take is a matter about which Shakespeare's contemporaries had conflicting feelings. One effect of England's break with the Catholic Church had been a spectacular change in official attitudes toward celibacy. While Catholics honored sexual renunciation and demanded that their clergy remain chaste, Protestants discouraged veneration of the Virgin Mary, abolished convents and monasteries, and urged clergy to marry. Despite these alterations, however, a powerful appreciation for virginity and belief in its semimagical powers persisted in Reformation England, cut loose from its explicitly religious moorings. The effect of Shakespeare's innovations on Whetstone, then, is both to heighten the ambivalence of the story and to focus the moral spotlight on Isabella's convictions and the choices that follow from them.

Isabella believes that she would damn herself by sleeping with Angelo.

> Better it were a brother died at once
> Than that a sister, by redeeming him,
> Should die for ever.
>
> (2.4.107–9)

Is she right? St. Augustine, the most influential Christian writer on sexual morality, insists that since sin is a property of the will, not a physical state, persons who are forced to perform sexual acts are blameless. If chastity is a state of mind, then the fate of Isabella's body is possibly independent of, and irrelevant to, the fate of her soul. Perhaps, in fact, by acquiescing to Angelo, Isabella would perform an act of charity, generously sacrificing her own preferences for Claudio's benefit. On the other hand, female "virtue" has traditionally been defined in physical as well as mental terms, so that chastity, the spiritual attitude, is hard to separate from virginity, the bodily condition. Moreover, Isabella is not exactly a rape victim; she must, as Angelo says, "fit her consent" to his proposal. Does that consent, however reluctant, contaminate her with his sin? Quite possibly. Would it permanently unsuit her for her religious vocation? Quite possibly. Clearly it is reasonable, then, for Isabella to be cautious; and no one, says Augustine, is obliged to put him- or herself in eternal peril merely in order to save the life of another person.

Since, however, Shakespeare characteristically translates sweeping moral questions into scrupulously personal terms, apparently reasonable general maxims do not entirely suffice to explain Isabella's motives. On one hand, her obstinacy seems justified after the fact, when Angelo decides to execute Claudio, because clearly her capitulation would not have saved her brother's life. On the other hand, Isabella's obsession with her own purity seems excessive, especially in 3.1, when it manifests itself in gross insensitivity to her plaintive, terrified brother. Moreover, her fervent yearning for constraint, like Angelo's, seems luridly imbued with sadomasochism.

> were I under the terms of death,
> Th'impression of keen whips I'd wear as rubies,
> And strip myself to death as to a bed
> That longing have been sick for, ere I'd yield
> My body up to shame.
>
> (2.4.100–04)

At such moments, Isabella seems not to be exterminating or transcending her own sexuality, but redirecting it in ways of which she is not entirely conscious. She not only shares Angelo's assumption that the sexual act is a defilement, but like him she finds discipline exciting. With all our disapproval of Angelo's abuse of power and our sympathy with Isabella's indignation, we can still see how their conflict arises as much from their similarities as from their differences.

Isabella's difficulty is hard to resolve because it is unclear how much her chastity is worth. Is it more valuable than her brother's life? Is it more valuable than her own life, which she would throw down for Claudio, she claims, "as frankly as a pin" (3.1.105)? Is it only fair, as Angelo claims, to yield him her body as compensation for overlooking Claudio's offense, or is "lawful mercy . . . nothing kin to foul redemption" (2.4.113–14)? Shakespeare provides no answer to these questions, but the conflict they produce yields the play's most vividly realized interactions. As the title suggests, *Measure for Measure* is obsessed with problems of substitution and commensurability—from the opening scene in which Angelo takes over as the Duke's deputy to Angelo's proposal that Isabella vindicate Claudio by committing his sin herself, to the bed trick that replaces Isabella with Mariana, to the Provost's exchange of Ragusine's head for Claudio's. Even the most apparently trivial comic interchanges persistently echo the concern with equivalence, proportionality, and relative priority: the Gentlemen argue about whether they are cut from lists or velvet; Pompey and Abhorson debate the relative standing of bawd and hangman.

Questions of equivalence seem to underlie the very possibility of justice, even the possibility of any ethical thinking. When a person commits a misdeed, restoring the status quo ante is usually impossible. Thus the wrongdoer ought, we feel, either to make adequate restitution or to suffer in rough proportion to the anguish he or she has caused, rendering, in the biblical phrase, measure for measure. In sexual matters, however, such problems of equivalence are murky, because there is no consensus regarding how apparently straightforward bodily acts ought to be interpreted. Angelo compares Claudio's offense to murder and counterfeiting; Lucio thinks it is trivial, "a game of tick-tack" (1.2.167). What seem to be the same actions can be evaluated in wildly different ways, depending on one's frame of reference: to the abstemious Angelo, Claudio's behavior looks like gross debauchery, while to Mistress Overdone's dissolute patrons, it looks positively restrained. Motives alter what seem to be the same actions, so that we are inclined to regard Claudio more leniently than Lucio, who abandoned his mistress after making her pregnant. So do outcomes: the bed trick means that Angelo, intending to commit an impermissible act, in fact performs a licit one, unknowingly laying the groundwork for his pardon in the final scene.

The commitment of several characters to a Christian religious vocation further complicates the possibility of establishing some kind of commensurability. Isabella, especially, assumes that spiritual goods like honor and purity are infinitely more important than secular, visible possessions. In her system of values, a promise of ardent prayer constitutes the most potent bribe she can offer Angelo, beside which gold is barren and trivial. The counterintuitive otherworldliness of Isabella's concept of commensurability is central to Christianity, a religion founded on the spectacularly lopsided substitution of the blameless Christ for sinful humanity in the system of God's justice. But since such religious convictions are not subject to the verification of the senses, they are open to challenge by those more firmly attached to the things of this world. For Claudio, any fate seems better than death. His hierarchy of priorities is different from Isabella's, and so, therefore, are his conceptions of commensurability.

How are such drastic discrepancies between the various characters' moral and social outlooks to be reconciled? The agent for bringing order and justice is Duke Vincentio, a concealed authority who learns everybody's secrets in the course of the play. Far from providing an authoritative solution to the play's ethical impasse, however, the Duke has elicited almost as much controversy as Isabella. Some critics see him as a version of God, "like power divine," as Angelo declares in the final scene. Some have suggested that the Duke was meant to compliment the diffident King James I, who at the time of the play's first performance had just ascended the English throne, after the death of his extroverted predecessor, Elizabeth I. More skeptical critics see the Duke as a schemer who foists his dirty work onto political subordinates and meddles impudently, even sacrilegiously, with the lives of his subjects.

The Duke's function as clergyman reflects the fact that the problems of *Measure for Measure* can only be solved by someone who can obtain access to the concealed realm of motives and intentions, a privilege usually reserved for a confessor. But merely knowing such information will not bring practical redress of injustice. So at the same time, unlike a clergyman, he must retain the secular ruler's ability to mandate changes in the world in order to bring matters to a satisfactory conclusion. A prince disguised as a friar, the Duke bridges, however unsteadily, the gap between knowledge and power. An actual sovereign with such prerogatives would approach tyranny—for that reason, the functions of priest and lay magistrate were ordinarily separated even in Shakespeare's time, when church and state were far more closely allied than they are today. In the play's fictional Vienna, however, the Duke's sweeping authority conveniently allows him to impose a resolution.

There are limits to Vincentio's power. Not even a Duke can sequester erotic fervor from the cruelty and disorder with which it has proven to be so intimately and insidiously allied. Not even a Duke can make passion tractable. The best he can manage is to introduce his subjects to some socially sanctioned medium between celibacy and abandon. Marriage in *Measure for Measure* is thus patently not a happy aspiration but a stopgap measure imposed on reluctant or noncommittal individuals, for whom the alternative in several cases is death. Indeed, Lucio, forthright as usual, complains that marriage is a worse fate than hanging; the others are distinctly muted in their response to the Duke's nuptial stratagems. Claudio and Juliet are given no lines in which to celebrate their reunion; nor do we hear that Angelo, who claims to "crave death more willingly than mercy" (5.1.470), is grateful to be preserved as Mariana's husband. Isabella remains silent in the face of the Duke's unexpected proposal of marriage, leaving it an open question whether she is overwhelmed with joy or gripped with horror, whether the Duke provides her with a socially and personally satisfying alternative to the cloister or merely recapitulates Angelo's harassment.

The pro forma quality of the coupling with which *Measure for Measure* concludes suggests that marital union is not, finally, the resolution toward which the play most convincingly moves. Most of the last scene is devoted to finding a way out of the difficulties posed by the radical moral incommensurabilities described above. In quick succession, the Duke's trial rehearses the normal outcome of Isabella's complaint—her condemnation and Angelo's exoneration—and then demonstrates that in this instance, almost miraculously, Angelo's secret vice will be made manifest after all. But this disclosure does not end the play, for the Duke's plan demands that Isabella plead for Angelo's life "against all sense," as the Sermon on the Mount commands her to do. The simple asceticism of the flesh with which *Measure for Measure* begins is displaced at last by a more subtle and exacting asceticism of the spirit, as Isabella renounces the hunger for vengeance in favor of a forgiveness that goes very much against the grain. Only this principled willingness to overlook injury and tolerate difference, the play seems to imply, can still the jostling among heterogeneous moral perspectives that endlessly complicate life in Vienna.

KATHARINE EISAMAN MAUS

TEXTUAL NOTE

The First Folio (1623, F) is the only authoritative text for most of *Measure for Measure,* and the *Norton Shakespeare* in general follows F closely. This text has some puzzling features. In F's 1.2, Claudio's imprisonment is first announced by Mistress Overdone, then shortly thereafter described by Pompey to Mistress Overdone, who seems unaware of the situation she has just related. The Oxford editors believe that *Measure for Measure* was adapted by Thomas Middleton for a performance after Shakespeare's death. In this scene, they argue, F reproduces in succession both the adapted text and the passage it was designed to replace. The same theory would explain some curious features of the action at the end of Act 3 and the beginning of Act 4: Mariana's song seems to have been taken from *The Bloody Brother,* a play first performed around 1617, and the Duke's soliloquy during the absence of Mariana and Isabella is irrelevant to its context. The adapter, in the course of rewriting the beginning of Act 4, probably switched this soliloquy with the one at the end of Act 3.

Because the line between adapted and original material is impossible to recover with any certainty, this edition does not attempt to restore a supposedly "Shakespearean" version of the play, but instead reconstructs the version presumably performed by the King's Men a few years before the printing of the Folio. This reconstruction departs from F only in omitting the short, redundant Shakespearean passage. The omitted passage is reproduced as an appendix, as is the soliloquy at the end of Act 3 as the Oxford editors believe Shakespeare originally wrote it (see Additional Passages). Mariana's song at the beginning of Act 4 has been collated with the authoritative manuscript originally belonging to John Wilson, the composer who set the lyric to music; as a result, F's "but" in line 6 has been emended to "though."

SELECTED BIBLIOGRAPHY

Adelman, Janet. "Bed Tricks: On Marriage as the End of Comedy in *All's Well That Ends Well* and *Measure for Measure.*" *Shakespeare's Personality.* Ed. Norman H. Holland, Sidney Homan, and Bernard J. Paris. Berkeley: University of California Press, 1989. 151–74. Sexuality as defilement and marriage as punishment in *Measure for Measure.*

Baines, Barbara. "Assaying the Power of Chastity in *Measure for Measure.*" *Studies in English Literature* 30 (1990): 248–98. Isabella's chastity as an active virtue in the Vienna of *Measure for Measure.*

Bennett, Josephine Waters. *"Measure for Measure" as Royal Entertainment.* New York: Columbia University Press, 1966. The play as it reflects James I's court, political philosophy, and royal persona.

Bloom, Harold, ed. *William Shakespeare's "Measure for Measure."* New York: Chelsea House, 1987. Anthology of critical essays.

Dollimore, Jonathan. "Transgression and Surveillance in *Measure for Measure.*" *Political Shakespeare: New Essays in Cultural Materialism.* Ed. Jonathan Dollimore and Alan Sinfield. Ithaca, N.Y.: Cornell University Press, 1985. 72–87.

Engle, Lars. "*Measure for Measure* and Modernity: The Problem of the Skeptic's Authority." *Shakespeare and Modernity: Early Modern to Millennium.* Ed. Hugh Grady. New York: Routledge, 2000. 85–104. Ethical relativism and difficulties of judgment.

Hawkins, Harriett. *Measure for Measure*. Boston: Twayne, 1987. Chapters on stage history, critical reception, and the play's major interpretive cruxes.

Knight, G. Wilson. "*Measure for Measure* and the Gospels." *The Wheel of Fire: Essays in Interpretation of Shakespeare's Sombre Tragedies*. London: Oxford University Press, 1930. 80–106. Duke Vincentio as godlike: *Measure for Measure* as a Christian play.

Maus, Katharine Eisaman. "Sexual Secrecy in *Measure for Measure*." *Inwardness and Theater in the English Renaissance*. Chicago: University of Chicago Press, 1995. 157–81. Sexual privacy as a challenge for legal supervision and as the grounds for character in *Measure for Measure*.

Shell, Marc. *The End of Kinship: "Measure for Measure," Incest, and the Ideal of Universal Siblinghood*. Stanford: Stanford University Press, 1988. Proper and improper exchanges in the Christian world of *Measure for Measure*, in which everyone is a brother or sister to everyone else.

Shuger, Debora Kuller. *Political Theologies in Shakespeare's England: The Sacred and the State in "Measure for Measure."* New York: Palgrave, 2001. *Measure for Measure* shows the intimate connection between problems of governance and religion in early modern Europe.

Wheeler, Richard P. *Shakespeare's Development and the Problem Comedies: Turn and Counter-Turn*. Berkeley: University of California Press, 1981. 1–33, 92–153. Detailed psychoanalytic interpretation.

FILM

Measure for Measure. 1979. Dir. Desmond Davis. UK. BBC-TV production. Nuanced performances from the entire ensemble, particularly Tim Pigott-Smith (Angelo), Kenneth Colley (Duke), Kate Nelligan (Isabella), and Frank Middlemass (Pompey).

Measure for Measure

THE PERSONS OF THE PLAY

Vincentio, the DUKE of Vienna
ANGELO, appointed his deputy
ESCALUS, an old lord, appointed Angelo's secondary
CLAUDIO, a young gentleman
JULIET, betrothed to Claudio
ISABELLA, Claudio's sister, novice to a sisterhood of nuns
LUCIO, a 'fantastic'
Two other such GENTLEMEN
FROTH, a foolish gentleman
MISTRESS OVERDONE, a bawd
POMPEY, her clownish servant
A PROVOST
ELBOW, a simple constable
A JUSTICE
ABHORSON, an executioner
BARNARDINE, a dissolute condemned prisoner
MARIANA, betrothed to Angelo
A BOY, attendant on Mariana
FRIAR PETER
FRANCESCA, a nun
VARRIUS, a lord, friend to the Duke
Lords, officers, citizens, servants

1.1

Enter DUKE, ESCALUS, [*and other*] *lords*

DUKE   Escalus.

ESCALUS   My lord.

DUKE   Of government the properties to unfold°   *explain*
Would seem in me t'affect° speech and discourse,   *love; show off*
5   Since I am put° to know that your own science°   *obliged / knowledge*
Exceeds in that the lists° of all advice   *limits*
My strength can give you. Then no more remains
But this: to° your sufficiency,° as your worth is able,   *rely on / ability*
And let them[1] work. The nature of our people,
10   Our city's institutions and the terms°   *procedures*
For common justice, you're as pregnant° in   *expert*
As art° and practice hath enrichèd any   *learning*
That we remember.
   [*He gives* ESCALUS *papers*]
                     There is our commission,
From which we would not have you warp.°   *deviate*
   [*To a lord*]   Call hither,
15   I say bid come before us, Angelo.   [*Exit lord*]

1.1 Location: The play takes place in Vienna. Some scene locations can merely be inferred. This scene may be set in the Duke's palace.

1. The referent of "them" is unclear. Perhaps a line is missing.

[*To* ESCALUS] What figure of us think you he will bear?[2]—
For you must know we have with special soul°   *deliberation*
Elected° him our absence to supply,°   *Chosen / make up for*
Lent him our terror, dressed him with our love,
20 And given his deputation° all the organs°   *deputyship / instruments*
Of our own power. What think you of it?
  ESCALUS   If any in Vienna be of worth
To undergo° such ample grace° and honour,   *sustain / favor*
It is Lord Angelo.
         Enter ANGELO
  DUKE   Look where he comes.
25 ANGELO   Always obedient to your grace's will,
I come to know your pleasure.
  DUKE   Angelo,
There is a kind of character[3] in thy life
That to th'observer doth thy history°   *life story*
Fully unfold. Thyself and thy belongings°   *endowments*
30 Are not thine own so proper° as to waste   *exclusively*
Thyself upon thy virtues, they on thee.
Heaven doth with us as we with torches do,
Not light them for themselves; for if our virtues
Did not go forth of° us, 'twere all alike   *from*
35 As if we had them not.[4] Spirits are not finely touched
But to fine issues;[5] nor nature never lends
The smallest scruple° of her excellence   *bit*
But, like a thrifty goddess, she determines°   *ordains*
Herself the glory of a creditor,
40 Both thanks and use.° But I do bend° my speech   *interest / direct*
To one that can my part in him advertise.°   *make known*
Hold[6] therefore, Angelo.
In our remove be thou at full ourself.
Mortality° and mercy in Vienna   *Power to kill*
45 Live in thy tongue and heart. Old Escalus,
Though first in question, is thy secondary.[7]
Take thy commission.
  ANGELO   Now good my lord,
Let there be some more test made of my metal°   *(variant of "mettle")*
Before so noble and so great a figure
Be stamped upon it.
50 DUKE   No more evasion.
We have with leavened° and preparèd choice   *fermented (mature)*
Proceeded to you; therefore take your honours.
     [ANGELO *takes his commission*]
Our haste from hence is of so quick condition
That it prefers itself, and leaves unquestioned[8]
55 Matters of needful value. We shall write to you
As time and our concernings° shall importune,°   *affairs / demand*
How it goes with us; and do look° to know   *expect*
What doth befall you here. So fare you well.

---

2. How do you think he will represent me (with the royal plural)? Angelo is imagined bearing his ruler's image like a coin; compare "metal" in line 48.
3. Handwriting; engraved pattern.
4. *Heaven . . . not:* similarly, Jesus, in Matthew 5:14–16, tells his followers not to hide their light under a bushel.

5. *Spirits . . . issues:* Spirits are not made fine except to do fine deeds.
6. Silence; take (this commission).
7. Though first to be addressed, is your subordinate.
8. That it takes precedence, and leaves unconsidered.

To th' hopeful execution do I leave you
Of your commissions.

60 ANGELO   Yet give leave, my lord,
That we may bring you something° on the way.   *some distance*

DUKE   My haste may not admit° it;   *permit*
Nor need you, on mine honour, have to do
With⁹ any scruple. Your scope is as mine own,

65 So to enforce or qualify° the laws   *mitigate*
As to your soul seems good. Give me your hand.
I'll privily away. I love the people,
But do not like to stage me° to their eyes.   *display myself*
Though it do well,° I do not relish well   *is politically useful*

70 Their loud applause and *aves*° vehement;   *salutations*
Nor do I think the man of safe discretion°   *sound judgment*
That does affect° it. Once more, fare you well.   *desire*

ANGELO   The heavens give safety to your purposes!

ESCALUS   Lead forth and bring you back in happiness!

75 DUKE   I thank you. Fare you well.   *Exit*

ESCALUS   I shall desire you, sir, to give me leave
To have free° speech with you; and it concerns me   *frank*
To look into the bottom of my place.¹
A power I have, but of what strength and nature

80 I am not yet instructed.°   *informed*

ANGELO   'Tis so with me. Let us withdraw together,
And we may soon our satisfaction have
Touching that point.

ESCALUS   I'll wait upon° your honour.   *Exeunt*   *accompany*

1.2

Enter LUCIO, *and two other* GENTLEMEN

LUCIO   If the Duke with the other dukes come not to composi-
tion° with the King of Hungary, why then, all the dukes fall   *agreement*
upon° the King.   *attack*

FIRST GENTLEMAN   Heaven grant us its peace, but not the King
5   of Hungary's!

SECOND GENTLEMAN   Amen.

LUCIO   Thou concludest like the sanctimonious pirate, that went
to sea with the Ten Commandments, but scraped° one out of   *erased*
the table.°   *tablet*

10 SECOND GENTLEMAN   'Thou shalt not steal'?

LUCIO   Ay, that he razed.

FIRST GENTLEMAN   Why, 'twas a commandment to command
the captain and all the rest from their functions: they put forth
to steal. There's not a soldier of us all that in the thanksgiving

15   before meat° do relish the petition well that prays for peace.   *food*

SECOND GENTLEMAN   I never heard any soldier dislike° it.   *express aversion to*

LUCIO   I believe thee, for I think thou never wast where grace
was said.

SECOND GENTLEMAN   No? A dozen times at least.

20 FIRST GENTLEMAN   What, in metre?

LUCIO   In any proportion,° or in any language.   *meter*

---

9. *have to do / With*: worry about.
1. To examine my duties thoroughly.
1.2. Location: A street or public place. In F, as here, the
scene begins with what is evidently an interpolation

introduced after Shakespeare's death. A reconstruction
of the original opening appears at the end of the play as
Additional Passage A.

FIRST GENTLEMAN   I think, or in any religion.

LUCIO   Ay, why not? Grace is grace despite of all controversy;[1] as
for example, thou thyself art a wicked villain despite of all
25   grace.

FIRST GENTLEMAN   Well, there went but a pair of shears between us.[2]

LUCIO   I grant—as there may between the lists° and the velvet.   *selvages*
Thou art the list.

FIRST GENTLEMAN   And thou the velvet. Thou art good velvet,
30   thou'rt a three-piled[3] piece, I warrant thee. I had as lief° be a   *had rather*
list of an English kersey° as be piled as thou art pilled,[4] for a   *wool cloth*
French velvet. Do I speak feelingly° now?   *to the point; painfully*

LUCIO   I think thou dost, and indeed with most painful feeling°   *conviction*
of thy speech. I will out of thine own confession learn to begin°   *drink to*
35   thy health, but whilst I live forget to drink after thee.°   *(to avoid infection)*

FIRST GENTLEMAN   I think I have done myself wrong,° have I   *laid myself open to that*
not?

SECOND GENTLEMAN   Yes, that thou hast, whether thou art
tainted or free.°   *sick or well*

Enter [MISTRESS OVERDONE]

40   LUCIO   Behold, behold, where Madam Mitigation° comes! I   *(of sexual desire)*
have purchased as many diseases under her roof as come to—

SECOND GENTLEMAN   To what, I pray?

LUCIO   Judge.°   *Guess*

SECOND GENTLEMAN   To three thousand dolours° a year?   *pains; dollars*

45   FIRST GENTLEMAN   Ay, and more.

LUCIO   A French crown° more.   *coin; syphilitic sore*

FIRST GENTLEMAN   Thou art always figuring° diseases in me, but   *imagining*
thou art full of error—I am sound.°   *healthy*

LUCIO   Nay not, as one would say, healthy, but so sound° as   *resounding*
50   things that are hollow—thy bones are hollow,[5] impiety° has   *wickedness*
made a feast of thee.

FIRST GENTLEMAN [*to* MISTRESS OVERDONE]   How now, which of
your hips has the most profound sciatica?[6]

MISTRESS OVERDONE   Well, well! There's one yonder arrested
55   and carried to prison was worth five thousand of you all.

SECOND GENTLEMAN   Who's that, I pray thee?

MISTRESS OVERDONE   Marry° sir, that's Claudio, Signor Claudio.   *By the Virgin Mary*

FIRST GENTLEMAN   Claudio to prison? 'Tis not so.

MISTRESS OVERDONE   Nay, but I know 'tis so. I saw him arrested,
60   saw him carried away; and, which is more, within these three
days his head to be chopped off.

LUCIO   But after° all this fooling, I would not have it so. Art thou   *despite*
sure of this?

MISTRESS OVERDONE   I am too sure of it, and it is for getting
65   Madame Julietta with child.

LUCIO   Believe me, this may be. He promised to meet me two
hours since and he was ever precise in promise-keeping.

---

1. Referring to the religious controversy over whether
human beings are saved by divine grace or by good works.
grace: divine favor; prayer before a meal.
2. We are cut from the same cloth.
3. Very plush; full of rectal sores (a symptom of syphilis).
Lucio accuses the First Gentleman of being a "list," a
selvage or edging of inferior cloth; the Gentleman retorts
that he'd rather be a plain selvage than an expensively

"piled" velvet like Lucio. Lucio then uses the Gentle-
man's knowledge of "piles" to score a point against him.
4. Ruined; made bald (a sign of syphilis, the "French
pox"). Syphilitic sores were covered with velvet patches.
5. Syphilis causes bones to become brittle.
6. Ache in the sciatic vein of the hip, associated with
venereal disease.

SECOND GENTLEMAN Besides, you know, it draws° something   *approaches*
  near to the speech we had to such a purpose.
70 FIRST GENTLEMAN But most of all agreeing with the proclamation.
LUCIO Away; let's go learn the truth of it.
                              Exeunt [LUCIO *and* GENTLEMEN]
MISTRESS OVERDONE Thus, what with the war, what with the
  sweat,° what with the gallows, and what with poverty, I am cus-   *plague*
  tom-shrunk.°   *short on customers*
        Enter [POMPEY *the*] *Clown*
75 How now, what's the news with you?
POMPEY You have not heard of the proclamation, have you?
MISTRESS OVERDONE What proclamation, man?
POMPEY All houses in the suburbs[7] of Vienna must be plucked° down.   *torn*
MISTRESS OVERDONE And what shall become of those in the city?
80 POMPEY They shall stand for seed.[8] They had gone down too,
  but that a wise burgher put in° for them.   *citizen interceded*
MISTRESS OVERDONE But shall all our houses of resort in the
  suburbs be pulled down?
POMPEY To the ground, mistress.
85 MISTRESS OVERDONE Why, here's a change indeed in the com-
  monwealth. What shall become of me?
POMPEY Come, fear not you. Good counsellors° lack no clients.   *attorneys*
  Though you change your place, you need not change your
  trade. I'll be your tapster still. Courage, there will be pity taken
90 on you. You that have worn your eyes almost out in the ser-
  vice,[9] you will be considered.°   *recompensed*
        [*A noise within*]
MISTRESS OVERDONE What's to do° here, Thomas Tapster?[1]   *the matter*
  Let's withdraw!
        Enter PROVOST,° CLAUDIO, JULIET,[2] [*and*] *officers*; LUCIO   *jailer*
        and [*the*] *two* GENTLEMEN
POMPEY Here comes Signor Claudio, led by the Provost to
95 prison; and there's Madame Juliet.
        Exeunt [MISTRESS OVERDONE *and* POMPEY]
CLAUDIO [*to the* PROVOST] Fellow, why dost thou show me thus
        to th' world?
  Bear me to prison, where I am committed.
PROVOST I do it not in evil disposition,
  But from Lord Angelo by special charge.
100 CLAUDIO Thus can the demigod Authority
  Make us pay down for our offence, by weight,°   *fully*
  The bonds of ° heaven. On whom it will, it will;[3]   *obligations to*
  On whom it will not, so; yet still 'tis just.
LUCIO Why, how now, Claudio? Whence comes this restraint?
105 CLAUDIO From too much liberty,° my Lucio, liberty.   *looseness*
  As surfeit is the father of much fast,°   *gluttony precedes fasting*
  So every scope,° by the immoderate use,   *freedom*
  Turns to restraint. Our natures do pursue,

---

7. London brothels ("houses") were located outside the
city walls, where civic authorities had difficulty control-
ling them.
8. Grain for the next crop; semen.
9. "Eye" was slang for "female genital"; blindness is
another symptom of syphilis.
1. Stock name for a tapster (bartender).

2. Claudio and Juliet are perhaps wearing white sheets of
penance; such public humiliations were common pun-
ishments for sexual transgressions.
3. Paul has God say in Romans 9:15: "I will have mercy
on him, to whom I will show mercy: and will have com-
passion on him, on whom I will have compassion."

Like rats that raven° down their proper bane,°   *devour / poison*
110   A thirsty evil; and when we drink, we die.
        LUCIO   If I could speak so wisely under an arrest, I would send
        for certain of my creditors.[4] And yet, to say the truth, I had as
        lief have the foppery° of freedom as the morality of imprison-   *folly*
        ment. What's thy offence, Claudio?
115   CLAUDIO   What but to speak of would offend again.
        LUCIO   What, is't murder?
        CLAUDIO   No.
        LUCIO   Lechery?
        CLAUDIO   Call it so.
        PROVOST   Away, sir; you must go.
        CLAUDIO   One word, good friend.
                  [*The* PROVOST *shows assent*]
        Lucio, a word with you.
120   LUCIO   A hundred, if they'll do you any good.
                  [CLAUDIO *and* LUCIO *speak apart*]
        Is lechery so looked after?
        CLAUDIO   Thus stands it with me. Upon a true contract,[5]
        I got possession of Julietta's bed.
        You know the lady; she is fast° my wife,   *nearly; entirely*
125   Save that we do the denunciation° lack   *declaration*
        Of outward order.° This we came not to   *public ceremony*
        Only for propagation° of a dower   *enlargement*
        Remaining in the coffer of her friends,°   *relatives*
        From whom we thought it meet° to hide our love   *appropriate*
130   Till time had made them for° us. But it chances   *favorably disposed to*
        The stealth of our most mutual° entertainment   *reciprocal; intimate*
        With character too gross° is writ on Juliet.   *writing too large*
        LUCIO   With child, perhaps?
        CLAUDIO   Unhapp'ly even so.
        And the new deputy now for the Duke—
135   Whether it be the fault and glimpse° of newness,   *glitter*
        Or whether that the body public be
        A horse whereon the governor doth ride,
        Who, newly in the seat, that it may know
        He can command, lets it straight° feel the spur—   *immediately*
140   Whether the tyranny be in his place,°   *office*
        Or in his eminence that fills it up—
        I stagger in.° But this new governor   *hesitate to say*
        Awakes me all the enrollèd° penalties   *recorded*
        Which have, like unscoured armour, hung by th' wall
145   So long that fourteen zodiacs° have gone round,   *years*
        And none of them been worn; and, for a name,°   *reputation*
        Now puts the drowsy and neglected act
        Freshly on me. 'Tis surely for a name.
        LUCIO   I warrant° it is; and thy head stands so tickle° on thy   *I'm sure / insecurely*
150   shoulders that a milkmaid, if she be in love, may sigh it off.[6]
        Send after the Duke, and appeal to him.

4. Who, Lucio implies, would have him arrested for
nonpayment of debts.
5. A secret plighting of troth, as opposed to public nup-
tials; in seventeenth-century England, such a contract
could constitute legal marriage if made in the present

tense ("I marry you" rather than "I will marry you") and
followed by sexual consummation. The nature of the
contract between Claudio and Juliet is unclear.
6. That a milkmaid's lovesick sigh may blow it off (with
wordplay on "maidenhead").

CLAUDIO   I have done so, but he's not to be found.
    I prithee, Lucio, do me this kind service.
    This day my sister should the cloister enter,
155 And there receive her approbation.°   *become a novice*
    Acquaint her with the danger of my state.
    Implore her in my voice that she make friends
    To the strict deputy. Bid herself assay° him.   *try*
    I have great hope in that, for in her youth
160 There is a prone° and speechless dialect   *eager; submissive*
    Such as move men; beside, she hath prosperous art°   *skill*
    When she will play with reason and discourse,
    And well she can persuade.
LUCIO   I pray she may—as well for the encouragement of thy
165 like,° which else would stand under grievous imposition,° as for   *those like you / burden*
    the enjoying of thy life, who I would be sorry should be thus
    foolishly lost at a game of tick-tack.[7] I'll to her.
CLAUDIO   I thank you, good friend Lucio.
LUCIO   Within two hours.
170 CLAUDIO   Come, officer; away.
                 Exeunt [LUCIO *and* GENTLEMEN *at one door;*
              CLAUDIO, JULIET, PROVOST, *and officers at another*]

1.3

    Enter DUKE *and* [*a*] FRIAR
DUKE   No, holy father, throw away that thought.
    Believe not that the dribbling[1] dart of love
    Can pierce a complete° bosom. Why I desire thee   *an invulnerable*
    To give me secret harbour hath a purpose
5   More grave and wrinkled° than the aims and ends   *(suggesting aged wisdom)*
    Of burning youth.
FRIAR   May your grace speak of it?
DUKE   My holy sir, none better knows than you
    How I have ever loved the life removed,°   *retired*
    And held in idle price° to haunt assemblies   *thought it frivolous*
10 Where youth and cost a witless bravery° keeps.   *pointless ostentation*
    I have delivered to Lord Angelo—
    A man of stricture° and firm abstinence—   *self-restraint*
    My absolute power and place here in Vienna;
    And he supposes me travelled to Poland—
15 For so I have strewed it in the common ear,°   *ears of common people*
    And so it is received.° Now, pious sir,   *believed*
    You will demand of me why I do this.
FRIAR   Gladly, my lord.
DUKE   We have strict statutes and most biting laws,
20 The needful bits and curbs to headstrong weeds,[2]
    Which for this fourteen years we have let slip;°   *slide*
    Even like an o'ergrown lion in a cave
    That goes not out to prey. Now, as fond° fathers,   *doting*
    Having bound up the threat'ning twigs of birch
25 Only to stick it in their children's sight
    For terror, not to use, in time the rod

---

7. A kind of backgammon scored by placing pegs into holes; with sexual innuendo.
1.3 Location: A Friar's cell.
1. Inadequate, like an arrow shot without sufficient force.

2. Since "bits and curbs" are parts of bridles, many editors emend "weeds" to "jades" or "steeds," but the Oxford English Dictionary records several instances of "weed" as a slang term for a worthless horse.

More mocked becomes than feared: so our decrees,
Dead to infliction,° to themselves are dead;   *Never inflicted*
And Liberty plucks Justice by the nose,[3]
30 The baby beats the nurse, and quite athwart
Goes all decorum.

FRIAR   It rested in° your grace   *remained possible for*
To unloose this tied-up Justice when you pleased,
And it in you more dreadful would have seemed
Than in Lord Angelo.

DUKE   I do fear, too dreadful.
35 Sith° 'twas my fault to give the people scope,   *Since*
'Twould be my tyranny to strike and gall° them   *chafe*
For what I bid them do—for we bid this be done
When evil deeds have their permissive pass,°   *unhindered passage*
And not the punishment. Therefore indeed, my father,
40 I have on Angelo imposed the office,
Who may in th'ambush° of my name strike home,   *under cover*
And yet my nature never in the fight
T'allow in slander.° And to behold his sway,°   *To permit slander / rule*
I will as 'twere a brother of your order
45 Visit both prince° and people. Therefore, I prithee,   *ruler*
Supply me with the habit, and instruct me
How I may formally in person bear°   *behave in character*
Like a true friar. More reasons for this action
At our more leisure shall I render you.
50 Only this one: Lord Angelo is precise,°   *puritanical*
Stands at a guard with envy,° scarce confesses   *on guard against desire*
That his blood flows, or that his appetite
Is more to bread than stone. Hence shall we see
If power change purpose, what our seemers be.   *Exeunt*

1.4

Enter ISABELLA, *and* FRANCESCA, *a nun*

ISABELLA   And have you nuns no farther privileges?
FRANCESCA   Are not these large° enough?   *generous*
ISABELLA   Yes, truly. I speak not as desiring more,
But rather wishing a more strict restraint
5 Upon the sisterhood, the votarists of Saint Clare.
LUCIO (*within*)   Ho, peace be in this place!
ISABELLA [*to* FRANCESCA]   Who's that which calls?
FRANCESCA   It is a man's voice. Gentle Isabella.
Turn you the key, and know° his business of° him.   *find out / from*
You may, I may not; you are yet unsworn.
10 When you have vowed, you must not speak with men
But in the presence of the prioress.
Then if you speak, you must not show your face;
Or if you show your face, you must not speak.
        [LUCIO *calls within*]
He calls again. I pray you answer him.
        [*She stands aside*][1]
15 ISABELLA   Peace and prosperity! Who is't that calls?
        [*She opens the door*]

---

3. Licentiousness insults the administration of law.
1.4 Location: A convent of St. Clare, an order known for
austere discipline.
1. Or Francesca may exit here.

[*Enter* LUCIO]

LUCIO Hail, virgin, if you be—as those cheek-roses°   *glowing cheeks*
Proclaim you are no less. Can you so stead° me   *help*
As bring me to the sight of Isabella,
A novice of this place, and the fair sister
20 To her unhappy° brother Claudio?   *unfortunate*

ISABELLA Why her unhappy brother? Let me ask,
The rather for I now must make you know
I am that Isabella, and his sister.

LUCIO Gentle and fair, your brother kindly greets you.
25 Not to be weary° with you, he's in prison.   *tedious*

ISABELLA Woe me! For what?

LUCIO For that which, if myself might be his judge,
He should receive his punishment in thanks.
He hath got his friend° with child.   *lover*

ISABELLA   Sir, make me not your story.°   *don't tell me tales*

30 LUCIO 'Tis true. I would not—though 'tis my familiar° sin   *habitual*
With maids to seem the lapwing,[2] and to jest
Tongue far from heart—play with all virgins so.
I hold you as a thing enskied° and sainted   *placed in heaven*
By your renouncement, an immortal spirit,
35 And to be talked with in sincerity
As with a saint.

ISABELLA You do blaspheme the good in mocking me.

LUCIO Do not believe it. Fewness° and truth, 'tis thus: *In few words*
Your brother and his lover have embraced.
40 As those that feed grow full, as blossoming time
That from the seedness° the bare fallow° brings   *sowing / plowland*
To teeming foison,° even so her plenteous womb   *abundance*
Expresseth his full tilth° and husbandry.[3]   *tillage*

ISABELLA Someone with child by him? My cousin Juliet?

45 LUCIO Is she your cousin?

ISABELLA Adoptedly,° as schoolmaids change° their names   *By choice / exchange*
By vain° though apt affection.   *foolish*

LUCIO   She it is.

ISABELLA O, let him marry her!

LUCIO   This is the point.
The Duke is very strangely gone from hence;
50 Bore many gentlemen—myself being one—
In hand and hope of action;[4] but we do learn,
By those that know the very nerves° of state,   *sinews (inward secrets)*
His giving out° were of an infinite distance   *What he proclaimed*
From his true-meant design. Upon° his place,   *In*
55 And with full line° of his authority,   *extent*
Governs Lord Angelo—a man whose blood
Is very snow-broth;° one who never feels   *melted snow*
The wanton stings and motions° of the sense,   *stimulants and impulses*
But doth rebate° and blunt his natural edge   *dull*
60 With profits of the mind, study, and fast.
He, to give fear to use° and liberty,   *custom*
Which have for long run by the hideous law

---

2. Bird that cries alarm when far from its nest, a common
figure for deception.
3. Cultivation (punning on "husband").

4. *Bore . . . action*: Deceived us into hoping for some
military action.

As mice by lions, hath picked out an act°   *a statute*
Under whose heavy° sense your brother's life   *oppressive*
65 Falls into forfeit. He arrests him on it,
And follows close the rigour of the statute
To make him an example. All hope is gone,
Unless you have the grace by your fair prayer
To soften Angelo. And that's my pith°   *essence*
70 Of business 'twixt you and your poor brother.
ISABELLA   Doth he so seek his life?
LUCIO   Has censured° him already,   *sentenced*
And, as I hear, the Provost hath a warrant
For's execution.
ISABELLA   Alas, what poor
Ability's in me to do him good?
75 LUCIO   Assay the power you have.
ISABELLA   My power? Alas, I doubt.
LUCIO   Our doubts are traitors,
And makes us lose the good we oft might win,
By fearing to attempt. Go to Lord Angelo;
80 And let him learn to know, when maidens sue,
Men give like gods, but when they weep and kneel,
All their petitions are as freely theirs
As° they themselves would owe° them.   *As if / were to own*
ISABELLA   I'll see what I can do.
LUCIO   But speedily.
ISABELLA   I will about it straight,°   *immediately*
85 No longer staying but to give the Mother°   *Mother Superior*
Notice of my affair.° I humbly thank you.   *business*
Commend me to my brother. Soon at night
I'll send him certain word of my success.°   *fortune (good or bad)*
LUCIO   I take my leave of you.
ISABELLA   Good sir, adieu.
Exeunt [ISABELLA *and* FRANCESCA *at one door,*
LUCIO *at another door*]

2.1
Enter ANGELO, ESCALUS, *and servants;* [*a*] JUSTICE
ANGELO   We must not make a scarecrow of the law,
Setting it up to fear° the birds of prey,   *frighten*
And let it keep one shape till custom make it
Their perch, and not their terror.
ESCALUS   Ay, but yet
5 Let us be keen, and rather cut a little
Than fall and bruise to death. Alas, this gentleman
Whom I would save had a most noble father.
Let but your honour know—
Whom I believe to be most strait° in virtue—   *rigorous*
10 That in the working of your own affections,°   *passions*
Had time cohered with place, or place with wishing,
Or that the resolute acting of your blood°   *desire*
Could have attained th'effect° of your own purpose—   *fulfillment*
Whether you had not sometime in your life

2.1 Location: The court of justice.

15   Erred in this point which now you censure° him,   *condemn in*
        And pulled the law upon you.
    ANGELO   'Tis one thing to be tempted, Escalus,
        Another thing to fall. I not° deny   *do not*
        The jury passing on the prisoner's life
20   May in the sworn twelve have a thief or two
        Guiltier than him they try. What knows the law[1]
        That thieves do pass on thieves? What's open° made to justice,   *evident*
        That justice seizes. 'Tis very pregnant:°   *clear*
        The jewel that we find, we stoop and take't
25   Because we see it, but what we do not see
        We tread upon and never think of it.
        You may not so extenuate his offence
        For° I have had such faults; but rather tell me,   *Because*
        When I that censure him do so offend,
30   Let mine own judgement pattern out° my death,   *give precedent for*
        And nothing come in partial.° Sir, he must die.   *no allowances be made*
    ESCALUS   Be it as your wisdom will.
    ANGELO   Where is the Provost?
          Enter PROVOST
    PROVOST   Here, if it like your honour.
    ANGELO   See that Claudio
        Be execute by nine tomorrow morning.
35   Bring him his confessor, let him be prepared,
        For that's the utmost of his pilgrimage.°   [*Exit* PROVOST]   *life's journey*
    ESCALUS   Well, heaven forgive him, and forgive us all!
        Some rise by sin, and some by virtue fall.
        Some run from brakes of vice,[2] and answer none;°   *not at all*
40   And some condemnèd for a fault alone.°   *single imperfection*
         Enter ELBOW, FROTH, POMPEY, *and officers*
    ELBOW   Come, bring them away. If these be good people in a
        commonweal, that do nothing but use their abuses° in com-   *do their bad deeds*
        mon houses,° I know no law. Bring them away.   *brothels*
    ANGELO   How now, sir? What's your name? And what's the matter?
45   ELBOW   If it please your honour, I am the poor Duke's constable,
        and my name is Elbow. I do lean° upon justice, sir; and do   *depend*
        bring in here before your good honour two notorious benefactors.[3]
    ANGELO   Benefactors? Well! What benefactors are they?
        Are they not malefactors?
50   ELBOW   If it please your honour, I know not well what they are;
        but precise[4] villains they are, that I am sure of, and void of all
        profanation° in the world that good Christians ought to have.   *(for "reverence")*
    ESCALUS [*to* ANGELO]   This comes off° well; here's a wise officer!   *turns out*
    ANGELO   Go to, what quality° are they of ? Elbow is your name?   *rank*
55   Why dost thou not speak, Elbow?
    POMPEY   He cannot, sir; he's out at elbow.[5]
    ANGELO   What are you, sir?
    ELBOW   He, sir? A tapster, sir, parcel bawd;° one that serves a bad   *part-time pimp*

---

1. What does the law know; who knows what law.
2. F has "brakes of ice," a famous crux; often amended as here. *brakes:* thickets.
3. Elbow comically misuses words; here he means "malefactors," criminals.
4. Elbow means "precious"; "precise" (morally scrupulous) is elsewhere applied to Angelo.
5. Ragged; perplexed at the sound of his name. Pompey loves to play on the double meanings of words.

woman whose house, sir, was, as they say, plucked down in the
60 suburbs; and now she professes a hot-house,° which I think is   *pretends to run a sauna*
a very ill house too.

ESCALUS How know you that?

ELBOW My wife, sir, whom I detest° before heaven and your   *(for "protest")*
honour—

65 ESCALUS How, thy wife?

ELBOW Ay, sir, whom I thank heaven is an honest woman—

ESCALUS Dost thou detest her therefor?

ELBOW I say, sir, I will detest myself also, as well as she, that this
house, if it be not a bawd's house, it is pity of her life,° for it is   *a great pity*
70 a naughty° house.   *wicked*

ESCALUS How dost thou know that, constable?

ELBOW Marry, sir, by my wife, who, if she had been a woman
cardinally° given, might have been accused in fornication,   *(for "carnally")*
adultery, and all uncleanliness there.

75 ESCALUS By the woman's means?

ELBOW Ay, sir, by Mistress Overdone's means. But as she° spit   *(Elbow's wife)*
in his° face, so she defied him.   *(Pompey's)*

POMPEY [to ESCALUS] Sir, if it please your honour, this is not so.

ELBOW Prove it before these varlets° here, thou honourable   *villains*
80 man, prove it.

ESCALUS [to ANGELO] Do you hear how he misplaces?°   *confuses his words*

POMPEY Sir, she came in great with child, and longing—saving
your honour's reverence°—for stewed prunes.⁶ Sir, we had but   *excuse the expression*
two in the house, which at that very distant° time stood, as it   *(for "instant")*
85 were, in a fruit dish⁷—a dish of some threepence; your honours
have seen such dishes; they are not china dishes, but very good
dishes.

ESCALUS Go to, go to, no matter for the dish, sir.

POMPEY No, indeed, sir, not of° a pin; you are therein in the   *worth*
90 right. But to the point. As I say, this Mistress Elbow, being, as I
say, with child, and being great-bellied, and longing, as I said,
for prunes; and having but two in the dish, as I said, Master
Froth here, this very man, having eaten the rest, as I said, and,
as I say, paying for them very honestly; for, as you know, Master
95 Froth, I could not give you threepence again.°   *in change*

FROTH No, indeed.

POMPEY Very well. You being, then, if you be remembered,
cracking the stones of the foresaid prunes—

FROTH Ay, so I did indeed.

100 POMPEY Why, very well.—I telling you then, if you be remem-
bered, that such a one and such a one were past cure of the
thing you wot of,⁸ unless they kept very good diet, as I told
you—

FROTH All this is true.

105 POMPEY Why, very well then—

ESCALUS Come, you are a tedious fool. To the purpose. What
was done to Elbow's wife that he hath cause to complain of?
Come me° to what was done to her.   *Get*

POMPEY Sir, your honour cannot come to that yet.⁹

---

6. Commonly served in brothels; also suggesting "testi-
cles" in the series of double entendres that follows.
7. Slang term for "female genital."

8. Euphemism for syphilis. *wot:* know.
9. Taking "done" in the sexual sense, Pompey pretends
shock at Escalus's salaciousness.

110   ESCALUS   No, sir, nor I mean it not.°   *I don't mean that*

      POMPEY   Sir, but you shall come to it, by your honour's leave.
      And I beseech you, look into° Master Froth here, sir, a man of   *consider*
      fourscore pound a year,[1] whose father died at Hallowmas°—   *Nov. 1, All Saint's Day*
      was't not at Hallowmas, Master Froth?

115   FROTH   All Hallow Eve.°   *Halloween*

      POMPEY   Why, very well. I hope here be truths. He, sir, sitting,
      as I say, in a lower° chair, sir—'twas in the Bunch of Grapes,[2]   *reclining?*
      where indeed you have a delight to sit, have you not?

      FROTH   I have so, because it is an open room,[3] and good for
120   winter.

      POMPEY   Why, very well then. I hope here be truths.

      ANGELO   This will last out a night in Russia,
      When nights are longest there. [*To* ESCALUS] I'll take my leave,
      And leave you to the hearing of the cause,°   *case*
125   Hoping you'll find good cause to whip them all.

      ESCALUS   I think no less. Good morrow to your lordship.

                                      Exit [ANGELO]
      Now, sir, come on, what was done to Elbow's wife, once more?

      POMPEY   Once, sir? There was nothing done to her once.

      ELBOW   I beseech you, sir, ask him what this man did to my wife.

130   POMPEY   I beseech your honour, ask me.

      ESCALUS   Well, sir, what did this gentleman to her?

      POMPEY   I beseech you, sir, look in this gentleman's face. Good
      Master Froth, look upon his honour. 'Tis for a good purpose.
      Doth your honour mark° his face?   *note*

135   ESCALUS   Ay, sir, very well.

      POMPEY   Nay, I beseech you, mark it well.

      ESCALUS   Well, I do so.

      POMPEY   Doth your honour see any harm in his face?

      ESCALUS   Why, no.

140   POMPEY   I'll be supposed° upon a book° his face is the worst   *(for "deposed") / Bible*
      thing about him. Good, then—if his face be the worst thing
      about him, how could Master Froth do the constable's wife any
      harm? I would know that of your honour.

      ESCALUS   He's in the right, constable; what say you to it?

145   ELBOW   First, an it like° you, the house is a respected[4] house;   *if it please*
      next, this is a respected fellow; and his mistress is a respected
      woman.

      POMPEY [*to* ESCALUS]   By this hand, sir, his wife is a more
      respected person than any of us all.

150   ELBOW   Varlet, thou liest; thou liest, wicked varlet. The time is
      yet to come that she was ever respected with man, woman, or
      child.

      POMPEY   Sir, she was respected with him before he married with her.

      ESCALUS   Which is the wiser here, justice or iniquity? [*To*
155   ELBOW] Is this true?

      ELBOW [*to* POMPEY]   O thou caitiff, O thou varlet, O thou wicked
      Hannibal![5] I respected with her before I was married to her?
      [*To* ESCALUS] If ever I was respected with her, or she with

---

1. Eighty pounds was a low income for a gentleman. The father's recent death means that Froth has just come into his inheritance.
2. A room in a tavern.

3. A public room (where fires were kept burning).
4. For "suspected."
5. Blunder for "cannibal"; also, both Hannibal and Pompey were famous generals of ancient times.

me, let not your worship think me the poor Duke's officer. [*To*
160 POMPEY] Prove this, thou wicked Hannibal,[6] or I'll have mine
action of battery° on thee. *(for "slander")*

ESCALUS   If he took° you a box o'th' ear you might have your
action of slander too.

ESCALUS   *struck*

ELBOW   Marry, I thank your good worship for it. What is't your
165 worship's pleasure I shall do with this wicked caitiff?° *knave*

ESCALUS   Truly, officer, because he hath some offences in him
that thou wouldst discover° if thou couldst, let him continue in *expose*
his courses° till thou knowest what they are. *conduct*

ELBOW   Marry, I thank your worship for it.—Thou seest, thou
170 wicked varlet now, what's come upon thee. Thou art to con-
tinue now, thou varlet, thou art to continue.

ESCALUS [*to* FROTH]   Where were you born, friend?

FROTH   Here in Vienna, sir.

ESCALUS   Are you of fourscore pounds a year?

175 FROTH   Yes, an't please you, sir.

ESCALUS   So. [*To* POMPEY] What trade are you of, sir?

POMPEY   A tapster, a poor widow's tapster.

ESCALUS   Your mistress's name?

POMPEY   Mistress Overdone.

180 ESCALUS   Hath she had any more than one husband?

POMPEY   Nine, sir—Overdone by the last.[7]

ESCALUS   Nine?—Come hither to me, Master Froth. Master
Froth, I would not have you acquainted with tapsters. They will
draw you,[8] Master Froth, and you will hang them.° Get you *get them hanged*
185 gone, and let me hear no more of you.

FROTH   I thank your worship. For mine own part, I never come
into any room in a tap-house but I am drawn in.

ESCALUS   Well, no more of it, Master Froth. Farewell.

[*Exit* FROTH]

Come you hither to me, Master Tapster. What's your name,
190 Master Tapster?

POMPEY   Pompey.

ESCALUS   What else?

POMPEY   Bum, sir.

ESCALUS   Troth, and your bum is the greatest thing about you;
195 so that, in the beastliest sense, you are Pompey the Great.[9]
Pompey, you are partly a bawd, Pompey, howsoever you colour
it in being a tapster, are you not? Come, tell me true; it shall
be the better for you.

POMPEY   Truly, sir, I am a poor fellow that would live.

200 ESCALUS   How would you live, Pompey? By being a bawd? What
do you think of the trade, Pompey? Is it a lawful trade?

POMPEY   If the law would allow it, sir.

ESCALUS   But the law will not allow it, Pompey; nor it shall not° *nor shall it*
be allowed in Vienna.

205 POMPEY   Does your worship mean to geld and spay all the youth
of the city?

ESCALUS   No, Pompey.

6. Ancient Carthaginian general who waged war
against Rome; possibly Escalus means "cannibal."
7. She takes her name from Overdone, her last hus-
band; her last husband wore her out.

8. Get you beer; steal your substance; convey you to exe-
cution.
9. The Roman general Pompey was surnamed "the
Great."

POMPEY   Truly, sir, in my poor opinion they will to't then. If your
worship will take order° for the drabs° and the knaves, you need   *measures / whores*
210   not to fear the bawds.

ESCALUS   There is pretty orders beginning, I can tell you. It is
but heading° and hanging.   *beheading*

POMPEY   If you head and hang all that offend that way but for
ten year together, you'll be glad to give out a commission° for   *an order*
215   more heads. If this law hold° in Vienna ten year, I'll rent the   *remain*
fairest house in it after threepence a bay.[1] If you live to see this
come to pass, say Pompey told you so.

ESCALUS   Thank you, good Pompey; and in requital of° your   *return for*
prophecy, hark you. I advise you, let me not find you before
220   me again upon any complaint whatsoever; no, not for° dwelling   *even for*
where you do. If I do, Pompey, I shall beat you to your tent,
and prove a shrewd Caesar to you;[2] in plain dealing, Pompey,
I shall have you whipped. So for this time, Pompey, fare you well.

POMPEY   I thank your worship for your good counsel; [*aside*] but
225   I shall follow it as the flesh and fortune shall better determine.
Whip me? No, no; let carman° whip his jade.°   *cart driver / horse*
The valiant heart's not whipped out of his trade.   *Exit*

ESCALUS   Come hither to me, Master Elbow; come hither, Mas-
ter Constable. How long have you been in this place of con-
230   stable?

ELBOW   Seven year and a half, sir.

ESCALUS   I thought, by the readiness in the office, you had con-
tinued in it some time. You say seven years together?

ELBOW   And a half, sir.

235   ESCALUS   Alas, it hath been great pains to you. They do you
wrong to put you so oft upon't. Are there not men in your ward
sufficient° to serve it?   *fit*

ELBOW   Faith, sir, few of any wit in such matters. As they are
chosen, they are glad to choose me for them. I do it for some
240   piece of money, and go through with all.

ESCALUS   Look° you bring me in the names of some six or seven,   *See that*
the most sufficient of your parish.

ELBOW   To your worship's house, sir?

ESCALUS   To my house. Fare you well.

    [*Exit* ELBOW *with officers*]

245   What's o'clock, think you?

JUSTICE   Eleven, sir.

ESCALUS   I pray you home to dinner with me.[3]

JUSTICE   I humbly thank you.

ESCALUS   It grieves me for the death of Claudio,
250   But there's no remedy.

JUSTICE   Lord Angelo is severe.

ESCALUS   It is but needful.
Mercy is not itself that oft looks so.
Pardon is still° the nurse of second woe.   *always*
255   But yet, poor Claudio! There is no remedy.
Come, sir.   *Exeunt*

---

1. Townhouse rental was based on the number of front
windows ("bays").
2. Julius Caesar defeated Pompey in 48 B.C.E. *shrewd:*
harsh.
3. Dinner was served at midday. *pray:* ask.

2.2

Enter PROVOST [*and a*] SERVANT

SERVANT   He's hearing of a cause;° he will come straight.°   *case / right away*
  I'll tell him of you.

PROVOST   Pray you do.   [*Exit* SERVANT]
                            I'll know
  His pleasure; maybe he will relent. Alas,
  He° hath but as offended in a dream.   *(Claudio)*
5   All sects,° all ages, smack° of this vice; and he   *kinds of people / partake*
  To die for't!

        Enter ANGELO

ANGELO   Now, what's the matter, Provost?
PROVOST   Is it your will Claudio shall die tomorrow?
ANGELO   Did not I tell thee yea? Hadst thou not order?
  Why dost thou ask again?
PROVOST   Lest I might be too rash.
10   Under your good correction, I have seen
  When after execution judgement hath
  Repented o'er his doom.°   *sentence*
ANGELO   Go to; let that be mine.°   *my concern*
  Do you your office, or give up your place,
  And you shall well be spared.°   *easily be done without*
PROVOST   I crave your honour's pardon.
15   What shall be done, sir, with the groaning Juliet?
  She's very near her hour.°   *(of childbirth)*
ANGELO   Dispose of her
  To some more fitter place, and that with speed.
        [*Enter* SERVANT]
SERVANT   Here is the sister of the man condemned
  Desires access to you.
ANGELO   Hath he a sister?
20   PROVOST   Ay, my good lord; a very virtuous maid,
  And to be shortly of a sisterhood,
  If not already.
ANGELO   Well, let her be admitted.   [*Exit* SERVANT]
  See you the fornicatress be removed.
  Let her have needful but not lavish means.
  There shall be order° for't.   *written direction*
        Enter LUCIO *and* ISABELLA
25   PROVOST   God save your honour.
ANGELO   Stay a little while. [*To* ISABELLA] You're welcome.
      What's your will?
ISABELLA   I am a woeful suitor to your honour.
  Please° but your honour hear me.   *If it please*
ANGELO   Well, what's your suit?
ISABELLA   There is a vice that most I do abhor,
30   And most desire should meet the blow of justice,
  For which I would not plead, but that I must;
  For which I must not plead, but that I am
  At war 'twixt will and will not.
ANGELO   Well, the matter?
ISABELLA   I have a brother is condemned to die.

2.2 Location: A room in the court of justice.

35   I do beseech you, let it be his fault,°   *his fault be condemned*
    And not my brother.
    PROVOST [*aside*]   Heaven give thee moving graces!°   *the gift of persuasion*
    ANGELO   Condemn the fault, and not the actor° of it?   *doer*
    Why, every fault's condemned ere it be done.
    Mine were the very cipher of a function,
40   To fine° the faults whose fine° stands in record,   *condemn / penalty*
    And let go by° the actor.   *leave unpunished*
    ISABELLA   O just but severe law!
    I had a brother, then. Heaven keep your honour.
    LUCIO [*aside to* ISABELLA]   Give't not o'er° so. To him again;   *Don't give up*
        entreat him.
    Kneel down before him; hang upon° his gown.   *cling to*
45   You are too cold. If you should need a pin,
    You could not with more tame a tongue desire it.
    To him, I say!
    ISABELLA [*to* ANGELO]   Must he needs° die?   *necessarily*
    ANGELO   Maiden, no remedy.
50   ISABELLA   Yes, I do think that you might pardon him,
    And neither heaven nor man grieve at the mercy.
    ANGELO   I will not do't.
    ISABELLA   But can you if you would?
    ANGELO   Look what° I will not, that I cannot do.   *Whatever*
    ISABELLA   But might you do't, and do the world no wrong,
55   If so your heart were touched with that remorse°   *pity*
    As mine is to him?
    ANGELO   He's sentenced; 'tis too late.
    LUCIO [*aside to* ISABELLA]   You are too cold.
    ISABELLA   Too late? Why, no; I that do speak a word
60   May call° it again. Well, believe this,   *retract*
    No ceremony° that to great ones 'longs,   *symbolic accessory*
    Not the king's crown, nor the deputed sword,
    The marshal's truncheon, nor the judge's robe,
    Become them with one half so good a grace
65   As mercy does.
    If he had been as you and you as he,
    You would have slipped like him, but he, like you,
    Would not have been so stern.
    ANGELO   Pray you be gone.
    ISABELLA   I would to heaven I had your potency,°   *power*
70   And you were Isabel! Should it then be thus?
    No; I would tell what 'twere to be a judge,
    And what a prisoner.
    LUCIO [*aside to* ISABELLA]   Ay, touch him;[1] there's the vein.°   *that's the style*
    ANGELO   Your brother is a forfeit of the law,
    And you but waste your words.
    ISABELLA   Alas, alas!
75   Why, all the souls that were were forfeit[2] once,
    And He that might the vantage° best have took   *advantage*
    Found out° the remedy.[3] How would you be   *Procured*
    If He which is the top° of judgement should   *highest pattern or source*
    But judge you as you are? O, think on that,

---

1. Influence him; but perhaps Isabella touches Angelo's arm or garment here.
2. Lost (as a result of Adam and Eve's disobedience).
3. By saving all mankind in the person of Christ.

80 And mercy then will breathe within your lips,
　　Like man new made.° .... *renewed by faith*
ANGELO　　　　　　　　　Be you content, fair maid.° .... *(with play on "new made")*
　　It is the law, not I, condemn your brother.
　　Were he my kinsman, brother, or my son,
　　It should be thus with him. He must die tomorrow.
85 ISABELLA　Tomorrow? O, that's sudden! Spare him, spare him!
　　He's not prepared for death. Even for our kitchens
　　We kill the fowl of season.° Shall we serve heaven .... *at the proper time*
　　With less respect than we do minister
　　To our gross selves? Good good my lord, bethink you:
90 Who is it that hath died for this offence?
　　There's many have committed it.
LUCIO [*aside*]　　　　　　　　Ay, well said.
ANGELO　The law hath not been dead, though it hath slept.
　　Those many had not dared to do that evil
　　If the first that did th'edict infringe
95 Had answered for his deed. Now 'tis awake,
　　Takes note of what is done, and, like a prophet,
　　Looks in a glass° that shows what future evils, ... *mirror*
　　Either raw,° or by remissness new conceived .... *unripe*
　　And so in progress to be hatched and born,
100 Are now to have no successive degrees,[4]
　　But ere they live, to end.
ISABELLA　　　　　　　　Yet show some pity.
ANGELO　I show it most of all when I show justice,
　　For then I pity those I do not know
　　Which a dismissed° offence would after gall,° .... *Whom a pardoned / hurt*
105 And do him right that, answering° one foul wrong, ... *paying for*
　　Lives not to act another. Be satisfied.
　　Your brother dies tomorrow. Be content.
ISABELLA　So you must be the first that gives this sentence,
　　And he that suffers. O, it is excellent
110 To have a giant's strength, but it is tyrannous
　　To use it like a giant.
LUCIO [*aside to* ISABELLA]　That's well said.
ISABELLA　　　　　Could great men thunder
　　As Jove[5] himself does, Jove would never be quiet,
115 For every pelting° petty officer .... *paltry*
　　Would use his heaven for thunder, nothing but thunder.
　　Merciful heaven,
　　Thou rather with thy sharp and sulphurous° bolt .... *fiery*
　　Split'st the unwedgeable and gnarlèd oak
120 Than the soft myrtle. But man, proud man,
　　Dressed in a little brief authority,
　　Most ignorant of what he's most assured,
　　His glassy° essence, like an angry ape[6] .... *fragile; illusory*
　　Plays such fantastic tricks before high heaven
125 As makes the angels weep, who, with our spleens,[7]
　　Would all themselves laugh mortal.

---

4. Future stages of development.　　　　　　6. A figure of grotesque mimicry.
5. King of the Roman gods, whose weapon was the thun-　7. Thought to be the seat of laughter.
derbolt.

LUCIO [*aside to* ISABELLA]   O, to him, to him, wench!° He will   girl
    relent.
    He's coming;° I perceive't.   yielding
PROVOST [*aside*]   Pray heaven she win him!
ISABELLA   We cannot weigh our brother with ourself.[8]
130 Great men may jest with saints; 'tis wit in them,
    But in the less,° foul profanation.   ordinary people
LUCIO [*aside to* ISABELLA]   Thou'rt i'th' right, girl. More o' that.
ISABELLA   That in the captain's but a choleric word,
    Which in the soldier is flat blasphemy.
135 LUCIO [*aside to* ISABELLA]   Art advised o' that?° More on't.   So you know about that
ANGELO   Why do you put° these sayings upon me?   impose
ISABELLA   Because authority, though it err like others,
    Hath yet a kind of medicine in itself
    That skins the vice o'th' top.[9] Go to your bosom;
140 Knock there, and ask your heart what it doth know
    That's like my brother's fault. If it confess
    A natural guiltiness, such as is his,
    Let it not sound a thought upon your tongue
    Against my brother's life.
ANGELO [*aside*]   She speaks, and 'tis such sense°   sound advice
145 That my sense breeds° with it. [*To* ISABELLA] Fare you well.   desire increases
ISABELLA   Gentle my° lord, turn back.   My gracious
ANGELO   I will bethink me.° Come again tomorrow.   consider
ISABELLA   Hark how I'll bribe you; good my lord, turn back.
ANGELO   How, bribe me?
150 ISABELLA   Ay, with such gifts that° heaven shall share with° you.   as / apportion to
LUCIO [*aside to* ISABELLA]   You had marred all else.
ISABELLA   Not with fond° shekels of the tested° gold,   foolish / refined
    Or stones,° whose rate° are either rich or poor   jewels / value
    As fancy values them; but with true prayers,
155 That shall be up at heaven and enter there
    Ere sunrise, prayers from preservèd° souls,   protected
    From fasting maids whose minds are dedicate
    To nothing temporal.
ANGELO   Well, come to me tomorrow.
160 LUCIO [*aside to* ISABELLA]   Go to;° 'tis well; away.   Come on
ISABELLA   Heaven keep your honour[1] safe.
ANGELO [*aside*]   Amen;
    For I am that way going to temptation,
    Where prayer is crossed.°   corrupted; frustrated
ISABELLA   At what hour tomorrow
    Shall I attend your lordship?
165 ANGELO   At any time fore noon.
ISABELLA   God save your honour.
ANGELO [*aside*]   From thee; even from thy virtue.
    [*Exeunt* ISABELLA, LUCIO, *and* PROVOST]
    What's this? What's this? Is this her fault or mine?
    The tempter or the tempted, who sins most, ha?
    Not she; nor doth she tempt; but it is I
170 That, lying by the violet in the sun,
    Do, as the carrion does, not as the flower,

8. We cannot judge others as we judge ourselves.
9. That causes a skin to grow over the sore.

1. Isabella calls Angelo "your honor" as a term of respect; Angelo understands the phrase as referring to his virtue.

Corrupt with virtuous season.° Can it be   *Rot in fine weather*
That modesty may more betray our sense°   *seduce our appetite*
Than woman's lightness?° Having waste ground enough,   *licentiousness*
175   Shall we desire to raze the sanctuary,
And pitch° our evils there? O, fie, fie, fie!   *hurl; set up*
What dost thou, or what art thou, Angelo?
Dost thou desire her foully for those things
That make her good? O, let her brother live!
180   Thieves for their robbery have authority,
When judges steal themselves. What, do I love her,
That I desire to hear her speak again,
And feast upon her eyes? What is't I dream on?
O cunning enemy,° that, to catch a saint,°   *(Satan) / holy person*
185   With saints dost bait thy hook! Most dangerous
Is that temptation that doth goad us on
To sin in loving virtue. Never could the strumpet,
With all her double vigour°—art and nature—   *twofold power*
Once stir my temper;° but this virtuous maid   *excite me*
190   Subdues me quite. Ever till now
When men were fond,° I smiled, and wondered how.   *Exit*   *infatuated*

2.3

Enter [at one door] the DUKE, *[disguised as a friar,] and*
[at another door, the] PROVOST
DUKE   Hail to you, Provost!—so I think you are.
PROVOST   I am the Provost. What's your will, good friar?
DUKE   Bound by my charity and my blest order,
I come to visit the afflicted spirits
5   Here in the prison.[1] Do me the common right°   *right of all clerics*
To let me see them, and to make me know
The nature of their crimes, that I may minister
To them accordingly.
PROVOST   I would do more than that, if more were needful.
Enter JULIET
10   Look, here comes one, a gentlewoman of mine,°   *in my care*
Who, falling in the flaws° of her own youth,   *faults; gusts of passion*
Hath blistered her report.° She is with child,   *reputation*
And he that got° it, sentenced—a young man   *begot*
More fit to do another such offence
15   Than die for this.
DUKE   When must he die?
PROVOST   As I do think, tomorrow.
[*To* JULIET] I have provided for you. Stay a while,
And you shall be conducted.
20   DUKE   Repent you, fair one, of the sin you carry?
JULIET   I do, and bear the shame most patiently.
DUKE   I'll teach you how you shall arraign° your conscience,   *accuse*
And try your penitence if it be sound
Or hollowly put on.
25   JULIET   I'll gladly learn.
DUKE   Love you the man that wronged you?
JULIET   Yes, as I love the woman that wronged him.

2.3 Location: The prison.
1. Echoing 1 Peter 3:19: "He . . . went, and preached unto the spirits that were in prison."

DUKE So then it seems your most offenceful act
    Was mutually committed?

JULIET   Mutually.

30 DUKE Then was your sin of heavier° kind than his.   *graver*

JULIET I do confess it and repent it, father.

DUKE 'Tis meet° so, daughter. But lest you do repent   *appropriate*
    As that° the sin hath brought you to this shame—   *Because*
    Which sorrow is always toward ourselves, not heaven,

35   Showing we would not spare heaven[2] as we love it,
    But as we stand in fear—

JULIET I do repent me as it is an evil,
    And take the shame with joy.

DUKE   There rest.°   *remain*
    Your partner, as I hear, must die tomorrow,

40   And I am going with instruction to him.
    Grace go with you. *Benedicite!*°   *Exit*   *Bless you*

JULIET Must die tomorrow? O injurious law,
    That respites me a life[3] whose very comfort
    Is still a dying horror!

PROVOST   'Tis pity of° him.   *Exeunt*   *for*

2.4

Enter ANGELO

ANGELO When I would pray and think, I think and pray
    To several° subjects: heaven hath my empty words,   *different*
    Whilst my invention,° hearing not my tongue,   *imagination*
    Anchors on Isabel; God in my mouth,

5   As if I did but only chew his name,
    And in my heart the strong and swelling evil
    Of my conception.[1] The state° whereon I studied   *statecraft; dignity*
    Is like a good thing, being often read,
    Grown seared° and tedious. Yea, my gravity,   *arid*

10   Wherein—let no man hear me—I take pride,
    Could I with boot° change for an idle plume[2]   *advantage*
    Which the air beats in vain. O place,° O form,°   *rank / formality*
    How often dost thou with thy case,° thy habit,°   *appearance / dress*
    Wrench awe from fools, and tie the wiser souls

15   To thy false seeming! Blood, thou art blood.[3]
    Let's write 'good angel'[4] on the devil's horn—
    'Tis now the devil's crest.°   *heraldic device*

    Enter SERVANT

                 How now? Who's there?

SERVANT One Isabel, a sister, desires access to you.

ANGELO Teach her the way.   [*Exit* SERVANT]
                 O heavens,

20   Why does my blood thus muster° to my heart,   *crowd*
    Making both it unable° for itself,   *weak*
    And dispossessing all my other parts
    Of necessary fitness?
    So play° the foolish throngs with one that swoons—   *act*

2. Relieve heaven from distress.
3. Pregnant women were spared the death penalty, at least until after childbirth.
2.4 Location: A room in the court of justice.
1. *the strong . . . conception:* the wickedness of my idea; original sin, inherited through the parents.

2. A frivolous feather, as worn in the hats of rakish youths.
3. That is, basic passions cannot be eradicated (contrasts with 1.4.56–58).
4. With pun on Angelo's name.

25   Come all to help him, and so stop the air
  By which he should revive—and even so
  The general subject° to a well-wished king   *common people*
  Quit their own part° and, in obsequious fondness,°   *place / foolish love*
  Crowd to his presence, where their untaught° love   *ignorant*
  Must needs appear offence.

        Enter ISABELLA

30   How now, fair maid?

ISABELLA   I am come to know your pleasure.

ANGELO [*aside*]   That you might know[5] it would much better please me
  Than to demand° what 'tis. [*To* ISABELLA] Your brother cannot live.   *ask*

ISABELLA   Even so.° Heaven keep your honour.[6]   *So be it*

35 ANGELO   Yet may he live a while, and it may be
  As long as you or I. Yet he must die.

ISABELLA   Under your sentence?

ANGELO   Yea.

ISABELLA   When, I beseech you?—that in his reprieve,
40   Longer or shorter, he may be so fitted°   *prepared*
  That his soul sicken not.

ANGELO   Ha, fie, these filthy vices! It were as good
  To pardon him that hath from nature stolen
  A man already made,[7] as to remit°   *excuse*
45   Their saucy sweetness that do coin God's image
  In stamps that are forbid.[8] 'Tis all as easy
  Falsely° to take away a life true° made   *Wrongly / legitimately*
  As to put metal[9] in restrainèd° moulds,   *forbidden*
  To make a false one.

50 ISABELLA   'Tis set down so in heaven, but not in earth.

ANGELO   Say you so? Then I shall pose° you quickly.   *ask*
  Which had you rather: that the most just law
  Now took your brother's life, or, to redeem him,
  Give up your body to such sweet uncleanness
  As she that he hath stained?

55 ISABELLA   Sir, believe this.
  I had rather give my body than my soul.

ANGELO   I talk not of your soul. Our compelled sins
  Stand more for number than for account.[1]

ISABELLA   How say you?

ANGELO   Nay, I'll not warrant that,[2] for I can speak
60   Against the thing I say. Answer to this.
  I now, the voice of the recorded law,
  Pronounce a sentence on your brother's life.
  Might there not be a charity in sin
  To save this brother's life?

ISABELLA   Please° you to do't,   *If it please*
65   I'll take it as a peril to my soul
  It is no sin at all, but charity.

ANGELO   Pleased you to do't at peril of your soul
  Were equal poise° of sin and charity.   *balance*

---

5. With pun on "carnal knowledge."
6. A form of farewell.
7. *hath . . . made*: has committed murder.
8. *coin . . . forbid*: counterfeit God's image (by begetting illegitimate children).

9. Variant spelling of "mettle" (spirit). Some thought the child's spirit was conveyed in its father's semen.
1. *Our . . . account*: Sins we are forced to commit fill out the list but are not held against us.
2. I'll not guarantee that to be true.

ISABELLA That I do beg his life, if it be sin,
70 Heaven let me bear it. You granting° of my suit,   *Supposing you grant*
If that be sin, I'll make it my morn prayer
To have it added to the faults of mine,
And nothing of your answer.

ANGELO   Nay, but hear me.
Your sense pursues not mine.[3] Either you are ignorant,
75 Or seem so craftily, and that's not good.

ISABELLA Let me be ignorant, and in nothing good
But graciously° to know I am no better.   *by God's grace*

ANGELO Thus wisdom wishes to appear most bright
When it doth tax° itself: as these black masks[4]   *reprove*
80 Proclaim an enshield° beauty ten times louder   *a shielded*
Than beauty could, displayed. But mark me.
To be receivèd° plain, I'll speak more gross.°   *understood / clearly*
Your brother is to die.

ISABELLA So.°   *Yes*

85 ANGELO And his offence is so, as it appears,
Accountant° to the law upon that pain.°   *Accountable / penalty*

ISABELLA True.

ANGELO Admit° no other way to save his life—   *Suppose*
As I subscribe not° that nor any other—   *agree to neither*
90 But, in the loss of question,[5] that you his sister,
Finding yourself desired of such a person
Whose credit with the judge, or own great place,°   *rank*
Could fetch your brother from the manacles
Of the all-binding law, and that there were
95 No earthly mean to save him, but that either
You must lay down the treasures of your body
To this supposed,° or else to let him suffer—   *supposed man*
What would you do?

ISABELLA As much for my poor brother as myself.
100 That is, were I under the terms° of death,   *sentence*
Th'impression of keen whips I'd wear as rubies,
And strip myself to death as to a bed
That longing have been sick for, ere I'd yield
My body up to shame.

105 ANGELO Then must your brother die.

ISABELLA And 'twere the cheaper way.
Better it were a brother died at once
Than that a sister, by redeeming him,
Should die for ever.°   *be eternally damned*

110 ANGELO Were not you then as cruel as the sentence
That you have slandered so?

ISABELLA Ignominy in ransom and free pardon
Are of two houses;° lawful mercy   *different families*
Is nothing kin to foul redemption.

115 ANGELO You seemed of late to make the law a tyrant,
And rather proved° the sliding of your brother   *argued*
A merriment than a vice.

ISABELLA O pardon me, my lord. It oft falls out
To have what we would° have, we speak not what we mean.   *wish to*

---

3. You don't follow my meaning; your desire is not
aroused by mine.

4. Worn at court entertainments.

5. For the sake of discussion.

120 I something° do excuse the thing I hate   *to some extent*
    For his advantage that I dearly love.
    ANGELO   We are all frail.[6]
    ISABELLA   Else° let my brother die—   *Otherwise*
    If not a federy,° but only he,   *confederate*
    Owe and succeed thy weakness.[7]
    ANGELO   Nay, women are frail too.
125 ISABELLA   Ay, as the glasses° where they view themselves,   *mirrors*
    Which are as easy broke as they make forms.
    Women? Help, heaven! Men their creation° mar   *origin*
    In profiting by them. Nay, call us ten times frail,
    For we are soft as our complexions are,
    And credulous to false prints.[8]
130 ANGELO   I think it well,°   *agree completely*
    And from this testimony of your own sex,
    Since I suppose we are made to be no stronger
    Than faults may shake our frames, let me be bold.°   *presumptuous*
    I do arrest° your words. Be that you are;   *seize upon*
135 That is, a woman. If you be more,° you're none.   *(that is, better)*
    If you be one, as you are well expressed°   *shown to be*
    By all external warrants,° show it now,   *evidence*
    By putting on the destined livery.[9]
    ISABELLA   I have no tongue° but one. Gentle my lord,   *speech*
140 Let me entreat you speak the former language.
    ANGELO   Plainly conceive, I love you.
    ISABELLA   My brother did love Juliet,
    And you tell me that he shall die for it.
    ANGELO   He shall not, Isabel, if you give me love.
145 ISABELLA   I know your virtue hath a licence[1] in't,
    Which seems a little fouler than it is,
    To pluck on° others.   *test; mislead*
    ANGELO   Believe me, on mine honour,
    My words express my purpose.
    ISABELLA   Ha, little honour to be much believed,
150 And most pernicious purpose! Seeming, seeming!
    I will proclaim° thee, Angelo; look for't.   *denounce*
    Sign me a present° pardon for my brother,   *an immediate*
    Or with an outstretched throat I'll tell the world aloud
    What man thou art.
    ANGELO   Who will believe thee, Isabel?
155 My unsoiled name, th'austereness of my life,
    My vouch° against you, and my place i'th' state,   *attestation*
    Will so your accusation overweigh
    That you shall stifle in your own report,°   *story; reputation*
    And smell of calumny. I have begun,
160 And now I give my sensual race the rein.
    Fit thy consent to my sharp appetite.
    Lay by all nicety and prolixious° blushes   *coyness and excessive*
    That banish what they sue for. Redeem thy brother
    By yielding up thy body to my will,

---

6. Echoing Ecclesiasticus 8:5: "We are all worthy blame."
7. Own and inherit the weakness under discussion, or the weakness that you possess.
8. And receptive to false impressions; referring to Angelo's counterfeiting imagery, lines 45ff.
9. That is, by accepting women's sexual destiny and subjection to men. *livery:* servant's uniform.
1. Liberty to seem licentious.

165   Or else he must not only die the death,
        But thy unkindness° shall his death draw out   *unnaturalness*
        To ling'ring sufferance.° Answer me tomorrow,   *torment*
        Or by the affection° that now guides me most,   *passion*
        I'll prove a tyrant to him. As for you,
170   Say what you can, my false o'erweighs your true.   *Exit*
    ISABELLA   To whom should I complain? Did I tell this,
        Who would believe me? O perilous mouths,
        That bear in them one and the selfsame tongue
        Either of condemnation or approof,°   *approval*
175   Bidding the law make curtsy° to their will,   *submit*
        Hooking both right and wrong to th'appetite,
        To follow as it draws! I'll to my brother.
        Though he hath fall'n by prompture° of the blood,   *instigation*
        Yet hath he in him such a mind of honour
180   That had he twenty heads to tender° down   *pay*
        On twenty bloody blocks, he'd yield them up
        Before his sister should her body stoop
        To such abhorred pollution.
        Then Isabel live chaste, and brother die:
185   More than our brother is our chastity.
        I'll tell him yet of Angelo's request,
        And fit his mind to death, for his soul's rest.   *Exit*

3.1

Enter DUKE *[disguised as a friar],* CLAUDIO, *and* PROVOST
    DUKE   So then you hope of pardon from Lord Angelo?
    CLAUDIO   The miserable have no other medicine
        But only hope.
        I've hope to live, and am prepared to die.
5   DUKE   Be absolute° for death. Either death or life   *resolved*
        Shall thereby be the sweeter. Reason thus with life.
        If I do lose thee, I do lose a thing
        That none but fools would keep. A breath thou art,
        Servile to all the skyey influences[1]
10   That dost this habitation where thou keep'st°   *live*
        Hourly afflict. Merely° thou art death's fool,°   *Utterly / dupe*
        For him thou labour'st by thy flight to shun,
        And yet runn'st toward him still.° Thou art not noble,   *always*
        For all th'accommodations° that thou bear'st   *material comforts*
15   Are nursed by baseness.[2] Thou'rt by no means valiant,
        For thou dost fear the soft and tender fork°   *forked tongue*
        Of a poor worm.° Thy best of rest is sleep,   *snake*
        And that thou oft provok'st,° yet grossly fear'st   *summon*
        Thy death, which is no more. Thou art not thyself,°   *self-contained*
20   For thou exist'st on many a thousand grains
        That issue out of dust.° Happy thou art not,   *grow from the ground*
        For what thou hast not, still thou striv'st to get,
        And what thou hast, forget'st. Thou art not certain,°   *stable*
        For thy complexion° shifts to strange effects   *temperament*
25   After° the moon. If thou art rich, thou'rt poor,[3]   *Following*

3.1 Location: The prison.
1. Subject to all the influences of the heavenly bodies.
2. Are grown from plants and animals; made by lower-class people.

3. From Revelation 3:17: "For thou sayest, I am rich and increased with goods, and have need of nothing, and knowest not how thou art wretched and miserable, and poor, and blind, and naked."

For like an ass whose back with ingots bows,
Thou bear'st thy heavy riches but a journey,
And death unloads thee. Friend hast thou none,
For thine own bowels,° which do call thee sire,   offspring
30   The mere effusion° of thy proper° loins,   very emission / own
Do curse the gout, serpigo,° and the rheum,°   skin disease / congestion
For ending thee no sooner. Thou hast nor youth nor age,
But as it were an after-dinner's sleep
Dreaming on both; for all thy blessèd youth
35   Becomes as agèd,° and doth beg the alms°   as if old / for money
Of palsied eld;° and when thou art old and rich,   old people
Thou hast neither heat,° affection, limb,° nor beauty,   desire / strength
To make thy riches pleasant. What's in this
That bears the name of life? Yet in this life
40   Lie hid more thousand° deaths; yet death we fear   a thousand more
That makes these odds° all even.   irregularities
CLAUDIO   I humbly thank you.
To sue° to live, I find I seek to die,   ask
And seeking death, find life.[4] Let it come on.
ISABELLA [within]   What ho! Peace here, grace, and good company!
45   PROVOST   Who's there? Come in; the wish deserves a welcome.
DUKE [to CLAUDIO]   Dear sir, ere long I'll visit you again.
CLAUDIO   Most holy sir, I thank you.
               Enter ISABELLA
ISABELLA   My business is a word or two with Claudio.
PROVOST   And very welcome. Look, signor, here's your sister.
DUKE   Provost, a word with you.
50   PROVOST   As many as you please.
     [The DUKE and PROVOST draw aside]
DUKE   Bring me to hear them speak where I may be concealed.
     [They conceal themselves]
CLAUDIO   Now sister, what's the comfort?
ISABELLA   Why, as all comforts are: most good, most good indeed.
Lord Angelo, having affairs to heaven,
55   Intends you for his swift ambassador,
Where you shall be an everlasting leiger.°   resident ambassador
Therefore your best appointment° make with speed.   preparation
Tomorrow you set on.°   forward
CLAUDIO   Is there no remedy?
ISABELLA   None but such remedy as, to save a head,
60   To cleave a heart in twain.
CLAUDIO   But is there any?
ISABELLA   Yes, brother, you may live.
There is a devilish mercy in the judge,
If you'll implore it, that will free your life,
But fetter you till death.
65   CLAUDIO   Perpetual durance?°   imprisonment
ISABELLA   Ay, just,° perpetual durance; a restraint,   exactly so
Though all the world's vastidity° you had,   vastness
To a determined scope.[5]
CLAUDIO   But in what nature?

4. Echoing Matthew 16:25: "For whosoever will save his   5. Constricted space (by the awareness of the means by
life, shall lose it: and whosoever shall lose his life for my   which he had been saved).
sake, shall find it."

ISABELLA   In such a one as you consenting to't
70   Would bark[6] your honour from that trunk° you bear,   *body; tree trunk*
And leave you naked.
CLAUDIO   Let me know the point.
ISABELLA   O, I do fear thee, Claudio, and I quake
Lest thou a feverous° life shouldst entertain,°   *feverish / cherish*
And six or seven winters more respect°   *esteem*
75   Than a perpetual honour. Dar'st thou die?
The sense° of death is most in apprehension,°   *awareness / anticipation*
And the poor beetle that we tread upon
In corporal sufferance° finds a pang as great   *bodily suffering*
As when a giant dies.
CLAUDIO   Why give you me this shame?
80   Think you I can a resolution fetch°   *derive*
From flow'ry° tenderness? If I must die,   *florid*
I will encounter darkness as a bride,
And hug it in mine arms.
ISABELLA   There spake my brother; there my father's grave
85   Did utter forth a voice. Yes, thou must die.
Thou art too noble to conserve a life
In base appliances.° This outward-sainted deputy,   *ignoble means*
Whose settled° visage and deliberate word   *composed*
Nips youth i'th' head[7] and follies doth enew°   *drive into hiding*
90   As falcon doth the fowl, is yet a devil.
His filth within being cast,[8] he would appear
A pond as deep as hell.
CLAUDIO   The precise[9] Angelo?
ISABELLA   O, 'tis the cunning livery of hell
The damnedest body to invest° and cover   *dress*
95   In precise guards!° Dost thou think, Claudio: *trimmings*
If I would yield him my virginity,
Thou might'st be freed!
CLAUDIO   O heavens, it cannot be!
ISABELLA   Yes, he would give't thee, from this rank offence,
So to offend him still.[1] This night's the time
100   That I should do what I abhor to name,
Or else thou diest tomorrow.
CLAUDIO   Thou shalt not do't.
ISABELLA   O, were it but my life,
I'd throw it down for your deliverance
As frankly° as a pin.   *freely*
105   CLAUDIO   Thanks, dear Isabel.
ISABELLA   Be ready, Claudio, for your death tomorrow.
CLAUDIO   Yes. Has he affections in him
That thus can make him bite the law by th' nose°   *flout the law*
When he would force it? Sure it is no sin,
110   Or of the deadly seven[2] it is the least.
ISABELLA   Which is the least?
CLAUDIO   If it were damnable, he being so wise,
Why would he for the momentary trick°   *trifle*

6. Strip off, like bark from a tree.
7. As a hawk kills a bird.
8. Cleaned out; measured; vomited.
9. F has "prenzie" here and in line 95; some editors emend (as here) to "precise," others to "princely."

1. *give't thee . . . still*: grant you freedom in return for his foul sin, so that you might continue offending him.
2. Seven deadly sins (pride, lechery, envy, anger, covetousness, gluttony, and sloth).

	Be perdurably fined?° O Isabel!	*eternally punished*
115	ISABELLA What says my brother?	
	CLAUDIO Death is a fearful thing.	
	ISABELLA And shamèd life a hateful.	
	CLAUDIO Ay, but to die, and go we know not where;	
	To lie in cold obstruction,° and to rot;	*congealment*
120	This sensible warm motion° to become	*conscious warm body*
	A kneaded clod, and the dilated° spirit	*expansive; released*
	To bath in fiery floods, or to reside	
	In thrilling° region of thick-ribbèd ice;	*bitterly cold*
	To be imprisoned in the viewless° winds,	*unseeing; invisible*
125	And blown with restless violence round about	
	The pendent° world; or to be worse than worst	*hanging in space*
	Of those that lawless and incertain thought[3]	
	Imagine howling—'tis too horrible!	
	The weariest and most loathèd worldly life	
130	That age, ache, penury, and imprisonment	
	Can lay on nature is a paradise	
	To what we fear of death.	
	ISABELLA Alas, alas!	
	CLAUDIO Sweet sister, let me live.	
135	What sin you do to save a brother's life,	
	Nature dispenses with° the deed so far	*excuses*
	That it becomes a virtue.	
	ISABELLA O, you beast!	
	O faithless coward, O dishonest wretch,	
	Wilt thou be made a man° out of my vice?	*given life*
140	Is't not a kind of incest to take life	
	From thine own sister's shame? What should I think?	
	Heaven shield° my mother played my father fair,	*forbid*
	For such a warpèd slip of wilderness°	*shoot of wild stock*
	Ne'er issued from his blood. Take my defiance,°	*rejection*
145	Die, perish! Might but my bending down	
	Reprieve thee from thy fate, it should proceed.	
	I'll pray a thousand prayers for thy death,	
	No word to save thee.	
	CLAUDIO Nay, hear me, Isabel.	
150	ISABELLA O fie, fie, fie!	
	Thy sin's not accidental,° but a trade.°	*casual / habit*
	Mercy to thee would prove itself a bawd.[4]	
	'Tis best that thou diest quickly.	
	[*She parts from* CLAUDIO]	
	CLAUDIO O hear me, Isabella.	
	DUKE [*coming forward to* ISABELLA] Vouchsafe a word, young	
155	sister, but one word.	
	ISABELLA What is your will?	
	DUKE Might you dispense with your leisure,° I would by and by	*spare the time*
	have some speech with you. The satisfaction I would require	
	is likewise your own benefit.	
160	ISABELLA I have no superfluous leisure; my stay must be stolen	
	out of other affairs; but I will attend° you a while.	*await*
	DUKE [*standing aside with* CLAUDIO] Son, I have overheard what	
	hath passed between you and your sister. Angelo had never the	

---

3. Of those whom unbridled and dubious conjecture.   4. By facilitating sinful behavior.

purpose to corrupt her; only he hath made an assay°   *a trial*
165 of her virtue, to practise his judgement with the disposition of
natures. She, having the truth of honour° in her, hath made   *chastity*
him that gracious° denial which he is most glad to receive. I   *virtuous*
am confessor to Angelo, and I know this to be true. Therefore
prepare yourself to death. Do not falsify° your resolution with   *corrupt*
170 hopes that are fallible. Tomorrow you must die. Go to your
knees and make ready.

CLAUDIO   Let me ask my sister pardon. I am so out of love with
life that I will sue to be rid of it.

DUKE   Hold you there.° Farewell.   *Remain so resolved*
     [CLAUDIO *joins* ISABELLA][5]

175 Provost, a word with you.

PROVOST [*coming forward*]   What's your will, father?

DUKE   That now you are come, you will be gone. Leave me a
while with the maid. My mind° promises with my habit° no   *intention / friar's gown*
loss shall touch her by my company.

180 PROVOST   In good time.°   *Exit* [*with* CLAUDIO]   *Very well*

DUKE   The hand that hath made you fair hath made you good.
The goodness that is cheap in beauty makes beauty brief in
goodness;[6] but grace,° being the soul of your complexion,° shall   *virtue / constitution*
keep the body of it ever fair. The assault that Angelo hath made
185 to you fortune hath conveyed to my understanding; and but
that frailty hath examples° for his falling, I should wonder at   *precedents*
Angelo. How will you do to content this substitute,° and to save   *deputy*
your brother?

ISABELLA   I am now going to resolve him. I had rather my
190 brother die by the law than my son should be unlawfully born.
But O, how much is the good Duke deceived in Angelo! If ever
he return and I can speak to him, I will open my lips in vain,
or discover° his government.[7]   *expose*

DUKE   That shall not be much amiss. Yet as the matter now
195 stands, he will avoid° your accusation: he made trial of you   *quash*
only. Therefore fasten your ear on my advisings. To the love I
have in doing good, a remedy presents itself. I do make myself
believe that you may most uprighteously do a poor wronged
lady a merited benefit, redeem your brother from the angry
200 law, do no stain to your own gracious person, and much please
the absent Duke, if peradventure he shall ever return to have
hearing of this business.

ISABELLA   Let me hear you speak farther. I have spirit to do any-
thing that appears not foul in the truth of my spirit.

205 DUKE   Virtue is bold, and goodness never fearful. Have you not
heard speak of Mariana, the sister of Frederick, the great soldier
who miscarried° at sea?   *perished*

ISABELLA   I have heard of the lady, and good words went with
her name.

210 DUKE   She should this Angelo have married, was affianced to her
oath, and the nuptial appointed;° between which time of the   *wedding day set*
contract and limit° of the solemnity, her brother Frederick was   *date*
wrecked at sea, having in that perished vessel the dowry of his

---

5. The Duke's conversation with the Provost provides an   makes beauty short-lived.
opportunity for a silent reconciliation.   7. Conduct; mode of governing.
6. The goodness that is little valued by the beautiful

sister. But mark how heavily this befell to the poor gentle-
215 woman. There she lost a noble and renowned brother, in his
love toward her ever most kind and natural; with him, the por-
tion and sinew° of her fortune, her marriage dowry; with both,   *mainstay*
her combinate° husband, this well-seeming Angelo.   *betrothed*

ISABELLA   Can this be so? Did Angelo so leave her?

220 DUKE   Left her in her tears, and dried not one of them with his
comfort; swallowed° his vows whole, pretending° in her discov-   *retracted / alleging*
eries of dishonour;° in few, bestowed her on her own lamenta-   *unchastity*
tion, which she yet wears for his sake; and he, a marble° to her   *impervious*
tears, is washed with them, but relents not.

225 ISABELLA   What a merit were it in death to take this poor maid
from the world! What corruption in this life, that it will let this
man live! But how out of this can she avail?°   *profit*

DUKE   It is a rupture that you may easily heal, and the cure of it
not only saves your brother, but keeps you from dishonour in
230 doing it.

ISABELLA   Show me how, good father.

DUKE   This forenamed maid hath yet in her the continuance of
her first affection.° His unjust unkindness, that in all reason   *passion*
should have quenched her love, hath, like an impediment in
235 the current, made it more violent and unruly. Go you to
Angelo, answer his requiring with a plausible obedience, agree
with his demands to the point;° only refer yourself to this advan-   *exactly*
tage: first, that your stay with him may not be long; that the
time may have all shadow° and silence in it; and the place   *darkness*
240 answer to convenience. This being granted in course, and now
follows all. We shall advise this wronged maid to stead up° your   *fulfill*
appointment, go in your place. If the encounter acknowledge
itself° hereafter, it may compel him to her recompense; and   *becomes known*
hear, by this is your brother saved, your honour untainted, the
245 poor Mariana advantaged, and the corrupt deputy scaled.[8] The
maid will I frame° and make fit for his attempt. If you think   *prepare*
well to carry this, as you may, the doubleness of the benefit
defends the deceit from reproof. What think you of it?

ISABELLA   The image of it gives me content already, and I trust
250 it will grow to a most prosperous perfection.°   *completion*

DUKE   It lies much in your holding up. Haste you speedily to
Angelo. If for this night he entreat you to his bed, give him
promise of satisfaction. I will presently to Saint Luke's; there
at the moated grange° resides this dejected[9] Mariana. At that   *country house*
255 place call upon me; and dispatch° with Angelo, that it may be   *settle*
quickly.

ISABELLA   I thank you for this comfort. Fare you well, good
father.   *Exit*

Enter ELBOW, [POMPEY *the*] *Clown, and officers*[1]

ELBOW   Nay, if there be no remedy for it but that you will needs°   *you must*
260 buy and sell men and women like beasts, we shall have all the
world drink brown and white bastard.°   *sweet wine (with pun)*

DUKE   O heavens, what stuff is here?

POMPEY   'Twas never merry world since, of two usuries,[2] the

---

8. Overreached; weighed (and found wanting).
9. Depressed; rejected.
1. The rest of the scene takes place on the street. Some

editors begin a new scene here, though the Duke remains
onstage.
2. Lending of money at interest; prostitution.

merriest was put down, and the worser allowed by order of law,[3]
265 a furred gown° to keep him warm—and furred with fox on   (*worn by usurers*)
lambskins too, to signify that craft,° being richer than inno-   *cunning*
cency, stands for the facing.[4]

ELBOW   Come your way, sir.—Bless you, good father friar.[5]

DUKE   And you, good brother father. What offence hath this man
270 made you, sir?

ELBOW   Marry, sir, he hath offended the law; and, sir, we take
him to be a thief, too, sir, for we have found upon him, sir, a
strange picklock,° which we have sent to the deputy.   *skeleton key*

DUKE [*to* POMPEY]   Fie, sirrah, a bawd,° a wicked bawd!   *pimp*
275 The evil that thou causest to be done,
That is thy means to live. Do thou but think
What 'tis to cram a maw or clothe a back
From such a filthy vice. Say to thyself,
'From their abominable and beastly touches
280 I drink, I eat, array° myself, and live'.   *dress*
Canst thou believe thy living is a life,
So stinkingly depending?° Go mend, go mend.   *dependent*

POMPEY   Indeed it does stink in some sort, sir. But yet, sir, I
would prove—

285 DUKE   Nay, if the devil have given thee proofs for sin,
Thou wilt prove° his.—Take him to prison, officer.   *prove to be*
Correction° and instruction must both work   *Punishment*
Ere this rude° beast will profit.°   *barbarous / improve*

ELBOW   He must before the deputy, sir; he has given him warn-
290 ing. The deputy cannot abide a whoremaster. If he be a whore-
monger and comes before him, he were as good go a mile on
his errand.[6]

DUKE   That° we were all as some would seem to be—   *Would that*
Free from our faults, or faults from seeming free.°   *free from seeming*

295 ELBOW   His neck will come to° your waist: a cord,[7] sir.   *end up like*
          Enter LUCIO

POMPEY   I spy comfort, I cry bail. Here's a gentleman, and a
friend of mine.

LUCIO   How now, noble Pompey? What, at the wheels of Cae-
sar? Art thou led in triumph?[8] What, is there none of Pygmali-
300 on's images[9] newly made woman to be had now, for putting
the hand in the pocket and extracting clutched?[1] What reply,
ha? What sayst thou to this tune, matter, and method?[2] Is't not
drowned i'th' last rain,[3] ha? What sayst thou, trot?° Is the world   *bawd*
as it was, man? Which is the way? Is it sad and few words? Or
305 how? The trick° of it?   *style*

DUKE   Still° thus and thus; still worse!   *Always*

LUCIO   How doth my dear morsel thy mistress? Procures she still, ha?

3. A statute of 1570 allowed interest of 10 percent or less.
4. Is used to trim the garment; displays itself to the world.
5. Absurd, since "friar" means "brother"; hence the Duke's reply.
6. *he were . . . errand:* he would be better doing anything rather than that.
7. Encircled by a rope, as the friar's cord encircles his waist.

8. After Roman victories, vanquished generals were paraded behind the chariot wheels of their conquerors.
9. In classical legend, the sculptor Pygmalion fell in love with one of his statues, who was given life by Venus, the goddess of love; with a play on "become a woman" (lose one's virginity).
1. Clenched, with money for bail.
2. This style, topic, and sequence of thought.
3. Overwhelmed with recent misfortune.

POMPEY Troth, sir, she hath eaten up° all her beef,° and she is   *worn out / prostitutes*
herself in the tub.[4]

310 LUCIO Why, 'tis good, it is the right of it, it must be so. Ever
your fresh whore and your powdered[5] bawd; an unshunned°   *unavoidable*
consequence, it must be so. Art going to prison, Pompey?

POMPEY Yes, faith, sir.

LUCIO Why 'tis not amiss, Pompey. Farewell. Go; say I sent thee
315 thither. For debt, Pompey, or how?

ELBOW For being a bawd, for being a bawd.

LUCIO Well then, imprison him. If imprisonment be the due of
a bawd, why, 'tis his right. Bawd is he doubtless, and of antiq-
uity° too—bawd born.° Farewell, good Pompey. Commend me   *long standing / at birth*
320 to the prison, Pompey. You will turn good husband° now, Pom-   *householder*
pey; you will keep the house.

POMPEY I hope, sir, your good worship will be my bail?

LUCIO No, indeed, will I not, Pompey; it is not the wear.° I will   *fashion*
pray, Pompey, to increase your bondage. If you take it not
325 patiently, why, your mettle° is the more. Adieu, trusty Pom-   *spirit; shackles*
pey.— Bless you, friar.

DUKE And you.

LUCIO Does Bridget paint° still, Pompey, ha?   *use cosmetics*

ELBOW [*to* POMPEY] Come your ways, sir, come.

330 POMPEY [*to* LUCIO] You will not bail me then, sir?

LUCIO Then, Pompey, nor now.—What news abroad,° friar,   *in the world*
what news?

ELBOW [*to* POMPEY] Come your ways, sir, come.

LUCIO Go to kennel, Pompey,[6] go.

[*Exeunt* ELBOW, POMPEY, *and officers*]

335 What news, friar, of the Duke?

DUKE I know none. Can you tell me of any?

LUCIO Some say he is with the Emperor of Russia; other some,°   *some others*
he is in Rome. But where is he, think you?

DUKE I know not where; but wheresoever, I wish him well.

340 LUCIO It was a mad, fantastical trick° of him to steal from the   *eccentric caprice*
state, and usurp the beggary he was never born to. Lord Angelo
dukes it° well in his absence; he puts transgression to't.[7]   *plays the Duke*

DUKE He does well in't.

LUCIO A little more lenity to lechery would do no harm in him.
345 Something too crabbed° that way, friar.   *Somewhat too harsh*

DUKE It is too general a vice, and severity must cure it.

LUCIO Yes, in good sooth, the vice is of a great° kindred, it is   *an extensive; powerful*
well allied.° But it is impossible to extirp° it quite, friar, till   *connected / extirpate*
eating and drinking be put down. They say this Angelo was not
350 made by man and woman, after this downright[8] way of cre-
ation. Is it true, think you?

DUKE How should he be made, then?

LUCIO Some report a sea-maid° spawned him, some that he was   *mermaid*
begot between two stockfishes.° But it is certain that when he   *dried fish*
355 makes water his urine is congealed ice; that I know to be true.
And he is a motion ungenerative;[9] that's infallible.°   *certain*

DUKE You are pleasant,° sir, and speak apace.°   *merry / unrestrainedly*

---

4. Pickling tub for preserving ("powdering") beef; sweat-
ing tub for curing venereal disease.
5. Pickled; covered with cosmetic powder.
6. "Pompey" was a common dog's name.

7. He prosecutes lawbreaking vigorously.
8. In accordance with this straightforward.
9. An impotent puppet.

LUCIO   Why, what a ruthless thing is this in him, for the rebel-
lion of a codpiece¹ to take away the life of a man! Would the
360   Duke that is absent have done this? Ere he would have hanged
a man for the getting° a hundred bastards, he would have paid   *begetting*
for the nursing a thousand. He had some feeling of the sport,
he knew the service,° and that instructed him to mercy.   *(of prostitution)*
DUKE   I never heard the absent Duke much detected° for   *accused*
365   women; he was not inclined that way.
LUCIO   O sir, you are deceived.
DUKE   'Tis not possible.
LUCIO   Who, not the Duke? Yes, your beggar of fifty; and his
use° was to put a ducat in her clack-dish.² The Duke had cro-   *custom*
370   chets° in him. He would be drunk too, that let me inform you.   *odd notions*
DUKE   You do him wrong, surely.
LUCIO   Sir, I was an inward° of his. A shy fellow was the Duke,   *intimate*
and I believe I know the cause of his withdrawing.
DUKE   What, I prithee, might be the cause?
375   LUCIO   No, pardon, 'tis a secret must be locked within the teeth
and the lips. But this I can let you understand. The greater file
of the subject° held the Duke to be wise.   *majority of the people*
DUKE   Wise? Why, no question but he was.
LUCIO   A very superficial, ignorant, unweighing° fellow.   *injudicious*
380   DUKE   Either this is envy° in you, folly, or mistaking. The very   *malice*
stream° of his life, and the business he hath helmed,° must,   *course / steered*
upon a warranted need,° give him a better proclamation.° Let   *necessarily / reputation*
him be but testimonied° in his own bringings-forth,° and he   *proven / public actions*
shall appear to the envious a scholar, a statesman, and a soldier.
385   Therefore you speak unskilfully,° or, if your knowledge be   *ignorantly*
more, it is much darkened in your malice.
LUCIO   Sir, I know him and I love him.
DUKE   Love talks with better knowledge, and knowledge with
dearer love.
390   LUCIO   Come, sir, I know what I know.
DUKE   I can hardly believe that, since you know not what you
speak. But if ever the Duke return, as our prayers are he may,
let me desire you to make your answer before him. If it be
honest you have spoke, you have courage to maintain it. I am
395   bound to call upon° you; and I pray you, your name?   *accuse*
LUCIO   Sir, my name is Lucio, well known to the Duke.
DUKE   He shall know you better, sir, if I may live to report you.
LUCIO   I fear you not.
DUKE   O, you hope the Duke will return no more, or you imag-
400   ine me too unhurtful an opposite.° But indeed I can do you   *adversary*
little harm; you'll forswear this again.°   *at another time*
LUCIO   I'll be hanged first. Thou art deceived in me, friar. But
no more of this. Canst thou tell if Claudio die tomorrow or no?
DUKE   Why should he die, sir?
405   LUCIO   Why? For filling a bottle with a tundish.° I would the   *funnel (with innuendo)*
Duke we talk of were returned again; this ungenitured agent°   *sexless deputy*
will unpeople the province with continency. Sparrows° must   *(proverbially lustful)*
not build in his house-eaves, because they are lecherous. The
Duke yet would have dark deeds darkly answered:° he would   *secretly requited*
410   never bring them to light. Would he were returned. Marry, this

---

1. Padded pouch worn over a man's breeches.   2. Begging bowl (with sexual innuendo).

Claudio is condemned for untrussing.° Farewell, good friar. I   *undoing his leggings*
prithee pray for me. The Duke, I say to thee again, would eat
mutton on Fridays.[3] He's not past it yet, and, I say to thee, he
would mouth° with a beggar, though she smelt° brown bread   *kiss / smelled of*
415 and garlic.[4] Say that I said so. Farewell.   *Exit*

DUKE   No might nor greatness in mortality°   *mortal existence*
Can censure scape;° back-wounding calumny[5]   *escape censure*
The whitest virtue strikes. What king so strong
Can tie the gall° up in the slanderous tongue?   *rancor*
      Enter ESCALUS, PROVOST, *and* [MISTRESS OVERDONE]
But who comes here?

420 ESCALUS [*to the* PROVOST]   Go, away with her to prison.

MISTRESS OVERDONE   Good my lord, be good to me. Your hon-
our is accounted a merciful man, good my lord.

ESCALUS   Double and treble admonition,[6] and still forfeit in the
same kind!° This would make mercy swear[7] and play the tyrant.   *way*

425 PROVOST   A bawd of eleven years' continuance, may it please
your honour.

MISTRESS OVERDONE   My lord, this is one Lucio's information°   *accusation*
against me. Mistress Kate Keepdown was with child by him in
the Duke's time; he promised her marriage. His child is a year
430 and a quarter old come Philip and Jacob.[8] I have kept it myself;
and see how he goes about° to abuse° me.   *out of his way / injure*

ESCALUS   That fellow is a fellow of much licence. Let him be
called before us. Away with her to prison. Go to, no more
words. Provost, my brother° Angelo will not be altered; Claudio   *colleague*
435 must die tomorrow. Let him be furnished with divines, and
have all charitable preparation.[9] If my brother wrought by° my   *acted according to*
pity, it should not be so with him.

PROVOST   So please you, this friar hath been with him and
advised him for th'entertainment° of death.   *acceptance*
      [*Exeunt* PROVOST *and* MISTRESS OVERDONE]

440 ESCALUS   Good even, good father.

DUKE   Bliss and goodness on you.

ESCALUS   Of whence are you?

DUKE   Not of this country, though my chance° is now   *fortune*
To use it for my time.° I am a brother   *dwell here at present*
445 Of gracious order, late come from the See°   *Vatican*
In special business from his Holiness.

ESCALUS   What news abroad i'th' world?

DUKE   None, but that there is so great a fever on goodness that
the dissolution of it must cure it.[1] Novelty is only in request,°   *alone in demand*
450 and it is as dangerous to be aged in° any kind of course as it is   *habituated to*
virtuous to be inconstant in any undertaking. There is scarce
truth° enough alive to make societies secure, but security[2]   *honesty; loyalty*
enough to make fellowships° accursed. Much upon° this riddle   *partnerships/According to*
runs the wisdom of the world. This news is old enough, yet it

---

3. *mutton:* prostitute (slang); it was forbidden to eat meat
on Fridays.
4. The food of the poor.
5. *back-wounding calumny:* slander ("calumny") is cow-
ardly because it is not done to the victim's face.
6. Exceeding that recommended by Paul in Titus 3:10:
"Reject him that is an heretic, after once or twice admo-
nition."
7. Varying the proverbial "make a saint swear."

8. May 1 was the Feast of St. Philip and St. James
(Jacob), but also the time of sexually licentious May Day
festivities, when the child was presumably conceived.
9. Spiritual preparation enjoined by Christian charity.
1. *there is . . . it:* that is, goodness is so sick that only
death will "cure" it.
2. Financial bonds liable to forfeit; blind trustfulness.
societies: association with others.

455 is every day's news. I pray you, sir, of what disposition was the Duke?

ESCALUS   One that, above all other strifes, contended especially
to know himself.[3]

DUKE   What pleasure was he given to?

ESCALUS   Rather rejoicing to see another merry than merry at
460 anything which professed° to make him rejoice; a gentleman   *attempted*
of all temperance. But leave we him to his events,° with a   *affairs*
prayer they may prove prosperous, and let me desire to know°   *ask*
how you find Claudio prepared. I am made to understand that
you have lent him visitation.°   *visited him*

465 DUKE   He professes to have received no sinister measure° from   *unjust treatment*
his judge, but most willingly humbles himself to the determi-
nation° of justice. Yet had he framed° to himself, by the instruc- *sentence / imagined*
tion of his frailty, many deceiving promises of life, which I, by
my good leisure,° have discredited to him; and now is he   *gradually*
470 resolved to die.

ESCALUS   You have paid the heavens your function, and the pris-
oner the very debt of your calling.[4] I have laboured for the
poor gentleman to the extremest shore° of my modesty, but my   *utmost limit*
brother-justice have I found so severe that he hath forced me
475 to tell him he is indeed Justice.[5]

DUKE   If his own life answer° the straitness° of his proceeding, it *correspond to / strictness*
shall become him well; wherein if he chance to fail, he hath
sentenced° himself.   *condemned*

ESCALUS   I am going to visit the prisoner. Fare you well.

480 DUKE   Peace be with you.   [*Exit* ESCALUS][6]
He who the sword of heaven[7] will bear
Should be as holy as severe,
Pattern in himself to know,
Grace to stand, and virtue go,[8]
485 More nor less to others paying
Than by self-offences° weighing.   *his own offenses*
Shame to him whose cruel striking
Kills for faults of his own liking!
Twice treble shame on Angelo,
490 To weed my vice,[9] and let his grow!
O, what may man within him hide,
Though angel on the outward side!
How may likeness made in crimes[1]
Make my practice on the times
495 To draw with idle spiders' strings
Most ponderous and substantial things?[2]
Craft against vice I must apply.
With Angelo tonight shall lie
His old betrothèd but despisèd.
500 So disguise shall, by th' disguisèd,[3]
Pay with falsehood false exacting,
And perform an old contracting.   *Exit*

3. "Know thyself" was proverbial advice.
4. You have repaid the heavens for giving you your voca-
tion, and given the prisoner all he can expect of a friar.
5. Absolute justice personified.
6. For a reconstruction of the following episodes as they
were originally written, see Additional Passage B.
7. The authority of a ruler, conferred by God.
8. When to stand firm, and when to take action (?).

9. The Duke speaks as a representative sinner.
1. How can the similarity between Claudio's and
Angelo's offenses.
2. *To draw . . . things:* the law was proverbially compared
to a spider's web, which caught small insects but which
large insects could break through. *idle:* ineffectual.
3. Mariana, "disguised" as Isabella.

4.1

MARIANA [*discovered with a*] BOY *singing*

BOY Take, O take those lips away
    That so sweetly were forsworn,°   *perjured*
    And those eyes, the break of day
    Lights° that do mislead° the morn;   *Suns / guide falsely*
5   But my kisses bring again, bring again,°   *return*
    Seals of love, though sealed in vain, sealed in vain.

Enter DUKE [*disguised as a friar*]

MARIANA Break off thy song, and haste thee quick away.
  Here comes a man of comfort, whose advice
  Hath often stilled my brawling° discontent. [*Exit* BOY] *clamorous*
10 I cry you mercy,° sir, and well could wish   *beg your pardon*
  You had not found me here so musical.
  Let me excuse me, and believe me so:°   *in this*
  My mirth it much displeased, but pleased my woe.[1]
DUKE 'Tis good; though music oft hath such a charm° *magic spell*
15 To make bad good,° and good provoke to harm. I pray you tell *bad appear good*
  me, hath anybody enquired for me here today? Much upon° *at about*
  this time have I promised here to meet.
MARIANA You have not been enquired after; I have sat here all day.

Enter ISABELLA

DUKE I do constantly° believe you; the time is come even now. *assuredly*
20 I shall crave your forbearance° a little. Maybe I will call upon *departure; patience*
  you anon, for some advantage to yourself.
MARIANA I am always bound to you.   *Exit*
DUKE Very well met, and welcome.
  What is the news from this good deputy?
25 ISABELLA He hath a garden circummured° with brick, *walled about*
  Whose western side is with a vineyard backed;
  And to that vineyard is a planckèd° gate,   *made of planks*
  That makes his opening with this bigger key.
  This other doth command a little door
30 Which from the vineyard to the garden leads.
  There have I made my promise
  Upon the heavy° middle of the night   *In the gloomy*
  To call upon him.
DUKE But shall you on your knowledge° find this way? *with this information*
35 ISABELLA I have ta'en a due and wary note upon't.
  With whispering and most guilty diligence,
  In action all of precept,° he did show me *With explanatory gestures*
  The way twice o'er.
DUKE   Are there no other tokens°   *signs*
  Between you 'greed concerning her observance?[2]
40 ISABELLA No, none, but only a repair° i'th' dark, *journey to the place*
  And that I have possessed° him my most° stay *informed / longest*
  Can be but brief, for I have made him know
  I have a servant comes with me along
  That stays upon° me, whose persuasion is   *waits for*
  I come about my brother.
45 DUKE   'Tis well borne up.°   *maintained*

4.1 Location: Mariana's house. Probably Mariana and the Boy are "discovered" by drawing back a curtain to reveal the characters within an alcove at the back of the stage.

1. The music drove away mirth but nurtured melancholy.
2. That she (Mariana) must observe.

I have not yet made known to Mariana
A word of this.—What ho, within! Come forth!

      Enter MARIANA

[*To* MARIANA] I pray you be acquainted with this maid.
She comes to do you good.

ISABELLA   I do desire the like.

50 DUKE [*to* MARIANA]   Do you persuade yourself° that I respect you?   *believe*

MARIANA   Good friar, I know you do, and so have found it.

DUKE   Take then this your companion° by the hand,   *partner*
Who hath a story ready for your ear.
I shall attend your leisure;° but make haste,   *wait until you are ready*
The vaporous night approaches.

55 MARIANA [*to* ISABELLA]   Will't please you walk aside?

      Exeunt [MARIANA *and* ISABELLA]

DUKE[3]   O place° and greatness, millions of false° eyes   *rank / misjudging*
Are stuck° upon thee; volumes of report°   *fixed / rumors*
Run with their false and most contrarious quest°   *misguided inquiry*
Upon thy doings; thousand escapes° of wit   *sallies*
60 Make thee the father° of their idle dream,°   *subject / fantasy*
And rack[4] thee in their fancies.

      Enter MARIANA *and* ISABELLA

                        Welcome. How agreed?

ISABELLA   She'll take the enterprise upon her, father,
If you advise it.

DUKE   It is not my consent,
But my entreaty too.

ISABELLA [*to* MARIANA]   Little have you to say
65 When you depart from him but, soft and low,
'Remember now my brother'.

MARIANA   Fear me not.[5]

DUKE   Nor, gentle daughter, fear you not at all.
He is your husband on a pre-contract.°   *formal betrothal*
To bring you thus together 'tis no sin,
70 Sith that° the justice of your title to him   *Since*
Doth flourish° the deceit. Come, let us go.   *give propriety to*
Our corn's to reap, for yet our tilth's° to sow.   *Exeunt*   *tilled land*

4.2

      Enter PROVOST *and* [POMPEY]

PROVOST   Come hither, sirrah. Can you cut off a man's head?

POMPEY   If the man be a bachelor, sir, I can; but if he be a mar-
ried man, he's his wife's head,[1] and I can never cut off a wom-
an's head.[2]

5 PROVOST   Come, sir, leave me° your snatches,° and yield me a   *stop / quips*
direct answer. Tomorrow morning are to die Claudio and Bar-
nardine. Here is in our prison a common executioner, who in
his office lacks a helper. If you will take it on you to assist him,
it shall redeem you from your gyves;° if not, you shall have   *fetters*

---

3. The following lines, which seem out of context, may have originally been part of the Duke's soliloquy at the end of Act 3.
4. Misrepresent (literally, "torture by stretching").
5. Rely upon me; but the Duke takes "fear" in its modern sense.

4.2 Location: The prison.
1. Alluding to Paul's doctrine "the husband is the wife's head," Ephesians 5:23.
2. Playing on "married woman's maidenhead," an improbability.

10 your full time of imprisonment, and your deliverance with an
unpitied° whipping; for you have been a notorious bawd.   *unmerciful*

POMPEY   Sir, I have been an unlawful bawd time out of mind,
but yet I will be content to be a lawful hangman. I would be
glad to receive some instruction from my fellow partner.

15 PROVOST   What ho, Abhorson! Where's Abhorson there?

Enter ABHORSON

ABHORSON   Do you call, sir?

PROVOST   Sirrah, here's a fellow will help you tomorrow in your
execution. If you think it meet, compound with him by the
year,[3] and let him abide here with you; if not, use him for the

20 present, and dismiss him. He cannot plead his estimation° with   *reputation*
you; he hath been a bawd.

ABHORSON   A bawd, sir? Fie upon him, he will discredit our mystery.[4]

PROVOST   Go to, sir, you weigh equally; a feather will turn the scale.

                                                                Exit

POMPEY   Pray, sir, by your good favour°—for surely, sir, a good   *permission*

25 favour° you have, but that you have a hanging look[5]—do you   *face*
call, sir, your occupation a mystery?

ABHORSON   Ay, sir, a mystery.

POMPEY   Painting,[6] sir, I have heard say is a mystery; and your
whores, sir, being members of my occupation, using painting,

30 do prove my occupation a mystery. But what mystery there
should be in hanging, if I should be hanged I cannot imagine.

ABHORSON   Sir, it is a mystery.

POMPEY   Proof.

ABHORSON   Every true man's apparel fits your thief[7]—

35 POMPEY   If it be too little for your thief, your true man thinks it
big enough.° If it be too big for your thief, your thief thinks it   *a big enough loss*
little enough.° So every true man's apparel fits your thief.   *a small enough gain*

Enter PROVOST

PROVOST   Are you agreed?

POMPEY   Sir, I will serve him, for I do find your hangman is

40 a more penitent trade than your bawd—he doth oftener ask
forgiveness.[8]

PROVOST [*to* ABHORSON]   You, sirrah, provide your block and
your axe tomorrow, four o'clock.

ABHORSON [*to* POMPEY]   Come on, bawd, I will instruct thee in

45 my trade. Follow.

POMPEY   I do desire to learn, sir, and I hope, if you have occasion
to use me for your own turn, you shall find me yare.° For truly,   *skillful; eager*
sir, for your kindness I owe you a good turn.[9]

PROVOST   Call hither Barnardine and Claudio.

                               Exeunt [ABHORSON *and* POMPEY]

50 Th'one has my pity; not a jot the other,
Being a murderer, though he were my brother.

Enter CLAUDIO

Look, here's the warrant, Claudio, for thy death.
'Tis now dead midnight, and by eight tomorrow
Thou must be made immortal. Where's Barnardine?

---

3. Settle regular terms of employment with him.
4. Profession, requiring specialized skills and training.
5. Downcast expression; hangman's face.
6. Artist's occupation; use of cosmetics.
7. Abhorson implies that the thief assumes the character of an honest man by stealing his clothing; he also
suggests an analogy between the thief and the hangman, who was awarded the clothes of his victims.
8. Executioners customarily asked forgiveness of their victims before killing them.
9. Favor; turning off the scaffold.

55 CLAUDIO   As fast locked up in sleep as guiltless labour
When it lies starkly° in the travailer's° bones.   *stiffly / worker's*
He will not wake.
PROVOST   Who can do good on him?
Well, go prepare yourself.
                    [*Knocking within*]
                                     But hark, what noise?
Heaven give your spirits comfort!   [*Exit* CLAUDIO]
                    [*Knocking again*]
                                     By and by!
60 I hope it is some pardon or reprieve
For the most gentle Claudio.
                    Enter DUKE [*disguised as a friar*]
                                     Welcome, father.
DUKE   The best and wholesom'st spirits of the night
Envelop you, good Provost! Who called here of late?
PROVOST   None since the curfew[1] rung.
65 DUKE   Not Isabel?
PROVOST   No.
DUKE   They will then, ere't be long.
PROVOST   What comfort is for Claudio?
DUKE   There's some in hope.
70 PROVOST   It is a bitter° deputy.   *cruel*
DUKE   Not so, not so; his life is paralleled
Even with the stroke and line[2] of his great justice.
He doth with holy abstinence subdue
That in himself which he spurs on his power
75 To qualify° in others. Were he mealed° with that   *moderate / stained*
Which he corrects, then were he tyrannous;
But this being so, he's just.
                    [*Knocking within*]
                                     Now are they come.
                    [*The* PROVOST *goes to a door*]
This is a gentle Provost. Seldom when°   *Rarely*
The steelèd° jailer is the friend of men.   *hard-hearted*
                    [*Knocking within*]
[*To* PROVOST] How now, what noise? That spirit's possessed
80   with haste
That wounds th'unlisting postern° with these strokes.   *unyielding door*
PROVOST   There he° must stay until the officer   *(the messenger)*
Arise to let him in. He° is called up.   *(the officer)*
DUKE   Have you no countermand for Claudio yet,
But he must die tomorrow?
85 PROVOST   None, sir, none.
DUKE   As near the dawning, Provost, as it is,
You shall hear more ere morning.
PROVOST   Happily°   *Perhaps*
You something know, yet I believe there comes
No countermand. No such example° have we;   *precedent*
90 Besides, upon the very siege° of justice   *seat*
Lord Angelo hath to the public ear
Professed the contrary.

1. Evening bell, rung at 9:00 P.M.
2. Exact course; also suggesting ax blows and hanging ropes.

Enter a MESSENGER

This is his lordship's man.

DUKE   And here comes Claudio's pardon.

95 MESSENGER [*giving a paper to* PROVOST]   My lord hath sent you
this note, and by me this further charge: that you swerve not
from the smallest article of it, neither in time, matter, or other
circumstance. Good morrow; for, as I take it, it is almost day.

PROVOST   I shall obey him.   [*Exit* MESSENGER]

100 DUKE [*aside*]   This is his pardon, purchased by such sin
For which the pardoner himself is in.
Hence hath offence his° quick celerity,   *its*
When it is borne in high authority.
When vice makes mercy, mercy's so extended

105 That for the fault's love[3] is th'offender friended.°—   *befriended*
Now sir, what news?

PROVOST   I told you: Lord Angelo, belike thinking me remiss in
mine office, awakens me with this unwonted putting-on;°   *urging*
methinks strangely, for he hath not used° it before.   *practiced*

110 DUKE   Pray you let's hear.

PROVOST [*reading the letter*]   'Whatsoever you may hear to the
contrary, let Claudio be executed by four of the clock, and in
the afternoon Barnardine. For my better satisfaction, let me
have Claudio's head sent me by five. Let this be duly per-

115 formed, with a thought that more depends on it than we must
yet deliver.° Thus fail not to do your office, as you will answer   *make known*
it at your peril.'
What say you to this, sir?

DUKE   What is that Barnardine, who is to be executed in th'afternoon?

120 PROVOST   A Bohemian born, but here nursed up and bred; one
that is a prisoner nine years old.°   *nine years a prisoner*

DUKE   How came it that the absent Duke had not either deliv-
ered him to his liberty or executed him? I have heard it was
ever his manner to do so.

125 PROVOST   His friends still° wrought reprieves for him; and indeed   *continually*
his fact,° till now in the government of Lord Angelo, came not   *crime*
to an undoubtful° proof.   *a certain*

DUKE   It is now apparent?

PROVOST   Most manifest, and not denied by himself.

130 DUKE   Hath he borne himself penitently in prison? How seems
he to be touched?°   *affected*

PROVOST   A man that apprehends death no more dreadfully but as
a drunken sleep; careless, reckless, and fearless of what's past,
present, or to come; insensible of mortality, and desperately

135 mortal.[4]

DUKE   He wants° advice.   *needs*

PROVOST   He will hear none. He hath evermore had the liberty
of the prison. Give him leave to escape hence, he would not.
Drunk many times a day, if not many days entirely° drunk. We   *continuously*

140 have very oft awaked him as if to carry him to execution, and
showed him a seeming warrant for it; it hath not moved him at all.

DUKE   More of him anon. There is written in your brow, Provost,
honesty and constancy. If I read it not truly, my ancient skill

---

3. For love of the fault.   4. Reckless of death, and in a state of mortal sin.

beguiles me. But in the boldness° of my cunning,° I will lay   *confidence / skill*
145   myself in hazard.[5] Claudio, whom here you have warrant to
    execute, is no greater forfeit to the law than Angelo who hath
    sentenced him. To make you understand this in a manifested
    effect,° I crave but four days' respite, for the which you are to   *clear demonstration*
    do me both a present° and a dangerous courtesy.°   *an immediate / favor*
150 PROVOST   Pray sir, in what?
    DUKE   In the delaying death.
    PROVOST   Alack, how may I do it, having the hour limited, and
    an express command under penalty to deliver his head in the
    view of Angelo? I may make my case as Claudio's to cross° this   *oppose*
155   in the smallest.
    DUKE   By the vow of mine order, I warrant you, if my instructions
    may be your guide, let this Barnardine be this morning exe-
    cuted, and his head borne to Angelo.
    PROVOST   Angelo hath seen them both, and will discover° the   *discern*
160   favour.
    DUKE   O, death's a great disguiser, and you may add to it. Shave
    the head and tie the beard, and say it was the desire of the
    penitent to be so bared before his death; you know the course
    is common. If anything fall to you upon° this more than thanks   *as a result of*
165   and good fortune, by the saint whom I profess,[6] I will plead
    against it with my life.
    PROVOST   Pardon me, good father, it is against my oath.
    DUKE   Were you sworn to the Duke or to the deputy?
    PROVOST   To him and to his substitutes.
170   DUKE   You will think you have made no offence if the Duke
    avouch° the justice of your dealing?   *vouch for*
    PROVOST   But what likelihood is in that?
    DUKE   Not a resemblance,° but a certainty. Yet since I see you   *likelihood*
    fearful, that neither my coat,° integrity, nor persuasion can with   *religious garb*
175   ease attempt you,° I will go further than I meant, to pluck all   *win you over*
    fears out of you. [*Showing a letter*] Look you, sir, here is the
    hand and seal of the Duke. You know the character,° I doubt   *handwriting*
    not, and the signet is not strange to you?
    PROVOST   I know them both.
180   DUKE   The contents of this is the return of the Duke. You shall
    anon° over-read it at your pleasure, where you shall find within   *right away*
    these two days he will be here. This is a thing that Angelo
    knows not, for he this very day receives letters of strange tenor,
    perchance of the Duke's death, perchance entering into some
185   monastery; but by chance nothing of what is writ.° Look, th'un-   *written here*
    folding star[7] calls up the shepherd. Put not yourself into amaze-
    ment° how these things should be. All difficulties are but easy   *perplexity*
    when they are known. Call your executioner, and off with Bar-
    nardine's head. I will give him a present shrift,° and advise him   *an immediate confession*
190   for a better place. Yet° you are amazed; but this° shall abso-   *Still / (the letter)*
    lutely resolve you.° Come away, it is almost clear dawn.   *free you from doubt*

                                               Exeunt

---

5. I will bet on it; I will put myself in peril.
6. The patron saint of my order.

7. Morning star (which tells the shepherd he may safely release the sheep from the fold).

4.3

Enter [POMPEY]

POMPEY   I am as well acquainted here as I was in our house of
profession.¹ One would think it were Mistress Overdone's own
house, for here be many of her old customers. First, here's
young Master Rash; he's in for a commodity² of brown paper
and old ginger, nine score and seventeen pounds, of which he
made five marks ready money.³ Marry, then ginger⁴ was not
much in request, for the old women were all dead.⁵ Then is
there here one Master Caper,° at the suit of Master Threepile⁶   *fashionable dance*
the mercer,° for some four suits of peach-coloured satin, which   *cloth dealer*
now peaches° him a beggar. Then have we here young Dizzy,   *impeaches; declares*
and young Master Deepvow, and Master Copperspur and Mas-
ter Starve-lackey⁷ the rapier and dagger man,⁸ and young Drop-
hair⁹ that killed lusty Pudding,° and Master Forthright the   *stuffed guts*
tilter,° and brave Master Shoe-tie the great traveller,¹ and wild   *fencer*
Half-can that stabbed Pots,² and I think forty more, all great
doers in our trade, and are now 'for the Lord's sake'.³

Enter ABHORSON

ABHORSON   Sirrah, bring Barnardine hither.

POMPEY   Master Barnardine! You must rise⁴ and be hanged,
Master Barnardine!

ABHORSON   What ho, Barnardine!

BARNARDINE   [*within*]   A pox o' your throats! Who makes that
noise there? What are you?

POMPEY   Your friends, sir; the hangman. You must be so good,
sir, to rise and be put to death.

BARNARDINE   Away, you rogue, away! I am sleepy.

ABHORSON   Tell him he must awake, and that quickly too.

POMPEY   Pray, Master Barnardine, awake till you are executed,
and sleep afterwards.

ABHORSON   Go in to him and fetch him out.

POMPEY   He is coming, sir, he is coming. I hear his straw rustle.

ABHORSON   Is the axe upon the block, sirrah?

POMPEY   Very ready, sir.

Enter BARNARDINE

BARNARDINE   How now, Abhorson, what's the news with you?

ABHORSON   Truly, sir, I would desire you to clap into⁵ your pray-
ers, for, look you, the warrant's come.

BARNARDINE   You rogue, I have been drinking all night. I am not
fitted for't.

POMPEY   O, the better, sir; for he that drinks all night, and is
hanged betimes° in the morning, may sleep the sounder all the   *early*
next day.

Enter DUKE [*disguised as a friar*]

4.3 Location: Scene continues.
1. Religious house ("nunnery" was slang for "brothel").
2. To evade the statutory limit on interest, usurers would
give borrowers part of their loan in practically worthless
"commodities," which they were supposed to sell for
ready money. *he's in for:* he's in for falling into debt over.
3. Rash paid 197 pounds for the "commodity," a very
large sum, and sold it for about 3.3 pounds.
4. Used to make warming tonics.
5. Presumably victims of the 1603 plague, mentioned
earlier by Mistress Overdone.

6. Richest sort of velvet.
7. One who fails to feed his servants.
8. Suggesting a reputation for brawling.
9. Premature baldness was a sign of syphilis.
1. Observer of foreign fashions (probably ironic).
2. Suggesting drinking cups.
3. The cry of prisoners begging from the prison grate.
Prisoners had to pay for their own food and lodging.
4. Get out of bed; mount the scaffold.
5. Immediately begin; join your hands for.

ABHORSON [*to* BARNARDINE]   Look you, sir, here comes your
    ghostly° father. Do we jest now, think you?   *spiritual*
DUKE [*to* BARNARDINE]   Sir, induced by my charity, and hearing
    how hastily you are to depart, I am come to advise you, comfort
45   you, and pray with you.
BARNARDINE   Friar, not I. I have been drinking hard all night,
    and I will have more time to prepare me, or they shall beat out
    my brains with billets.° I will not consent to die this day, that's   *thick sticks*
    certain.
50 DUKE   O sir, you must; and therefore, I beseech you,
    Look forward on the journey you shall go.
BARNARDINE   I swear I will not die today, for any man's persuasion.
DUKE   But hear you—
BARNARDINE   Not a word. If you have anything to say to me,
55   come to my ward,° for thence will not I today.   *Exit*   *cell*
DUKE   Unfit to live or die. O gravel° heart!   *(i.e., hard)*
    After him, fellows; bring him to the block.
                [*Exeunt* ABHORSON *and* POMPEY]
      Enter PROVOST
PROVOST   Now, sir, how do you find the prisoner?
DUKE   A creature unprepared, unmeet° for death;   *unfit*
60 And to transport° him in the mind he is   *execute (euphemistic)*
    Were damnable.
PROVOST   Here in the prison, father,
    There died this morning of a cruel fever
    One Ragusine, a most notorious pirate,
    A man of Claudio's years, his beard and head
65 Just of his colour. What if we do omit°   *disregard*
    This reprobate till he were well inclined,
    And satisfy the deputy with the visage
    Of Ragusine, more like to Claudio?
DUKE   O, 'tis an accident that heaven provides.
70 Dispatch it presently; the hour draws on
    Prefixed° by Angelo. See this be done,   *Fixed in advance*
    And sent according to command, whiles I
    Persuade this rude° wretch willingly to die.   *uncivilized*
PROVOST   This shall be done, good father, presently.
75 But Barnardine must die this afternoon;
    And how shall we continue° Claudio,   *maintain*
    To save me from the danger that might come
    If he were known alive?
DUKE   Let this be done:
    Put them in secret holds,° both Barnardine and Claudio.   *cells*
80 Ere twice the sun hath made his journal° greeting   *daily*
    To yonder generation,[6] you shall find
    Your safety manifested.
PROVOST   I am your free dependant.°   *willing servant*
DUKE   Quick, dispatch, and send the head to Angelo.
                Exit [PROVOST]
    Now will I write letters to Angelo[7]—
85 The Provost, he shall bear them—whose contents
    Shall witness to him I am near at home,

---

6. That is, the people outside the prison.
7. "Angelo" may be an error for "Varrius," whom the Duke meets outside the city in 4.5.

    And that by great injunctions° I am bound   *for compelling reasons*
    To enter publicly. Him I'll desire
    To meet me at the consecrated fount
90   A league below the city, and from thence,
    By cold gradation° and well-balanced form,   *deliberate degrees*
    We shall proceed with Angelo.
        Enter PROVOST [*with Ragusine's head*]
PROVOST   Here is the head; I'll carry it myself.
DUKE   Convenient° is it. Make a swift return,   *Suitable*
95   For I would commune° with you of such things   *confer*
    That want no ear but yours.
PROVOST   I'll make all speed.   *Exit*
ISABELLA [*within*]   Peace, ho, be here!
DUKE   The tongue of Isabel. She's come to know
100   If yet her brother's pardon be come hither;
    But I will keep her ignorant of her good,
    To make her heavenly comforts of° despair   *out of*
    When it is least expected.
ISABELLA [*within*]   Ho, by your leave!
        Enter ISABELLA
DUKE   Good morning to you, fair and gracious daughter.
105 ISABELLA   The better, given me° by so holy a man.   *so greeted*
    Hath yet the deputy sent my brother's pardon?
DUKE   He hath released him, Isabel, from the world.
    His head is off and sent to Angelo.
ISABELLA   Nay, but it is not so.
DUKE   It is no other.
110 Show your wisdom, daughter, in your close° patience. *silent*
ISABELLA   O, I will to° him and pluck out his eyes!   *will go to*
DUKE   You shall not be admitted to his sight.
ISABELLA [*weeping*]   Unhappy Claudio! Wretched Isabel!
    Injurious world! Most damnèd Angelo!
115 DUKE   This nor° hurts him, nor profits you a jot.   *neither*
    Forbear it, therefore; give your cause° to heaven.   *grievance*
    Mark what I say, which you shall find
    By every syllable a faithful verity.
    The Duke comes home tomorrow—nay, dry your eyes—
120 One of our convent, and his confessor,
    Gives me this instance.° Already he hath carried   *indication*
    Notice to Escalus and Angelo,
    Who do prepare to meet him at the gates,
    There to give up their power. If you can pace° your wisdom *train to walk*
125 In that good path that I would wish it go,
    And you shall have your bosom° on this wretch,   *desire*
    Grace° of the Duke, revenges to your heart,   *Favor*
    And general honour.
ISABELLA   I am directed by you.
DUKE   This letter, then, to Friar Peter give.
130 'Tis that he sent me of the Duke's return.
    Say by this token I desire his company
    At Mariana's house tonight. Her cause and yours
    I'll perfect° him withal, and he shall bring you   *fully instruct*
    Before the Duke, and to the head of° Angelo   *and directly to*
135 Accuse him home and home.° For my poor self,   *to the utmost*
    I am combinèd° by a sacred vow,   *bound*

And shall be absent. [*Giving the letter*] Wend you° with this letter.   *Depart*
Command these fretting° waters from your eyes   *agitated; corrosive*
With a light heart. Trust not my holy order
If I pervert° your course.   *lead astray*
      Enter LUCIO
                            Who's here?

140 LUCIO   Good even.°   *evening*
    Friar, where's the Provost?

DUKE   Not within, sir.

LUCIO   O pretty Isabella, I am pale at mine heart to see thine
eyes so red. Thou must be patient. I am fain to dine and sup
with water and bran;[8] I dare not for my head fill my belly; one
145   fruitful° meal would set me to't.[9] But they say the Duke will be   *plentiful*
here tomorrow. By my troth, Isabel, I loved thy brother. If the
old fantastical° Duke of dark corners° had been at home, he   *capricious/secret places*
had lived.   [*Exit* ISABELLA]

DUKE   Sir, the Duke is marvellous° little beholden to your   *remarkably*
150   reports; but the best is, he lives not° in them.   *is not to be found*

LUCIO   Friar, thou knowest not the Duke so well as I do. He's a
better woodman[1] than thou tak'st him for.

DUKE   Well, you'll answer° this one day. Fare ye well.   *account for*

LUCIO   Nay, tarry, I'll go along with thee. I can tell thee pretty
155   tales of the Duke.

DUKE   You have told me too many of him already, sir, if they be
true; if not true, none were enough.

LUCIO   I was once before him for getting a wench with child.

DUKE   Did you such a thing?

160 LUCIO   Yes, marry, did I; but I was fain to forswear it. They would
else° have married me to the rotten medlar.[2]   *otherwise*

DUKE   Sir, your company is fairer° than honest. Rest you well.   *more speciously pleasant*

LUCIO   By my troth, I'll go with thee to the lane's end. If bawdy
talk offend you, we'll have very little of it. Nay, friar, I am a
165   kind of burr; I shall stick.   *Exeunt*

4.4

    Enter ANGELO *and* ESCALUS

ESCALUS   Every letter he hath writ hath disvouched other.°   *repudiated the others*

ANGELO   In most uneven and distracted manner. His actions
show much like to madness. Pray heaven his wisdom be not
tainted.° And why meet him at the gates, and redeliver our   *impaired*
5   authorities there?

ESCALUS   I guess not.

ANGELO   And why should we proclaim it in an hour before his
entering, that if any crave redress of injustice, they should
exhibit° their petitions in the street?   *present*

10 ESCALUS   He shows his reason for that—to have a dispatch° of   *prompt settlement*
complaints, and to deliver us from devices° hereafter, which   *contrivances*
shall then have no power to stand against us.

ANGELO   Well, I beseech you let it be proclaimed.
Betimes° i'th' morn I'll call you at your house.   *Early*

---

8. Diet thought to suppress lust.
9. Would incite me to lechery.
1. Hunter (literally, of game; here, of women).

2. Kind of pear eaten when rotten; slang for "prostitute."
4.4 Location: Vienna.

15   Give notice to such men of sort and suit°   *rank and retinue*
      As are to meet him.
    ESCALUS   I shall, sir. Fare you well.
    ANGELO   Good night.   *Exit* [ESCALUS]
      This deed unshapes° me quite, makes me unpregnant°   *destroys/unready*
20   And dull to all proceedings. A deflowered maid,
      And by an eminent body¹ that enforced°   *exerted; raped*
      The law against it! But that her tender shame
      Will not proclaim against her maiden loss,°   *loss of virginity*
      How might she tongue° me! Yet reason dares her no,²   *reproach*
25   For my authority bears off a credent bulk,³
      That no particular° scandal once can touch   *private; single*
      But it confounds° the breather. He should have lived,   *confutes; overthrows*
      Save that his riotous youth, with dangerous sense,°   *sensibility; sensuality*
      Might in the times to come have ta'en revenge
30   By° so receiving a dishonoured life   *Because of*
      With ransom of such shame. Would yet he had lived.
      Alack, when once our grace we have forgot,
      Nothing goes right; we would, and we would not.   *Exit*

4.5

Enter DUKE, [*in his own habit*] *and* FRIAR PETER
    DUKE   These letters at fit time deliver me.
      The Provost knows our purpose and our plot.
      The matter being afoot, keep° your instruction,   *observe*
      And hold you ever to our special drift,°   *purpose*
5   Though sometimes you do blench° from this to that   *swerve*
      As cause doth minister.° Go call at Flavio's house,   *serve*
      And tell him where I stay. Give the like notice
      To Valentinus, Rowland, and to Crassus,
      And bid them bring the trumpets° to the gate.   *trumpeters*
      But send me Flavius first.
10 FRIAR PETER   It shall be speeded well.°   [*Exit*]   *quickly done*
        Enter VARRIUS
    DUKE   I thank thee, Varrius; thou hast made good haste.
      Come, we will walk.° There's other of our friends   *withdraw*
      Will greet us here anon. My gentle° Varrius!   *Exeunt*   *noble*

4.6

Enter ISABELLA *and* MARIANA
    ISABELLA   To speak so indirectly° I am loath—   *evasively*
      I would say the truth, but to accuse him so,
      That is your part—yet I am advised to do it,
      He says, to veil full purpose.
    MARIANA   Be ruled by him.
5 ISABELLA   Besides, he tells me that if peradventure
      He speak against me on the adverse side,
      I should not think it strange, for 'tis a physic°   *medicine*
      That's bitter to sweet end.
       Enter [FRIAR] PETER
    MARIANA   I would Friar Peter—

---

1. Person (also suggesting the physical body).   4.5 Location: Outside the city.
2. Makes her dare not.   4.6 Location: A street near the city gates.
3. Sustains such massive credibility.

10 ISABELLA   O, peace; the friar is come.
     FRIAR PETER   Come, I have found you out a stand° most fit,   *place*
     Where you may have such vantage° on the Duke   *advantageous position*
     He shall not pass you. Twice have the trumpets sounded.[1]
     The generous° and gravest citizens   *noble*
15 Have hent° the gates, and very near upon   *reached*
     The Duke is ent'ring; therefore hence, away.   *Exeunt*

5.1

Enter [at one door] DUKE, VARRIUS, *[and] lords; [at*
another door] ANGELO, ESCALUS, LUCIO, *citizens [and*
officers]

     DUKE [*to* ANGELO]   My very worthy cousin,° fairly met.   *fellow nobleman*
     [*To* ESCALUS] Our old and faithful friend, we are glad to see you.
     ANGELO *and* ESCALUS   Happy return be to your royal grace.
     DUKE   Many and hearty thankings to you both.
5   We have made enquiry of you, and we hear
     Such goodness of your justice that our soul
     Cannot but yield you forth to public thanks,
     Forerunning more requital.°   *greater reward*
     ANGELO   You make my bonds° still greater.   *obligations*
     DUKE   O, your desert speaks loud, and I should wrong it
10   To lock it in the wards° of covert bosom,   *prison cells*
     When it deserves with characters° of brass   *letters*
     A forted° residence 'gainst the tooth of time   *fortified*
     And razure° of oblivion. Give me your hand,   *erasure*
     And let the subject° see, to make them know   *people*
15   That outward courtesies would fain proclaim
     Favours that keep° within. Come, Escalus,   *dwell*
     You must walk by us on our other hand,
     And good supporters[1] are you.
                 [*They walk forward*]
                 Enter [FRIAR] PETER *and* ISABELLA
     FRIAR PETER   Now is your time. Speak loud, and kneel before him.
20   ISABELLA [*kneeling*]   Justice, O royal Duke! Vail your regard°   *Look down*
     Upon a wronged—I would fain° have said, a maid.   *like to*
     O worthy prince, dishonour not your eye
     By throwing it on any other object,
     Till you have heard me in my true complaint,
25   And given me justice, justice, justice, justice!
     DUKE   Relate your wrongs. In what? By whom? Be brief.
     Here is Lord Angelo shall give you justice.
     Reveal yourself° to him.   (*your complaint*)
     ISABELLA   O worthy Duke,
     You bid me seek redemption of the devil.
30   Hear me yourself, for that which I must speak
     Must either punish me, not being believed,
     Or wring redress from you. Hear me, O hear me, hear!
     ANGELO   My lord, her wits, I fear me, are not firm.
     She hath been a suitor to me for her brother,
     Cut off° by course of justice.   *Executed*
35   ISABELLA [*standing*]   By course of justice!

---

1. The third flourish will signal the Duke's arrival.
5.1 Location: The city gates.

1. Attendants; in heraldry, "supporters" are figures
depicted beside a shield, holding it up.

ANGELO And she will speak most bitterly and strange.

ISABELLA Most strange, but yet most truly, will I speak.
　　That Angelo's forsworn, is it not strange?
　　That Angelo's a murderer, is't not strange?
40　　That Angelo is an adulterous thief,
　　An hypocrite, a virgin-violator,
　　Is it not strange, and strange?

DUKE　　　　　　　　　　　　Nay, it is ten times strange!

ISABELLA It is not truer he is Angelo
　　Than this is all as true as it is strange.
45　　Nay, it is ten times true, for truth is truth
　　To th'end of reck'ning.[2]

DUKE　　　　　　　　　Away with her. Poor soul,
　　She speaks this in th'infirmity of sense.

ISABELLA O prince, I conjure° thee, as thou believ'st　　　　　　*appeal to*
　　There is another comfort than this world,
50　　That thou neglect me not with that opinion
　　That I am touched with madness. Make not impossible
　　That which but seems unlike.° 'Tis not impossible　　　　　*unlikely*
　　But° one, the wicked'st caitiff° on the ground,　　　　　*That/villain*
　　May seem as shy,° as grave, as just, as absolute,°　　*reserved/perfect*
55　　As Angelo; even so may Angelo,
　　In all his dressings, characts,[3] titles, forms,°　　　　　*formalities*
　　Be an arch-villain. Believe it, royal prince,
　　If he be less, he's nothing; but he's more,
　　Had I more name for badness.

DUKE　　　　　　　　　　　By mine honesty,
60　　If she be mad, as I believe no other,
　　Her madness hath the oddest frame° of sense,　　　　　*shape*
　　Such a dependency° of thing on thing　　　　*connected sequence*
　　As e'er I heard in madness.

ISABELLA　　　　　　　　　　O gracious Duke,
　　Harp not on that, nor do not banish reason
65　　For inequality;[4] but let your reason serve
　　To make the truth appear where it seems hid,
　　And hide the false seems° true.　　　　　　　　　*that seems*

DUKE　　　　　　　　　Many that are not mad
　　Have sure more lack of reason. What would you say?

ISABELLA I am the sister of one Claudio,
70　　Condemned upon the act of° fornication　　　　　*decree against*
　　To lose his head, condemned by Angelo.
　　I, in probation of a sisterhood,
　　Was sent to by my brother, one Lucio
　　As° then the messenger.　　　　　　　　　　　*Being*

LUCIO　　　　　　　That's I, an't like your grace.
75　　I came to her from Claudio, and desired her
　　To try her gracious fortune with Lord Angelo
　　For her poor brother's pardon.

ISABELLA　　　　　　　　　That's he indeed.

DUKE [*to* LUCIO] You were not bid to speak.

---

2. *for truth . . . reck'ning:* echoing 1 Esdras 4:38: "But
truth doth abide, and is strong forever, and liveth and
reigneth for ever and ever." *reck'ning:* day of reckoning.

3. Signs (of office).
4. Difference in rank (between Isabella and Angelo); dis-
crepancy (between my report and what seems true).

LUCIO   No, my good lord,
    Nor wished to hold my peace.

80   DUKE   I wish you now, then. Pray you take note of it;
    And when you have a business for yourself,
    Pray heaven you then be perfect.

LUCIO   I warrant° your honour.   *assure*

DUKE   The warrant's[5] for yourself; take heed to't.

ISABELLA   This gentleman told somewhat of my tale—

85   LUCIO   Right.

DUKE   It may be right, but you are i'the wrong
    To speak before your time. [*To* ISABELLA] Proceed.

ISABELLA   I went
    To this pernicious caitiff deputy—

DUKE   That's somewhat madly spoken.

ISABELLA   Pardon it;
    The phrase is to the matter.°   *appropriate*

90   DUKE   Mended again.
    The matter; proceed.

ISABELLA   In brief, to set the needless process by,[6]
    How I persuaded, how I prayed and kneeled,
    How he refelled° me, and how I replied—   *repelled*

95   For this was of much length—the vile conclusion
    I now begin with grief and shame to utter.
    He would not, but by gift of my chaste body
    To his concupiscible° intemperate lust,   *desirous*
    Release my brother; and after much debatement,

100 My sisterly remorse confutes° mine honour,   *overcomes*
    And I did yield to him. But the next morn betimes,
    His purpose surfeiting,° he sends a warrant   *satisfied*
    For my poor brother's head.

DUKE   This is most likely!

ISABELLA   O, that it were as like° as it is true!   *probable*

105 DUKE   By heaven, fond° wretch, thou knows't not what thou speak'st,   *foolish*
    Or else thou art suborned against his honour
    In hateful practice.° First, his integrity   *conspiracy*
    Stands without blemish. Next, it imports no reason°   *makes no sense*
    That with such vehemency he should pursue

110 Faults proper° to himself. If he had so offended,   *belonging*
    He would have weighed thy brother by himself,
    And not have cut him off. Someone hath set you on.°   *incited you*
    Confess the truth, and say by whose advice
    Thou cam'st here to complain.

ISABELLA   And is this all?

115 Then, O you blessèd ministers° above,   *angels*
    Keep me in patience, and with ripened time
    Unfold the evil which is here wrapped up
    In countenance![7] Heaven shield your grace from woe,
    As I, thus wronged, hence unbelievèd go.

120 DUKE   I know you'd fain be gone. An officer!
    To prison with her.
          [*An officer guards* ISABELLA]
               Shall we thus permit

---

5. That is, for arrest, punning on the verb in line 83.   7. In false appearance; in royal favor.
6. To skip unnecessary parts of the story.

A blasting° and a scandalous breath to fall   *blighting*
On him so near us? This needs must be a practice.°   *conspiracy*
Who knew of your intent and coming hither?

125 ISABELLA   One that I would were here, Friar Lodowick.[8]
                                                [*Exit, guarded*]
DUKE   A ghostly father, belike. Who knows that Lodowick?
LUCIO   My lord, I know him. 'Tis a meddling friar;
    I do not like the man. Had he been lay, my lord,
    For certain words he spake against your grace
130 In your retirement, I had swinged° him soundly.   *beat*
DUKE   Words against me? This'° a good friar, belike!   *This is*
    And to set on this wretched woman here
    Against our substitute! Let this friar be found.
                                        [*Exit one or more*]
LUCIO   But yesternight, my lord, she and that friar,
135 I saw them at the prison. A saucy friar,
    A very scurvy fellow.
FRIAR PETER   Blessed be your royal grace!
    I have stood by, my lord, and I have heard
    Your royal ear abused. First hath this woman
    Most wrongfully accused your substitute,
140 Who is as free from touch or soil with her
    As she from one ungot.°   *not yet begotten*
DUKE   We did believe no less.
    Know you that Friar Lodowick that she speaks of?
FRIAR PETER   I know him for a man divine and holy,
    Not scurvy, nor a temporary meddler,[9]
145 As he's reported by this gentleman;
    And, on my trust, a man that never yet
    Did, as he vouches,° misreport your grace.   *asserts*
LUCIO   My lord, most villainously; believe it.
FRIAR PETER   Well, he in time may come to clear himself;
150 But at this instant he is sick, my lord,
    Of a strange fever. Upon his mere° request,   *Solely at his*
    Being come to knowledge that there was complaint
    Intended 'gainst Lord Angelo, came I hither
    To speak, as from his mouth, what he doth know
155 Is true and false, and what he with his oath
    And all probation° will make up full clear   *proof*
    Whensoever he's convented.° First, for this woman: *summoned*
    To justify° this worthy nobleman,   *vindicate*
    So vulgarly and personally accused,
160 Her shall you hear disprovèd to her eyes,
    Till she herself confess it.
DUKE   Good friar, let's hear it.
                                        [*Exit* FRIAR PETER]
    Do you not smile at this, Lord Angelo?
    O heaven, the vanity of wretched fools!
    Give us some seats.
            [*Seats are brought in*]
                    Come, cousin Angelo,

---

8. Evidently the Duke's name when in disguise.   9. Meddler in temporal matters.

165 In this I'll be impartial; be you judge
     Of your own cause.[1]
          [*The* DUKE *and* ANGELO *sit*]
          Enter [FRIAR PETER *and*] MARIANA [*veiled*]
                    Is this the witness, friar?
     First let her show her face, and after speak.
MARIANA Pardon, my lord, I will not show my face
     Until my husband bid me.
170 DUKE What, are you married?
MARIANA No, my lord.
DUKE Are you a maid?°   unmarried woman; virgin
MARIANA No, my lord.
DUKE A widow then?
175 MARIANA Neither, my lord.
DUKE Why, you are nothing then; neither maid, widow, nor wife!
LUCIO My lord, she may be a punk,° for many of them are nei-   prostitute
     ther maid, widow, nor wife.
DUKE Silence that fellow. I would° he had some cause to prattle   wish
180   for himself.°   (in his own defense)
LUCIO Well, my lord.
MARIANA My lord, I do confess I ne'er was married,
     And I confess besides, I am no maid.
     I have known[2] my husband, yet my husband
185   Knows not that ever he knew me.
LUCIO He was drunk then, my lord, it can be no better.
DUKE For the benefit of silence, would thou wert so too.
LUCIO Well, my lord.
DUKE This is no witness for Lord Angelo.
190 MARIANA Now I come to't, my lord.
     She that accuses him of fornication
     In self-same manner doth accuse my husband,
     And charges him, my lord, with such a time
     When I'll depose° I had him in mine arms   testify
     With all th'effect° of love.   manifestations
195 ANGELO   Charges she more than me?
MARIANA Not that I know.
DUKE   No? You say your husband.
MARIANA Why just,° my lord, and that is Angelo,   just so
     Who thinks he knows that he ne'er knew my body,
     But knows, he thinks, that he knows Isabel's.
200 ANGELO This is a strange abuse.° Let's see thy face.   imposture
MARIANA [*unveiling*] My husband bids me; now I will unmask.
     This is that face, thou cruel Angelo,
     Which once thou swor'st was worth the looking on.
     This is the hand which, with a vowed contract,
205   Was fast belocked in thine. This is the body
     That took away the match° from Isabel,   assignation
     And did supply° thee at thy garden-house   satisfy
     In her imagined person.
DUKE [*to* ANGELO] Know you this woman?
210 LUCIO Carnally, she says.
DUKE Sirrah, no more!

---

1. Ironically recalling the principle that no one ought   2. Had sexual intercourse with.
to judge his or her own cause.

LUCIO   Enough, my lord.

ANGELO   My lord, I must confess I know this woman;
  And five years since there was some speech of marriage
215   Betwixt myself and her, which was broke off,
  Partly for that her promisèd proportions°   *dowry*
  Came short of composition,° but in chief   *the agreed sum*
  For that her reputation was disvalued°   *discredited*
  In levity;° since which time of five years   *For wantonness*
220   I never spake with her, saw her, nor heard from her,
  Upon my faith and honour.

MARIANA [*kneeling before the* DUKE]   Noble prince,
  As there comes light from heaven, and words from breath,
  As there is sense° in truth, and truth in virtue,   *significance*
  I am affianced this man's wife, as strongly
225   As words could make up vows. And, my good lord,
  But Tuesday night last gone, in's garden-house,
  He knew me as a wife. As this is true,
  Let me in safety raise me from my knees,
  Or else forever be confixèd° here,   *fixed firmly*
  A marble monument.

230   ANGELO   I did but smile till now.
  Now, good my lord, give me the scope° of justice.   *extent*
  My patience here is touched.° I do perceive   *irritated*
  These poor informal° women are no more   *disorderly*
  But instruments° of some more mightier member° *agents/power*
235   That sets them on. Let me have way, my lord,
  To find this practice out.

DUKE [*standing*]   Ay, with my heart,
  And punish them even to your height of pleasure.—
  Thou foolish friar, and thou pernicious woman
  Compact with° her that's gone, think'st thou thy oaths, *In league with*
240   Though they would swear down each particular saint,
  Were testimonies against his worth and credit
  That's sealed in approbation?° You, Lord Escalus, *ratified by proof*
  Sit with my cousin; lend him your kind pains
  To find out this abuse, whence 'tis derived.
245   There is another friar that set them on.
  Let him be sent for.
       [ESCALUS *sits*]

FRIAR PETER   Would he were here, my lord, for he indeed
  Hath set the women on to this complaint.
  Your Provost knows the place where he abides,
  And he may fetch him.

250   DUKE [*to one or more*]   Go, do it instantly.   [*Exit one or more*]
  [*To* ANGELO] And you, my noble and well-warranted cousin,
  Whom it concerns to hear this matter forth,°   *out*
  Do with your injuries as seems you best
  In any chastisement. I for a while will leave you,
255   But stir not you till you have well determined° *passed judgment*
  Upon these slanderers.

ESCALUS   My lord, we'll do it throughly.°   *thoroughly*
                         Exit [DUKE]
  Signor Lucio, did not you say you knew that Friar Lodowick to
  be a dishonest person?

LUCIO   *Cucullus non facit monachum:*[3] honest in nothing but in
260   his clothes; and one that hath spoke most villainous speeches
of the Duke.

ESCALUS   We shall entreat you to abide here till he come, and
enforce° them against him. We shall find this friar a notable   urge
fellow.

265   LUCIO   As any in Vienna, on my word.

ESCALUS   Call that same Isabel here once again; I would speak
with her.   [*Exit one or more*]

[*To* ANGELO] Pray you, my lord, give me leave to question. You
shall see how I'll handle her.

270   LUCIO   Not better than he, by her own report.

ESCALUS   Say you?

LUCIO   Marry, sir, I think if you handled her privately, she would
sooner confess; perchance publicly she'll be ashamed.

ESCALUS   I will go darkly° to work with her.   privately; soberly

275   LUCIO   That's the way, for women are light[4] at midnight.

                    Enter ISABELLA [*guarded*]

ESCALUS   [*to* ISABELLA]   Come on, mistress, here's a gentle-
woman denies all that you have said.

                    Enter DUKE [*disguised as a friar, hooded, and*] PROVOST

LUCIO   My lord, here comes the rascal I spoke of, here with the
Provost.

280   ESCALUS   In very good time. Speak not you to him till we call
upon you.

LUCIO   Mum.

ESCALUS   [*to the* DUKE]   Come, sir, did you set these women on
to slander Lord Angelo? They have confessed you did.

285   DUKE   'Tis false.

ESCALUS   How! Know you where you are?

DUKE   Respect to your great place, and let the devil
Be sometime honoured fore his burning throne.[5]
Where is the Duke? 'Tis he should hear me speak.

290   ESCALUS   The Duke's in° us, and we will hear you speak.   power is vested in
Look you speak justly.°   accurately

DUKE   Boldly at least.
[*To* ISABELLA *and* MARIANA]   But O, poor souls,
Come you to seek the lamb here of the fox,
Good night to your redress! Is the Duke gone?
Then is your cause gone too. The Duke's unjust

295   Thus to retort° your manifest appeal,°   cast back / accusation
And put your trial in the villain's mouth
Which here you come to accuse.

LUCIO   This is the rascal, this is he I spoke of.

ESCALUS   Why, thou unreverend and unhallowed° friar,   impious
300   Is't not enough thou hast suborned these women
To accuse this worthy man but, in foul mouth,
And in the witness of his proper° ear,   own
To call him villain, and then to glance° from him   ricochet
To th' Duke himself, to tax° him with injustice?   reproach

---

3. The hood does not make the monk (proverbial).
4. Licentious; exploiting the unintentional sexual sug-
gestion of Escalus's "go darkly to work."

5. *let . . . throne:* that is, the devil, too, seated on his
throne in hell, seems a figure of honor. *fore:* before.

305 Take him hence; to th' rack with him. We'll touse° you   *tear*
Joint by joint—but we will know his[6] purpose.
What, 'unjust'?

DUKE   Be not so hot. The Duke
Dare no more stretch this finger of mine than he
Dare rack his own. His subject am I not,
310 Nor here provincial.[7] My business in this state
Made me a looker-on here in Vienna,
Where I have seen corruption boil and bubble
Till it o'errun the stew;° laws for all faults,   *cauldron; brothel*
But faults so countenanced that the strong statutes
315 Stand like the forfeits[8] in a barber's shop,
As much in mock as mark.

ESCALUS   Slander to th' state!
Away with him to prison.

ANGELO   What can you vouch against him, Signor Lucio?
320 Is this the man that you did tell us of?

LUCIO   'Tis he, my lord.—Come hither, goodman Bald-pate.[9]
Do you know me?

DUKE   I remember you, sir, by the sound of your voice.[1] I met
you at the prison, in the absence of the Duke.

325 LUCIO   O, did you so? And do you remember what you said of
the Duke?

DUKE   Most notedly, sir.

LUCIO   Do you so, sir? And was the Duke a fleshmonger,° a fool,   *whoremaster*
and a coward, as you then reported him to be?

330 DUKE   You must, sir, change persons with me ere you make that
my report. You indeed spoke so of him, and much more, much
worse.

LUCIO   O, thou damnable fellow! Did not I pluck thee by the
nose° for thy speeches?   *(gesture of contempt)*

335 DUKE   I protest I love the Duke as I love myself.

ANGELO   Hark how the villain would close[2] now, after his trea-
sonable abuses.

ESCALUS   Such a fellow is not to be talked withal. Away with him
to prison. Where is the Provost? Away with him to prison. Lay
340 bolts° enough upon him. Let him speak no more. Away with   *fetters*
those giglets° too, and with the other confederate companion.[3]   *strumpets*
     [MARIANA *is raised to her feet, and is guarded.*
     The PROVOST *makes to seize the* DUKE]

DUKE   Stay, sir, stay a while.

ANGELO   What, resists he? Help him, Lucio.

LUCIO [*to the* DUKE]   Come, sir; come, sir; come, sir! Foh,° sir!   *(expression of disgust)*
345 Why, you bald-pated lying rascal, you must be hooded, must
you? Show your knave's visage, with a pox to you! Show your
sheep-biting face,[4] and be hanged an hour![5] Will't not off?
     [*He pulls off the friar's hood, and discovers the* DUKE.
     ANGELO *and* ESCALUS *rise*]

---

6. The friar's; the confusion of pronouns suggests Esca-
lus's fury.
7. Subject to local ecclesiastical authorities.
8. Jocular list of penalties for minor infractions.
9. Mr. Bald-head: "goodman" was a form of address for
a man below the rank of gentleman; friars shaved their
heads.
1. The friar's hood presumably covers his face so that he

cannot see Lucio.
2. Conclude; hide himself; come to a settlement.
3. Fellow (contemptuous).
4. Like the wolf in sheep's clothing.
5. Jocular way of saying "be hanged." Animals were
sometimes executed like human beings for destroying life
or property.

DUKE Thou art the first knave that e'er madest a duke.
First, Provost, let me bail these gentle three.
350 [*To* LUCIO] Sneak not away, sir, for the friar and you
Must have a word anon. [*To one or more*] Lay hold on him.
LUCIO This may prove worse than hanging.
DUKE [*to* ESCALUS] What you have spoke, I pardon. Sit you down.
We'll borrow place° of him.   seat; office
[ESCALUS *sits*]
[*To* ANGELO]   Sir, by your leave.
[*He takes Angelo's seat*]
355 Hast thou or° word or wit or impudence   either
That yet can do thee office?° If thou hast,   service
Rely upon it till my tale be heard,
And hold no longer out.
ANGELO   O my dread lord,
I should be guiltier than my guiltiness
360 To think I can be undiscernible,
When I perceive your grace, like power divine,
Hath looked upon my passes.[6] Then, good prince,
No longer session° hold upon my shame,   inquiry
But let my trial be mine own confession.
365 Immediate sentence then, and sequent° death,   thereafter
Is all the grace I beg.
DUKE   Come hither, Mariana.
[*To* ANGELO] Say, wast thou e'er contracted to this woman?
ANGELO I was, my lord.
DUKE Go, take her hence and marry her instantly.
370 Do you the office, friar; which consummate,°   finished
Return him here again. Go with him, Provost.
      Exeunt [ANGELO, MARIANA, FRIAR PETER, *and the* PROVOST]
ESCALUS My lord, I am more amazed at his dishonour
Than at the strangeness of it.°   (the situation)
DUKE   Come hither, Isabel.
Your friar is now your prince. As I was then
375 Advertising° and holy to your business,   Attentive
Not changing heart with habit I am still
Attorneyed° at your service.   Engaged as advocate
ISABELLA   O, give me pardon,
That I, your vassal, have employed and pained°   troubled
Your unknown sovereignty.
DUKE   You are pardoned, Isabel.
380 And now, dear maid, be you as free° to us.   generous
Your brother's death I know sits at your heart,
And you may marvel why I obscured myself,
Labouring to save his life, and would not rather
Make rash remonstrance° of my hidden power   demonstration
385 Than let him so be lost. O most kind maid,
It was the swift celerity of his death,
Which I did think with slower foot came on,
That brained° my purpose. But peace be with him!   killed
That life is better life, past fearing death,
390 Than that which lives to fear. Make it your comfort,
So happy is your brother.

6. Actions, trespasses; recalling Job 34:21: "For his eyes are upon the ways of man, and he seeth all his goings."

ISABELLA   I do, my lord.
    Enter ANGELO, MARIANA, [FRIAR] PETER, [*and*] PROVOST
DUKE   For this new-married man approaching here,
   Whose salt° imagination yet hath wronged   *salacious*
   Your well-defended honour, you must pardon
395   For Mariana's sake; but as he adjudged° your brother—   *condemned*
   Being criminal in double violation
   Of sacred chastity and of promise-breach,
   Thereon dependent, for your brother's life—
   The very mercy° of the law cries out   *Even the merciful aspect*
400   Most audible, even from his proper° tongue,   *its own*
   'An Angelo for Claudio, death for death'.
   Haste still° pays haste, and leisure° answers leisure; *always / deliberation*
   Like doth quit° like, and measure still for measure.   *requite*
   Then, Angelo, thy fault's thus manifested,
405   Which, though° thou wouldst deny, denies thee vantage.° *even if / (i.e., clemency)*
   We do condemn thee to the very block
   Where Claudio stooped to death, and with like haste.
   Away with him.
MARIANA   O my most gracious lord,
   I hope you will not mock me with a husband!
410 DUKE   It is your husband mocked you with a husband.
   Consenting to the safeguard of your honour,
   I thought your marriage fit; else imputation,°   *censure*
   For that he knew you, might reproach your life,
   And choke your good to come.° For his possessions, *ruin your prospects*
415   Although by confiscation they are ours,[7]
   We do enstate and widow you° with all,   *give you widow's rights*
   To buy you a better husband.
MARIANA   O my dear lord,
   I crave no other, nor no better man.
DUKE   Never crave him; we are definitive.°   *resolute*
MARIANA   Gentle my liege—
420 DUKE   You do but lose your labour.—
   Away with him to death. [*To* LUCIO] Now, sir, to you.
MARIANA [*kneeling*]   O my good lord!—Sweet Isabel, take my part;
   Lend me your knees, and all my life to come
   I'll lend you all my life to do you service.
425 DUKE   Against all sense you do importune her.
   Should she kneel down in mercy of this fact,°   *crime*
   Her brother's ghost his pavèd bed° would break, *stone-covered grave*
   And take her hence in horror.
MARIANA   Isabel,
   Sweet Isabel, do yet but kneel by me.
430   Hold up your hands; say nothing; I'll speak all.
   They say best men are moulded out of faults,
   And, for the most,° become much more the better *most part*
   For being a little bad. So may my husband.
   O Isabel, will you not lend a knee?
DUKE   He dies for Claudio's death.
435 ISABELLA [*kneeling*]   Most bounteous sir,
   Look, if it please you, on this man condemned
   As if my brother lived. I partly think

---

7. Because a felon's property was forfeit to the crown.

A due sincerity governed his deeds,
Till he did look on me. Since it is so,
440 Let him not die. My brother had but justice,
In that he did the thing for which he died.
For Angelo,
His act did not o'ertake his bad intent,
And must be buried° but as an intent   *(i.e., forgotten)*
445 That perished by the way. Thoughts are no subjects,⁸
Intents but merely thoughts.

MARIANA   Merely, my lord.

DUKE   Your suit's unprofitable. Stand up, I say.
        [MARIANA *and* ISABELLA *stand*]
I have bethought me of another fault.
Provost, how came it Claudio was beheaded
At an unusual hour?

450 PROVOST   It was commanded so.

DUKE   Had you a special warrant for the deed?

PROVOST   No, my good lord, it was by private message.

DUKE   For which I do discharge you of your office.
        Give up your keys.

PROVOST   Pardon me, noble lord.
455 I thought it was a fault, but knew it not,
Yet did repent me after more advice;°   *deliberation*
For° testimony whereof one in the prison   *As*
That should by private order else° have died   *otherwise*
I have reserved alive.

460 DUKE   What's he?

PROVOST   His name is Barnardine.

DUKE   I would thou hadst done so by Claudio.
        Go fetch him hither. Let me look upon him.   [*Exit* PROVOST]

ESCALUS   I am sorry one so learned and so wise
465 As you, Lord Angelo, have still° appeared,   *always*
Should slip so grossly, both in the heat of blood
And lack of tempered judgement afterward.

ANGELO   I am sorry that such sorrow I procure,°   *cause*
And so deep sticks it in my penitent heart
470 That I crave death more willingly than mercy.
'Tis my deserving, and I do entreat it.

        Enter BARNARDINE *and* PROVOST; CLAUDIO, [*muffled,*°   *with his face wrapped*
        and] JULIET

DUKE   Which is that Barnardine?

PROVOST   This, my lord.

DUKE   There was a friar told me of this man.
        [*To* BARNARDINE] Sirrah, thou art said to have a stubborn soul
475 That apprehends no further than this world,
And squar'st° thy life according. Thou'rt condemned;   *frames*
But, for those earthly faults,⁹ I quit° them all,   *pardon*
And pray thee take this mercy to provide
For better times to come.—Friar, advise him.
480 I leave him to your hand. [*To* PROVOST] What muffled fellow's that?

PROVOST   This is another prisoner that I saved,
Who should have died when Claudio lost his head,
As like almost to Claudio as himself.

---

8. Thoughts are not subject to prosecution.   9. Offenses subject to earthly punishment.

[*He unmuffles* CLAUDIO]

DUKE [*to* ISABELLA]   If he be like your brother, for his sake
485   Is he pardoned; and for your lovely sake
       Give me your hand, and say you will be mine.¹
       He is my brother° too. But fitter time for that.   *(as a brother-in-law)*
       By this Lord Angelo perceives he's safe.
       Methinks I see a quick'ning in his eye.
490   Well, Angelo, your evil quits° you well.   *recompenses*
       Look that you love your wife, her worth worth° yours.   *being equal to*
       I find an apt remission° in myself;   *inclination to mercy*
       And yet here's one in place° I cannot pardon.   *present*
       [*To* LUCIO] You, sirrah, that knew me for a fool, a coward,
495   One all of luxury,° an ass, a madman,   *lasciviousness*
       Wherein have I so deserved of you
       That you extol me thus?

LUCIO   Faith, my lord, I spoke it but according to the trick.°   *fashion*
       you will hang me for it, you may; but I had rather it would
500   please you I might be whipped.

DUKE   Whipped first, sir, and hanged after.
       Proclaim it, Provost, round about the city,
       If any woman wronged by this lewd fellow,
       As I have heard him swear himself there's one
505   Whom he begot with child, let her appear,
       And he shall marry her. The nuptial finished,
       Let him be whipped and hanged.

LUCIO   I beseech your highness, do not marry me to a whore.
       Your highness said even now I made you a duke; good my lord,
510   do not recompense me in making me a cuckold.

DUKE   Upon mine honour, thou shalt marry her.
       Thy slanders I forgive, and therewithal
       Remit thy other forfeits.°—Take him to prison,   *punishments*
       And see our pleasure herein executed.
515 LUCIO   Marrying a punk, my lord, is pressing to death,² whip-
       ping, and hanging.

DUKE   Slandering a prince deserves it.   [*Exit* LUCIO *guarded*]
       She, Claudio, that you wronged, look you restore.³
       Joy to you, Mariana. Love her, Angelo.
520   I have confessed her,° and I know her virtue.   *been her confessor*
       Thanks, good friend Escalus, for thy much goodness.
       There's more behind° that is more gratulate.°   *to come / gratifying*
       Thanks, Provost, for thy care and secrecy.
       We shall employ thee in a worthier place.
525   Forgive him, Angelo, that brought you home
       The head of Ragusine for Claudio's.
       Th'offence pardons itself. Dear Isabel,
       I have a motion° much imports your good,   *proposal*
       Whereto, if you'll a willing ear incline,
530   What's mine is yours, and what is yours is mine.
       [*To all*] So bring° us to our palace, where we'll show   *accompany*
       What's yet behind that's meet you all should know.   [*Exeunt*]

---

1. It is not clear how Isabella responds to the Duke's pro-
posal of marriage.   2. Executing by crushing under heavy weights.
       3. To her good name, by marrying her.

Additional Passages

The text of *Measure for Measure* given in this edition is probably that of an adapted version made for Shakespeare's company after his death. Adaptation seems to have affected two passages, printed below as the Oxford editors believe Shakespeare to have written them.

A. 1.2.0.1–104

The passage begins with seven lines that the adapter (believed to be Thomas Middleton) intended to be replaced by 1.2.52–71 of the play as printed here. The adapter must have contributed all of 1.2.0.1–74, which in the earliest and subsequent printed texts precede the discussion between the clown (Pompey) and the bawd (Mistress Overdone) about Claudio's arrest. Lucio's entry alone at line 36 below, some eleven lines after his reentry with the two Gentlemen and the Provost's party in the adapted text, probably represents Shakespeare's original intention. In his version, Juliet, present but silent in the adapted text both in 1.2 and 5.1, probably did not appear in either scene; accordingly, the words "and there's Madam Juliet" (1.2.95) must also be the reviser's work, and do not appear below.

> *Enter* POMPEY *and* MISTRESS OVERDONE, *meeting*
>
> MISTRESS OVERDONE   How now, what's the news with you?
> POMPEY   Yonder man is carried to prison.
> MISTRESS OVERDONE   Well! What has he done?
> POMPEY   A woman.
> 5   MISTRESS OVERDONE   But what's his offence?
> POMPEY   Groping for trouts[1] in a peculiar° river.   *private*
> MISTRESS OVERDONE   What, is there a maid[2] with child by him?
> POMPEY   No, but there's a woman with maid[3] by him: you have
>   not heard of the proclamation, have you?
> 10   MISTRESS OVERDONE   What proclamation, man?
> POMPEY   All houses in the suburbs of Vienna must be plucked down.
> MISTRESS OVERDONE   And what shall become of those in the city?
> POMPEY   They shall stand for seed. They had gone down too, but
>   that a wise burgher put in for them.
> 15   MISTRESS OVERDONE   But shall all our houses of resort in the
>   suburbs be pulled down?
> POMPEY   To the ground, mistress.
> MISTRESS OVERDONE   Why, here's a change indeed in the com-
>   monwealth. What shall become of me?
> 20   POMPEY   Come, fear not you. Good counsellors lack no clients.
>   Though you change your place, you need not change your
>   trade. I'll be your tapster still. Courage, there will be pity taken
>   on you. You that have worn your eyes almost out in the service,
>   you will be considered.
>   *A noise within*
> 25   MISTRESS OVERDONE   What's to do here, Thomas Tapster?
>   Let's withdraw!
>   *Enter the* PROVOST *and* CLAUDIO
> POMPEY   Here comes Signor Claudio, led by the Provost to
>   prison.   *Exeunt* MISTRESS OVERDONE *and* POMPEY
> CLAUDIO   Fellow, why dost thou show me thus to th' world?
> 30   Bear me to prison, where I am committed.
> PROVOST   I do it not in evil disposition,

---

1. Literally, a way of catching trout by tickling their bellies.
2. Young woman (but Pompey understands "virgin").
3. Pregnant with a baby girl.

But from Lord Angelo by special charge.
CLAUDIO   Thus can the demigod Authority
Make us pay down for our offence, by weight,
35   The bonds of heaven. On whom it will, it will;
On whom it will not, so; yet still 'tis just.
      Enter LUCIO
LUCIO   Why, how now, Claudio? Whence comes this restraint?

B. 3.1.479–4.1.65

Before revision, there would have been no act break and no song; the lines immediately
following the song would also have been absent. The Duke's soliloquies "He who the
sword of heaven will bear" and "O place and greatness" have evidently been transposed
in revision; in the original, the end of "O place and greatness" would have led straight
on to the Duke's meeting with Isabella and then Mariana.

ESCALUS   I am going to visit the prisoner. Fare you well.
DUKE   Peace be with you.   *Exit* ESCALUS
      O place and greatness, millions of false eyes
      Are stuck upon thee; volumes of report
5   Run with their false and most contrarious quest
      Upon thy doings; thousand escapes of wit
      Make thee the father of their idle dream,
      And rack thee in their fancies.
            Enter ISABELLA
DUKE   Very well met.
      What is the news from this good deputy?
10   ISABELLA   He hath a garden circummured with brick,
      Whose western side is with a vineyard backed;
      And to that vineyard is a planckèd gate,
      That makes his opening with this bigger key.
      This other doth command a little door
15   Which from the vineyard to the garden leads.
      There have I made my promise
      Upon the heavy middle of the night
      To call upon him.
DUKE   But shall you on your knowledge find this way?
20   ISABELLA   I have ta'en a due and wary note upon't.
      With whispering and most guilty diligence,
      In action all of precept, he did show me
      The way twice o'er.
DUKE   Are there no other tokens
      Between you 'greed concerning her observance?
25   ISABELLA   No, none, but only a repair i'th' dark,
      And that I have possessed him my most stay
      Can be but brief, for I have made him know
      I have a servant comes with me along
      That stays upon me, whose persuasion is
      I come about my brother.
30   DUKE   'Tis well borne up.
      I have not yet made known to Mariana
      A word of this.—What ho, within! Come forth!
            Enter MARIANA
      [*To* MARIANA] I pray you be acquainted with this maid.
      She comes to do you good.

ISABELLA   I do desire the like.

35 DUKE [to MARIANA]   Do you persuade yourself that I respect you?

MARIANA   Good friar, I know you do, and so have found it.

DUKE   Take then this your companion by the hand,
    Who hath a story ready for your ear.
    I shall attend your leisure; but make haste,
    The vaporous night approaches.

40 MARIANA   Will't please you walk aside.

Exeunt MARIANA *and* ISABELLA

DUKE   He who the sword of heaven will bear
    Should be as holy as severe,
    Pattern in himself to know,
    Grace to stand, and virtue go,
45 More nor less to others paying
    Than by self-offences weighing.
    Shame to him whose cruel striking
    Kills for faults of his own liking!
    Twice treble shame on Angelo,
50 To weed my vice, and let his grow!
    O, what may man within him hide,
    Though angel on the outward side!
    How may likeness made in crimes
    Make my practice on the times
55 To draw with idle spiders' strings
    Most ponderous and substantial things?
    Craft against vice I must apply.
    With Angelo tonight shall lie
    His old betrothed but despisèd.
60 So disguise shall, by th' disguisèd,
    Pay with falsehood false exacting,
    And perform an old contracting.

Enter MARIANA *and* ISABELLA

    Welcome. How agreed?

ISABELLA   She'll take the enterprise upon her, father,
65 If you advise it.

HISTORIES

Shakespearean History

by

JEAN E. HOWARD

In the 1590s, the first decade of his life as an actor and playwright for the London stage, Shakespeare poured much of his energy into dramatizing events from the prior several hundred years of England's past. At this time, he wrote or had a major hand in writing at least eight plays depicting English monarchical history of the late fourteenth and the fifteenth centuries. These included *The First Part of the Contention of the Two Famous Houses of York and Lancaster* (*2 Henry VI*), *The True Tragedy of Richard Duke of York and the Good King Henry the Sixth* (*3 Henry VI*), *The First Part of Henry the Sixth* (*1 Henry VI*), *The Tragedy of King Richard the Third*, *The Tragedy of King Richard the Second*, *The History of Henry the Fourth* (*1 Henry IV*), *The Second Part of Henry the Fourth* (*2 Henry IV*), and *The Life of Henry the Fifth*. Collectively, these plays dramatized the deposition of Richard II, the attempts of Henry IV and Henry V to rule England in the wake of this deposition, the civil war (the so-called War of the Roses) that subsequently broke out between the Lancastrian and Yorkist branches of the Plantagenet family to which Richard belonged, and finally the defeat by Henry Tudor, a Lancastrian, of the Yorkist king, Richard III, at the Battle of Bosworth Field in 1485. During this decade, Shakespeare also wrote *The Life and Death of King John* that examines the reign of the thirteenth-century monarch who struggled to be regarded as the legitimate King of England despite competing claims to that title, and later in his career (1613) he composed *All Is True* (*Henry VIII*) in collaboration with John Fletcher that dramatizes events from the reign of Henry VIII, the second of the Tudor kings of England. Recently, critics have once again begun to take seriously the possibility that parts of *King Edward the Third* (c. 1596) are also by Shakespeare. It depicts the impressive military victories achieved by the father and grandfather of Richard II over French and Scottish adversaries. In his fascination with dramatizing English history Shakespeare was dealing with events that had had a formative effect on the world in which he lived. When Henry Tudor kills Richard III at Bosworth Field, is crowned King of England, and marries Elizabeth of York, he not only unites the Lancastrian and Yorkist factions, but also inaugurates the Tudor dynasty that held the throne during Shakespeare's own lifetime. Elizabeth I, who ruled England from 1558 to 1603, was the granddaughter of Henry VII.

In these plays about English history, Shakespeare was also giving a distinctive stamp to one of the most important dramatic genres of the 1590s, but one whose exact parameters were somewhat undefined at the time and remain in dispute today. Elizabethan playwrights regularly staged plays based on historical events. Shakespeare's contemporary, Christopher Marlowe, for example, wrote a famous play, *Edward II* (1592), about the ill-fated reign of a fourteenth-century English king that may have sparked Shakespeare's interest in mining late medieval monarchical chronicles for dramatic subjects. Many playwrights, however, did not confine themselves to medieval English materials, but looked to classical Greece and Rome, ancient Britain, or contemporary France for historical subjects. Some plays based on historical events were not labeled as histories. If, for example, they focused on the life of a particular character, as in Shakespeare's own play about Richard III, they might simply be called tragedies. Generic categorizations at the time were fluid, and some plays could be categorized in more than one way. Moreover, historical plays differed widely in form and feel. Some dramas from the mid-sixteenth century, such as John Bale's vehemently anti-Catholic *King Johan* (1538), were often overtly polemical and, in Bale's case, warned against the dangers of the Roman Church to England's well-being. To drive home his point, Bale gave his characters allegorical names such as Sedition, Dissimulation, and Usurped Power (another name for the Pope). Other history plays, such as Thomas Heywood's two-part play on the life of Edward IV (1600), combined a fairly perfunctory depiction of political and military events of Edward's reign with a second, sentimental plot focusing on the suffering of Jane Shore, the citizen wife whom the king seduced. That part of the play feels like a domestic drama of citizen life and competes with the monarchical plot for the audience's attention.

The Elizabethan history play was, therefore, a capacious and somewhat indeterminate genre. The Shakespearean history play is a less elusive entity, partly because of the help given by the 1623 Folio edition of Shakespeare's works, prepared after his death by members of his acting company, the King's Men. There, all of Shakespeare's plays are divided into three categories: comedies, histories, and tragedies. Among the histories, the editors list ten Shakespeare plays, all defined by their subject matter—that is, their focus on monarchical history from post–Norman Conquest England (history about events after 1066). These include *King John* and *Henry VIII* plus the eight plays dealing with the reigns of Richard II to Henry VI. *Edward III*, whose authorship is even debated today, is not included on the list. In retrospect, critics, when speaking of the Elizabethan history play, tend to limit the genre to the kind of play Shakespeare made popular. This a testament to his achievement, but it nonetheless narrows our understanding of the many different kinds of plays that might be considered part of the early modern theater's romance with history.

In formal terms, Shakespeare's histories can be tragic, like *Richard II*, or comic, like *1 Henry IV*. In his own lifetime, at least three of the plays listed in the First Folio as histories were designed as tragedies on the title pages of the quarto or Octavo texts in which they were first published: *The True Tragedy of Richard Duke of York and the Good King Henry the Sixth* (3 *Henry VI*), *The Tragedy of King Richard the Third*, and *The Tragedy of King Richard the Second*. In regard to the latter two plays, each focuses on the rise and fall of a single major figure, unlike other histories in which attention is distributed across a range of characters and that often dramatize only part of a

The table of contents of the First Folio (1623). Note the division of the plays into the categories of comedies, histories, and tragedies.

particular king's reign. Even though Shakespeare wrote plays about Roman history, such as *Julius Caesar* and *Antony and Cleopatra,* and plays about England's ancient past, such as *Cymbeline* and *King Lear,* they are not typically now grouped with his English histories.

The ambiguities surrounding what was and was not a history play testify to the experimental nature of the genre in Shakespeare's day and the energies it captured. As early as 1592, if contemporary commentators are right, audiences were excited by plays that showed them their national past. Thomas Nashe, writing in that year, praised plays in which "our forefathers valiant acts (that have line long buried in rustie brasse and worm-eaten bookes) are revived, and they themselves raised from the Grave of Oblivion, and brought to pleade their aged Honours in open presence." He goes on to refer to events dramatized in Shakespeare's *1 Henry VI* in which the English hero, Talbot, and his son are killed heroically fighting the French and refusing to flee, even though they are vastly outnumbered. As Nashe says: "How would it have joyed brave *Talbot* (the terror of the French) to thinke that after he had lyne two hundred yeares in his Tombe, he should triumphe againe on the Stage, and have his bones newe embalmed with the teares of ten thousand spectators at least (at severall times), who, in the Tragedian that represents his person, imagine they behold him fresh bleeding?" Here, Nashe imagines Talbot receiving a kind of immortality through drama as his deeds and person are revivified (to his distinct pleasure) again and again on the contemporary stage. Theatergoers, in their turn, were reported to be moved to tears by this vivid reenactment of events two hundred years in the past but retaining the capacity to give pleasure in the present.

But the pleasure of history plays was not without its dangers. Because many history plays dealt with fairly recent historical events, and because audiences might read these plays with an eye to how they covertly commented on contemporary events, dramatists had to be careful about what they dramatized and how. For example, it was forbidden to refer on the stage to current affairs of state or to sitting monarchs and their representatives. Technically, all playbooks had to be submitted to the Office of the Master of the Revels to be reviewed for libelous or dangerous matter before a play could be performed, and sometimes parts of a play were ordered to be excised. A coauthored play on the life of Sir Thomas More, in which Shakespeare is believed to have a hand, provides one such example. This play dramatized what is known as the Ill May Day riots of 1517 against foreign workers in England. Edmund Tilney, then Master of the Revels, wrote on the playbook: "Leave out ye insurrection wholly and ye cause thereof." In the 1590s, there was considerable resentment toward foreign workers in London, and presumably a play that staged an anti-alien riot (even one that had occurred seventy years earlier) was considered too provocative to be allowed. More mysterious is the performance and print history of *Richard II.* In its fourth act, this play shows Richard II's abdication of the throne of England under pressure from his captor, Bolingbroke, soon to be Henry IV. In the First Folio, at least, the play shows these events. In the First Quarto (1597), these lines are missing. No one can definitively explain their absence. Perhaps they were simply added by Shakespeare after the first printing of the play. But it is also possible that this part of the play *did* exist in 1597 but was subject to censorship. We know the play could be controversial. In 1601, when the Earl of Essex led a rebellion against Elizabeth I, his supporters requested Shakespeare's company to perform a play about Richard II on the eve of their great undertaking. By legend, at least, a fearful Elizabeth is supposed to have said: "I am Richard II. Know you not that?" A sitting monarch was always afraid of a usurper, and staging Richard's ignominious descent from the throne could have been considered dangerous matter.

However tricky it was to stage history, Shakespeare's interest in the enterprise was shared with a number of his contemporaries. In the sixteenth century, there was widespread interest in the writing of history and a number of new developments in its practice. For many medieval historians, history was closely linked to theology and revealed God's divine plan for mankind. A providential sense that God was the first cause of historical events remained widespread well into the seventeenth century. However, many historians were also increasingly interested in the role that human actors play in shaping historical events and in the lessons that could be learned from reading accounts of the past. Many of the changes in historical practice originated in Italy as writers like Polydore Vergil began to question medieval historical narratives and to consult archives to determine the causes of historical changes and the circumstances surrounding particular events. In England in the late sixteenth century, an elite group of men, including William Camden, took pride in doing original research into the texts and objects of the past, rather than accepting received wisdom about them. Known as antiquarians, these scholars eschewed a providential view of history, studying antiquity for its own sake and not for its relevance to the present. While they constituted a distinct minority within the writers of history in Shakespeare's lifetime, they nonetheless pointed the way to modern research practices and showed how far some writers could move from the providentialism and reliance on prior authorities that was the dominant mode of medieval historical writing.

In England, the keen interest in the writing of history was probably partly due to the century of warfare and political strife that had preceded the establishment of the Tudor dynasty. Writers were eager to understand and make sense of these past events and to draw lessons from them that would lead to greater stability in the present. In writing his plays, Shakespeare made frequent use of several complex sixteenth-century chronicle histories that surveyed events in the reigns of England's kings. The first, Edward Hall's

The Union of the Two Noble and Illustre Famelies of Lancastre and Yorke (1548), painted a devastating picture of the chaos of the War of the Roses and presented the coming to power of the Tudors as the providential salvation of England. In writing his history plays, Shakespeare frequently drew upon details from Hall, but even more often from Raphael Holinshed's *Chronicles of England, Scotlande, and Irelande,* 2nd ed. (1587). This massive book, especially in the second edition published after Holinshed's death, incorporated writings by William Harrison, Richard Stanyhurst, John Hooker, Abraham Fleming, and many others in addition to Holinshed's own histories. While popularly attributed to a single author, it was in actuality a plural text that included competing accounts of some events and demon-

The title page of Raphael Holinshed's *Chronicles* (1587 ed.).

strated an array of styles and modes of historical practice. As was true for the chronicle writers, Shakespeare typically organized his representation of English history through the exploration of a particular king's reign.

Besides these enormous prose chronicles, Shakespeare was probably familiar as well with the practice of humanists writers of the mid-sixteenth century (men of letters dedicated to the revival of classical learning, to the editing and translation of classical texts, and to the reform of contemporary educational practices). The humanists were particularly concerned with the moral purposes to which the reading and writing of history could be put. They felt that reading history could inspire men to virtue and warn them from vice and that kings, for example, should learn from history how to avoid tyrannical deeds. Sir Thomas Elyot, a mid-sixteenth-century humanist interested in the role of education in preparing young men for lives of public service, wrote in his *The Boke Named the Governour* (1531) that "if a noble man do thus seriously and diligently rede histories, I dare affirme there is no study or science for him of equal commoditie and pleasure, havynge regarde to every tyme and age." Roger Ascham, schoolmaster to Elizabeth I, affirmed the utilitarian value of studying history, saying that it "could bring excellent learning and breed staid judgment in taking any like matter in hand." Among the humanist histories important to Shakespeare was Sir Thomas More's *History of King Richard the Thirde* (1513), which served as the basis for the accounts of Richard's reign in Hall and Holinshed. In this psychologically complex work, More included a number of vivid speeches that he attributes to the historical figures he discusses in order to heighten the rhetorical impact of his narrative. One can imagine the effect of this practice on a dramatist like Shakespeare, whose stock in trade was making history live through the speeches of his characters.

The writing of history was, then, in sixteenth-century England in a state of transition and ferment. A number of different assumptions and practices were in play, sometimes within a single work. Particular writers might, for example, intensely explore the human motives and the secular causes of particular events but still insist on the providential design undergirding all earthly actions. Shakespeare was familiar with a number of different kinds of historical texts, and aspects of many of them were incorporated into his plays. But drama was different from prose history. In the early modern period, history and poetry (or poesy), though not always clearly distinguished from one another, were beginning to be disentangled. There was growing consensus that writers of history were less at liberty than poets to embellish facts with fiction or to take liberties with chronology. Edmund Spenser, Shakespeare's contemporary and a fellow poet, described the difference between poets who deal with historical matter and historians primarily in terms of the order of presentation that each must employ. "An historiographer discourseth of affayres orderly as they were donne, accounting as well the times as the actions; but a poet thrusteth into the middest, even where it most concerneth him, and there recoursing to the thinges forepaste, and divining of thinges to come, maketh a pleasing analysis of all." If historians are to begin at the start of a reign and move through to its conclusion, a poet can begin anywhere he wishes and selectively dramatize events of particular interest. This is a practice everywhere evident in Shakespeare's history plays. He begins his play on the reign of Richard III not with Richard's birth, but with a soliloquy, both humorous and chilling, in which the grown prince confesses to the audience his desire for the throne and meditates on how he will snatch it from his older brothers. The play itself dramatizes only a handful of events from Richard's life but does so in a way that follows a tragic trajectory in which Richard schemes and murders his way to power, only to lose his touch and to fall prey to his own hubris and the accumulated anger of those whom he has injured, an ending piously presented as fulfilling the will of heaven.

Sir Philip Sidney, another poet and Shakespeare's contemporary, makes an even sharper distinction between historians and poets. In his *Apology for Poetry*, he defends poetry as superior to history in that historians are bound to tell "the particular truth of things," while historical poets can embellish the historical record, create more perfect examples of vice or virtue than history affords, and, through "the speaking picture" of poetry vividly embody for readers the moral lessons historians less effectively attempt to impart. As Sidney says:

> for whatsoever action, or faction, whatsoever counsel, policy, or war strategem the historian is bound to recite, that may the poet (if he list) with his imitation make his own, beautifying it both for further teaching, and more delighting, as it pleaseth him: having all, from Dante's heaven to his hell, under the authority of his pen.

Shakespeare used the poet's liberty liberally. While many modern readers obtain much of their "knowledge" about fifteenth-century English history from Shakespeare's plays, this may not be smart if those readers want to know what contemporary historians actually believe happened during those bloody decades. Everywhere, Shakespeare treats historical events with the freedom that is the poet's prerogative. He notoriously alters and adds to his sources, compresses into a single year events that took decades, and everywhere assigns speeches to characters that are entirely the creation of his own brain and not of any historical record. For example, a famous scene in one of his early history plays—Act 2, Scene 4, of *1 Henry VI*—is found in no historical record. In it, Shakespeare memorably depicts the followers of the Yorkists plucking white roses from bushes in the Temple Garden in London, while Lancastrians pluck red roses in order to show whose part each group takes in the acrimonious dispute over which branch of the Plantagenet line has a superior claim to the English throne. From this scene, the bloody fiasco of decades of civil war is imagined to have derived. The scene is typical of Shakespeare's practice in that it gives vivid physical embodiment to an abstraction— in this case, the War of the Roses—while allowing the audience to keep straight a large cast of characters by the flower badges that each faction wears.

There are innumerable examples of other occasions when Shakespeare takes liberties with the historical accounts he found in his sources. In his plays about the reign of Henry IV, for example, he makes the king's son, Prince Hal, the same age as Hotspur, the son of the king's former friend and now his great enemy, the Earl of Northumberland. In actuality, Hotspur was more than twenty years older than Hal. But Shakespeare wants to present the two young men as same-age rivals and as a study in contrasts: Hotspur is honor-driven, impetuous, and valiant in war; Hal is a seeming layabout who spends days in a London tavern with low-life companions, rather than at court learning from his father how to rule a kingdom or at war winning the honor Hotspur so strenuously pursues. Hal's father goes so far as to wish that these children had been switched at birth and that Hotspur were his own flesh and blood and heir to his kingdom. While Hal eventually vindicates himself and becomes a successful ruler, a great deal of the dramatic interest of *1 Henry IV* derives from the contrast Shakespeare creates between the chivalric Hotspur and the more calculating son of England's king.

In the *Henry IV* plays, Shakespeare also invents a memorable group of ordinary people who hang out in a London tavern. They aren't found in the chronicle sources; rather, they resemble contemporary residents of Shakespeare's own day. The group includes a tavernkeeper, Mistress Quickly; a woman of dubious virtue appropriately called Doll Tearsheet; a bombastic braggart, Pistol; and other characters suited to the low-life milieu of commercial London. By adding these figures to his account of England's past, Shakespeare greatly increased the social and temporal range of his history plays. This may in part have been done to enhance the appeal of those plays to contemporary theatergoers, who saw in these characters traces of the familiar world in which they lived. But they serve other purposes, including providing an ironic or contrasting perspective on issues broached elsewhere in the play. For example, in *Henry V* a Chorus figure claims that honor motivates all the soldiers who go with Prince Hal, now King Henry V, to fight against the French in pursuit of English claims to French territory. Pistol, however, urges his friends to join the French campaign for quite another reason. "Let us to France, like horseleeches, my boys, / To suck, to suck, the very blood to suck" (2.3.46–47). Pillage and plunder are his goals. The juxtaposition of the Chorus and Pistol undercuts the former's rosy picture of the unity of the English forces and calls attention to the gap between the Chorus's idealized view of the French campaign and the more sordid aspects of its execution. This counterpoint of voices and perspectives, present elsewhere as well, is what gives the play its ironic edge and keeps it from slipping over into a mythologized view of Henry's greatness and the unity of the "band of brothers" that he creates around him. The presence of these low-life characters also reminds the audience that while monarchical history is about monarchs, it affects ordinary people in crucial ways, not all of them beneficial. Some people die in Henry's campaign; some lose their homes; some are turned into scavengers for profit, like Pistol. On the edges of this and other plays, Shakespeare gives glimpses of the effects on the powerless of the events that the chronicles record, and these are nearly always his own invention.

Shakespeare, then, takes a poet's liberty with historical material, drawing repeatedly from prose sources but adding, changing, and embellishing in ways that make the plays more theatrical and more complex. A great deal of ink has been spilled trying to figure out whether Shakespeare himself took a particular view on history's unfolding. Did he see history in providential terms? By contrast, did he view history as a sequence of events motivated entirely by the actions of powerful individuals? Did he believe Tudor mythology that saw in Henry Tudor's defeat of Richard III and marriage to Elizabeth of York the working out of a divine plan for England's salvation after the chaos of civil war and the treasonous deposition of Richard II by Henry Bolingbroke? One difficulty in answering these questions with conviction rests in the considerable differences among his ten or so English histories. Shakespeare came of dramatic age in the 1590s, and his approach to the genre that he helped to make popular changed over time.

The first four plays dealing with the reign of Henry VI and of Richard III—commonly called the first tetralogy—were all written before 1594. They represent some of Shakespeare's very earliest dramatic efforts, and, as was common practice at the time, he may well have written several of them in collaboration with other dramatists. It is not clear that they were intended at first as a unified set of plays, and 2 Henry VI was probably written before 1 Henry VI. Collectively, they dramatize the origins and devastating effects of the War of the Roses. The three Henry VI plays suggest that civil war was largely caused by the weakness of Henry VI and by the self-centeredness of many of the English nobles who put their own private interests before the good of the Commonwealth. In regard to these three plays, it would be too grand, I think, to say that they embody a theory of history. What they reveal is the chaos that overtakes a kingdom that is weakly ruled and the dangerous anomalies that arise in those conditions, including the unprecedented power wielded by Henry's Amazonian queen, Margaret of Anjou, or by the lower-class rebel leader, Jack Cade. Richard III, by contrast, most powerfully of any of Shakespeare's histories, articulates a providential view of history's unfolding. Cursed by his victims and haunted by bad dreams, Richard's character is modeled in part on the Vice figure of medieval morality plays. The Vice, always clever and theatrically compelling, nonetheless embodies evil and is at war with virtue and the forces of good. In Richard III, the King is finally beaten at Bosworth Field by Henry Tudor, a man presented as Richard's antithesis. A virtuous figure who longs to unite England and end civil strife, he is blessed by dreams predicting his victory over the so-called "dog," Richard, and himself prays that his descendants will "enrich the time to come with smooth-faced peace, / With smiling plenty, and fair prosperous days" (5.8.33–34). Elizabeth I, of course, was one of those descendants. In this particular play, Shakespeare seems to intimate that England has been providentially rescued from chaos by the miraculous appearance of a savior bent on returning England to a state of peace and lawful rule.

King John is something of an anomaly. Set much earlier than Shakespeare's other histories, it deals with the reign of a monarch whom Protestant writers hailed as an early defender of England's freedom from the Church of Rome. There are several sixteenth-century plays dealing with John's reign, but Shakespeare's is distinguished by its relative indifference to the religious questions to which other dramatists devoted most of their attention. Instead, Shakespeare's play focuses with unusual realism on questions of legitimacy. John is a sitting king, but his nephew Arthur, son of his older brother Geoffrey, has a more legitimate dynastic claim to the throne. Arthur, however, is a child, raised in France, and ill suited to rule. The most talented potential claimant to the throne is the Bastard, Falconbridge, the illegitimate son of Richard the Lionheart. In such circumstances, who should rule? The play creates unusually strong parts for women, including Constance, Arthur's mother, and Eleanor, John's mother; and they play major roles in the play's inconclusive, but troubling meditation on the relative weight to be given to bloodlines, talent, and possession of the throne as factors in determining monarchical legitimacy.

The so-called second tetralogy, starting with *Richard II* (1596) and including the two parts of *Henry IV* (1597 and 1598) and *Henry V* (1599), differs in many ways from the plays dealing with the War of the Roses. Although written after those earlier plays, the second tetralogy nonetheless deals with the historical period that preceded the War of the Roses. It provides, in effect, the backstory to those plays. It begins with Richard II's ill-fated reign, including his deposition and death, and then in three successive plays dramatizes the struggles of the Lancastrian kings, Henry IV and Henry V, to maintain their power and win legitimacy in the wake of the deposition of this lawfully anointed king. Although in *Richard II* the Bishop of Carlisle warns that God will punish Richard's enemies, in truth the following three plays focus less on the theme of divine retribution and more on the skills needed for the successful performance of kingship, whatever the route that led to the throne. Prince Hal is an especially vivid example of a figure who, at his first appearance in *1 Henry IV*, does not seem suited to rule. He prefers to jest with Falstaff in

A late sixteenth-century portrait of Henry IV (1367–1413) by an unknown artist. National Portrait Gallery, London.

Mistress Quickly's tavern rather than to attend to statescraft. Gradually, however, Shakespeare reveals the calculation that guides his activities and the benefits that accrue to him from his tavern sojourn, including his ability to speak with any man "in his own language," a gift he finds crucial when he needs to lead common soldiers into battle in France. Prince Hal is a new kind of political being, one whose legitimacy depends less on his dubious genealogical claim to the throne than on the performative skills through which he crafts a public image and carefully manipulates those around him.

The plays in the second tetralogy also broaden their focus beyond that of the court and the nobility to include scenes that depict the common people of the realm, whether Mistress Quickly and Pistol, the Gloucestershire Justices of the Peace Silence and Shallow, or the common footsoldiers Michael Williams and John

Bates. Rather than just a kingdom, the England of the *Henry IV* and *Henry V* plays is also a nation, an entity defined by its status as a bounded territory with various inhabitants whose allegiance must be won and not assumed. In these later histories, Shakespeare displays less a theory of history than a keen interest in how power can be exercised well or badly and the particular skills one needs to be a leader of the many men who comprise the nation.

Henry VIII is different yet again, one of the very last plays Shakespeare's wrote and one dealing with events closest to the period in which he himself lived. Partly a melodrama based on the rise and fall of Henry's chief adviser, Cardinal Wolsey, *Henry VIII* shares features with Shakespeare's late romances in its episodic structure and its happy resolution with the birth of a daughter, Elizabeth, to Henry's second wife, Anne Boleyn. Though unusually sympathetic to the plight of Katherine, Henry's first wife, the play for the most part skates over the difficulties of Henry's long and eventful reign to conclude with the event that for the Tudors was the most important aspect of it: the birth of the woman that was to rule England from 1558 to 1603.

From this diverse body of dramatic material, it is difficult to generalize about Shakespeare's attitudes toward history. But it is clear that he found in the chronicles rich resources that he could use in creating compelling dramas about how power is won and lost, about how ambition for a throne can destroy (in the case of Richard III) those who experience it, or (as with Henry V) can sometimes transform a wastrel into a disciplined leader of men. It is often said that theatergoers in Shakespeare's time found his history plays compelling because they played to a general interest in the nation's history at a time, after the defeat of the Spanish Armada in 1588, when England was becoming increasingly self-conscious about its status as a national power alongside the other nations of Europe. London was a thriving commercial center; the Tudors had developed centralized administrative structures for the country; England was establishing trading routes to the East and soon was to be engaged in American colonization; national pride was running high. In such circumstances, it was undoubtedly true that Shakespeare's history plays had considerable popular appeal as windows into the past of a nation in a period of rapid and self-conscious change. Many theatergoers would not have been able to read or, if they could read, would not have been able to afford a book like Holinshed's *Chronicles of England, Scotlande, and Irelande*. Anyone, however, for a small fee could attend the public theater. Shakespeare's history plays reached people from every social class, gender, and level of literacy.

Yet the popular success of these plays also depended on the skill with which

A 1537 ink-and-watercolor portrait of Henry VIII (1491–1547) by Hans Holbein the Younger. National Portrait Gallery, London.

Shakespeare and his collaborators transformed the raw material of their sources into effective drama—the way, that is, they exercised the "liberty" of the poet to shape a pleasing fiction. Examining the range of his history plays reveals, in part, Shakespeare's increasing sophistication with the arts of stagecraft. The early histories have huge casts of characters: in terms of significant parts, there are 32 male characters and 3 women in *1 Henry VI*; 50 men and 4 women in *The First Part of the Contention*; 42 men and 3 women in *The True Tragedy of Richard Duke of York*; and 37 men and 5 women in *The Tragedy of King Richard The Third*. These plays also have complex plots. Yet Shakespeare quickly grew adept at distinguishing between characters and organizing the action through compelling juxtapositions and richly emblematic scenes that crystallize the essence of the action. The Temple Garden scene in *1 Henry VI* in which Yorkists and Lancastrians pluck red and white roses as emblems of their differing monarchical allegiances is one such scene. Amid the chaotic slaughter that dominates *The True Tragedy of Richard Duke of York,* Shakespeare inserts another such scene—Scene 5 of Act 2—in which the weak king, sitting on a molehill away from the battle being waged by his wife's army against his enemies, observes a father carry onstage the body of a man he has slain whom he discovers to be his own son and a son carry on stage the body of a man he has slain whom he discovers to be his father. This allegorical tableau captures the essence of civil war: the killing of son by father, father by son. Meanwhile, the king, who should control civil strife, sits helplessly by, wishing he were a shepherd and not the king of England. While Shakespeare came to eschew such highly emblematic scenes, he nonetheless learned from these complex early histories how to give dramatic shape to complicated narratives and much larger sets of characters than are found in his early comedies written at about the same time.

In *Richard II*, much of the theatrical tension comes from the telling juxtaposition of the poetic, loquacious, and ineffective Richard and his pragmatic, highly effective antagonist Harry Bolingbroke. They are studies in alternative modes of kingship, the one setting in high relief the qualities of the other. As early as *1 Henry VI*, Shakespeare had effectively juxtaposed Lord Talbot, the great English warrior who defends England's claims to French territory, against, on the one hand, the many English nobles, like Suffolk, who selfishly refuse to send him aid and, on the other hand, the French maid, Joan of Arc, who leads the French resistance to his assault on territories in France. Talbot embodies the best of chivalric English values. Unswerving in his service to Henry VI, his steadfastness sets in sharp relief the degeneracy of the other English nobles, while his gender, his nobility, and his fidelity to a code of chivalric honor (even if that means the certain death of himself and his young son) contrasts with the low-born Joan of Arc's femininity, her opportunism, and her desperate attempts to save her life at any cost. Talbot is singled out by Nashe as an especially memorable example of the kind of figure the historical drama could rescue from oblivion; he is also the fulcrum around which Shakespeare builds a play of telling juxtapositions.

By the time he wrote *1* and *2 Henry IV,* Shakespeare had developed what can only be called a rich contrapuntal style of dramatizing history in which the actions of one group of characters mirror, comment upon, and offer other alternatives to the actions of other groups of characters. In *1 Henry IV,* there is a particularly fine example of this dramatic technique. There are three distinct dramatic worlds evoked in this play: the prosaic world of Henry IV, struggling to keep control of his throne; the exotic world of the rebels who oppose him, a group including the Welsh magician Glyndŵr, the bold Scottish warrior the Earl of Douglas, and the hotheaded Hotspur, whose family hails from the wild northern territories of England; and, finally, the world of the Eastcheap tavern, where Falstaff, a fat, down-at-the-heels knight, presides over a festive world of eating, drinking, and practical pranks. The differences among these three worlds starkly dramatize the choices facing the young Prince Hal, who must choose whether he will be, as his actions seem to promise, a truant from the duty-driven world of court or rise to the challenge posed by Hotspur and strive for honor on the field of battle. Must he, if he chooses the path of duty, forfeit the spontaneous pleasures of the tavern, where people make stage plays about kings, using cushions for crowns, without actually having to assume the grinding burdens of the office? With a dramaturgy marvelously free of didacticism, Shakespeare invites the theatergoer to ponder the consequences of choice, to feel as well as to intellectualize what it means to follow one course of life and not another.

It is in his early history plays that Shakespeare also first revealed his magical ability to create characters that are not only memorable, but that do the work of making history intelligible and quietly suggesting the role that individuals play in its making. Everyone, of course, remembers Falstaff, one of the most popular dramatic characters ever created, and the hunchbacked villain Richard III, for whom, as for his father, Shakespeare created some of his first soliloquies, speeches that reveal the working of mind at play and not just a recitation of events. For example, in the middle of *The True Tragedy of Richard Duke of York*, the Duke's son, Richard of Gloucester, having just watched his brother, King Edward, fawn over a low-born woman whom he will soon take to wife, renounces the pleasures of love and declares his intention to seize the crown from this brother.

> Why, I can smile, and murder whiles I smile,
> And cry 'Content!' to that which grieves my heart,
> And wet my cheeks with artificial tears,
> And frame my face to all occasions.
> I'll drown more sailors than the mermaid shall;
> I'll slay more gazers than the basilisk;
> I'll play the orator as well as Nestor,
> Deceive more slyly than Ulysses could,
> And, like a Sinon, take another Troy.
> I can add colours to the chameleon,
> Change shapes with Proteus for advantages,
> And set the murderous Machiavel to school.
> Can I do this, and cannot get a crown?
> Tut, were it farther off, I'll pluck it down.
>   (3.2.182–95)

This litany of boasting claims captures Richard's hubris and his theatrical bent. He will take his example from the most treacherous figures of history and myth, and outdo them all. But what gives the speech its special character is the dismissive last line. Descending to a colloquial "Tut," breaking the iambic pentameter with an explosive opening syllable, Richard signals that he is prepared to do more than list precedents. He'll "pluck" the crown, no matter what the obstacles.

The early histories, though dominated by men like Richard, also contain some usually vivid roles for women; see especially Joan of Arc in *1 Henry VI*; Margaret of Anjou, who appears in all four plays of the first tetralogy; Constance and Eleanor in *King John*; and Mistress Quickly, Hotspur's wife, Kate, and the French Princess, Catherine, in the second tetralogy. Lingering a moment on Margaret's part shows how Shakespeare embellished his sources to create one of the most memorable women in any of his histories. In all of these plays, patriarchal rule is assumed. The crown passes lineally from father to son; women are vehicles for this reproductive continuity. Margaret of Anjou, however, is much more. At the end of *1 Henry VI,* she is brought from France to be the young Henry VI's bride, largely because her beauty made her irresistibly attractive to Suffolk, one of Henry's nobles and eventually Margaret's openly acknowledged lover. In *Part II,* as King Henry proves utterly incapable of rule, Margaret assumes a greater and greater role in public affairs, actually leading Lancastrian troops into battle against the Yorkist forces and ordering Henry to stay off the battlefield, so disheartening is his impact on his troops. In *Part III,* Henry goes so far as to make a bargain with the Yorkists that, if they will let him retain his crown in his lifetime, he will resign it to them upon his death, in effect disinheriting his young son, Edward. It is at this point that the paradoxical greatness and monstrosity of Margaret is fully revealed. In essence, she becomes the effective ruler of England, directing the course of the war and defending the rights of her son to his royal inheritance; paradoxically, she defends these traditional values while usurping her husband's prerogatives. Enacting what many considered an unnatural role for a woman, she reveals what she sees as the unnatural behavior of the King.

Shakespeare embellishes Margaret's historical role considerably. Early in *The True Tragedy of Richard Duke of York,* Shakespeare creates a scene in which Margaret cruelly exults over Richard, the Yorkist patriarch whom she has captured. In the chronicle sources, her ally, Clifford, cuts off the head of the already dead York, puts a paper crown on that head, and presents it to Margaret. In Shakespeare's version of the scene, York is still alive when brought to Margaret, and she mockingly makes him stand on a mole-hill, then gives him a napkin dipped in the blood of his youngest son, Rutland, for him to use to dry his tears, and finally has him crowned with the paper crown before herself being one of those who stabs him to death. Throughout this long scene, Margaret jeers and mocks her defeated foe, and he curses her, at one point asserting that she has a "tiger's heart wrapped in a woman's hide!" (1.4.138). Her villainy is impressively over the top, and the scene must have been a memorable one. When Robert Greene, one of Shakespeare's contemporaries, wanted to put down his rival playwright he called him "an upstart Crow, beautified with our feathers, that with his *Tygers hart wrapt in a Players hyde,* supposes he is as well able to bombast out a blanke verse as the best of you." Angry at Shakespeare for borrowing from his work or copying his style ("beautified with our feathers"), Greene uses Shakespeare's own memorable line about Margaret to suggest that Shakespeare himself is an unnatural overreacher. The final act for this crowd-pleasing character occurred in *Richard III,* in which, defeated and stripped of military power, she becomes a prophet of doom, calling down curses on her enemies, including Richard himself.

In his English histories, then, Shakespeare was learning his craft as well as meditating on historical causation and the role of chance and of personality and personal skills in historical events. After the 1590s, his interest in the genre waned, replaced by an intensified commitment to the writing of tragedies that drew on material other than the doings of England's late medieval kings. But in his decade of deep involvement with the English history play, Shakespeare created a body of work unmatched by his contemporaries in the sophistication with which it dramatized the interplay of chance, personality, skill, force, and perhaps even providence in the shaping of history. He began by dramatizing the chaotic War of the Roses and ended his histories of the 1590s by moving backward in time to the heroics of Henry V's French campaign, in the process creating plays strikingly different in form and feel. What remained constant was his commitment to exploring the complexity of events, sometimes looking at the compromises that for him seem to attend the work of rule and sometimes glancing, on the edges of the monarchical narrative, at the lives of ordinary people as they are affected, or not, by the strivings of the powerful. In the process, he created an origin story for his country and a picture of

The head of Margaret of Anjou, depicted on a medal. Victoria and Albert Museum, London.

late medieval England so powerful that we have to remind ourselves today that it is just a fiction, the work of a poet historical.

SELECTED BIBLIOGRAPHY

Calderwood, James L. *Metadrama in Shakespeare's Henriad: Richard II to Henry V.* Berkeley: University of California Press, 1979.

Dutton, Richard, and Jean E. Howard. *A Companion to Shakespeare's Works,* II: *The Histories.* Malden, Mass.: Blackwell, 2003.

Hodgdon, Barbara. *The End Crowns All: Closure and Contradiction in Shakespeare's Histories.* Princeton: Princeton University Press, 1991.

Howard, Jean E., and Phyllis Rackin. *Engendering a Nation: A Feminist Account of Shakespeare's English Histories.* London: Routledge, 1997.

Levine, Nina S. *Women's Matters: Politics, Gender, and Nation in Shakespeare's Early History Plays.* Newark: University of Delaware Press, 1998.

Levy, F. J. *Tudor Historical Thought.* San Marino, Calif.: Huntington Library, 1967.

Ornstein, Robert. *A Kingdom for a Stage: The Achievement of Shakespeare's History Plays.* Cambridge, Mass.: Harvard University Press, 1972.

Pugliatti, Paola. *Shakespeare the Historian.* Basingstoke, Eng.: Macmillan, 1996.

Rackin, Phyllis. *Stages of History: Shakespeare's English Chronicles.* Ithaca, N.Y.: Cornell University Press, 1990.

Ribner, Irving. *The English History Play in the Age of Shakespeare.* Princeton: Princeton University Press, 1957.

Tillyard, E. M. W. *Shakespeare's History Plays.* London: Chatto & Windus, 1944.

Richard III

Among the very few anecdotes about Shakespeare that date from his own lifetime is a ribald story recorded in 1602 in the diary of a London law student, John Manningham:

> Upon a time when Burbage played Richard III there was a citizen grew so far in liking with him, that before she went from the play she appointed him to come that night unto her by the name of Richard III. Shakespeare, overhearing their conclusion, went before, was entertained and at his game ere Burbage came. The message being brought that Richard III was at the door, Shakespeare caused return to be made that William the Conqueror was before Richard III.

Like most stories about celebrities, this one probably says more about those who circulated it than about those it describes. But it does at least suggest that Richard Burbage, the famous actor who first played Richard III (as well as such parts as Romeo and Hamlet), had not by virtue of his villainous role lost all of his glamour. Indeed, it is striking that Richard—the "elvish-marked, abortive, rooting hog" (1.3.225), the "poisonous bunch-backed toad" (1.3.244), the heartless cur sent, as he himself puts it, "deformed" and "unfinished" (1.1.20) into the world—has seemed weirdly and compellingly attractive to generations of playgoers. From the start, the play seems to have aroused intense interest: first performed in 1592 or 1593, *Richard III* was published in quarto no fewer than five times during Shakespeare's lifetime.

What can account for this attraction? It is not an obvious feature in the chronicle histories upon which Shakespeare relied, nor does Richard seem to have a comparable allure in another play of unknown authorship that dates from the same period, *The True Tragedy of Richard III*. In these works, Richard figures as the pitiless, treacherous villain of what has been called the "Tudor Myth"—that is, the officially sanctioned account of the origin and legitimacy of the Tudor dynasty. That dynasty was founded by Henry, Earl of Richmond, who defeated Richard III at the Battle of Bosworth Field (1485), reigned until his death in 1509 as Henry VII, and was the grandfather of Queen Elizabeth (1533–1603). It is hardly surprising that the new regime, whose claim to the throne was somewhat shaky, would wish to discredit the old. Modern historians emphasize Richard's solid administrative skills; Tudor apologists depict Richard not merely as venal or unscrupulous but as a monster of evil, a creature whose moral viciousness was vividly stamped on his twisted body.

The principal literary source for this spectacularly partisan depiction was not a piece of simple propaganda but an unusually subtle and complex *History of King Richard the Third* (c. 1513) by the great humanist Thomas More. Later sixteenth-century historians, notably Edward Halle in *The Union of the Two Noble and Illustre Famelies of Lancastre & Yorke* (1548) and Raphael Holinshed in *The Chronicles of England, Scotland, and Ireland* (1577, revised in 1587), followed closely in More's wake, repeating many of the details that Shakespeare in turn borrowed: Richard's habit of gnawing his lip, for example, or his restlessness, or the rumor that he was born with teeth. More and his followers deftly interwove three distinct explanatory accounts of Richard's behavior: political, psychological, and metaphysical. As a politician (a word with nasty connotations in the Renaissance), More's Richard is a particularly cunning player in a corrupt world, a schemer plotting to seize power and destroy all real or potential rivals. Psychologically, he is a strange blend of courage, wit, skillful dissembling, and fathomless malice. And on the metaphysical plane, he is a horrible instrument of God's wrath, a virtual devil incarnate.

Most sixteenth-century historians and chroniclers were, by our standards, far more interested in conveying moral meanings than in impartially recounting facts. Shakespeare allowed himself an even greater latitude, freely reshaping and condensing his historical materials in order to heighten dramatic effect and to intensify the political, psychological, and metaphysical dimensions of his villainous antihero. The play compresses events that in reality occurred over a long period of time, so that, for example, Richard's murderous plot against his brother George, Duke of Clarence (1478), is cleverly twined around his cynical courtship of Lady Anne (1472), which is in turn depicted as occurring during the funeral procession of King Henry (1471). The historical Lady Anne had only been betrothed to King Henry's son Edward, but Shakespeare writes as if she had actually been married to him; likewise, he folds Richmond's unsuccessful attempt to invade England in 1483 into his successful invasion of 1485, and he has old Queen Margaret, who was not even in England during most of the events that the play depicts, haunting the royal court like a bitter, half-crazed Greek tragic chorus.

Manipulating the insecurities, factional rivalries, and ambitions of everyone around him, Shakespeare's Richard is a consummate portrait of what sixteenth-century Englishmen termed a "machiavel"—that is, a person who acts on the immoral advice allegedly offered by the Florentine humanist Niccolò Machiavelli in *The Prince* (written in 1513, first printed in 1532). According to the period's lurid and grossly distorted account of this advice, Machiavelli had counseled princes to lie, cheat, and murder under the cover of hypocritical professions of virtue and piety. "I count Religion but a childish Toy," declares the character called Machevil, who speaks the prologue to Marlowe's *Jew of Malta* (c. 1590). Shakespeare's Richard, at first terrified by the apparition of the ghosts in Act 5, rallies to express comparable sentiments: "Conscience is but a word that cowards use, / Devised at first to keep the strong in awe" (5.6.39–40). These are sentiments that, for the most part, Richard keeps to himself—or, rather, shares only with the audience in a succession of gleeful asides—for he is highly skilled at assuming the pose of religious faith. Aided by his fellow hypocrite Buckingham, Richard appears in a memorable scene, prayer book in hand, miming "devotion and right Christian zeal" (3.7.103) while cynically stage-managing the supposedly popular call for his coronation.

Richard III. Portrait by unknown artist (c. 1590).

Shakespeare's vision of Richard as a consummate role-player goes back to a brilliant sketch of the same character in one of the three earlier plays he had written on fifteenth-century English history. Taken together, these plays—*The First Part of Henry the Sixth, The First Part of the Contention of the Two Famous Houses of York and Lancaster* (2 Henry VI), and *The True Tragedy of Richard Duke of York and the Good King Henry the Sixth* (3 Henry VI)—depict the chaotic, violent struggle known as the Wars of the Roses, between two noble houses, the Lancastrians and the Yorkists. At the close of *Richard Duke of York* (3 Henry VI), the Yorkist faction, led by the Duke of York's three surviving sons (Edward, George, and Richard), has triumphed. The last Lancastrian king, Henry VI, has been killed, and Richard's eldest brother has been crowned King Edward IV. But a shadow is cast across this decisive Yorkist victory by the ruthless and unsatisfied ambition of Richard.

Even though it can stand (and be performed) entirely on its own, *Richard III* may be regarded as the fourth part of a tetralogy, for it picks up directly from the turbulent events depicted in *Richard Duke of York* and, more particularly, from the project Richard announces in a long soliloquy. He declares that since nature has seen fit to deform his body and so exclude him from sensual pleasures, he will instead pursue the crown. "I can add colours to the chameleon," he boasts, "change shapes with Proteus for advantages, / And set the murderous Machiavel to school" (*Richard Duke of York* 3.2.191–93). Here Shakespeare is beginning to psychologize the machiavel, to provide inner motives for his violent ambition and his compulsive shape changing. *Richard III* continues and intensifies this process: as his opening soliloquy suggests, Richard feels that from birth he has been cruelly cheated by dissembling nature. Deprived of the normal satisfactions of nurturing and kindness—it is as if his mother's womb itself had rejected him—he tries to find compensatory satisfaction in cruelty and dissembling of his own. He seeks not only vengeance against an unloving world but also the pleasure of cherishing himself. Yet at the end, in a vigorous if crude moment of self-analysis, he discovers that even self-love eludes him: "I love myself. Wherefore? . . . O no, alas, I rather hate myself" (5.5.141–43).

Richard's self-hatred is psychologically revealing—evidently, he has internalized the loathing that he inspires in virtually everyone around him—but it is not simply generated from within: there is, the play's characters continually imply, a divinely sanctioned, objective moral order independent of both individuals and society, and by the fixed norms of this order Richard *is* hateful. It is possible for villains like Richard or the murderers of Clarence to close their ears to the admonitions of conscience, but all human actions are part of a larger design and will ultimately be judged by a heavenly power. From this higher perspective, Richard's deformity is less the *cause* of his evil nature than its *sign*. Similarly, the ghosts in Act 5 are not merely psychological projections but metaphysical emissaries. The dead do not simply rot and disappear, nor do they survive only in the memories and dreams of the living: they are an ineradicable presence, a part of the structure of reality, an uncanny age group capable of blessing and cursing. Richard tries to shake off their condemnation, as earlier he had jauntily deflected Margaret's elaborate curse, but their words bring beads of sweat to his trembling flesh. For while he may tell himself that his victims' words are merely the impotent weapons of the powerless, he cannot escape the play's pervasive sense that there is something eerie and disturbing about curses, as if through incantatory verbal ritual they magically touch the hidden order of things.

Despite Richard's disruptive mockery and unceremonious violence, an atmosphere of ritual lingers over much of *Richard III*, tingeing the rhetorically elaborate expressions of grief and

Henry VII. Portrait by Michael Sittow (1505).

"For they account his head upon the bridge" (3.2.67). London Bridge adorned with the heads of traitors. From Claes Jansz. Visscher, *Londinum florentissima Britanniae urbs* (1625).

anger, solemnizing formal ceremonies, and shaping the perceptions of the guilt-ridden characters. Although the play gives us historical figures with psychological motivations and political stratagems, often we seem less in the secular world of disenchanted politics than in the world of classical tragedy or medieval rite. Thus, for example, Clarence's terrible nightmare just before his murder recalls the hell of the Roman playwright Seneca and, still more, the hell of fourteenth-century Christian painting, with its howling fiends and damned souls. Clarence is haunted by the sense of an unappeasable God preparing to punish him for his crimes, and his dream discloses what he does not yet consciously know: that the agent of divine retribution is his own brother, Richard.

This ritual process—the inexorable working out, through the agency of Richard, of retributive justice or (as ancient tragedians personified it) Nemesis—is best conveyed perhaps by the chorus of grief-crazed women, above all by old Queen Margaret, who identifies Richard as "hell's black intelligencer" (4.4.71), or secret agent. In a series of stiff antiphonal laments (4.4.35ff.), Margaret (the widow of the slain Henry VI), Queen Elizabeth (the widow of Edward IV), and the Duchess of York (the widowed mother of Edward and his brothers, including Richard) tease out the strict eye-for-an-eye logic of the action. And at one startling moment, Richard himself comes close to acknowledging his role within this scheme: he likens himself to "the formal Vice, Iniquity" (3.1.82).

The character called the Vice is an inheritance of the medieval morality play: the busy enemy of mankind, the Vice was at once the agent of hell and the tool of divine providence, a master plotter and a puppet in a play that is not of his own making. Yet this fixed place in the divine plan did not preclude his acquiring an extraordinary theatrical power and resourcefulness, qualities that Shakespeare would later exploit in characters as different (and as magnificent) as Falstaff and Iago. Shakespeare constructs Richard out of many elements in the Vice tradition: a jaunty use of asides, a delight in sharing his schemes with the audience, a grotesque appearance, a penchant for disguise, a manic energy and humor, and a wickedly engaging ability to defer though not finally to escape well-deserved punishment. Richard's own allusion to the Vice calls attention to yet another element, a skill in playing with the doubleness of words and exploiting the slipperiness of language: "Thus like the formal Vice, Iniquity, / I moralize two meanings in one word" (3.1.82–83). *Richard III* puts the demonic master of this vicious skill on display and, in the end, stages his destruction: in a sense, the ritual that lingers over the play is an exorcism.

But, of course, *Richard III* is not in fact a ritual, and Shakespeare's subtle blending of psychological, metaphysical, and political perspectives carefully suspends any determination of their relative significance in the events he dramatizes. The psychological development of Richard is arrested by the intimation that psychology is itself the tool of a supernatural scheme; the supernatural is subverted (at least until the ghost scene) by the Machiavellian subordination of religion to power politics; but power politics is itself undermined by the suggestion that individuals act in the grip not of rational calculation but of psychological pressures and passions over which they have little or no control. The complex interplay of forces is reflected perhaps in an ambiguity about the play's genre: first appearing in print as *The Tragedy of King Richard the Third*, it was rechristened in the First Folio as one of Shakespeare's history plays, *The Life & Death of Richard the Third*.

That these multiple perspectives do not simply cancel each other out is the result of the extraordinary theatrical force of Richard himself. Only *Hamlet*, of all Shakespeare's plays, is comparably dominated by a single character, and only *Macbeth* is comparably structured around an evil hero. (The villains Richard most anticipates—Philip the Bastard in *King John*, Don John in *Much Ado About Nothing*, Iago in *Othello*, and Edmund in *King Lear*—are all at varying degrees of distance from the main protagonist.) Without for a moment concealing from the audience Richard's appalling, monstrous evil, Shakespeare makes his villain immensely captivating. In large part, his allure derives from what Keats called the "gusto," the overwhelming liveliness, of Shakespeare's characters: "Your eyes drop millstones when fools' eyes fall tears," says Richard to the murderers; "I like you, lads" (1.3.351–52). The startling frankness of this villainy has a comic charge, a charge renewed in the open wickedness of his plans for unsuspecting Hastings—"Chop off his head" (3.1.190)—or for the innocent young princes: "I wish the bastards dead" (4.2.19). There is gusto in Richard's slyness as well as in his frankness, a slyness that also is often comic: "So wise so young, they say, do never live long" (3.1.79).

The allure of such moments seems to be bound up with the allure of the theater itself, with its capacity for emotional intensification, surprise, deception, and heightened energy. The religious enemies of the theater in Shakespeare's age charged that this energy was essentially erotic—the playhouse, they complained, aroused sexual desire— and before dismissing their charges as preposterous, we might recall the comic anecdote from John Manningham's diary with which this introduction began. Shakespeare himself in *Richard III* seems to play with the seductive power of theatrical performance in the bizarre scene in which Richard successfully courts Lady Anne over the body of her father-in-law, the King, whom he has murdered: "Was ever woman in this humour wooed?" Richard exults; "Was ever woman in this humour won?" (1.2.215–16). Richard's wooing has nothing to do with tenderness, affection, sympathy, or even physical attraction; we witness an aggressive male assault upon Lady Anne's rooted, eloquently expressed, and eminently justified fear and loathing. Here, as elsewhere, Richard gets what he wants because he possesses greater power to control the scenario: more than Anne, more than anyone, he knows how to initiate action, conceal motives, threaten, intimidate, and hurt. He has killed Anne's husband as well as her father-in-law; he will, when she has served his purpose, kill Anne too. Anne knows this well enough—"Ill rest betide the chamber where thou liest" (1.2.112)—but she virtually invents uncertainties to mask the calculating murderousness she herself has perceived with cold clarity: "I would I knew thy heart," she muses, seconds after she has thoroughly inventoried Richard's villainous heart (1.2.180).

Anne is shallow, corruptible, naively ambitious, and, above all, frightened—all qualities that help to account for her spectacular surrender—but the scene's theatrical power rests less upon a depiction of her character than upon the spectacle of Richard's restless aggression transformed during the rapid-fire exchange of one-liners (called in rhetoric *stichomythia*) into a perverse form of sexual provocation and of Anne's verbal violence transformed, in spite of itself, into an erotic response. In light of this transformation, the misshapen Richard's celebration of his sexual attractiveness—

> I do mistake my person all this while.
> Upon my life she finds, although I cannot,
> Myself to be a marv'lous proper man—

is not wholly ironic, even if he himself thinks it is (1.2.239–50).

Eros has not been excluded from Richard's career; it has found a new and compelling form in his energetic, witty, and murderous chafing against the obstacles in his path. These obstacles are not simply set in opposition to his desire; rather they virtually constitute it, for it is the extent of his distance from power that generates Richard's craving for it. His politics, and hence the sexuality implied by that politics, is transgressive; it thrives on the violation of social and natural bonds. His is the psychology of the rapist, and the character in Shakespeare closest to Richard III is the rapist Tarquin (in *The Rape of Lucrece*), whose lust is excited precisely by the barriers he is forced to overcome. This chafing structure is why the violent verbal assaults upon Richard, most intense from the women in the play, seem only to intensify his aggressive energies. It is perhaps also why Richard seems to lose much of his erotic power as soon as he has established himself on the throne. When the obstacles in his path to the crown have been removed, when there is no legitimate authority to transgress, the erotic quality of his ambition immediately begins to wane.

The play has allowed Richard to be a perverse erotic champion—a role probably possible only in this highly theatrical vision of history—but the desire he embodies cannot be integrated into any viable social or natural order; nor does it constitute a coherent, stable inner life. By the play's end, he seems a hollow man, a set of theatrical masks that project grotesque shadows upon the world. Fittingly, when "shadows," in the form of those he has murdered, return to terrify him, he can only express his fear in histrionic terms, staging a miniature dialogue with himself and then imagining his conscience as the audience, with its thousand tongues condemning him for a villain.

Richard's manifest theatricality is only the extreme form of a theatricality diffused throughout the play. Virtually all of the speeches—lamentation, cursing, debate, persuasion—are cast as self-conscious performances: "What means this scene of rude impatience?" asks the Duchess of York; Queen Elizabeth replies, "To mark an act of tragic violence" (2.2.38–39). Moreover, there is a pervasive sense that the characters exist as figures in someone else's play: through most of the performance, they are figures, without knowing it, in Richard's play, but Richard himself is a figure in another play, larger than himself. That larger play is at once the drama of history, scripted (as Tudor ideology claimed) by God, and the historical drama or tragedy, scripted by Shakespeare. If the script obliges all of the characters to display the power of divine providence, it obliges them at the same time to display the power of the theater. For if the stage pays homage to the state, it also makes the state into a histrionic spectacle on the public stage. *Richard III* manages to imply that the whole vast enterprise of Tudor power exists to make this play, and the theater in which it is performed, possible.

STEPHEN GREENBLATT

TEXTUAL NOTE

Richard III first appeared in quarto (Q1) in 1597, without the playwright's name but with a very full title page:

> THE TRAGEDY OF King Richard the third. Containing, His treacherous Plots against his brother Clarence: the pittiefull murther of his iunocent nephewes: his tyrannicall vsurpation: with the whole course of his detested life, and most deserued death. As it hath beene lately Acted by the Right honourable the Lord Chamberlaine his seruants AT LONDON Printed by Valentine Sims, for Andrew Wise, dwelling in Paules Chu[r]chyard, at the Signe of the Angell. 1597.

The play proved to be a popular one: so much so that five more quarto versions came out before the appearance of the First Folio (F) in 1623. These quarto editions (Q2–Q6) can claim no textual authority, because of their means of composition; each was based on the text of the one immediately preceding it. Each not only carried forward, therefore, the accumulated errors of its predecessors but added some of its own. The main editorial questions revolve, then, about the authority of, and the relationship between, Q1 and F.

Certainly the quarto text influenced F. But the hundreds of differences between the two suggest that a further source, an independent manuscript, was also used in the construction of F. The Oxford editor Gary Taylor believes that this manuscript was probably a transcript, presumably done by a scribe, of Shakespeare's "foul papers," that is, a version of the play in Shakespeare's own hand, with whatever additions, corrections, and revisions he may have inserted in the course of its composition.

It appears that neither Q nor F derives directly from Shakespeare's own manuscript. It has, however, been proposed that Q, the shorter text, might represent a first draft of the play. Gary Taylor rejects this hypothesis. In his view, Q is a "bad" Quarto—that is, one reconstructed from memory of the play as performed. If so, it is a surprisingly thorough reconstruction, carried out, probably, not by one or two renegade players of minor roles but by Shakespeare's company itself, or rather by those members to hand when the reconstructed text was being written down. Some part of the company on tour in the provinces, for example, could have found itself without a prompt copy of *Richard III*. A text hurriedly assembled in such circumstances might be substantially complete, except for gaps in the minor roles, which would have been played by hired men. Such gaps, showing up as omissions and textual variants, do in fact occur in the quarto version of the play and therefore lend support to Taylor's theory. Given that the passages Q omits tend to slow down the dramatic action and that its only substantial additional passage is a particularly impressive one (the "clock" dialogue, 4.2.101–20), it seems to follow that Q is a later text—one more theatrically attuned, one trimmed of some superfluous bulk. Hence, Oxford adopts a substantial number of the quarto variants.

Other omissions appear to show the effects of censorship. The exclamation "Zounds" ("by His wounds") appears four times in Q but not in F, as does a reference to "Christ's dear blood shed for our grievous sins." The name "God," however, appears frequently in both texts. Political rather than purely religious concerns seem to have caused a further omission. Hastings's lines at the conclusion of 3.4, in which he prophesies "the fearful'st time" in a coming "miserable England," could well be seen as unsettling to an audience that laid great store by prophecy. These lines do not appear in F. But what of the inclusion only in Q of the "clock" dialogue mentioned above? In fact, this seeming anomaly (it is the only major passage not in F) adds weight to the early F hypothesis. The very singular nature of this passage leads Oxford to see it as "an inspired afterthought." No political considerations—far less theatrical ones—could justify its deletion. We might also note that in what was an already very long play, Shakespeare might have been more inclined to deletion than to addition.

F, we can see, is closer to its sources, Halle and Holinshed, and is manifestly the superior text. Many passages are better crafted in meter and meaning than their quarto counterparts. F, then, is the control text for substantive readings. Recalling, however, that the quarto reconstruction would have taken place at a time when Shakespeare himself was active in the company and may have had a hand in revision for the stage, an unusually large number of departures from the control text have been retained. The reader is thus presented, we hope, with the play in its most fully realized theatrical form.

In this edition, Folio passages that were omitted from Q and relegated in the *Oxford Shakespeare* to an appendix are printed inset and in italics.

SELECTED BIBLIOGRAPHY

Burnett, Mark Thornton. "'Monsters' and 'Molas': Body Politics in *Richard III*." *Constructing "Monsters" in Shakespearean Drama and Early Modern Culture*. New York: Palgrave Macmillan, 2002. 65–94. Fluctuating between images of monsters shaped and unfinished, Richard represents the anxieties of a barren Tudor line seeking new political form.

Carroll, William. " 'The Form of Law': Ritual and Succession in *Richard III*." *True Rites and Maimed Rites: Ritual and Anti-Ritual in Shakespeare and His Age*. Ed. Linda Woodbridge and Edward Berry. Urbana: University of Illinois Press, 1992. 203–19.

Howard, Jean E., and Phyllis Rackin. "Weak Kings, Warrior Women, and the Assault on Dynastic Authority." *Engendering a Nation: A Feminist Account of Shakespeare's English Histories*. London: Routledge, 1997. 100–18. Shifting from history to tragedy, *Richard III* ennobles and disempowers women as passive emblems of pity, while Richard appropriates their seductive theatrical energy.

Hunter, Robert G. *Shakespeare and the Mystery of God's Judgments*. Athens: University of Georgia Press, 1976. Poised between Augustinian and Calvinist conceptions of God's will, Richard's seemingly contradictory status as a tragic figures acting in a providential frame generates the complexity of Shakespeare's art.

Marche, Stephen. "Mocking Dead Bones: Historical Memory and the Theater of the Dead in *Richard III*." *Comparative Drama* 37.1 (2003): 37–57. The play's ambivalent generic status—between tragedy and history—is reflected in Richard's tragic inability to overcome history by silencing the dead who challenge his shaping narrative.

Moulton, Ian Frederick. " 'A Monster Great Deformed': The Unruly Masculinities of *Richard III*." *Shakespeare Quarterly* 47.3 (1996): 251–68. Shakespeare both critiques and celebrates masculine aggression, revealing the incoherence of masculinity as an early modern cultural concept.

Rossiter, A. P. *Angel with Horns, and Other Shakespeare Lectures*. Ed. Graham Storey. New York: Theatre Arts Books, 1961. Richard's demonic appeal as God's avenging angel makes the play less moral history than comic history built on paradoxical irony and inversion.

Targoff, Ramie. " 'Dirty' Amens: Devotion, Applause, and Consent in *Richard III*." *Renaissance Drama* 31 (2002): 61–84. The question of what constitutes true consent on the part of the English toward their King can be tracked through the play's odd use of the liturgical term "Amen," which both Richard and Richmond solicit in different ways from their audiences in order to legitimate their rule.

Torey, Michael. " 'The Plain Devil and Dissembling Looks': Ambivalent Physiognomy and Shakespeare's *Richard III*." *English Literary Renaissance* 30.2 (2000): 123–53. Richard's ability to deceive his victims and manipulate his corporal image complicates the seeming intelligibility of his deformity.

Wheeler, Richard P. "History, Character, and Conscience in *Richard III*." *Comparative Drama* 5 (1971–72): 301–21. The play dramatizes the struggle between divine and profane views of history, between conscience and egoism, that troubled the late Elizabethan era.

FILMS

Richard III. 1912. Dir. André Calmettes and James Keane. USA. 55 min. The silent film version, with Robert Gemp as Edward IV and Frederick Warde as Richard.

Richard III. 1955. Dir. Laurence Olivier. UK. 161 min. A deformed and morally twisted yet seductively charismatic Richard, played by Olivier, with John Gielgud as Clarence.

Richard III. 1995. Dir. Richard Loncraine. UK/USA. 104 min. Richard as a sly and ruthless fascist dictator in a stylishly corrupt 1930s Britain. Ian McKellan is Richard, Robert Downey, Jr. is Lord Rivers.

Looking for Richard. 1996. Dir. Al Pacino. USA. 111 min. Part adaptation, part behind-the-scenes documentary about bringing the Shakespeare play to modern audiences. With Pacino playing Richard and Kevin Spacey playing Buckingham.

The Tragedy of
King Richard the Third

THE PERSONS OF THE PLAY

KING EDWARD IV

DUCHESS OF YORK, his mother

PRINCE EDWARD

Richard, the young Duke of YORK } his sons

George, Duke of CLARENCE

RICHARD, Duke of GLOUCESTER, later KING RICHARD III } his brothers

Clarence's SON

Clarence's DAUGHTER

QUEEN ELIZABETH, King Edward's wife

Anthony Woodeville, Earl RIVERS, her brother

Marquis of DORSET }
Lord GRAY } her sons

Sir Thomas VAUGHAN

GHOST OF KING HENRY VI

QUEEN MARGARET, his widow

GHOST OF PRINCE EDWARD, his son

LADY ANNE, Prince Edward's widow

William, LORD HASTINGS, Lord Chamberlain

Lord STANLEY, Earl of Derby, his friend

HENRY EARL OF RICHMOND, later KING HENRY VII, Stanley's son-in-law

Earl of OXFORD }
Sir James BLUNT } Richmond's followers
Sir Walter HERBERT }

Duke of BUCKINGHAM }
Duke of NORFOLK }
Sir Richard RATCLIFFE }
Sir William CATESBY } Richard Gloucester's followers
Sir James TYRRELL }
Two MURDERERS }
A PAGE }

CARDINAL

BISHOP OF ELY

John, a PRIEST

SIR CHRISTOPHER, a Priest

Sir Robert BRACKENBURY, Lieutenant of the Tower of London

Lord MAYOR of London

A SCRIVENER

Hastings, a PURSUIVANT

SHERIFF

Aldermen and Citizens

Attendants, two bishops, messengers, soldiers

1.1

Enter RICHARD *Duke of* GLOUCESTER[1]

RICHARD GLOUCESTER   Now is the winter of our discontent
　　Made glorious summer by this son of York;[2]
　　And all the clouds that loured° upon our house°　　　　　　*glowered / family*
　　In the deep bosom of the ocean buried.
5　　Now are our brows bound with victorious wreaths,
　　Our bruisèd arms° hung up for monuments,°　　　　　　*armor / memorials*
　　Our stern alarums° changed to merry meetings,　　　　　　*call to arms*
　　Our dreadful marches to delightful measures.°　　　　　　*dances*
　　Grim-visaged war hath smoothed his wrinkled front,°　　　　　　*forehead*
10　　And now—instead of mounting barbèd° steeds　　　　　　*armored*
　　To fright the souls of fearful adversaries—
　　He capers[3] nimbly in a lady's chamber
　　To the lascivious pleasing of a lute.
　　But I, that am not shaped for sportive° tricks　　　　　　*amorous*
15　　Nor made to court an amorous looking-glass,
　　I that am rudely stamped[4] and want° love's majesty　　　　　　*lack*
　　To strut before a wanton ambling nymph,
　　I that am curtailed of this fair proportion,°　　　　　　*shape*
　　Cheated of feature° by dissembling nature,　　　　　　*good appearance*
20　　Deformed, unfinished, sent before my time
　　Into this breathing world scarce half made up—
　　And that so lamely and unfashionable°　　　　　　*badly formed*
　　That dogs bark at me as I halt° by them—　　　　　　*limp*
　　Why, I in this weak piping[5] time of peace
25　　Have no delight to pass away the time,
　　Unless to spy my shadow in the sun
　　And descant on° mine own deformity.　　　　　　*remark upon*
　　And therefore since I cannot prove° a lover　　　　　　*prove to be*
　　To entertain these fair well-spoken days,
30　　I am determinèd° to prove a villain　　　　　　*resolved; fated*
　　And hate the idle pleasures of these days.
　　Plots have I laid, inductions[6] dangerous,
　　By drunken prophecies, libels and dreams
　　To set my brother Clarence[7] and the King
35　　In deadly hate the one against the other.
　　And if King Edward be as true and just
　　As I am subtle false and treacherous,
　　This day should Clarence closely be mewed up°　　　　　　*caged (like a hawk)*
　　About a prophecy which says that 'G'[8]
40　　Of Edward's heirs the murderer shall be.

　　　　Enter [George Duke of] CLARENCE, *guarded, and [Sir
　　　　Robert]* BRACKENBURY

　　Dive, thoughts, down to my soul: here Clarence comes.
　　Brother, good day. What means this armèd guard
　　That waits upon your grace?

1.1 Location: A street in London.
1. Pronounced "Gloster."
2. *son of York*: Edward IV, son of Richard, Duke of York; with wordplay on Edward's emblem, a sun in splendor.
3. In court dances, men often made "capers," or showy leaps; also suggests a sexual escapade.
4 Roughly, imperfectly shaped (alluding to the stamping of a coin with an image).
5. Characterized by the music of a peaceful shepherd's

flute: shrill-voiced, like women or children.
6. Initial moves, prologues.
7. George, Duke of Clarence, Richard, Duke of Gloucester, and King Edward IV were brothers; Clarence, being older than Richard, would become King if Edward and his heirs died.
8. Which Edward interprets as "George," but which could—and does—mean "Gloucester."

CLARENCE His majesty,
Tend'ring° my person's safety, hath appointed   *Caring about*
45 This conduct° to convey me to the Tower.⁹   *escort*
RICHARD GLOUCESTER Upon what cause?
CLARENCE   Because my name is George.
RICHARD GLOUCESTER Alack, my lord, that fault is none of yours.
He should for that commit your godfathers.¹
Belike° his majesty hath some intent   *Probably*
50 That you should be new-christened in the Tower.
But what's the matter, Clarence? May I know?
CLARENCE Yea, Richard, when I know—for I protest
As yet I do not. But as I can learn
He hearkens after prophecies and dreams,
55 And from the cross-row° plucks the letter 'G'   *alphabet*
And says a wizard told him that by 'G'
His issue° disinherited should be.   *children*
And for my name of George begins with 'G',
It follows in his thought that I am he.
60 These, as I learn, and suchlike toys° as these,   *trifles*
Hath moved his highness to commit° me now.   *arrest*
RICHARD GLOUCESTER Why, this it is when men are ruled by women.
'Tis not the King that sends you to the Tower;
My Lady Gray,² his wife—Clarence, 'tis she
65 That tempts him to this harsh extremity.
Was it not she, and that good man of worship³
Anthony Woodeville her brother there,
That made him send Lord Hastings to the Tower,
From whence this present day he is delivered?
70 We are not safe, Clarence; we are not safe.
CLARENCE By heaven, I think there is no man secure
But the Queen's kindred, and night-walking heralds°   *secret go-betweens*
That trudge betwixt the King and Mrs Shore.⁴
Heard ye not what an humble suppliant
75 Lord Hastings was for his delivery?
RICHARD GLOUCESTER Humbly complaining to her deity⁵
Got my Lord Chamberlain⁶ his liberty.
I'll tell you what: I think it is our way,°   *strategy*
If we will keep in favour with the King,
80 To be her men and wear her livery.⁷
The jealous, o'erworn widow⁸ and herself,°   *(Jane Shore)*
Since that our brother dubbed them⁹ gentlewomen,
Are mighty gossips° in our monarchy.   *busybodies*
BRACKENBURY I beseech your graces both to pardon me.
85 His majesty hath straitly given in charge°   *has strictly ordered*

9. Tower of London, used to house noble prisoners as well as (in Elizabethan England) traitors and political agitators.
1. The godfather was responsible for the naming of a newborn child.
2. A sarcastic reference to the Queen, widow of Sir John Gray before her marriage to the King. Her maiden name was Elizabeth Woodeville (also Woodville).
3. Honor (here, a sarcastic phrase, more appropriate to a solid, middle-class citizen than to the Queen's brother, Anthony Woodeville, who succeeded his father as Earl Rivers).
4. Jane Shore, wife of a London goldsmith. Her liaison with Edward was notorious. *Mrs:* Mistress (here in both the polite and the abusive sense).
5. Jane Shore (ironically, by analogy with "her majesty").
6. Hastings's title. According to Shakespeare's sources, Jane Shore became his mistress when her affair with the King ended.
7. Servants ("men") in noble households wore the colors ("livery") of the family.
8. The Queen, a widow before she married Edward IV. *o'erworn:* faded.
9. Invested them with the status of (usually used of knights). Richard grossly exaggerates the lowly status of the Queen's family before her marriage.

That no man shall have private conference,
Of what degree soever,[1] with your brother.

RICHARD GLOUCESTER Even so. An't° please your worship, Brackenbury,   *If it*
You may partake of anything we say.

90 We speak no treason, man. We say the King
Is wise and virtuous, and his noble Queen
Well struck° in years, fair, and not jealous.   *advanced*
We say that Shore's wife hath a pretty foot,
A cherry lip,

95 A bonny eye, a passing° pleasing tongue,   *an exceedingly*
And that the Queen's kin are made gentlefolks.
How say you, sir? Can you deny all this?

BRACKENBURY With this, my lord, myself have naught° to do.   *nothing*

RICHARD GLOUCESTER Naught[2] to do with Mrs Shore? I tell thee, fellow:

100 He that doth naught with her—excepting one—
Were best to do it secretly alone.

BRACKENBURY What one, my lord?

RICHARD GLOUCESTER Her husband, knave. Wouldst thou betray me?

BRACKENBURY I beseech your grace to pardon me, and do withal°   *moreover*

105 Forbear your conference with the noble Duke.

CLARENCE We know thy charge, Brackenbury, and will obey.

RICHARD GLOUCESTER We are the Queen's abjects,° and must obey.   *base subjects*
Brother, farewell. I will unto the King,
And whatsoe'er you will employ me in—

110 Were it to call King Edward's widow° 'sister'—   *(Queen Elizabeth)*
I will perform it to enfranchise° you.   *free*
Meantime, this deep disgrace in brotherhood
Touches me dearer[3] than you can imagine.

CLARENCE I know it pleaseth neither of us well.

115 RICHARD GLOUCESTER Well, your imprisonment shall not be long.
I will deliver you or lie for you.[4]
Meantime, have patience.

CLARENCE   I must perforce.° Farewell.   *of necessity*
        Exeunt CLARENCE[, BRACKENBURY, *and guard, to the Tower*]

RICHARD GLOUCESTER Go tread the path that thou shalt ne'er return.
Simple plain Clarence, I do love thee so

120 That I will shortly send thy soul to heaven,
If heaven will take the present at° our hands.   *from*
But who comes here? The new-delivered° Hastings?   *newly released*
        Enter LORD HASTINGS [*from the Tower*]

LORD HASTINGS Good time of day unto my gracious lord.

RICHARD GLOUCESTER As much unto my good Lord Chamberlain.

125 Well are you welcome to the open air.
How hath your lordship brooked° imprisonment?   *tolerated*

LORD HASTINGS With patience, noble lord, as prisoners must.
But I shall live, my lord, to give them thanks
That were the cause of my imprisonment.

130 RICHARD GLOUCESTER No doubt, no doubt—and so shall Clarence too,
For they that were your enemies are his,
And have prevailed as much on him as you.

---

1. *no . . . soever*: that is, despite Richard's high rank
("degree"), he must not speak with the prisoner.
2. Wickedness; here, specifically sexual intercourse.
3. Wounds me more, but also (as a hidden meaning),

implicates me more.
4. In prison, in place of Clarence (with a pun on "lie"
as "tell falsehoods about"). "Deliver" and "lie for" rhyme.

LORD HASTINGS   More pity that the eagles should be mewed
 While kites° and buzzards prey at liberty.   *scavenger birds*
135 RICHARD GLOUCESTER   What news abroad?°   *circulating*
LORD HASTINGS   No news so bad abroad as this at home:
 The King is sickly, weak, and melancholy,
 And his physicians fear° him mightily.   *fear for*
RICHARD GLOUCESTER   Now by Saint Paul, that news is bad indeed.
140 O he hath kept an evil diet° long,   *way of life*
 And overmuch consumed his royal person.[5]
 'Tis very grievous to be thought upon.
 Where is he? In his bed?
LORD HASTINGS   He is.
RICHARD GLOUCESTER   Go you before and I will follow you.
                Exit HASTINGS
145 He cannot live, I hope, and must not die
 Till George be packed with post-haste° up to heaven. *by express*
 I'll in to urge his hatred more to Clarence,
 With lies well steeled° with weighty arguments. *made strong*
 And if I fail not in my deep intent,
150 Clarence hath not another day to live—
 Which done, God take King Edward to his mercy
 And leave the world for me to bustle in.
 For then I'll marry Warwick's youngest daughter.[6]
 What though I killed her husband and her father?[7]
155 The readiest way to make the wench amends
 Is to become her husband and her father,
 The which will I: not all so much for love,
 As for another secret close intent,°   *private purpose*
 By marrying her, which I must reach unto.
160 But yet I run before my horse to market.
 Clarence still breathes, Edward still lives and reigns;
 When they are gone, then must I count my gains. *Exit*

1.2

*Enter [gentlemen, bearing] the corpse of [King] Henry VI
[in an open coffin], with halberdiers[1] to guard it,*
 LADY ANNE *being the mourner*
LADY ANNE   Set down, set down your honourable load,
 If honour may be shrouded in a hearse,°   *an open coffin*
 Whilst I a while obsequiously° lament   *mournfully*
 Th'untimely fall of virtuous Lancaster.[2]
 [They set the coffin down]
5 Poor key-cold[3] figure of a holy king,
 Pale ashes of the house of Lancaster,
 Thou bloodless remnant of that royal blood:
 Be it lawful that I invocate thy ghost[4]
 To hear the lamentations of poor Anne,
10 Wife to thy Edward, to thy slaughtered son,

---

5. And has been weakened by extravagant living.
6. Lady Anne Neville, who had been betrothed (but not married) to Edward, Prince of Wales, the son of King Henry VI. Shakespeare, however, writes of Anne as Edward's widow.
7. *her father*: Henry VI (father-in-law).
1.2 Location: A street in London.
1. Men carrying halberds (a spearlike weapon with a

blade as well as a point).
2. Henry VI, of the house of Lancaster, was deposed and murdered by the Yorkists. The dynastic quarrel dates from the deposition of Richard II and is dramatized in Shakespeare's three *Henry VI* plays.
3. Proverbial for "cold as death."
4. Conjuring of spirits was generally condemned. *invocate*: invoke.

Stabbed by the selfsame hand that made these wounds.
Lo, in these windows⁵ that let forth thy life,
I pour the helpless° balm of my poor eyes.   *useless*
O cursèd be the hand that made these holes,
15 Cursèd the blood that let this blood from hence,
Cursèd the heart that had the heart to do it.
More direful hap betide° that hated wretch   *fate befall*
That makes us wretched by the death of thee
Than I can wish to wolves, to spiders, toads,
20 Or any creeping venomed thing that lives.
If ever he have child, abortive° be it,   *incompletely formed*
Prodigious,° and untimely brought to light,   *Monstrous*
Whose ugly and unnatural aspect°   *appearance*
May fright the hopeful mother at the view,
25 And that be heir to his unhappiness.⁶
If ever he have wife, let her be made
More miserable by the death of him
Than I am made by my young lord and thee.⁷—
Come now towards Chertsey° with your holy load,   *monastery near London*
30 Taken from Paul's⁸ to be interrèd there,
        [*The gentlemen lift the coffin*]
And still as° you are weary of this weight   *Whenever*
Rest you, whiles I lament King Henry's corpse.
        Enter RICHARD *Duke of* GLOUCESTER
RICHARD GLOUCESTER [*to the gentlemen*]   Stay, you that bear
        the corpse, and set it down.
LADY ANNE   What black magician conjures up this fiend
35   To stop devoted charitable deeds?
RICHARD GLOUCESTER [*to the gentlemen*]   Villains,° set down   *Scoundrels; peasants*
        the corpse, or by Saint Paul
        I'll make a corpse of him that disobeys.
HALBERDIER   My lord, stand back and let the coffin pass.
RICHARD GLOUCESTER   Unmannered dog, stand thou when I command.
40   Advance⁹ thy halberd higher than my breast,
        Or by Saint Paul I'll strike thee to my foot
        And spurn° upon thee, beggar, for thy boldness.   *kick*
        [*They set the coffin down*]
LADY ANNE [*to gentlemen and halberdiers*]   What, do you tremble?
        Are you all afraid?
        Alas, I blame you not, for you are mortal,
45   And mortal eyes cannot endure the devil.—
        Avaunt,° thou dreadful minister of hell.   *Be gone*
        Thou hadst but power over his mortal body;
        His soul thou canst not have; therefore be gone.
RICHARD GLOUCESTER   Sweet saint, for charity be not so cursed.° *bad-tempered*
50 LADY ANNE   Foul devil, for God's sake hence and trouble us not,
        For thou hast made the happy earth thy hell,
        Filled it with cursing cries and deep exclaims.
        If thou delight to view thy heinous deeds,
        Behold this pattern° of thy butcheries.—   *example*
55   O gentlemen, see, see! Dead Henry's wounds

---

5. Stab wounds (possibly referring to the custom of opening the windows to let a dying soul pass).
6. Evil nature; ill fortune.
7. By the deaths of Prince Edward and King Henry VI.
8. St. Paul's, cathedral of the City of London.
9. Raise upright (rather than hold it pointing at Richard).

Ope their congealèd mouths and bleed afresh.[1]—
Blush, blush, thou lump of foul deformity,
For 'tis thy presence that ex-hales° this blood   *calls forth*
From cold and empty veins where no blood dwells.
60   Thy deed, inhuman and unnatural,
Provokes this deluge supernatural.[2]
O God, which this blood mad'st, revenge his death.
O earth, which this blood drink'st, revenge his death.
Either heav'n with lightning strike the murd'rer dead,
65   Or earth gape open wide and eat him quick°   *alive*
As thou dost swallow up this good king's blood,
Which his hell-governed arm hath butcherèd.
RICHARD GLOUCESTER   Lady, you know no rules of charity,
Which renders good for bad, blessings for curses.
70   LADY ANNE   Villain, thou know'st no law of God nor man.
No beast so fierce but knows some touch of pity.
RICHARD GLOUCESTER   But I know none, and therefore am no beast.
LADY ANNE   O wonderful, when devils tell the truth![3]
RICHARD GLOUCESTER   More wonderful, when angels are so angry.
75   Vouchsafe,° divine perfection of a woman,   *Grant*
Of these supposèd crimes to give me leave
By circumstance° but to acquit myself.   *detailed argument*
LADY ANNE   Vouchsafe, diffused[4] infection of a man,
Of these known evils but to give me leave
80   By circumstance t'accuse thy cursèd self.
RICHARD GLOUCESTER   Fairer than tongue can name thee, let me have
Some patient leisure to excuse myself.
LADY ANNE   Fouler than heart can think thee, thou canst make
No excuse current° but to hang thyself.   *valid*
85   RICHARD GLOUCESTER   By such despair I should accuse myself.
LADY ANNE   And by despairing shalt thou stand excused,
For doing worthy vengeance on thyself
That didst unworthy slaughter upon others.
RICHARD GLOUCESTER   Say that I slew them not.
LADY ANNE   Then say they were not slain.
90   But dead they are—and, devilish slave, by thee.
RICHARD GLOUCESTER   I did not kill your husband.
LADY ANNE   Why, then he is alive.
RICHARD GLOUCESTER   Nay, he is dead, and slain by Edward's hand.
LADY ANNE   In thy foul throat thou liest. Queen Margaret saw
Thy murd'rous falchion° smoking in his blood,[5]   *curved sword*
95   The which thou once didst bend against° her breast,   *turn toward*
But that thy brothers beat aside the point.
RICHARD GLOUCESTER   I was provokèd by her sland'rous tongue,
That laid their guilt upon my guiltless shoulders.
LADY ANNE   Thou wast provokèd by thy bloody mind,
100   That never dream'st on aught° but butcheries.   *anything*
Didst thou not kill this king?
RICHARD GLOUCESTER   I grant ye.

---

1. A murdered victim's wounds were supposed to bleed again in the presence of the murderer.
2. Q, F: most unnatural. The emendation underscores Anne's call (in the next line) for divine intervention.
3. That is, Richard is a devil, not man or beast.

4. Misshapen, but also an infection whose harmful effects are dispersed widely.
5. In *Richard Duke of York* (3 *Henry VI*) 5.5, King Edward stabbed the Prince first, and Richard followed.

LADY ANNE   Dost grant me, hedgehog?[6] Then God grant me, too,
Thou mayst be damnèd for that wicked deed.
O he was gentle, mild, and virtuous.

105 RICHARD GLOUCESTER   The better for the King of Heaven that hath him.

LADY ANNE   He *is* in heaven, where thou shalt never come.

RICHARD GLOUCESTER   Let him thank me that holp° that help° to send him thither,   helped
For he was fitter for that place than earth.

LADY ANNE   And thou unfit for any place but hell.

110 RICHARD GLOUCESTER   Yes, one place else, if you will hear me name it.

LADY ANNE   Some dungeon.

RICHARD GLOUCESTER   Your bedchamber.

LADY ANNE   Ill rest betide° the chamber where thou liest.   befall

RICHARD GLOUCESTER   So will it, madam, till I lie with you.

LADY ANNE   I hope so.

RICHARD GLOUCESTER   I know so. But gentle Lady Anne,
115 To leave this keen encounter of our wits
And fall something into a slower method,[7]
Is not the causer of the timeless° deaths   untimely
Of these Plantagenets,[8] Henry and Edward,
As blameful as the executioner?

120 LADY ANNE   Thou wast the cause of that accursèd effect.

RICHARD GLOUCESTER   Your beauty was the cause of that effect—
Your beauty that did haunt me in my sleep
To undertake the death of all the world
So I might live one hour in your sweet bosom.

125 LADY ANNE   If I thought that, I tell thee, homicide,°   murderer
These nails should rend that beauty from my cheeks.

RICHARD GLOUCESTER   These eyes could not endure sweet beauty's wreck.
You should not blemish it if I stood by.
As all the world is cheerèd by the sun,
130 So I by that: it is my day, my life.

LADY ANNE   Black night o'ershade thy day, and death thy life.

RICHARD GLOUCESTER   Curse not thyself, fair creature: thou art both.

LADY ANNE   I would I were, to be revenged on thee.[9]

RICHARD GLOUCESTER   It is a quarrel most unnatural,
135 To be revenged on him that loveth you.

LADY ANNE   It is a quarrel just and reasonable,
To be revenged on him that killed my husband.

RICHARD GLOUCESTER   He that bereft thee, lady, of thy husband,
Did it to help thee to a better husband.

140 LADY ANNE   His better doth not breathe upon the earth.

RICHARD GLOUCESTER   He lives that loves thee better than he° could.   (Edward)

LADY ANNE   Name him.

RICHARD GLOUCESTER   Plantagenet.

LADY ANNE   Why, that was he.

RICHARD GLOUCESTER   The selfsame name, but one of better nature.

LADY ANNE   Where is he?

RICHARD GLOUCESTER   Here.

        She spits at him

                    Why dost thou spit at me?

145 LADY ANNE   Would it were mortal poison for thy sake.

6. Term of abuse applied to someone who pays no attention to others' feelings; alluding to Richard's humped back and his heraldic badge, the boar.
7. And argue somewhat less hastily.
8. The royal house from which both Lancastrians,

including Henry and his son Edward, and Yorkists, including Richard himself, descended.
9. That is, if Anne were Richard's day and his life, she could end both and thus be revenged on him.

RICHARD GLOUCESTER   Never came poison from so sweet a place.
LADY ANNE   Never hung poison on a fouler toad.[1]
    Out of my sight! Thou dost infect mine eyes.
RICHARD GLOUCESTER   Thine eyes, sweet lady, have infected mine.
150   LADY ANNE   Would° they were basilisks[2] to strike thee dead.   *I wish that*
RICHARD GLOUCESTER   I would they were, that I might die at once,°   *once and for all*
    For now they kill me with a living death.
    Those eyes of thine from mine have drawn salt tears,
    Shamed their aspects° with store of childish drops.[3]   *appearance*
154.1   *These eyes, which never shed remorseful tear—*
          No, when my father York and Edward[4] wept
          To hear the piteous moan that Rutland[5] made
          When black-faced° Clifford shook his sword at him;   *threatening*
154.5   *Nor when thy warlike father° like a child*   *(Warwick)*
          Told the sad story of my father's death
          And twenty times made pause to sob and weep,
          That all the standers-by had wet their cheeks
          Like trees bedashed with rain. In that sad time
154.10   *My manly eyes did scorn an humble tear,*
          And what these sorrows could not thence exhale°   *draw out*
          Thy beauty hath, and made them blind with weeping.
155   I never sued° to friend nor enemy;   *petitioned*
    My tongue could never learn sweet smoothing° word;   *flattering*
    But now thy beauty is proposed my fee,°   *recompense*
    My proud heart sues and prompts my tongue to speak.
        She looks scornfully at him
    Teach not thy lip such scorn, for it was made
160   For kissing, lady, not for such contempt.
    If thy revengeful heart cannot forgive,
        [He kneels and offers her his sword]
    Lo, here I lend thee this sharp-pointed sword,
    Which if thou please to hide in this true breast
    And let the soul forth that adoreth thee,
165   I lay it naked to the deadly stroke
    And humbly beg the death upon my knee.
        He lays his breast open;° she offers° at [it] with his sword   *bare / thrusts*
    Nay, do not pause, for I did kill King Henry;
    But 'twas thy beauty that provokèd me.
    Nay, now dispatch: 'twas I that stabbed young Edward;
170   But 'twas thy heavenly face that set me on.
        She lets fall the sword
    Take up the sword again, or take up me.
LADY ANNE   Arise, dissembler.
        [He rises]
                Though I wish thy death,
    I will not be thy executioner.
RICHARD GLOUCESTER   Then bid me kill myself, and I will do it.
LADY ANNE   I have already.
175   RICHARD GLOUCESTER   That was in thy rage.
    Speak it again, and even with the word

---

1. Toads were popularly regarded as "ugly and venomous" (*As You Like It* 2.1.13).
2. Legendary monsters, supposed to kill with a glance.
3. The indented passage that follows, 154.1–154.12, appears only in F.

4. His brother, now the King.
5. Historically, Rutland was Richard's older brother. Shakespeare unhistorically makes him a child. His death is dramatized in *Richard Duke of York* 1.3–2.1.

This hand—which for thy love did kill thy love—
Shall, for thy love, kill a far truer love.
To both their deaths shalt thou be accessary.

180 LADY ANNE   I would I knew thy heart.

RICHARD GLOUCESTER   'Tis figured in my tongue.

LADY ANNE   I fear me both are false.

RICHARD GLOUCESTER   Then never man was true.

LADY ANNE   Well, well, put up your sword.

185 RICHARD GLOUCESTER   Say then my peace is made.

LADY ANNE   That shalt thou know hereafter.

RICHARD GLOUCESTER   But shall I live in hope?

LADY ANNE   All men, I hope, live so.

RICHARD GLOUCESTER   Vouchsafe° to wear this ring.   Consent

190 LADY ANNE   To take is not to give.[6]

RICHARD GLOUCESTER   Look how my ring encompasseth° thy finger;   encircles
Even so thy breast encloseth my poor heart.
Wear both of them, for both of them are thine.
And if thy poor devoted servant° may   lover
195 But beg one favour at thy gracious hand,
Thou dost confirm his happiness for ever.

LADY ANNE   What is it?

RICHARD GLOUCESTER   That it may please you leave these sad designs°   affairs
To him that hath most cause to be a mourner,
200 And presently° repair to Crosby House,[7]   at once
Where—after I have solemnly interred
At Chertsey monast'ry this noble king,
And wet his grave with my repentant tears—
I will with all expedient° duty see you.   prompt
205 For divers unknown° reasons, I beseech you   various secret
Grant me this boon.°   favor

LADY ANNE   With all my heart—and much it joys me, too,
To see you are become so penitent.
Tressell and Berkeley, go along with me.

RICHARD GLOUCESTER   Bid me farewell.

210 LADY ANNE   'Tis more than you deserve.[8]
But since you teach me how to flatter you,
Imagine I have said farewell already.   *Exeunt two with* ANNE

RICHARD GLOUCESTER   Sirs, take up the corpse.

GENTLEMAN   Towards Chertsey, noble lord?

RICHARD GLOUCESTER   No, to Blackfriars; there attend° my coming.   await
Exeunt [with] corpse. Manet° GLOUCESTER   Remains
215 Was ever woman in this humour° wooed?   mood; manner
Was ever woman in this humour won?
I'll have her, but I will not keep her long.
What, I that killed her husband and his father,
To take her in her heart's extremest hate,
220 With curses in her mouth, tears in her eyes,
The bleeding witness of my hatred by,
Having God, her conscience, and these bars° against me,   obstacles
And I no friends to back my suit withal
But the plain devil and dissembling looks—
225 And yet to win her, all the world to nothing?° Ha!   against such odds

---

6. To take your ring is not to give myself.   8. That is, to fare well is more than you deserve.
7. One of Richard's London residences.

Hath she forgot already that brave prince,
Edward her lord, whom I some three months since
Stabbed in my angry mood at Tewkesbury?
A sweeter and a lovelier gentleman,
230 Framed in the prodigality of nature,[9]
Young, valiant, wise, and no doubt right royal,
The spacious world cannot again afford°—   *provide*
And will she yet abase° her eyes on me,   *lower; humble*
That cropped the golden prime[1] of this sweet prince
235 And made her widow to a woeful bed?
On me, whose all not equals Edward's moiety?°   *half*
On me, that halts° and am misshapen thus?   *limp*
My dukedom to a beggarly *denier*,[2]
I do mistake my person all this while.
240 Upon my life she finds, although I cannot,
Myself to be a marv'lous proper° man.   *handsome*
I'll be at charges for° a looking-glass   *I'll buy*
And entertain° a score or two of tailors   *hire*
To study fashions to adorn my body.
245 Since I am crept in° favour with myself,   *into*
I will maintain it with some little cost.
But first I'll turn yon fellow in his grave,
And then return lamenting to my love.
Shine out, fair sun, till I have bought a glass,
250 That I may see my shadow as I pass.   *Exit*

1.3

Enter QUEEN [ELIZABETH], *Lord* RIVERS, [*Marquis* DORSET],
and Lord GRAY

RIVERS [*to* ELIZABETH]   Have patience, madam. There's no doubt his majesty
Will soon recover his accustomed health.
GRAY [*to* ELIZABETH]   In that you brook it ill,° it makes him worse.   *take it badly*
Therefore, for God's sake entertain good comfort,
5 And cheer his grace with quick° and merry eyes.   *lively*
QUEEN ELIZABETH   If he were dead, what would betide on° me?   *befall*
RIVERS[1]   No other harm but loss of such a lord.
QUEEN ELIZABETH   The loss of such a lord includes all harms.
GRAY   The heavens have blessed you with a goodly son
10 To be your comforter when he is gone.
QUEEN ELIZABETH   Ah, he is young, and his minority
Is put unto the trust of Richard Gloucester,
A man that loves not me—nor none of you.
RIVERS   Is it concluded° he shall be Protector?   *officially decreed*
15 QUEEN ELIZABETH   It is determined,° not concluded yet;   *decided*
But so it must be, if the King miscarry.°   *die*

Enter [*the Duke of*] BUCKINGHAM *and* [*Lord* STANLEY
Earl of] *Derby*

GRAY   Here come the Lords of Buckingham and Derby.
BUCKINGHAM [*to* ELIZABETH]   Good time of day unto your royal grace.
STANLEY [*to* ELIZABETH]   God make your majesty joyful, as you have been.

---

9. Made when nature in its gift giving was being lavish.   to: against (as in betting).
1. Springtime (Richard "cropped," or harvested,   1.3 Location: The royal palace of Westminster.
Edward's life prematurely).   1. F: Gray. Rivers's role in the conversation is far fuller
2. French coin, one-twelfth of a sou (extremely little).   in Q than in F (see lines 30, 54).

20 QUEEN ELIZABETH   The Countess Richmond,[2] good my lord of Derby,
  To your good prayer will scarcely say 'Amen'.
  Yet, Derby—notwithstanding she's your wife,
  And loves not me—be you, good lord, assured
  I hate not you for her proud arrogance.
25 STANLEY   I do beseech you, either not believe
  The envious° slanders of her false accusers   *malicious*
  Or, if she be accused on true report,
  Bear with her weakness, which I think proceeds
  From wayward° sickness, and no grounded malice.   *not easily treated*
30 RIVERS   Saw you the King today, my lord of Derby?
  STANLEY   But° now the Duke of Buckingham and I   *Just*
  Are come from visiting his majesty.
  QUEEN ELIZABETH   With likelihood of his amendment,° lords?   *recovery*
  BUCKINGHAM   Madam, good hope: his grace speaks cheerfully.
35 QUEEN ELIZABETH   God grant him health. Did you confer with him?
  BUCKINGHAM   Ay, madam. He desires to make atonement°   *reconciliation*
  Between the Duke of Gloucester and your brothers,
  And between them and my Lord Chamberlain,°   *(Hastings)*
  And sent to warn° them to his royal presence.   *summon*
40 QUEEN ELIZABETH   Would all were well! But that will never be.
  I fear our happiness is at the height.[3]
    Enter RICHARD [*Duke of*] GLOUCESTER [*and* LORD
      HASTINGS]
  RICHARD GLOUCESTER   They do me wrong, and I will not endure it.
  Who are they that complain unto the King
  That I forsooth am stern and love them not?
45 By holy Paul, they love his grace but lightly
  That fill his ears with such dissentious rumours.
  Because I cannot flatter and look fair,
  Smile in men's faces, smooth,° deceive, and cog,°   *flatter / cheat*
  Duck with French nods[4] and apish° courtesy,   *imitative; clumsy*
50 I must be held a rancorous enemy.
  Cannot a plain man live and think no harm,
  But thus his simple truth must be abused
  With° silken, sly, insinuating jacks?°   *By / nobodies*
  RIVERS   To whom in all this presence° speaks your grace?   *present company*
55 RICHARD GLOUCESTER   To thee, that hast nor honesty nor grace.
  When have I injured thee? When done thee wrong?
  Or thee? Or thee? Or any of your faction?
  A plague upon you all! His royal grace—
  Whom God preserve better than you would wish—
60 Cannot be quiet scarce a breathing while[5]
  But you must trouble him with lewd° complaints.   *ignorant*
  QUEEN ELIZABETH   Brother of Gloucester, you mistake the matter.
  The King—on his own royal disposition,°   *inclination*
  And not provoked by any suitor else—
65 Aiming belike° at your interior hatred,   *Guessing probably*
  That in your outward action shows itself
  Against my children, brothers, and myself,

---

2. Lady Margaret Beaufort, Lord Stanley's wife, was (by an earlier marriage) the mother of Henry Tudor, Earl of Richmond, who at play's end succeeds Richard and becomes Henry VII. As a descendant of the house of Lancaster, she was unlikely to have friendly feelings toward the Yorkist King Edward IV or his family.
3. At its highest point on Fortune's proverbial wheel, and thus about to decline.
4. *French nods:* elaborate bows.
5. Long enough to catch his breath.

Makes[6] him to send, that he may learn the ground
Of your ill will, and thereby to remove it.

70 RICHARD GLOUCESTER   I cannot tell. The world is grown so bad
That wrens make prey where eagles dare not perch.
Since every jack became a gentleman,
There's many a gentle person made a jack.

QUEEN ELIZABETH   Come, come, we know your meaning, brother Gloucester.
75 You envy my advancement, and my friends'.
God grant we never may have need of you.

RICHARD GLOUCESTER   Meantime, God grants that I have need of you.
Our brother° is imprisoned by your means,   (Clarence)
Myself disgraced, and the nobility
80 Held in contempt, while great promotions
Are daily given to ennoble those
That scarce some two days since were worth a noble.[7]

QUEEN ELIZABETH   By him° that raised me to this care-full height   (God)
From that contented hap° which I enjoyed,   fortune; lot
85 I never did incense his majesty
Against the Duke of Clarence, but have been
An earnest advocate to plead for him.
My lord, you do me shameful injury
Falsely to draw me in these vile suspects.°   suspicions

90 RICHARD GLOUCESTER   You may deny that you were not the mean°   instigation
Of my Lord Hastings' late imprisonment.

RIVERS   She may, my lord, for—

RICHARD GLOUCESTER   She may, Lord Rivers; why, who knows not so?
She may do more, sir, than denying that.
95 She may help you to many fair preferments,°   lucrative positions
And then deny her aiding hand therein,
And lay those honours on[8] your high desert.
What may she not? She may—ay, marry,[9] may she.

RIVERS   What 'marry, may she'?

100 RICHARD GLOUCESTER   What marry, may she? Marry with a king:
A bachelor, and a handsome stripling,° too.   young man
Iwis your grandam had a worser match.[1]

QUEEN ELIZABETH   My lord of Gloucester, I have too long borne
Your blunt upbraidings and your bitter scoffs.
105 By heaven, I will acquaint his majesty
Of those gross taunts that oft I have endured.
I had rather be a country servant-maid
Than a great queen, with this condition:
To be so baited,° scorned, and stormèd at.   provoked

Enter old QUEEN MARGARET[2] [*unseen behind them*]

110 Small joy have I in being England's queen.

QUEEN MARGARET [*aside*]   And lessened be that small, God I beseech him.
Thy honour, state,° and seat° is due to me.   rank / throne

RICHARD GLOUCESTER [*to* ELIZABETH]   What? Threat you me
with telling of the King?
Tell him, and spare not. Look what° I have said,   Whatever

---

6. The grammatical subject is still "the King."
7. Gold coin, worth one-third of a pound sterling.
8. And attribute those honors to.
9. Indeed (originally, an oath on the Virgin Mary), with pun in nest line on "wed."
1. Your mother (and the Queen's) was born of a less

distinguished union. *Iwis:* Assuredly (already archaic).
2. Historically, Margaret—widow of the Lancastrian King Henry VI—was held prisoner in England for five years after her husband's defeat at the Battle of Tewkesbury and then exiled to France.

115   I will avouch't in presence of the King.
      I dare adventure to be° sent to th' Tower.   *I risk being*
      'Tis time to speak; my pains³ are quite forgot.
      QUEEN MARGARET [*aside*]   Out, devil! I remember them too well.
      Thou killed'st my husband Henry in the Tower,
120   And Edward, my poor son, at Tewkesbury.
      RICHARD GLOUCESTER [*to* ELIZABETH]   Ere you were queen—
          ay, or your husband king—
      I was a packhorse° in his great affairs,   *beast of burden*
      A weeder-out of his proud adversaries,
      A liberal rewarder of his friends.
125   To royalize his blood, I spent mine own.
      QUEEN MARGARET [*aside*]   Ay, and much better blood than his or thine.
      RICHARD GLOUCESTER [*to* ELIZABETH]   In all which time you
          and your husband Gray
      Were factious° for the house of Lancaster;   *partisan*
      And Rivers, so were you.—Was not your husband
130   In Margaret's battle° at Saint Albans slain?⁴   *army*
      Let me put in your minds, if you forget,
      What you have been ere this, and what you are;
      Withal,° what I have been, and what I am.   *In addition; also*
      QUEEN MARGARET [*aside*]   A murd'rous villain, and so still thou art.
135   RICHARD GLOUCESTER   Poor Clarence did forsake his father⁵ Warwick—
      Ay, and forswore himself, which Jesu pardon—
      QUEEN MARGARET [*aside*]   Which God revenge!
      RICHARD GLOUCESTER   To fight on Edward's party° for the crown,   *side*
      And for his meed,° poor lord, he is mewed up.   *reward*
140   I would to God my heart were flint like Edward's,
      Or Edward's soft and pitiful like mine.
      I am too childish-foolish for this world.
      QUEEN MARGARET [*aside*]   Hie° thee to hell for shame, and leave this world,   *Hurry*
      Thou cacodemon;° there thy kingdom is.   *evil spirit*
145   RIVERS   My lord of Gloucester, in those busy days
      Which here you urge° to prove us enemies,   *recall*
      We followed then our lord, our sovereign king.
      So should we you, if you should be our king.
      RICHARD GLOUCESTER   If I should be? I had rather be a pedlar.
150   Far be it from my heart, the thought thereof.
      QUEEN ELIZABETH   As little joy, my lord, as you suppose
      You should enjoy, were you this country's king,
      As little joy may you suppose in me,
      That I enjoy being the queen thereof.
155   QUEEN MARGARET [*aside*]   Ah, little joy enjoys the queen thereof,
      For I am she, and altogether joyless.
      I can no longer hold me patient.
          [*She comes forward*]
      Hear me, you wrangling pirates, that fall out
      In sharing that which you have pilled° from me.   *pillaged*
160   Which of you trembles not that looks on me?
      If not that I am Queen, you bow like subjects;

---

3. Efforts, trouble (on the King's behalf).
4. Queen Elizabeth's first husband, Sir John Gray, died fighting for the Lancastrian faction.
5. Father-in-law. Clarence married Warwick's daughter Isabella, sister of this play's Lady Anne, and for a time defied his brothers by supporting the Lancastrian faction. He "forswore himself" (line 136) by returning to fight for the Yorkish faction.

Yet that by you deposed, you quake like rebels.[6]
[*To* RICHARD] Ah, gentle villain,[7] do not turn away.
RICHARD GLOUCESTER   Foul wrinkled witch, what mak'st thou°   *what are you doing*
    in my sight?
165   QUEEN MARGARET   But repetition° of what thou hast marred: *recounting*
    That will I make before I let thee go.[8]
166.1   RICHARD GLOUCESTER   *Wert thou not banishèd on pain of death?*
      QUEEN MARGARET   *I was, but I do find more pain in banishment*
       Than death can yield me here by my abode.
    A husband and a son thou ow'st to me,
    [*To* ELIZABETH] And thou a kingdom; [*to the rest*] all of you allegiance.
    This sorrow that I have by right is yours,
170   And all the pleasures you usurp are mine.
RICHARD GLOUCESTER   The curse my noble father laid on thee—
    When thou didst crown his warlike brows with paper,
    And with thy scorns° drew'st rivers from his eyes,   *mocking speeches*
    And then, to dry them, gav'st the duke a clout°   *rag; handkerchief*
175   Steeped in the faultless° blood of pretty Rutland[9]—   *innocent*
    His curses then, from bitterness of soul
    Denounced against thee, are all fall'n upon thee,
    And God, not we, hath plagued thy bloody deed.
QUEEN ELIZABETH [*to* MARGARET]   So just is God to right the innocent.
LORD HASTINGS [*to* MARGARET]   O 'twas the foulest deed to slay
180   that babe,°   *(Rutland)*
    And the most merciless that e'er was heard of.
RIVERS [*to* MARGARET]   Tyrants themselves wept when it was reported.
DORSET [*to* MARGARET]   No man but prophesied revenge for it.
BUCKINGHAM [*to* MARGARET]   Northumberland, then present, wept to see it.
185   QUEEN MARGARET   What? Were you snarling all before I came,
    Ready to catch each other by the throat,
    And turn you all your hatred now on me?
    Did York's dread curse prevail so much with heaven
    That Henry's death, my lovely Edward's death,
190   Their kingdom's loss, my woeful banishment,
    Should all but answer for° that peevish brat?   *Should merely equal*
    Can curses pierce the clouds and enter heaven?
    Why then, give way, dull clouds, to my quick° curses!   *lively*
    Though not by war, by surfeit° die your king,   *high living*
195   As ours by murder to make him a king.
    [*to* ELIZABETH] Edward thy son, that now is Prince of Wales,
    For Edward my son, that was Prince of Wales,
    Die in his youth by like° untimely violence.   *similarly*
    Thyself, a queen, for me that was a queen,
200   Outlive thy glory like my wretched self.
    Long mayst thou live—to wail thy children's death,
    And see another, as I see thee now,
    Decked° in thy rights, as thou art 'stalled° in mine.   *Dressed / installed*
    Long die thy happy days before thy death,
205   And after many lengthened hours of grief
    Die, neither mother, wife, nor England's queen.—

6. *If . . . rebels:* Even if you do not bow because I am
Queen, at least you tremble like rebels because you
deposed me.
7. Well-born peasant; kindly scoundrel.
8. The indented passage that follows, 166.1–166.3,

appears only in F.
9. This is dramatized in *Richard Duke of York*
1.4.80–96, in which Margaret crowns the Duke of York
with a paper crown and waves a handkerchief dipped in
his son Rutland's blood in front of his eyes.

Rivers and Dorset, you were standers-by,
And so wast thou, Lord Hastings,[1] when my son
Was stabbed with bloody daggers. God I pray him,
210 That none of you may live his natural age,
But by some unlooked° accident cut off.   unlooked-for
RICHARD GLOUCESTER   Have done thy charm,° thou hateful,   spell; curse
       withered hag.
QUEEN MARGARET   And leave out thee? Stay, dog, for thou shalt hear me.
       If heaven have any grievous plague in store
215 Exceeding those that I can wish upon thee,
O let them keep it till thy sins be ripe,
And then hurl down their indignation
On thee, the troubler of the poor world's peace.
The worm of conscience still begnaw thy soul.
220 Thy friends suspect for° traitors while thou liv'st,   to be
And take deep traitors for thy dearest friends.
No sleep close up that deadly eye of thine,
Unless it be while some tormenting dream
Affrights thee with a hell of ugly devils.
225 Thou elvish-marked, abortive, rooting hog,[2]
Thou that wast sealed° in thy nativity   stamped
The slave of nature[3] and the son of hell,
Thou slander of thy heavy° mother's womb,   sorrowful
Thou loathèd issue of thy father's loins,
230 Thou rag of honour, thou detested—
RICHARD GLOUCESTER   Margaret.
QUEEN MARGARET   Richard.
RICHARD GLOUCESTER   Ha?
QUEEN MARGARET   I call thee not.
RICHARD GLOUCESTER   I cry thee mercy° then, for I did think   I beg your pardon
That thou hadst called me all these bitter names.
235 QUEEN MARGARET   Why so I did, but looked for no reply.
O let me make the period° to my curse.   full stop; finish
RICHARD GLOUCESTER   'Tis done by me, and ends in 'Margaret'.
QUEEN ELIZABETH [to MARGARET]   Thus have you breathed your
       curse against yourself.
QUEEN MARGARET   Poor painted Queen, vain flourish[4] of my fortune,
240 Why strew'st thou sugar on that bottled° spider   bottle-shaped; swollen
Whose deadly web ensnareth thee about?
Fool, fool, thou whet'st a knife to kill thyself.
The day will come that thou shalt wish for me
To help thee curse this poisonous bunch-backed° toad.   hunchbacked
245 LORD HASTINGS   False-boding° woman, end thy frantic curse,   Falsely prophesying
Lest to thy harm thou move our patience.
QUEEN MARGARET   Foul shame upon you, you have all moved mine.
RIVERS   Were you well served, you would be taught your duty.
QUEEN MARGARET   To serve me well you all should do me duty.°   show me deference
250 Teach me to be your queen, and you my subjects:
O serve me well, and teach yourselves that duty.
DORSET   Dispute not with her: she is lunatic.

1. Rivers, Dorset, and Hastings were not present at
Prince Edward's murder at Tewkesbury as dramatized in
Richard Duke of York 5.5, but they are in the chronicles
that served as Shakespeare's sources. The Prince, in fact,
was slain by unknown combatants during the battle.

2. Richard's emblem was the white boar. *elvish-
marked*: deformed by evil fairies. *abortive*: misshapen.
3. Because he was deformed from birth.
4. *painted*: counterfeit, with play on "use of cosmet-
ics." *vain flourish*: empty, meaningless decoration.

QUEEN MARGARET   Peace, master Marquis, you are malapert.°   *impertinent*
Your fire-new stamp of honour is scarce current.[5]
255   O that your young nobility could judge
What 'twere to lose it and be miserable.
They that stand high have many blasts to shake them,
And if they fall they dash themselves to pieces.
RICHARD GLOUCESTER   Good counsel, marry!—Learn it, learn it, Marquis.
260   DORSET   It touches you, my lord, as much as me.
RICHARD GLOUCESTER   Ay, and much more; but I was born so high.
Our eyrie[6] buildeth in the cedar's top,
And dallies with the wind, and scorns the sun.
QUEEN MARGARET   And turns the sun to shade. Alas, alas!
265   Witness my son, now in the shade of death,
Whose bright outshining beams thy cloudy wrath
Hath in eternal darkness folded up.
Your eyrie buildeth in our eyrie's nest.—
O God that seest it, do not suffer it;
270   As it was won with blood, lost be it so.
RICHARD GLOUCESTER   Peace, peace! For shame, if not for charity.
QUEEN MARGARET   Urge neither charity nor shame to me.
Uncharitably with me have you dealt,
And shamefully my hopes by you are butchered.
275   My charity is outrage; life, my shame;°   *my life is one of shame*
And in that shame still live my sorrow's rage.
BUCKINGHAM   Have done, have done.
QUEEN MARGARET   O princely Buckingham, I'll kiss thy hand
In sign of league and amity with thee.
280   Now fair befall° thee and thy noble house!   *good fortune to*
Thy garments are not spotted with our blood,
Nor thou within the compass° of my curse.   *scope*
BUCKINGHAM   Nor no one here, for curses never pass
The lips of those that breathe them in the air.[7]
285   QUEEN MARGARET   I will not think but they ascend the sky
And there awake God's gentle sleeping peace.
O Buckingham, take heed of yonder dog.
    [*She points at* RICHARD]
Look when he fawns, he bites; and when he bites,
His venom tooth will rankle[8] to the death.
290   Have naught to do with him; beware of him;
Sin, death, and hell have set their marks on him,
And all their ministers attend on him.
RICHARD GLOUCESTER   What doth she say, my lord of Buckingham?
BUCKINGHAM   Nothing that I respect, my gracious lord.
295   QUEEN MARGARET   What, dost thou scorn me for my gentle counsel,
And soothe the devil that I warn thee from?
O but remember this another day,
When he shall split thy very heart with sorrow,
And say, 'Poor Margaret was a prophetess'.—
300   Live each of you the subjects to his hate,
And he to yours, and all of you to God's.   *Exit*
HASTINGS   My hair doth stand on end to hear her curses.

---

5. Your recently acquired title is not yet secure (as
newly minted coins that have not yet achieved common
currency).
6. Eagle's brood (the sons of York).

7. *curses . . . air:* it is as if curses were never spoken or
afflict only the curser.
8. Will cause a wound that will fester.

RIVERS   And so doth mine. I muse why she's at liberty.

RICHARD GLOUCESTER   I cannot blame her, by God's holy mother.
305 She hath had too much wrong, and I repent
     My part thereof that I have done to her.

QUEEN ELIZABETH   I never did her any, to my knowledge.

RICHARD GLOUCESTER   Yet you have all the vantage of her wrong.⁹
     I was too hot° to do somebody good,   *eager*
310 That° is too cold° in thinking of it now.   *Who / ungrateful*
     Marry, as for Clarence, he is well repaid:
     He is franked up to fatting¹ for his pains.
     God pardon them that are the cause thereof.

RIVERS   A virtuous and a Christian-like conclusion,
315 To pray for them that have done scathe° to us.   *harm*

RICHARD GLOUCESTER   So do I ever—(*speaks to himself*) being well advised:
     For had I cursed now, I had cursed myself.

          Enter [Sir William] CATESBY

CATESBY   Madam, his majesty doth call for you,
     And for your grace, and you my gracious lords.

320 QUEEN ELIZABETH   Catesby, I come.—Lords, will you go with me?

RIVERS   We wait upon your grace.   *Exeunt. Manet RICHARD*

RICHARD GLOUCESTER   I do the wrong, and first begin to brawl.°   *complain; protest*
     The secret mischiefs that I set abroach°   *set in motion*
     I lay unto the grievous charge of² others.
325 Clarence, whom I indeed have cast in darkness,
     I do beweep to many simple gulls°—   *credulous fools*
     Namely to Derby, Hastings, Buckingham—
     And tell them, ''Tis the Queen and her allies
     That stir the King against the Duke my brother'.
330 Now they believe it, and withal whet me
     To be revenged on Rivers, Dorset, Gray;
     But then I sigh, and with a piece of scripture
     Tell them that God bids us do good for evil;
     And thus I clothe my naked villainy
335 With odd old ends,° stol'n forth of Holy Writ,   *old bits and pieces*
     And seem a saint when most I play the devil.

          Enter two MURDERERS

     But soft, here come my executioners.—
     How now, my hardy, stout, resolvèd° mates!   *resolute*
     Are you now going to dispatch this thing?

340 A MURDERER   We are, my lord, and come to have the warrant,
     That we may be admitted where he is.

RICHARD GLOUCESTER   Well thought upon; I have it here about me.

          [He gives them the warrant]

     When you have done, repair° to Crosby Place.   *return*
     But sirs, be sudden° in the execution,   *swift*
345 Withal obdurate; do not hear him plead,
     For Clarence is well spoken, and perhaps
     May move your hearts to pity, if you mark° him.   *listen to*

A MURDERER   Tut, tut, my lord, we will not stand to prate.
     Talkers are no good doers. Be assured,
350 We go to use our hands, and not our tongues.

---

9. All the benefits acquired as a result of the wrong she   2. I make into a serious accusation against.
has suffered.
1. He is penned up to fatten (for slaughter, like a pig).

RICHARD GLOUCESTER   Your eyes drop millstones when fools'
    eyes fall° tears.   *let fall*
    I like you, lads. About your business straight.°   *straightaway*
    Go, go, dispatch.
MURDERERS   We will, my noble lord.
    Exeunt [RICHARD *at one door, the* MURDERERS *at another*]

1.4

Enter [*George Duke of*] CLARENCE [*and Sir Robert*
    BRACKENBURY[1]]
BRACKENBURY   Why looks your grace so heavily° today?   *melancholy*
CLARENCE   O I have passed a miserable night,
    So full of fearful dreams, of ugly sights,
    That as I am a Christian faithful man,
5   I would not spend another such a night
    Though 'twere to buy a world of happy days,
    So full of dismal terror was the time.
BRACKENBURY   What was your dream, my lord? I pray you, tell me.
CLARENCE   Methoughts that I had broken from the Tower,
10   And was embarked to cross to Burgundy,
    And in my company my brother Gloucester,
    Who from my cabin tempted me to walk
    Upon the hatches;[2] there we looked toward England,
    And cited up° a thousand heavy times   *recalled*
15   During the wars of York and Lancaster
    That had befall'n us. As we paced along
    Upon the giddy footing of the hatches,
    Methought that Gloucester stumbled, and in falling
    Struck me—that sought to stay° him—overboard   *steady*
20   Into the tumbling billows of the main.
    O Lord! Methought what pain it was to drown,
    What dreadful noise of waters in my ears,
    What sights of ugly death within my eyes.
    Methoughts I saw a thousand fearful wrecks,
25   Ten thousand men that fishes gnawed upon,
    Wedges of gold, great ouches,[3] heaps of pearl,
    Inestimable° stones, unvalued° jewels,   *Countless / invaluable*
    All scattered in the bottom of the sea.
    Some lay in dead men's skulls; and in those holes
30   Where eyes did once inhabit, there were crept—
    As 'twere in scorn of eyes—reflecting gems,
    Which wooed the slimy bottom of the deep
    And mocked the dead bones that lay scattered by.
BRACKENBURY   Had you such leisure in the time of death,
35   To gaze upon these secrets of the deep?
CLARENCE   Methought I had, and often did I strive
    To yield the ghost,° but still° the envious° flood   *To die / always / malicious*
    Stopped-in° my soul and would not let it forth   *Stopped up*
    To find the empty, vast, and wand'ring air,
40   But smothered it within my panting bulk,°   *body*
    Who° almost burst to belch it in the sea.   *Which*

1.4 Location: In the Tower of London.
1. F gives this part to an anonymous keeper, Bracken-
bury not entering until line 72.

2. Planks laid across the hold of a ship, forming a tem-
porary deck.
3. Gold or silver brooches set with jewels. Q, F: anchors.

BRACKENBURY Awaked you not in this sore agony?

CLARENCE No, no, my dream was lengthened after life.[4]
O then began the tempest to my soul!
45 I passed, methought, the melancholy flood,[5]
With that sour ferryman which poets write of,
Unto the kingdom of perpetual night.
The first that there did greet my stranger soul
Was my great father-in-law, renownèd Warwick,
50 Who cried aloud, 'What scourge° for perjury   *punishment*
Can this dark monarchy afford false Clarence?'
And so he vanished. Then came wand'ring by
A shadow[6] like an angel, with bright hair,
Dabbled in blood, and he shrieked out aloud,
55 'Clarence is come: false, fleeting,° perjured Clarence,   *fickle*
That stabbed me in the field by Tewkesbury.
Seize on him, furies![7] Take him unto torment!'
With that, methoughts a legion of foul fiends
Environed° me, and howlèd in mine ears   *Surrounded*
60 Such hideous cries that with the very noise
I trembling waked, and for a season after
Could not believe but that I was in hell,
Such terrible impression made my dream.

BRACKENBURY No marvel, lord, though° it affrighted you;   *that*
65 I am afraid, methinks, to hear you tell it.

CLARENCE Ah, Brackenbury, I have done these things,
That now give evidence against my soul,
For Edward's sake; and see how he requites me.[8]
68.1 *O God! If my deep prayers cannot appease thee*
But thou wilt be avenged on my misdeeds,
Yet execute thy wrath in me alone.
O spare my guiltless wife and my poor children.
Keeper, I pray thee, sit by me awhile.
70 My soul is heavy, and I fain would° sleep.   *I desire to*

BRACKENBURY I will, my lord. God give your grace good rest.
[CLARENCE *sleeps*]
Sorrow breaks seasons and reposing hours,[9]
Makes the night morning and the noontide night.
Princes have but their titles for their glories,
75 An outward honour for an inward toil,
And for unfelt imaginations[1]
They often feel a world of restless cares;
So that, between their titles and low name,
There's nothing differs but the outward fame.
Enter two MURDERERS
80 FIRST MURDERER Ho, who's here?

BRACKENBURY What wouldst thou, fellow? And how cam'st thou hither?

SECOND MURDERER I would speak with Clarence, and I came
hither on my legs.

---

4. My dream also depicted my fate after death.
5. The river Styx, across which Charon (the "sour fer-
ryman" of the next line) ferried souls to Hades, the clas-
sical hell.
6. Shade, ghost (Edward, Prince of Wales—son of
Henry VI, and Clarence's brother-in-law—whom
Clarence helped to murder; see *Richard Duke of York*
5.5.40).

7. In Greek mythology, female spirits who enacted
vengeance for blood crimes against relatives.
8. The indented passage that follows, 68.1–68.4,
appears only in F. *requites*: repays.
9. Sorrow disrupts life's normal rhythms and disre-
gards the hours appropriate to sleep.
1. *for unfelt imaginations*: "for the sake of imaginary
and unreal gratifications" (Dr. Johnson).

BRACKENBURY What, so brief?

85 FIRST MURDERER 'Tis better, sir, than to be tedious. [*To* SECOND
MURDERER] Let him see our commission,° and talk no more.   *authorization*
    [BRACKENBURY] *reads*

BRACKENBURY I am in this commanded to deliver
The noble Duke of Clarence to your hands.
I will not reason what is meant hereby,
90 Because I will be° guiltless of the meaning.   *wish to be*
There lies the Duke asleep, and there the keys.
    [*He throws down the keys*]
I'll to the King and signify to him
That thus I have resigned to you my charge.°   *responsibility*

FIRST MURDERER You may, sir; 'tis a point of wisdom. Fare you
95 well.   *Exit* [BRACKENBURY]

SECOND MURDERER What, shall I stab him as he sleeps?

FIRST MURDERER No. He'll say 'twas done cowardly, when he
wakes.

SECOND MURDERER Why, he shall never wake until the great
100 judgement day.

FIRST MURDERER Why, then he'll say we stabbed him sleeping.

SECOND MURDERER The urging of that word 'judgement' hath
bred a kind of remorse in me.

FIRST MURDERER What, art thou afraid?

105 SECOND MURDERER Not to kill him, having a warrant, but to
be damned for killing him, from the which no warrant can
defend me.

FIRST MURDERER I thought thou hadst been resolute.

SECOND MURDERER So I am—to let him live.

110 FIRST MURDERER I'll back to the Duke of Gloucester and tell
him so.

SECOND MURDERER Nay, I pray thee. Stay a little. I hope this
passionate humour° of mine will change. It was wont to hold   *compassionate mood*
me but while one tells° twenty.   *counts*
    [*He counts to twenty*]

115 FIRST MURDERER How dost thou feel thyself now?

SECOND MURDERER Some certain dregs of conscience are yet
within me.

FIRST MURDERER Remember our reward, when the deed's done.

SECOND MURDERER 'Swounds,° he dies. I had forgot the reward.   *By God's wounds*

120 FIRST MURDERER Where's thy conscience now?

SECOND MURDERER O, in the Duke of Gloucester's purse.

FIRST MURDERER When he opens his purse to give us our
reward, thy conscience flies out.

SECOND MURDERER 'Tis no matter. Let it go. There's few or
125 none will entertain° it.   *host; employ*

FIRST MURDERER What if it come to thee again?

SECOND MURDERER I'll not meddle with it. It makes a man a cow-
ard. A man cannot steal but it accuseth him. A man cannot
swear but it checks him. A man cannot lie with his neighbour's
130 wife but it detects him. 'Tis a blushing, shamefaced spirit, that
mutinies in a man's bosom. It fills a man full of obstacles. It
made me once restore a purse of gold that by chance I found.
It beggars any man that keeps it. It is turned out of towns and
cities for a dangerous thing, and every man that means to live
135 well endeavours to trust to himself and live without it.

FIRST MURDERER 'Swounds, 'tis even now at my elbow, per-
suading me not to kill the Duke.

SECOND MURDERER   Take the devil in thy mind, and believe him°   *(conscience)*
not: he would insinuate with thee but to make thee sigh.²

140 FIRST MURDERER   I am strong framed; he cannot prevail with
me.

SECOND MURDERER   Spoke like a tall° man that respects thy rep-
utation. Come, shall we fall to work?   *valiant*

FIRST MURDERER   Take him on the costard with the hilts of thy

145 sword, and then throw him into the malmsey butt³ in the next
room.

SECOND MURDERER   O excellent device!—and make a sop⁴ of
him.

FIRST MURDERER   Soft,° he wakes.   *Hush*

150 SECOND MURDERER   Strike!

FIRST MURDERER   No, we'll reason with him.

CLARENCE   Where art thou, keeper? Give me a cup of wine.

SECOND MURDERER   You shall have wine enough, my lord, anon.

CLARENCE   In God's name, what art thou?

FIRST MURDERER   A man, as you are.

155 CLARENCE   But not as I am, royal.

FIRST MURDERER   Nor you as we are, loyal.

CLARENCE   Thy voice is thunder, but thy looks are humble.

FIRST MURDERER   My voice is now the King's;⁵ my looks, mine own.

CLARENCE   How darkly and how deadly dost thou speak.

160 Your eyes do menace me. Why look you pale?
Who sent you hither? Wherefore do you come?

SECOND MURDERER   To, to, to—

CLARENCE   To murder me.

BOTH MURDERERS   Ay, ay.

CLARENCE   You scarcely have the hearts to tell me so,
And therefore cannot have the hearts to do it.

165 Wherein, my friends, have I offended you?

FIRST MURDERER   Offended us you have not, but the King.

CLARENCE   I shall be reconciled to him again.

SECOND MURDERER   Never, my lord; therefore prepare to die.

CLARENCE   Are you drawn forth° among a world of men   *selected from*

170 To slay the innocent? What is my offence?
Where is the evidence that doth accuse me?
What lawful quest° have given their verdict up   *jury*
Unto the frowning judge, or who pronounced
The bitter sentence of poor Clarence' death?

175 Before I be convict by course of law,
To threaten me with death is most unlawful.
I charge you, as you hope to have redemption
By Christ's dear blood, shed for our grievous sins,
That you depart and lay no hands on me.

180 The deed you undertake is damnable.

FIRST MURDERER   What we will do, we do upon command.

SECOND MURDERER   And he that hath commanded is our king.

CLARENCE   Erroneous vassals,° the great King of Kings   *Misguided subjects*

---

2. *he . . . sight:* he (conscience) would ingratiate him-
self with you simply to cause you grief.
3. Wine barrel (malmsey is a strong, sweet wine).
costard: head (literally, a large apple).
4. Piece of bread or wafer soaked in wine.
5. I am now acting on the King's command.

	Hath in the table of his law° commanded	*the Ten Commandments*
185	That thou shalt do no murder. Will you then	
	Spurn at his edict, and fulfil a man's?	
	Take heed, for he holds vengeance in his hand	
	To hurl upon their heads that break his law.	

SECOND MURDERER And that same vengeance doth he hurl on thee,
190   For false forswearing, and for murder too.
      Thou didst receive the sacrament[6] to fight
      In quarrel of° the house of Lancaster.   *On the side of*
FIRST MURDERER And, like a traitor to the name of God,
      Didst break that vow, and with thy treacherous blade
195   Unripped'st the bowels of thy sov'reign's son.[7]
SECOND MURDERER Whom thou wast sworn to cherish and defend.
FIRST MURDERER How canst thou urge God's dreadful law to us,
      When thou hast broke it in such dear degree?
CLARENCE Alas, for whose sake did I that ill deed?
200   For Edward, for my brother, for his sake.
      He sends ye not to murder me for this,
      For in that sin he is as deep as I.
      If God will be avengèd for the deed,
      O know you yet, he doth it publicly.
205   Take not the quarrel from his pow'rful arm;
      He needs no indirect or lawless course
      To cut off those that have offended him.
FIRST MURDERER Who made thee then a bloody minister°   *agent*
      When gallant springing° brave Plantagenet,°   *sprightly / (Edward)*
210   That princely novice,° was struck dead by thee?   *youth*
CLARENCE My brother's love,° the devil, and my rage.   *My love for my brother*
FIRST MURDERER Thy brother's love, our duty, and thy faults
      Provoke us hither now to slaughter thee.
CLARENCE If you do love my brother, hate not me.
215   I am his brother, and I love him well.
      If you are hired for meed,° go back again,   *reward*
      And I will send you to my brother Gloucester,
      Who shall reward you better for my life
      Than Edward will for tidings of my death.
220   SECOND MURDERER You are deceived. Your brother Gloucester hates you.
CLARENCE O no, he loves me, and he holds me dear.
      Go you to him from me.
FIRST MURDERER   Ay, so we will.
CLARENCE Tell him, when that our princely father York
      Blessed his three sons with his victorious arm,
225   And charged us from his soul to love each other,
      He little thought of this divided friendship.
      Bid Gloucester think of this, and he will weep.
FIRST MURDERER Ay, millstones, as he lessoned° us to weep.   *taught*
CLARENCE O do not slander him, for he is kind.[8]
230   FIRST MURDERER As snow in harvest. Come, you deceive yourself.
      'Tis he that sends us to destroy you here.
CLARENCE It cannot be, for he bewept my fortune,

---

6. Take communion and in doing so swear by the body   Henry VI.
of God.   8. He is full of natural feelings (and hence a loving
7. That is, Prince Edward, son of the then sovereign,   brother).

And hugged me in his arms, and swore with sobs
That he would labour° my delivery.   *work for*
235   FIRST MURDERER   Why, so he doth, when he delivers you
From this earth's thraldom to the joys of heaven.
SECOND MURDERER   Make peace with God, for you must die, my lord.
CLARENCE   Have you that holy feeling in your souls
To counsel me to make my peace with God,
240   And are you yet to your own souls so blind
That you will war with God by murd'ring me?
O sirs, consider: they that set you on
To do this deed will hate you for the deed.
SECOND MURDERER [*to* FIRST]   What shall we do?
CLARENCE   Relent? and save your souls.
245   FIRST MURDERER   Relent? No. 'Tis cowardly and womanish.
CLARENCE   Not to relent is beastly, savage, devilish.—
My friend, I spy some pity in thy looks.
O if thine eye be not a flatterer,°   *deceiver (of Clarence)*
Come thou on my side, and entreat for me.
250   A begging prince, what beggar pities not?
Which of you, if you were a prince's son,
Being pent° from liberty as I am now,   *restrained*
If two such murderers as yourselves came to you,
Would not entreat for life? As you would beg
255   Were you in my distress—
SECOND MURDERER   Look behind you, my lord!
FIRST MURDERER   (*He stabs* [CLARENCE]) Take that, and that! If
      all this will not serve,
I'll drown you in the malmsey butt within.
                                                        Exit [*with Clarence's body*]
SECOND MURDERER   A bloody deed, and desperately dispatched!
260   How fain,° like Pilate, would I wash my hands   *gladly*
Of this most grievous, guilty murder done.
            Enter FIRST MURDERER
FIRST MURDERER   How now? What mean'st thou, that thou help'st me not?
By heaven, the Duke shall know how slack you have been.
SECOND MURDERER   I would he knew that I had saved his brother.
265   Take thou the fee, and tell him what I say,
For I repent me that the Duke is slain.   *Exit*
FIRST MURDERER   So do not I. Go, coward as thou art.—
Well, I'll go hide the body in some hole
Till that the Duke give order for his burial.
270   And, when I have my meed, I will away,
For this will out,⁹ and then I must not stay.   *Exit*

2.1

Flourish.° Enter KING [EDWARD], *sick*, QUEEN [ELIZA-   *Trumpet call*
BETH], *Lord Marquis* DORSET, [*Lord*] RIVERS, [*LORD*]
HASTINGS, [*Sir William*] CATESBY, [*the Duke of*] BUCK-
INGHAM [*and Lord Gray*]
KING EDWARD   Why, so! Now have I done a good day's work.
You peers, continue this united league.
I every day expect an embassage
From my redeemer to redeem me hence,

---

9. "Murder will out" was proverbial.   **2.1** Location: The palace, London.

5 And more in peace my soul shall part to heaven
Since I have made my friends at peace on earth.
Hastings and Rivers, take each other's hand.
Dissemble not[1] your hatred; swear your love.

RIVERS   By heaven, my soul is purged from grudging hate,
10 And with my hand I seal my true heart's love.
      [*He takes Hastings' hand*]

LORD HASTINGS   So thrive I,° as I truly swear the like.   *May I prosper*

KING EDWARD   Take heed you dally° not before your king,   *trifle*
Lest he that is the supreme King of Kings
Confound° your hidden falsehood, and award°   *Defeat / cause*
15 Either of you to be the other's end.[2]

LORD HASTINGS   So prosper I, as I swear perfect love.

RIVERS   And I, as I love Hastings with my heart.

KING EDWARD [*to* ELIZABETH]   Madam, yourself is not exempt from this,
Nor your son Dorset;—Buckingham, nor you.
20 You have been factious one against the other.
Wife, love Lord Hastings, let him kiss your hand—
And what you do, do it unfeignedly.

QUEEN ELIZABETH [*giving* HASTINGS *her hand to kiss*]   There,
    Hastings. I will never more remember
Our former hatred: so thrive I, and mine.°   *my family*

25 KING EDWARD   Dorset, embrace him. Hastings, love Lord Marquis.

DORSET   This interchange of love, I here protest,°   *affirm*
Upon my part shall be inviolable.

LORD HASTINGS   And so swear I.
      [*They embrace*]

KING EDWARD   Now, princely Buckingham, seal thou this league
30 With thy embracements to my wife's allies,
And make me happy in your unity.

BUCKINGHAM [*to* ELIZABETH]   Whenever Buckingham doth turn his hate
Upon your grace, but° with all duteous love   *nor*
Doth cherish you and yours, God punish me
35 With hate in those where I expect most love.
When I have most need to employ a friend,
And most assurèd that he is a friend,
Deep,° hollow, treacherous, and full of guile   *Crafty*
Be he unto me. This do I beg of heaven,
40 When I am cold in love to you or yours.
      [*They*] *embrace*

KING EDWARD   A pleasing cordial,° princely Buckingham,   *health-giving drink*
Is this thy vow unto my sickly heart.
There wanteth now our brother Gloucester here,
To make the blessèd period° of this peace.   *conclusion*
    Enter [*Sir Richard*] RATCLIFFE *and* [RICHARD *Duke of*]
    GLOUCESTER

45 BUCKINGHAM   And in good time,
Here comes Sir Richard Ratcliffe and the Duke.

RICHARD GLOUCESTER   Good morrow to my sovereign King and Queen.—
And princely peers, a happy time of day.

KING EDWARD   Happy indeed, as we have spent the day.
50 Brother, we have done deeds of charity,
Made peace of enmity, fair love of hate,

---

1. Do not merely disguise.   2. Each of you to cause the death of the other.

Between these swelling wrong-incensèd[3] peers.
RICHARD GLOUCESTER   A blessèd labour, my most sovereign lord.
Among this princely heap° if any here,   *company*
55   By false intelligence° or wrong surmise,   *information*
Hold me a foe,
If I unwittingly or in my rage
Have aught committed that is hardly borne°   *is deeply resented*
By any in this presence, I desire
60   To reconcile me to his friendly peace.
'Tis death to me to be at enmity.
I hate it, and desire all good men's love.—
First, madam, I entreat true peace of you,
Which I will purchase with my duteous service.—
65   Of you, my noble cousin Buckingham,
If ever any grudge were lodged between us.—
Of you, Lord Rivers, and Lord Gray of you,
That all without desert° have frowned on me.—   *entirely without cause*
Dukes, earls, lords, gentlemen, indeed of all!
70   I do not know that Englishman alive
With whom my soul is any jot at odds
More than the infant that is born tonight.
I thank my God for my humility.
QUEEN ELIZABETH   A holy day shall this be kept hereafter.
75   I would to God all strifes were well compounded.°—   *resolved*
My sovereign lord, I do beseech your highness
To take our brother Clarence to your grace.
RICHARD GLOUCESTER   Why, madam, have I offered love for this,
To be so flouted° in this royal presence?   *mocked*
80   Who knows not that the gentle Duke is dead?
They all start
You do him injury to scorn his corpse.[4]
RIVERS[5]   Who knows not he is dead? Who knows he is?
QUEEN ELIZABETH   All-seeing heaven, what a world is this?
BUCKINGHAM   Look I so pale, Lord Dorset, as the rest?
85   DORSET   Ay, my good lord, and no one in the presence°   *(of the King)*
But his red colour hath forsook his cheeks.
KING EDWARD   Is Clarence dead? The order was reversed.
RICHARD GLOUCESTER   But he, poor man, by your first order died,
And that a wingèd Mercury[6] did bear;
90   Some tardy cripple bore the countermand,
That came too lag° to see him buried.   *late*
God grant that some, less noble and less loyal,
Nearer in bloody thoughts, but not in blood,[7]
Deserve not worse than wretched Clarence did,
95   And yet go current from suspicion.[8]
Enter [Lord STANLEY] Earl of Derby
STANLEY [*kneeling*]   A boon,° my sovereign, for my service done.   *favor*
KING EDWARD   I pray thee, peace! My soul is full of sorrow.
STANLEY   I will not rise, unless your highness hear me.

---

3. *swelling:* inflated with anger and pride. *wrong-incensèd:* mistakenly provoked; provoked by wrongs, injuries.
4. *to scorn his corpse:* by (supposedly) speaking ironically of him.
5. F assigns this line to King Edward.

6. The speedy messenger of the gods in classical mythology.
7. That is, nearer to bloody plots than was the innocent Clarence, but not so near the King in blood (another dig at the Queen's upstart relatives).
8. And yet are accepted at face value without suspicion.

KING EDWARD   Then say at once, what is it thou requests?
100 STANLEY   The forfeit, sovereign, of my servant's life,⁹
    Who slew today a riotous gentleman,
    Lately attendant on the Duke of Norfolk.
    KING EDWARD   Have I a tongue to doom° my brother's death,   *order*
    And shall that tongue give pardon to a slave?
105   My brother slew no man; his fault was thought;
    And yet his punishment was bitter death.
    Who sued to me for him? Who in my wrath
    Kneeled at my feet, and bid me be advised?°   *consider carefully*
    Who spoke of brotherhood? Who spoke of love?
110   Who told me how the poor soul did forsake
    The mighty Warwick and did fight for me?
    Who told me, in the field at Tewkesbury,
    When Oxford had me down, he rescued me,
    And said, 'Dear brother, live, and be a king'?
115   Who told me, when we both lay in the field,
    Frozen almost to death, how he did lap° me   *wrap*
    Even in his garments, and did give himself
    All thin° and naked to the numb-cold night?   *thinly clad*
    All this from my remembrance brutish wrath
120   Sinfully plucked, and not a man of you
    Had so much grace to put it in my mind.
    But when your carters° or your waiting vassals   *cart drivers*
    Have done a drunken slaughter, and defaced
    The precious image¹ of our dear redeemer,
125   You straight° are on your knees for 'Pardon, pardon!'—   *straightaway*
    And I, unjustly too, must grant it you.
    But, for my brother, not a man would speak,
    Nor I, ungracious, speak unto myself
    For him, poor soul. The proudest of you all
130   Have been beholden to him in his life,
    Yet none of you would once beg for his life.
    O God, I fear thy justice will take hold
    On me—and you, and mine, and yours, for this.—
    Come, Hastings, help me to my closet.°   *private (bed)room*
135   Ah, poor Clarence!   *Exeunt some with* KING *and* QUEEN
    RICHARD GLOUCESTER   This is the fruits of rashness. Marked you not
    How that the guilty kindred of the Queen
    Looked pale, when they did hear of Clarence' death?
    O, they did urge it still unto the King.
140   God will revenge it. Come, lords, will you go
    To comfort Edward with our company?
    BUCKINGHAM   We wait upon your grace.   *Exeunt*

2.2

Enter the old DUCHESS OF YORK *with the two children of*
    *Clarence*¹
BOY   Good grannam, tell us, is our father dead?
DUCHESS OF YORK   No, boy.
GIRL   Why do you weep so oft, and beat your breast,

---

9. That is, the release of his servant from a sentence of
death.
1. A man, thought to be created in God's image.

2.2 Location: The palace, London.
1. Edward and Margaret Plantagenet (not to be confused
with King Edward, Prince Edward, or Queen Margaret).

And cry, 'O Clarence, my unhappy son'?

5 BOY Why do you look on us and shake your head,
And call us orphans, wretches, castaways,
If that our noble father were alive?
DUCHESS OF YORK My pretty cousins,° you mistake me both.   *kinsmen*
I do lament the sickness of the King,
10 As loath to lose him, not your father's death.
It were lost sorrow to wail one that's lost.
BOY Then you conclude, my grannam, he is dead.
The King mine uncle is to blame for this.
God will revenge it—whom I will importune°   *beg*
15 With earnest prayers, all to that effect.
GIRL And so will I.
DUCHESS OF YORK Peace, children, peace! The King doth love you well.
Incapable° and shallow innocents,   *Uncomprehending*
You cannot guess who caused your father's death.
20 BOY Grannam, we can. For my good uncle Gloucester
Told me the King, provoked to it by the Queen,
Devised impeachments° to imprison him,   *charges*
And when my uncle told me so he wept,
And pitied me, and kindly kissed my cheek,
25 Bade me rely on him as on my father,
And he would love me dearly as his child.
DUCHESS OF YORK Ah, that deceit should steal such gentle shapes,°   *appearances*
And with a virtuous visor° hide deep vice!   *mask*
He is my son, ay, and therein my shame;
30 Yet from my dugs° he drew not this deceit.   *breasts*
BOY Think you my uncle did dissemble, grannam?
DUCHESS OF YORK Ay, boy.
BOY I cannot think it. Hark, what noise is this?
Enter QUEEN [ELIZABETH] *with her hair about her ears*[2]
QUEEN ELIZABETH Ah, who shall hinder me to wail and weep?
35 To chide my fortune, and torment myself?
I'll join with black despair against my soul,
And to myself become an enemy.
DUCHESS OF YORK What means this scene of rude° impatience?   *violent*
QUEEN ELIZABETH To mark an act of tragic violence.
40 Edward, my lord, thy son, our king, is dead.[3]
Why grow the branches when the root is gone?
Why wither not the leaves that want° their sap?   *lack*
If you will live, lament; if die, be brief,
That our swift-wingèd souls may catch the King's,
45 Or like obedient subjects follow him
To his new kingdom of ne'er-changing night.
DUCHESS OF YORK Ah, so much interest° have I in thy sorrow   *right to share*
As I had title[4] in thy noble husband.
I have bewept a worthy husband's[5] death,
50 And lived with looking on his images.°   *likenesses (his sons)*
But now two mirrors[6] of his princely semblance

---

2. Disheveled hair was a conventional expression of grief on the Elizabethan stage. F adds "Rivers and Dorset after her" and gives them lines to speak later in the scene.
3. Shakespeare is telescoping events. Edward actually died some five years after Clarence.
4. Legal right (as Edward's mother, the Duchess of York has a right to mourn).
5. The Duke of York (whose death is dramatized in *Richard Duke of York*).
6. Clarence and King Edward.

Are cracked in pieces by malignant death,
And I for comfort have but one false glass,°   *(Richard)*
That grieves me when I see my shame in him.
55 Thou art a widow, yet thou art a mother,
And hast the comfort of thy children left.
But death hath snatched my husband from mine arms
And plucked two crutches from my feeble hands,
Clarence and Edward. O what cause have I,
60 Thine being but a moiety° of my moan,   *half*
To overgo° thy woes, and drown thy cries?   *exceed*
BOY [*to* ELIZABETH]   Ah, aunt, you wept not for our father's death.
How can we aid you with our kindred tears?°   *tears of relatives*
DAUGHTER [*to* ELIZABETH]   Our fatherless distress was left unmoaned;
65 Your widow-dolour° likewise be unwept.   *widow's grief*
QUEEN ELIZABETH   Give me no help in lamentation.
I am not barren to bring forth complaints.[7]
All springs reduce[8] their currents to mine eyes,
That I, being governed by the wat'ry moon,
70 May send forth plenteous tears to drown the world.
Ah, for my husband, for my dear Lord Edward!
CHILDREN   Ah, for our father, for our dear Lord Clarence!
DUCHESS OF YORK   Alas, for both, both mine, Edward and Clarence!
QUEEN ELIZABETH   What stay° had I but Edward, and he's gone?   *support*
75 CHILDREN   What stay had we but Clarence, and he's gone?
DUCHESS OF YORK   What stays had I but they, and they are gone?
QUEEN ELIZABETH   Was never widow had so dear° a loss!   *grievous*
CHILDREN   Were never orphans had so dear a loss!
DUCHESS OF YORK   Was never mother had so dear a loss!
80 Alas, I am the mother of these griefs.
Their woes are parcelled;° mine is general.   *inclusive*
She for an Edward weeps, and so do I;
I for a Clarence weep, so doth not she.
These babes for Clarence weep, and so do I;
85 I for an Edward weep, so do not they.
Alas, you three on me, threefold distressed,
Pour all your tears. I am your sorrow's nurse,
And I will pamper° it with lamentation.[9]   *(over)feed*
88.1   DORSET   *Comfort, dear mother. God is much displeased*
         That you take with unthankfulness his doing.
         In common worldly things 'tis called ungrateful
         With dull unwillingness to pay a debt
88.5   *Which with a bounteous hand was kindly lent;*
         Much more to be thus opposite with° heaven   *in opposition to*
         For it requires° the royal debt it lent you.   *calls back*
     RIVERS   *Madam, bethink you like a careful mother*
         Of the young Prince your son. Send straight for him;
88.10   *Let him be crowned. In him your comfort lives.*
         Drown desperate sorrow in dead Edward's grave
         And plant your joys in living Edward's throne.

---

7. I can deliver my own lamentations.
8. Lead back (as to the sea, which is governed by the moon).

9. The indented passage that follows, 88.1–88.12, appears only in F.

Enter RICHARD [*Duke of*] GLOUCESTER, *the* [*Duke of*]
BUCKINGHAM, [*Lord* STANLEY *Earl of*] *Derby*, [LORD]
HASTINGS, *and* [*Sir Richard*] RATCLIFFE

RICHARD GLOUCESTER [*to* ELIZABETH] Sister, have comfort. All of us have cause

90   To wail the dimming of our shining star,
       But none can help our harms by wailing them.—
       Madam, my mother, I do cry you mercy.°   *I beg your pardon*
       I did not see your grace. Humbly on my knee
       I crave your blessing.

95 DUCHESS OF YORK   God bless thee, and put meekness in thy breast,
       Love, charity, obedience, and true duty.

RICHARD GLOUCESTER   Amen. [*Aside*] 'And make me die a good old man.'
       That is the butt-end° of a mother's blessing;   *conclusion*
       I marvel that her grace did leave it out.

100 BUCKINGHAM   You cloudy° princes and heart-sorrowing peers   *sad; raining (tears)*
       That bear this heavy mutual load of moan,°   *lamentation*
       Now cheer each other in each other's love.
       Though we have spent our harvest of this king,
       We are to reap the harvest of his son.

105   The broken rancour[1] of your high-swoll'n hearts
       But lately° splinted, knit, and joined together,   *Only recently*
       Must gently be preserved, cherished, and kept.
       Meseemeth° good that, with some little train,°   *I think it / entourage*
       Forthwith from Ludlow[2] the young Prince be fet°   *fetched*

110   Hither to London to be crowned our king.[3]

110.1   RIVERS   *Why with some little train, my lord of Buckingham?*

       BUCKINGHAM   *Marry, my lord, lest by a multitude*°   *large entourage*
       The new-healed wound of malice should break out,
       Which would be so much the more dangerous

110.5   *By how much the estate is green and yet ungoverned.*[4]
       Where every horse bears his commanding rein[5]
       And may direct his course as please himself°   *as he pleases*
       As well the fear of harm as harm apparent°   *as actual harm*
       In my opinion ought to be prevented.

110.10 RICHARD GLOUCESTER   *I hope the King made peace with all of us,*
       And the compact is firm and true in me.

       RIVERS   *And so in me, and so I think in all.*
       Yet since it is but green, it should be put
       To no apparent likelihood of breach,

110.15   *Which haply*° *by much company might be urged.*   *perhaps*
       Therefore I say, with noble Buckingham,
       That it is meet° *so few should fetch the Prince.*   *fitting*

       HASTINGS   *And so say I.*

RICHARD GLOUCESTER   Then be it so, and go we to determine
       Who they shall be that straight shall post° to Ludlow.—   *ride speedily*
       Madam, and you my sister, will you go
       To give your censures° in this weighty business?   *opinions*

115 QUEEN ELIZABETH *and* DUCHESS OF YORK   With all our hearts.

Exeunt. Manent RICHARD *and* BUCKINGHAM

---

1. Bitterness that caused you to be divided (unnatu-
rally, like a broken limb).
2. Royal castle in Shropshire, near the Welsh border,
where Prince Edward, as Prince of Wales, was staying.
3. The indented passage that follows, 110.1–110.18,

appears only in F.
4. *By . . . ungoverned*: Considering that the govern-
ment is newly established and not yet in full control.
5. *bears . . . rein*: takes charge of the rein that should
restrain him.

BUCKINGHAM　My lord, whoever journeys to the Prince,
　　For God's sake let not us two stay at home,
　　For by the way I'll sort° occasion, *find*
　　As index° to the story we late° talked of, *prologue / lately*
120　To part the Queen's proud kindred from the Prince.
RICHARD GLOUCESTER　My other self, my counsel's consistory,° *council chamber*
　　My oracle, my prophet, my dear cousin!
　　I, as a child, will go by thy direction.
　　Towards Ludlow then, for we'll not stay behind.　　*Exeunt*

2.3
Enter one CITIZEN *at one door and another at the other*
FIRST CITIZEN　Good morrow, neighbour. Whither away so fast?
SECOND CITIZEN　I promise° you, I scarcely know myself. *assure*
　　Hear you the news abroad?
FIRST CITIZEN　　　　　　　Yes, that the King is dead.
SECOND CITIZEN　Ill news, by'r Lady;° seldom comes the better.[1] *by the Virgin Mary*
5　I fear, I fear, 'twill prove a giddy° world. *mad*
　　　　Enter another CITIZEN
THIRD CITIZEN　Neighbours, God speed.
FIRST CITIZEN　　　　　　　Give you good morrow, sir.
THIRD CITIZEN　Doth the news hold of good King Edward's death?
SECOND CITIZEN　Ay, sir, it is too true. God help the while.
THIRD CITIZEN　Then, masters,° look to see a troublous world. *sirs*
10　FIRST CITIZEN　No, no, by God's good grace his son shall reign.
THIRD CITIZEN　Woe to that land that's governed by a child.
SECOND CITIZEN　In him there is a hope of government,
　　Which in his nonage council under him,[2]
　　And in his full and ripened years himself,
15　No doubt shall then, and till then, govern well.
FIRST CITIZEN　So stood the state when Henry the Sixth
　　Was crowned in Paris but at nine months old.
THIRD CITIZEN　Stood the state so? No, no, good friends, God wot.° *knows*
　　For then this land was famously enriched
20　With politic,° grave counsel;° then the King *astute / advisers*
　　Had virtuous uncles to protect his grace.
FIRST CITIZEN　Why, so hath this, both by his father and mother.
THIRD CITIZEN　Better it were they all came by his father,
　　Or by his father there were none at all.
25　For emulation° who shall now be near'st[3] *competition*
　　Will touch us all too near, if God prevent not.
　　O full of danger is the Duke of Gloucester,
　　And the Queen's sons and brothers haught° and proud. *haughty*
　　And were they° to be ruled, and not to rule, *(both factions)*
30　This sickly land might solace° as before. *prosper*
FIRST CITIZEN　Come, come, we fear the worst. All will be well.
THIRD CITIZEN　When clouds are seen, wise men put on their cloaks;
　　When great leaves fall, then winter is at hand;
　　When the sun sets, who doth not look for night?
35　Untimely storms make men expect a dearth.

2.3 Location: A street in London.
1. Things rarely change for the better (proverbial).
2. The Privy Council governing in his name during the

years of his minority.
3. Most influential with the King.

All may be well, but if God sort° it so   *ordain*
'Tis more than we deserve, or I expect.
SECOND CITIZEN   Truly the hearts of men are full of fear.
You cannot reason° almost with a man   *converse*
40   That looks not heavily and full of dread.
THIRD CITIZEN   Before the days of change still is it so.
By a divine instinct men's minds mistrust°   *suspect*
Ensuing danger, as by proof° we see   *experience*
The water swell before a boist'rous storm.
45   But leave it all to God. Whither away?
SECOND CITIZEN   Marry, we were sent for to the justices.
THIRD CITIZEN   And so was I. I'll bear you company.   *Exeunt*

2.4

Enter [Lord] CARDINAL, *young [Duke of]* YORK, QUEEN
*[*ELIZABETH*], and the [old]* DUCHESS OF YORK

CARDINAL   Last night, I hear, they lay them at Northampton.
At Stony Stratford[1] they do rest tonight.
Tomorrow, or next day, they will be here.
DUCHESS OF YORK   I long with all my heart to see the Prince.
5   I hope he is much grown since last I saw him.
QUEEN ELIZABETH   But I hear, no. They say my son of York
Has almost overta'en him in his growth.
YORK   Ay, mother, but I would not have it so.
DUCHESS OF YORK   Why, my young cousin, it is good to grow.
10   YORK   Grandam, one night as we did sit at supper,
My uncle Rivers talked how I did grow
More than my brother. 'Ay', quoth my nuncle° Gloucester,   *uncle (colloquial)*
'Small herbs have grace; gross weeds do grow apace'.°   *rapidly*
And since, methinks I would not grow so fast,
15   Because sweet flow'rs are slow, and weeds make haste.
DUCHESS OF YORK   Good faith, good faith, the saying did not hold°   *hold true*
In him that did object° the same to thee.   *argue*
He was the wretched'st thing when he was young,
So long a-growing, and so leisurely,
20   That if his rule were true he should be gracious.
CARDINAL   Why, so no doubt he is, my gracious madam.
DUCHESS OF YORK   I hope he is, but yet let mothers doubt.
YORK   Now, by my troth, if I had been remembered,
I could have given my uncle's grace a flout[2]
25   To touch his growth, nearer than he touched° mine.   *hit*
DUCHESS OF YORK   How, my young York? I pray thee, let me hear it.
YORK   Marry, they say my uncle grew so fast
That he could gnaw a crust at two hours old.
'Twas full two years ere I could get a tooth.
30   Grannam, this would have been a biting jest.
DUCHESS OF YORK   I pray thee, pretty York, who told thee this?
YORK   Grannam, his nurse.
DUCHESS OF YORK   His nurse? Why, she was dead ere thou wast born.
YORK   If 'twere not she, I cannot tell who told me.

2.4 Location: The palace, London.   2. *if . . . flout:* if I had been told this, I could have
1. Town in Buckinghamshire (south of Northampton).   taunted my noble uncle.
F reverses the order of the towns.

35 QUEEN ELIZABETH   A parlous° boy! Go to,³ you are too shrewd.°   *mischievous / sharp*
CARDINAL   Good madam, be not angry with the child.
QUEEN ELIZABETH   Pitchers have ears.⁴
          Enter [Marquis] DORSET
CARDINAL   Here comes your son, Lord Dorset.
What news, Lord Marquis?
DORSET   Such news, my lord,
As grieves me to report.
QUEEN ELIZABETH   How doth the Prince?
DORSET   Well, madam, and in health.
40 DUCHESS OF YORK   What is thy news then?
DORSET   Lord Rivers and Lord Gray are sent to Pomfret,⁵
And with them Thomas Vaughan, prisoners.
DUCHESS OF YORK   Who hath committed them?
DORSET   The mighty dukes,
Gloucester and Buckingham.
CARDINAL   For what offence?
45 DORSET   The sum of all I can,° I have disclosed.   *know*
Why or for what the nobles were committed
Is all unknown to me, my gracious lord.
QUEEN ELIZABETH   Ay me! I see the ruin of our house.
The tiger now hath seized the gentle hind.°   *doe*
50 Insulting tyranny begins to jet°   *encroach; strut*
Upon the innocent and aweless⁶ throne.
Welcome destruction, blood, and massacre!
I see, as in a map, the end of all.
DUCHESS OF YORK   Accursèd and unquiet wrangling days,
55 How many of you have mine eyes beheld?
My husband lost his life to get the crown,
And often up and down my sons were tossed,
For me to joy and weep their gain and loss.
And being seated,° and domestic broils°   *enthroned / disorders*
60 Clean overblown,° themselves the conquerors   *Completely ended*
Make war upon themselves, brother to brother,
Blood to blood, self against self. O preposterous
And frantic outrage, end thy damnèd spleen,°   *malice*
Or let me die, to look on death no more.
65 QUEEN ELIZABETH [*to* YORK]   Come, come, my boy, we will to sanctuary.⁷—
Madam, farewell.
DUCHESS OF YORK   Stay, I will go with you.
QUEEN ELIZABETH   You have no cause.
CARDINAL [*to* ELIZABETH]   My gracious lady, go,
And thither bear your treasure and your goods.
For my part, I'll resign° unto your grace   *hand over*
70 The seal⁸ I keep, and so betide° to me   *and so may it happen*
As well I tender° you and all of yours.   *care for*
Go, I'll conduct you to the sanctuary.   *Exeunt*

---

3. Expression of disapproval.
4. Proverbially said of children who overhear remarks made by adults: "Little pitchers have big ears."
5. Modern Pontefract, in west Yorkshire, site of the castle where Richard II was murdered.
6. Not able to command respect (because the King is so young).

7. Anyone, including criminals, could claim the protection of the church ("sanctuary") and thus immunity from civil law, initially for forty days. The Queen sought sanctuary at Westminster Abbey.
8. An engraved stamp, signifying the authority of the bearer, used to authenticate legal documents; here, the Great Seal of England.

3.1[1]

The Trumpets sound. Enter young PRINCE [EDWARD],
the Dukes of GLOUCESTER *and* BUCKINGHAM, *Lord* CAR-
DINAL, *with others* [*including Lord* STANLEY *Earl of
Derby and Sir William* CATESBY]

BUCKINGHAM   Welcome, sweet Prince, to London, to your chamber.[2]
RICHARD GLOUCESTER [*to* PRINCE EDWARD]   Welcome, dear
    cousin, my thoughts' sovereign.°   *ruler of my thoughts*
  The weary way hath made you melancholy.
PRINCE EDWARD   No, uncle, but our crosses[3] on the way
5   Have made it tedious, wearisome, and heavy.
    I want° more uncles here to welcome me.   *lack; desire*
RICHARD GLOUCESTER   Sweet Prince, the untainted virtue of your years
    Hath not yet dived into the world's deceit,
    Nor more can you distinguish of a man
10   Than of his outward show, which God he knows
    Seldom or never jumpeth° with the heart.   *coincides*
    Those uncles[4] which you want were dangerous.
    Your grace attended to their sugared words,
    But looked not on the poison of their hearts.
15   God keep you from them, and from such false friends.
PRINCE EDWARD   God keep me from false friends; but they were none.
          Enter Lord MAYOR [*and his train*]
RICHARD GLOUCESTER   My lord, the Mayor of London comes to greet you.
MAYOR [*kneeling to* PRINCE EDWARD]   God bless your grace with
    health and happy days.
PRINCE EDWARD   I thank you, good my lord, and thank you all.—
20   I thought my mother and my brother York
    Would long ere this have met us on the way.
    Fie, what a slug° is Hastings, that he hastes not   *sluggard*
    To tell us whether they will come or no.
          Enter LORD HASTINGS
BUCKINGHAM   In happy time here comes the sweating lord.
25 PRINCE EDWARD [*to* HASTINGS]   Welcome, my lord. What, will
    our mother come?
LORD HASTINGS   On what occasion° God he knows, not I,   *For what reason*
    The Queen your mother, and your brother York,
    Have taken sanctuary. The tender° Prince   *young; affectionate*
    Would fain have° come with me to meet your grace,   *Would have liked to*
30   But by his mother was perforce° withheld.   *forcibly*
BUCKINGHAM   Fie, what an indirect and peevish° course   *perverse*
    Is this of hers!—Lord Cardinal, will your grace
    Persuade the Queen to send the Duke of York
    Unto his princely brother presently?°—   *immediately*
35   If she deny, Lord Hastings, go with him,
    And from her jealous° arms pluck him perforce.   *suspicious; mistrustful*
CARDINAL   My lord of Buckingham, if my weak oratory
    Can from his mother win the Duke of York,

3.1 Location: A street in London.
1. Either because of defects in the original manuscript or because of blunders in the printing house, the text of this scene, up to line 148, is exceptionally corrupt and has been editorially reconstructed.
2. Capital (London was known as *camera regis,* "the King's chamber").

3. Referring to the arrests of his uncle and half-brothers on the journey.
4. Of the two arrested, only Rivers, being Elizabeth's brother, was Prince Edward's real uncle; Gray, a son by Elizabeth's previous marriage, was therefore actually half brother to the Prince.

   Anon° expect him. But if she be obdurate   *Very soon*
40 To mild entreaties, God in heaven forbid
   We should infringe the sacred privilege
   Of blessèd sanctuary. Not for all this land
   Would I be guilty of so deep a sin.
  BUCKINGHAM You are too senseless-obstinate, my lord,
45 Too ceremonious° and traditional.   *rule-bound*
   Weigh it not with the grossness° of this age.   *coarseness*
   You break not sanctuary in seizing him.
   The benefit thereof is always granted
   To those whose dealings have deserved the place,
50 And those who have the wit to claim the place.
   This prince hath neither claimed it nor deserved it,
   And therefore, in my mind, he cannot have it.
   Then taking him from thence that 'longs not there,[5]
   You break thereby no privilege nor charter.
55 Oft have I heard of 'sanctuary men',[6]
   But 'sanctuary children' ne'er till now.
  CARDINAL My lord, you shall o'errule my mind for once.—
   Come on, Lord Hastings, will you go with me?
  LORD HASTINGS I come, my lord.
60 PRINCE EDWARD Good lords, make all the speedy haste you may.—
       Exeunt CARDINAL *and* HASTINGS
   Say, uncle Gloucester, if our brother come,
   Where shall we sojourn° till our coronation?   *stay*
  RICHARD GLOUCESTER Where it seems best unto your royal self.
   If I may counsel you, some day or two
65 Your highness shall repose you at the Tower,[7]
   Then where you please and shall be thought most fit
   For your best health and recreation.
  PRINCE EDWARD I do not like the Tower of any place.°—   *of all places*
   Did Julius Caesar build that place, my lord?
70 BUCKINGHAM He did, my gracious lord, begin that place,
   Which since succeeding ages have re-edified.°   *built further*
  PRINCE EDWARD Is it upon record, or else reported[8]
   Successively from age to age, he built it?
  BUCKINGHAM Upon record, my gracious liege.
75 PRINCE EDWARD But say, my lord, it were not registered,°   *documented*
   Methinks the truth should live from age to age,
   As 'twere retailed° to all posterity   *related orally*
   Even to the general all-ending day.°   *Day of Judgment*
  RICHARD GLOUCESTER [*aside*] So wise so young, they say, do
    never live long.
80 PRINCE EDWARD What say you, uncle?
  RICHARD GLOUCESTER I say, 'Without characters° fame lives long'.   *writing*
   [*Aside*] Thus like the formal Vice, Iniquity,[9]
   I moralize two meanings in one word.[1]
  PRINCE EDWARD That Julius Caesar was a famous man:

---

5. Taking the Prince from a place he has not claimed as sanctuary.
6. Criminals seeking to avoid prosecution.
7. It was customary for Kings of England (before James II) to spend the night before their coronation in the Tower, it being a royal palace and one of the strongest fortresses in the country. But Edward fears its other

aspect, as a prison.
8. Is it on written record or otherwise told orally.
9. The conventional Vice figure, called Iniquity, who in sixteenth-century morality plays symbolized all of the vices.
1. As the Vice often did, Richard makes the same phrase have a double meaning.

85 With what his valour did t'enrich his wit,
His wit set down to make his valour live.[2]
Death made no conquest of this conqueror,
For yet he lives in fame though not in life.
I'll tell you what, my cousin Buckingham.
90 BUCKINGHAM   What, my good lord?
PRINCE EDWARD   An if° I live until I be a man,   *An if = If*
I'll win our ancient right[3] in France again,
Or die a soldier, as I lived a king.
RICHARD GLOUCESTER [*aside*]   Short summers lightly have a
forward spring.[4]

*Enter young [Duke of] YORK, [LORD] HASTINGS, and
[Lord] CARDINAL*

95 BUCKINGHAM   Now in good time, here comes the Duke of York.
PRINCE EDWARD   Richard of York, how fares our loving brother?
YORK   Well, my dread[5] lord—so must I call you now.
PRINCE EDWARD   Ay, brother, to our grief, as it is yours.
Too late° he died that might have kept that title,   *recently*
100 Which by his death hath lost much majesty.
RICHARD GLOUCESTER   How fares our noble cousin, Lord of York?
YORK   I thank you, gentle uncle, well. O, my lord,
You said that idle° weeds are fast in growth;   *useless*
The Prince, my brother, hath outgrown me far.
105 RICHARD GLOUCESTER   He hath, my lord.
YORK   And therefore is he idle?
RICHARD GLOUCESTER   O my fair cousin, I must not say so.
YORK   He is more beholden to you then than I.
RICHARD GLOUCESTER   He may command me as my sovereign,
But you have power in me as a kinsman.
110 YORK   I pray you, uncle, render me this dagger.
RICHARD GLOUCESTER   My dagger, little cousin? With all my heart.
PRINCE EDWARD   A beggar, brother?
YORK   Of my kind uncle that I know will give,
It being but a toy° which is no grief to give.   *trifle*
115 RICHARD GLOUCESTER   A greater gift than that I'll give my cousin.
YORK   A greater gift? O, that's the sword to it.[6]
RICHARD GLOUCESTER   Ay, gentle cousin, were it light enough.
YORK   O, then I see you will part but° with light° gifts.   *only / trivial*
In weightier things you'll say a beggar nay.
120 RICHARD GLOUCESTER   It is too heavy for your grace to wear.
YORK   I'd weigh it lightly, were it heavier.[7]
RICHARD GLOUCESTER   What, would you have my weapon, little lord?
YORK   I would, that I might thank you as you call me.
RICHARD GLOUCESTER   How?
125 YORK   Little.
PRINCE EDWARD   My lord of York will still be cross° in talk.—   *perverse; quarrelsome*
Uncle, your grace knows how to bear with him.
YORK   You mean to bear me, not to bear with me.—
Uncle, my brother mocks both you and me.

---

2. *With . . . live:* The same valorous deeds that
enlivened Caesar's writing were themselves made
immortal by his retelling of them.
3. Right to the throne (claimed by Henry V and his son
Henry VI).
4. Proverbial: Those who die young ("forward") are

often ("lightly") precocious.
5. Held in awe (a common formula for addressing a
king).
6. *to it:* that is, to the dagger (the sword is to the dagger as the greater gift is to the lesser).
7. I'd consider it of little value, even if it were heavier.

130 Because that I am little like an ape,
    He thinks that you should bear me on your shoulders.[8]
BUCKINGHAM   With what a sharp, prodigal wit[9] he reasons.
    To mitigate the scorn he gives his uncle,
    He prettily and aptly taunts himself.
135 So cunning and so young is wonderful.°   *a cause of wonder*
RICHARD GLOUCESTER [*to* PRINCE EDWARD]   My lord, will't
    please you pass along?
    Myself and my good cousin Buckingham
    Will° to your mother to entreat of her   *Will go*
    To meet you at the Tower and welcome you.
140 YORK [*to* PRINCE EDWARD]   What, will you go unto the Tower, my lord?
PRINCE EDWARD   My Lord Protector needs will have it so.
YORK   I shall not sleep in quiet at the Tower.
RICHARD GLOUCESTER   Why, what should you fear there?
YORK   Marry, my uncle Clarence' angry ghost.
145 My grannam told me he was murdered there.
PRINCE EDWARD   I fear no uncles dead.
RICHARD GLOUCESTER   Nor none that live, I hope.
PRINCE EDWARD   An if they[1] live, I hope I need not fear.
    [*To* YORK] But come, my lord, and with a heavy heart,
    Thinking on them, go we unto the Tower.
    A sennet.[2]
          Exeunt. Manent RICHARD, BUCKINGHAM, *and* CATESBY
BUCKINGHAM [*to* RICHARD]   Think you, my lord, this little prating°   *chattering*
150   York
    Was not incensèd° by his subtle mother   *incited*
    To taunt and scorn you thus opprobriously?
RICHARD GLOUCESTER   No doubt, no doubt. O, 'tis a parlous° boy,   *shrewd*
    Bold, quick, ingenious, forward, capable.
155 He is all the mother's, from the top to toe.
BUCKINGHAM   Well, let them rest.—Come hither, Catesby. Thou art sworn
    As deeply° to effect what we intend   *cunningly*
    As closely° to conceal what we impart.   *secretly*
    Thou know'st our reasons, urged upon the way.[3]
160 What think'st thou? Is it not an easy matter
    To make Lord William Hastings of our mind,[4]
    For the instalment° of this noble duke   *enthroning*
    In the seat royal of this famous isle?
CATESBY   He for his father's sake so loves the Prince[5]
165 That he will not be won to aught against him.
BUCKINGHAM   What think'st thou then of Stanley?° Will not he?   *(Earl of Derby)*
CATESBY   He will do all-in-all as Hastings doth.
BUCKINGHAM   Well then, no more but this. Go, gentle Catesby,
    And, as it were far off, sound thou Lord Hastings
170 How he doth stand affected to our purpose.[6]
170.1   *And summon him tomorrow to the Tower*
          To sit about° the coronation.   *To discuss in council*
    If thou dost find him tractable° to us,   *compliant*

8. Alluding to Richard's hunched back, which is com-
pared to the saddle worn by jesters who carried mon-
keys about at carnivals and fairs.
9. A nimble wit (intelligence); a wit both sharp and
prodigal (abundant or excessive).
1. Richard meant himself; Edward refers to Rivers and
Gray.

2. Trumpet notes to signal a procession.
3. On the journey from London to Ludlow.
4. To have Hastings share in our opinion.
5. Hastings loves the Prince as the son of the beloved
King Edward.
6. The following indented passage, 170.1–170.2,
appears only in F. *stand affected to:* regard, like.

Encourage him, and tell him all our reasons.
If he be leaden, icy, cold, unwilling,
Be thou so too, and so break off your talk,
175   And give us notice of his inclination,
For we tomorrow hold divided counsels,[7]
Wherein thyself shalt highly° be employed.   *importantly*
RICHARD GLOUCESTER   Commend me to Lord William.° Tell   *(Hastings)*
      him, Catesby,
His ancient knot[8] of dangerous adversaries
180   Tomorrow are let blood° at Pomfret Castle,   *are executed*
And bid my lord, for joy of this good news,
Give Mrs Shore[9] one gentle kiss the more.
BUCKINGHAM   Good Catesby, go effect this business soundly.°   *thoroughly; well*
CATESBY   My good lords both, with all the heed I can.
185   RICHARD GLOUCESTER   Shall we hear from you, Catesby, ere we sleep?
CATESBY   You shall, my lord.
RICHARD GLOUCESTER   At Crosby House,° there shall you find   *(Richard's residence)*
      us both.   *Exit* CATESBY
BUCKINGHAM   My lord, what shall we do if we perceive
Lord Hastings will not yield to our complots?°   *plots*
190   RICHARD GLOUCESTER   Chop off his head. Something we will determine.
And look when° I am king, claim thou of me   *And as soon as*
The earldom of Hereford, and all the movables[1]
Whereof the King my brother was possessed.
BUCKINGHAM   I'll claim that promise at your grace's hand.
195   RICHARD GLOUCESTER   And look° to have it yielded with all kindness.   *And expect*
Come, let us sup betimes,° that afterwards   *early*
We may digest our complots in some form.[2]   *Exeunt*

3.2

Enter a MESSENGER *to the door of* LORD HASTINGS
MESSENGER [*knocking*]   My lord, my lord!
LORD HASTINGS [*within*]   Who knocks?
MESSENGER   One from Lord Stanley.
Enter LORD HASTINGS
LORD HASTINGS   What is't o'clock?
MESSENGER   Upon the stroke of four.
LORD HASTINGS   Cannot my Lord Stanley sleep these tedious nights?
MESSENGER   So it appears by that I have to say.
5   First he commends him to your noble self.
LORD HASTINGS   What then?
MESSENGER   Then certifies° your lordship that this night   *assures*
He dreamt the boar had razèd off his helm.[1]
Besides, he says there are two councils kept,
10   And that may be determined at the one
Which may make you and him to rue at° th'other.   *regret*
Therefore he sends to know your lordship's pleasure,
If you will presently° take horse with him,   *immediately*

---

7. There will be two separate council meetings, one
public to plan the Prince's coronation, the other private
to plot Richard's seizing of the crown.
8. Conspiracy, with additional meaning of "tumor,"
picked up in the next line in the image of bloodletting
as medical treatment.
9. After Edward's death, Jane Shore (see 1.1.71–77)
became Hastings's mistress.

1. Personal as opposed to real property: furnishings,
rather than land.
2. We may break plans down into an orderly system
(with pun on "digest").
3.2 Location: Outside Lord Hastings's house, in Lon-
don.
1. He dreamed the boar (Richard's emblem) had
sheared off his helmet (figuratively, cut off his head).

And with all speed post with him toward the north
15   To shun the danger that his soul divines.°   *prophesies*
LORD HASTINGS   Go, fellow, go, return unto thy lord.
  Bid him not fear the separated councils.
  His honour and myself are at the one,
  And at the other is my good friend Catesby,
20   Where nothing can proceed that toucheth° us   *concerns; harms*
  Whereof I shall not have intelligence.°   *secret information*
  Tell him his fears are shallow, without instance.°   *evidence*
  And for his dreams, I wonder he's so simple,°   *childish*
  To trust the mock'ry of unquiet slumbers.
25   To fly the boar before the boar pursues
  Were to incense the boar to follow us,
  And make pursuit where he did mean° no chase.   *intend*
  Go, bid thy master rise, and come to me,
  And we will both together to the Tower,
30   Where he shall see the boar will use us kindly.[2]
MESSENGER   I'll go, my lord, and tell him what you say.   *Exit*
      Enter CATESBY
CATESBY   Many good morrows to my noble lord.
LORD HASTINGS   Good morrow, Catesby. You are early stirring.
  What news, what news, in this our tott'ring state?
35 CATESBY   It is a reeling° world indeed, my lord,   *an unstable*
  And I believe will never stand upright
  Till Richard wear the garland of the realm.
LORD HASTINGS   How? 'Wear the garland'? Dost thou mean the crown?
CATESBY   Ay, my good lord.
40 LORD HASTINGS   I'll have this crown° of mine cut from my shoulders   *head*
  Before I'll see the crown so foul misplaced.
  But canst thou guess that he doth aim at it?
CATESBY   Ay, on my life, and hopes to find you forward°   *a strong supporter*
  Upon his party° for the gain thereof—   *On his side*
45   And thereupon he sends you this good news:
  That this same very day your enemies,
  The kindred of the Queen, must die at Pomfret.
LORD HASTINGS   Indeed I am no mourner for that news,
  Because they have been still my adversaries.
50   But that I'll give my voice on Richard's side
  To bar my master's heirs in true descent,
  God knows I will not do it, to the death.[3]
CATESBY   God keep your lordship in that gracious mind!
LORD HASTINGS   But I shall laugh at this a twelvemonth hence:
55   That they which brought me in my master's hate,[4]
  I live to look upon their tragedy.
  Well, Catesby, ere a fortnight make me older,
  I'll send some packing that yet think not on't.
CATESBY   'Tis a vile thing to die, my gracious lord,
60   When men are unprepared, and look not for it.
LORD HASTINGS   O monstrous, monstrous! And so falls it out
  With Rivers, Vaughan, Gray—and so 'twill do
  With some men else, that think themselves as safe

---

2. Gently (but also, with unintended irony, character-istically).
3. Even at the risk of death.

4. That those (Rivers, Vaughan, and Gray) who turned King Edward against me.

As thou and I, who as thou know'st are dear
65 To princely Richard and to Buckingham.
CATESBY   The Princes both make high account of° you—   *highly esteem*
[*Aside*] For they account° his head upon the bridge.[5]   *expect*
LORD HASTINGS   I know they do, and I have well deserved it.
Enter Lord STANLEY
Come on, come on, where is your boar-spear,[6] man?
70 Fear you the boar, and go so unprovided?[7]
STANLEY   My lord, good morrow.—Good morrow, Catesby.—
You may jest on, but by the Holy Rood°   *Cross*
I do not like these several° councils, I.   *separate*
LORD HASTINGS   My lord, I hold my life as dear as you do yours,
75 And never in my days, I do protest,
Was it so precious to me as 'tis now.
Think you, but° that I know our state secure,   *if it were not*
I would be so triumphant as I am?
STANLEY   The lords at Pomfret, when they rode from London,
80 Were jocund,° and supposed their states were sure,°   *merry / secure*
And they indeed had no cause to mistrust;
But yet you see how soon the day o'ercast.°   *became overcast*
This sudden stab of rancour I misdoubt.[8]
Pray God, I say, I prove a needless coward.
85 What, shall we toward the Tower? The day is spent.[9]
LORD HASTINGS   Come, come, have with you!° Wot° you what,   *I'll go with you / Know*
    my lord?
Today the lords you talked of are beheaded.
STANLEY   They for their truth° might better wear their heads   *honesty*
Than some that have accused them wear their hats.°   *retain their offices*
90 But come, my lord, let us away.
Enter a PURSUIVANT [*named*] *Hastings*[1]
LORD HASTINGS   Go on before; I'll follow presently.
Exeunt STANLEY *and* CATESBY
Well met, Hastings. How goes the world with thee?
PURSUIVANT   The better that your lordship please° to ask.   *is pleased*
LORD HASTINGS   I tell thee, man, 'tis better with me now
95 Than when I met thee last, where now we meet.
Then was I going prisoner to the Tower,
By the suggestion° of the Queen's allies;   *incitement*
But now, I tell thee—keep it to thyself—
This day those enemies are put to death,
100 And I in better state than e'er I was.
PURSUIVANT   God hold it[2] to your honour's good content.
LORD HASTINGS   Gramercy,° Hastings. There, drink that for me.   *Many thanks*
He throws him his purse
PURSUIVANT   God save your lordship.   *Exit*
Enter a PRIEST

---

5. London Bridge (where the heads of traitors were displayed high on poles).
6. Specialized hunting spear with a crossbar to prevent the impaled boar's tusks from wounding the hunter.
7. Do you fear the boar, and (yet) go unprepared?
8. I mistrust such sudden attacks (as those that befell Rivers, Vaughan, and Gray).
9. It's getting late (in the morning). The scene had opened at 4:00 A.M.
1. F omits his name (taken from Holinshed's *Chroni-*

cles), here and in the dialogue. The name may be important in calling attention to the significance of Lord Hastings's own name: the word means either "someone who hurries" (here, to his destruction) or "a fruit that ripens early or before its time." *pursuivant*: state messenger with authority to execute warrants (particularly of treason). Figuratively, a pursuivant was any summoner or messenger.
2. May God maintain your prosperity.

PRIEST   Well met, my lord. I am glad to see your honour.
105 LORD HASTINGS   I thank thee, good Sir³ John, with all my heart.
     I am in your debt for your last exercise.°   *sermon*
     Come the next sabbath, and I will content you.⁴
          He whispers in his ear.
          Enter BUCKINGHAM
     BUCKINGHAM   What, talking with a priest, Lord Chamberlain?
     Your friends at Pomfret, they do need the priest;
110 Your honour hath no shriving work⁵ in hand.
     LORD HASTINGS   Good faith, and when I met this holy man
     The men you talk of came into my mind.
     What, go you toward the Tower?
     BUCKINGHAM   I do, my lord, but long I cannot stay there;
115 I shall return before your lordship thence.
     LORD HASTINGS   Nay, like enough, for I stay dinner⁶ there.
     BUCKINGHAM [*aside*]   And supper° too, although thou⁷ know'st it not.   *evening meal*
     Come, will you go?
     LORD HASTINGS   I'll wait upon° your lordship.   *Exeunt*   *attend; go with*

                              3.3
          Enter Sir Richard RATCLIFFE *with halberdiers carrying
          Lords* RIVERS, GRAY, *and [Sir Thomas]* VAUGHAN *to
          death at Pomfret*¹
     RIVERS   Sir Richard Ratcliffe, let me tell thee this:
     Today shalt thou behold a subject die
     For truth, for duty, and for loyalty.
     GRAY [*to* RATCLIFFE]   God bless the Prince from all the pack of you!
5   A knot° you are of damnèd bloodsuckers.   *group*
     VAUGHAN [*to* RATCLIFFE]   You live, that shall cry woe for° this   *shall regret*
          hereafter.
     RATCLIFFE   Dispatch.° The limit of your lives is out.   *Be quick*
     RIVERS   O Pomfret, Pomfret! O thou bloody prison,
10   Fatal and ominous to noble peers!
     Within the guilty closure° of thy walls,   *enclosure*
     Richard the Second here was hacked to death,
     And, for more slander to thy dismal seat,²
     We give to thee our guiltless blood to drink.
     GRAY   Now Margaret's curse is fall'n upon our heads,
15   For standing by when Richard stabbed her son.
     RIVERS   Then cursed she Hastings; then cursed she Buckingham;
     Then cursed she Richard. O remember, God,
     To hear her prayer for them as now for us.
     And for° my sister and her princely sons,   *as for*
20   Be satisfied, dear God, with our true blood,
     Which, as thou know'st, unjustly must be spilt.
     RATCLIFFE   Make haste: the hour of death is expiate.°   *fully come*
     RIVERS   Come, Gray; come, Vaughan; let us here embrace.
     Farewell, until we meet again in heaven.   *Exeunt*

---

3. Courteous title of respect for clergymen.
4. I will pay your "debt" with a donation.
5. Confession and absolution (here, before execution).
6. I stay for dinner (eaten at about 11:00 A.M.).
7. Here, used contemptuously, as opposed to the formal "you" in line 118.

3.3 Location: Pontefract Castle.
1. Q has an extra opening line for this scene: RATCLIFFE Come, bring forth the prisoners.
2. And, in order to increase the notoriety of this gloomy place.

3.4

Enter [the Duke of] BUCKINGHAM, [Lord STANLEY Earl
of] Derby, [LORD] HASTINGS, BISHOP OF ELY, [the Duke
of] NORFOLK, [Sir William CATESBY,]¹ with others at a
table

LORD HASTINGS   Now, noble peers, the cause why we are met
Is to determine of° the coronation.   decide upon
In God's name, speak: when is the royal day?
BUCKINGHAM   Is all things ready for that solemn time?
5 STANLEY   It is, and wants but nomination.°   naming the day
BISHOP OF ELY   Tomorrow, then, I judge a happy° day.   suitable
BUCKINGHAM   Who knows the Lord Protector's mind herein?
Who is most inward° with the noble Duke?   intimate
BISHOP OF ELY   Your grace, methinks, should soonest know his mind.
10 BUCKINGHAM   We know each other's faces. For° our hearts,   As for
He knows no more of mine than I of yours,
Or I of his, my lord, than you of mine.—
Lord Hastings, you and he are near in love.
LORD HASTINGS   I thank his grace; I know he loves me well.
15 But for his purpose in the coronation,
I have not sounded him,° nor he delivered   sounded him out
His gracious pleasure any way therein.
But you, my honourable lords, may name the time,
And in the Duke's behalf I'll give my voice,°   vote
20 Which I presume he'll take in gentle part.°   he'll graciously approve
Enter [RICHARD Duke of] GLOUCESTER
BISHOP OF ELY   In happy time, here comes the Duke himself.
RICHARD GLOUCESTER   My noble lords, and cousins all, good morrow.
I have been long a sleeper, but I trust
My absence doth neglect no great design²
25 Which by my presence might have been concluded.
BUCKINGHAM   Had not you come upon your cue, my lord,
William Lord Hastings had pronounced your part—
I mean, your voice, for crowning of the King.
RICHARD GLOUCESTER   Than my Lord Hastings no man might be bolder.³
30 His lordship knows me well, and loves me well.—
My lord of Ely, when I was last in Holborn⁴
I saw good strawberries in your garden there.
I do beseech you send for some of them.
BISHOP OF ELY   Marry, and will, my lord, with all my heart. *Exit*
35 RICHARD GLOUCESTER   Cousin of Buckingham, a word with you.
[Aside] Catesby hath sounded Hastings in° our business,   in respect to
And finds the testy gentleman so hot
That he will lose his head ere give consent
His 'master's child'—as worshipful° he terms it—   reverentially
40 Shall lose the royalty° of England's throne.   sovereignty
BUCKINGHAM   Withdraw yourself a while; I'll go with you.
Exeunt [RICHARD and BUCKINGHAM]⁵
STANLEY   We have not yet set down this day of triumph.

3.4 Location: The Tower of London.
1. F has Ratcliffe and Lovell (Sir Thomas Lovell; see
4.4.449) instead of Catesby.
2. My absence delays no important project.
3. No one could more confidently speak for me than
Lord Hastings; but also, no one could be more pre-
sumptuous.
4. The Bishop of Ely's official London residence.
5. Q keeps Buckingham on, and changes "I'll go with
you" to "I'll follow you."

Tomorrow, in my judgement, is too sudden,
For I myself am not so well provided°   *well equipped*
45 As else I would be, were the day prolonged.°   *further off*
      Enter BISHOP OF ELY
BISHOP OF ELY   Where is my lord, the Duke of Gloucester?
    I have sent for these strawberries.
LORD HASTINGS   His grace looks cheerfully and smooth° this morning.   *untroubled*
    There's some conceit° or other likes° him well,   *thought / pleases*
50 When that he bids good morrow with such spirit.
    I think there's never a man in Christendom
    Can lesser hide his love or hate than he,
    For by his face straight° shall you know his heart.   *immediately*
STANLEY   What of his heart perceive you in his face
55 By any likelihood° he showed today?   *appearance*
LORD HASTINGS   Marry, that with no man here he is offended—
    For were he, he had shown it in his looks.
STANLEY   I pray God he be not.
      Enter RICHARD[6] *and* BUCKINGHAM
RICHARD GLOUCESTER   I pray you all, tell me what they deserve
60 That do conspire my death with devilish plots
    Of damnèd witchcraft, and that have prevailed
    Upon my body with their hellish charms?
LORD HASTINGS   The tender love I bear your grace, my lord,
    Makes me most forward in this princely presence
65 To doom th'offenders, whatsoe'er they be.
    I say, my lord, they have deservèd death.
RICHARD GLOUCESTER   Then be your eyes the witness of their evil:
    See how I am bewitched. Behold, mine arm
    Is like a blasted sapling withered up.
70 And this is° Edward's wife, that monstrous witch,   *this is the work of*
    Consorted° with that harlot, strumpet Shore,   *In league with*
    That by their witchcraft thus have markèd me.
LORD HASTINGS   If they have done this deed, my noble lord—
RICHARD GLOUCESTER   'If'? Thou protector of this damnèd strumpet,
75 Talk'st thou to me of 'ifs'? Thou art a traitor.—
    Off with his head. Now, by Saint Paul I swear,
    I will not dine until I see the same.
    Some see it done.
    The rest that love me, rise and follow me.
      Exeunt. Manent CATESBY[7] *with* HASTINGS
80 LORD HASTINGS   Woe, woe for England! Not a whit for me,
    For I, too fond,° might have prevented this.   *foolish*
    Stanley did dream the boar did raze our helms,
    But I did scorn it and disdain to fly.
    Three times today my footcloth horse[8] did stumble,
85 And started when he looked upon the Tower,
    As° loath to bear me to the slaughterhouse.   *As though*
    O now I need the priest that spake to me.
    I now repent I told the pursuivant,
    As too triumphing,° how mine enemies   *exulting*

---

6. According to Holinshed, "He returned into the chamber . . . with a wonderful sour, angry countenance, knitting the brows, frowning and fretting, and gnawing on his lips."

7. F calls for Ratcliffe and Lovell.
8. Horse draped with a richly ornamented covering reaching almost to the ground.

90   Today at Pomfret bloodily were butchered,
    And I myself secure in grace and favour.
    O Margaret, Margaret! Now thy heavy curse
    Is lighted on poor Hastings' wretched head.
    CATESBY Come, come, dispatch: the Duke would be at dinner.
95   Make a short shrift;° he longs to see your head.   *confession (to a priest)*
    LORD HASTINGS O momentary grace of mortal men,
    Which we more hunt for than the grace of God.
    Who builds his hope in th'air of your good looks[9]
    Lives like a drunken sailor on a mast,
100   Ready with every nod[1] to tumble down
    Into the fatal bowels of the deep.[2]
    CATESBY Come, come, dispatch. 'Tis bootless to exclaim.°   *pointless to protest*
    LORD HASTINGS O bloody Richard! Miserable England!
    I prophesy the fearful'st time to thee
105   That ever wretched age hath looked upon.—
    Come lead me to the block; bear him my head.
    They smile at me, who shortly shall be dead.   *Exeunt*

3.5

Enter RICHARD *Duke of* GLOUCESTER *and [the Duke of]*
    BUCKINGHAM *in rotten° armour, marvellous ill-favoured°*   *rusty / ugly*
    RICHARD GLOUCESTER Come, cousin, canst thou quake and change thy
        colour?
    Murder thy breath in middle of a word?
    And then again begin, and stop again,
    As if thou wert distraught and mad with terror?
5   BUCKINGHAM Tut, I can counterfeit the deep tragedian,
    Tremble and start at wagging of a straw,[1]
    Speak, and look back, and pry° on every side,   *peer*
    Intending° deep suspicion; ghastly looks   *Suggesting*
    Are at my service, like enforcèd smiles,
10   And both are ready in their offices[2]
    At any time to grace my stratagems.
        Enter the [Lord] MAYOR
    RICHARD GLOUCESTER *[aside to* BUCKINGHAM] Here comes the Mayor.
    BUCKINGHAM *[aside to* RICHARD] Let me alone to entertain him.—Lord Mayor—
    RICHARD GLOUCESTER *[calling as to one within]* Look to the drawbridge there!
15   BUCKINGHAM Hark, a drum!
    RICHARD GLOUCESTER *[calling as to one within]* Catesby, o'erlook°   *look (out) over*
        the walls!
    BUCKINGHAM Lord Mayor, the reason we have sent—
    RICHARD GLOUCESTER Look back, defend thee! Here are enemies.
    BUCKINGHAM God and our innocence defend and guard us.
        Enter [Sir William] CATESBY[3] *with Hastings' head*
20   RICHARD GLOUCESTER O, O, be quiet! It is Catesby.
    CATESBY Here is the head of that ignoble traitor,
    The dangerous and unsuspected Hastings.
    RICHARD GLOUCESTER So dear I loved the man that I must weep.

---

9. *Who . . . looks:* Anyone who puts his faith in your
seemingly favorable glances.
1. Complex play on words: Ready as he dozes off; as the
ship rolls; as the monarch, whose "good looks" upheld
him, condemns him with a silent nod.
2. Lines 102–07 appear only in F. Censorship or the
fear of censorship may well be why Hastings's ominous

prediction was omitted from Q.
3.5 Location: The Tower of London.
1. Act startled by the least movement or gesture.
2. Both are eager to perform their functions.
3. F calls for Ratcliffe and Lovell, and brings on
Catesby earlier, with the Mayor.

I took him for the plainest° harmless creature   *most manifestly*
25   That breathed upon the earth, a Christian,
Made him my book° wherein my soul recorded   *diary*
The history of all her secret thoughts.
So smooth he daubed his vice with show of virtue
That, his apparent open guilt omitted—
30   I mean, his conversation[4] with Shore's wife—
He lived from all attainture of suspect.[5]
BUCKINGHAM   The covert'st sheltered° traitor that ever lived.   *The most hidden*
[*To the* MAYOR] Would you imagine, or almost believe—
Were't not that, by great preservation,[6]
35   We live to tell it—that the subtle traitor
This day had plotted in the Council house
To murder me and my good lord of Gloucester?
MAYOR   Had he done so?
RICHARD GLOUCESTER   What, think you we are Turks or infidels,
40   Or that we would against the form of law
Proceed thus rashly in the villain's death
But that the extreme peril of the case,
The peace of England, and our persons' safety,
Enforced us to this execution?
45   MAYOR   Now fair befall you, he deserved his death,
And your good graces both have well proceeded,°   *acted*
To warn false traitors from the like° attempts.   *similar*
I never looked for better at his hands
After he once fell in with Mrs Shore.
50   RICHARD GLOUCESTER[7]   Yet had not we determined he should die,
Until your lordship came to see his end,
Which now the loving haste of these our friends°—   (*Catesby and Buckingham*)
Something against our meanings°—have prevented;   *intentions*
Because, my lord, we would have had you hear
55   The traitor speak, and timorously confess
The manner and the purpose of his treason,
That you might well have signified the same
Unto the citizens, who haply° may   *perhaps*
Misconster us in him,[8] and wail his death.
60   MAYOR   But, my good lord, your graces' word shall serve
As well as° I had seen and heard him speak.   *As well as = As if*
And do not doubt, right noble princes both,
But° I'll acquaint our duteous citizens   *That*
With all your just proceedings in this cause.°   *action*
65   RICHARD GLOUCESTER   And to that end we wished your lordship here,
T'avoid the censures of the carping° world.   *overcritical*
BUCKINGHAM   Which, since you come too late of our intent,°   *for what we intended*
Yet witness° what you hear we did intend,   *bear witness to*
And so, my good Lord Mayor, we bid farewell.   *Exit* MAYOR
70   RICHARD GLOUCESTER   Go after; after, cousin Buckingham!
The Mayor towards Guildhall[9] hies him in all post;°   *haste*
There, at your meetest vantage of the time,[1]
Infer° the bastardy of Edward's children.   *Allege*
Tell them how Edward put to death a citizen

4. Intercourse (in both senses).   Buckingham.
5. He lived free from all taint of suspicion.   8. Misunderstand our treatment of him.
6. By the most fortunate preservation (of our lives).   9. Center of municipal government in London.
7. F assigns this speech and the two preceding lines to   1. At your most appropriate and advantageous moment.

75 Only for saying he would make his son
'Heir to the Crown'—meaning indeed, his house,°   *tavern*
Which by the sign thereof was termèd so.
Moreover, urge his hateful luxury°   *lasciviousness*
And bestial appetite in change of lust,[2]
80 Which stretched unto their servants, daughters, wives,
Even where° his raging eye, or savage heart,   *Wherever*
Without control, listed° to make a prey.   *desired*
Nay, for a need, thus far come near my person:[3]
Tell them, when that my mother went with child
85 Of that insatiate Edward,[4] noble York,
My princely father, then had wars in France,
And by true computation of the time
Found that the issue° was not his begot—   *offspring*
Which well appearèd in his lineaments,°   *features*
90 Being nothing like the noble Duke my father.
Yet touch this sparingly, as 'twere far off,
Because, my lord, you know my mother lives.
BUCKINGHAM   Doubt not, my lord, I'll play the orator
As if the golden fee[5] for which I plead
95 Were for myself. And so, my lord, adieu.   [*He starts to go*]
RICHARD GLOUCESTER   If you thrive well, bring them to Baynard's Castle,[6]
Where you shall find me well accompanied
With reverend fathers and well-learnèd bishops.
BUCKINGHAM   I go, and towards three or four o'clock
100 Look for the news that the Guildhall affords.[7]   *Exit*
100.1   KING RICHARD   *Go, Lovell, with all speed to Doctor Shaw;*
[To RATCLIFFE*] Go thou to Friar Penker.[8] Bid them both*
Meet me within this hour at Baynard's Castle.
[*Exeunt* LOVELL *and* RATCLIFFE]
RICHARD GLOUCESTER   Now will I in, to take some privy order[9]
To draw the brats of Clarence[1] out of sight,
And to give notice that no manner[2] person
Have any° time recourse unto the Princes.   *Exeunt*   *at any*

3.6

Enter a SCRIVENER° *with a paper in his hand*   *scribe*
SCRIVENER   Here is the indictment of the good Lord Hastings,
Which in a set hand fairly is engrossed,[1]
That it may be today read o'er in Paul's[2]—
And mark how well the sequel° hangs together: *sequence of events*
5 Eleven hours I have spent to write it over,
For yesternight by Catesby was it sent me;
The precedent° was full as long a-doing;   *rough draft*
And yet, within these five hours, Hastings lived,

2. In continually shifting the object of his lust.
3. *for . . . person:* if necessary, impugn even to this
extent my own honor (by implying that his mother was
unfaithful).
4. *went . . . Edward:* was pregnant with dissolute
Edward. *insatiate:* impossible to satisfy.
5. The crown (punning on "lawyer's fee").
6. Richard's stronghold, between Blackfriars and London Bridge.
7. The indented passage that follows, 100.1–100.3,
appears only in F.
8. Dr. Shaw, brother to the Lord Mayor, and Friar

Perkins, provincial of the Augustinian Order, were
prominent clerics who made public speeches supporting Richard's claim to the throne.
9. To make some secret arrangements.
1. The two children seen in 2.2.
2. No kind of (in other words, of whatever status or
importance).
3.6 Location: Somewhere in London.
1. Which is written in official script (as opposed to a
draft copy) and in the format of a legal document.
2. St. Paul's Cathedral, which served as a secular as
well as sacred gathering place.

Untainted,° unexamined, free, at liberty.   *Unaccused*
10   Here's a good world the while! Who is so gross°   *stupid*
      That cannot see this palpable device?°   *obvious stratagem*
      Yet who so bold but says he sees it not?
      Bad is the world, and all will come to naught,°   *wickedness; nothing*
      When such ill dealing must be seen in thought.[3]   *Exit*

3.7

Enter RICHARD [*Duke of*] GLOUCESTER *at one door and*
[*the Duke of*] BUCKINGHAM *at another*

RICHARD GLOUCESTER   How now, how now! What say the citizens?
BUCKINGHAM   Now, by the holy mother of our Lord,
      The citizens are mum, say not a word.
RICHARD GLOUCESTER   Touched you° the bastardy of Edward's   *Did you touch on*
      children?
5   BUCKINGHAM   I did, with his contract with Lady Lucy,[1]
      And his contract by deputy[2] in France,
      Th'insatiate greediness of his desire,
      And his enforcement° of the city wives,   *violation*
      His tyranny for trifles, his own bastardy—
10   As being got° your father then in France,   *conceived*
      And his resemblance,° being not like the Duke.   *appearance*
      Withal, I did infer your lineaments°—   *lineage*
      Being the right idea° of your father   *true image*
      Both in your face[3] and nobleness of mind;
15   Laid open all your victories in Scotland,[4]
      Your discipline in war, wisdom in peace,
      Your bounty, virtue, fair humility—
      Indeed, left nothing fitting for your purpose
      Untouched or slightly handled° in discourse.   *lightly mentioned*
20   And when mine oratory grew toward end,
      I bid them that did love their country's good
      Cry 'God save Richard, England's royal king!'
RICHARD GLOUCESTER   And did they so?
BUCKINGHAM   No, so God help me. They spake not a word,
25   But, like dumb statues or breathing stones,
      Stared each on other and looked deadly pale—
      Which, when I saw, I reprehended them,
      And asked the Mayor, what meant this wilful silence?
      His answer was, the people were not used
30   To be spoke to but by the Recorder.°   *(a city official)*
      Then he was urged to tell my tale again:
      'Thus saith the Duke . . . thus hath the Duke inferred'°— *asserted*
      But nothing spoke in warrant from himself.°   *on his own authority*
      When he had done, some followers of mine own,
35   At lower end of the Hall, hurled up their caps,

3. Must be perceived but not spoken of.
3.7 Location: Baynard's Castle.
1. Lady Elizabeth Lucy bore Edward a child. If, as
Buckingham alleges, there had been a formal engage-
ment between them, Edward's subsequent marriage to
Elizabeth Gray would have been ruled invalid. His chil-
dren by that marriage would have been bastards and
hence ineligible to inherit the throne.
2. The Earl of Warwick, as deputy, had contracted with
Louis XI of France for the marriage of Edward to Bona

of Savoy, the French queen's sister (see *Richard Duke
of York* 3.3).
3. Q, F: forme. The Oxford editors observe that since
Richard is prominently deformed, "form" is inappropri-
ate; in the chronicles, it is Richard's *face* that is com-
pared with his father's.
4. In 1482, as leader of an English expeditionary force
against the Scots, Richard had advanced all the way to
Edinburgh.

And some ten voices cried 'God save King Richard!'
And thus I took the vantage of° those few: opportunity presented by
'Thanks, gentle citizens and friends', quoth I;
'This general applause and cheerful shout
40 Argues your wisdoms and your love to Richard'—
And even here brake off and came away.
RICHARD GLOUCESTER   What tongueless blocks were they!
    Would they not speak?
BUCKINGHAM[5]   No, by my troth, my lord.
RICHARD GLOUCESTER   Will not the Mayor then, and his brethren, come?
45 BUCKINGHAM   The Mayor is here at hand. Intend° some fear;   Pretend
And look you get a prayer book in your hand,
Be not you spoke with, but by mighty suit;[6]
And stand between two churchmen, good my lord,
For on that ground I'll build a holy descant.[7]
50 And be not easily won to our request.
Play the maid's part:[8] still answer 'nay'—and take it.
RICHARD GLOUCESTER   I go. An if you plead as well for them
As I can say nay to thee for myself,
No doubt we'll bring it to a happy issue.
    [One knocks within]
55 BUCKINGHAM   Go, go, up to the leads![9] The Lord Mayor knocks.—
    Exit [RICHARD]
    Enter the [Lord] MAYOR, [aldermen,] and citizens
Welcome, my lord. I dance attendance° here.   am kept waiting
I think the Duke will not be spoke withal.
    Enter CATESBY
Now Catesby, what says your lord to my request?
CATESBY   He doth entreat your grace, my noble lord,
60 To visit him tomorrow, or next day.
He is within with two right reverend fathers,
Divinely bent to meditation,
And in no worldly suits would he be moved,
To draw him from his holy exercise.
65 BUCKINGHAM   Return, good Catesby, to the gracious Duke.
Tell him myself, the Mayor, and aldermen,
In deep designs, in matter of great moment,
No less importing than[1] our general good,
Are come to have some conference with his grace.
70 CATESBY   I'll signify so much unto him straight.   Exit
BUCKINGHAM   Ah ha! My lord, this prince is not an Edward.
He is not lolling on a lewd day-bed,
But on his knees at meditation;
Not dallying with a brace° of courtesans,   pair
75 But meditating with two deep° divines;   profoundly learned
Not sleeping to engross° his idle body,   fatten
But praying to enrich his watchful° soul.   vigilant
Happy were England would this virtuous prince
Take on his grace the sovereignty thereof.
80 But, sure I fear, we shall not win him to it.

---

5. F omits this line.
6. Do not let them speak with you unless they beg you.
7. Comment; improvised musical variation, usually the highest part. *ground*: basis; musical theme or air, often the bass line.

8. Keep refusing, but at the same time take whatever is offered (proverbial, with sexual innuendo).
9. Flat roof covered with lead.
1. Of no less significance than.

MAYOR   Marry, God defend° his grace should say us nay.   *forbid*
BUCKINGHAM   I fear he will. Here Catesby comes again.
        Enter CATESBY
    Now Catesby, what says his grace?
CATESBY   He wonders to what end you have assembled
85   Such troops of citizens to come to him,
    His grace not being warned thereof before.
    He fears, my lord, you mean no good to him.
BUCKINGHAM   Sorry I am my noble cousin should
    Suspect me that I mean no good to him.
90   By heaven, we come to him in perfect love,
    And so once more return and tell his grace.   *Exit* CATESBY
    When holy and devout religious men
    Are at their beads,° 'tis much to draw them thence.   *prayers*
    So sweet is zealous contemplation.
        Enter RICHARD *aloft, between two bishops.* [*Enter*
        CATESBY *below*]
95   MAYOR   See where his grace stands 'tween two clergymen.
BUCKINGHAM   Two props of virtue for a Christian prince,
    To stay him from the fall of vanity;[2]
    And see, a book of prayer in his hand—
    True ornaments to know[3] a holy man.—
100   Famous Plantagenet, most gracious prince,
    Lend favourable ear to our request,
    And pardon us the interruption
    Of thy devotion and right Christian zeal.
RICHARD GLOUCESTER   My lord, there needs no such apology.
105   I do beseech your grace to pardon me,
    Who, earnest in the service of my God,
    Deferred the visitation of my friends.
    But leaving this, what is your grace's pleasure?
BUCKINGHAM   Even that, I hope, which pleaseth God above,
110   And all good men of this ungoverned isle.
RICHARD GLOUCESTER   I do suspect I have done some offence
    That seems disgracious° in the city's eye,   *displeasing*
    And that you come to reprehend my ignorance.
BUCKINGHAM   You have, my lord. Would it might please your grace
115   On our entreaties to amend your fault.
RICHARD GLOUCESTER   Else wherefore breathe I in a Christian land?[4]
BUCKINGHAM   Know then, it is your fault that you resign
    The supreme seat, the throne majestical,
    The sceptred office of your ancestors,
120   Your state of fortune[5] and your due of birth,
    The lineal glory of your royal house,
    To the corruption of a blemished stock,[6]
    Whiles in the mildness of your sleepy° thoughts—   *contemplative*
    Which here we waken to our country's good—
125   The noble isle doth want her proper° limbs: *lack her own*
    Her face defaced with scars of infamy,
    Her royal stock graft with ignoble plants
    And almost shouldered in° the swallowing gulf   *shoved into*

2. To prevent him from falling into the sin of vanity.
3. *True . . . know*: Prayer books (and also, perhaps, the
clergymen) by which to recognize.
4. Why else do I lead a Christian life?

5. The position that fortune has given you.
6. Edward's "family tree" is degraded by bastardy and
immorality.

Of dark forgetfulness and deep oblivion,
130 Which to recure° we heartily solicit   restore
Your gracious self to take on you the charge
And kingly government of this your land—
Not as Protector, steward, substitute,
Or lowly factor° for another's gain,   agent
135 But as successively,° from blood to blood,   in order of succession
Your right of birth, your empery,° your own.   absolute dominion
For this, consorted° with the citizens,   together
Your very worshipful° and loving friends,   respectful
And by their vehement instigation,
140 In this just cause come I to move your grace.
RICHARD GLOUCESTER   I cannot tell if to depart in silence
Or bitterly to speak in your reproof
Best fitteth my degree° or your condition.[7]   rank
143.1   *If not to answer, you might haply° think*   perhaps
              Tongue-tied ambition, not replying, yielded°   agreed
              To bear the golden yoke of sovereignty,
              Which fondly° you would here impose on me.   foolishly
143.5   *If to reprove you for this suit of yours,*
              So seasoned° with your faithful love to me,   made palatable
              Then on the other side I checked° my friends.   rebuked
              Therefore to speak, and to avoid the first,
              And then in speaking not to incur the last,
143.10   *Definitively thus I answer you.*
Your love deserves my thanks; but my desert,
145 Unmeritable,° shuns your high request.   Undeserving
First, if all obstacles were cut away
And that my path were even° to the crown,   smooth
As the ripe revenue and due of birth,
Yet so much is my poverty of spirit,
150 So mighty and so many my defects,
That I would rather hide me from my greatness—
Being a barque to brook° no mighty sea—   a boat to endure
Than in my greatness covet to be hid,[8]
And in the vapour of my glory smothered.
155 But God be thanked, there is no need of me,
And much I need° to help you, were there need.   lack (ability)
The royal tree hath left us royal fruit,
Which, mellowed by the stealing hours of time,
Will well become the seat of majesty
160 And make, no doubt, us happy by his reign.
On him I lay that° you would lay on me,   what
The right and fortune of his happy° stars,   auspicious
Which God defend that I should wring from him.
BUCKINGHAM   My lord, this argues conscience in your grace,
165 But the respects thereof are nice and trivial,[9]
All circumstances well considered.
You say that Edward is your brother's son;
So say we, too—but not by Edward's wife.
For first was he contract° to Lady Lucy—   betrothed

---

7. Social rank. The indented passage that follows,
143.1–143.10, appears only in F.
8. Than desire to be enveloped by my greatness.

9. But the reasons you advance are nit-picking (thus,
overscrupulous).

170   Your mother lives a witness to his vow[1]—
    And afterward, by substitute,° betrothed   *proxy*
    To Bona, sister to the King of France.
    These both put off, a poor petitioner,
    A care-crazed mother to a many sons,
175   A beauty-waning and distressèd widow
    Even in the afternoon of her best days,
    Made prize and purchase° of his wanton eye,   *booty*
    Seduced the pitch and height of his degree[2]
    To base declension° and loathed bigamy.   *degradation*
180   By her in his unlawful bed he got
    This Edward, whom our manners° call the Prince.   *we in politeness*
    More bitterly could I expostulate,
    Save that for reverence to some alive[3]
    I give a sparing limit to my tongue.
185   Then, good my lord, take to your royal self
    This proffered benefit° of dignity—   *bestowal*
    If not to bless us and the land withal,
    Yet to draw forth° your noble ancestry   *to rescue*
    From the corruption of abusing times,
190   Unto a lineal, true-derivèd course.
    MAYOR [*to* RICHARD]   Do, good my lord; your citizens entreat you.
    BUCKINGHAM [*to* RICHARD]   Refuse not, mighty lord, this proffered love.
    CATESBY [*to* RICHARD]   O make them joyful: grant their lawful suit.
    RICHARD GLOUCESTER   Alas, why would you heap this care on me?
195   I am unfit for state and majesty.
    I do beseech you, take it not amiss.
    I cannot, nor I will not, yield to you.
    BUCKINGHAM   If you refuse it—as, in love and zeal,
    Loath to depose the child, your brother's son,
200   As well we know your tenderness of heart
    And gentle, kind, effeminate remorse,[4]
    Which we have noted in you to your kindred,
    And equally indeed to all estates°—   *social classes*
    Yet know, whe'er° you accept our suit or no,   *whether*
205   Your brother's son shall never reign our king,
    But we will plant some other in the throne,
    To the disgrace and downfall of your house.
    And in this resolution here we leave you.—
    Come, citizens. 'Swounds,° I'll entreat no more.   *By God's wounds*
210   RICHARD GLOUCESTER   O do not swear, my lord of Buckingham.
                        Exeunt [BUCKINGHAM *and some others*]
    CATESBY   Call him again, sweet prince. Accept their suit.
    ANOTHER[5]   If you deny them, all the land will rue° it.   *suffer for*
    RICHARD GLOUCESTER   Will you enforce° me to a world of cares?   *condemn*
    Call them again.   [*Exit one or more*]
              I am not made of stone,
215   But penetrable to your kind entreats,°   *entreaties*
    Albeit against my conscience and my soul.

---

1. Buckingham draws attention to the Duchess of York's objection to her son Edward's marriage to Elizabeth Gray; Edward's supposed betrothals (see notes to lines 5–6), along with the fact of Elizabeth's widowhood, are put forward as evidence that the marriage should be considered bigamous and hence the offspring illegitimate.
2. Drew him down from the eminence appropriate to his noble rank.
3. Richard's own mother, the Duchess of York.
4. And natural, tender pity (feelings thought of at that time as primarily feminine).
5. One of the remaining citizens, city officials, or bishops. In F, Catesby speaks this line.

Enter BUCKINGHAM *and the rest*

    Cousin of Buckingham, and sage, grave men,
    Since you will buckle fortune on my back,
    To° bear her burden, whe'er I will or no,   *To make me*
220   I must have patience to endure the load.
    But if black scandal or foul-faced reproach
    Attend the sequel of your imposition,°   *what you impose on me*
    Your mere° enforcement shall acquittance° me   *outright / acquit*
    From all the impure blots and stains thereof;
225   For God doth know, and you may partly see,
    How far I am from the desire of this.
MAYOR   God bless your grace! We see it, and will say it.
RICHARD GLOUCESTER   In saying so, you shall but say the truth.
BUCKINGHAM   Then I salute you with this royal title:
230   Long live kind Richard, England's worthy king!
ALL BUT RICHARD[6]   Amen.
BUCKINGHAM   Tomorrow may it please you to be crowned?
RICHARD GLOUCESTER   Even when you please, for you will have it so.
BUCKINGHAM   Tomorrow then, we will attend your grace.
235   And so, most joyfully, we take our leave.
RICHARD GLOUCESTER [*to the bishops*]   Come, let us to our holy work again.—
    Farewell, my cousin. Farewell, gentle friends.

Exeunt [RICHARD *and bishops above, the rest below*]

4.1

Enter QUEEN [ELIZABETH], *the* [*old*] DUCHESS OF YORK,
and Marquis DORSET *at one door;* [LADY] ANNE *Duchess*
of Gloucester [*with Clarence's daughter*] *at another door*

DUCHESS OF YORK   Who meets us here? My niece° Plantagenet,   *granddaughter*
    Led in° the hand of her kind aunt of Gloucester?   *by*
    Now for° my life, she's wand'ring to the Tower,   *upon*
    On pure heart's love, to greet the tender° Prince.—   *young*
    Daughter,° well met.   *Daughter-in-law*
5 LADY ANNE   God give your graces both
    A happy and a joyful time of day.
QUEEN ELIZABETH   As much to you, good sister.° Whither away?   *sister-in-law*
LADY ANNE   No farther than the Tower, and—as I guess—
    Upon the like devotion° as yourselves: *devout duty*
10   To gratulate° the gentle princes there.   *greet*
QUEEN ELIZABETH   Kind sister, thanks. We'll enter all together—

Enter [*from the Tower* BRACKENBURY] *the Lieutenant*

    And in good time, here the Lieutenant comes.
    Master Lieutenant, pray you by your leave,
    How doth the Prince, and my young son of York?
15 BRACKENBURY   Right well, dear madam. By your patience,
    I may not suffer° you to visit them.   *permit*
    The King hath strictly charged the contrary.
QUEEN ELIZABETH   The King? Who's that?
BRACKENBURY   I mean, the Lord Protector.
QUEEN ELIZABETH   The Lord protect him from that kingly title.[1]
20   Hath he set bounds° between their love and me?   *barriers*

---

6. Q assigns this word to the Mayor only.
4.1 Location: Before the Tower.

1. May God prevent Richard from acquiring the title of
King.

I am their mother; who shall bar me from them?

DUCHESS OF YORK   I am their father's mother; I will see them.

LADY ANNE   Their aunt I am in law, in love their mother;
Then bring me to their sights. I'll bear thy blame,

25   And take thy office from thee on my peril.[2]

BRACKENBURY   No, madam, no; I may not leave it° so.   *give up my office*
I am bound by oath, and therefore pardon me.   *Exit*
    Enter Lord STANLEY [*Earl of Derby*]

STANLEY   Let me but meet you ladies one hour hence,
And I'll salute your grace of York as mother

30   And reverend looker-on° of two fair queens.[3]   *beholder*
[*To* ANNE] Come, madam, you must straight to Westminster,[4]
There to be crownèd Richard's royal queen.

QUEEN ELIZABETH   Ah, cut my lace asunder,[5] that my pent heart
May have some scope to beat, or else I swoon

35   With this dead-killing news.

LADY ANNE   Despiteful tidings! O unpleasing news!

DORSET [*to* ANNE]   Be of good cheer.—Mother, how fares your grace?

QUEEN ELIZABETH   O Dorset, speak not to me. Get thee gone.
Death and destruction dogs thee at thy heels.

40   Thy mother's name is ominous to children.[6]
If thou wilt outstrip death, go cross the seas,
And live with Richmond from[7] the reach of hell.
Go, hie thee! Hie thee from this slaughterhouse,
Lest thou increase the number of the dead,

45   And make me die the thrall° of Margaret's curses: *slave*
'Nor mother, wife, nor counted° England's Queen'.   *regarded as*

STANLEY   Full of wise care is this your counsel, madam.
[*To* DORSET] Take all the swift advantage of the hours.
You shall have letters from me to my son°   *stepson (Richmond)*

50   In your behalf, to meet you on the way.
Be not ta'en tardy by unwise delay.

DUCHESS OF YORK   O ill-dispersing° wind of misery!   *misfortune-scattering*
O my accursèd womb, the bed° of death!   *birthplace*
A cockatrice[8] hast thou hatched to the world,

55   Whose unavoided eye is murderous.

STANLEY [*to* ANNE]   Come, madam, come. I in all haste was sent.

LADY ANNE   And I in all unwillingness will go.
O would to God that the inclusive verge°   *enclosing rim*
Of golden metal that must round° my brow   *encircle*

60   Were red-hot steel, to sear me to the brains.
Anointed let me be with deadly venom,[9]
And die ere men can say 'God save the Queen'.

QUEEN ELIZABETH   Go, go, poor soul. I envy not thy glory.
To feed my humour,° wish thyself no harm.   *To humor me*

65   LADY ANNE   No? Why? When he that is my husband now
Came to me as I followed Henry's corpse,
When scarce the blood was well washed from his hands,

2. And take on the responsibilities of your position at my own risk.
3. Elizabeth, widow of Edward IV, and Anne, wife of Richard III.
4. To Westminster Abbey, where English monarchs are traditionally crowned.
5. Elizabethan women wore tightly laced bodices.

6. The fact that you are my son places you in danger.
7. Away from. Henry Tudor, Earl of Richmond, had fled to Brittany in 1472, when Edward IV secured his grasp on the throne.
8. Basilisk (see note to 1.2.150).
9. Instead of the holy oil used in the ceremony of coronation.

Which issued from my other angel husband
And that dear saint which then I weeping followed—
70 O when, I say, I looked on Richard's face,
This was my wish: 'Be thou', quoth I, 'accursed
For making me, so young, so old a widow,[1]
And when thou wedd'st, let sorrow haunt thy bed;
And be thy wife—if any be so mad—
75 More miserable made by the life of thee
Than thou hast made me by my dear lord's death.'
Lo, ere I can repeat this curse again,
Within so small a time, my woman's heart
Grossly° grew captive to his honey words   *Stupidly*
80 And proved the subject of mine own soul's curse,
Which hitherto hath held mine eyes from rest—
For never yet one hour in his bed
Did I enjoy the golden dew of sleep,
But with his timorous° dreams was still° awaked.   *fearful / continually*
85 Besides, he hates me for° my father Warwick,   *because of*
And will, no doubt, shortly be rid of me.
QUEEN ELIZABETH   Poor heart, adieu. I pity thy complaining.°   *lamenting*
LADY ANNE   No more than with my soul I mourn for yours.
DORSET   Farewell, thou woeful welcomer of glory.
90 LADY ANNE   Adieu, poor soul, that tak'st thy leave of it.
DUCHESS OF YORK [*to* DORSET] Go thou to Richmond, and good fortune guide thee.
[*To* ANNE, STANLEY, *and Clarence's daughter*] Go thou to Richard, and good angels
tend thee.
[*To* ELIZABETH] Go thou to sanctuary, and good thoughts possess thee.
I to my grave, where peace and rest lie with me.
95 Eighty odd years of sorrow have I seen,
And each hour's joy racked with a week of teen.[2]   [*Exit*]
96.1   QUEEN ELIZABETH   *Stay: yet look back with me unto the Tower.—*
Pity, you ancient stones, those tender babes,
Whom envy° hath immured within your walls.   *malice; jealousy*
Rough cradle for such little pretty ones,
96.5   *Rude ragged nurse, old sullen playfellow*
For tender princes: use my babies well.
So foolish sorrow bids your stones farewell.   *Exeunt*

4.2

Sound a sennet. Enter [KING] RICHARD *in pomp,* [*the
Duke of*] BUCKINGHAM, [*Sir William*] CATESBY, *other
nobles*[1] [*and a* PAGE]
KING RICHARD   Stand all apart.°—Cousin of Buckingham.   *aside*
BUCKINGHAM   My gracious sovereign?
KING RICHARD   Give me thy hand.
Sound [*a sennet*]. *Here he ascendeth the throne*
Thus high by thy advice
5 And thy assistance is King Richard seated.
But shall we wear these glories for a day?
Or shall they last, and we rejoice in them?
BUCKINGHAM   Still° live they, and for ever let them last.   *Perpetually*

---

1. Doomed to a long life of widowhood.
2. Grief. The indented passage that follows, 96.1–96.7, appears only in F; the other characters remain onstage.
4.2 Location: The palace, London.
1. In F, specifically Ratcliffe and Lovell.

KING RICHARD   Ah, Buckingham, now do I play the touch,[2]
10   To try if thou be current° gold indeed.   *real, genuine*
Young Edward lives. Think now what I would speak.
BUCKINGHAM   Say on, my loving lord.
KING RICHARD   Why, Buckingham, I say I would be king.
BUCKINGHAM   Why, so you are, my thrice-renownèd liege.
15   KING RICHARD   Ha? Am I king? 'Tis so. But Edward lives.
BUCKINGHAM   True, noble prince.
KING RICHARD   O bitter consequence,°   *conclusion; retort*
That Edward still should live 'true noble prince'.
Cousin, thou wast not wont° to be so dull.   *accustomed*
Shall I be plain? I wish the bastards dead,
20   And I would have it immediately performed.
What sayst thou now? Speak suddenly,° be brief.   *at once*
BUCKINGHAM   Your grace may do your pleasure.
KING RICHARD   Tut, tut, thou art all ice. Thy kindness freezes.
Say, have I thy consent that they shall die?
25   BUCKINGHAM   Give me some little breath, some pause, dear lord,
Before I positively speak in this.
I will resolve° you herein presently.°   *Exit*   *answer / shortly*
CATESBY [*to another, aside*]   The King is angry. See, he gnaws his lip.
KING RICHARD [*aside*]   I will converse with iron-witted fools
30   And unrespective° boys. None are for me   *unobservant*
That look into me with considerate° eyes.   *critical*
High-reaching° Buckingham grows circumspect.—   *Ambitious*
Boy.
PAGE   My lord?
35   KING RICHARD   Know'st thou not any whom corrupting gold
Will tempt unto a close° exploit of death?   *secret*
PAGE   I know a discontented gentleman
Whose humble means match not his haughty spirit.
Gold were as good as twenty orators,
40   And will no doubt tempt him to anything.
KING RICHARD   What is his name?
PAGE   His name, my lord, is Tyrrell.
KING RICHARD   I partly know the man. Go call him hither, boy.
                                                                Exit [PAGE]
[*Aside*] The deep-revolving,° witty° Buckingham   *deeply scheming / clever*
No more shall be the neighbour to my counsels.
45   Hath he so long held out° with me untired,   *kept up*
And stops he now for breath? Well, be it so.
            Enter [*Lord*] STANLEY [*Earl of*] *Derby*
How now, Lord Stanley? What's the news?
STANLEY   Know, my loving lord,
The Marquis Dorset, as I hear, is fled
50   To Richmond, in those parts beyond the seas
Where he abides.
KING RICHARD   Come hither, Catesby. [*Aside to* CATESBY] Rumour it abroad
That Anne, my wife, is very grievous sick.
I will take order for her keeping close.[3]
55   Enquire me out some mean-born gentleman,
Whom I will marry straight to Clarence' daughter.

---

2. Touchstone: a means of testing gold.   3. I will arrange to have her kept out of sight.

The boy⁴ is foolish,° and I fear not him.   *simpleminded*
Look how thou dream'st. I say again, give out
That Anne, my queen, is sick, and like to die.
60 About it, for it stands me much upon°   *is very important to me*
To stop all hopes whose growth may damage me.
                                                        [*Exit* CATESBY]
    [*Aside*] I must be married to my brother's daughter,⁵
    Or else my kingdom stands on brittle glass.
    Murder her brothers, and then marry her?
65 Uncertain way of gain, but I am in
    So far in blood that sin will pluck on° sin.   *incite*
    Tear-falling pity dwells not in this eye.—
            Enter [*Sir James*] TYRRELL; [*he kneels*]
    Is thy name Tyrrell?
TYRRELL   James Tyrrell, and your most obedient subject.
KING RICHARD   Art thou indeed?
70 TYRRELL   Prove° me, my gracious lord.   *Test*
KING RICHARD   Dar'st thou resolve to kill a friend of mine?
TYRRELL   Please you,° but I had rather kill two enemies.   *If you wish*
KING RICHARD   Why there thou hast it: two deep enemies,
    Foes to my rest, and my sweet sleep's disturbers,
75 Are they that I would have thee deal upon.°   *set to work upon*
    Tyrrell, I mean those bastards in the Tower.
TYRRELL   Let me have open means to come⁶ to them,
    And soon I'll rid you from the fear of them.
KING RICHARD   Thou sing'st sweet music. Hark, come hither, Tyrrell.
80 Go, by this token. Rise, and lend thine ear.
            [RICHARD] *whispers in his ear*
    'Tis no more but so.° Say it is done,   *That's all*
    And I will love thee, and prefer° thee for it.   *promote*
TYRRELL   I will dispatch it straight.
KING RICHARD   Shall we hear from thee, Tyrrell, ere we sleep?⁷
            Enter BUCKINGHAM
85 TYRRELL   Ye shall, my lord.   *Exit*
BUCKINGHAM   My lord, I have considered in my mind
    The late request that you did sound me in.
KING RICHARD   Well, let that rest. Dorset is fled to Richmond.
BUCKINGHAM   I hear the news, my lord.
90 KING RICHARD   Stanley, he° is your wife's son. Well, look to it.   *(Richmond)*
BUCKINGHAM   My lord, I claim the gift, my due by promise,
    For which your honour and your faith is pawned:
    Th'earldom of Hereford, and the movables
    Which you have promisèd I shall possess.
95 KING RICHARD   Stanley, look to your wife. If she convey
    Letters to Richmond, you shall answer it.°   *for it*
BUCKINGHAM   What says your highness to my just request?
KING RICHARD   I do remember me, Henry the Sixth
    Did prophesy that Richmond should be king,
100 When Richmond was a little peevish boy.
    A king . . . perhaps . . . perhaps.⁸
BUCKINGHAM   My lord?

---

4. Clarence's eldest son, Edward, Earl of Warwick.
5. To Edward's daughter, Elizabeth of York, who was later to unite the two houses by becoming queen to the Lancastrian Henry VII, formerly the Earl of Richmond.
6. Let me have free access.
7. F omits this and the following line.
8. The passage that follows, lines 101–119, appears only in Q.

KING RICHARD   How chance the prophet could not at that time
  Have told me, I being by, that I should kill him?
BUCKINGHAM   My lord, your promise for the earldom.
105 KING RICHARD   Richmond? When last I was at Exeter,
  The Mayor in courtesy showed me the castle,
  And called it 'Ruge-mount'⁹—at which name I started,
  Because a bard of Ireland¹ told me once
  I should not live long after I saw 'Richmond'.
110 BUCKINGHAM   My lord?
KING RICHARD   Ay? What's o'clock?
BUCKINGHAM   I am thus bold to put your grace in mind
  Of what you promised me.
KING RICHARD   But what's o'clock?
BUCKINGHAM   Upon the stroke of ten.
115 KING RICHARD   Well, let it strike!
BUCKINGHAM   Why 'let it strike'?
KING RICHARD   Because that, like a jack,² thou keep'st the stroke
  Betwixt thy begging and my meditation.
  I am not in the giving vein today.
120 BUCKINGHAM   Why then resolve me,° whe'er you will or no?   *answer me resolutely*
KING RICHARD   Thou troublest me. I am not in the vein.°   *mood*
  Exit [RICHARD, *followed by all but* BUCKINGHAM]
BUCKINGHAM   And is it thus? Repays he my deep° service   *i.e., rendered at great risk*
  With such contempt? Made I him king for this?
  O let me think on Hastings, and be gone
125 To Brecon,° while my fearful head is on.   *manor house in Wales*
           Exit [*at another door*]

4.3

    Enter Sir [*James*] TYRRELL
TYRRELL   The tyrannous and bloody act is done—
  The most arch° deed of piteous massacre   *preeminent*
  That ever yet this land was guilty of.
  Dighton and Forrest,¹ whom I did suborn°   *induce*
5 To do this piece of ruthless butchery,
  Albeit they were fleshed² villains, bloody dogs,
  Melted with tenderness and mild compassion,
  Wept like two children in their deaths' sad story.³
  'O thus', quoth Dighton, 'lay the gentle babes';
10 'Thus, thus', quoth Forrest, 'girdling° one another   *embracing*
  Within their alabaster° innocent arms.   *marble-white*
  Their lips were four red roses on a stalk,
  And in their summer beauty kissed each other.
  A book of prayers on their pillow lay,
15 'Which once', quoth Forrest, 'almost changed my mind.
  But O, the devil'—there the villain stopped,
  When° Dighton thus told on, 'We smotherèd   *At which point*
  The most replenishéd° sweet work of nature,   *complete*

---

9. Redhill (but punning on "Richmond").
1. Celtic bards, or poets, were also considered prophets.
2. A Jack was the mechanical figure who appeared to strike the hours in early clocks. By clockwork reiterations of his suit, Richard suggests, Buckingham is behaving like an annoying beggar and interfering with Richard's "meditation."
4.3 Location: The palace, London.

1. For the murder of the princes, Tyrrell recruited his servant, John Dighton, along with Myles Forrest and two others.
2. Experienced in killing; applied to hounds that had been fed part of their first kill in order to give them a taste for blood.
3. Wept in telling the sad story of the Princes' deaths.

That from the prime° creation e'er she framed.'   *first*
20   Hence both are gone,° with conscience and remorse.   *overcome*
They could not speak, and so I left them both,
To bear this tidings to the bloody king.
          Enter KING RICHARD
And here he comes.—All health, my sovereign lord.
      KING RICHARD   Kind Tyrrell, am I happy in thy news?
25   TYRRELL   If to have done the thing you gave in charge
Beget your happiness,⁴ be happy then,
For it is done.
      KING RICHARD   But didst thou see them dead?
      TYRRELL   I did, my lord.
      KING RICHARD   And buried, gentle Tyrrell?
      TYRRELL   The chaplain of the Tower hath buried them;
30   But where, to say the truth, I do not know.
      KING RICHARD   Come to me, Tyrrell, soon, at after-supper,°   *dessert*
When thou shalt tell the process° of their death.   *story*
Meantime, but think how I may do thee good,
And be inheritor of thy desire.⁵
Farewell till then.
35   TYRRELL   I humbly take my leave.   *Exit*
      KING RICHARD   The son of Clarence have I pent° up close.   *locked*
His daughter meanly have I matched in marriage.⁶
The sons of Edward sleep in Abraham's bosom,⁷
And Anne, my wife, hath bid this world goodnight.
40   Now, for° I know the Breton⁸ Richmond aims   *because*
At young Elizabeth, my brother's daughter,
And by that knot° looks proudly o'er the crown,   *marriage; alliance*
To her go I, a jolly thriving wooer⁹—
          Enter [Sir Richard] RATCLIFFE¹ [*running*]
      RATCLIFFE   My lord.
45   KING RICHARD   Good news or bad, that thou com'st in so bluntly?
      RATCLIFFE   Bad news, my lord. Ely° is fled to Richmond,   *(Bishop of Ely)*
And Buckingham, backed with the hardy Welshmen,
Is in the field, and still his power increaseth.
      KING RICHARD   Ely with Richmond troubles me more near°   *deeply*
50   Than Buckingham and his rash-levied strength.°   *hastily raised army*
Come, I have learned that fearful commenting
Is leaden servitor² to dull delay.
Delay leads impotent and snail-paced beggary.°   *ruin*
Then fiery expedition° be my wing: *speed*
55   Jove's Mercury,³ an herald for a king.
Go, muster men. My counsel is my shield.⁴
We must be brief, when traitors brave the field.⁵   *Exeunt*

4. *If . . . happiness:* If it pleases you to have accomplished what you ordered done.
5. *but . . . desire:* you have only to think what you want of me, and you will possess it.
6. I have married off to a poor man.
7. In heaven (see Luke 16:22–23).
8. Person from Brittany; Richmond spent fourteen years in exile there before returning to England to face Richard III in 1485.
9. It was widely rumored that Anne was poisoned in order to facilitate a plan by Richard to marry Elizabeth,

sister to the missing princes; modern historians believe that these allegations are probably untrue. Richard's alleged actions regarding Clarence's son and daughter (lines 36–37) are certainly untrue.
1. Q calls for Catesby.
2. *fearful . . . servitor:* frightened talk is the sluggish attendant.
3. The swift messenger of the gods.
4. *My . . . shield:* I do not talk, but arm myself to fight. *counsel:* adviser.
5. When traitors defy (us on) the battlefield.

4.4

Enter old QUEEN MARGARET

QUEEN MARGARET So now prosperity begins to mellow°   *ripen*
And drop into the rotten mouth of death.
Here in these confines slyly have I lurked
To watch the waning of mine enemies.
5   A dire induction° am I witness to,   *prologue (as to a play)*
And will to France, hoping the consequence°   *conclusion (as of a play)*
Will prove as bitter, black, and tragical.

Enter the [old] DUCHESS OF YORK *and* QUEEN [ELIZABETH]

Withdraw thee, wretched Margaret. Who comes here?

QUEEN ELIZABETH Ah, my poor princes! Ah, my tender babes!
10   My unblown° flowers, new-appearing sweets!°   *unopened / blooms*
If yet your gentle souls fly in the air,
And be not fixed in doom perpetual,[1]
Hover about me with your airy wings
And hear your mother's lamentation.

15 QUEEN MARGARET [*aside*] Hover about her, say that right for right
Hath dimmed your infant morn to agèd night.[2]

DUCHESS OF YORK[3] So many miseries have crazed° my voice   *cracked*
That my woe-wearied tongue is still and mute.
Edward Plantagenet, why art thou dead?

20 QUEEN MARGARET [*aside*] Plantagenet doth quit° Plantagenet;   *pay for (the deeds of)*
Edward for Edward pays a dying debt.[4]

QUEEN ELIZABETH Wilt thou, O God, fly from such gentle lambs
And throw them in the entrails of the wolf?
When° didst thou sleep, when such a deed was done?   *Whenever (up until now)*

25 QUEEN MARGARET [*aside*] When holy Harry[5] died, and my sweet son.

DUCHESS OF YORK Dead life, blind sight, poor mortal living ghost,[6]
Woe's scene, world's shame, grave's due by life usurped,[7]
Brief abstract° and record of tedious days,   *epitome; summary*
Rest thy unrest on England's lawful earth,
30   Unlawfully made drunk with innocents' blood.

[*They sit*]

QUEEN ELIZABETH Ah that thou[8] wouldst as soon afford a grave
As thou canst yield a melancholy seat.
Then would I hide my bones, not rest them here.
Ah, who hath any cause to mourn but we?

35 QUEEN MARGARET [*coming forward*] If ancient sorrow be most reverend,
Give mine the benefit of seniory,[9]
And let my griefs frown on the upper hand.[1]
If sorrow can admit society,
Tell o'er° your woes again by viewing mine.   *Count; narrate*
40   I had an Edward, till a Richard killed him;
I had a husband, till a Richard killed him.

4.4 Location: Before the palace.
1. *fixed in doom perpetual*: assigned by an irrevocable
sentence to your final place of punishment or reward.
2. *right for . . . night*: evenhanded justice has destroyed
the bright hopes of your young lives.
3. Q places this after line 34 (making it the last speech
before Margaret's intervention) and omits lines 20–21.
4. A debt for which payment is death. *Edward for
Edward*: Prince Edward (Elizabeth's son) for Prince
Edward (Margaret's son, whose murder is dramatized in
Richard Duke of York).

5. Henry VI (Margaret's husband).
6. *mortal living ghost*: a dead person doomed to exist
among the living.
7. *graves . . . usurped*: person who ought to be dead,
unlawfully alive.
8. Here, Elizabeth is addressing the earth directly.
9. Seniority; Q1–5 have "signorie," F "signeurie,"
which suggests that Margaret may mean "sovereignty"
or "lordship" ("seigniory").
1. *frown . . . hand*: have precedence in mourning.

[*To* ELIZABETH] Thou hadst an Edward, till a Richard killed him;
Thou hadst a Richard,[2] till a Richard killed him.
DUCHESS OF YORK [*rising*] I had a Richard too, and thou didst kill him;
I had a Rutland too,[3] thou holpst to kill him.
QUEEN MARGARET Thou hadst a Clarence too, and Richard killed him.
From forth the kennel of thy womb hath crept
A hell-hound that doth hunt us all to death:
That dog that had his teeth before his eyes,[4]
To worry° lambs and lap their gentle blood;   *tear apart*
That foul defacer of God's handiwork,
That reigns in gallèd° eyes of weeping souls;   *sore (from crying)*
That excellent grand tyrant of the earth
Thy womb let loose to chase us to our graves.
O upright, just, and true-disposing God,
How do I thank thee that this charnel[5] cur
Preys on the issue° of his mother's body,   *offspring*
And makes her pewfellow° with others' moan.   *companion at church*
DUCHESS OF YORK O Harry's wife, triumph not in my woes.
God witness with me, I have wept for thine.
QUEEN MARGARET Bear with me. I am hungry for revenge,
And now I cloy me° with beholding it.   *gorge myself*
Thy Edward, he is dead, that killed my Edward;
Thy other Edward dead, to quite° my Edward;   *requite*
Young York, he is but boot,[6] because both they
Matched not the high perfection of my loss;
Thy Clarence, he is dead, that stabbed my Edward,
And the beholders of this frantic° play—   *insane*
Th'adulterate° Hastings, Rivers, Vaughan, Gray—   *adulterous*
Untimely smothered° in their dusky graves.   *buried*
Richard yet lives, hell's black intelligencer,°   *spy*
Only reserved their factor[7] to buy souls
And send them thither; but at hand, at hand
Ensues his piteous and unpitied end.
Earth gapes, hell burns, fiends roar, saints pray,
To have him suddenly conveyed from hence.
Cancel his bond of life, dear God, I plead,
That I may live and say, 'The dog is dead'.
QUEEN ELIZABETH O thou didst prophesy the time would come
That I should wish for thee to help me curse
That bottled spider, that foul bunch-backed toad.
QUEEN MARGARET I called thee then 'vain flourish of my fortune';
I called thee then, poor shadow,° 'painted queen'[8]—   *semblance*
The presentation° of but what I was,   *copy*
The flattering index° of a direful pageant,°   *prologue / play*
One heaved a-high to be hurled down below,
A mother only mocked with two fair babes,
A dream of what thou wast, a garish flag

---

2. Edward and Richard were Queen Elizabeth's two sons (smothered in the Tower).
3. Her husband (Richard, Duke of York) and youngest son; both deaths are dramatized in Act 1 of *Richard Duke of York*.
4. His enemies rumored that the savage Richard was born with teeth.
5. Of the charnel house or tomb. Q, F print "carnal."
6. He is thrown in simply to make the bargain even.
7. *Only . . . factor*: Retained (or preserved from death) only in order to serve as hell's agent. *their*: the demonic inhabitants of hell.
8. See 1.3.239.

To be the aim of every dangerous shot,[9]
90 A sign° of dignity, a breath, a bubble,   *mere symbol*
A queen in jest, only to fill the scene.
Where is thy husband now? Where be thy brothers?
Where are thy two sons? Wherein dost thou joy?
Who sues, and kneels, and says 'God save the Queen'?
95 Where be the bending° peers that flattered thee?   *bowing; yielding*
Where be the thronging troops that followed thee?
Decline[1] all this, and see what now thou art:
For happy wife, a most distressèd widow;
For joyful mother, one that wails the name;
100 For queen, a very caitiff,° crowned with care;   *wretch*
For one being sued to, one that humbly sues;
For she that scorned at me, now scorned of° me;   *by*
For she being feared of all, now fearing one;
For she commanding all, obeyed of none.
105 Thus hath the course of justice whirled about,
And left thee but a very prey to time,
Having no more but thought of what thou wert
To torture thee the more, being what thou art.
Thou didst usurp my place, and dost thou not
110 Usurp the just proportion of my sorrow?
Now thy proud neck bears half my burdened° yoke—   *burdensome*
From which, even here, I slip my weary head,
And leave the burden of it all on thee.
Farewell, York's wife, and queen of sad mischance.
115 These English woes shall make me smile in France.
QUEEN ELIZABETH [*rising*]   O thou, well skilled in curses, stay a while,
And teach me how to curse mine enemies.
QUEEN MARGARET   Forbear to sleep the nights, and fast the days;
Compare dead happiness with living woe;
120 Think that thy babes were sweeter than they were,
And he that slew them fouler than he is.
Bett'ring° thy loss makes the bad causer worse.   *Magnifying*
Revolving° this will teach thee how to curse.   *Musing on*
QUEEN ELIZABETH   My words are dull. O quicken° them with   *enliven; sharpen*
thine!
QUEEN MARGARET   Thy woes will make them sharp and pierce
125 like mine.   *Exit*
DUCHESS OF YORK   Why should calamity be full of words?
QUEEN ELIZABETH   Windy attorneys to their client woes,[2]
Airy recorders of intestate joys,[3]
Poor breathing° orators of miseries.   *speaking*
130 Let them have scope. Though what they will impart
Help nothing else, yet do they ease the heart.
DUCHESS OF YORK   If so, then be not tongue-tied; go with me,
And in the breath of bitter words let's smother
My damnèd son, that thy two sweet sons smothered.
[*A march within*]
135 The trumpet sounds. Be copious in exclaims.°   *exclamation*

9. *garish . . . shot*: bearer of a brightly colored standard who draws the enemy fire.
1. Recite in order with the proper endings (as a noun in Latin grammar).
2. Words are long-winded pleaders for the sufferings that have hired them.
3. Words record joys that have died without bequeathing anything.

Enter KING RICHARD *and his train marching with*
drummers and trumpeters

KING RICHARD   Who intercepts me in my expedition?°   *haste; march*
DUCHESS OF YORK   O, she that might have intercepted thee,
By strangling thee in her accursèd womb,
From all the slaughters, wretch, that thou hast done.
140   QUEEN ELIZABETH   Hid'st thou that forehead with a golden crown,
Where should be branded—if that right were right—
The slaughter of the prince that owed° that crown,   *rightfully owned*
And the dire death of my poor sons and brothers?
Tell me, thou villain-slave, where are my children?
145   DUCHESS OF YORK   Thou toad, thou toad, where is thy brother Clarence?
And little Ned Plantagenet his son?
QUEEN ELIZABETH   Where is the gentle Rivers, Vaughan, Gray?
DUCHESS OF YORK   Where is kind Hastings?
KING RICHARD [*to his train*]   A flourish, trumpets! Strike
        alarum,° drums!   *Call to arms*
150   Let not the heavens hear these tell-tale women
Rail on the Lord's anointed. Strike, I say!
        Flourish. Alarums
[*To the women*] Either be patient and entreat me fair,°   *treat me courteously*
Or with the clamorous report° of war   *noise*
Thus will I drown your exclamations.
155   DUCHESS OF YORK   Art thou my son?
KING RICHARD   Ay, I thank God, my father, and yourself.
DUCHESS OF YORK   Then patiently hear my impatience.
KING RICHARD   Madam, I have a touch of your condition,°   *temperament*
That cannot brook the accent° of reproof.   *abide the language*
DUCHESS OF YORK   O let me speak!
160   KING RICHARD   Do, then; but I'll not hear.
DUCHESS OF YORK   I will be mild and gentle in my words.
KING RICHARD   And brief, good mother, for I am in haste.
DUCHESS OF YORK   Art thou so hasty? I have stayed° for thee,   *waited*
God knows, in torment and in agony—
165   KING RICHARD   And came I not at last to comfort you?
DUCHESS OF YORK   No, by the Holy Rood,° thou know'st it well.   *Cross*
Thou cam'st on earth to make the earth my hell.
A grievous burden was thy birth to me;
Tetchy° and wayward was thy infancy;   *Irritable*
170   Thy schooldays frightful,° desp'rate, wild, and furious;   *frightening*
Thy prime° of manhood daring, bold, and venturous;   *beginning*
Thy age confirmed,° proud, subtle, sly, and bloody;   *settled maturity*
More mild, but yet more harmful; kind in hatred.[4]
What comfortable hour canst thou name
175   That ever graced me[5] in thy company?
KING RICHARD   Faith, none but Humphrey Hewer,[6] that called your grace
To breakfast once, forth° of my company.   *out*
If I be so disgracious° in your eye,   *unpleasing*
Let me march on, and not offend you, madam.—
Strike up the drum.
180   DUCHESS OF YORK   I pray thee, hear me speak.

---

4. Concealing hatred under cover of kindness.
5. Gave me pleasure; but Richard interprets as "called me by the title 'your grace.'"
6. A proper name, based on "ewer" (a servant who waits at table), but also suggesting "huer" (someone who makes a hue or cry) and playing on "hour" (line 174). Proverbially, "to dine with Duke Humphrey" was not to dine at all.

KING RICHARD   You speak too bitterly.
DUCHESS OF YORK   Hear me a word,
  For I shall never speak to thee again.
KING RICHARD   So.
DUCHESS OF YORK   Either thou wilt die by God's just ordinance
185 Ere from this war thou turn° a conqueror,   *return*
  Or I with grief and extreme age shall perish,
  And never more behold thy face again.
  Therefore take with thee my most heavy curse,
  Which in the day of battle tire thee more
190 Than all the complete armour that thou wear'st.
  My prayers on the adverse party° fight,   *opposite side*
  And there the little souls of Edward's children
  Whisper° the spirits of thine enemies,   *Whisper to*
  And promise them success and victory.
195 Bloody thou art, bloody will be thy end;
  Shame serves° thy life, and doth thy death attend.   *Exit*   *accompanies*
QUEEN ELIZABETH   Though far more cause, yet much less spirit to curse
  Abides in me; I say 'Amen' to all.
KING RICHARD   Stay, madam. I must talk a word with you.
200 QUEEN ELIZABETH   I have no more sons of the royal blood
  For thee to slaughter. For my daughters, Richard,
  They shall be praying nuns, not weeping queens,
  And therefore level not to hit their lives.[7]
KING RICHARD   You have a daughter called Elizabeth,
205 Virtuous and fair, royal and gracious.
QUEEN ELIZABETH   And must she die for this? O let her live,
  And I'll corrupt her manners,° stain her beauty,   *morals*
  Slander myself as false to Edward's bed,
  Throw over her the veil of infamy.
210 So° she may live unscarred of bleeding slaughter,   *Provided that*
  I will confess she was not Edward's daughter.
KING RICHARD   Wrong not her birth. She is a royal princess.
QUEEN ELIZABETH   To save her life I'll say she is not so.
KING RICHARD   Her life is safest only in her birth.[8]
215 QUEEN ELIZABETH   And only in that safety died her brothers.
KING RICHARD   Lo, at their births good stars were opposite.°   *adverse*
QUEEN ELIZABETH   No, to their lives ill friends were contrary.°   *opposed*
KING RICHARD   All unavoided° is the doom° of destiny—   *unavoidable / sentence*
QUEEN ELIZABETH   True, when avoided grace[9] makes destiny.
220 My babes were destined to a fairer death,
  If grace had blessed thee with a fairer life.[1]
221.1   KING RICHARD   *You speak as if that I had slain my cousins.*
       QUEEN ELIZABETH   *Cousins indeed, and by their uncle cozened°*   *cheated*
         Of comfort, kingdom, kindred, freedom, life.
         Whose hand soever lanced their tender hearts,
221.5   *Thy head all indirectly gave direction.*[2]
         No doubt the murd'rous knife was dull and blunt
         Till it was whetted on thy stone-hard heart
         To revel in the entrails of my lambs.
         But that still° use of grief makes wild grief tame,   *Except that continual*

---

7. And therefore do not take aim to kill them.
8. Her life is safe only because of her high birth.
9. When a man who has rejected God's grace (that is, Richard).

1. The indented passage that follows, 221.1–221.14, appears only in F.
2. *Whose . . . direction:* No matter who killed them, it was you, though indirectly, who caused it.

221.10
> *My tongue should to thy ears not name my boys*
> *Till that my nails were anchored in thine eyes—*
> *And I in such a desp'rate bay[3] of death,*
> *Like a poor barque° of sails and tackling reft,°*   boat / deprived
> *Rush all to pieces on thy rocky bosom.*

KING RICHARD   Madam, so thrive I in my enterprise
And dangerous success of bloody wars,
As I intend more good to you and yours
225   Than ever you or yours by me were harmed.[4]

QUEEN ELIZABETH   What good is covered with the face of heaven,[5]
To be discovered, that can do me good?

KING RICHARD   Th'advancement of your children, gentle lady.

QUEEN ELIZABETH   Up to some scaffold, there to lose their heads.

230 KING RICHARD   Unto the dignity and height of fortune,
The high imperial type° of this earth's glory.   symbol

QUEEN ELIZABETH   Flatter my sorrow with report of it.
Tell me what state, what dignity, what honour,
Canst thou demise° to any child of mine?   transmit

235 KING RICHARD   Even all I have—ay, and myself and all,
Will I withal endow a child of thine,
So° in the Lethe[6] of thy angry soul   If
Thou drown the sad remembrance of those wrongs,
Which thou supposest I have done to thee.

240 QUEEN ELIZABETH   Be brief, lest that the process° of thy kindness   story
Last longer telling° than thy kindness' date.°   in the telling / duration

KING RICHARD   Then know that, from my soul,[7] I love thy daughter.

QUEEN ELIZABETH   My daughter's mother thinks that with her soul.

KING RICHARD   What do you think?

245 QUEEN ELIZABETH   That thou dost love my daughter *from* thy soul;
So *from* thy soul's love didst thou love her brothers,
And *from* my heart's love I do thank thee for it.

KING RICHARD   Be not so hasty to confound° my meaning.   deliberately misconstrue
I mean, that *with* my soul I love thy daughter,
250   And do intend to make her queen of England.

QUEEN ELIZABETH   Well then, who dost thou mean shall be her king?

KING RICHARD   Even he that makes her queen. Who else should be?

QUEEN ELIZABETH   What, thou?

KING RICHARD   Even so. How think you of it?

QUEEN ELIZABETH   How canst thou woo her?

KING RICHARD   That would I learn of you,
255   As one being best acquainted with her humour.°   temperament

QUEEN ELIZABETH   And wilt thou learn of me?

KING RICHARD   Madam, with all my heart.

QUEEN ELIZABETH   Send to her, by the man that slew her brothers,
A pair of bleeding hearts; thereon engrave
'Edward' and 'York'; then haply° will she weep.   perhaps
260   Therefore present to her—as sometimes° Margaret   once
Did to thy father, steeped in Rutland's blood[8]—
A handkerchief which, say to her, did drain

---

3. Inlet; the situation of a cornered animal when it turns to face its hunters.
4. *Madam . . . harmed:* (I pray) that the success of my upcoming battles be as certain as is my intention to do to you more good in the future than I have done you harm in the past. *success:* consequence.

5. What good is there on earth.
6. A river in the underworld whose waters induced forgetfulness.
7. With all my soul (but Queen Elizabeth takes it as "separated from," "at variance with").
8. Dramatized in *Richard Duke of York* 1.4.

The purple sap° from her sweet brother's body,   *blood*
And bid her wipe her weeping eyes withal.°   *with it*
265 If this inducement move her not to love,
Send her a letter of thy noble deeds.
Tell her thou mad'st away her uncle Clarence,
Her uncle Rivers—ay, and for her sake
Mad'st quick conveyance with° her good aunt Anne.   *Got rid of*
270 KING RICHARD You mock me, madam. This is not the way
To win your daughter.
QUEEN ELIZABETH   There is no other way,
Unless thou couldst put on some other shape,
And not be Richard, that hath done all this.⁹

273.1 KING RICHARD *Say that I did all this for love of her.*
  QUEEN ELIZABETH *Nay, then indeed she cannot choose but hate thee,*
   Having bought love with such a bloody spoil.°   *slaughter*
  KING RICHARD *Look what° is done cannot be now amended.* *Whatever*
273.5 *Men shall deal° unadvisedly sometimes,*   *act*
  Which after-hours gives leisure to repent.
  If I did take the kingdom from your sons,
  To make amends I'll give it to your daughter.
  If I have killed the issue of your womb,
273.10 *To quicken your increase¹ I will beget*
  Mine issue of your blood upon your daughter.
  A grandam's name is little less in love
  Than is the doting title of a mother.
  They are as children but one step below,
273.15 *Even of your mettall,° of your very blood:*   *spirit*
  Of all one pain, save for a night of groans
  Endured of her for whom you bid like sorrow.²
  Your children were vexation to your youth,
  But mine shall be a comfort to your age.
273.20 *The loss you have is but a son being king,*
  And by that loss your daughter is made queen.
  I cannot make you what amends I would,
  Therefore accept such kindness as I can.°   *can give*
  Dorset your son, that with a fearful soul
273.25 *Leads discontented steps in foreign soil,*
  This fair alliance quickly shall call home
  To high promotions and great dignity.
  The king that calls your beauteous daughter wife,
  Familiarly shall call thy Dorset brother.
273.30 *Again shall you be mother to a king,*
  And all the ruins of distressful times
  Repaired with double riches of content.
  What? We have many goodly days to see.
  The liquid drops of tears that you have shed
273.35 *Shall come again, transformed to orient° pearl,*   *shining*
  Advantaging° their loan with interest   *Augmenting*
  Of ten times double gain of happiness.
  Go then, my mother, to thy daughter go.
  Make bold her bashful years with your experience.

---

9. The indented passage that follows, 273.1–273.55, appears only in F.
1. To give (new) life to your offspring.

2. *Of all . . . sorrow:* Originating from a single bout of labor (Elizabeth's), with the addition of just one more night of pain by the daughter you bore.

273.40
Prepare her ears to hear a wooer's tale.
Put in her tender heart th'aspiring flame
Of golden sovereignty. Acquaint the Princess
With the sweet silent hours of marriage joys.
And when this arm of mine hath chastisèd

273.45
The petty rebel, dull-brained Buckingham,
Bound with triumphant garlands will I come
And lead thy daughter to a conqueror's bed—
To whom I will retail° my conquest won,   *relate*
And she shall be sole victoress: Caesar's Caesar.

273.50
QUEEN ELIZABETH   What were I best to say? Her father's brother
Would° be her lord?° Or shall I say her uncle?   *Wishes to / husband*
Or he that slew her brothers and her uncles?
Under what title shall I woo for thee,
That God, the law, my honour, and her love

273.55
Can make seem pleasing to her tender years?

KING RICHARD   Infer° fair England's peace by this alliance.   *Give as a reason*

275 QUEEN ELIZABETH   Which she shall purchase with still-lasting° war.   *perpetual*

KING RICHARD   Tell her the King, that may command, entreats.

QUEEN ELIZABETH   That at her hands which the King's King° forbids.   *(God)*

KING RICHARD   Say she shall be a high and mighty queen.

QUEEN ELIZABETH   To vail° the title,° as her mother doth.   *yield / (of Queen)*

280 KING RICHARD   Say I will love her everlastingly.

QUEEN ELIZABETH   But how long shall that title 'ever' last?

KING RICHARD   Sweetly in force unto her fair life's end.

QUEEN ELIZABETH   But how long fairly° shall her sweet life last?   *without foul play*

KING RICHARD   As long as heaven and nature lengthens it.

285 QUEEN ELIZABETH   As long as hell and Richard likes of it.

KING RICHARD   Say I, her sovereign, am her subject love.

QUEEN ELIZABETH   But she, your subject, loathes such sovereignty.

KING RICHARD   Be eloquent in my behalf to her.

QUEEN ELIZABETH   An honest tale speeds° best being plainly told.   *succeeds*

290 KING RICHARD   Then plainly to her tell my loving tale.

QUEEN ELIZABETH   Plain and not honest is too harsh a style.[3]

KING RICHARD   Your reasons are too shallow and too quick.[4]

QUEEN ELIZABETH   O no, my reasons are too deep and dead—
Too deep and dead, poor infants, in their graves.

295 KING RICHARD   Harp not on that string, madam. That is past.

QUEEN ELIZABETH   Harp on it still shall I, till heart-strings break.

KING RICHARD   Now by my George, my garter,[5] and my crown—

QUEEN ELIZABETH   Profaned, dishonoured, and the third usurped.

KING RICHARD   I swear—

QUEEN ELIZABETH   By nothing, for this is no oath.

300
Thy George, profaned, hath lost his° holy honour;   *its*
Thy garter, blemished, pawned his lordly virtue;
Thy crown, usurped, disgraced his kingly glory.
If something thou wouldst swear to be believed,
Swear then by something that thou hast not wronged.

KING RICHARD   Then by myself—

305 QUEEN ELIZABETH   Thy self is self-misused.

KING RICHARD   Now by the world—

---

3. The plain style (as in the proverb "Truth is plain"), unless it is truth telling, will be too harsh; lies need elaborate decoration.
4. Rash, ill considered; but Elizabeth's response plays on "quick" as "alive."
5. A garter and a jeweled pendant with the figure of St. George were parts of the insignia of the Order of the Garter, the highest order of knighthood.

QUEEN ELIZABETH   'Tis full of thy foul wrongs.

KING RICHARD   My father's death—

QUEEN ELIZABETH   Thy life hath that dishonoured.

KING RICHARD   Why then, by God—

QUEEN ELIZABETH   God's wrong is most of all.

     If thou didst fear to break an oath with him,
310   The unity the King my husband made[6]
     Thou hadst not broken, nor my brothers died.
     If thou hadst feared to break an oath by him,
     Th'imperial metal circling now thy head
     Had graced the tender temples of my child,
315   And both the princes had been breathing here,
     Which now—two tender bedfellows for dust—
     Thy broken faith hath made the prey for worms.
     What canst thou swear by now?

KING RICHARD   The time to come.

QUEEN ELIZABETH   That thou hast wrongèd in the time o'erpast,
320   For I myself have many tears to wash
     Hereafter time,° for time past wronged by thee.   *The future*
     The children live, whose fathers thou hast slaughtered—
     Ungoverned youth,[7] to wail it in their age.°   *when they grow older*
     The parents live, whose children thou hast butchered—
325   Old barren plants, to wail it with° their age.   *along with*
     Swear not by time to come, for that thou hast
     Misused ere used, by times ill-used o'erpast.[8]

KING RICHARD   As I intend[9] to prosper and repent,
     So thrive I in my dangerous affairs
330   Of hostile arms—myself myself confound,°   *may I ruin myself*
     Heaven and fortune bar me happy hours,
     Day yield me not thy light nor night thy rest;
     Be opposite, all planets of good luck,
     To my proceeding—if, with dear heart's love,
335   Immaculate devotion, holy thoughts,
     I tender° not thy beauteous, princely daughter.   *love*
     In her consists my happiness and thine.
     Without her follows—to myself and thee,
     Herself, the land, and many a Christian soul—
340   Death, desolation, ruin, and decay.
     It cannot be avoided but by this;
     It will not be avoided but by this.
     Therefore, good-mother°—I must call you so—   *mother-in-law*
     Be the attorney of my love to her.
345   Plead what I will be, not what I have been;
     Not my deserts, but what I will deserve.
     Urge the necessity and state of times,°   *state of affairs*
     And be not peevish-fond° in great designs.   *foolishly obstinate*

QUEEN ELIZABETH   Shall I be tempted of the devil thus?
350 KING RICHARD   Ay, if the devil tempt you to do good.

QUEEN ELIZABETH   Shall I forget myself to be myself?[1]

KING RICHARD   Ay, if yourself's remembrance wrong yourself.

---

6. The "reconciliation" staged in 2.1 between Queen
Elizabeth and her enemies.
7. Youth without a father's guidance.
8. *thou . . . o'erpast:* you have, by the continuing effects
of your past crimes, misused the future even before it

comes to pass.
9. *As I intend:* the formulation has the force of "I swear
that as I intend."
1. Am I to overlook all wrongs done me in order to
become Queen Mother (as I already have been)?

QUEEN ELIZABETH   Yet thou didst kill my children.

KING RICHARD   But in your daughter's womb I bury them,

355 Where, in that nest of spicery,[2] they will breed

Selves of themselves, to your recomfiture.°   *consolation*

QUEEN ELIZABETH   Shall I go win my daughter to thy will?

KING RICHARD   And be a happy mother by the deed.

QUEEN ELIZABETH   I go. Write to me very shortly,

360 And you shall understand from me her mind.

KING RICHARD   Bear her my true love's kiss,

    [*He kisses her*]   and so farewell—

                           Exit [ELIZABETH]

    Relenting fool, and shallow, changing woman.

       Enter [*Sir Richard*] RATCLIFFE

    How now, what news?

RATCLIFFE   Most mighty sovereign, on the western coast

365 Rideth a puissant° navy. To our shores   *mighty*

Throng many doubtful, hollow-hearted friends,

Unarmed and unresolved, to beat them back.

'Tis thought that Richmond is their° admiral,   *(the navy's)*

And there they hull,° expecting but the aid   *drift; wait*

370 Of Buckingham to welcome them ashore.

KING RICHARD   Some light-foot° friend post° to the Duke of   *swift-footed / hasten*

    Norfolk.

    Ratcliffe thyself, or Catesby—where is he?[3]

CATESBY   Here, my good lord.

KING RICHARD   Catesby, fly to the Duke.

CATESBY   I will, my lord, with all convenient° haste.   *due*

375 KING RICHARD   Ratcliffe, come hither. Post to Salisbury;

When thou com'st thither—[*to* CATESBY] dull, unmindful villain,

Why stay'st thou here, and goest not to the Duke?

CATESBY   First, mighty liege, tell me your highness' pleasure:

What from your grace I shall deliver to him?

380 KING RICHARD   O true, good Catesby. Bid him levy straight

The greatest strength and power that he can make,°   *raise*

And meet me suddenly° at Salisbury.   *without delay*

CATESBY   I go.   *Exit*

RATCLIFFE   What, may it please you, shall I do at Salisbury?

385 KING RICHARD   Why, what wouldst thou do there before I go?

RATCLIFFE   Your highness told me I should post before.

KING RICHARD   My mind is changed.

       Enter Lord STANLEY

                        Stanley, what news with you?

STANLEY   None, good my liege, to please you with the hearing,

Nor none so bad but well may be reported.

390 KING RICHARD   Hoyday,° a riddle! Neither good nor bad.   *(an exclamation)*

Why need'st thou run so many mile about

When thou mayst tell thy tale the nearest° way?   *most direct*

Once more, what news?

STANLEY   Richmond is on the seas.

KING RICHARD   There let him sink, and be the seas on him.

395 White-livered° renegade, what doth he there?   *Cowardly*

---

2. Fragrant spices—in contrast to the stench of other burial places; the spices on the phoenix's pyre. *nest:* place where eggs are hatched, but also specifically the nest or pyre on which the legendary phoenix burned itself and then rose from its own ashes.

3. Parts of lines 373–74 appear only in F.

STANLEY I know not, mighty sovereign, but by guess.

KING RICHARD Well, as you guess?

STANLEY Stirred up by Dorset, Buckingham, and Ely,
He makes for England, here to claim the crown.

400 KING RICHARD Is the chair° empty? Is the sword unswayed?   *throne*
Is the King dead? The empire° unpossessed?   *state*
What heir of York is there alive but we?
And who is England's king but great York's heir?
Then tell me, what makes he° upon the seas?   *what is he doing*

405 STANLEY Unless for that, my liege, I cannot guess.

KING RICHARD Unless for that° he comes to be your liege,   *because*
You cannot guess wherefore the Welshman⁴ comes.
Thou wilt revolt and fly to him, I fear.

STANLEY No, my good lord, therefore mistrust me not.

410 KING RICHARD Where is thy power then? To beat him back,
Where be thy tenants and thy followers?
Are they not now upon the western shore,
Safe-conducting the rebels from their ships?

STANLEY No, my good lord, my friends are in the north.

415 KING RICHARD Cold friends to me. What do they in the north,
When they should serve their sovereign in the west?

STANLEY They have not been commanded, mighty King.
Pleaseth° your majesty to give me leave,   *If it please*
I'll muster up my friends and meet your grace

420 Where and what time your majesty shall please.

KING RICHARD Ay, ay, thou wouldst be gone to join with Richmond.
But I'll not trust thee.

STANLEY   Most mighty sovereign,
You have no cause to hold my friendship doubtful.
I never was, nor never will be, false.

425 KING RICHARD Go then and muster men—but leave behind
Your son George Stanley. Look your heart be firm,
Or else his head's assurance is but frail.

STANLEY So deal with him as I prove true to you.   *Exit*

Enter a MESSENGER

MESSENGER My gracious sovereign, now in Devonshire,

430 As I by friends am well advertisèd,°   *well informed*
Sir Edward Courtenay and the haughty prelate,
Bishop of Exeter, his elder brother,
With many more confederates are in arms.

Enter another MESSENGER

SECOND MESSENGER In Kent, my liege, the Guildfords are in arms,

435 And every hour more competitors°   *associates*
Flock to the rebels, and their power grows strong.

Enter another MESSENGER

THIRD MESSENGER My lord, the army of great Buckingham—

KING RICHARD Out on ye, owls!⁵ Nothing but songs of death?

He striketh him

There, take thou that, till thou bring better news.

440 THIRD MESSENGER The news I have to tell your majesty
Is that, by sudden flood and fall of water,°   *rain*
Buckingham's army is dispersed and scattered,
And he himself wandered away alone,

---

4. Richmond's grandfather, Owen Tudor, was Welsh.   5. The cry of the owl was thought to portend evil.

No man knows whither.

KING RICHARD   I cry thee mercy.°—   *I beg your pardon*
445   Ratcliffe, reward him for the blow I gave him.—
Hath any well-advisèd° friend proclaimed   *foresighted*
Reward to him that brings the traitor in?

THIRD MESSENGER   Such proclamation hath been made, my lord.

Enter another MESSENGER

FOURTH MESSENGER   Sir Thomas Lovell and Lord Marquis Dorset—
450   'Tis said, my liege—in Yorkshire are in arms.
But this good comfort bring I to your highness:
The Breton navy is dispersed by tempest.
Richmond in Dorsetshire sent out a boat
Unto the shore, to ask those on the banks
455   If they were his assistants,° yea or no?   *allies*
Who answered him they came from Buckingham
Upon his party.° He, mistrusting them,   *faction*
Hoist sail and made his course again for Bretagne.°   *Brittany*

KING RICHARD   March on, march on, since we are up in arms,
460   If not to fight with foreign enemies,
Yet to beat down these rebels here at home.

Enter CATESBY

CATESBY   My liege, the Duke of Buckingham is taken.
That is the best news. That the Earl of Richmond
Is with a mighty power landed at Milford⁶
465   Is colder tidings, yet they must be told.

KING RICHARD   Away, towards Salisbury! While we reason° here,   *talk*
A royal battle might be won and lost.
Someone take order Buckingham be brought
To Salisbury. The rest march on with me.   *Flourish. Exeunt*

4.5

Enter [Lord STANLEY *Earl of] Derby and* SIR CHRISTO-
PHER *[a priest]*

STANLEY   Sir Christopher, tell Richmond this from me:
That in the sty of this most deadly boar
My son George Stanley is franked up in hold.¹
If I revolt, off goes young George's head.
5   The fear of that holds off my present aid.
But tell me, where is princely Richmond now?

SIR CHRISTOPHER   At Pembroke, or at Ha'rfordwest² in Wales.

STANLEY   What men of name° resort to him?   *rank*

SIR CHRISTOPHER   Sir Walter Herbert, a renownèd soldier,
10   Sir Gilbert Talbot, Sir William Stanley,³
Oxford, redoubted° Pembroke,⁴ Sir James Blunt,   *dreaded*
And Rhys-ap-Thomas with a valiant crew,
And many other of great name and worth—
And towards London do they bend their power,°   *lead their troops*

---

6. Milford Haven, a large, deep natural harbor on the
Welsh coast, far enough from centers of population to
be ideal for an invading army. The events of Rich-
mond's successful invasion at Milford in 1485 are tele-
scoped, in the mouths of the four messengers, with
those of his unsuccessful rebellion against Richard two
years earlier.

4.5 Location: A private place, perhaps Derby's house.
1. Is shut up (in a sty) in custody.
2. Haverford West, town at the northern end of Mil-
ford Haven. Pembroke was the county town of Pem-
brokeshire, situated on Milford Haven.
3. Lord Stanley, the Earl of Derby's brother.
4. Jasper Tudor, Richmond's uncle.

15   If by the way they be not fought withal.
    STANLEY   Well, hie° thee to thy lord. Commend me to him.   *hasten*
        Tell him the Queen hath heartily consented
        He should espouse Elizabeth her daughter.
        My letter will resolve him of my mind.[5]
20   Farewell.   *Exeunt [severally]*

5.1

Enter [the Duke of] BUCKINGHAM with halberdiers, led
[by a SHERIFF] to execution

    BUCKINGHAM   Will not King Richard let me speak with him?
    SHERIFF   No, my good lord, therefore be patient.
    BUCKINGHAM   Hastings, and Edward's children, Gray and Rivers,
        Holy King Henry and thy fair son Edward,
5   Vaughan, and all that have miscarried°   *died*
        By underhand, corrupted, foul injustice:
        If that your moody, discontented souls[1]
        Do through the clouds behold this present hour,
        Even for revenge mock my destruction.
10   This is All-Souls' day,[2] fellow, is it not?
    SHERIFF   It is.
    BUCKINGHAM   Why then All-Souls' day is my body's doomsday.
        This is the day which, in King Edward's time,
        I wished might fall on me,[3] when I was found
15   False to his children and his wife's allies.°   *kinsmen*
        This is the day wherein I wished to fall
        By the false faith of him whom most I trusted.
        This, this All-Souls' day to my fearful soul
        Is the determined respite of my wrongs.[4]
20   That high all-seer which I dallied with
        Hath turned my feignèd prayer on my head,
        And given in earnest what I begged in jest.
        Thus doth he force the swords of wicked men
        To turn their own points in their masters' bosoms.
25   Thus Margaret's curse falls heavy on my neck.
        'When he', quoth she, 'shall split thy heart with sorrow,
        Remember Margaret was a prophetess.'[5]
        Come lead me, officers, to the block of shame.
        Wrong hath but wrong, and blame the due of blame.   *Exeunt*

5.2

Enter [HENRY EARL OF] RICHMOND [with a letter, the
Earl of] OXFORD, [Sir James] BLUNT, [Sir Walter] HER-
BERT, and others, with drum and colours

    HENRY EARL OF RICHMOND   Fellows in arms, and my most loving friends,
        Bruised underneath the yoke of tyranny,
        Thus far into the bowels° of the land   *center*

---

5. Will make my intentions clear to him.
5.1 Location: Salisbury.
1. Because they are unable to rest in peace until their violent deaths have been avenged. *moody:* angry.
2. November 2, the day on which the Roman Catholic Church intercedes for all Christian souls and on which spirits were supposed to walk (as in the following scenes at Shrewsbury).

3. See Buckingham's prophetic speech in 2.1.32–40.
4. Is the preordained ending of my wrongdoing (but alluding to the more usual significance of All Souls' Day, "preordained final rest from suffering"). *respite:* day to which something is postponed.
5. See 1.3.298–99.
5.2 Location: Near Tamworth in Staffordshire.

Have we marched on without impediment,
5 And here receive we from our father[1] Stanley
Lines of fair comfort and encouragement.
The wretched, bloody, and usurping boar,
That spoils your summer fields and fruitful vines,
Swills your warm blood like wash,° and makes his trough   *pig fodder*
10 In your inboweled° bosoms, this foul swine   *disemboweled*
Lies now even in the centry° of this isle,   *center; sentry post*
Near to the town of Leicester, as we learn.
From Tamworth thither is but one day's march.
In God's name, cheerly° on, courageous friends,   *cheerfully*
15 To reap the harvest of perpetual peace
By this one bloody trial of sharp war.
OXFORD   Every man's conscience is a thousand swords
To fight against this guilty homicide.°   *murderer*
HERBERT   I doubt not but his friends will turn to us.
20 BLUNT   He hath no friends but what are friends for fear,
Which in his dearest° need will fly from him.   *most extreme*
HENRY EARL OF RICHMOND   All for our vantage.° Then, in God's   *advantage*
name, march.
True hope is swift, and flies with swallows' wings;
Kings it makes gods, and meaner° creatures kings.   *baser*
Exeunt [marching]

5.3

Enter KING RICHARD *in arms, with [the Duke of]* NOR-
FOLK, *[Sir Richard]* RATCLIFFE, *Sir William [*CATESBY,
and others][1]
KING RICHARD   Here pitch our tent, even here in Bosworth field.
[*Soldiers begin to pitch a tent*]
Why, how now, Catesby? Why look you so sad?
CATESBY   My heart is ten times lighter than my looks.
KING RICHARD   My lord of Norfolk.
NORFOLK   Here, most gracious liege.
5 KING RICHARD   Norfolk, we must have knocks.° Ha, must we not?   *blows*
NORFOLK   We must both give and take, my loving lord.
KING RICHARD   Up with my tent! Here will I lie tonight.
But where tomorrow? Well, all's one for that.°   *it makes no difference*
Who hath descried° the number of the traitors?   *discerned*
10 NORFOLK   Six or seven thousand is their utmost power.
KING RICHARD   Why, our battalia° trebles that account.°   *army / number*
Besides, the King's name is a tower of strength,
Which they upon the adverse faction want.°   *lack*
Up with the tent! Come, noble gentlemen,
15 Let us survey the vantage of the ground.[2]
Call for some men of sound direction.°   *military judgment*
Let's lack no discipline, make no delay—
For, lords, tomorrow is a busy day.   *Exeunt [at one door]*

1. Stepfather (Richmond was the son of Edmund Tudor
and Margaret Beaufort; Lord Stanley, Earl of Derby, was
his mother's third husband). *our:* royal plural.
5.3 Location: The rest of the play takes place on
Bosworth Field.

1. Instead of Catesby, the stage direction in F has the
Earl of Surrey, who speaks with Richard at line 3.
2. *vantage of the ground:* military advantages offered by
the spot chosen for battle.

5.4

Enter [at another door HENRY EARL OF] RICHMOND,
[Sir James BLUNT,] *Sir William Brandon, [the Earl of]*
OXFORD, *[Marquis]* DORSET *[and others]*[1]

HENRY EARL OF RICHMOND   The weary sun hath made a golden set,
And by the bright track of his fiery car[2]
Gives token of a goodly day tomorrow.
Sir William Brandon, you shall bear my standard.
5 The Earl of Pembroke keeps° his regiment;   *stays with*
Good Captain Blunt, bear my good night to him,
And by the second hour in the morning
Desire the Earl to see me in my tent.
Yet one thing more, good Captain, do for me:
10 Where is Lord Stanley quartered, do you know?
BLUNT   Unless I have mista'en his colours much,
Which well I am assured I have not done,
His regiment lies half a mile, at least,
South from the mighty power of the King.
15 HENRY EARL OF RICHMOND   If without peril it be possible,
Sweet Blunt, make some good means to speak with him,
And give him from me this most needful note.
BLUNT   Upon my life, my lord, I'll undertake it.
And so God give you quiet rest tonight.
HENRY EARL OF RICHMOND   Good night, good Captain Blunt.
                                                        [*Exit* BLUNT]
20   Come, gentlemen.
Give me some ink and paper in my tent.
I'll draw the form and model° of our battle,   *plan*
Limit° each leader to his several charge,°   *Appoint / separate duty*
And part° in just proportion our small power.   *divide*
25 Let us consult upon tomorrow's business.
Into my tent: the dew is raw and cold.
                                    They withdraw into the tent

5.5

[A table brought in.] Enter KING RICHARD, *[Sir
Richard]* RATCLIFFE, *[the Duke of]* NORFOLK, *[Sir
William]* CATESBY *[and others]*

KING RICHARD   What is't o'clock?
CATESBY   It's supper-time, my lord. It's nine o'clock.
KING RICHARD   I will not sup tonight. Give me some ink and paper.
What, is my beaver easier° than it was?   *my helmet visor looser*
5 And all my armour laid into my tent?
CATESBY   It is, my liege, and all things are in readiness.
KING RICHARD   Good Norfolk, hie thee° to thy charge.   *hasten*
Use careful watch; choose trusty sentinels.
NORFOLK   I go, my lord.
10 KING RICHARD   Stir with the lark tomorrow, gentle Norfolk.
NORFOLK   I warrant° you, my lord.   *Exit*   *assure; guarantee*
KING RICHARD   Catesby.
CATESBY   My lord?

5.4
1. Although Q and F are silent on the question of how many tents are onstage at the end of this scene, most editors direct these attendants to pitch another for Richmond during the following dialogue. Oxford and Dorset are specified in F but not in Q, which calls only for "the lords."
2. Chariot (of the sun god Phoebus).
5.5

KING RICHARD   Send out a pursuivant-at-arms°   *one who attends a herald*
          To Stanley's regiment. Bid him bring his power°   *forces*
          Before sun-rising, lest his son George fall
15   Into the blind cave of eternal night.   [*Exit* CATESBY]
          Fill me a bowl of wine. Give me a watch.[1]
          Saddle white Surrey[2] for the field tomorrow.
          Look that my staves° be sound, and not too heavy.   *lance shafts*
          Ratcliffe.
20 RATCLIFFE   My lord?
    KING RICHARD   Saw'st thou the melancholy Lord Northumberland?
    RATCLIFFE   Thomas the Earl of Surrey and himself,
          Much about cockshut° time, from troop to troop   *twilight*
          Went through the army, cheering up the soldiers.
25 KING RICHARD   So, I am satisfied. Give me some wine.
          I have not that alacrity of spirit,
          Nor cheer of mind, that I was wont to have.
                    [*The wine is brought*]
          Set it down. Is ink and paper ready?
    RATCLIFFE   It is, my lord.
    KING RICHARD   Leave me. Bid my guard watch.
30   About the mid of night come to my tent,
          Ratcliffe, and help to arm me. Leave me, I say.
          Exit RATCLIFFE [*with others.* RICHARD *writes, and later sleeps*]
                    Enter [*Lord* STANLEY *Earl of*] *Derby to* HENRY EARL
                    OF] RICHMOND [*and the lords*] *in his tent*
    STANLEY   Fortune and victory sit on thy helm!°   *helmet*
    HENRY EARL OF RICHMOND   All comfort that the dark night can afford
          Be to thy person, noble father-in-law.°   *stepfather*
35   Tell me, how fares our loving mother?
    STANLEY   I, by attorney,° bless thee from thy mother,   *by proxy*
          Who prays continually for Richmond's good.
          So much for that. The silent hours steal on,
          And flaky° darkness breaks within the east.   *streaked with light*
40   In brief—for so the season° bids us be—   *time of day*
          Prepare thy battle early in the morning,
          And put thy fortune to th'arbitrement°   *determination; verdict*
          Of bloody strokes and mortal-sharing[3] war.
          I, as I may—that which I would, I cannot—
45   With best advantage will deceive the time,[4]
          And aid thee in this doubtful shock° of arms.   *this uncertain clash*
          But on thy side I may not be too forward—
          Lest, being seen, thy brother,° tender° George,   *stepbrother / young*
          Be executed in his father's sight.
50   Farewell. The leisure° and the fearful time   *time available*
          Cuts off the ceremonious vows of love
          And ample interchange of sweet discourse,
          Which so long sundered friends should dwell upon.
          God give us leisure for these rights of love.
55   Once more, adieu. Be valiant, and speed well.

---

1. Probably a watch light (a slow-burning candle, to write by); possibly a special guard (see line 29).
2. The chroniclers report that Richard was mounted on a "great white course," but the name is Shakespeare's.
3. Apportioning to mortals their lot; shearing or cutting

down mortals. Q has "mortal staring," giving the commonplace image of war as both evil-looking and able to cause damage with its glance (like a basilisk).
4. *as . . . time:* as best I can—for I cannot fight openly on your side—I will mislead Richard.

HENRY EARL OF RICHMOND   Good lords, conduct him to his regiment.
I'll strive with° troubled thoughts to take a nap,   *despite*
Lest leaden slumber peise° me down tomorrow,   *weigh*
When I should mount with wings of victory.
60   Once more, good night, kind lords and gentlemen.
            Exeunt [STANLEY *and the lords*]. *Manet* RICHMOND
            [RICHMOND *kneels*]
O thou, whose captain I account myself,
Look on my forces with a gracious eye.
Put in their hands thy bruising irons° of wrath,   *swords*
That they may crush down with a heavy fall
65   Th'usurping helmets of our adversaries.
Make us thy ministers of chastisement,
That we may praise thee in the victory.
To thee I do commend my watchful° soul,   *alert*
Ere I let fall the windows° of mine eyes.   *eyelids*
70   Sleeping and waking, O defend me still!   [*He*] *sleeps*
            Enter the GHOST OF *young* PRINCE EDWARD [*above*][5]
GHOST OF PRINCE EDWARD (*to* RICHARD)   Let me sit heavy on
      thy soul tomorrow,
Prince Edward, son to Henry the Sixth.[6]
Think how thou stabbedst me in my prime of youth
At Tewkesbury. Despair, therefore, and die.
75   (*To* RICHMOND) Be cheerful, Richmond, for the wrongèd souls
Of butchered princes fight in thy behalf.
King Henry's issue,° Richmond, comforts thee.   [*Exit*][7]   *offspring*
            Enter [*above*] *the* GHOST OF [KING] HENRY VI
GHOST OF KING HENRY (*to* RICHARD)   When I was mortal, my
      anointed° body   (*with sacred oil*)
By thee was punchèd full of deadly holes.
80   Think on the Tower[8] and me. Despair and die.
Harry the Sixth bids thee despair and die.
(*To* RICHMOND) Virtuous and holy, be thou conqueror.
Harry that prophesied[9] thou shouldst be king
Comforts thee in thy sleep. Live and flourish!   [*Exit*]
            Enter [*above*] *the* GHOST OF [*George Duke of*] CLARENCE
85   GHOST OF CLARENCE [*to* RICHARD]   Let me sit heavy on thy soul tomorrow,
I that was washed to death with fulsome° wine,   *sickening*
Poor Clarence, by thy guile betrayed to death.
Tomorrow in the battle think on me,
And fall° thy edgeless sword. Despair and die.   *drop*
90   (*To* RICHMOND) Thou offspring of the house of Lancaster,
The wrongèd heirs of York do pray for thee.
Good angels guard thy battle.° Live and flourish!   [*Exit*]   *army*
            Enter [*above*] *the* GHOSTS OF [*Lords*] RIVERS, GRAY, *and*
            [*Sir Thomas*] VAUGHAN
GHOST OF RIVERS [*to* RICHARD]   Let me sit heavy on thy soul tomorrow,
Rivers that died at Pomfret. Despair and die.
95   GHOST OF GRAY [*to* RICHARD]   Think upon Gray, and let thy soul despair.

5. Q, F do not specify how or where the ghosts enter.
6. Line not present in Q, F; it is added here because
Edward is the one character not seen previously, and it is
possible that information originally intended as dialogue
ended up as the stage direction when the text was printed.
7. Exits not given in Q, F. The ghosts could exeunt
together at the end.

8. Where Henry VI was supposedly murdered.
9. See *Richard Duke of York* 4.7, in which King Henry
(sometimes "Harry"), declaring the young Richmond
"England's hope," foresees Richmond's accession to
the throne and the beginning of what was to become
the Tudor dynasty.

GHOST OF VAUGHAN [*to* RICHARD]   Think upon Vaughan, and with guilty fear
    Let fall thy pointless lance. Despair and die.
ALL THREE (*to* RICHMOND)   Awake, and think our wrongs in Richard's bosom
    Will conquer him. Awake, and win the day!   [*Exeunt* GHOSTS]
        Enter [*above*] *the* GHOSTS OF THE *two young* PRINCES
GHOSTS OF THE PRINCES (*to* RICHARD)   Dream on thy cousins,[1]
100   smothered in the Tower.
    Let us be lead within thy bosom, Richard,
    And weigh thee down to ruin, shame, and death.
    Thy nephews' souls bid thee despair and die.
    (*To* RICHMOND) Sleep, Richmond, sleep in peace and wake in joy.
105   Good angels guard thee from the boar's annoy.
    Live, and beget a happy race of kings!
    Edward's unhappy sons do bid thee flourish. [*Exeunt* GHOSTS]
        Enter [*above*] *the* GHOST OF *Lord* HASTINGS[2]
GHOST OF HASTINGS [*to* RICHARD]   Bloody and guilty, guiltily awake,
    And in a bloody battle end thy days.
110   Think on Lord Hastings, then despair and die.
    (*To* RICHMOND) Quiet, untroubled soul, awake, awake!
    Arm, fight, and conquer for fair England's sake.   [*Exit*]
        Enter [*above*] *the* GHOST OF LADY ANNE
GHOST OF LADY ANNE (*to* RICHARD)   Richard, thy wife, that wretched Anne thy wife,
    That never slept a quiet hour with thee,
115   Now fills thy sleep with perturbations.
    Tomorrow in the battle think on me,
    And fall thy edgeless sword. Despair and die.
    (*To* RICHMOND) Thou quiet soul, sleep thou a quiet sleep.
    Dream of success and happy victory.
120   Thy adversary's wife doth pray for thee.   [*Exit*]
        Enter [*above*] *the* GHOST [OF *the Duke*] *of* BUCKINGHAM
GHOST OF BUCKINGHAM (*to* RICHARD)   The first was I that helped thee to the crown;
    The last was I that felt thy tyranny.
    O in the battle think on Buckingham,
    And die in terror of thy guiltiness!
125   Dream on, dream on, of bloody deeds and death;
    Fainting,° despair; despairing, yield thy breath.   *Losing heart*
    (*To* RICHMOND) I died for hope[3] ere I could lend thee aid.
    But cheer thy heart, and be thou not dismayed.
    God and good angels fight on Richmond's side,
130   And Richard falls in height of all his pride.   [*Exit*]
        RICHARD *starteth up out of a dream*
KING RICHARD   Give me another horse! Bind up my wounds!
    Have mercy, Jesu!—Soft, I did but dream.
    O coward conscience, how dost thou afflict me?
    The lights burn blue.[4] It is now dead midnight.
135   Cold fearful drops stand on my trembling flesh.
    What do I fear? Myself? There's none else by.
    Richard loves Richard; that is, I am I.
    Is there a murderer here? No. Yes, I am.
    Then fly! What, from myself? Great reason. Why?

1. Nephews ("cousins" was a term used for any kins-
men).
2. Q has him enter before the princes, as he had died
before them.

3. I died hoping I could aid you.
4. Thought to indicate the presence of ghosts.

140   Lest I revenge. Myself upon myself?
       Alack, I love myself. Wherefore?° For any good   *Why*
       That I myself have done unto myself?
       O no, alas, I rather hate myself
       For hateful deeds committed by myself.
145   I am a villain. Yet I lie: I am not.
       Fool, of thyself speak well.—Fool, do not flatter.
       My conscience hath a thousand several° tongues,   *separate*
       And every tongue brings in a several tale,
       And every tale condemns me for a villain.
150   Perjury, perjury, in the high'st degree!⁵
       Murder, stern murder, in the dir'st degree!
       All several sins, all used in each degree,
       Throng to the bar,° crying all, 'Guilty, guilty!'   *(of the court)*
       I shall despair.⁶ There is no creature loves me,
155   And if I die no soul will pity me.
       Nay, wherefore should they?—Since that I myself
       Find in myself no pity to myself.
       Methought the souls of all that I had murdered
       Came to my tent, and every one did threat
160   Tomorrow's vengeance on the head of Richard.
              Enter RATCLIFFE
RATCLIFFE   My lord?
KING RICHARD   'Swounds, who is there?
RATCLIFFE   My lord, 'tis I. The early village cock
       Hath twice done salutation to the morn.
165   Your friends are up, and buckle on their armour.
KING RICHARD   O Ratcliffe, I have dreamed a fearful dream.
       What thinkest thou, will all our friends prove true?
RATCLIFFE   No doubt, my lord.
KING RICHARD   Ratcliffe, I fear, I fear.
RATCLIFFE   Nay, good my lord, be not afraid of shadows.°   *illusions; ghosts*
170 KING RICHARD   By the Apostle Paul, shadows tonight
       Have struck more terror to the soul of Richard
       Than can the substance of ten thousand soldiers
       Armèd in proof° and led by shallow Richmond.   *impenetrable armor*
       'Tis not yet near day. Come, go with me.
175   Under our tents I'll play the eavesdropper,
       To see if any mean to shrink from me.
                  Exeunt RICHARD *and* RATCLIFFE
              Enter the lords to [HENRY EARL OF] RICHMOND, *sitting
              in his tent*
LORDS   Good morrow, Richmond.
HENRY EARL OF RICHMOND   Cry mercy,° lords and watchful   *Beg your pardon*
              gentlemen,
       That you have ta'en a tardy sluggard here.
180 A LORD   How have you slept, my lord?
HENRY EARL OF RICHMOND   The sweetest sleep and fairest
              boding° dreams   *most propitious*
       That ever entered in a drowsy head
       Have I since your departure had, my lords.

___

5. Every kind of sin, from least to most wicked.
6. Despair was considered the only unforgivable sin; see 1.2.85–88.

Methought their souls whose bodies Richard murdered
185 Came to my tent and cried on[7] victory.
I promise you, my soul is very jocund°   *joyful*
In the remembrance of so fair a dream.
How far into the morning is it, lords?
A LORD   Upon the stroke of four.
190 HENRY EARL OF RICHMOND   Why then, 'tis time to arm, and give direction.
        His oration to his soldiers
Much that I could say, loving countrymen,
The leisure° and enforcement of the time   *time available*
Forbids to dwell on. Yet remember this:
God and our good cause fight upon our side.
195 The prayers of holy saints and wrongèd souls,
Like high-reared bulwarks, stand before our forces.
Richard except,° those whom we fight against   *excepted*
Had rather have us win than him they follow.
For what is he they follow? Truly, friends,
200 A bloody tyrant and a homicide;
One raised in blood, and one in blood established;[8]
One that made means° to come by what he hath,   *that contrived*
And slaughtered those that were the means to help him;
A base, foul stone, made precious by the foil[9]
205 Of England's chair, where he is falsely set;[1]
One that hath ever been God's enemy.
Then if you fight against God's enemy,
God will, in justice, ward° you as his soldiers.   *guard*
If you do sweat to put a tyrant down,
210 You sleep in peace, the tyrant being slain.
If you do fight against your country's foes,
Your country's foison° pays your pains the hire.   *abundance*
If you do fight in safeguard of your wives,
Your wives shall welcome home the conquerors.
215 If you do free your children from the sword,
Your children's children quites° it in your age.   *requites*
Then, in the name of God and all these rights,
Advance° your standards! Draw your willing swords!   *Raise*
For me, the ransom of this bold attempt
220 Shall be my cold corpse on the earth's cold face;[2]
But if I thrive,° to gain of my attempt,   *succeed*
The least of you shall share his part thereof.
Sound, drums and trumpets, bold and cheerfully!
God and Saint George!° Richmond and victory!   *patron saint of England*
        [*Exeunt to the sound of drums and trumpets*]

                        5.6
        Enter KING RICHARD, [*Sir Richard*] RATCLIFFE, [*Sir
        William*] CATESBY [*and others*]
KING RICHARD   What said Northumberland, as touching° Richmond?   *regarding*
RATCLIFFE   That he was never trainèd up in arms.

---

7. And called out (a hunting term); here, urged me on
to.
8. *One raised . . . established:* One who has come to the
throne by bloodshed and has held it through further
bloodshed.
9. Metal leaf was often placed under a jewel as a part

of its setting, in order to increase its radiance.
1. Of the throne of England, on which he is wrongly
placed; with a pun on "being set like a jewel."
2. *the ransom . . . face:* the only ransom I will give them
is my dead body.
5.6

KING RICHARD   He said the truth. And what said Surrey then?
RATCLIFFE   He smiled and said, 'The better for our purpose.'
5   KING RICHARD   He was in the right, and so indeed it is.
            Clock strikes
    Tell the clock there.¹ Give me a calendar.°   *an almanac*
    Who saw the sun today?
            [*A book is brought*]
RATCLIFFE   Not I, my lord.
KING RICHARD   Then he disdains to shine, for by the book°   *(the almanac)*
    He should have braved° the east an hour ago.   *made resplendent*
10   A black day will it be to somebody.
    Ratcliffe.
RATCLIFFE   My lord?
KING RICHARD   The sun will not be seen today.
    The sky doth frown and lour° upon our army.   *glower*
    I would these dewy tears were from° the ground.   *gone from*
15   Not shine today—why, what is that to me
    More than to Richmond? For the selfsame heaven
    That frowns on me looks sadly upon him.
            Enter [the Duke of] NORFOLK
NORFOLK   Arm, arm, my lord! The foe vaunts° in the field.   *flaunts his strength*
KING RICHARD   Come, bustle, bustle! Caparison° my horse.   *Put the trappings on*
            [RICHARD *arms*]
20   Call up Lord Stanley, bid him bring his power.°   [*Exit one*]   *forces*
    I will lead forth my soldiers to the plain,
    And thus my battle° shall be orderèd.   *army*
    My forward° shall be drawn out all in length,   *front rank*
    Consisting equally of horse and foot,
25   Our archers placèd strongly in the midst.
    John Duke of Norfolk, Thomas Earl of Surrey,
    Shall have the leading of this multitude.
    They thus directed,° we ourself will follow   *positioned*
    In the main battle, whose puissance° on both sides   *power*
30   Shall be well wingèd° with our chiefest horse.°   *flanked / best cavalry*
    This, and Saint George to boot!² What think'st thou, Norfolk?
NORFOLK   A good direction, warlike sovereign.
            He showeth him a paper
    This paper found I on my tent this morning.
            [*He reads*]
        'Jackie of Norfolk be not too bold,
35   For Dickon thy master is bought and sold.'³
KING RICHARD   A thing devisèd by the enemy.—
    Go, gentlemen, each man unto his charge.
    Let not our babbling dreams affright our souls.
    Conscience is but a word that cowards use,
40   Devised at first to keep the strong in awe.
    Our strong arms be our conscience; swords, our law.
    March on, join° bravely! Let us to't, pell mell—   *join battle*
    If not to heaven, then hand in hand to hell.
            His oration to his army
    What shall I say, more than I have inferred?°   *put forward*
45   Remember whom you are to cope withal:°   *with*

---

1. Count the clock's strokes.
2. *and . . . boot:* with the aid of our patron saint as a
bonus.

3. Is betrayed. *Jackie of Norfolk:* John, Duke of Nor-
folk. *Dickon:* Dick (that is, Richard).

A sort° of vagabonds, rascals and runaways,   *gang*
A scum of Bretons and base lackey° peasants,   *lowly*
Whom their o'ercloyèd° country vomits forth   *nauseously overfull*
To desperate ventures and assured destruction.

50 You sleeping safe, they bring to you unrest;
You having lands and blessed with beauteous wives,
They would distrain° the one, distain° the other.   *confiscate / dishonor*
And who doth lead them, but a paltry fellow?
Long kept in Bretagne at our mother's[4] cost;
55 A milksop; one that never in his life
Felt so much cold as over shoes in snow.[5]
Let's whip[6] these stragglers o'er the seas again,
Lash hence these overweening rags of France,
These famished beggars, weary of their lives,
60 Who—but for° dreaming on this fond° exploit—   *were it not for / foolish*
For want of means,° poor rats, had hanged themselves.   *livelihood*
If we be conquered, let *men* conquer us,
And not these bastard Bretons, whom our fathers
Have in their own land beaten, bobbed,° and thumped,   *pounded*
65 And in record left them the heirs of shame.[7]
Shall these enjoy our lands? Lie with our wives?
Ravish our daughters?
            Drum afar off
                              Hark, I hear their drum.
Fight, gentlemen of England! Fight, bold yeomen!
Draw, archers, draw your arrows to the head!
70 Spur your proud horses hard, and ride in blood!
Amaze the welkin° with your broken staves!   *sky*
            Enter a MESSENGER
What says Lord Stanley? Will he bring his power?
MESSENGER   My lord, he doth deny° to come.   *refuse*
KING RICHARD   Off with young George's head!
75 NORFOLK   My lord, the enemy is past the marsh.
After the battle let George Stanley die.
KING RICHARD   A thousand hearts are great within my bosom.
Advance our standards! Set upon our foes!
Our ancient word° of courage, fair Saint George,   *battle cry*
80 Inspire us with the spleen° of fiery dragons.   *anger*
Upon them! Victory sits on our helms!°   *Exeunt*   *helmets*

5.7

Alarum. Excursions.° Enter [*Sir William*] CATESBY   *Military sallies*
CATESBY [*calling*][1]   Rescue, my lord of Norfolk! Rescue, rescue!
[*To a soldier*] The King enacts more wonders than a man,[2]
Daring an opposite° to every danger.   *to oppose himself*
His horse is slain, and all on foot he fights,
5 Seeking for Richmond in the throat of death.
[*Calling*] Rescue, fair lord, or else the day is lost!

---

4. Apparently from a misprint in Holinshed, which should have read "brother's" (that is, Richard's brother-in-law, Charles, Duke of Burgundy, who supported Richmond in exile). Possibly: to the detriment of England, the mother country.
5. *as . . . snow*: as one does who walks in snow that covers the tops of his shoes.

6. English vagabonds were whipped out of the parish by a local official.
7. And gave them a shameful record in history.
5.7
1. Some editors bring Norfolk onstage, although the stage directions do not call for him in either Q or F.
2. More wonders than seems possible for a man.

Alarums. Enter [KING] RICHARD

KING RICHARD   A horse! A horse! My kingdom for a horse!

CATESBY   Withdraw, my lord. I'll help you to a horse.

KING RICHARD   Slave, I have set my life upon a cast,³

10   And I will stand the hazard of the die.
I think there be six Richmonds⁴ in the field.
Five have I slain today, instead of him.
A horse! A horse! My kingdom for a horse!   [*Exeunt*]

5.8

Alarum. Enter [KING] RICHARD [*at one door*] *and*
[HENRY EARL OF] RICHMOND [*at another*]. *They fight.*
RICHARD *is slain.* [*Exit* RICHMOND.] *Retreat*¹ *and flour-
ish. Enter* [HENRY EARL OF] RICHMOND *and* [*Lord* STAN-
LEY *Earl of*] *Derby, with divers other lords* [*and soldiers*]

HENRY EARL OF RICHMOND   God and your arms be praised, victorious friends!
The day is ours. The bloody dog is dead.

STANLEY [*bearing the crown*]   Courageous Richmond, well hast
   thou acquit° thee.   *acquitted; conducted*
Lo, here this long usurpèd royalty²

5   From the dead temples of this bloody wretch
Have I plucked off, to grace thy brows withal.°   *with*
Wear it, enjoy it, and make much of it.
[*He sets the crown on Henry's head*]

KING HENRY VII   Great God of heaven, say 'Amen' to all.
But tell me—young George Stanley, is he living?

10   STANLEY   He is, my lord, and safe in Leicester town,
Whither, if it please you, we may now withdraw us.

KING HENRY VII   What men of name are slain on either side?

STANLEY [*reads*]   John Duke of Norfolk, Robert Brackenbury,
Walter Lord Ferrers, and Sir William Brandon.

15   KING HENRY VII   Inter their bodies as becomes their births.°   *befits their rank*
Proclaim a pardon to the soldiers fled
That in submission will return to us,
And then—as we have ta'en the sacrament³—
We will unite the white rose and the red.⁴

20   Smile, heaven, upon this fair conjunction,°   *union*
That long have frowned upon their enmity.
What traitor hears me and says not 'Amen'?
England hath long been mad, and scarred herself;
The brother blindly shed the brother's blood;

25   The father rashly slaughtered his own son;
The son, compelled, been butcher to the sire;
All that divided York and Lancaster,
United in their dire division.⁵
O now let Richmond and Elizabeth,

30   The true succeeders of each royal house,
By God's fair ordinance° conjoin together,   *decree*

3. A throw of the die (one of a pair of dice) in line 10.
4. In addition to Richmond, five other men dressed and armed to resemble him (a common safety measure).
5.8
1. A trumpet signal for (Richard's) men to retire.
2. Emblem of sovereignty; here, the crown.
3. Referring to the oath, taken by Richmond in the cathedral at Rheims, that he would marry Princess

Elizabeth as soon as he was crowned.
4. The badges of the Yorkist (white) and Lancastrian (red) factions. The marriage of Richmond (Lancastrian) and Princess Elizabeth (Yorkist) brought to an end the so-called Wars of the Roses, dramatized in the three *Henry VI* plays.
5. Joined by hatred, having nothing in common but mutual antagonism.

And let their heirs—God, if his will be so—
Enrich the time to come with smooth-faced peace,
With smiling plenty, and fair prosperous days.
35　Abate° the edge of traitors, gracious Lord,   *Blunt*
That would reduce° these bloody days again   *bring back*
And make poor England weep forth streams of blood.
Let them not live to taste this land's increase,°   *prosperity*
That would with treason wound this fair land's peace.
40　Now civil wounds are stopped; peace lives again.
That she may long live here, God say 'Amen'.

　　　　　　　　　　　　　　　　[Flourish.] Exeunt

Richard II

In the first scene of *Richard II,* two armed noblemen face each other before the royal throne. They hurl insults at one another, their deadly antagonism barely held in check by the formality of the occasion. This is an "appeal for treason," a kind of trial already archaic in Shakespeare's time, in which plaintiff and defendant present their cases in their own persons before the king, who instantly dispenses justice. The structure of the situation suggests what the men themselves insist upon: that one lies and one tells the truth, that one is a traitor and one a true subject. But even while we are implicitly asked to judge between rival claims, we have no way of knowing what has happened or whom to trust.

In the ensuing scenes, we learn that Bolingbroke and Mowbray are fighting about the murder of Thomas of Woodstock, the uncle of King Richard II. Apparently Boling-broke knows that Richard secretly ordered Woodstock's death. Since he cannot say so, he picks Richard's agent Mowbray as his target, for Woodstock had been in Mowbray's safekeeping. Meanwhile, Mowbray, likewise unable to blame the true culprit openly, is outraged at being called a traitor when it was his allegiance to Richard that led him to acquiesce in the killing.

This is a far more tangled situation than the simple yes-or-no structure of the appeal for treason or, several scenes later, the "trial by combat" could allow anyone to acknowl-edge. Moreover, the King's participation in the crime upon which he is supposed to be passing judgment obviously compromises his impartiality. The institution of the appeal for treason is premised on the assumptions that, as Richard himself states emphatically, the king has no part in his subjects' quarrels and that it is in his best interests to have the truth revealed. Here, neither assumption is correct. The ceremonies of royal authority so colorfully staged in the first few scenes turn out to be inconclusive, post-poning rather than confronting real sources of discord.

As the play continues, we come to realize that the confusion of the first few scenes, a confusion Shakespeare forces his audience momentarily to share, results from an intractable problem in a system of monarchical government. Since the king's subjects are obliged to obey him, it is not clear how, short of direct divine intervention, his fol-lies or vices may be checked. To admit that subjects have a right to judge or even to remove their king threatens the stability of the realm, since any subject, discontented for any reason, might incite a revolt. But to allow the king to have his own way no mat-ter what opens the way to tyranny.

The proper extent of a monarch's power was a crucial, and unresolved, political issue in sixteenth- and early seventeenth-century England, when first the Tudors and then the Stuarts struggled to extend their traditional prerogatives. A few decades after Shakespeare's death, disagreement about the nature of royal authority would provoke the English Civil War. In the 1590s, when Shakespeare was writing his history plays, the lines of stress upon which the country would eventually fracture were already apparent, even though the disasters to come would not have seemed inevitable.

When Shakespeare wrote about the medieval reign of Richard II, in other words, he saw the conflicts of that reign through the lens of the late sixteenth century. His meticulous re-creation of antiquated judicial processes did not conceal from audi-ences in his own time the contemporary relevance of the play. In all sixteenth-century texts and perhaps in performance, the lines in which Richard gives up his crown were omitted: many scholars theorize that this episode was considered too inflammatory to print or stage. When the Earl of Essex rebelled against Elizabeth I in 1601, some of his supporters cited Richard's reign as providing a historical precedent for the deposition of a monarch. They paid Shakespeare's company to perform a play about Richard's reign—almost certainly Shakespeare's play—in an attempt to rally supporters to their cause. "I am Richard II," snapped the furious Queen. "Know you not that?"

To acknowledge the contemporary relevance of Richard's reign is not to claim that Shakespeare wrote his play purely as a means of commenting obliquely on the policies of Elizabeth I. Rather, the urgent contemporary task of defining a nation-state led Shakespeare to an extended historical inquiry into the institution of the English monarchy, an inquiry of which *Richard II* is a part. By looking at points at which the normal order of royal succession is challenged, Shakespeare illuminates interesting inconsistencies in Renaissance theories of kingship and political authority. Several years earlier, he had written the three *Henry VI* plays and *Richard III,* which while not originally conceived as a series eventually constituted what critics call the "first tetralogy": a group of plays that together present a continuous chronicle of the long Wars of the Roses in the fifteenth century. Soon after finishing *Richard III,* Shakespeare began writing another group of history plays, the "second tetralogy," which backtrack in time to treat the origins of the conflicts he had already brought to the stage.

As he had for his earlier history plays, Shakespeare turned to Raphael Holinshed's *Chronicles of England, Scotland, and Ireland* (1587). There he found in the reign of Richard II a remote cause of the war to be waged many years hence. Richard II was grandson of Edward III, whose formidable precedent haunts all the plays of the second tetralogy. King Edward had five sons who survived to adulthood, but his eldest, Edward the Black Prince, predeceased him. The Black Prince left a son of his own, however, the future Richard II, to whom the throne descended after Edward III's death. At the time of his accession, Richard was ten years old, and during his adolescence his powerful uncles, the younger brothers of the Black Prince, administered his kingdom on his behalf. After Richard reached young adulthood and began to rule in his own name, he found it difficult to gain the respect of his uncles, experienced middle-aged men who had become accustomed to command. His own rashness and ineffectuality only compounded his troubles. Shakespeare's play opens upon the young Richard, already complicit in the murder of one of his uncles; the remaining uncles, who scorn Richard's maladroit rule but realize they owe allegiance to him; and Richard's cousins Bolingbroke and Northumberland, who are more willing than their elders to act on the recognition of the ruler's weakness.

Early in the play, Richard reacts to Bolingbroke's veiled challenge by exiling him; shortly thereafter, he confiscates Bolingbroke's estate. When, exasperated, Bolingbroke invades England and successfully seizes the crown from his cousin, his action neatly ruptures two traditional sources of royal authority. Unquestionably, Bolingbroke is the more astute tactician, the more effective leader. Richard, however, is equally undoubtedly the rightful heir of Edward III, and as such has been anointed king in a sacred coronation ceremony. Thus

Richardus ii. From John Rastell, *The Pastyme of People* (1529).

"Like perspectives, which, rightly gazed upon, / Show nothing but confusion; eyed awry, / Distinguish form" (*Richard II* 2.2.18–20). The most famous Renaissance example of such a "perspective" or anamorphic picture is Hans Holbein's *The Ambassadors* (1533); when the painting is viewed from the side ("awry"), the elongated object in the foreground reveals itself to be a skull.

one character has all the advantages when considered from a material and practical point of view, while the other derives his claim to authority from the more abstract principle of divinely sanctioned hereditary right.

Shakespeare imagines the division between the two men not merely as a political issue but as a question of character. A vivid sense of Bolingbroke's personality emerges in his confrontation with Mowbray. Mowbray harps on Bolingbroke's lies, laments the damage Bolingbroke's accusation has done to his reputation, and experiences Bolingbroke's verbal accusation as a physical attack: he is "pierced to the soul with slander's venomed spear" (1.1.171). Bolingbroke, by contrast, trusts not words but physical strength: "What my tongue speaks my right-drawn sword may prove," he stoutly declares (1.1.46). Tellingly, his word "right" conflates his proficiency as a warrior with the uprightness of his cause, suggesting that he does not care to recognize the potential difference. Likewise, Bolingbroke repeatedly speaks of making his words *good*, by which he means backing them up by force. As a corollary, he is suspicious or dismissive of anything that seems merely imaginary, verbal, or abstract. When his father, Gaunt, encourages him to reconcile himself to his exile by renaming it an educational tour or a pleasure junket, Bolingbroke replies:

> O, who can hold a fire in his hand
> By thinking on the frosty Caucasus,
> Or cloy the hungry edge of appetite
> By bare imagination of a feast . . . ?
> (1.3.257–60)

As the play proceeds, this insistence on material facts rather than words or imagination comes to seem entirely characteristic of a man who has no legal claim on the throne, but who takes it because he is able to do so.

Unlike Bolingbroke, Richard is an inept manager of practical affairs. In the first act, most of his powerful kinfolk let him literally get away with murder; but in the second act, it becomes clear that they will not tolerate his infringement of property rights. Medieval kings were expected to cover most of the expenses of government from their own large estates, but to raise additional funds Richard "farms out" the realm—that is, grants the power to tax to private individuals who can confiscate subjects' property virtually as they please, provided the king gets a share of the spoils. Not surprisingly, such legalized theft produces widespread resentment. For the upper aristocracy, the last straw is Richard's seizure of the duchy of Lancaster upon John of Gaunt's death: the encroachment seems to them worse than homicide, because it directly threatens the social structure upon which their status depends. Inherited property distinguishes noblemen from "men of no name": in fact, noble names are derived from property, the lands of Lancaster, Gloucester, York, Northumberland, and so forth. In *Richard II*, both social disruptions and identity crises are marked by a struggle over such titles and the power they signify. Bolingbroke, returning to England, insists on being called "Lancaster," not "Hereford"; Northumberland presumptuously forgets to call Richard "King"; Richard himself laments, upon his deposition, that "I must nothing be . . . I have no name, no title" (4.1.191, 245).

Although technically aristocrats did not own their land outright but held it in trust from the sovereign, by Richard's time Magna Carta protected the right of property holders to pass their lands to their heirs. Only a conviction for treason could forfeit the family claim. Ironically, at the moment Richard commandeers the Lancastrian estates, Bolingbroke is apparently on the verge of invading England with an armed force, so he is actually a traitor and Richard could eventually have appropriated his property in a perfectly legal manner. But Richard's characteristic neglect of proper procedure makes Bolingbroke's return seem a response to dispossession and thus turns the nobility toward the rebel cause.

Richard does not imagine that he must earn the respect of the people he governs, or balance his budget, or follow laws. He does not believe that his authority depends on the consent of the governed or on the effective manipulation of material resources. Whereas Bolingbroke thinks of power as emanating from "below"—from the King's subjects, from the deployment of material resources—Richard thinks of it as descending from "above," from the God whose representative on earth he was born to be. His assertion in 3.2.50–53 is entirely characteristic:

> Not all the water in the rough rude sea
> Can wash the balm from an anointed king.
> The breath of worldly men cannot depose
> The deputy elected by the Lord.

Later in the same scene, deserted by all but a few supporters, he exclaims: "Is not the King's name forty thousand names? / Arm, arm, my name!" (3.2.81–82). What Richard needs now, of course, is not names but soldiers, but he deliberately refuses to acknowledge the difference.

Richard's drastic impracticalities derive from his conviction that the God who put him on the throne is immanent in the created universe and vigilant in defense of His deputy. Richard is not unique in this conviction: the assumption that God intervenes continuously in human affairs in order to guarantee just outcomes underlies the ritual of the trial by combat as it is staged in 1.3. The way spirit informs and controls the material world can render "dead matter" sympathetic to human beings. "This earth shall have a feeling," Richard claims (3.2.24). Thus he is confident that the earth will put toads in the way of traitors, and that angels will rush to save a king in trouble.

Medieval histories are full of such narratives: the ground opens up and swallows an atheist; lightning strikes a perjurer dead.

By Shakespeare's time, the trial by combat had been discredited and the conception of the world to which Richard adheres was beginning to seem obsolete. Some thinkers were increasingly discarding anthropocentric ways of thinking and conceiving of the material world as something alien to human consciousness, ruled by purely physical laws of cause and effect. This change in mentality affected historians, who were subjecting long-accepted myths to critical scrutiny; scientists, who began to place a new value on empirical experimentation; and theologians, who were becoming more skeptical of the continuation of miracles in postbiblical times. Political theorists such as Machiavelli pragmatically insisted on describing political power as it really was exercised, and not as God or moral scruples might dictate that it ought to be exercised. The pragmatic Bolingbroke, then, is associated with a new, effective, but not necessarily moral or satisfying way of thinking about the manipulation of men and matter.

Richard's assumptions about the world and his place in it turn out to be wrong. His naïveté about the relationship of language and power, spirit and matter, leaves him vulnerable to Bolingbroke's assault. Bolingbroke's supplanting of Richard, then, might be seen not merely as a personal or even a political victory, but as the uprooting of one worldview by another. Whether this displacement represents an advance or a deterioration is, however, another question. The second part of the play, in which Bolingbroke emerges victorious, reexamines the nature of the conflict between the two men and the principles they represent.

In a pivotal scene in Act 3, Bolingbroke, Northumberland, and York approach the castle in which Richard has sequestered himself. When Richard finally emerges on the battlements, Bolingbroke exclaims:

> See, see, King Richard doth himself appear,
> As doth the blushing discontented sun
> From out the fiery portal of the east
> When he perceives the envious clouds are bent
> To dim his glory and to stain the track
> Of his bright passage to the occident.
> (3.3.61–66)

Bolingbroke is untypically eloquent here, but interestingly, his extended simile works against his own interests. The comparison between king and sun, a traditional figure of speech, implies that the king is both unique and indispensable. Rebels are not rival suns; they are transient clouds that the mighty king will eventually burn away. Even while he mutinies against Richard's misgovernment, Bolingbroke seems unable to escape a conservative conception of monarchy in which rebellion is a form of envy doomed to failure.

Bolingbroke's linguistic slip suggests that it may be easier to amass an army and seize the throne than to put aside one's inherited convictions about the nature of royal authority. Bolingbroke does not have an alternative vocabulary in which to justify his own behavior. Thus, throughout the play, it is hard to be sure whether he is cunningly concealing his true motives or simply incapable of articulating them even to himself. In the opening scenes, although Richard recognizes Bolingbroke's challenge to his authority, Bolingbroke himself seems a bit obtuse about his own purposes, as if his accusation of Mowbray were merely an effect of his sturdy loyalty to Richard. Likewise, it is unclear whether he initially realizes that his return from exile commits him not merely to regaining the Lancastrian estates but to a more thorough attack on Richard's sovereignty. Bolingbroke never appears before us, alone or in company, to ponder his own conduct and motives. In this regard, he differs not only from the obsessively self-reflective Richard but from other Shakespearean usurpers: Richard III, Macbeth, *Hamlet*'s Claudius.

In Act 4, however unable he may be to justify the grounds of his own authority, Bolingbroke—now King Henry IV—astutely recognizes that he must convince his subjects that he is legitimately entitled to the crown. Henry needs, somehow, to transfer to himself that mysterious sense of royal sanctity in which Richard initially places so much confidence and to which Henry has no plausible claim. Henry and his followers thus attempt to paper over his gross procedural breach with procedural punctiliousness. Richard cannot be summarily imprisoned or executed; rather, he must seem voluntarily and publicly to resign his sovereignty to Henry.

Unfortunately for Henry, he is not good at managing such rituals, while Richard is in his element. In 4.1, Richard masterfully seizes the symbolic initiative from the apparent victors. "Now mark me how I will undo myself," he announces (line 193).

> I give this heavy weight from off my head,
> And this unwieldy sceptre from my hand,
> The pride of kingly sway from out my heart.
> With mine own tears I wash away my balm,
> With mine own hands I give away my crown,
> With mine own tongue deny my sacred state,
> With mine own breath release all duteous oaths.
> All pomp and majesty I do forswear.
> My manors, rents, revenues I forgo.
> My acts, decrees, and statutes I deny.
> (lines 194–203)

Richard's actions and words here are meant to recall a coronation ceremony, in which the king is invested with the crown and scepter as his insignia of office, anointed with balm as a sign that he is God's chosen, promised the allegiance of his subjects, given formal title to the royal domains. One of the main points of this ceremony is its permanence: it cannot be undone. By referring to this ritual at the moment of his deposition, Richard implies that giving up the crown is an impossible act, a kind of absurdity. Moreover, reversing the ceremonies—taking off the crown rather than putting it on, relinquishing rather than accepting the scepter—suggests a special scandal. In medieval and early modern Europe, as among some fundamentalist religious groups today, reversing beneficent ceremonies supposedly evoked their diabolical opposites. One called up devils by reciting Scripture passages backward, or bound oneself to Satan by performing an inversion of baptismal rites. Richard's enthusiastic self-dramatization of his plight does not quell doubts about the legitimacy of the usurpation, but encourages those doubts. Immediately after Richard departs, his friends begin to conspire on his behalf; and although their plot is eventually crushed, Henry's reign will never be quiet thereafter.

As the play proceeds, the view of politics associated with Bolingbroke, a view that initially seems hardheaded and realistic, begins to seem not very practical after all. An acceptable social order requires more than the brute force Henry deploys so expertly. It requires a common set of ideas and practices, a common language and attitude, a set of rituals—all the immaterial abstractions Henry had originally been inclined to disregard.

Just as Shakespeare, over the course of the play, alters our view of the political dilemma represented by the rebellion, so he manipulates our outlook on its main characters. As soon as Richard has lost his throne, we need no longer evaluate him in terms of his effectiveness as a ruler. Immediately his talents seem more obvious, his faults less reprehensible. Richard's extraordinary poetic and introspective gifts allow him to analyze his own situation with a delicacy and insight of which Bolingbroke is entirely incapable. He is acutely aware of the figure he cuts to the only audience that matters to him, himself; in fact, his self-destructive behavior might be seen as an unconscious quest for the expressive opportunities provided only by misery. Always preoccupied with analogies between kingship and godhead, Richard identifies more and more, as the play

Death of Phaeton. From Antonio Tempesta, *Ovid's "Metamorphoses"* (1606).

continues, with the suffering Christ, consoling himself with the comparison and deriving from it a certain sad grandeur. Obviously Richard's particular strengths are intrinsically connected to his weaknesses, but that does not mean that those strengths are negligible. They are especially hard to ignore in a *play*, in which poetic language, symbolic thought, and the effective deployment of spectacle are central concerns.

Our shifting view of Richard has produced, in both Shakespeare's time and our own, a certain ambiguity as to the play's genre. When Shakespeare's friends and fellow actors compiled his works in the First Folio, they grouped *Richard II* with the history plays—understandably, since it concerns itself with problems of rule and the legitimacy of rulers, is based on historical materials, and inaugurates a series of plays that deals with the reigns of three successive kings. Yet in its earliest printed version the play was called "The Tragedie of Richard II," a title that suggests a focus not on the fate of a nation but on the disastrous career of a fascinating, flawed individual.

Richard's case encourages us to reflect on the way the politics and the values of political life—the dominant concerns of history plays—constrain our evaluation of him. In *Richard II*, Shakespeare uses female characters to suggest the possibility of an alternative perspective on the events he depicts. In the second scene, the Duchess of Gloucester urges Gaunt to revenge Thomas of Woodstock, her husband and his brother. Gaunt refuses: in his view, the subject's duty to his monarch must outweigh his obligation to his kin. Their conversation reminds us that England's political crisis is also a familial disaster, and that construing it as one rather than the other has important consequences.

Throughout the play, the men, like Gaunt, tend to subordinate domestic concerns to civic ones, family bonds to the all-important relationship between king and subject. The women, like the Duchess of Gloucester, do the opposite. Although the historical Richard was married to a ten-year-old queen, Shakespeare makes Isabella a mature young woman and invents touching, wholly nonfactual scenes in which she intuitively senses her husband's trouble, then discovers the usurpation in a garden and suffers through an imposed parting from her husband. The pathos of these scenes derives from the Queen's utter helplessness. She is imagined as Richard's wife, a domestic function, not England's Queen, a public one. All her responses are thus founded on her singleminded loyalty to the marital tie, as sharply distinguished from the bonds of politics. "Banish us both, and send the King with me," she begs Northumberland, when he informs them that she will be exiled and her husband kept under house arrest in England. "That were some love, but little policy," Northumberland replies (5.1.83, 84). The last thing Bolingbroke needs is a legitimate child of Richard's to confuse his claims on the throne even more. But the Queen fails to grasp Northumberland's meaning, because she does not understand "policy"—that is, politics. It is not her sphere.

The difference between civic and domestic domains also appears in the scenes immediately following, which stage a dispute between the Duke and Duchess of York over their son, Aumerle. Here again Shakespeare altered his sources, unhistorically making Aumerle an only child and the Duchess his natural mother. Having discovered that Aumerle is involved in a plot to kill the new Henry IV and reinstate Richard, York feels bound to inform Henry of the treason. He puts what he sees as his civic duty above the ties of blood. The Duchess is outraged. "Wilt thou not hide the trespass of thine own?" she asks. "Have we more sons? Or are we like to have?" (5.2.89–90). For her, the familial relationship takes precedence over the public one.

This dividing of the "public" male role from the "private" female role is hardly a Shakespearean invention. But Shakespeare puts that division of perspective to thematic use in *Richard II*. In 2.2, when Isabella has a presentiment of ruin, Bushy tries to console her in an elaborate speech about perspective glasses and "anamorphic" paintings. These two Renaissance inventions encourage speculation about the difference between the "right" or "centered" way of seeing and an oblique outlook from which shapes look very different. Of course, Isabella's inexplicable presentiment of disaster turns out to be more apt than her male companions' optimism. Perhaps the women's different perspective implies that the history play's focus on traditionally masculine political concerns may exclude whole realms of human experience.

In the fifth act, Richard—weeping, enclosed, suffering, and excluded from authority—finds himself in the position the play has defined as a feminine one. Politically marginalized, he nonetheless dominates the closing moments of the play, first by his powerful soliloquizing and later by his courageous defiance of his murderers. In some respects, the final scenes of *Richard II* recall its opening. What seems to be a simple opposition turns out to be far more complex, as categories of expedience and impracticality, power and weakness, right and wrong mutate and change places. Once again, the apparent conclusion of a conflict merely postpones its resolution. The *Henry IV* plays will stage the aftermath.

KATHARINE EISAMAN MAUS

TEXTUAL NOTE

The first printed version of *Richard II* was a Quarto published in 1597 (Q1). The quality of the text is good, and most scholars have assumed that it was printed either directly from Shakespeare's manuscript or (because the stage directions are very brief) from a transcript of Shakespeare's manuscript not designed to provide the basis for theatrical performance. Two more Quartos, printed in 1598 (Q2 and Q3), mention Shakespeare as the author of the play on their title pages. In 1608, a fourth Quarto appeared (Q4), and in 1615, a fifth (Q5); each Quarto seems based on the one that had appeared before it. However, Q4 was the first to print the "new additions of the parliament scene, and the deposing of King Richard," scenes not present in the earlier Quartos.

The First Folio of 1623 (F) text was probably printed with reference to a promptbook, because it has much more detailed stage directions than the quarto texts. Editors disagree, however, over whether this promptbook text was based on Shakespeare's manuscript or on a corrected copy of Q1 or Q3. F includes a version of the abdication scene that is different, and better, than the one in Q4 and Q5. F omits some lines that are present in Q1, and there are also a number of single-word divergences between the two texts. In cases where only a single line is missing, the deletion may represent a compositor's error, so the Oxford editors have followed Q1. In cases where more substantial passages have been excluded, the editors assume that Shakespeare himself was responsible; these passages are indented in the text.

The most important difference between Q1 and F is F's inclusion of the deposition scene. Some scholars have argued that Elizabeth's censors considered the passage too provocative to stage and insisted that it be deleted; after Elizabeth's death, it was possible to reinstate the offending material. Others argue that Shakespeare revised the play during the first decade of the seventeenth century and wrote the deposition scene at that time.

The Oxford editors have generally based their text on Q1, except for the deposition scene, where they have followed F. They have, however, assimilated many of F's more complete stage directions and many of its single-word variants from Q1, when in the editors' opinion those variants represent Shakespeare's revisions to his own text rather than compositorial corruptions.

SELECTED BIBLIOGRAPHY

Calderwood, James L. "*Richard II* and the Fall of Speech." *Shakespearean Metadrama: The Argument of the Play in "Titus Andronicus," "Love's Labour's Lost," "Romeo and Juliet," and "Richard II."* Minneapolis: University of Minnesota Press, 1971. 149–86. The transfer of power from Richard to Bolingbroke as a version of Shakespeare's move from lyric stylization to a sparer dramatic language.

Doran, Madeline. "Imagery in *Richard II* and *Henry IV*." *Modern Language Review* 37 (1942): 113–22. Changes in handling metaphor and simile as key to the differences between *Richard II* and *Henry IV, Part 1*.

Gaudet, Paul. "The 'Parasitical Counselors' in Shakespeare's *Richard II*: A Problem in Dramatic Interpretation." *Shakespeare Quarterly* 33 (1982): 142–54. Bushy, Bagot, and Greene: innocent or guilty?

Hamilton, Donna. "The State of Law in *Richard II*." *Shakespeare Quarterly* 34 (1983): 5–17. The relation between monarchy and law in *Richard II* and in early modern political theory.

Kantorowicz, Ernst H. Chapter 2. *The King's Two Bodies: A Study in Mediaeval Political Theology*. Princeton: Princeton University Press, 1957. 24–41. Theory of kingship in *Richard II*.

Kastan, David. "Proud Majesty Made a Subject: Shakespeare and the Spectacle of Rule." *Shakespeare Quarterly* 37 (1986): 459–75. Theatrical representation destabilizes kingship in *Richard II*.

McMillin, Scott. "*Richard II*: Eyes of Sorrow, Eyes of Desire." *Shakespeare Quarterly* 35 (1984): 40–52. An impulse to self-expressiveness is at odds with the exercise of political power in *Richard II*.

Moore, Jeanie Grant. "Queen of Sorrow, King of Grief: Reflections and Perspectives in *Richard II*." *In Another Country: Feminist Perspectives on Renaissance Drama*. Ed. Dorothea Kehler and Susan Baker. Metuchen, N.J.: Scarecrow Press, 1991. 19–35. Special attention to imagery of mirrors and anamorphic pictures.

Saccio, Peter. *Shakespeare's English Kings: History, Chronicle, and Drama.* 2nd ed. New York: Oxford University Press, 2000. 17–35. Succinct account of the historical background to Shakespeare's play.
Tillyard, E. M. W. *Shakespeare's History Plays.* London: Chatto & Windus, 1944. 244–63. *Richard II* shows the transition from the medieval to the modern world.
Zitner, Sheldon. "Aumerle's Conspiracy." *Studies in English Literature* 14 (1974): 238–57. The importance of the Aumerle scenes for the end of *Richard II.*

FILM

King Richard the Second. 1978. Dir. David Giles, UK. 158 mins. In this BBC-TV production, Derek Jacobi as an effeminate Richard II confronts Jon Finch as the calculating Bolingbroke. John Gielgud is a notable John of Gaunt.

The Tragedy of King Richard the Second

THE PERSONS OF THE PLAY

KING RICHARD II
The QUEEN, his wife
JOHN OF GAUNT, Duke of Lancaster, Richard's uncle
Harry BOLINGBROKE, Duke of Hereford, John of Gaunt's son,
    later KING HENRY IV
DUCHESS OF GLOUCESTER, widow of Gaunt's and York's brother
Duke of YORK, King Richard's uncle
DUCHESS OF YORK
Duke of AUMERLE, their son
Thomas MOWBRAY, Duke of Norfolk
GREEN ⎫
BAGOT ⎬ followers of King Richard
BUSHY ⎭
Percy, Earl of NORTHUMBERLAND ⎫
HARRY PERCY, his son ⎪
Lord ROSS ⎬ of Bolingbroke's party
Lord WILLOUGHBY ⎭
Earl of SALISBURY ⎫
BISHOP OF CARLISLE ⎬ of King Richard's party
Sir Stephen SCROPE ⎭
Lord BERKELEY
Lord FITZWALTER
Duke of SURREY
ABBOT OF WESTMINSTER
Sir Piers EXTON
LORD MARSHAL
HERALDS
CAPTAIN of the Welsh army
LADIES attending the Queen
GARDENER
Gardener's MEN
Exton's MEN
KEEPER of the prison at Pomfret
GROOM of King Richard's stable
Lords, soldiers, attendants

1.1

Enter KING RICHARD, JOHN OF GAUNT, *with* [*the* LORD
    MARSHAL], *other nobles, and attendants*

KING RICHARD   Old John of Gaunt,[1] time-honoured Lancaster,
    Hast thou according to thy oath and bond
    Brought hither Henry Hereford, thy bold son,
    Here to make good the boist'rous late appeal,°   *violent recent accusation*

1.1. Location: Windsor Castle.
1. Named after his birthplace, Ghent (in Flanders); his
title was Duke of Lancaster. He was fifty-eight years
old.

5   Which then our leisure² would not let us hear,
        Against the Duke of Norfolk, Thomas Mowbray?
      JOHN OF GAUNT I have, my liege.
      KING RICHARD Tell me moreover, hast thou sounded° him   *inquired of*
        If he appeal the Duke on ancient malice³
10   Or worthily, as a good subject should,
        On some known ground of treachery in him?
      JOHN OF GAUNT As near as I could sift° him on that argument,° *discover from / topic*
        On some apparent° danger seen in him   *manifest*
        Aimed at your highness, no inveterate malice.
      KING RICHARD Then call them to our presence.
                            [Exit one or more]
15   Face to face
        And frowning brow to brow, ourselves will hear
        The accuser and the accusèd freely speak.
        High-stomached° are they both and full of ire;   *Haughty*
        In rage, deaf as the sea, hasty as fire.
        Enter BOLINGBROKE *[Duke of Hereford], and* MOWBRAY
        [Duke of Norfolk]
20   BOLINGBROKE Many years of happy days befall
        My gracious sovereign, my most loving liege!
      MOWBRAY Each day still better others' happiness,⁴
        Until the heavens, envying earth's good hap,°   *fortune*
        Add an immortal title to your crown!
25   KING RICHARD We thank you both. Yet one but flatters us,
        As well appeareth by the cause you come,
        Namely, to appeal each other of high treason.
        Cousin of Hereford, what dost thou object°   *charge*
        Against the Duke of Norfolk, Thomas Mowbray?
30   BOLINGBROKE First—heaven be the record to my speech—
        In the devotion of a subject's love,
        Tend'ring° the precious safety of my Prince,   *Having care for*
        And free from other misbegotten hate,
        Come I appellant° to this princely presence.   *as accuser*
35   Now, Thomas Mowbray, do I turn to thee;
        And mark my greeting° well, for what I speak   *address*
        My body shall make good upon this earth,
        Or my divine° soul answer it in heaven.   *Immortal*
        Thou art a traitor and a miscreant,
40   Too good° to be so, and too bad to live,   *wellborn*
        Since the more fair and crystal is the sky,
        The uglier seem the clouds that in it fly.
        Once more, the more to aggravate the note,°   *emphasize the reproach*
        With a foul traitor's name stuff I thy throat,
45   And wish, so please my sovereign, ere I move
        What my tongue speaks my right-drawn sword may prove.
      MOWBRAY Let not my cold words here accuse my zeal.° *cast doubt on my loyalty*
        'Tis not the trial of a woman's war,
        The bitter clamour of two eager° tongues,   *sharp*
50   Can arbitrate⁵ this cause betwixt us twain.
        The blood is hot that must be cooled for this.

---

2. That is, lack of leisure. Richard uses the royal "we."   4. May each day be better than the last.
3. Out of long-standing enmity.   5. Judge (without implying compromise).

Yet can I not of such tame patience boast
As to be hushed and naught at all to say.
First, the fair reverence of your highness curbs me
55 From giving reins and spurs to my free speech,
Which else would post° until it had returned   *ride fast*
These terms of treason doubled down his throat.
Setting aside his high blood's royalty,[6]
And let him be° no kinsman to my liege,   *And as if he were*
60 I do defy him, and I spit at him,
Call him a slanderous coward and a villain;
Which to maintain I would allow him odds,
And meet him, were I tied° to run afoot   *obliged*
Even to the frozen ridges of the Alps,
65 Or any other ground inhabitable,
Wherever Englishman durst set his foot.
Meantime let this defend my loyalty:
By all my hopes, most falsely doth he lie.
BOLINGBROKE [*throwing down his gage*][7] Pale trembling coward,
      there I throw my gage,
70 Disclaiming here the kindred of[8] the King,
And lay aside my high blood's royalty,
Which fear, not reverence, makes thee to except.°   *set aside*
If guilty dread have left thee so much strength
As to take up mine honour's pawn,° then stoop.   *(the gage)*
75 By that, and all the rites of knighthood else,
Will I make good against thee, arm to arm,
What I have spoke or thou canst worse devise.
MOWBRAY [*taking up the gage*] I take it up,[9] and by that sword I swear
Which gently laid my knighthood on my shoulder,
80 I'll answer thee in any fair degree°   *honorable manner*
Or chivalrous design of knightly trial;
And when I mount, alive may I not light°   *dismount*
If I be traitor or unjustly fight!
KING RICHARD [*to* BOLINGBROKE] What doth our cousin lay to
      Mowbray's charge?
85 It must be great that can inherit us°   *make us have*
So much as of a thought of ill in him.
BOLINGBROKE   Look what I speak, my life shall prove it true:
That Mowbray hath received eight thousand nobles°   *gold coins*
In name of lendings° for your highness' soldiers,   *As advances on pay*
90 The which he hath detained for lewd employments,°   *improper uses*
Like a false traitor and injurious villain.
Besides I say, and will in battle prove,
Or° here or elsewhere, to the furthest verge°   *Either / horizon*
That ever was surveyed by English eye,
95 That all the treasons for these eighteen years[1]
Complotted° and contrivèd in this land   *Plotted*
Fetch° from false Mowbray their first head° and spring.   *Derive / source*
Further I say, and further will maintain
Upon his bad life, to make all this good,

6. Bolingbroke as well as Richard was a grandson of   8. The privilege of kinship with.
Edward III.   9. Thereby accepting the challenge.
7. Pledge to combat—probably a glove.   1. Since the Peasants' Revolt of 1381.

100 That he did plot the Duke of Gloucester's death,[2]
     Suggest° his soon-believing° adversaries,   *Incite / credulous*
     And consequently,° like a traitor-coward,   *subsequently*
     Sluiced° out his innocent soul through streams of blood;   *Let flow*
     Which blood, like sacrificing Abel's,[3] cries
105 Even from the tongueless caverns of the earth
     To me for justice and rough chastisement.
     And, by the glorious worth of my descent,
     This arm shall do it or this life be spent.
     KING RICHARD   How high a pitch[4] his resolution soars!
110 Thomas of Norfolk, what sayst thou to this?
     MOWBRAY   O, let my sovereign turn away his face,
     And bid his ears a little while be deaf,
     Till I have told this slander of his blood°   *disgrace to his ancestry*
     How God and good men hate so foul a liar!
115 KING RICHARD   Mowbray, impartial are our eyes and ears.
     Were he my brother, nay, my kingdom's heir,
     As he is but my father's brother's son,
     Now by my sceptre's awe I make a vow
     Such neighbour-nearness to our sacred blood
120 Should nothing privilege him, nor partialize°   *bias*
     The unstooping firmness of my upright soul.
     He is our subject, Mowbray; so art thou.
     Free speech and fearless I to thee allow.
     MOWBRAY   Then, Bolingbroke, as low as to thy heart
125 Through the false passage of thy throat thou liest!
     Three parts of that receipt° I had for Calais   *money received*
     Disbursed I duly to his highness' soldiers.
     The other part reserved I by consent,
     For that my sovereign liege was in my debt
130 Upon remainder of a dear account[5]
     Since last I went to France to fetch his queen.
     Now swallow down that lie. For Gloucester's death,
     I slew him not, but to my own disgrace
     Neglected my sworn duty in that case.[6]
135 For you, my noble lord of Lancaster,
     The honourable father to my foe,
     Once did I lay an ambush for your life,
     A trespass that doth vex my grievèd soul;
     But ere I last received the Sacrament
140 I did confess it, and exactly° begged   *expressly*
     Your grace's pardon, and I hope I had it.
     This is my fault. As for the rest appealed,°   *accused*
     It issues from the rancour of a villain,
     A recreant° and most degenerate° traitor,   *faithless / cowardly*
145 Which in myself° I boldly will defend,   *my own person*
     [*He throws down his gage*]
     And interchangeably° hurl down my gage   *reciprocally*

---

2. Thomas of Woodstock, Duke of Gloucester, was
mysteriously murdered while in the custody of Mow-
bray. Richard had reason to hate him; earlier Wood-
stock had attempted to curtail the young King's power
by placing authority in the hands of a royal council, of
which Woodstock was the head.
3. In Genesis 4, Cain murders his brother Abel

because God prefers Abel's offering of sheep to Cain's
fruits of the ground.
4. Highest point of a falcon's flight.
5. For the balance of a large sum.
6. Mowbray is circumspect here; in the next scene,
Gaunt and the Duchess assert less ambiguously that
Richard ordered him to kill Woodstock.

Upon this overweening traitor's foot,
To prove myself a loyal gentleman
Even in the best blood chambered° in his bosom;   *enclosed*
150   In haste whereof° most heartily I pray   *To hasten which*
Your highness to assign our trial day.
      [BOLINGBROKE *takes up the gage*]
KING RICHARD   Wrath-kindled gentlemen, be ruled by me.
Let's purge this choler without letting blood.[7]
This we prescribe, though no physician:
155   Deep malice[8] makes too deep incision;
Forget, forgive, conclude,° and be agreed;   *come to terms*
Our doctors say this is no time to bleed.
Good uncle, let this end where it begun.
We'll calm the Duke of Norfolk, you your son.
160   JOHN OF GAUNT   To be a make-peace shall become my age.
Throw down, my son, the Duke of Norfolk's gage.[9]
KING RICHARD   And, Norfolk, throw down his.
JOHN OF GAUNT   When, Harry, when?
Obedience bids I should not bid again.
KING RICHARD   Norfolk, throw down! We bid; there is no boot.°   *help for it*
165   MOWBRAY [*kneeling*]   Myself I throw, dread sovereign, at thy foot.
My life thou shalt command, but not my shame.
The one my duty owes, but my fair name,
Despite of death that lives upon my grave,
To dark dishonour's use thou shalt not have.
170   I am disgraced, impeached, and baffled[1] here,
Pierced to the soul with slander's venomed spear,
The which no balm can cure but his heart blood
Which breathed° this poison.   *uttered*
KING RICHARD   Rage must be withstood.
Give me his gage. Lions make leopards tame.[2]
175   MOWBRAY [*standing*]   Yea, but not change his spots.[3] Take but my shame,
And I resign my gage. My dear dear lord,
The purest treasure mortal times° afford   *earthly lives*
Is spotless reputation; that away,
Men are but gilded loam, or painted clay.
180   A jewel in a ten-times barred-up chest
Is a bold spirit in a loyal breast.
Mine honour is my life. Both grow in one.°   *united*
Take honour from me, and my life is done.
Then, dear my liege, mine honour let me try.°   *put to the test*
185   In that I live, and for that will I die.
KING RICHARD   Cousin, throw down your gage. Do you begin.
BOLINGBROKE   O God defend my soul from such deep sin!
Shall I seem crest-fallen in my father's sight?
Or with pale beggar-fear impeach my height°   *disgrace my rank*
190   Before this out-dared dastard?° Ere my tongue   *coward*
Shall wound my honour with such feeble wrong,
Or sound so base a parle,° my teeth shall tear   *trumpet call for a truce*
The slavish motive° of recanting fear,   *instrument (the tongue)*

7. Let's expel the bile (thought to be the physiological
cause of anger) without bloodletting (in combat; as a
medical remedy).
8. Enmity; virulence (of a disease).
9. As a gesture of reconciliation.

1. Publicly stripped of knighthood (a chivalric term).
2. Lions were the King's emblem; leopards were Mow-
bray's. Heraldic banners are likely to be displayed
onstage in this scene.
3. Leopard spots; stains of reproach.

And spit it bleeding in his° high disgrace   *its*
195   Where shame doth harbour, even in Mowbray's face.

Exit [JOHN OF] GAUNT

KING RICHARD   We were not born to sue, but to command;
       Which since we cannot do to make you friends,
       Be ready, as your lives shall answer it,
       At Coventry upon Saint Lambert's day.°   *September 17*
200   There shall your swords and lances arbitrate
       The swelling difference of your settled hate.
       Since we cannot atone° you, we shall see   *reconcile*
       Justice design the victor's chivalry.⁴
       Lord Marshal, command our officers-at-arms
205   Be ready to direct these home alarms.°   *Exeunt*   *domestic disturbances*

1.2

Enter JOHN OF GAUNT [*Duke of Lancaster*], *with*
DUCHESS OF GLOUCESTER

JOHN OF GAUNT   Alas, the part I had in Gloucester's blood¹
       Doth more solicit me than your exclaims°   *exclamations*
       To stir against the butchers of his life.
       But since correction lieth in² those hands
5   Which made the fault that we cannot correct,
       Put we our quarrel to the will of heaven,
       Who, when they see the hours ripe on earth,
       Will rain hot vengeance on offenders' heads.
DUCHESS OF GLOUCESTER   Finds brotherhood in thee no sharper spur?
10   Hath love in thy old blood no living fire?
       Edward's° seven sons, whereof thyself art one,   *Edward III's*
       Were as seven vials of his sacred blood,
       Or seven fair branches springing from one root.
       Some of those seven are dried by nature's course,
15   Some of those branches by the destinies cut;
       But Thomas, my dear lord, my life, my Gloucester,
       One vial full of Edward's sacred blood,
       One flourishing branch of his most royal root,
       Is cracked, and all the precious liquor spilt;
20   Is hacked down, and his summer leaves all faded
       By envy's° hand and murder's bloody axe.   *hatred's*
       Ah, Gaunt, his blood was thine! That bed, that womb,
       That mettle,° that self° mould that fashioned thee,   *substance / same*
       Made him a man; and though thou liv'st and breathest,
25   Yet art thou slain in him. Thou dost consent
       In some large measure to thy father's death
       In that thou seest thy wretched brother die,
       Who was the model of thy father's life.
       Call it not patience, Gaunt, it is despair.
30   In suff'ring thus thy brother to be slaughtered
       Thou show'st the naked° pathway to thy life,   *defenseless; obvious*
       Teaching stern murder how to butcher thee.
       That which in mean° men we entitle patience   *common*
       Is pale cold cowardice in noble breasts.

---

4. Indicate the victor in knightly combat.   Gaunt's younger brother.
1.2 Location: John of Gaunt's house.   2. Since punishment depends on (Gaunt blames
1. Thomas of Woodstock, Duke of Gloucester, was   Richard for Woodstock's death).

35　What shall I say? To safeguard thine own life
　　The best way is to venge° my Gloucester's death.　　　　　　　　*avenge*
　JOHN OF GAUNT　God's is the quarrel; for God's substitute,
　　His deputy anointed in his sight,
　　Hath caused his death; the which if wrongfully,
40　Let heaven revenge, for I may never lift
　　An angry arm against his minister.°　　　　　　　　　　　　　*agent*
　DUCHESS OF GLOUCESTER　Where then, alas, may I complain myself?
　JOHN OF GAUNT　To God, the widow's champion and defence.
　DUCHESS OF GLOUCESTER　Why then, I will. Farewell, old Gaunt.
45　Thou goest to Coventry, there to behold
　　Our cousin° Hereford and fell° Mowbray fight.　　　　*Kinsman / ruthless*
　　O, set my husband's wrongs on Hereford's spear,
　　That it may enter butcher Mowbray's breast!
　　Or if misfortune miss the first career,³
50　Be Mowbray's sins so heavy in his bosom
　　That they may break his foaming courser's back
　　And throw the rider headlong in the lists,
　　A caitiff,° recreant° to my cousin Hereford!　　　　　*A wretch / yielding*
　　Farewell, old Gaunt. Thy sometimes° brother's wife　　　　　　*former*
55　With her companion, grief, must end her life.
　JOHN OF GAUNT　Sister, farewell. I must to Coventry.
　　As much good stay with thee as go with me.
　DUCHESS OF GLOUCESTER　Yet one word more. Grief boundeth⁴
　　　　where it falls,
　　Not with the empty hollowness, but weight.⁵
60　I take my leave before I have begun,
　　For sorrow ends not when it seemeth done.
　　Commend me to thy brother, Edmund York.
　　Lo, this is all.—Nay, yet depart not so!
　　Though this be all, do not so quickly go.
65　I shall remember more. Bid him—ah, what?—
　　With all good speed at Pleshey⁶ visit me.
　　Alack, and what shall good old York there see
　　But empty lodgings° and unfurnished walls,　　　　　　　　　*rooms*
　　Unpeopled offices,° untrodden stones,　　　　　　　　*servants' quarters*
70　And what hear there for welcome but my groans?
　　Therefore commend me; let him not come there
　　To seek out sorrow that dwells everywhere.
　　Desolate, desolate will I hence and die.
　　The last leave of thee takes my weeping eye. *Exeunt* [*severally*]°　*separately*

1.3

Enter LORD MARSHAL [*with officers setting out chairs*],
and Duke [*of*] AUMERLE

　LORD MARSHAL　My lord Aumerle, is Harry Hereford armed?
　AUMERLE　Yea, at all points,° and longs to enter in.　　　　　*completely*
　LORD MARSHAL　The Duke of Norfolk, sprightfully° and bold,　　*spiritedly*
　　Stays° but the summons of the appellant's° trumpet.　　*Awaits / accuser's*
5　AUMERLE　Why then, the champions are prepared, and stay
　　For nothing but his majesty's approach.

---

3. If (Mowbray's) downfall fail to occur at the first
encounter.
4. Rebounds (causing further sound; the Duchess
apologizes for continuing to speak).

5. Not because it is hollow, like a bouncing ball, but
because it is heavy.
6. Gloucester's house in Essex.
1.3 Location: The lists (tournament arena) at Coventry.

The trumpets sound, and KING [RICHARD] *enters with*
[JOHN OF] GAUNT, BUSHY, BAGOT, GREEN, *and other*
nobles. When they are set, enter MOWBRAY *Duke of Nor-*
folk, defendant, in arms, and a HERALD [*to Mowbray*]

KING RICHARD   Marshal, demand of yonder champion
    The cause of his arrival here in arms.
    Ask him his name, and orderly° proceed   *according to the rules*
10   To swear him in the justice of his cause.
LORD MARSHAL [*to* MOWBRAY]   In God's name and the King's,
    say who thou art,
    And why thou com'st thus knightly clad in arms,
    Against what man thou com'st, and what thy quarrel.
    Speak truly on thy knighthood and thy oath,
15   As so defend thee heaven and thy valour!
MOWBRAY   My name is Thomas Mowbray, Duke of Norfolk,
    Who hither come engagèd by my oath—
    Which God defend° a knight should violate—   *forbid*
    Both to defend my loyalty and truth
20   To God, my king, and my succeeding issue,
    Against the Duke of Hereford that appeals me;
    And by the grace of God and this mine arm
    To prove him, in defending of myself,
    A traitor to my God, my king, and me.
25   And as I truly fight, defend me heaven!
        [*He sits.*]
        The trumpets sound. Enter [BOLINGBROKE] *Duke of*
        Hereford, appellant, in armour, and HERALD
KING RICHARD   Marshal, ask yonder knight in arms
    Both who he is and why he cometh hither
    Thus plated in habiliments of war;[1]
    And formally, according to our law,
30   Depose° him in the justice of his cause.   *Take testimony from*
LORD MARSHAL [*to* BOLINGBROKE]   What is thy name? And
    wherefore com'st thou hither
    Before King Richard in his royal lists?
    Against whom comest thou? And what's thy quarrel?
    Speak like a true knight, so defend thee heaven!
35 BOLINGBROKE   Harry of Hereford, Lancaster, and Derby
    Am I, who ready here do stand in arms
    To prove by God's grace and my body's valour
    In lists on Thomas Mowbray, Duke of Norfolk,
    That he is a traitor foul and dangerous
40   To God of heaven, King Richard, and to me.
    And as I truly fight, defend me heaven!
        [*He sits*]
LORD MARSHAL   On pain of death, no person be so bold
    Or daring-hardy as to touch the lists
    Except the Marshal and such officers
45   Appointed to direct these fair designs.°   *procedures*
BOLINGBROKE [*standing*]   Lord Marshal, let me kiss my sovereign's hand
    And bow my knee before his majesty,
    For Mowbray and myself are like two men
    That vow a long and weary pilgrimage;

---

1. Wearing plated battle armor.

50   Then let us take a ceremonious leave
      And loving farewell of our several° friends.   *respective*
      LORD MARSHAL [*to* KING RICHARD]   The appellant in all duty
          greets your highness,
      And craves to kiss your hand and take his leave.
      KING RICHARD   We will descend and fold him in our arms.
          [*He descends from his seat and embraces* BOLINGBROKE]
55   Cousin of Hereford, as° thy cause is just,   *insofar as*
      So be thy fortune in this royal fight.
      Farewell, my blood, which if today thou shed,
      Lament we may, but not revenge thee dead.
      BOLINGBROKE   O, let no noble eye profane° a tear   *misuse*
60   For me if I be gored with Mowbray's spear.
      As confident as is the falcon's flight
      Against a bird do I with Mowbray fight.
      [*To the* LORD MARSHAL] My loving lord, I take my leave of you;
      [*To* AUMERLE] Of you, my noble cousin, Lord Aumerle;
65   Not sick, although I have to do with death,
      But lusty,° young, and cheerly drawing breath.   *vigorous*
      Lo, as at English feasts, so I regreet°   *greet*
      The daintiest[2] last, to make the end most sweet.
      [*To* GAUNT, *kneeling*] O thou, the earthly author of my blood,
70   Whose youthful spirit in me regenerate°   *reborn*
      Doth with a two-fold vigour lift me up
      To reach at victory above my head,
      Add proof° unto mine armour with thy prayers,   *invulnerability*
      And with thy blessings steel° my lance's point,   *harden*
75   That it may enter Mowbray's waxen° coat   *(that is, soft)*
      And furbish new the name of John a Gaunt
      Even in the lusty haviour° of his son.   *conduct*
      JOHN OF GAUNT   God in thy good cause make thee prosperous!
      Be swift like lightning in the execution,
80   And let thy blows, doubly redoublèd,
      Fall like amazing° thunder on the casque°   *stupefying / helmet*
      Of thy adverse pernicious enemy.
      Rouse up thy youthful blood, be valiant, and live.
      BOLINGBROKE [*standing*]   Mine innocence and Saint George
          to thrive!
85   MOWBRAY [*standing*]   However God or fortune cast my lot,
      There lives or dies, true to King Richard's throne,
      A loyal, just, and upright gentleman.
      Never did captive with a freer heart
      Cast off his chains of bondage and embrace
90   His golden uncontrolled enfranchisement°   *unrestrained liberation*
      More than my dancing soul doth celebrate
      This feast of battle with mine adversary.
      Most mighty liege, and my companion peers,
      Take from my mouth the wish of happy years.
95   As gentle and as jocund as to jest°   *take part in revels*
      Go I to fight. Truth hath a quiet breast.
      KING RICHARD   Farewell, my lord. Securely° I espy   *Confidently*
      Virtue with valour couchèd[3] in thine eye.—
      Order the trial, Marshal, and begin.

---

2. Finest thing, like a dessert.   3. Lodged; aimed in readiness (like a lance).

100 LORD MARSHAL   Harry of Hereford, Lancaster, and Derby,
    Receive thy lance; and God defend the right!
       [*An officer bears a lance to* BOLINGBROKE]
    BOLINGBROKE   Strong as a tower in hope, I cry 'Amen!'°   *from Psalm 61:3*
    LORD MARSHAL [*to an officer*]   Go bear this lance to Thomas,
    Duke of Norfolk.
       [*An officer bears a lance to* MOWBRAY]
    FIRST HERALD   Harry of Hereford, Lancaster, and Derby
105   Stands here for God, his sovereign, and himself,
    On pain to be found false and recreant,
    To prove the Duke of Norfolk, Thomas Mowbray,
    A traitor to his God, his king, and him,
    And dares him to set forward to the fight.
110 SECOND HERALD   Here standeth Thomas Mowbray, Duke of Norfolk,
    On pain to be found false and recreant,
    Both to defend himself and to approve°   *prove*
    Henry of Hereford, Lancaster, and Derby
    To God his sovereign and to him disloyal,
115   Courageously and with a free desire
    Attending but the signal to begin.
    LORD MARSHAL   Sound trumpets, and set forward combatants!
       [*A charge is sounded.*]
       [KING RICHARD *throws down his warder*]°   *staff*
    Stay, the King hath thrown his warder down.
    KING RICHARD   Let them lay by their helmets and their spears,
120   And both return back to their chairs again.
       [BOLINGBROKE *and* MOWBRAY *disarm and sit*]
    [*To the nobles*] Withdraw with us, and let the trumpets sound
    While we return° these dukes what we decree.   *Until we deliver to*
       A long flourish° [*during which* KING RICHARD *and his*   *extended trumpet call*
       nobles withdraw and hold council, then come forward.
       KING RICHARD *addresses* BOLINGBROKE *and* MOWBRAY]
    Draw near, and list what with our council we have done.
    For that° our kingdom's earth should not be soiled   *Because*
125   With that dear blood which it hath fosterèd,
    And for° our eyes do hate the dire aspect°   *because / spectacle*
    Of civil wounds ploughed up with neighbours' swords,[4]
127.1   *And for we think the eagle-wingèd pride*
      Of sky-aspiring and ambitious thoughts
      With rival-hating envy set on you°   *malice set you on*
      To wake our peace, which in our country's cradle
127.5   *Draws the sweet infant breath of gentle sleep,*
    Which, so roused up with boist'rous untuned drums,
    With harsh-resounding trumpets' dreadful bray,
130   And grating shock of wrathful iron arms,
    Might from our quiet confines fright fair peace
    And make us wade even in our kindred's blood,
    Therefore we banish you our territories.
    You, cousin Hereford, upon pain° of life,   *loss*
135   Till twice five summers have enriched our fields
    Shall not regreet° our fair dominions,   *greet again*
    But tread the stranger° paths of banishment.   *foreign*

---

4. The following indented passage (lines 127.1–127.5) appears in Q1 but not in F. Shakespeare probably deleted
it as part of his limited revisions to the text.

BOLINGBROKE   Your will be done. This must my comfort be:
That sun that warms you here shall shine on me,
140 And those his golden beams to you here lent
Shall point on me and gild my banishment.
KING RICHARD   Norfolk, for thee remains a heavier doom,°   sentence
Which I with some unwillingness pronounce.
The sly° slow hours shall not determinate°   stealthy / bring to an end
145 The dateless limit° of thy dear° exile.   limitless period / grievous
The hopeless word of 'never to return'
Breathe I against thee, upon pain of life.
MOWBRAY   A heavy sentence, my most sovereign liege,
And all unlooked-for from your highness' mouth.
150 A dearer merit,° not so deep a maim°   better reward / an injury
As to be cast forth in the common air,
Have I deservèd at your highness' hands.
The language I have learnt these forty years,
My native English, now I must forgo,
155 And now my tongue's use is to me no more
Than an unstringèd viol° or a harp,   six-stringed instrument
Or like a cunning° instrument cased up,   skillfully made
Or, being open, put into his hands
That knows no touch to tune the harmony.
160 Within my mouth you have enjailed my tongue,
Doubly portcullised° with my teeth and lips,   Shut in by an iron gate
And dull unfeeling barren ignorance
Is made my jailer to attend on me.
I am too old to fawn upon a nurse,
165 Too far in years to be a pupil now.
What is thy sentence then but speechless death,
Which robs my tongue from breathing native breath?
KING RICHARD   It boots° thee not to be compassionate.°   helps / sorrowful
After our sentence, plaining° comes too late.   lamenting
170 MOWBRAY   Then thus I turn me from my country's light,
To dwell in solemn shades of endless night.
KING RICHARD   Return again, and take an oath with thee.
[To both] Lay on our royal sword your banished hands.
Swear by the duty that you owe to God—
175 Our part therein⁵ we banish with yourselves—
To keep the oath that we administer.
You never shall, so help you truth and God,
Embrace each other's love in banishment,
Nor never look upon each other's face,
180 Nor never write, regreet, nor reconcile
This low'ring tempest of your home-bred hate,
Nor never by advisèd° purpose meet   deliberated
To plot, contrive, or complot any ill
'Gainst us, our state, our subjects, or our land.
BOLINGBROKE   I swear.
185 MOWBRAY   And I, to keep all this.
BOLINGBROKE   Norfolk, so far as to mine enemy
By this time, had the King permitted us,
One of our souls had wandered in the air,

5. Your allegiance to me as God's deputy.

Banished this frail sepulchre of our flesh,
190 As now our flesh is banished from this land.
Confess thy treasons ere thou fly the realm.
Since thou hast far to go, bear not along
The clogging° burden of a guilty soul.   encumbering
MOWBRAY   No, Bolingbroke, if ever I were traitor,
195 My name be blotted from the book of life,°   eternal life
And I from heaven banished as from hence.
But what thou art, God, thou, and I do know,
And all too soon I fear the King shall rue.
Farewell, my liege. Now no way can I stray:°   lose my way
200 Save back to England, all the world's my way.   *Exit*
KING RICHARD   Uncle, even in the glasses° of thine eyes   windows
I see thy grievèd heart. Thy sad aspect°   appearance
Hath from the number of his banished years
Plucked four away. [*To* BOLINGBROKE] Six frozen winters spent,
205 Return with welcome home from banishment.
BOLINGBROKE   How long a time lies in one little word!
Four lagging winters and four wanton° springs   luxuriant
End in a word: such is the breath of kings.
JOHN OF GAUNT   I thank my liege that in regard of me
210 He shortens four years of my son's exile.
But little vantage° shall I reap thereby,   profit
For ere the six years that he hath to spend
Can change their moons and bring their times about,
My oil-dried lamp and time-bewasted° light   extinguished by time
215 Shall be extinct with age and endless night.
My inch of taper will be burnt and done,
And blindfold⁶ death not let me see my son.
KING RICHARD   Why, uncle, thou hast many years to live.
JOHN OF GAUNT   But not a minute, King, that thou canst give.
220 Shorten my days thou canst with sudden sorrow,
And pluck nights from me, but not lend a morrow.
Thou canst help time to furrow me with age,
But stop no wrinkle in his pilgrimage.
Thy word is current° with him for my death,   valid
225 But dead, thy kingdom cannot buy my breath.
KING RICHARD   Thy son is banished upon good advice,
Whereto thy tongue a party verdict⁷ gave.
Why at our justice seem'st thou then to lour?°   frown
JOHN OF GAUNT   Things sweet to taste prove in digestion sour.
230 You urged me as a judge, but I had rather
You would have bid me argue like a father.
Alas, I looked when° some of you should say   I expected that
I was too strict to make mine own away,
But you gave leave to my unwilling tongue
235 Against my will to do myself this wrong.⁸
235.1   *O, had't been a stranger, not my child,*
             To smooth° his fault I should have been more mild.   To gloss over
             A partial slander° sought I to avoid,   A suspicion of partiality
             And in the sentence my own life destroyed.

---

6. Because death's emblem is a hooded figure or an eyeless skull, and because the dead cannot see.
7. A share in the joint verdict.

8. The following indented passage (lines 235.1–235.4) appears only in Q1.

KING RICHARD   Cousin, farewell; and uncle, bid him so.
Six years we banish him, and he shall go.
      Flourish. Exeunt [all but AUMERLE, *the* LORD MARSHAL,
      JOHN OF GAUNT, *and* BOLINGBROKE]
AUMERLE [*to* BOLINGBROKE]   Cousin, farewell. What presence
      must not know,[9]
From where you do remain° let paper show.   [*Exit*]   *stay*
LORD MARSHAL [*to* BOLINGBROKE]   My lord, no leave take I, for
240   I will ride
As far as land will let me by your side.
JOHN OF GAUNT [*to* BOLINGBROKE]   O, to what purpose dost
      thou hoard thy words,
That thou return'st no greeting to thy friends?
BOLINGBROKE   I have too few to take my leave of you,
245   When the tongue's office° should be prodigal   *function*
To breathe the abundant dolour of the heart.
JOHN OF GAUNT   Thy grief is but thy absence for a time.
BOLINGBROKE   Joy absent, grief is present for that time.
JOHN OF GAUNT   What is six winters? They are quickly gone.
250   BOLINGBROKE   To men in joy, but grief makes one hour ten.
JOHN OF GAUNT   Call it a travel that thou tak'st for pleasure.
BOLINGBROKE   My heart will sigh when I miscall it so,
Which finds it an enforcèd pilgrimage.
JOHN OF GAUNT   The sullen passage of thy weary steps
255   Esteem as foil[1] wherein thou art to set
The precious jewel of thy home return.[2]
256.1   BOLINGBROKE   *Nay, rather every tedious stride I make*
          Will but remember° what a deal° of world   *remind me / an extent*
          I wander from the jewels that I love.
          Must I not serve a long apprenticehood
256.5   *To foreign passages, and in the end,*
          Having my freedom, boast of nothing else
          But that I was a journeyman[3] to grief?
       JOHN OF GAUNT   *All places that the eye of heaven° visits*   *sun; God's presence*
          Are to a wise man ports and happy havens.
256.10   *Teach thy necessity to reason thus;*
          There is no virtue like necessity.
          Think not the King did banish thee,
          But thou the King. Woe doth the heavier sit
          Where it perceives it is but faintly° borne.   *faintheartedly*
256.15   *Go, say I sent thee forth to purchase° honour,*   *acquire*
          And not the King exiled thee; or suppose
          Devouring pestilence hangs in our air
          And thou art flying to a fresher clime.
          Look what° thy soul holds dear, imagine it   *Whatever*
256.20   *To lie that way thou goest, not whence thou com'st.*
          Suppose the singing birds musicians,
          The grass whereon thou tread'st the presence strewed,[4]
          The flowers fair ladies, and thy steps no more
          Than a delightful measure° or a dance;   *a stately dance*

---

9. What you cannot tell me personally because of your
absence.
1. Thin metal against which jewels were set to enhance
their luster.

2. The following indented passage (lines 256.1–256.26)
appears only in Q1.
3. Person who has finished an apprenticeship.
4. The royal presence chamber strewn with rushes.

<table>
<tr><td>256.25</td><td>For *gnarling°* sorrow hath less power to bite</td><td>*snarling*</td></tr>
<tr><td></td><td>The man that mocks at it and sets it *light.°*</td><td>*values it lightly*</td></tr>
</table>

BOLINGBROKE O, who can hold a fire in his hand
By thinking on the frosty Caucasus,[5]
Or cloy the hungry edge of appetite
260 By bare imagination of a feast,
Or wallow naked in December snow
By thinking on *fantastic°* summer's heat?   *imagined*
O no, the apprehension of the good
Gives but the greater feeling to the worse.
265 Fell sorrow's tooth doth never *rankle°* more   *irritate*
Than when he bites, but lanceth[6] not the sore.

JOHN OF GAUNT Come, come, my son, I'll bring thee on thy way.
Had I thy youth and cause, I would not *stay.°*   *linger*

BOLINGBROKE Then England's ground, farewell. Sweet soil, adieu,
270 My mother and my nurse that bears me yet!
Where'er I wander, boast of this I can:
Though banished, yet a trueborn Englishman.   *Exeunt*

1.4

*Enter KING [RICHARD] with GREEN and BAGOT at one
door, and the Lord AUMERLE at another*

KING RICHARD We did observe.[1]—Cousin Aumerle,
How far brought you high Hereford on his way?

AUMERLE I brought high Hereford, if you call him so,
But to the next highway, and there I left him.

5 KING RICHARD And say, what store of parting tears were shed?

AUMERLE Faith, none for *me,°* except the north-east wind,   *my part*
Which then grew bitterly against our faces,
Awaked the sleeping *rheum,°* and so by chance   *tears*
Did grace our hollow parting with a tear.

10 KING RICHARD What said our cousin when you parted with him?

AUMERLE 'Farewell.' And *for°* my heart disdainèd that my tongue   *because*
Should so profane the word, that[2] taught me craft
To counterfeit oppression of such grief
That words seemed buried in my sorrow's grave.
15 *Marry,°* would the word 'farewell' have lengthened hours   *Indeed*
And added years to his short banishment,
He should have had a volume of farewells;
But since it would not, he had none of me.

KING RICHARD He is our cousin, cousin;[3] but 'tis doubt,
20 When time shall call him home from banishment,
Whether our kinsman come to see his *friends.°*   *relatives*
Ourself and Bushy, Bagot here, and Green
Observed his courtship to the common people,
How he did seem to dive into their hearts
25 With humble and familiar courtesy,
What reverence he did throw away on slaves,
Wooing poor craftsmen with the craft of smiles
And patient *underbearing°* of his fortune,   *enduring*

5. Mountain range between the Black and Caspian seas.
6. Probes (to release the pus from an abscess).
1.4 Location: The court.
1. The scene begins in mid-conversation; the King is
replying to a remark by Bagot or Green.

2. His heart. Unwilling to give Hereford good wishes
insincerely, Aumerle pretends to be overwhelmed with
grief.
3 Richard, Bolingbroke, and Aumerle were sons of
three brothers.

As 'twere to banish their affects with him.[4]
30 Off goes his bonnet° to an oysterwench.   *cap*
A brace of draymen° bid God speed him well,   *A couple of cart drivers*
And had the tribute of his supple knee
With 'Thanks, my countrymen, my loving friends',
As were our England in reversion[5] his,
35 And he our subjects' next degree in hope.
GREEN   Well, he is gone, and with him go these thoughts.
Now for the rebels which stand out in Ireland.
Expedient manage° must be made, my liege,   *Hasty arrangements*
Ere further leisure yield them further means
40 For their advantage and your highness' loss.
KING RICHARD   We will ourself in person to this war,
And for° our coffers with too great a court   *because*
And liberal largess are grown somewhat light,
We are enforced to farm our royal realm,[6]
45 The revenue whereof shall furnish us
For our affairs in hand. If that come short,
Our substitutes° at home shall have blank charters,[7]   *deputies*
Whereto, when they shall know what men are rich,
They shall subscribe them° for large sums of gold,   *write down their names*
50 And send them after to supply our wants;
For we will make for Ireland presently.°   *at once*
        Enter BUSHY
Bushy, what news?
BUSHY   Old John of Gaunt is grievous sick, my lord,
55 Suddenly taken, and hath sent post-haste
To entreat your majesty to visit him.
KING RICHARD   Where lies he?
BUSHY   At Ely House.
KING RICHARD   Now put it, God, in his physician's mind
To help him to his grave immediately.
60 The lining[8] of his coffers shall make coats
To deck our soldiers for these Irish wars.
Come, gentlemen, let's all go visit him.
Pray God we may make haste and come too late!   *Exeunt*

2.1

Enter JOHN OF GAUNT [*Duke of Lancaster*], *sick,* [*carried
in a chair*], *with Duke of* YORK
JOHN OF GAUNT   Will the King come, that I may breathe my last
In wholesome counsel to his unstaid° youth?   *unruly*
YORK   Vex not yourself, nor strive not with your breath,
For all in vain comes counsel to his ear.
5 JOHN OF GAUNT   O, but they say the tongues of dying men
Enforce attention, like deep harmony.
Where words are scarce they are seldom spent in vain,
For they breathe truth that breathe their words in pain.
He that no more must say is listened more
10   Than they whom youth and ease have taught to glose.°   *talk speciously*

4. As if taking their affections with him into exile.
5. A legal term for property that reverts to the original owner on the expiring of a contract.
6. To lease the King's right to tax.
7. Documents enabling the King to raise money by forced loans; the deputies can fill in the blanks with any amount they see fit.
8. Contents (playing on "lining cloth").
2.1 Location: Ely House.

More are men's ends marked than their lives before.
   The setting sun, and music at the close,
As the last taste of sweets, is sweetest last,
Writ in remembrance more than things long past.
15 Though Richard my life's counsel would not hear,
My death's sad tale may yet undeaf his ear.
YORK No, it is stopped with other, flattering sounds,
As praises of whose taste the wise are feared,°   *wary*
Lascivious metres to whose venom sound
20 The open ear of youth doth always listen,
Report of fashions in proud Italy,
Whose manners still° our tardy-apish[1] nation   *always*
Limps after in base imitation.
Where doth the world thrust forth a vanity—
25 So° it be new there's no respect° how vile—   *Provided / regard for*
That is not quickly buzzed into his ears?
Then all too late comes counsel, to be heard
Where will doth mutiny with wit's regard.[2]
Direct not him whose way himself will choose:
30 'Tis breath thou lack'st, and that breath wilt thou lose.
JOHN OF GAUNT Methinks I am a prophet new-inspired,
And thus, expiring, do foretell of him.
His rash, fierce blaze of riot° cannot last,   *wastefulness*
For violent fires soon burn out themselves.
35 Small showers last long, but sudden storms are short.
He tires betimes° that spurs too fast betimes.   *soon*
With eager feeding food doth choke the feeder.
Light vanity, insatiate cormorant,[3]
Consuming means, soon preys upon itself.
40 This royal throne of kings, this sceptred isle,
This earth of majesty, this seat of Mars,°   *war god's dwelling*
This other Eden, demi-paradise,
This fortress built by nature for herself
Against infection° and the hand of war,   *disease; depravity*
45 This happy breed of men, this little world,
This precious stone set in the silver sea,
Which serves it in the office° of a wall,   *function*
Or as a moat defensive to a house
Against the envy° of less happier lands;   *malice*
50 This blessèd plot, this earth, this realm, this England,
This nurse, this teeming womb of royal kings,
Feared by their breed[4] and famous by their birth,
Renownèd for their deeds as far from home
For Christian service and true chivalry[5]
55 As is the sepulchre, in stubborn Jewry,[6]
Of the world's ransom, blessèd Mary's son;
This land of such dear souls, this dear dear land,
Dear for her reputation through the world,
Is now leased out—I die pronouncing it—
60 Like to a tenement° or pelting° farm.   *rental property / worthless*
England, bound in with the triumphant sea,

1. Imitative but outmoded.
2. Where willfulness overthrows sound judgment.
3. Glutton (literally, a bird that swallows fish whole).
4. For their inherited valor.

5. Alluding to the English kings' accomplishments in the Crusades.
6. Judaea, stubborn in its resistance to Christianity.

Whose rocky shore beats back the envious siege
Of wat'ry Neptune, is now bound in with shame,
With inky blots and rotten parchment bonds.[7]
65 That England that was wont to conquer others
Hath made a shameful conquest of itself.
Ah, would the scandal vanish with my life,
How happy then were my ensuing death!

Enter KING [RICHARD], QUEEN, [*Duke of*] AUMERLE,
BUSHY, GREEN, BAGOT, [*Lord*] ROSS, *and* [*Lord*]
WILLOUGHBY

YORK   The King is come. Deal mildly with his youth,
70 For young hot colts, being reined, do rage the more.
QUEEN   How fares our noble uncle Lancaster?
KING RICHARD   What comfort, man? How is't with agèd Gaunt?
JOHN OF GAUNT   O, how that name befits my composition!°   constitution
Old Gaunt indeed, and gaunt in being old.
75 Within me grief hath kept a tedious fast,
And who abstains from meat° that is not gaunt?   food
For sleeping England long time have I watched.°   stayed awake
Watching breeds leanness, leanness is all gaunt.
The pleasure that some fathers feed upon
80 Is my strict fast: I mean my children's looks.[8]
And therein fasting, hast thou made me gaunt.
Gaunt am I for the grave, gaunt as a grave,
Whose hollow womb inherits naught but bones.
KING RICHARD   Can sick men play so nicely° with their names?   subtly
85 JOHN OF GAUNT   No, misery makes sport to mock itself.
Since thou dost seek to kill my name in me,[9]
I mock my name, great King, to flatter thee.
KING RICHARD   Should dying men flatter with those that live?
JOHN OF GAUNT   No, no, men living flatter those that die.
90 KING RICHARD   Thou now a-dying sayst thou flatt'rest me.
JOHN OF GAUNT   O no: thou diest, though I the sicker be.
KING RICHARD   I am in health; I breathe, and see thee ill.
JOHN OF GAUNT   Now He that made me knows I see thee ill:
Ill in myself to see, and in thee seeing ill.[1]
95 Thy deathbed is no lesser than thy land,
Wherein thou liest in reputation sick;
And thou, too careless patient as thou art,
Committ'st thy anointed body to the cure
Of those physicians[2] that first wounded thee.
100 A thousand flatterers sit within thy crown,
Whose compass° is no bigger than thy head,   circumference
And yet, encagèd in so small a verge,[3]
The waste[4] is no whit lesser than thy land.
O, had thy grandsire with a prophet's eye
105 Seen how his son's son should destroy his sons,
From forth° thy reach he would have laid thy shame,   out of
Deposing thee before thou wert possessed,[5]
Which art possessed° now to depose thyself.   in a diabolical frenzy

7. Richard's "blank charters."
8. Since Bolingbroke is exiled.
9. Destroy my family (by exiling Bolingbroke).
1. Too ill to see well, and seeing evil in you.
2. Richard's favorites, or his own bad impulses.

3. Area; distance of 12 miles around the court, to which special rules applied.
4. Destruction (specifically, injury done to a property by a tenant); waist, narrowest part.
5. In possession of the crown.

Why, cousin,° wert thou regent° of the world   *kinsman / ruler*
110   It were a shame to let this land by lease.
But, for thy world, enjoying but this land,[6]
Is it not more than shame to shame it so?
Landlord of England art thou now, not king.
Thy state of law[7] is bondslave to the law,
115   And—
    KING RICHARD   And thou, a lunatic lean-witted fool,
Presuming on an ague's privilege,°   *the privilege of the sick*
Dar'st with thy frozen° admonition   *rigid; caused by a chill*
Make pale our cheek, chasing the royal blood
120   With fury from his native residence.°   *its natural place*
Now by my seat's° right royal majesty,   *throne's*
Wert thou not brother to great Edward's son,[8]
This tongue that runs so roundly° in thy head   *freely*
Should run thy head from thy unreverent shoulders.
125   JOHN OF GAUNT   O, spare me not, my brother Edward's son,
For that I was his father Edward's son.
That blood already, like the pelican,[9]
Hast thou tapped out[1] and drunkenly caroused.
My brother Gloucester, plain well-meaning soul—
130   Whom fair befall in heaven 'mongst happy souls—
May be a precedent and witness good
That thou respect'st not spilling° Edward's blood.   *don't hesitate to spill*
Join with the present sickness that I have,
And thy unkindness be like crookèd age,
135   To crop° at once a too-long withered flower.   *cut*
Live in thy shame, but die not shame with thee.[2]
These words hereafter thy tormentors be.
[*To attendants*] Convey me to my bed, then to my grave.
Love they to live that love and honour have.
                  Exit [*carried in a chair*]
140   KING RICHARD   And let them die that age and sullens° have,   *sulks*
For both hast thou, and both become the grave.
    YORK   I do beseech your majesty impute his words
To wayward sickliness and age in him.
He loves you, on my life, and holds you dear
145   As Harry Duke of Hereford, were he here.
    KING RICHARD   Right, you say true: as Hereford's love, so his.[3]
As theirs, so mine; and all be as it is.
            Enter [*Earl of*] NORTHUMBERLAND
    NORTHUMBERLAND   My liege, old Gaunt commends him to your majesty.
    KING RICHARD   What says he?
    NORTHUMBERLAND   Nay, nothing: all is said.
150   His tongue is now a stringless instrument.
Words, life, and all, old Lancaster hath spent.
    YORK   Be York the next that must be bankrupt so!
Though death be poor, it ends a mortal woe.
    KING RICHARD   The ripest fruit first falls, and so doth he.

---

6. Since this realm alone constitutes your world.
7. Legal status (as landlord, not King).
8. Edward the Black Prince, Edward III's son and Richard's father.
9. A mother pelican was thought to wound her breast so her ungrateful young could feed on her blood.

1. Let run as from a barrel tap.
2. May your shame outlive you.
3. York claims that Gaunt loves Richard as much as he loves his own son; Richard deliberately misconstrues York to mean Gaunt loves Richard as much as Hereford does.

155   His time is spent; our pilgrimage must be.°   *continue*
        So much for that. Now for our Irish wars.
        We must supplant those rough rug-headed kerns,[4]
        Which live like venom where no venom else
        But only they have privilege to live.[5]
160   And for° these great affairs do ask some charge,[6]   *because*
        Towards our assistance we do seize to us
        The plate, coin, revenues, and movables°   *personal property*
        Whereof our uncle Gaunt did stand possessed.
      YORK   How long shall I be patient? Ah, how long
165   Shall tender° duty make me suffer wrong?   *scrupulous*
        Not Gloucester's death, nor Hereford's banishment,
        Nor Gaunt's rebukes, nor England's private wrongs,[7]
        Nor the prevention of poor Bolingbroke
        About his marriage,[8] nor my own disgrace,
170   Have ever made me sour my patient cheek,
        Or bend one wrinkle° on my sovereign's face.   *one frown*
        I am the last of noble Edward's sons,
        Of whom thy father, Prince of Wales, was first.
        In war was never lion raged more fierce,
175   In peace was never gentle lamb more mild,
        Than was that young and princely gentleman.
        His face thou hast, for even so looked he,
        Accomplished with the number of thy hours.°   *When he was your age*
        But when he frowned it was against the French,
180   And not against his friends. His noble hand
        Did win what he did spend, and spent not that
        Which his triumphant father's hand had won.
        His hands were guilty of no kindred blood,
        But bloody with the enemies of his kin.
185   O, Richard, York is too far gone with grief,
        Or else he never would compare between.
      KING RICHARD   Why uncle, what's the matter?
      YORK   O my liege,
        Pardon me if you please; if not, I, pleased
        Not to be pardoned, am content withal.°   *nevertheless*
190   Seek you to seize and grip into your hands
        The royalties[9] and rights of banished Hereford?
        Is not Gaunt dead? And doth not Hereford live?
        Was not Gaunt just? And is not Harry true?
        Did not the one deserve to have an heir?
195   Is not his heir a well-deserving son?
        Take Hereford's rights away, and take from Time
        His° charters and his customary rights   *Its*
        Let not tomorrow then ensue° today;   *follow*
        Be not thyself, for how art thou a king
200   But by fair sequence and succession?
        Now afore God—God forbid I say true!—
        If you do wrongfully seize Hereford's rights,
        Call in° the letters patents that he hath   *Revoke*

---

4. Shaggy Irish foot soldiers.
5. Alluding to the legend that St. Patrick drove snakes out of Ireland.
6. Do demand some expenditure.
7. Wrongs committed against private individuals.

8. Richard intervened against Bolingbroke's proposed marriage to the King of France's cousin.
9. Privileges granted by a king through "letters patents" (line 203).

By his attorneys general to sue
205 His livery, and deny his offered homage,[1]
You pluck° a thousand dangers on your head,   *pull*
You lose a thousand well-disposèd hearts,
And prick my tender patience to those thoughts
Which honour and allegiance cannot think.
210 KING RICHARD   Think what you will, we seize into our hands
His plate, his goods, his money, and his lands.
YORK   I'll not be by the while.[2] My liege, farewell.
What will ensue hereof there's none can tell.
But by bad courses may be understood
215 That their events° can never fall out good.   *Exit*   *outcomes*
KING RICHARD   Go, Bushy, to the Earl of Wiltshire straight.
Bid him repair° to us to Ely House   *go*
To see° this business. Tomorrow next   *attend to*
We will for Ireland, and 'tis time, I trow.°   *think*
220 And we create, in absence of ourself,
Our uncle York Lord Governor of England;
For he is just and always loved us well.—
Come on, our Queen; tomorrow must we part.
Be merry, for our time of stay is short.
        Flourish. Exeunt KING [RICHARD], QUEEN[, AUMERLE,
        GREEN, *and* BAGOT *at one door,* BUSHY *at another door*].
        Manent° NORTHUMBERLAND, WILLOUGHBY, *and* ROSS   *Remain*
225 NORTHUMBERLAND   Well, lords, the Duke of Lancaster is dead.
ROSS   And living too, for now his son is Duke.
WILLOUGHBY   Barely in title, not in revenues.
NORTHUMBERLAND   Richly in both, if justice had her right.
ROSS   My heart is great,° but it must break with silence   *full of emotion*
230 Ere't be disburdened with a liberal° tongue.   *unrestrained*
NORTHUMBERLAND   Nay, speak thy mind, and let him ne'er
        speak more
That speaks thy words again to do thee harm.
WILLOUGHBY   Tends that that thou wouldst speak to[3] the Duke
        of Hereford?
If it be so, out with it boldly, man.
235 Quick is mine ear to hear of good towards him.
ROSS   No good at all that I can do for him,
Unless you call it good to pity him,
Bereft and gelded of his patrimony.
NORTHUMBERLAND   Now afore God, 'tis shame such wrongs are borne
240 In him, a royal prince, and many more
Of noble blood in this declining land.
The King is not himself, but basely led
By flatterers; and what they will inform
Merely in° hate 'gainst any of us all,   *Purely out of*
245 That will the King severely prosecute
'Gainst us, our lives, our children, and our heirs.
ROSS   The commons° hath he pilled° with grievous taxes,   *common people / stripped*
And quite lost their hearts. The nobles hath he fined
For ancient quarrels, and quite lost their hearts.

1. The letters patents allow Hereford, through his legal representatives ("attorneys general"), to make a legal claim for the inheritance of his land ("sue" for delivery), provided he swears allegiance to the King ("offers homage").
2. Present during the seizure.
3. Does what you would say concern.

250 WILLOUGHBY   And daily new exactions are devised,
   As blanks, benevolences,° and I wot° not what.   *forced loans / know*
   But what, a' God's name, doth become of this?°   *this money*
   NORTHUMBERLAND   Wars hath not wasted it; for warred he hath not,
   But basely yielded upon compromise
255 That which his ancestors achieved with blows.[4]
   More hath he spent in peace than they in wars.
   ROSS   The Earl of Wiltshire hath the realm in farm.[5]
   WILLOUGHBY   The King's grown bankrupt like a broken man.
   NORTHUMBERLAND   Reproach and dissolution hangeth over him.
260 ROSS   He hath not money for these Irish wars,
   His burdenous taxations notwithstanding,
   But by the robbing of the banished Duke.
   NORTHUMBERLAND   His noble kinsman. Most degenerate King!
   But, lords, we hear this fearful tempest sing,
265 Yet seek no shelter to avoid the storm.
   We see the wind sit sore° upon our sails,   *blow hard*
   And yet we strike[6] not, but securely° perish.   *heedlessly*
   ROSS   We see the very wreck that we must suffer,
   And unavoided° is the danger now   *unavoidable*
270 For suffering° so the causes of our wreck.   *enduring*
   NORTHUMBERLAND   Not so: even through the hollow eyes° of death   *eye sockets*
   I spy life peering; but I dare not say
   How near the tidings of our comfort is.
   WILLOUGHBY   Nay, let us share thy thoughts, as thou dost ours.
275 ROSS   Be confident to speak, Northumberland.
   We three are but thyself, and, speaking so,
   Thy words are but as thoughts. Therefore be bold.
   NORTHUMBERLAND   Then thus. I have from Port le Blanc,
   A bay in Brittaine,[7] received intelligence
280 That Harry Duke of Hereford, Reinold Lord Cobham,
   Thomas son and heir to the Earl of Arundel[8]
   That late broke from the Duke of Exeter,
   His[9] brother, Archbishop late° of Canterbury,   *until recently*
   Sir Thomas Erpingham, Sir Thomas Ramston,
285 Sir John Norbery,
   Sir Robert Waterton, and Francis Coint,
   All these well furnished by the Duke of Brittaine
   With eight tall ships, three thousand men of war,°   *soldiers*
   Are making hither with all due expedience,
290 And shortly mean to touch our northern shore.
   Perhaps they had ere this, but that they stay
   The first departing of the King[1] for Ireland.
   If then we shall shake off our slavish yoke,
   Imp out[2] our drooping country's broken wing,
295 Redeem from broking pawn° the blemished crown,   *pawnbrokers*
   Wipe off the dust that hides our sceptre's gilt,
   And make high majesty look like itself,
   Away with me in post° to Ravenspurgh.[3]   *speedily*

---

4. Referring to the ceding of Brest, a city in western France, to the Duke of Brittany.
5. *in farm:* on lease (as in 1.4.44–46).
6. Lower sails; deliver blows.
7. Brittany, in northwest France.
8. An editorial approximation of a line missing from

early texts. Shakespeare's source states that Arundel's son escaped from Exeter's custody.
9. The Earl of Arundel's.
1. *they stay . . . King:* they wait for the King to depart first.
2. Engraft new feathers on (from falconry).
3. Then a port on the river Humber, in Yorkshire.

But if you faint,° as fearing to do so,   *are fainthearted*
300   Stay, and be secret, and myself will go.
ROSS   To horse, to horse! Urge doubts to them that fear.
WILLOUGHBY   Hold out my horse,° and I will first be there.   *If my horse holds up*

                             Exeunt

2.2

Enter the QUEEN, BUSHY, *[and]* BAGOT

BUSHY   Madam, your majesty is too much sad.[1]
    You promised when you parted with the King
    To lay aside life-harming heaviness°   *melancholy*
    And entertain° a cheerful disposition.   *assume*
5   QUEEN   To please the King I did; to please myself
    I cannot do it. Yet I know no cause
    Why I should welcome such a guest as grief,
    Save bidding farewell to so sweet a guest
    As my sweet Richard. Yet again, methinks
10   Some unborn sorrow, ripe in fortune's womb,
    Is coming towards me; and my inward soul
    At nothing trembles. With something it grieves
    More than with parting from my lord the King.
    BUSHY   Each substance of a grief hath twenty shadows
15   Which shows like grief itself but is not so.
    For sorrow's eye, glazèd with blinding tears,
    Divides one thing entire to many objects—
    Like perspectives, which, rightly gazed upon,
    Show nothing but confusion; eyed awry,
20   Distinguish form.[2] So your sweet majesty,
    Looking awry upon your lord's departure,
    Find shapes° of grief more than himself to wail,°   *images / bewail*
    Which, looked on as it is, is naught but shadows
    Of what it is not. Then, thrice-gracious Queen,
25   More than your lord's departure weep not: more is not seen,
    Or if it be, 'tis with false sorrow's eye,
    Which for things true weeps things imaginary.
    QUEEN   It may be so, but yet my inward soul
    Persuades me it is otherwise. Howe'er it be,
30   I cannot but be sad: so heavy-sad
    As thought—on thinking on no thought I think[3]—
    Makes me with heavy nothing faint and shrink.
    BUSHY   'Tis nothing but conceit,° my gracious lady.   *imagination*
    QUEEN   'Tis nothing less:[4] conceit is still° derived   *always*
35   From some forefather grief; mine is not so;
    For nothing hath begot my something° grief—   *substantial*
    Or something hath the nothing that I grieve[5]—
    'Tis in reversion that I do possess[6]—

2.2. Location: Windsor Castle.
1. Shakespeare makes Richard's queen a mature young woman; the historical Isabella was married to Richard at seven years and was ten at the time of Bolingbroke's invasion.
2. *For . . . from:* Bushy compares the Queen's eye first to a perspective glass that multiplies one image into many, then to a perspective picture that looks distorted unless viewed at an angle ("awry").
3. *As thought . . . think:* a difficult line. The Oxford

editors adopt the Q1 version, "thought"; other editors adopt the F version, "though," which is hardly less obscure. The Queen is playing with the paradox that her premonition, a thought of nothing, or "no thought," is nonetheless almost physically oppressive.
4. Anything but conceit.
5. Or the grief that I feel apparently over nothing actually has some cause.
6. It will come at a later date (that is, her grief anticipates its occasion).

But what it is that is not yet known what,
40 I cannot name; 'tis nameless woe, I wot.
     Enter GREEN
GREEN   God save your majesty, and well met, gentlemen.
  I hope the King is not yet shipped for Ireland.
QUEEN   Why hop'st thou so? 'Tis better hope he is,
  For his designs crave° haste, his haste good hope.   *need*
45 Then wherefore dost thou hope he is not shipped?
GREEN   That he, our hope, might have retired his power,°   *brought back his forces*
  And driven into despair an enemy's hope,
  Who strongly hath set footing in this land.
  The banished Bolingbroke repeals° himself,   *recalls from exile*
50 And with uplifted arms° is safe arrived   *weapons*
  At Ravenspurgh.
QUEEN   Now God in heaven forbid!
GREEN   Ah madam, 'tis too true! And, that is worse,
  The Lord Northumberland, his son young Harry Percy,
  The Lords of Ross, Beaumont, and Willoughby,
55 With all their powerful friends, are fled to him.
BUSHY   Why have you not proclaimed Northumberland,
  And all the rest, revolted faction-traitors?°   *treasonous conspirators*
GREEN   We have; whereupon the Earl of Worcester
  Hath broke his staff,[7] resigned his stewardship,
60 And all the household servants fled with him
  To Bolingbroke.
QUEEN   So, Green, thou art the midwife to my woe,
  And Bolingbroke my sorrow's dismal heir.
  Now hath my soul brought forth her prodigy,°   *monstrous birth; portent*
65 And I, a gasping new-delivered mother,
  Have woe to woe, sorrow to sorrow joined.
BUSHY   Despair not, madam.
QUEEN   Who shall hinder me?
  I will despair, and be at enmity
  With cozening° hope. He° is a flatterer,   *cheating / (Hope)*
70 A parasite, a keeper-back of death,
  Who° gently would dissolve° the bonds of life,   *(Death) / loosen*
  Which false hope lingers in extremity.
     Enter [Duke of] YORK [*wearing a gorget*][8]
GREEN   Here comes the Duke of York.
QUEEN   With signs of war about his agèd neck.
75 O, full of careful business° are his looks!   *anxious preoccupation*
  Uncle, for God's sake speak comfortable° words.   *comforting*
YORK   Should I do so, I should belie my thoughts.
  Comfort's in heaven, and we are on the earth,
  Where nothing lives but crosses,° cares, and grief.   *misfortunes*
80 Your husband, he is gone to save far off,
  Whilst others come to make him lose at home.
  Here am I, left to underprop his land,
  Who, weak with age, cannot support myself.
  Now comes the sick hour that his surfeit made.
85 Now shall he try° his friends that flattered him.   *test*
     Enter a [SERVINGMAN]

---

7. Symbolically resigning his office as lord steward of
the King's household. Worcester is Northumberland's

brother.
8. Piece of armor protecting the throat.

SERVINGMAN   My lord, your son was gone before I came.

YORK   He was? Why so, go all which way it will.
    The nobles they are fled. The commons° they are cold,   *common people*
    And will, I fear, revolt on Hereford's side.
90   Sirrah, get thee to Pleshey, to my sister° Gloucester.   *sister-in-law*
    Bid her send me presently° a thousand pound—   *immediately*
    Hold; take my ring.[9]

SERVINGMAN   My lord, I had forgot to tell your lordship,
    Today as I came by I callèd there—
95   But I shall grieve you to report the rest.

YORK   What is't, knave?°   *fellow*

SERVINGMAN   An hour before I came, the Duchess died.

YORK   God for his mercy, what a tide of woes
    Comes rushing on this woeful land at once!
100   I know not what to do. I would to God,
    So my untruth° had not provoked him to it,   *disloyalty*
    The King had cut off my head with my brother's.
    What, are there no posts° dispatched for Ireland?   *fast messengers*
    How shall we do for money for these wars?
105   [*To the* QUEEN] Come, sister—cousin, I would say; pray pardon me.[1]
    [*To the* SERVINGMAN] Go, fellow, get thee home. Provide some carts,
    And bring away the armour that is there. [*Exit* SERVINGMAN]
    Gentlemen, will you go muster men?
    If I know how or which way to order these affairs
110   Thus disorderly thrust into my hands,
    Never believe me. Both are my kinsmen.
    T'one is my sovereign, whom both my oath
    And duty bids defend; t'other again
    Is my kinsman, whom the King hath wronged,
115   Whom conscience and my kindred bids to right.
    Well, somewhat we must do. [*To the* QUEEN] Come, cousin,
    I'll dispose of° you.—   *make arrangements for*
    Gentlemen, go muster up your men,
    And meet me presently at Berkeley Castle.[2]
120   I should to Pleshey too, but time will not permit.
    All is uneven,
    And everything is left at six and seven.°   *in confusion*

Exeunt Duke [*of* YORK *and*] QUEEN.
Manent BUSHY, GREEN [*and* BAGOT]

BUSHY   The wind sits fair[3] for news to go for Ireland,
    But none returns. For us to levy power
125   Proportionable to the enemy
    Is all unpossible.

GREEN   Besides, our nearness to the King in love
    Is near° the hate of those love not the King.   *Implies*

BAGOT   And that is the wavering commons; for their love
130   Lies in their purses, and whoso empties them
    By so much fills their hearts with deadly hate.

BUSHY   Wherein the King stands generally condemned.

BAGOT   If judgement lie in them,° then so do we,   *is in the people's hands*
    Because we ever have been near the King.

---

9. As proof that he comes with York's authorization.   2. In Gloucestershire, in western England.
1. The Duchess's death is uppermost in York's mind. 3. The wind blows from a favorable direction.

135 GREEN Well, I will for refuge straight to Bristol Castle.
     The Earl of Wiltshire is already there.
   BUSHY Thither will I with you; for little office°   service
     Will the hateful commoners perform for us,
     Except like curs to tear us all to pieces.
140 [*To* BAGOT] Will you go along with us?
   BAGOT No, I will to Ireland, to his majesty.
     Farewell: if heart's presages be not vain
     We three here part that ne'er shall meet again.
   BUSHY That's as York thrives[4] to beat back Bolingbroke.
145 GREEN Alas, poor Duke, the task he undertakes
     Is numb'ring sands and drinking oceans dry.
     Where one on his side fights, thousands will fly.
   BAGOT Farewell at once, for once, for all and ever.
   BUSHY Well, we may meet again.
   BAGOT   I fear me never.
            Exeunt [BUSHY *and* GREEN *at one door,*
                    and BAGOT *at another door*]

2.3

Enter [BOLINGBROKE *Duke of Lancaster and*] *Hereford,*
and [*the Earl of*] NORTHUMBERLAND

BOLINGBROKE How far is it, my lord, to Berkeley now?
NORTHUMBERLAND Believe me, noble lord,
     I am a stranger here in Gloucestershire.
     These high wild hills and rough uneven ways
5   Draws out our miles and makes them wearisome;
     And yet your fair discourse hath been as sugar,
     Making the hard way sweet and delectable.
     But I bethink me what a weary way
     From Ravenspurgh to Cotswold[1] will be found
10   In° Ross and Willoughby, wanting° your company,   By / lacking
     Which I protest hath very much beguiled
     The tediousness and process° of my travel.   tedious course
     But theirs is sweetened with the hope to have
     The present benefit which I possess;
15   And hope to joy is little less in joy
     Than hope enjoyed. By this° the weary lords   this expectation
     Shall make their way seem short as mine hath done
     By sight of what I have: your noble company.
BOLINGBROKE Of much less value is my company
     Than your good words.
            Enter HARRY PERCY
20   But who comes here?
NORTHUMBERLAND It is my son, young Harry Percy,[2]
     Sent from my brother Worcester, whencesoever.°   wherever he may be
     Harry, how fares your uncle?°   Worcester
HARRY PERCY I had thought, my lord, to have learned his
     health of you.
25 NORTHUMBERLAND Why, is he not with the Queen?
HARRY PERCY No, my good lord; he hath forsook the court,

---

4. That depends on York's success.
2.3 Location: Gloucestershire.
1. Hilly part of Gloucestershire.

2. Shakespeare makes Harry Percy, the Hotspur of
1 Henry IV, a boy here; the historical Percy was two
years older than Bolingbroke.

Broken his staff of office, and dispersed
The household of the King.
NORTHUMBERLAND   What was his reason?
He was not so resolved when last we spake together.
30   HARRY PERCY   Because your lordship was proclaimèd traitor.
But he, my lord, is gone to Ravenspurgh
To offer service to the Duke of Hereford,
And sent me over by Berkeley to discover
What power the Duke of York had levied there,
35   Then with directions to repair to Ravenspurgh.
NORTHUMBERLAND   Have you forgot the Duke of Hereford, boy?[3]
HARRY PERCY   No, my good lord, for that is not forgot
Which ne'er I did remember. To my knowledge,
I never in my life did look on him.
40   NORTHUMBERLAND   Then learn to know him now. This is the Duke.
HARRY PERCY   My gracious lord, I tender you my service,
Such as it is, being tender, raw, and young,
Which elder days shall ripen and confirm
To more approved° service and desert.   *more fully demonstrated*
45   BOLINGBROKE   I thank thee, gentle Percy, and be sure
I count myself in nothing else so happy
As in a° soul rememb'ring my good friends;   *my*
And as my fortune ripens with thy love,
It shall be still thy true love's recompense.
50   My heart this covenant makes; my hand thus seals it.
                    [*He gives* PERCY *his hand*]
NORTHUMBERLAND   How far is it to Berkeley, and what stir°   *activity*
Keeps good old York there with his men of war?
HARRY PERCY   There stands the castle, by yon tuft of trees,
Manned with three hundred men, as I have heard,
55   And in it are the Lords of York, Berkeley, and Seymour,
None else of name° and noble estimate.°   *title / reputation*
                    Enter [*Lord*] ROSS *and* [*Lord*] WILLOUGHBY
NORTHUMBERLAND   Here come the Lords of Ross and Willoughby,
Bloody with spurring, fiery red with haste.
BOLINGBROKE   Welcome, my lords. I wot° your love pursues   *know*
60   A banished traitor. All my treasury
Is yet but unfelt° thanks, which, more enriched,   *immaterial*
Shall be your love and labour's recompense.
ROSS   Your presence makes us rich, most noble lord.
WILLOUGHBY   And far surmounts our labour to attain it.
65   BOLINGBROKE   Evermore thank's the exchequer[4] of the poor,
Which till my infant fortune comes to years°   *of age*
Stands for° my bounty.   *in place of*
                    Enter BERKELEY
                              But who comes here?
NORTHUMBERLAND   It is my lord of Berkeley, as I guess.
BERKELEY   My lord of Hereford, my message is to you.
70   BOLINGBROKE   My lord, my answer is to 'Lancaster',[5]
And I am come to seek that name in England,

_____

3. Northumberland scolds his son for not greeting Bo-   5. I only reply to the title of Lancaster (which Richard
lingbroke respectfully.   took away).
4. Gratitude is always the treasury.

And I must find that title in your tongue
Before I make reply to aught you say.
BERKELEY   Mistake me not, my lord, 'tis not my meaning
75   To raze one title of your honour out.
To you, my lord, I come—what lord you will—
From the most gracious regent of this land,
The Duke of York, to know what pricks you on°   *incites you*
To take advantage of the absent time°   *time of absence*
80   And fright our native peace with self-borne⁶ arms.
           Enter [Duke of] YORK
BOLINGBROKE   I shall not need transport my words by you.
Here comes his grace in person.—My noble uncle!
     [He kneels]
YORK   Show me thy humble heart, and not thy knee,
Whose duty is deceivable° and false.   *deceptive*
85   BOLINGBROKE   My gracious uncle—
YORK   Tut, tut, grace me no grace, nor uncle me no uncle.
I am no traitor's uncle, and that word 'grace'
In an ungracious mouth is but profane.
Why have those banished and forbidden legs
90   Dared once to touch a dust° of England's ground?   *speck*
But then more 'why': why have they dared to march
So many miles upon her peaceful bosom,
Frighting her pale-faced villages with war
And ostentation° of despisèd arms?   *display*
95   Com'st thou because the anointed King is hence?
Why, foolish boy, the King is left behind,
And in my loyal bosom lies his power.
Were I but now the lord of such hot youth
As when brave Gaunt, thy father, and myself
100   Rescued the Black Prince, that young Mars of men,
From forth the ranks of many thousand French,
O then how quickly should this arm of mine,
Now prisoner to the palsy, chastise thee
And minister correction° to thy fault!   *administer punishment*
105   BOLINGBROKE   My gracious uncle, let me know my fault.
On what condition stands it and wherein?⁷
YORK   Even in condition of the worst degree:
In gross rebellion and detested treason.
Thou art a banished man, and here art come
110   Before the expiration of thy time
In braving° arms against thy sovereign.   *defiant*
BOLINGBROKE *[standing]*   As I was banished, I was banished Hereford;
But as I come, I come for Lancaster.
And, noble uncle, I beseech your grace,
115   Look on my wrongs with an indifferent° eye.   *impartial*
You are my father, for methinks in you
I see old Gaunt alive. O then, my father,
Will you permit that I shall stand condemned
A wandering vagabond, my rights and royalties
120   Plucked from my arms perforce and given away
To upstart unthrifts?° Wherefore was I born?   *spendthrifts*

---

6. Borne for oneself, not for the King; borne against   7. What is its nature, and in what does it consist?
fellow countrymen.

If that my cousin King be King in England,
It must be granted I am Duke of Lancaster.
You have a son, Aumerle my noble kinsman.
125 Had you first died and he been thus trod down,
He should have found his uncle Gaunt a father
To rouse his wrongs and chase them to the bay.[8]
I am denied to sue my livery[9] here,
And yet my letters patents give me leave.
130 My father's goods are all distrained° and sold,   *confiscated*
And these and all are all amiss employed.
What would you have me do? I am a subject,
And I challenge law;° attorneys are denied me;   *demand my rights*
And therefore personally I lay my claim
135 To my inheritance of free descent.°   *legal succession*
NORTHUMBERLAND The noble Duke hath been too much abused.
ROSS It stands your grace upon[1] to do him right.
WILLOUGHBY Base men by his endowments° are made great.   *property*
YORK My lords of England, let me tell you this.
140 I have had feeling of my cousin's wrongs,
And laboured all I could to do him right.
But in this kind° to come, in braving arms,   *manner*
Be his own carver,[2] and cut out his way
To find out right with wrong[3]—it may not be.
145 And you that do abet him in this kind
Cherish rebellion, and are rebels all.
NORTHUMBERLAND The noble Duke hath sworn his coming is
But for his own, and for the right of that
We all have strongly sworn to give him aid;
150 And let him never see joy that breaks that oath.
YORK Well, well, I see the issue° of these arms.   *consequence*
I cannot mend it, I must needs confess,
Because my power° is weak and all ill-left.   *army*
But if I could, by Him that gave me life,
155 I would attach° you all, and make you stoop   *arrest*
Unto the sovereign mercy of the King.
But since I cannot, be it known to you
I do remain as neuter.° So fare you well—   *neutral*
Unless you please to enter in the castle
160 And there repose you for this night.
BOLINGBROKE An offer, uncle, that we will accept.
But we must win° your grace to go with us   *persuade*
To Bristol Castle, which they say is held
By Bushy, Bagot, and their complices,°   *accomplices*
165 The caterpillars° of the commonwealth,   *devourers*
Which I have sworn to weed and pluck away.
YORK It may be I will go with you—but yet I'll pause,
For I am loath to break our country's laws.
Nor° friends nor foes, to me welcome you are.   *Neither*
170 Things past redress are now with me past care.   *Exeunt*

8. *rouse*: startle an animal from its cover. *bay*: point
where the animal turns on its pursuers.
9. See note to 2.1.205.

1. It is incumbent on your grace.
2. Help himself to meat (instead of waiting to be served).
3. To illegally obtain what he deserves.

2.4

Enter Earl of SALISBURY *and a* WELSH CAPTAIN

WELSH CAPTAIN My lord of Salisbury, we have stayed° ten days,   *waited*
   And hardly° kept our countrymen together,   *with difficulty*
   And yet we hear no tidings from the King.
   Therefore we will disperse ourselves. Farewell.
5 SALISBURY Stay yet another day, thou trusty Welshman.
   The King reposeth all his confidence in thee.
WELSH CAPTAIN 'Tis thought the King is dead. We will not stay.
   The bay trees in our country are all withered,
   And meteors fright the fixèd stars of heaven.
10   The pale-faced moon looks bloody on the earth,[1]
   And lean-looked prophets whisper fearful change.
   Rich men look sad, and ruffians dance and leap;
   The one in fear to lose what they enjoy,
   The other to enjoy° by rage and war.   *hoping to profit*
15   These signs forerun the death or fall of kings.
   Farewell. Our countrymen are gone and fled,
   As well assured Richard their king is dead.   *Exit*
SALISBURY Ah, Richard! With the eyes of heavy mind
   I see thy glory, like a shooting star,
20   Fall to the base earth from the firmament.
   Thy sun sets weeping in the lowly west,
   Witnessing° storms to come, woe, and unrest.   *Testifying to*
   Thy friends are fled to wait upon thy foes,
   And crossly° to thy good all fortune goes.   *Exit*   *adversely*

3.1

Enter BOLINGBROKE [*Duke of Lancaster and Hereford,*
Duke of] YORK, [*Earl of*] NORTHUMBERLAND, [*Lord*]
ROSS, [HARRY] PERCY, [*and Lord*] WILLOUGHBY
BOLINGBROKE Bring forth these men.
   [*Enter*] BUSHY *and* GREEN, [*guarded as*] *prisoners*
   Bushy and Green, I will not vex° your souls,   *afflict*
   Since presently° your souls must part your bodies,   *immediately*
   With too much urging° your pernicious lives,   *emphasizing*
5   For 'twere no charity. Yet to wash your blood
   From off my hands, here in the view of men
   I will unfold some causes of your deaths.
   You have misled a prince, a royal king,
   A happy° gentleman in blood and lineaments,[1]   *fortunate*
10   By you unhappied and disfigured clean.°   *utterly*
   You have, in manner,° with your sinful hours   *so to speak*
   Made a divorce betwixt his queen and him,
   Broke the possession of a royal bed,
   And stained the beauty of a fair queen's cheeks
15   With tears drawn from her eyes by your foul wrongs.[2]
   Myself—a prince by fortune of my birth,
   Near to the King in blood, and near in love
   Till you did make him misinterpret me—
   Have stooped my neck under your injuries,

2.4 Location: A camp in Wales.
1. Holinshed records the first of these omens (line 8); the others are poetic commonplaces.
3.1 Location: Before Bristol Castle.

1. In descent and qualities.
2. Bolingbroke implies that Bushy and Green had homosexual relations with Richard; Holinshed claims that they procured female paramours for him.

air

20 And sighed my English breath in foreign clouds,°   *air*
 Eating the bitter bread of banishment,
 Whilst you have fed upon my signories,°   *estates*
 Disparked my parks³ and felled my forest woods,
 From my own windows torn my household coat,⁴
25 Razed° out my imprese,° leaving me no sign, *Scraped / heraldic emblem*
 Save men's opinions and my living blood,
 To show the world I am a gentleman.
 This and much more, much more than twice all this,
 Condemns you to the death.—See them delivered over
30 To execution and the hand of death.
 BUSHY More welcome is the stroke of death to me
 Than Bolingbroke to England.
 GREEN My comfort is that heaven will take our souls,
 And plague injustice with the pains of hell.
35 BOLINGBROKE My lord Northumberland, see them dispatched.
   [*Exit* NORTHUMBERLAND, *with* BUSHY *and* GREEN, *guarded*]
 Uncle, you say the Queen is at your house.
 For God's sake, fairly° let her be intreated.° *courteously / treated*
 Tell her I send to her my kind commends.°   *greetings*
 Take special care my greetings be delivered.
40 YORK A gentleman of mine I have dispatched
 With letters of your love to her at large.° *fully described*
 BOLINGBROKE Thanks, gentle uncle.—Come, lords, away,
 To fight with Glyndŵr⁵ and his complices.
 A while to work, and after, holiday.   *Exeunt*

3.2

 Drums. Flourish. Enter [KING] RICHARD, [*Duke of*]
 AUMERLE, [BISHOP OF] CARLISLE, *and soldiers* [*with*]
 colours°   *flags*
 KING RICHARD Harlechly Castle call they this at hand?
 AUMERLE Yea, my lord. How brooks° your grace the air *enjoys*
 After your late° tossing on the breaking seas? *recent*
 KING RICHARD Needs must° I like it well. I weep for joy *Necessarily*
5 To stand upon my kingdom once again.
   [*He touches the ground*]
 Dear earth, I do salute thee with my hand,
 Though rebels wound thee with their horses' hoofs.
 As a long-parted mother with her child
 Plays fondly with her tears, and smiles in meeting,
10 So, weeping, smiling, greet I thee my earth,
 And do thee favours with my royal hands.
 Feed not thy sovereign's foe, my gentle earth,
 Nor with thy sweets° comfort his ravenous sense;¹ *bounty*
 But let thy spiders that suck up thy venom²
15 And heavy-gaited toads³ lie in their way,
 Doing annoyance to the treacherous feet
 Which with usurping steps do trample thee.
 Yield stinging nettles to mine enemies,

---

3. Put my hunting lands to other use.
4. Removed the stained glass bearing my coat of arms.
5. This character appears in *1 Henry IV* and is perhaps to be identified with the Welsh captain of 2.4.
3.2 Location: Near Harlech Castle, on the coast of

Gwynedd, Wales.
1. Appetite; intention.
2. It was thought that spiders drew their venom from the earth.
3. Also thought to be poisonous.

And when they from thy bosom pluck a flower
20 Guard it, I pray thee, with a lurking adder,
Whose double° tongue may with a mortal touch   *forked*
Throw death upon thy sovereign's enemies.—
Mock not my senseless conjuration,[4] lords.
This earth shall have a feeling, and these stones
25 Prove armèd soldiers, ere her native king°   *King entitled by birth*
Shall falter under foul rebellion's arms.
    BISHOP OF CARLISLE   Fear not, my lord. That power that made you king
    Hath power to keep you king in spite of all.[5]
28.1   *The means that heavens yield must be embraced*
            And not neglected; else° heaven would,   *otherwise*
            And we will not: heaven's offer we refuse,
            The proffered means of succour and redress.
    AUMERLE   He means, my lord, that we are too remiss,
30 Whilst Bolingbroke, through our security,°   *overconfidence*
    Grows strong and great in substance and in friends.
    KING RICHARD   Discomfortable° cousin, know'st thou not   *Disheartening*
    That when the searching eye of heaven is hid
    Behind the globe, that lights the lower world,
35 Then thieves and robbers range abroad unseen
    In murders and in outrage bloody here;
    But when from under this terrestrial ball
    He fires° the proud tops of the eastern pines,   *lights up*
    And darts his light through every guilty hole,
40 Then murders, treasons, and detested sins,
    The cloak of night being plucked from off their backs,
    Stand bare and naked, trembling at themselves?
    So when this thief, this traitor, Bolingbroke,
    Who all this while hath revelled in the night
45 Whilst we were wand'ring with the Antipodes,
    Shall see us rising in our throne, the east,[6]
    His treasons will sit blushing in his face,
    Not able to endure the sight of day,
    But, self-affrighted, tremble at his sin.
50 Not all the water in the rough rude sea
    Can wash the balm° from an anointed king.   *oil of consecration*
    The breath of worldly men cannot depose
    The deputy elected by the Lord.
    For every man that Bolingbroke hath pressed°   *drafted*
55 To lift shrewd° steel against our golden crown,   *wicked; sharp*
    God for his Richard hath in heavenly pay
    A glorious angel. Then if angels fight,
    Weak men must fall; for heaven still° guards the right.   *always*
        Enter [Earl of] SALISBURY
    Welcome, my lord. How far off lies your power?
60 SALISBURY   Nor nea'er° nor farther off, my gracious lord,   *Neither nearer*
    Than this weak arm. Discomfort guides my tongue,
    And bids me speak of nothing but despair.
    One day too late, I fear me, noble lord,
    Hath clouded all thy happy days on earth.

---

4. Injunction addressed to an insentient being (the earth).
5. The following indented passage (lines 28.1–28.4) appears only in Q1.
6. *That when . . . east:* Richard compares the sun ("the searching eye of heaven," line 33), the antipodes, or "lower world" on the other side of the globe, to himself leaving England to visit Ireland. Unlike the sun, however, Richard arrives from the west.

65   O, call back yesterday, bid time return,
      And thou shalt have twelve thousand fighting men.
      Today, today, unhappy day too late,
      Overthrows thy joys, friends, fortune, and thy state;°   *prosperity; nation*
      For all the Welshmen, hearing thou wert dead,
70   Are gone to Bolingbroke, dispersed, and fled.
  AUMERLE   Comfort, my liege. Why looks your grace so pale?
  KING RICHARD   But now° the blood of twenty thousand men   *A moment ago*
      Did triumph° in my face, and they are fled;   *shine*
      And till so much blood thither come again
75   Have I not reason to look pale and dead?
      All souls that will be safe fly from my side,
      For time hath set a blot upon my pride.
  AUMERLE   Comfort, my liege. Remember who you are.
  KING RICHARD   I had forgot myself. Am I not King?
80   Awake, thou sluggard majesty, thou sleep'st!
      Is not the King's name forty thousand names?
      Arm, arm, my name! A puny subject strikes
      At thy great glory. Look not to the ground,
      Ye favourites of a king: are we not high?
85   High be our thoughts. I know my uncle York
      Hath power enough to serve our turn.
          Enter SCROPE
                                              But who comes here?
  SCROPE   More health and happiness betide my liege
      Than can my care-tuned[7] tongue deliver° him.   *offer*
  KING RICHARD   Mine ear is open and my heart prepared.
90   The worst is worldly loss thou canst unfold.
      Say, is my kingdom lost? Why 'twas my care,°   *trouble*
      And what loss is it to be rid of care?
      Strives Bolingbroke to be as great as we?
      Greater he shall not be. If he serve God
95   We'll serve Him too, and be his fellow so.[8]
      Revolt our subjects? That we cannot mend.
      They break their faith to God as well as us.
      Cry° woe, destruction, ruin, loss, decay: *Though you may cry*
      The worst is death, and death will have his° day.   *its*
100 SCROPE   Glad am I that your highness is so armed
      To bear the tidings of calamity.
      Like an unseasonable stormy day,
      Which makes the silver rivers drown their shores
      As if the world were all dissolved to tears,
105   So high above his limits° swells the rage   *bounds; banks*
      Of Bolingbroke, covering your fearful° land   *alarmed*
      With hard bright steel, and hearts harder than steel.
      Whitebeards have armed their thin and hairless scalps
      Against thy majesty. Boys with women's voices
110   Strive to speak big, and clap their female° joints   *weak*
      In stiff unwieldy arms° against thy crown.   *armor*
      Thy very beadsmen[9] learn to bend their bows
      Of double-fatal[1] yew against thy state.

---

7. Tuned to the key sorrow.   praying for their benefactors' souls.
8. Be Bolingbroke's equal in that regard.   1. Because yew is poisonous, and its wood was used to
9. Poor elderly men who received charity in return for   make bows.

Yea, distaff-women° manage rusty bills[2]   *spinners*
115   Against thy seat.° Both young and old rebel,   *throne*
And all goes worse than I have power to tell.
KING RICHARD   Too well, too well thou tell'st a tale so ill.
Where is the Earl of Wiltshire? Where is Bagot?[3]
What is become of Bushy, where is Green,
120   That they have let the dangerous enemy
Measure our confines[4] with such peaceful° steps?   *unopposed*
If we prevail, their heads shall pay for it.
I warrant they have made peace with Bolingbroke.
SCROPE   Peace have they made with him indeed, my lord.
125   KING RICHARD   O villains, vipers damned without redemption!
Dogs easily won to fawn on any man!
Snakes in my heart-blood warmed, that sting my heart!
Three Judases, each one thrice-worse than Judas![5]
Would they make peace? Terrible hell make war
130   Upon their spotted° souls for this offence!   *blemished*
SCROPE   Sweet love, I see, changing his property,°   *its quality*
Turns to the sourest and most deadly hate.
Again uncurse their souls. Their peace is made
With heads, and not with hands. Those whom you curse
135   Have felt the worst of death's destroying wound,
And lie full low, graved in the hollow ground.
AUMERLE   Is Bushy, Green, and the Earl of Wiltshire dead?
SCROPE   Ay, all of them at Bristol lost their heads.
AUMERLE   Where is the Duke my father, with his power?
140   KING RICHARD   No matter where. Of comfort no man speak.
Let's talk of graves, of worms and epitaphs,
Make dust our paper, and with rainy eyes
Write sorrow on the bosom of the earth.
Let's choose executors and talk of wills—
145   And yet not so, for what can we bequeath
Save our deposèd° bodies to the ground?   *dethroned; prostrate*
Our lands, our lives, and all are Bolingbroke's;
And nothing can we call our own but death,
And that small model[6] of the barren earth
150   Which serves as paste[7] and cover to our bones.
[*Sitting*] For God's sake, let us sit upon the ground,
And tell sad stories of the death of kings—
How some have been deposed, some slain in war,
Some haunted by the ghosts they have deposed,
155   Some poisoned by their wives, some sleeping killed,
All murdered. For within the hollow crown
That rounds° the mortal temples of a king   *encircles*
Keeps Death his court; and there the antic° sits,   *jester*
Scoffing his state[8] and grinning at his pomp,
160   Allowing him a breath, a little scene,
To monarchize,° be feared, and kill with looks,[9]   *play the monarch*
Infusing him with self and vain conceit,[1]
As if this flesh which walls about our life

2. Spiked axes on long shafts.
3. Bagot is not one of the "three Judases" (line 128)
actually executed by Bolingbroke; he reappears in 4.1.
4. Travel over our territories.
5. Disciple who betrayed Jesus.

6. Microcosm (the body); enveloping shape (the grave).
7. Pastry shell (also known as "coffin").
8. Mocking the King's regality.
9. Order executions with a glance.
1. Instilling in him vain ideas about himself.

Were brass impregnable; and humoured thus,[2]
165 Comes at the last, and with a little pin
Bores through his castle wall; and farewell, king.
Cover your heads,[3] and mock not flesh and blood
With solemn reverence. Throw away respect,
Tradition, form, and ceremonious duty,
170 For you have but mistook me all this while.
I live with bread, like you; feel want,
Taste grief, need friends. Subjected thus,[4]
How can you say to me I am a king?

BISHOP OF CARLISLE   My lord, wise men ne'er wail their present woes,
175 But presently prevent the ways to wail.[5]
To fear the foe, since fear oppresseth° strength,   *suppresses*
Gives in your weakness strength unto your foe;
And so your follies fight against yourself.
Fear, and be slain. No worse can come to fight;°   *in fighting*
180 And fight and die is death destroying death,[6]
Where fearing dying pays death servile breath.

AUMERLE   My father hath a power.° Enquire of him,   *an army*
And learn to make a body of a limb.

KING RICHARD [*standing*]   Thou chid'st me well. Proud Boling-
broke, I come
185 To change blows with thee for our day of doom.[7]
This ague-fit° of fear is overblown.°   *chill / blown over*
An easy task it is to win our own.
Say, Scrope, where lies our uncle with his power?
Speak sweetly, man, although thy looks be sour.

190 SCROPE   Men judge by the complexion° of the sky   *appearance*
The state and inclination of the day.
So may you by my dull and heavy eye
My tongue hath but a heavier tale to say.
I play the torturer by small and small°   *little by little*
195 To lengthen out the worst that must be spoken.
Your uncle York is joined with Bolingbroke,
And all your northern castles yielded up,
And all your southern gentlemen° in arms   *men of rank*
Upon his faction.

KING RICHARD   Thou hast said enough.
200 [*To* AUMERLE] Beshrew° thee, cousin, which didst lead me forth   *Woe to*
Of that sweet way I was in to despair.
What say you now? What comfort have we now?
By heaven, I'll hate him everlastingly
That bids me be of comfort any more.
205 Go to Flint Castle;° there I'll pine away.   *Welsh castle near Chester*
A king, woe's slave, shall kingly woe obey.
That power I have, discharge, and let them go
To ear° the land that hath some hope to grow;   *till*
For I have none. Let no man speak again
210 To alter this, for counsel is but vain.

AUMERLE   My liege, one word.

KING RICHARD   He does me double wrong

2. And Death having thus amused himself.
3. Replace your hats (do not respectfully remain bare-
headed).
4. Made a subject to such needs (with pun).

5. But immediately vanquish the causes of grief.
6. To die fighting is to destroy death's power by dying.
7. To exchange blows with you in order to determine
our fates.

That wounds me with the flatteries of his tongue.
Discharge my followers. Let them hence away
From Richard's night to Bolingbroke's fair day.   *Exeunt*

3.3

Enter BOLINGBROKE [*Duke of Lancaster and Hereford,*
Duke of] YORK, [*Earl of*] NORTHUMBERLAND, [*and sol-*
diers] *with drum and colours*

BOLINGBROKE   So that by this intelligence° we learn   *information*
The Welshmen are dispersed, and Salisbury
Is gone to meet the King, who lately landed
With some few private friends upon this coast.

5   NORTHUMBERLAND   The news is very fair and good, my lord.
Richard not far from hence hath hid his head.

YORK   It would beseem the Lord Northumberland
To say 'King Richard'. Alack the heavy day
When such a sacred king should hide his head!

10   NORTHUMBERLAND   Your grace mistakes. Only to be brief
Left I his title out.

YORK   The time hath been,
Would you have been so brief with him, he would
Have been so brief with you to shorten you,
For taking so the head,¹ your whole head's length.

15   BOLINGBROKE   Mistake not, uncle, further than you should.

YORK   Take not, good cousin, further than you should,
Lest you mistake° the heavens are over our heads.   *forget*

BOLINGBROKE   I know it, uncle, and oppose not myself
Against their will.

Enter [HARRY] PERCY [*and a trumpeter*]
But who comes here?

20   Welcome, Harry. What, will not this castle yield?

HARRY PERCY   The castle royally is manned, my lord,
Against thy entrance.

BOLINGBROKE   Royally?
Why, it contains no king.

HARRY PERCY   Yes, my good lord,
It doth contain a king. King Richard lies

25   Within the limits of yon lime and stone,
And with him are the Lord Aumerle, Lord Salisbury,
Sir Stephen Scrope, besides a clergyman
Of holy reverence; who, I cannot learn.

NORTHUMBERLAND   O, belike° it is the Bishop of Carlisle.   *probably*

30   BOLINGBROKE [*to* NORTHUMBERLAND]   Noble lord,
Go to the rude ribs° of that ancient castle;   *rough walls*
Through brazen trumpet send the breath of parley
Into his ruined ears,° and thus deliver.   *its battered loopholes*
Henry Bolingbroke

35   Upon his knees doth kiss King Richard's hand,
And sends allegiance and true faith of heart
To his most royal person, hither come
Even at his feet to lay my arms and power,
Provided that my banishment repealed°   *revoked*

40   And lands restored again be freely granted.

3.3 Location: Before Flint Castle.   1. For omitting the title thus; for acting without restraint.

If not, I'll use the advantage of my power,
And lay° the summer's dust with showers of blood   *make settle*
Rained from the wounds of slaughtered Englishmen;
The which how far off from the mind of Bolingbroke
45   It is such crimson tempest should bedrench
The fresh green lap of fair King Richard's land,
My stooping duty° tenderly shall show.   *submissive kneeling*
Go, signify as much, while here we march
Upon the grassy carpet of this plain.
50   Let's march without the noise of threat'ning drum,
That from this castle's tottered° battlements   *dilapidated*
Our fair appointments° may be well perused.   *equipment*
Methinks King Richard and myself should meet
With no less terror than the elements
55   Of fire and water° when their thund'ring shock   *lightning and rain*
At meeting tears the cloudy cheeks of heaven.
Be he the fire, I'll be the yielding water.
The rage be his, whilst on the earth I rain°   *(punning on "reign"?)*
My waters: on the earth, and not on him.—
60   March on, and mark King Richard, how he looks.
          [*They march about the stage; then* BOLINGBROKE, YORK,
          PERCY, *and soldiers stand at a distance from the walls;*
          NORTHUMBERLAND *and a trumpeter advance to the
          walls.*] *The trumpets sound* [a] *parley without, and* [an]
          answer within; then a flourish [*within.* KING] RICHARD
          appeareth on the walls,[2] [*with* BISHOP OF] CARLISLE,
          [*Duke of*] AUMERLE, SCROPE, [*and Earl of*] SALISBURY
See, see, King Richard doth himself appear,
As doth the blushing[3] discontented sun
From out the fiery portal of the east
When he perceives the envious° clouds are bent   *malicious*
65   To dim his glory and to stain the track
Of his bright passage to the occident.
YORK   Yet looks he like a king. Behold, his eye,
As bright as is the eagle's, lightens forth[4]
Controlling majesty. Alack, alack for woe
70   That any harm should stain so fair a show!
KING RICHARD [*to* NORTHUMBERLAND]   We are amazed; and
                thus long have we stood
To watch° the fearful bending of thy knee,   *wait for*
Because we thought ourself thy lawful king.
An if° we be, how dare thy joints forget   *An if = If*
75   To pay their aweful° duty to our presence?   *reverential*
If we be not, show us the hand of God
That hath dismissed us from our stewardship.
For well we know no hand of blood and bone
Can grip° the sacred handle of our sceptre,   *seize*
80   Unless he do profane, steal, or usurp.
And though you think that all—as you have done—
Have torn° their souls by turning them from us,   *ruined (by disloyalty)*
And we are barren and bereft of friends,

2. That is, on the balcony of the tiring-house at the   weather).
back of the stage.   4. Flashes out (the eagle is a traditional royal symbol).
3. Red (proverbially, a red morning sky anticipates bad

threaten

Yet know my master, God omnipotent,
85 Is mustering in his clouds on our behalf
Armies of pestilence; and they shall strike
Your children yet unborn and unbegot,
That lift your vassal hands against my head
And threat° the glory of my precious crown. *threaten*
90 Tell Bolingbroke, for yon methinks he is,
That every stride he makes upon my land
Is dangerous treason. He is come to open
The purple testament° of bleeding war; *blood-red document*
But ere the crown he looks for live in peace
95 Ten thousand bloody crowns° of mothers' sons *heads*
Shall ill become the flower of England's face,[5]
Change the complexion of her maid-pale° peace *innocent white*
To scarlet indignation, and bedew
Her pastures' grass with faithful English blood.
    NORTHUMBERLAND [*kneeling*] The King of heaven forbid our
100   lord the King
Should so with civil and uncivil[6] arms
Be rushed upon. Thy thrice-noble cousin
Harry Bolingbroke doth humbly kiss thy hand,
And by the honourable tomb he swears,
105 That stands upon your royal grandsire's° bones, *(Edward III's)*
And by the royalties of both your bloods,
Currents that spring from one most gracious head,° *source*
And by the buried hand of warlike Gaunt,
And by the worth and honour of himself,
110 Comprising all that may be sworn or said,
His coming hither hath no further scope° *aim*
Than for his lineal royalties,° and to beg *hereditary rights*
Enfranchisement° immediate on his knees; *Recall from exile*
Which on thy royal party° granted once, *part*
115 His glittering arms he will commend° to rust, *commit*
His barbèd° steeds to stables, and his heart *armed*
To faithful service of your majesty.
This swears he as he is a prince and just,
And as I am a gentleman I credit° him. *believe*
120 KING RICHARD Northumberland, say thus the King returns:° *replies*
His noble cousin is right welcome hither,
And all the number of his fair demands
Shall be accomplished without contradiction.
With all the gracious utterance thou hast,
125 Speak to his gentle hearing kind commends.° *regards*
    [NORTHUMBERLAND *and the trumpeter return to*
      BOLINGBROKE]
    [*To* AUMERLE] We do debase ourself, cousin, do we not,
To look so poorly° and to speak so fair? *abjectly*
Shall we call back Northumberland, and send
Defiance to the traitor, and so die?
130 AUMERLE No, good my lord, let's fight with gentle words
Till time lend friends, and friends their helpful swords.
    KING RICHARD O God, O God, that e'er this tongue of mine,
That laid the sentence of dread banishment

---

5. Blooming surface of England; faces of England's choicest youth.
6. Of the same country and violent; playing on "civil" as "peaceful" and "uncivil" as "alien."

On yon proud man, should take it off again
135 With words of sooth!° O, that I were as great   *soothing words*
As is my grief, or lesser than my name,
Or that I could forget what I have been,
Or not remember what I must be now!
Swell'st thou, proud heart? I'll give thee scope to beat,
140 Since foes have scope to beat both thee and me.
            [NORTHUMBERLAND *advances to the walls*]
    AUMERLE   Northumberland comes back from Bolingbroke.
    KING RICHARD   What must the King do now? Must he submit?
The King shall do it. Must he be deposed?
The King shall be contented. Must he lose
145 The name of King? A° God's name, let it go.   *In*
I'll give my jewels for a set of beads,°   *rosary*
My gorgeous palace for a hermitage,
My gay apparel for an almsman's° gown,   *a beggar's*
My figured° goblets for a dish of wood,   *engraved*
150 My sceptre for a palmer's° walking staff,   *pilgrim's*
My subjects for a pair of carvèd saints,
And my large kingdom for a little grave,
A little, little grave, an obscure grave;
Or I'll be buried in the King's highway,°   *(as suicides were)*
155 Some way of common trade° where subjects' feet   *passage*
May hourly trample on their sovereign's head,
For on my heart they tread now, whilst I live,
And buried once, why not upon my head?
Aumerle, thou weep'st, my tender-hearted cousin.
160 We'll make foul weather with despisèd tears.
Our sighs and they shall lodge° the summer corn,   *beat down*
And make a dearth° in this revolting° land.   *famine / rebellious*
Or shall we play the wantons° with our woes,   *we frolic*
And make some pretty match° with shedding tears;   *clever game*
165 As thus to drop them still° upon one place   *continually*
Till they have fretted° us a pair of graves   *eroded for*
Within the earth, and therein laid? 'There lies
Two kinsmen digged their graves with weeping eyes.'
Would not this ill do well? Well, well, I see
170 I talk but idly° and you mock at me.   *foolishly*
Most mighty prince, my lord Northumberland,
What says King Bolingbroke? Will his majesty
Give Richard leave to live till Richard die?
You make a leg,° and Bolingbroke says 'Ay'.   *an obeisance*
175 NORTHUMBERLAND   My lord, in the base court° he doth attend   *outer courtyard*
To speak with you. May it please you to come down?
    KING RICHARD   Down, down I come like glist'ring Phaethon,[7]
Wanting the manage° of unruly jades.[8]   *Lacking control*
In the base court: base court where kings grow base
180 To come at traitors' calls, and do them grace.°   *favor them*
In the base court, come down: down court, down King,
For night-owls shriek where mounting larks should sing.
            [*Exeunt* KING RICHARD *and his party*]

---

7. In Greek mythology, the son of the sun god. He
attempted to drive his father's sun chariot but was too
weak to control the horses; Zeus, king of the gods,
struck him down with a thunderbolt to prevent him
from destroying the earth.
8. Horses (contemptuous).

[NORTHUMBERLAND *returns to* BOLINGBROKE]

BOLINGBROKE   What says his majesty?

NORTHUMBERLAND   Sorrow and grief of heart
Makes him speak fondly,° like a frantic° man.   *foolishly / an insane*
[*Enter* KING RICHARD *and his party below*]
Yet he is come.

185 BOLINGBROKE   Stand all apart,
And show fair duty to his majesty.
        He kneels down
My gracious lord.

KING RICHARD   Fair cousin, you debase your princely knee
To make the base earth proud with kissing it.

190 Me rather had° my heart might feel your love   *I had rather*
Than my unpleased eye see your courtesy.
Up, cousin, up. Your heart is up, I know,
Thus high at least,⁹ although your knee be low.

BOLINGBROKE   My gracious lord, I come but for mine own.

195 KING RICHARD   Your own is yours, and I am yours, and all.

BOLINGBROKE   So far be mine, my most redoubted° lord,   *dreaded*
As my true service shall deserve your love.

KING RICHARD   Well you deserve. They well deserve to have
That know the strong'st and surest way to get.
        [BOLINGBROKE *rises*]

200 [*To* YORK] Uncle, give me your hands. Nay, dry your eyes.
Tears show their love, but want their remedies.°   *do no good*
[*To* BOLINGBROKE] Cousin, I am too young to be your father,
Though you are old enough to be my heir.
What you will have I'll give, and willing too;

205 For do we must what force will have us do.
Set on towards London, cousin: is it so?

BOLINGBROKE   Yea, my good lord.

KING RICHARD   Then I must not say no.
        Flourish. Exeunt.

3.4

Enter the QUEEN *with her two* LADIES

QUEEN   What sport shall we devise here in this garden,
To drive away the heavy thought of care?

FIRST LADY   Madam, we'll play at bowls.°   *lawn bowling*

QUEEN   'Twill make me think the world is full of rubs,¹

5 And that my fortune runs against the bias.²

SECOND LADY   Madam, we'll dance.

QUEEN   My legs can keep no measure° in delight   *dance step*
When my poor heart no measure° keeps in grief;   *moderation*
Therefore no dancing, girl. Some other sport.

10 FIRST LADY   Madam, we'll tell tales.

QUEEN   Of sorrow or of joy?

FIRST LADY   Of either, madam.

QUEEN   Of neither, girl.
For if of joy, being altogether wanting,

15 It doth remember° me the more of sorrow.   *remind*

---

9. Richard touches his crown.
3.4 Location: The Duke of York's garden.
1. Impediments (a term from the game of bowls).

2. Runs askew. *bias:* literally, a lead weight in the bowl
that makes it run smoothly.

Or if of grief, being altogether had,°   *possessed*
It adds more sorrow to my want of joy.
For what I have I need not to repeat,
And what I want it boots° not to complain.   *helps*
SECOND LADY   Madam, I'll sing.
20   QUEEN   Tis well that thou hast cause;
But thou shouldst please me better wouldst thou weep.
SECOND LADY   I could weep, madam, would it do you good.
QUEEN   And I could sing, would weeping do me good,
And never borrow any tear of thee.
              Enter a GARDENER *and two* [MEN]
25   But stay; here come the gardeners.
Let's step into the shadow of these trees.
My wretchedness unto a row of pins[3]
They will talk of state, for everyone doth so
Against° a change. Woe is forerun with woe.   *In anticipation of*
        [*The* QUEEN *and her* LADIES *stand apart*]
30   GARDENER [*to* FIRST MAN]   Go, bind thou up young dangling apricots
Which, like unruly children, make their sire
Stoop with oppression of their prodigal° weight.   *excessive*
Give some supportance to the bending twigs.
[*To* SECOND MAN] Go thou, and, like an executioner,
35   Cut off the heads of too fast-growing sprays
That look too lofty in our commonwealth.
All must be even° in our government.   *equal*
You thus employed, I will go root away
The noisome° weeds which without profit suck   *harmful*
40   The soil's fertility from wholesome flowers.
FIRST MAN   Why should we, in the compass of a pale,[4]
Keep law and form and due proportion,
Showing as in a model our firm estate,°   *stable government*
When our sea-wallèd garden, the whole land,
45   Is full of weeds, her fairest flowers choked up,
Her fruit trees all unpruned, her hedges ruined,
Her knots[5] disordered, and her wholesome herbs
Swarming with caterpillars?
GARDENER   Hold thy peace.
He that hath suffered° this disordered spring   *permitted*
50   Hath now himself met with the fall of leaf.
The weeds which his broad spreading leaves did shelter,
That seemed in eating him to hold him up,
Are plucked up, root and all, by Bolingbroke—
I mean the Earl of Wiltshire, Bushy, Green.
SECOND MAN   What, are they dead?
55   GARDENER   They are; and Bolingbroke
Hath seized the wasteful King. O, what pity is it
That he had not so trimmed and dressed° his land   *cultivated*
As we this garden! We at time of year°   *in season*
Do wound the bark, the skin of our fruit trees,[6]
60   Lest, being over-proud in° sap and blood,   *excessively swollen with*
With too much riches it confound° itself.   *ruin*

---

3. I'll bet my great wretchedness against a trivial row
of pins.
4. In the limits of a fenced enclosure.

5. Intricate flower beds; social bonds.
6. *Do . . . trees:* this restricts the tree's food supply,
encouraging fruit buds to form.

Had he done so to great and growing men,
They might have lived to bear, and he to taste,
Their fruits of duty. Superfluous branches
65 We lop away, that bearing boughs may live.
Had he done so, himself had borne° the crown,[7]   retained
Which waste of idle hours hath quite thrown down.
FIRST MAN   What, think you then the King shall be deposed?
GARDENER   Depressed° he is already, and deposed   Brought low
70 'Tis doubt° he will be. Letters came last night   feared
To a dear friend of the good Duke of York's
That tell black tidings.
QUEEN   O, I am pressed to death through want of speaking![8]
      [*She comes forward*]
Thou, old Adam's[9] likeness, set to dress° this garden,   cultivate
75 How dares thy harsh rude° tongue sound this unpleasing news?   ignorant
What Eve, what serpent hath suggested° thee   tempted
To make a second fall of cursèd man?
Why dost thou say King Richard is deposed?
Dar'st thou, thou little better thing than earth,
80 Divine° his downfall? Say where, when, and how   Prophesy
Cam'st thou by this ill tidings? Speak, thou wretch!
GARDENER   Pardon me, madam. Little joy have I
To breathe this news, yet what I say is true.
King Richard he is in the mighty hold
85 Of Bolingbroke. Their fortunes both are weighed.
In your lord's scale is nothing but himself
And some few vanities that make him light.
But in the balance of great Bolingbroke,
Besides himself, are all the English peers,
90 And with that odds he weighs King Richard down.
Post° you to London and you will find it so.   Hasten
I speak no more than everyone doth know.
QUEEN   Nimble mischance that art so light of foot,
Doth not thy embassage° belong to me,   message
95 And am I last that knows it? O, thou think'st
To serve me last, that I may longest keep
Thy sorrow in my breast. Come, ladies, go
To meet at London London's king in woe.
What, was I born to this, that my sad look
100 Should grace the triumph° of great Bolingbroke?   triumphal procession
Gard'ner, for telling me these news of woe,
Pray God the plants thou graft'st may never grow.
                        Exit [with her LADIES]
GARDENER   Poor Queen, so that° thy state might be no worse   if as a result
I would my skill were subject to thy curse.
105 Here did she fall° a tear. Here in this place   drop
I'll set a bank of rue,[1] sour herb-of-grace.
Rue even for ruth° here shortly shall be seen   pity
In the remembrance of a weeping queen.   *Exeunt*

---

7. Playing on the "crown" of a tree.
8. In medieval and Renaissance England, indicted persons who refused to plead guilty or not guilty were

killed with weights laid on the stomach.
9. Adam was the first gardener.
1. Herb associated with compassion and repentance.

4.1

Enter, as to Parliament, BOLINGBROKE [*Duke of Lancaster and Hereford, Duke of*] AUMERLE, [*Earl of*] NORTHUMBERLAND, [HARRY] PERCY, [*Lord*] FITZWALTER, [*Duke of*] SURREY, [BISHOP OF] CARLISLE, [*and the*] ABBOT OF WESTMINSTER

BOLINGBROKE   Call forth Bagot.

Enter BAGOT, [*with*] *officers*

                                 Now, Bagot, freely speak thy mind:
What thou dost know of noble Gloucester's death,
Who wrought it with[1] the King, and who performed
The bloody office° of his timeless° end.   *deed / untimely*

5 BAGOT   Then set before my face the Lord Aumerle.

BOLINGBROKE [*to* AUMERLE]   Cousin, stand forth, and look
      upon that man.

          [AUMERLE *stands forth*]

BAGOT   My lord Aumerle, I know your daring tongue
Scorns to unsay° what once it hath delivered.   *deny*
In that dead° time when Gloucester's death was plotted *fatal; dark*
10 I heard you say 'Is not my arm of length,°   *long enough*
That reacheth from the restful English court
As far as Calais, to mine uncle's head?'
Amongst much other talk that very time[2]
I heard you say that you had rather refuse
15 The offer of an hundred thousand crowns
Than° Bolingbroke's return to England,   *Than accept*
Adding withal° how blest this land would be   *besides*
In this your cousin's death.

AUMERLE   Princes and noble lords,
What answer shall I make to this base man?
20 Shall I so much dishonour my fair stars°   *honorable birth*
On equal terms to give him chastisement?[3]
Either I must, or have mine honour soiled
With the attainder° of his slanderous lips.   *accusation*
         [*He throws down his gage*]
There is my gage, the manual seal of death
25 That marks thee out for hell. I say thou liest,
And will maintain° what thou hast said is false *will uphold in combat*
In thy heart blood, though being all too base
To stain the temper[4] of my knightly sword.

BOLINGBROKE   Bagot, forbear. Thou shalt not take it up.

30 AUMERLE   Excepting one,° I would he° were the best *(Bolingbroke) / (Bagot)*
In all this presence that hath moved° me so.   *angered*

FITZWALTER   If that thy valour stand on sympathy,[5]
There is my gage, Aumerle, in gage to thine.
         [*He throws down his gage*]
By that fair sun which shows me where thou stand'st,
35 I heard thee say, and vauntingly° thou spak'st it, *boastfully*
That thou wert cause of noble Gloucester's death.
If° thou deny'st it twenty times, thou liest,   *Even if*

4.1 Location: Westminster Hall.
1. Who persuaded; who collaborated with.
2. *that very time:* inconsistent, since Gloucester was killed long before Bolingbroke's exile.

3. Punishment (a lord could refuse to fight a lowborn man in the trial by combat).
4. Quality (literally, "hardness").
5. Insists on equality of rank.

And I will turn thy falsehood to thy heart,
Where it was forgèd, with my rapier's point.
40 AUMERLE   Thou dar'st not, coward, live to see that day.
FITZWALTER   Now by my soul, I would it were this hour.
AUMERLE   Fitzwalter, thou art damned to hell for this.
HARRY PERCY   Aumerle, thou liest. His honour is as true
In this appeal° as thou art all unjust;   *accusation*
45 And that thou art so, there I throw my gage
        [*He throws down his gage*]
To prove it on thee to the extremest point
Of mortal breathing. Seize it if thou dar'st.
AUMERLE   An if I do not, may my hands rot off,
And never brandish more° revengeful steel   *again*
50 Over the glittering helmet of my foe.⁶
50.1   ANOTHER LORD   *I task the earth to the like, forsworn Aumerle,*
            And spur thee on with full as many lies°   *accusations of lying*
            As may be hollowed° in thy treacherous ear   *shouted*
            From sun to sun.° There is my honour's pawn.   *sunrise to sunset*
50.5   *Engage it to⁷ the trial if thou darest.*
            [*He throws down his gage*]
         AUMERLE   *Who sets° me else? By heaven, I'll throw⁸ at all.*   *challenges (in gambling)*
            I have a thousand spirits in one breast
            To answer twenty thousand such as you.
SURREY   My lord Fitzwalter, I do remember well
The very time Aumerle and you did talk.
FITZWALTER   'Tis very true. You were in presence° then,   *were present*
And you can witness with me this is true.
55 SURREY   As false, by heaven, as heaven itself is true.
FITZWALTER   Surrey, thou liest.
SURREY   Dishonourable boy,
That lie shall lie so heavy on my sword
That it shall render vengeance and revenge,
Till thou, the lie-giver, and that lie do lie
60 In earth as quiet as thy father's skull;
In proof whereof, there is my honour's pawn.
        [*He throws down his gage*]
Engage it to the trial if thou dar'st.
FITZWALTER   How fondly dost thou spur a forward horse!
If I dare eat, or drink, or breathe, or live,
65 I dare meet Surrey in a wilderness
And spit upon him whilst I say he lies,
And lies, and lies.⁹ There is my bond of faith
To tie thee to my strong correction.
As I intend to thrive in this new world,
70 Aumerle is guilty of my true appeal.°   *accusation*
Besides, I heard the banished Norfolk° say   *(Mowbray)*
That thou, Aumerle, didst send two of thy men
To execute the noble Duke at Calais.
AUMERLE   Some honest Christian trust me with° a gage.   *lend me*
        [*He takes another's gage and throws it down*]

6. The following indented passage (lines 50.1–50.8)   8. Defeat (as by throwing dice).
appears only in Q1.   9. Fitzwalter may throw down another gage here.
7. Accept it as a pledge ("gage") for.

75 That Norfolk lies, here do I throw down this,
If he may be repealed,° to try his honour.   *recalled from exile*
BOLINGBROKE   These differences shall all rest under gage[1]
Till Norfolk be repealed. Repealed he shall be,
And, though mine enemy, restored again
80 To all his lands and signories.° When he is returned,   *estates*
Against Aumerle we will enforce his trial.
BISHOP OF CARLISLE   That honourable day shall never be seen.
Many a time hath banished Norfolk fought
For Jesu Christ in glorious Christian field,[2]
85 Streaming the ensign of the Christian cross
Against black pagans, Turks, and Saracens;
And, toiled° with works of war, retired himself   *exhausted*
To Italy, and there at Venice gave
His body to that pleasant country's earth,
90 And his pure soul unto his captain, Christ,
Under whose colours he had fought so long.
BOLINGBROKE   Why, Bishop of Carlisle, is Norfolk dead?
BISHOP OF CARLISLE   As surely as I live, my lord.
BOLINGBROKE   Sweet peace conduct his sweet soul to the bosom
95 Of good old Abraham![3] Lords appellants,
Your differences° shall all rest under gage   *disputes*
Till we assign you to your days of trial.
                    Enter [Duke of] YORK
YORK   Great Duke of Lancaster, I come to thee
From plume-plucked° Richard, who with willing soul   *humbled*
100 Adopts thee heir, and his high sceptre yields
To the possession of thy royal hand.
Ascend his throne, descending now from him,
And long live Henry, of that name the fourth!
BOLINGBROKE   In God's name I'll ascend the regal throne.
105 BISHOP OF CARLISLE   Marry, God forbid!
Worst° in this royal presence may I speak,   *Least worthy*
Yet best beseeming° me to speak the truth.   *fitting (as a clergyman)*
Would God that any in this noble presence
Were enough noble to be upright judge
110 Of noble Richard. Then true noblesse° would   *nobility*
Learn° him forbearance from so foul a wrong.   *Teach*
What subject can give sentence on his king?
And who sits here that is not Richard's subject?
Thieves are not judged but° they are by° to hear,   *except when / present*
115 Although apparent° guilt be seen in them;   *obvious*
And shall the figure° of God's majesty,   *image*
His captain, steward, deputy elect,°   *chosen*
Anointed, crownèd, planted many years,
Be judged by subject and inferior breath,
120 And he himself not present? O, forfend° it, God,   *prohibit*
That in a Christian climate souls refined[4]
Should show so heinous, black, obscene° a deed!   *odious*
I speak to subjects, and a subject speaks
Stirred up by God thus boldly for his king.

---

1. Shall remain as standing challenges.
2. In battle for the Christian cause.
3. *the bosom . . . Abraham:* that is, heavenly rest; see

Luke 16:22.

4. Spiritually improved; aristocratic.

125 My lord of Hereford here, whom you call king,
Is a foul traitor to proud Hereford's king;
And, if you crown him, let me prophesy
The blood of English shall manure the ground,
And future ages groan for this foul act.

130 Peace shall go sleep with Turks and infidels,
And in this seat° of peace tumultuous wars   region; throne
Shall kin with kin and kind with kind confound.[5]
Disorder, horror, fear, and mutiny
Shall here inhabit, and this land be called

135 The field of Golgotha[6] and dead men's skulls.
O, if you rear this house against this house°   (Lancaster against York)
It will the woefullest division prove
That ever fell upon this cursèd earth!
Prevent, resist it; let it not be so,

140 Lest child, child's children, cry against you woe.
NORTHUMBERLAND   Well have you argued, sir, and for your pains
Of capital treason we arrest you here.
My lord of Westminster, be it your charge
To keep him safely till his day of trial.[7]

145 May it please you, lords, to grant the Commons' suit?[8]
BOLINGBROKE   Fetch hither Richard, that in common° view   public
He may surrender.[9] So we shall proceed
Without suspicion.
YORK   I will be his conduct.°   escort
                                                        Exit
BOLINGBROKE   Lords, you that here are under our arrest,

150 Procure your sureties for your days of answer.[1]
Little are we beholden to your love,
And little looked for° at your helping hands.   expected
          Enter RICHARD and [Duke of] YORK [with attendants
          bearing the crown and sceptre]
RICHARD   Alack, why am I sent for to a king
Before I have shook off the regal thoughts

155 Wherewith I reigned? I hardly yet have learned
To insinuate, flatter, bow, and bend my knee.
Give sorrow leave awhile to tutor me
To this submission. Yet I well remember
The favours° of these men. Were they not mine?   faces; benefits

160 Did they not sometime cry 'All hail!' to me?
So Judas did to Christ. But He in twelve
Found truth in all but one; I, in twelve thousand, none.
God save the King! Will no man say 'Amen'?
Am I both priest and clerk?[2] Well then, Amen.

165 God save the King, although I be not he.
And yet Amen, if heaven do think him me.
To do what service am I sent for hither?
YORK   To do that office° of thine own good will   task; ceremony
Which tired majesty did make thee offer:

---

5. Shall destroy kinsman by fellow kinsman and coun-
tryman by fellow countryman.
6. Place of Christ's crucifixion, the name of which
means "place of dead men's skulls."
7. The passage that follows, to line 308, is not included
in the earliest texts. See Textual Note.
8. The House of Commons' request that Richard

should have judgment passed on him.
9. Abdicate (the legitimacy of the Commons' suit
depended on Richard's having given up the crown and
thus his royal immunity from prosecution).
1. Procure persons guaranteeing your appearance on
the day of trial.
2. Priest's assistant who utters the responses to prayers.

170 The resignation of thy state and crown
To Henry Bolingbroke.
RICHARD [*to an attendant*]   Give me the crown. [*To* BOLINGBROKE]
Here, cousin, seize the crown.
Here, cousin. On this side my hand, on that side thine.
Now is this golden crown like a deep well
175 That owes° two buckets filling one another,[3]   *has*
The emptier ever dancing in the air,
The other down, unseen, and full of water.
That bucket down and full of tears am I,
Drinking my griefs, whilst you mount up on high.
180 BOLINGBROKE   I thought you had been willing to resign.
RICHARD   My crown I am, but still my griefs are mine.
You may my glories and my state° depose,   *royal status*
But not my griefs; still° am I king of those.   *permanently*
BOLINGBROKE   Part of your cares you give me with your crown.
185 RICHARD   Your cares set up do not pluck my cares down.
My care is loss of care by old care done;
Your care is gain of care by new care won.[4]
The cares I give I have, though given away;
They 'tend° the crown, yet still with me they stay.   *attend; accompany*
190 BOLINGBROKE   Are you contented to resign the crown?
RICHARD   Ay, no; no, ay; for I must nothing be;[5]
Therefore no, no, for I resign to thee.
Now mark me how I will undo° myself.   *ruin; strip*
I give this heavy weight from off my head,
[BOLINGBROKE *accepts the crown*]
195 And this unwieldy sceptre from my hand,
[BOLINGBROKE *accepts the sceptre*]
The pride of kingly sway from out my heart.
With mine own tears I wash away my balm,
With mine own hands I give away my crown,
With mine own tongue deny my sacred state,°   *divine right to be King*
200 With mine own breath release all duteous oaths.°   *oaths of allegiance*
All pomp and majesty I do forswear.
My manors, rents, revenues I forgo.
My acts, decrees, and statutes I deny.°   *repudiate*
God pardon all oaths that are broke to me.
205 God keep all vows unbroke are made to thee.
Make me, that nothing have, with nothing grieved,[6]
And thou with all pleased, that hast all achieved.
Long mayst thou live in Richard's seat to sit,
And soon lie Richard in an earthy pit.
210 'God save King Henry,' unkinged Richard says,
'And send him many years of sunshine° days.'   *sunny*
What more remains?
NORTHUMBERLAND [*giving* RICHARD *papers*]
No more but that you read°   *read aloud*
These accusations and these grievous crimes
Committed by your person and your followers

3. That is, the raising of one causing the other to descend and fill.
4. *Your cares . . . won:* an extended wordplay on "care": Your assuming cares of state does not relieve me of grief. I mourn the loss of responsibility, by lack of dili- gence in the past; you concern yourself with gaining responsibility, won by effort.
5. Playing on "ay" (yes) and "I": since I am no thing, then "I," that is, "ay," is "no."
6. Grieved at nothing; grieved at having nothing.

215 Against the state and profit° of this land,   *established prosperity*
That by confessing them, the souls of men
May deem that you are worthily deposed.
RICHARD   Must I do so? And must I ravel out
My weaved-up follies? Gentle Northumberland,
220 If thy offences were upon record,
Would it not shame thee in so fair a troop°   *company*
To read a lecture° of them? If thou wouldst,   *give a public reading*
There shouldst thou find one heinous article
Containing the deposing of a king
225 And cracking the strong warrant of an oath,
Marked with a blot, damned in the book of heaven.
Nay, all of you that stand and look upon
Whilst that my wretchedness doth bait⁷ myself,
Though some of you, with Pilate, wash your hands,⁸
230 Showing an outward pity, yet you Pilates
Have here delivered me to my sour° cross,   *bitter*
And water cannot wash away your sin.
NORTHUMBERLAND   My lord, dispatch.° Read o'er these articles.   *hurry up*
RICHARD   Mine eyes are full of tears; I cannot see.
235 And yet salt water blinds them not so much
But they can see a sort° of traitors here.   *pack*
Nay, if I turn mine eyes upon myself
I find myself a traitor with the rest,
For I have given here my soul's consent
240 T'undeck the pompous° body of a king,   *splendidly dressed*
Made glory base and sovereignty a slave,
Proud majesty a subject, state° a peasant.   *royalty*
NORTHUMBERLAND   My lord—
RICHARD   No lord of thine, thou haught°-insulting man,   *haughty*
245 Nor no man's lord. I have no name, no title,
No, not that name was given me at the font,
But 'tis usurped. Alack the heavy day,
That I have worn so many winters out
And know not now what name to call myself!
250 O, that I were a mockery king of snow,
Standing before the sun of Bolingbroke
To melt myself away in water-drops!
Good king, great king—and yet not greatly good—
An if my word be sterling° yet in England,   *valid (like currency)*
255 Let it command a mirror hither straight,°   *immediately*
That it may show me what a face I have,
Since it is bankrupt of his° majesty.   *its*
BOLINGBROKE   Go some of you and fetch a looking-glass.
                   [*Exit one or more*]
NORTHUMBERLAND   Read o'er this paper while the glass° doth   *until the mirror*
     come.
260 RICHARD   Fiend, thou torment'st me ere I come to hell.
BOLINGBROKE   Urge it no more, my lord Northumberland.
NORTHUMBERLAND   The Commons will not then be satisfied.
RICHARD   They shall be satisfied. I'll read enough
     When I do see the very book indeed

---

7. Torment (as in bearbaiting).
8. Pilate, Jesus' judge, washed his hands to signify his

disclaiming of responsibility for the death sentence he
imposed at the request of the Jews.

265 Where all my sins are writ, and that's myself.
    Enter one with a glass
    Give me that glass, and therein will I read.
        [RICHARD *takes the glass and looks in it*]
    No deeper wrinkles yet? Hath sorrow struck
    So many blows upon this face of mine
    And made no deeper wounds? O flatt'ring glass,
270 Like to my followers in prosperity,
    Thou dost beguile me! Was this face the face
    That every day under his household roof
    Did keep ten thousand men? Was this the face
    That like the sun did make beholders wink?°   shut their eyes
275 Is this the face which faced⁹ so many follies,
    That was at last outfaced° by Bolingbroke?   stared down
    A brittle glory shineth in this face.
    As brittle as the glory is the face,
        [*He shatters the glass*]
    For there it is, cracked in an hundred shivers.
280 Mark, silent King, the moral of this sport:
    How soon my sorrow hath destroyed my face.
    BOLINGBROKE   The shadow¹ of your sorrow hath destroyed
    The shadow° of your face.   image
    RICHARD   Say that again:
    'The shadow of my sorrow'—ha, let's see.
285 'Tis very true: my grief lies all within,
    And these external manner of laments
    Are merely shadows to the unseen grief
    That swells with silence in the tortured soul.
    There lies the substance, and I thank thee, King,
290 For thy great bounty that not only giv'st
    Me cause to wail, but teachest me the way
    How to lament the cause. I'll beg one boon,°   favor
    And then be gone and trouble you no more.
    Shall I obtain it?
    BOLINGBROKE   Name it, fair cousin.
295 RICHARD   Fair cousin? I am greater than a king;
    For when I was a king my flatterers
    Were then but subjects; being now a subject,
    I have a king here to my flatterer.
    Being so great, I have no need to beg.
300 BOLINGBROKE   Yet ask.
    RICHARD   And shall I have?
    BOLINGBROKE   You shall.
    RICHARD   Then give me leave to go.
    BOLINGBROKE   Whither?
305 RICHARD   Whither you will, so° I were from your sights.   provided that
    BOLINGBROKE   Go some of you, convey° him to the Tower.   conduct
    RICHARD   O good, 'convey'!° Conveyors are you all,   steal
    That rise thus nimbly by a true king's fall.
                                        [*Exit, guarded*]
    BOLINGBROKE   On Wednesday next we solemnly set down

9. Countenanced; adorned (as a garment trimmed with "facings").
1. Darkness; outward display; image, reflection; un-
happiness (Richard plays on the word's various meanings in the following passage).

310   Our coronation. Lords, prepare yourselves.

Exeunt. Manent [ABBOT OF] WESTMINSTER,

[BISHOP OF] CARLISLE, [*and*] AUMERLE

ABBOT OF WESTMINSTER   A woeful pageant have we here beheld.

BISHOP OF CARLISLE   The woe's to come, the children yet unborn

    Shall feel this day as sharp to them as thorn.

AUMERLE   You holy clergymen, is there no plot

315   To rid the realm of this pernicious blot?

ABBOT OF WESTMINSTER   My lord, before I freely speak my

    mind herein,

    You shall not only take the sacrament[2]

    To bury mine intents,[3] but also to effect

    Whatever I shall happen to devise.

320   I see your brows are full of discontent,

    Your hearts of sorrow, and your eyes of tears.

    Come home with me to supper. I will lay

    A plot shall show us all a merry day.   *Exeunt*

5.1

Enter the QUEEN *with her* LADIES

QUEEN   This way the King will come. This is the way

    To Julius Caesar's ill-erected Tower,[1]

    To whose flint bosom my condemnèd lord

    Is doomed a prisoner by proud Bolingbroke.

5   Here let us rest, if this rebellious earth

    Have any resting for her true king's queen.

Enter RICHARD, *and guard*

    But soft,° but see—or rather do not see—   *wait*

    My fair rose wither. Yet look up, behold,

    That you in pity may dissolve to dew,

10   And wash him fresh again with true-love tears.—

    Ah, thou the model where old Troy did stand![2]

    Thou map° of honour, thou King Richard's tomb,   *epitome*

    And not King Richard! Thou most beauteous inn:

    Why should hard-favoured° grief be lodged in thee,   *ugly; unfortunate*

15   When triumph is become an alehouse[3] guest?

RICHARD   Join not with grief, fair woman, do not so,

    To make my end too sudden. Learn, good soul,

    To think our former state a happy dream,

    From which awaked, the truth of what we are

20   Shows us but this. I am sworn brother, sweet,

    To grim necessity, and he and I

    Will keep a league till death. Hie° thee to France,   *Hasten*

    And cloister thee in some religious house.°   *convent*

    Our holy lives must win a new world's° crown,   *(heaven's)*

25   Which our profane hours here have stricken down.

QUEEN   What, is my Richard both in shape and mind

    Transformed and weakenèd? Hath Bolingbroke

    Deposed thine intellect? Hath he been in thy heart?

    The lion dying thrusteth forth his paw

---

2. A solemn oath, accompanied by the rite of Communion.
3. To keep my intentions secret.
5.1 Location: A street near the Tower of London.
1. The Tower of London (popularly thought to have

been built by Caesar). *ill-erected:* poorly built; erected for evil ends.
2. The pattern of fallen greatness, like Troy.
3. Poorer class of lodging (referring to Bolingbroke) than an "inn."

30 And wounds the earth, if nothing else, with rage
To be° o'erpowered; and wilt thou, pupil-like,   *At being*
Take the correction, mildly kiss the rod,
And fawn on rage with base humility,
Which art a lion and the king of beasts?

35 RICHARD   A king of beasts[4] indeed! If aught but beasts,
I had been still a happy king of men.
Good sometimes° Queen, prepare thee hence for France.   *former*
Think I am dead, and that even here thou tak'st,
As from my death-bed, thy last living leave.

40 In winter's tedious nights, sit by the fire
With good old folks, and let them tell thee tales
Of woeful ages long ago betid;[5]
And ere thou bid goodnight, to quit their griefs°   *repay their sad tales*
Tell thou the lamentable fall of me,

45 And send the hearers weeping to their beds;
Forwhy the senseless brands will sympathize[6]
The heavy accent of thy moving[7] tongue,
And in compassion weep the fire out;
And some° will mourn in ashes, some coal black,   *(firebrands)*

50 For the deposing of a rightful king.
        Enter [Earl of] NORTHUMBERLAND

NORTHUMBERLAND   My lord, the mind of Bolingbroke is changed.
You must to Pomfret,° not unto the Tower.   *castle in Yorkshire*
And, madam, there is order ta'en[8] for you.
With all swift speed you must away to France.

55 RICHARD   Northumberland, thou ladder wherewithal
The mounting Bolingbroke ascends my throne,
The time shall not be many hours of age
More than it is ere foul sin, gathering head,
Shall break into corruption.[9] Thou shalt think,

60 Though he divide the realm and give thee half,
It is too little helping[1] him to all.
He shall think that thou, which know'st the way
To plant unrightful kings, wilt know again,
Being ne'er so little urged another way,

65 To pluck him headlong from the usurpèd throne.
The love of wicked friends converts to fear,
That fear to hate, and hate turns one or both
To worthy° danger and deservèd death.   *severe*

NORTHUMBERLAND   My guilt be on my head, and there an end.[2]

70 Take leave and part,° for you must part° forthwith.   *separate / depart*

RICHARD   Doubly divorced! Bad men, you violate
A twofold marriage: 'twixt my crown and me,
And then betwixt me and my married wife.
[*To the* QUEEN] Let me unkiss the oath 'twixt thee and me—

75 And yet not so, for with a kiss 'twas made.
Part us, Northumberland: I towards the north,
Where shivering cold and sickness pines the clime;°   *afflicts the region*

---

4. Lion (Richard's emblem); ruler of beastly men.
5. Woe that happened long ago.
6. Because even the insentient firewood will respond
empathetically.
7. Physically and emotionally.
8. Arrangements have been made.
9. Pus (the image is of a swelling abscess). *Henry IV,*

Parts 1 and 2, the sequels to *Richard II,* dramatize
Northumberland's rebellion against "the mounting Bo-
lingbroke."
1. *helping:* since you helped.
2. Recalling the cry of the Jews at Jesus' trial: "His
death be upon our heads, and the heads of our chil-
dren."

My queen to France, from whence set forth in pomp
She came adornèd hither like sweet May,
80   Sent back like Hallowmas° or short'st of day.[3]   *November 1*
QUEEN   And must we be divided? Must we part?
RICHARD   Ay, hand from hand, my love, and heart from heart.
QUEEN   Banish us both, and send the King with me.
NORTHUMBERLAND   That were some love, but little policy.°   *but politically naive*
85 QUEEN   Then whither he goes, thither let me go.
RICHARD   So two together weeping make one woe.
    Weep thou for me in France, I for thee here.
    Better far off than, near, be ne'er the nea'er.[4]
    Go count thy way with sighs, I mine with groans.
90 QUEEN   So longest way shall have the longest moans.
RICHARD   Twice for one step I'll groan, the way being short,
    And piece the way out° with a heavy heart.   *lengthen the way*
    Come, come, in wooing sorrow let's be brief,
    Since, wedding it, there is such length in grief.
95   One kiss shall stop our mouths, and dumbly° part.   *silently*
    Thus give I mine, and thus take I thy heart.
        [They kiss]
QUEEN   Give me mine own again. 'Twere no good part[5]
    To take on me to keep and kill thy heart.
        [They kiss]
    So now I have mine own again, be gone,
100   That I may strive to kill it with a groan.
RICHARD   We make woe wanton[6] with this fond delay.
    Once more, adieu. The rest let sorrow say.
       Exeunt [RICHARD, *guarded, and* NORTHUMBERLAND *at*
       one door, the QUEEN *and her* LADIES *at another door*]

5.2

    Enter DUKE *and* DUCHESS OF YORK
DUCHESS OF YORK   My lord, you told me you would tell the rest,
    When weeping made you break the story off,
    Of our two cousins'° coming into London.   *kinsmen's*
YORK   Where did I leave?
DUCHESS OF YORK   At that sad stop, my lord,
5   Where rude misgoverned° hands from windows' tops°   *unruly / upper windows*
    Threw dust and rubbish on King Richard's head.
YORK   Then, as I said, the Duke, great Bolingbroke,
    Mounted upon a hot and fiery steed,
    Which his aspiring rider[1] seemed to know,
10   With slow but stately pace kept on his course,
    Whilst all tongues cried 'God save thee, Bolingbroke!'
    You would have thought the very windows spake,
    So many greedy looks of young and old
    Through casements darted their desiring eyes
15   Upon his visage, and that all the walls
    With painted imagery[2] had said at once,
    'Jesu preserve thee! Welcome, Bolingbroke!'

---

3. Winter solstice.
4. Better to be far away than to be near but never
nearer to our happiness.
5. It would not be good of me.
6. We make our woe unrestrained; we make a sport of

our grief.
5.2 Location: The Duke of York's house.
1. Object of "seemed to know."
2. Painted cloths that were hung on walls in pageants;
figures in these sometimes had "speech bubbles."

Whilst he, from the one side to the other turning,
Bare-headed, lower than his proud steed's neck,
20　Bespake° them thus: 'I thank you, countrymen', *Addressed*
And thus still doing, thus he passed along.
DUCHESS OF YORK　Alack, poor Richard! Where rode he the whilst?
YORK　As in a theatre the eyes of men,
After a well-graced actor leaves the stage,
25　Are idly bent on him that enters next,
Thinking his prattle to be tedious,
Even so, or with much more contempt, men's eyes
Did scowl on gentle Richard. No man cried 'God save him!'
No joyful tongue gave him his welcome home;
30　But dust was thrown upon his sacred head,
Which with such gentle sorrow he shook off,
His face still combating° with tears and smiles, *continually struggling*
The badges° of his grief and patience, *emblems*
That had not God for some strong purpose steeled
35　The hearts of men, they must perforce have melted,
And barbarism itself have pitied him.
But heaven hath a hand in these events,
To whose high will we bound our calm contents.[3]
To Bolingbroke are we sworn subjects now,
40　Whose state and honour I for aye allow.° *forever acknowledge*
　　　Enter [Duke of] AUMERLE
DUCHESS OF YORK　Here comes my son Aumerle.
YORK　　　　　　　　　　　　　　Aumerle that was;[4]
But that is lost for being Richard's friend,
And, madam, you must call him 'Rutland' now.
I am in Parliament pledge for his truth° *guarantor of his loyalty*
45　And lasting fealty° to the new-made King. *fidelity*
DUCHESS OF YORK　Welcome, my son. Who are the violets now
That strew the green lap of the new-come spring?
AUMERLE　Madam, I know not, nor I greatly care not.
God knows I had as lief° be none as one. *had rather*
50　YORK　Well, bear you well in this new spring of time,
Lest you be cropped° before you come to prime. *cut*
What news from Oxford? Hold these jousts and triumphs?° *processions*
AUMERLE　For aught I know, my lord, they do.
YORK　You will be there, I know.
55　AUMERLE　If God prevent it not, I purpose so.
YORK　What seal is that that hangs without thy bosom?[5]
Yea, look'st thou pale? Let me see the writing.
AUMERLE　My lord, 'tis nothing.
YORK　　　　　　　　　No matter, then, who see it.
I will be satisfied. Let me see the writing.
60　AUMERLE　I do beseech your grace to pardon me.
It is a matter of small consequence,
Which for some reasons I would not have seen.
YORK　Which for some reasons, sir, I mean to see.
I fear, I fear!
DUCHESS OF YORK　What should you fear?

---

3. Bound ourselves to be calmly contented.
4. Aumerle has been deprived of his dukedom; he remains Earl of Rutland.

5. The document is in Aumerle's doublet, with the seal on a visibly dangling slip of attached paper.

65 'Tis nothing but some bond that he is entered into
For gay apparel 'gainst° the triumph day.   *in time for*
YORK   Bound to himself?[6] What doth he with a bond
That he is bound to? Wife, thou art a fool.
Boy, let me see the writing.
70 AUMERLE   I do beseech you, pardon me. I may not show it.
YORK   I will be satisfied. Let me see it, I say.
            He plucks it out of [Aumerle's] bosom, and reads it
Treason, foul treason! Villain, traitor, slave!
DUCHESS OF YORK   What is the matter, my lord?
YORK   Ho, who is within there? Saddle my horse.—
75 God for his mercy, what treachery is here!
DUCHESS OF YORK   Why, what is it, my lord?
YORK   Give me my boots, I say. Saddle my horse.—
Now by mine honour, by my life, my troth,
I will appeach° the villain.   *accuse*
80 DUCHESS OF YORK   What is the matter?
YORK   Peace, foolish woman.
DUCHESS OF YORK   I will not peace. What is the matter, son?
AUMERLE   Good mother, be content. It is no more
Than my poor life must answer.
DUCHESS OF YORK   Thy life answer?
85 YORK   Bring me my boots. I will unto the King.
            His man enters with his boots
DUCHESS OF YORK   Strike him,° Aumerle! Poor boy, thou art   *(the servant)*
      amazed.°   *distraught*
[*To York's man*]   Hence, villain! Never more come in my sight.
YORK   Give me my boots, I say.
DUCHESS OF YORK   Why, York, what wilt thou do?
Wilt thou not hide the trespass of thine own?
90 Have we more sons?[7] Or are we like to have?
Is not my teeming date° drunk up with time?   *my period of childbearing*
And wilt thou pluck my fair son from mine age,
And rob me of a happy mother's name?
Is he not like thee? Is he not thine own?
95 YORK   Thou fond,° mad woman,   *foolish*
Wilt thou conceal this dark conspiracy?
A dozen of them here have ta'en the sacrament,
And interchangeably set down their hands[8]
To kill the King at Oxford.
DUCHESS OF YORK   He shall be none.°   *not be one of them*
100 We'll keep him here, then what is that to him?
YORK   Away, fond woman! Were he twenty times my son
I would appeach him.
DUCHESS OF YORK   Hadst thou groaned° for him   *suffered labor pains*
As I have done thou wouldst be more pitiful.
But now I know thy mind: thou dost suspect
105 That I have been disloyal to thy bed,
And that he is a bastard, not thy son.
Sweet York, sweet husband, be not of that mind.
He is as like thee as a man may be,

---

6. If Aumerle had signed a bond to borrow money, the
creditor would have the bond.
7. Actually, Aumerle had a brother and a sister, and the

Duchess of York, the Duke's second wife, was Aumerle's
stepmother.
8. And mutually committed themselves in writing.

Not like to me or any of my kin,
And yet I love him.

110 YORK   Make way, unruly woman.

Exit [with his man]

DUCHESS OF YORK After, Aumerle! Mount thee upon his horse.
Spur, post,° and get before him to the King,   *Ride fast*
And beg thy pardon ere he do accuse thee.
I'll not be long behind—though I be old,
115 I doubt not but to ride as fast as York—
And never will I rise up from the ground
Till Bolingbroke have pardóned thee. Away, be gone!

Exeunt [severally]

5.3

Enter BOLINGBROKE, [*crowned* KING HENRY,] *with*
[HARRY] PERCY, *and other nobles*

KING HENRY Can no man tell of my unthrifty son?[1]
'Tis full three months since I did see him last.
If any plague hang over us, 'tis he.
I would to God, my lords, he might be found.
5 Enquire at London 'mongst the taverns there,
For there, they say, he daily doth frequent
With unrestrainèd loose companions—
Even such, they say, as stand in narrow lanes
And beat our watch° and rob our passengers°—   *watchmen / wayfarers*
10 Which he, young wanton and effeminate° boy,   *pleasure-seeking*
Takes on° the point of honour to support   *Makes it*
So dissolute a crew.

HARRY PERCY My lord, some two days since,° I saw the Prince,   *ago*
And told him of these triumphs held at Oxford.

15 KING HENRY And what said the gallant?

HARRY PERCY His answer was he would unto the stews,°   *brothels*
And from the common'st creature pluck a glove,
And wear it as a favour,[2] and with that
He would unhorse the lustiest° challenger.   *most vigorous*

20 KING HENRY As dissolute as desperate.° Yet through both   *reckless*
I see some sparks of better hope, which elder days
May happily[3] bring forth.

Enter [Duke of] AUMERLE, *amazed*

But who comes here?

AUMERLE Where is the King?

KING HENRY What means our cousin that he stares and looks so wildly?

25 AUMERLE [*kneeling*] God save your grace! I do beseech your majesty
To have some conference with your grace alone.

KING HENRY [*to lords*] Withdraw yourselves, and leave us here alone.

[*Exeunt all but* KING HENRY *and* AUMERLE]

What is the matter with our cousin now?

AUMERLE For ever may my knees grow° to the earth,   *be fixed*
30 My tongue cleave to the roof within my mouth,
Unless a pardon ere I rise or speak.

KING HENRY Intended or committed was this fault?

5.3 Location: Windsor Castle.
1. Henry's oldest son is Prince Hal of *1* and *2 Henry IV*,
later King Henry V. *unthrifty*: dissolute.

2. Lady's gift to a knight that is worn in combat.
3. Perhaps; with good fortune.

If on the first,° how heinous e'er it be,   *If only intended*
To win thy after-love I pardon thee.

35 AUMERLE[*rising*]   Then give me leave that I may turn the key,
That no man enter till my tale be done.

KING HENRY   Have thy desire.
[AUMERLE *locks the door.*]
The Duke of YORK *knocks at the door and crieth*

YORK [*within*]   My liege, beware! Look to thyself!
Thou hast a traitor in thy presence there.
[KING HENRY *draws his sword*]

KING HENRY [*to* AUMERLE]   Villain, I'll make thee safe.°   *harmless*

40 AUMERLE   Stay° thy revengeful hand! Thou hast no cause to fear.   *Restrain*

YORK [*knocking within*]   Open the door, secure° foolhardy King!   *overconfident*
Shall I for° love speak treason⁴ to thy face?   *out of*
Open the door, or I will break it open.
[KING HENRY *opens the door.*] *Enter* [*Duke of*] YORK

KING HENRY   What is the matter, uncle? Speak,
45 Recover breath, tell us how near is danger,
That we may arm us to encounter it.

YORK   Peruse this writing here, and thou shalt know
The treason that my haste⁵ forbids me show.°   *explain*
[*He gives* KING HENRY *the paper*]

AUMERLE   Remember, as thou read'st, thy promise past.
50 I do repent me. Read not my name there.
My heart is not confederate with my hand.°   *signature*

YORK   It was, villain, ere thy hand did set it down.
I tore it° from the traitor's bosom, King.   *(the bond)*
Fear, and not love, begets his penitence.
55 Forget to pity him, lest pity prove
A serpent that will sting thee to the heart.

KING HENRY   O, heinous, strong, and bold conspiracy!
O loyal father of a treacherous son!
Thou sheer,° immaculate, and silver fountain,   *clear*
60 From whence this stream through muddy passages
Hath held his current and defiled himself,
Thy overflow of good converts to bad,
And thy abundant goodness shall excuse
This deadly° blot in thy digressing⁶ son.   *damnable; death-dealing*

65 YORK   So shall my virtue be his vice's bawd,
And he shall spend mine honour with his shame,
As thriftless sons their scraping fathers' gold.
Mine honour lives when his dishonour dies,
Or my shamed life in his dishonour lies.
70 Thou kill'st me in his life: giving him breath
The traitor lives, the true man's put to death.

DUCHESS OF YORK [*within*]   What ho, my liege, for God's sake let me in!

KING HENRY   What shrill-voiced suppliant makes this eager cry?

DUCHESS OF YORK [*within*]   A woman, and thy aunt, great King; 'tis I.
75 Speak with me, pity me! Open the door!
A beggar begs that never begged before.

KING HENRY   Our scene is altered from a serious thing,
And now changed to 'The Beggar and the King'.°   *(the name of a ballad)*

---

4. Disrespectfully criticize (as "secure" and "foolhardy").   6. Diverging from course (as of a stream); transgressing.
5. York is out of breath.

My dangerous cousin, let your mother in.
80 I know she is come to pray for your foul sin.
   [AUMERLE *opens the door.*] *Enter* DUCHESS [OF YORK]
YORK If thou do pardon, whosoever pray,
  More sins for this forgiveness prosper may.
  This festered joint° cut off, the rest rest sound.   *infected limb*
  This let alone will all the rest confound.°   *destroy*
 DUCHESS OF YORK [*kneeling*] O King, believe not this
85   hard-hearted man.
  Love loving not itself, none other can.[7]
 YORK Thou frantic woman, what dost thou make° here?   *do*
  Shall thy old dugs° once more a traitor rear?   *breasts*
 DUCHESS OF YORK Sweet York, be patient.—Hear me, gentle liege.
 KING HENRY Rise up, good aunt.
90 DUCHESS OF YORK   Not yet, I thee beseech.
  Forever will I kneel upon my knees,
  And never see day that the happy sees,
  Till thou give joy, until thou bid me joy
  By pardoning Rutland, my transgressing boy.
95 AUMERLE [*kneeling*] Unto° my mother's prayers I bend my knee. *In support of*
 YORK [*kneeling*] Against them both my true joints bended be.
  Ill mayst thou thrive if thou grant any grace.
 DUCHESS OF YORK Pleads he in earnest? Look upon his face.
  His eyes do drop no tears, his prayers are in jest.
100   His words come from his mouth; ours from our breast.
  He prays but faintly, and would be denied;
  We pray with heart and soul, and all beside.
  His weary joints would gladly rise, I know;
  Our knees shall kneel till to the ground they grow.
105   His prayers are full of false hypocrisy;
  Ours of true zeal and deep integrity.
  Our prayers do outpray his; then let them have
  That mercy which true prayer ought to have.
 KING HENRY Good aunt, stand up.
 DUCHESS OF YORK   Nay, do not say 'Stand up'.
110 Say 'Pardon' first, and afterwards 'Stand up'.
  An if° I were thy nurse, thy tongue to teach,   *An if = If*
  'Pardon' should be the first word of thy speech.
  I never longed to hear a word till now.
  Say 'Pardon', King. Let pity teach thee how.
115 The word is short, but not so short as sweet;
  No word like 'Pardon' for kings' mouths so meet.°   *fit*
 YORK Speak it in French, King: say 'Pardonnez-moi'.[8]
 DUCHESS OF YORK Dost thou teach pardon pardon to destroy?[9]
  Ah, my sour° husband, my hard-hearted lord   *harsh*
120 That sets the word itself against the word!
  Speak 'Pardon' as 'tis current in our land;
  The chopping[1] French we do not understand.
  Thine eye begins to speak; set thy tongue there;
  Or in thy piteous heart plant thou thine ear,
125 That hearing how our plaints and prayers do pierce,

---

7. If one does not love one's own flesh and blood, one can love no one else (not even the King).
8. "Excuse me," a polite refusal.
9. Rhymes with "moi" in anglicized pronunciation.
1. Logic-chopping, changing the meaning.

Pity may move thee 'Pardon' to rehearse.°   *recite*
KING HENRY   Good aunt, stand up.
DUCHESS OF YORK   I do not sue to stand.
　　Pardon is all the suit I have in hand.
KING HENRY   I pardon him as God shall pardon me.
　　　　[YORK *and* AUMERLE *rise*]
130   DUCHESS OF YORK   O, happy vantage° of a kneeling knee!   *gain; position*
　　Yet am I sick for fear. Speak it again.
　　Twice saying pardon doth not pardon twain,°   *divide*
　　But makes one pardon strong.
KING HENRY   I pardon him
　　With all my heart.
DUCHESS OF YORK [*rising*]   A god on earth thou art.
135   KING HENRY   But for our trusty brother-in-law[2] and the Abbot,
　　With all the rest of that consorted° crew,   *confederated*
　　Destruction straight shall dog them at the heels.
　　Good uncle, help to order several powers°   *forces*
　　To Oxford, or where'er these traitors are.
140   They shall not live within this world, I swear,
　　But I will have them if I once know where.
　　Uncle, farewell; and cousin, so adieu.
　　Your mother well hath prayed; and prove you true.°   *loyal*
DUCHESS OF YORK   Come, my old[3] son. I pray God make thee new.
　　　　　　Exeunt [KING HENRY *at one door*; YORK,
　　　　　　　　　　DUCHESS OF YORK, *and* AUMERLE
　　　　　　　　　　　　at another door]

5.4

Enter Sir Piers EXTON, *and* [MEN]
EXTON   Didst thou not mark the King, what words he spake?
　　'Have I no friend will rid me of this living fear?'
　　Was it not so?
FIRST MAN   Those were his very words.
EXTON   'Have I no friend?' quoth he. He spake it twice,
5   And urged it twice together, did he not?
SECOND MAN   He did.
EXTON   And speaking it, he wishtly° looked on me,   *intently*
　　As who° should say 'I would thou wert the man   *As if he*
　　That would divorce this terror from my heart',
10   Meaning the King at Pomfret. Come, let's go.
　　I am the King's friend, and will rid° his foe.   *Exeunt*   *will get rid of*

5.5

Enter RICHARD, *alone*
RICHARD   I have been studying how I may compare
　　This prison where I live unto the world;
　　And for because the world is populous,
　　And here is not a creature but myself,
5   I cannot do it. Yet I'll hammer° it out.   *work*
　　My brain I'll prove the female° to my soul,   *(that is, receptive)*
　　My soul the father, and these two beget

2. The Duke of Exeter and Earl of Huntingdon, husband of Bolingbroke's sister; like Aumerle, he had been deprived of his dukedom.
3. Unregenerate (recalling the baptism service: "O

merciful God, grant that the old Adam in this child may be so buried that the new man may be raised up in him").
5.4 Location: Windsor Castle.
5.5 Location: Pomfret Castle.

A generation of still-breeding° thoughts;   *ever-breeding*
And these same thoughts people this little world
10   In humours[1] like the people of this world.°   *(the real world)*
For no thought is contented. The better sort,
As thoughts of things divine, are intermixed
With scruples,° and do set the faith itself   *doubts*
Against the faith,[2] as thus: 'Come, little ones',[3]
15   And then again,
'It is as hard to come as for a camel
To thread the postern of a small needle's eye.'[4]
Thoughts° tending to ambition, they do plot   *Other thoughts*
Unlikely wonders:° how these vain weak nails   *miracles*
20   May tear a passage through the flinty ribs
Of this hard world, my ragged° prison walls;   *rugged*
And for they cannot, die in their own pride.°   *prime of life; arrogance*
Thoughts tending to content° flatter themselves   *contentment*
That they are not the first of fortune's slaves,
25   Nor shall not be the last—like seely° beggars,   *simpleminded*
Who, sitting in the stocks, refuge[5] their shame
That many have, and others must, set there;
And in this thought they find a kind of ease,
Bearing their own misfortunes on the back
30   Of such as have before endured the like.
Thus play I in one person many people,
And none contented. Sometimes am I king;
Then treason makes me wish myself a beggar,
And so I am. Then crushing penury
35   Persuades me I was better when a king.
Then am I kinged again, and by and by
Think that I am unkinged by Bolingbroke,
And straight° am nothing. But whate'er I be,   *at once*
Nor I, nor any man that but° man is,   *merely*
40   With nothing shall be pleased till he be eased
With being nothing.
         The music plays
                    Music do I hear.
Ha; ha; keep time! How sour sweet music is
When time is broke and no proportion kept.
So is it in the music of men's lives.
45   And here have I the daintiness of ear
To check° time broke in a disordered string;°   *rebuke / string instrument*
But for the concord° of my state and time   *harmony*
Had not an ear to hear my true time broke.
I wasted time, and now doth time waste me,
50   For now hath time made me his numb'ring clock.[6]
My thoughts are minutes, and with sighs they jar
Their watches° on unto mine eyes, the outward watch[7]   *periods of vigil*
Whereto my finger, like a dial's point,°   *clock's hand*

---

1. Temperaments; caprices.
2. *the faith . . . faith*: scriptural passage against scriptural passage.
3. From Matthew 19:14, Mark 10:14, and Luke 18:25, implying the ease of obtaining salvation.
4. Adapting Matthew 19:24, Mark 10:25, or Luke

18:25, which describe the unlikeliness of the rich reaching heaven.
5. Find refuge for; rationalize.
6. Clock that counts hours and minutes, not an hourglass.
7. Clockface; mind's external watcher.

Is pointing still° in cleansing them from tears.[8]   *always*
55 Now, sir, the sounds that tell what hour it is
Are clamorous groans that strike upon my heart,
Which is the bell. So sighs, and tears, and groans
Show minutes, hours, and times. But my time
Runs posting° on in Bolingbroke's proud joy,   *speeding*
60 While I stand fooling here, his jack of the clock.[9]
This music mads° me. Let it sound no more,   *maddens*
For though it have holp° madmen to their wits,   *helped*
In me it seems it will make wise men mad.
          [*The music ceases*]
Yet blessing on his heart that gives it me,
65 For 'tis a sign of love, and love to Richard
Is a strange brooch° in this all-hating world.   *rare ornament*
          Enter a GROOM *of the stable*
GROOM   Hail, royal Prince!
RICHARD   Thanks, noble peer.
The cheapest of us is ten groats too dear.[1]
What art thou, and how com'st thou hither,
70 Where no man never comes but that sad dog
That brings me food to make misfortune live?
GROOM   I was a poor groom of thy stable, King,
When thou wert king; who, travelling towards York,
With much ado at length have gotten leave
75 To look upon my sometimes° royal master's face.   *former*
O, how it erned° my heart when I beheld   *grieved*
In London streets, that coronation day,
When Bolingbroke rode on roan Barbary,
That horse that thou so often hast bestrid,
80 That horse that I so carefully have dressed!°   *groomed*
RICHARD   Rode he on Barbary? Tell me, gentle friend,
How went he under him?
GROOM   So proudly as if he disdained the ground.
RICHARD   So proud that Bolingbroke was on his back.
85 That jade° hath eat bread from my royal hand;   *nag*
This hand hath made him proud with clapping° him.   *patting*
Would he not stumble, would he not fall down—
Since pride must have a fall—and break the neck
Of that proud man that did usurp his back?
90 Forgiveness, horse! Why do I rail on thee,
Since thou, created to be awed by man,
Wast born to bear? I was not made a horse,
And yet I bear a burden like an ass,
Spur-galled[2] and tired by jauncing° Bolingbroke.   *rough-riding*
          Enter KEEPER *to* RICHARD, *with meat*
95 KEEPER [*to* GROOM]   Fellow, give place.° Here is no longer stay.   *leave*
RICHARD [*to* GROOM]   If thou love me, 'tis time thou wert away.
GROOM   What my tongue dares not, that my heart shall say.
                                        Exit
KEEPER   My lord, will't please you to fall to?

---

8. Wiping tears from my eyes.
9. Manikin that strikes the clock's bell.
1. You have overpriced the cheaper of us (me, a prisoner) in calling me "royal." The difference between the coins "royal" (10 shillings) and "noble" (6 shillings 8 pence) is "ten groats" (40 pence). In other words, we are equal in worth.
2. Made sore by spurring.

RICHARD   Taste of it first,³ as thou art wont to do.

100 KEEPER   My lord, I dare not. Sir Piers of Exton,
    Who lately came from the King, commands the contrary.

RICHARD [*striking the* KEEPER]   The devil take Henry of Lancaster and thee!
    Patience is stale, and I am weary of it.

KEEPER   Help, help, help!

    EXTON *and his* [*men*] *rush in*

105 RICHARD   How now! What means death in this rude assault?
    [*He seizes a weapon from a man, and kills him*]
    Villain, thy own hand yields thy death's instrument.
    [*He kills another*]
    Go thou, and fill another room in hell.
    Here EXTON *strikes him down*

RICHARD   That hand shall burn in never-quenching fire
    That staggers thus my person.° Exton, thy fierce hand   *thus makes me stagger*
110   Hath with the King's blood stained the King's own land.
    Mount, mount, my soul; thy seat° is up on high,   *residence*
    Whilst my gross flesh sinks downward, here to die. [*He dies*]

EXTON   As full of valour as of royal blood.
    Both have I spilt. O, would the deed were good!
115   For now the devil that told me I did well
    Says that this deed is chronicled in hell.
    This dead King to the living King I'll bear.
    Take hence the rest, and give them burial here.
    Exeunt [EXTON *with Richard's body at one door, and*
    his men with the other bodies at another door]

5.6

Flourish. Enter [KING HENRY] *with* [*Duke of*] YORK, *with*
other lords and attendants

KING HENRY   Kind uncle York, the latest news we hear
    Is that the rebels have consumed with fire
    Our town of Ci'cester° in Gloucestershire;   *Cirencester*
    But whether they be ta'en or slain we hear not.

    Enter [*Earl of*] NORTHUMBERLAND

5   Welcome, my lord. What is the news?

NORTHUMBERLAND   First, to thy sacred state wish I all happiness.
    The next news is, I have to London sent
    The heads of Salisbury, Spencer, Blunt, and Kent.
    The manner of their taking may appear
10   At large discoursèd° in this paper here.   *Narrated in full*
    [*He gives the paper to* KING HENRY]

KING HENRY   We thank thee, gentle Percy, for thy pains,
    And to thy worth will add right worthy° gains.   *valuable; well-deserved*

    Enter Lord FITZWALTER

FITZWALTER   My lord, I have from Oxford sent to London
    The heads of Brocas and Sir Bennet Seely,
15   Two of the dangerous consorted° traitors   *confederated*
    That sought at Oxford thy dire overthrow.

KING HENRY   Thy pains, Fitzwalter, shall not be forgot.
    Right noble is thy merit, well I wot.°   *know*

    Enter HARRY PERCY [*with the* BISHOP OF] CARLISLE
    [*guarded*]

---

3. To make sure it is not poisoned.   **5.6** Location: Windsor Castle.

HARRY PERCY   The grand conspirator Abbot of Westminster,
20   With clog° of conscience and sour melancholy,   *burden*
Hath yielded up his body to the grave.
But here is Carlisle living, to abide
Thy kingly doom° and sentence of his pride.   *judgment*
KING HENRY   Carlisle, this is your doom.
25   Choose out some secret place, some reverent room
More than thou hast,¹ and with it joy° thy life.   *enjoy*
So as thou liv'st in peace, die free from strife.
For though mine enemy thou hast ever been,
High sparks of honour in thee have I seen.
        Enter EXTON *with [his men bearing] a coffin*
30   EXTON   Great King, within this coffin I present
Thy buried fear. Herein all breathless lies
The mightiest of thy greatest enemies,
Richard of Bordeaux, by me hither brought.
KING HENRY   Exton, I thank thee not, for thou hast wrought
35   A deed of slander° with thy fatal hand   *disgrace*
Upon my head and all this famous land.
EXTON   From your own mouth, my lord, did I this deed.
KING HENRY   They love not poison that do poison need;
Nor do I thee. Though I did wish him dead,
40   I hate the murderer, love him murderèd.
The guilt of conscience take thou for thy labour,
But neither my good word nor princely favour.
With Cain² go wander through the shades of night,
And never show thy head by day nor light.
        [Exeunt EXTON *and his men]*
45   Lords, I protest my soul is full of woe
That blood should sprinkle me to make me grow.
Come mourn with me for what I do lament,
And put on sullen black incontinent.°   *immediately*
I'll make a voyage to the Holy Land
50   To wash this blood off from my guilty hand.
March sadly after. Grace my mournings here
In weeping after this untimely bier.   *Exeunt [with the coffin]*

---

1. More reverent than the prison cell you inhabit now.
2. After Cain murdered his brother Abel, he was condemned to be a vagabond (Genesis 4:14).

I Henry IV

A roadside inn that fails to provide chamber pots for its customers, a castle in Wales where a magician summons spirits to be his musicians, the royal palace in London from which the King of England launches a campaign against rebel forces—these are but a few of the disparate venues where the action of *1 Henry IV* occurs. With this drama, the Shakespearean history play broadens out to encompass a rich diversity of languages, characters, and locales. Nothing in Shakespeare's earlier English histories quite anticipates this one. The great prose chronicles of the sixteenth century, such as Raphael Holinshed's *Chronicles of England, Scotland, and Ireland* (second edition, 1587), which Shakespeare consulted and whose materials he freely adapted and supplemented, stand behind all his history plays. The earlier plays, however, like the chronicles, focus primarily on the world of court and battlefield in which the monarch and his nobles appear as history's significant players, their rivalries and their achievements the focal point of the action. Common people such as Jack Cade have roles in these works, but their stories are typically subordinated to the monarchical plot. In *1 Henry IV*, something different happens. Several lines of action unfold at once, each connected to particular geographical locales, and each commenting upon, without simply displacing, the others. Henry IV, who had seized the throne from Richard II, is the play's title character, but from the start he is a beleaguered figure kept from his dream of making a Crusade to the Holy Land by discontent and rebellion among his nobles, especially the Percy family, and burdened with an oldest son, Prince Hal, who acts more like a prodigal child than the heir to the throne. The King appears in some key scenes, but for long stretches the action focuses on other characters and on places, like a common London tavern, that the King would never deign to visit.

Some events take place in the north of England, in the Northumberland stronghold of the Percy family. The play is set in the early fifteenth century, but even in the late sixteenth century the north of England was popularly regarded as lawless, wild, and linked to marginalized Catholic practices and beliefs, its nobility not fully incorporated into the increasingly centralized state being constructed by the Tudor monarchs. In 1569, members of the Percy family had been prominent in the Northern Rebellion, an attempt to overthrow Queen Elizabeth and put Mary Queen of Scots, a Catholic, on the throne. In drawing his portrait of the Percys, Shakespeare makes their champion, Hotspur, an impassioned embodiment of medieval chivalry, eager above all for honor and for the glory to be won in battle. While the historical Hotspur was actually much older than the King's son, Prince Hal, Shakespeare follows Samuel Daniel's poem *The Civile Wars Between the Two Houses of Lancaster and York* (1595) in making him Hal's coequal in years and his rival for preeminence in the kingdom. He is joined in rebellion by other figures from the threatening territories on the perimeter of England: by the Earl of Douglas, a formidable Scottish warrior, and by the Welshman Owain Glyndŵr, a self-proclaimed magician with a fiery temper, a lyrical temperament, and a daughter who marries Edmund Mortimer, the man presented in this play as Richard II's designated heir to the throne. Wales thus harbors both rebellion and the man who was arguably the legitimate King of England.

Another of the play's crucial locales is a tavern in Eastcheap, a commercial district in the east of London. This tavern is Prince Hal's second home where he comes to drink and amuse himself, and particularly to carouse with Falstaff, the dissipated knight who is the young Prince's tutor in folly, his intimate friend, and surrogate father. In Eastcheap, Hal rubs elbows with commoners such as Mistress Quickly, the Hostess,

The historical Owain Glyndŵr claimed the title of Prince of Wales. His great seal, both sides of which are shown here, bears the inscription "Owain, by the grace of God, prince of Wales" and depicts four upreared (rampant) lions, the coat of arms of the Gwynedd dynasty, to which Glyndŵr belonged.

and with Francis, the inarticulate apprentice tapster. Shakespeare took his cue about Hal's presence amid this crew from the many popular accounts of the Prince's dissolute youth, especially from a play printed in 1598 called *The Famous Victories of Henry the Fifth,* some version of which seems to have been staged in the late 1580s. It depicts not only episodes from Hal's madcap youth but also his eventual reformation and assumption of the throne. Shakespeare elaborated extensively on this story of youthful prodigality. Mistress Quickly, for example, is entirely his invention, and the character of Falstaff, while loosely modeled on a figure in *The Famous Victories,* is utterly transformed by Shakespeare into what has remained one of the great comic creations of the English theater. Witty, opportunistic, and utterly indifferent to the decorum expected of a knight of advanced years, Falstaff makes the tavern a place of perpetual play and the antithesis of the duty-driven world of the court. That the Prince seems irresistibly drawn to Eastcheap makes others, especially his father, question his fitness to rule, but the high-spirited playfulness of Falstaff's world suggests why the Prince might take refuge there from the demands of his public role and the exacting expectations of the King, his father.

One of the objections to English popular theater voiced by a contemporary poet, Sir Philip Sidney, was that it mingled clowns with kings in a way that violated codes of aesthetic and social decorum; these codes insisted on the strict separation of high and low subject matter, language, and people. In contrast to Sidney's dicta, *1 Henry IV* is thoroughly hybrid in its mingling of the high matter of rebellion and affairs of state with the low matter of drinking, jokes, and highway robbery. The play is also a temporal hybrid in that the tavern scenes seem to take place not in the early fifteenth century, when Henry IV was struggling to secure his rule, but more nearly in the late sixteenth century, when Shakespeare was actually writing his play. In the tavern scenes, for example, characters make fun of plays and modes of writing popular in the 1570s and 1580s, such as Thomas Preston's ranting tyrant play *Cambyses* (1569) and the baroquely ornate rhetoric popularized by John Lyly in his *Euphues* (1578). The tavern world is also filled with references to the commodities that passed through London's markets in the late sixteenth century. The characters there drink sack, Madeira, and bastard—popular alcoholic beverages, some (such as Madeira) imported from as far away as an island off the coast of west Africa; and they refer to articles of clothing, such as the Spanish-leather wallets and leather jerkins with crystal buttons, worn by London's aspiring mercantile classes. Eastcheap itself, where the tavern is located, was a major market street in Shakespeare's London, and the tavern scenes are steeped in references to the commercial culture, including the theatrical culture, of early modern England.

There is every indication, however, that if a Sidney would have found the hybridity of the play a problem, ordinary consumers did not. Judging by its publication history, in its own time *1 Henry IV* was one of Shakespeare's most popular plays. It appeared in two quarto versions in 1598 and then in five more before the First Folio was printed in 1623. Even after that, individual quarto editions of the play continued to appear. Part of its popularity undoubtedly derived from the fact that with *1 Henry IV*, the Shakespearean history play began to supplement chronicle history, which focuses on monarchs, nobles, and affairs of state, with chorography: that is, with a mode of writing popular in the late sixteenth century that described and surveyed the land of England focusing on the products, the terrain, and the customs of England's various regions. *1 Henry IV* is a chorography in the sense that while the play's distinct lines of action comment on one another, each is defined in relation to specific places, customs, and social groups. The commercial, bawdy world of the tavern, with its cast of lowlife characters and its rituals of drinking and play, is very different from the more formal milieu of Westminster, where the King and his nobles are immersed in the tasks of statecraft, and different again from the world of passion and magic centered in Glyndŵr's Welsh castle. Through the multiple plots, the spectator watching the play experiences the illusion of complex temporal simultaneity and social and geographic heterogeneity. Thus in successive scenes, the rebels, in Wales, plot the dismemberment of England and listen to a song sung in Welsh (3.1); King Henry, in Westminster, berates his wayward son (3.2); Falstaff, in Eastcheap, tries to cheat Mistress Quickly by claiming that his ring was stolen in her tavern (3.3). All these actions go on cotemporally but in widely disparate locales, creating a theatrical illusion of the diversity encompassed by the ongoing life of the nation and its bordering regions.

But the play's complex elaboration of difference also makes evident its monarch's central problem: how to maintain control over and enforce unity upon the territories over which he claims dominion but which threaten to break away or assert a worrisome autonomy. As in *Henry V,* Shakespeare here dramatizes the tension between efforts at nation building and the cultural, religious, and political differences that promote fragmentation. The problem of furthering national unity is especially pressing for Henry IV because he did not lineally inherit the throne; he seized it from Richard II. He is on shaky ground, then, should he attempt to unify England under the banner of his own legitimacy. In fact, for much of the play, Henry is a king in search of a strategy of rule. He had hoped to unify his people and quiet his conscience for his part in Richard's deposition and death by undertaking a Crusade to recover Jerusalem for European Christianity. But trouble at home keeps him from enacting his plan as rebellion bubbles up on the Scottish border, on the Welsh border, in the northern counties, and even in the Church, in the person of the Archbishop of York. The land seethes with the murmurings of rebels.

In the England of the 1590s, the monarch's most pressing problem of control was posed by Ireland; there, after 1595, the Earl of Tyrone led the challenge to English rule. Like Glyndŵr, Tyrone was educated in England and in some accounts was even Glyndŵr's descendant. While Ireland is not directly depicted in *1 Henry IV,* Hotspur verbally links Wales and Ireland. Urged to listen to a song sung in Welsh, he says that he would rather hear his hunting dog "howl in Irish" (3.1.232), thereby confirming the common English view that Welsh and Irish were equally barbarous languages. More important, Wales stands in the play as a displaced image of the contemporary Irish situation. In the popular imagination, Wales often seemed a foreign place of mystery and danger, even though it had been officially incorporated in England in the 1530s and the Welsh language banned as unnatural and barbarous. In *1 Henry IV,* Wales represents the threat not only of rebellion but also of effeminization and seduction. Mortimer, the supposed heir to the English throne, falls in love with Glyndŵr's daughter, promises to learn her language, and never appears on the battlefield against Henry's forces. In essence, he "goes native," a persistent fear voiced by the English concerning their soldiers and settlers in Ireland. The English had long worried that through prolonged contact with the Irish, English men and women might adopt their barbarous ways and forfeit their English identity. They even feared that their children, in drinking the milk of Irish wet nurses, could be transformed into people more Irish than English.

In *1 Henry IV*, the threat posed by the dangerous Welsh borderlands and by the northern Percy faction directly challenges the King's authority. Hampered by the questionable means by which he came to the throne, Henry ultimately finds force and guile the most effective instruments for maintaining his power. He can win battles, and he is willing to use deception to improve his position. At Shrewsbury, his major battle against the rebels, a number of Henry's nobles dress like the King, frustrating the enemy's ability to identify the true King and encouraging Henry's own forces by the seeming ubiquity of their monarch. Perpetual battle, however, is a costly way to rule, and having many nobles dress like him runs counter to Henry's stated belief that the King should be seldom seen in order to be the more wondered at when he does appear. To have many men marching in the King's clothing and answering to the King's name might, in fact, subversively suggest that "King" is a part any man could play, given the right accoutrements.

Prince Hal faces the pressing task of finding better strategies for ruling the changed world his father brought into being by his deposition of King Richard. He cannot assume that his kingship will be uncontested simply because he is Henry's son. A usurper's offspring has more legitimacy than a usurper, but not much. Rather, Hal must *make* himself King by a convincing performance of the part, and he must beat out those who would be his rivals, such as Harry Hotspur. Viewed one way, *1 Henry IV* is a study in the political and theatrical skills necessary for rule in a world where the inevitability and assumed legitimacy of inherited kingship has been called into question. In 1532, Niccolò Machiavelli's *The Prince*, a manual of practical statecraft, was published and quickly became notorious throughout Europe. Machiavelli taught rulers how to maintain their power through a mixture of guile, alliance, warfare, and personal force of character. Popularly viewed as irreligious and amoral, Machiavelli nonetheless was a byword for political pragmatism.

In his sophisticated manipulation of power, Hal shows himself a good student of Machiavelli, and the Machiavellian strand of his characterization has caused a split in critical assessments of him. To many, Hal personifies the ideal English king, the perfect mean between the self-indulgence of a Falstaff and the impassioned inflexibility of a Hotspur. He is thus an object of desire and emulation. Other critics focus on what they perceive as a lack of humanity at the heart of this consummate politician and recoil from his calculated use of other people to serve his own ends. For example, at the end of the first scene in which he appears, Hal in soliloquy speaks about his tavern mates:

> I know you all, and will a while uphold
> The unyoked humour of your idleness.
> Yet herein will I imitate the sun,
> Who doth permit the base contagious clouds
> To smother up his beauty from the world,
> That when he please again to be himself,
> Being wanted he may be more wondered at
> By breaking through the foul and ugly mists
> Of vapours that did seem to strangle him.
>
> (1.2.173–81)

These lines reveal the calculation that is one part of this character's representation. Comparing himself to the royal symbol, the sun, Hal casts his companions as the contaminating clouds and ugly mists that temporarily obscure his own radiance. Hal is chillingly disdainful of those he elsewhere treats as boon companions, but he also finds their baseness *useful,* since it will set in high relief his own glory, once he has cast them off.

Hal is an interesting dramatic character and not merely a personification of political expediency, however, precisely because his calculated use of his companions does not necessarily preclude his being attracted to them and to the world of play and good fellowship that they represent. In *1 Henry IV,* Hal is not yet King, and the moment of repudiation is not yet upon him. In this play, he can both enjoy his time in Eastcheap and also acquire skills there that he will need when he ascends his father's troubled throne. In the tavern, for example, he and Falstaff take turns playing King and Prince in a theatrical staging of the prodigal Hal's encounter with his reproving father. Hal rehearses the cadences and the sentiments of royal speech, trying out a part, learning to inhabit it convincingly. But it is not just his own part he masters. Unlike his father, Hal does not hold himself aloof from his would-be subjects. His ventures into Eastcheap are in part a mapping of one corner of England, a survey of the customs and strange languages of this locale. To Ned Poins he boasts that having been instructed by three tapsters in the terminology of drinking, "I can drink with any tinker in his own language during my life" (2.5.16–17).

In the tavern, Hal also meditates on the strange tongue of his great rival, Hotspur, whose impatient but impassioned speech Hal parodies:

> I am not yet of Percy's mind, the Hotspur of the North—he that kills me some six or seven dozen of Scots at a breakfast, washes his hands, and says to his wife, 'Fie upon this quiet life! I want work.' 'O my sweet Harry,' says she, 'how many hast thou killed today?' 'Give my roan horse a drench,' says he, and answers, 'Some fourteen,' an hour after; 'a trifle, a trifle.' I prithee call in Falstaff. I'll play Percy, and that damned brawn shall play Dame Mortimer his wife. (2.5.94–101)

Learning the language of others and rehearsing their tongues is, for Hal, one of the arts of power. He can—and later he will—repudiate some of those whose language and customs he has imbibed, making the repudiation a justification for his own rule. Knowing disorderliness, the King will use his office to punish it. He can also appropriate the language of others, as at Shrewsbury he appropriates the chivalric accents of Hotspur; or he can co-opt others to serve his own purposes by speaking to them in a tongue they can comprehend. By his own account, Hal is beloved of the tapsters who have taught him their language, and they have promised that when he is king, he "shall command all the good lads in Eastcheap" (2.5.12–13). Many of them he will eventually command in his wars in France. It can be argued, therefore, that there is a profound instrumentality to Hal's sojourn outside the court milieu that should be his "natural" home. He is acquiring theatrical skills, linguistic skills, and above all a knowledge of the diverse corners of an England he must rule by a mixture of charm, guile, and strategic severity—demonizing some subjects to win the loyalty of others, outstripping rivals by outdoing them at their own particular strengths.

Yet Hal is only part of this play, and *1 Henry IV*'s uniqueness consists in good part in the way it plays off one dramatic perspective, one line of action, against another. The young Prince is certainly the focus of the play's narrative of reform, and he is the only character who can move with seeming ease among the worlds of tavern, court, and battlefield. Yet even as he surveys and judges those around him, the play's structure of geographical juxtapositions and its vivid depiction of other characters and other modes of being invite the audience to submit the Prince himself to critical scrutiny. Consider, for example, 3.1 and 3.2, the scenes at the center of the play that take the audience first to Glyndŵr's castle in Wales, where he, Hotspur, Mortimer, and Worcester are plotting their rebellion, and then to the King's palace at Westminster to which Henry has summoned his son. The first scene graphically establishes the kingdom-cleaving threat posed by the rebels. They have a map and are planning how they will divide the territory of England into three parts. But the scene also establishes the danger, mystery, and beauty of this borderland. Glyndŵr is a man trained in occult arts who boasts that the earth shook at his birth and that he can summon spirits to do his bidding. Hotspur scoffs, but when Glyndŵr's daughter promises to sing in Welsh, Glyndŵr says:

> Do so, and those musicians that shall play to you
> Hang in the air a thousand leagues from hence,
> And straight they shall be here. Sit and attend.
>
> (3.1.220–22)

Three lines later, music plays, its origins a mystery. When Glyndŵr speaks, Wales seems a land of enchantment, haunted by spirits.

Wales is also a place where women are integral to the action as they seldom are elsewhere in the play. Except for Mistress Quickly, Kate Percy and Glyndŵr's daughter are the play's only two female characters; and 3.1, the play's only scene in which two women are onstage at the same time, is set in Wales and is largely Shakespeare's invention. In the chronicles, Glyndŵr, Mortimer, and Hotspur's proposed division of conquered territory is negotiated by representatives in the Archbishop of Bangor's house. By contrast, in *1 Henry IV* it occurs at Glyndŵr's home with the women present. In short, Shakespeare went to some trouble to link the rebels with women—more specifically, with wives and daughters. The question is why. In part, the choice portrays the rebels, unlike the Lancastrians, as having private as well as public lives. Glyndŵr is fond of his daughter and worries about her happiness. Mortimer dotes on this same daughter and seems to have married her for love as much as for political alliance. Hotspur's affection for his wife is displayed through the teasing banter with which he persistently addresses her. Scornful of mooning lovers, he nonetheless is careful to take his wife with him when he journeys to Wales.

The passions so nakedly on display in 3.1 clearly signal the rebels' vulnerabilities. In the patriarchal thought of the period, men were presented as superior to women because they were supposedly more rational and less subject to their passions. If men loved women too much, they risked becoming effeminate—that is, *like* a woman in placing desire above reason, especially if that desire kept a man from performing his public duties, such as going to war. Hotspur prizes his masculinity and the public honor to be won in battle. He is contemptuous of the affected courtier who appeared at Holmedon after the fighting, demanding Hotspur's prisoners (1.3.28–68). In his dealings with his wife, Hotspur seems to use banter and jokes to maintain control of his affection for her. He would not, for a woman, forgo the man-to-man erotics of battle when, "hot horse to horse" (4.1.123), he clashes against the bosom of Prince Hal. Mortimer, by contrast, simply succumbs to the charms of the Welsh woman. He never appears in battle: Wales and a wife swallow him up.

This Welsh world of danger, mystery, and passion sits strangely against the world of calculation that unfolds immediately thereafter, when in 3.2 King Henry castigates Prince Hal for his dissolute life and together they discuss strategies of monarchical self-presentation. The throne room is a place not of enchantment but of business. No women are shown at court, and passion manifests itself most strongly as the desire to rule. Father and son are both preoccupied with the tactics and strategies by which they can most effectively command the loyalty of subjects. While Henry fears his son misunderstands the task before him, Hal shows that he is every bit as astute as his father. But after the high emotions and alluring lyricism of the Welsh scene, the throne room at Westminster can seem a pragmatic and claustrophobic space. In concentrating their energies on rule, Henry and Hal here are divorced from many things that give the rebel world its charm.

Falstaff and the tavern pose a different challenge to the values of Westminster. As critics have shown, the fat man's tutoring of Hal in riotous living mimics the pedagogical relationship of master to student that was sometimes eroticized in the early modern period. Much of the poignancy of the play's depiction of the friendship between the two comes from the tension between their apparent intimacy and the Prince's stated intention to repudiate his companion. Falstaff's threat to monarchical values is obvious. Against the future-oriented calculations of Hal and his father, he insists on living in the present. As his huge body testifies, he demands the immediate gratification of physical desires. To eat, drink, and jest—these are pleasures that for Falstaff brook no delay. Hal can discipline himself. He is thin, as Falstaff points out, and he can plot a personal reformation sometime far in the future and work toward that end. Falstaff cannot or will not; and yet, while a figure of disorder, he has for many readers been the play's most interesting and memorable character. Aside from Hamlet, no other

Falstaff and Prince Hal. Pen and watercolor drawing on paper by William Blake (c. 1780).

Shakespearean figure has attracted as much critical attention as the fat knight.

When Shakespeare first wrote the play, he called this character Sir John Oldcastle. The choice was unfortunate, for the Cobham family, descendants of the historical Oldcastle, protested. William Brooke, the tenth Baron Cobham, had been Lord Chamberlain from August 1596 to March 1597, the very months when most scholars believe Shakespeare completed 1 Henry IV. Since the Lord Chamberlain oversaw the licensing of plays through the office of the Master of the Revels, Cobham was in an especially favorable position to object to this comic rendition of his ancestor. Shakespeare apparently changed the character's name in response to this act of censorship, though traces of his original intentions can be discerned, including the fact that in 1.2.37–38 Falstaff is still referred to as "my old lad of the castle." In addition, in the first complete Quarto of 1 Henry IV, there are a few traces of the fact that Peto once bore the name "Harvey," and Bardolph the name "Russell." Again, the objections of powerful figures may have forced changes. "Russell" was the family name of the prominent earls of Bedford, and "Harvey" the name of the stepfather of the Earl of Southampton.

Recently, some critics (including the editors of the Oxford text) have argued that the names "Peto," "Bardolph," and "Falstaff" should be replaced by the names Shakespeare originally intended—namely, "Harvey," "Russell," and "Oldcastle." They suggest that such a replacement would undo an act of censorship that thwarted Shakespeare's original intentions. This edition retains the substituted names primarily because these are the names Shakespeare consistently used after the initial act of censorship, and they have become part of the textual and dramatic history of this and other plays. While it is important to point out that an act of censorship occurred, to "undo" it creates new erasures in the textual and cultural history of the play. For Shakespeare, "Falstaff," not "Oldcastle," became the word linking the various textual manifestations of his fat knight as he appeared both in 1 and 2 Henry IV and then in The Merry Wives of Windsor.

It is of interest, however, to ask why Shakespeare first used the name "Oldcastle" in his play. The historical Oldcastle was a knight who served Henry IV in battle in both France and Wales, but who was also a Lollard; that is, he was connected with the religious group often seen as a forerunner of English Protestantism for its critiques of the Catholic Church and its advocacy of a vernacular Bible to be made available to lay people. At first, Henry IV treated Oldcastle's religious views leniently, but eventually Oldcastle was sent to the Tower of London and condemned as a heretic by the Archbishop of Canterbury. He escaped, and Henry was warned that Oldcastle was leading an armed force against him. Oldcastle was captured in 1417 and eventually hung in chains and then burned on the gallows.

This knight suggests Shakespeare's portrait of the chivalric heroes Prince Hal and Hotspur at the battle of Shrewsbury. From Henry Peacham's *Minerva Britanna* (1612).

In the sixteenth century, how one viewed Oldcastle depended largely on one's religious perspective. To many zealous Protestants, such as John Foxe, Oldcastle was a Protestant hero, a victim of Catholic oppression rather than a traitor; Foxe included Oldcastle in his *Book of Martyrs*. But by the 1590s, Lollards were also sometimes linked with "extremist" Protestant groups pushing for radical reforms in the Church of England. Making a well-known Lollard martyr a fat figure of disorder therefore did not necessarily signal Catholic sympathies. It might simply be a way of suggesting the hypocrisy of zealous reformers. In other plays, especially in his portrait of Malvolio in *Twelfth Night*, Shakespeare makes fun of "Puritans" who claimed a greater righteousness and strictness of life than their more moderate contemporaries. In *1 Henry IV*, Falstaff's language is liberally studded with biblical quotations, most of which he misapplies or contradicts by his behavior. Thus he tells Hal that one must labor in one's vocation (1.2.92–93), an injunction found in 1 Corinthians 7:20 and in Ephesians 4:1. But the vocation in which *he* would labor is that of thief—not exactly what Protestant divines meant when discussing the virtues of a vocation. Moreover, by making Falstaff so obviously a glutton and lover of sack, Shakespeare could be making fun of the hypocrisy of Puritans, as Ben Jonson was to do in *Bartholomew Fair* and Thomas Middleton in *A Chaste Maid in Cheapside*.

The name Shakespeare fastened upon to replace Oldcastle had its own history. The historical Fastolf (1378?–1459) was a courageous officer in Henry VI's war in France, though in some chronicles he appears erroneously to have been called a coward, a detail that Shakespeare repeats in *1 Henry VI*. Having once used the name without repercussion in the former play, Shakespeare may have felt it was safe to employ it as a replacement for "Oldcastle" and to play upon the figure's reputation for cowardice.

Yet it may be a mistake to connect Shakespeare's character too strictly to any historical counterpart. As scholarship has shown, Falstaff is a rich amalgam of popular and literary traditions. In part, he resembles the irreverent Vice figure from the medieval morality plays. Traditionally, the Vice, a comic and clever character, tempted the hero to sin while voices of virtue or duty tried to steer him along a more reputable path. In *1 Henry IV*, Hal is torn between his allegiances to Falstaff and his father, to vice and virtue, to the tavern and the court. Falstaff also conjures up the topsy-turvy world of Carnival in which rulers were temporarily displaced and the body's pleasures (eating, drinking, breaking wind, having sex) were celebrated before the arrival of abstemious Lent. The unending jokes about Falstaff's fat paunch highlight his symbolic connection to bodily excess, and his contempt for the law and for military duty make him the antithesis of the King and a perpetual emblem of disorder. In creating Falstaff, Shakespeare also drew on the figure from classical tradition of the braggart warrior who is really a coward. At Shrewsbury, Falstaff plays the coward, and yet he falsely claims credit for having killed Hotspur. The gap between his words and his deeds is enormous, though in this instance, as in many others, the Prince graciously does not reveal this lie for what it is. Above all, however, Falstaff embodies traditions of popular critique associated with the stage clown. In early productions, Will Kemp, the famous clown in Shakespeare's company, probably played the part. Sometimes speaking from a down-

stage position near the audience, the clown traditionally poked fun at upstage author-
ity figures. Falstaff does so in spades, whether mocking the elevated speech of King
Henry or twitting Hal for being so skinny. But Falstaff is more than a gadfly or a para-
site swollen fat on others' folly. He also embodies a mode of being in the world that
serves as a powerful alternative both to the calculations of Hal and to Hotspur's head-
long, death-courting pursuit of honor. For example, before the Battle of Shrewsbury
Falstaff meditates witheringly on just what honor means and on its value:

> Can honour set-to a leg? No. Or an arm? No. Or take away the grief of a wound?
> No. Honour hath no skill in surgery, then? No. What is honour? A word. What is in
> that word 'honour'? What is that 'honour'? Air. A trim reckoning! Who hath it?
> He that died o'Wednesday. Doth he feel it? No. Doth he hear it? No. 'Tis insensible
> then? Yea, to the dead. But will it not live with the living? No. Why? Detraction will
> not suffer it. Therefore I'll none of it. Honour is a mere scutcheon. And so ends my
> catechism. (5.1.130–39)

Others, like Hotspur, find honor worth dying for, and generations of men have gone
into battle believing the same thing. But for Falstaff, honor is worth the loss of neither
a leg nor a life. During the ensuing battle, Falstaff carries a bottle of sack in his pistol
case and ingloriously feigns death when attacked by Douglas. But though Hotspur and
others are slain, Falstaff rises up. He embraces neither honor nor death, but life, and
many readers and theatergoers have cheered his choice while others have been
repulsed by his opportunism and cowardice.

Shrewsbury, then, is not only the place where the play's disparate strands of action
come together as the King, Prince Hal, Hotspur, and even Falstaff assemble in one spot;
it is also where the audience is invited to judge the relative worth of the values
embraced by these different characters. Among those who fare well is Prince Hal.
Shrewsbury is perhaps his happiest hour. During the battle, he finds a way to redeem
his reputation and distinguish himself from Falstaff without being forced to repudiate
his friend, just as he kills Hotspur while paying homage to his courage. But the
equipoise of this battle's conclusion is precarious. Hal is not yet king and must still
delay his assumption of the throne. Falstaff has not reformed and probably never will.
And the rebels have not been destroyed. Hotspur is dead, but the Archbishop of York,
Glyndŵr, and Mortimer are still in arms. In other words, it is an illusion that Hal has
carried all before him. In the corners and crevices of the realm, dissension and differ-
ence remain. In such conditions, the work of rule is a performance with no end.

JEAN E. HOWARD

TEXTUAL NOTE

The first quarto edition of *1 Henry IV* was printed in 1598. Only a fragment, compris-
ing 1.3.199 through 2.3.19 of a single copy, now remains. This Quarto, usually desig-
nated as Q0 but in the Oxford edition called Q1, was the basis for a second quarto
edition printed later in 1598. This text, Q2, serves as the control text for most modern
editions. The manuscript behind Q1 does not seem to have been marked up for the the-
ater, so it was probably not the promptbook. The manuscript was either a corrected copy
of Shakespeare's "foul papers" or, more probably, a transcription of them made by a pro-
fessional scribe. This manuscript was prepared with unusual care, perhaps to show that
changes required by the Master of the Revels had been made in the text. Originally, the
characters Falstaff, Peto, and Bardolph had been assigned the names "Oldcastle," "Har-
vey," and "Russell." Objections from the Cobham family, descendants of Oldcastle, and
perhaps from other powerful people seem to have forced Shakespeare to change these
names (see the Introduction for a fuller discussion of this act of censorship).

Five other quarto editions were published, in 1599, 1604, 1608, 1613, and 1622, before the publication of the First Folio (F) in 1623. These all derive from Q2 and have no independent authority. The Folio text derives from the 1613 Quarto, but act and scene divisions were added, speech prefixes and stage directions altered, and oaths were softened or removed and biblical allusions altered in compliance with the 1606 edict forbidding profanity on the stage. The party responsible for these changes is uncertain. Some changes may have been made by the compositors who set the text or by someone acting as editor (perhaps John Heminges or Henry Condell, Shakespeare's fellow share-holders in the King's Men who oversaw the production of the First Folio). The Oxford editors plausibly argue that these changes may in part derive from a manuscript pre-pared by the same scribe who prepared a similarly "literary" manuscript for 2 Henry IV—that is, a manuscript less attuned to playhouse requirements than to the ration-alization of the text as a written document. This scribal manuscript may itself have derived from a promptbook whose theatrical features were largely obscured by the tran-scription. The Oxford editors also believe that a few of the changes made in F may reflect Shakespeare's own revisions of Q.

The act and scene divisions of F are followed except for the marking of new scenes at 2.3 and 5.3. The latter scene break, regularly inserted in most modern editions, indi-cates a clearing of the stage in the middle of the Battle of Shrewsbury; 2.3 is added to mark the moment at Gad's Hill when, Falstaff and his friends having led off the travel-ers they have captured, Hal and Poins come onstage disguised in their buckram suits.

As explained in the Introduction, for this play Norton is using the names "Falstaff," "Peto," and "Bardolph" (rather than Oxford's "Oldcastle," "Harvey," and "Russell"). Consequently, Oxford speech prefixes and stage directions, and in a few places the Oxford text, have been silently altered where these three characters are concerned in order to return to the names and language appearing in the printed quarto texts of 1598. Textual deviations from Q are marked in the variants, and Norton's standardiza-tion of quarto speech prefixes is delineated immediately before those variants. In par-ticular, "Falstaff," rather than Oxford's "Sir John," has been used in speech prefixes in this play as well as in 2 Henry IV.

SELECTED BIBLIOGRAPHY

Barber, C. L. "Rule and Misrule in Henry IV." Shakespeare's Festive Comedy: A Study of Dramatic Form and Its Relation to Social Custom. Princeton: Princeton University Press, 1959. 192–221. Explores the ritual subtext of Henry IV, Parts I and II, argu-ing that Falstaff becomes a scapegoat whose banishment rids the community of bad luck.

Barker, Roberta. "Tragical-Comical-Historical Hotspur." Shakespeare Quarterly 54 (2003): 288–307. Examines how Hotspur has been interpreted through the cen-turies and argues that the role is central to the play's examination of masculine hero-ism.

Greenblatt, Stephen. "Invisible Bullets." Shakespearean Negotiations: The Circulation of Social Energy in Renaissance England. Berkeley: University of California Press, 1988. 21–65. Discusses how Renaissance texts such as Thomas Hariot's A Brief and True Report of the New Found Land of Virginia and Shakespeare's 1 Henry IV sub-vert their culture's dominant values regarding religious belief and political author-ity and yet contain or mitigate the doubts they raise.

Greenfield, Matthew. "1 Henry IV: Metatheatrical Britain." British Identities and En-glish Renaissance Literature. Ed. David J. Baker and Willy Maley. New York: Cam-bridge University Press, 2002. 71–80. Discusses the interplay of different characters, locales, and genres in the play, arguing that it fails to create a single onstage community but instead reveals the distance between groups.

Highley, Christopher. "Wales, Ireland, and 1 Henry IV." Renaissance Drama, n.s., 21 (1990): 91–114. Discusses England's Elizabethan wars in Ireland as a subtext for

1 Henry IV and Glyndŵr as a displaced image of the Irish leader Hugh O'Neill, Earl of Tyrone.

Howard, Jean E., and Phyllis Rackin. "Gender and Nation: Anticipations of Modernity in the Second Tetralogy." *Engendering a Nation: A Feminist Account of Shakespeare's English Histories.* London: Routledge, 1997. 137–215. Focuses on the disruptive role of women in the play, both the Welsh women, including Glyndŵr's daughter, and the women of the Eastcheap tavern.

Kastan, David Scott. "'The King Hath Many Marching in His Coats'; or, What Did You Do During the War, Daddy?" *Shakespeare Left and Right.* Ed. Ivo Kamps. New York: Routledge, 1991. 241–58. Argues that the theater does not just reproduce the political ideologies of the powerful but instead makes space for unauthorized and heterogeneous views, including, in *Henry IV,* the view that kingship itself is just a role.

Laroque, François. "Shakespeare's 'Battle of Carnival and Lent': The Falstaff Scenes Reconsidered (*1* and *2 Henry IV*)." *Shakespeare and Carnival: After Bakhtin.* Ed. Ronald Knowles. New York: St. Martin's, 1998. 83–96. Discusses the connections between Shakespeare's *Henry IV* plays and the opposition in Carnival between the fat and the lean, Falstaff and the Prince.

McMillin, Scott. *Henry IV, Part One.* Shakespeare in Performance series. Manchester: Manchester University Press, 1991. Analyzes theatrical, film, and television performances of *1 Henry IV* in the second half of the twentieth century, arguing that this is the period when Hal, rather than Falstaff or Hotspur, became the focus of critical and theatrical attention.

Mullaney, Steven. "The Rehearsal of Cultures." *The Place of the Stage: License, Play, and Power in Renaissance England.* Chicago: University of Chicago Press, 1988. 60–87. Discusses the sixteenth-century fascination with collecting artifacts from distant cultures and argues that the stage also represented and rehearsed otherness.

FILMS

Chimes at Midnight. 1965. Dir. Orson Welles. UK. 115 min. In black and white, the film combines scenes from several plays to focus on Falstaff and his relationship with Prince Hal. An imaginative and moving adaptation, it boasts memorable performances by Welles as Falstaff, John Gielgud as Henry IV, and Keith Baxter as the Prince.

Henry IV, Part I. 1979. Dir. David Giles. UK. 155 min. A BBC-TV production with strong performances by Anthony Quayle as Falstaff and Tim Pigott-Smith as Hotspur in an otherwise dutifully faithful version of the play.

My Own Private Idaho. 1991. Dir. Gus Van Sant. USA. 102 min. Set in modern-day Portland, Oregon, and loosely based on the *Henry IV* plays, the film stars River Phoenix and Keanu Reeves as two young men who for a time join William Richert, the Falstaff figure, in a life of dissipation.

The History of Henry the Fourth

THE PERSONS OF THE PLAY

KING HENRY IV
PRINCE HARRY, Prince of Wales,
    familiarly known as Hal
Lord JOHN OF LANCASTER } King Henry's sons
Earl of WESTMORLAND
Sir Walter BLUNT

Earl of WORCESTER
Percy, Earl of NORTHUMBERLAND, his brother
Henry Percy, known as HOTSPUR,
    Northumberland's son
Kate, LADY PERCY, Hotspur's wife
Lord Edmund MORTIMER, called Earl of March,
    Lady Percy's brother
LADY MORTIMER, his wife } rebels against King Henry
Owain GLYNDŴR, Lady Mortimer's father
Earl of DOUGLAS
Sir Richard VERNON
Scrope, ARCHBISHOP of York
SIR MICHAEL, a member of the Archbishop's
    household

Sir John FALSTAFF
Edward (Ned) POINS
BARDOLPH
PETO
Mistress Quickly, HOSTESS of } associates of Prince Harry
    a tavern in Eastcheap
FRANCIS, a drawer
VINTNER
GADSHILL
CARRIERS
CHAMBERLAIN
OSTLER
TRAVELLERS
SHERIFF
MESSENGERS
SERVANT
Lords, soldiers

1.1

Enter KING [HENRY], *Lord* JOHN OF LANCASTER, [*and
the*] *Earl of* WESTMORLAND, *with other* [*lords*]

KING HENRY   So shaken as we are, so wan with care,
   Find we° a time for frighted peace to pant   *Let us find*
   And breathe short-winded accents° of new broils   *words*

1.1 Location: The palace, London.

To be commenced in strands afar remote.[1]
5　No more the thirsty entrance° of this soil　　　　　　　　　*parched mouth*
Shall daub her lips with her own children's blood.
No more shall trenching° war channel° her fields,　　　　　*cutting / furrow*
Nor bruise her flow'rets with the armèd hoofs
Of hostile paces.° Those opposèd eyes,　　　　　　　　　　*horses' footsteps*
10　Which, like the meteors of a troubled heaven,[2]
All of one nature, of one substance bred,
Did lately meet in the intestine° shock　　　　　　　　　　*internal*
And furious close° of civil butchery,　　　　　　　*hand-to-hand combat*
Shall now in mutual well-beseeming° ranks　　　　　　　　　*orderly*
15　March all one way, and be no more opposed
Against acquaintance, kindred, and allies.
The edge of war, like an ill-sheathèd knife,
No more shall cut his master. Therefore, friends,
As far as to the sepulchre of Christ—
20　Whose soldier now, under whose blessèd cross
We are impressèd° and engaged to fight—　　　　　　　　　*conscripted*
Forthwith a power of English shall we levy,
Whose arms were moulded in their mothers' womb
To chase these pagans in those holy fields
25　Over whose acres walked those blessèd feet
Which fourteen hundred years ago were nailed,
For our advantage, on the bitter cross.
But this our purpose now is twelve month old,
And bootless° 'tis to tell you we will go.　　　　　　　　　*useless*
30　Therefor° we meet not now. Then let me hear　　　　　*On that account*
Of you, my gentle cousin° Westmorland,　　　　　　　*my noble kinsman*
What yesternight our Council did decree
In forwarding this dear expedience.°　　　　　　　*urgent undertaking*
WESTMORLAND　My liege, this haste was hot in question,°　*under urgent debate*
35　And many limits of the charge[3] set down
But yesternight, when all athwart° there came　　　　*at cross-purposes*
A post° from Wales, loaden with heavy news,　　　　　　　*messenger*
Whose worst was that the noble Mortimer,
Leading the men of Herefordshire to fight
40　Against the irregular and wild Glyndŵr,[4]
Was by the rude hands of that Welshman taken,
A thousand of his people butcherèd,
Upon whose dead corpse'° there was such misuse,　　　　　*corpses*
Such beastly shameless transformation,[5]
45　By those Welshwomen done as may not be
Without much shame retold or spoken of.
KING HENRY　It seems then that the tidings of this broil
Brake° off our business for the Holy Land.　　　　　　　　*Broke*

---

1. On distant shores. King Henry is alluding to the
Holy Land, to which he vowed to lead a crusade at the
close of *Richard II*.
2. Unusual events in the sky, such as comets or shoot-
ing stars, were thought to portend strife and disaster.
3. Many particulars concerning responsibilities and
expenses.
4. In most editions, Glyndŵr's name is given as "Glen-
dower," an anglicized version of the Welsh word used in
this text. Glyndŵr is probably "irregular" in the sense of
using guerrilla tactics in his warfare; possibly, the word
alludes to his alleged sorcery.
5. Mutilation. Holinshed's 1587 *Chronicles*, one of
Shakespeare's sources, says the Welsh women's acts on
this occasion were too shameful to relate, but contem-
porary editor Abraham Fleming, in the same edition of
the *Chronicles*, includes an account of another battle in
which Welsh women cut off the sexual organs and the
noses of conquered enemies and put them, respectively,
in the mouths and anuses of those enemies.

WESTMORLAND   This matched with other did, my gracious lord,

50   For more uneven° and unwelcome news   *disturbing*
    Came from the north, and thus it did import:
    On Holy-rood day[6] the gallant Hotspur there—
    Young Harry Percy—and brave Archibald,
    That ever valiant and approvèd° Scot,   *worthy*
55   At Holmedon[7] met,
    Where they did spend a sad and bloody hour,
    As by° discharge of their artillery   *As judging by*
    And shape of likelihood° the news was told;   *And probable outcome*
    For he that brought them° in the very heat   *(the news)*
60   And pride° of their contention did take horse,   *height*
    Uncertain of the issue° any way.   *outcome*

KING HENRY   Here is a dear, a true industrious friend,
    Sir Walter Blunt,[8] new lighted from his horse,
    Stained with the variation of each soil
65   Betwixt that Holmedon and this seat° of ours;   *dwelling*
    And he hath brought us smooth° and welcome news. *agreeable*
    The Earl of Douglas is discomfited.
    Ten thousand bold Scots, two-and-twenty knights,
    Balked° in their own blood did Sir Walter see *Heaped up; thwarted*
70   On Holmedon's plains. Of prisoners Hotspur took
    Mordake the Earl of Fife and eldest son
    To beaten Douglas,[9] and the Earl of Athol,
    Of Moray, Angus, and Menteith;
    And is not this an honourable spoil?
75   A gallant prize? Ha, cousin, is it not?

WESTMORLAND   In faith, it is a conquest for a prince to boast of.

KING HENRY   Yea, there thou mak'st me sad, and mak'st me sin
    In envy that my lord Northumberland
    Should be the father to so blest a son—
80   A son who is the theme of honour's tongue,
    Amongst a grove the very straightest plant,
    Who is sweet Fortune's minion° and her pride—   *favorite*
    Whilst I by looking on the praise of him
    See riot and dishonour stain the brow
85   Of my young Harry. O, that it could be proved
    That some night-tripping fairy[1] had exchanged
    In cradle clothes our children where they lay,
    And called mine Percy, his Plantagenet![2]
    Then would I have his Harry, and he mine.
90   But let him° from my thoughts. What think you, coz,° *let him go / kinsman*
    Of this young Percy's pride? The prisoners
    Which he in this adventure hath surprised°   *captured*
    To his own use[3] he keeps, and sends me word

---

6. Holy Cross Day, September 14.
7. Holmedon (also spelled "Humbleton") in Northumberland was the site in 1402 of a Scottish invasion of England.
8. It is not clear whether Blunt comes onstage now. He could have entered at the beginning of the scene; alternatively, as in this edition, he may not come onstage at all. Blunt has no lines in the scene, and Henry could at this point receive a letter containing Blunt's news or could be reporting news he has already learned. "Here" would thus refer in a general way to Blunt's being at

court.
9. Mordake was not actually Douglas's son, but an understandable misreading of Holinshed led Shakespeare to believe he was.
1. It was popularly believed that fairies stole beautiful children and left bad or malformed ones in their place.
2. Henry was descended from the Plantagenet dynasty; and the Percys were a distinguished family from the north of England to which Hotspur belonged.
3. Prisoners were routinely used as a source of revenue.

I shall have none but Mordake Earl of Fife.
95 WESTMORLAND This is his uncle's teaching. This is Worcester,
Malevolent to you in all aspects,[4]
Which makes him prune[5] himself, and bristle up
The crest of youth against your dignity.
KING HENRY But I have sent for him to answer this;
100 And for this cause awhile we must neglect
Our holy purpose to Jerusalem.
Cousin, on Wednesday next our Council we
Will hold at Windsor. So inform the lords.
But come yourself with speed to us again,
105 For more is to be said and to be done
Than out of anger can be utterèd.
WESTMORLAND I will, my liege.

Exeunt [KING HENRY, LANCASTER, *and other lords
at one door*; WESTMORLAND *at another door*]

1.2

Enter [HARRY][1] *Prince of Wales and Sir John* FALSTAFF[2]
FALSTAFF Now, Hal, what time of day is it, lad?
PRINCE HARRY Thou art so fat-witted° with drinking of old   *thick-witted*
sack,[3] and unbuttoning thee after supper, and sleeping upon
benches after noon, that thou hast forgotten to demand that
5 truly which thou wouldst truly know. What a devil hast thou to
do with the time of the day? Unless hours were cups of sack, and
minutes capons,[4] and clocks the tongues of bawds, and dials°   *clock faces; sundials*
the signs of leaping-houses,° and the blessed sun himself a   *brothels*
fair hot wench in flame-coloured taffeta,[5] I see no reason why
10 thou shouldst be so superfluous° to demand the time of the day.   *needlessly curious*
FALSTAFF Indeed you come near me° now, Hal, for we that take   *are near the mark*
purses go by the moon and the seven stars,[6] and not 'By Phoe-
bus, he, that wand'ring knight so fair'.[7] And I prithee, sweet
wag,° when thou art a king, as God save thy grace—'majesty'   *mischievous boy*
15 I should say, for grace[8] thou wilt have none—
PRINCE HARRY What, none?
FALSTAFF No, by my troth, not so much as will serve to be pro-
logue to an egg and butter.[9]
PRINCE HARRY Well, how then? Come, roundly,° roundly.   *to the point*
20 FALSTAFF Marry° then, sweet wag, when thou art king let not   *By Mary (a mild oath)*
us that are squires of the night's body[1] be called thieves of the

---

4. Habitually hostile to you. The line suggests that Worcester is a planet whose influence is always harmful, whatever his position, or "aspect," in the sky.
5. A term from falconry suggesting the hawk's trimming of its feathers as preparation for action.
1.2 Location: A room in the Prince's apartments, London.
1. F's stage direction reads, "Henry Prince of Wales"; Q reads, "prince of Wales." Norton speech prefixes refer to this character as "Prince Harry," and the same designation is used, as here, in stage directions.
2. See Introduction and Textual Note for a discussion of Falstaff's name.
3. Spanish white wine.
4. Castrated male chickens (an Elizabethan delicacy).
5. Silk cloth, which in some contexts was associated with prostitutes.
6. The constellation known as the Pleiades. *go by the moon:* go about at moonlight; tell time by the light of the moon.
7. Evidently a line from a contemporary ballad or romance about Phoebus, the sun god of classical mythology.
8. Virtue; with a pun also on "grace" as meaning "God's favor" and "a prayer before meals." Falstaff asserts that Hal has none of these and so must be called "your majesty," rather than "your grace," which was also a title of honor.
9. *egg and butter:* a mere snack needing only the shortest grace.
1. Let not we who steal by night. Falstaff alludes to the attendants of knights known as "squires of the body."

day's beauty. Let us be 'Diana's foresters',[2] 'gentlemen of the
shade', 'minions of the moon', and let men say we be men of
good government,° being governed, as the sea is, by our noble   *conduct*
25   and chaste mistress the moon, under whose countenance° we   *face; protection*
steal.

PRINCE HARRY   Thou sayst well, and it holds well° too, for the   *the comparison is apt*
fortune of us that are the moon's men doth ebb and flow like
the sea, being governed as the sea is by the moon. As for proof
30   now: a purse of gold most resolutely snatched on Monday
night, and most dissolutely spent on Tuesday morning; got
with swearing 'lay by!',[3] and spent with crying 'bring in!';[4] now
in as low an ebb as the foot of the ladder, and by and by in as
high a flow as the ridge° of the gallows.[5]   *crossbar*

35   FALSTAFF   By the Lord, thou sayst true, lad; and is not my Host-
ess of the tavern a most sweet wench?

PRINCE HARRY   As the honey of Hybla,[6] my old lad of the cas-
tle;[7] and is not a buff jerkin[8] a most sweet robe of durance?°   *durability; imprisonment*

FALSTAFF   How now, how now, mad wag? What, in thy quips
40   and thy quiddities?° What a plague have I to do with a buff   *quibbles (wordplay)*
jerkin?

PRINCE HARRY   Why, what a pox[9] have I to do with my Hostess
of the tavern?

FALSTAFF   Well, thou hast called her to a reckoning[1] many a
45   time and oft.

PRINCE HARRY   Did I ever call for thee to pay thy part?[2]

FALSTAFF   No, I'll give thee thy due, thou hast paid all there.

PRINCE HARRY   Yea, and elsewhere so far as my coin would
stretch;[3] and where it would not, I have used my credit.

50   FALSTAFF   Yea, and so used it that were it not here apparent that
thou art heir apparent—but I prithee, sweet wag, shall there
be gallows standing in England when thou art king, and res-
olution thus fubbed[4] as it is with the rusty curb of old father
Antic° the law? Do not thou when thou art king hang a thief.   *buffoon*

55   PRINCE HARRY   No, thou shalt.

FALSTAFF   Shall I? O, rare! By the Lord, I'll be a brave° judge!   *fine; well-dressed*

PRINCE HARRY   Thou judgest false already. I mean thou shalt
have the hanging of the thieves, and so become a rare hang-
man.

60   FALSTAFF   Well, Hal, well; and in some sort it jumps° with my   *agrees*
humour° as well as waiting in the court,[5] I can tell you.   *temperament*

PRINCE HARRY   For obtaining of suits?[6]

---

2. Hunters by moonlight; thieves. In classical mythol-
ogy, Diana was goddess of the moon.
3. A thief's cry similar to "Hands up!"
4. A tavern customer's call for more food or wine.
5. The Prince's speech is riddled with sexual slang,
including "purse" (line 30) as meaning "vagina" or
"scrotum"; "snatched" (line 30) as "forcibly had sexual
relations with"; "spent" (line 31) as "exhausted by sex-
ual activity"; "lay by" (line 32) as "lie back"; "spent with"
(line 32) as "reached orgasm with"; and "low" (line 33)
and "high" (line 34) as referring to a penis, first limp
and then erect.
6. Region of Sicily renowned for its honey.
7. Slang for "roisterer"; also a play on the name "Old-

castle" (see Introduction).
8. Leather jacket often worn by jailers.
9. The equivalent of "what the devil." The pox literally
was plague or syphilis.
1. You have asked that she present the bill; asked that
she show her value sexually.
2. To pay your bill; to use your penis.
3. So far as my money would go; so far as my ability to
engender, or "coin," a child would take me.
4. And valor (of thieves) thus thwarted.
5. Being in attendance at the royal court or at the court
of justices.
6. Petitions; clothing. The hangman was entitled to
claim the victims' clothing.

FALSTAFF Yea, for obtaining of suits, whereof the hangman
hath no lean wardrobe. 'Sblood,[7] I am as melancholy as a gib
65 cat,° or a lugged bear.[8]   *tomcat*

PRINCE HARRY Or an old lion, or a lover's lute.

FALSTAFF Yea, or the drone of a Lincolnshire bagpipe.

PRINCE HARRY What sayst thou to a hare,[9] or the melancholy of
Moor-ditch?[1]

70 FALSTAFF Thou hast the most unsavoury similes, and art
indeed the most comparative,° rascalliest sweet young Prince.   *quick at comparisons*
But Hal, I prithee trouble me no more with vanity.° I would   *worthless things*
to God thou and I knew where a commodity° of good names°   *supply / reputations*
were to be bought. An old lord of the Council rated me the
75 other day in the street about you, sir, but I marked him not;
and yet he talked very wisely, but I regarded him not; and yet
he talked wisely, and in the street too.

PRINCE HARRY Thou didst well, for wisdom cries out in the
streets, and no man regards it.[2]

80 FALSTAFF O, thou hast damnable iteration,[3] and art indeed
able to corrupt a saint. Thou hast done much harm upon me,
Hal, God forgive thee for it. Before I knew thee, Hal, I knew
nothing; and now am I, if a man should speak truly, little bet-
ter than one of the wicked. I must give over this life, and I will
85 give it over. By the Lord, an° I do not, I am a villain. I'll be   *if*
damned for never a° king's son in Christendom.   *for no*

PRINCE HARRY Where shall we take a purse tomorrow, Jack?

FALSTAFF Zounds,[4] where thou wilt, lad! I'll make one;° an I do   *I'll take part*
not, call me villain and baffle me.[5]

90 PRINCE HARRY I see a good amendment of life in thee, from
praying to purse-taking.

FALSTAFF Why, Hal, 'tis my vocation,° Hal. 'Tis no sin for a   *calling*
man to labour in his vocation.[6]

   Enter POINS

Poins! Now shall we know if Gadshill[7] have set a match.° O,   *planned a theft*
95 if men were to be saved by merit,[8] what hole in hell were hot
enough for him? This is the most omnipotent villain that ever
cried 'Stand!' to a true° man.   *an honest*

PRINCE HARRY Good morrow, Ned.

POINS Good morrow, sweet Hal. [*To* FALSTAFF] What says
100 Monsieur Remorse? What says Sir John, sack-and-sugar
Jack?[9] How agrees the devil and thee about thy soul, that thou
soldest him on Good Friday[1] last, for a cup of Madeira[2] and a
cold capon's leg?

7. By His blood (an oath alluding to Christ's crucifix-
ion).
8. A baited bear. In a popular form of entertainment,
bears were led in chains and set upon by dogs.
9. The hare's sadness was proverbial. Its flesh, when
eaten, was supposed to generate melancholy.
1. An open sewer outside the walls of London.
2. A biblical allusion to Proverbs 1:20–24.
3. You have a soul-endangering way of reading Scrip-
ture. This is one of several speeches in which Falstaff
uses a language associated with Puritans.
4. By Christ's wounds (a strong oath).
5. And subject me to public disgrace. Falstaff alludes
to the practice of "baffling," in which perjured knights
or effigies of them were hung upside down in public
places.

6. Allusion to 1 Corinthians 7:20 and Ephesians 4:1.
Falstaff is misusing the biblical injunction to work at
one's vocation to justify robbery.
7. A thief named after Gad's Hill, the place where he
practices his robberies. This hill, near Rochester on the
road from Canterbury to London, was notorious for
highway robberies.
8. By good works (as opposed to salvation by God's
grace).
9. "Jack" is a nickname for "John," but the word also
means "a drinking vessel" or "a knave." Falstaff likes
sugar in his sack, or sweet white wine.
1. The strictest of fast days in the Christian calendar.
2. A white wine exported from Madeira, an island off
the coast of west Africa.

PRINCE HARRY   Sir John stands to° his word, the devil shall have   *keeps*
his bargain, for he was never yet a breaker of proverbs: he will
give the devil his due.
POINS [*to* FALSTAFF]   Then art thou damned for keeping thy
word with the devil.
PRINCE HARRY   Else he had been damned for cozening° the   *cheating*
devil.
POINS   But my lads, my lads, tomorrow morning by four o'clock
early, at Gads Hill, there are pilgrims going to Canterbury
with rich offerings, and traders riding to London with fat
purses. I have visors° for you all; you have horses for your-   *masks*
selves. Gadshill lies° tonight in Rochester. I have bespoke°   *lodges / ordered*
supper tomorrow night in Eastcheap.³ We may do it as secure°   *safely*
as sleep. If you will go, I will stuff your purses full of crowns;
if you will not, tarry at home and be hanged.
FALSTAFF   Hear ye, Edward, if I tarry at home and go not, I'll
hang you for going.
POINS   You will, chops?°   *fat cheeks*
FALSTAFF   Hal, wilt thou make one?
PRINCE HARRY   Who, I rob? I a thief? Not I, by my faith.
FALSTAFF   There's neither honesty,° manhood, nor good fel-   *honor*
lowship in thee, nor thou camest not of the blood royal, if
thou darest not stand for° ten shillings.⁴   *fight for; be worth*
PRINCE HARRY   Well then, once in my days I'll be a madcap.
FALSTAFF   Why, that's well said.
PRINCE HARRY   Well, come what will, I'll tarry at home.
FALSTAFF   By the Lord, I'll be a traitor then, when thou art king.
PRINCE HARRY   I care not.
POINS   Sir John, I prithee leave the Prince and me alone. I will
lay him down such reasons for this adventure that he shall go.
FALSTAFF   Well, God give thee the spirit of persuasion and him
the ears of profiting, that what thou speakest may move and
what he hears may be believed, that the true prince may, for
recreation' sake, prove a false thief; for the poor abuses of the
time want countenance.⁵ Farewell. You shall find me in
Eastcheap.
PRINCE HARRY   Farewell, the latter spring; farewell, All-hallow
summer.⁶   [*Exit* FALSTAFF]
POINS   Now, my good sweet honey lord, ride with us tomorrow.
I have a jest to execute that I cannot manage alone. Falstaff,
Peto, Bardolph, and Gadshill shall rob those men that we
have already waylaid—yourself and I will not be there—and
when they have the booty, if you and I do not rob them, cut
this head off from my shoulders.
PRINCE HARRY   But how shall we part with them in setting forth?
POINS   Why, we will set forth before or after them and appoint
them a place of meeting, wherein it is at our pleasure to fail.
And then will they adventure upon the exploit themselves,
which they shall have no sooner achieved but we'll set upon
them.

3. A street and market district in London, evidently the
location of the play's tavern.
4. A 10-shilling coin was called a "royal," thus punning
on the Prince's "blood royal."
5. Lack encouragement (from those of high rank).

6. Addressing Falstaff as youth in age (a second spring)
and likening him to a period of unusually mild weather
(a second summer) occurring around All Hallows' Day,
November 1.

PRINCE HARRY   Ay, but 'tis like that they will know us by our
155   horses, by our habits,° and by every other appointment,° to be   *clothing / item*
     ourselves.
POINS   Tut, our horses they shall not see—I'll tie them in the
     wood; our visors we will change after we leave them; and, sir-
     rah,[7] I have cases of buckram for the nonce,[8] to immask° our   *hide*
160   noted° outward garments.   *known*
PRINCE HARRY   But I doubt they will be too hard for us.[9]
POINS   Well, for two of them, I know them to be as true-bred
     cowards as ever turned back; and for the third, if he fight
     longer than he sees reason, I'll forswear arms. The virtue of
165   this jest will be the incomprehensible° lies that this same fat   *boundless*
     rogue will tell us when we meet at supper: how thirty at least
     he fought with, what wards,° what blows, what extremities he   *parries*
     endured; and in the reproof° of this lives the jest.   *disproof*
PRINCE HARRY   Well, I'll go with thee. Provide us all things nec-
170   essary, and meet me tomorrow night in Eastcheap; there I'll
     sup. Farewell.
POINS   Farewell, my lord.   *Exit*
PRINCE HARRY   I know you all, and will a while uphold
     The unyoked humour° of your idleness.   *unbridled whims*
175   Yet herein will I imitate the sun,
     Who doth permit the base contagious° clouds   *disease-carrying*
     To smother up his beauty from the world,
     That° when he please again to be himself,   *So that*
     Being wanted° he may be more wondered at   *Having been missed*
180   By breaking through the foul and ugly mists
     Of vapours that did seem to strangle him.
     If all the year were playing holidays,
     To sport would be as tedious as to work;
     But when they seldom come, they wished-for come,
185   And nothing pleaseth but rare accidents.°   *exceptional events*
     So when this loose behaviour I throw off
     And pay the debt I never promisèd,
     By how much better than my word I am,
     By so much shall I falsify men's hopes;°   *expectations*
190   And like bright metal on a sullen ground,°   *dull background*
     My reformation, glitt'ring o'er my fault,
     Shall show more goodly and attract more eyes
     Than that which hath no foil to set it off.
     I'll so offend to° make offence a skill,°   *as to / an art*
195   Redeeming time[1] when men think least I will.   *Exit*

1.3

Enter the KING, [*the Earls of*] NORTHUMBERLAND [*and*]
WORCESTER, HOTSPUR, *Sir Walter* BLUNT, *with other*
[*lords*]
KING HENRY [*to* HOTSPUR, NORTHUMBERLAND, *and* WORCESTER]
     My blood hath been too cold and temperate,
     Unapt° to stir at these indignities,   *Slow*

---

7. A familiar form of address, conventionally used with
social inferiors.
8. I have suits of coarse cloth for the purpose.
9. But I fear they will be more than we can manage.
1. Making amends for misspent time. Injunctions to

redeem time were both proverbial and biblical: see
Ephesians 5:16 or Colossians 4:5.
1.3. Location: A royal residence, probably Windsor
Castle.

And you have found me,° for accordingly   *discovered this fact*
You tread upon my patience; but be sure
5   I will from henceforth rather be myself,°   *(i.e., my royal self)*
Mighty and to be feared, than my condition,[1]
Which hath been smooth as oil, soft as young down,
And therefore lost that title of° respect   *claim to*
Which the proud soul ne'er pays but to the proud.
10 WORCESTER   Our house,[2] my sovereign liege, little deserves
The scourge of greatness to be used on it,
And that same greatness too, which our own hands
Have holp° to make so portly.°   *helped / majestic*
NORTHUMBERLAND [*to the* KING]   My lord—
KING HENRY   Worcester, get thee gone, for I do see
15 Danger and disobedience in thine eye.
O sir, your presence is too bold and peremptory,°   *proud*
And majesty might never yet endure
The moody frontier[3] of a servant brow.
You have good leave° to leave us. When we need   *full permission*
20 Your use and counsel we shall send for you. *Exit* WORCESTER
You were about to speak.
NORTHUMBERLAND   Yea, my good lord.
Those prisoners in your highness' name demanded,
Which Harry Percy here at Holmedon took,
Were, as he says, not with such strength denied
25 As was delivered° to your majesty,   *reported*
Who either through envy° or misprision°   *malice / error*
Was guilty of this fault, and not my son.
HOTSPUR [*to the* KING]   My liege, I did deny no prisoners;
But I remember, when the fight was done,
30 When I was dry° with rage and extreme toil,   *thirsty*
Breathless and faint, leaning upon my sword,
Came there a certain lord, neat and trimly dressed,
Fresh as a bridegroom, and his chin, new-reaped,[4]
Showed° like a stubble-land at harvest-home.[5]   *Looked*
35 He was perfumèd like a milliner,[6]
And 'twixt his finger and his thumb he held
A pouncet-box,[7] which ever and anon
He gave his nose and took't away again—
Who° therewith angry, when it next came there   *(the nose)*
40 Took it in snuff[8]—and still he smiled and talked;
And as the soldiers bore dead bodies by,
He called them untaught knaves, unmannerly
To bring a slovenly° unhandsome corpse   *base; nasty*
Betwixt the wind and his nobility.
45 With many holiday and lady° terms   *dainty and effeminate*
He questioned me; amongst the rest demanded
My prisoners in your majesty's behalf.
I then, all smarting with my wounds being cold—
To be so pestered with a popinjay!°—   *parrot; vain dandy*

1. My natural (mild) temperament.
2. The Percy family, which had supported Henry against Richard II.
3. The angry expression (punning on "frontier" as meaning both "forehead" and "military fortifications").
4. Newly trimmed. London in the 1590s witnessed a fashion for close-shaved beards.
5. At the end of harvest (when the fields are cut back to stubble).
6. Seller of finely scented apparel such as bonnets, ribbons, and gloves. The name derives from the fact that these goods were often imports from Milan.
7. Perfume box with a perforated lid.
8. Took offense at it; inhaled it.

50 Out of my grief° and my impatience   *pain*
   Answered neglectingly,° I know not what—   *negligently*
   He should, or should not—for he made me mad
   To see him shine so brisk, and smell so sweet,
   And talk so like a waiting gentlewoman
55 Of guns, and drums, and wounds, God save the mark!⁹
   And telling me the sovereign'st° thing on earth   *best*
   Was parmacity¹ for an inward bruise,
   And that it was great pity, so it was,
   This villainous saltpetre² should be digged
60 Out of the bowels of the harmless earth,
   Which many a good tall° fellow had destroyed   *brave*
   So cowardly, and but for these vile guns
   He would himself have been a soldier.
   This bald unjointed° chat of his, my lord,   *This trivial incoherent*
65 Made me to answer indirectly, as I said,
   And I beseech you, let not his report
   Come current° for an accusation   *Be taken as valid*
   Betwixt my love and your high majesty.
   BLUNT [*to the* KING]   The circumstance considered, good my lord,
70 Whate'er Lord Harry Percy then had said
   To such a person, and in such a place,
   At such a time, with all the rest retold,
   May reasonably die, and never rise
   To do him wrong or any way impeach
75 What then he said, so° he unsay it now.   *if*
   KING HENRY   Why, yet he doth deny° his prisoners,   *refuse to hand over*
   But with proviso and exception
   That we at our own charge shall ransom straight°   *immediately*
   His brother-in-law the foolish Mortimer,³
80 Who, on my soul, hath wilfully betrayed
   The lives of those that he did lead to fight
   Against that great magician, damned Glyndŵr—
   Whose daughter, as we hear, the Earl of March
   Hath lately married. Shall our coffers, then,
85 Be emptied to redeem a traitor home?
   Shall we buy treason, and indent with fears⁴
   When they have lost and forfeited themselves?
   No, on the barren mountains let him starve;
   For I shall never hold that man my friend
90 Whose tongue shall ask me for one penny cost
   To ransom home revolted° Mortimer—   *rebellious*
   HOTSPUR   Revolted Mortimer?
   He never did fall off,° my sovereign liege,   *change allegiance*
   But by the chance of war. To prove that true
95 Needs no more but one tongue for all those wounds,
   Those mouthèd° wounds, which valiantly he took   *gaping; eloquent*

---

9. God keep evil away (an expression of indignation).
1. Spermaceti, an oily substance from the sperm whale that was used in various medicines and potions. The spelling "parmacity" probably derives from the ointment's association with the Italian city of Parma.
2. The main ingredient of gunpowder.
3. Shakespeare follows Holinshed's *Chronicles* in confusing or conflating two Edmund Mortimers. One was

captured by Glyndŵr and later became Glyndŵr's son-in-law and Hotspur's brother-in-law. The other, the fifth Earl of March, was his nephew and claimed the English throne as a descendant of Lionel, Duke of Clarence, third son of Edward III. This Mortimer was the one named by Richard II as his presumptive heir.
4. And bargain with those whom we have reason to fear.

When on the gentle Severn's⁵ sedgy° bank,   *marshy*
In single opposition, hand to hand,
He did confound° the best part of an hour   *consume*
100   In changing hardiment° with great Glyndŵr.   *matching valor*
Three times they breathed,° and three times did they drink,   *rested*
Upon agreement, of swift Severn's flood,
Who, then affrighted with their bloody looks,
Ran fearfully among the trembling reeds,
105   And hid his crisp° head in the hollow bank,   *rippled*
Bloodstainèd with these valiant combatants.
Never did bare and rotten policy°   *cunning*
Colour° her working with such deadly wounds,   *Disguise*
Nor never could the noble Mortimer
110   Receive so many, and all willingly.
Then let not him be slandered with revolt.⁶
KING HENRY   Thou dost belie° him, Percy, thou dost belie him.   *misrepresent*
He never did encounter with Glyndŵr. I tell thee,
He durst as well have met the devil alone
115   As Owain Glyndŵr for an enemy.
Art thou not ashamed? But, sirrah, henceforth
Let me not hear you speak of Mortimer.
Send me your prisoners with the speediest means,
Or you shall hear in such a kind from me
120   As will displease you.—My lord Northumberland,
We license your departure with your son.
        [*To* HOTSPUR] Send us your prisoners, or you'll hear of it.
            Exeunt [*all but* HOTSPUR *and* NORTHUMBERLAND]
HOTSPUR   An if° the devil come and roar for them   *An if = If*
I will not send them. I will after straight°   *go after him at once*
125   And tell him so, for I will ease my heart,
Although it be with hazard of my head.
NORTHUMBERLAND   What, drunk with choler?° Stay and pause awhile.   *anger*
            Enter [*the Earl of*] WORCESTER
Here comes your uncle.
HOTSPUR   Speak of Mortimer?
Zounds, I will speak of him, and let my soul
130   Want mercy° if I do not join with him.   *Be damned*
In his behalf I'll empty all these veins,
And shed my dear blood drop by drop in the dust,
But I will lift the downfall° Mortimer   *downfallen*
As high in the air as this unthankful King,
135   As this ingrate and cankered° Bolingbroke.⁷   *corrupted*
NORTHUMBERLAND [*to* WORCESTER]   Brother, the King hath
        made your nephew mad.
WORCESTER   Who struck this heat up after I was gone?
HOTSPUR   He will forsooth have all my prisoners;
And when I urged the ransom once again
140   Of my wife's brother, then his cheek looked pale,
And on my face he turned an eye of death,°   *a menacing look*
Trembling even at the name of Mortimer.

5. The Severn River flows from Wales into Bristol   7. Henry's family name. Hotspur's use of it suggests his
Channel in England.   unwillingness to acknowledge Henry as King.
6. With the accusation of having revolted.

WORCESTER   I cannot blame him: was not he proclaimed
   By Richard, that dead is, the next of blood?°   *heir to the throne*
145 NORTHUMBERLAND   He was; I heard the proclamation.
   And then it was when the unhappy° King,   *unfortunate*
   Whose wrongs in us° God pardon, did set forth   *done by us*
   Upon his Irish expedition,[8]
   From whence he, intercepted,° did return   *interrupted*
150   To be deposed, and shortly murderèd.
WORCESTER   And for whose death we in the world's wide mouth
   Live scandalized° and foully spoken of.   *disgraced*
HOTSPUR   But soft,° I pray you; did King Richard then   *wait*
   Proclaim my brother° Edmund Mortimer   *brother-in-law*
   Heir to the crown?
155 NORTHUMBERLAND   He did; myself did hear it.
HOTSPUR   Nay, then I cannot blame his cousin[9] King
   That wished him on the barren mountains starve.
   But shall it be that you that set the crown
   Upon the head of this forgetful man,
160   And for his sake wear the detested blot
   Of murderous subornation,[1] shall it be
   That you a world of curses undergo,
   Being the agents or base second means,
   The cords, the ladder, or the hangman, rather?
165   O, pardon me that I descend so low
   To show the line and the predicament
   Wherein you range[2] under this subtle° King!   *cunning*
   Shall it for shame be spoken in these days,
   Or fill up chronicles in time to come,
170   That men of your nobility and power
   Did gage° them both in an unjust behalf,°   *pledge / cause*
   As both of you, God pardon it, have done:
   To put down Richard, that sweet lovely rose,
   And plant this thorn, this canker,[3] Bolingbroke?
175   And shall it in more shame be further spoken
   That you are fooled, discarded, and shook off
   By him for whom these shames ye underwent?
   No; yet time serves° wherein you may redeem   *is available*
   Your banished honours, and restore yourselves
180   Into the good thoughts of the world again,
   Revenge the jeering and disdained° contempt   *disdainful*
   Of this proud King, who studies day and night
   To answer° all the debt he owes to you   *satisfy*
   Even with the bloody payment of your deaths.
   Therefore, I say—
185 WORCESTER   Peace, cousin, say no more.
   And now I will unclasp a secret book,
   And to your quick-conceiving discontents
   I'll read you matter deep and dangerous,
   As full of peril and adventurous spirit

---

8. As Shakespeare dramatizes in *Richard II*, Boling-
broke returned to England from exile in France while
Richard was at war in Ireland.
9. Punning on "cozen" (cheat).
1. Of assisting with a murder.
2. *To . . . range*: To show the degree and category into
which you might be classified (with a pun on "line" as
meaning "hangman's rope" and on "predicament" as
meaning "an unpleasant situation").
3. Wild and inferior kind of rose; also, cankerworm
(which destroys plants), or ulcerated sore.

190   As to o'erwalk° a current roaring loud   *walk across*
        On the unsteadfast footing of a spear.
        HOTSPUR   If he fall in, good night, or sink or swim.[4]
        Send danger from the east unto the west,
        So° honour cross it from the north to south;   *Provided*
195   And let them grapple. O, the blood more stirs
        To rouse a lion than to start a hare!
        NORTHUMBERLAND [*to* WORCESTER]   Imagination of some great exploit
        Drives him beyond the bounds of patience.
        HOTSPUR   By heaven, methinks it were an easy leap
200   To pluck bright honour from the pale-faced moon,
        Or dive into the bottom of the deep,
        Where fathom-line[5] could never touch the ground,
        And pluck up drownèd honour by the locks,
        So he that doth redeem her thence might wear,
205   Without corrival,° all her dignities.   *competitor*
        But out upon this half-faced fellowship!°   *paltry sharing of honors*
        WORCESTER [*to* NORTHUMBERLAND]   He apprehends a world of
          figures[6] here,
        But not the form of what he should attend.°   *pay attention to*
        [*To* HOTSPUR] Good cousin, give me audience for a while,
210   And list° to me.   *listen*
        HOTSPUR   I cry you mercy.°   *I beg your pardon*
        WORCESTER   Those same noble Scots[7]
        That are your prisoners—
        HOTSPUR   I'll keep them all.
        By God, he shall not have a Scot of them;
        No, if a scot would save his soul he shall not.
        I'll keep them, by this hand.
215   WORCESTER   You start away,
        And lend no ear unto my purposes.
        Those prisoners you shall keep.
        HOTSPUR   Nay, I will; that's flat.
        He said he would not ransom Mortimer,
        Forbade my tongue to speak of Mortimer;
220   But I will find him when he lies asleep,
        And in his ear I'll hollo 'Mortimer!'
        Nay, I'll have a starling shall be taught to speak
        Nothing but 'Mortimer', and give it him
        To keep his anger still° in motion.   *constantly*
225   WORCESTER   Hear you, cousin, a word.
        HOTSPUR   All studies here I solemnly defy,°   *renounce*
        Save how to gall and pinch° this Bolingbroke.   *torture*
        And that same sword-and-buckler[8] Prince of Wales—
        But that I think his father loves him not
230   And would be glad he met with some mischance—
        I would have him poisoned with a pot of ale.[9]
        WORCESTER   Farewell, kinsman. I'll talk to you
        When you are better tempered to attend.

---

4. Farewell to him, whether he sinks or manages to swim for a short time.
5. A weighted line used in testing the depth of the sea.
6. Figures of speech; fantasies.
7. Inhabitants of Scotland (with a pun in the following lines on "scot" as meaning "a small sum").
8. In Elizabethan England, the sword and buckler, or small shield, were associated with ordinary fighting men. A prince should use rapier and dagger.
9. A drink associated with the common people.

NORTHUMBERLAND [*to* HOTSPUR] Why, what a wasp-stung and
          impatient fool
235   Art thou to break into this woman's mood,[1]
    Tying thine ear to no tongue but thine own!
HOTSPUR Why, look you, I am whipped and scourged with rods,
    Nettled and stung with pismires,° when I hear   *ants*
    Of this vile politician° Bolingbroke.   *schemer*
240   In Richard's time—what d'ye call the place?
    A plague upon't, it is in Gloucestershire.
    'Twas where the madcap Duke his uncle kept—
    His uncle York—where I first bowed my knee
    Unto this king of smiles, this Bolingbroke.[2]
245   'Sblood, when you and he came back from Ravenspurgh.[3]
NORTHUMBERLAND At Berkeley castle.
HOTSPUR   You say true.
    Why, what a candy deal of° courtesy   *quantity of sweet*
    This fawning greyhound then did proffer me!
    'Look when° his infant fortune came to age',   *Whenever; as soon as*
250   And 'gentle Harry Percy', and 'kind cousin'.
    O, the devil take such cozeners!°—God forgive me.   *cheaters*
    Good uncle, tell your tale; I have done.
WORCESTER Nay, if you have not, to't again.
    We'll stay° your leisure.   *await*
HOTSPUR   I have done, i'faith.
255 WORCESTER Then once more to your Scottish prisoners.
    Deliver them up° without their ransom straight;   *Release them*
    And make the Douglas'[4] son your only mean°   *agent; means*
    For powers° in Scotland, which, for divers reasons *raising an army*
    Which I shall send you written, be assured
260   Will easily be granted. [*To* NORTHUMBERLAND] You, my lord,
    Your son in Scotland being thus employed,
    Shall secretly into the bosom creep
    Of that same noble prelate well-beloved,
    The Archbishop.
HOTSPUR   Of York, is't not?
WORCESTER   True, who bears hard°   *resents*
265   His brother's death at Bristol, the Lord Scrope.[5]
    I speak not this in estimation,°   *as a guess*
    As what I think might be, but what I know
    Is ruminated, plotted, and set down,
    And only stays° but to behold the face   *waits*
270   Of that occasion that shall bring it on.
HOTSPUR I smell it; upon my life, it will do well!
NORTHUMBERLAND Before the game is afoot thou still lett'st slip.[6]
HOTSPUR Why, it cannot choose but be a noble plot—
    And then the power° of Scotland and of York   *army*
    To join with Mortimer, ha?
275 WORCESTER   And so they shall.

---

1. Alluding to the commonplace that women were, by nature, unable to hold their tongues.
2. This event is depicted in *Richard II* 2.3.20–56.
3. Bolingbroke's landing place at the mouth of the Humber River in Yorkshire upon his return from exile.
4. The "the" before Douglas's name indicates that he is head of a Scottish clan or noble family.
5. Richard Scroop (or le Scrope), the Archbishop of

York and an ally of the rebels in this play, was actually a distant cousin of William Scroop, Earl of Wiltshire, who was a favorite of Richard II and was executed by Henry IV in 1399. His death is mentioned in *Richard II* 3.2.
6. Before the quarry is even in the field, you always let loose the dogs. This image from hunting implies that Hotspur habitually jumps the gun.

HOTSPUR   In faith, it is exceedingly well aimed.

WORCESTER   And 'tis no little reason bids us speed
To save our heads by raising of a head;°   *an army*
For, bear ourselves as even° as we can,   *carefully*
280   The King will always think him in our debt,
And think we think ourselves unsatisfied
Till he hath found a time to pay us home.°   *repay us fully*
And see already how he doth begin
To make us strangers to his looks of love.
285   HOTSPUR   He does, he does. We'll be revenged on him.

WORCESTER   Cousin, farewell. No further go in this
Than I by letters shall direct your course.
When time is ripe, which will be suddenly,°   *soon*
I'll steal to Glyndŵr and Lord Mortimer,
290   Where you and Douglas and our powers at once,
As I will fashion it, shall happily meet,
To bear our fortunes in our own strong arms,
Which now we hold at° much uncertainty.   *with*

NORTHUMBERLAND   Farewell, good brother. We shall thrive, I
trust.
295   HOTSPUR [*to* WORCESTER]   Uncle, adieu. O, let the hours be short
Till fields° and blows and groans applaud our sport!   *battlefields*

Exeunt [WORCESTER *at one door,*
NORTHUMBERLAND *and* HOTSPUR *at another door*]

2.1

Enter a CARRIER,[1] *with a lantern in his hand*

FIRST CARRIER   Heigh-ho! An't° be not four by the day,° I'll be   *If it / in the morning*
hanged. Charles's Wain[2] is over the new chimney, and yet our
horse° not packed. What, ostler![3]   *horses*

OSTLER [*within*]   Anon,° anon!   *Right away*

5   FIRST CARRIER   I prithee, Tom, beat cut's saddle,[4] put a few
flocks in the point.[5] Poor jade is wrung in the withers,[6] out of
all cess.°   *measure*

Enter another CARRIER

SECOND CARRIER   Peas and beans° are as dank here as a dog,   *(horse feed)*
and that is the next way to give poor jades the bots.° This   *intestinal worms*
10   house is turned upside down since Robin Ostler died.

FIRST CARRIER   Poor fellow never joyed since the price of oats
rose; it was the death of him.

SECOND CARRIER   I think this be the most villainous house in all
London road for fleas. I am stung like a tench.[7]

15   FIRST CARRIER   Like a tench? By the mass, there is ne'er a king
christen° could be better bit than I have been since the first   *Christian king*
cock.°   *midnight*

2.1 Location: An innyard in Rochester, Kent.
1. One who transports goods for hire.
2. The constellation now known as the Plow or the Great Bear.
3. One who attends to horses at an inn.
4. Soften the horse's saddle. "Cut" was a term for a horse with a docked tail or a gelding; here, it may be the
horse's name.
5. Put a few tufts of wood in the saddle's pommel (to soften it).
6. The poor old horse is extremely sore in the ridge between its shoulder blades.
7. A spotted fish whose markings may have looked like flea bites.

SECOND CARRIER   Why, they will allow us ne'er a jordan,° and
then we leak° in your chimney, and your chamber-lye° breeds
20   fleas like a loach.⁸

chamber pot
urinate / urine

FIRST CARRIER   What, ostler! Come away, and be hanged, come
away!

SECOND CARRIER   I have a gammon of bacon° and two races°
of ginger to be delivered as far as Charing Cross.⁹

a ham / roots

25   FIRST CARRIER   God's body, the turkeys in my pannier° are
quite starved! What, ostler! A plague on thee, hast thou never
an eye in thy head? Canst not hear? An° 'twere not as good deed
as drink to break the pate° on thee, I am a very villain. Come,
and be hanged! Hast no faith° in thee?

basket

If
skull
responsibility

Enter GADSHILL

30   GADSHILL   Good morrow, carriers. What's o'clock?

FIRST CARRIER   I think it be two o'clock.

GADSHILL   I prithee lend me thy lantern to see my gelding in the
stable.

FIRST CARRIER   Nay, by God, soft.° I know a trick worth two of
35   that, i'faith.

wait

GADSHILL [*to* SECOND CARRIER]   I pray thee, lend me thine.

SECOND CARRIER   Ay, when? Canst tell?¹ 'Lend me thy lantern,'
quoth a.° Marry, I'll see thee hanged first.

says he

GADSHILL   Sirrah carrier, what time do you mean to come to
40   London?

SECOND CARRIER   Time enough to go to bed with a candle, I
warrant° thee.—Come, neighbour Mugs, we'll call up the
gentlemen. They will along° with company, for they have great
charge.°   *Exeunt* [CARRIERS]

assure
travel
have valuable cargo

45   GADSHILL   What ho, chamberlain!²

Enter CHAMBERLAIN

CHAMBERLAIN   'At hand' quoth Pickpurse.³

GADSHILL   That's even as fair° as "'At hand" quoth the cham-
berlain', for thou variest no more from picking of purses than
giving direction doth from labouring:⁴ thou layest the plot°
50   how.

good

plan

CHAMBERLAIN   Good morrow, Master Gadshill. It holds current
that° I told you yesternight. There's a franklin in the
Weald⁵ of Kent hath brought three hundred marks⁶ with him
in gold. I heard him tell it to one of his company last night at
55   supper—a kind of auditor, one that hath abundance of charge
too, God knows what. They are up already, and call for eggs
and butter; they will away presently.

holds true what

GADSHILL   Sirrah, if they meet not with Saint Nicholas's
clerks,⁷ I'll give thee this neck.

60   CHAMBERLAIN   No, I'll none of it; I pray thee keep that for the
hangman, for I know thou worshippest Saint Nicholas as truly
as a man of falsehood may.

8. A fish. The comparison means that urine breeds
fleas either as a loach breeds loaches or as a loach
breeds fleas. There was a popular belief that some fish
spawned flies or fleas.
9. A marketplace between London and Westminster.
1. A retort similar to "Never."
2. Bedroom attendant. In popular discourse, chamber-
lains were notorious for their complicity with thieves.
3. "I am at your disposal," as the thief said (evidently a

popular tag).
4. For you are not more different from a pickpocket
than an overseer is from a laborer.
5. There's a small landowner in the wooded region.
6. Coins worth two-thirds of a pound each.
7. Slang for "highway robbers." St. Nicholas was vari-
ously regarded as the patron saint of travelers and of
thieves.

GADSHILL   What talkest thou to me of the hangman? If I hang,
I'll make a fat pair of gallows, for if I hang, old Sir John hangs
65   with me, and thou knowest he's no starveling. Tut, there are
other Trojans⁸ that thou dreamest not of, the which° for sport'   who
sake are content to do the profession° some grace, that would,   (of robbery)
if matters should be looked into, for their own credit' sake
make all whole.° I am joined with no foot-landrakers,⁹ no   set things right
70   long-staff sixpenny strikers,¹ none of these mad mustachio
purple-hued maltworms,² but with nobility and tranquillity,
burgomasters and great 'oyez'-ers;³ such as can hold in,° such   can keep a secret
as will strike sooner than speak, and speak sooner than drink,
and drink sooner than pray. And yet, zounds, I lie, for they
75   pray continually to their saint the commonwealth; or rather,
not pray to her, but prey on her; for they ride up and down⁴
on her and make her their boots.°   booty; footwear
CHAMBERLAIN   What, the commonwealth their boots? Will she
hold out water in foul way?⁵
80   GADSHILL   She will, she will, justice hath liquored her.⁶ We steal
as in a castle,° cocksure; we have the recipe of fern-seed,⁷ we   in complete safety
walk invisible.
CHAMBERLAIN   Nay, by my faith, I think you are more beholden
to the night than to fern-seed for your walking invisible.
85   GADSHILL   Give me thy hand; thou shalt have a share in our
purchase,° as I am a true man.   plunder
CHAMBERLAIN   Nay, rather let me have it as you are a false thief.
GADSHILL   Go to, 'homo'° is a common name to all men. Bid the   man
ostler bring my gelding out of the stable. Farewell, you muddy°   stupid
90   knave.   Exeunt [severally]°   separately

2.2

Enter PRINCE [HARRY], POINS, PETO [*and* BARDOLPH]¹
POINS   Come, shelter, shelter!
     [*Exeunt* PETO *and* BARDOLPH *at another door*]
I have removed Falstaff's horse, and he frets° like a gummed   worries; frays
velvet.²
PRINCE HARRY   Stand close!°   [*Exit* POINS]   concealed
     Enter FALSTAFF
5   FALSTAFF   Poins! Poins, and be hanged! Poins!
PRINCE HARRY   Peace, ye fat-kidneyed rascal! What a brawling
dost thou keep!
FALSTAFF   Where's Poins, Hal?
PRINCE HARRY   He is walked up to the top of the hill. I'll go seek
10   him.   [*Exit*]

8. Slang for "roisterers."
9. Highwaymen who travel on foot (rather than on
horse).
1. Thieves who carried crude weapons and robbed for
small sums.
2. These drunkards with wild mustaches and purple
faces.
3. Court officials who cried "Oyez," or "Hear ye."
4. They travel (with a pun on "ride" as meaning "to
mount sexually").
5. Will she keep water out (off your feet) on a muddy

road; will she protect you in difficulty?
6. Greased her (as one waterproofs leather); bribed
her.
7. Popularly supposed to make those who wore it invis-
ible.
2.2 Location: The highway, Gad's Hill.
1. For a discussion of the names of "Bardolph" and
"Peto," see the Textual Note and Introduction.
2. Like cheap velvet treated with gum. Gummed velvet
was shiny but wore out quickly.

FALSTAFF   I am accursed to rob in that thief's company. The
rascal hath removed my horse and tied him I know not where.
If I travel but four foot by the square° further afoot, I shall   *(a measuring tool)*
break my wind.° Well, I doubt not but to die a fair death, for³   *be breathless; fart*
15   all this—if I scape hanging for killing that rogue. I have for-
sworn his company hourly any time this two-and-twenty
years, and yet I am bewitched with the rogue's company. If the
rascal have not given me medicines° to make me love him, I'll   *love potions*
be hanged. It could not be else: I have drunk medicines.
20   Poins! Hal! A plague upon you both! Bardolph! Peto! I'll starve
ere I'll rob a foot further. An 'twere not as good a deed as drink
to turn true man° and to leave these rogues, I am the veriest   *repent; turn informer*
varlet that ever chewed with a tooth. Eight yards of uneven
ground is threescore and ten miles afoot with me, and the
25   stony-hearted villains know it well enough. A plague upon't
when thieves cannot be true one to another!
   They whistle. [Enter PRINCE HARRY, POINS, PETO, *and*
   BARDOLPH]⁴
Whew! A plague upon you all! Give me my horse, you rogues,
give me my horse, and be hanged!
PRINCE HARRY   Peace, ye fat-guts. Lie down, lay thine ear close
30   to the ground, and list if thou canst hear the tread of trav-
ellers.
FALSTAFF   Have you any levers to lift me up again, being down?
'Sblood, I'll not bear my own flesh so far afoot again for all the
coin in thy father's exchequer. What a plague mean ye to colt°   *trick*
35   me thus?
PRINCE HARRY   Thou liest: thou art not colted, thou art
uncolted.°   *unhorsed*
FALSTAFF   I prithee, good Prince Hal, help me to my horse,
good king's son.
PRINCE HARRY   Out, ye rogue, shall I be your ostler?
40   FALSTAFF   Hang thyself in thine own heir-apparent garters!⁵ If
I be ta'en, I'll peach° for this. An I have not ballads made on   *inform against you*
you all and sung to filthy tunes,⁶ let a cup of sack be my poi-
son. When a jest is so forward, and afoot too!⁷ I hate it.
   Enter GADSHILL [*visored*]°   *wearing a mask*
GADSHILL   Stand!
45   FALSTAFF   So I do, against my will.
POINS   O, 'tis our setter,° I know his voice. Gadshill, what   *one who sets up a crime*
news?
GADSHILL⁸   Case ye,° case ye, on with your visors! There's   *Disguise yourselves*
money of the King's coming down the hill; 'tis going to the
50   King's exchequer.
FALSTAFF   You lie, ye rogue, 'tis going to the King's tavern.

---

3. Die a natural death, despite.
4. It is not clear exactly when the Prince and his com-
panions show themselves to the frustrated Falstaff.
They can all enter here, or the Prince and Poins could
enter at line 28 and Bardolph and Peto at the same time
as Gadshill at line 43.
5. Falstaff's version of the proverb "He may hang him-
self in his own garters." As the heir to the throne, the
Prince was a member of the Order of the Garter, the
highest order of English knighthood.
6. Ballads on topical themes were sung by ballad
singers and sold cheaply as broadsides in streets, the-

aters, and other public places.
7. When a plot (to rob) is so advanced and goes so well;
when a joke (on me) goes so far and makes me go on
foot.
8. In Q, this speech is assigned to Bardolph; but Poins
has just asked Gadshill a question, so one expects an
answer to come from him. It has been conjectured that
the confusion here may reflect confusion in Shake-
speare's foul papers about whether Bardolph and Gad-
shill were to be two characters or one. See note to
2.5.159.

GADSHILL   There's enough to make° us all.   *make fortunes for*
FALSTAFF   To be hanged.
          [*They put on visors*]
PRINCE HARRY   Sirs, you four shall front° them in the narrow   *confront*
55   lane. Ned Poins and I will walk lower. If they scape from your
          encounter, then they light on us.
PETO   How many be there of them?
GADSHILL   Some eight or ten.
FALSTAFF   Zounds, will they not rob us?
60   PRINCE HARRY   What, a coward, Sir John Paunch?
FALSTAFF   Indeed I am not John of Gaunt[9] your grandfather,
          but yet no coward, Hal.
PRINCE HARRY   Well, we leave that to the proof.°   *test*
POINS   Sirrah Jack, thy horse stands behind the hedge. When
65   thou needest him, there thou shalt find him. Farewell, and
          stand fast.
FALSTAFF   Now cannot I strike him if I should be hanged.
PRINCE HARRY [*aside to* POINS]   Ned, where are our disguises?
POINS [*aside to the* PRINCE]   Here, hard by. Stand close.
          [*Exeunt the* PRINCE *and* POINS]
70   FALSTAFF   Now, my masters, happy man be his dole,[1] say I;
          every man to his business.
          [*They stand aside.*]
          Enter the TRAVELLERS [*amongst them the* CARRIERS]
FIRST TRAVELLER   Come, neighbour, the boy shall lead our
          horses down the hill. We'll walk afoot a while, and ease their
          legs.
75   THIEVES [*coming forward*]   Stand!
SECOND TRAVELLER   Jesus bless us!
FALSTAFF   Strike, down with them, cut the villains' throats! Ah,
          whoreson caterpillars,[2] bacon-fed knaves! They hate us youth.
          Down with them, fleece them!
80   FIRST TRAVELLER   O, we are undone, both we and ours for ever!
FALSTAFF   Hang ye, gorbellied° knaves, are ye undone? No, ye   *potbellied*
          fat chuffs;[3] I would your store° were here. On, bacons,° on!   *all you own / fat men*
          What, ye knaves! Young men must live. You are grand-jurors,[4]
          are ye? We'll jure ye, faith.
          Here they rob them and bind them. Exeunt [*the* THIEVES
          with the TRAVELLERS]

2.3

          Enter PRINCE [HARRY] *and* POINS [*disguised in buckram
          suits*]
PRINCE HARRY   The thieves have bound the true° men; now   *honest*
          could thou and I rob the thieves, and go merrily to London. It
          would be argument° for a week, laughter for a month, and a   *topic for discussion*
          good jest for ever.
5   POINS   Stand close; I hear them coming.
          [*They stand aside*]
          Enter [FALSTAFF, BARDOLPH, PETO, *and* GADSHILL, *with
          the travellers' money*]

9. Henry IV's father. Falstaff puns on "Gaunt" as mean-
ing "lean"; in fact, his name is derived from "Ghent,"
his birthplace.
1. Proverbial expression meaning "Good luck to every-
one."
2. Parasites. *whoreson:* an insult derived from "whore's

son."
3. Rude, churlish fellows; misers.
4. Referring to the fact that only prosperous citizens
served on grand juries.
2.3 Location: Scene continues.

FALSTAFF Come, my masters, let us share, and then to horse
before day. An° the Prince and Poins be not two arrant cow-
ards, there's no equity stirring.° There's no more valour in that
Poins than in a wild duck.
     As they are sharing, the PRINCE *and* POINS *set upon*
     them
10 PRINCE HARRY Your money!
POINS Villains!
     They all [GADSHILL, BARDOLPH, *and* PETO] *run away*
     [*severally*] *and* FALSTAFF, *after a blow or two,* [*roars and*]
     runs away too, leaving the booty behind them
PRINCE HARRY Got with much ease. Now merrily to horse.
The thieves are all scattered, and possessed with fear
So strongly that they dare not meet each other.
15 Each takes his fellow for an officer.
Away, good Ned. Falstaff sweats to death,
And lards° the lean earth as he walks along.
Were't not for laughing, I should pity him.
POINS How the fat rogue roared!   *Exeunt* [*with the booty*]

If
justice to be found

drips fat on

2.4
     Enter HOTSPUR, *reading a letter*
HOTSPUR 'But for mine own part, my lord, I could be well con-
tented to be there, in respect of° the love I bear your house.'°—
He could be contented; why is he not then? In respect of the
love he bears our house! He shows in this he loves his own barn
5 better than he loves our house. Let me see some more.—'The
purpose you undertake is dangerous'— Why, that's certain: 'tis
dangerous to take a cold, to sleep, to drink; but I tell you, my
lord fool, out of this nettle danger we pluck this flower safety.—
'The purpose you undertake is dangerous, the friends you have
10 named uncertain, the time itself unsorted,° and your
whole plot too light for the counterpoise of° so great an
opposition.'— Say you so, say you so? I say unto you again, you
are a shallow, cowardly hind,° and you lie. What a lack-brain
is this! By the Lord, our plot is a good plot as ever was laid,
15 our friends true and constant; a good plot, good friends, and
full of expectation; an excellent plot, very good friends. What
a frosty-spirited rogue is this! Why, my lord of York° commends
the plot and the general course of the action. Zounds, an I
were now by this rascal, I could brain him with his lady's fan!
20 Is there not my father, my uncle, and myself? Lord Edmund
Mortimer, my lord of York, and Owain Glyndŵr? Is there not
besides the Douglas? Have I not all their letters, to meet me
in arms by the ninth of the next month? And are they not
some of them set forward already? What a pagan rascal is this,
25 an infidel! Ha, you shall see now, in very sincerity of fear and
cold heart will he to the King, and lay open all our proceed-
ings! O, I could divide myself and go to buffets[1] for moving°
such a dish of skim-milk with so honourable an action! Hang
him! Let him tell the King we are prepared; I will set forward
30 tonight.
     Enter his Lady [LADY PERCY]

because of / family

unsuitable
to counterbalance

peasant

(Archbishop Scrope)

urging

2.4 Location: The Percys' home, Warkworth Castle, in
Northumberland.

1. I could split myself into two and fall to blows with
myself.

How now, Kate? I must leave you within these two hours.
LADY PERCY   O my good lord, why are you thus alone?
For what offence have I this fortnight been
A banished woman from my Harry's bed?
35 Tell me, sweet lord, what is't that takes from thee
Thy stomach,° pleasure, and thy golden sleep?   appetite
Why dost thou bend thine eyes upon the earth,
And start so often when thou sitt'st alone?
Why hast thou lost the fresh blood in thy cheeks,
40 And given my treasures and my rights² of thee
To thick-eyed° musing and curst melancholy?   vacantly staring
In thy faint° slumbers I by thee have watched,   restless
And heard thee murmur tales of iron wars,
Speak terms of manège° to thy bounding steed,   horsemanship
45 Cry 'Courage! To the field!' And thou hast talked
Of sallies and retires,° of trenches, tents,   advances and retreats
Of palisadoes,³ frontiers,° parapets,   ramparts
Of basilisks, of cannon, culverin,⁴
Of prisoners ransomed, and of soldiers slain,
50 And all the currents of a heady° fight.   headlong
Thy spirit within thee hath been so at war,
And thus hath so bestirred thee in thy sleep,
That beads of sweat have stood upon thy brow
Like bubbles in a late-disturbèd° stream;   recently disturbed
55 And in thy face strange motions have appeared,
Such as we see when men restrain their breath
On some great sudden hest.° O, what portents are these?   command
Some heavy° business hath my lord in hand,   serious; sad
And I must know it, else he loves me not.
HOTSPUR   What ho!
    [Enter SERVANT]
60   Is Gilliams with the packet gone?
SERVANT   He is, my lord, an hour ago.
HOTSPUR   Hath Butler brought those horses from the sheriff?
SERVANT   One horse, my lord, he brought even now.
HOTSPUR   What horse? A roan, a crop-ear, is it not?
SERVANT   It is, my lord.
65 HOTSPUR   That roan shall be my throne.
Well, I will back him straight.—O, Esperance!⁵—
Bid Butler lead him forth into the park.
LADY PERCY   But hear you, my lord.
HOTSPUR   What sayst thou, my lady?
LADY PERCY   What is it carries you away?
HOTSPUR   Why, my horse,
My love, my horse.
70 LADY PERCY   Out, you mad-headed ape!
A weasel⁶ hath not such a deal of spleen°   impulsiveness; anger
As you are tossed with.
In faith, I'll know your business, Harry, that I will.

2. Marriage rights. Alluding to the belief that husbands and wives owe a mutual marriage debt that obliges them regularly to engage in sexual relations with one another.
3. Pointed stakes driven into the ground as defensive barriers.
4. *basilisks:* large cannons, named after a deadly mythological reptile. *culverin:* a name for both a kind of long cannon and a firearm noted for its ability to fire over a long range.
5. Referring to the Percy motto *Esperance ma comforte,* or "Hope is my reliance."
6. Weasels were proverbially quarrelsome.

I fear my brother Mortimer doth stir
75   About his title, and hath sent for you
To line° his enterprise; but if you go—   *strengthen*
HOTSPUR   So far afoot? I shall be weary, love.
LADY PERCY   Come, come, you paraquito,° answer me   *little parrot*
Directly to this question that I ask.
80   In faith, I'll break thy little finger,° Harry,   *(euphemism for "penis")*
An if thou wilt not tell me all things true.
HOTSPUR   Away, away, you trifler! Love? I love thee not,
I care not for thee, Kate. This is no world
To play with maumets[7] and to tilt° with lips.   *duel*
85   We must have bloody noses and cracked crowns,[8]
And pass them current,[9] too. God's me,° my horse!—   *God save me*
What sayst thou, Kate? What wouldst thou have with me?
LADY PERCY   Do you not love me? Do you not indeed?
Well, do not, then, for since you love me not
90   I will not love myself. Do you not love me?
Nay, tell me if you speak in jest or no.
HOTSPUR   Come, wilt thou see me ride?
And when I am a-horseback,[1] I will swear
I love thee infinitely. But hark you, Kate.
95   I must not have you henceforth question me
Whither I go, nor reason whereabout.°   *discuss about what*
Whither I must, I must; and, to conclude,
This evening must I leave you, gentle Kate.
I know you wise, but yet no farther wise
100   Than Harry Percy's wife; constant you are,
But yet a woman;[2] and for secrecy
No lady closer,° for I well believe   *more secretive*
Thou wilt not utter what thou dost not know.
And so far will I trust thee, gentle Kate.
105   LADY PERCY   How, so far?
HOTSPUR   Not an inch further. But hark you, Kate,
Whither I go, thither shall you go too.
Today will I set forth, tomorrow you.
Will this content you, Kate?
LADY PERCY   It must, of force.°   *Exeunt*   *of necessity*

2.5

Enter PRINCE [HARRY]
PRINCE HARRY   Ned, prithee come out of that fat° room, and   *stuffy*
lend me thy hand to laugh a little.
Enter POINS [*at another door*]
POINS   Where hast been, Hal?
PRINCE HARRY   With three or four loggerheads,° amongst three   *blockheads*
5   or fourscore hogsheads.° I have sounded the very bass-string of   *casks for liquor*
humility. Sirrah, I am sworn brother to a leash of drawers,° and   *group of three tapsters*
can call them all by their christen names, as 'Tom', 'Dick', and
'Francis'. They take it already, upon their salvation, that

7. Breasts; dolls; false gods. The term derived from "mahomet," whom English Protestants viewed as a false god worshipped by heathen peoples.
8. Punning on "cracked crowns" as meaning "broken heads" and "counterfeit currency." Hotspur may be alluding to the acts of rape associated with warfare: "nose" is slang for "penis," and a "cracked crown" can mean a "whore" or "deflowered woman."
9. Establish them as the norm; let them circulate.
1. On my horse; having sexual intercourse.
2. Women were assumed to be great talkers who could keep no secrets.
2.5 Location: An inn in Eastcheap, London.

though I be but Prince of Wales yet I am the king of courtesy,
10 and tell me flatly I am no proud jack° like Falstaff, but a   *fellow*
Corinthian,[1] a lad of mettle, a good boy—by the Lord, so they
call me; and when I am King of England I shall command all
the good lads in Eastcheap. They call drinking deep 'dyeing
scarlet',[2] and when you breathe in your watering[3] they cry
15 'Hem!' and bid you 'Play it off!'° To conclude, I am so good a   *Drink up*
proficient in one quarter of an hour that I can drink with any
tinker° in his own language during my life. I tell thee, Ned,   *itinerant pot mender*
thou hast lost much honour that thou wert not with me in this
action. But, sweet Ned—to sweeten which name of Ned I give
20 thee this penny-worth of sugar,[4] clapped even now into my
hand by an underskinker,° one that never spake other English   *assistant tapster*
in his life than 'Eight shillings and sixpence', and 'You are wel-
come', with this shrill addition, 'Anon,° anon, sir! Score° a   *At once / Chalk up*
pint of bastard[5] in the Half-moon!'[6] or so. But, Ned, to drive
25 away the time till Falstaff come, I prithee do thou stand in
some by-room, while I question my puny° drawer to what end   *inexperienced*
he gave me the sugar, and do thou never leave calling 'Fran-
cis!', that his tale to me may be nothing but 'Anon!' Step aside,
and I'll show thee a precedent.°   [*Exit* POINS]   *give you a foretaste*
30 POINS [*within*]   Francis!
PRINCE HARRY   Thou art perfect.
POINS [*within*]   Francis!
            Enter [FRANCIS, *a*] *drawer*
FRANCIS   Anon, anon, sir!—Look down into the Pomegranate,[7]
    Ralph!
35 PRINCE HARRY   Come hither, Francis.
FRANCIS   My lord.
PRINCE HARRY   How long hast thou to serve,[8] Francis?
FRANCIS   Forsooth, five years, and as much as to—
POINS [*within*]   Francis!
40 FRANCIS   Anon, anon, sir!
PRINCE HARRY   Five year! By'r Lady,[9] a long lease for the clink-
    ing of pewter. But Francis, darest thou be so valiant as to play
    the coward with thy indenture,° and show it a fair pair of   *contract*
    heels, and run from it?
45 FRANCIS   O Lord, sir, I'll be sworn upon all the books° in En-   *(Bibles)*
    gland, I could find in my heart—
POINS [*within*]   Francis!
FRANCIS   Anon, sir!
PRINCE HARRY   How old art thou, Francis?
50 FRANCIS   Let me see, about Michaelmas[1] next I shall be—
POINS [*within*]   Francis!
FRANCIS   Anon, sir! [*To the* PRINCE] Pray, stay a little, my lord.

---

1. A rich, licentious man. In contemporary texts, ancient Corinth was famous for wealth and sensuality.
2. Referring to the ruddy complexion associated with drunkards or to the fact that urine, a product of drink, was used to dye wool.
3. When you pause to breathe in your drink.
4. Tapsters sold sugar to sweeten wine.
5. A Spanish wine, so named because it was mixed or adulterated with honey.

6. Name of the inn room to which the wine is to be charged.
7. Name of another room in the inn.
8. Serve as apprentice. Apprenticeship typically began at age twelve or fourteen and lasted seven years.
9. By our Lady (an oath invoking the Virgin Mary).
1. September 29, a holy day honoring the archangel Michael and signifying to tradespeople the close of an accounting period.

PRINCE HARRY   Nay, but hark you, Francis. For the sugar thou
gavest me, 'twas a pennyworth, was't not?

55 FRANCIS   O Lord, I would it had been two!

PRINCE HARRY   I will give thee for it a thousand pound. Ask me
when thou wilt, and thou shalt have it—

POINS [*within*]   Francis!

FRANCIS   Anon, anon!

60 PRINCE HARRY   Anon, Francis? No, Francis, but tomorrow,
Francis; or, Francis, o' Thursday; or, indeed, Francis, when
thou wilt. But Francis.

FRANCIS   My lord.

PRINCE HARRY   Wilt thou rob this leathern-jerkin, crystal-

65 button, knot-pated, agate-ring, puke-stocking, caddis-garter,
smooth-tongue, Spanish-pouch?²

FRANCIS   O Lord, sir, who do you mean?

PRINCE HARRY   Why, then, your brown bastard is your only
drink!³ For look you, Francis, your white canvas doublet will

70 sully.° In Barbary,⁴ sir, it cannot come to° so much.   *get dirty / be worth*

FRANCIS   What, sir?

POINS [*within*]   Francis!

PRINCE HARRY   Away, you rogue! Dost thou not hear them call?
[*As he departs* POINS *and the* PRINCE] *both call him. The
Drawer stands amazed, not knowing which way to go.*
Enter VINTNER°   *Innkeeper*

VINTNER   What, standest thou still, and hearest such a calling?

75 Look to the guests within.   [*Exit* FRANCIS]
My lord, old Sir John with half a dozen more are at the door.
Shall I let them in?

PRINCE HARRY   Let them alone a while, and then open the door.
[*Exit* VINTNER]
Poins!

80 POINS [*within*]   Anon, anon, sir!
Enter POINS

PRINCE HARRY   Sirrah, Falstaff and the rest of the thieves are at
the door. Shall we be merry?

POINS   As merry as crickets, my lad. But hark ye, what cunning
match° have you made with this jest of the drawer? Come,   *game*

85 what's the issue?°   *outcome*

PRINCE HARRY   I am now of all humours that have showed
themselves humours⁵ since the old days of goodman° Adam to   *(title for a farmer)*
the pupil° age of this present twelve o'clock at midnight.   *youthful*
[*Enter* FRANCIS]
What's o'clock, Francis?

90 FRANCIS   Anon, anon, sir!   [*Exit at another door*]

---

2. Referring (satirically) to Francis's employer, who
would be robbed of Francis's labor if the apprentice
were to run away. This employer is imagined as dress-
ing in the manner of an upwardly mobile Londoner,
wearing a leather jacket ("jerkin") with crystal buttons
and keeping his hair close-cropped ("knot-pated"). He
also wears a signet ring with a carved agate, dark
("puke") stockings, and garters made from caddis rib-
bon (a cheaper alternative to silk). He has a simpering
style of speech and carries a vintner's pouch made of
Spanish leather.

3. The best of all drinks; the only drink you'll get (if you
stay in the tavern). This entire speech seems meant to
mystify Francis while obliquely warning him that he
will get dirty and be poor if he fulfills his apprentice-
ship.
4. North African region from which England acquired
sugar.
5. That is, I am in the mood for anything. Renaissance
medical theory held that four body fluids, or humors,
determined by their relative proportions the health,
temperament, and moods of an individual.

PRINCE HARRY   That ever this fellow should have fewer words than a parrot, and yet the son of a woman! His industry is upstairs and downstairs, his eloquence the parcel of a reckoning.° I am not yet of Percy's mind, the Hotspur of the North—he that kills me° some six or seven dozen of Scots at a breakfast, washes his hands, and says to his wife, 'Fie upon this quiet life! I want work.' 'O my sweet Harry,' says she, 'how many hast thou killed today?' 'Give my roan horse a drench,'° says he, and answers, 'Some fourteen,' an hour after; 'a trifle, a trifle.' I prithee call in Falstaff. I'll play Percy, and that damned brawn° shall play Dame Mortimer his wife. 'Rivo!'[6] says the drunkard. Call in Ribs, call in Tallow.°

items of a bill
he that slays

dose of medicine

fat boar
fat drippings

Enter FALSTAFF [*with sword and buckler,* BARDOLPH, PETO, *and* GADSHILL, *followed by* FRANCIS, *with wine*]

POINS   Welcome, Jack. Where hast thou been?

FALSTAFF   A plague of all cowards, I say, and a vengeance too, marry and amen!—Give me a cup of sack, boy.—Ere I lead this life long, I'll sew netherstocks,° and mend them and foot° them too. A plague of all cowards!—Give me a cup of sack, rogue. Is there no virtue extant?

stockings / making a new
foot for

He drinketh

PRINCE HARRY   Didst thou never see Titan° kiss a dish of butter— pitiful hearted Titan—that melted at the sweet tale of the sun's? If thou didst, then behold that compound.[7]

the sun

FALSTAFF [*to* FRANCIS]   You rogue, here's lime[8] in this sack too. There is nothing but roguery to be found in villainous man, yet a coward is worse than a cup of sack with lime in it.

[*Exit* FRANCIS][9]

A villainous coward! Go thy ways, old Jack, die when thou wilt. If manhood, good manhood, be not forgot upon the face of the earth, then am I a shotten herring.[1] There lives not three good men unhanged in England, and one of them is fat and grows old, God help the while.° A bad world, I say. I would I were a weaver[2]—I could sing psalms, or anything. A plague of all cowards, I say still.

these times

PRINCE HARRY   How now, woolsack, what mutter you?

FALSTAFF   A king's son! If I do not beat thee out of thy kingdom with a dagger of lath,[3] and drive all thy subjects afore thee like a flock of wild geese, I'll never wear hair on my face more. You, Prince of Wales!

PRINCE HARRY   Why, you whoreson round man, what's the matter?

FALSTAFF   Are not you a coward? Answer me to that. And Poins there?

POINS   Zounds, ye fat paunch, an ye call me coward, by the Lord I'll stab thee.

95
100
105
110
115
120
125
130

---

6. An exclamation associated with boisterous drinking.
7. Combination; that is, the melted butter (referring to Falstaff).
8. Often added to bad wine to make it dry and sparkling.
9. Neither Q nor F indicates when Francis leaves the stage. He plays no further part in the action after this, so an exit here avoids the problem of having a character onstage with no obvious function.

1. A herring that has spawned its roe and is thus very thin.
2. Weavers were reputed to sing the Psalms of the Bible at work. Many were Puritans, and some had emigrated from the zealously Protestant Low Countries.
3. A wooden dagger, which was the weapon associated with the Vice figure in medieval morality plays (see note to line 413).

FALSTAFF I call thee coward? I'll see thee damned ere I call
thee coward, but I would give a thousand pound I could run
135 as fast as thou canst. You are straight enough in the shoulders;
you care not who sees your back. Call you that backing of your
friends? A plague upon such backing! Give me them that will
face me. Give me a cup of sack. I am a rogue if I drunk today.
PRINCE HARRY O villain, thy lips are scarce wiped since thou
140 drunkest last.
FALSTAFF All is one for that.°   *It doesn't matter*
He drinketh
A plague of all cowards, still say I.
PRINCE HARRY What's the matter?
FALSTAFF What's the matter? There be four of us here have
145 ta'en a thousand pound this day morning.°   *this morning*
PRINCE HARRY Where is it, Jack, where is it?
FALSTAFF Where is it? Taken from us it is. A hundred upon
poor four of us.
PRINCE HARRY What, a hundred, man?
150 FALSTAFF I am a rogue if I were not at half-sword° with a dozen   *dueling closely*
of them, two hours together. I have scaped by miracle. I am
eight times thrust through the doublet,° four through the hose,° *short jacket / breeches*
my buckler° cut through and through, my sword hacked like   *shield*
a handsaw. *Ecce signum.*[4]
[*He shows his sword*]
155 I never dealt better since I was a man. All would not do.[5] A
plague of all cowards! [*Pointing to* GADSHILL, PETO, *and* BAR-
DOLPH] Let them speak. If they speak more or less than truth,
they are villains and the sons of darkness.
PRINCE HARRY[6] Speak, sirs, how was it?
160 GADSHILL We four set upon some dozen—
FALSTAFF [*to the* PRINCE] Sixteen at least, my lord.
GADSHILL And bound them.
PETO No, no, they were not bound.
FALSTAFF You rogue, they were bound every man of them, or
165 am a Jew else, an Hebrew Jew.
GADSHILL As we were sharing, some six or seven fresh men set
upon us.
FALSTAFF And unbound the rest; and then come in the other.
PRINCE HARRY What, fought you with them all?
170 FALSTAFF All? I know not what you call all, but if I fought not
with fifty of them, I am a bunch of radish. If there were not
two- or three-and-fifty upon poor old Jack, then am I no two-
legged creature.
PRINCE HARRY Pray God you have not murdered some of them.
175 FALSTAFF Nay, that's past praying for. I have peppered° two of   *made it hot for*
them. Two I am sure I have paid°—two rogues in buckram   *killed*
suits. I tell thee what, Hal, if I tell thee a lie, spit in my face,
call me horse. Thou knowest my old ward°—   *posture of defense*
[*He stands as to fight*]

---

4. Behold the evidence (Latin).
5. All I did was not enough; the whole group was insuf-
ficient opposition.
6. This is a second place (see 2.2.48) where textual
confusion surrounds the character of Gadshill. In Q,
this line is assigned to Gadshill and the following line
to Russell (whose name was changed to "Bardolph" as

a result of censorship; see Introduction). In F, this line
is assigned to the Prince and the following line to Gad-
shill. The next two speeches here assigned to Gadshill
were also given to Russell in Q. The F assignment of
these lines to Gadshill may indicate that at some point
Shakespeare divided between two characters a role
originally designed for one.

here I lay,° and thus I bore my point.° Four rogues in buckram   *stood / sword point*
180 let drive at me.
PRINCE HARRY   What, four? Thou saidst but two even now.
FALSTAFF   Four, Hal, I told thee four.
POINS   Ay, ay, he said four.
FALSTAFF   These four came all afront,° and mainly° thrust at me.   *abreast / mightily*
185 I made me no more ado, but took all their seven points in my
target,° thus.   *shield*
        [*He wards himself with his buckler*]
PRINCE HARRY   Seven? Why, there were but four even now.
FALSTAFF   In buckram?
POINS   Ay, four in buckram suits.
190 FALSTAFF   Seven, by these hilts,° or I am a villain else.   *sword handle*
PRINCE HARRY [*aside to* POINS]   Prithee, let him alone. We shall
have more anon.
FALSTAFF   Dost thou hear me, Hal?
PRINCE HARRY   Ay, and mark° thee too, Jack.   *pay attention to; count*
195 FALSTAFF   Do so, for it is worth the listening to. These nine in
buckram that I told thee of—
PRINCE HARRY [*aside to* POINS]   So, two more already.
FALSTAFF   Their points[7] being broken—
POINS [*aside to the* PRINCE]   Down fell their hose.
200 FALSTAFF   Began to give me ground. But I followed me° close,   *I followed*
came in foot and hand, and, with a thought,° seven of the eleven   *swift as thought*
I paid.
PRINCE HARRY [*aside to* POINS]   O monstrous! Eleven buckram
men grown out of two!
205 FALSTAFF   But, as the devil would have it, three misbegotten
knaves in Kendal green[8] came at my back and let drive at me;
for it was so dark, Hal, that thou couldst not see thy hand.
PRINCE HARRY   These lies are like their father that begets
them—gross as a mountain, open, palpable. Why, thou clay-
210 brained guts, thou knotty-pated° fool, thou whoreson obscene   *blockheaded*
greasy tallow-catch[9]—
FALSTAFF   What, art thou mad? Art thou mad? Is not the truth
the truth?
PRINCE HARRY   Why, how couldst thou know these men in
215 Kendal green when it was so dark thou couldst not see thy
hand? Come, tell us your reason. What sayst thou to this?
POINS   Come, your reason, Jack, your reason.
FALSTAFF   What, upon compulsion? Zounds, an I were at the
strappado,[1] or all the racks[2] in the world, I would not tell you
220 on compulsion. Give you a reason on compulsion? If reasons
were as plentiful as blackberries, I would give no man a rea-
son upon compulsion, I.
PRINCE HARRY   I'll be no longer guilty of this sin. This sanguine°   *red-faced*
coward, this bed-presser,° this horse-back-breaker, this huge hill   *licentious man*
225 of flesh—

---

7. Sword points, but Poins takes it as meaning "fasten-
ings for hose."
8. A coarse green cloth made in Kendal, Cumbria. It
was associated with poor country people, especially
forest dwellers, as well as outlaws.
9. Greasy lump of fat (gathered by butchers for candle

making).
1. A torture device in which victims were lifted off the
ground by ropes attached to their hands, which were
tied behind their backs, and then let fall.
2. A torture device in which victims' limbs were pulled
apart.

FALSTAFF 'Sblood, you starveling, you elf-skin, you dried neat's°   ox's
tongue, you bull's pizzle, you stock-fish[3]—O, for breath to utter
what is like thee!— you tailor's yard,[4] you sheath, you bow-
case, you vile standing tuck[5]—

230 PRINCE HARRY Well, breathe awhile, and then to't again, and
when thou hast tired thyself in base comparisons, hear me
speak but this.

POINS Mark, Jack.

PRINCE HARRY We two saw you four set on four, and bound
235 them, and were masters of their wealth.—Mark now how a
plain tale shall put you down.—Then did we two set on you
four, and, with a word, outfaced you from your prize, and have
it; yea, and can show it you here in the house. And Falstaff,
you carried your guts away as nimbly, with as quick dexterity,
240 and roared for mercy, and still run and roared, as ever I heard
bull-calf. What a slave art thou, to hack thy sword as thou
hast done, and then say it was in fight! What trick, what
device, what starting-hole° canst thou now find out to hide   refuge
thee from this open and apparent shame?

245 POINS Come, let's hear, Jack; what trick hast thou now?

FALSTAFF By the Lord, I knew ye as well as he that made ye.
Why, hear you, my masters. Was it for me to kill the heir-
apparent? Should I turn upon the true prince? Why, thou
knowest I am as valiant as Hercules;[6] but beware instinct. The
250 lion will not touch the true prince[7]—instinct is a great mat-
ter. I was now a coward on instinct. I shall think the better of
myself and thee during my life—I for a valiant lion, and thou
for a true prince. But by the Lord, lads, I am glad you have the
money.—[Calling] Hostess, clap to the doors.—Watch to-
255 night, pray tomorrow.[8] Gallants, lads, boys, hearts of gold, all
the titles of good fellowship come to you! What, shall we be
merry, shall we have a play extempore?

PRINCE HARRY Content, and the argument° shall be thy running   subject
away.

260 FALSTAFF Ah, no more of that, Hal, an thou lovest me.

Enter HOSTESS

HOSTESS O Jesu, my lord the Prince!

PRINCE HARRY How now, my lady the Hostess, what sayst thou
to me?

HOSTESS Marry, my lord, there is a nobleman of the court at door
265 would speak with you. He says he comes from your father.

PRINCE HARRY Give him as much as will make him a royal
man,[9] and send him back again to my mother.

FALSTAFF What manner of man is he?

HOSTESS An old man.

---

3. *bull's pizzle:* a bull's penis that when dried and
stretched was used as a whip. *stock-fish:* dried cod.
4. Tailors were popularly imagined to lack virility. Fal-
staff puns on "yard" as referring both to a tailor's mea-
suring stick and to his penis.
5. *sheath:* empty case (punning on "sheath" as meaning
"foreskin"). *bow-case:* a long, thin case for unstrung
bows. *standing tuck:* a stiff rapier (with a pun on "stand-
ing" as meaning "sexually erect").

6. In classical mythology, a hero who performed prodi-
gious acts of strength and courage.
7. A popular belief derived from classical texts.
8. Falstaff alludes here to Matthew 26:41: "Watch and
pray, that ye enter not into temptation." He puns on
"watch" as meaning "keep vigil" and "carouse" and on
"pray" as meaning "prey."
9. Punning on "nobles" and "royals" as names of coins,
the latter being more valuable.

270   FALSTAFF   What doth gravity out of his bed at midnight? Shall
I give him his answer?

PRINCE HARRY   Prithee do, Jack.

FALSTAFF   Faith, and I'll send him packing.   *Exit*

PRINCE HARRY   Now, sirs; [*to* GADSHILL] by'r Lady, you fought
275   fair—so did you, Peto, so did you, Bardolph. You are lions
too—you ran away upon instinct, you will not touch the true
prince; no, fie!

BARDOLPH   Faith, I ran when I saw others run.

PRINCE HARRY   Faith, tell me now in earnest, how came Fal-
280   staff's sword so hacked?

PETO   Why, he hacked it with his dagger, and said he would
swear truth out of England[1] but he would make you believe it
was done in fight, and persuaded us to do the like.

BARDOLPH   Yea, and to tickle our noses with speargrass,[2] to make
285   them bleed; and then to beslubber our garments with it, and
swear it was the blood of true men. I did that° I did not this   *what*
seven year before—I blushed to hear his monstrous devices.

PRINCE HARRY   O villain, thou stolest a cup of sack eighteen years
ago, and wert taken with the manner,° and ever since thou hast   *caught in the act*
290   blushed extempore.° Thou hadst fire[3] and sword on thy side,   *spontaneously*
and yet thou rannest away. What instinct hadst thou for it?

BARDOLPH [*indicating his face*]   My lord, do you see these mete-
ors? Do you behold these exhalations?[4]

PRINCE HARRY   I do.

295   BARDOLPH   What think you they portend?°   *signify*

PRINCE HARRY   Hot livers,[5] and cold° purses.   *empty*

BARDOLPH   Choler,[6] my lord, if rightly taken.°   [*Exit*][7]   *understood*

PRINCE HARRY   No, if rightly taken, halter.[8]

          Enter FALSTAFF

Here comes lean Jack; here comes bare-bone. How now, my
300   sweet creature of bombast?[9] How long is't ago, Jack, since
thou sawest thine own knee?

FALSTAFF   My own knee? When I was about thy years, Hal, I was
not an eagle's talon in the waist; I could have crept into any
alderman's thumb-ring. A plague of sighing and grief—it blows
305   a man up like a bladder. There's villainous news abroad. Here
was Sir John Bracy from your father; you must to the court in
the morning. That same mad fellow of the North, Percy, and
he of Wales that gave Amamon° the bastinado,° and made Luc-   *(a devil) / a beating*
ifer cuckold,[1] and swore the devil his true liegeman° upon the   *subject*
310   cross of a Welsh hook[2]—what a plague call you him?

---

1. Swear so excessively that Truth, imagined as an alle-
gorical figure, would run out of England to escape him.
2. A plant with sharply pointed leaves.
3. A reference to Bardolph's red face, the focus of the
jests that follow.
4. "Meteors" and "exhalations" refer to the red
blotches on Bardolph's face, here compared to distur-
bances in the heavens.
5. Short tempers; livers inflamed by drink.
6. The humor associated with an angry disposition.
7. Neither Q nor F marks an exit for Bardolph here,
but both indicate that he reenters at line 439. The nec-

essary exit might well follow this discussion of his
inflamed face.
8. No, if rightly arrested, a noose. The Prince forces a
legal reading on the previous line, playing on "choler"
as "collar," or "noose," and taking "taken" to mean
"arrested."
9. Cotton padding; pompous speech.
1. Slept with the devil's own wife; gave the devil his
horns (the proverbial sign of a cuckold).
2. A heavy weapon with a crooked end, lacking the
cross shape on which oaths were usually made.

POINS   Owain Glyndŵr.

FALSTAFF   Owain, Owain, the same; and his son-in-law Morti-
mer, and old Northumberland, and that sprightly Scot of Scots
Douglas, that runs a-horseback up a hill perpendicular—

315 PRINCE HARRY   He that rides at high speed and with his pistol
kills a sparrow flying.

FALSTAFF   You have hit it.

PRINCE HARRY   So did he never the sparrow.

FALSTAFF   Well, that rascal hath good mettle in him; he will not
320 run.

PRINCE HARRY   Why, what a rascal art thou, then, to praise him
so for running!

FALSTAFF   A-horseback, ye cuckoo, but afoot he will not budge
a foot.

325 PRINCE HARRY   Yes, Jack, upon instinct.

FALSTAFF   I grant ye, upon instinct. Well, he is there too, and
one Mordake, and a thousand blue-caps° more. Worcester is   *Scottish soldiers*
stolen away tonight. Thy father's beard is turned white with the
news. You may buy land now as cheap as stinking mackerel.

330 PRINCE HARRY   Why then, it is like, if there come a hot June and
this civil buffeting hold,° we shall buy maidenheads as they buy   *continue*
hobnails: by the hundreds.[3]

FALSTAFF   By the mass, lad, thou sayst true; it is like we shall
have good trading that way. But tell me, Hal, art not thou hor-
335 rible afeard? Thou being heir-apparent, could the world pick
thee out three such enemies again as that fiend Douglas, that
spirit Percy, and that devil Glyndŵr? Art thou not horribly
afraid? Doth not thy blood thrill° at it?   *shudder*

PRINCE HARRY   Not a whit, i'faith. I lack some of thy instinct.

340 FALSTAFF   Well, thou wilt be horribly chid tomorrow when thou
comest to thy father. If thou love me, practise an answer.

PRINCE HARRY   Do thou stand for° my father, and examine me   *impersonate*
upon the particulars of my life.

FALSTAFF   Shall I? Content. This chair shall be my state,° this   *throne*
345 dagger my sceptre, and this cushion my crown.
[*He sits*]

PRINCE HARRY   Thy state is taken for a joint-stool,[4] thy golden
sceptre for a leaden dagger, and thy precious rich crown for a
pitiful bald crown.

FALSTAFF   Well, an° the fire of grace be not quite out of thee,   *if*
350 now shalt thou be moved. Give me a cup of sack to make my
eyes look red, that it may be thought I have wept; for I must
speak in passion, and I will do it in King Cambyses' vein.[5]

PRINCE HARRY [*bowing*]   Well, here is my leg.°   *bow*

FALSTAFF   And here is my speech. [*To* PETO, POINS, *and* GADS-
355 HILL] Stand aside, nobility.

HOSTESS   O Jesu, this is excellent sport, i'faith.

FALSTAFF   Weep not, sweet Queen,[6] for trickling tears are vain.

---

3. Alluding to rape as a practice of war or to the notion
that women would be likely to relinquish their virginity
cheaply during wartime.
4. A stool made of wooden pieces fitted or joined
together.
5. In the exaggerated rhetorical style associated with

such early Elizabethan plays as *Cambyses,* a tragedy
about a despotic Persian king.
6. Possibly addressed to the Hostess, with a pun on
"quean" as slang for "whore."

HOSTESS O the Father, how he holds his countenance!° *keeps a straight face*

FALSTAFF For God's sake, lords, convey° my tristful° Queen, *lead away / sad*

360 For tears do stop° the floodgates of her eyes. *fill*

HOSTESS O Jesu, he doth it as like one of these harlotry° players *vagabond; scurvy*
as ever I see!

FALSTAFF Peace, good pint-pot; peace, good tickle-brain.[7]—
Harry, I do not only marvel where thou spendest thy time, but

365 also how thou art accompanied. For though the camomile,° *an herb*
the more it is trodden on, the faster it grows, yet youth, the
more it is wasted, the sooner it wears.[8] That thou art my son
I have partly thy mother's word, partly my own opinion, but
chiefly a villainous trick° of thine eye, and a foolish hanging *trait*

370 of thy nether° lip, that doth warrant° me. If then thou be son *lower / assure*
to me, here lies the point. Why, being son to me, art thou so
pointed at?° Shall the blessed sun of heaven prove a micher,° *criticized / truant*
and eat blackberries?—A question not to be asked. Shall the
son of England prove a thief, and take purses?—A question to

375 be asked. There is a thing, Harry, which thou hast often heard
of, and it is known to many in our land by the name of pitch.° *sticky, black tar*
This pitch, as ancient writers do report, doth defile.[9] So doth
the company thou keepest. For Harry, now I do not speak to
thee in drink, but in tears; not in pleasure, but in passion; not

380 in words only, but in woes also. And yet there is a virtuous
man whom I have often noted in thy company, but I know not
his name.

PRINCE HARRY What manner of man, an it like your majesty?

FALSTAFF A goodly, portly man, i'faith, and a corpulent; of a

385 cheerful look, a pleasing eye, and a most noble carriage;° and, *bearing*
as I think, his age some fifty, or, by'r Lady, inclining to three-
score. And now I remember me, his name is Falstaff. If that
man should be lewdly given,° he deceiveth me; for, Harry, I *be lustful*
see virtue in his looks. If, then, the tree may be known by the

390 fruit, as the fruit by the tree,[1] then peremptorily I speak it—
there is virtue in that Falstaff. Him keep with; the rest ban-
ish. And tell me now, thou naughty varlet, tell me, where hast
thou been this month?

PRINCE HARRY Dost thou speak like a king? Do thou stand for

395 me, and I'll play my father.

FALSTAFF [*standing*] Depose me. If thou dost it half so gravely,
so majestically both in word and matter, hang me up by the
heels for a rabbit sucker,° or a poulter's hare.[2] *an unweaned rabbit*

PRINCE HARRY [*sitting*] Well, here I am set.° *seated*

400 FALSTAFF And here I stand. [*To the others*] Judge, my masters.

PRINCE HARRY Now, Harry, whence come you?

FALSTAFF My noble lord, from Eastcheap.

PRINCE HARRY The complaints I hear of thee are grievous.

---

7. Slang term for a strong alcoholic drink, and hence
for the drinker.
8. Falstaff's entire speech is a parody of the previously
fashionable ornate rhetoric exemplified by John Lyly's
Euphues (1578).

9. See Ecclesiasticus 13:1 (also cited in Lyly's
Euphues).
1. An allusion to Matthew 12:33 (which also appears
in Lyly's *Euphues*).
2. A hare sold in a poultry shop.

FALSTAFF 'Sblood, my lord, they are false. [*To the others*] Nay,
405 I'll tickle ye for° a young prince, i'faith.   *amuse you as*
PRINCE HARRY Swearest thou, ungracious boy? Henceforth ne'er
look on me. Thou art violently carried away from grace. There
is a devil haunts thee in the likeness of an old fat man; a tun°   *large barrel*
of man is thy companion. Why dost thou converse° with that   *associate*
410 trunk of humours,[3] that bolting-hutch° of beastliness, that   *bin for coarse meal*
swollen parcel of dropsies,[4] that huge bombard° of sack, that   *leather wine vessel*
stuffed cloak-bag° of guts, that roasted Manningtree[5] ox with   *suitcase*
the pudding° in his belly, that reverend Vice,[6] that grey Iniquity,   *stuffing*
that father Ruffian, that Vanity in Years? Wherein is he good,°   *virtuous; proficient*
415 but to taste sack and drink it? Wherein neat and cleanly,° but   *deft*
to carve a capon and eat it? Wherein cunning, but in craft?
Wherein crafty, but in villainy? Wherein villainous, but in all
things? Wherein worthy, but in nothing?
FALSTAFF I would your grace would take me with you.° Whom   *explain what you mean*
420 means your grace?
PRINCE HARRY That villainous, abominable misleader of youth,
Falstaff; that old white-bearded Satan.
FALSTAFF My lord, the man I know.
PRINCE HARRY I know thou dost.
425 FALSTAFF But to say I know more harm in him than in myself
were to say more than I know. That he is old, the more the
pity, his white hairs do witness it. But that he is, saving your
reverence,[7] a whoremaster, that I utterly deny. If sack and
sugar be a fault, God help the wicked. If to be old and merry
430 be a sin, then many an old host° that I know is damned. If to   *innkeeper*
be fat be to be hated, then Pharaoh's lean kine[8] are to be
loved. No, my good lord, banish Peto, banish Bardolph, ban-
ish Poins, but for sweet Jack Falstaff, kind Jack Falstaff, true
Jack Falstaff, valiant Jack Falstaff, and therefore more valiant
435 being, as he is, old Jack Falstaff,
Banish not him thy Harry's company,
Banish not him thy Harry's company.
Banish plump Jack, and banish all the world.
PRINCE HARRY I do; I will.
[*Knocking within. Exit* HOSTESS.][9]
Enter BARDOLPH, *running*
440 BARDOLPH O my lord, my lord, the sheriff with a most mon-
strous watch° is at the door.   *group of constables*
FALSTAFF Out, ye rogue! Play out the play! I have much to say
in the behalf of that Falstaff.
Enter the HOSTESS

3. A chest full of body fluids, whose excess, according to Renaissance medical theory, was extremely unhealthy.
4. Diseases characterized by retention of water.
5. Market town in Essex, noted for the Manningtree Fair, where a roasted ox may have been part of the festivities.
6. An irreverent, comic, and (usually) youthful charac-ter representing evil and sin in the medieval morality plays. Sometimes named "Iniquity."
7. If you will excuse the expression.
8. In a biblical story in Genesis 41:18–21, Pharaoh dreams of seven lean cows ("kine") that portend seven years of famine.
9. Neither F nor Q marks an exit for the Hostess, but both indicate her reentry at line 443. It makes sense for her to exit here to see about the commotion at her door.

HOSTESS   O Jesu! My lord, my lord!

445   PRINCE HARRY   Heigh, heigh, the devil rides upon a fiddlestick!¹
What's the matter?

HOSTESS   The sheriff and all the watch are at the door. They are
come to search the house. Shall I let them in?

FALSTAFF   Dost thou hear, Hal? Never call a true piece of gold
450   a counterfeit—thou art essentially made, without seeming so.²

PRINCE HARRY   And thou a natural coward without instinct.

FALSTAFF   I deny your major.° If you will deny³ the sheriff, so.   *main premise*
If not, let him enter. If I become° not a cart° as well as another   *adorn / hangman's cart*
man, a plague on my bringing up. I hope I shall as soon be
455   strangled with a halter as another.

PRINCE HARRY   Go, hide thee behind the arras.° The rest walk up   *tapestry wall hanging*
above. Now, my masters, for a true face and good conscience.
[Exeunt POINS, BARDOLPH, *and* GADSHILL]

FALSTAFF   Both which I have had, but their date is out;° and   *has expired*
therefore I'll hide me.
[He withdraws behind the arras]

460   PRINCE HARRY *[to* HOSTESS]   Call in the sheriff.   *[Exit* HOSTESS]
Enter SHERIFF *and [a]* CARRIER
Now, master sheriff, what is your will with me?

SHERIFF   First, pardon me, my lord. A hue and cry⁴
Hath followed certain men unto this house.

PRINCE HARRY   What men?

465   SHERIFF   One of them is well known, my gracious lord,
A gross, fat man.

CARRIER   As fat as butter.

PRINCE HARRY   The man, I do assure you, is not here,
For I myself at this time have employed him.
And, sheriff, I will engage° my word to thee   *pledge*
470   That I will by tomorrow dinner-time
Send him to answer thee, or any man,
For anything he shall be charged withal.
And so let me entreat you leave the house.

SHERIFF   I will, my lord. There are two gentlemen
475   Have in this robbery lost three hundred marks.

PRINCE HARRY   It may be so. If he have robbed these men,
He shall be answerable. And so, farewell.

SHERIFF   Good night, my noble lord.

PRINCE HARRY   I think it is good morrow, is it not?

480   SHERIFF   Indeed, my lord, I think it be two o'clock.
*Exeunt [*SHERIFF *and* CARRIER]

PRINCE HARRY   This oily rascal is known as well as Paul's.°   *St. Paul's Cathedral*
Go call him forth.

PETO   Falstaff!
[He draws back the arras, revealing FALSTAFF *asleep]*
Fast asleep

---

1. That is, what a row about nothing.
2. A famously difficult passage. Falstaff may be insist-
ing he is true gold, not a counterfeit (and so should not
be turned over to the watch) just as Hal is a true Prince

("essentially made") despite appearances.
3. If you will refuse to let him in.
4. A group of citizens who pursue a criminal.

Behind the arras, and snorting like a horse.
PRINCE HARRY Hark how hard he fetches breath. Search his
485 pockets.
          [PETO] *searcheth his pocket and findeth certain papers.*
          [*He closeth the arras and cometh forward*]
     What hast thou found?
PETO   Nothing but papers, my lord.
PRINCE HARRY Let's see what they be. Read them.
PETO [*reads*] Item: a capon.   *2s. 2d.*
     Item: sauce.   *4d.*
490 Item: sack, two gallons.   *5s. 8d.*
     Item: anchovies and sack after supper.   *2s. 6d.*
     Item: bread.   *ob.*°   obolus (*halfpenny*)
PRINCE HARRY O monstrous! But one halfpennyworth of bread
     to this intolerable deal° of sack! What there is else, keep close;   *quantity*
495 we'll read it at more advantage.° There let him sleep till day.   *a better opportunity*
     I'll to the court in the morning. We must all to the wars, and
     thy place shall be honourable. I'll procure this fat rogue a
     charge of foot,[5] and I know his death will be a march of twelve
     score.[6] The money shall be paid back again, with advantage.°   *interest*
500 Be with me betimes° in the morning; and so good morrow,   *early*
     Peto.
PETO Good morrow, good my lord.   *Exeunt* [*severally*]

3.1

          Enter HOTSPUR, [*the Earl of*] WORCESTER, *Lord* MORTI-
          MER, [*and*] *Owain* GLYNDŴR [*with a map*]
MORTIMER These promises are fair, the parties sure,
     And our induction° full of prosperous hope.[1]   *beginning*
HOTSPUR Lord Mortimer and cousin Glyndŵr,
     Will you sit down? And uncle Worcester?
          [MORTIMER, GLYNDŴR, *and* WORCESTER *sit*]
5   A plague upon it, I have forgot the map!
GLYNDŴR No, here it is. Sit, cousin Percy, sit,
     Good cousin Hotspur;
          [HOTSPUR *sits*]
                              For by that name
     As oft as Lancaster[2] doth speak of you,
     His cheek looks pale, and with a rising sigh
     He wisheth you in heaven.
10 HOTSPUR   And you in hell,
     As oft as he hears Owain Glyndŵr spoke of.
GLYNDŴR I cannot blame him. At my nativity
     The front° of heaven was full of fiery shapes,   *forehead*
     Of burning cressets;[3] and at my birth

---

5. Command of an infantry company.
6. I know it will kill him to march twelve times twenty
yards or paces.
3.1 Location: Glyndŵr's castle, Wales. According to
Holinshed's *Chronicles,* the events of this scene take
place in the house of the Archdeacon of Bangor; but he
is not present in Shakespeare's scene, and Glyndŵr acts

as host throughout.
1. Full of the hope of prospering.
2. Referring to Henry's title as Duke and hence imply-
ing a denial of the legitimacy of his kingship.
3. Metal baskets of fire suspended from long poles;
meteors.

15 The frame and huge foundation of the earth
Shaked like a coward.

HOTSPUR   Why, so it would have done
At the same season if your mother's cat
Had but kittened, though yourself had never been born.

GLYNDŴR   I say the earth did shake when I was born.

20 HOTSPUR   And I say the earth was not of my mind
If you suppose as fearing you it shook.

GLYNDŴR   The heavens were all on fire, the earth did tremble—

HOTSPUR   O, then the earth shook to see the heavens on fire,
And not in fear of your nativity.

25 Diseasèd nature oftentimes breaks forth
In strange eruptions; oft the teeming° earth   *fertile*
Is with a kind of colic pinched and vexed
By the imprisoning of unruly wind
Within her womb, which for enlargement° striving   *release*
30 Shakes the old beldam° earth, and topples down   *grandmother*
Steeples and moss-grown towers. At your birth
Our grandam earth, having this distemp'rature,°   *disorder*
In passion shook.

GLYNDŴR   Cousin, of many men
I do not bear these crossings.° Give me leave   *contradictions*
35 To tell you once again that at my birth
The front of heaven was full of fiery shapes,
The goats ran from the mountains, and the herds
Were strangely clamorous to the frighted fields.
These signs have marked me extraordinary,
40 And all the courses of my life do show
I am not in the roll of common men.
Where is he living, clipped in with° the sea   *encircled by*
That chides the banks° of England, Scotland, Wales,   *shores*
Which° calls me pupil or hath read to° me?   *Who / tutored*
45 And bring him out° that is but woman's son   *show me any man*
Can trace° me in the tedious ways of art,[4]   *follow*
And hold me pace° in deep experiments.   *keep up with me*

HOTSPUR [*standing*]   I think there's no man speaketh better Welsh.[5]
I'll to dinner.

50 MORTIMER   Peace, cousin Percy, you will make him mad.

GLYNDŴR   I can call spirits from the vasty deep.°   *lower world*

HOTSPUR   Why, so can I, or so can any man;
But will they come when you do call for them?

GLYNDŴR   Why, I can teach you, cousin, to command the devil.

55 HOTSPUR   And I can teach thee, coz, to shame the devil,
By telling truth: 'Tell truth, and shame the devil'.
If thou have power to raise him, bring him hither,
And I'll be sworn I have power to shame him hence.
O, while you live, tell truth and shame the devil.

60 MORTIMER   Come, come, no more of this unprofitable chat.

GLYNDŴR   Three times hath Henry Bolingbroke made head°   *raised an army*
Against my power;° thrice from the banks of Wye   *army*

4. The long, laborious ways of magic.
5. The Welsh language was often described by English writers as a barbaric one, and "to speak Welsh" commonly meant to use a strange, unintelligible language. Hotspur implies that Glyndŵr speaks nonsense.

And sandy-bottomed Severn have I sent him
Bootless° home, and weather-beaten back.[6]   *Unsuccessful*
65   HOTSPUR   Home without boots, and in foul weather too!
How scapes he agues,° in the devil's name?   *fevers*
GLYNDŴR   Come, here's the map. Shall we divide our right,°   *what we are entitled to*
According to our threefold order ta'en?[7]
MORTIMER   The Archdeacon hath divided it
70   Into three limits° very equally.   *regions*
England from Trent and Severn hitherto°   *to here*
By south and east is to my part assigned;
All westward—Wales beyond the Severn shore
And all the fertile land within that bound—
75   To Owain Glyndŵr; [*to* HOTSPUR] and, dear coz, to you
The remnant northward lying off from Trent.
And our indentures tripartite° are drawn,   *in triplicate*
Which, being sealèd interchangeably[8]—
A business that this night may execute°—   *may be done tonight*
80   Tomorrow, cousin Percy, you and I
And my good lord of Worcester will set forth
To meet your father and the Scottish power,
As is appointed us, at Shrewsbury.
My father,° Glyndŵr, is not ready yet,   *father-in-law*
85   Nor shall we need his help these fourteen days.
Within that space you may have drawn together
Your tenants, friends, and neighbouring gentlemen.
GLYNDŴR   A shorter time shall send me to you, lords;
And in my conduct° shall your ladies come,   *escort*
90   From whom you now must steal and take no leave;
For there will be a world of water shed
Upon the parting of your wives and you.
HOTSPUR   Methinks my moiety° north from Burton here   *portion*
In quantity equals not one° of yours.   *either*
95   See how this river comes me cranking in,[9]
And cuts me from the best of all my land
A huge half-moon, a monstrous cantle,° out.   *piece*
I'll have the current in this place dammed up,
And here the smug° and silver Trent shall run   *smooth*
100   In a new channel fair and evenly.
It shall not wind with such a deep indent,
To rob me of so rich a bottom° here.   *lowland plain*
GLYNDŴR   Not wind? It shall, it must; you see it doth.
MORTIMER   Yea, but mark how he bears his course, and runs me up°   *turns upward*
105   With like advantage on the other side,
Gelding the opposèd continent[1] as much
As on the other side it takes from you.
WORCESTER   Yea, but a little charge° will trench° him here,   *expense / rechannel*
And on this north side win this cape of land,
110   And then he runs straight and even.
HOTSPUR   I'll have it so; a little charge will do it.

6. According to Holinshed, Glyndŵr used magic to raise storms that frustrated Henry's attacks.
7. *threefold:* either an agreement made in triplicate (see line 77) or an agreement having three parts (see the rebels' plan to divide the island into three pieces at

lines 68–76). *order ta'en:* agreement made.
8. Bearing the seals of all three nobles.
9. Comes bending in on my shores.
1. Cutting a vital piece from ("gelding") the opposite bank.

GLYNDŴR I'll not have it altered.

HOTSPUR Will not you?

GLYNDŴR No, nor you shall not.

115 HOTSPUR Who shall say me nay?

GLYNDŴR Why, that will I.

HOTSPUR Let me not understand you, then: speak it in Welsh.

GLYNDŴR I can speak English, lord, as well as you;
For I was trained up in the English court,
120 Where, being but young, I framèd to the harp
Many an English ditty lovely well,
And gave the tongue a helpful ornament²—
A virtue that was never seen in you.

HOTSPUR Marry, and I am glad of it, with all my heart.
125 I had rather be a kitten and cry 'mew'
Than one of these same metre ballad-mongers.³
I had rather hear a brazen canstick turned,⁴
Or a dry wheel grate on the axle-tree,°   axle
And that would set my teeth nothing on edge,
130 Nothing so much as mincing° poetry.   affected
'Tis like the forced gait of a shuffling° nag.   hobbled

GLYNDŴR Come, you shall have Trent turned.

HOTSPUR I do not care. I'll give thrice so much land
To any well-deserving friend;
135 But in the way of bargain—mark ye me—
I'll cavil on° the ninth part of a hair.   quibble about
Are the indentures drawn? Shall we be gone?

GLYNDŴR The moon shines fair. You may away by night.
I'll haste the writer, and withal°   simultaneously
140 Break with° your wives of your departure hence.   Inform
I am afraid my daughter will run mad,
So much she doteth on her Mortimer.   Exit

MORTIMER Fie, cousin Percy, how you cross my father!

HOTSPUR I cannot choose. Sometime he angers me
145 With telling me of the moldwarp⁵ and the ant,
Of the dreamer Merlin⁶ and his prophecies,
And of a dragon and a finless fish,
A clip-winged griffin⁷ and a moulten° raven,   moulted
A couching lion and a ramping cat,⁸
150 And such a deal of skimble-skamble° stuff   stupid
As puts me from my faith.⁹ I tell you what,
He held me last night at the least nine hours
In reckoning up the several devils' names
That were his lackeys. I cried, 'Hum!' and, 'Well, go to!',
155 But marked him not a word. O, he is as tedious
As a tired horse, a railing wife,
Worse than a smoky house. I had rather live

---

2. And gave the English language the ornament of a musical setting; and supplemented the English lyrics with pleasing music.
3. Sellers or writers of ballads.
4. A brazen candlestick scraped and polished on a lathe after casting. John Stow's *Survey of London* (1598) records contemporary complaints about the noise of candlestick making.
5. Mole. Holinshed records a prophecy whereby Henry, figured as a mole, would be overthrown by a

dragon, a lion, and a wolf, representing Glyndŵr, Percy, and Mortimer, respectively.
6. Legendary Welsh prophet, wizard, and bard at King Arthur's court.
7. A fabulous beast, part lion and part eagle.
8. Alluding to the heraldic terms "couchant" and "rampant," which mean "crouching" and "rearing fiercely." Hotspur is making fun of Glyndŵr's heraldic preoccupations.
9. As makes me a skeptic, even of religion.

With cheese and garlic, in a windmill, far,
Than feed on cates° and have him talk to me   *delicacies*
160   In any summer house° in Christendom.   *luxurious residence*
MORTIMER   In faith, he is a worthy gentleman,
Exceedingly well read, and profited°   *proficient*
In strange concealments,° valiant as a lion,   *In occult arts*
And wondrous affable, and as bountiful
165   As mines of India. Shall I tell you, cousin?
He holds your temper in a high respect,
And curbs himself even of his natural scope°   *freedom of speech*
When you come 'cross° his humour; faith, he does.   *contradict*
I warrant you, that man is not alive
170   Might so have tempted° him as you have done   *provoked*
Without the taste of danger and reproof.
But do not use it oft, let me entreat you.
WORCESTER [*to* HOTSPUR]   In faith, my lord, you are too wilful-blame,°   *stubborn*
And since your coming hither have done enough
175   To put him quite besides° his patience.   *out of*
You must needs learn, lord, to amend this fault.
Though sometimes it show greatness, courage, blood°—   *spirit; noble birth*
And that's the dearest grace° it renders you—   *best distinction*
Yet oftentimes it doth present° harsh rage,   *show*
180   Defect of manners, want of government,
Pride, haughtiness, opinion,° and disdain,   *self-conceit*
The least of which haunting a nobleman
Loseth men's hearts, and leaves behind a stain
Upon the beauty of all parts besides,°   *all other qualities*
185   Beguiling° them of commendation.   *Depriving*
HOTSPUR   Well, I am schooled. Good manners be your speed!°   *give you success*
Enter GLYNDŴR *with the Ladies* [LADY PERCY *and Morti-*
mer's wife]
Here come our wives, and let us take our leave.
[*Mortimer's wife weeps, and speaks to him in Welsh*]
MORTIMER   This is the deadly spite° that angers me: *vexation*
My wife can speak no English, I no Welsh.
190   GLYNDŴR   My daughter weeps she'll not part with you.
She'll be a soldier, too; she'll to the wars.
MORTIMER   Good father, tell her that she and my aunt Percy[1]
Shall follow in your conduct speedily.
GLYNDŴR *speaks to her in Welsh, and she answers*
him in the same
GLYNDŴR   She is desperate here,° a peevish self-willed harlotry,°   *on this point / hussy*
195   One that no persuasion can do good upon.
The lady speaks in Welsh
MORTIMER   I understand thy looks. That pretty Welsh°   *(i.e., her tears)*
Which thou down pourest from these swelling heavens°   *overflowing eyes*
I am too perfect° in, and but for shame   *proficient*
In such a parley° should I answer thee.   *In a similar language*
The lady [*kisses him, and speaks*] *again in Welsh*
200   MORTIMER   I understand thy kisses, and thou mine,
And that's a feeling disputation;[2]
But I will never be a truant, love,

1. Kate, Lady Percy. Her historical counterpart was the   2. A conversation rooted in emotions or in touch.
sister, not the aunt, of Glyndŵr's son-in-law.

Till I have learnt thy language, for thy tongue
Makes Welsh as sweet as ditties highly° penned,   *eloquently*
205   Sung by a fair queen in a summer's bower
With ravishing division,° to her lute.   *embellishments*
GLYNDŴR Nay, if you melt,° then will she run mad.   *weep*
            The lady [sits on the rushes³ and] speaks again in Welsh
MORTIMER O, I am ignorance itself in this!
GLYNDŴR She bids you on the wanton° rushes lay you down   *luxurious*
210   And rest your gentle head upon her lap,⁴
And she will sing the song that pleaseth you,
And on your eyelids crown the god of sleep,
Charming your blood with pleasing heaviness,°   *sleepiness*
Making such difference 'twixt wake and sleep
215   As is the difference betwixt day and night
The hour before the heavenly-harnessed team⁵
Begins his golden progress in the east.
MORTIMER With all my heart, I'll sit and hear her sing.
By that time will our book,° I think, be drawn.   *document*
            [He sits, resting his head on the Welsh lady's lap]
220   GLYNDŴR Do so, and those musicians that shall play to you
Hang in the air a thousand leagues from hence,
And straight they shall be here. Sit and attend.
HOTSPUR Come, Kate, thou art perfect in lying down.°   *expert at lovemaking*
Come, quick, quick, that I may lay my head in thy lap.⁶
225   LADY PERCY *[sitting]* Go, ye giddy goose!
            [HOTSPUR sits, resting his head on Lady Percy's lap.]
            The music plays⁷
HOTSPUR Now I perceive the devil understands Welsh;
And 'tis no marvel, he is so humorous.°   *eccentric; whimsical*
By'r Lady, he's a good musician.
LADY PERCY Then should you be nothing but musical,
230   For you are altogether governed by humours.°   *whims*
Lie still, ye thief, and hear the lady sing in Welsh.
HOTSPUR I had rather hear Lady my brach° howl in Irish.   *female hunting dog*
LADY PERCY Wouldst thou have thy head broken?
HOTSPUR No.
235   LADY PERCY Then be still.
HOTSPUR Neither—'tis a woman's fault.⁸
LADY PERCY Now God help thee!
HOTSPUR To the Welsh lady's bed.
LADY PERCY What's that?
240   HOTSPUR Peace; she sings.
            Here the lady sings a Welsh song
HOTSPUR Come, Kate, I'll have your song too.
LADY PERCY Not mine, in good sooth.°   *truth*
HOTSPUR Not yours, in good sooth! Heart,° you swear like a   *By God's heart*
comfit-maker's° wife: 'Not you, in good sooth!' and 'As true as   *confectioner's*
245   I live!' and
'As God shall mend me!' and 'As sure as day!';

---

3. Used as a floor covering, both in houses and on the theater stage.
4. Often a euphemism for the genitals.
5. The sun was supposedly carried in a chariot drawn by horses.
6. "Head" was slang for "penis" and "lap" for "vagina."

7. Instrumental music would probably be played in a so-called music house behind the upper stage in the Elizabethan theater and so might well seem to "hang in the air" (see lines 220–21).
8. No, I won't be still—it is a woman's trait (and I am a man).

And giv'st such sarcenet[9] surety for thy oaths
As if thou never walk'st further than Finsbury.[1]
Swear me, Kate, like a lady as thou art,
250 A good mouth-filling oath, and leave 'in sooth'
And such protest of pepper gingerbread[2]
To velvet-guards and Sunday citizens.[3]
Come, sing.
LADY PERCY　I will not sing.
255 HOTSPUR　'Tis the next° way to turn tailor,[4] or be redbreast   *quickest*
teacher.° [*Rising*] An the indentures be drawn, I'll away within   *or teach birds to sing*
these two hours; and so come in when ye will.   *Exit*
GLYNDŴR　Come, come, Lord Mortimer. You are as slow
As hot Lord Percy is on fire to go.
260 By this° our book is drawn. We'll but seal,   *now*
And then to horse immediately.
MORTIMER [*rising*]   With all my heart.
　　　　　　　[*The ladies rise, and all*] *exeunt*

3.2
Enter KING [HENRY], PRINCE [HARRY], *and* [*lords*]
KING HENRY　Lords, give us leave—the Prince of Wales and I
Must have some private conference—but be near at hand,
For we shall presently have need of you.   *Exeunt lords*
I know not whether God will have it so
5 For some displeasing service I have done,
That in his secret doom° out of my blood°   *judgment / lineage*
He'll breed revengement and a scourge for me,
But thou dost in thy passages° of life   *course*
Make me believe that thou art only marked
10 For° the hot vengeance and the rod of heaven   *To be*
To punish my mistreadings. Tell me else,
Could such inordinate° and low desires,   *unsuitable*
Such poor, such bare, such lewd, such mean attempts,°   *base undertakings*
Such barren pleasures,[1] rude society,
15 As thou art matched withal° and grafted to,   *with*
Accompany the greatness of thy blood,
And hold their level° with thy princely heart?   *And claim equality*
PRINCE HARRY　So please your majesty, I would I could
Quit° all offences with as clear excuse   *Clear myself of*
20 As well as I am doubtless° I can purge   *certain*
Myself of many I am charged withal;
Yet such extenuation let me beg
As, in reproof° of many tales devised—   *upon disproof*
Which oft the ear of greatness needs must hear
25 By smiling pickthanks° and base newsmongers°—   *flatterers / gossips*
I may, for some things true wherein my youth
Hath faulty wandered and irregular,
Find pardon on my true submission.°   *admission of guilt*
KING HENRY　God pardon thee! Yet let me wonder, Harry,

---

9. Flimsy (from the name of a fine silk).
1. Finsbury Fields, north of London, was a popular resort for London's middling classes. Hotspur implies that Kate's mild oaths make her sound like a burgher's wife.
2. Watered-down oaths. Gingerbread was cheaply available at fairs and markets, and sometimes pepper was used as an inexpensive substitute for ginger.

3. Citizens who doff their work clothes and dress up only on Sundays. *To velvet-guards*: To those, like citizens' wives, whose clothes are trimmed ("guarded") with velvet.
4. Tailors were noted for singing.
3.2 Location: The palace, London.
1. Unprofitable habits; nonreproductive erotic pursuits.

30   At thy affections,° which do hold a wing   *inclinations*
       Quite from² the flight of all thy ancestors.
       Thy place in Council thou hast rudely³ lost—
       Which by thy younger brother is supplied—
       And art almost an alien to the hearts
35   Of all the court and princes of my blood.
       The hope and expectation of thy time°   *time of life; youth*
       Is ruined, and the soul of every man
       Prophetically do forethink thy fall.
       Had I so lavish of my presence been,
40   So common-hackneyed⁴ in the eyes of men,
       So stale and cheap to vulgar company,
       Opinion,° that did help me to the crown,   *Public opinion*
       Had still kept loyal to possession,⁵
       And left me in reputeless° banishment,   *inglorious*
45   A fellow of no mark nor likelihood.°   *promise of success*
       By being seldom seen, I could not stir
       But, like a comet, I was wondered at,
       That men would tell their children 'This is he.'
       Others would say 'Where, which is Bolingbroke?'
50   And then I stole all courtesy from heaven,⁶
       And dressed myself in such humility
       That I did pluck allegiance from men's hearts,
       Loud shouts and salutations from their mouths,
       Even in the presence of the crownèd King.
55   Thus did I keep my person fresh and new,
       My presence like a robe pontifical°—   *churchman's rich dress*
       Ne'er seen but wondered at—and so my state,°   *magnificence; royalty*
       Seldom but sumptuous, showed like a feast,
       And won by rareness such solemnity.
60   The skipping King, he ambled up and down
       With shallow jesters and rash bavin° wits,   *brushwood*
       Soon kindled and soon burnt, carded his state,⁷
       Mingled his royalty with cap'ring fools,
       Had his great name profanèd with their scorns,°   *by their scornful manners*
65   And gave his countenance,° against his name,⁸   *approval*
       To laugh at gibing boys, and stand the push°   *tolerate the impudence*
       Of every beardless vain comparative;°   *wit*
       Grew a companion to the common streets,
       Enfeoffed° himself to popularity,   *Surrendered*
70   That, being daily swallowed by men's eyes,
       They surfeited with honey, and began
       To loathe the taste of sweetness, whereof a little
       More than a little is by much too much.
       So when he had occasion to be seen,
75   He was but as the cuckoo is in June,⁹
       Heard, not regarded, seen but with such eyes
       As, sick and blunted with community,°   *familiarity*

---

2. *which . . . from:* which do fly a course contrary to.
3. By violence. Perhaps alluding to the story, drama-
tized in *The Famous Victories of Henry V,* that Prince
Hal boxed the Lord Chief Justice on the ear and was
subsequently punished.
4. Cheapened. A hackney was a horse available for
common hire.
5. The possessor of the throne (Richard II).

6. That is, surpassed heaven itself for graciousness.
7. Adulterated his royal dignity. The term refers to a
process ("carding") whereby wool or liquids were mixed
with inferior substances.
8. To the detriment of his reputation.
9. Referring to a proverbial saying, "No one regards the
June cuckoo's song."

Afford no extraordinary gaze
Such as is bent on sun-like majesty
80 When it shines seldom in admiring eyes,
But rather drowsed and hung their eyelids down,
Slept in his face,° and rendered such aspect°   *before his eyes / looks*
As cloudy° men use to their adversaries,   *sullen*
Being with his presence glutted, gorged, and full.
85 And in that very line,° Harry, standest thou;   *category*
For thou hast lost thy princely privilege
With vile participation.° Not an eye   *base companionship*
But is a-weary of thy common sight,
Save mine, which hath desired to see thee more,
90 Which now doth that° I would not have it do—   *what*
Make blind itself with foolish tenderness.
    [*He weeps*]
PRINCE HARRY   I shall hereafter, my thrice-gracious lord,
Be more myself.
KING HENRY   For all the world,
As thou art to this hour was Richard then,
95 When I from France set foot at Ravenspurgh,
And even as I was then is Percy now.
Now by my sceptre, and my soul to boot,
He hath more worthy interest° to the state   *more claim by worth*
Than thou, the shadow° of succession;   *mere image*
100 For, of° no right, nor colour° like to right,   *having / pretext*
He doth fill fields with harness° in the realm,   *armor*
Turns head° against the lion's° armèd jaws,   *Leads a revolt / king's*
And, being no more in debt to years than thou,
Leads ancient lords and reverend bishops on
105 To bloody battles, and to bruising arms.
What never-dying honour hath he got
Against renownèd Douglas!—whose high deeds,
Whose hot incursions and great name in arms,
Holds from all soldiers chief majority°   *preeminence*
110 And military title capital[1]
Through all the kingdoms that acknowledge Christ.
Thrice hath this Hotspur, Mars° in swaddling-clothes,   *god of war*
This infant warrior, in his enterprises
Discomfited° great Douglas; ta'en him once;   *Defeated*
115 Enlargèd° him; and made a friend of him   *Released*
To fill the mouth of deep defiance up,[2]
And shake the peace and safety of our throne.
And what say you to this? Percy, Northumberland,
The Archbishop's grace of York, Douglas, Mortimer,
120 Capitulate° against us, and are up.°   *Combine / up in arms*
But wherefore do I tell these news to thee?
Why, Harry, do I tell thee of my foes,
Which° art my near'st and dearest enemy?—   *Who*
Thou that art like enough, through vassal° fear,   *servile*
125 Base inclination, and the start of spleen,°   *fit of temper*
To fight against me under Percy's pay,
To dog his heels, and curtsy at his frowns,

---

1. And claim to the title of principal (capital) warrior.
2. To add volume to the voice of deep defiance; to fill up the appetite of deep defiance.

To show how much thou art degenerate.

PRINCE HARRY   Do not think so; you shall not find it so.
130 And God forgive them that so much have swayed
Your majesty's good thoughts away from me.
I will redeem all this on Percy's head,
And in the closing of some glorious day
Be bold to tell you that I am your son;
135 When I will wear a garment all of blood,
And stain my favours° in a bloody mask,   *features*
Which, washed away, shall scour my shame with it.
And that shall be the day, whene'er it lights,°   *comes*
That this same child of honour and renown,
140 This gallant Hotspur, this all-praisèd knight,
And your unthought-of Harry chance to meet.
For every honour sitting on his helm,
Would they were multitudes, and on my head
My shames redoubled; for the time will come
145 That I shall make this northern youth exchange
His glorious deeds for my indignities.
Percy is but my factor,° good my lord,   *agent*
To engross up° glorious deeds on my behalf;   *amass*
And I will call him to so strict account
150 That he shall render every glory up,
Yea, even the slightest worship of his time,°   *honor of his life*
Or I will tear the reckoning from his heart.
This, in the name of God, I promise here,
The which if he be pleased I shall perform,
155 I do beseech your majesty may salve°   *heal*
The long-grown wounds of my intemperature;°   *disorder; intemperance*
If not, the end of life cancels all bonds,
And I will die a hundred thousand deaths
Ere break the smallest parcel of this vow.
160 KING HENRY   A hundred thousand rebels die in this.
Thou shalt have charge° and sovereign trust herein.   *military command*
        Enter [Sir Walter] BLUNT
How now, good Blunt? Thy looks are full of speed.

BLUNT   So hath the business that I come to speak of.
Lord Mortimer of Scotland[3] hath sent word
165 That Douglas and the English rebels met
The eleventh of this month at Shrewsbury.
A mighty and a fearful head° they are,   *army*
If promises be kept on every hand,
As ever offered foul play in a state.

170 KING HENRY   The Earl of Westmorland set forth today,
With him my son Lord John of Lancaster,
For this advertisement° is five days old.   *news*
On Wednesday next, Harry, you shall set forward.
On Thursday we ourselves will march.
175 Our meeting is Bridgnorth,[4] and, Harry, you
Shall march through Gloucestershire, by which account,°   *calculation*
Our business valuèd,° some twelve days hence   *taken into account*
Our general forces at Bridgnorth shall meet.

---

3. A Scottish lord who is unrelated to Glyndŵr's son-   4. A town about 20 miles southeast of Shrewsbury.
in-law.

Our hands are full of business; let's away.
180   Advantage feeds him fat[5] while men delay.   *Exeunt*

3.3

Enter FALSTAFF [*with a truncheon° at his waist*], *and*   *officer's club*
   BARDOLPH

FALSTAFF   Bardolph, am I not fallen away° vilely since this last   *shrunk*
  action?[1] Do I not bate?° Do I not dwindle? Why, my skin hangs   *grow thin*
  about me like an old lady's loose gown. I am withered like an
  old apple-john.[2] Well, I'll repent, and that suddenly, while I
5   am in some liking.° I shall be out of heart[3] shortly, and then I   *in the mood*
  shall have no strength to repent. An I have not forgotten what
  the inside of a church is made of, I am a peppercorn, a brewer's
  horse°—the inside of a church! Company, villainous company,   *an old workhorse*
  hath been the spoil of me.
10 BARDOLPH   Sir John, you are so fretful you cannot live long.
FALSTAFF   Why, there is it. Come, sing me a bawdy song, make
  me merry. I was as virtuously given° as a gentleman need to   *inclined*
  be: virtuous enough; swore little; diced not—above seven
  times a week; went to a bawdy-house not—above once in a
15   quarter—of an hour; paid money that I borrowed—three or
  four times; lived well, and in good compass.° And now I live   *limits*
  out of all order, out of all compass.
BARDOLPH   Why, you are so fat, Sir John, that you must needs be
  out of all compass,° out of all reasonable compass, Sir John.   *circumference; girth*
20 FALSTAFF   Do thou amend thy face, and I'll amend my life.
  Thou art our admiral,° thou bearest the lantern in the poop[4]—   *flagship*
  but 'tis in the nose of thee. Thou art the Knight of the Burn-
  ing Lamp.[5]
BARDOLPH   Why, Sir John, my face does you no harm.
25 FALSTAFF   No, I'll be sworn; I make as good use of it as many a
  man doth of a death's head,[6] or a *memento mori*.[7] I never see
  thy face but I think upon hell-fire and Dives that lived in
  purple—for there he is in his robes, burning, burning.[8] If thou
  wert any way given to virtue, I would swear by thy face; my
30   oath should be 'By this fire that's God's angel!' But thou art
  altogether given over,° and wert indeed, but for the light in thy   *dedicated to vice*
  face, the son of utter darkness. When thou rannest up Gads
  Hill in the night to catch my horse, if I did not think thou hadst
  been an *ignis fatuus* or a ball of wildfire,[9] there's no purchase
35   in money. O, thou art a perpetual triumph,° an everlasting   *torchlight procession*
  bonfire-light! Thou hast saved me a thousand marks[1] in links°   *small torches*
  and torches, walking with thee in the night betwixt tavern and

5. Opportunities (for rebellion) flourish; the superior position (of the rebels) improves.
3.3 Location: The inn in Eastcheap, London.
1. This last military engagement (referring to the Gad's Hill episode).
2. A kind of apple often eaten long after picking, when its skin was shriveled.
3. Disinclined; weary.
4. The ship's main deck.
5. Parodying figures from popular romance such as Amadis, the Knight of the Burning Sword.
6. A skull, or representation of a skull, such as was engraved as an emblem of mortality on seal rings.
7. An object serving as a reminder of mortality (Latin for "remember you must die").

8. Referring to a biblical parable about a rich man "clothed in purple and fine linen" who regularly refused to feed the beggar Lazarus and was ultimately forced to suffer in hell for his sin (Luke 16:19–23); also referring to Bardolph's body as bearing the signs of venereal disease. "Burning" implies "on fire with lust" as well as "infected with syphilitic sores."
9. A flaming explosive used in warfare or in fireworks; skin marked by erysipelas, an inflammatory disease. *ignis fatuus* (Latin for "foolish fire"): a phenomenon in which phosphorescent light appears on marshy ground; a false hope.
1. Considerable money (each mark was worth two-thirds of a pound).

tavern—but the sack that thou hast drunk me° would have   *drunk (at my cost)*
bought me lights as good cheap° at the dearest chandler's² in   *as cheaply*
40   Europe. I have maintained that salamander³ of yours with fire
any time this two-and-thirty years, God reward me for it.
BARDOLPH   'Sblood, I would my face were in your belly!⁴
FALSTAFF   God-a-mercy! So should I be sure to be heartburnt.
    Enter HOSTESS
How now, Dame Partlet⁵ the hen, have you enquired yet who
45   picked my pocket?
HOSTESS   Why, Sir John, what do you think, Sir John? Do you
think I keep thieves in my house? I have searched, I have
enquired; so has my husband, man by man, boy by boy, ser-
vant by servant. The tithe° of a hair was never lost in my house   *tenth part*
50   before.
FALSTAFF   Ye lie, Hostess: Bardolph was shaved and lost many
a hair,⁶ and I'll be sworn my pocket was picked. Go to, you are
a woman, go.
HOSTESS   Who, I? No, I defy thee! God's light, I was never
55   called so in mine own house before.
FALSTAFF   Go to, I know you well enough.
HOSTESS   No, Sir John, you do not know me,⁷ Sir John; I know
you, Sir John. You owe me money, Sir John, and now you pick
a quarrel to beguile me of it. I bought you a dozen of shirts to
60   your back.
FALSTAFF   Dowlas,° filthy dowlas. I have given them away to   *Coarse linen*
bakers' wives; they have made bolters° of them.   *sieves*
HOSTESS   Now as I am a true woman, holland° of eight shillings   *fine linen*
an ell.° You owe money here besides, Sir John: for your diet,   *a measure of 45 inches*
65   and by-drinkings,° and money lent you, four-and-twenty pound.   *drinks between meals*
FALSTAFF [*pointing at* BARDOLPH]   He had his part of it. Let him
pay.
HOSTESS   He? Alas, he is poor; he hath nothing.
FALSTAFF   How, poor? Look upon his face. What call you rich?
70   Let them coin his nose, let them coin his cheeks, I'll not pay
a denier.⁸ What, will you make a younker° of me? Shall I not   *novice; gull*
take mine ease in mine inn, but I shall have my pocket picked?
I have lost a seal-ring of my grandfather's worth forty mark.
HOSTESS   O Jesu, [*to* BARDOLPH] I have heard the Prince tell
75   him, I know not how oft, that that ring was copper.
FALSTAFF   How? The Prince is a jack,° a sneak-up.° [*Raising*   *rascal / sly villain*
his truncheon] 'Sblood, an he were here I would cudgel him
like a dog if he would say so.
    Enter PRINCE [HARRY *and* PETO], *marching; and* FAL-
    STAFF *meets* [*them*], *playing upon his truncheon like a*
    fife
How now, lad, is the wind in that door,° i'faith? Must we all   *quarter*
80   march?
BARDOLPH   Yea, two and two, Newgate fashion.⁹

2. The most expensive candle maker's.
3. A fabled lizard capable of living in fire. The implica-
tion is that Falstaff has maintained the salamander Bar-
dolph with the "fires" of sack or lust.
4. Equivalent to "Stick it down your throat" (a prover-
bial retort to an insult).
5. A traditional name for hens and for women sup-
posed to talk too much.

6. Had his beard cut; was cheated or robbed of his
money; lost his hair because of syphilis.
7. That is, you don't know how honest I am; you don't
have sexual knowledge of me.
8. French copper coin of little value.
9. Bound like convicts taken to and from London's
Newgate prison.

HOSTESS   My lord, I pray you hear me.

PRINCE HARRY   What sayst thou, Mistress Quickly? How doth
    thy husband?

    I love him well; he is an honest man.

85 HOSTESS   Good my lord, hear me!

FALSTAFF   Prithee, let her alone, and list to me.

PRINCE HARRY   What sayst thou, Jack?

FALSTAFF   The other night I fell asleep here behind the arras,
    and had my pocket picked. This house is turned bawdy-
90   house: they pick pockets.

PRINCE HARRY   What didst thou lose, Jack?

FALSTAFF   Wilt thou believe me, Hal, three or four bonds of
    forty pound apiece, and a seal-ring of my grandfather's.

PRINCE HARRY   A trifle, some eightpenny matter.

95 HOSTESS   So I told him, my lord; and I said I heard your grace
    say so; and, my lord, he speaks most vilely of you, like a foul-
    mouthed man as he is, and said he would cudgel you.

PRINCE HARRY   What? He did not!

HOSTESS   There's neither faith, truth, nor womanhood in me
100   else.

FALSTAFF   There's no more faith in thee than in a stewed
    prune,[1] nor no more truth in thee than in a drawn fox;[2] and,
    for womanhood, Maid Marian[3] may be the deputy's wife of
    the ward to° thee. Go, you thing,[4] go!   *compared to*

105 HOSTESS   Say, what thing, what thing?

FALSTAFF   What thing? Why, a thing to thank God on.

HOSTESS   I am no thing to thank God on. I would thou shouldst
    know it, I am an honest man's wife; and setting thy knight-
    hood aside, thou art a knave to call me so.

110 FALSTAFF   Setting thy womanhood aside, thou art a beast to say
    otherwise.

HOSTESS   Say, what beast, thou knave, thou?

FALSTAFF   What beast? Why, an otter.

PRINCE HARRY   An otter, Sir John? Why an otter?

115 FALSTAFF   Why? She's neither fish nor flesh;[5] a man knows not
    where to have her.[6]

HOSTESS   Thou art an unjust man in saying so. Thou or any
    man knows where to have me, thou knave, thou.

PRINCE HARRY   Thou sayst true, Hostess, and he slanders thee
120   most grossly.

HOSTESS   So he doth you, my lord, and said this other day you
    owed him a thousand pound.

PRINCE HARRY [*to* FALSTAFF]   Sirrah, do I owe you a thousand
    pound?

125 FALSTAFF   A thousand pound, Hal? A million! Thy love is worth
    a million; thou owest me thy love.

HOSTESS   Nay, my lord, he called you 'jack' and said he would
    cudgel you.

FALSTAFF   Did I, Bardolph?

---

1. Symbol of a bawd. Brothels often displayed a dish of stewed prunes in the window.
2. A hunted fox drawn out from its hiding spot; a dead fox dragged to lay a false trail.
3. A disreputable character, usually played by a cross-dressed man, in the boisterous May games and morris dances denounced by Puritan preachers. The figure is

here juxtaposed to the respectable wife of the deputy of the ward.
4. A euphemism for "female genitalia."
5. The otter's unusual appearance led to debates about whether it was a fish or an animal.
6. How to understand her; how to have sexual relations with her.

130   BARDOLPH   Indeed, Sir John, you said so.

        FALSTAFF   Yea, if he said my ring was copper.

        PRINCE HARRY   I say 'tis copper; darest thou be as good as thy
        word now?

        FALSTAFF   Why, Hal, thou knowest as thou art but man I dare,
135   but as thou art prince, I fear thee as I fear the roaring of the
        lion's whelp.°   *cub*

        PRINCE HARRY   And why not as the lion?

        FALSTAFF   The King himself is to be feared as the lion. Dost
        thou think I'll fear thee as I fear thy father? Nay, an I do, I pray
140   God my girdle break.

        PRINCE HARRY   O, if it should, how would thy guts fall about thy
        knees! But sirrah, there's no room for faith, truth, nor honesty
        in this bosom of thine; it is all filled up with guts and midriff.
        Charge an honest woman with picking thy pocket? Why, thou
145   whoreson impudent embossed rascal,[7] if there were anything
        in thy pocket but tavern reckonings, memorandums of bawdy-
        houses, and one poor pennyworth of sugar-candy to make thee
        long-winded°—if thy pocket were enriched with any other   *to give you energy*
        injuries[8] but these, I am a villain. And yet you will stand to it,°   *persist*
150   you will not pocket up° wrong. Art thou not ashamed?   *keep quiet about*

        FALSTAFF   Dost thou hear, Hal? Thou knowest in the state of
        innocency Adam fell, and what should poor Jack Falstaff do
        in the days of villainy? Thou seest I have more flesh than
        another man, and therefore more frailty. You confess, then,
155   you picked my pocket.

        PRINCE HARRY   It appears so by the story.

        FALSTAFF   Hostess, I forgive thee. Go make ready breakfast.
        Love thy husband, look to thy servants, cherish thy guests.
        Thou shalt find me tractable to any honest reason; thou seest
160   I am pacified still.° Nay, prithee, be gone.   *Exit* HOSTESS   *always*
        Now, Hal, to the news at court. For the robbery, lad, how is
        that answered?°   *settled*

        PRINCE HARRY   O, my sweet beef, I must still be good angel to
        thee. The money is paid back again.

165   FALSTAFF   O, I do not like that paying back; 'tis a double labour.

        PRINCE HARRY   I am good friends with my father, and may do
        anything.

        FALSTAFF   Rob me the exchequer the first thing thou dost, and
        do it with unwashed hands° too.   *do it at once*

170   BARDOLPH   Do, my lord.

        PRINCE HARRY   I have procured thee, Jack, a charge of foot.°   *an infantry command*

        FALSTAFF   I would it had been of horse! Where shall I find one°   *someone*
        that can steal well? O, for a fine thief of the age of two-and-
        twenty or thereabouts! I am heinously unprovided.° Well, God   *ill equipped*
175   be thanked for these rebels—they offend none but the virtuous.
        I laud them, I praise them.

        PRINCE HARRY   Bardolph.

        BARDOLPH   My lord?

        PRINCE HARRY   [*giving letters*]   Go bear this letter to Lord John
        of Lancaster,
180   To my brother John; this to my lord of Westmorland.

---

7. *embossed rascal*: bloated rogue; hunted deer,   8. Any other things whose loss causes you injury.
exhausted and foaming at the mouth.

[Exit BARDOLPH]
Go, Peto, to horse, to horse, for thou and I
Have thirty miles to ride yet ere dinner time.   *[Exit* PETO]
Jack, meet me tomorrow in the Temple Hall⁹
At two o'clock in the afternoon.
185　There shalt thou know thy charge, and there receive
Money and order for their furniture.°   *equipment*
The land is burning, Percy stands on high,
And either we or they must lower lie.   *[Exit]*
FALSTAFF   Rare words! Brave world! *[Calling]* Hostess, my
　　breakfast, come!—
190　O, I could wish this tavern were my drum!¹   *Exit*

4.1

Enter HOTSPUR *and [the Earls of]* WORCESTER *and*
DOUGLAS
HOTSPUR   Well said, my noble Scot! If speaking truth
In this fine age were not thought flattery,
Such attribution° should the Douglas have   *praise*
As not a soldier of this season's stamp°   *coinage*
5　Should go so general current° through the world.   *be so widely accepted*
By God, I cannot flatter, I do defy
The tongues of soothers,° but a braver place   *flatterers*
In my heart's love hath no man than yourself.
Nay, task° me to my word, approve° me, lord.   *hold / test*
10　DOUGLAS   Thou art the king of honour.
No man so potent breathes upon the ground
But I will beard° him.   *defy*
HOTSPUR   Do so, and 'tis well.
Enter a MESSENGER *with letters*
What letters hast thou there? I can but thank you.
MESSENGER   These letters come from your father.
15　HOTSPUR   Letters from him? Why comes he not himself?
MESSENGER   He cannot come, my lord, he is grievous sick.
HOTSPUR   Zounds, how has he the leisure to be sick
In such a jostling° time? Who leads his power?   *turbulent*
Under whose government° come they along?   *command*
20　MESSENGER   His letters bears his mind, not I, my lord.
　　[HOTSPUR *reads the letter*]
WORCESTER   I prithee tell me, doth he keep his bed?
MESSENGER   He did, my lord, four days ere I set forth;
And at the time of my departure thence
He was much feared° by his physicians.   *feared for*
25　WORCESTER   I would the state of time° had first been whole°   *of the times / healthy*
Ere he by sickness had been visited.
His health was never better worth° than now.   *of more value*
HOTSPUR   Sick now? Droop now? This sickness doth infect
The very life-blood of our enterprise.
30　'Tis catching° hither, even to our camp.   *infectious*
He writes me here that inward sickness stays him,
And that his friends by deputation°   *through deputies*

---

9. One of the Inns of Court, London's law schools.
1. A disputed passage. Perhaps Falstaff means he
wishes that he could stay at the tavern rather than go to
war or that he could make the tavern ring with the noise
of his departure. He puns on "taborn" (tabor), a kind of
drum used to call soldiers to battle.
4.1 Location: The rebel camp near Shrewsbury.

Could not so soon be drawn;° nor did he think it meet°   *assembled / suitable*
To lay so dangerous and dear a trust
35 On any soul removed° but on his own.   *not directly involved*
Yet doth he give us bold advertisement°   *counsel*
That with our small conjunction° we should on,   *joint force*
To see how fortune is disposed to us;
For, as he writes, there is no quailing now,
40 Because the King is certainly possessed°   *informed*
Of all our purposes. What say you to it?
WORCESTER   Your father's sickness is a maim to us.
HOTSPUR   A perilous gash, a very limb lopped off.
And yet, in faith, it is not. His present want°   *absence*
45 Seems more than we shall find it. Were it good
To set° the exact wealth of all our states°   *stake / resources*
All at one cast,° to set so rich a main[1]   *throw of the dice*
On the nice hazard° of one doubtful hour?   *precarious chance*
It were not good, for therein should we read
50 The very bottom and the sole[2] of hope,
The very list,° the very utmost bound,   *limit*
Of all our fortunes.
DOUGLAS   Faith, and so we should, where now remains
A sweet reversion°—we may boldly spend   *future inheritance*
55 Upon the hope of what is to come in.
A comfort of retirement[3] lives in this.
HOTSPUR   A rendezvous, a home to fly unto,
If that the devil and mischance look big°   *threateningly*
Upon the maidenhead° of our affairs.   *virgin state; start*
60 WORCESTER   But yet I would your father had been here.
The quality and hair° of our attempt   *character*
Brooks° no division. It will be thought   *Tolerates*
By some that know not why he is away
That wisdom, loyalty, and mere° dislike   *absolute*
65 Of our proceedings kept the Earl from hence;
And think how such an apprehension
May turn the tide of fearful faction,°   *timid support*
And breed a kind of question in our cause.
For, well you know, we of the off'ring° side   *challenging*
70 Must keep aloof from strict arbitrement,°   *rigorous judgment*
And stop all sight-holes, every loop° from whence   *loophole*
The eye of reason may pry in upon us.
This absence of your father's draws° a curtain   *opens*
That shows the ignorant a kind of fear
Before not dreamt of.
75 HOTSPUR   You strain too far.
I rather of his absence make this use:
It lends a lustre, and more great opinion,°   *prestige*
A larger dare° to our great enterprise,   *daring*
Than if the Earl were here; for men must think
80 If we without his help can make a head°   *raise an army*
To push against a kingdom, with his help
We shall o'erturn it topsy-turvy down.
Yet° all goes well, yet all our joints° are whole.   *So far / limbs*

1. A stake in gambling; an army.   3. Refuge to which one can retreat.
2. Undersurface (as of a shoe), with a pun on "soul."

DOUGLAS   As heart can think, there is not such a word
85   Spoke of in Scotland as this term of fear.
          Enter Sir Richard VERNON
HOTSPUR   My cousin Vernon! Welcome, by my soul!
VERNON   Pray God my news be worth a welcome, lord.
      The Earl of Westmorland, seven thousand strong,
      Is marching hitherwards; with him Prince John.
HOTSPUR   No harm. What more?
90   VERNON   And further I have learned
      The King himself in person is set forth,
      Or hitherwards intended speedily,
      With strong and mighty preparation.
HOTSPUR   He shall be welcome too. Where is his son,
95   The nimble-footed madcap Prince of Wales,
      And his comrades that daffed° the world aside   *tossed*
      And bid it pass?
VERNON   All furnished,° all in arms,   *equipped*
      All plumed like ostriches,⁴ that with the wind
      [   ]
100   Baiting° like eagles having lately bathed,   *Beating their wings*
      Glittering in golden coats like images,°   *gilded statues*
      As full of spirit as the month of May,
      And gorgeous as the sun at midsummer;
      Wanton° as youthful goats, wild as young bulls.   *Frisky*
105   I saw young Harry with his beaver° on,   *visor; helmet*
      His cuishes° on his thighs, gallantly armed,   *armor for the thighs*
      Rise from the ground like feathered Mercury,⁵
      And vaulted with such ease into his seat
      As if an angel dropped down from the clouds
110   To turn and wind° a fiery Pegasus,⁶   *wheel about*
      And witch° the world with noble horsemanship.   *bewitch*
HOTSPUR   No more, no more! Worse than the sun in March,
      This praise doth nourish agues.⁷ Let them come!
      They come like sacrifices in their trim,°   *fine trappings*
115   And to the fire-eyed maid of smoky war°   *Bellona, goddess of war*
      All hot and bleeding will we offer them.
      The mailèd° Mars shall on his altar sit   *dressed in armor*
      Up to the ears in blood. I am on fire
      To hear this rich reprisal° is so nigh,   *prize*
120   And yet not ours! Come, let me taste° my horse,   *test; try*
      Who is to bear me like a thunderbolt
      Against the bosom of the Prince of Wales.
      Harry to Harry shall, hot horse to horse,
      Meet and ne'er part till one drop down a corpse.
      O, that Glyndŵr were come!
125   VERNON   There is more news.
      I learned in Worcester, as I rode along,
      He cannot draw° his power this fourteen days.   *assemble*
DOUGLAS   That's the worst tidings that I hear of yet.

---

4. Some editors follow Q in printing "estridges"
(goshawks, a kind of hawk) here. Various emendations
have been proposed for this and the following lines.
The Oxford editors assume a line has been lost, as the
brackets indicate.
5. The Roman messenger of the gods, often repre-

sented as a young man with winged sandals or a winged
hat.
6. A winged horse of classical myth.
7. The March sun was popularly imagined as warm
enough to kindle feverish diseases ("agues") without
being strong enough to dispel them.

WORCESTER   Ay, by my faith, that bears a frosty sound.

130 HOTSPUR   What may the King's whole battle° reach unto?   *army*

VERNON   To thirty thousand.

HOTSPUR   Forty let it be.

My father and Glyndŵr being both away,

The powers° of us may serve so great a day.   *armies*

Come, let us take a muster speedily.

135 Doomsday is near: die all, die merrily.

DOUGLAS   Talk not of dying; I am out of° fear   *free from*

Of death or death's hand for this one half year.   *Exeunt*

4.2

Enter FALSTAFF *and* BARDOLPH

FALSTAFF   Bardolph, get thee before to Coventry; fill me a bot-
tle of sack. Our soldiers shall march through. We'll to Sutton
Coldfield[1] tonight.

BARDOLPH   Will you give me money, captain?

5 FALSTAFF   Lay out,° lay out.   *Use your own*

BARDOLPH   This bottle makes an angel.[2]

FALSTAFF   [*giving* BARDOLPH *money*]   An if° it do, take it for thy   *An if=If*
labour; an if it make twenty, take them all; I'll answer the
coinage.[3] Bid my lieutenant Peto meet me at town's end.

10 BARDOLPH   I will, captain. Farewell.   *Exit*

FALSTAFF   If I be not ashamed of my soldiers, I am a soused
gurnet.° I have misused the King's press[4] damnably. I have got   *a pickled fish*
in exchange of one hundred and fifty soldiers three hundred
and odd pounds. I press me° none but good householders, yeo-   *I draft*
15 men's sons, enquire me out contracted° bachelors, such as had   *engaged to be wed*
been asked twice on the banns,[5] such a commodity° of warm   *quantity*
slaves[6] as had as lief° hear the devil as a drum, such as fear the   *willingly*
report of a caliver° worse than a struck° fowl or a hurt wild   *musket / wounded*
duck. I pressed me none but such toasts and butter,° with hearts   *such weaklings*
20 in their bellies no bigger than pins' heads, and they have
bought out their services;[7] and now my whole charge consists
of ensigns, corporals, lieutenants, gentlemen of companies[8]—
slaves as ragged as Lazarus[9] in the painted cloth,° where the   *cheap wall hangings*
glutton's dogs licked his sores—and such as indeed were never
25 soldiers, but discarded unjust° servingmen, younger sons to   *dishonest*
younger brothers, revolted° tapsters, and ostlers trade-fallen,°   *runaway / out of work*
the cankers° of a calm world and a long peace, ten times more   *cankerworms; parasites*
dishonourable-ragged than an old feazed ensign;° and such   *tattered flag*
have I to fill up the rooms of them as° have bought out their   *places of those who*
30 services, that you would think that I had a hundred and fifty
tattered prodigals lately come from swine-keeping, from eating
draff and husks.[1] A mad fellow met me on the way and told me
I had unloaded all the gibbets° and pressed the dead bodies.   *gallows*

4.2 Location: The road approaching Coventry.
1. Town about 20 miles northwest of Coventry in War-
wickshire.
2. Brings my outlay to several shillings (an "angel").
Falstaff retorts by punning on "makes" as meaning
"earns a profit of."
3. I'll be responsible for the money coined.
4. Commission for conscripting soldiers.
5. Proclamations made on three consecutive Sundays
affirming one's intent to marry.

6. Well-off or comfort-loving cowards.
7. They have paid me to excuse them from military ser-
vice.
8. Gentlemen volunteers who were not officers.
9. For the story of Lazarus and the rich man, see note
to 3.3.28.
1. Alluding to the biblical parable of the prodigal son,
who longs to eat swill ("draff") and corn husks meant
for pigs after he has squandered his inheritance in
debauchery (see Luke 15:11–16).

No eye hath seen such scarecrows. I'll not march through Cov-
35 entry with them, that's flat. Nay, and the villains march wide
betwixt the legs, as if they had gyves° on, for indeed I had the   *fetters*
most of them out of prison. There's not a shirt and a half in all
my company; and the half-shirt is two napkins tacked together
and thrown over the shoulders like a herald's coat without
40 sleeves; and the shirt, to say the truth, stolen from my host° at   *innkeeper*
Saint Albans, or the red-nose innkeeper of Daventry.² But that's
all one; they'll find linen enough on every hedge.³
    Enter PRINCE [HARRY] *and the Lord[Earl] of* WESTMOR-
LAND
PRINCE HARRY How now, blown Jack?⁴ How now, quilt?
FALSTAFF What, Hal! How now, mad wag? What a devil dost
45 thou in Warwickshire? My good lord of Westmorland, I cry
you mercy!° I thought your honour had already been at   *I beg your pardon*
Shrewsbury.
WESTMORLAND Faith, Sir John, 'tis more than time that I were
there, and you too; but my powers are there already. The King,
50 I can tell you, looks for us all. We must away° all night.   *must march*
FALSTAFF Tut, never fear° me. I am as vigilant as a cat to steal   *worry about*
cream.
PRINCE HARRY I think to steal cream indeed, for thy theft hath
already made thee butter.⁵ But tell me, Jack, whose fellows are
55 these that come after?
FALSTAFF Mine, Hal, mine.
PRINCE HARRY I did never see such pitiful rascals.
FALSTAFF Tut, tut, good enough to toss,⁶ food for powder,° food   *cannon fodder*
for powder. They'll fill a pit as well as better. Tush, man, mor-
60 tal men, mortal men.
WESTMORLAND Ay, but Sir John, methinks they are exceeding
poor and bare,° too beggarly.   *threadbare*
FALSTAFF Faith, for their poverty, I know not where they had
that, and for their bareness, I am sure they never learned that
65 of me.
PRINCE HARRY No, I'll be sworn, unless you call three fingers in
the ribs⁷ bare. But sirrah, make haste. Percy is already in the
field.   *Exit*
FALSTAFF What, is the King encamped?
70 WESTMORLAND He is, Sir John. I fear we shall stay too long.
                                 [Exit]
FALSTAFF Well, to the latter end of a fray
    And the beginning of a feast
    Fits a dull fighter and a keen guest.   *Exit*

4.3
    Enter HOTSPUR, [*the Earls of*] WORCESTER [*and*] DOUG-
LAS, *and* [*Sir Richard*] VERNON
HOTSPUR We'll fight with him tonight.
WORCESTER   It may not be.

2. Saint Albans is a town north of London, Daventry a town southeast of Coventry.
3. Where laundresses set it out to dry.
4. Punning on "jack" as referring to what many Eliza-bethan soldiers wore: a quilted jacket covered with leather or cloth and worn over iron plates. *blown:* swollen; short-winded.
5. The riches ("cream") you have stolen have made you rich, or turned you into fat.
6. Good enough to be tossed on pikes.
7. Three fingers of fat over the ribs. A finger was a mea-sure of three-quarters of an inch.
4.3 Location: The rebels' camp, Shrewsbury.

DOUGLAS   You give him then advantage.
VERNON   Not a whit.
HOTSPUR   Why say you so? Looks he not for supply?°   reinforcements
VERNON   So do we.
HOTSPUR   His is certain; ours is doubtful.
5   WORCESTER   Good cousin, be advised. Stir not tonight.
VERNON [to HOTSPUR]   Do not, my lord.
DOUGLAS   You do not counsel well.
    You speak it out of fear and cold heart.
VERNON   Do me no slander, Douglas. By my life—
    And I dare well maintain it with my life—
10   If well-respected° honour bid me on,   well-considered
    I hold as little counsel with weak fear
    As you, my lord, or any Scot that this day lives.
    Let it be seen tomorrow in the battle
    Which of us fears.
15   DOUGLAS   Yea, or tonight.
VERNON   Content.
HOTSPUR   Tonight, say I.
VERNON   Come, come, it may not be. I wonder much,
    Being men of such great leading° as you are,   leadership
20   That you foresee not what impediments
    Drag back our expedition.° Certain horse°   rapid progress / cavalry
    Of my cousin Vernon's are not yet come up.
    Your uncle Worcester's horse came but today,
    And now their pride° and mettle is asleep,   spirit
25   Their courage with hard labour tame and dull,
    That not a horse is half the half himself.
HOTSPUR   So are the horses of the enemy
    In general journey-bated° and brought low.   weary from travel
    The better part of ours are full of rest.
30   WORCESTER   The number of the King exceedeth our.
    For God's sake, cousin, stay° till all come in.   wait
          The trumpet sounds a parley[1] [within]. Enter
          Sir Walter BLUNT
BLUNT   I come with gracious offers from the King,
    If you vouchsafe me hearing and respect.
HOTSPUR   Welcome, Sir Walter Blunt; and would to God
35   You were of our determination.°   on our side
    Some of us love you well, and even those some°   those same persons
    Envy your great deservings and good name,
    Because you are not of our quality,°   party
    But stand against us like an enemy.
40   BLUNT   And God defend° but still I should stand so,   forbid
    So long as out of limit° and true rule   bounds of allegiance
    You stand against anointed majesty.
    But to my charge. The King hath sent to know
    The nature of your griefs,° and whereupon   grievances
45   You conjure from the breast of civil peace
    Such bold hostility, teaching his duteous land
    Audacious cruelty. If that the King
    Have any way your good deserts forgot,
    Which he confesseth to be manifold,

---

1. Summons to a conference with the enemy.

50 He bids you name your griefs, and with all speed
   You shall have your desires, with interest,
   And pardon absolute for yourself and these
   Herein misled by your suggestion.°   *instigation*
   HOTSPUR The King is kind, and well we know the King
55 Knows at what time to promise, when to pay.
   My father and my uncle and myself
   Did give him that same royalty he wears;
   And when he was not six-and-twenty strong,
   Sick in the world's regard, wretched and low,
60 A poor unminded° outlaw sneaking home,   *insignificant*
   My father gave him welcome to the shore;
   And when he heard him swear and vow to God
   He came but to be Duke of Lancaster,
   To sue his livery,[2] and beg his peace
65 With tears of innocency and terms of zeal,
   My father, in kind heart and pity moved,
   Swore him assistance, and performed it too.
   Now when the lords and barons of the realm
   Perceived Northumberland did lean to him,
70 The more and less came in with cap and knee,[3]
   Met him in boroughs, cities, villages,
   Attended him on bridges, stood in lanes,[4]
   Laid gifts before him, proffered him their oaths,
   Gave him their heirs as pages, followed him,
75 Even at the heels, in golden° multitudes.   *resplendent*
   He presently, as greatness knows itself,°   *recognizes its power*
   Steps me° a little higher than his vow   *Steps*
   Made to my father while his blood° was poor   *spirit*
   Upon the naked shore at Ravenspurgh,
80 And now forsooth takes on him to reform
   Some certain edicts and some strait° decrees   *strict*
   That lie too heavy on the commonwealth,
   Cries out upon abuses, seems to weep
   Over his country's wrongs; and by this face,°   *outward show*
85 This seeming brow of justice, did he win
   The hearts of all that he did angle for;
   Proceeded further, cut me off° the heads   *cut off*
   Of all the favourites that the absent King
   In deputation° left behind him here   *As deputies*
90 When he was personal° in the Irish war.   *engaged in person*
   BLUNT Tut, I came not to hear this.
   HOTSPUR   Then to the point.
   In short time after, he deposed the King,
   Soon after that deprived him of his life,
   And in the neck of that tasked° the whole state;   *And immediately taxed*
95 To make that worse, suffered his kinsman March[5]—
   Who is, if every owner were well placed,[6]
   Indeed his king—to be engaged° in Wales,   *held hostage*
   There without ransom to lie forfeited;°   *unredeemed*

---

2. To plead for the restitution of his lands (which Rich-
ard II had seized when John of Gaunt, Bolingbroke's
father, died).
3. Those of both high and low social status deferen-
tially presented themselves (with cap in hand and
bended knee).

4. Stood in rows along the roadways.
5. The Earl of March. For his claim to the throne, see
note to 1.3.79.
6. If everyone had possessions according to his entitle-
ment.

Disgraced me in my happy victories,
100   Sought to entrap me by intelligence,°   *spying*
Rated° mine uncle from the Council-board,   *Drove away*
In rage dismissed my father from the court,
Broke oath on oath, committed wrong on wrong,
And in conclusion drove us to seek out
105   This head of safety,[7] and withal° to pry   *also*
Into his title, the which we find
Too indirect° for long continuance.   *irregular*
BLUNT   Shall I return this answer to the King?
HOTSPUR   Not so, Sir Walter. We'll withdraw awhile.
110   Go to the King, and let there be impawned°   *pledged*
Some surety for a safe return again;
And in the morning early shall mine uncle
Bring him our purposes. And so, farewell.
BLUNT   I would you would accept of grace and love.
HOTSPUR   And maybe so we shall.
115   BLUNT   Pray God you do.

Exeunt [HOTSPUR, WORCESTER, DOUGLAS, *and*
VERNON *at one door,* BLUNT *at another door*]

4.4

Enter the ARCHBISHOP *of York, and* SIR MICHAEL
ARCHBISHOP [*giving letters*]   Hie, good Sir Michael, bear this sealèd brief°   *dispatch*
With wingèd haste to the Lord Marshal,
This to my cousin Scrope, and all the rest
To whom they are directed. If you knew
5   How much they do import, you would make haste.
SIR MICHAEL   My good lord,
I guess their tenor.
ARCHBISHOP   Like enough you do.
Tomorrow, good Sir Michael, is a day
Wherein the fortune of ten thousand men
10   Must bide the touch;° for, sir, at Shrewsbury,   *stand the test*
As I am truly given to understand,
The King with mighty and quick-raisèd power
Meets with Lord Harry. And I fear, Sir Michael,
What with the sickness of Northumberland,
15   Whose power was in the first proportion,°   *magnitude*
And what with Owain Glyndŵr's absence thence,
Who with them was a rated sinew[1] too,
And comes not in, overruled by prophecies,
I fear the power of Percy is too weak
20   To wage an instant° trial with the King.   *immediate*
SIR MICHAEL   Why, my good lord, you need not fear; there is Douglas
And Lord Mortimer.
ARCHBISHOP   No, Mortimer is not there.
SIR MICHAEL   But there is Mordake, Vernon, Lord Harry Percy;
And there is my lord of Worcester, and a head°   *troop*
25   Of gallant warriors, noble gentlemen.
ARCHBISHOP   And so there is; but yet the King hath drawn
The special head of all the land together—

7. That is, safety in these gathered forces.   1. A much-valued source of strength.
4.4 Location: The Archbishop's palace, York.

The Prince of Wales, Lord John of Lancaster,
The noble Westmorland, and warlike Blunt,
30 And many more corrivals,° and dear° men   *associates / noble*
Of estimation° and command in arms.   *reputation*
SIR MICHAEL   Doubt not, my lord, they shall be well opposed.
ARCHBISHOP   I hope no less, yet needful 'tis to fear;
And to prevent the worst, Sir Michael, speed.
35 For if Lord Percy thrive not, ere the King
Dismiss his power he means to visit us,
For he hath heard of our confederacy,
And 'tis but wisdom to make strong against him;
Therefore make haste. I must go write again
40 To other friends; and so farewell, Sir Michael.   *Exeunt [severally]*

5.1

Enter KING [HENRY], PRINCE [HARRY], *Lord* JOHN OF LAN-
CASTER, [*the*] *Earl of* WESTMORLAND, *Sir Walter* BLUNT,
and FALSTAFF
KING HENRY   How bloodily the sun begins to peer
Above yon bulky hill! The day looks pale
At his distemp'rature.°   *sick appearance*
PRINCE HARRY   The southern wind
Doth play the trumpet to his° purposes,   *(the sun's)*
5 And by his hollow whistling in the leaves
Foretells a tempest and a blust'ring day.
KING HENRY   Then with the losers let it sympathize,°   *accord*
For nothing can seem foul to those that win.
    *The trumpet sounds [a parley within]. Enter [the Earl
    of] WORCESTER [and Sir Richard VERNON][1]*
How now, my lord of Worcester? 'Tis not well
10 That you and I should meet upon such terms
As now we meet. You have deceived our trust,
And made us doff our easy robes of peace
To crush our old limbs in ungentle steel.
This is not well, my lord, this is not well.
15 What say you to it? Will you again unknit
This churlish knot of all-abhorrèd war,
And move in that obedient orb[2] again
Where you did give a fair and natural light,
And be no more an exhaled meteor,[3]
20 A prodigy of fear,° and a portent   *A fearful omen*
Of broachèd mischief° to the unborn times?   *Of evil set flowing*
WORCESTER   Hear me, my liege.
For mine own part, I could be well content
To entertain the lag-end° of my life   *latter end*
25 With quiet hours; for I protest,
I have not sought the day of this dislike.°   *discord*
KING HENRY   You have not sought it? How comes it, then?
FALSTAFF   Rebellion lay in his way, and he found it.

5.1 Location: King Henry's camp at Shrewsbury.
1. Neither Q nor F indicates that Vernon accompanies
Worcester in this scene, but it seems lacking in ceremony
for Worcester to go to King Henry's camp alone. Also, in
the next scene, Worcester discusses with Vernon what the
King has said and whether to inform Hotspur, making it
appear that Vernon was present at this meeting.

2. Orbit. Henry, drawing on a conventional analogy
between social and cosmological order, compares
Worcester to a star or a planet that, in Ptolemaic cos-
mology, should move properly in its sphere (orbit)
around the earth.
3. Meteors were thought to be made of gas exhaled by
the sun and were considered bad omens.

PRINCE HARRY   Peace, chewet,° peace!   *jackdaw; chatterer*

30   WORCESTER [*to the* KING]   It pleased your majesty to turn your looks
Of favour from myself and all our house;
And yet I must remember° you, my lord,   *remind*
We were the first and dearest of your friends.
For you my staff of office did I break
35   In Richard's time, and posted° day and night   *rode swiftly*
To meet you on the way and kiss your hand
When yet you were in place° and in account°   *social status / esteem*
Nothing so strong and fortunate as I.
It was myself, my brother, and his son
40   That brought you home, and boldly did outdare
The dangers of the time. You swore to us,
And you did swear that oath at Doncaster,
That you did nothing purpose° 'gainst the state,   *intend*
Nor claim no further than your new-fall'n right,[4]
45   The seat° of Gaunt, dukedom of Lancaster.   *estate*
To this we swore our aid, but in short space
It rained down fortune show'ring on your head,
And such a flood of greatness fell on you,
What with our help, what with the absent King,
50   What with the injuries° of a wanton° time,   *evils / lawless*
The seeming sufferances° that you had borne,   *wrongs*
And the contrarious° winds that held the King   *adverse*
So long in his unlucky Irish wars
That all in England did repute him dead;
55   And from this swarm of fair advantages
You took occasion to be quickly wooed
To gripe° the general sway into your hand,   *seize*
Forgot your oath to us at Doncaster,
And being fed by us, you used us so
60   As that ungentle gull,° the cuckoo's bird,   *rude young bird*
Useth the sparrow[5]—did oppress our nest,
Grew by our feeding to so great a bulk
That even our love° durst not come near your sight   *we who loved you*
For fear of swallowing.° But with nimble wing   *being swallowed*
65   We were enforced for safety' sake to fly
Out of your sight, and raise this present head,
Whereby we stand opposèd° by such means   *in opposition to you*
As you yourself have forged against yourself,
By unkind usage, dangerous° countenance,   *threatening*
70   And violation of all faith and troth
Sworn to us in your younger enterprise.
KING HENRY   These things indeed you have articulate,°   *expressed*
Proclaimed at market crosses,[6] read in churches,
To face° the garment of rebellion   *adorn*
75   With some fine colour° that may please the eye   *hue; pretext*
Of fickle changelings° and poor discontents,   *turncoats*
Which gape and rub the elbow[7] at the news
Of hurly-burly innovation;°   *rebellion*

---

4. The right newly descended to you (upon the death
of your father).
5. The female cuckoo lays its eggs in the nests of
smaller birds such as the sparrow, who raises the
cockoo's young until they grow so large they threaten
the sparrow and her nest.

6. Crosses set up in marketplaces, often atop polygonal
structures with open archways on each of the sides and
vaulted within.
7. And hug themselves with crossed arms (conven-
tional expression of delight).

<blockquote>And never yet did insurrection want°</blockquote> *lack*

80 Such water-colours to impaint his cause,
Nor moody beggars starving for a time
Of pell-mell° havoc and confusion. *chaotic*

PRINCE HARRY   In both our armies there is many a soul
Shall pay full dearly for this encounter
85 If once they join in trial.° Tell your nephew *combat*
The Prince of Wales doth join with all the world
In praise of Henry Percy. By my hopes,
This present enterprise set off his head,° *not counted against him*
I do not think a braver gentleman,
90 More active-valiant or more valiant-young,
More daring, or more bold, is now alive
To grace this latter age with noble deeds.
For my part, I may speak it to my shame,
I have a truant been to chivalry;
95 And so I hear he doth account me too.
Yet this, before my father's majesty:
I am content that he shall take the odds° *have the advantage*
Of his great name and estimation,° *reputation*
And will, to save the blood on either side,
100 Try fortune with him in a single fight.

KING HENRY   And, Prince of Wales, so dare we venture thee,
Albeit° considerations infinite *Were it not that*
Do make against it. No, good Worcester, no.
We love our people well; even those we love
105 That are misled upon your cousin's° part; *kinsman's*
And will they take the offer of our grace,° *mercy*
Both he and they and you, yea, every man
Shall be my friend again, and I'll be his.
So tell your cousin, and bring me word
110 What he will do. But if he will not yield,
Rebuke and dread correction wait on° us, *serve*
And they shall do their office. So be gone.
We will not now be troubled with reply.
We offer fair; take it advisedly.

Exeunt WORCESTER [*and* VERNON]

115 **PRINCE HARRY**   It will not be accepted, on my life.
The Douglas and the Hotspur both together
Are confident against the world in arms.

KING HENRY   Hence, therefore, every leader to his charge,
For on their answer will we set on them,
120 And God befriend us as our cause is just!

Exeunt. Manent° Prince [HARRY] *and* FALSTAFF *Remain*

FALSTAFF   Hal, if thou see me down in the battle, and bestride
me,° so.° 'Tis a point of friendship. *stand over me / good*

PRINCE HARRY   Nothing but a colossus[8] can do thee that friend-
ship. Say thy prayers, and farewell.

125 **FALSTAFF**   I would 'twere bed-time, Hal, and all well.

PRINCE HARRY   Why, thou owest God a death.   [*Exit*]

FALSTAFF   'Tis not due yet. I would be loath to pay him before
his day. What need I be so forward with him that calls not on
me? Well, 'tis no matter; honour pricks° me on. Yea, but how *spurs*

---

8. Referring to a massive statue of Apollo that purportedly stood over the entrance to the harbor in ancient Rhodes and was referred to as the Colossus of Rhodes.

130   if honour prick me off[9] when I come on? How then? Can hon-
      our set-to° a leg? No. Or an arm? No. Or take away the grief   *mend*
      of a wound? No. Honour hath no skill in surgery, then? No.
      What is honour? A word. What is in that word 'honour'? What
      is that 'honour'? Air. A trim reckoning!° Who hath it? He that   *A nice summing up*
135   died o'Wednesday. Doth he feel it? No. Doth he hear it? No.
      'Tis insensible[1] then? Yea, to the dead. But will it not live with
      the living? No. Why? Detraction° will not suffer° it. Therefore   *Slander / allow*
      I'll none of it. Honour is a mere scutcheon.[2] And so ends my
      catechism.   *Exit*

5.2

Enter [the Earl of] WORCESTER *and Sir Richard*
      VERNON

WORCESTER   O no, my nephew must not know, Sir Richard,
      The liberal and kind offer of the king.
VERNON   'Twere best he did.
WORCESTER   Then are we all undone.
      It is not possible, it cannot be,
5   The King should keep his word in loving us.
      He will suspect us still,° and find a time   *always*
      To punish this offence in other faults.
      Supposition all our lives shall be stuck full of eyes,[1]
      For treason is but trusted like the fox,
10   Who, ne'er so° tame, so cherished, and locked up,   *no matter how*
      Will have a wild trick of his ancestors.
      Look how we can, or° sad or merrily,   *whether*
      Interpretation will misquote our looks,
      And we shall feed like oxen at a stall,
15   The better cherished still the nearer death.
      My nephew's trespass may be well forgot;
      It hath the excuse of youth and heat of blood,
      And an adopted name of privilege[2]—
      A hare-brained Hotspur, governed by a spleen.°   *hot temper*
20   All his offences live upon my head,
      And on his father's. We did train° him on,   *lead*
      And, his corruption being ta'en from us,
      We as the spring° of all shall pay for all.   *source*
      Therefore, good cousin, let not Harry know
25   In any case the offer of the King.
      VERNON   Deliver what you will; I'll say 'tis so.
            Enter HOTSPUR *[and the Earl of* DOUGLAS*]*
      Here comes your cousin.
HOTSPUR   My uncle is returned.
      Deliver up[3] my Lord of Westmorland.
      Uncle, what news?
30   WORCESTER   The King will bid you battle presently.
      DOUGLAS   Defy him by the Lord of Westmorland.
      HOTSPUR   Lord Douglas, go you and tell him so.

9. Selects me to die; marks me off the list.
1. Imperceptible to the senses.
2. Heraldic shield exhibited at funerals displaying the
deceased person's coat of arms.
5.2 Location: The rebels' camp.
1. The King's suspicion will cause him constantly to
spy on us. Worcester is referring to an allegorical rep-

resentation of Suspicion dressed in a coat of eyes or to
secret agents similar to those whom Elizabeth's gov-
ernment maintained.
2. A nickname, "Hotspur," which may excuse his rash-
ness.
3. Release (as the hostage for the safe return of
Worcester and Vernon).

DOUGLAS   Marry, and shall, and very willingly.   *Exit*
WORCESTER   There is no seeming° mercy in the King.   *semblance of*
35 HOTSPUR   Did you beg any? God forbid!
WORCESTER   I told him gently of our grievances,
   Of his oath-breaking, which he mended thus:
   By now forswearing that he is forsworn.
   He calls us 'rebels', 'traitors', and will scourge
40   With haughty arms this hateful name in us.
      Enter [the Earl of] DOUGLAS
DOUGLAS   Arm, gentlemen, to arms, for I have thrown
   A brave° defiance in King Henry's teeth—   *proud*
   And Westmorland that was engaged° did bear it—   *held as hostage*
   Which cannot choose but bring him quickly on.
WORCESTER [*to* HOTSPUR]   The Prince of Wales stepped forth
45   before the King
   And, nephew, challenged you to single fight.
HOTSPUR   O, would the quarrel lay upon our heads,
   And that no man might draw short breath today
   But I and Harry Monmouth![4] Tell me, tell me,
50   How showed his tasking?° Seemed it in contempt?   *challenge*
VERNON   No, by my soul, I never in my life
   Did hear a challenge urged more modestly,
   Unless a brother should a brother dare
   To gentle° exercise and proof of arms.[5]   *noble*
55   He gave you all the duties of° a man,   *respect due to*
   Trimmed up your praises[6] with a princely tongue,
   Spoke your deservings like a chronicle,
   Making you ever better than his praise
   By still° dispraising praise valued with you;[7]   *constantly*
60   And, which became him like a prince indeed,
   He made a blushing cital° of himself,   *mention*
   And chid his truant youth with such a grace
   As if he mastered there a double spirit
   Of teaching and of learning instantly.°   *simultaneously*
65   There did he pause; but let me tell the world,
   If he outlive the envy° of this day,   *malice*
   England did never owe° so sweet a hope,   *own*
   So much misconstrued in his wantonness.°   *self-indulgence*
HOTSPUR   Cousin, I think thou art enamourèd
70   On° his follies. Never did I hear   *Of*
   Of any prince so wild a liberty.°   *such unrestrained license*
   But be he as he will, yet once ere night
   I will embrace him with a soldier's arm,
   That he shall shrink under my courtesy.
75   Arm, arm, with speed! And fellows, soldiers, friends,
   Better consider what you have to do
   Than I, that have not well the gift of tongue,
   Can lift your blood[8] up with persuasion.
      Enter a MESSENGER
MESSENGER   My lord, here are letters for you.
80 HOTSPUR   I cannot read them now.   [*Exit* MESSENGER]

4. Harry of Monmouth, the town in Wales where the Prince was born.
5. Trial of skill at weapons.
6. Embellished his praises of you.
7. As measured against you (because your merit exceeds all praise).
8. Rebelliousness; self-indulgence.

O gentlemen, the time of life is short.
To spend that shortness basely were too long
If life did ride upon a dial's point,
Still ending at the arrival of an hour.⁹
85   An if we live, we live to tread on kings;
If die, brave death when princes die with us!
Now for our consciences: the arms are fair
When the intent of bearing them is just.

        Enter another MESSENGER

MESSENGER   My lord, prepare; the King comes on apace. [*Exit*]
90 HOTSPUR   I thank him that he cuts me from my tale,
For I profess not° talking, only this: *am not skilled at*
Let each man do his best. And here draw I
A sword whose temper° I intend to stain   *tempered steel*
With the best blood that I can meet withal
95   In the adventure of this perilous day.
Now *Esperance!*¹ Percy! And set on!
Sound all the lofty instruments of war,
And by that music let us all embrace,
For, heaven to earth,² some of us never shall
100   A second time do such a courtesy.

      The trumpets sound. Here they embrace. [*Exeunt*]

5.3

    KING [HENRY] *enters with his power. Alarum*¹ [*and exe-*
    unt] *to the battle. Then enter* [*the Earl of*] DOUGLAS,
    and Sir Walter BLUNT [*disguised as the* KING]

BLUNT   What is thy name, that in the battle thus
Thou crossest me? What honour dost thou seek
Upon my head?
DOUGLAS   Know then my name is Douglas,
And I do haunt thee in the battle thus
5   Because some tell me that thou art a king.
BLUNT   They tell thee true.
DOUGLAS   The Lord of Stafford dear today hath bought
Thy likeness,² for instead of thee, King Harry,
This sword hath ended him. So shall it thee,
10   Unless thou yield thee as my prisoner.
BLUNT   I was not born a yielder, thou proud Scot,
And thou shalt find a king that will revenge
Lord Stafford's death.

      They fight. DOUGLAS *kills* BLUNT. *Then enter* HOTSPUR

HOTSPUR   O Douglas, hadst thou fought at Holmedon thus,
15   I never had triumphed upon a Scot.
DOUGLAS   All's done, all's won: here breathless lies the King.
HOTSPUR   Where?
DOUGLAS   Here.
HOTSPUR   This, Douglas? No, I know this face full well.
20   A gallant knight he was; his name was Blunt—

---

9. *To spend . . . hour:* that is, If life only lasted an hour
(*dial's point:* hand of a clock), it would still be too long
if it were basely spent.
1. Hope (the Percy motto; see note to 2.4.66).
2. The odds are as great as the distance from heaven to
earth.

5.3 Location: The remaining scenes take place on the
battlefield at Shrewsbury.
1. A call to arms, usually sounded on drum or trum-
pets.
2. *hath . . . likeness:* has paid for impersonating you;
has paid for his resemblance to you.

Semblably furnished° like the King himself.   *Similarly equipped*
DOUGLAS [*to Blunt's body*]   A fool go with thy soul,[3] whither it goes!
A borrowed title hast thou bought too dear.
Why didst thou tell me that thou wert a king?
25   HOTSPUR   The king hath many marching in his coats.[4]
DOUGLAS   Now by my sword, I will kill all his coats.
I'll murder all his wardrobe, piece by piece,
Until I meet the King.
HOTSPUR   Up and away!
Our soldiers stand full fairly for the day.[5]
                    Exeunt [leaving Blunt's body]
                Alarum. Enter FALSTAFF
30   FALSTAFF   Though I could scape shot-free[6] at London, I fear
the shot here. Here's no scoring[7] but upon the pate.—Soft,
who are you?— Sir Walter Blunt. There's honour for you.
Here's no vanity. I am as hot as molten lead, and as heavy too.
God keep lead out of me; I need no more weight than mine
35   own bowels. I have led my ragamuffins where they are pep-
pered; there's not three of my hundred and fifty left alive, and
they are for the town's end,[8] to beg during life.
                Enter PRINCE [HARRY]
But who comes here?
PRINCE HARRY   What, stand'st thou idle here? Lend me thy sword.
40   Many a noble man lies stark and stiff
Under the hoofs of vaunting enemies,
Whose deaths as yet are unrevenged. I prithee
Lend me thy sword.
FALSTAFF   O Hal, I prithee give me leave to breathe awhile.
45   Turk Gregory[9] never did such deeds in arms
As I have done this day. I have paid° Percy,   *settled with (killed)*
I have made him sure.[1]
PRINCE HARRY   He is indeed,
And living to kill thee. I prithee
Lend me thy sword.
FALSTAFF   Nay, before God, Hal,
50   If Percy be alive thou gett'st not my sword;
But take my pistol if thou wilt.
PRINCE HARRY   Give it me. What, is it in the case?
FALSTAFF   Ay, Hal;
'Tis hot, 'tis hot. There's that will sack a city.
                The PRINCE *draws it out, and finds it to be a bottle of*
                sack
PRINCE HARRY   What, is it a time to jest and dally now?
                He throws the bottle at him. Exit
55   FALSTAFF   Well, if Percy be alive, I'll pierce him. If he do come
in my way, so; if he do not, if I come in his willingly, let him
make a carbonado[2] of me. I like not such grinning° honour as   *menacing*

---

3. May the title of "fool" go with your soul (for imper-
sonating the King).
4. In his surcoat, or loose robes of rich material,
embroidered with the royal coat of arms and worn over
armor.
5. Our soldiers look as though they will win the day.
6. Escape without paying the tavern bill ("shot"), with
a pun in the following line on "shot" as ammunition
(projectiles, cannon shot, etc.).
7. Recording of debts by means of "scores," or notches

on a board (customary in taverns); wounding or cutting.
8. By the town gates, where people often begged.
9. A conflation of the idea of the Turk, taken to be a
cruel and fierce fighter and an enemy of Protestant En-
gland, and either Pope Gregory VII or Pope Gregory
XIII, both regarded as violent and cruel by Protestant
writers.
1. I have killed him; but the Prince takes "sure" to
mean "secure."
2. Meat slashed to grill.

Sir Walter hath. Give me life, which if I can save, so; if not, hon-
our comes unlooked for, and there's an end.

Exit [with Blunt's body]

5.4

Alarum. Excursions. Enter KING [HENRY], PRINCE
[HARRY, *wounded*], *Lord* JOHN OF LANCASTER, *and* [*the*]
Earl of WESTMORLAND

KING HENRY   I prithee, Harry, withdraw thyself, thou bleed'st too much.
Lord John of Lancaster, go you with him.

JOHN OF LANCASTER   Not I, my lord, unless I did bleed too.

PRINCE HARRY [*to the* KING]   I beseech your majesty, make up,°   *go forward*
5   Lest your retirement do amaze° your friends.   *alarm*

KING HENRY   I will do so. My lord of Westmorland,
Lead him to his tent.

WESTMORLAND [*to the* PRINCE]   Come, my lord, I'll lead you to your tent.

PRINCE HARRY   Lead me, my lord? I do not need your help,
10   And God forbid a shallow scratch should drive
The Prince of Wales from such a field as this,
Where stained[1] nobility lies trodden on,
And rebels' arms triumph in massacres.

JOHN OF LANCASTER   We breathe° too long. Come, cousin Westmorland,   *rest*
15   Our duty this way lies. For God's sake, come.

[*Exeunt* LANCASTER *and* WESTMORLAND]

PRINCE HARRY   By God, thou hast deceived me, Lancaster;
I did not think thee lord of such a spirit.
Before I loved thee as a brother, John,
But now I do respect thee as my soul.

20 KING HENRY   I saw him hold Lord Percy at the point°   *sword point*
With lustier maintenance° than I did look for   *more valiant bearing*
Of such an ungrown warrior.

PRINCE HARRY   O, this boy lends mettle to us all!   *Exit*

Enter [the Earl of] DOUGLAS

DOUGLAS   Another king! They grow like Hydra's heads.[2]
25   I am the Douglas, fatal to all those
That wear those colours on them. What art thou
That counterfeit'st the person of a king?

KING HENRY   The King himself, who, Douglas, grieves at heart
So many of his shadows° thou hast met   *likenesses*
30   And not the very King. I have two boys
Seek° Percy and thyself about the field;   *Who seek*
But seeing thou fall'st on me so luckily,
I will assay° thee; and defend thyself.   *challenge*

DOUGLAS   I fear thou art another counterfeit;
35   And yet, in faith, thou bear'st thee like a king.
But mine° I am sure thou art, whoe'er thou be,   *(my prize of war)*
And thus I win thee.

They fight. The KING *being in danger, enter* PRINCE
[HARRY]

PRINCE HARRY   Hold up thy head, vile Scot, or thou art like
Never to hold it up again. The spirits

5.4
1. Bloodstained; disgraced by defeat.
2. A monster in classical mythology that grew two

heads whenever one was cut off. The hydra was a com-
mon image of political disorder.

40 Of valiant Shirley, Stafford, Blunt, are in my arms.
It is the Prince of Wales that threatens thee,
Who never promiseth but he means to pay.
            They fight. DOUGLAS *flieth*
Cheerly, my lord! How fares your grace?
Sir Nicholas Gawsey hath for succour sent,
45 And so hath Clifton. I'll to Clifton straight.
KING HENRY   Stay and breathe awhile.
Thou hast redeemed thy lost opinion,°   *reputation*
And showed thou mak'st some tender of° my life,   *have some regard for*
In this fair rescue thou hast brought to me.
50 PRINCE HARRY   O God, they did me too much injury
That ever said I hearkened for° your death.   *desired*
If it were so, I might have let alone
The insulting° hand of Douglas over you,   *scornful*
Which would have been as speedy in your end
55 As all the poisonous potions in the world,
And saved the treacherous labour of your son.
KING HENRY   Make up° to Clifton; I'll to Sir Nicholas Gawsey.   *Go forward*
                                                                Exit
        Enter HOTSPUR
HOTSPUR   If I mistake not, thou art Harry Monmouth.
PRINCE HARRY   Thou speak'st as if I would deny my name.
HOTSPUR   My name is Harry Percy.
60 PRINCE HARRY   Why then, I see
A very valiant rebel of the name.
I am the Prince of Wales; and think not, Percy,
To share with me in glory any more.
Two stars keep not their motion in one sphere,³
65 Nor can one England brook° a double reign   *endure*
Of Harry Percy and the Prince of Wales.
HOTSPUR   Nor shall it, Harry, for the hour is come
To end the one of us, and would to God
Thy name in arms were now as great as mine.
70 PRINCE HARRY   I'll make it greater ere I part from thee,
And all the budding honours on thy crest°   *helmet; coat of arms*
I'll crop° to make a garland for my head.   *cut*
HOTSPUR   I can no longer brook thy vanities.°   *empty boasts*
        They fight.
        Enter FALSTAFF
FALSTAFF   Well said, Hal! To it, Hal! Nay, you shall find no boy's
75 play here, I can tell you.
        Enter DOUGLAS. *He fighteth with* FALSTAFF, *who falls*
        down as if he were dead. [*Exit* DOUGLAS.] *The* PRINCE
        killeth [HOTSPUR]
HOTSPUR   O Harry, thou hast robbed me of my youth.
I better brook the loss of brittle life
Than those proud titles thou hast won of me.
They wound my thoughts worse than thy sword my flesh.
80 But thoughts, the slaves of life, and life, time's fool,
And time, that takes survey of all the world,
Must have a stop.° O, I could prophesy,   *an end*

---

3. Alluding to the theory that stars moved in concentric spheres around a center. Only one star could occupy a
single sphere.

But that the earthy and cold hand of death
Lies on my tongue. No, Percy, thou art dust,
85 And food for—   [He dies]
PRINCE HARRY   For worms, brave Percy. Fare thee well, great heart.
Ill-weaved ambition, how much art thou shrunk!
When that this body did contain a spirit,
A kingdom for it was too small a bound,
90 But now two paces of the vilest earth
Is room enough. This earth that bears thee dead
Bears not alive so stout° a gentleman.   valiant
If thou wert sensible° of courtesy,   conscious
I should not make so dear° a show of zeal;°   heartfelt / emotion
95 But let my favours⁴ hide thy mangled face,
[He covers Hotspur's face]
And even in thy behalf I'll thank myself
For doing these fair rites of tenderness.
Adieu, and take thy praise with thee to heaven.
Thy ignominy sleep with thee in the grave,
100 But not remembered in thy epitaph.
          He spieth FALSTAFF on the ground
What, old acquaintance! Could not all this flesh
Keep in a little life? Poor Jack, farewell.
I could have better spared a better man.
O, I should have a heavy° miss of thee,   sad; weighty
105 If I were much in love with vanity.
Death hath not struck so fat a deer today,
Though many dearer in this bloody fray.
Embowelled⁵ will I see thee by and by.
Till then, in blood by noble Percy lie.   Exit
          FALSTAFF riseth up
110 FALSTAFF   Embowelled? If thou embowel me today, I'll give you
leave to powder° me, and eat me too, tomorrow. 'Sblood, 'twas   pickle in salt
time to counterfeit, or that hot termagant⁶ Scot had paid me,
scot and lot° too. Counterfeit? I lie, I am no counterfeit. To   in full
die is to be a counterfeit, for he is but the counterfeit of a man
115 who hath not the life of a man. But to counterfeit dying when
a man thereby liveth is to be no counterfeit, but the true and
perfect image of life indeed. The better part of valour is dis-
cretion, in the which better part° I have saved my life. Zounds,   role
I am afraid of this gunpowder Percy, though he be dead. How
120 if he should counterfeit too, and rise? By my faith, I am afraid
he would prove the better counterfeit. Therefore I'll make him
sure; yea, and I'll swear I killed him. Why may not he rise as
well as I? Nothing confutes me but eyes,⁷ and nobody sees
me. Therefore, sirrah, [stabbing HOTSPUR] with a new wound
125 in your thigh, come you along with me.
          He takes up HOTSPUR on his back.
          Enter PRINCE [HARRY] and [Lord] JOHN OF LANCASTER
PRINCE HARRY   Come, brother John. Full bravely hast thou fleshed

4. Ornaments such as plumes or gloves worn into battle.
5. Prepared for embalming and burial as noblemen
were; disemboweled in the manner of a hunted deer.
6. A quarrelsome or shrewish person; the name of an

imaginary deity who, according to medieval morality
plays, was worshipped by followers of Mohammed.
7. No one could confute my story but an eyewitness.

Thy maiden sword.[8]

JOHN OF LANCASTER   But soft; whom have we here?
Did you not tell me this fat man was dead?

PRINCE HARRY   I did; I saw him dead,
Breathless and bleeding on the ground.
130   [*To* FALSTAFF]   Art thou alive?
Or is it fantasy° that plays upon our eyesight?   *hallucination*
I prithee speak; we will not trust our eyes
Without our ears. Thou art not what thou seem'st.

FALSTAFF   No, that's certain: I am not a double man.°   But if I   *ghost; two men*
135   be not Jack Falstaff, then am I a jack.° There is Percy. If your   *knave*
father will do me any honour, so; if not, let him kill the next
Percy himself. I look to be either earl or duke, I can assure you.

PRINCE HARRY   Why, Percy I killed myself, and saw thee dead.

FALSTAFF   Didst thou? Lord, Lord, how this world is given to
140   lying! I grant you I was down and out of breath, and so was he;
but we rose both at an instant,° and fought a long hour by   *simultaneously*
Shrewsbury clock. If I may be believed, so; if not, let them that
should reward valour bear the sin upon their own heads. I'll
take't on my death° I gave him this wound in the thigh. If the   *swear on my deathbed*
145   man were alive and would deny it, zounds, I would make him
eat a piece of my sword.

JOHN OF LANCASTER   This is the strangest tale that e'er I heard.

PRINCE HARRY   This is the strangest fellow, brother John.
[*To* FALSTAFF] Come, bring your luggage nobly on your back.
150   For my part, if a lie may do thee grace,°   *get you favor*
I'll gild it with the happiest° terms I have.   *most favorable*
    A retreat is sounded
The trumpet sounds retreat; the day is our.
Come, brother, let us to the highest° of the field   *highest ground*
To see what friends are living, who are dead.
                Exeunt [*the* PRINCE *and* LANCASTER]

155   FALSTAFF   I'll follow, as they say, for reward. He that rewards me,
God reward him. If I do grow great, I'll grow less; for I'll purge,[9]
and leave sack, and live cleanly, as a nobleman should do.
                Exit [*bearing Hotspur's body*]

5.5

The trumpets sound. Enter KING [HENRY], PRINCE
[HARRY], *Lord* JOHN OF LANCASTER, [*the*] *Earl of* WEST-
MORLAND, *with* [*the Earl of*] WORCESTER *and* [*Sir Rich-
ard*] VERNON, *prisoners* [*and soldiers*]

KING HENRY   Thus ever did rebellion find rebuke.
Ill-spirited Worcester, did not we send grace,
Pardon, and terms of love to all of you?
And wouldst thou turn our offers contrary,
5   Misuse the tenor° of thy kinsman's trust?   *Abuse the substance*
Three knights upon our party slain today,
A noble earl, and many a creature else,

---

8. *Full . . . sword:* How courageously or splendidly
have you initiated in bloodshed your untried weapon
(fought your first battle). The phrase alludes to hunting
practices in which hawks or hounds were "fleshed," or

made eager for prey by the taste of blood. Also alluding,
by way of the slang meaning of "sword" as "penis," to a
man's first sexual encounters with the flesh of others.
9. I'll take laxatives (to reduce my weight); I'll repent.

Had been alive this hour
If like a Christian thou hadst truly borne
10   Betwixt our armies true intelligence.°   *information*
WORCESTER   What I have done my safety urged me to,
And I embrace this fortune patiently,
Since not to be avoided it falls on me.
KING HENRY   Bear Worcester to the death, and Vernon too.
15   Other offenders we will pause upon.°   *reflect upon*
                          Exeunt WORCESTER *and* VERNON [*guarded*]
How goes the field?
PRINCE HARRY   The noble Scot Lord Douglas, when he saw
The fortune of the day quite turned from him,
The noble Percy slain, and all his men
20   Upon the foot of fear,° fled with the rest;   *Fleeing in fear*
And falling from a hill he was so bruised
That the pursuers took him. At my tent
The Douglas is, and I beseech your grace
I may dispose of him.
25   KING HENRY   With all my heart.
PRINCE HARRY   Then, brother John of Lancaster,
To you this honourable bounty° shall belong.   *act of generosity*
Go to the Douglas, and deliver him
Up to his pleasure ransomless and free.
30   His valours shown upon our crests° today   *helmets*
Have taught us how to cherish such high deeds
Even in the bosom of our adversaries.
JOHN OF LANCASTER   I thank your grace for this high courtesy,
Which I shall give away immediately.
35   KING HENRY   Then this remains, that we divide our power.
You, son John, and my cousin Westmorland,
Towards York shall bend you° with your dearest speed   *direct your course*
To meet Northumberland and the prelate Scrope,
Who, as we hear, are busily in arms.
40   Myself and you, son Harry, will towards Wales,
To fight with Glyndŵr and the Earl of March.
Rebellion in this land shall lose his sway,
Meeting the check of such another day;
And since this business so fair is done,
45   Let us not leave° till all our own be won.   *leave off*
                     Exeunt [*the* KING, *the* PRINCE, *and their power*
                        at one door, LANCASTER, WESTMORLAND, *and their*
                                      power at another door]

Henry V

From a military point of view, Henry V was perhaps the most capable king England ever had. In 1414, reviving an English royal claim on the French throne, Henry invaded France. The following year, he won the Battle of Agincourt against impossible odds, forcing the King of France to declare him his heir and marry him to his daughter. Not surprisingly, Henry's story was a favorite with his English compatriots. It was lovingly chronicled by the historians Raphael Holinshed (died c. 1580) and Edward Hall (d. 1547), and probably dramatized once or more by other playwrights before Shakespeare brought his own version to the stage in 1599.

Shakespeare's *Henry V* is the last written of a set of eight plays on medieval English history. His first four history plays had dealt with the tumultuous years between 1422 and 1485, when England was first at war with France and then, after 1455, embroiled in a civil war—the Wars of the Roses. Shakespeare wrote another four plays several years later, presenting the events of 1398 to 1420 that led up to these long wars over the royal succession. *Richard II* depicts Henry Bolingbroke's successful rebellion against Richard II and his coronation as Henry IV. The next two plays describe the troubled reign of the usurper, whose former allies turn against him and whose son keeps company with thieves. At the end of *2 Henry IV,* the King dies and young Prince Hal ascends the throne as Henry V, quickly belying his wastrel reputation and proving himself an astute leader in the play that bears his name. In the final lines of *Henry V,* however, the Chorus foresees Henry's imminent death, after which civil strife will break out once again.

Henry V is, therefore, one of a group of plays rather than a freestanding work. It refers constantly to events before and after its own temporal limits, events familiar to Shakespeare's audience from plays they had already seen performed. These references complicate the play's tone considerably. The Chorus's final predictions, for instance, darken the otherwise straightforwardly triumphal conclusion. Surely our awareness of the internecine strife that precedes and follows Henry's reign reinforces our admiration for him—he prospers where others have failed and will again fail, miserably. At the same time, *Henry V* is haunted by problems merely deferred, not resolved; in the long view, its hero's success looks transitory, even futile.

In 1599, such complexities may have seemed especially pertinent. England was mobilizing for a major campaign against Ireland to be led by Elizabeth's dashing young favorite, the Earl of Essex. *Henry V* registers both the patriotic excitement generated by the prospect of a military venture in foreign parts and the dread of war in a notoriously difficult environment (in the event, Essex's expedition was a disaster). These acutely mixed feelings were symptomatic of more general disputes about England's foreign policy. For much of the sixteenth century, England had attempted merely to defend its borders, but as it became wealthier and more powerful, expansion seemed feasible again. Ireland and the Netherlands beckoned; so did the New World, where France and Spain had already established colonies. Henry V's foray into France typified the kind of aggressive enterprise some of Shakespeare's contemporaries wished their nation to underwrite and others denounced as wasteful and dangerous.

Given the circumstances in which *Henry V* was originally written, it is not surprising that it has generated striking interpretive disagreements or that the play continues to be viewed through the lens of contemporary events. In Laurence Olivier's film version, made during World War II, *Henry V* is a vindication of England's excellence, and the victory at Agincourt a hopeful precedent for success in a justified

Henricus v. From John Rastell, *The Pastyme of People* (1529).

European war. Kenneth Branagh's 1989 film, on the other hand, reflects the murkier experience of more recent conflicts: the American intervention in Vietnam, the British in the Falkland Islands. Did Shakespeare intend the play as a paeon to militarism or as an exposé of war's pointless brutality? Is Henry supposed to be a heroic or a repellent character? Is the war in France justified or purely expedient?

Henry's impressive leadership is repeatedly emphasized by the Chorus, by his followers, and even occasionally by his enemies. He not merely copes with, but triumphs over, the difficult circumstances bequeathed him: uniting his disputatious people against an external enemy, spending their aggressions abroad instead of at home, and gaining himself a kingdom to boot. He displays unshakeable personal courage in the campaign in France, in the smaller skirmishes as well as in the desperate moments before Agincourt. His "Once more unto the breach" speech (3.1.1–34) and his prophetic vision of aged veterans boasting to their compatriots on St. Crispin's Day (4.3.41ff.) have often been held up as models of inspirational eloquence.

On the other hand, *Henry V* clear-sightedly acknowledges, as had *Richard II* and *1* and *2 Henry IV,* that the factors that render someone an effective king are not necessarily morally admirable ones. Even while Shakespeare displays Henry's charisma to the full, he refuses to be entirely dazzled by his allure. In the early sixteenth century, Machiavelli had introduced Renaissance political thinkers to the notion that success as a ruler might be separable from, or even inimical to, what was conventionally considered virtuous behavior. A successful leader, he argued, needed the traits of both the fox and the lion: in other words, he had to know how to use deception and violence to achieve his ends. Shakespeare's Henry is certainly no monster of iniquity, but his career poses some of the same questions that Machiavelli raised in *The Prince.* What is the relationship of political success to personal goodness? Should princes be judged by moral rules different from those that apply to the rest of mankind?

A closer look at *Henry V* reveals a play not only deeply equivocal but self-consciously so. The capstone of Shakespeare's years of experimentation in the history play form, *Henry V* seems profoundly aware of the way generic constraints bear in upon its hero. Comedy and tragedy form themselves upon the rhythms of an individual life, ending in marriage or in death. History plays, by contrast, even when they seem to concentrate on the fortunes of a single character, dramatize the life of a nation, or at least its governing class. Characters in history plays are conceived as an endless generational succession, inheriting a political and historical situation from their ancestors and passing it down to their descendants. When one person dies, another steps into his place. The King's marriage represents not merely a natural culmination of his personal story, but one episode in a family's attempt to perpetuate a dynasty.

The young King Henry V is, therefore, both more and less than a talented and intelligent individual. One of a series, like the play that bears his name, he must come to terms with what it means to be part of a family line, what it means for one's "career" to begin before birth and end long after death. And Henry's family line is, of course, a tangled matter. His dubious title to the English throne reflects some of the instabilities in the concept of inheritance: what can it mean to acquire name and title "legitimately" from a man who stole the throne? The passing of property and title from one generation to the next might seem to reflect facts of nature, but it is also, as the Archbishop of Canterbury's discussion of "Salic law" reveals in 1.2, a matter of custom, a cultural construction. Inheritance can be altered as well by force or by negotiation: Henry IV compelled Richard to abdicate, and Henry V's victory at Agincourt requires the French King to recognize an English conqueror rather than his own son as heir to the French throne.

Troubles over the way proper generational sequence ought to be defined resonate throughout the play. War, in particular, seems intimately tied up with questions of lineage. Battlefield heroics can reinforce and clarify the relationship between fathers and sons. King Charles of France, for instance, describes Henry's belligerence as his birthright:

> The kindred of him hath been fleshed upon us,
> And he is bred out of that bloody strain
> That haunted us in our familiar paths.
> Witness our too-much-memorable shame
> When Crécy battle fatally was struck,
> And all our princes captived by the hand
> Of that black name, Edward, Black Prince of Wales,
> Whiles that his mountant sire, on mountain standing,
> Up in the air, crowned with the golden sun,
> Saw his heroical seed and smiled to see him
> Mangle the work of nature and deface
> The patterns that by God and by French fathers
> Had twenty years been made.
>
> (2.4.50–62)

Henry's great-uncle, Edward the Black Prince, butchers the French while the Prince's father, King Edward III, gladly looks on. There seem to be no mothers in this entirely male domain, merely God and fathers in alliance, so that Edward III himself seems rather improbably deified, "up in the air, crowned with the golden sun." Henry, in his stirring speech to his troops at Harfleur, evidences a similar pattern of assumptions:

> On, on, you noblest English,
> Whose blood is fet from fathers of war-proof,
> Fathers that like so many Alexanders
> Have in these parts from morn till even fought,
> And sheathed their swords for lack of argument.
> Dishonor not your mothers; now attest
> That those whom you called fathers did beget you.
>
> (3.1.17–23)

Mothers get a mention from Henry, as they did not from the French King, but they contribute nothing of their own nature to their offspring: their function is merely to duplicate the fathers in the next generation. Any discrepancy between the achievement of the fathers and the achievement of the sons, in fact, "dishonors" the mothers by implying that they must have slept with men other than their husbands, because the only explanation for such an inconsistency is that the biological father must be different from the acknowledged one. Once again, fathers set demanding precedents for sons eager to emulate their exploits but inevitably threatened by the possibility of falling short. The French King and Henry imagine inheritance, which might seem a passive process, as a strenuous endeavor.

If battle clarifies the pedigrees of winners, it simultaneously obscures those of the losers. In practical terms, of course, Henry's victory debars the Dauphin, the French heir apparent, from assuming his father's title. More generally, however, as both Henry and the French King insist, defeat in battle disrupts familial affinity, defacing paternal patterns, dishonoring mothers. Negotiating with Harfleur's governor, Henry predicts the consequences of the town's refusal to surrender quietly:

> why, in a moment look to see
> The blind and bloody soldier with foul hand
> Defile the locks of your shrill-shrieking daughters;
> Your fathers taken by the silver beards,
> And their most reverend heads dashed to the walls;
> Your naked infants spitted upon pikes,
> Whiles the mad mothers with their howls confused
> Do break the clouds, as did the wives of Jewry
> At Herod's bloody-hunting slaughtermen.
>
> (3.3.110–18)

On the face of it, it might seem surprising for a general to characterize his own troops as rapists and murderers, or implicitly to compare himself with the infanticidal King Herod, one of the Bible's wickedest villains. Yet Henry's rhetorical tactics are entirely deliberate: by describing his soldiers' potential victims as members of families—as daughters, fathers, infants, mothers—he heightens the impact of their violence. The rampaging army, he implies, will shatter not merely individuals but whole networks of affiliation. The speech effectively intimidates his auditors, who give up without a fight.

Soldiers using a battering ram. From Flavius Vegetius Renatus, *The Foure Bookes of Flavius Vegetius Renatus: Briefelye contayninge a plaine forme, and perfect knowledge of martiall policye . . .* (1572).

Unfortunately, even soldiers in the "winning" camp, insofar as they are vulnerable to the enemy, are liable to similar familial disasters. Exeter's description of war's misfortunes exempts neither side from calamity, from

> the widows' tears, the orphans' cries,
> The dead men's blood, the pining maidens' groans,
> For husbands, fathers, and betrothèd lovers . . . .
> (2.4.106–08)

Although Henry's invasion leaves the French more bloodied and tearful than the English, the English, too, suffer emotional and practical losses. Henry's soldiers are wasted by disease, hanged, occasionally even killed in battle. In 4.1, the common soldier worries, in an age without veteran's benefits, of dying with "wives left poor behind them" and "children rawly left" (lines 132–34). Henry's insistence on his inheritance rights, in other words, may disrupt not only his enemies' but his subordinates'. If infants are slaughtered, daughters raped, fathers torn from dependents, how can families be reconstituted? How can legitimate inheritance possibly be determined?

The difficulties of succession and inheritance are issues for Shakespeare the playwright as well as for his protagonist. Just as the character Henry V must strive to match and excel the patterns set by his ancestors, so the play *Henry V* must concern itself with what it means to be a sequel in two different senses: the way in which it represents actual historical events in a necessarily diminished theatrical form, and the way in which it must struggle to gratify an audience whose expectations had been formed by three exceedingly popular plays in the same series. At the beginning of every act, a Chorus pointedly emphasizes the play's self-conscious lack of realism:

> Can this cock-pit hold
> The vasty fields of France? Or may we cram
> Within this wooden O the very casques
> That did affright the air at Agincourt?
> (Prologue, lines 11–14)

Of course, *Henry V* is no more implausible than most other Renaissance plays. But in a sense, the theatrical anxieties of *Henry V* are cognate with the personal anxieties of its hero; the play is afraid of degenerating from its precursors, proving an inadequate replica of a distinguished original. And just as Henry V seems to overcompensate, not merely living up to his illustrious predecessors but going beyond them, so, too, *Henry V*, like many sequels, copes with its belatedness by a strategy of overstatement. It exaggerates some of the themes and issues of the earlier plays. In *1 Henry IV*, Hotspur, Prince Hal's valiant antagonist, epitomized many of the traditional ideals of chivalry—a word derived from the French *cheval*, "horse." In *Henry V*, Bourbon, one of Henry's new opponents, writes a sonnet to his horse that begins "Wonder of nature"—for, he says, "my horse is my mistress" (3.7.36–37, 40). Hotspur's chivalry, caricatured to the point of ridiculousness, degenerates in *Henry V* into bestiality jokes made at the expense of a blustering fop.

Shakespeare dramatizes Henry's success, in other words, not merely by magnifying his exploits but by minimizing the threat from possible competitors. Although the enemies of Henry's adulthood are technically more formidable than the enemies of his adolescence, they are characterized as bumbling and laughable, so that Henry's victory over them seems virtually preordained. Henry's allies seem similarly diminished. Falstaff, who dominated much of *1* and *2 Henry IV*, dies without reappearing in *Henry V*, leaving his cronies Bardolph, Nim, and Pistol to accompany Henry to France. They are joined by Fluellen, a Welsh soldier; MacMorris, an Irish one; Jamy, a Scots one; and Williams, a rural English one. This miscellany is proof of Henry's charisma; while in the previous plays the Irish, Scots, and Welsh were up in arms, Henry V successfully enlists them in his cause—not by homogenizing their differences, but by inspiring their allegiance to him even as they quarrel furiously with one another. Henry's triumph at Agincourt, Shakespeare claims, involves all the peoples of the British Isles. At the same time, these loyal adherents are given little of Falstaff's subversive wit, presumably because Falstaff's wholesale critique of military valor would undercut too thoroughly the premises of Henry's royal magnetism. Even the bluff yeoman Williams, who complains of the disproportionate suffering common people undergo to satisfy the ambitions of their betters, does not dissent from the fundamental principle of social and military hierarchy: to disobey one's superiors, he claims, "were against all proportion of subjection" (4.1.138). For better or worse, everyone seems to agree, the subject's life is at the ruler's disposal.

Shakespeare's excision of Falstaff's skeptical intelligence from *Henry V* means that there is no one within the play to point out the ironies of many of the turns of the plot. Presumably, though no one comments explicitly upon it, the venality of the clerics who finance Henry's expedition to France is sufficiently clear to the audience. Likewise, when Gower loyally remarks that Henry, unlike Alexander, never killed any of his friends, we are likely to think back to Falstaff's death, attributed earlier to Henry's neglect, and also to reflect that of Henry's other Eastcheap chums only Pistol has survived the "great victory" at Agincourt. Elsewhere it is unclear how or even whether the audience is expected to grasp an irony. In 1.1, Henry decides to press his claim on the French throne through the female line of descent. Shortly thereafter, he executes three erstwhile friends for conspiring against his life. In fact their plot was inspired by the conviction that Henry's title to the English throne was obstructed by the Earl of Mortimer's daughter, the Earl of Cambridge's wife. In other words, Henry employs against the French a principle that, if it were enforced against him, would strip him of both English and French kingdoms. Yet the point is made so obliquely that only a spectator cognizant of the tangled Plantagenet genealogy is likely to catch it.

As the stature of Henry's foes and associates diminishes, the ethical problems posed by his exploits are correspondingly aggravated. As we have already seen, Henry's self-assertion necessarily occurs at the expense of others, thereby raising the question of the extent to which his interests ought to take precedence over competing claims. Neither we nor Henry can be certain whether his exceptional situation and abilities exempt him from the criteria by which common persons are judged. In fact, Henry's unusual gifts as a leader render the uncertainty more pointed. Richard II disregarded common folk, and Henry IV deliberately avoided them; but Henry V inspires them by his capacity to immerse himself sympathetically in their lives. His insistence upon his ordinariness becomes a strategy of rule—part of what he is loved for during his lifetime and what becomes legendary after his death. But then, when he insists on seeing himself as a unique case nonetheless, he seems not merely to be asserting a King's usual prerogatives, but to be inconsistently or hypocritically making special allowances for himself.

This unresolved ambivalence becomes obvious in 4.1, when Henry disguises himself as a commoner and ventures among his rank and file. Initially, he argues for the essential similarity between himself and his followers.

> I think the King is but a man, as I am. The violet smells to him as it doth to me; the element shows to him as it doth to me. All his senses have but human conditions. His ceremonies laid by, in his nakedness he appears but a man, and though his affections are higher mounted than ours, yet when they stoop, they stoop with the like wing. (lines 99–104)

The ordinary soldiers, Williams and Bates, are unconvinced, pointing out that if they lose the battle, the King will be ransomed while they will be killed. On the other hand, they note, because they are required to obey the King under any circumstances, they need not concern themselves with the justice of the King's cause: their blood will be on Henry's head if he is waging an unjust war. The common soldiers see the King as unlike themselves, with special responsibilities that compensate for his special privileges. Henry responds indignantly:

> The King is not bound to answer the particular endings of his soldiers, the father of his son, nor the master of his servant, for they purpose not their deaths when they propose their services. Besides, there is no king, be his cause never so spotless, if it come to the arbitrament of swords, can try it out with all unspotted soldiers. Some, peradventure, have on them the guilt of premeditated and contrived murder; some, of beguiling virgins with the broken seals of perjury; some, making the wars their bulwark, that have before gored the gentle bosom of peace with pillage and robbery. (lines 146–55)

Henry resists accepting the extraordinary moral burden his followers would confer upon him. Yet his refusal is based not on his earlier assertion of the shared humanity of king and subject, but on a conviction of the king's special position. He distinguishes sharply and problematically between the king's "superior" violence—the violence of war—and the violence of individual subjects, which is merely criminal. After the soldiers leave, Henry exclaims bitterly:

> Upon the King.
> 'Let us our lives, our souls, our debts, our care-full wives,
> Our children, and our sins, lay on the King.'
> We must bear all. O hard condition,
> Twin-born with greatness: subject to the breath
> Of every fool, whose sense no more can feel
> But his own wringing. What infinite heartsease
> Must kings neglect that private men enjoy?
> (lines 212–19)

It is hard to take this self-pity seriously, given that Henry attempts to deflect all blame for his actions onto enemies and inferiors, even while accepting as his due the rewards that accrue to him by virtue of his exceptional status.

On the other hand, Shakespeare also shows effectively the King's genuine isolation from ordinary pleasures of work and play that normal people can take for granted. Though he repudiates Falstaff, the King retains a distinctly sportive quality; but the moral and practical gap that yawns between the ascendant Henry and his correspondingly diminished associates complicates the effect of his playfulness. In 2.2, with a typical flourish, he pretends to hand the traitors Scrope, Grey, and Cambridge their military commissions, after feigning to inquire about mercy for traitors. Actually, he gives them letters showing that he knows of their plot. This is splendid theater, but it is also quite chilling: Henry plays with his guilty victims as a cat plays with a mouse. His joke signifies not true contest, but absolute control.

Elsewhere, too, Henry's power tips the balance of hostility and affection that usually characterizes practical jokes in a markedly aggressive direction. In disguise on the eve of the Battle of Agincourt, he argues with the commoner Williams, as we have already seen, over the question of the king's responsibility for his subjects. He and Williams exchange gloves so they will be able to resume the quarrel after the battle. In 4.7, with victory assured, Henry gives Williams's glove to Fluellen to see what Williams will do when he sees it again. When Williams attacks Fluellen, Henry stops the fight, pretending to be angry at the insult to himself. Williams—technically guilty of the capital crime of mutiny—defends himself boldly enough, and Henry, thinking to be generous, returns Williams's glove to him filled with coins. Yet Williams fails to thank Henry, and when Fluellen attempts to add to the gift, he spurns it angrily. It is unclear from the script whether Williams eventually accepts the gold; either way, Henry's power contaminates what he wants to see as a game. While in the earlier plays Prince Hal always had the advantage of rank, it was still possible for Falstaff to give him almost as

Game of tennis. From Johann Amos Comenius, *Orbis Sensualium Pictus* (1659).

good as he got. Now that Henry is king and Falstaff is dead, Henry is always the winner, and so the game is no game at all. Arguably, in fact, Henry goes to war with France because he misses a sense of *competition*—because the fate of the effective king is that he cannot find real opposition at home.

Henry's wooing of Catherine in 5.2 is typified by the same dubious sense of fun. This scene, often quite endearing onstage, is also entirely beside the point. We hear from the Chorus in 3.0 that the French King offered Catherine to Henry before his forces arrived in France, but he rejected the offer because the suggested dowry—some "petty and unprofitable dukedoms"—did not suffice. Nonetheless, in 5.2, Henry calls Catherine his "capital demand" and presents himself to her as a wooer. He pretends that Catherine is free to reject him, even though the marriage is already arranged as part of the peace treaty. Rather like Williams, Catherine refuses to play along: when he asks, "Canst thou love me?" she replies, "I cannot tell." "Wilt thou have me?" "Dat is as it shall please de *roi mon père*" (lines 183ff.). Is Catherine being coy, or is she simply speaking the literal truth? In the game as Henry constructs it, Catherine's refusals can as easily be interpreted as coquettishness as real denial. In other words, even if she refuses to play Henry's game, she necessarily plays it anyhow. In *Henry V,* Shakespeare must cope with a knotty dramatic problem: how to interest an audience in a man who has, or wins, everything—whose life seems an unbroken series of successes. In the final scene as in the rest of the play, Shakespeare fascinates us by exhibiting the inevitably equivocal nature of kingly glory.

KATHARINE EISAMAN MAUS

TEXTUAL NOTE

Henry V exists in the 1623 First Folio (F) version and in a quarto version first issued in 1600 and reprinted in 1602 and 1619. The Folio version is generally accepted as the most authoritative text and was probably derived from Shakespeare's "foul papers," or manuscript, but there are also signs that the compositor consulted the 1619 Quarto

(Q3) when setting up the Folio text. F is not, however, a wholly reliable source; it contains a fairly large number of readings rejected by modern editors, probably the result of a compositor misreading a handwritten text. The Oxford editors argue that Q, although printed much earlier than F and obviously corrupt in some respects, actually represents a later stage of the text and may therefore incorporate some of Shakespeare's second thoughts and modifications. They believe that Q is based on memorial reconstruction by actors who played the parts of Exeter and Gower, for the text is far more reliable when these characters are onstage than for other scenes.

The quarto text also has a slightly different cast of characters than Folio's: F's Bedford is Q's Clarence, F's Westmoreland is Q's Warwick, and speeches assigned in F to Britain and to the Dauphin in the Agincourt scenes are given to Bourbon in Q. The most important substitution is the last, Bourbon's replacement of the Dauphin in 3.7, 4.2, and 4.5. In F, the Dauphin's substantial role sets him up as Henry's personal adversary, much as Hotspur was in *1 Henry IV.* Also in F, the Dauphin's amply demonstrated folly seems to warrant his eventual displacement by Henry. The quarto speech assignments, on the other hand, are consistent with King Charles's order in 3.5 that the Dauphin remain with him at Rouen. In Q, the Dauphin's absence from the battlefield, rather than his extravagantly frivolous presence, implies his unfitness for rule.

Although most editors accept the Folio speech assignments, Gary Taylor, editor of the Oxford text, argues that Shakespeare in fact vacillated about whether to include the Dauphin in the Agincourt scenes and that Q represents his final decision not to do so. In consequence, although F remains the Oxford control text, Taylor adopts many more readings from Q than do most editors. In this respect, the Oxford *Henry V* seems to depart from the editors' usual policy of not conflating distinctly different texts of the same play (the policy that produces the two *King Lears* later in this volume). Taylor provides information on the tangled textual history of the play and a full explanation of his editorial choices in his single-volume edition of *Henry V* (Oxford: Clarendon, 1982).

SELECTED BIBLIOGRAPHY

Altman, Joel. "'Vile Participation': The Amplification of Violence in the Theatre of *Henry V.*" *Shakespeare Quarterly* 42 (1991): 1–32. *Henry V* in the context of contemporary political and religious issues—in particular, the debate over the nature of Communion.

Barton, Anne. "The King Disguised: Shakespeare's *Henry V* and the Comical History." *The Triple Bond: Plays, Mainly Shakespearean, in Performance.* Ed. Joseph G. Price. University Park: Pennsylvania State University Press, 1975. 92–117. Sees *Henry V* in a tradition of Elizabethan plays that combine history and comedy.

Cormack, Bradin. "'If We Be Conquered': Legal Nationalism and the France of Shakespeare's English Histories." *A Power to Do Justice: Jurisdiction and Early English Literature.* Chicago: University of Chicago Press, 2007. Shakespeare's treatment of France and the French language in terms of sixteenth-century English anxieties about national identity.

Danson, Lawrence. "*Henry V*: King, Chorus, and Critics." *Shakespeare Quarterly* 34 (1983): 27–43. King Henry as an actor; the Chorus as a means of drawing attention to the relationship between history and theater.

Dollimore, Jonathan, and Alan Sinfield. "History and Ideology, Masculinity and Miscegenation." *Faultlines: Cultural Materialism and the Politics of Dissident Reading.* By Alan Sinfield. Berkeley: University of California Press, 1992. 109–42. Imperialist and masculinist attitudes reinforce one another in the play.

Greenblatt, Stephen. "Invisible Bullets: Renaissance Authority and Its Subversion, *Henry IV* and *Henry V.*" *Political Shakespeare: New Essays in Cultural Materialism.* Ed. Jonathan Dollimore and Alan Sinfield. Manchester: Manchester University

Press, 1985. 18–47. Theater and the glamour of a royal power that incorporates what seems to undermine it.

Ornstein, Robert. "Henry V." A Kingdom for a Stage: The Achievement of Shakespeare's History Plays. Cambridge, Mass.: Harvard University Press, 1972. 175–202. Henry V as an equivocal celebration of the King's victories.

Quint, David. "Alexander the Pig: Shakespeare on History and Poetry." Boundary 2 10 (1982): 49–63. Shakespeare's relation to Renaissance humanists' conceptions of history.

Rabkin, Norman. "Rabbits, Ducks, and Henry V." Shakespeare Quarterly 28 (1977): 279–96. Henry V as an unresolvably ambiguous play.

Wells, Stanley, with Gary Taylor. Modernizing Shakespeare's Spelling [Wells], with Three Studies in the Text of "Henry V" [Taylor]. Oxford: Clarendon, 1979. Provides the scholarly rationale for the textual editing of the Oxford/Norton version of the play.

FILMS

Henry V. 1944. Dir. Laurence Olivier. UK. 137 min. Colorful, patriotic version made near the end of World War II, with Oliver as a very sympathetic king. Intelligently translates the play's theatrical self-consciousness to the film medium.

Henry V. 1979. Dir. David Giles. UK. 163 min. This BBC-TV production retains more features of a stage production than do the elaborate Olivier and Branagh versions. David Gwillim is a pleasant but resolute hero.

Henry V. 1989. Dir. Kenneth Branagh. UK. 137 min. Harsher and more violent than the Olivier version, with an elaborate reenactment of the Battle of Agincourt. Branagh stars as a grimly driven Henry.

The Life of Henry the Fifth

THE PERSONS OF THE PLAY

CHORUS
KING HARRY V of England, claimant to the French throne
Duke of GLOUCESTER ⎫
Duke of CLARENCE ⎬ his brothers
Duke of EXETER, his uncle
Duke of YORK
SALISBURY
WESTMORLAND
WARWICK
Archbishop of CANTERBURY
Bishop of ELY
Richard, Earl of CAMBRIDGE ⎫
Henry, Lord SCROPE of Masham ⎬ traitors
Sir Thomas GREY ⎭
PISTOL ⎫
NIM ⎬ formerly Falstaff's companions
BARDOLPH ⎭
BOY, formerly Falstaff's page
HOSTESS, formerly Mistress Quickly, now Pistol's wife
Captain GOWER, an Englishman
Captain FLUELLEN, a Welshman
Captain MACMORRIS, an Irishman
Captain JAMY, a Scot
Sir Thomas ERPINGHAM
John BATES ⎫
Alexander COURT ⎬ English soldiers
Michael WILLIAMS ⎭
HERALD
KING CHARLES VI of France
ISABEL, his wife and queen
The DAUPHIN, their son and heir
CATHERINE, their daughter
ALICE, an old gentlewoman
The CONSTABLE of France ⎫
Duke of BOURBON
Duke of ORLÉANS
Duke of BERRI ⎬ French noblemen at Agincourt
Lord RAMBURES
Lord GRANDPRÉ ⎭
Duke of BURGUNDY
MONTJOY, the French Herald
GOVERNOR of Harfleur
French AMBASSADORS to England

Prologue

*Enter [*CHORUS *as*] *Prologue*

CHORUS O for a muse of fire, that would ascend
    The brightest heaven of invention:°   *imagination*
    A kingdom for a stage, princes to act,
    And monarchs to behold the swelling° scene.   *expansive; splendid*
5   Then should the warlike Harry, like himself,
    Assume the port° of Mars,° and at his heels,   *bearing / god of war*
    Leashed in like hounds, should famine, sword, and fire
    Crouch for employment. But pardon, gentles° all,   *gentlefolk*
    The flat unraisèd° spirits that hath dared   *uninspired*
10   On this unworthy scaffold° to bring forth   *platform*
    So great an object. Can this cock-pit° hold   *small cockfighting arena*
    The vasty fields of France? Or may we cram
    Within this wooden O° the very casques°   *round theater / helmets*
    That did affright the air at Agincourt?[1]
15   O pardon: since a crookèd figure[2] may
    Attest° in little place a million,   *Represent*
    And let us, ciphers° to this great account,°   *zeroes / sum; story*
    On your imaginary forces° work.   *powers of imagination*
    Suppose within the girdle of these walls
20   Are now confined two mighty monarchies,
    Whose high uprearèd and abutting fronts°   *frontiers*
    The perilous narrow ocean° parts asunder.   *(English Channel)*
    Piece out our imperfections with your thoughts:
    Into a thousand parts divide one man,
25   And make imaginary puissance.°   *power*
    Think, when we talk of horses, that you see them,
    Printing their proud hoofs i'th' receiving earth;
    For 'tis your thoughts that now must deck° our kings,   *equip*
    Carry them here and there, jumping o'er times,
30   Turning th'accomplishment of many years
    Into an hourglass—for the which supply,°   *to supplement which*
    Admit me Chorus to this history,
    Who Prologue-like your humble patience pray
    Gently to hear, kindly to judge, our play.   *Exit*

1.1

Enter the [Archbishop] of CANTERBURY *and [the Bishop
of]* ELY

CANTERBURY My lord, I'll tell you. That self ° bill is urged   *same*
    Which in th'eleventh year of the last king's reign
    Was like,° and had indeed against us passed,   *likely*
    But that the scrambling and unquiet time
5   Did push it out of farther question.°   *consideration*
ELY But how, my lord, shall we resist it now?
CANTERBURY It must be thought on. If it pass against us,
    We lose the better half of our possession,
    For all the temporal lands[1] which men devout
10   By testament have given to the Church
    Would they strip from us—being valued thus:

---

1. Site of Henry's famous victory over the French in
1415.
2. A zero, which multiplies a digit's value by ten.

crookèd: curved.
1.1 Location: In Henry's court.
1. Land devoted to secular uses.

As much as would maintain, to the King's honour,
Full fifteen earls and fifteen hundred knights,
Six thousand and two hundred good esquires;[2]
15 And, to relief of lazars° and weak age,   *lepers*
Of indigent faint souls past corporal° toil,   *bodily*
A hundred almshouses right well supplied;
And to the coffers of the King beside
A thousand pounds by th' year. Thus runs the bill.
20 ELY   This would drink deep.
CANTERBURY   'Twould drink the cup and all.
ELY   But what prevention?
CANTERBURY   The King is full of grace and fair regard.°   *kindly inclination*
ELY   And a true lover of the holy Church.
25 CANTERBURY   The courses of his youth promised it not.
The breath no sooner left his father's body
But that his wildness, mortified° in him,   *struck dead*
Seemed to die too. Yea, at that very moment
Consideration° like an angel came   *Spiritual reflection*
30 And whipped th'offending Adam° out of him,   *innate depravity*
Leaving his body as a paradise
T'envelop and contain celestial spirits.
Never was such a sudden scholar made;
Never came reformation in a flood
35 With such a heady currance° scouring faults;   *headlong current*
Nor never Hydra-headed[3] wilfulness
So soon did lose his seat°—and all at once—   *throne*
As in this king.
ELY   We are blessèd in the change.
CANTERBURY   Hear him but reason in divinity°   *theology*
40 And, all-admiring, with an inward wish
You would desire the King were made a prelate;°   *an important clergyman*
Hear him debate of commonwealth affairs,
You would say it hath been all-in-all his study;
List° his discourse of war, and you shall hear   *Listen to*
45 A fearful battle rendered you in music;
Turn him to any cause of policy,°   *political issue*
The Gordian knot[4] of it he will unloose,
Familiar° as his garter—that when he speaks,   *Offhandedly*
The air, a chartered libertine,° is still,   *licensed freedman*
50 And the mute wonder lurketh in men's ears
To steal his sweet and honeyed sentences:
So that the art and practic part of life
Must be the mistress to this theoric.[5]
Which is a wonder how his grace should glean it,
55 Since his addiction° was to courses vain,   *inclination*
His companies° unlettered, rude, and shallow,   *companions*
His hours filled up with riots,° banquets, sports,   *reveling*
And never noted in him any study,
Any retirement, any sequestration°   *removal*
60 From open haunts and popularity.[6]

2. Gentlemen below knightly rank.
3. Many-headed (the Hydra was a monstrous snake, killed by Hercules).
4. It was foretold that whoever untied the intricate Gordian knot would rule Asia; Alexander the Great cut it with his sword.
5. *the art . . . theoric:* practical experience must have taught him the theory.
6. From public places and unrefined companions.

ELY   The strawberry grows underneath the nettle,
    And wholesome berries thrive and ripen best
    Neighboured by fruit of baser quality;
    And so the Prince obscured his contemplation
65   Under the veil of wildness—which, no doubt,
    Grew like the summer grass, fastest by night,
    Unseen, yet crescive in his faculty.[7]
CANTERBURY   It must be so, for miracles are ceased,[8]
    And therefore we must needs admit the means°   *natural causes*
    How things are perfected.
70 ELY   But, my good lord,
    How now for mitigation of this bill
    Urged by the Commons? Doth his majesty
    Incline to it, or no?
CANTERBURY   He seems indifferent,
    Or rather swaying more upon our part
75   Than cherishing th'exhibitors[9] against us;
    For I have made an offer to his majesty,
    Upon our spiritual convocation[1]
    And in regard of causes now in hand,
    Which I have opened° to his grace at large: *expounded*
80   As touching France, to give a greater sum
    Than ever at one time the clergy yet
    Did to his predecessors part withal.°   *with*
ELY   How did this offer seem received, my lord?
CANTERBURY   With good acceptance of his majesty,
85   Save that there was not time enough to hear,
    As I perceived his grace would fain° have done,   *gladly*
    The severals[2] and unhidden passages°   *channels of descent*
    Of his true titles to some certain dukedoms,
    And generally to the crown and seat of France,
90   Derived from Edward,° his great-grandfather.   *King Edward III*
ELY   What was th'impediment that broke this off?
CANTERBURY   The French ambassador upon that instant
    Craved audience—and the hour I think is come
    To give him hearing. Is it four o'clock?
95 ELY   It is.
CANTERBURY   Then go we in, to know his embassy°—   *message*
    Which I could with a ready guess declare
    Before the Frenchman speak a word of it.
ELY   I'll wait upon you, and I long to hear it.   *Exeunt*

1.2

Enter KING [HARRY, *the Dukes of* GLOUCESTER], CLARENCE, *and*
    EXETER, [*and the Earls of*] WARWICK [*and*] WESTMORLAND
KING HARRY   Where is my gracious lord of Canterbury?
EXETER   Not here in presence.
KING HARRY   Send for him, good uncle.
WESTMORLAND   Shall we call in th'ambassador, my liege?

---

7. Yet growing according to its natural ability.
8. Protestants believed that no miracles occurred after scriptural times (anachronistic in the mouth of a medieval archbishop).
9. Parliamentary sponsors of the bill.

1. On behalf of the assembled clergy.
2. Legal means by which land is conveyed in separate parts to different heirs.
1.2 Location: The royal court.

KING HARRY   Not yet, my cousin.[1] We would be resolved,
5   Before we hear him, of some things of weight
       That task° our thoughts, concerning us and France.   *exercise*
                 Enter [Archbishop of CANTERBURY *and Bishop of* ELY]
       CANTERBURY   God and his angels guard your sacred throne,
       And make you long become° it.   *adorn*
       KING HARRY   Sure we thank you.
       My learnèd lord, we pray you to proceed,
10   And justly and religiously unfold
       Why the law Salic[2] that they have in France
       Or° should or should not bar us in our claim.   *Either*
       And God forbid, my dear and faithful lord,
       That you should fashion, wrest, or bow your reading,[3]
15   Or nicely charge° your understanding soul   *foolishly burden*
       With opening titles miscreate,[4] whose right
       Suits not in native colours° with the truth;   *Does not accord*
       For God doth know how many now in health
       Shall drop their blood in approbation°   *confirmation*
20   Of what your reverence shall incite us to.
       Therefore take heed how you impawn° our person,   *pledge*
       How you awake our sleeping sword of war;
       We charge you in the name of God take heed.
       For never two such kingdoms did contend
25   Without much fall of blood, whose guiltless drops
       Are every one a woe, a sore complaint
       'Gainst him whose wrongs gives edge unto the swords
       That makes such waste in brief mortality.°   *short-lived humankind*
       Under this conjuration° speak, my lord,   *injunction*
30   For we will hear, note, and believe in heart
       That what you speak is in your conscience washed
       As pure as sin with baptism.
       CANTERBURY   Then hear me, gracious sovereign, and you peers
       That owe your selves, your lives, and services
35   To this imperial throne. There is no bar
       To make against your highness' claim to France
       But this, which they produce from Pharamond:°   *legendary French King*
       '*In terram Salicam mulieres ne succedant*'—
       'No woman shall succeed in Salic[5] land'—
40   Which 'Salic land' the French unjustly gloss°   *interpret*
       To be the realm of France, and Pharamond
       The founder of this law and female bar.[6]
       Yet their own authors faithfully affirm
       That the land Salic is in Germany,
45   Between the floods° of Saale and of Elbe,   *rivers*
       Where, Charles the Great having subdued the Saxons,
       There left behind and settled certain French
       Who, holding in disdain the German women
       For some dishonest° manners of their life,   *unchaste*
50   Established there this law: to wit, no female
       Should be inheritrix in Salic land—
       Which Salic, as I said, 'twixt Elbe and Saale,

---

1. Kinsman; complimentary form of address from King
to nobles.
2. Explained below, lines 35ff.
3. Should shape, pervert, or bend your interpretation.

4. With explicating false property rights.
5. Referring to an ancient Frankish tribe that lived
beside the Rhine River.
6. And prohibition of female inheritance.

Is at this day in Germany called Meissen.
Then doth it well appear the Salic Law
55 Was not devisèd for the realm of France.
Nor did the French possess the Salic land
Until four hundred one-and-twenty years
After defunction° of King Pharamond,   *death*
Idly° supposed the founder of this law,   *Foolishly*
60 Who died within the year of our redemption°   A.D.
Four hundred twenty-six; and Charles the Great°   *Charlemagne*
Subdued the Saxons, and did seat° the French   *establish*
Beyond the river Saale, in the year
Eight hundred five. Besides, their writers say,
65 King Pépin, which deposèd Childéric,
Did, as heir general⁷—being descended
Of Blithild, which was daughter to King Clotaire—
Make claim and title to the crown of France.
Hugh Capet also—who usurped the crown
70 Of Charles the Duke of Lorraine, sole heir male
Of the true line and stock of Charles the Great—
To fine° his title with some shows of truth,   *complete; purify*
Though in pure truth it was corrupt and naught,
Conveyed himself as heir to th' Lady Lingard,
75 Daughter to Charlemain, who was the son
To Louis the Emperor, and Louis the son
Of Charles the Great. Also, King Louis the Ninth,
Who was sole heir to the usurper Capet,
Could not keep quiet in his conscience,
80 Wearing the crown of France, till satisfied
That fair Queen Isabel, his grandmother,
Was lineal of ° the Lady Ermengarde,   *descended from*
Daughter to Charles, the foresaid Duke of Lorraine;
By the which marriage, the line of Charles the Great
85 Was reunited to the crown of France.
So that, as clear as is the summer's sun,
King Pépin's title and Hugh Capet's claim,
King Louis his° satisfaction, all appear   *(Louis's)*
To hold in right and title of the female;
90 So do the kings of France unto this day,
Howbeit they would hold up this Salic Law
To bar your highness claiming from the female,
And rather choose to hide them in a net°   *complexities*
Than amply to embar° their crookèd titles,   *frankly to rule out*
95 Usurped from you and your progenitors.
KING HARRY   May I with right and conscience make this claim?
CANTERBURY   The sin upon my head, dread sovereign.
For in the Book of Numbers° is it writ,   *Numbers 27:8*
'When the son dies, let the inheritance
100 Descend unto the daughter.' Gracious lord,
Stand for your own; unwind your bloody flag;
Look back into your mighty ancestors.
Go, my dread lord, to your great-grandsire's tomb,
From whom you claim;⁸ invoke his warlike spirit,

---

7. One who inherits through either the male or female
line.

8. Edward III claimed the French throne through his
mother, Isabella.

105 And your great-uncle's, Edward the Black Prince,
Who on the French ground played a tragedy,
Making defeat° on the full power of France,   *(at Crécy, in 1346)*
Whiles his most mighty father° on a hill   *(Edward III)*
Stood smiling to behold his lion's whelp
110 Forage in blood of French nobility.
O noble English, that could entertain°   *encounter*
With half their forces the full pride of France,
And let another half stand laughing by,
All out of work, and cold for° action.   *for want of*
115 ELY Awake remembrance of those valiant dead,
And with your puissant° arm renew their feats.   *powerful*
You are their heir, you sit upon their throne,
The blood and courage that renownèd them°   *made them famous*
Runs in your veins—and my thrice-puissant liege
120 Is in the very May-morn of his youth,
Ripe for exploits and mighty enterprises.
        EXETER Your brother kings and monarchs of the earth
Do all expect that you should rouse yourself
As did the former lions of your blood.
125 WESTMORLAND They know your grace hath cause; and means and might,
So hath your highness. Never king of England
Had nobles richer and more loyal subjects,
Whose hearts have left their bodies here in England
And lie pavilioned° in the fields of France.   *encamped*
130 CANTERBURY O let their bodies follow, my dear liege,
With blood and sword and fire, to win your right.
In aid whereof, we of the spiritualty°   *clergy*
Will raise your highness such a mighty sum
As never did the clergy at one time
135 Bring in to any of your ancestors.
        KING HARRY We must not only arm t'invade the French,
But lay down our proportions⁹ to defend
Against the Scot, who will make raid upon us
With all advantages.°   *Given any opportunity*
140 CANTERBURY They of those marches,° gracious sovereign, *borderlands*
Shall be a wall sufficient to defend
Our inland from the pilfering borderers.
        KING HARRY We do not mean the coursing snatchers° only, *mounted raiders*
But fear the main intendment° of the Scot,   *hostile intention*
145 Who hath been still a giddy° neighbour to us.   *always an unreliable*
For you shall read that my great-grandfather
Never unmasked his power unto France
But that the Scot on his unfurnished° kingdom   *unprotected*
Came pouring like the tide into a breach°   *gap in a dike*
150 With ample and brim fullness of his force
Galling° the gleanèd° land with hot assays,°   *Hurting / depleted / attacks*
Girding with grievous siege castles and towns,
That England, being empty of defence,
Hath shook and trembled at the bruit° thereof.   *noise*
155 CANTERBURY She hath been then more feared than harmed, my liege.
For hear her but exampled° by herself :   *given an example*
When all her chivalry hath been in France

---

9. Decide the distribution of our forces.

And she a mourning widow of her nobles,
She hath herself not only well defended
160 But taken and impounded as a stray
The King of Scots,[1] whom she did send to France
To fill King Edward's fame with prisoner kings
And make your chronicle as rich with praise
As is the ooze and bottom of the sea
165 With sunken wrack° and sumless treasures.[2]   *shipwrecks*
    A LORD   But there's a saying very old and true:
          'If that you will France win,
          Then with Scotland first begin.'
For once the eagle England being in prey,°   *out hunting*
170 To her unguarded nest the weasel Scot
Comes sneaking, and so sucks her princely eggs,
Playing the mouse in absence of the cat,
To 'tame[3] and havoc° more than she can eat.   *spoil*
    EXETER   It follows then the cat must stay at home.
175 Yet that is but a crushed° necessity,   *forced*
Since we have locks to safeguard necessaries
And pretty° traps to catch the petty thieves.   *clever*
While that the armèd hand doth fight abroad,
Th'advisèd° head defends itself at home.   *well-advised*
180 For government, though high and low and lower,[4]
Put into parts,[5] doth keep in one consent,°   *harmony*
Congreeing° in a full and natural close,°   *Coming together / cadence*
Like music.
    CANTERBURY   True. Therefore doth heaven divide
The state of man in divers functions,
185 Setting endeavour in continual motion;
To which is fixèd, as an aim or butt,°   *target*
Obedience. For so work the honey-bees,
Creatures that by a rule in nature teach
The act of order to a peopled kingdom.
190 They have a king,[6] and officers of sorts,
Where some like magistrates correct at home;
Others like merchants venture trade abroad;
Others like soldiers, armèd in their stings,
Make boot upon° the summer's velvet buds,   *Plunder*
195 Which pillage they with merry march bring home
To the tent royal of their emperor,
Who busied in his majesty surveys
The singing masons building roofs of gold,
The civil citizens lading° up the honey,   *weighing*
200 The poor mechanic° porters crowding in   *menial*
Their heavy burdens at his narrow gate,
The sad-eyed justice with his surly hum
Delivering o'er to executors° pale   *executioners*
The lazy yawning drone. I this infer:
205 That many things, having full reference
To one consent,[7] may work contrariously.°   *disparately*

---

1. David II of Scotland, taken prisoner in 1346, when Edward III was in France; actually, he was imprisoned in London.
2. Incalculable riches.
3. Attame, or meddle with.
4. That is, composed of three social classes.
5. Divided into different functions.
6. The queen bee was thought to be male.
7. *having . . . consent:* united by a common purpose.

As many arrows, loosèd several ways,°   *from different places*
Fly to one mark, as many ways meet in one town,
As many fresh streams meet in one salt sea,
210   As many lines close in the dial's° centre,   *sundial's*
So may a thousand actions once afoot
End in one purpose, and be all well borne
Without defect. Therefore to France, my liege.
Divide your happy England into four,
215   Whereof take you one quarter into France,
And you withal shall make all Gallia° shake.   *France*
If we with thrice such powers left at home
Cannot defend our own doors from the dog,
Let us be worried,° and our nation lose   *savaged*
220   The name° of hardiness and policy.[8]   *reputation*
    KING HARRY   Call in the messengers sent from the Dauphin.[9]
                               [Exit one or more]
Now are we well resolved, and by God's help
And yours, the noble sinews of our power,
France being ours we'll bend it to our awe,°   *make it submit to us*
225   Or break it all to pieces. Or° there we'll sit,   *Either*
Ruling in large and ample empery°   *sovereignty*
O'er France and all her almost kingly dukedoms,
Or lay these bones in an unworthy urn,
Tombless, with no remembrance over them.
230   Either our history shall with full mouth
Speak freely of our acts, or else our grave,
Like Turkish mute,[1] shall have a tongueless mouth,
Not worshipped with a waxen epitaph.[2]
            Enter AMBASSADORS *of France [with a tun]*°   *chest; barrel*
Now are we well prepared to know the pleasure
235   Of our fair cousin Dauphin, for we hear
Your greeting is from him, not from the King.
    AMBASSADOR   May't please your majesty to give us leave
Freely to render what we have in charge,
Or shall we sparingly show you far off [3]
240   The Dauphin's meaning and our embassy?
    KING HARRY   We are no tyrant, but a Christian king,
Unto whose grace our passion is as subject
As is our wretches fettered in our prisons.
Therefore with frank and with uncurbèd plainness
Tell us the Dauphin's mind.
245   AMBASSADOR   Thus then in few:°   *short*
Your highness lately sending into France
Did claim some certain dukedoms, in the right
Of your great predecessor, King Edward the Third.
In answer of which claim, the Prince our master
250   Says that you savour° too much of your youth,   *show traces*
And bids you be advised, there's naught in France
That can be with a nimble galliard° won: *lively dance*
You cannot revel into dukedoms there.
He therefore sends you, meeter° for your spirit,   *more appropriate*

8. Political discernment.
9. Title of the French heir apparent.
1. Turkish harem attendants were reportedly castrated

and deprived of speech.
2. Not dignified with (even) a perishable memorial.
3. Show you in an abridged and roundabout way.

255   This tun of treasure, and in lieu of this
        Desires you let the dukedoms that you claim
        Hear no more of you. This the Dauphin speaks.
    KING HARRY   What treasure, uncle?
    EXETER [*opening the tun*]   Tennis balls, my liege.
    KING HARRY   We are glad the Dauphin is so pleasant° with us.   *jocular*
260   His present and your pains we thank you for.
        When we have matched our rackets to these balls,
        We will in France, by God's grace, play a set
        Shall strike his father's crown° into the hazard.[4]   *royal crown; coin*
        Tell him he hath made a match with such a wrangler
265   That all the courts of France will be disturbed
        With chases.[5] And we understand him well,
        How he comes o'er° us with our wilder days,   *taunts*
        Not measuring what use we made of them.
        We never valued this poor seat° of England,   *throne*
270   And therefore, living hence,° did give ourself   *away from court*
        To barbarous licence—as 'tis ever common
        That men are merriest when they are from home.
        But tell the Dauphin I will keep my state,°   *dignity; territory*
        Be like a king, and show my sail of greatness
275   When I do rouse me in° my throne of France.   *about*
        For that have I laid by my majesty
        And plodded like a man for working days,
        But I will rise there with so full a glory
        That I will dazzle all the eyes of France,
280   Yea strike the Dauphin blind to look on us.
        And tell the pleasant Prince this mock of his
        Hath turned his balls to gunstones,° and his soul   *cannonballs*
        Shall stand sore chargèd° for the wasteful vengeance   *heavily burdened*
        That shall fly from them—for many a thousand widows
285   Shall this his mock mock out of their dear husbands,
        Mock mothers from their sons, mock castles down;
        Ay, some are yet ungotten and unborn
        That shall have cause to curse the Dauphin's scorn.
        But this lies all within the will of God,
290   To whom I do appeal, and in whose name
        Tell you the Dauphin I am coming on
        To venge me° as I may, and to put forth   *avenge myself*
        My rightful hand in a well-hallowed cause.
        So get you hence in peace. And tell the Dauphin
295   His jest will savour but of shallow wit
        When thousands weep more than did laugh at it.—
        Convey them with safe conduct.—Fare you well.
                                            Exeunt AMBASSADORS
    EXETER   This was a merry message.
    KING HARRY   We hope to make the sender blush at it.
300   Therefore, my lords, omit no happy hour
        That may give furth'rance to our expedition;
        For we have now no thought in us but France,
        Save those to God, that run before our business.

---

4. Jeopardy; aperture in the back wall of an Eliza-
bethan tennis court.
5. Military pursuit; in tennis, second impact of a

missed return, rated by its proximity to the back wall (a
disputable point, hence "wrangler" in line 264).

Therefore let our proportions for these wars
305 Be soon collected, and all things thought upon
That may with reasonable swiftness add
More feathers to our wings; for, God before,[6]
We'll chide this Dauphin at his father's door.
Therefore let every man now task his thought,
310 That this fair action may on foot be brought.

Exeunt. Flourish

2.0

Enter CHORUS

CHORUS   Now all the youth of England are on fire,
And silken° dalliance in the wardrobe lies;   *luxurious*
Now thrive the armourers, and honour's thought
Reigns solely in the breast of every man.
5 They sell the pasture now to buy the horse,
Following the mirror° of all Christian kings   *exemplar*
With wingèd heels, as English Mercuries.[1]
For now sits expectation in the air
And hides a sword from hilts unto the point
10 With crowns imperial, crowns° and coronets,   *titles; coins*
Promised to Harry and his followers.
The French, advised by good intelligence°   *espionage*
Of this most dreadful preparation,
Shake in their fear, and with pale policy°   *feeble intrigue*
15 Seek to divert the English purposes.
O England!—model° to thy inward greatness,   *small replica*
Like little body with a mighty heart,
What mightst thou do, that honour would thee do,
Were all thy children kind and natural?
20 But see, thy fault France hath in thee found out:
A nest of hollow[2] bosoms, which he fills
With treacherous crowns; and three corrupted men—
One, Richard, Earl of Cambridge; and the second
Henry, Lord Scrope of Masham; and the third
25 Sir Thomas Grey, knight, of Northumberland—
Have, for the gilt[3] of France—O guilt indeed!—
Confirmed conspiracy with fearful° France;   *frightened*
And by their hands this grace of kings must die,
If hell and treason hold° their promises,   *keep*
30 Ere he take ship for France, and in Southampton.
Linger your patience on, and we'll digest
Th'abuse of distance, force—perforce—a play.[4]
The sum is paid, the traitors are agreed,
The King is set from London, and the scene
35 Is now transported, gentles, to Southampton.
There is the playhouse now, there must you sit,
And thence to France shall we convey you safe,
And bring you back, charming the narrow seas
To give you gentle pass—for if we may
40 We'll not offend one stomach[5] with our play.

6. With God leading us; if God leads us.
2.0
1. Messenger of the gods; patron of thieves.
2. Hypocritical; empty (as receptacles for money).
3. Gold; gold leaf (suggesting superficiality).

4. *digest . . . play*: incorporate (and make acceptable) a violation of the unity of place, and stuff a play with events.
5. Offend anyone; make anyone seasick.

But till the King come forth, and not till then,
Unto Southampton do we shift our scene.   *Exit*

2.1
Enter Corporal NIM *and Lieutenant* BARDOLPH
BARDOLPH   Well met, Corporal Nim.
NIM   Good morrow, Lieutenant Bardolph.
BARDOLPH   What, are Ensign° Pistol and you friends yet?   *flag bearer*
NIM   For my part, I care not. I say little, but when time shall
5   serve, there shall be smiles—but that shall be as it may. I dare
not fight, but I will wink° and hold out mine iron.° It is a simple   *close my eyes / sword*
one, but what though?° It will toast cheese, and it will endure   *of that*
cold, as another man's sword will—and there's an end.
BARDOLPH   I will bestow a breakfast to make you friends, and
10   we'll be all three sworn brothers to France. Let't be so, good
Corporal Nim.
NIM   Faith, I will live so long as I may, that's the certain of it,
and when I cannot live any longer, I will do as I may. That is
my rest, that is the rendezvous° of it.   *last word?*
15 BARDOLPH   It is certain, corporal, that he is married to Nell
Quickly, and certainly she did you wrong, for you were troth-
plight° to her.   *betrothed*
NIM   I cannot tell. Things must be as they may. Men may sleep,
and they may have their throats about them at that time, and
20   some say knives have edges. It must be as it may. Though
Patience be a tired mare, yet she will plod. There must be con-
clusions. Well, I cannot tell.
Enter [Ensign] PISTOL *and* HOSTESS *Quickly*
BARDOLPH   Good morrow, Ensign Pistol.[1] [*To* NIM] Here comes
Ensign Pistol and his wife. Good Corporal, be patient here.
25 NIM   How now, mine host° Pistol?   *tavern keeper; pimp*
PISTOL   Base tick, call'st thou me host? Now by Gad's lugs°   *God's ears*
I swear I scorn the term. Nor shall my Nell keep lodgers.
HOSTESS   No, by my troth, not long, for we cannot lodge and
board a dozen or fourteen gentlewomen that live honestly by
30   the prick° of their needles, but it will be thought we keep a   *(unwittingly obscene)*
bawdy-house straight.
[NIM *draws his sword*]
O well-a-day,° Lady![2] If he be not hewn now, we shall see wilful   *alas*
adultery° and murder committed.   *(for "assault")*
[PISTOL *draws his sword*]
BARDOLPH   Good lieutenant, good corporal, offer nothing° here.   *don't fight*
35 NIM   Pish.
PISTOL   Pish for thee, Iceland dog.° Thou prick-eared cur of   *small, hairy breed*
Iceland.
HOSTESS   Good Corporal Nim, show thy valour, and put up°   *away*
your sword.
[*They sheathe their swords*]
NIM   Will you shog off ?° I would have you *solus*.[3]   *move along*
40 PISTOL   'Solus', egregious dog? O viper vile!
The *solus* in thy most marvellous face,

2.1 Location: Eastcheap, a slum section of London,
site of the tavern scenes in *1* and *2 Henry IV*. Bardolph,
Pistol, and Hostess Quickly were featured in the *Henry
IV* plays; Nim (slang for "thief") is a new character.

1. Sixteenth-century pistols were notoriously noisy and
inaccurate.
2. By our Lady, a mild oath.
3. Alone; unmarried.

The *solus* in thy teeth, and in thy throat,
And in thy hateful lungs, yea in thy maw pardie⁴—
And which is worse, within thy nasty mouth.
45 I do retort° the *solus* in thy bowels,   *send back*
For I can take,° and Pistol's cock is up,⁵   *take fire; strike*
And flashing fire will follow.
NIM   I am not Barbason,° you cannot conjure me.⁶ I have an   *(the name of a devil)*
humour° to knock you indifferently well. If you grow foul with   *inclination*
50 me, Pistol, I will scour you with my rapier, as I may, in fair
terms.° If you would walk off, I would prick your guts a little,   *pretty thoroughly*
in good terms, as I may, and that's the humour of it.
PISTOL   O braggart vile, and damnèd furious wight!°   *creature*
The grave doth gape and doting death is near.
55 Therefore ex-hale.°   *draw (your sword)*
        [PISTOL *and* NIM] *draw* [*their swords*]
BARDOLPH   Hear me, hear me what I say.
        [*He draws his sword*]
He that strikes the first stroke, I'll run him up to the hilts, as I
am a soldier.
PISTOL   An oath of mickle° might, and fury shall abate.   *great*
        [*They sheathe their swords*]
60 [*To* NIM] Give me thy fist,° thy forefoot to me give.   *(i.e., hand)*
Thy spirits are most tall.°   *valiant*
NIM   I will cut thy throat one time or other, in fair terms, that is
the humour of it.
PISTOL   *Couple a gorge,*⁷
65 That is the word. I thee defy again.
O hound of Crete, think'st thou my spouse to get?
No, to the spital⁸ go,
And from the powd'ring tub⁹ of infamy
Fetch forth the lazar kite of Cressid's kind,¹
70 Doll Tearsheet² she by name, and her espouse.
I have, and I will hold, the quondam° Quickly   *former*
For the only she, and—*pauca,*° there's enough. Go to.   *few (words)*
        Enter the BOY [*running*]
BOY   Mine host Pistol, you must come to my master,° and you,   *(Sir John Falstaff)*
hostess. He is very sick, and would to bed.—Good Bardolph,
75 put thy face between his sheets, and do the office of a warming-
pan.³—Faith, he's very ill.
BARDOLPH   Away, you rogue!
HOSTESS   By my troth, he'll yield the crow a pudding⁴ one of
these days. The King has killed his heart.⁵ Good husband,
80 come home presently.°   *Exit* [*with* BOY]   *right away*
BARDOLPH   Come, shall I make you two friends? We must to
France together. Why the devil should we keep knives to cut
one another's throats?
PISTOL   Let floods o'erswell,⁶ and fiends for food howl on!
85 NIM   You'll pay me the eight shillings I won of you at betting?

4. *in thy maw pardie*: in your stomach, indeed (old-fashioned).
5. Pistol's trigger is cocked (unwittingly obscene).
6. Frighten me with big words.
7. Corrupt French for "Cut the throat."
8. Hospital; in Elizabethan times, a filthy, disease-ridden place occupied by indigents near death.
9. Sweat bath, used in treating syphilis.

1. The diseased, scavenging whore (Cressida, a faithless Trojan woman, was a pattern of female wickedness).
2. A prostitute who appears in *2 Henry IV.*
3. Referring to Bardolph's "fiery" complexion.
4. He'll feed the crows (after his death).
5. By rejecting him, in the last scene of *2 Henry IV.*
6. Let destruction reign (perhaps an unidentified quotation).

PISTOL   Base is the slave that pays.

NIM   That now I will have. That's the humour of it.

PISTOL   As manhood shall compound.° Push home.   *valor will determine*
      [PISTOL *and* NIM] *draw* [*their swords*]

BARDOLPH [*drawing his sword*]   By this sword, he that makes the
90   first thrust, I'll kill him. By this sword, I will.

PISTOL   Sword is an oath,[7] and oaths must have their course.
      [*He sheathes his sword*]

BARDOLPH   Corporal Nim, an° thou wilt be friends, be friends.   *if*
      An thou wilt not, why then be enemies with me too. Prithee,
      put up.

95   NIM   I shall have my eight shillings?

PISTOL   A noble° shalt thou have, and present pay,[8]   *6 shillings 8 pence*
      And liquor likewise will I give to thee,
      And friendship shall combine, and brotherhood.
      I'll live by Nim, and Nim shall live by me.
100   Is not this just? For I shall sutler[9] be
      Unto the camp, and profits will accrue.
      Give me thy hand.

NIM   I shall have my noble?

PISTOL   In cash, most justly paid.

105   NIM   Well then, that's the humour of 't.
      [NIM *and* BARDOLPH *sheathe their swords*]
      Enter HOSTESS [*Quickly*]

HOSTESS   As ever you come of women, come in quickly to Sir
      John. Ah, poor heart, he is so shaked of a burning quotidian-
      tertian,[1] that it is most lamentable to behold. Sweet men, come
      to him.   [*Exit*]

110   NIM   The King hath run bad humours on° the knight, that's the   *shows ill will toward*
      even° of it.   *truth*

PISTOL   Nim, thou hast spoke the right.
      His heart is fracted° and corroborate.[2]   *broken*

NIM   The King is a good king, but it must be as it may. He passes
115   some humours and careers.°   *behaves strangely*

PISTOL   Let us condole° the knight—for, lambkins, we will live.   *console*
                                                                  Exeunt

2.2

Enter [*Duke of*] EXETER, [*Duke of* GLOUCESTER,] *and*
[*Earl of*] WESTMORLAND

GLOUCESTER   Fore God, his grace is bold to trust these traitors.

EXETER   They shall be apprehended by and by.

WESTMORLAND   How smooth and even they do bear themselves,
      As if allegiance in their bosoms sat,
5   Crownèd with faith and constant loyalty.

GLOUCESTER   The King hath note of all that they intend,
      By interception which they dream not of.

EXETER   Nay, but the man that was his bedfellow,[1]
      Whom he hath dulled and cloyed° with gracious favours—   *tired and sated*
10   That he should for a foreign purse so sell
      His sovereign's life to death and treachery.

---

7. Punning on " 's word," by God's word.
8. And immediate payment.
9. Seller of provisions (notoriously dishonest).
1. Dangerous fever (the Hostess conflates quotidian fever, which recurs daily, with tertian fever, which

recurs every third day).
2. Confirmed (error for "corrupted").
2.2 Location: Southampton, a port in the south of England.
1. It was common for men to share a bed.

Sound trumpets. Enter KING [HARRY, *Lord*] SCROPE,
[*Earl of*] CAMBRIDGE, *and* [*Sir Thomas*] GREY

KING HARRY   Now sits the wind fair, and we will aboard.
My lord of Cambridge, and my kind lord of Masham,
And you, my gentle knight, give me your thoughts.

15   Think you not that the powers we bear with us
Will cut their passage through the force of France,
Doing the execution° and the act   destruction
For which we have in head° assembled them?   an army

SCROPE   No doubt, my liege, if each man do his best.

20   KING HARRY   I doubt not that, since we are well persuaded
We carry not a heart with us from hence
That grows not in a fair consent with ours,
Nor leave not one behind that doth not wish
Success and conquest to attend on us.

25   CAMBRIDGE   Never was monarch better feared and loved
Than is your majesty. There's not, I think, a subject
That sits in heart-grief and uneasiness
Under the sweet shade of your government.

GREY   True. Those that were your father's enemies

30   Have steeped their galls° in honey, and do serve you   bitterness
With hearts create of duty and of zeal.

KING HARRY   We therefore have great cause of thankfulness,
And shall forget the office° of our hand   use
Sooner than quittance° of desert and merit,   payment

35   According to their weight and worthiness.

SCROPE   So service shall with steelèd sinews toil,
And labour shall refresh itself with hope,
To do your grace incessant services.

KING HARRY   We judge no less.—Uncle of Exeter,

40   Enlarge° the man committed° yesterday   Release / imprisoned
That railed against our person. We consider
It was excess of wine that set him on,
And on his more advice° we pardon him.   sober reconsideration

SCROPE   That's mercy, but too much security.°   complacency

45   Let him be punished, sovereign, lest example
Breed, by his sufferance,° more of such a kind.   by pardoning him

KING HARRY   O let us yet be merciful.

CAMBRIDGE   So may your highness, and yet punish too.

GREY   Sir, you show great mercy if you give him life,

50   After the taste of much correction.

KING HARRY   Alas, your too much love and care of me
Are heavy orisons° 'gainst this poor wretch.   weighty pleas
If little faults proceeding on distemper°   from drunkenness
Shall not be winked at,° how shall we stretch our eye   overlooked

55   When capital crimes, chewed, swallowed, and digested,[2]
Appear before us? We'll yet° enlarge that man,   nonetheless
Though Cambridge, Scrope, and Grey, in their dear° care   loving
And tender preservation of our person,
Would have him punished. And now to our French causes.
Who are the late[3] commissioners?

60   CAMBRIDGE   I one, my lord.
Your highness bade me ask for it° today.   (the commission)

---

2. That is, crimes thoroughly premeditated.   3. Newly appointed (to govern during Henry's absence).

SCROPE   So did you me, my liege.

GREY   And I, my royal sovereign.

KING HARRY   Then Richard, Earl of Cambridge, there is yours;
There yours, Lord Scrope of Masham, and sir knight,
65 Grey of Northumberland, this same is yours.
Read them, and know I know your worthiness.—
My lord of Westmorland, and Uncle Exeter,
We will aboard tonight.—Why, how now, gentlemen?
What see you in these papers, that you lose
70 So much complexion?—Look ye how they change:
Their cheeks are paper.—Why, what read you there
That have so cowarded and chased your blood
Out of appearance?°   sight

CAMBRIDGE   I do confess my fault,
And do submit me to your highness' mercy.

75 GREY *and* SCROPE   To which we all appeal.

KING HARRY   The mercy that was quick° in us but late   alive
By your own counsel is suppressed and killed.
You must not dare, for shame, to talk of mercy,
For your own reasons turn into your bosoms,
80 As dogs upon their masters, worrying° you.—   tearing
See you, my princes and my noble peers,
These English monsters?⁴ My lord of Cambridge here,
You know how apt our love was to accord°   agree
To furnish him with all appurtenants°   privileges
85 Belonging to his honour; and this vile man
Hath for a few light crowns lightly conspired
And sworn unto the practices° of France   plots
To kill us here in Hampton. To the which
This knight,° no less for bounty bound to us   (Grey)
90 Than Cambridge is, hath likewise sworn. But O
What shall I say to thee, Lord Scrope, thou cruel,
Ingrateful, savage, and inhuman creature?
Thou that didst bear the key of all my counsels,
That knew'st the very bottom of my soul,
95 That almost mightst ha' coined me into gold
Wouldst thou ha' practised on° me for thy use: conspired against
May it be possible that foreign hire
Could out of thee extract one spark of evil
That might annoy my finger? 'Tis so strange
100 That though the truth of it stands off as gross°   clearly
As black on white, my eye will scarcely see it.
Treason and murder ever kept together,
As two yoke-devils sworn to either's purpose,
Working so grossly in a natural° cause   (for devils)
105 That admiration° did not whoop° at them;   astonishment / cry out
But thou, 'gainst all proportion,° didst bring in   natural order
Wonder to wait on° treason and on murder.   consort with
And whatsoever cunning fiend it was
That wrought upon thee so preposterously°   unnaturally
110 Hath got the voice° in hell for excellence.   vote
And other devils that suggest° by treasons   seduce
Do botch and bungle up° damnation   clumsily conceal

---

4. "Monsters" were usually imported freaks.

	With patches, colours,° and with forms, being fetched°	*pretexts / derived*
	From glist'ring semblances of piety;	
115	But he that tempered° thee, bade thee stand up,°	*molded / rebel*
	Gave thee no instance° why thou shouldst do treason,	*motive*
	Unless to dub thee with the name[5] of traitor.	
	If that same demon that hath gulled° thee thus	*duped*
	Should with his lion gait walk the whole world,	
120	He might return to vasty Tartar° back	*to huge hell*
	And tell the legions,° 'I can never win	*armies of devils*
	A soul so easy as that Englishman's.'	
	O how hast thou with jealousy° infected	*suspicion*
	The sweetness of affiance.° Show men dutiful?	*trust*
125	Why so didst thou. Seem they grave and learned?	
	Why so didst thou. Come they of noble family?	
	Why so didst thou. Seem they religious?	
	Why so didst thou. Or are they spare in diet,	
	Free from gross passion, or° of mirth or anger,	*either*
130	Constant in spirit, not swerving with the blood,°	*passion*
	Garnished and decked in modest complement,°	*appearance*
	Not working with the eye without the ear,	
	And but in purgèd° judgement trusting neither?	*purified*
	Such, and so finely boulted,° didst thou seem.	*sifted*
135	And thus thy fall hath left a kind of blot	
	To mark the full-fraught° man, and best endowed,	*packed (with excellences)*
	With some suspicion. I will weep for thee,	
	For this revolt of thine methinks is like	
	Another fall of man.—Their faults are open.°	*obvious*
140	Arrest them to the answer of the law,	
	And God acquit them of their practices.	

EXETER   I arrest thee of high treason, by the name of Richard,
        Earl of Cambridge.—I arrest thee of high treason, by the name
        of Henry, Lord Scrope of Masham.—I arrest thee of high trea-
145   son, by the name of Thomas Grey, knight, of Northumberland.

	SCROPE Our purposes God justly hath discovered,°	*revealed*
	And I repent my fault more than my death,	
	Which I beseech your highness to forgive	
	Although my body pay the price of it.	
150	CAMBRIDGE For me, the gold of France did not seduce,	
	Although I did admit it as a motive	
	The sooner to effect what I intended.[6]	
	But God be thankèd for prevention,	
	Which heartily in sufferance° will rejoice,	*suffering punishment*
155	Beseeching God and you to pardon me.	
	GREY Never did faithful subject more rejoice	
	At the discovery of most dangerous treason	
	Than I do at this hour joy o'er myself,	
	Prevented from a damnèd enterprise.	
160	My fault, but not my body, pardon, sovereign.	
	KING HARRY God 'quit° you in his mercy. Hear your sentence.	*acquit*
	You have conspired against our royal person,	
	Joined with an enemy proclaimed and fixed,	

---

5. To knight you with the title.
6. The Earl of Cambridge was heir of Edmund Mortimer through his wife, Edmund's sister, and Mortimer arguably had a better claim to the English throne than did Henry himself. Henry's adherence to a principle of inheritance "through the female line" is hardly absolute.

And from his coffers
165 Received the golden earnest of° our death,   *advance payment for*
Wherein you would have sold your king to slaughter,
His princes and his peers to servitude,
His subjects to oppression and contempt,
And his whole kingdom into desolation.
170 Touching our person seek we no revenge,
But we our kingdom's safety must so tender,°   *regard*
Whose ruin you have sought, that to her laws
We do deliver you. Get ye therefore hence,
Poor miserable wretches, to your death;
175 The taste whereof, God of his mercy give
You patience to endure, and true repentance
Of all your dear° offences.—Bear them hence.   *grievous*
                    Exeunt [the traitors, guarded]
Now lords for France, the enterprise whereof
Shall be to you, as us, like° glorious.   *equally*
180 We doubt not of a fair and lucky war,
Since God so graciously hath brought to light
This dangerous treason lurking in our way
To hinder our beginnings. We doubt not now
But every rub° is smoothèd on our way.   *obstacle*
185 Then forth, dear countrymen. Let us deliver
Our puissance° into the hand of God,   *power*
Putting it straight in expedition.°   *at once in action*
Cheerly to sea, the signs° of war advance: *flags*
No king of England, if not king of France. *Flourish. Exeunt*

2.3
Enter [Ensign] PISTOL, *[Corporal]* NIM, *[Lieutenant]*
BARDOLPH, BOY, *and* HOSTESS *[Quickly]*

HOSTESS Prithee, honey, sweet husband, let me bring° thee to   *accompany*
Staines.[1]
PISTOL No, for my manly heart doth erne.° Bardolph,   *grieve*
Be blithe; Nim, rouse thy vaunting veins; boy, bristle
5 Thy courage up. For Falstaff he is dead,
And we must erne therefore.
BARDOLPH Would I were with him, wheresome'er he is, either
in heaven or in hell.
HOSTESS Nay, sure he's not in hell. He's in Arthur's bosom,[2] if
10 ever man went to Arthur's bosom. A° made a finer end, and   *He*
went away an° it had been any christom[3] child. A parted ev'n   *as if*
just between twelve and one, ev'n at the turning o'th' tide—for
after I saw him fumble with the sheets, and play with flowers,° *(on the bedclothes)*
and smile upon his finger's end, I knew there was but one way.
15 For his nose was as sharp as a pen, and a babbled of green
fields.[4] 'How now, Sir John?' quoth I. 'What, man! Be o' good
cheer.' So a cried out, 'God, God, God', three or four times.
Now I, to comfort him, bid him a should not think of God; I
hoped there was no need to trouble himself with any such

2.3 Location: Eastcheap.
1. Town on the road to Southampton.
2. Mistake for "Abraham's bosom," heaven.
3. Error for "chrisom," just christened.
4. Falstaff was reciting the Twenty-third Psalm ("The

Lord is my shepherd"), but Hostess Quickly does not
recognize it. The text is corrupt at this point, reading "a
Table of green fields," and was corrected by the
eighteenth-century editor Lewis Theobald in a famous
emendation.

20   thoughts yet. So a bade me lay more clothes on his feet. I put
    my hand into the bed and felt them, and they were as cold as
    any stone. Then I felt to his knees, and so up'ard and up'ard,
    and all was as cold as any stone.

    NIM   They say he cried out of sack.[5]

25   HOSTESS   Ay, that a did.

    BARDOLPH   And of women.

    HOSTESS   Nay, that a did not.

    BOY   Yes, that a did, and said they were devils incarnate.

    HOSTESS   A could never abide carnation, 'twas a colour he never

30   liked.

    BOY   A said once the devil would have him about women.

    HOSTESS   A did in some sort, indeed, handle° women—but then   *discuss*
    he was rheumatic,[6] and talked of the Whore of Babylon.[7]

    BOY   Do you not remember, a saw a flea stick upon Bardolph's

35   nose, and a said it was a black soul burning in hell-fire.

    BARDOLPH   Well, the fuel[8] is gone that maintained that fire.
    That's all the riches I got in his service.

    NIM   Shall we shog?° The King will be gone from Southampton.   *be off*

    PISTOL   Come, let's away.—My love, give me thy lips.
        [*He kisses her*]

40   Look to my chattels and my movables.°   *personal property*
    Let senses rule. The word is 'Pitch and pay'.°   *Cash down, no credit*
    Trust none, for oaths are straws, men's faiths are wafer-cakes,°   *fragile*
    And Holdfast is the only dog,[9] my duck.°   *darling*
    Therefore *caveto*° be thy counsellor.   *beware*

45   Go, clear thy crystals.°—Yokefellows in arms,   *wipe your eyes*
    Let us to France, like horseleeches, my boys,
    To suck, to suck, the very blood to suck!

    BOY [*aside*]   And that's but unwholesome food, they say.

    PISTOL   Touch her soft mouth, and march.

50   BARDOLPH   Farewell, hostess.
        [*He kisses her*]

    NIM   I cannot kiss, that is the humour of it, but adieu.

    PISTOL [*to* HOSTESS]   Let housewifery appear. Keep close,° I   *Stay indoors; be thrifty*
    thee command.

    HOSTESS   Farewell! Adieu!   *Exeunt* [*severally*]°   *separately*

2.4

Flourish. Enter KING [CHARLES *the Sixth of France*], *the*
DAUPHIN, [*the* CONSTABLE,] *and the Dukes of* BERRI *and*
[BOURBON]

    KING CHARLES   Thus comes the English with full power upon us,
    And more than carefully it us concerns
    To answer royally in our defences.
    Therefore the Dukes of Berri and of Bourbon,

5   Of Brabant and of Orléans shall make forth,
    And you Prince Dauphin, with all swift dispatch
    To line° and new-repair our towns of war   *garrison*

---

5. *of sack:* against wine, formerly one of Falstaff's great
indulgences.
6. Error for "lunatic," delirious.
7. The scarlet woman of Revelation, identified by
Protestants with the Catholic Church.

8. That is, Falstaff's liquor.
9. Alluding to the proverb "Brag is a good dog, but
Holdfast is better."
2.4 Location: France, where the remainder of the play
takes place. The King's court at Rouen.

With men of courage and with means defendant.°   *of defense*
For England° his approaches makes as fierce   *the King of England*
10 As waters to the sucking of a gulf.°   *whirlpool*
It fits us then to be as provident
As fear may teach us, out of late° examples   *recent*
Left by the fatal and neglected[1] English
Upon our fields.

DAUPHIN   My most redoubted° father,   *formidable*
15 It is most meet° we arm us 'gainst the foe,   *proper*
For peace itself should not so dull a kingdom—
Though war, nor no known quarrel, were in question—
But that defences, musters, preparations
Should be maintained, assembled, and collected
20 As° were a war in expectation.   *As if*
Therefore, I say, 'tis meet we all go forth
To view the sick and feeble parts of France.
And let us do it with no show of fear,
No, with no more than if we heard that England
25 Were busied with a Whitsun morris dance[2]
For, my good liege, she is so idly° kinged,   *frivolously*
Her sceptre so fantastically° borne   *irrationally*
By a vain, giddy, shallow, humorous° youth,   *capricious*
That fear attends her not.

CONSTABLE   O peace, Prince Dauphin.
30 You are too much mistaken in this king.
Question your grace the late° ambassadors   *recent*
With what great state he heard their embassy,
How well supplied with agèd counsellors,
How modest in exception,° and withal   *objecting*
35 How terrible° in constant resolution,   *fearsome*
And you shall find his vanities forespent°   *his former follies*
Were but the outside of the Roman Brutus,[3]
Covering discretion with a coat of folly,
As gardeners do with ordure° hide those roots   *manure*
40 That shall first spring and be most delicate.

DAUPHIN   Well, 'tis not so, my Lord High Constable.
But though° we think it so, it is no matter.   *if*
In cases of defence 'tis best to weigh°   *consider*
The enemy more mighty than he seems.
45 So the proportions of defence are filled[4]—
Which, of a weak and niggardly projection,°   *scale*
Doth like a miser spoil his coat with scanting°   *skimping*
A little cloth.

KING CHARLES   Think we King Harry strong.
And princes, look you strongly arm to meet him.
50 The kindred of him hath been fleshed[5] upon us,
And he is bred out of that bloody strain
That haunted us in our familiar paths.
Witness our too-much-memorable shame

---

1. The fatally underestimated, at the Battles of Crécy (1346) and Poitiers (1356).
2. Folk dance celebrating Whitsuntide, a summer holiday.
3. Lucius Junius Brutus pretended idiocy to disarm the tyrant Lucius Tarquinius Superbus, against whom he led a successful revolt.
4. A proper defense is mounted.
5. Have been given their first taste of blood.

When Crécy battle fatally was struck,°   *fought*
55   And all our princes captived by the hand
     Of that black name, Edward, Black Prince of Wales,
     Whiles that his mountant° sire, on mountain standing,   *ascendant*
     Up in the air, crowned with the golden sun,
     Saw his heroical seed and smiled to see him
60   Mangle the work of nature and deface
     The patterns that by God and by French fathers
     Had twenty years been made. This is a stem
     Of that victorious stock, and let us fear
     The native° mightiness and fate° of him.   *hereditary / fortune*
        Enter a MESSENGER
65   MESSENGER   Ambassadors from Harry, King of England,
     Do crave admittance to your majesty.
     KING CHARLES   We'll give them present audience. Go and bring them.
                                                    [*Exit* MESSENGER]
     You see this chase is hotly followed, friends.
     DAUPHIN   Turn head[6] and stop pursuit. For coward dogs
70   Most spend their mouths° when what they seem to threaten   *bark the loudest*
     Runs far before them. Good my sovereign,
     Take up the English short, and let them know
     Of what a monarchy you are the head.
     Self-love, my liege, is not so vile a sin
     As self-neglecting.
        Enter [Duke of] EXETER [*attended*]
75   KING CHARLES   From our brother England?
     EXETER   From him, and thus he greets your majesty:
     He wills you, in the name of God Almighty,
     That you divest yourself and lay apart°   *aside*
     The borrowed glories that by gift of heaven,
80   By law of nature and of nations, 'longs°   *belongs*
     To him and to his heirs, namely the crown,
     And all wide-stretchèd honours that pertain
     By custom and the ordinance of times°   *laws of ages*
     Unto the crown of France. That you may know
85   'Tis no sinister° nor no awkward° claim,   *illegitimate / oblique*
     Picked from the worm-holes of long-vanished days,
     Nor from the dust of old oblivion raked,
     He sends you this most memorable line,°   *pedigree*
     In every branch truly demonstrative,°   *conclusive*
90   Willing you over-look° this pedigree,   *Wishing you to look over*
     And when you find him evenly derived°   *directly descended*
     From his most famed of famous ancestors,
     Edward the Third, he bids you then resign
     Your crown and kingdom, indirectly° held   *unjustly*
95   From him, the native and true challenger.°   *claimant*
     KING CHARLES   Or else what follows?
     EXETER   Bloody constraint. For if you hide the crown
     Even in your hearts, there will he rake for it.
     Therefore in fierce tempest is he coming,
100 In thunder and in earthquake, like a Jove,
     That if requiring° fail, he will compel;   *requesting*

6. Make a stand (a hunting term).

And bids you, in the bowels° of the Lord,   *compassion*
Deliver up the crown, and to take mercy
On the poor souls for whom this hungry war
105 Opens his vasty jaws; and on your head
Turns he the widows' tears, the orphans' cries,
The dead men's blood, the pining maidens' groans,
For husbands, fathers, and betrothèd lovers
That shall be swallowed in this controversy.
110 This is his claim, his threat'ning, and my message—
Unless the Dauphin be in presence here,
To whom expressly I bring greeting too.
    KING CHARLES   For us, we will consider of this further.
Tomorrow shall you bear our full intent
Back to our brother England.
115   DAUPHIN   For the Dauphin,
I stand here for him. What to him from England?
    EXETER   Scorn and defiance, slight regard, contempt;
And anything that may not misbecome
The mighty sender, doth he prize° you at.   *assess*
120 Thus says my king: an if° your father's highness   *an if=if*
Do not, in grant° of all demands at large,°   *concession / in full*
Sweeten the bitter mock you sent his majesty,
He'll call you to so hot an answer for it
That caves and womby vaultages° of France   *hollow caverns*
125 Shall chide your trespass and return your mock
In second accent° of his ordinance.°   *echo / artillery*
    DAUPHIN   Say if my father render fair return
It is against my will, for I desire
Nothing but odds° with England. To that end,   *strife*
130 As matching to his youth and vanity,°   *frivolity*
I did present him with the Paris° balls.   *tennis*
    EXETER   He'll make your Paris Louvre° shake for it,   *French royal palace*
Were it the mistress° court of mighty Europe.   *principal (in tennis)*
And be assured, you'll find a diff'rence,
135 As we his subjects have in wonder found,
Between the promise of his greener° days   *younger*
And these he masters now: now he weighs time
Even to the utmost grain.° That you shall read   *smallest unit*
In your own losses, if he stay in France.
140   KING CHARLES [*rising*]   Tomorrow shall you know our mind at full.
       Flourish[7]
    EXETER   Dispatch us with all speed, lest that our king
Come here himself to question our delay—
For he is footed° in this land already.   *come ashore*
    KING CHARLES   You shall be soon dispatched with fair conditions.
145 A night is but small breath° and little pause   *small time*
To answer matters of this consequence.   *Exeunt. Flourish*

---

7. Fanfare (to signal the end of the interview; Exeter unceremoniously continues).

3.0

Enter CHORUS

CHORUS   Thus with imagined wing° our swift scene flies   *wings of imagination*
            In motion of no less celerity
            Than that of thought. Suppose that you have seen
            The well-appointed° king at Dover pier   *well-equipped*
5   Embark his royalty, and his brave fleet
            With silken streamers the young Phoebus fanning.[1]
            Play with your fancies,° and in them behold   *imagination*
            Upon the hempen tackle ship-boys climbing;
            Hear the shrill whistle,° which doth order give   *(of the ship's captain)*
10   To sounds confused; behold the threaden° sails,   *woven of thread*
            Borne with th'invisible and creeping wind,
            Draw the huge bottoms° through the furrowed sea,   *hulls*
            Breasting the lofty surge. O do but think
            You stand upon the rivage° and behold   *shore*
15   A city on th'inconstant billows dancing—
            For so appears this fleet majestical,
            Holding due course to Harfleur.[2] Follow, follow!
            Grapple° your minds to sternage° of this navy,   *Fasten / the sterns*
            And leave your England, as dead midnight still,
20   Guarded with grandsires, babies, and old women,
            Either past or not arrived to pith° and puissance.   *strength*
            For who is he, whose chin is but enriched
            With one appearing hair, that will not follow
            These culled° and choice-drawn cavaliers to France?   *select*
25   Work, work your thoughts, and therein see a siege.
            Behold the ordnance° on their carriages,   *cannons*
            With fatal mouths gaping on girded° Harfleur.   *encircled*
            Suppose th'ambassador from the French comes back,
            Tells Harry that the King doth offer him
30   Catherine his daughter, and with her, to° dowry,   *as*
            Some petty and unprofitable dukedoms.
            The offer likes° not, and the nimble gunner   *pleases*
            With linstock° now the devilish cannon touches,   *lighting stick*
                 Alarum, and chambers° go off   *small cannon*
            And down goes all before them. Still be kind,
35   And eke out our performance with your mind.   *Exit*

3.1

Alarum. Enter KING [HARRY *and the English army, with*]
            scaling ladders

KING HARRY   Once more unto the breach,[1] dear friends, once more,
            Or close the wall up with our English dead.
            In peace there's nothing so becomes a man
            As modest stillness and humility,
5   But when the blast of war blows in our ears,
            Then imitate the action of the tiger.
            Stiffen the sinews, conjure up the blood,
            Disguise fair nature with hard-favoured rage.
            Then lend the eye a terrible aspect,

3.0
1. *the . . . fanning:* fluttering toward the rising sun.
2. French port on the mouth of the Seine.

3.1 Location: Before Harfleur.
1. Gap in the fortifications, created by artillery bombardment.

10   Let it pry° through the portage² of the head   *peer*
      Like the brass cannon, let the brow o'erwhelm° it   *overhang*
      As fearfully as doth a gallèd° rock   *worn*
      O'erhang and jutty° his confounded° base,   *jut out over / ruined*
      Swilled° with the wild and wasteful° ocean.   *Washed / destructive*
15   Now set the teeth and stretch the nostril wide,
      Hold hard the breath, and bend up every spirit
      To his full height. On, on, you noblest English,
      Whose blood is fet° from fathers of war-proof,°   *fetched / proven in war*
      Fathers that like so many Alexanders³
20   Have in these parts from morn till even fought,
      And sheathed their swords for lack of argument.°   *opposition*
      Dishonour not your mothers; now attest
      That those whom you called fathers did beget you.
      Be copy° now to men of grosser° blood,   *example / less noble*
25   And teach them how to war. And you, good yeomen,° *men below noble rank*
      Whose limbs were made in England, show us here
      The mettle° of your pasture; let us swear   *quality*
      That you are worth your breeding—which I doubt not,
      For there is none of you so mean and base
30   That hath not noble lustre in your eyes.
      I see you stand like greyhounds in the slips,°   *leashes*
      Straining upon the start. The game's afoot.
      Follow your spirit, and upon this charge
      Cry, 'God for Harry! England and Saint George!'° *patron saint of England*
            Alarum, and chambers go off. [Exeunt]

3.2

Enter NIM, BARDOLPH, [*Ensign*] PISTOL, *and* BOY
BARDOLPH   On, on, on, on, on! To the breach, to the breach!
NIM   Pray thee corporal, stay. The knocks are too hot, and for
    mine own part I have not a case° of lives. The humour of it is   *set*
    too hot, that is the very plainsong° of it.   *plain truth*
5 PISTOL   'The plainsong' is most just,° for humours do abound. *apt*
    Knocks go and come, God's vassals drop and die,
    [*sings*]   And sword and shield
                  In bloody field
                  Doth win immortal fame.
10 BOY   Would I were in an alehouse in London. I would give all
    my fame for a pot of ale, and safety.
    PISTOL [*sings*]   And I.
              If wishes would prevail with me°   *in my case*
              My purpose should not fail with me
15   But thither would I hie.°   *go*
    BOY [*sings*]   As duly
                  But not as truly
                  As bird doth sing on bough.
        Enter [Captain] FLUELLEN *and beats them in*
FLUELLEN   God's plud!¹ Up to the breaches, you dogs! Avaunt,
20 you cullions!²
PISTOL   Be merciful, great duke, to men of mould.³

---

2. Portholes (that is, eye sockets).
3. Alexander the Great was said to have wept because no worlds remained for him to conquer.
3.2 Scene continues.

1. Blood (Fluellen's Welsh accent substitutes "p" for "b," and also "f" for "v" and "ch" for "j").
2. Be off, you wretches. *cullions*: testicles.
3. Earth (that is, mortal men).

Abate thy rage, abate thy manly rage,
Abate thy rage, great duke. Good bawcock,[4] bate
Thy rage. Use lenity,° sweet chuck.   *leniency*
25 NIM   These be good humours![5]
       [FLUELLEN *begins to beat* NIM]
       Your honour runs bad humours.°   *Exeunt [all but the* BOY]   *is ill tempered*
   BOY   As young as I am, I have observed these three swashers.° I   *swashbucklers*
       am boy to them all three, but all they three, though they should
       serve me, could not be man[6] to me, for indeed three such
30   antics° do not amount to a man. For Bardolph, he is white-   *buffoons*
       livered° and red-faced—by the means whereof a° faces it out,   *cowardly / he*
       but fights not. For Pistol, he hath a killing tongue and a quiet
       sword—by the means whereof a breaks words, and keeps whole
       weapons. For Nim, he hath heard that men of few words are
35   the best men, and therefore he scorns to say his prayers, lest a
       should be thought a coward. But his few bad words are
       matched with as few good deeds—for a never broke any man's
       head but his own, and that was against a post, when he was
       drunk. They will steal anything, and call it 'purchase'.[7] Bar-
40   dolph stole a lute case, bore it twelve leagues,° and sold it for   *about 36 miles*
       three halfpence. Nim and Bardolph are sworn brothers in
       filching,° and in Calais[8] they stole a fire shovel. I knew by that   *stealing*
       piece of service the men would carry coals.[9] They would have
       me as familiar with men's pockets as their gloves or their hand-
45   kerchiefs—which makes° much against my manhood, if I   *offends*
       should take from another's pocket to put into mine, for it is
       plain pocketing up of wrongs.[1] I must leave them, and seek
       some better service. Their villainy goes against my weak stom-
       ach, and therefore I must cast it up.°   *Exit*   *vomit it; leave it*

3.3

Enter [Captain] GOWER *[and Captain* FLUELLEN,
       meeting]
   GOWER   Captain Fluellen, you must come presently° to the   *immediately*
       mines.[1] The Duke of Gloucester would speak with you.
   FLUELLEN   To the mines? Tell you the Duke it is not so good to
       come to the mines. For look you, the mines is not according to
5   the disciplines° of the war. The concavities° of it is not suffi-   *tactics; art / depth*
       cient. For look you, th'athversary, you may discuss unto the
       Duke, look you, is digt° himself, four yard under, the coun-   *digged (dug)*
       termines.[2] By Cheshu,° I think a will plow° up all, if there is not   *Jesu / blow*
       better directions.
10 GOWER   The Duke of Gloucester, to whom the order° of the   *supervision*
       siege is given, is altogether directed by an Irishman, a very val-
       iant gentleman, i'faith.
   FLUELLEN   It is Captain MacMorris, is it not?
   GOWER   I think it be.
15 FLUELLEN   By Cheshu, he is an ass, as[3] in the world. I will verify

---

4. Fine chap (French *beau coq*).
5. This is fine behavior (sarcastic).
6. Punning on the sense "personal servant."
7. Booty (seized in combat).
8. French port town.
9. Do dirty work; tolerate insults.

1. Pocketing stolen goods; putting up with insults (unmanly behavior).
3.3 Location: Outside Harfleur.
1. Tunnels dug to undermine a besieged fortress.
2. Tunnels dug to undermine enemy "mines."
3. *he is an ass, as:* he is as big an ass as there is.

as much in his beard.° He has no more directions in the true   *to his face*
disciplines of the wars, look you—of the *Roman* disciplines—
than is a puppy dog.

       Enter [Captain] MACMORRIS *and Captain* JAMY

GOWER   Here a comes, and the Scots captain, Captain Jamy,
20   with him.

FLUELLEN   Captain Jamy is a marvellous falorous° gentleman,   *valorous*
    that is certain, and of great expedition° and knowledge in   *quick-wittedness*
    th'anciant wars, upon my particular knowledge of his directions.
    By Cheshu, he will maintain his argument as well as any mili-
25   tary man in the world, in the disciplines of the pristine wars of
    the Romans.

JAMY   I say gud day, Captain Fluellen.

FLUELLEN   Good e'en to your worship, good Captain James.

GOWER   How now, Captain MacMorris, have you quit the
30   mines? Have the pioneers given o'er?°   *diggers stopped work*

MACMORRIS   By Chrish law,[4] 'tish ill done. The work ish give
    over, the trumpet sound the retreat. By my hand I swear, and
    my father's soul, the work ish ill done, it ish give over. I would
    have blowed up the town, so Chrish save me law, in an hour.
35   O 'tish ill done, 'tish ill done, by my hand 'tish ill done.

FLUELLEN   Captain MacMorris, I beseech you now, will you
    vouchsafe° me, look you, a few disputations with you, as partly   *allow*
    touching or concerning the disciplines of the war, the Roman
    wars, in the way of argument, look you, and friendly communi-
40   cation? Partly to satisfy my opinion and partly for the satisfac-
    tion, look you, of my mind. As touching the direction of the
    military discipline, that is the point.

JAMY   It sall be vary gud, gud feith, gud captains bath,° and I sall   *both*
    quite° you with gud leve, as I may pick occasion. That sall I,   *requite; answer*
45   marry.

MACMORRIS   It is no time to discourse, so Chrish save me. The
    day is hot, and the weather and the wars and the King and the
    dukes. It is no time to discourse. The town is besieched. An the
    trumpet call us to the breach, and we talk and, be Chrish, do
50   nothing, 'tis shame for us all. So God sa'° me, 'tis shame to   *save*
    stand still, it is shame by my hand. And there is throats to be
    cut, and works to be done, and there ish nothing done, so
    Christ sa' me law.

JAMY   By the mess,° ere these eyes of mine take themselves to   *By the mass (an oath)*
55   slumber, ay'll de gud service, or I'll lig° i'th' grund for it. Ay   *lie*
    owe Got a death, and I'll pay't as valorously as I may, that sall I
    suirely do, that is the brief and the long. Marry, I wad full fain
    heard° some question 'tween you twae.°   *eagerly have heard / two*

FLUELLEN   Captain MacMorris, I think, look you, under your
60   correction, there is not many of your nation—

MACMORRIS   Of my nation? What ish my nation? Ish a villain
    and a bastard and a knave and a rascal? What ish my nation?
    Who talks of my nation?

FLUELLEN   Look you, if you take the matter otherwise than is
65   meant, Captain MacMorris, peradventure I shall think you do
    not use me with that affability as in discretion you ought to use

---

4. La (adds force to an utterance).

me, look you, being as good a man as yourself, both in the
disciplines of war and in the derivation of my birth, and in
other particularities.

70 MACMORRIS   I do not know you so good a man as myself. So
Chrish save me, I will cut off your head.

GOWER   Gentlemen both, you will mistake each other.

JAMY   Ah, that's a foul fault.

        A parley[5] *[is sounded]*

GOWER   The town sounds a parley.

75 FLUELLEN   Captain MacMorris, when there is more better
opportunity to be required, look you, I will be so bold as to tell
you I know the disciplines of war. And there is an end.   *Exit*

        [Flourish.] Enter KING [HARRY] *and all his train before*
        the gates

KING HARRY   How yet resolves the Governor of the town?
This is the latest parle° we will admit.   last parley
80 Therefore to our best mercy give yourselves,
Or like to men proud of° destruction   glorying in
Defy us to our worst. For as I am a soldier,
A name that in my thoughts becomes me best,
If I begin the batt'ry° once again   bombardment
85 I will not leave the half-achievèd Harfleur
Till in her ashes she lie burièd.
The gates of mercy shall be all shut up,
And the fleshed° soldier, rough and hard of heart,   inflamed
In liberty of bloody hand shall range
90 With conscience wide° as hell, mowing like grass   permissive
Your fresh fair virgins and your flow'ring infants.
What is it then to me if impious war
Arrayed in flames like to the prince of fiends
Do with his smirched complexion all fell° feats   cruel
95 Enlinked to waste° and desolation?   destruction
What is't to me, when you yourselves are cause,
If your pure maidens fall into the hand
Of hot and forcing violation?
What rein can hold licentious wickedness
100 When down the hill he holds° his fierce career?°   maintains / gallop
We may as bootless° spend our vain command   unprofitably
Upon th'enragèd soldiers in their spoil
As send precepts° to the leviathan°   summons / sea monster
To come ashore. Therefore, you men of Harfleur,
105 Take pity of your town and of your people
Whiles yet my soldiers are in my command,
Whiles yet the cool and temperate wind of grace
O'erblows° the filthy and contagious clouds[6]   Disperses
Of heady° murder, spoil, and villainy.   headstrong
110 If not—why, in a moment look to see
The blind and bloody soldier with foul hand
Defile the locks of your shrill-shrieking daughters;
Your fathers taken by the silver beards,
And their most reverend heads dashed to the walls;
115 Your naked infants spitted° upon pikes,   impaled
Whiles the mad mothers with their howls confused

---

5. Trumpet call requesting negotiation.   6. Pestilence was believed to drop from the sky.

Do break the clouds, as did the wives of Jewry[7]
At Herod's bloody-hunting slaughtermen.
What say you? Will you yield, and this avoid?
120 Or, guilty in defence, be thus destroyed?

Enter GOVERNOR [*on the wall*]

GOVERNOR   Our expectation hath this day an end.
The Dauphin, whom of succours we entreated,
Returns° us that his powers are yet not ready   Replies to
To raise so great a siege. Therefore, dread King,
125 We yield our town and lives to thy soft mercy.
Enter our gates, dispose of us and ours,
For we no longer are defensible.

KING HARRY   Open your gates.   [*Exit* GOVERNOR]
Come, Uncle Exeter,
Go you and enter Harfleur. There remain,
130 And fortify it strongly 'gainst the French.
Use mercy to them all. For us, dear uncle,
The winter coming on, and sickness growing
Upon our soldiers, we will retire to Calais.
Tonight in Harfleur will we be your guest;
135 Tomorrow for the march are we addressed.°   ready

[*The gates are opened.*] *Flourish, and* [*they*] *enter the town*

3.4

Enter [*Princess*] CATHERINE *and* ALICE, *an old gentle-
woman*

CATHERINE   Alice, tu as été en Angleterre, et tu bien parles
le langage.[1]
ALICE   Un peu, madame.
CATHERINE   Je te prie, m'enseignez. Il faut que j'apprenne à
5   parler. Comment appelez-vous la main en anglais?
ALICE   La main? Elle est appelée *de hand*.
CATHERINE   *De hand*. Et les doigts?
ALICE   Les doigts? Ma foi, j'oublie les doigts, mais je me souvien-
drai. Les doigts—je pense qu'ils sont appelés *de fingres*. Oui, *de
10   fingres*.
CATHERINE   La main, *de hand*; les doigts, *de fingres*. Je pense que
je suis la bonne écolière; j'ai gagné deux mots d'anglais vite-
ment. Comment appelez-vous les ongles?
ALICE   Les ongles? Nous les appelons *de nails*.
15 CATHERINE   *De nails*. Écoutez—dites-moi si je parle bien: *de
hand, de fingres*, et *de nails*.

---

7. Judaea; see Matthew 2:16–18.
3.4 Location: The French King's palace.
1. A translation of this French scene follows, with editorial comments in brackets.

CATHERINE   Alice, you've been in England, and you speak the language well.
ALICE   A little, madam.
CATHERINE   Please teach me. I must learn to speak it. What do you call *la main* in English?
ALICE   *La main*? It is called "de hand."
CATHERINE   De hand. And *les doigts*?
ALICE   *Les doigts*? Faith, I forget *les doigts*, but I'll remember. *Les doigts*—I think they're called "de fingres." Yes, de
fingres.
CATHERINE   *Le main*, de hand; *les doigts*, de fingres. I think I'm a good scholar; I've learned two words of English
quickly. What do you call *les ongles*?
ALICE   *Les ongles*? We call them "de nails."
CATHERINE   De nails. Listen—tell me if I speak well: de hand, de fingres, and de nails.

ALICE   C'est bien dit, madame. Il est fort bon anglais.

CATHERINE   Dites-moi l'anglais pour le bras.

ALICE   *De arma,* madame.

20 CATHERINE   Et le coude?

ALICE   *D'elbow.*

CATHERINE   *D'elbow.* Je m'en fais la répétition de tous les mots
que vous m'avez appris dès à présent.

ALICE   Il est trop difficile, madame, comme je pense.

25 CATHERINE   Excusez-moi, Alice. Écoutez: *d'hand, de fingre, de
nails, d'arma, de bilbow.*

ALICE   *D'elbow,* madame.

CATHERINE   O Seigneur Dieu, je m'en oublie! *D'elbow.* Com-
ment appelez-vous le col?

30 ALICE   *De nick,* madame.

CATHERINE   *De nick.* Et le menton?

ALICE   *De chin.*

CATHERINE   *De sin.* Le col, *de nick;* le menton, *de sin.*

ALICE   Oui. Sauf votre honneur, en vérité vous prononcez les

35 mots aussi droit que les natifs d'Angleterre.

CATHERINE   Je ne doute point d'apprendre, par la grâce de Dieu,
et en peu de temps.

ALICE   N'avez-vous y déjà oublié ce que je vous ai enseigné?

CATHERINE   Non, et je réciterai à vous promptement: *d'hand, de

40 fingre, de mailès—*

ALICE   *De nails,* madame.

CATHERINE   *De nails, de arma, de ilbow—*

ALICE   Sauf votre honneur, *d'elbow.*

CATHERINE   Ainsi dis-je. *D'elbow, de nick,* et *de sin.* Comment

45 appelez-vous les pieds et la robe?

ALICE   *De foot,* madame, et *de cown.*

CATHERINE   *De foot* et *de cown?* O Seigneur Dieu! Ils sont les
mots de son mauvais, corruptible, gros, et impudique, et non
pour les dames d'honneur d'user. Je ne voudrais prononcer ces

50 mots devant les seigneurs de France pour tout le monde. Foh!
De foot et *de cown!* Néanmoins, je réciterai une autre fois ma

---

ALICE   That's well said, madam. It is very good English.

CATHERINE   Tell me the English for *le bras.*

ALICE   "De arma," madam.

CATHERINE   And *le coude?*

ALICE   "D'elbow."

CATHERINE   D'elbow. I'll repeat all the words you have taught me so far.

ALICE   It is too difficult, madam, in my opinion.

CATHERINE   Excuse me, Alice. Listen: d'hand, de fingre, de nails, d'arma, de bilbow.

ALICE   D'elbow, madam.

CATHERINE   O Lord God, I forgot. D'elbow. What do you call *le col?*

ALICE   "De nick," madam.

CATHERINE   De nick. And *le menton?*

ALICE   "De chin."

CATHERINE   De sin. *Le col,* de nick; *le menton,* de sin.

ALICE   Yes. Saving your honor, to tell the truth you pronounce the words just as properly as the native English.

CATHERINE   I don't doubt that I'll learn, with God's help, and in a short time.

ALICE   Haven't you already forgotten what I have taught you?

CATHERINE   No, I shall recite to you right now: d'hand, de fingre, de mailès—

ALICE   De nails, madam.

CATHERINE   De nails, de arma, de ilbow—

ALICE   Saving your honor, d'elbow.

CATHERINE   That's what I said. D'elbow, de nick, and de sin. What do you call *les pieds* and *la robe?*

ALICE   "De foot," madam, and "de cown" [gown].

CATHERINE   De foot and de cown? O Lord God, those are evil-sounding words, easily misconstrued, vulgar, and
immodest, and not for respectable ladies to use. [They sound like the French *foutre,* "fuck," and *con,* "cunt."] I
wouldn't speak those words in front of French gentlemen for all the world. Ugh! de foot and de cown! Still, I shall

leçon ensemble. *D'hand, de fingre, de nails, d'arma, d'elbow, de nick, de sin, de foot, de cown.*

ALICE Excellent, madame!

55 CATHERINE *C'est assez pour une fois. Allons-nous à dîner.*

Exeunt

3.5

Enter KING [CHARLES *the Sixth*] *of France,* DAUPHIN,
CONSTABLE, [DUKE *of*] BOURBON, *and others*

KING CHARLES 'Tis certain he hath passed the River Somme.

CONSTABLE And if he be not fought withal,° my lord,   *with*
Let us not live in France; let us quit all
And give our vineyards to a barbarous people.

5 DAUPHIN *O Dieu vivant!*° Shall a few sprays[1] of us,   *O living God*
The emptying of our fathers' luxury,[2]
Our scions,° put in wild and savage stock,   *grafts*
Spirt° up so suddenly into the clouds   *Sprout*
And over-look their grafters?

10 BOURBON Normans, but bastard Normans, Norman bastards!
Mort de ma vie,° if they march along   *Death of my life*
Unfought withal, but I will sell my dukedom
To buy a slobb'ry° and a dirty farm   *muddy*
In that nook-shotten[3] isle of Albion.°   *England*

15 CONSTABLE *Dieu de batailles!*° Where° have they this mettle?   *God of battles / Whence*
Is not their climate foggy, raw, and dull,
On whom as in despite° the sun looks pale,   *contempt*
Killing their fruit with frowns? Can sodden° water,   *boiled; to make ale*
A drench for sur-reined jades[4]—their barley-broth—
20 Decoct° their cold blood to such valiant heat?   *Boil, to purify*
And shall our quick blood, spirited with wine,
Seem frosty? O for honour of our land
Let us not hang like roping° icicles   *ropelike*
Upon our houses' thatch, whiles a more frosty people
25 Sweat drops of gallant youth in our rich fields—
'Poor' may we call them,° in their native lords.   *(the fields)*

DAUPHIN By faith and honour,
Our madams mock at us and plainly say
Our mettle is bred out,° and they will give   *is exhausted*
30 Their bodies to the lust of English youth,
To new-store France with bastard warriors.

BOURBON They bid us, 'To the English dancing-schools,
And teach lavoltas° high and swift corantos'[5]—   *leaping dance*
Saying our grace is only in our heels,
35 And that we are most lofty runaways.

KING CHARLES Where is Montjoy the herald? Speed° him hence.   *Quickly send*
Let him greet England with our sharp defiance.
Up, princes, and with spirit of honour edged
More sharper than your swords, hie° to the field.   *go*
40 Charles Delabret, High Constable of France,
You Dukes of Orléans, Bourbon, and of Berri,
Alençon, Brabant, Bar, and Burgundy,

recite my entire lesson once more. D'hand, de fingre, de nails, d'arma, d'elbow, de nick, de sin, de foot, de cown.
ALICE Excellent, madam!
CATHERINE That's enough for one time. Let's go to dinner.
3.5 Location: The French King's court.   3. With an indented shore.
1. Offshoots (bastards).   4. A tonic for overworked horses.
2. The discharge ("emptying") of our forefathers' lust.   5. Running dance.

Jaques Châtillion, Rambures, Vaudemont,
Beaumont, Grandpré, Roussi, and Fauconbridge,
45   Foix, Lestrelles, Boucicault, and Charolais,
High dukes, great princes, barons, lords, and knights,
For your great seats now quit you° of great shames.   banners° (later line)
Bar Harry England, that sweeps through our land
With pennons° painted in the blood of Harfleur;   banners
50   Rush on his host, as doth the melted snow
Upon the valleys, whose low vassal seat
The Alps doth spit and void his rheum° upon.   empty its moisture
Go down upon him, you have power enough,
And in a captive chariot into Rouen
Bring him our prisoner.
55   CONSTABLE   This becomes the great.°   befits noblemen
Sorry am I his numbers are so few,
His soldiers sick and famished in their march,
For I am sure when he shall see our army
He'll drop his heart into the sink° of fear   pit
60   And, fore achievement,° offer us his ransom.   instead of battle
KING CHARLES   Therefore, Lord Constable, haste on Montjoy,
And let him say to England that we send
To know what willing ransom he will give.—
Prince Dauphin, you shall stay with us in Rouen.
65   DAUPHIN   Not so, I do beseech your majesty.
KING CHARLES   Be patient, for you shall remain with us.—
Now forth, Lord Constable, and princes all,
And quickly bring us word of England's fall. *Exeunt [severally]*

3.6
Enter Captains GOWER *and* FLUELLEN [*meeting*]

GOWER   How now, Captain Fluellen, come you from the bridge?
FLUELLEN   I assure you there is very excellent services commit-
ted at the bridge.
GOWER   Is the Duke of Exeter safe?
5   FLUELLEN   The Duke of Exeter is as magnanimous as Agamem-
non,[1] and a man that I love and honour with my soul and my
heart and my duty and my live and my living and my uttermost
power. He is not, God be praised and blessed, any hurt in the
world, but keeps the bridge most valiantly, with excellent disci-
10   pline. There is an ensign lieutenant there at the pridge, I think
in my very conscience he is as valiant a man as Mark Antony,
and he is a man of no estimation° in the world, but I did see   fame
him do as gallant service.
GOWER   What do you call him?
15   FLUELLEN   He is called Ensign Pistol.
GOWER   I know him not.
Enter Ensign PISTOL
FLUELLEN   Here is the man.
PISTOL   Captain, I thee beseech to do me favours.
The Duke of Exeter doth love thee well.
20   FLUELLEN   Ay, I praise God, and I have merited some love at his
hands.

---

6. *For . . . you:* In defense of your high ranks, now revenge   3.6 Location: The English camp.
yourselves.   1. Greek general in the Trojan War.

PISTOL   Bardolph, a soldier firm and sound of heart,
Of buxom° valour, hath by cruel fate   *lively*
And giddy Fortune's furious fickle wheel,
25   That goddess blind that stands upon the rolling restless stone—
FLUELLEN   By your patience, Ensign Pistol: Fortune is painted
blind, with a muffler° afore her eyes, to signify to you that For-   *blindfold*
tune is blind. And she is painted also with a wheel, to signify to
you—which is the moral of it—that she is turning and incon-
30   stant and mutability and variation. And her foot, look you, is
fixed upon a spherical stone, which rolls and rolls and rolls.
In good truth, the poet makes a most excellent description of
it; Fortune is an excellent moral.°   *symbolic emblem*
PISTOL   Fortune is Bardolph's foe and frowns on him,
35   For he hath stol'n a pax,² and hangèd must a° be.   *he*
A damnèd death—
Let gallows gape for dog, let man go free,
And let not hemp³ his windpipe suffocate.
But Exeter hath given the doom° of death   *sentence*
40   For pax of little price.
Therefore go speak, the Duke will hear thy voice,
And let not Bardolph's vital thread be cut
With edge of penny cord and vile reproach.
Speak, captain, for his life, and I will thee requite.
45   FLUELLEN   Ensign Pistol, I do partly understand your meaning.
PISTOL   Why then rejoice therefor.
FLUELLEN   Certainly, ensign, it is not a thing to rejoice at. For
if, look you, he were my brother, I would desire the Duke to
use his good pleasure, and put him to executions. For disci-
50   pline ought to be used.
PISTOL   Die and be damned! and *fico*⁴ for thy friendship.
FLUELLEN   It is well.
PISTOL   The fig of Spain.
FLUELLEN   Very good.
55   PISTOL   I say the fig within thy bowels and thy dirty maw.   *Exit*
FLUELLEN   Captain Gower, cannot you hear it lighten and
thunder?
GOWER   Why, is this the ensign you told me of? I remember him
now. A bawd, a cutpurse.°   *thief*
60   FLUELLEN   I'll assure you, a uttered as prave words at the pridge
as you shall see in a summer's day. But it is very well. What he
has spoke to me, that is well, I warrant you, when time is serve.
GOWER   Why 'tis a gull,° a fool, a rogue, that now and then goes   *simpleton*
to the wars, to grace himself at his return into London under
65   the form of a soldier. And such fellows are perfect in the great
commanders' names, and they will learn° you by rote where   *teach*
services were done— at such and such a sconce,° at such a   *fortification*
breach, at such a convoy, who came off bravely, who was shot,
who disgraced, what terms the enemy stood on—and this they
70   con° perfectly in the phrase of war, which they trick up° with   *memorize / adorn*
new-tuned° oaths. And what a beard of the General's cut and a   *newly coined*
horrid suit of the camp⁵ will do among foaming bottles and ale-

2. Small tablet with a crucifix stamped on it.   the thumb between two fingers.
3. Of which ropes were made.   5. *horrid . . . camp*: frightening soldier's attire.
4. Spanish for "fig"; obscene gesture made by thrusting

washed wits is wonderful to be thought on. But you must learn
to know such slanders° of the age, or else you may be marvel-   *disgraces*
75 lously mistook.

FLUELLEN   I tell you what, Captain Gower, I do perceive he is
not the man that he would gladly make show to the world he
is. If I find a hole in his coat,° I will tell him my mind.   *means of exposing him*
[*A drum is heard*]
Hark you, the King is coming, and I must speak with him from
80 the pridge.

Enter KING [HARRY] *and his poor soldiers,* [*with*] *drum
and colours*°   *drummer and flag bearer*
God pless your majesty.

KING HARRY   How now, Fluellen, com'st thou from the bridge?

FLUELLEN   Ay, so please your majesty. The Duke of Exeter has
very gallantly maintained the pridge. The French is gone off,
85 look you, and there is gallant and most prave passages.° Marry,   *altercations*
th'athversary was have possession of the pridge, but he is
enforced to retire, and the Duke of Exeter is master of the
pridge. I can tell your majesty, the Duke is a prave man.

KING HARRY   What men have you lost, Fluellen?

90 FLUELLEN   The perdition° of th'athversary hath been very great,   *loss*
reasonable great. Marry, for my part I think the Duke hath lost
never a man, but one that is like to be executed for robbing a
church, one Bardolph, if your majesty know the man. His face
is all bubuncles and whelks° and knobs and flames o' fire, and   *abscesses and pimples*
95 his lips blows at his nose, and it is like a coal of fire, sometimes
plue and sometimes red. But his nose is executed,⁶ and his
fire's out.

KING HARRY   We would have all such offenders so cut off, and
we here give express charge that in our marches through the
100 country there be nothing compelled from the villages, nothing
taken but° paid for, none of the French upbraided or abused in   *unless*
disdainful language. For when lenity° and cruelty play for a   *leniency*
kingdom, the gentler gamester is the soonest winner.

Tucket.° Enter MONTJOY   *Trumpet call*

MONTJOY   You know me by my habit.°   *herald's coat*

105 KING HARRY   Well then, I know thee. What shall I know of thee?

MONTJOY   My master's mind.

KING HARRY   Unfold it.

MONTJOY   Thus says my King:
'Say thou to Harry of England, though we seemed dead, we did
but sleep. Advantage° is a better soldier than rashness. Tell   *Circumspection*
him, we could have rebuked him at Harfleur, but that we
110 thought not good to bruise an injury° till it were full ripe. Now   *squeeze a pimple*
we speak upon our cue,° and our voice is imperial. England   *at the proper time*
shall repent his folly, see his weakness, and admire our suffer-
ance.° Bid him therefore consider of his ransom, which must   *wonder at our patience*
proportion the losses we have borne, the subjects we have lost,
115 the disgrace we have digested°—which in weight to re-answer,°   *endured / compensate*
his pettiness would bow under. For our losses, his exchequer°   *King's treasury*
is too poor; for th'effusion of our blood, the muster⁷ of his king-
dom too faint a number; and for our disgrace, his own person
kneeling at our feet but a weak and worthless satisfaction. To
120 this add defiance, and tell him for conclusion he hath betrayed

6. Slit (in the pillory before he is hanged).   7. Entire population, assembled for military service.

his followers, whose condemnation is pronounced.'
So far my King and master; so much my office.
KING HARRY   What is thy name? I know thy quality.°   rank
MONTJOY   Montjoy.
125   KING HARRY   Thou dost thy office fairly. Turn thee back
And tell thy king I do not seek him now,
But could be willing to march on to Calais
Without impeachment,° for to say the sooth°—   hindrance / truth
Though 'tis no wisdom to confess so much
130   Unto an enemy of craft and vantage°—   cunning and superiority
My people are with sickness much enfeebled,
My numbers lessened, and those few I have
Almost no better than so many French;
Who when they were in health—I tell thee herald,
135   I thought upon one pair of English legs
Did march three Frenchmen. Yet forgive me, God,
That I do brag thus. This your air of France
Hath blown that vice in me. I must repent.
Go, therefore, tell thy master here I am;
140   My ransom is this frail and worthless trunk,°   body
My army but a weak and sickly guard.
Yet, God before, tell him we will come on,
Though France himself and such another neighbour
Stand in our way. There's for thy labour, Montjoy.[8]
145   Go bid thy master well advise himself.
If we may pass, we will; if we be hindered,
We shall your tawny ground with your red blood
Discolour. And so, Montjoy, fare you well.
The sum of all our answer is but this:
150   We would not seek a battle as we are,
Nor as we are we say we will not shun it.
So tell your master.
MONTJOY   I shall deliver so. Thanks to your highness.   *Exit*
GLOUCESTER   I hope they will not come upon us now.
155   KING HARRY   We are in God's hand, brother, not in theirs.
March to the bridge. It now draws toward night.
Beyond the river we'll encamp ourselves,
And on tomorrow bid them march away.   *Exeunt*

3.7

Enter the CONSTABLE, *Lord* RAMBURES, [*Dukes of*]
ORLÉANS [*and*] BOURBON,[1] *with others*
CONSTABLE   Tut, I have the best armour of the world. Would it
were day.
ORLÉANS   You have an excellent armour. But let my horse have
his due.
5   CONSTABLE   It is the best horse of Europe.
ORLÉANS   Will it never be morning?
BOURBON   My lord of Orléans and my Lord High Constable, you
talk of horse and armour?
ORLÉANS   You are as well provided of both as any prince in the
10   world.
BOURBON   What a long night is this! I will not change my horse

---

8. Henry generously "tips" the enemy herald.
3.7 Location: The French camp near Agincourt.

1. As in Q; F has "Dauphin" in this scene and in 4.2
and 4.5. See Textual Note.

with any that treads but on four pasterns.° Ah ha! He bounds   *hooves*
from the earth as if his entrails were hares—*le cheval volant,*
the Pegasus, *qui a les narines de feu!*[2] When I bestride him, I
15 soar, I am a hawk; he trots the air, the earth sings when he
touches it,[3] the basest horn° of his hoof is more musical than   *lowest part (with pun)*
the pipe of Hermes.[4]

ORLÉANS   He's of the colour of the nutmeg.

BOURBON   And of the heat of the ginger.[5] It is a beast for Per-
20 seus. He is pure air and fire, and the dull elements of earth and
water never appear in him, but only in patient stillness while
his rider mounts him. He is indeed a horse, and all other jades°   *nags*
you may call beasts.

CONSTABLE   Indeed, my lord, it is a most absolute° and excellent   *perfect*
25 horse.

BOURBON   It is the prince of palfreys.° His neigh is the bidding   *warhorses*
of a monarch, and his countenance enforces homage.

ORLÉANS   No more, cousin.

BOURBON   Nay, the man hath no wit, that cannot from the ris-
30 ing of the lark to the lodging of the lamb vary deserved praise
on my palfrey. It is a theme as fluent° as the sea. Turn the sands   *flowing; abundant*
into eloquent tongues, and my horse is argument° for them all.   *subject*
'Tis a subject for a sovereign to reason on, and for a sovereign's
sovereign to ride on, and for the world, familiar to us and
35 unknown, to lay apart their particular functions, and wonder at
him. I once writ a sonnet in his praise, and began thus: 'Won-
der of nature!—'

ORLÉANS   I have heard a sonnet begin so to one's mistress.

BOURBON   Then did they imitate that which I composed to my
40 courser, for my horse is my mistress.

ORLÉANS   Your mistress bears well.[6]

BOURBON   *Me* well, which is the prescribed praise and perfection
of a good and particular° mistress.   *private*

CONSTABLE   Nay, for methought yesterday your mistress
45 shrewdly° shook your back.   *severely*

BOURBON   So perhaps did yours.

CONSTABLE   Mine was not bridled.

BOURBON   O then belike she was old and gentle, and you rode
like a kern° of Ireland, your French hose° off, and in your strait   *soldier / wide breeches*
50 strossers.°   *tights*

CONSTABLE   You have good judgement in horsemanship.

BOURBON   Be warned by me then: they that ride so, and ride not
warily, fall into foul bogs. I had rather have my horse to my
mistress.

55 CONSTABLE   I had as lief have my mistress a jade.°   *horse; whore*

BOURBON   I tell thee, Constable, my mistress wears his own
hair.[7]

CONSTABLE   I could make as true a boast as that, if I had a sow
to my mistress.

60 BOURBON   '*Le chien est retourné à son propre vomissement, et la*

---

2. The flying horse . . . with nostrils of fire. Pegasus was
a mythological flying horse, ridden by the hero Perseus.
3. When Pegasus struck Mount Helicon with his hoof,
the fountain of the Muses sprang forth.
4. Greek messenger god, whose sweet playing on the
pipe charmed the many-eyed guard Argus, allowing the
imprisoned Io to escape.

5. Horses' colors supposedly suggested their disposi-
tions: "nutmeg" meant "pleasant and nimble"; "ginger"
meant "hot and skittish."
6. Carries weight (with obscene innuendo).
7. Implying that the constable's mistress does not, hav-
ing lost it to syphilis.

truie lavée au bourbier.'[8] Thou makest use of anything.

CONSTABLE   Yet do I not use my horse for my mistress, or any such proverb so little kin to the purpose.

RAMBURES   My Lord Constable, the armour that I saw in your
65   tent tonight, are those stars or suns upon it?

CONSTABLE   Stars, my lord.

BOURBON   Some of them will fall tomorrow, I hope.

CONSTABLE   And yet my sky shall not want.

BOURBON   That may be, for you bear a many superfluously,
70   and 'twere more honour some were away.

CONSTABLE   Even as your horse bears your praises, who would trot as well were some of your brags dismounted.

BOURBON   Would I were able to load him with his desert! Will it never be day? I will trot tomorrow a mile, and my way shall
75   be paved with English faces.

CONSTABLE   I will not say so, for fear I should be faced out of my way.° But I would it were morning, for I would fain° be about   turned aside / gladly
the ears of the English.

RAMBURES   Who will go to hazard° with me for twenty prisoners?   wager

80   CONSTABLE   You must first go yourself to hazard, ere you have them.

BOURBON   'Tis midnight. I'll go arm myself.   *Exit*

ORLÉANS   The Duke of Bourbon longs for morning.

RAMBURES   He longs to eat the English.

85   CONSTABLE   I think he will eat all he kills.

ORLÉANS   By the white hand of my lady, he's a gallant prince.

CONSTABLE   Swear by her foot, that she may tread out° the oath.   erase with her foot

ORLÉANS   He is simply the most active gentleman of France.

CONSTABLE   Doing is activity, and he will still be doing.

90   ORLÉANS   He never did harm that I heard of.

CONSTABLE   Nor will do none tomorrow. He will keep that good name still.

ORLÉANS   I know him to be valiant.

CONSTABLE   I was told that by one that knows him better than
95   you.

ORLÉANS   What's he?

CONSTABLE   Marry, he told me so himself, and he said he cared not who knew it.

ORLÉANS   He needs not; it is no hidden virtue in him.

100   CONSTABLE   By my faith, sir, but it is. Never anybody saw it but his lackey.[9] 'Tis a hooded valour, and when it appears it will bate.[1]

ORLÉANS   'Ill will never said well.'

CONSTABLE   I will cap that proverb with 'There is flattery in
105   friendship.'

ORLÉANS   And I will take up that with 'Give the devil his due.'

CONSTABLE   Well placed! There stands your friend for the devil. Have at the very eye° of that proverb with 'A pox of the devil!'   bull's-eye

ORLÉANS   You are the better at proverbs by how much 'a fool's
110   bolt° is soon shot'.   short, blunt arrow

---

8. "The dog is turned to his own vomit again and the sow that was washed to her wallowing in the mire" (quoting 2 Peter 2:22).
9. That is, the only person he is brave enough to beat is his servant.
1. Beat its wings (like a hawk, which was kept "hooded" until prey was sighted); also, abate.

CONSTABLE   You have shot over.°   *overshot the target*
ORLÉANS   'Tis not the first time you were overshot.°   *defeated*
    Enter a MESSENGER
MESSENGER   My Lord High Constable, the English lie within
    fifteen hundred paces of your tents.
115 CONSTABLE   Who hath measured the ground?
MESSENGER   The Lord Grandpré.
CONSTABLE   A valiant and most expert gentleman.
                                   [*Exit* MESSENGER]
    Would it were day! Alas, poor Harry of England. He longs not
    for the dawning as we do.
120 ORLÉANS   What a wretched and peevish fellow is this King of
    England, to mope° with his fat-brained followers so far out of   *wander*
    his knowledge.
CONSTABLE   If the English had any apprehension,° they would   *sense*
    run away.
125 ORLÉANS   That they lack—for if their heads had any intellectual
    armour, they could never wear such heavy headpieces.
RAMBURES   That island of England breeds very valiant creatures.
    Their mastiffs are of unmatchable courage.
ORLÉANS   Foolish curs, that run winking° into the mouth of a   *with closed eyes*
130 Russian bear², and have their heads crushed like rotten apples.
    You may as well say, 'That's a valiant flea that dare eat his
    breakfast on the lip of a lion.'
CONSTABLE   Just,° just. And the men do sympathize with the   *True*
    mastiffs in robustious and rough coming on, leaving their wits
135 with their wives. And then, give them great meals of beef,³ and
    iron and steel, they will eat like wolves and fight like devils.
ORLÉANS   Ay, but these English are shrewdly° out of beef.   *badly*
CONSTABLE   Then shall we find tomorrow they have only stom-
    achs° to eat, and none to fight. Now is it time to arm. Come,   *appetite*
140 shall we about it?
ORLÉANS   It is now two o'clock. But let me see—by ten
    We shall have each a hundred Englishmen.   *Exeunt*

4.0

    [*Enter*] CHORUS
CHORUS   Now entertain conjecture of° a time   *imagine*
    When creeping murmur and the poring° dark   *pouring; eye-straining*
    Fills the wide vessel of the universe.
    From camp to camp through the foul womb of night
5 The hum of either army stilly sounds,
    That° the fixed sentinels almost receive   *So that*
    The secret whispers of each other's watch.
    Fire answers fire, and through their paly° flames   *pale*
    Each battle sees the other's umbered° face.   *shadowed*
10 Steed threatens steed, in high and boastful neighs
    Piercing the night's dull ear, and from the tents
    The armourers, accomplishing° the knights,   *equipping*
    With busy hammers closing rivets up,
    Give dreadful note of preparation.
15 The country cocks do crow, the clocks do toll

---

2. Referring to the sport of bearbaiting, in which dogs   3. A traditional English food.
were set upon bears chained to a post.   **4.0**

And the third hour of drowsy morning name.
Proud of their numbers and secure in soul,
The confident and overlusty French
Do the low-rated° English play at dice,[1]   *underrated*
20   And chide the cripple tardy-gaited night,
Who like a foul and ugly witch doth limp
So tediously away. The poor condemnèd English,
Like sacrifices, by their watchful fires
Sit patiently and inly° ruminate   *inwardly*
25   The morning's danger; and their gesture sad,
Investing° lank lean cheeks and war-worn coats,   *Accompanying*
Presented them unto the gazing moon
So many horrid ghosts. O now, who will behold
The royal captain of this ruined band
30   Walking from watch to watch, from tent to tent,
Let him cry, 'Praise and glory on his head!'
For forth he goes and visits all his host,°   *army*
Bids them good morrow with a modest smile
And calls them brothers, friends, and countrymen.
35   Upon his royal face there is no note°   *sign*
How dread an army hath enrounded° him;   *encircled*
Nor doth he dedicate° one jot of colour   *lose*
Unto the weary and all-watchèd night,
But freshly looks and overbears attaint[2]
40   With cheerful semblance and sweet majesty,
That every wretch, pining and pale before,
Beholding him, plucks comfort from his looks.
A largess universal,° like the sun,   *wealth available to all*
His liberal eye doth give to everyone,
45   Thawing cold fear, that mean and gentle° all   *lowborn and noble*
Behold, as may unworthiness define,[3]
A little touch of Harry in the night.
And so our scene must to the battle fly,
Where O for pity, we shall much disgrace,
50   With four or five most vile and ragged foils,°   *swords*
Right ill-disposed in brawl ridiculous,
The name of Agincourt. Yet sit and see,
Minding° true things by what their mock'ries be.   *Exit*   *Imagining*

4.1
Enter KING [HARRY] *and* [*Duke of*] GLOUCESTER [*then
the Duke of* CLARENCE]

KING HARRY   Gloucester, 'tis true that we are in great danger;
The greater therefore should our courage be.
Good morrow, brother Clarence. God Almighty!
There is some soul of goodness in things evil,
5   Would men observingly distil it out—
For our bad neighbour makes us early stirrers,
Which is both healthful and good husbandry.°   *economy*
Besides, they are our outward consciences,
And preachers to us all, admonishing
10   That we should dress us fairly° for our end.   *prepare adequately*

---

1. See 3.7.79.   3. As far as their limited capacities permit.
2. And suppresses signs of exhaustion.   4.1 Location: The English camp at Agincourt.

Thus may we gather honey from the weed
And make a moral of the devil himself.
       Enter [Sir Thomas] ERPINGHAM
Good morrow, old Sir Thomas Erpingham.
A good soft pillow for that good white head
15 Were better than a churlish turf of France.
ERPINGHAM   Not so, my liege. This lodging likes° me better,   *pleases*
    Since I may say, 'Now lie I like a king.'
KING HARRY   'Tis good for men to love their present pains
    Upon example.[1] So the spirit is eased,
20 And when the mind is quickened, out of doubt
    The organs, though defunct and dead before,
    Break up their drowsy grave and newly move
    With casted slough[2] and fresh legerity.°   *nimbleness*
    Lend me thy cloak, Sir Thomas.
        [He puts on Erpingham's cloak]
                          Brothers both,
25 Commend me to the princes in our camp.
    Do my good morrow° to them, and anon   *Say good morning*
    Desire them all to my pavilion.
GLOUCESTER   We shall, my liege.
ERPINGHAM   Shall I attend your grace?
30 KING HARRY   No, my good knight.
    Go with my brothers to my lords of England.
    I and my bosom must debate awhile,
    And then I would no other company.
ERPINGHAM   The Lord in heaven bless thee, noble Harry.
35 KING HARRY   God-a-mercy,° old heart, thou speak'st cheerfully.   *Thank you*
               Exeunt [all but KING HARRY*]*
        Enter PISTOL *[to him]*
PISTOL   *Qui vous là?*°   *Who goes there*
KING HARRY   A friend.
PISTOL   Discuss unto me: art thou officer,
    Or art thou base, common, and popular?°   *plebeian*
40 KING HARRY   I am a gentleman of a company.
PISTOL   Trail'st thou the puissant pike?°   *Are you an infantryman*
KING HARRY   Even so. What are you?
PISTOL   As good a gentleman as the Emperor.
KING HARRY   Then you are a better than the King.
45 PISTOL   The King's a bawcock and a heart-of-gold,
    A lad of life, an imp of fame,°   *a scion of noble stock*
    Of parents good, of fist most valiant.
    I kiss his dirty shoe, and from heartstring
    I love the lovely bully.° What is thy name?   *lovable swashbuckler*
50 KING HARRY   Harry *le roi.*°   *the King*
PISTOL   Leroi? A Cornish name. Art thou of Cornish crew?
KING HARRY   No, I am a Welshman.
PISTOL   Know'st thou Fluellen?
KING HARRY   Yes.
55 PISTOL   Tell him I'll knock his leek about his pate
    Upon Saint Davy's day.[3]
KING HARRY   Do not you wear your dagger in your cap that day,
    lest he knock that about yours.

---

1. By the pattern provided by others.
2. Old skin having been cast off (like a snake).

3. March 1, Welsh national holiday celebrating St. David's victory over the Saxons.

PISTOL   Art thou his friend?

60   KING HARRY   And his kinsman too.

PISTOL   The *fico*[4] for thee then.

KING HARRY   I thank you. God be with you.

PISTOL   My name is Pistol called.

KING HARRY   It sorts° well with your fierceness.   *Exit* [PISTOL]   agrees

Enter [*Captains*] FLUELLEN *and* GOWER [*severally.* KING

HARRY *stands apart*]

65   GOWER   Captain Fluellen!

FLUELLEN   So! In the name of Jesu Christ, speak fewer. It is the

greatest admiration° in the universal° world, when the true and   wonder / whole

ancient prerogatifs and laws of the wars is not kept. If you

would take the pains but to examine the wars of Pompey the

70   Great,[5] you shall find, I warrant you, that there is no tiddle-

taddle nor pibble-babble° in Pompey's camp. I warrant you,   chattering

you shall find the ceremonies of the wars, and the cares of it,

and the forms of it, and the sobriety of it, and the modesty of

it, to be otherwise.

75   GOWER   Why, the enemy is loud. You hear him all night.

FLUELLEN   If the enemy is an ass and a fool and a prating cox-

comb,° is it meet,° think you, that we should also, look you, be   yammering fool / proper

an ass and a fool and a prating coxcomb? In your own con-

science now?

80   GOWER   I will speak lower.

FLUELLEN   I pray you and beseech you that you will.

Exeunt [FLUELLEN *and* GOWER]

KING HARRY   Though it appear a little out of fashion,°   unconventional

There is much care and valour in this Welshman.

Enter three soldiers: John BATES, *Alexander* COURT, *and*

Michael WILLIAMS

COURT   Brother John Bates, is not that the morning which breaks

85   yonder?

BATES   I think it be. But we have no great cause to desire the

approach of day.

WILLIAMS   We see yonder the beginning of the day, but I think

we shall never see the end of it.—Who goes there?

90   KING HARRY   A friend.

WILLIAMS   Under what captain serve you?

KING HARRY   Under Sir Thomas Erpingham.

WILLIAMS   A good old commander and a most kind gentleman.

I pray you, what thinks he of our estate?°   situation

95   KING HARRY   Even as men wrecked upon a sand, that look to be

washed off the next tide.

BATES   He hath not told his thought to the King?

KING HARRY   No, nor it is not meet he should. For though I speak

it to you, I think the King is but a man, as I am. The violet

100   smells to him as it doth to me; the element shows° to him as it   the sky appears

doth to me. All his senses have but human conditions.° His   limitations

ceremonies laid by, in his nakedness he appears but a man,

and though his affections° are higher mounted than ours, yet   desires

when they stoop,[6] they stoop with the like wing. Therefore,

105   when he sees reason of fears,° as we do, his fears, out of doubt,   to fear

---

4. See 3.6.51.   6. Plummet down (term from falconry).
5. Roman general, defeated by Julius Caesar.

be of the same relish° as ours are. Yet, in reason, no man should   *taste; kind*
possess him with[7] any appearance of fear, lest he, by showing
it, should dishearten his army.

BATES   He may show what outward courage he will, but I
110   believe, as cold a night as 'tis, he could wish himself in Thames
up to the neck. And so I would he were, and I by him, at all
adventures,[8] so we were quit° here.   *away from*

KING HARRY   By my troth,° I will speak my conscience of the   *oath*
King. I think he would not wish himself anywhere but where
115   he is.

BATES   Then I would he were here alone. So should he be sure
to be ransomed, and a many poor men's lives saved.

KING HARRY   I dare say you love him not so ill to wish him here
alone, howsoever you speak this to feel° other men's minds.   *test*
120   Methinks I could not die anywhere so contented as in the
King's company, his cause being just and his quarrel honour-
able.

WILLIAMS   That's more than we know.

BATES   Ay, or more than we should seek after. For we know
125   enough if we know we are the King's subjects. If his cause be
wrong, our obedience to the King wipes the crime of it out of
us.

WILLIAMS   But if the cause be not good, the King himself hath a
heavy reckoning to make, when all those legs and arms and
130   heads chopped off in a battle shall join together at the latter
day,[9] and cry all, 'We died at such a place'—some swearing,
some crying for a surgeon, some upon their wives left poor
behind them, some upon the debts they owe, some upon their
children rawly° left. I am afeard there are few die well that die   *abruptly; poorly*
135   in a battle, for how can they charitably dispose of anything,
when blood is their argument?° Now, if these men do not die   *business*
well, it will be a black matter for the King that led them to it—
who° to disobey were against all proportion of subjection.[1]   *whom*

KING HARRY   So, if a son that is by his father sent about merchan-
140   dise do sinfully miscarry upon the sea, the imputation of° his   *blame for*
wickedness, by your rule, should be imposed upon his father,
that sent him. Or if a servant, under his master's command
transporting a sum of money, be assailed by robbers, and die in
many irreconciled iniquities,° you may call the business of the   *unatoned sins*
145   master the author of the servant's damnation. But this is not so.
The King is not bound to answer the particular endings of his
soldiers, the father of his son, nor the master of his servant, for
they purpose not their deaths when they propose their services.
Besides, there is no king, be his cause never so spotless, if it
150   come to the arbitrament° of swords, can try it out with all   *settlement*
unspotted° soldiers. Some, peradventure,° have on them the   *unblemished / perhaps*
guilt of premeditated and contrived murder; some, of beguiling
virgins with the broken seals of perjury; some, making the wars
their bulwark,° that have before gored the gentle bosom of   *defense (against the law)*
155   peace with pillage and robbery. Now, if these men have

---

7. Induce him to experience.
8. Whatever might happen.
9. Last Judgment, when human beings are to be

resurrected in the body.
1. *against . . . subjection*: to defy all proper relation-
ships of authority and subordination.

defeated the law and outrun native° punishment, though they   *at home*
can outstrip men, they have no wings to fly from God. War is
his beadle.° War is his vengeance. So that here men are pun-   *police officer*
ished for before-breach° of the King's laws, in now the King's   *earlier breaking*
160   quarrel. Where they feared the death, they have borne life
away; and where they would be safe, they perish. Then if they
die unprovided,° no more is the King guilty of their damnation   *unprepared*
than he was before guilty of those impieties for the which they
are now visited.° Every subject's duty is the King's, but every   *punished*
165   subject's soul is his own. Therefore should every soldier in the
wars do as every sick man in his bed: wash every mote° out of   *speck*
his conscience. And dying so, death is to him advantage;° or   *profit*
not dying, the time was blessedly lost wherein such preparation
was gained. And in him that escapes, it were not sin to think
170   that, making God so free an offer, he° let him outlive that day   *(God)*
to see his greatness and to teach others how they should pre-
pare.

BATES   'Tis certain, every man that dies ill,° the ill upon his own   *in sin*
head. The King is not to answer it. I do not desire he
175   should answer for me, and yet I determine to fight lustily for
him.

KING HARRY   I myself heard the King say he would not be ran-
somed.

WILLIAMS   Ay, he said so, to make us fight cheerfully, but when
180   our throats are cut he may be ransomed, and we ne'er the
wiser.

KING HARRY   If I live to see it, I will never trust his word after.

WILLIAMS   You pay him then! That's a perilous shot out of an
elder-gun,° that a poor and a private displeasure can do against   *a popgun*
185   a monarch. You may as well go about to turn the sun to ice
with fanning in his face with a peacock's feather. You'll never
trust his word after! Come, 'tis a foolish saying.

KING HARRY   Your reproof is something too round.° I should be   *blunt*
angry with you, if the time were convenient.

190 WILLIAMS   Let it be a quarrel between us, if you live.

KING HARRY   I embrace it.

WILLIAMS   How shall I know thee again?

KING HARRY   Give me any gage° of thine, and I will wear it in my   *token*
bonnet. Then if ever thou darest acknowledge it, I will make it
195   my quarrel.

WILLIAMS   Here's my glove. Give me another of thine.

KING HARRY   There.
    [*They exchange gloves*]

WILLIAMS   This will I also wear in my cap. If ever thou come to
me and say, after tomorrow, 'This is my glove', by this hand I
200   will take thee a box on the ear.

KING HARRY   If ever I live to see it, I will challenge it.

WILLIAMS   Thou darest as well be hanged.

KING HARRY   Well, I will do it, though I take thee in the King's
company.

205 WILLIAMS   Keep thy word. Fare thee well.

BATES   Be friends, you English fools, be friends. We have
French quarrels enough, if you could tell how to reckon.°   *count*

KING HARRY   Indeed, the French may lay twenty French crowns°   *coins; heads*
to one they will beat us, for they bear them on their shoulders.

210 But it is no English treason to cut French crowns,[2] and tomor-
row the King himself will be a clipper.   *Exeunt soldiers*
Upon the King.
'Let us our lives, our souls, our debts, our care-full wives,
Our children, and our sins, lay on the King.'
215 We must bear all. O hard condition,
Twin-born with greatness: subject to the breath
Of every fool, whose sense no more can feel
But his own wringing.° What infinite heartsease   *pain*
Must kings neglect that private men enjoy?
220 And what have kings that privates have not too,
Save ceremony, save general ceremony?
And what art thou, thou idol ceremony?
What kind of god art thou, that suffer'st more
Of mortal griefs than do thy worshippers?
225 What are thy rents?° What are thy comings-in?°   *revenues / income*
O ceremony, show me but thy worth.
What is thy soul of adoration?[3]
Art thou aught° else but place, degree, and form,   *anything*
Creating awe and fear in other men?
230 Wherein thou art less happy, being feared,
Than they in fearing.
What drink'st thou oft, instead of homage sweet,
But poisoned flattery? O be sick, great greatness,
And bid thy ceremony give thee cure.
235 Think'st thou the fiery fever will go out
With titles blown from adulation?
Will it give place to flexure° and low bending?   *bowing*
Canst thou, when thou command'st the beggar's knee,
Command the health of it? No, thou proud dream
240 That play'st so subtly with a king's repose;
I am a king that find° thee, and I know   *expose*
'Tis not the balm, the sceptre, and the ball,°   *orb (royal accessory)*
The sword, the mace, the crown imperial,
The intertissued robe of gold and pearl,
245 The farcèd° title running fore the king,   *stuffed*
The throne he sits on, nor the tide of pomp
That beats upon the high shore of this world—
No, not all these, thrice-gorgeous ceremony,
Not all these, laid in bed majestical,
250 Can sleep so soundly as the wretched slave
Who with a body filled and vacant mind
Gets him to rest, crammed with distressful bread;
Never sees horrid night, the child of hell,
But like a lackey° from the rise to set   *servant*
255 Sweats in the eye of Phoebus,° and all night   *the sun*
Sleeps in Elysium;° next day, after dawn   *classical paradise*
Doth rise and help Hyperion° to his horse,   *the sun's charioteer*
And follows so the ever-running year
With profitable labour to his grave.
260 And but for ceremony such a wretch,
Winding up days with toil and nights with sleep,

---

2. "Clipping" (line 211), or shaving, precious metal off   3. What is the secret of the adoration you inspire?
coins was punishable as treason.

Had the forehand° and vantage of a king.   *advantage*
The slave, a member of the country's peace,
Enjoys it, but in gross brain little wots°   *thinks*
265   What watch the King keeps to maintain the peace,
Whose hours the peasant best advantages.°   *profits most from*

         Enter [Sir Thomas] ERPINGHAM

ERPINGHAM   My lord, your nobles, jealous of° your absence,   *concerned about*
Seek through your camp to find you.
KING HARRY   Good old knight,
Collect them all together at my tent.
I'll be before thee.
270   ERPINGHAM   I shall do't, my lord.   *Exit*
KING HARRY   O God of battles, steel my soldiers' hearts.
Possess them not with fear. Take from them now
The sense of reck'ning,° ere th'opposèd numbers   *ability to count*
Pluck their hearts from them. Not today, O Lord,
275   O not today, think not upon the fault
My father made in compassing the crown.[4]
I Richard's body have interrèd new,°   *buried anew*
And on it have bestowed more contrite tears
Than from it issued forcèd drops of blood.
280   Five hundred poor have I in yearly pay
Who twice a day their withered hands hold up°   *(in prayer)*
Toward heaven to pardon blood. And I have built
Two chantries,[5] where the sad and solemn priests
Sing still for Richard's soul. More will I do,
285   Though all that I can do is nothing worth,
Since that my penitence comes after ill,°   *sin*
Imploring pardon.

         Enter the [Duke of] GLOUCESTER

GLOUCESTER   My liege.
KING HARRY   My brother Gloucester's voice? Ay.
290   I know thy errand, I will go with thee.
The day, my friends, and all things stay° for me.   *Exeunt*   *wait*

                         4.2

         Enter [Dukes of BOURBON *and]* ORLÉANS, *and [Lord]*
                     RAMBURES

ORLÉANS   The sun doth gild our armour. Up, my lords!
BOURBON   *Monte cheval!*° My horse! *Varlet, lacquais!*° Ha!   *To horse / valet*
ORLÉANS   O brave spirit!
BOURBON   *Via les eaux et terre!*
5   ORLÉANS   *Rien plus? L'air et feu!*[1]
BOURBON   *Cieux,*° Cousin Orléans!   *To the heavens*

         Enter CONSTABLE

Now, my Lord constable!
CONSTABLE   Hark how our steeds for present° service neigh.   *immediate*
BOURBON   Mount them and make incision in their hides,
10   That their hot blood may spin in English eyes
And dout° them with superfluous courage. Ha!   *extinguish*
RAMBURES   What, will you have them weep our horses' blood?

---

4. Henry's father usurped the throne from its rightful
possessor, Richard II.
5. Chapels where Masses for the dead were sung.
4.2. Location: The French camp.

1. Away over water and earth!
No more? Air and fire! (Playing on the four elements,
of which fire was the highest.)

How shall we then behold their natural tears?

Enter MESSENGER

MESSENGER   The English are embattled,[2] you French peers.
15   CONSTABLE   To horse, you gallant princes, straight to horse!
Do but behold yon poor and starvèd band,
And your fair show° shall suck away their souls,   *appearance*
Leaving them but the shells and husks of men.
There is not work enough for all our hands,
20   Scarce blood enough in all their sickly veins
To give each naked curtal-axe° a stain   *cutlass*
That our French gallants shall today draw out
And sheathe for lack of sport. Let us but blow on them,
The vapour of our valour will o'erturn them.
25   'Tis positive 'gainst all exceptions,° lords,   *'Tis definitely true*
That our superfluous lackeys and our peasants,
Who in unnecessary action swarm
About our squares of battle, were enough
To purge this field of such a hilding° foe,   *worthless*
30   Though we upon this mountain's basis by°   *foot nearby*
Took stand° for idle speculation,   *Stood still*
But that our honours must not. What's to say?
A very little little let us do
And all is done. Then let the trumpets sound
35   The tucket sonance° and the note to mount,   *trumpet signal*
For our approach shall so much dare the field
That England shall couch down in fear and yield.

Enter [Lord] GRANDPRÉ

GRANDPRÉ   Why do you stay so long, my lords of France?
Yon island carrions,° desperate of their bones,   *cadavers*
40   Ill-favouredly become the morning field.
Their ragged curtains° poorly are let loose   *banners*
And our air shakes them passing scornfully.
Big Mars° seems bankrupt in their beggared host   *god of war*
And faintly through a rusty beaver° peeps.   *visor*
45   The horsemen sit like fixèd candlesticks
With torchstaves° in their hands, and their poor jades   *tapers*
Lob° down their heads, drooping the hides and hips,   *Hang*
The gum down-roping° from their pale dead eyes,   *mucus dripping*
And in their palled° dull mouths the gimmaled° bit   *pale / jointed*
50   Lies foul with chewed grass, still and motionless.
And their executors,[3] the knavish crows,
Fly o'er them all impatient for their hour.
Description cannot suit itself in words
To demonstrate the life of° such a battle   *depict realistically*
55   In life so lifeless as it shows itself.
CONSTABLE   They have said their prayers, and they stay° for death.   *wait*
BOURBON   Shall we go send them dinners and fresh suits
And give their fasting horses provender,°   *food*
And after° fight with them?   *afterward*
60   CONSTABLE   I stay but for my guidon.° To the field!   *pennant*
I will the banner from a trumpet° take   *trumpeter*
And use it for my haste. Come, come away!
The sun is high, and we outwear° the day.   *Exeunt*   *waste*

---

2. Drawn into lines of battle.   3. Administrators of wills (who dispose of the remains
                                          of the dead).

4.3

Enter [Dukes of] GLOUCESTER, [CLARENCE, *and*] EXE-
TER, [*Earls of*] SALISBURY *and* [WARWICK, *and Sir*
Thomas] ERPINGHAM, *with all [the] host*

GLOUCESTER   Where is the King?

CLARENCE   The King himself is rode to view their battle.°   army

WARWICK   Of fighting men they have full threescore thousand.°   60,000

EXETER   There's five to one. Besides, they all are fresh.

5   SALISBURY   God's arm strike with us! 'Tis a fearful odds.
God b'wi' you, princes all. I'll to my charge.°   command post
If we no more meet till we meet in heaven,
Then joyfully, my noble Lord of Clarence,
My dear Lord Gloucester, and my good Lord Exeter,

10   And [*to* WARWICK] my kind kinsman, warriors all, adieu.

CLARENCE   Farewell, good Salisbury, and good luck go with thee.

EXETER   Farewell, kind lord. Fight valiantly today—
And yet I do thee wrong to mind° thee of it,   remind
For thou art framed of the firm truth of valour.

[*Exit* SALISBURY]

15   CLARENCE   He is as full of valour as of kindness,
Princely in both.

Enter KING; [HARRY, *behind*]

WARWICK   O that we now had here
But one ten thousand of those men in England
That do no work today.

KING HARRY   What's he that wishes so?
My cousin Warwick? No, my fair cousin.

20   If we are marked to die, we are enough
To do our country loss;° and if to live,   For our country to lose
The fewer men, the greater share of honour.
God's will, I pray thee wish not one man more.
By Jove, I am not covetous for gold,

25   Nor care I who doth feed upon my cost;
It ernes° me not if men my garments wear;   grieves
Such outward things dwell not in my desires.
But if it be a sin to covet honour
I am the most offending soul alive.

30   No, faith, my coz,° wish not a man from England.   kinsman
God's peace, I would not lose so great an honour
As one man more methinks would share° from me   deprive
For the best hope I have. O do not wish one more.
Rather proclaim it presently° through my host°   immediately / army

35   That he which hath no stomach° to this fight,   appetite; courage
Let him depart. His passport shall be made
And crowns for convoy° put into his purse.   money for transport
We would not die in that man's company
That fears his fellowship° to die with us.   duty as our companion

40   This day is called the Feast of Crispian.[1]
He that outlives this day and comes safe home
Will stand a-tiptoe when this day is named
And rouse him at the name of Crispian.
He that shall see this day and live t'old age

4.3 Location: The English camp.
1. October 25, dedicated to the martyred brothers Crispin and Crispianus (or Crispinian).

45 Will yearly on the vigil° feast his neighbours   *eve of the saint's day*
And say, 'Tomorrow is Saint Crispian.'
Then will he strip his sleeve and show his scars
And say, 'These wounds I had on Crispin's day.'
Old men forget; yet all shall be forgot,
50 But he'll remember, with advantages,°   *embellishments*
What feats he did that day. Then shall our names,
Familiar in his mouth as household words—
Harry the King, Bedford and Exeter,
Warwick and Talbot, Salisbury and Gloucester—
55 Be in their flowing cups freshly remembered.
This story shall the good man teach his son,
And Crispin Crispian shall ne'er go by
From this day to the ending of the world
But we in it shall be rememberèd,
60 We few, we happy few, we band of brothers.
For he today that sheds his blood with me
Shall be my brother; be he ne'er so vile,°   *lowborn*
This day shall gentle his condition.[2]
And gentlemen in England now abed
65 Shall think themselves accursed they were not here,
And hold their manhoods cheap whiles any speaks
That fought with us upon Saint Crispin's day.

       Enter [Earl of] SALISBURY

SALISBURY   My sovereign lord, bestow yourself° with speed.   *take your positions*
The French are bravely in their battles° set   *battle lines*
70 And will with all expedience° charge on us.   *speed*
KING HARRY   All things are ready if our minds be so.
WARWICK   Perish the man whose mind is backward now.
KING HARRY   Thou dost not wish more help from England, coz?
WARWICK   God's will, my liege, would you and I alone,
75 Without more help, could fight this royal battle.
KING HARRY   Why now thou hast unwished five thousand men,
Which likes° me better than to wish us one.—   *pleases*
You know your places. God be with you all.

       Tucket. Enter MONTJOY

MONTJOY   Once more I come to know of thee, King Harry,
80 If for thy ransom thou wilt now compound°   *make terms*
Before thy most assurèd overthrow.
For certainly thou art so near the gulf
Thou needs must be englutted.° Besides, in mercy   *swallowed*
The Constable desires thee thou wilt mind°   *remind*
85 Thy followers of repentance, that their souls
May make a peaceful and a sweet retire
From off these fields where, wretches, their poor bodies
Must lie and fester.
KING HARRY   Who hath sent thee now?
90 MONTJOY   The Constable of France.
KING HARRY   I pray thee bear my former answer back.
Bid them achieve° me, and then sell my bones.   *get*
Good God, why should they mock poor fellows thus?
The man that once did sell the lion's skin
95 While the beast lived, was killed with hunting him.[3]

---

2. Shall raise him to gentlemanly rank.   3. *The man . . . him:* alluding to one of Aesop's fables.

A many of our bodies shall no doubt
Find native° graves, upon the which, I trust,   (*English*)
Shall witness live in brass of this day's work.
And those that leave their valiant bones in France,
100   Dying like men, though buried in your dunghills
They shall be famed. For there the sun shall greet them
And draw their honours reeking° up to heaven,   *steaming; stinking*
Leaving their earthly parts to choke your clime,
The smell whereof shall breed a plague in France.
105   Mark then abounding valour in our English,
That, being dead, like to the bullets grazing°   *ricocheting*
Break out into a second course of mischief,
Killing in relapse of mortality.°   *another fatal outbreak*
Let me speak proudly. Tell the Constable
110   We are but warriors for the working day.°   *workaday warriors*
Our gayness and our gilt are all besmirched
With rainy marching in the painful field.
There's not a piece of feather° in our host—   *decorative plume*
Good argument, I hope, we will not fly—
115   And time hath worn us into slovenry.°   *filth*
But by the mass, our hearts are in the trim.°   *fine shape*
And my poor soldiers tell me, yet ere night
They'll be in fresher robes, as they will pluck
The gay new coats o'er your French soldiers' heads,
120   And turn them out of service.⁴ If they do this—
As if God please, they shall—my ransom then
Will soon be levied.⁵ Herald, save thou thy labour.
Come thou no more for ransom, gentle herald.
They shall have none, I swear, but these my joints—
125   Which if they have as I will leave 'em them,
Shall yield them little. Tell the Constable.
MONTJOY   I shall, King Harry. And so fare thee well.
Thou never shalt hear herald any more.
KING HARRY   I fear thou wilt once more come for a ransom.
                                             Exit [MONTJOY]
         Enter [*Duke of* YORK]
130   YORK   My lord, most humbly on my knee I beg
The leading of the vanguard.
KING HARRY   Take it, brave York.—Now soldiers, march away,
And how thou pleasest, God, dispose the day.   *Exeunt*

                    4.4
         Alarum. Excursions.° *Enter* PISTOL, [*a*] FRENCH SOL-   *Skirmishes*
         DIER, [*and the*] BOY
PISTOL   Yield, cur.
FRENCH SOLDIER   *Je pense que vous êtes le gentilhomme de bon*
*qualité.*¹
PISTOL   *Qualité? 'Calin o custure me!*²
5   Art thou a gentleman? What is thy name? Discuss.
FRENCH SOLDIER   *O Seigneur Dieu!*°   *O Lord God*
PISTOL [*aside*]   O Seigneur Dew should be a gentleman.—

---

4. Dismiss them, stripped of their servant's uniforms.
5. Collected (from the French themselves).
4.4. Location: The battlefield.

1. I think you are a gentleman of high rank.
2. The Irish refrain of a popular ballad, meaning "I am a girl from beside the Suir."

Perpend° my words, O Seigneur Dew, and mark: *Weigh*
O Seigneur Dew, thou diest, on point of fox,°   *sword*
10   Except, O Seigneur, thou do give to me
Egregious° ransom.   *Extraordinary*

FRENCH SOLDIER   *O prenez miséricorde! Ayez pitié de moi!*[3]

PISTOL   'Moy' shall not serve, I will have forty 'moys',[4]
Or I will fetch thy rim° out at thy throat   *stomach lining*
15   In drops of crimson blood.

FRENCH SOLDIER   *Est-il impossible d'échapper la force de ton bras?*[5]

PISTOL   Brass, cur? Thou damnèd and luxurious° mountain goat,   *lecherous*
Offer'st me brass?

FRENCH SOLDIER   *O pardonne-moi!*

20   PISTOL   Sayst thou me so? Is that a ton of moys?—
Come hither boy. Ask me this slave in French
What is his name.

BOY   *Écoutez: comment êtes-vous appelé?*[6]

FRENCH SOLDIER   *Monsieur le Fer.*

25   BOY   He says his name is Master Fer.

PISTOL   Master Fer? I'll fer him, and firk° him, and ferret° him.   *beat / savage*
Discuss the same in French unto him.

BOY   I do not know the French for fer and ferret and firk.

PISTOL   Bid him prepare, for I will cut his throat.

30   FRENCH SOLDIER   *Que dit-il, monsieur?*°   *What does he say, sir*

BOY   *Il me commande à vous dire que vous faites vous prêt, car ce*
soldat ici est disposé tout à cette heure de couper votre gorge.°   *(translates Pistol)*

PISTOL   *Oui, couper la gorge, par ma foi,*[7]
Peasant, unless thou give me crowns, brave crowns;
35   Or mangled shalt thou be by this my sword.

FRENCH SOLDIER   *O je vous supplie, pour l'amour de Dieu, me*
pardonner. Je suis le gentilhomme de bonne maison. Gardez ma
vie, et je vous donnerai deux cents écus°   *(translated by the boy)*

PISTOL   What are his words?

40   BOY   He prays you to save his life. He is a gentleman of a good
house, and for his ransom he will give you two hundred
crowns.

PISTOL   Tell him, my fury shall abate, and I the crowns will take.

FRENCH SOLDIER   *Petit monsieur, que dit-il?*[8]

45   BOY   *Encore qu'il est contre son jurement de pardonner aucun*
prisonnier; néanmoins, pour les écus que vous lui ci promettez, il
est content à vous donner la liberté, le franchisement.

FRENCH SOLDIER [*kneeling to* PISTOL]   *Sur mes genoux je vous*
donne mille remerciements, et je m'estime heureux que j'ai
50   *tombé entre les mains d'un chevalier, comme je pense, le plus*
brave, vaillant, et treis-distingué seigneur d'Angleterre.°   *(translated by the boy)*

PISTOL   Expound unto me, boy.

BOY   He gives you upon his knees a thousand thanks, and he
esteems himself happy that he hath fallen into the hands of
55   one, as he thinks, the most brave, valorous, and thrice-worthy
seigneur of England.

PISTOL   As I suck blood, I will some mercy show.
Follow me.

---

3. O take pity! Have pity on me!   6. Listen: what's your name?
4. Pistol mistakes *moi* for the name of a coin.   7. Yes, cut your throat, by my faith.
5. Is it impossible to escape the strength of your arm?   8. Little sir, what says he?

BOY   *Suivez-vous le grand capitaine.*[9]

[*Exeunt* PISTOL *and* FRENCH SOLDIER]

60   I did never know so full a voice issue from so empty a heart.
But the saying is true: 'The empty vessel makes the greatest
sound.' Bardolph and Nim had ten times more valour than this
roaring devil i'th' old play, that everyone may pare his nails
with a wooden dagger,[1] and they are both hanged, and so

65   would this be, if he durst steal anything adventurously.° I must   *recklessly*
stay with the lackeys with the luggage of our camp. The French
might have a good prey of us, if he knew of it, for there is none
to guard it but boys.   *Exit*

4.5

Enter CONSTABLE, [*Dukes of*] ORLÉANS [*and*] BOURBON,
and [*Lord*] RAMBURES

CONSTABLE   *O diable!*

ORLÉANS   *O Seigneur! Le jour est perdu, tout est perdu!*

BOURBON   *Mort de ma vie!*[1] All is confounded,° all.   *lost*
Reproach and everlasting shame

5   Sits mocking in our plumes.

A short alarum

O méchante fortune!°—[*To* RAMBURES] Do not run away.   *evil fate*

ORLÉANS   We are enough yet living in the field
To smother up the English in our throngs,
If any order might be thought upon.

10   BOURBON   The devil take order. Once more back again!
And he that will not follow Bourbon now,
Let him go home, and with his cap in hand
Like a base leno° hold the chamber door   *pimp*
Whilst by a slave no gentler° than my dog   *better born*

15   His fairest daughter is contaminated.

CONSTABLE   Disorder that hath spoiled° us friend° us now.   *ruined / befriend*
Let us on heaps go offer up our lives.

BOURBON   I'll to the throng.
Let life be short, else shame will be too long.[2]   *Exeunt*

4.6

Alarum. Enter KING [HARRY] *and his train,*° *with pris-*   *followers*
oners

KING HARRY   Well have we done, thrice-valiant countrymen.
But all's not done; yet keep the French the field.

[*Enter the Duke of* EXETER]

EXETER   The Duke of York commends him to your majesty.

KING HARRY   Lives he, good uncle? Thrice within this hour

5   I saw him down, thrice up again and fighting.
From helmet to the spur, all blood he was.

EXETER   In which array, brave soldier, doth he lie,
Larding° the plain. And by his bloody side,   *Moistening*
Yokefellow to his honour-owing° wounds,   *honorable*

10   The noble Earl of Suffolk also lies.

---

9. Follow the great captain.
1. Allegorical "Vice" characters in old-fashioned moral-
ity plays were typically armed with wooden daggers.
4.5 Location: The battlefield.
1. O the devil!

O God! The day is lost, all is lost!
Death of my life!
2. See Additional Passages at end of play for the Folio
and quarto versions of this scene.
4.6 Location: The battlefield.

Suffolk first died, and York, all haggled over,°   *hacked up*
Comes to him, where in gore he lay insteeped,°   *soaked*
And takes him by the beard, kisses the gashes
That bloodily did yawn upon his face,
15   And cries aloud, "Tarry, dear cousin Suffolk.
My soul shall thine keep company to heaven.
Tarry, sweet soul, for mine, then fly abreast,
As in this glorious and well-foughten field
We kept together in our chivalry.'
20   Upon these words I came and cheered him up.
He smiled me in the face, raught° me his hand,   *reached*
And with a feeble grip says, 'Dear my lord,
Commend my service to my sovereign.'
So did he turn, and over Suffolk's neck
25   He threw his wounded arm, and kissed his lips,
And so espoused to death, with blood he sealed
A testament of noble-ending love.
The pretty and sweet manner of it forced
Those waters from me which I would have stopped.
30   But I had not so much of man in me,
And all my mother° came into mine eyes   *(feminine) tenderness*
And gave me up to tears.
KING HARRY   I blame you not,
For hearing this I must perforce compound°   *come to terms*
With mistful eyes, or they will issue° too.   *weep*
     Alarum
35   But hark, what new alarum is this same?
The French have reinforced their scattered men.
Then every soldier kill his prisoners.
     [*The soldiers kill their prisoners*]¹
Give the word through.
PISTOL   *Coup' la gorge.*°   *Exeunt*   *Cut the throat*

4.7

Enter [Captains] FLUELLEN *and* GOWER

FLUELLEN   Kill the poys and the luggage! 'Tis expressly against
the law of arms. 'Tis as arrant a piece of knavery, mark you
now, as can be offert. In your conscience now, is it not?
GOWER   'Tis certain there's not a boy left alive. And the cowardly
5   rascals that ran from the battle ha' done this slaughter. Besides,
they have burned and carried away all that was in the King's
tent; wherefore the King most worthily hath caused every sol-
dier to cut his prisoner's throat. O 'tis a gallant king.
FLUELLEN   Ay, he was porn at Monmouth.° Captain Gower,   *(in Wales)*
10   what call you the town's name where Alexander the Pig was
born?
GOWER   Alexander the Great.
FLUELLEN   Why I pray you, is not 'pig' great? The pig or the
great or the mighty or the huge or the magnanimous are all
15   one reckonings, save the phrase is a little variations.°   *(for "varied")*
GOWER   I think Alexander the Great was born in Macedon. His
father was called Philip of Macedon, as I take it.
FLUELLEN   I think it is e'en Macedon where Alexander is porn.

---

1. This may or may not be done onstage.   **4.7** Location: Before Henry's pavilion.

I tell you, captain, if you look in the maps of the world I warrant
20   you sall find, in the comparisons between Macedon and Mon-
mouth, that the situations, look you, is both alike. There is a
river in Macedon, and there is also moreover a river at Mon-
mouth. It is called Wye at Monmouth, but it is out of my prains
what is the name of the other river—but 'tis all one, 'tis alike as
25   my fingers is to my fingers, and there is salmons in both. If you
mark Alexander's life well, Harry of Monmouth's life is come
after it indifferent well.[1] For there is figures° in all things. Alex-   comparisons
ander, God knows, and you know, in his rages and his furies
and his wraths and his cholers° and his moods and his displea-   angers
30   sures and his indignations, and also being a little intoxicates in
his prains, did in his ales and his angers, look you, kill his best
friend Cleitus—
GOWER   Our King is not like him in that. He never killed any of
his friends.
35   FLUELLEN   It is not well done, mark you now, to take the tales
out of my mouth ere it is made an end and finished. I speak
but in the figures and comparisons of it. As Alexander killed his
friend Cleitus, being in his ales and his cups, so also Harry
Monmouth, being in his right wits and his good judgements,
40   turned away the fat knight with the great-belly doublet—he was
full of jests and gipes° and knaveries and mocks—I have forgot   gibes
his name.
GOWER   Sir John Falstaff.
FLUELLEN   That is he. I'll tell you, there is good men porn at
45   Monmouth.
GOWER   Here comes his majesty.
         Alarum. Enter KING HARRY *and [the English army], with*
         [Duke of] BOURBON, *[Duke of* ORLÉANS, *and other] pris-*
         oners.[2] *Flourish*
KING HARRY   I was not angry since I came to France
Until this instant. Take a trumpet, herald;
Ride thou unto the horsemen on yon hill.
50   If they will fight with us, bid them come down,
Or void° the field: they do offend our sight.   leave
If they'll do neither, we will come to them,
And make them skirr° away as swift as stones   scurry
Enforcèd° from the old Assyrian slings.   Driven
55   Besides, we'll cut the throats of those we have,
And not a man of them that we shall take
Shall taste our mercy. Go and tell them so.
         Enter MONTJOY
EXETER   Here comes the herald of the French, my liege.
GLOUCESTER   His eyes are humbler than they used to be.
60   KING HARRY   How now, what means this, herald? Know'st thou not
That I have fined° these bones of mine for ransom?   pledged
Com'st thou again for ransom?
MONTJOY   No, great King.
I come to thee for charitable licence,°   permission
That we may wander o'er this bloody field
65   To book° our dead and then to bury them,   register

1. *is . . . well:* resembles it fairly well.
2. This is a second batch of prisoners, captured after the French counterattack.

To sort our nobles from our common men—
For many of our princes, woe the while,
Lie drowned and soaked in mercenary blood.[3]
So do our vulgar° drench their peasant limbs   *common people*
70   In blood of princes, and our wounded steeds
Fret fetlock°-deep in gore, and with wild rage   *ankle*
Jerk out their armèd heels at their dead masters,
Killing them twice. O give us leave, great King,
To view the field in safety, and dispose
Of their dead bodies.
75 KING HARRY   I tell thee truly, herald,
I know not if the day be ours or no,
For yet a many of your horsemen peer°   *appear*
And gallop o'er the field.
MONTJOY   The day is yours.
KING HARRY   Praisèd be God, and not our strength, for it.
80   What is this castle called that stands hard by?
MONTJOY   They call it Agincourt.
KING HARRY   Then call we this the field of Agincourt,
Fought on the day of Crispin Crispian.
FLUELLEN   Your grandfather of famous memory, an't° please   *if it*
85   your majesty, and your great-uncle Edward the Plack Prince of
Wales, as I have read in the chronicles, fought a most prave
pattle here in France.
KING HARRY   They did, Fluellen.
FLUELLEN   Your majesty says very true. If your majesties is
90   remembered of it, the Welshmen did good service in a garden
where leeks did grow, wearing leeks in their Monmouth caps,[4]
which your majesty know to this hour is an honourable badge
of the service. And I do believe your majesty takes no scorn to
wear the leek upon Saint Tavy's day.
95 KING HARRY   I wear it for a memorable honour,
For I am Welsh, you know, good countryman.
FLUELLEN   All the water in Wye° cannot wash your majesty's   *Welsh river*
Welsh plood out of your pody, I can tell you that. God pless it
and preserve it, as long as it pleases his grace, and his majesty
100   too.
KING HARRY   Thanks, good my countryman.
FLUELLEN   By Jeshu, I am your majesty's countryman. I care not
who know it, I will confess it to all the world. I need not to be
ashamed of your majesty, praised be God, so long as your maj-
105   esty is an honest man.
KING HARRY   God keep me so.
        Enter WILLIAMS [*with a glove in his cap*]
                Our heralds go with him.
Bring me just notice° of the numbers dead   *accurate record*
On both our parts.
       Exeunt [MONTJOY, GOWER, *and English*] *heralds*
          Call yonder fellow hither.
EXETER [*to* WILLIAMS]   Soldier, you must come to the King.
110 KING HARRY   Soldier, why wearest thou that glove in thy cap?
WILLIAMS   An't please your majesty, 'tis the gage° of one that I   *token*
should fight withal, if he be alive.

---

3. Common soldiers, unlike noblemen, fought for pay.   4. Tall, tapering caps without brims.

KING HARRY   An Englishman?

WILLIAMS   An't please your majesty, a rascal, that swaggered with
115   me last night—who, if a live, and ever dare to challenge this
glove, I have sworn to take him a box o'th' ear; or if I can see
my glove in his cap—which he swore, as he was a soldier, he
would wear if a lived—I will strike it out soundly.

KING HARRY   What think you, Captain Fluellen? Is it fit this sol-
120   dier keep his oath?

FLUELLEN   He is a craven° and a villain else, an't please your   coward
majesty, in my conscience.

KING HARRY   It may be his enemy is a gentleman of great sort,
quite from the answer of his degree.[5]

125   FLUELLEN   Though he be as good a gentleman as the devil is,
as Lucifer and Beelzebub° himself, it is necessary, look your   Satan
grace, that he keep his vow and his oath. If he be perjured, see
you now, his reputation is as arrant a villain and a Jack-sauce°   saucy knave
as ever his black shoe trod upon God's ground and his earth,
130   in my conscience, law.

KING HARRY   Then keep thy vow, sirrah, when thou meetest the
fellow.

WILLIAMS   So I will, my liege, as I live.

KING HARRY   Who serv'st thou under?

135   WILLIAMS   Under Captain Gower, my liege.

FLUELLEN   Gower is a good captain, and is good knowledge and
literatured° in the wars.   well read

KING HARRY   Call him hither to me, soldier.

WILLIAMS   I will, my liege.   *Exit*

140   KING HARRY   [*giving him Williams's other glove*]   Here, Fluellen,
wear thou this favour for me and stick it in thy cap. When
Alençon and myself were down together, I plucked this glove
from his helm. If any man challenge this, he is a friend to
Alençon and an enemy to our person. If thou encounter any
145   such, apprehend° him, an° thou dost me love.   arrest / if

FLUELLEN   Your grace does me as great honours as can be
desired in the hearts of his subjects. I would fain° see the man   gladly
that has but two legs that shall find himself aggriefed at this
glove, that is all; but I would fain see it once. An't please God
150   of his grace, that I would see.

KING HARRY   Know'st thou Gower?

FLUELLEN   He is my dear friend, an't please you.

KING HARRY   Pray thee, go seek him and bring him to my tent.

FLUELLEN   I will fetch him.   *Exit*

155   KING HARRY   My lord of Warwick and my brother Gloucester,
Follow Fluellen closely at the heels.
The glove which I have given him for a favour
May haply purchase him a box o'th' ear.
It is the soldier's. I by bargain should
160   Wear it myself. Follow, good cousin Warwick.
If that the soldier strike him, as I judge
By his blunt bearing he will keep his word,
Some sudden mischief may arise of it,
For I do know Fluellen valiant
165   And touched with choler,° hot as gunpowder,   made angry

5. Quite above responding to a challenge from one of Williams's rank.

And quickly will return an injury.°   *insult*
Follow, and see there be no harm between them.
Go you with me, uncle of Exeter.   *Exeunt [severally]*

4.8

Enter [Captain] GOWER *and* WILLIAMS

WILLIAMS   I warrant° it is to knight you, captain.   *I'm sure*

Enter [Captain] FLUELLEN

FLUELLEN   God's will and his pleasure, captain, I beseech you
now, come apace° to the King. There is more good toward you,   *quickly*
peradventure,° than is in your knowledge to dream of.   *perhaps*

5   WILLIAMS   Sir, know you this glove?
FLUELLEN   Know the glove? I know the glove is a glove.
WILLIAMS *[plucking the glove from Fluellen's cap]*   I know this,
     and thus I challenge it.
         *[He] strikes [*FLUELLEN*]*
FLUELLEN   God's plood, and his! An arrant traitor as any's in the

10   universal world, or in France, or in England.
GOWER *[to* WILLIAMS*]*   How now, sir? You villain!
WILLIAMS   Do you think I'll be forsworn?
FLUELLEN   Stand away, Captain Gower. I will give treason his
     payment into plows, I warrant you.

15   WILLIAMS   I am no traitor.
FLUELLEN   That's a lie in thy throat. I charge you in his majesty's
     name, apprehend him. He's a friend of the Duke Alençon's.

Enter [Earl of] WARWICK *and [Duke of]* GLOUCESTER

WARWICK   How now, how now, what's the matter?
FLUELLEN   My lord of Warwick, here is—praised be God for it—

20   a most contagious° treason come to light, look you, as you shall   *noxious*
     desire in a summer's day.

Enter KING [HARRY] *and [Duke of]* EXETER

Here is his majesty.
KING HARRY   How now, what is the matter?
FLUELLEN   My liege, here is a villain and a traitor that, look your

25   grace, has struck the glove which your majesty is take out of
     the helmet of Alençon.
WILLIAMS   My liege, this was my glove—here is the fellow° of   *mate*
     it—and he that I gave it to in change promised to wear it in his
     cap. I promised to strike him, if he did. I met this man with my

30   glove in his cap, and I have been as good as my word.
FLUELLEN   Your majesty hear now, saving your majesty's man-
     hood, what an arrant rascally beggarly lousy knave it is. I hope
     your majesty is pear° me testimony and witness, and will   *(for "will bear")*
     avouchment° that this is the glove of Alençon that your maj-   *(for "vouch")*

35   esty is give me, in your conscience now.
KING HARRY   Give me thy glove, soldier.
     Look, here is the fellow of it.
     'Twas I indeed thou promisèd'st to strike,
     And thou hast given me most bitter terms.°   *words*

40   FLUELLEN   An't please your majesty, let his neck answer for it, if
     there is any martial law in the world.
KING HARRY   How canst thou make me satisfaction?
WILLIAMS   All offences, my lord, come from the heart. Never
     came any from mine that might offend your majesty.

4.8 Location: Before Henry's pavilion.

45 KING HARRY It was ourself thou didst abuse.

WILLIAMS Your majesty came not like yourself. You appeared to
me but as a common man. Witness the night, your garments,
your lowliness. And what your highness suffered under that
shape, I beseech you take it for your own fault, and not mine,
50 for had you been as I took you for, I made no offence. There-
fore I beseech your highness pardon me.

KING HARRY Here, Uncle Exeter, fill this glove with crowns
And give it to this fellow.—Keep it, fellow,
And wear it for an honour in thy cap
55 Till I do challenge it.—Give him the crowns.
—And captain, you must needs be friends with him.

FLUELLEN By this day and this light, the fellow has mettle
enough in his belly.—Hold, there is twelve pence for you, and
I pray you to serve God, and keep you out of prawls and prab-
60 bles and quarrels and dissensions, and I warrant you it is the
better for you.

WILLIAMS I will none of your money.

FLUELLEN It is with a good will. I can tell you, it will serve you
to mend your shoes. Come, wherefore should you be so pash-
65 ful? Your shoes is not so good. 'Tis a good shilling, I warrant
you, or I will change it.[1]

Enter [an English] HERALD

KING HARRY Now, herald, are the dead numbered?

HERALD Here is the number of the slaughtered French.

KING HARRY What prisoners of good sort° are taken, uncle?   high rank
70 EXETER Charles, Duke of Orléans, nephew to the King;
Jean, Duke of Bourbon, and Lord Boucicault;
Of other lords and barons, knights and squires,
Full fifteen hundred, besides common men.

KING HARRY This note doth tell me of ten thousand French
75 That in the field lie slain. Of princes in this number
And nobles bearing banners,° there lie dead   coats of arms
One hundred twenty-six; added to these,
Of knights, esquires, and gallant gentlemen,
Eight thousand and four hundred, of the which
80 Five hundred were but yesterday dubbed knights.
So that in these ten thousand they have lost
There are but sixteen hundred mercenaries;
The rest are princes, barons, lords, knights, squires,
And gentlemen of blood and quality.
85 The names of those their nobles that lie dead:
Charles Delabret, High Constable of France;
Jaques of Châtillion, Admiral of France;
The Master of the Crossbows, Lord Rambures;
Great-Master of France, the brave Sir Guiscard Dauphin;
90 Jean, Duke of Alençon; Antony, Duke of Brabant,
The brother to the Duke of Burgundy;
And Édouard, Duke of Bar; of lusty earls,
Grandpré and Roussi, Fauconbridge and Foix,
Beaumont and Marle, Vaudemont and Lestrelles.
95 Here was a royal fellowship of death.

---

1. Williams may or may not take the money.

Where is the number of our English dead?
[*He is given another paper*]
Edward the Duke of York, the Earl of Suffolk,
Sir Richard Keighley, Davy Gam Esquire;
None else of name,° and of all other men   high rank
100   But five-and-twenty. O God, thy arm was here,
And not to us, but to thy arm alone
Ascribe we all. When, without stratagem,
But in plain shock° and even play of battle,   confrontation
Was ever known so great and little loss
105   On one part and on th'other? Take it God,
For it is none but thine.
EXETER   'Tis wonderful.
KING HARRY   Come, go we in procession to the village,
And be it death proclaimèd through our host
To boast of this, or take that praise from God
110   Which is his only.
FLUELLEN   Is it not lawful, an't please your majesty, to tell how
many is killed?
KING HARRY   Yes, captain, but with this acknowledgement,
That God fought for us.
115   FLUELLEN   Yes, in my conscience, he did us great good.
KING HARRY   Do we all holy rites:
Let there be sung *Non nobis* and *Te Deum*,[2]
The dead with charity enclosed in clay;°   buried with pious love
And then to Calais, and to England then,
120   Where ne'er from France arrived more-happy° men.   *Exeunt*   more fortunate

5.0

Enter CHORUS
CHORUS   Vouchsafe° to those that have not read the story   Allow
That I may prompt them—and of such as have,
I humbly pray them to admit th'excuse
Of time, of numbers, and due course of things,
5   Which cannot in their huge and proper life
Be here presented. Now we bear the King
Toward Calais. Grant him there; there seen,
Heave him away upon your wingèd thoughts
Athwart the sea. Behold, the English beach
10   Pales-in° the flood, with men, maids, wives, and boys,   Fences in
Whose shouts and claps out-voice the deep-mouthed sea,
Which like a mighty whiffler[1] fore the King
Seems to prepare his way. So let him land,
And solemnly see him set on to London.
15   So swift a pace hath thought, that even now
You may imagine him upon Blackheath,[2]
Where that his lords desire him to have borne
His bruisèd helmet and his bended sword
Before him through the city; he forbids it,
20   Being free from vainness and self-glorious pride,
Giving full trophy, signal, and ostent°   honor for the victory

---

2. *Non nobis* is Psalm 115, beginning "Not unto us, O
Lord, not unto us, but unto thy name give the glory." *Te
Deum* is a canticle of thanks beginning "We praise thee,
O God."

5.0
1. Official who cleared the way for a procession.
2. Open space outside London.

Quite from himself, to God. But now behold,
In the quick forge and working-house of thought,
How London doth pour out her citizens.
25 The Mayor and all his brethren, in best sort,°   clothing
Like to the senators of th'antique Rome
With the plebeians° swarming at their heels,   commoners
Go forth and fetch their conqu'ring Caesar in—
As, by a lower but high-loving likelihood,[3]
30 Were now the General of our gracious Empress[4]—
As in good time he may—from Ireland coming,
Bringing rebellion broachèd° on his sword,   impaled
How many would the peaceful city quit
To welcome him! Much more, and much more cause,
35 Did they this Harry. Now in London place him;
As yet the lamentation of the French
Invites the King of England's stay at home.
The Emperor's coming[5] in behalf of France,
To order peace between them [
40   ][6] and omit
All the occurrences, whatever chanced,
Till Harry's back-return again to France.[7]
There must we bring him, and myself have played
The interim by rememb'ring° you 'tis past.   reminding
45 Then brook° abridgement, and your eyes advance,   tolerate
After your thoughts, straight back again to France.   *Exit*

5.1

Enter [Captain] GOWER *and [Captain]* FLUELLEN *[with
a leek in his cap and a cudgel]*

GOWER Nay, that's right. But why wear you your leek today?
Saint Davy's day is past.
FLUELLEN There is occasions and causes why and wherefore in
all things. I will tell you, ass my friend, Captain Gower. The
5 rascally scald° beggarly lousy pragging knave Pistol—which you   scabby
and yourself and all the world know to be no petter than a
fellow, look you now, of no merits—he is come to me, and
prings me pread and salt yesterday,° look you, and bid me eat   (on St. Davy's Day)
my leek. It was in a place where I could not breed no con-
10 tention with him, but I will be so bold as to wear it in my cap
till I see him once again, and then I will tell him a little piece
of my desires.
Enter [Ensign] PISTOL
GOWER Why, here a° comes, swelling like a turkey-cock.   he
FLUELLEN 'Tis no matter for his swellings nor his turkey-
15 cocks.—God pless you Ensign Pistol, you scurvy lousy knave,
God pless you.
PISTOL Ha, art thou bedlam?° Dost thou thirst, base Trojan,°   crazy / villain
To have me fold up Parca's[1] fatal web?
Hence! I am qualmish° at the smell of leek.   nauseated

---

3. Lovingly anticipated probability.
4. *General . . . Empress:* Earl of Essex (see Introduc-
tion).
5. Sigismund; the Holy Roman Emperor, attempted,
and failed, to negotiate a peace between France and
England.

6. A line is evidently missing here.
7. Henry invaded France a second and third time, in
1417 and 1421; Act 5 begins in the latter year.
5.1 Location: The English camp.
1. The Parcae were the mythological Fates who spun
and cut the thread of life.

20 FLUELLEN I peseech you heartily, scurvy lousy knave, at my
desires and my requests and my petitions, to eat, look you, this
leek. Because, look you, you do not love it, nor your affections
and your appetites and your digestions does not agree with it, I
would desire you to eat it.

25 PISTOL Not for Cadwallader° and all his goats.   *last Welsh king*

FLUELLEN There is one goat for you. [*He*] *strikes* [PISTOL] Will
you be so good, scald° knave, as eat it?   *worthless*

PISTOL Base Trojan, thou shalt die.

FLUELLEN You say very true, scald knave, when God's will is. I
30 will desire you to live in the mean time, and eat your victuals.°   *food*
Come, there is sauce for it. [*He strikes him*] You called me
yesterday 'mountain-squire',° but I will make you today a   (*Wales is moutainous*)
'squire of low degree'. I pray you, fall to. If you can mock a leek
you can eat a leek.
        [*He strikes him*]

35 GOWER Enough, captain, you have astonished° him.   *stunned*

FLUELLEN By Jesu, I will make him eat some part of my leek, or
I will peat his pate° four days and four nights.—Bite, I pray you.   *head*
It is good for your green° wound and your ploody coxcomb.°   *fresh/head*

PISTOL Must I bite?

40 FLUELLEN Yes, certainly, and out of doubt and out of question
too, and ambiguities.

PISTOL By this leek, I will most horribly revenge—
        [FLUELLEN *threatens him*]
I eat and eat—I swear—

FLUELLEN Eat, I pray you. Will you have some more sauce to
45 your leek? There is not enough leek to swear by.

PISTOL Quiet thy cudgel,° thou dost see I eat.   *wooden club*

FLUELLEN Much good do you, scald knave, heartily. Nay, pray
you throw none away. The skin is good for your broken cox-
comb. When you take occasions to see leeks hereafter, I pray
50 you mock at 'em, that is all.

PISTOL Good.

FLUELLEN Ay, leeks is good. Hold you, there is a groat° to heal   *fourpence*
your pate.

PISTOL Me, a groat?

55 FLUELLEN Yes, verily,° and in truth you shall take it, or I have   *truly*
another leek in my pocket which you shall eat.

PISTOL I take thy groat in earnest° of revenge.   *advance payment*

FLUELLEN If I owe you anything, I will pay you in cudgels. You
shall be a woodmonger, and buy nothing of me but cudgels.
60 God b'wi' you, and keep you, and heal your pate.   *Exit*

PISTOL All hell shall stir for this.

GOWER Go, go, you are a counterfeit cowardly knave. Will you
mock at an ancient tradition, begun upon an honourable
respect and worn as a memorable trophy of predeceased
65 valour, and dare not avouch° in your deeds any of your words?   *prove*
I have seen you gleeking and galling° at this gentleman twice   *jesting and annoying*
or thrice. You thought, because he could not speak English in
the native garb, he could not therefore handle an English cud-
gel. You find it otherwise. And henceforth let a Welsh correc-
70 tion teach you a good English condition. Fare ye well.   *Exit*

PISTOL Doth Fortune play the hussy° with me now?   *whore*
News have I that my Nell is dead

I'th' spital of a malady of France,°   *venereal disease*
And there my rendezvous° is quite cut off.   *refuge*
75 Old I do wax, and from my weary limbs
Honour is cudgelled. Well, bawd° I'll turn,   *pimp*
And something lean to cutpurse of quick hand.
To England will I steal, and there I'll steal,
And patches will I get unto these cudgelled scars,
80 And swear I got them in the Gallia° wars.   *Exit*   *French*

5.2

Enter at one door KING [HARRY, *Dukes of*] EXETER [*and*
CLARENCE, *Earl of*] WARWICK, *and other lords; at
another,* KING [CHARLES *the Sixth*] *of France,* QUEEN ISA-
BEL, *the Duke of* BURGUNDY, *and other French,* [*among
them Princess*] CATHERINE [*and* ALICE]

KING HARRY   Peace to this meeting, wherefor° we are met.   *for which*
Unto our brother France and to our sister,
Health and fair time of day. Joy and good wishes
To our most fair and princely cousin Catherine;
5 And as a branch and member of this royalty,
By whom this great assembly is contrived,
We do salute you, Duke of Burgundy.
And princes French, and peers, health to you all.
KING CHARLES   Right joyous are we to behold your face.
10 Most worthy brother England, fairly met.
So are you, princes English, every one.
QUEEN ISABEL   So happy be the issue,° brother England,   *outcome*
Of this good day and of this gracious meeting,
As we are now glad to behold your eyes—
15 Your eyes which hitherto have borne in them,
Against the French that met them in their bent,°   *glance*
The fatal balls° of murdering basilisks.[1]   *eyeballs; cannonballs*
The venom of such looks we fairly hope
Have lost their quality,° and that this day   *nature*
20 Shall change all griefs and quarrels into love.
KING HARRY   To cry amen to that, thus we appear.
QUEEN ISABEL   You English princes all, I do salute you.
BURGUNDY   My duty to you both, on equal love,
Great Kings of France and England. That I have laboured
25 With all my wits, my pains, and strong endeavours,
To bring your most imperial majesties
Unto this bar° and royal interview,   *court*
Your mightiness on both parts best can witness.
Since, then, my office hath so far prevailed
30 That face to face and royal eye to eye
You have congreeted,° let it not disgrace me   *met*
If I demand, before this royal view,
What rub° or what impediment there is   *hindrance*
Why that the naked, poor, and mangled peace,
35 Dear nurse of arts, plenties, and joyful births,
Should not in this best garden of the world,
Our fertile France, put up her lovely visage?
Alas, she hath from France too long been chased,

5.2 Location: The French court.   1. Fabulous animals able to kill with a glance.

	And all her husbandry° doth lie on heaps,	*agriculture*
40	Corrupting in it° own fertility.	*its*
	Her vine, the merry cheerer of the heart,	
	Unprunèd dies; her hedges even-plashed°	*interwoven*
	Like prisoners wildly overgrown with hair	
	Put forth disordered twigs; her fallow leas°	*unplanted fields*
45	The darnel, hemlock, and rank fumitory°	*kinds of weeds*
	Doth root upon, while that the coulter° rusts	*plow*
	That should deracinate° such savagery.	*root out*
	The even mead°—that erst brought sweetly forth	*meadow*
	The freckled cowslip, burnet, and green clover—	
50	Wanting the scythe, all uncorrected, rank,	
	Conceives by idleness,° and nothing teems	*Breeds worthless things*
	But hateful docks, rough thistles, kecksies, burs,°	*(all are weeds)*
	Losing both beauty and utility.	
	An° all our vineyards, fallows, meads, and hedges,	*And if*
55	Defective in their natures, grow to wildness,	
	Even so our houses and ourselves and children	
	Have lost, or do not learn for want of time,	
	The sciences° that should become° our country,	*knowledge/adorn*
	But grow like savages—as soldiers will	
60	That nothing do but meditate on blood—	
	To swearing and stern looks, diffused° attire,	*disordered*
	And everything that seems unnatural.	
	Which to reduce into our former favour²	
	You are assembled, and my speech entreats	
65	That I may know the let° why gentle peace	*impediment*
	Should not expel these inconveniences	
	And bless us with her former qualities.	
	KING HARRY If, Duke of Burgundy, you would the peace	
	Whose want gives growth to th'imperfections	
70	Which you have cited, you must buy that peace	
	With full accord to all our just demands,	
	Whose tenors° and particular effects	*general principles*
	You have enscheduled briefly in your hands.	
	BURGUNDY The King hath heard them, to the which as yet	
	There is no answer made.	
75	KING HARRY Well then, the peace,	
	Which you before so urged, lies in his answer.	
	KING CHARLES I have but with a cursitory° eye	*cursory*
	O'erglanced the articles. Pleaseth your grace	
	To appoint some of your council presently	
80	To sit with us once more, with better heed	
	To re-survey them, we will suddenly	
	Pass our accept and peremptory° answer.	*approved and definite*
	KING HARRY Brother, we shall.—Go, Uncle Exeter	
	And brother Clarence, and you, brother Gloucester;	
85	Warwick and Huntingdon, go with the King,	
	And take with you free power to ratify,	
	Augment, or alter, as your wisdoms best	
	Shall see advantageable for our dignity,	
	Anything in or out of our demands,	
90	And we'll consign° thereto.—Will you, fair sister,	*agree*

2. To revert to our old appearance.

Go with the princes, or stay here with us?

QUEEN   Our gracious brother, I will go with them.
Haply° a woman's voice may do some good   *Perhaps*
When articles too nicely° urged be stood on.   *punctiliously*

95   KING HARRY   Yet leave our cousin Catherine here with us.
She is our capital° demand, comprised   *chief*
Within the fore-rank of our articles.

QUEEN   She hath good leave.
        Exeunt [all but] KING HARRY, CATHERINE, *and [*ALICE*]*
        the gentlewoman

KING HARRY   Fair Catherine, and most fair,
Will you vouchsafe to teach a soldier terms

100   Such as will enter at a lady's ear
And plead his love-suit to her gentle heart?

CATHERINE   Your majesty shall mock at me. I cannot speak your
England.

KING HARRY   O fair Catherine, if you will love me soundly with

105   your French heart, I will be glad to hear you confess it brokenly
with your English tongue. Do you like me, Kate?

CATHERINE *Pardonnez-moi,*° I cannot tell vat is 'like me'.   *Excuse me*

KING HARRY   An angel is like you, Kate, and you are like an
angel.

110   CATHERINE [*to* ALICE]   *Que dit-il?—que je suis semblable à les*
anges?

ALICE   *Oui, vraiment—sauf votre grâce—ainsi dit-il.*[3]

KING HARRY   I said so, dear Catherine, and I must not blush to
affirm it.

115   CATHERINE   *O bon Dieu!*° *Les langues des hommes sont pleines*   *O good God*
de tromperies.°   *(translated below)*

KING HARRY   What says she, fair one? That the tongues of men
are full of deceits?

ALICE   *Oui,* dat de tongeus of de mans is be full of deceits—dat

120   is de Princess.

KING HARRY   The Princess is the better Englishwoman. I'faith,
Kate, my wooing is fit for thy understanding. I am glad thou
canst speak no better English, for if thou couldst, thou wouldst
find me such a plain king that thou wouldst think I had sold

125   my farm to buy my crown. I know no ways to mince it in love,
but directly to say, 'I love you'; then if you urge me farther than
to say, 'Do you in faith?', I wear out my suit. Give me your
answer, i'faith do, and so clap° hands and a bargain. How say   *shake*
you, lady?

130   CATHERINE   *Sauf votre honneur,*° me understand well.   *Save your honor*

KING HARRY   Marry, if you would put me to verses, or to dance
for your sake, Kate, why, you undid me. For the one I have
neither words nor measure,° and for the other I have no   *meter*
strength in measure°—yet a reasonable measure in strength. If   *talent for dancing*

135   I could win a lady at leap-frog, or by vaulting into my saddle
with my armour on my back, under the correction of bragging
be it spoken, I should quickly leap into a wife. Or if I might
buffet° for my love, or bound my horse for her favours, I could   *box*
lay on like a butcher, and sit like a jackanapes,° never off. But   *monkey*

140   before God, Kate, I cannot look greenly,° nor gasp out my elo-   *abashed*

---

3. What does he say? That I am like an angel? Yes, truly, save your grace, he says that.

quence, nor I have no cunning in protestation—only down-
right oaths, which I never use till urged, nor never break for
urging. If thou canst love a fellow of this temper,° Kate, whose   *makeup*
face is not worth sunburning, that never looks in his glass° for   *mirror*
145 love of anything he sees there, let thine eye be thy cook. I speak
to thee plain soldier: if thou canst love me for this, take me. If
not, to say to thee that I shall die, is true—but for thy love, by
the Lord, no. Yet I love thee, too. And while thou livest, dear
Kate, take a fellow of plain and uncoined° constancy, for he   *not in common use*
150 perforce must do thee right, because he hath not the gift to
woo in other places. For these fellows of infinite tongue, that
can rhyme themselves into ladies' favours, they do always rea-
son themselves out again. What! A speaker is but a prater,° a   *chatterer*
rhyme is but a ballad; a good leg will fall, a straight back will
155 stoop, a black beard will turn white, a curled pate will grow
bald, a fair face will wither, a full eye will wax° hollow, but a   *become*
good heart, Kate, is the sun and the moon—or rather the sun
and not the moon, for it shines bright and never changes, but
keeps his course truly. If thou would have such a one, take me;
160 and take me, take a soldier; take a soldier, take a king. And
what sayst thou then to my love? Speak, my fair—and fairly, I
pray thee.

CATHERINE Is it possible dat I sould love de *ennemi* of France?

KING HARRY No, it is not possible you should love the enemy of
165 France, Kate. But in loving me, you should love the friend of
France, for I love France so well that I will not part with a
village of it, I will have it all mine; and Kate, when France is
mine, and I am yours, then yours is France, and you are mine.

CATHERINE I cannot tell vat is dat.

170 KING HARRY No, Kate? I will tell thee in French—which I am
sure will hang upon my tongue like a new-married wife about
her husband's neck, hardly to be shook off. *Je quand suis le
possesseur de France, et quand vous avez le possession de moi*—
let me see, what then? Saint Denis be my speed!—*donc vôtre
175 est France, et vous êtes mienne.*[4] It is as easy for me, Kate, to
conquer the kingdom as to speak so much more French. I shall
never move° thee in French, unless it be to laugh at me.   *persuade*

CATHERINE *Sauf votre honneur, le français que vous parlez, il est
meilleur que l'anglais lequel je parle.*[5]

180 KING HARRY No, faith, is't not, Kate. But thy speaking of my
tongue, and I thine, most truly-falsely, must needs be granted
to be much at one.° But Kate, dost thou understand thus much   *alike; united*
English? Canst thou love me?

CATHERINE I cannot tell.

185 KING HARRY Can any of your neighbours tell, Kate? I'll ask them.
Come, I know thou lovest me, and at night when you come
into your closet° you'll question this gentlewoman about me,   *bedchamber*
and I know, Kate, you will to her dispraise those parts° in me   *qualities*
that you love with your heart. But good Kate, mock me merci-
190 fully—the rather, gentle princess, because I love thee cruelly.
If ever thou be'st mine, Kate—as I have a saving faith within
me tells me thou shalt—I get thee with scrambling,° and thou   *fighting*

4. Translation of the last part of his previous speech.
5. Saving your honor, the French you speak is better than the English I speak.

must therefore needs prove a good soldier-breeder. Shall not
thou and I, between Saint Denis and Saint George,[6] com-
195 pound a boy, half-French half-English, that shall go to Con-
stantinople and take the Turk by the beard? Shall we not? What
sayst thou, my fair flower-de-luce?[7]

CATHERINE   I do not know dat.

KING HARRY   No, 'tis hereafter to know, but now to promise. Do
200 but now promise, Kate, you will endeavour for your French
part of such a boy, and for my English moiety° take the word   half
of a king and a bachelor. How answer you, *la plus belle Cather-*
ine du monde, mon très chère et divine déesse?[8]

CATHERINE   Your *majesté 'ave faux*° French enough to deceive   false
205 de most *sage demoiselle*° dat is *en France.*   maiden

KING HARRY   Now fie upon my false French! By mine honour,
in true English, I love thee, Kate. By which honour I dare not
swear thou lovest me, yet my blood° begins to flatter me that   instinct
thou dost, notwithstanding the poor and untempering° effect of   ungratiating
210 my visage. Now beshrew° my father's ambition! He was think-   curse
ing of civil wars when he got me; therefore was I created with
a stubborn outside, with an aspect° of iron, that when I come   a face
to woo ladies I fright them. But in faith, Kate, the elder I wax
the better I shall appear. My comfort is that old age, that ill
215 layer-up° of beauty, can do no more spoil upon my face. Thou   preserver
hast me, if thou hast me, at the worst, and thou shalt wear me,
if thou wear me, better and better; and therefore tell me, most
fair Catherine, will you have me? Put off your maiden blushes,
avouch the thoughts of your heart with the looks of an empress,
220 take me by the hand and say, 'Harry of England, I am thine'—
which word thou shalt no sooner bless mine ear withal, but I
will tell thee aloud, 'England is thine, Ireland is thine, France
is thine, and Henry Plantagenet is thine'—who, though I speak
it before his face, if he be not fellow° with the best king; thou   equal
225 shalt find the best king of good fellows. Come, your answer in
broken music°—for thy voice is music and thy English broken.   music in parts
Therefore, queen of all, Catherine, break thy mind to me in
broken English: wilt thou have me?

CATHERINE   Dat is as it shall please de *roi mon père.*°   King my father

230 KING HARRY   Nay, it will please him well, Kate. It shall please
him, Kate.

CATHERINE   Den it sall also content me.

KING HARRY   Upon that I kiss your hand, and I call you my
queen.

235 CATHERINE *Laissez, mon seigneur, laissez, laissez! Ma foi, je ne*
veux point que vous abbaissez votre grandeur en baisant la main
d'une de votre seigneurie indigne serviteur. Excusez-moi, je vous
supplie, mon treis-puissant seigneur.[9]

KING HARRY   Then I will kiss your lips, Kate.

240 CATHERINE   *Les dames et demoiselles pour être baisées devant*
leurs noces, il n'est pas la coutume de France.°   (translated below)

KING HARRY [*to* ALICE]   Madam my interpreter, what says she?

ALICE   Dat it is not be de *façon pour les*° ladies of France—I   fashion for the
cannot tell vat is *baiser en*° Anglish.   "kiss" in

---

6. Patron saints of France and England.
7. Fleur-de-lis, French national emblem.
8. The most beautiful Catherine in the world, my very
dear and divine goddess.

9. Stop, my lord, stop, stop! My faith, I do not want you
to lower your grandeur by kissing the hand of one of
your humble servants. Excuse me, I beseech you, my
very powerful lord.

245 KING HARRY   To kiss.

ALICE   Your *majesté entend* bettre *que moi.*[1]

KING HARRY   It is not a fashion for the maids in France to kiss
before they are married, would she say?

ALICE   *Oui, vraiment.*°   *Yes, truly*

250 KING HARRY   O Kate, nice° customs curtsy to great kings. Dear   *fastidious*
Kate, you and I cannot be confined within the weak list° of a   *barrier*
country's fashion. We are the makers of manners, Kate, and the
liberty that follows our places stops the mouth of all find-faults,
as I will do yours, for upholding the nice fashion of your coun-

255 try in denying me a kiss. Therefore, patiently and yielding. [*He
kisses her*] You have witchcraft in your lips, Kate. There is more
eloquence in a sugar touch of them than in the tongues of the
French Council, and they should sooner persuade Harry of
England than a general petition of monarchs. Here comes

260 your father.

           Enter KING [CHARLES, QUEEN ISABEL, *the Duke of* BUR-
           GUNDY,] *and the French* [*and*] *English lords*

BURGUNDY   God save your majesty. My royal cousin, teach you
our princess English?

KING HARRY   I would have her learn, my fair cousin, how per-
fectly I love her, and that is good English.

265 BURGUNDY   Is she not apt?

KING HARRY   Our tongue is rough, coz,° and my condition is not   *kinsman*
smooth, so that having neither the voice nor the heart of flattery
about me I cannot so conjure up the spirit of love in her that
he will appear in his true likeness.

270 BURGUNDY   Pardon the frankness of my mirth, if I answer you for
that. If you would conjure in her, you must make a circle;[2] if
conjure up love in her in his true likeness, he must appear
naked and blind.° Can you blame her then, being a maid yet   (*like Cupid, god of love*)
rosed over with the virgin crimson of modesty, if she deny the

275 appearance of a naked blind boy in her naked seeing self? It
were, my lord, a hard condition for a maid to consign to.

KING HARRY   Yet they do wink° and yield, as love is blind and   *close their eyes*
enforces.

BURGUNDY   They are then excused, my lord, when they see not

280 what they do.

KING HARRY   Then, good my lord, teach your cousin to consent
winking.

BURGUNDY   I will wink on her to consent, my lord, if you will
teach her to know my meaning. For maids, well summered

285 and warm kept, are like flies at Bartholomew-tide:° blind,   *August 24*
though they have their eyes. And then they will endure han-
dling, which before would not abide looking on.

KING HARRY   This moral ties me over to time and a hot summer,
and so I shall catch the fly, your cousin, in the latter end,[3] and

290 she must be blind too.

BURGUNDY   As love is, my lord, before that it loves.

KING HARRY   It is so. And you may, some of you, thank love for
my blindness, who cannot see many a fair French city for one
fair French maid that stands in my way.

---

1. Your majesty understands better than I.
2. By embracing her (sorcerers drew circles to call up
devils).
3. At last; in the backside.

295 KING CHARLES Yes, my lord, you see them perspectively,[4] the
 cities turned into a maid—for they are all girdled with maiden
 walls that war hath never entered.
KING HARRY Shall Kate be my wife?
KING CHARLES So please you.
300 KING HARRY I am content, so the maiden° cities you talk of may   *unconquered*
 wait on her: so the maid that stood in the way for my wish shall
 show me the way to my will.
KING CHARLES We have consented to all terms of reason.
KING HARRY Is't so, my lords of England?
305 WARWICK The King hath granted every article:
 His daughter first, and so in sequel all,
 According to their firm proposèd natures.
EXETER Only he hath not yet subscribèd° this: *signed to*
 where your majesty demands that the King of France, having
310 any occasion to write for matter of grant,° shall name your high-   *in formal documents*
 ness in this form and with this addition: [*reads*] in French,
 Notre très cher fils Henri, Roi d'Angleterre, Héritier de France,
 and thus in Latin, *Praeclarissimus filius noster Henricus, Rex
 Angliae et Haeres Franciae*.[5]
315 KING CHARLES Nor this I have not, brother, so denied,
 But your request shall make me let it pass.
KING HARRY I pray you then, in love and dear alliance,
 Let that one article rank with the rest,
 And thereupon give me your daughter.
320 KING CHARLES Take her, fair son, and from her blood raise up
 Issue° to me, that the contending kingdoms   *Offspring*
 Of France and England, whose very shores look pale
 With envy of each other's happiness,
 May cease their hatred, and this dear conjunction°   *loving union*
325 Plant neighbourhood° and Christian-like accord   *neighborliness*
 In their sweet bosoms, that never war advance
 His bleeding sword 'twixt England and fair France.
ALL Amen.
KING HARRY Now welcome, Kate, and bear me witness all
330 That here I kiss her as my sovereign Queen.
 Flourish
QUEEN ISABEL God, the best maker of all marriages,
 Combine your hearts in one, your realms in one.
 As man and wife, being two, are one in love,
 So be there 'twixt your kingdoms such a spousal
335 That never may ill office° or fell° jealousy,   *bad action / cruel*
 Which troubles oft the bed of blessèd marriage,
 Thrust in between the paction° of these kingdoms   *agreement*
 To make divorce of their incorporate league;
 That English may as French, French Englishmen,
340 Receive each other, God speak this 'Amen'.
ALL Amen.
KING HARRY Prepare we for our marriage. On which day,
 My lord of Burgundy, we'll take your oath,
 And all the peers', for surety of our leagues.

4. In a lens that produces optical illusions.
5. Our very dear son Henry, King of England, heir of France.

345 Then shall I swear to Kate, and you to me,
And may our oaths well kept and prosp'rous be.

Sennet.° Exeunt Ceremonial trumpet call

Epilogue

Enter chorus[1]

chorus   Thus far with rough and all-unable pen
Our bending° author hath pursued the story,   (over a desk)
In little room confining mighty men,
Mangling by starts the full course of their glory.
5   Small time, but in that small most greatly lived
This star of England. Fortune made his sword,
By which the world's best garden he achieved,
And of it left his son imperial lord.
Henry the Sixth, in infant bands° crowned king   swaddling clothes
10   Of France and England, did this king succeed,
Whose state so many had the managing
That they lost France and made his England bleed,
Which oft our stage hath shown[2]—and, for their sake,
In your fair minds let this acceptance take.°   [*Exit*]   this play find favor

Additional Passages

The Dauphin / Bourbon variant, which usually involves only the speech prefixes,
has several consequences for the dialogue and structure of 4.5. Following are the
edited Folio and quarto versions of this scene.

A. Folio

Enter constable, orléans, bourbon, dauphin, *and*
rambures

constable   *O diable!*
orléans   *O Seigneur! Le jour est perdu, tout est perdu.*
dauphin   *Mort de ma vie!* All is confounded, all.
Reproach and everlasting shame
5   Sits mocking in our plumes.

A short alarum

O méchante fortune! Do not run away.   [*Exit* rambures]
constable   Why, all our ranks are broke.
dauphin   O perdurable shame! Let's stab ourselves:
Be these the wretches that we played at dice for?
10   orléans   Is this the king we sent to for his ransom?
bourbon   Shame, an eternall shame, nothing but shame!
Let us die in pride. In once more, back again!
And he that will not follow Bourbon now,
Let him go home, and with his cap in hand
15   Like a base leno hold the chamber door,
Whilst by a slave no gentler than my dog
His fairest daughter is contaminated.
constable   Disorder that hath spoiled us, friend us now,
Let us on heaps go offer up our lives.
20   orléans   We are enough yet living in the field
To smother up the English in our throngs,

---

1. The following lines form a sonnet.
2. In *1 Henry VI, The First Part of the Contention* (*2*

Henry VI), *Richard Duke of York* (*3 Henry VI*), *and*
Richard III.

> If any order might be thought upon.
> BOURBON   The devil take order now. I'll to the throng.
> Let life be short, else shame will be too long.   *Exeunt*

B. Quarto

> *Enter the four French lords:* [*the* CONSTABLE, ORLÉANS,
>   BOURBON, *and* GEBON]
> GEBON   *O diabello!*°   devil
> CONSTABLE   *Mort de ma vie!*
> ORLÉANS   O what a day is this!
> BOURBON   *O jour de honte,*° all is gone, all is lost.   day of shame
> 5 CONSTABLE   We are enough yet living in the field
>   To smother up the English,
>   If any order might be thought upon.
> BOURBON   A plague of order! Once more to the field!
>   And he that will not follow Bourbon now,
> 10   Let him go home, and with his cap in hand,
>   Like a base leno hold the chamber door,
>   Whilst by a slave no gentler than my dog
>   His fairest daughter is contaminated.
>   CONSTABLE   Disorder that hath spoiled us, right us now.
> 15   Come we in heaps, we'll offer up our lives
>   Unto these English, or else die with fame.
> BOURBON   Come, come along.
>   Let's die with honour, our shame doth last too long.   *Exeunt*

TRAGEDIES

Shakespearean Tragedy

by

STEPHEN GREENBLATT

Seven years after Shakespeare's death, two of his repertory-company colleagues, John Heminges and Henry Condell, undertook to collect and print his plays in a single large volume, the First Folio. They chose not to present the plays in either chronological or alphabetical order but rather to organize them in three large genres or literary categories: comedies, histories, and tragedies. In the latter category, they included eleven plays: *Coriolanus, Titus Andronicus, Romeo and Juliet, Timon of Athens, Julius Caesar, Macbeth, Hamlet, King Lear, Othello, Antony and Cleopatra,* and *Cymbeline*. This last play, with a happy ending that resolves the dark dilemmas of a tangled plot, is now most often called a "romance," and it remains something of a surprise that the original editors did not include it with two roughly similar plays, *The Winter's Tale* and *The Tempest*, which they grouped with the comedies. The ten remaining plays in Heminges and Condell's tragedies category constitute the broadly accepted canon of Shakespearean tragedy.

The inclusion of *Cymbeline* among the Folio's tragedies signals the fact that there is nothing fixed or absolute about the boundaries of Shakespearean genres. During Shakespeare's lifetime three other of his plays—*3 Henry VI, Richard III,* and *Richard II*—were published as tragedies. Almost all modern editors follow the Folio editors in renaming and reclassifying them as histories. The classification does not mean that Shakespeare's tragedies are necessarily less historical than his histories or that his histories are necessarily less tragic than his tragedies; it only means that the plays Heminges and Condell termed "histories" are all based on English history after the Norman Conquest of 1066. Many, though not all, of the tragedies are also based on historical sources—classical history, pre-Conquest British history, Danish and Scottish history. (*King Lear* had been published before the Folio as a "history," and *Hamlet* had been printed twice as a "tragical history").

Generic boundaries were convenient, but they were easily crossed, and there was ample room, then as now, for disagreement and bafflement. *Troilus and Cressida* was printed first as a history. The Folio editors had their doubts: they renamed the play *The Tragedy of Troilus and Cressida*. But this renaming did not solve the problem of a play that seemed to call all generic categories into question: evidently perplexed and unable to come up with a solution, the editors decided not to list the play in any of the categories of the Folio's title page but instead simply to place it—unheralded—between the histories and the tragedies. Most modern editors now classify the play as a comedy, sometimes as a "problem comedy." But under enough pressure, all of Shakespeare's plays begin to seem like "problems."

More than two thousand years ago, in the *Poetics*, the Greek philosopher Aristotle came up with some of the key analytical terms for understanding the strange and compelling type of drama called tragedy. The core of a tragedy, Aristotle thought, was its action. Through the crafting of a plot of appropriate scale and coherence—neither too vast and complex nor too narrow—the successful playwright created the artful *mimesis*, or "imitation," of an action. The play's central character, a person of high rank, should be neither perfectly virtuous nor irremediably vicious; moral nature somewhere between the two extremes was best suited to engage the audience in a powerful way. The greatest tragedies—for Aristotle, the supreme example was Sophocles' *Oedipus*

Rex—featured a fatal *blunder* or character *flaw* that brings the hero to destruction; a sudden *reversal* of fortune; and a powerful moment of *recognition* in which ignorance gives way to a terrible knowledge. The effect for the audience was an intense emotional purging, or *catharsis,* in the experience of pity and fear.

Each of these terms has some purchase on Shakespeare's tragedies, with their remarkable array of flawed heroes, their powerful plot twists and painful bursts of psychological and moral illumination, and their wrenching emotional effects. Yet the playwright's great achievement as a whole does not comfortably fit the philosopher's influential descriptive account. The elegantly chiseled structural design in which Aristotle was most interested is powerfully present in Shakespeare—in the astonishing reversal of fortune brought about in *Julius Caesar* by Antony's funeral oration, for example, or in the blinded Gloucester's recognition in *King Lear* that the son he had trusted has betrayed him—but this design is often overshadowed by the sheer magnitude of the events and the passions directly represented onstage. Even an early play like *Titus Andronicus,* though set in the ancient world and full of classical allusions, pulls sharply away from the conception of tragedy formulated by Aristotle and elaborated by his followers into a set of rules. For Shakespeare, the form of tragedy, the element central to the *Poetics,* is only a slender, fragile bark bobbing on a chaotic, destructive, and ecstatic sea of suffering. The playwright who begins *Titus Andronicus* with the spectacle of an enraged father stabbing his son to death was directly in touch with energies in the tragic theater that the philosopher only saw through a glass darkly.

How did it happen? How did Shakespeare create a series of stupendous tragedies that continue to haunt audiences and readers? The answer certainly does not lie in any well-defined collective understanding, shared with his contemporaries, of what constituted a successful play in this genre. To be sure, in the late 1580s, Shakespeare's distinguished contemporary, Sir Philip Sidney, drew on Aristotle's *Poetics* to pen an important attack on the tragedies currently being performed on the English stage. These native tragedies, Sidney complained, fail to observe the proper "unities of place and time." Instead of depicting only a single, well-demarcated place, the stage typically represents so many different places—Asia on one side and Africa on the other, as he

Tamora pleading for her sons, the earliest illustration of a Shakespeare work. From Henry Peacham's woodcuts for *Titus Andronicus* (c. 1595).

puts it—that a performer, on entering, has to begin by saying where he is, or the audience will be completely lost. "Now ye shall have three ladies walk to gather flowers," Sidney writes, warming to his theme,

and then we must believe the stage to be a garden. By and by we hear news of shipwreck in the same place, and then we are to blame if we accept it not for a rock. . . . While in the meantime two armies fly in, represented with four swords and bucklers [shields], and then what hard heart will not receive it for a pitched [battle]field?

The same criticisms apply to the representation of time: in the course of the brief interval that the audience watches a play, a young prince and princess fall in love, marry, and have a child who grows up and himself falls in love, marries, and is ready to start a family of his own. "How absurd it is!" And to compound these errors, the aristocratic Sidney notes with disgust, English playwrights, by "mingling kings and clowns," do not even manage to write "right tragedies" or "right comedies." "Clowns"—country bumpkins fit only to laugh at—are thrust in "by head and shoulders, to play a part in majestical matters, with neither decency nor discretion, so as neither the admiration and commiseration, nor the right sportfulness, is by their mongrel tragicomedy obtained."

That Sidney, who was killed in battle in 1586, unwittingly describes important features of *King Lear, Antony and Cleopatra,* or *Cymbeline*—plays written years after his death—signals the fact that Shakespeare was indifferent to the classical norms for tragedy. In his tragedies (and comedies), Shakespeare was drawing on the native theatrical traditions disdained by Sidney, traditions that enabled the playwright, when he wished, to mingle kings and clowns and to use the bare stage to represent multiple places and variable stretches of time. The great medieval English "mystery cycles" had undertaken to stage the whole Christian vision of the world, from the Creation to the Crucifixion to the Last Judgment, and the secular dramas that arose in the mid-sixteenth century entertained English audiences with sprawling stories drawn from the chronicles of both national and world history.

In Shakespeare, the action shifts effortlessly in *Julius Caesar* from the Capitol in Rome to Sardis in western Turkey and then to the fateful battlefield near Philippi in Macedonia; *Othello* begins in Venice and moves to Cyprus, where the Venetian forces are bracing for a Turkish assault that never materializes; *Antony and Cleopatra* shuttles restlessly between Rome and Egypt, alighting as well in a bewildering array of army camps and ships moored off the Greek and Italian coasts. Time is comparably flexible: there are scenes—for example, the assassination of Duncan in *Macbeth*—in which the seconds seem to tick by with agonizing slowness; at other moments, years pass without notice. And in one celebrated instance—*Othello*—time seems both short and long, so that events are at once precipitous and drawn out. The audience disorientation that worries Sidney seems to Shakespeare to be of no concern whatever: the playwright is altogether confident that he can give the audience exactly what information it needs exactly when it needs it.

The aristocratic distaste for the mingling of kings and clowns is also entirely alien to Shakespeare, whose tragedies routinely bring together figures from the opposite ends of the social spectrum. Here, again, Shakespeare could draw upon the native theatrical tradition, with secular tales that interwove the lives of beggars and princes and religious dramas that emphasized the homely, often comic presence of simple folk in the presence of transcendent suffering. It is not that Shakespeare is indifferent to social status: on the contrary, most of his tragedies center on the fate of charismatic monarchs, princes, and military heroes. (The most significant exception, *Romeo and Juliet,* concerns the sole heirs to two of the wealthiest and most socially prominent families in their city.) But some of his most powerful tragic effects arise in such encounters as the ruined Roman general Titus Andronicus with the poor pigeon-bearing "clown," Hamlet with the gravediggers, Lear with the Fool, or Cleopatra with the rustic who brings her the poisonous snakes with which she will commit suicide.

Sidney feared that encounters of this kind would undermine the "majestical" dignity of tragedy and leave in its stead "mongrel tragicomedy." Shakespeare seems to have enthusiastically embraced the mongrelization of genres. His comedies are shot through with pain and the fear of death; his tragedies, even the direst of them, echo with strange laughter. In a characteristically ghastly moment in a ghastly play, Titus Andronicus is told that if he cuts off his hand and sends it to the emperor, the lives of his two sons will be spared. When a few moments later he gets back his severed hand, along with the heads of his sons, Shakespeare scripted for him this line: "Ha, ha, ha!" (3.1.263).

As this extreme example suggests, the laughter in Shakespearean tragedy is not only the incidental effect of the puns and antics of the clowns; it is pervasive and structural. The gulling of Othello—an older man (and an outlandish stranger) married to a beautiful young woman—is a traditional comic plot, as the conniving villain Iago understands. "It cannot be long that Desdemona should continue her love to the Moor," he confidently predicts; "She must change for youth" (1.3.335–36, 342). In *King Lear,* old Lear and Gloucester attempt to block the desires of their children, exactly as aged fathers always do in comedy. The illegitimate Edmond invites the audience to laugh at the cleverness with which he will topple his legitimate brother and deceive his foolish father:

> Well then,
> Legitimate Edgar, I must have your land.
> Our father's love is to the bastard Edmond
> As to th' legitimate. Fine word, 'legitimate'.
> Well, my legitimate, if this letter speed
> And my invention thrive, Edmond the base
> Shall top th' legitimate. I grow, I prosper.
> Now gods, stand up for bastards!
>
> *(Tragedy of King Lear* 1.2.15–22)

This is the stuff of comedy.

Yet *King Lear* and *Othello* are unmistakably tragedies; indeed, they are among the most searing, soul-searching tragedies ever written. The comic elements are real enough, but they serve only to enrich the human complexity, intensify the sense of irony, and highlight the suffering and loss that characterize these remarkable plays. Their impact derives not from any patrolling of generic boundaries but from an overwhelming emotional power.

Shakespeare's supreme confidence in his ability to wield this power seems bound up with the reckless daring with which he laces his tragedies with comedy. Near the end of the play, with his fate closing in upon him, Hamlet has time to exchange witticisms with the gravediggers and to tease the fatuous courtier Osric. In *Antony and Cleopatra,* the despairing hero, rapidly bleeding to death, has time to bestow one farewell kiss on the Egyptian queen for whom he has given up the whole world. But Cleopatra, safely locked inside her monument, refuses to come down, for fear that she will be captured. Instead, she and her women decide to pull Antony up—"O quick," he gasps, "or I am gone!"—and as they struggle to do so, Cleopatra makes a joke: "Here's sport indeed. How heavy weighs my lord! / Our strength is all gone into heaviness" (4.16.32–34). The playwright who could at that charged moment call attention to his aging hero's bulk and insert a pun on "heaviness" (at once weight and sadness) was not playing by any conventional generic rules. There survives an intriguing trace of Shakespeare's critical reflection on how far he could go in the mingling of genres. In 1672, long after the playwright's death, the poet John Dryden remarked that "Shakespeare showed the best of his skill in his Mercutio, and he said himself, that he was forced to kill him in the third Act, to prevent being killed by him." If the report that reached Dryden can be trusted, then Shakespeare registered the extent to which the mocking spirit of comedy, in the person of Mercutio, was threatening to subvert *Romeo and Juliet.*

What is perhaps most immediately striking about Shakespeare's tragedies, taken as a group, is how unlike one another they are. There is no sense of formula and startlingly little repetition. As critics have observed, the hero of any one of these plays, tormented by insoluble dilemmas, would have had no difficulty resolving the crises of another. Before the ghost had vanished from the ramparts, Macbeth would have unseamed Claudius from the nave to the chops, while Hamlet would in Act 5 still be brooding on whether or not to kill Scotland's king. It is not simply that the heroes are remarkably different in their passions, their fears, and their longings; the world that each of them inhabits is utterly distinct and incommensurable. Romeo and Juliet's Verona seems to belong to an entirely different universe from Lear's Britain or Hamlet's Elsinore; Coriolanus and Brutus are both inhabitants of Rome, but they would not recognize each other's city.

The tragedies are, to be sure, the works of the same person. Thus, for example, in *Antony and Cleopatra,* written fairly late in Shakespeare's career, we can identify themes that the play shares with some of the earlier tragedies:

- with *Romeo and Juliet,* a fascination with a passionate love that overwhelms traditional, deep-seated enmities before finally being overwhelmed by them
- with *Julius Caesar,* a fascination with the lives of those who ruled the world, men and women who are fully aware of their historical significance, even as they grapple with the familiar desires and fears, the egotism, insecurity, and jealousy of ordinary mortals
- with *Hamlet* and *Macbeth,* a fascination with dangerously ambiguous situations and an obsessive interest in the seductive, hidden power of female sexuality
- with *King Lear,* a fascination with the loss of power attendant on aging, and an inquiry into the nature of service
- with *Othello,* a fascination with the outsider, with the contrast of cultures, with the exotic

But the differences in the tragic territory marked off by *Antony and Cleopatra* are still more notable:

- The protagonists are decidedly not young lovers confined by their parents' choices for them.
- The possession of unlimited power is not finally the object of passion but gives way to something else.
- Ambiguity is not, or not necessarily, a mark of evil, and the power of female sexuality is more celebrated than feared.
- Aging is a sign not of weakening but of a shift of interest and mood.
- The exoticism is not tamed or destroyed but remains the object of longing.

The consequence is that this play feels entirely distinct—in its rhythms, its preoccupations, and its overarching mood—from anything that had gone before.

There is a very basic feature that the plays, taken together, do share: Shakespeare's tragedies all move toward an ending in death, just as his comedies move toward an ending in marriage. The death in question is principally, though usually not exclusively, the death of the hero; often there are others—on occasion, many others—who, in the course of the play, accompany him on the path to destruction. Some of the corpses of those who litter the stage are of those—Iago's pawn Roderigo in *Othello,* Goneril's repellent steward Oswald in *King Lear,* the hateful Demetrius and Chiron in *Titus Andronicus*—who have willingly served the malevolent designs of the major villains. The villains themselves end up either dead or, like Aaron the Moor and Iago, on their way to a gruesome execution.

But it is not only the evil who join the heroes of the tragedies in the ranks of death. There are many entirely innocent victims, from the mutilated Lavinia to the loving Des-

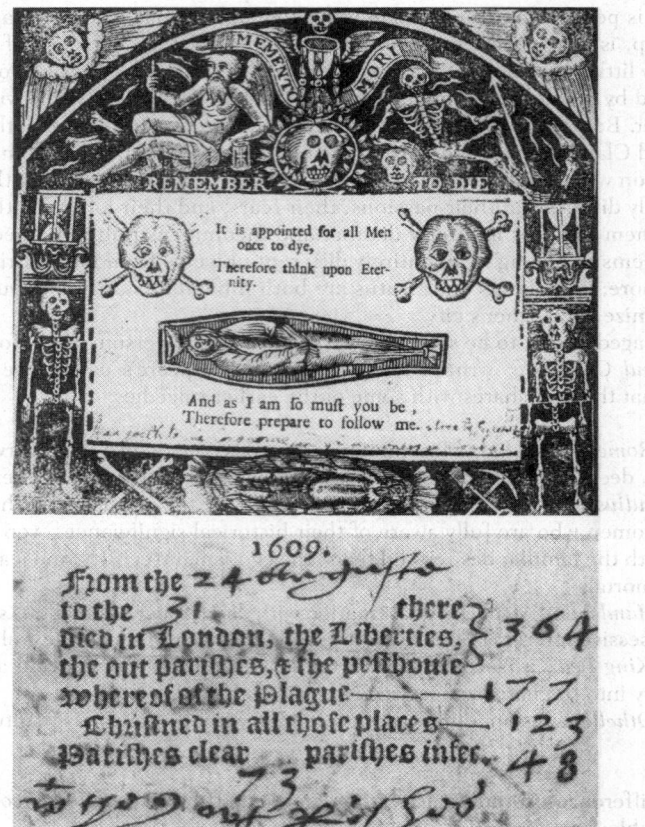

Top: Woodcut memento mori (seventeenth century). *Bottom:* Printed form for recording mortalities and christenings in London and environs (1609).

demona, from Cordelia to Lady Macduff and her sweet young children. These defenseless women and children are the objects of cunning plots and premeditated violence. There are others who simply find themselves at the wrong place at the wrong time: the simple rustic who brings the emperor a gift of pigeons in *Titus,* the wet nurse who carries Aaron's baby to him in that same play, Cinna the poet in *Julius Caesar,* and grieving Paris in *Romeo and Juliet,* who has come to strew flowers on Juliet's grave.

The heroes of several of Shakespeare's tragedies—Titus Andronicus, Macbeth, and Coriolanus—are virtual killing machines who are responsible for much of the mayhem around them. "I am in blood / Stepped in so far," says Macbeth halfway through the play, "that, should I wade no more, / Returning were as tedious as go o'er" (3.4.135–37). And the last words that Coriolanus hears, as the swords are thrust into his body, are the enraged cries of those he has irreparably harmed: "He killed my son! My daughter! He killed my cousin / Marcus! He killed my father!" (5.6.122–23). But even those tragic heroes who are not professional killers very often cause, directly or indirectly, the deaths of those around them. The sword that Hamlet blindly thrusts through the arras, in the hope of killing his wicked uncle, is a fit emblem: Hamlet's blow kills not his uncle but rather Polonius, whose death in turn leads to the miserable end of his daughter, Ophelia. Before the uncle is finally killed—both stabbed and poisoned by Hamlet—Ophelia's brother, Laertes, will also die, as will Hamlet's mother, Gertrude, and his school friends Rosencranz and Guildenstern. Hamlet, too, is fatally wounded, and his best friend, Horatio, determined to follow him to the grave, is stopped from suicide only by Hamlet's urgent plea:

Scenes from William Sampson's *The Vow Breaker* (1636).

> Absent thee from felicity a while,
> And in this harsh world draw thy breath in pain
> To tell my story.
>
> (5.2.289–91)

Hamlet evidently views death, his own and that of others, as "felicity." In the course of the play, he has somehow moved from tormented, anxious irresolution to a quiet acceptance of his own fate. "If it be now," he tells Horatio,

> 'tis not to come. If it be not to come, it will be now. If it be not now, yet it will come. The readiness is all.
>
> (5.2.158–60)

But is the audience of Shakespeare's tragedies meant share this view? In certain of the plays, the answer seems to be yes. At the end of *King Lear,* when the old man's heart finally fails, one of the bystanders tries desperately to revive him, but Kent, who has witnessed firsthand the whole course of Lear's atrocious sufferings, protests:

> O, let him pass. He hates him
> That would upon the rack of this tough world
> Stretch him out longer.
> (*The Tragedy of King Lear* 5.3.287–89)

If life is an instrument of torture, then death is the merciful cessation of pain. Something of the same could be said of Othello, for whom the only imaginable future is one of unendurable remorse, rage, and self-pity, or for Macbeth, whose life has become

> a tale
> Told by an idiot, full of sound and fury,
> Signifying nothing.
>
> (5.5.25–27)

So, too, Timon of Athens, in his miserable cave at the end of his life, feels only emptiness, contempt, and a longing for extinction. "Graves only be men's works," he declares in misanthropic disgust, "and death their gain" (5.2.107). And if, less despairing than these characters, Cleopatra can imagine a future, it is one in which she will be ruthlessly humiliated, paraded in the triumphal procession of her Roman conquerors and given over to the vulgar amusement of the mob. "Bravest at the last," Caesar says admiringly of her suicide, "She levelled at our purposes"—that is, she understood the fate that was in store for her—"and, being royal, / Took her own way" (5.2.325–27).

But this welcome death is by no means true for all of the tragic protagonists. It is not clear that it is even true of Hamlet. Ordering that the dead prince be lifted up "like a soldier," Fortinbras says that Hamlet was likely, "had he been put on"—that is, had he been put to the test—to have acted "most royally" (5.2.340–42). While we may doubt the assessment of Hamlet's military aptitude, Fortinbras's words remind us of the hero's thwarted ambition to succeed his father as king of Denmark and remind us, too, of the hopes that have been cut off by his death and of all that remains to be said. "O, I could tell you," the dying Hamlet begins to say to his friend, only to realize that there is no time left: "But let it be. Horatio, I am dead" (5.2.279–80).

Antony displaying Caesar's wounds. From the frontispiece of Shakespeare's *Julius Caesar* (Nicholas Rowe ed., 1709).

If in some of Shakespeare's tragedies, death comes as a relief or a welcome release, in others it comes as a shattering interruption. In *Julius Caesar*, Brutus, facing certain military defeat, chooses to end his life: "Our enemies have beat us to the pit," he acknowledges; "It is more worthy to leap in ourselves / Than tarry till they push us" (5.5.23–25). This end is neither the fulfillment of his deepest wish nor a release from his misery. It is the final, agonizing failure of his cherished dream to save the Roman Republic. And Hamlet's resignation or Lear's exhaustion are entirely alien to Romeo and Juliet, who are only beginning to savor the joys of their passionate love and whose death is precipitated by a series of ghastly accidents.

There is, then, no typical form of "tragic death" in Shakespeare: no characteristic end, no consistent stance, and no single audience response. Nor are all deaths represented: the death of the martyr, for example, sublimely fervent in religious belief, does not occur in Shakespearean tragedies, nor does the death of someone reduced to misery by abject poverty and illness. So, too, an entirely accidental end—the hero knocked down by a runaway horse or struck dead by lightning—is outside the range of ends regarded as tragic in the plays.

The death of the protagonists in these plays all bear a significant relation to everything that has come before—that is, to their choices, their suffering, their whole way of experiencing the world. Many of the heroes and heroines of Shakespearean tragedy actively choose death by committing suicide; and even when they do not kill themselves, they go to their deaths, like Macbeth or Coriolanus, as if they had chosen to do so. The principal figures seem to have a stake in "owning" their own deaths, as if they were determined to make their ends as expressive of their lives as all their other words and actions have been.

This determination does not preclude the sense of fatality that haunts many of the protagonists, from the "star-crossed lovers" Romeo and Juliet to Brutus, who senses Caesar's ghost haunting the battlefield at Philippi, to Macbeth, whose destiny in some obscure way is linked to the obscene connivance of the Weird Sisters. "The charm's wound up" (1.3.35), the Weird Sisters sing, just before Macbeth makes his first appearance: perhaps then the whole bloody sequence of events that follows is only the inexorable enactment of what they have predetermined and set in motion. That dismaying possibility is never laid to rest, and how could it be? After all, from a certain perspective, everything that happens in a Shakespearean tragedy has in reality been predetermined, set in motion by the master who has wound up the charm.

There are strange moments in these plays in which the principal characters seem to have an intimation of forces that are compelling them to act and react as they do, whether those forces are understood to be supernatural agents or some other invisible structural principle. "The time is out of joint," Hamlet cries, in the wake of his encounter with the ghost of his father; "O cursèd spite / That ever I was born to set it right!" (1.5.189–90). "As flies to wanton boys are we to th' gods," says the despairing Gloucester in King Lear;

The death of Pyramus and Thisbe. Woodcut from Ovid's *Metamorphoses* (Venice, 1538).

"They kill us for their sport" (*Tragedy* 4.1.37–38). But however intense these intimations may be, Shakespeare's protagonists do not passively submit to their fate, as if they were sleepwalking toward death. (There is in *Macbeth* a famous scene of sleepwalking, but it is not about fatalism but about nightmarish guilt.) Hamlet spends much of the play trying to establish for himself what he should do and on what grounds he should do it. Gloucester—who has always had a tendency to blame the gods or the stars for whatever goes wrong—attempts to take his fate in his own hands by throwing himself off Dover Cliff. And though at the end of his tragedy Macbeth grasps that he has been cunningly manipulated by the equivocations of witches who "palter with us in a double sense" (5.10.20), he does not even then simply conclude that he is the passive instrument of a malevolent fate. "Be these juggling fiends no more believed" (5.10.19), he says, and a moment later throws himself into a fight to the death: "Yet I will try the last" (5.10.32).

None of these actions precludes the possibility of a predetermined end, of course, but the characters themselves cannot and do not live as if they had no agency at all. They suffer intensely from what Hamlet calls the "slings and arrows of outrageous fortune" (3.1.60), but they are never merely victims. They always contribute to the catastrophe that befalls them, if only by setting in motion through some irreversible action an uncontrollable chain of events that brings devastation in its wake. This contribution reflects to a considerable degree the fact that almost all of Shakespeare's tragic protagonists are socially important people, people whose inherited rank, office, and wealth accustom them to the exercise of power. The power, as they learn to their cost, is never absolute—"They told me I was everything," the ruined Lear says, shivering from cold and fever—"'tis a lie, I am not ague-proof" (4.5.102). But they possess for the most part a quality that Kent, in disguise, claims to see in the face of Lear. "You have that in your countenance," Kent says, "which I would fain call master." "What's that?" Lear asks; and Kent's reply is a single word: "Authority" (*Tragedy* 1.4.24–27). The principal exceptions to this rule, Romeo and Juliet, do not possess such authority, and hence their fate seems more contingent than that of the other tragic heroes; but even here their determination to act upon their passion, whatever the cost, shapes their destiny.

The critic A. C. Bradley, whose 1904 book *Shakespearean Tragedy* remains the best single study of the subject, observes that in almost all of Shakespeare's tragic heroes there is "a marked one-sidedness, a predisposition in some particular direction; a total incapacity, in certain circumstances, of resisting the force which draws in this direction; a fatal tendency to identify the whole being with one interest, object, passion, or habit of mind." The heroes—most of them, at least—are driven to extremes, whether of love, ambition, generosity, anger, or some other intense emotion to which they devote the whole of their being.

"If there were reason for these miseries," cries Titus Andronicus, "Then into limits could I bind my woes" (3.1.218–19). But there are no limits: "I am the sea" (3.1.224). "But come what sorrow can," Romeo tells Friar Laurence,

> It cannot countervail the exchange of joy
> That one short minute gives me in her sight.
> Do thou but close our hands with holy words,
> Then love-devouring death do what he dare—
> It is enough I may but call her mine.
>
> (2.5.3–8)

Friar Laurence tries to rein in Romeo's reckless passion: "Love moderately" (2.5.14), he sagely advises. But such urgings of restraint, echoed in many of the plays, always fall on deaf ears.

The heroes are never figures of moderation; they are committed by nature and by choice to the experience of the absolute. "O my soul's joy," Othello exclaims, when he is reunited with Desdemona,

> If after every tempest come such calms,
> May the winds blow till they have wakened death,
> And let the labouring barque climb hills of seas
> Olympus-high, and duck again as low
> As hell's from heaven. If it were now to die
> 'Twere now to be most happy, for I fear
> My soul hath her content so absolute
> That not another comfort like to this
> Succeeds in unknown fate.
>
> (2.1.181–89)

Here as elsewhere the tragic hero exists in a world of immense heights and immense depths, a world in which they are willing to hazard everything: "and when I love thee not, / Chaos is come again" (3.3.92–93).

The chaos, when it comes, afflicts far more than the inner lives of the heroes. Shakespearean tragedies are political as well as psychological, the effect of brilliant plots as well as brilliant characters. They are concerned with dynastic struggles, as in *Hamlet, King Lear,* and *Macbeth;* with violent conflicts between social classes, as in *Coriolanus;* with world-historical events, as in *Julius Caesar;* with the clash of civilizations, as in *Antony and Cleopatra.* They are testing grounds for the nature and limits of fundamental human drives and values—love, hatred, revenge, generosity, the craving for power—and searching explorations of moral ambivalence.

The explorations center, of course, on the heroes, whose inward experience Shakespeare represents with unrivaled mastery. But they are by no means limited to these heroes. Each play is a complex hall of mirrors, cunningly constructed to examine certain key motivations and relationships from multiple perspectives. A son's fraught relationship to his father (and the memory of his father) is probed unforgettably in Hamlet's encounter with the ghost, but it is also explored in Laertes' and Fortinbras's dealings with their fathers. The mingled tyranny, gullibility, and suffering of Lear and his daughters are echoed in Gloucester and his sons. The political obsessions of Brutus are shared by Cassius, Casca, Trebonius, Decius, Metullus Cimber, and the other conspirators, each of whom, remarkably enough, is given just enough time to establish a distinct individual identity as historical agents.

The plays are not monologues: they all involve multiple subjectivities, and Shakespeare's amazing gifts enabled him to grant at least a touch of life to virtually anyone he brought onstage. We cannot reduce the plays to their title characters alone, any more than we can reduce the plays to a list of tragic themes. But it is obviously not an accident that while almost all of the comedies have playfully general titles like *The Comedy of Errors, As You Like It, Much Ado About Nothing,* and *All's Well That Ends Well,* the titles of the tragedies all insist on dominant individuals, as if intense individuation were itself part of the tragic burden of existence. So, too, among the multiple and tangled concerns of the plays, it is possible to identify certain recurrent preoccupations, even obsessions.

This introduction has dwelt on one of these, death, and anyone who reads the plays attentively can add others: an experience of radical vulnerability; an encounter with the intolerable; an ambivalent, destructive love; a seething hatred of beauty and goodness; a struggle against suicidal pessimism; a recognition of the strange, conjoined power and hollowness of language. A worthwhile account of a Shakespearean tragedy will depend not on ballooning generalizations but on a particular, local richness of apprehension, a grasp of the boundless intelligence with which these preoccupations are explored, and, above all perhaps, a savoring of the playwright's limitless poetic resources. At times, Shakespeare draws upon those resources to make his characters speak in an exalted idiom far removed from the language of the everyday, as when Othello speaks of himself as

924 ♦ SHAKESPEAREAN TRAGEDY

> one whose subdued eyes,
> Albeit unusèd to the melting mood,
> Drops tears as fast as the Arabian trees
> Their medicinable gum.
>
> (5.2.357–60)

At other times Shakespeare's characters, even when they are kings in a faraway land, speak in suffering accents that are as familiar and unbearable as one's own most intimate nightmares. At the close of *King Lear* (*Tragedy* 5.3.280–83), Shakespeare departed from all of his sources to provide a devastating vision of tragic desolation, the vision of a distraught father holding in his arms his dead child:

> No, no, no life?
> Why should a dog, a horse, a rat have life,
> And thou no breath at all? Thou'lt come no more.
> Never, never, never, never, never.

SELECTED BIBLIOGRAPHY

Belsey, Catherine. *The Subject of Tragedy: Identity and Difference in Renaissance Drama.* London: Methuen, 1985.

Bradley, A. C. *Shakespearean Tragedy: Lectures on "Hamlet," "Othello," "King Lear," "Macbeth."* 2nd ed. London: Macmillan, 1905.

Dollimore, Jonathan. *Radical Tragedy: Religion, Ideology, and Power in the Drama of Shakespeare and His Contemporaries.* 2nd ed. Durham, N.C.: Duke University Press, 1993.

Drakakis, John, ed. *Shakespearean Tragedy.* London: Longman, 1992.

Dutton, Richard, and Jean E. Howard, eds. *A Companion to Shakespeare's Works,* vol. I: *The Tragedies.* Malden, Mass.: Blackwell, 2003.

Frye, Northrop. *Fools of Time: Studies in Shakespearean Tragedy.* Toronto: University of Toronto Press, 1967.

Garner, Shirley Nelson, and Madelon Sprengnether eds. *Shakespearean Tragedy and Gender.* Bloomington: Indiana University Press, 1996.

Leggatt, Alexander. *Shakespeare's Tragedies: Violation and Identity.* Cambridge, Eng.: Cambridge University Press, 2005.

McEachern, Claire, ed. *The Cambridge Companion to Shakespearean Tragedy.* Cambridge, Eng.: Cambridge University Press, 2002.

Neill, Michael. *Issues of Death: Mortality and Identity in English Renaissance Tragedy.* Oxford: Clarendon, 1997.

Romeo and Juliet

Plato's dialogue *The Symposium* recounts a dinner party where the guests spent a long night in impassioned, brilliant philosophical conversation about love. By daybreak, most of the guests had fallen asleep, but Socrates, who had spoken with particularly luminous intelligence, was still awake, trying to prove that a single playwright was capable of writing both comedy and tragedy. As he clinched his case, his weary interlocutors nodded off to sleep. Thus we never learn the argument that Socrates was making for the convergence of the tragic and comic visions in one dramatist, and neither the ancient Greek nor the Roman world has left us an instance of that convergence. But we have its supreme embodiment in Shakespeare. The achievement is particularly striking in two plays probably written around 1595. Scholars have been unable to determine with certainty whether *Romeo and Juliet* was written before or after *A Midsummer Night's Dream;* one of Shakespeare's most delightful comedies and one of his most beloved tragedies appear to have been written at virtually the same time and out of some very similar materials.

In the entertainment performed for the newlyweds at the close of *A Midsummer Night's Dream,* the young lovers, Pyramus and Thisbe, are separated by a "vile wall." They attempt to elope together, but Pyramus, mistakenly thinking that Thisbe has been killed, rashly commits suicide, whereupon Thisbe in despair stabs herself. A strange way, it would seem, to celebrate festive nuptials, but Shakespeare's comedy continually triumphs over fears of rashness, mutability, and death by staging and laughing at them. The inept amateur actors call attention so crudely to the tragedy's artificiality and contrivance that it provokes derisive laughter: "This is the silliest stuff that ever I heard" (5.1.207).

In *Romeo and Juliet,* whose climax closely resembles that of Pyramus and Thisbe, Shakespeare does not shy away from artifice and contrivance. His tragedy is unusually dependent on coincidence, mischance, and accident to produce what the Chorus, in the sonnet that serves as the prologue, calls the lovers' "misadventured piteous overthrows." Nor does he forswear the note of witty, wicked parody that transformed the woes of Pyramus and Thisbe into an occasion for mirth. Romeo's friend Mercutio gives voice to an irrepressible spirit of mockery, a spirit that seems to challenge the very possibility of romantic love or tragic destiny. (There is a seventeenth-century report—it doesn't date from the playwright's own lifetime—that Shakespeare remarked that he was forced to kill Mercutio in the third act to prevent being killed by him.) But Shakespeare manages to make the story of his reckless, star-crossed lovers immensely moving, resistant at once to corrosive irony and to moralizing disapproval. He does so principally through his mastery of what the bumbling performers in *A Midsummer Night's Dream* conspicuously lack: the power of language to make and unmake the world.

It is this poetic power—"poetic" derives from the Greek word for "making"—that provides Shakespeare with the key to resolving the paradox addressed by Socrates in *The Symposium* and that enables him to transform his rather shopworn source materials into something rich and strange. The story of the ill-fated lovers from bitterly feuding families had been told many times in the sixteenth century by Italian and French writers and had already appeared more than once in English. Shakespeare's direct source is Arthur Brooke's *Tragicall Historye of Romeus and Juliet* (1562), a long, leaden English poem based on a French prose version by Pierre Boaistuau (1559), who was in turn adapting an Italian version by Bandello (1554), who in turn based his narrative on Luigi da Porto's version (1525) of a tale by Masuccio Salernitano (1476). Shakespeare follows the main outline of Brooke's narrative, although he makes many changes in the interests of theatrical compression and intensification. Hence the events that in Brooke take nine months are telescoped into a few days. The figure of Mercutio is brilliantly developed, as is the vulgar, meddling, earthy Nurse. Juliet, eighteen years old in Bandello's version and sixteen in Brooke's, is depicted as only thirteen, a young girl suddenly awakening to passionate desires that set her against the will of her family.

But it is principally by means of the incandescent brilliance of its language that *Romeo and Juliet* has earned its place as one of the greatest love stories in world literature. Shakespeare makes linguistic power figure thematically in the play by insisting on the crucial importance of naming and, more generally, by repeatedly calling attention to the force of verbal actions. This was by no means the playwright's private obsession. His play is the product of a rhetorical culture, a culture steeped in an awareness—in the philosopher J. L. Austin's phrase—of "how to do things with words." What are some of the things that characters do with words? For a start, they insult each other, a dangerous pastime of both servants and masters. They also invite one another (Capulet's favorite pastime); they confess (formally, to a priest; informally, to friends); they conjure; they curse; they make contracts; they vow; and, if they have the power of the prince, they banish. And through all of these verbal actions, no matter how serious or even deadly they may be, they constantly play with language.

Romeo and Juliet is saturated with language games: paradoxes, oxymorons, double entendres, rhyming tricks, verbal echoings, multiple puns. The obvious question is, why? One possible answer, proposed as early as the eighteenth century, is that Shakespeare could not resist: verbal wit was an addiction, an obsession, the object of an irrational passion. He could indulge this passion because a display of wit would appeal to those segments of the audience most attuned to rhetorical acrobatics. Another answer

Two gallants fight a duel in the street. From George Wither, *A Collection of Emblemes* (1635).

is that puns are a clarifying challenge, an assault on sentiments to test whether they are genuine or merely forced and empty. Hence Mercutio attempts to mock Romeo's passion with a set of ribald jests, jests that are reiterated unconsciously by the Nurse in such exclamations as "Stand up, stand up, stand an you be a man" (3.3.88). To survive the corrosive effect of such mockery is a measure of true love and a sign of authenticity: "He jests at scars that never felt a wound" (2.1.43).

But this explanation for the tragedy's pervasive wordplay is not wholly adequate, since at the height of both their love and their despair, Romeo and Juliet also pun. Romeo on the verge of suicide plays with the word "engrossing" (death as wholesaler; monopolist; lawyer); Juliet plays with the word "restorative" (the kiss as medicine; poison; death; resurrection); and both play with the Elizabethan "die" as a term for "orgasm." Here wordplay functions not to deflate but to cram into brief utterances more meanings than language would ordinarily hold and to force us to confront both unresolvable contradictions and hidden connections. That is, puns work to juxtapose or hold open possibilities that normally are viewed as mutually exclusive. Thus they may be said to reach both a psychological and a thematic level at which oppositions—pain and joy, loss and restoration, love and death, comedy and tragedy—are canceled.

Wordplay would be impossible in a language in which words were strictly bound to things in a perfect correspondence between naming and nature. Punning is possible only if there is some slippage in sound and meaning, so that one sign can refer to two or more objects or, as Mercutio wittily demonstrates in his Queen Mab speech, to nothing at all. Yet wordplay can also suggest surprising linkages and secret realities. Hence, for example, the punning in Romeo and Juliet's initial exchange at the Capulet ball derives its power from the lovers' conviction that there really is an essential relation between the touching of their hands and lips and a religious experience. This relation, invisible to the ordinary social world around them, is disclosed in the language game they spontaneously play, a game that takes the form of a shared sonnet.

Even to speak of this first exchange as a game is to risk diminishing its intense seriousness. For Mercutio, words are fantastic trifles in a world fit only for satire, sexual teasing, and make-believe. He is a young man in love with masks; indeed, as he readies himself for the masked ball, he seems to regard his own face as a mask: "Give me a case to put my visage in, / A visor for a visor" (1.4.29–30). The moment Romeo and Juliet meet, all masks seem to fall away, all prior emotions fade into nothingness, and all games become earnest. "Did my heart love till now?" asks Romeo, and Juliet, sending the Nurse to find out Romeo's name, declares, "If he be married, / My grave is like to be my wedding bed" (1.5.131–32).

At some moments in *Romeo and Juliet,* then, wordplay reveals the arbitrariness of language; at other moments, it seems to reveal a hidden reality, even a sacred truth. These contradictory revelations are explored in the famous balcony scene in Act 2. Mercutio's mockery gives way, after Romeo's abrupt, one-line dismissal, to incantatory language so intense as to create a new heaven and a new earth. A bare, daylit stage (as it would have been in the Elizabethan playhouse) becomes a dark garden above which Juliet appears like the sun. Visibility is canceled and then restored, by means of metaphor, to the "white upturnèd wond'ring eyes / Of mortals" (2.1.71–72). Romeo's ecstatic words are the poetic record of a revelation, a vision of a creature unique, perfect, and infinitely beautiful.

The visionary moment turns into a moment of auditory revelation as well, as Romeo, in an intense, eroticized version of what audiences routinely do, overhears Juliet's soliloquy. He has entered into her most intimate thoughts and longings and has an overpowering proof of their authenticity, since she speaks with no awareness of his presence. The inner world his lyrical utterance has conjured up is miraculously united with her own. But her words at once offer a complete fulfillment of this union and a shattering of fulfillment: "O Romeo, Romeo, wherefore art thou Romeo?" (2.1.75). Only if Romeo's name is an arbitrary sign, to be stripped away, discarded, and replaced, can her love be realized. But in a world in which words are divorced from reality, what

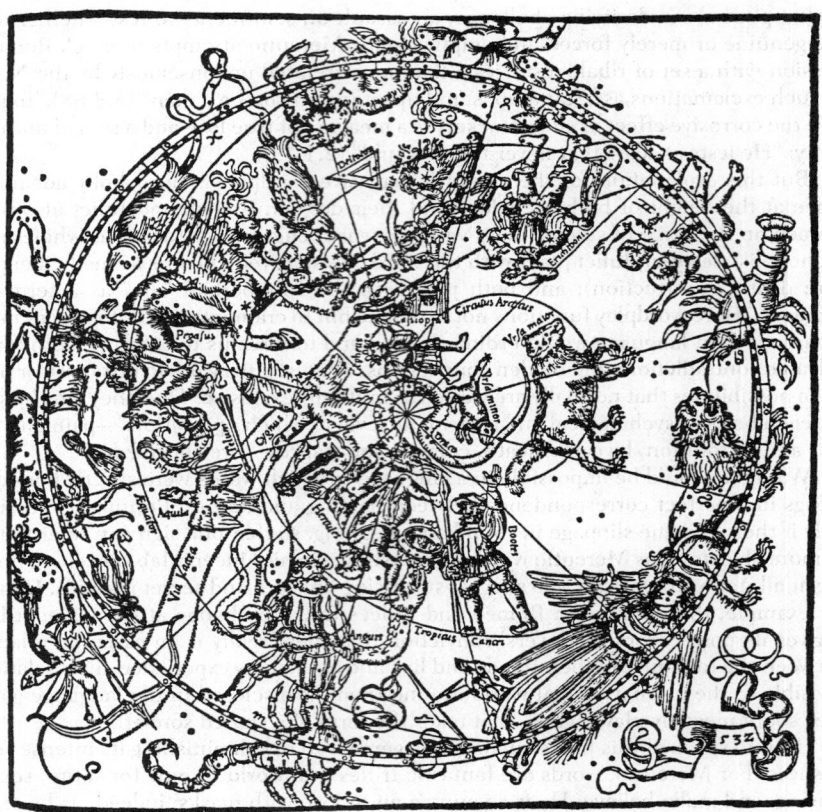

"Then I defy you, stars" (5.1.24). *Imagines Constellationum*. From Ptolemy, *Almagest* (1541 ed.), after Dürer.

would be the status of a love made by language? In a world in which names are mere empty signs, how could language create a new reality?

If words are arbitrary, then Romeo and Juliet's love, woven of words, is wedded to nothingness. If they are not arbitrary, if they cannot float free of the body and society, then their love will be destroyed by the rage of feuding parents—the parents who have bestowed proper names on their offspring—and by the whole daylight world of social exchange that gives ordinary language its normal meanings. Against the magical, passionate, transformative language of Romeo and Juliet is set not only Mercutio's mockery but the Nurse's garrulous evocation of the inescapable life cycle: birth, weaning, sexual maturity, and death.

In the Nurse's view, all lives have a certain interchangeability. Juliet's value can be measured in gold coins—"I tell you, he that can lay hold of her / Shall have the chinks" (1.5.113–14)—and an exiled husband can be replaced: Paris is "a lovely gentleman," she tells the grieving Juliet, "Romeo's a dishclout to him" (3.5.218–19). Romeo and Juliet insist by contrast on the absolute singularity of their love, on the stilling of cyclical time, and on the cancellation of the social network of form and compliment. For a moment on her balcony, Juliet regrets that Romeo has heard her declare her "true-love passion," but then she bids farewell to conventional restraint and boldly steps forward into the magical realm of reciprocal desire. This realm is not without its own solemn order: their love must be formally confirmed in honorable vows of holy matrimony spoken before the friar. But first in the garden, away from church and family and friends, the fullness of the lovers' matched longings finds expression in words that seem to possess mythic power, power to transform darkness into intense light and at the same time to block out the harsh, unforgiving light of the everyday.

The everyday has its own powerful resources, however, and forces its way back into the world that love has transformed. It does so through the ability of names like "Capulet" and "Montague" to conjure up bitter social rivalries. For, as *Romeo and Juliet* repeatedly discloses, words as we ordinarily use them are rarely wholly arbitrary or wholly mythic. They are social constructions, communal creations that are neither complete unto themselves nor empty and hence malleable by individuals. Both language as arbitrary and language as mythic are radical attempts to challenge this notion of words as shared creations carrying with them the tensions and resolutions present in communities, but the community in effect kills off the challenge—whether it comes from Mercutio, who tries to turn social hatred and love alike into a game about "nothing," or from Romeo and Juliet, who try to escape through darkness, subterfuge, and the language of love into a realm apart.

How does the communitarian spirit of language, and with it a sense of the inescapability of the social, manifest itself in *Romeo and Juliet*? It does so, first of all, through a series of characters such as those we glimpse in the opening moments of the play, when the Capulet servants, Samson and Gregory, provoke the absurd quarrel with the Montague servants, Abraham and Balthasar. The point is not only the foolishness of the social codes—"Do you bite your thumb at us, sir?" "I do bite my thumb, sir" (1.1.39–40)—but also their pervasiveness. In a tragedy memorable for its dreams of the most intense privacy—Juliet longs for Romeo to leap to her arms "untalked of and unseen" (3.2.7)— the bustling world makes its presence felt as insistently as the Nurse's voice calling again and again to Juliet as she stands at her window. Shakespeare is wonderfully resourceful in conveying this presence. There is, for example, the nameless servant whose inability to read the list of those invited to the Capulets' ball leads him to turn for assistance to Romeo and Benvolio, who chance at that moment to be walking by. The list itself deftly conjures up the social elite of Verona, with its network of kinship bonds:

> Signor Placentio and his lovely nieces,
> Mercutio and his brother Valentine,
> Mine uncle Capulet, his wife and daughters,

and so on through the whole "fair assembly" (1.2.63ff). At the ball itself, Shakespeare is careful to include a glimpse of the servants, hurrying to clear the dishes but finding time to put aside a piece of marzipan for themselves or arranging for a private party with Susan Grindstone and Nell. And, in the midst of the horror and lamenting when Juliet's cold and stiff body is discovered on the morning she was to be married to Paris, Shakespeare turns our attention to the musicians who had been hired to entertain the wedding guests and who now stand around cracking lame jokes and hoping for a bit of dinner (as if—to invert a celebrated line from *Hamlet*—the marriage-baked meats will coldly furnish forth the funeral table).

There are, besides the servants, other social units that carry the glacial weight of the collective norms and ordinary interests against which Romeo and Juliet struggle. The exclusiveness and intensity of their love is clearly in tension with the bond that links Romeo to his male friends. "Now art thou sociable," says Mercutio with evident relief, when Romeo briefly resumes the old mocking repartee; "now art thou Romeo" (2.3.77). But neither Romeo nor Juliet is any longer the same person, and the passionate love that divides Romeo from his friends sets both lovers still more decisively against the values of their powerful families. Those values involve a complex intertwining of honor, dignity, love, will, and property, a blend that can manifest itself as gracious hospitality or as murderous feuding, as gentle nostalgia or as cold calculation, as a father's indulgent affection for his daughter or as blind rage when she attempts to thwart his will. Romeo and Juliet's love and clandestine marriage can find no place

The city of Verona. From John Speed, *Prospect of the Most Famous Parts of the World* (1676).

in this familial order of things, just as its absoluteness is incompatible with the familial sense of cyclical time.

Beyond the structure of the family in the society of Verona, though linked to that structure by ties of kinship, lies the state, embodied in the figure of Prince Escalus. Formally, *Romeo and Juliet* is built around the well-meaning ruler's attempt to stop the "civil brawls" (1.1.82) at the play's beginning, his banishment of Romeo at its midpoint, and his final inquiry, to "clear these ambiguities" (5.3.216), at its close. But this necessary principle of civic order, even though it has important consequences, seems almost beside the point, as inadequate and uncomprehending as the statues in pure gold that the grieving fathers propose to erect.

A much deeper social principle is figured in Friar Laurence, who embodies the collective wisdom and sanctity of the community. Although set apart, the friar is not a hermit or a recluse; he is an active agent in the community's affairs. His attempt to use Romeo and Juliet's love as a means to resolve the feud between the Montagues and the Capulets disastrously backfires, and with his sleeping potions, his elaborate plots, and, at the close, his fatal cowardice, he has some of the qualities of the stereotypical meddling friar of anticlerical satire. But Friar Laurence is a more complex figure, with a subtle grasp of the doubleness—both poison and medicine—of the natural world and a thoughtful advocacy of moderation. This advocacy draws on an ancient and powerful critique of extremes in passion, which the play's tragic outcome would seem to endorse.

Yet few readers or spectators come away from *Romeo and Juliet* with the conviction that it would be better to love moderately. The intensity of the lovers' passion seems to have its own compelling, self-justifying force, which quietly brushes away all social obstacles and moralizing warnings: "Think true love acted simple modesty" (3.2.16). And the play's incantatory language of love—braiding together the wildly fanciful and the exquisitely simple—has after four hundred years an unforgettable freshness:

> Come, gentle night; come, loving, black-browed night,
> Give me my Romeo, and when I shall die
> Take him and cut him out in little stars,
> And he will make the face of heaven so fine
> That all the world will be in love with night
> And pay no worship to the garish sun.
>
> (3.2.20–25)

If the society of the play will not tolerate such ecstatic desire, if the contingencies of the ordinary world manage to destroy it, *Romeo and Juliet* offers us the consoling realization that the lovers themselves have all along been in love with night.

STEPHEN GREENBLATT

TEXTUAL NOTE

Romeo and Juliet was first published in quarto in 1597 (Q1). A second edition (Q2), advertised on the title page as "newly corrected, augmented, and amended," was published two years later. Q2 provided copy for a third quarto published in 1609 (Q3), from which in turn was printed another quarto (Q4) and the First Folio (F) text (both in 1623). Since Q3 and Q4, along with the Folio version of the play, all depend on Q2, the complex textual problems posed by *Romeo and Juliet* are focused on the precise nature of Q2 and its relation to the substantially different versions of the play, Q1.

Scholars generally agree that Q1 is a so-called bad Quarto, a defective text that derives not from the author's manuscript but from the recollection of actors. Since Elizabethan playing companies usually tried to keep the plays out of print, Q1 would in all likelihood have been an unauthorized and illicit transcript; modern analysis has directed suspicion on the actors who played Romeo and Paris. The title page identifies neither author nor publisher, and the text was evidently not licensed in the Stationers' Register.

Q2 is a fuller, more authoritative text. Certain of its features—inconsistent speech prefixes, "permissive" stage directions (e.g., "Enter three or four Citizens," 1.1.66 stage direction), and the preservation of lines that Shakespeare evidently meant to cross out after revision—indicate that Q2 was set from the author's own rough draft, or "foul papers." The draft appears to have posed difficulties for the printing house, for the compositors seem on a number of occasions to have had difficulty making sense of the manuscript. Moreover, perhaps because a page of the manuscript was missing, one passage in Q2—from 1.2.51 to 1.3.36—is taken directly from Q1. With the exception of this passage, for which Q1 serves as the control text, the text of *Romeo and Juliet* is based on Q2.

SELECTED BIBLIOGRAPHY

Belsey, Catherine. "The Name of the Rose in *Romeo and Juliet*." *Yearbook of English Studies* 23 (1993): 126–42. *Romeo and Juliet* dramatizes both the desire to transcend the realm of signifiers into a metaphysical ideal and the impossibility of attaining it.

Goldberg, Jonathan. "*Romeo and Juliet*'s Open Rs." *Queering the Renaissance*. Ed. Jonathan Goldberg. Durham, N.C.: Duke University Press, 1994. 218–35. Homosocial rivalry challenges the play's heterosexual order, implying the interchangeability of male and female love objects.

Kahn, Coppélia. "Coming of Age in Verona." *The Woman's Part: Feminist Criticism of Shakespeare*. Ed. Carolyn Ruth Swift Lenz, Gayle Greene, and Carol Thomas Neely. Urbana: University of Illinois Press, 1983. 171–93. The oppressive mores of a patriarchal society are chiefly responsible for the tragic determinism that suffocates the lovers.

Kristeva, Julia. "*Romeo and Juliet*: Love-Hatred in the Couple." *Shakespearean Tragedy*. Ed. John Drakakis. New York: Longman, 1992. 296–315. We benefit from a closer look, informed by Freud and Lacan, at the symptomatic (unconscious) response to transgressive and fantastic love as manifested in the characters, the playwright, and ourselves.

Liebler, Naomi Conn. " 'There is no world without Verona walls': The City in *Romeo and Juliet*." *A Companion to Shakespeare's Works*, vol. 1: *The Tragedies*. Ed. Richard Dutton and Jean E. Howard. Malden, Mass.: Blackwell, 2003. 303–18. Shakespeare's Verona is a matrix of violence and disorder, becoming the play's tragic protagonist as it collapses the ideal of the walled city.

Moisan, Thomas. " 'O Any Thing of Nothing, First Create!': Gender and Patriarchy and the Tragedy of *Romeo and Juliet*." *In Another Country: Feminist Perspectives on Renaissance Drama*. Ed. Dorothea Kehler and Susan Baker. Metuchen, N.J.: Scarecrow Press, 1991. 113–36. *Romeo and Juliet*'s tragic love story subverts patriarchy, but its gender prescriptions recuperate male authority.

Nevo, Ruth. "Tragic Form in *Romeo and Juliet*." *Studies in English Literature* 9 (1969): 241–58. Shakespeare develops a distinctive style of tragedy, predicated on the heroic embodiment of opposing forces, the subversion of appearances, the presence of the uncanny, and the complex ideal of sexual love.

Porter, Joseph A. *Shakespeare's Mercutio: His History and Drama*. Chapel Hill, N.C.: University of North Carolina Press, 1988. From a patchwork of sources, classical and contemporary, Shakespeare breathed life into the complex, subversive, homosexual Mercutio.

Snow, Edward. "Language and Sexual Difference in *Romeo and Juliet*." *Shakespeare's "Rough Magic": Renaissance Essays in Honor of C. L. Barber*. Ed. Peter Erickson and Coppélia Kahn. Newark: University of Delaware Press, 1985. 168–92. If the language of Juliet and Romeo articulates their profound interconnectedness, it also discloses ominous differences between them and suggests that gender difference is the tragedy's deepest dichotomy.

Snyder, Susan. "*Romeo and Juliet*: Comedy into Tragedy." *Essays in Criticism* 20 (1970): 391–402. At first possessing all the makings of a comedy, *Romeo and Juliet* morphs from one genre to another: the descent into tragedy becomes ineluctable upon the death of Mercutio.

FILMS

Romeo and Juliet. 1936. Dir. George Cukor. USA. 125 min. A lavish, big-studio release, Cukor's black-and-white film stars Leslie Howard, who was then forty-two, and Norma Shearer in the lead roles. John Barrymore plays Mercutio.

West Side Story. 1961. Dir. Jerome Robbins and Robert Wise. USA. 152 min. A musical, modernized adaptation of the play set in New York with rival ethnic gangs. Leonard Bernstein wrote the celebrated score.

Romeo and Juliet. 1968. Dir. Franco Zeffirelli. UK/Italy. 138 min. A flower-power, 1960s youth-culture interpretation of the play, featuring teenaged actors Leonard Whiting and Olivia Hussey in the title roles.

William Shakespeare's Romeo + Juliet. 1996. Dir. Baz Luhrmann. USA. 120 min. Starring Leonardo DiCaprio and Claire Danes, Luhrmann's frenetic update, set in modern-day "Verona Beach," explains the family feud in terms of a gang conflict.

Qing ren jie (*A Time to Love*). 2005. Dir. Jianqi Huo. China. 113 min. Set during the Cultural Revolution, two Chinese lovers read and watch versions of Shakespeare's play together, and enact the balcony scene. In Mandarin.

The Most Excellent and Lamentable Tragedy of Romeo and Juliet

THE PERSONS OF THE PLAY

CHORUS
ROMEO
MONTAGUE, his father
MONTAGUE'S WIFE
BENVOLIO, Montague's nephew
ABRAHAM, Montague's servingman
BALTHASAR, Romeo's man
JULIET
CAPULET, her father
CAPULET'S WIFE
TYBALT, her nephew
His page
PETRUCCIO
CAPULET'S COUSIN
Juliet's NURSE
PETER
SAMSON } servingmen of the Capulets
GREGORY
Other SERVINGMEN
MUSICIANS
Escalus, PRINCE of Verona
MERCUTIO
County PARIS } his kinsmen
PAGE to Paris
FRIAR LAURENCE
FRIAR JOHN
An APOTHECARY
CHIEF WATCHMAN
Other CITIZENS OF THE WATCH
Masquers, guests, gentlewomen, followers of the Montague and Capulet factions

Prologue

[*Enter*] CHORUS

CHORUS   Two households, both alike in dignity°   *status*
    In fair Verona, where we lay our scene,
    From ancient grudge break to new mutiny,°   *wrangling*
    Where civil blood makes civil hands unclean.[1]
5   From forth the fatal° loins of these two foes   *ill-fated*
    A pair of star-crossed[2] lovers take their life,
    Whose misadventured° piteous overthrows   *unfortunate*
    Doth with their death bury their parents' strife.

Prologue
1. Where citizens' hands are stained with the blood of their fellow citizens.

2. Thwarted by the adverse influence of the stars appearing at the time of their birth, which controlled their destinies.

933

The fearful passage of their death-marked love
10   And the continuance of their parents' rage—
Which but their children's end, naught could remove—
Is now the two-hours' traffic° of our stage;   *business; movement*
The which if you with patient ears attend,
What here shall miss, our toil shall strive to mend.[3]   [*Exit*]

1.1

Enter SAMSON *and* GREGORY, *of the house of Capulet,*
with swords and bucklers°   *small round shields*

SAMSON   Gregory, on my word, we'll not carry coals.[1]

GREGORY   No, for then we should be colliers.[2]

SAMSON   I mean an° we be in choler,° we'll draw.°   *if / anger / draw swords*

GREGORY   Ay, while you live, draw your neck out of collar.°   *a noose*

5   SAMSON   I strike quickly,° being moved.[3]   *vigorously*

GREGORY   But thou art not quickly° moved to strike.   *speedily*

SAMSON   A dog of the house of Montague moves me.

GREGORY   To move is to stir, and to be valiant is to stand,[4] there-
fore if thou art moved, thou runn'st away.

10 SAMSON   A dog of that house shall move me to stand. I will take
the wall of[5] any man or maid of Montague's.

GREGORY   That shows thee a weak slave, for the weakest goes to
the wall.[6]

SAMSON   'Tis true, and therefore women, being the weaker ves-
15 sels,[7] are ever thrust to the wall;° therefore I will push Mon-   *ravished*
tague's men from the wall, and thrust his maids to the wall.

GREGORY   The quarrel is between our masters and us their men.

SAMSON   'Tis all one.° I will show myself a tyrant: when I have   *the same*
fought with the men I will be civil with the maids—I will cut
20 off their heads.

GREGORY   The heads of the maids?

SAMSON   Ay, the heads of the maids, or their maidenheads, take
it in what sense thou wilt.

GREGORY   They must take it in sense° that feel it.   *through sensation*

25 SAMSON   Me they shall feel while I am able to stand, and 'tis
known I am a pretty piece of flesh.[8]

GREGORY   'Tis well thou art not fish. If thou hadst, thou hadst
been poor-john.[9]

Enter [ABRAHAM *and another servingman*] *of the Mon-*
tagues

Draw thy tool.[1] Here comes of the house of Montagues.

30 SAMSON   My naked weapon is out. Quarrel, I will back thee.

GREGORY   How—turn thy back and run?

SAMSON   Fear me not.[2]

GREGORY   No, marry[3]—I fear thee!

SAMSON   Let us take the law of our side. Let them begin.

---

3. *What . . . mind:* The actors will try to rectify what-
ever is missing or ill told in the Prologue.
1.1 Location: A street or public place in Verona.
1. We'll not suffer humiliation.
2. Professional coal porters, proverbially sneaky.
3. Being roused to anger.
4. Stand firm against assault. Playing, as with "strike"
and "stir," on sexual arousal.
5. I will assert superiority over. The sidewalk nearest
the wall was cleaner than that nearer the street.
6. Proverbial: The weakest are always pushed aside.

7. Paul's description of women in 1 Peter 3:7.
8. An attractive fellow possessed of an impressive
member.
9. Dried salted hake, appropriate as a taunt because
shriveled and cheap. "Neither fish nor flesh" was
proverbial for an uncategorizable oddity.
1. Weapon (and continuing the bawdy wordplay).
2. Do not doubt my fortitude; in the next line, Gregory
takes it in the modern sense of "Do not be afraid of me."
3. By the Virgin Mary, a mild oath with a meaning sim-
ilar to "indeed."

35 GREGORY   I will frown as I pass by, and let them take it as they
list.°   *like*

SAMSON   Nay, as they dare. I will bite my thumb at them,[4] which
is disgrace to them if they bear it.
        [*He bites his thumb*]
ABRAHAM   Do you bite your thumb at us, sir?
40 SAMSON   I do bite my thumb, sir.
ABRAHAM   Do you bite your thumb at us, sir?
SAMSON [*to* GREGORY]   Is the law of our side if I say 'Ay'?
GREGORY   No.
SAMSON [*to* ABRAHAM]   No, sir, I do not bite my thumb at you,
45 sir, but I bite my thumb, sir.
GREGORY [*to* ABRAHAM]   Do you quarrel, sir?
ABRAHAM   Quarrel, sir? No, sir.
SAMSON   But if you do, sir, I am for you.[5] I serve as good a man
as you.
50 ABRAHAM   No better.
SAMSON   Well, sir.
        Enter BENVOLIO
GREGORY   Say 'better'. Here comes one of my master's kinsmen.
SAMSON [*to* ABRAHAM]   Yes, better, sir.
ABRAHAM   You lie.
55 SAMSON   Draw, if you be men. Gregory, remember thy washing°   *slashing; violent*
blow.
        They [*draw and*] *fight*
BENVOLIO [*drawing*]   Part, fools. Put up your swords. You know
not what you do.
        Enter TYBALT
TYBALT [*drawing*]   What, art thou drawn among these heartless
hinds?[6]
60 Turn thee, Benvolio. Look upon thy death.
BENVOLIO   I do but keep the peace. Put up thy sword,
Or manage° it to part these men with me.   *wield*
TYBALT   What, drawn and talk of peace? I hate the word
As I hate hell, all Montagues, and thee.
65 Have at thee, coward.
        They fight. Enter three or four CITIZENS [OF THE
        WATCH], *with clubs or partisans*°   *broad-tipped spears*
CITIZENS OF THE WATCH   Clubs, bills° and partisans! Strike! Beat   *ax-bladed spears*
them down!
Down with the Capulets. Down with the Montagues.
        Enter old CAPULET *in his gown, and his* WIFE
CAPULET   What noise is this? Give me my long sword, ho!
CAPULET'S WIFE   A crutch, a crutch—why call you for a sword?
        Enter old MONTAGUE [*with his sword drawn*], *and his*
        WIFE
70 CAPULET   My sword, I say. Old Montague is come,
And flourishes his blade in spite° of me.   *defiance*
MONTAGUE   Thou villain Capulet!
        [*His* WIFE *holds him back*]
                                     Hold me not, let me go.

---

4. Flick the thumbnail from behind the upper teeth, an
insulting gesture.
5. I accept your invitation to fight.

6. These cowardly servants, punning on female deer
("hinds") unprotected by a stag ("hart/heart").

MONTAGUE'S WIFE   Thou shalt not stir one foot to seek a foe.
[*The* CITIZENS OF THE WATCH *attempt to*] *part them.*
Enter PRINCE *Escalus with his train*
PRINCE   Rebellious subjects, enemies to peace,
75   Profaners of this neighbour-stainèd steel[7]—
          Will they not hear? What ho, you men, you beasts,
          That quench the fire of your pernicious rage
          With purple° fountains issuing from your veins: crimson
          On pain of torture, from those bloody hands
80   Throw your mistempered[8] weapons to the ground,
          And hear the sentence of your movèd° Prince.   furious
          [MONTAGUE, CAPULET, *and their followers throw*
          down their weapons]
          Three civil brawls bred of an airy° word   unsubstantial
          By thee, old Capulet, and Montague,
          Have thrice disturbed the quiet of our streets
85   And made Verona's ancient° citizens   elderly
          Cast by° their grave-beseeming ornaments[9]   Cast away
          To wield old partisans in hands as old,
          Cankered° with peace, to part your cankered° hate.   Rusty / malignant
          If ever you disturb our streets again
90   Your lives shall pay the forfeit° of the peace.   ransom
          For this time all the rest depart away.
          You, Capulet, shall go along with me;
          And Montague, come you this afternoon
          To know our farther pleasure in this case
95   To old Freetown,[1] our common judgement-place.
          Once more, on pain of death, all men depart.
                              Exeunt [*all but* MONTAGUE,
                                  his WIFE, *and* BENVOLIO]
MONTAGUE   Who set this ancient quarrel new abroach?°   open
          Speak, nephew: were you by when it began?
BENVOLIO   Here were the servants of your adversary
100   And yours, close fighting ere I did approach.
          I drew to part them. In the instant came
          The fiery Tybalt with his sword prepared,
          Which, as he breathed° defiance to my ears,   uttered
          He swung about his head and cut the winds
105   Who, nothing hurt withal,° hissed him in scorn.   by that
          While we were interchanging thrusts and blows,
          Came more and more, and fought on part and part[2]
          Till the Prince came, who parted either part.
MONTAGUE'S WIFE   O where is Romeo—saw you him today?
110   Right glad I am he was not at this fray.
BENVOLIO   Madam, an hour before the worshipped sun
          Peered forth° the golden window of the east,   out from
          A troubled mind drive° me to walk abroad,   drove
          Where, underneath the grove of sycamore[3]
115   That westward rooteth° from this city side,   grows out

---

7. You who defile weapons with the stains of your
neighbors' blood.
8. Badly shaped and hardened, as well as unnecessar-
ily wrathful by disposition.
9. Attire and symbolic staffs appropriate to grave old
age. Possibly playing on the old men's proximity to the

grave.
1. In Brooke's translation from the Italian source, the
Capulet house is called Villa Franca.
2. Fought for one side and the other.
3. Associated with melancholy lovers, who are "sick-
amour."

So early walking did I see your son.
Towards him I made, but he was ware° of me,   *wary*
And stole into the covert° of the wood.   *covering*
I, measuring his affections° by my own—   *inclination*
120 Which then most sought where most might not be found,⁴
Being one too many by my weary self—
Pursued my humour° not pursuing his,   *mood*
And gladly shunned who gladly fled from me.
MONTAGUE   Many a morning hath he there been seen,
125 With tears augmenting the fresh morning's dew,
Adding to clouds more clouds with his deep sighs.
But all so soon as the all-cheering sun
Should in the farthest east begin to draw
The shady curtains from Aurora's⁵ bed,
130 Away from light steals home my heavy° son,   *melancholy*
And private in his chamber pens himself,
Shuts up his windows, locks fair daylight out,
And makes himself an artificial night.
Black and portentous° must this humour⁶ prove,   *ominous (of illness)*
135 Unless good counsel may the cause remove.
BENVOLIO   My noble uncle, do you know the cause?
MONTAGUE   I neither know it nor can learn of him.
BENVOLIO   Have you importuned him by any° means?   *all*
MONTAGUE   Both by myself and many other friends,
140 But he, his own affection's counsellor,°   *confidant*
Is to himself—I will not say how true,⁷
But to himself so secret and so close,°   *discreet*
So far from sounding and discovery,°   *fathoming and revelation*
As is the bud bit with an envious worm°   *a spiteful grub (larva)*
145 Ere he can spread his sweet leaves° to the air   *petals*
Or dedicate his beauty to the sun.
Could we but learn from whence his sorrows grow
We would as willingly give cure as know.
          Enter ROMEO
BENVOLIO   See where he comes. So please you° step aside,   *please you = please*
150 I'll know his grievance or be much denied.
MONTAGUE   I would° thou wert so happy° by thy stay   *wish / fortunate*
To hear true shrift.° Come, madam, let's away.   *confession*
          Exeunt [MONTAGUE *and his* WIFE]
BENVOLIO   Good morrow, cousin.
ROMEO   Is the day so young?
BENVOLIO   But new° struck nine.   *only just*
ROMEO   Ay me, sad hours seem long.
155 Was that my father that went hence so fast?
BENVOLIO   It was. What sadness lengthens Romeo's hours?
ROMEO   Not having that which, having, makes them short.
BENVOLIO   In love.
ROMEO   Out.
160 BENVOLIO   Of love?
ROMEO   Out of her favour where I am in love.

---

4. *where . . . found:* in a place where I was unlikely to
have company.
5. Goddess of the dawn in classical legend.
6. "Humors," essential bodily fluids, were considered
the basis of human beings' physical and psychological

constitution. Too much black bile caused melancholy
and a host of illnesses and derangements.
7. Loyal, but also invoking the proverbial wisdom that
only one who is "true to him- or herself" can be
upstanding in dealing with others.

BENVOLIO   Alas that love, so gentle in his view,°   *appearance*
Should be so tyrannous and rough in proof.°   *experience*
ROMEO   Alas that love, whose view is muffled still,[8]
165   Should without eyes see pathways to his will.°   *intention; lust*
Where shall we dine? [*Seeing blood*] O me! What fray was here?
Yet tell me not, for I have heard it all.
Here's much to do with hate, but more with love.
Why then, O brawling love, O loving hate,
170   O anything of nothing first create;[9]
O heavy lightness, serious vanity,
Misshapen chaos of well-seeming forms,
Feather of lead, bright smoke, cold fire, sick health,
Still-waking° sleep, that is not what it is!   *Always awake*
175   This love feel I, that feel no love in this.
Dost thou not laugh?
BENVOLIO   No, coz,° I rather weep.   *cousin*
ROMEO   Good heart, at what?
BENVOLIO   At thy good heart's oppression.°   *affliction*
ROMEO   Why, such is love's transgression.
Griefs of mine own lie heavy in my breast,
180   Which thou wilt propagate° to have it pressed[1]   *multiply*
With more of thine. This love that thou hast shown
Doth add more grief to too much of mine own.
Love is a smoke made with the fume of sighs,
Being purged,° a fire sparkling in lovers' eyes,   *clarified*
185   Being vexed,° a sea nourished with lovers' tears.   *stirred up*
What is it else? A madness most discreet,°   *wise*
A choking gall and a preserving sweet.
Farewell, my coz.
BENVOLIO   Soft,° I will go along;   *Wait*
An if° you leave me so, you do me wrong.   *An If = if*
190   ROMEO   Tut, I have lost myself. I am not here.
This is not Romeo; he's some other where.
BENVOLIO   Tell me in sadness,[2] who is that you love?
ROMEO   What, shall I groan and tell thee?
BENVOLIO   Groan? Why no; but sadly tell me who.
195   ROMEO   Bid a sick man in sadness make his will,
A word ill urged to one that is so ill.
In sadness, cousin, I do love a woman.
BENVOLIO   I aimed so near when I supposed you loved.
ROMEO   A right good markman; and she's fair I love.
200   BENVOLIO   A right fair mark,° fair coz, is soonest hit.   *target; vulva*
ROMEO   Well, in that hit you miss. She'll not be hit
With Cupid's arrow; she hath Dian's wit,[3]
And, in strong proof° of chastity well armed,°   *tested armor / covered*
From love's weak childish bow she lives unharmed.
205   She will not stay° the siege of loving terms,   *undergo*
Nor bide th'encounter of assailing eyes,[4]

8. Who cannot see. Cupid was often depicted as blind or blindfolded.
9. *create:* created. Inverting the proverb "Nothing can come of nothing" and also recalling the doctrine that God made the world out of nothing. Romeo catalogues the "miraculous" paradoxes of love.
1. Burdened; embraced.

2. Seriousness, although Romeo plays on the sense "melancholy."
3. The scruples and cleverness of Diana, the classical goddess of hunting and chastity.
4. *th'encounter of assailing eyes:* military metaphors for courtship conventionally used in Petrarchan love poetry.

Nor ope her lap to saint-seducing gold.[5]
O, she is rich in beauty, only poor
That when she dies, with beauty dies her store.°   *wealth*

210 BENVOLIO   Then she hath sworn that she will still° live chaste?   *always*
ROMEO   She hath, and in that sparing° makes huge waste;   *refraining; thrift*
For beauty starved with her severity
Cuts beauty off from all posterity.[6]
She is too fair, too wise, wisely too fair,°   *just*

215 To merit bliss° by making me despair.[7]   *heaven's blessing*
She hath forsworn to love, and in that vow
Do I live dead, that live to tell it now.
BENVOLIO   Be ruled by me; forget to think of her.
ROMEO   O, teach me how I should forget to think!

220 BENVOLIO   By giving liberty unto thine eyes.
Examine other beauties.
ROMEO   'Tis the way
To call hers, exquisite, in question more.[8]
These happy masks that kiss fair ladies' brows,
Being black, puts us in mind they hide the fair.

225 He that is strucken blind cannot forget
The precious treasure of his eyesight lost.
Show me a mistress that is passing° fair,   *surpassingly*
What doth her beauty serve but as a note
Where I may read who passed that passing fair?

230 Farewell, thou canst not teach me to forget.
BENVOLIO   I'll pay° that doctrine, or else die in debt.[9]   *Exeunt*   *impart*

1.2

Enter old CAPULET, *County*° PARIS, *and the Clown*   *Count*
[PETER, *a servingman*]
CAPULET   But Montague is bound° as well as I,   *under oath*
In penalty alike, and 'tis not hard, I think,
For men so old as we to keep the peace.
PARIS   Of honourable reckoning[1] are you both,

5 And pity 'tis you lived at odds so long.
But now, my lord: what say you to my suit?
CAPULET   But saying o'er what I have said before.
My child is yet a stranger in the world;
She hath not seen the change of fourteen years.

10 Let two more summers wither in their pride
Ere we may think her ripe to be a bride.
PARIS   Younger than she are happy mothers made.
CAPULET   And too soon marred are those so early made.[2]
But woo her, gentle Paris, get her heart;

15 My will to her consent is but a part,
And, she agreed, within her scope of choice
Lies my consent and fair-according voice.
This night I hold an old-accustomed feast

5. To golden gifts that are irresistibly persuasive. Also,
in classical legend, Jupiter descended upon Danaë as a
shower of gold.
6. *For . . . posterity*: Since she will not have children,
her beauty will die with her. *starved*: killed.
7. Despair of salvation, a grave sin.
8. *in question more*: more intensely to mind.
9. Die whatever the cost to me; die still owing you the

doctrine of forgetfulness.
1.2 Location: A street or plaza in Verona.
1. Repute, with a play on "accounting."
2. Q2 includes two more lines following line 13, prob-
ably rejected by Shakespeare in the writing process:
"Earth hath swallowed all my hopes but she, / She's the
hopeful Lady of my earth" (*earth*: body).

Whereto I have invited many a guest
20 Such as I love, and you among the store,
One more most welcome, makes my number more.
At my poor house look to behold this night
Earth-treading stars that make dark heaven light.
Such comfort as do lusty young men feel
25 When well-apparelled April on the heel
Of limping winter treads—even such delight
Among fresh female buds shall you this night
Inherit° at my house; hear all, all see,   *Enjoy*
And like her most whose merit most shall be,
30 Which on more view of many, mine, being one,
May stand in number, though in reck'ning none.[3]
Come, go with me. [*Giving* PETER *a paper*] Go, sirrah,° trudge   *(address to an inferior)*
    about;
Through fair Verona find those persons out
Whose names are written there, and to them say
35 My house and welcome on their pleasure stay.°   *wait*
                            Exeunt [CAPULET *and* PARIS]
PETER Find them out whose names are written here? It is writ-
ten that the shoemaker should meddle with his yard° and the   *yardstick*
tailor with his last,° the fisher with his pencil° and the painter   *shoe form / paintbrush*
with his nets; but I am sent to find those persons whose names
40 are here writ, and can never find° what names the writing per-   *figure out*
son hath here writ. I must to the learned.
                    Enter BENVOLIO *and* ROMEO
In good time.
BENVOLIO [*to* ROMEO] Tut, man, one fire burns out another's burning,
    One pain is lessened by another's anguish.
45 Turn giddy,° and be holp° by backward turning.   *Turn until dizzy / helped*
    One desperate grief cures with another's languish.[4]
Take thou some new infection[5] to thy eye,
And the rank poison of the old will die.
ROMEO Your plantain leaf[6] is excellent for that.
50 BENVOLIO For what, I pray thee?
ROMEO For your broken° shin.   *gashed*
BENVOLIO Why, Romeo, art thou mad?
ROMEO Not mad, but bound more than a madman is;
    Shut up in prison, kept without my food,
    Whipped and tormented and— [*to* PETER] Good e'en,° good   *evening (afternoon)*
55   fellow.
PETER God gi'° good e'en. I pray, sir, can you read?   *give you*
ROMEO Ay, mine own fortune in my misery.[7]
PETER Perhaps you have learned it without book.[8] But I pray,
    can you read anything you see?
60 ROMEO Ay, if I know the letters and the language.
PETER Ye say honestly. Rest you merry.[9]
ROMEO Stay, fellow, I can read.
                    He reads the letter

3. *Which . . . none:* Upon closer inspection of the
many young women, my daughter may make a part of
the gorgeous display, but be of no account by herself.
"One" was proverbially "no number."
4. Is displaced by the languishing pain of a new grief.
5. New object of passion, which causes a distortion of
sight in the lover.
6. The ordinary plaintain leaf, used to dress wounds or

bruises and thought to have curative powers.
7 Romeo takes "read" to mean "understand" or "per-
ceive," as in "to read one's fortune."
8. *without book:* from memory or by ear, as well as
through experience rather than education.
9. A farewell. Peter takes Romeo to mean "if only I
knew the letters and the language."

'Signor Martino and his wife and daughters,
County° Anselme and his beauteous sisters,
65 The lady widow of Vitruvio,
Signor Placentio and his lovely nieces,
Mercutio and his brother Valentine,
Mine uncle Capulet, his wife and daughters,
My fair niece Rosaline and Livia,
70 Signor Valentio and his cousin Tybalt,
Lucio and the lively Helena.'
A fair assembly. Whither should they come?
PETER   Up.[1]
ROMEO   Whither?
75 PETER   To supper to our house.
ROMEO   Whose house?
PETER   My master's.
ROMEO   Indeed, I should have asked thee that before.
PETER   Now I'll tell you without asking. My master is the great
80 rich Capulet, and if you be not of the house of Montagues, I
pray come and crush° a cup of wine. Rest you merry.   *Exit*   drink
BENVOLIO   At this same ancient° feast of Capulet's   traditional
Sups the fair Rosaline, whom thou so loves,
With all the admirèd beauties of Verona.
85 Go thither, and with unattainted° eye   unbiased
Compare her face with some that I shall show,
And I will make thee think thy swan a crow.
ROMEO   When the devout religion° of mine eye   pious belief
Maintains such falsehood, then turn tears to fires;
90 And these° who, often drowned, could never die,   these eyes
Transparent° heretics, be burnt for liars.   Obvious; self-evident
One fairer than my love!—the all-seeing sun
Ne'er saw her match since first the world begun.
BENVOLIO   Tut, you saw her fair, none else being by,
95 Herself poised with° herself in either eye;   balanced against
But in that crystal scales let there be weighed
Your lady's love against some other maid
That I will show you shining at this feast,
And she shall scant show well that now seems best.
100 ROMEO   I'll go along, no such sight to be shown,
But to rejoice in splendour of mine own.   [*Exeunt*]

1.3
Enter CAPULET'S WIFE *and* NURSE
CAPULET'S WIFE   Nurse, where's my daughter? Call her forth to me.
NURSE   Now, by my maidenhead at twelve year old,[1]
I bade her come. What,[2] lamb, what, ladybird—
God forbid[3]—where is this girl? What, Juliet!
Enter JULIET
5 JULIET   How now, who calls?
NURSE   Your mother.
JULIET   Madam, I am here. What is your will?

---

1. "Come up" is a phrase expression scorn.
1.3 Location: Capulet's house.
1. Presumably the latest date that the Nurse could swear by her virginity.

2. An expression of impatience.
3. Either an apology for the promiscuous connotation of "ladybrid" of fearing something amiss in Juliet's absence.

CAPULET'S WIFE   This is the matter.—Nurse, give leave° a while.   *excuse us*
We must talk in secret.—Nurse, come back again.

10 I have remembered me, thou's° hear our counsel.°   *you shall / secrets*
Thou knowest my daughter's of a pretty age.

NURSE   Faith, I can tell her age unto an hour.

CAPULET'S WIFE   She's not fourteen.

NURSE   I'll lay fourteen of my teeth—and yet, to my teen° be it   *sorrow*
15 spoken, I have but four—she's not fourteen. How long is it now
to Lammastide?[4]

CAPULET'S WIFE   A fortnight and odd days.

NURSE   Even or odd, of all days in the year
Come Lammas Eve at night shall she be fourteen.

20 Susan[5] and she—God rest all Christian souls!—
Were of an age. Well, Susan is with God;
She was too good for me. But, as I said,
On Lammas Eve at night shall she be fourteen,
That shall she, marry, I remember it well.

25 'Tis since the earthquake now eleven years,
And she was weaned—I never shall forget it—
Of all the days of the year upon that day,
For I had then laid wormwood[6] to my dug,°   *on my nipple*
Sitting in the sun under the dovehouse wall.

30 My lord and you were then at Mantua.
Nay, I do bear a brain!° But, as I said,   *memory*
When it did taste the wormwood on the nipple
Of my dug and felt it bitter, pretty fool,°   *(an endearment)*
To see it tetchy° and fall out wi'th' dug!   *peevish*

35 'Shake', quoth the dove-house![7] 'Twas no need, I trow,
To bid me trudge;°   *remove myself*
And since that time it is eleven years,
For then she could stand high-lone.° Nay, by th' rood,°   *upright alone / cross*
She could have run and waddled all about,

40 For even the day before, she broke her brow,°   *cut her forehead*
And then my husband—God be with his soul,
A° was a merry man!—took up the child.   *He*
'Yea,' quoth he, 'dost thou fall upon thy face?
Thou wilt fall backward when thou hast more wit,°   *knowledge*

45 Wilt thou not, Jule?' And, by my halidom,°   *holiness; holy relic*
The pretty wretch left° crying and said 'Ay'.   *stopped*
To see now how a jest shall come about!°   *come true*
I warrant an° I should live a thousand years   *if*
I never should forget it. 'Wilt thou not, Jule?' quoth he,

50 And, pretty fool, it stinted° and said 'Ay'.   *she ceased*

CAPULET'S WIFE   Enough of this. I pray thee hold thy peace.

NURSE   Yes, madam. Yet I cannot choose but laugh
To think it should leave crying and say 'Ay'.
And yet, I warrant,° it had upon it° brow   *assure you / its*

55 A bump as big as a young cock'rel's stone.°   *rooster's testicle*
A perilous knock, and it cried bitterly.
'Yea,' quoth my husband, 'fall'st upon thy face?
Thou wilt fall backward when thou com'st to age,

---

4. August 1, originally celebrated by the church as a
harvest festival.
5. The Nurse evidently suckled Juliet after her own

daughter died.
6. A proverbially bitter plant extract.
7. The dove house shook with the earthquake.

Wilt thou not, Jule?' It stinted and said 'Ay'.
60 JULIET   And stint thou too, I pray thee, Nurse, say I.
NURSE   Peace, I have done. God mark° thee to his grace,   *elect*
Thou wast the prettiest babe that e'er I nursed.
An° I might live to see thee married once,°   *If / one day*
I have my wish.
65 CAPULET'S WIFE   Marry,° that 'marry' is the very theme   *Truly*
I came to talk of. Tell me, daughter Juliet,
How stands your dispositions to be married?
JULIET   It is an honour that I dream not of.
NURSE   'An honour'! Were not I thine only nurse,
70 I would say thou hadst sucked wisdom from thy teat.[8]
CAPULET'S WIFE   Well, think of marriage now. Younger than you
Here in Verona, ladies of esteem,
Are made already mothers. By my count
I was your mother much upon these years
75 That you are now a maid. Thus then, in brief :
The valiant Paris seeks you for his love.
NURSE   A man, young lady, lady, such a man
As all the world—why, he's a man of wax.[9]
CAPULET'S WIFE   Verona's summer hath not such a flower.
80 NURSE   Nay, he's a flower, in faith, a very flower.
CAPULET'S WIFE [*to* JULIET]   What say you? Can you love the gentleman?
This night you shall behold him at our feast.
Read o'er the volume of young Paris' face,
And find delight writ there with beauty's pen.
85 Examine every married lineament,[1]
And see how one° another lends content;[2]   *one to*
And what obscured in this fair volume lies
Find written in the margin[3] of his eyes.
This precious book of love, this unbound° lover,   *single; unrestrained*
90 To beautify him only lacks a cover.
The fish lives in the sea, and 'tis much pride
For fair without the fair within to hide.[4]
That book in many's eyes doth share the glory
That in gold clasps locks in the golden story.[5]
95 So shall you share all that he doth possess
By having him, making yourself no less.
NURSE   No less, nay, bigger. Women grow° by men.   *swell with child*
CAPULET'S WIFE [*to* JULIET]   Speak briefly: can you like of Paris' love?
JULIET   I'll look° to like, if looking liking move;[6]   *expect; examine*
100 But no more deep will I endart[7] mine eye
Than your consent gives strength to make it fly.
          Enter a servingman [PETER]
PETER   Madam, the guests are come, supper served up, you
called, my young lady asked for, the Nurse cursed in the pantry,
and everything in extremity.° I must hence to wait.° I beseech   *a terrible state / serve*
105 you follow straight.°   *immediately*

8. From the teat that nourished you.
9. Model of perfection, as if sculpted rather than born.
1. Harroniously composed feature; a joined line of
flowing handwriting.
2. Meaning; happiness.
3. Glosses to difficult passage of text were set in the
margin.
4. For a lovely setting (Juliet) to frame and enrich the

fair Paris.
5. *That book . . . story:* Many esteem a book's golden
binding as highly as the story it contains. The speech
thoroughly confuses who is covering whom.
6. If looking can motivate liking.
7. Sink itself like an arrow into its target; shoot glances
that, like Cupid's arrows, inflame his passions.

CAPULET'S WIFE   We follow thee.   *Exit a servingman* [PETER]
                                Juliet, the County stays.°   *the Count awaits*
NURSE   Go, girl; seek happy nights to° happy days.   *Exeunt*   *at the end of*

1.4

Enter ROMEO, MERCUTIO, *and* BENVOLIO, [*as masquers,*]
with five or six other masquers[1] [*bearing a drum and
torches*]

ROMEO   What, shall this speech° be spoke for our excuse,   *prologue*
    Or shall we on without apology?
BENVOLIO   The date is out of° such prolixity.   *past for*
    We'll have no Cupid hoodwinked[2] with a scarf,
5   Bearing a Tartar's painted bow of lath,[3]
    Scaring the ladies like a crowkeeper,°   *scarecrow*
    Nor no without-book° Prologue faintly spoke   *memorized*
    After° the prompter for our entrance.   *Repeating after*
    But let them measure° us by what they will,   *judge*
10   We'll measure° them a measure,° and be gone.   *apportion / dance*
ROMEO   Give me a torch. I am not for this ambling;°   *dancing*
    Being but heavy,° I will bear the light.   *melancholy*
MERCUTIO   Nay, gentle° Romeo, we must have you dance.   *noble; softhearted*
ROMEO   Not I, believe me. You have dancing shoes
15   With nimble soles; I have a soul of lead
    So stakes me to the ground I cannot move.
MERCUTIO   You are a lover; borrow Cupid's wings,
    And soar with them above a common bound.[4]
ROMEO   I am too sore° empiercèd with his shaft   *deeply*
20   To soar with his light° feathers, and so bound   *cheery; agile; wanton*
    I cannot bound a pitch[5] above dull woe;
    Under love's heavy burden do I sink.
MERCUTIO   And to sink in it should you burden love—
    Too great oppression for a tender thing.[6]
25 ROMEO   Is love a tender thing? It is too rough,
    Too rude, too boist'rous, and it pricks like thorn.
MERCUTIO   If love be rough with you, be rough with love.
    Prick° love for pricking, and you beat love down.[7]   *Stab; sexually penetrate*
    Give me a case[8] to put my visage in,
30   A visor for a visor.[9] What care I
    What curious eye doth quote° deformity?   *notice*
    Here are the beetle brows° shall blush for me.   *protruding eyebrows*
    [*They put on visors*]
BENVOLIO   Come, knock and enter, and no sooner in
    But every man betake him to his legs.°   *to dancing; to flight*
35 ROMEO   A torch for me. Let wantons light of heart
    Tickle the sense-less rushes° with their heels,   *floor matting*
    For I am proverbed with a grandsire° phrase.   *an ancient*

1.4 Location: Before Capulet's house.
1. Performers or participants in an aristocratic masked entertainment, consisting of dances and sometimes dumb shows and set speeches.
2. Blindfolded and foolish Cupid, a typical costume for the presenter of the masque's theme.
3. Short bow shaped like the upper lip, made of the thin wood used for theatrical properties.

4. A normal limit; an average dancer's leap.
5. Height from which a hawk stoops to kill.
6. Suggesting a pudendum.
7. *Prick . . . down*: Playing on the sense "satiate desire by fulfilling it."
8. Literally, "mask," but also slang for the vagina.
9. Mask for an ugly face. Proverbial: "A well-favored visor to hide an ill-favored face."

I'll be a candle-holder and look on.[1]
The game was ne'er so fair, and I am done.[2]
[*He takes a torch*]

40 MERCUTIO   Tut, dun's the mouse,[3] the constable's own word.°   *phrase*
If thou art dun we'll draw thee from the mire[4]
Of—save your reverence[5]—love, wherein thou stickest
Up to the ears. Come, we burn daylight,° ho!   *waste time*
ROMEO   Nay, that's not so.
MERCUTIO   I mean, sir, in delay
45 We waste our lights in vain, like lights by day.
Take our good meaning, for our judgement sits
Five times in that ere once in our five wits.[6]
ROMEO   And we mean° well in going to this masque,   *intend*
But 'tis no wit° to go.   *intelligence*
MERCUTIO   Why, may one ask?
ROMEO   I dreamt a dream tonight.°   *last night*
50 MERCUTIO   And so did I.
ROMEO   Well, what was yours?
MERCUTIO   That dreamers often lie.
ROMEO   In bed asleep while they do dream things true.
MERCUTIO   O, then I see Queen Mab[7] hath been with you.
BENVOLIO   Queen Mab, what's she?
55 MERCUTIO   She is the fairies' midwife, and she comes
In shape no bigger than an agate stone[8]
On the forefinger of an alderman,
Drawn with a team of little atomi°   *atoms*
Athwart men's noses as they lie asleep.
60 Her wagon spokes made of long spinners'° legs;   *spiders'*
The cover, of the wings of grasshoppers;
Her traces, of the moonshine's wat'ry beams;
Her collars, of the smallest spider web;
Her whip, of cricket's bone, the lash of film;°   *spider's-web thread*
65 Her wagoner,° a small grey-coated gnat   *driver*
Not half so big as a round little worm
Pricked from the lazy finger of a maid.[9]
Her chariot is an empty hazelnut
Made by the joiner° squirrel or old grub,[1]   *carpenter*
70 Time out o' mind the fairies' coachmakers.
And in this state° she gallops night by night   *regal finery*
Through lovers' brains, and then they dream of love;
O'er courtiers' knees, that dream on curtsies straight;[2]
O'er ladies' lips, who straight on kisses dream,
75 Which oft the angry Mab with blisters plagues
Because their breaths with sweetmeats° tainted are.   *candies*
Sometime she gallops o'er a lawyer's lip,

1. Proverbial: "A good candleholder proves a good gamester. A spectator loses nothing."
2. Proverbial: "When play is best, it is time to leave."
3. Proverbial: Keep silent and unseen, like a mouse.
4. In the Christmas game "Dun is in the mire," players pantomimed drawing a log representing a horse out of a boggy road. Mercutio is suggesting that Romeo is a stick-in-the-mud.
5. An apology for crude language, here used mockingly.
6. *Take . . . wits:* Understand my intended good meaning using common sense ("judgement"), which is five times as trustworthy as the five senses.

7. Possibly Celtic, but probably Shakespeare's invention. "Queen" meant "whore," and "Mab" was a stereotypical name for prostitutes.
8. A small human figure was often carved on agate stones set in seal rings.
9. According to popular belief, worms generated in idle girls' fingers.
1. Grubs bore holes. Lines 68–70, from Q1, do not appear in Q2 at all; numerous other changes in the order and wording of his speech suggest that Q1 incorporated revisions that Q2 and later revisions did not.
2. Dream of respectful bows immediately.

And then dreams he of smelling out a suit;[3]
And sometime comes she with a tithe-pig's[4] tail

80   Tickling a parson's nose as a° lies asleep;   *he*
Then dreams he of another benefice.[5]
Sometime she driveth o'er a soldier's neck,
And then dreams he of cutting foreign throats,
Of breaches, ambuscados, Spanish blades,[6]

85   Of healths five fathom deep;[7] and then anon°   *soon*
Drums in his ear, at which he starts and wakes,
And being thus frighted, swears a prayer or two,
And sleeps again. This is that very Mab
That plaits° the manes of horses in the night,   *entangles*

90   And bakes the elf-locks[8] in foul sluttish° hairs,   *dirty*
Which once untangled much misfortune bodes.
This is the hag, when maids lie on their backs,
That presses them[9] and learns° them first to bear,   *teaches*
Making them women of good carriage.[1]
This is she—

95   ROMEO   Peace, peace, Mercutio, peace!
Thou talk'st of nothing.°   *imaginings; a vagina*
MERCUTIO   True. I talk of dreams,
Which are the children of an idle brain,
Begot of nothing but vain fantasy,°   *empty imagination*
Which is as thin of substance as the air,

100   And more inconstant than the wind, who woos
Even now the frozen bosom of the north,
And, being angered, puffs away from thence,
Turning his face to the dew-dropping south.
BENVOLIO   This wind you talk of blows us from ourselves.

105   Supper is done, and we shall come too late.
ROMEO   I fear too early, for my mind misgives°   *fears*
Some consequence yet hanging in the stars
Shall bitterly begin his fearful date°   *period*
With this night's revels, and expire° the term   *finish*

110   Of a despisèd life, closed in my breast,
By some vile forfeit of untimely death.[2]
But he° that hath the steerage of my course   *(God)*
Direct my sail! On, lusty gentlemen.
BENVOLIO   Strike, drum.
They march about the stage and [exeunt]

1.5

[PETER and other SERVINGMEN] come forth with napkins
PETER   Where's Potpan, that he helps not to take away? He shift
a trencher,° he scrape a trencher!   *wooden plate*
FIRST SERVINGMAN   When good manners shall lie all in one or
two men's hands, and they unwashed too, 'tis a foul° thing.   *bad; dirty*

---

3. A petition at court, which the lawyer could facilitate
for a fee.
4. Pig paid as a tithe to the parish for the support of the
priest.
5. Pluralism—holding multiple benefices simulta-
neously—was a common source of corruption in the
early modern Church.
6. *breaches:* burst fortifications. *ambuscados:*
ambushes. *Spanish blades:* swords made in Toledo were
famous for their quality.

7. Fantastically deep cups of liquor.
8. And hardens the tangles. According to folk legend,
unknotting them would anger the malicious elves.
9. Evil spirits were supposed to be responsible for
erotic dreams, taking the form of an illusory sexual
partner.
1. Excellent deportment; the capacity for carrying the
weight of a lover; childbearing.
2. As fate prematurely foreclosing on a mortgaged life.
1.5. Location: Capulet's house.

5   PETER   Away with the joint-stools,[1] remove the court-cupboard,°   *sideboard*
      look to the plate.° Good thou, save me a piece of marzipan,   *silverware*
      and, as thou loves me, let the porter let in Susan Grindstone
      and Nell. Anthony and Potpan!
    SECOND SERVINGMAN   Ay, boy, ready.
10   PETER   You are looked for and called for, asked for and sought
      for, in the great chamber.
    FIRST SERVINGMAN   We cannot be here and there too. Cheerly,
      boys! Be brisk a while, and the longest liver take all.[2]
        [They come and go, setting forth tables and chairs]
        Enter old CAPULET *[and family and] all the guests and*
        gentlewomen to the masquers
    CAPULET *[to the masquers]*   Welcome, gentlemen. Ladies that
      have their toes
15   Unplagued with corns will walk a bout° with you.   *dance a turn*
    Aha, my mistresses, which of you all
    Will now deny to dance? She that makes dainty,°   *coyly demurs*
    She, I'll swear, hath corns. Am I come near ye now?[3]
    Welcome, gentlemen. I have seen the day
20   That I have worn a visor, and could tell
    A whispering tale in a fair lady's ear
    Such as would please. 'Tis gone, 'tis gone, 'tis gone.
    You are welcome, gentlemen. Come, musicians, play.
        Music plays, and they dance. [ROMEO *stands apart*]
    A hall,[4] a hall! Give room, and foot it, girls.
25   [*To* SERVINGMEN]   More light, you knaves, and turn the tables up,[5]
    And quench the fire, the room is grown too hot.
    [*To his* COUSIN] Ah sirrah, this unlooked-for° sport comes well.   *unexpected*
    Nay, sit, nay, sit, good cousin° Capulet,   *kinsman*
    For you and I are past our dancing days.
        [CAPULET *and his* COUSIN *sit*]
30   How long is't now since last yourself and I
    Were in a masque?
    CAPULET'S COUSIN   By'r Lady, thirty years.
    CAPULET   What, man, 'tis not so much, 'tis not so much.
      'Tis since the nuptial of Lucentio,
      Come Pentecost[6] as quickly as it will,
35   Some five-and-twenty years; and then we masqued.
    CAPULET'S COUSIN   'Tis more, 'tis more. His son is elder, sir.
      His son is thirty.
    CAPULET   Will you tell me that?
      His son was but a ward[7] two years ago.
    ROMEO [*to a* SERVINGMAN]   What lady's that which doth enrich the hand
      Of yonder knight?
40   SERVINGMAN   I know not, sir.
    ROMEO   O, she doth teach the torches to burn bright!
      It seems she hangs upon the cheek of night
      As a rich jewel in an Ethiope's ear—
      Beauty too rich for use, for earth too dear.[8]

---

1. Stools made by a furniture maker, commonly used for seating at large banquets.
2. Proverbial, meaning "Life is short."
3. Does that strike home?
4. Make space in the hall.
5. Dismantle and stack the trestle tables.

6. The seventh Sunday after Easter, a standard reference point in the medieval and Renaissance calendar.
7. Subject to a guardian; a minor.
8. Too precious for this world; too valuable to die and be buried in earth.

45 So shows a snowy dove trooping° with crows   *flocking*
As yonder lady o'er her fellows shows.
The measure° done, I'll watch her place of stand,°   *dance / standing*
And, touching hers, make blessèd my rude hand.
Did my heart love till now? Forswear it, sight,
50 For I ne'er saw true beauty till this night.
TYBALT   This, by his voice, should be a Montague.
Fetch me my rapier, boy.   [*Exit* page]
           What, dares the slave
Come hither, covered with an antic face,⁹
To fleer° and scorn at our solemnity?°   *sneer / festivity*
55 Now, by the stock and honour of my kin,
To strike him dead I hold it not a sin.
CAPULET [*standing*]   Why, how now, kinsman? Wherefore storm you so?
TYBALT   Uncle, this is a Montague, our foe,
A villain° that is hither come in spite   *An ill-doer; a slave*
60 To scorn at our solemnity this night.
CAPULET   Young Romeo, is it?
TYBALT   'Tis he, that villain Romeo.
CAPULET   Content° thee, gentle coz, let him alone.   *Calm*
A bears him like a portly° gentleman,   *dignified*
And, to say truth, Verona brags of him
65 To be a virtuous and well-governed° youth.   *sensible*
I would not for the wealth of all this town
Here in my house do him disparagement.
Therefore be patient, take no note of him.
It is my will, the which if thou respect,
70 Show a fair presence° and put off these frowns,   *demeanor*
An ill-beseeming semblance° for a feast.   *expression*
TYBALT   It fits when such a villain is a guest.
I'll not endure him.
CAPULET   He shall be endured.
What, goodman¹ boy, I say he shall. Go to,²
75 Am I the master here or you? Go to—
You'll not endure him! God shall mend my soul.
You'll make a mutiny° among my guests,   *brawl*
You will set cock-a-hoop!³ You'll be the man!
TYBALT   Why, uncle, 'tis a shame.
CAPULET   Go to, go to,
80 You are a saucy boy. Is't so, indeed?
This trick° may chance to scathe° you. I know what,⁴   *stupidity / harm*
You must contrary me. Marry, 'tis time⁵—
     [*A dance ends.* JULIET *retires to her place of stand, where*
     ROMEO *awaits her*]
[*To the guests*] Well said,° my hearts! [*To* TYBALT] You are a   *done*
    princox,° go.   *cheeky boy*
Be quiet, or— [*to* SERVINGMEN] more light, more light!— [*to*
    TYBALT] for shame,
85 I'll make you quiet. [*To the guests*] What, cheerly, my hearts!
     [*The music plays again, and the guests dance*]

9. A grotesque mask; a playful mask.
1. Courtesy title applied to a commoner (and thus an insult to the noble Tybalt).
2. An expression of impatience.
3. You will abandon restraint, like a drinker who removes the tap ("cock") from the barrel or like a boastfully crowing rooster.
4. Know what I'll do; mean what I say.
5. Time to teach you a lesson; time that you became obedient.

TYBALT Patience perforce° with wilful choler° meeting   *enforced / rash anger*
      Makes my flesh tremble in their different° greeting.   *hostile*
      I will withdraw, but this intrusion shall,
      Now seeming sweet, convert to bitt'rest gall.   *Exit*
90 ROMEO [*to* JULIET, *touching her hand*] If I profane with my unworthiest hand[6]
      This holy shrine, the gentler sin is this:
      My lips, two blushing pilgrims,[7] ready stand
      To smooth that rough touch with a tender kiss.
    JULIET Good pilgrim, you do wrong your hand too much,
95   Which mannerly° devotion shows in this.   *seemly*
      For saints[8] have hands that pilgrims' hands do touch,
      And palm to palm is holy palmers'° kiss.   *pilgrims'*
    ROMEO Have not saints lips, and holy palmers, too?
    JULIET Ay, pilgrim, lips that they must use in prayer.
100 ROMEO O then, dear saint, let lips do what hands do:
      They pray; grant thou, lest faith turn to despair.
    JULIET Saints do not move, though grant for prayers' sake.[9]
    ROMEO Then move not while my prayer's effect I take.
      [*He kisses her*]
      Thus from my lips, by thine my sin is purged.
105 JULIET Then have my lips the sin that they have took.
    ROMEO Sin from my lips? O trespass sweetly urged![1]
      Give me my sin again.°   *back*
      [*He kisses her*]
    JULIET   You kiss by th' book.[2]
    NURSE Madam, your mother craves a word with you.
      [JULIET *departs to her mother*]
    ROMEO What is her mother?
    NURSE   Marry, bachelor,°   *young man*
110 Her mother is the lady of the house,
      And a good lady, and a wise and virtuous.
      I nursed her daughter that you talked withal.°   *with*
      I tell you, he that can lay hold of her
      Shall have the chinks.°   *plenty of coins*
    ROMEO [*aside*]   Is she a Capulet?
115 O dear account!° My life is my foe's debt.[3]   *costly reckoning*
    BENVOLIO Away, be gone, the sport is at the best.
    ROMEO Ay, so I fear, the more is my unrest.
    CAPULET Nay, gentlemen, prepare not to be gone.
      We have a trifling foolish banquet towards.[4]
      [*They whisper in his ear*]
120 Is it e'en so? Why then, I thank you all.
      I thank you, honest gentlemen. Good night.
      More torches here! Come on then, let's to bed.
      [*To his* COUSIN] Ah, sirrah, by my fay,° it waxes late.   *faith*
      I'll to my rest.

6. Romeo and Juliet here address each other in the form of a sonnet.
7. Florio's *World of Wordes* (1598) translates the Italian word *romeo* as "wanderer" or "palmer" (pilgrim to the Holy Land).
8. Statues or pictures of saints, which attracted Catholic pilgrims. The Elizabethan Anglican Church held that the worship of such images was blasphemy; to an English audience, therefore, Romeo's description of his love could sound like idolatry.

9. Again identifying the saint with her image. As a statue she does not move, but as a saint in heaven she can intercede with God on behalf of the worshipper.
1. Sweetly argued that the first kiss was a transgression, and sweetly advocated that the transgression of a second kiss is needed to take the sin of the first away.
2. According to the rules; implies "proficiently," "politely," or "with poetic flatteries."
3. A debt owing to my foe; in the power of my foe.
4. A trifling, paltry dessert coming.

Exeunt [CAPULET, *his* WIFE, *and his* COUSIN. *The*
guests, gentlewomen, masquers, musicians, and
servingmen begin to leave]

125 JULIET   Come hither, Nurse. What is yon gentleman?
NURSE   The son and heir of old Tiberio.
JULIET   What's he that now is going out of door?
NURSE   Marry, that, I think, be young Petruccio.
JULIET   What's he that follows here, that would not dance?
130 NURSE   I know not.
JULIET   Go ask his name.
          [NURSE *goes*]
                              If he be marrièd,
My grave is like° to be my wedding bed.   likely
NURSE [*returning*]   His name is Romeo, and a Montague,
The only son of your great enemy.
135 JULIET [*aside*]   My only love sprung from my only hate!
Too early seen unknown, and known too late!
Prodigious° birth of love it is to me   Monstrous; ominous
That I must love a loathèd enemy.
NURSE   What's tis?° what's tis?   this
JULIET   A rhyme I learnt even now
Of one I danced withal.
          One calls within 'Juliet!'
140 NURSE   Anon,° anon.   Right away
Come, let's away. The strangers all are gone.   *Exeunt*

2.0

[*Enter*] CHORUS
CHORUS   Now old° desire doth in his deathbed lie,   Romeo's former
     And young affection gapes° to be his heir.   longs
That fair for which love groaned for and would die,
     With tender Juliet matched,° is now not fair.   compared
Now Romeo is beloved and loves again,°   in return; once more
5   Alike bewitchèd by the charm of looks;[1]
But to his foe supposed° he must complain,[2]   presumed
And she steal love's sweet bait from fearful° hooks.   fearsome
Being held a foe, he may not have access
To breathe such vows as lovers use° to swear,   are accustomed
10 And she as much in love, her means much less
     To meet her new belovèd anywhere.
But passion lends them power, time means, to meet,
Temp'ring extremities° with extreme sweet.   [*Exit*]   Modifying dangers

2.1

Enter ROMEO *alone*[1]
ROMEO   Can I go forward when my heart is here?
Turn back, dull earth,[2] and find thy centre[3] out.
          [*He turns back and withdraws.*]
          Enter BENVOLIO *with* MERCUTIO

2.0
1. Appearances; desirous glances.
2. Conventionally, make lovesick speeches.
2.1 Location: Outside Capulet's house.
1. The main stage represents the area outside the wall of
Capulet's orchard and then the inside of the orchard
below the window of Juliet's room. Romeo is imagined to

leap over the garden wall when he withdraws at line 2.
2. Romeo's flesh, drawing on two traditional views of the
human body: animated dust or clay, and a "microcosm,"
or little world, which mirrors the order of the universe.
Earth was the most sluggish and immobile element.
3. The point in the earth toward which everything falls;
or Romeo's heart (metaphorically, Juliet).

BENVOLIO [*calling*]   Romeo, my cousin Romeo, Romeo!

MERCUTIO   He is wise, and, on my life, hath stol'n him° home to bed.   *himself*

5   BENVOLIO   He ran this way, and leapt this orchard wall.
Call, good Mercutio.

MERCUTIO   Nay, I'll conjure° too.   *summon as a spirit*
Romeo! Humours!⁴ Madman! Passion! Lover!
Appear thou in the likeness of a sigh.
Speak but one rhyme and I am satisfied.

10   Cry but 'Ay me!' Pronounce but 'love' and 'dove'.
Speak to my gossip° Venus one fair word,   *crony*
One nickname for her purblind° son and heir,   *dim-sighted; blind*
Young Adam⁵ Cupid, he that shot so trim°   *accurately*
When King Cophetua loved the beggar maid.⁶—

15   He heareth not, he stirreth not, he moveth not.
The ape⁷ is dead, and I must conjure him.—
I conjure thee by Rosaline's bright eyes,
By her high forehead and her scarlet lip,
By her fine foot, straight leg, and quivering thigh,

20   And the demesnes° that there adjacent lie,   *estates*
That in thy likeness thou appear to us.

BENVOLIO   An if he hear thee, thou wilt anger him.

MERCUTIO   This cannot anger him. 'Twould anger him
To raise a spirit⁸ in his mistress' circle

25   Of some strange° nature, letting it there stand   *other person's*
Till she had laid it and conjured it down.
That were some spite. My invocation
Is fair and honest. In his mistress' name,
I conjure only but to raise up him.

30   BENVOLIO   Come, he hath hid himself among these trees
To be consorted° with the humorous⁹ night.   *in company*
Blind is his love, and best befits the dark.

MERCUTIO   If love be blind, love cannot hit the mark.°   *target; vulva*
Now will he sit under a medlar¹ tree

35   And wish his mistress were that kind of fruit
As maids call medlars when they laugh alone.
O Romeo, that she were, O that she were
An open-arse,° and thou a popp'rin' pear.²   *medlar*
Romeo, good night. I'll to my truckle-bed.³

40   This field-bed⁴ is too cold for me to sleep.
Come, shall we go?

BENVOLIO   Go then, for 'tis in vain
To seek him here that means not to be found.

                    Exeunt [BENVOLIO *and* MERCUTIO]

ROMEO [*coming forward*]   He jests at scars that never felt a wound.⁵
But soft,° what light through yonder window breaks?   *wait; hush*

---

4. Pure moods, not mixed together to form an even "temper."
5. Probably alluding to Adam Bell, a famously accurate sixteenth-century archer.
6. The story of a king who falls in love with a beggar and makes her his queen was the subject of a popular ballad.
7. Foolish creature (a disrespectful endearment), or alluding to a magician's trick of "reviving" an ape that had been trained to play dead.
8. A word for "semen"; the entire speech is filled with obscene wordplay.
9. Damp; melancholy.

1. A fruit thought to resemble the female sex organs, with a play on "meddle" in the sense "have sexual intercourse with."
2. A pear from Poperinghe in Flanders, punning on "popper-in" or "pop her in."
3. Small bed, often for a child, which was stored under a larger one.
4. A lying place in the open, and a soldier's portable bed.
5. Rhymes with "found." This line precedes a scene change in most editions, although the location remains the same if both the inside and the outside of the orchard are supposed to be visible onstage.

45　　It is the east, and Juliet is the sun.
　　　Arise, fair sun, and kill the envious moon,[6]
　　　Who is already sick and pale with grief
　　　That thou, her maid, art far more fair than she.
　　　Be not her maid, since she is envious.
50　　Her vestal° livery is but sick and green,[7]　　　　　　　　*virginal*
　　　And none but fools do wear it; cast it off.
　　　　　　　[*Enter* JULIET *aloft*]
　　　It is my lady, O, it is my love.
　　　O that she knew she were!
　　　She speaks, yet she says nothing. What of that?
55　　Her eye discourses; I will answer it.
　　　I am too bold. 'Tis not to me she speaks.
　　　Two of the fairest stars in all the heaven,
　　　Having some business, do entreat her eyes
　　　To twinkle in their spheres[8] till they return.
60　　What if her eyes were there, they in her head?—
　　　The brightness of her cheek would shame those stars
　　　As daylight doth a lamp; her eye in heaven
　　　Would through the airy region° stream so bright　　　*ethereal sky*
　　　That birds would sing and think it were not night.
65　　See how she leans her cheek upon her hand.
　　　O, that I were a glove upon that hand,
　　　That I might touch that cheek!
　　JULIET　　　　　　　　　　　　Ay me.
　　ROMEO [*aside*]　　　　　　　　She speaks.
　　　O, speak again, bright angel; for thou art
　　　As glorious to this night, being o'er my head,
70　　As is a wingèd messenger° of heaven　　　　　　　　　*angel*
　　　Unto the white upturnèd[9] wond'ring eyes
　　　Of mortals that fall back to gaze[1] on him
　　　When he bestrides the lazy-passing clouds
　　　And sails upon the bosom of the air.
　　JULIET [*not knowing* ROMEO *hears her*]　O Romeo, Romeo,
75　　　　wherefore° art thou Romeo?　　　　　　　　　　　*why*
　　　Deny thy father and refuse thy name,
　　　Or if thou wilt not, be but sworn my love,
　　　And I'll no longer be a Capulet.
　　ROMEO [*aside*]　　Shall I hear more, or shall I speak at this?
80　　JULIET　'Tis but thy name that is my enemy.
　　　Thou art thyself, though° not a Montague.　　　　　　*even if*
　　　What's Montague? It is nor hand, nor foot,
　　　Nor arm, nor face, nor any other part
　　　Belonging to a man. O, be some other name!
85　　What's in a name? That which we call a rose
　　　By any other word would smell as sweet.
　　　So Romeo would, were he not Romeo called,
　　　Retain that dear perfection which he owes°　　　　　　*owns*
　　　Without that title. Romeo, doff° thy name,　　　　　　*shed*
90　　And for thy name—which is no part of thee—
　　　Take all myself.

---

6. Emblem of Diana, goddess of chastity.
7. Unfulfilled sexual desire was thought to cause green sickness (anemia) in adolescent girls; also alluding to the moon's pallor.

8. In Ptolemaic astrology, crystalline spheres around the earth that carried the heavenly bodies in their rotations.
9. Turned up, revealing the whites at the bottoms.
1. Fall backward in gazing.

ROMEO [*to* JULIET] I take thee at thy word.[2]
 Call me but love and I'll be new baptized.[3]
 Henceforth I never will be Romeo.
JULIET   What man art thou that, thus bescreened in night,
 So stumblest on my counsel?°   *private thoughts*
95 ROMEO   By a name
 I know not how to tell thee who I am.
 My name, dear saint, is hateful to myself
 Because it is an enemy to thee.
 Had I it written, I would tear the word.
100 JULIET   My ears have yet not drunk a hundred words
 Of thy tongue's uttering, yet I know the sound.
 Art thou not Romeo, and a Montague?
 ROMEO   Neither, fair maid, if either thee dislike.°   *displeases you*
 JULIET   How cam'st thou hither, tell me, and wherefore?
105 The orchard walls are high and hard to climb,
 And the place death, considering who thou art,
 If any of my kinsmen find thee here.
 ROMEO   With love's light wings did I o'erperch° these walls,   *fly over*
 For stony limits cannot hold love out,
110 And what love can do, that dares love attempt.
 Therefore thy kinsmen are no stop° to me.   *obstacle*
 JULIET   If they do see thee, they will murder thee.
 ROMEO   Alack, there lies more peril in thine eye
 Than twenty of their swords. Look thou but sweet,
115 And I am proof° against their enmity.   *armed*
 JULIET   I would not for the world they saw thee here.
 ROMEO   I have night's cloak to hide me from their eyes,
 And but° thou love me, let them find me here.   *unless*
 My life were better ended by their hate
120 Than death prorogued,° wanting of° thy love.   *deferred / lacking*
 JULIET   By whose direction found'st thou out this place?
 ROMEO   By love, that first did prompt me to enquire.
 He lent me counsel, and I lent him eyes.
 I am no pilot, yet wert thou as far
125 As that vast shore washed with the farthest sea,
 I should adventure° for such merchandise.   *voyage*
 JULIET   Thou knowest the mask of night is on my face,
 Else would a maiden blush bepaint my cheek
 For that which thou hast heard me speak tonight.
130 Fain° would I dwell on form,° fain, fain deny   *Gladly / propriety*
 What I have spoke; but farewell, compliment.°   *polite convention*
 Dost thou love me? I know thou wilt say 'Ay',
 And I will take thy word. Yet if thou swear'st
 Thou mayst prove false. At lovers' perjuries,
135 They say, Jove laughs. O gentle Romeo,
 If thou dost love, pronounce° it faithfully;   *utter*
 Or if thou think'st I am too quickly won,
 I'll frown, and be perverse,° and say thee nay,   *contrary*
 So thou wilt woo; but else,° not for the world.   *otherwise*
140 In truth, fair Montague, I am too fond,°   *infatuated*
 And therefore thou mayst think my 'haviour light.°   *licentious; capricious*

---

2. At face value; as you have asked me to.   3. Given a new name; born into a new persona.

But trust me, gentleman, I'll prove more true
Than those that have more cunning to be strange.°   *distant*
I should have been more strange, I must confess,
145   But that thou overheard'st, ere I was ware,°   *aware*
My true-love passion. Therefore pardon me,
And not° impute this yielding to light love,   *do not*
Which the dark night hath so discoverèd.°   *revealed*
ROMEO   Lady, by yonder blessèd moon I vow,
150   That tips with silver all these fruit-tree tops—
JULIET   O swear not by the moon, th'inconstant moon
That monthly changes in her circled orb,°   *orbital sphere*
Lest that thy love prove likewise variable.
ROMEO   What shall I swear by?
JULIET   Do not swear at all,
155   Or if thou wilt, swear by thy gracious self,
Which is the god of my idolatry,[4]
And I'll believe thee.
ROMEO   If my heart's dear love—
JULIET   Well, do not swear. Although I joy in thee,
I have no joy of this contract° tonight.   *exchange of vows*
160   It is too rash, too unadvised,° too sudden,   *undeliberated*
Too like the lightning which doth cease to be
Ere one can say it lightens. Sweet, good night.
This bud of love by summer's ripening breath
May prove a beauteous flower when next we meet.
165   Good night, good night. As sweet repose and rest
Come to thy heart as that within my breast.
ROMEO   O, wilt thou leave me so unsatisfied?
JULIET   What satisfaction canst thou have tonight?
ROMEO   Th'exchange of thy love's faithful vow for mine.
170   JULIET   I gave thee mine before thou didst request it,
And yet I would it were° to give again.   *were available*
ROMEO   Wouldst thou withdraw it? For what purpose, love?
JULIET   But to be frank° and give it thee again.   *generous; honest*
And yet I wish but for the thing I have.
175   My bounty is as boundless as the sea,
My love as deep. The more I give to thee
The more I have, for both are infinite.
    [NURSE] *calls within*
I hear some noise within. Dear love, adieu.—
Anon,° good Nurse!—Sweet Montague, be true.   *One moment*
180   Stay but a little; I will come again.   [*Exit*]
ROMEO   O blessèd, blessèd night! I am afeard,
Being in night, all this is but a dream,
Too flattering-sweet to be substantial.
    [*Enter* JULIET *aloft*]
JULIET   Three words, dear Romeo, and good night indeed.
185   If that thy bent of love be honourable,
Thy purpose marriage, send me word tomorrow,
By one that I'll procure to come to thee,
Where and what time thou wilt perform the rite,
And all my fortunes at thy foot I'll lay,
190   And follow thee, my lord, throughout the world.

4. Not only was loving a man more than God idolatrous, but so was swearing oaths by anything other than God.

NURSE(*within*)   Madam!
JULIET   I come, anon. [*To* ROMEO] But if thou mean'st not well,
   I do beseech thee—
NURSE(*within*)   Madam!
195 JULIET   By and by I come.—
   To cease thy strife° and leave me to my grief.   *striving*
   Tomorrow will I send.
ROMEO   So thrive my soul⁵—
JULIET   A thousand times good night.   *Exit*
200 ROMEO   A thousand times the worse to want° thy light.   *lack*
   Love goes toward love as schoolboys from their books,
   But love from love, toward school with heavy looks.
    [*He is going*]
    Enter JULIET [*aloft*] *again*
JULIET   Hist,° Romeo! Hist! O for a falconer's voice   (*falconer's call*)
   To lure this tassel-gentle⁶ back again.
205   Bondage⁷ is hoarse, and may not speak aloud,
   Else would I tear° the cave where Echo⁸ lies,   *split with cries*
   And make her airy tongue more hoarse than mine
   With repetition of my Romeo's name. Romeo!
ROMEO   It is my soul that calls upon my name.
210   How silver-sweet sound lovers' tongues by night,
   Like softest music to attending ears!
JULIET   Romeo!
ROMEO   My nyas?°   *young hawk*
JULIET   What o'clock tomorrow
   Shall I send to thee?
ROMEO   By the hour of nine.
JULIET   I will not fail; 'tis twenty year till then.
215   I have forgot why I did call thee back.
ROMEO   Let me stand here till thou remember it.
JULIET   I shall forget, to have thee still° stand there,   *always*
   Rememb'ring how I love thy company.
ROMEO   And I'll still stay, to have thee still forget,
220   Forgetting any other home but this.
JULIET   'Tis almost morning. I would have thee gone—
   And yet no farther than a wanton's° bird,   *spoiled child's*
   That lets it hop a little from his hand,
   Like a poor prisoner in his twisted gyves,°   *fetters*
225   And with a silk thread plucks it back again,
   So loving-jealous of his liberty.
ROMEO   I would° I were thy bird.   *wish*
JULIET   Sweet, so would I.
   Yet I should kill thee with much cherishing.
   Good night, good night. Parting is such sweet sorrow
230   That I shall say good night till it be morrow.
ROMEO   Sleep dwell upon thine eyes, peace in thy breast.
                         [*Exit* JULIET]
   Would I were sleep and peace, so sweet to rest.
   Hence will I to my ghostly° sire's close° cell,   *spiritual / small; private*
   His help to crave, and my dear hap° to tell.   *Exit*   *fortune*

---

5. On peril of damnation.
6. Tercel-gentle, a male peregrine falcon. Literally, a
noble ("gentle") hawk.
7. Confinement within her family's home; duty owed

her family.
8. In classical legend, a woman who, scorned by Narcissus, wasted away with grief until only a voice
remained to haunt empty caves.

2.2

Enter FRIAR [LAURENCE] *alone, with a basket*

FRIAR LAURENCE   The grey°-eyed morn smiles on the frowning night,   *pale blue*
    Chequ'ring the eastern clouds with streaks of light,
    And fleckled° darkness like a drunkard reels   *dappled*
    From forth° day's path and Titan's¹ fiery wheels.   *out of*
5 Now, ere the sun advance° his burning eye   *brings up*
    The day to cheer and night's dank dew to dry,
    I must up-fill this osier cage° of ours   *willow basket*
    With baleful weeds and precious-juicèd flowers.
    The earth, that's nature's mother, is her tomb.
10 What is her burying grave, that is her womb,
    And from her womb children of divers° kind   *several; varied*
    We sucking on her natural bosom find,
    Many for many virtues° excellent,   *healthful properties*
    None but for some,² and yet all different.
15 O mickle° is the powerful grace° that lies   *great / divine beneficence*
    In plants, herbs, stones, and their true qualities,
    For naught° so vile that on the earth doth live   *nothing is*
    But to the earth some special good doth give;
    Nor aught so good but, strained° from that fair use,   *twisted*
20 Revolts from true birth, stumbling on abuse.³
    Virtue itself turns vice being misapplied,
    And vice sometime's by action dignified.

      Enter ROMEO

    Within the infant rind of this weak flower
    Poison hath residence, and medicine power,
25 For this, being smelt, with that part° cheers each part;°   *act / bodily member*
    Being tasted, slays all senses with the heart.
    Two such opposèd kings encamp them still°   *always*
    In man as well as herbs—grace and rude will;
    And where the worser is predominant,
30 Full soon the canker° death eats up that plant.   *grub; cancer*
ROMEO   Good morrow, father.
FRIAR LAURENCE   *Benedicite.°*   *God bless you*
    What early tongue so sweet saluteth me?
    Young son, it argues a distempered head
    So soon to bid good morrow to thy bed.
35 Care keeps his watch in every old man's eye,
    And where care lodges, sleep will never lie,
    But where unbruisèd° youth with unstuffed° brain   *fresh / unanxious*
    Doth couch his limbs, there golden sleep doth reign.
    Therefore thy earliness doth me assure
40 Thou art uproused with some distemp'rature;
    Or if not so, then here I hit it right:
    Our Romeo hath not been in bed tonight.
ROMEO   That last is true; the sweeter rest was mine.
FRIAR LAURENCE   God pardon sin!—Wast thou with Rosaline?
45 ROMEO   With Rosaline, my ghostly father? No,
    I have forgot that name and that name's woe.
FRIAR LAURENCE   That's my good son; but where hast thou been then?

2.2 Location: A street in Verona.
1. Helios, a classical sun god, was descended from the
Titans. He traveled across the sky in a chariot.

2. None that is not excellent for some use.
3. Turns from its intended benefits if it happens to be
misused.

ROMEO   I'll tell thee ere thou ask it me again.
    I have been feasting with mine enemy,
50   Where on a sudden one hath wounded me
    That's by me wounded. Both our remedies
    Within thy help and holy physic° lies.   *medicine*
    I bear no hatred, blessèd man, for lo,
    My intercession° likewise steads° my foe.   *request / benefits*
55 FRIAR LAURENCE   Be plain, good son, and homely° in thy drift.   *direct*
    Riddling confession finds but riddling shrift.°   *absolution*
    ROMEO   Then plainly know my heart's dear love is set
    On the fair daughter of rich Capulet.
    As mine on hers, so hers is set on mine,
60   And all combined save what thou must combine
    By holy marriage. When and where and how
    We met, we wooed, and made exchange of vow
    I'll tell thee as we pass; but this I pray,
    That thou consent to marry us today.
65 FRIAR LAURENCE   Holy Saint Francis, what a change is here!
    Is Rosaline, that thou didst love so dear,
    So soon forsaken? Young men's love then lies
    Not truly in their hearts, but in their eyes.
    Jesu Maria, what a deal of brine
70   Hath washed thy sallow° cheeks for Rosaline!   *yellowed*
    How much salt water thrown away in waste
    To season° love, that of it doth not taste!   *preserve; flavor*
    The sun not yet thy sighs[4] from heaven clears.
    Thy old° groans yet ring in mine ancient ears.   *former*
75   Lo, here upon thy cheek the stain doth sit
    Of an old tear that is not washed off yet.
    If e'er thou wast thyself, and these woes thine,
    Thou and these woes were all for Rosaline.
    And art thou changed? Pronounce this sentence° then: *maxim; verdict*
80   Women may fall when there's no strength in men.
    ROMEO   Thou chidd'st me oft for loving Rosaline.
    FRIAR LAURENCE   For doting, not for loving, pupil mine.
    ROMEO   And bad'st me bury love.
    FRIAR LAURENCE   Not in a grave
    To lay one in, another out to have.
85 ROMEO   I pray thee, chide me not. Her I love now
    Doth grace for grace and love for love allow.
    The other did not so.
    FRIAR LAURENCE   O, she knew well
    Thy love did read by rote, that could not spell.[5]
    But come, young waverer, come, go with me.
90   In one respect I'll thy assistant be;
    For this alliance may so happy prove
    To turn your households' rancour to pure love.
    ROMEO   O, let us hence! I stand° on sudden haste.   *depend; insist*
    FRIAR LAURENCE   Wisely and slow. They stumble that run fast.
                                  Exeunt

---

4. The mist Romeo's exhalations produced.
5. Did recite the memorized phrases of love poetry, without understanding or meaning them.

2.3

Enter BENVOLIO *and* MERCUTIO

MERCUTIO   Where the devil should this Romeo be? Came he
    not home tonight?°   *last night*

BENVOLIO   Not to his father's. I spoke with his man.

MERCUTIO   Why, that same pale° hard-hearted wench, that   *fair-skinned; frigid*
    Rosaline,

5   Torments him so that he will sure run mad.

BENVOLIO   Tybalt, the kinsman to old Capulet,
    Hath sent a letter to his father's house.

MERCUTIO   A challenge, on my life.

BENVOLIO   Romeo will answer° it.   *accept*

MERCUTIO   Any man that can write may answer a letter.

10 BENVOLIO   Nay, he will answer the letter's master, how he dares,
    being dared.

MERCUTIO   Alas, poor Romeo, he is already dead—stabbed with
    a white wench's black eye, run through the ear with a love
    song, the very pin[1] of his heart cleft with the blind bow-boy's
15   butt-shaft;[2] and is he a man to encounter Tybalt?

BENVOLIO   Why, what is Tybalt?

MERCUTIO   More than Prince of Cats.[3] O, he's the courageous
    captain of compliments.° He fights as you sing pricksong:[4]   *formalities of dueling*
    keeps time, distance,[5] and proportion.° He rests his minim   *harmony; form*
20   rests:[6] one, two, and the third in your bosom; the very butcher
    of a silk button.[7] A duellist, a duellist; a gentleman of the very
    first house of the first and second cause.[8] Ah, the immortal
    passado, the *punto reverso*, the *hai*.[9]

BENVOLIO   The what?

25 MERCUTIO   The pox of° such antic,° lisping, affecting° phan-   *on / grotesque / affected*
    tasims,° these new tuners of accent![1] 'By Jesu, a very good blade,   *bizarrely mannered men*
    a very tall° man, a very good whore.' Why° is not this a lamen-   *valiant / Why, now*
    table thing, grandsire, that we should be thus afflicted with
    these strange[2] flies,° these fashionmongers, these 'pardon-   *gaudy buzzers*
30   me's',[3] who stand so much on the new form that they cannot
    sit at ease on the old bench?[4] O, their bones, their bones![5]

    Enter ROMEO

BENVOLIO   Here comes Romeo, here comes Romeo!

MERCUTIO   Without his roe, like a dried herring.[6] O flesh, flesh,

---

2.3 Location: Scene continues.

1. Peg in the center of an archery target.

2. Blunt practice arrow, fit for children and hence for
Cupid.

3. Called Tybalt or Tibert in medieval stories of Rey-
nard the fox. "Catso," from the Italian word for "penis,"
was also a slang term for a rogue.

4. Sung from sheet music and thus more precise and
invariable than extempore or remembered music.

5. Musical intervals between notes; also, a set space to
be kept between combatants.

6. Short musical rests, referring to the brief strategic
pauses in a duel.

7. Alluding to the boast of an Italian fencing master in
London that he could "hit any Englishman with a
thrust upon any button."

8. *gentleman . . . cause:* superior practitioner of taking
up quarrels as duels. *first house:* the best fencing school.
cause: a reason that according to the etiquette of fencing
would require an honorable gentleman to seek a duel.

9. Italian fencing terms for a lunging sword thrust,
backhanded thrust, and thrust that reaches through.

1. These faddishly novel speakers, such as those
importing foreign phrases. A typical Renaissance En-
glish satire, here seemingly unaffected by the fact that
Italian is the native tongue of Verona.

2. Newfangled; foreign.

3. *pardon-me's:* the fastidiously mannered, affecting
the French *pardonnez-moi*.

4. *who . . . bench:* as if both Mercutio and Benvolio
were elderly ("grandsire"), viewing the decline of the
young. *stand:* insist. *form:* etiquette; fashion; bench.

5. *O . . . bones:* Aching on the austere furniture of their
predecessors; infected with the "bone disease," syphilis.
Mercutio may also be satirizing the courtly habit of cry-
ing "Bon! Bon!" (French for "good") as a kind of inane
flattery.

6. Emaciated, since the roe is removed in curing. This
leaves Romeo's name a mournful wail, "Me, O." He is
also missing his roe deer (female, named Rosaline).

how art thou fishified![7] Now is he for the numbers° that *verses*
35 Petrarch[8] flowed in. Laura to° his lady was a kitchen wench— *compared to*
marry, she had a better love to berhyme her—Dido[9] a dowdy,
Cleopatra a gypsy,[1] Helen and Hero[2] hildings° and harlots, *hussies*
Thisbe[3] a grey° eye or so, but not to the purpose.° Signor *blue / of consequence*
Romeo, *bonjour*. There's a French salutation to your French
40 slop.° You gave us the counterfeit fairly last night. *loose breeches*
ROMEO   Good morrow to you both. What counterfeit did I give
you?
MERCUTIO   The slip,[4] sir, the slip. Can you not conceive?° *understand*
ROMEO   Pardon, good Mercutio. My business was great, and in
45 such a case as mine a man may strain° courtesy. *nearly abandon*
MERCUTIO   That's as much as to say such a case as yours con-
strains a man to bow in the hams.[5]
ROMEO   Meaning to curtsy.[6]
MERCUTIO   Thou hast most kindly hit[7] it.
50 ROMEO   A most courteous exposition.
MERCUTIO   Nay, I am the very pink° of courtesy. *nonpareil; carnation*
ROMEO   Pink for flower.° *dianthus; vulva*
MERCUTIO   Right.
ROMEO   Why, then is my pump° well flowered.[8] *shoe; penis*
55 MERCUTIO   Sure wit, follow me° this jest now till thou hast worn *chase; respond to*
out thy pump, that when the single° sole of it is worn, the jest *thin*
may remain, after the wearing, solely singular.° *utterly unique*
ROMEO   O single-soled° jest, solely° singular for the singleness!° *shoddy / only / foolishness*
MERCUTIO   Come between us, good Benvolio. My wits faints.[9]
60 ROMEO   Switch and spurs,[1] switch and spurs, or I'll cry a match.° *claim a victory*
MERCUTIO   Nay, if our wits run the wild-goose chase,[2] I am done,
for thou hast more of the wild goose° in one of thy wits than I *folly*
am sure I have in my whole five. Was I with° you there for the *even with*
goose?
65 ROMEO   Thou wast never with me for anything when thou wast
not there for the goose.[3]
MERCUTIO   I will bite thee by the ear[4] for that jest.
ROMEO   Nay, good goose, bite not.[5]
MERCUTIO   Thy wit is very bitter sweeting,° it is a most sharp *apple*
70 sauce.° *mockery*
ROMEO   And is it not then well served in to a sweet goose?
MERCUTIO   O, here's a wit of cheverel,° that stretches from an *kid leather*
inch narrow to an ell broad.[6]

---

7. Gone pale and limp, turned into a herring. Fish, thought weak and relatively unnourishing, was the substitute for "flesh" (meat) during fasts.
8. Petrarch's sonnets addressed to Laura were the model for an English love-sonnet craze.
9. The beautiful queen of Carthage who fell in love with Aeneas but was deserted by him in Virgil's *Aeneid*.
1. A term of abuse. Gypsies were supposed to have come from Egypt, where Cleopatra was queen and lover of Julius Caesar and Mark Antony.
2. Helen's abduction by Paris initiated the Trojan War. Hero was Leander's lover in a tragic legend.
3. Beloved of Pyramus in a classical legend that parallels *Romeo and Juliet*. The young lovers, coming from hostile families, die as a result of a missed meeting and misinterpreted evidence.
4. Counterfeit coin.

5. Playing on "business" as "sexual intercourse" and "case" as "vagina." Mercutio suggests that Romeo needs to flex his buttocks or he may wind up with a leg-weakening venereal disease.
6. Pronounced the same as "courtesy."
7. Most truly guessed it; most truly sexually penetrated it.
8. Pinked, or decoratively perforated.
9. Treating the exchange of wit as a duel.
1. Flog your wits to a full gallop; continue.
2. A cross-country horse race in which the leader chose the course and the rest had to follow.
3. Silliness; whore's company.
4. Usually suggesting affectionate nibbling.
5. A proverbial cry for mercy, here used ironically.
6. That spreads itself very thin (an ell was forty-five inches).

ROMEO   I stretch it out for that word 'broad', which, added to the
75   goose, proves thee far and wide a broad goose.[7]

MERCUTIO   Why, is not this better now than groaning for love?
    Now art thou sociable, now art thou Romeo, now art thou what
    thou art by art° as well as by nature, for this drivelling love is   *learning*
    like a great natural° that runs lolling up and down to hide his   *idiot*
80   bauble[8] in a hole.

BENVOLIO   Stop there, stop there.

MERCUTIO   Thou desirest me to stop in[9] my tale° against the   *story; penis*
    hair.[1]

BENVOLIO   Thou wouldst else have made thy tale large.

85   MERCUTIO   O, thou art deceived, I would have made it short, for
    I was come to the whole depth of my tale, and meant indeed
    to occupy the argument° no longer.   *topic*

            Enter NURSE, and her man [PETER]

ROMEO   Here's goodly gear.[2]

BENVOLIO   A sail, a sail![3]

90   MERCUTIO   Two, two—a shirt° and a smock.°   *man / woman*

NURSE   Peter.

PETER   Anon.°   *At your service*

NURSE   My fan, Peter.

MERCUTIO   Good Peter, to hide her face, for her fan's the fairer
95   face.

NURSE   God ye° good morrow,° gentlemen.   *give you / morning*

MERCUTIO   God ye good e'en,° fair gentlewoman.   *afternoon*

NURSE   Is it good e'en?

MERCUTIO   'Tis no less, I tell ye: for the bawdy hand of the dial
100   is now upon the prick° of noon.   *mark; penis*

NURSE   Out upon you,[4] what° a man are you!   *what sort of*

ROMEO   One, gentlewoman, that God hath made for himself to
    mar.[5]

NURSE   By my troth, it is well said. 'For himself to mar', quoth
105   a?° Gentlemen, can any of you tell me where I may find the   *he*
    young Romeo?

ROMEO   I can tell you, but young Romeo will be older when you
    have found him than he was when you sought him. I am the
    youngest of that name, for fault° of a worse.   *lack*

110   NURSE   You say well.

MERCUTIO   Yea, is the worst well? Very well took, i'faith, wisely,
    wisely.

NURSE   [*to ROMEO*]   If you be he, sir, I desire some confidence
    with you.

115   BENVOLIO   She will endite[6] him to some supper.

MERCUTIO   A bawd, a bawd, a bawd. So ho![7]

ROMEO   What hast thou found?°   *spotted; figured out*

---

7. A gross idiot; a licentious fellow; a goose fattened for
the table.
8. *that . . . bauble:* who runs with his tongue hanging
out to cover up a Jester's wand, at one end either
grotesquely carved or adorned with an inflated pig's
bladder; penis.
9. Cease; stuff in.
1. Against the grain; against the pubic hair.
2. Spoken ironically of Mercutio's witticisms or the
Nurse's voluminous appearance.
3. A sailor's cry upon sighting another ship.

4. An expression of indignation.
5. *One . . . mar:* combines two proverbial expressions.
"It is his to make or mar" suggests that Mercutio has
the free will to determine his own character. "He is a
man of God's making" places the blame for Mercutio's
character on God.
6. Deliberately substituted for "invite," to mock the
Nurse's erroneous use of "confidence" for "conference"
in the line above.
7. The cry of a hunter who has spotted his quarry.

MERCUTIO No hare,° sir, unless a hare, sir, in a lenten pie,[8] that   *prostitute*
is something stale and hoar ere it be spent.[9]
     He walks by them and sings
120   An old hare hoar
            And an old hare hoar
              Is very good meat in Lent.
            But a hare that is hoar
            Is too much for a score[1]
125   When it hoars° ere it be spent.   *turns moldy; whores*
Romeo, will you come to your father's? We'll to dinner thither.
ROMEO I will follow you.
MERCUTIO Farewell, ancient lady. Farewell, [*sings*] 'lady, lady,
lady'.[2]   *Exeunt* MERCUTIO [*and*] BENVOLIO
130 NURSE I pray you, sir, what saucy merchant° was this that was so   *commoner*
full of his ropery?°   *knavery*
ROMEO A gentleman, Nurse, that loves to hear himself talk, and
will speak more in a minute than he will stand to° in a month.   *perform*
NURSE An a° speak anything against me, I'll take him down° an   *If he / humble him*
135 a were lustier[3] than he is, and twenty such jacks;° an if I cannot,   *scoundrels*
I'll find those that shall. Scurvy knave! I am none of his flirt-
jills,° I am none of his skeans-mates.[4] [*To* PETER] And thou   *loose women*
must stand by, too, and suffer every knave to use me at his
pleasure.
140 PETER I saw no man use you at his pleasure. If I had, my weapon
should quickly have been out; I warrant you, I dare draw as
soon as another man if I see occasion in a good quarrel, and
the law on my side.
NURSE Now, afore God, I am so vexed that every part about me
145 quivers. Scurvy knave! [*To* ROMEO] Pray you, sir, a word; and,
as I told you, my young lady bid me enquire you out. What she
bid me say I will keep to myself, but first let me tell ye if ye
should lead her in a fool's paradise, as they say, it were a very
gross° kind of behaviour, as they say, for the gentlewoman is   *outrageous*
150 young; and therefore if you should deal double° with her, truly   *falsely; forcefully*
it were an ill thing to be offered to any gentlewoman, and very
weak° dealing.   *poor*
ROMEO Nurse, commend me to thy lady and mistress. I protest°   *swear*
unto thee—
155 NURSE Good heart, and i'faith I will tell her as much. Lord,
Lord, she will be a joyful woman.
ROMEO What wilt thou tell her, Nurse? Thou dost not mark°   *pay attention to*
me.
NURSE I will tell her, sir, that you do protest;[5] which as I take it
160 is a gentlemanlike offer.
ROMEO Bid her devise
Some means to come to shrift this afternoon,
And there she shall at Friar Laurence' cell
Be shrived° and married. [*Offering money*] Here is for thy pains.   *absolved after confession*
165 NURSE No, truly, sir, not a penny.

---

8. Meat illicitly eaten during Lent by disguising it in a pie, just as the Nurse's unattractiveness hides whatever promiscuity she may practice.
9. Somewhat stale and moldy by the time the last of the rationed luxury is consumed.
1. Is too much to pay for.

2. Refrain to a ballad about a perfectly chaste woman, intended derisively.
3. Stronger; hornier.
4. Knife-wielding rogues.
5. The Nurse takes this as a marriage offer, probably confusing "protest" with "propose."

ROMEO   Go to, I say, you shall.

NURSE [*taking the money*]   This afternoon, sir. Well, she shall be there.

ROMEO   And stay, good Nurse, behind the abbey wall.
  Within this hour my man shall be with thee
170 And bring thee cords made like a tackled stair,°   a knotted ladder
  Which to the high topgallant[6] of my joy
  Must be my convoy° in the secret night.   means of conveyance
  Farewell. Be trusty, and I'll quit° thy pains.   repay
  Farewell. Commend me to thy mistress.

175 NURSE   Now God in heaven bless thee! Hark you, sir.

ROMEO   What sayst thou, my dear Nurse?

NURSE   Is your man secret?° Did you ne'er hear say   discreet
  'Two may keep counsel, putting one away'?

ROMEO   I warrant thee my man's as true as steel.

180 NURSE   Well, sir, my mistress is the sweetest lady.
  Lord, Lord, when 'twas a little prating thing—
  O, there is a nobleman in town, one Paris,
  That would fain lay knife aboard;[7] but she, good soul,
  Had as lief° see a toad, a very toad,   gladly
185 As see him. I anger her sometimes,
  And tell her that Paris is the properer° man;   more handsome
  But I'll warrant you, when I say so she looks
  As pale as any clout° in the versal° world.   sheet / entire
  Doth not rosemary[8] and Romeo begin
190 Both with a° letter?   the same

ROMEO   Ay, Nurse, what of that? Both with an 'R'.

NURSE   Ah, mocker—that's the dog's name.[9] 'R' is for the—no, I
  know it begins with some other letter, and she hath the pret-
  tiest sententious[1] of it, of you and rosemary, that it would do
195 you good to hear it.

ROMEO   Commend me to thy lady.

NURSE   Ay, a thousand times. Peter!

PETER   Anon.

NURSE [*giving* PETER *her fan*]   Before,° and apace.°   Lead / quickly
                    Exeunt [PETER *and* NURSE *at one door,*
                               ROMEO *at another door*]

2.4

  Enter JULIET

JULIET   The clock struck nine when I did send the Nurse.
  In half an hour she promised to return.
  Perchance she cannot meet him. That's not so.
  O, she is lame! Love's heralds should be thoughts,
5 Which ten times faster glides than the sun's beams
  Driving back shadows over louring° hills.   dark; threatening
  Therefore do nimble-pinioned° doves draw Love,°   winged / Venus
  And therefore hath the wind-swift Cupid wings.
  Now is the sun upon the highmost hill°   zenith
10 Of this day's journey, and from nine till twelve
  Is three long hours, yet she is not come.
  Had she affections° and warm youthful blood   passions

6. The highest platform on a mast, from which the top-
gallant sail was handled.
7. One claimed a place at dinner by laying one's per-
sonal knife on the table ("board").
8. A token of remembrance, between lovers and also of

the dead.
9. "R"—the sound "arr"—was thought to resemble a
dog's snarl.
1. Blunder for "sentences"; sayings.
2.4 Location: Capulet's orchard.

She would be as swift in motion as a ball.
My words would bandy° her to my sweet love,   *volley (as in tennis)*
15 And his to me.
But old folks, many feign° as they were dead—   *act*
Unwieldy, slow, heavy, and pale as lead.
    Enter NURSE [*and* PETER]
O God, she comes! O honey Nurse, what news?
Hast thou met with him? Send thy man away.
20 NURSE   Peter, stay° at the gate.   [*Exit* PETER]   *wait*
JULIET   Now, good sweet Nurse—O Lord, why look'st thou sad?
Though news be sad, yet tell them merrily;
If good, thou sham'st the music of sweet news
By playing it to me with so sour a face.
25 NURSE   I am a-weary. Give me leave° a while.   *Let me alone*
Fie, how my bones ache. What a jaunce° have I!   *trotting about*
JULIET   I would thou hadst my bones and I thy news.
Nay, come, I pray thee speak, good, good Nurse, speak.
NURSE   Jesu, what haste! Can you not stay a while?
30 Do you not see that I am out of breath?
JULIET   How art thou out of breath when thou hast breath
To say to me that thou art out of breath?
The excuse that thou dost make in this delay
Is longer than the tale thou dost excuse.
35 Is thy news good or bad? Answer to that.
Say either, and I'll stay° the circumstance.°   *wait for / full details*
Let me be satisfied: is't good or bad?
NURSE   Well, you have made a simple° choice. You know not   *foolish*
how to choose a man. Romeo? No, not he; though his face be
40 better than any man's, yet his leg excels all men's, and for a
hand and a foot and a body, though they be not to be talked
on,° yet they are past compare. He is not the flower of cour   *worth mentioning*
tesy, but, I'll warrant him, as gentle as a lamb. Go thy ways,[1]
wench. Serve God. What, have you dined at home?
45 JULIET   No, no. But all this did I know before.
What says he of our marriage—what of that?
NURSE   Lord, how my head aches! What a head have I!
It beats as it would fall in twenty pieces.
My back—
    [JULIET *rubs her back*]
        a' t'other side—ah, my back, my back!
50 Beshrew° your heart for sending me about   *Curse (mild oath)*
To catch my death with jauncing up and down.
JULIET   I'faith, I am sorry that thou art not well.
Sweet, sweet, sweet Nurse, tell me, what says my love?
NURSE   Your love says, like an honest° gentleman, and a courte-   *honorable*
55 ous, and a kind,° and a handsome, and, I warrant, a virtuous—   *true*
where is your mother?
JULIET   Where is my mother? Why, she is within.
Where should she be? How oddly thou repliest!
'Your love says like an honest gentleman
"Where is your mother?"'
60 NURSE   O, God's Lady° dear!   *Mary, Mother of God*
Are you so hot?° Marry come up, I trow.[2]   *impatient; aroused*

---

1. Off you go; do as you will do.
2. *Marry . . . trow:* an expression of indignant or amused surprise and reproof.

Is this the poultice for my aching bones?
Henceforward do your messages yourself.

JULIET Here's such a coil!° Come, what says Romeo?   *to-do*

65 NURSE Have you got leave to go to shrift today?

JULIET I have.

NURSE Then hie° you hence to Friar Laurence' cell.   *hurry*
There stays a husband to make you a wife.
Now comes the wanton° blood up in your cheeks.   *fickle; lustful*

70 They'll be in scarlet straight° at any news.   *immediately*
Hie you to church. I must another way,
To fetch a ladder by the which your love
Must climb a bird's nest soon, when it is dark.
I am the drudge, and toil in your delight,

75 But you shall bear the burden³ soon at night.
Go, I'll to dinner. Hie you to the cell.

JULIET Hie to high fortune! Honest Nurse, farewell.

                               Exeunt [severally]°   *separately*

                               2.5

                Enter FRIAR [LAURENCE] *and* ROMEO

FRIAR LAURENCE So smile the heavens upon this holy act
That after-hours with sorrow chide us not!

ROMEO Amen, amen. But come what sorrow can,
It cannot countervail the exchange of joy

5 That one short minute gives me in her sight.
Do thou but close° our hands with holy words,   *join*
Then love-devouring death do what he dare—
It is enough I may but call her mine.

FRIAR LAURENCE These violent° delights have violent ends,   *sudden; intense*

10 And in their triumph die like fire and powder,¹
Which as they kiss consume. The sweetest honey
Is loathsome in his own deliciousness,
And in the taste confounds the appetite.²
Therefore love moderately. Long love doth so.

15 Too swift arrives as tardy as too slow.

                Enter JULIET *somewhat fast, and embraceth* ROMEO

Here comes the lady. O, so light³ a foot
Will ne'er wear out the everlasting flint.⁴
A lover may bestride the gossamers°   *spiders' threads*
That idles in the wanton° summer air,   *playful*

20 And yet not fall, so light is vanity.⁵

JULIET Good even° to my ghostly° confessor.   *evening / spiritual*

FRIAR LAURENCE Romeo shall thank thee, daughter, for us both.

JULIET As much to him,⁶ else is his thanks too much.

ROMEO Ah, Juliet, if the measure° of thy joy   *measuring vessel*

25 Be heaped like mine, and that thy skill be more
To blazon° it, then sweeten with thy breath°   *describe; trumpet / speech*
This neighbour air, and let rich music's tongue
Unfold the imagined° happiness that both   *unexpressed ideas of*

---

3. Do the work; carry a lover; sing the theme of a duet, alluding to the sounds of lovemaking.
2.5 Location: Friar Laurence's cell.
1. Gunpowder. *triumph:* victory; celebration.
2. *The sweetest . . . appetite:* from the proverb "Too much honey cloys the stomach." *his:* its. *confounds:*

overwhelms.
3. Swift; dainty; free of care; sexually open.
4. Will never endure or subdue the hard road of life.
5. Temporary worldly pleasure.
6. An equal amount. Both greetings consist of a kiss.

Receive in either by this dear encounter.

30 JULIET Conceit,° more rich in matter than in words,   *Imagination*
    Brags of his substance,[7] not of ornament.°   *rhetoric; form*
    They are but beggars that can count their worth,
    But my true love is grown to such excess
    I cannot sum up some of half my wealth.[8]

35 FRIAR LAURENCE Come, come with me, and we will make short work,
    For, by your leaves, you shall not stay alone
    Till Holy Church incorporate two in one.[9]   *Exeunt*

3.1

Enter MERCUTIO [*with his page*], BENVOLIO, *and men*

BENVOLIO I pray thee, good Mercutio, let's retire.
    The day is hot, the Capels are abroad,°   *about*
    And if we meet we shall not scape a brawl,
    For now, these hot days, is the mad blood stirring.

5 MERCUTIO Thou art like one of these fellows that, when he
    enters the confines of a tavern, claps me° his sword upon the   *claps me = claps*
    table and says 'God send me no need of thee', and by the oper-
    ation° of the second cup, draws him on the drawer[1] when   *effect*
    indeed there is no need.

10 BENVOLIO Am I like such a fellow?

MERCUTIO Come, come, thou art as hot a jack° in thy mood as   *rogue*
    any in Italy, and as soon moved° to be moody,° and as soon   *provoked / angry*
    moody to be° moved.   *at being*

BENVOLIO And what to?

15 MERCUTIO Nay, an there were two such, we should have none
    shortly, for one would kill the other. Thou—why, thou wilt
    quarrel with a man that hath a hair more or a hair less in his
    beard than thou hast. Thou wilt quarrel with a man for crack-
    ing nuts, having no other reason but because thou hast hazel
20   eyes. What eye but such an eye would spy out such a quarrel?
    Thy head is as full of quarrels as an egg is full of meat,° and yet   *foodstuff*
    thy head hath been beaten as addle° as an egg for quarrelling.   *rotten; confused*
    Thou hast quarrelled with a man for coughing in the street
    because he hath wakened thy dog that hath lain asleep in the
25   sun. Didst thou not fall out with a tailor for wearing his new
    doublet before Easter;[2] with another for tying his new shoes
    with old ribbon? And yet thou wilt tutor me from quarrelling!

BENVOLIO An I were so apt to quarrel as thou art, any man
    should buy the fee-simple[3] of my life for an hour and a quarter.

30 MERCUTIO The fee simple? O, simple!°   *foolish*

Enter TYBALT, PETRUCCIO, *and others*

BENVOLIO By my head, here comes the Capulets.

MERCUTIO By my heel, I care not.

TYBALT [*to* PETRUCCIO *and the others*] Follow me close, for I
    will speak to them.
    [*To the Montagues*] Gentlemen, good e'en. A word with one
    of you.

---

7. Wealth; content.
8. *I . . . wealth:* The amount is too large to be under-
stood precisely.
9. Literally, put two into one body. Marriage mystically
united man and woman in "one flesh" (Genesis 2:2).
3.1 Location: A street in Verona.

1. Draws his sword on the server.
2. New fashions came out at Easter, after the austere
penitence of Lent.
3. Outright possession of land, usually an inherited
right; here, the whole value of Benvolio's life.

35 MERCUTIO   And but one word with one of us? Couple it with
something: make it a word and a blow.

TYBALT   You shall find me apt enough to that, sir, an you will
give me occasion.

MERCUTIO   Could you not take some occasion without giving?

40 TYBALT   Mercutio, thou consort'st° with Romeo.   *associate*

MERCUTIO   'Consort'?° What, dost thou make us minstrels? An   *Play in a band*
thou make minstrels of us, look to hear nothing but discords.
[*Touching his rapier*] Here's my fiddlestick; here's that shall
make you dance. Zounds°—'Consort'!   *By God's wounds*

45 BENVOLIO   We talk here in the public haunt° of men.   *gathering place*
Either withdraw unto some private place,
Or reason coldly° of your grievances,   *dispassionately*
Or else depart.° Here all eyes gaze on us.   *separate*

MERCUTIO   Men's eyes were made to look, and let them gaze.
50 I will not budge for no man's pleasure, I.
         Enter ROMEO

TYBALT   Well, peace be with you, sir. Here comes my man.

MERCUTIO   But I'll be hanged, sir, if he wear your livery.[4]
Marry, go before to field, he'll be your follower.°   *servant; pursuer*
Your worship in that sense may call him 'man'.

55 TYBALT   Romeo, the love I bear thee can afford
No better term than this: thou art a villain.°   *base commoner; rogue*

ROMEO   Tybalt, the reason that I have to love thee
Doth much excuse the appertaining rage
To[5] such a greeting. Villain am I none.
60 Therefore, farewell. I see thou knowest me not.

TYBALT   Boy, this shall not excuse the injuries
That thou hast done me. Therefore turn and draw.

ROMEO   I do protest I never injured thee,
But love thee better than thou canst devise
65 Till thou shalt know the reason of my love.
And so, good Capulet—which name I tender°   *regard; love*
As dearly as mine own—be satisfied.

MERCUTIO [*drawing*]   O calm, dishonourable, vile submission!
Alla stoccado carries it away.[6]
70 Tybalt, you ratcatcher, come, will you walk?°   *withdraw to fight*

TYBALT   What wouldst thou have with me?

MERCUTIO   Good King of Cats, nothing but one of your nine
lives. That I mean to make bold withal,° and, as you shall use   *be so bold as to take*
me hereafter,[7] dry-beat° the rest of the eight. Will you pluck   *soundly thrash*
75 your sword out of his pilcher° by the ears? Make haste, lest mine   *leather scabbard*
be about your ears ere it be out.

TYBALT [*drawing*]   I am for you.

ROMEO   Gentle Mercutio, put thy rapier up.

MERCUTIO [*to* TYBALT]   Come, sir, your *passado*.°   *forward thrust*
[*They fight*]

80 ROMEO [*drawing*]   Draw, Benvolio. Beat down their weapons.
Gentlemen, for shame forbear this outrage.°   *violence*
Tybalt, Mercutio, the Prince expressly hath
Forbid this bandying° in Verona streets.   *strife*

---

4. Mercutio obnoxiously mistakes Tybalt's "my man"   appropriate anger at.
for "personal servant."   6. The rapier thrust wins the day.
5. *Doth . . . / To*: Permits me to put aside my otherwise   7. And, according to how you subsequently treat me.

Hold, Tybalt, good Mercutio.
[ROMEO *beats down their points and rushes between*
them.] TYBALT *under Romeo's arm thrusts* MERCUTIO *in*
85 PETRUCCIO   Away, Tybalt!
Exeunt TYBALT [PETRUCCIO, *and their followers*]
MERCUTIO   I am hurt.
A plague o' both your houses. I am sped.°   *finished*
Is he gone, and hath nothing?
BENVOLIO   What, art thou hurt?
MERCUTIO   Ay, ay, a scratch, a scratch; marry, 'tis enough.
90 Where is my page? Go, villain. Fetch a surgeon.
[*Exit page*]
ROMEO   Courage, man. The hurt cannot be much.
MERCUTIO   No, 'tis not so deep as a well, nor so wide as a church
door, but 'tis enough. 'Twill serve. Ask for me tomorrow, and
you shall find me a grave man. I am peppered,° I warrant, for   *done for*
95 this world. A plague o' both your houses! Zounds, a dog, a rat,
a mouse, a cat, to scratch a man to death! A braggart, a rogue,
a villain, that fights by the book of arithmetic![8] Why the devil
came you between us? I was hurt under your arm.
ROMEO   I thought all for the best.
100 MERCUTIO   Help me into some house, Benvolio,
Or I shall faint. A plague o' both your houses.
They have made worms' meat of me.
I have it, and soundly, too. Your houses!
Exeunt [*all but* ROMEO]
ROMEO   This gentleman, the Prince's near ally,°   *relative*
105 My very° friend, hath got this mortal hurt   *true*
In my behalf, my reputation stained
With Tybalt's slander—Tybalt, that an hour
Hath been my cousin! O sweet Juliet,
Thy beauty hath made me effeminate,
110 And in my temper[9] softened valour's steel.
Enter BENVOLIO
BENVOLIO   O Romeo, Romeo, brave Mercutio is dead!
That gallant spirit hath aspired° the clouds,   *ascended to*
Which too untimely here did scorn the earth.
ROMEO   This day's black fate on more days doth depend.°   *hang over*
115 This but begins the woe others must end.
Enter TYBALT
BENVOLIO   Here comes the furious Tybalt back again.
ROMEO   He gad° in triumph, and Mercutio slain?   *gallivanting*
Away to heaven, respective lenity,°   *respectful lenience*
And fire-eyed fury be my conduct° now.   *guide*
120 Now, Tybalt, take the 'villain' back again
That late thou gav'st me, for Mercutio's soul
Is but a little way above our heads,
Staying for thine to keep him company.
Either thou, or I, or both must go with him.
125 TYBALT   Thou, wretched boy, that didst consort° him here,   *accompany*
Shalt with him hence.

8. By the numbers; according to a fencing manual.
9. Emotional makeup, here suggesting the hardened
character of a fighting man (*temper:* to harden steel). It

was believed that too much time with or passion for
women would cause a man to become effeminate.

ROMEO   This shall determine that.
    They fight. TYBALT *falls [and dies]*
BENVOLIO   Romeo, away, be gone.
  The citizens are up,° and Tybalt slain.   *up in arms*
  Stand not amazed.° The Prince will doom° thee death   *stupefied / sentence*
130 If thou art taken. Hence, be gone, away.
ROMEO   O, I am fortune's fool!°   *dupe*
BENVOLIO   Why dost thou stay?
                               Exit ROMEO
    Enter CITIZENS [OF THE WATCH]
CITIZEN OF THE WATCH   Which way ran he that killed Mercutio?
  Tybalt, that murderer, which way ran he?
BENVOLIO   There lies that Tybalt.
CITIZEN OF THE WATCH   Up, sir, go with me.
135 I charge thee in the Prince's name, obey.
    Enter PRINCE, *old* MONTAGUE, CAPULET, *their* WIVES,
    and all
PRINCE   Where are the vile beginners of this fray?
BENVOLIO   O noble Prince, I can discover° all   *reveal*
  The unlucky manage° of this fatal brawl.   *handling*
  There lies the man, slain by young Romeo,
140 That slew thy kinsman, brave Mercutio.
CAPULET'S WIFE   Tybalt, my cousin, O, my brother's child!
  O Prince, O cousin, husband! O, the blood is spilled
  Of my dear kinsman! Prince, as thou art true,
  For blood of ours shed blood of Montague!
  O cousin, cousin!
145 PRINCE   Benvolio, who began this fray?
BENVOLIO   Tybalt, here slain, whom Romeo's hand did slay.
  Romeo, that spoke him° fair,° bid him bethink   *to him / courteously*
  How nice° the quarrel was, and urged withal°   *trivial / also*
  Your high displeasure. All this—utterèd
150 With gentle breath, calm look, knees humbly bowed—
  Could not take° truce with the unruly spleen°   *arrange / bitter mood*
  Of Tybalt deaf to peace, but that he tilts
  With piercing steel at bold Mercutio's breast,
  Who, all as hot, turns deadly point to point,
155 And, with a martial scorn, with one hand beats
  Cold death aside,[1] and with the other sends
  It back to Tybalt, whose dexterity
  Retorts° it. Romeo, he cries aloud,   *Returns*
  'Hold, friends, friends, part!' and swifter than his tongue
160 His agent° arm beats down their fatal points,   *effective*
  And 'twixt them rushes, underneath whose arm
  An envious° thrust from Tybalt hit the life   *A malicious*
  Of stout° Mercutio, and then Tybalt fled,   *courageous*
  But by and by comes back to Romeo,
165 Who had but newly entertained° revenge,   *considered*
  And to't they go like lightning; for ere I
  Could draw to part them was stout Tybalt slain,
  And as he fell did Romeo turn and fly.
  This is the truth, or let Benvolio die.

---

1. *with . . . aside:* the two would have been fighting either with daggers in or cloaks rolled about their second hand to ward off the other's weapon.

170 CAPULET'S WIFE He is a kinsman to the Montague.
    Affection makes him false; he speaks not true.
    Some twenty of them fought in this black strife,
    And all those twenty could but kill one life.
    I beg for justice, which thou, Prince, must give.
175   Romeo slew Tybalt; Romeo must not live.
    PRINCE Romeo slew him, he slew Mercutio.
    Who now the price of his° dear blood doth owe?   *(Mercutio's)*
    MONTAGUE Not Romeo, Prince. He was Mercutio's friend.
    His fault° concludes but what the law should end,   *offense*
    The life of Tybalt.
180 PRINCE   And for that offence
    Immediately we do exile him hence.
    I have an interest in your hate's proceeding;
    My blood° for your rude brawls doth lie a-bleeding.   *kinsman*
    But I'll amerce° you with so strong a fine   *penalize*
185   That you shall all repent the loss of mine.
    I will be deaf to pleading and excuses.
    Nor tears nor prayers shall purchase out° abuses.   *compensate for*
    Therefore use none. Let Romeo hence in haste,
    Else, when he is found, that hour is his last.
190   Bear hence this body, and attend our will.
    Mercy but murders, pardoning those that kill.
             Exeunt [with the body]

3.2

    Enter JULIET *alone*
JULIET Gallop apace,° you fiery-footed steeds,   *quickly*
    Towards Phoebus' lodging.[1] Such a waggoner°   *charioteer*
    As Phaëton[2] would whip you to the west
    And bring in cloudy night immediately.
5   Spread thy close° curtain, love-performing night,   *covering*
    That runaways'[3] eyes may wink,° and Romeo   *close*
    Leap to these arms untalked of and unseen.
    Lovers can see to do their amorous rites
    By their own beauties; or, if love be blind,
10 It best agrees with night. Come, civil° night,   *solemn*
    Thou sober-suited matron all in black,
    And learn me how to lose a winning match[4]
    Played for a pair of stainless maidenhoods.
    Hood my unmanned° blood, bating[5] in my cheeks,   *untamed; virgin*
15 With thy black mantle till strange° love grown bold   *shy*
    Think true love acted simple° modesty.   *mere; innocent*
    Come night, come Romeo; come, thou day in night,
    For thou wilt lie upon the wings of night
    Whiter than new snow on a raven's back.
20 Come, gentle night; come, loving, black-browed night,
    Give me my Romeo, and when I shall die

3.2 Location: Capulet's house.
1. Under the world to the west, where the sun god Phoebus Apollo was imagined to rest with his fiery chariot at night.
2. The son of Apollo, who rashly attempted to steer his father's chariot across the sky. To save the earth from scorching, Jupiter struck him down with a lightning bolt.
3. Either the runaway horses of the sun or roving and curious vagabonds.
4. *match*: competition. A husband and a marriage ("match") are won by surrendering.
5. Fluttering like a restless falcon before its eyes are covered with a "hood" to calm it.

Take him and cut him out in little stars,[6]
And he will make the face of heaven so fine
That all the world will be in love with night
25 And pay no worship to the garish sun.
O, I have bought the mansion of a love
But not possessed it, and though I am sold,[7]
Not yet enjoyed. So tedious is this day
As is the night before some festival
30 To an impatient child that hath new robes
And may not wear them.
            Enter NURSE, [*wringing her hands,*] *with the ladder of*
            cords in her lap°   *bodice fold*
                        O, here comes my Nurse,
And she brings news, and every tongue that speaks
But Romeo's name speaks heavenly eloquence.
Now, Nurse, what news? What, hast thou there
The cords that Romeo bid thee fetch?
35 NURSE [*putting down the cords*]   Ay, ay, the cords.
JULIET   Ay me, what news? Why dost thou wring thy hands?
NURSE   Ah, welladay!° He's dead, he's dead, he's dead!   *alas*
We are undone, lady, we are undone.
Alack the day, he's gone, he's killed, he's dead!
JULIET   Can heaven be so envious?°   *spiteful; jealous*
40 NURSE   Romeo can,
Though heaven cannot. O Romeo, Romeo,
Who ever would have thought it Romeo?
JULIET   What devil art thou that dost torment me thus?
This torture should be roared in dismal hell.
45 Hath Romeo slain himself? Say thou but 'Ay',
And that bare vowel 'I' shall poison more
Than the death-darting eye of cockatrice.[8]
I am not I if there be such an 'Ay',
Or those eyes shut that makes thee answer 'Ay'.
50 If he be slain, say 'Ay'; or if not, 'No'.
Brief sounds determine of my weal° or woe.   *welfare*
NURSE   I saw the wound, I saw it with mine eyes,
God save the mark,[9] here on his manly breast—
A piteous corpse, a bloody, piteous corpse—
55 Pale, pale as ashes, all bedaubed in blood,
All in gore° blood; I swoonèd at the sight.   *clotted*
JULIET   O, break, my heart, poor bankrupt, break at once!
To prison,[1] eyes; ne'er look on liberty.
Vile earth,[2] to earth resign; end motion° here,   *movement; emotion*
60 And thou and Romeo press[3] one heavy° bier!   *weighty; sad*
NURSE   O Tybalt, Tybalt, the best friend I had!
O courteous Tybalt, honest° gentleman,   *honorable*
That ever I should live to see thee dead!
JULIET   What storm is this that blows so contrary?
65 Is Romeo slaughtered, and is Tybalt dead?

---

6. *Take . . . stars*: an imagined tranformation, based on those in Ovid's *Metamorphoses*, whereby Romeo also dies and is immortalized. Q4's reading of "he" for "I" (line 21) makes more immediate sense and is often accepted. Also, "die" could mean "have an orgasm."
7. *O . . . sold*: the image is inverted: first Juliet buys the mansion, and then she becomes the "sold" house.
8. A mythical serpent that kills by merely looking.

9. An apology for mentioning something unpleasant, but also emphasizing the fatal "mark" of the rapier.
1. Bankruptcy—to "break" financially—was punishable by imprisonment.
2. The despised body, echoing Ecclesiastes 12:7: "Then shall the dust return to the earth as it was."
3. Burden; embrace.

My dearest cousin and my dearer lord?
Then, dreadful trumpet, sound the general doom,[4]
For who is living if those two are gone?
NURSE   Tybalt is gone and Romeo banishèd.
70 Romeo that killed him—he is banishèd.
JULIET   O God, did Romeo's hand shed Tybalt's blood?
NURSE   It did, it did, alas the day, it did.
JULIET   O serpent heart hid with° a flow'ring° face!   by / lovely; benign
Did ever dragon keep° so fair a cave?   guard
75 Beautiful tyrant, fiend angelical!
Dove-feathered raven, wolvish-ravening lamb!
Despisèd substance of divinest show!°   appearance
Just opposite to what thou justly° seem'st—   precisely; rightfully
A damnèd saint, an honourable villain.
80 O nature, what hadst thou to do[5] in hell
When thou didst bower[6] the spirit of a fiend
In mortal paradise of such sweet flesh?
Was ever book containing such vile matter
So fairly bound? O, that deceit should dwell
85 In such a gorgeous palace!
NURSE   There's no trust, no faith, no honesty in men;
All perjured, all forsworn, all naught,° dissemblers all.   wicked
Ah, where's my man? Give me some aqua vitae.°   brandy
These griefs, these woes, these sorrows make me old.
Shame come to Romeo!
90 JULIET   Blistered be thy tongue
For such a wish! He was not born to shame.
Upon his brow shame is ashamed to sit,
For 'tis a throne where honour may be crowned
Sole monarch of the universal earth.
95 O, what a beast was I to chide at him!
NURSE   Will you speak well of him that killed your cousin?
JULIET   Shall I speak ill of him that is my husband?
Ah, poor my° lord, what tongue shall smooth° thy name   my poor / praise
When I, thy three-hours wife, have mangled it?
100 But wherefore, villain, didst thou kill my cousin?
That villain cousin would have killed my husband.
Back, foolish tears, back to your native spring!
Your tributary[7] drops belong to woe,
Which you, mistaking, offer up to joy.[8]
105 My husband lives, that Tybalt would have slain;
And Tybalt's dead, that would have slain my husband.
All this is comfort. Wherefore° weep I then?   Why
Some word there was, worser than Tybalt's death,
That murdered me. I would forget it fain,°   gladly
110 But O, it presses to my memory
Like damnèd guilty deeds to sinners' minds!
'Tybalt is dead, and Romeo banishèd.'
That 'banishèd', that one word 'banishèd'
Hath slain ten thousand Tybalts. Tybalt's death
115 Was woe enough, if it had ended there;

4. The Last Judgment announced with angel's trumpets.
5. What were you doing.
6. Lodge or enclose, suggesting a surrounding garden.
7. Tribute-paying; in-flowing.
8. Offer up to a joyful (and thus inappropriate) occasion.

Or, if sour woe delights in fellowship
And needly° will be ranked with⁹ other griefs,   necessarily
Why followed not, when she said 'Tybalt's dead',
'Thy father', or 'thy mother', nay, or both,
120   Which modern° lamentation might have moved?°   ordinary / produced
But with a rearward¹ following Tybalt's death,
'Romeo is banishèd'—to speak that word
Is father, mother, Tybalt, Romeo, Juliet,
All slain, all dead. 'Romeo is banishèd'—
125   There is no end, no limit, measure, bound,
In that word's death. No words can that woe sound.°   utter; fathom
Where is my father and my mother, Nurse?
NURSE   Weeping and wailing over Tybalt's corpse.
Will you go to them? I will bring you thither.
130   JULIET   Wash they his wounds with tears; mine shall be spent
When theirs are dry, for Romeo's banishment.
Take up those cords. Poor ropes, you are beguiled,°   cheated
Both you and I, for Romeo is exiled.
He made you for a highway to my bed,
135   But I, a maid, die maiden-widowèd.
Come, cords; come, Nurse; I'll to my wedding bed,
And death, not Romeo, take my maidenhead!
NURSE [taking up the cords]   Hie to your chamber. I'll find Romeo
To comfort you. I wot° well where he is.   know
140   Hark ye, your Romeo will be here at night.
I'll to him. He is hid at Laurence' cell.
JULIET [giving her a ring]   O, find him! Give this ring to my true knight,
And bid him come to take his last farewell. Exeunt [severally]

3.3
Enter FRIAR [LAURENCE]
FRIAR LAURENCE   Romeo, come forth, come forth, thou fear-full man.
Affliction is enamoured of thy parts,°   qualities
And thou art wedded to calamity.
Enter ROMEO
ROMEO   Father, what news? What is the Prince's doom?°   sentence
5   What sorrow craves acquaintance at my hand
That I yet know not?
FRIAR LAURENCE   Too familiar
Is my dear son with such sour company.
I bring thee tidings of the Prince's doom.
ROMEO   What less than doomsday is the Prince's doom?
10   FRIAR LAURENCE   A gentler judgement vanished° from his lips: escaped
Not body's death, but body's banishment.
ROMEO   Ha, banishment? Be merciful, say 'death',
For exile hath more terror in his look,
Much more than death. Do not say 'banishment'.
15   FRIAR LAURENCE   Hence from Verona art thou banishèd.
Be patient,° for the world is broad and wide.   able to endure
ROMEO   There is no world without° Verona walls   outside
But purgatory, torture, hell itself.
Hence banishèd is banished from the world,
20   And world's exile is death. Then 'banishèd'

9. Will be accompanied by.   3.3 Location: Friar Laurence's cell.
1. rearward: rearguard action, with a pun on "afterword."

Is death mistermed. Calling death 'banishèd'
Thou cutt'st my head off with a golden axe,
And smil'st upon the stroke that murders me.
FRIAR LAURENCE   O deadly° sin, O rude unthankfulness!   *damnable*
25   Thy fault our law calls death,° but the kind Prince,   *a capital offense*
Taking thy part, hath rushed° aside the law   *forced*
And turned that black word 'death' to banishment.
This is dear mercy, and thou seest it not.
ROMEO   'Tis torture, and not mercy. Heaven is here
30   Where Juliet lives, and every cat and dog
And little mouse, every unworthy thing,
Live here in heaven and may look on her,
But Romeo may not. More validity,°   *health*
More honourable state, more courtship° lives   *courtly state; wooing*
35   In carrion flies than Romeo. They may seize
On the white wonder of dear Juliet's hand,
And steal immortal blessing from her lips,
Who, even in pure and vestal° modesty,   *virginal*
Still° blush, as thinking their own kisses¹ sin.   *Always*
40   But Romeo may not, he is banishèd.
Flies may do this, but I from this must fly.
They are free men, but I am banishèd.
And sayst thou yet that exile is not death?
Hadst thou no poison mixed, no sharp-ground knife,
45   No sudden mean° of death, though ne'er so mean,°   *method / ignoble*
But 'banishèd' to kill me—'banishèd'?
O friar, the damnèd use that word in hell.²
Howling attends it. How hast thou the heart,
Being a divine, a ghostly confessor,
50   A sin-absolver and my friend professed,
To mangle me with that word 'banishèd'?
FRIAR LAURENCE   Thou fond° mad man, hear me a little speak.   *foolish; infatuated*
ROMEO   O, thou wilt speak again of banishment.
FRIAR LAURENCE   I'll give thee armour to keep off that word—
55   Adversity's sweet milk, philosophy,
To comfort thee though thou art banishèd.
ROMEO   Yet 'banishèd'? Hang up° philosophy!   *Hang up = Hang*
Unless philosophy can make a Juliet,
Displant° a town, reverse a prince's doom,   *Uproot*
60   It helps not, it prevails not. Talk no more.
FRIAR LAURENCE   O, then I see that madmen have no ears.
ROMEO   How should they, when that wise men have no eyes?
FRIAR LAURENCE   Let me dispute° with thee of thy estate.°   *discuss / position*
ROMEO   Thou canst not speak of that thou dost not feel.
65   Wert thou as young as I, Juliet thy love,
An hour but° married, Tybalt murderèd,   *only*
Doting like me, and like me banishèd,
Then mightst thou speak, then mightst thou tear thy hair,
And fall upon the ground, as I do now,
    [*He falls upon the ground*]
70   Taking the measure of an unmade grave.
    Knock [*within*]
FRIAR LAURENCE   Arise, one knocks. Good Romeo, hide thyself.

---

1. Their touching each other in closing.   2. Because they are banished from heaven.

ROMEO   Not I, unless the breath of heartsick groans
  Mist-like enfold me from the search of eyes.
   Knock [within]
FRIAR LAURENCE   Hark, how they knock!—Who's there?—
  Romeo, arise.
75 Thou wilt be taken.—Stay a while.—Stand up.
   [*Still*] *knock [within]*
  Run to my study.—By and by!—God's will,°   *By providence*
  What simpleness° is this?   *stupidity*
   Knock [within]
         I come, I come.
  Who knocks so hard? Whence come you? What's your will?
NURSE [*within*]³   Let me come in, and you shall know my errand.
  I come from Lady Juliet.
80 FRIAR LAURENCE [*opening the door*] Welcome then.
   Enter NURSE
NURSE   O holy friar, O tell me, holy friar,
  Where is my lady's lord? Where's Romeo?
FRIAR LAURENCE   There on the ground, with his own tears
  made drunk.
NURSE   O, he is even° in my mistress' case,°   *exactly / condition; vagina*
85 Just in her case! O woeful sympathy,
  Piteous predicament! Even so lies she,
  Blubb'ring and weeping, weeping and blubb'ring.
  [*To* ROMEO]   Stand up, stand up, stand an° you be a man,   *if*
  For Juliet's sake, for her sake, rise and stand.
90 Why should you fall into so deep an O?°   *a groaning*
ROMEO [*rises*]   Nurse.
NURSE   Ah sir, ah sir, death's the end of all.⁴
ROMEO   Spak'st thou of Juliet? How is it with her?
  Doth not she think me an old° murderer,   *a practiced*
  Now I have stained the childhood of our joy
95 With blood removed but little from her own?
  Where is she, and how doth she, and what says
  My concealed lady° to our cancelled° love? *secret wife / invalidated*
NURSE   O, she says nothing, sir, but weeps and weeps,
  And now falls on her bed, and then starts up,
100 And 'Tybalt' calls, and then on Romeo cries,
  And then down falls again.
ROMEO   As if that name
  Shot from the deadly level° of a gun   *aim*
  Did murder her as that name's cursèd hand
  Murdered her kinsman. O tell me, friar, tell me,
105 In what vile part of this anatomy
  Doth my name lodge? Tell me, that I may sack
  The hateful mansion.
   He offers to stab himself, and NURSE *snatches the dagger*
   away
FRIAR LAURENCE   Hold° thy desperate hand.   *Restrain*
  Art thou a man? Thy form cries out thou art.
  Thy tears are womanish, thy wild acts denote
110 The unreasonable° fury of a beast.   *incapable of reason*

---

3. Behind one of the doors at the back of the stage, representing the door of the cell.   4. A proverbial consolation.

Unseemly° woman in a seeming man,   *Inappropriate; immodest*
And ill-beseeming beast in seeming both!⁵
Thou hast amazed me. By my holy order,
I thought thy disposition better tempered.
115 Hast thou slain Tybalt? Wilt thou slay thyself,
And slay thy lady that in thy life lives
By doing damnèd° hate upon thyself?   *sinful*
Why rail'st thou on thy birth, the heaven, and earth,
Since birth° and heaven° and earth,° all three, do meet   *nobility / soul / body*
120 In thee at once, which thou at once wouldst lose?
Fie, fie, thou sham'st thy shape, thy love, thy wit,
Which like a usurer abound'st in all,
And usest none in that true use indeed
Which should bedeck thy shape, thy love, thy wit.⁶
125 Thy noble shape is but a form° of wax,   *figure*
Digressing° from the valour of a man;   *If it deviates*
Thy dear love sworn but hollow perjury,
Killing that love which thou hast vowed to cherish;
Thy wit, that ornament° to shape and love,   *necessary accessory*
130 Misshapen° in the conduct° of them both,   *Inept / management*
Like powder in a skilless soldier's flask
Is set afire by thine own ignorance,
And thou dismembered with thine own defence.°   *weapon*
What, rouse thee, man! Thy Juliet is alive,
135 For whose dear sake thou wast but lately dead:
There art thou happy. Tybalt would kill thee,
But thou slewest Tybalt: there art thou happy.
The law that threatened death becomes thy friend,
And turns it to exile: there art thou happy.
140 A pack of blessings light upon thy back,
Happiness courts thee in her best array,
But, like a mishavèd° and sullen wench,   *misbehaved*
Thou pout'st upon thy fortune and thy love.
Take heed, take heed, for such die miserable.
145 Go, get thee to thy love, as was decreed.
Ascend her chamber; hence and comfort her.
But look thou stay not till the watch be set,⁷
For then thou canst not pass to Mantua,
Where thou shalt live till we can find a time
150 To blaze° your marriage, reconcile your friends,°   *make public / kin*
Beg pardon of the Prince, and call thee back
With twenty hundred thousand times more joy
Than thou went'st forth in lamentation.
Go before, Nurse. Commend me to thy lady,
155 And bid her hasten all the house to bed,
Which heavy sorrow makes them apt unto.
Romeo is coming.
NURSE   O Lord, I could have stayed here all the night
To hear good counsel! O, what learning is!
160 My lord, I'll tell my lady you will come.
ROMEO   Do so, and bid my sweet prepare to chide.

---

5. An unnatural beast in seeming both man and unrea-
soning animal, or both man and woman.
6. *thou sham'st . . . wit:* you abound in looks, love, and
intelligence ("wit"), but you do not use them judiciously

and are therefore like a usurer who acquires money for
its own sake, without putting it to good use.
7. Until the guards take up their positions (at the city
gates).

NURSE *offers to go in, and turns again*
NURSE [*giving the ring*]   Here, sir, a ring she bid me give you, sir.
Hie you,° make haste, for it grows very late.   *Hurry*
ROMEO   How well my comfort° is revived by this.   *Exit* NURSE   *happiness*
FRIAR LAURENCE   Go hence, good night, and here stands° all   *and on this depends*
165   your state.
Either be gone before the watch be set,
Or by the break of day disguised from hence.
Sojourn in Mantua. I'll find out your man,
And he shall signify from time to time
170   Every good hap° to you that chances here.   *event*
Give me thy hand. 'Tis late. Farewell. Good night.
ROMEO   But that a joy past joy calls out on me,
It were a grief so brief° to part with thee.   *hastily*
Farewell.   *Exeunt* [*severally*]

3.4

Enter old CAPULET, *his* WIFE, *and* PARIS
CAPULET   Things have fall'n out, sir, so unluckily
That we have had no time to move° our daughter.   *persuade*
Look you, she loved her kinsman Tybalt dearly,
And so did I. Well, we were born to die.
5   'Tis very late. She'll not come down tonight.
I promise you, but for your company
I would have been abed an hour ago.
PARIS   These times of woe afford no times to woo.
Madam, good night. Commend me to your daughter.
10   CAPULET'S WIFE   I will, and know her mind early tomorrow.
Tonight she's mewed up to¹ her heaviness.°   *sadness*
PARIS *offers to go in, and* CAPULET *calls him again*
CAPULET   Sir Paris, I will make a desperate tender°   *a reckless offer*
Of my child's love. I think she will be ruled
In all respects by me. Nay, more, I doubt it not.
15   Wife, go you to her ere you go to bed.
Acquaint her here of my son Paris' love,
And bid her—mark you me?—on Wednesday next—
But soft—what day is this?
PARIS   Monday, my lord.
CAPULET   Monday. Ha, ha! Well, Wednesday is too soon.
20   O' Thursday let it be. O' Thursday, tell her,
She shall be married to this noble earl.
Will you be ready? Do you like this haste?
We'll keep° no great ado—a friend or two.   *celebrate with*
For hark you, Tybalt being slain so late,°   *recently*
25   It may be thought we held° him carelessly,°   *regarded / indifferently*
Being our kinsman, if we revel much.
Therefore we'll have some half a dozen friends,
And there an end. But what say you to Thursday?
PARIS   My lord, I would° that Thursday were tomorrow.   *wish*
30   CAPULET   Well, get you gone. O' Thursday be it, then.
[*To his* WIFE]   Go you to Juliet ere you go to bed.
Prepare her, wife, against° this wedding day.—   *for*

3.4 Location: Capulet's house.   1. Shut in with. The "mews" are hawks' housing.

Farewell, my lord.—Light to my chamber, ho!—
Afore me,[2] it is so very late that we
35   May call it early by and by. Good night.

Exeunt [CAPULET *and his* WIFE *at
one door,* PARIS *at another door*]

3.5

Enter ROMEO *and* JULIET *aloft* [*with the ladder of cords*]

JULIET   Wilt thou be gone? It is not yet near day.
It was the nightingale, and not the lark,
That pierced the fear-full hollow of thine ear.
Nightly she sings on yon pom'granate tree.
5   Believe me, love, it was the nightingale.
ROMEO   It was the lark, the herald of the morn,
No nightingale. Look, love, what envious° streaks   *spiteful*
Do lace the severing° clouds in yonder east.   *parting*
Night's candles are burnt out, and jocund day
10   Stands tiptoe on the misty mountain tops.
I must be gone and live, or stay and die.
JULIET   Yon light is not daylight; I know it, I.
It is some meteor that the sun exhaled[1]
To be to thee this night a torchbearer
15   And light thee on thy way to Mantua.
Therefore stay yet. Thou need'st not to be gone.
ROMEO   Let me be ta'en, let me be put to death.
I am content, so° thou wilt have it so.   *as long as*
I'll say yon grey is not the morning's eye,
20   'Tis but the pale reflex° of Cynthia's° brow;   *reflection / the moon's*
Nor that is not the lark whose notes do beat
The vaulty heaven so high above our heads.
I have more care° to stay than will to go.   *desire*
Come, death, and welcome; Juliet wills it so.
25   How is't, my soul? Let's talk. It is not day.
JULIET   It is, it is. Hie hence, be gone, away.
It is the lark that sings so out of tune,
Straining° harsh discords and unpleasing sharps.[2]   *Distorting; tuning up*
Some say the lark makes sweet division;°   *variations on a melody*
30   This doth not so, for she divideth us.
Some say the lark and loathèd toad changed eyes.[3]
O, now I would they had changed voices, too,
Since arm from arm that voice doth us affray,°   *frighten*
Hunting thee hence with hunt's-up[4] to the day.
35   O, now be gone! More light and light it grows.
ROMEO   More light and light, more dark and dark our woes.

Enter NURSE *hastily*

NURSE   Madam.
JULIET   Nurse.
NURSE   Your lady mother is coming to your chamber.
40   The day is broke; be wary, look about.   [*Exit*]

---

2. *Afore me:* A mild oath, or possibly an address to the torchbearing servant to walk in front of him.
3.5 Location: The upper acting area represents Juliet's window or balcony. The main stage represents Capulet's orchard until line 59, then the interior of Capulet's house from line 64.
1. Breathed. Meteors were thought to be impure vapors that the sun had drawn up from the earth and ignited and were usually considered bad omens.
2. Harsh sounds, too-high tones.
3. A folk explanation for the supposed ugliness of the lark's eyes and the beauty of the toad's. *changed:* exchanged.
4. Morning song used to wake the bride after the wedding night.

JULIET   Then, window, let day in, and let life out.
ROMEO   Farewell, farewell! One kiss, and I'll descend.
          He [lets down the ladder of cords and] goes down
JULIET   Art thou gone so, love, lord, my husband, friend?°   *lover*
          I must hear from thee every day in the hour,
45   For in a minute there are many days.
          O, by this count I shall be much in years
          Ere I again behold my Romeo.
ROMEO   Farewell.
          I will omit no opportunity
50   That may convey my greetings, love, to thee.
JULIET   O, think'st thou we shall ever meet again?
ROMEO   I doubt it not, and all these woes shall serve
          For sweet discourses° in our times to come.   *conversations*
JULIET   O God, I have an ill-divining° soul!   *a misfortune-predicting*
55   Methinks I see thee, now thou art so low,
          As one dead in the bottom of a tomb.
          Either my eyesight fails, or thou look'st pale.
ROMEO   And trust me, love, in my eye so do you.
          Dry sorrow drinks our blood.⁵ Adieu, adieu.   *Exit*
JULIET *[pulling up the ladder and weeping]*   O fortune, fortune,
60   all men call thee fickle.
          If thou art fickle, what dost thou with him
          That is renowned for faith?° Be fickle, fortune,   *fidelity*
          For then I hope thou wilt not keep him long,
          But send him back.
                    Enter [CAPULET'S WIFE below]
CAPULET'S WIFE   Ho, daughter, are you up?
65 JULIET   Who is't that calls? It is my lady mother.
          Is she not down° so late, or up so early?   *in bed*
          What unaccustomed cause procures° her hither?   *brings*
                    She goes down [and enters below]
CAPULET'S WIFE   Why, how now, Juliet?
JULIET   Madam, I am not well.
CAPULET'S WIFE   Evermore weeping for your cousin's death?
70   What, wilt thou wash him from his grave with tears?
          An if thou couldst, thou couldst not make him live,
          Therefore have done. Some grief shows much of love,
          But much of grief shows still° some want° of wit.   *always / lack*
JULIET   Yet let me weep for such a feeling° loss.   *profound*
75 CAPULET'S WIFE   So shall you feel° the loss, but not the friend°   *experience; touch / kin*
          Which you so weep for.
JULIET   Feeling so the loss,
          I cannot choose but ever weep the friend.°   *lover*
CAPULET'S WIFE   Well, girl, thou weep'st not so much for his death
          As that the villain lives which slaughtered him.
JULIET   What villain, madam?
80 CAPULET'S WIFE   That same villain Romeo.
JULIET *[aside]*   Villain and he be many miles asunder.
          [To her mother] God pardon him—I do, with all my heart,
          And yet no man like° he doth grieve my heart.   *so much as; resembling*
CAPULET'S WIFE   That is because the traitor murderer lives.

---

5. *Dry . . . blood:* Each sigh supposedly cost the heart a drop of blood. Thus, the lovers are pale. *Dry:* Thirsty.

85	JULIET Ay, madam, from the reach of these my hands.	
	Would none but I might venge my cousin's death.	
	CAPULET'S WIFE We will have vengeance for it, fear thou not.	
	Then weep no more. I'll send to one in Mantua,	
	Where that same banished runagate° doth live,	*runaway; fugitive*
90	Shall give him such an unaccustomed dram	
	That he shall soon keep Tybalt company;	
	And then I hope thou wilt be satisfied.°	*sufficiently avenged*
	JULIET Indeed, I never shall be satisfied	
	With Romeo till I behold him, dead,	
95	Is my poor heart⁶ so for a kinsman vexed.	
	Madam, if you could find out but a man	
	To bear a poison, I would temper° it	*mix; dilute*
	That Romeo should, upon receipt thereof,	
	Soon sleep in quiet. O, how my heart abhors	
100	To hear him named and cannot come to him	
	To wreak the love I bore my cousin	
	Upon his body that hath slaughtered him!	
	CAPULET'S WIFE Find thou the means, and I'll find such a man.	
	But now I'll tell thee joyful tidings, girl.	
105	JULIET And joy comes well in such a needy time.	
	What are they, I beseech your ladyship?	
	CAPULET'S WIFE Well, well, thou hast a careful° father, child;	*solicitous*
	One who, to put thee from thy heaviness,	
	Hath sorted out a sudden° day of joy	*chosen an immediate*
110	That thou expect'st not, nor I looked not for.	
	JULIET Madam, in happy° time. What day is that?	*at a fortunate*
	CAPULET'S WIFE Marry, my child, early next Thursday morn	
	The gallant, young, and noble gentleman	
	The County Paris at Saint Peter's Church	
115	Shall happily make thee there a joyful bride.	
	JULIET Now, by Saint Peter's Church, and Peter too,	
	He shall not make me there a joyful bride.	
	I wonder° at this haste, that I must wed	*am astonished*
	Ere he that should be husband comes to woo.	
120	I pray you, tell my lord and father, madam,	
	I will not marry yet; and when I do, I swear	
	It shall be Romeo—whom you know I hate—	
	Rather than Paris. These are news indeed.	
	Enter old CAPULET *and* NURSE	
	CAPULET'S WIFE Here comes your father. Tell him so yourself,	
125	And see how he will take it at your hands.	
	CAPULET When the sun sets, the earth doth drizzle° dew,	*weep out*
	But for the sunset of my brother's son	
	It rains downright.	
	How now, a conduit,° girl? What, still in tears?	*fountain*
130	Evermore show'ring? In one little body	
	Thou counterfeit'st a barque,° a sea, a wind,	*represent a ship*
	For still thy eyes—which I may call the sea—	
	Do ebb and flow with tears. The barque thy body is,	
	Sailing in this salt flood; the winds thy sighs,	
135	Who,° raging with thy tears and they with them,	*Which*

6. *till . . . heart:* Juliet allows her mother to understand that she will not be satisfied "till I behold him dead," while privately meaning that until she beholds him, "dead is my poor heart."

Without a sudden calm will overset
Thy tempest-tossèd body.—How now, wife?
Have you delivered to her our decree?

CAPULET'S WIFE Ay, sir, but she will none,° she gives you thanks.   *not agree*
140   I would the fool° were married to her grave.   *peevish child*

CAPULET   Soft, take me with you,[7] take me with you, wife.
How, will she none? Doth she not give us thanks?
Is she not proud?° Doth she not count her blest,   *gratified*
Unworthy as she is, that we have wrought°   *contrived for*
145   So worthy a gentleman to be her bride?°   *bridegroom*

JULIET   Not proud you have, but thankful that you have.
Proud can I never be of what I hate,
But thankful even for hate° that is meant love.°   *a hateful thing / as love*

CAPULET   How, how, how, how—chopped logic?° What is this?   *mere sophistry*
150   'Proud', and 'I thank you', and 'I thank you not',
And yet 'not proud'? Mistress minion,° you,   *spoiled child*
Thank me no thankings, nor proud me no prouds,
But fettle° your fine joints 'gainst° Thursday next   *prepare / for*
To go with Paris to Saint Peter's Church,
155   Or I will drag thee on a hurdle[8] thither.
Out,[9] you green-sickness carrion! Out, you baggage,
You tallow-face!

CAPULET'S WIFE   Fie, fie, what, are you mad?

JULIET *(kneels down)*   Good father, I beseech you on my knees,
Hear me with patience but to speak a word.

160   CAPULET   Hang thee, young baggage, disobedient wretch!
I tell thee what: get thee to church o' Thursday,
Or never after look me in the face.
Speak not, reply not, do not answer me.
       [JULIET *rises*]
My fingers itch. Wife, we scarce thought us blest
165   That God had lent us but this only child,
But now I see this one is one too much,
And that we have a curse in having her.
Out on her, hilding!°   *hussy*

NURSE   God in heaven bless her!
You are to blame, my lord, to rate° her so.   *berate*

170   CAPULET   And why, my lady Wisdom? Hold your tongue,
Good Prudence. Smatter° with your gossips,° go!   *Chatter / cronies*

NURSE   I speak no treason.

CAPULET   O, God-i'-good-e'en!°   *for God's sake*

NURSE   May not one speak?

CAPULET   Peace, you mumbling fool,
Utter your gravity° o'er a gossip's bowl,°   *wisdom / drinking bowl*
For here we need it not.

175   CAPULET'S WIFE   You are too hot.°   *irascible, rash*

CAPULET   God's bread,° it makes me mad. Day, night;   *By the communion bread*
work, play;
Alone, in company, still my care° hath been   *business*
To have her matched; and having now provided
A gentleman of noble parentage,

---

7. Not so fast, let me understand you.   execution.
8. A sledge used to draw traitors through the streets to   9. An expression of disgust and impatience.

180 Of fair demesnes,° youthful, and nobly lined,°   *estates / descended*
    Stuffed, as they say, with honourable parts,°   *qualities*
    Proportioned as one's thought would wish a man¹—
    And then to have a wretched puling fool,
    A whining maumet,° in her fortune's tender,²   *puppet*
185 To answer 'I'll not wed, I cannot love;
    I am too young, I pray you pardon me'!
    But an you will not wed, I'll pardon you!°   *excuse you (to leave)*
    Graze where you will, you shall not house with me.
    Look to't, think on't. I do not use° to jest.   *make it customary*
190 Thursday is near. Lay hand on heart.³ Advise.°   *Consider*
    An you be mine, I'll give you to my friend.
    An you be not, hang, beg, starve, die in the streets,
    For, by my soul, I'll ne'er acknowledge thee,
    Nor what is mine shall never do thee good.
195 Trust to't. Bethink you. I'll not be forsworn.   *Exit*
JULIET   Is there no pity sitting in the clouds
    That sees into the bottom of my grief ?
    O sweet my° mother, cast me not away!   *my sweet*
    Delay this marriage for a month, a week;
200 Or if you do not, make the bridal bed
    In that dim monument° where Tybalt lies.   *sepulchre*
CAPULET'S WIFE   Talk not to me, for I'll not speak a word.
    Do as thou wilt, for I have done with thee.   *Exit*
JULIET   O, God—O Nurse, how shall this be prevented?
205 My husband is on earth, my faith° in heaven.   *marriage vows*
    How shall that faith return again to earth
    Unless that husband send it me from heaven
    By leaving earth?⁴ Comfort me, counsel me.
    Alack, alack, that heaven should practise stratagems
210 Upon so soft a subject as myself!
    What sayst thou? Hast thou not a word of joy?
    Some comfort, Nurse.
NURSE   Faith, here it is: Romeo
    Is banishèd, and all the world to nothing⁵
    That he dares ne'er come back to challenge you,
215 Or if he do, it needs must be by stealth.
    Then, since the case so stands as now it doth,
    I think it best you married with the County.
    O, he's a lovely gentleman!
    Romeo's a dishclout° to him. An eagle, madam,   *dishcloth*
220 Hath not so green, so quick, so fair an eye
    As Paris hath. Beshrew° my very heart,   *Curse*
    I think you are happy° in this second match,   *lucky*
    For it excels your first; or if it did not,
    Your first is dead, or 'twere as good he were
225 As living hence and you no use of him.
JULIET   Speak'st thou from thy heart?
NURSE   And from my soul, too, else beshrew them both.
JULIET   Amen.
NURSE   What?

---

1. Shaped as handsomely as you can imagine.
2. When good fortune is offered her.
3. Ascertain your feelings.
4. *How . . . earth:* How can I swear marriage vows

again unless Romeo dies first, thus releasing me from
my vows to him?
5. And it's a sure bet.

230 JULIET   Well, thou hast comforted me marvellous much.
        Go in; and tell my lady I am gone,
        Having displeased my father, to Laurence' cell
        To make confession and to be absolved.
    NURSE   Marry, I will; and this is wisely done.   [*Exit*]
235 JULIET (*looks after* NURSE)   Ancient damnation!⁶ O most wicked fiend!
        Is it more sin to wish me thus forsworn,
        Or to dispraise my lord with that same tongue
        Which she hath praised him with above compare
        So many thousand times? Go, counsellor!
240   Thou and my bosom° henceforth shall be twain.°   *heart's contents / divided*
        I'll to the friar, to know his remedy.
        If all else fail, myself have power to die.   *Exit*

4.1

Enter FRIAR [LAURENCE] *and County* PARIS

    FRIAR LAURENCE   On Thursday, sir? The time is very short.
    PARIS   My father Capulet will have it so,
        And I am nothing slow¹ to slack his haste.
    FRIAR LAURENCE   You say you do not know the lady's mind?
5   Uneven is the course.² I like it not.
    PARIS   Immoderately she weeps for Tybalt's death,
        And therefore have I little talked of love,
        For Venus smiles not in a house of tears.
        Now, sir, her father counts it dangerous
10   That she do give her sorrow so much sway,
        And in his wisdom hastes our marriage
        To stop the inundation of her tears,
        Which, too much minded° by herself alone,   *brooded over*
        May be put from her by society.°   *company*
15   Now do you know the reason of this haste.
    FRIAR LAURENCE [*aside*]   I would I knew not why it should be slowed.—
                  Enter JULIET
        Look, sir, here comes the lady toward my cell.
    PARIS   Happily met, my lady and my wife.
    JULIET   That may be, sir, when I may be a wife.
20 PARIS   That 'may be' must be, love, on Thursday next.
    JULIET   What must be shall be.
    FRIAR LAURENCE   That's a certain text.
    PARIS   Come you to make confession to this father?
    JULIET   To answer that, I should confess to you.
    PARIS   Do not deny to him that you love me.
25 JULIET   I will confess to you that I love him.
    PARIS   So will ye, I am sure, that you love me.
    JULIET   If I do so, it will be of more price,°   *value*
        Being spoke behind your back, than to your face.
    PARIS   Poor soul, thy face is much abused with tears.
30 JULIET   The tears have got small victory by that,
        For it was bad enough before their spite.°   *injury*
    PARIS   Thou wrong'st it more than tears with that report.
    JULIET   That is no slander, sir, which is a truth,
        And what I spake, I spake it to my face.

---

6. Damnable old woman (with a hint of "original sin").   1. Not reluctant; not trying to drag behind him.
4.1. Location: Friar Laurence's cell.   2. The plan is irregular; this is a tricky road to follow.

35 PARIS Thy face is mine, and thou hast slandered it.
  JULIET It may be so, for it is not mine own.[3]—
      Are you at leisure, holy father, now,
      Or shall I come to you at evening mass?
  FRIAR LAURENCE My leisure serves me, pensive° daughter, now.   *sorrowful*
40   My lord, we must entreat the time alone.
  PARIS God shield° I should disturb devotion!—   *forbid*
      Juliet, on Thursday early will I rouse ye.
      [*Kissing her*] Till then, adieu, and keep this holy kiss.   *Exit*
  JULIET O, shut the door, and when thou hast done so,
45   Come weep with me, past hope, past cure, past help!
  FRIAR LAURENCE O Juliet, I already know thy grief.°   *grievous situation*
      It strains me past the compass° of my wits.   *limit*
      I hear thou must, and nothing may prorogue° it,   *postpone*
      On Thursday next be married to this County.
50 JULIET Tell me not, friar, that thou hear'st of this,
      Unless thou tell me how I may prevent it.
      If in thy wisdom thou canst give no help,
      Do thou but call my resolution wise,
          [*She draws a knife*]
      And with this knife I'll help it presently.°   *immediately*
55   God joined my heart and Romeo's, thou our hands,
      And ere this hand, by thee to Romeo's sealed,
      Shall be the label[4] to another deed,
      Or my true heart with treacherous revolt
      Turn to another, this shall slay them both.
60   Therefore, out of thy long-experienced time,
      Give me some present counsel; or, behold,
      'Twixt my extremes° and me this bloody knife   *extreme difficulties*
      Shall play the umpire, arbitrating that
      Which the commission° of thy years and art°   *authority / learning*
65   Could to no issue of true honour bring.
      Be not so long to speak. I long to die
      If what thou speak'st speak not of remedy.
  FRIAR LAURENCE Hold, daughter, I do spy a kind of hope
      Which craves as desperate° an execution[5]   *reckless*
70   As that is desperate° which we would prevent.   *hopeless*
      If, rather than to marry County Paris,
      Thou hast the strength of will to slay thyself,
      Then is it likely thou wilt undertake
      A thing like death to chide away this shame,
75   That cop'st° with death himself to scape from it;°   *Who wrestles / (shame)*
      And, if thou dar'st, I'll give thee remedy.
  JULIET O, bid me leap, rather than marry Paris,
      From off the battlements of any tower,
      Or walk in thievish° ways, or bid me lurk   *thief-infested*
80   Where serpents are. Chain me with roaring bears,
      Or hide me nightly in a charnel house,°   *burial vault*
      O'ercovered quite with dead men's rattling bones,
      With reeky° shanks and yellow chapless[6] skulls;   *foully damp*

3. Because it belongs to Romeo; also because Juliet, in   and so a pledge confirming another marriage.
her ambiguous replies, is not showing Paris her true face.   5. A performance; a killing.
4. Ribbon attaching a seal to a legal document (deed),   6. Without a lower jaw.

Or bid me go into a new-made grave
85 And hide me with a dead man in his tomb—
Things that, to hear them told, have made me tremble—
And I will do it without fear or doubt,°   *dread; hesitation*
To live an unstained wife to my sweet love.
FRIAR LAURENCE   Hold, then; go home, be merry, give consent
90 To marry Paris. Wednesday is tomorrow.
Tomorrow night look° that thou lie alone.   *be sure*
Let not the Nurse lie with thee in thy chamber.
Take thou this vial, being then in bed,
And this distilling° liquor drink thou off,   *permeating*
95 When presently through all thy veins shall run
A cold and drowsy humour;° for no pulse   *bodily fluid*
Shall keep his° native progress, but surcease.°   *its / cease*
No warmth, no breath shall testify thou livest.
The roses in thy lips and cheeks shall fade
100 To wanny° ashes, thy eyes' windows° fall   *pale / lids*
Like death when he shuts up the day of life.
Each part, deprived of supple government,°   *control of movement*
Shall, stiff and stark and cold, appear like death;
And in this borrowed likeness of shrunk death
105 Thou shalt continue two-and-forty hours,
And then awake as from a pleasant sleep.
Now, when the bridegroom in the morning comes
To rouse thee from thy bed, there art thou dead.
Then, as the manner of our country is,
110 In thy best robes, uncovered on the bier
Thou shalt be borne to that same ancient vault
Where all the kindred of the Capulets lie.
In the meantime, against° thou shalt awake,   *in preparation for when*
Shall Romeo by my letters know our drift,°   *scheme*
115 And hither shall he come, and he and I
Will watch° thy waking, and that very night   *keep vigil for*
Shall Romeo bear thee hence to Mantua.
And this shall free thee from this present shame,
If no inconstant toy° nor womanish fear   *fickle whim*
120 Abate thy valour in the acting it.
JULIET   Give me, give me! O, tell not me of fear!
FRIAR LAURENCE *[giving her the vial]*   Hold, get you gone. Be
     strong and prosperous
In this resolve. I'll send a friar with speed
To Mantua with my letters° to thy lord.   *letter*
125 JULIET   Love give me strength, and strength shall help afford.
Farewell, dear father.   *Exeunt [severally]*

4.2

Enter old CAPULET, *his* WIFE, NURSE, *and two or three*
     SERVINGMEN
CAPULET *[giving a* SERVINGMAN *a paper]*   So many guests invite
     as here are writ.   *[Exit* SERVINGMAN*]*
     [To the other SERVINGMAN*]* Sirrah, go hire me twenty
     cunning° cooks.   *skillful*

4.2 Location: Capulet's house.

SERVINGMAN   You shall have none ill, sir, for I'll try° if they can   *test*
     lick their fingers.
5   CAPULET   How canst thou try them so?
SERVINGMAN   Marry, sir, 'tis an ill cook that cannot lick his own
     fingers, therefore he that cannot lick his fingers goes not with
     me.
CAPULET   Go, be gone.   [*Exit* SERVINGMAN]
10   We shall be much unfurnished° for this time.   *unprepared*
     [*To* NURSE] What, is my daughter gone to Friar Laurence?
NURSE   Ay, forsooth.
CAPULET   Well, he may chance to do some good on her.
     A peevish,° self-willed harlotry° it° is.   *An obstinate / brat / she*
          Enter JULIET
15   NURSE   See where she comes from shrift° with merry look.   *absolution*
CAPULET [*to* JULIET]   How now, my headstrong, where have you
          been gadding?
JULIET   Where I have learned me to repent the sin
     Of disobedient opposition
     To you and your behests, and am enjoined
20   By holy Laurence to fall prostrate here
     To beg your pardon. (*She kneels down*) Pardon, I beseech you.
     Henceforward I am ever ruled by you.
CAPULET [*to* NURSE]   Send for the County; go tell him of this.
     I'll have this knot knit up tomorrow morning.
25   JULIET   I met the youthful lord at Laurence' cell,
     And gave him what becoming° love I might,   *suitable*
     Not stepping o'er the bounds of modesty.
CAPULET   Why, I am glad on't.° This is well. Stand up.   *of it*
          [JULIET *rises*]
     This is as't should be. Let me see the County.
30   [*To* NURSE] Ay, marry, go, I say, and fetch him hither.
     Now, afore God, this reverend holy friar,
     All our whole city is much bound to him.
JULIET   Nurse, will you go with me into my closet°   *chamber*
     To help me sort such needful ornaments
35   As you think fit to furnish me tomorrow?
CAPULET'S WIFE   No, not till Thursday. There is time enough.
CAPULET   Go, Nurse, go with her. We'll to church tomorrow.
                              Exeunt JULIET *and* NURSE
CAPULET'S WIFE   We shall be short in our provision.
     'Tis now near night.
CAPULET   Tush, I will stir about,
40   And all things shall be well, I warrant thee, wife.
     Go thou to Juliet, help to deck up her.
     I'll not to bed tonight. Let me alone.
     I'll play the housewife for this once. What, ho!
     They are all forth. Well, I will walk myself
45   To County Paris to prepare up him
     Against tomorrow. My heart is wondrous light,
     Since this same wayward girl is so reclaimed.[1]
                              Exeunt [*severally*]

---

1. Reformed; claimed in marriage.

4.3

Enter JULIET *and* NURSE *[with garments]*[1]

JULIET Ay, those attires are best. But, gentle Nurse,
I pray thee leave me to myself tonight,
For I have need of many orisons°   *prayers*
To move the heavens to smile upon my state,

5 Which—well thou knowest—is cross° and full of sin.   *adverse*

Enter [CAPULET'S WIFE]

CAPULET'S WIFE What, are you busy, ho? Need you my help?
JULIET No, madam, we have culled such necessaries
As are behoveful° for our state° tomorrow.   *needful / ceremony*
So please° you, let me now be left alone,   *If it pleases*

10 And let the Nurse this night sit up with you,
For I am sure you have your hands full all
In this so sudden business.
CAPULET'S WIFE   Good night.
Get thee to bed, and rest, for thou hast need.

Exeunt [CAPULET'S WIFE *and* NURSE]

JULIET Farewell. God knows when we shall meet again.

15 I have a faint cold fear thrills° through my veins   *pierces*
That almost freezes up the heat of life.
I'll call them back again to comfort me.
Nurse!—What should she do here?

[She opens curtains, behind which is seen her bed]

My dismal° scene I needs must act alone.   *calamitous*

20 Come, vial. What if this mixture do not work at all?
Shall I be married then tomorrow morning?
No, no, this shall forbid it. Lie thou there.

[She lays down a knife]

What if it be a poison which the friar
Subtly hath ministered to have me dead,

25 Lest in this marriage he should be dishonoured
Because he married me before to Romeo?
I fear it is—and yet methinks it should not,°   *not be*
For he hath still° been tried° a holy man.   *always / proved*
How if, when I am laid into the tomb,

30 I wake before the time that Romeo
Come to redeem me? There's a fearful point.
Shall I not then be stifled in the vault,
To whose foul mouth no healthsome air breathes in,
And there die strangled° ere my Romeo comes?   *suffocated*

35 Or, if I live, is it not very like°   *likely*
The horrible conceit of death and night,
Together with the terror of the place—
As° in a vault, an ancient receptacle   *As it is*
Where for this many hundred years the bones

40 Of all my buried ancestors are packed;
Where bloody Tybalt, yet but green° in earth,   *newly*
Lies fest'ring in his shroud; where, as they say,
At some hours in the night spirits resort—
Alack, alack, is it not like that I,

45 So early waking—what with loathsome smells,

4.3 Location: Capulet's house.
1. Juliet's chamber may be represented by a bed onstage for this scene and the next.

And shrieks like mandrakes[2] torn out of the earth,
That living mortals, hearing them, run mad—
O, if I wake, shall I not be distraught,
Environèd with all these hideous fears,
50 And madly play with my forefathers' joints,
And pluck the mangled Tybalt from his shroud,
And, in this rage,° with some great kinsman's bone   *insanity*
As with a club dash out my desp'rate brains?
O, look! Methinks I see my cousin's ghost
55 Seeking out Romeo that did spit his body
Upon a rapier's point. Stay, Tybalt, stay!
Romeo, Romeo, Romeo! Here's drink. I drink to thee.
        [*She drinks from the vial and*] *falls upon her bed within*
        the curtains

4.4

Enter [CAPULET'S WIFE,] *and* NURSE *with herbs*
CAPULET'S WIFE   Hold, take these keys, and fetch more spices, Nurse.
NURSE   They call for dates and quinces in the pastry.°   *pastry kitchen*
        Enter old CAPULET
CAPULET   Come, stir, stir, stir! The second cock hath crowed.
The curfew bell[1] hath rung. 'Tis three o'clock.
5 Look to the baked meats, good Angelica.[2]
Spare not for cost.
NURSE   Go, you cot-quean,° go.   *old housewife*
Get you to bed. Faith, you'll be sick tomorrow
For this night's watching.°   *wakefulness*
CAPULET   No, not a whit. What, I have watched ere now
10 All night for lesser cause, and ne'er been sick.
CAPULET'S WIFE   Ay, you have been a mouse-hunt° in your time,   *skirt chaser*
But I will watch° you from such watching now.   *guard*
                    Exeunt [CAPULET'S WIFE] *and* NURSE
CAPULET   A jealous-hood,[3] a jealous-hood!
        Enter three or four SERVINGMEN, *with spits and logs and*
        baskets
                            Now, fellow, what is there?
FIRST SERVINGMAN   Things for the cook, sir, but I know not what.
CAPULET   Make haste, make haste.
        [*Exit* FIRST SERVINGMAN *and one or two others*]
15   Sirrah, fetch drier logs.
Call Peter. He will show thee where they are.
SECOND SERVINGMAN   I have a head, sir, that will find out logs[4]
And never trouble Peter for the matter.
CAPULET   Mass,° and well said! A merry whoreson,° ha!   *By the mass / rogue*
Thou shalt be loggerhead.°   *Exit* [SECOND SERVINGMAN]   *wooden-headed*
20   Good faith, 'tis day.
The County will be here with music straight,
For so he said he would.
        Play music [*within*]
                    I hear him near.

---

2. Plants with forked roots thought to resemble a man.
Popular belief held that they uttered a death- or
madness-producing shriek upon being pulled up.
4.4 Location: Scene continues.
1. Also rung at daybreak.
2. Unclear whether Capulet refers to his wife or the

nurse.
3. Jealousy; jealous woman.
4. I have a good head for finding things, so I can cer-
tainly find the logs; my head knows all about logs (I am
a blockhead).

Nurse! Wife! What ho, what, Nurse, I say!

    Enter NURSE

Go waken Juliet. Go and trim her up.

25   I'll go and chat with Paris. Hie, make haste,
Make haste, the bridegroom he is come already.
Make haste, I say.   *[Exit]*

NURSE   Mistress, what, mistress! Juliet! Fast,° I warrant her, she.   *Asleep*
Why, lamb, why, lady! Fie, you slug-abed!

30   Why, love, I say, madam, sweetheart, why, bride!
What, not a word? You take your pennyworths° now.   *bits (of sleep)*
Sleep for a week, for the next night, I warrant,
The County Paris hath set up his rest⁵
That you shall rest but little. God forgive me!

35   Marry, and amen. How sound is she asleep!
I needs must wake her. Madam, madam, madam!
Ay, let the County take° you in your bed.   *catch; sexually possess*
He'll fright you up, i'faith. Will it not be?

    [She draws back the curtains]

What, dressed and in your clothes, and down again?

40   I must needs wake you. Lady, lady, lady!
Alas, alas! Help, help! My lady's dead.
O welladay,° that ever I was born!   *alas*
Some aqua-vitae, ho! My lord, my lady!

    Enter [CAPULET'S WIFE]

CAPULET'S WIFE   What noise is here?

NURSE   O lamentable day!

CAPULET'S WIFE   What is the matter?

45   NURSE   Look, look. O heavy day!

CAPULET'S WIFE   O me, O me, my child, my only life!
Revive, look up, or I will die with thee.
Help, help, call help!

    Enter [CAPULET]

CAPULET   For shame, bring Juliet forth. Her lord is come.

50   NURSE   She's dead, deceased. She's dead, alack the day!

CAPULET'S WIFE   Alack the day, she's dead, she's dead, she's dead!

CAPULET   Ha, let me see her! Out,° alas, she's cold.   *Woe*
Her blood is settled,° and her joints are stiff.   *motionless*
Life and these lips have long been separated.

55   Death lies on her like an untimely frost
Upon the sweetest flower of all the field.

NURSE   O lamentable day!

CAPULET'S WIFE   O woeful time!

CAPULET   Death, that hath ta'en her hence to make me wail,
Ties up my tongue, and will not let me speak.

    Enter FRIAR [LAURENCE] *and* PARIS [*with Musicians*]

60   FRIAR LAURENCE   Come, is the bride ready to go to church?

CAPULET   Ready to go, but never to return.
[*To* PARIS] O son, the night before thy wedding day
Hath death lain with thy wife. See, there she lies,
Flower as she was, deflowerèd by him.

65   Death is my son-in-law, death is my heir.
My daughter he hath wedded. I will die,
And leave him all. Life, living,° all is death's.   *property*

---

5. Has resolved (from staking everything in the card game primero), with bawdy pun.

All at once wring their hands and cry out

PARIS   Have I thought° long to see this morning's face,   *expected*
    And doth it give me such a sight as this?
70   Beguiled,° divorcèd, wrongèd, spited,° slain!   *Cheated / injured*
    Most detestable death, by thee beguiled,
    By cruel, cruel thee quite overthrown.
    O love, O life: not life, but love in death.
CAPULET'S WIFE   Accursed, unhappy, wretched, hateful day!
75   Most miserable hour that e'er time saw
    In lasting° labour of his pilgrimage!   *eternal*
    But one, poor one, one poor and loving child,
    But one thing to rejoice and solace in,
    And cruel death hath catched° it from my sight!   *seized*
80 NURSE   O woe! O woeful, woeful, woeful day!
    Most lamentable day! Most woeful day
    That ever, ever, I did yet behold!
    O day, O day, O day, O hateful day,
    Never was seen so black a day as this!
85   O woeful day, O woeful day!
CAPULET   Despised, distressèd, hated, martyred, killed!
    Uncomfortable° time, why cam'st thou now   *Comfortless*
    To murder, murder our solemnity?°   *festivity*
    O child, O child, my soul and not my child!⁶
90   Dead art thou, alack, my child is dead,
    And with my child my joys are burièd.
FRIAR LAURENCE   Peace, ho, for shame! Confusion's° cure lives   *Destruction's*
      not
    In these confusions.° Heaven and yourself   *commotions*
    Had part in this fair maid. Now heaven hath all,
95   And all the better is it for the maid.
    Your part in her you could not keep from death,
    But heaven keeps his part in eternal life.
    The most you sought was her promotion,°   *social advancement*
    For 'twas your heaven° she should be advanced,   *highest ambition*
100   And weep ye now, seeing she is advanced
    Above the clouds as high as heaven itself?
    O, in this love you love your child so ill
    That you run mad, seeing that she is well.
    She's not well married that lives married long,
105   But she's best married that dies married young.
    Dry up your tears, and stick your rosemary
    On this fair corpse, and, as the custom is,
    All in her best array bear her to church;
    For though fond° nature° bids us all lament,   *foolish; doting / affection*
110   Yet nature's tears are reason's merriment.°   *laughable idiocy*
CAPULET   All things that we ordainèd festival
    Turn from their office° to black funeral.   *due function*
    Our instruments to melancholy bells,
    Our wedding cheer° to a sad burial feast,   *fare*
115   Our solemn° hymns to sullen° dirges change;   *ceremonial / mournful*
    Our bridal flowers serve for a buried corpse,
    And all things change them to the contrary.
FRIAR LAURENCE   Sir, go you in; and madam, go with him,
    And go, Sir Paris. Everyone prepare

6. *not my child*: because dead and only a corpse.

120   To follow this fair corpse unto her grave.
       The heavens do lour° upon you for some ill.°   *hang threatening / offense*
       Move° them no more by crossing their high will.   *Anger*
           All but NURSE *go forth, casting rosemary on* JULIET *and*
               shutting the curtains. Manent° NURSE *and* MUSICIANS   *Remain*
FIRST MUSICIAN   Faith, we may put° up our pipes and be gone.   *pack*
NURSE   Honest good fellows, ah, put up, put up,
125   For well you know this is a pitiful case.
FIRST MUSICIAN   Ay, by my troth, the case may be amended.⁷
                                                            Exit [NURSE]
           Enter PETER
PETER   Musicians, O, musicians! 'Heart's ease',° 'Heart's ease';   *(popular song)*
       O, an you will have me live, play 'Heart's ease'.
FIRST MUSICIAN   Why 'Heart's ease'?
130   PETER   O, musicians, because my heart itself plays 'My heart is
       full of woe'. O, play me some merry dump° to comfort me.   *sad tune*
FIRST MUSICIAN   Not a dump, we. 'Tis no time to play now.
PETER   You will not then?
FIRST MUSICIAN   No.
135   PETER   I will then give it you soundly.°   *thoroughly; in sound*
FIRST MUSICIAN   What will you give us?
PETER   No money, on my faith, but the gleek.⁸ I will give you
       the minstrel.⁹
FIRST MUSICIAN   Then will I give you the serving-creature.
140   PETER [*drawing his dagger*]   Then will I lay the serving-creature's
       dagger on your pate. I will carry° no crochets.¹ I'll re you, I'll   *bear; sing*
       fa you. Do you note° me?   *heed*
FIRST MUSICIAN   An you re us and fa us, you note° us.   *give notes to*
SECOND MUSICIAN   Pray you, put up your dagger and put out°   *show; quench*
145   your wit.
PETER   Then have at you with my wit. I will dry-beat° you with   *thrash*
       an iron° wit, and put up my iron dagger. Answer² me like men.   *a merciless*
       [*Sings*]   When griping grief the heart doth wound,
                   And doleful dumps° the mind oppress,   *melancholy*
150   Then music with her silver sound³—
       Why 'silver sound', why 'music with her silver sound'? What
       say you, Matthew Minikin?°   *small lute string*
FIRST MUSICIAN   Marry, sir, because silver hath a sweet sound.
PETER   Prates!° What say you, Hugh Rebec?⁴   *Chatter*
155   SECOND MUSICIAN   I say 'silver sound' because musicians sound
       for silver.
PETER   Prates too! What say you, Simon Soundpost?⁵
THIRD MUSICIAN   Faith, I know not what to say.
PETER   O, I cry you mercy,° you are the singer. I will say for you.   *beg your pardon*
160   It is 'music with her silver sound' because musicians have no
       gold for sounding.⁶
       [*Sings*]   Then music with her silver sound
                       With speedy help doth lend redress.   *Exit*
FIRST MUSICIAN   What a pestilent knave is this same!

7. Things could be better; the instrument case can be   3. Lines from the song "In Commendation of Music."
repaired.   4. Three-stringed instrument.
8. To "give the gleek" was to make a fool of or play a   5. Supporting peg fixed between the sounding board
trick on.   and back of a stringed instrument.
9. I will insultingly call you a minstrel.   6. Musicians are given no gold for playing; they are
1. Whimsy; quarter notes.   poor and have no gold to jingle.
2. Defy; respond to.

165   SECOND MUSICIAN   Hang him, jack! Come, we'll in here, tarry
     for the mourners, and stay° dinner.   *Exeunt*   *await*

5.1

     Enter ROMEO
   ROMEO   If I may trust the flattering° truth of sleep,   *encouraging*
     My dreams presage some joyful news at hand.
     My bosom's lord sits lightly in his throne,¹
     And all this day an unaccustomed spirit
5   Lifts me above the ground with cheerful thoughts.
     I dreamt my lady came and found me dead—
     Strange dream, that gives a dead man leave to think!—
     And breathed such life with kisses in° my lips   *into*
     That I revived and was an emperor.
10   Ah me, how sweet is love itself possessed°   *enjoyed in reality*
     When but love's shadows° are so rich in joy!   *dreams; images*
     Enter BALTHASAR, *his man, booted*²
     News from Verona! How now, Balthasar?
     Dost thou not bring me letters from the friar?
     How doth my lady? Is my father well?
15   How fares my Juliet? That I ask again,
     For nothing can be ill if she be well.
   BALTHASAR   Then she is well, and nothing can be ill.
     Her body sleeps in Capel's monument,
     And her immortal part with angels lives.
20   I saw her laid low in her kindred's vault,
     And presently° took post³ to tell it you.   *immediately*
     O, pardon me for bringing these ill news,
     Since you did leave it for my office,° sir.   *duty*
   ROMEO   Is it e'en so? Then I defy you, stars.
25   Thou knowest my lodging. Get me ink and paper,
     And hire posthorses. I will hence tonight.
   BALTHASAR   I do beseech you, sir, have patience.
     Your looks are pale and wild, and do import°   *signify*
     Some misadventure.   Tush, thou art deceived.
   ROMEO
30   Leave me, and do the thing I bid thee do.
     Hast thou no letters to me from the friar?
   BALTHASAR   No, my good lord.
   ROMEO   No matter. Get thee gone,
     And hire those horses. I'll be with thee straight.
                        Exit BALTHASAR
     Well, Juliet, I will lie with thee tonight.
35   Let's see for means. O mischief, thou art swift
     To enter in the thoughts of desperate men!
     I do remember an apothecary,
     And hereabouts a dwells, which late I noted,
     In tattered weeds,° with overwhelming° brows,   *clothes / overhanging*
40   Culling of simples.° Meagre were his looks.   *herbs*
     Sharp misery had worn him to the bones,
     And in his needy° shop a tortoise hung,   *poor*
     An alligator stuffed, and other skins

5.1 Location: A street in Mantua.   2. *booted*: as if he has just dismounted.
1. Love rules in the heart; the heart is at ease in the   3. Set out on post horses.
chest.

Of ill-shaped fishes; and about his shelves
45 A beggarly account° of empty boxes,   *A sparse collection*
Green earthen pots, bladders, and musty seeds,
Remnants of packthread,° and old cakes of roses⁴   *twine*
Were thinly scattered to make up a show.
Noting this penury, to myself I said
50 'An if a man did need a poison now,
Whose sale is present death⁵ in Mantua,
Here lives a caitiff ° wretch would sell it him.'   *pitiful*
O, this same thought did but forerun my need,
And this same needy man must sell it me.
55 As I remember, this should be the house.
Being holiday, the beggar's shop is shut.
What ho, apothecary!
    Enter APOTHECARY
APOTHECARY   Who calls so loud?
ROMEO   Come hither, man. I see that thou art poor.
    [*He offers money*]
Hold, there is forty ducats.⁶ Let me have
60 A dram of poison—such soon-speeding gear⁷
As will disperse itself through all the veins,
That the life-weary taker may fall dead,
And that the trunk° may be discharged of breath   *body*
As violently as hasty powder fired
65 Doth hurry from the fatal cannon's womb.
APOTHECARY   Such mortal drugs I have, but Mantua's law
Is death to any he° that utters° them.   *man / offers to sell*
ROMEO   Art thou so bare° and full of wretchedness,   *destitute*
And fear'st to die? Famine is in thy cheeks,
70 Need and oppression starveth in thy eyes,
Contempt and beggary hangs upon thy back.
The world is not thy friend, nor the world's law.
The world affords° no law to make thee rich.   *provides*
Then be not poor, but break it, and take this.
75 APOTHECARY   My poverty but not my will consents.
ROMEO   I pay thy poverty and not thy will.
APOTHECARY [*handing* ROMEO *poison*]   Put this in any liquid
thing you will
And drink it off, and if you had the strength
Of twenty men it would dispatch you straight.°   *immediately*
ROMEO [*giving money*]   There is thy gold—worse poison to
80 men's souls,
Doing more murder in this loathsome world,
Than these poor compounds that thou mayst not sell.
I sell thee poison; thou hast sold me none.
Farewell, buy food, and get thyself in flesh.°   *grow fatter*
    [*Exit* APOTHECARY]
85 Come, cordial° and not poison, go with me   *restorative; heart's ease*
To Juliet's grave, for there must I use thee.   *Exit*

4. Rose petals pressed into cake form and used as a
sachet.
5. Punishable by immediate death.
6. Various gold coins used at times in much of Europe,
and Shakespeare's usual currency for plays not set in
England.
7. Quick-working stuff; quick-killing stuff.

5.2

Enter FRIAR JOHN [*at one door*]

FRIAR JOHN   Holy Franciscan friar, brother, ho!

Enter FRIAR LAURENCE [*at another door*]

FRIAR LAURENCE   This same should be the voice of Friar John.
Welcome from Mantua! What says Romeo?
Or if his mind° be writ, give me his letter.   *thoughts*

5   FRIAR JOHN   Going to find a barefoot brother out—
One of our order—to associate me[1]
Here in this city visiting the sick,
And finding him, the searchers[2] of the town,
Suspecting that we both were in a house

10   Where the infectious pestilence did reign,
Sealed up the doors, and would not let us forth,
So that my speed to Mantua there was stayed.°   *stopped*

FRIAR LAURENCE   Who bare my letter then to Romeo?

FRIAR JOHN   I could not send it—here it is again—

15   Nor get a messenger to bring it thee,
So fearful were they of infection.°   *contagion*

FRIAR LAURENCE   Unhappy fortune! By my brotherhood,
The letter was not nice,° but full of charge,°   *trivial / importance*
Of dear import,° and the neglecting it   *serious consequence*

20   May do much danger. Friar John, go hence.
Get me an iron crow,° and bring it straight   *crowbar*
Unto my cell.

FRIAR JOHN   Brother, I'll go and bring it thee.   *Exit*

FRIAR LAURENCE   Now must I to the monument alone.
Within this three hours will fair Juliet wake.

25   She will beshrew° me much that Romeo   *curse*
Hath had no notice of these accidents.°   *events*
But I will write again to Mantua,
And keep her at my cell till Romeo come.
Poor living corpse, closed in a dead man's tomb!   *Exit*

5.3

Enter County PARIS *and his* PAGE, *with flowers, sweet°*   *perfumed*
water [*and a torch*]

PARIS   Give me thy torch, boy. Hence, and stand aloof.°   *stay apart*
Yet put it out, for I would not be seen.

[*His* PAGE *puts out the torch*]

Under yon yew trees lay thee all along,°   *stretched out*
Holding thy ear close to the hollow ground.

5   So shall no foot upon the churchyard tread,
Being° loose, unfirm, with digging up of graves,   *The ground being*
But thou shalt hear it. Whistle then to me
As signal that thou hear'st something approach.
Give me those flowers. Do as I bid thee. Go.

10   PAGE [*aside*]   I am almost afraid to stand alone
Here in the churchyard, yet I will adventure.°   *risk it*

[*He hides himself at a distance from* PARIS]

5.2 Location: Friar Laurence's cell.
1. Franciscan friars (barefoot because the order is
sworn to poverty) traveled only in pairs. *associate*:
accompany.

2. Health officers appointed to examine corpses and
identify houses infected with the plague.
5.3 Location: The Capulet mausoleum.

PARIS (*strews the tomb with flowers*)   Sweet flower, with flowers
    thy bridal bed I strew.
        [*He sprinkles water*]
    O woe! Thy canopy° is dust and stones,   *covering; bed hangings*
    Which with sweet water nightly I will dew,
15   Or, wanting that, with tears distilled by moans.
    The obsequies that I for thee will keep°   *perform*
    Nightly shall be to strew thy grave and weep.
        [PAGE *whistles*]
    The boy gives warning. Something doth approach.
    What cursèd foot wanders this way tonight
20   To cross° my obsequies and true love's rite?   *thwart*
        Enter ROMEO *and* BALTHASAR, *with a torch, a mattock,*°   *pickax*
        and a crow of iron
    What, with a torch? Muffle me, night, a while.
        [*He stands aside*]
ROMEO   Give me that mattock and the wrenching iron.
    Hold, take this letter. Early in the morning
    See thou deliver it to my lord and father.
25   Give me the light. Upon thy life I charge thee,
    Whate'er thou hear'st or seest, stand all aloof,
    And do not interrupt me in my course.
    Why I descend into this bed of death
    Is partly to behold my lady's face,
30   But chiefly to take thence from her dead finger
    A precious ring, a ring that I must use
    In dear° employment. Therefore hence, be gone.   *important; tender*
    But if thou, jealous,° dost return to pry   *suspicious*
    In what I farther shall intend to do,
35   By heaven, I will tear thee joint by joint,
    And strew this hungry churchyard with thy limbs.
    The time and my intents are savage-wild,
    More fierce and more inexorable far
    Than empty tigers or the roaring sea.
40 BALTHASAR   I will be gone, sir, and not trouble ye.
ROMEO   So shalt thou show me friendship. Take thou that.
        [*He gives money*]
    Live and be prosperous, and farewell, good fellow.
BALTHASAR [*aside*]   For all this same, I'll hide me hereabout.
    His looks I fear, and his intents I doubt.°   *suspect*
        [*He hides himself at a distance from* ROMEO.]
        ROMEO *begins to open the tomb*
45 ROMEO   Thou detestable maw, thou womb[1] of death,
    Gorged with the dearest morsel of the earth,
    Thus I enforce thy rotten jaws to open,
    And in despite° I'll cram thee with more food.   *defiant ill will*
PARIS [*aside*]   This is that banished haughty Montague
50   That murdered my love's cousin, with which grief
    It is supposèd the fair creature died;
    And here is come to do some villainous shame
    To the dead bodies. I will apprehend him.
    [*Drawing*] Stop thy unhallowed° toil, vile Montague!   *unholy*

---

1. Belly; also playing on the birthplace of Romeo's death.

55 Can vengeance be pursued further than death?
Condemnèd villain, I do apprehend thee.
Obey and go with me, for thou must die.
ROMEO I must indeed, and therefore came I hither.
Good gentle youth, tempt not a desp'rate° man.   *despairing; violent*
60 Fly hence, and leave me. Think upon these gone.
Let them affright thee. I beseech thee, youth,
Put not another sin upon my head
By urging me to fury. O, be gone.
By heaven, I love thee better than myself,
65 For I come hither armed against myself.
Stay not, be gone. Live, and hereafter say
A madman's mercy bid thee run away.
PARIS I do defy thy conjuration,°   *entreaty*
And apprehend thee for a felon here.
70 ROMEO [*drawing*] Wilt thou provoke me? Then have at thee, boy.
    They fight
PAGE O Lord, they fight! I will go call the watch.   [*Exit*]
PARIS O, I am slain! If thou be merciful,
Open the tomb, lay me with Juliet.
ROMEO In faith, I will.   [PARIS *dies*]
    Let me peruse this face.
75 Mercutio's kinsman, noble County Paris!
What said my man when my betossèd° soul   *storm-tossed*
Did not attend° him as we rode? I think   *listen to*
He told me Paris should have married Juliet.
Said he not so? Or did I dream it so?
80 Or am I mad, hearing him talk of Juliet,
To think it was so? O, give me thy hand,
One writ with me in sour misfortune's book.
I'll bury thee in a triumphant° grave.   *magnificent*
    [*He opens the tomb, revealing* JULIET]
A grave—O no, a lantern,° slaughtered youth,   *lighthouse*
85 For here lies Juliet, and her beauty makes
This vault a feasting presence² full of light.
    [*He bears the body of Paris to the tomb*]
Death, lie thou there, by a dead man interred.
How oft, when men are at the point of death,
Have they been merry, which their keepers° call   *sick nurses; jailors*
90 A lightning before death! O, how may I
Call this a lightning? O my love, my wife!
Death, that hath sucked the honey of thy breath,
Hath had no power yet upon thy beauty.
Thou art not conquered.° Beauty's ensign° yet   *overpowered; seduced / flag*
95 Is crimson in thy lips and in thy cheeks,
And death's pale flag is not advancèd there.
Tybalt, liest thou there in thy bloody sheet?
O, what more favour can I do to thee
Than with that hand that cut thy youth in twain
100 To sunder his° that was thine enemy?   *the youth of him*
Forgive me, cousin. Ah, dear Juliet,
Why art thou yet so fair? Shall I believe
That unsubstantial° death is amorous,   *immaterial*

2. Festive royal chamber for receiving guests.

And that the lean abhorrèd monster keeps
105   Thee here in dark to be his paramour?
For fear of that I still will stay with thee,
And never from this pallet of dim night
Depart again. Here, here will I remain
With worms that are thy chambermaids. O, here
110   Will I set up my everlasting rest,³
And shake the yoke of inauspicious stars
From this world-wearied flesh. Eyes, look your last.
Arms, take your last embrace, and lips, O you
The doors of breath, seal with a righteous kiss
115   A dateless° bargain to engrossing⁴ death.   *An eternal*
      [*He kisses* JULIET, *then pours poison into the cup*]
Come, bitter conduct°, come, unsavoury guide,   *conductor; leader*
Thou desperate pilot, now at once run on
The dashing rocks thy seasick weary° barque!   *travel-weary*
Here's to my love.
      [*He drinks the poison*]
              O true apothecary,
120   Thy drugs are quick!° Thus with a kiss I die.   *fast; vigorous*
      [*He kisses* JULIET,] *falls* [*and dies.*]
      Enter FRIAR [LAURENCE] *with lantern, crow,*
      and spade

FRIAR LAURENCE   Saint Francis be my speed!° How oft tonight   *help*
Have my old feet stumbled at graves? Who's there?
BALTHASAR   Here's one, a friend, and one that knows you well.
FRIAR LAURENCE   Bliss be upon you. Tell me, good my friend,
125   What torch is yon that vainly lends his light
To grubs and eyeless skulls? As I discern,
It burneth in the Capels' monument.
BALTHASAR   It doth so, holy sir, and there's my master,
One that you love.
FRIAR LAURENCE   Who is it?
BALTHASAR   Romeo.
FRIAR LAURENCE   How long hath he been there?
130   BALTHASAR   Full half an hour.
FRIAR LAURENCE   Go with me to the vault.
BALTHASAR   I dare not, sir.
My master knows not but I am gone hence,
And fearfully° did menace me with death   *fearsomely*
If I did stay to look on his intents.
135   FRIAR LAURENCE   Stay then, I'll go alone. Fear comes upon me.
O, much I fear some ill unthrifty° thing.   *unfortunate*
BALTHASAR   As I did sleep under this yew tree here
I dreamt my master and another fought,
And that my master slew him.
FRIAR LAURENCE   Romeo!
      [*He*] *stoops and looks on the blood and weapons*
140   Alack, alack, what blood is this which stains
The stony entrance of this sepulchre?
What mean these masterless and gory swords
To lie discoloured by this place of peace?

3. Make my final determination.
4. Buying up in large quantities to monopolize; writing a legal document.

Romeo! O, pale! Who else? What, Paris, too,
145   And steeped in blood? Ah, what an unkind° hour   *unnatural; a cruel*
Is guilty of this lamentable chance!°   *event*
      JULIET *[awakes and] rises*
      The lady stirs.
      JULIET   O comfortable° friar, where is my lord?   *solace-giving*
      I do remember well where I should be,
150   And there I am. Where is my Romeo?
      FRIAR LAURENCE   I hear some noise. Lady, come from that nest
      Of death, contagion, and unnatural sleep.
      A greater power than we can contradict
      Hath thwarted our intents. Come, come away.
155   Thy husband in thy bosom there lies dead,
      And Paris, too. Come, I'll dispose of thee
      Among a sisterhood of holy nuns.
      Stay not to question, for the watch is coming.
      Come, go, good Juliet. I dare no longer stay.   *Exit*
160   JULIET   Go, get thee hence, for I will not away.
      What's here? A cup closed in my true love's hand?
      Poison, I see, hath been his timeless° end.   *untimely; lasting*
      O churl!—drunk all, and left no friendly drop
      To help me after? I will kiss thy lips.
165   Haply° some poison yet doth hang on them,   *Perhaps*
      To make me die with a restorative.⁵
            [She kisses Romeo's lips]
      Thy lips are warm.
      CHIEF WATCHMAN *[within]*   Lead, boy. Which way?
      JULIET   Yea, noise? Then I'll be brief.
            [She takes Romeo's dagger]
                                    O happy° dagger,   *fortunate*
      This is thy sheath! There rust, and let me die.
            She stabs herself, falls [and dies]
            Enter [PAGE] *and* WATCH
170   PAGE   This is the place, there where the torch doth burn.
      CHIEF WATCHMAN   The ground is bloody. Search about the churchyard.
      Go, some of you. Whoe'er you find, attach.°   *arrest*
            [Exeunt some WATCHMEN*]*
      Pitiful sight! Here lies the County slain,
      And Juliet bleeding, warm, and newly dead,
175   Who here hath lain this two days burièd.
      Go tell the Prince. Run to the Capulets,
      Raise up the Montagues. Some others search.
            [Exeunt other WATCHMEN *severally]*
      We see the ground° whereon these woes do lie,   *earth*
      But the true ground° of all these piteous woes   *cause*
180   We cannot without circumstance° descry.   *a fuller account*
            Enter [WATCHMEN] *with Romeo's man* [BALTHASAR]
      SECOND WATCHMAN   Here's Romeo's man. We found him in
            the churchyard.
      CHIEF WATCHMAN   Hold him in safety° till the Prince come   *securely*
            hither.
            Enter another WATCHMAN WITH FRIAR [LAURENCE]
      THIRD WATCHMAN   Here is a friar that trembles, sighs, and weeps.

---

5. Both the kiss, which is healing, and the poison, which restores them to each other.

We took this mattock and this spade from him
185 As he was coming from this churchyard's side.⁶
CHIEF WATCHMAN   A great suspicion. Stay° the friar, too.   Hold
    Enter PRINCE *with others*
PRINCE   What misadventure is so early up,
    That calls our person from our morning rest?
    Enter old CAPULET *and his* WIFE
CAPULET   What should it be that is so shrieked abroad?
190 CAPULET'S WIFE   O, the people in the street cry 'Romeo',
    Some 'Juliet', and some 'Paris', and all run
    With open° outcry toward our monument.   public; open-mouthed
PRINCE   What fear is this which startles° in our ears?   bursts out
CHIEF WATCHMAN   Sovereign, here lies the County Paris slain,
195   And Romeo dead, and Juliet, dead before,
    Warm, and new killed.
PRINCE   Search, seek, and know how this foul murder comes.
CHIEF WATCHMAN   Here is a friar, and slaughtered Romeo's man,
    With instruments upon them fit to open
200   These dead men's tombs.
CAPULET   O heavens! O wife, look how our daughter bleeds!
    This dagger hath mista'en, for lo, his house°   scabbard
    Is empty on the back of Montague,
    And it mis-sheathèd in my daughter's bosom.
205 CAPULET'S WIFE   O me, this sight of death is as a bell
    That warns° my old age to a sepulchre.   summons
    Enter old MONTAGUE
PRINCE   Come, Montague, for thou art early up
    To see thy son and heir more early down.
MONTAGUE   Alas, my liege, my wife is dead tonight.
210   Grief of my son's exile hath stopped her breath.
    What further woe conspires against mine age?
PRINCE   Look, and thou shalt see.
MONTAGUE [*seeing Romeo's body*]   O thou untaught! What
    manners is in this,
    To press before° thy father to a grave?   To shove ahead of
215 PRINCE   Seal up the mouth of outrage⁷ for a while,
    Till we can clear these ambiguities
    And know their spring, their head, their true descent;
    And then will I be general of your woes,
    And lead you even to death. Meantime, forbear,
220   And let mischance be slave to° patience.   overruled by
    Bring forth the parties of suspicion.
FRIAR LAURENCE   I am the greatest,° able to do least,   most suspect
    Yet most suspected, as the time and place
    Doth make against me, of this direful murder;
225   And here I stand, both to impeach and purge
    Myself condemnèd and myself excused.⁸
PRINCE   Then say at once what thou dost know in this.
FRIAR LAURENCE   I will be brief, for my short date° of breath   duration
    Is not so long as is a tedious tale.
230   Romeo, there dead, was husband to that Juliet,
    And she, there dead, that Romeo's faithful wife.

6. This side of the churchyard.
7. Of impassioned exclamation.
8. *to . . . excused:* to accuse myself of what I am guilty of and clear myself of what I am not.

I married them, and their stol'n marriage day
Was Tybalt's doomsday, whose untimely death
Banished the new-made bridegroom from this city,
235   For whom, and not for Tybalt, Juliet pined.
You, to remove that siege of grief from her,
Betrothed and would have married her perforce°   *forcibly*
To County Paris. Then comes she to me,
And with wild looks bid me devise some mean°   *method*
240   To rid her from this second marriage,
Or in my cell there would she kill herself.
Then gave I her—so tutored by my art[9]—
A sleeping potion, which so took effect
As I intended, for it wrought on her
245   The form° of death. Meantime I writ to Romeo   *appearance*
That he should hither come as this° dire night   *as this = this*
To help to take her from her borrowed grave,
Being the time the potion's force should cease.
But he which bore my letter, Friar John,
250   Was stayed by accident, and yesternight
Returned my letter back. Then all alone,
At the prefixéd° hour of her waking,   *prearranged*
Came I to take her from her kindred's vault,
Meaning to keep her closely° at my cell   *secretly*
255   Till I conveniently° could send to Romeo.   *befittingly*
But when I came, some minute ere the time
Of her awakening, here untimely lay
The noble Paris and true Romeo dead.
She wakes, and I entreated her come forth
260   And bear this work of heaven with patience.
But then a noise did scare me from the tomb,
And she, too desperate, would not go with me,
But, as it seems, did violence on herself.
All this I know, and to the marriage
265   Her nurse is privy; and if aught in this
Miscarried by my fault, let my old life
Be sacrificed, some hour before his° time,   *its*
Unto the rigour of severest law.
PRINCE   We still° have known thee for a holy man.   *always*
270   Where's Romeo's man? What can he say to this?
BALTHASAR   I brought my master news of Juliet's death,
And then in post° he came from Mantua   *haste*
To this same place, to this same monument.
This letter he early bid me give his father,
275   And threatened me with death, going in the vault,
If I departed not and left him there.
PRINCE   Give me the letter. I will look on it.
      [He *takes the letter*]
Where is the County's page that raised the watch?
Sirrah, what made° your master in this place?   *did*
280 PAGE   He came with flowers to strew his lady's grave,
And bid me stand aloof, and so I did.
Anon° comes one with light to ope the tomb,   *Soon*

---

9. As I knew through my medical study to do.

And by and by my master drew on him,
And then I ran away to call the watch.
285   PRINCE   This letter doth make good the friar's words,
Their course of love, the tidings of her death;
And here he writes that he did buy a poison
Of a poor 'pothecary, and therewithal
Came to this vault to die, and lie with Juliet.
290   Where be these enemies? Capulet, Montague,
See what a scourge is laid upon your hate,
That heaven finds means to kill your joys° with love.   *happiness; children*
And I, for winking at° your discords, too   *closing my eyes to*
Have lost a brace of kinsmen. All are punishèd.
295   CAPULET   O brother Montague, give me thy hand.
This is my daughter's jointure,° for no more   *marriage portion*
Can I demand.
  MONTAGUE   But I can give thee more,
For I will raise her statue in pure gold,
That whiles Verona by that name is known
300   There shall no figure at such rate be set[1]
As that of true and faithful Juliet.
  CAPULET   As rich shall Romeo's by his lady's lie,
Poor sacrifices of our enmity.
  PRINCE   A glooming° peace this morning with it brings.   *frowning; dark*
305   The sun for sorrow will not show his head.
Go hence, to have more talk of these sad things.
Some shall be pardoned, and some punishèd;
For never was a story of more woe
Than this of Juliet and her Romeo.
                          [The tomb is closed.] Exeunt

---

1. No figure shall be so valued; no figure shall be erected at such a price.

Julius Caesar

In *Julius Caesar,* Shakespeare dramatizes incidents that seem not merely locally momentous but of world-historical significance. Indeed, one of the protagonists of his play, Caius Cassius, eagerly anticipates his own impersonated presence on Shakespeare's stage:

> How many ages hence
> Shall this our lofty scene be acted over,
> In states unborn and accents yet unknown!
> (3.1.112–14)

Cassius correctly predicts that his own actions, although they will eventually become ancient history, will nonetheless remain compelling to people far removed in time and place from the original events. When Shakespeare imagines ancient Romans, he imagines not people famous by accident, but people constantly aware that the eyes of the world are upon them, and will remain upon them for centuries to come.

The Romans' unbridled sense of self-importance results from the unprecedented scope of their political and military power. By 44 B.C.E., an astonishing sequence of conquests had made Rome, once an unremarkable Italian town, the center of an empire that stretched from North Africa to Britain, from Persia to Spain. The vastness of these domains magnifies the exploits of Rome's central political figures, because the consequences of their actions resonate across continents and down the centuries.

Yet as *Julius Caesar* opens, Rome's outsized ambitions are threatening to destroy it. For centuries, Rome had been governed not by a king or a dictator, but by elected officers, and its republican traditions had been a source of fierce civic pride. Yet as the city's military endeavors grow increasingly ambitious, its generals, with the might of their armies behind them, wield more power than the factionalized senate to which they supposedly owe allegiance. Of these generals, the charismatic and enterprising Julius Caesar, who had subdued much of northwest Europe even while consolidating his popularity among the poorer classes at home, seems particularly dangerous. When legal and military attempts to curb Caesar's growing power fail, a group of conspirators led by Caius Cassius and Marcus Brutus assassinate him. Yet the death of Caesar does not, as his killers had hoped, restore Rome to its tradition of republican government. Instead, civil war ensues, in which Caesar's friend Mark Antony and Caesar's adopted heir, Octavius, defeat the forces of the conspirators. Eventually, after a power struggle among the victors (recounted in Shakespeare's *Antony and Cleopatra*), Octavius is enthroned as the emperor Augustus. His ascendancy, consolidating immense power in a single individual, completes the political transformation that Julius Caesar's assassins had tried to prevent.

Even though these consequences took years to unfold, the assassination of Julius Caesar is historically important because it seems to mark the end of one epoch and the beginning of another. Similarly, Shakespeare's *Julius Caesar*, first performed in 1599, marks a watershed in his career as a playwright. On the one hand, it returns to, and reworks, some of the central political concerns of the series of eight English history plays that Shakespeare wrote in the 1590s. The questions with which the play grapples include: Who constitutes a political community—everybody in the state, both rich and poor, or only the elite and powerful among them? What limits can a community appropriately set on the activities of its most remarkable members? Are citizens allowed, or even obliged, to defend the rule of law against an exceptionally powerful individual by resorting to extralegal violence? When the demands of civic responsibility apparently conflict with those of personal loyalty, which ought to prevail? Ultimately, these are questions not about individual choices and behaviors, but about the future of a society: Does Rome's success as a military power eventually doom the republican political system that made that success possible in the first place?

The English history plays, especially the "second tetralogy" consisting of *Richard II, 1* and *2 Henry IV,* and *Henry V,* dramatize political change in a way that highlights the significance of individual characters. In *Julius Caesar,* the problem of character figures even more profoundly. In the conflicted, highly self-conscious Brutus, Shakespeare invents a kind of hero that resembles those of the tragedies that he will begin to write at the turn of the seventeenth century: the brooding Hamlet, the self-destructive Othello, the murderous but self-analytical Macbeth. Of course, distinctions between "personal" and "political" matters tend to be fuzzy and suspect, and, in a play about an assassination, are likely to be impossible to disentangle. Nonetheless, for all its acute analysis of human beings in groups, *Julius Caesar* turns on a question that seems more individual than social: What brings a man to destroy what he claims to love?

Shakespeare's source materials in *Julius Caesar* may well have encouraged this simultaneous attention to political dilemmas and psychological complexity. Virtually from the moment the conspirators pulled their swords from Caesar's bleeding corpse, the events that Shakespeare treats in *Julius Caesar* were amply documented and their rationale debated. Different commentators from antiquity to the Renaissance, depending on their own political convictions, viewed the assassination as an act of heroism or villainy and celebrated or denounced its perpetrators accordingly. While Michelangelo and Milton idealize Brutus as a selfless defender of human liberty, Dante plunges him, with Cassius, into the deepest pit of hell. It is not surprising that Shakespeare, ever alive to the dramatic possibilities inherent in multiple, conflicting perspectives, should choose to stage an incident that had been provoking debate for more than sixteen hundred years.

For Shakespeare's contemporaries, the political questions raised by Caesar's career were not merely of antiquarian interest. Throughout early modern Europe, strong monarchs were attempting, with varying degrees of success, to consolidate their power. In England, these efforts threatened the traditional prerogatives of the aristocracy and of elected representatives in the House of Commons. For thinkers and writers saturated by their classical education in the antique past, it was easy to see the shift toward strong monarchy as replaying the shift from republican to imperial Rome. In England in 1599, moreover, concerns over this general trend were exacerbated by more specific anxieties. Queen Elizabeth I had proven a remarkably durable queen—she had already survived several attempts on her life—but at sixty-six, she was a very old woman by Renaissance standards, and her reign was clearly soon to come to an end. Since, however, she had never begotten children or named an heir, it was unclear who would succeed her or how the new monarch would be selected. Conceivably, England would revert, upon her death, to the kind of civil chaos through which it had suffered in the fifteenth century. In a state in which censorship made direct commentary on contemporary political affairs virtually impossible, the story of Caesar's death and its calamitous aftermath provided an opportunity to reflect, at a suitably prudent distance, upon what might happen when accepted methods of allocating and transferring sovereign power disintegrated.

Julius Caesar. From Plutarch, *The Lives of the Noble Grecians and Romanes* (1595).

The most important source for Shakespeare's *Julius Caesar* is not, however, a political treatise but the biographies of Caesar and Brutus in Plutarch's *Lives of the Noble Grecians and Romanes,* translated into English by Thomas North. Writing in the first century C.E., Plutarch had construed the biographer's task as inextricable from the historian's, since in his view history recorded the achievements of great men. Shakespeare followed Plutarch in stressing the decisive roles played by the acknowledged leaders of Roman society, rather than dwelling on the frictions among larger social groups. Not that he was unaware of the latter: the testiness of *Julius Caesar*'s opening scene makes the internal divisions in Roman society abundantly clear. But throughout the play, commoners are largely imagined from an upper-class perspective—as a politically unsophisticated mob that hardly seems to deserve the scrupulous civic responsibility of its betters. The capacity for conscious and reflective political decision making rests in the hands of a small elite.

Plutarch's "great man" view of history conduces to compelling dramas involving a manageable number of psychologically complex characters. And Shakespeare's drastic condensation of narrative time frame in *Julius Caesar* has the effect of exaggerating Plutarch's emphases. In Plutarch, Caesar's triumph over Pompey's sons occurs in October, but Shakespeare makes it coincide with the Lupercalia in February, so that the assassination on the ides of March seems a direct response to a specific display of arrogance. Likewise, in Plutarch, Brutus and Cassius withdraw from Rome more than a year after Caesar's funeral, but in Shakespeare, their flight follows immediately upon Antony's brilliant incitement of the Roman mob. The effect is not only to escalate dramatic momentum but also to make the personal strengths and weaknesses of Rome's leaders seem matters of titanic consequence.

In the Roman Republic, Plutarch claimed, there was always more than one powerful person, but rarely more than a few. Shakespeare depicts the last days of the Republic in a drama that no single protagonist appropriates wholly to himself. Instead, *Julius Caesar* divides its attention among several characters, setting them off against one another, while the titular hero makes less claim upon the audience's attention than might be expected. Plutarch's biography emphasizes Caesar's military genius, his ruthless executive skill, and his astonishing capacity to rescue himself repeatedly from crushing adversity. Shakespeare's Caesar seems less outsized. His accomplishments are not shown or much alluded to, and much of what we do hear is filtered through the hostile reports of resentful observers. He wants supremacy less, apparently, because he has any particular vision for the Roman polity than because he yearns for the unqualified homage of others. His egotism seems ridiculous: despite his physical frailties, he imagines himself as embodying a godlike permanence, "unshaked of motion" (3.1.70):

> . . . I am constant as the Northern Star,
> Of whose true fixed and resting quality
> There is no fellow in the firmament.
> (3.1.60–62)

Shakespeare loads this moment of self-description with dramatic irony: even as Caesar speaks these lines, the conspirators encircle him, daggers in hand. Yet Caesar's weaknesses also make the conspirators' fears seem less plausible. Deaf, epileptic, doting over his wife, he seems an unlikely aspirant to tyrannical power.

Brutus, Caesar's friend and killer, is far more fully elaborated, and in fact the originality of Shakespeare's play lies in its concentration of attention on Brutus instead of upon the play's titular hero. Unlike the other characters, Brutus appears to us in several guises: as a public figure, a husband, a master of servants, a military leader. Thus he experiences painfully in his own person the value conflicts that are elsewhere dispersed among various antagonists. How is Brutus—and how are we—to reconcile his tender regard for his wife and servant with his willingness to commit political murder? Does Brutus's intimacy with Caesar make his decision to assassinate him truly noble, since it cannot be said to stem from self-interest? Or does it suggest a troubling insensitivity to the claims of friendship and to Caesar's genuinely exceptional character?

The soliloquies in which Brutus carefully deliberates upon his reasons for, and the possible consequences of, his actions provide abundant insight into his turbulent inner life. Yet the soliloquies raise as many questions about his motives as they resolve. They force the audience to wonder how Brutus's idealism and his commitment to principle is to be evaluated. Surely his habit of appealing to abstract moral and political tenets is an admirable trait, especially in a city in which selfishness seems the dominant passion. But repeatedly, this practice leads him to commit disastrous tactical errors. Concerned to minimize bloodshed, he refuses to countenance Cassius's suggestion that Antony be killed along with Caesar. Then—once again ignoring Cassius's advice—he permits Antony to deliver an unsupervised eulogy at Caesar's funeral, thus losing the "spin" on Caesar's death and unleashing the rage of the crowd against himself and his allies. Later, his indignation at what he believes to be Cassius's corrupt practices seriously endangers their alliance.

In all these cases, Brutus tries to diminish the extent to which any of his actions might conceivably serve his own self-interested ends, even though by doing so he risks and eventually dooms the cause he is attempting to serve. Brutus shares Caesar's admiration for the Stoic virtue of "constancy," framing it, however, less in terms of power over others than in terms of personal self-control. By behaving according to immovable principles, he tries to give his life a stern but reassuring fixity. Like Caesar, Brutus ends up paying for this aspiration with his life, and even before he does so, the desire to be, in Caesar's words, "constant as the Northern star" seems misplaced in a play in which character seems complex and highly mutable.

In comparison, the impulsive, unscrupulous Cassius is far more alert to the way the world really works, willingly stooping to expediency to get what he wants and what his cause needs. The contrast with Antony likewise clarifies the way in which Brutus's principles incapacitate him. Antony emerges as a formidable opponent not despite but because of traits that Brutus can see only as weaknesses: love of sensual indulgence, lack of principle, a tendency to live in the present without sufficient care for past or future. Antony's uninhibited, improvisatory nature suits him beautifully for swaying the plebeians. A marvelous actor, Antony exploits gestures, cunning rhetoric, props, and any other means that fully serve the particular moment in which he finds himself. In fact, his political astuteness seems to arise directly from his personal familiarity with passion, since much of politics is, as Brutus never quite realizes, a matter of assessing and responding to group desire. While Brutus naively believes that Caesar's death simply restores the Republic to its status quo ante, Antony immediately understands that the future of Rome and its institutions rests in the hands of Rome's populace and, thus—since that populace is fickle and violent—ultimately in the hands of whoever can sway that populace to his will.

Even while Shakespeare vividly differentiates his characters, he shows clearly how they derive from the particular social and intellectual culture they inhabit. Shakespeare was no antiquarian: he imagines the characters of *Julius Caesar* wearing Elizabethan doublet and hose, and he notoriously equips ancient Rome with a medieval invention, the mechanical clock. Nonetheless, his Romans share a set of distinctive values, ideals, and assumptions. When Antony, at the end of the play, calls Brutus "the noblest Roman of them all," he is not simply praising Brutus as an individual. Instead, he is locating Brutus in a tradition of specifically "Roman" virtue, a virtue associated with the particular strengths of the republican form of government that Brutus died attempting to defend.

What does this virtue entail? Brutus's willingness to identify his abstract principles with the common good, as well as his intense suspicion of anyone who appears self-aggrandizing, is wholly characteristic of an ethos that distinguishes sharply between duty and pleasure, between public good and private self-enrichment. The

Marc Antony. From Plutarch, *The Lives of the Noble Grecians and Romanes* (1595).

heroes of the Roman Republic had always been celebrated for their incorruptibility and for their preference for public service, however thankless, over private goods such as marriage, friendship, sensual pleasure, and personal enrichment. Many of them adhered to a Stoic code of personal conduct that mandated emotional self-control and self-sacrifice. At the same time, Rome was in fact a hotbed of nepotism and unscrupulousness, and its venality grew along with its power. Thus, pillars of the Roman Republic like Lucius Junius Brutus, Marcus Cato, Scipio Africanus, and Marcus Brutus himself were admired not merely because their civic-mindedness was socially valuable, but because such exemplars were rarer and more surprising than Romans liked to admit.

The sharp distinction that Roman culture made between public and private domains has important consequences in *Julius Caesar*. The public world is an all-male affair: bonds and rivalries provide both the glue that holds the Roman Republic together and a competitive petulancy that ordinarily precludes a single individual's gaining too much power. We are given a vivid picture of this complex interpersonal dynamic in Cassius's account of his swimming contest with Caesar. In this incident of pure bravado, friends test their toughness against one another, and one ends up saving the other's life; but because all neediness is imagined to be shameful, what seems like generosity or charity is shot through with contempt. The same rivalrous intensity characterizes the almost erotically charged quarrel and reconciliation between Brutus and Cassius in 4.2. These are people who will kill each other while loving them and, after killing them, will generously eulogize them.

Beside the fraught intensity of such relationships, the heterosexual connections in the play are rather pallid. Although Brutus is deeply attached to Portia, it does not occur to him to take her into his confidence until she struggles mightily for the privilege on the eve of the assassination; even then, all she requests is information, not permission to offer advice. Similarly, Decius easily shames Caesar into ignoring Calpurnia's foreboding dream:

> it were a mock
> Apt to be rendered for someone to say
> 'Break up the Senate till another time,
> When Caesar's wife shall meet with better dreams.'
> (2.2.96–99)

Even the most powerful man in the Roman Empire, apparently, cannot risk being seen to be influenced by a mere wife. Most tellingly, in what is perhaps a sign of textual corruption but more probably an instance of Shakespearean skill in delineating character, we are given two successive accounts of the way Brutus learns of Portia's suicide. In the first, Brutus divulges the loss himself to Cassius, expressing his grief in solitary conference with an old friend. Shortly thereafter, however, he tells his military subordinates that he has not received any news of Portia at all. Once informed that she has died "in strange manner," he affects a studied indifference, insisting that the tidings merely interfere with more important matters at hand. His ability to sequester domestic concerns from public and military ones elicits the admiration of those around him: for true "Romans" are willing to incur huge emotional costs for what they imagine is the greater good.

Since honor, in this conceptual system, is imagined to involve fierce commitment to the public sphere, and since that sphere is exclusively the domain of men, the women in *Julius Caesar* are weak and marginalized. Even within the confines of the household, they seem unable to cultivate an alternative form of social value. Maternity, for instance, is not a source of power here: Calpurnia is barren, and Portia, too, is apparently childless. The "feminine intuition" that both women possess in abundance has no practical effect. Their "nobility" requires them to internalize values that for them have little use. Portia proves what she calls her masculine courage to her husband by the bizarre means of stabbing herself deliberately in the thigh, a gesture that suggests a self-castration, as if a woman were at best a slashed man. For the virtue that she claims to possess is not truly her own possession; rather, it is a quality reflected from her male

Brutus falling on his sword. From Geffrey Whitney, A *Choice of Emblemes* (1586).

relatives that makes her superior to ordinary women. "Think you I am no stronger than my sex, / Being so fathered and so husbanded?" (2.1.295–96). Portia kills herself, typically, in an exceptionally painful way, by swallowing hot coals. While the fabled hardihood of Portia's father, Cato, or her husband, Brutus, has at least some military rationale, Portia's imitation of their fortitude seems pointlessly self-punishing, serving neither their ends nor her own.

The pressure of Roman values on the characters of *Julius Caesar* suggests that its protagonists are not entirely free to invent themselves; they are limited to the cultural materials at hand. Moreover the complexity of the situation in which they find themselves makes it difficult for them to know exactly why they behave as they do. Often in *Julius Caesar*, the same scene provides a character with a variety of motives, permitting alternative descriptions of a single action. Thus, when Brutus decides to participate in the conspiracy to kill Caesar, he believes that he has carefully sequestered his self-interest from his convictions about the common good. But Cassius has meanwhile been tossing flattering messages through his window, so the theater audience must consider the possibility that Brutus's appeal to principle is a rationalization, and that he is swayed by a personal ambition of which he may not be entirely aware.

Elsewhere, Shakespeare complicates his portraits by what might be called a technique of gradual release. By slowly making details available to the audience, he forces it to revise its previous impressions to take account of new information. For instance, Antony's bravura eulogy reaches a climax when he reads Caesar's will, thus harnessing the plebeians' greed to the end of revenging Caesar's death. A mere two scenes later, he is shown in conference with Lepidus and Octavius, giving brisk orders to minimize the cost of Caesar's generosity. The incongruity between the first scene and the second makes Antony's original celebration of his friend's magnanimity seem, in retrospect, less sincere or spontaneous. Nonetheless, the two scenes do not force the audience to a single obvious conclusion. Does Antony's later parsimony indicate that he was simply hypocritical when he used Caesar's will to provoke a riot? Perhaps, but not necessarily; he could simply have been caught up in a wave of loyalty to Caesar and in the pathos of the situation, or he could have had vaguely ambitious but not yet fully articulated plans. In such cases, Shakespeare's cunning dramatic presentation enhances the complexity of his characterizations. The realistic illusion depends as much on what he withholds from the audience as on what he provides it.

On other grounds, too, a reading focusing purely on character seems finally inadequate. In oft-cited lines, Cassius pronounces: "The fault, dear Brutus, is not in our stars, / But in ourselves, that we are underlings" (1.2.141–42). It is not at all clear, however, that he is right. Plutarch emphasizes how the fates of his biographical subjects fail to reflect their virtues. Caesar, who had miraculously survived so many strange adventures in hostile foreign lands, can be dispatched in a few minutes by his erstwhile friends just moments after leaving his own house. Cicero, whose oratory had held sway in Rome for so many years, is obliterated by Antony and Octavius practically as an afterthought. The gifted and honorable Brutus meets death after a military defeat that seems almost accidental. Cassius's suicide is even more haphazard. The inscrutable workings of fate play at least as great a role as personality does in determining the outcome of the action.

For this reason, virtually all the characters find it impossible to achieve a reliable perspective on events in which they are immersed. In the play's most literal case of limited vision, the "thick-sighted" Cassius misinterprets victory as defeat and kills himself moments before his triumphant soldiers arrive, hoping to congratulate him. Here and elsewhere, Shakespeare drums home the difference between the perspective of the theater audience, for whom the killing of Julius Caesar is an act centuries old, now replayed for its entertainment value, and the perspective of the characters within the play, for whom it is unfolding in the present moment, its consequences both dire and unknown. From our point of view, ironies are everywhere. Caesar pronounces upon his immovable constancy moments before being dispatched; his murderers, attempting to eliminate a potential tyrant, open the way for centuries of despotism. As Antony plots with Octavius to eliminate Lepidus, the audience knows as Antony cannot that the cold, noncommittal Octavius will ultimately annihilate both his triumviral associates.

To be alive to such ironies, the characters would need to be able to look into the future. Struggling to understand their own place in history, they continually resort to augury, attempting—usually incorrectly—to comprehend the omens that shadow forth their fates. In *Julius Caesar*, omens are always telling, but they are rarely intelligible except in retrospect. No one knows what to make of the lions loose in the streets; the soothsayer arrives too late; Caesar's dream is misinterpreted; Cassius notices carrion birds on his standards but decides to disregard them. By emphasizing the analogies among personal, political, and natural forms of disruption, omens on the one hand intensify the significance of the play's characters: their decisions, quirks, and flaws affect the structure of the universe itself. They are indeed, as they have imagined themselves, persons of unprecedented and enormous significance. On the other hand, the reliability of omens challenges the notion that history is the product of personal effort, since augury implies restrictions on free will, suggesting that individuals are caught in the toils of a historical process they cannot possibly control or understand. Undergirding the other questions of authority, responsibility, and agency in *Julius Caesar* are unanswerable questions about who creates history, and what that history can possibly mean.

KATHARINE EISAMAN MAUS

TEXTUAL NOTE

The 1623 First Folio (F) provides the only authoritative text for *Julius Caesar*. The fullness of the stage directions, which specify sound effects as well as actors' exits and entrances, and the absence of Shakespearean spellings suggest that the Folio text was derived from the theater company's official promptbook rather than from Shakespeare's manuscript.

Despite the general reliability of the Folio *Julius Caesar*, there are a few editorial puzzles. In Act 4, there is some confusion about the parts played by the minor characters Titinius, Lucillius, and Lucius, leading some scholars to believe that Shakespeare revised these scenes. Two conundrums have more significant consequences for the play's characterizations. In 1614 and again in 1625, Shakespeare's contemporary Ben Jonson ridiculed a line in 3.1 in which Caesar supposedly proclaims: "Know Caesar doth not wrong but with just cause." F omits the last four words, but the currency of Jonson's joke even after the publication of the Folio suggests that they were retained in performance. Indeed, the apparent illogic of Caesar's utterance (how can a wrong have a just cause?) seems to testify powerfully to the speaker's megalomaniac sense that he transcends the rules ordinary mortals must obey. The Oxford text restores the line as reported by Jonson rather than emending it to some more "reasonable" possibility. Some textual scholars see a similar lapse of logic in 4.2, in which Brutus's account of Portia's death to Cassius seems to contradict his claim, moments later, that he is ignorant of that death. Possibly Shakespeare revised the scene and forgot to cancel the rejected lines. However, as in 3.1, the seeming inconsistency might be justified as revealing an interesting aspect of Brutus's character or of Roman attitudes toward the difference between domestic and public domains.

SELECTED BIBLIOGRAPHY

Bloom, Harold, ed. *William Shakespeare's "Julius Caesar."* New York: Chelsea House, 1988. Anthology of critical essays.

Burckhardt, Sigurd. "How Not to Murder Caesar." *Shakespearean Meanings*. Princeton: Princeton University Press, 1968. 3–21. *Julius Caesar* and historical change.

Knights, L. C. "Shakespeare and Political Wisdom: A Note on the Personalism of *Julius Caesar* and *Coriolanus*." *Sewanee Review* 61 (1953): 43–55. Politics and individual character.

Miles, Gary B. "How Roman Are Shakespeare's 'Romans'?" *Shakespeare Quarterly* 40 (1989): 257–83. Shakespeare's adaptation and revision of his classical sources.

Miola, Robert S. "*Julius Caesar* and the Tyrannicide Debate." *Renaissance Quarterly* 38 (1985): 271–89. Renaissance political theorists disagreed over whether the killing of a king was ever justified; *Julius Caesar* shows Shakespeare's knowledge of this dispute.

Paster, Gail Kern. "'In the Spirit of Men There Is No Blood': Blood as a Trope of Gender in *Julius Caesar*." *Shakespeare Quarterly* 40 (1989): 284–98. Manliness and bloody bodies in the play.

Rebhorn, Wayne. "The Crisis of the Aristocracy in *Julius Caesar*." *Renaissance Quarterly* 43 (1990): 75–111. Shakespeare's Romans resemble sixteenth-century English aristocrats in their desire for self-mastery and competitiveness with one another.

Visser, Nicholas. "Plebeian Politics in Julius Caesar." *Shakespeare in Southern Africa* 7 (1994): 22–31. Contemporary South African performances offer insights into the play's concept of class relations and of the mob.

Wilson, Richard, ed. *Julius Caesar*. New York: Palgrave, 2002. Collection of recent essays on the play.

FILMS

Julius Caesar. 1953. Dir. Joseph L. Mankiewicz. USA. 120 min. This black-and-white Hollywood production features James Mason as a brooding, intense Brutus, John Gielgud as Cassius, and the young Marlon Brando, in an Oscar-nominated performance, as a charismatic Antony.

Julius Caesar. 1970. Dir. Stuart Burge. UK. 117 min. A brisk production, enlivened by colorful street and battle scenes. Jason Robards Plays Brutus, Charlton Heston is Antony, John Gielgud is Caesar, and Diana Rigg is Portia.

Julius Caesar. 1979. Dir. Herbert Wise. UK. 161 min. A BBC-TV production. Textually faithful but blandly acted. David Collings is, however, effective as Cassius.

The Tragedy of Julius Caesar

THE PERSONS OF THE PLAY

Julius CAESAR
CALPURNIA, his wife
Marcus BRUTUS, a noble Roman, opposed to Caesar
PORTIA, his wife
LUCIUS, his servant
Caius CASSIUS
CASCA
TREBONIUS
DECIUS Brutus } opposed to Caesar
METELLUS Cimber
CINNA
Caius LIGARIUS
Mark ANTONY
OCTAVIUS Caesar } rulers of Rome after Caesar's death
LEPIDUS
FLAVIUS
MURELLUS } tribunes of the people
CICERO
PUBLIUS } senators
POPILLIUS Laena
A SOOTHSAYER
ARTEMIDORUS
CINNA the Poet
PINDARUS, Cassius' bondman
TITINIUS, an officer in Cassius' army
LUCILLIUS
MESSALA
VARRUS
CLAUDIO
YOUNG CATO } officers and soldiers in Brutus' army
STRATO
VOLUMNIUS
FLAVIUS
DARDANIUS
CLITUS
A POET
A GHOST of Caesar
A COBBLER
A CARPENTER
Other PLEBEIANS
A MESSENGER
SERVANTS
Senators, soldiers, and attendants

1.1

Enter FLAVIUS, MURELLUS, *and certain commoners over the stage*

FLAVIUS Hence, home, you idle creatures, get you home!
Is this a holiday? What, know you not,
Being mechanical,° you ought not walk   *of the artisan class*
Upon a labouring day without the sign°   *tools and garments*
5 Of your profession?—Speak, what trade art thou?
CARPENTER Why, sir, a carpenter.
MURELLUS Where is thy leather apron and thy rule?
What dost thou with thy best apparel on?—
You, sir, what trade are you?
10 COBBLER Truly, sir, in respect of° a fine workman I am but, as   *in comparison with*
you would say, a cobbler.[1]
MURELLUS But what trade art thou? Answer me directly.
COBBLER A trade, sir, that I hope I may use with a safe con-
science, which is indeed, sir, a mender of bad soles.°   *(punning on "souls")*
15 FLAVIUS What trade, thou knave? Thou naughty° knave, what trade?   *wicked*
COBBLER Nay, I beseech you, sir, be not out[2] with me. Yet if
you be out, sir, I can mend you.
MURELLUS What mean'st thou by that? Mend me, thou saucy fellow?
COBBLER Why, sir, cobble you.
20 FLAVIUS Thou art a cobbler, art thou?
COBBLER Truly, sir, all that I live by is with the awl. I meddle
with no tradesman's matters, nor women's matters,° but withal[3]   *(a bawdy joke)*
I am indeed, sir, a surgeon to old shoes: when they are in great
danger I recover° them. As proper° men as ever trod upon   *resole; cure / fine*
25 neat's leather° have gone° upon my handiwork.   *cowhide / walked*
FLAVIUS But wherefore art not in thy shop today?
Why dost thou lead these men about the streets?
COBBLER Truly, sir, to wear out their shoes to get myself into
more work. But indeed, sir, we make holiday to see Caesar, and
30 to rejoice in his triumph.[4]
MURELLUS Wherefore rejoice? What conquest brings he home?
What tributaries° follow him to Rome   *ransom payers*
To grace in captive bonds his chariot wheels?[5]
You blocks, you stones, you worse than senseless° things!   *inanimate*
35 O, you hard hearts, you cruel men of Rome,
Knew you not Pompey?[6] Many a time and oft
Have you climbed up to walls and battlements,
To towers and windows, yea to chimney-tops,
Your infants in your arms, and there have sat
40 The livelong day with patient expectation
To see great Pompey pass the streets of Rome.
And when you saw his chariot but appear,
Have you not made an universal shout,
That Tiber[7] trembled underneath her banks
45 To hear the replication° of your sounds   *echo*
Made in her concave shores?

1.1 Location: A street in Rome.
1. Mender of shoes; bungler (the sense Murellus understands).
2. Angry; worn out, like shoes.
3. Nevertheless; punning on "awl."
4. Triumphal procession in honor of victory (by Roman custom, over foreign enemies, but here over Caesar's political adversaries, Pompey's sons).
5. Captives were tied to their conquerors' chariots.
6. Pompey the Great, who had shared rule of Rome with Caesar and Crassus; he was defeated by Caesar after their alliance disintegrated and was later assassinated.
7. River that flows through Rome.

And do you now put on your best attire?
And do you now cull out° a holiday?   *choose*
And do you now strew flowers in his way
50 That comes in triumph over Pompey's blood?°   *offspring*
Be gone!
Run to your houses, fall upon your knees,
Pray to the gods to intermit[8] the plague
That needs must light on this ingratitude.
55 FLAVIUS Go, go, good countrymen, and for this fault
Assemble all the poor men of your sort;°   *rank*
Draw them to Tiber banks, and weep your tears
Into the channel, till the lowest stream
Do kiss the most exalted shores of all.°   *tops of the riverbanks*
                    Exeunt all the commoners
60 See whe'er° their basest mettle be not moved.   *whether*
They vanish tongue-tied in their guiltiness.
Go you down that way towards the Capitol;[9]
This way will I. Disrobe the images
If you do find them decked with ceremonies.[1]
65 MURELLUS May we do so?
You know it is the Feast of Lupercal.[2]
FLAVIUS It is no matter. Let no images
Be hung with Caesar's trophies.° I'll about,   *ornaments*
And drive away the vulgar° from the streets;   *commoners*
70 So do you too where you perceive them thick.
These growing feathers plucked from Caesar's wing
Will make him fly an ordinary pitch,[3]
Who else° would soar above the view of men   *otherwise*
And keep us all in servile fearfulness.   *Exeunt*

1.2

[*Loud music.*] *Enter* CAESAR, ANTONY [*stripped*] *for the
course,*[1] CALPURNIA, PORTIA, DECIUS, CICERO, BRUTUS,
CASSIUS, CASCA, *a* SOOTHSAYER[, *a throng of citizens*];
after them, MURELLUS *and* FLAVIUS

CAESAR Calpurnia.
CASCA Peace, ho! Caesar speaks.
[*Music ceases*]
CAESAR Calpurnia.
CALPURNIA Here, my lord.
5 CAESAR Stand you directly in Antonio's way
When he doth run his course.—Antonio.
ANTONY Caesar, my lord.
CAESAR Forget not in your speed, Antonio,
To touch Calpurnia, for our elders say
10 The barren, touchèd in this holy chase,
Shake off their sterile curse.
ANTONY   I shall remember:
When Caesar says 'Do this', it is performed.

8. Withhold (plague was considered a divine punishment).
9. Hill on whose top was the Temple of Jupiter, where victorious generals in a triumph offered sacrifice.
1. Caesar's followers had put imperial crowns ("ceremonies") on his statues.
2. Lupercalia, a festival celebrated February 15. His-
torically, Caesar's triumph took place in October.
3. At a medium height (an image from falconry).
1.2 Location: A public place in Rome.
1. During the Lupercalia, two celebrants ran naked through Rome, striking those they met with goatskin thongs.

CAESAR Set on,° and leave no ceremony out.   *Proceed*

        [*Music*]

SOOTHSAYER Caesar!

15 CAESAR Ha! Who calls?

CASCA Bid every noise be still. Peace yet again.

        [*Music ceases*]

CAESAR Who is it in the press° that calls on me?   *crowd*

    I hear a tongue shriller than all the music

    Cry 'Caesar!' Speak. Caesar is turned to hear.

SOOTHSAYER Beware the ides[2] of March.

20 CAESAR   What man is that?

BRUTUS A soothsayer bids you beware the ides of March.

CAESAR Set him before me; let me see his face.

CASSIUS Fellow, come from the throng; look upon Caesar.

        [*The* SOOTHSAYER *comes forward*]

CAESAR What sayst thou to me now? Speak once again.

25 SOOTHSAYER Beware the ides of March.

CAESAR He is a dreamer. Let us leave him. Pass!°   *Onward*

        Sennet.° Exeunt. Manent° BRUTUS *and* CASSIUS   *Trumpet flourish / Remain*

CASSIUS Will you go see the order of the course?°   *running of the race*

BRUTUS Not I.

CASSIUS I pray you, do.

30 BRUTUS I am not gamesome;° I do lack some part   *fond of sport*

    Of that quick° spirit that is in Antony.   *lively*

    Let me not hinder, Cassius, your desires.

    I'll leave you.

CASSIUS Brutus, I do observe you now of late.

35 I have not from your eyes that gentleness

    And show of love as I was wont° to have.   *accustomed*

    You bear too stubborn and too strange° a hand[3]   *unfriendly*

    Over your friend that loves you.

BRUTUS   Cassius,

    Be not deceived. If I have veiled my look,°   *seemed less outgoing*

40 I turn the trouble of my countenance°   *my troubled looks*

    Merely° upon myself. Vexèd I am   *Wholly*

    Of late with passions of some difference,°   *conflicting kinds*

    Conceptions only proper° to myself,   *suitable*

    Which give some soil,° perhaps, to my behaviours.   *blemish*

45 But let not therefore my good friends be grieved—

    Among which number, Cassius, be you one—

    Nor construe any further° my neglect   *make any more of*

    Than that poor Brutus, with himself at war,

    Forgets the shows of love to other men.

50 CASSIUS Then, Brutus, I have much mistook your passion,° *feelings*

    By means whereof[4] this breast of mine hath buried°   *concealed*

    Thoughts of great value, worthy cogitations.

    Tell me, good Brutus, can you see your face?

BRUTUS No, Cassius, for the eye sees not itself

55 But by reflection, by some other things.

CASSIUS 'Tis just;°   *true*

    And it is very much lamented, Brutus,

---

2. The ides marked roughly the midpoint of every Roman month (usually the thirteenth); in March, the fifteenth.

3. Management of horse's reins (figurative).

4. In consequence of which mistake.

That you have no such mirrors as will turn
Your hidden worthiness into your eye,
60 That you might see your shadow.° I have heard   *reflection*
Where many of the best respect° in Rome—   *repute*
Except immortal Caesar—speaking of Brutus,
And groaning underneath this age's yoke,
Have wished that noble Brutus had his eyes.[5]
65 BRUTUS Into what dangers would you lead me, Cassius,
That you would have me seek into myself
For that which is not in me?
CASSIUS Therefor,° good Brutus, be prepared to hear.   *As to that*
And since you know you cannot see yourself
70 So well as by reflection, I, your glass,°   *mirror*
Will modestly discover° to yourself   *reveal*
That of yourself which you yet know not of.
And be not jealous on° me, gentle Brutus,   *suspicious of*
Were I a common laughter,° or did use   *object of ridicule*
75 To stale° with ordinary° oaths my love   *debase / cheap*
To every new protester;° if you know   *declarer of friendship*
That I do fawn on men and hug them hard,
And after scandal° them; or if you know   *defame*
That I profess myself° in banqueting   *declare friendship*
80 To all the rout:° then hold me dangerous.   *mob*
         Flourish, and shout [within]
BRUTUS What means this shouting? I do fear the people
Choose Caesar for their king.
CASSIUS   Ay, do you fear it?
Then must I think you would not have it so.
BRUTUS I would not, Cassius; yet I love him well.
85 But wherefore do you hold me here so long?
What is it that you would impart to me?
If it be aught toward the general good,
Set honour in one eye and death i'th' other,
And I will look on both indifferently;°   *impartially*
90 For let the gods so speed me as[6] I love
The name of honour more than I fear death.
CASSIUS I know that virtue to be in you, Brutus,
As well as I do know your outward favour.°   *appearance*
Well, honour is the subject of my story.
95 I cannot tell what you and other men
Think of this life; but for my single self,
I had as lief not be,° as live to be   *I had rather be dead*
In awe of such a thing as I myself.
I was born free as Caesar, so were you.
100 We both have fed as well, and we can both
Endure the winter's cold as well as he.
For once upon a raw and gusty day,
The troubled Tiber chafing with° her shores,   *raging against*
Said Caesar to me 'Dar'st thou, Cassius, now
105 Leap in with me into this angry flood,
And swim to yonder point?'° Upon the word,   *promontory*
Accoutred° as I was I plungèd in,   *Dressed in armor*
And bade him follow. So indeed he did.

---

5. That is, could see properly.   6. Make me fortunate insofar as.

The torrent roared, and we did buffet it
110 With lusty sinews, throwing it aside,
And stemming° it with hearts of controversy.°   *confronting / rivalry*
But ere we could arrive° the point proposed,   *reach*
Caesar cried 'Help me, Cassius, or I sink!'
Ay, as Aeneas[7] our great ancestor
115 Did from the flames of Troy upon his shoulder
The old Anchises bear, so from the waves of Tiber
Did I the tirèd Caesar. And this man
Is now become a god, and Cassius is
A wretched creature, and must bend his body°   *(must bow)*
120 If Caesar carelessly but nod on him.
He had a fever when he was in Spain,
And when the fit was on him, I did mark
How he did shake. 'Tis true, this god did shake.
His coward lips did from their colour fly;[8]
125 And that same eye whose bend° doth awe the world   *glance*
Did lose his° lustre. I did hear him groan,   *its*
Ay, and that tongue of his that bade the Romans
Mark him and write his speeches in their books,
'Alas!' it cried, 'Give me some drink, Titinius',
130 As a sick girl. Ye gods, it doth amaze me
A man of such a feeble temper° should   *constitution*
So get the start of° the majestic world,   *advantage over*
And bear the palm° alone!   *be victor*

Shout [within]. Flourish

BRUTUS   Another general shout!
I do believe that these applauses are
135 For some new honours that are heaped on Caesar.
CASSIUS Why, man, he doth bestride the narrow world
Like a Colossus,[9] and we petty men
Walk under his huge legs, and peep about
To find ourselves dishonourable graves.
140 Men at sometime° were masters of their fates.   *formerly*
The fault, dear Brutus, is not in our stars,
But in ourselves, that we are underlings.
Brutus and Caesar: what should be in that 'Caesar'?
Why should that name be sounded more than yours?
145 Write them together: yours is as fair a name.
Sound them: it doth become the mouth as well.
Weigh them: it is as heavy. Conjure with 'em:
'Brutus' will start[1] a spirit as soon as 'Caesar'.
Now in the names of all the gods at once,
150 Upon what meat° doth this our Caesar feed   *food*
That he is grown so great? Age, thou art shamed.
Rome, thou hast lost the breed of noble bloods.
When went there by an age since the great flood,[2]
But it was famed with° more than with one man?   *renowned for*
155 When could they say till now, that talked of Rome,

---

7. Legendary Trojan warrior and founder of Rome;
when the Greeks burned Troy, he carried his father,
Anchises, out on his back.
8. Did turn pale; did desert their flag (Caesar suffered
epileptic seizures).
9. Giant statue of Apollo, which straddled the harbor

of Rhodes.
1. Raise (only the names of the gods were thought to
be able to raise the dead).
2. A great flood was recorded in classical as well as bib-
lical accounts.

That her wide walls encompassed but one man?
Now is it Rome indeed, and room° enough   *(pronounced like "Rome")*
When there is in it but one only man.
O, you and I have heard our fathers say
160 There was a Brutus once³ that would have brooked°   *endured*
Th'eternal devil to keep his state° in Rome   *hold court*
As easily as a king.
BRUTUS   That you do love me I am nothing jealous.°   *not at all uncertain*
What you would work° me to I have some aim.°   *persuade / idea*
165 How I have thought of this and of these times
I shall recount hereafter. For this present,°   *present time*
I would not, so with love° I might entreat you,   *if in friendship*
Be any further moved.° What you have said   *persuaded*
I will consider. What you have to say
170 I will with patience hear, and find a time
Both meet° to hear and answer such high things.   *Fitting both*
Till then, my noble friend, chew upon this:
Brutus had rather be a villager
Than to repute himself a son of Rome
175 Under these hard conditions as this time
Is like to lay upon us.
CASSIUS   I am glad
That my weak words have struck but thus much show
Of fire from Brutus.
          [*Music.*] *Enter* CAESAR *and his train*°   *retinue*
BRUTUS   The games are done, and Caesar is returning.
180 CASSIUS   As they pass by, pluck Casca by the sleeve,⁴
And he will, after his sour fashion, tell you
What hath proceeded worthy° note today.   *worthy of*
BRUTUS   I will do so. But look you, Cassius,
The angry spot doth glow on Caesar's brow,
185 And all the rest look like a chidden° train.   *scolded*
Calpurnia's cheek is pale, and Cicero
Looks with such ferret⁵ and such fiery eyes
As we have seen him in the Capitol
Being crossed in conference° by some senators.   *opposed in debate*
190 CASSIUS   Casca will tell us what the matter is.
CAESAR   Antonio.
ANTONY   Caesar.
CAESAR   Let me have men about me that are fat,
Sleek-headed men, and such as sleep a-nights.
195 Yon Cassius has a lean and hungry look.
He thinks too much. Such men are dangerous.
ANTONY   Fear him not, Caesar, he's not dangerous.
He is a noble Roman, and well given.°   *well disposed*
CAESAR   Would he were fatter! But I fear him not.
200 Yet if my name⁶ were liable to fear,
I do not know the man I should avoid
So soon as that spare Cassius. He reads much,
He is a great observer, and he looks

3. Lucius Junius Brutus, an ancestor of Marcus Brutus
and a founder of the Roman Republic, famed for his role
in expelling the Tarquins, who had ruled Rome as Kings.
4. Like "cloak" (line 216), "doublet" (line 262), and

"unbracèd" (1.3.48), this suggests a performance in
Elizabethan dress.
5. Ferretlike (red and darting).
6. One of my name (that is, myself).

Quite through[7] the deeds of men. He loves no plays,
205 As thou dost, Antony; he hears no music.[8]
Seldom he smiles, and smiles in such a sort°   *manner*
As if he mocked himself, and scorned his spirit
That could be moved to smile at anything.
Such men as he be never at heart's ease
210 Whiles they behold a greater than themselves,
And therefore are they very dangerous.
I rather tell thee what is to be feared
Than what I fear, for always I am Caesar.
Come on my right hand, for this ear is deaf,
215 And tell me truly what thou think'st of him.

Sennet. Exeunt CAESAR *and his train.* [BRUTUS,
CASSIUS, *and* CASCA *remain*]

CASCA [*to* BRUTUS]   You pulled me by the cloak.° Would you   *pulled me aside*
speak with me?

BRUTUS   Ay, Casca. Tell us what hath chanced today,
That Caesar looks so sad.°   *serious*

220 CASCA   Why, you were with him, were you not?

BRUTUS   I should not then ask Casca what had chanced.

CASCA   Why, there was a crown offered him; and being offered
him, he put it by with the back of his hand, thus; and then the
people fell a-shouting.

225 BRUTUS   What was the second noise for?

CASCA   Why, for that too.

CASSIUS   They shouted thrice. What was the last cry for?

CASCA   Why, for that too.

BRUTUS   Was the crown offered him thrice?

230 CASCA   Ay, marry,° was't; and he put it by thrice, every time   *indeed*
gentler than other; and at every putting by, mine honest°   *(sarcastic)*
neighbours shouted.

CASSIUS   Who offered him the crown?

CASCA   Why, Antony.

BRUTUS   Tell us the manner of it, gentle° Casca.   *noble*

235 CASCA   I can as well be hanged as tell the manner of it. It was
mere foolery,° I did not mark it. I saw Mark Antony offer him   *utter absurdity*
a crown—yet 'twas not a crown neither, 'twas one of these coro-
nets—and as I told you he put it by once; but for all that, to my
thinking he would fain° have had it. Then he offered it to him   *gladly*
240 again; then he put it by again—but to my thinking he was very
loath to lay his fingers off it. And then he offered it the third
time; he put it the third time by. And still° as he refused it,   *continually*
the rabblement hooted, and clapped their chapped hands, and
threw up their sweaty nightcaps,[9] and uttered such a deal of
245 stinking breath because Caesar refused the crown that it had
almost choked Caesar; for he swooned and fell down at it. And
for mine own part, I durst not laugh for fear of opening my lips
and receiving the bad air.

CASSIUS   But soft, I pray you. What, did Caesar swoon?

250 CASCA   He fell down in the market-place, and foamed at mouth,
and was speechless.

---

7. Completely into the motives of.
8. This was regarded as a sign of wickedness; see *The*

Merchant of Venice.
9. Artisans wore felt hats on holidays.

BRUTUS 'Tis very like: he hath the falling sickness.[1]
CASSIUS No, Caesar hath it not; but you and I
    And honest Casca, we have the falling sickness.
255 CASCA I know not what you mean by that, but I am sure Caesar
    fell down. If the tag-rag people° did not clap him and hiss him,   *riffraff*
    according as he pleased and displeased them, as they use° to   *are accustomed*
    do the players in the theatre, I am no true man.
BRUTUS What said he when he came unto himself?
260 CASCA Marry, before he fell down, when he perceived the com-
    mon herd was glad he refused the crown, he plucked me ope[2]
    his doublet° and offered them his throat to cut. An° I had been   *jacket / If*
    a man of any occupation, if I would not have taken him at a°   *his*
    word, I would I might go to hell among the rogues. And so he
265   fell. When he came to himself again, he said, if he had done
    or said anything amiss, he desired their worships to think it was
    his infirmity. Three or four wenches where I stood cried 'Alas,
    good soul!' and forgave him with all their hearts. But there's no
    heed to be taken of them: if Caesar had stabbed[3] their mothers
270   they would have done no less.
BRUTUS And after that he came thus sad away?
CASCA Ay.
CASSIUS Did Cicero say anything?
CASCA Ay, he spoke Greek.
275 CASSIUS To what effect?
CASCA Nay, an I tell you that, I'll ne'er look you i'th' face again.
    But those that understood him smiled at one another, and
    shook their heads. But for mine own part, it was Greek to me.
    I could tell you more news, too. Murellus and Flavius, for pull-
280   ing scarves[4] off Caesar's images, are put to silence.° Fare you   *deprived of office*
    well. There was more foolery yet, if I could remember it.
CASSIUS Will you sup with me tonight, Casca?
CASCA No, I am promised forth.°   *elsewhere*
CASSIUS Will you dine with me tomorrow?
285 CASCA Ay, if I be alive, and your mind hold,° and your dinner   *does not change*
    worth the eating.
CASSIUS Good; I will expect you.
CASCA Do so. Farewell both.   *Exit*
BRUTUS What a blunt fellow is this grown to be!
290   He was quick mettle° when he went to school.   *of energetic spirit*
CASSIUS So is he now, in execution
    Of any bold or noble enterprise,
    However he puts on this tardy form.[5]
    This rudeness° is a sauce to his good wit,°   *harshness / intelligence*
295   Which gives men stomach° to digest his words   *relish*
    With better appetite.
BRUTUS And so it is. For this time I will leave you.
    Tomorrow, if you please to speak with me,
    I will come home to you; or if you will,
300   Come home to me and I will wait for you.
CASSIUS I will do so. Till then, think of the world.° *Exit* BRUTUS   *state of affairs*
    Well, Brutus, thou art noble; yet I see

---

1. Epilepsy (Cassius puns on "collapse from power").   4. Decorations (see 1.1.63–64).
2. Pulled open ("me" is colloquial).   5. Although he feigns this indolent manner.
3. Playing on "sexually penetrated."

Thy honourable mettle may be wrought
From that it is disposed.[6] Therefore it is meet°   *fitting*
305 That noble minds keep ever with their likes;
For who so firm that cannot be seduced?
Caesar doth bear me hard,° but he loves Brutus.   *ill will*
If I were Brutus now, and he were Cassius,
He should not humour° me. I will this night   *influence*
310 In several hands° in at his windows throw—   *various handwritings*
As if they came from several citizens—
Writings, all tending to° the great opinion   *intimating*
That Rome holds of his name, wherein obscurely°   *cryptically*
Caesar's ambition shall be glancèd° at.   *hinted*
315 And after this, let Caesar seat him sure,[7]
For we will shake him, or worse days endure.   *Exit*

1.3

Thunder and lightning. Enter CASCA, [*at one door, with
his sword drawn,*] *and* CICERO [*at another*]

CICERO   Good even, Casca. Brought° you Caesar home?   *Escorted*
Why are you breathless, and why stare you so?
CASCA   Are not you moved, when all the sway° of earth   *realm*
Shakes like a thing unfirm? O Cicero,
5 I have seen tempests when the scolding winds
Have rived° the knotty oaks, and I have seen   *split*
Th'ambitious ocean swell and rage and foam
To be exalted with° the threat'ning clouds;   *raised as high as*
But never till tonight, never till now,
10 Did I go through a tempest dropping fire.
Either there is a civil strife in heaven,
Or else the world, too saucy° with the gods,   *insolent*
Incenses them to send destruction.
CICERO   Why, saw you anything more° wonderful?   *else*
15 CASCA   A common slave—you know him well by sight—
Held up his left hand, which did flame and burn
Like twenty torches joined; and yet his hand,
Not sensible of° fire, remained unscorched.   *Not feeling*
Besides—I ha' not since put up° my sword—   *sheathed*
20 Against° the Capitol I met a lion   *Next to*
Who glazed° upon me, and went surly by   *stared*
Without annoying° me. And there were drawn   *harming*
Upon a heap[1] a hundred ghastly° women,   *pallid*
Transformèd with their fear, who swore they saw
25 Men all in fire walk up and down the streets.
And yesterday the bird of night° did sit   *screech owl*
Even at noonday upon the market-place,
Hooting and shrieking. When these prodigies°   *abnormalities*
Do so conjointly meet,° let not men say   *happen together*
30 'These are their reasons', 'they are natural',
For I believe they are portentous things
Unto the climate° that they point upon.   *region*
CICERO   Indeed it is a strange-disposèd time;

---

6. *wrought . . . disposed*: changed from its natural prop-
erty (alluding to the alchemical transmutation of metals).
7. Establish himself securely.

1.3 Location: A street in Rome.
1. Huddled in a crowd.

But men may construe things after their fashion,°   *in their own way*
35   Clean° from the purpose of the things themselves.   *Completely different*
    Comes Caesar to the Capitol tomorrow?
   CASCA   He doth, for he did bid Antonio
    Send word to you he would be there tomorrow.
   CICERO   Good night then, Casca. This disturbèd sky
    Is not to walk in.
40   CASCA   Farewell, Cicero.   *Exit* CICERO
            Enter CASSIUS [*unbraced*]°   *with open doublet*
   CASSIUS   Who's there?
   CASCA   A Roman.
   CASSIUS   Casca, by your voice.
   CASCA   Your ear is good. Cassius, what night is this?
   CASSIUS   A very pleasing night to honest men.
   CASCA   Who ever knew the heavens menace so?
45   CASSIUS   Those that have known the earth so full of faults.
    For my part, I have walked about the streets,
    Submitting me unto the perilous night;
    And thus unbracèd, Casca, as you see,
    Have bared my bosom to the thunder-stone;°   *thunderbolt*
50   And when the cross° blue lightning seemed to open   *forked; hostile*
    The breast of heaven, I did present myself
    Even° in the aim and very flash of it.   *Exactly*
   CASCA   But wherefore did you so much tempt the heavens?
    It is the part of men to fear and tremble
55   When the most mighty gods by tokens° send   *signs*
    Such dreadful heralds to astonish° us.   *dismay*
   CASSIUS   You are dull, Casca, and those sparks of life
    That should be in a Roman you do want,°   *lack*
    Or else you use not. You look pale, and gaze,
60   And put on fear, and cast yourself in wonder,
    To see the strange impatience of the heavens;
    But if you would consider the true cause
    Why all these fires, why all these gliding ghosts,
    Why birds and beasts from quality and kind[2]—
65   Why old men, fools, and children calculate°—   *prophesy*
    Why all these things change from their ordinance,°—   *usual order*
    Their natures, and preformèd faculties,
    To monstrous° quality—why, you shall find   *unnatural*
    That heaven hath infused them with these spirits
70   To make them instruments of fear and warning
    Unto some monstrous state.[3] Now could I, Casca,
    Name to thee a man most like this dreadful night,
    That thunders, lightens, opens graves, and roars
    As doth the lion in the Capitol;
75   A man no mightier than thyself or me
    In personal action, yet prodigious° grown,   *ominous*
    And fearful,° as these strange eruptions° are.   *terrifying / upheavals*
   CASCA   'Tis Caesar that you mean, is it not, Cassius?
   CASSIUS   Let it be who it is; for Romans now
80   Have thews° and limbs like to their ancestors.   *sinews*
    But woe the while!° Our fathers' minds are dead,   *alas for these times*

---

2. *from quality and kind*: behaving contrary to their   3. Abnormal situation; atrocious government.
nature.

And we are governed with our mothers' spirits.
Our yoke and sufferance° show us womanish.   *servitude and patience*

CASCA   Indeed they say the senators tomorrow
85   Mean to establish Caesar as a king,
And he shall wear his crown by sea and land
In every place save here in Italy.

CASSIUS [*drawing his dagger*]   I know where I will wear this dagger then:
Cassius from bondage will deliver Cassius.
90   Therein, ye gods, you make the weak most strong;
Therein, ye gods, you tyrants do defeat.
Nor stony tower, nor walls of beaten brass,
Nor airless dungeon, nor strong links of iron,
Can be retentive to° the strength of spirit;   *Can imprison*
95   But life, being weary of these worldly bars,°   *hindrances*
Never lacks power to dismiss itself.
If I know this, know all the world besides,
That part of tyranny that I do bear
I can shake off at pleasure.

            Thunder still

CASCA   So can I.
100   So every bondman in his own hand bears
The power to cancel his captivity.

CASSIUS   And why should Caesar be a tyrant then?
Poor man, I know he would not be a wolf
But that he sees the Romans are but sheep.
105   He were no lion, were not Romans hinds.°   *female deer; servants*
Those that with haste will make a mighty fire
Begin it with weak straws. What trash is Rome,
What rubbish, and what offal,° when it serves   *wood chips; refuse*
For the base° matter to illuminate   *underlying; despicable*
110   So vile a thing as Caesar! But, O grief,
Where hast thou led me? I perhaps speak this
Before a willing bondman; then I know
My answer must be made.⁴ But I am armed,°   *(physically and morally)*
And dangers are to me indifferent.°   *insignificant*
115 CASCA   You speak to Casca, and to such a man
That is no fleering° tell-tale. Hold.° My hand.   *sneering / Enough*
Be factious° for redress of all these griefs,   *Form a group*
And I will set this foot of mine as far
As who° goes farthest.   *whoever*
            [*They join hands*]

CASSIUS   There's a bargain made.
120   Now know you, Casca, I have moved° already   *persuaded*
Some certain of the noblest-minded Romans
To undergo° with me an enterprise   *undertake*
Of honourable-dangerous consequence.
And I do know by this° they stay° for me   *this time / wait*
125   In Pompey's Porch;⁵ for now, this fearful night,
There is no stir or walking in the streets,
And the complexion of the element°   *disposition of the sky*
In favour's° like the work we have in hand,   *In appearance is*
Most bloody, fiery, and most terrible.

            Enter CINNA

---

4. I must pay the penalty.   5. Portico of a theater commissioned by Pompey.

130   CASCA   Stand close° a while, for here comes one in haste.   *concealed*
      CASSIUS   'Tis Cinna; I do know him by his gait.
       He is a friend.—Cinna, where haste you so?
      CINNA   To find out you. Who's that? Metellus Cimber?
      CASSIUS   No, it is Casca, one incorporate°   *a party*
135   To our attempts. Am I not stayed for,° Cinna?   *awaited*
      CINNA   I am glad on't.[6] What a fearful night is this!
       There's two or three of us have seen strange sights.
      CASSIUS   Am I not stayed for? Tell me.
      CINNA   Yes, you are.
140   O Cassius, if you could
       But win the noble Brutus to our party—
      CASSIUS   Be you content. Good Cinna, take this paper,
           [*He gives* CINNA *letters*]
       And look you lay it in the Praetor's[7] Chair,
       Where Brutus may but° find it; and throw this   *must surely*
145   In at his window. Set this up with wax
       Upon old Brutus'° statue. All this done,   *Lucius Junius Brutus's*
       Repair° to Pompey's Porch where you shall find us.   *Proceed*
       Is Decius Brutus and Trebonius there?
      CINNA   All but Metellus Cimber, and he's gone
150   To seek you at your house. Well, I will hie,°   *hasten*
       And so bestow these papers as you bade me.
      CASSIUS   That done, repair to Pompey's Theatre.   *Exit* CINNA
       Come, Casca, you and I will yet ere day
       See Brutus at his house. Three parts° of him   *quarters*
155   Is ours already, and the man entire
       Upon the next encounter yields him ours.
      CASCA   O, he sits high in all the people's hearts,
       And that which would appear offence in us
       His countenance, like richest alchemy,[8]
160   Will change to virtue and to worthiness.
      CASSIUS   Him and his worth, and our great need of him,
       You have right well conceited.° Let us go,   *understood*
       For it is after midnight, and ere day
       We will awake him and be sure of him.   *Exeunt*

2.1

Enter BRUTUS *in his orchard*

      BRUTUS   What, Lucius, ho!—
       I cannot by the progress of the stars
       Give guess how near to day.—Lucius, I say!—
       I would it were my fault to sleep so soundly.—
5   When, Lucius, when?° Awake, I say! What, Lucius!   *(expressing impatience)*
           Enter LUCIUS
      LUCIUS   Called you, my lord?
      BRUTUS   Get me a taper° in my study, Lucius.   *candle*
       When it is lighted, come and call me here.
      LUCIUS   I will, my lord.   *Exit*
10   BRUTUS   It must be by his° death. And for my part   *(Caesar's)*
       I know no personal cause to spurn° at him,   *kick*

---

6. Cinna is responding to Cassius's information about Casca.
7. Brutus was one of sixteen praetors, or chief magistrates, subordinate only to the two consuls.

8. Alchemy attempted to change base metals into gold. *countenance:* approval; noble appearance.
2.1 Location: Outside Brutus's house.

But for the general.° He would be crowned.   *common good*
How that might change his nature, there's the question.
It is the bright day that brings forth the adder,
15   And that craves° wary walking. Crown him: that!   *calls for*
And then I grant we put a sting in him
That at his will he may do danger with.
Th'abuse of greatness is when it disjoins
Remorse° from power. And to speak truth of Caesar,   *Conscience*
20   I have not known when his affections swayed°   *passions ruled*
More than his reason. But 'tis a common proof°   *experience*
That lowliness° is young ambition's ladder,   *humility*
Whereto the climber-upward turns his face;
But when he once attains the upmost round,°   *rung*
25   He then unto the ladder turns his back,
Looks in the clouds, scorning the base degrees[1]
By which he did ascend. So Caesar may.
Then lest he may, prevent. And since the quarrel
Will bear no colour for the thing he is,[2]
30   Fashion° it thus: that what he is, augmented,   *Describe*
Would run to these and these extremities;
And therefore think him as a serpent's egg,
Which, hatched, would as his kind° grow mischievous,°   *by its nature / harmful*
And kill him in the shell.
     Enter LUCIUS [*with a letter*]
35   LUCIUS   The taper burneth in your closet,° sir.   *private room*
Searching the window for a flint, I found
This paper, thus sealed up, and I am sure
It did not lie there when I went to bed.
     [*He*] *gives him the letter*
BRUTUS   Get you to bed again; it is not day.
40   Is not tomorrow, boy, the ides of March?
LUCIUS   I know not, sir.
BRUTUS   Look in the calendar and bring me word.
LUCIUS   I will, sir.   *Exit*
BRUTUS   The exhalations° whizzing in the air   *meteors*
45   Give so much light that I may read by them.
     [*He*] *opens the letter and reads*
'Brutus, thou sleep'st. Awake, and see thyself.
Shall Rome, et cetera? Speak, strike, redress.'—
'Brutus, thou sleep'st. Awake.'
Such instigations have been often dropped
50   Where I have took them up.
'Shall Rome, et cetera?' Thus must I piece it out:
Shall Rome stand under one man's awe? What, Rome?
My ancestors did from the streets of Rome
The Tarquin drive when he was called a king.[3]
55   'Speak, strike, redress.' Am I entreated
To speak and strike? O Rome, I make thee promise,
If the redress will follow,[4] thou receivest
Thy full petition at the hand of Brutus.
     Enter LUCIUS
LUCIUS   Sir, March is wasted fifteen days.

---

1. Low rungs; contemptible means; lowly social ranks.   3. See note to 1.2.160.
2. Will find no plausible pretext in his conduct so far.   4. That is, if killing Caesar will restore the Republic.

Knock within

60 BRUTUS 'Tis good. Go to the gate; somebody knocks. [*Exit* LUCIUS]
Since Cassius first did whet° me against Caesar   *incite*
I have not slept.
Between the acting of a dreadful thing
And the first motion,° all the interim is   *impulse*
65 Like a phantasma° or a hideous dream.   *nightmare*
The genius° and the mortal instruments[5]   *immortal spirit*
Are then in counsel, and the state of man,
Like to a little kingdom, suffers then
The nature of an insurrection.[6]

Enter LUCIUS

70 LUCIUS Sir, 'tis your brother Cassius[7] at the door,
Who doth desire to see you.
BRUTUS   Is he alone?
LUCIUS No, sir, there are more with him.
BRUTUS   Do you know them?
LUCIUS No, sir; their hats are plucked about their ears,
And half their faces buried in their cloaks,
75 That by no means I may discover° them   *identify*
By any mark of favour.°   *distinctive feature*
BRUTUS   Let 'em enter.   [*Exit* LUCIUS]
They are the faction. O conspiracy,
Sham'st thou to show thy dang'rous brow by night,
When evils are most free?° O then by day   *uninhibited*
80 Where wilt thou find a cavern dark enough
To mask thy monstrous visage? Seek none, conspiracy.
Hide it in smiles and affability;
For if thou put thy native semblance on,[8]
Not Erebus° itself were dim enough   *dark underworld region*
85 To hide thee from prevention.[9]

Enter the conspirators [*muffled*]: CASSIUS, CASCA,
DECIUS, CINNA, METELLUS, *and* TREBONIUS

CASSIUS I think we are too bold[1] upon your rest.
Good morrow, Brutus. Do we trouble you?
BRUTUS I have been up this hour, awake all night.
Know I these men that come along with you?
90 CASSIUS Yes, every man of them; and no man here
But honours you; and every one doth wish
You had but that opinion of yourself
Which every noble Roman bears of you.
This is Trebonius.
BRUTUS   He is welcome hither.
CASSIUS This, Decius Brutus.
95 BRUTUS   He is welcome too.
CASSIUS This, Casca; Cinna, this; and this, Metellus Cimber.
BRUTUS They are all welcome.
What watchful° cares do interpose themselves   *sleep-preventing*
Betwixt your eyes and night?
CASSIUS   Shall I entreat a word?
[CASSIUS *and* BRUTUS *stand aside and*] *whisper*

---

5. Bodily powers.
6. *the state . . . insurrection:* referring to a common-place analogy between disorder in man, in the body politic, and in nature.
7. Cassius was married to Brutus's sister.
8. Display your natural appearance.
9. From being recognized and thwarted.
1. We intrude too presumptuously.

100 DECIUS Here lies the east. Doth not the day break here?
     CASCA No.
     CINNA O pardon, sir, it doth; and yon grey lines
       That fret° the clouds are messengers of day.   *interlace*
     CASCA You shall confess that you are both deceived.
       [*He points his sword*]
105 Here, as I point my sword, the sun arises,
       Which is a great way growing° on the south,   *encroaching*
       Weighing° the youthful season of the year.   *On account of*
       Some two months hence up higher toward the north
       He first presents his fire, and the high° east   *due*
110 Stands, as the Capitol, directly here.
       [*He points his sword*]
       [BRUTUS *and* CASSIUS *join the other conspirators*]
     BRUTUS Give me your hands all over, one by one.
       [*He shakes their hands*]
     CASSIUS And let us swear our resolution.
     BRUTUS No, not an oath. If not the face° of men,   *(grave) expressions*
       The sufferance° of our souls, the time's abuse²—   *suffering*
115 If these be motives weak, break off betimes,°   *at once*
       And every man hence to his idle° bed.   *unused; lazy*
       So let high-sighted° tyranny range on   *arrogant*
       Till each man drop by lottery.³ But if these,°   *these reasons*
       As I am sure they do, bear fire enough
120 To kindle cowards and to steel with valour
       The melting spirits of women, then, countrymen,
       What need we any spur but our own cause
       To prick us to redress? What other bond
       Than secret Romans,⁴ that have spoke the word
125 And will not palter?° And what other oath   *equivocate*
       Than honesty° to honesty engaged   *integrity*
       That this shall be or we will fall for it?
       Swear° priests and cowards and men cautelous,°   *Let swear / crafty; wary*
       Old feeble carrions,° and such suffering souls   *corpselike men*
130 That welcome wrongs;⁵ unto bad causes swear
       Such creatures as men doubt;° but do not stain   *suspect*
       The even° virtue of our enterprise,   *just; straightforward*
       Nor th'insuppressive° mettle of our spirits,   *the indomitable*
       To think that or° our cause or our performance   *either*
135 Did need an oath, when every drop of blood
       That every Roman bears, and nobly bears,
       Is guilty of a several bastardy⁶
       If he do break the smallest particle
       Of any promise that hath passed from him.
140 CASSIUS But what of Cicero? Shall we sound him?°   *find out his thoughts*
       I think he will stand very strong with us.
     CASCA Let us not leave him out.
     CINNA   No, by no means.
     METELLUS O, let us have him, for his silver hairs
       Will purchase us a good opinion,°   *reputation*

---

2. The corruption of the present time.
3. Chance (the tyrant's caprice).
4. Than that we are Romans capable of secrecy.

5. That gladly submit to oppression.
6. Will show itself individually to be adulterated by non-Roman blood.

145 And buy men's voices to commend our deeds.
It shall be said his judgement ruled our hands.
Our youths and wildness shall no whit appear,
But all be buried in his gravity.
BRUTUS   O, name him not! Let us not break with° him,   *disclose our plans to*
150 For he will never follow anything
That other men begin.
CASSIUS   Then leave him out.
CASCA   Indeed he is not fit.
DECIUS   Shall no man else be touched, but only Caesar?
155 CASSIUS   Decius, well urged.° I think it is not meet°   *suggested / proper*
Mark Antony, so well beloved of Caesar,
Should outlive Caesar. We shall find of him
A shrewd° contriver. And you know his means,   *malicious*
If he improve° them, may well stretch so far   *make the most of*
160 As to annoy° us all; which to prevent,   *harm*
Let Antony and Caesar fall together.
BRUTUS   Our course⁷ will seem too bloody, Caius Cassius,
To cut the head off and then hack the limbs,
Like wrath in death and envy° afterwards—   *malice*
165 For Antony is but a limb of Caesar.
Let's be sacrificers, but not butchers, Caius.
We all stand up against the spirit of Caesar,
And in the spirit of men there is no blood.
O, that we then could come by° Caesar's spirit,   *obtain*
170 And not dismember Caesar! But, alas,
Caesar must bleed for it. And, gentle friends,
Let's kill him boldly, but not wrathfully.
Let's carve him as a dish fit for the gods,
Not hew him as a carcass fit for hounds.
175 And let our hearts, as subtle° masters do,   *cunning*
Stir up their servants° to an act of rage,   *(that is, our hands)*
And after seem to chide 'em. This shall make
Our purpose necessary, and not envious;°   *malicious*
Which so appearing to the common eyes,
180 We shall be called purgers,° not murderers.   *purifiers*
And for Mark Antony, think not of him,
For he can do no more than Caesar's arm
When Caesar's head is off.
CASSIUS   Yet I fear him;
For in the engrafted° love he bears to Caesar—   *deep-rooted*
185 BRUTUS   Alas, good Cassius, do not think of him.
If he love Caesar, all that he can do
Is to himself: take thought,° and die for Caesar.   *succumb to melancholy*
And that were much he should,⁸ for he is given
To sports, to wildness, and much company.
190 TREBONIUS   There is no fear° in him. Let him not die;   *nothing to fear*
For he will live, and laugh at this hereafter.
          Clock strikes
BRUTUS   Peace, count the clock.⁹
CASSIUS   The clock hath stricken three.

---

7. Punning on "corse," meaning "corpse."   9. The clock is an anachronism, like sleeves and
8. And that is more than he is likely to do.   doublets.

TREBONIUS 'Tis time to part.

CASSIUS   But it is doubtful yet
Whether Caesar will come forth today or no;
195   For he is superstitious grown of late,
Quite from the main° opinion he held once   *Contrary to the strong*
Of fantasy, of dreams and ceremonies.
It may be these apparent° prodigies,   *manifest*
The unaccustomed terror of this night,
200   And the persuasion of his augurers,[1]
May hold him from the Capitol today.

DECIUS   Never fear that. If he be so resolved
I can o'ersway° him; for he loves to hear   *prevail upon*
That unicorns may be betrayed with trees,[2]
205   And bears with glasses,[3] elephants with holes,°   *pits*
Lions with toils,° and men with flatterers;   *nets*
But when I tell him he hates flatterers;
He says he does, being then most flattered. Let me work,
For I can give his humour the true bent,[4]
210   And I will bring him to the Capitol.

CASSIUS   Nay, we will all of us be there to fetch him.

BRUTUS   By the eighth hour. Is that the uttermost?°   *latest*

CINNA   Be that the uttermost, and fail not then.

METELLUS   Caius Ligarius doth bear Caesar hard,°   *ill will*
215   Who rated° him for speaking well of Pompey.   *rebuked*
I wonder none of you have thought of him.

BRUTUS   Now good Metellus, go along by him.°   *to his house*
He loves me well, and I have given him reasons.
Send him but hither, and I'll fashion° him.   *work upon*
220 CASSIUS   The morning comes upon's. We'll leave you, Brutus.
And, friends, disperse yourselves; but all remember
What you have said, and show yourselves true Romans.

BRUTUS   Good gentlemen, look fresh and merrily.
Let not our looks put on° our purposes;   *display*
225   But bear it as our Roman actors do,
With untired spirits and formal constancy.°   *decorous self-possession*
And so good morrow to you every one.

                     Exeunt. Manet° BRUTUS   *Remains*
Boy, Lucius!—Fast asleep? It is no matter.
Enjoy the honey-heavy dew of slumber.
230   Thou hast no figures° nor no fantasies   *imaginings*
Which busy care draws in the brains of men;
Therefore thou sleep'st so sound.

          Enter PORTIA

PORTIA   Brutus, my lord.

BRUTUS   Portia, what mean you? Wherefore rise you now?
It is not for° your health thus to commit   *good for*
235   Your weak condition to the raw cold morning.

PORTIA   Nor for yours neither. You've ungently,° Brutus,   *unkindly*
Stole from my bed; and yesternight at supper
You suddenly arose, and walked about

---

1. Priests who interpreted "auguries," or omens.
2. The unicorn could supposedly be caught by tricking
it into impaling its horn on a tree.

3. Mirrors (imagined to bewilder bears).
4. Give his disposition the right direction.

Musing and sighing, with your arms across;[5]
240 And when I asked you what the matter was,
You stared upon me with ungentle looks.
I urged you further; then you scratched your head,
And too impatiently stamped with your foot.
Yet I insisted; yet you answered not,
245 But with an angry wafture° of your hand   *gesture*
Gave sign for me to leave you. So I did,
Fearing to strengthen that impatience
Which seemed too much enkindled, and withal°   *besides*
Hoping it was but an effect of humour,°   *moodiness*
250 Which sometime hath his° hour with every man.   *its*
It will not let you eat, nor talk, nor sleep;
And could it work so much upon your shape
As it hath much prevailed on your condition,°   *disposition*
I should not know you° Brutus. Dear my lord,   *recognize you as*
255 Make me acquainted with your cause of grief.
BRUTUS   I am not well in health, and that is all.
PORTIA   Brutus is wise, and were he not in health
He would embrace the means to come by it.
BRUTUS   Why, so I do. Good Portia, go to bed.
260 PORTIA   Is Brutus sick? And is it physical°   *curative*
To walk unbracèd° and suck up the humours[6]   *with open doublet*
Of the dank morning? What, is Brutus sick?
And will he steal out of his wholesome bed
To dare the vile contagion of the night,
265 And tempt the rheumy and unpurgèd° air   *moist and impure*
To add unto his sickness? No, my Brutus,
You have some sick offence° within your mind,   *disturbance*
Which by the right and virtue° of my place°   *prerogative / (as a wife)*
I ought to know of. [*Kneeling*] And upon my knees,
270 I charm° you by my once-commended beauty,   *conjure*
By all your vows of love, and that great vow
Which did incorporate and make us one,
That you unfold to me, your self, your half,
Why you are heavy,° and what men tonight   *dejected*
275 Have had resort to you—for here have been
Some six or seven, who did hide their faces
Even from darkness.
BRUTUS   Kneel not, gentle Portia.
PORTIA [*rising*]   I should not need if you were gentle Brutus.
Within the bond of marriage, tell me, Brutus,
280 Is it excepted[7] I should know no secrets
That appertain to you? Am I your self
But as it were in sort or limitation?[8]
To keep with you at meals, comfort your bed,
And talk to you sometimes? Dwell I but in the suburbs[9]
285 Of your good pleasure? If it be no more,
Portia is Brutus' harlot, not his wife.
BRUTUS   You are my true and honourable wife,

---

5. Crossed (a sign of melancholy).
6. Inhale the mists.
7. Is it stipulated as a qualification that.
8. *in sort or limitation:* after a fashion or with restric-

tions (like "excepted," "limited" is a legal term).
9. Outlying areas (where brothels were located in Shakespeare's time).

As dear to me as are the ruddy drops
That visit° my sad heart.   *afflict; come to*

290   PORTIA   If this were true, then should I know this secret.
I grant I am a woman, but withal°   *still*
A woman that Lord Brutus took to wife.
I grant I am a woman, but withal
A woman well reputed, Cato's daughter.[1]

295   Think you I am no stronger than my sex,
Being so fathered and so husbanded?
Tell me your counsels;° I will not disclose 'em.   *secrets*
I have made strong proof of my constancy,
Giving myself a voluntary wound

300   Here in the thigh. Can I bear that with patience,
And not my husband's secrets?

BRUTUS   O ye gods,
Render me worthy of this noble wife!
            Knock[ing within]
Hark, hark, one knocks. Portia, go in a while,
And by and by thy bosom shall partake

305   The secrets of my heart.
All my engagements° I will construe° to thee,   *commitments / explain*
All the charactery[2] of my sad brows.
Leave me with haste.
                                        Exit PORTIA
            Lucius, who's that knocks?
Enter LUCIUS, *and* LIGARIUS [*with a kerchief round his
head*][3]

LUCIUS   Here is a sick man that would speak with you.

310   BRUTUS   Caius Ligarius, that Metellus spake of.—
Boy, stand aside.   [*Exit* LUCIUS]
            Caius Ligarius, how?°   *how are you*

LIGARIUS   Vouchsafe° good morrow from a feeble tongue.   *Deign to accept*

BRUTUS   O, what a time have you chose out, brave Caius,
To wear a kerchief! Would you were not sick!

315   LIGARIUS   I am not sick if Brutus have in hand
Any exploit worthy the name of honour.

BRUTUS   Such an exploit have I in hand, Ligarius,
Had you a healthful ear to hear of it.

LIGARIUS   By all the gods that Romans bow before,
I here discard my sickness.
            [*He pulls off his kerchief*]

320   Soul of Rome,
Brave son derived from honourable loins,
Thou like an exorcist° hast conjured up   *a magician*
My mortifièd° spirit. Now bid me run,   *deadened*
And I will strive with things impossible,

325   Yea, get the better of them. What's to do?

BRUTUS   A piece of work that will make sick men whole.°   *healthy*

LIGARIUS   But are not some whole that we must make sick?

BRUTUS   That must we also. What it is, my Caius,
I shall unfold to thee as we are going
To whom it must be done.

---

1. Marcus Porcius Cato was renowned for his strict
moral integrity; after Caesar's victory over Pompey, he
killed himself rather than submit to Caesar's rule.
2. Handwriting (the lines of care "inscribed" on his

forehead).
3. Kerchiefs were commonly worn by the sick in
Elizabethan England.

330 LIGARIUS   Set on° your foot,   *Advance*
　　　And with a heart new-fired I follow you
　　　To do I know not what; but it sufficeth
　　　That Brutus leads me on.
BRUTUS   Follow me then.   *Exeunt*

2.2

Thunder and lightning.
Enter Julius CAESAR *in his nightgown°*   *dressing gown*
CAESAR   Nor heaven nor earth have been at peace tonight.
　　　Thrice hath Calpurnia in her sleep cried out
　　　'Help, ho! They murder Caesar!'—Who's within?
　　　　　Enter a SERVANT
SERVANT   My lord.
5 CAESAR   Go bid the priests do present° sacrifice,   *immediate*
　　　And bring me their opinions of success.[1]
SERVANT   I will, my lord.   *Exit*
　　　　　Enter CALPURNIA
CALPURNIA   What mean you, Caesar? Think you to walk forth?
　　　You shall not stir out of your house today.
10 CAESAR   Caesar shall forth. The things that threatened me
　　　Ne'er looked but on my back; when they shall see
　　　The face of Caesar, they are vanishèd.
CALPURNIA   Caesar, I never stood on ceremonies,°   *heeded omens*
　　　Yet now they fright me. There is one within,
15 　　Besides the things that we have heard and seen,
　　　Recounts most horrid sights seen by the watch.[2]
　　　A lioness hath whelpèd in the streets,
　　　And graves have yawned and yielded up their dead.
　　　Fierce fiery warriors fight upon the clouds,
20 　　In ranks and squadrons and right form of war,°   *regular battle formation*
　　　Which drizzled blood upon the Capitol.
　　　The noise of battle hurtled in the air.
　　　Horses do neigh, and dying men did groan,
　　　And ghosts did shriek and squeal about the streets.
25 　　O Caesar, these things are beyond all use,°   *all normal experience*
　　　And I do fear them.
CAESAR   What can be avoided
　　　Whose end is purposed by the mighty gods?
　　　Yet Caesar shall go forth, for these predictions
　　　Are to° the world in general as to Caesar.   *Are as applicable to*
30 CALPURNIA   When beggars die there are no comets seen;
　　　The heavens themselves blaze forth° the death of princes.   *flame out; proclaim*
CAESAR   Cowards die many times before their deaths;
　　　The valiant never taste of death but once.
　　　Of all the wonders that I yet have heard,
35 　　It seems to me most strange that men should fear,
　　　Seeing that death, a necessary end,
　　　Will come when it will come.
　　　　　Enter SERVANT
　　　　　　　　　　What say the augurers?
SERVANT   They would not have you to stir forth today.

2.2 Location: Caesar's house.　　　　　　reading the entrails of the sacrificial animals.
1. Of the outcome (good or bad), as determined by　2. Night watchmen (another anachronism).

Plucking the entrails of an offering forth,
40 They could not find a heart within the beast.
CAESAR   The gods do this in shame of cowardice.°   *to put cowardice to shame*
Caesar should be a beast without a heart
If he should stay at home today for fear.
No, Caesar shall not. Danger knows full well
45 That Caesar is more dangerous than he.
We are two lions littered in one day,
And I the elder and more terrible.
And Caesar shall go forth.
CALPURNIA   Alas, my lord,
Your wisdom is consumed in confidence.°   *overconfidence*
50 Do not go forth today. Call it my fear
That keeps you in the house, and not your own.
We'll send Mark Antony to the Senate House,
And he shall say you are not well today.
Let me upon my knee prevail in this.
    [*She kneels*]
55 CAESAR   Mark Antony shall say I am not well,
And for thy humour° I will stay at home.   *whim*
    Enter DECIUS
Here's Decius Brutus; he shall tell them so.
    [CALPURNIA *rises*]
DECIUS   Caesar, all hail! Good morrow, worthy Caesar.
I come to fetch you to the Senate House.
60 CAESAR   And you are come in very happy° time   *opportune*
To bear my greeting to the senators
And tell them that I will not come today.
Cannot is false, and that I dare not, falser.
I will not come today; tell them so, Decius.
CALPURNIA   Say he is sick.
65 CAESAR   Shall Caesar send a lie?
Have I in conquest stretched mine arm so far,
To be afeard to tell greybeards the truth?
Decius, go tell them Caesar will not come.
DECIUS   Most mighty Caesar, let me know some cause,
70 Lest I be laughed at when I tell them so.
CAESAR   The cause is in my will; I will not come.
That is enough to satisfy the Senate.
But for your private satisfaction,
Because I love you, I will let you know.
75 Calpurnia here, my wife, stays° me at home.   *keeps*
She dreamt tonight° she saw my statue,   *last night*
Which like a fountain with an hundred spouts
Did run pure blood; and many lusty° Romans   *joyful*
Came smiling and did bathe their hands in it.
80 And these does she apply° for warnings and portents   *interpret*
Of evils imminent, and on her knee
Hath begged that I will stay at home today.
DECIUS   This dream is all amiss interpreted.
It was a vision fair and fortunate.
85 Your statue spouting blood in many pipes,
In which so many smiling Romans bathed,
Signifies that from you great Rome shall suck
Reviving blood, and that great men shall press

For tinctures, stains, relics, and cognizance.[3]
90   This by Calpurnia's dream is signified.
CAESAR   And this way have you well expounded it.
DECIUS   I have, when you have heard what I can say.
And know it now: the Senate have concluded
To give this day a crown to mighty Caesar.
95   If you shall send them word you will not come,
Their minds may change. Besides, it were a mock
Apt to be rendered[4] for someone to say
'Break up the Senate till another time,
When Caesar's wife shall meet with better dreams.'
100   If Caesar hide himself, shall they not whisper
'Lo, Caesar is afraid'?
Pardon me, Caesar; for my dear dear love
To your proceeding° bids me tell you this,   advancement
And reason to my love is liable.[5]
105   CAESAR   How foolish do your fears seem now, Calpurnia!
I am ashamèd I did yield to them.
Give me my robe, for I will go.
        Enter [CASSIUS,] BRUTUS, LIGARIUS, METELLUS, CASCA,
        TREBONIUS, *and* CINNA
And look where Cassius is come to fetch me.
CASSIUS   Good morrow, Caesar.
CAESAR   Welcome, Cassius.—
110   What, Brutus, are you stirred so early too?—
Good morrow, Casca.—Caius Ligarius,
Caesar was ne'er so much your enemy
As that same ague° which hath made you lean.   fever
What is't o'clock?
BRUTUS   Caesar, 'tis strucken eight.
115   CAESAR   I thank you for your pains and courtesy.
        Enter ANTONY
See, Antony that revels long a-nights
Is notwithstanding up. Good morrow, Antony.
ANTONY   So to most noble Caesar.
CAESAR [*to* CALPURNIA]   Bid them prepare within.
I am to blame to be thus waited for.   [*Exit* CALPURNIA]
120   Now, Cinna.—Now, Metellus.—What, Trebonius!
I have an hour's talk in store for you.
Remember that you call on me today.
Be near me, that I may remember you.
TREBONIUS   Caesar, I will, [*aside*] and so near will I be
125   That your best friends shall wish I had been further.
CAESAR   Good friends, go in and taste some wine with me,
And we, like[6] friends, will straightway go together.
BRUTUS [*aside*]   That every like is not the same, O Caesar,
The heart of Brutus ernes° to think upon.   *Exeunt*   grieves

2.3

Enter ARTEMIDORUS, *reading a letter*
ARTEMIDORUS   'Caesar, beware of Brutus. Take heed of Cassius.

3. Heraldic colors and emblems ("tinctures," "stains,"
and "cognizance"); venerated properties of saints ("tinc-
tures," "stains," and "relics").
4. *a mock . . . rendered:* a sarcastic reply likely to be made.

5. And prudence is subordinate to my affection.
6. As becomes (but Brutus plays on the senses "resem-
bling" and "equal to").
2.3 Location: A street near the Capitol.

Come not near Casca. Have an eye to Cinna. Trust not Trebo-
nius. Mark well Metellus Cimber. Decius Brutus loves thee
not. Thou hast wronged Caius Ligarius. There is but one mind
5   in all these men, and it is bent against Caesar. If thou beest not
immortal, look about you. Security gives way to° conspiracy.   *Overconfidence permits*
The mighty gods defend thee!

                                         Thy lover,°   *friend*
                                   Artemidorus.'

10   Here will I stand till Caesar pass along,
And as a suitor° will I give him this.   *petitioner*
My heart laments that virtue cannot live
Out of the teeth of emulation.[1]
If thou read this, O Caesar, thou mayst live.
15   If not, the fates with traitors do contrive.°   *Exit*   *conspire*

2.4

Enter PORTIA *and* LUCIUS

PORTIA   I prithee, boy, run to the Senate House.
Stay not to answer me, but get thee gone.—
Why dost thou stay?

LUCIUS   To know my errand, madam.

PORTIA   I would have had thee there and here again
5   Ere I can tell thee what thou shouldst do there.
[*Aside*] O constancy, be strong upon my side;
Set a huge mountain 'tween my heart and tongue.
I have a man's mind, but a woman's might.
How hard it is for women to keep counsel!°   *a secret*
[*To* LUCIUS] Art thou here yet?

10 LUCIUS   Madam, what should I do?
Run to the Capitol, and nothing else?
And so return to you, and nothing else?

PORTIA   Yes, bring me word, boy, if thy lord look well,
For he went sickly forth; and take good note
15   What Caesar doth, what suitors press to him.
Hark, boy, what noise is that?

LUCIUS   I hear none, madam.

PORTIA   Prithee, listen well.
I heard a bustling rumour,° like a fray,   *disturbed clamor*
20   And the wind brings it from the Capitol.

LUCIUS   Sooth,° madam, I hear nothing.   *In truth*

Enter the SOOTHSAYER

PORTIA   Come hither, fellow. Which way hast thou been?

SOOTHSAYER   At mine own house, good lady.

PORTIA   What is't o'clock?

25 SOOTHSAYER   About the ninth hour, lady.

PORTIA   Is Caesar yet gone to the Capitol?

SOOTHSAYER   Madam, not yet. I go to take my stand
To see him pass on to the Capitol.

PORTIA   Thou hast some suit to Caesar, hast thou not?

30 SOOTHSAYER   That I have, lady. If it will please Caesar
To be so good to Caesar as to hear me,
I shall beseech him to befriend himself.

PORTIA   Why, know'st thou any harms intended towards him?

---

1. Beyond the danger of ambitious envy.   **2.4** Location: Brutus's house.

SOOTHSAYER   None that I know will be; much that I fear may chance.
    Good morrow to you.
        [He moves away]
35   Here the street is narrow.
    The throng that follows Caesar at the heels,
    Of senators, of praetors, common suitors,
    Will crowd a feeble man almost to death.
    I'll get me to a place more void,° and there   *empty*
40   Speak to great Caesar as he comes along.   *Exit*
PORTIA *[aside]*   I must go in. Ay me! How weak a thing
    The heart of woman is! O Brutus,
    The heavens speed thee in thine enterprise!—
    Sure the boy heard me. *[To* LUCIUS*]* Brutus hath a suit
45   That Caesar will not grant. *[Aside]* O, I grow faint!
    [To LUCIUS*]* Run, Lucius, and commend me to my lord.
    Say I am merry.° Come to me again,   *in good spirits*
    And bring me word what he doth say to thee.
                             Exeunt [severally]°   *separately*

3.1

Enter [at one door] ARTEMIDORUS, *the* SOOTHSAYER *[and*
citizens]. Flourish. Enter [at another door] CAESAR, BRUTUS,
CASSIUS, CASCA, DECIUS, METELLUS, TREBONIUS, CINNA,
*[*LIGARIUS,*]* ANTONY, LEPIDUS, PUBLIUS*[*, POPILLIUS,
and other senators]

CAESAR *[to the* SOOTHSAYER*]*   The ides of March are come.
SOOTHSAYER   Ay, Caesar, but not gone.
ARTEMIDORUS   Hail, Caesar! Read this schedule.°   *document*
DECIUS *[to* CAESAR*]*   Trebonius doth desire you to o'er-read
5   At your best leisure this his humble suit.
ARTEMIDORUS   O Caesar, read mine first, for mine's a suit
    That touches° Caesar nearer. Read it, great Caesar.   *concerns*
CAESAR   What touches us ourself shall be last served.°   *attended to*
ARTEMIDORUS   Delay not, Caesar, read it instantly.
CAESAR   What, is the fellow mad?
10 PUBLIUS *[to* ARTEMIDORUS*]*   Sirrah, give place.
CASSIUS *[to* ARTEMIDORUS*]*   What, urge you your petitions in the street?
    Come to the Capitol.
        [They walk about the stage][1]
POPILLIUS *[aside to* CASSIUS*]*   I wish your enterprise today may thrive.
CASSIUS   What enterprise, Popillius?
POPILLIUS   Fare you well.
        [He leaves CASSIUS, *and makes to*° CAESAR*]*   *goes toward*
15 BRUTUS   What said Popillius Laena?
CASSIUS   He wished today our enterprise might thrive.
    I fear our purpose is discoverèd.
BRUTUS   Look how he makes to Caesar. Mark him.
CASSIUS   Casca, be sudden,° for we fear prevention.°—   *swift / being thwarted*
20   Brutus, what shall be done? If this be known,
    Cassius or Caesar never shall turn back,°   *return alive*
    For I will slay myself.
BRUTUS   Cassius, be constant.°   *resolute*

3.1 Location: At the Capitol.
1. Indicating a movement from the street outside to the interior of the Capitol.

Popillius Laena speaks not of our purposes,
For look, he smiles, and Caesar doth not change.

25 CASSIUS Trebonius knows his time, for look you, Brutus,
He draws Mark Antony out of the way. [*Exeunt* TREBONIUS *and* ANTONY]

DECIUS Where is Metellus Cimber? Let him go
And presently prefer° his suit to Caesar.   at once present
[CAESAR *sits*]

BRUTUS He is addressed.° Press near, and second him.   ready

30 CINNA Casca, you are the first that rears your hand.
[*The conspirators and the other senators
take their places*]

CAESAR Are we all ready? What is now amiss
That Caesar and his Senate must redress?

METELLUS [*coming forward and kneeling*] Most high, most
mighty, and most puissant Caesar,
Metellus Cimber throws before thy seat
An humble heart.

35 CAESAR   I must prevent° thee, Cimber.   thwart
These couchings° and these lowly courtesies°   stoopings / bows
Might fire the blood° of ordinary men,   passions
And turn preordinance and first decree²
Into the law of children.° Be not fond³   childish whims
40 To think that Caesar bears such rebel° blood   lawless
That will be thawed from the true quality°   proper constancy
With that which melteth fools: I mean sweet words,
Low-crookèd° curtsies, and base spaniel fawning.   Obsequious; dishonest
Thy brother by decree is banishèd.
45 If thou dost bend and pray and fawn for him,
I spurn thee like a cur out of my way.
Know Caesar doth not wrong but with just cause,⁴
Nor without cause will he be satisfied.

METELLUS Is there no voice more worthy than my own
50 To sound more sweetly in great Caesar's ear
For the repealing of my banished brother?

BRUTUS [*coming forward and kneeling*] I kiss thy hand, but not
in flattery, Caesar,
Desiring thee that Publius Cimber may
Have an immediate freedom of repeal.°   release from banishment

CAESAR What, Brutus?

CASSIUS [*coming forward and kneeling*]
55   Pardon, Caesar; Caesar, pardon.
As low as to thy foot doth Cassius fall
To beg enfranchisement° for Publius Cimber.   liberation

CAESAR I could be well moved if I were as you.
If I could pray to move,° prayers would move me.   make pleas
60 But I am constant as the Northern Star,°   polestar
Of whose true fixed and resting° quality   stationary
There is no fellow° in the firmament.   equal
The skies are painted with unnumbered sparks;
They are all fire, and every one doth shine;
65 But there's but one in all doth hold his place.
So in the world: 'tis furnished well with men,

---

2. Established precedent and original rulings.
3. Do not be so foolish as.

4. F reads merely, "Know Caesar doth not wrong." See
Textual Note.

And men are flesh and blood, and apprehensive;°   *capable of understanding*
Yet in the number I do know but one
That unassailable holds on his rank,°   *maintains his place*
70   Unshaked of motion;⁵ and that I am he
Let me a little show it even in this—
That I was constant° Cimber should be banished,   *resolute*
And constant do remain to keep him so.
CINNA [*coming forward and kneeling*]
     O Caesar!
CAESAR   Hence! Wilt thou lift up Olympus?⁶
DECIUS [*coming forward with* LIGARIUS *and kneeling*]
     Great Caesar!
75   CAESAR   Doth not Brutus bootless° kneel?   *in vain*
CASCA [*coming forward and kneeling*]
     Speak hands for me.⁷
         They stab CAESAR [CASCA *first*, BRUTUS *last*]
CAESAR   Et tu, Bruté?⁸—Then fall Caesar.
                 [*He*] *dies*
CINNA   Liberty! Freedom! Tyranny is dead!
     Run hence, proclaim, cry it about the streets.
CASSIUS   Some to the common pulpits,° and cry out   *public platforms (rostra)*
80   'Liberty, freedom, and enfranchisement!'
BRUTUS   People and senators, be not affrighted.
     [*Exeunt in a tumult* LEPIDUS, POPILLIUS, *other senators*,
             ARTEMIDORUS, SOOTHSAYER, *and citizens*]
     Fly not! Stand still! Ambition's debt is paid.
CASCA   Go to the pulpit, Brutus.
DECIUS   And Cassius too.
85   BRUTUS   Where's Publius?°   *(an elderly senator)*
CINNA   Here, quite confounded° with this mutiny.°   *confused / tumult*
METELLUS   Stand fast together, lest some friend of Caesar's
     Should chance—
BRUTUS   Talk not of standing.—Publius, good cheer!
90   There is no harm intended to your person,
     Nor to no Roman else—so tell them, Publius.
CASSIUS   And leave us, Publius, lest that the people,
     Rushing on us, should do your age some mischief.°   *injury*
BRUTUS   Do so; and let no man abide° this deed   *pay the penalty for*
95   But we the doers.   [*Exit* PUBLIUS]
       Enter TREBONIUS
CASSIUS   Where is Antony?
TREBONIUS   Fled to his house, amazed.
     Men, wives, and children stare, cry out, and run,
     As° it were doomsday.   *As if*
BRUTUS   Fates, we will know your pleasures.
100   That we shall die, we know; 'tis but the time
     And drawing days out that men stand upon.⁹
CASCA   Why, he that cuts off twenty years of life
     Cuts off so many years of fearing death.

---

5. Completely steady; unmoved by persuasion.
6. High mountain in Greece where the gods were supposed to dwell.
7. Let my hands beseech in prayer; let violent action take over where speech has failed.
8. Latin: And you, Brutus? According to Plutarch, Cae-

sar spoke these words in Greek and stopped defending himself when he saw Brutus among the conspirators.
9. *'tis . . . upon*: it is but the specific time of death and the possibility of extending their lives with which men concern themselves.

BRUTUS   Grant that, and then is death a benefit.
105 So are we Caesar's friends, that have abridged
His time of fearing death. Stoop, Romans, stoop,
And let us bathe our hands in Caesar's blood
Up to the elbows, and besmear our swords;
Then walk we forth even to the market-place,°   *the Roman Forum*
110 And, waving our red weapons o'er our heads,
Let's all cry 'peace, freedom, and liberty!'
CASSIUS   Stoop, then, and wash.
        [*They smear their hands with Caesar's blood*]
                                 How many ages hence
Shall this our lofty scene be acted over,
In states unborn and accents° yet unknown!   *languages*
115 BRUTUS   How many times shall Caesar bleed in sport,°   *for entertainment*
That now on Pompey's basis lies along,[1]
No worthier than the dust!
CASSIUS   So oft as that shall be,
So often shall the knot° of us be called   *group*
The men that gave their country liberty.
DECIUS   What, shall we forth?
120 CASSIUS   Ay, every man away.
Brutus shall lead, and we will grace° his heels   *honor*
With the most boldest and best hearts of Rome.
        Enter [*Antony's*] SERVANT
BRUTUS   Soft;° who comes here? A friend of Antony's.   *Wait*
SERVANT [*kneeling and falling prostrate*] Thus, Brutus, did my master
        bid me kneel.
125 Thus did Mark Antony bid me fall down,
And, being prostrate, thus he bade me say.
'Brutus is noble, wise, valiant, and honest.°   *honorable*
Caesar was mighty, bold, royal, and loving.
Say I love Brutus, and I honour him.
130 Say I feared Caesar, honoured him, and loved him.
If Brutus will vouchsafe that Antony
May safely come to him and be resolved°   *learn for certain*
How Caesar hath deserved to lie in death,
Mark Antony shall not love Caesar dead
135 So well as Brutus living, but will follow
The fortunes and affairs of noble Brutus
Thorough° the hazards of this untrod state[2]   *Through*
With all true faith.' So says my master Antony.
BRUTUS   Thy master is a wise and valiant Roman.
140 I never thought him worse.
Tell him, so° please him come unto this place,   *if it should*
He shall be satisfied, and, by my honour,
Depart untouched.
SERVANT [*rising*]   I'll fetch him presently.°   *Exit*   *at once*
BRUTUS   I know that we shall have him well to friend.°   *as a friend*
145 CASSIUS   I wish we may. But yet have I a mind
That fears him much; and my misgiving still
Falls shrewdly to the purpose.[3]
        Enter ANTONY

---

1. Lies stretched out on the pedestal ("basis") of Pompey's statue.
2. These unprecedented circumstances.

3. *my . . . purpose*: my suspicions always turn out to be unfortunately pertinent.

BRUTUS   But here comes Antony.—Welcome, Mark Antony.

ANTONY   O mighty Caesar! Dost thou lie so low?

150 Are all thy conquests, glories, triumphs, spoils,
Shrunk to this little measure? Fare thee well.—
I know not, gentlemen, what you intend—
Who else must be let blood, who else is rank.[4]
If I myself, there is no hour so fit

155 As Caesar's death's hour, nor no instrument
Of half that worth as those your swords, made rich
With the most noble blood of all this world.
I do beseech ye, if you bear me hard,°   *bear me ill will*
Now, whilst your purpled° hands do reek° and smoke,   *bloody / steam*

160 Fulfil your pleasure. Live° a thousand years,   *If I live*
I shall not find myself so apt° to die.   *ready*
No place will please me so, no mean° of death,   *manner*
As here by Caesar, and by you cut off,
The choice° and master spirits of this age.   *most select*

165 BRUTUS   O Antony, beg not your death of us!
Though now we must appear bloody and cruel,
As by our hands and this our present act
You see we do, yet see you but our hands,
And this the bleeding business they have done.

170 Our hearts you see not; they are pitiful;°   *full of pity*
And pity to the general wrong of Rome—
As fire drives out fire, so pity pity[5]—
Hath done this deed on Caesar. For your part,°   *As for you*
To you our swords have leaden° points, Mark Antony.   *blunt*

175 Our arms, unstrung of malice,[6] and our hearts
Of brothers' temper,° do receive you in   *disposition*
With all kind love, good thoughts, and reverence.

CASSIUS   Your voice° shall be as strong as any man's   *opinion*
In the disposing of new dignities.[7]

180 BRUTUS   Only be patient till we have appeased°   *calmed*
The multitude, beside themselves with fear,
And then we will deliver you the cause
Why I, that did love Caesar when I struck him,
Have thus proceeded.

ANTONY   I doubt not of your wisdom.

185 Let each man render me his bloody hand.
He shakes hands with the conspirators
First, Marcus Brutus, will I shake with you.—
Next, Caius Cassius, do I take your hand.—
Now, Decius Brutus, yours;—now yours, Metellus;—
Yours, Cinna;—and my valiant Casca, yours;—

190 Though last, not least in love, yours, good Trebonius.
Gentlemen all—alas, what shall I say?
My credit° now stands on such slippery ground   *credibility*
That one of two bad ways you must conceit° me: *judge*
Either a coward or a flatterer.

195 That I did love thee, Caesar, O, 'tis true.
If then thy spirit look upon us now,

---

4. Festering with disease; overgrown. *let blood:* have
blood drawn off medically (that is, killed).
5. That is, pity for the state has driven out pity for
Caesar.

6. Having given up their power to harm. (The image is
of a bow with its string loosened or removed.)
7. Conferring new offices of state.

Shall it not grieve thee dearer° than thy death   *more keenly*
To see thy Antony making his peace,
Shaking the bloody fingers of thy foes—
200   Most noble!—in the presence of thy corpse?
Had I as many eyes as thou hast wounds,
Weeping as fast as they stream forth thy blood,
It would become me better than to close°   *agree*
In terms of friendship with thine enemies.
205   Pardon me, Julius. Here wast thou bayed,° brave hart;[8]   *brought to bay*
Here didst thou fall, and here thy hunters stand
Signed° in thy spoil° and crimsoned in thy lethe.[9]   *Marked / slaughter*
O world, thou wast the forest to this hart;
And this indeed, O world, the heart of thee.
210   How like a deer strucken by many princes
Dost thou here lie!
    CASSIUS   Mark Antony.
    ANTONY   Pardon me, Caius Cassius.
The enemies of Caesar shall say this;
215   Then in a friend it is cold modesty.°   *moderation*
    CASSIUS   I blame you not for praising Caesar so;
But what compact° mean you to have with us?   *agreement*
Will you be pricked in number of° our friends,   *be counted among*
Or shall we on,° and not depend on you?   *proceed*
220   ANTONY   Therefore I took your hands, but was indeed
Swayed from the point by looking down on Caesar.
Friends am I with you all, and love you all
Upon this hope: that you shall give me reasons
Why and wherein Caesar was dangerous.
225   BRUTUS   Or else were this a savage spectacle.
Our reasons are so full of good regard,°   *sound considerations*
That were you, Antony, the son of Caesar,
You should be satisfied.
    ANTONY   That's all I seek;
And am, moreover, suitor° that I may   *petitioner*
230   Produce° his body to the market-place,   *Bring out*
And in the pulpit,° as becomes a friend,   *rostrum*
Speak in the order° of his funeral.   *ceremony*
    BRUTUS   You shall, Mark Antony.
    CASSIUS   Brutus, a word with you.
  [*Aside to* BRUTUS] You know not what you do. Do not consent
235   That Antony speak in his funeral.
Know you how much the people may be moved
By that which he will utter?
    BRUTUS [*aside to* CASSIUS]   By your pardon,°   *With your permission*
I will myself into the pulpit first,
And show the reason of our Caesar's death.
240   What Antony shall speak I will protest°   *proclaim*
He speaks by leave and by permission;
And that we are contented Caesar shall
Have all true° rites and lawful ceremonies,   *proper*
It shall advantage° more than do us wrong.   *benefit*
245   CASSIUS [*aside to* BRUTUS]   I know not what may fall.° I like it not.   *happen*

---

8. Stag (punning on "heart").
9. Lost lifeblood (Lethe was the river of forgetfulness in the classical underworld).

BRUTUS   Mark Antony, here, take you Caesar's body.
  You shall not in your funeral speech blame us;
  But speak all good you can devise of Caesar,
  And say you do't by our permission;
250   Else shall you not have any hand at all
  About° his funeral. And you shall speak   *In*
  In the same pulpit whereto I am going,
  After my speech is ended.
ANTONY   Be it so;
255   I do desire no more.
BRUTUS   Prepare the body then, and follow us.
                      Exeunt. Manet ANTONY
ANTONY   O pardon me, thou bleeding piece of earth,
  That I am meek and gentle with these butchers.
  Thou art the ruins of the noblest man
260   That ever livèd in the tide of times.°   *flow of history*
  Woe to the hand that shed this costly° blood!   *precious*
  Over thy wounds now do I prophesy—
  Which like dumb mouths do ope their ruby lips
  To beg the voice and utterance of my tongue—
265   A curse shall light upon the limbs of men;
  Domestic fury and fierce civil strife
  Shall cumber° all the parts of Italy;   *oppress*
  Blood and destruction shall be so in use,°   *so customary*
  And dreadful objects so familiar,
270   That mothers shall but smile when they behold
  Their infants quartered° with the hands of war,   *cut in pieces*
  All pity choked with custom of fell° deeds;   *familiarity with cruel*
  And Caesar's spirit, ranging° for revenge,   *roving like a wild beast*
  With Ate° by his side come hot from hell,   *goddess of discord*
275   Shall in these confines° with a monarch's voice   *regions*
  Cry 'havoc!'¹ and let slip° the dogs of war,   *unleash*
  That this foul deed shall smell above the earth
  With carrion men, groaning for burial.
                      Enter Octavius' SERVANT
  You serve Octavius Caesar, do you not?
280 SERVANT   I do, Mark Antony.
ANTONY   Caesar did write for him to come to Rome.
SERVANT   He did receive his letters, and is coming,
  And bid me say to you by word of mouth—
  [*Seeing the body*] O Caesar!
285 ANTONY   Thy heart is big.° Get thee apart and weep.   *swollen with grief*
  Passion,° I see, is catching, for mine eyes,   *Sorrow*
  Seeing those beads of sorrow stand in thine,
  Began to water. Is thy master coming?
SERVANT   He lies° tonight within seven leagues° of Rome.   *stays / 20 miles*
290 ANTONY   Post° back with speed and tell him what hath chanced.   *Ride quickly*
  Here is a mourning Rome, a dangerous Rome,
  No Rome of safety for Octavius yet.
  Hie° hence and tell him so.—Yet stay awhile.   *Hasten*
  Thou shalt not back till I have borne this corpse
295   Into the market-place. There shall I try°   *test*
  In my oration how the people take

---

1. Military order for slaughter and pillage.

The cruel issue° of these bloody men;   *deed*
According to the which thou shalt discourse
To young Octavius of the state of things.
300   Lend me your hand.   *Exeunt [with Caesar's body]*

3.2

Enter BRUTUS *and* CASSIUS, *with the* PLEBEIANS
ALL THE PLEBEIANS   We will be satisfied!° Let us be satisfied!   *given an explanation*
BRUTUS   Then follow me, and give me audience, friends.
    [*Aside to* CASSIUS] Cassius, go you into the other street,
    And part the numbers.°   *divide the multitude*
5   [*To the* PLEBEIANS] Those that will hear me speak, let 'em stay here;
    Those that will follow Cassius, go with him;
    And public reasons shall be renderèd
    Of Caesar's death.
              BRUTUS [*ascends to*] *the pulpit*
FIRST PLEBEIAN   I will hear Brutus speak.
SECOND PLEBEIAN   I will hear Cassius, and compare their reasons
10   When severally° we hear them renderèd.   *separately*
              [*Exit* CASSIUS, *with some* PLEBEIANS]
            [*Enter* BRUTUS *above in the pulpit*]
THIRD PLEBEIAN   The noble Brutus is ascended. Silence.
BRUTUS   Be patient till the last.°   *end of my address*
    Romans, countrymen, and lovers,° hear me for my cause, and   *dear friends*
    be silent that you may hear. Believe me for° mine honour, and   *on account of*
15   have respect to° mine honour, that you may believe. Censure°   *regard for / Judge*
    me in your wisdom, and awake your senses,° that you may the   *understanding*
    better judge. If there be any in this assembly, any dear friend
    of Caesar's, to him I say that Brutus' love to Caesar was no less
    than his. If then that friend demand why Brutus rose against
20   Caesar, this is my answer: not that I loved Caesar less, but that
    I loved Rome more. Had you rather Caesar were living, and
    die all slaves, than that Caesar were dead, to live all free men?
    As Caesar loved me, I weep for him. As he was fortunate, I
    rejoice at it. As he was valiant, I honour him. But as he was
25   ambitious, I slew him. There is tears for his love, joy for his
    fortune, honour for his valour, and death for his ambition. Who
    is here so base that would be a bondman? If any, speak, for him
    have I offended.° Who is here so rude° that would not be a   *wronged / barbarous*
    Roman? If any, speak, for him have I offended. Who is here so
30   vile that will not love his country? If any, speak, for him have I
    offended. I pause for a reply.
ALL THE PLEBEIANS   None, Brutus, none.
BRUTUS   Then none have I offended. I have done no more to
    Caesar than you shall do¹ to Brutus. The question of° his   *reasons for*
35   death is enrolled° in the Capitol, his glory not extenuated°   *recorded / diminished*
    wherein he was worthy, nor his offences enforced° for which   *unduly stressed*
    he suffered death.
           Enter Mark ANTONY, *with* [*others bearing*] *Caesar's*
           body [*in a coffin*]
    Here comes his body, mourned by Mark Antony, who, though
    he had no hand in his death, shall receive the benefit of his
40   dying: a place in the commonwealth—as which of you shall

---

3.2 Location: The Forum.   1. Should do (in such circumstances).

not? With this I depart: that as I slew my best lover° for the   *friend*
good of Rome, I have the same dagger for myself when it shall
please my country to need my death.

ALL THE PLEBEIANS   Live, Brutus, live, live!

45   FIRST PLEBEIAN   Bring him with triumph home unto his house.

FOURTH PLEBEIAN   Give him a statue with his ancestors.

THIRD PLEBEIAN   Let him be Caesar.

FIFTH PLEBEIAN   Caesar's better parts°   *faculties*
   Shall be crowned in Brutus.

FIRST PLEBEIAN   We'll bring him to his house with shouts and clamours.

BRUTUS   My countrymen.

50   FOURTH PLEBEIAN   Peace, silence. Brutus speaks.

FIRST PLEBEIAN   Peace, ho!

BRUTUS   Good countrymen, let me depart alone,
   And, for my sake, stay here with Antony.
   Do grace° to Caesar's corpse, and grace² his speech   *Pay respect*

55   Tending° to Caesar's glories, which Mark Antony,   *Relating*
   By our permission, is allowed to make.
   I do entreat you, not a man depart
   Save I alone till Antony have spoke.   *Exit*

FIRST PLEBEIAN   Stay, ho, and let us hear Mark Antony.

60   THIRD PLEBEIAN   Let him go up into the public chair.
   We'll hear him. Noble Antony, go up.

ANTONY   For Brutus' sake I am beholden to you.
      [ANTONY *ascends to the pulpit*]

FIFTH PLEBEIAN   What does he say of Brutus?

THIRD PLEBEIAN   He says, for Brutus' sake
   He finds himself beholden to us all.

65   FIFTH PLEBEIAN   'Twere best he speak no harm of Brutus here!

FIRST PLEBEIAN   This Caesar was a tyrant.

THIRD PLEBEIAN   Nay, that's certain.
   We are blessed that Rome is rid of him.
      [*Enter* ANTONY *in the pulpit*]

FOURTH PLEBEIAN   Peace, let us hear what Antony can say.

ANTONY   You gentle Romans.

ALL THE PLEBEIANS   Peace, ho! Let us hear him.

70   ANTONY   Friends, Romans, countrymen, lend me your ears.
   I come to bury Caesar, not to praise him.
   The evil that men do lives after them;
   The good is oft interrèd with their bones.
   So let it be with Caesar. The noble Brutus

75   Hath told you Caesar was ambitious.
   If it were so, it was a grievous fault,
   And grievously hath Caesar answered° it.   *paid the penalty for*
   Here, under leave° of Brutus and the rest—   *by permission*
   For Brutus is an honourable man,

80   So are they all, all honourable men—
   Come I to speak in Caesar's funeral.
   He was my friend, faithful and just to me.
   But Brutus says he was ambitious,
   And Brutus is an honourable man.

85   He hath brought many captives home to Rome,

---

2. Courteously hear.

Whose ransoms did the general coffers° fill.   *public treasury*
Did this in Caesar seem ambitious?
When that the poor have cried, Caesar hath wept.
Ambition should be made of sterner stuff.
90   Yet Brutus says he was ambitious,
And Brutus is an honourable man.
You all did see that on the Lupercal
I thrice presented him a kingly crown,
Which he did thrice refuse. Was this ambition?
95   Yet Brutus says he was ambitious,
And sure he is an honourable man.
I speak not to disprove what Brutus spoke,
But here I am to speak what I do know.
You all did love him once, not without cause.
100   What cause withholds you then to mourn for him?
O judgement, thou art fled to brutish beasts,
And men have lost their reason!
      [*He weeps*]
                     Bear with me.
My heart is in the coffin there with Caesar,
And I must pause till it come back to me.
105 FIRST PLEBEIAN   Methinks there is much reason in his sayings.
FOURTH PLEBEIAN   If thou consider rightly of the matter,
    Caesar has had great wrong.
THIRD PLEBEIAN   Has he not, masters?
    I fear there will a worse come in his place.
FIFTH PLEBEIAN   Marked ye his words? He would not take the crown,
110   Therefore 'tis certain he was not ambitious.
FIRST PLEBEIAN   If it be found so, some will dear abide° it.   *pay dearly for*
FOURTH PLEBEIAN   Poor soul, his eyes are red as fire with weeping.
THIRD PLEBEIAN   There's not a nobler man in Rome than Antony.
FIFTH PLEBEIAN   Now mark him; he begins again to speak.
115 ANTONY   But° yesterday the word of Caesar might   *Only*
Have stood against the world. Now lies he there,
And none so poor to do him reverence.[3]
O masters, if I were disposed to stir
Your hearts and minds to mutiny° and rage,   *rebellion*
120   I should do Brutus wrong, and Cassius wrong,
Who, you all know, are honourable men.
I will not do them wrong. I rather choose
To wrong the dead, to wrong myself and you,
Than I will wrong such honourable men.
125   But here's a parchment with the seal of Caesar.
I found it in his closet.° 'Tis his will.   *study*
Let but the commons° hear this testament—   *commoners*
Which, pardon me, I do not mean to read—
And they would go and kiss dead Caesar's wounds,
130   And dip their napkins[4] in his sacred blood,
Yea, beg a hair of him for memory,
And, dying, mention it within their wills,
Bequeathing it as a rich legacy
Unto their issue.°   *children*

---

3. And no one is so lowly as to owe obeisance to him.
4. Handkerchiefs (implying that Caesar is a martyr whose bloody relics should be regarded as holy).

135   FIFTH PLEBEIAN   We'll hear the will. Read it, Mark Antony.
     ALL THE PLEBEIANS   The will, the will! We will hear Caesar's will.
     ANTONY   Have patience, gentle friends, I must not read it.
     It is not meet° you know how Caesar loved you.   *fitting*
     You are not wood, you are not stones, but men;
140   And, being men, hearing the will of Caesar,
     It will inflame you, it will make you mad.
     'Tis good you know not that you are his heirs,
     For if you should, O what would come of it?
     FIFTH PLEBEIAN   Read the will. We'll hear it, Antony.
145   You shall read us the will, Caesar's will.
     ANTONY   Will you be patient? Will you stay a while?
     I have o'ershot myself⁵ to tell you of it.
     I fear I wrong the honourable men
     Whose daggers have stabbed Caesar; I do fear it.
150   FIFTH PLEBEIAN   They were traitors. Honourable men?
     ALL THE PLEBEIANS   The will, the testament!
     FOURTH PLEBEIAN   They were villains, murderers. The will, read
     the will!
     ANTONY   You will compel me then to read the will?
155   Then make a ring about the corpse of Caesar,
     And let me show you him that made the will.
     Shall I descend? And will you give me leave?
     ALL THE PLEBEIANS
     Come down.
     FOURTH PLEBEIAN   Descend.
     THIRD PLEBEIAN   You shall have leave.
         [ANTONY *descends from the pulpit*]
     FIFTH PLEBEIAN   A ring.
     Stand round.
     FIRST PLEBEIAN   Stand from the hearse.° Stand from the body.   *bier*
160   FOURTH PLEBEIAN   Room for Antony, most noble Antony!
         [*Enter* ANTONY *below*]
     ANTONY   Nay, press not so upon me. Stand farre° off.   *farther*
     ALL THE PLEBEIANS   Stand back! Room! Bear back!
     ANTONY   If you have tears, prepare to shed them now.
     You all do know this mantle. I remember
165   The first time ever Caesar put it on.
     'Twas on a summer's evening in his tent,
     That day he overcame the Nervii.⁶
     Look, in this place ran Cassius' dagger through.
     See what a rent the envious° Casca made.   *spiteful*
170   Through this the well-belovèd Brutus stabbed;
     And as he plucked his cursèd steel away,
     Mark how the blood of Caesar followed it,
     As° rushing out of doors to be resolved⁷   *As if*
     If Brutus so unkindly° knocked or no—   *cruelly; unnaturally*
175   For Brutus, as you know, was Caesar's angel.⁸
     Judge, O you gods, how dearly Caesar loved him!
     This was the most unkindest cut of all.
     For when the noble Caesar saw him stab,

---

5. I have gone too far (an image from archery).   7. To find out for sure.
6. Gallic tribe conquered by Caesar in 57 B.C.E.; it was   8. Attendant spirit (that is, dearest friend).
an important victory, extravagantly celebrated in Rome.

Ingratitude, more strong than traitors' arms,
180 Quite vanquished him. Then burst his mighty heart,
And in his mantle muffling up his face,
Even at the base of Pompey's statue,
Which all the while ran blood, great Caesar fell.
O, what a fall was there, my countrymen!
185 Then I, and you, and all of us fell down,
Whilst bloody treason flourished⁹ over us.
O now you weep, and I perceive you feel
The dint° of pity. These are gracious drops.   *impression*
Kind souls, what, weep you when you but behold
190 Our Caesar's vesture° wounded? Look you here.   *garment*
Here is himself, marred, as you see, with traitors.
          [*He uncovers Caesar's body*]
FIRST PLEBEIAN   O piteous spectacle!
FOURTH PLEBEIAN   O noble Caesar!
THIRD PLEBEIAN   O woeful day!
FIFTH PLEBEIAN   O traitors, villains!
FIRST PLEBEIAN   O most bloody sight!
195 FOURTH PLEBEIAN   We will be revenged.
ALL THE PLEBEIANS   Revenge! About!° Seek! Burn! Fire! Kill! Slay!   *To work*
Let not a traitor live!
ANTONY   Stay, countrymen.
FIRST PLEBEIAN   Peace there, hear the noble Antony.
FOURTH PLEBEIAN   We'll hear him, we'll follow him, we'll die
200 with him!
ANTONY   Good friends, sweet friends, let me not stir you up
To such a sudden flood of mutiny.
They that have done this deed are honourable.
What private griefs° they have, alas, I know not,   *personal grievances*
205 That made them do it. They are wise and honourable,
And will no doubt with reasons answer you.
I come not, friends, to steal away your hearts.
I am no orator as Brutus is,
But, as you know me all, a plain blunt man
210 That love my friend; and that they know full well
That gave me public leave to speak¹ of him.
For I have neither wit,° nor words, nor worth,°   *intelligence / stature*
Action,° nor utterance, nor the power of speech,   *Gesture*
To stir men's blood. I only speak right on.°   *straightforwardly*
215 I tell you that which you yourselves do know,
Show you sweet Caesar's wounds, poor poor dumb mouths,
And bid them speak for me. But were I Brutus,
And Brutus Antony, there were an Antony
Would ruffle° up your spirits, and put a tongue   *stir*
220 In every wound of Caesar that should move
The stones of Rome to rise and mutiny.°   *riot*
ALL THE PLEBEIANS   We'll mutiny.
FIRST PLEBEIAN   We'll burn the house of Brutus.
THIRD PLEBEIAN   Away then! Come, seek the conspirators.
ANTONY   Yet hear me, countrymen, yet hear me speak.
225 ALL THE PLEBEIANS   Peace, ho! Hear Antony, most noble Antony.
ANTONY   Why, friends, you go to do you know not what.

9. Shook its sword; triumphed.   1. Permission to speak in public.

Wherein hath Caesar thus deserved your loves?
Alas, you know not. I must tell you then.
You have forgot the will I told you of.

230 ALL THE PLEBEIANS Most true. The will. Let's stay and hear the will.
ANTONY Here is the will, and under Caesar's seal.
To every Roman citizen he gives—
To every several° man—seventy-five drachmas.²   *individual*
FOURTH PLEBEIAN Most noble Caesar! We'll revenge his death.
THIRD PLEBEIAN O royal Caesar!
ANTONY   Hear me with patience.
235 ALL THE PLEBEIANS   Peace,° ho!   *Silence*
ANTONY Moreover he hath left you all his walks,
His private arbours, and new-planted orchards,°   *gardens*
On this side Tiber. He hath left them you,
And to your heirs for ever—common pleasures°   *public parks*
240 To walk abroad and recreate yourselves.
Here was a Caesar. When comes such another?
FIRST PLEBEIAN Never, never! Come, away, away!
We'll burn his body in the holy place,
And with the brands fire the traitors' houses.
245 Take up the body.
FOURTH PLEBEIAN Go, fetch fire!
THIRD PLEBEIAN Pluck down benches!
FIFTH PLEBEIAN Pluck down forms,° windows,° anything!   *benches / shutters*
            Exeunt PLEBEIANS [*with Caesar's body*]
ANTONY Now let it work. Mischief, thou art afoot.
Take thou what course thou wilt.
           Enter [*Octavius'*] SERVANT
250   How now, fellow?
SERVANT Sir, Octavius is already come to Rome.
ANTONY Where is he?
SERVANT He and Lepidus are at Caesar's house.
ANTONY And thither will I straight° to visit him.   *at once*
255 He comes upon a wish.° Fortune is merry,   *just as I wished*
And in this mood will give us anything.
SERVANT I heard him say Brutus and Cassius
Are rid° like madmen through the gates of Rome.   *Have ridden*
ANTONY Belike° they had some notice° of the people,   *Probably / warning*
260 How I had moved them. Bring me to Octavius.   *Exeunt*

3.3

    Enter CINNA *the poet*
CINNA I dreamt tonight° that I did feast with Caesar,   *last night*
And things unlucky charge my fantasy.¹
I have no will to wander forth of doors,
Yet something leads me forth.
    [*Enter*] *the* PLEBEIANS
5 FIRST PLEBEIAN What is your name?
SECOND PLEBEIAN Whither are you going?
THIRD PLEBEIAN Where do you dwell?
FOURTH PLEBEIAN Are you a married man or a bachelor?
SECOND PLEBEIAN Answer every man directly.²

---

2. Greek silver coins.   1. And bad omens oppress my imagination.
3.3 Location: A street in Rome.   2. At once; speaking straightforwardly.

10   FIRST PLEBEIAN   Ay, and briefly.

      FOURTH PLEBEIAN   Ay, and wisely.

      THIRD PLEBEIAN   Ay, and truly, you were best.°   *you'd better*

      CINNA   What is my name? Whither am I going? Where do I
      dwell? Am I a married man or a bachelor? Then to answer
15   every man directly and briefly, wisely and truly: wisely, I say, I
      am a bachelor.

      SECOND PLEBEIAN   That's as much as to say they are fools that
      marry. You'll bear me a bang° for that, I fear. Proceed directly.   *get a blow from me*

      CINNA   Directly I am going to Caesar's funeral.

20   FIRST PLEBEIAN   As a friend or an enemy?

      CINNA   As a friend.

      SECOND PLEBEIAN   That matter is answered directly.

      FOURTH PLEBEIAN   For your dwelling—briefly.

      CINNA   Briefly, I dwell by the Capitol.

25   THIRD PLEBEIAN   Your name, sir, truly.

      CINNA   Truly, my name is Cinna.

      FIRST PLEBEIAN   Tear him to pieces! He's a conspirator.

      CINNA   I am Cinna the poet, I am Cinna the poet.

      FOURTH PLEBEIAN   Tear him for his bad verses, tear him for his
30   bad verses.

      CINNA   I am not Cinna the conspirator.

      FOURTH PLEBEIAN   It is no matter, his name's Cinna. Pluck but
      his name out of his heart, and turn him going.°   *send him packing*

      THIRD PLEBEIAN   Tear him, tear him!

            [*They set upon* CINNA]

35   Come, brands, ho! Firebrands! To Brutus', to Cassius'! Burn
      all! Some to Decius' house, and some to Casca's; some to Liga-
      rius'. Away, go!

            Exeunt all the PLEBEIANS [*with* CINNA]

4.1

      Enter ANTONY [*with papers*], OCTAVIUS, *and* LEPIDUS

      ANTONY   These many, then, shall die; their names are pricked.°   *marked down*

      OCTAVIUS [*to* LEPIDUS]   Your brother too must die. Consent you, Lepidus?

      LEPIDUS   I do consent.

      OCTAVIUS   Prick him down, Antony.

      LEPIDUS   Upon condition° Publius shall not live,   *Provided that*
5   Who is your sister's son, Mark Antony.

      ANTONY   He shall not live. Look, with a spot I damn him.[1]

      But Lepidus, go you to Caesar's house;
      Fetch the will hither, and we shall determine
      How to cut off some charge in legacies.[2]

10   LEPIDUS   What, shall I find you here?

      OCTAVIUS   Or° here or at the Capitol.   *Exit* LEPIDUS   *Either*

      ANTONY   This is a slight, unmeritable° man,   *undeserving*
      Meet° to be sent on errands. Is it fit,   *Fit*
      The three-fold world divided,[3] he should stand
      One of the three to share it?

15   OCTAVIUS   So you thought him,
      And took his voice° who should be pricked to die   *accepted his opinion*

4.1 Location: Antony's house in Rome.
1. With a mark I condemn him to death.
2. Reduce the amount paid out to beneficiaries of Caesar's will.

3. Antony, Octavius, and Lepidus, in the second triumvirate, or joint rule of three, parceled out rule of Rome's empire among themselves.

In our black° sentence and proscription.[4] °*death*
ANTONY Octavius, I have seen more days than you,
And though we lay these honours on this man
20 To ease ourselves of divers sland'rous loads,° °*burdens of reproach*
He shall but bear them as the ass bears gold,
To groan and sweat under the business,
Either led or driven as we point the way;
And having brought our treasure where we will,
25 Then take we down his load, and turn him off,
Like to the empty° ass, to shake his ears °*unladen*
And graze in commons.[5]
OCTAVIUS   You may do your will;
But he's a tried and valiant soldier.
ANTONY So is my horse, Octavius, and for that
30 I do appoint° him store of provender. °*provide*
It is a creature that I teach to fight,
To wind,° to stop, to run directly on, °*turn*
His corporal° motion governed by my spirit; °*bodily*
And in some taste° is Lepidus but so. °*measure*
35 He must be taught, and trained, and bid go forth—
A barren-spirited fellow, one that feeds
On objects, arts, and imitations,[6]
Which, out of use and staled° by other men, °*made uninteresting*
Begin his fashion.[7] Do not talk of him
40 But as a property.° And now, Octavius, °*tool*
Listen° great things. Brutus and Cassius °*Give ear to*
Are levying powers.° We must straight make head.[8] °*armies*
Therefore let our alliance be combined,
Our best friends made,° our meinies stretched,[9] °*mustered*
45 And let us presently go sit in council,
How covert matters° may be best disclosed, °*dangers*
And open perils surest answerèd.° °*most safely confronted*
OCTAVIUS Let us do so, for we are at the stake[1]
And bayed about with many enemies;
50 And some that smile have in their hearts, I fear,
Millions of mischiefs.° °*evils*

Exeunt

4.2

Drum. Enter BRUTUS, [LUCIUS,] *and the army.* LUCIL-
LIUS, TITINIUS, *and* PINDARUS *meet them*
BRUTUS Stand, ho!° °*Halt*
SOLDIER Give the word 'ho', and stand.[1]
BRUTUS What now, Lucillius: is Cassius near?
LUCILLIUS He is at hand, and Pindarus is come
5 To do you salutation from his master.
BRUTUS He greets me well.° Your master, Pindarus, °*with a worthy man*
In his own change or by ill officers,[2]

---

4. A "proscribed" person had a price on his head, his
property was confiscated, and his children were pre-
vented from holding office.
5. In the public pasture; among the common people.
6. On curiosities, contrivances, and counterfeits.
7. He then takes up as fashionable.
8. We must raise an army at once.
9. Our bands of followers augmented.

1. That is, like bears in the sport of bearbaiting, tied to
a stake and surrounded by baying hounds.
4.2 Location: Sardis, in what is now western Turkey.
Brutus's tent in his army's camp.
1. Pass the word, and halt.
2. By his own altered feelings or through the actions of
bad subordinates.

Hath given me some worthy° cause to wish   *justifiable*
Things done undone. But if he be at hand,
I shall be satisfied.³

10   PINDARUS   I do not doubt
But that my noble master will appear
Such as he is, full of regard⁴ and honour.

BRUTUS   He is not doubted.—A word, Lucillius.

       BRUTUS *and* LUCILLIUS *speak apart*

How he received you let me be resolved.°   *informed*

15   LUCILLIUS   With courtesy and with respect enough,
But not with such familiar instances,°   *tokens of friendship*
Nor with such free and friendly conference,°   *conversation*
As he hath used of old.

BRUTUS   Thou hast described
A hot friend cooling. Ever note, Lucillius:

20   When love begins to sicken and decay
It useth an enforcèd ceremony.°   *a strained formality*
There are no tricks° in plain and simple faith;   *artifices*
But hollow° men, like horses hot at hand,⁵   *insincere*
Make gallant show and promise of their mettle;
       Low march⁶ within

25   But when they should endure the bloody spur,
They fall their crests° and, like deceitful jades,°   *lower their necks / nags*
Sink° in the trial. Comes his army on?   *Fail*

LUCILLIUS   They mean this night in Sardis to be quartered.
The greater part, the horse in general,°   *all the cavalry*
Are come with Cassius.
       Enter CASSIUS *and his powers*°   *armies*

30   BRUTUS   Hark, he is arrived.
March gently° on to meet him.   *slowly*
     [*The armies march*]

CASSIUS   Stand, ho!

BRUTUS   Stand, ho! Speak the word along.

FIRST SOLDIER   Stand!

35   SECOND SOLDIER   Stand!

THIRD SOLDIER   Stand!

CASSIUS   Most noble brother, you have done me wrong.

BRUTUS   Judge me, you gods: wrong I mine enemies?
And if not so, how should I wrong a brother?

40   CASSIUS   Brutus, this sober form of yours hides wrongs,
And when you do them—

BRUTUS   Cassius, be content.°   *keep calm*
Speak your griefs° softly. I do know you well.   *grievances*
Before the eyes of both our armies here,
Which should perceive nothing but love from us,

45   Let us not wrangle. Bid them move away,
Then in my tent, Cassius, enlarge° your griefs,   *express fully*
And I will give you audience.

CASSIUS   Pindarus,
Bid our commanders lead their charges° off   *troops*
A little from this ground.

---

3. I shall receive a full explanation.
4. Respect for you; renown (for his own abilities).
5. Eager at the outset.

6. Soft drumbeat (as from a distance; the sound becomes louder as the army enters).

50 BRUTUS   Lucillius, do you the like; and let no man
    Come to our tent till we have done our conference.
    Let Lucius and Titinius guard our door.   *Exeunt [the armies]*
        Manent BRUTUS *and* CASSIUS [*with* TITINIUS *and*
            LUCIUS *guarding the door*][7]
    CASSIUS   That you have wronged me doth appear in this:
        You have condemned and noted° Lucius Pella   *publicly disgraced*
55   For taking bribes here of the Sardians,
        Wherein my letters praying on his side,
        Because I knew the man, was slighted off.°   *contemptuously ignored*
    BRUTUS   You wronged yourself to write in such a case.
    CASSIUS   In such a time as this it is not meet°   *appropriate*
60   That every nice° offence should bear his comment.°   *trivial / be criticized*
    BRUTUS   Let me tell you, Cassius, you yourself
        Are much condemned to have° an itching palm,   *for having*
        To sell and mart° your offices for gold   *traffic in*
        To undeservers.
    CASSIUS   I, an itching palm?
65   You know that you are Brutus that speaks this,
        Or, by the gods, this speech were else° your last.   *otherwise*
    BRUTUS   The name of Cassius honours this corruption,[8]
        And chastisement doth therefore hide his head.
    CASSIUS   Chastisement?
70 BRUTUS   Remember March, the ides of March, remember.
        Did not great Julius bleed for justice' sake?
        What villain touched his body, that did stab,
        And not for justice?[9] What, shall one of us,
        That struck the foremost man of all this world
75   But for supporting robbers,[1] shall we now
        Contaminate our fingers with base bribes,
        And sell the mighty space of our large honours°   *impressive reputations*
        For so much trash° as may be graspèd thus?   *money (contemptuous)*
        I had rather be a dog and bay° the moon   *howl at*
        Than such a Roman.
80 CASSIUS   Brutus, bay° not me.   *howl at; hold at bay*
        I'll not endure it. You forget yourself
        To hedge me in.° I am a soldier, I,   *limit my authority*
        Older in practice, abler than yourself
        To make conditions.°   *manage affairs*
85 BRUTUS   Go to, you are not, Cassius.
    CASSIUS   I am.
    BRUTUS   I say you are not.
    CASSIUS   Urge° me no more, I shall forget myself.   *Provoke*
        Have mind upon your health. Tempt me no farther.
90 BRUTUS   Away, slight man.
    CASSIUS   Is't possible?
    BRUTUS   Hear me, for I will speak.
        Must I give way and room to your rash choler?[2]
        Shall I be frighted when a madman stares?
95 CASSIUS   O ye gods, ye gods! Must I endure all this?
    BRUTUS   All this? Ay, more. Fret till your proud heart break.

---

7. Some editors begin a new scene at this point.
8. Makes this corruption appear honorable.
9. *What . . . justice?*: Who was so villainous as to stab
Caesar for any motive other than justice?

1. Caesar was accused of permitting, even encourag-
ing, corruption among his subordinates.
2. Must I allow free passage to your rash anger?

Go show your slaves how choleric° you are,   *enraged*
And make your bondmen tremble. Must I budge?°   *flinch*
Must I observe° you? Must I stand and crouch°   *defer to / cringe*
100   Under your testy humour?° By the gods,   *irritable temper*
You shall digest³ the venom of your spleen,°   *anger*
Though it do split you. For from this day forth
I'll use you for my mirth, yea for my laughter,
When you are waspish.

CASSIUS   Is it come to this?

105   BRUTUS   You say you are a better soldier.
Let it appear so, make your vaunting° true,   *boasting*
And it shall please me well. For mine own part,
I shall be glad to learn of° noble men.   *from*

CASSIUS   You wrong me every way, you wrong me, Brutus.
110   I said an elder soldier, not a better.
Did I say better?

BRUTUS   If you did, I care not.

CASSIUS   When Caesar lived he durst not thus have moved° me.   *angered*

BRUTUS   Peace, peace; you durst not so have tempted him.

CASSIUS   I durst not?

115   BRUTUS   No.

CASSIUS   What, durst not tempt him?

BRUTUS   For your life you durst not.

CASSIUS   Do not presume too much upon my love.
I may do that I shall be sorry for.

120   BRUTUS   You have done that you should be sorry for.
There is no terror, Cassius, in your threats,
For I am armed so strong in honesty°   *rectitude*
That they pass by me as the idle wind,
Which I respect not.° I did send to you   *pay no attention to*
125   For certain sums of gold, which you denied me;
For I can raise no money by vile means.
By heaven, I had rather coin my heart
And drop my blood for drachmas than to wring
From the hard hands of peasants their vile trash
130   By any indirection.° I did send   *devious means*
To you for gold to pay my legions,
Which you denied me. Was that done like Cassius?
Should I have answered Caius Cassius so?
When Marcus Brutus grows so covetous
135   To lock such rascal counters from his friends,
Be ready, gods, with all your thunderbolts;
Dash him to pieces.

CASSIUS   I denied you not.

BRUTUS   You did.

CASSIUS   I did not. He was but a fool
That brought my answer back. Brutus hath rived° my heart.   *broken*
140   A friend should bear his friend's infirmities,
But Brutus makes mine greater than they are.

BRUTUS   I do not, till you practise them on me.

CASSIUS   You love me not.

BRUTUS   I do not like your faults.

CASSIUS   A friendly eye could never see such faults.

---

3. Swallow (not give vent to).

145 BRUTUS   A flatterer's would not, though they do appear
    As huge as high Olympus.
    CASSIUS   Come, Antony and young Octavius, come,
    Revenge yourselves alone on Cassius;
    For Cassius is aweary of the world,
150   Hated by one he loves, braved° by his brother,   *defied*
    Checked° like a bondman; all his faults observed,   *Rebuked*
    Set in a notebook, learned and conned by rote,°   *memorized*
    To cast into my teeth. O, I could weep
    My spirit from mine eyes! There is my dagger,
155   And here my naked breast; within, a heart
    Dearer° than Pluto's[4] mine, richer than gold.   *More valuable*
    If that thou beest a Roman, take it forth.
    I that denied thee gold will give my heart.
    Strike as thou didst at Caesar; for I know
160   When thou didst hate him worst, thou loved'st him better
    Than ever thou loved'st Cassius.
    BRUTUS   Sheathe your dagger.
    Be angry when you will; it shall have scope.°   *room for exercise*
    Do what you will; dishonour shall be humour.[5]
    O Cassius, you are yokèd° with a lamb   *allied*
165   That carries anger as the flint bears fire,
    Who, much enforcèd,° shows a hasty spark   *struck*
    And straight° is cold again.   *immediately*
    CASSIUS   Hath Cassius lived
    To be but mirth and laughter to his Brutus
    When grief and blood ill-tempered[6] vexeth him?
170 BRUTUS   When I spoke that, I was ill-tempered too.
    CASSIUS   Do you confess so much? Give me your hand.
    BRUTUS   And my heart too.
        [*They embrace*]
    CASSIUS   O Brutus!
    BRUTUS   What's the matter?
    CASSIUS   Have not you love enough to bear with me
    When that rash humour° which my mother gave me   *temperament*
    Makes me forgetful?
175 BRUTUS   Yes, Cassius, and from henceforth,
    When you are over-earnest with your Brutus,
    He'll think your mother chides, and leave you so.°   *let you alone*
        Enter [LUCILLIUS *and*] *a* POET
    POET   Let me go in to see the generals.
    There is some grudge between 'em; 'tis not meet
    They be alone.
180 LUCILLIUS   You shall not come to them.
    POET   Nothing but death shall stay me.
    CASSIUS   How now! What's the matter?
    POET   For shame, you generals, what do you mean?
    Love and be friends, as two such men should be,
    For I have seen more years, I'm sure, than ye.
185 CASSIUS   Ha, ha! How vilely doth this cynic[7] rhyme!

---

4. Roman god of riches (Plutus; often conflated with Pluto, god of the underworld).
5. Dishonorable actions shall be ascribed to moodiness.
6. Literally, badly mixed blood (thought to produce anger and melancholy).
7. Member of a philosophical school that refused to respect differences in social class.

BRUTUS [*to the* POET] Get you hence, sirrah;° saucy fellow, (*contemptuous address*)
 hence!
CASSIUS Bear with him, Brutus, 'tis his fashion.
BRUTUS I'll know his humour when he knows his time.[8]
 What should the wars do with these jigging° fools? *incompetently versifying*
 [*To the* POET] Companion,° hence! (*contemptuous*)
190 CASSIUS [*to the* POET] Away, away, be gone!
 Exit POET
BRUTUS Lucillius and Titinius, bid the commanders
 Prepare to lodge their companies tonight.
CASSIUS And come yourselves, and bring Messala with you
 Immediately to us. [*Exeunt* LUCILLIUS *and* TITINIUS]
BRUTUS Lucius, a bowl of wine. [*Exit* LUCIUS]
195 CASSIUS I did not think you could have been so angry.
BRUTUS O Cassius, I am sick of° many griefs. *suffering from*
CASSIUS Of your philosophy you make no use,
 If you give place to accidental evils.[9]
BRUTUS No man bears sorrow better. Portia is dead.
200 CASSIUS Ha! Portia?
BRUTUS She is dead.
CASSIUS How scaped I killing° when I crossed you so? *being killed*
 O insupportable and touching loss!
 Upon what sickness?
BRUTUS Impatience of° my absence, *Inability to tolerate*
205 And grief that young Octavius with Mark Antony
 Have made themselves so strong—for with° her death *with the news of*
 That tidings came. With this, she fell distraught,
 And, her attendants absent, swallowed fire.[1]
CASSIUS And died so?
BRUTUS Even so.
CASSIUS O ye immortal gods!
 Enter [LUCIUS] *with wine and tapers°* *candles*
210 BRUTUS Speak no more of her. [*To* LUCIUS] Give me a bowl of wine.
 [*To* CASSIUS] In this I bury all unkindness, Cassius.
 [*He*] *drinks*
CASSIUS My heart is thirsty for that noble pledge.
 Fill, Lucius, till the wine o'erswell° the cup. *overflow*
 I cannot drink too much of Brutus' love.
 [*He drinks*] [*Exit* LUCIUS]
 Enter TITINIUS *and* MESSALA[2]
215 BRUTUS Come in, Titinius; welcome, good Messala.
 Now sit we close about this taper here,
 And call in question° our necessities. *discuss*
CASSIUS [*aside*] Portia, art thou gone?
BRUTUS No more, I pray you.
 [*They sit*]
 Messala, I have here receivèd letters
220 That young Octavius and Mark Antony
 Come down upon us with a mighty power,
 Bending their expedition° toward Philippi.[3] *Pressing hastily*

---

8. I'll tolerate his eccentricity when he finds an appropriate time for it.
9. Brutus admired the Stoics, who taught that the wise man should remain unaffected by circumstances outside himself. *evils:* misfortunes.

1. Portia committed suicide by swallowing live embers.
2. Lucillius, who ought logically to return at this point (see lines 193–94), is not mentioned, an inconsistency that suggests Shakespearean revision of this scene.
3. City in northeastern Greece.

MESSALA Myself have letters of the selfsame tenor.
BRUTUS With what addition?
225 MESSALA That by proscription[4] and bills of outlawry
    Octavius, Antony, and Lepidus
    Have put to death an hundred senators.
BRUTUS Therein our letters do not well agree.
    Mine speak of seventy senators that died
230   By their proscriptions, Cicero being one.
CASSIUS Cicero one?
MESSALA   Ay, Cicero is dead,
    And by that order of proscription.
    [To BRUTUS] Had you your letters from your wife, my lord?
BRUTUS No, Messala.
235 MESSALA Nor nothing in your letters writ of her?
BRUTUS Nothing, Messala.
MESSALA   That methinks is strange.
BRUTUS Why ask you? Hear you aught of her in yours?
MESSALA No, my lord.
BRUTUS Now as you are a Roman, tell me true.
240 MESSALA Then like a Roman bear the truth I tell;
    For certain she is dead, and by strange manner.
BRUTUS Why, farewell, Portia.[5] We must die, Messala.
    With meditating that she must die once,°   *at some time*
    I have the patience to endure it now.
245 MESSALA Even so great men great losses should endure.
CASSIUS I have as much of this in art[6] as you,
    But yet my nature could not bear it so.
BRUTUS Well, to our work alive.[7] What do you think
    Of marching to Philippi presently?°   *at once*
CASSIUS I do not think it good.
BRUTUS   Your reason?
250 CASSIUS   This it is:
    'Tis better that the enemy seek us;
    So shall he waste his means, weary his soldiers,
    Doing himself offence; whilst we, lying still,
    Are full of rest, defence, and nimbleness.
255 BRUTUS Good reasons must of force° give place to better.   *of necessity*
    The people 'twixt Philippi and this ground
    Do stand but in a forced affection,
    For they have grudged us contribution.[8]
    The enemy marching along by them
260   By them shall make a fuller number up,
    Come on refreshed, new added,° and encouraged;   *reinforced*
    From which advantage shall we cut him off,
    If at Philippi we do face him there,
    These people at our back.
CASSIUS   Hear me, good brother.
265 BRUTUS Under your pardon.° You must note beside   *Allow me to continue*
    That we have tried the utmost of our friends;
    Our legions are brim-full, our cause is ripe.
    The enemy increaseth every day;

4. See note to 4.1.17.
5. On the apparent conflict between this passage and lines 199–210, see the Introduction and the Textual Note.
6. I have learned as much of this philosophy.
7. *alive:* of concern to those now living.
8. Money to support the army.

We at the height are ready to decline.
270　There is a tide in the affairs of men
　　　Which, taken at the flood, leads on to fortune;
　　　Omitted,° all the voyage of their life　　　　　　　*Once missed*
　　　Is bound in° shallows and in miseries.　　　　　　*confined to*
　　　On such a full sea are we now afloat,
275　And we must take the current when it serves,
　　　Or lose our ventures.⁹
CASSIUS　　　　　　　　Then, with your will,° go on.　　*as you wish*
　　　We'll along ourselves, and meet them at Philippi.
BRUTUS　The deep of night is crept upon our talk,
　　　And nature must obey necessity,
280　Which we will niggard° with a little rest.　　　　　*stint*
　　　There is no more to say.
CASSIUS　　　　　　　No more. Good night.
　　　Early tomorrow will we rise and hence.°　　　　　*depart*
BRUTUS　Lucius.
　　　　　Enter LUCIUS
　　　　　My gown.°　　　　　[*Exit* LUCIUS]　　*dressing gown*
　　　　　　　　Farewell, good Messala.
　　　Good night, Titinius. Noble, noble, Cassius,
　　　Good night and good repose.
285　CASSIUS　　　　　　　O my dear brother,
　　　This was an ill beginning of the night!
　　　Never come such division 'tween our souls.
　　　Let it not, Brutus.
　　　　　Enter LUCIUS *with the gown*
BRUTUS　　　　　　Everything is well.
CASSIUS　Good night, my lord.
BRUTUS　　　　　　　Good night, good brother.
TITINIUS *and* MESSALA　Good night, Lord Brutus.
290　BRUTUS　　　　　　　　Farewell, every one.
　　　　　　　　Exeunt [CASSIUS, TITINIUS, *and* MESSALA]
　　　Give me the gown.
　　　　　[*He puts on the gown*]
　　　　　　　Where is thy instrument?°　　　(*probably a lute*)
LUCIUS　Here in the tent.
BRUTUS　　　　　　What, thou speak'st drowsily.
　　　Poor knave,° I blame thee not; thou art o'erwatched.¹　*lad*
　　　Call Claudio and some other of my men.
295　I'll have them sleep on cushions in my tent.
LUCIUS　Varrus and Claudio!
　　　　　Enter VARRUS *and* CLAUDIO
VARRUS　　　　　　Calls my lord?
BRUTUS　I pray you, sirs, lie in my tent and sleep.
　　　It may be I shall raise you° by and by　　　　*get you up*
　　　On business to my brother Cassius.
300　VARRUS　So please you, we will stand and watch your pleasure.²
BRUTUS　I will not have it so. Lie down, good sirs.
　　　It may be I shall otherwise bethink me.°　　　*change my mind*
　　　　　[VARRUS *and* CLAUDIO *lie down to sleep*]
　　　Look, Lucius, here's the book I sought for so.

---

9. Investments (in trading voyages).　　　　2. And stay awake to attend to your wishes.
1. You have stayed up too long.

I put it in the pocket of my gown.

305 LUCIUS I was sure your lordship did not give it me.

BRUTUS Bear with me, good boy, I am much forgetful.
Canst thou hold up thy heavy eyes a while,
And touch thy instrument a strain or two?

LUCIUS Ay, my lord, an't° please you.   *if it*

BRUTUS   It does, my boy.

310 I trouble thee too much, but thou art willing.

LUCIUS It is my duty, sir.

BRUTUS I should not urge thy duty past thy might.
I know young bloods° look for a time of rest.   *youthful spirits*

LUCIUS I have slept, my lord, already.

315 BRUTUS It was well done, and thou shalt sleep again.
I will not hold thee long. If I do live,
I will be good to thee.

　　　　　[LUCIUS *plays*] *music and* [*sings*] *a song* [*and so falls
　　　　　asleep*]

This is a sleepy tune. O murd'rous slumber,
Lay'st thou thy leaden mace° upon my boy   *heavy staff of office*

320 That plays thee music?—Gentle knave, good night.
I will not do thee so much wrong to wake thee.
If thou dost nod thou break'st thy instrument;
I'll take it from thee, and, good boy, good night.

　　　　　[*He takes away Lucius' instrument, then opens the book*]

Let me see, let me see, is not the leaf turned down

325 Where I left reading? Here it is, I think.

　　　　　Enter the GHOST *of Caesar*

How ill this taper burns!³ Ha! Who comes here?
I think it is the weakness of mine eyes
That shapes this monstrous apparition.
It comes upon° me. Art thou any thing?   *toward*

330 Art thou some god, some angel, or some devil,
That mak'st my blood cold and my hair to stare?°   *stand on end*
Speak to me what thou art.

GHOST Thy evil spirit, Brutus.

BRUTUS Why com'st thou?

335 GHOST To tell thee thou shalt see me at Philippi.

BRUTUS Well; then I shall see thee again?

GHOST   Ay, at Philippi.

BRUTUS Why, I will see thee at Philippi then.   *Exit* GHOST
Now I have taken heart, thou vanishest.
Ill spirit, I would hold more talk with thee.—

340 Boy, Lucius, Varrus, Claudio, sirs, awake!
Claudio!

LUCIUS   The strings, my lord, are false.°   *out of tune*

BRUTUS He thinks he still is at his instrument.—
Lucius, awake!

LUCIUS My lord.

345 BRUTUS Didst thou dream, Lucius, that thou so cried'st out?

LUCIUS My lord, I do not know that I did cry.

BRUTUS Yes, that thou didst. Didst thou see anything?

LUCIUS Nothing, my lord.

BRUTUS Sleep again, Lucius.—Sirrah Claudio!

---

3. The dimming of a flame was held to indicate a ghost's presence.

[*To* VARRUS]   Fellow,
350   Thou, awake!
VARRUS   My lord.
CLAUDIO   My lord.
BRUTUS   Why did you so cry out, sirs, in your sleep?
BOTH   Did we, my lord?
BRUTUS   Ay. Saw you anything?
VARRUS   No, my lord, I saw nothing.
355   CLAUDIO   Nor I, my lord.
BRUTUS   Go and commend me° to my brother Cassius.   *send my regards*
      Bid him set on his powers betimes before,[4]
      And we will follow.
BOTH   It shall be done, my lord.
                Exeunt [VARRUS *and* CLAUDIO *at one door,* BRUTUS
                            and LUCIUS *at another door*]

                            5.1

                Enter OCTAVIUS, ANTONY, *and their army*
OCTAVIUS   Now, Antony, our hopes are answerèd.
      You said the enemy would not come down,
      But keep the hills and upper regions.
      It proves not so; their battles° are at hand.   *forces*
5   They mean to warn° us at Philippi here,   *challenge*
      Answering before we do demand of them.
ANTONY   Tut, I am in their bosoms,[1] and I know
      Wherefore they do it. They could be content
      To visit other places;° and come down   *To go elsewhere*
10   With fearful bravery,[2] thinking by this face°   *pretense; defiance*
      To fasten in our thoughts that they have courage;
      But 'tis not so.
                Enter a MESSENGER
MESSENGER   Prepare you, generals.
      The enemy comes on in gallant show.
      Their bloody sign° of battle is hung out,   *red flag*
15   And something to° be done immediately.   *is to*
ANTONY   Octavius, lead your battle softly° on   *your army warily*
      Upon the left hand of the even field.
OCTAVIUS   Upon the right hand, I; keep thou the left.
ANTONY   Why do you cross° me in this exigent?°   *thwart / critical moment*
20   OCTAVIUS   I do not cross you,[3] but I will do so.
                [*Drum.* ANTONY *and* OCTAVIUS] *march* [*with their army*].
                Drum [*within*]. *Enter* [*marching*] BRUTUS, CASSIUS, *and*
                their army [*amongst them* TITINIUS, LUCILLIUS, *and* MES-
                SALA]
                [*Octavius' and Antony's army makes a stand*]
BRUTUS   They stand, and would have parley.
CASSIUS   Stand fast, Titinius. We must out° and talk.   *go forward*
                [*Brutus' and Cassius' army makes a stand*]
OCTAVIUS   Mark Antony, shall we give sign of battle?
ANTONY   No, Caesar, we will answer on their charge.[4]

---

4. March off with his army before me.   terrifying display.
5.1 Location: The remainder of the play takes place on   3. March on the right side; dispute with you in the
the battlefield near Philippi.   future.
1. I know their secret thoughts.   4. We will meet them when they attack.
2. With a show of courage that conceals fear; with a

25   Make forth,° the generals would have some words.   *Go forward*
    OCTAVIUS [*to his army*]   Stir not until the signal.
        [ANTONY *and* OCTAVIUS *meet* BRUTUS *and* CASSIUS]
    BRUTUS   Words before blows: is it so, countrymen?
    OCTAVIUS   Not that we love words better, as you do.
    BRUTUS   Good words are better than bad strokes, Octavius.
30   ANTONY   In your° bad strokes, Brutus, you give good words.   *As you deliver*
    Witness the hole you made in Caesar's heart,
    Crying 'Long live, hail Caesar'.
    CASSIUS   Antony,
    The posture° of your blows are yet unknown;   *quality*
    But for your words, they rob the Hybla⁵ bees,
35   And leave them honeyless.
    ANTONY   Not stingless too.
    BRUTUS   O yes, and soundless too,
    For you have stolen their buzzing, Antony,
    And very wisely threat before you sting.
40   ANTONY   Villains, you did not so when your vile daggers
    Hacked one another in the sides of Caesar.
    You showed your teeth like apes,° and fawned like hounds,   *You imitated smiles*
    And bowed like bondmen, kissing Caesar's feet,
    Whilst damnèd Casca, like a cur, behind,
45   Struck Caesar on the neck. O you flatterers!
    CASSIUS   Flatterers? Now, Brutus, thank yourself.
    This tongue had not offended so today
    If Cassius might have ruled.°   *had his way*
    OCTAVIUS   Come, come, the cause.° If arguing make us sweat,   *matter in hand*
50   The proof° of it will turn to redder drops.   *testing*
        [*He draws*]
    Look, I draw a sword against conspirators.
    When think you that the sword goes up again?
    Never till Caesar's three and thirty wounds
    Be well avenged, or till another Caesar⁶
55   Have added slaughter to⁷ the swords of traitors.
    BRUTUS   Caesar, thou canst not die by traitors' hands,
    Unless thou bring'st them with thee.°   *(Unless by your hand)*
    OCTAVIUS   So I hope.
    I was not born to die on Brutus' sword.
    BRUTUS   O, if thou wert the noblest of thy strain,°   *family*
60   Young man, thou couldst not die more honourable.
    CASSIUS   A peevish° schoolboy, worthless of such honour,   *silly*
    Joined with a masquer and a reveller!⁸
    ANTONY   Old Cassius still.
    OCTAVIUS   Come, Antony, away.
    Defiance, traitors, hurl we in your teeth.
65   If you dare fight today, come to the field.
    If not, when you have stomachs.°   *inclination; courage*
        Exeunt OCTAVIUS, ANTONY, *and* [*their*] *army*
    CASSIUS   Why, now blow wind, swell billow, and swim bark.°   *ship*
    The storm is up, and all is on the hazard.°   *at risk*
    BRUTUS   Ho, Lucillius! Hark, a word with you.

---

5. Sicilian town famous for honey.   8. That is, Antony, who was noted for his love of extrav-
6. That is, Octavius Caesar himself.   agant entertainments and banquets.
7. Has increased the slaughter committed by.

LUCILLIUS   My lord.

    [*He*] *stand*[*s*] *forth*° [*and speaks with* BRUTUS]   *comes forward*

CASSIUS   Messala.

MESSALA [*standing forth*]   What says my general?

70 CASSIUS   Messala,

    This is my birthday; as° this very day   *on*

    Was Cassius born. Give me thy hand, Messala.

    Be thou my witness that, against my will,

    As Pompey was, am I compelled to set

75   Upon one battle all our liberties.

    You know that I held Epicurus strong,

    And his opinion.[9] Now I change my mind,

    And partly credit things that do presage.

    Coming from Sardis, on our former ensigns°   *foremost banners*

80   Two mighty eagles fell,° and there they perched,   *alighted*

    Gorging and feeding from our soldiers' hands,

    Who to Philippi here consorted° us.   *accompanied*

    This morning are they fled away and gone,

    And in their steads do ravens, crows, and kites[1]

85   Fly o'er our heads and downward look on us,

    As° we were sickly prey. Their shadows seem   *As if*

    A canopy most fatal,° under which   *ominous*

    Our army lies ready to give° the ghost.   *give up*

MESSALA   Believe not so.

CASSIUS   I but believe it partly,

90   For I am fresh of spirit, and resolved

    To meet all perils very constantly.°   *resolutely*

BRUTUS   Even so, Lucillius.

CASSIUS [*joining* BRUTUS]   Now, most noble Brutus,

    The gods° today stand friendly, that we may,   *May the gods*

    Lovers° in peace, lead on our days to age.   *Close friends*

95   But since the affairs of men rest still° incertain, *always remain*

    Let's reason with° the worst that may befall.   *consider*

    If we do lose this battle, then is this

    The very last time we shall speak together.

    What are you then determinèd to do?

100 BRUTUS   Even by the rule of that philosophy[2]

    By which I did blame Cato[3] for the death

    Which he did give himself—I know not how,

    But I do find it cowardly and vile

    For fear of what might fall° so to prevent°   *happen / anticipate*

105   The time° of life—arming myself with patience *natural limit*

    To stay° the providence of some high powers   *await*

    That govern us below.

CASSIUS   Then if we lose this battle,

    You are contented to be led in triumph[4]

    Thorough° the streets of Rome?   *Through*

110 BRUTUS   No, Cassius, no.

    Think not, thou noble Roman,

    That ever Brutus will go bound to Rome.

---

9. Epicurus, a Greek philosopher, thought the gods
indifferent to human affairs and therefore disbelieved
omens.
1. These are all scavenger birds, considered bad omens.

2. Brutus admired Plato, who rejected suicide.
3. See note to 2.1.294.
4. As a captive in a triumphal procession; see note to
1.1.30.

He bears too great a mind. But this same day
Must end that work the ides of March begun;
115 And whether we shall meet again I know not.
Therefore our everlasting farewell take.
For ever and for ever farewell, Cassius.
If we do meet again, why, we shall smile.
If not, why then, this parting was well made.
120 CASSIUS   For ever and for ever farewell, Brutus.
If we do meet again, we'll smile indeed.
If not, 'tis true this parting was well made.
BRUTUS   Why then, lead on. O that a man might know
The end of this day's business ere it come!
125 But it sufficeth that the day will end,
And then the end is known.—Come, ho, away!   *Exeunt*

5.2

Alarum.° Enter BRUTUS *and* MESSALA   *Offstage call to battle*
BRUTUS   Ride, ride, Messala, ride, and give these bills°   *written orders*
Unto the legions on the other side.°   *(Cassius's wing)*
Loud alarum
Let them set on° at once, for I perceive   *advance*
But cold demeanour° in Octavio's wing,   *lack of fighting spirit*
5 And sudden push gives them the overthrow.
Ride, ride, Messala; let them all come down.
Exeunt [severally]

5.3

Alarums. Enter CASSIUS [*with an ensign,°*] *and* TITINIUS   *a banner*
CASSIUS   O look, Titinius, look: the villains° fly.   *(Cassius's own men)*
Myself have to mine own turned enemy:
This ensign° here of mine was turning back;   *standard-bearer*
I slew the coward, and did take it° from him.   *(the standard)*
5 TITINIUS   O Cassius, Brutus gave the word too early,
Who, having some advantage on Octavius,
Took it too eagerly. His soldiers fell to spoil,°   *looting*
Whilst we by Antony are all enclosed.
Enter PINDARUS
PINDARUS   Fly further off, my lord, fly further off!
10 Mark Antony is in your tents, my lord;
Fly therefore, noble Cassius, fly farre° off.   *farther*
CASSIUS   This hill is far enough. Look, look, Titinius,
Are those my tents where I perceive the fire?
TITINIUS   They are, my lord.
CASSIUS   Titinius, if thou lovest me,
15 Mount thou my horse, and hide thy spurs in him
Till he have brought thee up to yonder troops
And here again, that I may rest assured
Whether yon troops are friend or enemy.
TITINIUS   I will be here again even with° a thought.   *Exit*   *as fast as*
20 CASSIUS   Go, Pindarus, get higher on that hill.
My sight was ever thick.° Regard, Titinius,   *dim*
And tell me what thou not'st about the field.   [*Exit* PINDARUS]
This day I breathèd first. Time is come round,

And where I did begin, there shall I end.
My life is run his compass.°   *its circuit*
    [*Enter* PINDARUS *above*]°   (*on the stage balcony*)
25   Sirrah, what news?
  PINDARUS   O my lord!
  CASSIUS   What news?
  PINDARUS   Titinius is enclosèd round about
    With horsemen, that make to him on the spur.[1]
30   Yet he spurs on. Now they are almost on him.
  Now Titinius. Now some light.° O, he lights too.   *alight*
  He's ta'en.°   *taken*
    Shout [*within*]
  And hark, they shout for joy.
  CASSIUS   Come down; behold no more.
                         [*Exit* PINDARUS]
  O coward that I am, to live so long
35   To see my best friend ta'en before my face!
    Enter PINDARUS [*below*]
  Come hither, sirrah. In Parthia° did I take thee prisoner,   (*modern Iran*)
  And then I swore thee, saving of[2] thy life,
  That whatsoever I did bid thee do
  Thou shouldst attempt it. Come now, keep thine oath.
40   Now be a freeman, and, with this good sword
  That ran through Caesar's bowels, search° this bosom.   *penetrate*
  Stand° not to answer. Here, take thou the hilts,°   *Delay / sword handle*
    [PINDARUS *takes the sword*]
  And when my face is covered, as 'tis now,
  Guide thou the sword.
    [PINDARUS *stabs him*]
                  Caesar, thou art revenged,
45   Even with the sword that killed thee.   [*He dies*]
  PINDARUS   So, I am free, yet would not so have been
  Durst° I have done my will. O Cassius!   *Dared*
  Far from this country Pindarus shall run,
  Where never Roman shall take note of him.   *Exit*
    Enter TITINIUS [*wearing a wreath of victory*°] *and* MES-   (*made of laurel leaves*)
    SALA
50   MESSALA   It is but change,° Titinius, for Octavius   *an even exchange*
  Is overthrown by noble Brutus' power,
  As Cassius' legions are by Antony.
  TITINIUS   These tidings will well comfort Cassius.
  MESSALA   Where did you leave him?
  TITINIUS   All disconsolate,
55   With Pindarus his bondman, on this hill.
  MESSALA   Is not that he that lies upon the ground?
  TITINIUS   He lies not like the living.—O my heart!
  MESSALA   Is not that he?
  TITINIUS   No, this was he, Messala;
  But Cassius is no more. O setting sun,
60   As in thy red rays thou dost sink tonight,
  So in his red blood Cassius' day is set.
  The sun of Rome is set. Our day is gone.

5.3
1. Who approach him at a gallop.   2. I made you swear, when I spared.

Clouds, dews, and dangers come. Our deeds are done.
Mistrust of my success³ hath done this deed.
65 MESSALA Mistrust of good success hath done this deed.
O hateful Error, Melancholy's child,⁴
Why dost thou show to the apt° thoughts of men   *impressionable*
The things that are not? O Error, soon conceived,
Thou never com'st unto a happy birth,
70 But kill'st the mother° that engendered thee.   *(the melancholy person)*
TITINIUS What, Pindarus! Where art thou, Pindarus?
MESSALA Seek him, Titinius, whilst I go to meet
The noble Brutus, thrusting this report
Into his ears. I may say 'thrusting' it,
75 For piercing steel and darts° envenomèd   *spears*
Shall be as welcome to the ears of Brutus
As tidings of this sight.
TITINIUS   Hie you, Messala,
And I will seek for Pindarus the while.   [*Exit* MESSALA]
Why didst thou send me forth, brave Cassius?
80 Did I not meet thy friends, and did not they
Put on my brows this wreath of victory,
And bid me give it thee? Didst thou not hear their shouts?
Alas, thou hast misconstrued everything.
But hold thee, take this garland on thy brow.
85 Thy Brutus bid me give it thee, and I
Will do his bidding. Brutus, come apace,°   *quickly*
And see how I regarded° Caius Cassius.   *esteemed*
By your leave, gods, this is a Roman's part:
Come Cassius' sword, and find Titinius' heart.
                              [*He stabs himself, and*] *dies*
    Alarum. Enter BRUTUS, MESSALA, YOUNG CATO,⁵ STRATO,
        VOLUMNIUS, LUCILLIUS[, LABIO, *and* FLAVIO]
90 BRUTUS Where, where, Messala, doth his body lie?
MESSALA Lo yonder, and Titinius mourning it.
BRUTUS Titinius' face is upward.
CATO   He is slain.
BRUTUS O Julius Caesar, thou art mighty yet.
Thy spirit walks abroad, and turns our swords
In our own proper° entrails.   *our very own*
        Low° *Alarums*   *Soft*
95 CATO   Brave Titinius,
Look whe'er° he have not crowned dead Cassius.   *whether*
BRUTUS Are yet two Romans living such as these?
The last of all the Romans, fare thee well.
It is impossible that ever Rome
100 Should breed thy fellow. Friends, I owe more tears
To this dead man than you shall see me pay.—
I shall find time, Cassius, I shall find time.—
Come, therefore, and to Thasos° send his body.   *an island near Philippi*
His funerals shall not be in our camp,
105 Lest it discomfort° us. Lucillius, come;   *dishearten*
And come, young Cato. Let us to the field.
Labio and Flavio, set our battles° on.   *forces*

---

3. Doubt about the outcome of my mission.   5. The son of Marcus Portius Cato.
4. That is, bred from melancholy thoughts.

'Tis three o'clock, and, Romans, yet ere night
We shall try fortune in a second fight.

Exeunt [with the bodies]

5.4

Alarum. Enter BRUTUS, MESSALA, YOUNG CATO, LUCIL-
LIUS, *and* FLAVIUS

BRUTUS   Yet, countrymen, O yet hold up your heads.

[Exit with MESSALA *and* FLAVIUS*]*

CATO   What bastard° doth not? Who will go with me?   *untrue Roman*
    I will proclaim my name about the field.
    I am the son of Marcus Cato, ho!

5   A foe to tyrants, and my country's friend.
    I am the son of Marcus Cato, ho!

Enter SOLDIERS, *and fight*

LUCILLIUS   And I am Brutus, Marcus Brutus, I,
    Brutus, my country's friend. Know me for Brutus.

*[*SOLDIERS *kill* CATO*]*

    O young and noble Cato, art thou down?

10   Why, now thou diest as bravely as Titinius,
    And mayst be honoured, being Cato's son.

FIRST SOLDIER   Yield, or thou diest.

LUCILLIUS   Only I yield to die.[1]
    There is so much,[2] that thou wilt kill me straight:°   *immediately*
    Kill Brutus, and be honoured in his death.

15 FIRST SOLDIER   We must not.—A noble prisoner.

SECOND SOLDIER   Room, ho! Tell Antony Brutus is ta'en.

Enter ANTONY

FIRST SOLDIER   I'll tell the news. Here comes the general.—
    [To ANTONY*]* Brutus is ta'en, Brutus is ta'en, my lord.

ANTONY   Where is he?

20 LUCILLIUS   Safe, Antony, Brutus is safe enough.
    I dare assure thee that no enemy
    Shall ever take alive the noble Brutus.
    The gods defend him from so great a shame.
    When you do find him, or° alive or dead,   *either*

25   He will be found like Brutus, like himself.°   *true to his noble nature*

ANTONY *[to* FIRST SOLDIER*]*   This is not Brutus, friend, but, I assure you,
    A prize no less in worth. Keep this man safe.
    Give him all kindness. I had rather have
    Such men my friends than enemies.
    [To another SOLDIER*]*   Go on,

30   And see whe'er Brutus be alive or dead,
    And bring us word unto Octavius' tent
    How everything is chanced.°   *has happened*

Exeunt [the SOLDIER *at one door,* ANTONY,
LUCILLIUS *and other* SOLDIERS, *some bearing*
Cato's body, at another door]

5.4
1. I yield only so that I may die.   2. There is enough inducement.

5.5

Enter BRUTUS, DARDANIUS, CLITUS, STRATO, *and*
VOLUMNIUS

BRUTUS Come, poor remains of friends, rest on this rock.
      [*He sits.* STRATO *rests and falls asleep*]
CLITUS Statillius¹ showed the torchlight, but, my lord,
      He came not back. He is or ta'en° or slain.   *either captured*
BRUTUS Sit thee down, Clitus. Slaying is the word:
5   It is a deed in fashion. Hark thee, Clitus.
      [*He whispers*]
CLITUS What I, my lord? No, not for all the world.
BRUTUS Peace, then, no words.
CLITUS   I'll rather kill myself.
      [*He stands apart*]
BRUTUS Hark thee, Dardanius.
      [*He whispers*]
DARDANIUS   Shall I do such a deed?
      [*He joins* CLITUS]
CLITUS O Dardanius!
10   DARDANIUS O Clitus!
CLITUS What ill request did Brutus make to thee?
DARDANIUS To kill him, Clitus. Look, he meditates.
CLITUS Now is that noble vessel full of grief,
      That it runs over even at his eyes.
15   BRUTUS Come hither, good Volumnius. List° a word.   *Listen to*
VOLUMNIUS What says my lord?
BRUTUS   Why this, Volumnius.
      The ghost of Caesar hath appeared to me
      Two several° times by night—at Sardis once,   *different*
      And this last night, here in Philippi fields.
      I know my hour is come.
20   VOLUMNIUS   Not so, my lord.
BRUTUS Nay, I am sure it is, Volumnius.
      Thou seest the world, Volumnius, how it goes.
      Our enemies have beat° us to the pit,²   *driven*
      Low alarums
      It is more worthy to leap in ourselves
25   Than tarry till they push us. Good Volumnius,
      Thou know'st that we two went to school together.
      Even for that, our love of old, I prithee,
      Hold thou my sword hilts whilst I run on it.
VOLUMNIUS That's not an office for a friend, my lord.
      Alarum still
30   CLITUS Fly, fly, my lord! There is no tarrying here.
BRUTUS Farewell to you, and you, and you, Volumnius.—
      Strato, thou hast been all this while asleep.
      [STRATO *wakes*]
      Farewell to thee too, Strato. Countrymen,
      My heart doth joy that yet in all my life
35   I found no man but he was true to me.

5.5
1. A soldier sent ahead with instructions to signal by torchlight if all is well.
2. Animal trap; grave.

I shall have glory by this losing day,
More than Octavius and Mark Antony
By this vile conquest shall attain unto.
So fare you well at once, for Brutus' tongue
40 Hath almost ended his life's history.
Night hangs upon mine eyes. My bones would rest,
That have but laboured³ to attain this hour.
    Alarum. Cry within: 'Fly, fly, fly!'
CLITUS   Fly, my lord, fly!
BRUTUS   Hence; I will follow.
    [*Exeunt* CLITUS, DARDANIUS, *and* VOLUMNIUS]
I prithee, Strato, stay thou by thy lord.
45 Thou art a fellow of a good respect.°   *reputation*
Thy life hath had some smatch° of honour in it.   *relish*
Hold then my sword, and turn away thy face
While I do run upon it. Wilt thou, Strato?
STRATO   Give me your hand first. Fare you well, my lord.
BRUTUS   Farewell, good Strato.
    [STRATO *holds the sword, while* BRUTUS *runs on it*]
50   Caesar, now be still.
I killed not thee with half so good a will.   [*He*] *dies*
    *Alarum. Retreat.*⁴ *Enter* ANTONY, OCTAVIUS, MESSALA,
    LUCILLIUS, *and the army*
OCTAVIUS   What man is that?
MESSALA   My master's man. Strato, where is thy master?
STRATO   Free from the bondage you are in, Messala.
55 The conquerors can but make a fire of him,°   *burn his body*
For Brutus only overcame himself,⁵
And no man else hath honour by his death.
LUCILLIUS   So Brutus should be found. I thank thee, Brutus,
That thou hast proved Lucillius' saying true.
60 OCTAVIUS   All that served Brutus, I will entertain them.°   *take them into service*
    [*To* STRATO] Fellow, wilt thou bestow° thy time with me?   *spend*
STRATO   Ay, if Messala will prefer° me to you.   *recommend*
OCTAVIUS   Do so, good Messala.
MESSALA   How died my master, Strato?
STRATO   I held the sword, and he did run on it.
65 MESSALA   Octavius, then take him to follow° thee,   *serve*
That did the latest° service to my master.   *last*
ANTONY   This was the noblest Roman of them all.
All the conspirators save only he
Did that° they did in envy of great Caesar.   *what*
70 He only in a general honest thought⁶
And common good to all⁷ made one of them.
His life was gentle,° and the elements⁸   *noble*
So mixed in him that nature might stand up
And say to all the world 'This was a man'.
75 OCTAVIUS   According° to his virtue let us use him,   *In accordance with*
With all respect and rites of burial.
Within my tent his bones tonight shall lie,
Most like a soldier, ordered° honourably.   *treated*

---

3. Labored for no other purpose than.
4. Trumpet signal to cease pursuit.
5. For only Brutus conquered Brutus.
6. With a virtuous, principled conviction.

7. And desire for the common good.
8. The four bodily humors, different combinations of which supposedly affected temperament; in the ideal individual, no single humor predominated.

So call the field to rest, and let's away
80 To part° the glories of this happy day.   *share*

Exeunt [with Brutus' body]

Hamlet

"Who's there?" Shakespeare's most famous play begins. The question, turned back on the tragedy itself, has haunted actors, audiences and readers for centuries. *Hamlet* is an enigma. Mountains of feverish speculation have only deepened the interlocking mysteries: Why does Hamlet delay avenging the murder of his father by Claudius, his father's brother? How much guilt does Hamlet's mother, Gertrude, who has since married Claudius, bear in this crime? How trustworthy is the ghost of Hamlet's father, who has returned from the grave to demand that Hamlet avenge his murder? Is vengeance morally justifiable in this play, or is it to be condemned? What exactly *is* the ghost, and where has it come from? Why is the ghost, visible to everyone in the first act, visible only to Hamlet in Act 3? Is Hamlet's madness feigned or true, a strategy masquerading as a reality or a reality masquerading as a strategy? Does Hamlet, who once loved Ophelia, continue to love her in spite of his apparent cruelty? Does Ophelia, crushed by that cruelty and driven mad by Hamlet's murder of her father, Polonius, actually intend to drown herself, or does she die accidentally? What enables Hamlet to pass from thoughts of suicide to faith in God's providence, from "To be, or not to be" to "Let be"? What was Hamlet trying to say before death stopped his speech at the close?

Shakespeare probably wrote *Hamlet* in 1600 (shortly after *Julius Caesar,* to which Polonius seems to allude at 3.2.93), but the precise date of composition is uncertain, and this uncertainty is compounded by the exceptionally complex state of the text. *The Tragedie of Hamlet, Prince of Denmarke* is included in the First Folio of 1623, but most editions of the play since the eighteenth century have incorporated passages that appear only in an earlier text, the Second Quarto, dated 1604 and entitled *The Tragicall Historie of Hamlet, Prince of Denmarke.* In the present edition of the play, based on the Folio text, lines that appear only in the Second Quarto are indented and numbered separately, so that readers will be able to assess the difference between the two versions. (Further information on these texts and on the First or so-called Bad Quarto is given in the Textual Note.) *Hamlet* is a monument of world literature, but it is a monument built on shifting sands.

With a text so fraught with uncertainty, it is tempting to think that our unresolved questions are largely the result of the perplexities that must inevitably come with the passage of time and the vagaries of editors. Yet the play in all its versions seems designed to provoke such perplexities. "What art thou?" Horatio asks the Ghost, and the question, unanswered, is echoed again and again until it seems to touch on everything: "Is it not like the King?" (1.1.57); "Why seems it so particular with thee?" (1.2.75); "What does this mean, my lord?" (1.4.8); "Whither wilt thou lead me?" (1.5.1); "What's Hecuba to him, or he to Hecuba, / That he should weep for her?" (2.2.536–37); "Why wouldst thou be a breeder of sinners?" (3.1.122–23); "What should such fellows as I do crawling between heaven and earth?" (3.1.127–28); "Do you see nothing there?" (3.4.122); "What is it ye would see?" (5.2.306). The dream of getting answers to such questions tantalizes many of the play's characters and drives them to scrutinize one another. But the task is maddeningly difficult. When Hamlet repeatedly asks Guildenstern, one of the school friends whom his uncle has set to spy on him, to play the recorder, Guildenstern protests that he does not know how. "You would play upon me," Hamlet returns, "you would seem to know my stops, you would pluck out the heart of my mystery. . . . do you think I am easier to be played on than a pipe?" (3.2.335–40).

Hamlet at once invites and resists interrogation. He is, more than any theatrical

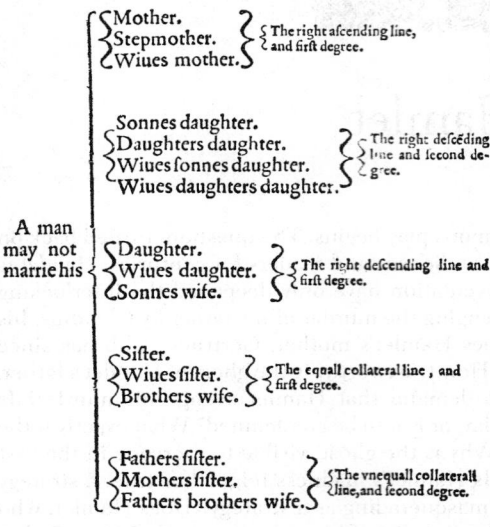

Table of prohibited marriages. From William Clerke, *The Triall of Bastardie* (London, 1594).

character before and perhaps since, a figure constructed around an unseen or secret core. Such a figure in the theater is something of a paradox, since all that exists of any character onstage is what is seen and heard there. But from his place onstage at the center of a courtly world in which he is "the observed of all observers" and hence a person allowed virtually no privacy, Hamlet insists that he has "that within which passeth show" (1.2.85). What is it that he has "within"? In the nineteenth century, following a suggestion by the German poet Johann Wolfgang von Goethe, critics frequently argued that Hamlet has within him the soul of a poet, too sensitive, delicate, and complex to endure the cruel pressures of a coarse world. In the twentieth century, following a suggestion by the founder of psychoanalysis, Sigmund Freud, many critics have speculated that Hamlet has within him an unresolved Oedipus complex, a sexual desire for his mother that prevents him from taking decisive action against the man who has done in reality the thing that Hamlet unconsciously desires to do: kill his father and marry his mother. On occasion, this psychological speculation has been challenged by a political one: Hamlet hides within himself a spirit of political resistance, a subversive challenge to a corrupt, illegitimate regime shored up by lies, spies, and treachery.

These recurrent attempts to pluck out the heart of Hamlet's mystery are a modern continuation of an interpretive activity that goes on throughout the play itself. Attempting to solve the riddle of Hamlet's strange behavior, Polonius speculates that the Prince is desperately lovesick for his daughter, but Claudius concludes, after spying on Hamlet's conversation with Ophelia, that "his affections do not that way tend" (3.1.161). Rosencrantz and Guildenstern propose that Hamlet is suffering from ambition—after all, though Denmark is an elective monarchy, the Prince could have hoped to succeed his father on the throne—but Hamlet vehemently refutes the charge: "O God, I could be bounded in a nutshell and count myself a king of infinite space, were it not that I have bad dreams" (2.2.248–50). Claudius doubts that Hamlet is mad and, even though he never directly articulates this suspicion, seems to fear that the Prince somehow knows of his secret crime. But Hamlet's painful interiority, his melancholy insistence that he has something "within," is already clear from his first appearance, before the Ghost's revelation. Gertrude therefore seems wiser to argue that her son's distemper at least originates in "his father's death and our o'er-hasty marriage" (2.2.57).

As we first encounter him, Hamlet is a young man in deep mourning, which his mother and uncle both urge him to cease. The death of fathers is natural and inevitable, they point out, and while it is customary to grieve, it is unreasonable to persist obstinately in sorrow. Hamlet responds that his grief is not a theatrical performance, a mere costume to be put on and then discarded. When he is alone onstage a few moments later, he discloses, in the first of his famous soliloquies, a near-suicidal despair and a corrosive bitterness centered on the haste with which his mother has remarried. This bitterness is intensified by Hamlet's idealized image of his father and by painful memories of what had seemed to him his parents' perfect mutual love. As he broods on the brief time between his father's death and his mother's remarriage, Hamlet's mind convulsively shortens the interval: "two months," "nay, not so much, not two," "within a month."

At such moments—and there are many in the play—the audience seems to have direct access to the protagonist's tormented inner life. That life appears startlingly raw and unscripted, but the impression is actually the consequence of Shakespeare's sophisticated poetic skills. Hamlet's soliloquies are carefully crafted rhetorical performances. Thus, for example, the celebrated lines that begin "To be, or not to be; that is the question" (3.1.58ff.) have the structure of a formal academic debate on the subject of suicide: prudently considering both sides of the question and rehearsing venerable commonplaces, Hamlet does not once use the words "I" or "me." Yet here and elsewhere his words manage with astonishing vividness to convey the spontaneous rhythms of a mind in motion. Shakespeare had anticipated this achievement in such plays as *Richard II, 1 Henry IV,* and *Julius Caesar:* King Richard, Prince Hal, and Brutus all have intimate moments in which they seem to disclose the troubled faces that are normally hidden behind expressionless social masks. But in its moral complexity, psychological depth, and philosophical power, *Hamlet* seems to mark an epochal shift not only in Shakespeare's own career but in Western drama; it is as if the play were giving birth to a whole new kind of literary subjectivity. This subjectivity—the sense of being inside a character's psyche and following its twists and turns—is to a large degree an effect of language, the product of dramatic poetry and prose of unprecedented intensity. In order to convey a traumatized mind struggling to articulate perceptions of a shattered world, Shakespeare developed a complex syntax and a remarkably expanded diction. Take the moment, for example, in which Hamlet broods about the spectacle of Fortinbras's army marching off to fight to the death for a worthless piece of ground. Hamlet is struck by the absurd waste of lives and wealth, but then his agonized consciousness of his failure to act more quickly to avenge his father's death begins to transform his thinking. The strain in the syntax reflects the strain of a mind queasily in motion:

> Rightly to be great
> Is not to stir without great argument,
> But greatly to find quarrel in a straw
> When honour's at the stake.
> (4.4.9.43–9.46)

So, too, by one scholar's count, Shakespeare introduced over six hundred words in *Hamlet* that he had not used before. Many of these words—"self-slaughter," "unweeded," "fanged," "malefaction," "unpolluted," "compulsive," and so on—do not appear, at least in the form or with the meaning they have here, in any previous English text. The innovative inwardness is not restricted to scenes in which Hamlet is alone onstage, nor is it restricted to the Prince himself; indeed, many of the deepest psychic revelations in the play are conveyed not in moments of isolation but in disturbing exchanges, intimate encounters in which love and poison are intertwined.

These innovations are not called for by the story itself. In *Hamlet,* as in so many of his plays, Shakespeare was recycling narratives long in circulation. The legendary tale of Hamlet (Amleth) was already recounted at length in the late twelfth-century *Danish History* compiled in Latin by Saxo the Grammarian. (The tale was retold in French in François de Belleforest's 1570 collection *Histoires Tragiques.*) In Saxo's version, the unscrupulous Feng ambushes and kills his brother Horwendil and marries Horwendil's wife, Gerutha. Horwendil and Gerutha had a son, Amleth, who undertakes to avenge his father. In doing so, the son suffers no pangs of conscience, since in pre-Christian Denmark revenge was not a violation of the moral or religious law but a filial obligation. And he needs no ghost to inform him of what happened and experiences no sickening uncertainty about his uncle's guilt, since the murder is public knowledge. Amleth's problem is survival: young and surrounded by Feng's henchmen, his every move is carefully watched. In order to avert suspicion and buy time, the cunning avenger pretends to be feebleminded. His strategy works: with the active assistance of his mother, Amleth eventually succeeds in killing his uncle, along with the uncle's followers, and is enthusiastically proclaimed King of Denmark.

This is the rough outline of the story that Shakespeare inherited, along, it seems, with at least one other version about which we know tantalizingly little: by 1589, English audiences had evidently seen a play, now lost, on the theme of Hamlet. Apparently, this play—which scholars call the Ur (original)-*Hamlet*—featured a ghost who cried, "Hamlet, revenge!" On the basis of the barest shreds of contemporary evidence, scholars have constructed elaborate theories about this supposed source play, but there is little agreement among them. Assuming that there was an Elizabethan staging of the story that preceded Shakespeare's, its author remains unknown. Many scholars have assigned it to Thomas Kyd, who wrote *The Spanish Tragedy* (c. 1587), one of the most successful and enduring Elizabethan plays. *The Spanish Tragedy* itself has features that strikingly anticipate Shakespeare's tragedy, including a ghost impatient for revenge, a secret crime, a hero tormented by uncertainty and self-reproach, the strategic feigning of a madness that seems disturbingly close to the real thing, a woman who goes mad from grief and commits suicide, a play within the play, and a final slaughter that wipes out much of the royal family and court, along with the avenger himself. Kyd's play is entirely structured around the problem of revenge—"wild justice," in Francis Bacon's haunting phrase—and gave rise to a whole genre of revenge plays in which *Hamlet* participates.

These plays generally share certain conventional assumptions. First, revenge is an individual response to an intolerable wrong or a public insult. It is an unauthorized, violent action in a world whose institutions seem unable or unwilling to satisfy a craving for justice. Second, since institutional channels are closed and since the criminal is usually either hidden or well protected, revenge almost always follows a devious path toward its violent end. Third, the revenger is in the grip of an inner compulsion: his course of action may be motivated by institutional failure—for example, the mechanisms of justice are in the hands of the criminals themselves—but even if these mechanisms were operating perfectly, they would not allow the psychic satisfactions of revenge. Fourth, revengers generally need their victims to know what is happening and why: satisfaction depends on a moment of declaration and vindication. And fifth, revenge is a universal imperative more powerful than the pious injunctions of any particular belief system, including Christianity itself.

Shakespeare had already produced a sensationally violent version of these conventions in *Titus Andronicus*. In *Hamlet,* he at once reproduces them and calls them into question. The audience knows for certain—from Claudius's tortured attempt to pray in Act 3—that there has been a "foul murder," a fratricide successfully covered over by the story that a serpent stung the sleeping King. But Hamlet does not overhear Claudius's confession and has only the questionable testimony of the Ghost. That testimony is open to question because the nature of the Ghost is open to question. The Ghost speaks as if he were condemned to a term of suffering in the realm Catholics called purgatory:

> Doomed for a certain term to walk the night,
> And for the day confined to fast in fires
> Till the foul crimes done in my days of nature
> Are burnt and purged away.
>
> (1.5.10–13)

But Protestant theologians vehemently denied that purgatory existed and argued that spirits thought to be ghosts were in fact devils sent to lure humans into sinful actions. Hamlet responds at first as if he believes the Ghost to be the authentic spirit of his

The man in prayer. By Mair von Landshut (1499).

father returned from the dead, but he subsequently expresses serious doubts—"The spirit that I have seen / May be the devil" (2.2.575–76)—and in the play's most famous soliloquy he speaks of death as "the undiscovered country from whose bourn / No traveller returns" (3.1.81–82).

The theatrical test Hamlet devises to authenticate the Ghost's accusation—carefully watching the reaction of his uncle to *The Mousetrap*—appears to resolve any doubts: "I'll take the Ghost's word," Hamlet exults, after the King has stormed out in a rage, "for a thousand pound" (3.2.263–64). Yet even here Shakespeare introduces an occasion for uncertainty: after all, the murderer in the play within the play is "one Lucianus, nephew to the King" (3.2.223). Claudius's anger could have arisen from the spectacle of the player-nephew killing his player-uncle and not from the spectacle of his own hidden crime. The effect on the audience is not so much to cast doubt on the Ghost's word as to uncouple Hamlet's inner life once again from the external world, even at the moment that he himself thinks they are at last securely linked.

This uncoupling, this sense of inward thoughts and feelings painfully cut off from the world around him, haunts virtually all of Hamlet's relationships. When he speaks with his old school friends Rosencrantz and Guildenstern, with the courtier Osric, or with Polonius, he is deliberately evasive, but his exchanges with Ophelia are equally oblique and baffling. Even with his intimate friend Horatio, there is some gap across which Hamlet struggles to speak: "There are more things in heaven and earth, Horatio," Hamlet says after his first encounter with the Ghost, "than are dreamt of in our philosophy" (1.5.168–69). (The quarto variant—"in your philosophy"—marks the gap between them still more sharply.) When Hamlet directly confronts his mother with the charge of murder, she reacts with astonishment. The painful words that follow, Hamlet's weird, tormented admonition to his mother to shun her husband's bed, do indeed seem to strike home: "These words like daggers," Gertrude exclaims, "enter in mine ears" (3.4.85). But the Ghost's sudden reappearance, visible this time only to Hamlet (and, of course, to the audience), convinces his mother that her son is mad. "Do you see nothing there?" asks Hamlet, to which his mother, certain that her son is hallucinating, replies steadfastly, "Nothing at all, yet all that is I see" (3.4.122–23).

Ironically, the distance between what Hamlet sees and what those around him see is smallest in the case of Claudius, since both share a knowledge of the secret crime that has poisoned the kingdom, and each maneuvers against the other throughout the play. But their fatal opposition never rises to full, open view until the final violent seconds, nor does Hamlet ever establish unequivocal, unambiguous public confirmation of his uncle's guilt. It would have been easy for Shakespeare to provide such confirmation—for example, in a last speech by the mortally wounded usurper—but he chooses instead to leave what Horatio calls "th' yet unknowing world" (5.2.323) in the dark. Until the explosion of treason and murder, the horrified bystanders know only a court in which the loving Claudius appeals to Hamlet as his "son" and wagers on his skill in fencing. Hamlet begins an explanation—"O I could tell you"—but he is cut short by death. The effect is to extend Hamlet's tragic isolation, his gnawing inward pain, all the way to his final silence.

What would it take to get rid of this pain? The possibility of cleansing, definitive action at once continually tantalizes and eludes the Prince. Such action is embodied in the soldier Fortinbras, but if Hamlet finds some way of easing his mental anguish, it is not through any comparable martial exploit, nor is it through the secret plotting undertaken by Laertes. The fact that both Fortinbras and Laertes are also attempting

Swordsmen. From *Vincentio Saviolo his Practise* (London, 1595).

to avenge the deaths of fathers underscores the shared crisis of dynastic succession but only intensifies the contrast with Hamlet's spiritual journey. The calm to which he gives voice near the play's close—"There's a special providence in the fall of a sparrow. If it be now, 'tis not to come. If it be not to come, it will be now. If it be not now, yet it will come. The readiness is all" (5.2.157–60)—descends upon him *before,* not as a result of, his revenge. The act of revenge itself happens in a flash of rage, without planning, without any self-vindicating declaration by Hamlet to Claudius, and without any public confession of guilt by the usurper. Revenge leaves the Prince not with inner satisfaction but with intense anxiety over his "wounded name."

Standing on a stage littered with corpses, Horatio promises to fulfill Hamlet's dying request to tell his story, but his account of "carnal, bloody, and unnatural acts," though it may be accurate, must be inadequate to the play we have just witnessed. For *Hamlet* situates the need for revenge in a context that goes beyond any crime, however heinous, and that seems resistant to violent solutions. Before the Ghost disclosed his uncle's villainy, Hamlet was suffering from the traumas of mortality: the searing pain of his father's death, a troubled recognition of his mother's sexuality, a sickening awareness of the vulnerability and corruptibility of the flesh. There was a time, the play implies, when Hamlet embodied all the hopes and aspirations of his age and his own vision of human possibility was unbounded—"What a piece of work is a man!"—but that vision has given way to bitter disillusionment: "And yet to me what is this quintessence of dust?" (2.2.293–94, 297–98).

Renaissance psychologists had a word for Hamlet's condition: melancholy, a state of spiritual desolation akin to madness but also to the literary and artistic genius. In Hamlet's melancholy consciousness, human existence has been reduced to dust at its dustiest. Although Claudius's secret crime is a political act that has poisoned the public sphere, the roots of Hamlet's despair seem to lie in a more intractably inward place, a place perhaps less consonant with revenge than with suicide. If there were only the evil usurper to depose, Hamlet might compass a straightforward course of action, but his soul-sickness has receding layers: beyond political corruption, there is the time-serving shallowness of his friends Rosencrantz and Guildenstern, and beyond this there is Ophelia's dismayingly compliant obedience to her father, and beyond this there is his mother's disturbing carnality, and beyond this there is the ongoing, endlessly transformative, morally indifferent cycle of life itself. For Hamlet, the quintessence of dust is not only the cold, inert matter produced by the nauseating triumph of death—the flesh of Alexander the Great metamorphosed into a plug of dirt stopping up a beer barrel—but also living matter pullulating with tenacious, meaningless vitality, produced by the equally nauseating triumph of life. "We fat all creatures else to fat us," Hamlet tells Claudius, "and we fat ourselves for maggots" (4.3.22–23).

In a world pervaded by decay, the process of natural renewal has come to seem grotesque and disgusting:

> 'Tis an unweeded garden
> That grows to seed; things rank and gross in nature
> Possess it merely.
>
> (1.2.135–37)

These lines immediately give way to bitter reflections on his mother's sexual appetite: in Hamlet's diseased consciousness, the spectacle of nature run riot, of uncontrolled breeding and feeding, centers on the body of woman. His bitterness at his mother's remarriage spreads like a stain to include all women, including the woman he had once ardently courted. "Get thee to a nunnery," Hamlet urges Ophelia, as if the only virtuous course of action were renunciation of the flesh. "Why wouldst thou be a breeder of sinners?" (3.1.122–23) Even this desperate advice seems to be undermined by Hamlet's obsessive sense of rampant female sexuality and of his own corruption, since in Elizabethan slang "nunnery" could also be a term for "brothel."

The fragile Ophelia begins to crack under the strain of Hamlet's misogynistic revulsion. Gertrude, who takes the full force of this revulsion, does not lose her wits, but when confronted alone by her son, she fears for her life. Both women sense the violence and despair seething in Hamlet beneath what he calls his "antic disposition" (1.5.173). That disposition, manifested in his disordered dress and in the "wild and whirling words" (1.5.137) that he begins to speak after encountering the Ghost, casts Hamlet in the strange role of jester in the court in which he is the mourning son and the heir apparent. Of all Shakespeare's tragic heroes, he is at once the saddest and the funniest. His blend of sarcasm, riddling, and sly wordplay initially strikes those around him as folly, but this first impression continually gives way to an uneasy awareness of hidden meanings: Claudius, alert to danger, notes that "there's something in his soul / O'er which his melancholy sits on brood" (3.1.163–64). The "something" Claudius senses is in part the murderous design of the revenger, but it is also the philosophical meditation on life and death that haunts Hamlet throughout the play. This meditation reaches a climax in the graveyard, where Hamlet, trading zany quibbles with one of the gravediggers, directly confronts the corruption and decay that had obsessed him ever since his father's death. If there is any release for Hamlet from this obsession—and it is not clear that there is—it comes from an unflinching gaze at a skull, the skull of the jester Yorick, but also, by extension, his father's skull and his own.

Stephen Greenblatt

TEXTUAL NOTE

Hamlet exists in three distinct early texts. The relationship among these texts, along with a mountain of speculation about an earlier theatrical version of the story, now lost, have occupied scholars for decades. These are some of the bare facts. A printer named James Roberts placed an entry in the Stationers' Register on July 26, 1602, for "A booke called the Revenge of Hamlett Prince Denmarke as yt was latelie Acted by the Lord Chamberleyne his servantes." The first known edition (Q1) is a Quarto dated 1603, printed not by Roberts but by Nicholas Ling and John Trundell. This edition, "*The Tragicall Historie of HAMLET Prince of Denmarke By William Shake-speare*," is a text markedly inferior, except for a few details, to the others and, at 2,200 type lines long, markedly shorter. Generally regarded as a highly suspect version of the play, it is often referred to as the "bad Quarto"—often differing markedly even when it overlaps with the other versions. (The Prince's most famous soliloquy, for example, begins "To be or not to be, ay there's the point.") Only two copies of this Quarto, first identified in 1823, are known to exist; one is in the British Library in London, the other in the Huntington Library in San Marino, California.

A second edition (Q2), dated 1604, was printed by James Roberts. The title page advertises itself as "Newly imprinted and enlarged to almost as much againe as it was, according to the true and perfect Coppie." At 3,800 type lines, Q2 makes good on its claim to substantial enlargement, and scholars tend to agree that the printer's shop set the text from the playwright's own handwritten draft, or "foul papers," occasionally supplemented by consultation with Q1. Q2 was reprinted once, without significant alteration, during Shakespeare's lifetime.

If Shakespeare's manuscript is behind Q2, what is the source of the substantially different Q1? The most widely accepted theory, first proposed in 1941 by G. I. Duthie (*The 'Bad' Quarto of Hamlet*), is that Q1 is the product of memorial reconstruction. That is, one or more actors in the play reported what they remembered to a scribe, who prepared copy for the printer. Scholars have conjectured that the principal reporter was the actor who played Marcellus and probably doubled as Valtemand and Lucianus, since the accuracy of the text, as measured by the subsequent editions, greatly improves whenever those characters are onstage. Along with virtually every other aspect of the textual history of *Hamlet*, this appeal to memorial reconstruction is a subject of continuing scholarly debate.

The third major version of the play appeared in 1623 in the First Folio (F), where it is entitled *The Tragedie of Hamlet, Prince of Denmarke*. This edition differs in important ways from Q2: there are a great many small changes, along with some substantial cuts and additions. Most recent editors believe that F was set not from the author's own draft but from a scribal transcript, possibly from a promptbook prepared while Shakespeare was still active in the company. Such a promptbook would normally have been made by annotating a fair copy of the author's foul papers. In other words, the text of *Hamlet* in F is probably closer than Q2 to the play as it was performed in the theater when Shakespeare was alive.

Traditionally, many editors regarded any changes introduced in the passage from the author's own draft to the transcript prepared for the prompter (and thus in the case of *Hamlet* from Q2 to F) as corruptions of the text. Their goal, then, was to remove the corruptions and restore the play to its original state, the text as the author had conceived it. But most if not all of the passages that appear in F and not in Q2 seem unmistakably by Shakespeare himself, while the passages that appear in Q2 and not in F seem equally authentic. Consequently, editors were forced to conjecture that the compositors of Q2 had in 1604 unaccountably omitted the passages that appear in F, while the compositors of the Folio had similarly omitted those passages that only appear in Q2. As early as the eighteenth century, *Hamlet*'s editors routinely conflated Q2 and F, incorporating in a single text as much as possible of both versions of the play.

The Oxford editors broke with this tradition. They observed that since Shakespeare was an active member of his company, the passage from foul papers to promptbook was not necessarily a corruption of his text. Rather, it could as easily have been the occasion for deliberate authorial revision, drawing upon his own second thoughts as well as the suggestions of his trusted professional colleagues. Close study of the differences between Q2 and F suggests the strong possibility of such revision, reflecting a coherent strategy. The Oxford editors hypothesized that Shakespeare himself prepared a fair copy of the foul papers from which Q2 was set, that in making that fair copy he revised the text in a number of ways, and that F derives, at one or possibly more removes, from that fair copy. Therefore, since the Oxford editors concluded that Shakespeare's own revisions are reflected in F, they adopted F as the control text.

In keeping with this decision, the *Oxford Shakespeare* relegated passages from Q2 that do not appear in F to an appendix. This format enables readers to imagine more readily the version of *Hamlet* thought to have been revised for performance during Shakespeare's own lifetime, but it has certain disadvantages, the principal of which is that only a reader extremely familiar with the play can easily imagine exactly how the Q2 passages functioned in what everyone agrees was a version of the play also written by Shakespeare. Moreover, since several of these passages have long been regarded as integral parts of the play, their relegation to an appendix makes it difficult for readers to participate fully in the great cultural conversation about *Hamlet* that has occupied artists, critics, and scholars for generations. Accordingly, the *Norton Shakespeare,* while following the Oxford text, has moved the Q2 passages from the appendix to the body of the play. But in order not to once again produce a conflated text, the Q2 passages are indented, printed in a different typeface, and numbered in such a way as to make clear their provenance. Also, at the points where the Folio and the Q2 passages directly overlap (3.4.70, 3.4.151, and 5.2.154), the overlapping lines are repeated. Those who wish to read the Folio version of *Hamlet* can thus simply skip over the offset Q2 passages, while at the same time it is possible for readers to see clearly the place that the Q2 passages occupy.

The First Quarto (Q1) of *Hamlet,* published in 1603, was evidently cobbled together from the memory of one or more of the actors in a production of Shakespeare's play. The text is notoriously defective, as its version of Hamlet's most famous soliloquy suggests:*

Q1 [cf. 3.1.58ff.]

To be, or not to be; ay, there's the point.
To die, to sleep: is that all? Ay all.
No, to sleep; to dream; ay marry, there it goes.
For in that dream of death, when we awake
And borne before an everlasting judge
From whence no passenger ever returned,
The undiscovered country at whose sight
The happy smile and the accursed damned—
But for this, the joyful hope of this,
Who'd bear the scorns and flattery of the world,
Scorned by the right rich, the rich cursed of the poor,
The widow being oppressed, the orphan wronged,
The taste of hunger or a tyrant's reign,
And thousand more calamities besides,
To grunt and sweat under this weary life,
When that he may his full quietus make
With a bare bodkin? Who would this endure,
But for a hope of something after death,
Which puzzles the brain and doth confound the sense,
Which makes us rather bear those evils we have
Than fly to others that we know not of?
Ay that. O, this conscience makes cowards of us all.—
Lady, in thy orisons be all my sins remembered.

Between the two authoritative versions of the play, the Second Quarto (Q2: 1604) and the Folio (F: 1623), there are many substantial differences, most notably the Q2-only passages that this edition indents and prints in a different typeface. In addition to these major alterations, apparently the consequence of Shakespeare's own revision of his play, there are many other small but suggestive differences between Q2 and F that also seem to reflect shifting authorial intentions. A sampling of these follows:

2.2.212ff.

Q2:
HAMLET You cannot take from me anything that I will not more willingly part withal: except my life, except my life, except my life.

F:
HAMLET You cannot, sir, take from me anything that I will more willingly part withal: except my life, my life.

5.1.166ff.

Q2:
FIRST CLOWN This same skull, sir, was sir Yorick's skull, the King's jester.

F:
FIRST CLOWN This same skull, sir, this same skull, sir, was Yorick's skull, the King's jester.

---

*Modernization from Kathleen O. Irace, ed., *The First Quarto of Hamlet* (New York: Cambridge University Press, 1998).

HAMLET This?
FIRST CLOWN E'en that.
HAMLET Alas, poor Yorick. I knew him, Horatio—a fellow of infinite jest, of most excellent fancy. He hath bore me on his back a thousand times; and now how abhorred in my imagination it is! My gorge rises at it. Here hung those lips that I have kissed I know not how oft. Where be your gibes now, your gambols, your songs, your flashes of merriment that were wont to set the table on a roar? Not one now to mock your own grinning?

HAMLET This?
FIRST CLOWN E'en that.
HAMLET Let me see. Alas, poor Yorick. I knew him, Horatio—a fellow of infinite jest, of most excellent fancy. He hath borne me on his back a thousand times; and how abhorred my imagination is! My gorge rises at it. Here hung those lips that I have kissed I know not how oft. Where be your gibes now, your gambols, your songs, your flashes of merriment that were wont to set the table on a roar? No one now to mock your own jeering?

5.1.196ff.

Q2:
HAMLET Imperious Caesar, dead and turned to clay,
Might stop a hole to keep the wind away.
O, that the earth which kept the world in awe
Should patch a wall t'expel the water's flaw.
But soft, but soft, awhile. Here comes the King.

F:
HAMLET Imperial Caesar, dead and turned to clay,
Might stop a hole to keep the wind away.
O, that the earth which kept the world in awe
Should patch a wall t'expel the winter's flaw.
But soft, but soft; aside. Here comes the King.

5.2.297ff.

Q2:
HAMLET But I do prophecy th'election lights
On Fortinbras. He has my dying voice.
So tell him, with th'occurants, more and less,
Which have solicited. The rest is silence.
HORATIO Now cracks a noble heart.

F:
HAMLET But I do prophecy th'election lights
On Fortinbras. He has mydying voice.
So tell him, with th'occurants, more and less,
Which have solicited. The rest is silence.
O, O, O, O!
HORATIO Now crack a noble heart.

SELECTED BIBLIOGRAPHY

Adelman, Janet. "Man and His Wife Is One Flesh: *Hamlet* and the Confrontation with the Maternal Body." *Suffocating Mothers: Fantasies of Maternal Origin in Shakespeare's Plays, "Hamlet" to "The Tempest."* New York: Routledge, 1992. 11–37. For Shakespeare, fully realized female sexuality (in the form of Gertrude) gives birth not only to fallen and contaminated man, but also to tragedy itself.

Bradley, A. C. *Shakespearean Tragedy: Lectures on "Hamlet," "Othello," "King Lear," "Macbeth."* 1904. 3rd ed. Basingstoke, Eng.: Macmillan, 1992. Hamlet's character—at the center of the tragedy that bears his name—is dominated by a morbid melancholy that weakens his ability to love and impedes his ability to act.

De Grazia, Margreta. *"Hamlet" Without Hamlet.* Cambridge, Mass.: Cambridge University Press, 2007. The elusiveness of Hamlet's inner life is a largely modern critical invention, obscuring the dispossession that Renaissance audiences would have seen as the tragedy's central crisis.

Eliot, T. S. "Hamlet and His Problems." *The Sacred Wood: Essays on Poetry and Criticism*. London: Methuen, 1920. *Hamlet* proves deficient as a work of art: the prince's disproportionate confusion about his condition reflects Shakespeare's own confusion concerning the proper assembly of his diverse literary materials.

Garber, Marjorie. "*Hamlet*: Giving Up the Ghost." *Shakespeare's Ghost Writers: Literature as Uncanny Causality*. New York: Methuen, 1987. 124–76. Simultaneously constituting and dissolving the self, the Ghost haunts the unstable relationship between action and memory; Shakespeare himself has a similarly haunting purchase on the modern imagination.

Greenblatt, Stephen. *Hamlet in Purgatory*. Princeton: Princeton University Press, 2001. *Hamlet* exploits and transforms into theatrical ritual the fears and desires generated by the Catholic cult of purgatory, a cult banned by Tudor Protestantism.

Maguire, Laurie. "'Actions that a man might play': Mourning, Memory, Editing." *Performance Research* 7 (2002): 66–76. Editors of Shakespeare searching for one "true" text of the play should take a hint from Hamlet himself: single viewpoints (whether ontological or editorial) ultimately bow to the daunting yet rich reality of multiplicity.

McGee, Arthur. *The Elizabethan Hamlet*. New Haven: Yale University Press, 1987. Hamlet emerges as a sophisticated manifestation of Vice from the medieval morality-play tradition.

Showalter, Elaine. "Representing Ophelia: Women, Madness, and the Responsibilities of Feminist Criticism." *Shakespeare and the Question of Theory*. Ed. Patricia Parker and Geoffrey Hartman. New York: Methuen, 1985. 77–94. A survey of shifting cultural attitudes toward the representation of Ophelia serves as a barometer of ideological conflict and as a contribution to the evolving discourse of feminist criticism.

Targoff, Ramie. "The Performance of Prayer: Sincerity and Theatricality in Early Modern England." *Representations* 60 (1997): 49–69. Hamlet's misreading of Claudius's prayer is neither accidental nor further evidence of his inability to act; rather, it is symptomatic of early modern Protestant anxieties over how to determine sincerity and hypocrisy.

Wilson, J. Dover. *What Happens in "Hamlet."* 3rd ed. Cambridge, Mass.: Cambridge University Press, 1951. In grappling with the play's dramatic difficulties, especially the problematic "Mouse-trap" scene, we more nearly approach "the secret of Hamlet's character."

See also the creative uses of *Hamlet* in Johann Wolfgang von Goethe's *Wilhelm Meister's Apprenticeship* (1796); James Joyce's *Ulysses* (1922); Tom Stoppard's *Rosencrantz and Guildenstern Are Dead* (1967); Heiner Müller's *Die Hamletmaschine* (1978); and John Updike's *Gertrude and Claudius* (2000).

Films

Hamlet. 1948. Dir. Laurence Olivier. UK. 155 min. In this black-and-white film, Olivier's Hamlet is an oedipal prince, tormented by a desire to kill his father and sleep with his mother (played in the film by an actress only two years older than Olivier).

Gamlet. 1964. Dir. Grigori Kozintsev and Iosif Shapiro. Soviet Union. 148 min. A black-and-white Cold-war *Hamlet*, in Russian, set in a prisonlike Elsinore.

Hamlet. 1990. Dir. Franco Zeffirelli. UK. 130 min. Naturalistic medieval scenes, with Glenn Close's strong Gertrude in an oedipally charged relationship with Mel Gibson's Hamlet.

Hamlet. 1996. Dir. Kenneth Branagh. UK. 242 min. (cut version 150 min.). Opulent, full-text epic rendered in the mirrored halls of a palatial nineteenth-century Austrian court.

Hamlet. 2000. Dir. Michael Almereyda. USA. 112 min. Inspired by director Akira Kurosawa, Almereyda updates the play to modern New York and draws on communications technologies such as videocameras, fax machines, and computers.

The Tragedy of Hamlet,
Prince of Denmark

THE PERSONS OF THE PLAY

GHOST of Hamlet, the late King of Denmark
KING CLAUDIUS, his brother
QUEEN GERTRUDE of Denmark, widow of King Hamlet, now
    wife of Claudius
Prince HAMLET, son of King Hamlet and Queen Gertrude
POLONIUS, a lord
LAERTES, son of Polonius
OPHELIA, daughter of Polonius
REYNALDO, servant of Polonius
HORATIO
ROSENCRANTZ } friends of Prince Hamlet
GUILDENSTERN
FRANCISCO
BARNARDO } soldiers
MARCELLUS
VALTEMAND
CORNELIUS
OSRIC } courtiers
GENTLEMEN
A SAILOR
Two CLOWNS, a gravedigger and his companion
A PRIEST
FORTINBRAS, Prince of Norway
A CAPTAIN in his army
AMBASSADORS from England
PLAYERS, who play the parts of the PROLOGUE, PLAYER KING,
    PLAYER QUEEN, and LUCIANUS, in *The Mousetrap*
Lords, messengers, attendants, guards, soldiers, followers of
    Laertes, sailors

1.1

Enter BARNARDO *and* FRANCISCO, *two sentinels* [*at several*° *doors*]   *separate*

BARNARDO Who's there?
FRANCISCO Nay, answer me.[1] Stand and unfold° yourself.   *identify*
BARNARDO Long live the King!
FRANCISCO   Barnardo?
BARNARDO   He.
FRANCISCO You come most carefully° upon your hour.   *dutifully; cautiously*
5 BARNARDO 'Tis now struck twelve. Get thee to bed, Francisco.
FRANCISCO For this relief much thanks. 'Tis bitter cold,
And I am sick at heart.

1.1 Location: A guard platform at Elsinore Castle, Denmark.

1. Francisco, as sentry on duty, is responsible for challenging anyone who appears.

BARNARDO	Have you had quiet guard?	
FRANCISCO	Not a mouse stirring.	
BARNARDO	Well, good night.	

If you do meet Horatio and Marcellus,
10 The rivals° of my watch, bid them make haste.   *partners*
      Enter HORATIO *and* MARCELLUS

FRANCISCO I think I hear them—Stand! Who's there?

HORATIO   Friends to this ground.°   *country*

MARCELLUS And liegemen° to the Dane.²   *sworn servants*

FRANCISCO   Give° you good night.   *God give*

MARCELLUS O farewell, honest soldier. Who hath relieved you?

FRANCISCO Barnardo has my place. Give you good night. *Exit*

15 MARCELLUS Holla, Barnardo!

BARNARDO Say—what, is Horatio there?

HORATIO A piece of him.

BARNARDO Welcome, Horatio. Welcome, good Marcellus.

MARCELLUS³ What, has this thing appeared again tonight?

20 BARNARDO I have seen nothing.

MARCELLUS Horatio says 'tis but our fantasy,
    And will not let belief take hold of him
    Touching this dreaded sight twice seen of us.
    Therefore I have entreated him along
25 With us to watch the minutes of this night,
    That if again this apparition come
    He may approve° our eyes and speak to it.⁴   *verify the evidence of*

HORATIO Tush, tush, 'twill not appear.

BARNARDO   Sit down a while,
    And let us once again assail your ears,
30 That are so fortified against our story,
    What we two nights have seen.

HORATIO   Well, sit we down,
    And let us hear Barnardo speak of this.

BARNARDO Last night of all,°   *Just last night*
    When yon same star that's westward from the pole°   *polestar*
35 Had made his° course t'illume that part of heaven   *its*
    Where now it burns, Marcellus and myself,
    The bell then beating one—
        Enter the GHOST [*in complete armour, holding a trun-*
        cheon, with his beaver up]⁵

MARCELLUS Peace, break thee off. Look where it comes again.

BARNARDO In the same figure like the King that's dead.

40 MARCELLUS [*to* HORATIO] Thou art a scholar—speak to it, Horatio.

BARNARDO Looks it not like the King?—Mark it, Horatio.

HORATIO Most like. It harrows me with fear and wonder.

BARNARDO It would° be spoke to.   *wishes to*

MARCELLUS   Question it, Horatio.

HORATIO [*to the* GHOST] What art thou that usurp'st⁶ this time of night,
45 Together with that fair and warlike form
    In which the majesty of buried Denmark°   *the buried King*

---

2. King of Denmark.
3. Q2 gives this line to Horatio.
4. A ghost was believed to speak only when spoken to. As a precaution, the experiment will be conducted by an educated man (Horatio) who knows Latin (the language effective for exorcising demonic spirits).

5. Holding a baton (military commander's sign of office), with his visor ("beaver") raised.
6. Wrongfully seize (both the night and the shape of the King). The familiar "thou" would be an inappropriate form of address for a real King.

Did sometimes° march? By heaven, I charge thee speak.   *formerly*

MARCELLUS   It is offended.

BARNARDO   See, it stalks away.

HORATIO [*to the* GHOST]   Stay, speak, speak, I charge thee speak.

Exit GHOST

50   MARCELLUS   'Tis gone, and will not answer.

BARNARDO   How now, Horatio? You tremble and look pale.

Is not this something more than fantasy?

What think you on't?°   *of it*

HORATIO   Before my God, I might not this believe

55   Without the sensible° and true avouch°   *sensory / testimony*

Of mine own eyes.

MARCELLUS   Is it not like the King?

HORATIO   As thou art to thyself.

Such was the very armour he had on

60   When he th'ambitious Norway° combated.   *King of Norway*

So frowned he once when in an angry parley°   *debate*

He smote the sledded Polacks[7] on the ice.

'Tis strange.

MARCELLUS   Thus twice before, and just at this dead hour,

65   With martial stalk hath he gone by our watch.

HORATIO   In what particular thought to work[8] I know not,

But in the gross and scope of my opinion[9]

This bodes some strange eruption° to our state.   *calamity*

MARCELLUS   Good now,° sit down, and tell me, he that knows,   *(an entreaty: Good sir, now)*

70   Why this same strict and most observant watch

So nightly toils the subject of the land,[1]

And why such daily cast° of brazen cannon,   *production*

And foreign mart° for implements of war,   *trade*

Why such impress° of shipwrights, whose sore task   *drafting*

75   Does not divide the Sunday from the week:

What might be toward° that this sweaty haste   *impending*

Doth make the night joint-labourer with the day,

Who is't that can inform me?

HORATIO   That can I—

At least the whisper goes so: our last king,

80   Whose image even but now appeared to us,

Was as you know by Fortinbras of Norway,

Thereto pricked° on by a most emulate° pride,   *spurred / rivalrous*

Dared to the combat; in which our valiant Hamlet—

For so this side of our known world esteemed him—

85   Did slay this Fortinbras, who by a sealed compact[2]

Well ratified by law and heraldry[3]

Did forfeit with his life all those his lands

Which he stood seized on° to the conqueror;   *held possession of*

Against the which a moiety competent°   *an equal portion*

90   Was gagèd° by our King, which had returned[4]   *staked*

To the inheritance° of Fortinbras   *ownership*

Had he been vanquisher, as by the same cov'nant

And carriage of the article designed[5]

---

7. Poles who traveled by sled.
8. *In . . . work:* What precise theory to follow.
9. But in my general opinion.
1. *So . . . land:* Requires the country's subjects to toil every night.
2. A mutually agreed-upon contract ("compact") to

which each set his seal.
3. Properly ratified in accordance with civil law and the law of arms.
4. Which would have gone.
5. And execution of the contract's provision.

His fell to Hamlet. Now sir, young Fortinbras,
95 Of unimprovèd° mettle hot and full,   untested; untrained
Hath in the skirts° of Norway here and there   outlying parts
Sharked up a list[6] of landless[7] resolutes
For food and diet to some enterprise
That hath a stomach in't,[8] which is no other—
100 And it doth well° appear unto our state—   obviously
But to recover of us by strong hand[9]
And terms compulsative° those foresaid lands   forcible
So by his father lost. And this, I take it,
Is the main motive of our preparations,
105 The source of this our watch, and the chief head°   source
Of this post-haste and rummage[1] in the land.[2]
106.1   BARNARDO   *I think it be no other but e'en so.*
                   Well may it sort° that this portentous figure   *be fitting*
                   Comes armèd through our watch so like the king
                   That was and is the question° of these wars.   *cause*
106.5   HORATIO   *A mote° it is to trouble the mind's eye.*   *speck of dust*
                   In the most high and palmy° state of Rome,   *flourishing*
                   A little ere the mightiest Julius fell,
                   The graves stood tenantless, and the sheeted° dead   *shrouded*
                   Did squeak and gibber in the Roman streets
106.10   *At stars with trains of fire,[3] and dews of blood,*
                   Disasters[4] in the sun; and the moist star,[5]
                   Upon whose influence Neptune's empire stands,°   *depends*
                   Was sick almost to doomsday with eclipse.[6]
                   And even the like precurse° of feared events,   *forerunner*
106.15   *As harbingers preceding still° the fates,*   *always*
                   And prologue to the omen° coming on,   *disastrous event*
                   Have heaven and earth together demonstrated
                   Unto our climature° and countrymen.   *region*
                   Enter the GHOST [*as before*]
But soft,° behold—lo where it comes again!   hush
I'll cross[7] it though it blast° me.—Stay, illusion.   wither
                   [*The* GHOST] *spreads his arms*
If thou hast any sound or use of voice,
110 Speak to me.
If there be any good thing to be done
That may to thee do ease and grace to me,
Speak to me.
If thou art privy to thy country's fate
115 Which happily° foreknowing may avoid,   perhaps; fortunately
O speak!
Or if thou hast uphoarded in thy life
Extorted treasure in the womb of earth—

---

6. Gathered together indiscriminately (as a shark takes prey) a band ("list").
7. Q1, Q2 print "lawless," which accurately conveys Horatio's view of these men; F's "landless," however, provides a more specific motive for their enlistment.
8. *For . . . in't:* The men will "feed" his enterprise; they are fed in return for their service. *stomach:* courageous action; challenge to the pride (of both the Prince and his men).
9. By main force (punning on the name "Fortinbras," literally "strong arm").
1. Of this feverish activity and commotion.

2. After this line, Q2 contains the following passage, 106.1–106.18, omitted in F.
3. "At" is emended from Q2's "As," which would require another verb.
4. Malevolent influences (astrological term).
5. The moon, thought to control tides by drawing water out of the sea ("Neptune's empire," line 106.12).
6. Eclipses of sun and moon would accompany Christ's return to earth on Judgment Day (see Revelation 6:12).
7. Confront, cross its path; also, make the sign of the cross (to counter its evil influence).

For which, they say, you spirits oft walk in death—
    The cock crows

120   Speak of it, stay and speak.—Stop it, Marcellus.

MARCELLUS   Shall I strike at it with my partisan?°   *spear-handled blade*

HORATIO   Do, if it will not stand.

BARNARDO   'Tis here.

HORATIO   'Tis here.
                                       Exit GHOST

MARCELLUS   'Tis gone.
  We do it wrong, being so majestical,

125   To offer it the show of violence,
  For it is as the air invulnerable,
  And our vain blows malicious mockery.

BARNARDO   It was about to speak when the cock crew.

HORATIO   And then it started like a guilty thing

130   Upon a fearful summons. I have heard
  The cock, that is the trumpet to the morn,
  Doth with his lofty and shrill-sounding throat
  Awake the god of day,[8] and at his warning,
  Whether in sea or fire, in earth or air,

135   Th'extravagant and erring[9] spirit hies°   *hurries*
  To his confine;° and of the truth herein   *enclosure*
  This present object° made probation.°   *example / proof*

MARCELLUS   It faded on the crowing of the cock.
  Some say that ever 'gainst° that season comes   *always when*

140   Wherein our saviour's birth is celebrated
  The bird of dawning singeth all night long;
  And then, they say, no spirit can walk abroad,
  The nights are wholesome; then no planets strike,[1]
  No fairy takes,° nor witch hath power to charm,   *bewitches*

145   So hallowed and so gracious° is the time.   *full of God's grace*

HORATIO   So have I heard, and do in part believe it.
  But look, the morn in russet mantle clad
  Walks o'er the dew of yon high eastern hill.
  Break we our watch up, and by my advice

150   Let us impart what we have seen tonight
  Unto young Hamlet; for upon my life,
  This spirit, dumb to us, will speak to him.
  Do you consent we shall acquaint him with it,
  As needful in our loves,[2] fitting our duty?

155 MARCELLUS   Let's do't, I pray; and I this morning know
  Where we shall find him most conveniently.   *Exeunt*

1.2

Flourish. Enter CLAUDIUS, *King of Denmark,* GERTRUDE
the Queen, [members of the] Council, [such] as POLON-
IUS, *his son* LAERTES *and [daughter]* OPHELIA, *[Prince]*
HAMLET *[dressed in black], cum aliis*°   *with others*

KING CLAUDIUS   Though yet of Hamlet our[1] dear brother's death
  The memory be green, and that it us befitted

---

8. The sun god, Phoebus Apollo.
9. Wandering out of its boundaries.
1. When they were in certain unfavorable astrological positions, heavenly bodies were thought to exercise a negative influence on earthly events.

2. As necessary because of the love we have for him.
1.2 Location: The castle.
1. My. (Kings often referred to themselves in the plural, the royal "we," although in the lines that follow, Claudius may also be talking about Danes in general.)

To bear our hearts in grief and our whole kingdom
To be contracted in one brow of woe,[2]
5   Yet so far hath discretion fought with nature°   *natural love*
That we with wisest sorrow think on him
Together with remembrance of ourselves.[3]
Therefore our sometime° sister, now our queen,[4]   *former*
Th'imperial jointress° of this warlike state,   *joint possessor*
10   Have we as 'twere with a defeated joy,
With one auspicious and one dropping eye,[5]
With mirth in funeral and with dirge in marriage,
In equal scale weighing delight and dole,°   *sorrow*
Taken to wife. Nor have we herein barred°   *excluded; contradicted*
15   Your better wisdoms, which have freely gone
With this affair along. For all, our thanks.
Now follows that you know° young Fortinbras,   *should be informed that*
Holding a weak supposal° of our worth,   *a poor opinion*
Or thinking by our late dear brother's death
20   Our state to be disjoint° and out of frame,°   *fractured / order*
Co-leagued with the dream of his advantage,[6]
He hath not failed to pester us with message
Importing° the surrender of those lands   *Concerning*
Lost by his father, with all bonds° of law,   *legal procedures*
25   To our most valiant brother. So much for him.
      Enter VALTEMAND *and* CORNELIUS
Now for ourself, and for this time of meeting,
Thus much the business is: we have here writ
To Norway, uncle of young Fortinbras—
Who, impotent and bed-rid, scarcely hears
30   Of this his nephew's purpose—to suppress
His further gait° herein, in that the levies,   *progress*
The lists, and full proportions are all made
Out of his subject;[7] and we here dispatch
You, good Cornelius, and you, Valtemand,
35   For bearers of this greeting to old Norway,
Giving to you no further personal power
To business with the King more than the scope
Of these dilated° articles allow.   *lengthy*
Farewell, and let your haste commend your duty.[8]
40 VALTEMAND   In that and all things will we show our duty.
  KING CLAUDIUS   We doubt it nothing,° heartily farewell.   *not at all*
      Exeunt VALTEMAND *and* CORNELIUS
And now, Laertes, what's the news with you?
You told us of some suit. What is't, Laertes?
You cannot speak of reason to the Dane°   *the Danish King*
45   And lose your voice. What wouldst thou beg, Laertes,

---

2. To be drawn together into a collective expression of
mourning (playing on "the frowning brow of a
mourner").
3. *we . . . ourselves:* "He is not wise that is not wise for
himself" was proverbial.
4. English canon law forbade marriage between former
brother- and sister-in-law (Leviticus 18:16; Book of
Common Prayer); it was on this ground that Henry VIII
annulled his marriage to his brother's widow and mar-
ried Anne Boleyn, Queen Elizabeth's mother. The rela-
tionship between Claudius and Gertrude could thus be
regarded as incestuous. In some early Germanic soci-

eties, however, a new King customarily married the late
King's widow.
5. One eye looking hopefully, the other downcast, or
"dropping" tears.
6. Reinforced by the illusion of his own advantageous
position.
7. *in that . . . subject:* since the moneys, enlistments,
and forces are made up of his (the King of Norway's)
subjects.
8. Let your swift departure (rather than elaborate
speeches) show your loyalty.

That shall not be my offer, not thy asking?[9]
The head is not more native[1] to the heart,
The hand more instrumental to the mouth,
Than is the throne of Denmark to thy father.
What wouldst thou have, Laertes?

50 LAERTES   Dread my° lord,   *My revered*
Your leave° and favour° to return to France,   *permission / approval*
From whence though willingly I came to Denmark
To show my duty in your coronation,
Yet now I must confess, that duty done,
55 My thoughts and wishes bend again towards France
And bow them to your gracious leave and pardon.[2]
KING CLAUDIUS   Have you your father's leave? What says Polonius?
POLONIUS   He hath, my lord, wrung from me my slow leave
By laboursome petition, and at last
60 Upon his will° I sealed my hard° consent.   *desire / reluctant*
I do beseech you give him leave to go.
KING CLAUDIUS   Take thy fair hour,[3] Laertes. Time be thine,
And thy best graces spend it at thy will.[4]
But now, my cousin[5] Hamlet, and my son—
65 HAMLET   A little more than kin and less than kind[6]
KING CLAUDIUS   How is it that the clouds still hang on you?
HAMLET   Not so, my lord, I am too much i'th' sun.[7]
QUEEN GERTRUDE   Good Hamlet, cast thy nightly colour[8] off,
And let thine eye look like a friend on Denmark.[9]
70 Do not for ever with thy vailèd lids°   *downcast eyes*
Seek for thy noble father in the dust.
Thou know'st 'tis common—all that lives must die,
Passing through nature to eternity.
HAMLET   Ay, madam, it is common.[1]
QUEEN GERTRUDE   If it be,
75 Why seems it so particular° with thee?   *personal*
HAMLET   Seems, madam? Nay, it *is*. I know not 'seems'.
'Tis not alone my inky cloak, good-mother,[2]
Nor customary suits of solemn black,
Nor windy suspiration° of forced breath,   *sighs*
80 No, nor the fruitful° river in the eye,   *copious*
Nor the dejected haviour° of the visage,   *expression*
Together with all forms, moods, shows of grief
That can denote me truly. These indeed 'seem',
For they are actions that a man might play;
85 But I have that within which passeth show—
These but the trappings and the suits of woe.

---

9. *What wouldst . . . asking:* What could you ask of me that I would not offer before you asked?
1. Naturally connected; an allusion to the "body politic," headed by the King and having as its heart the King's council.
2. And humbly ask you to grant permission to depart.
3. Opportunity (while you are young).
4. *Time . . . will:* Your time is your own; use it in accordance with your best qualities.
5. Kinsman (outside one's immediate family).
6. "The nearer in kin the less in kindness" was proverbial. Hamlet's riddling comment indicates first that there is little warmth in their new, only nominally closer

relationship. Playing on "kind" in the sense of natural type or offspring, however, he also refers to the incestuousness of the marriage that has produced their unnatural kinship.
7. In the sunshine of Claudius's favor; also, punning on "son."
8. Black mourning garments and melancholic behavior.
9. Both the King of Denmark and the country.
1. Commonplace (?); crude (?).
2. Stepmother. The hyphen, an editorial addition to F's "good Mother," calls attention to the ironic implication of Hamlet's words.

KING CLAUDIUS 'Tis sweet and commendable in your nature, Hamlet,
To give these mourning duties to your father;
But you must know your father lost a father;
90 That father lost, lost his; and the survivor bound
In filial obligation for some term
To do obsequious sorrow.[3] But to persever
In obstinate condolement° is a course   *lamenting*
Of impious stubbornness, 'tis unmanly grief,
95 It shows a will most incorrect° to heaven,   *unsubmissive*
A heart unfortified, a mind impatient,[4]
An understanding simple° and unschooled;   *childish*
For what we know must be, and is as common
As any the most vulgar thing to sense,[5]
100 Why should we in our peevish opposition
Take it to heart? Fie, 'tis a fault to heaven,
A fault against the dead, a fault to nature,
To reason most absurd, whose common theme
Is death of fathers, and who still° hath cried   *always*
105 From the first corpse[6] till he that died today,
'This must be so'. We pray you throw to earth
This unprevailing° woe, and think of us   *unavailing*
As of a father; for let the world take note
You are the most immediate° to our throne,   *next in succession*
110 And with no less nobility° of love   *purity; generosity*
Than that which dearest father bears his son
Do I impart towards you. For your intent
In going back to school in Wittenberg,[7]
It is most retrograde° to our desire,   *contrary*
115 And we beseech you bend you° to remain   *yield; agree*
Here in the cheer and comfort of our eye,
Our chiefest courtier, cousin, and our son.
QUEEN GERTRUDE Let not thy mother lose her prayers, Hamlet.
I pray thee stay with us, go not to Wittenberg.
120 HAMLET I shall in all my best obey you, madam.
KING CLAUDIUS Why, 'tis a loving and a fair reply.
Be as ourself in Denmark. [*To* GERTRUDE] Madam, come.
This gentle and unforced accord of Hamlet
Sits smiling to° my heart; in grace° whereof,   *Pleases / honor*
125 No jocund health that Denmark° drinks today   *the King*
But the great cannon to the clouds shall tell,°   *sound*
And the King's rouse[8] the heavens shall bruit again,°   *loudly echo*
Re-speaking earthly thunder. Come, away.
                    Flourish. Exeunt all but HAMLET
HAMLET O that this too too solid[9] flesh would melt,
130 Thaw, and resolve° itself into a dew,   *dissolve*
Or that the Everlasting had not fixed
His canon° 'gainst self-slaughter! O God, O God,   *law*
How weary, stale, flat, and unprofitable

3. To mourn as befits obsequies, or funeral cere-
monies.
4. A heart not strengthened (against emotion or mis-
fortune), a mind unprepared to suffer.
5. As the most obvious and ordinary thing we perceive
using our senses.
6. That of Abel, the first human to die, murdered by his
brother, Cain.

7. The birthplace of Protestantism, the university of
Luther and Faustus; many Danes studied there.
8. Bout of drinking.
9. F's reading; Q2 has "sallied," a possible spelling of
"sullied." Editors have seen wordplay on "sallied,"
assailed, or, alternatively, salty, tear-soaked (salting was
a method of preserving meat), and "sullied," or con-
taminated, ill used. "Solid" accords best with "melt."

Seem to me all the uses° of this world!   *customs; business*
135 Fie on't, ah fie, fie! 'Tis an unweeded garden
That grows to seed; things rank and gross in nature
Possess it merely.° That it should come to this—   *entirely*
But two months dead—nay, not so much, not two—
So excellent a king, that was to this
140 Hyperion to a satyr,[1] so loving to my mother
That he might not beteem° the winds of heaven   *permit*
Visit her face too roughly! Heaven and earth,
Must I remember? Why, she would hang on him
As if increase of appetite had grown
145 By what it fed on, and yet within a month—
Let me not think on't; frailty, thy name is woman—
A little month, or ere° those shoes were old   *before*
With which she followed my poor father's body,
Like Niobe, all tears,[2] why she, even she—
150 O God, a beast that wants discourse of reason[3]
Would have mourned longer!—married with mine uncle,
My father's brother, but no more like my father
Than I to Hercules; within a month,
Ere yet the salt of most unrighteous tears
155 Had left the flushing of her gallèd° eyes,   *inflamed*
She married. O most wicked speed, to post°   *hurry*
With such dexterity to incestuous sheets!
It is not, nor it cannot come to good.
But break, my heart, for I must hold my tongue.

Enter HORATIO, MARCELLUS, *and* BARNARDO

HORATIO   Hail to your lordship.
160 HAMLET   I am glad to see you well.
Horatio—or I do forget myself.
HORATIO   The same, my lord, and your poor servant ever.
HAMLET   Sir, my good friend; I'll change° that name with you.   *exchange*
And what make you from[4] Wittenberg, Horatio?—
Marcellus.
165 MARCELLUS   My good lord.
HAMLET   I am very glad to see you. [*To* BARNARDO]   Good even, sir.—
But what in faith make you from Wittenberg?
HORATIO   A truant disposition, good my lord.
HAMLET   I would not have your enemy say so,
170 Nor shall you do mine ear that violence
To make it truster° of your own report   *believer*
Against yourself. I know you are no truant.
But what is your affair in Elsinore?
We'll teach you to drink deep ere you depart.
175 HORATIO   My lord, I came to see your father's funeral.
HAMLET   I prithee do not mock me, fellow-student;
I think it was to see my mother's wedding.
HORATIO   Indeed, my lord, it followed hard upon.
HAMLET   Thrift, thrift, Horatio. The funeral baked meats°   *meat pies and pastries*
180 Did coldly° furnish forth the marriage tables.   *when cold*
Would I had met my dearest° foe in heaven   *most hated*

---

1. *So . . . satyr:* That King was to this as the sun god
(Hyperion, a Titan) is to a lustful half goat (mythologi-
cal companion of the wine god, Bacchus).
2. Niobe's fourteen children were killed by Apollo and
Artemis to punish her for boasting about them. She

continued to weep bitterly even after she was turned to
stone.
3. That lacks the faculty of rational thought.
4. What are you doing away from.

Ere I had ever seen that day, Horatio.
My father—methinks I see my father.

HORATIO   O where, my lord?

HAMLET   In my mind's eye, Horatio.

185 HORATIO   I saw him once. A° was a goodly king.   *He*

HAMLET   A was a man. Take him for all in all,
I shall not look upon his like again.

HORATIO   My lord, I think I saw him yesternight.

HAMLET   Saw? Who?

190 HORATIO   My lord, the King your father.

HAMLET   The King my father?

HORATIO   Season° your admiration° for a while   *Moderate / amazement*
With an attent° ear till I may deliver,   *attentive*
Upon the witness of these gentlemen,
This marvel to you.

195 HAMLET   For God's love let me hear!

HORATIO   Two nights together had these gentlemen,
Marcellus and Barnardo, on their watch,
In the dead waste° and middle of the night,   *stillness*
Been thus encountered. A figure like your father,

200 Armed at all points° exactly, cap-à-pie,°   *details / head to foot*
Appears before them, and with solemn march
Goes slow and stately by them. Thrice he walked
By their oppressed and fear-surprisèd eyes
Within his truncheon's⁵ length, whilst they distilled°   *dissolved*

205 Almost to jelly with the act° of fear   *effect*
Stand dumb and speak not to him. This to me
In dreadful secrecy impart they did,
And I with them the third night kept the watch,
Where, as they had delivered, both in time,

210 Form of the thing, each word made true and good,
The apparition comes. I knew your father;
These hands are not more like.⁶

HAMLET   But where was this?

MARCELLUS   My lord, upon the platform where we watched.

HAMLET   Did you not speak to it?

HORATIO   My lord, I did,

215 But answer made it none; yet once methought
It lifted up it° head and did address   *its*
Itself to motion like as it would speak,⁷
But even° then the morning cock crew loud,   *just*
And at the sound it shrunk in haste away
And vanished from our sight.

220 HAMLET   'Tis very strange.

HORATIO   As I do live, my honoured lord, 'tis true,
And we did think it writ down° in our duty   *prescribed*
To let you know of it.

HAMLET   Indeed, indeed, sirs; but this troubles me.—
Hold you the watch tonight?

225 BARNARDO *and* MARCELLUS   We do, my lord.

HAMLET   Armed, say you?

BARNARDO *and* MARCELLUS   Armed, my lord.

---

5. Officer's baton (see stage direction at 1.1.37).
6. These hands are not more like each other than the apparition was like King Hamlet.

7. *address . . . speak:* start to move as though it wished to speak.

HAMLET   From top to toe?

BARNARDO *and* MARCELLUS   My lord, from head to foot.

HAMLET   Then saw you not his
    face.

HORATIO   O yes, my lord, he wore his beaver up.

HAMLET   What° looked he? Frowningly?   *How*

HORATIO   A countenance more
    In sorrow than in anger.

230 HAMLET   Pale or red?

HORATIO   Nay, very pale.

HAMLET   And fixed his eyes upon you?

HORATIO   Most constantly.

HAMLET   I would I had been there.

HORATIO   It would have much amazed you.

235 HAMLET   Very like, very like. Stayed it long?

HORATIO   While one with moderate haste might tell° a hundred.   *count*

BARNARDO *and* MARCELLUS   Longer, longer.

HORATIO   Not when I saw't.

HAMLET   His beard was grizzly,° no?   *gray*

240 HORATIO   It was as I have seen it in his life,
    A sable silvered.[8]

HAMLET   I'll watch tonight. Perchance
    'Twill walk[9] again.

HORATIO   I warrant° you it will.   *guarantee*

HAMLET   If it assume my noble father's person
    I'll speak to it though hell itself should gape

245   And bid me hold my peace. I pray you all,
    If you have hitherto concealed this sight,
    Let it be treble[1] in your silence still,
    And whatsoever else shall hap° tonight,   *occur*
    Give it an understanding but no tongue.

250   I will requite your loves. So fare ye well.
    Upon the platform 'twixt eleven and twelve
    I'll visit you.

ALL THREE   Our duty to your honour.

HAMLET   Your love, as mine to you. Farewell.

                        Exeunt [all but HAMLET]
    My father's spirit in arms! All is not well.

255   I doubt° some foul play. Would the night were come.   *suspect*
    Till then, sit still, my soul. Foul deeds will rise,
    Though all the earth o'erwhelm them, to men's eyes.   *Exit*

1.3

Enter LAERTES *and* OPHELIA, *his sister*

LAERTES   My necessaries are inbarqued.° Farewell.   *aboard ship*
    And, sister, as the winds give benefit
    And convoy is assistant,[1] do not sleep
    But let me hear from you.

OPHELIA   Do you doubt that?

5 LAERTES   For Hamlet and the trifling of his favour,

---

8. Black sprinkled with white.
9. "Wake," F's reading, suggests a return to consciousness.
1. Triply (F's reading); most editors follow Q2's "ten-

able" (that is, able to be held).
1.3 Location: Polonius's apartments in the castle.
1. And means of transport is available.

Hold it a fashion and a toy in blood,
A violet in the youth of primy nature,
Forward[2] not permanent, sweet not lasting,
The perfume and suppliance° of a minute,　　　　　　　　　　*diversion*
No more.

OPHELIA　　No more but so?

10　LAERTES　　　　　　　　　Think it no more.
For nature crescent° does not grow alone　　　　　　　*growing*
In thews° and bulk, but as his temple° waxes　　*muscles / body*
The inward service° of the mind and soul　　　　*responsibility*
Grows wide withal.° Perhaps he loves you now,　　*along with it*
15　And now no soil° nor cautel° doth besmirch　　*stain / deception*
The virtue of his will;° but you must fear,　　*intentions; desires*
His greatness weighed,[3] his will is not his own,
For he himself is subject to his birth.
He may not, as unvalued° persons do,　　　　　　　　　*common*
20　Carve for himself,[4] for on his choice depends
The sanity[5] and health of the whole state;
And therefore must his choice be circumscribed
Unto the voice° and yielding° of that body[6]　　*vote / consent*
Whereof he is the head. Then if he says he loves you,
25　It fits° your wisdom so far to believe it　　　　　　*befits*
As he in his peculiar sect and force[7]
May give his saying deed,[8] which is no further
Than the main° voice of Denmark goes withal.　　　*collective*
Then weigh what loss your honour may sustain
30　If with too credent° ear you list° his songs,　　*trusting / listen to*
Or lose your heart, or your chaste treasure open
To his unmastered° importunity.　　　　　　　　　　*uncontrolled*
Fear it, Ophelia, fear it, my dear sister,
And keep within the rear of your affection,[9]
35　Out of the shot and danger of desire.
The chariest° maid is prodigal enough　　　*most careful; modest*
If she unmask her beauty to the moon.[1]
Virtue itself scapes not calumnious strokes.
The canker galls the infants[2] of the spring
40　Too oft before their buttons be disclosed,°　　*buds are open*
And in the morn and liquid dew of youth
Contagious blastments° are most imminent.　　　　　*blights*
Be wary then; best safety lies in fear;
Youth to itself rebels, though none else near.[3]
45　OPHELIA　I shall th'effect of this good lesson keep
As watchman to my heart; but, good my brother,
Do not, as some ungracious° pastors do,　　　　　　　*ungodly*
Show me the steep and thorny way to heaven
Whilst like a puffed° and reckless libertine　　　　*proud*

---

2. *a toy . . . / Forward:* a passing sexual fancy, a flower of his natural impulses in their prime, early blooming ("forward").
3. When his high rank is considered.
4. Help himself to his own choice of the roast (proverbially, to choose for himself).
5. Well-being, emended from F's "sanctity"; Q2 prints "safety."
6. Body politic; nation.
7. His special rank and power (F). Q2 (and most editors) give "particular act and place," which has been interpreted as "power of action and social position."

8. May act on his promise.
9. And be restrained, despite the forward march of your feelings.
1. *prodigal . . . moon:* risk-taking enough if she exposes herself to the chaste moon. (Upper-class women wore masks to screen their complexions from the sun.) Q2 introduces lines 36, 38, and 39 with quotation marks, identifying these sentences as proverbial or noteworthy.
2. The cankerworm injures the shoots.
3. Young people are naturally rebellious, even without provocation.

50   Himself the primrose path of dalliance treads

       And recks° not his own rede.°   *heeds / advice*

    LAERTES   O fear me not.°   *fear not for me*

        Enter POLONIUS

       I stay too long—but here my father comes.

       A double blessing is a double grace;

       Occasion smiles upon a second leave.[4]

55   POLONIUS   Yet here, Laertes? Aboard, aboard, for shame!

       The wind sits in the shoulder° of your sail,   *at the back*

       And you are stayed° for. There—my blessing with thee,   *waited*

       And these few precepts in thy memory

       See thou character.° Give thy thoughts no tongue,   *inscribe*

60   Nor any unproportioned° thought his act.   *unruly*

       Be thou familiar° but by no means vulgar.[5]   *friendly*

       The friends thou hast, and their adoption tried,°   *their friendship tested*

       Grapple them to thy soul with hoops of steel,

       But do not dull° thy palm with entertainment[6]   *callous*

65   Of each new-hatched unfledged comrade. Beware

       Of entrance to a quarrel, but being in,

       Bear't° that th'opposèd may beware of thee.   *Manage it so*

       Give every man thine ear but few thy voice.

       Take each man's censure,° but reserve thy judgement.   *opinion*

70   Costly thy habit° as thy purse can buy,   *dress*

       But not expressed in fancy;° rich not gaudy;   *bizarre excess*

       For the apparel oft proclaims the man,

       And they in France of the best rank and station

       Are of all most select and generous chief in that.[7]

75   Neither a borrower nor a lender be,

       For loan oft loses both itself and friend,

       And borrowing dulls the edge of husbandry.°   *economy*

       This above all—to thine own self be true,

       And it must follow, as the night the day,

80   Thou canst not then be false to any man.

       Farewell—my blessing season° this in thee.   *mature*

    LAERTES   Most humbly do I take my leave, my lord.

    POLONIUS   The time invites you. Go; your servants tend.°   *wait*

    LAERTES   Farewell, Ophelia, and remember well

       What I have said to you.

85   OPHELIA   'Tis in my memory locked,

       And you yourself shall keep the key of it.

    LAERTES   Farewell.   *Exit*

    POLONIUS   What is't, Ophelia, he hath said to you?

    OPHELIA   So please you, something touching the Lord Hamlet.

90   POLONIUS   Marry,[8] well bethought.

       'Tis told me he hath very oft of late

       Given private time to you, and you yourself

       Have of your audience° been most free and bounteous.   *attention*

       If it be so—as so 'tis put on° me,   *suggested to*

95   And that in way of caution—I must tell you

       You do not understand yourself so clearly

---

4. Favorable circumstances provide us with a second farewell.

5. Indiscriminately social.

6. Greeting (handshaking).

7. Are of all people the most adept at displaying rank in fine appearance.

8. By the Virgin Mary, a mild oath.

As it behoves my daughter and your honour.
What is between you? Give me up the truth.
OPHELIA   He hath, my lord, of late made many tenders°   *offers*
100   Of his affection to me.
POLONIUS   Affection, pooh! You speak like a green girl
Unsifted° in such perilous circumstance.   *Inexperienced*
Do you believe his 'tenders' as you call them?
OPHELIA   I do not know, my lord, what I should think.
105   POLONIUS   Marry, I'll teach you: think yourself a baby
That you have ta'en his tenders for true pay,
Which are not sterling.⁹ Tender° yourself more dearly,   *Value; protect*
Or—not to crack the wind of the poor phrase,
Running it thus¹—you'll tender me a fool.²
110   OPHELIA   My lord, he hath importuned me with love
In honourable fashion—
POLONIUS   Ay, fashion° you may call it. Go to,³ go to.   *conventional flattery*
OPHELIA   And hath given countenance° to his speech, my lord,   *authority*
With all the vows of heaven.
115   POLONIUS   Ay, springes to catch woodcocks.⁴ I do know
When the blood burns how prodigal° the soul   *lavishly*
Lends the tongue vows. These blazes, daughter,
Giving more light than heat, extinct° in both   *extinguished*
Even in their promise as it is a-making,
120   You must not take for fire. From this time, daughter,
Be somewhat scanter of your maiden presence.
Set your entreatments at a higher rate
Than a command to parley.⁵ For Lord Hamlet,
Believe so much in° him, that he is young,   *concerning*
125   And with a larger tether may he walk
Than may be given you. In few,° Ophelia,   *brief*
Do not believe his vows, for they are brokers,°   *go-betweens*
Not of the dye which their investments° show,   *clerical vestments*
But mere imploratators° of unholy suits,   *solicitors*
130   Breathing° like sanctified and pious bawds   *Speaking*
The better to beguile. This is for all—
I would not, in plain terms, from this time forth
Have you so slander° any moment leisure   *disgrace*
As to give words or talk with the Lord Hamlet.
135   Look to't, I charge you. Come your ways.°   *Come along*
OPHELIA   I shall obey, my lord.   *Exeunt*

1.4

Enter [Prince] HAMLET, HORATIO, *and* MARCELLUS
HAMLET   The air bites shrewdly,° it is very cold.   *sharply*
HORATIO   It is a nipping and an eager° air.   *a bitter*
HAMLET   What hour now?
HORATIO   I think it lacks of twelve.
5   MARCELLUS   No, it is struck.
HORATIO   Indeed? I heard it not. Then it draws near the season°   *time*
Wherein the spirit held his wont° to walk.   *was accustomed*

9. Genuine currency.
1. *crack . . . thus*: ruin the phrase with overworking (like a "broken-winded" horse).
2. A multiple pun: make me look foolish; seem yourself a fool; show me a baby (idiomatically, a "fool").
3. That's enough; come, come.
4. (Obvious) traps for proverbially gullible birds.
5. *Set . . . parley*: Do not negotiate a surrender (of your chastity) just because he asks to speak with you.
1.4 Location: The castle's battlements.

A flourish of trumpets, and two pieces [of ordnance]°   cannons
goes off

What does this mean, my lord?

10 HAMLET   The King doth wake tonight and takes his rouse,
Keeps wassail, and the swagg'ring upspring reels,[1]
And as he drains his draughts of Rhenish° down   Rhine wine
The kettle-drum and trumpet thus bray out
The triumph of his pledge.[2]

HORATIO   Is it a custom?

15 HAMLET   Ay, marry is't,
And to my mind, though I am native here
And to the manner° born, it is a custom   custom
More honoured in the breach than the observance.[3]

18.1 *This heavy-headed revel east and west*
Makes us traduced and taxed of other nations.
They clepe° us drunkards, and with swinish phrase   call
Soil our addition;° and indeed it takes   reputation
18.5 *From our achievements, though performed at height,°*   excellently
The pith° and marrow of our attribute.°   heart / attributed glory
So, oft itchances in particular men
That, for some vicious mole of nature[4] in them—
As in their birth,° wherein they are not guilty,   parentage
18.10 *Since nature cannot choose his° origin,*   its
By the o'ergrowth of some complexion,[5]
Oft breaking down the pales° and forts of reason,   fences; boundaries
Or by some habit that too much o'erleavens
The form of plausive manners[6]—that these men,
18.15 *Carrying, I say, the stamp of one defect,*
Being nature's livery or fortune's star,[7]
His virtues else be they as pure as grace,
As infinite as man may undergo,°   sustain
Shall in the general censure° take corruption   the public opinion
18.20 *From that particular fault. The dram of evil[8]*
Doth all the noble substance over-daub[9]
To his own scandal.°   shame

Enter GHOST [*as before*]

HORATIO   Look, my lord, it comes.

20 HAMLET   Angels and ministers of grace defend us!
Be thou a spirit of health or goblin° damned,   demon
Bring with thee airs° from heaven or blasts[1] from hell,   gentle breezes
Be thy intents wicked or charitable,
Thou com'st in such a questionable shape
25 That I will speak to thee. I'll call thee Hamlet,
King, father, royal Dane. O answer me!

---

1. *The King . . . reels*: The King revels and carouses rather than sleeping, has a drinking party ("wassail"), and staggers ("reels") through a wild German dance.
2. His success in draining his cup upon making a toast.
3. Which is more honored in being broken than in being observed. After this line, Q2 has the following passage, 18.1–18.22, omitted in F (possibly in deference to the English Queen, Anne of Denmark).
4. Natural blemish that tends to vice.
5. By the disproportionate amount of one humor (see note to 2.2.310–11), and thus an unbalanced personality.
6. *o'erleavens . . . manners*: changes the whole effect of otherwise pleasing ("plausive") manners for the worse (as

too much yeast ruins a batch of bread).
7. Being a congenital defect (the "livery," or clothing, given by nature) or a blemish caused by fortune (the influence of chance astrological events).
8. Tiny amount (eighth of an ounce) of bad qualities. This is a conjectural emendation of Q2's "eale," although there is no consensus on the correct reading.
9. *Doth . . . over-daub*: Obscures the virtuous essence with adhering dirt. Emended from Q2's "of a doubt," an incomplete thought; "often dout" (extinguish) is another plausible correction.
1. Pestilent gusts.

Let me not burst in ignorance, but tell
Why thy canonized° bones, hearsèd° in death,   *consecrated / coffined*
Have burst their cerements,° why the sepulchre   *grave clothes*
30   Wherein we saw thee quietly enurned°   *entombed*
Hath oped his ponderous and marble jaws
To cast thee up again. What may this mean,
That thou, dead corpse, again in complete steel,°   *armor*
Revisitst thus the glimpses of the moon,[2]
35   Making night hideous, and we fools of nature[3]
So horridly to shake our disposition°   *mental foundations*
With thoughts beyond the reaches of our souls?
Say, why is this? Wherefore? What should we do?
      GHOST *beckons* HAMLET
HORATIO   It beckons you to go away with it
40   As if it some impartment° did desire   *communication*
To you alone.
MARCELLUS [*to* HAMLET]   Look with what courteous action
It wafts° you to a more removèd ground.   *beckons*
But do not go with it.
HORATIO [*to* HAMLET]   No, by no means.
HAMLET   It will not speak. Then will I follow it.
HORATIO   Do not, my lord.
45   HAMLET   Why, what should be the fear?
I do not set my life at a pin's fee,°   *value*
And for my soul, what can it do to that,
Being a thing immortal as itself?
      [GHOST *beckons* HAMLET]
It waves me forth again. I'll follow it.
50   HORATIO   What if it tempt you toward the flood,° my lord,   *sea*
Or to the dreadful summit of the cliff
That beetles o'er° his base into the sea,   *overhangs*
And there assume some other horrible form
Which might deprive your sovereignty of reason
55   And draw you into madness? Think of it.[4]
55.1   *The very place puts toys of desperation,*[5]
      Without more motive,° into every brain   *cause*
      That looks so many fathoms to the sea
      And hears it roar beneath.
      [GHOST *beckons* HAMLET]
HAMLET   It wafts me still. [*To* GHOST] Go on, I'll follow thee.
MARCELLUS   You shall not go, my lord.
HAMLET   Hold off your hand.
HORATIO   Be ruled. You shall not go.
HAMLET   My fate cries out,
And makes each petty artere° in this body   *artery*
60   As hardy as the Nemean lion's[6] nerve.
      [GHOST *beckons* HAMLET]
Still am I called. Unhand me, gentlemen.
By heav'n, I'll make a ghost of him that lets° me.   *hinders*
I say, away! [*To* GHOST] Go on, I'll follow thee.
      Exeunt GHOST *and* HAMLET

---

2. *glimpses of the moon:* (earth lit by) flickering moon-light.
3. Mere mortals (terrified by encounters with the supernatural).

4. After this line, Q2 has the following passage, 55.1–55.4, omitted in F.
5. Imaginings of despair and suicide.
6. A ferocious beast killed by Hercules.

HORATIO   He waxes desperate with imagination.
65 MARCELLUS   Let's follow. 'Tis not fit thus to obey him.
HORATIO   Have after.° To what issue° will this come?   *Go on / end*
MARCELLUS   Something is rotten in the state of Denmark.
HORATIO   Heaven will direct it.
MARCELLUS   Nay, let's follow him.   *Exeunt*

1.5

Enter GHOST, *and* [Prince] HAMLET [following]

HAMLET   Whither wilt thou lead me? Speak. I'll go no further.
GHOST   Mark me.
HAMLET   I will.
GHOST   My hour is almost come
When I to sulph'rous and tormenting flames
Must render up myself.
HAMLET   Alas, poor ghost!
5 GHOST   Pity me not, but lend thy serious hearing
To what I shall unfold.
HAMLET   Speak, I am bound to hear.
GHOST   So art thou to revenge when thou shalt hear.
HAMLET   What?
GHOST   I am thy father's spirit,
10 Doomed for a certain term to walk the night,
And for the day confined to fast° in fires   *do penance*
Till the foul crimes done in my days of nature°   *my natural life*
Are burnt and purged away. But that I am forbid
To tell the secrets of my prison-house
15 I could a tale unfold whose lightest word
Would harrow up thy soul, freeze thy young blood,
Make thy two eyes like stars start from their spheres,
Thy knotty and combinèd locks to part,
And each particular hair to stand on end
20 Like quills upon the fretful porcupine.
But this eternal blazon[1] must not be
To ears of flesh and blood. List,° Hamlet, list, O list!   *Listen*
If thou didst ever thy dear father love—
HAMLET   O God!
25 GHOST   Revenge his foul and most unnatural murder.
HAMLET   Murder?
GHOST   Murder most foul, as in the best it is,
But this most foul, strange, and unnatural.
HAMLET   Haste, haste me to know it, that with wings as swift
30 As meditation or the thoughts of love
May sweep to my revenge.
GHOST   I find thee apt,
And duller shouldst thou be than the fat° weed   *gross*
That rots itself[2] in ease on Lethe wharf[3]
Wouldst thou not stir in this. Now, Hamlet, hear.
35 'Tis given out that, sleeping in mine orchard,
A serpent stung me. So the whole ear of Denmark
Is by a forgèd process° of my death   *a fabricated account*

1.5 Location: Scene continues.
1. Catalogue or display of the afterlife's mysteries.
2. Decays under its own excessive growth (F). Q1, Q2

print "roots itself," another possible reading.
3. In classical mythology, Lethe was the river of forget-fulness in Hades.

Rankly abused.° But know, thou noble youth,   *deceived*
The serpent that did sting thy father's life
40   Now wears his crown.
     HAMLET   O my prophetic soul! Mine uncle?
     GHOST   Ay, that incestuous, that adulterate° beast,   *adulterous*
     With witchcraft of his wit, with traitorous gifts°—   *abilities; presents*
     O wicked wit and gifts, that have the power
45   So to seduce!—won to his shameful lust
     The will of my most seeming-virtuous queen.
     O Hamlet, what a falling off was there!—
     From me, whose love was of that dignity
     That it went hand-in-hand even with the vow
50   I made to her in marriage, and to decline
     Upon a wretch whose natural gifts were poor
     To° those of mine.   *Compared to*
     But virtue, as it never will be moved,
     Though lewdness court it in a shape of heaven,
55   So lust, though to a radiant angel linked,
     Will sate itself[4] in a celestial bed,
     And prey on garbage.
     But soft, methinks I scent the morning's air.
     Brief let me be. Sleeping within mine orchard,
60   My custom always in the afternoon,
     Upon my secure hour thy uncle stole
     With juice of cursèd hebenon[5] in a vial,
     And in the porches° of mine ears did pour   *entranceways*
     The leperous distilment,[6] whose effect
65   Holds such an enmity with blood of man
     That swift as quicksilver it courses through
     The natural gates and alleys of the body,
     And with a sudden vigour it doth posset°   *curdle*
     And curd, like eager° droppings into milk,   *acid (like wine)*
70   The thin and wholesome blood. So did it mine;
     And a most instant tetter° barked about,[7]   *scaly rash*
     Most lazar-like,° with vile and loathsome crust,   *leperlike*
     All my smooth body.
     Thus was I, sleeping, by a brother's hand
75   Of life, of crown, of queen at once dispatched,°   *deprived*
     Cut off even in the blossoms of my sin,[8]
     Unhouseled, dis-appointed, unaneled,[9]
     No reck'ning made, but sent to my account
     With all my imperfections on my head.[1]
80   O horrible, O horrible, most horrible!
     If thou hast nature° in thee, bear it not.   *natural feeling*
     Let not the royal bed of Denmark be
     A couch for luxury° and damnèd incest.   *lechery*
     But howsoever thou pursuest this act,
85   Taint not thy mind,[2] nor let thy soul contrive
     Against thy mother aught.° Leave her to heaven,   *any punishment*

4. Will become satiated (and unable to find further plea-
sure).
5. A poison, possibly henbane.
6. Distillation causing skin to become scaly (as in lep-
rosy, a disease familiar in Elizabethan England).
7. Covered the body like bark.
8. Cut off when my sins were full-blown, flourishing.

9. Without the sacrament of the Eucharist, without
death-bed confession and absolution, and without
extreme unction, the ritual anointing of those who are
close to death.
1. No . . . head: Without having made restitution for my
sins, but sent to the Last Judgment liable for all my faults.
2. Do not let yourself be corrupted.

And to those thorns that in her bosom lodge
To prick and sting her. Fare thee well at once.
The glow-worm shows the matin° to be near,   *morning*
90 And gins° to pale his uneffectual fire.   *begins*
Adieu, adieu, Hamlet. Remember me.   *Exit*
HAMLET O all you host of heaven! O earth! What else?
And shall I couple° hell? O fie! Hold, hold, my heart,   *add*
And you, my sinews, grow not instant old,
95 But bear me stiffly up. Remember thee?
Ay, thou poor ghost, while memory holds a seat
In this distracted globe.³ Remember thee?
Yea, from the table° of my memory   *tablet; book*
I'll wipe away all trivial fond° records,   *foolish*
100 All saws of books, all forms, all pressures past,⁴
That youth and observation copied there,
And thy commandment all alone shall live
Within the book and volume of my brain
Unmixed with baser matter. Yes, yes, by heaven.
105 O most pernicious woman!
O villain, villain, smiling, damnèd villain!
My tables,⁵
My tables—meet it is I set it down
That one may smile and smile and be a villain.
110 At least I'm sure it may be so in Denmark.
        [*He writes*]
So, uncle, there you are. Now to my word:°   *watchword; motto*
It is 'Adieu, adieu, remember me'.
I have sworn't.
HORATIO *and* MARCELLUS [*within*] My lord, my lord.
        Enter HORATIO *and* MARCELLUS
115 MARCELLUS [*calling*] Lord Hamlet!
HORATIO Heaven secure him.
HAMLET So be it.
HORATIO [*calling*] Illo, ho, ho, my lord.
HAMLET Hillo, ho, ho, boy; come, bird, come.⁶
120 MARCELLUS How is't, my noble lord?
HORATIO [*to* HAMLET] What news, my lord?
HAMLET O wonderful!
HORATIO Good my lord, tell it.
HAMLET   No, you'll reveal it.
HORATIO Not I, my lord, by heaven.
MARCELLUS   Nor I, my lord.
125 HAMLET How say you then, would heart of man once think it?
But you'll be secret?
HORATIO *and* MARCELLUS Ay, by heav'n, my lord.
HAMLET There's ne'er a villain dwelling in all Denmark
But he's an arrant° knave.   *a downright*
HORATIO There needs no ghost, my lord, come from the grave
To tell us this.
130 HAMLET   Why, right, you are i'th' right,
And so without more circumstance° at all   *elaborate speech*

---

3. Confused head; disordered world; often also taken as
a reference to the Globe Theatre and the audience.
4. All adages from books, all images or customs, all past
impressions.

5. Scholars and others might carry two writing tables
hinged together, as a notebook.
6. Hamlet parodies a falconer's call.

I hold it fit that we shake hands and part,
You as your business and desires shall point you—
For every man has business and desire,
135 Such as it is—and for mine own poor part,
Look you, I'll go pray.

HORATIO   These are but wild and whirling words, my lord.

HAMLET   I'm sorry they offend you, heartily,
Yes, faith, heartily.

HORATIO   There's no offence, my lord.

140 HAMLET   Yes, by Saint Patrick,[7] but there is, Horatio,
And much offence, too. Touching this vision here,
It is an honest° ghost, that let me tell you.   *a reliable; a genuine*
For your desire to know what is between us,
O'ermaster't as you may. And now, good friends,
145 As you are friends, scholars, and soldiers,
Give me one poor request.

HORATIO   What is't, my lord? We will.

HAMLET   Never make known what you have seen tonight.

HORATIO *and* MARCELLUS   My lord, we will not.

HAMLET   Nay, but swear't.

HORATIO   In faith, my lord, not I.[8]

MARCELLUS   Nor I, my lord, in faith.

HAMLET   Upon my sword.[9]

150 MARCELLUS   We have sworn, my lord, already.

HAMLET   Indeed, upon my sword, indeed.
        GHOST *cries under the stage*

GHOST   Swear.

HAMLET   Ah ha, boy, sayst thou so? Art thou there, truepenny?°—   *trusty fellow*
Come on. You hear this fellow in the cellarage.
Consent to swear.

HORATIO   Propose the oath, my lord.

155 HAMLET   Never to speak of this that you have seen,
Swear by my sword.

GHOST [*under the stage*]   Swear.
        [*They swear*]

HAMLET   *Hic et ubique?*[1] Then we'll shift our ground.—
Come hither, gentlemen,
160 And lay your hands again upon my sword.
Never to speak of this that you have heard,
Swear by my sword.

GHOST [*under the stage*]   Swear.
        [*They swear*]

HAMLET   Well said, old mole. Canst work i'th' earth so fast?
165 A worthy pioneer.[2]—Once more remove,° good friends.   *move*

HORATIO   O day and night, but this is wondrous strange!

HAMLET   And therefore as a stranger give it welcome.[3]
There are more things in heaven and earth, Horatio,
Than are dreamt of in our philosophy.[4] But come,

---

7. Perhaps because Patrick was thought to be keeper of purgatory.
8. I will indeed not reveal it.
9. Swearing on a sword was a fairly common practice because the hilt and blade form a cross.
1. Here and everywhere (Latin).

2. Army trench digger.
3. As if it had a guest's right to courteous hospitality.
4. Human speculative knowledge. Q2 and most editors print "your philosophy"; F's "our" shows Hamlet himself still trying to reconcile his own understanding with the supernatural revelations.

170 Here as before, never, so help you mercy,
How strange or odd soe'er I bear myself—
As I perchance hereafter shall think meet
To put an antic disposition on⁵—
That you at such time seeing me never shall,
175 With arms encumbered° thus, or this headshake,   *folded*
Or by pronouncing of some doubtful° phrase   *ambiguous*
As 'Well, we know' or 'We could an if° we would',   *an if=if*
Or 'If we list° to speak', or 'There be, an if they might',⁶   *liked*
Or such ambiguous giving out, to note
180 That you know aught° of me—this not to do,   *anything*
So grace and mercy at your most need help you, swear.
GHOST [*under the stage*]   Swear.
        [*They swear*]
HAMLET   Rest, rest, perturbèd spirit.—So, gentlemen,
With all my love I do commend me to you,
185 And what so poor a man as Hamlet is
May do t'express his love and friending° to you,   *friendship*
God willing, shall not lack.° Let us go in together,   *be left undone*
And still° your fingers on your lips, I pray.   *always*
The time is out of joint.° O cursèd spite   *dislocated; disordered*
190 That ever I was born to set it right!
Nay, come,⁷ let's go together.   *Exeunt*

2.1

Enter old POLONIUS *with his man* REYNALDO

POLONIUS   Give him this money and these notes, Reynaldo.
REYNALDO   I will, my lord.
POLONIUS   You shall do marv'lous wisely, good Reynaldo,
Before you visit him to make enquire
Of his behaviour.
5 REYNALDO   My lord, I did intend it.
POLONIUS   Marry, well said, very well said. Look you, sir,
Enquire me° first what Danskers° are in Paris,   *for me / Danes*
And how, and who, what means,° and where they keep,°   *wealth; income / lodge*
What company, at what expense; and finding
10 By this encompassment and drift of question¹
That they do know my son, come you more nearer
Than your particular demands will touch it.²
Take you,° as 'twere, some distant knowledge of him,   *Pretend*
As thus: 'I know his father and his friends,
15 And in part him'—do you mark this, Reynaldo?
REYNALDO   Ay, very well, my lord.
POLONIUS   'And in part him, but', you may say, 'not well,
But if't be he I mean, he's very wild,
Addicted so and so'; and there put on him°   *attribute to him*
20 What forgeries° you please—marry, none so rank³   *made-up tales*
As may dishonour him, take heed of that—
But, sir, such wanton,° wild, and usual slips   *unrestrained*

---

5. To assume the behavior of a madman.
6. There are those who would speak if they were allowed.
7. The others are politely waiting for Hamlet, the Prince, to lead the way; he insists on informality.
2.1 Location: Polonius's apartments in the castle.

1. By this roundabout and indirect way of inquiry.
2. *come . . . it*: you will come closer to the truth than by direct questions.
3. Excessive; foul.

As are companions noted and most known
To youth and liberty.

25 REYNALDO   As gaming, my lord?
POLONIUS   Ay, or drinking, fencing, swearing,
Quarrelling, drabbing°—you may go so far.   *whoring*
REYNALDO   My lord, that would dishonour him.
POLONIUS   Faith, no, as you may season° it in the charge.   *mitigate*
30 You must not put another scandal on him,
That he is open° to incontinency.°   *inclined / sexual excess*
That's not my meaning—but breathe his faults so quaintly
That they may seem the taints of liberty,[4]
The flash and outbreak of a fiery mind,
35 A savageness in unreclaimèd° blood,   *unchecked*
Of general assault.[5]
REYNALDO   But, my good lord—
POLONIUS   Wherefore should you do this?
REYNALDO   Ay, my lord.
I would know that.
POLONIUS   Marry, sir, here's my drift,
And I believe it is a fetch of warrant:[6]
40 You laying these slight sullies on my son,
As 'twere a thing a little soiled i'th' working,[7]
Mark you, your party° in converse, him you would sound,°   *partner / sound out*
Having° ever seen in the prenominate crimes[8]   *If he has*
The youth you breathe of guilty, be assured
45 He closes° with you in this consequence:[9]   *confides*
'Good sir', or so, or 'friend', or 'gentleman',
According to the phrase° and the addition[1]   *expression*
Of man and country.
REYNALDO   Very good, my lord.
POLONIUS   And then, sir, does a° this—a does—   *he*
50 what was I about to say? By the mass, I was about to say some-
thing. Where did I leave?
REYNALDO   At 'closes in the consequence', at 'friend,
Or so', and 'gentleman'.
POLONIUS   At 'closes in the consequence'—ay, marry,
55 He closes with you thus: 'I know the gentleman,
I saw him yesterday'—or t'other day,
Or then, or then—'with such and such, and, as you say,
There was a° gaming, there o'ertook in 's rouse,   *he*
There falling out° at tennis', or perchance   *quarreling*
60 'I saw him enter such a house of sale',
Videlicet,° a brothel, or so forth. See you now,   *That is to say*
Your bait of falsehood takes this carp of truth;
And thus do we of wisdom and of reach°   *wide understanding*
With windlasses and with assays of bias[2]
65 By indirections find directions° out.   *real tendencies*
So, by my former° lecture and advice,   *preceding*
Shall you my son. You have me,° have you not?   *my meaning*

4. Faults resulting from freedom of action.
5. Which afflicts all young men.
6. *fetch of warrant:* justifiable trick (F). Q2 has "fetch of wit" (clever scheme).
7. Stained by education in the ways of the world, "shop soiled."
8. Aforesaid faults.
9. To the following effect.
1. Title of address.
2. And with indirect tests, like the curved line, or "bias," that a weighted bowling ball describes. *windlasses:* roundabout paths (a hunter's circuit to intercept game).

REYNALDO   My lord, I have.

POLONIUS   God b'wi' ye. Fare ye well.

70   REYNALDO   Good my lord.

POLONIUS   Observe his inclination in° yourself.   *for*

REYNALDO   I shall, my lord.

POLONIUS   And let him ply° his music.   *work at*

REYNALDO   Well, my lord.

      Enter OPHELIA

POLONIUS   Farewell.   *Exit* REYNALDO

75   How now, Ophelia, what's the matter?

OPHELIA   Alas, my lord, I have been so affrighted.

POLONIUS   With what, i'th' name of God?

OPHELIA   My lord, as I was sewing in my chamber,

    Lord Hamlet, with his doublet all unbraced,°   *jacket all unfastened*

80   No hat upon his head, his stockings fouled,

    Ungartered, and down-gyvèd to his ankle,[3]

    Pale as his shirt, his knees knocking each other,

    And with a look so piteous in purport

    As if he had been loosèd out of hell

85   To speak of horrors, he comes before me.

POLONIUS   Mad for thy love?

OPHELIA   My lord, I do not know,

    But truly I do fear it.

POLONIUS   What said he?

OPHELIA   He took me by the wrist and held me hard,

    Then goes he to the length of all his arm,

90   And with his other hand thus o'er his brow

    He falls to such perusal of my face

    As a° would draw it. Long stayed he so.   *As if he*

    At last, a little shaking of mine arm,

    And thrice his head thus waving up and down,

95   He raised a sigh so piteous and profound

    That it did seem to shatter all his bulk

    And end his being. That done, he lets me go,

    And, with his head over his shoulder turned,

    He seemed to find his way without his eyes,

100   For out o' doors he went without their help,

    And to the last bended their light[4] on me.

POLONIUS   Come, go with me. I will go seek the King.

    This is the very ecstasy° of love,   *insanity*

    Whose violent property fordoes° itself   *nature destroys*

105   And leads the will to desperate undertakings

    As oft as any passion under heaven

    That does afflict our natures. I am sorry—

    What, have you given him any hard words of late?

OPHELIA   No, my good lord, but as you did command

110   I did repel his letters and denied

    His access to me.

POLONIUS   That hath made him mad.

    I am sorry that with better speed and judgement

    I had not quoted° him. I feared he did but trifle   *observed*

---

3. Fallen round his ankles, like a prisoner's fetters, or "gyves."

4. Sight was thought to result from both sending light out and taking it in through the eyes.

And meant to wreck thee.[5] But beshrew my jealousy![°]   *curse my suspicion*
115 By heaven, it is as proper to our age
To cast beyond ourselves[6] in our opinions
As it is common for the younger sort
To lack discretion. Come, go we to the King.
This must be known, which, being kept close, might move
120 More grief to hide than hate to utter love.[7]   *Exeunt*

2.2

Flourish. Enter KING [CLAUDIUS] *and* QUEEN [GER-
TRUDE], ROSENCRANTZ *and* GUILDENSTERN,[1] *cum aliis*

KING CLAUDIUS Welcome, dear Rosencrantz and Guildenstern.
Moreover° that we much did long to see you,   *Beyond the fact*
The need we have to use you did provoke
Our hasty sending.° Something have you heard   *summons*
5 Of Hamlet's transformation—so I call it,
Since not th'exterior nor the inward man
Resembles that° it was. What it should be,   *what*
More than his father's death, that thus hath put him
So much from th'understanding of himself,
10 I cannot deem of.[2] I entreat you both
That, being of so young days[3] brought up with him,
And since so neighboured° to his youth and humour,°   *familiar / temperament*
That you vouchsafe your rest[4] here in our court
Some little time, so by your companies
15 To draw him on to pleasures, and to gather,
So much as from occasions° you may glean,   *opportunities*
Whether aught to us unknown afflicts him thus
That, opened,° lies within our remedy.   *if disclosed*
QUEEN GERTRUDE Good gentlemen, he hath much talked of you,
20 And sure I am two men there is not living
To whom he more adheres.[5] If it will please you
To show us so much gentry° and good will   *courtesy*
As to expend your time with us a while
For the supply and profit of our hope,[6]
25 Your visitation shall receive such thanks
As fits a king's remembrance.
ROSENCRANTZ   Both your majesties
Might, by the sovereign power you have of° us,   *over*
Put your dread° pleasures more into command   *reverend*
Than to entreaty.
GUILDENSTERN   But we both obey,
30 And here give up ourselves in the full bent[7]
To lay our service freely at your feet
To be commanded.
KING CLAUDIUS Thanks, Rosencrantz and gentle Guildenstern.

---

5. To ruin you through seduction.
6. *as proper . . . ourselves:* as natural to us old men to go too far and (like hunting dogs) lose the scent, thus erring out of caution.
7. *which . . . love:* we may incur hatred by revealing (Hamlet's) love, but to conceal it may cause greater suffering. *close:* secret.
2.2 Location: A stateroom in the castle.
1. Historical figures with these names are mentioned

in an ambassador's report to Queen Elizabeth sent from Elsinore in 1588.
2. Judge (F). Q2 prints "dream."
3. From such an early age.
4. That you agree to stay.
5. To whom he is more attached.
6. *For . . . hope:* To provide support for and furtherance of our hope.
7. To the fullest extent (like an archer's bow, fully drawn).

QUEEN GERTRUDE Thanks, Guildenstern and gentle Rosencrantz.
35 And I beseech you instantly to visit
My too-much changèd son.—Go, some of ye,
And bring the gentlemen where Hamlet is.
GUILDENSTERN Heavens make our presence and our practices
Pleasant and helpful to him.
QUEEN GERTRUDE   Ay, amen!
        Exeunt ROSENCRANTZ *and* GUILDENSTERN [*with others*]
        Enter POLONIUS
40 POLONIUS Th'ambassadors from Norway, my good lord,
Are joyfully returned.
KING CLAUDIUS Thou still° hast been the father of good news.   *always*
POLONIUS Have I, my lord? Assure you, my good liege,
I hold my duty, as I hold my soul,
45 Both to my God and to my gracious King.
And I do think—or else this brain of mine
Hunts not the trail of policy° so sure   *cleverness*
As it hath used to do—that I have found
The very cause of Hamlet's lunacy.
50 KING CLAUDIUS O speak of that, that I do long to hear!
POLONIUS Give first admittance to th'ambassadors.
My news shall be the fruit° to that great feast.   *dessert*
KING CLAUDIUS Thyself do grace to them, and bring them in.
                                    [*Exit* POLONIUS]
He tells me, my sweet queen, that he hath found
55 The head° and source of all your son's distemper.   *origin; chief part*
QUEEN GERTRUDE I doubt[8] it is no other but the main°—   *main matter*
His father's death and our o'er-hasty marriage.
KING CLAUDIUS Well, we shall sift him.°   *interrogate (Polonius)*
        Enter POLONIUS, VALTEMAND, *and* CORNELIUS
                Welcome, my good friends.
Say, Valtemand, what from our brother° Norway?   *fellow monarch*
60 VALTEMAND Most fair return of greetings and desires.°   *good wishes*
Upon our first[9] he sent out to suppress
His nephew's levies, which to him appeared
To be a preparation 'gainst the Polack;°   *King of Poland*
But better looked into, he truly found
65 It was against your highness; whereat grieved
That so his sickness, age, and impotence
Was falsely borne in hand,[1] sends out arrests
On Fortinbras,[2] which he, in brief, obeys,
Receives rebuke from Norway, and, in fine,°   *conclusion*
70 Makes vow before his uncle never more
To give th'essay of arms[3] against your majesty;
Whereon old Norway, overcome with joy,
Gives him three thousand crowns in annual fee°   *income*
And his commission to employ those soldiers
75 So levied as before, against the Polack,
With an entreaty herein further shown,
        [*He gives a letter to* CLAUDIUS]
That it might please you to give quiet pass

8. Fear, suspect. *distemper:* unbalanced mind.
9. When we first raised the matter.
1. Disloyally taken advantage of, tricked.
2. *arrests / On Fortinbras:* orders commanding Fortin-

bras to stop his preparations and (presumably) present
himself to explain them.
3. To mount a military challenge.

Through your dominions for his enterprise
On such regards of safety and allowance[4]
As therein are set down.

80 KING CLAUDIUS   It likes° us well,   *pleases*
And at our more considered° time we'll read,   *suitable for thought*
Answer, and think upon this business.
Meantime we thank you for your well-took labour.
Go to your rest; at night we'll feast together.
85 Most welcome home.

Exeunt [VALTEMAND *and* CORNELIUS]

POLONIUS   This business is very well ended.
My liege, and madam, to expostulate°   *debate*
What majesty should be, what duty is,
Why day is day, night night, and time is time,
90 Were nothing but to waste night, day, and time.
Therefore, since brevity is the soul of wit,
And tediousness the limbs and outward flourishes,°   *rhetorical devices*
I will be brief. Your noble son is mad—
'Mad' call I it, for to define true madness,
95 What is't but to be nothing else but mad?
But let that go.

QUEEN GERTRUDE   More matter with less art.

POLONIUS   Madam, I swear I use no art at all.
That he is mad, 'tis true; 'tis true 'tis pity,
And pity 'tis 'tis true—a foolish figure,°   *figure of speech*
100 But farewell it, for I will use no art.
Mad let us grant him, then; and now remains
That we find out the cause of this effect—
Or rather say 'the cause of this *defect*',
For this effect defective[5] comes by cause.
105 Thus it remains, and the remainder thus.
Perpend.°   *Consider*
I have a daughter—have whilst she is mine°—   *until she marries*
Who in her duty and obedience, mark,
Hath given me this. Now gather and surmise.

[*He reads a*] *letter*

110 'To the celestial and my soul's idol, the most beautified Ophe-
lia'—that's an ill phrase, a vile phrase, 'beautified' is a vile
phrase. But you shall hear—'these in° her excellent white   *these words unto*
bosom, these'.

QUEEN GERTRUDE   Came this from Hamlet to her?

115 POLONIUS   Good madam, stay° a while. I will be faithful.[6]   *wait*
                    'Doubt thou the stars are fire,
                        Doubt that the sun doth move,
                    Doubt° truth to be a liar,   *Suspect*
                        But never doubt I love.
120 O dear Ophelia, I am ill at these numbers.[7] I have not art to
reckon my groans.[8] But that I love thee best, O most best,
believe it. Adieu.
                    Thine evermore, most dear lady, whilst this
                        machine is° to him,   *this body belongs*

---

4. *On . . . allowance:* Conditions regarding your realm's
safety, subject to your approval.
5. This consequence showing a lack of something (Ham-
let's reason).

6. I will accurately read out the letter's contents.
7. Hamlet is both bad at writing verse and lovesick while
he is writing.
8. Count my groans; also, number my groans metrically.

Hamlet.'

125 This in obedience hath my daughter showed me,
And more above° hath his solicitings,   *in addition*
As they fell out° by time, by means, and place,   *occurred*
All given to mine ear.

KING CLAUDIUS   But how hath she
Received his love?

POLONIUS   What do you think of me?

130 KING CLAUDIUS   As of a man faithful and honourable.

POLONIUS   I would fain° prove so. But what might you think,   *be glad to*
When I had seen this hot love on the wing,
As I perceived it—I must tell you that—
Before my daughter told me, what might you,

135 Or my dear majesty your queen here, think,
If I had played the desk or table-book,⁹
Or given my heart a winking mute and dumb,¹
Or looked upon this love with idle sight—
What might you think? No, I went round° to work,   *directly*

140 And my young mistress thus I did bespeak:°   *address*
'Lord Hamlet is a prince out of thy star.°   *above your sphere*
This must not be'. And then I precepts gave her,
That she should lock herself from his resort,°   *visits*
Admit no messengers, receive no tokens;

145 Which done, she took the fruits of my advice,
And he, repulsèd—a short tale to make—
Fell into a sadness, then into a fast,
Thence to a watch,° thence into a weakness,   *an insomnia*
Thence to a lightness,° and, by this declension,°   *dizziness / decline*

150 Into the madness wherein now he raves,
And all we° wail for.   *of us*

KING CLAUDIUS [*to* GERTRUDE]   Do you think 'tis this?

QUEEN GERTRUDE   It may be; very likely.

POLONIUS   Hath there been such a time—I'd fain know that—

155 That I have positively said ''Tis so'
When it proved otherwise?

KING CLAUDIUS   Not that I know.

POLONIUS [*touching his head, then his shoulder*]
Take this from this if this be otherwise.
If circumstances lead me I will find
Where truth is hid, though it were hid indeed
Within the centre.°   *middle of the earth*

160 KING CLAUDIUS   How may we try° it further?   *test*

POLONIUS   You know sometimes he walks four hours together
Here in the lobby.

QUEEN GERTRUDE   So he does indeed.

POLONIUS   At such a time I'll loose my daughter to him.
[*To* CLAUDIUS] Be you and I behind an arras° then.   *a tapestry*

165 Mark the encounter. If he love her not,
And be not from his reason fall'n thereon,°   *on that account*

---

9. If I had recorded the perception (in my memory) but   1. Or made my heart close its eyes and remain silent.
kept it hidden.

Let me be no assistant for a state,
But keep a farm and carters.°   *wagon drivers*
KING CLAUDIUS   We will try it.

Enter [Prince] HAMLET, *[madly attired,] reading on a
book*[2]

QUEEN GERTRUDE   But look where sadly° the poor wretch comes   *gravely*
    reading.
170   POLONIUS   Away, I do beseech you both, away.
    I'll board him presently.° O give me leave.[3]   *accost him immediately*

Exit KING *and* QUEEN

    How does my good Lord Hamlet?
    HAMLET   Well, God-'a'-mercy.[4]
    POLONIUS   Do you know me, my lord?
175   HAMLET   Excellent, excellent well. You're a fishmonger.
    POLONIUS   Not I, my lord.
    HAMLET   Then I would you were so honest a man.
    POLONIUS   Honest, my lord?
    HAMLET   Ay, sir. To be honest, as this world goes, is to be one
180   man picked out of ten thousand.
    POLONIUS   That's very true, my lord.
    HAMLET   For if the sun breed maggots in a dead dog, being a
    good kissing carrion[5]—have you a daughter?
    POLONIUS   I have, my lord.
185   HAMLET   Let her not walk i'th' sun.[6] Conception[7] is a blessing,
    but not as your daughter may conceive. Friend, look to't.°   *take care*
    POLONIUS   [*aside*]   How say you by that? Still harping on my
    daughter. Yet he knew me not at first—a° said I was a fish-   *he*
    monger. A is far gone, far gone, and truly, in my youth I suf-
190   fered much extremity for love, very near this. I'll speak to him
    again.—What do you read, my lord?
    HAMLET   Words, words, words.
    POLONIUS   What is the matter,[8] my lord?
    HAMLET   Between who?
195   POLONIUS   I mean the matter you read, my lord.
    HAMLET   Slanders, sir; for the satirical slave° says here that old   *scoundrel*
    men have grey beards, that their faces are wrinkled, their eyes
    purging° thick amber° or plum-tree gum, and that they have a   *discharging / resin*
    plentiful lack of wit,° together with most weak hams.° All which,   *intellect / thighs*
200   sir, though I most powerfully and potently believe, yet I hold
    it not honesty° to have it thus set down; for you yourself, sir,   *honorable*
    should be old as I am—if, like a crab, you could go backward.
    POLONIUS   [*aside*]   Though this be madness, yet there is method
    in't.—Will you walk out of the air,[9] my lord?
205   HAMLET   Into my grave.
    POLONIUS   Indeed, that is out o'th' air. [*Aside*] How pregnant°   *meaningful*
    sometimes his replies are! A happiness° that often madness hits   *An appropriateness*

---

2. Hamlet possibly has two entrances here, the first at
the inner stage ("lobby," line 162) and the second at the
outer stage representing the audience chamber, where
Claudius, Gertrude, and Polonius are talking. Hamlet
would thus have overheard Polonius's plan before they
notice him reading (line 169). (See 2.1.79–82 for
Ophelia's description of Hamlet's attire.)
3. Excuse me (politely asking the King and Queen to
leave).
4. Thank you (used with inferiors).

5. Piece of flesh good for kissing. Dead matter was
thought to breed maggots, especially in sunlight.
6. Walk out in public or (as in 1.2.67) expose herself too
much to a Prince's (or son's) love.
7. The ability to form ideas; pregnancy.
8. Content, although Hamlet deliberately takes it as
"subject of a quarrel."
9. Outdoor air was regarded as a hazard for the sick;
Polonius may mean "out of the draughts," since the
scene seems to be set indoors.

on, which reason and sanity could not so prosperously° be   *successfully*
delivered of. I will leave him, and suddenly° contrive the means   *immediately*
210   of meeting between him and my daughter.—My lord, I will
take my leave of you.

HAMLET   You cannot, sir, take from me anything that I will more
willingly part withal°—except my life, my life, my life.   *with*

POLONIUS [*going*]   Fare you well, my lord.

215   HAMLET   These tedious old fools!

> *Enter* GUILDENSTERN *and* ROSENCRANTZ[1]

POLONIUS   You go to seek the Lord Hamlet. There he is.

ROSENCRANTZ   God save you, sir.

GUILDENSTERN [*to* POLONIUS]   Mine honoured lord.

> [*Exit* POLONIUS]

ROSENCRANTZ [*to* HAMLET]   My most dear lord.

220   HAMLET   My ex'llent good friends. How dost thou, Guilden-
stern? Ah, Rosencrantz—good lads, how do ye both?

ROSENCRANTZ   As the indifferent° children of the earth.   *ordinary*

GUILDENSTERN   Happy° in that we are not over-happy,   *Fortunate*
On Fortune's cap we are not the very button.°   *highest point*

225   HAMLET   Nor the soles of her shoe?

ROSENCRANTZ   Neither, my lord.

HAMLET   Then you live about her waist, or in the middle of her
favour?

GUILDENSTERN   Faith, her privates[2] we.

230   HAMLET   In the secret parts of Fortune? O, most true, she is a
strumpet.° What's the news?   *whore*

ROSENCRANTZ   None, my lord, but that the world's grown
honest.

HAMLET   Then is doomsday near. But your news is not true. Let
235   me question more in particular. What have you, my good
friends, deserved at the hands of Fortune that she sends you to
prison hither?

GUILDENSTERN   Prison, my lord?

HAMLET   Denmark's a prison.

240   ROSENCRANTZ   Then is the world one.

HAMLET   A goodly[3] one, in which there are many confines,°   *enclosures*
wards,° and dungeons, Denmark being one o'th' worst.   *cells*

ROSENCRANTZ   We think not so, my lord.

HAMLET   Why, then 'tis none to you, for there is nothing either
245   good or bad but thinking makes it so. To me it is a prison.

ROSENCRANTZ   Why, then your ambition makes it one; 'tis too
narrow for your mind.

HAMLET   O God, I could be bounded in a nutshell and count
myself a king of infinite space, were it not that I have bad
250   dreams.

GUILDENSTERN   Which dreams indeed are ambition; for the very
substance of the ambitious is merely the shadow of a dream.

HAMLET   A dream itself is but a shadow.

ROSENCRANTZ   Truly, and I hold ambition of so airy and light a
255   quality that it is but a shadow's shadow.

---

1. In F, Rosencrantz and Guildenstern enter after line
215; in Q1, after line 211; in Q2, after line 213. Because
Polonius addresses them at line 216, this seems the best
place for their entry.

2. A triple pun: private persons holding no office; inti-
mate friends; private parts, genitalia.
3. Spacious; fine.

HAMLET   Then are our beggars bodies, and our monarchs and outstretched heroes the beggars' shadows.⁴ Shall we to th' court? For, by my fay,° I cannot reason.   *faith*

ROSENCRANTZ *and* GUILDENSTERN   We'll wait upon° you.   *accompany*

260   HAMLET   No such matter.° I will not sort° you with the rest of my   *Certainly not / class* servants, for, to speak to you like an honest man, I am most dreadfully attended.° But in the beaten way⁵ of friendship, what   *waited upon* make you° at Elsinore?   *are you doing*

ROSENCRANTZ   To visit you, my lord, no other occasion.

265   HAMLET   Beggar that I am, I am even poor in thanks, but I thank you; and sure, dear friends, my thanks are too dear a halfpenny.⁶ Were you not sent for? Is it your own inclining? Is it a free° visitation? Come, deal justly with me. Come, come. Nay,   *voluntary* speak.

270   GUILDENSTERN   What should we say, my lord?

HAMLET   Why, anything—but to th' purpose. You were sent for, and there is a kind of confession in your looks which your modesties⁷ have not craft enough to colour.° I know the good King   *disguise* and Queen have sent for you.

275   ROSENCRANTZ   To what end, my lord?

HAMLET   That you must teach me. But let me conjure° you by   *solemnly request* the rights of our fellowship, by the consonancy° of our youth,   *harmonious friendship* by the obligation of our ever-preserved love, and by what more dear a better proposer could charge you withal, be even° and   *level* 280   direct with me whether you were sent for or no.

ROSENCRANTZ [*to* GUILDENSTERN]   What say you?

HAMLET   Nay then, I have an eye of° you—if you love me, hold   *on* not off.

GUILDENSTERN   My lord, we were sent for.

285   HAMLET   I will tell you why. So shall my anticipation prevent°   *forestall* your discovery, and your secrecy to the King and Queen moult no feather.⁸ I have of late—but wherefore I know not—lost all my mirth, forgone all custom of exercise; and indeed it goes so heavily with my disposition⁹ that this goodly frame,° the earth,   *structure* 290   seems to me a sterile promontory. This most excellent canopy the air, look you, this brave o'erhanging,¹ this majestical roof fretted° with golden fire—why, it appears no other thing to me   *adorned* than a foul and pestilent congregation° of vapours. What a   *mass* piece of work is a man! How noble in reason, how infinite in 295   faculty,° in form and moving how express² and admirable, in   *natural powers* action how like an angel, in apprehension how like a god—the beauty of the world, the paragon of animals! And yet to me what is this quintessence of dust?³ Man delights not me—no,

4. *Then . . . shadows:* Then beggars, being without ambition, are not shadows but have substance; if monarchs and heroes (who ambitiously "stretch" too far) are shadows and only substantial bodies can cast shadows, they must be the beggars' shadows.
5. Well-worn track (plain words).
6. Too expensive at a halfpenny (not worth a halfpenny); perhaps also, too expensive by a halfpenny for me to give in return for such worthless information.
7. Senses of decency.
8. Remain unimpaired. To pull the feathers off a reputation meant to detract from it.
9. *it goes . . . disposition:* I am so heavy with melancholy.

F, however, prints "heavenly" for Q2's "heavily," which, if accepted, gives a startling image of Hamlet's impatient world-weariness.
1. This splendid overhang (F). Most editions give Q2's "o'erhanging firmament" (heavens). In either case, the image may refer to the "heavens," the roof overhanging the Elizabethan stage, which was decorated with stars.
2. Precise; expressive.
3. It was thought that the heavenly bodies were composed of a fifth element ("quintessence"), superior to the other four (earth, air, fire, and water) and also the purest distillation of earthly objects. Hamlet thinks of humanity as dust at its dustiest.

nor woman neither, though by your smiling you seem to say

300 so.

ROSENCRANTZ   My lord, there was no such stuff in my thoughts.

HAMLET   Why did you laugh, then, when I said 'Man delights not me'?

ROSENCRANTZ   To think, my lord, if you delight not in man what

305 lenten entertainment[4] the players shall receive from you. We coted° them on the way, and hither are they coming to offer   *passed* you service.

HAMLET   He that plays the King shall be welcome; his majesty shall have tribute of me. The adventurous Knight shall use his

310 foil° and target,° the Lover shall not sigh gratis,° the Humorous   *sword / shield / for free* Man shall end his part in peace,[5] the Clown shall make those laugh whose lungs are tickled o'th' sear,[6] and the Lady shall say her mind freely, or the blank verse shall halt for't.[7] What players are they?

315 ROSENCRANTZ   Even those you were wont to take delight in, the tragedians° of the city.   *actors*

HAMLET   How chances it they travel? Their residence° both in   *(in the city)* reputation and profit was better both ways.

ROSENCRANTZ   I think their inhibition comes by the means of

320 the late innovation.[8]

HAMLET   Do they hold the same estimation° they did when I was   *esteem* in the city? Are they so followed?

ROSENCRANTZ   No, indeed, they are not.

HAMLET   How comes it? Do they grow rusty?

325 ROSENCRANTZ   Nay, their endeavour keeps° in the wonted° pace.   *continues / accustomed* But there is, sir, an eyrie of children, little eyases,[9] that cry out on the top of question[1] and are most tyrannically° clapped for't.   *outrageously* These are now the fashion, and so berattle° the common   *noisily abuse* stages[2]—so they call them—that many wearing rapiers are

330 afraid of goose-quills,[3] and dare scarce come thither.

HAMLET   What, are they children? Who maintains 'em? How are they escoted?° Will they pursue the quality° no longer than   *provided for / profession* they can sing?[4] Will they not say afterwards, if they should grow themselves to common players—as it is like° most will, if their   *likely*

335 means° are not better—their writers do them wrong to make   *financial options* them exclaim against their own succession?°   *later employment*

ROSENCRANTZ   Faith, there has been much to-do on both sides, and the nation° holds it no sin to tarre° them to controversy.   *populace / goad* There was for a while no money bid for argument unless the

340 poet and the player went to cuffs in the question.[5]

HAMLET   Is't possible?

---

4. Welcome. Lent was a period of penitence and fasting (when London theaters were closed).

5. *the Humorous . . . peace:* the eccentric (governed by excess of one humor, or mood-influencing bodily fluid) should be allowed to rant on without disturbance.

6. Whose lungs are primed to laugh. (The "sear" is the part of a gun holding back the hammer until the trigger releases it.)

7. *and the Lady . . . for't:* if the lady is not allowed to speak all her part, the poetry will "halt," or limp (fail to scan).

8. Comes from recent fashion (probably the rage for boy-acting companies). An "inhibition" could be either a hindrance or an official prohibition. (Elizabethan theaters were commonly closed at signs of political instability.)

9. Young hawks. A company of boy actors flourished at the private Blackfriars Theatre, leased from the Burbages, from 1600 to 1608. *eyrie:* nest for a bird of prey.

1. That yell over their critics' voices.

2. Public theaters (such as the Globe).

3. That gentlemen are afraid of the poet's satirical pen.

4. Only until their voices break.

5. *no money . . . question:* nothing offered for the plot (or draft) of a play unless it added to the dispute between the children's dramatists and the public theater companies. *went to cuffs:* came to blows.

GUILDENSTERN   O, there has been much throwing about of
brains.[6]

HAMLET   Do the boys carry it° away?   *(the victory)*

345   ROSENCRANTZ   Ay, that they do, my lord, Hercules and his load
too.[7]

HAMLET   It is not strange; for mine uncle is King of Denmark,
and those that would make mows° at him while my father lived   *grimaces*
give twenty, forty, an hundred ducats apiece for his picture in

350   little.° 'Sblood,[8] there is something in this more than natural,   *miniature*
if philosophy could find it out.

A *flourish*[9] *for the* PLAYERS

GUILDENSTERN   There are the players.

HAMLET   Gentlemen, you are welcome to Elsinore. Your hands,
come. Th'appurtenance° of welcome is fashion and ceremony.   *fitting accompaniment*

355   Let me comply with you in the garb,[1] lest my extent° to the   *offering (of welcome)*
players—which, I tell you, must show fairly° outward—should   *courteously*
more appear like entertainment° than yours.   *(warm) welcome*

[*He shakes hands with them*]

You are welcome. But my uncle-father and aunt-mother are
deceived.

360   GUILDENSTERN   In what, my dear lord?

HAMLET   I am but mad north-north-west;[2] when the wind is
southerly, I know a hawk from a handsaw.[3]

Enter POLONIUS

POLONIUS   Well be with you, gentlemen.

HAMLET [*aside*]   Hark you, Guildenstern, and you too—at each

365   ear a hearer—that great baby you see there is not yet out of
his swathing-clouts.°   *swaddling clothes*

ROSENCRANTZ [*aside*]   Haply° he's the second time come to   *Perhaps*
them, for they say an old man is twice a child.

HAMLET [*aside*]   I will prophesy he comes to tell me of the play-

370   ers. Mark it.—You say right, sir, for o' Monday morning, 'twas
so indeed.

POLONIUS   My lord, I have news to tell you.

HAMLET   My lord, I have news to tell you. When Roscius[4] was
an actor in Rome—

375   POLONIUS   The actors are come hither, my lord.

HAMLET   Buzz, buzz.[5]

POLONIUS   Upon mine honour—

HAMLET   Then came each actor on his ass.

POLONIUS   The best actors in the world, either for tragedy, com-

380   edy, history, pastoral, pastorical-comical, historical-pastoral,
tragical-historical, tragical-comical-historical-pastoral, scene
individable[6] or poem unlimited.[7] Seneca cannot be too heavy,

---

6. A great battle of wits.
7. In the course of one of his labors, Hercules held up
the world on his shoulders while Atlas (its usual support)
ran an errand; Hercules bearing the world was the sign of
the Globe.
8. By God's blood.
9. Trumpet flourishes often heralded dramatic perfor-
mances.
1. Let me follow accepted forms in the recognized
manner (by shaking hands).
2. The smallest compass point away from true north,
and thus not far from sane; or possibly, only mad on

occasions when the wind blows from the north-
northwest.
3. A small saw, and possibly a variant of "heronshaw"
(heron).
4. The most famous ancient Roman actor, a rather dated
news item.
5. A response to stale news.
6. Probably, play with no breaks in performance, or play
observing the unity of place (and presumably the other
classical unities). Shakespeare parodies the classifica-
tions of contemporary dramatic theorists.
7. (Dramatic) poem unrestricted by classical rules.

nor Plautus too light.[8] For the law of writ and the liberty,[9] these
are the only men.

385 HAMLET   O Jephthah, judge of Israel, what a treasure hadst
thou![1]

POLONIUS   What a treasure had he, my lord?

HAMLET   Why,
       'One fair daughter and no more,

390   The which he lovèd passing° well'.   *surpassingly*

POLONIUS   [*aside*]   Still on my daughter.

HAMLET   Am I not i'th' right, old Jephthah?

POLONIUS   If you call me Jephthah, my lord, I have a daughter
that I love passing well.

395 HAMLET   Nay, that follows not.[2]

POLONIUS   What follows then, my lord?

HAMLET   Why
                       'As by lot°   *chance*
                       God wot',°   *knows*

400 and then you know
                       'It came to pass
                       As most like° it was'—   *probable*
the first row° of the pious chanson° will show you more, for   *stanza / ballad*
look where my abridgements[3] come.

            Enter four or five PLAYERS

405 You're welcome, masters, welcome all.—I am glad to see thee
well.—Welcome, good friends.—O, my old friend! Thy face is
valanced° since I saw thee last. Com'st thou to beard° me in   *fringed (with beard) / defy*
Denmark?—What, my young lady and mistress.[4] By'r Lady,
your ladyship is nearer heaven than when I saw you last by the

410 altitude of a chopine.° Pray God your voice, like a piece of   *high platform shoe*
uncurrent gold, be not cracked within the ring.[5]—Masters, you
are all welcome. We'll e'en to't like French falc'ners,[6] fly at
anything we see. We'll have a speech straight.° Come, give us   *right away*
a taste of your quality.° Come, a passionate speech.   *professional skill*

415 FIRST PLAYER   What speech, my good lord?

HAMLET   I heard thee speak me a speech once, but it was never
acted, or, if it was, not above once; for the play, I remember,
pleased not the million. 'Twas caviare to the general.° But it   *populace*
was—as I received it, and others whose judgements in such

420 matters cried in the top of[7] mine—an excellent play, well
digested° in the scenes, set down with as much modesty° as   *organized / restraint*
cunning. I remember one said there was no sallets[8] in the lines
to make the matter savoury, nor no matter in the phrase that
might indict the author of affectation, but called it an honest

425 method, as wholesome as sweet, and by very much more hand-
some than fine.[9] One speech in it I chiefly loved, 'twas Aeneas'
tale to Dido, and thereabout of it especially where he speaks of

---

8. The best-known Roman playwrights, masters of
tragedy and comedy, respectively.
9. For plays where classical rules are either observed or
abandoned.
1. Jephthah vowed that if he defeated the Ammonites,
he would sacrifice the first living thing he saw on his
return. He won, and his daughter became the sacrificial
victim (Judges 11). "Jephthah, Judge of Israel" was the
title of a popular ballad, the "pious chanson" from
which Hamlet subsequently quotes or sings.
2. Polonius's having a daughter is not a logical conse-
quence of Hamlet's calling him Jephthah.

3. Those who cut me short; also, entertainments.
4. The boy who played female roles.
5. A coin was no longer legal tender if the circle or ring
enclosing the monarch's head was broken (by "clip-
ping," or trimming off small amounts of gold).
6. We'll go to work at once. (French falconers seem to
have been regarded as experts, willing to try any potential
prey.)
7. *cried . . . of*: outweighed.
8. Literally, salads (seasoned dishes); highly flavored, or
"salty" (lecherous).
9. Beautifully crafted rather than showy.

Priam's slaughter.[1] If it live in your memory, begin at this
line—let me see, let me see:

430   'The rugged° Pyrrhus,[2] like th'Hyrcanian beast'°—   *savage / tiger*
'tis not so. It begins with Pyrrhus—
'The rugged Pyrrhus, he whose sable° arms,   *black*
Black as his purpose, did the night resemble
When he lay couchèd° in the ominous horse,[3]   *hidden*

435   Hath now this dread and black complexion° smeared   *appearance*
With heraldry° more dismal. Head to foot   *heraldic colors*
Now is he total gules,° horridly tricked°   *all red / inked over*
With blood of fathers, mothers, daughters, sons,
Baked and impasted with° the parching° streets,   *encrusted by / fiery*

440   That lend a tyrranous and damnèd light
To their vile murders. Roasted in wrath and fire,
And thus o'er-sizèd[4] with coagulate gore,
With eyes like carbuncles[5] the hellish Pyrrhus
Old grandsire Priam seeks.'

445   So, proceed you.

POLONIUS   Fore God, my lord, well spoken, with good accent
and good discretion.

FIRST PLAYER   'Anon° he finds him,   *Soon*
Striking too short at Greeks. His antique sword,

450   Rebellious to his arm, lies where it falls,
Repugnant° to command. Unequal match,   *Resistant*
Pyrrhus at Priam drives, in rage strikes wide;
But with the whiff and wind of his fell° sword   *fierce*
Th'unnervèd° father falls. Then senseless Ilium,[6]   *strengthless*

455   Seeming to feel his blow, with flaming top
Stoops to his° base, and with a hideous crash   *its*
Takes prisoner Pyrrhus' ear. For lo, his sword,
Which was declining° on the milky° head   *descending / white*
Of reverend Priam, seemed i'th' air to stick.

460   So, as a painted tyrant,[7] Pyrrhus stood,
And, like a neutral to his will and matter,[8]
Did nothing.
But as we often see against° some storm   *before*
A silence in the heavens, the rack° stand still,   *cloud banks*

465   The bold winds speechless, and the orb° below   *earth*
As hush as death, anon the dreadful thunder
Doth rend the region:° so, after Pyrrhus' pause,   *sky*
A rousèd vengeance sets him new a-work;
And never did the Cyclops'[9] hammers fall

470   On Mars his° armour, forged for proof eterne,[1]   *(Mars's)*
With less remorse° than Pyrrhus' bleeding sword   *pity; hesitation*
Now falls on Priam.
Out, out, thou strumpet Fortune! All you gods,
In general synod, take away her power,

---

1. The murder of the Trojan King Priam, at the end of
the Trojan War; adapted from Virgil's *Aeneid*, possibly
via Christopher Marlowe's *Dido, Queen of Carthage*.
Aeneas recounts the story of Priam's slaughter to his
beloved, Dido.
2. Also known as Neoptolemus, he came to Troy to
avenge the death of his father, the Greek hero Achilles.
3. The Trojan horse, full of Greek warriors.
4. As though coated with sizing, the thick liquid used
to prepare a canvas for painting.

5. Gems supposed to glow with their own light.
6. The citadel of Troy.
7. Tyrant depicted in a painting and so incapable of
moving.
8. And as one indifferent toward his intention and the
action at hand.
9. The three one-eyed giants who served as armorers to
the classical gods and heroes.
1. To remain impenetrable forever.

475 Break all the spokes and fellies from her wheel,[2]
And bowl the round nave° down the hill of heaven,°   *wheel hub / Mt. Olympus*
As low as to the fiends!'

POLONIUS   This is too long.

HAMLET   It shall to the barber's, with your beard.°   [*To* FIRST   *It shall be cut short*
480 PLAYER] Prithee, say on. He's for a jig[3] or a tale of bawdry, or
he sleeps. Say on, come to Hecuba.

FIRST PLAYER   'But who, O who had seen the mobbled°   *veiled; muffled*
queen'—

HAMLET   'The mobbled queen'?

POLONIUS   That's good; 'mobbled queen' is good.

485 FIRST PLAYER   'Run barefoot up and down, threat'ning the flames
With bisson rheum;° a clout° upon that head   *blinding tears / cloth*
Where late the diadem stood, and for a robe,
About her lank and all o'er-teemèd[4] loins,
A blanket in th'alarm of fear caught up—
490 Who this had seen, with tongue in venom steeped,
'Gainst Fortune's state° would treason have pronounced.   *rule*
But if the gods themselves did see her then,
When she saw Pyrrhus make malicious sport
In mincing with his sword her husband's limbs,
495 The instant burst of clamour that she made—
Unless things mortal move them not at all—
Would have made milch° the burning eyes of heaven,   *milky; moist*
And passion° in the gods.'   *suffering; pity*

POLONIUS   Look whe'er° he has not turned his colour, and has   *whether*
500 tears in 's eyes. [*To* FIRST PLAYER] Prithee, no more.

HAMLET [*to* FIRST PLAYER]   'Tis well. I'll have thee speak out the
rest soon. [*To* POLONIUS] Good my lord, will you see the play-
ers well bestowed?° Do ye hear?—let them be well used,° for   *lodged / treated*
they are the abstracts° and brief chronicles of the time. After   *summaries*
505 your death you were better have a bad epitaph than their ill
report while you live.

POLONIUS   My lord, I will use them according to their desert.

HAMLET   God's bodykins,° man, much better. Use every man   *By God's dear body*
after° his desert, and who should scape whipping? Use them   *according to*
510 after your own honour and dignity—the less they deserve, the
more merit is in your bounty. Take them in.

POLONIUS [*to* PLAYERS]   Come, sirs.   *Exit*

HAMLET [*to* PLAYERS]   Follow him, friends. We'll hear a play
tomorrow. Dost thou hear me, old friend? Can you play the
515 murder of Gonzago?

PLAYERS   Ay, my lord.

HAMLET   We'll ha't° tomorrow night. You could for a need° study   *have it / if necessary*
a speech of some dozen or sixteen lines which I would set down
and insert in't, could ye not?

520 PLAYERS   Ay, my lord.

HAMLET   Very well. Follow that lord, and look you mock him
not.

Exeunt PLAYERS[5]

---

2. The power of Fortune's ever-turning wheel, raising
and lowering men in succession, was proverbial. *fellies:*
curved sections of a wooden wheel rim.
3. A ridiculous piece of poetry, or the dance that followed
many plays (unrelated to the drama).
4. Completely worn out with childbearing. (Hecuba was

supposed to have borne seventeen or more children.)
5. In F and Q1, the players leave after line 524. In Q2,
they leave with Polonius after line 512. Their exit has
been relocated here to coincide with Hamlet's command
that they follow Polonius.

My good friends, I'll leave you till night. You are welcome to
Elsinore.

525 ROSENCRANTZ   Good my lord.

HAMLET   Ay, so. God b'wi'° ye.   *Exeunt [all but]* HAMLET   *be with*
                              Now I am alone.
O, what a rogue and peasant slave am I!
Is it not monstrous that this player here,
But° in a fiction, in a dream of passion,   *Merely*
530 Could force his soul so to his whole conceit[6]
That from her° working all his visage wanned,°   *(the soul's)* / *grew pale*
Tears in his eyes, distraction in 's aspect,
A broken voice, and his whole function suiting
With forms to his conceit?[7] And all for nothing.
535 For Hecuba!
What's Hecuba to him, or he to Hecuba,
That he should weep for her? What would he do
Had he the motive and the cue for passion
That I have? He would drown the stage with tears,
540 And cleave the general ear[8] with horrid speech,
Make mad the guilty and appal the free,°   *innocent*
Confound the ignorant, and amaze° indeed   *bewilder*
The very faculty of eyes and ears. Yet I,
A dull and muddy-mettled° rascal, peak°   *dull-spirited* / *mope*
545 Like John-a-dreams,° unpregnant of[9] my cause,   *a sleepy idler*
And can say nothing—no, not for a king
Upon whose property° and most dear life   *rightful sovereignty*
A damned defeat[1] was made. Am I a coward?
Who calls me villain, breaks my pate° across,   *head*
550 Plucks off my beard and blows it in my face,
Tweaks me by th' nose, gives me the lie i'th' throat
As deep as to the lungs?[2] Who does me this?
Ha? 'Swounds,° I should take it; for it cannot be   *By God's wounds*
But I am pigeon-livered and lack gall[3]
555 To make oppression bitter, or ere this
I should 'a' fatted all the region kites[4]
With this slave's offal. Bloody, bawdy villain!
Remorseless, treacherous, lecherous, kindless villain!
O, vengeance!—
560 Why, what an ass am I? Ay, sure, this is most brave,°   *fine*
That I, the son of the dear murderèd,°   *the dear murdered man*
Prompted to my revenge by heaven and hell,
Must, like a whore, unpack my heart with words
And fall a-cursing like a very drab,°   *whore*
565 A scullion![5] Fie upon't, foh!—About,° my brain.   *Into action*
I have heard that guilty creatures sitting at a play
Have by the very cunning° of the scene   *artfulness*
Been struck so to the soul that presently°   *immediately*
They have proclaimed their malefactions;
570 For murder, though it have no tongue, will speak

---

6. Could make his innermost being conform so well with
his imagined situation.
7. *his whole . . . conceit:* the action of his whole body in
outward accord with his imagination.
8. The ears of people generally.
9. Not quickened into action by.

1. An act of overthrow worthy of damnation.
2. *gives . . . lungs:* calls me a thoroughgoing liar.
3. Pigeons were thought not to secrete gall, a bitter fluid
produced by the liver and the supposed source of anger.
4. All the kites (birds of prey) in the sky ("region").
5. Kitchen servant.

With most miraculous organ. I'll have these players
Play something like the murder of my father
Before mine uncle. I'll observe his looks,
I'll tent° him to the quick. If a° but blench,   *probe (a wound)* / *he*
575   I know my course. The spirit that I have seen
May be the devil, and the devil hath power
T'assume a pleasing shape; yea, and perhaps,
Out of my weakness and my melancholy—
As he is very potent with such spirits⁶—
580   Abuses° me to damn me. I'll have grounds   *Deceives*
More relative° than this. The play's the thing   *relevant*
Wherein I'll catch the conscience of the King.   *Exit*

3.1

Enter KING [CLAUDIUS], QUEEN [GERTRUDE], POLONIUS,
OPHELIA, ROSENCRANTZ, GUILDENSTERN, *and lords*

KING CLAUDIUS   [*to* ROSENCRANTZ *and* GUILDENSTERN]
And can you by no drift of circumstance¹
Get from him why he puts on this confusion,
Grating so harshly all his days of quiet
With turbulent and dangerous lunacy?
5   ROSENCRANTZ   He does confess he feels himself distracted,°   *confused; agitated*
But from what cause a will by no means speak.
GUILDENSTERN   Nor do we find him forward° to be sounded,°   *eager* / *probed*
But with a crafty madness keeps aloof
When we would bring him on to some confession
10   Of his true state.
QUEEN GERTRUDE   Did he receive you well?
ROSENCRANTZ   Most like a gentleman.
GUILDENSTERN   But with much forcing of his disposition.°   *mood*
ROSENCRANTZ   Niggard of question,² but of° our demands   *to*
Most free in his reply.
15   QUEEN GERTRUDE   Did you assay° him   *try to persuade*
To any pastime?
ROSENCRANTZ   Madam, it so fell out that certain players
We o'er-raught° on the way. Of these we told him,   *passed*
And there did seem in him a kind of joy
20   To hear of it. They are about the court,
And, as I think, they have already order
This night to play before him.
POLONIUS   'Tis most true,
And he beseeched me to entreat your majesties
To hear and see the matter.
25   KING CLAUDIUS   With all my heart; and it doth much content me
To hear him so inclined.—Good gentlemen,
Give him a further edge,° and drive his purpose on   *stimulus; appetite*
To these delights.
ROSENCRANTZ   We shall, my lord.
                        Exeunt ROSENCRANTZ *and* GUILDENSTERN
30   KING CLAUDIUS   Sweet Gertrude, leave us too,
For we have closely° sent for Hamlet hither,   *privately*

---

6. *Out of . . . spirits:* It was thought that those afflicted
with too much black bile, a humor (fluid), or "spirit"
(distillation) became melancholy and subject to halluci-
nations, which in turn made them easily tricked by the
devil. *potent with:* powerful over.
3.1 Location: The castle.
1. By no carefully directed conversation.
2. Reluctant to offer conversation.

That he, as 'twere by accident, may here
Affront° Ophelia.   *Confront*
Her father and myself, lawful espials,°   *spies*
35 Will so bestow ourselves that, seeing unseen,
We may of their encounter frankly judge,
And gather by him, as he is behaved,
If't be th'affliction of his love or no
That thus he suffers for.

QUEEN GERTRUDE   I shall obey you.
40 And for your part, Ophelia, I do wish
That your good beauties be the happy cause
Of Hamlet's wildness; so shall I hope your virtues
Will bring him to his wonted° way again,   *customary*
To both your honours.

OPHELIA   Madam, I wish it may.

[*Exit* GERTRUDE]

45 POLONIUS   Ophelia, walk you here.—Gracious,° so please you,   *Your Grace*
We will bestow ourselves.—Read on this book,
That show of such an exercise may colour
Your loneliness.³ We are oft to blame in this:
'Tis too much proved° that with devotion's visage   *true in experience*
50 And pious action we do sugar o'er
The devil himself.

KING CLAUDIUS   O, 'tis too true.
[*Aside*] How smart° a lash that speech doth give my conscience.   *sharp*
The harlot's cheek, beautied with plast'ring° art,   *cosmetic; healing*
Is not more ugly to the thing that helps it⁴
55 Than is my deed to my most painted word.
O heavy burden!

POLONIUS   I hear him coming. Let's withdraw, my lord.

Exeunt [CLAUDIUS *and* POLONIUS]

Enter [*Prince*] HAMLET

HAMLET   To be, or not to be; that is the question:
Whether 'tis nobler in the mind to suffer
60 The slings and arrows of outrageous fortune,
Or to take arms against a sea of troubles,
And, by opposing, end them. To die, to sleep—
No more, and by a sleep to say we end
The heartache and the thousand natural shocks
65 That flesh is heir to—'tis a consummation
Devoutly to be wished. To die, to sleep.
To sleep, perchance to dream. Ay, there's the rub,⁵
For in that sleep of death what dreams may come
When we have shuffled° off this mortal coil°   *cast / turmoil; flesh*
70 Must give us pause. There's the respect°   *consideration*
That makes calamity of so long life,⁶
For who would bear the whips and scorns of time,
Th'oppressor's wrong, the proud man's contumely,°   *scornful abuse*
The pangs of disprized° love, the law's delay,   *unvalued*
75 The insolence of office,° and the spurns⁷   *bureaucrats*

---

3. *may . . . loneliness:* may explain your solitude, and also give it a virtuous or pious look. The "book" is a prayer book or devotional text.
4. *to . . . it:* compared to the artificially beautiful surface that covers it.
5. Obstacle in the game of bowls, an impediment to the ball's intended path.
6. Makes adversity so long-lived (as opposed to quickly ended in suicide).
7. Kicks, insults.

That patient merit of th'unworthy takes,[8]
When he himself might his quietus make[9]
With a bare bodkin?° Who would these fardels° bear,   *mere dagger / burdens*
To grunt and sweat under a weary life,
80   But that the dread of something after death,
The undiscovered country from whose bourn°   *border*
No traveller returns, puzzles the will,
And makes us rather bear those ills we have
Than fly to others that we know not of?
85   Thus conscience[1] does make cowards of us all,
And thus the native hue° of resolution   *ruddy complexion*
Is sicklied o'er with the pale cast° of thought,   *tint*
And enterprises of great pith and moment[2]
With this regard° their currents turn awry,   *consideration*
90   And lose the name of action. Soft you, now,[3]
The fair Ophelia!—Nymph, in thy orisons°   *prayers*
Be all my sins remembered.

OPHELIA   Good my lord,
How does your honour for this many a day?

HAMLET   I humbly thank you, well, well, well.

95   OPHELIA   My lord, I have remembrances of yours
That I have longèd long to redeliver.
I pray you now receive them.

HAMLET   No, no, I never gave you aught.

OPHELIA   My honoured lord, you know right well you did,
100   And with them words of so sweet breath composed
As made the things more rich. Their perfume lost,
Take these again; for to the noble mind
Rich gifts wax° poor when givers prove unkind.   *grow*
There, my lord.

105   HAMLET   Ha, ha? Are you honest?°   *chaste; truthful*

OPHELIA   My lord.

HAMLET   Are you fair?

OPHELIA   What means your lordship?

HAMLET   That if you be honest and fair, your honesty should
110   admit no discourse to[4] your beauty.

OPHELIA   Could beauty, my lord, have better commerce° than   *dealings*
with honesty?

HAMLET   Ay, truly, for the power of beauty will sooner transform
honesty from what it is to a bawd than the force of honesty can
115   translate beauty into his° likeness. This was sometime a par-   *its (honesty's)*
adox, but now the time[5] gives it proof. I did love you once.

OPHELIA   Indeed, my lord, you made me believe so.

HAMLET   You should not have believed me, for virtue cannot so
inoculate our old stock but we shall relish of it.[6] I loved you
120   not.

OPHELIA   I was the more deceived.

HAMLET   Get thee to a nunnery.[7] Why wouldst thou be a breeder

8. That the deserving has to accept patiently from the unworthy.
9. A paid-off account was marked "Quietus est" ("laid to rest").
1. Both consciousness (introspective knowledge) and moral conscience.
2. Of profundity and importance (F). Q2 gives "pitch," meaning "height" (in the context of a falcon's flight).
3. Wait a moment (an expression of surprise).

4. No familiar conversation with.
5. This was formerly an uncredited opinion, but now the present age.
6. *You . . . it*: Virtue grafted onto fallen human nature cannot eradicate completely the taste ("relish") of original sin.
7. By entering a nunnery, Ophelia will take a vow of lifelong chastity. But in Elizabethan slang, "nunnery" could also mean "brothel."

of sinners? I am myself indifferent honest,° but yet I could   *moderately virtuous*
accuse me of such things that it were better my mother had not
125   borne me. I am very proud, revengeful, ambitious, with more
offences at my beck° than I have thoughts to put them in, imag-   *command*
ination to give them shape, or time to act them in. What should
such fellows as I do crawling between heaven and earth? We
are arrant° knaves, all. Believe none of us. Go thy ways to a   *downright*
130   nunnery. Where's your father?
    OPHELIA   At home, my lord.
    HAMLET   Let the doors be shut upon him, that he may play the
fool nowhere but in 's own house. Farewell.
    OPHELIA   O help him, you sweet heavens!
135   HAMLET   If thou dost marry, I'll give thee this plague for thy
dowry: be thou as chaste as ice, as pure as snow, thou shalt not
escape calumny. Get thee to a nunnery, go, farewell. Or if thou
wilt needs marry, marry a fool; for wise men know well enough
what monsters[8] you° make of them. To a nunnery, go, and   *you women*
140   quickly, too. Farewell.
    OPHELIA   O heavenly powers, restore him!
    HAMLET   I have heard of your paintings,° too, well enough. God   *cosmetics*
hath given you one face, and you make yourselves another. You
jig, you amble, and you lisp,[9] and nickname God's creatures,[1]
145   and make your wantonness your ignorance.[2] Go to, I'll no
more on't.° It hath made me mad. I say we will have no more   *of it*
marriages. Those that are married already—all but one—shall
live. The rest shall keep as they are. To a nunnery, go.   *Exit*
    OPHELIA   O what a noble mind is here o'erthrown!
150   The courtier's, soldier's, scholar's eye, tongue, sword,
Th'expectancy and rose of the fair state,
The glass° of fashion and the mould of form,[3]   *mirror image*
Th'observed of all observers, quite, quite, down!
And I, of ladies most deject and wretched,
155   That sucked the honey of his music vows,
Now see that noble and most sovereign reason
Like sweet bells jangled out of tune and harsh;
That unmatched form and feature of blown° youth   *fully blossoming*
Blasted° with ecstasy.° O woe is me,   *Withered / madness*
160   T'have seen what I have seen, see what I see!
        Enter KING [CLAUDIUS] *and* POLONIUS
    KING CLAUDIUS   Love? His affections° do not that way tend,   *emotions*
Nor what he spake, though it lacked form a little,
Was not like madness. There's something in his soul
O'er which his melancholy sits on brood,
165   And I do doubt° the hatch and the disclose[4]   *fear*
Will be some danger; which to prevent
I have in quick determination
Thus set it down:° he shall with speed to England   *resolved it*
For the demand of our neglected tribute.[5]

---

8. Alluding to the belief that cuckolds grew horns, but Hamlet may mean a more spiritual or psychological transformation as well.
9. *You jig . . . lisp*: You dance (or sing), walk with an affectedly easy gait, and speak artificially.
1. Use new and fashionable names instead of the God-given ones.

2. *make . . . ignorance*: "play dumb" to excuse your (seductive) affectations.
3. Pattern of decorum.
4. Public disclosure.
5. Although the play is set in a Renaissance world, Claudius's words invoke a distant medieval past, when England paid tribute to Denmark.

170   Haply° the seas and countries different,   *Perhaps; with luck*
      With variable objects,[6] shall expel
      This something-settled° matter in his heart,   *somewhat rooted*
      Whereon his brains still° beating puts him thus   *constantly*
      From fashion of himself.[7] What think you on't?
175   POLONIUS   It shall do well. But yet do I believe
      The origin and commencement of this grief
      Sprung from neglected° love.—How now, Ophelia?   *unrequited*
      You need not tell us what Lord Hamlet said;
      We heard it all.—My lord, do as you please,
180   But, if you hold it fit, after the play
      Let his queen mother all alone entreat him
      To show his griefs. Let her be round° with him,   *blunt*
      And I'll be placed, so please you, in the ear°   *within earshot*
      Of all their conference. If she find him not,[8]
185   To England send him, or confine him where
      Your wisdom best shall think.
      KING CLAUDIUS   It shall be so.
      Madness in great ones must not unwatched go.   *Exeunt*

3.2

Enter [Prince] HAMLET *and two or three of the* PLAYERS

      HAMLET   Speak the speech, I pray you, as I pronounced it to
      you—trippingly on the tongue; but if you mouth it,[1] as many
      of your players do, I had as lief° the town-crier had spoke my   *willingly*
      lines. Nor do not saw the air too much with your hand, thus,
5   but use all gently; for in the very torrent, tempest, and as I may
      say the whirlwind of your passion, you must acquire and beget
      a temperance that may give it smoothness. O, it offends me to
      the soul to hear a robustious,° periwig-pated° fellow tear a pas- *bombastic / wig-wearing*
      sion to tatters, to very rags, to split the ears of the groundlings,[2]
10   who for the most part are capable of nothing but inexplicable
      dumb shows[3] and noise. I would have such a fellow whipped
      for o'erdoing Termagant. It out-Herods Herod.[4] Pray you avoid
      it.
      A PLAYER   I warrant your honour.[5]
15   HAMLET   Be not too tame, neither; but let your own discretion
      be your tutor. Suit the action to the word, the word to the
      action, with this special observance: that you o'erstep not the
      modesty° of nature. For anything so overdone is from° the pur-   *moderation / opposed to*
      pose of playing, whose end, both at the first and now, was and
20   is to hold as 'twere the mirror up to nature, to show virtue her
      own feature, scorn her own image, and the very age and body
      of the time his form and pressure.[6] Now this overdone, or come
      tardy° off, though it make the unskilful[7] laugh, cannot but   *faultily*
      make the judicious grieve; the censure of the which one[8] must

6. With different sights or interests.
7. *puts . . . himself:* makes him unlike his normal self.
8. If she fails to discover his secret.
3.2 Location: A stateroom of the castle.
1. If you speak exaggeratedly.
2. Spectators standing on the ground before the stage (the cheapest area).
3. Brief mimed scenes giving the plot of the scene to follow (see 3.2.122ff.). By Shakespeare's time, this once-common device was out of fashion.
4. It surpasses the excesses of Herod, who, as a char-

acter in medieval cycle plays, was famous for his ranting. Termagant, an imaginary deity supposedly worshipped by Muslims, takes the form of a violent speaking idol in medieval drama.
5. I assure your Honor (that we will avoid it).
6. *the very . . . pressure:* the true state of things at present, in shape ("form") and likeness (as a stamp pressed in wax).
7. Undiscriminating.
8. The judgment of one of whom (judicious persons).

25 in your allowance o'erweigh a whole theatre of others. O, there
be players that I have seen play, and heard others praise, and
that highly, not to speak it profanely,[9] that neither having the
accent of Christians nor the gait of Christian, pagan, nor no
man, have so strutted and bellowed that I have thought some
30 of nature's journeymen[1] had made men, and not made them
well, they imitated humanity so abominably.

A PLAYER   I hope we have reformed that indifferently° with us,   *moderately well*
sir.

HAMLET   O, reform it altogether. And let those that play your
35 clowns speak no more than is set down for them; for there be
of° them that will themselves laugh to set° on some quantity of   *some of / urge*
barren° spectators to laugh too, though in the mean time some   *unthinking*
necessary question of the play be then to be considered. That's
villainous, and shows a most pitiful ambition in the fool that
40 uses it. Go make you ready.   *Exeunt* PLAYERS

Enter POLONIUS, GUILDENSTERN, *and* ROSENCRANTZ
[*To* POLONIUS] How now, my lord? Will the King hear this
piece of work?

POLONIUS   And the Queen too, and that presently.°   *immediately*

HAMLET   Bid the players make haste.   *Exit* POLONIUS
Will you two help to hasten them?

45 ROSENCRANTZ *and* GUILDENSTERN   We will, my lord.   *Exeunt*

HAMLET   What ho, Horatio!

Enter HORATIO

HORATIO   Here, sweet lord, at your service.

HAMLET   Horatio, thou art e'en as just° a man   *honest; balanced*
As e'er my conversation coped withal.[2]

HORATIO   O my dear lord—

HAMLET   Nay, do not think I flatter;
50 For what advancement° may I hope from thee,   *political favors*
That no revenue hast but thy good spirits
To feed and clothe thee? Why should the poor be flattered?
No, let the candied° tongue lick absurd pomp,   *flattering*
And crook the pregnant° hinges of the knee   *ready (to bow)*
55 Where thrift may follow feigning.[3] Dost thou hear?—
Since my dear soul was mistress of her choice
And could of° men distinguish, her election   *between*
Hath sealed thee for herself;[4] for thou hast been
As one in suff'ring all that suffers nothing,
60 A man that Fortune's buffets and rewards
Hath ta'en with equal thanks; and blest are those
Whose blood° and judgement are so well commingled   *passion*
That they are not a pipe for Fortune's finger
To sound what stop° she please. Give me that man   *finger holes; notes*
65 That is not passion's slave, and I will wear him
In my heart's core, ay, in my heart of heart,
As I do thee. Something too much of this.
There is a play tonight before the King.
One scene of it comes near the circumstance

---

9. Meaning no blasphemy (by implying as he goes on
to do that some humans were not created by God).
1. Hired assistants to the master craftsmen, still learn-
ing their trade.
2. As I ever encountered in my dealings with men.

3. Where prosperity may result from (flattering) lies.
Most editions follow Q2's "fawning."
4. Has marked you as her own (on a document, a legal
sign of possession).

70   Which I have told thee of my father's death.
I prithee, when thou seest that act afoot,
Even with the very comment of thy soul⁵
Observe mine uncle. If his occulted° guilt   *hidden*
Do not itself unkennel in one speech,
75   It is a damnèd ghost that we have seen,
And my imaginations are as foul
As Vulcan's stithy.⁶ Give him heedful note,
For I mine eyes will rivet to his face,
And after, we will both our judgements join
To censure of his seeming.⁷
80 HORATIO   Well, my lord.
If a° steal aught the whilst this play is playing   *he*
And scape detecting, I will pay the theft.
       Enter trumpets and kettle drums. Sound a flourish
HAMLET   They are coming to the play. I must be idle.°   *mad; unoccupied*
Get you a place.
       Danish march. Enter KING [CLAUDIUS], QUEEN [GER-
       TRUDE], POLONIUS, OPHELIA, ROSENCRANTZ, GUILDEN-
       STERN, *and other lords attendant, with* [*the King's*]
       guard carrying torches
KING CLAUDIUS   How fares⁸ our cousin° Hamlet?   *kinsman*
85 HAMLET   Excellent, i'faith, of the chameleon's dish. I eat the air,
    promise-crammed.⁹ You cannot feed capons¹ so.
KING CLAUDIUS   I have nothing with this answer, Hamlet. These
    words are not mine.
HAMLET   No, nor mine now. [*To* POLONIUS] My lord, you played
90   once i'th' university, you say.
POLONIUS   That I did, my lord, and was accounted a good actor.
HAMLET   And what did you enact?
POLONIUS   I did enact Julius Caesar. I was killed i'th' Capitol.²
    Brutus killed me.
95 HAMLET   It was a brute part of him to kill so capital a calf°   *such a prize fool*
    there.—Be the players ready?
ROSENCRANTZ   Ay, my lord, they stay° upon your patience.   *wait*
QUEEN GERTRUDE   Come hither, my good Hamlet. Sit by me.
HAMLET   No, good-mother,° here's mettle³ more attractive.   *stepmother*
    [*He sits by* OPHELIA]
100 POLONIUS [*aside*]   O ho, do you mark that?
HAMLET [*to* OPHELIA]   Lady, shall I lie in your lap?
OPHELIA   No, my lord.
HAMLET   I mean my head upon your lap?
OPHELIA   Ay, my lord.
105 HAMLET   Do you think I meant country matters?⁴
OPHELIA   I think nothing, my lord.
HAMLET   That's a fair thought to lie between maids' legs.

---

5. With your utmost critical faculty.
6. Smithy, or forge, of Vulcan, the Roman blacksmith god.
7. To judge by his outward reaction.
8. How does; Hamlet's response puns on "fare" as food and drink.
9. The chameleon was supposed to live on air. Hamlet puns on "heir," referring to Claudius's insubstantial promise of the succession.
1. Castrated cocks, crammed or fattened for the table

(and a term for a fool).
2. Perhaps an allusion to Shakespeare's own *Julius Caesar;* the actor who first played Polonius may also have played the part of Caesar.
3. A disposition (punning on magnetically attractive "metal").
4. Rustic doings (with an obscene pun on "cunt"). The punning continues in the following lines, where "nothing" suggests the female genitals (often linked to the shape of a zero), and "thing" the male genitals.

OPHELIA   What is, my lord?

HAMLET   No thing.

110   OPHELIA   You are merry, my lord.

HAMLET   Who, I?

OPHELIA   Ay, my lord.

HAMLET   O God, your only jig-maker![5] What should a man do
but be merry? For look you how cheerfully my mother looks,

115   and my father died within 's° two hours.   *these*

OPHELIA   Nay, 'tis twice two months, my lord.

HAMLET   So long? Nay then, let the devil wear black, for I'll have
a suit of sables.[6] O heavens, die two months ago and not forgot-
ten yet! Then there's hope a great man's memory may outlive

120   his life half a year. But, by'r Lady, a must build churches then,
or else shall a suffer not thinking on,[7] with the hobby-horse,
whose epitaph is 'For O, for O, the hobby-horse is forgot.'[8]

> *Hautboys° play. The dumb show enters. Enter a* KING   *Oboes*
> *and a* QUEEN *very lovingly, the* QUEEN *embracing him.*
> *She kneels and makes show of protestation unto him. He*
> *takes her up and declines° his head upon her neck. He*   *leans*
> *lays him down upon a bank of flowers. She, seeing him*
> *asleep, leaves him. Anon comes in a fellow, takes off his*
> *crown, kisses it, and pours poison in the King's ears, and*
> *exits. The* QUEEN *returns, finds the* KING *dead, and*
> *makes passionate action. The poisoner, with some two or*
> *three mutes,° comes in again, seeming to lament with*   *nonspeaking actors*
> *her. The dead body is carried away. The poisoner woos*
> *the* QUEEN *with gifts. She seems loath and unwilling a*
> *while, but in the end accepts his love. Exeunt [the*
> PLAYERS]

OPHELIA   What means this, my lord?

HAMLET   Marry, this is miching *malhecho*.° That means mis-   *sneaking wrongdoing*

125   chief.

OPHELIA   Belike this show imports the argument° of the play.   *plot*

> *Enter* PROLOGUE

HAMLET   We shall know by this fellow. The players cannot keep
counsel,° they'll tell all.   *a secret*

OPHELIA   Will a tell us what this show meant?

130   HAMLET   Ay, or any show that you'll show him. Be not you
ashamed to show, he'll not shame to tell you what it means.

OPHELIA   You are naught,° you are naught. I'll mark the play.   *indecent*

PROLOGUE   For us and for our tragedy

> Here stooping to your clemency,

135   We beg your hearing patiently.   *[Exit]*

HAMLET   Is this a prologue, or the posy of a ring?[9]

OPHELIA   'Tis brief, my lord.

HAMLET   As woman's love.

> *Enter the* [PLAYER] KING *and his* QUEEN

PLAYER KING   Full thirty times hath Phoebus' cart[1] gone round

---

5. The leading comic actor often devised and performed the farcical song and dance concluding a play. *only:* unrivaled.

6. Sable is both an expensive fur for cloaks and trim and the heraldic term for "black"; Hamlet simultaneously forswears his ascetic mourning and vows to continue it.

7. He shall have to endure being forgotten.

8. The hobbyhorse, a man with a mock horse's body strapped round his waist, was a figure in May Day morris dances (under attack in Shakespeare's time by religious reformers). "The hobby horse is forgot" seems to have been a ballad refrain.

9. The motto engraved in a ring.

1. Apollo's chariot (the sun).

140 Neptune's salt wash and Tellus' orbèd ground,[2]
And thirty dozen moons with borrowed sheen°   *reflected light*
About the world have times twelve thirties been
Since love our hearts and Hymen° did our hands   *goddess of marriage*
Unite commutual in most sacred bands.

145 PLAYER QUEEN   So many journeys may the sun and moon
Make us again count o'er ere love be done.
But woe is me, you are so sick of late,
So far from cheer and from your former state,
That I distrust° you. Yet, though I distrust,   *am worried about*
150 Discomfort° you my lord it nothing must.   *Sadden*
For women's fear and love holds quantity,[3]
In neither aught, or in extremity.[4]
Now what my love is, proof° hath made you know,   *experience*
And as my love is sized,° my fear is so.[5]   *in quantity*
154.1   *Where love is great, the littlest doubts are fear:*
     Where little fears grow great, great love grows there.

155 PLAYER KING   Faith, I must leave thee, love, and shortly too.
My operant° powers their functions leave° to do,   *vital / cease*
And thou shalt live in this fair world behind,
Honoured, beloved; and haply° one as kind   *perhaps*
For husband shalt thou—
PLAYER QUEEN   O, confound the rest!
160 Such love must needs be treason in my breast.
In second husband let me be accurst;
None wed the second but who killed the first.
HAMLET   Wormwood,[6] wormwood.
PLAYER QUEEN   The instances° that second marriage move°   *motives / prompt*
165 Are base respects of thrift,° but none of love.   *considerations of profit*
A second time I kill my husband dead
When second husband kisses me in bed.
PLAYER KING   I do believe you think what now you speak;
But what we do determine oft we break.
170 Purpose is but the slave to[7] memory,
Of violent birth but poor validity,°   *enduring strength*
Which now like fruit unripe sticks on the tree,
But fall unshaken when they mellow be.
Most necessary 'tis that we forget
175 To pay ourselves what to ourselves is debt.[8]
What to ourselves in passion we propose,
The passion ending, doth the purpose lose.
The violence of either grief or joy
Their own enactures with themselves destroy.[9]
180 Where joy most revels, grief doth most lament;
Grief joys, joy grieves, on slender accident.[1]
This world is not for aye,° nor 'tis not strange   *eternity*
That even our loves should with our fortunes change;

2. *Neptune's . . . ground:* The salty flood of the sea god and the round foundation of Tellus (the earth).
3. Are in equal proportions. Q2 includes one other line before this one: "For women fear too much, even as they love / And women's fear . . ."
4. *In . . . extremity:* Either love and fear are both absent, or both are extremely strong.
5. After this line, Q2 has a couplet, 154.1–154.2, omitted in F.
6. A bitter herb taken medicinally (hence, "a bitter pill to

swallow").
7. Our intentions serve and depend on.
8. *Most . . . debt:* It is inevitable (or necessary for our well-being) that we neglect to fulfill those promises made to ourselves.
9. *The violence . . . destroy:* Extreme grief and joy destroy themselves, and the motive for action vanishes with them.
1. On account of a small, unforeseen event.

For 'tis a question left us yet to prove
185   Whether love lead fortune or else fortune love.
The great man down, you mark his favourite flies;
The poor advanced° makes friends of enemies.   *promoted*
And hitherto° doth love on fortune tend,°   *to this extent / attend*
For who not needs shall never lack a friend,
190   And who in want a hollow friend doth try°   *test*
Directly seasons him² his enemy.
But orderly to end where I begun,
Our wills and fates do so contrary run³
That our devices still° are overthrown;   *our plans always*
195   Our thoughts are ours, their ends° none of our own.   *results*
So think thou wilt no second husband wed;
But die thy thoughts when thy first lord is dead.
PLAYER QUEEN   Nor earth to me give food, nor heaven light,
Sport and repose lock from me day and night,⁴
199.1   *To desperation turn my trust and hope;*
An anchor's cheer⁵ in prison be my scope.°   *extent (of good)*
200   Each opposite⁶ that blanks° the face of joy   *makes pale*
Meet what I would have well and it destroy,
Both here and hence pursue me lasting strife
If, once a widow, ever I be wife.
HAMLET   If she should break it now!
PLAYER KING [*to* PLAYER QUEEN]
205   'Tis deeply sworn. Sweet, leave me here a while.
My spirits grow dull, and fain° I would beguile   *gladly*
The tedious day with sleep.
PLAYER QUEEN   Sleep rock thy brain,
And never come mischance between us twain.
          [PLAYER KING] *sleeps. Exit* [PLAYER QUEEN]
HAMLET [*to* GERTRUDE]   Madam, how like you this play?
210   QUEEN GERTRUDE   The lady protests too much, methinks.
HAMLET   O, but she'll keep her word.
KING CLAUDIUS   Have you heard the argument?° Is there no   *plot*
   offence in't?
HAMLET   No, no, they do but jest, poison in jest. No offence i'th'
215   world.
KING CLAUDIUS   What do you call the play?
HAMLET   *The Mousetrap.* Marry, how? Tropically.⁷ This play is
   the image of a murder done in Vienna. Gonzago is the Duke's
   name, his wife Baptista.⁸ You shall see anon. 'Tis a knavish
220   piece of work; but what o' that? Your majesty, and we that have
   free° souls, it touches⁹ us not. Let the galled jade wince, our   *guiltless*
   withers are unwrung.¹
          Enter [PLAYER] LUCIANUS
   This is one Lucianus, nephew to the King.

---

2. Immediately hardens him, as timber is seasoned for
use.
3. What we desire and what is destined to happen are so
opposed.
4. After this line, Q2 has a couplet omitted in F, 199.1–
199.2.
5. Food for an anchorite (ascetic religious hermit).
6. Each adverse force.
7. As a trope, or rhetorical figure (perhaps punning on

"trap").
8. That is, the Player King and Queen (called "Duke"
and "Duchess" throughout Q1). Shakespeare seems to
base *The Mousetrap* on an extremely muddled version
of the Duke of Urbino's alleged 1538 murder by Luigi
Gonzaga.
9. Wounds; concerns.
1. Let the chafed horse wince, our shoulders are not
rubbed sore.

OPHELIA You are as good as a chorus,[2] my lord.
225 HAMLET I could interpret between you and your love if I could
see the puppets dallying.[3]
OPHELIA You are keen,° my lord, you are keen.   *sharply satirical*
HAMLET It would cost you a groaning to take off mine edge.[4]
OPHELIA Still better, and worse.[5]
230 HAMLET So you mis-take your husbands.[6] [*To* LUCIANUS] Begin,
murderer. Pox, leave thy damnable° faces and begin. Come: *grimacing*
'the croaking raven doth bellow for revenge'.[7]
PLAYER LUCIANUS Thoughts black, hands apt, drugs fit, and time
agreeing,
Confederate° season, else no creature seeing;   *Complicit*
235 Thou mixture rank° of midnight weeds collected,   *foul*
With Hecate's ban[8] thrice blasted, thrice infected,
Thy natural magic and dire property°   *quality*
On wholesome life usurp immediately.
[*He*] *pours the poison in* [*the Player King's*] *ears*
HAMLET A poisons him i'th' garden for 's estate.° His name's *position; state*
240 Gonzago. The story is extant, and writ in choice Italian. You
shall see anon how the murderer gets the love of Gonzago's
wife.
OPHELIA The King rises.
HAMLET What, frighted with false fire?[9]
245 QUEEN GERTRUDE [*to* CLAUDIUS] How fares my lord?
POLONIUS Give o'er the play.
KING CLAUDIUS Give me some light. Away.
COURTIERS Lights, lights, lights![1]
Exeunt all but HAMLET *and* HORATIO
HAMLET Why, let the stricken deer go weep,[2]
250 The hart ungallèd° play,   *unafflicted*
For some must watch,° while some must sleep,   *stay awake*
So runs the world away.[3]
Would not this,° sir, and a forest of feathers,[4] if the rest of my (The Mousetrap)
fortunes turn Turk° with me, with two Provençal roses on my *renegade*
255 razed[5] shoes, get me a fellowship in a cry of players,[6] sir?
HORATIO Half a share.
HAMLET A whole one, I.
For thou dost know, O Damon[7] dear,
This realm dismantled° was   *deprived*
260 Of Jove himself, and now reigns here
A very, very—pajock.[8]

2. The Chorus explained the forthcoming action. In pup-
pet shows, a choric narrator, or "interpreter," announced
the characters' names and spoke the dialogue.
3. Flirting. Hamlet uses "interpret" here in the sense of
acting as the go-between, or pander, for two lovers.
4. To satisfy my sexual appetite (leading to groaning in
either sexual intercourse or childbirth).
5. Wittier, and more obscene.
6. With these false promises ("for better and for worse"),
you take your husbands in marriage and cheat on them.
7. Misquoted from *The True Tragedy of Richard III* (c.
1591; not to be confused with Shakespeare's own *Rich-
ard III*).
8. Curse by the goddess of witchcraft.
9. Fireworks or blank cartridges.
1. This line is spoken by Polonius in Q2 and by "All"

in F.
2. A deer was thought to weep when mortally wounded.
These four lines are probably from a lost ballad.
3. That's the way of the world.
4. Plumes, worn often onstage.
5. Decorated with slashes. *Provençal roses*: large rosettes
concealing shoelaces.
6. *a fellowship . . . players*: a profit-sharing partnership in
a pack ("cry") of actors (such as Shakespeare had in the
Lord Chamberlain's Men).
7. Damon and Pythias were legendary ideals of friend-
ship.
8. "Patchock" (rare, meaning something like "oaf"), or
"peacock," emblem of the sin of pride. (The expected
rhyme word would be "ass.")

HORATIO   You might have rhymed.

HAMLET   O good Horatio, I'll take the Ghost's word for a thou-
sand pound. Didst perceive?

265 HORATIO   Very well, my lord.

HAMLET   Upon the talk of the pois'ning?

HORATIO   I did very well note him.

Enter ROSENCRANTZ *and* GUILDENSTERN

HAMLET   Ah ha! Come, some music, come, the recorders,
For if the King like not the comedy,

270   Why then, belike he likes it not, pardie.°   indeed (pardieu)
Come, some music.

GUILDENSTERN   Good my lord, vouchsafe me a word with you.

HAMLET   Sir, a whole history.

GUILDENSTERN   The King, sir—

275 HAMLET   Ay, sir, what of him?

GUILDENSTERN   Is in his retirement° marvellous distempered.   withdrawal

HAMLET   With drink, sir?

GUILDENSTERN   No, my lord, rather with choler.[9]

HAMLET   Your wisdom should show itself more richer° to signify   resourceful

280   this to his doctor, for for me to put him to his purgation[1] would
perhaps plunge him into far more choler.

GUILDENSTERN   Good my lord, put your discourse into some
frame,° and start° not so wildly from my affair.   order / jump away

HAMLET   I am tame, sir. Pronounce.

285 GUILDENSTERN   The Queen your mother, in most great afflic-
tion of spirit, hath sent me to you.

HAMLET   You are welcome.

GUILDENSTERN   Nay, good my lord, this courtesy is not of the
right breed.° If it shall please you to make me a wholesome°   kind; nobility / sane

290   answer, I will do your mother's commandment; if not, your
pardon° and my return shall be the end of my business.   permission to go

HAMLET   Sir, I cannot.

GUILDENSTERN   What, my lord?

HAMLET   Make you a wholesome answer. My wit's diseased. But,

295   sir, such answers as I can make, you shall command; or rather,
as you say, my mother. Therefore no more, but to the matter.
My mother, you say?

ROSENCRANTZ   Then thus she says: your behaviour hath struck
her into amazement and admiration.°   bewilderment

300 HAMLET   O wonderful son, that can so astonish a mother! But is
there no sequel at the heels of this mother's admiration?

ROSENCRANTZ   She desires to speak with you in her closet° ere   private chamber
you go to bed.

HAMLET   We shall obey, were she ten times our mother. Have

305   you any further trade with us?

ROSENCRANTZ   My lord, you once did love me.

HAMLET   So I do still, by these pickers and stealers.[2]

ROSENCRANTZ   Good my lord, what is your cause of distemper?

---

9. Both anger (Guildenstern's meaning) and indiges-
tion (Hamlet's). In Renaissance medical psychology,
each was a symptom of too much yellow bile—an
imbalance ("distemper") of the bodily fluids (humors).
1. A complicated pun: bloodletting; spiritual purging
(confession and absolution); legal purging (clearing one-

self of a crime).
2. Hands. (The catechism in the Book of Common
Prayer includes a promise to "keep my hands from pick-
ing and stealing, and my tongue from evil speaking,
lying, and slandering.")

You do freely° bar the door of your own liberty if you deny your   *voluntarily*
310   griefs to your friend.

HAMLET   Sir, I lack advancement.

ROSENCRANTZ   How can that be when you have the voice of the
  King himself for your succession in Denmark?

HAMLET   Ay, but 'while the grass grows . . .'³—the proverb is
315   something° musty.   *somewhat*

       *Enter one with a recorder*⁴

  O, the recorder. Let me see. [*To* ROSENCRANTZ *and* GUILDEN-
  STERN, *taking them aside*] To withdraw° with you, why do you   *speak privately*
  go about to recover the wind of me as if you would drive me
  into a toil?⁵

320 GUILDENSTERN   O my lord, if my duty be too bold, my love is
  too unmannerly.⁶

HAMLET   I do not well understand that. Will you play upon this
  pipe?

GUILDENSTERN   My lord, I cannot.

325 HAMLET   I pray you.

GUILDENSTERN   Believe me, I cannot.

HAMLET   I do beseech you.

GUILDENSTERN   I know no touch of it, my lord.

HAMLET   'Tis as easy as lying. Govern these ventages° with your   *finger holes*
330   fingers and thumb, give it breath with your mouth, and it will
  discourse most excellent music. Look you, these are the stops.°   *finger holes; notes*

GUILDENSTERN   But these cannot I command to any utterance
  of harmony. I have not the skill.

HAMLET   Why, look you now, how unworthy a thing you make
335   of me! You would play upon me, you would seem to know my
  stops, you would pluck out the heart of my mystery, you would
  sound° me from my lowest note to the top of my compass;° and   *fathom; play on / range*
  there is much music, excellent voice in this little organ,° yet   *musical instrument*
  cannot you make it speak. 'Sblood, do you think I am easier to
340   be played on than a pipe? Call me what instrument you will,
  though you can fret⁷ me, you cannot play upon me.

       Enter POLONIUS

  God bless you, sir.

POLONIUS   My lord, the Queen would speak with you, and pres-
  ently.

345 HAMLET   Do you see yonder cloud that's almost in shape of a
  camel?

POLONIUS   By th' mass, and 'tis: like a camel, indeed.

HAMLET   Methinks it is like a weasel.

POLONIUS   It is backed like a weasel.

350 HAMLET   Or like a whale.

POLONIUS   Very like a whale.

HAMLET   Then will I come to my mother by and by. [*Aside*]
  They fool me to the top of my bent.⁸ [*To* POLONIUS] I will come
  by and by.

355 POLONIUS   I will say so.

HAMLET   'By and by' is easily said.   *Exit* [POLONIUS]

---

3. "While the grass grows, the horse starves."
4. Q2 has "Enter the Players with Recorders."
5. *go . . . toil:* both conspire and take a roundabout
course in order to get to the windward (like a hunter
using his own smell to drive quarry to a waiting snare,
or "toil").

6. If I have been discourteous in pursuing what is my
duty, my love for you is to blame.
7. Irritate, punning on "frets of stringed instruments,"
which regulate fingering and pitch.
8. They go along with my foolishness to its limit, or to
the limit of my endurance.

Leave me, friends. [*Exeunt* ROSENCRANTZ *and* GUILDENSTERN]
'Tis now the very witching time of night,
When churchyards yawn, and hell itself breathes out
360 Contagion to this world. Now could I drink hot blood,
And do such bitter business as the day
Would quake to look on. Soft, now to my mother.
O heart, lose not thy nature!° Let not ever   *natural affection*
The soul of Nero⁹ enter this firm° bosom.   *resolved*
365 Let me be cruel, not unnatural.
I will speak daggers to her, but use none.
My tongue and soul in this be hypocrites¹—
How in my words somever² she be shent,°   *rebuked*
To give them seals³ never my soul consent.   *Exit*

3.3

Enter KING [CLAUDIUS], ROSENCRANTZ, *and* GUILDEN-
STERN
KING CLAUDIUS   I like him not, nor stands it safe with us
To let his madness range. Therefore prepare you.
I your commission will forthwith dispatch,
And he to England shall along with you.
5 The terms of our estate¹ may not endure
Hazard so dangerous as doth hourly grow
Out of his lunacies.²
GUILDENSTERN   We will ourselves provide.
Most holy and religious fear° it is   *care*
To keep those many many bodies safe
10 That live and feed upon your majesty.
ROSENCRANTZ   The single° and peculiar° life is bound   *individual / private*
With all the strength and armour of the mind
To keep itself from noyance;° but much more   *harm*
That spirit upon whose weal° depends and rests   *well-being*
15 The lives of many. The cease° of majesty   *decease*
Dies not alone, but like a gulf° doth draw   *whirlpool*
What's near it with it. It is a massy° wheel   *massive*
Fixed on the summit of the highest mount,
To whose huge spokes ten thousand lesser things
20 Are mortised° and adjoined, which° when it falls   *affixed / so that*
Each small annexment, petty consequence,
Attends° the boist'rous ruin. Never alone   *Accompanies*
Did the King sigh, but with a general groan.
KING CLAUDIUS   Arm° you, I pray you, to this speedy voyage,   *Prepare*
25 For we will fetters put upon this fear
Which now goes too free-footed.
ROSENCRANTZ *and* GUILDENSTERN   We will haste us.
                                           Exeunt [*both*]

Enter POLONIUS
POLONIUS   My lord, he's going to his mother's closet.
Behind the arras° I'll convey myself   *wall tapestry*
To hear the process.° I'll warrant she'll tax him home.³   *proceedings*

---

9. The Roman Emperor Nero reputedly murdered his
mother, in one account, by cutting open her womb.
1. Let me appear and speak as if I intended violence
(though I do not).
2. However much by my words.
3. To confirm them with visible deeds.

3.3 Location: The castle.
1. The responsibilities of our position.
2. Mad actions, apparently a revision in F of Q2's
"browes" (an ambiguous term suggesting "brain,"
"expressions," or "effrontery").
3. I'm sure she will rebuke him thoroughly.

30　And, as you said—and wisely was it said—
　　'Tis meet° that some more audience than a mother, 　　　　*fitting*
　　Since nature makes them partial, should o'erhear
　　The speech of vantage.° Fare you well, my liege. 　　　　*in addition*
　　I'll call upon you ere you go to bed,
　　And tell you what I know.

35　KING CLAUDIUS　　　　　　　Thanks, dear my lord.

Exit [POLONIUS]

　　O, my offence is rank! It smells to heaven.
　　It hath the primal eldest curse[4] upon't,
　　A brother's murder. Pray can I not.
　　Though inclination be as sharp as will,[5]
40　My stronger guilt defeats my strong intent,
　　And like a man to double business bound[6]
　　I stand in pause where I shall first begin,
　　And both neglect. What if this cursèd hand
　　Were thicker than itself with brother's blood,[7]
45　Is there not rain enough in the sweet heavens
　　To wash it white as snow?[8] Whereto serves mercy
　　But to confront the visage of offence?[9]
　　And what's in prayer but this twofold force,
　　To be forestallèd° ere we come to fall, 　　　　*prevented*
50　Or pardoned being down? Then I'll look up.
　　My fault is past—but O, what form of prayer
　　Can serve my turn? 'Forgive me my foul murder'?
　　That cannot be, since I am still possessed
　　Of those effects for which I did the murder—
55　My crown, mine own ambition, and my queen.
　　May one be pardoned and retain th'offence?[1]
　　In the corrupted currents of this world
　　Offence's gilded° hand may shove by justice, 　　　　*bribing*
　　And oft 'tis seen the wicked prize[2] itself
60　Buys out the law. But 'tis not so above.
　　There is no shuffling,° there the action lies 　　　　*evasion*
　　In his true nature,[3] and we ourselves compelled
　　Even to the teeth and forehead of[4] our faults
　　To give in evidence.[5] What then? What rests?° 　　　　*remains to be done*
65　Try what repentance can. What can it not?
　　Yet what can it when one cannot repent?
　　O wretched state, O bosom black as death,
　　O limèd[6] soul that, struggling to be free,
　　Art more engaged!° Help, angels! Make assay.° 　　　　*entangled / some attempt*
70　Bow, stubborn knees; and heart with strings of steel,

---

4. The first, oldest curse (God's curse on Cain for mur-
dering his brother, Abel; see Genesis 4:10–12).
5. Though my desire (to pray) is as strong as my deter-
mination to do so.
6. Committed to two different goals.
7. Were covered with a layer of brother's blood deeper
than the hand's thickness.
8. Compare Isaiah 1:15–18: "And though ye make
many prayers, I will not hear: for your hands are full of
blood. Wash you, make you clean; take away the evil of
your works from before mine eyes. . . . though your
sins were as crimson, they shall be made white as
snow."

9. *Whereto . . . offence:* What purpose has mercy if not
to oppose sin face to face?
1. And keep what was gained from the crime.
2. The profits from wickedness.
3. *the action . . . nature:* the deed appears in its true
form; legal proceedings are properly conducted.
4. *Even . . . of:* Even face to face with. (English law pro-
vided for the confrontation of the accused and the wit-
nesses.)
5. To testify. In English law, one cannot be forced to give
evidence against oneself; heavenly justice is different.
6. Caught as if in birdlime, a sticky substance smeared
on twigs to catch birds.

Be soft as sinews of the new-born babe.
All may be well.
    [*He kneels.*]
    Enter [*Prince*] HAMLET [*behind him*]
HAMLET   Now might I do it pat,° now a° is praying,   *neatly / he*
And now I'll do't,
    [*He draws his sword*]
                and so a goes to heaven,
75   And so am I revenged. That would be scanned.[7]
A villain kills my father, and for that
I, his sole son, do this same villain send
To heaven.
O, this is hire and salary, not revenge!
80   A took my father grossly, full of bread,[8]
With all his crimes broad blown,[9] as flush° as May;   *vigorously thriving*
And how his audit° stands, who knows save heaven?   *spiritual account*
But in our circumstance and course of thought[1]
'Tis heavy with him. And am I then revenged
85   To take him in the purging of his soul,
When he is fit and seasoned° for his passage?   *made ready*
No.
    [*He sheathes his sword*]
Up, sword, and know thou a more horrid hint.°   *occasion*
When he is drunk asleep, or in his rage,
90   Or in th'incestuous pleasure of his bed,
At gaming, swearing, or about some act
That has no relish° of salvation in't,   *trace*
Then trip him that his heels may kick at heaven,
And that his soul may be as damned and black
95   As hell whereto it goes. My mother stays.°   *waits*
This physic[2] but prolongs thy sickly days.   *Exit*
KING CLAUDIUS   My words fly up, my thoughts remain below.
Words without thoughts never to heaven go.   *Exit*

3.4

Enter QUEEN GERTRUDE *and* POLONIUS
POLONIUS   A will come straight.° Look you lay home to him.[1]   *immediately*
Tell him his pranks have been too broad° to bear with,   *outrageous*
And that your grace hath screened and stood between
Much heat and him. I'll silence me e'en here.
5   Pray you be round° with him.   *blunt*
HAMLET (*within*)   Mother, mother, mother!
QUEEN GERTRUDE   I'll warr'nt you. Fear° me not. Withdraw; I   *Doubt*
    hear him coming.
    [POLONIUS *hides behind the arras.*]
    Enter [*Prince*] HAMLET
HAMLET   Now, mother, what's the matter?
QUEEN GERTRUDE   Hamlet, thou hast thy father much offended.
10   HAMLET   Mother, you have my father much offended.

---

7. That needs careful evaluation.
8. Not spiritually prepared. Compare Ezekiel 16:49:
"Behold, this was the iniquity of thy sister Sodom, pride,
fullness of bread, and abundance of idleness."
9. With all his sins in full bloom.
1. But in our indirect and limited way of knowing on
earth.
2. Medicine (both Claudius's prayer and Hamlet's
postponement of the revenge).
3.4 Location: The Queen's private chamber.
1. Be sure to rebuke him thoroughly.

QUEEN GERTRUDE	Come, come, you answer with an idle tongue.	
HAMLET	Go, go, you question with a wicked tongue.	
QUEEN GERTRUDE	Why, how now,° Hamlet?	*what's this*
HAMLET	What's the matter now?	
QUEEN GERTRUDE	Have you forgot me?²	
HAMLET	No, by the rood,° not so.	*Cross of Christ*

15 You are the Queen, your husband's brother's wife.
But—would you were not so—you are my mother.

QUEEN GERTRUDE   Nay, then, I'll set those to you that can speak.³

HAMLET   Come, come, and sit you down. You shall not budge.
You go not till I set you up a glass°   *mirror*
20 Where you may see the inmost part of you.

QUEEN GERTRUDE   What wilt thou do? Thou wilt not murder me?
Help, help, ho!

POLONIUS [*behind the arras*]   What ho! Help, help, help!

HAMLET   How now, a rat? Dead for a ducat, dead.⁴
[*He thrusts his sword through the arras.*] *Kills* POLONIUS

POLONIUS   O, I am slain!

QUEEN GERTRUDE [*to* HAMLET]   O me, what hast thou done?

25 HAMLET   Nay, I know not. Is it the King?

QUEEN GERTRUDE   O, what a rash and bloody deed is this!

HAMLET   A bloody deed—almost as bad, good-mother,°   *stepmother*
As kill a king and marry with his brother.

QUEEN GERTRUDE   As kill a king?

HAMLET   Ay, lady, 'twas my word.
30 [*To* POLONIUS] Thou wretched, rash, intruding fool, farewell.
I took thee for thy better. Take thy fortune.
Thou find'st to be too busy° is some danger.—   *nosy*
Leave wringing of your hands. Peace, sit you down,
And let me wring your heart; for so I shall
35 If it be made of penetrable stuff,
If damnèd custom° have not brassed it so   *sinful habit*
That it is proof and bulwark against sense.⁵

QUEEN GERTRUDE   What have I done, that thou dar'st wag thy tongue
In noise so rude against me?

HAMLET   Such an act
40 That blurs the grace and blush of modesty,
Calls virtue hypocrite, takes off the rose
From the fair forehead of an innocent love
And sets a blister there,⁶ makes marriage vows
As false as dicers' oaths—O, such a deed
45 As from the body of contraction° plucks   *marriage contract*
The very soul, and sweet religion makes
A rhapsody⁷ of words. Heaven's face doth glow,°   *blush*
Yea, this solidity and compound mass⁸
With tristful° visage, as against the doom,⁹   *sad*
Is thought-sick at the act.

50 QUEEN GERTRUDE   Ay me, what act,

---

2. Forgotten the respect you owe to me as your mother.
3. *that can speak:* who can deal with someone as impossibly rude as you.
4. I bet a ducat I have killed it.
5. *brassed . . . sense:* made it so brasslike (or brazen) that it is impenetrably fortified against natural feeling ("sense").

6. Prostitutes, among other criminals, were branded on the forehead during the sixteenth and seventeenth centuries.
7. Meaningless jumble.
8. Solid earth (a compound of the four elements).
9. As if preparing for the Last Judgment.

That roars so loud and thunders in the index?[1]
HAMLET   Look here upon this picture, and on this,
The counterfeit presentment° of two brothers.   *painted portrayal*
See what a grace was seated on this brow—
55   Hyperion's° curls, the front° of Jove himself,   *The sun god's / forehead*
An eye like Mars,° to threaten or command,   *the god of war*
A station like the herald Mercury[2]
New lighted° on a heaven-kissing hill;   *alighted*
A combination and a form indeed
60   Where every god did seem to set his seal
To give the world assurance of a man.
This *was* your husband. Look you now what follows.
Here *is* your husband, like a mildewed ear°   *ear of grain*
Blasting° his wholesome brother. Have you eyes?   *Infesting*
65   Could you on this fair mountain leave° to feed,   *cease*
And batten on this moor?[3] Ha, have you eyes?
You cannot call it love, for at your age
The heyday in the blood[4] is tame, it's humble,
And waits° upon the judgement; and what judgement   *follows*
70   Would step from this to this?[5]
70.1   *Sense[6] sure you have,*
                   Else could you not have motion; but sure that sense
                   Is apoplexed,° for madness would not err,   *paralyzed*
                   Nor sense to ecstasy was ne'er so thralled
70.5   *But it reserved some quantity of choice*
                   To serve in such a difference.[7] What devil was't
                   That thus hath cozened you at hoodman-blind?[8]
                   Eyes without feeling, feeling without sight,
                   Ears without hands or eyes, smelling sans all,[9]
70.10   *Or but a sickly part of one true sense*
                   Could not so mope.[1]
                          What devil was't
That thus hath cozened you at hood-man blind?[2]
O shame, where is thy blush? Rebellious hell,
If thou canst mutine° in a matron's bones,   *mutiny*
To flaming youth let virtue be as wax
75   And melt in her° own fire. Proclaim no shame   *(youth's)*
When the compulsive ardour gives the charge,°   *order to attack*
Since frost itself as actively doth burn,
And reason panders will.[3]
QUEEN GERTRUDE   O Hamlet, speak no more!
Thou turn'st mine eyes into my very soul,
80   And there I see such black and grainèd° spots   *engrained*
As will not leave their tinct.°   *lose their color*
HAMLET   Nay, but to live
In the rank sweat of an enseamèd° bed,   *a greasy*

1. Table of contents; preface.
2. A stance like the winged herald of the gods.
3. And glut yourself on this poor pastureland (possibly punning on "blackamoor").
4. The excitement of sexual passion.
5. After "this?" Q2 has a longer version, 70.1–70.11, of Hamlet's subsequent one and a half lines.
6. Sensation; the five senses (sight, smell, hearing, taste, and touch).
7. *ne'er . . . difference:* never so enslaved by madness that it did not retain some ability to choose between such different men ("sense" connoting "reason").
8. See note to line 71.
9. *sans all:* without any other sense. Cf. Psalm 115:5–6 on idolaters: "Eyes have they, but they see not: They have ears but they hear not: noses have they, but they smell not."
1. Could not be so obtuse.
2. That in this way has cheated you in blindman's buff (as if her second husband had been put in her way while she was groping blindfolded).
3. And mature reason abets lust (rather than restraining it).

Stewed in corruption, honeying and making love
Over the nasty sty—

QUEEN GERTRUDE   O, speak to me no more!
85   These words like daggers enter in mine ears.
No more, sweet Hamlet.

HAMLET   A murderer and a villain,
A slave that is not twenti'th part the tithe°   *one-tenth*
Of your precedent° lord, a vice[4] of kings,   *previous*
A cutpurse° of the empire and the rule,   *pickpocket*
90   That from a shelf the precious diadem stole
And put it in his pocket—

QUEEN GERTRUDE   No more.

HAMLET   A king of shreds and patches[5]—
Enter GHOST *in his nightgown*[6]
Save me and hover o'er me with your wings,
95   You heavenly guards! [*To* GHOST] What would you, gracious figure?

QUEEN GERTRUDE   Alas, he's mad.

HAMLET [*to* GHOST]   Do you not come your tardy son to chide,
That, lapsed in time and passion,[7] lets go by
Th'important° acting of your dread command?   *urgent*
O, say!

100   GHOST   Do not forget. This visitation
Is but to whet thy almost blunted purpose.
But look, amazement on thy mother sits.
O, step between her and her fighting soul.
Conceit° in weakest bodies strongest works.   *Imagination*
105   Speak to her, Hamlet.

HAMLET   How is it with you, lady?

QUEEN GERTRUDE   Alas, how is't with you,
That you do bend your eye on vacancy,
And with th'incorporal° air do hold discourse?   *bodiless*
110   Forth at your eyes your spirits wildly peep,
And, as the sleeping soldiers in th'alarm,°   *call to arms*
Your bedded hair, like life in excrements,[8]
Start up and stand on end. O gentle son,
Upon the heat and flame of thy distemper°   *unbalanced mind*
115   Sprinkle cool patience! Whereon do you look?

HAMLET   On him, on him. Look you how pale he glares.
His form and cause conjoined,[9] preaching to stones,
Would make them capable. [*To* GHOST] Do not look
upon me,
Lest with this piteous action you convert°   *change (to mercy)*
120   My stern effects.° Then what I have to do,   *intended acts*
Will want true colour[1]—tears perchance° for blood.   *perhaps*

QUEEN GERTRUDE   To whom do you speak this?

HAMLET   Do you see nothing there?

QUEEN GERTRUDE   Nothing at all, yet all that is I see.

HAMLET   Nor did you nothing hear?

QUEEN GERTRUDE   No, nothing but ourselves.

---

4. In morality plays, the buffoon who personified evil.
5. *shreds and patches:* motley, the costume of a jester.
6. The nightgown is specified only in Q1; Q2 and F
leave open the possibility that the Ghost is appearing
again in his armor.
7. *lapsed . . . passion:* having allowed time to pass and

passionate dedication (to revenge) to fade.
8. In insensate outgrowths (used of nails and hair).
bedded: (formerly) flat and inert.
9. His appearance joined with his reason for appearing.
1. Will not be as it should (since he cries colorless tears
instead of shedding red blood).

125 HAMLET Why, look you there. Look how it steals away.
My father, in his habit² as° he lived. _when; as if_
Look where he goes even now out at the portal.

Exit GHOST

QUEEN GERTRUDE This is the very coinage of your brain.
This bodiless creation ecstasy
Is very cunning in.³

130 HAMLET Ecstasy?
My pulse as yours doth temperately keep time,
And makes as healthful music. It is not madness
That I have uttered. Bring me to the test,
And I the matter will reword,° which madness _repeat exactly_

135 Would gambol° from. Mother, for love of grace _skitter away_
Lay not a flattering unction⁴ to your soul
That not your trespass but my madness speaks.
It will but skin° and film the ulcerous place _cover_
Whilst rank corruption, mining° all within, _undermining_

140 Infects unseen. Confess yourself to heaven;
Repent what's past, avoid what is to come,
And do not spread the compost o'er the weeds
To make them ranker. Forgive me this my virtue,° _virtuous exhortation_
For in the fatness° of these pursy° times _grossness / flatulent_

145 Virtue itself of vice must pardon beg,
Yea, curb° and woo for leave° to do him good. _bow / permission_

QUEEN GERTRUDE O Hamlet, thou hast cleft my heart in twain!

HAMLET O, throw away the worser part of it,
And live the purer with the other half!

150 Good night—but go not to mine uncle's bed.
Assume° a virtue if you have it not.⁵ _Put on (actions of)_

151.1 _That monster custom, who all sense doth eat,_
Of habits devilish,⁶ is angel yet in this:
That to the use° of actions fair and good _habitual practice_
He likewise gives a frock or livery

151.5 _That aptly° is put on. Refrain tonight,_ _quickly_
And that shall lend a kind of easiness
To the next abstinence, the next more easy—
For use almost can change the stamp of nature—
And either in° the devil, or throw him out _let in_

151.10 _With wondrous potency._

Refrain tonight,
And that shall lend a kind of easiness
To the next abstinence. Once more, good night;

155 And when you are desirous to be blest,
I'll blessing beg of you. For this same lord,
I do repent. But heaven hath pleased it so
To punish me with this, and this with me,
That I must be their scourge and minister.⁷

160 I will bestow° him, and will answer well⁸ _dispose of_
The death I gave him. So, again, good night.

---

2. Dress and bearing.
3. _This bodiless . . . in:_ This type of hallucination is a
particular skill ("cunning") of madness.
4. Do not apply an ointment that relieves pain but does
not heal (contrasted to a sacramental unction that
blesses the soul).

5. Q2 has the following longer version (151.1–151.10)
of lines 152–54 (_Refrain . . . abstinence_).
6. Emended from Q2's "devil," apparently in compressed
opposition to "angel."
7. Heaven's agent of punishment.
8. Will take responsibility for.

I must be cruel only to be kind.
Thus bad begins, and worse remains behind.[9]

QUEEN GERTRUDE   What shall I do?

165   HAMLET   Not this, by no means, that I bid you do:
Let the bloat King tempt you again to bed,
Pinch wanton on your cheek, call you his mouse,
And let him for a pair of reechy° kisses,   *filthy*
Or paddling° in your neck with his damned fingers,   *fondly fingering*
170   Make you to ravel° all this matter out,   *disclose*
That I essentially am not in madness,
But mad in craft.° 'Twere good you let him know,   *cunning*
For who that's but° a queen, fair, sober, wise,   *only*
Would from a paddock,° from a bat, a gib,°   *toad / tomcat*
175   Such dear concernings° hide? Who would do so?   *Such vital affairs*
No, in despite of sense and secrecy,
Unpeg the basket on the house's top,
Let the birds fly, and, like the famous ape,
To try conclusions in the basket creep,
180   And break your own neck down.[1]

QUEEN GERTRUDE   Be thou assured, if words be made of breath,
And breath of life, I have no life to breathe
What thou hast said to me.

HAMLET   I must to England.
You know that?

QUEEN GERTRUDE   Alack, I had forgot.
185   'Tis so concluded on.[2]

185.1   HAMLET   *There's letters sealed, and my two schoolfellows—*
Whom I will trust as I will adders fanged—
They bear the mandate, they must sweep my way
And marshal me to knavery[3] Let it work,°   *proceed*
185.5   *For 'tis the sport to have the engineer[4]*
Hoised with his own petard;[5] and't shall go hard
But I will delve one yard below their mines°   *military tunnels*
And blow them at the moon. O, 'tis most sweet
When in one line two crafts directly meet.[6]

HAMLET   This man shall set me packing.
I'll lug the guts into the neighbour room.
Mother, good night indeed. This counsellor
Is now most still, most secret, and most grave,
Who was in life a foolish prating knave.—
190   Come, sir, to draw toward an end with you.[7]—
Good night, mother.   *Exit, tugging in* POLONIUS

---

9. To follow. Q2 here adds, "One word more good
Lady."
1. *like . . . down:* a tale presumably involving an ape who
opened a wicker cage full of birds and released them from
the rooftop; after climbing into the basket, he tried to imi-
tate their flight to freedom but died in the fall. *try con-
clusions:* test the results.
2. Q2 contains the following additional passage.
3. *sweep . . . knavery:* prepare my path and escort me

into a trap (also, and provoke me to crime).
4. Designer and builder of "engines" (military devices).
5. Blown skyward by his own bomb (for breaching
enemy fortifications).
6. That is, when two devious plots ("crafts") meet along
the same path of tunneling (a standard technique in siege
warfare).
7. To conclude my dealings with you (punning on
"draw" as "drag").

4.1

Enter KING CLAUDIUS *to* QUEEN GERTRUDE[1]

KING CLAUDIUS   There's matter in these sighs, these profound heaves;
You must translate. 'Tis fit we understand them.
Where is your son?[2]

3.1   QUEEN GERTRUDE   *Bestow this place on us a little while*
                    Exeunt [ROSENCRANTZ *and* GUILDENSTERN]
Ah, my good lord, what have I seen tonight!

5   KING CLAUDIUS   What, Gertrude? How does Hamlet?

QUEEN GERTRUDE   Mad as the sea and wind when both contend
Which is the mightier. In his lawless fit,
Behind the arras hearing something stir,
He whips his rapier out and cries 'A rat, a rat!',

10   And in his brainish apprehension° kills   *brain-sick notion*
The unseen good old man.

KING CLAUDIUS   O heavy deed!
It had been so with us° had we been there.   *me (royal "we")*
His liberty is full of threats to all—
To you yourself, to us, to everyone.

15   Alas, how shall this bloody deed be answered?°   *accounted for*
It will be laid to° us, whose providence°   *blamed on / foresight*
Should have kept short,° restrained, and out of haunt[3]   *closely tethered*
This mad young man. But so much was our love,
We would not understand what was most fit,

20   But, like the owner° of a foul disease,   *victim*
To keep it from divulging,° let it feed   *being seen*
Even on the pith of life. Where is he gone?

QUEEN GERTRUDE   To draw apart the body he hath killed,
O'er whom—his very madness, like some ore°   *vein of gold*

25   Among a mineral° of metals base,   *mine*
Shows itself pure—a° weeps for what is done.   *he*

KING CLAUDIUS   O Gertrude, come away!
The sun no sooner shall the mountains touch
But we will ship him hence; and this vile deed

30   We must with all our majesty and skill
Both countenance° and excuse.—Ho, Guildenstern!   *condone*
                    Enter ROSENCRANTZ *and* GUILDENSTERN
Friends both, go join you with some further aid.
Hamlet in madness hath Polonius slain,
And from his mother's closet hath he dragged him.

35   Go seek him out, speak fair, and bring the body
Into the chapel. I pray you haste in this.
                    Exeunt [ROSENCRANTZ *and* GUILDENSTERN]
Come, Gertrude, we'll call up our wisest friends
To let them know both what we mean to do
And what's untimely done.[4]

39.1   *So envious slander,*[5]
          Whose whisper o'er the world's diameter,°   *whole extent*

4.1 Location: The castle.
1. The action continues, Gertrude remaining onstage.
(Act divisions in the play are not authorial.) In Q2,
Rosencrantz and Guildenstern enter with Claudius.
2. In Q2, Rosencrantz and Guildenstern, having entered
with Claudius and Gertrude, can exit here (see line 3.1).

3. Public gatherings.
4. After "done," Q2 has the following passage,
39.1–39.5, omitted in F.
5. The phrase is conjectural. Q2 is missing a half line
that contains the subject of the sentence.

As level as the cannon to his blank,[6]
Transports his poisoned shot, may miss our name
39.5 And hit the woundless° air. *invulnerable*
O, come away!
40 My soul is full of discord and dismay. *Exeunt*

4.2

Enter [Prince] HAMLET
HAMLET   Safely stowed.
ROSENCRANTZ *and* GUILDENSTERN (*within*) Hamlet, Lord Hamlet!
HAMLET   What noise? Who calls on Hamlet?
Enter ROSENCRANTZ *and* GUILDENSTERN
O, here they come.
ROSENCRANTZ   What have you done, my lord, with the dead body?
5 HAMLET   Compounded° it with dust, whereto 'tis kin. *Mixed*
ROSENCRANTZ   Tell us where 'tis, that we may take it thence
And bear it to the chapel.
HAMLET   Do not believe it.
ROSENCRANTZ   Believe what?
10 HAMLET   That I can keep your counsel and not mine own.[1]
Besides, to be demanded of° a sponge—what replication° *questioned by / reply*
should be made by the son of a king?
ROSENCRANTZ   Take you me for a sponge, my lord?
HAMLET   Ay, sir, that soaks up the King's countenance,° his *favor*
15 rewards, his authorities. But such officers do the King best ser-
vice in the end. He keeps them, like an ape an apple in the
corner of his jaw, first mouthed to be last swallowed. When he
needs what you have gleaned, it is but squeezing you, and,
sponge, you shall be dry again.
20 ROSENCRANTZ   I understand you not, my lord.
HAMLET   I am glad of it. A knavish speech sleeps in a foolish
ear.[2]
ROSENCRANTZ   My lord, you must tell us where the body is, and
go with us to the King.
25 HAMLET   The body is with the King, but the King is not with the
body.[3] The King is a thing—
GUILDENSTERN   A thing, my lord?
HAMLET   Of nothing. Bring me to him. Hide fox, and all after.[4]
[*Exit running, pursued by the others*]

4.3

Enter KING [CLAUDIUS][1]
KING CLAUDIUS   I have sent to seek him, and to find the body.
How dangerous is it that this man goes loose!
Yet must not we put the strong law on him.
He's loved of° the distracted° multitude, *by / unreasonable*

---

6. As straight as the cannon at a target at point-blank
range. (The cannon would be tilted to aim at a distant
target.)
4.2 Location: Scene continues.
1. Hamlet plays on two senses of "counsel": That I can
follow your advice and not keep my secret.
2. An insulting remark is not perceived by a fool.
3. A riddle. Hamlet may mean that Polonius is gone to
the afterlife with King Hamlet but Claudius is still alive;
or he may refer to the legal theory of the "king's two bod-

ies" (one the king's natural body, the other the immortal
abstract body of the state).
4. From the children's game fox-and-hounds, similar to
hide-and-seek.
4.3 Location: Scene continues.
1. Q2 reads, "Enter King and two or three," thus allow-
ing the ensuing lines to be spoken to other characters
rather than treating them as a soliloquy or directed to
the audience.

5   Who like not in their judgement but their eyes,[2]

And where 'tis so, th'offender's scourge° is weighed,   *punishment*

But never the offence. To bear° all smooth and even,   *manage*

This sudden sending him away must seem

Deliberate pause.° Diseases desperate grown   *Careful planning*

10   By desperate appliance° are relieved,   *remedy*

Or not at all.

        Enter ROSENCRANTZ

           How now, what hath befall'n?

ROSENCRANTZ   Where the dead body is bestowed, my lord,

We cannot get from him.

KING CLAUDIUS   But where is he?

ROSENCRANTZ   Without, my lord, guarded to know your pleasure.

15   KING CLAUDIUS   Bring him before us.

ROSENCRANTZ   Ho, Guildenstern! Bring in my lord.

        Enter [Prince] HAMLET *and* GUILDENSTERN

KING CLAUDIUS   Now, Hamlet, where's Polonius?

HAMLET   At supper.

KING CLAUDIUS   At supper? Where?

20   HAMLET   Not where he eats, but where a is eaten.[3] A certain

convocation of politic° worms are e'en° at him. Your worm is   *cunning / now*

your only emperor for diet.[4] We fat all creatures else° to fat us,   *besides ourselves*

and we fat ourselves for maggots. Your fat king and your lean

beggar is but variable service°—two dishes, but to one table.   *different courses*

25   That's the end.

KING CLAUDIUS   Alas, alas!

HAMLET   A man may fish with the worm that hath eat of a king,

and eat of the fish that hath fed of that worm.

KING CLAUDIUS   What dost thou mean by this?

30   HAMLET   Nothing but to show you how a king may go a progress°   *royal journey*

through the guts of a beggar.

KING CLAUDIUS   Where is Polonius?

HAMLET   In heaven. Send thither to see. If your messenger find

him not there, seek him i'th' other place yourself. But indeed,

35   if you find him not this month, you shall nose him as you go

up the stairs into the lobby.

KING CLAUDIUS *[to* ROSENCRANTZ*]*   Go seek him there.

HAMLET *[to* ROSENCRANTZ*]*   A will stay till ye come.

                   [Exit ROSENCRANTZ*]*

KING CLAUDIUS   Hamlet, this deed of thine, for thine especial safety—

40   Which we do tender° as we dearly grieve   *value*

For that which thou hast done—must send thee hence

With fiery quickness. Therefore prepare thyself.

The barque is ready, and the wind at help,

Th'associates tend,° and everything is bent°   *companions wait / poised*

45   For England.

HAMLET   For England?

KING CLAUDIUS   Ay, Hamlet.

---

2. Who choose not by reason but by external appearance.
3. Possibly an allusion to the Eucharist (Lord's Supper), in which the body of Christ is consumed in the form of bread.
4. *Your worm . . . diet*: The average worm is the only creature with a diet superior to a King's. The Diet

(Council) of Emperor Charles V at Worms in 1521 called on Luther to defend his new doctrine. A scholar at Hamlet's university at Wittenberg, Luther maintained that faith alone, rather than sacramental ritual, was the basis of salvation.

HAMLET   Good.

KING CLAUDIUS   So is it if thou knew'st our purposes.

50   HAMLET   I see a cherub⁵ that sees them. But come, for England.
Farewell, dear mother.

KING CLAUDIUS   Thy loving father, Hamlet.

HAMLET   My mother. Father and mother is man and wife, man
and wife is one flesh,⁶ and so my mother. Come, for England.

$\qquad\qquad\qquad\qquad\qquad\qquad\qquad\qquad$ *Exit*

55   KING CLAUDIUS [*to* GUILDENSTERN]   Follow him at foot.° Tempt $\qquad$ *his heel*
him with speed aboard.
Delay it not. I'll have him hence tonight.
Away, for everything is sealed and done
That else leans° on th'affair. Pray you, make haste. $\qquad$ *bears*

$\qquad\qquad\qquad\qquad\qquad\qquad$ [*Exit* GUILDENSTERN]

And, England,⁷ if my love thou hold'st at aught°— $\qquad$ *any value*
60   As my great power thereof may give thee sense,⁸
Since yet thy cicatrice° looks raw and red $\qquad$ *scar*
After the Danish sword, and thy free awe⁹
Pays homage to us—thou mayst not coldly set° $\qquad$ *indifferently view*
Our sovereign process, which imports at full,¹
65   By letters conjuring to that effect,
The present° death of Hamlet. Do it, England, $\qquad$ *immediate*
For like the hectic° in my blood he rages, $\qquad$ *fever*
And thou must cure me. Till I know 'tis done,
Howe'er my haps,° my joys were ne'er begun. $\qquad$ *Exit* $\qquad$ *fortunes*

4.4

Enter FORTINBRAS *with a drum and his army over the
stage*

FORTINBRAS   Go, captain, from me greet the Danish king.
Tell him that by his licence° Fortinbras $\qquad$ *permission*
Claims the conveyance of° a promised march $\qquad$ *escort for*
Over his kingdom. You know the rendezvous.
5   If that his majesty would aught with us,
We shall express our duty in his eye,° $\qquad$ *presence*
And let him know so.

CAPTAIN   I will do't, my lord. $\qquad\qquad\qquad$ [*Exit*]

FORTINBRAS   Go safely¹ on. $\qquad\qquad\qquad$ *Exeunt* [*marching*]

Enter [*Prince*] HAMLET, ROSENCRANTZ, [GUILDENSTERN,] *etc.*

9.1   HAMLET [*to the* CAPTAIN]   *Good sir, whose powers*° *are these?* $\qquad$ *forces*

CAPTAIN   *They are of Norway, sir.*

HAMLET $\qquad\qquad\qquad\qquad$ *How purposed, sir, I pray you?*

CAPTAIN   *Against some part of Poland.*

HAMLET $\qquad\qquad\qquad\qquad\qquad$ *Who commands them, sir?*

CAPTAIN   *The nephew to old Norway, Fortinbras.*

9.5   HAMLET   *Goes it against the main*° *of Poland, sir,* $\qquad$ *heart*
Or for some frontier?

CAPTAIN   *Truly to speak, and with no addition,*° $\qquad$ *exaggeration*

---

5. The keen-sighted second order of angels, cherubim symbolized heavenly knowledge.
6. As stated in Genesis 2:23 and the marriage rite of the Book of Common Prayer.
7. King of England.
8. May give you a reason to feel the value of that love.
9. Your respect unconstrained (by an army of occupa-

tion).
1. Our sovereign command, which signifies in detailed instructions.
4.4 Location: The Danish coast.
1. In Q2, "softly" (that is, slowly, circumspectly). In Q2, the captain remains onstage, and the scene continues with the following passage, 9.1–9.56.

We go to gain a little patch of ground
That hath in it no profit but the name.

9.10 To pay five ducats, five, I would not farm° it,   *lease*
Nor will it yield to Norway or the Pole
A ranker rate, should it be sold in fee.²

HAMLET Why then, the Polack never will defend it.

CAPTAIN Yes, it is already garrisoned.

9.15 HAMLET Two thousand souls and twenty thousand ducats
Will now³ debate the question of this straw.°   *trifle*
This is th'imposthume° of much wealth and peace,   *abscess*
That inward breaks and shows no cause without⁴
Why the man dies. I humbly thank you, sir.

CAPTAIN God buy° you, sir.   [*Exit*]   *be with*

9.20 ROSENCRANTZ   Will't please you go, my lord?

HAMLET I'll be with you straight. Go a little before
                                                          [*Exeunt all but* HAMLET]

How all occasions do inform against° me   *accuse*
And spur my dull revenge! What is a man
If his chief good and market° of his time   *profit*
9.25 Be but to sleep and feed?—a beast, no more.
Sure, he that made us with such large discourse,°   *reasoning faculty*
Looking before and after,⁵ gave us not
That capability° and god-like reason   *intelligence*
To fust° in us unused. Now whether it be   *grow moldy*
9.30 Bestial oblivion,⁶ or some craven scruple
Of thinking too precisely on th'event—
A thought which, quartered, hath but one part wisdom
And ever three parts coward—I do not know
Why yet I live to say 'This thing's to do',
9.35 Sith° I have cause, and will, and strength, and means,   *Since*
To do't. Examples gross as earth exhort me,
Witness this army of such mass and charge,°   *cost*
Led by a delicate and tender° prince,   *young*
Whose spirit with divine ambition puffed°   *inspired*
9.40 Makes mouths at the invisible event,⁷
Exposing what is mortal and unsure
To all that fortune, death, and danger dare,
Even for an eggshell. Rightly to be great
Is not to stir without great argument,
9.45 But greatly to find quarrel in a straw
When honour's at the stake.⁸ How stand I, then,
That have a father killed, a mother stained,
Excitements° of my reason and my blood,   *Urgings*
And let all sleep while, to my shame, I see
9.50 The imminent death of twenty thousand men
That, for a fantasy and trick° of fame,   *fragile trifle*
Go to their graves like beds, fight for a plot
Whereon the numbers cannot try the cause,⁹

---

2. Sold outright as a freehold. *ranker rate:* more generous
return.
3. Oxford's emendation of Q2's "Will not."
4. That ruptures internally without external symptom.
5. Able to see past and future.
6. Animal-like inability to remember.

7. Shows a scornful face to unforeseeable outcomes.
8. *Rightly . . . stake:* These lines, syntactically ambiguous, seem to mean that true greatness lies not in rational restraint but in noble action. *the stake:* post to which a bull or bear was fastened for baiting.
9. Which is not big enough for the armies to fight on.

Which is not tomb enough and continent°   *container*
9.55   To hide the slain. O, from this time forth
My thoughts be bloody or be nothing worth!   Exit

4.5

Enter QUEEN GERTRUDE *and* HORATIO

QUEEN GERTRUDE   I will not speak with her.

HORATIO[1]   She is importunate,
Indeed distraught. Her mood will needs be pitied.

QUEEN GERTRUDE   What would she have?

HORATIO   She speaks much of her father, says she hears
5   There's tricks i'th' world, and hems, and beats her heart,
Spurns enviously at straws,[2] speaks things in doubt°   *obscurely*
That carry but half sense. Her speech is nothing,
Yet the unshapèd use° of it doth move   *incoherent manner*
The hearers to collection.° They aim° at it,   *inference / guess*
10   And botch° the words up fit to° their own thoughts,   *patch / to match*
Which,° as her winks and nods and gestures yield them,   *(words)*
Indeed would make one think there might be thought,
Though nothing sure, yet much unhappily.[3]

QUEEN GERTRUDE   'Twere good she were spoken with, for she may strew
15   Dangerous conjectures in ill-breeding minds.
Let her come in.

      [HORATIO *withdraws to admit* OPHELIA]

QUEEN GERTRUDE   To my sick soul, as sin's true nature is,
Each toy° seems prologue to some great amiss.°   *triviality / calamity*
So full of artless jealousy° is guilt,   *uncontrolled suspicion*
20   It spills itself in fearing to be spilt.

Enter OPHELIA *distracted, playing on a lute, and her
hair down, singing*[4]

OPHELIA   Where is the beauteous majesty of Denmark?

QUEEN GERTRUDE   How now,° Ophelia?   *What's this*

OPHELIA (*sings*) How should I your true love know
            From another one?—
25   By his cockle hat and staff,
           And his sandal shoon.[5]

QUEEN GERTRUDE   Alas, sweet lady, what imports° this song?   *means*

OPHELIA   Say you? Nay, pray you, mark.°   *listen*
   (*Song*)   He is dead and gone, lady,
30   He is dead and gone.
          At his head a grass-green turf,
          At his heels a stone.

QUEEN GERTRUDE   Nay, but Ophelia—

OPHELIA   Pray you, mark.
35   (*Song*)   White his shroud as the mountain snow—

Enter KING [CLAUDIUS]

QUEEN GERTRUDE   Alas, look here, my lord.

4.5 Location: A public room of the castle.
1. As in F. In Q2, lines 1–2 and 4–13 are spoken by a
"Gent.," while Horatio comments on them in lines
14–15 (assigned in F to Gertrude).
2. Kicks bitterly (takes offense) at the slightest thing.
3. Though they reveal nothing for certain, her words

could lead to unfortunate impressions.
4. F simply notes that Ophelia enters distracted; the
additional details are taken from Q1.
5. Shoes. *cockle hat*: a cockle-shell badge worn in the
hat was a pilgrim's memento of St. James's shrine at
Compostela in Spain.

OPHELIA *(Song)*   Larded° with sweet flowers,   *Garnished*
                   Which bewept to the grave did—not[6]—go
                   With true-love showers.°   *tears*
40 KING CLAUDIUS   How do ye, pretty lady?
OPHELIA   Well, God'ield° you. They say the owl was a baker's   *God yield (reward)*
    daughter.[7] Lord, we know what we are, but know not what we
    may be. God be at your table!
    KING CLAUDIUS *[to* GERTRUDE*]*   Conceit° upon her father.   *Brooding imagination*
45 OPHELIA   Pray you, let's have no words of this, but when they ask
    you what it means, say you this.
                   (Song)   Tomorrow is Saint Valentine's day,
                   All in the morning betime,°   *early*
                   And I a maid at your window
50   To be your Valentine.
                   Then up he rose, and donned his clothes,
                   And dupped° the chamber door;   *unlatched*
                   Let in the maid, that out a maid
                   Never departed more.
55 KING CLAUDIUS   Pretty Ophelia—
OPHELIA   Indeed, la? Without an oath, I'll make an end on't.°   *of it*
    (Song)   By Gis,° and by Saint Charity,   *Jesus*
               Alack, and fie for shame!
               Young men will do't if they come to't,
60   By Cock,[8] they are to blame.
               Quoth she 'Before you tumbled me,
               You promised me to wed.'
               So would I 'a' done, by yonder sun,
               An° thou hadst not come to my bed.   *If*
65 KING CLAUDIUS *[to* GERTRUDE*]*   How long hath she been thus?
OPHELIA   I hope all will be well. We must be patient. But I can-
    not choose but weep to think they should lay him i'th' cold
    ground. My brother shall know of it. And so I thank you for
    your good counsel. Come, my coach! Good night, ladies, good
70 night, sweet ladies, good night, good night.   *Exit*
    KING CLAUDIUS *[to* HORATIO*]*   Follow her close. Give her good
                   watch, I pray you.   *[Exit* HORATIO*]*
    O, this is the poison of deep grief! It springs
    All from her father's death. O Gertrude, Gertrude,
    When sorrows come they come not single spies,°   *scouts*
75 But in battalions. First, her father slain;
    Next, your son gone, and he most violent author
    Of his own just remove; the people muddied,°   *confused*
    Thick and unwholesome in their thoughts and whispers
    For good Polonius' death; and we have done but greenly°   *naively*
80 In hugger-mugger° to inter him; poor Ophelia   *secrecy*
    Divided from herself and her fair judgement,
    Without the which we are pictures or mere beasts;
    Last, and as much containing° as all these,   *and as important*
    Her brother is in secret come from France,

---

6. By adding "not," Ophelia changes the song's words and meter to fit the circumstances of Polonius's burial (see lines 79–80).
7. A folktale: Christ turned a baker's daughter into an owl because when he asked for food, she would give him only a small loaf.
8. A corruption of "God" in very mild swearing (playing on "penis").

85 Feeds on this wonder, keeps himself in clouds,°   *unverified suspicion*
And wants° not buzzers° to infect his ear   *lacks / scandal mongers*
With pestilent speeches of his father's death;
Wherein necessity, of matter beggared,
Will nothing stick our persons to arraign
90 In ear and ear.⁹ O my dear Gertrude, this,
Like to a murd'ring-piece,¹ in many places
Gives me superfluous° death.   *redundant*
    A noise within

QUEEN GERTRUDE   Alack, what noise is this?
KING CLAUDIUS   Where is my Switzers?² Let them guard the door.
    Enter a MESSENGER
What is the matter?
MESSENGER   Save yourself, my lord.
95 The ocean, overpeering of his list,³
Eats not the flats with more impetuous⁴ haste
Than young Laertes, in a riotous head,°   *insurrection; tidal wave*
O'erbears your officers. The rabble call him lord,
And, as° the world were now but° to begin,   *as if / only now*
100 Antiquity forgot, custom not known,
The ratifiers and props of every word,⁵
They cry 'Choose we! Laertes shall be king.'
Caps, hands, and tongues applaud it to the clouds,
'Laertes shall be king, Laertes king.'
105 QUEEN GERTRUDE   How cheerfully on the false trail they cry!⁶
    A noise within
O, this is counter,⁷ you false Danish dogs!
KING CLAUDIUS   The doors are broke.
    Enter LAERTES *with* [*his* FOLLOWERS *at the door*]
LAERTES   Where is the King?—Sirs, stand you all without.
ALL HIS FOLLOWERS   No, let's come in.
110 LAERTES   I pray you, give me leave.
ALL HIS FOLLOWERS   We will, we will.
LAERTES   I thank you. Keep the door.   [*Exeunt* FOLLOWERS]
                       O thou vile king,
Give me my father.
QUEEN GERTRUDE   Calmly, good Laertes.
LAERTES   That drop of blood that's calm proclaims me bastard,
115 Cries cuckold to my father, brands the harlot
Even here between the chaste unsmirchèd brow
Of my true mother.
KING CLAUDIUS   What is the cause, Laertes,
That thy rebellion looks so giant-like?—
Let him go, Gertrude. Do not fear° our person.   *fear for*
120 There's such divinity doth hedge a king

---

9. *Wherein . . . ear:* In which affair, because they have no
real information and need to give some account, they will
not hesitate to whisper accusations against us.
1. Small cannon that fired shrapnel.
2. Company of Swiss mercenaries (employed as royal
bodyguards in many European countries).
3. Rising over its boundary at the shore.
4. Spelled "impittious" in F and "impitious" in Q2, prob-
ably meaning "merciless" as well as "rash." *flats:* low-
lying countryside.
5. *Antiquity . . . word:* Ignoring history and traditional
precedents, which give meaning, order, and stability to
society by fixing the agreed-upon meaning of political
contracts (and of any truth expressed in language).
6. How enthusiastically they run after the wrong scent
(like a pack of hounds hunting the murderer of Polonius).
7. This is following the quarry's trail, but in the wrong
direction.

That treason can but peep to what it would,[8]
Acts little of his will.—Tell me, Laertes,
Why thou art thus incensed.—Let him go, Gertrude.—
Speak, man.

LAERTES　　　　Where is my father?

KING CLAUDIUS　　　　　　　　Dead.

QUEEN GERTRUDE [*to* LAERTES]　　But not by him.

125 KING CLAUDIUS　　　　　　Let him demand his fill.

LAERTES　How came he dead? I'll not be juggled with.°　　　　*deceived*
To hell, allegiance! Vows to the blackest devil!
Conscience and grace to the profoundest pit!
I dare damnation. To this point° I stand,　　　　*resolve*
130 That both the worlds I give to negligence,[9]
Let come what comes. Only I'll be revenged
Most throughly° for my father.　　　　*thoroughly*

KING CLAUDIUS　Who shall stay° you?　　　　*prevent*

LAERTES　My will, not all the world;
135 And for my means, I'll husband them so well
They shall go far with little.

KING CLAUDIUS　　　　　　Good Laertes,
If you desire to know the certainty
Of your dear father's death, is't writ in your revenge
That, sweepstake,[1] you will draw° both friend and foe,　　　　*take from*
140 Winner and loser?

LAERTES　None but his enemies.

KING CLAUDIUS　Will you know them then?

LAERTES　To his good friends thus wide I'll ope my arms,
And, like the kind life-rend'ring pelican,
Repast them with my blood.[2]

145 KING CLAUDIUS　　　　　　Why, now you speak
Like a good child and a true gentleman.
That I am guiltless of your father's death,
And am most sensibly° in grief for it,　　　　*sympathetically*
It shall as level° to your judgement pierce　　　　*directly*
150 As day does to your eye.

　　　　A noise within

VOICES [*within*]　Let her come in.[3]

LAERTES How now, what noise is that?

　　　　Enter OPHELIA [*as before*]

O heat dry up my brains! Tears seven times salt
Burn out the sense and virtue° of mine eye!　　　　*natural power*
155 By heaven, thy madness shall be paid by weight
Till our scale turns the beam.[4] O rose of May,
Dear maid, kind sister, sweet Ophelia!
O heavens, is't possible a young maid's wits
Should be as mortal as an old man's life?
160 Nature is fine in love, and where 'tis fine

---

8. That treason can only glance furtively at what it would like to do.
9. That both this world and the next do not matter to me.
1. Indiscriminately. (The winner of a sweepstake gained the stakes of all other players.)
2. The female pelican was supposed to feed, and even revive, its young with blood from a wound it pecked in its

own breast. *Repast:* Feed.
3. This line is assigned to no one in F but rather appears in italic following the stage direction "A noise within." Q2 gives the line to Laertes.
4. *shall . . . beam:* shall be atoned for until vengeance outweighs the injury of madness (thus tilting the "scale" of justice).

It sends some precious instance of itself
After the thing it loves.[5]

OPHELIA *(Song)*   They bore him barefaced on the bier,
                    Hey non nony, nony, hey nony,
165   And on his grave rained many a tear—
Fare you well, my dove.

LAERTES   Hadst thou thy wits and didst persuade° revenge,   *argue for*
It could not move thus.

OPHELIA   You must sing 'Down, a-down', and you, 'Call him a
170 down-a'. O, how the wheel[6] becomes it! It is the false steward
that stole his master's daughter.[7]

LAERTES   This nothing's more than matter.[8]

OPHELIA   There's rosemary, that's for remembrance. Pray, love,
remember. And there is pansies; that's for thoughts.[9]

175 LAERTES   A document in madness—thoughts and remembrance
fitted.

OPHELIA   There's fennel for you, and columbines.[1] There's rue
for you, and here's some for me. We may call it herb-grace o'
Sundays. O, you must wear your rue with a difference.[2] There's
180 a daisy. I would give you some violets,[3] but they withered all
when my father died. They say a made a good end.

(Song)   For bonny sweet Robin is all my joy.

LAERTES   Thought and affliction, passion, hell itself
She turns to favour° and to prettiness.   *beauty*

185 OPHELIA *(Song)*   And will a not come again,
                       And will a not come again?
                       No, no, he is dead,
                       Go to thy death-bed,
                       He never will come again.

190   His beard as white as snow,
                       All flaxen° was his poll.°   *white / head*
                       He is gone, he is gone,
                       And we cast away moan.
                       God 'a' mercy on his soul.
195 And of all Christian souls, I pray God. God b'wi' ye.

         Exeunt OPHELIA [*and* GERTRUDE]

LAERTES   Do you see this, O God?

KING CLAUDIUS   Laertes, I must commune with your grief,
Or you deny me right. Go but apart,
Make choice of whom° your wisest friends you will,   *whichever of*
200 And they shall hear and judge 'twixt you and me.
If by direct or by collateral° hand   *an agent's*
They find us touched,° we will our kingdom give,   *involved in guilt*

---

5. *Nature . . . loves:* Human nature is made most ethere-
ally pure by love and sends a precious token ("instance")
of itself after the object of its love. Laertes struggles to say
that because of Ophelia's great love for her father, her
sanity departed with him.
6. Probably refrain, although possibly spinning wheel (at
which women sang ballads) or Fortune's wheel. "Down,
a-down" resembles the refrain of recorded ballads.
7. *false . . . daughter:* the tale is unknown; Laertes seems
to recognize it.
8. This nonsense signifies more than coherent speech.
9. *There's . . . thoughts:* Ophelia, recalling the flowers'

symbolic significance, distributes them to Laertes,
Gertrude, and Claudius.
1. Columbines were associated with ingratitude or
marital infidelity, fennel with flattery.
2. In heraldry, minor branches of a family were distin-
guished by a "difference," a variation or addition to the
coat of arms. Ophelia probably means "for a different
reason." Rue is associated with repentance, and Ophelia
identifies it with the "herb of grace" (wormwood), since
penitence depended on and enabled God's blessing.
3. Representing faithfulness; daisies could symbolize
dissembling seduction.

Our crown, our life, and all that we call ours,
To you in satisfaction.° But if not,   *recompense*
205 Be you content to lend your patience to us,
And we shall jointly labour with your soul
To give it due content.
LAERTES   Let this be so.
His means of death, his obscure burial—
No trophy, sword, nor hatchment[4] o'er his bones,
210 No noble rite nor formal ostentation°—   *rite of grief*
Cry to be heard, as 'twere from heaven to earth,
That I must call't in question.[5]
KING CLAUDIUS   So you shall;
And where th'offence is, let the great axe fall.
I pray you go with me.   *Exeunt*

4.6

Enter HORATIO *with* [*a* SERVANT]
HORATIO   What are they that would speak with me?
SERVANT   Sailors, sir. They say they have letters for you.
HORATIO   Let them come in.   [*Exit* SERVANT]
I do not know from what part of the world
5   I should be greeted if not from Lord Hamlet.
Enter SAILOR[S]
A SAILOR   God bless you, sir.
HORATIO   Let him bless thee too.
A SAILOR   A shall, sir, an't° please him. There's a letter for you,   *if it*
sir. It comes from th'ambassador that was bound for England—
10   if your name be Horatio, as I am let to know it is.
HORATIO (*reads*) 'Horatio, when thou shalt have overlooked°   *read*
this, give these fellows some means° to the King. They have   *access*
letters for him. Ere we were two days old at sea, a pirate of very
warlike appointment° gave us chase. Finding ourselves too slow   *equipment*
15   of sail, we put on a compelled valour, and in the grapple I
boarded them. On the instant they got clear of our ship, so I
alone became their prisoner. They have dealt with me like
thieves of mercy; but they knew what they did:[1] I am to do a
good turn for them. Let the King have the letters I have sent,
20   and repair thou° to me with as much haste as thou wouldst fly   *come*
death. I have words to speak in thine ear will make thee dumb,
yet are they much too light for the bore° of the matter. These   *caliber; size*
good fellows will bring thee where I am. Rosencrantz and
Guildenstern hold their course for England. Of them I have
25   much to tell thee. Farewell.
He that thou knowest thine,
Hamlet.'
Come, I will give you way° for these your letters,   *means of delivery*
And do't the speedier that you may direct me
30   To him from whom you brought them.   *Exeunt*

---

4. Lozenge-shaped tablet bearing a coat of arms, carried in funeral processions and deposited near the tomb. *trophy:* memorial (often consisting of real or symbolic weapons and armor).
5. I must demand an explanation of it.
4.6 Location: The castle.

1. *They have . . . did:* They have been merciful, but with the expectation of a return. Hamlet recalls the thieves crucified next to Christ (one of whom he blessed) and Christ's plea of forgiveness for those who "know not what they do" (Luke 23:34–43).

4.7

Enter KING [CLAUDIUS] *and* LAERTES

KING CLAUDIUS   Now must your conscience my acquittance seal,[1]
And you must put me in your heart for friend,
Sith° you have heard, and with a knowing ear,   *Since*
That he which hath your noble father slain
Pursued my life.

5   LAERTES   It well appears. But tell me
Why you proceeded not against these feats,°   *acts*
So crimeful and so capital° in nature,   *punishable by death*
As by your safety, wisdom, all things else,
You mainly° were stirred up.   *greatly*

KING CLAUDIUS   O, for two special reasons,
10   Which may to you perhaps seem much unsinewed,°   *uncompelling*
And yet to me they're strong. The Queen his mother
Lives almost by his looks; and for myself—
My virtue or my plague, be it either which—
She's so conjunctive to my life and soul
15   That, as the star moves not but in his sphere,[2]
I could not but by her. The other motive
Why to a public count° I might not go   *accounting*
Is the great love the general gender° bear him,   *the common people*
Who, dipping all his faults in their affection,
20   Would, like the spring that turneth wood to stone,[3]
Convert his guilts to graces; so that my arrows,
Too slightly timbered for so loud a wind,
Would have reverted to my bow again,
And not where I had aimed them.

25   LAERTES   And so have I a noble father lost,
A sister driven into desp'rate terms,
Who has, if praises may go back again,[4]
Stood challenger, on mount, of all the age
For her perfections.[5] But my revenge will come.

30   KING CLAUDIUS   Break not your sleeps for that. You must not think
That we are made of stuff so flat and dull
That we can let our beard be shook with danger,[6]
And think it pastime. You shortly shall hear more.
I loved your father, and we love ourself.
35   And that, I hope, will teach you to imagine—

Enter a MESSENGER *with letters*

How now? What news?

MESSENGER   Letters, my lord, from Hamlet.
This to your majesty; this to the Queen.

KING CLAUDIUS   From Hamlet? Who brought them?

MESSENGER   Sailors, my lord, they say. I saw them not.
40   They were given me by Claudio. He received them.

KING CLAUDIUS   Laertes, you shall hear them.—Leave us.

Exit MESSENGER

4.7 Location: Claudius's private apartments.
1. *my acquittance seal*: affirm my innocence (of Polonius's death).
2. According to Ptolemeic astronomy, heavenly bodies moved in hollow spheres. *conjunctive* (line 14): closely united (as two planets were said astronomically to be "in conjunction" when they appeared close).
3. In limestone-rich areas (such as south Warwickshire),

concentrations in spring water may be great enough to petrify absorbent objects.
4. May refer to what was (but is no longer).
5. *Stood . . . perfections*: Conspicuously challenged the world to match her perfections.
6. That I can allow anyone to endanger me with contemptuous behavior.

[*Reads*] 'High and mighty, you shall know I am set naked° on   destitute
your kingdom. Tomorrow shall I beg leave to see your kingly
eyes, when I shall, first asking your pardon,° thereunto recount   permission
45   th'occasions of my sudden and more strange return.
                                                      Hamlet.'
        What should this mean? Are all the rest come back?
        Or is it some abuse,° and no such thing?   deception
        LAERTES   Know you the hand?
        KING CLAUDIUS   'Tis Hamlet's character.°   handwriting
50   'Naked'—and in a postscript here he says
        'Alone'. Can you advise me?
        LAERTES   I'm lost in it, my lord. But let him come.
        It warms the very sickness in my heart
        That I shall live and tell him to his teeth,
        'Thus diddest thou'.[7]
55   KING CLAUDIUS   If it be so, Laertes—
        As how should it be so, how otherwise?[8]—
        Will you be ruled by me?
        LAERTES   If so° you'll not o'errule me to a peace.   Provided that
        KING CLAUDIUS   To thine own peace. If he be now returned,
60   As checking at[9] his voyage, and that he means
        No more to undertake it, I will work him
        To an exploit, now ripe in my device,°   planning
        Under the which he shall not choose but fall;
        And for his death no wind of blame shall breathe;
65   But even his mother shall uncharge° the practice°   not accuse / connivance
        And call it accident.[1]
66.1   LAERTES   *My lord, I will be ruled,*
                The rather if you could devise it so
                That I might be the organ.°   agent
            KING CLAUDIUS   *It falls right.*
                You have been talked of, since your travel, much,
66.5   *And that in Hamlet's hearing, for a quality*
                Wherein they say you shine. Your sum of parts°   abilities
                Did not together pluck such envy from him
                As did that one, and that, in my regard,
                Of the unworthiest siege.°   lowest rank
            LAERTES   *What part is that, my lord?*
66.10   KING CLAUDIUS   *A very ribbon in the cap of youth,*
                Yet needful too, for youth no less becomes°   is suited by
                The light and careless livery that it wears
                Than settled age his sables and his weeds
                Importing health and graveness.[2]
                                              Some two months since
        Here was a gentleman of Normandy.
        I've seen myself, and served against, the French,
        And they can well° on horseback; but this gallant   are skilled
70   Had witchcraft in't. He grew into his seat,
        And to such wondrous doing brought his horse

---

7. This which I do now to you, you did to my father.   1. After "accident," Q2 has the following passage,
8. *As . . . otherwise*: How could Hamlet be returning,   66.1–66.14, omitted in F.
and yet how else could he have sent this letter?   2. *his . . . graveness*: its rich gowns trimmed with sable,
9. As one who has been diverted from ("checking at" is   garments ("weeds") signifying concern for prosperity
a term from falconry).   and dignity.

As had he been incorpsed and demi-natured[3]
With the brave beast. So far he passed my thought
That I in forgery of shapes and tricks[4]
Come short of what he did.

75 LAERTES   A Norman was't?

KING CLAUDIUS   A Norman.

LAERTES   Upon my life, Lamord.

KING CLAUDIUS   The very same.

LAERTES   I know him well. He is the brooch° indeed,   ornament
And gem, of all the nation.

KING CLAUDIUS   He made confession° of you,   testimonial
80 And gave you such a masterly report
For art and exercise in your defence,
And for your rapier most especially,
That he cried out 'twould be a sight indeed
If one could match you.[5]

84.1   *Th'escrimers° of their nation*   *fencers*
                    He swore had neither motion, guard, nor eye
                    If you opposed them.

                                        Sir, this report of his
85 Did Hamlet so envenom with his envy
That he could nothing do but wish and beg
Your sudden° coming o'er to play with him.   immediate
Now, out of this—

LAERTES   What out of this, my lord?

KING CLAUDIUS   Laertes, was your father dear to you?
90 Or are you like the painting of a sorrow,
A face without a heart?

LAERTES   Why ask you this?

KING CLAUDIUS   Not that I think you did not love your father,
But that I know love is begun by time,°   circumstance
And that I see, in passages of proof,[6]
95 Time qualifies° the spark and fire of it.[7]   moderates

95.1   *There lives within the very flame of love*
                    A kind of wick or snuff[8] that will abate it,
                    And nothing is at a like° goodness still,°   *an equal / always*
                    For goodness, growing to a plurisy,[9]
95.5   *Dies in his own too much.° That we would do*   *overabundance*
                    We should do when we would, for this 'would' changes,
                    And hath abatements and delays as many
                    As there are tongues, are hands, are accidents;
                    And then this 'should' is like a spendthrift's sigh,
95.10   *That hurts by easing.[1] But to the quick° of th'ulcer—*   *center*

Hamlet comes back. What would you undertake
To show yourself your father's son in deed
More than in words?

LAERTES   To cut his throat i'th' church.

3. As if he had been in the same body and had half the
nature of (the image of a centaur).
4. That I in my very imagination ("forgery") of figures
and skillful feats of horsemanship.
5. After "you," Q2 has the following passage, 84.1–84.3,
omitted in F.
6. From experiences that have tested this.
7. After this line, Q2 has the following passage, 95.1–

95.10, omitted in F.
8. Burned part of the wick (which causes smoke and
reduces light if not removed).
9. A chest inflammation, metaphorically like a fire in the
heart; thought to take its name from the Latin for "more"
(*plus*) and to be caused by an excess of humors (and so
playing on "excess").
1. A sigh was thought to use up a drop of blood.

KING CLAUDIUS   No place indeed should murder sanctuarize.[2]
100 Revenge should have no bounds. But, good Laertes,
Will you do this?—keep close within your chamber.
Hamlet returned shall know you are come home.
We'll put on those shall[3] praise your excellence,
And set a double varnish on the fame
105 The Frenchman gave you; bring you, in fine,° together,   *conclusion*
And wager on your heads. He, being remiss,°   *unwary*
Most generous,° and free from all contriving,   *noble*
Will not peruse the foils; so that with ease,
Or with a little shuffling, you may choose
110 A sword unbated, and, in a pass of practice,[4]
Requite him for your father.
LAERTES   I will do't,
And for that purpose I'll anoint my sword.
I bought an unction° of a mountebank°   *ointment / quack*
So mortal that, but dip a knife in it,
115 Where it draws blood no cataplasm° so rare,   *poultice*
Collected from all simples° that have virtue°   *herbs / potency*
Under the moon, can save the thing from death
That is but scratched withal.° I'll touch my point   *with it*
With this contagion, that if I gall° him slightly,   *prick*
It may be death.
120 KING CLAUDIUS   Let's further think of this;
Weigh what convenience both of time and means
May fit us to our shape.[5] If this should fail,
And that our drift look° through our bad performance,   *our intention be seen*
'Twere better not essayed. Therefore this project
125 Should have a back or second[6] that might hold
If this should blast in proof.[7] Soft, let me see.
We'll make a solemn wager on your cunnings . . . °   *skills*
I ha't! When in your motion° you are hot and dry—   *exercise*
As make your bouts more violent to that end—
130 And that he calls for drink, I'll have prepared him
A chalice for the nonce,° whereon but sipping,   *occasion*
If he by chance escape your venomed stuck,°   *thrust*
Our purpose may hold there.—
        Enter QUEEN [GERTRUDE]
                                    How now, sweet Queen?
QUEEN GERTRUDE   One woe doth tread upon another's heel,
135 So fast they follow. Your sister's drowned, Laertes.
LAERTES   Drowned? O, where?
QUEEN GERTRUDE   There is a willow grows aslant a brook
That shows his hoar leaves[8] in the glassy stream.
Therewith fantastic garlands did she make
140 Of crow-flowers, nettles, daisies, and long purples,[9]

---

2. Give sanctuary to a murderer. In English tradition, a
criminal remained invulnerable to secular authority for
most crimes (save sacrilege and treason) as long as he
took refuge in a church.
3. *We'll . . . shall:* I shall incite some people to.
4. In a treacherous thrust. *unbated:* unblunted (as recre-
ational or practice foils were).
5. May make us ready to put into effect our plot and to
assume the roles we are to play.
6. Should have reserve soldiers (military metaphor for

the plotting).
7. Should blow up in our faces when put to the test (like
a cannon).
8. The willow leaf is gray-white ("hoar") on the under-
sides (reflected from below by the water). The willow
was an emblem of mourning and of forsaken love.
9. Early purple orchises. *crow-flowers:* common name for
several wildflowers, including Ragged Robin and blue-
bells (often appearing beside long purples in woodland
and sharing their association with fertility).

That liberal shepherds give a grosser¹ name,
But our cold° maids do dead men's fingers call them.   chaste
There on the pendent boughs her crownet° weeds   garlanded
Clamb'ring to hang,² an envious sliver° broke,   a malicious twig
145   When down the weedy trophies and herself
Fell in the weeping brook. Her clothes spread wide,
And mermaid-like a while they bore her up;
Which time she chanted snatches of old tunes,
As one incapable° of her own distress,   uncomprehending
150   Or like a creature native and endued
Unto that element.³ But long it could not be
Till that her garments, heavy with their drink,
Pulled the poor wretch from her melodious lay°   song
To muddy death.

155 LAERTES   Alas, then is she drowned.
   QUEEN GERTRUDE   Drowned, drowned.
   LAERTES   Too much of water hast thou, poor Ophelia,
And therefore I forbid my tears. But yet
It is our trick;° nature her custom holds,   characteristic way
Let shame say what it will.
          [He weeps]
160   When these are gone,
The woman will be out.⁴ Adieu, my lord.
I have a speech of fire that fain° would blaze,   gladly
But that this folly douts° it.   Exit   extinguishes
   KING CLAUDIUS   Let's follow, Gertrude.
How much I had to do to calm his rage!
165   Now fear I this will give it start again;
Therefore let's follow.   Exeunt

5.1

Enter two CLOWNS° *carrying a spade and a pickaxe*   rustics; peasants
   FIRST CLOWN   Is she to be buried in Christian burial that wilfully
seeks her own salvation?¹
   SECOND CLOWN   I tell thee she is, and therefore make her grave
straight.° The coroner hath sat on her,² and finds it Christian   right away
5 burial.³
   FIRST CLOWN   How can that be unless she drowned herself in
her own defence?
   SECOND CLOWN   Why, 'tis found so.
   FIRST CLOWN   It must be *se offendendo*,⁴ it cannot be else; for
10 here lies the point: if I drown myself wittingly, it argues an act;
and an act hath three branches: it is to act, to do, and to per-
form. Argal⁵ she drowned herself wittingly.

---

1. More indecent. Among the recorded names for the purple orchis are "priest's-pintle" (penis), "dog's cullions" (testicles), "goat's cullions," and "fool's ballochs." *liberal:* free-spoken.
2. Deserted lovers proverbially hung garlands on willows.
3. *native . . . element:* naturally fit to live in water.
4. *When . . . out:* When I have cried my tears, the feminine side of my nature will be gone with them.
5.1 Location: A churchyard.
1. Probably a mistake for "damnation"; suicide was a mortal sin. Ordinarily, suicides would not receive a "Christian burial" (in consecrated ground with the

church's blessing and ritual).
2. Conducted an inquest on the cause of her death.
3. And has given the verdict that she is eligible for a Christian burial (in effect, a decision that Ophelia did not drown herself).
4. A mangled version of *se defendendo*, the term for "killing in self-defense."
5. For "ergo," or "therefore." The argument parodies a famous law case of 1554 concerning suicide by drowning, in which the act was said to have three parts: imagination, resolution, and perfection (accomplishment).

SECOND CLOWN   Nay, but hear you, Goodman Delver.[6]
FIRST CLOWN   Give me leave. Here lies the water—good. Here
15 stands the man—good. If the man go to this water and drown
himself, it is, will he nill he,° he goes. Mark you that. But if the   *willy-nilly*
water come to him and drown him, he drowns not himself;
argal he that is not guilty of his own death shortens not his own
life.
20 SECOND CLOWN   But is this law?
FIRST CLOWN   Ay, marry, is't: coroner's quest° law.   *inquest*
SECOND CLOWN   Will you ha' the truth on't? If this had not been
a gentlewoman, she should have been buried out o' Christian
burial.
25 FIRST CLOWN   Why, there thou sayst,° and the more pity that   *how right you are*
great folk should have count'nance° in this world to drown or   *privilege*
hang themselves more than their even° Christian. Come, my   *fellow*
spade. There is no ancient gentlemen but gardeners, ditchers,
and gravemakers; they hold up° Adam's profession.   *carry on*
[FIRST CLOWN *digs*]
30 SECOND CLOWN   Was he a gentleman?
FIRST CLOWN   A was the first that ever bore arms.[7]
SECOND CLOWN   Why, he had none.
FIRST CLOWN   What, art a heathen? How dost thou understand
the Scripture? The Scripture says Adam digged. Could he dig
35 without arms? I'll put another question to thee. If thou answer-
est me not to the purpose, confess thyself[8]—
SECOND CLOWN   Go to.[9]
FIRST CLOWN   What is he that builds stronger than either the
mason, the shipwright, or the carpenter?
40 SECOND CLOWN   The gallows-maker; for that frame° outlives a   *structure*
thousand tenants.
FIRST CLOWN   I like thy wit well, in good faith. The gallows does°   *serves*
well. But how does it well? It does well to those that do ill. Now
thou dost ill to say the gallows is built stronger than the church,
45 argal the gallows may do well to thee. To't again, come.
SECOND CLOWN   'Who builds stronger than a mason, a ship-
wright, or a carpenter?'
FIRST CLOWN   Ay, tell me that, and unyoke.[1]
SECOND CLOWN   Marry, now I can tell.
50 FIRST CLOWN   To't.
SECOND CLOWN   Mass,° I cannot tell.   *By the Mass*
Enter [*Prince*] HAMLET *and* HORATIO *afar off*
FIRST CLOWN   Cudgel thy brains no more about it, for your dull
ass will not mend° his pace with beating; and when you are   *improve*
asked this question next, say 'a grave-maker'; the houses that he
55 makes lasts till doomsday. Go, get thee to Johan.[2] Fetch me a
stoup° of liquor.   [*Exit* SECOND CLOWN]   *flagon*
(*Sings*) In youth when I did love, did love,
Methought it was very sweet

6. Master Digger ("Goodman" was the ordinary title in addressing a man by his occupation).
7. Those bearing a family coat of arms were officially recognized as gentlemen; playing on "limbs."
8. "Confess thyself and be hanged" was proverbial.
9. An expression of impatience.
1. Rest your wits from work (like draft animals).
2. *Johan:* unknown (presumably a neighborhood ale-house keeper).

To contract°-O-the time for-a-my behove,°   *shorten / advantage*
60   O methought there-a-was nothing-a-meet.[3]

HAMLET   Has this fellow no feeling of his business that a sings at grave-making?

HORATIO   Custom hath made it in him a property of easiness.[4]

HAMLET   'Tis e'en so; the hand of little employment hath the
65   daintier sense.[5]

FIRST CLOWN *(sings)* But age with his stealing steps
    Hath caught me in his clutch,
    And hath shipped me intil the land,°   *into the earth*
    As if I had never been such.
    [He throws up a skull]

70 HAMLET   That skull had a tongue in it and could sing once. How
the knave jowls° it to th' ground as if 'twere Cain's jawbone,   *slams*
that did the first murder! This might be the pate of a politician
which this ass o'er-offices,[6] one that would circumvent God,
might it not?

75 HORATIO   It might, my lord.

HAMLET   Or of a courtier, which could say 'Good morrow, sweet
lord. How dost thou, good lord?' This might be my lord such a
one, that praised my lord such a one's horse when a meant to
beg it, might it not?

80 HORATIO   Ay, my lord.

HAMLET   Why, e'en so, and now my lady Worm's, chapless,° and   *lacking a lower jaw*
knocked about the mazard° with a sexton's spade. Here's fine   *head*
revolution,[7] an° we had the trick° to see't. Did these bones cost   *if / ability*
no more the breeding but to play at loggats with 'em?[8] Mine
85 ache to think on't.

FIRST CLOWN *(sings)* A pickaxe and a spade, a spade,
    For and° a shrouding-sheet;   *And also*
    O, a pit of clay for to be made
    For such a guest is meet.
    [He throws up another skull]

90 HAMLET   There's another. Why might not that be the skull of a
lawyer? Where be his quiddits[9] now, his quillets,° his cases, his   *quibbles*
tenures,° and his tricks? Why does he suffer this rude knave   *property titles*
now to knock him about the sconce° with a dirty shovel, and   *head*
will not tell him of his action of battery?[1] H'm! This fellow
95 might be in 's time a great buyer of land, with his statutes, his
recognizances, his fines, his double vouchers, his recoveries.[2]
Is this the fine° of his fines and the recovery° of his recoveries,   *end / profit*
to have his fine° pate full of fine° dirt? Will his vouchers vouch[3]   *subtle / fine-grained*
him no more of his purchases, and double ones too, than the

---

3. *meet:* suitable. The Clown sings garbled snatches of Thomas Lord Vaux's poem "The Aged Lover Renounceth Love," printed in *Tottel's Miscellany* (1557). The extrametrical "O"s and "A"s are probably grunts while digging.
4. *a property of easiness:* something he can do without distress.
5. Has more delicate feeling (because not hardened by calluses).
6. *o'er-offices:* lords it over because of his position, pulls rank on. A "politician" was a schemer for political advantage.
7. Reversal of fortune (literally, the turning of Fortune's

wheel).
8. Was it so inexpensive and easy to bring these bones to maturity that they can be treated as loggats (small wooden clubs thrown at a stake)?
9. Subtle distinctions.
1. Legal prosecution for assault.
2. Fines and recoveries were both kinds of lawsuits brought to make legal an agreement to transfer land ownership. The "double voucher" summoned two witnesses to attest to the land's ownership in these cases. *statutes:* mortgages on land, often linked with "recognizances" (bonds acknowledging a particular debt).
3. Guarantee.

100 length and breadth of a pair of indentures?[4] The very convey-
ances° of his lands will hardly lie in this box;° and must th'in- *deeds / deed box; coffin*
heritor° himself have no more, ha? *owner*

HORATIO   Not a jot more, my lord.

HAMLET   Is not parchment made of sheepskins?

105 HORATIO   Ay, my lord, and of calf-skins too.

HAMLET   They are sheep and calves° that seek out assurance[5] in *simpletons and fools*
that. I will speak to this fellow. [*To the* FIRST CLOWN] Whose
grave's this, sirrah?[6]

FIRST CLOWN   Mine, sir.

110 (*Sings*)   O, a pit of clay for to be made
                    For such a guest is meet.

HAMLET   I think it be thine indeed, for thou liest in't.

FIRST CLOWN   You lie out on't, sir, and therefore it is not yours.
For my part, I do not lie in't, and yet it is mine.

115 HAMLET   Thou dost lie in't, to be in't and say 'tis thine. 'Tis for
the dead, not for the quick;° therefore thou liest. *living*

FIRST CLOWN   'Tis a quick° lie, sir, 'twill away again from me to *nimble*
you.

HAMLET   What man dost thou dig it for?

120 FIRST CLOWN   For no man, sir.

HAMLET   What woman, then?

FIRST CLOWN   For none, neither.

HAMLET   Who is to be buried in't?

FIRST CLOWN   One that was a woman, sir; but, rest her soul, she's
125 dead.

HAMLET   How absolute° the knave is! We must speak by the *precise*
card,[7] or equivocation will undo us. By the Lord, Horatio, these
three years I have taken note of it. The age is grown so picked° *punctilious*
that the toe of the peasant comes so near the heel of the court-
130 ier he galls his kibe.° [*To the* FIRST CLOWN] How long hast thou *chafes his heel sore*
been a grave-maker?

FIRST CLOWN   Of all the days i'th' year I came to't that day that
our last King Hamlet o'ercame Fortinbras.

HAMLET   How long is that since?

135 FIRST CLOWN   Cannot you tell that? Every fool can tell that. It
was the very day that young Hamlet was born—he that was
mad and sent into England.

HAMLET   Ay, marry, why was he sent into England?

FIRST CLOWN   Why, because a was mad. A shall recover his wits
140 there; or if a do not, 'tis no great matter there.

HAMLET   Why?

FIRST CLOWN   'Twill not be seen in him there. There the men
are as mad as he.

HAMLET   How came he mad?

145 FIRST CLOWN   Very strangely, they say.

HAMLET   How strangely?

FIRST CLOWN   Faith, e'en with losing his wits.

HAMLET   Upon what ground?[8]

---

4. The two copies of a document (written on one sheet
and separated by an irregular cut so that they could later
be proved to be part of one transaction). The dead man's
property (his grave) is hardly bigger than these elaborate
papers.
5. Security, playing on the legal conveyance of a property

title.
6. An address used with inferiors.
7. With precisely defined meanings (literally, by the
directions marked on a mariner's compass card).
8. From what cause? (The Clown takes him to mean "In
what country?")

FIRST CLOWN   Why, here in Denmark. I have been sexton here,
150   man and boy, thirty years.

HAMLET   How long will a man lie i'th' earth ere he rot?

FIRST CLOWN   I'faith, if a be not rotten before a die—as we have
    many pocky corpses nowadays, that will scarce hold the laying
    in[9]—a will last you some eight year or nine year. A tanner will
155   last you nine year.

HAMLET   Why he more than another?

FIRST CLOWN   Why, sir, his hide is so tanned with his trade that
    a will keep out water a great while, and your water is a sore
    decayer of your whoreson° dead body. Here's a skull, now. This   °vile
160   skull has lain in the earth three-and-twenty years.

HAMLET   Whose was it?

FIRST CLOWN   A whoreson mad fellow's it was. Whose do you
    think it was?

HAMLET   Nay, I know not.

165   FIRST CLOWN   A pestilence on him for a mad rogue—a poured a
    flagon of Rhenish° on my head once! This same skull, sir, was   °Rhine wine
    Yorick's skull, the King's jester.

HAMLET   This?

FIRST CLOWN   E'en that.

170   HAMLET   Let me see.
    [He takes the skull]
    Alas, poor Yorick. I knew him, Horatio—a fellow of infinite
    jest, of most excellent fancy. He hath borne me on his back a
    thousand times; and now, how abhorred my imagination is! My
    gorge rises at it. Here hung those lips that I have kissed I know
175   not how oft. Where be your gibes now, your gambols, your
    songs, your flashes of merriment that were wont to set the table
    on a roar? Not one now to mock your own grinning? Quite
    chop-fallen?[1] Now get you to my lady's chamber and tell her,
    let her paint an inch thick, to this favour° she must come. Make   °appearance
180   her laugh at that. Prithee, Horatio, tell me one thing.

HORATIO   What's that, my lord?

HAMLET   Dost thou think Alexander looked o' this fashion i'th'
    earth?

HORATIO   E'en so.

185   HAMLET   And smelt so? Pah!
    [He throws the skull down]

HORATIO   E'en so, my lord.

HAMLET   To what base uses we may return, Horatio! Why may
    not imagination trace the noble dust of Alexander till a find it
    stopping a bung-hole?°   °opening of a cask

190   HORATIO   'Twere to consider too curiously° to consider so.   °oversubtly

HAMLET   No, faith, not a jot; but to follow him thither with mod-
    esty° enough, and likelihood to lead it, as thus: Alexander died,   °reasonable speculation
    Alexander was buried, Alexander returneth into dust, the dust
    is earth, of earth we make loam,[2] and why of that loam whereto
195   he was converted might they not stop a beer-barrel?
    Imperial Caesar, dead and turned to clay,
    Might stop a hole to keep the wind away.
    O, that that earth which kept the world in awe

---

9. *pocky . . . in:* bodies riddled with venereal disease that
hardly keep from disintegrating during their burial rites.

1. Dejected; also, with a dropped or lost lower jaw.
2. A mix of clay and straw used as plaster.

Should patch a wall t'expel the winter's flaw!°   *violent wind*
But soft, but soft; aside.
    [HAMLET *and* HORATIO *stand aside.*] *Enter* KING [CLAU-
    DIUS], QUEEN [GERTRUDE], LAERTES, *and a coffin, with*
    [*a* PRIEST *and*] *lords attendant*
200   Here comes the King,
The Queen, the courtiers—who is that they follow,
And with such maimèd rites?[3] This doth betoken
The corpse they follow did with desp'rate hand
Fordo it° own life. 'Twas of some estate.°   *Bring down its / rank*
Couch we° a while, and mark.   *Let's lie low*
205 LAERTES   What ceremony else?
HAMLET [*aside to* HORATIO]   That is Laertes, a very noble youth. Mark.
LAERTES   What ceremony else?
PRIEST   Her obsequies have been as far enlarged
As we have warrantise.° Her death was doubtful,[4]   *proper sanction*
210 And but that great command o'ersways the order[5]
She should in ground unsanctified have lodged
Till the last trumpet. For° charitable prayers,   *Rather than*
Shards, flints, and pebbles should be thrown on her,
Yet here she is allowed her virgin rites,
215 Her maiden strewments,[6] and the bringing home
Of bell and burial.[7]
LAERTES   Must there no more be done?
PRIEST   No more be done.
We should profane the service of the dead
220 To sing sage° requiem and such rest to her   *solemn*
As to peace-parted° souls.   *peacefully deceased*
LAERTES   Lay her i'th' earth,
And from her fair and unpolluted flesh
May violets spring. I tell thee, churlish priest,
A minist'ring angel shall my sister be
225 When thou liest howling.°   *(in hell)*
HAMLET [*aside*]   What, the fair Ophelia!
QUEEN GERTRUDE [*scattering flowers*]   Sweets to the sweet. Farewell.
I hoped thou shouldst have been my Hamlet's wife.
I thought thy bride-bed to have decked, sweet maid,
And not t'have strewed thy grave.
230 LAERTES   O, treble woe
Fall ten times treble on that cursèd head
Whose wicked deed thy most ingenious sense[8]
Deprived thee of!—Hold off the earth a while,
Till I have caught her once more in mine arms.
    [LAERTES] *leaps into the grave*
235 Now pile your dust upon the quick and dead
Till of this flat a mountain you have made
To o'ertop old Pelion, or the skyish head
Of blue Olympus.[9]

---

3. Truncated ceremonies (ordinarily grand for a court funeral).
4. That is, possibly suicide.
5. And if royal authority had not prevailed over the usual ecclesiastical procedure.
6. Flowers strewed over the casket or grave. Throughout northern Europe, funerary flowers of an unmarried girl often included a special wreath that was sometimes afterward hung in the church. (Q2's "crants" [garlands] for F's "rites" specifically evokes this practice.)
7. *the bringing . . . burial*: the taking her to her resting place with the ritual passing bells and funeral service.
8. Quick, perceptive intelligence.
9. In Greek mythology, giants piled Pelion (a mountain in Thessaly) on top of Mount Ossa in an attempt to climb Mount Olympus.

HAMLET [*coming forward*]   What is he whose grief
 Bears such an emphasis,[1] whose phrase° of sorrow   *rhetoric*
240 Conjures the wand'ring stars° and makes them stand   *planets*
 Like wonder-wounded° hearers? This is I,   *awestruck*
 Hamlet the Dane.[2]
    HAMLET *leaps in after* LAERTES
LAERTES The devil take thy soul.
HAMLET Thou pray'st not well.
245 I prithee take thy fingers from my throat,
 For though I am not splenative° and rash,   *quick-tempered*
 Yet have I something in me dangerous,
 Which let thy wiseness fear. Away thy hand.
KING CLAUDIUS [*to* LORDS] Pluck them asunder.
QUEEN GERTRUDE   Hamlet, Hamlet!
ALL THE LORDS Gentlemen!
250 HORATIO [*to* HAMLET]   Good my lord, be quiet.
HAMLET Why, I will fight with him upon this theme
 Until my eyelids will no longer wag.°   *blink*
QUEEN GERTRUDE O my son, what theme?
HAMLET I loved Ophelia. Forty thousand brothers
255 Could not, with all their quantity of love,
 Make up my sum.—What wilt thou do for her?
KING CLAUDIUS O, he is mad, Laertes.
QUEEN GERTRUDE [*to* LAERTES] For love of God, forbear him.° *let him alone*
HAMLET [*to* LAERTES] 'Swounds,° show me what thou'lt do. *By Christ's wounds*
260 Woot° weep, woot fight, woot fast, woot tear thyself, *Wilt thou*
 Woot drink up eisel,° eat a crocodile?   *vinegar*
 I'll do't. Dost thou come here to whine,
 To outface me with leaping in her grave?
 Be buried quick with her, and so will I.
265 And if thou prate of mountains, let them throw
 Millions of acres on us, till our ground,
 Singeing his pate° against the burning zone,° *his head / sun's sphere*
 Make Ossa[3] like a wart. Nay, an° thou'lt mouth,° *if / speak excessively*
 I'll rant as well as thou.
KING CLAUDIUS [*to* LAERTES] This is mere madness,
270 And thus a while the fit will work on him.
 Anon,° as patient as the female dove   *Soon*
 When that her golden couplets are disclosed,° *chicks are hatched*
 His silence will sit drooping.
HAMLET [*to* LAERTES]   Hear you, sir,
 What is the reason that you use me thus?
275 I loved you ever. But it is no matter.
 Let Hercules himself do what he may,
 The cat will mew, and dog will have his day.[4]   *Exit*
KING CLAUDIUS I pray you, good Horatio, wait upon him.
          [*Exit*] HORATIO
 [*To* LAERTES] Strengthen your patience in° our last night's *with*
   speech.
280 We'll put the matter to the present push.°— *the immediate trial*
 Good Gertrude, set some watch over your son.—

---

1. A violent expression.
2. Normally the title of the King of Denmark.
3. Greek mountain (see note to line 238).

4. *Let . . . day:* Despite Laertes' Herculean ranting, my
day will come.

This grave shall have a living monument.[5]
An hour of quiet shortly shall we see;
Till then, in patience our proceeding be.   *Exeunt*

5.2

Enter [Prince] HAMLET *and* HORATIO

HAMLET   So much for this, sir. Now, let me see, the other.°   *other matter*
   You do remember all the circumstance?°   *state of things then*
HORATIO   Remember it, my lord!
HAMLET   Sir, in my heart there was a kind of fighting
5 That would not let me sleep. Methought I lay
   Worse than the mutines in the bilboes.[1] Rashly°—   *Impulsively*
   And praised be rashness for it: let us know°   *acknowledge*
   Our indiscretion° sometime serves us well   *unreasoned action*
   When our dear plots do pall,° and that should teach us   *grow weak*
10 There's a divinity that shapes our ends,
   Rough-hew them° how we will—   *Form them roughly*
HORATIO   That is most certain.
HAMLET   Up from my cabin,
   My sea-gown scarfed about me in the dark,
15 Groped I to find out them, had my desire,
   Fingered° their packet, and in fine° withdrew   *Stole / finally*
   To mine own room again, making so bold,
   My fears forgetting manners, to unseal
   Their grand commission; where I found, Horatio—
20 O royal knavery!—an exact command,
   Larded° with many several° sorts of reasons   *Elaborated / different*
   Importing° Denmark's health, and England's, too,   *Concerning*
   With ho! such bugs and goblins in my life,[2]
   That on the supervise,° no leisure bated,°   *reading / allowed*
25 No, not to stay° the grinding of the axe,   *await*
   My head should be struck off.
HORATIO   Is't possible?
HAMLET [*giving it to him*]   Here's the commission. Read it at more leisure.
   But wilt thou hear me how I did proceed?
HORATIO   I beseech you.
30 HAMLET   Being thus benetted round with villainies—
   Ere I could make a prologue to my brains,
   They had begun the play[3]—I sat me down,
   Devised a new commission, wrote it fair.[4]
   I once did hold it, as our statists° do,   *statesmen*
35 A baseness to write fair, and laboured much
   How to forget that learning;[5] but, sir, now
   It did me yeoman's service.[6] Wilt thou know
   Th'effect of what I wrote?
HORATIO   Ay, good my lord.

5. A lasting memorial; hinting that Hamlet, now "living," will soon be sacrificed to Ophelia's memory.
5.2 Location: A stateroom of the castle.
1. Worse than the mutineers in the ankle fetters.
2. Such fanciful horrors that would result were I to remain alive. *bugs:* bugbears.
3. *Ere . . . play:* Hamlet's brains "acted" before he consciously thought out a plan.
4. In the professional handwriting of finished (published) documents.

5. *I once . . . learning:* In the sixteenth century, the upper echelons of government became increasingly professionalized; Hamlet implies that these newly elevated officials are prone to snobbish pretensions, covering up their education as common clerks, and he confesses that he once shared their snobbery.
6. It served me valiantly. English yeomen (free landholders) were famous for military strength, supposedly because they fought for their national interest rather than for base pay.

HAMLET   An earnest conjuration° from the King,   *appeal*
40   As England was his faithful tributary,
         As love between them like the palm should flourish,
         As peace should still her wheaten garland⁷ wear
         And stand a comma⁸ 'tween their amities,
         And many such like 'as'es of great charge,⁹
45   That on the view and know of these contents,
         Without debatement further more or less,
         He should the bearers put to sudden death,
         Not shriving-time¹ allowed.
HORATIO   How was this sealed?
HAMLET   Why, even in that was heaven ordinant.°   *guiding*
50   I had my father's signet in my purse,
         Which was the model of that Danish seal;
         Folded the writ up in the form of th'other,
         Subscribed° it, gave't th'impression,° placed it safely,   Signed / seal (*in wax*)
         The changeling² never known. Now the next day
55   Was our sea-fight; and what to this was sequent°   *subsequent*
         Thou know'st already.
HORATIO   So Guildenstern and Rosencrantz go to't.
HAMLET   Why, man, they did make love to this employment.
         They are not near my conscience. Their defeat°   *destruction*
60   Doth by their own insinuation grow.
         'Tis dangerous when the baser nature comes
         Between the pass and fell incensèd points³
         Of mighty opposites.°   *opponents*
HORATIO   Why, what a king is this!
HAMLET   Does it not, think'st thee, stand me now upon⁴—
65   He that hath killed my king and whored my mother,
         Popped in between th'election and my hopes,
         Thrown out his angle° for my proper° life,   *fishhook/own*
         And with such coz'nage°—is't not perfect conscience   *trickery*
         To quit° him with this arm? And is't not to be damned   *requite*
70   To let this canker° of our nature come   *cancerous sore*
         In° further evil?   *Into*
HORATIO   It must be shortly known to him from England
         What is the issue° of the business there.   *result*
HAMLET   It will be short. The interim's mine,
75   And a man's life's no more than to say 'one'.⁵
         But I am very sorry, good Horatio,
         That to Laertes I forgot myself;
         For by the image° of my cause I see   *mirror's reflection*
         The portraiture of his. I'll court his favours.
80   But sure, the bravery° of his grief did put me   *ostentation*
         Into a tow'ring passion.
HORATIO   Peace, who comes here?
         Enter young OSRIC, *a courtier* [*taking off his hat*]

---

7. Like the palm tree, an emblem of peace and prosperity.
8. And hold their interests separate but still connected (unlike a period, which would cut off "amity").
9. Weighty clauses beginning with "as"; asses bearing heavy loads.
1. Time for final confession and absolution, a part of the state ritual of legal executions.

2. A malicious elf child substituted for an infant, as Hamlet swaps his counterfeit letter for their authentic one.
3. *the pass . . . points:* fencing language; the thrust ("pass") and fiercely angry ("fell") rapiers.
4. Rest incumbent upon me.
5. And life lasts no longer than it takes to pronounce ("say") the monosyllable "one."

OSRIC   Your lordship is right welcome back to Denmark.

HAMLET   I humbly thank you, sir. [*To* HORATIO] Dost know this
water-fly?

85   HORATIO   No, my good lord.

HAMLET   Thy state is the more gracious,° for 'tis a vice to know   *blessed*
him. He hath much land, and fertile. Let a beast be lord of
beasts, and his crib shall stand at the king's mess.[6] 'Tis a chuff,°   *rich boor; jackdaw*
but, as I say, spacious in the possession of dirt.

90   OSRIC   Sweet lord, if your friendship were at leisure I should
impart a thing to you from his majesty.

HAMLET   I will receive it, sir, with all diligence of spirit. Put your
bonnet° to his right use; 'tis for the head.   *hat*

OSRIC   I thank your lordship, 'tis very hot.

95   HAMLET   No, believe me, 'tis very cold. The wind is northerly.

OSRIC   It is indifferent° cold, my lord, indeed.   *rather*

HAMLET   Methinks it is very sultry and hot for my complexion.°   *constitution*

OSRIC   Exceedingly, my lord. It is very sultry, as 'twere—I cannot
tell how. But, my lord, his majesty bade me signify to you that

100   a° has laid a great wager on your head. Sir, this is the matter.   *he*

HAMLET   I beseech you, remember.[7]

OSRIC   Nay, good my lord, for mine ease, in good faith.[8]

102.1   *Sir here is newly come to court Laertes, believe me, an*
absolute gentleman, full of most excellent differences,°   *superior qualities*
of very soft° society and great showing.° Indeed, to speak   *pleasing / appearance*
feelingly° of him, he is the card or calendar of gentry,[9]   *appreciatively*
102.5   *for you shall find in him the continent of what part[1] a*
gentleman would see.

HAMLET   *Sir, his definement suffers no perdition in you,[2]*
though I know to divide him inventorially would dizzy
th'arithmetic of memory, and yet but yaw neither in
102.10   *respect of his quick sail.[3] But in the verity of extolment,°*   *in truthful praise*
I take him to be a soul of great article,[4] and his infusion°   *inborn essence*
of such dearth° and rareness as, to make true diction[5] of   *preciousness*
him, his semblable° is his mirror, and who else would   *likeness*
trace him his umbrage, nothing more.[6]

102.15   OSRIC   *Your lordship speaks most infallibly of him.*

HAMLET   *The concernancy,° sir? Why do we wrap the gen-*   *relevance (to us)*
tleman in our more rawer breath?[7]

OSRIC   *Sir?*

HORATIO   *Is't not possible to understand in another*
102.20   *tongue? You will to't, sir, rarely.[8]*

HAMLET   *What imports the nomination° of this gentleman?*   *mention*

OSRIC   *Of Laertes?*

6. *Let . . . mess:* If an animal owned enough herds, even
it might find a place at the King's table. *crib:* manger.
7. "Remember your courtesy," the conventional expres-
sion inviting a subordinate to put his hat back on.
8. A conventional expression declining Hamlet's invita-
tion. Q2 adds the following passage, lines 102.1–102.34,
in place of lines 103–4, placing a comma instead of a
period after "faith."
9. The model of gentlemanly behavior. *card:* chart or
map. *calendar:* account book, directory.
1. Attribute or quality, playing on "region" (to which
Laertes is the "card"). *continent:* embodiment, contin-
uing the geographical pun.
2. Your picture of him ("definement") loses none of the
man's real excellence.

3. *to divide . . . sail:* to list his qualities individually would
confuse the memory's reckoning up (through recount-
ing vast numbers), and yet only steer erratically ("yaw")
around Laertes' skills—that is, the description would
only approximate his virtues.
4. Large scope (?); excellent qualities (?).
5. To speak truly.
6. And whoever imitates him is like his shadow
("umbrage"), not the real thing at all.
7. Our less refined words (since we are so much infe-
rior to Laertes).
8. *Is't . . . rarely:* Can't he understand his words in
another man's mouth? You will have your joke, sir, splen-
didly.

HORATIO [*aside to* HAMLET] *His purse is empty already; all
's golden words are spent.*

102.25   HAMLET [*to* OSRIC] Of him, sir.

OSRIC *I know you are not ignorant—*

HAMLET *I would you did, sir; yet, in faith, if you did it
would not much approve° me. Well, sir?*   *commend*

OSRIC *You are not ignorant of what excellence Laertes is.*

102.30   HAMLET I dare not confess that, lest I should compare
with him in excellence.[9] But to know a man well were
to know himself.[1]

OSRIC *I mean, sir, for his weapon. But in the imputation
laid on him by them, in his meed° he's unfellowed.°*   *merit / unmatched*

Sir, you are not ignorant of what excellence Laertes is at his
weapon.

105   HAMLET What's his weapon?

OSRIC Rapier and dagger.

HAMLET That's two of his weapons. But well.

OSRIC The King, sir, hath wagered with him six Barbary horses,
against the which he imponed,° as I take it, six French rapiers   *staked*

110   and poniards, with their assigns° as girdle,° hanger,[2] or so.   *accessories / sword belt*
Three of the carriages, in faith, are very dear to fancy, very
responsive to the hilts, most delicate carriages, and of very lib-
eral conceit.[3]

HAMLET What call you the carriages?[4]

114.1   HORATIO [*aside to* HAMLET] *I know you must be edified
by the margin[5] ere you had done.*

115   OSRIC The carriages, sir, are the hangers.

HAMLET The phrase would be more germane to the matter if we
could carry cannon by our sides. I would it might be hangers
till then. But on: six Barbary horses against six French swords,
their assigns, and three liberal-conceited carriages—that's the

120   French bet against the Danish. Why is this 'imponed', as you
call it?

OSRIC The King, sir, hath laid,° sir, that in a dozen passes   *placed his bet*
between you and him he shall not exceed you three hits.[6] He
hath on't twelve for nine,[7] and it would come to immediate

125   trial if your lordship would vouchsafe the answer.[8]

HAMLET How if I answer no?

OSRIC I mean, my lord, the opposition of your person in trial.

HAMLET Sir, I will walk here in the hall. If it please his majesty,
'tis the breathing° time of day with me. Let the foils be brought;   *exercising*

130   the gentleman willing, an° the King hold his purpose, I will   *if*
win for him an I can. If not, I'll gain nothing but my shame
and the odd hits.

OSRIC Shall I re-deliver you e'en so?

HAMLET To this effect, sir; after what flourish your nature will.

---

9. Claim to match him (since, proverbially, only excel-
lence recognizes excellence).
1. For in order to know another man truly, one must
know oneself.
2. Attaching straps.
3. *are . . . conceit:* capture the imagination ("fancy")
and match or echo ("respond to") the ornamentation on
the rapiers' hilts; further, they are finely wrought ("del-
icate") and of an elaborate ("liberal") design.
4. Osric's inflated term for "hangers," or straps. Here Q2
adds the following aside by Horatio, lines 114.1–114.2.

5. Must be informed by an explanatory note (from the
margin of a book).
6. Laertes must score three more "hits" than Hamlet
out of twelve bouts of swordplay to win the wager.
7. If "he" is Laertes, Osric may mean "He has bet twelve
passes for nine hits" (a greater challenge than the King's
terms, by which he would only need eight hits to win).
8. Would accept the challenge (Osric's meaning, and
the only honorable response). In the next line, Hamlet
deliberately misunderstands "answer" as "(any) reply."

135 OSRIC I commend my duty° to your lordship.   *dedicate my service*

HAMLET Yours, yours.   [*Exit* OSRIC]

He does well to commend° it himself; there are no tongues   *recommend*

else for 's turn.°   *purpose*

HORATIO This lapwing runs away with the shell on his head.[9]

140 HAMLET A did comply with his dug[1] before a sucked it. Thus
has he—and many more of the same bevy that I know the
drossy° age dotes on—only got the tune of the time and out-   *worthless*
ward habit of encounter,[2] a kind of yeasty collection which
carries them through and through the most fanned and win-

145 nowed opinions;[3] and do but blow them to their trial, the
bubbles are out.[4]

Enter a LORD

146.1 LORD [*to* HAMLET] *My lord, his majesty commended him
to you by young Osric, who brings back to him that you
attend him in the hall. He sends to know if your pleasure
hold to play with Laertes, or that you will take longer*

146.5 *time.*

HAMLET *I am constant to my purposes; they follow the
King's pleasure. If his fitness speaks, mine is ready, now
or whensoever, provided I be so able as now.*

LORD *The King and Queen and all are coming down.*

146.10 HAMLET *In happy time.*

LORD *The Queen desires you to use some gentle enter-
tainment[5] to Laertes before you fall to play.*

HAMLET *She well instructs me.*   [*Exit* LORD]

HORATIO *You will lose, my lord.*

HORATIO You will lose this wager, my lord.

HAMLET I do not think so. Since he went into France, I have
been in continual practice. I shall win at the odds. But thou

150 wouldst not think how all here about my heart—but it is no
matter.

HORATIO Nay, good my lord—

HAMLET It is but foolery, but it is such a kind of gain-giving° as   *misgiving*
would perhaps trouble a woman.

155 HORATIO If your mind dislike anything, obey it. I will forestall
their repair° hither, and say you are not fit.   *coming*

HAMLET Not a whit. We defy augury. There's a special provi-
dence[6] in the fall of a sparrow. If it be now, 'tis not to come.
If it be not to come, it will be now. If it be not now, yet it will

160 come. The readiness is all. Since no man has aught of what he
leaves, what is't to leave betimes?[7]

9. The newly hatched chicks of the plover ("lapwing")
were supposed to scurry about still wearing their
eggshells, a reference to the bonnet that Osric has finally
put back on as well as to the courtier's brainless chirping.
1. He bowed politely to his mother's breast.
2. *the tune . . . encounter:* the fashionable turns of
speech ("tune of the time") and the formulas ('habit')
of courteous conversation ("encounter").
3. *a kind of . . . opinions:* their empty clichés get them
through or pass for the most carefully considered wis-
dom (which is "fanned and winnowed" like wheat sep-
arated from chaff during threshing). *yeasty collection:* a
frothy and inflated repertoire of speech and behavior.
4. And if you test them by blowing on them—as Ham-
let does by speaking to Osric—they pop and dissolve. In
Q2, the following passage, lines 146.1–146.14, replaces
Horatio's line in F, "You will lose this wager, my lord."

5. To behave with conciliatory courtesy. Shakespeare
seems to have considered two alternative explanations
for Hamlet's final graciousness toward Laertes; here, in
Q2, the Queen's maternal guidance nudges him to it,
while F instead supplies Hamlet's own regret for his
graveside brawling in 5.2.76–81.
6. God's direction for a specific event (over and above
"general providence," the whole shape of God's design).
Compare Matthew 10:29. The specifically Protestant
theology of God's predestinating power is more explicit
in Q1's version of this line: "There's a predestinate prov-
idence / In the fall of a sparrow."
7. Since man does not truly possess what he must leave
behind him (worldly things and earthly flesh), why does
it matter to leave them sooner ("betimes")? Q2 reads
"Since no man of ought he leaves, knows what is't to
leave betimes, let be."

Enter KING [CLAUDIUS], QUEEN [GERTRUDE], LAERTES,
and lords, with [OSRIC *and*] *other attendants with trum-*
pets, drums, cushions, foils, and gauntlets; a table, and
flagons of wine on it

KING CLAUDIUS   Come, Hamlet, come, and take this hand from me.
HAMLET [*to* LAERTES]   Give me your pardon, sir. I've done you wrong;
  But pardon't as you are a gentleman.
165 This presence° knows,   *royal company*
  And you must needs have heard, how I am punished
  With sore distraction.° What I have done   *agitation; insanity*
  That might your nature, honour, and exception°   *disapproval*
  Roughly awake, I here proclaim was madness.
170 Was't Hamlet wronged Laertes? Never Hamlet.
  If Hamlet from himself be ta'en away,
  And when he's not himself does wrong Laertes,
  Then Hamlet does it not, Hamlet denies it.
  Who does it then? His madness. If't be so,
175 Hamlet is of the faction that is wronged.
  His madness is poor Hamlet's enemy.
  Sir, in this audience
  Let my disclaiming from a purposed evil[8]
  Free me so far in your most generous thoughts
180 That I have shot mine arrow o'er the house
  And hurt my brother.[9]
LAERTES   I am satisfied in nature,
  Whose motive in this case should stir me most
  To my revenge. But in my terms of honour[1]
  I stand aloof, and will no reconcilement
185 Till by some elder masters of known honour
  I have a voice and precedent of peace[2]
  To keep my name ungored;° but till that time   *my reputation intact*
  I do receive your offered love like love,
  And will not wrong it.
HAMLET   I do embrace it freely,
190 And will this brothers' wager frankly° play.—   *freely*
  [*To attendants*]   Give us the foils. Come on.
LAERTES [*to attendants*]   Come, one for me.
HAMLET   I'll be your foil,[3] Laertes. In mine ignorance
  Your skill shall, like a star i'th' darkest night,
  Stick° fiery off indeed.   *Sparkle; jab*
195 LAERTES   You mock me, sir.
HAMLET   No, by this hand.
KING CLAUDIUS   Give them the foils, young Osric. Cousin Hamlet,
  You know the wager?
HAMLET   Very well, my lord.
  Your grace hath laid the odds o'th' weaker side.
200 KING CLAUDIUS   I do not fear it; I have seen you both.
  But since he is bettered,° we have therefore odds.° *favored / handicapping*
LAERTES   [*taking a foil*]   This is too heavy; let me see another.

8. Let my disavowal of evil intention.
9. F's reading is "mother."
1. But where my social standing as a man of honor is
concerned.
2. *Till . . . peace:* Until the consensus of men of author-
itative standing, judging by the standards of tradition
(precedent), holds that I can make an honorable peace.
3. Flattering contrast. Jewels were often set with a
piece of metal foil under them to increase their glitter.

HAMLET [*taking a foil*]   This likes° me well. These foils have all   *pleases*
       a° length?   *the same*
OSRIC   Ay, my good lord.
     [HAMLET *and* LAERTES] *prepare to play*
KING CLAUDIUS [*to attendants*]   Set me the stoups° of wine upon   *flagons*
205   that table.
    If Hamlet give the first or second hit,
    Or quit in answer of the third exchange,[4]
    Let all the battlements their ordnance° fire.   *canons*
    The King shall drink to Hamlet's better breath,°   *energy*
210   And in the cup an union[5] shall he throw
    Richer than that which four successive kings
    In Denmark's crown have worn. Give me the cups,
    And let the kettle° to the trumpet speak,   *kettledrum*
    The trumpet to the cannoneer without,
215   The cannons to the heavens, the heaven to earth,
    'Now the King drinks to Hamlet'.
       Trumpets the while [*he drinks*]
                   Come, begin.
    And you, the judges, bear a wary eye.
HAMLET [*to* LAERTES]   Come on, sir.
LAERTES   Come, my lord.
     They play
220 HAMLET   One.
LAERTES   No.
HAMLET [*to* OSRIC]   Judgement.
OSRIC   A hit, a very palpable hit.
LAERTES   Well, again.
225 KING CLAUDIUS   Stay.° Give me drink. Hamlet, this pearl is thine.   *Stop*
    Here's to thy health.—
       Drum [*and*] *trumpets sound, and shot goes off*
                 Give him the cup.
HAMLET   I'll play this bout first. Set it by a while.—
    Come.
     They play again
     Another hit. What say you?
LAERTES   A touch, a touch, I do confess.
KING CLAUDIUS   Our son shall win.
230 QUEEN GERTRUDE   He's fat° and scant of breath.—   *sweaty*
    Here, Hamlet, take my napkin.° Rub thy brows.   *handkerchief*
    The Queen carouses to thy fortune, Hamlet.
HAMLET   Good madam.
KING CLAUDIUS   Gertrude, do not drink.
QUEEN GERTRUDE   I will, my lord, I pray you pardon me.
     She drinks [*then offers the cup to* HAMLET]
235 KING CLAUDIUS [*aside*]   It is the poisoned cup; it is too late.
HAMLET   I dare not drink yet, madam; by and by.
QUEEN GERTRUDE [*to* HAMLET]   Come, let me wipe thy face.
LAERTES [*aside to* CLAUDIUS]   My lord, I'll hit him now.
KING CLAUDIUS [*aside to* LAERTES]   I do not think't.
240 LAERTES [*aside*]   And yet 'tis almost 'gainst my conscience.

---

4. Or repay Laertes' victories by winning the third
bout.
5. A pearl, of exceptional quality. Claudius is perhaps
proposing to dissolve the gem, as Cleopatra did in a
much-repeated legend.

HAMLET   Come for the third, Laertes, you but dally.
I pray you pass° with your best violence.   *thrust*
I am afeard you make a wanton° of me.   *spoiled child*
LAERTES   Say you so? Come on.
    [They] play
OSRIC   Nothing neither way.
LAERTES *[to* HAMLET*]*   Have at you now!
    *[*LAERTES *wounds* HAMLET.*] In scuffling, they change
    rapiers*[6] *[and* HAMLET *wounds* LAERTES*]*
245   KING CLAUDIUS *[to attendants]*   Part them, they are incensed.
HAMLET *[to* LAERTES*]*   Nay, come again.
    The QUEEN *falls down*[7]
OSRIC   Look to the Queen there, ho!
HORATIO   They bleed on both sides. *[To* HAMLET*]* How is't, my lord?
OSRIC   How is't, Laertes?
LAERTES   Why, as a woodcock to mine own springe,° Osric.   *snare*
250   I am justly killed with mine own treachery.
HAMLET   How does the Queen?
KING CLAUDIUS   She swoons to see them bleed.
QUEEN GERTRUDE   No, no, the drink, the drink! O my dear Hamlet,
The drink, the drink—I am poisoned.   *[She dies]*
HAMLET   O villainy! Ho! Let the door be locked!   *[Exit* OSRIC*]*
255   Treachery, seek it out.
LAERTES   It is here, Hamlet. Hamlet, thou art slain.
No med'cine in the world can do thee good.
In thee there is not half an hour of life.
The treacherous instrument is in thy hand,
260   Unbated° and envenomed. The foul practice   *Not blunted*
Hath turned itself on me. Lo, here I lie,
Never to rise again. Thy mother's poisoned.
I can no more. The King, the King's to blame.
HAMLET   The point envenomed too? Then, venom, to thy work.
    [He] hurts KING *[*CLAUDIUS*]*
265   ALL THE COURTIERS   Treason, treason!
KING CLAUDIUS   O yet defend me, friends! I am but hurt.
HAMLET   Here, thou incestuous, murd'rous, damnèd Dane,
Drink off this potion. Is thy union[8] here?
Follow my mother.   KING *[*CLAUDIUS*] dies*
LAERTES   He is justly served.
270   It is a poison tempered° by himself.   *mixed*
Exchange forgiveness with me, noble Hamlet.
Mine and my father's death come not upon thee,[9]
Nor thine on me.   LAERTES *dies*
HAMLET   Heaven make thee free of it! I follow thee.
275   I am dead, Horatio. Wretched Queen, adieu!
You that look pale and tremble at this chance,
That are but mutes° or audience to this act,   *nonspeaking actors*
Had I but time—as this fell sergeant[1] Death
Is strict in his arrest—O, I could tell you—

---

6. *In . . . rapiers:* from F. While Q2 lacks any stage direc-
tion here, Q1 has "They catch one another's Rapiers,"
suggesting that each combatant is trying to disarm the
other with his free hand. Q1 also supplies daggers at line
161; these would presumably have been dropped so
that each man would have a free hand.
7. This stage direction and the one at line 253 are taken
from Q1, where they occur together.
8. Referring to both the pearl and his incestuous mar-
riage to Gertrude.
9. May your soul not be judged accountable for our
murders.
1. As this fierce sheriff's officer.

280 But let it be. Horatio, I am dead,
Thou liv'st. Report me and my cause aright
To the unsatisfied.
HORATIO   Never believe it.
I am more an antique Roman than a Dane.[2]
Here's yet some liquor left.
HAMLET   As thou'rt a man,
285 Give me the cup. Let go. By heaven, I'll ha't.
O God, Horatio, what a wounded name,
Things standing thus unknown, shall live behind me!
If thou didst ever hold me in thy heart,
Absent thee from felicity a while,
290 And in this harsh world draw thy breath in pain
To tell my story.
          March afar off, and shout within
                    What warlike noise is this?
          Enter OSRIC
OSRIC   Young Fortinbras, with conquest come from Poland,
To th'ambassadors of England gives
This warlike volley.°   *military salute*
HAMLET   O, I die, Horatio!
295 The potent poison quite o'ercrows[3] my spirit.
I cannot live to hear the news from England,
But I do prophesy th'election lights
On Fortinbras. He has my dying voice.[4]
So tell him, with th'occurrents,° more and less,   *events*
300 Which have solicited.[5] The rest is silence.
O, O, O, O![6]   HAMLET *dies*
HORATIO   Now cracks a noble heart. Good night, sweet prince,
And flights of angels sing thee to thy rest.—
Why does the drum come hither?
          Enter FORTINBRAS *with the English* AMBASSADORS, *with*
          drumme[r], colours, and attendants
305 FORTINBRAS   Where is this sight?
HORATIO   What is it ye would see?
If aught of woe or wonder, cease your search.
FORTINBRAS   This quarry cries on havoc.[7] O proud death,
What feast is toward° in thine eternal cell   *preparing*
310 That thou so many princes at a shot
So bloodily hast struck!
AMBASSADOR   The sight is dismal,
And our affairs from England come too late.
The ears are senseless that should give us hearing
To tell him° his commandment is fulfilled,   *(Claudius)*
315 That Rosencrantz and Guildenstern are dead.
Where should we have our thanks?
HORATIO   Not from his mouth,
Had it th'ability of life to thank you.

---

2. Ancient ("antique") Romans generally regarded sui-
cide as preferable to dishonor; in particular, they believed
that servants or retainers should not outlive their mas-
ter's overthrow.
3. Announces triumph over, like the victorious rooster in
a cockfight.
4. Vote. Because Denmark is an elective monarchy, For-
tinbras can only become King by receiving the "voice,"
or vote, of electors like Hamlet.

5. Some editors assume that the sentence is grammat-
ically incomplete, broken off by death. Hamlet seems to
refer to the events that have moved ("solicited") him to
have his story told and to give his support to Fortinbras.
6. These exclamations, omitted from Q2, might be
suggestive stage directions for death throes, rather than
scripted cries.
7. All this slaughtered game ("quarry") proclaims a
massacre.

He never gave commandment for their death.
But since so jump° upon this bloody question°   *immediately / matter*
320 You from the Polack wars, and you from England,
Are here arrived, give order that these bodies
High on a stage be placèd to the view;
And let me speak to th' yet unknowing world
How these things came about. So shall you hear
325 Of carnal, bloody, and unnatural acts,
Of accidental judgements,° casual° slaughters,   *retributions / chance*
Of deaths put on° by cunning and forced cause;   *instigated*
And, in this upshot, purposes mistook
Fall'n on th'inventors' heads. All this can I
Truly deliver.
330 FORTINBRAS   Let us haste to hear it,
And call the noblest to the audience.
For me, with sorrow I embrace my fortune.
I have some rights of memory⁸ in this kingdom,
Which now to claim my vantage° doth invite me.   *favorable opportunity*
335 HORATIO   Of that I shall have also cause to speak,
And from his mouth whose voice will draw on more.⁹
But let this same be presently performed,
Even whiles men's minds are wild, lest more mischance
On° plots and errors happen.   *On top of*
FORTINBRAS   Let four captains
340 Bear Hamlet like a soldier to the stage,
For he was likely, had he been put on,°   *put to the test*
To have proved° most royally; and for his passage,   *shown himself; acted*
The soldiers' music and the rites of war
Speak loudly for him.
345 Take up the body. Such a sight as this
Becomes the field,¹ but here shows° much amiss.   *appears*
Go, bid the soldiers shoot.

*Exeunt, marching [with the bodies]; after
the which, a peal of ordnance are shot off*

---

8. *of memory:* unforgotten; traditional.
9. Whose choice will induce more votes of support.

1. Is most appropriate to a battlefield.

Othello

"The problem of the twentieth century is the problem of the color-line." So prophesied the African American intellectual and activist W. E. B. Du Bois in his classic study *The Souls of Black Folk* (1903) just as the century began. Du Bois's prediction may have been premature with respect to Shakespearean tragedy, where *Hamlet, King Lear,* and *Macbeth* continued to dominate critical attention throughout most of the twentieth century. But today, *Othello* (1602–03) speaks to readers and audiences alike with unusual power, largely because it explores race and racism in unsettling fashion. Does this emphasis, centered on the dark skin of the title character, belatedly recognize a crucial issue previously neglected or misconstrued? Alternatively, does the recent preoccupation with race impose contemporary concerns on material with a different orientation?

Yes, to both questions. Interpretation is always influenced by both past and present—here by the play itself, together with its theatrical and critical heritage, and by the current preoccupations of contemporary audiences and readers. A complex work elicits different responses in different times or places: in *Othello,* to oversimplify, one issue (jealousy) was formerly more prominent, while another (race) has emerged—or reemerged—only recently. Neither race nor jealousy is the play's sole concern. *Othello* provocatively investigates gender and sexuality. It is preoccupied with class conflict, morality, and metaphysics. And it sets its central domestic disaster against the international conflict between Venetians and Turks over the island of Cyprus—a religious, political, and military antagonism that subtly informs the characters' catastrophic personal relationships.

This thematic range can be investigated by looking at Shakespeare's handling of his sources, at his unusual manipulation of dramatic genres and, hence, of audience expectations, at the psychology of Iago and Othello as well as their interaction, and, finally, at race itself. Much of *Othello*'s plot—but little of its outlook, characterization, or language—derives from Giovanbattista Giraldi Cinthio's *De gli hecatommithi* ("Hundred Tales," third decade, seventh story, 1565). In Shakespeare's version, racial issues are more persistent. The play here draws primarily on the 1600 translation of *A Geographical Historie of Africa* by Leo Africanus, a Moroccan Muslim who had been captured by Christian pirates and brought to Rome, where he converted to Catholicism. The public world of Venetian-Turkish affairs, absent from Cinthio, probably derives from Richard Knolles's *Generall Historie of the Turkes* (1603). Minor characters are given interesting twists. For instance, Emilia, the wife of Iago, the story's villain, is passive in Cinthio but in Shakespeare speaks for the rights of women, stands by Desdemona, Othello's wife, and ultimately brings her own husband down—at the cost of her life. The changes to Iago and Othello are even more consequential. Unlike *De gli hecatommithi*'s malefactor, who is motivated by unrequited lust for Desdemona and anger that she has refused his advances, Shakespeare's Iago loathes Othello and is determined to destroy him. His manipulative mastery is given greater scope, thereby enhancing a sense of his power as well as his fathomless viciousness. Similarly, by making Othello Desdemona's killer (Iago's job in Cinthio) and by having him publicly acknowledge his responsibility for the act, Shakespeare increases the character's guilt as well as his grandeur—the latter further enhanced by an elevation in social status from his position in the source. Thus *Othello,* unlike *De gli hecatommithi*, ties everything to the central murder.

The manipulation of generic expectations in *Othello* produces multiple perspectives on the plot. Though familiar with the classical dramatic genres of comedy and tragedy, Shakespeare was also influenced by late medieval–early Renaissance morality plays and

Two views of "the Moor" (one Arab or Berber, the other sub-Saharan), suggesting the range of images Shakespeare may have had in mind. Left: the Moroccan ambassador to Queen Elizabeth I (1600); right: "a Moor," from Cesare Vecellio, *De gli habiti antichi et moderni* (1590).

by Renaissance experimentation with hybrid forms. Hence, all of his plays are mixtures. The distinctiveness of *Othello,* however, lies not in the copresence of comic and tragic elements—a common feature in Shakespearean drama—but in the work's daring experiments with shifting generic frameworks. Its opening act, probably Shakespeare's invention, employs a strategy of studied indirection. It is night in a city—Venice, we are later told (1.1.107). Plot and character are presented in nonspecific terms: Roderigo is irritated that Iago "shouldst know of this," "of such a matter"—a matter concerning a "him" (1.1.3, 5, 6), an unnamed personage invoked only by pronouns until the snide reference to "his Moorship" (1.1.32). The play's first audiences might have connected this character with the titular figure, even though Othello himself does not appear on stage until scene 2 and is not named until scene 3. Iago tells Roderigo to "call up her father" (1.1.67), again without identifying "her" or "her father." The two men provoke Brabanzio, "her father," in similarly oblique fashion, only gradually revealing that Roderigo's "this" is a sexual relationship and, still later, that it is a marriage. Their imprecision about "this" encourages the audience to wonder what kind of play they are watching. It turns out to be a romantic comedy. Iago and Roderigo's strategy is aimed at persuading Brabanzio to nullify the union. They do get Brabanzio's aid, but they do not get what they want. Against the cultural norms of Shakespeare's time and subsequent centuries, the play celebrates Othello's grandeur, Desdemona's assertive autonomy (she wooed him), and the result—marriage between Moor and Venetian, old and young, black and white. The initial suppression of the names of the lovers renders them as character types to which stylized attributes, however misleading, can be attached before their individuality emerges. The darkness and the urban setting point to romantic concerns. The villain's machinations fail; the opposition of the old father, a standard blocking figure in stage comedy, proves ineffectual; the Duke, the play's highest ranking character, ratifies the marriage. It has all been so easy. Midway through the third scene, the story is over.

Except, of course, that it isn't. A new obstacle to marital bliss has arisen—the Turkish fleet's threat to Cyprus. The Venetian Senate dispatches Othello there to defend the interests of the state. To these vicissitudes of war the play adds the trial of separation. Although Desdemona will join Othello, she travels separately—with Iago. Before Venetian ships reach Cyprus, however, a storm destroys the Turkish armada. But by removing one danger, the storm creates two others. Will Desdemona be safe at sea? Will Othello? Romantic comedy has modulated into romance in the manner of late antique Greek and Roman prose fiction: faithful lovers, separated by storms, must undergo prolonged suffering before their final reunion. But Desdemona soon arrives unharmed; Othello promptly follows. By early in the second act, the play has apparently resolved issues of race and ethnicity, love and sexuality, religious and military hostilities. But less than halfway through the play, romantic comedy and romance both give way to domestic tragedy, a popular dramatic form of the time, usually set in England, in which female marital infidelity leads to disaster. Since there is no adultery, however, this third generic movement does not automatically occur. Iago must fabricate pretexts for Othello's sexual jealousy, a sensibility often associated on the Renaissance English stage with modern Italy and the Mediterranean. Accordingly, as we'll later see, neither comedy nor romance is ever definitively rejected.

These multiple formal perspectives—comedy, romance, domestic tragedy—help generate a correspondingly complex treatment of the characters and their interaction. The play begins with Iago. We quickly learn that "his Moorship," presumably a foreigner to Venice, has chosen as his lieutenant Cassio, an unproven gentleman from Florence and, hence, also a foreigner of sorts. Iago, the battle-tested, homegrown common soldier, deeply resents the slight. Out for himself and passed over for promotion, Iago is a young man on the make driven by class, regional, and ethnic resentment and willing to use others as means to his ends. Moreover, he has no illusions about those means. For instance, he anticipates that Brabanzio's opposition to his daughter's marriage will fail because of Othello's military importance to Venice (1.1.145–60). But Iago is more than a cool calculator; he is also tortured by a superheated sexual jealousy. Although he lacks any evidence, he believes that Othello has become Emilia's lover. He invents the sexual liaison between Cassio and Desdemona in order to supplant Cassio as lieutenant and make Othello jealous, arguing to himself that the charge of adultery he knows he has simply made up is actually real. Here, perhaps, we glimpse Iago's own sexual anxieties. Thus, he acknowledges his lust for Desdemona, explaining, however, that it is motivated by a desire to do to Othello what he assumes Othello has already done to him. And he converts his careerist resentment of Cassio into a fear that Cassio, too, will become Emilia's lover (2.1.273–99).

Furthermore, Iago enjoys the sport of ruining Othello's life. In this respect, he descends from a key figure of the earlier English morality plays—the Vice, a semisecularized devil who employs his comic verve to try to destroy his virtuous antagonists and whose colloquial intimacy with the audience often half-succeeds in winning that audience over. His diabolism is emphasized throughout the play. As he explains,

> When devils will the blackest sins put on,
> They do suggest at first with heavenly shows,
> As I do now.
>
> (2.3.325–27)

Similarly, Othello concludes:

> OTHELLO I look down towards his feet, but that's a fable.
> [*To* IAGO] If that thou beest a devil I cannot kill thee.
> [*He wounds* IAGO]
> . . . .
> IAGO   I bleed, sir, but not killed.
>
> (5.2.292–94)

The "fable" is that the devil's feet are cloven hooves. If Iago is the devil, he cannot die, a point he mockingly makes by insisting he is "not killed."

For more than a century, *Othello* in performance has often been Iago's show, partly because he wittily speaks to—not just before—the audience. Iago is also extremely talkative, uttering two hundred more lines than Othello himself—indeed, more than any other Shakespearean character except Hamlet. Thus, he potentially dominates a play that deploys the smallest cast in Shakespearean tragedy and that, after the first act, conforms to the Aristotelian unities of time, place, and action that Shakespeare normally ignores. As a matter of fact, his prominence has proven a recurrent problem, since it runs the risk of belittling Othello.

On the other hand, Iago's various motives help the play offer multiple accounts of Othello as well. Why does Othello move from nobly loving husband to insanely jealous murderer? If Iago is driven by resentment and jealousy, Othello is a savage fool. But if Iago is devilish, the play acquires a religious cast. Othello's soul hangs in the balance; in repudiating his good "angel" (5.2.140) and succumbing to temptation, he reenacts the fall. Faced with a supernatural adversary, Othello is less culpable. Hence, the long-standing debate about the protagonist's character cannot be resolved: Othello is noble victim and barbaric dupe.

Indeed, the disastrous outcome partly results from Iago's ability to turn Desdemona's and Othello's very nobility against them. Desdemona's bold, generous spirit becomes evidence of her affair with Cassio. Othello's "free and open nature" enables him to "be led by th' nose" (1.3.381, 383). Iago can also count on Othello's military resoluteness. Before Othello becomes jealous, he has staked everything on Desdemona: "My life upon her faith" (1.3.293). His grief at Desdemona's supposed betrayal, combining the martial and the marital, is at first moving in its stately repetitions:

> Farewell the tranquil mind, farewell content,
> Farewell the plumèd troops and the big wars
> That makes ambition virtue! O, farewell,
> Farewell the neighing steed and the shrill trump.
> (3.3.353–56)

But as Othello's psyche breaks down, incoherent prose supplants measured verse: "Handkerchief—confessions—handkerchief. . . . Pish! Noses, ears, and lips! Is't possible? Confess? Handkerchief? O devil! *He falls down in a trance*" (4.1.36–41, s.d.).

Put another way, Othello is out of his element. A soldier since childhood, he knows little of peacetime urban existence. He should feel at home on Cyprus, a military prize. But when the Turkish threat dissipates, the island becomes the typical other world of Shakespearean drama, where all characters are displaced and fundamental change occurs. In particular, Cyprus's ancient association with sexual license emerges. Although this seems antithetical to republican Venice's sobriety, we come to suspect that Venice is no better. As a result, Othello is more vulnerable to Iago's influence than he would be on the battlefield. He accepts narratives about himself and Desdemona composed from the repugnant sexual—and especially misogynist—stereotypes of European society that also torment Iago. Brabanzio warns Othello: "She has deceived her father, and may thee" (1.3.292). Iago retrieves the thought:

> IAGO She did deceive her father, marrying you.
> . . . .
> OTHELLO   And so she did.
> (3.3.210–12)

As Iago's thinking has revealed, sexual guilt need be merely plausible. "'Tis probable, and palpable to thinking," Brabanzio argues, that Othello used magic on Desdemona (1.2.77). The Duke rejects mere assertion and "poor likelihoods" (1.3.108). But Iago gets away with "imputation, and strong circumstances" (3.3.411) rather than "ocular proof" (3.3.365), because Othello cannot challenge Iago's cynical view of sexuality:

"In Venice they do let God see the pranks / They dare not show their husbands" (3.3.206–07). Hence, Iago's description of Cassio and Desdemona in the play's recurrent animal imagery—"as prime as goats, as hot as monkeys" (3.3.408)—returns in Othello's "Goats and monkeys!" (4.1.260). This outcome seems to depend, however, on Iago's ability to elicit Othello's own sexual anxieties.

The sexual loathing Othello reveals here may also be inspired by Desdemona's directness:

> That I did love the Moor to live with him,
> My downright violence and storm of fortunes
> May trumpet to the world.
>
> (1.3.247–49)

Othello registers the allure and the threat of such erotic boldness when he and Desdemona are reunited on Cyprus: "If it were now to die / 'Twere now to be most happy," where "to die" also means to have an orgasm (2.1.186–87). Christian doctrine sometimes considered excessive marital sexual pleasure a form of adultery. Earlier, Iago plots "after some time to abuse Othello's ears / That he is too familiar with his wife" (1.3.377–78). "He" is presumably Cassio, to whom Iago has recently referred. But the nearer mention of Othello and the pronoun confusion—since "his" must refer to Othello—suggest that Othello experiences his own sexual desire as adulterous, that following sexual consummation of his marriage (if that actually occurs) he projects this desire onto Cassio, and that he punishes his sexual feelings by killing Desdemona.

Not surprisingly, the conclusion also encourages an ambivalent view of Othello. Shakespeare emphasizes Desdemona's innocent victimization by dramatizing her obedience to her husband.

> DESDEMONA O, falsely, falsely murdered!
> . . . .
> A guiltless death I die.
> EMILIA O, who hath done this deed?
> DESDEMONA Nobody, I myself. Farewell.
> Commend me to my kind lord. O, farewell!
>
> (5.2.126–34)

A loyally subordinate Desdemona is more conventionally reassuring than the Desdemona who flouted convention to marry Othello. This diminution of female autonomy retreats from Desdemona's bolder position early in the play, which is itself echoed by Emilia's brave, principled defiance at the end. Yet Desdemona's final words may indicate a masochistic submissiveness as unsettling as her previous behavior or perhaps, taken from a Christian perspective, a paradox—the simultaneous assertion of suicide (a mortal sin) and guiltlessness. Her words also increase Othello's guilt and underscore the mistreatment of women that we see as well in both Iago's relationship with Emilia and Cassio's with Bianca, the courtesan who loves him.

Othello himself believes he is administering secular justice or performing a religious ritual in killing Desdemona. But his rage forces him to "call what I intend to do / A murder, which I thought a sacrifice" (5.2.69–70). Confronted with Desdemona's innocence, he assumes the same role—this time, however, executing himself. But suicide evokes Christian despair and certainty of damnation as well as disinterested justice and ancient Stoic heroism. Similarly, one may disagree with Othello's conviction that he is "an honourable murderer," "one not easily jealous" (5.2.300, 354).

The persistence of a comic outlook further complicates our judgment. As in Shakespeare's earlier romantic comedy *Much Ado About Nothing* (1598), information sufficient to unmask the villain's slandering of female sexual propriety has always been available. Further, Othello speculates that Desdemona's infidelity arises because "I am declined / Into the vale of years" (3.3.269–70), thereby invoking farce's standard cuckolding of old man by young woman, of January by May. Similarly, Emilia oxymoronically calls Othello a "murderous coxcomb" (fool) and asks a familiar comic question: "What should such a fool / Do with so good a wife?" (5.2.240–41). The play then concludes by literalizing the metaphorical destination of romantic comedy—the marriage bed, here present in grimly parodic form.

A pervasive association between sex and death also promotes ambivalence. The fatal "napkin," or handkerchief, indicative of aristocratic privilege but important because of its very triviality, symbolically captures these feelings. Presented, according to Othello, to his mother by "an Egyptian . . . charmer," the handkerchief combines the magic and ethnic exoticism Othello earlier repudiates in defending his marriage to Desdemona. It enabled his mother to "subdue my father / Entirely to her love" (3.4.57–58). Or perhaps not. Othello ultimately offers a more prosaic account: "It was a handkerchief, an antique token / My father gave my mother" (5.2.223–24). "Spotted with strawberries" (3.3.440), it may evoke the blood Desdemona loses with her virginity on the marriage bed. Desdemona has Emilia "lay on my bed my wedding sheets" (4.2.108); Othello anticipates that "thy bed, lust-stained, shall with lust's blood be spotted" (5.1.37). This association between sexual pleasure and death is then enacted. Attracted by his sleeping wife, Othello cannot resist kissing her: "Be thus when thou art dead, and I will kill thee / And love thee after" (5.2.18–19). He recalls this necrophilic perversity at his own death: "I kissed thee ere I killed thee. No way but this: / Killing myself, to die upon a kiss" (5.2.368–69), where "die" once again carries a secondary sexual sense. Romance's movement toward reuniting long-separated lovers takes the form of a postmortem embrace. Furthermore, this concluding tableau includes not only Othello and Desdemona but perhaps Emilia as well, whose dying wish is to "lay me by my mistress' side!" (5.2.244). If so, we witness the very ménage à trois or intimate bedroom relationship between Emilia and Othello that Iago invoked to motivate his revenge.

What, then, of race? It is there from the start. Iago warns Brabanzio that "an old black ram / Is tupping your white ewe" (1.1.88–89). The arousal of Brabanzio's fear of miscegenation works. The old man cannot believe that his daughter would ever "run . . . to the sooty bosom / Of such a thing as thou" (1.2.71–72). He is wrong, however, not just about Desdemona but also about the sympathies of the Venetian Senate. As the Duke explains, "Your son-in-law is far more fair than black" (1.3.289). Yet this victory is uncomfortable: the praise arises from the negative connotations of blackness. Hence, when Othello seeks to understand his wife's betrayal, he adopts these connotations literally—"Haply for I am black" (3.3.267)—and metaphorically—"My name . . . is now begrimed and black / As mine own face" (3.3.391–93).

The language of color in the play draws on the biblical association of blackness and evil, Elizabethan prejudice toward black Africans resident in England,

The manner of Turkish tyrannie over Christian slaves.

Compare Othello's last speech before killing himself (5.2.361–65). Woodcut, from F. Knight, *A Relation of Seavan Yeares Slaverie Under the Turkes of Argeire . . .* (1640).

ethnographic accounts of passionately jealous Africans, and the early stages of the slave trade. Yet it lacks the full racist import it subsequently acquired. Renaissance thought was innocent of the biological view of ethnic difference that triumphed in the nineteenth century. Othello's mention of being "sold to slavery" (1.3.137), given its Mediterranean context, has more to do with social hierarchy and religious difference than skin color. Until the late seventeenth century, *Othello*'s commentators make little of Othello's appearance, although they assume, in line with most of the play's language, that he is black—a position rejected in the nineteenth century and still sometimes challenged today. (See the two renderings of Moors on page 1170.) Shakespeare also followed less prominent, more sympathetic accounts of Moors, deriving from subordinate strains in both travel literature and the religious tradition. The racial issues of *Othello* are, therefore, both like and unlike those of the present, with which they are connected partly by the unbroken influence of the play itself.

These issues have produced powerful contradictory reactions on the stage, where *Othello* has always been one of Shakespeare's most popular works. Well into the twentieth century, audiences and critics often agreed with Brabanzio, seeing in the conclusion the triumph of Othello's barbaric African essence over his civilized European surface. When they defended his nobility, they denied he was black. "Othello *was a white* man," Mary Preston of Baltimore wrote in 1869. A compromise resolution offered by the actor Herbert Beerbohm Tree in 1912 suggests the underlying racist agreement between antithetical conclusions about Othello's skin color: "Othello was an Oriental, not a Negro: a stately Arab of the best caste."

But especially when Othello is played by an actor of sub-Saharan descent, performances have seemed to strike a blow for freedom—on the Continent following the revolutions of 1848, in czarist Russia on the eve of the liberation of the serfs, after 1863 and the emancipation of American slaves, in World War II America, and in the final years of South African apartheid. The 1943 American *Othello,* featuring what may have been the American theater's first kiss between a black actor (Paul Robeson) and a white actress, was at the time the longest-running production of any Shakespearean play in the United States. Yet commentators of African descent have sometimes taken the opposite view—that a black actor as Othello runs the risk of reinforcing racial stereotypes. The problem for a white actor is even graver. With the recent return on the stage to the pre-1800 conviction that Othello is black, productions have steered away from white performers in the part, fearing that they would produce minstrel-show figures in blackface reminiscent of nineteenth-century burlesques of the play—precisely the charge sometimes made against Laurence Olivier's 1965 portrayal.

This history inevitably affects contemporary understanding of the conclusion of the play, when race seems to return literally with a vengeance. The alien connotations of the handkerchief are echoed by the ethnic rhetoric of Othello's last long speech, in which the conflict of civilizations reemerges in the Moor's identification with the exotic non-European, non-Christian world. In the quarto version (see the Textual Note), Othello is "like the base Indian" who "threw a pearl away / Richer than all his tribe" (5.2.356–57). But the Folio reads "base Iudean" (Judean) and hence may allude to Judas, betrayer of Christ, or to Herod the Great, murderer of his wife, Mariamne, out of jealousy. Othello "drops tears as fast as the Arabian trees / Their medicinable gum" (5.2.359–60). He asks his listeners to remind the Venetian state

> that in Aleppo once,
> Where a malignant and a turbaned Turk
> Beat a Venetian and traduced the state,
> I took by th' throat the circumcisèd dog
> And smote him thus.
> *He stabs himself*
>
> (5.2.361–65, s.d.)

In Act 1, Othello, an orthodox Christian and loyal servant of the state, agrees to defend Venice from the Turks—to protect Christianity from a Muslim people with whom Moors were linked on religious, political, and military grounds. By having Venice send Othello to that island to protect Christian interests from the forces of Islam, Shakespeare inserts his protagonist into a defining struggle of the age. In Act 5, Othello remembers that he defended Venice from the Turks once before. This recollection is the occasion for his suicide, a deed that splits him in two. Othello is agent and object of justice, servant and enemy of the Christian state. As a "base Iudean" and "circumcisèd dog," he is a Jew. Circumcision also makes him a Turk. The external military conflict returns as internal division within Othello's soul. Othello half assumes an ethnic and religious otherness to exorcise his guilt. The development of the plot both undermines and validates ethnocentric and racist stereotypes. But is this conclusion really about race, or does it turn instead on religious—and, hence, cultural—antagonism? The question resonates in today's world, where the "problem of the color-line" seems both related to and distinct from the persistence, in the eastern Mediterranean and beyond, of the very religious and military conflicts evoked by *Othello*. Hence, the uneasiness of the ending, where the unwarranted projection of guilt entirely beyond the confines of Europe is the precondition of that noble acceptance of responsibility with which Othello so memorably leaves the world and the play.

WALTER COHEN

TEXTUAL NOTE

The Tragedy of Othello, the Moore of Venice survives in two early authoritative versions—the First Quarto of 1622 (Q) and the First Folio of the following year (F). Extensive study of the background and relationship of the two texts has yet to produce anything close to a consensus. The Oxford editors hypothesize that F uses a scribal copy of Shakespeare's own revision of his earlier manuscript preserved in Q. On the other hand, Q more accurately preserves Shakespeare's characteristic spelling and punctuation, its stage directions are fuller and more authorial (although some were probably added later), and it contains more than fifty oaths excluded from F presumably in response to the Profanity Act of 1606. It is also the only Shakespearean Quarto with act divisions. In order to capture these features, the version printed here uses Q for these details. But it includes the roughly 160 lines from F not found in Q, and it usually prefers F to Q in the over one thousand places where their wording differs. In general, then, F is the primary source for the language, whereas Q provides the spelling, punctuation, oaths, and to some extent stage directions. Act divisions are the same in the two versions. Other modern editions of the play, although differing in their assumptions and in many details, produce broadly similar texts.

The passages unique to F fall into three main categories. In Act 1, Roderigo's and Brabanzio's accusations against Othello are longer. Second, beginning in Act 3, F provides Othello with greater opportunity to express his anguish. Finally and most important, the last two acts of F provide fuller parts for Desdemona (mainly by giving her the willow song in 4.3) and Emilia. These passages tend to place F further away from cynicism and disillusionment than is Q. Some of the more extensive or striking differences from Q are mentioned in the notes. By contrast, differences in Iago's role between Q and F are minor and incidental. The excision of oaths places the scribal transcript for F after 1606. Perhaps the Profanity Act necessitated certain limited revisions for a revival in 1606 or later. Perhaps then or at another time, the Oxford editors hypothesize, Shakespeare introduced more substantive changes—occasionally in the oaths, more often in the characters themselves.

Various alternatives to this approach appear in the scholarly literature on the play. One recent explanation is worthy of particular note, however. According to this argument, the 160 lines found only in F are part of the original text. Q represents an abridgment designed for performance and, for the most part, dictated to a scribe by the actors who initially played the parts. If this is so (and it currently seems the most persuasive hypothesis), the thematic differences between Q and F suggested above would represent not two distinct stages in Shakespeare's career but two different versions of the same play—the *Othello* performed for some or all audiences in the early seventeenth century and the version available to readers and potentially to spectators at least from 1623 on, though perhaps earlier as well.

SELECTED BIBLIOGRAPHY

Barthelemy, Anthony Gerard, ed. *Critical Essays on Shakespeare's "Othello."* New York: Hall, 1994. A collection of important essays (including Boose, Fineman, Loomba, Neely, Neill, Newman), mainly from the 1970s and 1980s, focusing on race and gender.

Danson, Lawrence. "England, Islam, and the Mediterranean Drama: *Othello* and Others." *Journal for Early Modern Cultural Studies* 2.2 (2002): 1–25. Contextual study of East and West, showing the instability of standard distinctions among Moor, Turk, Jew, and Christian.

Greenblatt, Stephen. *Renaissance Self-Fashioning: From More to Shakespeare.* Chicago: University of Chicago Press, 1980. 222–54. Othello's narrative self-fashioning and its subversion by Desdemona's submission and Iago's malice; a central essay for modern *Othello* scholarship and for New Historicist criticism generally.

Hankey, Julie, ed. *Othello.* 2nd ed. New York: Cambridge University Press, 2005. History of performance (stage, film, and television), with an extensive list of productions over 400 years and a text of the play with theatrical annotations.

Neill, Michael, ed. *Othello, the Moor of Venice.* Oxford: Clarendon, 2006. Outstanding scholarly edition with a book-length critical introduction.

Nostbakken, Faith, ed. *Understanding "Othello": A Student Casebook to Issues, Sources, and Historical Documents.* Westport, Conn.: Greenwood Press, 2000. Extensive excerpts from Renaissance sources, including Cinthio and Knowles; briefer selections from literary and performance criticism; suggestions of contemporary relevance (O.J. Simpson, Bill Clinton, etc.).

Orlin, Lena Cowen, ed. *Othello.* New York: Palgrave Macmillan, 2004. Leading essays since 1990, mostly on gender and marriage (Berger, Bristol, Sinfield) or race and reception (Bartels, Singh, Hodgdon, Albanese).

Pechter, Edward. *"Othello" and Interpretive Traditions.* Iowa City: University of Iowa Press, 1999. Relatively traditional account of the play's power that recognizes the inextricable link between text and interpretation while arguing for the continuing influence of earlier critical debates on current scholarship.

Potter, Lois. *Othello.* Shakespeare in Performance series. Manchester: Manchester University Press, 2002. Manchester: Manchester University Press, 2002. Focus on recent stagings, live or electronic, seeing Paul Robeson's performances from the 1930s to the 1950s as the defining events in modern productions of the play.

Wain, John, ed. *Shakespeare, "Othello": A Casebook.* London: Macmillan, 1971. Classic essays by Rymer, Johnson, Coleridge, Bradley, Eliot, Knight, Empson, Leavis, Gardner, Bayley, Auden, Coghill.

FILMS

Othello. 1952. Dir. Orson Welles. USA. 93 min. This black-and-white film stars Welles as Othello. Famous for its innovative and disorienting camera work more than for its acting.

Othello. 1965. Dir. Stuart Burge and John Dexter. UK. 165 min. Film of a stage performance, with Laurence Olivier as Othello and Maggie Smith as Desdemona. Notable not only for the white actor's effort fully to impersonate a black African—seen at the time as both troubling and moving—but also for Smith's spirited Desdemona, a break with the prior stage tradition of representing the character as a passive victim.

Othello. 1988. Dir. Janet Suzman. South Africa/UK. 187 min. Film of the controversial South African stage performance (the first with a black African actor and a white actress) that became a form of antiapartheid protest.

Othello. 1995. Dir. Oliver Parker. USA/UK. 123 min. First version made for film with an African American, Laurence Fishburne, as Othello. Kenneth Branagh as Iago dominates the play (as often happens with Iago). Ironically, racial issues are muted.

O. 2001. Dir. Tim Blake Nelson. USA. 95 min. Set in a contemporary high school, centered on a basketball player, Odin (Mekhi Phifer), in love with Desi (Julia Stiles), undone by Hugo (Josh Hartnett); also with Martin Sheen.

The Tragedy of Othello, the Moor of Venice

THE PERSONS OF THE PLAY

OTHELLO, the Moor of Venice
DESDEMONA, his wife
Michael CASSIO, his lieutenant
BIANCA, a courtesan, in love with Cassio
IAGO, the Moor's ensign
EMILIA, Iago's wife
A CLOWN, a servant of Othello
The DUKE of Venice
BRABANZIO, Desdemona's father, a senator of Venice
GRAZIANO, Brabanzio's brother
LODOVICO, kinsman of Brabanzio
SENATORS of Venice
RODERIGO, a Venetian gentleman, in love with Desdemona
MONTANO, Governor of Cyprus
A HERALD
A MESSENGER
Attendants, officers, sailors, gentlemen of Cyprus, musicians

1.1

Enter IAGO[1] *and* RODERIGO

RODERIGO   Tush, never tell me!° I take it much unkindly   *(Annoyance; disbelief)*
    That thou, Iago, who hast had my purse
    As if the strings were thine, shouldst know of this.
IAGO   'Sblood,° but you'll not hear me!   *By Christ's blood*
5   If ever I did dream of such a matter, abhor me.
RODERIGO   Thou told'st me thou didst hold him in thy hate.
IAGO   Despise me
    If I do not. Three great ones of the city,
    In personal suit to make me his lieutenant,
10   Off-capped° to him; and by the faith of man   *Took off their caps*
    I know my price, I am worth no worse a place.
    But he, as loving his own pride and purposes,
    Evades them with a bombast circumstance[2]
    Horribly stuffed with epithets of war,°   *military jargon*
15   Nonsuits° my mediators; for 'Certes,'° says he,   *Denies / Certainly*
    'I have already chose my officer.'
    And what was he?
    Forsooth, a great arithmetician,[3]
    One Michael Cassio, a Florentine,

1.1 Location: A street in Venice.
1. Iago's name may be related to Santiago Matamoros, St. James the Moor Slayer, the patron saint of Spain.
2. With an inflated circumlocution. *bombast*: cotton pad-
ding in clothes, a metaphor picked up by "stuffed" (line 14) and possibly "suit" (line 9) and "Nonsuits" (line 15).
3. Implying that Cassio's knowledge of war is purely theoretical.

20	A fellow almost damned in a fair wife,⁴	
	That° never set a squadron in the field	*Who*
	Nor the division° of a battle° knows	*ordering / battalion*
	More than a spinster°—unless the bookish theoric,°	*housewife / learning*
	Wherein the togaed consuls can propose⁵	
25	As masterly as he. Mere prattle without practice	
	Is all his soldiership; but he, sir, had th'election,	
	And I—of whom his eyes had seen the proof	
	At Rhodes, at Cyprus, and on other grounds	
	Christened and heathen—must be beleed° and calmed°	*without wind / becalmed*
30	By debitor and creditor. This counter-caster,⁶	
	He in good time° must his lieutenant be,	*indeed (scornful)*
	And I—God bless the mark!°—his Moorship's ensign.⁷	*God help us*

RODERIGO   By heaven, I rather would have been his hangman.

IAGO   Why, there's no remedy. 'Tis the curse of service.

35	Preferment goes by letter and affection,⁸	
	And not by old gradation,° where each second	*traditional seniority*
	Stood heir to th' first. Now, sir, be judge yourself	
	Whether I in any just term am affined°	*am bound in any just way*
	To love the Moor.⁹	

40	RODERIGO I would not follow him then.	
	IAGO O sir, content you.°	*be content*
	I follow him to serve my turn upon him.	
	We cannot all be masters, nor all masters	
	Cannot be truly followed. You shall mark	
45	Many a duteous and knee-crooking knave	
	That, doting on his own obsequious bondage,	
	Wears out his time much like his master's ass	
	For naught but provender,° and when he's old, cashiered.°	*animal feed / fired*
	Whip me° such honest knaves. Others there are	*The hell with*
50	Who, trimmed° in forms and visages of duty,	*outwardly decorated*
	Keep yet their hearts attending on themselves,	
	And, throwing but shows of service on their lords,	
	Do well thrive by 'em, and when they have lined their coats,	
	Do themselves homage. These fellows have some soul,	
55	And such a one do I profess myself—for, sir,	
	It is as sure as you are Roderigo,	
	Were I the Moor I would not be Iago.	
	In following him I follow but myself.	
	Heaven is my judge, not I for° love and duty,	*I am not driven by*
60	But seeming so for my peculiar° end.	*personal*
	For when my outward action doth demonstrate	
	The native act and figure¹ of my heart	

4. Obscure. Cassio has not yet met Bianca and is unmarried, although in Shakespeare's source he is. Perhaps Shakespeare's error, a reference to Cassio as a ladies' man, or an oblique, debatable anticipation of the main plot.
5. In which the toga-wearing senators can debate.
6. *debitor and creditor, counter-caster:* pejorative terms for an accountant (Cassio).
7. As "ensign," Iago is something like a standard-bearer or third-in-command. He clearly ranks below "lieutenant" Cassio, the second-in-command. This reference to "his Moorship" is also the first indication about whom Iago has been complaining.

8. Promotion comes through connections and favoritism.
9. A Moor was a Muslim of the mixed Berber and Arab people inhabiting northwest Africa. This term, like the comparison of Othello to a "Barbary horse" (an Arab, line 113), formerly led to the denial of Othello's blackness. But the passages describing Othello's appearance—"thick-lips," "black ram," "sooty bosom," "black Othello," "I am black," "black / As mine own face" (1.1.66, 1.1.88, 1.2.71, 2.3.27–28, 3.3.267, 3.3.392–93)—seem to have greater weight. "Moor" often meant sub-Saharan African in the Renaissance.
1. The innate operation (or motivation) and shape (or nature).

In compliment extern,° 'tis not long after   *outward appearance*
But I will wear my heart upon my sleeve
65   For daws° to peck at. I am not what I am.   *crowlike birds*
RODERIGO   What a full fortune does the thick-lips owe°   *own*
    If he can carry't thus!
IAGO   Call up her father,
    Rouse him, make after him, poison his delight,
    Proclaim him in the streets; incense her kinsmen,
70   And, though he in a fertile climate dwell,
    Plague him with flies. Though that his joy be joy,
    Yet throw such chances of vexation on't
    As it may lose some colour.
RODERIGO   Here is her father's house. I'll call aloud.
75   IAGO   Do, with like timorous accent° and dire yell   *frightening tone*
    As when, by night and negligence, the fire
    Is spied in populous cities.
RODERIGO [*calling*]   What ho, Brabanzio, Signor Brabanzio, ho!
IAGO [*calling*]   Awake, what ho, Brabanzio, thieves, thieves, thieves!
80   Look to your house, your daughter, and your bags.
    Thieves, thieves!

       [*Enter*] BRABANZIO [*in his nightgown*] *at a window*
           above

BRABANZIO   What is the reason of this terrible summons?
    What is the matter there?
RODERIGO   Signor, is all your family within?
IAGO   Are your doors locked?
85   BRABANZIO   Why, wherefore ask you this?
IAGO   'Swounds,° sir, you're robbed. For shame, put on your   *By Christ's wounds*
    gown.
    Your heart is burst, you have lost half your soul.
    Even now, now, very now, an old black ram
    Is tupping° your white ewe. Arise, arise!   *copulating with*
90   Awake the snorting° citizens with the bell,   *snoring*
    Or else the devil will make a grandsire of you.
    Arise, I say.
BRABANZIO   What, have you lost your wits?
RODERIGO   Most reverend signor, do you know my voice?
BRABANZIO   Not I. What are you?
95   RODERIGO   My name is Roderigo.
BRABANZIO   The worser welcome.
    I have charged thee not to haunt about my doors.
    In honest plainness thou hast heard me say
    My daughter is not for thee, and now in madness,
100   Being full of supper and distempering° draughts,   *destabilizing*
    Upon malicious bravery° dost thou come   *defiance*
    To start° my quiet.   *upset*
RODERIGO   Sir, sir, sir.
BRABANZIO   But thou must needs be sure
105   My spirits and my place° have in their power   *rank*
    To make this bitter to thee.
RODERIGO   Patience, good sir.
BRABANZIO   What tell'st thou me of robbing? This is Venice.
    My house is not a grange.°   *country house*
RODERIGO   Most grave Brabanzio,

In simple and pure soul I come to you.

110 IAGO [*to* BRABANZIO] 'Swounds, sir, you are one of those that will
not serve God if the devil bid you. Because we come to do you
service and you think we are ruffians, you'll have your daughter
covered with a Barbary horse,[2] you'll have your nephews° neigh   grandsons
to you, you'll have coursers for cousins and jennets for ger-
115 mans.[3]

BRABANZIO What profane wretch art thou?

IAGO I am one, sir, that comes to tell you your daughter and the
Moor are now making the beast with two backs.°   copulating

BRABANZIO Thou art a villain.

IAGO   You are a senator.

120 BRABANZIO This thou shalt answer.° I know thee, Roderigo.   account for

RODERIGO Sir, I will answer anything. But I beseech you,
If 't be your pleasure and most wise consent[4]—
As partly I find it is—that your fair daughter,
At this odd-even° and dull watch o'th' night,   late (around midnight)
125 Transported with no worse nor better guard
But with a knave of common° hire, a gondolier,   public
To the gross clasps of a lascivious Moor—
If this be known to you, and your allowance,°   allowed by you
We then have done you bold and saucy wrongs.
130 But if you know not this, my manners tell me
We have your wrong rebuke. Do not believe
That, from° the sense of all civility,   in opposition to
I thus would play and trifle with your reverence.
Your daughter, if you have not given her leave,
135 I say again hath made a gross revolt,
Tying her duty, beauty, wit, and fortunes
In an extravagant and wheeling stranger[5]
Of here and everywhere. Straight° satisfy yourself.   Immediately
If she be in her chamber or your house,
140 Let loose on me the justice of the state
For thus deluding you.

BRABANZIO [*calling*]   Strike on the tinder,° ho!   A light
Give me a taper,° call up all my people.   candle
This accident° is not unlike my dream;   event
Belief of it oppresses me already.
Light, I say, light!   *Exit*

145 IAGO   Farewell, for I must leave you.
It seems not meet° nor wholesome to my place   proper
To be producted°—as, if I stay, I shall—   presented as witness
Against the Moor, for I do know the state,
However this may gall him with some check,°   reprimand
150 Cannot with safety cast° him, for he's embarked°   dismiss / committed
With such loud reason° to the Cyprus wars,   vociferous, just support
Which even now stands in act,° that, for their souls,   are taking place
Another of his fathom° they have none   caliber
To lead their business, in which regard—

---

2. Horse from northwest coastal Africa; an Arab; sug-
gesting barbarism.
3. *coursers:* strong horses. *cousins:* kinsmen. *jennets:*
small Spanish horses. *germans:* close relatives.

4. Lines 122–38 do not appear in Q.
5. In a vagrant and vagabond foreigner (perhaps sug-
gesting a planet wandering off course).

155   Though I do hate him as I do hell pains—
    Yet for necessity of present life
    I must show out a flag and sign of love,
    Which is indeed but sign. That you shall surely find him,
    Lead to the Sagittary⁶ the raisèd search,°   *awakened searchers*
160   And there will I be with him. So farewell.   *Exit*

    Enter [below] BRABANZIO *in his nightgown, and servants*
        with torches

BRABANZIO   It is too true an evil. Gone she is,
    And what's to come of my despisèd time°   *lifetime*
    Is naught but bitterness. Now, Roderigo,
    Where didst thou see her?—O unhappy girl!—
165   With the Moor, sayst thou?—Who would be a father?—
    How didst thou know 'twas she?—O, she deceives me
    Past thought!—What said she to you? *[To servants]* Get more tapers,
    Raise all my kindred.   *[Exit one or more]*
    [To RODERIGO*]*   Are they married, think you?
RODERIGO   Truly, I think they are.
170 BRABANZIO   O heaven, how got she out? O, treason of the blood!
    Fathers, from hence trust not your daughters' minds
    By what you see them act. Is there not charms°   *magic*
    By which the property° of youth and maidhood°   *attribute / virginity*
    May be abused? Have you not read, Roderigo,
    Of some such thing?
175 RODERIGO   Yes, sir, I have indeed.
BRABANZIO *[to servants]*   Call up my brother. *[To* RODERIGO*]* O,
        would you had had her.
    [To servants] Some one way, some another.   *[Exit one or more]*
    [To RODERIGO*]*   Do you know
    Where we may apprehend her and the Moor?
RODERIGO   I think I can discover him, if you please
180   To get good guard and go along with me.
BRABANZIO   Pray you lead on. At every house I'll call;
    I may command° at most. *[Calling]* Get weapons, ho,   *demand help*
    And raise some special officers of night.
    On, good Roderigo. I will deserve° your pains.   *Exeunt*   *reward*

1.2

    Enter OTHELLO, IAGO, *and attendants with torches*

IAGO   Though in the trade of war I have slain men,
    Yet do I hold it very stuff ° o'th' conscience   *essence*
    To do no contrived° murder. I lack iniquity,   *premeditated*
    Sometime, to do me service. Nine or ten times
5   I had thought to've yerked him° here, under the ribs.   *stabbed (Roderigo)*
OTHELLO   'Tis better as it is.
IAGO   Nay, but he prated,
    And spoke such scurvy and provoking terms
    Against your honour
    That, with the little godliness I have,

---

6. Perhaps indicating an inn named for the astrological sign Sagitarius, where Othello and Desdemona are staying. It may also suggest Othello himself, since Sagitarius is depicted as a centaur (a mythological being part man, part horse), and Iago has already likened Othello to a "Barbary horse."

1.2 Location: Another street in Venice, before Othello's lodgings.

10   I did full hard forbear him.[1] But I pray you, sir,
    Are you fast° married? Be assured of this: *legitimately*
    That the magnifico° is much beloved,   *(Brabanzio)*
    And hath in his effect a voice potential°   *powerful*
    As double as the Duke's. He will divorce you,
15   Or put upon you what restraint or grievance
    The law, with all his might to enforce it on,
    Will give him cable.°   *scope*
    OTHELLO   Let him do his spite.
    My services which I have done the signory°   *Venetian government*
    Shall out-tongue his complaints. 'Tis yet to know°— *not publicly known*
20   Which, when I know that boasting is an honour,
    I shall promulgate—I fetch my life and being
    From men of royal siege,° and my demerits°   *rank / deserts*
    May speak unbonneted[2] to as proud a fortune
    As this that I have reached. For know, Iago,
25   But that I love the gentle Desdemona
    I would not my unhousèd° free condition   *unconfined*
    Put into circumscription and confine
    For the seas' worth.
            Enter CASSIO *and officers, with torches*
                But look, what lights come yond?
    IAGO   Those are the raisèd father and his friends.
    You were best go in.
30   OTHELLO   Not I. I must be found.
    My parts,° my title, and my perfect soul[3]   *qualities*
    Shall manifest me rightly. Is it they?
    IAGO   By Janus,° I think no.   *two-faced Roman god*
    OTHELLO   The servants of the Duke, and my lieutenant!
35   The goodness of the night upon you, friends.
    What is the news?
    CASSIO   The Duke does greet you, general,
    And he requires your haste-post-haste appearance
    Even on the instant.
    OTHELLO   What is the matter, think you?
    CASSIO   Something from Cyprus, as I may divine;
40   It is a business of some heat.° The galleys   *urgency*
    Have sent a dozen sequent° messengers   *successive*
    This very night at one another's heels,
    And many of the consuls, raised and met,
    Are at the Duke's already. You have been hotly called for,
45   When, being not at your lodging to be found,
    The senate sent about three several quests
    To search you out.
    OTHELLO   'Tis well I am found by you.
    I will but spend a word here in the house
    And go with you.   *[Exit]*
    CASSIO   Ensign, what makes he here?
50   IAGO   Faith, he tonight hath boarded a land-carrack.° *large merchant ship*
    If it prove lawful prize, he's made for ever.
    CASSIO   I do not understand.

---

1. I barely restrained myself from attacking him.   3. My clear conscience.
2. Without deference; modestly.

IAGO   He's married.

CASSIO   To who?

Enter BRABANZIO, RODERIGO, *and* OFFICERS, *with lights*
and weapons

IAGO   Marry,° to—   *By Mary (mild oath)*
   [*Enter* OTHELLO]
   [*To* OTHELLO] Come, captain, will you go?

OTHELLO   Have with you.°   *Let's go*

55   CASSIO   Here comes another troop to seek for you.

IAGO   It is Brabanzio. General, be advised.
   He comes to bad intent.

OTHELLO   Holla, stand, there!

RODERIGO [*to* BRABANZIO]   Signor, it is the Moor.

BRABANZIO   Down with him, thief!

IAGO [*drawing his sword*]   You, Roderigo? Come, sir, I am for you.

60   OTHELLO   Keep up° your bright swords, for the dew will rust 'em.   *Put away*
   [*To* BRABANZIO] Good signor, you shall more command with years
   Than with your weapons.

BRABANZIO   O thou foul thief, where hast thou stowed my daughter?
   Damned as thou art, thou hast enchanted her,

65   For I'll refer me to all things of sense,[4]
   If she in chains of magic were not bound,
   Whether a maid so tender, fair, and happy,
   So opposite to marriage that she shunned
   The wealthy curlèd darlings of our nation,

70   Would ever have, t'incur a general mock,
   Run from her guardage to the sooty bosom
   Of such a thing as thou—to fear, not to delight.
   Judge me the world if 'tis not gross in sense[5]
   That thou hast practised on her with foul charms,

75   Abused her delicate youth with drugs or minerals
   That weakens motion. I'll have't disputed on.°   *argued by experts*
   'Tis probable, and palpable to thinking.
   I therefore apprehend and do attach° thee   *arrest*
   For an abuser of the world, a practiser

80   Of arts inhibited and out of warrant.°   *prohibited and illegal*
   [*To* OFFICERS] Lay hold upon him. If he do resist,
   Subdue him at his peril.

OTHELLO   Hold your hands,
   Both you of my inclining° and the rest.   *following*
   Were it my cue to fight, I should have known it

85   Without a prompter. Whither will you that I go
   To answer this your charge?

BRABANZIO   To prison, till fit time
   Of law and course of direct session
   Call thee to answer.

OTHELLO   What if I do obey?
   How may the Duke be therewith satisfied,

90   Whose messengers are here about my side
   Upon some present business of the state
   To bring me to him?

OFFICER [*to* BRABANZIO]   'Tis true, most worthy signor.

---

4. For I'll ask, relying on common sense.
5. If it is not patently obvious. Lines 73–78 do not appear in Q.

The Duke's in council, and your noble self,
I am sure, is sent for.

BRABANZIO   How, the Duke in council?
95   In this time of the night? Bring him away.°   *along*
     Mine's not an idle cause. The Duke himself,
     Or any of my brothers of the state,
     Cannot but feel this wrong as 'twere their own;
     For if such actions may have passage free,
100 Bondslaves and pagans shall our statesmen be.   *Exeunt*

1.3

Enter [the] DUKE *and* SENATORS *set at a table, with*
lights and OFFICERS

DUKE   There is no composition in these news
       That gives them credit.[1]

FIRST SENATOR   Indeed, they are disproportioned.°   *inconsistent*
       My letters say a hundred and seven galleys.

DUKE   And mine a hundred-forty.

SECOND SENATOR   And mine two hundred.
5   But though they jump not on a just account°—   *don't exactly agree*
       As, in these cases, where the aim reports
       'Tis oft with difference[2]—yet do they all confirm
       A Turkish fleet, and bearing up to Cyprus.

DUKE   Nay, it is possible enough to judgement.
10   I do not so secure me in the error,
       But the main article I do approve
       In fearful sense.[3]

SAILOR *(within)*   What ho, what ho, what ho!

                    Enter [a] SAILOR

OFFICER   A messenger from the galleys.

DUKE   Now, what's the business?

SAILOR   The Turkish preparation° makes for Rhodes.   *battle-ready fleet*
15   So was I bid report here to the state
       By Signor Angelo.[4]

DUKE *[to* SENATORS]   How say you by this change?

FIRST SENATOR   This cannot be,
       By no assay° of reason—'tis a pageant   *test*
20   To keep us in false gaze. When we consider
       The importancy of Cyprus to the Turk,
       And let ourselves again but understand
       That, as it more concerns the Turk than Rhodes,
       So may he with more facile question bear it,[5]
25   For that it stands not in such warlike brace,
       But altogether lacks th'abilities
       That Rhodes is dressed in—if we make thought of this,
       We must not think the Turk is so unskilful
       To leave that latest° which concerns him first,   *last*
30   Neglecting an attempt of ease and gain
       To wake and wage° a danger profitless.   *risk*

1.3 Location: A Venetian council room.
1. *There . . . credit:* The reports lack the consistency
that would make them believable.
2. *where . . . difference:* where the reports are esti-
mates, there are often discrepancies among them.
3. *I do not . . . sense:* I am not so reassured by the dis-
crepancies as to dismiss the main concern—the

approach of the Turkish fleet.
4. Not mentioned elsewhere in the play, Angelus Sori-
anus was a Venetian sea captain who received the Ve-
netian ambassador bearing from Constantinople the
Turkish ultimatum to surrender Cyprus shortly before
its capture by the Turks in 1571.
5. So also can the Turkish fleet more easily win it.

DUKE   Nay, in all confidence, he's not for Rhodes.
OFFICER   Here is more news.
      Enter a MESSENGER
MESSENGER   The Ottomites,° reverend and gracious,   *Ottoman Turks*
35   Steering with due course toward the Isle of Rhodes,
    Have there injointed them with an after° fleet.   *joined with another*
FIRST SENATOR   Ay, so I thought. How many, as you guess?
MESSENGER   Of thirty sail, and now they do restem°   *retrace*
    Their backward course, bearing with frank appearance
40   Their purposes toward Cyprus. Signor Montano,
    Your trusty and most valiant servitor,
    With his free duty recommends you thus,[6]
    And prays you to believe him.
DUKE   'Tis certain then for Cyprus.
    Marcus Luccicos,[7] is not he in town?
45 FIRST SENATOR   He's now in Florence.
DUKE   Write from us to him post-post-haste. Dispatch.
      Enter BRABANZIO, OTHELLO, RODERIGO, IAGO, CASSIO,
      and officers
FIRST SENATOR   Here comes Brabanzio and the valiant Moor.
DUKE   Valiant Othello, we must straight° employ you   *immediately*
    Against the general enemy° Ottoman.   *(of all Christendom)*
50   [*To* BRABANZIO] I did not see you. Welcome, gentle° signor.   *noble*
    We lacked your counsel and your help tonight.
BRABANZIO   So did I yours. Good your grace, pardon me.
    Neither my place,° nor aught I heard of business,   *official duty*
    Hath raised me from my bed, nor doth the general care
55   Take hold on me; for my particular grief
    Is of so floodgate and o'erbearing nature
    That it engluts and swallows other sorrows,
    And it is still itself.[8]
DUKE   Why, what's the matter?
BRABANZIO   My daughter, O, my daughter!
SENATORS   Dead?
BRABANZIO   Ay, to me.
60   She is abused,° stol'n from me, and corrupted   *deluded*
    By spells and medicines bought of mountebanks.°   *quacks*
    For nature so preposterously to err,
    Being not deficient, blind, or lame of sense,
    Sans° witchcraft could not.   *Without*
65 DUKE   Whoe'er he be that in this foul proceeding
    Hath thus beguiled your daughter of herself
    And you of her, the bloody book of law
    You shall yourself read in the bitter letter
    After your own sense, yea, though our proper son
    Stood in your action.[9]
70 BRABANZIO   Humbly I thank your grace.
    Here is the man, this Moor, whom now it seems
    Your special mandate for the state affairs
    Hath hither brought.
SENATORS   We are very sorry for't.

---

6. With his freely given loyalty reports to you thus.
7. Not mentioned elsewhere in the play.
8. *That . . . itself*: That my "grief" can incorporate other "sorrows" without being affected.

9. *You shall . . . action:* You yourself shall interpret the law as you see fit even if my own son is the one you accuse.

DUKE [*to* OTHELLO]   What in your own part can you say to this?

75   BRABANZIO   Nothing but this is so.

OTHELLO   Most potent, grave, and reverend signors,
My very noble and approved good masters,
That I have ta'en away this old man's daughter,
It is most true, true I have married her.

80   The very head and front° of my offending   *height and breadth*
Hath this extent, no more. Rude° am I in my speech,   *Unpolished*
And little blessed with the soft phrase of peace,
For since these arms of mine had seven years' pith°   *strength*
Till now some nine moons wasted,° they have used   *Nine months ago*

85   Their dearest° action in the tented field,   *most valued*
And little of this great world can I speak
More than pertains to feats of broils° and battle.   *combats*
And therefore little shall I grace my cause
In speaking for myself. Yet, by your gracious patience,

90   I will a round° unvarnished tale deliver   *plain*
Of my whole course of love, what drugs, what charms,
What conjuration and what mighty magic—
For such proceeding I am charged withal°—   *with*
I won his daughter.

BRABANZIO   A maiden never bold,

95   Of spirit so still and quiet that her motion
Blushed at herself[1]—and she in spite of nature,
Of years, of country, credit,° everything,   *reputation*
To fall in love with what she feared to look on!
It is a judgement maimed and most imperfect

100 That will confess perfection so could err
Against all rules of nature, and must° be driven   *(we therefore) must*
To find out practices of cunning hell
Why this should be. I therefore vouch again
That with some mixtures powerful o'er the blood,°   *passions*

105 Or with some dram conjured° to this effect,   *enchanted dose*
He wrought upon her.

DUKE   To vouch this is no proof
Without more wider and more overt test
Than these thin habits and poor likelihoods
Of modern seeming do prefer against him.[2]

110 A SENATOR   But Othello, speak.
Did you by indirect and forcèd courses°   *means*
Subdue and poison this young maid's affections,
Or came it by request and such fair question°   *conversation*
As soul to soul affordeth?

OTHELLO   I do beseech you,

115 Send for the lady to the Sagittary,
And let her speak of me before her father.
If you do find me foul in her report,
The trust, the office I do hold of you
Not only take away, but let your sentence
Even fall upon my life.

120 DUKE [*to* OFFICERS]   Fetch Desdemona hither.

---

1. *her . . . herself*: she blushed at herself at the slightest provocation.
2. *Without . . . him*: Without fuller and more direct testimony than mere appearances and conjecture based on currently popular beliefs against him.

OTHELLO   Ensign, conduct them. You best know the place.

Exit [IAGO *with*] *two or three* [*officers*]

    And till she come, as truly as to heaven

    I do confess the vices of my blood,°   *sins of passion*

    So justly to your grave ears I'll present

125   How I did thrive in this fair lady's love,

    And she in mine.

DUKE   Say it, Othello.

OTHELLO   Her father loved me, oft invited me,

    Still° questioned me the story of my life   *Constantly*

    From year to year, the battles, sieges, fortunes

130   That I have passed.

    I ran it through even from my boyish days

    To th' very moment that he bade me tell it,

    Wherein I spoke of most disastrous chances,°   *events*

    Of moving accidents° by flood and field,   *events*

135   Of hair-breadth scapes i'th' imminent deadly breach,³

    Of being taken by the insolent foe

    And sold to slavery, of my redemption thence,

    And portance° in my traveller's history,   *conduct*

    Wherein of antres° vast and deserts idle,   *caves*

140   Rough quarries, rocks, and hills whose heads touch heaven,

    It was my hint° to speak. Such was my process,°   *occasion / story*

    And of the cannibals that each other eat,

    The Anthropophagi,⁴ and men whose heads

    Do grow beneath their shoulders. These things to hear

145   Would Desdemona seriously incline,

    But still the house affairs would draw her thence,

    Which ever as° she could with haste dispatch   *Whenever*

    She'd come again, and with a greedy ear

    Devour up my discourse; which I observing,

150   Took once a pliant° hour, and found good means   *convenient*

    To draw from her a prayer of earnest heart

    That I would all my pilgrimage dilate,°   *relate*

    Whereof by parcels she had something heard,

    But not intentively.° I did consent,   *continuously*

155   And often did beguile her of her tears

    When I did speak of some distressful stroke

    That my youth suffered. My story being done,

    She gave me for my pains a world of kisses.⁵

    She swore in faith 'twas strange, 'twas passing° strange, *exceptionally*

160   'Twas pitiful, 'twas wondrous pitiful.

    She wished she had not heard it, yet she wished

    That heaven had made her such a man.⁶ She thankèd me,

    And bade me, if I had a friend that loved her,

    I should but teach him how to tell my story,

165   And that would woo her. Upon this hint I spake.

    She loved me for the dangers I had passed,

    And I loved her that she did pity them.

    This only is the witchcraft I have used.

---

3. In the deadly gaps in a fortification.

4. Man-eaters. The term is from the ancient Roman writer Pliny the Elder. Shakespeare was also indebted to the travel literature of the Middle Ages (*Mandeville's Travels*) and the Renaissance (Hakluyt's *Principal*

Navigations, among others).

5. F reads "kisses," Q "sighs." It is hard to explain "kisses" as a textual error.

6. Made such a man for her; made her into such a man.

Enter DESDEMONA, IAGO, *and attendants*
Here comes the lady. Let her witness it.

170 DUKE   I think this tale would win my daughter, too.—
Good Brabanzio,
Take up this mangled matter at the best.°   *Make the best of this*
Men do their broken weapons rather use
Than their bare hands.

BRABANZIO   I pray you hear her speak.

175 If she confess that she was half the wooer,
Destruction on my head if my bad blame
Light on the man! Come hither, gentle mistress.
Do you perceive in all this noble company
Where most you owe obedience?

DESDEMONA   My noble father,

180 I do perceive here a divided duty.
To you I am bound for life and education.
My life and education both do learn° me   *teach*
How to respect you. You are the lord of duty,
I am hitherto your daughter. But here's my husband,

185 And so much duty as my mother showed
To you, preferring you before her father,
So much I challenge° that I may profess   *assert*
Due to the Moor my lord.

BRABANZIO   God b'wi'you, I ha' done.
Please it your grace, on to the state affairs.

190 I had rather to adopt a child than get° it.   *beget*
Come hither, Moor.
I here do give thee that° with all my heart   *that which*
Which, but° thou hast already, with all my heart   *except that*
I would keep from thee. [*To* DESDEMONA] For your sake, jewel,

195 I am glad at soul I have no other child,
For thy escape would teach me tyranny,
To hang clogs[7] on 'em. I have done, my lord.

DUKE   Let me speak like yourself, and lay a sentence°   *draw a moral*
Which, as a grece° or step, may help these lovers   *step*

200 Into your favour.
When remedies are past, the griefs are ended
By seeing the worst which late on hopes depended.[8]
To mourn a mischief that is past and gone
Is the next way to draw new mischief on.

205 What cannot be preserved when fortune takes,
Patience her injury a mockery makes.[9]
The robbed that smiles steals something from the thief;
He robs himself that spends a bootless° grief.   *pointless*

BRABANZIO   So let the Turk of Cyprus us beguile,

210 We lose it not so long as we can smile.
He bears the sentence° well that nothing bears   *saying; judgment*
But the free comfort which from thence he hears,
But he bears both the sentence and the sorrow
That, to pay grief, must of poor patience borrow.

215 These sentences, to sugar or to gall,°   *both sweet and bitter*

---

7. Blocks of wood tied to criminals' legs to keep them
from escaping.
8. By seeing those things come to pass that caused
grief in anticipation. The Duke paints the moral in

rhyming couplets, to which Brabanzio replies in kind.
9. Patience laughs at what cannot be helped (and thus
reduces the "injury").

Being strong on both sides, are equivocal.
But words are words. I never yet did hear
That the bruised heart was piercèd¹ through the ear. I humbly
beseech you proceed to th'affairs of state.

220 DUKE The Turk with a most mighty preparation makes for
Cyprus. Othello, the fortitude of the place is best known to
you, and though we have there a substitute of most allowed
sufficiency,° yet opinion, a more sovereign mistress of effects,   *known ability*
throws a more safer voice on you.² You must therefore be con-

225 tent to slubber° the gloss of your new fortunes with this more   *soil*
stubborn° and boisterous expedition.   *rougher*

OTHELLO The tyrant custom, most grave senators,
Hath made the flinty and steel couch of war
My thrice-driven° bed of down. I do agnize°   *sifted / acknowledge*

230 A natural and prompt alacrity
I find in hardness,° and do undertake   *hardship*
This present wars against the Ottomites.
Most humbly therefore bending to your state,°   *authority*
I crave fit disposition for my wife,

235 Due reference of place and exhibition,³
With such accommodation and besort°   *suitable attendance*
As levels with her breeding.

DUKE Why, at her father's!

BRABANZIO I will not have it so.

240 OTHELLO Nor I.

DESDEMONA Nor would I there reside,
To put my father in impatient thoughts
By being in his eye. Most gracious Duke,
To my unfolding° lend your prosperous° ear,   *proposal / receptive*

245 And let me find a charter° in your voice   *an authorization*
T'assist my simpleness.

DUKE   What would you, Desdemona?

DESDEMONA That I did love the Moor to live with him,
My downright violence and storm of fortunes⁴
May trumpet to the world. My heart's subdued

250 Even to the very quality of my lord.⁵
I saw Othello's visage in his mind,
And to his honours and his valiant parts°   *qualities*
Did I my soul and fortunes consecrate;
So that, dear lords, if I be left behind,

255 A moth of peace, and he go to the war,
The rites° for why I love him are bereft me,   *(of love); (of war?)*
And I a heavy interim shall support
By his dear absence. Let me go with him.

OTHELLO [*to the* DUKE] Let her have your voice.

260 Vouch with me heaven, I therefor beg it not
To please the palate of my appetite,
Nor to comply with heat°—the young affects⁶   *sexual passion*
In me defunct—and proper° satisfaction,   *personal; fitting*

---

1. Surgically lanced (and presumably cured).
2. *opinion . . . you:* public opinion, which determines
what gets done, finds greater security with you.
3. Proper accommodation and maintenance.
4. My outright defiance of custom.
5. *My heart's . . . lord:* I love him for what he is (military,

adventurous). Q reads "utmost pleasure" for "very
quality"—an openly sexual formulation that makes
Desdemona's response one of subordination rather
than of identification, sexual and otherwise.
6. The youthful desires.

But to be free° and bounteous to her mind;   *liberal*
265   And heaven defend your good souls that you think
      I will your serious and great business scant
      When she is with me. No, when light-winged toys°   *diversions*
      Of feathered Cupid seel° with wanton dullness   *blind*
      My speculative and officed instruments,[7]
270   That my disports° corrupt and taint my business,   *sexual pleasures*
      Let housewives make a skillet of my helm,
      And all indign° and base adversities   *undignified*
      Make head against my estimation.[8]
DUKE   Be it as you shall privately determine,
275   Either for her stay or going. Th'affair cries haste,
      And speed must answer it.
A SENATOR [*to* OTHELLO]   You must away tonight.
DESDEMONA   Tonight, my lord?
DUKE   This night.
OTHELLO   With all my heart.
DUKE   At nine i'th' morning here we'll meet again.
      Othello, leave some officer behind,
280   And he shall our commission bring to you,
      And such things else of quality and respect°   *weight and importance*
      As doth import° you.   *concern*
OTHELLO   So please your grace, my ensign.
      A man he is of honesty[9] and trust.
      To his conveyance I assign my wife,
285   With what else needful your good grace shall think
      To be sent after me.
DUKE   Let it be so.
      Good night to everyone. [*To* BRABANZIO] And, noble signor,
      If virtue no delighted° beauty lack,   *delightful*
      Your son-in-law is far more fair than black.
290   A SENATOR   Adieu, brave Moor. Use Desdemona well.
BRABANZIO   Look to her,° Moor, if thou hast eyes to see.   *Watch her carefully*
      She has deceived her father, and may thee.
                  Exeunt [DUKE, BRABANZIO, CASSIO, SENATORS,
                                                and officers]
OTHELLO   My life upon her faith. Honest Iago,
      My Desdemona must I leave to thee.
295   I prithee let thy wife attend on her,
      And bring them after in the best advantage.[1]
      Come, Desdemona. I have but an hour
      Of love, of worldly matter and direction
      To spend with thee. We must obey the time.
                  Exeunt [OTHELLO *the*] *Moor and* DESDEMONA
300   RODERIGO   Iago.
IAGO   What sayst thou, noble heart?
RODERIGO   What will I do, think'st thou?
IAGO   Why, go to bed and sleep.
RODERIGO   I will incontinently° drown myself.   *immediately*
305   IAGO   If thou dost, I shall never love thee after. Why, thou silly
      gentleman!

---

7. My duty-bound faculties of sense.   of them deeply ironic, some unwittingly so.
8. Raise an army against my good reputation.   1. And bring them along at the most favorable moment.
9. The first of many references to Iago's "honesty," all

RODERIGO   It is silliness to live when to live is torment; and then
have we a prescription° to die when death is our physician.   *right; doctor's order*

IAGO   O, villainous!° I ha' looked upon the world for four times   *absurd; immoral?*
310   seven years, and since I could distinguish betwixt a benefit and
an injury I never found man that knew how to love himself.
Ere I would say I would drown myself for the love of a guinea-
hen,° I would change my humanity with a baboon.   *woman*

RODERIGO   What should I do? I confess it is my shame to be so
315   fond, but it is not in my virtue° to amend it.   *native ability*

IAGO   Virtue? A fig!° 'Tis in ourselves that we are thus or thus.   *(an obscenity)*
Our bodies are our gardens, to the which our wills are garden-
ers; so that if we will plant nettles or sow lettuce, set hyssop° and   *mint herb*
weed up thyme, supply it with one gender of herbs or distract it
320   with many, either to have it sterile with idleness° or manured   *noncultivation*
with industry, why, the power and corrigible authority° of this   *ability to decide*
lies in our wills. If the beam° of our lives had not one scale of   *(as on a scale)*
reason to peise° another of sensuality, the blood and baseness   *counterweigh*
of our natures would conduct us to most preposterous conclu-
325   sions. But we have reason to cool our raging motions,° our car-   *appetites*
nal stings, our unbitted° lusts; whereof I take this that you call   *unrestrained*
love to be a sect or scion.°   *offshoot*

RODERIGO   It cannot be.

IAGO   It is merely a lust of the blood and a permission of the will.
330   Come, be a man. Drown thyself? Drown cats and blind pup-
pies. I have professed me thy friend, and I confess me knit to
thy deserving with cables of perdurable° toughness. I could   *durable*
never better stead° thee than now. Put money in thy purse.   *help*
Follow thou the wars, defeat thy favour with an usurped beard.[2]
335   I say, put money in thy purse. It cannot be long that Desde-
mona should continue her love to the Moor—put money in
thy purse—nor he his to her. It was a violent commencement°   *an abruptly begun affair*
in her, and thou shalt see an answerable sequestration[3]—put
but money in thy purse. These Moors are changeable in their
340   wills—fill thy purse with money. The food that to him now
is as luscious as locusts[4] shall be to him shortly as bitter as
coloquintida.[5] She must change for youth. When she is sated
with his body, she will find the error of her choice. Therefore
put money in thy purse. If thou wilt needs° damn thyself, do it   *If you must*
345   a more delicate way than drowning. Make all the money thou
canst. If sanctimony° and a frail vow betwixt an erring° barbar-   *holy rite / a wandering*
ian and a super-subtle° Venetian be not too hard for my wits   *highly sensitive*
and all the tribe of hell, thou shalt enjoy her; therefore make
money. A pox o' drowning thyself—it is clean out of the way.°   *of no use*
350   Seek thou rather to be hanged in compassing° thy joy than to   *encompassing*
be drowned and go without her.

RODERIGO   Wilt thou be fast° to my hopes if I depend on the   *duty bound*
issue?°   *outcome*

IAGO   Thou art sure of me. Go, make money. I have told thee
355   often, and I re-tell thee again and again, I hate the Moor. My
cause is hearted,° thine hath no less reason. Let us be conjunc-   *heartfelt*
tive° in our revenge against him. If thou canst cuckold him,   *joined*

---

2. Disguise your appearance with a fake beard.   5. Colocynth, a purgative—one of Iago's many refer-
3. A correspondingly abrupt separation.   ences to the digestive tract.
4. A sweet, exotic fruit, perhaps carob or honeysuckle.

thou dost thyself a pleasure, me a sport. There are many events
in the womb of time, which will be delivered. Traverse,° go,   *Go (to arms)*
360   provide thy money. We will have more of this tomorrow.
Adieu.

RODERIGO   Where shall we meet i'th' morning?

IAGO   At my lodging.

RODERIGO   I'll be with thee betimes.°   *early*

IAGO   Go to, farewell—
Do you hear, Roderigo?

RODERIGO   I'll sell all my land.   *Exit*

365   IAGO   Thus do I ever make my fool my purse—
For I mine own gained knowledge should profane
If I would time expend with such a snipe°   *fool*
But for my sport and profit. I hate the Moor,
And it is thought abroad° that 'twixt my sheets   *rumored*
370   He has done my office. I know not if't be true,
But I, for mere suspicion in that kind,
Will do° as if for surety. He holds° me well: *act / esteems*
The better shall my purpose work on him.
Cassio's a proper° man. Let me see now,   *handsome*
375   To get his place, and to plume up° my will   *gratify*
In double knavery—how, how? Let's see.
After some time to abuse Othello's ears
That he is too familiar with his wife;⁶
He hath a person and a smooth dispose°   *manner*
380   To be suspected, framed to make women false.
The Moor is of a free° and open nature,   *liberal*
That thinks men honest that but seem to be so,
And will as tenderly° be led by th' nose   *easily*
As asses are.
385   I ha't. It is ingendered. Hell and night
Must bring this monstrous birth to the world's light.   *Exit*

2.1

Enter [below] MONTANO, *Governor of Cyprus; two other*
GENTLEMEN *[above]*

MONTANO   What from the cape can you discern at sea?

FIRST GENTLEMEN   Nothing at all. It is a high-wrought flood.°   *very rough sea*
I cannot 'twixt the heaven and the main°   *sea*
Descry° a sail.   *Discern*

5   MONTANO   Methinks the wind hath spoke aloud at land.
A fuller blast ne'er shook our battlements.
If it ha' ruffianed° so upon the sea,   *raged*
What ribs of oak, when mountains melt on them,
Can hold the mortise?¹ What shall we hear of this?

10   SECOND GENTLEMEN   A segregation° of the Turkish fleet;   *separation*
For do but stand upon the foaming shore,
The chidden billow² seems to pelt the clouds,
The wind-shaked surge with high and monstrous mane

---

6. "He" is Cassio (as in line 379), but "his" refers to
Othello—a potential confusion of pronouns.
2.1 Location: A seaport in Cyprus; outdoors near the
harbor.
1. *What . . . mortise:* What ship (with "ribs of oak")

can hold its joints ("mortise") together when "moun-
tains" of water pour on it?
2. The surging ocean, rebuked ("chidden") by the wind
(or repulsed by the land).

Seems to cast water on the burning Bear
15 And quench the guards of th'ever-fixèd Pole.³
I never did like molestation view°   *see such a tumult*
On the enchafèd flood.
MONTANO   If that the Turkish fleet
Be not ensheltered and embayed, they are drowned.
It is impossible to bear it out.

Enter a THIRD GENTLEMEN

20 THIRD GENTLEMEN   News, lads! Our wars are done.
The desperate tempest hath so banged the Turks
That their designment° halts. A noble ship of Venice   *plan*
Hath seen a grievous wrack and sufferance
On most part of their fleet.
25 MONTANO   How, is this true?
THIRD GENTLEMEN   The ship is here put in,
A Veronessa.⁴ Michael Cassio,
Lieutenant to the warlike Moor Othello,
Is come on shore; the Moor himself at sea,
30 And is in full commission here for Cyprus.
MONTANO   I am glad on't; 'tis a worthy governor.
THIRD GENTLEMEN   But this same Cassio, though he speak of comfort
Touching the Turkish loss, yet he looks sadly,°   *seriously*
And prays the Moor be safe, for they were parted
With foul and violent tempest.
35 MONTANO   Pray heavens he be,
For I have served him, and the man commands
Like a full soldier. Let's to the sea-side, ho!—
As well to see the vessel that's come in
As to throw out our eyes for brave Othello,
40 Even till we make the main and th'aerial blue
An indistinct regard.⁵
THIRD GENTLEMEN   Come, let's do so,
For every minute is expectancy
Of more arrivance.

Enter CASSIO

CASSIO   Thanks, you the valiant of this warlike isle
45 That so approve the Moor! O, let the heavens
Give him defence against the elements,
For I have lost him on a dangerous sea.
MONTANO   Is he well shipped?
CASSIO   His barque is stoutly timbered, and his pilot
50 Of very expert and approved allowance.°   *known ability*
Therefore my hopes, not surfeited to death,°   *not excessive*
Stand in bold cure.°   *likely to be rewarded*
VOICES (*within*)   A sail, a sail, a sail!
CASSIO   What noise?
A GENTLEMAN   The town is empty. On the brow° o'th' sea   *cliff at the edge*
55 Stand ranks of people, and they cry 'A sail!'
CASSIO   My hopes do shape him° for the governor.   *make it out to be*
A *shot*

---

3. *burning Bear:* the constellation Ursa Minor. *guards:*
probably two stars in the constellation that point in a
line to the polestar, also in Ursa Minor.
4. Meaning unclear: originally from Verona, though now

used by the Venetians; a cutter; possibly meant to modify
not "ship" but Cassio, although he is Florentine (1.1.19).
5. *Even . . . regard:* Until we can't distinguish sea from
sky.

A GENTLEMAN   They do discharge their shot of courtesy—
Our friends, at least.

CASSIO   I pray you, sir, go forth,
And give us truth who 'tis that is arrived.

60 A GENTLEMAN   I shall.   *Exit*

MONTANO   But, good lieutenant, is your general wived?

CASSIO   Most fortunately. He hath achieved a maid
That paragons° description and wild fame,   *stands above*
One that excels the quirks of blazoning° pens,   *praise-giving*
65 And in th'essential vesture of creation
Does tire the engineer.[6]

Enter GENTLEMAN

                          How now, who has put in?

GENTLEMAN   'Tis one Iago, ensign to the general.

CASSIO   He's had most favourable and happy speed.
Tempests themselves, high seas, and howling winds,
70 The guttered° rocks and congregated° sands,   *jagged / accumulated*
Traitors ensteeped° to enclog the guiltless keel,   *underwater*
As having sense of beauty do omit°   *forgo*
Their mortal° natures, letting go safely by   *deadly*
The divine Desdemona.

MONTANO   What is she?

75 CASSIO   She that I spake of, our great captain's captain,
Left in the conduct of the bold Iago,
Whose footing here anticipates our thoughts
A sennight's speed.[7] Great Jove, Othello guard,
And swell his sail with thine own powerful breath,
80 That he may bless this bay with his tall ship,
Make love's quick pants in Desdemona's arms,
Give renewed fire to our extincted spirits,
And bring all Cyprus comfort.

Enter DESDEMONA, IAGO, EMILIA, *and* RODERIGO

                          O, behold,
The riches of the ship is come on shore!
85 You men of Cyprus, let her have your knees.

[MONTANO *and the* GENTLEMEN *make curtsy to*
DESDEMONA]

Hail to thee, lady, and the grace of heaven
Before, behind thee, and on every hand
Enwheel thee round!

DESDEMONA   I thank you, valiant Cassio.
What tidings can you tell me of my lord?

90 CASSIO   He is not yet arrived, nor know I aught
But that he's well and will be shortly here.

DESDEMONA   O, but I fear—how lost you company?

CASSIO   The great contention of the sea and skies
Parted our fellowship.

95 VOICES (*within*)   A sail, a sail!

CASSIO   But hark, a sail.

[*A shot*]

A GENTLEMAN   They give their greeting to the citadel.
This likewise is a friend.

---

6. *in . . . engineer:* whose natural beauty exhausts the
poet's capacity to invent praise.

7. *Whose . . . speed:* Whose arrival predates our expec-
tations by a week.

CASSIO   See for the news. [*Exit* GENTLEMAN]
       Good ensign, you are welcome. [*Kissing* EMILIA] Welcome, mistress.
100   Let it not gall your patience, good Iago,
       That I extend my manners. 'Tis my breeding
       That gives me this bold show of courtesy.
       IAGO   Sir, would she give you so much of her lips
       As of her tongue she oft bestows on me,
105   You would have enough.
       DESDEMONA   Alas, she has no speech![8]
       IAGO   In faith, too much.
       I find it still when I ha' leave to sleep.
       Marry, before your ladyship, I grant,
110   She puts her tongue a little in her heart,[9]
       And chides with thinking.
       EMILIA   You ha' little cause to say so.
       IAGO   Come on, come on. You are pictures out of door,
       Bells in your parlours; wildcats in your kitchens,
       Saints in your injuries; devils being offended,
115   Players in your housewifery, and hussies in your beds.[1]
       DESDEMONA   O, fie upon thee, slanderer!
       IAGO   Nay, it is true, or else I am a Turk.
       You rise to play and go to bed to work.
       EMILIA   You shall not write my praise.
       IAGO   No, let me not.
120   DESDEMONA   What wouldst write of me, if thou shouldst praise me?
       IAGO   O, gentle lady, do not put me to't,
       For I am nothing if not critical.
       DESDEMONA   Come on, essay°—there's one gone to the harbour?   *try*
       IAGO   Ay, madam.
125   DESDEMONA   I am not merry, but I do beguile°   *disguise*
       The thing I am° by seeming otherwise.   *(worried for Othello)*
       Come, how wouldst thou praise me?
       IAGO   I am about it, but indeed my invention
       Comes from my pate as birdlime[2] does from frieze°—   *coarse wool cloth*
130   It plucks out brains and all. But my muse labours,°   *(in childbirth)*
       And thus she is delivered:
       If she be fair and wise, fairness and wit,
       The one's for use, the other useth it.[3]
       DESDEMONA   Well praised! How if she be black and witty?
135   IAGO   If she be black and thereto have a wit,
       She'll find a white that shall her blackness fit.[4]
       DESDEMONA   Worse and worse.
       EMILIA   How if fair and foolish?
       IAGO   She never yet was foolish that was fair,
       For even her folly° helped her to an heir.   *foolishness; lechery*
140   DESDEMONA   These are old fond° paradoxes, to make fools laugh   *foolish*
       i'th' alehouse.

---

8. Perhaps: Alas, the accused scolding chatterbox is not even rising to her own defense (both a defense of Emilia and a prod for her to speak).
9. She keeps her (critical) thoughts to herself.
1. *You are . . . beds:* Iago shifts from Emilia to women generally in this speech. *pictures:* models of silent propriety. *Bells:* Noisy. *kitchens:* perhaps domestic affairs generally, rather than a specific room. *Saints:* Martyrs.

Players in your housewifery: Deceptive in managing household expenses. *hussies:* wanton (perhaps businesslike, or sparing of sexual favors).
2. Sticky substance used to trap small birds.
3. *The one's . . . it:* Intelligence makes use of beauty.
4. *black:* dark-haired or dark-complexioned. *white:* fair-skinned person ("wight" means "person"). *fit:* (sexual).

What miserable praise hast thou for her
That's foul° and foolish?   ugly

IAGO   There's none so foul and foolish thereunto,°   to boot
145   But does foul° pranks which fair and wise ones do.   lascivious

DESDEMONA   O heavy ignorance! Thou praisest the worst best.
But what praise couldst thou bestow on a deserving woman
indeed—one that, in the authority of her merit, did justly put
on the vouch° of very malice itself?   compel the approval

150   IAGO   She that was ever fair and never proud,
Had tongue at will and yet was never loud,
Never lacked gold and yet went never gay,°   lavishly clothed
Fled from her wish, and yet said 'Now I may';⁵
She that, being angered, her revenge being nigh,
155   Bade her wrong stay° and her displeasure fly;   sense of injury end
She that in wisdom never was so frail
To change the cod's head for the salmon's tail;⁶
She that could think and ne'er disclose her mind,
See suitors following, and not look behind—
160   She was a wight, if ever such wights were—

DESDEMONA   To do what?

IAGO   To suckle fools, and chronicle small beer.⁷

DESDEMONA   O most lame and impotent conclusion! Do not
learn of him, Emilia, though he be thy husband. How say you,
165   Cassio, is he not a most profane and liberal° counsellor?   outspoken

CASSIO   He speaks home, madam. You may relish him more in°   as
the soldier than in the scholar.

[CASSIO *and* DESDEMONA *talk apart*]

IAGO [*aside*]   He takes her by the palm. Ay, well said°—whisper.   well done
With as little a web as this will I ensnare as great a fly as Cassio.
170   Ay, smile upon her, do. I will gyve° thee in thine own court-   shackle
ship.° You say true, 'tis so indeed. If such tricks as these strip   courtliness
you out of your lieutenantry, it had been better you had not
kissed your three fingers⁸ so oft, which now again you are most
apt to play the sir° in. Very good, well kissed, an excellent   gentleman
175   curtsy, 'tis so indeed; yet again your fingers to your lips? Would
they were clyster-pipes° for your sake.   enema tubes

Trumpets within

[*Aloud*] The Moor—I know his trumpet.

CASSIO   'Tis truly so.

DESDEMONA   Let's meet him and receive him.

CASSIO   Lo where he comes!

Enter OTHELLO *and attendants*

OTHELLO [*to* DESDEMONA]   O my fair warrior!

DESDEMONA   My dear Othello.

180   OTHELLO   It gives me wonder great as my content
To see you here before me. O my soul's joy,
If after every tempest come such calms,
May the winds blow till they have wakened death,
And let the labouring barque° climb hills of seas   small ship

---

5. Voluntarily withstood temptation even when given
the choice.
6. To make an unworthy exchange. Probably also sug-
gesting sexual infidelity: "cod" means "penis," and "tail"
equals "vulva."

7. To breast-feed babies and keep track of trivial
domestic goods. That is, such perfect virtue suits only a
dull, complacent, decidedly ungenteel housewife.
8. Kissing one's own hand was a common courtly ges-
ture from a gentleman to a lady.

185   Olympus-high,⁹ and duck again as low
      As hell's from heaven. If it were now to die¹
      'Twere now to be most happy, for I fear
      My soul hath her content so absolute
      That not another comfort like to this
      Succeeds° in unknown fate.°   *will follow / future*
190 DESDEMONA   The heavens forbid
      But that our loves and comforts should increase
      Even as our days do grow.
      OTHELLO   Amen to that, sweet powers!
      I cannot speak enough of this content.
      It stops me here, it is too much of joy.
195   And this, *(they kiss)* and this, the greatest discords be
      That e'er our hearts shall make.
      IAGO [*aside*]   O, you are well tuned now,
      But I'll set down the pegs that make this music,²
      As honest as I am.
      OTHELLO   Come, let us to the castle.
      News, friends: our wars are done, the Turks are drowned.
200   How does my old acquaintance of this isle?—
      Honey, you shall be well desired° in Cyprus,   *welcomed*
      I have found great love amongst them. O my sweet,
      I prattle out of fashion, and I dote
      In mine own comforts. I prithee, good Iago,
205   Go to the bay and disembark my coffers.
      Bring thou the master° to the citadel.   *captain*
      He is a good one, and his worthiness
      Does challenge° much respect. Come, Desdemona.—   *deserve*
      Once more, well met at Cyprus!
                          Exeunt OTHELLO *and* DESDEMONA
                        [*with all but* IAGO *and* RODERIGO]
210 IAGO [*to an attendant as he goes out*]   Do thou meet me pres-
      ently at the harbour. [*To* RODERIGO] Come hither. If thou beest
      valiant—as they say base° men being in love have then a nobil-   *lowly born*
      ity in their natures more than is native to them—list³ me. The   *listen to*
      lieutenant tonight watches on the court of guard.³ First, I
215   must tell thee this: Desdemona is directly in love with him.
      RODERIGO   With him? Why, 'tis not possible!
      IAGO   Lay thy finger thus,° and let thy soul be instructed. Mark   *Be silent*
      me with what violence she first loved the Moor, but for brag-
      ging and telling her fantastical lies. To love him still for prat-
220   ing?—let not thy discreet heart think it. Her eye must be fed,
      and what delight shall she have to look on the devil? When the
      blood is made dull with the act of sport, there should be again
      to inflame it, and to give satiety a fresh appetite, loveliness in
      favour,° sympathy in years, manners, and beauties, all which   *looks*
225   the Moor is defective in. Now, for want of these required con-
      veniences,° her delicate tenderness will find itself abused,°   *compatibilities / revolted*
      begin to heave the gorge,° disrelish and abhor the Moor. Very   *feel nausea*
      nature will instruct her in it and compel her to some second
      choice. Now, sir, this granted—as it is a most pregnant° and   *obvious; (sexual)*

---

9. Mt. Olympus, home of the Greek gods and hence
too high for mortals.
1. To perish; to have an orgasm.

2. I'll untune (by loosening) the "pegs" that hold the
strings of a musical instrument taut.
3. Cassio is in charge of the watch at the guardhouse.

230 unforced position—who stands so eminent in the degree of[4]
this fortune as Cassio does?—a knave very voluble,° no further   *facile*
conscionable° than in putting on the mere form of civil and   *no more ethical*
humane seeming for the better compass° of his salt° and most   *achievement / lewd*
hidden loose affection. Why, none; why, none—a slipper° and   *slippery*
235 subtle knave, a finder of occasion, that has an eye can stamp
and counterfeit advantages,[5] though true advantage never pre-
sent itself, a devilish knave! Besides, the knave is handsome,
young, and hath all those requisites in him that folly° and green   *wantonness*
minds look after. A pestilent° complete knave, and the woman   *damnably*
240 hath found him already.

RODERIGO   I cannot believe that in her. She's full of most blessed
condition.

IAGO   Blessed fig's end!° The wine she drinks is made of grapes.   *(obscene)*
If she had been blessed, she would never have loved the Moor.
245 Blessed pudding!° Didst thou not see her paddle with the palm   *sausage*
of his hand? Didst not mark that?

RODERIGO   Yes, that I did, but that was but courtesy.

IAGO   Lechery, by this hand; an index and obscure prologue to
the history of lust and foul thoughts.[6] They met so near with
250 their lips that their breaths embraced together. Villainous
thoughts, Roderigo! When these mutualities so marshal the
way, hard at hand comes the master and main exercise,[7] th'in-
corporate° conclusion. Pish! But, sir, be you ruled by me. I have   *in the flesh*
brought you from Venice. Watch you tonight. For the com-
255 mand, I'll lay't upon you.[8] Cassio knows you not; I'll not be far
from you. Do you find some occasion to anger Cassio, either
by speaking too loud, or tainting° his discipline, or from what   *insulting*
other course you please, which the time shall more favourably
minister.°   *provide*

260 RODERIGO   Well.

IAGO   Sir, he's rash and very sudden in choler, and haply° may   *perhaps*
strike at you. Provoke him that he may, for even out of that will
I cause these of Cyprus to mutiny, whose qualification shall
come into no true taste again[9] but by the displanting of Cassio.
265 So shall you have a shorter journey to your desires by the means
I shall then have to prefer° them, and the impediment most   *promote*
profitably removed, without the which there were no expecta-
tion of our prosperity.

RODERIGO   I will do this, if you can bring it to any opportunity.

270 IAGO   I warrant thee. Meet me by and by at the citadel. I must
fetch his necessaries° ashore. Farewell.   *Othello's possessions*

RODERIGO   Adieu.   *Exit*

IAGO   That Cassio loves her, I do well believe it.
That she loves him, 'tis apt and of great credit.°   *likely and believable*
275 The Moor—howbe't that I endure him not—
Is of a constant, loving, noble nature,
And I dare think he'll prove to Desdemona
A most dear° husband. Now I do love her too,   *affectionate; costly*
Not out of absolute lust—though peradventure

---

4. *in the degree of*: as next in line for.
5. Who can (like a counterfeiter) create his own oppor-
tunities.
6. *an . . . thoughts*: the analogy is to a dirty book. *index*:
table of contents. *obscure*: encoded. *history*: story.

7. When these intimacies have cleared the way, the
main event follows close behind. Here, the analogy is to
an official procession.
8. Stand watch tonight. I'll see that you receive orders.
9. *whose . . . again*: who will not be adequately appeased.

280	I stand accountant° for as great a sin—	accountable
	But partly led to diet° my revenge	feed
	For that I do suspect the lusty Moor	
	Hath leapt into my seat,° the thought whereof	slept with my wife
	Doth, like a poisonous mineral, gnaw my inwards;°	innards
285	And nothing can or shall content my soul	
	Till I am evened with him, wife for wife—	
	Or failing so, yet that I put the Moor	
	At least into a jealousy so strong	
	That judgement cannot cure, which thing to do,	
290	If this poor trash of Venice whom I trace	
	For his quick hunting stand the putting on,[1]	
	I'll have our Michael Cassio on the hip,°	at my mercy
	Abuse° him to the Moor in the rank garb°—	Slander / "hot" manner
	For I fear Cassio with my nightcap,° too—	(as sexual rival)
295	Make the Moor thank me, love me, and reward me	
	For making him egregiously an ass,	
	And practising upon° his peace and quiet	undermining
	Even to madness. 'Tis here,° but yet confused.	My plan is here
	Knavery's plain face is never seen till used. *Exit*	

2.2

Enter Othello's HERALD *reading a proclamation*

	HERALD It is Othello's pleasure—our noble and valiant gen-	
	eral—that, upon certain tidings now arrived importing the	
	mere perdition° of the Turkish fleet, every man put himself	entire loss
	into triumph: some to dance, some to make bonfires, each man	
5	to what sport and revels his addiction° leads him; for besides	inclination
	these beneficial news, it is the celebration of his nuptial. So	
	much was his pleasure should be proclaimed. All offices° are	storehouses
	open, and there is full liberty of feasting from this present hour	
	of five till the bell have told eleven. Heaven bless the isle of	
10	Cyprus and our noble general, Othello! *Exit*	

2.3

Enter OTHELLO, DESDEMONA, CASSIO, *and attendants*

	OTHELLO Good Michael, look you to the guard tonight.	
	Let's teach ourselves that honourable stop°	self-restraint
	Not to outsport° discretion.	pass the limits of
	CASSIO Iago hath direction what to do,	
5	But notwithstanding, with my personal eye	
	Will I look to't.	
	OTHELLO Iago is most honest.	
	Michael, good night. Tomorrow with your earliest	
	Let me have speech with you. [*To* DESDEMONA] Come, my dear love,	
	The purchase made, the fruits are to ensue.	
10	That profit's yet to come 'tween me and you.[1]	
	[*To* CASSIO] Good night.	
	Exeunt OTHELLO, DESDEMONA [*and attendants*]	
	Enter IAGO	

---

1. *If . . . on:* If Roderigo, whom I follow (?), train (?),
put weights on to slow him down (?), is successfully set
on the hunt when incited.

2.2 Location: A street in Cyprus.
2.3 Location: The citadel at Cyprus.
1. We haven't yet consummated our marriage.

CASSIO   Welcome, Iago. We must to the watch.

IAGO   Not this hour, lieutenant; 'tis not yet ten o'th' clock. Our
general cast° us thus early for the love of his Desdemona, who   *dismissed*
15   let us not therefore blame. He hath not yet made wanton the
night with her, and she is sport for Jove.

CASSIO   She's a most exquisite lady.

IAGO   And I'll warrant her full of game.

CASSIO   Indeed, she's a most fresh and delicate creature.

20   IAGO   What an eye she has! Methinks it sounds a parley° to prov-   *(military) call*
ocation.

CASSIO   An inviting eye, and yet, methinks, right modest.

IAGO   And when she speaks, is it not an alarum° to love?   *a call (to arms)*

CASSIO   She is indeed perfection.

25   IAGO   Well, happiness to their sheets. Come, lieutenant. I have
a stoup° of wine, and here without are a brace° of Cyprus gal-   *two quarts / pair*
lants that would fain have a measure° to the health of black   *would like to drink*
Othello.

CASSIO   Not tonight, good Iago. I have very poor and unhappy
30   brains for drinking. I could well wish courtesy would invent
some other custom of entertainment.

IAGO   O, they are our friends! But one cup. I'll drink for you.

CASSIO   I ha' drunk but one cup tonight, and that was craftily
qualified,° too, and behold what innovation° it makes here! I   *well diluted / disorder*
35   am infortunate in the infirmity, and dare not task my weakness
with any more.

IAGO   What, man, 'tis a night of revels, the gallants desire it!

CASSIO   Where are they?

IAGO   Here at the door. I pray you call them in.

40   CASSIO   I'll do't, but it dislikes me.°   *Exit*   *I don't like doing it*

IAGO   If I can fasten but one cup upon him,
With that which he hath drunk tonight already
He'll be as full of quarrel and offence
As my young mistress' dog. Now my sick fool Roderigo,
45   Whom love hath turned almost the wrong side out,
To Desdemona hath tonight caroused
Potations pottle-deep, and he's to watch.[2]
Three else of Cyprus—noble swelling° spirits   *proud*
That hold their honours in a wary distance,[3]
50   The very elements° of this warlike isle—   *typical residents*
Have I tonight flustered with flowing cups,
And they watch too. Now 'mongst this flock of drunkards
Am I to put our Cassio in some action
That may offend the isle.

      Enter MONTANO, CASSIO, GENTLEMEN, *and* [*servants
with wine*]

                    But here they come.
55   If consequence do but approve my dream,[4]
My boat sails freely both with wind and stream.°   *current*

CASSIO   Fore God, they have given me a rouse° already.   *full draft*

MONTANO   Good faith, a little one; not past a pint,
As I am a soldier.

IAGO   Some wine, ho!

---

2. *caroused . . . watch:* consumed drink to the bottom
of the tankard, and he's assigned guard duty.

3. Who are touchy about their honor.
4. If events turn out as I hope.

60   [*Sings*]   And let me the cannikin° clink, clink,   *drinking vessel*
               And let me the cannikin clink.
                   A soldier's a man,
                   O, man's life's but a span,
               Why then, let a soldier drink.

65   Some wine, boys!

CASSIO   Fore God, an excellent song.

IAGO   I learned it in England, where indeed they are most potent
    in potting.⁵ Your Dane, your German, and your swag°-bellied   *hanging*
    Hollander—drink, ho!—are nothing to your English.

70 CASSIO   Is your Englishman so exquisite in his drinking?

IAGO   Why, he drinks you with facility your Dane dead drunk.
    He sweats not to overthrow your Almain.° He gives your Hol-   *German*
    lander a vomit ere the next pottle° can be filled.   *tankard*

CASSIO   To the health of our general!

75 MONTANO   I am for it, lieutenant, and I'll do you justice.°   *match your drinking*

IAGO   O sweet England!
    [*Sings*]   King Stephen was and a worthy peer,
                 His breeches cost him but a crown;
                 He held them sixpence all too dear,
80   With that he called the tailor lown.°   *lout*
               He was a wight of high renown,
                 And thou art but of low degree.
               'Tis pride° that pulls the country down,   *ostentatious clothing*
               Then take thy auld cloak about thee.

85   Some wine, ho!

CASSIO   Fore God, this is a more exquisite song than the other.

IAGO   Will you hear't again?

CASSIO   No, for I hold him to be unworthy of his place that does
    those things. Well, God's above all, and there be souls must be
90   saved, and there be souls must not be saved.⁶

IAGO   It's true, good lieutenant.

CASSIO   For mine own part—no offence to the general, nor any
    man of quality°—I hope to be saved.   *rank*

IAGO   And so do I too, lieutenant.

95 CASSIO   Ay, but, by your leave, not before me. The lieutenant is
    to be saved before the ensign. Let's ha' no more of this. Let's to
    our affairs. God forgive us our sins. Gentlemen, let's look to
    our business. Do not think, gentlemen, I am drunk. This is my
    ensign, this is my right hand, and this is my left. I am not drunk
100   now. I can stand well enough, and I speak well enough.

GENTLEMEN   Excellent well.

CASSIO   Why, very well then. You must not think then that I am
    drunk.   *Exit*

MONTANO   To th' platform, masters. Come, let's set the watch.
                                   [*Exeunt* GENTLEMEN]

105 IAGO   You see this fellow that is gone before—
    He's a soldier fit to stand by Caesar
    And give direction; and do but see his vice.
    'Tis to his virtue a just equinox,°   *of equal size*
    The one as long as th'other. 'Tis pity of him.
110   I fear the trust Othello puts him in,

---

5. Most adept at drinking.   held by Calvinist Protestants that some souls are des-
6. Referring to the idea of predestination, the belief   tined from the outset to be saved and others damned.

On some odd time of his infirmity,
Will shake this island.
MONTANO   But is he often thus?
IAGO 'Tis evermore his prologue to his sleep.
He'll watch the horologe a double set[7]
If drink rock not his cradle.
115 MONTANO   It were well
The general were put in mind of it.
Perhaps he sees it not, or his good nature
Prizes the virtue that appears in Cassio,
And looks not on his evils. Is not this true?
                Enter RODERIGO
120 IAGO [*aside*] How now, Roderigo!
I pray you after the lieutenant, go.   *Exit* RODERIGO
MONTANO And 'tis great pity that the noble Moor
Should hazard such a place as his own second
With one of an engraffed° infirmity.   ingrained
125 It were an honest action to say so
To the Moor.
IAGO   Not I, for this fair island!
I do love Cassio well, and would do much
To cure him of this evil.
VOICES (*within*) Help, help!
IAGO   But hark, what noise?
                Enter CASSIO, *driving in* RODERIGO
130 CASSIO 'Swounds, you rogue, you rascal!
MONTANO What's the matter, lieutenant?
CASSIO A knave teach me my duty?—I'll beat the knave into a
twiggen° bottle.   wicker-cased
RODERIGO Beat me?
135 CASSIO Dost thou prate, rogue?
MONTANO Nay, good lieutenant, I pray you, sir, hold your hand.
CASSIO Let me go, sir, or I'll knock you o'er the mazard.°   head
MONTANO Come, come, you're drunk.
CASSIO Drunk?
                They fight
140 IAGO [*to* RODERIGO] Away, I say. Go out and cry a mutiny.
                                        [*Exit* RODERIGO]
Nay, good lieutenant. God's will, gentlemen!
Help, ho! Lieutenant! Sir! Montano! Sir!
Help, masters. Here's a goodly watch indeed.
                A bell rung
Who's that which rings the bell? Diablo,° ho!   The devil
145 The town will rise. God's will, lieutenant, hold.
You'll be ashamed for ever.
                Enter OTHELLO *and attendants, with weapons*
OTHELLO   What is the matter here?
MONTANO 'Swounds, I bleed still. I am hurt to th' death.
                [*Attacking* CASSIO] He dies.
OTHELLO Hold, for your lives!
IAGO Hold, ho, lieutenant, sir, Montano, gentlemen!
150 Have you forgot all place of sense and duty?
Hold, the general speaks to you. Hold, hold, for shame.

---

7. He'll stay up twice around the clock.

OTHELLO Why, how now, ho? From whence ariseth this?
Are we turned Turks, and to ourselves do that
Which heaven hath forbid the Ottomites?°   (*by raising a storm*)
For Christian shame, put by this barbarous brawl.
He that stirs next to carve for his own rage°   *draw a sword in anger*
Holds his soul light. He dies upon his motion.
Silence that dreadful bell—it frights the isle
From her propriety.
        [*Bell stops*]
                                What is the matter, masters?
Honest Iago, that looks dead with grieving,
Speak. Who began this? On thy love I charge thee.
IAGO I do not know. Friends all but now, even now,
In quarter° and in terms like bride and groom   *Under control*
Devesting them° for bed; and then but now—   *Getting undressed*
As if some planet° had unwitted men—   *astrological influence*
Swords out, and tilting one at others' breasts
In opposition bloody. I cannot speak
Any beginning to this peevish odds,°   *silly quarrel*
And would in action glorious I had lost
Those legs that brought me to a part of it.
OTHELLO How comes it, Michael, you are thus forgot?
CASSIO I pray you pardon me. I cannot speak.
OTHELLO Worthy Montano, you were wont be° civil.   *you used to be*
The gravity and stillness of your youth
The world hath noted, and your name is great
In mouths of wisest censure.° What's the matter,   *judgment*
That you unlace your reputation thus,
And spend your rich opinion° for the name   *reputation*
Of a night-brawler? Give me answer to it.
MONTANO Worthy Othello, I am hurt to danger.
Your officer Iago can inform you,
While I spare speech—which something now offends me°—   *somewhat now pains me*
Of all that I do know; nor know I aught
By me that's said or done amiss this night,
Unless self-charity° be sometimes a vice,   *care of oneself*
And to defend ourselves it be a sin
When violence assails us.
OTHELLO   Now, by heaven,
My blood begins my safer guides to rule,
And passion, having my best judgement collied,°   *darkened*
Essays to lead the way. 'Swounds, if I stir,
Or do but lift this arm, the best of you
Shall sink in my rebuke. Give me to know
How this foul rout began, who set it on,
And he that is approved in this offence,
Though he had twinned with me, both at a birth,
Shall lose me. What, in a town of war
Yet° wild, the people's hearts brimful of fear,   *Still*
To manage° private and domestic quarrel   *carry on*
In night, and on the court and guard of safety!⁸
'Tis monstrous. Iago, who began't?
MONTANO [*to* IAGO] If partially affined° or leagued in office   *biased (for Cassio)*

___

8. And at the place where safety and security are at stake (on the night watch).

Thou dost deliver more or less than truth,
Thou art no soldier.

IAGO   Touch me not so near.
  I had rather ha' this tongue cut from my mouth
205   Than it should do offence to Michael Cassio.
  Yet I persuade myself to speak the truth
  Shall nothing wrong him. This it is, general.
  Montano and myself being in speech,
  There comes a fellow crying out for help,
210   And Cassio following him with determined sword
  To execute upon° him. Sir, this gentleman   *To attack*
  Steps in to Cassio, and entreats his pause.
  Myself the crying fellow did pursue,
  Lest by his clamour, as it so fell out,
215   The town might fall in fright. He, swift of foot,
  Outran my purpose, and I returned, the rather
  For that I heard the clink and fall of swords
  And Cassio high in oath, which till tonight
  I ne'er might say before. When I came back—
220   For this was brief—I found them close together
  At blow and thrust, even as again they were
  When you yourself did part them.
  More of this matter cannot I report,
  But men are men. The best sometimes forget.
225   Though Cassio did some little wrong to him,
  As men in rage strike those that wish them best,
  Yet surely Cassio, I believe, received
  From him that fled some strange indignity
  Which patience could not pass.°   *let pass*

OTHELLO   I know, Iago,
230   Thy honesty and love doth mince° this matter,   *minimize*
  Making it light to Cassio. Cassio, I love thee,
  But never more be officer of mine.

          Enter DESDEMONA, *attended*

  Look if my gentle love be not raised up.
  I'll make thee an example.
235 DESDEMONA   What is the matter, dear?
OTHELLO   All's well now, sweeting.
  Come away to bed. [*To* MONTANO] Sir, for your hurts
  Myself will be your surgeon. [*To attendants*] Lead him off.

          [*Exeunt attendants with* MONTANO]

  Iago, look with care about the town,
240   And silence those whom this vile brawl distracted.
  Come, Desdemona. 'Tis the soldier's life
  To have their balmy slumbers waked with strife.

        Exeunt [OTHELLO *the*] *Moor,* DESDEMONA,
                     and attendants

IAGO   What, are you hurt, lieutenant?
CASSIO   Ay, past all surgery.
245 IAGO   Marry, God forbid.
CASSIO   Reputation, reputation, reputation—O, I ha' lost my rep-
  utation, I ha' lost the immortal part of myself, and what remains
  is bestial! My reputation, Iago, my reputation.
IAGO   As I am an honest man, I thought you had received some
250   bodily wound. There is more sense in that than in reputation.

Reputation is an idle and most false imposition,° oft got without   *artificial notion*
merit and lost without deserving. You have lost no reputation
at all unless you repute yourself such a loser. What, man, there
are more ways to recover the general again. You are but now
255 cast in his mood—a punishment more in policy⁹ than in mal-
ice, even so as one would beat his offenceless dog to affright an
imperious lion. Sue to° him again, and he's yours.   *Petition*

CASSIO I will rather sue to be despised than to deceive so good
a commander with so slight, so drunken, and so indiscreet an
260 officer. Drunk, and speak parrot,° and squabble? Swagger,   *rant on*
swear, and discourse fustian° with one's own shadow? O thou   *nonsense*
invisible spirit of wine, if thou hast no name to be known by,
let us call thee devil.

IAGO What was he that you followed with your sword? What had
265 he done to you?

CASSIO I know not.

IAGO Is't possible?

CASSIO I remember a mass of things, but nothing distinctly; a
quarrel, but nothing wherefore.° O God, that men should put   *but not why*
270 an enemy in their mouths° to steal away their brains! That we   *should drink*
should with joy, pleasance, revel, and applause transform our-
selves into beasts!

IAGO Why, but you are now well enough. How came you thus
recovered?

275 CASSIO It hath pleased the devil drunkenness to give place to
the devil wrath. One unperfectness shows me another, to make
me frankly despise myself.

IAGO Come, you are too severe a moraller. As the time, the
place, and the condition of this country stands, I could heartily
280 wish this had not befallen; but since it is as it is, mend it for
your own good.

CASSIO I will ask him for my place again. He shall tell me I am
a drunkard. Had I as many mouths as Hydra,¹ such an answer
would stop them all. To be now a sensible man, by and by a
285 fool, and presently a beast! O, strange! Every inordinate cup is
unblessed, and the ingredient is a devil.

IAGO Come, come. Good wine is a good familiar creature, if it
be well used. Exclaim no more against it. And, good lieutenant,
I think you think I love you.

290 CASSIO I have well approved° it, sir—I drunk?   *tested*

IAGO You or any man living may be drunk at a time, man. I'll
tell you what you shall do. Our general's wife is now the gen-
eral. I may say so in this respect, for that he hath devoted and
given up himself to the contemplation, mark, and denotement°   *observation*
295 of her parts° and graces. Confess yourself freely to her. Impor-   *qualities*
tune her help to put you in your place again. She is of so free,°   *generous*
so kind, so apt, so blessed a disposition, she holds it a vice in
her goodness not to do more than she is requested. This broken
joint between you and her husband entreat her to splinter,°   *heal with a splint*
300 and, my fortunes against any lay° worth naming, this crack of   *wager*
your love shall grow stronger than it was before.

CASSIO You advise me well.

---

9. *cast . . . policy:* dismissed in anger—a matter of   1. A mythical serpent with many heads who grew two
policy (of public example).   more when one was cut off.

IAGO   I protest,° in the sincerity of love and honest kindness.   *insist*

CASSIO   I think it freely, and betimes° in the morning I will   *early*
305   beseech the virtuous Desdemona to undertake for me. I am
desperate of my fortunes if they check° me here.   *stop*

IAGO   You are in the right. Good night, lieutenant. I must to the
watch.

CASSIO   Good night, honest Iago.   *Exit*

310   IAGO   And what's he then that says I play the villain,
When this advice is free I give, and honest,
Probal° to thinking, and indeed the course   *Wise*
To win the Moor again? For 'tis most easy
Th'inclining° Desdemona to subdue   *The well-disposed*
315   In any honest suit. She's framed as fruitful°   *generous*
As the free elements; and then for her
To win the Moor, were't to renounce his baptism,
All seals and symbols of redeemèd sin,
His soul is so enfettered to her love
320   That she may make, unmake, do what she list,
Even as her appetite° shall play the god   *wishes*
With his weak function.° How am I then a villain,   *faculties*
To counsel Cassio to this parallel° course   *suitable*
Directly to his good? Divinity° of hell: *Theology*
325   When devils will the blackest sins put on,
They do suggest at first with heavenly shows,
As I do now; for whiles this honest fool
Plies Desdemona to repair his fortune,
And she for him pleads strongly to the Moor,
330   I'll pour this pestilence into his ear:
That she repeals him° for her body's lust,   *appeals for him*
And by how much she strives to do him good
She shall undo her credit with the Moor.
So will I turn her virtue into pitch,²
335   And out of her own goodness make the net
That shall enmesh them all.
                    Enter RODERIGO
                    How now, Roderigo?

RODERIGO   I do follow here in the chase, not like a hound that
hunts, but one that fills up the cry.° My money is almost spent,   *a pack follower*
I ha' been tonight exceedingly well cudgelled, and I think the
340   issue will be I shall have so much° experience for my pains: *only so much*
and so, with no money at all and a little more wit, return again
to Venice.

IAGO   How poor are they that ha' not patience!
What wound did ever heal but by degrees?
345   Thou know'st we work by wit and not by witchcraft,
And wit depends on dilatory° time.   *drawn-out*
Does't not go well? Cassio hath beaten thee,
And thou by that small hurt hast cashiered° Cassio.   *dismissed*
Though other things grow fair against the sun,
350   Yet fruits that blossom first will first be ripe.³
Content thyself a while. By the mass,° 'tis morning.   *(a mild oath)*

2. Black, sticky substance used as a snare. The more   3. *Though . . . ripe:* Although others may appear to be
the thing caught in it tries to escape, the more stuck it   prospering, your plan will be successful soonest
becomes.   because started first.

Pleasure and action make the hours seem short.
Retire thee. Go where thou art billeted.
Away, I say. Thou shalt know more hereafter.
Nay, get thee gone.   *Exit* RODERIGO
355   Two things are to be done.
My wife must move for Cassio to her mistress.
I'll set her on.
Myself a while to draw the Moor apart,
And bring him jump° when he may Cassio find   *exactly*
360 Soliciting his wife. Ay, that's the way.
Dull not device by coldness and delay.⁴   *Exit*

3.1

Enter CASSIO *with* MUSICIANS

CASSIO   Masters, play here—I will content° your pains—   *reward*
         Something that's brief, and bid 'Good morrow, general'.
         [*Music.*] *Enter* CLOWN
CLOWN   Why, masters, ha' your instruments been in Naples,
         that they speak i'th' nose thus?¹
5   MUSICIAN   How, sir, how?
CLOWN   Are these, I pray you, wind instruments?²
MUSICIAN   Ay, marry are they, sir.
CLOWN   O, thereby hangs a tail.
MUSICIAN   Whereby hangs a tale, sir?
10   CLOWN   Marry, sir, by many a wind instrument that I know. But
         masters, here's money for you, and the general so likes your
         music that he desires you, for love's sake, to make no more
         noise with it.
MUSICIAN   Well, sir, we will not.
15   CLOWN   If you have any music that may not° be heard, to't again;   *cannot*
         but, as they say, to hear music the general does not greatly care.
MUSICIAN   We ha' none such, sir.
CLOWN   Then put up your pipes in your bag, for I'll away. Go,
         vanish into air, away.   *Exeunt* MUSICIANS
20   CASSIO   Dost thou hear, my honest friend?
CLOWN   No, I hear not your honest friend, I hear you.
CASSIO   Prithee, keep up thy quillets.° There's a poor piece of   *pack up your puns*
         gold for thee. If the gentlewoman that attends the general's wife
         be stirring, tell her there's one Cassio entreats her a little favour
25   of speech. Wilt thou do this?
CLOWN   She is stirring, sir. If she will stir hither, I shall seem° to   *arrange*
         notify unto her.
CASSIO   Do, good my friend.   *Exit* CLOWN
         Enter IAGO
                In happy time,° Iago.   *Well met*
IAGO   You ha' not been abed, then.
CASSIO   Why, no. The day had broke
30   Before we parted. I ha' made bold, Iago,
         To send in to your wife. My suit to her

---

4. Don't let sluggishness and slowness to act weaken
the plot.
3.1 Location: Outside Othello and Desdemona's room.
1. That they sound so nasal; perhaps a reference to
venereal disease, often associated with Naples, or a

phallic or anal joke.
2. The exchange that follows depends on the connec-
tions between wind instruments, flatulence, and
"tale/tail."

Is that she will to virtuous Desdemona
Procure me some access.

IAGO   I'll send her to you presently,°   *immediately*
35   And I'll devise a mean to draw the Moor
Out of the way, that your converse and business
May be more free.

CASSIO   I humbly thank you for't.   *Exit* IAGO
I never knew a Florentine more kind and honest.

      Enter EMILIA

EMILIA   Good morrow, good lieutenant. I am sorry
40   For your displeasure, but all will sure be well.
The general and his wife are talking of it,
And she speaks for you stoutly. The Moor replies
That he you hurt is of great fame in Cyprus,
And great affinity,° and that in wholesome wisdom   *well connected*
45   He might not but refuse you. But he protests he loves you,
And needs no other suitor but his likings
To take the saf'st occasion by the front°   *forelock*
To bring you in again.

CASSIO   Yet I beseech you,
If you think fit, or that it may be done,
50   Give me advantage of some brief discourse
With Desdemon alone.

EMILIA   Pray you come in.
I will bestow you where you shall have time
To speak your bosom° freely.   *heart*

CASSIO   I am much bound to you.

                            Exeunt

3.2

      Enter OTHELLO, IAGO, *and* GENTLEMEN

OTHELLO   These letters give, Iago, to the pilot,
And by him do my duties° to the senate.   *send my respects*
That done, I will be walking on the works.°   *fortifications*
Repair there to me.

IAGO   Well, my good lord, I'll do't.   [*Exit*]
5   OTHELLO   This fortification, gentlemen—shall we see't?

A GENTLEMAN   We'll wait upon your lordship.   *Exeunt*

3.3

      Enter DESDEMONA, CASSIO, *and* EMILIA

DESDEMONA   Be thou assured, good Cassio, I will do
All my abilities in thy behalf.

EMILIA   Good madam, do. I warrant it grieves my husband
As if the cause were his.

5   DESDEMONA   O, that's an honest fellow. Do not doubt, Cassio,
But I will have my lord and you again
As friendly as you were.

CASSIO   Bounteous madam,
Whatever shall become of Michael Cassio
He's never anything but your true servant.

10   DESDEMONA   I know't. I thank you. You do love my lord.
You have known him long, and be you well assured

3.2 Location: The citadel.   3.3 Location: The citadel's garden.

He shall in strangeness stand no farther off
Than in a politic distance.[1]

CASSIO   Ay, but, lady,
That policy may either last so long,
15   Or feed upon such nice and wat'rish diet,
Or breed itself so out of circumstance,[2]
That, I being absent and my place supplied,°   *filled*
My general will forget my love and service.

DESDEMONA   Do not doubt° that. Before Emilia here   *fear*
20   I give thee warrant° of thy place. Assure thee,   *assurance*
If I do vow a friendship I'll perform it
To the last article. My lord shall never rest.
I'll watch him tame, and talk him out of patience.[3]
His bed shall seem a school, his board a shrift.°   *confessional*
25   I'll intermingle everything he does
With Cassio's suit. Therefore be merry, Cassio,
For thy solicitor° shall rather die   *advocate*
Than give thy cause away.°   *up*

                    Enter OTHELLO *and* IAGO

EMILIA   Madam, here comes my lord.
CASSIO   Madam, I'll take my leave.
DESDEMONA   Why, stay, and hear me speak.
30   CASSIO   Madam, not now. I am very ill at ease,
Unfit for mine own purposes.
DESDEMONA   Well, do your discretion.   *Exit* CASSIO
IAGO   Ha! I like not that.
OTHELLO   What dost thou say?
35   IAGO   Nothing, my lord. Or if, I know not what.
OTHELLO   Was not that Cassio parted from my wife?
IAGO   Cassio, my lord? No, sure, I cannot think it,
That he would steal away so guilty-like
Seeing your coming.
40   OTHELLO   I do believe 'twas he.
DESDEMONA   How now, my lord?
I have been talking with a suitor here,
A man that languishes in your displeasure.
OTHELLO   Who is't you mean?
45   DESDEMONA   Why, your lieutenant, Cassio; good my lord,
If I have any grace or power to move you,
His present reconciliation take;°   *Accept him now*
For if he be not one that truly loves you,
That errs in ignorance and not in cunning,°   *not knowingly*
50   I have no judgement in an honest face.
I prithee call him back.
OTHELLO   Went he hence now?
DESDEMONA   Yes, faith, so humbled
That he hath left part of his grief with me
55   To suffer with him. Good love, call him back.
OTHELLO   Not now, sweet Desdemon. Some other time.
DESDEMONA   But shall't be shortly?
OTHELLO   The sooner, sweet, for you.

---

1. *He . . . distance*: He will distance himself from you
only as much as good diplomacy requires.
2. *Or feed . . . circumstance*: Or persist based on such
unimportant and poor justifications, or continue by
chance.
3. I'll keep him awake until he obeys me, and talk to
him beyond his endurance.

	DESDEMONA	Shall't be tonight at supper?	
	OTHELLO	No, not tonight.	
	DESDEMONA	Tomorrow dinner,° then?	*midday meal*
	OTHELLO	I shall not dine at home.	
60		I meet the captains at the citadel.	
	DESDEMONA	Why then, tomorrow night, or Tuesday morn,	

DESDEMONA   Why then, tomorrow night, or Tuesday morn,
On Tuesday noon, or night, on Wednesday morn—
I prithee name the time, but let it not
Exceed three days. In faith, he's penitent,
65   And yet his trespass, in our common reason°—   *normal judgment*
Save that, they say, the wars must make example
Out of her° best—is not almost a fault   *(war's)*
T'incur a private check.[4] When shall he come?
Tell me, Othello. I wonder in my soul
70   What you would ask me that I should deny,
Or stand so mamm'ring° on? What, Michael Cassio,   *hesitating*
That came a-wooing with you, and so many a time
When I have spoke of you dispraisingly
Hath ta'en your part—to have so much to-do
75   To bring him in?° By'r Lady, I could do much.[5]   *into favor*

OTHELLO   Prithee, no more. Let him come when he will.
I will deny thee nothing.

DESDEMONA   Why, this is not a boon.
'Tis as I should entreat you wear your gloves,
Or feed on nourishing dishes, or keep you warm,
80   Or sue to you to do a peculiar° profit   *particular*
To your own person. Nay, when I have a suit
Wherein I mean to touch your love indeed,
It shall be full of poise° and difficult weight,   *balanced judgment*
And fearful to be granted.

OTHELLO   I will deny thee nothing,
85   Whereon I do beseech thee grant me this:
To leave me but a little to myself.

DESDEMONA   Shall I deny you? No. Farewell, my lord.

OTHELLO   Farewell, my Desdemona. I'll come to thee straight.°   *immediately*

DESDEMONA   Emilia, come. [*To* OTHELLO] Be as your fancies
teach° you.   *as your whims lead*
90   Whate'er you be, I am obedient.

Exeunt DESDEMONA *and* EMILIA

OTHELLO   Excellent wretch!° Perdition catch my soul   *(affectionate)*
But I do love thee, and when I love thee not,
Chaos is come again.

IAGO   My noble lord.
95   OTHELLO   What dost thou say, Iago?

IAGO   Did Michael Cassio, when you wooed my lady,
Know of your love?

OTHELLO   He did, from first to last. Why dost thou ask?

IAGO   But for a satisfaction of my thought,
No further harm.
100   OTHELLO   Why of thy thought, Iago?

IAGO   I did not think he had been acquainted with her.

OTHELLO   O yes, and went between us very oft.

IAGO   Indeed?

4. *is . . . check*: is barely worth even private criticism.   5. Do much to make you regret your reluctance (?).

OTHELLO   Indeed? Ay, indeed. Discern'st thou aught in that?
105   Is he not honest?
IAGO   Honest, my lord?
OTHELLO   Honest? Ay, honest.
IAGO   My lord, for aught I know.
OTHELLO   What dost thou think?
IAGO   Think, my lord?
110 OTHELLO   'Think, my lord?' By heaven, thou echo'st me
         As if there were some monster in thy thought
         Too hideous to be shown! Thou dost mean something.
         I heard thee say even now thou liked'st not that,
         When Cassio left my wife. What didst not like?
115   And when I told thee he was of my counsel°   in my confidence
         In my whole course of wooing, thou cried'st 'Indeed?'
         And didst contract and purse thy brow together
         As if thou then hadst shut up in thy brain
         Some horrible conceit.° If thou dost love me,   thought
120   Show me thy thought.
IAGO   My lord, you know I love you.
OTHELLO   I think thou dost,
         And for° I know thou'rt full of love and honesty,   since
         And weigh'st thy words before thou giv'st them breath,
125   Therefore these stops° of thine fright me the more;   reluctances
         For such things in a false disloyal knave
         Are tricks of custom,° but in a man that's just,   habitual
         They're close dilations,⁶ working from the heart
         That passion cannot rule.°   control
IAGO   For Michael Cassio,
130   I dare be sworn I think that he is honest.
OTHELLO   I think so too.
IAGO   Men should be what they seem,
         Or those that be not, would they might seem none.⁷
OTHELLO   Certain, men should be what they seem.
IAGO   Why then, I think Cassio's an honest man.
135 OTHELLO   Nay, yet there's more in this.
         I prithee speak to me as to thy thinkings,
         As thou dost ruminate, and give thy worst of thoughts
         The worst of words.
IAGO   Good my lord, pardon me.
         Though I am bound to every act of duty,
140   I am not bound to that all slaves are free to.⁸
         Utter my thoughts? Why, say they are vile and false,
         As where's that palace whereinto foul things
         Sometimes intrude not? Who has that breast so pure
         But some uncleanly apprehensions
145   Keep leets and law-days, and in sessions sit
         With meditations lawful?⁹
OTHELLO   Thou dost conspire against thy friend,° Iago,   (Othello)
         If thou but think'st him wronged and mak'st his ear
         A stranger to thy thoughts.
IAGO   I do beseech you,

6. Involuntary revelations of interior, close-kept secrets.
7. Or . . . none: If only those who are not what they
seem didn't seem to be what they are not.
8. I am not obligated to reveal my inner thoughts,
something about which even slaves have a choice.
9. uncleanly . . . lawful: illegitimate thoughts meet in
court ("leets") from time to time (on "law-days") and
debate (in court "sessions") with legitimate ones.

150   Though I perchance am vicious° in my guess—   *mistaken*
         As I confess it is my nature's plague
         To spy into abuses, and oft my jealousy
         Shapes faults that are not—that your wisdom then,
         From one that so imperfectly conceits,°   *imagines*
155   Would take no notice, nor build yourself a trouble
         Out of his scattering° and unsure observance.   *incoherent*
         It were not for your quiet nor your good,
         Nor for my manhood, honesty, and wisdom,
         To let you know my thoughts.
     OTHELLO   What dost thou mean?
160   IAGO   Good name in man and woman, dear my lord,
         Is the immediate jewel of their souls.
         Who steals my purse steals trash; 'tis something, nothing;
         'Twas mine, 'tis his, and has been slave to thousands.
         But he that filches from me my good name
165   Robs me of that which not enriches him
         And makes me poor indeed.
     OTHELLO   By heaven, I'll know thy thoughts.
     IAGO   You cannot, if my heart were in your hand;
         Nor shall not whilst 'tis in my custody.
     OTHELLO   Ha!
     IAGO   O, beware, my lord, of jealousy.
170   It is the green-eyed monster which doth mock
         The meat it feeds on.[1] That cuckold lives in bliss
         Who, certain of his fate, loves not his wronger.[2]
         But O, what damnèd minutes tells he o'er
         Who dotes yet doubts, suspects yet fondly loves!
175   OTHELLO   O misery!
     IAGO   Poor and content is rich, and rich enough,
         But riches fineless° is as poor as winter   *boundless*
         To him that ever fears he shall be poor.
         Good God the souls of all my tribe defend
         From jealousy!
180   OTHELLO   Why, why is this?
         Think'st thou I'd make a life of jealousy,
         To follow still the changes of the moon°   *To renew endlessly*
         With fresh suspicions? No, to be once in doubt
         Is once to be resolved.° Exchange me for a goat   *to be finally settled*
185   When I shall turn the business of my soul
         To such exsufflicate and blowed° surmises   *inflated and blown-up*
         Matching thy inference. 'Tis not to make me jealous
         To say my wife is fair, feeds well, loves company,
         Is free of speech, sings, plays, and dances well.
190   Where virtue is, these are more virtuous,
         Nor from mine own weak merits will I draw
         The smallest fear or doubt of her revolt,°   *or fear of her betrayal*
         For she had eyes and chose me. No, Iago,
         I'll see before I doubt; when I doubt, prove;
195   And on the proof, there is no more but this:
         Away at once with love or jealousy.

---

1. which . . . on: that tortures, as it consumes, the   2. Who, knowing it is his fate to be cuckolded, doesn't
heart of the jealous person.   love his wife.

IAGO   I am glad of this, for now I shall have reason
　　　 To show the love and duty that I bear you
　　　 With franker spirit. Therefore, as I am bound,
200　　Receive it from me. I speak not yet of proof.
　　　 Look to your wife. Observe her well with Cassio.
　　　 Wear your eyes thus: not jealous, nor secure.
　　　 I would not have your free and noble nature
　　　 Out of self-bounty be abused.³ Look to't.
205　　I know our country disposition well.
　　　 In Venice they do let God see the pranks
　　　 They dare not show their husbands; their best conscience
　　　 Is not to leave't undone, but keep't unknown.
OTHELLO　　Dost thou say so?
210　IAGO　She did deceive her father, marrying you,
　　　 And when she seemed to shake and fear your looks
　　　 She loved them most.
OTHELLO　　　　　　　　And so she did.
IAGO　　　　　　　　　　　Why, go to,° then.　　　　　　*that's it*
　　　 She that so young could give out such a seeming,
　　　 To seel her father's eyes up close as oak,⁴
215　　He thought 'twas witchcraft! But I am much to blame.
　　　 I humbly do beseech you of your pardon
　　　 For too much loving you.
OTHELLO　　　　　　　　I am bound to thee for ever.
IAGO　I see this hath a little dashed your spirits.
OTHELLO　Not a jot, not a jot.
IAGO　　　　　　　　　　　I'faith, I fear it has.
220　　I hope you will consider what is spoke
　　　 Comes from my love. But I do see you're moved.
　　　 I am to pray you not to strain my speech
　　　 To grosser issues,° nor to larger reach　　　　*greater conclusions*
　　　 Than to suspicion.
225　OTHELLO　I will not.
IAGO　　Should you do so, my lord,
　　　 My speech should fall into such vile success
　　　 Which my thoughts aimed not. Cassio's my worthy friend.
　　　 My lord, I see you're moved.
OTHELLO　　　　　　　　No, not much moved.
230　　I do not think but Desdemona's honest.
IAGO　Long live she so, and long live you to think so!
OTHELLO　And yet how nature, erring from itself—
IAGO　Ay, there's the point; as, to be bold with you,
　　　 Not to affect° many proposèd matches　　　　*desire*
235　　Of her own clime, complexion, and degree,
　　　 Whereto we see in all things nature tends.
　　　 Foh, one may smell in such a will most rank,
　　　 Foul disproportions, thoughts unnatural!
　　　 But pardon me. I do not in position°　　　　*argument*
240　　Distinctly speak of her, though I may fear
　　　 Her will,° recoiling° to her better judgement,　*desire / submitting*
　　　 May fall to match you with her country forms⁵
　　　 And happily° repent.　　　　　　　　*perhaps*

3. Be deceived on account of your own goodness.　father's eyes as tightly as oak (a fine-grained wood).
4. Perhaps: To cover ("seel" means "to blind") her　5. May happen to compare you with Venetian standards.

OTHELLO   Farewell, farewell.
  If more thou dost perceive, let me know more.
245   Set on thy wife to observe. Leave me, Iago.
IAGO [*going*]   My lord, I take my leave.
OTHELLO   Why did I marry? This honest creature doubtless
  Sees and knows more, much more, than he unfolds.
IAGO [*returning*]   My lord, I would I might entreat your honour
250   To scan this thing no farther. Leave it to time.
  Although 'tis fit that Cassio have his place—
  For sure he fills it up with great ability—
  Yet, if you please to hold him off a while,
  You shall by that perceive him and his means.[6]
255   Note if your lady strain his entertainment°   *urge his reception*
  With any strong or vehement importunity.
  Much will be seen in that. In the mean time,
  Let me be thought too busy° in my fears—   *meddlesome*
  As worthy cause I have to fear I am—
260   And hold her free,° I do beseech your honour.   *believe her innocent*
OTHELLO   Fear not my government.°   *self-conduct*
IAGO   I once more take my leave.
                             Exit
OTHELLO   This fellow's of exceeding honesty,
  And knows all qualities° with a learned spirit   *(human) types*
  Of human dealings. If I do prove her haggard,°   *wild (falconry)*
265   Though that her jesses were my dear heart-strings
  I'd whistle her off and let her down the wind
  To prey at fortune.[7] Haply for° I am black,   *Perhaps because*
  And have not those soft parts of conversation°   *easy manners*
  That chamberers° have; or for I am declined   *gallants*
270   Into the vale of years—yet that's not much—
  She's gone. I am abused,° and my relief   *deceived*
  Must be to loathe her. O curse of marriage,
  That we can call these delicate creatures ours
  And not their appetites! I had rather be a toad
275   And live upon the vapour of a dungeon
  Than keep a corner in the thing I love
  For others' uses. Yet 'tis the plague of great ones;
  Prerogatived° are they less than the base.°   *Privileged / lowborn*
  'Tis destiny unshunnable, like death.
280   Even then this forkèd plague is fated to us
  When we do quicken.[8]
        Enter DESDEMONA *and* EMILIA
                  Look where she comes.
  If she be false, O then heaven mocks itself!
  I'll not believe't.
DESDEMONA   How now, my dear Othello?
  Your dinner, and the generous° islanders   *noble*
285   By you invited, do attend° your presence.   *wait for*
OTHELLO   I am to blame.
DESDEMONA   Why do you speak so faintly? Are you not well?
OTHELLO   I have a pain upon my forehead here.°   *(from cuckold's horns)*

6. Method (for restoring himself to favor).
7. *Though . . . fortune*: Even if what tied her ("jesses" were leg straps put on a hawk) were my own heartstrings, I'd set her loose downwind forever to hunt on her own.

8. *Even . . . quicken*: The "plague" of horns (imagined to grow from the forehead of a cuckold) is our fate as soon as we live.

DESDEMONA   Faith, that's with watching.° 'Twill away again.   *from lack of sleep*
290   Let me but bind it hard, within this hour
       It will be well.
OTHELLO   Your napkin° is too little.   *handkerchief*
       [*He puts the napkin from him. It drops*]
       Let it alone. Come, I'll go in with you.
DESDEMONA   I am very sorry that you are not well.
                    Exeunt OTHELLO *and* DESDEMONA
EMILIA [*taking up the napkin*]   I am glad I have found this napkin.
295   This was her first remembrance from the Moor.
       My wayward husband hath a hundred times
       Wooed me to steal it, but she so loves the token—
       For he conjured her⁹ she should ever keep it—
       That she reserves it evermore about her
300   To kiss and talk to. I'll ha' the work ta'en out,°   *embroidery copied*
       And give't Iago. What he will do with it,
       Heaven knows, not I.
       I nothing,° but to please his fantasy.   *intend nothing*
                    Enter IAGO
IAGO   How now, what do you here alone?
305   EMILIA   Do not you chide. I have a thing for you.
IAGO   You have a thing for me? It is a common thing.¹
EMILIA   Ha?
IAGO   To have a foolish wife.
EMILIA   O, is that all? What will you give me now
310   For that same handkerchief?
IAGO   What handkerchief?
EMILIA   What handkerchief?
       Why, that the Moor first gave to Desdemona,
       That which so often you did bid me steal.
315   IAGO   Hast stol'n it from her?
EMILIA   No, faith, she let it drop by negligence,
       And to th'advantage° I, being here, took't up.   *taking the occasion*
       Look, here 'tis.
IAGO   A good wench! Give it me.
EMILIA   What will you do with it, that you have been so earnest
       To have me filch it?
320   IAGO   Why, what is that to you?
       [*He takes the napkin*]
EMILIA   If it be not for some purpose of import,
       Give't me again. Poor lady, she'll run mad
       When she shall lack it.
IAGO   Be not acknown on't.° I have use for it. Go, leave me.   *Don't let it be known*
                    Exit EMILIA
325   I will in Cassio's lodging lose this napkin,
       And let him find it. Trifles light as air
       Are to the jealous confirmations strong
       As proofs of holy writ. This may do something.
       The Moor already changes with my poison.
330   Dangerous conceits° are in their natures poisons,   *ideas*
       Which at the first are scarce found to distaste,
       But, with a little act° upon the blood,   *effect*

9. Made her swear; perhaps also an unwitting back-   employed witchcraft to win Desdemona.
ward glance at Brabanzio's charge in 1.3 that Othello   1. It is a vagina ("thing") available to all.

Burn like the mines of sulphur.[2]
Enter OTHELLO
I did say so.
Look where he comes. Not poppy nor mandragora[3]
335 Nor all the drowsy syrups of the world
Shall ever medicine thee to that sweet sleep
Which thou owedst° yesterday.   *owned*
OTHELLO   Ha, ha, false to me?
IAGO   Why, how now, general? No more of that.
340 OTHELLO   Avaunt, be gone. Thou hast set me on the rack.
I swear 'tis better to be much abused°   *mistreated; deceived*
Than but to know't a little.
IAGO   How now, my lord?
OTHELLO   What sense had I of her stol'n hours of lust?
I saw't not, thought it not; it harmed not me.
345 I slept the next night well, fed well, was free and merry.
I found not Cassio's kisses on her lips.
He that is robbed, not wanting° what is stol'n,   *missing*
Let him not know't and he's not robbed at all.
IAGO   I am sorry to hear this.
350 OTHELLO   I had been happy if the general camp,
Pioneers° and all, had tasted her sweet body,   *Manual laborers*
So° I had nothing known. O, now for ever   *If*
Farewell the tranquil mind, farewell content,
Farewell the plumèd troops and the big wars
355 That makes ambition virtue! O, farewell,
Farewell the neighing steed and the shrill trump,
The spirit-stirring drum, th'ear-piercing fife,
The royal banner, and all quality,°   *aspects*
Pride,° pomp, and circumstance° of glorious war!   *Magnificence / ceremony*
360 And O, you mortal engines° whose rude throats   *deadly cannons*
Th'immortal Jove's dread clamours° counterfeit,   *thunderclaps*
Farewell! Othello's occupation's gone.
IAGO   Is't possible, my lord?
OTHELLO [*taking* IAGO *by the throat*]   Villain, be sure thou prove
my love a whore.
365 Be sure of it. Give me the ocular proof,
Or, by the worth of mine eternal soul,
Thou hadst been better have been born a dog
Than answer my waked wrath.
IAGO   Is't come to this?
OTHELLO   Make me to see't, or at the least so prove it
370 That the probation° bear no hinge nor loop   *proof*
To hang a doubt on, or woe upon thy life.
IAGO   My noble lord.
OTHELLO   If thou dost slander her and torture me,
Never pray more; abandon all remorse,
375 On horror's head horrors accumulate,
Do deeds to make heaven weep, all earth amazed,
For nothing canst thou to damnation add
Greater than that.

---

2. Pliny the Elder describes two islands of sulfur between mainland Italy and Sicily that were rumored to be always on fire.

3. A sleep-inducing substance made from the mandrake root.

IAGO   O grace, O heaven forgive me!
Are you a man? Have you a soul or sense?
380 God buy you, take mine office.[4] O wretched fool,°   *(to himself)*
That lov'st to make thine honesty a vice!°   *fault*
O monstrous world, take note, take note, O world,
To be direct and honest is not safe!
I thank you for this profit,° and from hence   *profitable lesson*
385 I'll love no friend, sith° love breeds such offence.   *since*
OTHELLO   Nay, stay. Thou shouldst be honest.
IAGO   I should be wise, for honesty's a fool,
And loses that° it works for.   *what*
OTHELLO   By the world,[5]
I think my wife be honest, and think she is not.
390 I think that thou art just, and think thou art not.
I'll have some proof. My name, that was as fresh
As Dian's[6] visage, is now begrimed and black
As mine own face. If there be cords, or knives,
Poison, or fire, or suffocating streams,
395 I'll not endure it. Would I were satisfied!
IAGO   I see, sir, you are eaten up with passion.
I do repent me that I put it to you.
You would be satisfied?
OTHELLO   Would? Nay, and I will.
IAGO   And may. But how, how satisfied, my lord?
400 Would you, the supervisor,° grossly gape on,   *observer*
Behold her topped?
OTHELLO   Death and damnation! O!
IAGO   It were a tedious° difficulty, I think,   *painful*
To bring them to that prospect. Damn them then
If ever mortal eyes do see them bolster°   *share a pillow*
405 More° than their own!° What then, how then?   *Other / own eyes*
What shall I say? Where's satisfaction?
It is impossible you should see this,
Were they as prime° as goats, as hot as monkeys,   *lustful*
As salt as wolves in pride,[7] and fools as gross
410 As ignorance made drunk. But yet I say,
If imputation, and strong circumstances[8]
Which lead directly to the door of truth,
Will give you satisfaction, you might ha't.
OTHELLO   Give me a living reason she's disloyal.
415 IAGO   I do not like the office,
But sith I am entered in this cause so far,
Pricked to't° by foolish honesty and love,   *Prodded on*
I will go on. I lay with Cassio lately,
And being troubled with a raging tooth,
420 I could not sleep. There are a kind of men
So loose of soul that in their sleeps
Will mutter their affairs. One of this kind is Cassio.
In sleep I heard him say 'Sweet Desdemona,
Let us be wary, let us hide our loves',
425 And then, sir, would he grip and wring my hand,

---

4. Good-bye, I resign my official position (ensign).
5. Othello's speech (lines 388–95) does not appear in Q.
6. Diana, goddess of chastity and of the (pale) moon.
The Second Quarto (1630) replaces "My" (line 391)

with "Her," a plausible but arguably less powerful reading that lacks textual authority.
7. As lecherous as wolves in heat.
8. If inference and strong circumstantial evidence.

Cry 'O, sweet creature!', then kiss me hard,
As if he plucked up kisses by the roots,
That grew upon my lips, lay his leg o'er my thigh,
And sigh, and kiss, and then cry 'Cursèd fate,
430   That gave thee to the Moor!'
OTHELLO   O, monstrous, monstrous!
IAGO   Nay, this was but his dream.
OTHELLO   But this denoted a foregone conclusion.°   *an earlier event*
IAGO   'Tis a shrewd doubt,° though it be but a dream,   *reasonable fear*
435   And this may help to thicken other proofs
That do demonstrate thinly.
OTHELLO   I'll tear her all to pieces.
IAGO   Nay, yet be wise; yet we see nothing done.
She may be honest yet. Tell me but this:
Have you not sometimes seen a handkerchief
440   Spotted with strawberries in your wife's hand?
OTHELLO   I gave her such a one. 'Twas my first gift.
IAGO   I know not that, but such a handkerchief—
I am sure it was your wife's—did I today
See Cassio wipe his beard with.
OTHELLO   If it be that—
445   IAGO   If it be that, or any that was hers,
It speaks against her with the other proofs.
OTHELLO   O that the slave° had forty thousand lives!   *(Cassio)*
One is too poor, too weak for my revenge.
Now do I see 'tis true. Look here, Iago.
450   All my fond love thus do I blow to heaven—'tis gone.
Arise, black vengeance, from the hollow hell.
Yield up, O love, thy crown and hearted throne°   *rule of the heart*
To tyrannous hate! Swell, bosom, with thy freight,°   *burden*
For 'tis of aspics'° tongues.   *poison snakes'*
IAGO   Yet be content.
OTHELLO   O, blood, blood, blood!
455   IAGO   Patience, I say. Your mind may change.
OTHELLO   Never, Iago. Like to the Pontic Sea,°   *Black Sea*
Whose icy current and compulsive course
Ne'er knows retiring ebb, but keeps due on
To the Propontic and the Hellespont,[9]
460   Even so my bloody thoughts with violent pace
Shall ne'er look back, ne'er ebb to humble love,
Till that a capable° and wide revenge   *capacious*
Swallow them up.
[*He kneels*]
                              Now, by yon marble heaven,
In the due reverence of a sacred vow
I here engage my words.
465   IAGO   Do not rise yet.
          IAGO *kneels*[1]
Witness you ever-burning lights above,
You elements that clip° us round about,   *embrace (sexual?)*
Witness that here Iago doth give up

---

9. The Propontic was the body of water bounded by the straits of Bosphorus and the Dardanelles (Hellespont), the latter strait leading to the Aegean.
1. Parody of the marriage ceremony.

The execution° of his wit, hands, heart   *command*
470 To wronged Othello's service. Let him command,
And to obey shall be in me remorse,°   *pity (for Othello)*
What bloody business ever.°   *soever*
    [*They rise*]
OTHELLO   I greet thy love,
Not with vain thanks, but with acceptance bounteous,
And will upon the instant put thee to't.°   *immediately test it*
475 Within these three days let me hear thee say
That Cassio's not alive.
IAGO   My friend is dead.
'Tis done at your request; but let her live.
OTHELLO   Damn her, lewd minx!° O, damn her, damn her!   *wanton*
Come, go with me apart. I will withdraw
480 To furnish me with some swift means of death
For the fair devil. Now art thou my lieutenant.
IAGO   I am your own for ever.   *Exeunt*

3.4

Enter DESDEMONA, EMILIA, *and the* CLOWN

DESDEMONA   Do you know, sirrah,[1] where Lieutenant Cassio
lies?
CLOWN   I dare not say he lies anywhere.
DESDEMONA   Why, man?
5 CLOWN   He's a soldier, and for me to say a soldier lies, 'tis stab-
bing.
DESDEMONA   Go to. Where lodges he?
CLOWN   To tell you where he lodges is to tell you where I lie.
DESDEMONA   Can anything be made of this?
10 CLOWN   I know not where he lodges, and for me to devise a
lodging and say he lies here, or he lies there, were to lie in
mine own throat.°   *lie outrageously*
DESDEMONA   Can you enquire him out, and be edified by
report?
15 CLOWN   I will catechize the world for him; that is, make ques-
tions, and by them answer.
DESDEMONA   Seek him, bid him come hither, tell him I have
moved° my lord on his behalf, and hope all will be well.   *petitioned*
CLOWN   To do this is within the compass° of man's wit, and   *scope*
20 therefore I will attempt the doing it.   *Exit*
DESDEMONA   Where should° I lose the handkerchief, Emilia?   *did*
EMILIA   I know not, madam.
DESDEMONA   Believe me, I had rather have lost my purse
Full of crusadoes,° and but° my noble Moor   *gold coins / but that*
25 Is true of mind, and made of no such baseness
As jealous creatures are, it were enough
To put him to ill thinking.
EMILIA   Is he not jealous?
DESDEMONA   Who, he? I think the sun where he was born
Drew all such humours from him.
    Enter OTHELLO
EMILIA   Look where he comes.
30 DESDEMONA   I will not leave him now till Cassio

3.4 Location: Before the citadel.   1. A form of address to an inferior.

Be called to him. How is't with you, my lord?

OTHELLO   Well, my good lady. [*Aside*] O hardness to dissemble!—
How do you, Desdemona?

DESDEMONA   Well, my good lord.

OTHELLO   Give me your hand. This hand is moist, my lady.

35   DESDEMONA   It hath felt no age, nor known no sorrow.

OTHELLO   This argues fruitfulness and liberal heart.[2]
Hot, hot and moist—this hand of yours requires
A sequester from liberty; fasting, and prayer,
Much castigation, exercise devout,

40   For here's a young and sweating devil here
That commonly rebels. 'Tis a good hand,
A frank° one.   *(sexually) open*

DESDEMONA   You may indeed say so,
For 'twas that hand that gave away my heart.

OTHELLO   A liberal hand. The hearts of old gave hands,

45   But our new heraldry is hands, not hearts.[3]

DESDEMONA   I cannot speak of this. Come now, your promise.

OTHELLO   What promise, chuck?°   *woodchuck (affectionate)*

DESDEMONA   I have sent to bid Cassio come speak with you.

OTHELLO   I have a salt and sorry rheum° offends me.   *badly watering eyes*
Lend me thy handkerchief.

50   DESDEMONA [*offering a handkerchief*]   Here, my lord.

OTHELLO   That which I gave you.

DESDEMONA   I have it not about me.

OTHELLO   Not?

DESDEMONA   No, faith, my lord.

OTHELLO   That's a fault. That handkerchief
Did an Egyptian to my mother give.

55   She was a charmer,° and could almost read   *sorceress*
The thoughts of people. She told her, while she kept it
'Twould make her amiable,° and subdue my father   *desirable*
Entirely to her love; but if she lost it,
Or made a gift of it, my father's eye

60   Should hold her loathèd, and his spirits should hunt
After new fancies. She, dying, gave it me,
And bid me, when my fate would have me wived,
To give it her.° I did so, and take heed on't.   *to my wife*
Make it a darling, like your precious eye.

65   To lose't or give't away were such perdition°   *loss; damnation*
As nothing else could match.

DESDEMONA   Is't possible?

OTHELLO   'Tis true. There's magic in the web of it.
A sibyl° that had numbered in the world   *female prophet*
The sun to course two hundred compasses[4]

70   In her prophetic fury sewed the work.
The worms were hallowed that did breed the silk,
And it was dyed in mummy,[5] which the skilful
Conserved of° maidens' hearts.   *Preserved out of*

DESDEMONA   I'faith, is't true?

---

2. This demonstrates fertility (perhaps, by implication, lust) and a generous (loose) heart. A moist hand was thought to be a sign of active desire.
3. These days the joining of hands doesn't signify the joining of hearts.
4. *that . . . compasses*: who was two hundred years old.
5. Fluid drained from mummified bodies, supposedly magical.

OTHELLO   Most veritable. Therefore look to't well.
75 DESDEMONA   Then would to God that I had never seen it!
OTHELLO   Ha, wherefore?
DESDEMONA   Why do you speak so startingly and rash?
OTHELLO   Is't lost? Is't gone? Speak, is't out o'th' way?
DESDEMONA   Heaven bless us!
80 OTHELLO   Say you?
DESDEMONA   It is not lost, but what an if° it were?   *an if=if*
OTHELLO   How?
DESDEMONA   I say it is not lost.
OTHELLO   Fetch't, let me see't.
DESDEMONA   Why, so I can, sir, but I will not now.
85   This is a trick to put me from my suit.
        Pray you let Cassio be received again.
OTHELLO   Fetch me the handkerchief. My mind misgives.
DESDEMONA   Come, come, you'll never meet a more sufficient° man.   *complete*
OTHELLO   The handkerchief.
DESDEMONA   I pray, talk me of Cassio.
OTHELLO   The handkerchief.
90 DESDEMONA   A man that all his time
        Hath founded his good fortunes on your love,
        Shared dangers with you—
OTHELLO   The handkerchief.
DESDEMONA   I'faith, you are to blame.
95 OTHELLO   'Swounds!   *Exit*
EMILIA   Is not this man jealous?
DESDEMONA   I ne'er saw this before.
        Sure there's some wonder in this handkerchief.
        I am most unhappy in the loss of it.
EMILIA   'Tis not a year or two shows us a man.[6]
100   They are all but° stomachs, and we all but food.   *nothing but*
        They eat us hungrily, and when they are full,
        They belch us.
                Enter IAGO *and* CASSIO
                     Look you, Cassio and my husband.
IAGO [*to* CASSIO]   There is no other way. 'Tis she must do't,
        And lo, the happiness![7] Go and importune her.
105 DESDEMONA   How now, good Cassio? What's the news with you?
CASSIO   Madam, my former suit. I do beseech you
        That by your virtuous means I may again
        Exist and be a member of his love
        Whom I, with all the office of my heart,
110   Entirely honour. I would not be delayed.
        If my offence be of such mortal° kind   *deadly*
        That nor° my service past, nor present sorrows,   *neither*
        Nor purposed merit in futurity
        Can ransom me into his love again,
115   But to know so° must be my benefit.   *Even to know this*
        So° shall I clothe me in a forced content,   *If so*
        And shut° myself up in some other course   *give*
        To fortune's alms.
DESDEMONA   Alas, thrice-gentle Cassio!

6. Probably: It doesn't take long to see what men are   7. What a happy coincidence (seeing Desdemona).
made of.

My advocation is not now in tune.[8]
My lord is not my lord, nor should I know him
Were he in favour° as in humour altered.   *appearance*
So help me every spirit sanctified
As I have spoken for you all my best,
And stood within the blank of° his displeasure   *in the aim of*
For my free speech! You must a while be patient.
What I can do I will, and more I will
Than for myself I dare. Let that suffice you.

IAGO   Is my lord angry?

EMILIA   He went hence but now,
And certainly in strange unquietness.

IAGO   Can he be angry? I have seen the cannon
When it hath blown his ranks into the air,
And, like the devil, from his very arm
Puffed his own brother;[9] and is he angry?
Something of moment then. I will go meet him.
There's matter in't indeed, if he be angry.

DESDEMONA   I prithee do so.   *Exit* IAGO
                  Something sure of state,[1]
Either from Venice or some unhatched practice°   *unfinished plot*
Made demonstrable here in Cyprus to him,
Hath puddled his clear spirit; and in such cases
Men's natures wrangle with inferior things,
Though great ones are their object. 'Tis even so;
For let our finger ache and it indues°   *induces*
Our other, healthful members even to a sense
Of pain. Nay, we must think men are not gods,
Nor of them look for such observancy°   *careful attention*
As fits the bridal.° Beshrew me° much, Emilia,   *wedding / (mild curse)*
I was—unhandsome° warrior as I am—   *unskilled*
Arraigning his unkindness with my soul;
But now I find I had suborned the witness,
And he's indicted falsely.[2]

EMILIA   Pray heaven it be
State matters, as you think, and no conception
Nor no jealous toy° concerning you.   *whim*

DESDEMONA   Alas the day, I never gave him cause.

EMILIA   But jealous souls will not be answered so.
They are not ever jealous for the cause,
But jealous for they're jealous. It is a monster
Begot upon itself, born on itself.

DESDEMONA   Heaven keep the monster from Othello's mind.

EMILIA   Lady, amen.

DESDEMONA   I will go seek him. Cassio, walk here about.
If I do find him fit I'll move your suit,
And seek to effect it to my uttermost.

CASSIO   I humbly thank your ladyship.
             Exeunt DESDEMONA *and* EMILIA

---

8. My advocacy isn't working properly.
9. Blew up his own brother (and Othello wasn't angry even then).

1. Surely some official business.
2. *suborned . . . falsely*: made the witness lie and so accused Othello falsely.

Enter BIANCA[3]

BIANCA   Save you,° friend Cassio.   *God save you*

CASSIO   What make° you from home?   *brings*

165   How is't with you, my most fair Bianca?
       I'faith, sweet love, I was coming to your house.

BIANCA   And I was going to your lodging, Cassio.
       What, keep a week away? Seven days and nights,
       Eightscore-eight hours, and lovers' absent hours

170   More tedious than the dial eightscore times![4]
       O weary reckoning!°   *calculating*

CASSIO   Pardon me, Bianca,
       I have this while with leaden thoughts been pressed,
       But I shall in a more continuate° time   *opportune*
       Strike off° this score of absence. Sweet Bianca,   *Make up*
       Take me this work out.°   *Copy this embroidery*

       [*He gives her Desdemona's napkin*]

175   BIANCA   O Cassio, whence came this?
       This is some token from a newer friend.
       To the felt absence now I feel a cause.
       Is't come to this? Well, well.

CASSIO   Go to,° woman.   *Stop it*
       Throw your vile guesses in the devil's teeth,

180   From whence you have them. You are jealous now
       That this is from some mistress, some remembrance.
       No, by my faith, Bianca.

BIANCA   Why, whose is it?

CASSIO   I know not, neither. I found it in my chamber.
       I like the work well. Ere it be demanded°—   *sought out*

185   As like° enough it will—I would have it copied.   *likely*
       Take it, and do't, and leave me for this time.

BIANCA   Leave you? Wherefore?

CASSIO   I do attend here on the general,
       And think it no addition,° nor my wish,   *(to my cause)*
       To have him see me womaned.

190   BIANCA   Why, I pray you?

CASSIO   Not that I love you not.

BIANCA   But that you do not love me.
       I pray you bring me on the way a little,
       And say if I shall see you soon at night.

CASSIO   'Tis but a little way that I can bring you,

195   For I attend here; but I'll see you soon.

BIANCA   'Tis very good. I must be circumstanced.[5]

                                                      Exeunt

                          4.1

       Enter IAGO *and* OTHELLO

IAGO   Will you think so?

OTHELLO   Think so, Iago?

IAGO   What, to kiss in private?

OTHELLO   An unauthorized kiss.

---

3. "Bianca" means "white" in Italian—perhaps part of the play's ironic reversal of conventional color imagery, given that Bianca is a "customer" (courtesan, 4.1.117).
4. *lovers' . . . times:* each hour lovers are parted is eight

score (160) times more tedious than normal clock time.
5. Content with what circumstances offer.
4.1 Location: Before the citadel.

IAGO   Or to be naked with her friend in bed
    An hour or more, not meaning any harm?
5 OTHELLO   Naked in bed, Iago, and not mean harm?
    It is hypocrisy against the devil.[1]
    They that mean virtuously and yet do so,
    The devil their virtue tempts, and they tempt heaven.[2]
  IAGO   If they do nothing, 'tis a venial slip.°   *an excusable sin*
10 But if I give my wife a handkerchief—
  OTHELLO   What then?
  IAGO   Why then, 'tis hers, my lord, and being hers,
    She may, I think, bestow't on any man.
  OTHELLO   She is protectress of her honour, too.
15 May she give that?
  IAGO   Her honour is an essence that's not seen.
    They° have it very oft that have it not.   *They are reputed to*
    But for the handkerchief—
  OTHELLO   By heaven, I would most gladly have forgot it.
20 Thou said'st—O, it comes o'er my memory
    As doth the raven o'er the infectious house,[3]
    Boding to all!—he had my handkerchief.
  IAGO   Ay, what of that?
  OTHELLO   That's not so good now.
  IAGO   What if I had said I had seen him do you wrong,
25 Or heard him say—as knaves be such abroad,[4]
    Who having by their own importunate suit
    Or voluntary dotage of some mistress
    Convincèd or supplied° them, cannot choose   *Seduced or satisfied*
    But they must blab—
  OTHELLO   Hath he said anything?
30 IAGO   He hath, my lord. But, be you well assured,
    No more than he'll unswear.
  OTHELLO   What hath he said?
  IAGO   Faith, that he did—I know not what he did.
  OTHELLO   What, what?
  IAGO   Lie—
  OTHELLO   With her?
  IAGO   With her, on her, what
      you will.
  OTHELLO   Lie with her? Lie on her? We say 'lie on her' when
35 they belie° her. Lie with her? 'Swounds, that's fulsome!°   *slander / nauseating*
    Handkerchief—confessions—handkerchief. To[5] confess and be
    hanged for his labour. First to be hanged and then to confess!
    I tremble at it. Nature would not invest herself in such shadow-
    ing passion without some instruction.[6] It is not words that
40 shakes me thus. Pish! Noses, ears, and lips! Is't possible? Con-
    fess? Handkerchief? O devil!
        He falls down in a trance

1. *Naked . . . devil:* By showing every sign of commit-
ting adultery but then stopping just in time, they delib-
erately mislead the devil, who wrongly takes their
apparent intention to sin at face value (just as an ordi-
nary hypocrite deceives by professing virtue).
2. *They . . . heaven:* Those who mean well ("virtuously")
but act in this lascivious fashion ("so") make it easy for the
devil successfully to tempt them, and they push heaven to
the point where it may not be able to forgive them (?).

3. The raven was thought to be an ill omen and a car-
rier of plague. *infectious:* plague-infested.
4. As such knaves do exist in the world.
5. Lines 36–41 do not appear in Q. Arguably, these
lines provide more time for Othello to drive himself to
distraction and hence make his collapse more plausible.
6. *Nature . . . instruction:* It isn't natural that I would
feel such overwhelming ("shadowing") emotion (jeal-
ousy) unless there were some cause for it.

IAGO   Work on; my medicine works. Thus credulous fools are caught,
    And many worthy and chaste dames even thus,
    All guiltless, meet reproach. What ho, my lord!
    My lord, I say. Othello!
          Enter CASSIO

45   How now, Cassio?
CASSIO   What's the matter?
IAGO   My lord is fall'n into an epilepsy.
    This is his second fit. He had one yesterday.
CASSIO   Rub him about the temples.
IAGO   No, forbear.
50   The lethargy° must have his° quiet course.   *trance / its*
    If not, he foams at mouth, and by and by
    Breaks out to savage madness. Look, he stirs.
    Do you withdraw yourself a little while,
    He will recover straight.° When he is gone   *immediately*
55   I would on great occasion° speak with you.   [*Exit* CASSIO]   *important matters*
    How is it, general? Have you not hurt your head?[7]
OTHELLO   Dost thou mock me?
IAGO   I mock you not, by heaven.
    Would you would bear your fortune like a man.
OTHELLO   A hornèd man's a monster and a beast.
60 IAGO   There's many a beast then in a populous city,
    And many a civil° monster.   *city-dwelling*
OTHELLO   Did he confess it?
IAGO   Good sir, be a man.
    Think every bearded fellow that's but yoked
65   May draw with you.[8] There's millions now alive
    That nightly lie in those unproper beds
    Which they dare swear peculiar.[9] Your case is better.
    O, 'tis the spite of hell, the fiend's arch-mock,°   *devil's greatest mock*
    To lip° a wanton in a secure° couch   *kiss / an unsuspected*
70   And to suppose her chaste! No, let me know,
    And knowing what I am,° I know what she shall be.   *(a cuckold)*
OTHELLO   O, thou art wise, 'tis certain.
IAGO   Stand you a while apart.
    Confine yourself but in a patient list.°   *boundary*
    Whilst you were here, o'erwhelmèd with your grief—
75   A passion most unsuiting such a man—
    Cassio came hither. I shifted him away,
    And laid good 'scuse upon your ecstasy,°   *for your fit*
    Bade him anon return and here speak with me,
    The which he promised. Do but encave° yourself,   *hide*
80   And mark the fleers,° the gibes and notable scorns   *sneers*
    That dwell in every region of his face.
    For I will make him tell the tale anew,
    Where, how, how oft, how long ago, and when
    He hath and is again to cope° your wife.   *copulate with*
85   I say, but mark his gesture. Marry, patience,
    Or I shall say you're all-in-all in spleen,°   *completely impulsive*
    And nothing of a man.

---

7. Othello takes this as suggesting that he has grown
cuckold's horns.
8. *every . . . you:* every married man ("yoked," like an
ox, to his wife and hence to cuckoldry) labors ("draws")
under the same fate.
9. *That . . . peculiar:* Who lie in beds that don't belong
entirely to them but that they would swear are exclu-
sively their own.

OTHELLO   Dost thou hear, Iago?
I will be found most cunning in my patience,
But—dost thou hear?—most bloody.

IAGO   That's not amiss,
90   But yet keep time° in all. Will you withdraw?   *maintain control*
        [OTHELLO *stands apart*]
Now will I question Cassio of Bianca,
A hussy that by selling her desires
Buys herself bread and cloth. It is a creature
That dotes on Cassio—as 'tis the strumpet's plague
95   To beguile many and be beguiled by one.
He, when he hears of her, cannot restrain
From the excess of laughter.
        Enter CASSIO
                                        Here he comes.
As he shall smile, Othello shall go mad;
And his unbookish° jealousy must conster°   *ignorant / construe*
100 Poor Cassio's smiles, gestures, and light behaviours
Quite in the wrong. How do you now, lieutenant?

CASSIO   The worser that you give me the addition
Whose want even kills me.

IAGO   Ply Desdemona well and you are sure on't.
105 Now, if this suit lay in Bianca's power,
How quickly should you speed!

CASSIO [*laughing*]   Alas, poor caitiff!°   *wretch*

OTHELLO [*aside*]   Look how he laughs already.

IAGO   I never knew a woman love man so.

110 CASSIO   Alas, poor rogue! I think i'faith she loves me.

OTHELLO [*aside*]   Now he denies it faintly, and laughs it out.

IAGO   Do you hear, Cassio?

OTHELLO [*aside*]   Now he importunes him
To tell it o'er. Go to, well said, well said.

IAGO   She gives it out that you shall marry her.
Do you intend it?

115 CASSIO   Ha, ha, ha!

OTHELLO [*aside*]   Do ye triumph, Roman,[1] do you triumph?

CASSIO   I marry! What, a customer?° Prithee, bear some charity   *courtesan*
to my wit°—do not think it so unwholesome. Ha, ha, ha!   *sense*

OTHELLO [*aside*]   So, so, so, so. They laugh that wins.

120 IAGO   Faith, the cry goes that you marry her.

CASSIO   Prithee, say true.

IAGO   I am a very villain else.°   *if it's not true*

OTHELLO [*aside*]   Ha' you scored° me? Well.   *scored off*

CASSIO   This is the monkey's own giving out.° She is persuaded   *Bianca's own story*
125 I will marry her out of her own love and flattery, not out of my
promise.

OTHELLO [*aside*]   Iago beckons me. Now he begins the story.
        [OTHELLO *draws closer*]

CASSIO   She was here even now. She haunts me in every place.
I was the other day talking on the sea-bank with certain Vene-
130 tians, and thither comes the bauble,° and falls me thus about   *toy*
my neck.

---

1. Perhaps Othello draws on associations either with Rome's imperial successes (and subsequent collapse) or with the
Roman practice of holding celebratory processions.

OTHELLO [*aside*]   Crying 'O dear Cassio!' as it were. His gesture
imports° it.   *indicates*

CASSIO   So hangs and lolls and weeps upon me, so shakes and
135   pulls me—ha, ha, ha!

OTHELLO [*aside*]   Now he tells how she plucked him to my
chamber. O, I see that nose of yours, but not that dog I shall
throw it to!²

CASSIO   Well, I must leave her company.

Enter BIANCA

140   IAGO   Before me, look where she comes.

CASSIO   'Tis such another fitchew!³ Marry, a perfumed one. [*To*
BIANCA] What do you mean by this haunting of me?

BIANCA   Let the devil and his dam° haunt you. What did you   *mother*
mean by that same handkerchief you gave me even now? I was
145   a fine fool to take it. I must take out° the whole work—a likely   *copy*
piece of work,° that you should find it in your chamber and   *an implausible story*
know not who left it there. This is some minx's token, and I
must take out the work. There, give it your hobby-horse.° [*Giv-*   *loose woman*
ing CASSIO *the napkin*] Wheresoever you had it, I'll take out
150   no work on't.

CASSIO   How now, my sweet Bianca, how now, how now?

OTHELLO [*aside*]   By heaven, that should° be my handkerchief.   *must*

BIANCA   An° you'll come to supper tonight, you may. An you will   *If*
not, come when you are next prepared for.⁴   *Exit*

155   IAGO   After her, after her.

CASSIO   Faith, I must, she'll rail in the streets else.

IAGO   Will you sup there?

CASSIO   Faith, I intend so.

IAGO   Well, I may chance to see you, for I would very fain speak
160   with you.

CASSIO   Prithee, come, will you?

IAGO   Go to, say no more.   *Exit* CASSIO

OTHELLO   How shall I murder him, Iago?

IAGO   Did you perceive how he laughed at his vice?

165   OTHELLO   O Iago!

IAGO   And did you see the handkerchief?

OTHELLO   Was that mine?

IAGO   Yours, by this hand. And to see how he prizes the foolish
woman your wife. She gave it him, and he hath given it his
170   whore.

OTHELLO   I would have him nine years a-killing.⁵ A fine woman,
a fair woman, a sweet woman.

IAGO   Nay, you must forget that.

OTHELLO   Ay, let her rot and perish, and be damned tonight, for
175   she shall not live. No, my heart is turned to stone; I strike it,
and it hurts my hand. O, the world hath not a sweeter creature!
She might lie by an emperor's side, and command him tasks.

IAGO   Nay, that's not your way.°   *(the way to think)*

OTHELLO   Hang her, I do but say what she is—so delicate with
180   her needle, an admirable musician. O, she will sing the savage-
ness out of a bear! Of so high and plenteous wit and invention.°   *imagination*

---

2. *I see . . . to:* I'm envisioning my revenge, but the time
is not yet quite right. Cutting off the enemy's nose was
understood as a form of retribution.
3. Polecat, associated with prostitutes because of its

bad smell and presumed lecherousness.
4. Come next time I prepare for you (never).
5. I would spend nine years killing him.

IAGO   She's the worse for all this.

OTHELLO   O, a thousand, a thousand times! And then of so gen-
tle° a condition.   *highly born*

185   IAGO   Ay, too gentle.°   *generous (sexually)*

OTHELLO   Nay, that's certain. But yet the pity of it, Iago. O, Iago,
the pity of it, Iago!

IAGO   If you are so fond° over her iniquity, give her patent° to   *foolish / license*
offend; for if it touch not you, it comes near nobody.

190   OTHELLO   I will chop her into messes.° Cuckold me!   *pieces of food*

IAGO   O, 'tis foul in her.

OTHELLO   With mine officer.

IAGO   That's fouler.

OTHELLO   Get me some poison, Iago, this night. I'll not expostu-
195   late with her, lest her body and beauty unprovide my mind°   *weaken my resolve*
again. This night, Iago.

IAGO   Do it not with poison. Strangle her in her bed, even the
bed she hath contaminated.

OTHELLO   Good, good, the justice of it pleases, very good.

200   IAGO   And for Cassio, let me be his undertaker.° You shall hear   *murderer*
more by midnight.

OTHELLO   Excellent good.

       A trumpet

What trumpet is that same?

IAGO   I warrant, something from Venice.

       Enter LODOVICO, DESDEMONA, *and attendants*

205   'Tis Lodovico. This comes from the Duke. See, your wife's with
him.

LODOVICO   God save the worthy general.

OTHELLO   With all my heart,° sir.   *Thank you*

LODOVICO   [*giving* OTHELLO *a letter*]   The Duke and the senators
210   of Venice greet you.

OTHELLO   I kiss the instrument° of their pleasures.°   *bearer / commands*

       [*He reads the letter*]

DESDEMONA   And what's the news, good cousin Lodovico?

IAGO   [*to* LODOVICO]   I am very glad to see you, signor. Welcome
to Cyprus.

215   LODOVICO   I thank you. How does Lieutenant Cassio?

IAGO   Lives, sir.

DESDEMONA   Cousin, there's fall'n between him and my lord
An unkind° breach. But you shall make all well.   *unnatural*

OTHELLO   Are you sure of that?

220   DESDEMONA   My lord.

OTHELLO   [*reads*]   'This fail you not to do as you will'—

LODOVICO   He did not call, he's busy in the paper.
Is there division 'twixt my lord and Cassio?

DESDEMONA   A most unhappy one. I would do much
225   T'atone° them, for the love I bear to Cassio.   *To reconcile*

OTHELLO   Fire and brimstone!

DESDEMONA   My lord?

OTHELLO   Are you wise?

DESDEMONA   What, is he angry?

LODOVICO   Maybe the letter moved him,
For, as I think, they do command him home,
Deputing Cassio in his government.°   *official position*

230   DESDEMONA   By my troth, I am glad on't.

OTHELLO   Indeed!

DESDEMONA   My lord?

OTHELLO [*to* DESDEMONA]   I am glad to see you mad.[6]

DESDEMONA   Why, sweet Othello!

235   OTHELLO   Devil!

[*He strikes her*]

DESDEMONA   I have not deserved this.

LODOVICO   My lord, this would not be believed in Venice,
    Though I should swear I saw't. 'Tis very much.°   *going too far*
    Make her amends, she weeps.

OTHELLO   O, devil, devil!

240   If that the earth could teem with° woman's tears,   *become pregnant by*
    Each drop she falls would prove a crocodile.[7]
    Out of my sight!

DESDEMONA [*going*]   I will not stay to offend you.

LODOVICO   Truly, an obedient lady.
    I do beseech your lordship call her back.

245   OTHELLO   Mistress!

DESDEMONA [*returning*]   My lord?

OTHELLO [*to* LODOVICO]   What would you° with her, sir?   *do you wish*

LODOVICO   Who, I, my lord?

OTHELLO   Ay, you did wish that I would make her turn.°   *return*

250   Sir, she can turn and turn,° and yet go on   *(sexually)*
    And turn again, and she can weep, sir, weep,
    And she's obedient, as you say, obedient,
    Very obedient. [*To* DESDEMONA] Proceed you in your tears.
    [*To* LODOVICO] Concerning this, sir—[*To* DESDEMONA] O well
        painted passion!
    [*To* LODOVICO] I am commanded home. [*To* DESDEMONA] Get
255   you away.
    I'll send for you anon. [*To* LODOVICO] Sir, I obey the mandate,
    And will return to Venice. [*To* DESDEMONA] Hence, avaunt!°   *begone*

                              [*Exit* DESDEMONA]

    [*To* LODOVICO] Cassio shall have my place, and, sir, tonight
    I do entreat that we may sup together.

260   You are welcome, sir, to Cyprus. Goats and monkeys![8]   *Exit*

LODOVICO   Is this the noble Moor whom our full senate
    Call all-in-all sufficient? Is this the nature
    Whom passion could not shake, whose solid virtue
    The shot of accident nor dart of chance
    Could neither graze nor pierce?

265   IAGO   He is much changed.

LODOVICO   Are his wits safe? Is he not light of brain?

IAGO   He's that he is. I may not breathe my censure
    What he might be. If what he might he is not,
    I would to heaven he were.[9]

LODOVICO   What, strike his wife!

270   IAGO   Faith, that was not so well. Yet would I knew

---

6. Perhaps Othello is pleased that she's rejoicing in
Cassio's promotion and hence revealing their adulter-
ous affair, which she would be "mad" to do in public
and in front of him.
7. Each drop would cause the earth to conceive a croc-
odile (crocodiles proverbially wept false tears for their

victims).
8. Symbols of lust.
9. *I may . . . were:* I won't express my judgment on
whether he is sane. If he is sane, I wish he were insane
(because only that would excuse his bad behavior); if he
is not sane, I wish he were.

That stroke would prove the worst.

LODOVICO   Is it his use,°   *custom*
     Or did the letters work upon his blood°   *passions*
     And new-create his fault?

IAGO   Alas, alas.
     It is not honesty in me to speak
275   What I have seen and known. You shall observe him,
     And his own courses° will denote him so   *actions*
     That I may save my speech. Do but go after,
     And mark how he continues.

LODOVICO   I am sorry that I am deceived in him.   *Exeunt*

4.2

Enter OTHELLO *and* EMILIA

OTHELLO   You have seen nothing then?

EMILIA   Nor ever heard, nor ever did suspect.

OTHELLO   Yes, you have seen Cassio and she together.

EMILIA   But then I saw no harm, and then I heard
5   Each syllable that breath made up between 'em.

OTHELLO   What, did they never whisper?

EMILIA   Never, my lord.

OTHELLO   Nor send you out o'th' way?

EMILIA   Never.

10 OTHELLO   To fetch her fan, her gloves, her mask, nor nothing?

EMILIA   Never, my lord.

OTHELLO   That's strange.

EMILIA   I durst, my lord, to wager she is honest,
     Lay down my soul at stake. If you think other,
15   Remove your thought; it doth abuse your bosom.
     If any wretch ha' put this in your head,
     Let heaven requite it with the serpent's curse,[1]
     For if she be not honest, chaste, and true,
     There's no man happy; the purest of their wives
     Is foul as slander.

20 OTHELLO   Bid her come hither. Go.   *Exit* EMILIA
     She says enough, yet she's a simple bawd
     That cannot say as much.[2] This is a subtle whore,
     A closet lock and key° of villainous secrets,   *A hider*
     And yet she'll kneel and pray—I ha' seen her do't.

        Enter DESDEMONA *and* EMILIA

DESDEMONA   My lord, what is your will?

25 OTHELLO   Pray you, chuck, come hither.

DESDEMONA   What is your pleasure?

OTHELLO   Let me see your eyes.
     Look in my face.

DESDEMONA   What horrible fancy's this?

OTHELLO [*to* EMILIA]   Some of your function,[3] mistress.
30   Leave procreants° alone, and shut the door,   *copulators*
     Cough or cry 'Hem' if anybody come.
     Your mystery, your mystery°—nay, dispatch.   *Exit* EMILIA   *profession*

DESDEMONA   Upon my knees, what doth your speech import?

4.2 Location: The citadel.
1. In Genesis, the curse that God laid on the serpent who deceived Eve.

2. *yet . . . much:* yet it would be a simpleminded go-between who can't say as much as she did.
3. Fulfill your bawd's function by guarding the door.

I understand a fury in your words,
But not the words.

35 OTHELLO   Why, what art thou?

DESDEMONA   Your wife, my lord, your true and loyal wife.

OTHELLO   Come, swear it, damn thyself,
Lest, being° like one of heaven, the devils themselves   *appearing*
Should fear to seize thee. Therefore be double-damned:
Swear thou art honest.

40 DESDEMONA   Heaven doth truly know it.

OTHELLO   Heaven truly knows that thou art false as hell.

DESDEMONA   To whom, my lord? With whom? How am I false?

OTHELLO [*weeping*]   Ah, Desdemon, away, away, away!

DESDEMONA   Alas, the heavy day! Why do you weep?

45 Am I the motive of these tears, my lord?
If haply° you my father do suspect   *perhaps*
An instrument of this your calling back,
Lay not your blame on me. If you have lost him,
I have lost him too.

OTHELLO   Had it pleased God
50 To try me with affliction; had He rained
All kind of sores and shames on my bare head,
Steeped me in poverty to the very lips,
Given to captivity me and my utmost hopes,
I should have found in some place of my soul
55 A drop of patience. But, alas, to make me
The fixèd figure for the time of scorn
To point his slow and moving finger at⁴—
Yet could I bear that too, well, very well.
But there where I have garnered° up my heart,   *stored*
60 Where either I must live or bear no life,
The fountain⁵ from the which my current runs
Or else dries up—to be discarded thence,
Or keep it as a cistern for foul toads
To knot and gender° in! Turn thy complexion there,   *To couple and engender*
65 Patience,⁶ thou young and rose-lipped cherubin,
Ay, here look grim as hell.

DESDEMONA   I hope my noble lord esteems me honest.

OTHELLO   O, ay—as summer flies are in the shambles,°   *slaughterhouse*
That quicken even with blowing.⁷ O thou weed,
70 Who art so lovely fair, and smell'st so sweet,
That the sense aches at thee—would thou hadst ne'er been born!

DESDEMONA   Alas, what ignorant sin have I committed?

OTHELLO   Was this fair paper, this most goodly book,
Made to write 'whore' upon? What committed?
75 Committed?⁸ O thou public commoner,°   *prostitute*
I should make very forges of my cheeks,
That would to cinders burn up modesty,
Did I but speak thy deeds. What committed?

---

4. *The fixed . . . at:* The designated object of scorn for this scornful time to point (as on a clock face) its slowly moving hand at.
5. Spring. The language here imagines Desdemona as the source of Othello's potential offspring.
6. *Turn . . . / Patience:* Change color at the thought of that, Patience. Or perhaps Patience and the "cherubin"

(end of line) are Desdemona, whom Othello directs to gaze at his own face or a mirror.
7. Who come to life (or bring their offspring to life and hence make the meat foul) as soon as the eggs are deposited. The point seems to be the speed of breeding, inferred from Desdemona's supposed infidelity.
8. Lines 75–78 do not appear in Q.

Heaven stops the nose at it, and the moon winks;°   *closes its eyes*
80   The bawdy° wind, that kisses all it meets,   *promiscuous*
     Is hushed within the hollow mine of earth°   *within a cave*
     And will not hear't. What committed?
DESDEMONA   By heaven, you do me wrong.
OTHELLO   Are not you a strumpet?
85   DESDEMONA   No, as I am a Christian.
     If to preserve this vessel for my lord
     From any other foul unlawful touch
     Be not to be a strumpet, I am none.
OTHELLO   What, not a whore?
DESDEMONA   No, as I shall be saved.
90   OTHELLO   Is't possible?
DESDEMONA   O heaven forgive us!
OTHELLO   I cry you mercy° then.   *I beg your pardon*
     I took you for that cunning whore of Venice
     That married with Othello. [*Calling*] You, mistress,
95   That have the office opposite to Saint Peter
     And keeps the gate of hell,
          Enter EMILIA
                              you, you, ay, you.
     We ha' done our course.° [*Giving money*] There's money for your pains.   *business*
     I pray you, turn the key and keep our counsel.   *Exit*
EMILIA   Alas, what does this gentleman conceive?°   *believe*
100 How do you, madam? How do you, my good lady?
DESDEMONA   Faith, half asleep.
EMILIA   Good madam, what's the matter with my lord?
DESDEMONA   With who?
EMILIA   Why, with my lord, madam.
DESDEMONA   Who is thy lord?
EMILIA   He that is yours, sweet lady.
105 DESDEMONA   I ha' none. Do not talk to me, Emilia.
     I cannot weep, nor answers have I none
     But what should go by water.° Prithee tonight   *appear in tears*
     Lay on my bed my wedding sheets, remember.
     And call thy husband hither.
EMILIA   Here's a change indeed.   *Exit*
110 DESDEMONA   'Tis meet° I should be used so, very meet.   *fitting*
     How have I been behaved, that he might stick
     The small'st opinion on my least misuse?[9]
          Enter IAGO *and* EMILIA
IAGO   What is your pleasure, madam? How is't with you?
DESDEMONA   I cannot tell. Those that do teach young babes
115 Do it with gentle means and easy tasks.
     He might ha' chid me so, for, in good faith,
     I am a child to chiding.
IAGO   What is the matter, lady?
EMILIA   Alas, Iago, my lord hath so bewhored her,°   *called her whore*
     Thrown such despite° and heavy terms upon her,   *spite*
120 That true hearts cannot bear it.
DESDEMONA   Am I that name, Iago?
IAGO   What name, fair lady?
DESDEMONA   Such as she said my lord did say I was.

---

9. *that . . . misuse:* perhaps, which would cause him to suspect even slightly the least fault.

EMILIA   He called her whore. A beggar in his drink
125   Could not have laid such terms upon his callet.°   *whore*
IAGO   Why did he so?
DESDEMONA   I do not know. I am sure I am none such.
IAGO   Do not weep, do not weep. Alas the day!
EMILIA   Hath she forsook so many noble matches,
130   Her father and her country and her friends,
    To be called whore? Would it not make one weep?
DESDEMONA   It is my wretched fortune.
IAGO   Beshrew° him for't.   *Curse*
    How comes this trick° upon him?   *behavior*
DESDEMONA   Nay, heaven doth know.
EMILIA   I will be hanged if some eternal villain,
135   Some busy° and insinuating rogue,   *meddling*
    Some cogging,° cozening° slave, to get some office,   *deceiving / cheating*
    Have not devised this slander. I will be hanged else.
IAGO   Fie, there is no such man. It is impossible.
DESDEMONA   If any such there be, heaven pardon him.
140   EMILIA   A halter° pardon him, and hell gnaw his bones!   *hangman's noose*
    Why should he call her whore? Who keeps her company?
    What place, what time, what form, what likelihood?
    The Moor's abused by some most villainous knave,
    Some base, notorious knave, some scurvy fellow.
145   O heaven, that such companions thou'dst unfold,°   *reveal*
    And put in every honest hand a whip
    To lash the rascals naked through the world,
    Even from the east to th' west!
IAGO   Speak within door.°   *more softly*
EMILIA   O, fie upon them. Some such squire° he was   *fellow*
150   That turned your wit the seamy side without,°   *wrong side out*
    And made you to suspect me with the Moor.
IAGO   You are a fool. Go to.
DESDEMONA   O God, Iago,
    What shall I do to win my lord again?
    Good friend, go to him; for by this light of heaven,
    I know not how I lost him.
        [*She kneels*]
155   Here I kneel.[1]
    If e'er my will did trespass 'gainst his love,
    Either in discourse of thought or actual deed,
    Or that mine eyes, mine ears, or any sense
    Delighted them in any other form,[2]
160   Or that I do not yet,° and ever did,   *still*
    And ever will—though he do shake me off
    To beggarly divorcement—love him dearly,
    Comfort forswear me.° Unkindness may do much,   *Deny me divine solace*
    And his unkindness may defeat my life,
    But never taint my love.
        [*She rises*]
165   I cannot say 'whore'.
    It does abhor me[3] now I speak the word.

1. Lines 155–68 (beginning with "Here") do not appear in Q.
2. Took pleasure in anyone but him.
3. Fill me with abhorrence; make me abhorrent, with a pun on "ab-whore."

To do the act that might the addition° earn,   *label*
Not the world's mass of vanity° could make me.   *all worldly splendor*
IAGO   I pray you, be content. 'Tis but his humour.°   *mood*
170   The business of the state does him offence,
And he does chide with you.
DESDEMONA   If 'twere no other!
IAGO   It is but so, I warrant.
        [*Flourish within*]
Hark how these instruments summon you to supper.
175   The messengers of Venice stays the meat.°   *are waiting to eat*
Go in, and weep not. All things shall be well.
                    Exeunt DESDEMONA *and* EMILIA
        Enter RODERIGO
How now, Roderigo?
RODERIGO   I do not find that thou deal'st justly with me.
IAGO   What in the contrary?
180   RODERIGO   Every day thou daff'st me with some device,[4] Iago,
and rather, as it seems to me now, keep'st from me all conve-
niency° than suppliest me with the least advantage of hope. I   *opportunity*
will indeed no longer endure it, nor am I yet persuaded to put
up in peace what already I have foolishly suffered.
185   IAGO   Will you hear me, Roderigo?
RODERIGO   Faith, I have heard too much, for your words and
performances are no kin together.
IAGO   You charge me most unjustly.
RODERIGO   With naught but truth. I have wasted myself out of
190   my means. The jewels you have had from me to deliver Desde-
mona would half have corrupted a votarist.° You have told me   *nun*
she hath received 'em, and returned me expectations and com-
forts of sudden respect and acquaintance, but I find none.
IAGO   Well, go to,° very well.   *(expresses remonstrance)*
195   RODERIGO   'Very well', 'go to'! I cannot go to,° man, nor 'tis not   *succeed sexually*
very well. Nay, I think it is scurvy, and begin to find myself
fopped° in it.   *made a fool*
IAGO   Very well.
RODERIGO   I tell you 'tis not very well. I will make myself known
200   to Desdemona. If she will return me my jewels, I will give
over my suit and repent my unlawful solicitation. If not, assure
yourself I will seek satisfaction of you.
IAGO   You have said° now.   *finished*
RODERIGO   Ay, and said nothing but what I protest intendment
205   of doing.
IAGO   Why, now I see there's mettle in thee, and even from this
instant do build on thee a better opinion than ever before. Give
me thy hand, Roderigo. Thou hast taken against me a most just
exception, but yet I protest I have dealt most directly in thy
210   affair.
RODERIGO   It hath not appeared.
IAGO   I grant, indeed, it hath not appeared, and your suspicion
is not without wit and judgement. But, Roderigo, if thou hast
that in thee indeed which I have greater reason to believe now
215   than ever—I mean purpose, courage, and valour—this night
show it. If thou the next night following enjoy not Desdemona,

---

4. You put me off with some trick.

take me from this world with treachery, and devise engines
for° my life.   *plots against*

RODERIGO   Well, what is it? Is it within reason and compass?°   *possibility*

220   IAGO   Sir, there is especial commission come from Venice to
depute Cassio in Othello's place.

RODERIGO   Is that true? Why then, Othello and Desdemona
return again to Venice.

IAGO   O no, he goes into Mauritania,⁵ and takes away with him

225   the fair Desdemona, unless his abode be lingered here by some
accident, wherein none can be so determinate° as the remov-   *effectual*
ing of Cassio.

RODERIGO   How do you mean 'removing' of him?

IAGO   Why, by making him uncapable of Othello's place—

230   knocking out his brains.

RODERIGO   And that you would have me to do.

IAGO   Ay, if you dare do yourself a profit and a right. He sups
tonight with a harlotry, and thither will I go to him. He knows
not yet of his honourable fortune.° If you will watch his going   *his promotion*

235   thence, which I will fashion° to fall out between twelve and   *arrange*
one, you may take him at your pleasure. I will be near, to sec-
ond your attempt, and he shall fall between us. Come, stand
not amazed at it, but go along with me. I will show you such a
necessity in his death that you shall think yourself bound to put

240   it on him. It is now high supper-time, and the night grows to
waste. About it.

RODERIGO   I will hear further reason for this.

IAGO   And you shall be satisfied.   *Exeunt*

4.3

Enter OTHELLO, DESDEMONA, LODOVICO, EMILIA, *and*
attendants

LODOVICO   I do beseech you, sir, trouble yourself no further.

OTHELLO   O, pardon me, 'twill do me good to walk.

LODOVICO [*to* DESDEMONA]   Madam, good night. I humbly thank
your ladyship.

DESDEMONA   Your honour is most welcome.

OTHELLO   Will you walk, sir?

5   O, Desdemona!

DESDEMONA   My lord?

OTHELLO   Get you to bed on th'instant. I will be returned forth-
with. Dismiss your attendant there. Look't be done.

DESDEMONA   I will, my lord.

Exeunt [OTHELLO, LODOVICO, *and attendants*]

10   EMILIA   How goes it now? He looks gentler than he did.

DESDEMONA   He says he will return incontinent.°   *immediately*
He hath commanded me to go to bed,
And bid me to dismiss you.

EMILIA   Dismiss me?

DESDEMONA   It was his bidding. Therefore, good Emilia,

15   Give me my nightly wearing, and adieu.
We must not now displease him.

EMILIA   I would you had never seen him.

DESDEMONA   So would not I. My love doth so approve him

---

5. Country in the western Sahara.   **4.3** Location: Scene continues.

That even his stubbornness, his checks, his frowns—
20 Prithee unpin me—have grace and favour in them.
    [EMILIA *helps* DESDEMONA *to undress*]
EMILIA   I have laid those sheets you bade me on the bed.
DESDEMONA   All's one.° Good faith, how foolish are our minds!   *It doesn't matter*
If I do die before thee, prithee shroud me
In one of these same sheets.
EMILIA   Come, come, you talk.
25 DESDEMONA   My mother had a maid called Barbary.[1]
She was in love, and he she loved proved mad
And did forsake her. She had a song of willow.
An old thing 'twas, but it expressed her fortune,
And she died singing it. That song tonight
30 Will not go from my mind. I[2] have much to do
But to[3] go hang my head all at one side
And sing it, like poor Barbary. Prithee, dispatch.
EMILIA   Shall I go fetch your nightgown?
DESDEMONA   No. Unpin me here.
This Lodovico is a proper man.
EMILIA   A very handsome man.
35 DESDEMONA   He speaks well.
EMILIA   I know a lady in Venice would have walked barefoot to
Palestine for a touch of his nether lip.
DESDEMONA [*sings*]   'The poor soul sat sighing by a sycamore tree,
    Sing all a green willow.[4]
40 Her hand on her bosom, her head on her knee,
    Sing willow, willow, willow.
The fresh streams ran by her and murmured her moans,
    Sing willow, willow, willow.
Her salt tears fell from her and softened the stones,
45   Sing willow'—
Lay by these.—
            'willow, willow.'
Prithee, hie thee.° He'll come anon.   *hurry*
'Sing all a green willow must be my garland.
50 Let nobody blame him, his scorn I approve'—
Nay, that's not next. Hark, who is't that knocks?
EMILIA   It's the wind.
DESDEMONA [*sings*]   'I called my love false love, but what said he then?[5]
    Sing willow, willow, willow.
55 If I court more women, you'll couch with more men.'
So, get thee gone. Good night. Mine eyes do itch.
Doth that bode weeping?
EMILIA   'Tis neither here nor there.
DESDEMONA   I have heard it said so. O, these men, these men![6]
Dost thou in conscience think—tell me, Emilia—
60 That there be women do abuse their husbands
In such gross kind?°   *fashion*
EMILIA   There be some such, no question.
DESDEMONA   Wouldst thou do such a deed for all the world?
EMILIA   Why, would not you?

---

1. Iago compares Othello to a "Barbary horse" in 1.1.113.
2. Lines 30–51 ("I . . . next") do not appear in Q.
3. I can barely bring myself not to.
4. A conventional symbol of disappointed love.
5. Lines 53–55 do not appear in Q.
6. Lines 58–61 do not appear in Q.

DESDEMONA   No, by this heavenly light.

EMILIA   Nor I neither, by this heavenly light. I might do't as well
65   i'th' dark.

DESDEMONA   Wouldst thou do such a deed for all the world?

EMILIA   The world's a huge thing. It is a great price for a small
vice.

DESDEMONA   In truth, I think thou wouldst not.

70   EMILIA   In truth, I think I should, and undo't when I had done.
Marry, I would not do such a thing for a joint ring,[7] nor for
measures of lawn,° nor for gowns, petticoats, nor caps, nor any   *linen*
petty exhibition;° but for all the whole world? Ud's° pity, who   *gift / God's*
would not make her husband a cuckold to make him a mon-
75   arch? I should venture purgatory for't.

DESDEMONA   Beshrew me if I would do such a wrong
For the whole world.

EMILIA   Why, the wrong is but a wrong i'th' world, and having
the world for your labour, 'tis a wrong in your own world, and
80   you might quickly make it right.

DESDEMONA   I do not think there is any such woman.

EMILIA   Yes, a dozen, and as many
To th' vantage as would store the world they played for.[8]
But I do think it is their husbands' faults[9]
85   If wives do fall. Say that they slack their duties,°   *marital duties*
And pour our treasures into foreign laps,[1]
Or else break out in peevish jealousies,
Throwing restraint upon us; or say they strike us,
Or scant our former having in despite:[2]
90   Why, we have galls;° and though we have some grace,   *tempers*
Yet have we some revenge. Let husbands know
Their wives have sense like them. They see, and smell,
And have their palates both for sweet and sour,
As husbands have. What is it that they do
95   When they change us for others? Is it sport?
I think it is. And doth affection° breed it?   *lust*
I think it doth. Is't frailty that thus errs?
It is so, too. And have not we affections,
Desires for sport, and frailty, as men have?
100 Then let them use us well, else let them know
The ills we do, their ills instruct us so.

DESDEMONA   Good night, good night. God me such uses° send   *habits*
Not to pick bad from bad, but by bad mend![3]   *Exeunt*

5.1

Enter IAGO *and* RODERIGO

IAGO   Here, stand behind this bulk.° Straight° will he come.   *shop stall / Right away*
Wear thy good rapier bare, and put it home.°   *drive it into him*
Quick, quick, fear nothing. I'll be at thy elbow.
It makes us or it mars us. Think on that,
5   And fix most firm thy resolution.

RODERIGO   Be near at hand. I may miscarry in't.

---

7. A cheap ring in separable halves.
8. *and . . . for:* and as many more as it would take to
populate the world they gained by doing it.
9. Lines 84–101 do not appear in Q.
1. And give the semen that belongs to us to other women.

2. Or reduce our allowances out of spite.
3. Not to take bad behavior as an example, but to know
what to avoid.
5.1 Location: A street in Cyprus.

IAGO   Here at thy hand. Be bold, and take thy stand.
RODERIGO [*aside*]   I have no great devotion to the deed,
    And yet he hath given me satisfying reasons.
10   'Tis but a man gone. Forth my sword—he dies!
IAGO [*aside*]   I have rubbed this young quat° almost to the sense,°   *pimple / to the quick*
    And he grows angry. Now, whether he kill Cassio
    Or Cassio him, or each do kill the other,
    Every way makes my gain. Live Roderigo,°   *If Roderigo lives*
15   He calls me to a restitution large
    Of gold and jewels that I bobbed from him°   *defrauded him of*
    As gifts to Desdemona.
    It must not be. If Cassio do remain,
    He hath a daily beauty in his life
20   That makes me ugly; and besides, the Moor
    May unfold° me to him—there stand I in much peril.   *reveal*
    No, he must die. But so, I hear him coming.
        Enter CASSIO
RODERIGO   I know his gait, 'tis he. [*Attacking* CASSIO] Villain, thou diest.
CASSIO   That thrust had been mine enemy indeed,
25   But that my coat is better° than thou know'st.   *thicker; more armored*
    I will make proof of° thine.   *test*
        [*He stabs* RODERIGO, *who falls*]
RODERIGO   O, I am slain!
        [IAGO *wounds* CASSIO *in the leg from behind. Exit* IAGO]
CASSIO [*falling*]   I am maimed for ever. Help, ho, murder, murder!
        Enter OTHELLO [*above*]
OTHELLO   The voice of Cassio. Iago keeps his word.
RODERIGO   O, villain that I am!
30 OTHELLO   It is even so.
CASSIO   O, help, ho! Light, a surgeon!
OTHELLO   'Tis he. O brave Iago, honest and just,
    That hast such noble sense of thy friend's wrong—
    Thou teachest me. Minion,° your dear lies dead,   *Hussy*
35   And your unblessed fate hies.° Strumpet, I come.   *damnation hurries on*
    Forth of° my heart those charms, thine eyes, are blotted.   *Out of*
    Thy bed, lust-stained, shall with lust's blood be spotted. *Exit*
        Enter LODOVICO *and* GRAZIANO
CASSIO   What ho, no watch, no passage?° Murder, murder!   *passersby*
GRAZIANO   'Tis some mischance. The voice is very direful.
40 CASSIO   O, help!
LODOVICO   Hark.
RODERIGO   O wretched villain!
LODOVICO   Two or three groan. 'Tis heavy° night.   *dark*
    These may be counterfeits. Let's think't unsafe
45   To come into° the cry without more help.   *go near*
RODERIGO   Nobody come? Then shall I bleed to death.
        Enter IAGO *with a light*
LODOVICO   Hark.
GRAZIANO   Here's one comes in his shirt, with light and weapons.
IAGO   Who's there? Whose noise is this that cries on murder?
LODOVICO   We do not know.
50 IAGO   Do not you hear a cry?
CASSIO   Here, here. For heaven's sake, help me.
IAGO   What's the matter?
GRAZIANO [*to* LODOVICO]   This is Othello's ensign, as I take it.

LODOVICO   The same indeed, a very valiant fellow.

IAGO [to CASSIO]   What are you here that cry so grievously?

55 CASSIO   Iago—O, I am spoiled, undone by villains.
Give me some help.

IAGO   O me, lieutenant, what villains have done this?

CASSIO   I think that one of them is hereabout
And cannot make away.

IAGO   O treacherous villains!
[To LODOVICO and GRAZIANO] What are you there? Come in
60   and give some help.

RODERIGO   O, help me there!

CASSIO   That's one of 'em.

IAGO [stabbing RODERIGO]   O murderous slave! O villain!

RODERIGO   O damned Iago! O inhuman dog!

65 IAGO   Kill men i'th' dark? Where be these bloody thieves?
How silent is this town! Ho, murder, murder!
[To LODOVICO and GRAZIANO] What may you be? Are you of
good or evil?

LODOVICO   As you shall prove us, praise us.

IAGO   Signor Lodovico.

LODOVICO   He, sir.

70 IAGO   I cry you mercy. Here's Cassio hurt by villains.

GRAZIANO   Cassio?

IAGO   How is't, brother?

CASSIO   My leg is cut in two.

IAGO   Marry, heaven forbid!

75   Light, gentlemen. I'll bind it with my shirt.
                    Enter BIANCA

BIANCA   What is the matter, ho? Who is't that cried?

IAGO   Who is't that cried?

BIANCA   O my dear Cassio,
My sweet Cassio, O, Cassio, Cassio!

IAGO   O notable strumpet! Cassio, may you suspect
80   Who they should be that have thus mangled you?

CASSIO   No.

GRAZIANO   I am sorry to find you thus. I have been to seek you.

IAGO   Lend me a garter. So. O for a chair,°   litter
To bear him easily hence!

85 BIANCA   Alas, he faints. O, Cassio, Cassio, Cassio!

IAGO   Gentlemen all, I do suspect this trash
To be a party in this injury.
Patience a while, good Cassio. Come, come,
Lend me a light. [Going to RODERIGO] Know we this face or no?
90   Alas, my friend, and my dear countryman.
Roderigo? No—yes, sure—O heaven, Roderigo!

GRAZIANO   What, of Venice?

IAGO   Even he, sir. Did you know him?

GRAZIANO   Know him? Ay.

95 IAGO   Signor Graziano, I cry your gentle pardon.
These bloody accidents must excuse my manners
That so neglected you.

GRAZIANO   I am glad to see you.

IAGO   How do you, Cassio? O, a chair, a chair!

GRAZIANO   Roderigo.

IAGO   He, he, 'tis he.

[*Enter attendants with a chair*]

100 O, that's well said, the chair!
Some good man bear him carefully from hence.
I'll fetch the general's surgeon. [*To* BIANCA] For you, mistress,
Save you your labour. He that lies slain here, Cassio,
Was my dear friend. What malice was between you?
105 CASSIO   None in the world, nor do I know the man.
IAGO [*to* BIANCA]   What, look you pale? [*To attendants*] O, bear
        him out o'th' air.[1]
    [*To* LODOVICO *and* GRAZIANO] Stay you, good gentlemen.
            [*Exeunt attendants with* CASSIO *in the chair
                    and with Roderigo's body*]
    [*To* BIANCA]   Look you pale, mistress?
    [*To* LODOVICO *and* GRAZIANO] Do you perceive the ghastness° of her eye?   terror
    [*To* BIANCA] Nay, an° you stare we shall hear more anon.   if
110 [*To* LODOVICO *and* GRAZIANO] Behold her well; I pray you look upon her.
    Do you see, gentlemen? Nay, guiltiness
    Will speak, though tongues were out of use.
            Enter EMILIA
EMILIA   Alas, what is the matter? What is the matter, husband?
IAGO   Cassio hath here been set on in the dark
115 By Roderigo and fellows that are scaped.
    He's almost slain, and Roderigo dead.
EMILIA   Alas, good gentleman! Alas, good Cassio!
IAGO   This is the fruits of whoring. Prithee, Emilia,
    Go know of Cassio where he supped tonight.
120 [*To* BIANCA] What, do you shake at that?
BIANCA   He supped at my house, but I therefore shake not.
IAGO   O, did he so? I charge you go with me.
EMILIA [*to* BIANCA]   O, fie upon thee, strumpet!
BIANCA   I am no strumpet, but of life as honest
    As you that thus abuse me.
125 EMILIA   As I? Fough, fie upon thee!
IAGO   Kind gentlemen, let's go see poor Cassio dressed.
    [*To* BIANCA] Come, mistress, you must tell's another tale.
    Emilia, run you to the citadel
    And tell my lord and lady what hath happed.
    Will you go on afore?   [*Exit* EMILIA]
130 [*Aside*]   This is the night
    That either makes me or fordoes° me quite.   *Exeunt*   undoes

5.2

            Enter OTHELLO *with a light.* [*He draws back a curtain,
                    revealing*] DESDEMONA [*asleep*] *in her bed*
OTHELLO   It is the cause,[1] it is the cause, my soul.
    Let me not name it to you, you chaste stars.
    It is the cause. Yet I'll not shed her blood,
    Nor scar that whiter skin of hers than snow,
5   And smooth as monumental alabaster.°   stone used in tombs
    Yet she must die, else she'll betray more men.
    Put out the light, and then put out the light.[2]

---

1. Out of the open air (thought to be bad for wounds).
5.2 Location: Desdemona and Othello's bedroom.
1. What matters is Desdemona's infidelity; the "cause"
of justice, which Othello sees himself defending, as in
the subsequent lines.
2. This and the following lines compare the light of
Othello's lamp or torch to Desdemona's "light" of life.

If I quench thee, thou flaming minister,°   *light that serves me*
I can again thy former light restore
10   Should I repent me; but once put out thy light,
Thou cunning'st pattern of excelling nature,[3]
I know not where is that Promethean heat[4]
That can thy light relume.° When I have plucked thy rose   *relight*
I cannot give it vital growth again.
15   It needs must wither. I'll smell thee on the tree.
      [*He kisses her*]
O balmy breath, that dost almost persuade
Justice to break her sword! One more, one more.
Be thus when thou art dead, and I will kill thee
And love thee after. One more, and that's the last.
      He kisses her
20   So sweet was ne'er so fatal. I must weep,
But they are cruel tears. This sorrow's heavenly,
It strikes where it doth love.[5] She wakes.
DESDEMONA   Who's there? Othello?
OTHELLO   Ay, Desdemona.
25   DESDEMONA   Will you come to bed, my lord?
OTHELLO   Have you prayed tonight, Desdemon?
DESDEMONA   Ay, my lord.
OTHELLO   If you bethink yourself of any crime
    Unreconciled as yet to heaven and grace,
30   Solicit° for it straight.   *Ask forgiveness*
DESDEMONA   Alack, my lord, what may you mean by that?
OTHELLO   Well, do it, and be brief. I will walk by.
    I would not kill thy unpreparèd spirit.
    No, heavens forfend! I would not kill thy soul.
DESDEMONA   Talk you of killing?
OTHELLO   Ay, I do.
35   DESDEMONA   Then heaven
    Have mercy on me.
OTHELLO   Amen, with all my heart.
DESDEMONA   If you say so, I hope you will not kill me.
OTHELLO   Hum!
DESDEMONA   And yet I fear you, for you're fatal then
40   When your eyes roll so. Why I should fear I know not,
    Since guiltiness I know not, but yet I feel I fear.
OTHELLO   Think on thy sins.
DESDEMONA   They are loves I bear to you.
OTHELLO   Ay, and for that thou diest.
45   DESDEMONA   That death's unnatural that kills for loving.
    Alas, why gnaw you so your nether lip?
    Some bloody passion shakes your very frame.
    These are portents, but yet I hope, I hope
    They do not point on me.
OTHELLO   Peace, and be still.
DESDEMONA   I will so. What's the matter?
50   OTHELLO   That handkerchief
    Which I so loved and gave thee, thou gav'st to Cassio.

---

3. You most cleverly wrought example of nature's work.
4. Life-giving fire. In Greek mythology, Prometheus stole fire from heaven to give it to humankind; in a different tradition, he is credited with animating humankind from clay.
5. See Hebrews 12:6: "For whom the Lord loveth, he chasteneth."

DESDEMONA   No, by my life and soul. Send for the man
And ask him.

OTHELLO   Sweet soul, take heed, take heed of perjury.
55   Thou art on thy deathbed.

DESDEMONA   Ay, but not yet to die.

OTHELLO   Presently.°   *Immediately*
Therefore confess thee freely of thy sin,
For to deny each article with oath
60   Cannot remove nor choke the strong conception
That I do groan withal.⁶ Thou art to die.

DESDEMONA   Then Lord have mercy on me.

OTHELLO   I say amen.

DESDEMONA   And have you mercy, too. I never did
Offend you in my life, never loved Cassio
65   But with such general warranty of heaven
As I might love. I never gave him token.

OTHELLO   By heaven, I saw my handkerchief in's hand.
O perjured woman! Thou dost stone° my heart,   *harden*
And makes me call what I intend to do
70   A murder, which I thought a sacrifice.
I saw the handkerchief.

DESDEMONA   He found it, then.
I never gave it him. Send for him hither.
Let him confess a truth.

OTHELLO   He hath confessed.

DESDEMONA   What, my lord?

OTHELLO   That he hath usèd thee.

75   DESDEMONA   How, unlawfully?

OTHELLO   Ay.

DESDEMONA   He will not say so.

OTHELLO   No, his mouth is stopped.
Honest Iago hath ta'en order for't.

80   DESDEMONA   O, my fear interprets! What, is he dead?

OTHELLO   Had all his hairs been lives, my great revenge
Had stomach for 'em all.

DESDEMONA [*weeping*]   Alas, he is betrayed, and I undone.

OTHELLO   Out, strumpet! Weep'st thou for him to my face?

85   DESDEMONA   O, banish me, my lord, but kill me not.

OTHELLO [*attacking her*]   Down, strumpet.

DESDEMONA   Kill me tomorrow; let me live tonight.

OTHELLO   Nay, an you strive—

DESDEMONA   But half an hour.

90   OTHELLO   Being done, there is no pause.⁷

DESDEMONA   But while I say one prayer.

OTHELLO   It is too late.
He smothers her

DESDEMONA   O Lord, Lord, Lord!
EMILIA *at the door*

EMILIA (*within*)   My lord, my lord, what ho, my lord, my lord!

95   OTHELLO   What noise is this? Not dead? Not yet quite dead?
I that am cruel am yet merciful.

---

6. *Cannot . . . withal:* Cannot stop the strong conviction   makes me groan so. The metaphor is from childbirth.
I have in your guilt (or the firm plan to kill you), which   7. Now that I've started, there's no stopping.

I would not have thee linger in thy pain.
So, so.
EMILIA [*within*]   What ho, my lord, my lord!
OTHELLO   Who's there?
EMILIA [*within*]   O, good my lord, I would speak a word with you.
OTHELLO [*calling*]   Yes.—'Tis Emilia. [*Calling*] By
100   and by!—She's dead.
'Tis like she comes to speak of Cassio's death.
The noise was high.° Ha! No more moving.   *commotion was loud*
Still as the grave. Shall she come in? Were't good?
I think she stirs again. No. What's best to do?
105   If she come in, she'll sure speak to my wife.
My wife, my wife! What wife? I ha' no wife.
O insupportable, O heavy hour!
Methinks it should be now a huge eclipse
Of sun and moon, and that th'affrighted globe
Should yawn at alteration.[8]
110   EMILIA [*within*]   I do beseech you
That I may speak with you. O, good my lord!
OTHELLO   I had forgot thee.—O, come in, Emilia.—
Soft,° by and by. Let me the curtains draw.   *Quiet*
[*He closes the bed-curtains*]
Where art thou?
[*He opens the door.*] *Enter* EMILIA
                    What's the matter with thee now?
115   EMILIA   O my good lord, yonder's foul murder's done.
OTHELLO   What, now?
EMILIA   But° now, my lord.   *Just*
OTHELLO   It is the very error° of the moon,   *deviation*
She comes more nearer earth than she was wont,
120   And makes men mad.
EMILIA   Cassio, my lord, hath killed a young Venetian
Called Roderigo.
OTHELLO   Roderigo killed
And Cassio killed?
EMILIA   No, Cassio is not killed.
OTHELLO   Not Cassio killed? Then murder's out of tune,
125   And sweet revenge grows harsh.
DESDEMONA   O, falsely, falsely murdered!
EMILIA   O Lord, what cry is that?
OTHELLO   That? What?
EMILIA   Out and alas, that was my lady's voice!
[*She opens the bed-curtains*]
130   Help, help, ho, help! O lady, speak again!
Sweet Desdemona, O sweet mistress, speak!
DESDEMONA   A guiltless death I die.
EMILIA   O, who hath done this deed?
DESDEMONA   Nobody, I myself. Farewell.
Commend me to my kind lord. O, farewell!   *She dies*
OTHELLO   Why, how should she be murdered?
135   EMILIA   Alas, who knows?
OTHELLO   You heard her say herself it was not I.
EMILIA   She said so, I must needs report the truth.

8. Should gape at the change. Earthquakes were associated with eclipses.

OTHELLO   She's like a liar gone to burning hell.
'Twas I that killed her.

140 EMILIA   O, the more angel she, and you the blacker devil!

OTHELLO   She turned to folly,° and she was a whore.   *wantonness*

EMILIA   Thou dost belie her, and thou art a devil.

OTHELLO   She was false as water.

EMILIA   Thou art rash as fire
To say that she was false. O, she was heavenly true!

145 OTHELLO   Cassio did top her. Ask thy husband else.°   *if you doubt it*
O, I were damned beneath all depth in hell
But that I did proceed upon just grounds
To this extremity! Thy husband knew it all.

EMILIA   My husband?

OTHELLO   Thy husband.

EMILIA   That she was false to wedlock?

150 OTHELLO   Ay, with Cassio. Had she been true,
If heaven would make me such another world
Of one entire and perfect chrysolite°   *topaz*
I'd not have sold her for it.

EMILIA   My husband?

OTHELLO   Ay, 'twas he that told me on her first.

155 An honest man he is, and hates the slime
That sticks on filthy deeds.

EMILIA   My husband?

OTHELLO   What needs this iterance?° Woman, I say thy husband.   *repetition*

EMILIA   O mistress, villainy hath made mocks with° love.⁹   *at*
My husband say she was false?

OTHELLO   He, woman.

160 I say thy husband. Dost understand the word?
My friend, thy husband, honest, honest Iago.

EMILIA   If he say so, may his pernicious soul
Rot half a grain a day. He lies to th' heart.
She was too fond of her most filthy bargain.

165 OTHELLO   Ha?

EMILIA   Do thy worst.
This deed of thine is no more worthy heaven
Than thou wast worthy her.

OTHELLO   Peace, you were best.°   *it would be best for you*

EMILIA   Thou hast not half that power to do me harm

170 As I have to be hurt. O gull,° O dolt,   *fool*
As ignorant as dirt! Thou hast done a deed—
I care not for thy sword, I'll make thee known
Though I lost twenty lives. Help, help, ho! Help!
The Moor hath killed my mistress. Murder, murder!

                Enter MONTANO, GRAZIANO, *and* IAGO

175 MONTANO   What is the matter? How now, general?

EMILIA   O, are you come, Iago? You have done well,
That men must lay their murders on your neck.

GRAZIANO   What is the matter?

EMILIA [*to* IAGO]   Disprove this villain if thou beest a man.

180 He says thou told'st him that his wife was false.
I know thou didst not. Thou'rt not such a villain.
Speak, for my heart is full.

---

9. Lines 158–61 do not appear in Q.

IAGO   I told him what I thought, and told no more
Than what he found himself was apt and true.
185 EMILIA   But did you ever tell him she was false?
IAGO   I did.
EMILIA   You told a lie, an odious, damnèd lie,
Upon my soul a lie, a wicked lie.
She false with Cassio? Did you say with Cassio?
190 IAGO   With Cassio, mistress. Go to, charm° your tongue.   *silence*
EMILIA   I will not charm my tongue. I am bound to speak.
My mistress here lies murdered in her bed.[1]
MONTANO *and* GRAZIANO   O heavens forfend!
EMILIA [*to* IAGO]   And your reports have set the murder on.
195 OTHELLO   Nay, stare not, masters. It is true indeed.
GRAZIANO   'Tis a strange truth.
MONTANO   O monstrous act!
EMILIA   Villainy, villainy, villainy!
I think upon't, I think. I smell't. O villainy!
I thought so then. I'll kill myself for grief.
200 O villainy, villainy!
IAGO   What, are you mad? I charge you get you home.
EMILIA   Good gentlemen, let me have leave to speak.
'Tis proper I obey him, but not now.
Perchance, Iago, I will ne'er go home.
OTHELLO   O, O, O!

OTHELLO *falls on the bed*
205 EMILIA   Nay, lay thee down and roar,
For thou hast killed the sweetest innocent
That e'er did lift up eye.°   (*to heaven*)
OTHELLO [*rising*]   O, she was foul!
[*To* GRAZIANO] I scarce did know you, uncle. There lies your niece,
Whose breath indeed these hands have newly stopped.
210 I know this act shows° horrible and grim.   *appears*
GRAZIANO   Poor Desdemon, I am glad thy father's dead.
Thy match was mortal to him, and pure grief
Shore his old thread in twain.[2] Did he live now
This sight would make him do a desperate turn,°   *act*
215 Yea, curse his better angel from his side,
And fall to reprobance.[3]
OTHELLO   'Tis pitiful. But yet Iago knows
That she with Cassio hath the act of shame
A thousand times committed. Cassio confessed it,
220 And she did gratify his amorous works
With that recognizance° and pledge of love   *token*
Which I first gave her. I saw it in his hand.
It was a handkerchief, an antique token
My father gave my mother.
EMILIA   O God! O heavenly God!
IAGO   'Swounds, hold your peace!
225 EMILIA   'Twill out, 'twill out. I peace?
No, I will speak as liberal as the north.[4]
Let heaven, and men, and devils, let 'em all,
All, all cry shame against me, yet I'll speak.

1. Lines 192–200 do not appear in Q.
2. Cut the thread of his life.
3. Suicide, the unforgivably sinful act of despair.
4. As freely as the north wind.

IAGO   Be wise and get you home.

230 EMILIA   I will not.

[IAGO *draws his sword*]

GRAZIANO [*to* IAGO]   Fie, your sword upon a woman?

EMILIA   O thou dull Moor, that handkerchief thou speak'st of
　　I found by fortune and did give my husband,
　　For often, with a solemn earnestness—

235 　　More than indeed belonged to such a trifle—
　　He begged of me to steal't.

IAGO 　　　　　　　　　Villainous whore!

EMILIA   She give it Cassio? No, alas, I found it,
　　And I did give't my husband.

IAGO 　　　　　　　　Filth, thou liest.

EMILIA   By heaven I do not, I do not, gentlemen.

240 　　O murderous coxcomb!° What should such a fool　　　　　　　*fool*
　　Do with so good a wife?

OTHELLO 　　　　　　　Are there no stones° in heaven　　　*thunderbolts*
　　But what serves for the thunder? Precious° villain!　　　*Absolute*

The Moor runs at IAGO. [MONTANO *disarms* OTHELLO.]

IAGO [*wounds*] *his wife*

GRAZIANO   The woman falls. Sure he hath killed his wife.

EMILIA   Ay, ay. O, lay me by my mistress' side!　　　*Exit* IAGO

245 GRAZIANO   He's gone, but his wife's killed.

MONTANO   'Tis a notorious villain. Take you this weapon
　　Which I have here recovered from the Moor.
　　Come, guard the door without. Let him not pass,
　　But kill him rather. I'll after that same villain,
　　For 'tis a damnèd slave.　　　*Exeunt* MONTANO *and* GRAZIANO

250 OTHELLO 　　　　　　　I am not valiant neither,
　　But every puny whipster° gets my sword.　　　*insignificant person*
　　But why should honour outlive honesty?[5]
　　Let it go all.

EMILIA 　　　　　What did thy song bode, lady?[6]
　　Hark, canst thou hear me? I will play the swan,

255 　　And die in music. [*Sings*] 'Willow, willow, willow.'—
　　Moor, she was chaste. She loved thee, cruel Moor.
　　So come my soul to bliss as I speak true.
　　So, speaking as I think, alas, I die.　　　*She dies*

OTHELLO   I have another weapon in this chamber.

260 　　It was a sword of Spain, the ice-brook's temper.°　　　*tempered in icy water*
　　O, here it is. [*Calling*] Uncle, I must come forth.

GRAZIANO (*within*)   If thou attempt it, it will cost thee dear.
　　Thou hast no weapon, and perforce must suffer.

OTHELLO   Look in upon me then, and speak with me,

265 　　Or, naked° as I am, I will assault thee.　　　*unarmed*

[*Enter* GRAZIANO]

GRAZIANO   What is the matter?

OTHELLO 　　　　　　　Behold, I have a weapon;
　　A better never did itself sustain
　　Upon a soldier's thigh. I have seen the day
　　That, with this little arm and this good sword,

270 　　I have made my way through more impediments

5. Why should military reputation outlive integrity?
6. Lines 253–55 ("What . . . willow.'—") do not appear in Q.

Than twenty times your stop.° But O, vain boast!   *power to stop*
Who can control his fate? 'Tis not so now.
Be not afraid, though you do see me weaponed.
Here is my journey's end, here is my butt⁷
275　And very sea-mark° of my utmost sail.   *beacon*
Do you go back dismayed? 'Tis a lost° fear.   *an unnecessary*
Man but a rush° against Othello's breast   *Aim even a reed*
And he retires. Where should Othello go?
　　[*To* DESDEMONA] Now, how dost thou look now? O ill-starred wench,
280　Pale as thy smock! When we shall meet at count°   *Judgment Day*
This look of thine will hurl my soul from heaven,
And fiends will snatch at it.
　　　　　[*He touches her*]
　　　　　　　　　　　Cold, cold, my girl,
Even like thy chastity. O cursèd, cursèd slave!
Whip me, ye devils,
285　From the possession of this heavenly sight.
Blow me about in winds, roast me in sulphur,
Wash me in steep-down gulfs of liquid fire!
O Desdemon! Dead Desdemon! Dead! O! O!
　　　　　Enter LODOVICO, MONTANO, IAGO [*guarded by*] *officers,*
　　　　　with CASSIO *in a chair*
LODOVICO　Where is this rash and most unfortunate man?
290　OTHELLO　That's he that was Othello. Here I am.
LODOVICO　Where is that viper? Bring the villain forth.
OTHELLO　I look down towards his feet,⁸ but that's a fable.
　　　　　[*To* IAGO] If that thou beest a devil I cannot kill thee.
　　　　　[*He wounds* IAGO]
LODOVICO　Wrench his sword from him.
　　　　　[*Officers disarm* OTHELLO]
IAGO　　　　　　　　　　　I bleed, sir, but not killed.
295　OTHELLO　I am not sorry, neither. I'd have thee live,
For in my sense° 'tis happiness to die.   *state of feeling*
LODOVICO　O thou Othello, that was once so good,
Fall'n in the practice° of a cursèd slave,   *plot*
What shall be said to thee?
OTHELLO　　　　　　　　Why, anything;
300　An honourable murderer, if you will,
For naught I did in hate, but all in honour.
LODOVICO　This wretch hath part confessed his villainy.
Did you and he consent in Cassio's death?
OTHELLO　Ay.
305　CASSIO　Dear general, I never gave you cause.
OTHELLO　I do believe it, and I ask your pardon.
Will you, I pray, demand that demi-devil
Why he hath thus ensnared my soul and body?
IAGO　Demand me nothing. What you know, you know.
310　From this time forth I never will speak word.
LODOVICO [*to* IAGO]　What, not to pray?
GRAZIANO [*to* IAGO]　Torments° will ope your lips.   *Tortures*
OTHELLO　Well, thou dost best.
LODOVICO　Sir, you shall understand what hath befall'n,
315　Which as, I think, you know not. Here is a letter,

---

7. Goal. Lines 273–79 do not appear in Q.　　　　8. To look for the devil's cloven feet.

Found in the pocket of the slain Roderigo,
And here another. The one of them imports
The death of Cassio, to be undertook
By Roderigo.

320 OTHELLO   O villain!
CASSIO   Most heathenish and most gross.°   *monstrous*
LODOVICO   Now here's another discontented paper
Found in his pocket too, and this it seems
Roderigo meant to've sent this damnèd villain,
325 But that, belike,° Iago in the interim   *most likely*
Came in and satisfied him.
OTHELLO [*to* IAGO]   O thou pernicious caitiff!°   *wretch*
How came you, Cassio, by that handkerchief
That was my wife's?
CASSIO   I found it in my chamber,
330 And he himself confessed it, but even now,
That there he dropped it for a special purpose
Which wrought to his desire.
OTHELLO   O fool, fool, fool!
CASSIO   There is besides in Roderigo's letter
How he upbraids Iago, that he made him
335 Brave° me upon the watch, whereon it came   *Defy*
That I was cast;° and even but now he spake   *dismissed*
After long seeming dead, Iago hurt him,
Iago set him on.
LODOVICO [*to* OTHELLO]   You must forsake this room and go with us.
340 Your power and your command is taken off,
And Cassio rules in Cyprus. For this slave,
If there be any cunning cruelty
That can torment him much and hold him° long,   *(alive)*
It shall be his. You shall close° prisoner rest   *tightly confined*
345 Till that the nature of your fault be known
To the Venetian state. [*To officers*] Come, bring away.
OTHELLO   Soft you,° a word or two before you go.   *Wait*
I have done the state some service, and they know't.
No more of that. I pray you, in your letters,
350 When you shall these unlucky deeds relate,
Speak of me as I am. Nothing extenuate,
Nor set down aught in malice. Then must you speak
Of one that loved not wisely but too well,
Of one not easily jealous but, being wrought,
355 Perplexed in the extreme; of one whose hand,
Like the base Indian, threw a pearl away
Richer than all his tribe;⁹ of one whose subdued° eyes,   *(by grief)*
Albeit unusèd to the melting mood,
Drops tears as fast as the Arabian trees
360 Their medicinable gum.° Set you down this,   *myrrh*
And say besides that in Aleppo once,
Where a malignant and a turbaned Turk
Beat a Venetian and traduced the state,
I took by th' throat the circumcisèd dog

9. Othello supposes an uncivilized "Indian" unaware of the value of a pearl. Compare this reading from Q with F's "Judean," which may suggest malice rather than ignorance by alluding to Judas (betrayer of Christ) or perhaps Herod (who killed his wife Mariamne out of jealousy). "Judean" also anticipates "circumcisèd" (line 364) and hence an identification of Othello with Jews.

365   And smote him thus.

He stabs himself

LODOVICO   O bloody period!°   *conclusion; sentence*

GRAZIANO   All that is spoke is marred.

OTHELLO [*to* DESDEMONA]   I kissed thee ere I killed thee. No way but this:

Killing myself, to die upon a kiss.[1]   *He [kisses* DESDEMONA *and] dies*

370 CASSIO   This did I fear, but thought he had no weapon,

For he was great of heart.

LODOVICO [*to* IAGO]   O Spartan dog,°   *notoriously savage*

More fell° than anguish, hunger, or the sea,   *cruel*

Look on the tragic loading of this bed.

This is thy work. The object poisons sight.

Let it be hid.

[They close the bed-curtains]

375   Graziano, keep the house,

And seize upon the fortunes of the Moor,

For they succeed on you. [*To* CASSIO] To you, Lord Governor,

Remains the censure° of this hellish villain.   *sentence*

The time, the place, the torture, O, enforce it!

380 Myself will straight aboard, and to the state

This heavy act with heavy heart relate.   *Exeunt [with Emilia's body]*

---

1. At 5.2.244, the dying Emilia says, "O, lay me by my mistress' side!" She then addresses Desdemona in a way that suggests that her wish has been granted. If it has, however, the presence of her body intrudes upon the concluding tableau of the dead Desdemona being kissed by the dying Othello, where "die" in line 369, as earlier, has the secondary sense of "orgasm."

King Lear

You have, King James told his eldest son a few years before Shakespeare wrote *King Lear,* a double obligation to love God: first because He made you a man, and second because He made you "a little God to sit on his Throne, and rule over other men." Whatever the realities of Renaissance kingship—realities that included the stern necessity of compromise, reciprocity, and restraint—the idea of sovereignty was closely linked to fantasies of divine omnipotence. From his exalted height, the sovereign looked down upon the tiny figures of the ordinary mortals below him. Their hopes, the material conditions of their miserable existence, their names, were of little interest, and yet the King knew that they too were looking back up at him. "For kings being public persons," James uneasily acknowledged, are set "upon a public stage, in the sight of all the people; where all the beholders' eyes are attentively bent to look and pry in the least circumstance of their secretist drifts." Under such circumstances, the sovereign's dream was to command, like God, not only unquestioning obedience but unqualified love.

In *King Lear,* Shakespeare explores the dark consequences of this dream not only in the state but also in the family, where the Renaissance father increasingly styled himself "a little God." If, as the play opens, the aged Lear, exercising his imperious will and demanding professions of devotion, is "every inch a king," he is also by the same token every inch a father, the absolute ruler of a family that conspicuously lacks the alternative authority of a mother. Shakespeare's play invokes this royal and paternal sovereignty only to chronicle its destruction in scenes of astonishing cruelty and power. The very words "every inch a king" are spoken not by the confident figure of supreme authority whom we glimpse in the first moments but by the ruined old man who perceives in his feverish rage and madness that the fantasy of omnipotence is a fraud: "When the rain came to wet me once, and the wind to make me chatter; when the thunder would not peace at my bidding; there I found 'em, there I smelt 'em out. Go to, they are not men o' their words! They told me I was everything. 'Tis a lie, I am not ague-proof" (4.6.98–103).

"They told me I was everything": Shakespeare's culture continually staged public rituals of deference to authority. These rituals—kneeling, bowing, uncovering the head, and so forth—enacted respect for wealth, caste, power, and, at virtually every level of society, age. Jacobean England had a strong official regard for the rights and privileges of age. It told itself that, by the will of God and the natural order of things, authority gravitated to the old, particularly to old men, and it contrived to ensure that this proper, sanctified arrangement of society be everywhere respected.

" 'Tis a lie": Shakespeare's culture continually told itself at the same time that without the control of property and the threat of punishment, any claim to authority was chillingly vulnerable to the ruthless ambitions of the young, the restless, and the discontented. The incessant, ritualized spectacles of sovereignty have a nervous air, as if no one quite believed all the grand claims to divine sanction for the rule of Kings and fathers, as if those who ruled both states and families secretly feared that the elaborate hierarchical structure could vanish like a mirage, exposing their shivering, defenseless bodies. *King Lear* relentlessly stages this horrifying descent toward what the ruined King, contemplating the filthy, naked body of a mad beggar, calls "the thing itself": "unaccommodated man is no more but such a poor, bare forked animal as thou art" (3.4.98–100). Lear and the Earl of Gloucester, another old man whose terrible fate closely parallels Lear's, repeatedly look up at the heavens and call upon the gods for help, but the gods are silent. The despairing Gloucester concludes that the universe is actively malevolent—"As flies to wanton boys are we to the gods; / They kill us for their sport" (4.1.37–38)—but the awful silence of the gods may equally be a sign of their indifference or their nonexistence.

The story of King Lear and his three daughters had been often told when Shakespeare undertook to make it the subject of a tragedy. The play, performed at court in December 1605, was probably written and first performed somewhat earlier, though not before 1603, since it contains allusions to a florid piece of anti-Catholic propaganda published in that year: Samuel Harsnett's *Declaration of Egregious Popish Imposture* (the source of the colorful names of the "foul fiends" by whom Shakespeare's mad beggar claims to be possessed). Thus scholars generally assign Shakespeare's composition of *King Lear* to 1604–05, shortly after *Othello* (c. 1603–04) and before *Macbeth* (c. 1606): an astounding succession of tragic masterpieces.

King Lear first appeared in print in a Quarto published in 1608 entitled *M. William Shak-speare: His True Chronicle Historie of the life and death of King Lear*; a substantially different text, entitled *The Tragedie of King Lear* and grouped with the other tragedies, was printed in the 1623 First Folio. From the eighteenth century, when the difference between the two texts was first noted, editors, assuming that they were imperfect versions of the identical play, customarily conflated them, blending together the approximately one hundred Folio lines not printed in the Quarto with the approximately three hundred quarto lines not printed in the Folio and selecting as best they could among the hundreds of particular alternative readings. But there is a growing scholarly consensus that the 1608 text of *Lear* represents the play as Shakespeare first wrote it and that the 1623 text represents a substantial revision. (See the Textual Note for further discussion.) We provide a sampling, on facing pages, of the different versions, and readers who wish to pursue the issues raised by the differences are urged to consult the full texts included in the complete *Norton Shakespeare*.

When *King Lear* was first performed, it may have struck contemporaries as strangely timely in the wake of a lawsuit that had occurred in late 1603. The two elder daughters of a doddering gentleman named Sir Brian Annesley attempted to get their father legally certified as insane, thereby enabling themselves to take over his estate, while his youngest daughter vehemently protested on her father's behalf. The youngest daughter's name happened to be Cordell, a name uncannily close to that of Lear's youngest daughter, Cordelia, who tries to save her father from the malevolent designs of her older sisters.

The Annesley case is worth invoking not only because it may have caught Shakespeare's attention but also because it directs our own attention to the ordinary family tensions and fears around which *King Lear*, for all of its wildness, violence, and strangeness, is constructed. Though the Lear story has the mythic quality of a folktale (specifically, it resembles both the tale of Cinderella and the tale told in many cultures of a daughter who falls into disfavor for telling her father she loves him as much as salt), it was rehearsed in Shakespeare's time as a piece of authentic British history from the very ancient past (c. 800 B.C.E.) and as an admonition to contemporary fathers not to put too much trust in the flattery of their children: "Remember what happened to old King Lear . . ." In some versions of the story, including Shakespeare's, the warning centers on a decision to retire.

Cordeilla Queene. From Raphael Holinshed, *The Firste Volume of the Chronicles of England, Scotlande, and Irelande* (1577).

Retirement has come to seem a routine event, but in the patriarchal, gerontocratic culture of Tudor and Stuart England, it was generally shunned. When through illness or extreme old age it became unavoidable, retirement put a severe strain on the politics and psychology of deference by driving a wedge between status—what Lear at society's pinnacle calls "The name, and all the additions to a king" (1.1.136)—and power. In both the state and the family, the strain could be somewhat eased by transferring power to the eldest legitimate male successor, but as the families of both the legendary Lear and the real Brian Annesley showed, such a successor did not always exist. In the absence of a male heir, the aged Lear, determined to "shake all cares and business" from himself and confer them on "younger strengths," attempts to divide his kingdom equally among his daughters so that, as he puts it, "future strife / May be prevented now" (1.1.37–38, 42–43). But this attempt is a disastrous failure. Critics have often argued that the roots of the failure lie in the division of the kingdom, that any parceling out of the land on a map would itself have provoked in the audience an ominous shudder, as it is clearly meant to do when the rebels spread out a map in anticipation of a comparable division in *1 Henry IV*. But the principal focus of Shakespeare's tragedy seems to lie elsewhere: Lear's folly is not (or not only) that he retires or even that he divides his kingdom—the play opens with the Earl of Gloucester and the Earl of Kent commenting without apparent disapproval on the scrupulous equality of the shares—but rather that he rashly disinherits the only child who truly loves him, his youngest daughter.

Shakespeare contrives moreover to show that the problem with which his characters are grappling does not simply result from the absence of a son and heir. In his most brilliant and complex use of a double plot, he intertwines the story of Lear and his three daughters with the story of Gloucester and his two sons, a tale he adapted from an episode in Philip Sidney's prose romance *Arcadia*. Gloucester has a legitimate heir, his elder son, Edgar, as well as an illegitimate son, Edmond, and in this family the tragic conflict originates not in an unusual manner of transferring property from one generation to another but rather in the reverse: Edmond seethes with murderous resentment at the disadvantage entirely customary for someone in his position, both as a younger son and as what was called a "base" or "natural" child. "Thou, nature, art my goddess," he declares:

> Wherefore should I
> Stand in the plague of custom, and permit
> The curiosity of nations to deprive me,
> For that I am some twelve or fourteen moonshines
> Lag of a brother? Why bastard? wherefore base?
> (1.2.1–6)

For the seductive and ruthlessly ambitious Edmond, the social order and the language used to articulate it are merely arbitrary constraints, obstacles to the triumph of his will. He schemes to tear down the obstacles by playing on his father's fears, cleverly planting a forged letter in which his older brother appears to be plotting against his father's life. The letter's chilling sentences express Edmond's own impatience, his hatred of the confining power of custom, his disgusted observation of "the oppression of aged tyranny; who sways, not as it hath power, but as it is suffered" (1.2.48–49). Gloucester is predictably horrified and incensed; these are, as Edmond cunningly knows, the cold sentiments that the aged fear lie just beneath the surface of deference and flattery. The forged letter reflects back as well on the scene in which Gloucester himself has just participated: a scene in which everyone, with the exception of the Earl of Kent, has tamely suffered a tyrannical old man to banish his youngest daughter for her failure to flatter him.

Why does Lear, who has already drawn up the map dividing the kingdom, stage the love test? In Shakespeare's principal source, an anonymous play called *The True Chronicle History of King Leir* (published in 1605 but dating from 1594 or earlier), there is a gratifyingly clear answer. Leir's strong-willed daughter Cordella has vowed that she will only marry a man whom she herself loves; Leir wishes her to marry the man

Stargazing. From John Cypriano, *A Most Strange and Wonderfull Prophesie* (1595). "I should have been that I am had the maidenliest star in the firmament twinkled on my bastardizing" (1.2.120–122).

he chooses for his own dynastic purposes. He stages the love test, anticipating that in competing with her sisters Cordella will declare that she loves her father best, at which point Leir will demand that she prove her love by marrying the suitor of his choice. The stratagem backfires, but its purpose is clear.

By stripping his character of a comparable motive, Shakespeare makes Lear's act seem stranger, at once more arbitrary and more rooted in deep psychological needs. His Lear is a man who has determined to retire from power but who cannot endure dependence. Unwilling to lose his identity as an absolute authority both in the state and in the family, he arranges a public ritual—"Which of you shall we say doth love us most?" (1.1.49)—whose aim seems to be to allay his own anxiety by arousing it in his children. Since the shares have already been apportioned, Lear evidently wants his daughters to engage in a competition for his bounty without having to endure any of the actual consequences of such a competition; he wants, that is, to produce in them something like the effect of theater, where emotions run high and their practical effects are negligible. But in this absolutist theater Cordelia refuses to perform: "What shall Cordelia speak? Love, and be silent" (1.1.60). When she says "Nothing," a word that echoes darkly throughout the play, Lear hears what he most dreads: emptiness, loss of respect, the extinction of identity. And when, under further interrogation, she declares that she loves her father "according to my bond" (1.1.92), Lear understands these words too to be the equivalent of "nothing."

As Cordelia's subsequent actions demonstrate, his youngest daughter's bond is in reality a sustaining, generous love, but it is a love that ultimately leads to her death. Here Shakespeare makes an even more startling departure not only from *The True Chronicle History of King Leir* but from all his known sources. The earliest of these, the account in Geoffrey of Monmouth's twelfth-century *Historia Regum Britanniae*, sets the pattern repeated in John Higgins's *Mirour for Magistrates* (1574 edition), William Warner's *Albions England* (1586), Raphael Holinshed's *Chronicles of England, Scotlande, and Irelande* (2nd ed., 1587), and Edmund Spenser's *Faerie Queene* (1590, 2.10.27–32): the aged Lear is overthrown by his wicked daughters and their husbands, but he is restored to the throne by the army of his good daughter's husband, the King of France. The story then is one of loss and restoration: Lear resumes his reign, and when, "made ripe for death" by old age, as Spenser puts it, he dies, he is succeeded by Cordelia. The conclusion is not unequivocally happy; in all of the known chronicles, Cordelia rules worthily for several years and then, after being deposed and imprisoned by her nephews, in despair commits suicide. But Shakespeare's ending is unprecedented in its tragic devastation. When in Act 5 Lear suddenly enters with the lifeless body of Cordelia in his arms, the original audience, secure in the expectation of a very different resolution, must have been doubly shocked, a shock cruelly reinforced when the signs that she might be reviving—"This feather stirs; She lives!" (5.3.264)—all prove false. Lear apparently dies in the grip of the illusion that he detects some breath on his daughter's lips, but we know that Cordelia will, as he says a moment earlier, "come no more; / Never, never, never, never, never!" (5.3.306–07).

Those five reiterated words, the bleakest pentameter line Shakespeare ever wrote, are the climax of an extraordinary poetics of despair that is set in motion when Lear disinherits Cordelia and when Gloucester credits Edmond's lies about Edgar. *King Lear* has seemed to many modern readers and audiences the greatest of Shakespeare's tragedies precisely because of its anguished look into the heart of darkness, but its vision of suffering and evil has not always commanded unequivocal admiration. In the eighteenth century, Samuel Johnson wrote, "I was many years ago so shocked by Cordelia's death that I know not whether I ever endured to read again the last scenes of the play till I undertook to revise them as an editor." Johnson's contemporaries preferred a revision of Shakespeare's tragedy undertaken in 1681 by Nahum Tate. Finding the play "a Heap of Jewels, unstrung, and unpolisht," Tate proceeded to restring them in order to save Cordelia's life and to produce the unambiguous and happy triumph of the forces of good.

Only in the nineteenth century was Shakespeare's deeply pessimistic ending—the old generation dead or dying, the survivors shaken to the core, the ruling families all broken with no impending marriage to promise renewal—generally restored to theatrical performance and the tragedy's immense power fully acknowledged. Even passionate admirers of *King Lear,* however, continued to express deep uneasiness, repeatedly noting not only its unbearably painful close but also what Johnson first called the "improbability of Lear's conduct" and Samuel Taylor Coleridge termed the plot's "glaring absurdity." Above all, critics questioned whether the tragedy was suitable for the stage. Coleridge compared the suffering Lear to one of Michelangelo's titanic figures, but the grandeur invoked by the comparison led his contemporary Charles Lamb to conclude flatly that "Lear is essentially impossible to be represented on stage." "To see Lear acted," Lamb wrote, "to see an old man tottering about the stage with a walking stick, turned out of doors by his daughters in a rainy night, has nothing in it but what is painful and disgusting." In such a view, *King Lear* could only be staged successfully in the imagination; there alone would Lear's passion be perceived not like ordinary human suffering but rather, in the marvelous characterization of another Romantic critic, William Hazlitt, "like a sea, swelling, chafing, raging, without bound, without hope, without beacon, or anchor." In the theater of the mind, Shakespeare's play could assume its true, stupendous proportions, enabling the reader to grasp its ultimate meaning. That meaning, the great early twentieth-century critic A. C. Bradley wrote, is that we must "renounce the world, hate it, and lose it gladly. The only real thing in it is the soul, with its courage, patience, devotion. And nothing outward can touch that." These are stirring words, but what about the body?

Brilliant modern stage performances and, more recently, films belying the view that *King Lear* is unactable have underscored not only the play's acute theatrical sophistication and self-awareness but also its emphasis on the body's inescapable centrality. If Shakespeare explores the extremes of the mind's anguish and the soul's devotion, he never forgets that his characters have bodies as well, bodies that have needs, cravings, and terrible vulnerabilities. When in this tragedy characters fall from high station, they plunge unprotected into a world of violent storms, murderous cruelty, and physical horror. The old King wanders raging on the heath, through a wild night of thunder and rain. Disguised as Poor Tom, a mad beggar possessed by demons, Gloucester's son Edgar enacts a life of utmost degradation: "Poor Tom, that eats the swimming frog, the toad, the tadpole, the wall-newt and the water; that in the fury of his heart, when the foul fiend rages, eats cow-dung for sallats; swallows the old rat and the ditch-dog; drinks the green mantle of the standing-pool" (3.4.119–23). Gloucester's fate is even more terrible: betrayed by his son Edmond, he is seized in his own house by Lear's sadistic daughter Regan and her husband, Cornwall, tied to a chair, brutally interrogated, blinded, and then thrust bleeding out of doors.

Mental anguish in *King Lear,* then, is closely intertwined with physical anguish; the terrifying forces that are released by Lear's folly crash down upon both body and soul, just as the storm that rages on the heath seems at once an objective event and a symbolic representation of Lear's innermost being. The greatest expression of this intertwining in the play is Lear's madness, which brings together a devastating loss of identity, a relentless, radical assault on the hypocrisies of authority, and a demented, nauseated loathing of female sexuality. The loathing culminates in a fit of retching—"Fie, fie, fie; pah, pah!"—followed by Lear's delusional attempt to find a physical remedy for his psychic pain: "Fie, fie, fie! pah! pah! / Give me an ounce of civet, good apothecary, / To sweeten my imagination" (4.6.126–28). In fact, relief from the chaotic rage of madness comes in the wake of a deep, restorative sleep and a change of garments.

The body in *King Lear* is a site not only of abject misery, nausea, and pain but of care and a nascent moral awareness. In the midst of his mad ravings, Lear turns to the shivering Fool and asks, "Art cold?" (3.2.66). The simple question anticipates his recognition a few moments later that there is more suffering in the world than his own:

> Poor naked wretches, whereso'er you are,
> That bide the pelting of this pitiless storm,
> How shall your houseless heads and unfed sides
> Your looped and windowed raggedness, defend you
> From seasons such as these? O, I have ta'en
> Too little care of this!
>
> (3.4.29–34)

And if the world seems largely unjust and indifferent to human suffering, there are nonetheless throughout the play constant manifestations of generosity of body as well

Tom Durie (1614). By Marcus Gheeraerts the Younger. Durie was the jester of Anne of Denmark, who was married to James I.

as soul. "Help me, help me!" cries the frightened Fool, to which Kent (disguised in order to serve the King who has banished him) says simply, "Give me thy hand" (3.4.41–42). "What are you?" says the blind Gloucester to the son he has unjustly disinherited, to which the son, also in disguise, replies similarly, "Give me your hand" (4.6.215, 218). (In a moving moment from the *History of . . . King Lear,* absent from the Folio version, two of Gloucester's servants not only react with horror to their master's blinding but also resolve to assist him: "Go thou; I'll fetch some flax and whites of eggs/To apply to his bleeding face. Now, heaven help him!" [3.7.110–11].) Such signs of goodness and empathy do not outweigh the harshness of the physical world of the play, let alone cancel out the vicious cruelty of certain of its inhabitants, but they do qualify its moral bleakness.

It is possible to detect in *King Lear* one of the great structural rhythms of Christianity: a passage through suffering, humiliation, and pain to a transcendent wisdom and love. Lear's initial actions were blind and selfish, but he comes to acknowledge his folly and, in an immensely poignant scene, to kneel down before the daughter he has wronged. Gloucester too learns that he was blind, even when his eyes could see, and he passes, by means of Edgar's strange deception at the imaginary cliff, from suicidal despair to patient resignation. "Men must endure / Their going hence, even as their coming hither," Edgar wisely counsels his father. "Ripeness is all" (5.2.9–11). For a time, evil seems to flourish in the world, but the wicked do not ultimately triumph. The sadistic Duke of Cornwall is fatally wounded by his own morally upright servant, Edmond is killed by the brother he had tried to destroy, the loathsome Oswald is clubbed to death trying to murder Gloucester, one wicked sister poisons the other and then kills herself. Against self-interest and in the face of intolerable pressure, goodness shines forth. The Earl of Kent, banished by the rash Lear, dons a disguise in order to serve his King and master, and there are comparable acts of devoted service and self-sacrificing love from Edgar, Cordelia, and that remarkable figure the Fool. In one of the comic masterpieces of the sixteenth century, *The Praise of Folly,* the great Dutch humanist Erasmus used the fool as an emblem of the deepest Christian wisdom, revealed only when the pride, cruelty, and ambition of the world are shattered by a cleansing laughter. The shattering in *King Lear* is tragically violent and deadly, but the presence of the truth-telling Fool seems to point toward a comparable revelation.

Yet *King Lear,* set in a pagan world, resists the redemptive optimism that underlies the Christian vision (an optimism that led Dante to call his poem of damnation and salvation *The Divine Comedy*). The Fool's unnervingly perceptive observations sound far more corrosive than loving—he is, in Lear's words, "a bitter fool" (1.4.125)—and he disappears altogether in the third act. His moments of insight and those of all the other characters in the play are radically unstable, like brilliant flashes of lightning in a vast, dark landscape. Hence, for example, Lear's recognition of his folly in banishing Cordelia for her "most small fault" (1.4.243) is immediately followed by his hideous cursing of Goneril. His moving acknowledgment of the suffering of the poor, naked wretches is immediately followed by his inability to see the poor naked wretch before him in any terms but his own: "Hast thou given all to thy two daughters? And art thou come to this?" (3.4.49–50). And his appeal to patient resignation—"When we are born, we cry that we are come / To this great stage of fools" (4.6.176–77)—is immediately followed by a mad fantasy of revenge: "Then kill, kill, kill, kill, kill, kill!" (4.6.181). Every time we seem to have reached firm moral ground, the ground shifts, and we are kept, as Johnson observed, in "a perpetual tumult of indignation, pity, and hope." There are moments of apparent resolution: "Let's away to prison," says Lear to the weeping Cordelia, when they are captured by the enemy. "We two alone will sing like birds i' the cage" (5.3.8–9). But a more terrible fate lies before them. "Some good I mean to do," says the dying Edmond, "despite of mine own nature" (5.3.242–43). But his attempt to send a reprieve and therefore in some measure to redeem himself comes too late. The play's nightmarish events continually lurch ahead of intentions, and even efforts to say "I have seen the worst" are frustrated.

The tragedy is not only that the intervals of moral resolution, mental lucidity, and spiritual calm are so brief, continually giving way to feverish grief and rage, but also that the modest human understandings, moving in their simplicity, cost such an enormous amount of pain. Edgar saves his father from despair but also in some sense breaks his father's heart. Cordelia's steadfast honesty, her refusal to flatter the father she loves, may be admirable but has disastrous consequences, and her attempt to save Lear only leads to her own death. For a sublime moment, Lear actually *sees* his daughter, understands her separateness, acknowledges her existence—

> Do not laugh at me;
> For, as I am a man, I think this lady
> To be my child Cordelia

but it has taken the destruction of virtually his whole world for him to reach this recognition (4.7.69–71).

An apocalyptic dream of last judgment and redemption hovers over the entire tragedy, but it is a dream forever deferred. At the sight of the howling Lear with the dead Cordelia in his arms, the bystanders can only ask a succession of stunned questions:

> KENT   Is this the promised end?
> EDGAR   Or image of that horror?
>
>   (5.3.261–62)

Lear's own question a moment later seems the most terrible and the most important: "Why should a dog, a horse, a rat have life, / And thou no breath at all?" (5.3.305–06). It is a sign of *King Lear*'s astonishing freedom from orthodoxy that it refuses to offer any of the conventional answers to this question, answers that largely serve to conceal or deflect the mourner's anguish. Shakespeare's tragedy asks us not to turn away from evil, folly, and unbearable human pain but, seeing them face-to-face, to strengthen our capacity to speak the truth, to endure, and to love.

STEPHEN GREENBLATT

TEXTUAL NOTE

The textual traces of *King Lear* have probably given scholars more cause for debate than any of Shakespeare's other works. The debate centers on the relative authority of the two early texts of the tragedy, the First Quarto (Q1) and the First Folio (F), and the relationship between them. Q1 contains approximately three hundred lines that do not appear in F; F prints approximately one hundred lines that are not in Q1. There are also hundreds of individual variants, some apparently negligible but others highly significant. To take a single instance, the closing lines of the play—by convention assigned to the person who will now govern the state—are in Q1 spoken by Albany, in F spoken by Edgar.

Q1 was first printed in December and January of 1607–08 in the shop of Nicholas Okes, a London printer, under the following title:

> M. William Shak-speare: His True Chronicle Historie of the life and death of King Lear and his three Daughters. With the vnfortunate life of Edgar, sonne and heire to the Earle of Gloster, and his sullen and assumed humor of Tom of Bedlam: As it was played before the Kings Maiestie at Whitehall vpon S. Stephans night in Christmas Hollidayes. By his Maiesties seruants playing vsually at the Gloabe on the Banckeside. London, Printed for Nathaniel Butter, and are to be sold at his shop in Pauls Church-yard at the signe of the Pide Bull neere St. Austins Gate. 1608.

Of the print run, only twelve copies have been found. Q1 was set, most scholars agree, from Shakespeare's own draft, his "foul papers." That Q1 was printed from such a draft and not from a scribe's copy or a promptbook promises strong authority. However, there are difficulties.

Peculiarities within the text and variations among the twelve copies suggest that Okes's printing shop was not quite up to the task set by this long, complex play. *King Lear* appears indeed to have been the first play Okes attempted. There was clearly a shortage of typeface, particularly of full stops and colons: this may help to explain anomalous aspects of lineation and punctuation. Evidently, two compositors worked together on the play, one perhaps reading aloud while the other set the type; this may have caused what often appear to be aural errors in the text. And these errors, which may have been compounded by difficulties in reading the copy, might have been avoided had the printer's copy come from an experienced scribe rather than from Shakespeare's own handwriting, which appears at some points to have been illegible. The result is a text of great importance but tantalizing uncertainty. While no critics doubt that Q1 represents a legitimate early version of *King Lear,* it is a version whose authority is compromised by a succession of readings that are often confusing and sometimes nonsensical.

At a time when it was generally accepted that Q1 and F were, for all their differences, derived from one original text, now lost, these textual difficulties were relatively easily handled: the editor would conflate the two texts, weaving together the lines that appear in only one or the other version and correcting Q1 with reference to F or (in a much smaller number of instances) F with reference to Q1. The Oxford editors broke decisively with this tradition of conflation. Instead, they edited and printed Q1 and F as separate and distinct texts. This edition offers a sampling of the different texts but prints a conflated version, edited by Barbara K. Lewalski of Harvard University.

SELECTED BIBLIOGRAPHY

Booth, Stephen. "On the Greatness of *King Lear*." *"King Lear," "Macbeth," Indefinition and Tragedy*. New Haven: Yale University Press, 1983. 1–57. Shakespeare's tragedy compels readers and audience through its power of indefiniteness: the play's characters, categories, and boundaries melt and blur, disclosing the instability of all attempts to impose order on the world.

Cavell, Stanley. "The Avoidance of Love: A Reading of *King Lear*." *Disowning Knowledge in Six Plays of Shakespeare*. Cambridge: Cambridge University Press, 1987. 39–124. To face the frightening isolation of all humans, to grasp the difference between the knowledge of love and the acknowledgment of love, to understand that in order to see one must also allow oneself to be seen, to endure the shame of exposure—these are among *King Lear*'s radical insights.

De Grazia, Margreta. "The Ideology of Superfluous Things: *King Lear* as Period Piece." *Subject and Object in Renaissance Culture*. Ed. Margreta de Grazia, Maureen Quilligan, and Peter Stallybrass. Cambridge: Cambridge University Press, 1996. 17–42. Far from being protomodern, the play depicts a world where persons and things cannot be separated and superfluity is a sign of apocalypse.

Greenblatt, Stephen. "Shakespeare and the Exorcists." *Shakespearean Negotiations: The Circulation of Social Energy in Renaissance England*. Berkeley: University of California Press, 1988. 94–128. Shakespeare draws theatrical energy from the contemporary practice of exorcism, a ritualized encounter with evil attacked by Protestant officials as a vicious, histrionic fraud.

Holland, Peter, ed. *King Lear and Its Afterlife: Shakespeare Survey* 55 (2002): 1–180. Treating four centuries of adaptations, appropriations, performances, and interpretations, this essay collection focuses on plays, songs, and novels that draw on *King Lear*.

Jones, John. *Shakespeare at Work*. Oxford: Oxford University Press, 1995. Close attention to the Folio revisions of the quarto text of the play discloses a cunning symbolic design that links Lear's craziness with an obsession with quantity.

Kronenfeld, Judy. *"King Lear" and the Naked Truth: Rethinking the Language of Religion and Resistance*. Durham, N.C.: Duke University Press, 1998. The play should be understood not through deconstruction or new historicism but through the common Christian culture that gave its terms meaning outside a polemical context.

Leggatt, Alexander. *King Lear*. 2nd ed. Manchester: Manchester University Press, 2004. Interpretive problems are explored through the history of twentieth-century stage and film productions.

Nuttall, A. D. "King Lear." *Why Does Tragedy Give Pleasure?* Oxford: Clarendon, 1996. 81–105. The play gives pleasure not by sealing off suffering in poetic form but by destroying the expected recognition and closure of tragedy.

Taylor, Gary, and Michael Warren, eds. *The Division of the Kingdoms: Shakespeare's Two Versions of "King Lear."* Oxford: Clarendon, 1983. This essay collection presents the case for the quarto and Folio texts as distinct works and explores the consequences for interpreting *King Lear*.

FILMS

Korol Lir. 1969. Dir. Grigori Kozintsev and Iosif Shapiro. Soviet Union. 139 min. This black-and-white film presents a wizened but childlike Lear in a peasant-filled wasteland; a romantic fable in the Christian Middle Ages.

King Lear. 1971. Dir. Peter Brook. UK. 137 min. Men in pelts wander in a primitive tundra. Breaks in cinematic realism signal Lear's decline. With Paul Scofield and Jack MacGowran.

King Lear. 1983. Dir. Michael Elliott. UK. 158 min. Laurence Olivier, nearly eighty, in his final *Lear*. A television production that opens at Stonehenge.

Ran. 1985. Dir. Akira Kurosawa. Japan. 160 min. Set in sixteenth-century feudal Japan, the story, loosely adapted from Shakespeare, is noted for its elegaic battle sequences and orgies of red. In Japanese. With Tatsuya Nakadai and Akira Terao.

King Lear. 1998. Dir. Richard Eyre. UK. 150 min. Garish hues and torch-lit interiors for an especially cruel Lear, with equally vicious Regan and Goneril. With Ian Holm and Victoria Hamilton.

King Lear

A CONFLATED TEXT

THE PERSONS OF THE PLAY

LEAR, King of Britain
GONERIL, Lear's eldest daughter
Duke of ALBANY, her husband
REGAN, Lear's second daughter
Duke of CORNWALL, her husband
CORDELIA, Lear's youngest daughter
King of FRANCE   }
Duke of BURGUNDY } suitors of Cordelia
Earl of KENT, later disguised as Caius
Earl of GLOUCESTER
EDGAR, elder son of Gloucester, later disguised as Tom o' Bedlam
EDMUND, bastard son of Gloucester
OLD MAN, Gloucester's tenant
CURAN, Gloucester's retainer
Lear's FOOL
OSWALD, Goneril's steward
A DOCTOR
A CAPTAIN
A GENTLEMAN
A HERALD
SERVANTS to Cornwall
Knights, officers, messengers, soldiers, attendants

1.1

Enter KENT, GLOUCESTER,[1] *and* EDMUND

KENT   I thought the king had more affected° the Duke of   *favored*
  Albany° than Cornwall.   *Scotland*
GLOUCESTER   It did always seem so to us; but now, in the divi-
  sion of the kingdom, it appears not° which of the dukes he   *is not clear*
5 values most; for equalities° are so weighed,° that curiosity in   *shares / equal*
  neither can make choice of either's moiety.[2]
KENT   Is not this your son, my lord?
GLOUCESTER   His breeding,° sir, hath been at my charge.[3] I have   *upbringing*
  so often blushed to acknowledge him, that now I am brazed°   *hardened*
10 to it.
KENT   I cannot conceive° you.   *comprehend*
GLOUCESTER   Sir, this young fellow's mother could;[4] whereupon
  she grew round-wombed, and had, indeed, sir, a son for her
  cradle ere she had a husband for her bed. Do you smell a
15 fault?[5]

1.1 Location: King Lear's court.
1. Pronounced "Gloster."
2. *that . . . moiety:* that careful scrutiny ("curiosity") of both parts cannot determine which portion ("moiety") is

preferable.
3. My responsibility; at my cost.
4. Could conceive; punning on biological conception.
5. Sin, wrongdoing; female genitals.

KENT   I cannot wish the fault undone, the issue° of it being so   *offspring; result*
proper.°   *handsome; right*
GLOUCESTER   But I have, sir, a son by order of law,° some year   *legitimate son*
elder than this, who yet is no dearer in my account.° Though   *estimation*
20   this knave° came something saucily⁶ into the world before he   *scamp; fellow*
was sent for, yet was his mother fair; there was good sport at his
making, and the whoreson° must be acknowledged. Do you   *rogue; bastard*
know this noble gentleman, Edmund?
EDMUND   No, my lord.
25   GLOUCESTER   My lord of Kent. Remember him hereafter as my
honorable friend.
EDMUND   My services to your lordship.
KENT   I must love you, and sue° to know you better.   *seek*
EDMUND   Sir, I shall study deserving.°   *shall learn to deserve*
30   GLOUCESTER   He hath been out° nine years, and away he shall   *away; abroad*
again. (*Sound a sennet*)° The king is coming.   *fanfare of trumpets*
      Enter one bearing a coronet, then King LEAR, CORN-
      WALL, ALBANY, GONERIL, REGAN, CORDELIA, *and atten-*
      dants
LEAR   Attend the lords of France and Burgundy, Gloucester.
GLOUCESTER   I shall, my liege.°   *feudal superior*
      Exeunt GLOUCESTER *and* EDMUND
LEAR   Meantime we° shall express our darker° purpose.   *(royal "we") / more secret*
35   Give me the map there. Know that we have divided
In three our kingdom; and 'tis our fast° intent   *fixed*
To shake all cares and business from our age,
Conferring them on younger strengths, while we
Unburthened crawl toward death. Our son° of Cornwall,   *son-in-law*
40   And you, our no less loving son of Albany,
We have this hour a constant will to publish⁷
Our daughters' several dowers,° that future strife   *individual dowries*
May be prevented now. The princes, France and Burgundy,
Great rivals in our youngest daughter's love,
45   Long in our court have made their amorous sojourn,
And here are to be answered. Tell me, my daughters—
Since now we will divest us, both of rule,
Interest° of territory, cares of state—   *Legal title*
Which of you shall we say doth love us most?
50   That° we our largest bounty° may extend   *So that / generosity*
Where nature doth with merit challenge.⁸ Goneril,
Our eldest-born, speak first.
GONERIL   Sir, I love you more than words can wield° the matter;   *convey*
Dearer than eye-sight, space,° and liberty;   *freedom of movement*
55   Beyond what can be valued, rich or rare;
No less than life, with grace, health, beauty, honor;
As much as child e'er loved, or father found;
A love that makes breath° poor, and speech unable;   *language*
Beyond all manner of so much° I love you.   *Beyond all comparison*
60   CORDELIA (*aside*)   What shall Cordelia speak? Love, and be silent.
LEAR   Of all these bounds,° even from this line to this,   *regions*
With shadowy forests and with champains riched,°   *enriched plains*
With plenteous rivers and wide-skirted meads,°   *broad meadows*

---

6. Somewhat rudely; somewhat shamefully.
7. A fixed determination to announce publicly.

8. *Where . . . challenge:* To the one whose natural love
and deserving lay claim (to our generosity).

We make thee lady: to thine and Albany's issue°   children; heirs
65   Be this perpetual. What says our second daughter,
     Our dearest Regan, wife to Cornwall? Speak.
     REGAN   Sir, I am made
     Of the self-same metal° that my sister is,   spirit; substance
     And prize me at her worth.° In my true heart   believe myself her equal
70   I find she names my very deed of love;
     Only she comes too short, that° I profess   in that
     Myself an enemy to all other joys,
     Which the most precious square of sense possesses,⁹
     And find I am alone felicitate°   am only made happy
     In your dear highness' love.
75   CORDELIA (aside)   Then poor Cordelia!
     And yet not so; since, I am sure, my love's
     More ponderous° than my tongue.   weighty
     LEAR   To thee and thine hereditary ever
     Remain this ample third of our fair kingdom;
80   No less in space, validity,° and pleasure,   value
     Than that conferred on Goneril. Now, our joy,
     Although our last and least;° to whose young love   youngest; smallest
     The vines of France and milk of Burgundy
     Strive to be interessed,° what can you say to draw   admitted
85   A third more opulent than your sisters? Speak.
     CORDELIA   Nothing, my lord.
     LEAR   Nothing?
     CORDELIA   Nothing.
     LEAR   Nothing will come of nothing,¹ speak again.
90   CORDELIA   Unhappy that I am, I cannot heave
     My heart into my mouth. I love your majesty
     According to my bond;° nor more nor less.   filial duty
     LEAR   How, how, Cordelia! mend your speech a little,
     Lest it may mar your fortunes.
     CORDELIA   Good my lord,
95   You have begot me, bred me, loved me; I
     Return those duties back as are right fit,
     Obey you, love you, and most honor you.
     Why have my sisters husbands, if they say
     They love you all°? Haply,° when I shall wed,   completely / Perhaps; if lucky
100 That lord whose hand must take my plight° shall carry   marriage vow; condition
     Half my love with him, half my care and duty.
     Sure, I shall never marry like my sisters,
     To love my father all.
     LEAR   But goes thy heart with this?
105 CORDELIA   Ay, good my lord.
     LEAR   So young, and so untender?
     CORDELIA   So young, my lord, and true.°   honest; faithful
     LEAR   Let it be so! Thy truth, then, be thy dower!
     For, by the sacred radiance of the sun,
110 The mysteries of Hecate,² and the night;

---

9. Which . . . possesses: That the body can enjoy. precious
square of sense: measure of sensibility; or, perhaps, bal-
anced and sensitive perception. The square may repre-
sent the even mixture of the body's four fluids, or humors.
1. Ex nihilo nihil fit, a maxim derived from Aristotle, was
accepted by the Christian Middle Ages with the single

exception of God having created the world out of
nothing.
2. A classical goddess of the moon and the patron of
witchcraft, she was associated with the underworld,
Hades.

By all the operation of the orbs
From whom we do exist and cease to be;[3]
Here I disclaim all my paternal care,
Propinquity° and property of blood,°   *Closeness / kinship*
115 And as a stranger to my heart and me
Hold thee, from this,° for ever. The barbarous Scythian,[4]   *this time*
Or he that makes his generation messes[5]
To gorge his appetite, shall to my bosom
Be as well neighbored, pitied, and relieved,
As thou my sometime° daughter.   *former*
120 KENT   Good my liege—
LEAR   Peace, Kent!
Come not between the dragon and his wrath.
I loved her most, and thought to set my rest[6]
On her kind nursery.° Hence, and avoid my sight!   *care*
125 So be my grave my peace,[7] as here I give
Her father's heart from her! Call France; who stirs?[8]
Call Burgundy. Cornwall and Albany,
With my two daughters' dowers digest° this third: *incorporate*
Let pride, which she calls plainness,° marry her.   *directness*
130 I do invest you jointly with my power,
Pre-eminence, and all the large effects°   *outward shows; trappings*
That troop with° majesty. Ourself, by monthly course,   *accompany*
With reservation of° an hundred knights,   *legal right to retain*
By you to be sustained, shall our abode
135 Make with you by due turns. Only we still retain
The name, and all the additions° to a king;   *prerogatives*
The sway,° revenue, execution of the rest,   *power*
Beloved sons, be yours; which to confirm,
This coronet[9] part betwixt you.
KENT   Royal Lear,
140 Whom I have ever honored as my king,
Loved as my father, as my master followed,
As my great patron thought on in my prayers—
LEAR   The bow is bent and drawn, make from° the shaft.   *get clear of*
KENT   Let it fall° rather, though the fork° invade   *strike home / arrowhead*
145 The region of my heart: be Kent unmannerly,
When Lear is mad. What wilt thou do, old man?
Think'st thou that duty shall have dread to speak,
When power to flattery bows? To plainness° honor's bound,   *plain speaking*
When majesty stoops to folly. Reverse thy doom,°   *Revoke your sentence*
150 And, in thy best consideration, check°   *halt*
This hideous rashness. Answer my life my judgment,[1]
Thy youngest daughter does not love thee least;
Nor are those empty-hearted whose low sounds
Reverb no hollowness.°   *Echo no insincerity*
LEAR   Kent, on thy life, no more.
155 KENT   My life I never held but as a pawn°   *chess piece; stake*

3. *By all . . . be:* Referring to the belief that the move-
ments of stars and planets ("orbs") corresponded to phys-
ical and spiritual motions in a person and thus controlled
his or her fate.
4. Notoriously savage Crimean nomads of classical
antiquity.
5. *he . . . messes:* he who makes meals of his parents or
his children.

6. To secure my repose; to stake my all, as in the card
game known as primero.
7. So may I rest in peace (probably an oath).
8. Does nobody stir? An order, with the force of "Get
moving."
9. Cordelia's crown, symbol of the endowment she has
forsworn.
1. *Answer . . . judgment:* I'll stake my life on my opinion.

To wage° against thy enemies; nor fear to lose it,   *wager*
Thy safety being the motive.

LEAR   Out of my sight!

KENT   See better, Lear; and let me still° remain   *always*
The true blank° of thine eye.   *precise bull's-eye*

LEAR   Now, by Apollo—

160   KENT   Now, by Apollo, king,
Thou swear'st thy gods in vain[2]

LEAR   O, vassal! miscreant!°   *villain; unbeliever*

Laying his hand on his sword

ALBANY   ⎫
CORNWALL   ⎬ Dear sir, forbear.

KENT   Do;
Kill thy physician, and the fee bestow

165   Upon thy foul disease.[3] Revoke thy doom;
Or, whilst I can vent clamor from my throat,
I'll tell thee thou dost evil.

LEAR   Hear me, recreant!°   *traitor*
On thine allegiance, hear me!
Since thou hast sought to make us break our vow,

170   Which we durst never yet, and with strained° pride   *overblown*
To come between our sentence and our power,
Which nor our nature nor our place[4] can bear,
Our potency made good,° take thy reward.   *demonstrated*
Five days we do allot thee, for provision

175   To shield thee from diseases of the world;
And on the sixth to turn thy hated back
Upon our kingdom: if, on the tenth day following,
Thy banished trunk° be found in our dominions,   *body*
The moment is thy death. Away! by Jupiter,

180   This shall not be revoked.

KENT   Fare thee well, king. Sith° thus thou wilt appear,   *Since*
Freedom lives hence, and banishment is here.
(*To* CORDELIA) The gods to their dear shelter take thee, maid,
That justly think'st, and hast most rightly said!

185   (*To* REGAN *and* GONERIL) And your large speeches may your deeds approve,[5]
That good effects may spring from words of love.
Thus Kent, O princes, bids you all adieu;
He'll shape his old course in a country new.   *Exit*

Flourish.° Re-enter GLOUCESTER, *with* FRANCE, BUR-   *Fanfare of trumpets*
GUNDY, *and attendants*

GLOUCESTER   Here's France and Burgundy, my noble lord.

190   LEAR   My lord of Burgundy,
We first address towards you, who with this king
Hath rivaled for our daughter. What, in the least,
Will you require in present dower with her,
Or cease your quest of love?

BURGUNDY   Most royal majesty,

195   I crave no more than what your highness offered,
Nor will you tender° less.   *offer*

LEAR   Right noble Burgundy,

---

2. You invoke your gods falsely and without effect.
3. *Kill . . . disease:* You would not only kill the doctor but hand his fee over to the disease.

4. Which neither my temperament nor my royal position.
5. And let your actions live up to your fine words.

When she was dear to us, we did hold her so;
But now her price is fallen. Sir, there she stands;
If aught within that little seeming substance,[6]
200　Or all of it, with our displeasure pieced,°　　　　　　　　　　*joined*
And nothing more, may fitly like° your grace,　　　　　　　*please*
She's there, and she is yours.
BURGUNDY　　　　　　　　I know no answer.
LEAR　Will you, with those infirmities she owes,°　　　　　　*owns*
Unfriended, new-adopted to our hate,
205　Dowered with our curse, and strangered° with our oath,　*estranged*
Take her, or leave her?
BURGUNDY　　　　　　　　Pardon me, royal sir;
Election makes not up on such conditions.[7]
LEAR　Then leave her, sir; for, by the power that made me,
I tell you° all her wealth. (*To* FRANCE) For° you, great king,　*inform you of / As for*
210　I would not from your love make such a stray°　　　　　　*stray so far*
To° match you where I hate; therefore beseech you　　　　*As to*
To avert your liking° a more worthier way　　　　　　　*To turn your affections*
Than on a wretch whom nature is ashamed
Almost to acknowledge hers.
FRANCE　　　　　　　　This is most strange,
215　That she, whom even but now was your best object,
The argument° of your praise, balm of your age,　　　　　*theme*
Most best, most dearest, should in this trice° of time　　　*moment*
Commit a thing so monstrous, to dismantle°　　　　*as to strip off; disrobe*
So many folds of favor. Sure, her offense
220　Must be of such unnatural degree,
That monsters it,° or your fore-vouched affection　　　*makes it monstrous*
Fall'n into taint;[8] which to believe of her,
Must be a faith that reason without miracle
Could never plant in me.
CORDELIA　　　　　　　　I yet beseech your majesty—
225　If for I want° that glib and oily art,　　　　　　　　*because I lack*
To speak and purpose not°—since what I well intend,　*and not intend*
I'll do't before I speak—that you make known
It is no vicious blot, murder, or foulness,
No unchaste action, or dishonored step,
230　That hath deprived me of your grace and favor;
But even for want of that for which I am richer,
A still-soliciting° eye, and such a tongue　　　　　　*An always-begging*
As I am glad I have not, though not to have it
Hath lost me in your liking.
LEAR　　　　　　　　Better thou
235　Hadst not been born than not to have pleased me better.
FRANCE　Is it but this—a tardiness in nature
Which often leaves the history unspoke
That it intends to do?[9] My lord of Burgundy,
What say you to the lady? Love's not love
240　When it is mingled with regards° that stands　　　　*considerations*

6. *little seeming substance*: one who appears insubstantial; one who will not pretend.
7. A choice cannot be made under those terms.
8. *or . . . taint*: or else the love you earlier swore for Cordelia must be regarded with suspicion. "Or" may also

mean "before," in which case the phrase would mean "before the love you once proclaimed could have decayed."
9. *a tardiness . . . do*: a natural reserve that inhibits voicing one's intentions.

Aloof from th' entire point. Will you have her?
She is herself a dowry.
BURGUNDY   Royal Lear,
Give but that portion which yourself proposed,
And here I take Cordelia by the hand,
245   Duchess of Burgundy.
LEAR   Nothing! I have sworn; I am firm.
BURGUNDY   I am sorry, then, you have so lost a father
That you must lose a husband.
CORDELIA   Peace be with Burgundy!
Since that respects of fortune are his love,
250   I shall not be his wife.
FRANCE   Fairest Cordelia, that art most rich, being poor;
Most choice, forsaken; and most loved, despised!
Thee and thy virtues here I seize upon:
Be it lawful I take up what's cast away.
255   Gods, gods! 't is strange that from their cold'st neglect
My love should kindle to inflamed respect.°   ardent regard
Thy dowerless daughter, king, thrown to my chance,
Is queen of us, of ours, and our fair France.
Not all the dukes of waterish° Burgundy   irrigated; watery; weak
260   Can buy this unprized° precious maid of me.   unappreciated
Bid them farewell, Cordelia, though unkind;°   though they are unkind
Thou losest here,° a better where° to find.   this place / place
LEAR   Thou hast her, France; let her be thine; for we
Have no such daughter, nor shall ever see
265   That face of hers again. Therefore be gone
Without our grace, our love, our benison.°   blessing
Come, noble Burgundy.
            Flourish. Exeunt all but FRANCE, GONERIL, REGAN, *and*
                CORDELIA
FRANCE   Bid farewell to your sisters.
CORDELIA   The jewels of our father, with washed eyes
270   Cordelia leaves you. I know you what you are,
And like a sister am most loath to call
Your faults as they are named.° Love well our father.   are properly called
To your professed bosoms° I commit him;   publicly proclaimed love
But yet, alas, stood I within his grace,
275   I would prefer° him to a better place.   promote; recommend
So, farewell to you both.
REGAN   Prescribe not us our duties.
GONERIL   Let your study
Be to content your lord, who hath received you
At fortune's alms.[1] You have obedience scanted,°   neglected
280   And well are worth the want that you have wanted.[2]
CORDELIA   Time shall unfold what pleated cunning hides:
Who cover faults, at last shame them derides.[3]
Well may you prosper!
FRANCE   Come, my fair Cordelia.
                Exeunt FRANCE *and* CORDELIA

---

1. As a charitable gift from Dame Fortune.
2. And you deserve to get no more love (from your hus-
band) than you have given (to your father). "Want" plays
on its alternative meanings of "lack" and "desire."
3. Those who hide their faults will in the end be put to
shame.

GONERIL   Sister, it is not a little I have to say of what most nearly
285   appertains to us both. I think our father will hence to-night.
REGAN   That's most certain, and with you; next month with us.
GONERIL   You see how full of changes° his age is; the observation   *fickleness*
we have made of it hath not been little:[4] he always loved our
sister most; and with what poor judgment he hath now cast her
290   off appears too grossly.°   *blatantly*
REGAN   'Tis the infirmity of his age; yet he hath ever but slen-
derly known himself.
GONERIL   The best and soundest of his time hath been but rash;[5]
then° must we look to receive from his age, not alone the   *therefore*
295   imperfections of long-engraffed condition,° but therewithal the   *deep-rooted habit*
unruly waywardness that infirm and choleric years bring with
them.
REGAN   Such unconstant starts[6] are we like° to have from him as   *likely*
this of Kent's banishment.
300   GONERIL   There is further compliment° of leave-taking between   *ceremony*
France and him. Pray you, let's hit° together: if our father carry   *join; strike*
authority with such dispositions[7] as he bears, this last surren-
der° of his will but offend° us.   *abdication / harm*
REGAN   We shall further think on 't.
305   GONERIL   We must do something, and i' the heat.°   *Exeunt*   *quickly*

1.2

Enter EDMUND, *with a letter*

EDMUND   Thou, nature, art my goddess; to thy law
My services are bound.[1] Wherefore° should I   *Why*
Stand in the plague of custom,[2] and permit
The curiosity° of nations to deprive me,   *legal niceties*
5   For that° I am some twelve or fourteen moonshines°   *Because / months*
Lag of° a brother? Why bastard? wherefore base?   *Younger than*
When my dimensions are as well compact,°   *composed*
My mind as generous° and my shape as true,   *noble*
As honest° madam's issue? Why brand they us   *married; chaste*
10   With base? with baseness? bastardy? base, base?
Who, in the lusty stealth of nature, take
More composition and fierce quality[3]
Than doth, within a dull, stale, tired bed,
Go to creating a whole tribe of fops,°   *fools*
15   Got° 'tween asleep and wake? Well, then,   *Begotten*
Legitimate Edgar, I must have your land.
Our father's love is to° the bastard Edmund   *as much to*
As to the legitimate. Fine word—'legitimate'!
Well, my legitimate, if this letter speed,°   *succeed*
20   And my invention° thrive, Edmund the base   *plot*

---

4. We have observed it more than a little.
5. *The . . . rash:* Even in the prime of his life he was
impetuous.
6. Such impulsive outbursts.
7. Frame of mind.
1.2 Location: The Earl of Gloucester's house.
1. Edmund declares the raw force of unsocialized and
unregulated existence, as opposed to human law, to be
his ruler; ironically, "nature" also means "natural filial
affection." A "natural" was another word for "bastard"
(illegitimate child).

2. Submit to the imposition of inheritance law.
3. *Who . . . quality:* Whose begetting, by reason of its
furtiveness and heightened excitement, requires better
execution and more vigor. Alternatively (with "take"
meaning "give"), whose begetting produces (a person of)
more mixture and vigor. "Composition," or mixture, may
refer to the belief that the perfect offspring was conceived
from an equal quantity of male and female essence and
that physical and mental abnormalities were caused by a
predominance of one or the other.

Shall top° the legitimate. I grow; I prosper.   *overcome; usurp*
Now, gods, stand up for bastards!
　　　　Enter GLOUCESTER
GLOUCESTER   Kent banished thus? and France in choler
　　parted?°   *in anger departed*
　　And the king gone tonight?° subscribed° his power?   *last night / limited*
25　　Confirmed to exhibition?⁴ All this done
　　Upon the gad?° Edmund, how now! what news?   *spur of the moment*
EDMUND   So please your lordship, none. *Putting up the letter*
GLOUCESTER   Why so earnestly seek you to put up that letter?
EDMUND   I know no news, my lord.
30　GLOUCESTER   What paper were you reading?
EDMUND   Nothing, my lord.
GLOUCESTER   No? What needed, then, that terrible dispatch° of   *frightened haste*
　　it into your pocket? The quality of nothing hath not such need
　　to hide itself. Let's see. Come, if it be nothing, I shall not need
35　　spectacles.
EDMUND   I beseech you, sir, pardon me. It is a letter from my
　　brother, that I have not all o'er-read; and for so much as I have
　　perused, I find it not fit for your o'er-looking.
GLOUCESTER   Give me the letter, sir.
40　EDMUND   I shall offend, either to detain or give it. The contents,
　　as in part I understand them, are to blame.
GLOUCESTER   Let's see, let's see.
EDMUND   I hope, for my brother's justification, he wrote this but
　　as an essay or taste⁵ of my virtue.
45　GLOUCESTER (*reads*) "This policy and reverence of age makes
　　the world bitter to the best of our times;⁶ keeps our fortunes
　　from us till our oldness cannot relish them. I begin to find an
　　idle and fond° bondage in the oppression of aged tyranny; who   *a useless and foolish*
　　sways, not as it hath power, but as it is suffered.⁷ Come to me,
50　　that of this I may speak more. If our father would sleep till I
　　waked him, you should enjoy half his revenue for ever, and live
　　the beloved of your brother, Edgar."
　　Hum—conspiracy!—"Sleep till I waked him—you should
　　enjoy half his revenue"—My son Edgar! Had he a hand to
55　　write this? a heart and brain to breed it in?—When came this
　　to you? who brought it?
EDMUND   It was not brought me, my lord; there's the cunning of
　　it; I found it thrown in at the casement° of my closet.°   *window / private room*
GLOUCESTER   You know the character° to be your brother's?   *handwriting*
60　EDMUND   If the matter° were good, my lord, I durst swear it were   *content*
　　his; but, in respect of that, I would fain° think it were not.   *gladly*
GLOUCESTER   It is his.
EDMUND   It is his hand, my lord; but I hope his heart is not in
　　the contents.
65　GLOUCESTER   Hath he never heretofore sounded you° in this   *sounded you out*
　　business?
EDMUND   Never, my lord. But I have heard him oft maintain it
　　to be fit, that, sons at perfect age,° and fathers declining, the   *at maturity*

---

4. Established as mere show; relegated to pension. the prime of our lives. *policy:* statecraft; craftiness;
5. *but . . . taste:* simply as a proof or test. Both terms established order.
derive from metallurgy.   7. *who . . . suffered:* which rules not because it is power-
6. The established primacy of the elderly embitters us at ful but because it is permitted to ("suffered").

father should be as ward[8] to the son, and the son manage his
70   revenue.
GLOUCESTER   O villain, villain! His very opinion in the letter!
Abhorred villain! Unnatural, detested, brutish villain! worse
than brutish! Go, sirrah,[9] seek him. I'll apprehend him. Abom-
inable villain! Where is he?
75   EDMUND   I do not well know, my lord. If it shall please you to
suspend your indignation against my brother till you can derive
from him better testimony of his intent, you shall run a certain°   safe; reliable
course; where,° if you violently proceed against him, mistaking   whereas
his purpose, it would make a great gap in your own honor and
80   shake in pieces the heart of his obedience. I dare pawn down°   I dare stake
my life for him that he hath wrote this to feel° my affection to   feel out
your honor, and to no further pretense of danger.[1]
GLOUCESTER   Think you so?
EDMUND   If your honor judge it meet,° I will place you where   appropriate
85   you shall hear us confer of this, and by an auricular° assurance   audible
have your satisfaction; and that without any further delay than
this very evening.
GLOUCESTER   He cannot be such a monster—
EDMUND   Nor is not, sure.
90   GLOUCESTER   To his father, that so tenderly and entirely loves
him. Heaven and earth! Edmund, seek him out; wind me into
him,[2] I pray you; frame° the business after your own wisdom. I   arrange
would unstate myself, to be in a due resolution.[3]
EDMUND   I will seek him, sir, presently;° convey° the business as   immediately / carry out
95   I shall find means, and acquaint you withal.°   therewith
GLOUCESTER   These late° eclipses in the sun and moon portend   recent
no good to us.[4] Though the wisdom of nature can reason it
thus and thus, yet nature finds itself scourged by the sequent
effects.[5] Love cools, friendship falls off, brothers divide; in
100   cities, mutinies; in countries, discord; in palaces, treason; and
the bond cracked 'twixt son and father. This villain of mine
comes under the prediction; there's son against father. The
king falls from bias of nature;[6] there's father against child. We
have seen the best of our time. Machinations, hollowness,°   insincerity
105   treachery, and all ruinous disorders, follow us disquietly to our
graves. Find out this villain, Edmund; it shall lose thee noth-
ing; do it carefully. And the noble and true-hearted Kent ban-
ished! his offence, honesty! 'Tis strange.   *Exit*
EDMUND   This is the excellent foppery° of the world, that, when   foolishness
110   we are sick in fortune, often the surfeit° of our own behavior,   excesses
we make guilty of° our disasters the sun, the moon, and the   we hold responsible for
stars; as if we were villains by necessity; fools by heavenly com-
pulsion; knaves, thieves, and treachers,° by spherical predomi-   traitors

8. A child under eighteen years who was legally depen-
dent, often orphaned.
9. A form of address used with children or social infe-
riors.
1. No further intention to do harm.
2. Worm your way into his confidence (with "me" as an
intensifier); worm your way into his confidence for me
("me" as a term of respect).
3. I would give up everything to have my doubts resolved.
4. Lunar and solar eclipses that were seen in London

about a year before the play's first recorded performance
would have added spice to this superstitious belief in
the role of heavenly bodies as augurs of misfortune.
5. *Though . . . effects:* Though natural science may
explain the eclipses this way or that, nature (and family
bonds) suffers in the effects that follow.
6. The King deviates from his natural inclination. In the
game of bowls, the "bias" ("course") is the eccentric
path taken by the weighted ball when thrown.

nance;[7] drunkards, liars, and adulterers, by an enforced obe-
dience of planetary influence; and all that we are evil in, by a
divine thrusting on.° An admirable° evasion of whore-master   *imposition / amazing*
man, to lay his goatish disposition to the charge of a star![8] My
father compounded° with my mother under the dragon's tail,   *coupled*
and my nativity was under Ursa Major,[9] so that it follows, I am
rough and lecherous. Fut!° I should have been that° I am, had   *By Christ's foot / what*
the maidenliest star in the firmament twinkled on my bas-
tardizing. Edgar—

    Enter EDGAR

and pat° he comes like the catastrophe° of the old comedy. My   *on cue / resolution*
cue is villainous melancholy, with a sigh like Tom o' Bedlam.[1]
O, these eclipses do portend these divisions! Fa, sol, la, mi.[2]

EDGAR How now, brother Edmund? What serious contempla-
tion are you in?

EDMUND I am thinking, brother, of a prediction I read this
other day, what should follow these eclipses.

EDGAR Do you busy yourself about that?

EDMUND I promise you, the effects he writes of succeed° unhap-   *follow*
pily; as of unnaturalness between the child and the parent;
death, dearth, dissolutions of ancient amities; divisions in state,
menaces and maledictions against king and nobles; needless
diffidences,° banishment of friends, dissipation of cohorts,[3]   *baseless suspicions*
nuptial breaches, and I know not what.

EDGAR How long have you been a sectary astronomical?°   *a devotee of astrology*

EDMUND Come, come! When saw you my father last?

EDGAR Why, the night gone by.

EDMUND Spake you with him?

EDGAR Ay, two hours together.

EDMUND Parted you in good terms? Found you no displeasure
in him by word or countenance?°   *appearance; demeanor*

EDGAR None at all.

EDMUND Bethink yourself wherein you may have offended him;
and at my entreaty forbear° his presence till some little time   *avoid*
hath qualified° the heat of his displeasure; which at this instant   *moderated*
so rageth in him, that with the mischief of your person it would
scarcely allay.[4]

EDGAR Some villain hath done me wrong.

EDMUND That's my fear. I pray you, have a continent forbear-
ance° till the speed of his rage goes slower; and, as I say, retire   *restrained absence*
with me to my lodging, from whence I will fitly° bring you to   *when suitable*
hear my lord speak. Pray ye, go! There's my key. If you do stir
abroad, go armed.

EDGAR Armed, brother?

EDMUND Brother, I advise you to the best. Go armed. I am no
honest man if there be any good meaning towards you. I have

---

7. By the ascendancy of a particular planet. In the uni-
verse as conceived by Ptolemy, the planets revolved about
the earth on crystalline spheres.
8. *to lay . . . star:* to hold a star responsible for his lustful
desires. In Greek mythology, the satyr, a creature with
goatlike characteristics, was notoriously lecherous.
9. Constellations: *Dragon's tail* = Draco and *Ursa
Major* = Great Bear.
1. The usual name for lunatic beggars; "Bethlehem,"
shortened to "Bedlam," was the name of the oldest and

best-known London madhouse.
2. The portion of the scale Edmund sings is an aug-
mented fourth, an interval considered at this time very
discordant; it was sometimes referred to as "the devil in
music." *divisions:* social fractures; melodic embellish-
ments.
3. Scattering of forces.
4. *with . . . allay:* even harming you bodily would hardly
relieve his anger; alternatively, with the irritant of your
presence, it (Gloucester's anger) would not be abated.

told you what I have seen and heard; but faintly, nothing like
160 the image and horror of it. Pray you, away!
EDGAR   Shall I hear from you anon?
EDMUND   I do serve you in this business.   *Exit* EDGAR
A credulous father, and a brother noble,
Whose nature is so far from doing harms,
165 That he suspects none; on whose foolish honesty
My practices° ride easy! I see the business.⁵   plots
Let me, if not by birth, have lands by wit:°   intelligence
All with me's meet that I can fashion fit.⁶   *Exit*

1.3

Enter GONERIL, *and* OSWALD, *her steward*
GONERIL   Did my father strike my gentleman for chiding of his fool?
OSWALD   Yes, madam.
GONERIL   By day and night he wrongs me; every hour
He flashes into one gross crime° or other,   offense
5   That sets us all at odds. I'll not endure it.
His knights grow riotous, and himself upbraids us
On every trifle. When he returns from hunting,
I will not speak with him. Say I am sick.
If you come slack of former services,¹
10   You shall do well; the fault of it I'll answer.°   answer for
OSWALD   He's coming, madam; I hear him.
Horns within°   Hunting horns offstage
GONERIL   Put on what weary negligence you please,
You and your fellows.° I'd have it come to question.   servants
If he dislike it, let him to our sister,
15   Whose mind and mine, I know, in that are one,
Not to be overruled. Idle° old man,   Foolish
That still would manage those authorities
That he hath given away! Now, by my life,
Old fools are babes again, and must be used
20   With checks as flatteries, when they are seen abused.²
Remember what I tell you.
OSWALD   Well, madam.
GONERIL   And let his knights have colder looks among you.
What grows of it, no matter; advise your fellows so.
I would breed from hence occasions, and I shall,
25   That I may speak.³ I'll write straight° to my sister,   straightaway
To hold my very° course. Prepare for dinner.   *Exeunt*   exact

1.4

Enter KENT, *disguised*
KENT   If but as well¹ I other accents borrow,
That can my speech defuse,° my good intent   disguise
May carry through itself to that full issue°   result
For which I razed my likeness.² Now, banished Kent,

---

5. It is now clear to me what needs to be done.
6. Anything is fine by me as long as I can make it serve
my purpose. *meet:* justifiable; appropriate.
1.3 Location: The Duke of Albany's castle.
1. If you offer him less service (and respect) than before.
2. *Old . . . abused:* When foolish old men act like chil-
dren, rebukes are the kindest treatment when kind treat-

ment is abused.
3. *I would . . . speak:* I wish to foster situations, and I
shall, in which to speak my mind.
1.4 Location: As before.
1. As well as disguising my appearance.
2. Disguised my appearance; shaved off my beard (with
a pun on "razor").

5   If thou canst serve where thou dost stand condemned,
    So may it come,° thy master, whom thou lovest,   *come to pass*
    Shall find thee full of labors.°   *helpful; keen*

             Horns within. Enter LEAR, KNIGHTS, *and attendants*[3]

LEAR   Let me not stay° a jot for dinner; go get it ready.   *wait*

                                 Exit an attendant

    How now! What° art thou?   *Who*

10 KENT   A man, sir.

LEAR   What dost thou profess?[4] What wouldst thou with us?

KENT   I do profess to be no less than I seem; to serve him truly
that will put me in trust; to love him that is honest; to converse°   *associate*
with him that is wise and says little; to fear judgment; to fight

15   when I cannot choose;° and to eat no fish.[5]   *when I must*

LEAR   What art thou?

KENT   A very honest-hearted fellow, and as poor as the king.

LEAR   If thou be as poor for a subject as he is for a king, thou art
poor enough. What wouldst thou?

20 KENT   Service.

LEAR   Who wouldst thou serve?

KENT   You.

LEAR   Dost thou know me, fellow?

KENT   No, sir; but you have that in your countenance which I

25   would fain° call master.   *gladly*

LEAR   What's that?

KENT   Authority.

LEAR   What services canst thou do?

KENT   I can keep honest counsel,° ride, run, mar a curious tale   *keep secrets*

30   in telling it,[6] and deliver a plain message bluntly. That which
ordinary men are fit for, I am qualified in; and the best of me
is diligence.

LEAR   How old art thou?

KENT   Not so young, sir, to love a woman for singing, nor so old

35   to dote on her for anything. I have years on my back forty-eight.

LEAR   Follow me; thou shalt serve me. If I like thee no worse
after dinner, I will not part from thee yet. Dinner, ho dinner!
Where's my knave? my fool? Go you, and call my fool hither.

                                 Exit an attendant

             Enter OSWALD

    You, you, sirrah, where's my daughter?

40 OSWALD   So please you—   *Exit*

LEAR   What says the fellow there? Call the clotpoll° back. (*Exit*   *blockhead*
a KNIGHT) Where's my fool, ho? I think the world's asleep.

             Re-enter KNIGHT

    How now! where's that mongrel?

KNIGHT   He says, my lord, your daughter is not well.

45 LEAR   Why came not the slave back to me when I called him?

KNIGHT   Sir, he answered me in the roundest° manner, he would   *bluntest; rudest*
not.

LEAR   He would not!

KNIGHT   My lord, I know not what the matter is; but, to my judg-

---

3. Critics of James I complained that he devalued honors by granting too many knighthoods and that he squandered too much time in hunting.
4. What is your job (profession)? Kent, in reply, uses "profess" punningly to mean "claim."

5. And not to be a Catholic or penitent (Catholics were obliged to eat fish on specified occasions and as penance); alternatively, to be a manly man, a meat eater.
6. That is, Kent's plain, blunt speech would make him ill suited to tell a convoluted ("curious") tale.

50 ment, your highness is not entertained with that ceremonious
affection as you were wont,° there's a great abatement of kind-   *accustomed to*
ness appears as well in the general dependants° as in the duke   *servants*
himself also and your daughter.

LEAR Ha! sayest thou so?

55 KNIGHT I beseech you pardon me, my lord, if I be mistaken; for
my duty cannot be silent when I think your highness wronged.

LEAR Thou but rememberest° me of mine own conception.° I   *remind / perception*
have perceived a most faint neglect of late; which I have
rather blamed as mine own jealous curiosity[7] than as a very

60 pretense° and purpose of unkindness. I will look further into 't.   *a true intention*
But where's my fool? I have not seen him this two days.

KNIGHT Since my young lady's going into France, sir, the fool
hath much pined away.

LEAR No more of that; I have noted it well. Go you and tell my

65 daughter I would speak with her.   *Exit* KNIGHT
Go you, call hither my fool.   *Exit an attendant*
          Re-enter OSWALD
O, you sir, you! Come you hither, sir. Who am I, sir?

OSWALD My lady's father.

LEAR "My lady's father"! My lord's knave! You whoreson dog!

70 you slave! you cur!

OSWALD I am none of these, my lord; I beseech your pardon.

LEAR Do you bandy looks with me, you rascal? (*Striking him*)

OSWALD I'll not be struck, my lord.

KENT Nor tripped neither, you base foot-ball player.[8]
          Tripping up his heels

75 LEAR I thank thee, fellow; thou servest me, and I'll love thee.

KENT Come, sir, arise, away! I'll teach you differences.° Away,   *(of rank)*
away! If you will measure your lubber's length again,[9] tarry; but
away! Go to! Have you wisdom? so.   *Pushes* OSWALD *out*

LEAR Now, my friendly knave, I thank thee: there's earnest of°   *downpayment for*

80 thy service. (*Giving* KENT *money*)
          Enter FOOL

FOOL Let me hire him too. Here's my coxcomb.°   *fool's cap*
          Offering KENT *his cap*

LEAR How now, my pretty knave! How dost thou?

FOOL Sirrah, you were best take my coxcomb.

KENT Why, fool?

85 FOOL Why, for taking one's part that's out of favor. Nay, an thou
canst not smile as the wind sits, thou'lt catch cold shortly.[1]
There, take my coxcomb! Why, this fellow has banished two
on's daughters,[2] and did the third a blessing against his will. If
thou follow him, thou must needs wear my coxcomb. How

90 now, nuncle!° Would I had two coxcombs and two daughters!   *(mine) uncle*

LEAR Why, my boy?

FOOL If I gave them all my living,° I'd keep my coxcombs   *goods*
myself.[3] There's mine; beg another of thy daughters.

LEAR Take heed, sirrah; the whip.

95 FOOL Truth's a dog must to° kennel; he must be whipped out,   *go to*

---

7. *jealous curiosity:* paranoid concern with niceties.
8. Football was a rough street game played by the poor.
9. If you will be stretched out by me again. *lubber:*
clumsy oaf.
1. *an . . . shortly:* if you can't keep in favor with those

in power, you will soon find yourself left out in the cold.
2. By abdicating, Lear has in effect prevented his el-
dest daughters from any longer being his subjects, just
as if he had "banished" them.
3. I'd be twice as much a fool.

when Lady the brach[4] may stand by the fire and stink.

LEAR A pestilent gall° to me!   *annoyance; bitterness*

FOOL Sirrah, I'll teach thee a speech.

LEAR Do.

100 FOOL Mark it, nuncle:

       Have more than thou showest,

       Speak less than thou knowest,

       Lend less than thou owest,°   *own*

       Ride more than thou goest,°   *walk*

105   Learn° more than thou trowest,°   *Hear / believe*

       Set less than thou throwest,[5]

       Leave thy drink and thy whore,

       And keep in-a-door,

       And thou shalt have more

110   Than two tens to a score.[6]

KENT This is nothing, fool.

FOOL Then 'tis like the breath° of an unfeed° lawyer; you gave   *speech / unpaid*
me nothing for 't. Can you make no use of nothing, nuncle?

LEAR Why, no, boy; nothing can be made out of nothing.

115 FOOL (*to* KENT) Prithee, tell him, so much the rent of his land
comes to.[7] He will not believe a fool.

LEAR A bitter fool!

FOOL Dost thou know the difference, my boy, between a bitter
fool and a sweet fool?

120 LEAR No, lad; teach me.

FOOL   That lord that counseled thee

         To give away thy land,

       Come place him here by me,

       Do thou for him stand:°   *represent him*

125   The sweet and bitter fool

         Will presently appear;

       The one in motley[8] here,

       The other found out there.

LEAR Dost thou call me fool, boy?

130 FOOL All thy other titles thou hast given away; that thou wast
born with.

KENT This is not altogether fool,[9] my lord.

FOOL No, faith, lords and great men will not let me; if I had a
monopoly out, they would have part on 't: and ladies too, they

135 will not let me have all fool to myself; they'll be snatching.
Give me an egg, nuncle, and I'll give thee two crowns.

LEAR What two crowns shall they be?

FOOL Why, after I have cut the egg i' the middle, and eat up the
meat,° the two crowns of the egg. When thou clovest° thy   *edible part / cleaved*

140 crown i' the middle, and gavest away both parts, thou borest°   *you carried*
thy ass on thy back o'er the dirt. Thou hadst little wit° in thy   *sense*
bald crown, when thou gavest thy golden one away. If I speak
like myself° in this, let him be whipped that first finds it so.[1]   *(like a fool)*

---

4. *Lady the bitch.* Pet dogs were often called "Lady"
such and such. The allusion is to Regan and Goneril,
who are now being preferred to truthful Cordelia.
5. Don't gamble everything on a single cast of the
dice.
6. *And thou . . . score:* And there will be more than two
tens in your twenty—that is, you will become richer.

7. Remind him that no land means no rent; with a pun
on "rent" meaning "torn," "divided."
8. Multicolored dress of a court jester.
9. Foolish, folly. In the next line, the Fool takes "altogether
fool" to mean "one who has cornered the market on folly."
1. *that . . . so:* who first discovers for himself that this
is true; who first considers this to be foolish.

Singing

Fools had ne'er less wit in a year;

145   For wise men are grown foppish,[2]

They know not how their wits to wear,

Their manners are so apish.°   *stupid; imitative*

LEAR   When were you wont° to be so full of songs, sirrah?   *accustomed*

FOOL   I have used° it, nuncle, ever since thou madest thy daugh-   *practiced*

150 ters thy mother; for when thou gavest them the rod, and put'st

down thine own breeches,

Singing

Then they for sudden joy did weep,

And I for sorrow sung,

That such a king should play bo-peep,°   *a child's game*

155   And go the fools among.

Prithee, nuncle, keep a schoolmaster that can teach thy fool

to lie. I would fain learn to lie.

LEAR   An° you lie, sirrah, we'll have you whipped.   *If*

FOOL   I marvel what kin° thou and thy daughters are. They'll   *how alike*

160 have me whipped for speaking true, thou'lt have me whipped

for lying; and sometimes I am whipped for holding my peace.

I had rather be any kind o' thing than a fool; and yet I would

not be thee, nuncle; thou hast pared thy wit o' both sides, and

left nothing i' the middle. Here comes one o' the parings.

Enter GONERIL

165 LEAR   How now, daughter! What makes that frontlet[3] on?

Methinks you are too much of late i' the frown.

FOOL   Thou wast a pretty fellow when thou hadst no need to

care for her frowning; now thou art an O without a figure.[4] I

am better than thou art now; I am a fool, thou art nothing.   [*To*

170 GONERIL] Yes, forsooth, I will hold my tongue; so your face bids

me, though you say nothing. Mum, mum,

He that keeps nor crust nor crum,

Weary of all, shall want° some.   *lack; be in need of*

(*Pointing to* LEAR) That's a shealed peascod.°   *empty pea pod; nothing*

175 GONERIL   Not only, sir, this your all-licensed° fool,   *unrestrained*

But other of your insolent retinue

Do hourly carp and quarrel, breaking forth

In rank° and not-to-be-endured riots. Sir,   *foul; spreading*

I had thought, by making this well known unto you,

180 To have found a safe° redress; but now grow fearful,   *sure*

By what yourself too late° have spoke and done,   *recently*

That you protect this course, and put it on°   *encourage it*

By your allowance; which if you should, the fault

Would not 'scape censure, nor the redresses sleep,

185 Which, in the tender of a wholesome weal,

Might in their working do you that offense,

Which else were shame, that then necessity

Will call discreet proceeding.[5]

---

2. *Fools . . . foppish:* Professional fools have never been as witless since wise men have lately outdone them in idiocy.
3. Band worn on the forehead; here, a metaphor for "frown."
4. A zero without a preceding digit; nothing.
5. *which if you . . . proceeding:* if you do approve (of your

attendants' behavior), you will not escape criticism, nor will it be without retribution, which for the common good will cause you pain. While this would otherwise be improper, it will be seen as a prudent ("discreet") action under the circumstances. *tender of:* concern for. *weal:* state, commonwealth. *then necessity:* the demands of the time.

FOOL   For, you know, nuncle,
190   The hedge-sparrow fed the cuckoo⁶ so long,
                That it had it° head bit off by it young.°   *its / (the young cuckoo)*
         So, out went the candle, and we were left darkling.°   *in the dark*
LEAR   Are you our daughter?
GONERIL   Come, sir.
195   I would° you would make use of that good wisdom,   *wish*
         Whereof I know you are fraught,° and put away   *full*
         These dispositions,° that of late transform you   *moods; attitudes*
         From what you rightly are.
FOOL   May not an ass know when the cart draws the horse?
200   Whoop, Jug!⁷ I love thee.
LEAR   Doth any here know me? This is not Lear.
         Doth Lear walk thus? speak thus? Where are his eyes?
         Either his notion° weakens, his discernings   *intellect*
         Are lethargied—Ha! waking?° 'Tis not so.   *am I awake*
205   Who is it that can tell me who I am?
FOOL   Lear's shadow.
LEAR   I would° learn that; for, by the marks° of sovereignty,   *wish to / evidence*
         knowledge, and reason, I should be false persuaded I had
         daughters.
210 FOOL   Which° they will make an obedient father.   *Whom*
LEAR   Your name, fair gentlewoman?
GONERIL   This admiration,° sir, is much o' the savor   *excessive amazement*
         Of other your new pranks. I do beseech you
         To understand my purposes aright.
215   As you are old and reverend, you should be wise.
         Here do you keep a hundred knights and squires;
         Men so disordered,° so deboshed° and bold,   *disorderly / debauched*
         That this our court, infected with their manners,
         Shows° like a riotous inn. Epicurism° and lust   *Appears / Gluttony*
220   Make it more like a tavern or a brothel
         Than a graced° palace. The shame itself doth speak   *an honored*
         For instant remedy; be then desired
         By her, that else will take the thing she begs,
         A little to disquantity your train;°   *to reduce your retinue*
225   And the remainder that shall still depend,°   *be retained*
         To be such men as may besort° your age,   *befit*
         And know themselves° and you.   *know their place*
LEAR   Darkness and devils!
         Saddle my horses! call my train together!
         Degenerate bastard! I'll not trouble thee.
230   Yet° have I left a daughter.   *Still*
GONERIL   You strike my people, and your disordered rabble
         Make servants of their betters.
                Enter ALBANY
LEAR   Woe that° too late repents!—(*To* ALBANY)   *Woe to him who*
         O, sir, are you come?
235   Is it your will? Speak, sir. Prepare my horses!
         Ingratitude, thou marble-hearted fiend,
         More hideous when thou show'st thee in a child
         Than the sea-monster!

---

6. The cuckoo lays its eggs in other birds' nests.   7. Nickname for "Joan"; sobriquet for a whore.

ALBANY   Pray, sir, be patient.
  LEAR *(to* GONERIL)   Detested kite!° thou liest: *carrion-eating hawk*
240 My train are men of choice and rarest parts,°   *qualities*
That all particulars of duty know,
And in the most exact regard support
The worships of° their name. O most small fault,   *honors accorded*
How ugly didst thou in Cordelia show!
245 That, like an engine, wrench'd my frame of nature
From the fixed place;⁸ drew from my heart all love,
And added to the gall. O Lear, Lear, Lear!
Beat at this gate, that let thy folly in, *(striking his head)*
And thy dear° judgment out! Go, go, my people.   *precious*
250 ALBANY   My lord, I am guiltless, as I am ignorant
Of what hath moved you.
  LEAR   It may be so, my lord.
Hear, Nature, hear! dear goddess, hear!
Suspend thy purpose, if thou didst intend
To make this creature fruitful!
255 Into her womb convey sterility!
Dry up in her the organs of increase;
And from her derogate° body never spring   *debased*
A babe to honor her! If she must teem,°   *breed*
Create her child of spleen,° that it may live   *malice*
260 And be a thwart, disnatured° torment to her!   *a perverse, unnatural*
Let it stamp wrinkles in her brow of youth;
With cadent° tears fret° channels in her cheeks;   *flowing / carve*
Turn all her mother's pains and benefits°   *cares and kind actions*
To laughter and contempt, that she may feel
265 How sharper than a serpent's tooth it is
To have a thankless child! Away, away!   *Exit*
  ALBANY   Now, gods that we adore, whereof comes this?
  GONERIL   Never afflict yourself to know the cause;
But let his disposition have that scope
270 That dotage gives it.
          Re-enter LEAR
  LEAR   What, fifty of my followers at a clap?
Within a fortnight?
  ALBANY   What's the matter, sir?
  LEAR   I'll tell thee. *(To* GONERIL*)* Life and death! I am ashamed
That thou hast power to shake my manhood thus;
275 That these hot tears, which break from me perforce,°   *against my will*
Should make thee worth them. Blasts and fogs upon thee!
The untented woundings° of a father's curse   *The undressed wounds*
Pierce every sense about thee! Old fond° eyes,   *foolish*
Beweep° this cause again, I'll pluck ye out,   *If you weep over*
280 And cast you, with the waters that you lose,
To temper° clay. Yea, is it come to this?   *soften*
Let it be so. Yet have I left a daughter,
Who, I am sure, is kind and comfortable.°   *comforting*
When she shall hear this of thee, with her nails
285 She'll flay thy wolvish visage. Thou shalt find
That I'll resume the shape which thou dost think
I have cast off for ever; thou shalt, I warrant thee.

8. *like . . . place:* as a machine (or lever) dislocated my natural affections from their proper foundations.

Exeunt LEAR, KENT, *and attendants*

GONERIL. Do you mark that, my lord?

ALBANY   I cannot be so partial,° Goneril,   *biased*

290   To° the great love I bear you—   *Because of*

GONERIL   Pray you, content.° What, Oswald, ho! (*To the* FOOL)   *be quiet*
    You sir, more knave than fool, after your master!

FOOL   Nuncle Lear, nuncle Lear, tarry and take the fool with
    thee.

295   A fox, when one has caught her,
                And such a daughter,
                Should sure° to the slaughter,   *surely be sent*
                If my cap would buy a halter:°   *collar; noose*
                So the fool follows after.   *Exit*

GONERIL   This man hath had good counsel!—a hundred

300   knights?
    'Tis politic° and safe to let him keep   *prudent*
    At point° a hundred knights? Yes, that on every dream,   *Armed*
    Each buzz,° each fancy, each complaint, dislike,   *rumor*
    He may enguard° his dotage with their powers,   *protect*

305   And hold our lives in mercy. Oswald, I say!

ALBANY   Well, you may fear too far.

GONERIL   Safer than trust too far:
    Let me still° take away the harms I fear,   *always*
    Not° fear still to be taken. I know his heart.   *Rather than*
    What he hath uttered I have writ my sister.

310   If she sustain him and his hundred knights,
    When I have showed the unfitness—
                Re-enter OSWALD
                         How now, Oswald!
    What, have you writ that letter to my sister?

OSWALD   Yes, madam.

GONERIL   Take you some company, and away to horse!

315   Inform her full of my particular fear,
    And thereto add such reasons of your own
    As may compact° it more. Get you gone,   *compound*
    And hasten your return.   *Exit* OSWALD
    No, no, my lord,

320   This milky gentleness and course of yours
    Though I condemn not, yet, under pardon,°   *begging your pardon*
    You are much more attaxed° for want of wisdom   *taken to task; censured*
    Than praised for harmful mildness.

ALBANY   How far your eyes may pierce° I cannot tell: *foresee*

325   Striving to better, oft we mar what's well.

GONERIL   Nay, then—

ALBANY   Well, well; the event.°   *Exeunt*   *let's see the outcome*

1.5

Enter LEAR, KENT, *and* FOOL

LEAR Go you before° to Gloucester[1] with these letters. Acquaint   *on ahead*
my daughter no further with any thing you know than comes
from her demand out of the letter.[2] If your diligence be not
speedy, I shall be there afore you.

5   KENT I will not sleep, my lord, till I have delivered your letter.

                                                         Exit

FOOL If a man's brains were in 's heels, were't not in danger of
kibes?°   *chilblains*

LEAR Ay, boy.

FOOL Then, I prithee, be merry; thy wit shall ne'er go slip-shod.[3]

10 LEAR Ha, ha, ha!

FOOL Shalt° see thy other daughter will use thee kindly; for   *Thou shalt*
though she's as like this as a crab's° like an apple, yet I can tell   *crab apple; sour apple*
what I can tell.

LEAR Why, what canst thou tell, my boy?

15 FOOL She will taste as like this as a crab does to a crab. Thou
canst tell why one's nose stands i' the middle on's° face?   *of one's*

LEAR No.

FOOL Why, to keep one's eyes of either side's nose, that what a
man cannot smell out, 'a° may spy into.   *he*

20 LEAR I did her wrong—

FOOL Canst tell how an oyster makes his shell?

LEAR No.

FOOL Nor I neither; but I can tell why a snail has a house.

LEAR Why?

25 FOOL Why, to put his head in; not to give it away to his daugh-
ters, and leave his horns without a case.[4]

LEAR I will forget my nature.[5] So kind a father! Be my horses
ready?

FOOL Thy asses° are gone about 'em. The reason why the seven   *(servants)*
30 stars° are no more than seven is a pretty reason.   *the Pleiades*

LEAR Because they are not eight?

FOOL Yes, indeed. Thou wouldst make a good fool.

LEAR To take 't again perforce![6] Monster ingratitude!

FOOL If thou wert my fool, nuncle, I'd have thee beaten for
35 being old before thy time.

LEAR How's that?

FOOL Thou shouldst not have been old till thou hadst been wise.

LEAR O, let me not be mad, not mad, sweet heaven!
Keep me in temper;° I would not be mad!   *sane*

        Enter GENTLEMEN

40 How now! Are the horses ready?

GENTLEMEN Ready, my lord.

LEAR Come, boy.

FOOL She that's a maid now, and laughs at my departure,

1.5 Location: Before Albany's castle.
1. To Gloucestershire, where Cornwall and Regan
reside.
2. *than . . . letter:* other than such questions as are
prompted by the letter.
3. Literally, your brains will not wear slippers (to warm
feet that are afflicted with chilblains); feet of any intel-
ligence would not walk toward Regan.

4. Protective covering for his head or concealment for his
horns (horns were the conventional sign of a cuckold).
The Fool reflects the cynical view, common in the
period, that all married men are inevitably cuckolded.
5. Lose my fatherly feelings. *nature:* character.
6. To take it back by force. Lear may refer to Goneril's
treachery, or he may be contemplating resuming his
authority.

Shall not be a maid long, unless things be cut shorter.[7]

Exeunt

2.1

Enter EDMUND *and* CURAN *meeting*

EDMUND   Save° thee, Curan.   *God save*

CURAN   And you, sir. I have been with your father, and given
him notice that the Duke of Cornwall and Regan his duchess
will be here with him this night.

5   EDMUND   How comes that?

CURAN   Nay, I know not. You have heard of the news abroad—
I mean the whispered ones, for they are yet but ear-bussing
arguments?[1]

EDMUND   Not I. Pray you, what are they?

10   CURAN   Have you heard of no likely wars toward,° 'twixt the   *impending*
Dukes of Cornwall and Albany?

EDMUND   Not a word.

CURAN   You may do, then, in time. Fare you well, sir.   *Exit*

EDMUND   The duke be here tonight? The better! best!

15   This weaves itself perforce° into my business.   *necessarily*
My father hath set guard to take my brother;
And I have one thing, of a queasy question,[2]
Which I must act. Briefness and fortune, work!°   *be with me*
Brother, a word! Descend! Brother, I say!

Enter EDGAR

20   My father watches. O sir, fly this place!
Intelligence is given where you are hid.
You have now the good advantage of the night.
Have you not spoken 'gainst the Duke of Cornwall?
He's coming hither; now, i' the night, i' the haste,

25   And Regan with him: have you nothing said
Upon his party° 'gainst the Duke of Albany?   *On his (Cornwall's) side*
Advise yourself.°   *Consider carefully*

EDGAR   I am sure on't,° not a word.   *of it*

EDMUND   I hear my father coming. Pardon me!
In cunning I must draw my sword upon you:

30   Draw; seem to defend yourself; now quit you° well.   *acquit yourself*
Yield! Come before my father. Light, ho, here!
Fly, brother. Torches, torches! So farewell.   *Exit* EDGAR
Some blood drawn on me would beget opinion°   *produce the impression*
(*wounds his arm*)
Of my more fierce endeavor. I have seen drunkards

35   Do more than this in sport. Father, father!
Stop, stop! No help?

Enter GLOUCESTER, *and servants with torches*

GLOUCESTER   Now, Edmund, where's the villain?

EDMUND   Here stood he in the dark, his sharp sword out,
Mumbling of wicked charms, conjuring the moon
To stand° auspicious mistress,—   *To act as his*

40   GLOUCESTER   But where is he?

EDMUND   Look, sir, I bleed.

---

7. *She . . . shorter:* A girl who would laugh at my leav-
ing would be so foolish that she could not remain a vir-
gin for long; "things" refers both to the unfolding event
and to penises.

2.1 Location: Gloucester's castle.
1. Barely whispered affairs. *bussing:* buzzing.
2. And I have a hazardous and delicate problem.

GLOUCESTER   Where is the villain, Edmund?

EDMUND   Fled this way, sir. When by no means he could—

GLOUCESTER   Pursue him, ho! Go after.   *Exeunt some servants*

    By no means what?

45   EDMUND   Persuade me to the murder of your lordship;

    But that° I told him, the revenging gods   *In response to that*

    'Gainst parricides did all their thunders bend;

    Spoke, with how manifold and strong a bond

    The child was bound to the father; sir, in fine,°   *finally*

50   Seeing how loathly opposite° I stood   *opposed*

    To his unnatural purpose, in fell° motion,   *deadly*

    With his prepared sword, he charges home°   *strikes to the heart of*

    My unprovided° body, lanched° mine arm: *unprotected / struck*

    But when he saw my best alarumed spirits,

55   Bold in the quarrel's right,[3] roused to the encounter,

    Or whether gasted° by the noise I made,   *frightened*

    Full suddenly he fled.

GLOUCESTER   Let him fly far.

    Not in this land shall he remain uncaught;

    And found—dispatch.° The noble duke my master,   *And once found—killed*

60   My worthy arch° and patron, comes to-night: *lord*

    By his authority I will proclaim it,

    That he which finds him shall deserve our thanks,

    Bringing the murderous caitiff° to the stake;[4]   *wretch*

    He that conceals him, death.

65   EDMUND   When I dissuaded him from his intent,

    And found him pight° to do it, with curst° speech   *resolved / bitter*

    I threatened to discover° him. He replied,   *expose*

    "Thou unpossessing bastard! dost thou think

    If I would stand against thee, would the reposal°   *placing*

70   Of any trust, virtue, or worth in thee

    Make thy words faithed?° No. What I should deny—   *credible*

    As this I would; ay, though thou didst produce

    My very character[5]—I'd turn it all

    To[6] thy suggestion, plot, and damned practice:°   *scheming*

75   And thou must make a dullard of the world,

    If they not thought the profits of my death

    Were very pregnant and potential spurs

    To make thee seek it."[7]

GLOUCESTER   Strong° and fast'ned° villain!   *Flagrant / incorrigible*

    Would he deny his letter? I never got° him.   *begot*

    Tucket° within   *Flourish of trumpets*

80   Hark, the Duke's trumpets! I know not why he comes.

    All ports° I'll bar; the villain shall not 'scape;   *seaports; exits*

    The duke must grant me that. Besides, his picture[8]

    I will send far and near, that all the kingdom

    May have due note of him; and of my land,

85   Loyal and natural° boy, I'll work the means   *loving; illegitimate*

    To make thee capable.°   *legally able to inherit*

---

3. *my best . . . right:* that I was fully roused to action, made brave by righteousness.

4. Treachery and rebellion were crimes for which one could be burned.

5. Handwriting; but also, a true summary of my character.

6. *I'd . . . / To:* I'd blame it all on.

7. *And thou . . . it:* And do you think the world so stupid that it could not see the benefit you would get from my death (and thus a motive for plotting to kill me)? *pregnant:* full. *potential spurs:* powerful temptations.

8. Likenesses of outlaws were drawn up, printed, and publicly displayed, sometimes with an offer of reward as in "Wanted" posters.

Enter CORNWALL, REGAN, *and attendants*

CORNWALL   How now, my noble friend! Since I came hither,
(Which I can call but now) I have heard strange news.
REGAN   If it be true, all vengeance comes too short
90   Which can pursue the offender. How dost, my lord?
GLOUCESTER   O, madam, my old heart is cracked, is cracked!
REGAN   What, did my father's godson seek your life?
He whom my father named? Your Edgar?
GLOUCESTER   O, lady, lady, shame would have it hid!
95 REGAN   Was he not companion with the riotous knights
That tend° upon my father?   attend
GLOUCESTER   I know not, madam. 'Tis too bad, too bad!
EDMUND   Yes, madam, he was of that consòrt.°   company
REGAN   No marvel, then, though° he were ill affected.°   that / ill disposed
100 'Tis they have put him on° the old man's death,   have urged him to seek
To have th' expense° and waste of his revènues.   use
I have this present evening from my sister
Been well informed of them; and with such cautions
That if they come to sojourn at my house,
I'll not be there.
105 CORNWALL   Nor I, assure thee, Regan.
Edmund, I hear that you have shown your father
A child-like office.°   filial service
EDMUND   'Twas my duty, sir.
GLOUCESTER   He did bewray his practice,° and received   uncover his (Edgar's) plot
This hurt you see, striving to apprehend him.
CORNWALL   Is he pursued?
110 GLOUCESTER   Ay, my good lord.
CORNWALL   If he be taken, he shall never more
Be feared of doing harm. Make your own purpose,
How in my strength you please.⁹ For you, Edmund,
Whose virtue and obedience doth this instant
115 So much commend itself, you shall be ours.
Natures of such deep trust we shall much need;
You we first seize on.
EDMUND   I shall serve you, sir,
Truly, however else.°   if nothing else
GLOUCESTER   For him I thank your grace.
CORNWALL   You know not why we came to visit you—
120 REGAN   Thus out of season, threading dark-eyed night.
Occasions, noble Gloucester, of some poise,°   weight
Wherein we must have use of your advice:
Our father he hath writ, so hath our sister,
Of differences,° which I least thought of fit   quarrels
125 To answer from our home. The several° messengers   various
From hence attend° dispatch. Our good old friend,   await
Lay comforts to your bosom, and bestow
Your needful° counsel to our business,   badly needed
Which craves the instant use.¹
GLOUCESTER   I serve you, madam.
130 Your graces are right welcome.   *Exeunt*

---

9. *Make . . . please:* Devise your plots making use of my forces and authority as you see fit.   1. Which requires immediate attention.

2.2

Enter KENT *and* OSWALD, *severally°*   *separately*

OSWALD Good dawning to thee, friend. Art° of this house?   *Are you a servant*

KENT Ay.

OSWALD Where may we set our horses?

KENT I' the mire.

5 OSWALD Prithee, if thou lovest me,° tell me.   *if you will be so kind*

KENT I love thee not.

OSWALD Why, then, I care not for thee.

KENT If I had thee in Lipsbury pinfold,[1] I would make thee care
for me.

10 OSWALD Why dost thou use° me thus? I know thee not.   *treat*

KENT Fellow, I know thee.

OSWALD What dost thou know me for?

KENT A knave; a rascal; an eater of broken meats;° a base, proud,   *scraps*
shallow, beggarly, three-suited, hundred-pound, filthy, worsted-

15 stocking knave;[2] a lily-livered, action-taking knave; a whoreson,
glass-gazing, superserviceable, finical rogue; one-trunk-inher-
iting slave;[3] one that wouldst be a bawd in way of good service,[4]
and art nothing but the composition° of a knave, beggar, cow-   *combination*
ard, pandar, and the son and heir of a mongrel bitch; one

20 whom I will beat into clamorous whining, if thou deniest the
least syllable of thy addition.[5]

OSWALD Why, what a monstrous fellow art thou, thus to rail on
one that is neither known of° thee nor knows thee!   *by*

KENT What a brazen-faced varlet° art thou, to deny thou   *rascal*

25 knowest me! Is it two days ago since I tripped up thy heels, and
beat thee before the king? Draw, you rogue! For, though it be
night, yet the moon shines. I'll make a sop of the moonshine[6]
of you. Draw, you whoreson cullionly barber-monger,[7] draw!

Drawing his sword

OSWALD Away! I have nothing to do with thee.

30 KENT Draw, you rascal! You come with letters against the king,
and take Vanity the puppet's part against the royalty of her
father.[8] Draw, you rogue, or I'll so carbonado[9] your shanks!
Draw, you rascal! Come your ways!°   *Come forward*

OSWALD Help, ho! murther! help!

35 KENT Strike, you slave! Stand, rogue! Stand, you neat° slave!   *elegant; foppish*
Strike! [*Beating him*]

OSWALD Help, ho! muther! murther!

Enter EDMUND *with his rapier drawn,* CORNWALL,
REGAN, GLOUCESTER, *and servants*

2.2 Location: Before Gloucester's house.
1. If I had you in the enclosure of my mouth (gripped in my teeth). Lipsbury is probably an invented place-name. *pinfold:* pen, animal enclosure.
2. *three-suited . . . knave:* Oswald is being called a poor imitation of a gentleman. Servants were permitted three suits a year; one hundred pounds was the minimum qualification for the purchase of one of King James's knighthoods; a gentleman would wear silk, not "worsted" (of thick woolen material), stockings.
3. *lily-livered:* cowardly. *action-taking:* litigious, one who would rather use the law than his fists. *glass-gazing:* mirror-gazing. *superserviceable:* overly officious, or too ready to serve. *finical:* finicky, fastidious. *one-trunk-inheriting:* owning only what would fill one trunk.

4. *one that . . . service:* one who would even be a pimp if called upon.
5. Of the descriptions Kent has just applied to him. *addition:* title (used ironically).
6. Kent proposes so to skewer and pierce Oswald that his body might soak up moonlight. *sop:* piece of bread to be steeped or dunked in soup.
7. *cullionly barber-monger:* despicable frequenter of hairdressers. *cullion:* testicle.
8. *and take . . . father:* and support Goneril, here depicted as a dressed-up doll whose pride is contrasted with Lear's kingliness.
9. Slash or score as one would the surface of meat in preparation for broiling.

EDMUND   How now! What's the matter?
　　　　Parts them

KENT   With you, goodman boy, an° you please! Come, I'll flesh   *if*
40　　ye!¹ Come, on, young master!

GLOUCESTER   Weapons! arms! What's the matter here?

CORNWALL   Keep peace, upon your lives!
　　He dies that strikes again. What is the matter?

REGAN   The messengers from our sister and the king.

45　CORNWALL   What is your difference?° Speak.   *quarrel*

OSWALD   I am scarce in breath, my lord.

KENT   No marvel, you have so bestirred your valor. You cowardly
　　rascal, nature disclaims° in thee; a tailor made thee.   *disowns her part*

CORNWALL   Thou art a strange fellow. A tailor² make a man?

50　KENT   Ay, a tailor, sir. A stone-cutter or a painter could not have
　　made him so ill,° though he had been but two hours at the   *so badly*
　　trade.

CORNWALL   Speak yet, how grew your quarrel?

OSWALD   This ancient ruffian, sir, whose life I have spared at suit
55　of° his gray beard—   *on account of*

KENT   Thou whoreson zed!³ thou unnecessary letter! My lord, if
　　you will give me leave, I will tread this unbolted° villain into   *unsifted; coarse*
　　mortar, and daub the walls of a jakes° with him. Spare my gray   *privy; toilet*
　　beard, you wagtail?⁴

60　CORNWALL   Peace, sirrah!
　　You beastly knave, know you no reverence?°   *respect*

KENT   Yes, sir, but anger hath a privilege.

CORNWALL   Why art thou angry?

KENT   That such a slave as this should wear a sword,
65　Who wears no honesty. Such smiling rogues as these,
　　Like rats, oft bite the holy cords⁵ a-twain
　　Which are too intrinse° t' unloose; smooth° every passion   *intricate / flatter*
　　That in natures of their lords rebel;
　　Bring oil to fire, snow to their colder moods;
70　Renege,° affirm, and turn their halcyon beaks⁶   *Deny*
　　With every gale and vary° of their masters,   *mood*
　　Knowing nought, like dogs, but following.
　　A plague upon your epileptic° visage!   *distorted; grimacing*
　　Smile you° my speeches, as° I were a fool?   *Do you smile at / as if*
75　Goose, if I had you upon Sarum plain
　　I'ld drive ye cackling home to Camelot.⁷

CORNWALL   What, art thou mad, old fellow?

GLOUCESTER   How fell you out? say that.

KENT   No contraries° hold more antipathy   *opposites*
80　Than I and such a knave.

CORNWALL   Why dost thou call him knave? What's his offense?

KENT   His countenance likes° me not.   *pleases*

CORNWALL   No more, perchance, does mine, nor his, nor hers.

1. I'll initiate you into fighting, as a hunting dog is given
the taste of blood to rouse it for the chase.
2. Tailors, considered effeminate, were stock objects of
mockery.
3. The letter Z (zed) was considered superfluous and
omitted from many dictionaries.
4. A common English bird that takes its name from the
up-and-down flicking of its tail; this, and its characteristic
hopping from foot to foot, causes it to appear nervous.

5. Bonds of kinship, affection, marriage, or rank.
6. It was believed that the kingfisher (in Greek, *halcyon*)
could be used as a weather vane when dead: suspended
by a fine thread, its beak would turn whatever way the
wind blew.
7. *Goose . . . Camelot:* Comparing him to a cackling
goose, Kent tells Oswald that if he had him on Salisbury
Plain, he would drive him all the way to Camelot, leg-
endary home of King Arthur.

KENT   Sir, 'tis my occupation to be plain.
85   I have seen better faces in my time
Than stands on any shoulder that I see
Before me at this instant.
CORNWALL   This is some fellow,
Who, having been praised for bluntness, doth affect
A saucy roughness, and constrains the garb
90   Quite from his nature.[8] He cannot flatter, he,
An honest mind and plain, he must speak truth!
An they will take it, so; if not, he's plain.[9]
These kind of knaves I know, which in this plainness
Harbor more craft and more corrupter ends
95   Than twenty silly ducking observants
That stretch their duties nicely.[1]
KENT   Sir, in good sooth, in sincere verity,
Under the allowance of your great aspect,[2]
Whose influence, like the wreath of radiant fire
On flickering Phoebus' front,°   *the sun god's forehead*
100 CORNWALL   What mean'st by this?
KENT   To go out of my dialect,° which you discommend so   *normal mode of speech*
much. I know, sir, I am no flatterer. He that beguiled you in a
plain accent was a plain knave; which for my part I will not be,
though I should win your displeasure to entreat me to 't.[3]
105 CORNWALL   What was the offense you gave him?
OSWALD   I never gave him any:
It pleased the king his master very late°   *lately*
To strike at me, upon his misconstruction,°   *misunderstanding (me)*
When he, conjunct,° and flattering his displeasure,   *in league with*
110   Tripped me behind; being down, insulted,° railed,   *I being down, he insulted*
And put upon him such a deal of man,
That worthied him,[4] got praises of the king
For him attempting who was self-subdued;[5]
And, in the fleshment° of this dread exploit,   *excitement; flush*
Drew on me here again.
115 KENT   None of these rogues and cowards
But Ajax is their fool.[6]
CORNWALL   Fetch forth the stocks!
You stubborn miscreant knave, you reverent° braggart,   *old; revered*
We'll teach you—
KENT   Sir, I am too old to learn.
120   Call not your stocks for me. I serve the king;
On whose employment I was sent to you:
You shall do small respect, show too bold malice
Against the grace° and person° of my master,   *majesty / personal honor*

8. *and constrains . . . nature:* and assumes the appearance though it is untrue to his real self. Alternatively (with "his" meaning "its"), and distorts the true shape of plainness from what it naturally is (by turning it into disrespect).
9. If they will accept (Kent's attitude), well and good; if not, he is a plainspoken man (and does not care).
1. *Than . . . nicely:* Than twenty obsequious attendants who constantly bow idiotically, and who perform their functions with excessive diligence ("nicely").
2. With the permission of your great countenance. "Aspect" also refers to the astrological position of a planet; Kent's bombastic language here raises Cornwall

to the mock-heroic proportions of a heavenly body.
3. *He that . . . to 't:* The person who tried to hoodwink you with plain speaking was, indeed, a pure knave—something I won't be, even if you were to beg me to be one (a plain knave, or flatterer).
4. *And put . . . him:* And put on such a show of manliness that he was thought a worthy fellow.
5. For attacking a man who had already surrendered (Kent attacking Oswald).
6. *None . . . fool:* Such rogues and cowards as these talk as if they were greater warriors (and blusterers) than Ajax; such rogues always make even mighty Ajax out to be a fool.

Stocking° his messenger.   *By stocking*

125 CORNWALL   Fetch forth the stocks! As I have life and honor.
There shall he sit till noon.

REGAN   Till noon? Till night, my lord, and all night too!

KENT   Why, madam, if I were your father's dog,
You should not use me so.

REGAN   Sir, being° his knave, I will.   *since you are*

130 CORNWALL   This is a fellow of the self-same color°   *character*
Our sister° speaks of. Come, bring away the stocks!   *sister-in-law*
         Stocks brought out

GLOUCESTER   Let me beseech your grace not to do so.
His fault is much, and the good king his master
Will check° him for't. Your purposed° low correction   *reprimand / intended*

135 Is such as basest and contemnèd'st wretches
For pilferings and most common trespasses
Are punished with: the king must take it ill,
That he, so slightly valued in his messenger,
Should have him thus restrained.

CORNWALL   I'll answer° that.   *be responsible for*

140 REGAN   My sister may receive it much more worse,
To have her gentleman abused, assaulted,
For following° her affairs. Put in his legs.   *carrying out*
         KENT *is put in the stocks*
Come, my good lord, away.
         Exeunt all but GLOUCESTER *and* KENT

GLOUCESTER   I am sorry for thee, friend: 'tis the duke's pleasure,

145 Whose disposition, all the world well knows,
Will not be rubbed° nor stopped: I'll entreat for thee.   *obstructed*

KENT   Pray, do not sir. I have watched° and traveled hard;   *gone without sleep*
Some time I shall sleep out, the rest I'll whistle.
A good man's fortune may grow out at heels:[7]

150 Give° you good morrow!   *God give*

GLOUCESTER   The duke's to blame in this; 't will be ill-taken.
                                        Exit

KENT   Good king, that must approve° the common saw,°   *prove / saying*
Thou out of heaven's benediction comest
To the warm sun![8]

155 Approach, thou beacon[9] to this under globe,
That by thy comfortable beams I may
Peruse this letter! Nothing almost sees miracles
But misery.[1] I know 'tis from Cordelia,
Who hath most fortunately been informed

160 Of my obscurèd° course; (*reads*) "and shall find time   *hidden; disguised*
From this enormous state,° seeking to give   *awful state of affairs*
Losses their remedies." All weary and o'er-watched,°   *too long awake*
Take vantage,° heavy eyes, not to behold   *the opportunity*
This shameful lodging.

165 Fortune, good night; smile once more; turn thy wheel![2]
                                        Sleeps

---

7. The fortunes of even good men sometimes wear thin.
8. *Thou . . . sun:* You come from the blessing of heaven into the heat of the sun (go from good to bad).
9. It is arguable whether Kent here refers to the sun or the moon.
1. *Nothing . . . misery:* Only those suffering misery are

granted miracles; any comfort seems miraculous to those who are miserable.
2. The goddess Fortune was traditionally depicted with a wheel to signify her mutability and caprice. She was believed to take pleasure in arbitrarily lowering those at the top of her wheel and raising those at the bottom.

2.3

Enter EDGAR

EDGAR I heard myself proclaimed;°   *declared an outlaw*
And by the happy° hollow of a tree   *opportune*
Escaped the hunt. No port° is free; no place,   *seaport; exit*
That guard, and most unusual vigilance,
5   Does not attend my taking.° Whiles° I may 'scape,   *await my capture / Until*
I will preserve myself; and am bethought°   *resolved*
To take the basest and most poorest shape
That ever penury, in contempt of° man,   *for*
Brought near to beast. My face I'll grime with filth,
10 Blanket my loins, elf[1] all my hair in knots,
And with presented° nakedness out-face   *exposed*
The winds and persecutions of the sky.
The country gives me proof and precedent
Of Bedlam beggars, who, with roaring voices,
15 Strike° in their numbed and mortified° bare arms   *Stick / deadened*
Pins, wooden pricks, nails, sprigs of rosemary;
And with this horrible object,° from low farms,   *spectacle*
Poor pelting° villages, sheep-cotes, and mills,   *paltry; contemptible*
Sometime with lunatic bans,° sometime with prayers,   *curses*
20 Enforce their charity. Poor Turlygod![2] poor Tom!
That's something yet! Edgar I nothing am.[3]   *Exit*

2.4

Enter LEAR, FOOL, *and* GENTLEMAN

LEAR 'Tis strange that they should so depart from home,
And not send back my messenger.
GENTLEMAN   As I learned,
The night before there was no purpose in them°   *they had no intention*
Of this remove.°   *change of residence*
KENT   Hail to thee, noble master!
5 LEAR Ha!
Makest thou this shame thy pastime?
KENT   No, my lord.
FOOL Ha, ha! he wears cruel garters.[1] Horses are tied by the
heads, dogs and bears by the neck, monkeys by the loins, and
men by the legs. When a man's over-lusty at legs,[2] then he
10 wears wooden nether-stocks.°   *knee socks*
LEAR What's° he that hath so much thy place° mistook   *Who's / position*
To set thee here?
KENT   It is both he and she;
Your son° and daughter.   *son-in-law*
LEAR No.
15 KENT Yes.
LEAR No, I say.
KENT I say, yea.
LEAR No, no, they would not!
KENT Yes, yes, they have!

2.3 Location: As before.
1. Tangle the hair into "elf locks," supposed to be a
favorite trick of malicious elves.
2. A word of unknown origin.
3. Edgar, I am nothing; I am no longer Edgar.

2.4 Location: As before.
1. Worsted garters, punning on "crewel," a thin yarn.
The Fool is actually referring to the stocks in which
Kent's feet are held.
2. When a man's liable to run away.

20	LEAR	By Jupiter, I swear, no!	
	KENT	By Juno,³ I swear, aye!	

LEAR   They durst not do 't;
They would not, could not do 't. 'Tis worse than murder,
To do upon respect⁴ such violent outrage.
Resolve° me, with all modest° haste, which way   *Inform / reasonable*
25   Thou mightst deserve, or they impose, this usage,
    Coming from us.

KENT   My lord, when at their home
I did commend° your highness' letters to them,   *deliver*
Ere I was risen from the place that showed
My duty kneeling, came there a reeking° post,°   *steaming / messenger*
30   Stewed in his haste, half breathless, panting forth
From Goneril his mistress, salutations;
Delivered letters, spite of intermission,⁵
Which presently° they read; on whose contènts,   *immediately*
They summoned up their meiny,° straight° took horse;   *retinue / straightaway*
35   Commanded me to follow, and attend
The leisure of their answer, gave me cold looks,
And meeting here the other messenger,
Whose welcome, I perceived, had poisoned mine—
Being the very° fellow that of late   *same*
40   Displayed so saucily° against your highness—   *Acted so insolently*
Having more man° than wit° about me, drew.   *courage / sense*
He raised the house with loud and coward cries.
Your son and daughter found this trespass worth°   *deserving of*
The shame which here it suffers.
45 FOOL   Winter's not gone yet, if the wild-geese fly that way.⁶
         Fathers that wear rags
           Do make their children blind;⁷
         But fathers that bear bags
           Shall see their children kind.
50   Fortune, that arrant whore,
           Ne'er turns the key° to the poor.   *opens the door*
But, for all this, thou shalt have as many dolors⁸ for thy daugh-
ters as thou canst tell° in a year.   *count*
LEAR   O, how this mother° swells up toward my heart!   *hysteria*
55 Hysterica passio, down, thou climbing sorrow,⁹
Thy element's° below! Where is this daughter?   *natural place is*
KENT   With the earl, sir, here within.
LEAR   Follow me not; stay here.
                             Exit

GENTLEMAN   Made you no more offenses but what you speak of?
KENT   None. How chance the king comes with so small a train?
60 FOOL   An° thou hadst been set i' the stocks for that question,   *If*
thou hadst well deserved it.
KENT   Why, fool?
FOOL   We'll set thee to school to an ant, to teach thee there's no

3. Queen of the Roman gods and wife of Jupiter, with whom she constantly quarreled.
4. To do to one who deserves respect.
5. Regardless of interrupting me; despite the interruptions in his account (as he gasped for breath).
6. That is, things will get worse before they get better.
7. Blind to their father's needs.
8. Pains, sorrows; punning on "dollar," the English term

for the German "thaler," a large silver coin.
9. Hysterica . . . sorrow: Hysterica passio (a Latin expression originating in the Greek steiros, "suffering in the womb") was an inflammation of the senses. In Renaissance medicine, vapors from the abdomen were thought to rise up through the body, and in women, the uterus itself to wander around.

laboring i' the winter.[1] All that follow their noses are led by
their eyes but blind men, and there's not a nose among twenty
but can smell him that's stinking.° Let go thy hold when a great   *(as his fortunes decay)*
wheel runs down a hill,[2] lest it break thy neck with following
it; but the great one that goes up the hill, let him draw thee
after. When a wise man gives thee better counsel, give me
mine again. I would have none but knaves follow it, since a
fool gives it.
> That sir which serves and seeks for gain,
>   And follows but for form,
> Will pack° when it begins to rain,   *pack up and go*
>   And leave thee in the storm.
> But I will tarry; the fool will stay,
>   And let the wise man fly.
> The knave turns fool that runs away;[3]
>   The fool no knave, perdy.°   *by God (pardieu)*

KENT   Where learned you this, fool?
FOOL   Not i' the stocks, fool.
> *Re-enter* LEAR, *with* GLOUCESTER

LEAR   Deny to speak with me? They are sick? they are weary?
They have traveled all the night? Mere fetches;°   *ruses; pretexts*
The images of revolt and flying off.[4]
Fetch me a better answer.
GLOUCESTER   My dear lord,
You know the fiery quality° of the duke;   *disposition*
How unremoveable and fixed he is
In his own course.
LEAR   Vengeance! plague! death! confusion!°   *destruction*
Fiery? what quality? Why, Gloucester, Gloucester,
I'd speak with the Duke of Cornwall and his wife.
GLOUCESTER   Well, my good lord, I have informed them so.
LEAR   Informed them! Dost thou understand me, man?
GLOUCESTER   Ay, my good lord.
LEAR   The king would speak with Cornwall; the dear father
Would with his daughter speak, commands her service.
Are they informed of this? My breath and blood!
Fiery? the fiery duke? Tell the hot duke that—
No, but not yet. May be he is not well.
Infirmity doth still° neglect all office°   *always / obligation*
Whereto our health is bound; we are not ourselves
When nature, being oppressed, commands the mind
To suffer with the body. I'll forbear;
And am fallen out with my more headier will,[5]
To take° the indisposed and sickly fit   *mistake*
For the sound man. Death on my state![6] Wherefore°   *Why*
> *looking on* KENT
Should he sit here? This act persuades me
That this remotion° of the duke and her   *remoteness, aloofness*
Is practice° only. Give me my servant forth.   *trickery*

---

1. Ants, proverbially prudent, do not work in winter.
Implicitly, a wise person should know better than to look
for sustenance to an old man who has fallen on wintry
times.
2. A great wheel is a figure for Lear and of Fortune's
wheel itself, which has swung downward.
3. The scoundrel who runs away is the real fool.
4. *images of:* signs of. *flying off:* desertion; insurrection.
5. And disagree with my (earlier) more rash intention.
6. May my royal authority end (an oath). Ironically, this
has already happened.

110　Go tell the duke and 's wife I'd speak with them,
　　　Now, presently!° Bid them come forth and hear me,　　　　　　　*at once*
　　　Or at their chamber-door I'll beat the drum
　　　Till it cry sleep to death.[7]
　　GLOUCESTER　I would have all well betwixt you.　　　　　*Exit*
115　LEAR　O me, my heart, my rising heart! but, down!
　　FOOL　Cry to it, nuncle, as the cockney° did to the eels when she　　*Londoner (city woman)*
　　　put 'em i' the paste° alive; she knapped 'em o' the coxcombs°　　*pie; pastry / heads*
　　　with a stick, and cried "Down, wantons,° down!" 'Twas her　　*rogues*
　　　brother that, in pure kindness to his horse, buttered his hay.[8]
　　　　Enter CORNWALL, REGAN, GLOUCESTER, *and servants*
　　LEAR　Good morrow to you both.
120　CORNWALL　　　　　　　　　　Hail to your grace!
　　　　　KENT *is set at liberty*
　　REGAN　I am glad to see your highness.
　　LEAR　Regan, I think you are; I know what reason
　　　I have to think so. If thou shouldst not be glad,
　　　I would divorce me from thy mother's tomb,
125　Sepulchring° an adultress. (*To* KENT) O, are you free?　　*Because it entombed*
　　　Some other time for that. Belovèd Regan,
　　　Thy sister's naught.° O Regan, she hath tied　　　　　　*wicked; nothing*
　　　Sharp-toothed unkindness, like a vulture, here!
　　　　Points to his heart
　　　I can scarce speak to thee; thou'lt not believe
130　With how depraved a quality—O Regan!
　　REGAN　I pray you, sir, take patience. I have hope
　　　You less know how to value her desert
　　　Than she to scant her duty.[9]
　　LEAR　　　　　　　　　Say, how is that?
　　REGAN　I cannot think my sister in the least
135　Would fail her obligation. If, sir, perchance
　　　She have restrained the riots of your followers,
　　　'Tis on such ground, and to such wholesome end,
　　　As clears her from all blame.
　　LEAR　My curses on her!
　　REGAN　　　　　　　　O, sir, you are old;
140　Nature° in you stands on the very verge　　　　　　　　*Life*
　　　Of her confine.° You should be ruled and led　　　　　　*Of its limit*
　　　By some discretion,° that discerns your state　　　　*discreet person*
　　　Better than you yourself. Therefore, I pray you,
　　　That to our sister you do make return;
　　　Say you have wronged her, sir.
145　LEAR　　　　　　　　Ask her forgiveness?
　　　Do you but mark how this becomes the house:[1]
　　　"Dear daughter, I confess that I am old; (*kneeling*)
　　　Age° is unnecessary. On my knees I beg　　　　　　　　*An old man*
　　　That you'll vouchsafe me raiment,° bed, and food."　　*promise me clothing*
150　REGAN　Good sir, no more! These are unsightly tricks.
　　　Return you to my sister.

---

7. Till the noise kills sleep.
8. Like that of his sister (who wanted to make eel pie without killing the eels), his kindness was misplaced: horses will not eat buttered hay.
9. *I have . . . duty:* I expect that you are worse at valuing her deservings than she is at neglecting her duty. The double negative here ("less," "scant") is acceptable Jacobean usage.
1. Do you see how appropriate this is among members of a family (spoken ironically)?

LEAR (*rising*)   Never, Regan!
     She hath abated° me of half my train;   *deprived*
     Looked black upon me; struck me with her tongue
     Most serpent-like, upon the very heart.
155   All° the stored vengeances of heaven fall   *Let all*
     On her ingrateful top!° Strike her young bones,   *head*
     You taking° airs, with lameness!   *infectious; malignant*
CORNWALL   Fie, sir, fie!
LEAR   You nimble lightnings, dart your blinding flames
     Into her scornful eyes! Infect her beauty,
160   You fen-sucked fogs, drawn by the powerful sun,[2]
     To fall and blast her pride!
REGAN   O the blest gods! so will you wish on me,
     When the rash mood is on.
LEAR   No, Regan, thou shalt never have my curse.
165   Thy tender-hefted[3] nature shall not give
     Thee o'er to harshness. Her eyes are fierce; but thine
     Do comfort and not burn. 'Tis not in thee
     To grudge my pleasures, to cut off my train,
     To bandy hasty words, to scant my sizes,°   *reduce my allowances*
170   And in conclusion to oppose the bolt°   *to lock the door*
     Against my coming in. Thou better know'st
     The offices° of nature, bond of childhood,   *duties*
     Effects° of courtesy, dues of gratitude;   *Actions*
     Thy half o' the kingdom hast thou not forgot,
     Wherein I thee endowed.
175 REGAN   Good sir, to the purpose.°   *get to the point*
LEAR   Who put my man i' the stocks?
        Tucket within
CORNWALL   What trumpet's that?
REGAN   I know't, my sister's. This approves° her letter,   *confirms*
     That she would soon be here.
        Enter OSWALD
                 Is your lady come?
LEAR   This is a slave, whose easy-borrowed pride[4]
180   Dwells in the fickle grace of her he follows.
     Out varlet,° from my sight!   *wretch*
CORNWALL   What means your grace?
LEAR   Who stocked my servant? Regan, I have good hope
     Thou didst not know on 't.°   *of it*
        Enter GONERIL
     Who comes here? O heavens,
185   If you do love old men, if your sweet sway
     Allow obedience, if yourselves are old,
     Make it your cause! Send down, and take my part!
     (*To* GONERIL) Art not ashamed to look upon this beard?
     O Regan, wilt thou take her by the hand?
190 GONERIL   Why not by the hand, sir? How have I offended?
     All's not offense that indiscretion finds
     And dotage terms so.
LEAR   O sides,[5] you are too tough!

---

2. The sun was thought to suck poisonous vapors from marshy ground.
3. Tenderly placed; firmly set in a tender disposition (as a knife blade into its haft).
4. Unmerited and unpaid-for arrogance; "pride" may also refer to Oswald's fine clothing received for his services to Goneril.
5. Chest, where Lear's heart is swelling with emotion.

Will you yet hold? How came my man i' the stocks?

CORNWALL   I set him there, sir; but his own disorders°   *disorderly behavior*
Deserved much less advancement.[6]

195 LEAR   You! did you?

REGAN   I pray you, father, being weak, seem so.°   *behave so*
If, till the expiration of your month,
You will return and sojourn with my sister,
Dismissing half your train, come then to me.

200 I am now from home, and out of that provision
Which shall be needful for your entertainment.

LEAR   Return to her, and fifty men dismissed?
No, rather I abjure all roofs, and choose
To wage against the enmity o' the air;

205 To be a comrade with the wolf and owl—
Necessity's sharp pinch![7] Return with her?
Why, the hot-blooded France, that dowerless took
Our youngest born, I could as well be brought
To knee° his throne, and, squire-like, pension beg   *kneel to*

210 To keep base life afoot. Return with her?
Persuade me rather to be slave and sumpter°   *packhorse*
To this detested groom. (*Pointing at* OSWALD)

GONERIL   At your choice, sir.

LEAR   I prithee, daughter, do not make me mad.
I will not trouble thee, my child; farewell.

215 We'll no more meet, no more see one another.
But yet thou art my flesh, my blood, my daughter;
Or rather a disease that's in my flesh,
Which I must needs call mine. Thou art a boil,
A plague-sore, an embossed° carbuncle,   *a swollen*

220 In my corrupted blood. But I'll not chide thee;
Let shame come when it will, I do not call° it.   *call upon*
I do not bid the Thunder-bearer° shoot,   *(Jove)*
Nor tell tales of thee to high-judging Jove.
Mend° when thou canst; be better at thy leisure.   *Make amends*

225 I can be patient, I can stay with Regan,
I and my hundred knights.

REGAN   Not altogether so.
I looked not for° you yet, nor am provided   *I did not expect*
For your fit welcome. Give ear, sir, to my sister;
For those that mingle reason with your passion[8]

230 Must be content to think you old, and so—
But she knows what she does.

LEAR   Is this well° spoken?   *earnestly*

REGAN   I dare avouch° it, sir. What, fifty followers?   *vouch for*
Is it not well? What should you need of more?
Yea, or so many, sith° that both charge° and danger   *since / expense*

235 Speak 'gainst so great a number? How, in one house,
Should many people, under two commands,
Hold amity? 'T is hard; almost impossible.

GONERIL   Why might not you, my lord, receive attendance
From those that she calls servants, or from mine?

---

6. Deserved far worse treatment.
7. *To wage . . . pinch:* To counter, like predators, the harshness of the elements with the hardness brought on

by necessity. *pinch:* stress, pressure.
8. For those who temper your passionate argument with their own calm reasoning.

240   REGAN   Why not, my lord? If then they chanced to slack° you,   *neglect*
        We could control them. If you will come to me—
        For now I spy a danger—I entreat you
        To bring but five-and-twenty. To no more
        Will I give place or notice.°   *acknowledgment*
  LEAR   I gave you all—
245   REGAN   And in good time° you gave it.   *it was about time*
  LEAR   Made you my guardians, my depositaries;°   *trustees*
        But kept a reservation° to be followed   *reserved a right*
        With such a number. What, must I come to you
        With five-and-twenty, Regan? Said you so?
250   REGAN   And speak't again, my lord; no more with me.
  LEAR   Those wicked creatures yet do look well-favored,°   *attractive*
        When others are more wicked; not being the worst
        Stands in some rank of praise.[9] (*To* GONERIL) I'll go with thee:
        Thy fifty yet doth double five-and-twenty,
        And thou art twice her love.
255   GONERIL   Hear me, my lord.
        What need you five-and-twenty, ten, or five,
        To follow in a house where twice so many
        Have a command to tend you?
  REGAN   What need one?
  LEAR   O, reason not the need! Our basest beggars
260   Are in the poorest thing superfluous.[1]
        Allow not° nature more than nature needs,   *If you don't allow*
        Man's life's as cheap as beast's. Thou art a lady;
        If only to go warm were gorgeous,
        Why, nature needs not what thou gorgeous wear'st,
265   Which scarcely keeps thee warm.[2] But, for true need—
        You heavens, give me that patience,° patience I need!   *endurance*
        You see me here, you gods, a poor old man,
        As full of grief as age; wretched in both!
        If it be you that stirs these daughters' hearts
270   Against their father, fool me not so much
        To bear it tamely;[3] touch me with noble anger,
        And let not women's weapons, water-drops,
        Stain my man's cheeks! No, you unnatural hags,
        I will have such revenges on you both,
275   That all the world shall—I will do such things—
        What they are, yet I know not; but they shall be
        The terrors of the earth! You think I'll weep;
        No, I'll not weep.
        I have full cause of weeping, but this heart
280   Shall break into a hundred thousand flaws°   *fragments*
        Or ere° I'll weep. O fool, I shall go mad!   *Before*
              Exeunt LEAR, GLOUCESTER, KENT, *and* FOOL.
                    Storm and tempest
  CORNWALL   Let us withdraw; 't will be a storm.
  REGAN   This house is little; the old man and his people
        Cannot be well bestowed.°   *lodged*

9. Deserves some degree ("rank") of praise.
1. *Our . . . superfluous:* Even the lowliest beggars have
something more than the barest minimum.
2. *If . . . thee warm:* If gorgeousness in clothes is mea-
sured by the warmth they provide, your elaborate clothes
are superfluous, for they barely cover your body.
3. *fool . . . tamely:* do not make me so foolish as to accept
it meekly.

285 GONERIL 'Tis his own blame; hath put himself from° rest,　　　　　　*deprived himself of*
　　　　　And must needs taste his folly.
　　　REGAN For his particular,° I'll receive him gladly,　　　　　　　*single self*
　　　　　But not one follower.
　　　GONERIL　　　　　　　So am I purposed.
　　　　　Where is my lord of Gloucester?
290 CORNWALL Followed the old man forth. He is returned.
　　　　　Re-enter GLOUCESTER
　　　GLOUCESTER The king is in high rage.
　　　CORNWALL　　　　　　　　　　Whither is he going?
　　　GLOUCESTER He calls to horse, but will° I know not whither.　　*will go*
　　　CORNWALL 'Tis best to give him way; he leads himself.
　　　GONERIL My lord, entreat him by no means to stay.
295 GLOUCESTER Alack, the night comes on, and the bleak winds
　　　　　Do sorely ruffle.° For many miles about　　　　　　　　　*bluster*
　　　　　There's scarce a bush.
　　　REGAN　　　　　　　O, sir, to willful men,
　　　　　The injuries that they themselves procure
　　　　　Must be their schoolmasters. Shut up your doors.
300　　　He is attended with a desperate° train;　　　　　　　　　　*violent*
　　　　　And what they may incense° him to, being apt　　　　　　　*incite*
　　　　　To have his ear abused,° wisdom bids fear.　　　　　　　　*deceived*
　　　CORNWALL Shut up your doors, my lord; 'tis a wild night.
　　　　　My Regan counsels well. Come out o' the storm.　　*Exeunt*

3.1

　　　　　Storm still. Enter KENT *and a* GENTLEMAN, *at several*°　　*separate*
　　　　　doors
　　　KENT Who's there, besides foul weather?
　　　GENTLEMAN One minded like the weather, most unquietly.
　　　KENT I know you. Where's the king?
　　　GENTLEMAN Contending with the fretful elements;
5　　　Bids the wind blow the earth into the sea,
　　　　　Or swell the curlèd waters 'bove the main,°　　　　　　　*mainland*
　　　　　That things might change or cease; tears his white hair,
　　　　　Which the impetuous blasts, with eyeless rage,
　　　　　Catch in their fury, and make nothing of;
10　　　Strives in his little world of man to out-scorn
　　　　　The to-and-fro-conflicting wind and rain.
　　　　　This night, wherein the cub-drawn bear would couch,[1]
　　　　　The lion and the belly-pinchèd wolf
　　　　　Keep their fur dry, unbonneted° he runs,　　　　　　　　*hatless; uncrowned*
15　　　And bids what will take all.
　　　KENT　　　　　　　　But who is with him?
　　　GENTLEMAN None but the fool, who labors to out-jest
　　　　　His heart-struck injuries.[2]
　　　KENT　　　　　　　Sir, I do know you;
　　　　　And dare, upon the warrant of my note,[3]
　　　　　Commend a dear° thing to you. There is division,　　　*Entrust a crucial*
20　　　Although as yet the face of it be covered

3.1 Location: Bare, open country.
1. In which even the bear, though starving, having been
sucked dry ("drawn") by its cub, would not go out to
forage.

2. *to out-jest*: to relieve with laughter; to exorcise through
ridicule. *heart-struck injuries*: injuries (from the betrayal
of his paternal love) that penetrated to the heart.
3. On the basis of my skill (at judging people).

With mutual cunning, 'twixt Albany and Cornwall;
Who have—as who have not, that their great stars
Throned and set high?⁴—servants, who seem no less,°   *who appear as such*
Which are to France the spies and speculations°   *observers*
25   Intelligent of⁵ our state. What hath been seen,
Either in snuffs and packings° of the dukes,   *quarrels and plots*
Or the hard rein° which both of them have borne   *treatment*
Against the old kind king; or something deeper,
Whereof perchance these are but furnishings;°   *pretexts*
30   But, true it is, from France there comes a power
Into this scattered kingdom; who already,
Wise in° our negligence, have secret feet   *Aware of*
In some of our best ports, and are at point°   *ready*
To show their open banner. Now to you:
35   If on my credit you dare build° so far   *If you trust me*
To make your speed to Dover, you shall find
Some that will thank you, making just° report   *accurate*
Of how unnatural and bemadding° sorrow   *maddening*
The king hath cause to plain.°   *complain*
40   I am a gentleman of blood and breeding;
And, from some knowledge and assurance, offer
This office° to you.   *role; duty*
    GENTLEMAN   I will talk further with you.
    KENT   No, do not.
For confirmation that I am much more
45   Than my out-wall,° open this purse, and take   *outward appearance*
What it contains. If you shall see Cordelia—
As fear not but you shall—show her this ring,
And she will tell you who your fellow° is   *(Kent himself)*
That yet you do not know. Fie on this storm!
50   I will go seek the king.
    GENTLEMAN   Give me your hand. Have you no more to say?
    KENT   Few words, but, to effect,° more than all yet;   *in importance*
That, when we have found the king—in which your pain
That way, I'll this⁶—he that first lights on him
55   Holla the other.   *Exeunt severally*

3.2

Enter LEAR *and* FOOL. *Storm still*

    LEAR   Blow, winds, and crack your cheeks! rage! blow!
You cataracts and hurricanoes,¹ spout
Till you have drenched our steeples, drowned the cocks!°   *weather vanes*
You sulphurous and thought-executing fires,²
5   Vaunt-couriers° to oak-cleaving thunderbolts,   *Forerunners*
Singe my white head! And thou, all-shaking thunder,
Smite flat the thick rotundity o' the world!
Crack Nature's molds, all germens° spill at once,   *seeds*
That make ingrateful man!

---

4. *as . . . high:* as has everybody who has been favored by
destiny.
5. Supplying intelligence about; too well informed of.
6. *in which . . . this:* in which effort you will go that way
and I this way.

3.2 Location: As before.
1. *cataracts:* floodgates of the heavens. *hurricanoes:*
waterspouts (water from both sky and sea).
2. *thought-executing fires:* lightning that strikes as swiftly
as thought.

10 FOOL O nuncle, court holy-water[3] in a dry house is better than
this rain-water out o' door. Good nuncle, in, and ask thy daugh-
ters' blessing! Here's a night pities neither wise man nor fool.

LEAR Rumble thy bellyful! Spit, fire! spout, rain!
Nor rain, wind, thunder, fire, are my daughters:
15 I tax° not you, you elements, with unkindness;   *blame*
I never gave you kingdom, called you children,
You owe me no subscription.° Then let fall   *obedience; allegiance*
Your horrible pleasure. Here I stand, your slave,
A poor, infirm, weak, and despised old man.
20 But yet I call you servile ministers,°   *agents*
That have with two pernicious daughters joined
Your high engendered battles° 'gainst a head   *heaven-bred forces*
So old and white as this. O! O! 't is foul!

FOOL He that has a house to put 's head in has a good head-
25 piece.°   *hat; brain*
            The cod-piece that will house
               Before the head has any,
            The head and he shall louse;
               So beggars marry many.[4]
30   The man that makes his toe
               What he his heart should make
            Shall of a corn cry woe,
               And turn his sleep to wake.[5]
For there was never yet fair woman but she made mouths in a
35 glass.[6]

LEAR No, I will be the pattern of all patience; I will say nothing.
            Enter KENT
KENT Who's there?
FOOL Marry, here's grace and a cod-piece; that's a wise man and
a fool.[7]
40 KENT Alas, sir, are you here? things that love night
Love not such nights as these; the wrathful skies
Gallow° the very wanderers of the dark,   *Frighten*
And make them keep° their caves. Since I was man,   *keep inside*
Such sheets of fire, such bursts of horrid thunder,
45 Such groans of roaring wind and rain, I never
Remember to have heard. Man's nature cannot carry°   *bear*
The affliction nor the fear.
LEAR   Let the great gods,
That keep this dreadful pother° o'er our heads,   *commotion*
Find out their enemies now. Tremble, thou wretch,
50 That hast within thee undivulgèd crimes,
Unwhipped of° justice. Hide thee, thou bloody hand;   *Unpunished by*
Thou perjured, and thou simular° of virtue   *simulator; pretender*

---

3. Sprinkled blessings of a courtier; flattery.
4. *The cod-piece . . . many:* Whoever finds his penis a
lodging before providing shelter for his head will end up
in lice-infested poverty and live in married beggary. *cod-
piece:* a pouchlike covering for the male genitals, often
conspicuous, particularly in the costume of a fool.
5. *The man . . . wake:* The man who values an inferior
part of his body over the part that is truly valuable will
suffer from and lose sleep over that inferior part.

6. She practiced making pretty faces in a mirror. The
Fool probably refers to Regan's and Goneril's vanity, or
the line may be thrown in to soften the harshness of his
satire.
7. The supposedly wise King is symbolized by royal
grace, the Fool by his codpiece (here, slang for "penis").
The Fool speaks ironically: the King, as he has pointed
out, is now the foolish one. *Marry:* By the Virgin Mary (a
mild oath).

That are incestuous. Caitiff,° to pieces shake,   *Wretch*
That under covert and convenient seeming°   *fitting hypocrisy*
55 Hast practiced on° man's life. Close° pent-up guilts   *against / Secret*
Rive° your concealing continents,° and cry   *Split open / coverings*
These dreadful summoners grace.[8] I am a man
More sinned against than sinning.

KENT   Alack, bare-headed?
Gracious my lord, hard by here is a hovel;
60 Some friendship will it lend you 'gainst the tempest.
Repose you there, while I to this hard house°—   *household*
More harder than the stones whereof 'tis raised,
Which° even but now, demanding° after you,   *Who / I demanding*
Denied me to come in—return, and force
Their scanted° courtesy.   *niggardly*
65 LEAR   My wits begin to turn.
Come on, my boy. How dost, my boy? Art cold?
I am cold myself. Where is this straw, my fellow?
The art° of our necessities is strange,   *skill; alchemy*
That can make vile things precious. Come, your hovel.
70 Poor fool and knave, I have one part in my heart
That's sorry yet for thee.

FOOL (*singing*)[9]
     He that has and° a little tiny wit°—   *even / sense*
     With hey, ho, the wind and the rain—
     Must make content with his fortunes fit,
75   Though the rain it raineth every day.

LEAR   True, boy. Come, bring us to this hovel.

                  Exeunt LEAR and KENT

FOOL   This is a brave night to cool a courtesan.[1]
I'll speak a prophecy ere I go:[2]
     When priests are more in word than matter;°   *real virtue*
80   When brewers mar their malt with water;
     When nobles are their tailors' tutors;[3]
     No heretics burned, but wenches' suitors;[4]
     When every case in law is right;°   *just*
     No squire in debt, nor no poor knight;
85   When slanders do not live in tongues,
     Nor cutpurses° come not to throngs;   *pickpockets*
     When usurers tell their gold i' the field,[5]
     And bawds and whores do churches build;
     Then shall the realm of Albion°   *Britain*
90   Come to great confusion.°   *decay*
Then comes the time, who lives to see 't,
That going° shall be used° with feet.   *walking / practiced*
This prophecy Merlin shall make; for I live before his time.[6]

                     Exit

---

8. *and cry . . . grace:* and pray for mercy from these elements that bring you to justice.
9. The following song is an adaptation of one sung by Feste at the end of *Twelfth Night.*
1. To cool even the hot lusts of a prostitute.
2. What follows is a parody of the pseudo-Chaucerian "Merlin's Prophecy" from *The Arte of English Poesie.*
3. When noblemen follow fashion more closely than their tailors do.
4. When the only heretics burned are faithless lovers, who burn from venereal disease.
5. When usurers can count their profits openly (because they have no shady dealings to hide).
6. Merlin was the great wizard at the legendary court of King Arthur. Lear's Britain is set in an even more distant past.

3.3

Enter GLOUCESTER *and* EDMUND

GLOUCESTER   Alack, alack, Edmund, I like not this unnatural
dealing. When I desired their leave that I might pity° him, they   *relieve*
took from me the use of mine own house; charged me, on pain
of their perpetual displeasure, neither to speak of him, entreat
5   for him, nor any way sustain him.

EDMUND   Most savage and unnatural!

GLOUCESTER   Go to;° say you nothing. There's a division betwixt   *(an expletive)*
the dukes, and a worse matter than that. I have received a letter
this night; 'tis dangerous to be spoken; I have locked the letter
10   in my closet.° These injuries the king now bears will be   *private chamber*
revenged home;° there's part of a power already footed;[1] we   *to the hilt*
must incline to[2] the king. I will seek him, and privily° relieve   *secretly; privately*
him. Go you and maintain talk with the duke, that my charity
be not of him perceived if he ask for me, I am ill, and gone to
15   bed. Though I die for it, as no less is threatened me, the king
my old master must be relieved. There is some strange thing
toward,° Edmund; pray you, be careful.   *Exit*   *coming*

EDMUND   This courtesy,° forbid° thee, shall the duke   *act of kindness / forbidden*
Instantly know, and of that letter too.
20   This seems a fair deserving,[3] and must draw me
That which my father loses—no less than all.
The younger rises when the old doth fall.   *Exit*

3.4

Enter LEAR, KENT, *and* FOOL

KENT   Here is the place, my lord; good my lord, enter:
The tyranny of the open night's too rough
For nature° to endure.   *human weakness*
        Storm still

LEAR   Let me alone.

KENT   Good my lord, enter here.

5   LEAR   Wilt break my heart?

KENT   I had rather break mine own. Good my lord, enter.

LEAR   Thou think'st 'tis much that this contentious storm
Invades us to the skin. So 'tis to thee;
But where the greater malady is fixed,°   *rooted*
10   The lesser is scarce felt. Thou'dst shun a bear;
But if thy flight lay toward the raging sea,
Thou'dst meet the bear i' the mouth. When the mind's free,°   *unburdened*
The body's delicate.° The tempest in my mind   *sensitive*
Doth from my senses take all feeling else
15   Save° what beats there. Filial ingratitude!   *Except*
Is it not as° this mouth should tear this hand   *as if*
For lifting food to 't? But I will punish home.°   *thoroughly*
No, I will weep no more. In such a night
To shut me out! Pour on; I will endure.
20   In such a night as this! O Regan, Goneril!
Your old kind father, whose frank heart gave all—
O, that way madness lies; let me shun that;
No more of that.

3.3 Location: At Gloucester's castle.
1. Part of an army already landed.
2. We must take the side of.

3. This seems an action that deserves to be rewarded.
3.4 Location: Open country, before a cattle shed.

KENT	Good my lord, enter here.	
LEAR	Prithee, go in thyself; seek thine own ease:	
25	This tempest will not give me leave to° ponder	*allow me to*
On things would hurt me more. But I'll go in.	
(*To the* FOOL) In, boy; go first. You houseless poverty°—	*poor*
Nay, get thee in. I'll pray, and then I'll sleep.	

FOOL *goes in*

Poor naked wretches, whereso'er you are,
30 That bide° the pelting of this pitiless storm,   *endure; dwell in*
How shall your houseless heads and unfed sides,°   *starved ribs*
Your looped and windowed[1] raggedness, defend you
From seasons such as these? O, I have ta'en
Too little care of this! Take physic, pomp;[2]
35 Expose thyself to feel what wretches feel,
That thou mayst shake the superflux[3] to them,
And show the heavens more just.

EDGAR (*within*)   Fathom and half,[4] fathom and half!
Poor Tom!

The FOOL *runs out from the hovel*

40 FOOL   Come not in here, nuncle, here's a spirit.
Help me, help me!
KENT   Give me thy hand. Who's there?
FOOL   A spirit, a spirit! He says his name's poor Tom.
KENT   What art thou that dost grumble there i' the straw? Come
45 forth.

Enter EDGAR *disguised as a madman*

EDGAR   Away! the foul fiend follows me!
Through the sharp hawthorn blows the cold wind.[5]
Humh! go to thy cold bed, and warm thee.[6]
LEAR   Hast thou given all to thy two daughters? And art thou
50 come to this?
EDGAR   Who gives any thing to poor Tom? whom the foul fiend
hath led through fire and through flame, through ford and
whirlpool, o'er bog and quagmire; that hath laid knives under
his pillow and halters in his pew; set ratsbane by his porridge;[7]
55 made him proud of heart, to ride on a bay trotting-horse over
four-inched bridges,[8] to course° his own shadow for° a traitor.   *hunt / as*
Bless thy five wits![9] Tom's a-cold—O, do, de, do de, do de.
Bless thee from whirlwinds, star-blasting, and taking![1] Do poor
Tom some charity, whom the foul fiend vexes: there could I
60 have him now—and there—and there again, and there.[2]

Storm still

LEAR   What, has his daughters brought him to this pass?
Couldst thou save nothing? Didst thou give them all?

---

1. *looped and windowed:* full of holes and vents; "windowed" could also refer to cloth worn through to semi-transparency, like the oilcloth window "panes" of the poor.
2. Cure yourself, pompous person.
3. Superfluity; bodily discharge, suggested by "physic" (which also has the meaning of "purgative") in line 34. Excess here is also excess of wealth.
4. "Nine feet," a sailor's cry when taking soundings to gauge the depth of water.
5. *Through . . . wind:* Perhaps a fragment from a ballad.
6. *go . . . thee:* this expression is also used by the drunken beggar Christopher Sly in *The Taming of the Shrew*, Induction 1.

7. *laid knives . . . porridge:* these are all means by which the foul fiend tempts Tom to commit suicide. *halters:* nooses. *ratsbane:* rat poison.
8. Impossibly narrow, and probably suicidal to attempt without diabolical help.
9. The five wits were common wit, imagination, fantasy, estimation, and memory (from medieval and Renaissance cognitive theory).
1. *whirlwinds, star-blasting:* malign astrological influences capable of causing sickness or death. *taking:* infection; bewitchment.
2. As Edgar speaks this sentence, he might kill vermin on his body as if they were devils.

FOOL   Nay, he reserved a blanket, else we had been all shamed.

LEAR   Now, all the plagues that in the pendulous° air   *overhanging; portentous*
65   Hang fated o'er men's faults light on thy daughters!

KENT   He hath no daughters, sir.

LEAR   Death, traitor! nothing could have subdued nature
        To such a lowness but his unkind daughters.
        Is it the fashion that discarded fathers
70   Should have thus little mercy on their flesh?
        Judicious punishment! 't was this flesh begot
        Those pelican³ daughters.

EDGAR   Pillicock sat on Pillicock-hill.
        Halloo, halloo, loo, loo!⁴

75   FOOL   This cold night will turn us all to fools and madmen.

EDGAR   Take heed o' the foul fiend; obey thy parents; keep thy
        word justly; swear not; commit not with man's sworn spouse;
        set not thy sweet heart on proud array.⁵ Tom's a-cold.

LEAR   What hast thou been?

80   EDGAR   A serving-man, proud in heart and mind; that curled my
        hair; wore gloves in my cap;⁶ served the lust of my mistress'
        heart, and did the act of darkness with her; swore as many oaths
        as I spake words, and broke them in the sweet face of heaven:
        one that slept in the contriving of lust, and waked to do it. Wine
85   loved I deeply, dice dearly; and in woman out-paramoured the   *rumor-hungry*
        Turk.⁷ False of heart, light of ear,° bloody of hand; hog in sloth,
        fox in stealth, wolf in greediness, dog in madness, lion in prey.
        Let not the creaking of shoes⁸ nor the rustling of silks betray
        thy poor heart to woman. Keep thy foot⁹ out of brothels, thy
90   hand out of plackets,¹ thy pen from lenders' books, and defy
        the foul fiend. Still through the hawthorn blows the cold wind:
        Says suum, mun, ha, no, nonny. Dolphin my boy, my boy,
        sessa! let him trot by.²

        Storm still

LEAR   Why, thou wert better in thy grave than to answer° with thy   *encounter*
95   uncovered body this extremity of the skies.° Is man no more than   *violent weather*
        this? Consider him well. Thou owest the worm no silk, the beast
        no hide, the sheep no wool, that cat³ no perfume. Ha! here's
        three on's° are sophisticated! Thou art the thing itself; unac-   *of us*
        commodated⁴ man is no more but such a poor, bare, forked°   *two-legged*
100   animal as thou art. Off, off, you lendings!° come unbutton   *borrowed clothes*
        here.

        Tearing off his clothes

FOOL   Prithee, nuncle, be contented; 'tis a naughty° night to   *foul*
        swim in. Now a little fire in a wild° field were like an old lech-   *barren; lustful*
        er's heart; a small spark, all the rest on's° body cold. Look, here   *of his*
105   comes a walking fire.

        Enter GLOUCESTER, *with a torch*

3. Greedy. Young pelicans were reputed to feed on blood
from the wounds they made in their mother's breast; in
some versions, they first killed their father.
4. A fragment of an old rhyme, followed by hunting cries
or a ballad refrain; "Pillicock" was both a term of endear-
ment and a euphemism for "penis."
5. *obey . . . array*: these are fragments from the Ten Com-
mandments.
6. Favors from his mistress. In Petrarchan poetry, wooers
are "servants" to their ladies.
7. And had more women than the sultan had in his royal

harem.
8. Creaking shoes were a fashionable affectation.
9. Punning on the French *foutre* ("fuck").
1. Slits in skirts or petticoats.
2. These phrases are probably snatches from songs and
proverbs. "Dolphin" is an imagined animal or devil or the
heir to the French throne ("dauphin," which Shakespeare
usually Anglicized), or all three.
3. Civet cat, in Shakespeare's time the major source of
musk for perfume.
4. Naked; without the trappings of civilization.

EDGAR This is the foul fiend Flibbertigibbet.[5] He begins at cur-   *9:00 P.M. / midnight*
few,° and walks till the first cock.° He gives the web and the
pin,[6] squinies[7] the eye, and makes the hare-lip; mildews the
white° wheat, and hurts the poor creature of earth.   *near-ripe*

110   St. Withold footed thrice the old;[8]
        He met the night-mare and her nine-fold;[9]
        Bid her alight,
        And her troth plight,°   *And gave her word*
        And, aroint thee,° witch, aroint thee!   *begone*

115 KENT How fares your grace?

LEAR What's° he?   *Who's*

KENT Who's there? What is't you seek?

GLOUCESTER What are you there? Your names?

EDGAR Poor Tom, that eats the swimming frog, the toad, the

120 tadpole, the wall-newt and the water;° that in the fury of his   *water newt*
heart, when the foul fiend rages, eats cow-dung for sallets;°   *savories*
swallows the old rat and the ditch-dog;[1] drinks the green man-
tle° of the standing-pool; who is whipped from tithing to tith-   *scum*
ing,° and stock-punished,° and imprisoned; who hath had three   *parish / put in stocks*

125 suits to his back, six shirts to his body, horse to ride, and weapon
to wear;
        But mice and rats, and such small deer,[2]
        Have been Tom's food for seven long year.
      Beware my follower. Peace, Smulkin;° peace, thou fiend!   *a Harsnett devil*

130 GLOUCESTER What, hath your grace no better company?

EDGAR The prince of darkness is a gentleman. Modo he's call'd,
and Mahu.[3]

GLOUCESTER Our flesh and blood is grown so vile, my lord,
That it doth hate what gets° it.   *begets*

135 EDGAR Poor Tom's a-cold.

GLOUCESTER Go in with me. My duty cannot suffer°   *permit me*
To obey in all your daughters' hard commands:
Though their injunction be to bar my doors,
And let this tyrannous night take hold upon you

140 Yet have I ventured to come seek you out.
And bring you where both fire and food is ready.

LEAR First let me talk with this philosopher.
What is the cause of thunder?

KENT Good my lord, take his offer; go into the house.

145 LEAR I'll take a word with this same learned Theban.°   *Greek sage*
What is your study?°   *field of expertise*

EDGAR How to prevent the fiend, and to kill vermin.

LEAR Let me ask you one word in private.

KENT Importune him once more to go, my lord;
His wits begin to unsettle.

150 GLOUCESTER   Canst thou blame him?
       Storm still

---

5. A devil drawn from folk beliefs but famous for his prominent place in Samuel Harsnett's *Declaration of Egregious Popish Impostures* (1603); the frequent borrowings from Harsnett in *King Lear* set the earliest possible composition date for the play.
6. *web and the pin*: cataract.
7. Causes squints in.
8. St. Withold traversed the hilly countryside three times. *old*: wold, uplands.

9. *night-mare*: a demon that is not necessarily in the shape of a horse. *fold*: familiar, demon.
1. A dog found dead in a ditch.
2. *deer*: animals. These verses are adapted from a romance popular in Shakespeare's time, *Bevis of Hampton*.
3. Modo and Mahu, more Harsnett devils, were commanding generals of the hellish troops.

His daughters seek his death; ah, that good Kent!
He said it would be thus, poor banished man!
Thou say'st the king grows mad; I'll tell thee, friend,
I am almost mad myself. I had a son,
155   Now outlawed° from my blood. He sought my life.   *disowned*
But lately, very late.° I loved him, friend;   *recently*
No father his son dearer. True to tell thee,
The grief hath crazed my wits. What a night's this!
I do beseech your grace—
LEAR   O, cry you mercy,° sir.   *beg your pardon*
160   Noble philosopher, your company.
EDGAR   Tom's a-cold.
GLOUCESTER   In, fellow, there, into the hovel; keep thee warm.
LEAR   Come, let's in all.
                This way, my lord.
KENT   With him!
LEAR   I will keep still with my philosopher.
165 KENT   Good my lord, soothe° him; let him take the fellow.   *humor*
GLOUCESTER   Take him you on.°   *on ahead*
KENT   Sirrah, come on; go along with us.
LEAR   Come, good Athenian.°   *Greek philosopher*
GLOUCESTER   No words, no words: hush.
170 EDGAR   Child Rowland[4] to the dark tower came,
His word° was still°—Fie, foh, and fum,   *motto / always*
I smell the blood of a British[5] man.   *Exeunt*

3.5

Enter CORNWALL *and* EDMUND

CORNWALL   I will have my revenge ere I depart his house.
EDMUND   How, my lord, I may be censured,° that nature° thus   *judged / kinship*
gives way to loyalty, something fears me° to think of.   *I am somewhat afraid*
CORNWALL   I now perceive, it was not altogether your brother's
5   evil disposition made him seek his° death; but a provoking   *(Gloucester's)*
merit, set a-work by a reproveable badness in himself.[1]
EDMUND   How malicious is my fortune, that I must repent to
be just! This is the letter he spoke of, which approves him an
intelligent party to the advantages of France.[2] O heavens! that
10   this treason were not, or not I the detector!
CORNWALL   Go with me to the duchess.
EDMUND   If the matter of this paper be certain, you have mighty
business in hand.
CORNWALL   True or false, it hath made thee Earl of Gloucester.
15   Seek out where thy father is, that he may be ready for our
apprehension.°   *arrest*
EDMUND *(aside)*   If I find him comforting the king, it will stuff
his° suspicion more fully.—I will persèver in my course of loy-   *(Cornwall's)*
alty, though the conflict be sore between that and my blood.°   *filial duty*
20 CORNWALL   I will lay trust upon thee, and thou shalt find a
dearer father in my love.   *Exeunt*

---

4. *Child:* an aspirant to knighthood. Roland is the
famous hero of the Charlemagne legends.
5. "An Englishman" usually appears in this rhyme from
the cycle of tales of which "Jack and the Beanstalk" is the
best known. The alteration befits Lear's ancient Britain.
3.5 Location: At Gloucester's castle.

1. *a provoking . . . himself:* Gloucester's own wickedness
deservedly triggered the blameworthy evil in Edgar.
2. *which . . . France:* which proves him a spy and
informer in the aid of France; "party," or faction, was usu-
ally a term of opprobrium in the Renaissance.

3.6

Enter GLOUCESTER, LEAR, KENT, FOOL, *and* EDGAR

GLOUCESTER Here is better than the open air; take it thankfully.
I will piece out° the comfort with what addition I can; I will   *augment*
not be long from you.

KENT All the power of his wits have given sway to his impa-
5   tience:[1] the gods° reward your kindness! *Exit* GLOUCESTER   *may the gods*

EDGAR Frateretto° calls me; and tells me Nero is an angler in the   *a Harsnett devil*
lake of darkness.[2] Pray, innocent, and beware the foul fiend.

FOOL Prithee, nuncle, tell me whether a madman be a gentle-
man or a yeoman?[3]

10   LEAR A king, a king!

FOOL No, he's a yeoman that has a gentleman to° his son; for   *for*
he's a mad yeoman that sees his son a gentleman before him.

LEAR To have a thousand with red burning spits
Come hissing in upon 'em—

15   EDGAR The foul fiend bites my back.

FOOL He's mad that trusts in the tameness of a wolf, a horse's
health, a boy's love, or a whore's oath.

LEAR It shall be done; I will arraign° them straight.°   *prosecute / immediately*
(*To* EDGAR) Come, sit thou here, most learned justicer;

20   (*to the* FOOL) Thou, sapient sir, sit here. Now, you she foxes!

EDGAR Look, where he stands and glares! Wantest thou eyes° at   *observers*
trial, madam?

FOOL   Come o'er the bourn, Bessy, to me[4]—
              Her boat hath a leak,[5]

25   And she must not speak
              Why she dares not come over to thee.

EDGAR The foul fiend haunts poor Tom in the voice of a night-
ingale. Hopdance° cries in Tom's belly for two white° herring.   *a demon / fresh*
Croak° not, black angel; I have no food for thee.   *Growl*

30   KENT How do you, sir? Stand you not so amazed:
Will you lie down and rest upon the cushions?

LEAR I'll see their trial first. Bring in the evidence.
(*To* EDGAR) Thou robed man of justice, take thy place;
(*to the* FOOL) And thou, his yoke-fellow of equity,°   *partner of law*

35   Bench° by his side. (*To* KENT) You are o' the commission,°   *Sit / judiciary*
Sit you too.

EDGAR Let us deal justly.
              Sleepest or wakest thou, jolly shepherd?
              Thy sheep be in the corn;°   *grain*

40   And for one blast of thy minikin° mouth,   *dainty*
              Thy sheep shall take no harm.
Pur! the cat[6] is gray.

LEAR Arraign her first; 'tis Goneril. I here take my oath before
this honorable assembly, she kicked the poor king her father.

45   FOOL Come hither, mistress. Is your name Goneril?

LEAR She cannot deny it.

3.6 Location: Within an outbuilding of Gloucester's.
1. Rage; inability to bear more suffering.
2. In Chaucer's *Monk's Tale*, the infamously cruel
Roman Emperor Nero is found fishing in hell (lines 485–
86).
3. A free landowner but not a member of the gentry, lack-
ing official family arms and the distinctions they confer.

Shakespeare seems to have procured a coat of arms for
his father in 1596.
4. From an old song. *bourn:* a small stream.
5. She has venereal disease; punning on "boat" as body
and "burn" as genital discomfort.
6. Pur the cat is another devil; such devils in the shape
of cats were the familiars of witches.

FOOL   Cry you mercy, I took you for a joint-stool.[7]
LEAR   And here's another, whose warped looks proclaim
    What store° her heart is made on.° Stop her there!   *material / of*
50 Arms, arms, sword, fire! Corruption in the place!
    False justicer, why hast thou let her 'scape?
EDGAR   Bless thy five wits!
KENT   O pity! Sir, where is the patience now,
    That you so oft have boasted to retain?
55 EDGAR (*aside*)   My tears begin to take his part so much,
    They'll mar my counterfeiting.
LEAR   The little dogs and all,°   *Even the little dogs*
    Tray, Blanch, and Sweet-heart, see, they bark at me.
EDGAR   Tom will throw his head at° them. Avaunt,° you curs!   *will threaten? / Begone*
60   Be thy mouth or° black or white,   *either*
          Tooth that poisons° if it bite;   *gives rabies*
          Mastiff, greyhound, mongrel grim,
          Hound or spaniel, brach° or him,   *bitch*
          Or bobtail tike or trundle-tail.[8]
65   Tom will make them weep and wail:
          For, with throwing thus my head,
          Dogs leap the hatch,[9] and all are fled.
    Do de, de, de. Sessa![1] Come, march to wakes° and fairs and   *parish festivals*
    market-towns. Poor Tom, thy horn is dry.[2]
70 LEAR   Then let them anatomize° Regan; see what breeds about   *dissect*
    her heart. Is there any cause in nature that makes these hard
    hearts? (*To* EDGAR) You, sir, I entertain° for one of my hundred;   *retain*
    I do not like the fashion of your garments. You will say they are
    Persian;° but let them be changed.   *oriental; splendid*
75 KENT   Now, good my lord, lie there and rest awhile.
LEAR   Make no noise, make no noise; draw the curtains.° So, so,   *bed curtains*
    so. We'll go to supper i' the morning.
FOOL   And I'll go to bed at noon.
        [*Re-enter* GLOUCESTER]
GLOUCESTER   Come hither, friend. Where is the king my master?
80 KENT   Here, sir; but trouble him not; his wits are gone.
GLOUCESTER   Good friend, I prithee, take him in thy arms;
    I have o'erheard a plot of death upon° him: *against*
    There is a litter ready; lay him in 't
    And drive towards Dover, friend, where thou shalt meet
85 Both welcome and protection. Take up thy master.
    If thou shouldst dally half an hour, his life,
    With thine, and all that offer to defend him,
    Stand in assured loss.° Take up, take up!   *Are certainly doomed*
    And follow me, that will to some provision
    Give thee quick conduct.[3]
90 KENT   Oppressèd nature sleeps:
    This rest might yet have balmed° thy broken sinews,°   *soothed / nerves*
    Which, if convenience will not allow,

---

7. I beg your pardon, I mistook you for a stool. An idiom
of the day expressing annoyance at being slighted. Here
the part of Goneril is actually being played by a stool.
8. Short-tailed mongrel or long-tailed.
9. Dogs leap over the lower half of a divided door.
1. Apparently nonsense, although "Sessa" may be a ver-

sion of the French *cessez* ("stop" or "hush").
2. A begging formula that refers to the horn vessel that
vagabonds carried for drink; the covert sense is that Edgar
has run out of Bedlamite inspiration.
3. *that . . . conduct*: who will quickly guide you to some
supplies.

Stand in hard cure.° (*To the* FOOL) Come, help to bear thy   *Will be hard to cure*
    master:
Thou must not stay behind.
GLOUCESTER   Come come, away.

                         Exeunt all but EDGAR

95   EDGAR   When we our betters see bearing our° woes,   *our same*
We scarcely think our miseries our foes.
Who alone suffers suffers most i' the mind,
Leaving free° things and happy shows° behind: *carefree / scenes*
But then the mind much sufferance doth o'erskip
100 When grief hath mates, and bearing° fellowship.   *pain; suffering*
How light and portable my pain seems now,
When that which makes me bend makes the king bow;
He° childed as I fathered! Tom, away!   *He is*
Mark the high noises,° and thyself bewray°   *important rumors / reveal*
105 When false opinion, whose wrong thought defiles thee,
In thy just proof repeals and reconciles thee.[4]
What° will hap° more tonight, safe 'scape the king!   *Whatever / chance*
Lurk, lurk.   *Exit*

3.7

     Enter CORNWALL, REGAN, GONERIL, EDMUND, *and ser-*
     vants
CORNWALL (*to* GONERIL) Post° speedily to my lord your hus-   *Ride*
band; show him this letter. The army of France is landed. Seek
out the villain Gloucester.   *Exeunt some of the servants*
REGAN   Hang him instantly.
5   GONERIL   Pluck out his eyes.
CORNWALL   Leave him to my displeasure. Edmund, keep you
our sister° company. The revenges we are bound[1] to take   *sister-in-law*
upon your traitorous father are not fit for your beholding.
Advise the duke, where you are going, to a most festinate prep-
10 aration.[2] We are bound° to the like. Our posts° shall be swift and   *committed / messengers*
intelligent° betwixt us. Farewell, dear sister: farewell, my lord of   *well informed*
Gloucester.
     Enter OSWALD
How now! Where's the king?
OSWALD   My lord of Gloucester hath conveyed him hence.
15 Some five or six and thirty of his° knights,   *(Lear's)*
Hot questrists° after him, met him at gate;   *searchers*
Who, with some other of the lords° dependants,   *(Gloucester's)*
Are gone with him towards Dover; where they boast
To have well-armed friends.
CORNWALL   Get horses for your mistress.
20 GONERIL   Farewell, sweet lord, and sister.
CORNWALL   Edmund, farewell.
     Exeunt GONERIL, EDMUND, *and* OSWALD
Go seek the traitor Gloucester,
Pinion him° like a thief, bring him before us.   *Tie his arms*
     Exeunt other servants
Though well we may not pass° upon his life   *pass sentence*

---

4. *In . . . thee:* When true evidence pardons you and
reconciles you (with your father).
3.7 Location: At Gloucester's castle.

1. Bound by duty; expected by destiny.
2. *Advise . . . preparation:* When you reach Albany, tell
the Duke to prepare quickly.

25 Without the form° of justice, yet our power   *official proceedings*
   Shall do a courtesy³ to our wrath, which men
   May blame, but not control. Who's there? the traitor?
        Enter GLOUCESTER, *brought in by two or three*
REGAN   Ingrateful fox! 'tis he.
CORNWALL   Bind fast his corky° arms.   *withered*
30 GLOUCESTER   What mean your graces? Good my friends, consider
   You are my guests. Do me no foul play, friends.
CORNWALL   Bind him, I say.
        Servants bind him
REGAN   Hard, hard. O filthy traitor!
GLOUCESTER   Unmerciful lady as you are, I'm none.
CORNWALL   To this chair bind him. Villain, thou shalt find—
        REGAN *plucks his beard*°   *(an extreme insult)*
35 GLOUCESTER   By the kind gods, 'tis most ignobly done
   To pluck me by the beard.
REGAN   So white,° and such a traitor!   *white-haired; venerable*
GLOUCESTER   Naughty° lady,   *Wicked*
   These hairs, which thou dost ravish from my chin,
   Will quicken,° and accuse thee. I am your host.   *come alive*
40 With robbers' hands my hospitable favors°   *features*
   You should not ruffle° thus. What will you do?   *snatch at*
CORNWALL   Come, sir, what letters had you late° from France?   *lately*
REGAN   Be simple° answered, for we know the truth.   *straightforwardly*
CORNWALL   And what confederacy have you with the traitors
45 Late footed° in the kingdom?   *landed*
REGAN   To whose hands have you sent the lunatic king? Speak.
GLOUCESTER   I have a letter guessingly set down,⁴
   Which came from one that's of a neutral heart,
   And not from one opposed.
CORNWALL   Cunning.
REGAN   And false.
50 CORNWALL   Where hast thou sent the king?
GLOUCESTER   To Dover.
REGAN   Wherefore° to Dover? Wast thou not charged° at peril—   *Why / commanded*
CORNWALL   Wherefore to Dover? Let him first answer that.
GLOUCESTER   I am tied to the stake, and I must stand the
55 course.⁵
REGAN   Wherefore to Dover?
GLOUCESTER   Because I would not see thy cruel nails
   Pluck out his poor old eyes; nor thy fierce sister
   In his anointed⁶ flesh stick boarish fangs.
60 The sea, with such a storm as his bare head
   In hell-black night endured, would have buoyed° up,   *risen*
   And quenched the stellèd° fires.   *stars'*
   Yet, poor old heart, he holp° the heavens to rage.   *helped*
   If wolves had at thy gate howled that dern° time,   *dreary; dreadful*
65 Thou shouldst have said "Good porter, turn the key."°   *(to open the door)*
   All cruels else subscribed.⁷ But I shall see
   The wingèd vengeance⁸ overtake such children.

---

3. Shall allow a courtesy or indulgence; shall bow to.
4. Written without confirmation; speculative.
5. An image from bearbaiting, in which a bear on a short tether had to fight off the assault of dogs.
6. Consecrated with holy oils (as part of a King's corona-

tion).
7. All other cruel creatures yielded to compassion.
8. Swift or heaven-sent revenge; either an angel of God or the Furies, who were flying executors of divine vengeance in classical mythology.

CORNWALL   See 't shalt thou never. Fellows,° hold the chair.   *Servants*
        Upon these eyes of thine I'll set my foot.
70 GLOUCESTER   He that will think° to live till he be old,   *Whoever hopes*
        Give me some help! O cruel! O ye gods! [CORNWALL *pulls out*
        one of GLOUCESTER'*s eyes and stamps on it*]
    REGAN   One side will mock another. The other too!
    CORNWALL   If you see vengeance—
    FIRST SERVANT   Hold your hand, my lord;
        I have served you ever since I was a child;
75   But better service have I never done you
        Than now to bid you hold.
    REGAN   How now, you dog!
    FIRST SERVANT   If you did wear a beard upon your chin,
        I'd shake it on this quarrel.[9]
80 REGAN   What do you mean?°
    CORNWALL   My villain!°   *servant; villain*
    FIRST SERVANT   Why, then, come on, and take the chance of anger.[1]
    REGAN   Give me thy sword. A peasant stand up thus!
            CORNWALL *is wounded.*
            Takes a sword, and runs at him behind
    FIRST SERVANT   O, I am slain! My lord, you have one eye left
85   To see some mischief° on him. O!   *Dies*   *injury*
    CORNWALL   Lest it see more, prevent it. Out, vile jelly! [*He pulls
        out* GLOUCESTER'*s other eye*]
        Where is thy luster now?
    GLOUCESTER   All dark and comfortless. Where's my son Edmund?
        Edmund, enkindle all the sparks of nature,[2]
        To quit° this horrid act.   *requite; avenge*
90 REGAN   Out, treacherous villain!
        Thou call'st on him that hates thee. It was he
        That made the overture° of thy treasons to us;   *revelation*
        Who is too good to pity thee.
    GLOUCESTER   O my follies! Then Edgar was abused.°   *slandered*
95   Kind gods, forgive me that, and prosper him!
    REGAN   Go thrust him out at gates, and let him smell
        His way to Dover.   *Exit one with* GLOUCESTER
        How is't, my lord? how look you?°   *how do you feel*
    CORNWALL   I have received a hurt. Follow me, lady;
100   Turn out that eyeless villain. Throw this slave
        Upon the dunghill. Regan, I bleed apace.
        Untimely comes this hurt. Give me your arm.
                        Exit CORNWALL *led by* REGAN
    SECOND SERVANT   I'll never care what wickedness I do,
        If this man come to good.[3]
    THIRD SERVANT   If she live long,
105   And in the end meet the old° course of death,   *usual*
        Woman will all turn monsters.
    SECOND SERVANT   Let's follow the old earl, and get the Bedlam°   *madman*
        To lead him where he would. His roguish madness
        Allows itself to any thing.
110 THIRD SERVANT   Go thou; I'll fetch some flax and whites of eggs

9. I'd pluck it over this point; I'd issue a challenge.
1. Take the risk of fighting when angry; take the fortune
of one who is governed by his anger.
2. All the warmth of filial love; all the anger that your

father has received such treatment.
3. *I'll . . . good:* because this may be a sign that evil goes
unpunished. *this man:* Cornwall.

To apply to his bleeding face. Now, heaven help him!

Exeunt severally

4.1

Enter EDGAR

EDGAR Yet better thus, and known to be contemned°   *despised*
Than still° contemned and flattered. To be worst,   *always*
The lowest and most dejected thing of fortune,
Stands still in esperance, lives not in fear.[1]
5 The lamentable change is from the best;
The worst returns to laughter.[2] Welcome, then,
Thou unsubstantial air that I embrace!
The wretch that thou hast blown unto the worst
Owes nothing° to thy blasts. But who comes here?   *(because he can't pay)*

Enter GLOUCESTER, *led by an* OLD MAN

10 My father, parti-eyed?[3] World, world, O world!
But that thy strange mutations make us hate thee,
Life would not yield to age.[4]

OLD MAN O, my good lord, I have been your tenant, and your
father's tenant, these fourscore years.

15 GLOUCESTER Away, get thee away! Good friend, be gone.
Thy comforts° can do me no good at all;   *assistance*
Thee they may hurt.

OLD MAN Alack, sir, you cannot see your way.

GLOUCESTER I have no way, and therefore want no eyes;
20 I stumbled when I saw. Full oft 'tis seen,
Our means secure us, and our mere defects
Prove our commodities.[5] O dear son Edgar,
The food° of thy abusèd° father's wrath!   *fuel; prey / despised*
Might I but live to see thee in° my touch,   *through*
I'd say I had eyes again!

25 OLD MAN   How now! Who's there?

EDGAR *(aside)* O gods! Who is't can say "I am at the worst"?
I am worse than e'er I was.

OLD MAN   'Tis poor mad Tom.

EDGAR *(aside)* And worse I may be yet: the worst is not
So long as we can say "This is the worst."

OLD MAN Fellow, where goest?

30 GLOUCESTER   Is it a beggar-man?

OLD MAN Madman and beggar too.

GLOUCESTER He has some reason, else he could not beg.
I' the last night's storm I such a fellow saw;
Which made me think a man a worm. My son
35 Came then into my mind, and yet my mind
Was then scarce friends with him. I have heard more since.
As flies to wanton° boys are we to the gods;   *playful; careless*
They kill us for their sport.

EDGAR *(aside)*   How should this be?
Bad is the trade that must play fool to sorrow,[6]

4.1 Location: Open country.
1. *Stands . . . fear:* Remains in hope ("esperance") because there is no fear of falling further.
2. *The lamentable . . . laughter:* The change to be lamented is one that alters the best of circumstances; the worst luck can only improve.
3. Multicolored like a fool's costume (red with blood under white dressings).

4. *But . . . age:* If there were no strange reversals of fortune to make the world hateful, we would not consent to aging and death.
5. *Our means . . . commodities:* Our wealth makes us overconfident, and our utter deprivation proves to be beneficial.
6. It is a bad business to have to play the fool in the face of sorrow.

40   Angering itself and others.—Bless thee, master!

GLOUCESTER   Is that the naked fellow?

OLD MAN   Ay, my lord.

GLOUCESTER   Then, prithee, get thee gone. If, for my sake,
    Thou wilt o'ertake us, hence a mile or twain,
    I' the way toward Dover, do it for ancient love;[7]
45   And bring some covering for this naked soul,
    Who I'll entreat to lead me.

OLD MAN   Alack, sir, he is mad.

GLOUCESTER   'Tis the times' plague, when[8] madmen lead the blind.
    Do as I bid thee, or rather do thy pleasure;
    Above the rest, be gone.

50 OLD MAN   I'll bring him the best 'parel° that I have,   *apparel; clothing*
    Come on 't what will.   *Exit*

GLOUCESTER   Sirrah, naked fellow—

EDGAR   Poor Tom's a-cold. (*Aside*) I cannot daub it further.[9]

GLOUCESTER   Come hither, fellow.

55 EDGAR (*aside*)   And yet I must.—Bless thy sweet eyes, they bleed.

GLOUCESTER   Know'st thou the way to Dover?

EDGAR   Both stile and gate, horse-way and foot-path. Poor Tom
    hath been scared out of his good wits. Bless thee, good man's
    son, from the foul fiend! Five fiends have been in Poor Tom at
60   once; of lust, as Obidicut; Hobbididance, prince of dumbness;
    Mahu, of stealing; Modo, of murder; Flibbertigibbet, of mop-
    ping and mowing,° who since possesses chambermaids and   *making faces*
    waiting-women. So, bless thee, master!

GLOUCESTER   Here, take this purse, thou whom the heavens' plagues
65   Have humbled to all strokes.° That I am wretched   *to accept all blows*
    Makes thee the happier. Heavens, deal so still!°   *always*
    Let the superfluous and lust-dieted man,[1]
    That slaves° your ordinance,° that will not see   *defers to / authority*
    Because he doth not feel, feel your power quickly;
70   So distribution should undo excess,
    And each man have enough. Dost thou know Dover?

EDGAR   Ay, master.

GLOUCESTER   There is a cliff, whose high and bending° head   *overhanging*
    Looks fearfully in the confinèd deep.[2]
75   Bring me but to the very brim of it,
    And I'll repair the misery thou dost bear
    With something rich about me. From that place
    I shall no leading need.

EDGAR   Give me thy arm.
    Poor Tom shall lead thee.   *Exeunt*

4.2

Enter GONERIL *and* EDMUND

GONERIL   Welcome, my lord. I marvel our mild husband
    Not° met us on the way.   *Has not*

Enter OSWALD

               Now where's your master?

OSWALD   Madam, within, but never man so changed.
    I told him of the army that was landed;

---

7. For the sake of our long and loyal relationship (as master and servant).
8. The time is truly sick when.
9. I cannot continue the charade. *daub*: mask, plaster.

1. Let the overprosperous man who indulges his appetite.
2. Looks fearsomely into the straits below.
4.2 Location: Before Albany's castle.

5   He smiled at it. I told him you were coming;
    His answer was "The worse." Of Gloucester's treachery,
    And of the loyal service of his son,
    When I informed him, then he called me sot,°   *fool*
    And told me I had turned the wrong side out.[1]
10   What most he should dislike seems pleasant to him;
    What like, offensive.
  GONERIL (*to* EDMUND)   Then shall you go no further.
    It is the cowish° terror of his spirit,   *cowardly*
    That dares not undertake. He'll not feel wrongs
    Which tie him to an answer.[2] Our wishes on the way
15   May prove effects.[3] Back, Edmund, to my brother;°   *brother-in-law*
    Hasten his musters° and conduct his powers.°   *call-up of troops / armies*
    I must change arms at home, and give the distaff[4]
    Into my husband's hands. This trusty servant
    Shall pass between us. Ere long you are like° to hear,   *likely*
20   If you dare venture in your own behalf,
    A mistress's° command. Wear this; spare speech;   *(playing on "lover's")*
       (*giving a favor*)
    Decline your head. This kiss, if it durst speak,
    Would stretch thy spirits up into the air.
    Conceive,° and fare thee well.   *Understand my meaning*
  EDMUND   Yours in° the ranks of death.   *even in*
25   GONERIL   My most dear Gloucester!

                                  Exit EDMUND
    O, the difference of man and man!
    To thee a woman's services are due:
    My fool usurps my body.[5]
  OSWALD   Madam, here comes my lord.   *Exit*
     Enter ALBANY
  GONERIL   I have been worth the whistling.[6]
30   ALBANY   O Goneril!
    You are not worth the dust which the rude wind
    Blows in your face. I fear your disposition.
    That nature, which contemns it° origin,   *despises its*
    Cannot be bordered certain° in itself.   *be defended securely*
35   She that herself will sliver and disbranch°   *split*
    From her material sap, perforce must wither
    And come to deadly use.[7]
  GONERIL   No more; the text is foolish.
  ALBANY   Wisdom and goodness to the vile seem vile;
40   Filths savor but themselves. What have you done?
    Tigers, not daughters, what have you performed?
    A father, and a gracious aged man,
    Whose reverence even the head-lugged° bear would lick, *dragged by the head*
    Most barbarous, most degenerate, have you madded°   *driven mad*
45   Could my good brother° suffer you to do it?   *brother-in-law*
    A man, a prince, by him so benefited!

---

1. I had reversed things (by mistaking loyalty for treachery).
2. *He'll . . . answer:* He'll ignore insults that would provoke him to retaliate.
3. May be put into action.
4. A device used in spinning and so emblematic of the female role. To "change arms," therefore, is to swap the insignia of male and female identity.
5. My idiot husband presumes to possess me.

6. At one time, you would have come to welcome me home; referring to the proverb "It is a poor dog that is not worth the whistling."
7. *She . . . use:* The allusion is probably biblical: "But that which beareth thorns and briers is reproved, and is near unto cursing; whose end is to be burned" (Hebrews 6:8). *come to deadly use:* be destroyed; be used for burning.

If that the heavens do not their visible spirits
Send quickly down to tame these vild° offenses,   *wild; vile*
It will come,
50   Humanity must perforce° prey on itself,   *inevitably*
Like monsters of the deep.
GONERIL   Milk-livered° man!   *Cowardly*
That bear'st a cheek for blows, a head for wrongs:[8]
Who hast not in thy brows an eye discerning
Thine honor from thy suffering;[9] that not know'st
55   Fools do those villains pity who are punished
Ere they have done their mischief. Where's thy drum?°   *(to muster troops)*
France spreads his banners in our noiseless° land,   *peaceful*
With plumèd helm thy state begins to threat;
Whiles thou, a moral° fool, sit'st still, and criest   *moralizing*
"Alack, why does he so?"
60   ALBANY   See thyself, devil!
Proper deformity shows not in the fiend
So horrid as in woman.[1]
GONERIL   O vain° fool!   *useless*
ALBANY   Thou changèd and self-covered[2] thing, for shame,
Be-monster not thy feature. Were't my fitness°   *If it were appropriate*
65   To let these hands obey my blood,
They are apt enough to dislocate and tear
Thy flesh and bones. Howe'er° thou art a fiend,   *Although*
A woman's shape doth shield thee.
GONERIL   Marry, your manhood! mew![3]
      Enter a MESSENGER
70   ALBANY   What news?
MESSENGER   O, my good lord, the Duke of Cornwall's dead;
    Slain by his servant, going to put out
    The other eye of Gloucester.
ALBANY   Gloucester's eyes?
MESSENGER   A servant that he bred, thrilled with remorse,°   *shaken with pity*
75   Opposed against the act, bending° his sword   *directing*
To° his great master; who, thereat enraged,   *Against*
Flew on him, and amongst them felled him dead;
But not without that harmful stroke, which since
Hath plucked him after.[4]
ALBANY   This shows you are above,
80   You justicers,° that these our nether crimes[5]   *judges*
So speedily can venge! But, O poor Gloucester!
Lost he his other eye?
MESSENGER   Both, both, my lord.
This letter, madam, craves a speedy answer;
'T is from your sister.
85   GONERIL *(aside)*   One way I like this well;[6]
But being° a widow, and my Gloucester with her,   *her being*

---

8. *for wrongs:* fit for abuse; ready for cuckold's horns.
9. *discerning . . . suffering:* that can distinguish between an insult to your honor and something you should patiently endure.
1. *Proper . . . woman:* Deformity (of morals) is appropriate in the devil and so less horrid than in woman, from whom virtue is expected. Albany may hold a mirror in front of Goneril, since Jacobean women sometimes wore small mirrors attached to their dresses.

2. Altered and with your true (womanly) self concealed.
3. Some manhood! (spoken derisively). *Marry:* By the Virgin Mary. *mew:* a derisive catcall.
4. Has sent him to follow his servant into death.
5. Lower crimes, and so committed on earth, but also suggesting that the deeds smack of the netherworld of hell.
6. Because a political rival has been eliminated.

May all the building in my fancy pluck
Upon my hateful life.[7] Another way,
The news is not so tart.°—I'll read, and answer.   *Exit*   *bitter*

90 ALBANY   Where was his son when they did take his eyes?
MESSENGER   Come with my lady hither.
ALBANY   He is not here.
MESSENGER   No, my good lord; I met him back° again.   *returning*
ALBANY   Knows he the wickedness?
MESSENGER   Ay, my good lord; 'twas he informed against him;
95   And quit the house on purpose, that their punishment
Might have the freer course.
ALBANY   Gloucester, I live
To thank thee for the love thou show'dst the king,
And to revenge thine eyes. Come hither, friend.
Tell me what more thou know'st.   *Exeunt*

4.3

Enter KENT *and a* GENTLEMAN

KENT   Why the King of France is so suddenly gone back know
you the reason?
GENTLEMAN   Something he left imperfect° in the state, which   *unsettled*
since his coming forth is thought of;° which imports° to the   *remembered / portends*
5   kingdom so much fear and danger, that his personal return was
most required and necessary.
KENT   Who hath he left behind him general?
GENTLEMAN   The Marshall of France, Monsieur LaFar.
KENT   Did your letters pierce the queen to any demonstration of grief?
10 GENTLEMAN   Ay, sir. She took them, in my presence;
And now and then an ample tear trilled down
Her delicate cheek. It seemed she was a queen
Over her passion, who,° most rebel-like,   *which*
Sought to be king o'er her.
KENT   O, then it moved her.
15 GENTLEMAN   Not to a rage. Patience and sorrow strove
Who should express her goodliest.[1] You have seen
Sunshine and rain at once: her smiles and tears
Were like a° better way. Those happy smilets,   *Were similar in a*
That played on her ripe lip, seemed not to know
20 What guests were in her eyes, which parted thence,
As pearls from diamonds dropped. In brief,
Sorrow would be a rarity° most beloved,   *gem*
If all could so become it.[2]
KENT   Made she no verbal question?
GENTLEMAN   'Faith, once or twice she heaved the name of "father"
25   Pantingly forth, as if it pressed her heart;
Cried "Sisters! sisters! Shame of ladies! sisters!
Kent! father! sisters! What, i' the storm? i' the night?
Let pity not be believed!"[3] There she shook
The holy water from her heavenly eyes,
30   And clamor moistened.[4] Then away she started°   *sprang*
To deal with grief alone.

---

7. *May . . . life:* May pull down all of my built-up fan-
tasies and thus make my life hateful.
4.3 Location: Near the French camp at Dover.
1. Which should best express her feelings.

2. If everyone wore it so beautifully.
3. Never believe in pity; compassion cannot exist.
4. And moistened her anguish (with tears).

KENT   It is the stars,
  The stars above us, govern our conditions;
  Else one self mate and make⁵ could not beget
  Such different issues.° You spoke not with her since?   *offspring*
35 GENTLEMAN   No.
KENT   Was this before the king returned?
GENTLEMAN   No, since.
KENT   Well, sir, the poor distressed Lear's i' the town;
  Who sometime, in his better tune,° remembers   *state of mind*
  What we are come about, and by no means
  Will yield° to see his daughter.   *consent*
40 GENTLEMAN   Why, good sir?
KENT   A sovereign shame so elbows° him; his own unkindness,   *prods; nudges*
  That stripped her from his benediction, turned her
  To foreign casualties,° gave her dear rights   *risks*
  To his dog-hearted daughters, these things sting
45 His mind so venomously, that burning shame
  Detains him from Cordelia.
GENTLEMAN   Alack, poor gentleman!
KENT   Of Albany's and Cornwall's powers you heard not?
GENTLEMAN   'Tis so, they are afoot.
KENT   Well, sir, I'll bring you to our master Lear,
50 And leave you to attend him. Some dear cause°   *Some important reason*
  Will in concealment wrap me up awhile;
  When I am known aright, you shall not grieve°   *repent*
  Lending me this acquaintance.° I pray you, go   *news*
  Along with me.   *Exeunt*

4.4

Enter, with drum and colors, CORDELIA, DOCTOR, *and*
  soldiers

CORDELIA   Alack, 'tis he! Why, he was met even now
  As mad as the vexed sea; singing aloud;
  Crowned with rank fumiter and furrow-weeds,¹
  With hor-docks, hemlock, nettles, cuckoo-flowers,
5 Darnel, and all the idle° weeds that grow   *useless*
  In our sustaining corn. A century° send forth;   *battalion (100 men)*
  Search every acre in the high-grown field,
  And bring him to our eye.   *Exit an officer*
  What can man's wisdom
10 In the restoring° his bereaved sense?   *Do to restore*
  He that helps him take all my outward° worth.   *material*
DOCTOR   There is means, madam.
  Our foster-nurse of nature² is repose,
  The which he lacks. That to provoke in him,
15 Are many simples operative,³ whose power
  Will close the eye of anguish.
CORDELIA   All blest secrets,
  All you unpublished virtues° of the earth,   *obscure healing plants*
  Spring with my tears! be aidant and remediate°   *healing and remedial*

---

5. Or else the same pair of spouses; "mate" and "make"
may describe either partner.
4.4 Location: The French camp at Dover.
1. Fumiter was used against brain sickness. Furrow-
weeds, like the other weeds in the following lines, grow
in the furrows of plowed fields.
2. *Our . . . nature:* That which comforts and nourishes
human nature.
3. *That . . . operative:* To induce that ("repose") in him,
there are many effective medicinal herbs.

In the good man's distress! Seek, seek for him;
20   Lest his ungoverned rage dissolve the life
That wants° the means to lead it.   lacks
           Enter a MESSENGER
MESSENGER   News, madam;
The British powers° are marching hitherward.   armies
CORDELIA   'Tis known before; our preparation stands
In expectation of them. O dear father,
25   It is thy business that I go about;[4]
Therefore great France
My mourning and importuned° tears hath pitied.   importunate; solicitous
No blown° ambition doth our arms incite,   inflated
But love, dear love, and our aged father's right.[5]
30   Soon may I hear and see him!   *Exeunt*

4.5

           Enter REGAN *and* OSWALD
REGAN   But are my brother's powers° set forth?   (Albany's forces)
OSWALD   Ay, madam.
REGAN   Himself in person there?
OSWALD   Madam, with much ado.°   trouble
Your sister is the better soldier.
5   REGAN   Lord Edmund spake not with your lord at home?
OSWALD   No, madam.
REGAN   What might import° my sister's letter to him?   mean
OSWALD   I know not, lady.
REGAN   Faith, he is posted° hence on serious matter.   hurried
10   It was great ignorance, Gloucester's eyes being out,
To let him live. Where he arrives he moves
All hearts against us. Edmund, I think, is gone,
In pity of his misery,° to dispatch   (ironic)
His nighted° life; moreover, to descry°   darkened / investigate
15   The strength o' the enemy.
OSWALD   I must needs after° him, madam, with my letter.   go after
REGAN   Our troops set forth tomorrow. Stay with us;
The ways are dangerous.
OSWALD   I may not, madam:
My lady charged° my duty in this business.   commanded
20   REGAN   Why should she write to Edmund? Might not you
Transport her purposes by word? Belike,°   Perhaps
Something—I know not what. I'll love° thee much,   reward
Let me unseal the letter.
OSWALD   Madam, I had rather—
REGAN   I know your lady does not love her husband;
25   I am sure of that; and at her late° being here   recently
She gave strange oeillades° and most speaking looks   amorous glances
To noble Edmund. I know you are of her bosom.°   in her confidence
OSWALD   I, madam?
REGAN   I speak in understanding;° y'are, I know't.   with certainty
30   Therefore I do advise you, take this note:°   take note of this
My lord is dead; Edmund and I have talked;

4. The line echoes Christ's explanation of his mission in
Luke 2:49: "I must go about my father's business."
5. *No . . . right:* 1 Corinthians 13:4–5 in the Bishops'

Bible (1568) says that love "swelleth not, dealeth not
dishonestly, seeketh not her own."
4.5 Location: At Gloucester's castle.

And more convenient° is he for my hand   appropriate
Than for your lady's. You may gather° more.   infer
If you do find him, pray you, give him this;[1]
35 And when your mistress hears thus much from you,
I pray, desire her call her wisdom to her.[2]
So, fare you well.
If you do chance to hear of that blind traitor,
Preferment falls on him that cuts him off.°   cuts his life short
40 OSWALD Would I could meet him, madam! I should show
What party I do follow.
REGAN Fare thee well.   *Exeunt*

4.6

Enter GLOUCESTER, *and* EDGAR *dressed like a peasant*

GLOUCESTER When shall we come to the top of that same° hill?   agreed-upon
EDGAR You do climb up it now. Look how we labor.
GLOUCESTER Methinks the ground is even.
EDGAR   Horrible steep.
Hark, do you hear the sea?
GLOUCESTER   No, truly.
5 EDGAR Why, then, your other senses grow imperfect
By your eyes' anguish.
GLOUCESTER   So may it be, indeed.
Methinks thy voice is altered, and thou speakest
In better phrase and matter° than thou didst.   sense
EDGAR Y'are much deceived. In nothing am I changed
But in my garments.
10 GLOUCESTER   Methinks y'are better spoken.
EDGAR Come on, sir; here's the place. Stand still. How fearful
And dizzy 'tis, to cast one's eyes so low!
The crows and choughs° that wing the midway air[1]   jackdaws
Show° scarce so gross° as beetles. Halfway down   Appear / big
15 Hangs one that gathers sampire,° dreadful trade!   seaweed
Methinks he seems no bigger than his head.
The fishermen, that walk upon the beach,
Appear like mice; and yond tall anchoring bark,°   ship
Diminished to her cock;° her cock, a buoy   dinghy
20 Almost too small for sight. The murmuring surge,
That on the unnumbered° idle pebble chafes,   innumerable
Cannot be heard so high. I'll look no more,
Lest my brain turn, and the° deficient sight   my
Topple° down headlong.   Topple me
GLOUCESTER   Set me where you stand.
25 EDGAR Give me your hand. You are now within a foot
Of th' extreme verge. For all beneath the moon
Would I not leap upright.[2]
GLOUCESTER   Let go my hand.
Here, friend, 's another purse; in it a jewel
Well worth a poor man's taking. Fairies and gods
30 Prosper it[3] with thee! Go thou farther off;
Bid me farewell, and let me hear thee going.

---

1. This information, but possibly another letter or token.
2. *desire . . . to her:* tell her to come to her senses.
4.6 Location: Near Dover.
1. The air between cliff and sea.

2. I would not jump up and down (for fear of losing my balance).
3. Make it increase. Fairies were sometimes held to hoard and multiply treasure.

EDGAR Now fare you well, good sir.

GLOUCESTER   With all my heart.

EDGAR (*aside*) Why I do trifle thus with his despair
Is done to cure it.

GLOUCESTER (*kneeling*) O you mighty gods!

35 This world I do renounce, and, in your sights,
Shake patiently my great affliction off.
If I could bear it longer, and not fall
To quarrel° with your great opposeless wills,   *Into conflict*
My snuff and loathèd part of nature[4] should

40 Burn itself out. If Edgar live, O, bless him!
Now, fellow, fare thee well.

                    He falls forward and swoons

EDGAR   Gone, sir; farewell.—
And yet I know not how conceit may rob
The treasury of life, when life itself
Yields to the theft.[5] Had he been where he thought,

45 By this° had thought been past. Alive or dead?   *now*
Ho, you sir! friend! Hear you, sir? speak!
Thus might he pass° indeed. Yet he revives.   *pass away*
What are you, sir?

GLOUCESTER   Away, and let me die.

EDGAR Hadst thou been aught° but gossamer, feathers, air,   *anything*

50 So many fathom down precipitating,°   *plunging*
Thou'dst shivered° like an egg; but thou dost breathe;   *shattered*
Hast heavy substance; bleed'st not; speak'st; art sound.
Ten masts at each° make not the altitude   *end to end*
Which thou hast perpendicularly fell.

55 Thy life's a miracle. Speak yet again.

GLOUCESTER But have I fallen, or no?

EDGAR From the dread summit of this chalky bourn.[6]
Look up a-height; the shrill-gorged° lark so far   *shrill-throated*
Cannot be seen or heard. Do but look up.

60 GLOUCESTER Alack, I have no eyes.
Is wretchedness deprived° that benefit,   *deprived of*
To end itself by death? 'Twas yet some comfort,
When misery could beguile° the tyrant's rage,   *cheat*
And frustrate his proud will.

EDGAR   Give me your arm.

65 Up—so. How is 't? Feel you your legs? You stand.

GLOUCESTER Too well, too well.

EDGAR   This is above all strangeness.
Upon the crown o' the cliff, what thing was that
Which parted from you?

GLOUCESTER   A poor unfortunate beggar.

EDGAR As I stood here below, methought his eyes

70 Were two full moons; he had a thousand noses,
Horns whelked° and waved like the enridgèd sea: *twisted*
It was some fiend. Therefore, thou happy father,°   *lucky old man*
Think that the clearest° gods, who make them honors   *purest; most illustrious*
Of men's impossibilities,[7] have preserved thee.

4. The scorched and hateful remnant of my lifetime. *snuff:* end of a candlewick.
5. *And yet . . . theft:* Edgar worries that the imagined scenario ("conceit") he has invented may be enough to kill his father, particularly as Gloucester wishes for ("yields"

to") his own death.
6. The white chalk cliffs of Dover, which make a boundary ("bourn") between land and sea.
7. *who . . . impossibilities:* who attain honor for themselves by performing deeds impossible to men.

75 GLOUCESTER   I do remember now. Henceforth I'll bear
Affliction till it do cry out itself
"Enough, enough," and die. That thing you speak of,
I took it for a man; often 't would say
"The fiend, the fiend"—he led me to that place.

80 EDGAR   Bear free and patient thoughts. But who comes here?
Enter LEAR, *fantastically dressed with wild flowers*
The safer sense will ne'er accommodate
His master thus.[8]

LEAR   No, they cannot touch me for coining;[9] I am the king
himself.

85 EDGAR   O thou side-piercing sight!

LEAR   Nature's above art in that respect.[1] There's your press-
money.[2] That fellow handles his bow like a crow-keeper.[3] Draw
me a clothier's yard.[4] Look, look, a mouse! Peace, peace; this
piece of toasted cheese will do 't.°   (*lure the mouse*) There's my gauntlet; I'll
90 prove it on a giant.[5] Bring up the brown bills.[6] O, well flown,
bird!° i' the clout,° i' the clout. Hewgh! Give the word.°   *arrow / bull's-eye / password*

EDGAR   Sweet marjoram.[7]

LEAR   Pass.

GLOUCESTER   I know that voice.

95 LEAR   Ha! Goneril, with a white beard! They flattered me like a
dog;° and told me I had white hairs in my beard ere the black   *fawningly*
ones were there.[8] To say "aye" and "no" to everything that I
said!—"Aye" and "no" too was no good divinity.[9] When the
rain came to wet me once, and the wind to make me chatter;
100 when the thunder would not peace at my bidding; there I
found° 'em, there I smelt 'em out. Go to, they are not men o'   *understood*
their words! They told me I was everything. 'Tis a lie, I am not
ague-proof.°   *immune to illness*

GLOUCESTER   The trick° of that voice I do well remember.   *peculiarity*
Is 't not the king?

105 LEAR   Aye, every inch a king!
When I do stare, see how the subject quakes.
I pardon that man's life. What was thy cause?°   *crime*
Adultery?
Thou shalt not die. Die for adultery? No.
110 The wren goes to 't, and the small gilded fly
Does lecher in my sight.
Let copulation thrive; for Gloucester's bastard son
Was kinder to his father than my daughters
Got 'tween the lawful sheets. To 't luxury,° pell-mell!   *lechery*
115 For I lack soldiers. Behold yond simpering dame,
Whose face between her forks presages snow;[1]

8. *The . . . thus:* A sane mind would never allow its pos-
sessor to dress up this way.
9. Because minting money was the prerogative of the
King, nobody could overtake or equal ("touch") him.
1. My true feelings will always outvalue others' hypocrisy;
my natural supremacy surpasses any attempt to create a
false new reign. This image may also be based on coining
(see note 9, above).
2. Fee paid to a soldier impressed, or forced, into the
army.
3. A person hired as a scarecrow, and thus unfit for any-
thing else.
4. Draw the bowstring the full length of the arrow (a
standard English arrow was a cloth yard [37 inches]

long).
5. I'll defend my stand even against a giant. To throw
down an armored glove ("gauntlet") was to issue a chal-
lenge.
6. Brown painted pikes; the soldiers carrying them.
7. Used medicinally against madness.
8. Told me I had wisdom before age.
9. *no good divinity:* poor theology (because insincere);
from James 5:12, "Let your yea be yea; nay, nay."
1. Whose expression implies cold chastity. "Face" refers
to the area between her legs ("forks"), as well as to her
literal facial expression as framed by the aristocratic
lady's starched headpiece, also called a "fork."

That minces° virtue, and does shake the head   *affects*
To hear of° pleasure's name;   *even of*
The fitchew, nor the soilèd horse,[2] goes to 't
120 With a more riotous appetite.
Down from the waist they are Centaurs,[3]
Though women all above.
But° to the girdle° do the gods inherit.°   *Only / waist / own*
Beneath is all the fiends'; there's hell,[4] there's darkness,
125 There's the sulphurous pit, burning, scalding,
Stench, consumption! Fie, fie, fie! pah! pah!
Give me an ounce of civet,[5] good apothecary,
To sweeten my imagination.
There's money for thee.
130 GLOUCESTER   O, let me kiss that hand!
LEAR   Let me wipe it first; it smells of mortality.
GLOUCESTER   O ruined piece° of nature! This great world   *masterpiece*
Shall so wear out to nought.[6] Dost thou know me?
LEAR   I remember thine eyes well enough. Dost thou squiny° at   *squint*
135 me? No, do thy worst, blind Cupid; I'll not love. Read thou this
challenge; mark but the penning of it.
GLOUCESTER   Were all the letters suns, I could not see one.
EDGAR (*aside*)   I would not take° this from report. It is,   *believe*
And my heart breaks at it.
140 LEAR   Read.
GLOUCESTER   What, with the case° of eyes?   *socket*
LEAR   O, ho, are you there with me?[7] No eyes in your head, nor
no money in your purse? Your eyes are in a heavy case,[8] your
purse in a light. Yet you see how this world goes.
145 GLOUCESTER   I see it feelingly.°   *by touch; painfully*
LEAR   What, art mad? A man may see how this world goes with
no eyes. Look with thine ears. See how yond justice rails upon
yond simple° thief. Hark, in thine ear. Change places and,   *lowly; innocent*
handy-dandy,[9] which is the justice, which is the thief? Thou
150 hast seen a farmer's dog bark at a beggar?
GLOUCESTER   Aye, sir.
LEAR   And the creature° run from the cur? There thou mightst   *wretch*
behold the great image of authority: a dog's obeyed in office.
Thou rascal beadle,[1] hold° thy bloody hand!   *restrain*
155 Why dost thou lash that whore? Strip thine own back;
Thou hotly lusts to use her in that kind°   *way*
For which thou whipp'st her. The usurer hangs the cozener.[2]
Through tattered clothes small vices do appear;
Robes and furred gowns hide all. Plate° sin with gold,   *Armor; gild*
160 And the strong lance of justice hurtless° breaks;   *harmlessly*
Arm it in rags, a pigmy's straw does pierce it.
None does offend, none, I say, none; I'll able° 'em;   *authorize*
Take that of me, my friend, who have the power
To seal the accuser's lips. Get thee glass eyes;

2. Neither the polecat nor a horse full of fresh grass.
3. Lecherous mythological creatures that have a human body to the waist and the legs and torso of a horse below.
4. Shakespeare's frequent term for female genitals.
5. Exotic perfume derived from the sex glands of the civet cat.
6. Shall decay to nothing in the same way. In Renaissance philosophy, humans were perfectly analogous to the cosmos, standing for the whole in miniature and as its masterpiece.
7. Is that what you are telling me?
8. In a sad condition; playing on "case" as "sockets."
9. Pick a hand, as in a child's game.
1. The parish officer responsible for whippings.
2. The ruinous moneylender, prosperous enough to be made a judge, convicts the ordinary cheat.

165 And, like a scurvy politician,[3] seem
To see the things thou dost not. Now, now, now, now!
Pull off my boots. Harder, harder! So.

EDGAR   O, matter and impertinency° mixed!   *sense and nonsense*
Reason in madness!

170 LEAR   If thou wilt weep my fortunes, take my eyes.
I know thee well enough; thy name is Gloucester:
Thou must be patient. We came crying hither;
Thou knows't, the first time that we smell the air,
We wail and cry. I will preach to thee. Mark.

LEAR takes off his crown of weeds and flowers[4]

175 GLOUCESTER   Alack, alack the day!

LEAR   When we are born, we cry that we are come
To this great stage of fools. This'° a good block;[5]   *This is*
It were a delicate° stratagem, to shoe   *subtle*
A troop of horse with felt.[6] I'll put 't in proof;°   *to the test*
180 And when I have stol'n upon these sons-in-law,
Then, kill, kill, kill, kill, kill, kill!

Enter a GENTLEMAN, *with attendants*

GENTLEMAN   O, here he is; lay hand upon him. Sir,
Your most dear daughter—

LEAR   No rescue? What, a prisoner? I am even
185 The natural fool[7] of fortune. Use° me well;   *Treat*
You shall have ransom. Let me have surgeons;
I am cut to the brains.

GENTLEMAN   You shall have any thing.

LEAR   No seconds?° all myself?   *supporters*
Why, this would make a man a man of salt,[8]
190 To use his eyes for garden water-pots,
Aye, and laying° autumn's dust.   *settling*

GENTLEMAN   Good sir—

LEAR   I will die bravely,[9] like a smug° bridegroom. What!   *an elegant*
I will be jovial. Come, come; I am a king,
My masters, know you that?

195 GENTLEMAN   You are a royal one, and we obey you.

LEAR   Then there's life° in't. Nay, if you get it, you shall get it   *hope*
with running. Sa, sa, sa, sa.[1]   (*Exit running; attendants follow*)

GENTLEMAN   A sight most pitiful in the meanest wretch,
Past speaking of in a king! Thou hast one daughter,
200 Who redeems nature from the general curse
Which twain have brought her to.[2]

EDGAR   Hail, gentle° sir.   *noble*

GENTLEMAN   Sir, speed you.° What's your will?   *God speed you*

EDGAR   Do you hear aught, sir, of a battle toward?°   *coming*

GENTLEMAN   Most sure and vulgar.° Everyone hears that,   *commonly known*
Which° can distinguish sound.   *Who*

---

3. A vile schemer. In early modern England, "politician" meant an ambitious, even Machiavellian, upstart.
4. Like a preacher, removing his hat in the pulpit.
5. Stage (often called "scaffold" and hence linked to executioner's block); block used to shape a felt hat (such as the hat removed by a preacher before a sermon); mounting block (such as the stump or stock Lear may have sat on to remove his boots).
6. Hat material, to muffle the sound of the approaching cavalry.
7. Born plaything; playing on "natural" as "mentally

deficient."
8. A man reduced to nothing but the salt his tears deposit.
9. With courage; showily. "Die" plays on the Renaissance sense of "have an orgasm."
1. A cry to encourage dogs in the hunt.
2. *Who . . . to:* Who restores proper meaning and order to a universe plagued by the crimes of the other two daughters; alluding to the fall of humankind and the natural world caused by the sin of Adam and Eve and to the universal redemption brought about by Christ's sacrifice.

205 EDGAR But, by your favor,
How near's the other army?
GENTLEMAN Near and on speedy foot. The main descry°   *appearance*
Stands on the hourly thought.°   *Is expected forthwith*
EDGAR I thank you, sir. That's all.
210 GENTLEMAN Though that the queen on° special cause° is here,   *for / reason*
Her army is moved on.
EDGAR   I thank you, sir.   *Exit* GENTLEMAN
GLOUCESTER You ever-gentle gods, take my breath from me;
Let not my worser spirit³ tempt me again
To die before you please!
EDGAR   Well pray you, father.⁴
215 GLOUCESTER Now, good sir, what are you?
EDGAR A most poor man, made tame to fortune's blows;
Who, by the art of known and feeling° sorrows,   *profound*
Am pregnant to° good pity. Give me your hand,   *disposed to feel*
I'll lead you to some biding.°   *resting place*
GLOUCESTER   Hearty thanks.
220 The bounty and the benison of heaven
To boot, and boot!⁵
        Enter OSWALD
OSWALD A proclaimed prize!⁶ Most happy!°   *lucky*
That eyeless head of thine was first framed° flesh   *made of*
To raise my fortunes. Thou old unhappy traitor,
225 Briefly thyself remember.⁷ The sword is out
That must destroy thee.
GLOUCESTER   Now let thy friendly hand
Put strength enough to 't.
        EDGAR *interposes*
OSWALD   Wherefore, bold peasant.
Darest thou support a published° traitor? Hence,   *proclaimed*
Lest that the infection° of his fortune take   *(deathly) sickness*
230 Like° hold on thee. Let go his arm.   *The same*
EDGAR Chill⁸ not let go, zir, without vurther 'casion.°   *further occasion*
OSWALD Let go, slave, or thou diest!
EDGAR Good gentleman, go your gait,° and let poor volk pass.   *walk on*
An chud ha'° bin zwaggered out of my life, 't would not ha' bin   *If I could have*
235 zo long as 'tis by a vortnight. Nay, come not near th' old man;
keep out, che vor ye, or ise try whether your costard or my
ballow be the harder.⁹ Chill be plain with you.
OSWALD Out, dunghill!
EDGAR Chill pick your teeth, zir. Come! No matter vor your
240 foins.°   *sword thrusts*
        They fight, and EDGAR *knocks him down*
OSWALD Slave, thou hast slain me. Villain, take my purse.
If ever thou wilt thrive, bury my body;
And give the letters which thou find'st about me
To Edmund earl of Gloucester. Seek him out
245 Upon° the British party. O, untimely death!   *Within*
Death!   *He dies*

---

3. Wicked inclination; bad angel.
4. A term of respect for an elderly man.
5. In addition to my thanks, and may it bring you some worldly reward.
6. A wanted man, with a bounty on his life.
7. Recollect and pray forgiveness for your sins.

8. I will; dialect from Somerset was a stage convention for peasant dialogue.
9. *che vor ye . . . harder:* I warrant you, or I shall test whether your head or my cudgel is harder. *costard:* a kind of apple.

EDGAR   I know thee well: a serviceable° villain;   *an officious*
    As duteous to the vices of thy mistress
    As badness would desire.
GLOUCESTER   What, is he dead?
250 EDGAR   Sit you down, father; rest you.
    Let's see his pockets; the letters that he speaks of
    May be my friends. He's dead; I am only sorry
    He had no other death's man.° Let us see.   *executioner*
    Leave,° gentle wax;[1] and, manners blame us not.   *By your leave*
255 To know our enemies' minds, we'd rip their hearts;
    Their° papers, is more lawful.   *To rip their*
    (*Reads*) "Let our reciprocal vows be remembered. You have
    many opportunities to cut him off. If your will want° not, time   *lacks*
    and place will be fruitfully offered. There is nothing done,° if   *accomplished*
260 he return the conqueror. Then am I the prisoner, and his bed my
    jail; from the loathed warmth whereof deliver me, and supply°   *fill*
    the place for your labor.[2]
               Your—wife, so I would say—
                    Affectionate servant,
265   Goneril."
    O undistinguished space of woman's will![3]
    A plot upon her virtuous husband's life;
    And the exchange° my brother! Here, in the sands,   *substitute*
    Thee I'll rake up,° the post unsanctified°   *cover up / unholy messenger*
270 Of murderous lechers; and in the mature time°   *when the time is ripe*
    With this ungracious° paper strike the sight   *ungodly*
    Of the death-practiced duke.[4] For him 'tis well
    That of thy death and business I can tell.
GLOUCESTER   The king is mad. How stiff is my vile sense,[5]
275 That I stand up, and have ingenious feeling[6]
    Of my huge sorrows! Better I were distract;°   *mad*
    So should my thoughts be severed from my griefs,
    And woes by wrong° imaginations lose   *false*
    The knowledge of themselves.
         Drum afar off
EDGAR   Give me your hand.
280 Far off, methinks, I hear the beaten drum.
    Come, father, I'll bestow° you with a friend.   *Exeunt*   *lodge*

4.7

Enter CORDELIA, KENT, DOCTOR, *and a* GENTLEMAN
CORDELIA   O thou good Kent, how shall I live and work,
    To match thy goodness? My life will be too short,
    And every measure° fail me.   *attempt*
KENT   To be acknowledged, madam, is o'erpaid.°   *is more than enough*
5   All my reports go[1] with the modest truth;
    Nor more nor clipped, but so.[2]
CORDELIA   Be better suited.°   *attired*
    These weeds° are memories of those worser hours.   *clothes*
    I prithee, put them off.

---

1. The wax seal on the letter.
2. *for your labor:* as a reward for your endeavors, and
for further sexual exertion.
3. Limitless extent of woman's willfulness. As with "hell"
in line 124, "will" might also refer to a woman's genitals.
4. Of the Duke whose death is plotted.
5. How obstinate is my unwanted power of reason.

6. That I remain upright and firm in my sanity and
have rational perceptions.
4.7 Location: The French camp at Dover.
1. May all accounts of me agree.
2. Not greater or less, but exactly the modest amount I
deserve.

KENT   Pardon me, dear madam;
Yet to be known shortens my made intent.³
10 My boon I make it,⁴ that you know° me not   *acknowledge*
Till time and I think meet.°   *suitable*
CORDELIA Then be 't so, my good lord. (*To the* DOCTOR) How
 does the king?
DOCTOR Madam, sleeps still.
CORDELIA O you kind gods,
15 Cure this great breach in his abusèd nature!
The untuned and jarring senses, O, wind up⁵
Of this child-changèd⁶ father!
DOCTOR   So please your majesty
That we may wake the king? He hath slept long.
CORDELIA Be governed by your knowledge, and proceed
20 I' the sway° of your own will. Is he arrayed?° *By the authority / clothed*
  Enter LEAR *in a chair carried by servants*
GENTLEMAN Aye, madam. In the heaviness of his sleep
We put fresh garments on him.
DOCTOR Be by, good madam, when we do awake him;
I doubt not of his temperance.°   *calmness*
CORDELIA   Very well.
  Music
25 DOCTOR Please you, draw near. Louder the music there!
CORDELIA O my dear father! Restoration hang
Thy medicine on my lips; and let this kiss
Repair those violent harms that my two sisters
Have in thy reverence° made!   *aged dignity*
KENT   Kind and dear princess!
30 CORDELIA Had you not⁷ been their father, these white flakes° *locks of hair*
Had challenged° pity of them. Was this a face *Would have provoked*
To be opposed against the warring winds?
To stand against the deep dread-bolted thunder?
In the most terrible and nimble stroke
35 Of quick, cross lightning? to watch°—poor perdu!⁸— *to stand guard*
With this thin helm?° Mine enemy's dog,   *helmet (of hair)*
Though he had bit me, should have stood that night
Against my fire; and wast thou fain,° poor father,   *glad*
To hovel thee with swine, and rogues forlorn,
40 In short° and musty straw? Alack, alack!   *scant; broken*
'Tis wonder that thy life and wits at once
Had not concluded all.° He wakes; speak to him.   *altogether*
DOCTOR Madam, do you; 'tis fittest.
CORDELIA How does my royal lord? How fares your majesty?
45 LEAR You do me wrong to take me out o' the grave.
Thou art a soul in bliss; but I am bound
Upon a wheel of fire, that mine own tears
Do scald like molten lead.⁹
CORDELIA   Sir, do you know me?
LEAR You are a spirit, I know. When did you die?
50 CORDELIA Still, still, far wide!°   *unbalanced*

---

3. Revealing myself now would abort my designs.
4. The reward I beg is.
5. *The . . . up*: Reorder his confused and delirious mind. The image is of tightening the strings of a lute.
6. Changed by his children; changed into a child; playing on a musical key change.

7. Even if you had not.
8. Lost one; in military terms, a dangerously exposed sentry.
9. *but I . . . lead*: Lear puts himself in either hell or purgatory, both places of such punishment in medieval accounts.

DOCTOR   He's scarce awake. Let him alone awhile.

LEAR   Where have I been? Where am I? Fair daylight?
I am mightily abused.° I should e'en die with pity,   *wronged; deceived*
To see another thus. I know not what to say.
55   I will not swear these are my hands. Let's see.
I feel this pin prick. Would I were assured
Of my condition!

CORDELIA   O, look upon me, sir,
And hold your hands in benediction o'er me:
No, sir, you must not kneel.

60   LEAR   Pray, do not mock me.
I am a very foolish fond° old man,   *silly*
Fourscore and upward, not an hour more nor less;
And, to deal plainly,
I fear I am not in my perfect mind.
65   Methinks I should know you, and know this man;
Yet I am doubtful; for I am mainly° ignorant   *entirely*
What place this is; and all the skill I have
Remembers not these garments; nor I know not
Where I did lodge last night. Do not laugh at me;
70   For, as I am a man, I think this lady
To be my child Cordelia.

CORDELIA   And so I am, I am.

LEAR   Be your tears wet?¹ Yes, faith. I pray, weep not.
If you have poison for me, I will drink it.
I know you do not love me; for your sisters
75   Have, as I do remember, done me wrong.
You have some cause, they have not.

CORDELIA   No cause, no cause.

LEAR   Am I in France?

KENT   In your own kingdom, sir.

LEAR   Do not abuse° me.   *deceive; mock*

DOCTOR   Be comforted, good madam. The great rage,
80   You see, is killed in him; and yet it is danger
To make him even o'er° the time he has lost.   *go over*
Desire him to go in. Trouble him no more
Till further settling.°   *Until his mind eases*

CORDELIA   Will't please your highness walk?

LEAR   You must bear with me:
85   Pray you now, forget and forgive. I am old and foolish.

Exeunt all but KENT *and* GENTLEMAN

GENTLEMAN   Holds it true, sir, that the Duke of Cornwall was so
slain?

KENT   Most certain, sir.

GENTLEMAN   Who is conductor° of his people?   *commander*

90   KENT   As 'tis said, the bastard son of Gloucester.

GENTLEMAN   They say Edgar, his banished son, is with the Earl
of Kent in Germany.

KENT   Report° is changeable. 'Tis time to look about.° The pow-   *Rumor / prepare defenses*
ers of the kingdom approach apace.

95   GENTLEMAN   The arbitrement° is like to be bloody. Fare you   *encounter*
well, sir.   *Exit*

KENT   My point and period² will be throughly wrought,
Or° well or ill, as this day's battle's fought.   *Exit*   *For*

---

1. Are your tears real?; is this really happening?   2. The purpose and end of my life; literally, the full stop.

5.1

Enter, with drum and colors,° EDMUND, REGAN, GENTLE-   *regimental flags*
MAN, *and soldiers*

EDMUND   Know° of the duke if his last purpose hold,[1]   *Inquire*
Or whether since he is advised by aught[2]
To change the course. He's full of alteration°   *indecision*
And self-reproving. Bring his constant pleasure.°   *his settled intent*
                    To a GENTLEMAN, *who goes out*
5   REGAN   Our sister's man is certainly miscarried.[3]
EDMUND   'Tis to be doubted,° madam.   *feared*
REGAN   Now, sweet lord,
You know the goodness I intend upon you.
Tell me—but truly—but then speak the truth,
Do you not love my sister?
EDMUND   In honored° love.   *honorable*
10   REGAN   But have you never found my brother's way
To the forfended[4] place?
EDMUND   That thought abuses° you.   *deceives*
REGAN   I am doubtful° that you have been conjunct°   *suspicious / complicit*
And bosomed with° her, as far as we call hers.[5]   *enamored of*
EDMUND   No, by mine honor, madam.
15   REGAN   I never shall endure her. Dear my lord,
Be not familiar° with her.   *intimate*
EDMUND   Fear° me not.   *Doubt*
She and the duke her husband!
                    Enter, with drum and colors, ALBANY, GONERIL, *and*
                    soldiers
GONERIL (*aside*)   I had rather lose the battle than that sister
Should loosen° him and me.   *disunite*
20   ALBANY   Our very loving sister, well be-met.
Sir, this I hear: the king is come to his daughter,
With others whom the rigor° of our state°   *harshness / government*
Forced to cry out. Where I could not be honest,°   *honorable*
I never yet was valiant. For this business,
25   It toucheth° us, as France invades our land,   *concerns*
Not bolds the king, with others, whom, I fear,
Most just and heavy causes make oppose.[6]
EDMUND   Sir, you speak nobly.
REGAN   Why is this reasoned?[7]
GONERIL   Combine together 'gainst the enemy;
30   For these domestic and particular broils°   *minor details*
Are not the question here.
ALBANY   Let's then determine
With the ancient° of war on our proceeding.   *experienced officer*
EDMUND   I shall attend you presently° at your tent.   *in a moment*
REGAN   Sister, you'll go with us?[8]
35   GONERIL   No.
REGAN   'Tis most convenient;° pray you, go with us.   *suitable*
GONERIL (*aside*)   O, ho, I know the riddle.°—I will go.   *disguised meaning*
                    As they are going out, enter EDGAR *disguised*

5.1 Location: The British camp near Dover.
1. If his previous intention (to wage war) remains firm.
2. Since then anything has persuaded him.
3. Has surely come to grief by some accident.
4. Forbidden (to Edmund, because it is adulterous).
5. In total intimacy; all the way.
6. *It . . . oppose:* This is of concern to us because France

lands on our soil, not because it emboldens the King and
others, who, I am afraid, have been provoked for good
and solid reasons.
7. What is the point of this kind of speech?
8. Regan wants Goneril to go with Albany and her,
rather than with Edmund.

EDGAR If e'er your grace had speech with man so poor,
Hear me one word.

ALBANY   I'll overtake you. Speak.

Exeunt all but ALBANY *and* EDGAR

40 EDGAR Before you fight the battle, ope this letter.
If you have victory, let the trumpet sound
For him that brought it. Wretched though I seem,
I can produce a champion that will prove°   *defend*
What is avouched° there. If you miscarry,°   *asserted / perish*
45 Your business of the world hath so an end,
And machination° ceases. Fortune love you!   *plotting*

ALBANY Stay till I have read the letter.

EDGAR   I was forbid it.
When time shall serve, let but the herald cry,
And I'll appear again.

50 ALBANY Why, fare thee well. I will o'erlook thy paper.

Exit EDGAR

Re-enter EDMUND

EDMUND The enemy 's in view; draw up your powers.°   *troops*
Here is the guess° of their true strength and forces   *estimate*
By diligent discovery;° but your haste   *spying*
Is now urged on you.

ALBANY   We will greet the time.⁹   *Exit*

55 EDMUND To both these sisters have I sworn my love;
Each jealous° of the other, as the stung   *suspicious*
Are of the adder. Which of them shall I take?
Both? one? or neither? Neither can be enjoyed,
If both remain alive. To take the widow
60 Exasperates, makes mad her sister Goneril;
And hardly° shall I carry out my side,°   *with difficulty / plan*
Her husband being alive. Now then we'll use
His countenance¹ for the battle; which being done,
Let her who would be rid of him devise
65 His speedy taking off. As for the mercy
Which he intends to Lear and to Cordelia,
The battle done, and they within our power,
Shall° never see his pardon; for my state°   *They shall / condition*
Stands on° me to defend, not to debate.   *Exit*   *Obliges*

5.2

*Alarum within.*¹ *Enter, with drum and colors,* LEAR, COR-
DELIA, *and soldiers, over the stage; and exeunt.*
Enter EDGAR *and* GLOUCESTER

EDGAR Here, father,² take the shadow of this tree
For your good host;° pray that the right may thrive: *shelter*
If ever I return to you again,
I'll bring you comfort.

GLOUCESTER   Grace go with you, sir!   *Exit* EDGAR

Alarum and retreat° within. Re-enter EDGAR   *trumpet signal*

5 EDGAR Away, old man! give me thy hand! away!

---

9. We will be ready to meet the occasion.
1. Authority or backing; also suggesting "face," to be
used like a mask for Edmund's ambition.
5.2 Location: The rest of the play takes place near the
battlefield.
1. Trumpet call to battle (backstage).
2. See note to 4.6.214.

King Lear hath lost, he and his daughter ta'en.
Give me thy hand! come on!

GLOUCESTER   No farther, sir; a man may rot even° here.   *right*

EDGAR   What, in ill thoughts again? Men must endure
10   Their going hence, even as their coming hither;
Ripeness is all.³ Come on!

GLOUCESTER   And that's true, too.   *Exeunt*

5.3

Enter, in conquest, with drum and colors, EDMUND;
LEAR *and* CORDELIA, *prisoners;* CAPTAIN, SOLDIERS, *etc.*

EDMUND   Some officers take them away. Good guard,
Until their greater pleasures¹ first be known
That are to censure° them.   *judge*

CORDELIA   We are not the first
Who, with best meaning,° have incurred the worst.   *intention*
5   For thee, oppressèd king, am I cast down;°   *(into unhappiness)*
Myself could else out-frown false Fortune's frown.²
Shall we not see these daughters and these sisters?

LEAR   No, no, no, no! Come, let's away to prison.
We two alone will sing like birds i' the cage.
10   When thou dost ask me blessing, I'll kneel down,
And ask of thee forgiveness. So we'll live,
And pray, and sing, and tell old tales, and laugh
At gilded butterflies,³ and hear poor rogues
Talk of court news; and we'll talk with them too,
15   Who loses and who wins; who's in, and who's out;
And take upon's the mystery of things,
As if we were Gods' spies; and we'll wear out,°   *outlast*
In a walled prison, packs and sects of great ones,
That ebb and flow by the moon.⁴

EDMUND   Take them away.
20   LEAR   Upon such sacrifices,⁵ my Cordelia,
The gods themselves throw incense. Have I caught thee?
He that parts us shall bring a brand from heavens,
And fire us hence like foxes.⁶ Wipe thine eyes;
The good-years shall devour them, flesh and fell,⁷
25   Ere they shall make us weep! We'll see 'em starved first.
Come.   *Exeunt* LEAR *and* CORDELIA, *guarded*

EDMUND   Come hither, captain; hark.
Take thou this note (*giving a paper*). Go follow them to prison:
One step I have advanced° thee. If thou dost   *promoted*
30   As this instructs thee, thou dost make thy way
To noble fortunes. Know thou this, that men
Are as the time is. To be tender-minded
Does not become a sword.° Thy great employment   *befit a swordsman*

---

3. To await the destined time is the most important thing, as fruit falls only when ripe (playing on Gloucester's "rot," line 8); readiness for death is our only duty (compare *Hamlet* 5.2.160, "The readiness is all").

5.3
1. *Good . . . pleasures:* Guard them well until the desires of those greater persons.
2. Otherwise, I could be defiant in the face of bad fortune.
3. Gaudy courtiers.

4. *packs . . . moon:* followers and factions of important people whose positions at court vary as the tide.
5. Upon such sacrifices as we are or as you have made.
6. *shall . . . foxes:* must have divine aid to do so. The image is of using a torch to smoke foxes out of their holes, or, in the case of Lear and Cordelia, prison cells.
7. *flesh and fell:* meat and skin; entirely. The precise meaning of "good-years" has not been explained; it may signify simply the passage of time or may suggest some ominous, destructive power.

Will not bear question.° Either say thou'lt do 't,   *discussion*
Or thrive by other means.

35 CAPTAIN   I'll do 't, my lord.

EDMUND   About it; and write happy when thou hast done.[8]
Mark, I say, instantly; and carry it° so   *carry it out*
As I have set it down.

CAPTAIN   I cannot draw a cart, nor eat dried oats;°   *(like a horse)*
40 If it be a man's work, I'll do it.   *Exit*

    Flourish. Enter ALBANY, GONERIL, REGAN, *another* CAP-
    TAIN, *and soldiers*

ALBANY   Sir, you have showed today your valiant strain,°   *qualities; birth*
And fortune led you well. You have the captives
That were the opposites° of this day's strife.   *opponents*
I do require them of you, so to use° them   *treat*
45 As we shall find their merits and our safety
May equally determine.

EDMUND   Sir, I thought it fit
To send the old and miserable king
To some retention° and appointed guard;   *confinement*
Whose° age has charms in it, whose title more,   *(Lear's)*
50 To pluck the common bosom[9] on his side,
And turn our impressed lances° in our eyes   *conscripted lancers*
Which[1] do command them. With him I sent the queen;
My reason all the same; and they are ready
Tomorrow, or at further space,° t' appear   *at a future point*
55 Where you shall hold your session.° At this time   *court of judgment*
We sweat and bleed; the friend hath lost his friend;
And the best quarrels, in the heat, are cursed
By those that feel their sharpness.[2]
The question of Cordelia and her father
Requires a fitter place.

60 ALBANY   Sir, by your patience,
I hold you but a subject of° this war,   *in waging*
Not as a brother.

REGAN   That's as we list° to grace him.   *choose*
Methinks our pleasure might have been demanded,[3]
Ere you had spoken so far. He led our powers;°   *armies*
65 Bore the commission of my place and person;
The which immediacy° may well stand up,   *close connection*
And call itself your brother.

GONERIL   Not so hot!°   *Not so fast*
In his own grace° he doth exalt himself,   *merit*
More than in your addition.[4]

REGAN   In my rights,
70 By me invested, he compeers° the best.   *equals*

GONERIL   That were the most,[5] if he should husband you.

REGAN   Jesters do oft prove prophets.

GONERIL   Holla, holla!
That eye that told you so looked but a-squint.[6]

8. Go to it, and call yourself happy when you are done.
9. To garner the affection of the populace.
1. *in our eyes / Which:* in the eyes of us who.
2. *And . . . sharpness:* And in the heat of battle, even the most just wars are cursed by those who must suffer the fighting.
3. I think you should have inquired into my wishes.
4. In the honors you confer upon him.
5. That investiture would be complete.
6. Squinting was a proverbial effect of jealousy, because of the tendency to look suspiciously at potential rivals.

REGAN   Lady, I am not well; else I should answer
75   From a full-flowing stomach.° General,   *anger*
     Take thou my soldiers, prisoners, patrimony:
     Dispose of them, of me; the walls° are thine.   *fortress of my heart*
     Witness the world, that I create thee here
     My lord and master.
GONERIL   Mean you to enjoy him?
80 ALBANY   The let-alone° lies not in your good will.   *veto*
     EDMUND   Nor in thine, lord.
     ALBANY   Half-blooded° fellow, yes.   *Bastard*
     REGAN (*to* EDMUND)   Let the drum strike,[7] and prove my title thine.
     ALBANY   Stay yet; hear reason. Edmund, I arrest thee
     On capital treason; and, in thine attaint,[8]
     This gilded serpent (*pointing to* GONERIL). For your claim, fair
85   sister,°   *sister-in-law*
     I bar it in the interest of my wife;
     'Tis she is sub-contracted to this lord,
     And I, her husband, contradict your banes.°   *announcement of marriage*
     If you will marry, make your loves to me,
     My lady is bespoke.
90 GONERIL   An interlude!°   *A farce*
     ALBANY   Thou art armed, Gloucester. Let the trumpet sound.
     If none appear to prove upon thy head
     Thy heinous, manifest, and many treasons,
     There is my pledge (*throwing down a glove*); I'll prove it on thy heart,
95   Ere I taste bread, thou art in nothing less°   *in no way less guilty*
     Than I have proclaimed thee.
     REGAN   Sick, O, sick!
     GONERIL (*aside*)   If not, I'll ne'er trust medicine.°   *poison (euphemistic)*
     EDMUND   There's my exchange (*throwing down a glove*). What° *Whoever*
       in the world he is
     That names me traitor, villain-like he lies.
100   Call by thy trumpet. He that dares approach,
     On him, on you, who not? I will maintain
     My truth and honor firmly.
     ALBANY   A herald, ho!
     EDMUND   A herald, ho, a herald!
     ALBANY   Trust to thy single virtue;° for thy soldiers,   *your unassisted power*
105   All levied in my name, have in my name
     Took their discharge.
     REGAN   My sickness grows upon me.
     ALBANY   She is not well; convey her to my tent.   *Exit* REGAN, *led*
     Enter a HERALD
     Come hither, herald—Let the trumpet sound—
     And read out this.
     CAPTAIN   Sound, trumpet! (*A trumpet sounds*)
110 HERALD [*reads*]   "If any man of quality or degree within the
     lists of the army will maintain upon Edmund, supposed Earl of
     Gloucester, that he is a manifold traitor, let him appear by the
     third sound of the trumpet. He is bold in his defense."
     EDMUND   Sound! (*First trumpet*)
115 HERALD   Again! (*Second trumpet*)

---

7. Perhaps to announce the betrothal, or a challenge.
8. And in order to accuse you; and as one who shares your corruption or crime.

HERALD   Again! (*Third trumpet*)
    Trumpet answers within
    Enter EDGAR, *at the third sound, armed, with a trumpet*
    before him

ALBANY   Ask him his purposes, why he appears
    Upon this call o' the trumpet.

HERALD   What° are you?   *Who*
    Your name, your quality?° and why you answer   *degree; rank*
    This present summons?

120 EDGAR   Know, my name is lost;
    By treason's tooth bare-gnawn and canker-bit.°   *worm-eaten*
    Yet am I noble as the adversary
    I come to cope.°   *to encounter*

ALBANY   Which is that adversary?

EDGAR   What's he that speaks for Edmund Earl of Gloucester?

EDMUND   Himself. What say'st thou to him?

125 EDGAR   Draw thy sword,
    That,° if my speech offend a noble heart,   *So that*
    Thy arm may do thee justice. Here is mine.
    Behold, it is the privilege of mine honors,
    My oath, and my profession. I protest,
130   Maugre° thy strength, youth, place, and eminence,   *Despite*
    Despite thy victor sword and fire-new° fortune,   *newly minted*
    Thy valor and thy heart,° thou art a traitor;   *courage*
    False to thy gods, thy brother, and thy father;
    Conspirant 'gainst this high-illustrious prince;
135   And, from the extremest upward° of thy head   *top*
    To the descent° and dust below thy foot,   *lowest part; sole*
    A most toad-spotted⁹ traitor. Say thou "No,"
    This sword, this arm, and my best spirits, are bent°   *ready*
    To prove upon thy heart, whereto I speak,
    Thou liest.

140 EDMUND   In wisdom I should ask thy name;
    But, since thy outside looks so fair and warlike
    And that thy tongue some say of breeding breathes,
    What safe and nicely I might well delay
    By rule of knighthood, I disdain and spurn.¹
145   Back do I toss these treasons to thy head;
    With the hell-hated° lie o'erwhelm thy heart;   *hated as much as hell*
    Which, for° they yet glance by and scarcely bruise,   *since*
    This sword of mine shall give them instant way,°   *access*
    Where they shall rest for ever. Trumpets, speak!
    Alarums. They fight. EDMUND *falls*

ALBANY   Save° him, save him!   *Spare*
150 GONERIL   This is practice,° Gloucester: *trickery*
    By the law of arms thou wast not bound to answer
    An unknown opposite.° Thou art not vanquished,   *opponent*
    But cozened and beguiled.°   *cheated and deceived*

ALBANY   Shut your mouth, dame,
    Or with this paper shall I stople° it.   *plug*
155   Thou worse than any name, read thine own evil.
    No tearing, lady! I perceive you know it.

---

9. Venomous, like a toad; spotted with disgrace.
1. *And . . . spurn:* And since your speech may suggest high birth, I will not stick safely and meticulously to the rules of knighthood (which do not require a knight to fight an unknown opponent) and refuse to fight you.

Gives the letter to EDMUND

GONERIL   Say, if I do, the laws are mine, not thine.
Who can arraign° me for 't?   prosecute
ALBANY   Most monstrous! oh!
Know'st thou this paper?
GONERIL   Ask me not what I know.   *Exit*
160 ALBANY   Go after her: she's desperate; govern° her.   restrain
EDMUND   What you have charged me with, that have I done;
And more, much more; the time will bring it out.
'Tis past, and so am I. But what art thou
That hast this fortune on me?² If thou 'rt noble,
I do forgive thee.
165 EDGAR   Let's exchange charity.°   forgiveness
I am no less in blood than thou art, Edmund;
If more, the more thou hast wronged me.
My name is Edgar, and thy father's son.
The gods are just, and of our pleasant vices
170 Make instruments to plague us.
The dark and vicious place where thee he got³
Cost him his eyes.
EDMUND   Thou hast spoken right, 'tis true;
The wheel° is come full circle! I am here.⁴   Fortune's wheel
ALBANY   Methought thy very gait did prophesy
175 A royal nobleness. I must embrace thee.
Let sorrow split my heart, if ever I
Did hate thee or thy father!
EDGAR   Worthy prince. I know 't.
ALBANY   Where have you hid yourself?
How have you known the miseries of your father?
180 EDGAR   By nursing them, my lord. List° a brief tale;   Listen to
And when 'tis told, O, that my heart would burst!
The bloody proclamation to escape,⁵
That followed me so near—O, our lives' sweetness!
That we the pain of death would hourly die
185 Rather than die at once!⁶—taught me to shift
Into a madman's rags; to assume a semblance
That very° dogs disdained; and in this habit   even
Met I my father with his bleeding rings,°   sockets
Their precious stones° new lost; became his guide,   eyes
190 Led him, begged for him, saved him from despair;
Never—O fault!—revealed myself unto him,
Until some half-hour past, when I was armed:
Not sure, though hoping, of this good success,°   conclusion
I asked his blessing, and from first to last
195 Told him my pilgrimage. But his flawed° heart—   cracked
Alack, too weak the conflict to support!—
'Twixt two extremes of passion, joy and grief,
Burst smilingly.
EDMUND   This speech of yours hath moved me,
And shall perchance do good; but speak you on;
200 You look as you had something more to say.

2. Who have this good fortune at my expense.
3. The adulterous bed in which you were born; or, pos-
sibly, the vagina. *got*: begot.
4. Back at the lowest point.

5. In order to escape the sentence of death.
6. *our . . . once*: how sweet must life be that we prefer
the constant pain of dying to death itself.

ALBANY   If there be more, more woeful, hold it in;
  For I am almost ready to dissolve,°   *melt into tears*
  Hearing of this.
EDGAR   This would have seemed a period°   *conclusion*
  To such as love not sorrow; but another,
205 To amplify° too much would make much more,   *enlarge; extend*
  And top extremity.
  Whilst I was big in clamor° came there in a man, *lamenting loudly*
  Who, having seen me in my worst estate,
  Shunned my abhorred society; but then, finding
210 Who 'twas that so endured, with his strong arms
  He fastened on my neck, and bellowed out
  As he'd burst heaven; threw him on my father;
  Told the most piteous tale of Lear and him°   *himself*
  That ever ear received; which in recounting
215 His grief grew puissant,° and the strings of life *powerful*
  Began to crack. Twice then the trumpets sounded,
  And there I left him tranced.
ALBANY   But who was this?
EDGAR Kent, sir, the banished Kent; who in disguise
  Followed his enemy king,[7] and did him service
220 Improper° for a slave.   *Unfit even*
    Enter a GENTLEMAN, *with a bloody knife*
GENTLEMAN Help, help, O, help!
EDGAR   What kind of help?
ALBANY   Speak, man.
EDGAR What means that bloody knife?
GENTLEMAN   'Tis hot, it smokes,
  It came even from the heart of—O, she's dead!
ALBANY Who dead? speak, man.
225 GENTLEMAN Your lady, sir, your lady! and her sister
  By her is poisoned; she hath confessed it.
EDMUND I was contracted to them both. All three
  Now marry° in an instant.   *unite (in death)*
    Enter KENT
EDGAR   Here comes Kent.
ALBANY Produce their bodies, be they alive or dead:
230 This judgment of the heavens, that makes us tremble,
  Touches us not with pity.   *Exit* GENTLEMAN
          O, is this he?
  The time will not allow the compliment
  Which very manners urges.[8]
KENT   I am come
  To bid my king and master aye° good night.   *forever*
  Is he not here?
235 ALBANY   Great thing of° us forgot!   *by*
  Speak, Edmund, where's the king? and where's Cordelia?
  See'st thou this object,° Kent?   *spectacle*
    The bodies of GONERIL *and* REGAN *are brought in*
KENT Alack, why thus?
EDMUND   Yet° Edmund was beloved. *Despite all*

---

7. Because Lear had previously banished him. *enemy:*
hostile.   8. *the compliment . . . urges:* the ceremony that barest
             custom demands.

The one the other poisoned for my sake,
240 And after slew herself.
ALBANY   Even so. Cover their faces.
EDMUND   I pant for life. Some good I mean to do,
Despite of mine own nature. Quickly send,
Be brief° in it, to the castle; for my writ[9]   *speedy*
245 Is on the life of Lear and on Cordelia:
Nay, send in time.
ALBANY   Run, run, O, run!
EDGAR   To who, my lord? Who hath the office?° send   *commission*
Thy token of reprieve.
EDMUND   Well thought on. Take my sword,
Give it the° captain.   *to the*
250 ALBANY   Haste thee for thy life.   *Exit* EDGAR
EDMUND   He hath commission from thy wife and me
To hang Cordelia in the prison, and
To lay the blame upon her own despair,
That she fordid herself.[1]
255 ALBANY   The gods defend her! Bear him hence awhile.
                                                EDMUND *is borne off*
          Re-enter LEAR, *with* CORDELIA *dead in his arms;* EDGAR,
          CAPTAIN, *and others following*
LEAR   Howl, howl, howl, howl! O, you are men of stones:
Had I your tongues and eyes, I'd use them so
That heaven's vault should crack. She's gone forever!
I know when one is dead, and when one lives;
260 She's dead as earth. Lend me a looking-glass;
If that her breath will mist or stain the stone,[2]
Why, then she lives.
KENT   Is this the promised end?[3]
EDGAR   Or image of that horror?
ALBANY   Fall, and cease![4]
LEAR   This feather stirs; she lives! If it be so,
265 It is a chance which does redeem all sorrows
That ever I have felt.
KENT (*kneeling*)   O my good master!
LEAR   Prithee, away.
EDGAR   'Tis noble Kent, your friend.
LEAR   A plague upon you, murderers, traitors all!
I might have saved her; now she's gone for ever!
270 Cordelia, Cordelia! stay a little. Ha!
What is 't thou say'st? Her voice was ever soft,
Gentle, and low, an excellent thing in woman.
I killed the slave that was a-hanging thee.
GENTLEMAN   'Tis true, my lords, he did.
LEAR   Did I not, fellow?
275 I have seen the day, with my good biting falchion°   *light sword*
I would have made them skip: I am old now,

9. Order of execution.
1. Destroyed herself. In most of Shakespeare's source texts for the play, Cordelia does in fact kill herself after reigning for some years.
2. Mica, or stone polished to a mirror finish.

3. Doomsday; expected end of the play. In no version of the story previous to Shakespeare's does Cordelia die at this point.
4. Let the world collapse and end.

And these same crosses spoil me.⁵ Who are you?
Mine eyes are not o' the best. I'll tell you straight.°　　　*recognize you soon*

KENT　If fortune brag of two she loved and hated,
280　One of them we behold.⁶

LEAR　This is a dull sight.⁷ Are you not Kent?

KENT　　　　　　　　　　　　　　　The same,
Your servant Kent. Where is your servant Caius?°　　*(Kent's pseudonym)*

LEAR　He's a good fellow, I can tell you that;
He'll strike, and quickly too. He's dead and rotten.

285　KENT　No, my good lord; I am the very man—

LEAR　I'll see that straight.⁸

KENT　That, from your first of difference and decay,⁹
Have followed your sad steps.

LEAR　　　　　　　　　　You are welcome hither.

KENT　Nor no man else.¹ All's cheerless, dark, and deadly.°　　*deathly*
290　Your eldest daughters have fordone° themselves,　　*destroyed*
And desperately° are dead.　　　　　　　　　　　*in despair*

LEAR　　　　　　　　　Aye, so I think.

ALBANY　He knows not what he says; and vain° it is　　*in vain*
That we present us to him.

EDGAR　　　　　　　Very bootless.°　　　　　　　*futile*

Enter a CAPTAIN

CAPTAIN　Edmund is dead, my lord.

ALBANY　　　　　　　　That's but a trifle here.
295　You lords and noble friends, know our intent.
What comfort to this great decay° may come　　*ruin; destruction*
Shall be applied. For us, we will resign,
During the life of this old majesty,
To him our absolute power; (*to* EDGAR *and* KENT) you, to your
rights;
300　With boot,° and such addition° as your honors　　*reward / distinction*
Have more than merited. All friends shall taste
The wages of their virtue, and all foes
The cup of their deserving. O, see, see!

LEAR　And my poor fool² is hanged! No, no, no life!
305　Why should a dog, a horse, a rat, have life,
And thou no breath at all? Thou'lt come no more,
Never, never, never, never, never!
Pray you, undo this button. Thank you, sir.
Do you see this? Look on her, look, her lips,
Look there, look there!　　　　　　　　*Dies*

310　EDGAR　　　　　　He faints! My lord, my lord!

KENT　Break, heart; I prithee, break!

EDGAR　　　　　　　Look up, my lord.

KENT　Vex not his ghost.³ O, let him pass! He hates him much
That would upon the rack⁴ of this tough world
Stretch him out longer.

EDGAR　　　　　　He is gone, indeed.

5. And these recent adversities have weakened me; and these parries I could once match would now destroy me.
6. *If . . . behold:* If there were only two supreme examples in the world of Fortune's ability to raise up and cast down, Lear would be one; alternatively, we are each of us one (Lear and Kent are here looking at each other).
7. This is a sad sight; my vision is failing.
8. I'll attend to that shortly; I'll comprehend that in a moment.

9. Who from the beginning of your alteration and deterioration.
1. No, neither I nor anyone else is welcome. Alternatively, I am that man, not disguised as anyone else.
2. A term of endearment, here used for Cordelia, though it also recalls the disappearance of Lear's Fool after 3.6.
3. Do not disturb his departing soul.
4. Instrument of torture, used to stretch its victims.

315   KENT   The wonder is, he hath endured so long.
        He but usurped his life.[5]
    ALBANY   Bear them from hence. Our present business
        Is general woe. (*To* KENT *and* EDGAR) Friends of my soul, you twain
        Rule in this realm, and the gored° state sustain.   *wounded; bloody*
320   KENT   I have a journey, sir, shortly to go;
        My master calls me, I must not say no.
    EDGAR   The weight of this sad time we must obey;
        Speak what we feel, not what we ought to say.
        The oldest hath borne most; we that are young
325   Shall never see so much, nor live so long.

Exeunt, with dead march

---

5. From death, which already had a claim on it.

The History of King Lear

Scene 8

[*Storm.*] *Enter* KENT [*disguised,*] *and* [FIRST] GENTLE-
MAN, *at several° doors*   separate

KENT   What's here, beside foul weather?
FIRST GENTLEMAN   One minded like the weather,
Most unquietly.
KENT   I know you. Where's the King?
FIRST GENTLEMAN   Contending with the fretful element;
Bids the wind blow the earth into the sea
5   Or swell the curlèd waters 'bove the main,°   mainland
That things might change or cease; tears his white hair,
Which the impetuous blasts, with eyeless rage,
Catch in their fury and make nothing of;
Strives in his little world of man to outstorm
10   The to-and-fro-conflicting wind and rain.
This night, wherein the cub-drawn bear would couch,¹
The lion and the belly-pinchèd wolf
Keep their fur dry, unbonneted° he runs,   hatless; uncrowned
And bids what will take all.
KENT   But who is with him?
15   FIRST GENTLEMAN   None but the fool, who labours to outjest
His heart-struck injuries.²
KENT   Sir, I do know you,
And dare upon the warrant of my art³
Commend a dear° thing to you. There is division,   Entrust a crucial
Although as yet the face of it be covered
20   With mutual cunning, 'twixt Albany and Cornwall;
But true it is. From France there comes a power
Into this scattered kingdom, who already,
Wise in° our negligence, have secret feet   Aware of
In some of our best ports, and are at point°   ready
25   To show their open banner. Now to you:
If on my credit you dare build° so far   If you trust me
To make your speed to Dover, you shall find
Some that will thank you, making just° report   accurate
Of how unnatural and bemadding° sorrow   maddening
30   The King hath cause to plain.°   complain
I am a gentleman of blood and breeding,
And from some knowledge and assurance offer
This office° to you.   role; duty
FIRST GENTLEMAN   I will talk farther with you.
35   KENT   No, do not.
For confirmation that I am much more
Than my out-wall,° open this purse, and take   outward appearance
What it contains. If you shall see Cordelia—
As fear not but you shall—show her this ring
40   And she will tell you who your fellow° is,   (Kent himself)

Scene 8 Location: Bare, open country.
1. In which even the bear, though starving, having
been sucked dry ("drawn") by its cub, would not go out
to forage.

2. *to outjest:* to relieve with laughter; to exorcise through
ridicule. *heart-struck injuries:* injuries (from the betrayal
of his paternal love) that penetrated to the heart.
3. On the basis of my skill (at judging people).

The Tragedy of King Lear

3.1

Storm still. Enter KENT *[disguised] and [the* FIRST] GEN-
TLEMAN, *severally°*   separately

KENT Who's there, besides foul weather?

FIRST GENTLEMAN   One minded like the weather,
Most unquietly.

KENT   I know you. Where's the King?

FIRST GENTLEMAN Contending with the fretful elements;
Bids the wind blow the earth into the sea

5   Or swell the curlèd waters 'bove the main,°   mainland
That things might change or cease.

KENT   But who is with him?

FIRST GENTLEMAN None but the Fool, who labours to outjest
His heart-struck injuries.[1]

KENT   Sir, I do know you,
And dare upon the warrant of my note[2]

10   Commend a dear° thing to you. There is division,   Entrust a crucial
Although as yet the face of it is covered
With mutual cunning, 'twixt Albany and Cornwall,
Who have—as who have not that their great stars
Throned and set high[3]—servants, who seem no less,°   who appear as such

15   Which are to France the spies and speculations°   observers
Intelligent of[4] our state. What hath been seen,
Either in snuffs and packings° of the Dukes,   quarrels and plots
Or the hard rein° which both of them hath borne   treatment
Against the old kind King; or something deeper,

20   Whereof perchance these are but furnishings°—   pretexts

FIRST GENTLEMAN I will talk further with you.

KENT   No, do not.
For confirmation that I am much more
Than my out-wall,° open this purse, and take   outward appearance
What it contains. If you shall see Cordelia—

25   As fear not but you shall—show her this ring
And she will tell you who that fellow° is   (Kent himself)

3.1 Location: Bare, open country.
1. *to outjest:* to relieve with laughter; to exorcise through
ridicule. *heart-struck injuries:* injuries (from the betrayal
of his paternal love) that penetrated to the heart.

2. On the basis of my skill (at judging people).
3. *as . . . high:* as has everybody who has been favored
by destiny.
4. Supplying intelligence about; too well informed of.

That yet you do not know. Fie on this storm!
I will go seek the King.

FIRST GENTLEMAN   Give me your hand.
Have you no more to say?

KENT   Few words, but to effect°   *but in importance*
More than all yet: that when we have found the King—
45   In which endeavour I'll° this way, you that—   *I'll go*
He that first lights on him holla the other.   *Exeunt severally*

That yet you do not know. Fie on this storm!
I will go seek the King.
FIRST GENTLEMAN   Give me your hand. Have you no more to say?
30   KENT   Few words, but to effect° more than all yet: *but in importance*
That when we have found the King—in which your pain
That way, I'll this⁵—he that first lights on him
Holla the other.   *Exeunt [severally]*

Macbeth

On May 19, 1603, a scant two months after the death of Queen Elizabeth and the accession to the English throne of the Scottish King James, Shakespeare's company, the Lord Chamberlain's Men, was formally declared to be the King's Men. The players had every reason to be grateful to their new royal master for this lucrative distinction and attentive to his pleasure and interest. It has long been argued that one of the most striking signs of their gratitude is *Macbeth,* based on a story from Scottish history particularly apt for a monarch who traced his line back to Banquo, the noble thane whose murder Macbeth orders after he has killed King Duncan.

In Shakespeare's principal historical source, Raphael Holinshed's *Chronicles of England, Scotland, and Ireland* (1587), Banquo aids Macbeth in the murder of the King. Shakespeare suppresses this complicity. The witches (or "weird sisters") who tell Macbeth that he will be king tell Banquo that he will be the father of kings, but Banquo seems determined not to be drawn into any conspiratorial attempt to realize these prophecies. When, just before Duncan's assassination, Macbeth indirectly asks for his support, Banquo speaks of keeping his "allegiance clear" (2.1.27). Macbeth's only co-conspirator, then, is his wife. Innocent of the crime against Duncan, Banquo is killed because Macbeth fears and envies him and because he wishes to keep the crown he has seized from passing, as the witches had prophesied, to Banquo's heirs. Other significant changes Shakespeare made in his source materials further intensify Macbeth's isolation and his evil: in Holinshed's *Chronicles,* Duncan is a relatively young and feeble ruler, and Macbeth, having dispatched him, goes on to reign brilliantly for ten years. As Shakespeare staged the story, Duncan is a mature and virtuous king, and Scotland under the tyrant Macbeth is in the grip of a nightmare from which it will eventually awaken into the happy rule of Banquo's descendants.

As is so often the case with Shakespeare, we do not have a secure date for either the composition or the first performance of *Macbeth.* The first printed text is in the 1623 First Folio, but the play, usually dated 1606, has always seemed the most topical of Shakespeare's great tragedies, cannily alert at once to King James's personal obsessions and to contemporary events. The most unnerving of those events was the Gunpowder Plot, an attempt by a small group of conspirators, embittered by what they perceived as James's unwillingness to extend toleration to Roman Catholics, to set off a massive explosion that would blow up the King and his family along with most of the government. On the night before the intended attempt, the plot was foiled by the arrest of one of the principal conspirators, Guy Fawkes, who revealed under torture the names of his collaborators.

Among those hunted down, brought to trial, and executed for the Gunpowder Plot was Father Henry Garnet, head of the clandestine Jesuit mission in England. Garnet pleaded innocent, but the government prosecutors made much of the fact that he was the author of *A Treatise of Equivocation,* a book showing how to give misleading or ambiguous answers under oath. At a harrowing moment in *Macbeth,* in the immediate wake of the murder of the sleeping King Duncan, an insistent knocking is heard at the castle gate. (The knocking is a simple device, but in performance it almost always has a thrilling effect, famously characterized by the Romantic critic Thomas De Quincey as the reflux of the human upon the fiendish.) A porter, roused by the hammering on the door but still half drunk from the evening's revelry, appears. As he grumblingly goes to unlock the gate, he imagines that he is the gatekeeper in hell, opening the door to new arrivals. "Here's an equivocator," he says of one of these imaginary sinners, "that could swear in both the scales against either scale, who committed treason enough for God's sake, yet could not equivocate to heaven. O, come in, equivocator" (2.3.8–11). This treasonous equivocator knocking on hell's gate is almost certainly an allusion to the recently executed Henry Garnet.

The Gunpowder Plot was only one of the King's sources of anxiety. Not surprising for someone whose mother and father had both been killed, James had a horror of assassination and was convinced that there were many plots against his life. He also held a powerful conviction that a king was a sacred figure, God's own representative on earth. Regicide, in this view, was close to the ultimate crime, a demonic assault not simply on an individual and a community but on the fundamental order of the universe. James, who had written a learned book on witchcraft, suspected the hand of the devil in any plot against an anointed king, believed that witches had at various points in his own life conspired to harm him or render him impotent, and feared the existence of occult, invisible forces bent on bringing all things to ruin.

In several of his earlier plays, most notably in *Richard II*, Shakespeare's characters give voice to the theory that the King is God's deputy on earth and, consequently, that attacks upon him are evil, but kingship's claim to sacred authority is voiced exceptionally powerfully in *Macbeth* (not in Scotland alone, but also in neighboring England, where, as Malcolm tells Macduff, the touch of the pious King Edward cures disease). Exceptionally powerful, too, in this play is the metaphysical horror of regicide. The murder of Duncan is marked in the natural world with dreadful signs and portents and in the human world with an overpowering sense of devastation ironically given its most eloquent expression by the murderer Macbeth:

Henry IV of France (1553–1610) administers the royal touch, thought to cure scrofula. An etching by Pierre Firens, in André Du Laurens's *De mirabilii strumas sanandi vi solis Galliae regibus . . .* (Paris, 1609). See *Macbeth* 4.3.142–60.

Renown and grace is dead.
The wine of life is drawn, and the mere lees
Is left this vault to brag of.

(2.3.90–92)

Macbeth is speaking hypocritically—"look like the innocent flower," his wife had earlier counseled him, "but be the serpent under't" (1.5.63–64)—and yet, at least in one interpretation of the part, he is saying what he himself knows to be the grim truth. Far more than any other of Shakespeare's villains, more than the homicidal Richard III, the treacherous Claudius in *Hamlet*, and the cold-hearted Iago in *Othello,* Macbeth is fully aware of the wickedness of his deeds and is tormented by this awareness. Endowed with a clear-eyed grasp of the difference between good and evil, he chooses evil, even though the choice horrifies and sickens him.

Before he has taken the irrevocable step, Macbeth tries to recover his moral bearings. The deed he is contemplating, he begins by telling himself, would work only if he could control all consequences, so that his blow "might be the be-all and the end-all" (1.7.5). But he grasps that there is no possibility of such complete control and therefore no hope of practical success. His thoughts then turn to the overwhelming ethical arguments against the murder: he is not only the King's kinsman and subject but also his host, "who should against his murderer shut the door, / Not bear the knife myself" (1.7.15–16). And from these considerations, practical and ethical, Macbeth's restless, brooding mind rises higher, imagining that the murdered Duncan's virtues will plead like angels against the "deep damnation of his taking-off,"

And pity, like a naked new-born babe,
Striding the blast, or heaven's cherubin, horsed
Upon the sightless couriers of the air,
Shall blow the horrid deed in every eye
That tears shall drown the wind.

(1.7.21–25)

No one else in the play has a moral sensibility so intense or so visionary, no one else imagines so vividly the forces that lie beyond the ordinary and familiar horizon of human experience. Macbeth understands exactly what is at stake and what he must do: "We will," he tells his wife decisively, "proceed no further in this business" (1.7.31).

Why, then, does he change his mind and commit a crime he cannot even contemplate without horror? A significant part of the answer lies in the instigation of his formidable wife. When we first glimpse Lady Macbeth, she is reading a letter. (Reading was by no means a universal achievement for women of the early seventeenth century, let alone the eleventh, when the play's events are set, but Shakespeare frequently represents it in his plays in a variety of contexts.) The letter makes her burn with visions of the "golden round" that "fate and metaphysical aid" (1.5.26–27) seem to have conferred upon her husband. But even though she speaks of the crown as if it were already on Macbeth's head, she fears that he is too full of the "milk of human kindness" (1.5.15) to seize what has been promised him. She resolves then to "chastise" her husband, to urge him, in a phrase taken from archery that has a strong sexual undercurrent, to screw his courage to the sticking place. Lady Macbeth manipulates him in two principal ways. The first is through sexual taunting:

Art thou afeard
To be the same in thine own act and valour
As thou art in desire?
. . . .
When you durst do it, then you were a man

(1.7.39–41, 49)

And the second is through the terrible force of her determination:

> I have given suck, and know
> How tender 'tis to love the babe that milks me.
> I would, while it was smiling in my face,
> Have plucked my nipple from his boneless gums
> And dashed the brains out, had I so sworn
> As you have done to this.
>
> (1.7.54–59)

These words, and the gestures that viscerally intensify them onstage, cannot by themselves account for Macbeth's decision. He counters his wife's sexual taunting with a clear sense of the proper boundaries of his identity as a male and as a human being: "I dare do all that may become a man; / Who dares do more is none" (1.7.46–47). As for Lady Macbeth's fantasy of murdering her infant, its horror might have served rather to deter Macbeth from his unnatural crime than to spur him toward it. Virtually everyone is subject to terrible dreams and lawless fantasies—"Merciful powers," Banquo prays, "restrain in me the cursèd thoughts that nature / Gives way to in repose" (2.1.7–9)—but not everyone crosses the fatal line from criminal desire to criminal act.

That in crossing this line Macbeth murders a man toward whom he should be grateful, loyal, and protective, deepens the mystery of his crime, linking it to a long current of theological and philosophical brooding on the nature of evil. For St. Augustine, the great fourth-century church father, evil in its most radical form is gratuitous—that is, without an explicable rationale or motivation—and this notion of gratuitousness haunts subsequent thinkers, including those far from Christian orthodoxy. Thus the Florentine Niccolò Machiavelli, notorious in the sixteenth century for freethinking, writes in Chapter 37 of his *Discourses* that "when men are no longer obliged to fight from necessity, they fight from ambition, which passion is so powerful in the hearts of men that it never leaves them, no matter to what height they may rise." The reason for this, Machiavelli proposes, is that "nature has created men so that they desire everything, but are unable to attain it; desire being thus always greater than the faculty of acquiring, discontent with what they have and dissatisfaction with themselves result from it."

Macbeth and Lady Macbeth act on ambition, restless desire, and a will to power normally kept in check by the pragmatic, ethical, and religious considerations to which the wavering Macbeth initially gives voice. Lady Macbeth in effect works to liberate that will to power in her husband, freeing him from his "sickly" fears of damnation so that he can act with a ruthless blend of murderous violence and cunning. In her radically disenchanted, coolly skeptical view, the murder of the King can be undertaken without fear of guilty conscience, vengeful ghosts, or divine judgment: "The sleeping and the dead," she tells her shaken husband, "are but as pictures. 'Tis the eye of childhood / That fears a painted devil" (2.2.51–53).

This reassurance, Shakespeare's tragedy shows, is hopelessly shallow. As the spectral dagger, the ghost sitting in Macbeth's chair, and the indelible bloodstains on Lady Macbeth's hands all chillingly demonstrate, the secure distinction between representation and reality, the dead and the living, repeatedly breaks down, not simply for the characters but for the spectators as well. In most productions, the dagger and the blood are visible only to the diseased minds of the murderers, but Banquo's ghost is almost always palpably present onstage, visible to the audience as well as to the unhinged Macbeth, though invisible to everyone around him. Moreover, the dream of a "clean" regicide proves psychologically untenable: the seizure of the crown leads to feverish sleeplessness, brooding anxiety about security, and an overwhelming sense of defilement. Macbeth and Lady Macbeth are equally devastated, but the psychological trajectory in the wake of the crime is not the same for the two conspirators. Initially frozen in moral numbness, Lady Macbeth experiences a gradual decomposition, a growing horror that breaks forth unforgettably in the sleepwalking scene with her compulsive attempts to free herself of the smell and stain of blood: "All the perfumes of Arabia will not sweeten this little hand" (5.1.42–43). Initially gripped by a heightened sensitivity to fear, a dread that threatens inward decomposition, Macbeth experiences a gradual hardening and deadening of the self until he reaches a state of absolute numbness:

> Tomorrow, and tomorrow, and tomorrow
> Creeps in this petty pace from day to day
> To the last syllable of recorded time.
> (5.5.18–20)

The assassination also proves, as Macbeth had foreseen, politically untenable. There is always someone who escapes the murderer's net, someone who poses a threat or seeks to redress an injury or simply remembers what it felt like to be free and unafraid. It is impossible to tie up all the loose ends, to break the chain of action and reaction, to reach a stable resting place. There are no clean murders. One crime leads to another and then to another without bringing the criminal any closer to the security or contentment that each desperate act is meant to achieve. Macbeth cannot stop the bloody acts; instead he must multiply and extend them. Where Lady Macbeth had only fantasized the murder of children, Macbeth actually undertakes that and other crimes until he dreams, in his half-crazed words to the "secret, black, and midnight hags" (4.1.64), of universal destruction.

It is Macbeth's first encounter with these hags—the weird (or, in the original spelling, "weyward" or "weyard") sisters—that seems to initiate his descent toward murder and tyranny. But what kind of power do these malevolent bearded women have over Macbeth? Are they responsible, by magical influence or by planting the idea in his mind, for his decision to kill Duncan? Are they somehow privy to a predestined fate, as if they have seen the script of the tragedy before it is performed? Or, alternatively, are they uncanny emblems of Macbeth's psychological condition, a kind of screen onto which he projects his "horrible imaginings" (1.3.137)? The word "weird," in one of its etymologies, derives from the Old English word for "fate," but do the women Shakespeare depicts, trafficking in ambiguous prophecies, fretting over village squabbles, mumbling charms, actually control destiny (or, what amounts to the same thing, the

Macbeth and Banquo encounter the weird sisters (1.3). From Raphael Holinshed, *The Firste Volume of the Chronicles of England, Scotlande, and Irelande* (1577).

tragedy's plot)? What is the nature of these strange creatures that "look not like th'inhabitants o'th' earth," as Banquo observes, "and yet are on't" (1.3.39–40)?

Actors' responses to these questions have ranged wildly, though virtually all productions have recognized that the witches' scenes are among the most theatrically powerful and compelling in the play and that it matters a great deal whether they are made up to look grotesque or stately, perversely comical or terrifying. Scholarly responses have been complicated by the high probability that not all of the witchcraft scenes are by Shakespeare himself: it appears that 3.5 and part of 4.1, the scenes featuring the goddess Hecate, were added to the play some time after its first performance and incorporate songs derived from Thomas Middleton's play *The Witch*. (The Folio text of *Macbeth* cites only the first words of these songs, which are given in full in this edition.) But even if we set aside the problems raised by these interpolated scenes, the status of the witches in Shakespeare's play remains uncertain and seems to be so by design. "What are you?" asks Macbeth when he first encounters the eerie, sexually ambiguous figures, and he receives in reply his own name: "All hail, Macbeth" (1.3.45–46). Banquo urgently renews the inquiry, asking the creatures before his eyes if they truly exist or are only figments of his imagination; but his question, too, remains unanswered. When Macbeth and Banquo demand to know more, the witches vanish: "what seemed corporal / Melted as breath into the wind" (1.3.79–80). "As breath into the wind"—*Macbeth* is a tragedy of meltings, vanishing boundaries, and liminal states.

Much of the play transpires on the border between fantasy and reality, a sickening betwixt and between where a "horrid image" in the mind has the uncanny power to produce bodily effects "against the use of nature" (1.3.134, 136), where one mind is present to the innermost fantasies of another, where manhood threatens to vanish and murdered men walk and blood cannot be washed off. If these effects could be unequivocally attributed to the agency of the witches, the audience would at least have the security of a defined and focused fear. Alternatively, if the witches could be definitively dismissed as fantasy or fraud, the audience would at least have the clear-eyed certainty of witnessing human causes in an altogether secular world. But instead, Shakespeare achieves the remarkable effect of a nebulous infection, a bleeding of the demonic into the secular and the secular into the demonic.

The most famous instance of this effect is Lady Macbeth's great invocation of the "spirits / That tend on mortal thoughts" (1.5.38–39) to unsex her, fill her with cruelty, make thick her blood, and exchange her milk for gall. The speech appears to be a conjuration of demonic powers, an act of witchcraft in which the "murd'ring ministers" (1.5.46) are directed to bring about a set of changes in her body. She calls these ministers "sightless substances" (1.5.47): though invisible, they are—as she conceives them—not figures of speech or projections of her mind, but objective, substantial beings or forces. (Macbeth similarly seems to imagine invisible but objective forces when he speaks of "the sightless couriers of the air," 1.7.23.) But the fact that the spirits she invokes are "sightless" already moves this passage away from the literal existence of the weird sisters and toward the metaphorical use of "spirits" in her speech of a few moments earlier: "Hie thee hither, / That I may pour my spirits in thine ear" (1.5.23–24). The spirits she speaks of here are manifestly figurative—they refer to the bold words, the undaunted mettle, and the sexual taunts with which she intends to incite Macbeth to murder Duncan—but, like all of her expressions of will and passion, they strain toward bodily realization, even as they convey a psychic and hence invisible inwardness. That is, there is something uncannily literal about Lady Macbeth's influence on her husband, as if marital intimacy were akin to demonic possession, as if she had contrived to inhabit his mind, as if, in other words, she had literally poured her spirits in his ear. Conversely, there is something uncannily figurative about the "sightless substances" she invokes, as if the spirit world, the realm of "fate and metaphysical aid," were only a metaphor for her blind and murderous desires, as if the weird sisters were condensations of her own breath.

Witchcraft in Scotland. From *Newes from Scotland* (1591).

In Shakespeare's plays, as in those of his contemporaries, evildoers may wreak havoc for a time, but in the final restoration of order and justice, they and their principal accomplices are almost inevitably punished. Thus, at the close of *Macbeth*, not only are Macbeth and Lady Macbeth dead, but the victorious Malcolm also speaks of settling scores with "the cruel ministers / Of this dead butcher and his fiend-like queen" (5.11.34–35). Yet though the play has deeply implicated the witches in Macbeth's monstrous assault on the fabric of civilized life, there is no gesture toward punishing them, no sign that the victors are even aware of their existence. This omission is the more striking if we recall that at the time Shakespeare wrote his play, the authorities in England and Scotland were bringing women to trial on charges of witchcraft and executing them. The theatrical power of *Macbeth* seems bound up with its refusal to resolve the questions raised by the witches. At once marginal and central to the play, they are only briefly and intermittently onstage, but they are still suggestively present when we cannot see them, when the threats they embody are absorbed in the ordinary relations of everyday life.

"There's no art / To find the mind's construction in the face" (1.4.11–12), says the baffled Duncan about a man who had betrayed his trust, but Macbeth confronts a deeper perplexity, an appalling mystery within himself:

> My thought, whose murder yet is but fantastical,
> Shakes so my single state of man that function
> Is smothered in surmise, and nothing is
> But what is not.
>
> (1.3.138–41)

The witches have something to do with this inner torment, but what that something is remains as elusive as the dagger that Macbeth sees before him, handle toward his hand. Scotland is sick, "almost afraid to know itself" (4.3.166). But the sickness cannot be isolated in a conspiracy of witches. If violence stirs in the hinterlands, where marauding armies struggle, it breeds more murderously still in the inmost circles of the realm, where the ruler feels most secure: "This castle hath a pleasant seat," says Duncan, going unwittingly to his death:

> The air
> Nimbly and sweetly recommends itself
> Unto our gentle senses.
>
> (1.6.1–3)

If the mind is subject to "supernatural soliciting" (1.3.129) from some bizarre place, it is gripped still more terribly and irresistibly by "horrible imaginings" (1.3.137) from within. If there is sexual disturbance out on the heath, where the bearded hags stir the ingredients of their hideous caldron, there is deeper sexual disturbance at home, in the murderous intimacy of the marriage bond: "When you durst do it, then you were a man" (1.7.49). If you are worried about losing your manhood, it is not enough to hunt for witches; look to your wife. If you are anxious about your future, scrutinize your best friends: "He was a gentleman on whom I built / An absolute trust" (1.4.13–14). If you are worried about interior temptation, fear your own dreams:

> Merciful powers,
> Restrain in me the cursèd thoughts that nature
> Gives way to in repose.
>
> (2.1.7–9)

And if you fear spiritual desolation, turn your eyes on the contents not only of the hideous caldron but of your skull: "O, full of scorpions is my mind, dear wife!" (3.2.37).

The men who persecuted witches in Shakespeare's age were determined to compel full confessions, to pass judgment, and to escape from the terror of the inexplicable, the unforeseen, the aimlessly malignant. In *Macbeth,* the audience is given something better than confession, for it has visible proof of the demonic in action, but this visibility turns out to be as maddeningly equivocal or frustrating as the witches' riddling words. The "wayward" witches appear and disappear, their promises and prophecies all tricks, like practical jokes with appalling consequences. The language of the play subverts the illusory certainties of sight, and the forces of renewed order, Malcolm and Macduff, are themselves strangely unstable. Malcolm, who spins an elaborate fantasy of his own viciousness, and Macduff, who abandons his wife and children to their slaughter, are peculiar emblems of a renewed, divinely sanctioned order. Shakespeare may have set out to flatter the King, but it is difficult to see how the King, if he paid any attention to the tragedy that the King's Men offered him, could be reassured. The ambiguities of demonic agency are never resolved, and its horror spreads like a mist through a murky landscape. "What is't you do?" Macbeth asks the weird sisters. "A deed without a name" (4.1.65).

By the play's close, Macbeth has begun "to doubt th'equivocation of the fiend, / That lies like truth" (5.5.41–42). Equivocations are lies with mental reservations, words with double meanings, puns, twists of emphasis, and plays on false interpretations (such as the meaning of the phrase "not of woman born"). Like the witches—and, for that matter, like concepts of gender and authority and social order—language in *Macbeth* is a boundary stalker, neither a trustworthy guide nor a manifest illusion. Words sit dangerously in a middle ground; they must be brought under control, but they always threaten to slide into lies or magic charms or riddles or sheer emptiness. It is this emptiness with which Macbeth seems haunted at the end, with his vision of life as

> a tale
> Told by an idiot, full of sound and fury,
> Signifying nothing.
>
> (5.5.25–27)

If the closing moments of the play invite us to recoil from this black hole—after all, the tyrant is killed—they invite us to recoil from too confident and simple a celebration of the triumph of grace. For somewhere beyond the immediate circle of order restored, the witches are dancing around the caldron, and, the play seems to imply, the caldron is in every one of us.

STEPHEN GREENBLATT

TEXTUAL NOTE

The only authoritative text of *Macbeth* is the First Folio (1623), which consequently serves as the control text in this edition. Scholars generally agree that the Folio version (F) was based on a promptbook, a transcript derived, in all likelihood, from Shakespeare's rough draft of the play. F appears to be a fairly reliable record of its manuscript source, the promptbook.

There are, however, signs that this source was itself an abbreviated version of the play as first written and performed, for the text in F is considerably shorter than that of any of the other major tragedies. Moreover, the Folio's *Macbeth* appears to be a version of the play revised, sometime after Shakespeare had ceased to be active with the King's Men, for a court performance in the presence of King James. Scholars have long suspected that it contains material not by Shakespeare. In particular, the two songs referred to in 3.5 and 4.1 of F only by their opening phrases ("Come away, come away, &c.," "Blacke Spirits, &c.") are very likely by the playwright Thomas Middleton. Songs with the same opening phrases appear in a manuscript of Middleton's unsuccessful play *The Witch* (c. 1613) and are restored in full in this edition of *Macbeth*.

Middleton may have been personally responsible for the revision of *Macbeth* reflected in the Folio text. He could, in addition to the songs, have added all of 3.5 (which seems to diverge stylistically from the rest of the play) as well as parts of 4.1, particularly Hecate's speeches.

SELECTED BIBLIOGRAPHY

Adelman, Janet. "'Born of Woman': Fantasies of Maternal Power in *Macbeth*." *Cannibals, Witches, and Divorce: Estranging the Renaissance*. Ed. Marjorie Garber. Baltimore: Johns Hopkins University Press, 1987. 90–121. *Macbeth* represents dueling fantasies of absolute, destructive female power and of escape from that power; masculine authority is consolidated in the end by eliminating the feminine.

Bradley, A. C. *Shakespearean Tragedy: Lectures on "Hamlet," "Othello," "King Lear," "Macbeth."* London: Macmillan, 1905. The most concentrated, classical, and fast-paced of Shakespeare's great tragedies, *Macbeth* produces unequaled dread with its dark atmosphere and sublime central characters.

Calderwood, James L. *If It Were Done: "Macbeth" and Tragic Action.* Amherst: University of Massachusetts Press, 1986. *Macbeth* subverts the models of *Hamlet* and Aristotelian poetics, interrogating the nature of tragedy and the role of violence as both a threat to and a source of social order.

Greenblatt, Stephen. "Shakespeare Bewitched." *New Historical Literary Study: Essays on Reproducing Texts, Representing History.* Ed. Jeffrey N. Cox and Larry J. Reynolds. Princeton: Princeton University Press, 1993. 108–35. In writing *Macbeth*, Shakespeare drew both upon the King's belief in witchcraft and upon a skeptical critique of such belief by Reginald Scot.

Howard, Jean E. "Shakespeare, Geography, and the Work of Genre on the Early Modern Stage." *Modern Language Quarterly* 64.3 (2003): 299–322. Scotland's mingled contemporary reputation for nobility and savagery allowed Shakespeare to desacralize kingship.

Kastan, David Scott. "Macbeth and the 'Name of the King.'" *Shakespeare After Theory*. New York: Routledge, 1999. 165–82. Insistent doubling, blending the figures of the king and tyrant, undermines the attempt in *Macbeth* to contain violence by restoring moral order.

Mullaney, Steven. "Lying Like Truth: Riddle, Representation, and Treason." *The Place of the Stage: License, Play, and Power in Renaissance England*. Chicago: University of Chicago Press, 1988. 116–34. Like the Jacobean spectacle of a traitor on the scaffold, *Macbeth* reveals the generative power of equivocation, challenging the absolutes of royal authority.

Norbrook, David. "Macbeth and the Politics of Historiography." *Politics of Discourse: The Literature and History of Seventeenth-Century England*. Ed. Kevin Sharpe and Steven N. Zwicker. Berkeley: University of California Press, 1987. 78–116. Embroiled in seventeenth-century debates over writing Scottish history, Shakespeare raised the specter of justified regicide even as he drew on King James's monarchist views.

Orgel, Stephen. "*Macbeth* and the Antic Round." *The Authentic Shakespeare, and Other Problems of the Early Modern Stage*. New York: Routledge, 2002. 159–72. Revisions to the witches' scenes link theatrical spectacle to psychological inwardness and heighten the paradoxical role of women.

Wells, Robin Headlam. "'Arms and the Man': *Macbeth*." *Shakespeare on Masculinity*. New York: Cambridge University Press, 2000. 117–43. *Macbeth* blurs Gospel and classical epic conceptions of manhood, questioning the terms of King James's rule.

FILMS

Macbeth. 1948. Dir. Orson Welles. USA. 107 min. Expressionist, low-budget production, starring Welles and Jeanette Nolan.

Throne of Blood. 1957. Dir. Akira Kurosawa. Japan. 105 min. Kabuki-influenced production set in feudal Japan stars Toshirô Mifune and Isuzu Yamada.

Macbeth. 1971. Dir. Roman Polanski. UK/USA. 140 min. Bleak, misty, bloody vision, with strikingly young leads Jon Finch and Francesca Annis.

Macbeth. 1979. Dir. Philip Casson. UK. 146 min. Minimalist production for television with doubling actors and simple sets. Ian McKellen and Judi Dench star.

Scotland, PA. 2001. Dir. Billy Morrissette. USA. 104 min. Comic recasting in a 1970s American fast-food joint.

The Tragedy of Macbeth

THE PERSONS OF THE PLAY

KING DUNCAN of Scotland
MALCOLM ⎱ his sons
DONALBAIN ⎰
A CAPTAIN in Duncan's army
MACBETH, Thane of Glamis, later Thane of Cawdor, then King of Scotland
A PORTER at Macbeth's castle
Three MURDERERS attending on Macbeth
SEYTON, servant of Macbeth
LADY MACBETH, Macbeth's wife
A DOCTOR of Physic ⎱ attending on Lady Macbeth
A Waiting-GENTLEWOMAN ⎰
BANQUO, a Scottish thane
FLEANCE, his son
MACDUFF, Thane of Fife
LADY MACDUFF, his wife
MACDUFF'S SON
LENNOX
ROSS
ANGUS ⎱ Scottish Thanes
CAITHNESS ⎰
MENTEITH
SIWARD, Earl of Northumberland
YOUNG SIWARD, his son
An English DOCTOR
HECATE, Queen of the Witches
Six WITCHES
Three APPARITIONS, one an armed head, one a bloody child, one a child crowned
A SPIRIT LIKE A CAT
Other SPIRITS
An OLD MAN
A MESSENGER
MURDERERS
SERVANTS
A show of eight kings; Lords and Thanes, attendants, soldiers, drummers

1.1

Thunder and lightning. Enter three WITCHES

FIRST WITCH   When shall we three meet again?
  In thunder, lightning, or in rain?[1]
SECOND WITCH   When the hurly-burly's° done,   *tumult is*
  When the battle's lost and won.
5   THIRD WITCH   That will be ere the set of sun.

1.1 Location: An open place.   1. Witches were thought to be able to cause bad weather.

FIRST WITCH   Where the place?
SECOND WITCH   Upon the heath.
THIRD WITCH   There to meet with Macbeth.
FIRST WITCH   I come, Grimalkin.
SECOND WITCH   Paddock² calls.
THIRD WITCH   Anon.°   *At once*
10   ALL   Fair is foul, and foul is fair,
      Hover through the fog and filthy air.   *Exeunt*

1.2

Alarum within. Enter KING [DUNCAN], MALCOLM, DON-
ALBAIN, LENNOX, *with attendants, meeting a bleeding*
      CAPTAIN°   *staff officer*
KING DUNCAN   What bloody man is that? He can report,
      As seemeth by his plight, of the revolt
      The newest state.
MALCOLM   This is the sergeant
      Who like a good and hardy soldier fought
5   'Gainst my captivity. Hail, brave friend.
      Say to the King the knowledge of the broil°   *battle*
      As thou didst leave it.
CAPTAIN   Doubtful it stood,
      As two spent° swimmers that do cling together   *exhausted*
      And choke their art.¹ The merciless Macdonald—
10   Worthy to be a rebel, for to that°   *that end*
      The multiplying villainies of nature²
      Do swarm upon him—from the Western Isles°   *Hebrides and Ireland*
      Of kerns and galloglasses³ is supplied,
      And fortune on his damnèd quarry⁴ smiling
15   Showed° like a rebel's whore. But all's too weak,   *Appeared*
      For brave Macbeth—well he deserves that name!°—   *epithet*
      Disdaining fortune, with his brandished steel
      Which smoked with bloody execution,
      Like valour's minion°   *favorite*
20   Carved out his passage till he faced the slave,°   *(Macdonald)*
      Which° ne'er shook hands nor bade farewell to him   *Who*
      Till he unseamed him from the nave to th' chops·⁵
      And fixed his head upon our battlements.
KING DUNCAN   O valiant cousin,° worthy gentleman!   *kinsman*
25   CAPTAIN   As whence the sun 'gins his reflection⁶
      Shipwrecking storms and direful thunders break,
      So from that spring° whence comfort seemed to come   *source; (season)*
      Discomfort swells.° Mark, King of Scotland, mark.   *wells up*
      No sooner justice had, with valour armed,
30   Compelled these skipping° kerns to trust their heels   *mobile; fleeing*
      But the Norwegian lord, surveying vantage,°   *seeing his chance*
      With furbished° arms and new supplies of men   *polished*
      Began a fresh assault.
KING DUNCAN   Dismayed not this our captains, Macbeth and Banquo?

2. Paddock, a toad, and Grimalkin, a gray cat, are the
witches' familiars, or attendant evil spirits.
1.2 Location: A camp near the battlefield.
1. And confound their skill in swimming.
2. The evil aspects of his own nature; the villainous
progeny of nature (the mercenaries).
3. *kerns*: lightly armed Irish foot soldiers. *galloglasses*:
ax-wielding horsemen.

4. Its condemned victim. Fortune smiled temporarily
on Macdonald, although it had already marked him for
destruction. Many editions emend "quarry" to "quarrel."
5. Ripped him open from the navel to the jaw, as one
would rip open the seam of a garment.
6. Begins its return after the spring equinox, thought to
cause turbulent weather.

35   CAPTAIN   Yes, as sparrows eagles, or the hare the lion!
        If I say sooth I must report they were
        As cannons overcharged with double cracks,[7]
        So they doubly redoubled strokes upon the foe.
        Except° they meant to bathe in reeking wounds   *Unless*
40   Or memorize another Golgotha,[8]
        I cannot tell—
        But I am faint. My gashes cry for help.
  KING DUNCAN   So well thy words become thee as thy wounds:
        They smack of honour both.—Go get him surgeons.
                  [*Exit* CAPTAIN *with attendants*]
          Enter ROSS *and* ANGUS
        Who comes here?
45   MALCOLM   The worthy Thane[9] of Ross.
  LENNOX   What haste looks through his eyes! So should he look
        That seems to° speak things strange.   *seems about to*
  ROSS   God save the King.
  KING DUNCAN   Whence cam'st thou, worthy thane?
  ROSS   From Fife, great King,
        Where the Norwegian banners flout° the sky   *mock*
50   And fan our people cold.°   *cold with fear*
        Norway° himself, with terrible numbers,   *The King of Norway*
        Assisted by that most disloyal traitor
        The Thane of Cawdor, began a dismal° conflict,   *an ominous*
        Till that° Bellona's bridegroom,[1] lapped in proof,[2]   *Until*
55   Confronted him with self-comparisons,°   *comparable deeds*
        Point° against point, rebellious arm 'gainst arm,   *Swordpoint*
        Curbing his lavish° spirit; and to conclude,   *wild*
        The victory fell on us—
  KING DUNCAN   Great happiness.
  ROSS   That now
        Sweno, the Norways'° king, craves composition;°   *Norwegians' / a truce*
60   Nor would we deign him burial of his men
        Till he disbursèd at Saint Colum's inch[3]
        Ten thousand dollars[4] to our general use.
  KING DUNCAN   No more that Thane of Cawdor shall deceive
        Our bosom interest.[5] Go pronounce his present° death, *immediate*
65   And with his former title greet Macbeth.
  ROSS   I'll see it done.
  KING DUNCAN   What he hath lost, noble Macbeth hath won.
                      Exeunt severally°   *separately*

1.3

Thunder. Enter the three WITCHES

  FIRST WITCH   Where hast thou been, sister?
  SECOND WITCH   Killing swine.
  THIRD WITCH   Sister, where thou?
  FIRST WITCH   A sailor's wife had chestnuts in her lap,
        And munched, and munched, and munched. 'Give me,' quoth I.

---

7. Overloaded with double charges of gunpowder.
8. Or make the battlefield as memorable as Golgotha, the "place of skulls" where Jesus was crucified.
9. Title of Scottish nobility.
1. Macbeth, imagined as husband to Bellona, the Roman goddess of war.
2. Clad in tested armor.

3. Incholm, the island of St. Columba in the Firth of Forth.
4. German and Spanish coins (first minted in the sixteenth century, five hundred years after the events of the play).
5. Our closest concerns.
1.3 Location: An open place.

5   'Aroint thee,° witch,' the rump-fed runnion¹ cries.   *Begone*
       Her husband's to Aleppo gone, master o'th' *Tiger*.
       But in a sieve I'll thither sail,
       And like a rat without a tail
       I'll do, I'll do, and I'll do.
10   SECOND WITCH   I'll give thee a wind.
       FIRST WITCH   Thou'rt kind.
       THIRD WITCH   And I another.
       FIRST WITCH   I myself have all the other,°   *others*
       And the very ports they blow,°   *blow from*
15   All the quarters° that they know   *directions*
       I'th' shipman's card.°   *compass card*
       I'll drain him dry as hay.
       Sleep shall neither night nor day
       Hang upon his penthouse lid.²
20   He shall live a man forbid.°   *cursed*
       Weary sennights° nine times nine   *weeks*
       Shall he dwindle, peak,° and pine.   *waste away*
       Though his barque cannot be lost,
       Yet it shall be tempest-tossed.
       Look what I have.
25   SECOND WITCH   Show me, show me.
       FIRST WITCH   Here I have a pilot's thumb,
       Wrecked as homeward he did come.
                    Drum within
       THIRD WITCH   A drum, a drum—
       Macbeth doth come.
30   ALL [*dancing in a ring*]   The weird³ sisters hand in hand,
       Posters° of the sea and land,   *Swift travelers*
       Thus do go about, about,
       Thrice to thine, and thrice to mine,
       And thrice again to make up nine.
35   Peace! The charm's wound up.
                    Enter MACBETH *and* BANQUO
       MACBETH   So foul and fair a day I have not seen.
       BANQUO   How far is't called° to Forres?—What are these,   *said to be*
       So withered, and so wild in their attire,
       That look not like th'inhabitants o'th' earth
40   And yet are on't?—Live you, or are you aught
       That man may question?° You seem to understand me   *converse with*
       By each at once her choppy° finger laying   *chapped*
       Upon her skinny lips. You should be women,
       And yet your beards forbid me to interpret
       That you are so.
45   MACBETH [*to the* WITCHES]   Speak, if you can. What are you?
       FIRST WITCH   All hail, Macbeth! Hail to thee, Thane of Glamis.
       SECOND WITCH   All hail, Macbeth! Hail to thee, Thane of Cawdor.
       THIRD WITCH   All hail, Macbeth, that shalt be king hereafter!
       BANQUO   Good sir, why do you start and seem to fear
50   Things that do sound so fair? [*To the* WITCHES] I'th' name of truth,
       Are ye fantastical° or that indeed   *imaginary*

---

1. The fat-rumped, mangy slut.   3. F: "weyward," from the Old English "wyrd," meaning
2. Eyelid, which projects out over the eye like the slop-   "fate."
ing roof of a penthouse.

Which outwardly ye show? My noble partner
You greet with present grace° and great prediction   *title*
Of noble having° and of royal hope,   *estate*
55   That he seems rapt withal.⁴ To me you speak not.
If you can look into the seeds of time
And say which grain will grow and which will not,
Speak then to me, who neither beg nor fear
Your favours nor your hate.
60   FIRST WITCH   Hail!
SECOND WITCH   Hail!
THIRD WITCH   Hail!
FIRST WITCH   Lesser than Macbeth, and greater.
SECOND WITCH   Not so happy,° yet much happier.   *fortunate*
65   THIRD WITCH   Thou shalt get° kings, though thou be none.   *beget*
So all hail, Macbeth and Banquo!
FIRST WITCH   Banquo and Macbeth, all hail!
MACBETH   Stay, you imperfect° speakers, tell me more.   *incomplete*
By Sinel's° death I know I am Thane of Glamis,   *Macbeth's father*
70   But how of Cawdor? The Thane of Cawdor lives,
A prosperous gentleman, and to be king
Stands not within the prospect of belief,
No more than to be Cawdor. Say from whence
You owe° this strange intelligence,° or why   *possess / information*
75   Upon this blasted° heath you stop our way   *blighted*
With such prophetic greeting. Speak, I charge you.
              [*The*] WITCHES *vanish*
BANQUO   The earth hath bubbles, as the water has,
And these are of them. Whither are they vanished?
MACBETH   Into the air, and what seemed corporal°   *corporeal*
80   Melted as breath into the wind. Would they had stayed.
BANQUO   Were such things here as we do speak about,
Or have we eaten on the insane root⁵
That takes the reason prisoner?
MACBETH   Your children shall be kings.
BANQUO   You shall be king.
85   MACBETH   And Thane of Cawdor too. Went it not so?
BANQUO   To th' self-same tune and words. Who's here?
              Enter ROSS *and* ANGUS
ROSS   The King hath happily received, Macbeth,
The news of thy success, and when he reads°   *considers*
Thy personal venture° in the rebels' sight   *exploits*
90   His wonders and his praises do contend
Which should be thine or his; silenced with that,⁶
In viewing o'er the rest o'th' self-same day
He finds thee in the stout Norwegian ranks,
Nothing° afeard of what thyself didst make,   *Not at all*
95   Strange images° of death. As thick as hail   *forms*
Came post° with post, and every one did bear   *messenger*
Thy praises in his kingdom's great defence,
And poured them down before him.
ANGUS [*to* MACBETH]   We are sent

---

4. He seems entranced by these predictions.
5. Of the root causing insanity, possibly hemlock.
6. *His wonders . . . that:* Duncan does not know whether

to speak of his astonishment or his admiration, and so
is silent.

To give thee from our royal master thanks;
100   Only to herald thee into his sight,
    Not pay thee.
    ROSS   And, for an earnest° of a greater honour,   *a pledge*
    He bade me from him call thee Thane of Cawdor,
    In which addition,° hail, most worthy thane,   *title*
    For it is thine.
105   BANQUO   What, can the devil speak true?
    MACBETH   The Thane of Cawdor lives. Why do you dress me
    In borrowed robes?
    ANGUS   Who was the thane lives yet,
    But under heavy judgement bears that life
    Which he deserves to lose. Whether he was combined°   *allied*
110 With those of Norway, or did line the rebel°   *support Macdonald*
    With hidden help and vantage,° or that with both   *benefit*
    He laboured in his country's wrack,⁷ I know not;
    But treasons capital, confessed, and proved
    Have overthrown him.
    MACBETH [*aside*]   Glamis, and Thane of Cawdor.
115 The greatest is behind.° [*To* ROSS *and* ANGUS] Thanks for your pains.   *to come*
    [*To* BANQUO] Do you not hope your children shall be kings
    When those that gave the thane of Cawdor to me
    Promised no less to them?
    BANQUO   That, trusted home,°   *completely*
    Might yet enkindle° you unto the crown,   *encourage*
120 Besides the thane of Cawdor. But 'tis strange,
    And oftentimes to win us to our harm
    The instruments of darkness tell us truths,
    Win us with honest trifles to betray's°   *betray us*
    In deepest consequence.
125 [*To* ROSS *and* ANGUS] Cousins, a word, I pray you.
    MACBETH [*aside*]   Two truths are told
    As happy prologues to the swelling act⁸
    Of the imperial theme [*To* ROSS *and* ANGUS] I thank you, gentlemen.
    [*Aside*] This supernatural soliciting°   *temptation*
130 Cannot be ill, cannot be good. If ill,
    Why hath it given me earnest of success
    Commencing in a truth? I am Thane of Cawdor.
    If good, why do I yield to that suggestion
    Whose horrid image doth unfix my hair
135 And make my seated heart knock at my ribs
    Against the use° of nature? Present fears   *custom*
    Are less than horrible imaginings.
    My thought, whose murder yet is but fantastical,⁹
    Shakes so my single state of man¹ that function°   *capacity to act*
140 Is smothered in surmise,° and nothing is   *speculation*
    But what is not.
    BANQUO [*to* ROSS *and* ANGUS]
        Look how our partner's rapt.
    MACBETH [*aside*]   If chance will have me king, why, chance may crown me
    Without my stir.°   *effort*

---

7. He worked to bring about his country's ruin.
8. To the developing action, or climactic dramatic action.
9. In which murder is so far only a fantasy.

1. My undivided self. Macbeth feels that his wholeness is coming apart under the pressure of his criminal thought.

BANQUO [*to* ROSS *and* ANGUS]
        New honours come upon him,
  Like our strange° garments, cleave not to their mould°   *new / wearer's form*
  But with the aid of use.
145 MACBETH [*aside*]   Come what come may,
  Time and the hour runs through the roughest day.[2]
  BANQUO Worthy Macbeth, we stay° upon your leisure.   *wait; attend*
  MACBETH Give me your favour.° My dull brain was wrought°   *pardon / agitated*
  With things forgotten. [*To* ROSS *and* ANGUS] Kind gentlemen,
      your pains
150 Are registered° where every day I turn   *recorded (in my memory)*
  The leaf to read them. Let us toward the King.
  [*Aside to* BANQUO] Think upon what hath chanced, and at
      more time,
  The interim having weighed it, let us speak
  Our free hearts° each to other.   *unconcealed thoughts*
155 BANQUO Very gladly.
  MACBETH Till then, enough. [*To* ROSS *and* ANGUS] Come, friends.
                                      Exeunt

1.4

Flourish. Enter KING [DUNCAN], LENNOX, MALCOLM,
DONALBAIN, *and attendants*
KING DUNCAN Is execution done on Cawdor? Are not
  Those in commission[1] yet returned?
MALCOLM   My liege,
  They are not yet come back. But I have spoke
  With one that saw him die, who did report
5 That very frankly he confessed his treasons,
  Implored your highness' pardon, and set forth
  A deep repentance. Nothing in his life
  Became him like the leaving it. He died
  As one that had been studied° in his death   *practiced*
10 To throw away the dearest thing he owed°   *owned*
  As 'twere a careless° trifle.   *an uncared-for*
  KING DUNCAN   There's no art
  To find the mind's construction in the face.
  He was a gentleman on whom I built
  An absolute trust.
      Enter MACBETH, BANQUO, ROSS, *and* ANGUS
  [*To* MACBETH] O worthiest cousin,
15 The sin of my ingratitude even now
  Was heavy on me! Thou art so far before°   *ahead*
  That swiftest wing of recompense is slow
  To overtake thee. Would thou hadst less deserved,
  That the proportion both of thanks and payment
20 Might have been mine.[2] Only I have left to say,
  'More is thy due than more than all can pay'.
  MACBETH The service and the loyalty I owe,
  In doing it, pays itself. Your highness' part
  Is to receive our duties, and our duties

---

2. *Come . . . day:* What must happen will happen one
way or another.
1.4 Location: A camp near the battlefield.

1. Those charged to execute Cawdor.
2. *That . . . mine:* That the King's rewards would be gen-
erously proportional to Macbeth's dessert.

25 Are to your throne and state children and servants
    Which do but what they should by doing everything
    Safe toward° your love and honour.   *To safeguard*
KING DUNCAN   Welcome hither.
    I have begun to plant thee, and will labour
    To make thee full of growing.—Noble Banquo,
30 That hast no less deserved, nor must be known
    No less to have done so, let me enfold thee
    And hold thee to my heart.
BANQUO   There if I grow
    The harvest is your own.
KING DUNCAN   My plenteous joys,
    Wanton° in fullness, seek to hide themselves   *Unrestrained*
35 In drops of sorrow. Sons, kinsmen, thanes,
    And you whose places are the nearest,° know   *nearest to the throne*
    We will establish our estate³ upon
    Our eldest, Malcolm, whom we name hereafter
    The Prince of Cumberland;⁴ which honour must
40 Not unaccompanied invest him only,⁵
    But signs of nobleness, like stars, shall shine
    On all deservers. [*To* MACBETH] From hence to Inverness,°   *Macbeth's estate*
    And bind us further to you.⁶
MACBETH   The rest is labour which is not used for you.⁷
45 I'll be myself the harbinger,⁸ and make joyful
    The hearing of my wife with your approach;
    So humbly take my leave.
KING DUNCAN   My worthy Cawdor.
MACBETH [*aside*]   The Prince of Cumberland—that is a step
    On which I must fall down or else o'erleap,
50 For in my way it lies. Stars, hide your fires,
    Let not light see my black and deep desires;
    The eye wink at the hand;⁹ yet let that be°   *be done*
    Which the eye fears, when it is done, to see.   *Exit*
KING DUNCAN   True, worthy Banquo, he is full so valiant,¹
55 And in his commendations I am fed.
    It is a banquet to me. Let's after him,
    Whose care is gone before to bid us welcome.
    It is a peerless kinsman.   *Flourish. Exeunt*

1.5

Enter [LADY MACBETH,] *with a letter*

LADY MACBETH [*reading*]   'They met me in the day of success,
    and I have learned by the perfect'st° report they have more in   *most accurate*
    them than mortal knowledge. When I burned in desire to ques-
    tion them further, they made themselves air, into which they
5   vanished. Whiles I stood rapt in the wonder of it came missives°   *messengers*
    from the King, who all-hailed me "Thane of Cawdor", by
    which title before these weird sisters saluted me, and referred
    me to the coming on of time with "Hail, King that shalt be!"

3. We will settle the succession of the kingdom. At the time, the Scottish crown was not hereditary.
4. Title of the Scottish heir apparent.
5. *which . . . only:* honors will not be bestowed on Malcolm alone.
6. And make me further indebted to you by your hospitality.
7. Even repose seems wearisome when it is not dedicated to your purposes.
8. Forerunner; messenger sent ahead to arrange royal lodgings.
9. Let the eye deliberately ignore what the hand does.
1. As valiant as you say.
1.5 Location: Inverness, Macbeth's castle.

This have I thought good to deliver° thee, my dearest partner   *inform*
10   of greatness, that thou mightst not lose the dues of rejoicing
by being ignorant of what greatness is promised thee. Lay it
to thy heart, and farewell.'
Glamis thou art, and Cawdor, and shalt be
What thou art promised. Yet do I fear° thy nature.   *doubt*
15   It is too full o'th' milk of human kindness
To catch the nearest° way. Thou wouldst be great,   *most expedient*
Art not without ambition, but without
The illness° should attend it. What thou wouldst highly,   *wickedness (that)*
That wouldst thou holily; wouldst not play false,
20   And yet wouldst wrongly win. Thou'dst have, great Glamis,
That which cries 'Thus thou must do' if thou have it,
And that which rather thou dost fear to do
Than wishest should be undone. Hie° thee hither,   *Hasten*
That I may pour my spirits in thine ear
25   And chastise with the valour of my tongue
All that impedes thee from the golden round°   *crown*
Which fate and metaphysical° aid doth seem   *supernatural*
To have thee crowned withal.°   *with*
    Enter [a SERVANT*]*
                          What is your tidings?
SERVANT   The King comes here tonight.
LADY MACBETH   Thou'rt mad to say it.
30   Is not thy master with him, who, were't so,
Would have informed for preparation?
SERVANT   So please you, it is true. Our thane is coming,
One of my fellows had the speed of° him,   *outdistanced*
Who, almost dead for breath, had scarcely more
Than would make up his message.
35   LADY MACBETH   Give him tending;
He brings great news.   *Exit [*SERVANT*]*
                The raven[1] himself is hoarse
That croaks the fatal entrance of Duncan
Under my battlements. Come, you spirits
That tend on mortal° thoughts, unsex me here,   *attend deadly*
40   And fill me from the crown to the toe top-full
Of direst cruelty. Make thick my blood,
Stop up th'access and passage to remorse,°   *pity*
That no compunctious visitings of nature
Shake my fell° purpose, nor keep peace° between   *cruel / intervene*
45   Th'effect and it.[2] Come to my woman's breasts,
And take my milk for° gall, you murd'ring ministers,°   *in exchange for / agents*
Wherever in your sightless° substances   *invisible*
You wait on° nature's mischief. Come, thick night,   *assist*
And pall° thee in the dunnest° smoke of hell,   *envelop / darkest*
50   That my keen knife see not the wound it makes,
Nor heaven peep through the blanket of the dark
To cry 'Hold, hold!'
    Enter MACBETH
                Great Glamis, worthy Cawdor,
Greater than both by the all-hail hereafter,

---

1. The raven was considered a bird of ill omen.   2. My purpose and its accomplishment.

Thy letters have transported me beyond
55 This ignorant present, and I feel now
The future in the instant.

MACBETH   My dearest love,
Duncan comes here tonight.

LADY MACBETH   And when goes hence?

MACBETH   Tomorrow, as he purposes.

LADY MACBETH   O never
Shall sun that morrow see.
60 Your face, my thane, is as a book where men
May read strange matters. To beguile the time,
Look like the time;³ bear welcome in your eye,
Your hand, your tongue; look like the innocent flower,
But be the serpent under't. He that's coming
65 Must be provided for; and you shall put
This night's great business into my dispatch,°   management
Which shall to all our nights and days to come
Give solely sovereign sway and masterdom.

MACBETH   We will speak further.

LADY MACBETH   Only look up clear.°   appear innocent
70 To alter favour⁴ ever is to fear.
Leave all the rest to me.   *Exeunt*

1.6

Hautboys° and torches. Enter KING [DUNCAN], MAL-   Oboes
COLM, DONALBAIN, BANQUO, LENNOX, MACDUFF, ROSS,
ANGUS, *and attendants*

KING DUNCAN   This castle hath a pleasant seat.° The air   location
Nimbly and sweetly recommends itself
Unto our gentle senses.

BANQUO   This guest of summer,
The temple-haunting martlet,¹ does approve°   prove
5 By his loved mansionry° that the heavens' breath   nest building
Smells wooingly here. No jutty,° frieze,   projection
Buttress, nor coign of vantage° but this bird   convenient corner
Hath made his pendant bed and procreant° cradle;   for breeding
Where they most breed and haunt I have observed
The air is delicate.

Enter LADY [MACBETH]

10 KING DUNCAN   See, see, our honoured hostess!
The love that follows us sometime is our trouble,
Which still we thank as love.² Herein I teach you
How you shall bid God 'ield us for your pains,
And thank us for your trouble.³

LADY MACBETH   All our service
15 In every point twice done, and then done double,
Were° poor and single° business to contend   Would be / small
Against those honours deep and broad wherewith
Your majesty loads our house. For those of old,
And the late dignities heaped up to them,

---

3. *To . . . like the time:* To deceive the world, match your
expression to the occasion.
4. To alter your facial expression and thereby arouse
suspicion.
1.6 Location: Outside Macbeth's castle.

1. A bird, the martin, that often built its nest in churches.
2. *The . . . love:* Love bestowed upon us sometimes
causes us inconvenience, but we are still grateful for it.
3. *How . . . trouble:* Ask God to reward ("yield") me for
the trouble I cause you.

We rest your hermits.[4]

20 KING DUNCAN   Where's the Thane of Cawdor?
We coursed him at the heels,° and had a purpose   *followed him closely*
To be his purveyor;[5] but he rides well,
And his great love, sharp as his spur, hath holp° him   *helped*
To his home before us. Fair and noble hostess,
We are your guest tonight.

25 LADY MACBETH   Your servants ever
Have theirs, themselves, and what is theirs in count°   *in trust*
To make their audit at your highness' pleasure,
Still to return your own.[6]

KING DUNCAN   Give me your hand.
Conduct me to mine host. We love him highly,
30 And shall continue our graces towards him.
By your leave,[7] hostess.   *Exeunt*

1.7

Hautboys. Torches. Enter a sewer° and divers servants   *butler*
with dishes and service over the stage. Then enter MACBETH

MACBETH   If it were done when 'tis done, then 'twere well
It were done quickly. If th'assassination
Could trammel up the consequence, and catch
With his surcease success:[1] that but this blow
5 Might be the be-all and the end-all, here,°   *in this world*
But here upon this bank and shoal[2] of time,
We'd jump° the life to come. But in these cases   *risk*
We still have judgement[3] here, that° we but teach   *in that*
Bloody instructions which, being taught, return
10 To plague th'inventor. This even-handed° justice   *impartial*
Commends th'ingredience° of our poisoned chalice   *contents*
To our own lips. He's here in double trust:
First, as I am his kinsman and his subject,
Strong both against the deed; then, as his host,
15 Who should against his murderer shut the door,
Not bear the knife myself. Besides, this Duncan
Hath borne his faculties° so meek, hath been   *authority*
So clear° in his great office, that his virtues   *blameless*
Will plead like angels, trumpet-tongued against
20 The deep damnation of his taking-off,°   *murder*
And pity, like a naked new-born babe,
Striding the blast,[4] or heaven's cherubin, horsed
Upon the sightless couriers[5] of the air,
Shall blow the horrid deed in every eye

---

4. We remain your beadsmen (monks hired to pray for their employers).
5. Attendant who preceded the King when he traveled and procured foodstuffs for the royal party.
6. *Your servants . . . own:* Your servants hold all that they have in trust from you, and they are always ready to settle accounts and return to you what is yours.
7. By your permission. A request for permission to leave or perhaps for a formal kiss.
1.7 Location: A courtyard or an anteroom in Macbeth's castle.
1. *If th'assassination . . . success:* If only I could gain

success with Duncan's death (his "surcease"); if only the assassination were the end of the matter. *trammel up the consequence:* restrain the subsequent sequence of events, as in a trammel, or net.
2. Sandbar. The mortal span is seen as a narrow piece of land in the river of time. F has "Schoole," and "bank" may also mean "bench," suggesting that life is a time of instruction and probation.
3. We are invariably punished.
4. Astride the storm provoked by Duncan's death.
5. The invisible runners, the winds.

25   That tears shall drown the wind.[6] I have no spur
    To prick the sides of my intent, but only
    Vaulting ambition which o'erleaps itself
    And falls on th'other.[7]

          Enter LADY [MACBETH]

                    How now? What news?

LADY MACBETH   He has almost supped. Why have you left the chamber?

MACBETH   Hath he asked for me?

30 LADY MACBETH   Know you not he has?

MACBETH   We will proceed no further in this business.
    He hath honoured me of late, and I have bought°   *won*
    Golden opinions from all sorts of people,
    Which would be worn now in their newest gloss,
    Not cast aside so soon.

35 LADY MACBETH   Was the hope drunk
    Wherein you dressed yourself? Hath it slept since?
    And wakes it now to look so green° and pale   *sickly*
    At what it did so freely? From this time
    Such I account thy love. Art thou afeard
40   To be the same in thine own act and valour
    As thou art in desire? Wouldst thou have that°   *(the crown)*
    Which thou esteem'st the ornament of life,
    And live a coward in thine own esteem,
    Letting 'I dare not' wait upon 'I would',
    Like the poor cat i'th' adage?[8]

45 MACBETH   Prithee, peace.
    I dare do all that may become a man;
    Who dares do more is none.

LADY MACBETH   What beast was't then
    That made you break° this enterprise to me?   *broach*
    When you durst do it, then you were a man;
50   And to be more than what you were, you would
    Be so much more the man. Nor time nor place
    Did then adhere,° and yet you would make both.   *agree*
    They have made themselves, and that their fitness now
    Does unmake you. I have given suck, and know
55   How tender 'tis to love the babe that milks me.
    I would, while it was smiling in my face,
    Have plucked my nipple from his boneless gums
    And dashed the brains out, had I so sworn
    As you have done to this.

MACBETH   If we should fail?

LADY MACBETH   We fail![9]
60   But screw your courage to the sticking-place[1]
    And we'll not fail. When Duncan is asleep—
    Whereto the rather shall his day's hard journey
    Soundly invite him—his two chamberlains°   *bedroom attendants*
    Will I with wine and wassail° so convince°   *carousing / overpower*
65   That memory, the warder° of the brain,   *guard*
    Shall be a fume, and the receipt° of reason   *receptacle*

---

6. Tears will fall like heavy rain, which was believed to still the wind.
7. The other side. The image is of a rider vaulting over his horse instead of into his saddle, or of a horseman who clears a high obstacle but falls on the other side.

8. Proverbial: "The cat would eat fish but does not dare to wet her feet."
9. F: "faile?"
1. The notch on a crossbow that holds the string, which is cranked or screwed taut.

A limbeck² only. When in swinish sleep
Their drenchèd natures lies as in a death,
What cannot you and I perform upon
70 Th'unguarded Duncan? What not put upon
His spongy officers, who shall bear the guilt
Of our great quell?°   murder
MACBETH   Bring forth men-children only,
For thy undaunted mettle° should compose   substance
Nothing but males. Will it not be received,°   believed
75 When we have marked with blood those sleepy two
Of his own chamber and used their very daggers,
That they have done't?
LADY MACBETH   Who dares receive it other,
As we shall make our griefs and clamour roar
Upon his death?
MACBETH   I am settled, and bend up
80 Each corporal° agent to this terrible feat.   bodily
Away, and mock° the time with fairest show.   deceive
False face must hide what the false heart doth know.

                                                    Exeunt

                              2.1
              Enter BANQUO *and* FLEANCE, *with a torch*
              before him
BANQUO   How goes the night, boy?¹
FLEANCE   The moon is down. I have not heard the clock.
BANQUO   And she goes down at twelve.
FLEANCE   I take't 'tis later, sir.
BANQUO [*giving* FLEANCE *his sword*] Hold, take my sword.
       There's husbandry° in heaven,   thrift
5   Their candles are all out. Take thee that,² too.
A heavy summons° lies like lead upon me,   summons to sleep
And yet I would not sleep. Merciful powers,³
Restrain in me the cursèd thoughts that nature
Gives way to in repose.
              Enter MACBETH, *and a servant with a torch*
                      Give me my sword. Who's there?
10   MACBETH   A friend.
BANQUO   What, sir, not yet at rest? The King's a-bed.
He hath been in unusual pleasure, and
Sent forth great largesse° to your offices.⁴   gifts
This diamond he greets your wife withal
15   By the name of most kind hostess, and shut up°   concluded
In measureless content.
MACBETH   Being unprepared
Our will became the servant to defect,
Which else should free have wrought.⁵
BANQUO   All's well.
I dreamt last night of the three weird sisters.
To you they have showed some truth.

---

2. Alembic, the upper part of a still to which fumes rise.
The wine will make the memory a fume that will fill and
cloud the brain, the "receptacle of reason."
2.1 Location: The courtyard of Macbeth's castle.
1. How much of the night has passed?
2. Some article of clothing or armor.

3. Angels invoked as protection against demons.
4. Household departments.
5. *Being . . . wrought:* Our desire to entertain the King
liberally was constrained by the fact that we were unpre-
pared. *defect:* deficiency. *free:* freely.

20 MACBETH   I think not of them;
      Yet, when we can entreat an hour to serve,
      We would spend it in some words upon that business
      If you would grant the time.
      BANQUO   At your kind'st leisure.
      MACBETH   If you shall cleave to my consent when 'tis,[6]
      It shall make honour for you.
25 BANQUO   So° I lose none   *Provided*
      In seeking to augment it, but still keep
      My bosom franchised° and allegiance clear,°   *guiltless / unstained*
      I shall be counselled.°   *receptive*
      MACBETH   Good repose the while.
30 BANQUO   Thanks, sir. The like to you.
                             Exeunt BANQUO [*and* FLEANCE]
      MACBETH [*to the Servant*]   Go bid thy mistress, when my drink is ready,
      She strike upon the bell. Get thee to bed.   *Exit* [*Servant*]
      Is this a dagger which I see before me,
      The handle toward my hand? Come, let me clutch thee.
35 I have thee not, and yet I see thee still.
      Art thou not, fatal vision, sensible°   *perceptible*
      To feeling as to sight? Or art thou but
      A dagger of the mind, a false creation
      Proceeding from the heat-oppressèd° brain?   *fevered*
40 I see thee yet, in form as palpable
      As this which now I draw.
      Thou marshall'st° me the way that I was going,   *guide*
      And such an instrument I was to use.
      Mine eyes are made the fools o'th' other senses,
45 Or else worth all the rest. I see thee still,
      And on thy blade and dudgeon gouts° of blood,   *and handle drops*
      Which was not so before. There's no such thing.
      It is the bloody business which informs°   *creates shapes*
      Thus to mine eyes. Now o'er the one half-world
50 Nature seems dead, and wicked dreams abuse°   *deceive*
      The curtained sleep. Witchcraft celebrates
      Pale Hecate's offerings,[7] and withered murder,
      Alarumed° by his sentinel the wolf,   *Roused*
      Whose howl's his watch,° thus with his stealthy pace,   *watchword*
55 With Tarquin's[8] ravishing strides, towards his design°   *prey*
      Moves like a ghost. Thou sure and firm-set earth,
      Hear not my steps which way they walk, for fear
      Thy very stones prate of my whereabout,
      And take the present horror° from the time,   *terrible stillness*
60 Which now suits with it. Whiles I threat, he lives.
      Words to the heat of deeds too cold breath gives.
                    A bell rings
      I go, and it is done. The bell invites me.
      Hear it not, Duncan; for it is a knell
      That summons thee to heaven or to hell.   *Exit*

---

6. If you will support my opinion or my cause when the
time comes.
7. Sacrificial rites offered to Hecate, Greek goddess of
witchcraft and of the moon.

8. A Roman prince who ravished the chaste matron
Lucrece. Shakespeare tells the story in *The Rape of
Lucrece.*

2.2

Enter LADY [MACBETH]

LADY MACBETH   That which hath made them drunk hath made me bold.
What hath quenched them hath given me fire. Hark, peace!—
It was the owl that shrieked, the fatal bellman°   *night watchman*
Which gives the stern'st good-night.¹ He is about it.
5   The doors are open, and the surfeited grooms°   *attendants*
Do mock their charge° with snores. I have drugged their   *duty*
    possets°   *mulled milk and wine*
That death and nature do contend about them
Whether they live or die.
        Enter MACBETH [*above*]
MACBETH   Who's there? What ho?   [*Exit*]
LADY MACBETH   Alack, I am afraid they have awaked,
10   And 'tis not done. Th'attempt and not the deed
Confounds° us. Hark!—I laid their daggers ready;   *Ruins*
He could not miss 'em. Had he not resembled
My father as he slept, I had done't.
       [*Enter* MACBETH *below*]
                             My husband!
MACBETH   I have done the deed. Didst thou not hear a noise?
15 LADY MACBETH   I heard the owl scream and the crickets cry.
Did not you speak?
MACBETH   When?
LADY MACBETH   Now.
MACBETH   As I descended?
LADY MACBETH   Ay.
MACBETH   Hark!—Who lies i'th' second chamber?
LADY MACBETH   Donalbain.
MACBETH [*looking at his hands*]   This is a sorry sight.
LADY MACBETH   A foolish thought, to say a sorry sight.
20 MACBETH   There's one did laugh in's sleep, and one cried 'Murder!'
That they did wake each other. I stood and heard them.
But they did say their prayers and addressed them°   *settled themselves*
Again to sleep.
LADY MACBETH   There are two lodged together.
MACBETH   One cried 'God bless us' and 'Amen' the other,
25   As° they had seen me with these hangman's² hands.   *As if*
List'ning their fear I could not say 'Amen'
When they did say 'God bless us.'
LADY MACBETH   Consider it not so deeply.
MACBETH   But wherefore could not I pronounce 'Amen'?
30   I had most need of blessing, and 'Amen'
Stuck in my throat.
LADY MACBETH   These deeds must not be thought°   *thought on*
After these ways. So, it will make us mad.
MACBETH   Methought I heard a voice cry 'Sleep no more,
Macbeth does murder sleep'—the innocent sleep,
35   Sleep that knits up the ravelled sleave° of care,   *tangled skein*
The death of each day's life, sore labour's bath,

2.2 Location: Scene continues with only a brief pause.
1. A bell was rung outside the cells of condemned pris-
oners the night before they were to be executed.

2. Bloodstained. The hangman had to disembowel and
quarter his victims.

Balm of hurt minds, great nature's second course,[3]
Chief nourisher in life's feast—
LADY MACBETH   What do you mean?
MACBETH   Still it cried 'Sleep no more' to all the house,
40   'Glamis hath murdered sleep, and therefore Cawdor
Shall sleep no more, Macbeth shall sleep no more.'
LADY MACBETH   Who was it that thus cried? Why, worthy thane,
You do unbend° your noble strength to think   *slacken*
So brain-sickly of things. Go get some water
45   And wash this filthy witness° from your hand.   *evidence*
Why did you bring these daggers from the place?
They must lie there. Go, carry them, and smear
The sleepy grooms with blood.
MACBETH   I'll go no more.
I am afraid to think what I have done,
Look on't again I dare not.
50   LADY MACBETH   Infirm of purpose!
Give me the daggers. The sleeping and the dead
Are but as pictures. 'Tis the eye of childhood
That fears a painted devil. If he do bleed
I'll gild[4] the faces of the grooms withal,
For it must seem their guilt.   *Exit*
        Knock within
55   MACBETH   Whence is that knocking?—
How is't with me when every noise appals me?
What hands are here! Ha, they pluck out mine eyes.
Will all great Neptune's ocean wash this blood
Clean from my hand? No, this my hand will rather
60   The multitudinous seas incarnadine,°   *turn red*
Making the green one red.[5]
      Enter LADY [MACBETH]
LADY MACBETH   My hands are of your colour, but I shame
To wear a heart so white.
      Knock [*within*]
             I hear a knocking
At the south entry. Retire we to our chamber.
65   A little water clears us of this deed.
How easy is it then! Your constancy
Hath left you unattended.[6]
      Knock [*within*]
             Hark, more knocking.
Get on your nightgown, lest occasion call us
And show us to be watchers.[7] Be not lost
70   So poorly in your thoughts.
MACBETH   To know my deed 'twere best not know myself.[8]
      Knock [*within*]
Wake Duncan with thy knocking. I would thou couldst.
                 Exeunt

---

3. Second, and most nourishing, course of a meal; second, or alternative, habit or practice.
4. Coat as if with gold leaf. Gold was often called red; compare 2.3.109.
5. *one red*: entirely red.

6. *Your . . . unattended*: Your resolve has deserted you.
7. Those who have stayed awake.
8. It is better that I lose consciousness altogether than face my deed.

2.3

Enter a PORTER. *Knocking within*

PORTER   Here's a knocking indeed! If a man were porter of hell-
gate he should have old° turning the key.   *plenty of*

Knock [within]

Knock, knock, knock. Who's there, i'th' name of Beelzebub?°   *name of a devil*
Here's a farmer that hanged himself on th'expectation of
5   plenty.[1] Come in time![2] Have napkins° enough about you; here   *handkerchiefs*
you'll sweat for't.

Knock [within]

Knock, knock. Who's there, in th'other devil's name? Faith,
here's an equivocator[3] that could swear in both the scales
against either scale, who committed treason enough for God's
10   sake, yet could not equivocate to heaven. O, come in, equiv-
ocator.

Knock [within]

Knock, knock, knock. Who's there? 'Faith, here's an English
tailor come hither for stealing out of a French hose.[4] Come in,
tailor. Here you may roast your goose.[5]

Knock [within]

15   Knock, knock. Never at quiet. What are you?—But this place
is too cold for hell. I'll devil-porter it no further. I had thought
to have let in some of all professions that go the primrose way
to th'everlasting bonfire.

Knock [within]

Anon, anon!

[He opens the gate]

20   I pray you remember the porter.

Enter MACDUFF *and* LENNOX

MACDUFF   Was it so late, friend, ere you went to bed
That you do lie so late?

PORTER   Faith, sir, we were carousing till the second cock,° and   *3:00 A.M.*
drink, sir, is a great provoker of three things.

25   MACDUFF   What three things does drink especially provoke?

PORTER   Marry,° sir, nose-painting,[6] sleep, and urine. Lechery,   *Indeed*
sir, it provokes and unprovokes: it provokes the desire but it
takes away the performance. Therefore much drink may be
said to be an equivocator with lechery: it makes him and it
30   mars him; it sets him on and it takes him off; it persuades him
and disheartens him, makes him stand to° and not stand to; in   *maintain an erection*
conclusion, equivocates him in a sleep,[7] and, giving him the
lie,[8] leaves him.

MACDUFF   I believe drink gave thee the lie last night.

35   PORTER   That it did, sir, i'the very throat on me;[9] but I requited

---

2.3 Location: Scene continues, perhaps after a short
pause.
1. *Here's . . . plenty:* A farmer had hoarded grain to sell at
high prices but was ruined by a crop surplus that forced
prices down.
2. Good timing.
3. One who speaks ambiguously. An allusion to the Jesuit
doctrine that a seemingly false statement was not a lie
(and therefore not repugnant to God) if the speaker had
in mind a different meaning in which the utterance was
true. Possibly an allusion to the 1606 trial of the Jesuit
Henry Garnet for involvement in the Gunpowder Plot to
blow up the Houses of Parliament; Father Garnet had

written a treatise defending equivocation for Catholics
being persecuted for their beliefs.
4. Tight-fitting breeches, which would easily reveal the
tailor's attempt to skimp on the cloth supplied him for
their manufacture. He had apparently been able to do so
undetected when loose-fitting breeches were in fashion.
5. Heat your smoothing iron.
6. Reddening of the nose through drink.
7. Gives him an erotic experience in dreams only.
8. An elaborate pun: calling him a liar; laying him out
flat; making him urinate ("lye," or urine).
9. *i'the . . . me:* provoking a duel by insulting me with
a deliberate lie.

him for his lie, and, I think, being too strong for him, though
he took up my legs sometime, yet I made a shift to cast him.[1]

MACDUFF   Is thy master stirring?

Enter MACBETH

Our knocking has awaked him: here he comes.   [*Exit* PORTER]

LENNOX [*to* MACBETH]   Good morrow, noble sir.

40 MACBETH   Good morrow, both.

MACDUFF   Is the King stirring, worthy thane?

MACBETH   Not yet.

MACDUFF   He did command me to call timely° on him.   early
I have almost slipped the hour.

MACBETH   I'll bring you to him.

MACDUFF   I know this is a joyful trouble to you,
45 But yet 'tis one.

MACBETH   The labour we delight in physics pain.[2]
This is the door.

MACDUFF   I'll make so bold to call,
For 'tis my limited° service.   *Exit* MACDUFF   appointed

LENNOX   Goes the King hence today?

MACBETH   He does; he did appoint so.

50 LENNOX   The night has been unruly. Where we lay
Our chimneys were blown down, and, as they say,
Lamentings heard i'th' air, strange screams of death,
And prophesying with accents terrible
Of dire combustion° and confused events   tumult
55 New-hatched to th' woeful time. The obscure bird[3]
Clamoured the livelong night. Some say the earth
Was feverous and did shake.

MACBETH   'Twas a rough night.

LENNOX   My young remembrance cannot parallel
A fellow to it.

Enter MACDUFF

MACDUFF   O horror, horror, horror!
60 Tongue nor heart cannot conceive nor name thee.

MACBETH *and* LENNOX   What's the matter?

MACDUFF   Confusion° now hath made his masterpiece.   Ruin
Most sacrilegious murder hath broke ope
The Lord's anointed temple° and stole thence   (the King's body)
65 The life o'th' building.

MACBETH   What is't you say—the life?

LENNOX   Mean you his majesty?

MACDUFF   Approach the chamber and destroy your sight
With a new Gorgon.[4] Do not bid me speak.
See, and then speak yourselves. *Exeunt* MACBETH *and* LENNOX
70   Awake, awake!
Ring the alarum bell. Murder and treason!
Banquo and Donalbain, Malcolm, awake!
Shake off this downy sleep, death's counterfeit,
And look on death itself. Up, up, and see
75 The great doom's image.° Malcolm, Banquo,   replica of Doomsday
As from your graves rise up, and walk like sprites

---

1. *being . . . cast him*: the effects of drunkenness are
described in the language of a wrestling match. *cast*:
throw off; vomit.
2. Pleasure in labor mitigates its laboriousness.

3. The owl, bird of darkness.
4. A mythical monster with a woman's figure and snakes
for hair, the sight of whose face turned beholders to
stone. Medusa was one of the three Gorgons.

To countenance° this horror.   *suit; behold*

Bell rings. Enter LADY [MACBETH]

LADY MACBETH   What's the business,
That such a hideous trumpet calls to parley
The sleepers of the house? Speak, speak.

MACDUFF   O gentle lady,

80   'Tis not for you to hear what I can speak.
The repetition° in a woman's ear   *report*
Would murder as it fell.

Enter BANQUO

O Banquo, Banquo,
Our royal master's murdered!

LADY MACBETH   Woe, alas—
What, in our house?

BANQUO   Too cruel anywhere.

85   Dear Duff, I prithee contradict thyself,
And say it is not so.

Enter MACBETH, LENNOX, *and* ROSS

MACBETH   Had I but died an hour before this chance°   *occurrence*
I had lived a blessèd time, for from this instant
There's nothing serious in mortality.°   *worth living for*

90   All is but toys.° Renown and grace is dead.   *trifles*
The wine of life is drawn, and the mere lees
Is left this vault° to brag of.   *wine vault; world*

Enter MALCOLM *and* DONALBAIN

DONALBAIN   What is amiss?

MACBETH   You are, and do not know't.

95   The spring, the head, the fountain of your blood
Is stopped, the very source of it is stopped.

MACDUFF   Your royal father's murdered.

MALCOLM   O, by whom?

LENNOX   Those of his chamber, as it seemed, had done't.
Their hands and faces were all badged° with blood,   *marked*

100   So were their daggers, which, unwiped, we found
Upon their pillows. They stared and were distracted.
No man's life was to be trusted with them.

MACBETH   O, yet I do repent me of my fury
That I did kill them.

MACDUFF   Wherefore did you so?

105   MACBETH   Who can be wise, amazed, temp'rate and furious,
Loyal and neutral in a moment? No man.
Th'expedition° of my violent love   *haste*
Outran the pauser,° reason. Here lay Duncan,   *delayer*
His silver skin laced with his golden blood,

110   And his gashed stabs looked like a breach in nature
For ruin's wasteful° entrance; there the murderers,   *destructive*
Steeped in the colours of their trade, their daggers
Unmannerly breeched⁵ with gore. Who could refrain,
That had a heart to love, and in that heart
Courage to make 's love known?

115   LADY MACBETH   Help me hence, ho!

MACDUFF   Look to the lady.

MALCOLM [*aside to* DONALBAIN] Why do we hold our tongues,

5. Covered—as if with breeches—with blood.

That most may claim this argument° for ours?   *subject*
DONALBAIN [*aside to* MALCOLM]   What should be spoken here,
    where our fate,
Hid in an auger-hole,° may rush and seize us?   *in a cranny; in ambush*
Let's away. Our tears are not yet brewed.
120 MALCOLM [*aside to* DONALBAIN]   Nor our strong sorrow
Upon the foot of motion.[6]
BANQUO   Look to the lady;
                  [*Exit* LADY MACBETH, *attended*]
And when we have our naked frailties hid,°   *clothed*
That suffer in exposure, let us meet
And question° this most bloody piece of work,   *discuss*
125 To know it further. Fears and scruples° shake us.   *doubts*
In the great hand of God I stand, and thence
Against the undivulged pretence I fight
Of treasonous malice.[7]
MACDUFF   And so do I.
ALL   So all.
MACBETH   Let's briefly° put on manly readiness,°   *quickly / clothes; resolve*
And meet i'th' hall together.
130 ALL   Well contented.
            Exeunt [*all but* MALCOLM *and* DONALBAIN]
MALCOLM   What will you do? Let's not consort with them.
To show an unfelt sorrow is an office
Which the false man does easy. I'll to England.
DONALBAIN   To Ireland, I. Our separated fortune
135 Shall keep us both the safer. Where we are
There's daggers in men's smiles. The nea'er in blood,
The nearer bloody.[8]
MALCOLM   This murderous shaft that's shot
Hath not yet lighted,° and our safest way   *fallen*
Is to avoid the aim. Therefore to horse,
140 And let us not be dainty of° leave-taking,   *polite about*
But shift° away. There's warrant° in that theft   *slip / justification*
Which steals itself[9] when there's no mercy left.   *Exeunt*

2.4

Enter ROSS *with an* OLD MAN
OLD MAN   Threescore and ten I can remember well,
Within the volume of which time I have seen
Hours dreadful and things strange, but this sore night
Hath trifled former knowings.[1]
ROSS   Ha, good father,
5 Thou seest the heavens, as troubled with man's act,
Threatens his bloody stage. By th' clock 'tis day,
And yet dark night strangles the travelling lamp.°   *sun*
Is't night's predominance° or the day's shame   *ascendancy*
That darkness does the face of earth entomb
When living light should kiss it?
10 OLD MAN   'Tis unnatural,

---

6. *Nor . . . motion:* Nor has our strong sorrow yet begun
to express itself.
7. *Against . . . malice:* I will fight against the hidden pur-
pose behind this treasonous act.
8. *The nea'er . . . bloody:* The closer the kinship, the

nearer the danger of murder.
9. *Which steals itself:* Malcolm alludes to the fact that he
and Donalbain intend to "steal" away from the castle.
2.4 Location: Not far from Macbeth's castle.
1. Has made previous experiences seem trifling.

Even like the deed that's done. On Tuesday last
A falcon, tow'ring in her pride of place,[2]
Was by a mousing owl[3] hawked at and killed.

ROSS   And Duncan's horses— a thing most strange and certain—

15   Beauteous and swift, the minions° of their race,   *darlings*
Turned wild in nature, broke their stalls, flung out,
Contending 'gainst obedience, as° they would   *as if*
Make war with mankind.

OLD MAN   'Tis said they ate each other.

ROSS   They did so, to th'amazement of mine eyes
That looked upon't.

Enter MACDUFF

20   Here comes the good Macduff.
How goes the world, sir, now?

MACDUFF   Why, see you not?

ROSS   Is't known who did this more than bloody deed?

MACDUFF   Those that Macbeth hath slain.

ROSS   Alas the day,
What good could they pretend?[4]

MACDUFF   They were suborned.°   *bribed*

25   Malcolm and Donalbain, the King's two sons,
Are stol'n away and fled, which puts upon them
Suspicion of the deed.

ROSS   'Gainst nature still.
Thriftless ambition, that will raven up°   *devour*
Thine own life's means! Then 'tis most like

30   The sovereignty will fall upon Macbeth.

MACDUFF   He is already named and gone to Scone[5]
To be invested.

ROSS   Where is Duncan's body?

MACDUFF   Carried to Colmekill,[6]

35   The sacred storehouse of his predecessors,
And guardian of their bones.

ROSS   Will you to Scone?

MACDUFF   No, cousin, I'll to Fife.[7]

ROSS   Well, I will thither.

MACDUFF   Well, may you see things well done there. Adieu,
Lest our old robes sit easier than our new.

40   ROSS   Farewell, father.

OLD MAN   God's benison° go with you, and with those   *blessing*
That would make good of bad, and friends of foes.

Exeunt severally

3.1

Enter BANQUO

BANQUO   Thou hast it now: King, Cawdor, Glamis, all
As the weird women promised; and I fear
Thou played'st most foully for't. Yet it was said
It should not stand in thy posterity,[1]

5   But that myself should be the root and father

---

2. Mounting to her highest point in the sky before
swooping down.
3. An owl that usually feeds on mice.
4. What good could they expect to gain from the murder?
5. Ancient royal city where Scottish Kings were invested

with the ceremonial symbols of authority.
6. Iona, the burial place of Scottish Kings.
7. Macduff is the Thane of Fife.
3.1 Location: The royal palace at Forres.
1. It should not pass to your descendants.

Of many kings. If there come truth from them—
As upon thee, Macbeth, their speeches shine°—   *smile favorably*
Why by the verities on thee made good
May they not be my oracles as well,
10   And set me up in hope? But hush, no more.

      Sennet° sounded. Enter MACBETH *as King,* LADY MAC-   *Trumpet call*
      BETH *as Queen,* LENNOX, ROSS, *lords, and attendants*

MACBETH   Here's our chief guest.
LADY MACBETH   If he had been forgotten
   It had been as a gap in our great feast,
   And all-thing° unbecoming.   *entirely*
MACBETH [*to* BANQUO]   Tonight we hold a solemn° supper, sir,   *formal*
   And I'll request your presence.
15 BANQUO   Let your highness
   Command upon me, to the which my duties
   Are with a most indissoluble tie
   For ever knit.
MACBETH   Ride you this afternoon?
20 BANQUO   Ay, my good lord.
MACBETH   We should have else desired your good advice,
   Which still° hath been both grave° and prosperous,   *always / weighty*
   In this day's council; but we'll talk tomorrow.
   Is't far you ride?
25 BANQUO   As far, my lord, as will fill up the time
   'Twixt this and supper. Go not my horse the better,[2]
   I must become a borrower of the night
   For a dark hour or twain.
MACBETH   Fail not our feast.
30 BANQUO   My lord, I will not.
MACBETH   We hear our bloody cousins are bestowed°   *lodged*
   In England and in Ireland, not confessing
   Their cruel parricide, filling their hearers
   With strange invention.° But of that tomorrow,   *falsehood*
35   When therewithal we shall have cause of state
   Craving us jointly.[3] Hie you to horse. Adieu,
   Till you return at night. Goes Fleance with you?
BANQUO   Ay, my good lord. Our time does call upon 's.
MACBETH   I wish your horses swift and sure of foot,
40   And so I do commend° you to their backs.   *entrust*
   Farewell.   *Exit* BANQUO
   Let every man be master of his time
   Till seven at night. To make society
   The sweeter welcome, we will keep ourself
45   Till supper-time alone. While° then, God be with you.   *Till*

      Exeunt [*all but* MACBETH *and a* SERVANT]

   Sirrah, a word with you. Attend those men
   Our pleasure?
SERVANT   They are, my lord, without° the palace gate.   *outside*
MACBETH   Bring them before us.   *Exit* SERVANT
                  To be thus is nothing
50   But to be safely thus.[4] Our fears in° Banquo   *of*

---

2. If my horse does not go faster than I expect.
3. *cause . . . jointly:* state business demanding our joint attention.

4. *To be thus . . . thus:* To be a King is no good unless one can reign in safety ("thus" refers to "King").

	Stick° deep, and in his royalty of nature°	*Prick / natural nobility*
	Reigns that which would be feared. 'Tis much he dares,	
	And to° that dauntless temper of his mind	*added to*
	He hath a wisdom that doth guide his valour	
55	To act in safety. There is none but he	
	Whose being I do fear, and under him	
	My genius° is rebuked as, it is said,[5]	*tutelary spirit*
	Mark Antony's was by Caesar.° He chid the sisters	*Octavius Caesar*
	When first they put the name of king upon me,	
60	And bade them speak to him. Then, prophet-like,	
	They hailed him father to a line of kings.	
	Upon my head they placed a fruitless crown,	
	And put a barren sceptre in my grip,	
	Thence to be wrenched with° an unlineal hand,	*by*
65	No son of mine succeeding. If't be so,	
	For Banquo's issue have I filed° my mind,	*defiled*
	For them the gracious° Duncan have I murdered,	*full of grace*
	Put rancours° in the vessel of my peace	*bitterness*
	Only for them, and mine eternal jewel°	*soul*
70	Given to the common enemy of man°	*(the devil)*
	To make them kings, the seeds of Banquo kings.	
	Rather than so, come fate into the list°	*arena*
	And champion me to th'utterance.[6] Who's there?	

Enter Servant and two MURDERERS

[*To the Servant*] Now go to the door, and stay there till we call.

Exit Servant

75	Was it not yesterday we spoke together?	
	MURDERERS It was, so please your highness.	
	MACBETH Well then, now	
	Have you considered of my speeches? Know	
	That it was he in the times past which held you	
	So under° fortune, which you thought had been	*out of favor with*
80	Our innocent self. This I made good to you	
	In our last conference, passed in probation° with you	*reviewed the proof*
	How you were borne in hand,° how crossed,° the instruments,[7]	*deceived / thwarted*
	Who wrought with them, and all things else that might	
	To half a soul, and to a notion crazed,[8]	
	Say 'Thus did Banquo'.	
85	FIRST MURDERER You made it known to us.	
	MACBETH I did so, and went further, which is now	
	Our point of second meeting. Do you find	
	Your patience so predominant in your nature	
	That you can let this go? Are you so gospelled[9]	
90	To pray for this good man and for his issue,	
	Whose heavy hand hath bowed you to the grave	
	And beggared yours° for ever?	*your family*
	FIRST MURDERER We are men, my liege.	
	MACBETH Ay, in the catalogue ye go for men,	
	As hounds and greyhounds, mongrels, spaniels, curs,	
95	Shoughs, water-rugs, and demi-wolves[1] are clept°	*called*

---

5. Said by Plutarch. Shakespeare paraphrases him in *Antony and Cleopatra* (2.3).
6. And fight with me in single combat to the death.
7. Agents.

8. Even to a half-wit or to a crazed mind.
9. Imbued with the gospel spirit.
1. Shaggy lapdogs, water dogs (for fowling), and cross-breeds between wolf and dog.

All by the name of dogs. The valued file[2]
Distinguishes the swift, the slow, the subtle,
The housekeeper,° the hunter, every one   watchdog
According to the gift which bounteous nature
100   Hath in him closed;° whereby he does receive   enclosed
Particular addition from the bill
That writes them all alike.[3] And so of men.
Now, if you have a station° in the file,   position
Not i'th' worst rank of manhood, say't,
105   And I will put that business in your bosoms
Whose execution takes your enemy off,
Grapples you to the heart and love of us,
Who wear our health but sickly in his life,
Which in his death were perfect.

SECOND MURDERER   I am one, my liege,
110   Whom the vile blows and buffets of the world
Hath so incensed that I am reckless what
I do to spite the world.

FIRST MURDERER   And I another,
So weary with disasters, tugged with° fortune,   mauled by
That I would set° my life on any chance   risk
To mend it or be rid on't.

115 MACBETH   Both of you
Know Banquo was your enemy.

MURDERERS   True, my lord.

MACBETH   So is he mine, and in such bloody distance°   enmity
That every minute of his being thrusts
Against my near'st of life;[4] and though I could
120   With barefaced power sweep him from my sight
And bid my will avouch° it, yet I must not,   warrant
For° certain friends that are both his and mine,   Because of
Whose loves I may not drop, but wail° his fall   must bewail
Who I myself struck down. And thence it is
125   That I to your assistance do make love,°   I crave your aid
Masking the business from the common eye
For sundry weighty reasons.

SECOND MURDERER   We shall, my lord,
Perform what you command us.

FIRST MURDERER   Though our lives—

MACBETH   Your spirits shine through you. Within this hour at most
130   I will advise you where to plant yourselves,
Acquaint you with the perfect spy o'th' time,
The moment on't;[5] for't must be done tonight,
And something° from the palace; always thought°   at some distance / remember
That I require a clearness;[6] and with him,
135   To leave no rubs° nor botches in the work,   flaws
Fleance, his son, that keeps him company—
Whose absence is no less material to me
Than is his father's—must embrace the fate
Of that dark hour. Resolve yourselves apart.[7]
I'll come to you anon.

2. List specifying the value of the cataloged items.
3. *Particular . . . alike:* Distinction apart from a catalog
that lists them indiscriminately.
4. My most vital part, the heart.

5. *Acquaint . . . on't:* I will give you full and precise
instructions as to when it is to be done.
6. A clearance (from suspicion).
7. Make up your minds privately.

140 MURDERERS   We are resolved, my lord.
    MACBETH   I'll call upon you straight. Abide within.
                                            [*Exeunt* MURDERERS]
        It is concluded. Banquo, thy soul's flight,
        If it find heaven, must find it out tonight.   *Exit*

3.2

        Enter LADY [MACBETH] *and a* SERVANT
    LADY MACBETH   Is Banquo gone from court?
    SERVANT   Ay, madam, but returns again tonight.
    LADY MACBETH   Say to the King I would attend his leisure
        For a few words.
5   SERVANT   Madam, I will.   *Exit*
    LADY MACBETH   Naught's had, all's spent,
        Where our desire is got without content.°   *happiness*
        'Tis safer to be that which we destroy
        Than by destruction dwell in doubtful joy.
            Enter MACBETH
10   How now, my lord, why do you keep alone,
        Of sorriest° fancies your companions making,   *most wretched*
        Using° those thoughts which should indeed have died   *Entertaining*
        With them they think on? Things without all remedy
        Should be without regard.° What's done is done.   *not considered*
15 MACBETH   We have scorched° the snake, not killed it.   *slashed*
        She'll close° and be herself, whilst our poor malice   *heal*
        Remains in danger of her former tooth.[1]
        But let the frame of things disjoint, both the worlds suffer,[2]
        Ere we will eat our meal in fear, and sleep
20   In the affliction of these terrible dreams
        That shake us nightly. Better be with the dead,
        Whom we to gain our peace have sent to peace,
        Than on the torture° of the mind to lie   *rack*
        In restless ecstasy.° Duncan is in his grave.   *frenzy*
25   After life's fitful fever he sleeps well.
        Treason has done his worst. Nor steel nor poison,
        Malice domestic, foreign levy,[3] nothing
        Can touch him further.
    LADY MACBETH   Come on, gentle my lord,
        Sleek o'er your rugged looks, be bright and jovial
        Among your guests tonight.
30 MACBETH   So shall I, love,
        And so I pray be you. Let your remembrance
        Apply° to Banquo. Present him eminence°   *Be given / favor*
        Both with eye and tongue; unsafe the while that we
        Must lave our honours in these flattering streams[4]
35   And make our faces visors° to our hearts,   *masks*
        Disguising what they are.
    LADY MACBETH   You must leave this.
    MACBETH   O, full of scorpions is my mind, dear wife!
        Thou know'st that Banquo and his Fleance lives.

3.2 Location: The palace.
1. *our . . . tooth:* we remain in danger of her fangs, which
are as dangerous as they were before she was slashed.
poor malice: weak enmity.
2. Let the universe fall apart, and heaven and earth

suffer destruction.
3. An army levied abroad against Scotland.
4. *unsafe . . . streams:* we are unsafe at present, so we
must make our reputations look clean by flattering oth-
ers; we are unsafe as long as we must flatter.

LADY MACBETH But in them nature's copy's[5] not eterne.°   *everlasting*
40 MACBETH There's comfort yet, they are assailable.
   Then be thou jocund. Ere the bat hath flown
   His cloistered° flight, ere to black Hecate's summons   *restricted*
   The shard-borne[6] beetle with his drowsy hums
   Hath rung night's yawning peal,[7] there shall be done
   A deed of dreadful note.
45 LADY MACBETH   What's to be done?
MACBETH Be innocent of the knowledge, dearest chuck,[8]
   Till thou applaud the deed.—Come, seeling[9] night,
   Scarf up° the tender eye of pitiful day,   *Blindfold*
   And with thy bloody and invisible hand
50   Cancel and tear to pieces that great bond°   (Banquo's lease on life)
   Which keeps me pale. Light thickens, and the crow
   Makes wing to th' rooky° wood.   *full of rooks*
   Good things of day begin to droop and drowse,
   Whiles night's black agents to their preys do rouse.
55   Thou marvell'st at my words; but hold thee still.
   Things bad begun make strong themselves by ill.
   So prithee go with me.   *Exeunt*

3.3

Enter three MURDERERS

FIRST MURDERER [*to* THIRD MURDERER] But who did bid thee
   join with us?
THIRD MURDERER Macbeth.
SECOND MURDERER [*to* FIRST MURDERER] He needs not our mis-
   trust, since he delivers
   Our offices and what we have to do
   To the direction just.[1]
FIRST MURDERER [*to* THIRD MURDERER] Then stand with us.
5   The west yet glimmers with some streaks of day.
   Now spurs the lated° traveller apace   *belated*
   To gain the timely inn, and near approaches
   The subject of our watch.
THIRD MURDERER   Hark, I hear horses.
BANQUO [*within*] Give us a light there, ho!
SECOND MURDERER   Then 'tis he. The rest
10   That are within the note of expectation°   *list of expected guests*
   Already are i'th' court.
FIRST MURDERER   His horses go about.[2]
THIRD MURDERER Almost a mile; but he does usually,
   So all men do, from hence to th' palace gate
   Make it their walk.
       Enter BANQUO *and* FLEANCE *with a torch*
SECOND MURDERER [*aside*] A light, a light.
THIRD MURDERER [*aside*]   'Tis he.
15 FIRST MURDERER [*aside*] Stand to't.

---

5. Lease on life (a copyhold lease was subject to cancellation and therefore "not eterne"); the individual human cast from nature's mold.
6. Carried on scaly wings; born in dung ("shards").
7. Macbeth likens the beetle's humming to a bell, signaling the time for sleep.
8. Chick (term of endearment).

9. Eye-closing. Falcons' eyelids were sewn shut ("seeled") as part of their training.
3.3 Location: Near the palace.
1. *He . . . just:* We need not mistrust this man, since he knows perfectly Macbeth's instructions to us.
2. Are led (by servants) to the stables.

BANQUO   It will be rain tonight.
FIRST MURDERER   Let it come down.
    [FIRST MURDERER *strikes out the torch. The others attack*
    BANQUO]
BANQUO   O, treachery! Fly, good Fleance, fly, fly, fly!
    Thou mayst revenge.—O slave!   [*He dies. Exit* FLEANCE]
THIRD MURDERER   Who did strike out the light?
20 FIRST MURDERER   Was't not the way?°   *proper thing*
THIRD MURDERER   There's but one down. The son is fled.
SECOND MURDERER   We have lost best half of our affair.
FIRST MURDERER   Well, let's away and say how much is done.
                          Exeunt [*with Banquo's body*]

3.4

Banquet prepared. Enter MACBETH [*as King*], LADY [MAC-
BETH *as Queen*], ROSS, LENNOX, *Lords, and attendants.*
    [LADY MACBETH *sits*]
MACBETH   You know your own degrees;° sit down. At first and last¹   *ranks; places*
    The hearty welcome.
LORDS   Thanks to your majesty.
    [*They sit*]
MACBETH   Ourself will mingle with society
    And play the humble host. Our hostess keeps her state,°   *chair of state*
5   But in best time we will require° her welcome.   *request*
LADY MACBETH   Pronounce it for me, sir, to all our friends,
    For my heart speaks they are welcome.
                Enter FIRST MURDERER [*to the door*]
MACBETH   See, they encounter° thee with their hearts' thanks.   *answer*
    Both sides are even. Here I'll sit, i'th' midst.
10 Be large° in mirth. Anon we'll drink a measure   *unrestrained*
    The table round. [*To* FIRST MURDERER]   There's blood upon thy face.
FIRST MURDERER   [*aside to* MACBETH]   'Tis Banquo's, then.
MACBETH   'Tis better thee without than he within.²
    Is he dispatched?
15 FIRST MURDERER   My lord, his throat is cut. That I did for him.
MACBETH   Thou art the best o'th' cut-throats. Yet he's good
    That did the like for Fleance. If thou didst it,
    Thou art the nonpareil.°   *paragon (without equal)*
FIRST MURDERER   Most royal sir,
    Fleance is scaped.
20 MACBETH   Then comes my fit again; I had else been perfect,
    Whole as the marble, founded° as the rock,   *immovable*
    As broad and general° as the casing° air,   *unconstrained / surrounding*
    But now I am cabined, cribbed,° confined, bound in   *penned up*
    To saucy° doubts and fears. But Banquo's safe?   *importunate*
25 FIRST MURDERER   Ay, my good lord. Safe in a ditch he bides,
    With twenty trenchèd gashes on his head,
    The least a death to nature.
MACBETH   Thanks for that.
    There the grown serpent lies. The worm° that's fled   *young serpent*
    Hath nature that in time will venom breed,

3.4 Location: The palace.   2. Better on you than inside him.
1. To one and all.

30 No teeth for th' present. Get thee gone. Tomorrow

We'll hear ourselves° again. *Exit* [FIRST] MURDERER °*confer*

LADY MACBETH   My royal lord,

You do not give the cheer.° The feast is sold °*entertain*

That is not often vouched, while 'tis a-making,

'Tis given with welcome.³ To feed° were best at home. °*Mere eating*

35 From thence° the sauce to meat is ceremony, °*Away from home*

Meeting were° bare without it. °*Company would be*

Enter the Ghost of Banquo, and sits in Macbeth's place

MACBETH   Sweet remembrancer.° °*reminder*

Now good digestion wait on appetite,

And health on both.

LENNOX   May't please your highness sit?

MACBETH Here had we now our country's honour roofed⁴

40 Were the graced person of our Banquo present,

Who may I rather challenge for° unkindness °*accuse of*

Than pity for mischance.

ROSS   His absence, sir,

Lays blame upon his promise. Please't your highness

To grace us with your royal company?

MACBETH The table's full.

45 LENNOX   Here is a place reserved, sir.

MACBETH Where?

LENNOX Here, my good lord. What is't that moves your highness?

MACBETH Which of you have done this?

LORDS   What, my good lord?

MACBETH [*to the Ghost*] Thou canst not say I did it. Never shake

50 Thy gory locks at me.

ROSS [*rising*] Gentlemen, rise. His highness is not well.

LADY MACBETH [*rising*] Sit, worthy friends. My lord is often thus,

And hath been from his youth. Pray you, keep seat.

The fit is momentary. Upon a thought° °*In a moment*

55 He will again be well. If much you note him

You shall offend him, and extend his passion.° °*prolong his suffering*

Feed, and regard him not.

[*She speaks apart with* MACBETH]

Are you a man?

MACBETH Ay, and a bold one, that dare look on that

Which might appal the devil.

LADY MACBETH   O proper stuff!° °*mere nonsense*

60 This is the very painting of your fear;

This is the air-drawn dagger⁵ which you said

Led you to Duncan. O, these flaws° and starts, °*outbursts*

Impostors to° true fear, would well become °*compared with*

A woman's story at a winter's fire

65 Authorized by her grandam. Shame itself,

Why do you make such faces? When all's done

You look but on a stool.

MACBETH Prithee see there. Behold, look, lo—how say you?

Why, what care I? If thou canst nod, speak, too!

70 If charnel-houses and our graves must send

---

3. *The . . . welcome:* A feast is like a purchased meal if   4. All the Scottish nobility under one roof.
the guests are not assured often that they are welcome.   5. The dagger made of, or carried on, the air.

Those that we bury back, our monuments
Shall be the maws of kites.[6]   [*Exit Ghost*]
LADY MACBETH   What, quite unmanned in folly?
MACBETH   If I stand here, I saw him.
LADY MACBETH   Fie, for shame!
MACBETH   Blood hath been shed ere now, i'th' olden time,
75   Ere human statute purged the gentle weal;[7]
Ay, and since, too, murders have been performed
Too terrible for the ear. The time has been
That, when the brains were out, the man would die,
And there an end. But now they rise again
80   With twenty mortal murders° on their crowns,°   *deadly wounds / heads*
And push us from our stools. This is more strange
Than such a murder is.
LADY MACBETH [*aloud*]   My worthy lord,
Your noble friends do lack you.
MACBETH   I do forget.
Do not muse° at me, my most worthy friends.   *wonder*
85   I have a strange infirmity which is nothing
To those that know me. Come, love and health to all,
Then I'll sit down.
To an [*attendant*]   Give me some wine. Fill full.
              Enter Ghost
I drink to th' general joy of th'whole table,
And to our dear friend Banquo, whom we miss.
90   Would he were here. To all and him we thirst,°   *drink*
And all to all.[8]
LORDS   Our duties, and the pledge.°   *toast*
              [*They drink*]
MACBETH [*seeing the Ghost*]   Avaunt, and quit my sight! Let the
              earth hide thee.
Thy bones are marrowless, thy blood is cold.
Thou hast no speculation° in those eyes   *sight*
Which thou dost glare with.
95   LADY MACBETH   Think of this, good peers,
But as a thing of custom. 'Tis no other;
Only it spoils the pleasure of the time.
MACBETH   What man dare, I dare.
Approach thou like the ruggèd Russian bear,
100   The armed° rhinoceros, or th'Hyrcan[9] tiger;   *armored*
Take any shape but that,° and my firm nerves°   *(Banquo's) / sinews*
Shall never tremble. Or be alive again,
And dare me to the desert° with thy sword.   *deserted place*
If trembling I inhabit then,[1] protest me
105   The baby of a girl.[2] Hence, horrible shadow,
Unreal mock'ry, hence!   [*Exit Ghost*]
                        Why so, being gone,
I am a man again. Pray you sit still.
LADY MACBETH   You have displaced the mirth, broke the good meeting
With most admired° disorder.   *wondered at*

6. *If . . . kites:* If the dead return from their graves, noth-
ing will prevent them from being consumed by birds of
prey.
7. Before human or humane (Elizabethans did not spell
the two words differently) law cleansed the common-
wealth and made it peaceable.
8. All good wishes to everyone.
9. From Hyrcania, a region near the Caspian Sea.
1. If then I tremble; if, trembling, I stay indoors.
2. A baby girl; a girl's doll.

MACBETH   Can such things be
110   And overcome° us like a summer's cloud,   *pass over*
      Without our special wonder? You make me strange
      Even to the disposition that I owe,[3]
      When now I think you can behold such sights
      And keep the natural ruby of your cheeks
      When mine is blanched with fear.
115   ROSS   What sights, my lord?
      LADY MACBETH   I pray you, speak not. He grows worse and worse.
      Question enrages° him. At once, good night.   *Talk aggravates*
      Stand not upon the order of your going,
      But go at once.[4]
      LENNOX   Good night, and better health
      Attend his majesty.
120   LADY MACBETH   A kind good-night to all.   *Exeunt Lords*
      MACBETH   It will have blood, they say. Blood will have blood.
      Stones have been known to move, and trees to speak,
      Augurs° and understood relations[5] have   *Auguries*
      By maggot-pies and choughs and rooks[6] brought forth°   *revealed*
125   The secret'st man of blood.° What is the night?[7]   *murderer*
      LADY MACBETH   Almost at odds with morning, which is which.
      MACBETH   How sayst thou[8] that Macduff denies his person
      At our great bidding?
      LADY MACBETH   Did you send to him, sir?
      MACBETH   I hear it by the way,° but I will send.   *indirectly*
130   There's not a one of them but in his house
      I keep a servant fee'd.° I will° tomorrow,   *paid to spy / will go*
      And betimes° I will, to the weird sisters.   *early*
      More shall they speak, for now I am bent° to know   *determined*
      By the worst means the worst. For mine own good
135   All causes° shall give way. I am in blood   *other concerns*
      Stepped in so far that, should I° wade no more,°   *were I to / no farther*
      Returning were° as tedious as go° o'er.   *would be / going*
      Strange things I have in head that will to hand,
      Which must be acted ere they may be scanned.[9]
140   LADY MACBETH   You lack the season° of all natures, sleep.   *preservative*
      MACBETH   Come, we'll to sleep. My strange and self-abuse°   *self-delusion*
      Is the initiate fear that wants hard use.[1]
      We are yet but young in deed.°   *Exeunt*   *crime*

3.5

Thunder. Enter the three WITCHES *meeting* HECATE

      FIRST WITCH   Why, how now, Hecate? You look angerly.
      HECATE   Have I not reason, beldams° as you are?   *hags*
      Saucy and over-bold, how did you dare
      To trade and traffic with Macbeth
5   In riddles and affairs of death,
      And I, the mistress of your charms,
      The close° contriver of all harms,   *secret*

---

3. *You . . . owe:* You make me a stranger to my own nature, which I had supposed brave.
4. *Stand . . . once:* Do not follow the order of precedence in departing, but all go at once.
5. Formerly hidden, now revealed relationships between causes and effects.
6. Magpies, traditionally sacrificed by augurers, and birds (choughs and rooks) of the crow family.

7. What time of night is it?
8. What do you think of the fact that.
9. *ere . . . scanned:* at once, before they can be considered.
1. Is the fear of a novice who lacks toughening experience.
3.5 Location: An open place.

Was never called to bear my part
Or show the glory of our art?—

10 And, which is worse, all you have done
Hath been but for a wayward son,
Spiteful and wrathful, who, as others do,
Loves for his own ends, not for you.
But make amends now. Get you gone,

15 And at the pit of Acheron°   *river in hell*
Meet me i'th' morning. Thither he
Will come to know his destiny.
Your vessels and your spells provide,
Your charms and everything beside.

20 I am for th'air. This night I'll spend
Unto a dismal and a fatal end.[1]
Great business must be wrought ere noon.
Upon the corner of the moon
There hangs a vap'rous drop profound.[2]

25 I'll catch it ere it come to ground,
And that, distilled by magic sleights,
Shall raise such artificial sprites[3]
As by the strength of their illusion
Shall draw him on to his confusion.

30 He shall spurn fate, scorn death, and bear
His hopes 'bove wisdom, grace, and fear;
And you all know security°   *overconfidence*
Is mortals' chiefest enemy.

SPIRITS [*singing dispersedly within*]° Come away, come away.   *offstage*
35   Hecate, Hecate, come away.
HECATE   Hark, I am called! My little spirit, see,
Sits in a foggy cloud and stays for me.
                              [*The Song*]
SPIRITS [*within*]   Come away, come away,[4]
      Hecate, Hecate, come away.
40 HECATE   I come, I come, I come, I come,
      With all the speed I may,
      With all the speed I may.
      Where's Stadlin?
SPIRIT [*within*]   Here.
HECATE   Where's Puckle?
ANOTHER SPIRIT [*within*]   Here.
OTHER SPIRITS [*within*]   And Hoppo, too, and Hellwain, too,
45   We lack but you, we lack but you.
      Come away, make up the count.
HECATE   I will but 'noint,[5] and then I mount.
         [*Spirits appear above. A* SPIRIT LIKE A CAT *descends*]
SPIRITS [*above*]   There's one comes down to fetch his dues,
      A kiss, a coll,° a sip of blood,   *an embrace*
50   And why thou stay'st so long I muse,° I muse,   *wonder*
      Since the air's so sweet and good.
HECATE   O, art thou come? What news, what news?

---

1. Working toward a disastrous and fateful end.
2. Of deep or hidden significance; ready to fall.
3. Spirits produced by magic art.
4. The Folio only includes the first line of this song: the remaining lines, supplied here, come from a song with the same opening words from Thomas Middleton's play *The Witch* (c. 1613). See Textual Note.
5. Anoint myself, perhaps with an ointment to enable flying.

SPIRIT LIKE A CAT All goes still to our delight.
　　　　　　Either come, or else refuse, refuse.
55 HECATE Now I am furnished° for the flight.　　　　　　　*provided*
　　　　　[*She ascends with the* SPIRIT *and sings*]
　　　　　Now I go, now I fly,
　　　　　Malkin my sweet spirit and I.
SPIRITS *and* HECATE O what a dainty pleasure 'tis
　　　　　　To ride in the air
60　　　　　When the moon shines fair,
　　　　　And sing, and dance, and toy,° and kiss.　　　　　　*play amorously*
　　　　　Over woods, high rocks and mountains,
　　　　　Over seas and misty fountains,
　　　　　Over steeples, towers and turrets,
65　　　　　We fly by night 'mongst troops of spirits.
　　　　　No ring of bells to our ears sounds,
　　　　　No howls of wolves, no yelps of hounds.
　　　　　No, not the noise of waters-breach°　　　　　*breaking waves*
　　　　　Or cannons' throat our height can reach.
70 SPIRITS [*above*] No ring of bells to our ears sounds,
　　　　　No howls of wolves, no yelps of hounds.
　　　　　No, not the noise of waters-breach
　　　　　Or cannons' throat our height can reach.
　　　　　　[*Exeunt into the heavens the*
　　　　　　SPIRIT LIKE A CAT *and* HECATE]
FIRST WITCH Come, let's make haste. She'll soon be back again.
　　　　　　　　　　　　　　　　　　Exeunt

3.6

Enter LENNOX *and another* LORD

LENNOX My former speeches have but hit your thoughts,
　　Which can interpret farther.[1] Only I say
　　Things have been strangely borne.° The gracious Duncan　*carried on*
　　Was pitied of Macbeth: marry, he was dead;[2]
5　　And the right valiant Banquo walked too late,
　　Whom you may say, if 't please you, Fleance killed,
　　For Fleance fled: men must not walk too late.
　　Who cannot want the thought° how monstrous　　*can help thinking*
　　It was for Malcolm and for Donalbain
10　　To kill their gracious father? Damnèd fact,°　　　　　*deed*
　　How it did grieve Macbeth! Did he not straight
　　In pious° rage the two delinquents tear,　　　　　　　*loyal*
　　That were the slaves of drink, and thralls° of sleep?　　*slaves*
　　Was not that nobly done? Ay, and wisely too,
15　　For 'twould have angered any heart alive
　　To hear the men deny 't. So that I say
　　He has borne all things well, and I do think
　　That had he Duncan's sons under his key—
　　As, an 't° please heaven, he shall not—they should find　*if it*
20　　What 'twere to kill a father. So should Fleance.
　　But peace, for from broad words,[3] and 'cause he failed
　　His presence at the tyrant's feast, I hear

3.6 Location: Somewhere in Scotland.
1. *My . . . farther:* What I have said has coincided with
your thoughts. I need not say more; you can draw your
own further conclusions.

2. *The . . . dead:* Macbeth pitied Duncan after he was
dead, but not before. *of:* by.
3. As a result of his plain speaking.

Macduff lives in disgrace. Sir, can you tell
Where he bestows himself?°   *lodges*
LORD   The son of Duncan
25 From whom this tyrant holds° the due of birth°   *withholds / birthright*
    Lives in the English court, and is received
    Of the most pious Edward[4] with such grace
    That the malevolence of fortune nothing
    Takes from his high respect.[5] Thither Macduff
30 Is gone to pray the holy King upon his aid°   *in aid of Malcolm*
    To wake Northumberland and warlike Siward,
    That by the help of these—with Him above
    To ratify the work—we may again
    Give to our tables meat,° sleep to our nights,   *food*
35 Free from our feasts and banquets bloody knives,[6]
    Do faithful homage, and receive free[7] honours,
    All which we pine for now. And this report
    Hath so exasperate their king° that he   *exasperated (Macbeth)*
    Prepares for some attempt of war.
40 LENNOX   Sent he to Macduff?
    LORD   He did, and with° an absolute 'Sir, not I,'   *on receiving*
    The cloudy messenger turns me his back
    And hums, as who should say 'You'll rue the time
    That clogs me with this answer.'[8]
    LENNOX   And that well might
45 Advise him to a caution t'hold what distance
    His wisdom can provide.[9] Some holy angel
    Fly to the court of England and unfold
    His message ere he come, that a swift blessing
    May soon return to this our suffering country
    Under a hand accursed.[1]
50 LORD   I'll send my prayers with him.
                                                              Exeunt

                        4.1
    [*A Cauldron.*] *Thunder. Enter the three* WITCHES
    FIRST WITCH   Thrice the brinded° cat hath mewed.   *brindled; streaked*
    SECOND WITCH   Thrice, and once the hedge-pig° whined.   *hedgehog*
    THIRD WITCH   Harpier° cries ''Tis time, 'tis time.'   *(her familiar)*
    FIRST WITCH   Round about the cauldron go,
5   In the poisoned entrails throw.
    Toad that under cold stone
    Days and nights has thirty-one
    Sweltered venom sleeping got,[1]
    Boil thou first i'th' charmèd pot.
10 ALL   Double, double, toil and trouble,
    Fire burn, and cauldron bubble.

4. *received . . . Edward:* received by the saintly King Edward (Edward the Confessor, reigned 1042–66).
5. Does not deprive Malcolm of respect.
6. Free our feasts from bloody knives.
7. Freely given; enjoyed in freedom.
8. *He did . . . answer:* Macduff says, "Sir, not I." The scowling ("cloudy") messenger from Macbeth turns his back and hums. His rudeness seems to say ominously, "You'll rue the time that burdens ('clogs') me with this answer."
9. *And . . . provide:* Warn Macduff to keep as far from Macbeth as he can.
1. *country . . . accursed:* country suffering under an accursed hand.
4.1 Location: A cave with a boiling caldron.
1. *has . . . got:* has for thirty-one days and nights exuded poison formed during sleep.

SECOND WITCH   Fillet° of a fenny° snake,   *Slice / from the swamps*
In the cauldron boil and bake.
Eye of newt and toe of frog,
15   Wool of bat and tongue of dog,
Adder's fork° and blind-worm's sting,   *forked tongue*
Lizard's leg and owlet's wing,
For a charm of powerful trouble,
Like a hell-broth boil and bubble.
20   ALL   Double, double, toil and trouble,
Fire burn, and cauldron bubble.
THIRD WITCH   Scale of dragon, tooth of wolf,
Witches' mummy,° maw and gulf²   *mummified flesh*
Of the ravined° salt-sea shark,   *ravenous; glutted*
25   Root of hemlock digged i'th' dark,
Liver of blaspheming Jew,
Gall of goat, and slips of yew
Slivered° in the moon's eclipse,   *Cut off*
Nose of Turk, and Tartar's³ lips,
30   Finger of birth-strangled babe
Ditch-delivered by a drab,°   *whore*
Make the gruel thick and slab.°   *viscous*
Add thereto a tiger's chaudron°   *entrails*
For th'ingredience of our cauldron.
35   ALL   Double, double, toil and trouble,
Fire burn, and cauldron bubble.
SECOND WITCH   Cool it with a baboon's blood,
Then the charm is firm and good.
      Enter HECATE *and the other three* WITCHES
HECATE   O, well done! I commend your pains,
40   And everyone shall share i'th' gains.
And now about the cauldron sing
Like elves and fairies in a ring,
Enchanting all that you put in.
            Music and a song
HECATE   Black spirits and white, red spirits and grey,⁴
45   Mingle, mingle, mingle, you that mingle may.
FOURTH WITCH   Titty,⁵ Tiffin, keep it stiff in;
Firedrake, Puckey, make it lucky;
      Liard, Robin, you must bob in.
ALL   Round, around, around, about, about,
50   All ill come running in, all good keep out.
FOURTH WITCH   Here's the blood of a bat.
HECATE   Put in that, O put in that!
FIFTH WITCH   Here's leopard's bane.
HECATE   Put in a grain.
55   FOURTH WITCH   The juice of toad, the oil of adder.
FIFTH WITCH   Those will make the younker° madder.   *fashionable young man*
HECATE   Put in, there's all, and rid the stench.
A WITCH   Nay, here's three ounces of a red-haired wench.
ALL   Round, around, around, about, about,
60   All ill come running in, all good keep out.

2. Stomach and gullet.   song; see Textual Note.
3. Both thought of as cruel pagans.   5. The proper names are the names of spirits.
4. As in 3.5, the Folio only includes the first line of this

SECOND WITCH   By the pricking of my thumbs,
  Something wicked this way comes.
  [*Knock within*]
  Open, locks, whoever knocks.
  Enter MACBETH
MACBETH   How now, you secret, black, and midnight hags,
  What is't you do?
65 ALL THE WITCHES   A deed without a name.
MACBETH   I conjure you by that which you profess,°   *the black arts*
  Howe'er you come to know it, answer me.
  Though you untie the winds and let them fight
  Against the churches, though the yeasty° waves   *foamy*
70 Confound° and swallow navigation up,   *Defeat*
  Though bladed corn° be lodged° and trees blown down,   *ripe wheat / beaten down*
  Though castles topple on their warders' heads,
  Though palaces and pyramids do slope°   *bend*
  Their heads to their foundations, though the treasure
75 Of nature's germens⁶ tumble all together
  Even till destruction sicken,° answer me   *be surfeited*
  To what I ask you.
FIRST WITCH   Speak.
SECOND WITCH   Demand.
THIRD WITCH   We'll answer.
FIRST WITCH   Say if thou'dst rather hear it from our mouths
  Or from our masters.
MACBETH   Call 'em, let me see 'em.
80 FIRST WITCH   Pour in sow's blood that hath eaten
  Her nine farrow;° grease that's sweaten°   *litter of nine / sweated*
  From the murderer's gibbet° throw   *gallows*
  Into the flame.
ALL THE WITCHES   Come high or low,
  Thyself and office° deftly show.   *function*
  Thunder. FIRST APPARITION: *an armed° head*   *armored*
MACBETH   Tell me, thou unknown power—
85 FIRST WITCH   He knows thy thought.
  Hear his speech, but say thou naught.
FIRST APPARITION   Macbeth, Macbeth, Macbeth, beware Macduff,
  Beware the Thane of Fife. Dismiss me. Enough.
  [APPARITION] *descends*
MACBETH   Whate'er thou art, for thy good caution thanks.
90 Thou hast harped° my fear aright. But one word more—   *guessed*
FIRST WITCH   He will not be commanded. Here's another,
  More potent than the first.
    Thunder. SECOND APPARITION: *a bloody child*
SECOND APPARITION   Macbeth, Macbeth, Macbeth.
MACBETH   Had I three ears I'd hear thee.
95 SECOND APPARITION   Be bloody, bold, and resolute. Laugh to scorn
  The power of man, for none of woman born
  Shall harm Macbeth.
    [APPARITION] *descends*
MACBETH   Then live, Macduff—what need I fear of thee?
  But yet I'll make assurance double sure,

6. Seeds from which all nature grows. According to Renaissance theories of biology, if they were tumbled together, they would become barren or produce only monsters.

100　And take a bond of fate thou shalt not live,[7]
　　　That I may tell pale-hearted fear it lies,
　　　And sleep in spite of thunder.
　　　　　　　Thunder. THIRD APPARITION: *a child crowned, with a*
　　　　　　　tree in his hand[8]
　　　　　　　　　　　　　　　What is this
　　　That rises like the issue of a king,
　　　And wears upon his baby-brow the round
　　　And top° of sovereignty?　　　　　　　　　　　　　　　*crown*
105　ALL THE WITCHES　　　　　Listen, but speak not to't.
　　　THIRD APPARITION　　Be lion-mettled, proud, and take no care
　　　Who chafes, who frets, or where conspirers are.
　　　Macbeth shall never vanquished be until
　　　Great Birnam Wood to high Dunsinane Hill
　　　Shall come against him.
　　　　　　　[APPARITION] *descends*
110　MACBETH　　　　　　　That will never be.
　　　Who can impress° the forest, bid the tree　　　*force into service*
　　　Unfix his earth-bound root? Sweet bodements,° good!　　*omens*
　　　Rebellious dead,[9] rise never till the wood
　　　Of Birnam rise, and on's high place Macbeth
115　Shall live the lease of nature,° pay his breath　　*natural life span*
　　　To time and mortal custom.[1] Yet my heart
　　　Throbs to know one thing. Tell me, if your art
　　　Can tell so much, shall Banquo's issue ever
　　　Reign in this kingdom?
　　　ALL THE WITCHES　　　　Seek to know no more.
120　MACBETH　　I will be satisfied. Deny me this,
　　　And an eternal curse fall on you! Let me know.
　　　　　　　[*The cauldron sinks.*] *Hautboys*
　　　Why sinks that cauldron? And what noise° is this?　　*music*
　　　FIRST WITCH　　Show.
　　　SECOND WITCH　　Show.
125　THIRD WITCH　　Show.
　　　ALL THE WITCHES　　Show his eyes and grieve his heart,
　　　Come like shadows, so depart.
　　　　　　　A show of eight kings, [the] last with a glass° in his　　*mirror*
　　　　　　　hand; and BANQUO
　　　MACBETH　　Thou art too like the spirit of Banquo. Down!
　　　Thy crown does sear mine eyeballs. And thy hair,
130　Thou other gold-bound brow, is like the first.
　　　A third is like the former. Filthy hags,
　　　Why do you show me this?—A fourth? Start,° eyes!　　*Bulge out*
　　　What, will the line stretch out to th' crack of doom?
　　　Another yet? A seventh? I'll see no more—
135　And yet the eighth appears, who bears a glass
　　　Which shows me many more; and some I see
　　　That twofold balls and treble sceptres[2] carry.

---

7. By killing Macduff, Macbeth hopes to bind fate to its
promise that no man of woman born shall harm Mac-
beth.
8. Signifying Malcolm. The tree anticipates 5.5.31ff.
9. Perhaps Banquo. Some editors emend to "Rebellious
head" or "Rebellion's head," where "head" means
"army."

1. The custom of mortality; natural death.
2. James I was crowned twice, once as King of Scotland
and later as King of England. He carried one orb at each
coronation. "Treble sceptres" refers to the fact that he
held two scepters in the English coronation and one in
the Scottish, or perhaps to his claim to be King of
Britain, France, and Ireland.

Horrible sight! Now I see 'tis true,
For the blood-baltered[3] Banquo smiles upon me,
And points at them for his.[4]
                                    [*Exeunt kings and* BANQUO]
140   What, is this so?
HECATE   Ay, sir, all this is so. But why
       Stands Macbeth thus amazedly?°   *entranced*
       Come, sisters, cheer we up his sprites,°   *spirits*
       And show the best of our delights.
145   I'll charm the air to give a sound
       While you perform your antic round,°   *fantastic dance*
       That this great king may kindly say
       Our duties did his welcome pay.[5]
              Music. The WITCHES *dance, and vanish*
MACBETH   Where are they? Gone? Let this pernicious hour
150   Stand aye° accursèd in the calendar.   *ever*
       Come in, without there.
              Enter LENNOX
LENNOX   What's your grace's will?
MACBETH   Saw you the weird sisters?
LENNOX   No, my lord.
MACBETH   Came they not by you?
LENNOX   No, indeed, my lord.
MACBETH   Infected be the air whereon they ride,
155   And damned all those that trust them. I did hear
       The galloping of horse. Who was't came by?
LENNOX   'Tis two or three, my lord, that bring you word
       Macduff is fled to England.
MACBETH   Fled to England?
LENNOX   Ay, my good lord.
160 MACBETH [*aside*]   Time, thou anticipat'st° my dread exploits.   *forestall*
       The flighty purpose never is o'ertook
       Unless the deed go with it.[6] From this moment
       The very firstlings° of my heart shall be   *first notions*
       The firstlings° of my hand. And even now,   *first acts*
165   To crown my thoughts with acts, be it thought and done:
       The castle of Macduff I will surprise,
       Seize upon Fife, give to th'edge o'th' sword
       His wife, his babes, and all unfortunate souls
       That trace him in his line. No boasting like a fool;
170   This deed I'll do before this purpose cool.
       But no more sights! [*To* LENNOX] where are these gentlemen?
       come bring me where they are.   *Exeunt*

4.2
              Enter MACDUFF'S WIFE, *her* SON, *and* ROSS
LADY MACDUFF   What had he done to make him fly the land?
ROSS   You must have patience, madam.
LADY MACDUFF   He had none.

---

3. Having hair matted with blood.
4. Banquo was the legendary founder of the Stuart
dynasty.
5. Our service repaid the welcome he gave us.

6. *The flighty . . . it:* The fleeting intention is never real-
ized unless the deed is done immediately.
4.2 Location: Macduff's castle in Fife.

His flight was madness. When our actions do not,
Our fears do make us traitors.[1]

ROSS   You know not
5   Whether it was his wisdom or his fear.

LADY MACDUFF   Wisdom—to leave his wife, to leave his babes,
His mansion, and his titles° in a place   estates
From whence himself does fly? He loves us not,
He wants° the natural touch,° for the poor wren,   lacks / affection
10   The most diminutive of birds, will fight,
Her young ones in her nest, against the owl.
All is the fear and nothing is the love;
As little is the wisdom, where the flight
So runs against all reason.

ROSS   My dearest coz,°   kinswoman
15   I pray you school° yourself. But for your husband,   control
He is noble, wise, judicious, and best knows
The fits o'th' season.[2] I dare not speak much further,
But cruel are the times when we are traitors
And do not know ourselves;[3] when we hold rumour
20   From what we fear, yet know not what we fear,[4]
But float upon a wild and violent sea
Each way and none.[5] I take my leave of you;
Shall° not be long but° I'll be here again.   It shall / before
Things at the worst will cease, or else climb upward
25   To what they were before. My pretty cousin,°   (Macduff's son)
Blessing upon you!

LADY MACDUFF   Fathered he is, and yet he's fatherless.

ROSS   I am so much a fool, should I stay longer
It would be my disgrace and your discomfort.[6]
I take my leave at once.   *Exit*

30   LADY MACDUFF   Sirrah, your father's dead,
And what will you do now? How will you live?

MACDUFF'S SON   As birds do, mother.

LADY MACDUFF   What, with worms and flies?

MACDUFF'S SON   With what I get, I mean, and so do they.

LADY MACDUFF   Poor° bird, thou'dst never fear the net nor lime,[7]   Pitiful
35   The pitfall nor the gin.°   snare

MACDUFF'S SON   Why should I, mother? Poor° birds they are not   Worthless
set for.
My father is not dead, for all your saying.

LADY MACDUFF   Yes, he is dead. How wilt thou do for a father?

MACDUFF'S SON   Nay, how will you do for a husband?

40   LADY MACDUFF   Why, I can buy me twenty at any market.

MACDUFF'S SON   Then you'll buy 'em to sell again.

LADY MACDUFF   Thou speak'st with all thy wit, and yet, i'faith,
with wit enough for thee.

MACDUFF'S SON   Was my father a traitor, mother?

45   LADY MACDUFF   Ay, that he was.

---

1. *When . . . traitors:* Even when we have committed no treason, our fear of suspicion makes us behave as though we are guilty.
2. The violent convulsions of the present time; what befits the time.
3. *we . . . ourselves:* we are denounced as traitors but do not know why; we have no self-knowledge.

4. *when . . . fear:* when we believe rumors inspired by our fears, but those fears are themselves vague.
5. In every direction, and so finally in none.
6. I would disgrace myself and embarrass you by weeping (or perhaps by lingering).
7. Birdlime, a sticky substance smeared on twigs to catch small birds.

MACDUFF'S SON　What is a traitor?

LADY MACDUFF　Why, one that swears and lies.[8]

MACDUFF'S SON　And be all traitors that do so?

50 LADY MACDUFF　Everyone that does so is a traitor, and must be hanged.

MACDUFF'S SON　And must they all be hanged that swear° and lie?　　　　　　　　　　　　　　　　　　　*speak profanely*

LADY MACDUFF　Every one.

MACDUFF'S SON　Who must hang them?

55 LADY MACDUFF　Why, the honest men.

MACDUFF'S SON　Then the liars and swearers are fools, for there are liars and swearers enough to beat the honest men and hang up them.

LADY MACDUFF　Now God help thee, poor monkey! But how wilt
60 thou do for a father?

MACDUFF'S SON　If he were dead you'd weep for him. If you would not, it were a good sign that I should quickly have a new father.

LADY MACDUFF　Poor prattler, how thou talk'st!

Enter a MESSENGER

65 MESSENGER　Bless you, fair dame. I am not to you known,
Though in your state of honour I am perfect.[9]
I doubt° some danger does approach you nearly.　　　　　　　*fear*
If you will take a homely° man's advice,　　　　　　　　　　*plain*
Be not found here. Hence with your little ones!
70 To fright you thus methinks I am too savage,
To do worse to you were fell cruelty,[1]
Which is too nigh your person.[2] Heaven preserve you.
I dare abide no longer.　　　　　　　　　　*Exit* MESSENGER

LADY MACDUFF　　　　　　　　Whither should I fly?
I have done no harm. But I remember now
75 I am in this earthly world, where to do harm
Is often laudable, to do good sometime
Accounted dangerous folly. Why then, alas,
Do I put up that womanly defence
To say I have done no harm?

Enter MURDERERS

　　　　　　　　　　　　What are these faces?

80 A MURDERER　Where is your husband?

LADY MACDUFF　I hope in no place so unsanctified
Where such as thou mayst find him.

A MURDERER　　　　　　　　　　　He's a traitor.

MACDUFF'S SON　Thou liest, thou shag-haired villain.

A MURDERER [*stabbing him*]　　　　　　What, you egg!
Young fry° of treachery!　　　　　　　　　　　　　　　*spawn*

MACDUFF'S SON　　　　　　He has killed me, mother.
85 Run away, I pray you.

[*He dies.*] *Exit* [MACDUFF'S WIFE] *crying 'Murder!'*
[*followed by* MURDERERS *with the Son's body*]

---

8. Takes an oath and breaks it.
9. Though I know perfectly well your high rank (an apology for bursting in).
1. *To fright . . . cruelty*: Even to frighten you by speaking

of such danger is savage; actually to harm you would be brutal ("fell") cruelty.
2. Such cruelty is already too near you.

4.3

Enter MALCOLM *and* MACDUFF

MALCOLM Let us seek out some desolate shade, and there
Weep our sad bosoms empty.

MACDUFF   Let us rather
 Hold fast the mortal° sword, and like good men   *deadly*
 Bestride our downfall birthdom.[1] Each new morn
5 New widows howl, new orphans cry, new sorrows
 Strike heaven on the face that° it resounds   *so that*
 As if it felt with Scotland and yelled out
 Like syllable of dolour.°   *A similar cry of pain*

MALCOLM   What I believe I'll wail,
 What know believe; and what I can redress,
10 As I shall find the time to friend,° I will.   *favorable*
 What you have spoke it may be so, perchance.
 This tyrant, whose sole° name blisters our tongues,   *mere*
 Was once thought honest. You have loved him well.
 He hath not touched° you yet. I am young, but something *injured*
15 You may discern of him through me:[2] and wisdom° *it's prudent*
 To offer up a weak poor innocent lamb
 T'appease an angry god.

MACDUFF I am not treacherous.

MALCOLM But Macbeth is.
20 A good and virtuous nature may recoil
 In an imperial charge.[3] But I shall crave your pardon.
 That which you are my thoughts cannot transpose.° *transform*
 Angels are bright still, though the brightest° fell.   *(Lucifer)*
 Though all things foul would wear the brows of grace,
 Yet grace must still look so.[4]

25 MACDUFF   I have lost my hopes.[5]

MALCOLM Perchance even there where I did find my doubts.[6]
 Why in that rawness° left you wife and child, *unprotected condition*
 Those precious motives,° those strong knots of love, *inducements to devotion*
 Without leave-taking? I pray you,
30 Let not my jealousies° be your dishonours,   *suspicions*
 But mine own safeties.° You may be rightly just, *safeguards*
 Whatever I shall think.

MACDUFF   Bleed, bleed, poor country!
 Great tyranny, lay thou thy basis° sure,   *foundation*
 For goodness dare not check thee. Wear thou thy wrongs;° *wrongful gains*
35 The title is affeered.° Fare thee well, lord.   *confirmed*
 I would not be the villain that thou think'st
 For the whole space that's in the tyrant's grasp,
 And the rich east to boot.°   *as well*

MALCOLM   Be not offended.
 I speak not as in absolute fear° of you.   *complete distrust*
40 I think our country sinks beneath the yoke.
 It weeps, it bleeds, and each new day a gash
 Is added to her wounds. I think withal°   *nonetheless*

4.3 Location: England, before King Edward's palace.
1. Stand in defense over our downtrodden native land.
2. *I . . . me:* I am inexperienced, but you might gain favor with Macbeth by betraying me. Many editions emend "discern" to "deserve."
3. *recoil . . . charge:* give way to a royal command.

4. *Though . . . so:* Though everything evil disguises itself as virtue, virtue still looks like itself.
5. Hopes of Malcolm's help in a campaign against Macbeth.
6. Doubts of Macduff's loyalty, because he has left his wife and children.

There would be hands uplifted in my right,
And here from gracious England° have I offer   *the King of England*
45   Of goodly thousands. But for all this,
When I shall tread upon the tyrant's head,
Or wear it on my sword, yet my poor country
Shall have more vices than it had before,
More suffer, and more sundry° ways, than ever,   *in more various*
By him that shall succeed.
50   MACDUFF   What° should he be?   *Who*
MALCOLM   It is myself I mean, in whom I know
All the particulars° of vice so grafted   *varieties*
That when they shall be opened° black Macbeth   *disclosed*
Will seem as pure as snow, and the poor state
55   Esteem him as a lamb, being compared
With my confineless° harms.   *infinite*
MACDUFF   Not in the legions
Of horrid hell can come a devil more damned
In evils to top Macbeth.
MALCOLM   I grant him bloody,
Luxurious,° avaricious, false, deceitful,   *Lecherous*
60   Sudden,° malicious, smacking of every sin   *Violent*
That has a name. But there's no bottom, none,
In my voluptuousness. Your wives, your daughters,
Your matrons, and your maids could not fill up
The cistern of my lust, and my desire
65   All continent° impediments would o'erbear   *restraining; chaste*
That did oppose my will. Better Macbeth
Than such an one to reign.
MACDUFF   Boundless intemperance
In nature° is a tyranny. It hath been   *human nature*
Th'untimely emptying of the happy throne,
70   And fall of many kings. But fear not yet°   *nevertheless*
To take upon you what is yours. You may
Convey° your pleasures in a spacious plenty   *Manage secretly*
And yet seem cold.° The time° you may so hoodwink.°   *indifferent / age / deceive*
We have willing dames enough. There cannot be
75   That vulture in you to devour so many
As will to greatness dedicate themselves,
Finding it so inclined.
MALCOLM   With this there grows
In my most ill-composed affection° such   *character*
A staunchless° avarice that were I king   *An insatiable*
80   I should cut off the nobles for their lands,
Desire his jewels and this other's house,
And my more having would be as a sauce
To make me hunger more, that I should forge
Quarrels unjust against the good and loyal,
Destroying them for wealth.
85   MACDUFF   This avarice
Sticks deeper, grows with more pernicious root
Than summer-seeming⁷ lust, and it hath been
The sword° of our slain kings. Yet do not fear.   *undoing*
Scotland hath foisons° to fill up your will   *plenty*

---

7. Appropriate to youth ("summer") but passing with age, unlike avarice; summerlike.

90   Of your mere own.[8] All these are portable,°   *bearable*
     With other graces weighed.
     MALCOLM   But I have none. The king-becoming graces,
     As justice, verity, temp'rance, stableness,
     Bounty, perseverance, mercy, lowliness,°   *humility*
95   Devotion, patience, courage, fortitude,
     I have no relish° of them, but abound   *trace*
     In the division° of each several° crime,   *variations / separate*
     Acting it many ways. Nay, had I power I should
     Pour the sweet milk of concord into hell,
100 Uproar the universal peace, confound
     All unity on earth.
     MACDUFF   O Scotland, Scotland!
     MALCOLM   If such a one be fit to govern, speak.
     I am as I have spoken.
     MACDUFF   Fit to govern?
     No, not to live. O nation miserable,
105 With an untitled° tyrant bloody-sceptered,   *a usurping*
     When shalt thou see thy wholesome days again,
     Since that the truest issue of thy throne
     By his own interdiction° stands accursed   *declaration of unfitness*
     And does blaspheme his breed?° Thy royal father   *disgrace his heritage*
110 Was a most sainted king. The Queen that bore thee,
     Oft'ner upon her knees than on her feet,
     Died[9] every day she lived. Fare thee well.
     These evils thou repeat'st upon thyself
     Hath banished me from Scotland. O, my breast—
     Thy hope ends here!
115 MALCOLM   Macduff, this noble passion,
     Child of integrity, hath from my soul
     Wiped the black scruples,° reconciled my thoughts   *dark suspicions*
     To thy good truth and honour. Devilish Macbeth
     By many of these trains° hath sought to win me   *stratagems*
120 Into his power, and modest wisdom° plucks me   *prudent moderation*
     From over-credulous haste; but God above
     Deal between thee and me, for even now
     I put myself to thy direction and
     Unspeak° mine own detraction, here abjure   *Retract*
125 The taints and blames I laid upon myself
     For° strangers to my nature. I am yet   *As*
     Unknown to woman, never was forsworn,
     Scarcely have coveted what was mine own,
     At no time broke my faith, would not betray
130 The devil to his fellow, and delight
     No less in truth than life. My first false-speaking
     Was this upon myself. What I am truly
     Is thine and my poor country's to command,
     Whither indeed, before thy here-approach,
135 Old Siward with ten thousand warlike men,
     Already at a point,° was setting forth.   *prepared*
     Now we'll together; and the chance of goodness

---

8. *Scotland . . . own:* Scotland is bountiful enough to satisfy your greed with your own royal property alone.

9. Dead to the world. ("By your rejoicing which I have in Christ Jesus our Lord, I die daily," 1 Corinthians 15:31).

Be like our warranted quarrel!¹—Why are you silent?

MACDUFF Such welcome and unwelcome things at once
140 'Tis hard to reconcile.

Enter a DOCTOR

MALCOLM Well, more anon. [*To the* DOCTOR] Comes the King
forth, I pray you?

DOCTOR Ay, sir. There are a crew of wretched souls
That stay° his cure. Their malady convinces   °await
The great essay of art,² but at his touch,
145 Such sanctity hath Heaven given his hand,
They presently amend.°   °heal

MALCOLM   I thank you, doctor. *Exit* [DOCTOR]

MACDUFF What's the disease he means?

MALCOLM   'Tis called the evil³—
A most miraculous work in this good King,
Which often since my here-remain in England
150 I have seen him do. How he solicits° heaven   °moves by entreaty
Himself best knows, but strangely visited° people,   °afflicted
All swoll'n and ulcerous, pitiful to the eye,
The mere° despair of surgery, he cures,   °utter
Hanging a golden stamp° about their necks,   °coin
155 Put on with holy prayers; and 'tis spoken,
To the succeeding royalty he leaves
The healing benediction. With this strange virtue°   °power
He hath a heavenly gift of prophecy,
And sundry blessings hang about his throne
That speak him full of grace.°   °divine grace

Enter ROSS

160 MACDUFF   See who comes here.

MALCOLM My countryman, but yet I know° him not.   °recognize

MACDUFF My ever gentle cousin, welcome hither.

MALCOLM I know him now. Good God betimes° remove   °quickly
The means that makes us strangers!

ROSS   Sir, amen.

MACDUFF Stands Scotland where it did?

165 ROSS   Alas, poor country,
Almost afraid to know itself. It cannot
Be called our mother, but our grave, where nothing
But who knows nothing is once seen to smile;⁴
Where sighs and groans and shrieks that rend the air
170 Are made, not marked;° where violent sorrow seems   °noticed
A modern ecstasy.° The dead man's knell   °commonplace emotion
Is there scarce asked for who,⁵ and good men's lives
Expire before the flowers in their caps,
Dying or ere° they sicken.   °before

MACDUFF   O relation°   °report
Too nice° and yet too true!   °detailed

175 MALCOLM   What's the newest grief?

ROSS That of an hour's age doth hiss the speaker;⁶
Each minute teems° a new one.   °yields

---

1. *the . . . quarrel:* may the chance of success be equal to
the justice of our cause.
2. *convinces . . . art:* defeats the best efforts of medical
skill.
3. "The king's evil," scrofula, thought to be cured by the
royal touch.
4. No one smiles except he who knows nothing.
5. Scarcely anyone asks for whom it is rung.
6. Cause the speaker to be hissed for telling old news.

MACDUFF　　　　　　　　　　　　　How does my wife?
ROSS　Why, well.
MACDUFF　　　　　　　　And all my children?
ROSS　　　　　　　　　　　　　　　Well, too.
MACDUFF　The tyrant has not battered at their peace?
180　ROSS　No, they were well at peace when I did leave 'em.
MACDUFF　Be not a niggard of your speech. How goes't?
ROSS　When I came hither to transport the tidings
　　Which I have heavily° borne, there ran a rumour　　　　　　　　　*gravely*
　　Of many worthy fellows that were out,°　　　　　　　　　　　　*in arms*
185　Which was to my belief witnessed the rather°　　　　　*made more credible*
　　For that I saw the tyrant's power° afoot.　　　　　　　　　　　*army*
　　Now is the time of° help. [*To* MALCOLM] Your eye in scotland　　*moment for*
　　Would create soldiers, make our women fight
　　To doff° their dire distresses.　　　　　　　　　　　　　　*remove*
MALCOLM　　　　　　　　　　Be't their comfort
190　We are coming thither. Gracious England hath
　　Lent us good Siward and ten thousand men;
　　An older and a better soldier none°　　　　　　　　　　　*there is none*
　　That Christendom gives out.°　　　　　　　　　*proclaims; provides*
ROSS　　　　　　　　　　Would I could answer
　　This comfort with the like. But I have words
195　That would be howled out in the desert air
　　Where hearing should not latch° them.　　　　　　　　　　*catch*
MACDUFF　　　　　　　　　　What concern they—
　　The general cause, or is it a fee-grief°　　　　　　　　*private woe*
　　Due to° some single breast?　　　　　　　　　　　*Owned by*
ROSS　　　　　　　　　No mind that's honest
　　But in it shares some woe, though the main part
　　Pertains to you alone.
200　MACDUFF　　　　　　　　If it be mine,
　　Keep it not from me; quickly let me have it.
ROSS　Let not your ears despise my tongue for ever,
　　Which shall possess them with the heaviest sound
　　That ever yet they heard.
MACDUFF　　　　　　　　H'm, I guess at it.
205　ROSS　Your castle is surprised, your wife and babes
　　Savagely slaughtered. To relate the manner
　　Were on the quarry of these murdered deer
　　To add the death of you.⁷
MALCOLM　　　　　　　　Merciful heaven!
　　[*To* MACDUFF] What, man, ne'er pull your hat upon your
　　　　brows.°　　　　　　　　　　　　　　　*conceal your grief*
210　Give sorrow words. The grief that does not speak
　　Whispers the o'erfraught° heart and bids it break.　　　*overburdened*
MACDUFF　My children too?
ROSS　　　　　　　　Wife, children, servants, all
　　That could be found.
MACDUFF　　　　　　　　And I must be° from thence!　　　*had to be*
　　My wife killed too?
ROSS　　　　　　　　I have said.
MALCOLM　　　　　　　　Be comforted.

---

7. To tell how they were murdered would be to add your death to the heap of slaughtered game ("quarry").

215   Let's make us medicines of our great revenge
    To cure this deadly grief.
  MACDUFF   He has no children. All my pretty ones?
    Did you say all? O hell-kite! All?
    What, all my pretty chickens and their dam
220   At one fell swoop?
  MALCOLM   Dispute° it like a man.   *Fight*
  MACDUFF   I shall do so,
    But I must also feel it as a man.
    I cannot but remember such things were
225   That were most precious to me. Did heaven look on
    And would not take their part? Sinful Macduff,
    They were all struck for° thee. Naught° that I am,   *on account of / Wicked*
    Not for their own demerits but for mine
    Fell slaughter on their souls. Heaven rest them now.
230 MALCOLM   Be this the whetstone of your sword. Let grief
    Convert° to anger: blunt not the heart, enrage it.   *Be changed*
  MACDUFF   O, I could play the woman with mine eyes
    And braggart with my tongue! But gentle heavens
    Cut short all intermission.° Front to front°   *delay / Face-to-face*
235   Bring thou this fiend of Scotland and myself.
    Within my sword's length set him. If he scape,
    Heaven forgive him too.
  MALCOLM   This tune goes manly.
    Come, go we to the King. Our power° is ready;   *army*
    Our lack is nothing but our leave.[8] Macbeth
240   Is ripe for shaking, and the powers above
    Put on their instruments.[9] Receive what cheer you may:
    The night is long that never finds the day.   *Exeunt*

5.1

Enter a DOCTOR *of Physic° and a Waiting-*   *Physician*
GENTLEWOMAN
  DOCTOR   I have two nights watched with you, but can perceive
  no truth in your report. When was it she last walked?
  GENTLEWOMAN   Since his majesty went into the field° I have   *battlefield*
  seen her rise from her bed, throw her nightgown upon her,
5   unlock her closet,° take forth paper, fold it, write upon't, read   *chest*
  it, afterwards seal it, and again return to bed, yet all this while
  in a most fast sleep.
  DOCTOR   A great perturbation in nature, to receive at once the
  benefit of sleep and do the effects of watching°. In this slum-   *act as if awake*
10   bery agitation° besides her walking and other actual° perfor-   *movement / active*
  mances, what at any time have you heard her say?
  GENTLEWOMAN   That, sir, which I will not report after her.
  DOCTOR   You may to me; and 'tis most meet° you should.   *proper*
  GENTLEWOMAN   Neither to you nor anyone, having no witness to
15   confirm my speech.
             Enter LADY [MACBETH] *with a taper*
  Lo you, here she comes. This is her very guise,° and, upon my   *exact habit*
  life, fast asleep. Observe her. Stand close.°   *concealed*

---

8. We have only to take leave of the King.   **5.1** Location: Macbeth's castle in Dunsinane.
9. Arm themselves; set us to work as their agents.

DOCTOR   How came she by that light?

GENTLEWOMAN   Why, it stood by her. She has light by her con-
20   tinually. 'Tis her command.

DOCTOR   You see her eyes are open.

GENTLEWOMAN   Ay, but their sense are shut.

DOCTOR   What is it she does now? Look how she rubs her hands.

GENTLEWOMAN   It is an accustomed action with her, to seem
25   thus washing her hands. I have known her continue in this a
quarter of an hour.

LADY MACBETH   Yet here's a spot.

DOCTOR   Hark, she speaks. I will set down what comes from her
to satisfy° my remembrance the more strongly.   *support*

30   LADY MACBETH   Out, damned spot; out, I say. One, two,—why,
then 'tis time to do't. Hell is murky. Fie, my lord, fie, a soldier
and afeard? What need we fear who knows it when none can
call our power to account? Yet who would have thought the
old man to have had so much blood in him?

35   DOCTOR   Do you mark that?

LADY MACBETH   The Thane of Fife had a wife. Where is she
now? What, will these hands ne'er be clean? No more o' that,
my lord, no more o' that. You mar all with this starting.°   *startled movement*

DOCTOR   Go to, go to.° You have known what you should not.   *(expression of reproof)*

40   GENTLEWOMAN   She has spoke what she should not, I am sure of
that. Heaven knows what she has known.

LADY MACBETH   Here's the smell of the blood still. All the per-
fumes of Arabia will not sweeten this little hand. O, O, O!

DOCTOR   What a sigh is there! The heart is sorely charged.°   *burdened*

45   GENTLEWOMAN   I would not have such a heart in my bosom for
the dignity° of the whole body.   *worth*

DOCTOR   Well, well, well.

GENTLEWOMAN   Pray God it be, sir.

DOCTOR   This disease is beyond my practice.° Yet I have known   *skill*
50   those which have walked in their sleep who have died holily in
their beds.

LADY MACBETH   Wash your hands, put on your nightgown, look
not so pale. I tell you yet again, Banquo's buried. He cannot
come out on's° grave.   *of his*

55   DOCTOR   Even so?

LADY MACBETH   To bed, to bed. There's knocking at the gate.
Come, come, come, come, give me your hand. What's done
cannot be undone. To bed, to bed, to bed.   *Exit*

DOCTOR   Will she go now to bed?

60   GENTLEWOMAN   Directly.

DOCTOR   Foul whisp'rings are abroad. Unnatural deeds
Do breed unnatural troubles; infected minds
To their deaf pillows will discharge their secrets.
More needs she the divine° than the physician.   *priest*
65   God, God forgive us all! Look after her.
Remove from her the means of all annoyance,°   *self-injury*
And still keep eyes upon her. So, good night.
My mind she has mated,° and amazed my sight.   *bewildered*
I think, but dare not speak.

GENTLEWOMAN   Good night, good doctor. *Exeunt*

5.2

Enter MENTEITH, CAITHNESS, ANGUS, LENNOX, *soldiers,*
[*with a drummer*] *and colours*

MENTEITH   The English power is near, led on by Malcolm,
His uncle Siward, and the good Macduff.
Revenges burn in them, for their dear causes
Would to the bleeding° and the grim alarm°   *bloody / call to battle*
Excite° the mortified° man.   *Rouse / insensible; dead*

5   ANGUS   Near Birnam Wood
Shall we well° meet them. That way are they coming.   *doubtless*

CAITHNESS   Who knows if Donalbain be with his brother?

LENNOX   For certain, sir, he is not. I have a file°   *roster*
Of all the gentry. There is Siward's son,

10   And many unrough° youths that even now   *beardless*
Protest their first of manhood.[1]

MENTEITH   What does the tyrant?

CAITHNESS   Great Dunsinane he strongly fortifies.
Some say he's mad, others that lesser hate him
Do call it valiant fury; but for certain

15   He cannot buckle his distempered° cause   *disease-swollen*
Within the belt of rule.°   *restraint*

ANGUS   Now does he feel
His secret murders sticking on his hands.
Now minutely° revolts upbraid his faith-breach.   *every minute*
Those he commands move only in command,°   *under constraint*

20   Nothing in love. Now does he feel his title
Hang loose about him, like a giant's robe
Upon a dwarfish thief.

MENTEITH   Who then shall blame
His pestered° senses to recoil and start   *tormented*
When all that is within him does condemn
Itself for being there?

25   CAITHNESS   Well, march we on
To give obedience where 'tis truly owed.
Meet we the medicine° of the sickly weal,°   *(Malcolm) / state*
And with him pour we in our country's purge,
Each drop of us.

LENNOX   Or so much as it needs

30   To dew° the sovereign° flower and drown the weeds.   *bedew / royal; curative*
Make we our march towards Birnam.   *Exeunt, marching*

5.3

Enter MACBETH, [*the*] DOCTOR [*of Physic*], *and attendants*

MACBETH   Bring me no more reports. Let them fly all.°   *Let all thanes desert*
Till Birnam Wood remove to Dunsinane
I cannot taint° with fear. What's the boy Malcolm?   *be infected*
Was he not born of woman? The spirits that know

5   All mortal consequences° have pronounced me thus: *human destinies*
'Fear not, Macbeth. No man that's born of woman
Shall e'er have power upon thee.' Then fly, false thanes,
And mingle with the English epicures.[1]
The mind I sway° by and the heart I bear   *rule myself*

5.2 Location: The country near Dunsinane.   5.3 Location: Macbeth's castle in Dunsinane.
1. Declare for the first time that they are men.   1. Lovers of easy, luxurious living.

10   Shall never sag with doubt nor shake with fear.
                    Enter SERVANT
     The devil damn thee black, thou cream-faced loon!°   *rogue*
     Where gott'st thou that goose look?
SERVANT   There is ten thousand—
MACBETH   Geese, villain?
SERVANT   Soldiers, sir.
15 MACBETH   Go prick thy face and over-red thy fear,²
     Thou lily-livered³ boy. What soldiers, patch?°   *fool*
     Death of° thy soul, those linen cheeks of thine   *on*
     Are counsellors to fear.° What soldiers, whey-face?   *Teach others to fear*
SERVANT   The English force, so please you.
MACBETH   Take thy face hence.   [*Exit* SERVANT]
20   Seyton!—I am sick at heart
     When I behold—Seyton, I say!—This push°   *crisis*
     Will cheer⁴ me ever or disseat° me now.   *dethrone*
     I have lived long enough. My way of life
     Is fall'n into the sere,° the yellow leaf,   *withered state*
25   And that which should accompany old age,
     As° honour, love, obedience, troops of friends,   *Such as*
     I must not look to have, but in their stead
     Curses, not loud but deep, mouth-honour,° breath   *lip service*
     Which the poor heart would fain deny and dare not.
30   Seyton!
                    Enter SEYTON
SEYTON   What's your gracious pleasure?
MACBETH   What news more?
SEYTON   All is confirmed, my lord, which was reported.
MACBETH   I'll fight till from my bones my flesh be hacked.
     Give me my armour.
35 SEYTON   'Tis not needed yet.
MACBETH   I'll put it on.
     Send out more horses. Skirr° the country round.   *Scour*
     Hang those that talk of fear. Give me mine armour.
     How does your patient, doctor?
DOCTOR   Not so sick, my lord,
40   As she is troubled with thick-coming fancies
     That keep her from her rest.
MACBETH   Cure her of that.
     Canst thou not minister to a mind diseased,
     Pluck from the memory a rooted sorrow,
     Raze out the written troubles of⁵ the brain,
45   And with some sweet oblivious° antidote   *causing forgetfulness*
     Cleanse the fraught bosom of that perilous stuff
     Which weighs upon the heart?
DOCTOR   Therein the patient
     Must minister to himself.
MACBETH   Throw physic° to the dogs; I'll none of it.   *medicine*
50   [*To an attendant*] Come, put mine armour on. Give me my staff.°   *lance*
     Seyton, send out. Doctor, the thanes fly from me.

---

2. Redden your fearful pallor.
3. Lacking blood in your liver (thought to be the seat of courage); cowardly.
4. Comfort; enthrone or establish (punning on "cheer/ chair").
5. Erase the troubles engraved in.

[*To an attendant*] Come, sir, dispatch.°—If thou couldst, doctor, cast   *hurry*
The water⁶ of my land, find her disease,
And purge it to a sound and pristine health,

55   I would applaud thee to the very echo,
That should applaud again.   [*To an attendant*] Pull't off, I say.⁷
[*To the* DOCTOR] what rhubarb, cyme,° or what purgative drug   *senna (medicinal plant)*
Would scour° these English hence? Hear'st thou of them?   *purge*

DOCTOR   Ay, my good lord. Your royal preparation
Makes us hear something.

60   MACBETH [*to an attendant*]   Bring it⁸ after me.
I will not be afraid of death and bane°   *destruction*
Till Birnam Forest come to Dunsinane.

DOCTOR [*aside*]   Were I from Dunsinane away and clear,
Profit again should hardly draw me here.⁹   *Exeunt*

5.4

Enter MALCOLM, SIWARD, MACDUFF, SIWARD'S SON, MEN-
TEITH, CAITHNESS, ANGUS, *and* SOLDIERS, *marching,*
[*with a drummer*] *and colours*

MALCOLM   Cousins, I hope the days are near at hand
That chambers° will be safe.   *bedrooms*

MENTEITH   We doubt it nothing.°   *not at all*

SIWARD   What wood is this before us?

MENTEITH   The wood of Birnam.

MALCOLM   Let every soldier hew him down a bough

5   And bear't before him. Thereby shall we shadow°   *conceal*
The numbers of our host, and make discovery°   *reconnaissance*
Err in report of us.

A SOLDIER   It shall be done.

SIWARD   We learn no other but the confident tyrant
Keeps still in Dunsinane, and will endure
Our setting down before°'t.   *laying siege to*

10   MALCOLM   'Tis his main hope,
For where there is advantage° to be gone,   *opportunity*
Both more and less° have given him the revolt,   *great and lowly*
And none serve with him but constrainèd things,
Whose hearts are absent too.

MACDUFF   Let our just censures

15   Attend the true event,¹ and put we on
Industrious soldiership.

SIWARD   The time approaches
That will with due decision make us know
What we shall say we have, and what we owe.
Thoughts speculative their unsure hopes relate,

20   But certain issue strokes must arbitrate;²
Towards which, advance the war.   *Exeunt, marching*

---

6. *cast / The water:* analyze the urine as a method of
diagnosis.
7. A piece of armor is not properly fitted; Macbeth
orders the attendant to take it off.
8. The armor not yet on Macbeth.
9. No large fees could lure me back.

5.4 Location: The country near Birnam Wood.
1. *Let . . . event:* Let our judgments await the actual
outcome.
2. *Thoughts . . . arbitrate:* Speculation produces hopes
and unconfirmed optimism, but the issue will only be
decided by action.

5.5

Enter MACBETH, SEYTON, *and soldiers, with* [*a drummer*]
and colours

MACBETH Hang out our banners on the outward walls.
The cry is still 'They come.' Our castle's strength
Will laugh a siege to scorn. Here let them lie
Till famine and the ague eat them up.
5 Were they not forced° with those that should be ours   *reinforced*
We might have met them dareful,° beard to beard,   *boldly*
And beat them backward home.
      A cry within of women
                          What is that noise?
SEYTON It is the cry of women, my good lord.   [*Exit*]
MACBETH I have almost forgot the taste of fears.
10 The time has been my senses would have cooled°   *been chilled with terror*
To hear a night-shriek, and my fell of hair°   *hair on my skin*
Would at a dismal treatise° rouse and stir   *story*
As life were in't. I have supped full with horrors.
Direness, familiar to my slaughterous thoughts,
Cannot once start° me.   *startle*
      [*Enter* SEYTON]
15   Wherefore was that cry?
SEYTON The Queen, my lord, is dead.
MACBETH   She should have died hereafter.[1]
There would have been a time for such a word.
Tomorrow, and tomorrow, and tomorrow
Creeps in this petty pace from day to day
20 To the last syllable of recorded time,
And all our yesterdays have lighted fools
The way to dusty death. Out, out, brief candle.
Life's but a walking shadow, a poor player
That struts and frets his hour upon the stage,
25 And then is heard no more. It is a tale
Told by an idiot, full of sound and fury,
Signifying nothing.
      Enter a MESSENGER
                Thou com'st to use
Thy tongue: thy story quickly.
MESSENGER   Gracious my lord,
I should report that which I say I saw,
But know not how to do't.
30 MACBETH   Well, say, sir.
MESSENGER As I did stand my watch upon the hill
I looked toward Birnam, and anon methought
The wood began to move.
MACBETH   Liar and slave!
MESSENGER Let me endure your wrath if't be not so.
35 Within this three mile may you see it coming.
I say, a moving grove.
MACBETH   If thou speak'st false
Upon the next tree shall thou hang alive
Till famine cling° thee. If thy speech be sooth,°   *wither / truth*

5.5 Location: Macbeth's castle.
1. She would certainly have died someday; she should have died at another, more peaceful time.

I care not if thou dost for me as much.
40 I pall° in resolution, and begin   *fail*
To doubt th'equivocation of the fiend,
That lies like truth. 'Fear not till Birnam Wood
Do come to Dunsinane'—and now a wood
Comes toward Dunsinane. Arm, arm, and out.
45 If this which he avouches does appear
There is nor flying hence nor tarrying here.
I 'gin to be aweary of the sun,
And wish th'estate° o'th' world were now undone.   *ordered structure*
Ring the alarum bell. [*Alarums*] Blow wind, come wrack,°   *ruin*
50 At least we'll die with harness° on our back.   *Exeunt*   *armor*

5.6

Enter MALCOLM, SIWARD, MACDUFF, *and their army with*
boughs, [with a drummer] and colours
MALCOLM   Now near enough. Your leafy screens throw down,
And show° like those you are.   *appear*
   [*They throw down the boughs*]
                              You, worthy uncle,
Shall with my cousin, your right noble son,
Lead our first battle.° Worthy Macduff and we   *battalion*
5 Shall take upon's what else remains to do
According to our order.°   *battle plan*
SIWARD   Fare you well.
Do we but find the tyrant's power° tonight,   *army*
Let us be beaten if we cannot fight.
MACDUFF   Make all our trumpets speak, give them all breath,
10 Those clamorous harbingers of blood and death.
                              Exeunt. Alarums continued

5.7

Enter MACBETH
MACBETH   They have tied me to a stake. I cannot fly,
But bear-like I must fight the course.[1] What's he
That was not born of woman? Such a one
Am I to fear, or none.
   Enter YOUNG SIWARD
5 YOUNG SIWARD   What is thy name?
MACBETH   Thou'lt be afraid to hear it.
YOUNG SIWARD   No, though thou call'st thyself a hotter name
Than any is in hell.
MACBETH   My name's Macbeth.
YOUNG SIWARD   The devil himself could not pronounce a title
More hateful to mine ear.
10 MACBETH   No, nor more fearful.
YOUNG SIWARD   Thou liest, abhorrèd tyrant. With my sword
I'll prove the lie thou speak'st.
   [*They*] *fight, and* YOUNG SIWARD [*is*] *slain*
MACBETH   Thou wast born of woman,

5.6 Location: As before.
5.7 Location: As before.
1. Referring to the practice of bearbaiting, in which a

bear was tied to a stake and set upon by dogs. *course:*
round of bearbaiting.

But swords I smile at, weapons laugh to scorn,
Brandished by man that's of a woman born.

Exit [with the body]

5.8

Alarums. Enter MACDUFF

MACDUFF   That way the noise is. Tyrant, show thy face!
If thou beest slain and with° no stroke of mine,   *by*
My wife and children's ghosts will haunt me still.°   *always*
I cannot strike at wretched kerns,° whose arms   *Irish foot soldiers*
5 Are hired to bear their staves.° Either thou, Macbeth,   *spears*
Or else my sword with an unbattered edge
I sheathe again undeeded.¹ There thou shouldst be;
By this great clatter one of greatest note
Seems bruited.° Let me find him, fortune,   *announced*
10 And more I beg not.   *Exit. Alarums*

5.9

Enter MALCOLM *and* SIWARD

SIWARD   This way, my lord. The castle's gently rendered.°   *surrendered*
The tyrant's people on both sides do fight.
The noble thanes do bravely in the war.
The day almost itself professes yours,
And little is to do.
5 MALCOLM   We have met with foes
That strike beside us.¹
SIWARD   Enter, sir, the castle.   *Exeunt. Alarum*

5.10

Enter MACBETH

MACBETH   Why should I play the Roman fool,° and die   *the suicide*
On mine own sword? Whiles I see lives, the gashes
Do better upon them.

Enter MACDUFF

MACDUFF   Turn, hell-hound, turn.
MACBETH   Of all men else I have avoided thee.
5 But get thee back. My soul is too much charged
With blood of thine already.
MACDUFF   I have no words;
My voice is in my sword, thou bloodier villain
Than terms can give thee out.°   *words can describe*

[They] fight; alarum

MACBETH   Thou losest labour.°   *waste effort*
As easy mayst thou the intrenchant° air   *incapable of being cut*
10 With thy keen sword impress° as make me bleed.   *mark*
Let fall thy blade on vulnerable crests;
I bear a charmèd life, which must not yield
To one of woman born.
MACDUFF   Despair° thy charm,   *Despair of*
And let the angel° whom thou still hast served   *(evil) spirit*

5.8 Location: Before Macbeth's castle; the battle continues.
1. Having accomplished no deeds.
5.9 Location: Before Macbeth's castle.
1. Fight on our side; deliberately miss us.
5.10 Location: Scene continues.

15   Tell thee Macduff was from his mother's womb
    Untimely° ripped.   *Prematurely*
MACBETH   Accursèd be that tongue that tells me so,
    For it hath cowed° my better part of man;   *intimidated*
    And be these juggling fiends no more believed,
20   That palter° with us in a double sense,   *equivocate*
    That keep the word of promise to our ear
    And break it to our hope. I'll not fight with thee.
MACDUFF   Then yield thee, coward,
    And live to be the show and gaze° o'th' time.   *spectacle*
25   We'll have thee as our rarer monsters° are,   *prodigies*
    Painted upon a pole,¹ and underwrit
    'Here may you see the tyrant.'
MACBETH   I will not yield
    To kiss the ground before young Malcolm's feet,
    And to be baited° with the rabble's curse.   *harassed*
30   Though Birnam Wood be come to Dunsinane,
    And thou opposed being of no woman born,
    Yet I will try the last.° Before my body   *the last resort*
    I throw my warlike shield. Lay on, Macduff,
    And damned be him that first cries 'Hold, enough!'
                         Exeunt fighting. Alarums
    [*They*] *enter fighting, and* MACBETH [*is*] *slain.* [*Exit* MAC-
    DUFF *with Macbeth's body*]

5.11

*Retreat*¹ *and flourish. Enter with* [*a drummer*] *and col-
ours* MALCOLM, SIWARD, ROSS, *thanes, and soldiers*
MALCOLM   I would° the friends we miss were safe arrived.   *wish*
SIWARD   Some must go off;° and yet by these² I see   *die*
    So great a day as this is cheaply bought.
MALCOLM   Macduff is missing, and your noble son.
5 ROSS [*to* SIWARD]   Your son, my lord, has paid a soldier's debt.
    He only lived but till he was a man,
    The which no sooner had his prowess confirmed
    In the unshrinking station³ where he fought,
    But like a man he died.
SIWARD   Then he is dead?
10 ROSS   Ay, and brought off the field. Your cause of sorrow
    Must not be measured by his worth, for then
    It hath no end.
SIWARD   Had he his hurts before?°   *on his front*
ROSS   Ay, on the front.
SIWARD   Why then, God's soldier be he.
    Had I as many sons as I have hairs
15   I would not wish them to a fairer death;
    And so his knell is knolled.
MALCOLM   He's worth more sorrow,
    And that I'll spend for him.
SIWARD   He's worth no more.

---

1. Painted on a cloth or board supported by a pole as a
form of advertisement.
5.11 Location: Within the castle.

1. A trumpet call signaling the end of the battle.
2. To judge from those who are present.
3. Post from which he did not shrink.

They say he parted° well and paid his score,   departed
And so God be with him. Here comes newer comfort.
           Enter MACDUFF *with Macbeth's head*
20 MACDUFF [*to* MALCOLM]   Hail, King, for so thou art. Behold where stands[4]
Th'usurper's cursèd head. The time is free.°   *free from tyranny*
I see thee compassed with thy kingdom's pearl,[5]
That speak my salutation in their minds,
Whose voices I desire aloud with mine:
Hail, King of Scotland!
25 ALL BUT MALCOLM   Hail, King of Scotland!
      Flourish
MALCOLM We shall not spend a large expense of time
Before we reckon with° your several loves   *make an accounting of*
And make us even with you.° My thanes and kinsmen,   *reward your loyalty*
Henceforth be earls, the first that ever Scotland
30 In such an honour named. What's more to do
Which would be planted newly with the time,[6]
As calling home our exiled friends abroad,
That fled the snares of watchful tyranny,
Producing forth[7] the cruel ministers°   *agents*
35 Of this dead butcher and his fiend-like queen—
Who, as 'tis thought, by self and violent hands°   *her own violent hands*
Took off her life—this and what needful else
That calls upon us, by the grace of grace
We will perform in measure, time, and place.[8]
40 So thanks to all at once, and to each one,
Whom we invite to see us crowned at Scone.
                    Flourish. Exeunt Omnes°   *all*

---

4. Presumably upon a pole or lance.
5. I see you surrounded by your nobles, here called the "pearl" of the kingdom.
6. Which should be performed at the beginning of this

new era.
7. Bringing forward for trial.
8. In due order, at the proper time and place.

Antony and Cleopatra

What if Shakespeare had had second thoughts about *Romeo and Juliet*? He might have tried something a little different. In this version, the lovers, neither youthful nor married to each other, are involved in a long-standing, adulterous relationship. Romeo, thinking Juliet dead because she has sent a messenger with that lie, kills himself—though with a sword rather than poison. He partly bungles the job, however, and hence takes a while to die. Juliet resolves to follow him, but she delays for the entire fifth act before killing herself—though with poison rather than a sword. And when they are both finally dead, the audience may be less likely to lament the loss of "star-crossed lovers" than celebrate the fulfillment of a heroic passion.

In the event Shakespeare did have second thoughts about *Romeo and Juliet*; he called these second thoughts *Antony and Cleopatra* (late 1606–early 1607). The last of Shakespeare's three love tragedies, the play also rewrites *Othello*, the middle work of this group, converting its threat from the East, there represented by the Turks, into both a threat and an opportunity from the East, here represented by the Egyptians. All three tragedies set their domestic concerns thematically against the backdrop of bloody political conflict, but formally against the expectations of romantic comedy. All three seem like comedies that somehow get derailed. But *Antony and Cleopatra* replaces the emphasis on youth of romantic comedy, of *Romeo and Juliet*, and even of Desdemona in *Othello* with the most sustained, complex portrayal of mature love in Shakespeare's dramatic career.

In Shakespeare's romantic comedies, problem plays, and romances, the female protagonist often dominates the scene. But in the tragedies that Shakespeare composed from roughly 1599 to 1608, *Antony and Cleopatra* is the only such candidate. Moreover, following a series of tragedies—*Hamlet*, *Othello*, *King Lear*, and *Macbeth*—in which the protagonist's psychology is consistently probed, *Antony and Cleopatra* almost completely avoids soliloquy. Antony's and Cleopatra's motives often remain opaque—arguably, even to themselves. We never definitively learn why Antony thinks marriage to Octavia will solve his political problems, why Cleopatra flees at Actium, why she negotiates with Caesar in the last act. Instead of self-revelation, the play offers contradictory framing commentary by minor figures. These external perspectives help impart an epic feel, as do the geographical and scenic shifts, which also produce a loose, fragmentary, and capacious structure alien to classically inspired notions of proper dramatic form. *Antony and Cleopatra* is thus a new, transitional kind of tragedy. Its restlessness is of a piece with that of *Pericles*, perhaps the next play Shakespeare wrote and the first of his late romances. And the intimations of transcendence with which *Antony and Cleopatra* ends point toward the magical or supernatural resolutions of the romances more generally.

The play may also be compared to Shakespeare's other Roman tragedies, *Julius Caesar* and *Coriolanus*. All are based on Thomas North's translation of *Plutarch's Lives of the Noble Grecians and Romanes* (1579)—Shakespeare's favorite source, with the exception of Raphael Holinshed's *Chronicles of England, Scotland, and Ireland*, and one that he follows closely here. All three plays rely heavily on blank verse while almost entirely avoiding rhyme. Here Shakespeare may have followed the Earl of Surrey's sixteenth-century blank-verse translation of part of the *Aeneid* (19 B.C.E.), Virgil's epic of the legendary founding of Rome, itself understood as an allegory of the city-state's bloody transition from republic (rule by senatorial aristocracy) to empire (monarchical power) in the poet's own day.

Octavius Caesar, later known as Augustus, as on this medal. From Guillaume Du Choul, *Discours de la Religion des Anciens Romains* (1567 ed.).

It is this transition that Shakespeare dramatizes in *Julius Caesar* and *Antony and Cleopatra*. Chronologically, *Antony* picks up where *Julius Caesar* leaves off. That earlier play focuses on Caesar's assassination by republicans, led by Brutus and Cassius, and the assassins' subsequent defeat at the hands of Mark Antony (Caesar's lieutenant) and Octavius Caesar (Caesar's young grandnephew and adoptive son). *Antony and Cleopatra,* which covers the period from 40 to 30 B.C.E., completes the narrative of Roman civil war and the final destruction of the Republic. The dominant military power throughout the Mediterranean and beyond, Rome is ruled by the triumvirate of Lepidus, Octavius Caesar, and Mark Antony, who govern, respectively, the Mediterranean portions of Africa, Europe, and Asia. Accordingly, *Antony and Cleopatra* partly turns away from *Julius Caesar*'s emphasis on the struggle over Rome's internal political system, looking instead to Rome's external imperial domains. Correspondingly, the stylistic restraint fitted to Brutus's republican restraint gives way to an extravagant, hyperbolic verse in accord with the empire's expansive grandeur. This would thus seem the theater for heroic, legendary, even mythic performance: Antony is associated with Hercules, and Antony and Cleopatra are repeatedly compared to Mars and Venus.

Yet *Antony and Cleopatra* actually investigates the possibility of such performance in a postheroic world. It offers an epic view of the political arena but deprives that arena of heroic significance. Mark Antony and Octavius Caesar contend for political supremacy, but the love between Antony and Cleopatra increasingly occupies center stage. The work then asks whether heroic meaning can be transplanted to the ostensibly private terrain of love. Much of the play's fascination arises from this intertwining of empire and sexuality. Plutarch and other classical writers were preoccupied with what for them was the opposition between the political and moral virtue of the conquering West, and the luxurious, feminized sexuality of the older civilizations of the subjugated East. This understanding of empire reemerged in the Renaissance during a new era of Western expansion, marked by an increasingly racialized and still sexualized view of non-European peoples. Just months before the probable first performance of the play, King James authorized the establishment of an English colony in North America—an undertaking that resulted in the founding of Jamestown the following year. As in other western European countries at the time, Rome was the central model of imperial greatness. The view of Egypt was more mixed, however: it was both the preeminent source of ancient wisdom and a land that, even though Rome had defeated it, threatened to transmit its decadence to the victors.

Accordingly, *Antony and Cleopatra* itself seems designed to elicit complicated judgments. This has often proven difficult in performance. Long supplanted on the stage by John Dryden's *All for Love* (1678), which recasts Shakespeare's story as a tragedy of private life, the play came into its own only after 1800 in the heyday of the British Empire, with Cleopatra routinely embodying Oriental sexual vice. The text initially seems to justify this interpretation: Rome is contrasted to Egypt, West to East, the conquerors to the conquered. Rapid shifts of scene across enormous distances accentuate this division. A sober, masculine military ethos opposes a frivolous, feminized, and sexualized court. Political opportunism drives Antony's marriage to Octavia, love and sexual desire his relationship with Cleopatra; he chooses between fidelity to a chaste, white wife and adultery with a promiscuous, "tawny," "black" seductress (1.1.6, 1.5.28). That seductress has a smaller political role than in Plutarch—a change which accentuates the basic conflict. Where Caesar employs rational self-interest (he is the "universal landlord," 3.13.72), Antony revels in extravagant generosity and challenges Caesar to one-on-one combat. Young Caesar is a bureaucrat of the future, old Antony a warrior of the past. Caesar's concerns are public, Antony's private. Antony is guilty by association with his brother and his previous wife, Fulvia, who attack Caesar. By contrast, Caesar promises that "the time of universal peace is near" (4.6.4), an assertion that anticipates the *Pax Romana* (Roman peace) he instituted throughout the Empire and the birth of Christ in a Roman province during his long rule.

Yet the play seems to create such dichotomies only to undermine them. Antony boasts of his valor at Philippi, while Caesar "alone / Dealt on lieutenantry" (battled exclusively through his officers; 3.11.38–39). Earlier, however, Antony's "officer" Ventidius remarks, "Caesar and Antony have ever won / More in their officer than person" (3.1.16–17). Caesar's promise of "universal peace" is anticipated in a version of Christ's Last Supper that Antony shares with his followers.

> Tend me tonight.
> Maybe it is the period of your duty.
> Haply you shall not see me more; or if,
> A mangled shadow. Perchance tomorrow
> You'll serve another master.
> (4.2.24–28)

Enobarbus, who functions like a skeptical chorus, criticizes Antony for moving his friends to tears. But that skepticism is itself challenged. It leads Enobarbus to become a Judas figure who betrays his master by defecting to Caesar and who dies shortly thereafter, his heart broken by Antony's generosity.

Even the geographical contrast of the play partly dissolves into parallelisms: Roman war is eroticized, Egyptian love is militarized. The external representation of the lovers' relationship, the absence of scenes of them alone, and their pride in exhibiting their affair intensify the feeling that love and war influence each other, that there is no distinction between public and private. Furthermore, love is on both sides of the divide. Late in the play, Antony, focused exclusively on Cleopatra, is heroically preceded in suicide by his aptly named servant Eros (love), a figure from Plutarch. But when the work opens, Antony's neglect of military command is criticized as "this dotage of our General's" by Philo (again, "love"; 1.1.1), a figure invented by Shakespeare.

The eroticization of Rome also takes the form of powerful feelings directed toward Antony. Octavius Caesar at times acts almost as if he were the son—rather than grandnephew and adopted son—of Cleopatra's former lover, Julius Caesar, whose paternal role Antony has usurped. Octavius Caesar is disgusted by Antony and Cleopatra's theatrical coronation:

> At the feet sat
> Caesarion, whom they call my father's son,
> And all the unlawful issue that their lust
> Since then hath made between them.
> (3.6.5–8)

Here, there is a possible confusion between Antony and the older Caesar and a definite one between Caesarion and the younger Caesar, both of whom are "my father's son." At Antony's death, Caesar movingly recalls his foe:

> . . . thou, my brother, my competitor
> In top of all design, my mate in empire,
> Friend and companion in the front of war,

> The arm of mine own body, and the heart
> Where mine his thoughts did kindle.
> (5.1.42–46)

This outpouring of emotion leads in contradictory directions. By calling Antony his "brother" and "mate," and by invoking a meeting of "heart" and mind, Caesar on the one hand suggests an intimacy between the two men that recalls Renaissance celebrations of close male friendship but that also borders on the erotic. On the other hand, he neutralizes any filial anxiety he may feel by describing Antony first as "my brother" and then as a subordinate, "the arm of mine own body."

Most important, this strategy of undermining apparent distinctions has the effect of draining the political world of meaning. *Julius Caesar's* struggle between republic and empire arises only peripherally in *Antony and Cleopatra*, where it is voiced by Pompey (2.6.15–19), who is bought off, attacked, and finally murdered by the triumvirs. The Republic is thus all but dead when *Antony and Cleopatra* opens. Egypt's independence is at stake, although this occurs only to Cleopatra—belatedly and perhaps duplicitously. That leaves only the conflict between Antony and Caesar, a conflict, however, that simply concerns the desires of two ambitious men. The end of the Roman civil war is also important, but it is hard either to celebrate the victory of Caesar or lament the defeat of Antony. The disabused view of political power that emerges could be construed as an implicit critique of the centralizing monarchs of Shakespeare's own time.

On the other hand, the political symbolism of the two men is certainly antithetical. Caesar astutely adopts republican style, whereas Antony offends Roman sensibilities by taking on monarchical trappings (3.6.1–19). Antony's antagonist does not emulate the older Caesar, whose sexual and military conquests were intertwined (3.13.82–85). Hence the younger Caesar represents not the preservation but the diminution of traditional Roman values, a constriction of a heroic culture of which Antony is the last survivor. The play insists that politics and sex (or any kind of grandeur) are irrevocably sundered, that one can no longer have it both ways.

Certainly, Antony and Cleopatra cannot. The play characterizes Antony and Cleopatra through a language of greatness, shared by the protagonists and minor figures alike, only to subvert that rhetoric through still other commentary and, even more, through the behavior of Antony and Cleopatra themselves. Although Shakespeare makes them more sympathetic than they are in Plutarch, they remain maddeningly self-absorbed and self-destructive—lying, ignoring urgent business, acting impulsively, bullying underlings, reveling in vulgarity, apparently betraying each other. They are also militarily peripheral, as the fighting scenes, except for the first Battle of Alexandria, testify. Shakespeare's uncharacteristic decision to follow the practice of classical theater and keep all combat offstage leaves only a feeling of being let down, as helpless observers report on the debacle. Thus, Enobarbus laments at Actium:

> Naught, naught, all naught! I can behold no longer.
> Th'*Antoniad*, the Egyptian admiral,
> With all their sixty, fly and turn the rudder.
> (3.10.1–3)

At the last battle of the play, it is Antony's turn:

> All is lost.
> This foul Egyptian hath betrayèd me.
> My fleet hath yielded to the foe, and yonder
> They cast their caps up, and carouse together
> Like friends long lost.
> (4.13.9–13)

But this is not the whole story or even, in the end, most of it. Antony and Cleopatra are great not despite their failings but because of them. Inability to fit into Caesar's narrowed world of self-discipline sets them apart. Their outsized grandeur can be described only through paradoxical hyperbole. Antony's heart "is become the bellows and the fan / To cool a gipsy's lust": his heart is a fan that cools Cleopatra's lust by satisfying it, but in so doing he rekindles her passion, as if his heart were also a bellows (1.1.9–10). Similarly, when Cleopatra meets Antony, "pretty dimpled boys" (2.2.208) attend her

> With divers-coloured fans whose wind did seem
> To glow the delicate cheeks which they did cool,
> And what they undid did.
>
> (2.2.209–11)

And when told that marriage to Octavia will force Antony to abandon Cleopatra, Enobarbus demurs in the play's most famous lines:

> Never. He will not.
> Age cannot wither her, nor custom stale
> Her infinite variety. Other women cloy
> The appetites they feed, but she makes hungry
> Where most she satisfies.
>
> (2.2.239–43)

These passages might be considered accounts of insatiable middle-aged lust. The trick of the play is to convince the audience that they are really about love. Antony's feelings may seem easier to believe than Cleopatra's: he is the one who gives up an empire. By contrast, Cleopatra's combination of teasing frivolity, comic jealousy, and cold calculation have rendered her motives suspect. Yet Shakespeare gives her passages of extraordinary dignity early in the play, when Antony decides to leave her upon hearing of his wife Fulvia's death.

> Courteous lord, one word.
> Sir, you and I must part; but that's not it.
> Sir, you and I have loved; but there's not it;
> That you know well. Something it is I would—
> O, my oblivion is a very Antony,
> And I am all forgotten.
>
> (1.3.87–92)

Cleopatra experiences something more than she can express. Its articulation, therefore, initially takes the form of a failure to articulate. There is an echo of this later, when Enobarbus attempts to describe her to his fellow Romans: "her own person . . . beggared all description" (2.2.203–04). Here, however, Cleopatra tries to convey her meaning through a witticism: her forgetfulness makes her like Antony, who is forgetful of her. She forgets and is forgotten. But when Antony misses the point, thinking he has merely witnessed idle wordplay, she corrects him.

> 'Tis sweating labour
> To bear such idleness so near the heart
> As Cleopatra this. But sir, forgive me,
> . . . .
> . . . be deaf to my unpitied folly,
> And all the gods go with you.
>
> (1.3.94–100)

In short, Cleopatra's playfulness is the mere surface of her essential depth, a depth that involves a "sweating labour" like that of childbirth.

The last two acts put that depth to the test, ultimately making Cleopatra the play's central character. *Antony and Cleopatra*'s geographical restlessness diminishes as the protagonists' sphere of activity is reduced to Alexandria. Cleopatra sends Antony a fabricated, manipulative report of her death, he botches his suicide in response, and she then refuses to leave her monument to attend him as he lies dying. Instead, she hoists him up to her with the comment, "Here's sport indeed. How heavy weighs my lord!" (4.16.33), where "sport" is both playful and bitter, where "weighs" carries both physical and psychological meaning, and, hence, where the scene as a whole combines grotesque comedy with genuine pathos. Structurally, Antony's presumably climactic death becomes a mere false ending that shifts the burden of significance to the final act. Egypt and Cleopatra are what matter. Egypt has been associated throughout with the overflowing that Antony is faulted for at the outset. Antony declares his love for Cleopatra by rejecting the state he rules: "Let Rome in Tiber melt, and the wide arch / Of the ranged empire fall" (1.1.35–36). Upon hearing of Antony's marriage to Octavia, Cleopatra prays, "Melt Egypt into Nile, and kindly creatures / Turn all to serpents!" (2.5.78–79). This apocalyptic imagery, which dissolves all distinction, anticipates Antony's loss of self when he thinks Cleopatra has betrayed him. His body seems to him as "indistinct / As water is in water" (4.15.10–11). The language of liquefaction is also connected to the confusion of gender identity. Antony

> is not more manlike
> Than Cleopatra, nor the queen of Ptolemy
> More womanly than he.
>
> (1.4.5–7)

And Cleopatra reports, "I . . . put my tires and mantles on him whilst / I wore his sword Philippan" (2.5.21–23). Depending on one's perspective, this behavior either dangerously confuses gender roles, thereby leading to Antony's ignominious flight at Actium, or overcomes a destructive opposition.

Cleopatra herself, who metaphorically overflows boundaries, is literally linked to Egypt throughout the play. In particular, she is specifically identified with the Egyptian goddess Isis (3.6.17), who is invoked several times in the play, probably on the basis of Plutarch's *On Isis and Osiris*. Isis is the sister-wife of Osiris, whom she restores after he is pursued to his death by his brother-rival, Typhon. The conclusion thus seeks the regenerative powers of the Nile in Cleopatra. It asks whether she really is the equivalent of Isis, whether she really is the wife of Antony (Osiris), whether she really does restore him after he is pursued to his death by his brother (Caesar).

This is the work of Cleopatra's suicide, which makes good on these imagistic patterns, retrospectively justifying Antony's decision to die for her. We may desire the protagonists' deaths in Shakespeare's earlier tragedies, perhaps because life no longer has any meaning for these characters. But *Antony and Cleopatra* goes further: it convinces us that the suicides of the two lovers is a heroic achievement, that anything less would constitute abject failure. The ending also evokes the synthesis precluded by the play's dichotomies but implied by its more subtle patterns. Cleopatra dies the death of a Roman man:

> My resolution's placed, and I have nothing
> Of woman in me. Now from head to foot
> I am marble-constant. Now the fleeting moon
> No planet is of mine.
>
> (5.2.234–37)

She also dies the death of a faithful Roman wife:

> . . . methinks I hear
> Antony call. I see him rouse himself
> To praise my noble act. . . .
> . . . .
> . . . Husband, I come.
> Now to that name my courage prove my title.
>
> (5.2.274–79)

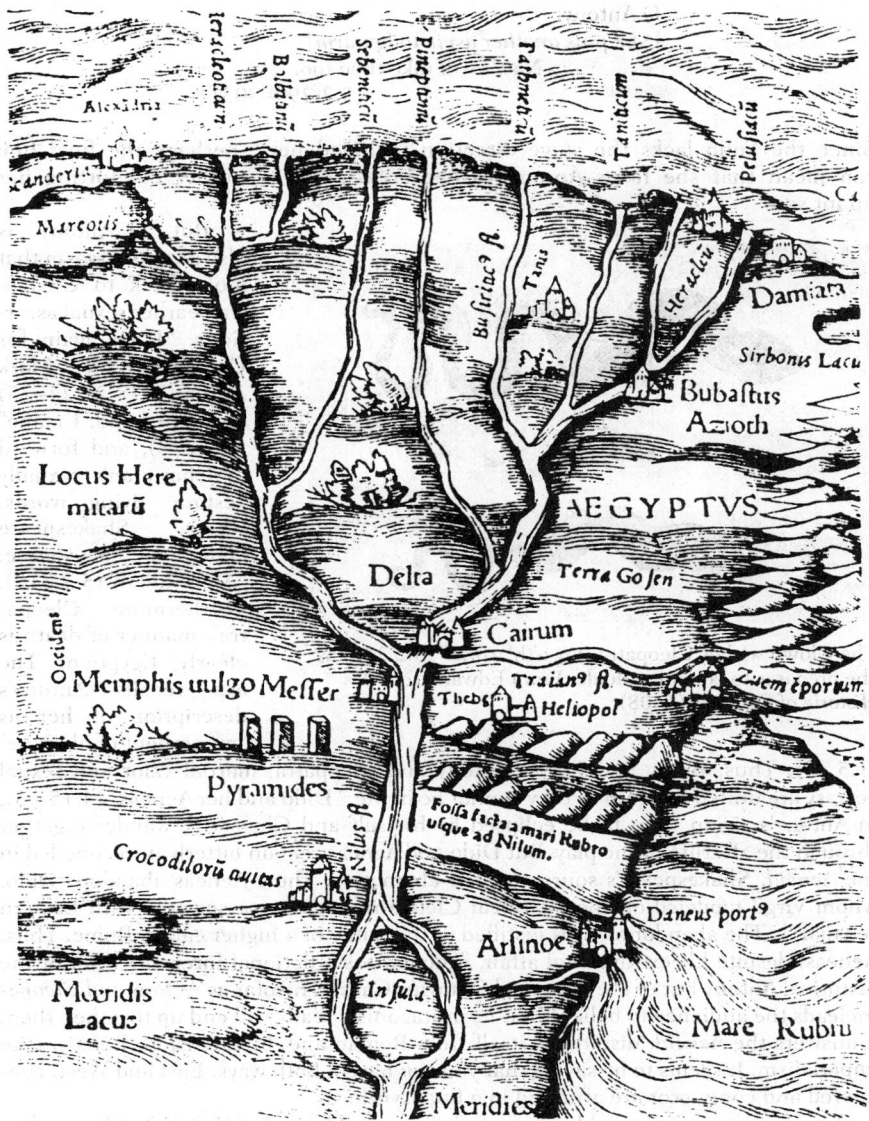

The Nile delta, showing the northern end of the river as it flows into the Mediterranean Sea. Alexandria is visible near the upper left-hand corner. From a map in Sebastian Münster's *Cosmographiae universalis* (1550).

And in taking the poisonous asp to her breast, she may become a Roman mother as well, in a passage that recalls her earlier representation of intense feeling in the language of childbirth:

> Peace, peace.
> Dost thou not see my baby at my breast,
> That sucks the nurse asleep?
> . . . .
> As sweet as balm, as soft as air, as gentle.

O Antony!
[*She puts another aspic to her arm*]
Nay, I will take thee too.
(5.2.299–303)

Since the Folio lacks the stage direction included here, perhaps the final line can mean that she takes Antony to her breast, like a mother comforting her infant son.

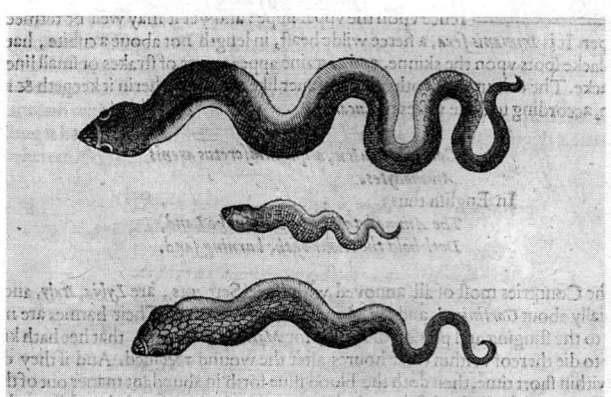

The Clown wishes Cleopatra "joy o'th' worm" (5.2.270) as she prepares to commit suicide. From Edward Topsell's *Historie of Serpents* (1608).

But "O Antony" is also a cry of orgasm that looks back to Cleopatra's earlier sexual assertions, "I am again for Cydnus / To meet Mark Antony" (5.2.224–25) and "Husband, I come" (5.2.278), and forward to Charmian's sexually ecstatic dying words, which Shakespeare added to his source: "Ah, soldier!" (5.2.319). Furthermore, Cleopatra's manner of death is clearly Egyptian. The asp recalls Antony's description of her as "my serpent of old Nile" (1.5.25). Thus, Rome and Egypt, Antony and Cleopatra, martial valor and sexual ecstasy are united in death as they cannot be in life. "Dido and her Aeneas" (4.15.53), in Antony's vision soon to be eclipsed by himself and Cleopatra, wander together through the afterlife of the play. But Dido and Aeneas remain bitterly unreconciled in the *Aeneid*, Shakespeare's source for the characters. There Aeneas abandons Dido, whom Virgil modeled on the historical Cleopatra and thus associated with Eastern sensuality. The abandonment is justified in the name of a higher cause, Rome. Thus, Aeneas, despite his extramarital affair, functions as a fictional forerunner not of the historical Antony but of the historical Octavius Caesar. Insofar as *Antony and Cleopatra* leads the audience to believe that its protagonists really will end up together, then, it answers the *Aeneid*, distancing itself from Roman and, by extension, Renaissance imperialism. It seems to be saying that you *can* have it both ways. East and West, conquered and conqueror are affirmed in a final synthesis.

Yet countercurrents trouble Cleopatra's "immortal longings" (5.2.272). She resolves on suicide not when she learns that Antony killed himself for her but when she becomes certain that Caesar plans to lead her in a humiliating triumph in Rome. Recognizing that her suicide will ruin Caesar's plans, she takes pleasure in imagining that Antony will "mock / The luck of Caesar," that the asp will "call great Caesar ass / Unpolicied" (5.2.276–77, 298–99). The concluding triumphant rhetoric thus cleans up earlier dubious behavior and puts the best face on defeat. Heroic aristocratic individualism can act in the world only by leaving it. Moreover, the domestic Cleopatra of the conclusion might seem the reduction to a conventional gender role of a woman who challenged sexual hierarchy. At her death, Cleopatra "lies / A lass unparalleled" (5.2.305–06). This alliterative eulogy juxtaposes the Latinate "unparalleled," typical of the extravagant rhetoric of the play, with the homespun "lass." Both stylistically and semantically, that humble word also matches Cleopatra's own rhetoric—"Husband," "baby," and "nurse." Moreover, in echoing her contempt for "Caesar [the] ass / Unpolicied," the phrase praises her at his expense. Alternatively, however, has *Antony and Cleopatra* instead presented "lies alas unparalleled?"

The answer depends on the relationship between the ending and the partly incompatible material that has preceded it. Most, though not all, critics have found the conclusion affirmative. But the work registers ambivalence to the last. This duality is captured in Cleopatra's account of the response she expects in Rome:

> The quick comedians
> Extemporally will stage us, and present
> Our Alexandrian revels. Antony
> Shall be brought drunken forth, and I shall see
> Some squeaking Cleopatra boy my greatness
> I'th' posture of a whore.
>
> (5.2.212–17)

Cleopatra shudders at the absurdity of a boy actor badly impersonating her, yet the part of Cleopatra in *Antony and Cleopatra* was originally performed by a boy. This reminder punctures the dramatic illusion just when it seems most essential. It looks back to Cleopatra's deliberate blurring of gender division. And it emphasizes the artifice of Cleopatra herself, a veteran actress in her final performance. Shakespeare here flaunts the power of his medium. But if it is impossible to "boy" Cleopatra's "greatness," to represent her adequately, perhaps that is an invitation, as she has earlier suggested, to look beyond what can be shown, to take seriously her "immortal longings."

WALTER COHEN

TEXTUAL NOTE

The Tragedie of Anthonie, and Cleopatra was published in the First Folio of 1623 (F), which also gives the forms *Anthony and Cleopater* in other references to the title of the play. "Anthony & Cleopatra" was entered on May 20, 1608, in the Stationers' Register, a listing of books intended for legal publication. As it happened, the play went unpublished; this entry may have been designed to prevent someone else from printing it. Both stylistic tests and probable verbal echoes in other plays suggest a date of late 1606 or possibly early 1607. The Folio version is ultimately based on an authorial manuscript but perhaps by way of a transcript. There is no evidence of the revisions necessary for theatrical performance. Thus, the stage directions list characters who have no role in the scene or even the entire play (characters excluded from the present edition); are insufficient at various points, especially in the closing scenes at Cleopatra's monument; and (like the speech prefixes) contain some authorial errors.

The play presents problems in modernizing proper names and in verse lineation. In addition, but less problematically, it has no act or scene divisions after an initial "Actus Primus. Scoena Prima." The ones supplied here follow editorial practice standard since the eighteenth century, except in starting a new scene after 4.7.3 (because the stage is cleared). This decision, of course, changes the scene numbering for the remainder of the act.

SELECTED BIBLIOGRAPHY

Archer, John Michael. "Antiquity and Degeneration in *Antony and Cleopatra*." *Race, Ethnicity, and Power in the Renaissance*. Ed. Joyce Green MacDonald. Madison, N.J.: Fairleigh Dickinson University Press, 1997. 145–64. The ambivalent image of

Egypt in the Renaissance, combining reverence for its antique wisdom with anxiety about contagious decadence.

Bloom, Harold, ed. *William Shakespeare's "Antony and Cleopatra."* New York: Chelsea House, 1988. Eight heterogeneous essays by important critics from the 1970s and 1980s.

Deats, Sara Munson, ed. *Antony and Cleopatra: New Critical Essays.* New York: Routledge, 2005. Fourteen new essays, including a long opening survey of criticism and performance by the editor.

Drakakis, John, ed. *"Antony and Cleopatra," William Shakespeare.* New York: St. Martin's, 1994. Twelve heterogeneous essays by leading critics, mainly from the 1970s and 1980s.

Holderness, Graham, Bryan Loughrey, and Andrew Murphy, eds. *Shakespeare: The Roman Plays.* London: Longman, 1996. Three essays on *Antony and Cleopatra* from the 1980s and 1990s, focusing on psychoanalytical and political issues.

Loomba, Ania. *Shakespeare, Race, and Colonialism.* Oxford: Oxford University Press, 2002. 112–34. Links of empire, gender ambiguity, skin color, gypsies, and role playing.

Madeleine, Richard, ed. *Antony and Cleopatra.* Cambridge: Cambridge University Press, 1998. Book-length history of productions of *Antony and Cleopatra*, combined with an edition of the play annotated with accounts of various performance decisions.

Rose, Mark, ed. *Twentieth Century Interpretations of "Antony and Cleopatra": A Collection of Critical Essays.* Englewood Cliffs, N.J.: Prentice-Hall, 1977. A dozen statements and essays from major critics, from 1945 to 1975, mostly formalist in character, with some attention to historical background.

Wofford, Susanne L. *Shakespeare's Late Tragedies: A Collection of Critical Essays.* Upper Saddle River, N.J.: Prentice Hall, 1996. Five essays on *Antony and Cleopatra* from the 1980s and 1990s, plus substantial discussion of the play in three other more general pieces; primarily issues of subjectivity, race, gender, empire, and performance.

Wood, Nigel, ed. *Antony and Cleopatra.* Buckingham, Eng.: Open University Press, 1996. Four essays connecting theory to interpretation, from the perspectives of mimetic rivalry, postcolonialism, polysemous gynocentrism, and genre.

FILM

Antony and Cleopatra. 1974. Dir. Jon Scoffield. UK. 161 min. Based on the 1972 Royal Shakespeare Company performance, starring Janet Suzman as an intelligent, tawny, feminist Cleopatra. Focuses on love at the expense of politics.

The Tragedy of
Antony and Cleopatra

THE PERSONS OF THE PLAY

MARK ANTONY (Marcus Antonius), triumvir of Rome

DEMETRIUS
PHILO
Domitius ENOBARBUS
VENTIDIUS
SILIUS } friends and followers of Antony
EROS
CAMIDIUS
SCARUS
DECRETAS

Octavius CAESAR, triumvir of Rome
OCTAVIA, his sister

MAECENAS
AGRIPPA
TAURUS
DOLABELLA } friends and followers of Caesar
THIDIAS
GALLUS
PROCULEIUS

LEPIDUS, triumvir of Rome
Sextus POMPEY (Pompeius)

MENECRATES
MENAS } friends of Pompey
VARRIUS

CLEOPATRA, Queen of Egypt

CHARMIAN
IRAS
ALEXAS
MARDIAN, a eunuch } attending on Cleopatra
DIOMED
SELEUCUS

A SOOTHSAYER
An AMBASSADOR
MESSENGERS
A BOY who sings
A SENTRY and men of his WATCH
Men of the GUARD
An EGYPTIAN
A CLOWN
SERVANTS
SOLDIERS
Eunuchs, attendants, captains, soldiers, servants

1.1

Enter DEMETRIUS *and* PHILO

PHILO   Nay, but this dotage° of our General's   absurd infatuation
O'erflows the measure.[1] Those his goodly eyes,
That o'er the files and musters°of the war   lines of troops
Have glowed like plated° Mars, now bend, now turn   armored
5   The office° and devotion of their view   duty
Upon a tawny front.[2] His captain's heart,
Which in the scuffles of great fights hath burst
The buckles on his breast, reneges all temper,[3]
And is become the bellows and the fan
To cool a gipsy's° lust.   Egyptian's; hussy's
   Flourish.° Enter ANTONY, CLEOPATRA, *her ladies, the*   Trumpet fanfare
   train,° with eunuchs fanning her   retinue
10   Look where they come.
Take but good note, and you shall see in him
The triple pillar of the world[4] transformed
Into a strumpet's fool. Behold and see.
CLEOPATRA [*to* ANTONY]   If it be love indeed, tell me how much.
15   ANTONY   There's beggary° in the love that can be reckoned.   little value
CLEOPATRA   I'll set a bourn° how far to be beloved.   boundary
ANTONY   Then must thou needs find out new heaven, new earth.[5]
   Enter a MESSENGER
MESSENGER   News, my good lord, from Rome.
ANTONY   Grates° me: the sum.°   Irks / summary
20   CLEOPATRA   Nay, hear them, Antony.
Fulvia° perchance is angry; or who knows   Antony's wife
If the scarce-bearded Caesar[6] have not sent
His powerful mandate to you: 'Do this, or this,
Take in° that kingdom and enfranchise° that.   Annex / liberate
25   Perform't, or else we damn thee.'
ANTONY   How,° my love?   What
CLEOPATRA   Perchance? Nay, and most like.[7]
You must not stay here longer. Your dismission°   marching orders
Is come from Caesar, therefore hear it, Antony.
30   Where's Fulvia's process°—Caesar's, I would say—both?   summons
Call in the messengers. As I am Egypt's queen,
Thou blushest, Antony, and that blood of thine
Is Caesar's homager;° else so thy cheek pays shame   Pays Caesar homage
When shrill-tongued Fulvia scolds. The messengers!
35   ANTONY   Let Rome in Tiber melt, and the wide arch
Of the ranged° empire fall. Here is my space.   orderly; extensive
Kingdoms are clay. Our dungy° earth alike   made of manure
Feeds beast as man. The nobleness of life
Is to do thus;° when such a mutual pair   act as we do; embrace
40   And such a twain can do't—in which I bind

1.1 Location: Cleopatra's palace, Alexandria.
1. Goes beyond suitable bounds.
2. A face or forehead of dark complexion (referring to Cleopatra; see the Introduction); military "front," or battle line.
3. Abandons all temperance ("temper" is also the hardness of tempered steel).
4. Antony, Octavius Caesar, and Lepidus were the three triumvirs ruling the Roman Empire (most of the known world, for Romans).

5. Alluding anachronistically to Revelation 21:1 ("I saw a new heaven, and a new earth") and to the discovery of the New World. This second meaning may connect to the imperial theme of the play—its sense of geographical expansiveness and European geographical expansion.
6. The opening of the play is set in 40 B.C.E., when Octavius Caesar was twenty-three; Antony was almost twenty years his senior.
7. It is most likely, rather than merely possible, that Fulvia is angry.

On pain of punishment the world to weet°—   *recognize*
We stand up peerless.
CLEOPATRA [*aside*]   Excellent falsehood!
Why did he marry Fulvia and not love her?
I'll seem the fool I am not. [*To* ANTONY] Antony
Will be himself.[8]
45   ANTONY   But stirred[9] by Cleopatra.
Now, for the love of Love and her soft hours
Let's not confound° the time with conference° harsh.   *ruin / conversation*
There's not a minute of our lives should stretch
Without some pleasure now. What sport° tonight?   *entertainment*
CLEOPATRA   Hear the ambassadors.
50   ANTONY   Fie, wrangling queen,
Whom everything becomes—to chide, to laugh,
To weep; how every passion fully strives
To make itself, in thee, fair and admired![1]
No messenger but thine;[1] and all alone
55 Tonight we'll wander through the streets and note
The qualities of people. Come, my queen.
Last night you did desire it. [*To the* MESSENGER] Speak not to us.
         Exeunt [ANTONY *and* CLEOPATRA] *with the train*
             [*and by another door the* MESSENGER]
DEMETRIUS   Is Caesar with° Antonius prized° so slight?   *by / esteemed*
PHILO   Sir, sometimes when he is not Antony
60 He comes too short of that great property°   *unique characteristic*
Which still° should go with Antony.   *always*
DEMETRIUS   I am full sorry
That he approves° the common liar who   *proves correct*
Thus speaks of him at Rome; but I will hope
Of better deeds tomorrow. Rest you happy.   *Exeunt*

1.2

Enter ENOBARBUS, *a* SOOTHSAYER, CHARMIAN, IRAS, MAR-
DIAN *the eunuch,* ALEXAS [*and attendants*]
CHARMIAN   Lord Alexas, sweet Alexas, most anything Alexas,
almost most absolute° Alexas, where's the soothsayer that you   *perfect*
praised so to th' Queen?
O that I knew this husband, which you say
Must charge his horns[1] with garlands!
5   ALEXAS   Soothsayer!
SOOTHSAYER   Your will?
CHARMIAN   Is this the man? Is't you, sir, that know things?
SOOTHSAYER   In nature's infinite book of secrecy
A little I can read.
10   ALEXAS [*to* CHARMIAN]   Show him your hand.
ENOBARBUS [*calling*]   Bring in the banquet° quickly,   *light meal; dessert*
Wine enough Cleopatra's health to drink.
    [*Enter servants with food and wine, and exeunt*]
CHARMIAN [*to* SOOTHSAYER]   Good sir, give me good fortune.
SOOTHSAYER   I make not, but foresee.

---

8. *I'll . . . himself*: I'll appear to believe Antony's false-
hood, although I am really not so credulous; he will con-
tinue in his folly. (But Antony construes the words he
hears as a compliment. It is also possible that Antony
hears Cleopatra's entire speech.)

9. Aroused; motivated; disturbed.
1. I will hear only what you have to say.
1.2 Location: Scene continues.
1. Must adorn his (proverbial) cuckold's horns.

CHARMIAN   Pray then, foresee me one.

15 SOOTHSAYER   You shall be yet
    Far fairer than you are.

CHARMIAN   He means in flesh.°   *(by getting fatter)*

IRAS   No, you shall paint° when you are old.   *use cosmetics*

CHARMIAN   Wrinkles forbid!

ALEXAS   Vex not his prescience. Be attentive.

CHARMIAN   Hush!

SOOTHSAYER   You shall be more beloving than beloved.

20 CHARMIAN   I had rather heat my liver with drinking.²

ALEXAS   Nay, hear him.

CHARMIAN   Good now,° some excellent fortune! Let me be mar-   *Please; fine; begin*
    ried to three kings in a forenoon and widow them all. Let me
    have a child at fifty to whom Herod of Jewry³ may do homage.

25 Find° me to marry me with Octavius Caesar, and companion   *Find in my palm*
    me° with my mistress.   *make me equal*

SOOTHSAYER   You shall outlive the lady whom you serve.

CHARMIAN   O, excellent! I love long life better than figs.⁴

SOOTHSAYER   You have seen and proved° a fairer former fortune   *undergone*
30 Than that which is to approach.

CHARMIAN   Then belike° my children shall have no names.°   *likely / be bastards*
    Prithee, how many boys and wenches must I have?

SOOTHSAYER   If every of your wishes had a womb,
    And fertile every wish, a million.

35 CHARMIAN   Out, fool—I forgive thee for a witch.⁵

ALEXAS   You think none but your sheets are privy to your wishes.

CHARMIAN *[to the* SOOTHSAYER*]*   Nay, come, tell Iras hers.

ALEXAS   We'll know all our fortunes.

ENOBARBUS   Mine, and most of our fortunes, tonight shall be
40 drunk to bed.

IRAS *[showing her hand to the* SOOTHSAYER*]*   There's a palm
    presages chastity,° if nothing else.   *(a dry palm)*

CHARMIAN   E'en as the o'erflowing Nilus presageth famine.⁶

IRAS   Go, you wild° bedfellow, you cannot soothsay.   *licentious*

45 CHARMIAN   Nay, if an oily palm° be not a fruitful prognostica-   *(sign of sensuality)*
    tion,° I cannot scratch mine ear. *[To the* SOOTHSAYER*]* Prithee,   *sign of fertility*
    tell her but a workaday° fortune.   *an everyday*

SOOTHSAYER   Your fortunes are alike.

IRAS   But how, but how? Give me particulars.

50 SOOTHSAYER   I have said.

IRAS   Am I not an inch of fortune better than she?

CHARMIAN   Well, if you were but an inch of fortune better than
    I, where would you choose it?

IRAS   Not in my husband's nose.°   *(sexual innuendo)*

55 CHARMIAN   Our worser° thoughts heavens mend! Alexas—come,   *lascivious*
    his fortune, his fortune. O, let him marry a woman that cannot
    go, sweet Isis,⁷ I beseech thee, and let her die too, and give him

---

2. Both falling in love and excessive drinking were
thought to inflame the liver, the seat of the passions.
3. Anachronistic: Charmian wants homage to her child
even from Herod, Cleopatra's enemy, who was to become
proverbial for his brutality to children when he slaugh-
tered the Holy Innocents in an effort to kill the infant
Jesus.
4. Genitalia (possibly proverbial); lines 27–28 also fore-
shadow 5.2.229–319.

5. Since you are a soothsayer, I will let you speak freely
and will not persecute you as a witch; I will forgive your
outlandish prognostications because they are unlikely to
come true.
6. Ironic: the silt brought down by the flooding Nile each
year gave Egypt its fertile soil.
7. Egyptian goddess of fertility, as well as of the earth and
moon. For the comparison of Cleopatra to Isis, see the
Introduction. *go:* come (sexual); bear children.

a worse, and let worse follow worse till the worst of all follow
him laughing to his grave, fiftyfold a cuckold. Good Isis, hear
60 me this prayer, though thou deny me a matter of more weight;
good Isis, I beseech thee.
IRAS Amen, dear goddess, hear that prayer of the people. For as
it is a heart-breaking to see a handsome man loose-wived,° so it   *wedded to an adulteress*
is a deadly sorrow to behold a foul knave uncuckolded. There-
65 fore, dear Isis, keep decorum,° and fortune him accordingly.   *do the right thing*
CHARMIAN Amen.
ALEXAS Lo now, if it lay in their hands to make me a cuckold,
they would make themselves whores but they'd do't.[8]

        Enter CLEOPATRA

ENOBARBUS Hush, here comes Antony.
CHARMIAN   Not he, the Queen.
CLEOPATRA Saw you my lord?
ENOBARBUS   No, lady.
70 CLEOPATRA   Was he not here?
CHARMIAN No, madam.
CLEOPATRA He was disposed to mirth, but on the sudden
A Roman° thought hath struck him. Enobarbus!   *of Rome; serious*
ENOBARBUS Madam?
75 CLEOPATRA Seek him, and bring him hither. Where's Alexas?
ALEXAS Here at your service. My lord approaches.

        Enter ANTONY *with a* MESSENGER

CLEOPATRA We will not look upon him. Go with us.

        Exeunt [all but ANTONY *and the* MESSENGER]

MESSENGER Fulvia thy wife first came into the field.°   *battlefield*
ANTONY Against my brother Lucius?[9]
80 MESSENGER Ay, but soon that war had end, and the time's state°   *situation at the time*
Made friends of them, jointing their force 'gainst Caesar,
Whose better issue° in the war from Italy   *greater success*
Upon the first encounter drave them.°   *drove them out*
ANTONY   Well, what worst?
MESSENGER The nature of bad news infects the teller.[1]
85 ANTONY When it concerns the fool or coward. On.
Things that are past are done. With me 'tis thus:
Who tells me true, though in his tale lie death,
I hear him as° he flattered.   *as if*
MESSENGER   Labienus[2]—
This is stiff news—hath with his Parthian force
90 Extended° Asia; from Euphrates   *Seized*
His conquering banner shook, from Syria
To Lydia and to Ionia,
Whilst—
ANTONY   Antony, thou wouldst say—
MESSENGER   O, my lord!
ANTONY Speak to me home.° Mince not the general tongue.[3]   *plainly*
95 Name Cleopatra as she is called in Rome.

8. *but they'd do't:* in order to do so.
9. Lucius Antonius, Roman consul.
1. Makes the teller hated by the hearer. For examples,
see 2.5 and 3.1.
2. Quintus Labienus, who was sent by Brutus and Cas-
sius following their killing of Julius Caesar (see *Julius
Caesar*) to garner support from the Parthians, an Asian
people whose empire came to include much of Meso-

potamia (Iraq) and Persia (Iran) and who regularly warred
with Rome. After Brutus's and Cassius's defeat at Philippi
by Antony, Octavius Caesar, and Lepidus, Labienus
defected to take command of the Parthian army and
began a war against the Romans, conquering some of
their provinces in the Middle East (lines 90–92)—prov-
inces Antony was supposed to protect.
3. Do not play down common opinion.

Rail thou in Fulvia's phrase,° and taunt my faults   *words*
With such full licence as both truth and malice
Have power to utter. O, then we bring forth weeds
When our quick° winds lie still, and our ills told us   *living; fertile*
100   Is as our earing.[4] Fare thee well a while.
MESSENGER   At your noble pleasure.   *Exit* MESSENGER
                    Enter another MESSENGER
ANTONY   From Sicyon,[5] ho, the news? Speak there.
SECOND MESSENGER   The man from Sicyon—
ANTONY   Is there such a one?
SECOND MESSENGER   He stays upon° your will.   *He attends*
ANTONY   Let him appear.
                    [*Exit* SECOND MESSENGER]
105   These strong Egyptian fetters I must break,
        Or lose myself in dotage.
                    Enter another MESSENGER *with a letter*
                                    What are you?
THIRD MESSENGER   Fulvia thy wife is dead.
ANTONY   Where died she?
THIRD MESSENGER   In Sicyon.
        Her length of sickness, with what else more serious
        Importeth thee° to know, this bears.   *Is important for you*
                    [*He gives* ANTONY *the letter*]
110   ANTONY   Forbear° me.   *Leave*
                    [*Exit* THIRD MESSENGER]
        There's a great spirit gone. Thus did I desire it.
        What our contempts doth often hurl from us
        We wish it ours again. The present pleasure,
        By revolution low'ring,[6] does become
115   The opposite of itself. She's° good being gone;   *Fulvia is*
        The hand could° pluck her back that shoved her on.   *would wish to*
        I must from this enchanting° queen break off.   *spellbinding*
        Ten thousand harms more than the ills I know
        My idleness doth hatch. How now, Enobarbus!
                    Enter ENOBARBUS
120   ENOBARBUS   What's your pleasure, sir?
ANTONY   I must with haste from hence.
ENOBARBUS   Why, then we kill[7] all our women. We see how
        mortal an unkindness is to them; if they suffer our departure,
        death's the word.
ANTONY   I must be gone.
125   ENOBARBUS   Under a compelling occasion let women die. It
        were pity to cast them away for nothing, though between them
        and a great cause they should be esteemed nothing. Cleopatra
        catching but the least noise of this dies instantly. I have seen
        her die twenty times upon far poorer moment.° I do think there   *for far less reason*
130   is mettle° in death, which commits some loving act upon her,   *(sexual) potency; courage*
        she hath such a celerity° in dying.   *speed*
ANTONY   She is cunning past man's thought.

---

4. O . . . *earing*: Antony compares his recent behavior to
an unplowed field: just as the field sprouts weeds when it
remains untilled (by hand or) by a "quick" (fertile) wind,
he falls into "ill" habits when he is not forced to face crit-
icism (to undergo "earing," plowing).
5. City in Greece where Antony left Fulvia.

6. Growing lower by turning (as of a wheel, such as For-
tune's).
7. Alluding to achieving an orgasm. Throughout the
scene "kill," "death," and "dying" all carry this bawdy res-
onance. "Nothing," which Enobarbus repeats, may refer
to the female genitals.

ENOBARBUS   Alack, sir, no. Her passions are made of nothing but
the finest part of pure love. We cannot call her winds and
135   waters sighs and tears; they are greater storms and tempests than
almanacs can report. This cannot be cunning in her; if it be,
she makes a shower of rain as well as Jove.[8]

ANTONY   Would I had never seen her!

ENOBARBUS   O, sir, you had then left unseen a wonderful piece
140   of work,° which not to have been blessed withal° would have   *masterpiece / with*
discredited your travel.[9]

ANTONY   Fulvia is dead.

ENOBARBUS   Sir.

ANTONY   Fulvia is dead.

145   ENOBARBUS   Fulvia?

ANTONY   Dead.

ENOBARBUS   Why, sir, give the gods a thankful sacrifice. When it
pleaseth their deities to take the wife of a man from him, it
shows to man the tailors of the earth; comforting therein that
150   when old robes° are worn out there are members[1] to make new.   *clothes; women*
If there were no more women but Fulvia, then had you indeed
a cut, and the case to be lamented. This grief is crowned with
consolation; your old smock brings forth a new petticoat, and
indeed the tears live in an onion that should water this sorrow.[2]

155   ANTONY   The business she hath broachèd in the state
Cannot endure my absence.

ENOBARBUS   And the business you have broached here cannot
be without you, especially that of Cleopatra's, which wholly
depends on your abode.°   *staying on here*

160   ANTONY   No more light answers. Let our officers
Have notice what we purpose. I shall break
The cause of our expedience° to the Queen,   *haste*
And get her leave to part; for not alone
The death of Fulvia, with more urgent touches,°   *concerns*
165   Do strongly speak to us, but the letters too
Of many our contriving friends[3] in Rome
Petition us at home.° Sextus Pompeius   *to go home*
Hath given the dare to Caesar and commands
The empire of the sea.[4] Our slippery° people,   *inconstant*
170   Whose love is never linked to the deserver
Till his deserts are past, begin to throw°   *ascribe (the title of)*
Pompey the Great and all his dignities
Upon his son, who—high in name and power,
Higher than both in blood and life°—stands up   *vitality and energy*
175   For the main soldier;[5] whose quality, going on,
The sides o'th' world may danger.[6] Much is breeding
Which, like the courser's hair, hath yet but life,
And not a serpent's poison.[7] Say our pleasure,

---

8. Jupiter; ruler of the gods: one of his duties was govern-
ing rain.
9. Would have cast doubt on your success as a traveler.
Travel also suggests travail, or work, as in "piece of work"
(lines 139–40).
1. Limbs; sexual organs. The sexual innuendo is contin-
ued in "cut" (line 152: severe blow; slash in a garment;
vagina, "case" (line 152: situation; set of clothes; vagina),
and "broachèd" (line 155, 157: opened or pricked).
2. the tears . . . sorrow: real tears are not called for.
3. Of many friends acting on our behalf.

4. Sextus Pompey was the younger son of Pompey the
Great, who was a foe of Julius Caesar (see *Julius Caesar*
1.1). Previously an outlaw, the Pompey of the play had
gained control of the shipping routes around Sicily.
5. stands . . . soldier: acts like the leading soldier.
6. whose . . . danger: whose accomplishments and charac-
ter, should they continue to succeed, might endanger the
entire arrangement of the world.
7. A horse's ("courser's," line 177) hair was believed to
become a live snake if put in water.

To such whose place° is under us, requires   *rank*
Our quick remove from hence.

180 ENOBARBUS   I shall do't. [*Exeunt severally*]

1.3

Enter CLEOPATRA, CHARMIAN, ALEXAS, *and* IRAS

CLEOPATRA   Where is he?

CHARMIAN   I did not see him since.°   *recently*

CLEOPATRA [*to* ALEXAS]   See where he is, who's with him, what he does.
I did not send you.[1] If you find him sad,°   *serious*
Say I am dancing; if in mirth, report

5   That I am sudden sick. Quick, and return.   [*Exit* ALEXAS]

CHARMIAN   Madam, methinks, if you did love him dearly,
You do not hold the method° to enforce   *act appropriately*
The like from him.

CLEOPATRA   What should I do I do not?°   *What else should I do*

CHARMIAN   In each thing give him way; cross him in nothing.

10 CLEOPATRA   Thou teachest like a fool, the way to lose him.

CHARMIAN   Tempt° him not so too far. Iwis,° forbear.   *Test / Indeed*
In time we hate that which we often fear.

        Enter ANTONY

But here comes Antony.

CLEOPATRA   I am sick and sullen.°   *dispirited*

ANTONY   I am sorry to give breathing° to my purpose.   *voice*

15 CLEOPATRA   Help me away, dear Charmian, I shall fall.
It cannot be thus long—the sides of nature[2]
Will not sustain it.

ANTONY   Now, my dearest queen.

CLEOPATRA   Pray you, stand farther from me.

ANTONY   What's the matter?

CLEOPATRA   I know by that same eye there's some good news.

20 What says the married woman°—you may go?   (*Fulvia*)
Would she had never given you leave to come.
Let her not say 'tis I that keep you here.
I have no power upon you; hers you are.

ANTONY   The gods best know—

CLEOPATRA   O, never was there queen

25 So mightily betrayed! Yet at the first
I saw the treasons planted.

ANTONY   Cleopatra—

CLEOPATRA   Why should I think you can be mine and true—
Though you in swearing shake the thronèd gods[3]—
Who have been false to Fulvia? Riotous madness,

30 To be entangled with those mouth-made° vows   *hypocritical*
Which break themselves in swearing.°   *as they are made*

ANTONY   Most sweet queen—

CLEOPATRA   Nay, pray you, seek no colour° for your going,   *excuse*
But bid farewell and go. When you sued staying,°   *entreated to remain*
Then was the time for words; no going then.

35 Eternity was in our[4] lips and eyes,
Bliss in our brow's bent;° none our parts so poor   *curve*

1.3 Location: Scene continues.
1. Do not say I sent you.
2. This cannot go on much longer—the bodily frame.
3. When Jupiter swore an oath, Olympus was supposed

to shake.
4. My (royal plural); possibly also the conventional first person plural.

But was a race of heaven.[5] They are so still,
Or thou, the greatest soldier of the world,
Art turned the greatest liar.

ANTONY   How now, lady!

40 CLEOPATRA   I would I had thy inches.° Thou shouldst know   size (phallic)
There were a heart in Egypt.[6]

ANTONY   Hear me, Queen.
The strong necessity of time commands
Our services a while, but my full heart
Remains in use° with you. Our Italy   in trust
45 Shines o'er with civil swords.° Sextus Pompeius   swords of civil war
Makes his approaches to the port of Rome.[7]
Equality of two domestic powers
Breed scrupulous faction.° The hated, grown to strength,   distrustful dissent
Are newly grown to love.° The condemned° Pompey,   popularity / banished
50 Rich in his father's honour, creeps° apace   insinuates himself
Into the hearts of such as have not thrived
Upon the present state,° whose numbers threaten;   government
And quietness, grown sick of rest, would purge
By any desperate change.[8] My more particular,°   personal motivation
55 And that which most with you should safe° my going,   sanction
Is Fulvia's death.

CLEOPATRA   Though age from folly could not give me freedom,
It does from childishness. Can Fulvia die?

ANTONY   She's dead, my queen.
         [He offers letters]
60 Look here, and at thy sovereign leisure read
The garboils° she awaked. At the last, best,[9]   upheavals
See when and where she died.

CLEOPATRA   O most false love!
Where be the sacred vials[1] thou shouldst fill
With sorrowful water? Now I see, I see,
65 In Fulvia's death how mine received shall be.

ANTONY   Quarrel no more, but be prepared to know
The purposes I bear, which are° or cease   continue
As you shall give th'advice. By the fire°   sun
That quickens Nilus' slime,[2] I go from hence
70 Thy soldier-servant, making peace or war
As thou affects.°   choose

CLEOPATRA   Cut my lace,[3] Charmian, come.
But let it be. I am quickly ill and well;
So[4] Antony loves.

ANTONY   My precious queen, forbear,
And give true evidence° to his love, which stands   be an honest witness
An honourable trial.

75 CLEOPATRA   So Fulvia told me.

---

5. *none . . . heaven:* Even my poorest attributes were heavenly.
6. There were courage (to respond to such insults) in the country (Queen) of Egypt.
7. Ostia (16 miles from Rome).
8. *And . . . change:* And peace, made ill by inactivity, wishes to purge itself of impurities by a violently acting remedy.
9. The best news last; Fulvia was at her best at the end of her life.

1. Renaissance writers thought that the Romans filled small bottles with tears to place in graves; also, where are your sad and watery eyes ("vials")?
2. That causes plants to grow in the silt that the Nile deposits.
3. Cutting the strings would be quicker than untying the lace on her bodice to relieve her from her feigned fainting spell.
4. Thus (falsely); as long as.

I prithee turn aside and weep for her,
Then bid adieu to me, and say the tears
Belong to Egypt.° Good now, play one scene   *Cleopatra*
Of excellent dissembling, and let it look
Like perfect honour.

80 ANTONY   You'll heat my blood.° No more.   *make me angry*

CLEOPATRA   You can do better yet; but this is meetly.°   *fairly good (acting)*

ANTONY   Now by my sword—

CLEOPATRA   And target.⁵ Still he mends.°   *improves*
But this is not the best. Look, prithee, Charmian,
How this Herculean Roman does become
85   The carriage of his chafe.⁶

ANTONY   I'll leave you, lady.

CLEOPATRA   Courteous lord, one word.
Sir, you and I must part; but that's not it.
Sir, you and I have loved; but there's not it;
90   That you know well. Something it is I would—
O, my oblivion is a very Antony,
And I am all forgotten.⁷

ANTONY   But that your royalty
Holds idleness your subject, I should take you
For idleness itself.⁸

CLEOPATRA   'Tis sweating labour°   *work; birth pains*
95   To bear such idleness° so near the heart   *flippancy; laziness*
As Cleopatra this. But sir, forgive me,
Since my becomings° kill me when they do not   *transformations; graces*
Eye° well to you. Your honour calls you hence,   *Look*
Therefore be deaf to my unpitied folly,
100   And all the gods go with you. Upon your sword
Sit laurel victory,⁹ and smooth success
Be strewed before your feet.

ANTONY   Let us go.
Come. Our separation so abides and flies¹
That thou residing here goes yet with me,
105   And I hence fleeting, here remain with thee.
Away.   *Exeunt [severally]*

1.4

Enter Octavius CAESAR *reading a letter,* LEPIDUS, *and their train*

CAESAR   You may see, Lepidus, and henceforth know,
It is not Caesar's natural vice to hate
Our great competitor.° From Alexandria   *ally; rival*
This is the news: he fishes, drinks, and wastes
5   The lamps of night in revel; is not more manlike
Than Cleopatra, nor the queen of Ptolemy¹

---

5. Shield. Cleopatra parodies the blustering oaths of heroic drama.
6. *does . . . chafe:* emulates Hercules, his heroic ancestor, with his posture of rage.
7. *my . . . forgotten:* my memory has deserted me as you are doing, and I have forgotten everything (am totally forgotten—by Antony).
8. *But . . . itself:* If you were not queen over your flippancy and hence in full control of it, I would think that you were flippancy itself.

9. *Upon . . . victory:* May your military exploits receive the laurel wreath as the reward for victory.
1. Consists so much of both remaining together and being separated (in that we are united by the shared experience of it).
1.4 Location: Rome.
1. Julius Caesar had commanded Cleopatra to marry her half brother Ptolemy XIV (acceptable within the Egyptian royal family); she was said to have had Ptolemy poisoned.

More womanly than he; hardly gave audience[2]
Or vouchsafed to think he had partners. You shall find there°   *(the letter); (Egypt)*
A man who is the abstract° of all faults   *paradigm*
That all men follow.

10 LEPIDUS   I must not think there are
    Evils enough to darken all his goodness.
    His faults in him seem as the spots of heaven,°   *stars*
    More fiery by night's blackness; hereditary
    Rather than purchased;° what he cannot change   *acquired*
15   Than° what he chooses.   *Rather than*

CAESAR   You are too indulgent. Let's grant it is not
    Amiss to tumble on the bed of Ptolemy,
    To give a kingdom for a mirth,° to sit   *joke*
    And keep the turn of° tippling with a slave,   *take turns at*
20   To reel the streets at noon, and stand the buffet°   *come to blows*
    With knaves that smells of sweat. Say° this becomes him—   *Even if*
    As his composure° must be rare indeed   *And his character*
    Whom these things cannot blemish—yet must Antony
    No way excuse his foils° when we do bear   *faults*
25   So great weight in° his lightness. If he filled   *as a result of*
    His vacancy° with his voluptuousness,   *leisure*
    Full surfeits and the dryness of his bones[3]
    Call on° him for't. But to confound° such time   *Afflict / waste*
    That drums° him from his sport, and speaks as loud   *summons*
30   As his own state° and ours— 'tis to be chid   *public responsibility*
    As we rate° boys who, being mature in knowledge,   *upbraid*
    Pawn their experience to their present pleasure,
    And so rebel to judgement.[4]

    Enter a MESSENGER

LEPIDUS   Here's more news.

MESSENGER   Thy biddings have been done, and every hour,
35   Most noble Caesar, shalt thou have report
    How 'tis abroad. Pompey is strong at sea,
    And it appears he is beloved of those
    That only have feared Caesar.[5] To the ports
    The discontents° repair, and men's reports   *discontented people*
    Give him° much wronged.   *[Exit]*   *Say he is*
40 CAESAR   I should have known no less.
    It hath been taught us from the primal state[6]
    That he which is was wished until he were,[7]
    And the ebbed° man, ne'er loved till ne'er worth love,   *fallen*
    Comes deared° by being lacked. This common body,°   *Is loved / The people*
45   Like to a vagabond flag° upon the stream,   *drifting reed*
    Goes to, and back, lackeying° the varying tide,   *following slavishly*
    To rot itself with motion.

    [Enter a SECOND MESSENGER]

SECOND MESSENGER   Caesar, I bring thee word
    Menecrates and Menas, famous pirates,°   *(allied with Pompey)*
    Makes the sea serve them, which they ear° and wound   *plow*
50   With keels of every kind. Many hot inroads

---

2. Hardly listened (to Octavius's messengers, in 1.1).
3. *Full . . . bones:* Ill health caused by overeating and venereal disease.
4. *being . . . judgement:* old enough to know better, abandon their wisdom in favor of momentary pleasure, and thus act against their better judgment.
5. That obeyed Caesar only out of fear.
6. Since the first society was organized.
7. That man who rules was supported until he began to rule.

They make in Italy. The borders maritime°   *coastal territories*
Lack blood° to think on't, and flush° youth revolt. *Go pallid / spirited*
No vessel can peep forth but 'tis as soon
Taken as seen; for Pompey's name strikes more
Than could his war resisted.[8]   [*Exit*]

55 CAESAR   Antony,
Leave thy lascivious wassails.° When thou once   *drunken revels*
Was beaten from Modena,[9] where thou slew'st
Hirtius and Pansa, consuls, at thy heel
Did famine follow, whom thou fought'st against—
60 Though daintily brought up—with patience more
Than savages could suffer. Thou didst drink
The stale° of horses, and the gilded° puddle   *urine / slime-covered*
Which beasts would cough at.° Thy palate then did deign°   *refuse (to drink) / accept*
The roughest berry on the rudest hedge.
65 Yea, like the stag when snow the pasture sheets,°   *covers*
The barks of trees thou browsed.° On the Alps   *fed upon*
It is reported thou didst eat strange flesh,
Which some did die to look on; and all this—
It wounds thine honour that I speak it now—
70 Was borne so like a soldier that thy cheek
So much as lanked° not.   *grew thin*
LEPIDUS   'Tis pity of him.
CAESAR   Let his shames quickly
Drive him to Rome. 'Tis time we twain
75 Did show ourselves i'th' field; and to that end
Assemble we immediate council. Pompey
Thrives in our idleness.
LEPIDUS   Tomorrow, Caesar,
I shall be furnished to inform you rightly
Both what° by sea and land I can be able°   *what forces / assemble*
To front° this present time.   *To confront the enemy at*
80 CAESAR   Till which encounter
It is my business, too. Farewell.
LEPIDUS   Farewell, my lord. What you shall know meantime
Of stirs° abroad I shall beseech you, sir,   *incidents*
To let me be partaker.
85 CAESAR   Doubt not, sir. I knew it for my bond.°   *Exeunt*   *responsibility*

1.5

Enter CLEOPATRA, CHARMIAN, IRAS, *and* MARDIAN

CLEOPATRA   Charmian!
CHARMIAN   Madam?
CLEOPATRA   [*yawning*] Ha, ha. Give me to drink mandragora.[1]
CHARMIAN   Why, madam?
5 CLEOPATRA   That I might sleep out this great gap of time
My Antony is away.
CHARMIAN   You think of him too much.
CLEOPATRA   O, 'tis treason!
CHARMIAN   Madam, I trust not so.
CLEOPATRA   Thou, eunuch Mardian!

8. *Pompey's . . . resisted:* Pompey's name alone is more
powerful than his forces would be if confronted in battle.
9. Site of a battle in which Antony was defeated by the
combined armies of Octavius Caesar and the Roman Sen-
ate, at the instigation of Cicero.
1.5 Location: Alexandria.
1. A narcotic, made from the mandrake plant.

MARDIAN   What's your highness' pleasure?
CLEOPATRA   Not now to hear thee sing.[2] I take no pleasure
10   In aught[3] an eunuch has. 'Tis well for thee
        That, being unseminared,° thy freer thoughts   *castrated*
        May not fly forth of Egypt. Hast thou affections?°   *desires*
MARDIAN   Yes, gracious madam.
CLEOPATRA   Indeed?
15 MARDIAN   Not in deed, madam, for I can do° nothing   *(sexually)*
        But what indeed is honest° to be done.   *chaste; moral*
        Yet have I fierce affections, and think
        What Venus did with Mars.[4]
CLEOPATRA   O, Charmian,
        Where think'st thou he is now? Stands he or sits he?
20   Or does he walk? Or is he on his horse?
        O happy horse, to bear the weight of Antony!
        Do bravely, horse, for wot'st° thou whom thou mov'st?—   *know*
        The demi-Atlas[5] of this earth, the arm°   *champion*
        And burgonet° of men. He's speaking now,   *helmet; guardian*
25   Or murmuring 'Where's my serpent of old Nile?'[6]—
        For so he calls me. Now I feed myself
        With most delicious poison. Think on me,
        That am with Phoebus'° amorous pinches black,   *the sun god*
        And wrinkled deep in time. Broad-fronted° Caesar,°   *Broad-browed / (Julius)*
30   When thou wast here above the ground I was
        A morsel for a monarch, and great Pompey[7]
        Would stand and make his eyes grow in my brow.
        There would he anchor his aspect,° and die°   *gaze / (sexual)*
        With looking on his life.
                Enter ALEXAS
ALEXAS   Sovereign of Egypt, hail!
35 CLEOPATRA   How much unlike art thou Mark Antony!
        Yet, coming from him, that great medicine[8] hath
        With his tinct° gilded thee. How goes it   *power; color*
        With my brave° Mark Antony?   *magnificent*
ALEXAS   Last thing he did, dear Queen,
        He kissed—the last of many doubled kisses—
40   This orient[9] pearl. His speech sticks in my heart.
CLEOPATRA   Mine ear must pluck it thence.
ALEXAS   'Good friend,' quoth he,
        'Say the firm° Roman to great Egypt° sends   *loyal; resolute / Cleopatra*
        This treasure of an oyster; at whose foot,
        To mend° the petty present, I will piece°   *improve / add to*
45   Her opulent throne with kingdoms. All the East,
        Say thou, shall call her mistress.' So he nodded,
        And soberly did mount an arm-jaunced steed,[1]

---

2. Castrati were used in Italian music from the end of the sixteenth century, and Shakespeare associates singing eunuchs with the eastern Mediterranean in *Twelfth Night* and *A Midsummer Night's Dream*; they are not thought to have been used as singers in ancient Rome.
3. In anything; in the nothing. The eunuch has nothing instead of testicles.
4. Venus, goddess of love (married to Vulcan), and Mars, god of war, were lovers.
5. Octavius and Antony between them rule the world—Lepidus having conveniently been forgotten—as Atlas bore it on his shoulders.

6. See 2.7.25–26 for the superstition that snakes formed spontaneously in the Nile mud; the asp in particular was associated with Isis, with whom Cleopatra identifies herself.
7. Gnaeus Pompey, older brother of Sextus Pompey (the character in this play) and son of Pompey the Great. But Cleopatra's phrasing makes him sound like the father.
8. Elixir of life: sought by alchemists, it was thought to be able to turn base metals to gold and cure all disease.
9. From India (more lustrous than European pearls).
1. Steed jolted by one in armor (or by its own armor).

Who neighed so high that what I would have spoke
Was beastly dumbed° by him.   *drowned out*

CLEOPATRA   What, was he sad or merry?

50 ALEXAS   Like to the time o'th' year between the extremes
Of hot and cold, he was nor° sad nor merry.   *neither*

CLEOPATRA   O well divided° disposition! Note him,   *balanced*
Note him, good Charmian, 'tis the man; but note him.
He was not sad, for he would shine on those
55 That make their looks by his;[2] he was not merry,
Which seemed to tell them his remembrance lay
In Egypt with his joy; but between both.
O heavenly mingle! Be'st thou sad or merry,
The violence of either thee becomes;
60 So does it no man else. Met'st thou my posts?°   *messengers*

ALEXAS   Ay, madam, twenty several° messengers.   *separate*
Why do you send so thick?

CLEOPATRA   Who's° born that day   *Whoever is*
When I forget to send to Antony
Shall die a beggar. Ink and paper, Charmian!
65 Welcome, my good Alexas. Did I, Charmian,
Ever love Caesar so?

CHARMIAN   O, that brave Caesar!

CLEOPATRA   Be choked with such another emphasis!
Say 'the brave Antony'.

CHARMIAN   The valiant Caesar.

CLEOPATRA   By Isis, I will give thee bloody teeth
70 If thou with Caesar paragon° again   *compare*
My man of men.

CHARMIAN   By your most gracious pardon,
I sing but after you.

CLEOPATRA   My salad days,
When I was green° in judgement, cold in blood,°   *immature / feeling*
To say as I said then. But come, away,
75 Get me ink and paper.
He shall have every day a several greeting,
Or I'll unpeople Egypt.[3]   *Exeunt*

2.1

Enter POMPEY, MENECRATES, *and* MENAS, *in warlike
manner*

POMPEY   If the great gods be just, they shall assist
The deeds of justest men.

MENECRATES   Know, worthy Pompey,
That what they do delay they not deny.

POMPEY   Whiles we are suitors to their throne, decays
The thing we sue for.[1]

5 MENECRATES   We, ignorant of ourselves,
Beg often our own harms, which the wise powers
Deny us for our° good; so find we profit   *our own*
By losing of our prayers.

POMPEY   I shall do well.

---

2. Who are dependent on his mood; who reflect his
appearance in their own.
3. If not, it will be only because I have run out of Egyp-
tians to act as messengers (or, because I have killed all

Egyptians).
2.1 Location: Pompey's headquarters (in Sicily).
1. *Whiles . . . for:* While we are beseeching the gods, what
we request is losing its value.

The people love me, and the sea is mine.

10 My powers are crescent,° and my auguring° hope   *growing / prophesying*

Says it° will come to th' full.² Mark Antony   *(my military power)*

In Egypt sits at dinner, and will make

No wars without doors.³ Caesar gets money where

He loses hearts. Lepidus flatters both,

15 Of° both is flattered; but he neither loves,°   *By / loves neither*

Nor either cares for him.

MENAS   Caesar and Lepidus

Are in the field; a mighty strength they carry.

POMPEY   Where have you this? 'Tis false.

MENAS   From Silvius, sir.

POMPEY   He dreams. I know they are in Rome together,

20 Looking° for Antony. But all the charms° of love,   *Waiting / incantations*

Salt° Cleopatra, soften thy waned⁴ lip.   *Lecherous*

Let witchcraft join with beauty, lust with both

Tie up the libertine, in a field of feasts

Keep his brain fuming;° Epicurean⁵ cooks   *drunk*

25 Sharpen with cloyless sauce⁶ his appetite,

That sleep and feeding may prorogue° his honour   *postpone*

Even till a Lethe'd dullness⁷—

         Enter VARRIUS

                   How now, Varrius?

VARRIUS   This is most certain that I shall deliver:

Mark Antony is every hour in Rome

30 Expected. Since he went from Egypt, 'tis

A space for farther travel.⁸

POMPEY   I could have given less° matter   *less crucial*

A better ear. Menas, I did not think

This amorous surfeiter would have donned his helm°   *helmet*

For such a petty war. His soldiership

35 Is twice the other twain. But let us rear°   *elevate*

The higher our opinion,° that our stirring   *(of ourselves)*

Can from the lap of Egypt's widow⁹ pluck

The ne'er lust-wearied Antony.

MENAS   I cannot hope°   *suppose*

Caesar and Antony shall well greet together.

40 His wife that's dead did trespasses to° Caesar,   *offended against*

His brother warred upon him, although, I think,

Not moved° by Antony.   *prompted*

POMPEY   I know not, Menas,

How lesser enmities may give way to greater.

Were't not that we stand up against them all,

45 'Twere pregnant° they should square° between themselves,   *evident / argue*

For they have entertainèd° cause enough   *sustained*

To draw their swords. But how the fear of us

May cement their divisions,° and bind up   *unite them*

---

2. Like the "crescent" moon.

3. Outside doors. Antony is concerned only with the wars of love, conducted indoors.

4. Withered; decreased, like the moon, perhaps in implicit contrast to the "crescent" and potentially "full" moon of Pompey's "powers" (lines 10–11).

5. The philosopher Epicurus and his followers believed that the gods took no interest in men's actions and that the only aim of life was to seek pleasure.

6. Sauce that never wearies or disgusts.

7. Drinking the water of Lethe, one of the rivers bounding Hades, caused total loss of memory.

8. Sufficient time to have traveled even farther (than between Egypt and Rome).

9. Cleopatra had married one of her brothers, Ptolemy XIV, whom she later seems to have had murdered. See note to 1.4.6.

The petty difference, we yet not know.
50　Be't as our gods will have't; it only stands
Our lives upon to use[1] our strongest hands.
Come, Menas.　　　　　　　　　　　　　　*Exeunt*

2.2

Enter ENOBARBUS *and* LEPIDUS

LEPIDUS　Good Enobarbus, 'tis a worthy deed,
And shall become you well, to entreat your captain
To soft and gentle speech.
ENOBARBUS　　　　　I shall entreat him
To answer like himself.[1] If Caesar move° him,　　　　　　°angers
5　Let Antony look over Caesar's head
And speak as loud as Mars. By Jupiter,
Were I the wearer of Antonio's beard
I would not shave't today.[2]
LEPIDUS　　　　　　　'Tis not a time
For private stomaching.°　　　　　　　　　　　　　°quarrels
ENOBARBUS　　　　　　　　　Every time
10　Serves for the matter that is then born in't.
LEPIDUS　But small to greater matters must give way.
ENOBARBUS　Not if the small come first.
LEPIDUS　　　　　　　　　　Your speech is passion.°　　　°not reasoned
But pray you, stir no embers° up. Here comes　　　　　°old resentments
The noble Antony.
Enter [at one door] ANTONY *and* VENTIDIUS
ENOBARBUS　　　　　And yonder Caesar.
Enter [at another door] CAESAR, MAECENAS, *and* AGRIPPA
15　ANTONY [*to* VENTIDIUS]　If we compose° well here, to Parthia.　°reach agreement
Hark, Ventidius.
CAESAR　　　　　　　I do not know,
Maecenas; ask Agrippa.
LEPIDUS[*to* CAESAR *and* ANTONY]　Noble friends,
That which combined us was most great; and let not
A leaner° action rend us. What's amiss,　　　　　　　°less important
20　May it be gently heard. When we debate
Our trivial difference loud,° we do commit　　　　　　°loudly; violently
Murder in° healing wounds. Then, noble partners,　°in the process of
The rather for° I earnestly beseech,　　　　　　　°Especially because
Touch you the sourest points with sweetest terms,
Nor curstness grow° to th' matter.　　　　　　°Do not let ill temper add
25　ANTONY　　　　　　　　　　'Tis spoken well.
Were we° before our armies, and to° fight,　　　　°If we were / about to
I should do thus.[3]
　　　[ANTONY *and* CAESAR *embrace.*] *Flourish*
CAESAR　Welcome to Rome.
ANTONY　Thank you.
30　CAESAR　Sit.
ANTONY　Sit, sir.
CAESAR　Nay then.

1. it . . . use: our lives depend entirely on the use of.
2.2 Location: Rome.
1. To answer in a manner appropriate to his character (greatness?; dissipation?).
2. Plucking a man's beard was an insult; Enobarbus

wants Antony to give Octavius the chance to insult him. Possibly, Enobarbus is suggesting not that Antony act heroically but that he merely look the part.
3. Formally embrace you, as I do now; possibly, speak as you request.

[They sit]

ANTONY   I learn you take things ill which are not so,
Or being,° concern you not.   *being ill*

CAESAR   I must be laughed at

35   If or° for nothing or a little I   *either*
Should say myself offended, and with you
Chiefly i'th'° world; more laughed at that I should   *Of all the*
Once name you derogately,° when to sound your name *censoriously*
It not concernèd me.

40 ANTONY   My being in Egypt, Caesar, what was't to you?

CAESAR   No more than my residing here at Rome
Might be to you in Egypt. Yet if you there
Did practise on° my state, your being in Egypt   *scheme against*
Might be my question.°   *concern*

ANTONY   How intend you 'practised'?

45 CAESAR   You may be pleased to catch at° mine intent   *grasp*
By what did here befall me. Your wife and brother
Made wars upon me, and their contestation
Was theme for you. You were the word of war.[4]

ANTONY   You do mistake the business. My brother never

50   Did urge me in his act.[5] I did enquire° it,   *inquire into*
And have my learning from some true reports°   *reliable sources*
That drew their swords with you. Did he not rather
Discredit my authority with yours,
And make the wars alike against my stomach,°   *wish*

55   Having alike° your cause? Of this, my letters   *Since I shared*
Before did satisfy you. If you'll patch a quarrel,
As matter whole you have to make it with,[6]
It must not be with this.

CAESAR   You praise yourself
By laying defects of judgement to me, but
You patched up your excuses.

60 ANTONY   Not so, not so.
I know you could not lack, I am certain on't,
Very necessity of this thought,[7] that I,
Your partner in the cause 'gainst which he fought,
Could not with graceful eyes attend[8] those wars

65   Which fronted° mine own peace. As for my wife,   *opposed*
I would you had her spirit in such another.
The third o'th' world is yours, which with a snaffle[9]
You may pace° easy, but not such a wife.   *train to walk*

ENOBARBUS   Would we had all such wives, that the men might

70   go to wars with the women.

ANTONY   So much uncurbable,° her garboils,° Caesar, *uncontrollable / tumults*
Made out of her impatience—which not wanted°   *did not lack*
Shrewdness of policy too—I grieving grant
Did you too much disquiet, for that you must
But° say I could not help it.   *Only*

75 CAESAR   I wrote to you

---

4. *contestation . . . war*: war was meant as an example for you to follow (had you as its theme); Your name was the war cry (war was waged in your name).
5. Claimed to be acting as my proxy.
6. *If . . . with*: If you'll patch together an old quarrel with trivia, when you have enough material to make a new one

(or, possibly, as if you had enough material to make one).
7. *I know . . . thought*: I'm confident that you must have been aware.
8. Could not look with approval on.
9. Bridle (one without a curb, for good-tempered horses).

When, rioting in Alexandria, you
Did pocket up my letters, and with taunts
Did gibe my missive out of audience.[1]

ANTONY   Sir, he fell upon° me ere admitted, then.   *broke in on*
80   Three kings I had newly feasted, and did want
Of what I was[2] i'th' morning; but next day
I told him of myself,° which was as much   *my situation*
As to have asked him pardon. Let this fellow
Be nothing° of our strife. If we contend,   *Be no part*
Out of our question° wipe him.   *dispute*
85   CAESAR   You have broken
The article° of your oath, which you shall never   *terms*
Have tongue to charge me with.
LEPIDUS   Soft, Caesar.
ANTONY   No, Lepidus, let him speak.
90   The honour is sacred which he talks on now,
Supposing that I lacked it.[3] But on, Caesar:
The article of my oath—
CAESAR   To lend me arms and aid when I required them,
The which you both denied.
ANTONY   Neglected, rather,
95   And then when poisoned hours had bound me up
From mine own knowledge.[4] As nearly as I may
I'll play the penitent to you, but mine honesty
Shall not make poor my greatness, nor my power
Work without it.[5] Truth is that Fulvia,
100   To have me out of Egypt, made wars here,
For which myself, the ignorant motive, do
So far ask pardon as befits mine honour°   *dignity*
To stoop in such a case.
LEPIDUS   'Tis noble spoken.
MAECENAS   If it might please you to enforce no further
105   The griefs° between ye; to forget them quite   *grievances*
Were to remember that the present need
Speaks to atone you.°   *Is to reconcile you*
LEPIDUS   Worthily spoken, Maecenas.
ENOBARBUS   Or if you borrow one another's love for the instant,
you may, when you hear no more words of Pompey, return it
110   again. You shall have time to wrangle in when you have noth-
ing else to do.
ANTONY   Thou art a soldier only. Speak no more.
ENOBARBUS   That truth should be silent I had almost forgot.
ANTONY   You wrong this presence,° therefore speak no more.   *(noble) company*
115   ENOBARBUS   Go to, then; your considerate stone.[6]
CAESAR   I do not much dislike the matter,° but   *content*
The manner of his speech, for't cannot be
We shall remain in friendship, our conditions°   *dispositions*
So diff'ring in their acts. Yet if I knew
120   What hoop should hold us staunch,° from edge to edge   *watertight; bound*

1. Scoffed my messenger out of your (public) hearing (referring to 1.1).
2. *did . . . was*: was not myself.
3. *The honour . . . it*: What Caesar speaks of now is my sacred honor, which he assumes I lack (even assuming I lack it).
4. *bound . . . knowledge*: prevented me from realizing what I was doing.
5. *mine . . . it*: my honorable behavior (in admitting a fault) will not diminish my power, nor shall my power operate without honor.
6. Very well, then; still and silent, but capable of thought.

O'th' world I would pursue it.
AGRIPPA   Give me leave, Caesar.
CAESAR   Speak, Agrippa.
AGRIPPA   Thou hast a sister by the mother's side,
125   Admired Octavia. Great Mark Antony
Is now a widower.
CAESAR   Say not so, Agrippa.
If Cleopatra heard you, your reproof
Were well deserved of rashness.[7]
ANTONY   I am not married, Caesar. Let me hear
130   Agrippa further speak.
AGRIPPA   To hold you in perpetual amity,
To make you brothers, and to knit your hearts
With an unslipping knot, take Antony°   *let Antony take*
Octavia to° his wife; whose beauty claims   *for*
135   No worse a husband than the best of men;
Whose virtue and whose general graces speak
That which none else can utter.[8] By this marriage
All little jealousies° which now seem great,   *mistrusts*
And all great fears which now import° their dangers,   *bring along*
140   Would then be nothing. Truths would be tales
Where now half-tales be truths.[9] Her love to both
Would each to other and all loves to both
Draw after her. Pardon what I have spoke,
For 'tis a studied, not a present° thought,   *sudden*
By duty ruminated.
145   ANTONY   Will Caesar speak?
CAESAR   Not till he hears how Antony is touched°   *reacts*
With° what is spoke already.   *To*
ANTONY   What power is in Agrippa,
If I would say 'Agrippa, be it so',
To make this good?
150   CAESAR   The power of Caesar,
And his power unto Octavia.
ANTONY   May I never
To this good purpose, that so fairly shows,
Dream of impediment![1] Let me have thy hand.
Further this act of grace, and from this hour
155   The heart of brothers govern in our loves
And sway our great designs.
CAESAR   There's my hand.
    [ANTONY *and* CAESAR *clasp hands*]
A sister I bequeath° you whom no brother   *hand over to*
Did ever love so dearly. Let her live
To join our kingdoms and our hearts; and never
Fly off our loves again.[2]
160   LEPIDUS   Happily, amen.
ANTONY   I did not think to draw my sword 'gainst Pompey,
For he hath laid strange° courtesies and great   *uncommon*

7. *your . . . rashness*: the reproof you would receive would befit your rashness.
8. *speak . . . utter*: speak for themselves; speak more powerfully than in any other woman.
9. *Truths . . . truths*: True reports, even if they were disturbing, could be passed over, regarded as hearsay, where now incomplete rumors are accepted as truth.

1. *May . . . impediment*: alluding to the Anglican marriage service, as does sonnet 116: "Let me not to the marriage of true minds / Admit impediments." *so fairly shows*: appears so attractive.
2. *never . . . again*: may our love for each other never again desert us.

Of late upon me. I must thank him only,°   *at least*
Lest my remembrance° suffer ill report;   *gratitude*
At heel of° that, defy him.   *Right after*

165 LEPIDUS   Time calls upon's.
Of° us must Pompey presently° be sought,   *By / immediately*
Or else he seeks out us.

ANTONY   Where lies he?

CAESAR   About the Mount Misena.³

ANTONY   What is his strength
By land?

CAESAR   Great and increasing, but by sea
He is an absolute master.

170 ANTONY   So is the fame.°   *report*
Would we had spoke together.° Haste we for it;   *(earlier)*
Yet ere we put ourselves in arms, dispatch we
The business we have talked of.

CAESAR   With most gladness,
And do° invite you to my sister's view,   *I do*
Whither straight I'll lead you.

175 ANTONY   Let us, Lepidus,
Not lack your company.

LEPIDUS   Noble Antony,
Not sickness should detain me.

        Flourish. Exeunt. Manent ENOBARBUS, AGRIPPA,
                  and MAECENAS

MAECENAS [*to* ENOBARBUS]   Welcome from Egypt, sir.

ENOBARBUS   Half the heart° of Caesar, worthy Maecenas! My   *Beloved friend*
180   honourable friend, Agrippa!

AGRIPPA   Good Enobarbus!

MAECENAS   We have cause to be glad that matters are so well
digested.° You stayed well by't⁴ in Egypt.   *settled*

ENOBARBUS   Ay, sir, we did sleep day out of countenance,⁵ and
185   made the night light° with drinking.   *bright; merry*

MAECENAS   Eight wild boars roasted whole at a breakfast and but
twelve persons there—is this true?

ENOBARBUS   This was but as a fly by° an eagle. We had much   *compared with*
more monstrous matter of feast, which worthily deserved noting.

190 MAECENAS   She's a most triumphant° lady, if report be square° to   *magnificent / fair*
her.

ENOBARBUS   When she first met Mark Antony, she pursed up
his heart upon the river of Cydnus.⁶

AGRIPPA   There she appeared indeed, or my reporter devised° well   *imagined*
195   for her.

ENOBARBUS   I will tell you.
The barge° she sat in, like a burnished throne   *oar-driven ship*
Burned on the water. The poop° was beaten gold;   *upper deck*
Purple° the sails, and so perfumèd that   *(royal dye)*
200 The winds were love-sick with them. The oars were silver,
Which to the tune of flutes kept stroke, and made
The water which they beat to follow faster,
As° amorous of their strokes. For° her own person,   *As if / As for*

---

3. Misenum, a hilly outcropping at the north end of the
Bay of Naples.
4. You hung in there; you had a high old time.
5. We disconcerted day by sleeping through it, and did

not see what it looked like.
6. She took possession of his heart on the Cydnus River
in Cilicia, Asia Minor (Turkey), on which the city of Tar-
sus stood.

It beggared all description. She did lie
205 In her pavilion—cloth of gold, of tissue[7]—
O'er-picturing that Venus where we see
The fancy outwork nature.[8] On each side her
Stood pretty dimpled boys, like smiling Cupids,
With divers-coloured fans whose wind did seem
210 To glow° the delicate cheeks which they did cool,   *make glow*
And what they undid did.

AGRIPPA   O, rare for Antony!

ENOBARBUS Her gentlewomen, like the Nereides,°   *sea nymphs*
So many mermaids, tended her i'th' eyes,°   *under her watchful eyes*
And made their bends adornings.[9] At the helm
215 A seeming mermaid steers. The silken tackle°   *sails and ropes*
Swell with the touches of those flower-soft hands
That yarely frame° the office. From the barge   *artfully carry out*
A strange invisible perfume hits the sense
Of the adjacent wharfs.° The city cast   *banks*
220 Her people out upon° her, and Antony,   *toward*
Enthroned i'th' market-place, did sit alone,
Whistling to th'air, which but for vacancy[1]
Had° gone to gaze on Cleopatra too,   *Would have*
And made a gap in nature.

AGRIPPA   Rare Egyptian!

225 ENOBARBUS Upon her landing Antony sent to her,
Invited her to supper. She replied
It should be better he became her guest,
Which she entreated. Our courteous Antony,
Whom ne'er the word of 'No' woman heard speak,
230 Being barbered ten times o'er, goes to the feast,
And for his ordinary° pays his heart   *public meal at an inn*
For what his eyes eat only.

AGRIPPA   Royal wench!
She made great Caesar° lay his sword to bed.   *(Julius)*
He ploughed her, and she cropped.[2]

ENOBARBUS   I saw her once
235 Hop forty paces through the public street,
And having lost her breath, she spoke and panted,
That° she did make defect° perfection,   *So that / her panting*
And breathless, pour breath forth.

MAECENAS   Now Antony
Must leave her utterly.

ENOBARBUS   Never. He will not.
240 Age cannot wither her, nor custom stale°   *familiarity diminish*
Her infinite variety. Other women cloy
The appetites they feed, but she makes hungry
Where most she satisfies. For vilest things
Become themselves° in her, that° the holy priests   *Are becoming / so that*
245 Bless her when she is riggish.°   *acts like a slut*

7. Fabric interwoven with gold thread.
8. *O'er-picturing . . . nature:* Outdoing even the picture
of Venus in which the artist outdid nature.
9. Made their curtsies additions to the decoration.
1. Which if not for the fact that its absence would have
left a vacuum (already in Shakespeare's time proverbially
impossible in nature).
2. She bore Caesarion. After the assassination of Julius

Caesar in 44 B.C.E., Cleopatra returned from Rome,
where she had accompanied him, to Egypt. There she
reigned with their son, who became Ptolemy XV, after
she ordered the death of her half brother and previous
co-ruler Ptolemy XIV. On Ptolemy XIV, see 1.4.6 with
note and 2.1.37 with note. On Antony and Cleopatra's
plans for Ptolemy XV, see 3.6.1–16. On Ptolemy XV's fate,
see note to 5.2.352.

MAECENAS   If beauty, wisdom, modesty can settle
 The heart of Antony, Octavia is
 A blessèd lottery° to him.   *prize*

AGRIPPA   Let us go.
 Good Enobarbus, make yourself my guest
 Whilst you abide here.

250   ENOBARBUS   Humbly, sir, I thank you. *Exeunt*

2.3

Enter ANTONY [*and*] CAESAR; OCTAVIA *between them*

ANTONY   The world and my great office will sometimes
 Divide me from your bosom.

OCTAVIA   All which time,
 Before the gods my knee shall bow my prayers
 To them for you.

ANTONY   Good night, sir. My Octavia,
5 Read not my blemishes in the world's report.
 I have not kept my square,° but that° to come   *stayed in line / what's*
 Shall all be done by th' rule.[1] Good night, dear lady.
 Good night, sir.

CAESAR   Good night.   *Exeunt* [CAESAR *and* OCTAVIA]

Enter SOOTHSAYER

10   ANTONY   Now, sirrah.[2] You do wish yourself in Egypt?

SOOTHSAYER   Would I had never come from thence, nor you
 Gone thither.

ANTONY   If you can, your reason?

SOOTHSAYER   I see it in my motion,° have it not in my tongue. *intuition*
 But yet hie° you to Egypt again.   *hurry*

ANTONY   Say to me
15 Whose fortunes shall rise higher: Caesar's or mine?

SOOTHSAYER   Caesar's. Therefore, O Antony, stay not by his side.
 Thy daemon, that thy spirit[3] which keeps thee, is
 Noble, courageous, high, unmatchable,
 Where Caesar's is not. But near him thy angel
20 Becomes afeard, as° being o'erpowered. Therefore *as if*
 Make space enough between you.

ANTONY   Speak this no more.

SOOTHSAYER   To none but thee; no more but when[4] to thee.
 If thou dost play with him at any game
 Thou art sure to lose; and of° that natural luck   *by*
25 He beats thee 'gainst the odds. Thy lustre thickens° *Your brightness dims*
 When he shines by. I say again, thy spirit
 Is all afraid to govern thee near him;
 But he away, 'tis noble.

ANTONY   Get thee gone.
 Say to Ventidius I would speak with him. *Exit* [SOOTHSAYER]
30 He shall to Parthia; be it art or hap,°   *talent or luck*
 He° hath spoken true. The very dice obey him,° *(the soothsayer)* / *(Caesar)*
 And in our sports my better cunning° faints   *capability*
 Under his chance.° If we draw lots, he speeds.° *luck / succeeds*

2.3 Location: Rome.
1. Regulation; ruler, as unit of measure (picking up
"square," line 6, a measuring tool).
2. Term by which a subordinate or social inferior is
addressed.
3. *Thy daemon . . . spirit*: Your guardian angel, which is
the spirit.
4. *no more but when*: only.

His cocks do win the battle still of° mine   *always against*
35 When it is all to nought, and his quails ever
Beat mine, inhooped, at odds.⁵ I will to Egypt;
And though I make this marriage for my peace,
I'th' East my pleasure lies.
     Enter VENTIDIUS
               O, come, Ventidius.
You must to Parthia, your commission's ready.
40 Follow me, and receive't.   *Exeunt*

2.4

    Enter LEPIDUS, MAECENAS, *and* AGRIPPA
LEPIDUS   Trouble yourselves no further. Pray you, hasten
Your generals after.¹
AGRIPPA   Sir, Mark Antony
Will e'en but° kiss Octavia, and we'll follow.   *merely*
LEPIDUS   Till I shall see you in your soldier's dress,
Which will become you both, farewell.
5 MAECENAS   We shall,
As I conceive the journey, be at the Mount°   *Mount Misenum*
Before you, Lepidus.
LEPIDUS   Your way is shorter.
My purposes do draw me° much about.   *force me to go*
You'll win two days upon me.
MAECENAS *and* AGRIPPA   Sir, good success.
10 LEPIDUS   Farewell.   *Exeunt* [MAECENAS *and* AGRIPPA *at one*
                    door, LEPIDUS *at another*]

2.5

   Enter CLEOPATRA, CHARMIAN, IRAS, *and* ALEXAS
CLEOPATRA   Give me some music—music, moody° food   *melancholy*
Of us that trade in love.
CHARMIAN, IRAS, *and* ALEXAS   The music, ho!
     Enter MARDIAN, *the eunuch*
CLEOPATRA   Let it alone. Let's to billiards. Come, Charmian.
CHARMIAN   My arm is sore. Best play with Mardian.
5 CLEOPATRA   As well a woman with an eunuch played
As with a woman. Come, you'll play with me, sir?
MARDIAN   As well as I can, madam.
CLEOPATRA   And when good will is showed, though't come too short¹
The actor may plead pardon. I'll none now.°   *I won't play now*
10 Give me mine angle.° We'll to th' river. There,   *fishing rod*
My music playing far off, I will betray°   *catch*
Tawny-finned fishes. My bended hook shall pierce
Their slimy jaws, and as I draw them up
I'll think them every one an Antony,
And say 'Ah ha, you're caught!'
15 CHARMIAN   'Twas merry when
You wagered on your angling, when your diver

---

5. *When . . . odds:* When the odds completely favor me, and when our quails are placed in a round enclosure to make them fight, his always beat mine, against all odds. **2.4** Location: Rome.

1. *hasten . . . after:* follow your leaders. **2.5** Location: Alexandria. 1. Referring to Mardian's sexual incapacity.

Did hang a salt° fish on his hook, which he   *preserved*
With fervency drew up.

CLEOPATRA   That time—O times!—
    I laughed him out of patience, and that night
20   I laughed him into patience, and next morn,
    Ere the ninth hour, I drunk him to his bed,
    Then put my tires and mantles° on him whilst   *headdresses and robes*
    I wore his sword Philippan.²

       Enter a MESSENGER

                   O, from Italy.
    Ram thou thy fruitful tidings in mine ears,
    That long time have been barren.

25 MESSENGER   Madam, madam!

CLEOPATRA   Antonio's dead. If thou say so, villain,
    Thou kill'st thy mistress; but well and free,
    If thou so yield° him, there is gold, and here   *report*
    My bluest veins to kiss—a hand that kings
    Have lipped, and trembled kissing.

30 MESSENGER   First, madam, he is well.

CLEOPATRA   Why, there's more gold. But, sirrah, mark: we use
    To say the dead are well. Bring it to that,
    The gold I give thee will I melt and pour
    Down thy ill-uttering throat.

35 MESSENGER   Good madam, hear me.

CLEOPATRA   Well, go to, I will.
    But there's no goodness in thy face. If Antony
    Be free and healthful, so tart a favour°   *so sour an expression*
    To trumpet such good tidings! If not well,
40   Thou shouldst come like a Fury³ crowned with snakes,
    Not like a formal° man.   *Not in the shape of a*

MESSENGER   Will't please you hear me?

CLEOPATRA   I have a mind to strike thee ere thou speak'st.
    Yet if thou say Antony lives, is well,
    Or friends with Caesar, or not captive to him,
45   I'll set thee in a shower of gold, and hail
    Rich pearls upon thee.

MESSENGER   Madam, he's well.

CLEOPATRA   Well said.

MESSENGER   And friends with Caesar.

CLEOPATRA   Thou'rt an honest man.

MESSENGER   Caesar and he are greater friends than ever.

CLEOPATRA   Make thee a fortune from me.

MESSENGER   But yet, madam—

50 CLEOPATRA   I do not like 'But yet'; it does allay°   *dissipate*
    The good precedence.° Fie upon 'But yet'.   *preceding good news*
    'But yet' is as a jailer to bring forth
    Some monstrous malefactor. Prithee, friend,
    Pour out the pack of matter to mine ear,°   *Give me all the news*
55   The good and bad together. He's friends with Caesar,
    In state of health, thou sayst; and, thou sayst, free.

MESSENGER   Free, madam? No, I made no such report.
    He's bound unto Octavia.

---

2. The sword with which Antony had beaten Brutus   3. In Greek mythology, a female avenging spirit.
and Cassius at Philippi.

CLEOPATRA   For what good turn?°   *good deed*
MESSENGER   For the best turn i'th' bed.
CLEOPATRA   I am pale, Charmian.
60   MESSENGER   Madam, he's married to Octavia.
CLEOPATRA   The most infectious pestilence upon thee!
    [She] strikes him down
MESSENGER   Good madam, patience!
CLEOPATRA   What say you?
    [She] strikes him
Hence, horrible villain, or I'll spurn° thine eyes   *kick*
Like balls before me. I'll unhair thy head,
    She hales° him up and down   *drags*
65   Thou shalt be whipped with wire and stewed in brine,
Smarting in ling'ring pickle.°   *salt water*
MESSENGER   Gracious madam,
I that do bring the news made not the match.
CLEOPATRA   Say 'tis not so, a province I will give thee,
And make thy fortunes proud. The blow thou hadst
70   Shall make thy peace for moving me to rage,
And I will boot° thee with what° gift beside   *compensate / whatever*
Thy modesty can beg.
MESSENGER   He's married, madam.
CLEOPATRA   Rogue, thou hast lived too long.
    [She] draw[s] a knife
MESSENGER   Nay then, I'll run.
What mean you, madam? I have made no fault.   *Exit*
75   CHARMIAN   Good madam, keep yourself within yourself.°   *restrain yourself*
The man is innocent.
CLEOPATRA   Some innocents 'scape not the thunderbolt.
Melt Egypt into Nile, and kindly° creatures   *harmless*
Turn all to serpents! Call the slave again.
80   Though I am mad I will not bite him. Call!
CHARMIAN   He is afeard to come.
CLEOPATRA   I will not hurt him.
    [Exit CHARMIAN*]*
These hands do lack nobility that they strike
A meaner° than myself, since I myself   *One of lower rank*
Have given myself the cause.°   *(by loving Antony)*
    Enter the MESSENGER *again [with* CHARMIAN*]*
Come hither, sir.
85   Though it be honest, it is never good
To bring bad news. Give to a gracious message
An host° of tongues, but let ill tidings tell   *A multitude*
Themselves when they be felt.[4]
MESSENGER   I have done my duty.
90   CLEOPATRA   Is he married?
I cannot hate thee worser than I do
If thou again say 'Yes'.
MESSENGER   He's married, madam.
CLEOPATRA   The gods confound° thee! Dost thou hold there still?   *destroy*
MESSENGER   Should I lie, madam?
CLEOPATRA   O, I would thou didst,
95   So° half my Egypt were submerged and made   *Even if*
A cistern° for scaled snakes. Go, get thee hence.   *reservoir; chamber pot*

4. *let . . . felt:* bad news is best revealed by letting the victim feel the effects.

Hadst thou Narcissus[5] in thy face, to me
Thou wouldst appear most ugly. He is married?

MESSENGER I crave your highness' pardon.

CLEOPATRA   He is married?

100 MESSENGER Take no offence that I would not° offend you.   do not want to
To punish me for what you make me do
Seems much unequal.° He's married to Octavia.   most unfair

CLEOPATRA O that his fault should make a knave° of thee,   villain
That act not what thou'rt sure of!°[6] Get thee hence.

105 The merchandise which thou hast brought from Rome
Are all too dear for me. Lie they upon thy hand,[7]
And be undone° by 'em.   [Exit MESSENGER]   ruined (financially)

CHARMIAN   Good your highness, patience.

CLEOPATRA In praising Antony I have dispraised Caesar.

CHARMIAN Many times, madam.

110 CLEOPATRA I am paid for't now. Lead me from hence.
I faint. O Iras, Charmian—'tis no matter.
Go to the fellow, good Alexas, bid him
Report the feature° of Octavia: her years,   appearance
Her inclination;° let him not leave out   disposition

115 The colour of her hair. Bring me word quickly.   [Exit ALEXAS]
Let him for ever go—let him not, Charmian;
Though he be painted one way like a Gorgon,
The other way's a Mars.[8] [To MARDIAN] Bid you Alexas
Bring me word how tall she is. Pity me, Charmian,

120 But do not speak to me. Lead me to my chamber.   Exeunt

2.6

Flourish. Enter POMPEY [*and*] MENAS *at one door, with*
[*a*] *drum*[*mer*] *and* [*a*] *trumpet*[*er*]; *at another,* CAESAR,
LEPIDUS, ANTONY, ENOBARBUS, MAECENAS, AGRIPPA, *with*
soldiers marching

POMPEY Your hostages I have, so have you mine,
And we shall talk before we fight.

CAESAR   Most meet°   fitting
That first we come to words, and therefore have we
Our written purposes° before us sent,   offers
5   Which if thou hast considered, let us know
If 'twill tie up° thy discontented sword   lead you to put aside
And carry back to Sicily much tall° youth   courageous
That else must perish here.

POMPEY   To you all three,
The senators alone° of this great world,   sole governors
10   Chief factors° for the gods: I do not know   agents
Wherefore° my father[1] should revengers want,°   why / lack

---

5. In Greek mythology, a surprisingly beautiful young man.
6. Who do not commit the offense you know about; who do not report the information you know.
7. Leave with your goods unsold.
8. Cleopatra imagines Antony as a figure in a perspective painting: popular in Shakespeare's time, they showed different images according to the angle from which they were viewed. In classical mythology, a Gorgon was one of three female monsters with snakes for hair whose horrific appearance could turn others to stone.
2.6 Location: Near Misenum, Italy.
1. Pompey the Great. The allusion in the following lines

is primarily to the events dramatized by Shakespeare in *Julius Caesar*. After being defeated by Julius Caesar at Pharsalia, Pompey the Great fled to Egypt and was there assassinated by agents of Ptolemy, Cleopatra's half brother (prior to the events in *Julius Caesar*). Julius Caesar was then himself assassinated by the Roman republican conspirators, who included Cassius and Brutus. The triumvirs Antony, Octavius, and Lepidus defeated and killed Brutus and Cassius at Philippi in revenge (see note to 1.2.88). The younger Pompey thus believes that by making war on the triumvirate, he avenges his father's death and the deaths of Brutus and Cassius (and, therefore, he fights for the Republic).

Having a son and friends, since Julius Caesar,
Who at Philippi the good Brutus ghosted,[2]
There saw you labouring for him.° What was't   *on his behalf*
15   That moved pale Cassius to conspire? And what
Made the all-honoured, honest° Roman Brutus,   *honorable*
With the armed rest, courtiers° of beauteous freedom,   *seekers*
To drench° the Capitol but that they would   *(in blood)*
Have one man but a man?° And that is it   *(and not a king)*
20   Hath made me rig° my navy, at whose burden   *equip*
The angered ocean foams; with which I meant
To scourge th'ingratitude that despiteful Rome
Cast on my noble father.
    CAESAR   Take your time.
    ANTONY   Thou canst not fear° us, Pompey, with thy sails.   *intimidate*
25   We'll speak with° thee at sea. At land thou know'st   *engage*
How much we do o'ercount° thee.   *outnumber*
    POMPEY   At land indeed
Thou dost o'ercount me of my father's house,[3]
But since the cuckoo builds not for himself,[4]
Remain in't as thou mayst.°   *as long as you can*
    LEPIDUS   Be pleased to tell us—
30   For this is from the present°—how you take   *beside the point*
The offers we have sent you.
    CAESAR   There's the point.
    ANTONY   Which do not be entreated to,° but weigh   *convinced unfairly of*
What it is worth, embraced.°   *if you consent*
    CAESAR   And what may follow,
To try a larger fortune?[5]
    POMPEY   You have made me offer
35   Of Sicily, Sardinia; and I must
Rid all the sea of pirates; then to send
Measures of wheat to Rome; this 'greed upon,
To part with unhacked edges,° and bear back   *unused swords*
Our targes undinted.°   *shields untouched*
    CAESAR, ANTONY, *and* LEPIDUS   That's our offer.
    POMPEY   Know, then,
40   I came before you here a man prepared
To take this offer. But Mark Antony
Put me to some impatience. Though I lose
The praise of it by telling, you must know,
When Caesar and your brother were at blows,
45   Your mother came to Sicily, and did find
Her welcome friendly.
    ANTONY   I have heard it, Pompey,
And am well studied for° a liberal thanks   *intend to offer*
Which I do owe you.
    POMPEY   Let me have your hand.
       [POMPEY *and* ANTONY *shake hands*]
I did not think, sir, to have met you here.

---

2. Caesar appeared as a ghost to Brutus at the Battle of Philippi.
3. Plutarch records that Antony agreed to buy the elder Pompey's house but ultimately refused to pay for it.
4. The cuckoo lays eggs in the nests of other birds, rather than building a nest of its own.
5. If you try (by fighting us) for a still larger fortune than we have offered.

50 ANTONY   The beds i'th' East are soft; and thanks to you,
      That called me timelier° than my purpose° hither;   *earlier / intention*
      For I have gained by't.
   CAESAR [*to* POMPEY]   Since I saw you last
      There is a change upon you.
   POMPEY   Well, I know not
      What counts harsh fortune casts upon my face,[6]
55   But in my bosom shall she never come
      To make my heart her vassal.
   LEPIDUS   Well met here.
   POMPEY   I hope so, Lepidus. Thus we are agreed.
      I crave our composition° may be written   *pact*
      And sealed between us.
   CAESAR   That's the next to do.
60 POMPEY   We'll feast each other ere we part, and let's
      Draw lots who shall begin.°   *act as host*
   ANTONY   That will I, Pompey.
   POMPEY   No, Antony, take the lot.
      But, first or last, your fine Egyptian cookery
65   Shall have the fame. I have heard that Julius Caesar
      Grew fat with feasting there.
   ANTONY   You have heard much.
   POMPEY   I have fair° meanings, sir.   *amicable*
   ANTONY   And fair° words to them.   *(ironic)*
   POMPEY   Then so much have I heard,
70   And I have heard Apollodorus carried[7]—
   ENOBARBUS   No more o' that, he did so.
   POMPEY   What, I pray you?
   ENOBARBUS   A certain queen to Caesar in a mattress.
   POMPEY   I know thee now. How far'st thou, soldier?
   ENOBARBUS   Well, and well am like to do, for I perceive
      Four feasts are toward.°   *to come*
75 POMPEY   Let me shake thy hand.
            [POMPEY *and* ENOBARBUS *shake hands*]
      I never hated thee. I have seen thee fight
      When I have envied thy behaviour.
   ENOBARBUS   Sir, I never loved you much, but I ha' praised ye
      When you have well deserved ten times as much
80   As I have said you did.
   POMPEY   Enjoy thy plainness.° It nothing ill becomes thee.   *matter-of-fact speech*
      Aboard my galley I invite you all.
      Will you lead, lords?
   CAESAR, ANTONY, *and* LEPIDUS   Show's the way, sir.
   POMPEY   Come.
            Exeunt. Manent ENOBARBUS *and* MENAS
   MENAS [*aside*]   Thy father, Pompey, would ne'er have made this treaty.
85   [*To* ENOBARBUS] You and I have known,° sir.   *met each other*
   ENOBARBUS   At sea, I think.
   MENAS   We have, sir.
   ENOBARBUS   You have done well by water.

6. What accounts cruel fortune calculates (by marking
notches, like wrinkles).
7. Alluding to the story that Cleopatra gained access to

her lover, Julius Caesar, by having herself rolled up in a
sleeping mat (told in Plutarch).

MENAS   And you by land.

90 ENOBARBUS   I will praise any man that will praise me, though it
cannot be denied what I have done by land.

MENAS   Nor what I have done by water.

ENOBARBUS   Yes, something you can deny for your own safety.
You have been a great thief by sea.

95 MENAS   And you by land.

ENOBARBUS   There I deny my land service; but give me your
hand, Menas. If our eyes had authority,° here they might take   *(to make an arrest)*
two thieves kissing.[8]

    [They shake hands]

MENAS   All men's faces are true,° whatsome'er their hands are.   *honest*

100 ENOBARBUS   But there is never a fair woman has a true° face.   *(without makeup)*

MENAS   No slander;° they steal hearts.   *That's true*

ENOBARBUS   We came hither to fight with you.

MENAS   For my part, I am sorry it is turned to a drinking. Pompey
doth this day laugh away his fortune.

105 ENOBARBUS   If he do, sure he cannot weep't back again.

MENAS   You've said,° sir. We looked not for Mark Antony here.   *spoken truly*
Pray you, is he married to Cleopatra?

ENOBARBUS   Caesar's sister is called Octavia.

MENAS   True, sir. She was the wife of Caius Marcellus.

110 ENOBARBUS   But she is now the wife of Marcus Antonius.

MENAS   Pray ye, sir?

ENOBARBUS   'Tis true.

MENAS   Then is Caesar and he for ever knit together.

ENOBARBUS   If I were bound to divine° of this unity I would not   *make predictions*
115 prophesy so.

MENAS   I think the policy of that purpose made more[9] in the
marriage than the love of the parties.

ENOBARBUS   I think so, too. But you shall find the band that
seems to tie their friendship together will be the very strangler
120 of their amity. Octavia is of a holy, cold, and still conversation.°   *disposition*

MENAS   Who would not have his wife so?

ENOBARBUS   Not he that himself is not so, which is Mark Antony.
He will to his Egyptian dish again; then shall the sighs of
Octavia blow the fire up in Caesar, and, as I said before, that
125 which is the strength of their amity shall prove the immediate
author° of their variance.° Antony will use his affection where   *cause / enmity*
it is. He married but his occasion here.[1]

MENAS   And thus it may be. Come, sir, will you aboard? I have a
health for you.

130 ENOBARBUS   I shall take it, sir. We have used our throats in
Egypt.

MENAS   Come, let's away.   *Exeunt*

---

8. Arrest two thieves embracing; catch two thieving
hands in a handshake, plotting together.
9. I think the politics of that "unity" weighed more
heavily.

1. *Antony . . . here:* Antony will act on his desire where it
really is located (Egypt). He married out of self-interest
here.

2.7

Music plays. Enter two or three SERVANTS *with a ban-*
quet[1]

FIRST SERVANT   Here they'll be, man. Some o' their plants are ill
rooted[2] already; the least wind i'th' world will blow them down.

SECOND SERVANT   Lepidus is high-coloured.

FIRST SERVANT   They have made him drink alms-drink.[3]

5 SECOND SERVANT   As they pinch one another by the disposition,[4]
he cries out 'No more!'—reconciles them to his entreaty° and   *(to stop arguing)*
himself to th' drink.

FIRST SERVANT   But it raises the greater war between him and his
discretion.

10 SECOND SERVANT   Why, this it is to have a name° in great men's   *only a nominal place*
fellowship. I had as lief° have a reed that will do me no service   *just as soon*
as a partisan I could not heave.[5]

FIRST SERVANT   To be called into a huge sphere and not to be
seen to move in't, are the holes where eyes should be which
15 pitifully disaster the cheeks.[6]

A sennet° *sounded. Enter* CAESAR, ANTONY, POMPEY,   *flourish of trumpets*
LEPIDUS, AGRIPPA, MAECENAS, ENOBARBUS, [*and*]
MENAS, *with other captains* [*and a boy*]

ANTONY   [*to* CAESAR]   Thus do they, sir: they take the flow° o'th'   *measure the depth*
Nile
By certain scales i'th'° pyramid. They know   *marks on the*
By th' height, the lowness, or the mean,° if dearth   *middle position*
Or foison° follow. The higher Nilus swells   *abundance*
20 The more it promises; as it ebbs, the seedsman
Upon the slime and ooze scatters his grain,
And shortly comes to harvest.

LEPIDUS   You've strange serpents there?

ANTONY   Ay, Lepidus.

25 LEPIDUS   Your serpent of Egypt is bred now of your mud by the
operation of your sun; so is your crocodile.

ANTONY   They are so.

POMPEY   Sit, and some wine. A health to Lepidus!
[ANTONY, POMPEY, *and* LEPIDUS *sit*]

LEPIDUS   I am not so well as I should be, but I'll ne'er out.°   *leave; miss a round*

30 ENOBARBUS   Not till you have slept—I fear me you'll be in° till   *remain; be drunk*
then.

LEPIDUS   Nay, certainly, I have heard the Ptolemies' pyramises[7]
are very goodly things: without contradiction I have heard that.

MENAS [*aside to* POMPEY]   Pompey, a word.

POMPEY [*aside to* MENAS]   Say in mine ear; what is't?

35 MENAS [*aside to* POMPEY]   Forsake thy seat, I do beseech thee, captain,
And hear me speak a word.

POMPEY [*aside to* MENAS]   Forbear° me till anon.   *Wait for*
[*Aloud*] This wine for Lepidus!

2.7 Location: Pompey's galley, off Misenum.
1. One of the courses of the feast, possibly dessert.
2. *their . . . rooted:* the soles of the feet of the (drunken)
leaders are unsteady; the alliance between Antony and
Caesar is shaky.
3. Drink given out of charity; in this case, extra rounds
given to reconcile the parties each time they quarrel; one
too many.
4. As they irritate one another according to their natures.

5. As a spear I could not lift (position without power).
6. *To be . . . cheeks:* To be placed in high circles in which
one is incapable of moving is like having, instead of eyes,
empty eye sockets that disfigure one's face. (In Ptolemaic
astronomy, a planet "moves" within its "sphere," one of a
series of concentric circles of which the universe is
formed, with the earth at the center. A planet's ill influ-
ence causes "disaster," which literally means "bad star.")
7. Pyramids (drunken speech).

[MENAS] *whispers in [Pompey's] ear*
LEPIDUS   What manner o' thing is your crocodile?
ANTONY   It is shaped, sir, like itself, and it is as broad as it hath
40   breadth. It is just so high as it is, and moves with it° own organs.   *its*
It lives by that which nourisheth it, and the elements once out
of it, it transmigrates.[8]
LEPIDUS   What colour is it of?
ANTONY   Of it own colour, too.
45   LEPIDUS   'Tis a strange serpent.
ANTONY   'Tis so, and the tears of it are wet.[9]
CAESAR [*to* ANTONY]   Will this description satisfy him?
ANTONY   With the health that Pompey gives him; else he is a
very epicure.°   *an insatiable glutton*
50   POMPEY [*aside to* MENAS]   Go hang, sir, hang! Tell me of that? Away,
Do as I bid you. [*Aloud*] Where's this cup I called for?
MENAS [*aside to* POMPEY]   If for the sake of merit° thou wilt hear me,   *past deeds*
Rise from thy stool.
POMPEY [*rising*]   I think thou'rt mad. The matter?
                    [MENAS *and* POMPEY *stand apart*]
MENAS   I have ever held my cap off to° thy fortunes.   *ever served*
55   POMPEY   Thou hast served me with much faith. What's else to say?
Be jolly, lords.
ANTONY   These quicksands, Lepidus,
Keep off them, for you sink.
MENAS   Wilt thou be lord of all the world?
POMPEY   What sayst thou?
MENAS   Wilt thou be lord of the whole world? That's twice.
POMPEY   How should that be?
60   MENAS   But entertain° it   *consider*
And, though thou think me poor, I am the man
Will give thee all the world.
POMPEY   Hast thou drunk well?
MENAS   No, Pompey, I have kept me from the cup.
Thou art, if thou dar'st be, the earthly Jove.
65   Whate'er the ocean pales° or sky inclips°   *encloses / embraces*
Is thine, if thou wilt ha't.
POMPEY   Show me which way!
MENAS   These three world-sharers, these competitors,°   *allies*
Are in thy vessel. Let me cut the cable;
And when we are put off,° fall to their throats.   *(from shore)*
All there is thine.
70   POMPEY   Ah, this thou shouldst have done
And not have spoke on't. In me 'tis villainy,
In thee 't had been good service. Thou must know
'Tis not my profit that does lead mine honour;
Mine honour, it.[1] Repent that e'er thy tongue
75   Hath so betrayed thine act.[2] Being done unknown,
I should have found it afterwards well done,
But must condemn it now. Desist, and drink.

---

8. Passes into other forms of life: referring to Pythagoras's
theory, apparently of Egyptian origin, that at death the
soul moves into another newborn living thing.
9. Continuing the pattern of comically uninformative
self-identity, this line may also refer to hypocritical croco-
dile tears and hence to Pompey, as his ensuing exchange

with Menas suggests. See also 3.2.54–60 and 5.1.26–49.
1. *'Tis . . . it*: It is my honor that precedes or is the basis
of my profit.
2. Treacherously disclosed your intentions and so made
it impossible to carry them out.

[*He returns to the others*]

MENAS [*aside*]   For this, I'll never follow thy palled° fortunes more.   *diminished*
  Who seeks and will not take when once 'tis offered,
  Shall never find it more.

80 POMPEY   This health to Lepidus!

ANTONY   Bear him ashore.—I'll pledge it° for him, Pompey.   *drink the toast*

ENOBARBUS   Here's to thee, Menas!

MENAS   Enobarbus, welcome.

POMPEY   Fill till the cup be hid.

[*One lifts* LEPIDUS, *drunk, and carries him off*]

ENOBARBUS   There's a strong fellow, Menas.

MENAS   Why?

85 ENOBARBUS   A° bears the third part of the world, man; seest not?   *He*

MENAS   The third part then is drunk. Would it were all,
  That it might go on wheels.°   *easily; out of control*

ENOBARBUS   Drink thou, increase the reels.°   *revels; spinning*

MENAS   Come.

POMPEY   This is not yet an Alexandrian feast.

90 ANTONY   It ripens towards it. Strike the vessels,° ho!   *Open more casks*
  Here's to Caesar!

CAESAR   I could well forbear't.
  It's monstrous° labour when I wash my brain,   *unnatural*
  An° it grow fouler.   *If as a result*

ANTONY   Be a child o'th' time.

95 CAESAR   Possess it, I'll make answer.³
  But I had rather fast from all, four days,
  Than drink so much in one.

ENOBARBUS [*to* ANTONY]   Ha, my brave Emperor,
  Shall we dance now the Egyptian bacchanals,⁴
  And celebrate our drink?

100 POMPEY   Let's ha't, good soldier.

ANTONY   Come, let's all take hands
  Till that the conquering wine hath steeped our sense
  In soft and delicate Lethe.°   *oblivion*

ENOBARBUS   All take hands.
  Make battery to° our ears with the loud music.   *Besiege*

105 The while I'll place you, then the boy shall sing.
  The holding° every man shall beat° as loud   *refrain / beat out*
  As his strong sides can volley.°   *fire off*

Music plays. ENOBARBUS *places them hand in hand*

BOY [*sings*]   Come, thou monarch of the vine,
         Plumpy Bacchus, with pink⁵ eyne!

110   In thy vats our cares be drowned,
         With thy grapes our hairs be crowned!
         Cup us till the world go round,
         Cup us till the world go round!

CAESAR   What would you more? Pompey, good night.
[*To* ANTONY]   Good-brother,°   *Brother-in-law*

115 Let me request you off.° Our graver business   *to come ashore*
  Frowns at this levity. Gentle lords, let's part.
  You see we have burnt° our cheeks. Strong Enobarb   *flushed*

---

3. Take it, and I'll drink, too; be in command of the time,   and revelry.
I say.
4. Wild, drunken revels in honor of Bacchus, god of wine   5. Half-closed and red from drinking.

Is weaker than the wine, and mine own tongue
Splits° what it speaks. The wild disguise° hath almost   *Deforms / drunkenness*
120   Anticked us° all. What needs more words? Good night.   *Made us clowns*
Good Antony, your hand.
POMPEY   I'll try you° on the shore.   *test your drinking*
ANTONY   And shall, sir. Give's your hand.
POMPEY   O Antony,
You have my father's house. But what, we are friends!
Come down into the boat.
                [*Exeunt all but* ENOBARBUS *and* MENAS]
ENOBARBUS   Take heed you fall not, Menas.
125   MENAS   I'll not° on shore.   *not go*
No, to my cabin. These drums, these trumpets, flutes, what!
Let Neptune hear we bid a loud farewell
To these great fellows. Sound and be hanged, sound out!
        Sound a flourish, with drums
ENOBARBUS [*throwing his cap in the air*]   Hoo, says a!° There's   *he*
  my cap.
MENAS   Ho, noble captain, come!   *Exeunt*

3.1

Enter VENTIDIUS [*with* SILIUS *and other Roman soldiers*]
  as it were in triumph; the dead body of Pacorus borne
  before him

VENTIDIUS   Now, darting Parthia,[1] art thou struck; and now
Pleased fortune does of Marcus Crassus'[2] death
Make me revenger. Bear the King's son's body
Before our army. Thy° Pacorus, Orodes,   *Your son*
Pays this for Marcus Crassus.
5   SILIUS   Noble Ventidius,
Whilst yet with Parthian blood thy sword is warm,
The fugitive Parthians follow.[3] Spur through Media,[4]
Mesopotamia, and the shelters whither
The routed fly. So thy grand captain, Antony,
10   Shall set thee on triumphant° chariots and   *triumphal*
Put garlands on thy head.
VENTIDIUS   O Silius, Silius,
I have done enough. A lower place,° note well,   *man of low rank*
May make too great an act. For learn this, Silius:
Better to leave undone than by our deed
15   Acquire too high a fame when him we serve's away.
Caesar and Antony have ever won
More in their officer than person.[5] Sossius,
One of my place in Syria, his° lieutenant,   *(Antony's)*
For quick accumulation of renown,
20   Which he achieved by th' minute,° lost his favour.   *more every minute*
Who does i'th' wars more than his captain can
Becomes his captain's captain; and ambition,

3.1 Location: Syria.
1. Parthian cavalry advanced flinging darts, then re-
treated shooting arrows. "Parthia" here refers to both the
nation and its King, Orodes.
2. A member, with Pompey the Great and Julius Caesar,
of the first triumvirate, treacherously and cruelly killed in
defeat by Orodes in 53 B.C.E.
3. Chase the fleeing Parthians.
4. The land between Persia and Armenia, east of
Mesopotamia—part of the Parthian Empire.
5. Owing more to the skill of their officers than to their
own skill.

The soldier's virtue, rather makes choice of loss
Than gain which darkens him.° *eclipses his renown*
25 I could do more to do Antonius good,
But 'twould offend him, and in his offence
Should my performance perish.° *lose its value*
SILIUS   Thou hast, Ventidius, that° *(discretion)*
Without the which a soldier and his sword
Grants scarce° distinction. Thou wilt write to Antony? *Scarcely admits of*
30 VENTIDIUS   I'll humbly signify what in his name,
That magical word of war, we have effected;
How, with his banners and his well-paid ranks,
The ne'er-yet-beaten horse° of Parthia *cavalry*
We have jaded° out o'th' field. *chased like tired nags*
SILIUS   Where is he now?
35 VENTIDIUS   He purposeth to Athens; whither, with what haste
The weight we must convey with's will permit,
We shall appear before him.—On there; pass along.   *Exeunt*

3.2

Enter AGRIPPA *at one door,* ENOBARBUS *at another*
AGRIPPA   What, are the brothers parted?° *brothers-in-law gone*
ENOBARBUS   They have dispatched° with Pompey; he is gone. *finished the business*
The other three are sealing.° Octavia weeps *signing their pact*
To part from Rome, Caesar is sad, and Lepidus
5 Since Pompey's feast, as Menas says, is troubled
With the green-sickness.[1]
AGRIPPA   'Tis a noble Lepidus.
ENOBARBUS   A very fine one. O, how he loves Caesar!
AGRIPPA   Nay, but how dearly he adores Mark Antony!
ENOBARBUS   Caesar? Why, he's the Jupiter of men.
10 AGRIPPA   What's Antony—the god of Jupiter?
ENOBARBUS   Spake you of Caesar? How, the nonpareil?° *incomparable*
AGRIPPA   O Antony, O thou Arabian bird![2]
ENOBARBUS   Would you praise Caesar, say 'Caesar'; go no further.
AGRIPPA   Indeed, he plied them both with excellent praises.
15 ENOBARBUS   But he loves Caesar best; yet he loves Antony—
Hoo! Hearts, tongues, figures,° scribes, bards, poets, cannot *(of speech); numbers*
Think, speak, cast,° write, sing, number°—hoo!— *calculate / make verses*
His love to Antony. But as for Caesar—
Kneel down, kneel down, and wonder.
AGRIPPA   Both he loves.
ENOBARBUS   They are his shards,[3] and he their beetle.
      [*Trumpet within*]
20   So,
This is° to horse. Adieu, noble Agrippa. *calls us*
AGRIPPA   Good fortune, worthy soldier, and farewell.
     Enter CAESAR, ANTONY, LEPIDUS, *and* OCTAVIA
ANTONY [*to* CAESAR]   No further, sir.

3.2 Location: Rome.
1. Anemia in adolescent, lovesick girls (hence, a feminizing attribute): here, used humorously for Lepidus's hangover and its effect, as well as ironically for his overblown affection for Caesar and Antony.
2. The phoenix, a legendary, self-resurrecting bird, only

one of which existed at a time. It was believed to live for several centuries, to die in flames, and to be reborn from its own ashes.
3. Dung patches (between which the beetle crawls to feed and breed); perhaps, wing cases (with which the beetle flies).

CAESAR   You take from me a great part of myself.
25   Use me well in't. Sister, prove such a wife
As my thoughts make thee, and as my farthest bond
Shall pass on thy approof.⁴ Most noble Antony,
Let not the piece° of virtue which is set   *paragon*
Betwixt us as the cement of our love
30   To keep it builded, be the ram to batter
The fortress of it; for better might we
Have loved without this mean° if on both parts   *intermediary*
This be not cherished.
ANTONY   Make me not offended
In° your distrust.   *By*
CAESAR   I have said.
ANTONY   You shall not find,
35   Though you be therein curious,° the least cause   *overly probing*
For what you seem to fear. So, the gods keep you,
And make the hearts of Romans serve your ends.
We will here part.
CAESAR   Farewell, my dearest sister, fare thee well.
40   The elements be kind to thee, and make
Thy spirits all of comfort. Fare thee well.
OCTAVIA [*weeping*]   My noble brother!
ANTONY   The April's in her eyes;° it is love's spring,   *She weeps*
And these the showers to bring it on. Be cheerful.
45   OCTAVIA   Sir, look well to my husband's° house, and—   *(Antony's)*
CAESAR   What, Octavia?
OCTAVIA   I'll tell you in your ear.
[*She whispers to* CAESAR]
ANTONY   Her tongue will not obey her heart, nor can
Her heart inform her tongue—the swan's-down feather,
That stands upon the swell at full of tide,
50   And neither way inclines.⁵
ENOBARBUS [*aside to* AGRIPPA]   Will Caesar weep?
AGRIPPA [*aside to* ENOBARBUS]   He has a cloud in's face.
ENOBARBUS [*aside to* AGRIPPA]   He were the worse for that were he a horse;⁶
So is he, being a man.
AGRIPPA [*aside to* ENOBARBUS]   Why, Enobarbus,
55   When Antony found Julius Caesar dead
He cried almost to roaring, and he wept
When at Philippi he found Brutus slain.
ENOBARBUS [*aside to* AGRIPPA]   That year indeed he was trou-
bled with a rheum.°   *flu; watery eyes*
What willingly he did confound° he wailed,°   *destroy / mourned*
Believe't, till I wept too.
60   CAESAR   No, sweet Octavia,
You shall hear from me still.° The time shall not   *constantly*
Outgo⁷ my thinking on° you.   *of*
ANTONY   Come, sir, come,
I'll wrestle with you in my strength of love.

4. *and as . . . approof:* and (such a wife) as to make my largest contractual commitment (also, my closest tie of affection: here, Caesar's to Octavia) approved on the basis of what you will prove to be.
5. *the swan's-down . . . inclines:* (she is like) the feather of a swan's down that floats in still water, unmoving (just as she can't speak) when the tide is about to turn. Octavia's emotions, balanced between brother and husband, are too strong to allow speech.
6. A horse with a cloud—a dark rather than a white star on its face—was supposedly ill tempered.
7. *The . . . / Outgo:* Even time will not endure beyond.

Look, here I have you [*embracing* CAESAR]; thus I let you go,
And give you to the gods.

65 CAESAR   Adieu, be happy.

LEPIDUS   Let all the number of the stars give light
To thy fair way.

CAESAR   Farewell, farewell.

      [*He*] *kisses* OCTAVIA

ANTONY   Farewell.

        Trumpets sound. Exeunt [ANTONY, OCTAVIA, *and*
          ENOBARBUS *at one door*, CAESAR, LEPIDUS, *and*
                      AGRIPPA *at another*]

3.3

Enter CLEOPATRA, CHARMIAN, IRAS, *and* ALEXAS

CLEOPATRA   Where is the fellow?

ALEXAS   Half afeard to come.

CLEOPATRA   Go to, go to.

      Enter the MESSENGER *as before*

                    Come hither, sir.

ALEXAS   Good majesty,
Herod of Jewry[1] dare not look upon you
But when you are well pleased.

CLEOPATRA   That Herod's head

5 I'll have; but how, when Antony is gone,
Through whom I might command it?

  [*To the* MESSENGER]   Come thou near.

MESSENGER   Most gracious majesty!

CLEOPATRA   Didst thou behold
Octavia?

MESSENGER   Ay, dread Queen.

CLEOPATRA   Where?

MESSENGER   Madam, in Rome.
I looked her in the face, and saw her led

10 Between her brother and Mark Antony.

CLEOPATRA   Is she as tall as me?

MESSENGER   She is not, madam.

CLEOPATRA   Didst hear her speak? Is she shrill-tongued or low?

MESSENGER   Madam, I heard her speak. She is low-voiced.

CLEOPATRA   That's not so good.° He cannot like her long.   *favorable to Octavia*

15 CHARMIAN   Like her? O Isis, 'tis impossible!

CLEOPATRA   I think so, Charmian. Dull of tongue, and dwarfish.
What majesty is in her gait? Remember
If e'er thou looked'st on majesty.

MESSENGER   She creeps.
Her motion and her station° are as one.   *standing still*

20 She shows° a body rather than a life,   *seems to be*
A statue than° a breather.   *rather than*

CLEOPATRA   Is this certain?

MESSENGER   Or I have no observance.°   *powers of observation*

CHARMIAN   Three in Egypt
Cannot make better note.[2]

CLEOPATRA   He's very knowing,

3.3 Location: Alexandria.
1. Renowned for his irrational cruelty. See note to 1.2.24.

2. *Three . . . note*: There are not three better witnesses in
all Egypt.

I do perceive't. There's nothing in her yet.
The fellow has good judgement.

25 CHARMIAN   Excellent.

CLEOPATRA [*to the* MESSENGER]   Guess at her years, I prithee.

MESSENGER   Madam,
  She was a widow—

CLEOPATRA   Widow? Charmian, hark.

MESSENGER   And I do think she's thirty.°   *(Cleopatra was 38)*

CLEOPATRA   Bear'st thou her face in mind? Is't long or round?

30 MESSENGER   Round, even to faultiness.

CLEOPATRA   For the most part, too, they are foolish that are so.
  Her hair—what colour?

MESSENGER   Brown, madam; and her forehead
  As low as she would wish it.³

CLEOPATRA [*giving money*]   There's gold for thee.
  Thou must not take my former sharpness ill.

35 I will employ thee back° again. I find thee   *to go back to Rome*
  Most fit for business. Go, make thee ready.
  Our letters are prepared.   [*Exit* MESSENGER]

CHARMIAN   A proper° man.   *An admirable*

CLEOPATRA   Indeed he is so. I repent me much
  That so I harried him. Why, methinks, by him,°   *by his account*
  This creature's no such thing.°   *nothing special*

40 CHARMIAN   Nothing, madam.

CLEOPATRA   The man hath seen some majesty, and should know.

CHARMIAN   Hath he seen majesty? Isis else defend,
  And serving you so long!⁴

CLEOPATRA   I have one thing more to ask him yet, good Charmian.

45 But 'tis no matter. Thou shalt bring him to me
  Where I will write. All may be well enough.

CHARMIAN   I warrant you, madam.   *Exeunt*

3.4

Enter ANTONY *and* OCTAVIA

ANTONY   Nay, nay, Octavia, not only that,
  That were excusable, that and thousands more
  Of semblable° import; but he hath waged   *like*
  New wars 'gainst Pompey, made his will and read it

5 To public ear,¹ spoke scantly° of me;   *meanly*
  When perforce he could not
  But pay me terms of honour, cold and sickly
  He vented them, most narrow measure° lent me.   *little credit*
  When the best hint° was given him, he not took't,   *opportunity*
  Or did it from his teeth.°   *insincerely*

10 OCTAVIA   O my good lord,
  Believe not all, or if you must believe,
  Stomach° not all. A more unhappy lady,   *Resent*
  If this division chance, ne'er stood between,
  Praying for both parts.

15 The good gods will mock me presently,°   *at once*

---

3. So that she would wish it no lower: high foreheads
were admired.
4. *Isis . . . long:* He surely has, considering how long he's
served you. *else defend:* prohibit that it not be so. There
may be a double irony in the lines, with Charmian appar-

ently denying that anyone who has long served Cleopatra
could recognize true majesty but not really meaning it.
3.4 Location: Athens.
1. Caesar's act implies promises to the public.

When I shall pray 'O, bless my lord and husband!',
Undo that prayer by crying out as loud
'O, bless my brother!' Husband win, win brother
Prays and destroys the prayer; no midway
'Twixt these extremes at all.

20 ANTONY   Gentle Octavia,
Let your best love draw to that point which seeks
Best to preserve it.[2] If I lose mine honour,
I lose myself. Better I were not yours
Than yours so branchless.° But, as you requested,   *amputated*
25 Yourself shall go between's. The meantime, lady,
I'll raise the preparation of a war
Shall stain your brother.° Make your soonest haste;   *hurt his reputation*
So° your desires are yours.   *In this way*

OCTAVIA   Thanks to my lord.
The Jove of power make me most weak, most weak,
30 Your reconciler! Wars 'twixt you twain would be
As if the world should cleave, and that slain men
Should solder° up the rift.   *close*

ANTONY   When it appears to you where this begins,°   *who started this*
Turn your displeasure that way, for our faults
35 Can never be so equal that your love
Can equally move with° them. Provide° your going,   *judge / Prepare for*
Choose your own company, and command what cost
Your heart has mind to.   *Exeunt*

3.5
Enter ENOBARBUS *and* EROS [*meeting*]

ENOBARBUS   How now, friend Eros?
EROS   There's strange news come, sir.
ENOBARBUS   What, man?
EROS   Caesar and Lepidus have made wars upon Pompey.
5 ENOBARBUS   This is old. What is the success?°   *outcome*
EROS   Caesar, having made use of him° in the wars 'gainst Pom-   *(Lepidus)*
pey, presently denied him rivality,° would not let him partake   *equal partnership*
in the glory of the action, and, not resting° here, accuses him   *stopping*
of letters he had formerly wrote to Pompey; upon his° own   *(Caesar's)*
10 appeal° seizes him; so the poor third is up,° till death enlarge   *accusation / imprisoned*
his confine.
ENOBARBUS   Then, world, thou hast a pair of chops,° no more,°   *jaws / (than two)*
And throw° between them all the food thou hast,   *if you should throw*
They'll grind the one the other. Where's Antony?
15 EROS   He's walking in the garden, thus, and spurns°   *kicks*
The rush° that lies before him, cries 'Fool Lepidus!'   *rushes*
And threats the throat of that his officer°   *that officer of his*
That murdered Pompey.[1]
ENOBARBUS   Our great navy's rigged.°   *prepared*
EROS   For Italy and Caesar. More,° Domitius: *There's more (to say)*
20 My lord desires you presently. My news
I might have told hereafter.

---

2. *Let . . . it:* Choose the one of us (Antony or Caesar) who best strives to preserve your love.
3.5 Location: Athens.
1. Historically, though Shakespeare leaves Antony's re-

sponsibility for the killing unclear, Pompey was said to have been murdered at the command of Antony, who here regrets the death because Pompey might have been a useful ally against Caesar.

ENOBARBUS   'Twill be naught.[2]
But let it be; bring me to Antony.
EROS   Come, sir.   *Exeunt*

3.6

Enter AGRIPPA, MAECENAS, *and* CAESAR

CAESAR   Contemning° Rome, he has done all this and more   *Despising*
In Alexandria. Here's the manner of 't:
I'th' market place on a tribunal° silvered,   *platform*
Cleopatra and himself in chairs of gold
5   Were publicly enthroned. At the feet sat
Caesarion, whom they call my father's[1] son,
And all the unlawful issue that their lust
Since then hath made between them. Unto her
He gave the stablishment° of Egypt; made her   *full possession*
10   Of lower Syria, Cyprus, Lydia,[2]
Absolute queen.
MAECENAS   This in the public eye?
CAESAR   I'th' common showplace, where they exercise.[3]
His sons he there proclaimed the kings of kings;
Great Media, Parthia, and Armenia
15   He gave to Alexander. To Ptolemy he assigned
Syria, Cilicia, and Phoenicia. She
In th'habiliments° of the goddess Isis   *costume*
That day appeared, and oft before gave audience,
As 'tis reported, so.°   *in this costume*
MAECENAS   Let Rome be thus informed.
20   AGRIPPA   Who, queasy with° his insolence already,   *sick of*
Will their good thoughts call° from him.   *remove*
CAESAR   The people knows it,
And have now received his accusations.
AGRIPPA   Who does he accuse?
CAESAR   Caesar, and that having in Sicily
25   Sextus Pompeius spoiled,° we had not rated° him   *ransacked / allotted*
His part o'th' isle.° Then does he say he lent me   *Sicily*
Some shipping, unrestored.° Lastly, he frets   *not returned (by me)*
That Lepidus of the triumvirate
Should be deposed; and being,° that we detain   *being deposed*
All his revenue.
30   AGRIPPA   Sir, this should be answered.
CAESAR   'Tis done already, and the messenger gone.
I have told him Lepidus was grown too cruel,
That he his high authority abused
And did deserve his change. For° what I have conquered,   *As for*
35   I grant him part; but then in his Armenia,
And other of his conquered kingdoms,
I demand the like.
MAECENAS   He'll never yield to that.
CAESAR   Nor must not then be yielded to in this.
Enter OCTAVIA *with her train*

---

2. Of no consequence; extremely harmful.
3.6 Location: Rome.
1. Julius Caesar (who adopted his grandnephew Octavius as his son). See 2.2.233–34 with note and note to 5.2.352.

2. District on the west coast of Asia Minor. Shakespeare took the name from North's translation of Plutarch, but the original has Libya.
3. In the arena (theater), where they engage in sports (perform).

	OCTAVIA	Hail, Caesar, and my lord; hail, most dear Caesar!	
40	CAESAR	That ever I should call thee castaway!	
	OCTAVIA	You have not called me so, nor have you cause.	
	CAESAR	Why have you stol'n upon us thus? You come not	

Like Caesar's sister. The wife of Antony
Should have an army for an usher, and

45 The neighs of horse to tell of her approach
Long ere she did appear. The trees by th' way
Should have borne men, and expectation fainted,
Longing for what it had not. Nay, the dust
Should have ascended to the roof of heaven,

50 Raised by your populous troops. But you are come
A market maid to Rome, and have prevented°   (by coming too early)
The ostentation° of our love; which, left unshown,   public display
Is often left unloved.⁴ We should have met you
By sea and land, supplying every stage°   (of the voyage)
With an augmented greeting.

55 OCTAVIA   Good my lord,
To come thus was I not constrained, but did it
On my free will. My lord, Mark Antony,
Hearing that you prepared for war, acquainted
My grievèd ear withal, whereon I begged
His pardon for° return.   permission to

60 CAESAR   Which soon he granted,
Being an obstruct 'tween his lust and him.

OCTAVIA   Do not say so, my lord.

CAESAR   I have eyes upon him,
And his affairs come to me on the wind.
Where is he now?

OCTAVIA   My lord, in Athens.

65 CAESAR   No, my most wrongèd sister. Cleopatra
Hath nodded him to her. He hath given his empire
Up to a whore; who° now are levying   both of them
The kings o'th' earth for war. He hath assembled
Bocchus, the King of Libya; Archelaus

70 Of Cappadocia; Philadelphos, King
Of Paphlagonia; the Thracian King Adallas;
King Malchus of Arabia; King of Pont;
Herod of Jewry; Mithridates, King
Of Comagene; Polemon and Amyntas,

75 The Kings of Mede and Lycaonia;⁵
With a more larger° list of sceptres.   yet longer

OCTAVIA   Ay me most wretched,
That have my heart parted betwixt two friends
That does afflict each other!

CAESAR   Welcome hither.
Your letters did withhold our° breaking forth   restrain me from

80 Till we perceived both how you were wrong° led   wrongly
And we in negligent danger.° Cheer your heart.   danger from negligence
Be you not troubled with the time,° which drives   present business
O'er your content° these strong necessities;   contentment

---

4. Is often thought not to be love at all. Or, *which . . .*   leads to its actual decline.
unloved: lack of opportunity to demonstrate love often   5. All kings from the East.

But let determined things to destiny
85 Hold unbewailed their way.⁶ Welcome to Rome;
Nothing more dear to me. You are abused
Beyond the mark° of thought, and the high gods,   *limits*
To do you justice, makes their ministers°   *agents*
Of us and those that love you. Best of comfort,
And ever welcome to us.
90 AGRIPPA   Welcome, lady.
MAECENAS   Welcome, dear madam.
Each heart in Rome does love and pity you.
Only th'adulterous Antony, most large°   *unlimited*
In his abominations, turns you off,
95 And gives his potent regiment° to a trull°   *powerful rule / whore*
That noises it° against us.   *cries out*
OCTAVIA   Is it so, sir?
CAESAR   Most certain. Sister, welcome. Pray you
Be ever known to patience. My dear'st sister!   *Exeunt*

3.7

Enter CLEOPATRA *and* ENOBARBUS
CLEOPATRA   I will be even with thee, doubt it not.
ENOBARBUS   But why, why, why?
CLEOPATRA   Thou hast forspoke° my being in these wars,   *opposed*
And sayst it is not fit.
ENOBARBUS   Well, is it, is it?
5 CLEOPATRA   Is't not denounced° against us? Why should not we   *Isn't war declared*
Be there in person?
ENOBARBUS [*aside*]   Well, I could reply
If we should serve with horse and mares together,
The horse were merely lost;¹ the mares would bear°   *seduce; carry*
A soldier and his horse.
CLEOPATRA   What is't you say?
10 ENOBARBUS   Your presence needs must puzzle° Antony,   *distract*
Take from his heart, take from his brain, from's time
What should not then be spared. He is already
Traduced° for levity; and 'tis said in Rome   *Slandered*
That Photinus, an eunuch, and your maids
Manage this war.
15 CLEOPATRA   Sink Rome,° and their tongues rot   *To hell with Rome*
That speak against us! A charge° we bear i'th' war,   *An expense; duty*
And as the president of my kingdom will
Appear there for° a man. Speak not against it.   *as if I were*
I will not stay behind.
Enter ANTONY *and* CAMIDIUS
ENOBARBUS   Nay, I have done.
Here comes the Emperor.
20 ANTONY   Is it not strange, Camidius,
That from Tarentum and Brundisium²
He could so quickly cut° the Ionian° Sea   *Cut across / Adriatic*
And take in° Toryne?°—You have heard on't, sweet?   *overrun / (near Actium)*

---

6. *let . . . way:* let predetermined events go to their destined conclusions without complaint.
3.7 Location: Antony's camp, near Actium, Greece.
1. *If . . . lost:* If we take both male and female horses

(whores) to the wars, the males would have no hope of triumphing, because of the females ("merely" equals "mare-ly").
2. Ports in southeast Italy.

CLEOPATRA   Celerity is never more admired°   *wondered at*
        Than by the negligent.
25 ANTONY   A good rebuke,
        Which might have well becomed the best of men
        To taunt at slackness. Camidius, we
        Will fight with him by sea.
    CLEOPATRA   By sea—what else?
    CAMIDIUS   Why will my lord do so?
    ANTONY   For that he dares us to't.
30 ENOBARBUS   So hath my lord dared him to single fight.
    CAMIDIUS   Ay, and to wage this battle at Pharsalia,°   *(near Actium)*
        Where Caesar fought with Pompey. But these offers
        Which serve not for his vantage, he shakes off,
        And so should you.
    ENOBARBUS   Your ships are not well manned,
35   Your mariners are muleters,° reapers, people   *mule drivers*
        Engrossed° by swift impress.° In Caesar's fleet   *Amassed / conscription*
        Are those that often have 'gainst Pompey fought.
        Their ships are yare,° yours heavy. No disgrace   *smooth running*
        Shall fall° you for refusing him at sea,   *befall*
        Being prepared for land.
40 ANTONY   By sea, by sea.
    ENOBARBUS   Most worthy sir, you therein throw away
        The absolute soldiership you have by land;
        Distract° your army, which doth most consist   *Divert*
        Of war-marked footmen; leave unexecuted°   *untapped*
45   Your own renownèd knowledge; quite forgo
        The way which promises assurance,° and   *victory*
        Give up yourself merely° to chance and hazard   *completely*
        From firm security.
    ANTONY   I'll fight at sea.
    CLEOPATRA   I have sixty sails, Caesar none better.
50 ANTONY   Our overplus of shipping will we burn,[3]
        And with the rest full-manned, from th'head° of Actium   *promontory*
        Beat th'approaching Caesar. But if we fail,
        We then can do't at land.
                Enter a MESSENGER
                            Thy business?
    MESSENGER   The news is true, my lord. He is descried.°   *He has been seen*
55   Caesar has taken Toryne.
    ANTONY   Can he be there in person? 'Tis impossible;
        Strange that his power° should be. Camidius,   *his entire army*
        Our nineteen legions thou shalt hold by land,
        And our twelve thousand horse. We'll to our ship.
        Away, my Thetis![4]
                Enter a SOLDIER
60   How now, worthy soldier?
    SOLDIER   O noble Emperor, do not fight by sea.
        Trust not to rotten planks. Do you misdoubt
        This sword and these my wounds? Let th'Egyptians

---

3. Antony seems to have burned his excess ("overplus")   taken by Octavius Caesar.
ships because he did not have enough sailors to man   4. Sea goddess, mother of the Greek hero Achilles.
them adequately and feared that they could easily be

And the Phoenicians go a-ducking;° we   *to sea*
65   Have used to conquer standing on the earth,
      And fighting foot to foot.
  ANTONY   Well, well; away!
                Exeunt ANTONY, CLEOPATRA, *and* ENOBARBUS
  SOLDIER   By Hercules, I think I am i'th' right.
  CAMIDIUS   Soldier, thou art; but his whole action grows
      Not in the power on't.⁵ So our leader's led,
      And we are women's men.
70 SOLDIER   You keep by land
      The legions and the horse whole, do you not?
  CAMIDIUS   Marcus Octavius, Marcus Justeius,
      Publicola and Caelius are for sea,
      But we keep whole° by land. This speed of Caesar's   *stay undivided*
      Carries beyond° belief.   *Exceeds*
75 SOLDIER   While he was yet in Rome
      His power went out in such distractions°   *separate detachments*
      As beguiled all spies.
  CAMIDIUS   Who's his lieutenant, hear you?
  SOLDIER   They say, one Taurus.
  CAMIDIUS   Well I know the man.
                Enter a MESSENGER
  MESSENGER   The Emperor calls Camidius.
80 CAMIDIUS   With news the time's in labour, and throws forth
      Each minute some.⁶   *Exeunt*

                        3.8
        Enter CAESAR *with his army, marching [and* TAURUS]
  CAESAR   Taurus!
  TAURUS   My lord?
  CAESAR   Strike not by land. Keep whole.° Provoke not battle   *Stay in reserve*
      Till we have done at sea. [*Giving a scroll*] Do not exceed
5   The prescript° of this scroll. Our fortune lies   *written orders*
      Upon this jump.°   *ploy*
        Exit [CAESAR *and his army at one door,* TAURUS *at another*]

                        3.9
              Enter ANTONY *and* ENOBARBUS
  ANTONY   Set we our squadrons on yon side o'th' hill
      In eye° of Caesar's battle,° from which place   *view / battle line*
      We may the number of the ships behold,
      And so proceed accordingly.   *Exeunt*

                        3.10
        CAMIDIUS *marcheth with his land army one way over the
        stage, and* TAURUS, *the lieutenant of Caesar, [with his
        army] the other way. After their going in is heard the
        noise of a sea-fight. Alarum. Enter* ENOBARBUS
  ENOBARBUS   Naught, naught, all naught!° I can behold no longer.   *lost; ruined*
      Th'*Antoniad,* the Egyptian admiral,°   *flagship*
      With all their sixty, fly and turn the rudder.

---

5. His entire plan is made without taking into account   3.8 Location: Near Actium.
his resources.   3.9 Location: Scene continues.
6. *throws . . . some:* each minute, more news is born.   3.10 Location: Scene continues.

To see't mine eyes are blasted.°   *(as if by lightning)*
    Enter SCARUS

SCARUS   Gods and goddesses—
  All the whole synod° of them!   *assembly*

5 ENOBARBUS   What's° thy passion?   *What provokes*

SCARUS   The greater cantle° of the world is lost   *corner; portion*
  With° very ignorance;° we have kissed away   *Through / idiocy*
  Kingdoms and provinces.

ENOBARBUS   How appears the fight?

SCARUS   On our side like the tokened pestilence,[1]
10   Where death is sure. Yon riband-red[2] nag of Egypt—
  Whom leprosy o'ertake!—i'th' midst o'th' fight—
  When vantage like a pair of twins appeared,[3]
  Both as the same, or rather ours the elder°—   *ours likely the stronger*
  The breese upon her,[4] like a cow in June,
  Hoists sails and flies.

15 ENOBARBUS   That I beheld.
  Mine eyes did sicken at the sight, and could not
  Endure a further view.

SCARUS   She once being luffed,[5]
  The noble ruin° of her magic, Antony,   *casualty*
  Claps on his sea-wing° and, like a doting mallard,°   *sails / male duck*
20   Leaving the fight in° height, flies after her.   *at its*
  I never saw an action of such shame.
  Experience, manhood, honour, ne'er before
  Did violate so itself.

ENOBARBUS   Alack, alack!
    Enter CAMIDIUS

CAMIDIUS   Our fortune on the sea is out of breath,
25   And sinks most lamentably. Had our general
  Been what he knew himself,° it had gone well.   *(to be)*
  O, he has given example for our flight
  Most grossly by his own.

ENOBARBUS   Ay, are you thereabouts?° Why then, good night   *of the same mind*
    indeed!

30 CAMIDIUS   Toward Peloponnesus are they fled.

SCARUS   'Tis easy to't,° and there I will attend   *to reach that place*
  What further comes.

CAMIDIUS   To Caesar will I render
  My legions and my horse. Six kings already
  Show me the way of yielding.

ENOBARBUS   I'll yet follow
35   The wounded chance° of Antony, though my reason   *fortune*
  Sits in the wind against me.°   *[Exeunt severally]*   *Opposes*

                    3.11
    Enter ANTONY *with Attendants*

ANTONY   Hark, the land bids me tread no more upon't,
  It is ashamed to bear me. Friends, come hither.

---

1. Plague manifested in tokens (red spots presaging death).
2. Decked in red ribbons. This emendation of F's "ribaudred"—a word of unclear meaning, if any—juxtaposes the image of Cleopatra bedecked like a horse or a whore with the red tokens of the plague.
3. When the fight could have gone either way.
4. Bitten by a gadfly; driven by a breeze.
5. Having prepared the ship's head to sail close to the wind (ready to leave).
3.11 Location: Alexandria.

I am so lated° in the world that I   *lost in the dark*
Have lost my way for ever. I have a ship
5 Laden with gold. Take that; divide it, fly,
And make your peace with Caesar.
ATTENDANTS   Fly? Not we.
ANTONY I have fled myself, and have instructed cowards
To run and show their shoulders.° Friends, be gone. *backs*
I have myself resolved upon a course
10 Which has no need of you. Be gone.
My treasure's in the harbour. Take it. O,
I followed that° I blush to look upon.   *that which*
My very hairs do mutiny, for the white
Reprove the brown for rashness, and they them° *they the others*
15 For fear and doting. Friends, be gone. You shall
Have letters from me to some friends that will
Sweep° your way for you. Pray you, look not sad, *Clear*
Nor make replies of loathness.° Take the hint° *reluctance / chance*
Which my despair proclaims. Let that be left
20 Which leaves° itself. To the seaside straightway! *ceases to be*
I will possess you of that ship and treasure.
Leave me, I pray, a little.° Pray you now,   *for a brief time*
Nay, do so; for indeed I have lost command.° *authority*
Therefore I pray you; I'll see you by and by.
             [Exeunt attendants]
   [He] sits down.
   Enter CLEOPATRA *led by* CHARMIAN, [IRAS,] *and* EROS
25 EROS Nay, gentle madam, to him. Comfort him.
IRAS Do, most dear Queen.
CHARMIAN Do. Why, what else?
CLEOPATRA Let me sit down. O Juno!
   [She sits down]
ANTONY No, no, no, no, no.
30 EROS *[to* ANTONY] See you here, sir?
ANTONY O fie, fie, fie!
CHARMIAN Madam.
IRAS Madam. O good Empress!
EROS Sir, sir.
35 ANTONY Yes, my lord, yes. He° at Philippi kept *(Octavius)*
His sword e'en like a dancer,° while I struck *(for decoration only)*
The lean and wrinkled Cassius; and 'twas I
That the mad Brutus ended.° He alone   *defeated*
Dealt on lieutenantry,° and no practice had *Fought through others*
40 In the brave squares° of war. Yet now—no matter. *fine formations*
CLEOPATRA *[rising, to* CHARMIAN *and* IRAS] Ah, stand by.
EROS The Queen, my lord, the Queen.
IRAS Go to him, madam.
Speak to him. He's unqualitied°   *lost his sense of self*
With very shame.
45 CLEOPATRA   Well then, sustain me. O!
EROS Most noble sir, arise. The Queen approaches.
Her head's declined, and death will seize her but° *unless*
Your comfort makes the rescue.
ANTONY I have offended reputation;
A most unnoble swerving.°   *slippage*
50 EROS   Sir, the Queen.

ANTONY [*rising*]   O, whither hast thou led me, Egypt? See
How I convey° my shame out of thine eyes°   *steal back / sight*
By looking back° what I have left behind   *back on*
'Stroyed° in dishonour.   *Destroyed*

CLEOPATRA   O, my lord, my lord,
55 Forgive my fearful sails! I little thought
You would have followed.

ANTONY   Egypt, thou knew'st too well
My heart was to thy rudder tied by th' strings,
And thou shouldst tow me after. O'er my spirit
Thy full supremacy thou knew'st, and that
60 Thy beck° might from the bidding of the gods   *call*
Command me.

CLEOPATRA   O, my pardon!

ANTONY   Now I must
To the young man[1] send humble treaties,° dodge   *appeals*
And palter in the shifts of lowness,[2] who
With half the bulk o'th' world played as I pleased,
65 Making and marring fortunes. You did know
How much you were my conqueror, and that
My sword, made weak by my affection,° would   *desire*
Obey it on all cause.°   *for any reason*

CLEOPATRA   Pardon, pardon!

ANTONY   Fall° not a tear, I say. One of them rates°   *Weep / is worth*
70 All that is won and lost. Give me a kiss.
            [*He kisses her*]
Even this repays me. [*To an Attendant*]   We sent our school-
master;°   *tutor to our children*
Is a° come back? [*To* CLEOPATRA] Love, I am full of lead.   *he*
[*Calling*] Some wine
Within there, and our viands!° Fortune knows   *food*
We scorn her most when most she offers blows.   *Exeunt*

3.12

Enter CAESAR, AGRIPPA, THIDIAS, *and* DOLABELLA, *with
others*

CAESAR   Let him appear that's come from Antony.
Know you him?

DOLABELLA   Caesar, 'tis his schoolmaster;
An argument° that he is plucked, when hither   *A proof*
He sends so poor a pinion° of his wing,   *an outer feather*
5   Which° had superfluous kings for messengers   *He who*
Not many moons gone by.

Enter AMBASSADOR *from Antony*

CAESAR   Approach and speak.

AMBASSADOR   Such as I am, I come from Antony.
I was of late as petty° to his ends   *inconsequential*
As is the morn-dew on the myrtle leaf
To his grand sea.[1]

10 CAESAR   Be't so. Declare thine office.°   *business*

AMBASSADOR   Lord of his fortunes he salutes thee, and

---

1. Octavius Caesar at this time (31 B.C.E.) was thirty-two,
Antony fifty-one.
2. *dodge . . . lowness:* shuffle and play fast and loose in
the shifty ways of a man brought low.

3.12 Location: Caesar's camp, Egypt.
1. In relation to the great sea, ultimate source of dew,
that is Antony.

Requires° to live in Egypt; which not granted,   *Asks*
He lessens his requests, and to thee sues
To let him breathe between the heavens and earth,
15 A private man in Athens. This for him.
Next, Cleopatra does confess thy greatness,
Submits her to thy might, and of thee craves
The circle° of the Ptolemies for her heirs,   *crown*
Now hazarded to thy grace.°   *placed at your mercy*
CAESAR   For Antony,
20 I have no ears to his request. The Queen
Of audience nor desire shall fail, so² she
From Egypt drive her all-disgracèd friend,
Or take his life there. This if she perform
She shall not sue unheard. So to them both.
AMBASSADOR   Fortune pursue thee!
25 CAESAR   Bring° him through the bands.°   *Escort / ranks*
                    [Exit AMBASSADOR, *attended]*
[*To* THIDIAS] To try thy eloquence now 'tis time. Dispatch.
From Antony win Cleopatra. Promise,
And in our name, what she requires. Add more
As thine invention° offers. Women are not   *imagination*
30 In° their best fortunes strong, but want will perjure   *While in*
The ne'er-touched vestal.³ Try thy cunning, Thidias.
Make thine own edict° for thy pains, which we   *Command your reward*
Will answer as a law.
THIDIAS   Caesar, I go.
CAESAR   Observe how Antony becomes his flaw,°   *reacts to his fall*
35 And what thou think'st his very action speaks
In every power that moves.⁴
THIDIAS   Caesar, I shall.
        Exeunt [CAESAR *and his train at one door, and*
                THIDIAS *at another*]

3.13

   Enter CLEOPATRA, ENOBARBUS, CHARMIAN, AND IRAS
CLEOPATRA   What shall we do, Enobarbus?
ENOBARBUS   Think,° and die.   *(about our misery)*
CLEOPATRA   Is Antony or we in fault for this?
ENOBARBUS   Antony only, that would make his will°   *lust*
Lord of his reason. What though° you fled   *What if*
5 From that great face of war, whose several ranges°   *battle lines*
Frighted each other? Why should he follow?
The itch of his affection should not then
Have nicked° his captainship, at such a point,   *bettered (gambling term)*
When half to half the world opposed, he being
10 The mooted° question. 'Twas a shame no less   *disputed*
Than was his loss, to course° your flying flags   *chase*
And leave his navy gazing.
CLEOPATRA   Prithee, peace.
     Enter the AMBASSADOR *with* ANTONY

---

2. Shall not fail to receive either a hearing or fulfillment
of her wishes, as long as.
3. *want . . . vestal:* need will make the purest virgin break
her vows.

4. *his very . . . moves:* his actions themselves reveal in
every move he makes.
3.13 Location: Alexandria.

ANTONY   Is that his answer?

AMBASSADOR   Ay, my lord.

ANTONY   The Queen shall then have courtesy, so° she   *as long as*

  Will yield us up.

AMBASSADOR   He says so.

15 ANTONY   Let her know't.

  [*To* CLEOPATRA] To the boy Caesar send this grizzled head,

  And he will fill thy wishes to the brim

  With principalities.

CLEOPATRA   That head, my lord?

ANTONY [*to the* AMBASSADOR]   To him again. Tell him he wears the rose

20 Of youth upon him, from which the world should note

  Something particular.° His coin, ships, legions,   *A success of his own*

  May be a coward's, whose ministers° would prevail   *aides; underlings*

  Under the service of a child as soon°   *as well*

  As i'th' command of Caesar. I dare him therefore

25 To lay his gay caparisons° apart   *showy adornments*

  And answer me declined,[1] sword against sword,

  Ourselves alone. I'll write it. Follow me.

              [*Exeunt* ANTONY *and* AMBASSADOR]

ENOBARBUS [*aside*]   Yes, like enough, high-battled° Caesar will   *with many troops*

  Unstate° his happiness and be staged to th' show[2]   *Overthrow*

30 Against a sworder! I see men's judgements are

  A parcel of° their fortunes, and things outward   *Consistent with*

  Do draw the inward quality after them

  To suffer all alike.° That he should dream,   *To decay together*

  Knowing all measures,[3] the full Caesar will

35 Answer° his emptiness! Caesar, thou hast subdued   *Fight; reply to*

  His judgement, too.

        Enter a SERVANT

SERVANT   A messenger from Caesar.

CLEOPATRA   What, no more ceremony? See, my women:

  Against the blown° rose may they stop their nose,   *decaying*

  That° kneeled unto the buds. Admit him, sir. [*Exit* SERVANT]   *Who once*

40 ENOBARBUS [*aside*]   Mine honesty° and I begin to square.°   *honor / square off; argue*

  The loyalty well held° to fools does make   *given*

  Our faith mere° folly; yet he that can endure   *complete*

  To follow with allegiance a fall'n lord

  Does conquer him that did his master conquer,

  And earns a place i'th' story.

        Enter THIDIAS

45 CLEOPATRA   Caesar's will?

THIDIAS   Hear it apart.

CLEOPATRA   None but friends; say boldly.

THIDIAS   So haply° are they friends to Antony.   *possibly*

ENOBARBUS   He needs as many, sir, as Caesar has,

  Or needs not us.[4] If Caesar please, our master

50 Will leap to be his friend. For us, you know,

  Whose he is, we are: and that is Caesar's.

---

1. And meet me past my prime, in my misfortune.
2. Be displayed to the public gaze (as in the London theater or Roman gladiatorial combat).
3. Having known the best and worst of times ("all mea-sures" of fortune, both "full[ness]" and "emptiness," line 35).
4. *Or needs not us:* If the situation is truly hopeless, he doesn't even need our friendship.

THIDIAS So. [*To* CLEOPATRA] Thus, then, thou most renowned:
    Caesar entreats
    Not to consider° in what case thou stand'st   *be concerned*
    Further than he is Caesar.[5]
  CLEOPATRA   Go on; right royal.°   *most generous*
55 THIDIAS He knows that you embraced not Antony
    As you did love, but as you fearèd him.
  CLEOPATRA O.
  THIDIAS The scars upon your honour therefore he
    Does pity as constrainèd° blemishes,   *involuntary*
    Not as deserved.
60 CLEOPATRA   He is a god, and knows
    What is most right. Mine honour was not yielded,
    But conquered merely.
  ENOBARBUS [*aside*]   To be sure of that
    I will ask Antony. Sir, sir, thou art so leaky
    That we must leave thee to thy sinking, for
    Thy dearest quit thee.   *Exit*
65 THIDIAS   Shall I say to Caesar
    What you require° of him?—For he partly begs   *request*
    To be desired to give. It much would please him
    That of his fortunes you should make a staff
    To lean upon. But it would warm his spirits
70   To hear from me you had left Antony,
    And put your self under his shroud,°   *protection; burial sheet*
    The universal landlord.
  CLEOPATRA   What's your name?
  THIDIAS My name is Thidias.
  CLEOPATRA   Most kind messenger,
    Say to great Caesar this in deputation:° *as my representative*
75   I kiss his conqu'ring hand. Tell him I am prompt
    To lay my crown at's feet, and there to kneel
    Till from his all-obeying° breath I hear   *which all obey*
    The doom of Egypt.[6]
  THIDIAS 'Tis your noblest course.
    Wisdom and fortune combating together,
80   If that the former dare but what it can,[7]
    No chance may shake it. Give me grace to lay
    My duty on your hand.
    [*He kisses Cleopatra's hand*]
  CLEOPATRA   Your Caesar's father oft,
    When he hath mused of taking kingdoms in,° *subduing kingdoms*
    Bestowed his lips on that unworthy place,
    As° it rained kisses.   *As if*
    Enter ANTONY *and* ENOBARBUS
85 ANTONY   Favours, by Jove that thunders!
    What art thou, fellow?
  THIDIAS   One that but performs
    The bidding of the fullest[8] man, and worthiest
    To have command obeyed.
  ENOBARBUS   You will be whipped.

---

5. Beyond remembering that he is Caesar—and hence nobly generous in forgiving insult and injury (but with a more sinister undertone as well).

6. What he destines for Egypt and its Queen.
7. If the wise man confines his daring to what is possible.
8. Most complete; most successful.

ANTONY [*calling*]   Approach, there!—Ah, you kite!⁹ Now, gods and devils,
90   Authority melts from me of late. When I cried 'Ho!',
        Like boys unto a muss¹ kings would start forth,
        And cry 'Your will?'—Have you no ears? I am
        Antony yet.
                Enter servant[s]
                    Take hence this jack,° and whip him.   knave
ENOBARBUS [*aside to* THIDIAS]   'Tis better playing with a lion's whelp°   cub
        Than with an old one dying.
95 ANTONY   Moon and stars!
        Whip him! Were't twenty of the greatest tributaries
        That do acknowledge Caesar, should I find them
        So saucy with the hand of she here—what's her name
        Since she was Cleopatra?² Whip him, fellows,
100   Till like a boy you see him cringe° his face,   distort
        And whine aloud for mercy. Take him hence.
THIDIAS   Mark Antony—
ANTONY   Tug him away. Being whipped,
        Bring him again. This jack of Caesar's shall
        Bear us an errand to him.   *Exeunt [servants] with* THIDIAS
105   You were half blasted° ere I knew you. Ha,   decayed
        Have I my pillow left unpressed in Rome,
        Forborne the getting° of a lawful race,   begetting
        And by a gem of women, to be abused
        By one that looks on feeders?°   parasites; servants
110 CLEOPATRA   Good my lord—
ANTONY   You have been a boggler° ever.   fickle one
        But when we in our viciousness grow hard—
        O misery on't!—the wise gods seel³ our eyes,
        In our own filth drop our clear judgements, make us
115   Adore our errors, laugh at's while we strut
        To our confusion.
CLEOPATRA   O, is't come to this?
ANTONY   I found you as a morsel cold upon
        Dead Caesar's trencher;° nay, you were a fragment°   plate / leftover
        Of Gnaeus Pompey's,⁴ besides what hotter hours
120   Unregistered in vulgar fame° you have   base gossip
        Luxuriously° picked out. For I am sure,   Wantonly
        Though you can guess what temperance should be,
        You know not what it is.
CLEOPATRA   Wherefore is this?
ANTONY   To let a fellow that will take rewards
125   And say 'God quit° you' be familiar with   repay
        My playfellow your hand, this kingly seal
        And plighter° of high hearts! O that I were   pledger
        Upon the hill of Basan to outroar
        The hornèd herd!⁵ For I have savage cause,
130   And to proclaim it civilly were like
        A haltered° neck which does the hangman thank   in the noose

9. Predator or whore, addressed to either Cleopatra or
Thidias.
1. Game in which small items were tossed to the ground
for children to snatch and grab.
2. Antony's question suggests that since Cleopatra's be-
havior has changed, her name must have changed as well.
3. Blind: hawks' eyes were sealed (sewn up) to tame

them.
4. Older brother of the Pompey of the play and son of
Pompey the Great. See note to 1.5.31.
5. Alluding to the bulls of the hill of Basan (Bashan) in
Psalms 68:15 and 22:12; Antony sees himself as a cuck-
old (a man whose wife has committed adultery), conven-
tionally imagined with horns.

For being yare° about him.   *swift*

Enter a SERVANT *with* THIDIAS

Is he whipped?

SERVANT   Soundly, my lord.

ANTONY   Cried he, and begged a° pardon?   *he*

135   SERVANT   He did ask favour.

ANTONY [*to* THIDIAS]   If that thy father live, let him repent
Thou wast not made his daughter; and be thou sorry
To follow Caesar in his triumph, since
Thou hast been whipped for following him. Henceforth

140   The white hand of a lady fever thee,⁶
Shake thou to look on't. Get thee back to Caesar;
Tell him thy entertainment.° Look° thou say   *treatment / See that*
He makes me angry with him, for he seems
Proud and disdainful, harping on what I am,

145   Not what he knew I was. He makes me angry,
And at this time most easy 'tis to do't,
When my good stars that were my former guides
Have empty left their orbs,° and shot their fires   *spheres*
Into th'abyss of hell. If he mislike

150   My speech and what is done, tell him he has
Hipparchus, my enfranchèd° bondman, whom   *emancipated*
He may at pleasure whip, or hang, or torture,
As he shall like, to quit° me. Urge it thou.   *requite*
Hence, with thy stripes,° be gone!   *Exit* [SERVANT *with*] THIDIAS   *wounds*

155   CLEOPATRA   Have you done yet?

ANTONY   Alack, our terrene moon⁷
Is now eclipsed, and it portends alone
The fall of Antony.

CLEOPATRA [*aside*]   I must stay his time.⁸

ANTONY   To flatter Caesar would you mingle eyes
With one that ties his points?⁹

160   CLEOPATRA   Not know me yet?

ANTONY   Cold-hearted toward me?

CLEOPATRA   Ah, dear, if I be so,
From my cold heart let heaven engender hail,
And poison it in the source, and the first stone
Drop in my neck: as it determines,° so   *turns to liquid*

165   Dissolve my life! The next Caesarion smite,
Till by degrees the memory of my womb,°   *my children*
Together with my brave Egyptians all,
By the discandying° of this pelleted storm   *dissolving*
Lie graveless till the flies and gnats of Nile
Have buried them for prey!

170   ANTONY   I am satisfied.
Caesar sits down in° Alexandria, where   *besieges*
I will oppose his fate.¹ Our force by land
Hath nobly held; our severed navy too
Have knit again, and fleet,° threat'ning most sea-like.   *are afloat*

175   Where hast thou been, my heart?° Dost thou hear, lady?   *bravery*
If from the field I shall return once more

---

6. May the white hand of a lady make you feverish.
7. Terrestrial moon goddess—Cleopatra.
8. I must hold my tongue until he is over his rage.

9. *would . . . points:* would you flirt with one of his servants? *points:* laces (attaching stockings to other clothing).
1. I will resist his apparently destined victory.

To kiss these lips, I will appear in blood.°   *bloody; vigorous*
I and my sword will earn our chronicle.°   *historical reputation*
There's hope in't yet.

CLEOPATRA   That's my brave lord.

180 ANTONY   I will be treble-sinewed, hearted, breathed,
And fight maliciously;° for when mine hours   *furiously*
Were nice² and lucky, men did ransom° lives   *buy their*
Of° me for jests;° but now I'll set my teeth,   *From / trinkets*
And send to darkness all that stop me. Come,

185 Let's have one other gaudy° night. Call to me   *merry*
All my sad captains. Fill our bowls once more.
Let's mock the midnight bell.³

CLEOPATRA   It is my birthday.
I had thought to've held it poor,° but since my lord   *modestly commemorated it*
Is Antony again, I will be Cleopatra.

190 ANTONY   We will yet do well.

CLEOPATRA   Call all his noble captains to my lord!

ANTONY   Do so. We'll speak to them, and tonight I'll force
The wine peep through their scars. Come on, my queen,
There's sap in't° yet. The next time I do fight   *vigor in (our cause)*
195 I'll make death love me, for I will contend°   *do battle*
Even with his pestilent° scythe. *Exeunt [all but* ENOBARBUS*]*   *plague-dealing*

ENOBARBUS   Now he'll outstare° the lightning. To be furious   *stare down*
Is to be frighted out of fear, and in that mood
The dove will peck the estridge;° and I see still°   *a kind of hawk / always*
200 A diminution in our captain's brain
Restores his heart. When valour preys on reason,
It eats the sword it fights with. I will seek
Some way to leave him.   *Exit*

4.1

Enter CAESAR, *reading a letter, with* AGRIPPA, MAECENAS,
and his army

CAESAR   He calls me boy, and chides as° he had power   *as though*
To beat me out of Egypt. My messenger
He hath whipped with rods, dares me to personal combat,
Caesar to Antony. Let the old ruffian know
5 I have many other ways to die; meantime,
Laugh at° his challenge.   *Mock*

MAECENAS   Caesar must think,
When one so great begins to rage, he's hunted
Even to falling. Give him no breath,° but now   *time to catch breath*
Make boot° of his distraction.° Never anger   *Take advantage / fury*
Made good guard for itself.

10 CAESAR   Let our best heads°   *officers*
Know that tomorrow the last of many battles
We mean to fight. Within our files° there are,   *troops*
Of those that served Mark Antony but late,
Enough to fetch him in.° See it done,   *capture him*
15 And feast the army. We have store to do't,
And they have earned the waste.° Poor Antony!   *Exeunt*   *expense*

---

2. *Were nice*: Permitted me to pick and choose, to act with noble generosity; were lascivious; were pampered.   3. Let's make a mockery of the hour by revelry; let's mock the death knell that fate seems to ring for us.   **4.1** Location: Caesar's camp, before Alexandria.

4.2

Enter ANTONY, CLEOPATRA, ENOBARBUS, CHARMIAN,
  IRAS, ALEXAS, *with others*

ANTONY He will not fight with me, Domitius?

ENOBARBUS   No.

ANTONY Why should he not?

ENOBARBUS He thinks, being twenty times of better fortune,
  He is twenty men to one.

ANTONY   Tomorrow, soldier,

5 By sea and land I'll fight. Or° I will live   Either
  Or bathe my dying honour in the blood
  Shall make it live again. Woot thou° fight well?   Will you

ENOBARBUS I'll strike, and cry 'Take all!'°   Winner take all

ANTONY   Well said. Come on!
  Call forth my household servants. Let's tonight
  Be bounteous at our meal.

              Enter SERVITORS

10   Give me thy hand.
  Thou hast been rightly honest; so hast thou,
  Thou, and thou, and thou; you have served me well,
  And kings have been your fellows.°   companions

CLEOPATRA [*to* ENOBARBUS]   What means this?

ENOBARBUS [*to* CLEOPATRA]   'Tis one of those odd tricks which
      sorrow shoots
  Out of the mind.

15 ANTONY [*to a* SERVITOR] And thou art honest too.
  I wish I could be made° so many men,   split up into
  And all of you clapped up together in
  An Antony, that I might do you service
  So good as you have done.

SERVITORS   The gods forbid!

20 ANTONY Well, my good fellows, wait on me tonight.
  Scant not my cups, and make as much of me
  As when mine empire was your fellow° too,   fellow servant
  And suffered° my command.   obeyed

CLEOPATRA [*aside to* ENOBARBUS] What does he mean?

ENOBARBUS [*aside to* CLEOPATRA]
  To make his followers weep.

ANTONY   Tend me tonight.

25 Maybe it is the period° of your duty.   end
  Haply° you shall not see me more; or if,°   Maybe / if you do
  A mangled shadow.° Perchance tomorrow   phantom
  You'll serve another master. I look on you
  As one that takes his leave. Mine honest friends,

30 I turn you not away, but, like a master
  Married to your good service, stay till death.
  Tend me tonight two hours. I ask no more;
  And the gods yield° you for't!   reward

ENOBARBUS   What mean you, sir,
  To give them this discomfort? Look, they weep,

35 And I, an ass, am onion-eyed.° For shame,   weepy
  Transform us not to women.

4.2 Location: Alexandria.

ANTONY   Ho, ho, ho,
Now the witch take° me if I meant it thus!   *bewitch*
Grace grow where those drops fall. My hearty friends,
You take me in too dolorous a sense;
40   For I spake to you for your comfort, did desire you
To burn this night with torches. Know, my hearts,
I hope well of tomorrow, and will lead you
Where rather I'll expect victorious life
Than death and honour. Let's to supper, come,
45   And drown consideration.°   *Exeunt*   *serious thoughts*

4.3

Enter a company of SOLDIERS

FIRST SOLDIER   Brother, good night. Tomorrow is the day.
SECOND SOLDIER   It will determine one way. Fare you well.°   *Good luck*
Heard you of nothing strange about° the streets?   *in*
FIRST SOLDIER   Nothing. What news?
5   SECOND SOLDIER   Belike° 'tis but a rumour. Good night to you.   *Most likely*
FIRST SOLDIER   Well, sir, good night.
          [Enter] other SOLDIERS, *meet[ing them]*
SECOND SOLDIER   Soldiers, have careful watch.
THIRD SOLDIER   And you. Good night, good night.
          They place themselves in every corner of the stage
SECOND SOLDIER   Here we;[1] an if° tomorrow   *an if=if*
Our navy thrive, I have an absolute hope
Our landmen will stand up.°   *make a stand*
FIRST SOLDIER   'Tis a brave army,
And full of purpose.
        Music of the hautboys° is under the stage   *oboes*
SECOND SOLDIER   Peace, what noise?
10   FIRST SOLDIER   List, list!
SECOND SOLDIER   Hark!
FIRST SOLDIER   Music i'th' air.
THIRD SOLDIER   Under the earth.
FOURTH SOLDIER   It signs° well, does it not?   *bodes*
THIRD SOLDIER   No.
FIRST SOLDIER   Peace, I say!
What should this mean?
SECOND SOLDIER   'Tis the god Hercules, whom Antony loved,
Now leaves him.
15   FIRST SOLDIER   Walk. Let's see if other watchmen
Do hear what we do.
SECOND SOLDIER   How now, masters?°   *good sirs*
ALL *(speak[ing] together)*[2]   How now?
How now? Do you hear this?
FIRST SOLDIER   Ay. Is't not strange?
THIRD SOLDIER   Do you hear, masters? Do you hear?
FIRST SOLDIER   Follow the noise so far as we have quarter.[3]
Let's see how it will give off.°   *end*
20   ALL   Content. 'Tis strange.   *Exeunt*

4.3 Location: Outside Cleopatra's palace, Alexandria.
1. Here are our positions.
2. Individual soldiers probably address different questions
and comments to one another rather than speaking in chorus.
3. As far as the limit of our watch.

4.4

Enter ANTONY *and* CLEOPATRA, *with* [CHARMIAN *and*]
others

ANTONY [*calling*]   Eros, mine armour, Eros!
CLEOPATRA   Sleep a little.
ANTONY   No, my chuck.° Eros, come, mine armour, Eros!   *my dear*
      Enter EROS [*with armour*]
      Come, good fellow, put thine iron on.¹
      If fortune be not ours today, it is
      Because we brave° her. Come.   *dare*
5 CLEOPATRA   Nay, I'll help, too.
      What's this for?
ANTONY   Ah, let be, let be! Thou art
      The armourer of my heart. False, false!° This, this!   *wrong*
CLEOPATRA   Sooth, la, I'll help. Thus it must be.
      [*She helps* ANTONY *to arm*]
ANTONY   Well, well,
      We shall thrive now. Seest thou, my good fellow?
      Go put on thy defences.°   *armor*
10 EROS   Briefly,° sir.   *Soon*
CLEOPATRA   Is not this buckled well?
ANTONY   Rarely, rarely.
      He that unbuckles this, till we do please
      To doff't° for our repose, shall hear a storm.   *remove it*
      Thou fumblest, Eros, and my queen's a squire°   *an attendant to a knight*
15   More tight° at this than thou. Dispatch.° O love,   *able / Finish*
      That thou couldst see my wars today, and knew'st
      The royal occupation! Thou shouldst see
      A workman° in't.   *An expert*
      Enter an armed SOLDIER
                     Good morrow to thee. Welcome.
      Thou look'st like him that knows a warlike charge.°   *purpose*
20   To business that we love we rise betime,°   *early*
      And go to't with delight.
SOLDIER   A thousand, sir,
      Early though't be, have on their riveted trim,°   *armor*
      And at the port expect you.
      Shout [*within*]. *Trumpets flourish. Enter* CAPTAINS *and*
      SOLDIERS
CAPTAIN   The morn is fair. Good morrow, General.
SOLDIERS   Good morrow, General.
25 ANTONY   'Tis well blown,² lads.
      This morning, like the spirit of a youth
      That means to be of note, begins betimes.
      So, so. Come, give me that. This way. Well said.°   *Well done*
      Fare thee well, dame. Whate'er becomes of me,
      This is a soldier's kiss.
      [*He kisses* CLEOPATRA]
30   Rebukable
      And worthy shameful check° it were to stand   *reprimand*
      On more mechanic° compliment. I'll leave thee   *coarse*
      Now like a man of steel. You that will fight,

4.4 Location: Cleopatra's palace.
1. Clad me in that piece of armor of mine that you have.
2. Well sounded (of the trumpet); well started (of the morning).

Follow me close. I'll bring you to't. Adieu.

Exeunt [all but CLEOPATRA *and* CHARMIAN]

CHARMIAN   Please you retire to your chamber?

35 CLEOPATRA   Lead me.
He goes forth gallantly. That he and Caesar might
Determine this great war in single fight!
Then, Antony—but now! Well, on.   *Exeunt*

4.5

Trumpets sound. Enter ANTONY *and* EROS [*meeting a*
SOLDIER]

SOLDIER   The gods make this a happy° day to Antony!   fortunate
ANTONY   Would thou and those thy scars had once° prevailed   earlier
To make me fight at land!

SOLDIER   Hadst thou done so,
The kings that have revolted,° and the soldier   deserted

5 That has this morning left thee, would have still
Followed thy heels.

ANTONY   Who's gone this morning?

SOLDIER   Who? One ever near thee. Call for Enobarbus,
He shall not hear thee, or from Caesar's camp
Say 'I am none of thine'.

ANTONY   What sayest thou?

SOLDIER   Sir, he is with Caesar.

10 EROS [*to* ANTONY]   Sir, his chests and treasure
He has not with him.

ANTONY   Is he gone?

SOLDIER   Most certain.

ANTONY   Go, Eros, send his treasure after. Do it.
Detain no jot, I charge thee. Write to him—
I will subscribe°—gentle adieus and greetings.   sign my name

15 Say that I wish he never find more cause
To change a master. O, my fortunes have
Corrupted honest men! Dispatch. Enobarbus!   *Exeunt*

4.6

Flourish. Enter AGRIPPA, CAESAR, *with* ENOBARBUS *and*
DOLABELLA

CAESAR   Go forth, Agrippa, and begin the fight.
Our will is Antony be took alive.
Make it so known.

AGRIPPA   Caesar, I shall.   [*Exit*]

CAESAR   The time of universal peace is near.[1]

5 Prove this° a prosp'rous day, the three-nooked world[2]   If this proves
Shall bear the olive° freely.   sign of peace

Enter a MESSENGER

MESSENGER   Antony
Is come into the field.

CAESAR   Go charge Agrippa

4.5 Location: Antony's camp, Alexandria.
4.6 Location: Caesar's camp, Alexandria.
1. Octavius Caesar, later the Emperor Augustus, was known for the *Pax Romana*—Roman peace—of his reign; the phrase also alludes to the birth of Christ, which occurred while Augustus was emperor. See the Introduction.

2. Three-cornered world. Referring (in descending order of probability) to Europe, Asia, Africa (the triumvirate's holdings); the three races descended from Noah's sons (Japhet, Shem, Ham); earth, sea, sky. The three races of Noah can to an extent be superimposed on the three continents and may connect with the later religious connotations of the Roman Empire. See the previous note.

Plant those that have revolted in the van,°   *front lines*
That Antony may seem to spend his fury
10   Upon himself.°   *On his former troops*

*Exeunt [*MESSENGER *at one door,* CAESAR *and*
DOLABELLA *at another]*

ENOBARBUS   Alexas did revolt, and went to Jewry on
Affairs of Antony; there did dissuade°   *persuade*
Great Herod to incline himself to Caesar
And leave his master, Antony. For this pains,
15   Caesar hath hanged him. Camidius and the rest
That fell away have entertainment° but   *employment*
No honourable trust. I have done ill,
Of which I do accuse myself so sorely
That I will joy no more.

Enter a SOLDIER *of Caesar's*

SOLDIER   Enobarbus, Antony
20   Hath after thee sent all thy treasure, with
His bounty overplus. The messenger
Came on my guard,° and at thy tent is now   *on my watch*
Unloading of his mules.
ENOBARBUS   I give it you.
25   SOLDIER   Mock not, Enobarbus,
I tell you true. Best you safed the bringer
Out of the host.³ I must attend mine office,°   *look after my duties*
Or would have done't myself. Your Emperor
Continues still a Jove.   *Exit*
30   ENOBARBUS   I am alone the° villain of the earth,   *the single greatest*
And feel I am so most.° O Antony,   *I feel it most*
Thou mine of bounty, how wouldst thou have paid
My better service, when my turpitude
Thou dost so crown with gold! This blows° my heart.   *swells; bursts*
35   If swift thought° break it not, a swifter mean°   *regret / means (suicide)*
Shall outstrike thought; but thought will do't, I feel.
I fight against thee? No, I will go seek
Some ditch wherein to die. The foul'st best fits
My latter part of life.   *Exit*

4.7

Alarum. Enter AGRIPPA *[with] drum[mer]s and trum-*
pet[er]s
AGRIPPA   Retire!° We have engaged our selves too far.   *Sound the retreat*
Caesar himself has work,° and our oppression   *is sorely challenged*
Exceeds what we expected.   *Exeunt*

4.8

Alarums. Enter ANTONY, *and* SCARUS *wounded*
SCARUS   O my brave Emperor, this is fought indeed!
Had we done so at first, we had droven them home
With clouts° about their heads.   *bandages; blows*
ANTONY   Thou bleed'st apace.

---

3. *Best . . . host:* It would be best if you ensured safe con-
duct through the lines for the messenger who brought
the treasure.

4.7 Location: The battlefield, Alexandria.
4.8 Location: Scene continues.

SCARUS I had a wound here that was like a T,
But now 'tis made an H.[1]
　　　　　[*Retreat sounded*] *far off*
5　ANTONY　　　　　　　They do retire.
SCARUS We'll beat 'em into bench-holes.° I have yet　　*latrine holes*
Room for six scotches° more.　　　　　　　　　*gashes*
　　　　Enter EROS
EROS They are beaten, sir, and our advantage serves
For a fair victory.
SCARUS　　　　　Let us score° their backs　　　　*slash*
10　And snatch 'em up as° we take hares, behind.　　*in the same way as*
'Tis sport to maul a runner.°　　　　　　　*coward*
ANTONY [*to* EROS]　　　I will reward thee
Once for thy sprightly° comfort, and tenfold　　　*cheerful*
For thy good valour. Come thee on.
SCARUS　　　　　　　　I'll halt° after.　*Exeunt*　*limp*

4.9

Alarum. Enter ANTONY *again in a march;* [*drummers
and trumpeters;*] SCARUS, *with others*
ANTONY　We have beat him to his camp. Run one before,
And let the Queen know of our gests.°　　[*Exit a soldier*]　*deeds*
　　　　　　　　　　　　　　　Tomorrow,
Before the sun shall see's, we'll spill the blood
That has today escaped. I thank you all,
5　For doughty-handed° are you, and have fought　　*brave*
Not as° you served the cause, but as't had been　　*as though*
Each man's like mine. You have shown all Hectors.[1]
Enter the city, clip° your wives, your friends,　　*embrace*
Tell them your feats whilst they with joyful tears
10　Wash the congealment from your wounds, and kiss
The honoured gashes whole.
　　　　　Enter CLEOPATRA
[*To* SCARUS]　　　　　　Give me thy hand.
To this great fairy° I'll commend thy acts,　　　*enchantress*
Make her thanks bless thee.
[*To* CLEOPATRA, *embracing her*]　O thou day° o'th' world,　*light*
Chain mine armed neck; leap thou, attire and all,
15　Through proof of harness° to my heart, and there　*impenetrable armor*
Ride on the pants° triumphing.　　　　　　*heartbeats*
CLEOPATRA　　　　　　Lord of lords!
O infinite virtue,° com'st thou smiling from　　*valor*
The world's great snare uncaught?
ANTONY　　　　　　　My nightingale,
We have beat them to their beds. What, girl, though grey
20　Do something° mingle with our younger brown, yet ha' we　*somewhat*
A brain that nourishes our nerves,° and can　　*muscles*
Get goal for goal of youth.[2] Behold this man.
Commend unto his lips thy favouring hand;
Kiss it, my warrior.

---

1. *wound . . . H:* the wound was originally shaped like a
T, but another gash across its bottom has made it look like
an H turned sideways (punning on "ache," pronounced
"aitch").
4.9 Location: Scene continues.

1. You have all fought like Hector (the greatest of the
Trojan warriors).
2. Compete with any youth. Antony is clearly referring
here to the "boy" Caesar, but also, possibly, to his own
boyhood.

[SCARUS *kisses Cleopatra's hand*]
                                He hath fought today
25 As if a god, in hate of mankind, had
     Destroyed in such a shape.
CLEOPATRA   I'll give thee, friend,
     An armour all of gold. It was a king's.
ANTONY He has deserved it, were it carbuncled°   *bejeweled*
     Like holy Phoebus' car.° Give me thy hand.   *the sun god's chariot*
30 Through Alexandria make a jolly march.
     Bear our hacked targets like° the men that owe° them.   *shields as befits / own*
     Had our great palace the capacity
     To camp° this host, we all would sup together   *put up*
     And drink carouses to the next day's fate,
35 Which promises royal° peril. Trumpeters,   *great*
     With brazen din blast you the city's ear;
     Make mingle with our rattling taborins,°   *small drums*
     That heaven and earth may strike their sounds together,
     Applauding our approach.   [*Trumpets sound.*] *Exeunt*

4.10
Enter a SENTRY *and his company;* ENOBARBUS *follows*
SENTRY   If we be not relieved within this hour
     We must return to th' court of guard.° The night   *guardroom*
     Is shiny,° and they say we shall embattle°   *bright / go to battle*
     By th' second hour i'th' morn.
FIRST WATCH   This last day was
     A shrewd° one to's.   *bad*
5 ENOBARBUS   O bear me witness, night—
SECOND WATCH   What man is this?
FIRST WATCH   Stand close,° and list° him.   *hidden / listen to*
ENOBARBUS Be witness to me, O thou blessèd moon,
     When men revolted° shall upon record   *deserters*
     Bear hateful memory, poor Enobarbus did
     Before thy face repent.
SENTRY   Enobarbus?
10 SECOND WATCH   Peace; hark further.
ENOBARBUS O sovereign mistress of true melancholy,°   *(the moon)*
     The poisonous damp of night disponge° upon me,   *pour down*
     That life, a very rebel to my will,
     May hang no longer on me. Throw my heart
15 Against the flint and hardness of my fault,
     Which,° being dried with grief, will break to powder,   *(his heart)*
     And finish all foul thoughts. O Antony,
     Nobler than my revolt is infamous,
     Forgive me in thine own particular,[1]
20 But let the world rank me in register°   *its records*
     A master-leaver and a fugitive.°   *deserter*
     O Antony! O Antony!   [*He dies*][2]
FIRST WATCH   Let's speak to him.

4.10 Location: Caesar's camp.
1. In whatever aspects of this business concern only you.
2. Depending on how this moment is played, Enobar-

bus's death may not be obvious either to those onstage
or to the audience.

SENTRY   Let's hear him, for the things he speaks
    May concern Caesar.

25   SECOND WATCH   Let's do so. But he sleeps.

SENTRY   Swoons, rather; for so bad a prayer as his
    Was never yet for° sleep.   *in preparation for*

FIRST WATCH   Go we to him.

SECOND WATCH   Awake, sir, awake; speak to us.

FIRST WATCH   Hear you, sir?

SENTRY   The hand of death hath raught° him.   *taken*
    Drums afar off

                                 Hark, the drums

30   Demurely° wake the sleepers. Let us bear him   *With subdued sound*
    To th' court of guard; he is of note. Our hour
    Is fully out.°   *expired*

SECOND WATCH   Come on, then. He may recover yet.
                                Exeunt [with the body]

4.11

Enter ANTONY *and* SCARUS *with their army*

ANTONY   Their preparation is today by sea;
    We please them not by land.

SCARUS   For both, my lord.

ANTONY   I would they'd fight i'th' fire or i'th' air;
    We'd fight there too.[1] But this it is: our foot°   *foot soldiers*

5   Upon the hills adjoining to the city
    Shall stay with us. Order for sea is given.
    They have put forth° the haven—   *departed from*
    Where their appointment° we may best discover,   *purpose; battle plan*
    And look on their endeavour.   *Exeunt*

4.12

Enter CAESAR *and his army*

CAESAR   But being° charged, we will be still° by land—   *unless we're / inactive*
    Which, as I take't, we shall, for his best force
    Is forth to man his galleys. To the vales,°   *valleys*
    And hold our best advantage.°   *Exeunt*   *take the best position*

4.13

Alarum afar off, as at a sea fight.
Enter ANTONY *and* SCARUS

ANTONY   Yet they are not joined.° Where yon pine does stand   *(in battle)*
    I shall discover all. I'll bring thee word
    Straight° how 'tis like° to go.   *Exit*   *Promptly / likely*

SCARUS   Swallows have built
    In Cleopatra's sails their nests. The augurs°   *soothsayers*

5   Say they know not, they cannot tell, look grimly,
    And dare not speak their knowledge. Antony
    Is valiant, and dejected, and by starts
    His fretted° fortunes give him hope and fear   *diminished*
    Of what he has and has not.
    Enter ANTONY

4.11 Location: This and the next two scenes take place   1. As well as in the other elements, earth and water.
on the battlefield.   4.12
                                                                        4.13

ANTONY   All is lost.

10   This foul Egyptian hath betrayèd me.
      My fleet hath yielded to the foe, and yonder
      They cast their caps up, and carouse together
      Like friends long lost. Triple-turned whore![1] 'Tis thou
      Hast sold me to this novice, and my heart
15   Makes only wars on thee. Bid them all fly;
      For when I am revenged upon my charm,°   sorceress
      I have done all. Bid them all fly. Be gone.   [*Exit* SCARUS]
      O sun, thy uprise shall I see no more.
      Fortune and Antony part here; even here
20   Do we shake hands.° All come to this? The hearts   (*before parting*)
      That spanieled° me at heels, to whom I gave   *fawned upon*
      Their wishes, do discandy,° melt their sweets   *melt*
      On blossoming Caesar; and this pine° is barked[2]   (*Antony*)
      That overtopped them all. Betrayed I am.
25   O this false soul of Egypt! This grave° charm,   *deadly*
      Whose eye becked° forth my wars and called them home,   *beckoned*
      Whose bosom was my crownet,° my chief end,°   *coronet / reward*
      Like a right° gipsy hath at fast and loose[3]   *true*
      Beguiled° me to the very heart of loss.°   *cheated / ruin*
      What, Eros, Eros!
           Enter CLEOPATRA
30   Ah, thou spell! Avaunt.°   *Leave me*
      CLEOPATRA   Why is my lord enraged against his love?
      ANTONY   Vanish, or I shall give thee thy deserving
      And blemish Caesar's triumph.° Let him take thee   *triumphal procession*
      And hoist thee up to the shouting plebeians;
35   Follow his chariot, like the greatest spot°   *taint*
      Of all thy sex; most monster-like be shown
      For poor'st diminutives,[4] for dolts, and let
      Patient Octavia plough thy visage up
      With her preparèd° nails.   *Exit* CLEOPATRA   *specially sharpened*
                               'Tis well thou'rt gone,
40   If it be well to live. But better 'twere
      Thou fell'st into° my fury, for one death   *a victim to*
      Might have prevented many. Eros, ho!
      The shirt of Nessus[5] is upon me. Teach me,
      Alcides, thou mine ancestor, thy rage.
45   Let me lodge Lichas on the horns o'th' moon,
      And with those hands that grasped the heaviest club
      Subdue my worthiest self. The witch shall die.
      To the young Roman boy she hath sold me, and I fall
      Under this plot. She dies for't. Eros, ho!   *Exit*

1. Cleopatra is "triple-turned" because disloyal to three (Julius Caesar, Pompey, and Antony); alluding to her changing political allegiances.
2. Stripped of its bark (and so killed).
3. *fast and loose:* a cheating game played by gypsies.
4. For the benefit of (in place of) the lowest people (dwarfs).
5. Hercules, also known as Alcides (line 44), with

whom Antony is repeatedly compared, fatally wounded the centaur Nessus for trying to rape his wife, Deianira. Nessus gave her some of his blood, falsely claiming that it would act as a love potion. Years later, she smeared some of the deadly blood on a shirt and sent it to Hercules. Blaming Lichas (line 45), who had brought the shirt, Hercules cast him into the sea. When she realized what she had done, Deianira killed herself.

4.14

Enter CLEOPATRA, CHARMIAN, IRAS, MARDIAN

CLEOPATRA   Help me, my women! O, he's more mad
Than Telamon for his shield;[1] the boar of Thessaly[2]
Was never so embossed.[3]

CHARMIAN   To th' monument![4]
There lock yourself, and send him word you are dead.

5   The soul and body rive° not more in parting   *separate*
Than greatness going off.°   *leaving someone*

CLEOPATRA   To th' monument!
Mardian, go tell him I have slain myself.
Say that the last I spoke was 'Antony',
And word it, prithee, piteously. Hence, Mardian,

10   And bring me° how he takes my death. To th' monument!   *bring me word*

                                                      Exeunt

4.15

Enter ANTONY *and* EROS

ANTONY   Eros, thou yet behold'st me?

EROS   Ay, noble lord.

ANTONY   Sometime we see a cloud that's dragonish,°   *in a dragon's shape*
A vapour sometime like a bear or lion,
A towered citadel, a pendent° rock,   *hanging*

5   A forkèd mountain, or blue promontory
With trees upon't that nod unto the world
And mock our eyes with air. Thou hast seen these signs;
They are black vesper's pageants.[1]

EROS   Ay, my lord.

ANTONY   That which is now a horse even with a thought

10   The rack distains,° and makes it indistinct   *cloud dims*
As water is in water.

EROS   It does, my lord.

ANTONY   My good knave° Eros, now thy captain is   *boy*
Even such a body. Here I am Antony,
Yet cannot hold this visible shape, my knave.

15   I made these wars for Egypt, and the Queen—
Whose heart I thought I had, for she had mine,
Which whilst it was mine had annexed unto't
A million more, now lost—she, Eros, has
Packed cards° with Caesar, and false-played my glory   *Stacked the deck*

20   Unto an enemy's triumph.°   *victory; trump card*
Nay, weep not, gentle Eros. There is left us
Ourselves to end ourselves.

        Enter MARDIAN
                        O thy vile lady,
She has robbed me of my sword!°   *valor; manhood*

MARDIAN   No, Antony,

4.14 Location: Alexandria.
1. Ajax, also known as Telemon, went mad and killed himself after the capture of Troy when he was not awarded Achilles' shield.
2. Sent by Diana to lay waste Calydon (killed by Meleager).
3. Was never so exhaustedly foaming at the mouth—that is, was never driven to such extremity (a hunting term).

4. The tomb that Cleopatra, forseeing her death, had built.
4.15 Location: Alexandria.
1. Illusory spectacles heralding the approach of night—with a probable allusion to funerals and death. (Pageants were originally moving stages on which miracle plays were presented.)

My mistress loved thee, and her fortunes mingled
With thine entirely.

25 ANTONY   Hence, saucy° eunuch, peace!   *disrespectful*
She hath betrayed me, and shall die the death.

MARDIAN   Death of one person can be paid but once,
And that she has discharged. What thou wouldst do
Is done unto thy hand.° The last she spake   *for you*
30 Was 'Antony, most noble Antony!'
Then in the midst a tearing groan did break
The name of Antony. It was divided
Between her heart and lips.² She rendered° life,   *gave up*
Thy name so buried in her.

ANTONY   Dead, then?

MARDIAN   Dead.

35 ANTONY   Unarm, Eros.³ The long day's task is done,
And we must sleep. [*To* MARDIAN] That thou depart'st hence safe
Does pay thy labour richly. Go.   *Exit* MARDIAN
                                        Off, pluck off.
        [EROS *helps* ANTONY *to unarm*]
The seven-fold shield⁴ of Ajax cannot keep
The battery° from my heart. O, cleave, my sides!   *onslaught*
40 Heart, once be stronger than thy continent;°   *container*
Crack thy frail case. Apace,° Eros, apace.   *Quickly*
No more a soldier. Bruisèd pieces,° do;   *of armor*
You have been nobly borne.—From me a while.   *Exit* EROS
I will o'ertake thee, Cleopatra, and
45 Weep for my pardon. So it must be, for now
All length° is torture. Since the torch° is out,   *longer life / (Cleopatra)*
Lie down, and stray no farther. Now all labour
Mars what it does; yea, very force entangles
Itself with strength.⁵ Seal,° then, and all is done.   *Finish the deed*
50 Eros!—I come, my queen.—Eros!—Stay for me.
Where souls do couch on flowers⁶ we'll hand in hand,
And with our sprightly port° make the ghosts gaze.   *cheerful stance*
Dido and her Aeneas shall want troops,⁷
And all the haunt° be ours. Come, Eros, Eros!   *place; ghosts*
                Enter EROS

EROS   What would my lord?

55 ANTONY   Since Cleopatra died
I have lived in such dishonour that the gods
Detest my baseness. I, that with my sword
Quartered the world, and o'er green Neptune's back°   *on the sea*
With ships made cities,⁸ condemn myself to lack°   *for lacking*
60 The courage of a woman; less noble mind
Than she which by her death our Caesar tells
'I am conqueror of myself.' Thou art sworn, Eros,

---

2. *It . . . lips:* It was half-uttered.
3. Here and in the following lines, the symbolic appropriateness of this historical figure's name ("Eros" means "love") is stressed.
4. A shield made of brass lined with six thicknesses of oxhide.
5. *very . . . strength:* strength defeats itself by its own exertions.
6. Lie ("couch") in the Elysian Fields of the blessed dead in the mythological underworld.

7. Shall lack followers. Dido, Queen of Carthage, commits suicide after being abandoned by her lover Aeneas, legendary Trojan founder of Rome, in Virgil's *Aeneid*; they are not reconciled in the underworld. Dido, who originally hailed from Phoenicia, is meant to recall Cleopatra. In leaving her, Aeneas places public responsibility above personal desire—unlike Antony but very much like Octavius Caesar, whom Virgil intended him to resemble.
8. Put so many ships to sea that the fleet resembled a city.

That when the exigent° should come, which now   *urgent need*
Is come indeed—when I should see behind me
65 Th'inevitable prosecution° of   *pursuit*
Disgrace and horror—that on my command
Thou then wouldst kill me. Do't. The time is come.
Thou strik'st not me; 'tis Caesar thou defeat'st.
Put colour in thy cheek.
EROS   The gods withhold me!°   *God forbid*
70 Shall I do that which all the Parthian darts,
Though enemy, lost aim and could not?
ANTONY   Eros,
Wouldst thou be windowed° in great Rome and see   *looking from a window*
Thy master thus with pleached° arms, bending down   *tied*
His corrigible° neck, his face subdued   *submissive*
75 To penetrative° shame, whilst the wheeled seat°   *piercing / chariot*
Of fortunate Caesar, drawn before him, branded
His baseness that ensued?⁹
EROS   I would not see't.
ANTONY   Come then; for with a wound I must be cured.
Draw that thy honest° sword, which thou hast worn   *honorable*
Most useful for thy country.
80 EROS   O sir, pardon me!
ANTONY   When I did make thee free, swor'st thou not then
To do this when I bade thee? Do it at once,
Or thy precedent° services are all   *earlier*
But accidents unpurposed.° Draw, and come.   *But pointless events*
85 EROS   Turn from me then that noble countenance
Wherein the worship° of the whole world lies.   *esteem; worth*
ANTONY [*turning away*]   Lo thee!
EROS   My sword is drawn.
ANTONY   Then let it do at once
The thing why thou hast drawn it.
EROS   My dear master,
90 My captain, and my Emperor: let me say,
Before I strike this bloody stroke, farewell.
ANTONY   'Tis said, man; and farewell.
EROS   Farewell, great chief. Shall I strike now?
ANTONY   Now, Eros.
    [EROS *stabs himself*]
EROS   Why, there then, thus I do escape the sorrow
Of Antony's death.   [*He dies*]
95 ANTONY   Thrice nobler than myself,
Thou teachest me, O valiant Eros, what
I should and thou couldst not. My queen and Eros
Have by their brave instruction got upon° me   *gained ahead of*
A nobleness in record.° But I will be   *history*
100 A bridegroom in my death, and run into't
As to a lover's bed.¹ Come then, and, Eros,
Thy master dies thy scholar. To do thus
I learned of thee.

---

9. *branded . . . ensued*: indicated, as if by a criminal's brand, the humiliation of the man who followed.
1. *But . . . bed*: Death is here treated as a form of erotic union or climax, with Antony as the bridegroom and death (and Cleopatra) the bride.

        [He stabs] himself
            How, not dead? Not dead?
  The guard, ho! O, dispatch° me!   *finish*
         Enter a GUARD *[and* DECRETAS*]*
FIRST GUARD   What's the noise?

105 ANTONY I have done my work ill, friends. O, make an end
  Of what I have begun!
SECOND GUARD   The star is fall'n.
FIRST GUARD And time is at his period.°   *its end*
ALL THE GUARDS   Alas
  And woe!
ANTONY Let him that loves me strike me dead.
FIRST GUARD   Not I.
SECOND GUARD   Nor I.
THIRD GUARD   Nor anyone. *Exeunt [the* GUARD*]*

110 DECRETAS Thy death and fortunes bid thy followers fly.
       [He takes Antony's sword]
  This sword but shown to Caesar, with this tidings,
  Shall enter me° with him.   *gain me favor*
       Enter DIOMEDES
DIOMEDES   Where's Antony?
DECRETAS There, Diomed, there.
DIOMEDES   Lives he? Wilt thou not answer, man?
                   [Exit DECRETAS*]*
ANTONY Art thou there, Diomed? Draw thy sword, and give me
  Sufficing° strokes for death.   *Enough*
115 DIOMEDES   Most absolute lord,
  My mistress Cleopatra sent me to thee.
ANTONY When did she send thee?
DIOMEDES   Now, my lord.
ANTONY   Where is she?
DIOMEDES Locked in her monument. She had a prophesying fear
  Of what hath come to pass; for when she saw—
120 Which never shall be found°—you did suspect   *(to be true)*
  She had disposed° with Caesar, and that your rage   *made an alliance*
  Would not be purged, she sent word she was dead;
  But fearing since how it might work, hath sent
  Me to proclaim the truth; and I am come,
125 I dread, too late.
ANTONY Too late, good Diomed. Call my guard, I prithee.
DIOMEDES What ho, the Emperor's guard! The guard, what ho!
  Come, your lord calls.
       Enter four or five of the GUARD *of Antony*
ANTONY Bear me, good friends, where Cleopatra bides.°   *waits; dwells*
130 'Tis the last service that I shall command you.
FIRST GUARD Woe, woe are we, sir, you may not live to wear
  All your true followers out.°   *outlive them*
ALL THE GUARDS   Most heavy day!
ANTONY Nay, good my fellows, do not please sharp fate
  To grace° it with your sorrows. Bid that welcome   *By gracing*
135 Which comes to punish us, and we punish it,
  Seeming to bear it lightly. Take me up.
  I have led you oft; carry me now, good friends,
  And have my thanks for all. *Exeunt bearing* ANTONY *[and* EROS*]*

4.16

Enter CLEOPATRA *and her maids aloft, with*
         CHARMIAN *and* IRAS

CLEOPATRA   O Charmian, I will never go from hence.

CHARMIAN   Be comforted, dear madam.

CLEOPATRA   No, I will not.
All strange and terrible events are welcome,
But comforts we despise. Our size of sorrow,
5 Proportioned to our cause, must be as great
As that which makes it.
         Enter DIOMEDES [*below*]
                        How now? Is he dead?

DIOMEDES   His death's upon him, but not dead.
Look out o'th' other side your monument.
His guard have brought him thither.
         Enter [*below*] ANTONY, [*borne by*] *the guard*

CLEOPATRA   O sun,
10 Burn the great sphere thou mov'st in; darkling¹ stand
The varying shore o'th' world! O Antony,
Antony, Antony! Help, Charmian,
Help, Iras, help, help, friends below!
Let's draw him hither.

ANTONY   Peace. Not Caesar's valour
15 Hath o'erthrown Antony, but Antony's
Hath triumphed on itself.

CLEOPATRA   So it should be,
That none but Antony should conquer Antony.
But woe 'tis so!

ANTONY   I am dying, Egypt, dying. Only
20 I here importune death° awhile until   ask death to wait
Of many thousand kisses the poor last
I lay upon thy lips.

CLEOPATRA   I dare not,° dear,   dare not come down
Dear, my lord, pardon. I dare not,
Lest I be taken. Nor th'imperious show°   triumphal procession
25 Of the full-fortuned Caesar ever shall
Be brooched° with me, if knife, drugs, serpents, have   decorated
Edge, sting, or operation.° I am safe.   power
Your wife, Octavia, with her modest eyes
And still conclusion,° shall acquire no honour   silent judgment
30 Demuring° upon me. But come, come, Antony.—   Gazing solemnly
Help me, my women.—We must draw thee up.
Assist, good friends.

ANTONY   O quick, or I am gone!

CLEOPATRA   Here's sport indeed. How heavy weighs my lord!
Our strength is all gone into heaviness,°   sadness; weight
35 That makes the weight. Had I great Juno's power
The strong-winged Mercury should fetch thee up
And set thee by Jove's side. Yet come a little.
Wishers were ever fools. O come, come, come!

4.16 Location: Cleopatra's monument, Alexandria.
1. *O . . . darkling:* For the spheres in which the sun, like
the planets and stars, was thought to move around the

earth, see note to 2.7.15. If the sun burned its sphere,
presumably it would move out of orbit, thus leaving the
earth in darkness ("darkling").

They heave ANTONY *aloft to* CLEOPATRA
And welcome, welcome! Die when thou hast lived,°   *lived again*
40   Quicken° with kissing. Had my lips that power,   *Revive*
Thus would I wear them out.
                    [*They kiss*]
ALL THE LOOKERS-ON   A heavy sight.
ANTONY   I am dying, Egypt, dying.
Give me some wine, and let me speak a little.
45   CLEOPATRA   No, let me speak, and let me rail so high
That the false hussy Fortune break her wheel,
Provoked by my offence.°   *insults*
ANTONY   One word, sweet queen.
Of Caesar seek your honour, with your safety. O!
CLEOPATRA   They do not go together.
ANTONY   Gentle, hear me.
50   None about Caesar trust but Proculeius.
CLEOPATRA   My resolution and my hands I'll trust,
None about Caesar.
ANTONY   The miserable change now at my end
Lament° nor sorrow at, but please your thoughts   *Neither lament*
55   In feeding them with those my former fortunes,
Wherein I lived the greatest prince o'th' world,
The noblest; and do now not basely die,
Not cowardly put off my helmet to
My countryman; a Roman by a Roman
60   Valiantly vanquished. Now my spirit is going;
I can no more.
CLEOPATRA   Noblest of men, woot die?°   *will you*
Hast thou no care of me? Shall I abide
In this dull world, which in thy absence is
No better than a sty?
                    [ANTONY *dies*]
                              O see, my women,
65   The crown o'th' earth doth melt. My lord!
O, withered is the garland° of the war.   *crowning glory*
The soldier's pole² is fall'n. Young boys and girls
Are level now with men. The odds° is gone,   *distinction among humans*
And there is nothing left remarkable
70   Beneath the visiting moon.
                    [*She falls*]
CHARMIAN   O, quietness, lady!
IRAS   She's dead, too, our sovereign.
CHARMIAN   Lady!
IRAS   Madam!
CHARMIAN   O, madam, madam, madam!
IRAS   Royal Egypt, Empress!
CHARMIAN   Peace, peace, Iras!
CLEOPATRA [*recovering*]   No more but e'en° a woman, and   *just (no longer Queen)*
75   commanded
By such poor passion as the maid that milks
And does the meanest chores. It were for° me   *would befit*
To throw my sceptre at the injurious gods,

---

2. Polestar; military standard; phallus.

To tell them that this world did equal theirs
80 Till they had stol'n our jewel. All's but naught.
Patience is sottish,° and impatience does   *foolish*
Become a dog that's mad. Then is it sin
To rush into the secret house of death
Ere death dare come to us? How do you, women?
85 What, what, good cheer! Why, how now, Charmian?
My noble girls! Ah, women, women! Look,
Our lamp is spent, it's out. Good sirs,° take heart;   *(to the women)*
We'll bury him, and then what's brave,° what's noble,   *fine*
Let's do it after the high Roman fashion,
90 And make death proud to take us. Come, away.
This case of that huge spirit now is cold.
Ah, women, women! Come. We have no friend
But resolution, and the briefest° end.   *fastest*

Exeunt [those above] bearing off Antony's body

5.1

Enter CAESAR *with his council of war:* AGRIPPA, DOLA-
BELLA, [MAECENAS, GALLUS, PROCULEIUS]

CAESAR Go to him, Dolabella, bid him yield.
Being so frustrate, tell him, he but mocks
The pauses that he makes.[1]
DOLABELLA   Caesar, I shall.   [*Exit*]

Enter DECRETAS *with the sword of Antony*

CAESAR Wherefore is that? And what art thou that dar'st
Appear thus° to us?   *with a drawn weapon*
5 DECRETAS   I am called Decretas.
Mark Antony I served, who best was worthy
Best to be served. Whilst he stood up and spoke
He was my master, and I wore my life
To spend° upon his haters. If thou please   *expend*
10 To take me to thee, as I was to him
I'll be to Caesar; if thou pleasest not,
I yield thee up my life.
CAESAR   What is't thou sayst?
DECRETAS I say, O Caesar, Antony is dead.
CAESAR The breaking° of so great a thing should make   *end; telling*
15 A greater crack.° The rivèd° world   *noise; fracture / split*
Should have shook lions into civil° streets,   *city*
And citizens to their° dens. The death of Antony   *(the lions')*
Is not a single doom; in that name lay
A moiety° of the world.   *half*
DECRETAS   He is dead, Caesar,
20 Not by a public minister of justice,
Nor by a hirèd knife; but that self° hand   *same*
Which writ his honour in the acts it did
Hath, with the courage which the heart did lend it,
Splitted the heart. This is his sword;
25 I robbed his wound of it. Behold it stained
With his most noble blood.
CAESAR [*weeping*]   Look you, sad friends,

5.1 Location: Caesar's camp.   1. *he but . . . makes:* his delays are a mere mockery.

The gods rebuke me;° but it is a tidings   *(for his tears)*
To wash the eyes of kings.
AGRIPPA   And strange it is
That nature must compel us to lament
Our most persisted deeds.°   *What we persevered in*
30 MAECENAS   His taints and honours
Waged° equal with° him.   *Fought as if / in*
AGRIPPA   A rarer spirit never
Did steer humanity;° but you gods will give us   *govern (any) man*
Some faults to make us men. Caesar is touched.
MAECENAS   When such a spacious mirror's set before him
He needs must see himself.
35 CAESAR   O Antony,
I have followed° thee to this. But we do lance°   *pursued / wound to cure*
Diseases in our bodies. I must perforce
Have shown to thee such a declining day,²
Or look on thine. We could not stall° together   *live in peace*
40 In the whole world. But yet let me lament,
With tears as sovereign³ as the blood of hearts,
That thou, my brother, my competitor°   *comrade; foe*
In top of all design,° my mate in empire,   *In the greatest ventures*
Friend and companion in the front of war,
45 The arm of mine own body, and the heart
Where mine his° thoughts did kindle—that our stars,   *its*
Unreconciliable, should divide
Our equalness° to this. Hear me, good friends—   *partnership*
          Enter an EGYPTIAN
But I will tell you at some meeter season.°   *fitter time*
50 The business of this man looks out of him;
We'll hear him what he says.—Whence are you?
EGYPTIAN   A poor Egyptian, yet the Queen my mistress,
Confined in all she has, her monument,
Of thy intents desires instruction,
55 That she preparèdly may frame herself
To th' way she's forced to.
CAESAR   Bid her have good heart.
She soon shall know of us, by some of ours,
How honourable and how kindly we
Determine for her. For Caesar cannot live
To be ungentle.
60 EGYPTIAN   So; the gods preserve thee!   *Exit*
CAESAR   Come hither, Proculeius. Go, and say
We purpose her no shame. Give her what comforts
The quality° of her passion° shall require,   *strength / grief*
Lest in her greatness, by some mortal stroke,
65 She do defeat us; for her life in Rome
Would be eternal in our triumph.⁴ Go,
And with your speediest bring us what she says
And how you find of her.
PROCULEIUS   Caesar, I shall.   *Exit*

---

2. *I must . . . day:* I would have had to exhibit my demise   bloodletting).
to you. *perforce:* necessarily.   4. *her life . . . triumph:* her presence alive in Rome would
3. As efficacious (weeping seems to be paralleled with   bring eternal renown to my triumphal procession.

CAESAR   Gallus, go you along.   [*Exit* GALLUS]
                          Where's Dolabella,
  To second Proculeius?
70 ALL BUT CAESAR   Dolabella!
  CAESAR   Let him alone; for I remember now
  How he's employed. He shall in time be ready.
  Go with me to my tent, where you shall see
  How hardly° I was drawn into this war,   *unwillingly*
75 How calm and gentle I proceeded still
  In all my writings.° Go with me, and see   *letters to Antony*
  What I can show in this.   *Exeunt*

5.2

Enter CLEOPATRA, CHARMIAN, IRAS, *and* MARDIAN
  CLEOPATRA   My desolation does begin to make
  A better life. 'Tis paltry to be Caesar.
  Not being Fortune, he's but Fortune's knave,°   *servant*
  A minister of her will. And it is great
5 To do that thing° that ends all other deeds,   *(suicide)*
  Which shackles accidents and bolts up change,
  Which sleeps and never palates more the dung,
  The beggar's nurse, and Caesar's.[1]
        Enter PROCULEIUS[2]
  PROCULEIUS   Caesar sends greeting to the Queen of Egypt,
10 And bids thee study on° what fair demands   *give thought to*
  Thou mean'st to have him grant thee.
  CLEOPATRA   What's thy name?
  PROCULEIUS   My name is Proculeius.
  CLEOPATRA   Antony
  Did tell me of you, bade me trust you; but
  I do not greatly care to be deceived,
15 That° have no use for trusting.[3] If your master   *Because I*
  Would have a queen his beggar, you must tell him
  That majesty, to keep decorum, must
  No less beg than a kingdom. If he please
  To give me conquered Egypt for my son,
20 He gives me so much of mine own as° I   *that*
  Will kneel to him with thanks.
  PROCULEIUS   Be of good cheer.
  You're fall'n into a princely hand; fear nothing.
  Make your full reference° freely to my lord,   *case*
  Who is so full of grace that it flows over
25 On all that need. Let me report to him
  Your sweet dependency,° and you shall find   *meek obeisance*
  A conqueror that will pray in aid for kindness,[4]
  Where he for grace is kneeled to.
  CLEOPATRA   Pray you, tell him
  I am his fortune's vassal, and I send him
30 The greatness he has got.[5] I hourly learn

5.2 Location: Cleopatra's monument.
1. *Which sleeps . . . Caesar's:* Which brings a sleep in which we no longer taste the produce of the earth (dung), nourisher of all from beggar to emperor.
2. Cleopatra and her women are inside the monument, the others outside it.
3. Cleopatra claims not to care whether she is deceived, in the hope that Proculeius will relax his guard and reveal

Caesar's intentions. But she may also mean that she doesn't like being deceived, knowing as she does the perils of misplaced trust.
4. Who will beg help in finding new ways to be kind.
5. *I am . . . got:* I do homage to his good fortune, and acknowledge the great position he has won. "Send him" may suggest Cleopatra's sense of superiority in conferring greatness upon Caesar.

A doctrine of obedience, and would gladly
Look him i'th' face.
PROCULEIUS   This I'll report, dear lady;
Have comfort, for I know your plight is pitied
Of° him that caused it.   By
          [*Enter Roman soldiers from behind*]
35   PROCULEIUS [*to the soldiers*]   You see how easily she may be surprised.
Guard her till Caesar come.
IRAS   Royal Queen—
CHARMIAN   O Cleopatra, thou art taken, Queen!
CLEOPATRA [*drawing a dagger*]   Quick, quick, good hands!
PROCULEIUS [*disarming* CLEOPATRA]   Hold,
          worthy lady, hold!
Do not yourself such wrong, who are in this
Relieved° but not betrayed.   *Rescued*
40   CLEOPATRA   What, of° death too,   *deprived of*
That rids our dogs of languish?⁶
PROCULEIUS   Cleopatra,
Do not abuse my master's bounty by
Th'undoing of yourself. Let the world see
His nobleness well acted, which your death
Will never let come forth.°   *allow to be displayed*
45   CLEOPATRA   Where art thou, death?
Come hither, come. Come, come, and take a queen
Worth many babes and beggars.⁷
PROCULEIUS   O temperance, lady!
CLEOPATRA   Sir, I will eat no meat.° I'll not drink, sir.   *food*
If idle talk will once be necessary,⁸
50   I'll not sleep, neither. This mortal house° I'll ruin,   *My body*
Do Caesar what he can. Know, sir, that I
Will not wait pinioned⁹ at your master's court,
Nor once be chastised with the sober eye
Of dull Octavia. Shall they hoist me up
55   And show me to the shouting varletry°   *rabble*
Of censuring Rome? Rather a ditch in Egypt
Be gentle grave unto me; rather on Nilus' mud
Lay me stark naked, and let the waterflies
Blow me into abhorring;¹ rather make
60   My country's high pyramides my gibbet,°   *gallows*
And hang me up in chains.
PROCULEIUS   You do extend
These thoughts of horror further than you shall
Find cause in Caesar.
          Enter DOLABELLA
DOLABELLA   Proculeius,
What thou hast done thy master Caesar knows,
65   And he hath sent for thee. For the Queen,
I'll take her to my guard.
PROCULEIUS   So, Dolabella,
It shall content me best. Be gentle to her.

---

6. Which rids even our dogs of protracted demise.
7. *babes and beggars*: death's cheapest victims; those most
often "relieved" (line 39) by the great.
8. (Even) if useless words are at times needed (to keep
me awake); if I am forced to engage in pointless chatter.

9. Will not serve shackled (or, will not wait like a bird
with clipped wings).
1. Lay their eggs on me (thereby breeding maggots) so
that I become disgusting, abhorrent.

    [*To* CLEOPATRA] To Caesar I will speak what° you shall please,   *whatever*
    If you'll employ me to him.

CLEOPATRA   Say I would die. *Exit* PROCULEIUS

70   DOLABELLA   Most noble Empress, you have heard of me.

    CLEOPATRA   I cannot tell.

    DOLABELLA   Assurèdly you know me.

    CLEOPATRA   No matter, sir, what I have heard or known.
    You laugh when boys or women tell their dreams;
    Is't not your trick?°   *custom*

    DOLABELLA   I understand not, madam.

75   CLEOPATRA   I dreamt there was an Emperor Antony.
    O, such another sleep, that I might see
    But such another man!

    DOLABELLA   If it might please ye—

    CLEOPATRA   His face was as the heav'ns, and therein stuck°   *were stuck*
    A sun and moon, which kept their course and lighted
    The little O o'th' earth.

80   DOLABELLA   Most sovereign creature—

    CLEOPATRA   His legs bestrid° the ocean; his reared arm   *straddled*
    Crested[2] the world. His voice was propertied
    As all the tunèd spheres,[3] and that to friends;
    But when he meant to quail° and shake the orb,°   *awe / globe*

85   He was as rattling thunder. For his bounty,
    There was no winter in't; an autumn 'twas,
    That grew the more by reaping. His delights
    Were dolphin-like; they showed his back above°   *they rose above*
    The element they lived in. In his livery°   *service*

90   Walked crowns and crownets.° Realms and islands were   *kings and princes*
    As plates° dropped from his pocket.   *silver coins*

    DOLABELLA   Cleopatra—

    CLEOPATRA   Think you there was, or might be, such a man
    As this I dreamt of?

    DOLABELLA   Gentle madam, no.

    CLEOPATRA   You lie, up to the hearing of the gods.

95   But if there be, or ever were one such,
    It's past the size of dreaming.[4] Nature wants stuff
    To vie strange forms with fancy; yet t'imagine
    An Antony were nature's piece 'gainst fancy,
    Condemning shadows quite.[5]

    DOLABELLA   Hear me, good madam:

100   Your loss is as yourself, great, and you bear it
    As answering to[6] the weight. Would I might never
    O'ertake° pursued success but° I do feel,   *Achieve / unless*
    By the rebound° of yours, a grief that smites   *reflection*
    My very heart at root.

    CLEOPATRA   I thank you, sir.

105   Know you what Caesar means to do with me?

    DOLABELLA   I am loath to tell you what I would you knew.

    CLEOPATRA   Nay, pray you, sir.

---

2. Formed a crest over (as in heraldry).
3. *was . . . spheres:* sounded like the music of the spheres, supposedly produced by the harmonious structure of the universe. See note to 2.7.15.
4. My vision of him surpasses what can be dreamed.
5. *Nature . . . quite:* Nature lacks material to compete

with the remarkable visions of the imagination in creating fantastic forms; but by imaging and creating Antony, nature has produced a masterpiece that outstrips even fancy and thus discredits imaginary conceptions.
6. *you . . . to:* you do justice to.

DOLABELLA   Though he be honourable—
CLEOPATRA   He'll lead me then in triumph.
DOLABELLA   Madam, he will, I know't.
       Flourish. Enter CAESAR, [*with*] PROCULEIUS, GALLUS,
       MAECENAS, *and others of his train*
ALL°   Make way, there! Caesar!   *(Caesar's train)*
CAESAR   Which is the Queen of Egypt?
DOLABELLA [*to* CLEOPATRA]
    It is the Emperor, madam.
       CLEOPATRA *kneels*
110   CAESAR   Arise! You shall not kneel.
    I pray you rise, rise, Egypt.
CLEOPATRA [*rising*]   Sir, the gods
    Will have it thus.° My master and my lord   *that I obey you*
    I must obey.
CAESAR   Take to you no hard thoughts.
    The record of what injuries you did us,
115   Though written in our flesh, we shall remember
    As things but done by chance.
CLEOPATRA   Sole sir° o'th' world,   *lord*
    I cannot project° mine own cause so well   *lay out*
    To make it clear,° but do confess I have   *innocent seeming*
    Been laden with like frailties which before
    Have often shamed our sex.
120   CAESAR   Cleopatra, know
    We will extenuate rather than enforce.°   *emphasize (faults)*
    If you apply yourself° to our intents,   *conform*
    Which towards you are most gentle, you shall find
    A benefit in this change; but if you seek
125   To lay on me a cruelty° by taking   *charge of cruelty*
    Antony's course, you shall bereave yourself
    Of my good purposes and put your children
    To that destruction which I'll guard them from,
    If thereon you rely. I'll take my leave.
130   CLEOPATRA   And may through all the world!⁷ 'Tis yours, and we,
    Your scutcheons° and your signs of conquest, shall   *captured shields*
    Hang in what place you please. [*Giving a paper*] Here, my good lord.
CAESAR   You shall advise me in all for° Cleopatra.   *concerning*
CLEOPATRA   This is the brief° of money, plate, and jewels   *summary*
135   I am possessed of. 'Tis exactly valued,
    Not petty things admitted.° Where's Seleucus?   *Except trivial things*
       [*Enter* SELEUCUS]
SELEUCUS   Here, madam.
CLEOPATRA [*to* CAESAR]   This is my treasurer. Let him speak, my lord,
    Upon his peril, that I have reserved
140   To myself nothing. Speak the truth, Seleucus.
SELEUCUS   Madam, I had rather seal° my lips   *sew up*
    Than to my peril speak that which is not.
CLEOPATRA   What have I kept back?
SELEUCUS   Enough to purchase what you have made known.
145   CAESAR   Nay, blush not, Cleopatra. I approve
    Your wisdom in the deed.
CLEOPATRA   See, Caesar! O, behold

---

7. As you may (take your leave and go) anywhere (as ruler of the world).

How pomp is followed![8] Mine° will now be yours,   *My followers*
And should we shift estates,° yours would be mine.   *change positions*
The ingratitude of this Seleucus does
150 Even make me wild.—O slave, of no more trust
Than love that's hired! What, goest thou back? Thou shalt
Go back, I warrant thee; but I'll catch thine eyes
Though° they had wings. Slave, soulless villain, dog!   *Even if*
O rarely° base!   *exceptionally*

CAESAR   Good Queen, let us entreat you.

155 CLEOPATRA   O Caesar, what a wounding shame is this,
That thou vouchsafing° here to visit me,   *stooping to come*
Doing the honour of thy lordliness
To one so meek—that mine own servant should
Parcel° the sum of my disgraces by   *Particularize; add to*
160 Addition of his envy.° Say, good Caesar,   *spite*
That I some lady° trifles have reserved,   *ladylike*
Immoment toys,° things of such dignity   *Worthless trinkets*
As we greet modern° friends withal;° and say   *everday / with*
Some nobler token I have kept apart
165 For Livia° and Octavia, to induce   *Caesar's wife*
Their mediation—must I be unfolded
With° one that I have bred? The gods! It smites me   *Turned in by*
Beneath the fall I have. [*To* SELEUCUS] Prithee, go hence,
Or I shall show the cinders° of my spirits   *smoldering coals*
170 Through th'ashes of my chance.° Wert thou a man°   *fortune / (not a eunuch)*
Thou wouldst have mercy on me.

CAESAR   Forbear, Seleucus.

[*Exit* SELEUCUS]

CLEOPATRA   Be it known that we, the greatest, are misthought°   *misjudged*
For things that others do; and when we fall
We answer others' merits in our name,[9]
Are therefore to be pitied.

175 CAESAR   Cleopatra,
Not what you have reserved nor what acknowledged
Put we i'th' roll of conquest. Still be't yours.
Bestow° it at your pleasure, and believe   *Dispense*
Caesar's no merchant, to make prize° with you   *haggle*
180 Of things that merchants sold. Therefore be cheered.
Make not your thoughts your prisons.[1] No, dear Queen;
For we intend so to dispose you as
Yourself shall give us counsel. Feed and sleep.
Our care and pity is so much upon you
185 That we remain your friend; and so adieu.

CLEOPATRA   My master and my lord!

CAESAR   Not so. Adieu.

Flourish. Exeunt CAESAR *and his train*

CLEOPATRA   He words me, girls, he words me, that I should not
Be noble to myself.[2] But hark thee, Charmian.

[*She whispers to* CHARMIAN]

---

8. How the great are served.
9. We are responsible for the deeds committed by others
in our names (an effort to shift the blame to Seleucus).
1. Don't think yourself a prisoner; don't be imprisoned
by (or in) your thoughts.
2. *He words . . . myself:* He puts me off from committing
suicide with mere words.

IRAS Finish, good lady. The bright day is done,
And we are for the dark.

190 CLEOPATRA [*to* CHARMIAN] Hie thee again.° *Hurry back*
I have spoke already, and it is provided.
Go put it to the haste.° *Do it quickly*

CHARMIAN Madam, I will.

Enter DOLABELLA

DOLABELLA Where's the Queen?

CHARMIAN Behold, sir. [*Exit*]

CLEOPATRA Dolabella!

DOLABELLA Madam, as thereto sworn by your command—

195 Which my love makes religion° to obey— *compels me*
I tell you this: Caesar through Syria
Intends his journey, and within three days
You with your children will he send before.
Make your best use of this. I have performed
Your pleasure, and my promise.

200 CLEOPATRA Dolabella,
I shall remain your debtor.

DOLABELLA I your servant.
Adieu, good Queen. I must attend on Caesar.

CLEOPATRA Farewell, and thanks. *Exit* [DOLABELLA]
Now, Iras, what think'st thou?
Thou, an Egyptian puppet shall be shown

205 In Rome, as well as I. Mechanic slaves° *Laborers*
With greasy aprons, rules,° and hammers shall *measuring sticks*
Uplift us to the view. In their thick° breaths, *foul*
Rank° of gross diet,° shall we be enclouded, *Stinking / coarse food*
And forced to drink° their vapour. *inhale*

IRAS The gods forbid!

210 CLEOPATRA Nay, 'tis most certain, Iras. Saucy lictors° *Insolent law officers*
Will catch at us like strumpets, and scald° rhymers *scurvy*
Ballad us out o' tune. The quick comedians
Extemporally° will stage us, and present *In improvised manner*
Our Alexandrian revels. Antony

215 Shall be brought drunken forth, and I shall see
Some squeaking Cleopatra boy³ my greatness
I'th' posture of a whore.

IRAS O, the good gods!

CLEOPATRA Nay, that's certain.

IRAS I'll never see't! For I am sure my nails
Are stronger than mine eyes.

220 CLEOPATRA Why, that's the way
To fool their preparation and to conquer
Their most absurd intents.

Enter CHARMIAN

Now, Charmian!
Show° me, my women, like a queen. Go fetch *Dress*
My best attires. I am again for Cydnus

225 To meet Mark Antony.⁴ Sirrah Iras, go.
Now, noble Charmian, we'll dispatch° indeed, *hurry; finish*

---

3. Cleopatra's part will be played by a boy (as it was in   4. See 2.2.192–232.
Shakespeare's day).

And when thou hast done this chore I'll give thee leave
To play till doomsday.—Bring our crown and all.   [*Exit* IRAS]
　　　　A noise within
Wherefore's this noise?
　　　　Enter a GUARDSMAN
GUARDSMAN　　　　　　　　Here is a rural fellow
230　That will not be denied your highness' presence.
　　He brings you figs.
　　CLEOPATRA　Let him come in.　　　　　　*Exit* GUARDSMAN
　　　　　　　　　　　　　What° poor an instrument　　　　*How*
　　May do a noble deed! He brings me liberty.
　　My resolution's placed,° and I have nothing　　　　　*unwavering*
235　Of woman in me. Now from head to foot
　　I am marble-constant. Now the fleeting° moon　　　*changeable*
　　No planet is of mine.
　　　　　Enter GUARDSMAN, *and* CLOWN° [*with a basket*]　　*rustic*
　　GUARDSMAN　　　　　　　This is the man.
　　CLEOPATRA　Avoid,° and leave him.　　　　　*Exit* GUARDSMAN　*Withdraw*
　　　　　　　　　　　　Hast thou the pretty worm[5]
　　Of Nilus there, that kills and pains not?
240　CLOWN　Truly, I have him; but I would not be the party that
　　　should desire you to touch him, for his biting is immortal;[6]
　　　those that do die of it do seldom or never recover.
　　CLEOPATRA　Remember'st thou any that have died on't?
　　CLOWN　Very many, men, and women too. I heard of one of
245　them no longer than yesterday, a very honest° woman, but　　*truthful; chaste*
　　　something given to lie,° as a woman should not do but in the　　*fib; lie with men*
　　　way of honesty, how she died° of the biting of it, what pain she　*perished; had an orgasm*
　　　felt. Truly, she makes a very good report o'th' worm; but he
　　　that will believe all that they say shall never be saved by half
250　that they do;[7] but this is most falliable:° the worm's an odd　*(error for "infallible")*
　　　worm.
　　CLEOPATRA　Get thee hence, farewell.
　　CLOWN　I wish you all joy of the worm.
　　CLEOPATRA　Farewell.
255　CLOWN　You must think this, look you, that the worm will do his
　　　kind.°　　　　　　　　　　　　　　　　　　　*what's in its nature*
　　CLEOPATRA　Ay, ay; farewell.
　　CLOWN　Look you, the worm is not to be trusted but in the keep-
　　　ing of wise people; for indeed there is no goodness in the worm.
260　CLEOPATRA　Take thou no care; it shall be heeded.
　　CLOWN　Very good. Give it nothing, I pray you, for it is not worth
　　　the feeding.
　　CLEOPATRA　Will it eat me?
　　CLOWN　You must not think I am so simple but I know the devil
265　himself will not eat a woman; I know that a woman is a dish
　　　for the gods, if the devil dress° her not. But truly, these same　*prepare (food); clothe*
　　　whoreson° devils do the gods great harm in their women; for in　*accursed*
　　　every ten that they make, the devils mar five.

---

5. Snake or serpent. In the Clown's description (lines
244–51), the "worm" also suggests the penis.
6. Comic error: the Clown means the opposite, but as so
often with such malapropisms in Shakespeare, the mis-
take reveals an unintended truth. See Cleopatra's "Im-
mortal longings" (line 272).

7. Perhaps the point is that a woman "given to lie" (line
246) is not to be believed. If Cleopatra acts on this "good
report o'th' worm," she will "never be saved" (lines 248–
49): she will die and, in Christian terms, will lose hope of
salvation by committing suicide.

CLEOPATRA   Well, get thee gone, farewell.
270   CLOWN   Yes, forsooth. I wish you joy o'th' worm.
                                    Exit [leaving the basket]
           [*Enter* IRAS *with a robe, crown, and other jewels*]
     CLEOPATRA   Give me my robe. Put on my crown. I have
       Immortal longings in me. Now no more
       The juice of Egypt's grape shall moist this lip.
           [CHARMIAN *and* IRAS *help her to dress*]
       Yare,° yare, good Iras, quick—methinks I hear   *Briskly*
275   Antony call. I see him rouse himself
       To praise my noble act. I hear him mock
       The luck of Caesar, which the gods give men
       To excuse their° after wrath. Husband, I come.   *(the gods')*
       Now to that name my courage prove my title.
280   I am fire and air; my other elements
       I give to baser life.[8] So, have you done?
       Come then, and take the last warmth of my lips.
           [*She kisses them*]
       Farewell, kind Charmian. Iras, long farewell.
           [IRAS *falls and dies*]
       Have I the aspic° in my lips? Dost fall?   *asp*
285   If thou and nature can so gently part,
       The stroke of death is as a lover's pinch,
       Which hurts and is desired. Dost thou lie still?
       If thus thou vanishest, thou tell'st the world
       It is not worth leave-taking.
290   CHARMIAN   Dissolve, thick cloud, and rain, that I may say
       The gods themselves do weep.
     CLEOPATRA   This proves me base.°   *ignoble*
       If she first meet the curlèd° Antony   *curly-haired*
       He'll make demand of° her, and spend that kiss   *question; (sexual)*
       Which is my heaven to have.
           [*She takes an aspic from the basket and puts it to her
           breast*]
                                    Come, thou mortal wretch,°   *deadly creature*
295   With thy sharp teeth this knot intrinsicate°   *intricate*
       Of life at once untie. Poor venomous fool,
       Be angry, and dispatch. O, couldst thou speak,
       That I might hear thee call great Caesar ass
       Unpolicied!°   *Outsmarted*
     CHARMIAN   O eastern star!°   *Venus; Cleopatra*
     CLEOPATRA   Peace, peace.
300   Dost thou not see my baby at my breast,
       That sucks the nurse asleep?
     CHARMIAN   O, break! O, break!
     CLEOPATRA   As sweet as balm, as soft as air, as gentle.
       O Antony!
           [*She puts another aspic to her arm*]
                  Nay, I will take thee too.
       What° should I stay—   [*She*] *dies*   *Why*

<hr>

8. *I am . . . life:* The "other elements" (line 280) are earth and water, the lower and heavier elements traditionally linked to women and thought to explain their fickleness. Cleopatra is particularly associated with these elements through her equation with (the mud of) Egypt. By asserting that she is only "fire and air," she is claiming to be manly (as in lines 234–35) and is also referring to the separation of the soul from the body at death.

CHARMIAN   In this vile world? So, fare thee well.
305   Now boast thee, death, in thy possession lies
      A lass unparalleled. Downy windows,° close,   *eyelids*
      And golden Phoebus never be beheld
      Of eyes again so royal. Your crown's awry.
      I'll mend it,° and then play—   *set it right*
            Enter the GUARD, *rustling*° *in*   *clattering*
310   FIRST GUARD   Where's the Queen?
      CHARMIAN   Speak softly. Wake her not.
      FIRST GUARD   Caesar hath sent—
      CHARMIAN   Too slow a messenger.
            [*She applies an aspic*]
      O come apace, dispatch! I partly feel thee.
      FIRST GUARD   Approach, ho! All's not well. Caesar's beguiled.°   *deceived*
315   SECOND GUARD   There's Dolabella sent from Caesar. Call him.
                                          [*Exit a* GUARDSMAN]
      FIRST GUARD   What work is here, Charmian? Is this well done?
      CHARMIAN   It is well done, and fitting for a princess
      Descended of so many royal kings.
      Ah, soldier!   CHARMIAN *dies*
            Enter DOLABELLA
      DOLABELLA   How goes it here?
      SECOND GUARD   All dead.
320   DOLABELLA   Caesar, thy thoughts
      Touch their effects° in this. Thyself art coming   *Are realized*
      To see performed the dreaded act which thou
      So sought'st to hinder.
      ALL   A way there, a way for Caesar!
            Enter CAESAR *and all his train, marching*
      DOLABELLA [*to* CAESAR]   O sir, you are too sure an augurer.
      That° you did fear is done.   *What*
325   CAESAR   Bravest at the last,
      She levelled at° our purposes, and, being royal,   *discerned rightly*
      Took her own way. The manner of their deaths?
      I do not see them bleed.
      DOLABELLA [*to a* GUARDSMAN]   Who was last with them?
      FIRST GUARD   A simple countryman that brought her figs.
      This was his basket.
      CAESAR   Poisoned, then.
330   FIRST GUARD   O Caesar,
      This Charmian lived but now; she stood and spake.
      I found her trimming up the diadem
      On her dead mistress; tremblingly she stood,
      And on the sudden dropped.
      CAESAR   O, noble weakness!
335   If they had swallowed poison, 'twould appear
      By external swelling; but she looks like sleep,
      As° she would catch another Antony   *As if*
      In her strong toil° of grace.   *snare*
      DOLABELLA   Here on her breast
      There is a vent of blood, and something blown.°   *emitted; swollen*
      The like is on her arm.
340   FIRST GUARD   This is an aspic's trail,
      And these fig-leaves have slime upon them such
      As th'aspic leaves upon the caves of Nile.

CAESAR   Most probable
That so she died; for her physician tells me
345   She hath pursued conclusions° infinite   *trial outcomes*
Of easy ways to die. Take up her bed,
And bear her women from the monument.
She shall be buried by her Antony.
No grave upon the earth shall clip° in it   *embrace*
350   A pair so famous. High events as these
Strike° those that make° them, and their story is   *Afflict / cause*
No less in pity than his glory⁹ which
Brought them to be lamented. Our army shall
In solemn show attend this funeral,
355   And then to Rome. Come, Dolabella, see
High order in this great solemnity.
                    Exeunt all [soldiers bearing CLEOPATRA *on her
                              bed,* CHARMIAN, *and* IRAS]

---

9. *their . . . glory:* there is no less pity in their story than there is glory in the exploits of Caesar. The immodesty of these lines, in the guise of praise, recalls Caesar's ambiguous grief, his combination of calculation and sentiment, at the news of Antony's death in 5.1. The historical Octavius Caesar went on to order the murder of Ptolemy XV (Caesarion), Cleopatra's son with Julius Caesar. Since Julius Caesar was Octavius's great-uncle and adoptive father, this act, which ended the Ptolemaic dynasty, might be seen as fraticide. See 2.1.37 with note, 2.2.233–34 with note, and 3.6.1–16 with note to line 6. By contrast, after Antony and Cleopatra's deaths, the historical Octavia, over her brother Octavius's objections, raised Anthony's children by Fulvia and Cleopatra, as well as her own five children with Antony and a previous husband.

ROMANCES

Shakespearean Romance
by
WALTER COHEN

What is a romance? Renaissance playwrights inherited two main genres from classical antiquity: comedy and tragedy. Shakespearean drama, however, has never been parceled out into just these two groups. The first relatively complete edition of Shakespeare's plays was published in 1623, seven years after the dramatist's death. John Heminges and Henry Condell, two of Shakespeare's colleagues in the King's Men, the theater company to which he belonged, collected and printed the plays in a single large volume that became known as the First Folio. While the Folio adopted the classical categories of comedy and tragedy, it also added a third division: history. Under "Histories," the editors included Shakespeare's works on English history that take place from the thirteenth to the sixteenth centuries. The Folio's three resulting rubrics—"Comedies," "Tragedies," "Histories"—have considerable value, but they make for a certain conceptual messiness. A Shakespearean history designates a narrowly defined subject matter that may be comic or tragic or neither. Shakespearean comedy and tragedy suggest both a prevailing tone (light or somber) and a likely outcome (happy or sad). None of these designations, however, fits particularly well with the plays included here under the heading of "Romance"—plays that do not concern medieval English history and that often combine a somber feel with a happy ending. The First Folio deals with these plays in three ways. *The Tempest* (1611) opens and *The Winter's Tale* (1609–11) closes the comedies, *Cymbeline* (1609–10) appears last among the tragedies, and *Pericles* (1607–08) and *The Two Noble Kinsmen* (1613–14) are excluded entirely—presumably because they are coauthored works. This essay, however, brings together these five works while also drawing on two other collaborative Shakespearean productions: the lost *Cardenio* (1612–13) and the English history play *All Is True* (*Henry VIII*, 1613). After briefly reviewing their relationship to earlier European literature and theater, it considers them from the three main perspectives that have emerged in modern scholarship. The late plays may accordingly be viewed as the culmination of Shakespearean comedy, as the members of the distinct genre of romance, or as two different versions of tragicomedy.

Although Heminges and Condell did not use the term, the notion of romance was well established by the Renaissance. Based on the word *Rome*, romance was used originally as the collective name for the everyday speech derived from Latin and now called the Romance languages. The books written in those languages came to be known as romances. Beginning in the twelfth century *romance* was used to indicate a literary genre, although the genre so indicated differed among the countries—primarily present-day Italy, France, Spain, and Portugal—where Romance languages were spoken. The most influential variation of the romance as a literary form occurred in Old French, where *roman* originally meant "a courtly, or chivalric, narrative." Medieval French romance spread across Europe, inspiring both learned and popular emulation. For their collaborative work *The Two Noble Kinsmen*, Shakespeare and John Fletcher looked to the late fourteenth century and one of Geoffrey Chaucer's *Canterbury Tales*, "The Knight's Tale," itself an adaptation of Giovanni Boccaccio's Italian original from a few decades before.

Such narratives, in prose as well as verse, continued to be composed in the sixteenth century: Ludovico Ariosto's *Orlando Furioso,* Torquato Tasso's *Jerusalem Liberated,* Sir Philip Sidney's *Arcadia,* and Edmund Spenser's *Faerie Queene* are among the most influential contributions to the genre. Like their medieval predecessors, these chivalric romances and many others invited dramatic adaptation.

A second narrative form that had an impact on Shakespearean romance is late classical Greek and, to a lesser extent, Latin prose fiction. A number of these works were translated into English in the late sixteenth century—Heliodorus's *Aethiopica,* the anonymous *Daphnis and Chloe,* and Achilles Tatius's *Clitophon and Leucippe*—and were exploited by Sidney as well as various playwrights. In such tales, faithful lovers are separated and often driven back and forth across the Mediterranean by bad people, bad weather, and bad luck. Ultimately, however, the virtuous couple earns a triumphant reunion that sometimes expands to include the restoration of the relationship between parent and child as well. In *Pericles,* Shakespeare and George Wilkins turned to Chaucer's contemporary John Gower for a story in his *Confessio Amantis* that is taken from an earlier Latin version that, in turn, goes back to a lost fifth-or sixth-century Greek original. In *The Winter's Tale,* Shakespeare borrowed from *Pandosto* (1588), a romance by his contemporary Robert Greene that is generally inspired by Greek fiction.

Along with classical and medieval sources, Shakespeare's final plays were influenced by important predecessors in English drama. Although few texts remain, their titles often survive. The romantic plays of the 1570s and 1580s seem to have combined a certain naïveté with theatrically effective plot twists and concluding scenes of recognition and reconciliation. In the anonymous *Rare Triumphes of Love and Fortune* (1580s), the Olympian gods intervene to set human affairs right. Shakespeare may have drawn on this play in both *Cymbeline* and *The Tempest.* A second legacy from the English theater is the saint's life, a dramatic form that dates from the late medieval period through the 1560s, after which it was suppressed by Protestant authorities. The anonymous work *Mary Magdalene,* preserved in a fifteenth-century manuscript, anticipates *Pericles* in sending a queen to her death at sea, only to be saved, along with her child, by the prayers of the titular character.

Late sixteenth-century Italian pastoral tragicomedy provided yet another dramatic model for Shakespearean romance. Tasso's *Aminta* (1573) is probably the best-known specimen of the genre. Of central importance here is Battista Guarini's *Il pastor fido* (*The Faithful Shepherd,* 1590). Unlike either narrative or dramatic romance, *Il pastor fido* directly engages both Aristotle's *Poetics* (fourth century B.C.E.), the profoundly influential work of theatrical theory, and Sophocles' tragedy *Oedipus Rex* (fifth century B.C.E.). One of Guarini's innovations was to subvert Sophocles' tragic plot at the very last moment, thereby allowing his protagonist to avoid incest and its catastrophic consequences. Shakespeare may have learned of Guarini through Fletcher's unsuccessful adaptation, *The Faithful Shepherdess* (1608–09). Although Shakespeare never borrows as directly as Fletcher did and is more circumspect than his Italian predecessors in finding a providential design in human affairs, most of his romances are indebted either to Guarini or to Italian pastoral tragicomedy in general for their overall shape, settings, and much more.

The most traditional approach to Shakespearean romance approximates the logic of the First Folio's editors in treating the playwright's romantic comedies, problem plays (*Measure for Measure, All's Well That Ends Well*), and romances all as variations on a comic movement from disorder to harmony. Beginning in 1893, when the critic Edward Dowden first applied the term *romance* to *Pericles* and the final three solely authored plays (*Cymbeline, The Winter's Tale,* and *The Tempest*), this first view has gradually been eclipsed by a second, now-dominant paradigm—that the romances differ from the comedies and, indeed, constitute a distinct form within Shakespeare's dramatic oeuvre. That form is marked by its vertical or longitudinal perspective, by a retrospective view that nonetheless leaves room for the future.

Separation and long suffering of families, perilous sea journeys beset by storms that form part of a symbolic geography, near-death experiences followed by spiritual rebirths, the cultivation of patience, the healing power of time, the eventual reunion of royal families whose children (primarily daughters) have been separated from their parents (primarily fathers) at birth, the power of those daughters to redeem their fathers—all these are recurrent motifs. Plot complications are unraveled in ultimate scenes of recognition and reconciliation, where music and visionary spectacle herald the appearance of Greco-Roman gods, who perhaps stand in for a mysterious Christian providence that guides human beings through the labyrinth of life. A third view of the late plays, developed by scholars in recent decades, gives new weight to the three heterogeneous tragicomic works—*Cardenio*, *All Is True*, and *The Two Noble Kinsmen*—on which Shakespeare collaborated with John Fletcher. *The Two Noble Kinsmen* is the only romance extant from this collaboration. *All Is True* is a national history play that treats some of the key events and personalities from the monarchy of King Henry VIII (reigned 1509–47). But it draws on the tone and many of the motifs of romance, with the presumed fictiveness of the standard romance story replaced by a narrative in which all is true. And in the lost *Cardenio*, abandoned lovers are reduced to despair before heaven brings about a romance-style reunion. The two playwrights apparently extracted the plot from an interpolated tale in Miguel de Cervantes's *Don Quixote*, Part 1 (1605, English translation by Thomas Shelton, 1612). In general, the coauthored plays seem to constitute a more pessimistic corrective to the core romances.

Each of these three views of the plays is worth considering in greater detail. Like the romantic comedies, the romances have their roots in seasonal festivity, emblematized in some of the titles: *The Winter's Tale* recalls *A Midsummer Night's Dream* and *Twelfth Night*. In all these plays, the seasonal cycle underlies a movement toward regeneration that is celebrated in the resolution of the plot. Shakespearean romantic comedy is indebted to classical New Comedy, a form invented in ancient Greece whose main surviving examples are the plays of the ancient Roman dramatists Plautus and Terence. With plots confined to the private lives of well-to-do citizens, New Comedy features a series of stock situations (hidden identity) and stock characters (young lovers, restrictive fathers, clever servants, braggart soldiers). The comic action turns on the young man's pursuit of the apparently unsuitable young woman, in the course of which various obstacles must be—and are—overcome. The legacy of Plautus and Terence was revised and elaborated upon in sixteenth-century Italian drama, which introduced to it elements of the Italian novella, or short story, beginning with Boccaccio's *Decameron* in the mid-fourteenth century. Nearly all of Shakespeare's romantic comedies, problem comedies, and romances are indebted to Italian narrative or drama, either directly or via French, Spanish, and English translation. Among the romances, *Cymbeline* borrows from the *Decameron*, *The Winter's Tale* exploits Sicily's association with literary pastoral in its setting, *The Tempest* resembles some of the scenarios from Italian popular theater (the commedia dell'arte), *Cardenio* presumably adapts a Cervantine novella that is itself influenced by Boccaccio and his successors, and, as we've seen, *The Two Noble Kinsmen* also goes back to Boccaccio's narrative poetry.

But Shakespearean comedy and romance depart from classical and Renaissance models in important ways that also sharply distinguish the plays from the classically minded satiric comedy of Shakespeare's contemporary, Ben Jonson. Shakespeare replaces the prosperous private citizens of earlier comedy with aristocrats and rulers, thereby blurring the traditional division between the private concerns of comedy and the public affairs of tragedy. Special attention is accorded to the fate of virtuous young women, whose marriages are crucial to the happy resolution of the plot. That resolution is complicated by a feature common to comedy and romance alike—a paternal or political decree that initially thwarts the romantic aspirations of the young lovers. Such a decree figures in the comedies from *The Two Gentlemen of Verona* through *Love's Labour's Lost* to *Measure for*

Measure, and in the late plays from *Pericles* through *The Tempest* to *All Is True.* To avoid its force, the characters flee the society of sanctioned public power for a world of disorder, license, and confused sexual identity. Geographically, this is the pastoral or green world that represents a physical and symbolic alternative to the city or, more often, the court. It is the setting for most of *As You Like It,* for the concluding resolution of both plots of *The Merry Wives of Windsor,* and, indeed, for much else in the romantic comedies. It is also a recurrent locale in the romances, above all in *The Tempest* but to some extent in each of them. The pastoral world is marked by a series of motifs shared by comedy and romance alike. The dreamlike madness of *The Comedy of Errors* and *A Midsummer Night's Dream* is echoed by *The Tempest, Cardenio,* and *The Two Noble Kinsmen.* The male disguise adopted by numerous women in the romantic comedies is also donned by Innogen in *Cymbeline* and, ineffectually, by Dorotea/Violante in *Cardenio* (where the first name, Dorotea, comes from Shelton's translation of Cervantes, while the second, Violante, is from the imitation of *Cardenio* by Lewis Theobald in his tragicomedy *Double Falsehood; or, The Distrest Lovers,* 1728). A lower-class theatrical performance honors the Athenian wedding of Theseus and Hippolyta in both *A Midsummer Night's Dream* and *The Two Noble Kinsmen.*

Both the comedies and the romances also erect barriers to young love very different from the initial prohibition. First, lovers create problems for themselves through their own defects. Katherine's shrewishness in *The Taming of the Shrew* belongs here, but more frequently the difficulty is the failings of men. Proteus comes close to raping Silvia in *The Two Gentlemen of Verona.* Similarly, in *Cardenio,* Ferdinando/Theobald promises his love to Dorotea/Violante, rapes her, abandons her for Luscinda/Leonora, and later abducts Luscinda/Leonora from a nunnery. Just as Claudio doesn't question the slanderous attack on Hero's sexual virtue in *Much Ado About Nothing,* so Posthumus believes the worst of Innogen in *Cymbeline*—outdoing Claudio, however, by ordering his wife's death. In *The Winter's Tale,* King Leontes does not need to be deceived: for no reason he becomes convinced that his wife, Hermione, has been unfaithful. A second barrier is very different, however. The triumph of heterosexual love entails the loss of something valuable, intimacy with another member of one's own sex. In *The Merchant of Venice,* Bassanio must learn to choose Portia over Antonio. In *The Winter's Tale,* Polixenes nostalgically recalls the innocence of his youthful friendship with Leontes. And in *The Two Noble Kinsmen,* the mere sight of Emilia tears apart the kinsmen, Palamon and Arcite, while Emilia herself sadly recalls her childhood love for Flavina, who died when the two girls were eleven.

Nonetheless, the pastoral experience as a whole usually leads to festivity and reconciliation at a deeper level that, through forgiveness, transforms character and restores community. The concluding reconciliation enables some of the characters to get more than they deserve. Just as Proteus is allowed to marry Julia in *The Two Gentlemen of Verona,* Fernando/Henriquez is paired off with Dorotea/Violante in *Cardenio.* Claudio wins Hero in *Much Ado About Nothing,* Posthumus regains Innogen in *Cymbeline,* and Leontes recovers Hermione in *The Winter's Tale.* While the plot mechanisms of the concluding resolutions tend to strain credulity, the happy outcome reveals the power of timely human intervention—whether of Portia in *The Merchant of Venice,* Duke Vincentio in *Measure for Measure,* Prospero in *The Tempest,* or Henry VIII in *All Is True.*

If comedy and romance share so many characteristics, where are the distinctive qualities of romance to be found? One answer lies in the intervening experience of tragedy. During the 1590s, Shakespeare wrote the majority of his romantic comedies. For most of the next decade, he focused on tragedy. The romances depart from the romantic comedies in their incorporation of a tragic perspective, which in most instances is ultimately transcended. Both the storms and the redemptive reconciliation of father and daughter in *Pericles* hark back to *King Lear,* a work that is itself based on a dramatic romance and that seems headed in the

Le Naufrage (The Shipwreck). Etching by Claude Lorrain (1600–82).

same direction until catastrophe intervenes. The jealousy of Posthumus in *Cymbeline* and of Leontes in *The Winter's Tale* reprises the fatal behavior of Othello. *All Is True* seems to have raided *Macbeth* for its Porter at the christening of the baby Elizabeth in Act 5. *The Tempest* echoes *Richard II, Julius Caesar, Hamlet,* and *Macbeth* in its concern with usurpation, *Hamlet* in its recourse to a play within a play, and *Othello* and *King Lear* in its dramatization of a father's difficulty in letting go of his daughter. In *The Two Noble Kinsmen,* both Emilia's comparison of pictures and the Jailer's Daughter's madness go back to *Hamlet,* the Daughter's willow song is borrowed from Desdemona in *Othello,* and the Doctor's effort to cure her and the enigmatic prophecies that provide false comfort to the protagonists come from *Macbeth.*

Shakespeare's incorporation of tragic elements in the romances often represents less a break with comedy than a shift in relative weight. Thus, the storm and shipwreck that wash Viola up on the coast of Illyria in *Twelfth Night* anticipate similar scenes not just in *Pericles* but also in *The Winter's Tale* and *The Tempest.* Similarly, the threat of rape that Silvia faces in *The Two Gentlemen of Verona* returns not only for Dorotea/Violante in *Cardenio* but also for Marina in *Pericles,* Innogen in *Cymbeline,* and Miranda in *The Tempest.*

But sometimes in the romances, tragedy is felt more strongly—as a rupture rather than a shift. This is true in the case of mortality—rare in the comedies, routine in the romances. The incestuous Antiochus and his Daughter, like Cleon and his murderous wife, Dionyza, are spectacularly dispatched in *Pericles.* In *Cymbeline,* death comes to both the murderous Queen and her sexually predatory son, Cloten. In *The Winter's Tale,* Leontes' jealousy costs him both his son and Antigonus, the courtier who saves Leontes' daughter, Perdita, from death only at the expense of his own life. In *Cardenio,* a hearse comes by at a crucial moment. *All Is True* chronicles the decline and death of the possibly treasonous Duke of Buckingham, the virtuous Katherine of Aragon, and the corrupt Cardinal Wolsey. It celebrates the corresponding rise of Cromwell, More, Cranmer, and Anne Boleyn, all of whom, however—as at least some of the audience would have known—went on to meet violent deaths as a result of the bloody controversy between Protestants and Catholics in sixteenth-century England. And in *The Two Noble Kinsmen,* only one of the kinsmen can survive: Arcite, the apparent victor over Palamon in a struggle to the death, is fatally injured when thrown from his horse.

While some romance characters die, others experience a quasi-ritualistic symbolic or metaphorical death. This is the fate of Thaisa and Marina in *Pericles*; Innogen in *Cymbeline*; Perdita and Hermione in *The Winter's Tale*; Prospero, Miranda, and Ferdinand in *The Tempest*; Cardenio/Julio in *Cardenio*; and Palamon in *The Two Noble Kinsmen*. The characteristic romance movement from symbolic death to spiritual rebirth is hardly automatic, however. First, it requires time. The passage of the years is necessary if the tragic dimension of life is to be overcome. In general, the romances possess far greater temporal spans than the romantic comedies. In *Pericles* and *The Winter's Tale*, events stretch out over the better part of a generation. *Cymbeline* and *The Tempest* conjure up crucial experiences in the past from the perspective of the present. Reversing the strategy of these two plays, *All Is True* anticipates the supposed triumphs of the audience's present but the play's future from the perspective of the audience's past but the play's present.

Emphasis on the workings of time is tied to a shift in the portrayal of virtuous young women. Shakespeare's romance heroines are less involved in getting their men than are their predecessors in the comedies, and their prospective or reconstituted marriages are less crucial to the restoration of the community. More generally, compared to the comedies the romances arguably feature fewer multiple-plot narratives and certainly stage fewer multiple-marriage conclusions. Both the reduced activity of these women and the reduced significance of their marriages may seem paradoxical, since the redemptive role of the romance heroines tends to exceed that of their predecessors in romantic comedy. But whatever their intentions, that role is directed less toward marriage than toward intergenerational restoration, and usually in particular toward the repair of their parents' suffering or misdeeds. An older man may recover both wife and daughter (Pericles, Leontes in *The Winter's Tale*), a daughter and two sons (Cymbeline), or a son (Alonso in *The Tempest*). Although Marina delivers her father, Pericles, from his misery, that moment of deliverance is just a prelude to the actual climax, in which Pericles is reunited with his wife, Thaisa, while Marina stands mutely by. Similarly, *The Winter's Tale* seems headed toward Perdita's return to the court of her father, Leontes, but the anticipated occasion is narrated rather than dramatized so that the stage can be reserved for the miraculous revival of the statue of her mother, Hermione, and hence for the reconciliation of father and mother, of husband and wife, while Perdita characteristically stands silently by. In *Cymbeline*, Innogen's reconciliation with husband and father alike after comparatively brief separations is followed by Cymbeline's recovery of his long-lost sons, Guiderius and Arviragus. In *The Tempest*, however important the dynastic implications of Miranda's upcoming marriage to Ferdinand may be, the work's conclusion is devoted primarily to her father Prospero's settling of accounts with men of his own age. Finally, rather than displacing the young woman's impact back to the previous generation, *All Is True* projects it forward to the next one. Anne Boleyn matters only as the mother of the future Queen Elizabeth, whose reign unfolds long after the end of the play.

This temporal, intergenerational logic may be understood structurally. *The Winter's Tale* perhaps represents the paradigmatic case. Although in Shakespeare's career comedy precedes tragedy, in this play it is the other way around. The first three acts revive *Othello*, the fourth *As You Like It*. A generation passes between these two movements of the plot. In other words, courtly tragedy is ultimately set in the past, so that its crimes and errors can be redeemed by pastoral comedy, peopled with the rural lower classes, located in the present. The rebirth, recognition, and reconciliation of Act 5 are made possible by the preceding sequence. One kind of variation on this pattern appears in both *Cymbeline* and *The Tempest*. The represented action is confined to the present, but part of what happens in *Cymbeline* and all of what happens in *The Tempest* depend on events as remote as those of the opening acts of *The Winter's Tale*. In all three instances, the potentially tragic moment is located at the birth or during the very early childhood of the youths who, now on the verge of adulthood, will prove crucial to the transcendence of tragedy. In still another variation on the paradigm of *The Winter's*

Tale, Pericles and *All Is True* present a sequence of minitragedies. In *Pericles,* these concern both the protagonist and his victimizers, the crucial difference being that Pericles' suffering can be overcome after a generation, whereas the others simply meet their deserved fate. The multiple tragedies of *All Is True* dramatize the fall of one illustrious personage after another from a position of eminence, with the jump forward in time relegated to a concluding prophecy inspired by the birth of the future Queen Elizabeth. Finally, *The Two Noble Kinsmen,* like *The Winter's Tale,* combines a relatively tragic work with a comic one. Like *Troilus and Cressida,* it draws on Chaucer for an account of violently destructive sexuality. Like *A Midsummer Night's Dream,* as we've seen, it offers a popular theatrical performance in the context of Theseus and Hippolyta's wedding. Here, however, the order seems to replicate, not reverse, that of Shakespeare's career. Rather than *A Midsummer Night's Dream* lightening the experience of *Troilus and Cressida,* the latter play seems to darken the outlook of the former.

As these examples suggest, the recapitulation characteristic of the romances places enormous structural pressure on the dramatic narrative. In the 1580s, Sidney's *Apology for Poetry* criticized tragicomedy for its violation of morally appropriate emotional effects in its indifference to the classical separation of styles—of comedy from tragedy.

> But besides these gross absurdities, how all their plays be neither right tragedies, nor right comedies, mingling kings and clowns, not because the matter so carrieth it, but thrust in clowns by head and shoulders, to play a part in majestical matters, with decency nor discretion, so as neither the admiration and commiseration, nor the right sportfulness, is by their mongrel tragicomedy obtained.

This criticism sounds as if it were directed toward Shakespearean drama in general. Sidney also disparages romantic drama for its violation of probability in its indifference to the classical unities of time (a play should last no more than a day) and place (it should take place in a single location).

> You shall have Asia of the one side, and Afric of the other . . . the player, when he cometh in, must ever begin with telling where he is, or else the tale will not be conceived. . . . By and by we hear news of shipwreck. . . . Upon the back of that comes out a hideous monster, . . . and then the miserable beholders are bound to take it for a cave. While in the meantime two armies fly in, represented with four swords and bucklers, and then what hard heart will not receive it for a pitched field? . . . two young princes fall in love. After many traverses, she is got with child, delivered of a fair boy; he is lost, groweth a man, falls in love, and is ready to get another child; and all this in two hours' space.

Here, it is as if Sidney were attacking the late plays in particular—Asia and Africa in *Antony and Cleopatra* (1606–07) and *Pericles;* shipwreck in *Pericles* and *The Tempest;* the hideous monster also in *The Tempest;* the cave in *Cymbeline* and *The Tempest;* the armies in *Antony and Cleopatra, Coriolanus* (1608), and *Cymbeline;* the love affairs followed by children lost for a generation in *Pericles, Cymbeline,* and *The Winter's Tale.*

A generation later Ben Jonson actually did attack Shakespeare's own romances on similar grounds. (See the introduction to *The Winter's Tale.*) It is easy to see why. Shakespeare goes out of his way to flaunt the primitivism of his materials and methods. Beyond employing Gower as narrator, *Pericles* repeatedly resorts to the outmoded dramatic device of the dumb show. *The Winter's Tale* ostentatiously rings out the old by having Antigonus, savior of Perdita, "*Exit, pursued by a bear*" (3.3.57, stage direction). It brings in the new by sending Time on stage as a Chorus to apologize for the sixteen-year gap in the action. *Cymbeline* goes well beyond the normal range of Shakespearean anachronism by combining ancient Britain, classical Rome, and Renaissance Italy. In the long final-recognition scene, Shakespeare delays the improbable revelations to such an extent that the audience, although more in the know than the characters, sympathizes with Cymbeline's impatience:

> I had rather thou shouldst live while nature will
> Than die ere I hear more. Strive, man, and speak.
> (5.6.151–52)

> I stand on fire.

> Come to the matter.
> (5.6.168–69)

> Nay, nay, to th' purpose.
> (5.6.178)

In *The Tempest*, where adherence to the unities of time and place requires Prospero to narrate the back story to his daughter Miranda, the conventionality of the device is again laid bare, as Prospero repeatedly accuses Miranda of not listening: "Dost thou attend me?" "Thou attend'st not!" "Dost thou hear?" (1.2.78, 87, 106). And earlier in the same scene, the audience learns that the play's opening storm is nothing more than a trick of the magician's art—nothing more, that is, than a trick of the dramatist's art.

In other words, much of the sophistication of the romances consists in Shakespeare's deliberate recourse to a threadbare stagecraft, in his undermining of the illusion of reality. He wants the audience to see and hear the creaking machinery, to recognize the labor of incorporating incompatible experiences, and nonetheless to find something moving and new. This is an art, however, that for all its artificiality also cooperates with the natural world. But the character of the cooperation between art and nature remains unclear. In Act 4 of *The Winter's Tale*, Perdita speaks against the improvement of nature by art in the cultivation of flowers. King Polixenes disagrees, arguing that

> we marry
> A gentler scion to the wildest stock,
> And make conceive a bark of baser kind
> By bud of nobler race.
> (4.4.92–95)

But when he discovers that his son is in love with Perdita, whom he believes to be a shepherdess, he violently opposes the marriage of a "gentler scion to the wildest stock" that he has just advocated.

The conflict between Polixenes and Perdita points away from impersonal structures. In the romances, regeneration depends on more than time and artful dramaturgy. It requires a patience often accompanied by suffering and sometimes by repentance. Wronged aristocrats—Belarius in *Cymbeline*, Prospero in *The Tempest*—must spend the better part of a generation in distant rural exile from the court. Pericles is separated from his daughter for a similar period of time, during the last part of which he also grieves over her, believing her dead. The time of mourning lasts an entire generation for Leontes, who justly holds himself responsible for the real death of his son, the supposed death of his daughter, and the apparent death of his wife in *The Winter's Tale*. In *Cymbeline*, Posthumus has to confront his guilt for what he believes is the murder of his wife. And much the same goes for Fernando/Henriquez in *Cardenio*.

The complement of remorse is a self-mastery on the part of the wronged characters that issues in forgiveness far more difficult to offer than in the romantic comedies because there is so much more to forgive. This is the forgiveness Wolsey receives from his enemies at the moment of his fall in *All Is True*. Such forgiveness is linked to the acceptance of social responsibility near the end of *The Tempest*, when in a gesture at once appalling, enigmatic, and moving, Prospero says of the semihuman Caliban, native of the island and would-be rapist of Prospero's daughter and murderer of Prospero himself, "This thing of darkness I / Acknowledge mine" (5.1.278–79). The acknowledgment here seems connected to Prospero's concluding renunciation of magic, emphasis on his own weakness, and consequent humility in the Epilogue he delivers, where the standard appeal for the audience's benevolence takes a sudden religious turn:

> And my ending is despair
> Unless I be relieved by prayer,
> Which pierces so, that it assaults
> Mercy itself, and frees all faults.
> As you from crimes would pardoned be,
> Let your indulgence set me free.
>
> (lines 15–20)

The moment is significant because Prospero is more in control of his own destiny than is any other character in Shakespeare. But in the end, even he must depend on others. The terms of that dependence, moreover, only underscore the infirmity of mortal creatures. Far more than the romantic comedies, the romances reduce the efficacy of human agency. Their virtuous, redemptive young women are less activist than emblematic. They are part of the pattern rather than its creator. Their symbolic names tell the story: in *Pericles,* Marina is of the sea; in *The Winter's Tale,* Perdita is lost; and in *The Tempest,* Miranda is to be wondered at.

All of these features of the romances—violence and literal or metaphorical death, the passage of time, an intergenerational orientation, suffering and repentance, forgiveness and the acknowledgment of human frailty—result in a more encompassing final reconciliation than in the romantic comedies. In those earlier plays, one or two characters often remain unincorporated at the end, less because they are cast out than because they find the terms of inclusion unpalatable. Shakespeare thereby signals the incomplete character of his festive endings, the continuing presence of melancholy, critique, skepticism, or isolation. In the romances, insistence on the partial, provisional nature of the resolution is carried by the previous losses, including, of course, death itself. Hence, all survivors are included regardless of their prior behavior and regardless of whether they have undergone a long period of repentance (Leontes in *The Winter's Tale*), only belatedly confessed their sins (Giacomo, slanderer of Innogen in *Cymbeline*), or not reformed at all (Antonio and Sebastian, murderous usurpers in *The Tempest;* arguably Gardiner, the overly zealous Catholic bishop of *All Is True*).

This inclusive spirit is possible because in the romances' conclusions the natural world with which art cooperates seems connected with an invisible supernatural reality. Like the incorporation of tragedy and the long temporal perspective, the providential guidance of mortal affairs is a signature of Shakespearean romance. The plays opt for resolutions that are rationally inexplicable (*The Winter's Tale, The Tempest*), accessible only through inspired Christian prophecy (*All Is True*), produced by luck but retrospectively coded as Christian providence (*Cardenio*), or manifestly generated by divine intervention that is classical in nomenclature (Diana in *Pericles;* Jupiter in *Cymbeline;* Mars, Venus, and Diana in *The Two Noble Kinsmen*) but Christian in nature (except, perhaps, in *The Two Noble Kinsmen*). The characters wander in a spiritual labyrinth, often stumbling as they go. But the fall is usually a fortunate one, a *felix culpa* that replicates the foundational failure of Adam and Eve, opening the way to earthly redemption and a fleeting glimpse of eternal reality. This vision, often in the form of a dream, is granted only to a character who strives to be worthy of it. Yet the plays suggest that these efforts alone may not be enough. It is the intertwining of divine and human agency that leads to the comic resolution.

Behind this outlook lies the dramaturgy of late-sixteenth-century Italy, based in the religious movement known as the Catholic Counter-Reformation. That dramaturgy also drew on a philosophical tradition known today as Renaissance Neoplatonism for a mystical belief in the unity of opposites, the cosmic harmony that gives meaning to the apparently random vicissitudes of earthly existence. This does not necessarily imply that the romances are Catholic in outlook. It does mean that "the music of the spheres"

Venus and Jupiter (astride an eagle). Engraving by Philips Galle (1585). The classical deities play crucial roles in the resolutions of *Pericles, Cymbeline,* and *The Two Noble Kinsmen.*

(*Pericles,* Scene 21, line 214), indication of divine harmony, is audible to the privileged. It is heard by Pericles ("I hear most heav'nly music," Scene 21, line 218). Cardenio/Julio believes he detects it in the singing of Dorotea/Violante. The revival of Hermione at the end of *The Winter's Tale* is accompanied by music. So, too, is Posthumus's vision of his family in *Cymbeline* and the appearance of the classical deities in *The Tempest.* "Some heavenly music" brings the shipwrecked nobility to their senses in Prospero's charmed circle toward the end of the same play (5.1.52). And music is also heard at the altars of Venus and Diana in Act 5 of *The Two Noble Kinsmen.*

In all these respects, the romances represent a logical development of Shakespeare's earlier dramatic practice and arguably the culmination of his career in the theater. They are also part of a more general movement on the English stage, although it is possible that Shakespeare himself initiated that movement. The romances seem to respond to a series of additional developments, however. One is institutional. In 1608, Shakespeare's company began performing during the winter at the Blackfriars, an indoor, "private" theater that catered to a more uniformly upscale audience than the patrons of the outdoor, "public" Globe, where the King's Men had been playing since 1599. The Blackfriars provided more elaborate theatrical machinery than was available in an open-air theater, and some of the romances take advantage of these resources. For instance, *The Tempest* and *All Is True* adapt the masque, a newly fashionable court theatrical that demanded complex special effects. The shift toward the Blackfriars may be seen as part of an elitist turn in Shakespeare's late plays, also noticeable in the declining role of the clown, a characteristic figure in the romantic comedies often integral to a subplot that comments on the central action. Yet members of the lower classes continue to be prominent in the romances. Such figures include the fishermen and the managers of the house of prostitution in *Pericles;* the Old Shepherd, the Clown, and Autolycus in *The Winter's Tale;* the Boatswain, Caliban, Stefano, and Trinculo in *The Tempest;* the Citizens, the shepherds, and their vicious but witty Master in *Cardenio;* the Porter and unruly citizens in *All Is True;* and the Jailer's Daughter, in addition to the country actors in *The Two Noble Kinsmen.* Equally important, *Pericles,* the earliest of the romances, predates the King's

Men's lease of the Blackfriars. The company continued to use the Globe in the warmer months, and it is certain that *The Winter's Tale* was performed there in 1611 and *All Is True* in 1613. In short, it is easy to make too much of the distinction between playhouses and probably best to view romance as an institutionally transitional form, with one foot in the "public" theater and the other in the "private."

A second motive behind the romances may be biographical. In 1607, Shakespeare's daughter Susanna got married. The next year she had a daughter, Elizabeth, and Shakespeare's own mother died. Thus, the romances coincide with a generational shift in the dramatist's family. The emphasis in the plays on daughters who both marry and help redeem their aging fathers seems compatible with this moment. So, too, does the celebration of the birth of a baby Elizabeth at the end of *All Is True*.

Political changes may also have influenced the romances. Upon assuming the throne in 1603, King James placed each of London's professional acting troupes under the patronage of a member of his immediate family. As the most successful of these troupes, Shakespeare's company, the Lord Chamberlain's Men, became the King's Men. The late plays seem to register this increased proximity to the crown. Just as the romantic comedies shift the focus from the middle class of New Comedy to the aristocracy, so the romances further elevate the social status of the protagonists by concerning themselves with royalty—Pericles, Prince of Tyre; Cymbeline, King of Britain; Leontes, King of Sicilia, in *The Winter's Tale*; Prospero, Duke of Milan, in *The Tempest*; Henry VIII, King of England, in *All Is True*; Theseus, Duke of Athens, in *The Two Noble Kinsmen*; and, more ambiguously, Duke Angelo and his elder son, Roderick, in *Cardenio*. The attention to the younger generation in relation to the older may also respond to the cult that grew up around James's children. The Welsh setting of the cave of Guiderius and Arviragus, Cym-

beline's lost sons, may glance at the 1610 investiture of James's first son, Henry, as Prince of Wales. *All Is True* enthusiastically alludes to the marriage of James's daughter Elizabeth in 1613. Perhaps the same event lies behind the far more somber concluding union of Emilia and Palamon in *The Two Noble Kinsmen,* in this case, however, with Arcite's apparently meaningless fatal fall paralleling the death the previous year of her brother Henry, symbol of the revival of chivalry and martial valor that the play nostalgically evokes. It is unclear if these allusions are flattering to the royal family. And, of course, the point is not to ascertain whether the romances are secretly allegories of that family—they are not—but to understand that the family's prominence, following the long rule of the unmarried and childless Queen Elizabeth, could have helped turn Shakespeare's imagination in a new direction.

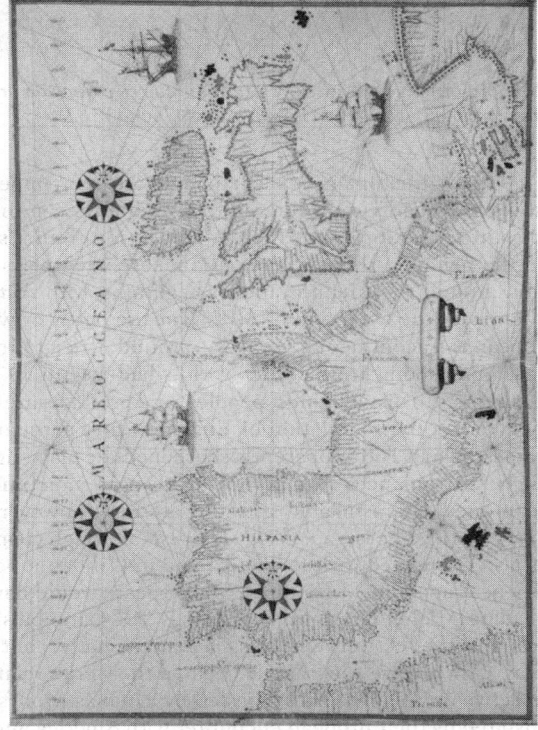

The Mediterranean, western Europe, and the northwest coast of Africa. By Joan Oliva (fl. 1580–1615).

Mapping the New World. From *Americae sive quartae orbis partis nova et exactissima descriptio*, engraved by Hieronymous Cock (1562).

Finally, the romances seem to meditate upon imperial expansion. English merchant ships had aggressively entered the Mediterranean in the 1570s, trading directly with the Ottoman Empire and thereby cutting into Venice's traditional economic dominance in the region. Although many of Shakespeare's plays throughout his career are set in and around the Mediterranean, beginning with *Antony and Cleopatra* (1606) all of them with the exception of *All Is True* are partly or wholly located there. Western European extracontinental voyages—around Africa to India, across the Atlantic to America, and, soon, around the world—had begun in the late fifteenth century, and references to distant lands, peoples, and products are dotted throughout Shakespeare's oeuvre. Yet the foundation of England's first permanent colony in the New World at Jamestown in 1607 apparently sharpened the playwright's interest in the topic. Accordingly, the romances' Mediterranean voyages sometimes feel as if they were also American ones. Unmistakable allusions are rare, however. *All Is True* overtly refers to the New World. The island of *The Tempest*, although clearly located in the Mediterranean, is also connected with Bermuda, and in Caliban it possesses a character whose name is a near anagram of cannibal. Shakespeare would have made the link to America from reading Michel de Montaigne's essay "Of Cannibals" (1580). Prospero colonizes the island and effectively enslaves Caliban, its native, but leaves it behind at the end of the play. Critics have accordingly debated the work's relationship to colonialism. One perspective on this issue is suggested by Thomas More's *Utopia* (1516), which was itself inspired by the European encounter with America and its peoples. In *The Tempest*, the good-hearted, loyal Gonzalo, cast upon the island, presents a utopian vision that is effectively ridiculed by the most treacherous characters in the play. But the redemptive structure of *The Tempest* and the other romances, the providential triumph over adversity following a long period of suffering, is itself a utopian scenario. This scenario distinguishes the late plays from their comic predecessors. If America significantly influences the romances, it does so not through incidental references but at the level of conceptual and dramatic structure.

Most discussions of the romances concentrate on *Pericles, Cymbeline, The Winter's Tale,* and *The Tempest*—and with good reason. Of Shakespeare's three subsequent plays, one is lost (*Cardenio*), another is a history play (*All Is True*), and the third seems very different from the four standard romances (*The Two Noble Kinsmen*). Yet in one obvious respect, the three plays belong together. As already noted, *Cardenio, All Is True,* and *The Two Noble Kinsmen* all are collaborations with Fletcher. English Renaissance playwrights routinely coauthored plays, and early and late in his career Shakespeare was no exception. By 1595, he had probably collaborated on at least *Titus Andronicus, Sir Thomas More,* and *Edward III;* after 1605, he jointly wrote *Timon of Athens* and, as we have seen, *Pericles, Cardenio, All Is True,* and *The Two Noble Kinsmen.* Coauthored works arguably have a less uniformly "Shakespearean" quality than the plays that Shakespeare composed by himself. One effect of attending to the final three plays, then, is to loosen the definition of the romances, to align them with the more general interest in romantic tragicomedy on the English stage at the time, and to underscore the uniquenesss of each of the late plays, the extent to which each deviates from the norms of even such capacious generic categories as romance or tragicomedy.

The Fletcherian collaborations might also be seen as a second stage of Shakespearean romance. Although these last plays share with the earlier romances the assertion of a providential plan, they transmute or eliminate the long temporal vistas previously necessary to the transcendence of tragedy. The final three works thus reduce the thematic depth of divine guidance, the sense that redemption is granted for effort, patience, and suffering, that though the bad may not always be punished, the good are always rewarded. The *Cardenio* story urges patience and the need to trust in time, but the assertions are metaphorical: things are quickly tidied up. *The Two Noble Kinsmen* offers a world of timeless serenity when Palamon and Arcite are first imprisoned, but the ordinary world of time means suffering without redemption. The two works lack the vertical perspective of the preceding romances, instead reverting to the horizontal structure of the still earlier problem plays. *All Is True* seems different. The passage of the years is instrumental in delivering the happy ending, as in the first four romances. But for whom is the ending happy? Not for anyone who has suffered along the way, with the limited and temporary exception of Archbishop Cranmer. Certainly not for Henry VIII, who always gets what he wants, who both does and does not seem responsible for what goes wrong, and whose tortured conscience over his marriage to Katherine is treated with amused skepticism. In other words, *All Is True* is a romance on the model of the earlier plays only if its protagonist is England itself. This plausible conclusion implies, however, the workings of a more austerely impersonal providence than is found in *Pericles, Cymbeline, The Winter's Tale,* and *The Tempest.*

What is true of time also holds for space. The problematic providentialism and foreshortened temporality of the final three plays may be connected to a geographical narrowing of the plot. Each of these works is confined to a single country. Gone, except metaphorically, are the perilous sea journeys of the immediately preceding years. Spatial breadth thus goes the way of temporal depth. The characters' problems are as grave as those in the previous romances, but both human and providential action seems constricted. These landlocked plays may suggest that the initial enthusiasm over the Virginia colony proved difficult to sustain. In retrospect, *The Tempest* appears both to justify and repudiate colonialism. Prospero's decision to leave the island parallels his rejection of magic: both acknowledge limits. Thereafter, although the colonial enterprise may be celebrated, as it is in *All Is True,* it is no longer represented. *Cardenio, All Is True,* and *The Two Noble Kinsmen* accordingly constitute a second movement within Shakespearean romance that reconfigures the entire sequence of plays that begins with *Pericles.*

The same point can be made of the characterization. In *The Tempest,* Prospero, despite his failings, is clearly associated with providence. In the succeeding plays, he is replaced by far weaker providential figures—Duke Angelo in *Cardenio;* Henry VIII in *All Is True;* Duke Theseus in *The Two Noble Kinsmen.* Similarly, daughters lose their redemptive role. Their marriages fail to connote the projection forward, much less the dynastic projection forward, of the family in time. In *Cardenio,* although the fathers are gladdened by the return of their children, the emotional force of the resolution arises overwhelmingly from the pairing off of the young lovers. In *The Two Noble Kinsmen,* Emilia becomes an object of contention and hence a source of destruction rather than reconciliation. Even Elizabeth doesn't save Henry in *All Is True.* He doesn't need saving, and in any case she's a mere babe at the end of the play and never marries. *All Is True* instead proceeds by homonyms, celebrating the marriage of King James's daughter Elizabeth as a substitute for actual familial continuity.

Symptomatically, the actual weddings are transformed from festive into tearful affairs. The hearse in *Cardenio* arrives just before the lovers' reunion. Henry's marriage to Anne in *All Is True* entails the rejection of Katherine and in the event her death. *The Two Noble Kinsmen* opens with the interruption of Theseus and Hippolyta's nuptials by the lamentations of the three widowed queens, is followed by the appearance of Palamon and Arcite on "two hearses" (biers, 1.4.0 s.d.), and ends by echoing its beginning, as the marriage of Palamon and Emilia competes with the mourning for Arcite. The scaling back of the young women's symbolic significance also accords with a casual attitude toward premarital sex. If *Cardenio* follows Cervantes, Dorotea consents to intercourse because she believes the false promises of a cad; if it corresponds to Theobald, she is raped. Either way, she loses her virginity. In the subplot of *The Two Noble Kinsmen,* the Doctor cures the Jailer's Daughter of madness by sending her to bed with someone she mistakenly believes to be Palamon. And in *All Is True,* Anne Boleyn's sexual modesty is treated with irreverence by the Old Lady who waits on her— an irreverence the audience is invited to share.

The last three plays also offer a darker view of violence and death than the previous romances. In *The Tempest,* no one dies. The same is true of *Cardenio.* But the near rape of Miranda by Caliban is replaced by the real rape of Dorotea/Violante by Fernando/Henriquez—a rape for which the perpetrator suffers mild pangs of conscience, fleeting public embarrassment, and the felicity of familial approval and wedded bliss. In *Pericles* and *Cymbeline,* although all who are vicious do not necessarily die, all who die are necessarily vicious. In *The Winter's Tale,* Leontes' son perishes because Leontes must be punished, and Antigonus dies because he has nobly risked everything to save Leontes' daughter, Perdita. Here, too, then, death is part of an ethical calculus. In *All Is True,* however, morality and mortality are randomly related. Buckingham, Wolsey, and Katherine must be removed so that Elizabeth can come to power. Katherine is the finest person in the play, but her death represents neither a voluntary sacrifice for the benefit of England nor a punishment of Henry for his misdeeds. And in *The Two Noble Kinsmen,* Palamon and Arcite seem morally equivalent. Hence, Arcite's death feels at best random, at worst a cruel trick played by providence on shell-shocked mortals. Theseus's assertion of divine wisdom accordingly seems desperate and unconvincing.

In short, the final three plays reveal a growing pessimism, a bleaker outlook, a grimmer universe, a declining belief in the possibility of transcending tragedy. It is unclear how this development relates to the apparently greater tolerance for Catholicism suggested by the Spanish setting of *Cardenio,* unique in Shakespeare's oeuvre, and the admiring treatment of Katherine of Aragon in *All Is True.* Perhaps the point is that all is true, that everyone is right. Both Katherine and Anne are celebrated. But Anne's victory comes in this world, Katherine's only in the next. In other words, this is merely a disguised form of the either-or logic characteristic of all three of the final plays: either Anne or Katherine, either Palamon or Arcite, either Protestants or Catholics. And in an additional sign of the reduced capaciousness of these works, their inability to integrate all the virtuous characters and more, the losers must die.

Finally, the successive views presented here of Shakespearean romance—as a continuation of the comedies, as a distinct and coherent category, and as an internally divided one—are by no means incompatible. They merely provide different ways into the subject. A broad approach to the romances should be open to all of these perspectives—and more.

SELECTED BIBLIOGRAPHY

Adelman, Janet. *Suffocating Mothers: Fantasies of Maternal Origin in Shakespeare's Plays, "Hamlet" to "The Tempest."* New York: Routledge, 1992. 193–238. The four main romances as efforts to recover the ideal parental couple lost in the tragedies that must nonetheless choose, alternately, either the mother or the father.

Bloom, Harold. *Shakespeare: The Invention of the Human.* New York: Riverhead, 1998. A major critic's personal, sometimes deliberately idiosyncratic, play-by-play analysis that rejects generic categorization of the four main romances, *All Is True* (*Henry VIII*), and *The Two Noble Kinsmen.*

Brown, John Russell, ed. *Later Shakespeare.* New York: St. Martin's, 1967. Ten essays, partly on the late tragedies but mainly on the four main romances and *All Is True* (*Henry VIII*), including both general approaches to the plays from diverse perspectives and readings of individual works.

Frye, Northrop. *A Natural Perspective: The Development of Shakespearean Comedy and Romance.* New York: Harcourt, Brace and World, 1965. Important argument for continuity between the romantic comedies and the romances.

Henke, Robert. *Pastoral Transformations: Italian Tragicomedy and Shakespeare's Late Plays.* Newark: University of Delaware Press, 1997. Compares Italian pastoral tragicomedy to *Cymbeline*, *The Winter's Tale*, and *The Tempest*, focusing primarily on parallels, while also attending to certain influences.

Jordan, Constance. *Shakespeare's Monarchies: Ruler and Subject in the Romances.* Ithaca, N.Y.: Cornell University Press, 1997. The four main romances as meditations on contemporary debates over the power of the crown, depicting misrule by the monarch and the political and psychological corrections necessary to restore proper government.

Kay, Carol McGinnis, and Henry E. Jacobs, eds. *Shakespeare's Romances Reconsidered.* Lincoln: University of Nebraska Press, 1978. Eleven essays from the 1970s, including readings of individual plays, comparisons to the work of other dramatists, and general studies of Shakespearean romance, with consideration of fathers and daughters and the relation of romance to masque (Frye, Leech), among other topics.

Leggatt, Alexander, ed. *The Cambridge Companion to Shakespearean Comedy.* Cambridge, Eng.: Cambridge University Press, 2002. Essays by Clubb on Italian backgrounds of romantic comedy and romance, and by O'Connell on the innovations of romance.

Palfrey, Simon. *Late Shakespeare: A New World of Words.* Oxford: Clarendon Press, 1997. Argues against conventional readings that stress the providentialism, elitism, and royalism of the four main romances in favor of emphasis on verbal, generic, and political complexity and dissonance.

Richards, Jennifer, and James Knowles, ed. *Shakespeare's Late Plays: New Readings.* Edinburgh: Edinburgh University Press, 1999. A collection distinctive for its insistence on taking into account not only the four standard romances but also the three collaborations with Fletcher—*The Two Noble Kinsmen*, *All Is True*, and *Cardenio.*

The Winter's Tale

In his induction to *Bartholomew Fair* (1614), Ben Jonson complained of plays that "make Nature afraid" and "beget Tales, Tempests, and such like Drolleries." His remarks seem aimed directly at his contemporary William Shakespeare, who, in the last years of his theatrical career, had written a number of plays, including *The Winter's Tale* (1609–11) and *The Tempest* (1611), that by some accounts might be said to "make Nature afraid." Jonson implies that such plays, eschewing realism, present fantastic or impossible events that defy the laws of nature. While Jonson found such concoctions unpalatable, most of Shakespeare's contemporaries did not. In prose romances popular throughout the period, characters regularly undertake impossible quests, encounter marvels, and are unexpectedly reunited with lost children. Shakespeare's late plays participate fully in this taste for the marvelous, reveling in, rather than being embarrassed by, the strange and the improbable. In the case of *The Winter's Tale*, we possess a rather full description of the play by Simon Forman, a London astrologer and doctor, who saw it performed on May 15, 1611, and described its complicated plot with no hint that he found either its events absurd or the play defective. On the contrary, Forman's detailed description suggests him to have been fully absorbed by what he saw. Concluding with an account of the deceptive tricks of the play's rogue, Autolycus, Forman moralized: "Beware trusting feigned beggars or fawning fellows."

Modern editors often group *Pericles, The Winter's Tale, Cymbeline*, and *The Tempest* together under the label "romances," although this is not a category used in the Folio (1623). There Shakespeare's plays are divided into comedies, tragedies, and histories. *Pericles* is not included in the Folio; *Cymbeline* is placed at the end of the tragedies; *The Tempest* appears as the first of the comedies and *The Winter's Tale* as the last. These placements are suggestive of the mixed tragicomic nature of these particular dramas. Like Shakespeare's earlier comedies, they all end happily, with families reunited and marriages in prospect; but the late plays also engage with the tragic dimensions of human life to a degree not customary for the early comedies. Before the characters in these plays reach safe harbor, they encounter tyranny, incest, the loss of wives and children, and the treachery of brothers. The protagonists suffer intensely, both because of fortune's blows and because of their own folly. Only by what is experienced as miracle does tragedy turn to mirth and suffering cease. While the miraculous quality of these reversals binds these plays together as a group, it is also at the heart of Jonson's objections. Improbable occurrences and unexpected transformations of sorrow into joy can affront sober common sense, but they also make romance emotionally and theatrically appealing. In defiance of probability, these plays construct a world in which (at least for some fortunate characters) second chances are possible.

By its very title *The Winter's Tale* signals its affiliations with popular storytelling. Within the play, Mamillius, the King of Sicilia's young son, informs his mother that "a sad tale's best for winter" (2.1.27) and offers to tell her one "of sprites and goblins" (2.1.28). The only sprites and goblins in Shakespeare's play turn out to be the internal demons of jealousy and suspicion that erupt in the mind of its protagonist, King Leontes, but *The Winter's Tale* is permeated by sadness, even during its festive conclusion, and its plot is full of wonders. Its starting point is King Leontes' sudden certainty that his wife, Hermione, is pregnant not with his own child, but with that of his childhood friend, King Polixenes of Bohemia, a visitor at Leontes' Sicilian court. Warned of Leontes' jealousy, Polixenes flees back to Bohemia, leaving the King to vent his wrath on Hermione. Imprisoned, she gives birth to a daughter, Perdita, whom Leontes orders

The Bloudy Mother.

OR

The most inhumane murthers, committed by *Iane Hatterslie* vpon diuers Infants, the issue of her owne bodie: & the priuate burying of them in an Orchard with her Araignment and execution.

As also, The most loathsome and lamentable end of *Adam Adamson* her Master, the vnlawfull begetter of those vnfortunate Babes; being eaten and consumed aliue with Wormes and Lice.

At East *Grinsted* in *Sussex* neere London, in Iuly last. 1609.

Printed for *Iohn Busbie*, and are to be soldby *Arthur Iohnson* in Paules Churchyard at the signe of the White Horse.

In the early seventeenth century, popular pamphlet literature circulated sensational stories of parents, especially unmarried women, who murdered or abandoned their children. In this title page from *The Bloudy Mother* (1609), a serving woman and her master bury the illegitimate child she has killed. On the right, for his part in begetting and disposing of the child, the master is consumed by lice and worms.

to be abandoned in the countryside far from Sicilia. Even when the oracle of Apollo subsequently declares Hermione innocent, Leontes continues to insist on her guilt. As he does, the death of his only son, Mamillius, is announced, and Hermione appears to die of grief. The first three acts of *The Winter's Tale* thus enact a miniature tragedy (not unlike Shakespeare's tragedy of the jealous Othello) in which Leontes' actions result in the loss of wife, daughter, and son. His personal tragedy also affects his kingdom. The oracle proclaims: "the King shall live without an heir if that which is lost be not found" (3.2.133–34). A kingdom without an heir to the throne is a kingdom in danger.

But then something extraordinary happens. The character Time appears onstage, informing the audience that sixteen years have passed and that Perdita, abandoned on the seacoast of Bohemia, has survived. Suddenly, instead of the wintry world of Leontes' Sicilian court, the play bursts with the energies of a Bohemian summer. The

Old Shepherd who rescued Perdita is about to hold a sheepshearing festival, and Florizel, King Polixenes' son, has fallen in love with Perdita. A series of extraordinary events returns the young couple to Leontes' court, where Perdita's true status as his child and heir is revealed. More wonders follow. Taken to see what they believe to be a statue of the long-dead Hermione, the King and his newly recovered daughter witness the seeming miracle of the statue's transformation into flesh and blood.

Shakespeare's chief source for this tale was Robert Greene's popular prose romance *Pandosto*, first published in 1588. Greene provided Shakespeare with the story of a jealous King who loses Queen and daughter but eventually has his daughter restored to him. But the differences between Shakespeare's play and Greene's prose tale are as striking as the similarities. For example, Shakespeare carefully changed the names of most of the characters he borrowed from Greene. In *Pandosto*, the King's lost daughter is Fawnia, but Shakespeare names her Perdita, a word that in Latin means "that which is lost." In Shakespeare's hands, Perdita's lover ceases to be Dorastus and becomes, instead, Florizel, which suggests the young prince's connection with the flowers of spring. Greene's protagonist, Pandosto, is transformed into Leontes, evoking the leonine or lionlike nature of his wrath. Shakespeare also reversed the kingdoms ruled by Greene's Kings. In *Pandosto*, the protagonist is King of Bohemia and his childhood friend rules Sicilia. In *The Winter's Tale*, the reverse is true, and one reason may be the association of Sicilia with the myth of Proserpina, the beautiful daughter of Ceres abducted by Dis, the god of the underworld, as she was picking flowers. Her mother attempted to free Proserpina, but she was allowed to return to the upper world only six months of each year. During that period, spring and summer came to the earth, but winter reigned when Proserpina returned to Dis's kingdom. The sixteen years of mourning Leontes undergoes in Perdita's absence provide a counterpart to aspects of this myth.

Shakespeare, however, made much larger changes in Greene's romance. For example, he enhanced the role of Leontes' son, who is barely mentioned by Greene; he added the characters of Paulina, Emilia, Antigonus, Autolycus, Clown, Time, and rustics such as Dorcas and Mopsa (in *Pandosto*, Mopsa was the name of the Old Shepherd's wife; in *The Winter's Tale*, that wife is long dead). The magnificent sheepshearing festival is Shakespeare's invention; nothing like it exists in *Pandosto*. Most importantly, Greene's romance ends on a tragic note. Although the King and his daughter are finally reunited, Pandosto's wife is never restored to him, and overcome with desire for his grown daughter, he attempts incest and later takes his own life.

Shakespeare clearly saw in Greene's grim tale the basis for a much more resonant narrative of loss and redemption. The play is a diptych of winter and summer, hinged by the appearance of Time. It is probably a mistake to account for this structure by using only one interpretive framework, for the play's elegant simplicity resonates with many narratives of renewal. Some have read the play in Christian terms, seeing Leontes as a sinner who, after a period of suffering and repentance, receives the gift of God's grace through the return of his daughter and the Christlike resurrection of his wife. The play loosely traces the liturgical calendar, moving from the hospitality associated with Christmas to the Lenten period of deprivation and repentance to the joyous celebration of Easter and the Maying festivals associated with Whitsuntide, which occurs seven weeks after Easter. Other critics have stressed the mythic qualities of the play, its resemblance, for example, to the myth of Proserpina, or to fertility rites in which the coming of spring and sexual fulfillment depend on the sacrifice of a figure, usually an old King, associated with winter. In *The Winter's Tale*, Leontes does not die, but he does mourn for sixteen years; and his servant Antigonus, who takes the babe to Bohemia and there names her Perdita, becomes Leontes' sacrificial substitute. Once he has deposited Perdita, Antigonus is mauled and eaten by a bear. As the Old Shepherd who rescues Perdita says to his son, who has witnessed this death, "Thou metst with things dying, I with things new-born" (3.3.104–05), the latter event seemingly dependent on the former. Other critics stress the pattern of generational renewal informing the play as the sins of the father, Leontes, give way to the innocent goodness of Florizel and Perdita. In some productions, the actress playing Hermione also plays Perdita (although a double for one of them usually has to be employed in the statue scene when they are both on stage together), deepening the sense that it is through their children that parents have a second life. Resonating with all these interpretive paradigms, *The Winter's Tale* draws richly on the many narratives and structures of belief through which Western culture has produced and sustained its desire for transcendence and renewal.

In modern productions, the symbolic power of the play's diptych structure is often highlighted by contrasts in the costumes and sets used to distinguish Sicilia and Bohemia. Sicilia, for example, is often a snow kingdom, dominated by white clothing and metallic props; Bohemia is a summer kingdom, the stage carpeted in green, the characters at the sheepshearing festival a riot of variegated colors. When the Bohemian party comes to Sicilia, the winter landscape is literally overwritten with the colorful clothes associated with Whitsuntide.

The play, however, is not simply about the triumph of the young, the rebirth of a world of possibility. *The Winter's Tale*, as befits a tragicomedy, moves from sorrow to joy, but that joy is bittersweet. However important the younger generation is to this old tale, the focus in this and the other romances stays resolutely on the older generation. It is Leontes who sins and must repent, Leontes whose family is reconstituted. Crucially, that reconstitution is only partial and imperfect. Mamillius, the young son, dies, the ultimate sacrifice to Leontes' tyrannous actions; and in the play's last scene, the playwright is at pains to stress that the "statue" of Hermione has wrinkles, the mark of time on her body. Traduced while a fertile wife and mother, Hermione returns as a woman past childbearing. Time, whose appearance marks the hinge of the play, may heal old sorrows and bring new births to pass, but it also shuts down possibilities and destroys youth and strength. The ending of Shakespeare's old tale induces wonder and joy, but it cannot make an old man young or erase all the consequences of rash deeds. Shakespeare's late plays achieve their rich emotional effects from the deep strains of melancholia that underwrite their measured celebrations of the return of love and hope to a chastened social order.

Nor, despite the archaic quality that permeates these plays, are they simple enactments of timeless patterns and narratives. The precipitating event of the play—the eruption of Leontes' jealousy—is a symptom of the faultlines in a particular patriarchal culture. Often said to be "irrational," this jealousy in actuality has its roots in the cultural practices that in Jacobean England made men the heads of families, lineages, and kingdoms, but at the same time made them crucially dependent on women's reproductive powers to generate legitimate heirs. As *The Winter's Tale* opens, Leontes asks Polixenes to extend his stay in Sicilia. Polixenes refuses, but when Hermione entreats him, he agrees. This event, and the sight of his pregnant wife conversing with his friend and holding him by the hand, triggers in Leontes so deep a suspicion of his wife's fidelity that he plans to have Polixenes killed and doubts the legitimacy of his son as well. In part, what disturbs Leontes is the unknowability of the biological origins of his children. Men theoretically had dominion over their wives, but as Leontes says, "No barricado for a belly" (1.2.205)—that is, no absolute defense of a woman's chastity but her own honor, and that lies in her control, not her husband's.

A deep ambivalence toward women and sexuality, moreover, surfaces earlier in the same scene when, reminiscing about his boyhood friendship with Leontes, Polixenes describes the two of them as twinned lambs who experienced a fall from paradise only when they felt sexual passion and had their first encounters with women. In this conversation, the two men echo a strand of early modern thought that viewed men's friendships with men as of greater worth than what were seen as men's more dangerous and unpredictable relations with women, an idea examined as early in Shakespeare's work as *The Two Gentlemen of Verona*. Construed as physically imperfect and as intellectually inferior to men, women were supposedly ruled by their passions and could in turn evoke dangerous and degrading emotions in men. Yet men were enjoined to marry these irrational creatures to procreate and to continue family lineage. Leontes' rage at Hermione seems to stem in part from his dependence on her to give him legitimate heirs.

Other tensions permeate the opening scenes. If in their younger days Polixenes and Leontes were like twinned lambs, in adulthood their friendship is tinged with competitiveness, with Hermione gradually becoming the focus of their rivalry. Polixenes' attendant Archidamus opens the play expressing uneasiness about repaying the generous hospitality provided by Leontes and suggesting rivalry as well as friendship between the two kingdoms; in 1.2 Leontes asks Polixenes if he loves *his* son as dearly as Leontes loves Mamillius, again suggesting competitiveness between the two Kings at the level of paternal affection for their sons. In this general context of subterranean rivalry, Leontes' command that Hermione entreat Polixenes to stay not only expresses his ostentatious generosity (he will even share his wife's attentions with his friend), but also calls forth his rivalrous jealousy (perhaps his friend has taken advantage of his generosity and assumed Leontes' place in Hermione's bed).

Once his jealousy has been triggered, Leontes gives the rein to a deadly rage that finds its chief object in Hermione's pregnant body. This anger is played out in part through Leontes' increasing identification with his young son, Mamillius. In Mamillius, Leontes sees himself as he once was, a young boy not yet wearing either the breeches or the sharp phallic dagger associated with adult manhood (1.2.157–58). It is an image of innocence but also of vulnerability. The name Mamillius, another of Shakespeare's brilliant inventions, suggests one source of that vulnerability. *Mamilla* is the word for the nipple on a breast or a diminutive form of *mamma,* the Latin word for the breast itself. His name thus connects Mamillius to the lactating breast and to the world of women, who in early modern culture presided over childbirth and the early years of children's lives. In a culture in which baby formula did not exist, infants depended utterly on women, either wet nurses or mothers, to provide the crucial sustenance, breast milk. As was often true of women from the upper class, Hermione does not herself seem to have nursed Mamillius. As Leontes bitterly exclaims: "I am glad you did not nurse him" (2.1.58). Nonetheless, the young boy's name and his appearance in 2.1 with his pregnant mother and her waiting women clearly associate him with the feminine sphere of birth, lactation, and early childhood. In identifying with Mamillius, a boy so young his nurse's milk is scarcely out of him, Leontes seems to feel both the vulnerability of the infant dependent on the lactating body of woman and the vulnerability of the adult husband dependent on the pregnant body and the chastity of his wife for legitimate offspring. As if to deny these dependencies, Leontes banishes Mamillius from his mother's presence, and he banishes Hermione to prison. Mamillius dies; Leontes appears to lose all that would link him to the future: wife, son, daughter.

The Winter's Tale makes Leontes a dangerous tyrant in Acts 1 to 3 and portrays his anger and paranoia as forces that torture his speech and profoundly isolate him. In the first three acts, Leontes' most characteristic action is to turn away from those who love or attempt to help him. He sends his wife to prison; casts out his infant daughter; refuses the good counsel of his courtiers; rages in misogynistic fury at Paulina, who brings Perdita to him from prison; and finally defies the oracle of Apollo. Lacking trust in his wife and in all those around him, Leontes condemns himself to deathlike isolation. As in Shakespeare's other late plays, much of the language of *The Winter's Tale* is difficult and dense. Normal word order is inverted; speeches begin and end in the middle of a line; figurative language is given elliptical expression. During his period of intense jealousy, Leontes' language becomes even more dense and compressed than is typical of the rest of the play. Looking at his son, he exclaims:

> Can thy dam—may't be?—
> Affection, thy intention stabs the centre.
> Thou dost make possible things not so held,
> Communicat'st with dreams—how can this be?—

With what's unreal thou coactive art,
And fellow'st nothing. Then 'tis very credent
Thou mayst co-join with something, and thou dost—
And that beyond commission; and I find it—
And that to the infection of my brains
And hard'ning of my brows.

(1.2.139–48)

In this difficult passage, Leontes wrestles with the knowledge that his "affection" (the passions of rage, jealousy, and suspicion released in him) wounds him and perhaps leads him to imagine things to be true that are not. On the other hand, his suspicions *may* be justified; he may already be a cuckold. In this horrible state of uncertainty, Leontes' speech verges on incoherence. He interrupts the flow of his own thoughts with questions and ejaculations; his mind darts from boy to mother to his own pain; he realizes he may be wrong, but returns, obsessively, to the coarse and shameful image of his forehead disfigured with the horns of a cuckold.

The inner disorder suggested by this language finds its outward manifestation in Leontes' increasingly tyrannical actions. In the early modern period, the ruler of a king-

In the early modern period, childbirth was largely the affair of women. In this picture from Jakob Rüff's *De conceptu et generatione hominis* (Concerning the conception and birth of man) (1580), several women attend to a woman in labor while, in the background, two men cast the child's horoscope.

dom was often compared to the head of a family. Good order in the commonwealth had its foundation in a well-ordered domestic realm. In *The Winter's Tale*, Leontes oversteps his just authority in both domains, refusing to take counsel from his courtiers, defying the gods, and condemning his wife for adultery with no evidence but his own suspicions. Nowhere, however, does he more certainly exceed his patriarchal authority than when he orders Hermione to stand trial before the proper period of her lying-in has passed. In the Renaissance, childbirth was recognized as an event both important and dangerous. Women gave birth surrounded by other women, usually a hired midwife, as well as by neighbors and female family members. The laboring female body, opened to let the child pass into the world, was considered to be in a particularly vulnerable state, needing to be protected from the unhealthful air that might enter the open womb. Consequently, birthing took place in a closed chamber, and after birth had occurred, women lay in their chambers for an extended period, recovering strength and purging their bodies of the blood and other fluids associated with pregnancy. At the end of this period, often lasting a month but sometimes longer, the woman came out of her house and returned to her normal routines. This occasion was marked by a "churching" ceremony, a rite of purification and celebration in which thanks were given for the safe delivery of a child and the woman's body declared cleansed of the impurities of pregnancy and birth.

When Hermione is made to stand trial, the pathos of her dignified defense of herself is heightened by her weakened state. In many productions, she appears on stage unattended, almost unable to stand. Among the wrongs done her, she accuses Leontes of having "with immodest hatred / The childbed privilege denied, which 'longs / To women of all fashion; lastly, hurried / Here, to this place, i'th' open air, before / I have got strength of limit" (3.2.100–04). Leontes' fury against the maternal body extends to denying that body the privileges of the lying-in period and exposing it to the dangers of the open air of a public place. This is domestic tyranny of a hideous sort.

After such cruelty, what recovery? Bohemia seems to be the place of hope in the play, and that feeling is conveyed in part by the vast expansion of character and event in that pastoral locale. After the claustrophobic focus on Leontes, the action unfolds to encompass the tricks of a wily rogue, Autolycus (whose name links him to the Autolycus of classical mythology, a crafty thief and grandfather of Ulysses; Autolycus's own father, Mercury, was the god of thieves); the sports of a sheepshearing festival; the courtship of Florizel and Perdita; and the intrigues that take many of these players back to Sicilia. The scene depicting the festival at the Old Shepherd's farm, 4.4, is one of the longest in Shakespeare's canon (810 lines), is entirely his own invention, and is a great feast of languages and events. It includes the singing of ballads, a dance of twelve satyrs, Perdita's lyrical catalog of the flowers appropriate to each stage of life, and the painful moment when Polixenes forbids his son's marriage.

As this last moment shows, although Bohemia is a place of healing, it is not a paradise. In Bohemia, "great creating nature" for a time replaces Apollo as the deity who presides over the action. The fertility of the earth and, by extension, the fertility of woman may here seem to be redeemed from the curse laid upon them by Leontes' suspicion of his wife; and Florizel's staunch commitment to Perdita in the face of mounting obstacles to their love augers well. But Polixenes just as staunchly opposes their union, threatening to use his patriarchal power in a way that, as with Leontes, would separate him from his son and from the possibility of future lineage. Bohemia also contains the rogue Autolycus, picking the pockets of country bumpkins and hiding his identity by a series of disguises. Further, Bohemian life is marked by enormous disparities of wealth. The Old Shepherd is rich, in part because of the money he found with Perdita. For the sheepshearing feast, Perdita can afford ingredients—raisins, rice, and spices, for example—that were exotic luxury goods, foodstuffs in excess of the subsistence diet of bread, beer, and cheese that was still the staple for many. It also possible that some of the Old Shepherd's wealth comes from the new profitability of raising sheep. Throughout the sixteenth and seventeenth centuries, land was increasingly enclosed—that is,

In this late seventeenth-century woodcut from the Pepysian collection of early modern ballads, a peddler carries a huge pack and holds several rabbits, or conies, which suggests that he is also a cony-catcher—that is, a con man (like Autolycus), whose victims were popularly called conies.

fenced off for grazing sheep rather than available for communal use in raising food and feeding cattle. These enclosures were popularly blamed for perceived increases in rural poverty and for the creation of masterless men, poor folk who roamed the countryside without fixed places of residence and who were believed to feign sickness or deformity in order to enforce charity from those they met. Autolycus, pretending to have lost his clothes to a highwayman, is a comic version of such a masterless man, yet his presence in the play, juxtaposed to that of the rich shepherd, is a reminder of the social tensions and economic stratifications that permeate the rural landscape with widespread enclosures and other changes in rural life.

Bohemia is also the locale of one of the great set pieces of the play—the debate between Polixenes and Perdita concerning the relative values of art and nature and the relationship between them. This was an ancient debate and one that could give off a decidedly musty odor, even though it was dusted off by a number of Shakespeare's contemporaries. At the heart of this debate lay the question of artifice. Was it a good thing? Did it distort or enhance nature? Given the imperfections of the fallen world and humankind's weaknesses, could art be instrumental in calling into being a better world, or was it merely a temptation to pride or to competition with the divine creator? The refreshing thing about the handling of these issues in *The Winter's Tale* is that the play comes to no abstract resolution concerning them. Rather, it encases the actual debate between Polixenes and Perdita in multiple ironies, and it complexly connects this debate to the actions of characters who seemingly have no involvement with it. For Perdita, product of the pastoral landscape, art is a bad thing. She wants no grafted or hybrid flowers in her garden. Yet even as she speaks her condemnation of art, Perdita is reluctantly dressed as Queen of the sheepshearing feast, a bit of artifice that reveals a truth she herself cannot know: namely, that she is a Queen's daughter. Polixenes, for his part, champions art, declaring that the practice of mixing wild and cultivated plants produces sturdy hybrids and that the art of grafting is itself a gift of nature. Yet when his son wishes to graft himself to a shepherd's daughter, Polixenes finds such a practice abhorrent.

Besides making the obvious point that people don't always act on their stated beliefs, this exchange shows the extreme pressure the play puts on the art-nature dichotomy. In Perdita's case, her "natural" condition as princess is revealed only by means of two kinds of artifice: her dress as Queen of the feast and the role Camillo creates for her as Florizel's Libyan Princess when he devises a way for the two young lovers to return to Leontes' court. Camillo even goes so far as to provide lines for the two to speak. His goal is ameliorative: to satisfy the desires of the young (as well as his own deep longings to again see his homeland) and to heal the breach between the two dissevered kingdoms. The point seems to be not whether in some abstract sense "art" violates "nature," but how artfulness, defined broadly as the representation of the world through painting, statuary, plays, and song, can open new possibilities for imagining what nature is or could be.

This is not an inconsequential point, for in the badly flawed world depicted in *The Winter's Tale* art gradually emerges as one of the resources people can use, either badly or well, to affect the world around them: to correct old mistakes and to forge new realities. Its effects are determined and limited, of course, by the skill and intentions of the artist and by the receptiveness of the audience. Autolycus is a subversive con man who uses disguises and deceptions to fleece money from gulls. By contrast, in the play's final movement, Paulina emerges as the chief representative of the ameliorative artist who uses her skills to make better the world around her. Once reviled by Leontes as a witch, Paulina becomes the King's spiritual guide in the last half of the play (her name linking her to the New Testament evangelist, St. Paul). This strikingly outspoken woman spends sixteen years preparing Leontes to be a fit spectator to the tableau of resurrection and renewal enacted in the last scene. When she had first brought the infant to Leontes from prison, Paulina had seemed to believe in the self-evident nature of truth. Laying the babe at Leontes' feet, she proclaimed that the "good goddess Nature" (2.3.104) had made it an exact copy of the father. Leontes had only to read what nature had written in the face of his child. But distorting jealousy and rage at his wife had bleared the King's vision. He would not or could not see himself in the female child he had fathered. So for sixteen years Paulina worked another way, fueling Leontes' remorse and artfully withholding both from him and from the theater audience the knowledge that Hermione lived. When the disguised Princess returns to Sicilia, Leontes gets a second chance. Looking at Perdita, he is finally able to see—not so much himself as the unslandered image of his wife in the young girl before him. Having admired Perdita, Leontes says to Paulina, "I thought of her [Hermione] / Even in these looks I made" (5.1.226–27). When he can believe in the potential goodness of women, and specifically in the chastity of the young woman who is the simulacrum of his wife, then Leontes can help to create the reality in which Perdita is truly a Princess and his wife a living being rather than the corpse into which his rage and distrust had transformed her.

The statue scene itself is one of the most moving dramatic moments in any of Shakespeare's plays. Like Leontes, the untutored audience does not know that Hermione lives. Consequently, under Paulina's careful guidance, the spectators both onstage and off seem to participate in willing the statue into life. When Hermione descends from her pedestal, the audience can feel itself present at the miraculous resurrection of the dead. In theological terms, this scene touches on controversial matters. Protestants repudiated what they characterized as Catholic idolatry, which involved the veneration of images, including statues of the Virgin Mary. Protestants, by contrast, typically stressed the ear over the eye, words over images, faith over works. In the wake of the Reformation, more radical Protestants went so far as to smash stained-glass windows and the statues of saints that had for many centuries adorned Catholic churches. The final moments of *The Winter's Tale* gesture toward this repudiated world of images and their veneration. While Paulina insists that the audience awaken its faith, she does so in a scene that is visually organized to focus all eyes on a statue that in its chapel setting might well evoke memories of prior Catholic practices. In his characteristic way, Shakespeare seems to have things two ways: drawing on the emotional power of Catholic rituals centered on the image, he simultaneously suggests that there is no statue on the stage at all, only a living woman roused to new vigor by the recovery of a long-lost daughter.

However ambiguous the theological implications of the final scene, ultimately the old tale ends happily, or mostly so. At the end of the play, patriarchy has been reformed, but its potential for abuses has hardly been eradicated. In the final scene, the highly charged image of the pregnant female body is nowhere to be seen. Perdita is not yet a wife; both Paulina and Hermione are probably too old for childbearing. For Perdita and Florizel perhaps the greatest tests of faith and mutuality lie ahead, when Perdita's transformation from maid into wife and mother will present new occasions for jealousy and distrust. Moreover, in *The Winter's Tale* the remembrance of things that were lost and can never be regained intrudes even on the celebration of the return of Perdita and of Hermione. Paulina pointedly recalls her husband, Antigonus, lost in carrying Perdita to Bohemia; Hermione speaks to Perdita of the sixteen long years of their separation; her wrinkles attest to other losses; Mamillius is gone forever. The point of *The Winter's Tale* hardly seems to be that folly has no consequences or that earthly paradise is possible. Those claims would indeed make nature afraid. Rather, the play celebrates the true miracle of partial restorations, of moments of exquisite joy wrested by work, art, and good fortune from the pains of the imperfect world that men and women have made.

JEAN E. HOWARD

TEXTUAL NOTE

The Winter's Tale was first printed in the Folio of 1623 at the end of the group of comedies. Simon Forman, a London doctor, saw a performance at the Globe on May 15, 1611, and it was performed at court on November 11 of that year. Its exact date of composition, however, is unknown. Largely on stylistic evidence and because *The Winter's Tale* is at several points indebted to Plutarch, a principal source for Shakespeare's classical tragedies such as *Coriolanus* (1608), the Oxford editors place the date of composition in 1609, before *Cymbeline*. Other editors believe the play was written late in 1610 or early in 1611 before the May performance witnessed by Forman. In Act 4, Scene 4, working men at the sheepshearing festival perform a satyr dance that resembles a dance in Ben Jonson's *Masque of Oberon*, which was performed at court on January 1, 1611. In Shakespeare's play, the Old Shepherd remarks that three of the performers had "danced before the King" (4.4.324). This reference has been used to suggest that Shakespeare either was writing *The Winter's Tale* in January of 1611 and so incorporated a contemporary court event into his play, or that he composed the bulk of the play after that date. It is also possible that Shakespeare—or someone else—added this dance to *The Winter's Tale* after the play had already been written and was in performance in order to capitalize on the glamour attached to court occasions, especially if, as the Old Shepherd indicates, members of Shakespeare's company performed in Jonson's masque. If so, the dance would have been recorded in the promptbook but not necessarily in Shakespeare's original manuscript.

The Folio text of the play was probably set from a transcript prepared by Ralph Crane, a scrivener who transcribed a number of plays associated with the King's Men. In many of the manuscripts prepared by Crane, and this is true for *The Winter's Tale,* all the characters who appear in certain scenes, regardless of when they actually come on stage, are listed in the opening stage direction. Crane sometimes modified stage directions in the interest of clarity and imposed his own punctuation and spelling on the playscripts, showing a decided preference for the heavy use of parentheses, hyphens, and apostrophes. The changes Crane made while copying the plays make it difficult to recognize what kind of manuscript lay behind his transcriptions: promptbook or foul papers. As with other plays set from Crane's transcriptions, the Folio *Winter's Tale* is a relatively clean text. Act and scene divisions are carefully and consistently noted, although stage directions are sparse. There are only forty-three in the Folio, and they are regularly supplemented in modern editions.

SELECTED BIBLIOGRAPHY

Adelman, Janet. "Masculine Authority and the Maternal Body: The Return to Origins in the Romances." *Suffocating Mothers: Fantasies of Maternal Origin in Shakespeare's Plays, "Hamlet" to "The Tempest."* New York: Routledge, 1992. 193–238. Argues that the romances attempt to redress the loss of the idealized parents enacted in *Hamlet* and that *The Winter's Tale* dramatizes the positive restoration of the sexualized mother in the person of Hermione.

Dolan, Frances. "Finding What Has Been 'Lost': Representations of Infanticide and *The Winter's Tale*." *Dangerous Familiars: Representations of Domestic Crime in England, 1550–1700.* Ithaca, N.Y.: Cornell University Press, 1994. 121–70. Connects *The Winter's Tale* to early modern stories of child abandonment and murder, arguing that the play ultimately forgives the tyrannous father, Leontes, for the exposure of Perdita.

Egan, Robert. "'The Art Itself Is Nature': *The Winter's Tale*." *Drama Within Drama: Shakespeare's Sense of His Art in "King Lear," "The Winter's Tale," and "The Tempest."* New York: Columbia University Press, 1975. 56–89. Discusses the role of art in rectifying the disordered world of *The Winter's Tale*.

Frye, Northrop. "The Triumph of Time." *A Natural Perspective: The Development of Shakespearean Comedy and Romance.* New York: Columbia University Press, 1965. 72–117. Discusses structures of action and conventions common across Shakespeare's comedies and romances.

Hunt, Maurice. "'Bearing Hence' Shakespeare's *The Winter's Tale*." *Studies in English Literature 1500–1900* 44 (2004): 333–46. Explores Shakespeare's creative play with the words "bear" and "bear away" in a play in which a bear appears on stage and is often associated with the tyrannous King Leontes.

Mowat, Barbara A. "Rogues, Shepherds, and the Counterfeit Distressed: Texts and Infracontexts of *The Winter's Tale* 4.3." *Shakespeare Studies* 22 (1994): 58–76. Examines the cultural contexts that help make sense of the figure of Autolycus, rogue and con man, in *The Winter's Tale*.

Newcomb, Lori H. "'If That Which Is Lost Be Not Found': Monumental Bodies, Spectacular Bodies in *The Winter's Tale*." *Ovid and the Renaissance Body.* Ed. Goran V. Stanivukovic. Toronto: University of Toronto Press, 2001. Analyzes the tension between the monumental (stasis and constraint) and the spectacular (metamorphosis and performative freedom) in both the text of *The Winter's Tale* and in its material history as book and as theater piece.

O'Connor, Marion. "'Imagine Me, Gentle Spectators': Iconomachy and *The Winter's Tale*." *A Companion to Shakespeare's Works. IV: The Poems, Problem Comedies, Late Plays.* Ed. Richard Dutton and Jean E. Howard. Malden, Mass.: Blackwell, 2003. 365–88. Discusses the Renaissance theological debate about the value and truth of images as it bears on a number of early modern plays, including *The Winter's Tale*, in which statues are staged. Argues that Shakespeare insists on the collaboration of word and image, eschewing a total embrace of Reformation logocentrism or Catholic image-worship.

Paster, Gail Kern. "Quarreling with the Dug, or 'I Am Glad You Did Not Nurse Him'." *The Body Embarrassed: Drama and the Disciplines of Shame in Early Modern England.* Ithaca, N.Y.: Cornell University Press, 1993. 215–80. Sets *The Winter's Tale* in an array of Shakespearean texts that anxiously explore early modern cultural practices surrounding reproduction and infant care, especially the practice of wet-nursing.

Wilson, Richard. "The Statue of Our Queen: Shakespeare's Open Secret." *Secret Shakespeare: Studies in Theatre, Religion and Resistance.* Manchester: Manchester University Press, 2004. 246–70. Argues for *The Winter's Tale*'s connection to recusant culture, especially the play's emphasis on the importance of secret spaces dominated by women.

FILM

The Winter's Tale. 1999. Dir. Robin Lough. UK. 170 min. A dark and moving Royal Shakespeare Company production with Anthony Sher as a Leontes truly made mad by jealousy and an impressively dignified Alexandra Gilbreath as Hermione. Imaginative staging of the bear and riveting statue scene as Hermione very slowly comes to life.

The Winter's Tale

THE PERSONS OF THE PLAY

LEONTES, King of Sicilia
HERMIONE, his wife
MAMILLIUS, his son
PERDITA, his daughter
CAMILLO
ANTIGONUS
CLEOMENES } Lords at Leontes' court
DION
PAULINA, Antigonus's wife
EMILIA, a lady attending on Hermione
A JAILER
A MARINER
Other Lords and Gentlemen, Ladies, Officers, and Servants at
     Leontes' court
POLIXENES, King of Bohemia
FLORIZEL, his son, in love with Perdita; known as Doricles
ARCHIDAMUS, a Bohemian lord
AUTOLYCUS, a rogue, once in the service of Florizel
OLD SHEPHERD
CLOWN, his son
MOPSA
DORCAS } shepherdesses
SERVANT of the Old Shepherd
Other Shepherds and Shepherdesses
Twelve countrymen disguised as satyrs
TIME, as chorus

1.1

Enter CAMILLO *and* ARCHIDAMUS

ARCHIDAMUS If you shall chance, Camillo, to visit Bohemia on
the like occasion whereon my services are now on foot,[1] you
shall see, as I have said, great difference betwixt our Bohemia
and your Sicilia.

5   CAMILLO I think this coming summer the King of Sicilia means
to pay Bohemia the visitation which he justly owes him.
ARCHIDAMUS Wherein our entertainment shall shame us, we
will be justified in our loves;[2] for indeed—
CAMILLO Beseech you—
10   ARCHIDAMUS Verily, I speak it in the freedom of my knowledge.
We cannot with such magnificence—in so rare— I know not
what to say.—We will give you sleepy drinks,° that your senses, *drinks to make you drowsy*
unintelligent of our insufficience,[3] may, though they cannot
praise us, as little accuse us.
15   CAMILLO You pay a great deal too dear for what's given freely.

1.1 Location: Sicilia. The palace of Leontes.
1. On an occasion similar to the one in which I am now
engaged (that is, as attendant lord to a visiting King).
2. Insofar as our less elaborate hospitality will put us to
shame, we will compensate by (the depth of) our love.
3. Unaware of our inadequacy.

ARCHIDAMUS Believe me, I speak as my understanding instructs
me, and as mine honesty puts it to utterance.

CAMILLO Sicilia cannot show himself over-kind to Bohemia.
They were trained together in their childhoods, and there
20 rooted betwixt them then such an affection which cannot
choose but branch⁴ now. Since their more mature dignities
and royal necessities made separation of their society,° their   *forced them apart*
encounters—though not personal— hath been royally attor-
neyed⁵ with interchange of gifts, letters, loving embassies, that°   *so that*
25 they have seemed to be together, though absent; shook hands
as over a vast;° and embraced as it were from the ends of   *wide expanse*
opposed winds.⁶ The heavens continue their loves.

ARCHIDAMUS I think there is not in the world either malice or
matter to alter it. You have an unspeakable° comfort of° your   *inexpressible / in*
30 young prince, Mamillius. It° is a gentleman of the greatest   *(He)*
promise that ever came into my note.

CAMILLO I very well agree with you in the hopes of him. It is a
gallant child; one that, indeed, physics the subject,⁷ makes old
hearts fresh. They that went on crutches ere he was born desire
35 yet their life° to see him a man.   *hope to live long enough*

ARCHIDAMUS Would they else be content to die?

CAMILLO Yes—if there were no other excuse why they should
desire to live.

ARCHIDAMUS If the King had no son they would desire to live on
40 crutches till he had one.   *Exeunt*

1.2

Enter LEONTES, HERMIONE, MAMILLIUS, POLIXENES, *and*
CAMILLO¹

POLIXENES Nine changes of the wat'ry star hath been
The shepherd's note² since we³ have left our throne
Without a burden.° Time as long again   *an occupant*
Would be filled up, my brother, with our thanks,
5 And yet we should for perpetuity
Go hence in debt.⁴ And therefore, like a cipher,
Yet standing in rich place,⁵ I multiply
With one 'We thank you' many thousands more
That go before it.

LEONTES   Stay° your thanks a while,   *Postpone*
And pay them when you part.

10 POLIXENES   Sir, that's tomorrow.
I am questioned by my fears° of what may chance⁶   *I am afraid*
Or breed upon° our absence, that may blow   *develop because of*
No sneaping winds at home to make us say

---

4. Flourish and spread (as a tree does when it puts
forth branches); divide.
5. Performed by deputies.
6. From opposite ends of the earth. Early modern
atlases often showed the four "corners" of the earth as
the source of the winds.
7. Restores the health of the King's subjects.
1.2 Location: Sicilia. The palace of Leontes.
1. Though listed in the stage direction in F, Camillo has
no part in this scene until line 210, when Leontes says,
"What, Camillo there!" Camillo may be a silent observer

for the first 210 lines, or, as some editors believe, his first
entrance may be marked by Leontes' exclamation.
2. The shepherd has observed nine changes of the
moon (that is, nine months). The moon is "the wat'ry
star" because it governs the tides.
3. Both Kings employ the royal "we," speaking of them-
selves in the plural.
4. And even then we would depart forever in your debt.
5. Like a zero ("cipher"), which is worthless in itself,
but valuable when it follows another number.
6. Happen by chance.

'This is put forth too truly.'[7] Besides, I have stayed
To tire your royalty.

15 LEONTES   We are tougher, brother,
Than you can put us to't.[8]

POLIXENES   No longer stay.

LEONTES   One sennight° longer.   *week*

POLIXENES   Very sooth,° tomorrow.   *In truth (a mild oath)*

LEONTES   We'll part the time° between's, then; and in that   *split the difffference*
I'll no gainsaying.°   *allow no contradiction*

POLIXENES   Press me not, beseech you, so.

20 There is no tongue that moves, none, none i'th' world
So soon as yours, could win me. So it should now,
Were there necessity in your request, although
'Twere needful I denied it. My affairs
Do even drag me homeward; which to hinder
25 Were, in your love, a whip to me;[9] my stay
To you a charge and trouble. To save both,
Farewell, our brother.

LEONTES   Tongue-tied, our queen? Speak you.

HERMIONE   I had thought, sir, to have held my peace until
You had drawn oaths from him not to stay. You, sir,
30 Charge him too coldly. Tell him you are sure
All in Bohemia's well. This satisfaction
The bygone day proclaimed.[1] Say this to him,
He's beat from his best ward.[2]

LEONTES   Well said, Hermione!

HERMIONE   To tell° he longs to see his son were strong.   *assert*
35 But let him say so then, and let him go.
But let him swear so and he shall not stay,
We'll thwack him hence with distaffs.[3]
[*To* POLIXENES] Yet of your royal presence I'll adventure°   *risk*
The borrow° of a week. When at Bohemia   *loan*
40 You take my lord, I'll give him my commission°   *permission*
To let him there a month behind the gest
Prefixed for's parting.[4]—Yet, good deed,° Leontes,   *indeed*
I love thee not a jar° o'th' clock behind   *tick*
What lady she her lord.[5]—You'll stay?

POLIXENES   No, madam.

45 HERMIONE   Nay, but you will?

POLIXENES   I may not, verily.

HERMIONE   Verily?
You put me off with limber° vows. But I,   *weak*
Though you would seek t'unsphere the stars[6] with oaths,
50 Should yet say 'Sir, no going.' Verily
You shall not go. A lady's 'verily''s
As potent as a lord's. Will you go yet?

---

7. *"that may . . . too truly,":* an obscure passage. Fearing
the worst, Polixenes hopes that no biting ("sneaping")
winds may blow (that is, no envious forces be active) at
home to make him conclude that his worries were jus-
tified.
8. Than any test you put us to.
9. That is, "To hinder me from going home, though lov-
ingly done, would be a punishment ('whip') to me."
1. This good news was announced yesterday.
2. He's forced to relinquish his strongest position. A

fencing metaphor.
3. Wooden sticks, usually about 3 feet long, which
were used in spinning wool. Proverbially, they were
female tools and symbols of female authority.
4. To remain there a month longer than the time
("gest") appointed in advance for his departure.
5. That is, "I love you no less than any noblewoman
loves her husband."
6. To disorder the cosmos. Alluding to the idea that the
stars move in fixed orbits around the earth.

Force me to keep you as a prisoner,
Not like a guest: so you shall pay your fees
55 When you depart,[7] and save your thanks. How say you?
My prisoner? or my guest? By your dread 'verily',
One of them you shall be.

POLIXENES   Your guest then, madam.
To be your prisoner should import offending,°   *mean I have offended you*
Which is for me less easy to commit
Than you to punish.

60 HERMIONE   Not your jailer then,
But your kind hostess. Come, I'll question you
Of my lord's tricks and yours when you were boys.
You were pretty lordings° then?   *young lords*

POLIXENES   We were, fair Queen,
Two lads that thought there was no more behind°   *(in the future)*
65 But such a day tomorrow as today,
And to be boy eternal.

HERMIONE   Was not my lord
The verier wag° o'th' two?   *greater mischief-maker*

POLIXENES   We were as twinned° lambs that did frisk i'th' sun,   *identical*
70 And bleat the one at th'other. What we changed°   *exchanged*
Was innocence for innocence. We knew not
The doctrine of ill-doing, nor dreamed
That any did. Had we pursued that life,
And our weak spirits ne'er been higher reared
75 With stronger blood,° we should have answered heaven   *With more mature passions*
Boldly, 'Not guilty', the imposition cleared
Hereditary ours.[8]

HERMIONE   By this we gather
You have tripped° since.   *sinned*

POLIXENES   O my most sacred lady,
Temptations have since then been born to's; for
80 In those unfledged[9] days was my wife a girl.
Your precious self had then not crossed the eyes
Of my young playfellow.

HERMIONE   Grace to boot!°   *Heaven help me!*
Of this make no conclusion,[1] lest you say
Your queen and I are devils. Yet go on.
85 Th'offences we have made you do we'll answer,°   *answer for*
If you first sinned with us, and that with us
You did continue fault, and that you slipped not
With any but with us.

LEONTES   Is he won yet?

HERMIONE   He'll stay, my lord.

LEONTES   At my request he would not.
90 Hermione, my dearest, thou never spok'st
To better purpose.

HERMIONE   Never?

LEONTES   Never but once.

HERMIONE   What, have I twice said well? When was't before?

---

7. In early modern England, prisoners were required to pay fees to jailers both for provisions and upon their release.
8. Freed even of the charge of original sin. The doctrine of original sin held that everyone at birth was tainted by sin because the first humans, Adam and Eve, disobeyed God in the Garden of Eden. Here original sin is linked to the sexual desires that come with maturity.
9. Youthful. An unfledged, or young, bird is one as yet lacking the feathers necessary for flight.
1. Do not follow out this line of reasoning.

I prithee tell me. Cram's° with praise, and make's   *Stuff us; overfeed us*
As fat as tame things. One good deed dying tongueless
95   Slaughters a thousand waiting upon that.[2]
Our praises are our wages. You may ride's
With one soft kiss a thousand furlongs ere
With spur we heat° an acre.[3] But to th' goal.°   *race over / purpose*
My last good deed was to entreat his stay.
100   What was my first? It has an elder sister,
Or I mistake you. O, would her name were Grace![4]
But once before I spoke to th' purpose? When?
Nay, let me have't. I long.

LEONTES   Why, that was when
Three crabbèd° months had soured themselves to death   *bitter*
105   Ere I could make thee open thy white hand
And clap° thyself my love. Then didst thou utter,   *pledge*
'I am yours for ever.'

HERMIONE   'Tis grace indeed.
Why lo you now; I have spoke to th' purpose twice.
The one for ever earned a royal husband;
Th'other, for some while a friend.[5]

[*She gives her hand to* POLIXENES.[6]
They stand aside]

110 LEONTES [*aside*]   Too hot, too hot:
To mingle friendship farre is mingling bloods.[7]
I have *tremor cordis*[8] on me. My heart dances,
But not for joy, not joy. This entertainment°   *hospitality*
May a free° face put on, derive a liberty   *innocent*
115   From heartiness, from bounty, fertile bosom,°   *generous affection*
And well become the agent.[9] 'T may, I grant.
But to be paddling° palms and pinching fingers,[1]   *caressing*
As now they are, and making practised smiles
As in a looking-glass; and then to sigh, as 'twere
120   The mort o'th' deer[2]—O, that is entertainment
My bosom likes not, nor my brows.[3]—Mamillius,
Art thou my boy?

MAMILLIUS   Ay, my good lord.

LEONTES   I'fecks,°   *In faith (a mild oath)*
Why, that's my bawcock.° What? Hast smutched° thy nose?   *fine fellow / dirtied*
They say it is a copy out of mine. Come, captain,
125   We must be neat—not neat,[4] but cleanly, captain.
And yet the steer, the heifer, and the calf

---

2. If one virtuous act goes unremarked, then the thousand more that might have been inspired by it will not come to be.
3. That is, "You'll go much farther with us if you will treat us kindly," with a pun on "ride" as meaning "enjoy us sexually."
4. Would that my first good act were virtuous (full of God's Grace). Hermione may be countering Polixenes' earlier suggestion that she first caused Leontes to sin. With a possible allusion to the Three Graces (Aglaia, Euphrosyne, and Thalia) of classical mythology. Usually depicted nude and dancing in a circle, the three women represented the epitome of earthly beauty and harmony.
5. "Friend" could also mean "lover," a meaning that Leontes takes up in his next speech.
6. It is not certain when Hermione and Polixenes join hands, but by line 117 Leontes remarks that they are

"paddling palms and pinching fingers." Joined hands—or hands separated from one another—are an important and recurring visual motif in the play, culminating at 5.3.107, when Paulina commands Leontes to "present your hand" to Hermione as she ceases to appear a statue.
7. Uniting in passion; having sexual intercourse.
8. A malady marked by an erratic heart rate.
9. And makes the actor of these deeds (Hermione) appear attractive.
1. Early modern texts often represent hands as erotic body parts. Moist palms were believed to be signs of sexual arousal; finger games may suggest sexual penetration.
2. To sigh as loudly as the horn blast that proclaims the death of a hunted deer.
3. Alluding to the proverbial notion that a cuckold sprouted horns from his brow.
4. Punning on neat as meaning both "clean" and "cattle with horns."

Are all called neat.—Still virginalling
Upon his palm?[5]—How now, you wanton° calf— — *playful*
Art thou my calf?

MAMILLIUS   Yes, if you will, my lord.

130 LEONTES Thou want'st a rough pash° and the shoots° that I have, — *shaggy head / horns*
To be full° like me. Yet they say we are — *entirely; fully*
Almost as like as eggs. Women say so,
That will say anything. But were they false
As o'er-dyed blacks,[6] as wind, as waters, false

135 As dice are to be wished by one that fixes
No bourn° 'twixt his and mine, yet were it true — *boundary; limit*
To say this boy were like me. Come, sir page,
Look on me with your welkin° eye. Sweet villain, — *sky blue*
Most dear'st, my collop![7] Can thy dam°—may't be?— — *mother*

140 Affection, thy intention stabs the centre.[8]
Thou dost make possible things not so held,° — *things held as impossible*
Communicat'st with dreams—how can this be?—
With what's unreal thou coactive art,° — *you collaborate*
And fellow'st° nothing. Then 'tis very credent° — *are companion to / believable*

145 Thou mayst co-join with something, and thou dost—
And that beyond commission;° and I find it— — *what is permitted*
And that to the infection of my brains
And hard'ning of my brows.° — *(with cuckold's horns)*

POLIXENES   What means Sicilia?

HERMIONE He something seems° unsettled. — *seems somewhat*

POLIXENES   How, my lord!

LEONTES What cheer? How is't with you, best brother?

150 HERMIONE   You look
As if you held a brow of much distraction.
Are you moved,° my lord? — *angry*

LEONTES   No, in good earnest.
How sometimes nature will betray its folly,
Its tenderness, and make itself a pastime° — *source of amusement*

155 To harder bosoms! Looking on the lines
Of my boy's face, methoughts I did recoil° — *go back*
Twenty-three years, and saw myself unbreeched,[9]
In my green velvet coat; my dagger muzzled,° — *in its sheath; blunted*
Lest it should bite its master, and so prove,

160 As ornament oft does, too dangerous.
How like, methought, I then was to this kernel,
This squash,° this gentleman.—Mine honest friend, — *unripe peapod*
Will you take eggs for money?[1]

MAMILLIUS   No, my lord, I'll fight.

LEONTES You will? Why, happy man be's dole![2]—My brother,

---

5. Still caressing his hand as if playing the virginal, a legless keyboard instrument played on the lap; still acting chastely (like a virgin).
6. Referring to textiles dyed black. Such black cloth was made "false" or weakened by the harsh chemicals in the dye. With a possible reference to Africans, whose dark skin was said to result from overexposure to the sun. It was a commonplace that Africans were prone to licentiousness and were thus sexually "false."
7. That is, "my own flesh." A "collop" is a portion of meat.
8. Passion (probably the passion of jealousy), your

intensity ("intention") pierces my heart or to the core of my being.
9. Not yet old enough to wear men's clothing ("breeches"). Before about the age of six, both girls and boys in early modern England wore a dresslike garment. Giving a boy breeches was a sign of his passage out of childhood and out of the care of women into the world of men.
1. A proverbial expression meaning "Will you accept a trifle in place of something valuable?"
2. Proverbial for "May you have good luck!"

165 Are you so fond of your young prince as we
Do seem to be of ours?

POLIXENES   If at home, sir,
He's all my exercise, my mirth, my matter;°   concern
Now my sworn friend, and then mine enemy;
My parasite, my soldier, statesman, all.
170 He makes a July's day short as December,
And with his varying childness° cures in me   youthful ways
Thoughts that would thick my blood.³

LEONTES   So stands this squire
Officed with me.⁴ We two will walk, my lord,
And leave you to your graver steps. Hermione,
175 How thou lov'st us show in our brother's welcome.
Let what is dear in Sicily be cheap.
Next to thyself and my young rover, he's
Apparent° to my heart.   Heir apparent

HERMIONE   If you would seek us,
We are yours i'th' garden. Shall's attend you there?
180 LEONTES   To your own bents° dispose you. You'll be found,   inclinations
Be you beneath the sky. [Aside] I am angling° now,   fishing; scheming
Though you perceive me not how I give line.
Go to, go to!
How she holds up the neb, the bill to him,⁵
185 And arms her° with the boldness of a wife   herself
To her allowing° husband!   approving

[Exeunt POLIXENES and HERMIONE]
Gone already.
Inch-thick, knee-deep, o'er head and ears a forked° one!—   horned
Go play, boy, play. Thy mother plays,° and I   dallies sexually
Play° too; but so disgraced a part, whose issue⁶   Play a role
190 Will hiss me to my grave. Contempt and clamour
Will be my knell. Go play, boy, play. There have been,
Or I am much deceived, cuckolds ere now,
And many a man there is, even at this present,
Now, while I speak this, holds his wife by th'arm,
195 That little thinks she has been sluiced⁷ in's absence,
And his pond⁸ fished by his next neighbour, by
Sir Smile, his neighbour.⁹ Nay, there's comfort in't,
Whiles other men have gates,¹ and those gates opened,
As mine, against their will. Should all despair
200 That have revolted° wives, the tenth of mankind   rebellious; unfaithful
Would hang themselves. Physic° for't there's none.   Medicine
It is a bawdy planet, that will strike
Where 'tis predominant;² and 'tis powerful. Think it:

3. Ideas that would make me melancholy, a physical and emotional malady connected with a supposed excess of "thick blood."
4. So this young man performs the same duty for me.
5. How she holds up her face, her mouth to him (to be kissed).
6. Outcome, with puns on "issue" as also meaning "offspring" and "the exit an actor makes from a stage." Leontes' words imply that in playing the part of a cuckold, the result of his role will be disgrace; the illegitimate offspring produced by his wife will bring him disgrace; and his exit from the stage (at death) will be a disgraceful one.
7. Little thinks she has had sexual relations. A sluice

was a trough or channel through which water could be directed. To be sluiced was to have water poured down one's "channel," here probably referring to the vagina where sperm entered.
8. Slang term for the sexual organs of his wife.
9. It is possible that "Sir Smile" is a reference to Polixenes, who may be laughing or smiling in his conversation with Hermione.
1. Another slang term for female genitalia. Leontes imagines the vulva as a gateway that ought to be entered only by a husband.
2. Alluding to the notion that planets control human actions and may exercise malign influences ("strike") when they are in certain "predominant" positions.

From east, west, north, and south, be it concluded,
205 No barricado for a belly.³ Know't,
It will let in and out the enemy
With bag and baggage.⁴ Many thousand on's°   *of us*
Have the disease and feel't not.—How now, boy?

MAMILLIUS   I am like you, they say.

LEONTES   Why, that's some comfort.
What, Camillo there!

210 CAMILLO [*coming forward*]   Ay, my good lord.

LEONTES   Go play, Mamillius, thou'rt an honest man.

[*Exit* MAMILLIUS]

Camillo, this great sir will yet stay longer.

CAMILLO   You had much ado to make his anchor hold.
When you cast out, it still came home.°   *always failed to hold*

LEONTES   Didst note it?

215 CAMILLO   He would not stay at your petitions, made
His business more material.°   *important*

LEONTES   Didst perceive it?
[*Aside*] They're here with me⁵ already, whisp'ring, rounding,°   *murmuring*
'Sicilia is a so-forth'. 'Tis far gone
When I shall gust° it last.—How came't, Camillo,   *perceive; taste*
That he did stay?

220 CAMILLO   At the good Queen's entreaty.

LEONTES   'At the Queen's' be't. 'Good' should be pertinent,
But so° it is, it is not. Was this taken°   *as / perceived*
By any understanding pate but thine?
For thy conceit is soaking,° will draw in   *your wit is quick*
225 More than the common blocks.° Not noted, is't,   *dimwits*
But of° the finer natures? By some severals°   *by / individuals*
Of head-piece° extraordinary? Lower messes⁶   *intellect*
Perchance are to this business purblind?° Say.   *blind*

CAMILLO   Business, my lord? I think most understand
230 Bohemia stays here longer.

LEONTES   Ha?

CAMILLO   Stays here longer.

LEONTES   Ay, but why?

CAMILLO   To satisfy your highness, and the entreaties
Of our most gracious mistress.

235 LEONTES   Satisfy?⁷
Th'entreaties of your mistress? Satisfy?
Let that suffice. I have trusted thee, Camillo,
With all the near'st things to my heart, as well
My chamber-counsels,° wherein, priest-like, thou   *secret matters*
240 Hast cleansed my bosom, I from thee departed
Thy penitent reformed. But we have been
Deceived in thy integrity, deceived
In that which seems so.

CAMILLO   Be it forbid, my lord.

LEONTES   To bide° upon't: thou art not honest; or   *dwell*
245 If thou inclin'st that way, thou art a coward,

---

3. No means of defending a womb.
4. With full military (or sexual) equipment.
5. They know my secret.
6. Those of lower social status at the dining table. A

"mess" refers to a group of four people who share meals together.
7. Punning on "satisfy" as meaning both "appease" and "give sexual pleasure to."

Which hoxes honesty behind,[8] restraining
From course required.[9] Or else thou must be counted
A servant grafted in my serious trust[1]
And therein negligent, or else a fool
250 That seest a game played home,° the rich stake drawn,°   *in earnest / won*
And tak'st it all for jest.
CAMILLO   My gracious lord,
I may be negligent, foolish, and fearful.
In every one of these no man is free,°   *guiltless*
But that his negligence, his folly, fear,
255 Among the infinite doings of the world
Sometime puts forth.° In your affairs, my lord,   *reveals itself*
If ever I were wilful-negligent,
It was my folly. If industriously°   *deliberately*
I played the fool, it was my negligence,
260 Not weighing well the end. If ever fearful
To do a thing where I the issue° doubted,   *outcome*
Whereof the execution did cry out
Against the non-performance,[2] 'twas a fear
Which oft infects the wisest. These, my lord,
265 Are such allowed infirmities that honesty
Is never free of. But beseech your grace
Be plainer with me, let me know my trespass
By its own visage. If I then deny it,
'Tis none of mine.
LEONTES   Ha' not you seen, Camillo—
270 But that's past doubt; you have, or your eye-glass°   *the lens of your eye*
Is thicker than a cuckold's horn—or heard—
For, to a vision° so apparent, rumour   *sight*
Cannot be mute—or thought—for cogitation
Resides not in that man that does not think—
275 My wife is slippery? If thou wilt confess—
Or else be impudently negative°   *shamelessly deny*
To have nor eyes, nor ears, nor thought—then say
My wife's a hobby-horse,[3] deserves a name
As rank° as any flax-wench[4] that puts to°   *indecent / has sexual relations*
280 Before her troth-plight.° Say't, and justify't.   *betrothal*
CAMILLO   I would not be a stander-by to hear
My sovereign mistress clouded so without
My present° vengeance taken. 'Shrew° my heart,   *immediate / Curse*
You never spoke what did become you less
285 Than this, which to reiterate° were sin   *repeat*
As deep as that, though true.[5]
LEONTES   Is whispering nothing?
Is leaning cheek to cheek? Is meeting noses?
Kissing with inside lip? Stopping the career°   *full gallop*
Of laughter with a sigh?—a note° infallible   *sign*

8. Which ensures that frankness is shackled.
9. Keeping (honesty) from the path it must take (to find out truth).
1. A servant who has grown into my confidence as a cutting is grafted onto a plant.
2. Even when the need to do the deed protested against its nonperformance.
3. Whore. The image is of a woman, who, like a horse,

can be mounted. F has "Holy-Horse," an obscure phrase nearly all modern editors emend to "hobby-horse."
4. A girl or woman, usually of low social status, who worked with flax, a fibrous plant used to make candlewicks, clothing, and linen.
5. That is, "As grave as is the sin that you accuse your wife of, even if it were true (which it is not)."

290   Of breaking honesty.° Horsing foot on foot?[6]   *violating chastity*
        Skulking in corners? Wishing clocks more swift,
        Hours minutes, noon midnight? And all eyes
        Blind with the pin and web° but theirs, theirs only,   *cataract disease*
        That would unseen be wicked? Is this nothing?
295   Why then the world and all that's in't is nothing,
        The covering sky is nothing, Bohemia nothing,
        My wife is nothing, nor nothing have these nothings[7]
        If this be nothing.
        CAMILLO   Good my lord, be cured
        Of this diseased opinion, and betimes,°   *quickly*
        For 'tis most dangerous.
300   LEONTES   Say it be, 'tis true.
        CAMILLO   No, no, my lord.
        LEONTES   It is. You lie, you lie.
        I say thou liest, Camillo, and I hate thee,
        Pronounce thee a gross lout, a mindless slave,
        Or else a hovering° temporizer, that   *irresolute*
305   Canst with thine eyes at once see good and evil,
        Inclining to them both. Were my wife's liver
        Infected as her life, she would not live
        The running of one glass.°   *hourglass*
        CAMILLO   Who does infect her?
        LEONTES   Why, he that wears her like her medal,[8] hanging
310   About his neck, Bohemia, who, if I
        Had servants true about me, that bare° eyes   *possessed*
        To see alike mine honour as their profits,
        Their own particular thrifts,° they would do that   *personal gain*
        Which should undo° more doing.° Ay, and thou   *stop / sexual acts*
315   His cupbearer,[9] whom I from meaner form°   *lower rank or place*
        Have benched, and reared to worship,[1] who mayst see
        Plainly as heaven sees earth and earth sees heaven,
        How I am galled,° mightst bespice a cup   *sorely vexed*
        To give mine enemy a lasting wink,[2]
        Which draught to me were cordial.[3]
320   CAMILLO   Sir, my lord,
        I could do this, and that with no rash° potion,   *quick-acting*
        But with a ling'ring° dram, that should not work   *slow-working*
        Maliciously,° like poison. But I cannot   *Violently*
        Believe this crack° to be in my dread mistress,   *flaw*
325   So sovereignly being honourable.
        I have loved thee—
        LEONTES   Make that thy question,° and go rot!   *concern*
        Dost think I am so muddy, so unsettled,
        To appoint° myself in this vexation?   *put*
        Sully the purity and whiteness of my sheets—
330   Which to preserve is sleep, which being spotted
        Is goads, thorns, nettles, tails of wasps—

---

6. Mounting or rubbing one foot on another. A sexually titillating pastime.
7. Alluding to the proverbial notion that nothing can come of nothing.
8. As though she were a miniature portrait of herself. Ornate lockets containing miniature portraits were popular love tokens among courtiers.
9. In a noble household a male servant whose respon-sibilities included serving wine to his master.
1. Given authority and elevated to a dignified position. Referring to his "bench" or place at the dining table as a sign of his high rank.
2. To close my enemy's eyes forever.
3. Which drink would be medicinal to me; which drink would cure my heartsickness (perhaps the *"tremor cordis"* to which Leontes referred at 1.2.112).

Give scandal to the blood o'th' prince, my son—
Who I do think is mine, and love as mine—
Without ripe moving° to't? Would I do this?   *good reason*
Could man so blench?°   *stray (from sense)*

335 CAMILLO   I must believe you, sir.
I do, and will fetch off° Bohemia for't,   *kill; rescue*
Provided that when he's removed your highness
Will take again your queen as yours at first,
Even for your son's sake, and thereby for sealing°   *silencing*
340 The injury of tongues in courts and kingdoms
Known and allied to yours.

LEONTES   Thou dost advise me
Even so as I mine own course have set down.
I'll give no blemish to her honour, none.

CAMILLO   My lord, go then, and with a countenance as clear
345 As friendship wears at feasts, keep° with Bohemia   *associate*
And with your queen. I am his cupbearer.
If from me he have wholesome beverage,
Account me not your servant.

LEONTES   This is all.
Do't, and thou hast the one half of my heart;
Do't not, thou splitt'st thine own.

350 CAMILLO   I'll do't, my lord.

LEONTES   I will seem friendly, as thou hast advised me.   *Exit*

CAMILLO   O miserable lady. But for me,
What case stand I in? I must be the poisoner
Of good Polixenes, and my ground to do't
355 Is the obedience to a master—one
Who in rebellion with himself, will have
All that are his so too. To do this deed,
Promotion follows. If I could find example
Of thousands that had struck anointed kings
360 And flourished after, I'd not do't. But since
Nor° brass, nor stone, nor parchment⁴ bears not one,   *Neither*
Let villainy itself forswear't.° I must   *swear not to do it*
Forsake the court. To do't, or no, is certain
To me a break-neck.°   *(death)*

Enter POLIXENES

                    Happy° star reign now!   *Lucky*
Here comes Bohemia.

365 POLIXENES [*aside*]   This is strange. Methinks
My favour here begins to warp. Not speak?—
Good day, Camillo.

CAMILLO   Hail, most royal sir.

POLIXENES   What is the news i'th' court?

CAMILLO   None rare,° my lord.   *noteworthy*

POLIXENES   The King hath on him such a countenance
370 As° he had lost some province, and a region   *As if*
Loved as he loves himself. Even now I met him
With customary compliment, when he,
Wafting his eyes to th' contrary,° and falling   *Shifting his gaze away*
A lip of much contempt,° speeds from me, and   *sneering*

---

4. That is, since no form of historical record (brass monuments, stone markers, or paper manuscripts) shows an
example of a man who flourished after killing a King.

375	So leaves me to consider what is breeding	
	That changes thus his manners.	
	CAMILLO I dare not know, my lord.	
	POLIXENES How, 'dare not'? Do not? Do you know, and dare not?	
	Be intelligent° to me. 'Tis thereabouts.[5]	*informative*
	For to yourself what you do know you must,°	*(know)*
380	And cannot say you 'dare not'. Good Camillo,	
	Your changed complexions are to me a mirror	
	Which shows me mine changed, too; for I must be	
	A party in this alteration,° finding	*(of Leontes' manner)*
	Myself thus altered with't.	
	CAMILLO There is a sickness	
385	Which puts some of us in distemper, but	
	I cannot name th' disease, and it is caught	
	Of you that yet are well.	
	POLIXENES How caught of me?	
	Make me not sighted like the basilisk.[6]	
	I have looked on thousands who have sped° the better	*fared*
390	By my regard, but killed none so. Camillo,	
	As you are certainly a gentleman, thereto	
	Clerk-like experienced,[7] which no less adorns	
	Our gentry° than our parents' noble names,	*status as gentlemen*
	In whose success we are gentle:[8] I beseech you,	
395	If you know aught which does behove my knowledge	
	Thereof to be informed,[9] imprison't not	
	In ignorant concealment.[1]	
	CAMILLO I may not answer.	
	POLIXENES A sickness caught of me, and yet I well?	
	I must be answered. Dost thou hear, Camillo,	
400	I conjure thee, by all the parts° of man	*duties*
	Which honour does acknowledge, whereof the least	
	Is not this suit of mine, that thou declare	
	What incidency° thou dost guess of harm	*event*
	Is creeping toward me; how far off, how near,	
405	Which way to be prevented, if to be;	
	If not, how best to bear it.	
	CAMILLO Sir, I will tell you,	
	Since I am charged in honour, and by him	
	That I think honourable. Therefore mark my counsel,	
	Which must be e'en as swiftly followed as	
410	I mean to utter it; or both yourself and me	
	Cry lost, and so good night!°	*good-bye forever*
	POLIXENES On, good Camillo.	
	CAMILLO I am appointed him to murder you.	
	POLIXENES By whom, Camillo?	
	CAMILLO By the King.	
	POLIXENES For what?	
	CAMILLO He thinks, nay, with all confidence he swears	
415	As he had seen't, or been an instrument	
	To vice° you to't, that you have touched his queen	*force*
	Forbiddenly.	

---

5. That is, "I'm more or less right (that you are afraid to tell me)."
6. A mythical serpent whose glance was said to be fatal.
7. Also having the experience of an educated man.

8. By succession from whom we are made noble.
9. Which it is necessary for me to know.
1. In concealment that keeps me ignorant; in concealment on the pretense that you are ignorant.

POLIXENES   O, then my best blood turn
To an infected jelly, and my name
Be yoked with his° that did betray the Best!°   *(Judas's) name / Christ*
420   Turn then my freshest reputation to
A savour° that may strike the dullest nostril   *foul odor*
Where I arrive, and my approach be shunned,
Nay hated, too, worse than the great'st infection
That e'er was heard or read.
CAMILLO   Swear his thought over²
425   By each particular star in heaven, and
By all their influences,³ you may as well
Forbid the sea for to obey the moon
As or° by oath remove or counsel shake   *either*
The fabric of his folly, whose foundation
430   Is piled upon his faith, and will continue
The standing of his body.°   *As long as he lives*
POLIXENES   How should this grow?°   *come to be*
CAMILLO   I know not, but I am sure 'tis safer to
Avoid what's grown than question how 'tis born.
If therefore you dare trust my honesty,
435   That lies enclosèd in this trunk° which you   *body*
Shall bear along impawned,⁴ away tonight!
Your followers I will whisper to the business,
And will by twos and threes at several posterns°   *city gates*
Clear them o'th' city. For myself, I'll put
440   My fortunes to your service, which are here
By this discovery° lost. Be not uncertain,   *revelation*
For by the honour of my parents, I
Have uttered truth; which if you seek to prove,
I dare not stand by; nor shall you be safer
445   Than one condemnèd by the King's own mouth,
Thereon his execution sworn.
POLIXENES   I do believe thee,
I saw his heart in's face. Give me thy hand.
Be pilot to me, and thy places° shall   *your position*
Still neighbour° mine. My ships are ready, and   *Always be near*
450   My people did expect my hence departure
Two days ago. This jealousy
Is for a precious creature. As she's rare
Must it be great; and as his person's mighty
Must it be violent; and as he does conceive
455   He is dishonoured by a man which ever
Professed° to him, why, his revenges must   *Professed love*
In that be made more bitter. Fear o'ershades me.
Good expedition° be my friend and comfort   *Let speed (in leaving)*
The gracious Queen, part of his theme, but nothing
460   Of his ill-ta'en suspicion.⁵ Come, Camillo,
I will respect thee as a father if
Thou bear'st my life off hence. Let us avoid.°   *be gone*

---

2. You may swear that his allegations are false.
3. Substances that, according to contemporary astro-
logical theories, were emitted by stars and helped to
shape human destiny.

4. Shall carry with you as a pledge (of my faith).
5. And make easier the situation of the virtuous Queen,
who is a part of Leontes' accusation, but who is not
guilty of his unjustified suspicion.

CAMILLO   It is in mine authority to command
The keys of all the posterns. Please your highness
465   To take the urgent hour.° Come, sir, away.   *Exeunt*   seize the moment

2.1

Enter HERMIONE, MAMILLIUS, [*and*] LADIES

HERMIONE   Take the boy to you. He so troubles me
'Tis past enduring.
FIRST LADY   Come, my gracious lord,
Shall I be your play-fellow?
MAMILLIUS   No, I'll none of you.
5   FIRST LADY   Why, my sweet lord?
MAMILLIUS   You'll kiss me hard, and speak to me as if
I were a baby still. [*To* SECOND LADY] I love you better.
SECOND LADY   And why so, my lord?
MAMILLIUS   Not for because
Your brows° are blacker—yet black brows they say   eyebrows
10   Become some women best, so that there be not
Too much hair there, but in a semicircle,
Or a half-moon made with a pen.
SECOND LADY   Who taught° 'this?   taught you
MAMILLIUS   I learned it out of women's faces. Pray now,
What colour are your eyebrows?
FIRST LADY   Blue, my lord.
15   MAMILLIUS   Nay, that's a mock. I have seen a lady's nose
That has been blue,[1] but not her eyebrows.
FIRST LADY   Hark ye,
The Queen your mother rounds apace.° We shall   grows round quickly
Present our services to a fine new prince
One of these days, and then you'd wanton° with us,   play
If we would have you.
20   SECOND LADY   She is spread of late
Into a goodly bulk, good time encounter her.°   good fortune be with her
HERMIONE   What wisdom stirs amongst you? Come sir, now
I am for you again. Pray you sit by us,
And tell's a tale.
25   MAMILLIUS   Merry or sad shall't be?
HERMIONE   As merry as you will.
MAMILLIUS   A sad tale's best for winter. I have one
Of sprites and goblins.
HERMIONE   Let's have that, good sir.
Come on, sit down, come on, and do your best
30   To fright me with your sprites. You're powerful at it.
MAMILLIUS   There was a man—
HERMIONE   Nay, come sit down, then on.
MAMILLIUS [*sitting*]   Dwelt by a churchyard.—I will tell it softly,
Yon crickets° shall not hear it.   (the other women)
HERMIONE   Come on then, and give't me in mine ear.
[*Enter apart* LEONTES, ANTIGONUS, *and* LORDS][2]

2.1 Location: Sicilia. The palace of Leontes.
1. It is unclear whether Mamillius is making a joke here or possibly referring to noses made "blue" by the cold or disfigured by venereal disease.
2. As with many scenes in this play, Ralph Crane, the scrivener who probably prepared the manuscript for the printer, massed all the entrances for 2.1 in the initial stage direction, regardless of when individual characters actually appeared on stage. Though it is clear that Leontes, Antigonus, and the other Lords enter only at 2.1.34, in F no entrance is marked for them here, and their names are included in the direction preceding 2.1.1.

35   LEONTES   Was he met there? His train?° Camillo with him?   *retinue*
    A LORD   Behind the tuft of pines I met them. Never
      Saw I men scour° so on their way. I eyed them   *hurry*
      Even to their ships.
    LEONTES   How blest am I
      In my just censure,° in my true opinion!   *judgment*
40   Alack, for lesser knowledge°—how accursed   *Would I knew less*
      In being so blest! There may be in the cup
      A spider steeped, and one may drink, depart,
      And yet partake no venom, for his knowledge
      Is not infected;³ but if one present
45   Th'abhorred ingredient to his eye, make known
      How he hath drunk, he cracks his gorge,° his sides,   *throat*
      With violent hefts.° I have drunk, and seen the spider.   *retching*
      Camillo was his help in this, his pander.
      There is a plot against my life, my crown.
50   All's true that is mistrusted.° That false villain   *suspected*
      Whom I employed was pre-employed by him.
      He has discovered° my design, and I   *revealed*
      Remain a pinched° thing, yea, a very trick   *tormented*
      For them to play at will. How came the posterns
      So easily open?
55   A LORD   By his great authority,
      Which often hath no less prevailed than so
      On your command.
    LEONTES   I know't too well.
      [*To* HERMIONE] Give me the boy. I am glad you did not nurse him.⁴
      Though he does bear some signs of me, yet you
      Have too much blood in him.
60   HERMIONE   What is this? Sport?
    LEONTES [*to a* LORD]   Bear the boy hence. He shall not come about her.
      Away with him, and let her sport herself
      With that she's big with, [*to* HERMIONE] for 'tis Polixenes
      Has made thee swell thus.   [*Exit one with* MAMILLIUS]
    HERMIONE   But I'd say he had not,
65   And I'll be sworn you would believe my saying,
      Howe'er you lean to th' nayward.°   *the contrary*
    LEONTES   You, my lords,
      Look on her, mark her well. Be but about
      To say she is a goodly lady, and
      The justice of your hearts will thereto add
70   ''Tis pity she's not honest,° honourable.'   *chaste*
      Praise her but for this her without-door° form—   *external*
      Which on my faith deserves high speech—and straight°   *immediately*
      The shrug, the 'hum' or 'ha', these petty brands°   *expressions; stigmas*
      That calumny° doth use—O, I am out,°   *slander / wrong*
75   That mercy does, for calumny will sear°   *stigmatize*
      Virtue itself⁵—these shrugs, these 'hum's' and 'ha's',
      When you have said she's goodly, come between
      Ere you can say she's honest. But be't known

---

3. Alluding to the belief that a spider consumed with food or drink would be poisonous only if its presence were known to the consumer.
4. Women who breast-fed infants were believed to shape an infant's character by substances transmitted in their milk.

5. Leontes seems to mean that calumny (slander) will openly attack virtue, and since Hermione is not virtuous, it is not calumny to attack her. Rather, it is mercy who speaks in indirect "hum's" and "ha's" about her behavior.

From him that has most cause to grieve it should be,
She's an adultress.

80 HERMIONE   Should a villain say so,
The most replenished° villain in the world,   °complete
He were as much more° villain. You, my lord,   °by so much more a
Do but mistake.

LEONTES   You have mistook,° my lady—   °erred; improperly taken
Polixenes for Leontes. O, thou thing,
85 Which I'll not call a creature of thy place[6]
Lest barbarism,° making me the precedent,   °uncivilized rudeness
Should a like° language use to all degrees,°   °the same / all ranks
And mannerly distinguishment° leave out   °proper distinction
Betwixt the prince and beggar. I have said
90 She's an adultress, I have said with whom.
More, she's a traitor, and Camillo is
A federary° with her, and one that knows   °confederate
What she should shame to know herself,
But with her most vile principal:° that she's   °partner
95 A bed-swerver,° even as bad as those   °adultress
That vulgars give bold'st titles;[7] ay, and privy
To this their late° escape.   °recent

HERMIONE   No, by my life,
Privy to none of this. How will this grieve you
When you shall come to clearer knowledge, that
100 You thus have published° me? Gentle my° lord,   °proclaimed / My noble
You scarce can right me throughly° then to say   °fully do me justice
You did mistake.

LEONTES   No. If I mistake
In those foundations which I build upon,
The centre° is not big enough to bear   °earth
105 A schoolboy's top.—Away with her to prison!
He who shall speak for her is afar-off° guilty,   °indirectly
But that he speaks.°   °Merely for speaking

HERMIONE   There's some ill planet reigns.
I must be patient till the heavens look
With an aspect more favourable.[8] Good my° lords,   °My good
110 I am not prone to weeping, as our sex
Commonly are; the want of which vain dew
Perchance shall dry your pities. But I have
That honourable grief lodged here which burns
Worse than tears drown. Beseech you all, my lords,
115 With thoughts so qualified° as your charities   °tempered
Shall best instruct you, measure me; and so
The King's will be performed.

LEONTES   Shall I be heard?

HERMIONE   Who is't that goes with me? Beseech your highness
My women may be with me, for you see
120 My plight requires it.—Do not weep, good fools,°   °dear ones
There is no cause. When you shall know your mistress
Has deserved prison, then abound in tears
As I come out. This action I now go on

6. To whom I'll not give the title of your (high) social position.
7. That common people call by the coarsest names.

8. Another allusion to the belief that planets can have an evil effect or "aspect" when situated in certain positions.

Is for my better grace.[9]—Adieu, my lord.
125　　I never wished to see you sorry; now
　　　　I trust I shall. My women, come, you have leave.° 　　　　　　　*permission*

LEONTES　Go, do our bidding. Hence!

　　　　　[*Exit* HERMIONE, *guarded, with* LADIES]

A LORD　Beseech your highness, call the Queen again.

ANTIGONUS [*to Leontes*]　Be certain what you do, sir, lest your justice
130　　Prove violence, in the which three great ones suffer—
　　　　Yourself, your queen, your son.

A LORD [*to* LEONTES]　　　　　　　　For her, my lord,
　　　　I dare my life lay down, and will do't, sir,
　　　　Please you t'accept it, that the Queen is spotless
　　　　I'th' eyes of heaven and to you—I mean
　　　　In this which you accuse her.

ANTIGONUS [*to* LEONTES]　　　　　　If it prove
135
　　　　She's otherwise, I'll keep my stables where
　　　　I lodge my wife,[1] I'll go in couples with her;[2]
　　　　Than when I feel and see her, no farther trust her.
　　　　For every inch of woman in the world,
140　　Ay, every dram° of woman's flesh is false 　　　　　　　*smallest piece*
　　　　If she be.

LEONTES　　　Hold your peaces.

A LORD　　　　　　　　　　Good my lord—

ANTIGONUS [*to* LEONTES]　It is for you we speak, not for ourselves.
　　　　You are abused, and by some putter-on° 　　　　　　　*instigator*
　　　　That will be damned for't. Would I knew the villain—
145　　I would land-damn him.[3] Be she honour-flawed—
　　　　I have three daughters: the eldest is eleven;
　　　　The second and the third nine and some five;
　　　　If this prove true, they'll pay for't. By mine honour,
　　　　I'll geld 'em all.[4] Fourteen they shall not see,
150　　To bring false generations.° They are co-heirs, 　　　　*illegitimate children*
　　　　And I had rather glib° myself than they 　　　　　　　*castrate*
　　　　Should not produce fair issue.° 　　　　　　　　　　　*legitimate offspring*

LEONTES　　　　　　　　Cease, no more!
　　　　You smell this business with a sense as cold
　　　　As is a dead man's nose. But I do see't and feel't
155　　As you feel doing thus;[5] and see withal
　　　　The instruments that feel.[6]

ANTIGONUS　　　　　　　　If it be so,
　　　　We need no grave to bury honesty;° 　　　　　　　　　*chastity*
　　　　There's not a grain of it the face to sweeten° 　　　　*to sweeten the face*
　　　　Of the whole dungy° earth. 　　　　　　　　　　　　　*foul*

LEONTES　　　　　　　　What? Lack I credit?

160　A LORD　I had rather you did lack than I, my lord,
　　　　Upon this ground;° and more it would content me 　*In this affair*

---

9. This trial I am enduring is for my greater honor (when vindicated); *or* This suffering I am enduring is to refine and purge me, leading to greater virtue.
1. An obscure passage, meaning that he'll guard his wife's lodgings as vigilantly as he guards his horses *or* that he will treat his wife's lodgings as he does his stables, where mares are separated from stallions.
2. Have her tied to me (as hounds were leashed together for the hunt).
3. A term of abuse whose exact meaning is unclear. It

may be a dialect form of "lamback" or "lambaste," which means "thrash."
4. I'll make them all barren. Literally, I'll cut out their organs of generation.
5. Leontes here probably does some action (touching a courtier or rubbing his hands together) that shows the immediacy of his sensory reactions.
6. I see the fingers ("instruments") with which I touch things; I see the sinners, Hermione and Polixenes, who touch one another.

To have her honour true than your suspicion,
Be blamed for't how you might.

LEONTES   Why, what need we
Commune with you of this, but rather follow
165 Our forceful instigation?° Our prerogative   *Our own powerful impulse*
Calls not your counsels,[7] but our natural goodness
Imparts this;° which, if you—or° stupefied   *this information / either*
Or seeming so in skill°—cannot or will not   *cunningly*
Relish° a truth like us, inform yourselves   *Appreciate*
170 We need no more of your advice. The matter,
The loss, the gain, the ord'ring on't,° is all   *of it*
Properly ours.

ANTIGONUS   And I wish, my liege,
You had only in your silent judgement tried it
Without more overture.°   *public disclosure*

LEONTES   How could that be?
175 Either thou art most ignorant by age
Or thou wert born a fool. Camillo's flight
Added to their familiarity,
Which was as gross as ever touched conjecture
That lacked sight only, naught for approbation
180 But only seeing,[8] all other circumstances
Made up to th' deed°—doth push on this proceeding.[9]   *Pointed to the deed*
Yet for a greater confirmation—
For in an act of this importance 'twere
Most piteous to be wild°—I have dispatched in post°   *rash / haste*
185 To sacred Delphos,[1] to Apollo's temple,
Cleomenes and Dion, whom you know
Of stuffed sufficiency.° Now from the oracle   *ample competence*
They will bring all, whose spiritual counsel had°   *obtained*
Shall stop or spur me. Have I done well?

190 A LORD Well done, my lord.

LEONTES   Though I am satisfied, and need no more
Than what I know, yet shall the oracle
Give rest to th' minds of others such as he,
Whose ignorant credulity will not
195 Come up to th' truth. So have we thought it good
From our free° person she should be confined,   *openly accessible*
Lest that the treachery of the two fled hence
Be left her to perform. Come, follow us.
We are to speak in public; for this business
Will raise° us all.   *rouse (to action)*

200 ANTIGONUS [aside] To laughter, as I take it,
If the good truth were known.   *Exeunt*

2.2

Enter PAULINA, a Gentleman[, and attendants]

PAULINA The keeper of the prison, call to him.
Let him have knowledge who I am.   [*Exit Gentleman*]

---

7. My privileges as King do not require that I seek your
advice.
8. As obvious ("gross") as any suspicion ("conjecture")
ever was that only lacked eyewitnesses ("sight" and
"seeing") to confirm its truth.
9. Does urge on this course of action.

1. Delos, often called Delphos by Renaissance writers,
was the island where Apollo, the sun god, was suppos-
edly buried. It is here conflated with Delphi, the Greek
mainland town where the oracle of Apollo could be con-
sulted.
2.2 Location: Sicilia. A prison.

Good lady,
No court in Europe is too good for thee.
What dost thou then in prison?
                    [*Enter* JAILER *and Gentleman*]
                                          Now, good sir,
You know me, do you not?

5   JAILER   For a worthy lady,
And one who much I honour.

  PAULINA   Pray you then,
Conduct me to the Queen.

  JAILER   I may not, madam. To the contrary
I have express commandment.

10   PAULINA   Here's ado,°   *Here's such a fuss*
To lock up honesty and honour from
Th'access of gentle° visitors. Is't lawful, pray you,   *noble; kind*
To see her women? Any of them? Emilia?

  JAILER   So please you, madam,
15 To put apart these your attendants, I
Shall bring Emilia forth.

  PAULINA   I pray now call her.—
Withdraw yourselves.   [*Exeunt Gentleman and attendants*]

  JAILER   And, madam,
20 I must be present at your conference.

  PAULINA   Well, be't so, prithee.   [*Exit* JAILER]
Here's such ado, to make no stain a stain
As passes colouring.[1]
                    [*Enter* JAILER *and* EMILIA]
                              Dear gentlewoman,
How fares our gracious lady?

25   EMILIA   As well as one so great and so forlorn
May hold together. On° her frights and griefs,   *Because of*
Which never tender lady hath borne greater,
She is, something° before her time, delivered.   *somewhat*

  PAULINA   A boy?

  EMILIA   A daughter, and a goodly babe,
30 Lusty,° and like° to live. The Queen receives   *Vigorous / likely*
Much comfort in't; says, 'My poor prisoner,
I am innocent as you.'

  PAULINA   I dare be sworn.
These dangerous, unsafe lunes° i'th' King, beshrew them!   *fits of lunacy*
He must be told on't, and he shall. The office°   *job*
35 Becomes a woman best. I'll take't upon me.
If I prove honey-mouthed, let my tongue blister,[2]
And never to my red-looked° anger be   *red-faced*
The trumpet[3] any more. Pray you, Emilia,
Commend° my best obedience to the Queen.   *Send*
40 If she dares trust me with her little babe
I'll show't the King, and undertake to be
Her advocate to th' loud'st. We do not know
How he may soften at the sight o'th' child.

---

1. To make from no stain at all a stain that exceeds
what the art of dyeing can do; to make of no sin a sin
that surpasses all attempts to justify it.
2. Alluding to the proverb that deceitfulness causes
blisters on the tongue.

3. In early modern warfare, a "trumpet" was a soldier
who, bearing a trumpet, went before the red-coated
herald who carried messages, often angry ones, to the
enemy camp.

The silence often of pure innocence
Persuades when speaking fails.
45 EMILIA   Most worthy madam,
Your honour and your goodness is so evident
That your free° undertaking cannot miss   *generous*
A thriving issue.[4] There is no lady living
So meet° for this great errand. Please your ladyship   *suitable*
50 To visit the next room, I'll presently
Acquaint the Queen of your most noble offer,
Who but today hammered of° this design   *mused upon*
But durst not tempt a minister of honour[5]
Lest she should be denied.
PAULINA   Tell her, Emilia,
55 I'll use that tongue I have. If wit flow from't
As boldness from my bosom, let't not be doubted
I shall do good.
EMILIA   Now be you blest for it!
I'll to the Queen. Please you come something° nearer.   *somewhat*
JAILER   Madam, if't please the Queen to send the babe
60 I know not what° I shall incur to pass it,[6]   *what (risk)*
Having no warrant.
PAULINA   You need not fear it, sir.
This child was prisoner to the womb, and is
By law and process of great nature thence
Freed and enfranchised, not a party to
65 The anger of the King, nor guilty of—
If any be—the trespass of the Queen.
JAILER   I do believe it.
PAULINA   Do not you fear. Upon mine honour,
I will stand twixt you and danger.   *Exeunt*

2.3

Enter LEONTES
LEONTES   Nor° night nor day, no rest! It is but weakness   *Neither*
To bear the matter thus, mere weakness. If
The cause were not in being°—part o'th' cause,   *alive*
She, th'adultress; for the harlot° King   *lewd*
5 Is quite beyond mine arm, out of the blank°   *target*
And level° of my brain, plot-proof; but she   *aim*
I can hook to me. Say that she were gone,
Given to the fire,[1] a moiety° of my rest   *portion*
Might come to me again. Who's there?
        [*Enter a* SERVANT]
SERVANT   My lord.
LEONTES   How does the boy?
10 SERVANT   He took good rest tonight.
'Tis hoped his sickness is discharged.
LEONTES   To see his nobleness!
Conceiving° the dishonour of his mother   *Realizing*
He straight° declined, drooped, took it deeply,   *immediately*
15 Fastened and fixed the shame on't° in himself;   *of it*

---

4. A successful outcome, with a pun on "issue" as "off-
spring."
5. But dared not risk asking a person of higher rank.
6. To let it pass (out of the prison).
2.3 Location: Sicilia. The palace of Leontes.
1. Burned at the stake (for treason against the King).

Threw off his spirit, his appetite, his sleep,
And downright languished. Leave me solely.° Go,   *alone*
See how he fares.   [*Exit* SERVANT]
                    Fie, fie, no thought of him.°   *(Polixenes)*
The very thought of my revenges that way
20 Recoil upon me. In himself too mighty,
And in his parties,° his alliance.° Let him be   *supporters / allies*
Until a time may serve. For present vengeance,
Take it on her. Camillo and Polixenes
Laugh at me, make their pastime at my sorrow.
25 They should not laugh if I could reach them, nor
Shall she, within my power.
                    Enter PAULINA [*carrying a babe, with* ANTIGONUS,
                    LORDS, *and the* SERVANT, *trying to restrain her*]
A LORD   You must not enter.
PAULINA   Nay rather, good my lords, be second to me.°   *help me*
Fear you his tyrannous passion more, alas,
Than the Queen's life?—a gracious, innocent soul,
More free° than he is jealous.   *innocent*
30 ANTIGONUS   That's enough.
SERVANT   Madam, he hath not slept tonight, commanded
None should come at him.
PAULINA   Not so hot, good sir.
I come to bring him sleep. 'Tis such as you,
That creep like shadows by him, and do sigh
35 At each his needless heavings, such as you
Nourish the cause of his awaking.° I   *wakefulness*
Do come with words as medicinal as true,
Honest as either, to purge him of that humour°   *mental disorder*
That presses him from sleep.
LEONTES   What noise there, ho?
40 PAULINA   No noise, my lord, but needful conference
About some gossips[2] for your highness.
LEONTES   How?
Away with that audacious lady! Antigonus,
I charged thee that she should not come about me.
I knew she would.
ANTIGONUS   I told her so, my lord,
45 On your displeasure's peril° and on mine,   *At the risk of your anger*
She should not visit you.
LEONTES   What, canst not rule her?
PAULINA   From all dishonesty he can. In this,
Unless he take the course that you have done—
Commit° me for committing honour—trust it,   *Imprison*
He shall not rule me.
50 ANTIGONUS   La you now, you hear.
When she will take the rein I let her run,
But she'll not stumble.
PAULINA [*to* LEONTES]   Good my liege, I come—
And I beseech you hear me, who professes
Myself your loyal servant, your physician,
55 Your most obedient counsellor; yet that dares
Less appear so in comforting° your evils   *condoning*

2. Godparents or sponsors at a child's baptism.

Than such as most seem yours³—I say, I come
From your good queen.

LEONTES   Good queen?

60 PAULINA   Good queen, my lord, good queen, I say good queen,
And would by combat make her good,⁴ so were I
A man, the worst about° you.   °lowest in rank of

LEONTES [to LORDS]   Force her hence.

PAULINA   Let him that makes but trifles of his eyes
First hand° me. On mine own accord, I'll off.   °touch

65 But first I'll do my errand. The good Queen—
For she is good—hath brought you forth a daughter—
Here 'tis—commends it to your blessing.
            [She lays down the babe]

LEONTES   Out!
A mankind° witch! Hence with her, out o'door—   °manlike
A most intelligencing bawd.°   °spying go-between

PAULINA   Not so.

70 I am as ignorant in that as you
In so entitling me,° and no less honest   °In calling me that
Than you are mad, which is enough, I'll warrant,
As this world goes, to pass for honest.

LEONTES [to LORDS]   Traitors,
Will you not push her out?
[To ANTIGONUS]   Give her the bastard.

75 Thou dotard, thou art woman-tired,⁵ unroosted
By thy Dame Partlet here.⁶ Take up the bastard,
Take't up, I say. Give't to thy crone.°   °old woman

PAULINA [to ANTIGONUS]   For ever
Unvenerable° be thy hands if thou   °Unworthy of respect
Tak'st up the princess by that forcèd baseness⁷
Which he has put upon't.

80 LEONTES   He dreads° his wife.   °fears

PAULINA   So I would you did. Then 'twere past all doubt
You'd call your children yours.

LEONTES   A nest of traitors.

ANTIGONUS   I am none, by this good light.

PAULINA   Nor I, nor any
But one that's here, and that's himself, for he

85 The sacred honour of himself, his queen's,
His hopeful son's, his babe's, betrays to slander,
Whose sting is sharper than the sword's; and will not—
For as the case now stands, it is a curse
He cannot be compelled to't—once remove

90 The root of his opinion, which is rotten
As ever oak or stone was sound.

LEONTES [to LORDS]   A callat°   °scold; harlot
Of boundless tongue, who late° hath beat her husband,   °recently
And now baits° me! This brat is none of mine.   °provokes
It is the issue° of Polixenes.   °offspring

---

3. Than those who (wrongly) seem most loyal.
4. Prove her to be innocent. Alluding to the chivalric
trials by combat in which knights would establish inno-
cence or guilt by means of duels.
5. You are pecked at by women. A metaphor from fal-

conry referring to tearing of flesh with the beak.
6. Expelled from your "roost" or "perch," the position
of domestic authority assigned to men. In medieval
tales, "Partlett" is a traditional name for a hen.
7. Under that wrongful name of bastard.

95   Hence with it, and together with the dam
        Commit them to the fire.
PAULINA   It is yours,
        And might we lay th'old proverb to your charge,°   *apply the proverb to you*
        So like you 'tis the worse. Behold, my lords,
        Although the print° be little, the whole matter   *copy*
100   And copy of the father: eye, nose, lip,
        The trick° of's frown, his forehead, nay, the valley,[8]   *distinctive character*
        The pretty dimples of his chin and cheek, his smiles,
        The very mould and frame of hand, nail, finger.
        And thou good goddess Nature, which hast made it
105   So like to him that got° it, if thou hast   *begot*
        The ordering of the mind too, 'mongst all colours
        No yellow[9] in't, lest she suspect, as he does,
        Her children not her husband's.
LEONTES [*to* ANTIGONUS]   A gross hag!—
        And lozel,° thou art worthy to be hanged,   *scoundrel*
        That wilt not stay her tongue.
110 ANTIGONUS   Hang all the husbands
        That cannot do that feat, you'll leave yourself
        Hardly one subject.
LEONTES   Once more, take her hence.
PAULINA   A most unworthy and unnatural lord
        Can do no more.
LEONTES   I'll ha' thee burnt.
PAULINA   I care not.
115   It is an heretic that makes the fire,
        Not she which burns in't.[1] I'll not call you tyrant;
        But this most cruel usage of your queen—
        Not able to produce more accusation
        Than your own weak-hinged fancy—something savours
120   Of tyranny, and will ignoble make you,
        Yea, scandalous to the world.
LEONTES [*to* ANTIGONUS]   On your allegiance,
        Out of the chamber with her! Were I a tyrant,
        Where were her life? She durst not call me so
        If she did know me one. Away with her!
125 PAULINA   I pray you do not push me, I'll be gone.
        Look to your babe, my lord; 'tis yours. Jove°   *(King of the gods)*
        A better guiding spirit. What needs these hands?[2]
        You that are thus so tender o'er° his follies   *gentle with*
        Will never do him good, not one of you.
130   So, so. Farewell, we are gone.   *Exit*
LEONTES [*to* ANTIGONUS]   Thou, traitor, hast set on thy wife to this.
        My child? Away with't! Even thou, that hast
        A heart so tender o'er it, take it hence
        And see it instantly consumed with fire.
135   Even thou, and none but thou. Take it up straight.°   *at once*
        Within this hour bring me word 'tis done,
        And by good testimony,° or I'll seize thy life,   *with good evidence*

---

8. Referring to an indentation in the lip or a cleft in the chin.
9. Proverbially, the color of jealousy.
1. The heretic is the one who unjustly makes the fire (Leontes), not the woman who burns in it (Hermione).
2. Why is it necessary for you to push me out? (spoken to Leontes' attendant lords).

With what thou else call'st thine. If thou refuse
And wilt encounter with my wrath, say so.
140 The bastard brains with these my proper° hands   *own*
Shall I dash out. Go, take it to the fire;
For thou set'st on thy wife.
ANTIGONUS   I did not, sir.
These lords, my noble fellows, if they please
Can clear me in't.
LORDS   We can. My royal liege,
145 He is not guilty of her coming hither.
LEONTES You're liars all.
A LORD Beseech your highness, give us better credit.° *think us more honorable*
We have always truly served you, and beseech
So to esteem of us. And on our knees we beg,
150 As recompense of our dear services
Past and to come, that you do change this purpose
Which, being so horrible, so bloody, must
Lead on to some foul issue. We all kneel.
LEONTES I am a feather for each wind that blows.
155 Shall I live on, to see this bastard kneel
And call me father? Better burn it now
Than curse it then. But be it. Let it live.
It shall not neither.
[*To* ANTIGONUS]   You, sir, come you hither,
You that have been so tenderly officious
160 With Lady Margery³ your midwife there,
To save this bastard's life—for 'tis a bastard,
So sure as this beard's grey. What will you adventure° *risk*
To save this brat's life?
ANTIGONUS   Anything, my lord,
That my ability may undergo,
165 And nobleness impose. At least thus much,
I'll pawn the little blood which I have left⁴
To save the innocent; anything possible.
LEONTES It shall be possible. Swear by this sword
Thou wilt perform my bidding.
ANTIGONUS   I will, my lord.
170 LEONTES Mark, and perform it. Seest thou? For the fail° *failure*
Of any point in't shall not only be
Death to thyself but to thy lewd-tongued wife,
Whom for this time we pardon. We enjoin thee,
As thou art liegeman° to us, that thou carry *loyal servant*
175 This female bastard hence, and that thou bear it
To some remote and desert place, quite out
Of our dominions; and that there thou leave it,
Without more mercy, to it° own protection *its*
And favour of the climate. As by strange fortune⁵
180 It came to us, I do in justice charge thee,
On thy soul's peril and thy body's torture,
That thou commend it strangely to some place⁶
Where chance may nurse° or end it. Take it up. *nurture; help*

---

3. A contemptuous name (like "Dame Partlett") for a disorderly woman. "Margery-prater" is a slang term for "hen."
4. Aging was thought to reduce the amount of blood in the body.
5. Since by some unusual chance; since by the act of a foreigner (Polixenes).
6. That you take it to some foreign land.

ANTIGONUS   I swear to do this, though a present death
185   Had been more merciful. Come on, poor babe,
Some powerful spirit instruct the kites° and ravens   *birds of prey*
To be thy nurses. Wolves and bears, they say,
Casting their savageness aside, have done
Like° offices of pity. Sir, be prosperous   *Similar*
190   In more than this deed does require;[7] [*to the babe*] and blessing
Against° this cruelty, fight on thy side,   *To counteract*
Poor thing, condemned to loss.°   *Exit* [*with the babe*]   *ruin*
LEONTES   No, I'll not rear
Another's issue.
                    Enter a SERVANT
SERVANT   Please your highness, posts°   *messengers*
From those you sent to th'oracle are come
195   An hour since. Cleomenes and Dion,
Being well arrived from Delphos, are both landed,
Hasting to th' court.
A LORD [*to* LEONTES]   So please you, sir, their speed
Hath been beyond account.°   *without precedent*
LEONTES   Twenty-three days
They have been absent. 'Tis good speed, foretells
200   The great Apollo suddenly° will have   *at once*
The truth of this appear. Prepare you, lords.
Summon a session,° that we may arraign   *trial*
Our most disloyal lady; for as she hath
Been publicly accused, so shall she have
205   A just and open trial. While she lives
My heart will be a burden to me. Leave me,
And think upon my bidding.   *Exeunt* [*severally*]°   *separately*

3.1

                    Enter CLEOMENES *and* DION
CLEOMENES   The climate's delicate, the air most sweet;
Fertile the isle,[1] the temple much surpassing
The common praise it bears.
DION   I shall report,
For most it caught° me, the celestial habits—°   *charmed / garments*
5   Methinks I so should term them—and the reverence
Of the grave wearers. O, the sacrifice—
How ceremonious, solemn, and unearthly
It was i'th' off'ring!
CLEOMENES   But of all, the burst°   *blast (of thunder)*
And the ear-deaf'ning voice o'th' oracle,
10   Kin to Jove's thunder, so surprised my sense
That I was nothing.
DION   If th'event° o'th' journey   *outcome*
Prove as successful to the Queen—O, be't so!—
As it hath been to us rare, pleasant, speedy,
The time is worth the use on't.[2]
CLEOMENES   Great Apollo

---

7. To a greater extent or in more ways than this action
deserves.
3.1 Location: A road in Sicilia.
1. The island of Delphos (Delos), Apollo's birthplace,
here conflated with Delphi, where Apollo's oracle was
located. See note to 2.1.185.
2. The time will have been well spent.

15 Turn all to th' best! These proclamations,
So forcing faults upon Hermione,
I little like.
DION   The violent carriage° of it   *rash handling*
Will clear or end the business. When the oracle,
Thus by Apollo's great divine° sealed up,   *priest*
20 Shall the contents discover,° something rare   *reveal*
Even then will rush to knowledge. Go. Fresh horses!
And gracious be the issue.°   *Exeunt   result; the child*

3.2

Enter LEONTES, LORDS, [*and*] OFFICERS

LEONTES   This sessions, to our great grief we pronounce,
Even pushes 'gainst our heart: the party tried
The daughter of a king, our wife, and one
Of us° too much beloved. Let us be cleared   *By us*
5 Of being tyrannous since we so openly
Proceed in justice, which shall have due course
Even to the guilt or the purgation.°   *acquittal*
Produce the prisoner.
OFFICER   It is his highness' pleasure
That the Queen appear in person here in court.

[*Enter* HERMIONE *guarded, with* PAULINA *and Ladies*]

10 Silence.[1]
LEONTES   Read the indictment.
OFFICER [*reads*]   Hermione, queen to the worthy Leontes, King
of Sicilia, thou art here accused and arraigned of high treason
in committing adultery with Polixenes, King of Bohemia, and
15 conspiring with Camillo to take away the life of our sovereign
lord the King, thy royal husband; the pretence° whereof being   *purpose*
by circumstances partly laid open, thou, Hermione, contrary to
the faith and allegiance of a true subject, didst counsel and aid
them for their better safety to fly away by night.
20 HERMIONE   Since what I am to say must be but° that   *only*
Which contradicts my accusation, and
The testimony on my part no other
But what comes from myself, it shall scarce boot° me   *profit*
To say 'Not guilty'. Mine integrity
25 Being counted falsehood shall, as I express it,
Be so received. But thus: if powers divine
Behold our human actions—as they do—
I doubt not then but innocence shall make
False accusation blush, and tyranny
30 Tremble at patience. You, my lord, best know—
Who least will seem to do so—my past life
Hath been as continent, as chaste, as true
As I am now unhappy; which° is more   *which unhappiness*
Than history can pattern,[2] though devised
35 And played to take° spectators. For behold me,   *captivate*
A fellow of the royal bed, which owe°   *who owns*
A moiety° of the throne; a great king's daughter,   *A portion*

3.2 Location: Sicilia. A court of justice.
1. In F, the word "Silence" is printed in italics and set
as a stage direction. Here it is treated as an imperative

and assigned to the Officer who announces the Queen's
entrance.
2. Than story or drama can show a precedent for.

The mother to a hopeful prince, here standing
To prate and talk for life and honour, fore°   before
40   Who please to come and hear. For° life, I prize° it   As for / value
As I weigh° grief, which I would spare.° For honour,   value / do without
'Tis a derivative³ from me to mine,°   (my children)
And only that I stand° for. I appeal   fight
To your own conscience, sir, before Polixenes
45   Came to your court how I was in your grace,
How merited to be so; since he came,
With what encounter so uncurrent° I   conduct so unacceptable
Have strained° t'appear thus.° If one jot beyond   transgressed / (on trial)
The bound of honour, or in act or will
50   That way inclining, hardened be the hearts
Of all that hear me, and my near'st of kin
Cry 'Fie' upon my grave.
LEONTES   I ne'er heard yet
That any of these bolder vices wanted
Less° impudence to gainsay° what they did   Were more lacking in / deny
Than to perform it first.
55   HERMIONE   That's true enough,
Though 'tis a saying, sir, not due° to me.   relevant
LEONTES   You will not own it.
HERMIONE   More than mistress of
Which comes to me in name of fault, I must not
At all acknowledge.⁴ For Polixenes,
60   With whom I am accused, I do confess
I loved him as in honour he required;°   was his due
With such a kind of love as might become
A lady like me; with a love, even such,
So, and no other, as yourself commanded;
65   Which not to have done I think had been in me
Both disobedience and ingratitude
To you and toward your friend, whose love had spoke
Even since it could speak, from an infant, freely
That it was yours. Now for conspiracy,
70   I know not how it tastes, though it be dished°   served
For me to try how. All I know of it
Is that Camillo was an honest man;
And why he left your court, the gods themselves,
Wotting° no more than I, are ignorant.   If they know
75   LEONTES   You knew of his departure, as you know
What you have underta'en to do in's absence.
HERMIONE   Sir,
You speak a language that I understand not.
My life stands in the level of your dreams,⁵
Which I'll lay down.
80   LEONTES   Your actions are my 'dreams'.
You had a bastard by Polixenes,
And I but° dreamed it. As you were past all shame—   merely
Those of your fact° are so—so past all truth;   (guilty) of your crime

---

3. Something handed on.
4. I must not answer for ("acknowledge") more than
those faults that I actually possess (am "mistress of").
Hermione is denying she possesses the "bolder vices" of

which Leontes accuses her in line 53.
5. As the target ("level") of your delusions. A metaphor
from archery.

Which to deny concerns more than avails;[6] for as
85 Thy brat hath been cast out, like to itself,°   *as it should be*
No father owning it—which is indeed
More criminal in thee than it—so thou
Shalt feel our justice, in whose easiest passage
Look for no less than death.[7]

HERMIONE   Sir, spare your threats.
90 The bug° which you would fright me with, I seek.   *horrible object*
To me can life be no commodity.°   *profit; comfort*
The crown and comfort of my life, your favour,
I do give° lost, for I do feel it gone   *reckon*
But know not how it went. My second joy,°   *(Mamillius)*
95 And first fruits of my body, from his presence
I am barred, like one infectious. My third comfort,
Starred most unluckily,[8] is from my breast,
The innocent milk in it° most innocent mouth,   *its*
Haled° out to murder; myself on every post[9]   *Dragged*
100 Proclaimed a strumpet, with immodest° hatred   *excessive*
The childbed privilege[1] denied, which 'longs°   *belongs*
To women of all fashion;° lastly, hurried   *ranks*
Here, to this place, i'th' open air,[2] before
I have got strength of limit.[3] Now, my liege,
105 Tell me what blessings I have here alive,
That I should fear to die. Therefore proceed.
But yet hear this—mistake me not—no life,
I prize it not a straw; but for mine honour,
Which I would free:° if I shall be condemned   *vindicate*
110 Upon surmises, all proofs sleeping else°   *except*
But what your jealousies awake, I tell you
'Tis rigour, and not law.[4] Your honours all,
I do refer me° to the oracle.   *appeal*
Apollo be my judge.

A LORD   This your request
115 Is altogether just. Therefore bring forth,
And in Apollo's name, his oracle.   *[Exeunt certain Officers]*

HERMIONE   The Emperor of Russia[5] was my father.
O that he were alive, and here beholding
His daughter's trial; that he did but see
120 The flatness° of my misery—yet with eyes   *boundlessness*
Of pity, not revenge.
           [Enter OFFICERS with CLEOMENES and DION]

OFFICER   You here shall swear upon this sword of justice
That you, Cleomenes and Dion, have
Been both at Delphos, and from thence have brought
125 This sealed-up oracle, by the hand delivered

---

6. Your denial of the truth costs you more effort than
it's worth.
7. In the mildest course of justice, you can expect
death. The implication is that death may well be pre-
ceded by torture.
8. Born under most unlucky stars.
9. Alluding to the early modern practice of nailing
proclamations to posts in public places.
1. The right to enjoy a period of bedrest and seclusion
after childbirth.
2. Exposure to air outside the domestic space was con-
sidered unsafe for women weakened by childbirth.
3. Before I have the strength that follows the custom-
ary period of confinement.
4. Playing on the expression "the rigor of the law,"
Hermione implies that judgment against her would be
mere tyranny ("rigor") and not law.
5. Possibly a reference to the legendary Czar Ivan the
Terrible, who died in 1584. Many London merchants
were interested in trade with Russia, especially after the
formation of the Muscovy Company in 1553.

Of great Apollo's priest; and that since then
You have not dared to break the holy seal,
Nor read the secrets in't.
CLEOMENES *and* DION   All this we swear.
130 LEONTES   Break up the seals, and read.
OFFICER [*reads*]   Hermione is chaste, Polixenes blameless, Ca-
millo a true subject, Leontes a jealous tyrant, his innocent babe
truly begotten, and the King shall live without an heir if that
which is lost be not found.
LORDS   Now blessèd be the great Apollo!
135 HERMIONE   Praised!
LEONTES   Hast thou read truth?
OFFICER   Ay, my lord, even so as it is here set down.
LEONTES   There is no truth at all i'th' oracle.
The sessions shall proceed. This is mere falsehood.
                    [*Enter a* SERVANT]
SERVANT   My lord the King! The King!
140 LEONTES   What is the business?
SERVANT   O sir, I shall be hated to report it.
The prince your son, with mere conceit° and fear   thought
Of the Queen's speed,° is gone.   fortune
LEONTES   How, 'gone'?
SERVANT   Is dead.
LEONTES   Apollo's angry, and the heavens themselves
Do strike at my injustice.
                    [HERMIONE *falls to the ground*]
145   How now there?
PAULINA   This news is mortal to the Queen. Look down
And see what death is doing.
LEONTES   Take her hence.
Her heart is but o'ercharged.° She will recover.   overburdened (by emotion)
I have too much believed mine own suspicion.
150 Beseech you, tenderly apply to her
Some remedies for life.
                    [*Exeunt* PAULINA *and Ladies, carrying* HERMIONE]
                              Apollo, pardon
My great profaneness 'gainst thine oracle.
I'll reconcile me to Polixenes,
New woo my queen, recall the good Camillo,
155 Whom I proclaim a man of truth, of mercy;
For being transported by my jealousies
To bloody thoughts and to revenge, I chose
Camillo for the minister to poison
My friend Polixenes, which had° been done,   would have
160 But that the good mind of Camillo tardied°   delayed
My swift command. Though I with death and with
Reward did threaten and encourage him,
Not doing it, and being done,[6] he, most humane
And filled with honour, to my kingly guest
165 Unclasped my practice,° quit his fortunes here—   Revealed my plot
Which you knew great—and to the certain hazard
Of all incertainties himself commended,°   consigned himself

---

6. That is, "Though I threatened him with death if he did not do it and encouraged him with the promise of reward
if he did do it."

No richer than his honour.[7] How he glisters
Through my rust![8] And how his piety
Does my deeds make the blacker!
    [Enter PAULINA]

170 PAULINA   Woe the while!
    O cut my lace,[9] lest my heart, cracking it,
    Break too.
A LORD   What fit is this, good lady?
PAULINA [*to* LEONTES]   What studied° torments, tyrant, hast for me?   *expertly devised*
    What wheels, racks, fires? What flaying, boiling
175   In leads or oils?[1] What old or newer torture
    Must I receive, whose every word deserves
    To taste of thy most worst? Thy tyranny,
    Together working with thy jealousies—
    Fancies too weak for boys, too green and idle°   *immature and foolish*
180   For girls of nine—O think what they have done,
    And then run mad indeed, stark mad, for all
    Thy bygone fooleries were but spices° of it.   *slight tastes*
    That thou betrayed'st Polixenes, 'twas nothing.
    That did but show thee, of° a fool, inconstant,   *for*
185   And damnable° ingrateful. Nor was't much   *damnably; cursedly*
    Thou wouldst have poisoned good Camillo's honour
    To have him kill a king—poor° trespasses,   *minor*
    More monstrous standing by,[2] whereof I reckon
    The casting forth to crows thy baby daughter
190   To be or° none or little, though a devil   *either*
    Would have shed water out of fire ere done't.[3]
    Nor is't directly laid to thee the death
    Of the young prince, whose honourable thoughts—
    Thoughts high for one so tender°—cleft the heart   *young*
195   That could conceive a gross° and foolish sire   *stupid*
    Blemished his gracious dam.° This is not, no,   *mother*
    Laid to thy answer.[4] But the last—O lords,
    When I have said,° cry woe! The Queen, the Queen,   *finished speaking*
    The sweet'st, dear'st creature's dead, and vengeance for't
    Not dropped down yet.
200 A LORD   The higher powers forbid!
PAULINA   I say she's dead. I'll swear't. If word nor oath
    Prevail not, go and see. If you can bring
    Tincture° or lustre in her lip, her eye,   *Color*
    Heat outwardly or breath within, I'll serve you
205   As I would do the gods. But O thou tyrant,
    Do not repent these things, for they are heavier
    Than all thy woes° can stir.° Therefore betake thee   *grief / remove*
    To nothing but despair. A thousand knees,
    Ten thousand years together, naked, fasting,
210   Upon a barren mountain, and still° winter   *always*

---

7. Possessing no fortune but his honor.
8. How he shines ("glisters") in comparison with my rust. The image alludes to polished and rusty armor.
9. It was believed that fainting might be prevented by cutting the stays on the tight bodices characteristic of female dress in this period.
1. A list of early modern forms of torture. The wheel was a device to which a person was tied and his or her limbs broken, usually by beating. The rack typically

consisted of a frame with a roller at each end; a person was attached to this frame and his or her limbs stretched by turning the rollers. To "flay" was to strip off someone's skin while he or she was still alive.
2. In comparison with more monstrous ones near at hand.
3. A devil would have shed tears from his fiery eyes (or from hellfires) before he had done it.
4. Presented as a charge you must answer.

In storm perpetual, could not move the gods
To look that way thou wert.°   *in your direction*

LEONTES   Go on, go on.
Thou canst not speak too much. I have deserved
All tongues to talk their bitt'rest.

A LORD [*to* PAULINA]   Say no more.
215 Howe'er the business goes, you have made fault
I'th' boldness of your speech.

PAULINA   I am sorry for't.
All faults I make, when I shall come to know them
I do repent. Alas, I have showed too much
The rashness of a woman. He is touched
220 To th' noble heart. What's gone and what's past help
Should be past grief.
[*To* LEONTES]   Do not receive affliction
At my petition.° I beseech you, rather   *Because of my injunction*
Let me be punished, that have minded° you   *reminded*
Of what you should forget. Now, good my liege,
225 Sir, royal sir, forgive a foolish woman.
The love I bore your queen—lo, fool again!
I'll speak of her no more, nor of your children.
I'll not remember you of my own lord,
Who is lost too. Take your patience to you,°   *Be patient*
And I'll say nothing.

230 LEONTES   Thou didst speak but well
When most the truth, which I receive much better
Than to be pitied of° thee. Prithee bring me   *by*
To the dead bodies of my queen and son.
One grave shall be for both. Upon them shall
235 The causes of their death appear, unto
Our shame perpetual. Once a day I'll visit
The chapel where they lie, and tears shed there
Shall be my recreation.[5] So long as nature°   *my bodily being*
Will bear up with this exercise, so long
240 I daily vow to use it. Come, and lead me
To these sorrows.   *Exeunt*

3.3

Enter ANTIGONUS, [*carrying the*] *babe,* [*with*] *a* MARINER

ANTIGONUS   Thou art perfect° then our ship hath touched upon   *certain*
The deserts of Bohemia?

MARINER   Ay, my lord, and fear
We have landed in ill time. The skies look grimly
And threaten present blusters.° In my conscience,°   *impending storms / opinion*
5   The heavens with that we have in hand are angry,
And frown upon's.

ANTIGONUS   Their sacred wills be done. Go get aboard.
Look to thy barque.° I'll not be long before   *ship*
I call upon thee.

MARINER   Make your best haste, and go not
10   Too far i'th' land. 'Tis like to be loud° weather.   *stormy*

5. My only diversion; my spiritual renewal or re-
creation.
3.3 Location: Bohemia. The seacoast. This play, as
does Greene's *Pandosto,* credits Bohemia with a coast.

Only for two brief periods in the late Middle Ages may
Bohemia have controlled a small piece of territory on
the Adriatic Sea, but it was otherwise landlocked.

Besides, this place is famous for the creatures
Of prey that keep° upon't.   *live*
ANTIGONUS   Go thou away.
I'll follow instantly.
MARINER   I am glad at heart
To be so rid o'th' business.   *Exit*
ANTIGONUS   Come, poor babe.
15   I have heard, but not believed, the spirits o'th' dead
May walk again. If such thing be, thy mother
Appeared to me last night, for ne'er was dream
So like a waking. To me comes a creature,
Sometimes her head on one side, some another.
20   I never saw a vessel° of like sorrow,   *person; receptacle*
So filled and so becoming.[1] In pure white robes
Like very sanctity she did approach
My cabin where I lay, thrice bowed before me,
And, gasping to begin some speech, her eyes
25   Became two spouts. The fury spent, anon°   *soon*
Did this break from her: 'Good Antigonus,
Since fate, against thy better disposition,
Hath made thy person for the thrower-out
Of my poor babe according to thine oath,
30   Places remote enough are in Bohemia.
There weep, and leave it crying; and for° the babe   *because*
Is counted lost for ever, Perdita[2]
I prithee call't. For this ungentle° business   *unkind; ignoble*
Put on thee by my lord, thou ne'er shalt see
35   Thy wife Paulina more.' And so with shrieks
She melted into air. Affrighted much,
I did in time collect myself, and thought
This was so, and no slumber. Dreams are toys,°   *trifles*
Yet for this once, yea superstitiously,
40   I will be squared° by this. I do believe   *ruled*
Hermione hath suffered death, and that
Apollo would—this being indeed the issue°   *child*
Of King Polixenes—it should here be laid,
Either for life or death, upon the earth
45   Of its right father. Blossom, speed° thee well!   *fare*
        [*He lays down the babe and a scroll*]
There lie, and there thy character.[3]
        [*He lays down a box*]
                              There these,[4]
Which may, if fortune please, both breed thee, pretty,
And still rest thine.[5]
        [*Thunder*]
                      The storm begins. Poor wretch,
That for thy mother's fault art thus exposed
50   To loss and what may follow! Weep I cannot,
But my heart bleeds, and most accursed am I
To be by oath enjoined to this. Farewell.

---

1. So filled with sorrow and so beautiful.
2. Latin for "lost one."
3. The written account of your history and parentage.
4. The gold and jewels with which the Old Shepherd grows rich and which are later used to identify the

Princess. See 5.2.29–36.
5. Which may, if you are lucky, be sufficient to pay for your upbringing, pretty child, and still leave you with something besides.

The day frowns more and more. Thou'rt like to have
A lullaby too rough. I never saw
55 The heavens so dim by day. A savage clamour!
Well may I get aboard. This is the chase.°   hunt
I am gone for ever!   *Exit, pursued by a bear*[6]
                    [*Enter an* OLD SHEPHERD]
OLD SHEPHERD   I would there were no age between ten and
three-and-twenty, or that youth would sleep out the rest; for
60 there is nothing in the between but getting wenches with child,
wronging the ancientry,° stealing, fighting—hark you now,   elderly people
would any but these boiled-brains° of nineteen and two-and-   lunatics
twenty hunt this weather? They have scared away two of my
best sheep, which I fear the wolf will sooner find than the mas-
65 ter. If anywhere I have them, 'tis by the seaside, browsing of°   on
ivy. Good luck, an't° be thy will!   if it
                    [*He sees the babe*]
What have we here? Mercy on's, a bairn!° A very pretty bairn.   child
A boy or a child,° I wonder? A pretty one, a very pretty one.   girl
Sure some scape.[7] Though I am not bookish,° yet I can read   not familiar with books
70 'waiting-gentlewoman' in the scape. This has been some stair-
work, some trunk-work, some behind-door-work.[8] They were
warmer that got° this than the poor thing is here. I'll take it up   begot
for pity; yet I'll tarry till my son come. He hallooed but even
now. Whoa-ho-hoa!
                    Enter CLOWN°   Bumpkin
75 CLOWN   Hilloa, loa!
OLD SHEPHERD   What, art so near? If thou'lt see a thing to talk
on° when thou art dead and rotten, come hither. What ail'st   about
thou, man?
CLOWN   I have seen two such sights, by sea and by land! But I
80 am not to say it is a sea, for it is now the sky. Betwixt the fir-
mament and it you cannot thrust a bodkin's° point.   needle's
OLD SHEPHERD   Why, boy, how is it?
CLOWN   I would you did but see how it chafes, how it rages, how
it takes up the shore. But that's not to the point. O, the most
85 piteous cry of the poor souls! Sometimes to see 'em, and not to
see 'em; now the ship boring° the moon with her mainmast,   piercing
and anon swallowed with yeast° and froth, as you'd thrust a cork   foam
into a hogshead.° And then for the land-service,[9] to see how the   cask of liquor
bear tore out his shoulder-bone, how he cried to me for help,
90 and said his name was Antigonus, a nobleman! But to make an
end of the ship—to see how the sea flap-dragoned it![1] But first,
how the poor souls roared, and the sea mocked them, and how

---

6. One of the most famous stage directions in English drama. A real bear, rather than a man in a bear suit, might have been used in this scene, perhaps discreetly led on a rope by the fleeing Antigonus. There were reports of tame bears in Shakespeare's London, and bearbaiting (setting dogs on chained bears) was a popular Elizabethan sport, sometimes occurring in the same amphitheaters used at other times for stage plays. It is more likely, however, that the bear was impersonated by an actor in a bear costume. Modern productions vary significantly in their representation of the bear. Some strive for realism, having a bearskin-clad actor or a mechanical likeness of a bear pass across a darkened stage illuminated only by the occasional lightning bolt. Others productions are more stylized, suggesting a bear by the obvious artifice of a mask or symbol.
7. Sexual transgression. English ballads and other popular literature of the period offer numerous accounts of female servants who abandon or kill children born out of wedlock.
8. Some secret sexual affair conducted on back stairs, in chests, or behind doors.
9. Punning on the military and culinary meanings of "service" to suggest both "combat on land" and "food to be served up on land."
1. Devoured it as if it were a flapdragon, a raisin floating on flaming brandy.

the poor gentleman roared, and the bear mocked him, both
roaring louder than the sea or weather.

95 OLD SHEPHERD Name of mercy, when was this, boy?

CLOWN Now, now. I have not winked° since I saw these sights. — blinked an eye
The men are not yet cold under water, nor the bear half dined
on the gentleman. He's at it now.

OLD SHEPHERD Would I had been by to have helped the old
100 man!

CLOWN I would you had been by the ship side, to have helped
her. There your charity would have lacked footing.²

OLD SHEPHERD Heavy° matters, heavy matters. But look thee — Sad
here, boy. Now bless thyself. Thou metst with things dying, I
105 with things new-born. Here's a sight for thee. Look thee, a bear-
ing-cloth³ for a squire's child.
[*He points to the box*]
Look thee here, take up, take up, boy. Open't. So, let's see. It
was told me I should be rich by the fairies. This is some
changeling.⁴ Open't. What's within, boy?

110 CLOWN [*opening the box*] You're a made° old man. If the sins of — prosperous
your youth are forgiven you, you're well to live.° Gold, all gold! — well off; virtuous

OLD SHEPHERD This is fairy gold,⁵ boy, and 'twill prove so. Up
with't, keep it close.° Home, home, the next° way. We are — secret / nearest
lucky, boy, and to be so still° requires nothing but secrecy. Let — always
115 my sheep go. Come, good boy, the next way home.

CLOWN Go you the next way with your findings. I'll go see if the
bear be gone from the gentleman, and how much he hath
eaten. They are never curst° but when they are hungry. If there — vicious
be any of him left, I'll bury it.

120 OLD SHEPHERD That's a good deed. If thou mayst discern by that
which is left of him what he is,° fetch me to th' sight of him. — his identity or rank

CLOWN Marry⁶ will I; and you shall help to put him i'th' ground.

OLD SHEPHERD 'Tis a lucky day, boy, and we'll do good deeds
on't.   *Exeunt*

4.1

Enter TIME,¹ *the Chorus*

TIME I that please some, try° all; both joy and terror — test
Of good and bad; that makes and unfolds error,
Now take upon me in the name° of Time — with the authority
To use my wings. Impute it not a crime
5 To me or my swift passage that I slide
O'er sixteen years and leave the growth untried° — development unexamined
Of that wide gap, since it is in my power
To o'erthrow law, and in one self-born° hour — selfsame
To plant and o'erwhelm° custom. Let me pass — establish and overthrow
10 The same I am ere ancient'st order was

2. There you would not have had a secure place to
stand, with a pun on "footing" as meaning "a founda-
tion" (upon which a charity might be founded).
3. The blanket used to wrap an infant in preparation
for baptism. A squire's child, being of a fairly high
social position, would have a rich bearing-cloth.
4. A child secretly substituted for another by fairies. The
term could apply to the abducted child (usually beautiful)
or to the one (often ugly or deformed) left in its place.
5. Riches left by fairies were unreliable. If not kept
secret, they brought bad luck.

6. A mild oath derived from the name of the Virgin
Mary.
4.1 Location: Scene continues.
1. In early modern texts, Time was conventionally rep-
resented as an old bald man with wings, signifying how
swiftly time passes. He often carried an hourglass and
a scythe, symbol of the power of time to destroy life. A
common saying was that Time was the revealer of
Truth, or that Truth was the daughter of Time. Robert
Greene's *Pandosto*, Shakespeare's chief source for *The
Winter's Tale*, was subtitled *The Triumph of Time*.

Or what is now received.[2] I witness to
The times that brought them in; so shall I do
To th' freshest things now reigning, and make stale
The glistering° of this present as my tale   *glittering shine*
15   Now seems to it.[3] Your patience this allowing,
I turn my glass,° and give my scene such growing   *hourglass*
As° you had slept between. Leontes leaving   *As if*
Th'effects of his fond° jealousies, so grieving   *foolish*
That he shuts up himself, imagine me,
20   Gentle spectators, that I now may be
In fair Bohemia, and remember well
I mentionèd a son o'th' King's, which Florizel
I now name to you; and with speed so pace°   *proceed*
To speak of Perdita, now grown in grace
25   Equal with wond'ring.[4] What of her ensues
I list not° prophesy, but let Time's news   *do not wish to*
Be known when 'tis brought forth. A shepherd's daughter
And what to her adheres,° which follows after,   *pertains*
Is th'argument° of Time. Of this allow,   *subject matter*
30   If ever you have spent time worse ere now.
If never, yet that Time himself doth say
He wishes earnestly you never may.   *Exit*

4.2

Enter POLIXENES *and* CAMILLO

POLIXENES   I pray thee, good Camillo, be no more importunate.
'Tis a sickness denying° thee anything, a death to grant this.   *to deny*
CAMILLO   It is sixteen[1] years since I saw my country. Though I
have for the most part been aired abroad,° I desire to lay my   *breathed foreign air*
5   bones there. Besides, the penitent King, my master, hath sent
for me, to whose feeling° sorrows I might be some allay°—or I   *deeply felt / relief*
o'erween° to think so—which is another spur to my departure.   *am bold enough*
POLIXENES   As thou lov'st me, Camillo, wipe not out the rest of
thy services by leaving me now. The need I have of thee thine
10   own goodness hath made. Better not to have had thee than thus
to want° thee. Thou, having made me businesses[2] which none   *be without*
without thee can sufficiently manage, must either stay to exe-
cute them thyself or take away with thee the very services thou
hast done; which if I have not enough considered°—as too   *rewarded*
15   much I cannot—to be more thankful to thee shall be my study,
and my profit therein, the heaping friendships.[3] Of that fatal°   *deadly*
country Sicilia, prithee speak no more, whose very naming
punishes me with the remembrance of that penitent—as thou
callest him—and reconciled King my brother, whose loss of his
20   most precious queen and children are even now to be afresh°   *newly*
lamented. Say to me, when sawest thou the Prince Florizel,
my son? Kings are no less unhappy, their issue° not being gra-   *children*
cious,° than they are in losing them when they have ap-   *not proving virtuous*
proved° their virtues.   *demonstrated*

---

2. Let me remain as I have been from before the begin-
nings of civilization even to the time of present customs.
3. As my tale now seems stale in comparison with the
present.
4. Now grown so gracious as to inspire admiration.
4.2 Location: Bohemia. The palace of Polixenes.

1. F reads "fifteene." At 4.1.6, Time says that sixteen
years have passed. This apparent error may be due to
carelessness on Shakespeare's part or to a misreading of
a Roman numeral by a compositor or scribe.
2. Performed services for me.
3. The accumulation of your kindnesses.

25 CAMILLO   Sir, it is three days since I saw the Prince. What his
happier affairs may be are to me unknown; but I have missingly
noted° he is of late much retired from court, and is less fre-   *noted by his absence*
quent to° his princely exercises than formerly he hath   *less often engaged in*
appeared.
30 POLIXENES   I have considered so much, Camillo, and with some
care, so far that I have eyes under my service° which look upon   *spies in my employ*
his removedness,° from whom I have this intelligence: that he   *retirement (from court)*
is seldom from the house of a most homely° shepherd, a man,   *simple*
they say, that from very nothing, and beyond the imagination
35 of his neighbours, is grown into an unspeakable estate.°   *untold wealth*
CAMILLO   I have heard, sir, of such a man, who hath a daughter
of most rare note.° The report of her is extended more than can   *quality*
be thought to begin° from such a cottage.   *originate*
POLIXENES   That's likewise part of my intelligence; but, I fear,
40 the angle° that plucks our son thither. Thou shalt accompany   *fishhook*
us to the place, where we will, not appearing what we are, have
some question with the shepherd; from whose simplicity I
think it not uneasy° to get the cause of my son's resort thither.   *difficult*
Prithee, be my present partner in this business, and lay aside
45 the thoughts of Sicilia.
CAMILLO   I willingly obey your command.
POLIXENES   My best Camillo! We must disguise ourselves.
Exeunt

4.3

Enter AUTOLYCUS *singing*

AUTOLYCUS
   When daffodils begin to peer,
      With heigh, the doxy° over the dale,   *beggar's wench*
   Why then comes in the sweet° o'the year,   *sweetest part*
      For the red blood reigns in the winter's pale.°   *skin made pale by winter*

5 The white sheet bleaching on the hedge,[1]
      With heigh, the sweet birds, O how they sing!
   Doth set my pugging° tooth on edge,   *thieving*
      For a quart of ale is a dish for a king.

   The lark, that tirra-lirra chants,
10   With heigh, with heigh, the thrush and the jay,
   Are summer songs for me and my aunts[2]
      While we lie tumbling in the hay.

I have served Prince Florizel, and in my time wore three-pile,[3]
but now I am out of service.

15   But shall I go mourn for that, my dear?
         The pale moon shines by night,
      And when I wander here and there
         I then do most go right.

      If tinkers[4] may have leave° to live,   *permission*
20   And bear the sow-skin budget,[5]

4.3 Location: Bohemia. Near the cottage where the
Old Shepherd, the Clown, and Perdita live.
1. It was common practice to set clothes out to dry on
hedges.
2. Another slang term for women who take beggars or
vagabonds for lovers.

3. A rich velvet cloth with a thick nap or "pile."
4. Menders of metal pots and kettles. The term was
also applied to itinerant beggars and thieves.
5. Pigskin bag. Bag in which a tinker carried his tools;
hence, a sign of his trade.

Then my account I well may give,
And in the stocks avouch it.°   *acknowledge (my crime)*
My traffic° is sheets. When the kite builds, look to lesser linen.⁶   *trade*
My father named me Autolycus,⁷ who being, as I am, littered
25   under Mercury,⁸ was likewise a snapper-up of unconsidered
trifles. With die and drab° I purchased this caparison, and my   *dice and whores*
revenue is the silly cheat.⁹ Gallows and knock° are too power-   *beatings*
ful on the highway.¹ Beating and hanging are terrors to me. For°   *As for*
the life to come, I sleep out the thought of it. A prize, a prize!

    Enter CLOWN

30   CLOWN   Let me see. Every 'leven wether tods,² every tod yields
pound and odd° shilling. Fifteen hundred shorn, what comes   *one*
the wool to?
AUTOLYCUS [*aside*]   If the springe° hold, the cock's³ mine.   *trap*
CLOWN   I cannot do't without counters.⁴ Let me see, what am I
35   to buy for our sheep-shearing feast?⁵ Three pound of sugar, five
pound of currants, rice—what will this sister of mine do with
rice? But my father hath made her mistress of the feast, and she
lays it on. She hath made me four-and-twenty nosegays for the
shearers—three-man-song-men,⁶ all, and very good ones—but
40   they are most of them means° and basses, but one Puritan   *tenors*
amongst them, and he sings psalms to hornpipes.⁷ I must have
saffron to colour the warden° pies; mace; dates, none—that's   *winter pear*
out of my note;° nutmegs, seven; a race° or two of ginger—but   *not on my list / root*
that I may beg; four pound of prunes, and as many of raisins
45   o'th' sun.°   *sun-dried*
AUTOLYCUS   [*grovelling on the ground*] O, that ever I was born!
CLOWN   I'th' name of me!
AUTOLYCUS   O help me, help me! Pluck but off these rags, and
then death, death!
50   CLOWN   Alack, poor soul, thou hast need of more rags to lay on
thee rather than have these off.
AUTOLYCUS   O sir, the loathsomeness of them offend me more
than the stripes° I have received, which are mighty ones and   *blows*
millions.
55   CLOWN   Alas, poor man, a million of beating may come to a
great matter.⁸
AUTOLYCUS   I am robbed, sir, and beaten; my money and apparel
ta'en from me, and these detestable things put upon me.
CLOWN   What, by a horseman, or a footman?°   *man on foot*
60   AUTOLYCUS   A footman, sweet sir, a footman.
CLOWN   Indeed, he should be a footman, by the garments he has
left with thee. If this be a horseman's coat it hath seen very hot

---

6. The kite, a small bird of prey, supposedly stole small pieces of linen to make its nest. Autolycus steals sheets, larger pieces of linen, probably those left to dry on hedges.
7. In classical mythology, a crafty thief and grandfather of Ulysses; Autolycus's own father, Mercury, was the god of thieves.
8. Fathered by Mercury; born when the planet Mercury was ascendant.
9. I was reduced to wearing this garb, and my income derives from petty swindles.
1. Autolycus fears the penalties meted out to highwaymen. He would rather be a petty thief.
2. Every eleven rams will yield 28 pounds (a "tod") of wool. The Clown and his father could expect to earn a substantial amount of money (almost 150 pounds) for

their wool.
3. Woodcock, a bird easily caught and hence proverbial for its stupidity.
4. Disks used in calculating sums.
5. In rural England, a traditional summer event in which people of different ranks took part in feasting and revelry.
6. Men who sing three-part songs.
7. Shrill-sounding musical instruments often played at country dances and hardly appropriate to accompany the singing of psalms. Shakespeare may here be satirizing Puritans, who were notorious for their opposition to music and dancing.
8. A million blows can be a serious affair, with a pun on "matter" as "pus," the sign of an infection caused by open wounds.

service. Lend me thy hand, I'll help thee. Come, lend me thy
hand.

[*He helps* AUTOLYCUS *up*]

65 AUTOLYCUS   O, good sir, tenderly. O!

CLOWN   Alas, poor soul!

AUTOLYCUS   O, good sir, softly,° good sir! I fear, sir, my shoulder-   *gently*
blade is out.

CLOWN   How now? Canst stand?

70 AUTOLYCUS   Softly, dear sir. Good sir, softly.

[*He picks the* CLOWN's *pocket*]⁹

You ha' done me a charitable office.°   *service*

CLOWN [*reaching for his purse*]   Dost lack any money? I have a
little money for thee.

AUTOLYCUS   No, good sweet sir, no, I beseech you, sir.¹ I have a

75 kinsman not past three-quarters of a mile hence, unto whom I
was going. I shall there have money, or anything I want. Offer
me no money, I pray you. That kills° my heart.   *touches*

CLOWN   What manner of fellow was he that robbed you?

AUTOLYCUS   A fellow, sir, that I have known to go about with

80 troll-madams.° I knew him once a servant of the Prince. I can-   *whores*
not tell, good sir, for which of his virtues it was, but he was
certainly whipped out of the court.

CLOWN   His vices, you would say. There's no virtue whipped out
of the court. They cherish it to make it stay there; and yet it

85 will no more but abide.°   *stay there only briefly*

AUTOLYCUS   Vices, I would say, sir. I know this man well. He
hath been since an ape-bearer,² then a process-server—a bai-
liff—then he compassed a motion° of the Prodigal Son,³ and   *devised a puppet show*
married a tinker's wife within a mile where my land and living°   *property*

90 lies, and having flown over many knavish professions, he settled
only in rogue. Some call him Autolycus.

CLOWN   Out upon him! Prig,° for my life, prig! He haunts   *Thief*
wakes,° fairs, and bear-baitings.   *festivals*

AUTOLYCUS   Very true, sir. He, sir, he. That's the rogue that put

95 me into this apparel.

CLOWN   Not a more cowardly rogue in all Bohemia. If you had
but looked big and spit at him, he'd have run.

AUTOLYCUS   I must confess to you, sir, I am no fighter. I am false
of heart° that way, and that he knew, I warrant him.   *without courage*

100 CLOWN   How do you now?

AUTOLYCUS   Sweet sir, much better than I was. I can stand, and
walk. I will even take my leave of you, and pace softly towards
my kinsman's.

CLOWN   Shall I bring thee° on the way?   *escort you*

105 AUTOLYCUS   No, good-faced sir, no, sweet sir.

CLOWN   Then fare thee well. I must go buy spices for our sheep-
shearing.

AUTOLYCUS   Prosper you, sweet sir.   *Exit* [*the* CLOWN]

---

9. It is uncertain when Autolycus actually picks the
Clown's pocket, but it adds to the humor if Autolycus's
next line, "You ha' done me a charitable office," can
refer both to the kindness the Clown has knowingly
shown Autolycus *and* to the kindness the Clown has
unwittingly done him in making available a purse for
the wily rogue to steal.
1. Autolycus does not want the Clown to find out he

has picked his pocket and so left him with no money.
He may here restrain the Clown from putting his hand
into his pocket.
2. One who carried about a trained monkey.
3. Alluding to the New Testament story of a spendthrift
son who squandered his money only to be forgiven by
his father.

Your purse is not hot° enough to purchase your spice. I'll be   *full*
110 with you at your sheep-shearing, too. If I make not this cheat°   *deception*
bring out° another, and the shearers prove sheep, let me be   *lead to*
unrolled[4] and my name put in the book of virtue.
[*Sings*]   Jog on, jog on, the footpath way,
          And merrily hent° the stile[5]-a.   *grab (to leap over)*
115   A merry heart goes all the day,
          Your sad tires in a mile-a.   *Exit*

4.4

Enter FLORIZEL [*dressed as Doricles a countryman*],
[*and*] PERDITA [*as Queen of the Feast*][1]

FLORIZEL   These your unusual weeds° to each part of you   *garments*
Does give a life; no shepherdess, but Flora°   *goddess of flowers*
Peering in April's front.[2] This your sheep-shearing
Is as a meeting of the petty gods,
And you the queen on't.°   *of it*
5 PERDITA   Sir, my gracious lord,
To chide at your extremes° it not becomes me—   *extravagances*
O, pardon that I name them! Your high self,
The gracious mark o'th' land,[3] you have obscured
With a swain's wearing,° and me, poor lowly maid,   *shepherd's costume*
10 Most goddess-like pranked up.° But that our feasts   *adorned*
In every mess[4] have folly, and the feeders°   *those who eat*
Digest it with a custom,[5] I should blush
To see you so attired; swoon, I think,
To show myself a glass.°   *mirror*
FLORIZEL   I bless the time
15 When my good falcon made her flight across
Thy father's ground.
PERDITA   Now Jove afford you cause!
To me the difference° forges dread; your greatness   *(in rank)*
Hath not been used to fear. Even now I tremble
To think your father by some accident
20 Should pass this way, as you did. O, the fates!
How would he look to see his work,° so noble,   *offspring; writings*
Vilely bound up?[6] What would he say? Or how
Should I, in these my borrowed flaunts,° behold   *rich garments*
The sternness of his presence?
FLORIZEL   Apprehend
25 Nothing but jollity. The gods themselves,
Humbling their deities to love, have taken
The shapes of beasts upon them. Jupiter
Became a bull, and bellowed; the green Neptune
A ram, and bleated; and the fire-robed god,
30 Golden Apollo, a poor humble swain,

---

4. Let my name be taken off the list (of thieves and vagabonds).
5. Steps by which people pass over a fence or hedge.
4.4 Location: Bohemia. In front of the cottage where the Old Shepherd, the Clown, and Perdita live.
1. Again, F lists in the initial stage direction all the major characters who appear in this very long scene. Florizel and Perdita seem, however, to have a private conversation before the Old Shepherd, Polixenes, and

others enter to them at line 54.
2. Peeping out in early April.
3. The one whose graces make him admired by all.
4. A group of four served at table together. See note to 1.2.227.
5. Tolerate it because they have grown used to it.
6. Outfitted in such an inferior way. A bookbinding metaphor.

As I seem now.[7] Their transformations
Were never for a piece° of beauty rarer,   *person*
Nor in a way so chaste,[8] since my desires
Run not before mine honour, nor my lusts
Burn hotter than my faith.

35   PERDITA   O, but sir,
Your resolution cannot hold when 'tis
Opposed, as it must be, by th' power of the King.
One of these two must be necessities,
Which then will speak that you must change this purpose,
Or I my life.[9]

40   FLORIZEL   Thou dearest Perdita,
With these forced° thoughts I prithee darken not   *unnatural; farfetched*
The mirth o'th' feast. Or° I'll be thine, my fair,   *Either*
Or not my father's. For I cannot be
Mine own, nor anything to any, if
45   I be not thine. To this I am most constant,
Though destiny say no. Be merry, gentle;
Strangle such thoughts as these with anything
That you behold the while. Your guests are coming.
Lift up your countenance as° it were the day   *as if*
50   Of celebration of that nuptial which
We two have sworn shall come.

PERDITA   O Lady Fortune,[1]
Stand you auspicious!

FLORIZEL   See, your guests approach.
Address° yourself to entertain them sprightly,   *Prepare*
And let's be red with mirth.
       [*Enter the* OLD SHEPHERD, *with* POLIXENES *and* CA-
       MILLO, *disguised, the* CLOWN, MOPSA, DORCAS, *and
       others*]

55   OLD SHEPHERD [*to* PERDITA]   Fie, daughter, when my old wife lived, upon
This day she was both pantler,° butler, cook,   *pantry maid*
Both dame° and servant, welcomed all, served all,   *mistress of the house*
Would sing her song and dance her turn, now here
At upper end o'th' table, now i'th' middle,
60   On his° shoulder, and his,° her face afire   *one person's / another's*
With labour, and the thing she took to quench it
She would to each one sip. You are retired
As if you were a feasted one° and not   *a guest*
The hostess of the meeting. Pray you bid
65   These unknown friends to's welcome, for it is
A way to make us better friends, more known.
Come, quench your blushes, and present yourself
That which you are, mistress o'th' feast. Come on,
And bid us welcome to your sheep-shearing,
As your good flock shall prosper.

70   PERDITA [*to* POLIXENES]   Sir, welcome.
It is my father's will I should take on me

---

7. In classical mythology, Jupiter transformed himself into a bull and abducted Europa; Neptune took on the shape of a ram to carry off Theopane; and the sun god Apollo disguised himself as a shepherd to court Alcestis.
8. Nor ever conducted with so chaste a purpose.

9. One of two things will become necessary: either you must change your plans, or I must change my life (that is, risk death).
1. In classical and Renaissance mythology, a woman of fickle disposition whose favors cannot be relied upon.

The hostess-ship o'th' day.
[*To* CAMILLO]   You're welcome, sir.
Give me those flowers there, Dorcas. Reverend sirs,
For you there's rosemary and rue. These keep°   *retain*
75   Seeming° and savour° all the winter long.   *Color / scent*
Grace and remembrance² be to you both,
And welcome to our shearing.
POLIXENES   Shepherdess,
A fair one are you. Well you fit our ages
With flowers of winter.
PERDITA   Sir, the year growing ancient,
80   Not yet on summer's death, nor on the birth
Of trembling winter, the fairest flowers o'th' season
Are our carnations and streaked gillyvors,³
Which some call nature's bastards. Of that kind
Our rustic garden's barren, and I care not
To get slips of them.
85   POLIXENES   Wherefore, gentle maiden,
Do you neglect them?
PERDITA   For I have heard it said
There is an art⁴ which in their piedness° shares   *streaked color*
With great creating nature.
POLIXENES   Say there be,
Yet nature is made better by no mean°   *means*
90   But nature makes that mean. So over that art
Which you say adds to nature is an art
That nature makes. You see, sweet maid, we marry
A gentler scion to the wildest stock,
And make conceive a bark of baser kind
95   By bud of nobler race.⁵ This is an art
Which does mend nature—change it rather; but
The art itself is nature.
PERDITA   So it is.
POLIXENES   Then make your garden rich in gillyvors,
And do not call them bastards.
PERDITA   I'll not put
100   The dibble° in earth to set° one slip of them,   *trowel / plant*
No more than, were I painted,° I would wish   *wearing cosmetics*
This youth should say 'twere well, and only therefore
Desire to breed by me. Here's flowers for you:
Hot⁶ lavender, mints, savory, marjoram,
105   The marigold, that goes to bed wi'th' sun,
And with him rises, weeping.⁷ These are flowers
Of middle summer, and I think they are given
To men of middle age. You're very welcome.
      [*She gives them flowers*]

2. Grace ("repentance") and remembrance are quali-
ties associated with rue and rosemary, respectively.
3. Gillyflowers or multicolored carnations. Their vari-
ations in color were thought to result from crossbreed-
ing with other flowers, which may be why Perdita calls
them "nature's bastards." They were proverbially asso-
ciated with sexual license.
4. The art of crossbreeding or grafting.
5. We unite a cutting from a highly cultivated plant to
the stem of a lesser one and cause the lesser plant to

bring forth a highly cultivated flower, that puns on
"gentler scion," "wildest stock," "baser kind," and
"nobler race" to suggest a successful union between a
highborn heir and a member of the lower social orders.
6. Herbs were divided into "hot" and "cold" varieties
based on their supposed temperatures.
7. The marigold, sometimes called "the spouse of the
sun," supposedly closed at sunset and opened, filled
with dew, in the morning when the sun came up.

CAMILLO   I should leave grazing were I of your flock,
And only live by gazing.

110 PERDITA   Out, alas,
You'd be so lean that blasts of January
Would blow you through and through.
[*To* FLORIZEL]   Now, my fair'st friend,
I would I had some flowers o'th' spring that might
Become your time of day; [*to* MOPSA *and* DORCAS] and yours, and yours,
115 That wear upon your virgin branches yet
Your maidenheads growing. O Proserpina,⁸
For the flowers now that, frighted, thou letst fall
From Dis's wagon!°—daffodils,   *chariot*
That come before the swallow dares, and take°   *charm*
120 The winds of March with beauty; violets, dim,°   *with hanging head*
But sweeter than the lids of Juno's eyes
Or Cytherea's breath;⁹ pale primroses,
That die unmarried ere they can behold
Bright Phoebus° in his strength—a malady   *the sun god*
125 Most incident to maids;¹ bold oxlips, and
The crown imperial;² lilies of all kinds,
The flower-de-luce³ being one. O, these I lack,
To make you garlands of, and my sweet friend,
To strew him o'er and o'er.

FLORIZEL   What, like a corpse?
130 PERDITA   No, like a bank, for love to lie and play on,
Not like a corpse—or if, not to be buried,
But quick° and in mine arms. Come, take your flowers.   *living*
Methinks I play as I have seen them do
In Whitsun pastorals.⁴ Sure this robe of mine
Does change my disposition.

135 FLORIZEL   What you do
Still° betters what is done. When you speak, sweet,   *Always*
I'd have you do it ever; when you sing,
I'd have you buy and sell so, so give alms,
Pray so; and for the ord'ring° your affairs,   *arranging for*
140 To sing them too. When you do dance, I wish you
A wave o'th' sea, that you might ever do
Nothing but that, move still, still so,
And own° no other function. Each your doing,°   *have / Each thing you do*
So singular° in each particular,   *distinctive*
145 Crowns what you are doing in the present deeds,
That all your acts are queens.

PERDITA   O Doricles,⁵
Your praises are too large. But that your youth
And the true blood which peeps so fairly through't

8. In Ovid's *Metamorphoses*, Proserpina, the daughter of Ceres, is abducted by Dis, or Pluto, as she gathers flowers and is taken in his chariot ("wagon") to his underworld kingdom. Sought out by Ceres, Proserpina is allowed to return to earth for six months each year. Her sojourn on earth coincides with spring and summer, her return to the underworld with fall and winter.
9. Juno was queen of the gods; "Cytherea" was another name for Venus, the goddess of love.
1. Alluding to the superstition that women who died of a kind of anemia known as green sickness would be transformed into primroses. Green sickness was espe-

cially associated with young virginal women; vigorous sexual activity was sometimes advocated as a cure.
2. A lily first imported into England from Turkey in the late sixteenth century.
3. Fleur-de-lis, the national flower of France.
4. English rural festivities traditionally held at Whitsuntide, a religious festival occurring in the spring, seven weeks after Easter. The festivities, often organized under a festival King and Queen, included morris dances and Robin Hood plays.
5. The name Florizel has assumed.

Do plainly give you out an unstained shepherd,
150 With wisdom I might fear, my Doricles,
You wooed me the false way.

FLORIZEL   I think you have
As little skill° to fear as I have purpose   *reason*
To put you to't. But come, our dance, I pray;
Your hand, my Perdita. So turtles[6] pair,
That never mean to part.
155 PERDITA   I'll swear for 'em.
POLIXENES [*to* CAMILLO]   This is the prettiest low-born lass that ever
Ran on the greensward.° Nothing she does or seems   *grassy turf*
But smacks of something greater than herself,
Too noble for this place.
CAMILLO   He tells her something
160 That makes her blood look out.° Good sooth, she is   *makes her blush*
The queen of curds and cream.[7]
CLOWN   Come on, strike up!
DORCAS   Mopsa must be your mistress. Marry, garlic to mend
her kissing with![8]
MOPSA   Now, in good time!
165 CLOWN   Not a word, a word, we stand upon our manners. Come,
strike up!
            [*Music.*] *Here a dance of shepherds and shepherdesses*
POLIXENES   Pray, good shepherd, what fair swain is this
Which dances with your daughter?
OLD SHEPHERD   They call him Doricles, and boasts himself°   *he boasts*
170 To have a worthy feeding;° but I have it   *good pasture land*
Upon his own report, and I believe it.
He looks like sooth.° He says he loves my daughter.   *appears to be honest*
I think so, too, for never gazed the moon
Upon the water as he'll stand and read,
175 As 'twere, my daughter's eyes; and to be plain,
I think there is not half a kiss to choose
Who loves another° best.   *the other*
POLIXENES   She dances featly.°   *nimbly*
OLD SHEPHERD   So she does anything, though I report it
That° should be silent. If young Doricles   *Who*
180 Do light upon her, she shall bring him that
Which he not dreams of.
            Enter [a] SERVANT
SERVANT   O, master, if you did but hear the pedlar at the door,
you would never dance again after a tabor and pipe.[9] No, the
bagpipe could not move you. He sings several° tunes faster than   *different*
185 you'll tell° money. He utters them as he had eaten ballads,[1]   *count*
and all men's ears grew° to his tunes.   *listened intently*
CLOWN   He could never come better.° He shall come in. I love   *at a better time*
a ballad but even too well, if it be doleful matter merrily set
down, or a very pleasant thing indeed, and sung lamentably.
190 SERVANT   He hath songs for man or woman, of all sizes. No milli-
ner[2] can so fit his customers with gloves. He has the prettiest

---

6. Turtledoves, which proverbially mate for life.
7. Referring perhaps to a cream custard known as "white pot." In some May games, a woman was chosen as Queen of white-pot cream.
8. To make her breath sweet (said ironically).
9. A small drum and fife used for morris dancing.

1. Alluding to the broadside ballads that were sung and sold by peddlers who traveled throughout the country.
2. One who sells fashionable articles of clothing such as hats and gloves. Originally, the word meant one who sells items imported from Milan.

love songs for maids, so without bawdry, which is strange, with
such delicate burdens° of dildos and fadings, 'Jump her, and *refrains*
thump her';³ and where some stretch-mouthed° rascal would, *obscene*
195 as it were, mean mischief and break a foul gap into the matter,⁴
he makes the maid to answer, 'Whoop, do me no harm, good
man'; puts him off, slights him, with 'Whoop, do me no harm,
good man!'

POLIXENES This is a brave° fellow. *fine*
200 CLOWN Believe me, thou talkest of an admirable conceited° fel- *very witty*
low. Has he any unbraided° wares? *new; not shopworn*

SERVANT He hath ribbons of all the colours i'th' rainbow; points⁵
more than all the lawyers in Bohemia can learnedly handle,
though they come to him by th' gross; inkles, caddises, cam-
205 brics, lawns⁶—why, he sings 'em over as they were gods or god-
desses. You would think a smock° were a she-angel, he so *a woman's undergarment*
chants to the sleeve-hand° and the work about the square on't.⁷ *wristband*

CLOWN Prithee bring him in, and let him approach singing.

PERDITA Forewarn him that he use no scurrilous words in's
210 tunes. [*Exit* SERVANT]

CLOWN You have of these° pedlars that have more in them than *There are some*
you'd think, sister.

PERDITA Ay, good brother, or go about° to think. *intend*

 Enter AUTOLYCUS [*wearing a false beard, carrying his*
 pack, and] *singing*

AUTOLYCUS Lawn as white as driven snow,
215 Cypress⁸ black as e'er was crow,
  Gloves as sweet° as damask roses, *perfumed*
  Masks for faces, and for noses;⁹
  Bugle-bracelet,¹ necklace amber,
  Perfume for a lady's chamber;
220 Golden coifs,° and stomachers² *caps*
  For my lads to give their dears;
  Pins and poking-sticks of steel,³
  What maids lack from head to heel
  Come buy of me, come, come buy, come buy,
225 Buy, lads, or else your lasses cry. Come buy!

CLOWN If I were not in love with Mopsa thou shouldst take no
money of me, but being enthralled as I am, it will also be the
bondage of certain ribbons and gloves.⁴

MOPSA I was promised them against° the feast, but they come *in time for*
230 not too late now.

DORCAS He hath promised you more than that,⁵ or there be
liars.

---

3. Though the servant claims that the songs are with-
out bawdiness, the refrains are in fact full of sexual
puns that the servant may not understand. "Dildos" are
artificial penises; "fadings" can mean "orgasms"; and
"jump her and thump her" denotes sexual relations with
a woman.
4. Would interrupt the song with an indecent insertion.
5. Laces for fastening garments, with a pun on "points"
as meaning "legal arguments."
6. "Inkles" were linen tapes; "caddises" were worsted
tapes used for garters; "cambrics" and "lawns" were
heavy and sheer linens.
7. The stitching about the yoke of the garment.
8. A crepe material imported from Cyprus and used for

mourning clothes.
9. Many upper-class English women wore masks to
protect their skin from exposure to the sun. Some
women's noses being eaten away by syphilis, and masks
would also cover this deformity.
1. A bracelet of shiny black beads.
2. Embroidered bodices for dresses.
3. Metal rods used to iron the ruffs or stiff collars worn
by both men and women. The term is also slang for
"penis."
4. Because I am the prisoner of love, certain ribbons
and gloves must also be put in bondage (bound up in a
parcel).
5. (Perhaps he has promised marriage.)

MOPSA   He hath paid° you all he promised you. Maybe he has   given; had sex with
   paid you more, which will shame you to give him again.⁶

235   CLOWN   Is there no manners left among maids? Will they wear
   their plackets where they should bear their faces?⁷ Is there not
   milking-time, when you are going to bed, or kiln-hole,° to whis-   fireplace
   tle of these secrets, but you must be tittle-tattling before all our
   guests? 'Tis well they are whispering. Clammer your tongues,⁸

240   and not a word more.

MOPSA   I have done. Come, you promised me a tawdry-lace⁹ and
   a pair of sweet gloves.

CLOWN   Have I not told thee how I was cozened by the way,°   cheated on the road
   and lost all my money?

245   AUTOLYCUS   And indeed, sir, there are cozeners abroad, therefore
   it behoves men to be wary.

CLOWN   Fear not thou, man, thou shalt lose nothing here.

AUTOLYCUS   I hope so, sir, for I have about me many parcels of
   charge.°   valuable goods

250   CLOWN   What hast here? Ballads?

MOPSA   Pray now, buy some. I love a ballad in print, alife,° for   on my life
   then we are sure they are true.

AUTOLYCUS   Here's one to a very doleful tune, how a usurer's
   wife was brought to bed of twenty money-bags at a burden,° and   in one childbirth

255   how she longed to eat adders' heads and toads carbonadoed.°   cut and grilled

MOPSA   Is it true, think you?

AUTOLYCUS   Very true, and but a month old.

DORCAS   Bless me from marrying a usurer!

AUTOLYCUS   Here's the midwife's name to't, one Mistress Tail-

260   Porter,¹ and five or six honest° wives' that were present. Why   truthful; chaste
   should I carry lies abroad?

MOPSA [to CLOWN]   Pray you now, buy it.

CLOWN   Come on, lay it by, and let's first see more ballads. We'll
   buy the other things anon.

265   AUTOLYCUS   Here's another ballad, of a fish that appeared upon
   the coast on Wednesday the fourscore° of April, forty thousand   eightieth day
   fathom° above water, and sung this ballad against the hard   measurement of six feet
   hearts of maids. It was thought she was a woman, and was
   turned into a cold fish for she would not exchange flesh° with   have sex

270   one that loved her. The ballad is very pitiful, and as true.

DORCAS   Is it true too, think you?

AUTOLYCUS   Five justices' hands at it,° and witnesses more than   signatures on it
   my pack will hold.

CLOWN   Lay it by, too. Another.

275   AUTOLYCUS   This is a merry ballad, but a very pretty one.

MOPSA   Let's have some merry ones.

AUTOLYCUS   Why, this is a passing° merry one, and goes to the   very
   tune of 'Two Maids Wooing a Man'. There's scarce a maid
   westward° but she sings it. 'Tis in request, I can tell you.   in the west

---

6. "More" may allude to a pregnancy that will result in
an illegitimate child that she will give to the Clown.
7. That is, "Will they reveal their most private affairs in
public?" There is a pun on "placket," which refers to
both an opening in a petticoat and female genitals.
8. An obscure phrase. The Clown clearly means they
are to be quiet. "To clammer" is a term from bell ring-
ing that means to make the jangling sound characteris-
tic of bells before they grow silent. In F, the phrase is
printed as "clamor your tongues." Many emendations
have been proposed.
9. A cheap, brightly colored scarf associated with St.
Audrey's Fair. St. Audrey was the founder of Ely Cathe-
dral; she died of a petticoat throat tumor that she believed was a
punishment for wearing gay neckerchiefs in her youth.
1. The name punningly suggests one who reports gos-
sip ("tales") as well as one who handles genitalia (slang
meaning of "tail").

280 MOPSA We can both sing it. If thou'lt bear a part² thou shalt
hear; 'tis in three parts.

DORCAS We had the tune on't° a month ago.   *of it*

AUTOLYCUS I can bear my part, you must know, 'tis my occu-
pation.° Have at it with you.   *job; act of copulation*

[*They sing*]

285 AUTOLYCUS Get you hence, for I must go³
Where it fits not you to know.

DORCAS   Whither?

MOPSA   O whither?

DORCAS   Whither?

MOPSA It becomes thy oath full well
Thou to me thy secrets tell.

290 DORCAS Me too. Let me go thither.

MOPSA Or thou go'st to th' grange° or mill,   *farm*

DORCAS If to either, thou dost ill.

AUTOLYCUS   Neither.

DORCAS   What neither.

AUTOLYCUS   Neither.

DORCAS Thou hast sworn my love to be.

295 MOPSA Thou hast sworn it more to me.
Then whither goest? Say, whither?

CLOWN We'll have this song out anon by ourselves. My father
and the gentlemen are in sad° talk, and we'll not trouble them.   *serious*
Come, bring away thy pack after me. Wenches, I'll buy for you
300 both. Pedlar, let's have the first choice. Follow me, girls.

[*Exit with* DORCAS *and* MOPSA]

AUTOLYCUS And you shall pay well for 'em.

[*Sings*]   Will you buy any tape,
Or lace for your cape,
My dainty duck, my dear-a?
305   Any silk, any thread,
Any toys° for your head,   *small ornaments*
Of the new'st and fin'st, fin'st wear-a?
Come to the pedlar,
Money's a meddler,
310   That doth utter° all men's ware-a.   *Exit*   *put on sale*

[*Enter* SERVANT]

SERVANT Master, there is three carters,° three shepherds, three   *drivers of carts*
neatherds,° three swineherds that have made themselves all   *keepers of cows*
men of hair.⁴ They call themselves saultiers,° and they have a   *jumpers*
dance which the wenches say is a gallimaufry of gambols,°   *jumble of jumps*
315 because they are not in't. But they themselves are o'th' mind,
if it be not too rough for some that know little but bowling,° it   *(a more sedate sport)*
will please plentifully.

OLD SHEPHERD Away. We'll none on't. Here has been too much
homely° foolery already. [*To* POLIXENES] I know, sir, we weary   *rough*
320 you.

POLIXENES You weary those that° refresh us. Pray, let's see these   *who*
four threes° of herdsmen.   *trios*

SERVANT One three of them, by their own report, sir, hath

---

2. Sing a part in the song; play a role (in a sexual
encounter with the two women).
3. F prints "Song" before this line and "Autolycus"
before the next.

4. Probably they have disguised themselves in animal
skins in order to resemble satyrs—mythical woodland
figures, part man, part beast, having the pointed ears,
legs, and short horns of a goat.

danced before the King,⁵ and not the worst of the three but
325   jumps twelve foot and a half by th' square.°   *exactly*

OLD SHEPHERD   Leave your prating. Since these good men are
    pleased, let them come in—but quickly, now.

SERVANT   Why, they stay at door, sir.
        Here a dance of twelve satyrs

POLIXENES [*to the* OLD SHEPHERD]   O, father, you'll know more of that hereafter.
330   [*To* CAMILLO] Is it not too far gone? 'Tis time to part them.
    He's simple, and tells much.
    [*To* FLORIZEL]   How now, fair shepherd,
    Your heart is full of something that does take
    Your mind from feasting. Sooth, when I was young
    And handed love° as you do, I was wont   *pledged love*
335   To load my she with knacks.° I would have ransacked   *small gifts; trifles*
    The pedlar's silken treasury, and have poured it
    To her acceptance.° You have let him go,   *For her to choose*
    And nothing marted° with him. If your lass   *bought from*
    Interpretation should abuse,° and call this   *Should misinterpret*
340   Your lack of love or bounty, you were straited°   *hard-pressed*
    For a reply, at least if you make a care
    Of happy holding her.°   *Of keeping her happy*

FLORIZEL   Old sir, I know
    She prizes not such trifles as these are.
    The gifts she looks° from me are packed and locked   *expects*
345   Up in my heart, which I have given already,
    But not delivered.
    [*To* PERDITA]   O, hear me breathe my life°   *make vows of eternal love*
    Before this ancient sir, who, it should seem,
    Hath sometime loved. I take thy hand, this hand
    As soft as dove's down, and as white as it,
350   Or Ethiopian's tooth, or the fanned snow that's bolted°   *sifted*
    By th' northern blasts twice o'er.

POLIXENES   What follows this?
    How prettily the young swain seems to wash
    The hand was° fair before! I have put you out.°   *that was / interrupted you*
    But to your protestation. Let me hear
355   What you profess.

FLORIZEL   Do, and be witness to't.

POLIXENES   And this my neighbour too?

FLORIZEL   And he, and more
    Than he; and men, the earth, the heavens, and all,
    That were I crowned the most imperial monarch,
    Thereof most worthy, were I the fairest youth
360   That ever made eye swerve,° had force and knowledge   *commanded attention*
    More than was ever man's, I would not prize them
    Without her love; for her employ them all,
    Commend them and condemn them to her service
    Or to their own perdition.⁶

POLIXENES   Fairly offered.

CAMILLO   This shows a sound affection.

---

5. This may be a reference to a court performance of Ben Jonson's *Masque of Oberon*, which included a dance of twelve satyrs. It was first put on in January of 1611.

6. Either dedicate my attributes to her service or sentence them to destruction, with a pun on "perdition" and "Perdita."

365	OLD SHEPHERD But, my daughter,	

<pre>
365   OLD SHEPHERD   But, my daughter,
        Say you the like to him?
      PERDITA   I cannot speak
        So well, nothing so well, no, nor mean better.
        By th' pattern of mine own thoughts I cut out
        The purity of his.⁷
      OLD SHEPHERD   Take hands, a bargain;
370   And, friends unknown, you shall bear witness to't.
        I give my daughter to him, and will make
        Her portion° equal his.   dowry
      FLORIZEL   O, that must be
        I'th' virtue of your daughter. One° being dead,   Someone
        I shall have more than you can dream of yet,
375   Enough then for your wonder. But come on,
        Contract us fore these witnesses.⁸
      OLD SHEPHERD   Come, your hand;
        And, daughter, yours.
      POLIXENES   Soft,° swain, a while, beseech you.   Go slowly
        Have you a father?
      FLORIZEL   I have. But what of him?
380   POLIXENES   Knows he of this?
      FLORIZEL   He neither does nor shall.
      POLIXENES   Methinks a father
        Is at the nuptial of his son a guest
        That best becomes the table. Pray you once more,
385   Is not your father grown incapable
        Of reasonable affairs?⁹ Is he not stupid
        With age and alt'ring rheums?° Can he speak, hear,   debilitating disease
        Know man from man? Dispute° his own estate?°   Discuss / condition
        Lies he not bed-rid, and again does nothing
        But what he did being childish?
390   FLORIZEL   No, good sir.
        He has his health, and ampler strength indeed
        Than most have of his age.
      POLIXENES   By my white beard,
        You offer him, if this be so, a wrong
        Something unfilial.° Reason my son¹   Somewhat unbecoming a son
395   Should choose himself a wife, but as good reason
        The father, all whose joy is nothing else
        But fair posterity, should hold some counsel
        In such a business.
      FLORIZEL   I yield° all this;   grant
        But for some other reasons, my grave sir,
400   Which 'tis not fit you know, I not acquaint
        My father of this business.
      POLIXENES   Let him know't.
      FLORIZEL   He shall not.
      POLIXENES   Prithee let him.
      FLORIZEL   No, he must not.
      OLD SHEPHERD   Let him, my son. He shall not need to grieve
        At knowing of thy choice.
</pre>

---

7. By my pure thoughts I recognize the purity of his. A dressmaking metaphor.
8. A pledge of marriage spoken before two witnesses was legally binding.

9. Unfit to handle matters requiring reason and good sense.
1. It is reasonable that my son.

FLORIZEL   Come, come, he must not.
   Mark our contract.
405 POLIXENES [*removing his disguise*]   Mark your divorce, young sir,
   Whom son I dare not call. Thou art too base
   To be acknowledged. Thou a sceptre's heir,
   That thus affects° a sheep-hook?   *desires*
   [*To the* OLD SHEPHERD]   Thou, old traitor,
   I am sorry that by hanging thee I can but
   Shorten thy life one week.
410 [*To* PERDITA]   And thou, fresh piece
   Of excellent witchcraft,[2] who of force° must know   *of necessity*
   The royal fool thou cop'st° with—   *you deal; you have sex*
OLD SHEPHERD   O, my heart!
POLIXENES   I'll have thy beauty scratched with briers and made
   More homely than thy state.
   [*To* FLORIZEL]   For thee, fond° boy,   *foolish*
415 If I may ever know thou dost but sigh
   That thou no more shalt see this knack,° as never   *worthless thing*
   I mean thou shalt, we'll bar thee from succession,
   Not hold thee of our blood, no, not our kin,
   Farre than Deucalion off.[3] Mark thou my words.
   Follow us to the court.
420 [*To the* OLD SHEPHERD]   Thou churl, for this time,
   Though full of our displeasure, yet we free thee
   From the dead° blow of it.   *deadly*
   [*To* PERDITA]   And you, enchantment,
   Worthy enough a herdsman—yea, him° too,   *(Florizel)*
   That makes himself, but for our honour therein,
425 Unworthy thee[4]—if ever henceforth thou
   These rural latches to his entrance open,
   Or hoop° his body more with thy embraces,   *encircle*
   I will devise a death as cruel for thee
   As thou art tender to't.   *Exit*
PERDITA   Even here undone.
430 I was not much afeard, for once or twice
   I was about to speak, and tell him plainly
   The selfsame sun that shines upon his court
   Hides not his visage from our cottage, but
   Looks on alike.° Will't please you, sir, be gone?   *both alike*
435 I told you what would come of this. Beseech you,
   Of your own state take care. This dream of mine
   Being now awake, I'll queen it no inch farther,°   *play the queen no further*
   But milk my ewes and weep.
CAMILLO [*to the* OLD SHEPHERD]   Why, how now, father?
   Speak ere thou diest.
OLD SHEPHERD   I cannot speak, nor think,
   Nor dare to know that which I know.
440 [*To* FLORIZEL]   O sir,
   You have undone a man of fourscore-three,°   *eighty-three*

2. You beautiful young woman skilled in witchcraft.
Some people believed that witches could induce love by
potions.
3. Less linked in kinship than Deucalion, who accord-
ing to classical mythology was, along with his wife, the
only person to escape a flood sent by Zeus. He thus was
the ancestor of humankind and the most distant rela-
tion one might have.
4. A difficult passage. Polixenes seems to mean that
Florizel, by his actions, has made himself unworthy of
even a shepherd's daughter were it not for the fact that
he is a King's son and so would harm his father's honor
by such a marriage.

That thought to fill his grave in quiet, yea,
To die upon the bed my father died,
To lie close by his honest bones. But now
445 Some hangman must put on my shroud, and lay me
Where no priest shovels in dust.[5]
[*To* PERDITA]   O cursed wretch,
That knew'st this was the Prince, and wouldst adventure
To mingle faith° with him. Undone, undone!   *exchange vows*
If I might die within this hour, I have lived
To die when I desire.   *Exit*

450 FLORIZEL [*to* PERDITA]   Why look you so upon me?
I am but sorry, not afeard; delayed,
But nothing altered. What I was, I am,
More straining on for plucking back,[6] not following
My leash unwillingly.[7]
CAMILLO   Gracious my lord,
455 You know your father's temper. At this time
He will allow no speech—which I do guess
You do not purpose° to him; and as hardly°   *intend / unwillingly*
Will he endure your sight as yet, I fear.
Then till the fury of his highness settle,
Come not before him.
460 FLORIZEL   I not purpose it.
I think, Camillo?[8]
CAMILLO   Even he, my lord.
PERDITA [*to* FLORIZEL]   How often have I told you 'twould be thus?
How often said my dignity would last
But° till 'twere known?   *Only*
FLORIZEL   It cannot fail but by
465 The violation of my faith, and then
Let nature crush the sides o'th' earth together
And mar the seeds° within. Lift up thy looks.   *sources of life*
From my succession wipe me, father! I
Am heir to my affection.
CAMILLO   Be advised.°   *prudent*
470 FLORIZEL   I am, and by my fancy.° If my reason   *love*
Will thereto be obedient, I have reason.[9]
If not, my senses, better pleased with madness,
Do bid it° welcome.   *(madness)*
CAMILLO   This is desperate, sir.
FLORIZEL   So call it. But it does fulfil my vow.
475 I needs must think it honesty. Camillo,
Not for Bohemia, nor the pomp that may
Be thereat gleaned; for all the sun sees, or
The close° earth wombs,° or the profound seas hides   *secret / holds in her womb*
In unknown fathoms, will I break my oath
480 To this my fair beloved. Therefore, I pray you,
As you have ever been my father's honoured friend,
When he shall miss me—as, in faith, I mean not
To see him any more—cast your good counsels

---

5. As a criminal, he would be buried without ritual under the gallows. In regular funeral rites, the priest customarily placed the first shovelful of dirt on the grave.
6. More eager to go forward because of being pulled back.
7. Not following this course of action unwillingly (like a dog dragged by its leash).
8. Camillo may here have taken off his disguise or been recognized by Florizel even with it on.
9. If my reason will obey love, I will embrace reason.

Upon his passion.° Let myself and fortune   *anger*
485 Tug° for the time to come. This you may know,   *Contend*
And so deliver:° I am put to sea   *report*
With her who here I cannot hold on shore;
And most opportune to her need, I have
A vessel rides fast by,° but not prepared   *anchored nearby*
490 For this design. What course I mean to hold
Shall nothing benefit your knowledge, nor
Concern me the reporting.[1]

CAMILLO   O my lord,
I would your spirit were easier for advice,°   *to advise*
Or stronger for your need.

FLORIZEL   Hark, Perdita—
[*To* CAMILLO] I'll hear you by and by.

495 CAMILLO [*aside*]   He's irremovable,°   *unyielding*
Resolved for flight. Now were I happy if
His going I could frame to serve my turn,
Save him from danger, do him love and honour,
Purchase the sight again of dear Sicilia
500 And that unhappy king, my master, whom
I so much thirst to see.

FLORIZEL   Now, good Camillo,
I am so fraught with curious business° that   *matters requiring care*
I leave out ceremony.

CAMILLO   Sir, I think
You have heard of my poor services i'th' love
That I have borne your father?

505 FLORIZEL   Very nobly
Have you deserved. It is my father's music
To speak your deeds, not little of his care
To have them recompensed as thought on.[2]

CAMILLO   Well, my lord,
If you may please to think I love the King,
510 And through him what's nearest to him, which is
Your gracious self, embrace but my direction,°   *simply follow my advice*
If your more ponderous° and settled project   *weighty*
May suffer° alteration. On mine honour,   *permit*
I'll point you where you shall have such receiving
515 As shall become your highness, where you may
Enjoy your mistress—from the whom I see
There's no disjunction° to be made but by,   *separation*
As heavens forfend,° your ruin—marry her,   *forbid*
And with my best endeavours in your absence
520 Your discontenting° father strive to qualify°   *discontented / appease*
And bring him up to liking.°   *to giving approval*

FLORIZEL   How, Camillo,
May this, almost a miracle, be done?—
That I may call thee something more than man,
And after that trust to thee.

CAMILLO   Have you thought on°   *of*
A place whereto you'll go?

525 FLORIZEL   Not any yet.

---

1. Would not benefit you to know nor me to report.
2. And no small matter among his affairs to reward your deeds as fully as he values them.

But as th'unthought-on accident is guilty
To what we wildly do,[3] so we profess
Ourselves to be the slaves of chance, and flies
Of every wind that blows.[4]

CAMILLO   Then list to me.
530 This follows, if you will not change your purpose
But undergo this flight: make for Sicilia,
And there present yourself and your fair princess,
For so I see she must be, fore Leontes.
She shall be habited° as it becomes   *dressed*
535 The partner of your bed. Methinks I see
Leontes opening his free° arms and weeping   *generous*
His welcomes forth; asks thee there 'Son, forgiveness!'
As 'twere i'th' father's person,[5] kisses the hands
Of your fresh princess; o'er and o'er divides him
540 'Twixt his unkindness and his kindness.[6] Th'one
He chides° to hell, and bids the other grow   *rebukes*
Faster than thought or time.

FLORIZEL   Worthy Camillo,
What colour° for my visitation shall I   *pretext*
Hold up before him?

CAMILLO   Sent by the King your father
545 To greet him, and to give him comforts. Sir,
The manner of your bearing towards him, with
What you, as from your father, shall deliver—°   *say*
Things known betwixt us three—I'll write you down,
The which shall point you forth° at every sitting   *direct you*
550 What you must say, that he shall not perceive
But that you have your father's bosom° there,   *trust*
And speak his very heart.

FLORIZEL   I am bound to you.
There is some sap° in this.   *life*

CAMILLO   A course more promising
Than a wild dedication of yourselves
555 To unpathed waters, undreamed shores; most certain,
To miseries enough—no hope to help you,
But as you shake off one, to take another;
Nothing so certain° as your anchors, who   *certain (to detain you)*
Do their best office if they can but stay° you   *keep*
560 Where you'll be loath to be. Besides, you know,
Prosperity's the very bond of love,
Whose fresh complexion and whose heart together
Affliction alters.°   *changes for the worse*

PERDITA   One of these is true.
I think affliction may subdue the cheek°   *make one pale*
But not take in° the mind.   *conquer*

565 CAMILLO   Yea, say you so?
There shall not at your father's house these seven years[7]
Be born another such.

FLORIZEL   My good Camillo,

---

3. But as the unexpected event (Polixenes' discovery of our love) is responsible for our rash behavior now.
4. And like flies blown about by the winds.
5. As if he were your father; *or* as if you were your father.

6. That is, he divides his speech between his past unkindness to your father and the kindness he is eager to perform now.
7. Proverbial expression meaning "for a long time."

She's as forward of her breeding as
She is i'th' rear our birth.[8]

CAMILLO   I cannot say 'tis pity

570   She lacks instructions,° for she seems a mistress°   *schooling / teacher*
To most that teach.

PERDITA   Your pardon, sir. For this
I'll blush you thanks.

FLORIZEL   My prettiest Perdita!
But O, the thorns we stand upon! Camillo,
Preserver of my father, now of me,

575   The medicine of our house, how shall we do?
We are not furnished° like Bohemia's son,   *dressed; equipped*
Nor shall appear so in Sicilia.

CAMILLO   My lord,
Fear none of this. I think you know my fortunes

580   Do all lie there. It shall be so my care
To have you royally appointed° as if   *outfitted*
The scene you play were mine.° For instance, sir,   *written by me*
That you may know you shall not want—one word.
     [*They speak apart.*]
     Enter AUTOLYCUS

AUTOLYCUS   Ha, ha! What a fool honesty is, and trust—his sworn

585   brother—a very simple gentleman! I have sold all my trumpery;
not a counterfeit stone, not a ribbon, glass, pomander,[9] brooch,
table-book,° ballad, knife, tape, glove, shoe-tie, bracelet, horn-   *notebook*
ring[1] to keep my pack from fasting.° They throng who should   *from going empty*
buy first, as if my trinkets had been hallowed,° and brought a   *blessed; made sacred*

590   benediction to the buyer; by which means I saw whose purse
was best in picture;° and what I saw, to my good use I remem-   *looked best (to steal)*
bered. My clown, who wants but something° to be a reasonable   *lacks only one thing*
man, grew so in love with the wenches' song that he would not
stir his pettitoes° till he had both tune and words, which so   *feet (pigs' toes)*

595   drew the rest of the herd to me that all their other senses stuck
in ears.° You might have pinched a placket, it was sense-   *were devoted to hearing*
less.° 'Twas nothing to geld a codpiece of a purse.[2] I could have   *felt nothing*
filed keys off that hung in chains. No hearing, no feeling but
my sir's song, and admiring the nothing of it.[3] So that in this

600   time of lethargy I picked and cut most of their festival purses,
and had not the old man come in with a hubbub against his
daughter and the King's son, and scared my choughs° from the   *jackdaws (silly birds)*
chaff, I had not left a purse alive in the whole army.
     [CAMILLO, FLORIZEL, *and* PERDITA *come forward*]

CAMILLO   Nay, but my letters by this means being there

605   So soon as you arrive shall clear that doubt.

FLORIZEL   And those that you'll procure from King Leontes—

CAMILLO   Shall satisfy your father.

PERDITA   Happy be you!
All that you speak shows fair.

CAMILLO [*seeing* AUTOLYCUS]   Who have we here?

---

8. That is, "She is as superior to her lowly upbringing
as she is inferior to our noble birth."
9. A mixture of sweet-smelling substances made into a
ball and carried about for ornament or to prevent infec-
tion.
1. A ring made from horn, which was said to possess

magical qualities.
2. It was easy to cut a purse loose from a codpiece, the
baglike article of dress attached to the front of a man's
hose and covering his genitals.
3. The silliness of it, with a pun on "nothing" and "not-
ing" (meaning "tune"), which were similarly pronounced.

We'll make an instrument of this, omit

610 Nothing° may give us aid.   *Nothing that*

AUTOLYCUS [*aside*] If they have overheard me now—why,
    hanging!

CAMILLO How now, good fellow? Why shakest thou so? Fear
    not, man. Here's no harm intended to thee.

615 AUTOLYCUS I am a poor fellow, sir.

CAMILLO Why, be so still.° Here's nobody will steal that from   *always*
    thee. Yet for the outside of thy poverty,° we must make an   *your ragged clothes*
    exchange. Therefore discase° thee instantly— thou must think   *undress*
    there's a necessity in't—and change garments with this gentle-

620   man. Though the pennyworth° on his side be the worst, yet   *bargain*
    hold thee, [*giving him money*] there's some boot.°   *something more*

AUTOLYCUS I am a poor fellow, sir. [*Aside*] I know ye well
    enough.

CAMILLO Nay prithee, dispatch°—the gentleman is half flayed[4]   *hurry*

625   already.

AUTOLYCUS Are you in earnest,[5] sir? [*Aside*] I smell the trick on't.

FLORIZEL Dispatch, I prithee.

AUTOLYCUS Indeed, I have had earnest, but I cannot with con-
    science take it.

630 CAMILLO Unbuckle, unbuckle.
        [FLORIZEL *and* AUTOLYCUS *exchange clothes*]
    [*To* PERDITA] Fortunate mistress—let my prophecy
    Come home to ye![6]—you must retire yourself
    Into some covert,° take your sweetheart's hat   *hiding place*
    And pluck it o'er your brows, muffle your face,

635   Dismantle you,° and, as you can, dislikon°   *Take off your cloak / disguise*
    The truth of your own seeming,° that you may—   *appearance*
    For I do fear eyes°—over to shipboard   *spies*
    Get undescried.

PERDITA   I see the play so lies
    That I must bear a part.

CAMILLO   No remedy.
    [*To* FLORIZEL] Have you done there?

640 FLORIZEL   Should I now meet my father
    He would not call me son.

CAMILLO   Nay, you shall have no hat.
    [*He gives the hat to* PERDITA]
    Come, lady, come. Farewell, my friend.

AUTOLYCUS   Adieu, sir.

FLORIZEL O Perdita, what have we twain forgot!
    Pray you, a word.
        [*They speak aside*]

645 CAMILLO [*aside*] What I do next shall be to tell the King
    Of this escape, and whither they are bound;
    Wherein my hope is I shall so prevail
    To force him after, in whose company
    I shall re-view Sicilia, for whose sight
    I have a woman's longing.[7]

---

4. Half undressed (skinned).
5. "Serious," with a pun on "earnest" as meaning both "sincere" and "an advance payment." See line 628.
6. Let my prophecy (that she be fortunate) be fulfilled.
7. Women, especially pregnant women, were said to be vulnerable to irrational and very intense cravings.

650 FLORIZEL   Fortune speed us!
Thus we set on, Camillo, to th' seaside.
CAMILLO   The swifter speed the better.
                    Exeunt [FLORIZEL, PERDITA, *and* CAMILLO][8]
AUTOLYCUS   I understand the business, I hear it. To have an open
ear, a quick eye, and a nimble hand is necessary for a cutpurse.
655 A good nose is requisite also, to smell out work for th'other
senses. I see this is the time that the unjust man doth thrive.
What an exchange had this been without boot!° What a boot[9]   *even without payment*
is here with this exchange! Sure the gods do this year connive
at° us, and we may do anything extempore.° The Prince him-   *indulge / spontaneously*
660 self is about a piece of iniquity, stealing away from his father
with his clog° at his heels. If I thought it were a piece of honesty   *encumbrance (Perdita)*
to acquaint the King withal,° I would not do't. I hold it the   *with it*
more knavery to conceal it, and therein am I constant° to my   *faithful*
profession.
                    Enter [*the*] CLOWN *and* [*the* OLD] SHEPHERD[, *carrying a*
                    fardel° *and a box*]   *bundle*
665 Aside, aside! Here is more matter for a hot brain. Every lane's
end, every shop, church, session,° hanging, yields a careful   *court session*
man work.
CLOWN   See, see, what a man you are now! There is no other
way but to tell the King she's a changeling,[1] and none of your
670 flesh and blood.
OLD SHEPHERD   Nay, but hear me.
CLOWN   Nay, but hear *me.*
OLD SHEPHERD   Go to,° then.   *Go ahead*
CLOWN   She being none of your flesh and blood, your flesh and
675 blood has not offended the King, and so your flesh and blood
is not to be punished by him. Show those things you found
about her, those secret things, all but what she has with her.
This being done, let the law go whistle, I warrant you.
OLD SHEPHERD   I will tell the King all, every word, yea, and his
680 son's pranks, too, who, I may say, is no honest man, neither to
his father nor to me, to go about to make me the King's brother-
in-law.
CLOWN   Indeed, brother-in-law was the farthest off'° you could   *most remote relation*
have been to him, and then your blood had been the dearer by
685 I know not how much an ounce.
AUTOLYCUS [*aside*]   Very wisely, puppies.
OLD SHEPHERD   Well, let us to the King. There is that in this
fardel will make him scratch his beard.
AUTOLYCUS [*aside*]   I know not what impediment this complaint
690 may be to the flight of my master.°   *(Florizel)*
CLOWN   Pray heartily he be at'° palace.   *at the*
AUTOLYCUS [*aside*]   Though I am not naturally honest, I am so
sometimes by chance. Let me pocket up my pedlar's excre-
ment.°   *hair*
                    [*He removes his false beard*]
695 —How now, rustics, whither are you bound?
OLD SHEPHERD   To th' palace, an° it like your worship.   *if*

---

8. F marks a single *"Exit"* here for Camillo, but Florizel
and Perdita undoubtedly exit also, leaving Autolycus
alone on stage to comment on what he has witnessed.

9. Benefit; shoe.
1. A child left or abducted by fairies. See note to
3.3.109.

AUTOLYCUS   Your affairs there? What? With whom? The condi-
    tion of that fardel?° The place of your dwelling? Your names?   *nature of that bundle*
    Your ages? Of what having,° breeding,° and anything that is   *property / upbringing*
700   fitting to be known, discover.°   *reveal*
CLOWN   We are but plain° fellows, sir.   *simple; smooth*
AUTOLYCUS   A lie, you are rough and hairy. Let me have no
    lying. It becomes none but tradesmen, and they often give us
    soldiers the lie,[2] but we pay them for it with stamped coin, not
705   stabbing steel, therefore they do not *give* us the lie.[3]
CLOWN   Your worship had like to have given us one° if you had   *(the lie)*
    not taken yourself with the manner.[4]
OLD SHEPHERD   Are you a courtier, an't like you, sir?
AUTOLYCUS   Whether it like me or no, I am a courtier. Seest thou
710   not the air of the court in these enfoldings?° Hath not my gait   *garments*
    in it the measure° of the court? Receives not thy nose court   *stately walk*
    odour from me? Reflect I not on thy baseness court-contempt?
    Thinkest thou, for that I insinuate° to toze° from thee thy busi-   *subtly work / tease out*
    ness, I am therefore no courtier? I am courtier cap-à-pie,° and   *from head to foot*
715   one that will either push on or pluck back thy business there.
    Whereupon I command thee to open° thy affair.   *reveal*
OLD SHEPHERD   My business, sir, is to the King.
AUTOLYCUS   What advocate hast thou to him?
OLD SHEPHERD   I know not, an't like you.
720 CLOWN [*aside to the* OLD SHEPHERD]   'Advocate' 's the court
    word for a pheasant.[5] Say you have none.
OLD SHEPHERD   None, sir. I have no pheasant, cock nor hen.
AUTOLYCUS [*aside*]   How blessed are we that are not simple men!
    Yet nature might have made me as these are,
725   Therefore I will not disdain.
CLOWN   This cannot be but° a great courtier.   *anyone but*
OLD SHEPHERD   His garments are rich, but he wears them not
    handsomely.
CLOWN   He seems to be the more noble in being fantastical.° A   *eccentric*
730   great man, I'll warrant. I know by the picking on's teeth.[6]
AUTOLYCUS   The fardel there, what's i'th' fardel? Wherefore that
    box?
OLD SHEPHERD   Sir, there lies such secrets in this fardel and box
    which none must know but the King, and which he shall know
735   within this hour, if I may come to th' speech of him.
AUTOLYCUS   Age,° thou hast lost thy labour.   *Old man*
OLD SHEPHERD   Why, sir?
AUTOLYCUS   The King is not at the palace, he is gone aboard a
    new ship to purge° melancholy and air himself; for if thou   *rid himself of*
740   beest capable of° things serious, thou must know the King is   *can understand*
    full of grief.
OLD SHEPHERD   So 'tis said, sir; about his son, that should have
    married a shepherd's daughter.
AUTOLYCUS   If that shepherd be not in handfast,° let him fly. The   *arrested*

---

2. They call us soldiers liars; they cheat us soldiers.
3. Punning on "give the lie" as meaning both "cheat"
and "insult me in a way that requires a challenge to a
duel." The point seems to be that since soldiers pay
with good currency rather than by stabbing (the appro-
priate response to an insult), vendors can't claim to
have given anything—including the lie—to anyone, and
a duel can be successfully avoided.

4. If you had not stopped yourself in the middle.
5. The Clown thinks "advocate" means "bribe" or
"gift," of which a pheasant would be an example. He is
confusing the King's court with a law court in which
game birds were supposedly given as bribes to local
magistrates.
6. Ornate toothpicks were considered fashionable
accessories.

745 curses he shall have, the tortures he shall feel, will break the
back of man, the heart of monster.

CLOWN   Think you so, sir?

AUTOLYCUS   Not he alone shall suffer what wit can make heavy
and vengeance bitter, but those that are germane° to him,   related
750 though removed fifty times, shall all come under the hangman,
which, though it be great pity, yet it is necessary. An old sheep-
whistling rogue,⁷ a ram-tender, to offer to have his daughter
come into grace!° Some say he shall be stoned; but that death   favor (at court)
is too soft for him, say I. Draw our throne into a sheepcote?°   pen for sheep
755 All deaths are too few, the sharpest too easy.

CLOWN   Has the old man e'er a son, sir, do you hear, an't like
you, sir?

AUTOLYCUS   He has a son, who shall be flayed alive, then
'nointed over with honey, set on the head of a wasps' nest, then
760 stand till he be three-quarters-and-a-dram° dead, then recov-   a tiny bit
ered again with aqua-vitae,° or some other hot infusion, then,   brandy
raw as he is, and in the hottest day prognostication° proclaims,   almanac prediction
shall he be set against a brick wall, the sun looking with a
southward eye upon him, where he is to behold him with flies
765 blown° to death. But what talk we of these traitorly rascals,   swollen
whose miseries are to be smiled at, their offences being so
capital? Tell me, for you seem to be honest plain men, what
you have° to the King. Being something gently considered,⁸ I'll   have to say
bring you where he is aboard, tender° your persons to his pres-   deliver
770 ence, whisper him in your behalfs, and if it be in man, besides
the King, to effect your suits, here is man shall do it.

CLOWN [to the OLD SHEPHERD]   He seems to be of great author-
ity. Close° with him, give him gold; and though authority be a   Make a deal
stubborn bear, yet he is oft led by the nose with gold. Show the
775 inside of your purse to the outside of his hand, and no more
ado. Remember—'stoned', and 'flayed alive'.

OLD SHEPHERD   An't please you, sir, to undertake the business
for us, here is that° gold I have. I'll make it as much more, and   what
leave this young man in pawn° till I bring it you.   as security
780 AUTOLYCUS   After I have done what I promised?

OLD SHEPHERD   Ay, sir.

AUTOLYCUS   Well, give me the moiety.° [To the CLOWN] Are you   half
a party in this business?

CLOWN   In some sort, sir. But though my case° be a pitiful one,   condition; skin
785 I hope I shall not be flayed out of it.

AUTOLYCUS   O, that's the case of the shepherd's son. Hang him,
he'll be made an example.

CLOWN [to the OLD SHEPHERD]   Comfort, good comfort. We
must to the King, and show our strange sights. He must
790 know 'tis none of your daughter, nor my sister. We are gone°   lost (dead)
else.° [To AUTOLYCUS] Sir, I will give you as much as this old   otherwise
man does when the business is performed, and remain, as he
says, your pawn till it be brought you.

AUTOLYCUS   I will trust you. Walk before° toward the seaside. Go   ahead of me
795 on the right hand. I will but look upon the hedge,⁹ and follow
you.

7. An old rascal who whistles while he tends sheep.   will give me a bribe worthy of my high rank.
8. As I am a highly regarded gentleman at court; if you   9. Slang for "relieve myself."

CLOWN [*to the* OLD SHEPHERD]   We are blessed in this man, as I
    may say, even blessed.
OLD SHEPHERD   Let's before, as he bids us. He was provided to
800   do us good.   [*Exit with the* CLOWN]
AUTOLYCUS   If I had a mind to be honest, I see fortune would
    not suffer° me. She drops booties° in my mouth. I am courted   *permit / prizes*
    now with a double occasion:° gold, and a means to do the   *opportunity*
    Prince my master good, which who knows how that may turn
805   back to my advancement? I will bring these two moles, these
    blind ones, aboard him.° If he think it fit to shore them[1] again,   *(his ship)*
    and that the complaint they have to the King concerns him
    nothing, let him call me rogue for being so far officious, for I
    am proof against° that title, and what shame else belongs to't.   *impervious to*
810   To him will I present them. There may be matter in it.   *Exit*

5.1
Enter LEONTES, CLEOMENES, DION, [*and*] PAULINA
CLEOMENES [*to* LEONTES]   Sir, you have done enough, and have performed
    A saint-like sorrow. No fault could you make
    Which you have not redeemed, indeed, paid down
    More penitence than done trespass.[1] At the last
5   Do as the heavens have done, forget your evil.
    With them, forgive yourself.
LEONTES   Whilst I remember
    Her and her virtues I cannot forget
    My blemishes in them,° and so still think of   *in relation to them*
    The wrong I did myself, which was so much
10   That heirless it hath made my kingdom, and
    Destroyed the sweet'st companion that e'er man
    Bred his hopes out of. True?
PAULINA   Too true, my lord.
    If one by one you wedded all the world,
    Or from the all that are took something good
15   To make a perfect woman, she you killed
    Would be unparalleled.
LEONTES   I think so. Killed?
    She I killed? I did so. But thou strik'st me
    Sorely to say I did; it is as bitter
    Upon thy tongue as in my thought. Now, good now,°   *if you would*
    Say so but seldom.
20 CLEOMENES   Not at all,° good lady.   *Never (say these things)*
    You might have spoke a thousand things that would
    Have done the time more benefit,[2] and graced°   *showed*
    Your kindness better.
PAULINA   You are one of those
    Would have him wed again.
DION   If you would not so
25   You pity not the state,° nor the remembrance   *kingdom*
    Of his most sovereign name,[3] consider little
    What dangers, by his highness' fail of issue,°   *lack of offspring*
    May drop upon his kingdom and devour

1. Put them ashore.
5.1 Location: Sicilia. The palace of Leontes.
1. Performed more penance than your sin warranted.
2. That would have been more useful in these times.
3. Nor the perpetuation of his royal lineage (through a new child).

Incertain lookers-on.⁴ What were more holy
30 Than to rejoice the former queen is well?°   *(in heaven)*
What holier, than for royalty's repair,
For present comfort and for future good,
To bless the bed of majesty again
With a sweet fellow to't?

PAULINA   There is none worthy
35 Respecting° her that's gone. Besides, the gods   *In comparison to*
Will have fulfilled their secret purposes.⁵
For has not the divine Apollo said?
Is't not the tenor of his oracle
That King Leontes shall not have an heir
40 Till his lost child be found? Which that it shall
Is all as monstrous° to our human reason   *incredible*
As my Antigonus to break his grave
And come again to me, who, on my life,
Did perish with the infant. 'Tis your counsel
45 My lord should to the heavens be contrary,
Oppose against their wills.
[*To* LEONTES]   Care not for issue.
The crown will find an heir. Great Alexander
Left his to th' worthiest,⁶ so his successor
Was like to be the best.

LEONTES   Good Paulina,
50 Who hast the memory of Hermione,
I know, in honour—O, that ever I
Had squared me° to thy counsel! Then even now   *conformed my actions*
I might have looked upon my queen's full eyes,
Have taken treasure from her lips.

PAULINA   And left them
More rich for what they yielded.

55 LEONTES   Thou speak'st truth.
No more such wives, therefore no wife. One worse,
And better used,° would make her sainted spirit   *treated*
Again possess her° corpse, and on this stage,   *(Hermione's)*
Where we offenders mourn, appear soul-vexed,°   *with troubled soul*
And begin, 'Why° to me?'   *Why offer this insult*

60 PAULINA   Had she such power
She had just cause.

LEONTES   She had, and would incense me
To murder her I married.

PAULINA   I should so.
Were I the ghost that walked I'd bid you mark
Her eye, and tell me for what dull part in't
65 You chose her. Then I'd shriek that even your ears
Should rift° to hear me, and the words that followed   *split*
Should be, 'Remember mine'.°   *(my eyes)*

LEONTES   Stars, stars,
And all eyes else,° dead coals! Fear thou no wife.   *all other eyes*
I'll have no wife, Paulina.

4. And destroy those subjects who are bewildered (by the matter of his successor).
5. Will ensure that their secret purposes are fulfilled.
6. Alexander the Great (356–323 B.C.E.), conqueror of Greece, Persia, and Egypt, died before his own son was born and reportedly urged his followers simply to choose the worthiest man as his successor.

PAULINA   Will you swear

70   Never to marry but by my free leave?

LEONTES   Never, Paulina, so be blest my spirit.

PAULINA   Then, good my lords, bear witness to his oath.

CLEOMENES   You tempt him over-much.

PAULINA   Unless another

    As like Hermione as is her picture

    Affront° his eye—   *Confront*

75 CLEOMENES   Good madam, I have done.[7]

PAULINA   Yet if my lord will marry—if you will, sir;

    No remedy but you will—give me the office

    To choose your queen. She shall not be so young

    As was your former, but she shall be such

80   As, walked your first queen's ghost,[8] it should take joy

    To see her in your arms.

LEONTES   My true Paulina,

    We shall not marry till thou bidd'st us.

PAULINA   That

    Shall be when your first queen's again in breath.°   *alive*

    Never till then.

        Enter a SERVANT

85 SERVANT   One that gives out himself° Prince Florizel,   *claims to be*

    Son of Polixenes, with his princess—she

    The fairest I have yet beheld—desires access

    To your high presence.

LEONTES   What° with him? He comes not   *Who comes*

    Like to° his father's greatness. His approach,   *As befits*

90   So out of circumstance° and sudden, tells us   *informal*

    'Tis not a visitation framed,° but forced   *planned*

    By need and accident. What train?°   *retinue*

SERVANT   But few,

    And those but mean.°   *of low rank*

LEONTES   His princess, say you, with him?

SERVANT   Ay, the most peerless piece of earth, I think,

    That e'er the sun shone bright on.

95 PAULINA   O, Hermione,

    As every present time doth boast itself

    Above a better, gone, so must thy grave

    Give way to what's seen now![9]

    [*To the* SERVANT]   Sir, you yourself

    Have said and writ so; but your writing now

100   Is colder than that theme. She had not been

    Nor was not to be equalled—thus your verse

    Flowed with her beauty once. 'Tis shrewdly° ebbed   *grievously*

    To say you have seen a better.

SERVANT   Pardon, madam.

    The one° I have almost forgot—your pardon!   *(Hermione)*

105   The other, when she has obtained your eye,

    Will have your tongue too. This is a creature,

---

7. Many editors emend this line to assign "I have done" to Paulina, rather than Cleomenes. As it stands, the line suggests Cleomenes' exasperation that Paulina will not listen to him. If emended to assign the last three words to Paulina, the exchange may suggest that Paulina is at least minimally responsive to the pleas of Leontes' courtiers that she mitigate her opposition to his remarriage.
8. If Hermione appeared as a ghost.
9. As each present time boasts itself to be superior to a time better than itself, but gone from view, so you, in your grave, must be superseded by what is now seen.

Would she begin a sect, might quench the zeal
Of all professors else;[1] make proselytes°   *converts*
Of who° she but bid follow.   *Of those who*

PAULINA   How? Not women!

110   SERVANT   Women will love her that she is a woman
More worth° than any man; men, that she is   *worthy*
The rarest of all women.

LEONTES   Go, Cleomenes.
Yourself, assisted with your honoured friends,
Bring them to our embracement.   *Exit* [CLEOMENES]
                     Still 'tis strange
He thus should steal upon us.

115   PAULINA   Had our prince,
Jewel of children, seen this hour, he had paired
Well with this lord. There was not full a month°   *a full month*
Between their births.

LEONTES   Prithee no more, cease. Thou know'st
He dies to me again when talked of. Sure,
120   When I shall see this gentleman thy speeches
Will bring me to consider that which may
Unfurnish me of reason.° They are come.   *Make me go mad*
     Enter FLORIZEL, PERDITA, CLEOMENES, *and others*
Your mother was most true to wedlock, Prince,
For she did print your royal father off,[2]
125   Conceiving you. Were I but twenty-one,
Your father's image is so hit° in you,   *exact*
His very air, that I should call you brother,
As I did him, and speak of something wildly
By us performed before. Most dearly welcome,
130   And your fair princess—goddess! O, alas,
I lost a couple that 'twixt heaven and earth
Might thus have stood, begetting wonder, as
You, gracious couple, do; and then I lost—
All mine own folly—the society,
135   Amity too, of your brave° father, whom,   *stouthearted*
Though bearing misery, I desire my life[3]
Once more to look on him.

FLORIZEL   By his command
Have I here touched Sicilia, and from him
Give you all greetings that a king at friend°   *in friendship*
140   Can send his brother; and but° infirmity,   *were it not that*
Which waits upon worn times,° hath something seized   *accompanies old age*
His wished ability,[4] he had himself
The lands and waters 'twixt your throne and his
Measured° to look upon you, whom he loves—   *Journeyed across*
145   He bade me say so—more than all the sceptres,
And those that bear them, living.

LEONTES   O, my brother!
Good gentleman, the wrongs I have done thee stir
Afresh within me, and these thy offices,°   *greetings*
So rarely° kind, are as interpreters   *extraordinarily*

---

1. Of all those who professed other religions.
2. Made an exact copy of Polixenes, as a printer produces a book.

3. Whom, though I am suffering, I wish to live long enough.
4. Has somewhat deprived him of his desired strength.

150   Of my behindhand slackness.⁵ Welcome hither,
          As is the spring to th'earth! And hath he too
          Exposed this paragon to th' fearful usage—
          At least ungentle—of the dreadful Neptune°   *god of the sea*
          To greet a man not worth her pains, much less
          Th'adventure° of her person?   *risk*
155 FLORIZEL   Good my lord,
          She came from Libya.
     LEONTES   Where the warlike Smalus,⁶
          That noble honoured lord, is feared and loved?
     FLORIZEL   Most royal sir, from thence; from him whose daughter
          His tears proclaimed his, parting with her. Thence,
160   A prosperous south wind friendly, we have crossed,
          To execute the charge my father gave me
          For visiting your highness. My best train
          I have from your Sicilian shores dismissed;
          Who for Bohemia bend,° to signify   *make their way*
165   Not only my success in Libya, sir,
          But my arrival, and my wife's, in safety
          Here where we are.
     LEONTES   The blessèd gods
          Purge all infection from our air whilst you
          Do climate° here! You have a holy father,   *reside*
170   A graceful gentleman, against whose person,
          So sacred as it is, I have done sin,
          For which the heavens, taking angry note,
          Have left me issueless; and your father's blessed,
          As he from heaven merits it, with you,
175   Worthy his goodness. What might I have been,
          Might I a son and daughter now have looked on,
          Such goodly things as you?
                  Enter a LORD
     LORD   Most noble sir,
          That which I shall report will bear no credit
          Were not the proof so nigh. Please you, great sir,
180   Bohemia greets you from himself by me;
          Desires you to attach° his son, who has,   *arrest*
          His dignity and duty⁷ both cast off,
          Fled from his father, from his hopes, and with
          A shepherd's daughter.
     LEONTES   Where's Bohemia? Speak.
185 LORD   Here in your city. I now came from him.
          I speak amazedly,° and it becomes°   *confusedly / befits*
          My marvel° and my message. To your court   *astonishment*
          Whiles he was hast'ning—in the chase, it seems,
          Of this fair couple—meets he on the way
190   The father of this seeming° lady and   *apparent; false*
          Her brother, having both their country quitted
          With this young prince.
     FLORIZEL   Camillo has betrayed me,

---

5. Are reminders of my slowness (in greeting you).   Plutarch.
6. An obscure allusion. The name may be a misprint   7. His royal status and his duty to his father.
for "Synalus," a soldier from Carthage mentioned by

Whose honour and whose honesty till now
Endured all weathers.

LORD   Lay't so to his charge.°   *Accuse him directly*
He's with the King your father.

LEONTES   Who, Camillo?

LORD   Camillo, sir. I spake with him, who now
Has these poor men in question. Never saw I
Wretches so quake. They kneel, they kiss the earth,
Forswear° themselves as often as they speak.   *Perjure*
Bohemia stops his ears, and threatens them
With divers deaths in death.°   *With diverse tortures*

PERDITA   O, my poor father!
The heaven sets spies upon us, will not have
Our contract celebrated.

LEONTES   You are married?

FLORIZEL   We are not, sir, nor are we like to be.
The stars, I see, will kiss the valleys first.
The odds for high and low's alike.[8]

LEONTES   My lord,
Is this the daughter of a king?

FLORIZEL   She is,
When once she is my wife.

LEONTES   That 'once', I see, by your good father's speed
Will come on very slowly. I am sorry,
Most sorry, you have broken from his liking
Where you were tied in duty; and as sorry
Your choice is not so rich in worth° as beauty,   *rank*
That you might well enjoy her.

FLORIZEL [*to* PERDITA]   Dear, look up.
Though fortune, visible an enemy,
Should chase us with my father, power no jot
Hath she to change our loves.[9]—Beseech you, sir,
Remember since you owed no more to time
Than I do now.° With thought of such affections,   *when you were my age*
Step forth mine advocate. At your request
My father will grant precious things as trifles.

LEONTES   Would he do so, I'd beg your precious mistress,
Which he counts but a trifle.

PAULINA   Sir, my liege,
Your eye hath too much youth in't. Not a month
Fore your queen died she was more worth such gazes
Than what you look on now.

LEONTES   I thought of her
Even in these looks I made.
[*To* FLORIZEL]   But your petition
Is yet unanswered. I will to your father.
Your honour not o'erthrown by your desires,[1]
I am friend to them and you. Upon which errand
I now go toward him. Therefore follow me,
And mark what way I make. Come, good my lord.   *Exeunt*

---

8. That is, "Chance treats those of high and low rank
identically."
9. Even if Lady Fortune were to make herself apparent
as our enemy and join my father in pursuit, she would

remain powerless to change our love.
1. So long as you have not allowed passion to destroy
your virtue.

5.2

Enter AUTOLYCUS *and a* GENTLEMAN

AUTOLYCUS Beseech you, sir, were you present at this relation?°   *when this was told*

FIRST GENTLEMAN I was by at the opening of the fardel, heard
the old shepherd deliver the manner how he found it; where-
upon, after a little amazedness, we were all commanded out of
5   the chamber. Only this, methought I heard the shepherd say
he found the child.

AUTOLYCUS I would most gladly know the issue° of it.   *outcome*

FIRST GENTLEMAN I make a broken delivery° of the business, but   *confused report*
the changes I perceived in the King and Camillo were very
10   notes of admiration.[1] They seemed almost, with staring on one
another, to tear the cases° of their eyes. There was speech in   *burst the sockets*
their dumbness, language in their very gesture. They looked as°   *as if*
they had heard of a world ransomed, or one destroyed. A
notable passion of wonder appeared in them, but the wisest
15   beholder, that knew no more but seeing, could not say if
th'importance were joy or sorrow. But in the extremity of the
one,° it must needs be.   *of the one or the other*

Enter another GENTLEMAN

Here comes a gentleman that happily° knows more. The news,   *perhaps*
Ruggiero!

20 SECOND GENTLEMAN Nothing but bonfires. The oracle is ful-
filled. The King's daughter is found. Such a deal° of wonder is   *a great quantity*
broken out within this hour, that ballad-makers cannot be able
to express it.[2]

Enter another GENTLEMAN

Here comes the Lady Paulina's steward. He can deliver you
25   more.—How goes it now, sir? This news which is called true is
so like an old tale that the verity of it is in strong suspicion. Has
the King found his heir?

THIRD GENTLEMAN Most true, if ever truth were pregnant by cir-
cumstance.° That which you hear you'll swear you see, there is   *proven by evidence*
30   such unity in the proofs. The mantle of Queen Hermione's,
her jewel about the neck of it, the letters of Antigonus found
with it, which they know to be his character;° the majesty of   *handwriting*
the creature, in resemblance of the mother; the affection of°   *instinct toward*
nobleness which nature shows above° her breeding,° and many *in excess of / upbringing*
35   other evidences proclaim her with all certainty to be the King's
daughter. Did you see the meeting of the two kings?

SECOND GENTLEMAN No.

THIRD GENTLEMAN Then have you lost a sight which was to be
seen, cannot be spoken of. There might you have beheld one
40   joy crown another, so and in such manner that it seemed sor-
row wept to take leave of them, for their joy waded in tears.
There was casting up of eyes, holding up of hands, with counte-
nance° of such distraction[3] that they were to be known by gar-   *face*
ment, not by favour.° Our king being ready to leap out of   *features*
45   himself for joy of his found daughter, as if that joy were now
become a loss cries, 'O, thy mother, thy mother!', then asks
Bohemia forgiveness, then embraces his son-in-law, then again

---

5.2 Location: Sicilia. The palace of Leontes.   scandals and sensations.
1. Were the very marks of wonder.   3. So altered by emotion.
2. Ballads often provided accounts of contemporary

worries he° his daughter with clipping° her. Now he thanks the   *he agitates / embracing*
old shepherd, which stands by like a weather-bitten conduit of
50 many kings' reigns.[4] I never heard of such another encounter,
which lames report to follow it,[5] and undoes° description to do°   *defies / express*
it.

SECOND GENTLEMAN What, pray you, became of Antigonus, that
carried hence the child?

55 THIRD GENTLEMAN Like an old tale still, which will have matter
to rehearse° though credit° be asleep and not an ear open. He   *relate / belief*
was torn to pieces with a bear. This avouches° the shepherd's   *vows*
son, who has not only his innocence,° which seems much, to   *simplemindedness*
justify him, but a handkerchief and rings of his,° that Paulina   *(of Antigonus)*
60 knows.

FIRST GENTLEMAN What became of his barque° and his fol-   *ship*
lowers?

THIRD GENTLEMAN Wrecked the same instant of their master's
death, and in the view of the shepherd; so that all the instru-
65 ments which aided to expose the child were even then lost
when it was found. But O, the noble combat that 'twixt joy and
sorrow was fought in Paulina! She had one eye declined for
the loss of her husband, another elevated[6] that the oracle was
fulfilled. She lifted the Princess from the earth, and so locks
70 her in embracing as if she would pin her to her heart, that she
might no more be in danger of losing.°   *of being lost*

FIRST GENTLEMAN The dignity of this act was worth the audi-
ence of kings and princes, for by such was it acted.

THIRD GENTLEMAN One of the prettiest touches of all, and that
75 which angled for mine eyes—caught the water,° though not   *(my tears)*
the fish—was when at the relation of the Queen's death, with
the manner how she came to't bravely confessed and lamented
by the King, how attentiveness° wounded his daughter till from   *intent listening*
one sign of dolour° to another she did, with an 'Alas', I would   *grief*
80 fain say bleed tears; for I am sure my heart wept blood. Who
was most marble° there changed colour. Some swooned, all   *unfeeling*
sorrowed. If all the world could have seen't, the woe had been
universal.

FIRST GENTLEMAN Are they returned to the court?

85 THIRD GENTLEMAN No. The Princess, hearing of her mother's
statue, which is in the keeping of Paulina, a piece many years
in doing, and now newly performed° by that rare Italian master   *completed*
Giulio Romano,[7] who, had he himself eternity and could put
breath into his work, would beguile° nature of her custom,° so   *cheat / business*
90 perfectly he is her ape.° He so near to Hermione hath done   *imitator*
Hermione that they say one would speak to her and stand in
hope of answer. Thither with all greediness of affection are
they gone, and there they intend to sup.

SECOND GENTLEMAN I thought she had some great matter there
95 in hand, for she hath privately twice or thrice a day, ever since
the death of Hermione, visited that removed° house. Shall we   *distant; hidden*
thither, and with our company piece° the rejoicing?   *join*

4. Who stands by weeping like a waterspout that has
been around for the reigns of many Kings. Some large
buildings had "conduits" or waterpipes in the form of
gargoyles or gnarled human faces.
5. Which makes any account of it seem deficient.
6. That is, Paulina simultaneously cried and laughed.

7. An Italian painter, a follower of Raphael, who died in
1546 and was most famous for a series of erotic draw-
ings illustrating sexual positions, or "postures." It is not
clear whether Shakespeare, in fact, had ever seen any of
his work.

FIRST GENTLEMAN   Who would be thence, that has the benefit
of access? Every wink of an eye some new grace will be born.
100   Our absence makes us unthrifty to our knowledge.[8] Let's
along.   *Exeunt* [GENTLEMEN]

AUTOLYCUS   Now, had I not the dash° of my former life in me, | stain; touch
would preferment° drop on my head. I brought the old man | royal favor
and his son aboard the° Prince; told him I heard them talk of a | aboard the ship of the
105   fardel, and I know not what. But he at that time over-fond of
the shepherd's daughter—so he then took her to be—who
began to be much sea-sick, and himself little better, extremity
of weather continuing, this mystery remained undiscovered.
But 'tis all one to me, for had I been the finder-out of this secret
110   it would not have relished° among my other discredits. | appeared well
        Enter [*the* OLD] SHEPHERD *and* [*the*] CLOWN [*dressed as
        gentlemen*]
Here come those I have done good to against my will, and
already appearing in the blossoms of their fortune.

OLD SHEPHERD   Come, boy; I am past more children, but thy
sons and daughters will be all gentlemen born.

115   CLOWN [*to* AUTOLYCUS]   You are well met, sir. You denied to
fight with me this other° day because I was no gentleman born. | the other
See you these clothes? Say you see them not, and think me
still no gentleman born. You were best say these robes are not
gentlemen born. Give me the lie,[9] do, and try whether I am
120   not now a gentleman born.

AUTOLYCUS   I know you are now, sir, a gentleman born.

CLOWN   Ay, and have been so any time these four hours.

OLD SHEPHERD   And so have I, boy.

CLOWN   So you have; but I was a gentleman born before my
125   father, for the King's son took me by the hand and called me
brother; and then the two kings called my father brother; and
then the Prince my brother and the Princess my sister called
my father father; and so we wept; and there was the first gentle-
man-like tears that ever we shed.

130   OLD SHEPHERD   We may live, son, to shed many more.

CLOWN   Ay, or else 'twere hard luck, being in so preposterous
estate[1] as we are.

AUTOLYCUS   I humbly beseech you, sir, to pardon me all the
faults I have committed to your worship, and to give me your
135   good report to the Prince my master.

OLD SHEPHERD   Prithee, son, do, for we must be gentle° now we | act nobly
are gentlemen.

CLOWN   Thou wilt amend thy life?

AUTOLYCUS   Ay, an it like your good worship.

140   CLOWN   Give me thy hand. I will swear to the Prince thou art as
honest a true fellow as any is in Bohemia.

OLD SHEPHERD   You may say it, but not swear it.

CLOWN   Not swear it now I am a gentleman? Let boors° and | peasants
franklins° say it; I'll swear it. | small farmers

145   OLD SHEPHERD   How if it be false, son?

CLOWN   If it be ne'er so false,° a true gentleman may swear it in | Even if it is false

---

8. Makes us squander an opportunity to add to our knowledge.
9. Insult me so that I must respond with the challenge of a duel.
1. The Clown probably means "prosperous," but "pre-

posterous" is a nice blunder for it suggests that their new status as gentlemen is preposterous in the sense of (1) contrary to nature or (2) putting last what should be first—that is, inverting the social order by putting "real" gentlemen behind "false" gentlemen like themselves.

the behalf of his friend, [*to* AUTOLYCUS] and I'll swear to the
Prince thou art a tall fellow of thy hands° and that thou wilt not   *a brave man of action*
be drunk; but I know thou art no tall fellow of thy hands and
150   that thou wilt be drunk; but I'll swear it, and I would thou
wouldst be a tall fellow of thy hands.

AUTOLYCUS   I will prove so, sir, to my power.°   *as well as I can*

CLOWN   Ay, by any means prove a tall fellow. If I do not wonder
how thou dar'st venture to be drunk, not being a tall fellow,
155   trust me not.
       [*Flourish within*]
Hark, the kings and princes, our kindred, are going to see the
Queen's picture.° Come, follow us. We'll be thy good masters.   *likeness*
                              Exeunt

5.3

Enter LEONTES, POLIXENES, FLORIZEL, PERDITA, CA-
MILLO, PAULINA, LORDS [*and attendants*][1]

LEONTES   O grave and good Paulina, the great comfort
That I have had of thee!

PAULINA   What,° sovereign sir,   *Whatever*
I did not well, I meant well. All my services
You have paid home,° but that you have vouchsafed°   *fully rewarded / vowed*
5   With your crowned brother and these young contracted
Heirs of your kingdoms my poor house to visit,
It is a surplus° of your grace which never   *an additional sign*
My life may last to answer.

LEONTES   O Paulina,
We honour you with trouble.[2] But we came
10   To see the statue of our queen. Your gallery
Have we passed through, not without much content
In many singularities;° but we saw not   *In seeing many rarities*
That which my daughter came to look upon,
The statue of her mother.

PAULINA   As she lived peerless,
15   So her dead likeness I do well believe
Excels what ever yet you looked upon,
Or hand of man hath done. Therefore I keep it
Lonely,° apart. But here it is. Prepare   *Alone*
To see the life as lively mocked° as ever   *realistically imitated*
20   Still° sleep mocked death. Behold, and say 'tis well.   *Quiet*
       [*She draws a curtain and reveals the figure of* HERMI-
       ONE, *standing like a statue*]
I like your silence; it the more shows off
Your wonder. But yet speak; first you, my liege.
Comes it not something° near?   *somewhat*

LEONTES   Her natural posture.
Chide me, dear stone, that I may say indeed
25   Thou art Hermione; or rather, thou art she
In thy not chiding, for she was as tender

5.3 Location: Sicilia. Paulina's house.
1. In F, the stage direction reads: "*Enter Leontes, Polix-
enes, Florizell, Perdita, Camillo, Paulina: Hermione (like
a Statue:) Lords, etc.*" For a reader of the play, this direc-
tion suggests that Hermione is a living character pre-
tending to be a statue. For a theatergoer unacquainted

with the play, by contrast, the immobile female figure
seen on stage is probably first assumed to be an actual
statue of the dead Queen.
2. The honor we pay to you demands much of you (by
way of hospitality).

As infancy and grace. But yet, Paulina,
Hermione was not so much wrinkled, nothing°   *not at all*
So agèd as this seems.
POLIXENES   O, not by much.
30 PAULINA   So much the more our carver's excellence,
Which lets go by some sixteen years, and makes her
As° she lived now.   *As if*
LEONTES   As now she might have done,
So much to my good comfort as it is
Now piercing to my soul. O, thus she stood,
35 Even with such life of majesty—warm life,
As now it coldly stands—when first I wooed her.
I am ashamed. Does not the stone rebuke me
For being more stone° than it? O royal piece!°   *hard-hearted / work of art*
There's magic in thy majesty, which has
40 My evils conjured° to remembrance, and   *summoned*
From thy admiring° daughter took the spirits,   *wondering*
Standing like stone with thee.
PERDITA   And give me leave,
And do not say 'tis superstition, that
I kneel and then implore her blessing.³ Lady,
45 Dear Queen, that ended when I but began,
Give me that hand of yours to kiss.
PAULINA   O, patience!
The statue is but newly fixed;° the colour's   *painted*
Not dry.
CAMILLO [*to* LEONTES]   My lord, your sorrow was too sore° laid on,   *painfully*
50 Which sixteen winters cannot blow away,
So many summers dry.⁴ Scarce any joy
Did ever so long live; no sorrow
But killed itself much sooner.
POLIXENES [*to* LEONTES]   Dear my brother,
Let him that was the cause of this have power
55 To take off so much grief from you as he
Will piece up in himself.⁵
PAULINA [*to* LEONTES]   Indeed, my lord,
If I had thought the sight of my poor image
Would thus have wrought you°—for the stone is mine—   *made you distraught*
I'd not have showed it.
[*She makes to draw the curtain*]
LEONTES   Do not draw the curtain.
60 PAULINA   No longer shall you gaze on't, lest your fancy
May think anon it moves.
LEONTES   Let be, let be!
Would I were dead but that methinks already.⁶
What was he that did make it? See, my lord,
Would you not deem it breathed, and that those veins
Did verily bear blood?
65 POLIXENES   Masterly done.
The very life seems warm upon her lip.
LEONTES   The fixture of her eye has motion in't,⁷

---

3. A possible reference to the Protestant attack on the
Catholic practice of kneeling before images of the Vir-
gin Mary.
4. And an equal number of summers cannot dry up.
5. Will make a part of himself.
6. May I die if I do not think it already moves.
7. The setting ("fixture") of her eye gives the appear-
ance of motion.

As° we are mocked with art.   *In such a way that*
PAULINA   I'll draw the curtain.
 My lord's almost so far transported that
 He'll think anon it lives.
70 LEONTES   O sweet Paulina,
 Make me to think so twenty years together.
 No settled senses° of the world can match   *calm state of mind*
 The pleasure of that madness. Let's alone.
PAULINA I am sorry, sir, I have thus far stirred you; but
 I could afflict you farther.
75 LEONTES   Do, Paulina,
 For this affliction has a taste as sweet
 As any cordial° comfort. Still methinks   *restorative*
 There is an air comes from her.° What fine chisel *she seems to breathe*
 Could ever yet cut breath? Let no man mock me,
 For I will kiss her.
80 PAULINA   Good my lord, forbear.
 The ruddiness upon her lip is wet.
 You'll mar it if you kiss it, stain your own
 With oily painting.° Shall I draw the curtain?   *paint*
LEONTES No, not these twenty years.
PERDITA   So long could I
 Stand by, a looker-on.
85 PAULINA   Either forbear,
 Quit presently° the chapel, or resolve you   *immediately*
 For more amazement. If you can behold it,
 I'll make the statue move indeed, descend,
 And take you by the hand. But then you'll think—
90 Which I protest against—I am assisted
 By wicked powers.
LEONTES   What you can make her do
 I am content to look on; what to speak,
 I am content to hear; for 'tis as easy
 To make her speak as move.
PAULINA   It is required
95 You do awake your faith. Then, all stand still.
 Or those that think it is unlawful business
 I am about, let them depart.
LEONTES   Proceed.
 No foot shall stir.
PAULINA   Music; awake her; strike!°   *strike up!*
   [*Music*]
   [*To* HERMIONE] 'Tis time. Descend. Be stone no more. Approach.
100 Strike all that look upon with marvel. Come,
 I'll fill your grave up. Stir. Nay, come away.
 Bequeath to death your numbness, for from him°   *(death)*
 Dear life redeems you.
 [*To* LEONTES]   You perceive she stirs.
   [HERMIONE *slowly descends*]
 Start not. Her actions shall be holy as
105 You hear my spell is lawful. Do not shun her
 Until you see her die again, for then
 You kill her double.[8] Nay, present your hand.
 When she was young, you wooed her. Now, in age,

---

8. That is, "If you were to shun her in this new life, you would kill her again."

Is she become the suitor?

LEONTES   O, she's warm!

110   If this be magic, let it be an art
Lawful as eating.

POLIXENES   She embraces him.

CAMILLO   She hangs about his neck.
If she pertain to life,° let her speak too.   *be truly alive*

115 POLIXENES   Ay, and make it manifest where she has lived,
Or how stol'n from the dead.

PAULINA   That she is living,
Were it but told you, should be hooted at
Like an old tale. But it appears she lives,
Though yet she speak not. Mark a little while.

120   [*To* PERDITA] Please you to interpose, fair madam. Kneel,
And pray your mother's blessing.—Turn, good lady,
Our Perdita is found.

HERMIONE   You gods, look down,
And from your sacred vials pour your graces
Upon my daughter's head.—Tell me, mine own,

125   Where hast thou been preserved? Where lived? How found
Thy father's court? For thou shalt hear that I,
Knowing by Paulina that the oracle
Gave hope thou wast in being,° have preserved   *alive*
Myself to see the issue.°   *the outcome; the child*

PAULINA   There's time enough for that,

130   Lest they desire upon this push to trouble
Your joys with like relation.[9] Go together,
You precious winners all; your exultation
Partake° to everyone. I, an old turtle,[1]   *Spread your happiness*
Will wing me to some withered bough, and there

135   My mate, that's never to be found again,
Lament till I am lost.°   *dead*

LEONTES   O peace, Paulina!
Thou shouldst a husband take by my consent,
As I by thine a wife. This is a match,
And made between's by vows. Thou hast found mine,

140   But how is to be questioned, for I saw her,
As I thought, dead, and have in vain said many
A prayer upon her grave. I'll not seek far—
For him, I partly know his mind—to find thee
An honourable husband. Come, Camillo,

145   And take her by the hand, whose worth and honesty
Is richly noted, and here justified°   *testified to*
By us, a pair of kings. Let's from this place.
[*To* HERMIONE] What, look upon my brother. Both your pardons,
That e'er I put between your holy looks

150   My ill suspicion. This'° your son-in-law   *This is*
And son unto the King, whom heavens directing
Is troth-plight° to your daughter. Good Paulina,   *betrothed*
Lead us from hence, where we may leisurely
Each one demand and answer to his part

155   Performed in this wide gap of time since first
We were dissevered. Hastily lead away.   *Exeunt*

---

9. Lest they (bystanders?) desire at this crucial moment to trouble your happiness with similar stories.
1. I.e., turtledove, a symbol of faithful love.

Is she become the suitor?

LEONTES   O, she's warm!
If this be magic, let it be an art   110
Lawful as eating.

POLIXENES   She embraces him.

CAMILLO   She hangs about his neck.
If she pertain to life, let her speak too.

POLIXENES   Ay, and make it manifest where she has lived,   115
Or how stol'n from the dead.

PAULINA   That she is living,
Were it but told you, should be hooted at
Like an old tale. But it appears she lives,
Though yet she speak not. Mark a little while.
[To Perdita] Please you to interpose, fair madam. Kneel,   120
And pray your mother's blessing.—Turn, good lady,
Our Perdita is found.

HERMIONE   You gods, look down,
And from your sacred vials pour your graces
Upon my daughter's head.—Tell me, mine own,
Where hast thou been preserved? Where lived? How found   125
Thy father's court? For thou shalt hear that I,
Knowing by Paulina that the oracle
Gave hope thou wast in being, have preserved
Myself to see the issue.

PAULINA   There's time enough for that,
Lest they desire upon this push to trouble   130
Your joys with like relation. Go together,
You precious winners all; your exultation
Partake to everyone. I, an old turtle,
Will wing me to some withered bough, and there
My mate, that's never to be found again,   135
Lament till I am lost.

LEONTES   O peace, Paulina!
Thou shouldst a husband take by my consent,
As I by thine a wife. This is a match,
And made between's by vows. Thou hast found mine,
But how is to be questioned, for I saw her,   140
As I thought, dead, and have in vain said many
A prayer upon her grave. I'll not seek far—
For him, I partly know his mind—to find thee
An honourable husband. Come, Camillo,
And take her by the hand, whose worth and honesty   145
Is richly noted, and here justified
By us, a pair of kings. Let's from this place.
What, look upon my brother. Both your pardons,
That e'er I put between your holy looks
My ill suspicion. This your son-in-law,   150
And son unto the King, whom heavens directing,
Is troth-plight to your daughter. Good Paulina,
Lead us from hence, where we may leisurely
Each one demand and answer to his part
Performed in this wide gap of time since first   155
We were dissevered. Hastily lead away.
Exeunt

8. Lest they (the winners) desire at this social moment to trouble your happiness with similar sorrow.
1. The turtledove, a symbol of faithful love.

The Tempest

Near the close of *King Lear*, the ruined old king, stripped of the last vestiges of his power, dreams of being locked away happily in prison with his beloved Cordelia. Father and daughter have a more tragic fate in store for them, but Shakespeare returns to the dream in *The Tempest*. The play opens on a remote island of exile where Prospero, deposed from power and thrust out of Milan by his wicked brother, has found shelter with his only daughter, Miranda. Unlike many of Shakespeare's plays, *The Tempest* does not appear to have a single dominant source for its plot, but it is a kind of echo chamber of Shakespearean motifs. Its story of loss and recovery and its air of wonder link it closely to the group of late plays that modern editors generally call "romances" (*Pericles, The Winter's Tale, Cymbeline*), but it resonates as well with issues that haunted Shakespeare's imagination throughout his career: the painful necessity for a father to let his daughter go (*Othello, King Lear*); the treacherous betrayal of a legitimate ruler (*Richard II, Julius Caesar, Hamlet, Macbeth*); the murderous hatred of one brother for another (*Richard III, As You Like It, Hamlet, King Lear*); the passage from court society to the wilderness and the promise of a return (*A Midsummer Night's Dream, As You Like It*); the young heiress, torn from her place in the social hierarchy (*Twelfth Night, Pericles, The Winter's Tale*); the dream of manipulating others by means of art, especially by staging miniature plays within plays (*1 Henry IV, Much Ado About Nothing, Hamlet*); the threat of a radical loss of identity (*The Comedy of Errors, Richard II, King Lear*); the relationship between nature and nurture (*Pericles, The Winter's Tale*); the harnessing of magical powers (*The First Part of the Contention [2 Henry VI], A Midsummer Night's Dream, Macbeth*).

Though it is the first play printed in the First Folio (1623), *The Tempest* is probably one of the last that Shakespeare wrote. It can be dated fairly precisely: it uses material that was not available until late 1610, and there is a record of a performance before the king on Hallowmas Night, 1611. Since Shakespeare retired soon after to Stratford, *The Tempest* has seemed to many to be his valedictory to the theater. In this view, Prospero's strangely anxious and moving epilogue—"Now my charms are all o'erthrown, / And what strength I have's mine own"—is the expression of Shakespeare's own professional leave-taking. There are reasons to be skeptical: after finishing *The Tempest*, he collaborated on at least two other plays, *All Is True (Henry VIII)* and *The Two Noble Kinsmen*, and it is perilous to identify Shakespeare too closely with any of his characters, let alone an exiled, embittered, manipulative princely wizard. Yet the echo-chamber effect is striking, and when Prospero and others speak of his powerful "art," it is difficult not to associate the skill of the great magician with the skill of the great playwright. Near the end of the play, the association is made explicit when Prospero uses his magic powers to produce what he terms "some vanity of mine art" (4.1.41), a betrothal masque performed by spirits whom he calls forth "to enact / My present fancies" (4.1.121–22). The masque, typically a lavish courtly performance with music and dancing, may have seemed particularly appropriate on the occasion of another early performance: *The Tempest* was one of fourteen plays provided as part of the elaborate festivities in honor of the betrothal and marriage of King James's daughter Elizabeth to Frederick, the elector palatine. As Prospero's gift of the beautiful spectacle displays his magnificence and authority, so *The Tempest* and the other plays commanded by the king for his daughter's wedding would have enhanced his own prestige.

The Tempest opens with a spectacular storm that recalls *King Lear* not only in its violence but in its indifference to the ruler's authority: "What cares these roarers for

Magical storm. From Olaus Magnus, *Historia de Gentibus Septentrionalibus* (1555 ed.).

the name of king?" (1.1.15–16), shouts the exasperated Boatswain at the aristocrats who are standing in his way. The Boatswain's outburst seems unanswerable: like the implacable thunder in *King Lear*, the tempest marks the point at which exalted titles are revealed to be absurd pretensions, substanceless in the face of the elemental forces of nature and the desperate struggle for survival. But we soon learn that this tempest is not in fact natural and that it emphatically does hear and respond to human power, a power that is terrifying but, at least by its own account, benign: "The direful spectacle of the wreck," Prospero tells his daughter, "I have with such provision in mine art / So safely ordered" (1.2.26, 28–29) that no one on board has been harmed.

Shakespeare's contemporaries were fascinated by the figure of the magus, the great magician who by dint of deep learning, ascetic discipline, and patient skill could command the secret forces of the natural and supernatural world. Distinct from the village witch and "cunning man," figures engaged in local acts of healing and malice, and distinct, too, from alchemical experimenters bent on turning base metal into gold, the magus, cloaked in a robe covered with mysterious symbols, pronounced his occult charms, called forth spirits, and ranged in his imagination through the heavens and the earth, conjoining contemplative wisdom with virtuous action in order to confer great benefits upon his age. But there was a shiver of fear mingled with the popular admiration: when the person in Shakespeare's time most widely identified as a magus, the wizard John Dee, was away from his house, his library, one of the greatest private collections of books in England, was set on fire and burned to the ground.

Book, costume, powerful language, the ability to enact the fancies of the brain: these are key elements of both magic and theater. "I have bedimmed / The noontide sun," Prospero declares (5.1.41–42), beginning an enumeration of extraordinary accomplishments that culminates with the revelation that

> graves at my command
> Have waked their sleepers, oped, and let 'em forth
> By my so potent art.
>
> (5.1.48–50)

For the playwright who conjured up the ghosts of Caesar and old Hamlet, the claim does not seem extravagant, but for a magician it amounts to an extremely dangerous confession. Necromancy—communing with the spirits of the dead—was the very essence of black magic, the hated practice from which Prospero is careful to distinguish himself throughout the play. Before his exile, the island had been the realm of the "damned witch Sycorax," who was banished there "for mischiefs manifold and sorceries terrible" (1.2.265–66). The legitimacy of Prospero's power, including power over his slave Caliban, Sycorax's son, depends on his claims to moral authority, but for one disturbing moment it is difficult to see the difference between "foul witch" and princely magician. Small wonder that as soon as he has disclosed that he has trafficked with the dead, Prospero declares that he abjures his "rough magic" (5.1.50).

Prospero does not give an explicit reason for this abjuration, but it appears to be a key stage in the complex process that has led, before the time of the play, to his overthrow and will lead, after the play's events are over, to his return to power. This process in its entirety requires years to unfold, but the play depicts only a small, though crucially important, fragment of it. Together with his early *Comedy of Errors, The Tempest* is unusual among Shakespeare's plays in observing what literary critics of the age called the unities of time and place; unlike *Antony and Cleopatra,* for example, which ranges over a huge territory, or *The Winter's Tale,* which covers a huge span of time, the actions of *The Tempest* all take place in a single locale, the island, during the course of a single day. In a long scene of exposition just after the spectacular opening storm, Prospero tells Miranda that he is at a critical moment; everything depends on his seizing the opportunity that fortune has granted him. The whole play, then, is the spectacle of his timing, timing that might be cynically termed political opportunism or theatrical cunning but that Prospero himself associates with the working out of "providence divine" (1.2.160). The opportunity he seizes has its tangled roots in what he calls "the dark backward and abyss of time" (1.2.50). Many years before, when he was Duke of Milan, Prospero's preoccupation with "secret studies" gave his ambitious and unscrupulous brother Antonio the opportunity to topple him from power. Now those same studies, perfected during his long exile, have enabled Prospero to cause

The conjurer. Engraving by Theodore de Bry after a drawing by John White. From Thomas Hariot, *A Briefe and True Report of the New Found Land of Virginia* (1590).

Antonio and his shipmates, sailing back to Italy from Tunis, to be shipwrecked on his island, where they have fallen unwittingly under his control. His magic makes it possible not only to wrest back his dukedom but to avenge himself for the terrible wrong that his brother and his brother's principal ally, Alonso, the King of Naples, have done him: "They now are in my power" (3.3.90). Audiences in Shakespeare's time would have had an all too clear image of how horrendous the vengeance of enraged princes usually was. That Prospero restrains himself from the full exercise of his power to harm his enemies, that he breaks his magic staff and drowns his book, is his highest moral achievement, a triumphant display of self-mastery: "The rarer action is / In virtue than in vengeance" (5.1.27–28).

All of those who are shipwrecked on the island undergo the same shock of terror and unexpected survival, but their experiences, as they cross the yellow sands and make their way toward the interior of the island, differ markedly. The least affected are the mariners, including the feisty Boatswain; after their exhausting labors in the storm, they have sunk into a strange, uneasy sleep, only to be awakened in time to sail the miraculously restored ship back to Italy. The others are put through more complex trials; exposed to varying degrees of anxiety, temptation, grief, fear, and penitence, they are in effect subjects in a psychological experiment carefully conducted by Prospero, who attempts to instill in them moral self-control and work-discipline. The most generously treated is Ferdinand, the only son of the King of Naples, whom Prospero, in what is essentially a carefully planned dynastic alliance, has secretly chosen to be his son-in-law. As Ferdinand bewails what he assumes is his father's death by drowning, he hears strange, haunting music, including the remarkable song of death and metamorphosis, "Full fathom five thy father lies" (1.2.400). Ferdinand is the only one of the shipwrecked company, until the play's final scene, to encounter Prospero directly; the magician makes the experience menacing, humiliating, and frustrating, but this is the modest, salutary price the young man must pay to win the hand of the beautiful Miranda, who seems to him a goddess and who, for her part, has fallen in love with him at first sight.

Prospero directs the experience of the rest as well, but not in person; instead they principally encounter his diligent servant, Ariel. Ariel is not human, although at a crucial moment he is able to imagine what he would feel "were I human" (5.1.20). He is, as the cast of characters describes him, an "airy spirit," capable of moving at immense speed, altering the weather, and producing vivid illusions. We learn that Ariel possesses an inherent moral "delicacy," a delicacy that in the past (that is, before the time depicted in the play) has brought him pain. For, as Prospero reminds him, he had been Sycorax's servant and was, for refusing "to act her earthy and abhorred commands" (1.2.275), imprisoned by the witch for many years in a cloven pine. Prospero freed him from confinement and now demands in return a fixed term of service, which Ariel provides with a mixture of brilliant alacrity and grumbling. Prospero responds in turn with mingled affection and anger, alternating warm praises and dire threats. Although Prospero's "art," through which he commands Ariel and the lesser spirits, seems to foresee and control everything, this control is purchased by constant discipline.

And, for all his godlike powers, there are limits to what Prospero can do. He can make the loathed Antonio and the others know something of the bitterness of loss and isolation; he can produce in them irresistible drowsiness and startled awakenings; he can command Ariel to lay before them a splendid banquet and then make it suddenly vanish; he can drive them to desperation and madness. But in the case of his own brother and Alonso's similarly wicked brother Sebastian, Prospero cannot reshape their inner lives and effect a moral transformation. The most he can do with these men without conscience is to limit through continual vigilance any further harm they might do and to take back what is rightfully his. When, with an obvious effort, Prospero declares that he forgives his brother's "rankest fault" (5.1.134), Antonio is conspicuously silent.

But the higher moral purpose of Prospero's art is not all a failure. With Alonso, the project of provoking repentance by generating intense grief and fear succeeds admirably: Alonso not only gives up his power over the dukedom of Milan but begs Prospero's pardon for the wrong he committed in conspiring to overthrow him. (Both rulers, Alonso and Prospero, can look forward to a unification of their states in the next generation, through the marriage of Ferdinand and Miranda.) Moreover, Prospero's carefully contrived scenarios succeed in confirming the decency, loyalty, and goodness of Alonso's counselor, Gonzalo, who had years before provided the exiled Duke and his daughter with the means necessary for their survival.

It is Gonzalo's goodness that at the end of the play enables him to grasp the dynastic providence in the bewildering tangle of events—"Was Milan thrust from Milan, that his issue / Should become kings of Naples?" (5.1.208–09)—and that earlier inspires him to sense the miraculous nature of their survival. Indifferent to the contemptuous mockery of the cynical Antonio and Sebastian, Gonzalo responds to shipwreck on the strange island by speculating on how he would govern it were he responsible for its "plantation":

> I'th' commonwealth I would by contraries
> Execute all things. For no kind of traffic
> Would I admit, no name of magistrate;
> Letters should not be known; riches, poverty,
> And use of service, none; contract, succession,
> Bourn, bound of land, tilth, vineyard, none;
> No use of metal, corn, or wine, or oil;
> No occupation, all men idle, all.
>
> (2.1.147–54)

Shakespeare adapted Gonzalo's utopian speculations from a passage in "Of Cannibals" (1580), a remarkably free-spirited essay by the French humanist Michel de Montaigne. The Brazilian Indians, Montaigne admiringly writes (in John Florio's 1603 translation), have "no kind of traffic, no knowledge of letters, no intelligence of numbers, no name

America. Engraving by Theodor Galle after a drawing by Jan van der Straet (c. 1580).

of magistrate nor of politic superiority, no use of service, of riches or of poverty, no contracts, no successions . . . no occupation but idle, no respect of kindred but common, no apparel but natural, no manuring of lands, no use of wine, corn, or metal." For Montaigne, the European adventurers and colonists, confident in their cultural superiority, are the real barbarians, while the American natives, with their cannibalism and free love, live in accordance with nature.

The issues raised by Montaigne, and more generally by New World voyages, may have been particularly interesting to *The Tempest*'s early audiences as news reached London of the extraordinary adventures of the Virginia Company's colony at Jamestown. Shakespeare seems to have read a detailed account of these adventures in a letter written by the colony's secretary, William Strachey; although the letter was not printed until 1625, it was evidently circulating in manuscript in 1610. In 1609, a fleet carrying more than four hundred persons sent out to reinforce the colony was struck by a hurricane near the Virginia coast. Two of the vessels reached their destination, but the third, the ship carrying the governor, Sir Thomas Gates, ran aground on an uninhabited island in the Bermudas. Remarkably enough, all of the passengers and crew survived; but their tribulations were not over. By forcing everyone to labor side by side in order to survive, the violence of the storm had weakened the governor's authority, and both the natural abundance and the isolation of the island where they were shipwrecked weakened it further. Gates ordered the company to build new ships in order to sail to Jamestown, but his command met with ominous grumblings and threats of mutiny. According to Strachey's letter, the main troublemaker directly challenged Gates's authority: "therefore let the Governour (said he) kiss, etc." In response, Gates had the troublemaker shot to death. New ships were built, and in an impressive feat of navigation, the entire company reached Jamestown. The group found the settlement deeply demoralized: illness was rampant, food was scarce, and relations with the neighboring Indians, once amicable, had completely broken down. Only harsh military discipline kept the English colony from falling apart.

With the possible exception of some phrases from Strachey's description of the storm and a few scattered details, *The Tempest* does not directly use any of this vivid narrative. Prospero's island is evidently in the Mediterranean, and the New World is only mentioned as a far-off place, "the still-vexed Bermudas" (1.2.230), where the swift Ariel flies to fetch dew. Yet Shakespeare's play seems constantly to echo precisely the issues raised by the Bermuda shipwreck and its aftermath. What does it take to survive? How do men of different classes and moral character react during a state of emergency? What is the proper relation between theoretical understanding and practical experience or between knowledge and power? Is obedience to authority willing or forced? How can those in power protect themselves from the conspiracies of malcontents? Is it possible to detect a providential design in what looks at first like a succession of accidents? If there are natives to contend with, how should colonists establish friendly and profitable relations with them? What is to be done if relations turn sour? How can those who rule prevent an alliance between hostile natives and the poorer colonists, often disgruntled and themselves exploited? And—Montaigne's more radical questions—what is the justification of one person's rule over another? Who is the civilized man, and who is the barbarian?

The unregenerate nastiness of Antonio and Sebastian, conjoined with the goodness of Gonzalo, might seem indirectly to endorse Montaigne's critique of the Europeans and his praise of the cannibals, were it not for the disturbing presence in *The Tempest* of the character whose name is almost an anagram for "cannibal," Caliban. Caliban, whose god Setebos is mentioned in accounts of Magellan's voyages as a Patagonian deity, is anything but a noble savage. Shakespeare does not shrink from the darkest European fantasies about the Wild Man. Indeed, he exaggerates them: Caliban is deformed, lecherous, evil-smelling, treacherous, naive, drunken, lazy, rebellious, violent, and devil-worshipping. According to Prospero, he is not even human: "A devil, a born devil, on whose nature / Nurture can never stick" (4.1.188–89). When he first came to the island, Prospero recalls, he treated Caliban "with human care" (1.2.349), lodging him in his own cell until the savage tried to rape Miranda. The arrival of the other Europeans brings out still worse qualities. Encountering the basest of the company, Alonso's jester, Trinculo, and drunken butler, Stefano, Caliban falls at their feet in brutish worship and then devises a conspiracy to murder Prospero in his sleep. Were the conspiracy to succeed, Caliban would get neither the girl for whom he lusts nor the freedom for which he shouts—he would become "King" Stefano's "foot-licker" (4.1.218)—but he would satisfy the enormous hatred he feels for Prospero.

Prospero's power, Caliban reasons, derives from his superior knowledge. "Remember / First to possess his books," he urges the louts, "for without them / He's but a sot as I am. . . . Burn but his books" (3.2.86–90). The strategy is a canny one, in recognizing an underlying link between literacy and authority, but the problem is not only that Stefano and Trinculo are hopeless fools but also that Prospero, like all Renaissance princes, has a diligent spy network: the invisible Ariel overhears the conspirators and warns his master of the approaching danger. Prospero's sudden recollection of the warning leads him to break off the betrothal masque with one of the most famous speeches in all of Shakespeare, "Our revels now are ended" (4.1.148ff.). This brooding meditation on the theatrical insubstantiality of the entire world and the dreamlike nature of human existence has seemed to many the pinnacle of the play's visionary wisdom. But it does not subsume in its rich cadences the other voices in *The Tempest*; specifically, it does not silence the surprising power of Caliban's voice.

That voice has been amplified in the centuries that followed the first performances of *The Tempest*, as European colonialism saw its grand political, moral, and economic claims disputed and, after violent struggles, dismantled. During these struggles, many anticolonial writers and critics rewrote Shakespeare's play, casting Prospero as a smugly racist, sexist oppressor, Ariel as a native coopted and corrupted by his colonial master, and Caliban as a victimized hero. "Prospero invaded the islands," declared the Cuban writer Roberto Fernández Retamar, "killed our ancestors, enslaved Caliban, and taught him his language to make himself understood. What else can Caliban do but use that same language—today he has no other—to curse him, to wish that the 'red plague' would fall on him?"

Shakespeare, who wrote when the colonialist project was still in its early stages, could not have anticipated this afterlife, and some scholars have argued that the relevance to *The Tempest* of the New World voyages has been greatly exaggerated. But, as the Barbadian writer George Lamming puts it, "Caliban keeps answering back." Caliban enters the play cursing, grumbling, and, above all, disputing Prospero's authority: "This island's mine, by Sycorax my mother, / Which thou tak'st from me" (1.2.334–35). By the close, his attempt to kill Prospero foiled and his body racked with cramps and bruises, Caliban declares that he will "be wise hereafter, / And seek for grace" (5.1.298–99). Yet it is not his mumbled reformation but his vehement protests that leave an indelible mark on *The Tempest*. The play may depict Caliban, in Prospero's ugly term, as "filth," but it gives him a remarkable, unforgettable eloquence. To Miranda's taunting reminder that she taught him to speak, Caliban retorts, "You taught me language, and my profit on't / Is I know how to curse" (1.2.366–67). It is not only in cursing, however, that Caliban is gifted: in richly sensuous poetry, he speaks of the island's natural resources and of his dreams. Caliban can be beaten into submission, but the master cannot eradicate his slave's desires, his pleasures, and his inconsolable pain. And across the vast gulf that divides the triumphant prince and the defeated savage, there is a momentary, enigmatic glimpse of a hidden bond: "This thing of darkness," Prospero says of Caliban, "I / Acknowledge mine" (5.1.278–79). The words need only be a claim of ownership, but they seem to hint at a deeper, more disturbing link between father and monster, legitimate ruler and savage, judge and criminal. Perhaps the link is only an illusion, a trick of the imagination on a strange island, but as Prospero leaves the island, it is he who begs for pardon.

Stephen Greenblatt

TEXTUAL NOTE

The only authoritative printed text of *The Tempest* is in the First Folio of 1623 (F), where it appears as the first play, at the head of the comedies. The text seems to have been prepared with care. It includes a list of characters *("Names of the Actors")* printed at the end of the play and supplies act and scene divisions that this edition follows. There are also unusually full stage directions, although scholars have argued about whether these were written entirely by Shakespeare or were supplied or elaborated by the person who transcribed the author's manuscript for the compositors. Certain features of this transcription have led scholars to the conclusion that it was done by Ralph Crane, an experienced scribe who was responsible for the preparation of at least four other Shakespeare plays.

Most of the songs in *The Tempest* are preserved in early to mid-seventeenth-century manuscripts. These manuscripts indicate repeats and refrains, which have accordingly been accepted in the text of this edition.

SELECTED BIBLIOGRAPHY

Albanese, Denise. "Admiring Miranda and Enslaving Nature." *New Science, New World.* Durham, N.C.: Duke University Press, 1996. 59–91. Miranda as the feminine locus of the play's exploration of nature and culture.

Barker, Francis, and Peter Hulme. "Nymphs and Reapers Heavily Vanish: The Discursive Con-texts of *The Tempest.*" *Alternative Shakespeares.* Vol. I. Ed. John Drakakis. London: Methuen, 1985. 191–205. English colonialism as a discursive context for the play's interest in the usurpation of power.

Brotton, Jerry. "'This Tunis, sir, was Carthage': Contesting Colonialism in *The Tempest.*" *Post-Colonial Shakespeares.* Ed. Ania Loomba and Martin Orkin. London: Routledge, 1998. 23–42. The play's Mediterranean geography exposes a bifurcated interest in both the Old and the New Worlds.

Brown, Paul. "'This Thing of Darkness I Acknowledge Mine': *The Tempest* and the Discourse of Colonialism." *Political Shakespeare: New Essays in Cultural Materialism.* Ed. Jonathan Dollimore and Alan Sinfield. Ithaca, N.Y.: Cornell University Press, 1985. 48–71. Shakespeare's ambivalent depictions of political, social, and sexual authority read in relation to contemporary colonial practice.

Callaghan, Dympna. "Irish Memories in *The Tempest.*" *Shakespeare Without Women: Representing Gender and Race on the Renaissance Stage.* London: Routledge, 2000. 97–138. Using the play's Irish echoes, considers how selective colonial recollection suppresses the cultural memory of the colonized.

Cartelli, Thomas. "Prospero in Africa: *The Tempest* as Colonialist Text and Pretext." *Repositioning Shakespeare: National Formations, Postcolonial Appropriations.* London: Routledge, 1999. 87–104. *The Tempest* can be made to operate both for and against the interests of modern Western ideology.

Greenblatt, Stephen. "Martial Law in the Land of Cockaigne." *Shakespearean Negotiations: The Circulation of Social Energy in Renaissance England.* Berkeley: University of California Press, 1988. 129–63. The play apparently celebrates the restoration of patriarchal order yet also ironically scrutinizes the political manipulation of anxiety.

Hulme, Peter, and William H. Sherman, eds. *"The Tempest" and Its Travels.* Philadelphia: University of Pennsylvania Press, 2000. A range of critical and creative materials, situating the play amid the local and global contexts of its time and beyond.

Orgel, Stephen. *The Illusion of Power: Political Theater in the English Renaissance.* Berkeley: University of California Press, 1975. Compares public and court theater practice, highlighting the masque's role in the allegorized expression of sovereign power.

Vaughan, Virginia Mason, and Alden T. Vaughan. *Critical Essays on Shakespeare's "The Tempest."* New York: Hall, 1998. Eleven essays illustrating the breadth and diversity of critical and cultural engagement with the play.

FILMS

Forbidden Planet. 1956. Dir. Fred M. Wilcox. USA. 98 min. A science-fiction cult classic in which Ariel is a robot and Caliban a monster of the id.

The Tempest. 1960. Dir. George Schaefer. USA. 76 min. A made-for-TV, one-camera film of a solid, though short stage rendition, with Richard Burton standing out as Caliban.

The Tempest. 1979. Dir. Derek Jarman. UK. 95 min. Part Gothic, part punk. Renders Juno's masque as a Broadway musical number.

Tempest. 1982. Dir. Paul Mazursky. USA. 140 min. Disenchanted New York architect escapes to a Greek island to reexamine his life.

Prospero's Books. 1991. Dir. Peter Greenaway. UK. 129 min. Surreal and baroque, focusing on the imagined contents of Prospero's library. John Gielgud stars.

The Tempest

THE PERSONS OF THE PLAY

PROSPERO, the rightful Duke of Milan
MIRANDA, his daughter
ANTONIO, his brother, the usurping Duke of Milan
ALONSO, King of Naples
SEBASTIAN, his brother
FERDINAND, Alonso's son
GONZALO, an honest old counsellor of Naples
ADRIAN
FRANCISCO } lords
ARIEL, an airy spirit attendant upon Prospero
CALIBAN, a savage and deformed native of the island, Prospero's slave
TRINCULO, Alonso's jester
STEFANO, Alonso's drunken butler
The MASTER of a ship
BOATSWAIN
MARINERS
SPIRITS
 The Masque
Spirits appearing as:
IRIS
CERES
JUNO
Nymphs, reapers

1.1

A tempestuous noise of thunder and lightning heard.
Enter a SHIPMASTER *and a* BOATSWAIN[1] [*at separate*
doors]

MASTER Boatswain!
BOATSWAIN Here, Master. What cheer?
MASTER Good,[2] speak to th' mariners. Fall to't yarely,° or we run   *promptly*
 ourselves aground. Bestir, bestir!   *Exit*
 Enter MARINERS
5 BOATSWAIN Heigh, my hearts!° Cheerly, cheerly, my hearts!   *hearties*
 Yare, yare! Take in the topsail![3] Tend° to th' Master's whistle!— *Attend*
 Blow till thou burst thy wind, if room enough.[4]
  Enter ALONSO, SEBASTIAN, ANTONIO, FERDINAND, GON-
  ZALO, *and others*
ALONSO Good Boatswain, have care. Where's the Master?
 [*To the* MARINERS] Play the men!°   *Act like men*
10 BOATSWAIN I pray now, keep below.
ANTONIO Where is the Master, Boatswain?

1.1 Location: A ship at sea.
1. The Boatswain probably enters after the shipmaster calls him; the latter is perhaps on the upper stage.
2. Acknowledging the Boatswain's presence; or perhaps short for "good man."

3. To reduce the surface area of the sail, and thereby lessen the force of the wind pushing the ship toward the island.
4. The wind may blow until it splits itself, provided there is enough sea room to maneuver in.

BOATSWAIN   Do you not hear him? You mar our labour. Keep
your cabins; you do assist the storm.

GONZALO   Nay, good,° be patient.   *good man*

15   BOATSWAIN   When the sea is. Hence! What cares these roarers
for the name of king?[5] To cabin! Silence; trouble us not.

GONZALO   Good, yet remember whom thou hast aboard.

BOATSWAIN   None that I more love than myself. You are a coun-
cillor;[6] if you can command these elements to silence and work

20   peace of the present,[7] we will not hand° a rope more. Use your   *handle*
authority. If you cannot, give thanks you have lived so long and
make yourself ready in your cabin for the mischance of the
hour, if it so hap.° [*To the* MARINERS] Cheerly, good hearts! [*To*   *happen*
GONZALO] Out of our way, I say!   *Exit*

25   GONZALO   I have great comfort from this fellow. Methinks he
hath no drowning mark[8] upon him; his complexion is perfect
gallows.[9] Stand fast, good Fate, to his hanging. Make the rope
of his destiny our cable,[1] for our own doth little advantage.° If   *use*
he be not born to be hanged, our case is miserable.

Exit [Courtiers]

Enter BOATSWAIN

30   BOATSWAIN   Down with the topmast![2] Yare! Lower, lower! Bring
her to try wi'th' main-course![3]

A cry within

A plague upon this howling! They are louder than the weather,
or our office.[4]

Enter SEBASTIAN, ANTONIO, *and* GONZALO

Yet again? What do you here? Shall we give o'er° and drown?   *up*

35   Have you a mind to sink?

SEBASTIAN   A pox o'your throat, you bawling, blasphemous,
incharitable dog!

BOATSWAIN   Work you, then.

ANTONIO   Hang, cur, hang, you whoreson insolent noisemaker.

40   We are less afraid to be drowned than thou art.

[*Exeunt* MARINERS]

GONZALO   I'll warrant him for drowning,[5] though° the ship were   *even if*
no stronger than a nutshell and as leaky as an unstanched°   *a freely menstruating*
wench.

BOATSWAIN   Lay her a-hold, a-hold! Set her two courses![6] Off to

45   sea again! Lay her off!

Enter MARINERS, *wet*

MARINERS   All lost! To prayers, to prayers! All lost!

[*Exeunt* MARINERS]

BOATSWAIN   What, must our mouths be cold?[7]

GONZALO   The King and Prince at prayers! Let's assist them,
For our case is as theirs.

---

5. "Roarers," referring here to the waves, was also a
term for riotous people.
6. Member of the King's council; also an adviser or per-
suader.
7. Of the present circumstances.
8. Birthmark whose position was held to portend death
by drowning. "He that was born to be hanged will never
be drowned" was proverbial.
9. His physiognomy, appearance, shows that he will
certainly be hanged.
1. Anchor cable (an anchor is actually useless in a storm).

2. To reduce the top weight of the ship and make it
more stable.
3. Bring the ship close to the wind sailing only with the
mainsail.
4. Duties (in shouting orders).
5. I'll guarantee him against drowning.
6. Set the foresail in addition to the mainsail.
7. To be cold in the mouth—to be dead—was prover-
bial; may also suggest that the mariners warm their
mouths with liquor (line 50).

SEBASTIAN   I'm out of patience.
50 ANTONIO   We are merely° cheated of our lives by drunkards.   *utterly*
     This wide-chopped° rascal—would thou mightst lie drowning   *large-mouthed*
     The washing of ten tides.[8]
GONZALO   He'll be hanged yet,
     Though every drop of water swear against it
     And gape at wid'st to glut° him.   *its widest to swallow*
          A confused noise within
MARINERS [*within*]   Mercy on us!
55   We split, we split! Farewell, my wife and children!
     Farewell, brother! We split, we split, we split!
                                   [*Exit* BOATSWAIN]
ANTONIO   Let's all sink wi'th' King.
SEBASTIAN   Let's take leave of him.
          Exit [ANTONIO *and* SEBASTIAN]
GONZALO   Now would I give a thousand furlongs of sea for an
     acre of barren ground: long heath, broom, furze,[9] anything.
60   The wills above be done, but I would fain die a dry death.
                                                              Exit

1.2

Enter PROSPERO [*in his magic cloak, with a staff*], *and*
          MIRANDA

MIRANDA[1]   If by your art,[2] my dearest father, you have
     Put the wild waters in this roar, allay them.
     The sky, it seems, would pour down stinking pitch,
     But that the sea, mounting to th' welkin's° cheek,   *sky's*
5   Dashes the fire out. O, I have sufferèd
     With those that I saw suffer! A brave° vessel,   *splendid*
     Who had, no doubt, some noble creature in her,
     Dashed all to pieces! O, the cry did knock
     Against my very heart! Poor souls, they perished.
10   Had I been any god of power, I would
     Have sunk the sea within the earth, or ere°   *before*
     It should the good ship so have swallowed and
     The fraughting souls[3] within her.
PROSPERO[4]   Be collected.
     No more amazement.° Tell your piteous° heart   *consternation / pitying*
     There's no harm done.
MIRANDA   O woe the day!
15 PROSPERO   No harm.
     I have done nothing but in care of thee,
     Of thee, my dear one, thee, my daughter, who
     Art ignorant of what thou art, naught knowing
     Of whence I am, nor that I am more better°   *higher in rank*

---

8. Pirates were hanged on the shore at low-water mark
and left there for the ebbing and flowing of three tides.
9. Heather, yellow shrubs, and gorse—all shrubs that
grow in poor soil.
1.2 Location: The rest of the play is set in various parts
of Prospero's island.
1. *Miranda* in Latin means "admirable" or "wonder-

ing." Miranda uses the formal "you," contrasting with
Prospero's more familiar "thou."
2. Skill; magic; learning; science.
3. Souls constituting the freight; perhaps also suggest-
ing "burdened."
4. *Prospero* in Italian and Spanish means "fortunate" or
"prosperous."

20   Than Prospero, master of a full poor cell[5]
      And thy no greater father.

MIRANDA   More to know
      Did never meddle with° my thoughts.   *intrude upon*

PROSPERO   'Tis time
      I should inform thee farther. Lend thy hand,
      And pluck my magic garment from me.

      [MIRANDA *removes Prospero's cloak, and he lays it on the*
      ground]

                                   So.

25   Lie there, my art.—Wipe thou thine eyes; have comfort.
      The direful spectacle of the wreck, which touched
      The very virtue of compassion in thee,
      I have with such provision° in mine art   *foresight*
      So safely ordered that there is no soul—

30   No, not so much perdition° as an hair   *loss*
      Betid° to any creature in the vessel,   *Happened*
      Which° thou heard'st cry, which thou saw'st sink. Sit down, *Whom*
      For thou must now know farther.

      [MIRANDA *sits*]

MIRANDA   You have often
      Begun to tell me what I am, but stopped

35   And left me to a bootless inquisition,°   *profitless inquiry*
      Concluding 'Stay; not yet'.

PROSPERO   The hour's now come.
      The very minute bids thee ope° thine ear,   *open*
      Obey, and be attentive. Canst thou remember
      A time before we came unto this cell?

40   I do not think thou canst, for then thou wast not
      Out° three years old.   *Fully*

MIRANDA   Certainly, sir, I can.

PROSPERO   By° what? By any other house or person?   *About*
      Of anything the image tell me that
      Hath kept with thy remembrance.

MIRANDA   'Tis far off,

45   And rather like a dream than an assurance°   *a certainty*
      That my remembrance warrants.° Had I not   *guarantees is true*
      Four or five women once that tended me?

PROSPERO   Thou hadst, and more, Miranda. But how is it
      That this lives in thy mind? What seest thou else

50   In the dark backward° and abyss of time?   *past*
      If thou rememb'rest aught° ere thou cam'st here,   *anything*
      How thou cam'st here thou mayst.

MIRANDA   But that I do not.

PROSPERO   Twelve year since, Miranda, twelve year since,
      Thy father was the Duke of Milan,[6] and
      A prince of power—

55 MIRANDA   Sir, are not you my father?

PROSPERO   Thy mother was a piece° of virtue,° and   *perfect example / chastity*
      She said thou wast my daughter; and thy father
      Was Duke of Milan, and his only heir
      And princess no worse issued.°   *no less nobly born*

---

5. Suggesting a hermit's or a poor man's dwelling. *full:*   6. Pronounced with stress on the first syllable.
very.

MIRANDA   O the heavens!
60   What foul play had we that we came from thence?
     Or blessèd° was't we did?   *providential*
PROSPERO   Both, both, my girl.
     By foul play, as thou sayst, were we heaved thence,
     But blessedly holp° hither.   *helped*
MIRANDA   O, my heart bleeds
     To think o'th' teen° that I have turned you to,   *sorrow; trouble*
65   Which is from° my remembrance. Please you, farther.   *out of*
PROSPERO   My brother and thy uncle called Antonio—
     I pray thee mark me, that a brother should
     Be so perfidious—he whom next° thyself   *after*
     Of all the world I loved, and to him put
70   The manage° of my state—as at that time   *control*
     Through all the signories° it was the first,   *lordships*
     And Prospero the prime° duke—being so reputed   *foremost*
     In dignity, and for the liberal arts[7]
     Without a parallel—those being all my study,
75   The government I cast upon my brother,
     And to my state grew stranger, being transported[8]
     And rapt in secret studies. Thy false uncle—
     Dost thou attend me?
MIRANDA   Sir, most heedfully.
PROSPERO   Being once perfected how to grant suits,[9]
80   How to deny them, who t'advance and who
     To trash for over-topping,[1] new created
     The creatures° that were mine, I say—or changed 'em   *dependents*
     Or else new formed 'em;[2] having both the key°   *control*
     Of officer and office, set all hearts i'th' state
85   To what tune pleased his ear, that° now he was   *so that*
     The ivy which had hid my princely trunk
     And sucked my verdure° out on't. Thou attend'st not! *vitality; power*
MIRANDA   O good sir, I do.
PROSPERO   I pray thee mark me.
     I, thus neglecting worldly ends, all dedicated
90   To closeness° and the bettering of my mind   *seclusion*
     With that which but° by being so retired   *merely*
     O'er-priced all popular rate,[3] in my false brother
     Awaked an evil nature; and my trust,
     Like a good parent,[4] did beget of him
95   A falsehood, in its contrary° as great   *inverse qualities*
     As my trust was, which had indeed no limit,
     A confidence sans° bound. He being thus lorded   *without*
     Not only with what my revenue yielded
     But what my power might else exact, like one
100 Who having into° truth, by telling oft,   *unto*
     Made such a sinner of his memory
     To credit his own lie,[5] he did believe

---

7. As opposed to the "mechanical arts," the "liberal arts" encompassed the trivium (grammar, logic, and rhetoric) and the quadrivium (arithmetic, geometry, music, and astronomy).
8. Enraptured, with suggestions of "conveyed to another place." *grew stranger:* grew alienated from; became a foreigner to.
9. Having mastered handling formal requests.
1. For rising too high. *trash:* restrain, hold back (as by a leash).
2. *changed . . . 'em:* changed the duties and allegiance of existing officials, or created new ones.
3. Became too precious for the people to value, or understand.
4. From the colloquial "Good parents breed bad children."
5. *like one . . . lie:* like someone who comes to believe his own repeatedly stated lie. *To:* So as to.

He was indeed the Duke. Out o'th'° substitution,   *As a consequence of the*
And executing° th'outward face° of royalty   *portraying / image*
105 With all prerogative, hence his ambition growing—
Dost thou hear?
MIRANDA   Your tale, sir, would cure deafness.
PROSPERO   To have no screen between this part he played
And him he played it for, he needs will be
Absolute Milan.[6] Me,° poor man—my library   *As for me*
110 Was dukedom large enough—of temporal royalties°   *rule*
He thinks me now incapable; confederates,°   *(he) plots*
So dry° he was for sway,° wi'th' King of Naples   *thirsty / power*
To give him annual tribute, do him homage,
Subject his coronet to his crown,[7] and bend
115 The dukedom, yet unbowed—alas, poor Milan—
To most ignoble stooping.[8]
MIRANDA   O the heavens!
PROSPERO   Mark his condition° and th'event,° then tell me   *treaty / outcome*
If this might be a brother.
MIRANDA   I should sin
To think but° nobly of my grandmother.   *anything but*
Good wombs have borne bad sons.[9]
120 PROSPERO   Now the condition.
This King of Naples, being an enemy
To me inveterate, hearkens my brother's suit;
Which was that he, in lieu o'th' premises[1]
Of homage and I know not how much tribute,
125 Should presently extirpate me and mine
Out of the dukedom, and confer fair Milan,
With all the honours, on my brother. Whereon,
A treacherous army levied, one midnight
Fated to th' purpose did Antonio open
130 The gates of Milan; and, i'th' dead of darkness,
The ministers° for th' purpose hurried thence   *agents*
Me and thy crying self.
MIRANDA   Alack, for pity!
I, not rememb'ring how I cried out then,
Will cry it o'er again; it is a hint°   *an occasion*
That wrings mine eyes to't.
135 PROSPERO [*sitting*]   Hear a little further,
And then I'll bring thee to the present business
Which now's upon's, without the which this story
Were most impertinent.°   *irrelevant*
MIRANDA   Wherefore did they not
That hour destroy us?
PROSPERO   Well demanded, wench;[2]
140 My tale provokes that question. Dear, they durst not,
So dear the love my people bore me; nor set
A mark so bloody on the business, but
With colours fairer painted their foul ends.
In few,° they hurried us aboard a barque,°   *short / ship*

---

6. *To have . . . Milan:* He wanted to be the Duke of
Milan in actual fact, rather than merely exercising power
as the Duke's proxy. *screen:* partition, barrier.
7. Subject Antonio's coronet to Alonso's crown. *coronet:*
a lesser crown indicating the wearer's inferiority to the
sovereign.
8. *and bend . . . stooping:* by making Milan, previously

free, a tributary subject of Naples.
9. Antonio's character need not imply that his mother
was a bad parent (see line 94).
1. In return for the conditions agreed upon.
2. A young woman; also term of endearment to wife,
daughter, or sweetheart.

145 Bore us some leagues to sea, where they prepared
     A rotten carcass of a butt,³ not rigged,
     Nor tackle, sail, nor mast—the very rats
     Instinctively have quit it. There they hoist us,
     To cry to th' sea that roared to us, to sigh
150 To th'winds, whose pity, sighing back again,
     Did us but loving wrong.⁴

MIRANDA   Alack, what trouble
     Was I then to you!

PROSPERO   O, a cherubin
     Thou wast that did preserve me. Thou didst smile,
     Infusèd with a fortitude from heaven,
155 When I have decked° the sea with drops° full salt,   covered; adorned / tears
     Under my burden groaned;⁵ which° raised in me   (Miranda's smile)
     An undergoing stomach,° to bear up   A courage to endure
     Against what should ensue.

MIRANDA   How came we ashore?
160 PROSPERO   By providence divine.
     Some food we had, and some fresh water, that
     A noble Neapolitan, Gonzalo,
     Out of his charity—who being then appointed
     Master of this design—did give us; with
165 Rich garments, linens, stuffs, and necessaries
     Which since have steaded° much. So, of his gentleness,⁶   been useful
     Knowing I loved my books, he furnished me
     From mine own library with volumes that
     I prize above my dukedom.

MIRANDA   Would I might
     But ever see that man!

170 PROSPERO   Now I arise.⁷
     [He stands and puts on his cloak]⁸
     Sit still,° and hear the last of our sea-sorrow.   Continue to sit
     Here in this island we arrived, and here
     Have I thy schoolmaster made thee more profit°   profit more
     Than other princes⁹ can, that have more time
175 For vainer hours and tutors not so careful.°   caring

MIRANDA   Heavens thank you for't. And now I pray you, sir—
     For still 'tis beating in my mind—your reason
     For raising this sea-storm.

PROSPERO   Know thus far forth.
     By accident most strange, bountiful Fortune,
180 Now my dear lady,¹ hath mine enemies
     Brought to this shore; and by my prescience
     I find my zenith² doth depend upon
     A most auspicious star,³ whose influence
     If now I court not, but omit,° my fortunes   disregard

3. Cask or tub: here, deprecatory for "boat."
4. The winds, responding sympathetically to our sighs, only blew us farther out to sea.
5. The secondary sense provides an image of giving birth.
6. Nobility; kindness.
7. Referring to the action of standing; or to Prospero's rising fortunes (as in lines 179–85). The former might visually reinforce the latter, especially if Prospero also resumes his magical powers by putting on his cloak.

8. This direction, necessary before Prospero can charm Miranda to sleep, follows naturally from the reference to Prospero's books, his other source of power.
9. *princes*: a generic plural for "princes and princesses."
1. Traditional characterization of Fortune as a woman changeable in her affections.
2. Highest point, as of a star in the sky.
3. Referring to the belief that celestial bodies had astrological influence on people and events.

185   Will ever after droop. Here cease more questions.

Thou art inclined to sleep; 'tis a good dullness,°   *drowsiness*

And give it way. I know thou canst not choose.

      [MIRANDA *sleeps*]

Come away,° servant, come! I am ready now.   *Come here*

Approach, my Ariel,⁴ come!

      Enter ARIEL

190 ARIEL   All hail, great master, grave sir, hail. I come

To answer thy best pleasure. Be't to fly,

To swim, to dive into the fire, to ride

On the curled clouds, to thy strong bidding task

Ariel and all his quality.°   *cohorts; faculties*

 PROSPERO   Hast thou, spirit,

195 Performed to point° the tempest that I bade thee?   *in detail*

 ARIEL   To every article.

I boarded the King's ship. Now on the beak,°   *prow*

Now in the waste,° the deck,° in every cabin,   *midship / poop*

I flamed amazement.⁵ Sometime I'd divide,

200 And burn in many places;⁶ on the top-mast,

The yards, and bowsprit, would I flame distinctly;

Then meet and join. Jove's lightning, the precursors

O'th' dreadful thunderclaps, more momentary

And sight-outrunning° were not. The fire and cracks   *quicker than the eye*

205 Of sulphurous⁷ roaring the most mighty Neptune

Seem to besiege, and make his bold waves tremble,

Yea, his dread trident shake.

 PROSPERO   My brave spirit!

Who was so firm, so constant, that this coil°   *turmoil*

Would not infect his reason?

 ARIEL   Not a soul

210 But felt a fever of the mad,° and played   *such as madmen feel*

Some tricks of desperation. All but mariners

Plunged in the foaming brine and quit the vessel,

Then all afire with me. The King's son Ferdinand,

With hair upstaring°—then like reeds, not hair—   *standing on end*

215 Was the first man that leaped; cried 'Hell is empty,

And all the devils are here'.

 PROSPERO   Why, that's my spirit!

But was not this nigh shore?

 ARIEL   Close by, my master.

 PROSPERO   But are they, Ariel, safe?

 ARIEL   Not a hair perished.

On their sustaining⁸ garments not a blemish,

220 But fresher than before. And, as thou bad'st° me,   *commanded*

In troops° I have dispersed them 'bout the isle.   *groups*

The King's son have I landed by himself,

Whom I left cooling of ° the air with sighs   *cooling*

In an odd angle° of the isle, and sitting,   *corner*

His arms in this sad knot.⁹

---

4. Ariel's name, along with sounding like "airy," also means "lion of God." The name appears as a magical spirit in various occult texts.
5. I appeared as flames, causing terror.
6. The phosphorescent effect of St. Elmo's fire, caused in a thunderstorm by the charge of static electricity that builds up particularly around metal projections.
7. Sulphur was popularly associated with thunder and lightning.
8. Buoying up, and thus suggesting "life-giving."
9. Folded sadly, like this (folded arms implied sorrow).

225 PROSPERO   Of the King's ship,
     The mariners, say how thou hast disposed,
     And all the rest o'th' fleet.
     ARIEL   Safely in harbour
     Is the King's ship, in the deep nook where once
     Thou called'st me up at midnight to fetch dew
230 From the still-vexed° Bermudas, there she's hid;   *ever-stormy*
     The mariners all under hatches stowed,
     Who, with° a charm joined to° their suffered labour,   *by virtue of / with*
     I have left asleep. And for the rest o'th' fleet,
     Which I dispersed, they all have met again,
235 And are upon the Mediterranean float°   *billow; sea*
     Bound sadly home for Naples,
     Supposing that they saw the King's ship wrecked,
     And his great person perish.
     PROSPERO   Ariel, thy charge
     Exactly is performed; but there's more work.
     What is the time o'th' day?
240 ARIEL   Past the mid season.°   *noon*
     PROSPERO   At least two glasses.° The time 'twixt six and now   *hourglasses*
     Must by us both be spent most preciously.
     ARIEL   Is there more toil? Since thou dost give me pains,°   *tasks*
     Let me remember° thee what thou hast promised   *remind*
     Which is not yet performed me.
245 PROSPERO   How now? Moody?
     What is't thou canst demand?
     ARIEL   My liberty.
     PROSPERO   Before the time be out? No more!
     ARIEL   I prithee,
     Remember I have done thee worthy service,
     Told thee no lies, made thee no mistakings, served
250 Without or° grudge or grumblings. Thou did promise   *either*
     To bate° me a full year.   *remit; excuse*
     PROSPERO   Dost thou forget
     From what a torment I did free thee?
     ARIEL   No.
     PROSPERO   Thou dost, and think'st it much to tread the ooze
     Of the salt deep,
255 To run upon the sharp wind of the north,
     To do me business in the veins¹ o'th' earth
     When it is baked° with frost.   *dried and hardened*
     ARIEL   I do not, sir.
     PROSPERO   Thou liest, malignant thing. Hast thou forgot
     The foul witch Sycorax, who with age and envy
260 Was grown into a hoop?° Hast thou forgot her?   *bent over with age*
     ARIEL   No, sir.
     PROSPERO   Thou hast. Where was she born? Speak, tell me!
     ARIEL   Sir, in Algiers.
     PROSPERO   O, was she so! I must
     Once in a month recount what thou hast been,
265 Which thou forget'st. This damned witch Sycorax,
     For mischiefs manifold and sorceries terrible
     To enter human hearing, from Algiers

---

1. Mineral veins or subterranean rivers.

Thou know'st was banished. For one thing she did
They would not take her life.[2] Is not this true?

270 ARIEL Ay, sir.

PROSPERO This blue-eyed[3] hag was hither brought with child,
And here was left by th' sailors. Thou, my slave,
As thou report'st thyself, was then her servant;
And for° thou wast a spirit too delicate   *because*
275 To act her earthy[4] and abhorred commands,
Refusing her grand hests,° she did confine thee   *commands*
By help of her more potent ministers,°   *agents; slaves*
And in her most unmitigable rage,
Into a cloven pine; within which rift
280 Imprisoned thou didst painfully remain
A dozen years, within which space she died
And left thee there, where thou didst vent thy groans
As fast as mill-wheels strike.° Then was this island—   *hit the water*
Save for the son that she did litter° here,   *give birth to*
285 A freckled whelp, hag-born—not honoured with
A human shape.

ARIEL   Yes, Caliban her son.

PROSPERO Dull thing, I say so:[5] he, that Caliban
Whom now I keep in service. Thou best know'st
What torment I did find thee in. Thy groans
290 Did make wolves howl, and penetrate° the breasts   *arouse sympathy in*
Of ever-angry bears; it was a torment
To lay upon the damned, which Sycorax
Could not again undo. It was mine art,
When I arrived and heard thee, that made gape
The pine and let thee out.

295 ARIEL   I thank thee, master.

PROSPERO If thou more murmur'st, I will rend an oak,
And peg thee in his° knotty entrails till   *its*
Thou hast howled away twelve winters.

ARIEL   Pardon, master.
I will be correspondent° to command,   *compliant*
300 And do my spriting gently.°   *graciously*

PROSPERO Do so, and after two days
I will discharge thee.[6]

ARIEL   That's my noble master!
What shall I do? Say what, what shall I do?

PROSPERO Go make thyself like to a nymph o'th' sea. Be subject
305 To no sight but thine and mine, invisible
To every eyeball else.[7] Go take this shape,°   *appearance; disguise*
And hither come in't. Go; hence with diligence! *Exit* [ARIEL]
Awake, dear heart, awake! Thou hast slept well;
Awake.

MIRANDA [*awaking*] The strangeness of your story put
Heaviness° in me.   *Sleepiness*
310 PROSPERO   Shake it off. Come on;

---

2. *For . . . life:* Only because she got pregnant. Capital sentences were commuted for pregnant women; ordinarily, condemned witches were either hanged or burned at the stake.
3. Blue eyelids were thought to be a sign of pregnancy.
4. Difficult for Ariel, whose element is air; also, grossly material, coarse.
5. You dullard, that's just what I said.
6. Prospero reduces this to within two days at line 425 and actually releases Ariel in about four hours' time.
7. *Be . . . else:* Ariel may wear a conventional costume, indicating his invisibility to other characters onstage.

We'll visit Caliban my slave, who never
Yields us kind answer.

MIRANDA   'Tis a villain, sir,
I do not love to look on.

PROSPERO   But as 'tis,
We cannot miss° him. He does make our fire,   avoid; do without
315   Fetch in our wood, and serves in offices°   capacities; duties
That profit us.—What ho! Slave, Caliban!
Thou earth, thou, speak!

CALIBAN (within)   There's wood enough within.

PROSPERO   Come forth, I say! There's other business for thee.
Come, thou tortoise! When?

            Enter ARIEL, like a water-nymph
320   Fine apparition! My quaint[8] Ariel,
Hark in thine ear.
        [He whispers]

ARIEL   My lord, it shall be done.   Exit

PROSPERO   Thou poisonous slave, got° by the devil[9] himself   begot
Upon thy wicked dam,° come forth!   harmful, foul mother

            Enter CALIBAN

CALIBAN   As wicked dew as e'er my mother brushed[1]
325   With raven's feather from unwholesome fen°   bog
Drop on you both! A southwest[2] blow on ye,
And blister you all o'er!

PROSPERO   For this be sure tonight thou shalt have cramps,
Side-stitches that shall pen thy breath up. Urchins[3]
330   Shall forth at vast of° night, that they may work   during the boundless
All exercise on thee.[4] Thou shalt be pinched
As thick as honeycomb,[5] each pinch more stinging
Than bees that made 'em.°   (honeycomb cells)

CALIBAN   I must eat my dinner.
This island's mine, by Sycorax my mother,
335   Which thou tak'st from me. When thou cam'st first,
Thou strok'st me and made much of me, wouldst give me
Water with berries in't, and teach me how
To name the bigger light, and how the less,[6]
That burn by day and night; and then I loved thee,
340   And showed thee all the qualities o'th' isle,
The fresh springs, brine-pits, barren place and fertile—
Cursed be I that did so! All the charms°   spells
Of Sycorax, toads, beetles, bats, light on you;
For I am all the subjects that you have,
345   Which first was mine own king, and here you sty me°   pen me up
In this hard rock, whiles you do keep from me
The rest o'th' island.

PROSPERO   Thou most lying slave,
Whom stripes° may move, not kindness! I have used° thee,   lashes / treated

8. The term could simultaneously mean "ingenious," "curious in appearance," and "elegant."
9. Not merely an insult, but also an allusion to Caliban's birth from the devil (incubus) and witch.
1. Brushed up, collected. Dew was a common ingredient of magical potions.
2. A southerly wind was considered plague-bearing.
3. Hedgehogs; but here indicates spirits disguised as hedgehogs.

4. that . . . thee: in order that they may perform their habitual activity.
5. Thou . . . honeycomb: The pinch marks will be as closely packed as, and of similar texture to, the cells of a honeycomb.
6. Recalls Genesis 1:16: "God then made two great lights: the greater light to rule the day, and the less light to rule the night."

Filth as thou art, with human care, and lodged thee
350 In mine own cell, till thou didst seek to violate
The honour of my child.
CALIBAN   O ho, O ho! Would't had been done!
Thou didst prevent me; I had peopled else
This isle with Calibans.
MIRANDA[7]   Abhorrèd slave,
355 Which any print° of goodness wilt not take,   *impression*
Being capable of° all ill! I pitied thee,   *susceptible to*
Took pains to make thee speak, taught thee each hour
One thing or other. When thou didst not, savage,
Know thine own meaning, but wouldst gabble like
360 A thing most brutish, I endowed thy purposes
With words that made them known. But thy vile race,°   *hereditary nature*
Though thou didst learn, had that in't which good natures
Could not abide to be with; therefore wast thou
Deservedly confined into this rock,
365 Who hadst deserved more than a prison.
CALIBAN   You taught me language, and my profit on't
Is I know how to curse. The red plague rid you[8]
For learning me your language!
PROSPERO   Hag-seed,° hence!   *Offspring of a hag*
Fetch us in fuel. And be quick, thou'rt best,
370 To answer other business.°—Shrug'st thou, malice?   *perform other tasks*
If thou neglect'st or dost unwillingly
What I command, I'll rack thee with old[9] cramps,
Fill all thy bones with aches,[1] make thee roar,
That beasts shall tremble at thy din.
CALIBAN   No, pray thee.
375 [*Aside*] I must obey. His art is of such power
It would control my dam's god Setebos,[2]
And make a vassal of him.
PROSPERO   So, slave, hence!   *Exit* CALIBAN
                Enter FERDINAND *and* ARIEL, *invisible, playing and
                singing.*[3] [PROSPERO *and* MIRANDA *stand aside*]

Song

ARIEL   Come unto these yellow sands,
                And then take hands;
380   Curtsied when you have and kissed—
                The wild waves whist[4]—
                Foot it featly° here and there,   *Dance nimbly*
                And, sweet sprites, bear°   *sing*
                The burden.° Hark, hark.   *refrain*
385 SPIRITS (*dispersedly* [*within*]) Bow-wow!
ARIEL   The watch-dogs bark.
SPIRITS [*within*] Bow-wow!

---

7. Many editors assign this speech to Prospero, believing
it to be out of character for Miranda.
8. The plague that gives red sores destroy, kill you.
9. As of aged people; long-accustomed.
1. As a noun, this was probably pronounced "aitches."
2. A name found in travel narratives as a god of the Pata-
gonians.

3. This probably does not imply that Ferdinand enters
first, even though such a staging is possible if Ferdinand
is bewildered as to where this music is coming from. Ariel
is invisible to all but Prospero and the audience. He is
probably still dressed as a water nymph.
4. Become hushed and attentive.

ARIEL   Hark, hark, I hear
                   The strain of strutting Chanticleer
390   Cry 'cock-a-diddle-dow'.
FERDINAND   Where should this music be? I'th' air or th'earth?
It sounds no more; and sure it waits° upon   *attends*
Some god o'th' island. Sitting on a bank,
Weeping again the King my father's wreck,
395 This music crept by me upon the waters,
Allaying both their fury and my passion°   *grief*
With its sweet air.° Thence I have followed it—   *melody*
Or it hath drawn me rather. But 'tis gone.
No, it begins again.

Song

400 ARIEL   Full fathom five thy father lies.
                       Of his bones are coral made;
                   Those are pearls that were his eyes;
                       Nothing of him that doth fade
                   But doth suffer a sea-change
405   Into something rich and strange.
                   Sea-nymphs hourly ring his knell:
SPIRITS [*within*]   Ding dong.
ARIEL   Hark, now I hear them.
SPIRITS [*within*]   Ding-dong bell. [*etc.*]
FERDINAND   The ditty does remember[5] my drowned father.
410 This is no mortal° business, nor no sound   *human; of death*
That the earth owes.°   *owns*
                   [*Music*]
                   I hear it now above me.
PROSPERO [*to* MIRANDA]   The fringèd curtains of thine eye advance,°   *raise*
And say what thou seest yon.
MIRANDA   What is't? A spirit?
Lord, how it looks about! Believe me, sir,
415 It carries a brave° form. But 'tis a spirit.   *splendid; gallant*
PROSPERO   No, wench, it eats and sleeps, and hath such senses
As we have, such. This gallant° which thou seest   *fine gentleman*
Was in the wreck, and but° he's something° stained   *except that / somewhat*
With grief, that's beauty's canker,[6] thou mightst call him
420 A goodly person. He hath lost his fellows,
And strays about to find 'em.
MIRANDA   I might call him
A thing divine, for nothing natural
I ever saw so noble.
PROSPERO [*aside*][7]   It° goes on, I see,   *(My plan)*
As my soul prompts it. [*To* ARIEL] Spirit, fine spirit, I'll free thee
Within two days for this.
425 FERDINAND [*aside*]   Most sure the goddess
On whom these airs attend.[8] [*To* MIRANDA] Vouchsafe° my prayer   *Grant*
May know if you remain° upon this island,   *dwell*

---

5. Commemorate. *ditty:* the words of the song.
6. Cankerworm; caterpillar ("beauty" being seen as a flower); spreading sore.
7. Prospero's asides here and at lines 442, 454, and 497 may be either private utterances or addressed to Ariel. If the former, Ariel may nevertheless hear them; Prospero

speaks to Ariel after all these instances. Their import may well be purposefully enigmatic.
8. *Most . . . attend:* Probably spoken aside, but possibly an invocation. *Most sure the goddess:* Echoes Aeneas's reaction to seeing Venus after his shipwreck, "o dea certe" (*Aeneid* I.328). *airs:* Ariel's melodies.

And that you will some good instruction give
How I may bear me° here. My prime request,   *conduct myself*
430   Which I do last pronounce, is—O you wonder⁹—
        If you be maid¹ or no?
MIRANDA   No wonder, sir,
        But certainly a maid.
FERDINAND   My language! Heavens!
        I am the best² of them that speak this speech,
        Were I but where 'tis spoken.
PROSPERO   How, the best?
435   What wert thou if the King of Naples heard thee?
FERDINAND   A single³ thing, as I am now that wonders
        To hear thee speak of Naples. He does hear me,⁴
        And that he does I weep. Myself am Naples,°   *King of Naples*
        Who with mine eyes, never since at ebb,° beheld   *ceasing to flow*
        The King my father wrecked.
440   MIRANDA   Alack, for mercy!
FERDINAND   Yes, faith, and all his lords, the Duke of Milan
        And his brave son⁵ being twain.
PROSPERO [*aside*]   The Duke of Milan
        And his more braver daughter could control⁶ thee,
        If now 'twere fit to do't. At the first sight
445   They have changed eyes.⁷—Delicate° Ariel,   *Graceful; artful*
        I'll set thee free for this. [*To* FERDINAND] A word, good sir.
        I fear you have done yourself some wrong.⁸ A word.
MIRANDA [*aside*]   Why speaks my father so ungently?° This   *discourteously*
        Is the third man that e'er I saw, the first
450   That e'er I sighed for. Pity move my father
        To be inclined my way.
FERDINAND   O, if a virgin,
        And your affection not gone forth,⁹ I'll make you
        The Queen of Naples.
PROSPERO   Soft, sir! One word more.
        [*Aside*] They are both in either's powers. But this swift business
455   I must uneasy° make, lest too light¹ winning   *difficult*
        Make the prize light. [*To* FERDINAND] One word more. I charge thee
        That thou attend me. Thou dost here usurp
        The name thou ow'st° not; and hast put thyself   *own*
        Upon this island as a spy, to win it
        From me the lord on't.°   *of it*
460   FERDINAND   No, as I am a man.
MIRANDA   There's nothing ill can dwell in such a temple.²
        If the ill spirit have so fair a house,
        Good things will strive to dwell with't.
PROSPERO [*to* FERDINAND]   Follow me.
        [*To* MIRANDA] Speak not you for him; he's a traitor. [*To* FERDINAND] Come!

---

9. Miracle, punning on the meaning of Miranda's name.
1. Unmarried virgin; made (human).
2. Highest in rank, assuming he has succeeded his father.
3. Weak and helpless; solitary; one and the same.
4. "He" and "me" both refer to Ferdinand. Presuming his father to be dead, Ferdinand takes himself to be the new King of Naples (and as such, he hears himself speaking). Alternatively, Ferdinand thinks his father's spirit hears him.
5. The only instance in which Antonio is mentioned as

having a son.
6. Challenge; take to task; exercise power over.
7. Exchanged loving glances; fallen in love at first sight.
8. Euphemistic for "told a lie about yourself."
9. Given over to someone else.
1. Easy; playing on the meanings of "little valued" and also "promiscuous" in line 456.
2. A common metaphor for the body; also a conventional Renaissance notion that moral qualities were physically manifest.

465 I'll manacle thy neck and feet together.
Sea-water shalt thou drink; thy food shall be
The fresh-brook mussels,³ withered roots, and husks
Wherein the acorn cradled. Follow!
FERDINAND   No.
I will resist such entertainment° till   *treatment*
Mine enemy has more power.
He draws, and is charmed from moving
470 MIRANDA   O dear father,
Make not too rash a trial of him, for
He's gentle, and not fearful.⁴
PROSPERO   What, I say,
My foot° my tutor? Put thy sword up, traitor,   *inferior*
Who mak'st a show but dar'st not strike, thy conscience
475 Is so possessed with guilt. Come from thy ward,°   *defensive stance*
For I can here disarm thee with this stick°   *magician's wand*
And make thy weapon drop.
MIRANDA   Beseech you, father!
PROSPERO   Hence! Hang not on my garments.
MIRANDA   Sir, have pity.
I'll be his surety.
PROSPERO   Silence! One word more
480 Shall make me chide thee, if not hate thee. What,
An advocate for an impostor? Hush!
Thou think'st there is no more such shapes° as he,   *forms; men*
Having seen but him and Caliban. Foolish wench!
To° th' most of men this is a Caliban,   *Compared to*
And they to him are angels.
485 MIRANDA   My affections
Are then most humble. I have no ambition
To see a goodlier man.
PROSPERO [*to* FERDINAND]   Come on; obey.
Thy nerves° are in their infancy again,   *sinews*
And have no vigour in them.
FERDINAND   So they are.
490 My spirits,° as in a dream, are all bound up.   *mental powers*
My father's loss, the weakness which I feel,
The wreck of all my friends, nor this man's threats
To whom I am subdued, are but light to me,
Might I but through my prison once a day
495 Behold this maid. All corners else o'th' earth
Let liberty make use of; space enough
Have I in such a prison.
PROSPERO [*aside*]   It works. [*To* ARIEL] Come on.—
Thou hast done well, fine Ariel. [*To* FERDINAND] Follow me.
[*To* ARIEL] Hark what thou else shalt do me.
MIRANDA [*to* FERDINAND]   Be of comfort.
500 My father's of a better nature, sir,
Than he appears by speech. This is unwonted°   *unusual*
Which now came from him.
PROSPERO [*to* ARIEL]   Thou shalt be as free
As mountain winds; but then° exactly do   *until then*
All points of my command.

---

3. Freshwater mussels are inedible.   4. He's noble and, therefore, not cowardly. Alternatively,
                                                not fearsome.

505 ARIEL To th' syllable.

PROSPERO [*to* FERDINAND] Come, follow. [*To* MIRANDA] Speak
  not for him.   *Exeunt*

2.1

Enter ALONSO, SEBASTIAN, ANTONIO, GONZALO, ADRIAN,
  and FRANCISCO

GONZALO [*to* ALONSO] Beseech you, sir, be merry. You have cause,
  So have we all, of joy; for our escape
  Is much beyond our loss. Our hint° of woe   occasion
  Is common; every day some sailor's wife,
5 The masters of some merchant, and the merchant,[1]
  Have just° our theme of woe. But for the miracle,   exactly
  I mean our preservation, few in millions
  Can speak like us. Then wisely, good sir, weigh
  Our sorrow with° our comfort.   against
ALONSO   Prithee, peace.[2]
10 SEBASTIAN [*to* ANTONIO] He receives comfort like cold porridge.°   broth
ANTONIO The visitor[3] will not give him o'er so.°   leave him alone
SEBASTIAN Look, he's winding up the watch of his wit. By and
  by it will strike.
GONZALO [*to* ALONSO] Sir—
15 SEBASTIAN [*to* ANTONIO] One: tell.°   keep count
GONZALO [*to* ALONSO] When every grief is entertained° that's   harbored
  offered,
  Comes to th'entertainer[4]—
SEBASTIAN A dollar.[5]
GONZALO Dolour° comes to him indeed. You have spoken truer   Sorrow
20 than you purposed.
SEBASTIAN You have taken it wiselier than I meant you should.
GONZALO [*to* ALONSO] Therefore my lord—
ANTONIO [*to* SEBASTIAN] Fie, what a spendthrift is he of his
  tongue!
25 ALONSO [*to* GONZALO] I prithee, spare.°   spare your words
GONZALO Well, I have done. But yet—
SEBASTIAN [*to* ANTONIO] He will be talking.
ANTONIO Which of he or Adrian, for a good wager, first begins
  to crow?[6]
30 SEBASTIAN The old cock.
ANTONIO The cockerel.[7]
SEBASTIAN Done. The wager?
ANTONIO A laughter.[8]
SEBASTIAN A match!
35 ADRIAN [*to* GONZALO] Though this island seem to be desert°—   uninhabited
ANTONIO [*to* SEBASTIAN] Ha, ha, ha!
SEBASTIAN So, you're paid.[9]
ADRIAN Uninhabitable, and almost inaccessible—
SEBASTIAN [*to* ANTONIO] Yet—
40 ADRIAN Yet—

2.1
1. The chief officers of some merchant ship and its
owner.
2. Sebastian takes this as "pease," as in "pease porridge."
3. Antonio compares Gonzalo with one who visits and
comforts the sick and distressed.
4. There comes to the person who accepts that grief.

5. *dollar*: English name for the German thaler.
6. Which of the two will first begin to speak ("crow")?
7. "The young cock crows as the old hears" was prover-
bial. "Old cock" refers to Gonzalo and "cockerel" to
Adrian.
8. From the proverb "He laughs that wins."
9. Antonio's laugh is his prize.

ANTONIO [*to* SEBASTIAN] He could not miss't.

ADRIAN It must needs be of subtle, tender, and delicate[1]
    temperance.°   *climate*

ANTONIO [*to* SEBASTIAN] Temperance was a delicate wench.[2]

45   SEBASTIAN Ay, and a subtle, as he most learnedly delivered.[3]

ADRIAN [*to* GONZALO] The air breathes upon us here most
    sweetly.

SEBASTIAN [*to* ANTONIO] As if it had lungs, and rotten ones.

ANTONIO Or as 'twere perfumed by a fen.°   *bog*

50   GONZALO [*to* ADRIAN] Here is everything advantageous to life.

ANTONIO [*to* SEBASTIAN] True, save° means to live.   *except*

SEBASTIAN Of that there's none, or little.

GONZALO [*to* ADRIAN] How lush and lusty° the grass looks! *tender and luxuriant*
    How green!

55   ANTONIO The ground indeed is tawny.

SEBASTIAN With an eye[4] of green in't.

ANTONIO He misses not much.

SEBASTIAN No, he doth but mistake the truth totally.

GONZALO [*to* ADRIAN] But the rarity[5] of it is, which is indeed
60   almost beyond credit—

SEBASTIAN [*to* ANTONIO] As many vouched° rarities are. *alleged, accepted*

GONZALO [*to* ADRIAN] That our garments being, as they were,
    drenched in the sea, hold notwithstanding their freshness and
    glosses, being rather new-dyed than stained with salt water.

65   ANTONIO [*to* SEBASTIAN] If but one of his pockets[6] could speak,
    would it not say he lies?

SEBASTIAN Ay, or very falsely pocket up his report.[7]

GONZALO [*to* ADRIAN] Methinks our garments are now as fresh
    as when we put them on first in Afric, at the marriage of the
70   King's fair daughter Claribel to the King of Tunis.

SEBASTIAN 'Twas a sweet marriage, and we prosper well in our
    return.

ADRIAN Tunis was never graced before with such a paragon to°   *for*
    their queen.

75   GONZALO Not since widow Dido's[8] time.

ANTONIO [*to* SEBASTIAN] Widow?[9] A pox o'that! How came that
    'widow' in? Widow Dido!

SEBASTIAN What if he had said 'widower Aeneas' too? Good
    Lord, how you take° it!   *fuss about*

80   ADRIAN [*to* GONZALO] 'Widow Dido' said you? You make me
    study of ° that: she was of Carthage, not of Tunis.   *examine*

GONZALO This Tunis, sir, was Carthage.[1]

ADRIAN Carthage?

GONZALO I assure you, Carthage.

---

1. Exquisite, but in Antonio's usage (line 44), "given to
pleasure." *subtle:* fine, but in Sebastian's usage (line 45),
"sexually expert" or "crafty."
2. Antonio takes "Temperance" to be the name of a girl.
delicate: voluptuous, given to pleasure.
3. "Learnedly delivered" was a popular phrase among
Puritans who wanted to appear pious.
4. A tinge. In Antonio's reply, an "eye of green" refers to
Gonzalo's optimistic capacity to see green.
5. Exceptional quality; but in Sebastian's usage (line 61),
"uncommon thing."
6. Seen as the garments' "mouth"; also implying that

Gonzalo's pockets are stained.
7. The evidence of stained pockets would confute Gon-
zalo's words and reputation for honesty. *pocket up:* sup-
press, or keep silent; also, receive unprotestingly.
8. Queen of ancient Carthage, whose tragic love affair
with Aeneas is related in Virgil's *Aeneid.*
9. Antonio picks on this designation for a woman aban-
doned by her lover as being either irrelevant or conspicu-
ously prudish. Dido, however, was in fact a widow when
she met Aeneas.
1. The city of Tunis was actually built 10 miles from the
site of Carthage.

85 ANTONIO [*to* SEBASTIAN] His word is more than the miraculous harp.[2]

SEBASTIAN He hath raised the wall, and houses too.

ANTONIO What impossible matter will he make easy next?

SEBASTIAN I think he will carry this island home in his pocket,
90 and give it his son for an apple.

ANTONIO And sowing the kernels° of it in the sea, bring forth   seeds
more islands.

GONZALO [*to* ADRIAN] Ay.[3]

ANTONIO [*to* SEBASTIAN] Why, in good time.

95 GONZALO [*to* ALONSO] Sir, we were talking that our garments
seem now as fresh as when we were at Tunis, at the marriage
of your daughter, who is now queen.

ANTONIO And the rarest that e'er came there.

SEBASTIAN Bate,[4] I beseech you, widow Dido.

100 ANTONIO O, widow Dido? Ay, widow Dido.

GONZALO [*to* ALONSO] Is not, sir, my doublet as fresh as the first
day I wore it? I mean in a sort.[5]

ANTONIO [*to* SEBASTIAN] That 'sort' was well fished for.

GONZALO [*to* ALONSO] When I wore it at your daughter's
105 marriage.

ALONSO You cram these words into mine ears against
The stomach of my sense.[6] Would I had never
Married my daughter there! For, coming thence,
My son is lost; and, in my rate,° she too,   consideration
110 Who is so far from Italy removed
I ne'er again shall see her. O thou mine heir
Of Naples and of Milan, what strange fish
Hath made his meal on thee?

FRANCISCO   Sir, he may live.
I saw him beat the surges under him
115 And ride upon their backs. He trod the water,
Whose enmity he flung aside, and breasted
The surge, most swoll'n, that met him. His bold head
'Bove the contentious waves he kept, and oared
Himself with his good arms in lusty° stroke   vigorous
120 To th' shore, that o'er his wave-worn basis bowed,[7]
As° stooping to relieve him. I not° doubt   As if / do not
He came alive to land.

ALONSO   No, no; he's gone.

SEBASTIAN [*to* ALONSO] Sir, you may thank yourself for this great loss,
That would not bless our Europe with your daughter,
125 But rather loose° her to an African,   lose; release
Where she, at least, is banished from your eye,
Who° hath cause to wet the grief° on't.   (Claribel) / weep

ALONSO   Prithee, peace.

SEBASTIAN You were kneeled to and importuned otherwise[8]
By all of us, and the fair soul herself
130 Weighed between loathness and obedience at

2. Referring to Amphion's harp, to the music of which
the walls (but not the houses) of Thebes arose.
3. Affirming his belief that Tunis was Carthage; Antonio
mocks the length of time this took.
4. Except (as a verb); don't mention.
5. Comparatively speaking; Antonio plays on "drawing

lots."
6. *You . . . sense:* The image is of one being force-fed
words against the appetite ("stomach") for hearing them.
7. *that . . . bowed:* that extended out and drooped over
the foot of the cliff, which had been eroded by waves.
8. *otherwise:* to act differently.

Which end o'th' beam should bow.[9] We have lost your son,
I fear, for ever. Milan and Naples have
More widows in them of this business' making
Than we bring men to comfort them. The fault's your own.

ALONSO   So is the dear'st o'th' loss.[1]

135 GONZALO   My lord Sebastian,
The truth you speak doth lack some gentleness
And time to speak it in. You rub the sore[2]
When you should bring the plaster.

SEBASTIAN *[to* ANTONIO*]*   Very well.

140 ANTONIO   And most chirurgeonly.°   *surgeonlike*

GONZALO *[to* ALONSO*]*   It is foul weather in us all, good sir,
When you are cloudy.

SEBASTIAN *[to* ANTONIO*]*   Fowl weather?[3]

ANTONIO   Very foul.

GONZALO *[to* ALONSO*]*   Had I plantation[4] of this isle, my lord—

ANTONIO *[to* SEBASTIAN*]*   He'd sow't with nettle-seed.

SEBASTIAN   Or docks,
or mallows.[5]

145 GONZALO   And were the king on't, what would I do?

SEBASTIAN *[to* ANTONIO*]*   Scape being drunk, for want of wine.

GONZALO   I'th' commonwealth I would by contraries
Execute all things.[6] For no kind of traffic°   *commerce*
Would I admit, no name of magistrate;

150 Letters° should not be known; riches, poverty,   *Writing; erudition*
And use of service,° none; contract, succession,[7]   *servants*
Bourn,° bound of land, tilth,° vineyard, none;   *Boundary / tillage*
No use of metal, corn,° or wine, or oil;   *grain*
No occupation, all men idle, all;

155 And women too—but innocent and pure;[8]
No sovereignty—

SEBASTIAN *[to* ANTONIO*]*   Yet he would be king on't.

ANTONIO   The latter end of his commonwealth forgets the
beginning.

GONZALO *[to* ALONSO*]*   All things in common° nature should   *for communal use*
produce

160 Without sweat or endeavour. Treason, felony,
Sword, pike, knife, gun, or need of any engine,°   *weapon*
Would I not have; but nature should bring forth
Of it° own kind all foison,° all abundance,   *its / plenty*
To feed my innocent people.

165 SEBASTIAN *[to* ANTONIO*]*   No marrying[9] 'mong his subjects?

ANTONIO   None, man, all idle: whores and knaves.

GONZALO *[to* ALONSO*]*   I would with such perfection govern, sir,
T'excel the Golden Age.[1]

---

9. *Weighed . . . bow:* Weighed loathness to marry against
obedience to her father to find out which end of the
scales' beam would sink.
1. That is, the most grievous, or costliest, part of the loss
is also my own.
2. "To rub the sore" was proverbial. *plaster* (line 138): a
soothing remedy.
3. Perhaps recalling lines 28–31.
4. Had I responsibility for colonization of the island, but
also interpreted as "planting" by Antonio and Sebastian.
5. Cited as wild plants prone to grow on uncultivated
land; but dock is a traditional soother of nettle stings, and

mallow roots were used to make soothing ointment.
6. *I would . . . things:* I would advance the opposite to
what would be usual. This speech is based on a passage
in John Florio's translation of Montaigne's essay "Of the
Cannibals."
7. Inheritance of property.
8. Idleness proverbially begets lust.
9. Seen as irrelevant to sexually innocent people; also a
form of contract (line 151).
1. In classical mythology, the earliest of the ages—a time
without strife, labor, or injustice, when abundant food
grew without cultivation.

SEBASTIAN   Save° his majesty!   *God save*
ANTONIO   Long live Gonzalo!
GONZALO [*to* ALONSO]   And—do you mark me, sir?
170   ALONSO   Prithee, no more. Thou dost talk nothing to me.
GONZALO   I do well believe your highness, and did it to minister
   occasion² to these gentlemen, who are of such sensible° and   *sensitive*
   nimble lungs that they always use° to laugh at nothing.   *are accustomed*
ANTONIO   'Twas you we laughed at.
175   GONZALO   Who, in this kind of merry fooling, am nothing to
   you. So you may continue, and laugh at nothing still.
ANTONIO   What a blow was there given!
SEBASTIAN   An it had not fallen flat-long.³
GONZALO   You are gentlemen of brave mettle.⁴ You would lift
180   the moon out of her sphere, if she would continue in it five
   weeks without changing.⁵
            Enter ARIEL, [*invisible,*] *playing solemn music*
SEBASTIAN   We would so, and then go a-bat-fowling.⁶
ANTONIO [*to* GONZALO]   Nay, good my lord, be not angry.
GONZALO   No, I warrant you, I will not adventure my discretion
185   so weakly.⁷ Will you laugh me asleep? For I am very heavy.°   *tired; serious*
ANTONIO   Go sleep, and hear us.
            [GONZALO, ADRIAN, *and* FRANCISCO *sleep*]
ALONSO   What, all so soon asleep? I wish mine eyes
   Would, with themselves, shut up my thoughts.—I find
   They are inclined to do so.
SEBASTIAN   Please you, sir,
190   Do not omit° the heavy offer° of it.   *neglect / opportunity*
   It seldom visits sorrow; when it doth,
   It is a comforter.
ANTONIO   We two, my lord,
   Will guard your person while you take your rest,
   And watch your safety.
ALONSO   Thank you. Wondrous heavy.
            [*He sleeps. Exit* ARIEL]
195   SEBASTIAN   What a strange drowsiness possesses them!
ANTONIO   It is the quality o'th' climate.
SEBASTIAN   Why
   Doth it not then our eyelids sink? I find
   Not myself disposed to sleep.
ANTONIO   Nor I; my spirits are nimble.
   They fell together all, as by consent;°   *consensus*
200   They dropped as by a thunderstroke. What might,
   Worthy Sebastian, O, what might—? No more!—
   And yet methinks I see it in thy face.
   What thou shouldst be th'occasion speaks° thee, and   *opportunity reveals to*
   My strong imagination sees a crown
   Dropping upon thy head.
205   SEBASTIAN   What, art thou waking?°   *awake*
ANTONIO   Do you not hear me speak?

---

2. *minister occasion:* afford opportunity.
3. If it had not fallen on the flat, harmless side of the
sword.
4. Courage; punning on "metal," as of a sword blade.
5. *You would . . . changing:* If the moon were to remain
in her orbit ("sphere") one week longer than usual (five
weeks), you would steal her from her place.
6. Trapping birds by using light to attract them and bats
to strike them down; may also mean swindling and vic-
timizing the simple.
7. I will not put my sound judgment at risk so foolishly.

SEBASTIAN   I do, and surely
    It is a sleepy language, and thou speak'st
    Out of thy sleep. What is it thou didst say?
    This is a strange repose, to be asleep
210   With eyes wide open; standing, speaking, moving,
    And yet so fast asleep.
ANTONIO   Noble Sebastian,
    Thou letst thy fortune sleep, die rather; wink'st°   *shut your eyes*
    Whiles thou art waking.
SEBASTIAN   Thou dost snore distinctly;°   *meaningfully*
    There's meaning in thy snores.
215 ANTONIO   I am more serious than my custom. You
    Must be so too if heed° me, which to do   *if you heed*
    Trebles thee o'er.
SEBASTIAN   Well, I am standing water.[8]
ANTONIO   I'll teach you how to flow.
SEBASTIAN   Do so; to ebb
    Hereditary sloth[9] instructs me.
ANTONIO   O,
220   If you but knew how you the purpose cherish
    Whiles thus you mock it;[1] how in stripping it
    You more invest° it! Ebbing° men, indeed,   *clothe / Declining*
    Most often do so near the bottom run
    By their own fear or sloth.
SEBASTIAN   Prithee, say on.
225   The setting° of thine eye and cheek proclaim   *fixed look*
    A matter° from thee, and a birth, indeed,   *Something important*
    Which throes[2] thee much to yield.
ANTONIO   Thus, sir.
    Although this lord° of weak remembrance,° this,   *(Gonzalo) / memory*
    Who shall be of as little memory°   *remembered*
230   When he is earthed,° hath here almost persuaded—   *buried*
    For he's a spirit of persuasion, only
    Professes[3] to persuade—the King his son's alive,
    'Tis as impossible that he's undrowned
    As he that sleeps here swims.
SEBASTIAN   I have no hope
    That he's undrowned.
235 ANTONIO   O, out of that 'no hope'
    What great hope have you! No hope that way° is   *(that he's not drowned)*
    Another way so high a hope that even
    Ambition cannot pierce a wink° beyond,   *catch a glimpse*
    But doubt discovery there.[4] Will you grant with me
    That Ferdinand is drowned?
SEBASTIAN   He's gone.
240 ANTONIO   Then tell me,
    Who's the next heir of Naples?
SEBASTIAN   Claribel.

---

8. Between tides, and thus open to suggestion; also asso-
ciated with being slothful. *Trebles thee o'er:* Makes you
three times as great.
9. Inherited laziness, or the slowness to attain prosperity
arising from being born a younger brother.
1. *If . . . it:* If you only understood that your mockery
reveals how great your aspirations really are; also, the

hereditary position you mock is actually to your advan-
tage. *cherish:* hold dear; cultivate.
2. Which puts in agony, as in childbirth.
3. *only / Professes:* his sole vocation is.
4. Doubt that there is anything to achieve beyond the
high hope of the crown.

ANTONIO She that is Queen of Tunis; she that dwells
Ten leagues beyond man's life;° she that from Naples   *lifetime journey*
Can have no note°—unless the sun were post°—   *information / messenger*
245 The man i'th' moon's too slow—till new-born chins
Be rough and razorable; she that from° whom   *returning from*
We all were sea-swallowed, though some cast again⁵—
And by that destiny, to perform an act
Whereof what's past is prologue, what to come
In yours and my discharge.°   *performance*
250 SEBASTIAN   What stuff is this? How say you?
'Tis true my brother's daughter's Queen of Tunis;
So is she heir of Naples; 'twixt which regions
There is some space.
ANTONIO   A space whose every cubit°   *about 18 to 22 inches*
Seems to cry out 'How shall that Claribel
255 Measure us° back to Naples? Keep° in Tunis,   *(the cubits) / Stay*
And let Sebastian wake.'° Say this were death   *(to his opportunity)*
That now hath seized them; why, they were no worse
Than now they are. There be that° can rule Naples   *those that*
As well as he that sleeps, lords that can prate
260 As amply and unnecessarily
As this Gonzalo; I myself could make
A chough of as deep chat.⁶ O, that you bore
The mind that I do, what a sleep were this
For your advancement! Do you understand me?
SEBASTIAN Methinks I do.
265 ANTONIO   And how does your content
Tender° your own good fortune?   *Regard; care for*
SEBASTIAN   I remember
You did supplant your brother Prospero.
ANTONIO   True;
And look how well my garments sit upon me,
Much feater° than before. My brother's servants   *more trimly*
270 Were then my fellows; now they are my men.
SEBASTIAN But for your conscience.
ANTONIO Ay, sir, where lies that? If 'twere a kibe⁷
'Twould put me to° my slipper; but I feel not   *make me wear*
This deity in my bosom. Twenty consciences
275 That stand 'twixt me and Milan, candied⁸ be they,
And melt ere they molest. Here lies your brother,
No better than the earth he lies upon
If he were that which now he's like—that's dead;
Whom I with this obedient steel,° three inches of it,   *sword*
280 Can lay to bed for ever; whiles you, doing thus,
To the perpetual wink for aye° might put   *sleep forever*
This ancient morsel, this Sir Prudence, who
Should not upbraid our course. For all the rest,
They'll take suggestion° as a cat laps milk;   *prompting to evil*
285 They'll tell the clock° to any business that   *chime; agree*
We say befits the hour.
SEBASTIAN   Thy case, dear friend,

5. Regurgitated, cast ashore; also, possibly, theatrical
role-playing.
6. *I . . . chat:* I could train a jackdaw (known for imitat-
ing speech) to speak as profoundly.
7. Chilblain; sore on the heel.
8. Turned to sugar; crystallized in sugar.

Shall be my precedent. As thou got'st Milan,
I'll come by Naples. Draw thy sword. One stroke
Shall free thee from the tribute which thou payest,
And I the King shall love thee.

290 ANTONIO   Draw together,
And when I rear my hand, do you the like
To fall it on Gonzalo.
        [*They draw*]
SEBASTIAN   O, but one word.
        Enter ARIEL, [*invisible,*] *with music and song*
ARIEL [*to* GONZALO]   My master through his art foresees the danger
That you his friend are in—and sends me forth,
295 For else° his project dies, to keep them⁹ living.   *otherwise*
        [*He*] *sings in Gonzalo's ear*
            While you here do snoring lie,
            Open-eyed conspiracy
                His time° doth take.   *opportunity*
            If of life you keep a care,
300   Shake off slumber, and beware.
                Awake, awake!
ANTONIO [*to* SEBASTIAN]   Then let us both be sudden.
GONZALO [*awaking*]   Now good angels
Preserve the King!
ALONSO [*awaking*]   Why, how now? Ho, awake!
        [*The others awake*]
[*To* ANTONIO *and* SEBASTIAN]   Why are you° drawn?   *your weapons*
[*To* GONZALO] Wherefore this ghastly° looking?   *fearful*
305 GONZALO   What's the matter?
SEBASTIAN   Whiles we stood here securing° your repose,   *guarding*
Even now we heard a hollow burst of bellowing,
Like bulls, or rather lions. Did't not wake you?
It struck mine ear most terribly.
ALONSO   I heard nothing.
310 ANTONIO   O, 'twas a din to fright a monster's ear,
To make an earthquake! Sure it was the roar
Of a whole herd of lions.
ALONSO   Heard you this, Gonzalo?
GONZALO   Upon mine honour, sir, I heard a humming,
And that a strange one too, which did awake me.
315 I shaked you, sir, and cried.° As mine eyes opened   *called out*
I saw their weapons drawn. There was a noise,
That's verily.° 'Tis best we stand upon our guard,   *the truth*
Or that we quit this place. Let's draw our weapons.
ALONSO   Lead off this ground, and let's make further search
For my poor son.
320 GONZALO   Heavens keep him from these beasts!
For he is sure i'th' island.
ALONSO   Lead away. [*Exeunt all but* ARIEL]¹
ARIEL   Prospero my lord shall know what I have done.
So, King, go safely on to seek thy son.   *Exit*

---

9. Gonzalo and Alonso.
1. Ariel's following lines are spoken as the other characters depart; he probably exits in another direction.

2.2

Enter CALIBAN, *[wearing a gaberdine,[1] and] with a bur-*
den of wood

CALIBAN *[throwing down his burden]*   All the infections that the
sun sucks up
From bogs, fens, flats,° on Prosper fall, and make him   marshes
By inch-meal° a disease!   inch by inch
[A noise of thunder heard][2]
              His spirits hear me,
And yet I needs must curse. But they'll nor pinch,
5   Fright me with urchin-shows,[3] pitch me i'th' mire,
Nor lead me like a fire-brand in the dark
Out of my way, unless he bid 'em. But
For every trifle are they set upon me;
Sometime like apes, that mow° and chatter at me   grimace
10   And after bite me; then like hedgehogs, which
Lie tumbling in my barefoot way and mount
Their pricks at my footfall; sometime am I
All wound with° adders, who with cloven tongues   entwined by
Do hiss me into madness.
        Enter TRINCULO[4]
                 Lo now, lo!
15   Here comes a spirit of his, and to torment me
For bringing wood in slowly. I'll fall flat.
Perchance he will not mind° me.   notice
    [He lies down]

TRINCULO Here's neither bush nor shrub to bear off° any   ward off
weather at all, and another storm brewing. I hear it sing i'th'
20 wind. Yon same black cloud, yon huge one, looks like a foul
bombard[5] that would shed his liquor. If it should thunder as it
did before, I know not where to hide my head. Yon same cloud
cannot choose but fall by pailfuls. *[Seeing* CALIBAN*]* What have
we here, a man or a fish? Dead or alive?—A fish, he smells
25 like a fish; a very ancient and fish-like smell; a kind of not-of-
the-newest poor-john.[6] A strange fish! Were I in England now,
as once I was, and had but this fish painted,[7] not a holiday-fool
there but would give a piece of silver. There would this mon-
ster make a man.[8] Any strange beast there makes a man. When
30 they will not give a doit° to relieve a lame beggar, they will lay   small coin
out ten to see a dead Indian.[9] Legged like a man, and his fins
like arms! Warm, o' my troth! I do now let loose my opinion,
hold it no longer. This is no fish, but an islander that hath
lately suffered by a thunderbolt.
    [Thunder]
35 Alas, the storm is come again. My best way is to creep under
his gaberdine; there is no other shelter hereabout. Misery
acquaints a man with strange bedfellows. I will here shroud°   take cover
till the dregs[1] of the storm be past.

2.2
1. A loose smock made of coarse material.
2. Caliban takes this as a response to his curse; in F, the direction comes before Caliban speaks.
3. With the sight of hedgehoglike spirits.
4. Trinculo is probably dressed in traditional fool's motley (many-colored garment).
5. Large leather drinking vessel; stone-throwing military

engine.
6. Dried hake, a poor person's staple.
7. On a sign to attract spectators.
8. Make a fortune for a man; become a man.
9. An allusion to exhibitions of American Indians in London.
1. Drinks, as from a "bombard" of wine.

[*He hides under Caliban's gaberdine.*]
Enter STEFANO, *singing* [*with a wooden bottle in his hand*]

STEFANO   I shall no more to sea, to sea,
40   Here shall I die ashore—
This is a very scurvy tune to sing at a man's funeral.
Well, here's my comfort.
   [*He*] *drinks,* [*then*] *sings*
   The master, the swabber, the boatswain, and I,
    The gunner and his mate,
45   Loved Mall, Meg, and Marian, and Margery,
    But none of us cared for Kate.
    For she had a tongue with a tang,°   *sting*
    Would cry to a sailor 'Go hang!'
   She loved not the savour of tar nor of pitch,
50   Yet a tailor might scratch her where'er she did itch.[2]
    Then to sea, boys, and let her go hang!
    Then to sea [*etc.*].
This is a scurvy tune, too. But here's my comfort.
   [*He*] *drinks*

CALIBAN [*to* TRINCULO] Do not torment me! O!
55 STEFANO What's the matter?° Have we devils here? Do you put *What's going on?*
tricks upon's with savages and men of Ind,° ha? I have not *India*
scaped drowning to be afeard now of your four legs. For it hath
been said: 'As proper a man as ever went on four legs[3] cannot
make him give ground.' And it shall be said so again, while
60 Stefano breathes at'° nostrils.   *at the*
CALIBAN The spirit torments me. O!
STEFANO This is some monster of the isle with four legs, who
hath got, as I take it, an ague.° Where the devil should he learn *a fit of fever*
our language? I will give him some relief, if it be but for that.
65 If I can recover° him and keep him tame and get to Naples *cure*
with him, he's a present for any emperor that ever trod on neat's
leather.°   *cowhide; shoes*
CALIBAN [*to* TRINCULO] Do not torment me, prithee! I'll bring
my wood home faster.
70 STEFANO He's in his fit now, and does not talk after° the wisest. *in the manner of*
He shall taste of my bottle. If he have never drunk wine afore,
it will go near to° remove his fit. If I can recover him and keep *almost*
him tame, I will not take too much for him.[4] He shall pay for
him that hath° him, and that soundly.   *gets*
75 CALIBAN [*to* TRINCULO] Thou dost me yet but little hurt. Thou
wilt anon, I know it by thy trembling. Now Prosper works upon
thee.
STEFANO Come on your ways.° Open your mouth. Here is that *Come on*
which will give language to you, cat.[5] Open your mouth. This
80 will shake° your shaking, I can tell you, and that soundly. You *dislodge*
cannot tell who's your friend. Open your chaps again.
   [CALIBAN *drinks*]

2. Implying sexual desire and gratification. Tailors were often mocked for supposed lack of virility.
3. Comically varying "on two legs" (upright); also sug-gesting "on crutches."
4. No sum can be too high for him.
5. "Ale will make a cat speak" was proverbial.

TRINCULO   I should know that voice. It should be—but he is
drowned, and these are devils. O, defend me!

STEFANO   Four legs and two voices—a most delicate° monster!   °exquisitely made

85   His forward voice now is to speak well of his friend; his back-
ward voice is to utter foul speeches and to detract. If all the
wine in my bottle will recover him,[6] I will help his ague.
Come.

[CALIBAN *drinks*]

Amen.°   I will pour some in thy other mouth.   °Enough

90   TRINCULO   Stefano!

STEFANO   Doth thy other mouth call me? Mercy, mercy! This is
a devil, and no monster. I will leave him. I have no long
spoon.[7]

TRINCULO   Stefano! If thou beest Stefano, touch me and speak

95   to me, for I am Trinculo. Be not afeard. Thy good friend Trin-
culo.

STEFANO   If thou beest Trinculo, come forth. I'll pull thee by
the lesser legs. If any be Trinculo's legs, these are they.

[*He pulls out* TRINCULO *by the legs*]

Thou art very° Trinculo indeed! How cam'st thou to be the   °actual

100   siege° of this moon-calf?[8] Can he vent° Trinculos?   °excrement / defecate

TRINCULO [*rising*]   I took him to be killed with a thunderstroke.
But art thou not drowned, Stefano? I hope now thou art not
drowned. Is the storm overblown? I hid me under the dead
moon-calf 's gaberdine for fear of the storm. And art thou living,

105   Stefano? O Stefano, two Neapolitans scaped!

[*He dances* STEFANO *round*]

STEFANO   Prithee, do not turn me about. My stomach is not
constant.

CALIBAN   These be fine things, an if ° they be not spirits.   °an if = if
That's a brave° god, and bears celestial liquor.   °an excellent; a fine

110   I will kneel to him.

[*He kneels*]

STEFANO [*to* TRINCULO]   How didst thou scape? How cam'st thou
hither? Swear by this bottle how thou cam'st hither. I escaped
upon a butt of sack[9] which the sailors heaved o'erboard, by this
bottle—which I made of the bark of a tree with mine own

115   hands since I was cast ashore.

CALIBAN   I'll swear upon that bottle to be thy true subject, for
the liquor is not earthly.

STEFANO [*offering* TRINCULO *the bottle*]   Here. Swear then how
thou escapedst.

120   TRINCULO   Swum ashore, man, like a duck. I can swim like a
duck, I'll be sworn.

STEFANO   Here, kiss the book.[1]

[TRINCULO *drinks*]

Though thou canst swim like a duck, thou art made like a
goose.[2]

---

6. If it takes all the wine in my bottle to cure him.
7. From the proverbial "He should have a long spoon
that sups with the devil."
8. Deformed creature; miscarriage, owing to the sup-
posed detrimental influence of the moon.
9. Cask of Spanish or Canary wine.

1. Confirming an oath by kissing the Bible; or the prover-
bial "Kiss the cup" ("Drink").
2. Probably alluding to Trinculo's outstretched neck with
the bottle as a beak; also a byword for giddiness and
unsteadiness on the feet.

125 TRINCULO   O Stefano, hast any more of this?
    STEFANO   The whole butt, man. My cellar is in a rock by th' sea-
        side, where my wine is hid.
        [CALIBAN rises]
    How now, moon-calf? How does thine ague?
    CALIBAN   Hast thou not dropped from heaven?
130 STEFANO   Out o'th' moon, I do assure thee. I was the man i'th'
        moon when time was.°   *once upon a time*
    CALIBAN   I have seen thee in her, and I do adore thee.
        My mistress° showed me thee, and thy dog and thy bush.³   *(Miranda)*
    STEFANO   Come, swear to that. Kiss the book. I will furnish it
135   anon with new contents. Swear.
        [CALIBAN drinks]
    TRINCULO   By this good light,° this is a very shallow monster! I   *sun*
        afeard of him? A very weak monster! The man i'th' moon? A
        most poor, credulous monster! Well drawn,° monster, in good   *drunk*
        sooth!
140 CALIBAN [to STEFANO]   I'll show thee every fertile inch o'th' island,
        And I will kiss thy foot. I prithee, be my god.
    TRINCULO   By this light, a most perfidious and drunken monster!
        When's god's asleep, he'll rob his bottle.
    CALIBAN [to STEFANO]   I'll kiss thy foot. I'll swear myself thy subject.
145 STEFANO   Come on then; down, and swear.
        [CALIBAN kneels]
    TRINCULO   I shall laugh myself to death at this puppy-headed
        monster. A most scurvy monster! I could find in my heart to
        beat him—
    STEFANO [to CALIBAN]   Come, kiss.
        [CALIBAN kisses his foot]
150 TRINCULO   But that the poor monster's in drink.° An abominable   *drunk*
        monster!
    CALIBAN   I'll show thee the best springs; I'll pluck thee berries;
        I'll fish for thee, and get thee wood enough.
        A plague upon the tyrant that I serve!
155   I'll bear him no more sticks, but follow thee,
        Thou wondrous man.
    TRINCULO   A most ridiculous monster, to make a wonder of a
        poor drunkard!
    CALIBAN [to STEFANO]   I prithee, let me bring thee where crabs°   *crab apples*
        grow,
160   And I with my long nails will dig thee pig-nuts,°   *edible tubers*
        Show thee a jay's nest, and instruct thee how
        To snare the nimble marmoset. I'll bring thee
        To clust'ring filberts, and sometimes I'll get thee
        Young seamews° from the rock. Wilt thou go with me?   *seagulls*
165 STEFANO   I prithee now, lead the way without any more talk-
        ing.—Trinculo, the King and all our company else being
        drowned, we will inherit here.—Here, bear my bottle.⁴—Fel-
        low Trinculo, we'll fill him° by and by again.   *it*
    CALIBAN (sings drunkenly)⁵   Farewell, master, farewell, farewell!
170 TRINCULO   A howling monster, a drunken monster!

---

3. A dog and a thornbush were traditional attributes of the man in the moon; cf. *A Midsummer Night's Dream* 5.1.248–49.

4. Probably spoken to Caliban.
5. This stage direction may be misplaced and may actu-ally refer to the following song, "No more dams."

CALIBAN [*sings*]   No more dams I'll make for° fish,   to trap
                    Nor fetch in firing°   firewood
                    At requiring,
                    Nor scrape trenchering,⁶ nor wash dish.
175   'Ban, 'ban, Cacaliban
                    Has a new master.—Get a new man!⁷
        Freedom, high-day!° High-day, freedom! Freedom, high-day,   holiday
        freedom!

STEFANO   O brave° monster! Lead the way.   *Exeunt*   excellent; fine

3.1

Enter FERDINAND, *bearing a log*

FERDINAND   There be some sports are painful, and their labour
        Delight in them sets off.¹ Some kinds of baseness
        Are nobly undergone, and most poor matters
        Point to rich ends. This my mean° task   lowly
5   Would be as heavy to me as odious, but°   except that
        The mistress which I serve quickens° what's dead,   enlivens
        And makes my labours pleasures. O, she is
        Ten times more gentle than her father's crabbed,
        And he's composed of harshness. I must remove
10   Some thousands of these logs and pile them up,
        Upon a sore° injunction. My sweet mistress   harsh
        Weeps when she sees me work, and says such baseness
        Had never like executor. I forget,
        But these sweet thoughts do even refresh my labours,
        Most busil'est² when I do it.°   (labor)

Enter MIRANDA, *and* PROSPERO [*following at a distance*]

15 MIRANDA   Alas now, pray you
        Work not so hard. I would the lightning had
        Burnt up those logs that you are enjoined to pile.
        Pray set it down, and rest you. When this burns
        'Twill weep³ for having wearied you. My father
20   Is hard at study. Pray now, rest yourself.
        He's safe° for these three hours.   We are safe from him

FERDINAND   O most dear mistress,
        The sun will set before I shall discharge
        What I must strive to do.

MIRANDA   If you'll sit down
        I'll bear your logs the while. Pray give me that;
        I'll carry it to the pile.

25 FERDINAND   No, precious creature.
        I had rather crack my sinews, break my back,
        Than you should such dishonour undergo
        While I sit lazy by.

MIRANDA   It would become me
        As well as it does you; and I should do it
30   With much more ease, for my good will is to it,
        And yours it is against.

---

6. Trenchers, or wooden plates.
7. Addressed to the old master, Prospero.
3.1
1. *their . . . off:* the greater effort invested amounts to

more pleasure; the labor of painful activities ("sports") is
offset by whatever delight we take in them.
2. Most busily (giving a double superlative).
3. By exuding drops of resin.

PROSPERO [*aside*]   Poor worm, thou art infected.[4]
This visitation[5] shows it.
MIRANDA [*to* FERDINAND]   You look wearily.
FERDINAND   No, noble mistress, 'tis fresh morning with me
When you are by at night. I do beseech you,
35   Chiefly that I might set it in my prayers,
What is your name?
MIRANDA   Miranda. O my father,
I have broke your hest° to say so!   *disobeyed your command*
FERDINAND   Admired[6] Miranda!
Indeed the top of admiration, worth
What's dearest to the world. Full many a lady
40   I have eyed with best regard, and many a time
Th'harmony of their tongues hath into bondage
Brought my too diligent° ear. For several virtues   *attentive*
Have I liked several° women; never any   *various*
With so full soul but some defect in her
45   Did quarrel with the noblest grace she owed°   *owned*
And put it to the foil.[7] But you, O you,
So perfect and so peerless, are created
Of every creature's best.
MIRANDA   I do not know
One of my sex, no woman's face remember
50   Save from my glass° mine own; nor have I seen   *mirror*
More that I may call men than you, good friend,
And my dear father. How features are abroad[8]
I am skilless° of ; but, by my modesty,°   *ignorant / virginity*
The jewel in my dower,° I would not wish   *dowry*
55   Any companion in the world but you;
Nor can imagination form a shape
Besides° yourself to like of. But I prattle   *Other than*
Something° too wildly, and my father's precepts   *Somewhat*
I therein do forget.
FERDINAND   I am in my condition°   *rank*
60   A prince, Miranda, I do think a king—
I would° not so—and would no more endure   *wish it were*
This wooden slavery[9] than to suffer
The flesh-fly[1] blow my mouth. Hear my soul speak.
The very instant that I saw you did
65   My heart fly to your service; there resides
To make me slave to it. And for your sake
Am I this patient log-man.
MIRANDA   Do you love me?
FERDINAND   O heaven, O earth, bear witness to this sound,
And crown what I profess with kind event°   *favorable outcome*
70   If I speak true! If hollowly,° invert   *falsely*
What best is boded° me to mischief !° I,   *foretold to / misfortune*
Beyond all limit of what° else i'th' world,   *whatsoever*
Do love, prize, honour you.

4. Inflicted with lovesickness. *worm:* an expression of
tenderness; but a worm was often thought to carry dis-
ease.
5. Suggesting a pastoral or charitable visit to the sick; or
may indicate a visit by the plague, here lovesickness.
6. Playing on the meaning of Miranda's name.

7. Foiled it, or made it ineffectual; challenged it, as in a
fencing match (compare "quarrel" in line 45).
8. What people look like elsewhere.
9. The log as a symbol of Prospero's oppression.
1. Species of fly that deposits its eggs ("blows") in dead
flesh.

MIRANDA [*weeping*]   I am a fool
    To weep at what I am glad of.
PROSPERO [*aside*]   Fair encounter
75 Of two most rare affections! Heavens rain grace
    On that which breeds between 'em.
FERDINAND [*to* MIRANDA]   Wherefore weep you?
MIRANDA   At mine unworthiness, that dare not offer
    What I desire to give, and much less take
    What I shall die to want.² But this is trifling,
80 And all the more it seeks to hide itself
    The bigger bulk it shows.³ Hence, bashful cunning,°   *artful shyness*
    And prompt me, plain and holy innocence.
    I am your wife, if you will marry me.
    If not, I'll die your maid.° To be your fellow°   *virgin; servant / equal*
85 You may deny me, but I'll be your servant
    Whether you will or no.
FERDINAND [*kneeling*]   My mistress,° dearest;   *sweetheart*
    And I thus humble ever.
MIRANDA   My husband then?
FERDINAND   Ay, with a heart as willing°   *desirous*
90 As bondage e'er of freedom. Here's my hand.⁴
MIRANDA   And mine, with my heart in't. And now farewell
    Till half an hour hence.
FERDINAND   A thousand thousand.°   *(farewells)*
                    Exeunt [*severally*° MIRANDA *and* FERDINAND]   *separately*
PROSPERO   So glad of this as they I cannot be,
    Who are surprised with all;° but my rejoicing   *overwhelmed by all*
95 At nothing can be more. I'll to my book,°   *book of magic*
    For yet ere supper-time must I perform
    Much business appertaining.   *Exit*

3.2

Enter CALIBAN, STEFANO, *and* TRINCULO

STEFANO [*to* CALIBAN]   Tell not me. When the butt is out we will
    drink water, not a drop before. Therefore bear up and board
    'em.¹ Servant monster, drink to me.
TRINCULO   Servant monster? The folly° of this island! They say   *absurdity*
5   there's but five upon this isle. We are three of them; if th'other
    two be brained° like us, the state totters.   *have brains*
STEFANO   Drink, servant monster, when I bid thee. Thy eyes are
    almost set° in thy head.   *fixed by drunkenness*
TRINCULO   Where should they be set° else? He were a brave   *placed*
10 monster indeed if they were set in his tail.
STEFANO   My man-monster hath drowned his tongue in sack.
    For my part, the sea cannot drown me. I swam, ere I could
    recover the shore, five and thirty leagues,° off and on.² By this   *about 100 miles*

2. *At . . . want:* Miranda is not at liberty to bestow her
virginity nor to obtain the consummation that she desires
and lacs.
3. *all . . . shows:* an image of secret pregnancy.
4. *I am your wife . . . hand:* Such an exchange could
actually have constituted a marriage ceremony. In
Shakespeare's time, weddings did not need to be wit-

nessed and performed in a church to be valid (compare
4.1.14–19).
3.2
1. Force a way aboard, continuing the naval-warfare
terminology; take onboard (drink). *bear up:* sail to the
attack.
2. Tacking away from and toward the shore.

light, thou shalt be my lieutenant, monster, or my standard.[3]

15 TRINCULO Your lieutenant if you list;° he's no standard.   *wish*

STEFANO We'll not run, Monsieur Monster.

TRINCULO Nor go° neither; but you'll lie[4] like dogs, and yet say   *walk*
nothing neither.

STEFANO Moon-calf, speak once in thy life, if thou beest a good
20 moon-calf.

CALIBAN How does thy honour? Let me lick thy shoe.
I'll not serve him; he is not valiant.

TRINCULO Thou liest, most ignorant monster! I am in case° to   *prepared*
jostle a constable. Why, thou debauched fish, thou, was there
25 ever man a coward that hath drunk so much sack as I today?
Wilt thou tell a monstrous lie, being but half a fish and half a
monster?

CALIBAN [*to* STEFANO] Lo, how he mocks me! Wilt thou let him,
my lord?

30 TRINCULO 'Lord' quoth he? That a monster should be such a
natural![5]

CALIBAN [*to* STEFANO] Lo, lo, again! Bite him to death, I prithee.

STEFANO Trinculo, keep a good tongue in your head. If you
prove a mutineer, the next tree.° The poor monster's my sub-   *(for a gallows)*
35 ject, and he shall not suffer indignity.

CALIBAN I thank my noble lord. Wilt thou be pleased
To hearken once again to the suit I made to thee?

STEFANO Marry, will I. Kneel and repeat it. I will stand, and so
shall Trinculo.

[CALIBAN *kneels*.]

Enter ARIEL, *invisible*

40 CALIBAN As I told thee before, I am subject to a tyrant, a sor-
cerer, that by his cunning hath cheated me of the island.

ARIEL Thou liest.

CALIBAN [*to* TRINCULO] Thou liest, thou jesting monkey, thou.
I would my valiant master would destroy thee.
45 I do not lie.

STEFANO Trinculo, if you trouble him any more in's tale, by this
hand, I will supplant° some of your teeth.   *uproot*

TRINCULO Why, I said nothing.

STEFANO Mum, then, and no more. [*To* CALIBAN] Proceed.

50 CALIBAN I say by sorcery he got this isle;
From me he got it. If thy greatness will
Revenge it on him—for I know thou dar'st,
But this thing[6] dare not—

STEFANO That's most certain.

55 CALIBAN Thou shalt be lord of it, and I'll serve thee.

STEFANO How now shall this be compassed?° Canst thou bring   *accomplished*
me to the party?°   *person concerned*

CALIBAN Yea, yea, my lord. I'll yield him thee asleep
Where thou mayst knock a nail into his head.[7]

60 ARIEL Thou liest, thou canst not.

---

3. Standard-bearer, but in Trinculo's reply "one who can
stand up."
4. Lie (down); tell lies; excrete.
5. An idiot, punning on the idea that monsters were

unnatural.
6. Trinculo; or perhaps Caliban himself.
7. As Jael murdered sleeping Sisera in Judges 4:21 and
5:26.

CALIBAN   What a pied ninny's° this! [*To* TRINCULO] Thou scurvy   *fool in motley*
    patch!°   *jester; idiot*
    [*To* STEFANO] I do beseech thy greatness give him blows,
    And take his bottle from him. When that's gone
    He shall drink naught but brine, for I'll not show him
65   Where the quick freshes° are.   *fast-flowing springs*
STEFANO   Trinculo, run into no further danger. Interrupt the
    monster one word further, and, by this hand, I'll turn my mercy
    out o'doors and make a stockfish of thee.[8]
TRINCULO   Why, what did I? I did nothing. I'll go farther off.
70 STEFANO   Didst thou not say he lied?
ARIEL   Thou liest.
STEFANO   Do I so? [*Striking* TRINCULO] Take thou that. As you
    like this, give me the lie° another time.   *call me a liar*
TRINCULO   I did not give the lie. Out o'your wits and hearing
75   too? A pox o'your bottle! This can sack and drinking do. A
    murrain° on your monster, and the devil take your fingers.   *plague*
CALIBAN   Ha, ha, ha!
STEFANO   Now forward with your tale. [*To* TRINCULO] Prithee,
    stand further off.
80 CALIBAN   Beat him enough; after a little time
    I'll beat him too.
STEFANO [*to* TRINCULO]
              Stand farther. [*To* CALIBAN] Come, proceed.
CALIBAN   Why, as I told thee, 'tis a custom with him
    I'th' afternoon to sleep. There° thou mayst brain him,   *Then*
    Having first seized his books; or with a log
85   Batter his skull, or paunch° him with a stake,   *disembowel*
    Or cut his weasand° with thy knife. Remember   *windpipe*
    First to possess his books, for without them
    He's but a sot° as I am, nor hath not   *stupid fool*
    One spirit to command—they all do hate him
90   As rootedly as I. Burn but his books.
    He has brave utensils,[9] for so he calls them,
    Which when he has a house he'll deck withal.
    And that most deeply to consider is
    The beauty of his daughter. He himself
95   Calls her a nonpareil.° I never saw a woman   *one without equal*
    But only Sycorax my dam and she,
    But she as far surpasseth Sycorax
    As great'st does least.
STEFANO   Is it so brave° a lass?   *excellent; fine*
CALIBAN   Ay, lord. She will become thy bed, I warrant,
100   And bring thee forth brave brood.
STEFANO   Monster, I will kill this man. His daughter and I will
    be king and queen—save° our graces!—and Trinculo and thy-   *God save*
    self shall be viceroys. Dost thou like the plot, Trinculo?
TRINCULO   Excellent.
105 STEFANO   Give me thy hand. I am sorry I beat thee. But while
    thou liv'st, keep a good tongue in thy head.

8. Proverbial allusion to the beating of dried fish before   9. Perhaps confusing implements for magic and house-
cooking it.   hold goods.

CALIBAN   Within this half hour will he be asleep.
    Wilt thou destroy him then?
STEFANO   Ay, on mine honour.
110 ARIEL [aside]   This will I tell my master.
CALIBAN   Thou mak'st me merry; I am full of pleasure.
    Let us be jocund. Will you troll° the catch°   *sing / round; song*
    You taught me but while-ere?°   *a short time ago*
STEFANO   At thy request, monster, I will do reason, any rea-
115 son.°—Come on, Trinculo, let us sing.   *anything reasonable*
   (Sings)   Flout 'em and cout[1] 'em,
           And scout° 'em and flout 'em.   *mock*
              Thought is free.
CALIBAN   That's not the tune.
    ARIEL plays the tune on a tabor and pipe[2]
120 STEFANO   What is this same?
TRINCULO   This is the tune of our catch, played by the picture
    of Nobody.[3]
STEFANO [calls towards ARIEL]   If thou beest a man, show thyself
    in thy likeness. If thou beest a devil, take't as thou list.°   *wish*
125 TRINCULO   O, forgive me my sins!
STEFANO   He that dies pays all debts.[4] [Calls] I defy thee.—
    Mercy upon us![5]
CALIBAN   Art thou afeard?
STEFANO   No, monster, not I.
130 CALIBAN   Be not afeard. The isle is full of noises,
    Sounds, and sweet airs,° that give delight and hurt not.   *tunes*
    Sometimes a thousand twangling instruments
    Will hum about mine ears, and sometime voices
    That if I then had waked after long sleep
135   Will make me sleep again; and then in dreaming
    The clouds methought would open and show riches
    Ready to drop upon me, that when I waked
    I cried to dream again.
STEFANO   This will prove a brave kingdom to me, where I shall
140 have my music for nothing.[6]
CALIBAN   When Prospero is destroyed.
STEFANO   That shall be by and by.° I remember the story.   *very soon*
               [Exit ARIEL, playing music]
TRINCULO   The sound is going away. Let's follow it, and after do
    our work.
145 STEFANO   Lead, monster; we'll follow.—I would I could see this
    taborer. He lays it on.[7]
TRINCULO [to CALIBAN]   Wilt come? I'll follow Stefano.   *Exeunt*

---

1. Probably a dialectal form of "colt" (cheat). The stage direction ("Sings") suggests that the others cannot manage the catch and remain in bewildered silence. But Trinculo, and perhaps Caliban, may attempt to join in.
2. The tabor was a small drum slung on the left-hand side of the body; the tabor pipe was a long narrow pipe played with the left hand. The combination was associated with rustic dances and merrymaking.
3. "Nobody" was a character in a comedy who was depicted on the title page of the printed text. Large

breeches up to his neck made him appear to have no trunk.
4. Varying the proverbial "Death pays all debts."
5. Stefano's defiance comically collapses.
6. James I spent large sums on court music, but not typically of the popular kind Ariel now plays.
7. He sets himself to his music vigorously. Stefano deserts Caliban in order to follow the music. Trinculo and Caliban in turn follow Stefano (line 147).

3.3

Enter ALONSO, SEBASTIAN, ANTONIO, GONZALO, ADRIAN, *and* FRANCISCO

GONZALO [*to* ALONSO]   By'r la'kin,¹ I can go no further, sir.
My old bones ache. Here's a maze trod indeed
Through forthrights and meanders.° By your patience,   *direct and winding paths*
I needs must rest me.

ALONSO   Old lord, I cannot blame thee,
5   Who am myself attached° with weariness   *seized*
To th' dulling of my spirits. Sit down and rest.
Even° here I will put off my hope, and keep it   *Exactly*
No longer for° my flatterer. He is drowned   *as*
Whom thus we stray to find, and the sea mocks
10   Our frustrate° search on land. Well, let him go.   *vain*
[*They sit*]

ANTONIO [*aside to* SEBASTIAN]   I am right glad that he's so out of hope.
Do not for° one repulse forgo the purpose   *on account of*
That you resolved t'effect.

SEBASTIAN [*aside to* ANTONIO] The next advantage
Will we take throughly.°   *thoroughly*

ANTONIO [*aside to* SEBASTIAN] Let it be tonight,
15   For now they are oppressed with travel.° They   *journey; travail*
Will not nor cannot use such vigilance
As when they are fresh.

SEBASTIAN [*aside to* ANTONIO] I say tonight. No more.
Solemn and strange music. [*Enter*] PROSPERO *on the
top,² invisible*

ALONSO   What harmony is this? My good friends, hark.

GONZALO   Marvellous sweet music.
Enter [*spirits, in*] *several strange shapes, bringing in* [*a
table and*] *a banquet, and dance about it with gentle
actions of salutations, and, inviting the King and* [*his
companions*] *to eat, they depart*

20 ALONSO   Give us kind keepers,° heavens! What were these?   *guardian angels*

SEBASTIAN   A living drollery.³ Now I will believe
That there are unicorns; that in Arabia
There is one tree, the phoenix' throne, one phoenix⁴
At this hour reigning there.

ANTONIO   I'll believe both;
25   And what does else want credit° come to me,   *lack belief*
And I'll be sworn 'tis true. Travellers ne'er did lie,⁵
Though fools at home condemn 'em.

GONZALO   If in Naples
I should report this now, would they believe me—
If I should say I saw such islanders?
30   For certes° these are people of the island,   *certainly*
Who though they are of monstrous shape, yet note
Their manners are more gentle-kind than of
Our human generation you shall find
Many, nay, almost any.

3.3
1. Ladykin: a colloquial form of reference to the Virgin
Mary.
2. A small acting area above the upper stage.
3. A puppet show with live actors.

4. The unicorn and phoenix, a bird, were two mytholog-
ical creatures that sometimes figured in travelers' tales.
Only one pheonix was said to exist in the world at any one
time.
5. Proverbially, "A traveler may lie with authority."

PROSPERO [*aside*]   Honest lord,
35 Thou hast said well, for some of you there present
Are worse than devils.

ALONSO   I cannot too much muse.°   *marvel*
Such shapes, such gesture, and such sound, expressing—
Although they want the use of tongue°—a kind   *language*
Of excellent dumb discourse.

PROSPERO [*aside*]   Praise in departing.[6]

FRANCISCO   They vanished strangely.

40 SEBASTIAN   No matter, since
They have left their viands° behind, for we have stomachs.°   *food / good appetites*
Will't please you taste of what is here?

ALONSO   Not I.

GONZALO   Faith, sir, you need not fear. When we were boys,
Who would believe that there were mountaineers°   *mountain dwellers*
45 Dewlapped like bulls, whose throats had hanging at 'em
Wallets° of flesh? Or that there were such men   *Pouches*
Whose heads stood in their breasts? Which now we find
Each putter-out of five for one[7] will bring us
Good warrant of.

ALONSO [*rising*]   I will stand to and feed,°   *begin eating*
50 Although my last—no matter, since I feel
The best is past. Brother, my lord the Duke,
Stand to, and do as we.

     [ALONSO, SEBASTIAN, *and* ANTONIO *approach the table.*]
     Thunder and lightning. Enter ARIEL [*descending*] *like a*
     harpy,[8] *claps his wings upon the table, and, with a*
     quaint device,° *the banquet vanishes*[9]   *an ingenious mechanism*

ARIEL   You are three men of sin, whom destiny—
That hath to° instrument this lower world   *as its*
55 And what is in't—the never-surfeited sea
Hath caused to belch up you, and on this island
Where man doth not inhabit, you 'mongst men
Being most unfit to live. I have made you mad,
And even with suchlike valour[1] men hang and drown
Their proper selves.°   *Themselves*
     [ALONSO, SEBASTIAN, *and* ANTONIO *draw*][2]
60   You fools! I and my fellows
Are ministers of fate. The elements
Of whom your swords are tempered[3] may as well
Wound the loud winds, or with bemocked-at stabs
Kill the still-closing[4] waters, as diminish
65 One dowl° that's in my plume.° My fellow ministers   *featherlet / plumage*
Are like° invulnerable. If you could hurt,   *similarly*

6. Reserve your praise until the end of the event.
7. A traveler could profit from a voyage by laying down a sum with a broker before departing and undertaking to bring back evidence of having reached his destination; if successful, he was repaid fivefold.
8. A mythological monster with a vulture's wings and claws and a woman's face. Aeneas and his companions encountered these harpies, who stole their meals and threatened to punish them with slow starvation. *Thunder and lightning:* Both spectacular and functional for disguising the mechanics of the "quaint device."
9. The simplest effective staging is by means of a rotating tabletop with the vessels of the banquet fixed to its surface. Leg-to-leg planks supporting the tabletop or a hang-

ing cloth would conceal the vanished banquet. The harpy's wings would hide the mechanics from the audience, and clapping them would provide a visual distraction.
1. *suchlike valour:* fearlessness that comes from madness.
2. Ariel perhaps ascends beyond their reach here. Aeneas's companions, like Alonso here, similarly attempted to kill the harpies with swords.
3. Compounded and hardened. Metal was sometimes thought of as being compounded of earth and fire, here contrasted with winds and waters.
4. Self-healing, since they close immediately once parted.

Your swords are now too massy° for your strengths   *heavy*
And will not be uplifted.
    [ALONSO, SEBASTIAN, *and* ANTONIO *stand amazed*°] *crazed; bewildered*
         But remember,
   For that's my business to you, that you three
70 From Milan did supplant good Prospero;
   Exposed unto the sea, which hath requit it,
   Him and his innocent child; for which foul deed,
   The powers, delaying not forgetting,[5] have
   Incensed the seas and shores, yea, all the creatures,[6]
75 Against your peace. Thee of thy son, Alonso,
   They have bereft, and do pronounce by me
   Ling'ring perdition[7]—worse than any death
   Can be at once—shall step by step attend
   You and your ways; whose[8] wraths to guard you from—
80 Which here in this most desolate[9] isle else falls
   Upon your heads—is nothing° but heart's sorrow   *there is no alternative*
   And a clear life° ensuing.   *a life innocent of sin*
     He [*ascends and*] *vanishes*[1] *in thunder. Then, to soft*
     music, enter the [*spirits*] *again, and dance with mocks*
     and mows,° *and* [*they depart,*] *carrying out the table* *grimaces*
  PROSPERO Bravely the figure of this harpy hast thou
   Performed, my Ariel; a grace it had devouring.[2]
85 Of my instruction hast thou nothing bated°   *omitted*
   In what thou hadst to say. So with good life[3]
   And observation strange[4] my meaner ministers°   *lesser spirits*
   Their several kinds° have done.° My high charms work, *various roles / performed*
   And these mine enemies are all knit up
90 In their distractions. They now are in my power;
   And in these fits I leave them, while I visit
   Young Ferdinand, whom they suppose is drowned,
   And his and mine loved darling.   [*Exit*]
    [GONZALO, ADRIAN, *and* FRANCISCO *go towards the*
    others]
  GONZALO I'th' name of something holy, sir, why stand you
   In this strange stare?
95 ALONSO   O, it is monstrous, monstrous!
   Methought the billows spoke and told me of it,
   The winds did sing it to me, and the thunder,
   That deep and dreadful organ-pipe, pronounced
   The name of Prosper. It did bass my trespass.[5]
100 Therefor° my son i'th' ooze is bedded, and   *For that*
   I'll seek him deeper than e'er plummet sounded,
   And with him there lie mudded.   *Exit*
  SEBASTIAN   But one fiend at a time,
   I'll fight their legions o'er.°   *from beginning to end*

---

5. Related to the proverb "God stays long but strikes at last."
6. Compare Genesis 1:21: "Then God created . . . everything living and moving."
7. Slow starvation; hell on earth of spiritual suffering. The phrase is first the object of "pronounce" and then the subject of "shall . . . attend."
8. Refers to "the powers" in line 73.
9. Joyless, wretched; barren, deserted.

1. Ariel is raised out of sight into the canopy.
2. In clapping his wings, Ariel has created the illusion of having devoured the banquet.
3. Convincingly; with vitality. *So:* In the same way.
4. Remarkable attention to the requirements of their parts, or instructions.
5. The thunder proclaimed my sin ("trespass") in a bass voice, or with a bass background; perhaps wordplay on the "utter baseness" of trespass.

ANTONIO   I'll be thy second.

Exeunt [SEBASTIAN *and* ANTONIO]

GONZALO   All three of them are desperate.° Their great guilt,   *in despair; reckless*

105   Like poison given to work° a great time after,   *take effect*
    Now 'gins to bite the spirits. I do beseech you
    That are of suppler joints, follow them swiftly,
    And hinder them from what this ecstasy°   *madness*
    May now provoke them to.

ADRIAN   Follow, I pray you.   *Exeunt*

4.1

Enter PROSPERO, FERDINAND, *and* MIRANDA

PROSPERO [*to* FERDINAND]   If I have too austerely punished you,
    Your compensation makes amends, for I
    Have given you here a third¹ of mine own life—
    Or that for which I live—who° once again   *whom*
5   I tender° to thy hand. All thy vexations   *offer*
    Were but my trials of thy love, and thou
    Hast strangely° stood the test. Here, afore heaven,   *wonderfully*
    I ratify this my rich gift. O Ferdinand,
    Do not smile at me that I boast of her,
10   For thou shalt find she will outstrip all praise,
    And make it halt° behind her.   *limp*

FERDINAND   I do believe it
    Against an oracle.²

PROSPERO   Then, as my gift and thine own acquisition
    Worthily purchased,° take my daughter. But   *Gained by effort*
15   If thou dost break her virgin-knot° before   *virginity*
    All sanctimonious° ceremonies may   *holy*
    With full and holy rite be ministered,
    No sweet aspersion° shall the heavens let fall   *shower of grace*
    To make this contract grow; but barren hate,
20   Sour-eyed disdain, and discord, shall bestrew
    The union of your bed with weeds³ so loathly
    That you shall hate it both. Therefore take heed,
    As Hymen's⁴ lamps shall light you.

FERDINAND   As I hope
    For quiet days, fair issue,° and long life   *children*
25   With such love as 'tis now, the murkiest den,°   *cave*
    The most opportune place, the strong'st suggestion°   *temptation*
    Our worser genius can,⁵ shall never melt
    Mine honour into lust to take away
    The edge° of that day's celebration;   *unblunted desire*
30   When I shall think or° Phoebus' steeds are foundered⁶   *either*
    Or night kept chained below.

PROSPERO   Fairly spoke.

4.1
1. Miranda. The usual poetic conceit was a half; commentators variously conjecture the other third to be his dukedom, his books, or his late wife.
2. *I . . . oracle:* I would believe it even if an oracle said otherwise.
3. Weeds in place of the flowers traditionally strewn on the marriage bed; wordplay on both "marriage bed" and

"seed-bed."
4. Classical god of marriage.
5. Is capable of. *worser genius:* evil spirit corresponding to a guardian angel.
6. Collapsed and made lame. *Phoebus' steeds:* the mythological horses that drew the chariot of the sun. Ferdinand anticipates that on his wedding day he will in his impatience think that the night will never come.

Sit, then, and talk with her. She is thine own.

[FERDINAND *and* MIRANDA *sit and talk together*]

What,° Ariel, my industrious servant Ariel!   *Now, then*

Enter ARIEL

ARIEL   What would my potent master? Here I am.

35   PROSPERO   Thou and thy meaner° fellows your last service   *lesser*
    Did worthily perform, and I must use you
    In such another trick. Go bring the rabble,[7]
    O'er whom I give thee power, here to this place.
    Incite them to quick motion, for I must
40   Bestow upon the eyes of this young couple
    Some vanity[8] of mine art. It is my promise,
    And they expect it from me.

ARIEL   Presently?°   *At once*

PROSPERO   Ay, with a twink.[9]

ARIEL   Before you can say 'Come' and 'Go',
45   And breathe twice, and cry 'So, so',
             Each one tripping on his toe
             Will be here with mop and mow.[1]
             Do you love me, master? No?

PROSPERO   Dearly, my delicate Ariel. Do not approach
    Till thou dost hear me call.

50   ARIEL   Well; I conceive.°   *Exit*   *understand*

PROSPERO [*to* FERDINAND]   Look thou be true.[2] Do not give dalliance
    Too much the rein.[3] The strongest oaths are straw
    To th' fire i'th' blood. Be more abstemious,
    Or else, good night your vow.

FERDINAND   I warrant you, sir,
55   The white cold virgin snow upon my heart
    Abates the ardour of my liver.[4]

PROSPERO   Well.—
    Now come, my Ariel! Bring a corollary°   *surplus*
    Rather than want° a spirit. Appear, and pertly.°   *lack / briskly*
        Soft music

[*To* FERDINAND *and* MIRANDA] No tongue, all eyes! Be silent.

Enter IRIS[5]

60   IRIS   Ceres, most bounteous lady, thy rich leas[6]
    Of wheat, rye, barley, vetches,[7] oats, and peas;
    Thy turfy mountains where live nibbling sheep,
    And flat meads° thatched with stover,[8] them to keep;   *meadows*
    Thy banks with peonied and twillèd[9] brims
65   Which spongy° April at thy hest betrims[1]   *wet*
    To make cold nymphs chaste crowns; and thy broom-groves,[2]
    Whose shadow the dismissèd bachelor° loves,   *rejected suitor*

---

7. Troupe of lesser spirits: *trick:* theatrical device, or clever artifice.
8. Trifle; conceit; illusion; display.
9. In the twinkling of an eye.
1. With derisive and grimacing gestures.
2. Take care that you remain faithful to your promise. Prospero may have caught the lovers just indulging in dalliance.
3. To "give the rein" is to make a horse gallop.
4. *The . . . liver:* Virgin snow lies on his heart because he has remained chaste, never having given in to his ardent liver. The liver was held to be the seat of passion.

5. Goddess of the rainbow and messenger of Juno; her apparel is in the colors of the rainbow, and she wears "saffron wings" (line 78).
6. Arable land. Ceres was the Roman goddess of agriculture and generative nature.
7. Pealike plants grown for fodder.
8. Hay for winter fodder.
9. Reinforced with entwined branches to prevent riverbank erosion. *peonied:* covered with peonies.
1. Adorns with flowers; recalls the colloquial "April showers bring forth May flowers."
2. Thickets of gorse, yellow-flowered shrubs. *cold:* chaste.

Being lass-lorn; thy pole-clipped vineyard,[3]
And thy sea-marge,° sterile and rocky-hard,   *seashore*
70 Where thou thyself dost air:° the Queen o'th' Sky,°   *take fresh air / Juno*
Whose wat'ry arch° and messenger am I,   *rainbow*
Bids thee leave these, and with her sovereign grace
      JUNO [*appears in the air*][4]
Here on this grass-plot,[5] in this very place,
To come and sport.—Her peacocks fly amain.[6]
75 Approach, rich Ceres, her to entertain.
      Enter [ARIEL *as*] CERES[7]

CERES   Hail, many-coloured messenger, that ne'er
Dost disobey the wife of Jupiter;°   *Juno*
Who with thy saffron wings upon my flowers
Diffusest honey-drops, refreshing showers,
80 And with each end of thy blue bow dost crown
My bosky[8] acres and my unshrubbed down,
Rich scarf[9] to my proud earth. Why hath thy queen
Summoned me hither to this short-grassed green?

IRIS   A contract of true love to celebrate,
85 And some donation freely to estate°   *bestow*
On the blest lovers.

CERES   Tell me, heavenly bow,°   *rainbow*
If Venus or her son,[1] as° thou dost know,   *as far as*
Do now attend the Queen. Since they did plot
The means that dusky Dis[2] my daughter got,
90 Her and her blind boy's scandalled° company   *scandalous; notorious*
I have forsworn.

IRIS   Of her society
Be not afraid. I met her deity
Cutting the clouds towards Paphos,[3] and her son
Dove-drawn[4] with her. Here thought they to have done
95 Some wanton charm upon[5] this man and maid,
Whose vows are that no bed-right[6] shall be paid
Till Hymen's torch be lighted[7]—but in vain.
Mars's hot minion° is returned again.   *lover; Venus*
Her waspish-headed[8] son has broke his arrows,
100 Swears he will shoot no more, but play with sparrows,[9]
And be a boy right out.°   *an ordinary boy*
      [*Music.* JUNO *descends to the stage*][1]

CERES   Highest queen of state,
Great Juno, comes; I know her by her gait.°   *majestic bearing*

---

3. Vineyard with vines embracing, twined around, their supporting poles; pruned vineyard. "Vineyard" was pronounced as three syllables. *lass-lorn:* abandoned by the girl he wooed.
4. Juno was queen of the heavens and goddess of women, held to protect marriages and preside over childbirth. Her chair is ornamented with a peacock motif. She descends by a "flight" mechanism to a position suspended in the air above the stage. Music may be played. Juno remains in view aloft until line 101. If, however, F's direction here is misplaced, she may not appear until line 101.
5. Compare "this short-grassed green" (line 83) and "this green land" (line 130): a green carpet on the acting area is indicated.
6. In haste. Peacocks, sacred to Juno, drew her chariot.
7. Her part is probably played by Ariel (see line 167).
8. Covered with bushes and thickets.
9. Ornamental and hung across the body rather than

around the neck.
1. Cupid, proverbially blind.
2. King of the underworld in classical mythology. Venus and her son Cupid made him fall in love with Ceres' daughter Proserpine, whom he abducted (Ovid, *Metamorphoses* 5.395ff.).
3. City in Cyprus: associated with Venus.
4. Doves were sacred to Venus and drew her chariot.
5. *done . . . upon:* cast a lustful spell upon.
6. Right to consummate the marriage; also suggesting a rite, as in line 17.
7. Until the wedding ceremony is performed.
8. Peevish, irritable, and with arrows like the wasp's sting.
9. Sparrows were associated with Venus because they were proverbially lustful.
1. This completes Juno's flight to the stage; again, music may be played.

JUNO   How does my bounteous sister? Go with me
    To bless this twain, that they may prosperous be,
105   And honoured in their issue.
          [CERES *joins* JUNO, *and*] *they sing*²

JUNO   Honour, riches, marriage-blessing,
          Long continuance and increasing,
          Hourly joys be still° upon you!   *always*
          Juno sings her blessings on you.
110 CERES   Earth's increase, and foison° plenty,   *abundance*
          Barns and garners° never empty,   *granaries*
          Vines with clust'ring bunches growing,
          Plants with goodly burden bowing;
          Spring come to you at the farthest,
115   In the very end of harvest.³
          Scarcity and want shall shun you,
          Ceres' blessing so is on you.
FERDINAND This is a most majestic vision, and
    Harmonious charmingly.⁴ May I be bold°   *Would I be right*
    To think these spirits?
120 PROSPERO   Spirits, which by mine art
    I have from their confines⁵ called to enact
    My present fancies.
FERDINAND   Let me live here ever!
    So rare a wondered° father and a wise   *endowed with wonders*
    Makes this place paradise.
          JUNO *and* CERES *whisper, and send* IRIS *on employment*
PROSPERO   Sweet° now, silence.   *Softly*
125   Juno and Ceres whisper seriously.
    There's something else to do. Hush, and be mute,
    Or else our spell is marred.
IRIS   You nymphs called naiads of the wind'ring⁶ brooks,
    With your sedged crowns° and ever-harmless looks,   *garlands of reeds*
130   Leave your crisp channels, and on this green land
    Answer your summons; Juno does command.
    Come, temperate nymphs, and help to celebrate
    A contract of true love. Be not too late.
          Enter certain nymphs
    You sunburned sicklemen,° of August weary,   *harvesters*
135   Come hither from the furrow and be merry;
    Make holiday, your rye-straw hats put on,
    And these fresh nymphs encounter every one
    In country footing.
          *Enter certain reapers, properly habited.*⁷ *They join with*
          the nymphs in a graceful dance; towards the end whereof
          PROSPERO *starts suddenly, and speaks*
PROSPERO [*aside*]   I had forgot that foul conspiracy
140   Of the beast Caliban and his confederates
    Against my life. The minute of their plot

---

2. Ceres and Juno might be raised together in the flight apparatus and sing suspended above the stage. They would then vanish (line 142 stage direction) by being raised into the heavens.
3. Let spring return immediately after harvest, without any intervening winter. (In Greek mythology, winter was originally caused by Ceres abandoning the earth in search of Proserpine.)
4. Delightfully; magically; harmoniously.
5. Regions of dwelling. Word is accented on the second syllable.
6. Perhaps a conflation of "wandering" and "winding." The naiads were mythical river nymphs.
7. Either properly or finely dressed.

Is almost come. [*To the spirits*] Well done! Avoid;° no more!   *Begone*
    To a strange, hollow, and confused noise, the [*spirits in*
    the pageant] *heavily vanish.*[8]
    [FERDINAND *and* MIRANDA *rise*]

FERDINAND [*to* MIRANDA]   This is strange. Your father's in some passion
    That works° him strongly.   *agitates*

MIRANDA   Never till this day
145   Saw I him touched with anger so distempered.°   *troubled; distracted*

PROSPERO   You do look, my son, in a moved sort,°   *disturbed manner*
    As if you were dismayed. Be cheerful, sir.
    Our revels[9] now are ended. These our actors,
    As I foretold you,° were all spirits, and   *told you before*
150   Are melted into air, into thin air;[1]
    And like the baseless fabric[1] of this vision,
    The cloud-capped towers, the gorgeous palaces,
    The solemn temples, the great globe[2] itself,
    Yea, all which it inherit,[3] shall dissolve;
155   And, like this insubstantial pageant faded,
    Leave not a rack° behind. We are such stuff   *wisp of cloud*
    As dreams are made on,° and our little life   *of*
    Is rounded[4] with a sleep. Sir, I am vexed.
    Bear with my weakness. My old brain is troubled.
160   Be not disturbed with my infirmity.
    If you be pleased, retire into my cell,
    And there repose. A turn or two I'll walk
    To still my beating mind.

FERDINAND *and* MIRANDA   We wish your peace.
                        Exeunt [FERDINAND *and* MIRANDA]

PROSPERO   Come with a thought![5] I thank thee, Ariel. Come!
            Enter ARIEL

ARIEL   Thy thoughts I cleave to. What's thy pleasure?

165 PROSPERO   Spirit,
    We must prepare to meet with Caliban.

ARIEL   Ay, my commander. When I presented[6] Ceres
    I thought to have told thee of it, but I feared
    Lest I might anger thee.

170 PROSPERO   Say again: where didst thou leave these varlets?°   *ruffians*

ARIEL   I told you, sir, they were red-hot with drinking;
    So full of valour that they smote the air
    For breathing in their faces, beat the ground
    For kissing of their feet; yet always bending°   *aiming*
175   Towards their project. Then I beat my tabor,°   *side drum*
    At which like unbacked° colts they pricked their ears,   *never-ridden*
    Advanced° their eyelids, lifted up their noses   *Opened*
    As° they smelt music. So I charmed their ears   *As if*
    That calf-like they my lowing° followed, through   *mooing*
180   Toothed briars, sharp furzes, pricking gorse,° and thorns,   *prickly shrubs*
    Which entered their frail shins. At last I left them
    I'th' filthy-mantled[7] pool beyond your cell,

---

8. Sorrowfully depart (probably not implying a trick of staging).
9. Entertainment, in both festive and theatrical senses.
1. An edifice or substance without foundations; insubstantial, alluding to buildings in masque scenery.
2. World; also with a passing allusion to the Globe Theatre.

3. All who come into possession of it.
4. Rounded off; surrounded; or, possibly, crowned.
5. Come as fast as thought, a colloquial simile.
6. Acted; produced the masque of; introduced while playing Iris.
7. Covered with filthy scum.

There dancing up to th' chins, that° the foul lake   *so that*
O'er-stunk[8] their feet.
PROSPERO   This was well done, my bird.°   *chick; dear*
185   Thy shape invisible retain thou still.
The trumpery° in my house, go bring it hither   *cheap goods*
For stale° to catch these thieves.   *decoy; bait*
ARIEL   I go, I go.   *Exit*
PROSPERO   A devil, a born devil, on whose nature
Nurture can never stick; on whom my pains,
190   Humanely taken, all, all lost, quite lost,
And, as with age his body uglier grows,
So his mind cankers.° I will plague them all,   *festers*
Even to roaring.
                 Enter ARIEL, *laden with glistening apparel, etc.*
                    Come, hang them on this lime.[9]
             [ARIEL *hangs up the apparel. Exeunt* PROSPERO *and*
                                                            ARIEL]
            Enter CALIBAN, STEFANO, *and* TRINCULO, *all wet*
CALIBAN   Pray you, tread softly, that the blind mole may
195   Not hear a foot fall. We now are near his cell.
STEFANO   Monster, your fairy, which you say is a harmless fairy,
has done little better than played the Jack° with us.   *knave; will-o'-the-wisp*
TRINCULO   Monster, I do smell° all horse-piss, at which my   *smell of*
nose is in great indignation.
200   STEFANO   So is mine. Do you hear, monster? If I should take a
displeasure against you, look you—
TRINCULO   Thou wert but a lost monster.
CALIBAN   Good my lord, give me thy favour still.
Be patient, for the prize I'll bring thee to
205   Shall hoodwink[1] this mischance. Therefore speak softly.
All's hushed as midnight yet.
TRINCULO   Ay, but to lose our bottles in the pool!
STEFANO   There is not only disgrace and dishonour in that,
monster, but an infinite loss.
210   TRINCULO   That's more to me than my wetting. Yet this is your
harmless fairy, monster.
STEFANO   I will fetch off[2] my bottle, though I be o'er ears° for   *drowned*
my labour.
CALIBAN   Prithee, my king, be quiet. Seest thou here;
215   This is the mouth o'th' cell. No noise, and enter.
Do that good mischief which may make this island
Thine own for ever, and I thy Caliban
For aye° thy foot-licker.   *ever*
STEFANO   Give me thy hand.
I do begin to have bloody thoughts.
220   TRINCULO [*seeing the apparel*]   O King Stefano, O peer! O wor-
thy Stefano, look what a wardrobe here is for thee![3]
CALIBAN   Let it alone, thou fool, it is but trash.
TRINCULO [*putting on a gown*]   O ho, monster, we know what
belongs to a frippery!° O King Stefano!   *old-clothes shop*

---

8. Made smelly; smelled worse than.
9. Lime tree, indicating a stage property.
1. Blind with a hood, as was done to pacify a hawk—
hence, make harmless; also, put out of sight.

2. Recover; rescue; drink off.
3. Recalling "King Stephen was and a worthy peer, / His
breeches cost him but a crown," a popular ballad about
King Stephen, sung in part in *Othello* 2.3.77ff.

225 STEFANO Put off that gown, Trinculo. By this hand, I'll have that
gown.

TRINCULO Thy grace shall have it.

CALIBAN The dropsy⁴ drown this fool! What do you mean
To dote thus on such luggage?° Let't alone,   *encumbrances*

230 And do the murder first. If he awake,
From toe to crown he'll fill our skins with pinches,
Make us° strange stuff.   *Turn us into*

STEFANO Be you quiet, monster.—Mistress lime, is not this my
jerkin?° Now is the jerkin under the line.⁵ Now, jerkin, you are   *leather jacket*

235 like to lose your hair and prove a bald jerkin.⁶

[STEFANO *and* TRINCULO *take garments*]

TRINCULO Do, do! We steal by line and level,⁷ an't like° your   *if it please*
grace.

STEFANO I thank thee for that jest. Here's a garment for't. Wit
shall not go unrewarded while I am king of this country. 'Steal

240 by line and level' is an excellent pass of pate.⁸ There's another
garment for't.

TRINCULO Monster, come, put some lime upon your fingers,⁹
and away with the rest.

CALIBAN I will have none on't. We shall lose our time,

245 And all be turned to barnacles,¹ or to apes
With foreheads villainous° low.   *wretchedly*

STEFANO Monster, lay to° your fingers. Help to bear this away   *apply*
where my hogshead of wine is, or I'll turn you out of my king-
dom. Go to, carry this.

250 TRINCULO And this.

STEFANO Ay, and this.

[*They load* CALIBAN *with apparel.*]

A noise of hunters heard. Enter divers° spirits in shape of   *various*
dogs and hounds, hunting them about; PROSPERO *and*
ARIEL *setting them on*

PROSPERO Hey, Mountain, hey!

ARIEL   Silver! There it goes, Silver!

PROSPERO Fury, Fury! There, Tyrant, there! Hark, hark!

[*Exeunt* STEFANO, TRINCULO, *and* CALIBAN, *pursued by spirits*]

[*To* ARIEL] Go, charge my goblins that they grind their joints

255 With dry convulsions,² shorten up their sinews
With agèd cramps, and more pinch-spotted³ make them
Than pard or cat o'mountain.⁴

[*Cries within*]

ARIEL   Hark, they roar!

PROSPERO Let them be hunted soundly.° At this hour   *thoroughly*
Lies at my mercy all mine enemies.

---

4. A disease characterized by the accumulation of fluid
in connective tissue.
5. Below the lime tree; south of the equator; below the
waist. Also a possible allusion to the proverb "Thou hast
stricken the ball under the line," meaning "You have
cheated." Stefano has taken the jerkin from the lime tree.
6. Baldness caused either through tropical disease or by
sailors who customarily shaved the heads of passengers
when they crossed the line of the equator for the first
time. "Under the [waist]line" (line 234) could also be an
allusion to baldness from syphilis.
7. An idiomatic expression for "properly, by the rules"—
literally, "by plumb line and carpenter's level"; also pun-

ning on "lime." *Do, do*: an expression of approval.
8. Thrust of wit (fencing term).
9. Be "lime-fingered," sticky-fingered (alluding to bird-
lime, a gluey substance used to catch birds).
1. Barnacle geese, also known as "tree geese" and sup-
posed to begin life as barnacle shells.
2. Afflicting "sapless," or old, people.
3. Spotted with bruises from pinches. *agèd cramps*: the
convulsions of old age.
4. Both terms are synonymous with "leopard"; the second
is from Jeremiah 13:23: "May a man of Ind change his
skin, and the cat of the mountain her spots?" (Bishops'
Bible).

260   Shortly shall all my labours end, and thou
      Shalt have the air at freedom. For a little,
      Follow, and do me service.   *Exeunt*

                              5.1
      Enter PROSPERO, *in his magic robes, and* ARIEL
      PROSPERO   Now does my project gather to a head.[1]
      My charms crack not, my spirits obey, and time
      Goes upright with his carriage.[2] How's the day?
      ARIEL   On the sixth hour; at which time, my lord,
      You said our work should cease.
5   PROSPERO   I did say so
      When first I raised the tempest. Say, my spirit,
      How fares the King and's° followers?   *and his*
      ARIEL   Confined together
      In the same fashion as you gave in charge,
      Just as you left them; all prisoners, sir,
10   In the lime-grove which weather-fends[3] your cell.
      They cannot budge till your release.° The King,   *you release them*
      His brother, and yours, abide all three distracted,°   *out of their wits*
      And the remainder mourning over them,
      Brimful of sorrow and dismay; but chiefly
15   Him that you termed, sir, the good old lord Gonzalo:
      His tears run down his beard like winter's drops
      From eaves of reeds.° Your charm so strongly works 'em   *thatched roofs*
      That if you now beheld them your affections°   *feelings*
      Would become tender.
      PROSPERO   Dost thou think so, spirit?
      ARIEL   Mine would, sir, were I human.
20   PROSPERO   And mine shall.
      Hast thou, which art but air, a touch,° a feeling   *sense*
      Of their afflictions, and shall not myself,
      One of their kind, that relish all as sharply
      Passion as they,[4] be kindlier[5] moved than thou art?
25   Though with their high° wrongs I am struck to th' quick,   *great*
      Yet with my nobler reason 'gainst my fury
      Do I take part.° The rarer action is   *side*
      In virtue than in vengeance. They being penitent,
      The sole drift of my purpose doth extend
30   Not a frown further. Go release them, Ariel.
      My charms I'll break, their senses I'll restore,
      And they shall be themselves.
      ARIEL   I'll fetch them, sir.   *Exit*
      [PROSPERO *draws a circle with his staff*][6]
      PROSPERO[7]   Ye elves of hills, brooks, standing lakes and groves,
      And ye that on the sands with printless foot
35   Do chase the ebbing Neptune, and do fly him
      When he comes back; you demi-puppets[8] that

5.1
1. Draw to its fulfillment. "Project" suggests an alchemi-
cal projection or "experiment."
2. Because his carriage, or burden, is now light.
3. Which protects from the weather.
4. *that . . . they:* who feel as much strong emotion as they
do.
5. More tenderly; more naturally.
6. The original text does not indicate when the circle is

drawn. Other possibilities are at the beginning of the
scene or before the entry at line 57.
7. Prospero's speech closely follows Ovid's *Metamorpho-
ses* 7.265–77, in Arthur Golding's translation (1567); the
speaker in Ovid is the sorceress Medea, who uses her
witchcraft to vengeful ends.
8. Puppets; elves; quasi puppets.

By moonshine do the green sour ringlets[9] make
Whereof the ewe not bites; and you whose pastime
Is to make midnight° mushrooms, that rejoice   *springing up overnight*
40   To hear the solemn curfew;[1] by whose aid,
Weak masters[2] though ye be, I have bedimmed
The noontide sun, called forth the mutinous winds,
And 'twixt the green sea and the azured vault°   *the sky*
Set roaring war—to the dread rattling thunder
45   Have I given fire, and rifted° Jove's stout oak   *split*
With his own bolt;° the strong-based promontory   *lightning bolt*
Have I made shake, and by the spurs° plucked up   *roots*
The pine and cedar; graves at my command
Have waked their sleepers, oped, and let 'em forth
50   By my so potent art. But this rough[3] magic
I here abjure. And when I have required°   *summoned*
Some heavenly music—which even now I do—
To work mine end upon their senses that°   *the senses of whom*
This airy[4] charm is for, I'll break my staff,
55   Bury it certain° fathoms in the earth,   *several*
And deeper than did ever plummet sound
I'll drown my book.

> *Solemn music. Here enters [first]* ARIEL *[invisible]; then*
> ALONSO, *with a frantic gesture, attended by* GONZALO;
> SEBASTIAN *and* ANTONIO, *in like manner, attended by*
> ADRIAN *and* FRANCISCO. *They all enter the circle which*
> PROSPERO *had made, and there stand charmed; which*
> PROSPERO *observing, speaks*

[*To* ALONSO][5] A solemn air,° and° the best comforter   *song / which is*
To an unsettled fancy,° cure thy brains,   *imagination*
Now useless, boiled within thy skull.
60   [*To* SEBASTIAN *and* ANTONIO][6]   There stand,
For you are spell-stopped.—
Holy Gonzalo, honourable man,
Mine eyes, ev'n sociable° to the show° of thine,   *sympathetic / appearance*
Fall fellowly drops. [*Aside*] The charm dissolves apace,
65   And as the morning steals upon the night,
Melting the darkness, so their rising senses
Begin to chase the ignorant fumes[7] that mantle°   *envelop*
Their clearer° reason.—O good Gonzalo,   *growing clearer*
My true preserver, and a loyal sir°   *gentleman*
70   To him thou follow'st, I will pay° thy graces   *requite*
Home° both in word and deed.—Most cruelly   *Fully*
Didst thou, Alonso, use me and my daughter.
Thy brother was a furtherer° in the act.—   *an accomplice*
Thou art pinched° for't now, Sebastian.   *tortured; afflicted*
[*To* ANTONIO]   Flesh and blood,
75   You, brother mine, that entertained ambition,
Expelled remorse and nature,[8] whom,° with Sebastian—   *who*

---

9. Fairy rings: distinctive circles of grass supposed to be caused by dancing fairies but actually caused by mushrooms.
1. The bell rung at nightfall, indicating the time when spirits are abroad.
2. Ineffectual when acting independently; without supernatural power; subordinate spirits.
3. Violent; discordant; crudely approximate.

4. Wrought by spirits of the air.
5. Prospero remains invisible and inaudible to Alonso and his party until he greets Alonso at line 108.
6. Or perhaps to all the shipwrecked lords.
7. Fogs of ignorance; the image is of the sun ("rising senses") dissipating morning mist.
8. Pity and brotherly affection.

Whose inward pinches therefore are most strong,—
Would here have killed your king, I do forgive thee,
Unnatural though thou art. [*Aside*] Their understanding
80 Begins to swell,° and the approaching tide   (*as does a tide*)
Will shortly fill the reasonable shores
That now lie foul and muddy. Not° one of them   *There is not*
That yet looks on me, or would know me.—Ariel,
Fetch me the hat and rapier⁹ in my cell.
85 I will discase° me, and myself present   *undress*
As I was sometime Milan.¹ Quickly, spirit!
Thou shalt ere long be free.
                    ARIEL *sings and helps to attire him* [*as Duke of Milan*]
ARIEL   Where the bee sucks, there suck I:
          In a cowslip's bell I lie;
90   There I couch when owls do cry.
          On the bat's back I do fly
          After summer merrily.
          Merrily, merrily shall I live now
          Under the blossom that hangs on the bough.
95   Merrily, merrily shall I live now
          Under the blossom that hangs on the bough.
PROSPERO   Why, that's my dainty Ariel! I shall miss thee,
But yet thou shalt have freedom.—So, so, so.²—
To the King's ship, invisible as thou art!
100 There shalt thou find the mariners asleep
Under the hatches. The Master and the Boatswain
Being awake, enforce them to this place,
And presently,° I prithee.   *immediately*
ARIEL   I drink the air before me, and return
105 Or ere° your pulse twice beat.   *Exit*   *Before*
GONZALO   All torment, trouble, wonder, and amazement°   *bewilderment*
Inhabits here. Some heavenly power guide us
Out of this fearful° country!   *fearsome*
PROSPERO   Behold, sir King,
The wrongèd Duke of Milan, Prospero.
110 For more assurance that a living prince
Does now speak to thee, I embrace thy body;
And to thee and thy company I bid
A hearty welcome.
                    [*He embraces* ALONSO]
ALONSO   Whe'er° thou beest he or no,   *Whether*
Or some enchanted trifle³ to abuse° me,   *delude; maltreat*
115 As late I have been, I not know. Thy pulse
Beats as of flesh and blood; and since I saw thee
Th'affliction of my mind amends, with which
I fear a madness held me. This must crave°—   *requires, as explanation*
An if this be at all⁴—a most strange story.
120 Thy dukedom⁵ I resign, and do entreat

---

9. Elements of normal aristocratic dress.   tion."
1. Formerly, when Duke of Milan.   4. If this is really happening.
2. Prospero arranges his attire approvingly.   5. Alonso's rights of homage and tribute from it.
3. With a suggestion of the old sense of "trifle" as "decep-

Thou pardon me my wrongs. But how should Prospero
Be living and be here?

PROSPERO [*to* GONZALO]   First, noble friend,
Let me embrace thine age,° whose honour cannot   *old body*
Be measured or confined.
          [*He embraces* GONZALO]

GONZALO   Whether this be
Or be not, I'll not swear.

125   PROSPERO   You do yet taste
Some subtleties⁶ o'th' isle that will not let you
Believe things certain.—Welcome, my friends all.
[*Aside to* SEBASTIAN *and* ANTONIO]
But you, my brace° of lords, were I so minded,   *pair*
I here could pluck his highness' frown upon you

130   And justify° you traitors. At this time   *prove*
I will tell no tales.

SEBASTIAN [*to* ANTONIO] The devil speaks in him.

PROSPERO   No.
[*To* ANTONIO]   For you, most wicked sir, whom° to call brother   *who*
Would even infect my mouth, I do forgive
Thy rankest fault, all of them, and require

135   My dukedom of thee, which perforce° I know   *necessarily*
Thou must restore.

ALONSO   If thou beest Prospero,
Give us particulars of thy preservation,
How thou hast met us here, whom three hours since
Were wrecked upon this shore, where I have lost—

140   How sharp the point of this remembrance is!—
My dear son Ferdinand.

PROSPERO   I am woe° for't, sir.   *I grieve*

ALONSO   Irreparable is the loss, and patience
Says it is past her cure.

PROSPERO   I rather think
You have not sought her help, of° whose soft grace°   *by / mercy*

145   For the like loss I have her sovereign aid,
And rest myself content.

ALONSO   You the like loss?

PROSPERO   As great to me as late;° and supportable   *recent*
To make the dear loss⁷ have I means much weaker
Than you may call to comfort you, for I
Have lost my daughter.⁸

150   ALONSO   A daughter?
O heavens, that they were living both in Naples,
The king and queen there! That they were, I wish
Myself were mudded in that oozy bed
Where my son lies. When did you lose your daughter?

155   PROSPERO   In this last tempest. I perceive these lords
At this encounter do so much admire°   *wonder*
That they devour their reason,⁹ and scarce think
Their eyes do offices of truth,° these words   *function accurately*

6. *You . . . subtleties:* You still experience some of the illu-
sions. "Subtleties" were also sweet confections shaped
like castles, temples, beasts, allegorical figures, etc., and
arranged like a pageant.
7. *supportable . . . loss:* in order to make the heartfelt loss

bearable.
8. Prospero apparently means that Alonso still has a
child, his daughter Claribel, to comfort him.
9. "Reason" has the additional sense of "discourse";
hence the phrase is an extension of "swallow their words."

Are natural breath. But howsoe'er you have
160 Been jostled from your senses, know for certain
That I am Prospero, and that very Duke
Which was thrust forth of Milan, who most strangely,
Upon this shore where you were wrecked, was landed
To be the lord on't. No more yet of this,
165 For 'tis a chronicle of day by day,
Not a relation for a breakfast, nor
Befitting this first meeting. Welcome, sir.
This cell's my court. Here have I few attendants,
And subjects none abroad.¹ Pray you, look in.
170 My dukedom since you have given me again,
I will requite you with as good a thing;
At least bring forth a wonder to content ye
As much as me my dukedom.

           Here PROSPERO *discovers*² FERDINAND *and* MIRANDA,
           playing at chess

MIRANDA   Sweet lord, you play me false.°   *trick me*
175 FERDINAND   No, my dearest love,
    I would not for the world.
MIRANDA   Yes, for a score of kingdoms you should wrangle,
    An I would call it fair play.³
ALONSO   If this prove
    A vision of the island, one dear son
    Shall I twice lose.
180 SEBASTIAN   A most high miracle.
FERDINAND [*coming forward*]   Though the seas threaten, they are merciful.
    I have cursed them without cause.
        [*He kneels*]
ALONSO   Now all the blessings
    Of a glad father compass thee about.°   *surround you*
    Arise and say how thou cam'st here.
        [FERDINAND *rises*]
MIRANDA [*coming forward*]   O wonder!
185 How many goodly creatures are there here!
How beauteous mankind is! O brave new world
That has such people in't!
PROSPERO   'Tis new to thee.
ALONSO [*to* FERDINAND]   What is this maid with whom thou
    wast at play?
    Your eld'st° acquaintance cannot be three hours.   *longest*
190 Is she the goddess that hath severed us,
    And brought us thus together?
FERDINAND   Sir, she is mortal;
    But by immortal providence she's mine.
    I chose her when I could not ask my father
    For his advice, nor thought I had one. She
195 Is daughter to this famous Duke of Milan,
    Of whom so often I have heard renown,
    But never saw before; of whom I have

---

1. Elsewhere about the island; beyond the cell.
2. Reveals by drawing back a curtain hanging in front of the discovery space.
3. *for . . . play:* if I would not accuse you of cheating, you would quarrel for twenty kingdoms. Other editions read "And" for "An" (i.e., you could quarrel for twenty kingdoms, and I would still call it fair play.)

Received a second life; and second father
This lady makes him to me.
ALONSO   I am hers.[4]
200 But O, how oddly will it sound, that I
Must ask my child° forgiveness!   (Miranda)
PROSPERO   There, sir, stop.
Let us not burden our remembrance with
A heaviness° that's gone.   sorrow
GONZALO   I have inly wept,
Or should have spoke ere this. Look down, you gods,
205 And on this couple drop a blessèd crown,
For it is you that have chalked forth° the way   marked out
Which brought us hither.
ALONSO   I say amen, Gonzalo.
GONZALO Was Milan° thrust from Milan, that his issue   the Duke of Milan
Should become kings of Naples? O rejoice
210 Beyond a common joy! And set it down
With gold on lasting pillars:[5] in one voyage
Did Claribel her husband find at Tunis,
And Ferdinand her brother found a wife
Where he himself was lost; Prospero his dukedom
215 In a poor isle; and all of us ourselves,
When no man was his own.[6]
ALONSO [to FERDINAND and MIRANDA] Give me your hands.
Let grief and sorrow still° embrace his heart   always
That° doth not wish you joy.   Who
GONZALO   Be it so! Amen!
          Enter ARIEL, with the MASTER and BOATSWAIN amazedly
          following
O look, sir, look, sir, here is more of us!
220 I prophesied if a gallows were on land
This fellow could not drown. [To the BOATSWAIN] Now,
    blasphemy,°   blasphemer
That swear'st grace o'erboard: not an oath on shore?
Hast thou no mouth by land? What is the news?
BOATSWAIN The best news is that we have safely found
225 Our King and company. The next, our ship,
Which but three glasses° since we gave out° split,   hourglasses / declared
Is tight and yare[7] and bravely rigged, as when
We first put out to sea.
ARIEL [aside to PROSPERO] Sir, all this service
Have I done since I went.
PROSPERO [aside to ARIEL]   My tricksy° spirit!   capricious; neat
230 ALONSO These are not natural events; they strengthen°   increase
From strange to stranger. Say, how came you hither?
BOATSWAIN   If I did think, sir, I were well awake
I'd strive to tell you. We were dead of° sleep,   with
And—how we know not—all clapped° under hatches,   shut up
235 Where but even now, with strange and several° noises   various
Of roaring, shrieking, howling, jingling chains,
And more diversity of sounds, all horrible,

---

4. I will be her second father, Alonso's assent to the
betrothal.
5. Suggesting, perhaps, the triumphal arches commis-

sioned to celebrate notable occasions.
6. When we all had lost our senses.
7. Is sound and ready to sail.

We were awaked; straightway at liberty;
Where we in all her trim freshly beheld
240 Our royal, good, and gallant ship, our Master
Cap'ring to eye° her. On° a trice, so please you,   *Dancing to see / In*
Even in a dream, were we divided from them,
And were brought moping° hither.   *dazed*

ARIEL [*aside to* PROSPERO]   Was't well done?

PROSPERO [*aside to* ARIEL]   Bravely, my diligence. Thou shalt be free.

245 ALONSO   This is as strange a maze as e'er men trod,
And there is in this business more than nature
Was ever conduct° of. Some oracle   *conductor*
Must rectify our knowledge.

PROSPERO   Sir, my liege,
Do not infest° your mind with beating on[8]   *trouble*
250 The strangeness of this business. At picked leisure,
Which shall be shortly, single° I'll resolve you,   *in private*
Which to you shall seem probable,° of every   *plausible*
These happened accidents;° till when be cheerful,   *occurrences*
And think of each thing well. [*Aside to* ARIEL] Come hither, spirit.
255 Set Caliban and his companions free.
Untie the spell.   [*Exit* ARIEL]
[*To* ALONSO]   How fares my gracious sir?
There are yet missing of your company
Some few odd lads that you remember not.

     Enter ARIEL, *driving in* CALIBAN, STEFANO, *and* TRIN-
     CULO, *in their stolen apparel*

STEFANO   Every man shift for all the rest, and let no man take
260 care for himself,[9] for all is but fortune. Coragio, bully-monster,[1]
coragio!

TRINCULO   If these° be true spies which I wear in my head, here's   *these eyes*
a goodly sight.

CALIBAN   O Setebos, these be brave spirits indeed!
265 How fine° my master is! I am afraid   *splendidly dressed*
He will chastise me.

SEBASTIAN   Ha, ha! What things are these, my lord Antonio?
Will money buy 'em?

ANTONIO   Very like;° one of them   *likely*
Is a plain° fish, and no doubt marketable.   *mere*
270 PROSPERO   Mark but the badges[2] of these men, my lords,
Then say if they° be true. This misshapen knave,   *(the men); (the badges)*
His mother was a witch, and one so strong
That could control the moon, make flows and ebbs,
And deal in her command without her power.[3]
275 These three have robbed me, and this demi-devil,[4]
For he's a bastard one, had plotted with them
To take my life. Two of these fellows you
Must know and own.[5] This thing of darkness I
Acknowledge mine.

CALIBAN   I shall be pinched to death.
280 ALONSO   Is not this Stefano, my drunken butler?

---

8. With repeatedly worrying about.
9. Stefano drunkenly confuses the saying "Every man for himself."
1. Gallant monster. *Coragio:* Take courage (Italian).
2. Livery. Servants often wore their master's emblem,

but Prospero probably refers to the stolen apparel.
3. And wield her (the moon's) power without her authority, or beyond the reach of her might.
4. Being the offspring of Sycorax and the devil.
5. And acknowledge to be yours.

SEBASTIAN   He is drunk now. Where had he wine?

ALONSO   And Trinculo is reeling ripe.° Where should they   *drunk*
Find this grand liquor that hath gilded⁶ 'em?
[*To* TRINCULO] How cam'st thou in this pickle?⁷

285   TRINCULO   I have been in such a pickle since I saw you last that,
I fear me, will never out of my bones. I shall not fear flyblowing.⁸

SEBASTIAN   Why, how now, Stefano?

STEFANO   O, touch me not! I am not Stefano, but a cramp.

290   PROSPERO   You'd be king o'the isle, sirrah?

STEFANO   I should have been a sore° one, then.   *an inept; severe; pained*

ALONSO [*pointing to* CALIBAN]   This is a strange thing as e'er I
looked on.

PROSPERO   He is as disproportioned in his manners⁹

295   As in his shape. [*To* CALIBAN] Go, sirrah, to my cell.
Take with you your companions. As you look
To have my pardon, trim° it handsomely.   *tidy; decorate*

CALIBAN   Ay, that I will; and I'll be wise hereafter,
And seek for grace. What a thrice-double ass

300   Was I to take this drunkard for a god,
And worship this dull fool!

PROSPERO   Go to, away!   [*Exit* CALIBAN]¹

ALONSO [*to* STEFANO *and* TRINCULO]
Hence, and bestow your luggage where you found it.

SEBASTIAN   Or stole it, rather.   [*Exeunt* STEFANO *and* TRINCULO]

PROSPERO [*to* ALONSO]   Sir, I invite your highness and your train

305   To my poor cell, where you shall take your rest
For this one night; which part of it° I'll waste°   *part of which / spend*
With such discourse as I not doubt shall make it
Go quick away: the story of my life,
And the particular accidents° gone by   *events*

310   Since I came to this isle. And in the morn
I'll bring you to your ship, and so to Naples,
Where I have hope to see the nuptial
Of these our dear-belovèd solemnized;
And thence retire me to my Milan, where
Every third thought shall be my grave.

315   ALONSO   I long
To hear the story of your life, which must
Take° the ear strangely.   *Captivate*

PROSPERO   I'll deliver° all,   *relate*
And promise you calm seas, auspicious gales,
And sail so expeditious that shall° catch   *it will*

320   Your royal fleet far off. [*Aside to* ARIEL] My Ariel, chick,
That is thy charge. Then to the elements
Be free, and fare thou well.   [*Exit* ARIEL]
Please you, draw near.°   *go in*
Exeunt [*all but* PROSPERO]²

Epilogue

PROSPERO   Now my charms are all o'erthrown,
And what strength I have's mine own,
Which is most faint. Now 'tis true
I must be here confined by you
5   Or sent to Naples. Let me not,
Since I have my dukedom got,
And pardoned the deceiver, dwell
In this bare island° by your spell;   (the stage)
But release me from my bands°   fetters
10   With the help of your good hands.°   (applause)
Gentle breath° of yours my sails   Favorable comment
Must fill, or else my project fails,
Which was to please. Now I want°   lack
Spirits to enforce, art to enchant;
15   And my ending¹ is despair
Unless I be relieved by prayer,
Which pierces so, that it assaults
Mercy itself, and frees all faults.
As you from crimes would pardoned be,
20   Let your indulgence² set me free.
                        [*He awaits applause, then*] *exit*

Epilogue
1. Punning on the sense "death."   2. Approval; appeasement; remission for sin.

The Sonnets

Shakespeare's plays often seem indifferent to high-cultural rules of construction. His sonnets (composed from about 1591 to 1604, possibly revised thereafter, and published in 1609) are the opposite: they faithfully adhere to the norms of an international tradition inspired by the fourteenth-century Italian poet Petrarch. Paradoxically, the very strictness of sonnet structure is the condition of possibility for Shakespeare's originality. The rigor of the form encourages a logical, rationalist approach to the standard topic of the Renaissance sonnet—love and its attendant emotions (desire, jealousy, and the like). The conflict between passionate feelings and a mobile intellect often skeptical of those feelings accordingly becomes a central theme of the poems. And that mobility is conveyed through a linguistic virtuosity marked by metaphors and puns that can work either with or against the larger structure of the sonnet.

Thematically, the sonnets are equally distinctive. The typical object of love—the unapproachable, exalted lady—is displaced so as to make room for a daring representation of homoerotic and adulterous passions. Almost the entire sequence can be divided along these lines. Sonnets 1–126 recount the speaker's idealized, sometimes painful love for a femininely beautiful, well-born male youth; 127–52 his unidealized, ultimately bitter affair with a darkly attractive, unaristocratic "mistress"—where this term invokes, however ironically, the vocabulary of courtly love rather than the derogatory modern meaning. The two love relationships are complicated by a lovers' triangle (40–42, 133–34, 144) and a poetic rival for the youth's affections (78–80, 82–86). These topics provide the occasion for a complex meditation upon a range of issues— time, nature, human mortality, economics, perhaps class and race, and, not least, an artistic immortality. And this self-referential reflection upon the sonnets' very composition is heightened by the reader's intense proximity to a speaker who is and is not Shakespeare.

The poems are best approached by locating their formal specificity against the background of two artistic practices through which Shakespeare came to the poems: his work in the theater, and the prior tradition of the sonnet. The standard verse line of Shakespearean drama and Shakespearean sonnet alike is iambic pentameter. But there the similarity ends. Roughly two-thirds of all lines in the plays are composed in unrhymed iambic pentameter, or blank verse; less than 10 percent employ rhyme. By contrast, Shakespeare's sonnets almost always consist of fourteen rhyming iambic-pentameter lines. Blank verse easily accommodates enjambment, the runover of sense from one line to the next. Rhyme encourages congruence between syntax and verse line: a unit of meaning ends when the line does. Blank verse supports the narrative logic of Shakespearean drama, rhyme the lyric impulse of the Shakespearean sonnet. You watch a play to see what happens next; you read a sonnet to discover the original expression of feelings and thoughts. Language is thus more obtrusively part of meaning in poetry than in drama.

It is easy to find exceptions to these claims. The crucial consideration, however, is the significance for Shakespeare of inherited conventions. The sonnet originated in Italy a century before Petrarch. Petrarch's decisive poetic sequence chronicles the author's passionately complex emotions in relation to his beloved Laura. The Petrarchan sonnet is divided into two frequently contrasting units, an octave (eight lines) and a sestet (six lines), by its rhyme scheme—*abbaabba cdecde*, where each letter represents a line and a repeated letter indicates a rhyme. The Petrarchan mode reached England by the early sixteenth century in the works of Wyatt and Surrey, whose modified rhyme scheme (*abab cdcd efef gg*), later taken over by Shakespeare, divides the sonnet into three quatrains (four-line groupings) and a couplet. This organization offers greater conceptual range than does the Petrarchan model. The quatrains can operate in parallel, represent steps in a logical argument, or contradict each other. They may be grouped into larger units of eight-and-four lines or eight-and-six lines (if the couplet is included) that are set against each other, with the result in the latter case that the Petrarchan octave-sestet structure is approximated. In turn, the epigrammatic concluding couplet, whose analytical tendencies contrast with the more experiential approach of at least the first two quatrains, can summarize the preceding lines, generalize from them, draw appropriate inferences, contribute a new thought, or even reverse the preceding argument.

Sonnet structure often guides Shakespeare's pervasive use of imagery and metaphor. In Sonnet 73, each quatrain pursues a different metaphor as part of a single argument:

> That time of year thou mayst in me behold
> When yellow leaves, or none, or few, do hang
> Upon those boughs which shake against the cold,
> Bare ruined choirs where late the sweet birds sang.
> In me thou seest the twilight of such day
> As after sunset fadeth in the west,
> Which by and by black night doth take away,
> Death's second self, that seals up all in rest.
> In me thou seest the glowing of such fire
> That on the ashes of his youth doth lie
> As the death-bed whereon it must expire,
> Consumed with that which it was nourished by.
>> This thou perceiv'st, which makes thy love more strong,
>> To love that well which thou must leave ere long.

The evocation of fall in the opening quatrain nostalgically communicates the sadness of aging. Enjambment supports the imagistic pattern: it causes meaning to "hang" in the balance at the end of the line, just as "yellow leaves . . . do hang / Upon those boughs." The "yellow leaves" are also leaves of a book, "bare ruined choirs," or quires (manuscript gatherings). Similarly, the birds' former song, together with the primary meaning of "choirs" (the part of a church where the choir sings), may refer to the speaker's own voice and hence to a lost poetic creativity. In short, the experience of aging is compared to the annual movement toward colder seasons and to the decline of artistic inspiration. In the second quatrain, the unit of time constricts: "That time of year" is replaced by "the twilight of such day." Although, like autumn, sunset is a natural process, it is not an organic one. Emphasis accordingly shifts away from bodily degeneration. These lines also look forward in a way the first quatrain does not. Twilight is taken away by "black night . . . , / Death's second self, that seals up all in rest." The rest that night brings is a source of comfort, but night is compared with death, and the syntax, at odds with the literal meaning, suggests that it is death rather than night "that seals up all in [eternal] rest."

The third quatrain opens like the second, with "In me thou seest," a phrase also partly anticipated in the first line of the poem. This repetition reinforces the parallelism among the quatrains and suggests that the poem proceeds less by narrative progression than by thematic variation. Yet this quatrain, while highlighting the transition from aging to mortality, narrows time further, to the "glowing" fire, in effect abandoning the temporal model of the first two quatrains for a spatial metaphor. Only the ashes remain from the fire's and, by implication, the speaker's "youth" (line 10); they are also the fire's and the speaker's "death-bed" (line 11). The earlier idealization of youth, now reduced to "ashes," has disappeared; conversely, although the fire of old age no longer rages, it is still "glowing"—it still gives off heat. The present is thus a continuation of the past. Furthermore, the metaphorical relationship is reversed. The dying fire is a metaphor for human aging, but that aging becomes a metaphor for the dying fire.

Paradoxically, the fire is "Consumed with that which it was nourished by"; it is "consumed" (or choked) by—and along with—the very ashes that, as fuel, previously "nourished" it. Normally, the fire consumes the fuel, not the other way around. Both "consumed" and "nourished" metaphorically explain the already metaphorical fire, which they connect back to humanity through their allusions to eating. The speaker's fiery passion for the youth he addresses nourished him when he was young but consumes him now. Indeed, the line structurally enacts the tacit thematic rejection of a temporal model of decline. It is an example of chiasmus, in which the elements of the first half ("Consumed . . . that") are repeated in reverse order in the second half ("which . . . nourished"), thus producing an *abba* semantic pattern. Accordingly, this quatrain has no equivalent to the earlier "cold" or "night," which are metaphorically responsible for the approach of death. Life and death have the same source.

All three quatrains employ cyclical metaphors of life, death, and rebirth. But the cycle remains incomplete. Autumn does not lead to spring or night to day. The "long-lived phoenix" (19.4), the legendary self-resurrecting bird that dies in flames and is reborn from the ashes, doesn't quite appear. Perhaps these suppressed allusions to cyclical patterns raise and then frustrate expectations, denying the consolation of the future. The concluding couplet, which moves away from metaphor and toward a new idea, suggests this interpretation. Recognizing the speaker's literally consuming passion makes the youth's "love more strong" (line 13). The youth, therefore, loves well what he "must leave ere long" (line 14)—explicitly, the speaker; implicitly, his own life, partly because that leaving recalls the "yellow leaves" with which the poem opened. There is no answer to the destructive power of time, but that power is partly counteracted by love.

Sonnet 73 suggests how conformity to sonnet convention can enable a thoughtful interplay among time, love, death, and art. Sonnet 81, on the other hand, offers a radical disjunction of syntax and rhyme scheme: almost any two consecutive lines can produce a complete sentence, depending on how you punctuate:

> And toungs to be, your beeing shall rehearse,
> When all the breathers of this world are dead,
> You still shall liue (such vertue hath my Pen).
> (81.11–13)

This three-line sequence, presented as it appears in the first edition of 1609, runs over the end of a quatrain but nonetheless produces two possible sentences that are grammatically correct and semantically effective (lines 11 and 12 or 12 and 13). Conceptually, the unorthodox move here is the implicit equation of the speaker with his social superior, the youth. The poet's literary prowess promises enduring renown for both the writer and his subject. Or does it? If you take lines 11 and 12 together, as modern editions do, the emphasis falls on "dead." But if you instead take lines 12 and 13 as a unit, the center of interest becomes "liue" and "my Pen." The poem thus promises both death and immortality, just as the wordplay on "rehearse" (line 11) predicts a future in which the youth is both still spoken about and literally re-hearsed.

The relationship between formal and thematic innovation can also be approached by considering the sonnets as a sequence. English enthusiasm for such sequences was triggered by the posthumous printing of Sir Philip Sidney's collection *Astrophel and Stella* (1591). Sonnets also circulated in manuscript form, since print culture was often considered beneath the dignity of (would-be) gentlemen or courtier-poets. The vogue for sonnet sequences responded to poets' ambitions as well as to the gender politics of the late Elizabethan court. Middle-class writers, for instance, sought financial assistance for their work by praising their aristocratic patrons. Expressions of love in this hierarchical relationship may be less indications of deep feeling than competitive strategies of advancement. Shakespeare's rival poet sonnets seem to convert this competition into literary theme. In general, then, it is often hard to determine where authentic senti-ment ends and professional calculation begins.

Shakespeare's sonnets first appeared in print in the Quarto of 1609. It seems unlikely, however, that Shakespeare authorized its publication. If this conclusion is cor-rect, questions arise about the internal organization of the sonnets as well (although not about their authorship). It has been suggested that the division of the sequence into two main groups is unwarranted. Most of the poems are not explicitly about either the youth or the mistress and do not even designate the sex of the person discussed. Only their relative position in the collection has produced the standard simplification adopted here. Furthermore, the sequence as a whole is relatively uninterested in plot. The poems to the mistress in particular show little sign of organization or process, com-bining occasional affection with chaos, bitterness, self-abasement, shame, unwilling sexual desire, and self-loathing. Perhaps, in 1609, they had not yet been placed in a par-ticular order; perhaps they were intended for a separate collection. But the first 126 sonnets, too, evince only intermittent interest in linear movement, emphasizing long-ing, jealousy, and a fear of separation, while anticipating both the desire and the anguish of the subsequent poems.

Nonetheless, many of the sonnets are carefully ordered in pairs or longer groups. More important, the two main sections of the sequence are of compelling thematic interest. For the two centuries ending about a generation ago, the homoerotic attach-ment to the youth, now a routine part of critical discussion, provoked revulsion or denial. Sonnet 20 was—and still is—at the center of the debate:

> A woman's face with nature's own hand painted
> Hast thou, the master-mistress of my passion;
> A woman's gentle heart, but not acquainted
> With shifting change as is false women's fashion;
> An eye more bright than theirs, less false in rolling,
> Gilding the object whereupon it gazeth;
> A man in hue, all hues in his controlling,
> Which steals men's eyes and women's souls amazeth.
> And for a woman wert thou first created,
> Till nature as she wrought thee fell a-doting,
> And by addition me of thee defeated
> By adding one thing to my purpose nothing. [one thing = a penis]
>> But since she pricked thee out for women's pleasure,
>> Mine be thy love and thy love's use their treasure.

Nature originally intended the youth to be a woman (the octave). But she fell in love with her creation and hence turned him into a male, a change that benefited her but forced the speaker to limit his relationship to the youth to love without sexual con-summation (the sestet). Thus, the poem wittily plays with gender boundaries—"mas-ter-mistress," "A woman's face," "one thing," "A man in hue" (with a further sexual reference if "hue" was pronounced like "you"; lines 2, 1, 12, 7). "Acquainted" and "controlling" pun on "cunt"; "nothing" and "treasure" refer to the female sexual organ as well (lines 3, 7, 12, 14). As someone "pricked . . . out for women's pleasure" (line 13), the youth is equipped to give women pleasure but also to be "pricked" and hence experience women's pleasure. Even the form gets into the act: this is the only sonnet where all the rhymes have "feminine" endings—the term since the Renaissance for a two-syllable rhyme with the second syllable unstressed. Finally, the misogyny of the poem's complaint about "false" women (lines 4, 5) is consistent with its homoeroti-cism. Women are to be resented because the speaker prefers males, or at least the youth, and also because they get to enjoy "love's use," while he must content himself merely with "love" (line 14)—where the contrast suggests that "love" carries both its

Renaissance meaning of "friendship" and its modern sense of romantic and sexual desire.

Sonnet 20 looks forward to poems that express passionate, erotic love for the youth, apparently without sexual fulfillment. But they also look back to the opening seventeen sonnets, in which the speaker urges the youth to marry and produce an heir. Hence, the speaker solicits the youth's love for someone else, since the point is procreation and, therefore, an immortality comparable to the artistic immortality promised later in the sequence. The exhortation cuts against both the conventional aspiration of the love sonnet and the speaker's unconventional aim of winning the youth. But this is because the multiple possible meanings of "love" in Sonnet 20 characterize the poems to the youth more generally.

"Thy beauty's form in table of my heart" (24.2). Here a man is holding a "table" (tablet) in front of his heart while another man engraves the first man's portrait on it. From Geffrey Whitney, *A Choice of Emblemes* (1586).

How the case for marriage is argued is instructive. Shakespeare's reversal of the metaphorical relationship in sonnet 73, it will be recalled, removes any fixed point of reference. A comparable reversal also marks economic imagery of the first seventeen sonnets. As in Sonnet 20 (line 14), that imagery frequently turns on usury. Long subject to denunciation, usury in Renaissance England was just beginning its conversion into the respectable financial category of interest. Shakespeare shared the prevailing repugnance at the idea of making money out of money. Thus, the speaker condemns his mistress for her affair with the young man, represented as collecting a debt:

> The statute of thy beauty thou wilt take,
> Thou usurer that putt'st forth all to use.
> (134.9–10)

She will "take" the full amount owed to her financially (sexually) because, like a "usurer," she employs "all" her wealth (her body) for profit ("use" means both "engage in usury" and "engage in sexual activity"). Elsewhere, more ambivalently, the youth is criticized for being, paradoxically, both "unthrifty" and a "niggard" (4.1, 5):

> Profitless usurer, why dost thou use
> So great a sum of sums yet canst not live?
> (4.7–8)

Here, "use" antithetically means both "use up" and "lend at interest." Literally, how can the youth lend vast "sums" for profit and be unable to support himself? Metaphorically, he acts in a "profitless" manner in wasting his endowments. Hence, he cannot "live" on in his children. By implication, a usurer is always without value.

But the lines also imagine the opposite. If there is a profitless usurer, there might be a profitable one. This good usurer predominates in the sonnets:

> That use is not forbidden usury
> Which happies those that pay the willing loan.
> (6.5–6)

Is "forbidden" an attribute of all, or just unallowable, usury? Keeping one's "treasure" to oneself merits only "thriftless praise"; "beauty's use" deserves "much more praise" if a child results (2.6–9). At least "an unthrift" allows the world to enjoy his wealth;

"beauty's waste" is indefensible—"kept unused, the user so destroys it" (9.9–12). And sonnet 20 ends, as we've seen, with the speaker declaring, as if to console himself: "Mine be thy love and thy love's use their treasure" (line 14). The speaker gets the youth's love, whereas the "treasure" women get is merely the "use" (metaphorically, children) of that love. He obtains the principal, they the interest. These passages activate metaphorical meanings of "use" to promote marriage and family. But in so doing, they connect the proper use of beauty with usury, which comes to be understood as the economic equivalent of human reproduction, the early sonnet's highest ideal. The neo-feudal celebration of tradition as lineage smuggles in a defense of economic behavior destructive of tradition. Usury is transformed into a potentially noble activity. Through metaphor, then, Shakespeare entertains ideas that might have been less accessible as bald statements.

The poems to the speaker's mistress are also scandalously unconventional—in their focus on a sordid, adulterous affair with an unfaithful woman that is marked by passionate desire and equally passionate recrimination. Even the relatively serene sonnets in this section self-consciously undermine convention:

> My mistress' eyes are nothing like the sun;
> . . . .
> And yet, by heaven, I think my love as rare
> As any she belied with false compare.
> (130.1, 13–14)

Here the target is the standard Petrarchan mode of praise. More generally, the aim is to dismantle falsely idealizing rhetoric:

> When my love swears that she is made of truth
> I do believe her though I know she lies,
> . . . .
> Therefore I lie with her, and she with me,
> And in our faults by lies we flattered be.
> (138.1–2, 13–14)

In Sonnet 130, true love requires the speaker to reject "false compare." In Sonnet 138, love paradoxically requires the speaker to "credit . . . false-speaking," to suppress "simple truth" (lines 7–8), and to embrace "lies." The sequence ends, however, with the bitter deployment of the same rhetoric against speaker and woman alike:

> For I have sworn thee fair—more perjured eye
> To swear against the truth so foul a lie.
> (152.13–14)

This concluding couplet recalls the opening of the sequence on the mistress:

> In the old age black was not counted fair,
> . . . .
> But now is black beauty's successive heir.
> (127.1, 3)

Black is the color of the woman's eyes, eyebrows, breasts, hair (127.9–10, 132.3, 130.3–4), and skin:

> Then I will swear beauty herself is black,
> And all they foul that thy complexion lack.
> (132.13–14)

As in other poetry of the time, this paradoxical, anticonventional praise of blackness echoes the biblical Song of Songs as well as sixteenth-century Continental and English poetry, including Sidney's. The praise is often inseparable from a misogynistic denunciation of the use of cosmetics to produce artificial beauty (127.4–12). Black hair and eyes gained prestige in the 1590s through a shift in fashion from blond hair to dark. Thus the speaker's personal views accord with broader social change.

The mistress's color may or may not be racialized, however, since even dark skin might merely distinguish her from falsely idealized women or aristocratic ladies able to avoid the sun. Nonetheless, *Titus Andronicus, Othello, Antony and Cleopatra*, and *The Tempest* feature actual or threatened interracial coupling. The mistress's combination of blackness and promiscuity may provoke both desire and fear of powerfully exotic female sexuality. The valence of blackness accordingly moves from the paradoxical to the conventional: "In nothing art thou black save in thy deeds" (131.13); "For I have sworn thee fair, and thought thee bright, / Who art as black as hell, and dark as night" (147.13–14). Like usury, then, blackness oscillates between conventional norms and radical innovation. Such is the case with the sonnets more generally.

Finally, the intense emotion here and elsewhere, the psychological complexity with which it is scrutinized, the unconventional subject matter, the sense that one is over-hearing snatches of conversation, the first-person speaker, that speaker's self-conscious identification with Shakespeare (135–136)—all encourage a biographical interpretation of the sonnets. For two centuries, such interpretation has proven risky either to under-take or to avoid. There has been a major but unsuccessful scholarly effort to discover the real people whom Shakespeare discusses but does not name. The youth has most often been identified with Henry Wriothesley, Earl of Southampton, or William Herbert, Earl of Pembroke. The sonnets' dedication is to "Mr. W. H.," Pembroke's initials and the reverse of Southampton's. But neither is likely to have been addressed as "Mr." Proposals about the identity of the mistress are much shakier. Christopher Marlowe and George Chap-man are among those suggested as the rival poet—on the basis of no real evidence. This inconclusiveness led mid-twentieth-century critics to focus on formal concerns. But the resulting advances often entailed evading the disconcerting biographical material that the poems do seem to provide. Shakespeare's sonnets, like his plays, combine verbal artistry and conceptual unorthodoxy with psychological exploration. Their special fascination, however, is that the soul they examine is apparently Shakespeare's own.

WALTER COHEN

TEXTUAL NOTE

The sonnets were printed for the first time in "SHAKESPEARES SONNETS," a Quarto that appeared in 1609 and also included "A Lover's Complaint," a poem attributed to Shake-speare but probably by John Davies. The type for the volume was set by two composi-tors, who probably worked from a scribal transcript of an authorial manuscript. It is likely that the arrangement of the sonnets is primarily, or perhaps entirely, Shake-spearean. But since the compositors punctuated in different ways, the Quarto's punc-tuation cannot be regarded as authorial. Indeed, it is unlikely that Shakespeare had anything to do with the printing of the Quarto; it is also unlikely that this was an author-ized edition—although the second point is more controversial than the first.

The Quarto was reprinted in *Poems: Written by W. Shakespeare, Gent.* (1640), in which the sonnets (with eight omitted) and "A Lover's Complaint" were joined by addi-tional poetry of Shakespeare and other writers, individual sonnets were run together to produce longer works, the sonnets were titled, their order was rearranged, and a few pronouns were changed or (in the titles) invented. This collection has no independent textual value. *The Passionate Pilgrim* (first edition, 1599 or earlier; second edition, 1599–1600), an unauthorized volume attributed to Shakespeare by its publisher, is a different matter. The second edition includes twenty poems—three from *Love's Labour's Lost* (the 1598 Quarto of which presumably had already appeared in print), four others more reliably attributed to other writers, eleven pieces by unknown authors, and versions of sonnets 138 and 144 that seem to be both erroneous and unrevised.

Another dozen sonnets survive in various manuscripts, all from 1620 or later. Although many derive from the Quarto, a few may preserve—amid mistakes in transcription—authentically Shakespearean phrasing from versions earlier than those in the 1609 edition. It is possible that one or more of these transcripts derive directly from an authorial manuscript and in that sense are closer to what Shakespeare wrote than is the Quarto. The Alternative Versions include manuscript renditions of sonnets 2 (the most popular, judging by the number of extant copies) and 106, as well as sonnets 138 and 144 as they appeared in *The Passionate Pilgrim*. Sonnets 8 and 128, for which additional versions are not included here, could also possibly derive from authorial manuscripts. From the four included in the Alternative Versions, one may perhaps learn something of Shakespeare's process of revision.

The poems were probably composed over more than a decade. *The Passionate Pilgrim* and, more inferentially, some of the manuscripts show that Shakespeare wrote a number of the sonnets in the 1590s at the latest. So, too, does Francis Meres's reference in 1598 to Shakespeare's "sugred Sonnets among his priuate friends." The circulation of manuscripts was a common form of "publication" at the time. It should be noted, however, that a "sonnet" could be any short lyric poem. The best candidate for early composition is probably 145, on the basis of its vocabulary, its use of tetrameters rather than pentameters, and the words "hate away" (line 13)—a possible pun on the name of the poet's wife, Anne Hathaway. Further chronological hints are provided by the boom in love-sonnet sequences during the 1590s as well as by Shakespeare's own plays from 1594 to 1596—*Love's Labour's Lost, A Midsummer Night's Dream, Romeo and Juliet*, and *Richard II*—plays that, despite belonging to a variety of genres, are all linked to the sonnets in vocabulary, lyrical feel, and (by the standards of Shakespearean drama) high incidence of rhyme.

Recent scholarship, however, has suggested a later composition or revision for a considerable number of the sonnets. Although no consensus currently exists, a plausible recent estimate is as follows:

1–60:	c. 1595–1596 (later revised?)
61–103:	c. 1594–1595
104–26:	c. 1598–1604
127–54:	c. 1591–1595

Even if this dating is only roughly accurate, it indicates that the sequence of the sonnets as published in 1609 sharply deviates from the chronology of composition. Beyond revealing that Shakespeare—and perhaps not Shakespeare alone—rearranged the sonnets according to other criteria, this conclusion also implies a disconnect between autobiographical impulse and chronological narrative (unless the sonnets that were composed later uniformly refer back to an earlier time). If the poems are in fact autobiographical, they cannot provide a linear account of events. This nonnarrative hypothesis is supported by internal evidence, specifically the references to the love triangle involving the speaker, the youth, and the mistress both early and late in the sequence (40–42, 133–34, 144). Alternatively, if the sequence does provide a linear narrative, it cannot be autobiographical. And, of course, the sequence may offer neither chronological narrative nor actual autobiography.

SELECTED BIBLIOGRAPHY

Bloom, Harold, ed. *Shakespeare's Sonnets*. New York: Chelsea House, 1987. Five leading critical essays from 1960 to 1985.

Booth, Stephen. *An Essay on Shakespeare's Sonnets*. New Haven: Yale University Press, 1969. Detailed evidence for multiple overlapping structures within individual sonnets, structures that expand possible meaning without cohering into a unified whole.

————, ed. *Shakespeare's Sonnets*. New Haven: Yale University Press, 1977. Same argument as above, but in the form of a detailed poem-by-poem commentary, together with both the 1609 Quarto of the sonnets and a modernized version.

Fineman, Joel. *Shakespeare's Perjured Eye: The Invention of Poetic Subjectivity in the Sonnets*. Berkeley: University of California Press, 1986. Psychoanalytical study that distinguishes the narcissistic, homosexual visual identification of sonnets 1–126 from the misogynistic heterosexual desire and conflict of 127–52, the latter being the founding moment of modern subjectivity.

Halpern, Richard. *Shakespeare's Perfume: Sodomy and Sublimity in the Sonnets, Wilde, Freud, and Lacan*. Philadelphia: University of Pennsylvania Press, 2002. 11–31. Links sodomy, aesthetics, sublimation, and the sublime.

Hernstein, Barbara, ed. *Discussions of Shakespeare's Sonnets*. Boston: Heath, 1964. Brief pre-twentieth-century accounts plus thirteen important essays from 1930 to 1960.

Schoenfeldt, Michael, ed. *A Companion to Shakespeare's Sonnets*. Malden, Mass.: Blackwell, 2007. The sonnets and "A Lover's Complaint" together with twenty-three essays from the current century plus contributions from Booth (1969) and Vendler (1997).

Vendler, Helen. *The Art of Shakespeare's Sonnets*. Cambridge, Mass.: Belknap Press, 1997. Detailed sonnet-by-sonnet interpretation, focusing on formal considerations, together with the 1609 Quarto and a modernized version of the text, as well as a CD-ROM of Vendler reading the poems.

Willen, Gerald, and Victor B. Reed, eds. *A Casebook on Shakespeare's Sonnets*. New York: Crowell, 1964. Annotated modern edition of the sonnets together with six major critical essays from the 1930s to the early 1950s and very brief explications of a few individual sonnets.

Sonnets

TO.THE.ONLY.BEGETTER.OF.
THESE.ENSUING.SONNETS.
M^R. W. H.[1] ALL.HAPPINESS.
AND.THAT.ETERNITY.
PROMISED.
BY.
OUR.EVER-LIVING.POET.[2]
WISHETH.
THE.WELL-WISHING.
ADVENTURER.IN.
SETTING.
FORTH.
T. T.[3]

1

From fairest creatures we desire increase,°   *offspring*
That thereby beauty's rose[1] might never die,
But as the riper should by time decease,
His tender[2] heir might bear his memory;
5   But thou, contracted° to thine own bright eyes,   *engaged; reduced*
Feed'st thy light's flame with self-substantial fuel,[3]
Making a famine where abundance lies,
Thyself thy foe, to thy sweet self too cruel.
Thou that art now the world's fresh ornament
10 And only herald to the gaudy° spring   *brilliant*
Within thine own bud buriest thy content,°   *substance; happiness*
And, tender churl,° mak'st waste in niggarding.   *young old miser*
    Pity the world, or else this glutton be:
    To eat the world's due, by the grave and thee.[4]

Dedication
1. The identity of W. H. has generated much speculation. As "the only begetter of these ensuing sonnets," "W. H." is probably a misprint for "W. S." or "W. SH." (William Shakespeare). Other candidates include the person who obtained the manuscript for the publisher and the youth who apparently inspired most of the poems. For biographical speculation about the sonnets, see the Introduction.
2. God, literally "ever-living," who promises eternity to Shakespeare (if, as suggested in the previous note, "W.H." refers to Shakespeare); or, less probably, Shakespeare, who promises "eternity" to the young man.
3. Thomas Thorpe, the printer, is the "well-wishing adventurer."
Sonnet 1
1. In Q, "rose," unlike most other nouns, is always capitalized (35.2; 54.3, 6, 11; 67.8; 95.2; 98.10; 99.8; 109.14; and 130.5, 6). Here, it is also italicized. These printing conventions, combined with the placement of the word near the beginning of the first sonnet and its frequent repetition thereafter, suggest that "rose" is the poet's name for the object of his desire, on the model of, for instance, Stella in Sir Philip Sidney's influential sonnet sequence *Astrophel and Stella* (published 1591). The rose had long been associated with female genitalia, most notably in the thirteenth-century French narrative poem *The Romance of the Rose*, by Guillaume de Lorris and Jean de Meun. In Shakespeare's case, however, the object of desire is male. He is most frequently referred to as "youth," almost never as "boy" or "man." Shakespeare's "mistress" in the later sonnets is contrasted with "roses" (130.5, 6).
2. The rose's (the youth's) young.
3. Are consuming yourself like a candle.
4. *this . . . thee:* be a glutton by causing what is due to the world (your posterity) to be consumed both by the grave and within yourself.

2[1]

When forty winters shall besiege thy brow
And dig deep trenches in thy beauty's field,
Thy youth's proud livery,° so gazed on now,   *uniform; appearance*
Will be a tattered weed,° of small worth held.   *clothing; plant*
5 Then being asked where all thy beauty lies,
Where all the treasure of thy lusty days,
To say within thine own deep-sunken eyes
Were an all-eating shame and thriftless praise.[2]
How much more praise deserved thy beauty's use[3]
10 If thou couldst answer 'This fair child of mine
Shall sum my count, and make my old excuse',[4]
Proving his beauty by succession thine.°   *inherited from you*
   This were° to be new made when thou art old,   *would be*
   And see thy blood warm when thou feel'st it cold.

3

Look in thy glass,° and tell the face thou viewest   *mirror*
Now is the time that face should form another,
Whose fresh repair° if now thou not renewest   *state*
Thou dost beguile° the world, unbless° some mother.   *swindle / leave childless*
5 For where is she so fair whose uneared° womb   *unplowed*
Disdains the tillage of thy husbandry?[1]
Or who is he so fond will be the tomb
Of his self-love to stop posterity?[2]
Thou art thy mother's glass, and she in thee
10 Calls back the lovely April of her prime;
So thou through windows of thine age[3] shalt see,
Despite of wrinkles, this thy golden time.
   But if thou live remembered not to be,[4]
   Die single, and thine image dies with thee.

4

Unthrifty loveliness, why dost thou spend
Upon thyself thy beauty's legacy?
Nature's bequest gives nothing, but doth lend,
And being frank, she lends to those are free.[1]
5 Then, beauteous niggard, why dost thou abuse
The bounteous largess given thee to give?
Profitless usurer, why dost thou use°   *lend for profit; spend*
So great a sum of sums yet canst not live?[2]
For having traffic° with thyself alone,   *(commercial); (sexual)*
10 Thou of thyself thy sweet self dost deceive.°   *defraud*
Then how when nature calls thee to be gone:
What acceptable audit canst thou leave?
   Thy unused[3] beauty must be tombed with thee,
   Which usèd, lives th'executor to be.

Sonnet 2
1. See *Spes Altera* in the Alternative Versions.
2. Would be a shameful admission of gluttony and boast of excessive expenditure.
3. How much more would the use (employment; investment or usurious lending) of your beauty merit.
4. Shall make my accounts balance and defend (absolve) me in my age.
Sonnet 3
1. Cultivation; acting as a husband.

2. *who . . . posterity:* who is so foolish that he will selfishly deny posterity a child?
3. Eyes weakened by old age; your children.
4. But if you live to be forgotten.
Sonnet 4
1. And being generous, she lends to those who (also) are generous.
2. Make a living; live on in your children.
3. Not put to use; not interest-bearing.

5

Those hours that with gentle work did frame°   *form*
The lovely gaze° where every eye doth dwell   *face*
Will play the tyrants to the very same,
And that unfair which fairly doth excel;[1]
5 For never-resting time leads summer on
To hideous winter, and confounds° him there,   *destroys*
Sap checked with frost, and lusty leaves quite gone,
Beauty o'er-snowed, and bareness everywhere.
Then were not summer's distillation left
10 A liquid prisoner pent in walls of glass,
Beauty's effect with beauty were bereft,[2]
Nor° it nor no remembrance what it was.   *Neither*
　　But flowers distilled, though they with winter meet,
　　Lose[3] but their show; their substance still lives sweet.

6[1]

Then let not winter's ragged° hand deface   *rough*
In thee thy summer ere thou be distilled.
Make sweet some vial,° treasure° thou some place   *womb / enrich*
With beauty's treasure ere it be self-killed.
5 That use° is not forbidden usury   *lending for profit*
Which happies those that pay the willing loan:[2]
That's for thyself° to breed another thee,   *So you would do*
Or ten times happier, be it ten for one;°   *1,000% interest*
Ten times thyself were happier than thou art,
10 If ten of thine ten times refigured° thee.   *copied*
Then what could death do if thou shouldst depart,
Leaving thee living in posterity?
　　Be not self-willed,[3] for thou art much too fair
　　To be death's conquest and make worms thine heir.

7

Lo, in the orient° when the gracious light°   *east / sun*
Lifts up his burning head, each under° eye   *earthly*
Doth homage to his new-appearing sight,
Serving with looks his sacred majesty,
5 And having climbed the steep-up heavenly hill,
Resembling strong youth in his middle age,°   *noon*
Yet mortal looks adore his beauty still,
Attending on his golden pilgrimage.
But when from highmost pitch, with weary car,°   *sun god's chariot*
10 Like feeble age he reeleth from the day,
The eyes, 'fore duteous, now converted° are   *turned*
From his low tract,° and look another way.   *path*
　　So thou, thyself outgoing in thy noon,
　　Unlooked on diest unless thou get° a son.°   *beget / (sun)*

Sonnet 5
1. Will make unattractive that which now excels in beauty.
2. *Then . . . bereft:* Then if there were no perfume distilled from flowers bottled in glass vials, both beauty and its effect would be lost.
3. Q has "Leese," understood in this edition as a cognate of "lose." This is Shakespeare's only use of "Leese," which

allows a pun on "lease." See 13.5.
Sonnet 6
1. This sonnet links with 5.
2. Which makes happy those who willingly lend, or who willingly repay the loan with interest (in the form of children).
3. Stubborn; leaving everything in a will to yourself alone.

8

Music to hear,[1] why hear'st thou music sadly?
Sweets° with sweets war not, joy delights in joy.   *Sweet things*
Why lov'st thou that which thou receiv'st not gladly,
Or else receiv'st with pleasure thine annoy?
5   If the true concord of well-tunèd sounds
By unions° married do offend thine ear,   *harmony*
They do but sweetly chide thee, who confounds°   *destroys*
In singleness the parts[2] that thou shouldst bear.
Mark how one string, sweet husband to another,
10   Strikes each in each° by mutual ordering,   *Resonates*
Resembling sire and child and happy mother,
Who all in one one pleasing note do sing;
   Whose speechless° song, being many, seeming one,   *The strings' wordless*
   Sings this to thee: 'Thou single wilt prove none.'[3]

9

Is it for fear to wet a widow's eye
That thou consum'st thyself in single life?
Ah, if thou issueless° shalt hap to die,   *childless*
The world will wail thee like a makeless° wife.   *widowed*
5   The world will be thy widow, and still° weep   *continually*
That thou no form of thee hast left behind,
When every private° widow well may keep   *individual*
By children's eyes her husband's shape in mind.
Look what° an unthrift in the world doth spend   *Whatever*
10   Shifts but his° place, for still the world enjoys it;   *its*
But beauty's waste hath in the world an end,
And kept unused, the user° so destroys it.   *spender; lender*
   No love toward others in that bosom sits
   That on himself such murd'rous shame commits.

10

For shame deny that thou bear'st love to any,
Who for thyself art so unprovident.
Grant, if thou wilt, thou art beloved of many,
But that thou none lov'st is most evident;
5   For thou art so possessed with murd'rous hate
That 'gainst thyself thou stick'st not to conspire,°   *don't balk at conspiring*
Seeking that beauteous roof to ruinate
Which to repair should be thy chief desire.
O, change thy thought, that I may change my mind!°   *judgment*
10   Shall hate be fairer lodged than gentle love?
Be as thy presence° is, gracious and kind,   *appearance*
Or to thyself at least kind-hearted prove.
   Make thee another self for love of me,
   That beauty still may live in thine or thee.

Sonnet 8
1. You whose voice is music.
2. Musical parts; roles as husband and father.

3. Without an heir, death will render you nothing (alluding to the proverb "One is no number").

11

As fast as thou shalt wane, so fast thou grow'st
In one of thine from that which thou departest,[1]
And that fresh blood which youngly thou bestow'st
Thou mayst call thine when thou from youth convertest.° *turn away*
5 Herein lives wisdom, beauty, and increase;
Without this, folly, age, and cold decay.
If all were minded so, the times should cease,
And threescore year would make the world away.
Let those whom nature hath not made for store,° *breeding*
10 Harsh,° featureless,° and rude,° barrenly perish. *ugly (all three words)*
Look whom she best endowed she gave the more,[2]
Which bounteous gift thou shouldst in bounty° cherish. *by using bountifully*
 She carved thee for her seal,[3] and meant thereby
 Thou shouldst print more, not let that copy die.

12

When I do count the clock° that tells the time, *hours as they strike*
And see the brave° day sunk in hideous night; *fine*
When I behold the violet past prime,
And sable° curls ensilvered o'er with white; *black*
5 When lofty trees I see barren of leaves,
Which erst° from heat did canopy the herd, *once*
And summer's green all girded up in sheaves
Borne on the bier with white and bristly beard:[1]
Then of thy beauty do I question make
10 That thou among the wastes of time must go,
Since sweets° and beauties do themselves forsake, *sweet things*
And die as fast as they see others grow;
 And nothing 'gainst time's scythe can make defence
 Save breed to brave him° when he takes thee hence. *children to defy time*

13

O that you were yourself![1] But, love, you are
No longer yours than you yourself here live.
Against° this coming end you should prepare, *For*
And your sweet semblance to some other give.
5 So should that beauty which you hold in lease
Find no determination;° then you were° *never end / would be*
Yourself again after your self's decease,
When your sweet issue your sweet form should bear.
Who lets so fair a house fall to decay,
10 Which husbandry[2] in honour might uphold
Against the stormy gusts of winter's day,
And barren rage of death's eternal cold?
 O, none but unthrifts,° dear my love, you know. *spendthrifts*
 You had a father; let your son say so.

Sonnet 11
1. In a child begotten in youth (with suggestions of sexual intercourse and of death).
2. To whomever nature gave most (made best-looking) she gave even more (extra reproductive abilities). The near circularity of "best endowed" and "more" alludes to Matthew 25:29, the paradoxical parable of the talents: "For unto every man that hath, it shall be given."

3. Literally, a stamp of authority.
Sonnet 12
1. *An . . . beard:* And sheaves of mature ("bearded") grain carried away on the harvest cart; old man borne on a funeral bier.
Sonnet 13
1. If only you could remain your (eternal) self.
2. Stewardship; being a husband.

14

Not from the stars do I my judgement pluck,
And yet methinks I have astronomy;°   *astrological knowledge*
But not to tell of good or evil luck,
Of plagues, of dearths, or seasons' quality.
5 Nor can I fortune to brief minutes° tell,   *precisely*
'Pointing to each his thunder, rain, and wind,
Or say with princes if it shall go well
By oft predict° that I in heaven find;   *numerous signs*
But from thine eyes my knowledge I derive,
10 And, constant stars, in them I read such art
As¹ truth and beauty shall together thrive
If from thyself to store thou wouldst convert.²
    Or else of thee this I prognosticate:
    Thy end is truth's and beauty's doom and date.°   *final judgment and end*

15

When I consider every thing that grows
Holds° in perfection but a little moment,   *Remains*
That this huge stage presenteth naught but shows
Whereon the stars in secret influence° comment;   *(astrologically)*
5 When I perceive that men as plants increase,
Cheerèd and checked even by the selfsame sky;
Vaunt° in their youthful sap,° at height decrease,   *Gloat / strength*
And wear their brave state out of memory:¹
Then the conceit° of this inconstant stay°   *imagination / (on earth)*
10 Sets you most rich in youth before my sight,
Where wasteful time debateth° with decay   *competes*
To change your day of youth to sullied night;
    And all in war with time for love of you,
    As he takes from you, I engraft you new.²

16¹

But wherefore do not you a mightier way
Make war upon this bloody tyrant, time,
And fortify yourself in your decay
With means more blessèd than my barren rhyme?
5 Now stand you on the top of happy hours,°   *in your prime*
And many maiden gardens yet unset°   *unplanted*
With virtuous wish would bear your living flowers,
Much liker than your painted counterfeit.°   *image in art or poetry*
So should the lines of life² that life repair°   *restore*
10 Which this time's pencil or my pupil pen³
Neither in inward worth nor outward fair
Can make you live yourself° in eyes of men.°   *as yourself*
    To give away yourself keeps yourself still,°   *(as children)*
    And you must live drawn by your own sweet skill.

Sonnet 14
1. *such art / As:* such predictions as that.
2. If you would provide for the future.
Sonnet:15
1. Wear their splendid clothing until they are forgotten (with a sense of "wearing out").
2. *And . . . new:* And I, in competition with time because

I love you, restore you with my verse.
Sonnet 16
1. This sonnet links with 15.
2. Lineage; living lines (unlike those of poet or painter).
3. Neither today's painters ("pencil" means "paintbrush") nor I, who imitate painting in my verse.

17

Who will believe my verse in time to come
If it were filled with your most high deserts?—
Though yet, heaven knows, it is but as a tomb
Which hides your life, and shows not half your parts.°   attributes
5   If I could write the beauty of your eyes
And in fresh numbers° number all your graces,   lively verses
The age to come would say 'This poet lies;
Such heavenly touches ne'er touched earthly faces.'
So should my papers, yellowed with their age,
10 Be scorned, like old men of less truth than tongue,
And your true rights° be termed a poet's rage°   praises / hyperbole
And stretchèd metre° of an antique song.   overwrought poetry
    But were some child of yours alive that time,
    You should live twice: in it, and in my rhyme.

18

Shall I compare thee to a summer's day?
Thou art more lovely and more temperate.
Rough winds do shake the darling buds of May,
And summer's lease° hath all too short a date.   fixed span of time
5   Sometime too hot the eye of heaven shines,
And often is his gold complexion dimmed,
And every fair from fair¹ sometime declines,
By chance or nature's changing course untrimmed;°   rendered ordinary
But thy eternal summer shall not fade
10 Nor lose possession of that fair thou ow'st,°   own
Nor shall death brag thou wander'st in his shade
When in eternal lines to time thou grow'st.²
    So long as men can breathe or eyes can see,
    So long lives this, and this gives life to thee.

19

Devouring time, blunt thou the lion's paws,
And make the earth devour her own sweet brood;
Pluck the keen teeth from the fierce tiger's jaws,
And burn the long-lived phoenix¹ in her blood.°   alive
5   Make glad and sorry seasons as thou fleet'st,
And do whate'er thou wilt, swift-footed time,
To the wide world and all her fading sweets.°   sweet things
But I forbid thee one most heinous crime:
O, carve not with thy hours my love's fair brow,
10 Nor draw no lines there with thine antique° pen.   old; capricious
Him in thy course untainted do allow
For beauty's pattern to succeeding men.
    Yet do thy worst, old time; despite thy wrong
    My love shall in my verse ever live young.

Sonnet 18
1. Lovely thing from loveliness.
2. When in immortal poetry you become engrafted to
time.

Sonnet 19
1. Legendary, self-resurrecting bird believed to live in
cycles of several centuries, dying in flames and reborn
from the ashes. See also 73.9–12.

20

A woman's face with nature's own hand° painted   *(without cosmetics)*
Hast thou, the master-mistress[1] of my passion;[2]
A woman's gentle heart, but not acquainted°   *(pun on "quaint," "cunt")*
With shifting change as is false women's fashion;
5   An eye more bright than theirs, less false in rolling,°   *wandering (sexually)*
Gilding the object whereupon it gazeth;
A man in hue, all hues in his controlling,[3]
Which steals men's eyes and women's souls amazeth.°   *overwhelms*
And for° a woman wert thou first created,   *to be; to be with*
10   Till nature as she wrought thee fell a-doting,°   *behaved foolishly*
And by addition me of thee defeated°   *cheated me of you*
By adding one thing to my purpose nothing.[4]
    But since she pricked° thee out for women's pleasure,[5]   *chose; (sexual)*
    Mine be thy love and thy love's use their treasure.[6]

21

So is it not with me as with that muse°   *poet*
Stirred by a painted° beauty to his verse,   *(with cosmetics)*
Who heaven itself for ornament° doth use,   *poetic imagery*
And every fair with his fair doth rehearse,[1]
5   Making a couplement of proud compare[2]
With sun and moon, with earth, and sea's rich gems,
With April's first-born flowers, and all things rare
That heaven's air in this huge rondure hems.°   *globe surrounds*
O let me, true in love, but truly write,
10   And then believe me my love is as fair
As any mother's child, though not so bright
As those gold candles° fixed in heaven's air.   *(the stars)*
    Let them say more that like of hearsay° well;   *clichés*
    I will not praise that purpose not° to sell.   *since I don't intend*

22

My glass° shall not persuade me I am old   *mirror*
So long as youth and thou are of one date;°   *While you're young*
But when in thee time's furrows I behold,
Then look I° death my days should expiate.°   *I expect / conclude*
5   For all that beauty that doth cover thee
Is but the seemly° raiment of my heart,   *fitting*
Which in thy breast doth live, as thine in me;
How can I then be elder than thou art?
O therefore, love, be of thyself so wary
10   As I, not for myself, but for thee will,
Bearing thy heart, which I will keep so chary°   *cautiously*
As tender nurse her babe from faring ill.

Sonnet 20
1. Both patron and sexual mistress (hence, homoerotic); referring to the youth's feminine looks.
2. Object of my love; controller of my feelings; controller of my passionate poetry.
3. A man whose looks enable him to attract and dominate all others; a man whose looks encompass all other appearances (both male and female). "Hue" may pun on "you" with possible sexual connotations. "Hues" may pun on "use"; see line 14 and note. "Controlling" puns on "cunt." 4. *one . . . nothing*: something (a penis) of no use to me;

"thing" meant sexual organ; "nothing" meant female sexual organ.
5. To give women pleasure; to have the pleasure women have.
6. I'll have the main part of your love (the capital or principal), while women get just the "use" (interest; pleasure; children) of it (or, while you use women sexually).
Sonnet 21
1. And compares every beautiful thing with his beloved.
2. Making a link in proud comparison.

Presume not on[1] thy heart when mine is slain:
Thou gav'st me thine not to give back again.

23

As an unperfect actor on the stage
Who with his fear is put besides° his part,   *forgets*
Or some fierce thing replete with too much rage
Whose strength's abundance weakens his own heart,
5 So I, for fear of trust,° forget to say   *lack of confidence*
The perfect ceremony of love's rite,[1]
And in mine own love's strength seem to decay,
O'er-charged with burden of mine own love's might.
O let my books be then the eloquence
10 And dumb presagers° of my speaking breast,   *mute presenters*
Who plead for love, and look for recompense
More than that tongue that more hath more expressed.[2]
    O learn to read what silent love hath writ;
    To hear with eyes belongs to love's fine wit.

24

Mine eye hath played the painter,[1] and hath steeled[2]
Thy beauty's form in table° of my heart.   *the painted tablet*
My body is the frame wherein 'tis held,
And perspective[3] it is best painter's art;
5 For through the painter must you see his skill
To find where your true image pictured lies,
Which in my bosom's shop° is hanging still,   *heart's workshop*
That hath his windows glazèd with thine eyes.[4]
Now see what good turns eyes for eyes have done:
10 Mine eyes have drawn thy shape, and thine for me
Are windows to my breast, wherethrough the sun
Delights to peep, to gaze therein on thee.
    Yet eyes this cunning want° to grace their art: *lack this talent*
    They draw but what they see, know not the heart.

25

Let those who are in favour with their stars
Of public honour and proud titles boast,
Whilst I, whom fortune of such triumph bars,
Unlooked-for joy in that I honour most.[1]
5 Great princes' favourites their fair leaves spread°   *bloom*
But as the marigold at the sun's eye,[2]
And in themselves their pride lies° buried,   *will lie*
For at a frown they in their glory die.
The painful warrior famousèd for might,

Sonnet 22
1. Do not expect to get back.
Sonnet 23
1. Q reads "right," suggesting love's due as well as ritual.
2. More than that (rival) speaker who has more often said more.
Sonnet 24
1. The running conceit is of the speaker and addressee looking into one another's eyes, seeing both the other and himself reflected.
2. Engraved. Editors often emend Q's "steeld" to "stell'd" (fixed, placed) for a better fit with "painter."
3. Seen from the proper angle, through the painter's

eyes. A "perspective" was a distorted painting that looked right only if viewed from the correct angle.
4. The addressee looks into the speaker's eyes ("windows"), which seem fitted with glass ("glazèd") by the reflection there of the addressee's own eyes. The eyes are the heart's ("his" [its], referring to "bosom's," line 7) windows, through which the addressee can therefore see his own image in the speaker's heart.
Sonnet 25
1. Unexpectedly (privately) take pleasure in what I most esteem (the youth).
2. Only at the prince's pleasure or whim.

10   After a thousand victories once foiled
       Is from the book of honour razèd° quite,   *deleted*
       And all the rest forgot for which he toiled.
          Then happy I, that love and am beloved
          Where I may not remove nor be removed.

26

       Lord of my love, to whom in vassalage°   *feudal allegiance*
       Thy merit hath my duty strongly knit,
       To thee I send this written embassage°   *missive*
       To witness duty, not to show my wit;
5   Duty so great which wit so poor as mine
       May make seem bare in wanting° words to show it,   *lacking*
       But that I hope some good conceit° of thine   *opinion*
       In thy soul's thought, all naked,[1] will bestow° it,   *provide a place for*
       Till whatsoever star that guides my moving°   *actions*
10   Points on me graciously with fair aspect,°   *astrological influence*
       And puts apparel on my tattered loving
       To show me worthy of thy sweet respect.
          Then may I dare to boast how I do love thee;
          Till then, not show my head where thou mayst prove° me.   *test*

27

       Weary with toil I haste me to my bed,
       The dear repose for limbs with travel° tired;   *work; journeying*
       But then begins a journey in my head
       To work my mind when body's work's expired;
5   For then my thoughts, from far where I abide,
       Intend a zealous pilgrimage to thee,
       And keep my drooping eyelids open wide,
       Looking on darkness which the blind do see:
       Save that my soul's imaginary sight
10   Presents thy shadow° to my sightless view,   *picture*
       Which like a jewel hung in ghastly night
       Makes black night beauteous and her old face new.
          Lo, thus by day my limbs, by night my mind,
          For° thee, and for myself, no quiet find.   *Because of*

28[1]

       How can I then return in happy plight,°   *condition*
       That am debarred the benefit of rest,
       When day's oppression is not eased by night,
       But day by night and night by day oppressed,
5   And each, though enemies to either's° reign,   *each other's*
       Do in consent shake hands to torture me,
       The one by toil, the other to complain[2]
       How far I toil, still farther off from thee?
       I tell the day to please him thou art bright,
10   And do'st him grace when clouds do blot the heaven;[3]
       So flatter I the swart°-complexioned night   *dark*
       When sparkling stars twire not thou gild'st the even.[4]

Sonnet 26
1. Refers to his "bare"-seeming "duty."
Sonnet 28
1. This sonnet links with 27.

2. *one:* day. *other:* night, making me "complain."
3. And confer beauty on him as a substitute for the sun.
4. By saying that when stars aren't twinkling, you brighten the evening.

But day doth daily draw my sorrows longer,
And night doth nightly make grief's strength seem stronger.

29

When, in disgrace with fortune and men's eyes,
I all alone beweep my outcast state,
And trouble deaf heaven with my bootless° cries,   *unavailing*
And look upon myself and curse my fate,
5 Wishing me like to one more rich in hope,
Featured like him, like him with friends possessed,[1]
Desiring this man's art° and that man's scope,°   *skill / range*
With what I most enjoy° contented least: *like; own*
Yet in these thoughts myself almost despising,
10 Haply[2] I think on thee, and then my state,°   *mood; fortunes*
Like to the lark at break of day arising
From sullen earth, sings hymns at heaven's gate;
    For thy sweet love remembered such wealth brings
    That then I scorn to change my state with kings'.

30

When to the sessions° of sweet silent thought   *court sittings*
I summon up remembrance of things past,
I sigh° the lack of many a thing I sought,   *mourn*
And with old woes new wail my dear time's waste.[1]
5 Then can I drown an eye unused to flow
For precious friends hid in death's dateless° night,   *endless*
And weep afresh love's long-since-cancelled° woe,   *repaid (with sorrow)*
And moan th'expense° of many a vanished sight.   *passing*
Then can I grieve at grievances foregone,°   *bygone*
10 And heavily° from woe to woe tell° o'er   *sadly / say; count*
The sad account° of fore-bemoanèd moan,   *story; finances*
Which I new pay as if not paid before.
    But if the while I think on thee, dear friend,
    All losses are restored, and sorrows end.

31

Thy bosom is endearèd with° all hearts   *loved by; enriched by*
Which I by lacking have supposèd dead,
And there reigns love, and all love's loving parts,
And all those friends which I thought buried.
5 How many a holy and obsequious° tear   *dutifullly mourning*
Hath dear religious° love stol'n from mine eye   *devoted*
As interest of° the dead, which° now appear   *due payment to / who*
But things removed° that hidden in thee lie!   *absent*
Thou art the grave where buried love doth live,
10 Hung with the trophies° of my lovers gone,   *memorials*
Who all their parts° of me to thee did give: *shares*
That due of many[1] now is thine alone.

Sonnet 29
1. *Wishing . . . possessed:* Three people he wants to be like—"like to one" with better prospects, better looking "like him," and having friends "like him."
2. By chance; also, pun on "happily."

Sonnet 30
1. *my . . . waste:* the frittering or wasting away of my precious time.

Sonnet 31
1. What was owed to many (myself).

Their images I loved I view in thee,
And thou, all they,[2] hast all the all of me.

32

If thou survive my well-contented day[1]
When that churl death my bones with dust shall cover,
And shalt by fortune° once more resurvey   *chance*
These poor rude° lines of thy deceasèd lover,   *rough*
5 Compare them with the bett'ring° of the time,   *progress; better art*
And though they be outstripped by every pen,
Reserve them for my love, not for their rhyme
Exceeded by the height of happier men.[2]
O then vouchsafe me but this loving thought:
10 'Had my friend's muse grown with this growing age,
A dearer birth° than this his love had brought   *worthier poem*
To march in ranks of better equipage;°   *poems*
   But since he died, and poets better prove,°   *have improved*
   Theirs for their style I'll read, his for his love.'

33

Full many a glorious morning have I seen
Flatter the mountain tops with sovereign eye,°   *sunlight*
Kissing with golden face the meadows green,
Gilding pale streams with heavenly alchemy;
5 Anon° permit the basest° clouds to ride   *(But) soon / darkest*
With ugly rack° on his celestial face,   *cloudy mask*
And from the forlorn world his visage hide,
Stealing unseen to west with this disgrace.
Even so my sun one early morn did shine
10 With all triumphant splendour on my brow;
But out, alack,° he was but one hour mine;   *alas*
The region° cloud hath masked him from me now.   *high*
   Yet him for this my love no whit disdaineth:
   Suns of the world may stain° when heaven's sun staineth.   *darken*

34[1]

Why didst thou promise such a beauteous day
And make me travel forth without my cloak,
To let base clouds o'ertake me in my way,
Hiding thy brav'ry° in their rotten smoke?°   *finery / noxious mists*
5 'Tis not enough that through the cloud thou break
To dry the rain on my storm-beaten face,
For no man well of such a salve can speak
That heals the wound and cures not the disgrace.[2]
Nor can thy shame° give physic to° my grief;   *remorse / cure*
10 Though thou repent, yet I have still the loss.
Th'offender's sorrow lends but weak relief
To him that bears the strong offence's cross.°   *consequences*

2. And you, who are made up of all of them.
Sonnet 32
1. Day of my death, which I shall willingly accept.
2. *Reserve . . . men:* Keep them because you love me, not
for their value as poetry, which is surpassed by poets more
fortunate in their talent than I.
Sonnet 34
1. This sonnet links with 33.
2. Disfigurement; dishonor done the poet by the youth's
neglect.

Ah, but those tears are pearl which thy love sheds,
And they are rich, and ransom° all ill deeds.   *atone for*

35

No more be grieved at that which thou hast done:
Roses have thorns, and silver fountains mud.
Clouds and eclipses stain° both moon and sun,   *darken*
And loathsome canker° lives in sweetest bud.   *(worm)*
5   All men make faults, and even I in this,
Authorizing thy trespass with compare,[1]
Myself corrupting salving thy amiss,[2]
Excusing thy sins more than thy sins are;[3]
For to thy sensual fault I bring in sense[4]—
10   Thy adverse party is thy advocate—
And 'gainst myself a lawful plea commence.
Such civil war is in my love and hate
     That I an accessory needs must be
     To that sweet thief which sourly robs from me.

36

Let me confess that we two must be twain[1]
Although our undivided loves are one;
So shall those blots° that do with me remain   *flaws; sources of shame*
Without thy help by me be borne alone.
5   In our two loves there is but one respect,°   *focus of attention*
Though in our lives a separable spite[2]
Which, though it alter not love's sole° effect,   *single-minded*
Yet doth it steal sweet hours from love's delight.
I may not evermore acknowledge thee
10   Lest my bewailèd guilt should do thee shame,
Nor thou with public kindness honour me
Unless thou take° that honour from thy name.   *lose*
     But do not so. I love thee in such sort°   *such a way*
     As, thou being mine, mine is thy good report.[3]

37

As a decrepit father takes delight
To see his active child do deeds of youth,
So I, made lame by fortune's dearest° spite,   *direst*
Take all my comfort of° thy worth and truth;   *in*
5   For whether beauty, birth, or wealth, or wit,
Or any of these all, or all, or more,
Entitled in thy parts[1] do crownèd sit,
I make my love engrafted to this store.[2]
So then I am not lame, poor, nor despised,
10   Whilst that this shadow° doth such substance give   *idea*
That I in thy abundance am sufficed

Sonnet 35
1. Justifying your offense with comparisons.
2. Corrupting myself in minimizing your transgression.
3. Excusing you (overindulgently) from worse sins than the ones you've committed.
4. I use reason to defend your sensual offense.
Sonnet 36
1. Separated; but also, paradoxically, two of a kind or bound together.

2. Separation that causes vexation; vexation that causes separation.
3. Reputation. This couplet also ends 96.
Sonnet 37
1. Enrolled among your good qualities.
2. I engraft my love onto this abundance (of good qualities).

And by a part of all thy glory live.
    Look what° is best, that best I wish in thee;   *whatever*
    This° wish I have, then ten times happy me.   *When this*

38

How can my muse want subject to invent°   *lack subject matter*
While thou dost breathe, that pour'st into my verse
Thine own sweet argument,° too excellent   *theme*
For every vulgar paper to rehearse?¹
5 O, give thyself the thanks if aught in me
Worthy perusal stand against thy sight;²
For who's so dumb that cannot write to thee,
When thou thyself dost give invention light?
Be thou the tenth muse, ten times more in worth
10 Than those old nine which rhymers invocate,
And he that calls on thee, let him bring forth
Eternal numbers° to outlive long° date.   *verses / a distant*
    If my slight muse do please these curious° days,   *finicky*
    The pain° be mine, but thine shall be the praise.   *pains; effort*

39

O, how thy worth with manners° may I sing   *modesty*
When thou art all the better part of me?
What can mine own praise to mine own self bring,
And what is't but mine own when I praise thee?
5 Even for° this let us divided live,   *Because of*
And our dear love lose name of single one,°   *the reputation of unity*
That by this separation I may give
That due to thee which thou deserv'st alone.
O absence, what a torment wouldst thou prove
10 Were it not thy sour leisure gave sweet leave
To entertain° the time with thoughts of love,   *enliven*
Which time and thoughts so sweetly doth deceive,
    And that thou teachest how to make one twain
    By praising him here° who doth hence remain!   *in this poem*

40¹

Take all my loves, my love, yea, take them all:
What hast thou then more than thou hadst before?
No love, my love, that thou mayst true love call—
All mine was thine before thou hadst this more.
5 Then if for my love thou my love receivest,²
I cannot blame thee for my love thou usest;³
But yet be blamed if thou this self⁴ deceivest
By wilful taste of what thyself° refusest.   *your better nature*
I do forgive thy robb'ry, gentle thief,
10 Although thou steal thee all my poverty;°   *what little I own*
And yet love knows it is a greater grief

Sonnet 38
1. Every ordinary, commonplace piece of writing to set forth.
2. *if . . . sight:* if you see anything in my writing worth reading.
Sonnet 40
1. Sonnets 40–42 concern a situation that may be identical to the love triangle described in 133–34 and 144.
2. Then if for love of me you take my beloved.
3. *for . . . usest:* because you use my beloved (sexually).
4. The poet (often emended, perhaps rightly, to "thyself").

To bear love's wrong than hate's known injury.
    Lascivious grace,° in whom all ill well shows,   *Charming wanton*
    Kill me with spites,° yet we must not be foes.   *offenses*

41

Those pretty° wrongs that liberty° commits   *minor / licentiousness*
When I am sometime absent from thy heart
Thy beauty and thy years full well befits,
For still° temptation follows where thou art.   *continually*
5 Gentle° thou art, and therefore to be won;   *Tender; upper-class*
Beauteous thou art, therefore to be assailed;
And when a woman woos, what woman's son
Will sourly leave her till he have prevailed?[1]
Ay me, but yet thou mightst my seat[2] forbear,
10 And chide thy beauty and thy straying youth
Who lead thee in their riot° even there   *depraved conduct*
Where thou art forced to break a two-fold troth:
    Hers, by thy beauty tempting her to thee,
    Thine, by thy beauty being false to me.

42

That thou hast her, it is not all my grief,
And yet it may be said I loved her dearly;
That she hath thee is of my wailing chief,°   *chief reason*
A loss in love that touches me more nearly.
5 Loving offenders, thus I will excuse ye:
Thou dost love her because thou know'st I love her,
And for my sake even so doth she abuse° me,   *mistreat*
Suff'ring my friend for my sake to approve her.[1]
If I lose thee, my loss is my love's gain,
10 And losing° her, my friend hath found that loss: *I losing*
Both find each other, and I lose both twain,
And both for my sake lay on me this cross.°   *affliction*
    But here's the joy: my friend and I are one.
    Sweet flattery!° Then she loves but me alone.   *Pleasing delusion*

43

When most I wink,° then do mine eyes best see,   *shut my eyes*
For all the day they view things unrespected;°   *unheeded; unworthy*
But when I sleep, in dreams they look on thee,
And, darkly bright, are bright in dark directed.[1]
5 Then thou, whose shadow shadows doth make bright,[2]
How would thy shadow's form° form happy show°   *substance / sight*
To the clear day with thy much clearer light,
When to unseeing eyes[3] thy shade shines so!
How would, I say, mine eyes be blessèd made
10 By looking on thee in the living day,
When in dead night thy fair imperfect° shade   *incorporeal*

Sonnet 41
1. Until he has had his way. But Q's "he" could easily be a misprint for "she."
2. Rightful place (my mistress).
Sonnet 42
1. To put her to the test (sexually).

Sonnet 43
1. (My eyes) seeing in the dark turn toward your bright eyes in the dark.
2. Whose image lightens darkness.
3. Because closed in sleep.

Through heavy sleep on sightless eyes doth stay!
　　All days are nights to see till I see thee,
　　And nights bright days when dreams do show thee me.°　　　　　*to me*

44

If the dull° substance of my flesh were thought,　　　　　*heavy*
Injurious distance should not stop my way;
For then, despite of space, I would be brought
From limits° far remote where° thou dost stay.　　　　　*places / to where*
5　No matter then although my foot did stand
Upon the farthest earth removed from thee;
For nimble thought can jump both sea and land
As soon as think the place where he° would be.　　　　　*(thought)*
But ah, thought kills me that I am not thought,
10　To leap large lengths of miles when thou art gone,
But that, so much of earth and water wrought,[1]
I must attend time's leisure[2] with my moan,
　　Receiving naught by elements so slow
　　But heavy tears, badges of either's woe.[3]

45[1]

The other two,[2] slight° air and purging fire,　　　　　*light*
Are both with thee wherever I abide;
The first my thought, the other my desire,
These present-absent[3] with swift motion slide;
5　For when these quicker° elements are gone　　　　　*livelier*
In tender embassy of love to thee,
My life, being made of four, with two alone
Sinks down to death, oppressed with melancholy,
Until life's composition be recured°　　　　　*renewed*
10　By those swift messengers returned from thee,
Who even but now come back again assured
Of thy fair health, recounting it to me.
　　This told, I joy; but then no longer glad,
　　I send them back again and straight° grow sad.　　　　　*suddenly*

46

Mine eye and heart are at a mortal° war　　　　　*lethal*
How to divide the conquest of thy sight.[1]
Mine eye my heart thy picture's sight would bar,
My heart, mine eye the freedom° of that right.　　　　　*free enjoyment*
5　My heart doth plead that thou in him dost lie,
A closet° never pierced with crystal eyes;　　　　　*room*
But the defendant doth that plea deny,
And says in him thy fair appearance lies.
To 'cide° this title is empanellèd°　　　　　*decide / enrolled*
10　A quest° of thoughts, all tenants to the heart,

Sonnet 44
1. Being compounded of so much earth and water (the heavy elements).
2. I must wait humbly (as if on a great man) for time to reunite us.
3. Emblems of the grief of each of the poet's elements (of earth because heavy [sad], of water because wet).
Sonnet 45
1. This sonnet links with 44.

2. Of the poet's four elements. See 44.11.
3. Now present, now absent; constantly coming and going.
Sonnet 46
1. The spoils of the sight of you (possibly in a painting; see 47.5–14).

And by their verdict is determinèd   *jury*
The clear eye's moiety° and the dear heart's part,   *share*
  As thus: mine eye's due is thy outward part,
  And my heart's right thy inward love of heart.

47[1]

Betwixt mine eye and heart a league is took,°   *truce is made*
And each doth good turns now unto the other.
When that mine eye is famished for a look,
Or heart in love with sighs himself doth smother,[2]
5 With my love's picture then my eye doth feast,
And to the painted banquet bids my heart.
Another time mine eye is my heart's guest
And in his thoughts of love doth share a part.
So either by thy picture or my love,
10 Thyself away art present still with me;
For thou no farther than my thoughts canst move,
And I am still° with them, and they with thee;   *constantly*
  Or if they sleep, thy picture in my sight
  Awakes my heart to heart's and eye's delight.

48

How careful was I when I took my way°   *set off*
Each trifle under truest° bars to thrust,   *most reliable*
That to my use° it might unusèd stay   *benefit*
From hands of falsehood, in sure wards° of trust.   *safe places*
5 But thou, to° whom my jewels trifles are,   *compared to*
Most worthy comfort, now my greatest grief,[1]
Thou best of dearest and mine only care
Art left the prey of every vulgar thief.
Thee have I not locked up in any chest
10 Save where thou art not, though I feel thou art—
Within the gentle closure of my breast,
From whence at pleasure thou mayst come and part;°   *go*
  And even thence thou wilt be stol'n, I fear,
  For truth° proves thievish for a prize so dear.   *even honesty*

49

Against° that time—if ever that time come—   *In preparation for*
When I shall see thee frown on my defects,
Whenas thy love hath cast his utmost sum,[1]
Called to that audit by advised respects;°   *judicious reasons*
5 Against that time when thou shalt strangely° pass   *as a stranger*
And scarcely greet me with that sun, thine eye,
When love converted from the thing it was
Shall reasons find of settled gravity:[2]
Against that time do I ensconce me° here   *secure myself*
10 Within the knowledge of mine own desert,[3]
And this my hand against myself uprear°   *testify against myself*

Sonnet 47
1. This sonnet links with 46.
2. Or when my loving heart smothers itself with sighs.
Sonnet 48
1. Because absent and in danger of being stolen.

Sonnet 49
1. When your love has calculated the bottom line.
2. Shall find reasons for a dignified reserve; shall find reasons of well-established seriousness (for leaving me).
3. My (lack of?) worthiness to be loved.

To guard the lawful reasons on thy part.°   defend your case
　　To leave poor me thou hast the strength of laws,
　　Since why to love° I can allege no cause.   why you should love

50

How heavy° do I journey on the way,   wearily
When what I seek—my weary travel's end—
Doth teach that ease and that repose to say[1]
'Thus far the miles are measured from thy friend.'
5　The beast that bears me, tired with my woe,
Plods dully on to bear° that weight in me,   while bearing
As if by some instinct the wretch did know
His rider loved not speed, being made[2] from thee.
The bloody spur cannot provoke him on
10　That sometimes anger thrusts into his hide,
Which heavily he answers with a groan
More sharp to me than spurring to his side;
　　For that same groan doth put this in my mind:
　　My grief lies onward and my joy behind.

51[1]

Thus can my love excuse the slow offence°   offense of slowness
Of my dull bearer when from thee I speed:
From where thou art why should I haste me thence?
Till I return, of posting° is no need.   riding quickly
5　O what excuse will my poor beast then find
When swift extremity° can seem but slow?   extreme (return) speed
Then should I spur, though mounted on the wind;
In wingèd speed no motion shall I know.[2]
Then can no horse with my desire keep pace;
10　Therefore desire, of perfect'st love being made,
Shall rein° no dull flesh in his fiery race;   curb
But love, for love,° thus shall excuse my jade: on love's behalf
　　Since from thee going he went wilful-slow,
　　Towards thee I'll run and give him leave to go.°   walk

52

So am I as the rich° whose blessèd key   rich man
Can bring him to his sweet up-lockèd treasure,
The which he will not ev'ry hour survey,
For° blunting the fine point of seldom° pleasure.   To avoid / occasional
5　Therefore are feasts° so solemn° and so rare   feast days / dignified
Since, seldom coming, in the long year set
Like stones of worth they thinly placèd are,
Or captain° jewels in the carcanet.°   chief / jeweled collar
So is the time that keeps you as° my chest,°   like / jewel case
10　Or as the wardrobe which the robe doth hide,
To make some special instant special blest

Sonnet 50
1. Teach the comforts at the end of the road to remind me that.
2. *speed, being made*: hastening away; haste, when and because it is.
Sonnet 51
1. This sonnet links with 50.

2. I will feel no motion when desire carries me back through the air. See line 11 and sonnets 44–45 for the association of fire and air with desire and thought, and of earth and water with dull, slow flesh.

By new unfolding his imprisoned pride.
   Blessèd are you whose worthiness gives scope,
   Being had, to triumph; being lacked, to hope.[1]

53

What is your substance, whereof are you made,
That millions of strange shadows on you tend?°   *attend*
Since every one hath, every one, one shade,[1]
And you, but one, can every shadow lend.[2]
5   Describe° Adonis, and the counterfeit°   *Draw / likeness*
Is poorly imitated after you.
On Helen's cheek all art of beauty set,
And you in Grecian tires are painted new.[3]
Speak of the spring and foison° of the year: *harvest time*
10 The one doth shadow of your beauty show,
The other as your bounty doth appear;
And you in every blessèd shape we know.°   *recognize*
   In all external grace you have some part,
   But you like none, none you, for constant heart.

54

O how much more doth beauty beauteous seem
By° that sweet ornament which truth doth give!   *Because of*
The rose looks fair, but fairer we it deem
For that sweet odour which doth in it live.
5   The canker blooms[1] have full as deep a dye
As the perfumèd tincture° of the roses,   *color*
Hang on such thorns, and play as wantonly°   *flatter as playfully*
When summer's breath their maskèd buds discloses;
But for° their virtue only is° their show   *since / lies wholly in*
10 They live unwooed and unrespected° fade,   *unappreciated*
Die to themselves.° Sweet roses do not so;   *alone; without influence*
Of their sweet deaths are sweetest odours made:
   And so of you, beauteous and lovely youth,
   When that° shall fade, by verse distils your truth.[2]   *beauty*

55

Not marble nor the gilded monuments
Of princes shall outlive this powerful rhyme,
But you shall shine more bright in these contents
Than unswept stone besmeared with sluttish° time.   *slovenly*
5   When wasteful war shall statues overturn,
And broils° root out the work of masonry,   *battles*
Nor Mars his° sword nor war's quick fire shall burn   *Neither Mars's*
The living record of your memory.
'Gainst death and all oblivious enmity
10 Shall you pace forth; your praise shall still find room

Sonnet 52
1. *gives . . . hope:* allows me to exult when with you and to hope when not with you.
Sonnet 53
1. Since each person has an individual shadow.
2. Can cast all shadows (are visible in every image).
3. *On . . . new:* If one were to use every art to reproduce the beauty of Helen of Troy (or use artful cosmetics

on Helen's cheek) it would look like you in Grecian headgear.
Sonnet 54
1. Dog roses (having little scent).
2. See sonnet 5. Q's "vade" is a variant of "fade," the reading adopted here, but it probably has the secondary meaning of "depart," from the Latin *vadere.*

Even in the eyes of all posterity
That wear this world out to the ending doom.[1]
   So, till the judgement that yourself arise,
   You live in this, and dwell in lovers' eyes.

56

Sweet love,[1] renew thy force. Be it not said
Thy edge should blunter be than appetite,
Which but° today by feeding is allayed,   *merely for*
Tomorrow sharpened in his former might.
5 So, love, be thou; although today thou fill
Thy hungry eyes even till they wink° with fullness,   *close (to sleep)*
Tomorrow see again, and do not kill
The spirit of love with a perpetual dullness.
Let this sad int'rim like the ocean be
10 Which parts the shore where two contracted new
Come daily to the banks, that when they see
Return of love, more blessed may be the view;[2]
   Or call it winter, which, being full of care,
   Makes summer's welcome, thrice more wished, more rare.°   *valuable*

57

Being your slave, what should I do but tend°   *wait*
Upon the hours and times of your desire?
I have no precious time at all to spend,
Nor services to do, till you require;
5 Nor dare I chide the world-without-end° hour   *endless*
Whilst I, my sovereign, watch the clock for you,
Nor think the bitterness of absence sour
When you have bid your servant once adieu.
Nor dare I question with my jealous thought
10 Where you may be, or your affairs suppose,°   *speculate on*
But like a sad slave stay and think of naught
Save, where you are, how happy you make those.
   So true a fool is love that in your will,[1]
   Though you do anything, he thinks no ill.

58[1]

That god forbid, that made me first your slave,
I should in thought control your times of pleasure,
Or at your hand th'account of hours to crave,[2]
Being your vassal° bound to stay° your leisure.   *slave / wait upon*
5 O let me suffer, being at your beck,
Th'imprisoned absence of your liberty,[3]
And patience, tame to sufferance, bide each check,[4]
Without accusing you of injury.

Sonnet 55
1. Doomsday: in Christianity, the Day of Judgment, when dead bodies are supposed to "arise" (line 13) from the grave and be united with their souls.
Sonnet 56
1. The feeling (not the beloved).
2. *Let . . . view:* The "sad" interval between periods of feeling love is like an ocean dividing shores where two lovers come daily hoping for the (emotionally renewing) sight of a boat bringing the other. *contracted new:* newly betrothed.

Sonnet 57
1. Desire (including sexual desire); capitalized in Q, perhaps punning on Shakespeare's name. See 135–36.
Sonnet 58
1. This sonnet links with 57.
2. Or should seek an account of how you pass your time.
3. The imprisoned feeling caused by your licentiousness when you're away.
4. And (let me) patient, acquiescent in suffering, endure each setback.

Be where you list,° your charter° is so strong   *wish / freedom*
10 That you yourself may privilege° your time   *allocate*
   To what you will; to you it doth belong
   Yourself to pardon of self-doing° crime.   *committed by you*
     I am to wait, though waiting so be hell,
     Not blame your pleasure, be it ill or well.

59

   If there be nothing new, but that which is
   Hath been before, how are our brains beguiled,°   *cheated*
   Which, labouring° for invention, bear amiss   *working; giving birth*
   The second burden of a former child![1]
5 O that record° could with a backward look   *recollection*
   Even of five hundred courses of the sun
   Show me your image in some antique book
   Since mind at first in character was done,[2]
   That I might see what the old world could say
10 To this composèd wonder of your frame;[3]
   Whether we are mended° or whe'er better they,   *improved*
   Or whether revolution be the same.[4]
     O, sure I am the wits° of former days   *clever writers*
     To subjects worse have given admiring praise.

60

   Like as the waves make towards the pebbled shore,
   So do our minutes hasten to their end,
   Each changing place with that which goes before;
   In sequent toil all forwards do contend.[1]
5 Nativity,° once in the main of light,°   *A newborn / in the world*
   Crawls to maturity, wherewith being crowned
   Crookèd° eclipses 'gainst his glory fight,   *Pernicious*
   And time that gave doth now his gift confound.°   *ruin*
   Time doth transfix the flourish[2] set on youth,
10 And delves the parallels° in beauty's brow;   *carves the wrinkles*
   Feeds on the rarities of nature's truth,[3]
   And nothing stands but for his scythe to mow.
     And yet to times in hope° my verse shall stand,   *future days*
     Praising thy worth despite his cruel hand.

61

   Is it thy will thy image should keep open
   My heavy eyelids to the weary night?
   Dost thou desire my slumbers should be broken
   While shadows° like to thee do mock my sight?   *visions*
5 Is it thy spirit that thou send'st from thee
   So far from home into my deeds to pry,
   To find out shames and idle hours in me,
   The scope and tenor of thy jealousy?[1]
     O no; thy love, though much, is not so great.

Sonnet 59
1. *bear . . . child:* mistakenly ("amiss") give birth for a second time to a child that has already been born.
2. Since writing was invented.
3. To the wonderful composition of your form (perhaps referring to the sonnet itself as well).
4. Whether the revolving of the ages makes no difference.

Sonnet 60
1. Toiling one after the other, all seek to move forward.
2. Time pierces and destroys the ornament (beauty).
3. On the most precious products of nature's perfection.
Sonnet 61
1. The object and intent of your distrust (that is, "shames and idle hours," line 7).

10   It is my love that keeps mine eye awake,
      Mine own true love that doth my rest defeat,
      To play the watchman ever for thy sake.
        For thee watch I° whilst thou dost wake elsewhere,   *I remain awake*
        From me far off, with others all too near.

62

      Sin of self-love possesseth all mine eye,
      And all my soul, and all my every part;
      And for this sin there is no remedy,
      It is so grounded inward in my heart.
5   Methinks no face so gracious is as mine,
      No shape so true,° no truth of such account,   *perfect*
      And for myself mine own worth do define
      As° I all other° in all worths surmount.   *As if / others*
      But when my glass° shows me myself indeed,   *mirror*
10   Beated and chapped with tanned antiquity,
      Mine own self-love quite contrary I read;
      Self so self-loving were iniquity.
        'Tis thee, my self,° that for° myself I praise,   *you, my other self / as*
        Painting my age with beauty of thy days.

63

      Against° my love shall be as I am now,   *Preparing for when*
      With time's injurious hand crushed and o'erworn;
      When hours have drained his blood and filled his brow
      With lines and wrinkles; when his youthful morn
5   Hath travelled° on to age's steepy¹ night,   *progressed; toiled*
      And all those beauties whereof now he's king
      Are vanishing, or vanished out of sight,
      Stealing away the treasure of his spring:
      For such a time do I now fortify
10   Against confounding° age's cruel knife,   *devastating*
      That he shall never cut from memory
      My sweet love's beauty, though° my lover's life.   *though he will sever*
        His beauty shall in these black lines be seen,
        And they shall live, and he in them still green.°   *perpetually youthful*

64

      When I have seen by time's fell° hand defaced   *fierce*
      The rich proud cost° of outworn buried age;   *expense*
      When sometime°-lofty towers I see down razed,   *once*
      And brass eternal slave to mortal rage;¹
5   When I have seen the hungry ocean gain
      Advantage on the kingdom of the shore,
      And the firm soil win of° the wat'ry main,   *win ground from*
      Increasing store with loss and loss with store;²
      When I have seen such interchange of state,
10   Or state³ itself confounded to decay,°   *reduced to ruins*
      Ruin hath taught me thus to ruminate:

Sonnet 63
1. Precipitous (like the path of the setting sun).
Sonnet 64
1. And eternal brass forever succumbs to death's violence.

2. Adding to the stock of one by loss of the other, and vice versa.
3. *state* (line 9): condition; sovereign territory. *state* (line 10): pomp.

That time will come and take my love away.
  This thought is as a death, which° cannot choose   *since thought*
  But weep to have° that which it fears to lose.   *at having*

65

Since° brass, nor stone, nor earth, nor boundless sea,   *Since there is neither*
But sad mortality o'ersways their power,
How with this rage shall beauty hold a plea,[1]
Whose action is no stronger than a flower?
5 O how shall summer's honey breath hold out
Against the wrackful° siege of battering days   *damaging*
When rocks impregnable are not so stout,
Nor gates of steel so strong, but time decays?°   *decays them*
O fearful meditation! Where, alack,
10 Shall time's best jewel° from time's chest[2] lie hid,   *(the beloved)*
Or what strong hand can hold his swift foot back,
Or who his spoil° of beauty can forbid?   *destruction*
  O none, unless this miracle have might:
  That in black ink my love may still shine bright.

66

Tired with all these°, for restful death I cry: *(the ensuing wrongs)*
As,° to behold desert° a beggar born,   *For example / merit*
And needy nothing trimmed in jollity,[1]
And purest faith unhappily forsworn,°   *betrayed; perjured*
5 And gilded honour shamefully misplaced,
And maiden virtue rudely strumpeted,
And right perfection wrongfully disgraced,
And strength by limping sway° disablèd,   *feeble leaders*
And art made tongue-tied° by authority,   *learning silenced*
10 And folly, doctor-like, controlling skill,[2]
And simple truth miscalled simplicity,°   *naïveté*
And captive good attending° captain ill.   *serving*
  Tired with all these, from these would I be gone,
  Save that to die I leave my love alone.

67

Ah, wherefore with infection[1] should he live
And with his presence grace impiety,
That° sin by him advantage should achieve   *So that*
And lace° itself with his society?   *decorate*
5 Why should false painting imitate his cheek,
And steal dead seeming of[2] his living hue?
Why should poor° beauty indirectly seek   *lesser*
Roses of shadow,° since his rose is true?   *Cosmetic beauty*
Why should he live now nature bankrupt is,
10 Beggared of blood to blush through lively veins,
For she hath no exchequer° now but his,   *treasury*

Sonnet 65
1. How can beauty make a (legal) case against such a power to destroy?
2. Treasure chest; coffin.
Sonnet 66
1. And ungifted (or impoverished) worthlessness adorned with finery.

2. And folly, feigning erudition, dominating true wisdom or ability. Before modern medicine, doctors were often portrayed as fools or con artists.
Sonnet 67
1. The world's ills (as in 66).
2. *dead seeming of*: an inanimate outward resemblance from.

And proud of many, lives upon his gains?[3]
    O, him she stores° to show what wealth she had   *keeps*
    In days long since, before these last so bad.

68[1]

Thus is his cheek the map° of days outworn,   *image*
When beauty lived and died as flowers do now,
5 Before these bastard signs of fair° were borne°   *cosmetics / worn; born*
Or durst inhabit on a living brow;
Before the golden tresses of the dead,
The right of sepulchres,[2] were shorn away
To live a second life on second head;
Ere beauty's dead fleece made another gay.
In him those holy antique hours° are seen   *good old days*
10 Without all ornament, itself and true,
Making no summer of another's green,
Robbing no old to dress his beauty new;
    And him as for a map doth nature store,°   *keep*
    To show false art what beauty was of yore.

69

Those parts of thee that the world's eye doth view
Want° nothing that the thought of hearts can mend.°   *Lack / imagine better*
All tongues, the voice of souls, give thee that due,
Utt'ring bare truth even so as foes commend.[1]
5 Thy outward thus with outward praise is crowned,
But those same tongues that give thee so thine own°   *your due*
In other accents° do this praise confound°   *words / undermine*
By seeing farther than the eye hath shown.
They look into the beauty of thy mind,
10 And that in guess they measure by thy deeds.
Then, churls, their thoughts—although their eyes were kind—
To thy fair flower add the rank smell of weeds.
    But why thy odour matcheth not thy show,°   *appearance*
    The soil is this: that thou dost common grow.[2]

70[1]

That thou are blamed shall not be thy defect,
For slander's mark° was ever yet the fair.   *target*
The ornament of beauty is suspect,°   *suspicion*
A crow that flies in heaven's sweetest air.
5 So° thou be good, slander doth but approve   *So long as*
Thy worth the greater, being wooed of time;[2]
For canker vice[3] the sweetest buds doth love,
And thou present'st a pure unstainèd prime.°   *youth*
Thou hast passed by the ambush of young days
10 Either not assailed, or victor being charged;

3. Though (falsely) taking pride in her abundance (of offspring?), lives off the interest he earns (from his endowment of beauty).
Sonnet 68
1. This sonnet links with 67.
2. Properly belonging to tombs (wigs were made from the hair of corpses).
Sonnet 69
1. Uttering minimal truth, in the way that enemies

praise.
2. The ground (reason; also, stain) is this: you are becoming low (promiscuous).
Sonnet 70
1. This sonnet links with 69.
2. *slander . . . time*: the gossip merely proves that you're so popular ("wooed of time") that you're worth even more.
3. Slander, like a cankerworm.

Yet this thy praise cannot be so° thy praise   *enough*
To tie up envy, evermore enlarged.°   *forever at large*
  If some suspect of ill masked not thy show,°   *appearance*
  Then thou alone kingdoms of hearts shouldst owe.°   *own*

71

No longer mourn for me when I am dead
Than you shall hear the surly sullen bell
Give warning to the world that I am fled
From this vile world with vilest[1] worms to dwell.
5 Nay, if you read this line, remember not
The hand that writ it; for I love you so
That I in your sweet thoughts would be forgot
If thinking on me then should make you woe.
O, if, I say, you look upon this verse
10 When I perhaps compounded am° with clay,   *am mixed*
Do not so much as my poor name rehearse,°   *repeat; rebury*
But let your love even with my life decay,
  Lest the wise world should look into your moan
  And mock you with me° after I am gone.   *for loving me*

72

O, lest the world should task you to recite
What merit lived in me that you should love,
After my death, dear love, forget me quite;
For you in me can nothing worthy prove—
5 Unless you would devise some virtuous lie
To do more for me than mine own desert,
And hang more praise upon deceasèd I
Than niggard truth would willingly impart.
O, lest your true love may seem false in this,
10 That you for love speak well of me untrue,°   *untruthfully*
My° name be buried where my body is,   *Let my*
And live no more to shame nor me nor you;
  For I am shamed by that which I bring forth,[1]
  And so should you,° to love things nothing worth.   *you be*

73

That time of year thou mayst in me behold
When yellow leaves, or none, or few, do hang
Upon those boughs which shake against the cold,
Bare ruined choirs where late the sweet birds sang.[1]
5 In me thou seest the twilight of such day
As after sunset fadeth in the west,
Which by and by black night doth take away,
Death's second self, that seals up all in rest.
In me thou seest the glowing of such fire
10 That° on the ashes of his youth[2] doth lie   *As*

Sonnet 71
1. Q's "vildest" is an archaic form of "vilest" that may also carry the connotation of "most reviled."
Sonnet 72
1. Presumably alluding to the writer's poems or to his profession as actor and playwright.
Sonnet 73
1. *choirs:* the area in a church where the choir ("sweet birds") sings; gatherings of manuscript "leaves" (line 2), or quires ("quiers" in Q).
2. Perhaps referring to the phoenix, a legendary self-resurrecting bird believed to live in cycles of several centuries, dying in flames and being reborn from the ashes. See also 19.4.

As the death-bed whereon it must expire,
Consumed with that which it was nourished by.[3]
   This thou perceiv'st, which makes thy love more strong,
   To love that° well which thou must leave ere long.   *(the speaker); (life)*

74[1]

But be contented when that fell arrest°   *fearful death*
Without all bail shall carry me away.
My life hath in this line° some interest,°   *verse / legal claim*
Which for memorial still with thee shall stay.
5 When thou reviewest° this, thou dost review   *reread*
The very part° was consecrate to thee.   *part of me that*
The earth can have but earth, which is his due;
My spirit is thine, the better part of me.
So then thou hast but lost the dregs of life,
10 The prey of worms, my body being dead,
The coward conquest of a wretch's knife,[2]
Too base of° thee to be rememberèd.   *by*
The worth of that° is that which it contains,   *(the body)*
And that is this,° and this with thee remains.   *this spirit (his poetry)*

75

So are you to my thoughts as food to life,
Or as sweet-seasoned° showers are to the ground;   *spring*
And for the peace of you° I hold such strife   *you provide*
As 'twixt a miser and his wealth is found:
5 Now proud as an enjoyer, and anon
Doubting the filching age[1] will steal his treasure;
Now counting° best to be with you alone,   *estimating*
Then bettered° that the world may see my pleasure;   *better contented*
Sometime all full with feasting on your sight,
10 And by and by clean° starvèd for a look;   *wholly*
Possessing or pursuing no delight
Save what is had or must from you be took.
   Thus do I pine and surfeit day by day,
   Or° gluttoning on all, or all away.°   *Either / having nothing*

76

Why is my verse so barren of new pride,°   *adornments*
So far from variation or quick° change?   *lively*
Why, with the time,° do I not glance aside   *following the fashion*
To new-found methods and to compounds[1] strange?
5 Why write I still all one, ever the same,
And keep invention in a noted weed,[2]
That every word doth almost tell my name,
Showing their birth and where° they did proceed?   *whence*
O know, sweet love, I always write of you,

---

3. Ironically, the fire is choked ("consumed") by (along with) the ashes, which are the residue of the fuel that the fire previously fed upon ("was nourished by").
Sonnet 74
1. This sonnet links with 73.
2. The cowardly conquest of a wretch such as Death (who was thought to carry a scythe).

Sonnet 75
1. Fearing that these dishonest times.
Sonnet 76
1. *compounds:* stylistic or formal mixtures; compound words; elaborate medicines (with "methods," which also refers to both literary and medical treatments).
2. And keep literary creativity in such familiar clothing.

10 And you and love are still my argument;°   *always my topic*
    So all my best is dressing old words new,
    Spending again what is already spent;
        For as the sun is daily new and old,
        So is my love, still telling what is told.

77[1]

Thy glass° will show thee how thy beauties wear,[2]   *mirror*
Thy dial° how thy precious minutes waste,   *sundial*
The vacant leaves thy mind's imprint° will bear,   *written ideas*
And of this book this learning mayst thou taste:
5   The wrinkles which thy glass will truly show
Of mouthèd° graves will give thee memory;°   *gaping / remind you*
Thou by thy dial's shady stealth° mayst know   *stealing shadow*
Time's thievish progress to eternity;
Look what° thy memory cannot contain   *Whatever*
10 Commit to these waste blanks,° and thou shalt find   *empty pages*
Those children nursed,° delivered from thy brain,   *preserved*
To take a new acquaintance of thy mind.°   *strike you afresh*
    These offices° so oft as thou wilt look   *functions*
    Shall profit thee and much enrich thy book.

78[1]

So oft have I invoked thee for my muse
And found such fair assistance in my verse
As every alien pen hath got my use,[2]
And under thee° their poesy disperse.   *with you as patron*
5   Thine eyes, that taught the dumb on high° to sing   *aloud*
And heavy ignorance aloft to fly,
Have added feathers to the learned's wing[3]
And given grace° a double majesty.   *excellence*
Yet be most proud of that which I compile,°   *write*
10 Whose influence° is thine and born of thee.   *power to move*
In others' works thou dost but mend° the style,   *improve*
And arts° with thy sweet graces gracèd be;   *(their) artistry*
    But thou art all my art, and dost advance
    As high as learning my rude ignorance.

79

Whilst I alone did call upon thy aid
My verse alone had all thy gentle grace;
But now my gracious numbers are decayed,
And my sick muse doth give another place.°   *way to another poet*
5   I grant, sweet love, thy lovely argument[1]
Deserves the travail° of a worthier pen,   *labor*
Yet what of thee thy poet doth invent
He robs thee of, and pays it thee again.
He lends thee virtue, and he stole that word
10 From thy behaviour; beauty doth he give,
And found it in thy cheek: he can afford°   *extend*

Sonnet 77
1. This sonnet appears to have accompanied the gift of a notebook.
2. Last; wear away; "were" (Q's spelling).
Sonnet 78
1. This sonnet begins the rival poet sequence (78–80,

82–86).
2. That every other poet imitates me.
3. Have improved the poetic "flights" of even accomplished poets.
Sonnet 79
1. The subject of your loveliness.

No praise to thee but what in thee doth live.
Then thank him not for that which he doth say,
Since what he owes thee thou thyself dost pay.

80

O, how I faint° when I of you do write,   *get discouraged*
Knowing a better spirit° doth use your name,   *(the rival poet)*
And in the praise thereof spends all his might,
To make me tongue-tied, speaking of your fame!
5   But since your worth, wide as the ocean is,
The humble as° the proudest sail doth bear,   *as well as*
My saucy barque,° inferior far to his,   *impudent boat*
On your broad main° doth wilfully appear.   *waters*
Your shallowest help will hold me up afloat
10 Whilst he upon your soundless° deep doth ride;   *bottomless*
Or, being wrecked, I am a worthless boat,
He of tall building[1] and of goodly pride.°   *magnificence*
    Then if he thrive and I be cast away,
    The worst was this: my love was my decay.

81[1]

Or° I shall live your epitaph to make,   *Either*
Or you survive when I in earth am rotten.
From hence° your memory death cannot take,   *the world; my poetry*
Although in me each part° will be forgotten.   *each of my attributes*
5   Your name from hence° immortal life shall have,   *henceforth; my poetry*
Though I, once gone, to all the world must die.
The earth can yield me but a common grave
When you entombèd in men's eyes shall lie.
Your monument shall be my gentle verse,
10 Which eyes not yet created shall o'er-read,
And tongues to be° your being shall rehearse°   *future tongues / recite*
When all the breathers of this world are dead.
    You still shall live—such virtue° hath my pen—   *power*
    Where breath most breathes, even in° the mouths of men.   *right in*

82

I grant thou wert not married to my muse,
And therefore mayst without attaint o'erlook°   *dishonor read*
The dedicated[1] words which writers° use   *other writers*
Of their fair subject, blessing every book.
5   Thou art as fair in knowledge as in hue,°   *appearance*
Finding thy worth a limit° past my praise,   *region*
And therefore art enforced to seek anew
Some fresher stamp of these time-bettering days.[2]
And do so, love; yet when they have devised
10 What strainèd touches rhetoric can lend,
Thou, truly fair, wert truly sympathized[3]
In true plain words by thy true-telling friend;

Sonnet 80
1. Tall, strong build.
Sonnet 81
1. Except for lines 2–3 and 10–11, any two consecutive lines in this sonnet form a complete sentence.

Sonnet 82
1. Devoted; referring to a prefatory dedication.
2. Some more recent imprint (commendation) of these culturally progressive times.
3. Would be accurately represented.

And their gross painting° might be better used   °cosmetics; flattery
Where cheeks need blood: in thee it is abused.°   °used wrongly

83

I never saw that you did painting° need,   °cosmetics
And therefore to your fair° no painting set.   °beauty
I found—or thought I found—you did exceed
The barren tender° of a poet's debt;   °payment
5 And therefore have I slept in your report:[1]
That° you yourself, being extant, well might show   °So that
How far a modern° quill doth come too short,   °trite; fashionable
Speaking of worth, what worth[2] in you doth grow.
This silence for° my sin you did impute,   °to be
10 Which shall be most my glory, being dumb;
For I impair not beauty, being mute,
When others would give life, and bring a tomb.[3]
   There lives more life in one of your fair eyes
   Than both your poets can in praise devise.

84

Who is it that says most which[1] can say more
Than this rich praise: that you alone are you,[2]
In whose confine immurèd is the store
Which should example where your equal grew?[3]
5 Lean penury within that pen doth dwell
That to his subject lends not some small glory;
But he that writes of you, if he can tell
That you are you, so dignifies his story.
Let him but copy what in you is writ,
10 Not making worse what nature made so clear,°   °purely excellent
And such a counterpart shall fame° his wit,   °copy will make famous
Making his style admirèd everywhere.
   You to your beauteous blessings add a curse,[4]
   Being fond on praise, which makes your praises worse.[5]

85

My tongue-tied muse in manners holds her still°   °tactfully says nothing
While comments of° your praise, richly compiled,   °commentaries in
Reserve thy character° with golden quill   °Hoard up your features
And precious phrase by all the muses filed.°   °polished
5 I think good thoughts whilst other° write good words,   °others
And like unlettered clerk still cry 'Amen'
To every hymn[1] that able spirit affords°   °offers
In polished form of well-refinèd pen.
Hearing you praised I say ''Tis so, 'tis true,'

Sonnet 83
1. Neglected to sing your praises.
2. In speaking of value of the worth that.
3. When others who try to make you live in their writings only end up burying you.
Sonnet 84
1. *Who . . . which:* What hyperbolical enthusiast.
2. The line is a poetical in-joke, echoing a passage in Gervase Markham's *Devoreux* (published 1597) that addresses and praises Penelope Rich, a famous beauty of the Elizabethan court. Like *Devoreux*, Q has "Rich" rather than "rich." See also 85.2.

3. *In . . . grew:* Within whom is contained the stock that would be needed to produce your equal?
4. Personality flaw; vexation (for those who would praise you).
5. Being (too) fond of praise, which makes the praise seem like flattery; being (too) fond of the sort of praise that detracts from you.
Sonnet 85
1. *like . . . hymn:* like an illiterate parish clerk reflexively approve ("cry 'Amen'" after) every poem ("hymn") of praise.

10   And to the most° of praise add something more;   *highest*
        But that is in my thought,° whose love to you,   *unspoken*
        Though words come hindmost, holds his rank before.°   *before all others*
         Then others for the breath of words respect,°   *regard*
         Me for my dumb thoughts, speaking in effect.°   *in reality*

86

Was it the proud full sail of his° great verse   *(a rival poet's)*
Bound for the prize° of all-too-precious you   *pirate's spoils*
That did my ripe thoughts in my brain inhearse,°   *bury*
Making their tomb the womb wherein they grew?
5   Was it his spirit, by spirits taught to write
Above a mortal pitch,° that struck me dead?   *height*
No, neither he nor his compeers[1] by night
Giving him aid my verse astonishèd.°   *made silent*
He nor that affable familiar ghost°   *spirit*
10   Which nightly gulls° him with intelligence,°   *fools / ideas*
As victors, of my silence cannot boast;
I was not sick of any fear from thence.
     But when your countenance filled up[2] his line,
     Then lacked I matter; that enfeebled mine.

87

Farewell—thou art too dear° for my possessing,   *costly*
And like° enough thou know'st thy estimate.°   *it is likely / value*
The charter of thy worth gives thee releasing;[1]
My bonds in thee are all determinate.°   *terminated*
5   For how do I hold thee but by thy granting,
And for that riches where is my deserving?
The cause of this fair gift in me is wanting,
And so my patent back again is swerving.[2]
Thyself thou gav'st, thy own worth then not knowing,
10   Or me to whom thou gav'st it else mistaking;°   *overestimating*
So thy great gift, upon misprision growing,°   *based on error*
Comes home again, on better judgement making.[3]
     Thus have I had thee as a dream doth flatter:°   *creates an illusion*
     In sleep a king, but waking no such matter.

88

When thou shalt be disposed to set me light°   *value me little*
And place my merit in the eye of scorn,
Upon thy side against myself I'll fight,
And prove thee virtuous though thou art forsworn.
5   With mine own weakness being best acquainted,
Upon thy part I can set down a story
Of faults concealed wherein I am attainted,
That thou in losing me shall win much glory;
And I by this will be a gainer too;
10   For bending all my loving thoughts on thee,
The injuries that to myself I do,
Doing thee vantage, double vantage me.

Sonnet 86
1. Colleagues (the "spirits" in line 5).
2. Your features gave subject matter to; your approval made up for any lack in.

Sonnet 87
1. The privilege you derive from your worth releases you from love's bonds.
2. My rights of possession revert to you.
3. *on . . . making:* when you realize your error.

Such is my love, to thee I so belong,
That for thy right myself will bear all wrong.

89

Say that thou didst forsake me for some fault,
And I will comment° upon that offence;   *elaborate*
Speak of my lameness, and I straight will halt,[1]
Against thy reasons making no defence.
Thou canst not, love, disgrace me half so ill,   5
To set a form upon desirèd change,[2]
As I'll myself disgrace, knowing thy will.
I will acquaintance strangle and look strange,[3]
Be absent from thy walks,° and in my tongue   *familiar places*
Thy sweet belovèd name no more shall dwell,   10
Lest I, too much profane, should do it wrong,
And haply° of our old acquaintance tell.   *by chance*
   For thee, against myself I'll vow debate;°   *combat*
   For I must ne'er love him whom thou dost hate.

90[1]

Then hate me when thou wilt, if ever, now,
Now while the world is bent my deeds to cross,°   *foil*
Join with the spite of fortune, make me bow,
And do not drop in for an after-loss.[2]
Ah do not, when my heart hath scaped this sorrow,   5
Come in the rearward of a conquered woe;[3]
Give not a windy night a rainy morrow
To linger out a purposed overthrow.[4]
If thou wilt leave me, do not leave me last,
When other petty griefs have done their spite,   10
But in the onset come; so shall I taste
At first the very worst of fortune's might,
   And other strains° of woe, which now seem woe,   *types; burdens*
   Compared with loss of thee will not seem so.

91

Some glory in their birth, some in their skill,
Some in their wealth, some in their body's force,
Some in their garments (though new-fangled ill),°   *fashionably ugly*
Some in their hawks and hounds, some in their horse,°   *horses*
And every humour hath his° adjunct pleasure   5   *temperament has its*
Wherein it finds a joy above the rest.
But these particulars are not my measure;°   *(of joy)*
All these I better° in one general best.   *exceed*
Thy love is better than high birth to me,
Richer than wealth, prouder than garments' cost,   10
Of more delight than hawks or horses be,
And having thee of all men's pride[1] I boast,

Sonnet 89
1. Talk of my disability (perhaps alluding to the lame meter of line 2), and I at once will limp (stop objecting).
2. To lend justification to the change you seek.
3. I will end our familiarity and act like a stranger.
Sonnet 90
1. This sonnet links with 89.

2. Do not fall upon me to inflict a later disaster.
3. Assault me again after I have overcome my present grief.
4. *To . . . overthrow:* By protracting or delaying your intended assault.
Sonnet 91
1. Of everything in which others take pride.

Wretched in this alone: that thou mayst take
All this away, and me most wretched make.

92[1]

But do thy worst to steal thyself away,
For term of° life thou art assurèd mine,   *the duration of my*
And life no longer than thy love will stay,
For it depends upon that love of thine.
5 Then need I not to fear the worst of wrongs
When in the least of them[2] my life hath end.
I see a better state to me belongs
Than that which on thy humour doth depend.
Thou canst not vex me with inconstant mind,
10 Since that my life on thy revolt doth lie.[3]
O, what a happy title[4] do I find—
Happy to have thy love, happy to die!
    But what's so blessèd fair that fears no blot?
    Thou mayst be false, and yet I know it not.

93[1]

So shall I live supposing thou art true
Like a deceivèd husband; so love's face°   *appearance*
May still seem love to me, though altered new—
Thy looks with me, thy heart in other place.
5 For there can live no hatred in thine eye,
Therefore in that I cannot know thy change.
In many's looks the false heart's history
Is writ in moods and frowns and wrinkles strange,[2]
But heaven in thy creation did decree
10 That in thy face sweet love should ever dwell;
Whate'er thy thoughts or thy heart's workings be,
Thy looks should nothing thence but sweetness tell.
    How like Eve's apple doth thy beauty grow
    If thy sweet virtue answer not thy show![3]

94

They that have power to hurt and will do none,
That do not do the thing they most do show,[1]
Who moving others are themselves as stone,
Unmovèd, cold,° and to temptation slow—   *composed*
5 They rightly° do inherit heaven's graces,   *truly*
And husband nature's riches from expense;[2]
They are the lords and owners of their faces,
Others but stewards° of their excellence.   *hired managers*
The summer's flower is to the summer sweet
10 Though to itself it only live and die,[3]
But if that flower with base infection meet

Sonnet 92
1. This sonnet links with 91.
2. In the slightest sign of your displeasure.
3. Since change in your affections would kill me.
4. What a claim to be considered happy.
Sonnet 93
1. This sonnet links with 92.
2. In signs of anger and frowns and displeased

expressions.
3. Does not correspond to your looks.
Sonnet 94
1. *they most do show:* that their appearance implies.
2. And protect nature's rich endowment from waste.
3. *is . . . die:* emits its sweetness to others even though it lives and dies in apparent isolation (unpollinated: compare 54.5–11).

The basest weed outbraves his dignity;[4]
  For sweetest things turn sourest by their deeds:
  Lilies that fester smell far worse than weeds.[5]

95

How sweet and lovely dost thou make the shame
Which, like a canker° in the fragrant rose,   *cankerworm*
Doth spot the beauty of thy budding name!°   *fame*
O, in what sweets dost thou thy sins enclose!
5 That tongue that tells the story of thy days,
Making lascivious comments on thy sport,°   *amorous adventures*
Cannot dispraise, but in a kind of praise,
Naming thy name, blesses° an ill report.   *makes positive*
O, what a mansion have those vices got
10 Which for their habitation chose out thee,
Where beauty's veil doth cover every blot
And all things turns to fair that eyes can see!
    Take heed, dear heart, of this large privilege:
    The hardest knife ill used doth lose his° edge.   *its*

96

Some say thy fault is youth, some wantonness;° *promiscuity; frivolity*
Some say thy grace is youth and gentle sport.[1]
Both grace and faults are loved of more and less;° *by people of all ranks*
Thou mak'st faults graces that to thee resort.
5 As on the finger of a thronèd queen
The basest jewel will be well esteemed,
So are those errors that in thee are seen
To truths translated° and for true things deemed.   *converted*
How many lambs might the stern° wolf betray   *vicious*
10 If like° a lamb he could his looks translate!   *into*
How many gazers mightst thou lead away
If thou wouldst use the strength of all thy state!°   *power*
    But do not so: I love thee in such sort°   *such a way*
    As, thou being mine, mine is thy good report.[2]

97

How like a winter hath my absence been
From thee, the pleasure of the fleeting year!
What freezings have I felt, what dark days seen,
What old December's bareness everywhere!
5 And yet this time removed° was summer's time,   *away*
The teeming autumn big° with rich increase,   *pregnant*
Bearing the wanton burden of the prime°   *harvest of wanton spring*
Like widowed wombs after their lords' decease.
Yet this abundant issue seemed[1] to me
10 But hope of orphans and unfathered fruit,
For summer and his pleasures wait° on thee,   *attend*
And thou away, the very birds are mute;

---

4. Exceeds the flower in magnificence.
5. This line also occurs in *The Reign of King Edward III*, a play printed anonymously in 1596 and sometimes attributed, in whole or in part, to Shakespeare.

Sonnet 96
1. A gentleman's sexual prerogative.
2. Reputation. The same couplet ends 36.
Sonnet 97
1. Offspring seemed in prospect, before the beloved's absence.

Or if they sing, 'tis with so dull a cheer°   *such a dismal mood*
That leaves look pale, dreading the winter's near.

98

From you have I been absent in the spring
When proud-pied° April, dressed in all his trim,°   *multicolored / finery*
Hath put a spirit of youth in everything,
That heavy Saturn[1] laughed and leapt with him.
5   Yet nor the lays° of birds nor the sweet smell   *not the songs*
Of different flowers° in odour and in hue   *flowers differing*
Could make me any summer's story tell,°   *speak (write) happily*
Or from their proud lap° pluck them where they grew;   *(the ground)*
Nor did I wonder at the lily's white,
10   Nor praise the deep vermilion in the rose.
They were but sweet, but figures° of delight   *merely emblems*
Drawn after you, you pattern of all those;
    Yet seemed it winter still, and, you away,
    As with your shadow I with these did play.[2]

99[1]

The forward° violet thus did I chide: *early*
Sweet thief, whence didst thou steal thy sweet° that smells,   *perfume*
If not from my love's breath? The purple pride°   *beauty*
Which on thy soft cheek for complexion dwells
5   In my love's veins thou hast too grossly° dyed.   *obviously*
The lily I condemnèd for thy hand,[2]
And buds of marjoram[3] had stol'n thy hair;
The roses fearfully on thorns did stand,
One blushing shame, another white despair;
10   A third, nor red nor white, had stol'n of both,°   *(making it pink)*
And to° his robb'ry had annexed thy breath;   *in addition to*
But for his theft in pride of all his growth
A vengeful canker° ate him up to death.   *cankerworm*
    More flowers I noted, yet I none could see
    But sweet° or colour it had stol'n from thee.   *perfume*

100

Where are thou, muse, that thou forget'st so long
To speak of that which gives thee all thy might?
Spend'st thou thy fury[1] on some worthless song,
Dark'ning° thy power to lend base subjects light?   *Debasing*
5   Return, forgetful muse, and straight° redeem   *immediately*
In gentle numbers° time so idly spent;   *noble poetry*
Sing to the ear that doth thy lays esteem
And gives thy pen both skill and argument.°   *substance*
Rise, resty° muse, my love's sweet face survey   *lazy*
10   If° time have any wrinkle graven there.   *To see if*
If any, be a satire to° decay   *satirist of*
And make time's spoils despisèd everywhere.

Sonnet 98
1. The planet Saturn was regarded as cold and slow, exerting a melancholy influence.
2. As if with your image I played with these flowers.
Sonnet 99
1. This sonnet has an extra opening line.

2. For stealing whiteness from your (the beloved's) hand.
3. The herb, sweet of scent and auburn in color.
Sonnet 100
1. Inspiration (the "poet's rage" of 17.11).

Give my love fame faster than time wastes life;
So, thou prevene'st° his scythe and crookèd knife.   *impede*

101[1]

O truant muse, what shall be thy amends
For thy neglect of truth in beauty dyed?
Both truth and beauty on my love depends;
So dost thou too, and therein° dignified.   *therein are you*
5   Make answer, muse. Wilt thou not haply° say   *perhaps*
'Truth needs no colour with his colour fixed,[2]
Beauty no pencil beauty's truth to lay,[3]
But best is best if never intermixed'?°   *(with cosmetics)*
Because he needs no praise wilt thou be dumb?
10 Excuse not silence so, for't lies in thee
To make him much outlive a gilded tomb,
And to be praised of° ages yet to be.   *by*
      Then do thy office,° muse; I teach thee how   *duty*
      To make him seem long° hence as he shows° now.   *a long time / appears*

102

My love is strengthened, though more weak in seeming.°   *appearance*
I love not less, though less the show appear.
That love is merchandized[1] whose rich esteeming°   *appraisal*
The owner's tongue doth publish everywhere.
5   Our love was new and then but in the spring°   *just beginning*
When I was wont to greet it with my lays,
As Philomel[2] in summer's front° doth sing,   *beginning*
And stops her pipe in growth of riper days—
Not that the summer is less pleasant now
10 Than when her mournful hymns did hush the night,
But that wild music burdens[3] every bough,
And sweets grown common lose their dear delight.
      Therefore like her I sometime hold my tongue,
      Because I would not dull° you with my song.   *overfeed*

103

Alack, what poverty my muse brings forth
That, having such a scope to show her pride,[1]
The argument all bare° is of more worth   *subject by itself*
Than when it hath my added praise beside!
5   O blame me not if I no more can write!
Look in your glass° and there appears a face   *mirror*
That overgoes my blunt invention[2] quite,
Dulling° my lines and doing me disgrace.   *(by contrast)*
Were it not sinful then, striving to mend,°   *improve*
10 To mar the subject that before was well?—
For to no other pass° my verses tend   *end*

Sonnet 101
1. This sonnet links with 100.
2. Truth needs no artificial color to be added to his natural coloring.
3. True beauty need apply no (cosmetic) brush.
Sonnet 102
1. (Debased by being) turned into merchandise for sale.
2. Nightingale; with ambiguous hints of the myth of Philomel, whose brother-in-law raped her and ripped out her tongue to ensure her silence. See Book 6 of Ovid's *Metamorphoses*.
3. Loads; provides a musical refrain (probably from many other poets) on.
Sonnet 103
1. Considering that she has such opportunity (in you) to display her skill (her pride in you).
2. That surpasses my dull powers of invention.

Than of your graces and your gifts to tell;
   And more, much more, than in my verse can sit
   Your own glass shows you when you look in it.

104

To me, fair friend, you never can be old;
For as you were when first your eye I eyed,
Such seems your beauty still. Three winters cold
Have from the forests shook three summers' pride;°   *splendor*
5 Three beauteous springs to yellow autumn turned
In process° of the seasons have I seen,   *the progress*
Three April perfumes in three hot Junes burned
Since first I saw you fresh, which yet° are green.   *who still*
Ah yet doth beauty, like a dial hand,
10 Steal from his figure and no pace perceived;[1]
So your sweet hue,° which methinks still doth stand,   *appearance*
Hath motion, and mine eye may be deceived.
   For fear of which, hear this, thou age unbred:°   *future age*
   Ere you were born was beauty's summer dead.

105

Let not my love be called idolatry,
Nor my belovèd as an idol show,
Since all alike my songs and praises be
To one, of one, still° such, and ever so.   *continually*
5 Kind is my love today, tomorrow kind,
Still constant in a wondrous excellence.
Therefore my verse, to constancy confined,
One thing expressing, leaves out difference.°   *diversity (of theme)*
'Fair, kind, and true' is all my argument,
10 'Fair, kind, and true' varying to other words,
And in this change is my invention spent,[1]
Three themes in one, which wonderous scope affords.
   Fair, kind, and true have often lived alone,°   *separately*
   Which three till now never kept seat° in one.   *dwelt permanently*

106[1]

When in the chronicle of wasted° time   *past*
I see descriptions of the fairest wights,°   *people*
And beauty making beautiful old rhyme
In praise of ladies dead and lovely knights;
5 Then in the blazon[2] of sweet beauty's best,
Of hand, of foot, of lip, of eye, of brow,
I see their antique pen would have expressed
Even such a beauty as you master° now.   *possess*
So all their praises are but prophecies
10 Of this our time, all you prefiguring,
And for° they looked but with divining° eyes   *as / prophetic*
They had not skill enough your worth to sing;   *want to*

Sonnet 104
1. *doth . . . perceived*: beauty imperceptibly "steals" (departs stealthily from; robs from) the youthful appearance ("figure") of the beloved as the hand of the watch ("dial") stealthily progresses ("steals") away from the number ("figure") on the watch face.

Sonnet 105
1. And in varying the words alone my inventiveness is expended.
Sonnet 106
1. See "On his Mistress' Beauty" in the Alternative Versions.
2. Poetic catalog of virtues.

For we° which now behold these present days   *even we*
Have eyes to wonder, but lack tongues to praise.

107

Not mine own fears nor the prophetic soul
Of the wide world dreaming on things to come
Can yet the lease° of my true love control,   *allotted term*
Supposed as forfeit to a confined doom.[1]
5 The mortal moon hath her eclipse endured,[2]
And the sad augurs mock their own presage;[3]
Incertainties now crown themselves assured,[4]
And peace proclaims olives of endless age.[5]
Now with the drops[6] of this most balmy time
10 My love looks fresh, and death to me subscribes,°   *submits*
Since spite of him I'll live in this poor rhyme
While he insults° o'er dull and speechless tribes,[7]   *prevails*
     And thou in this shalt find thy monument
     When tyrants' crests and tombs of brass are spent.°   *ruined*

108

What's in the brain that ink may character°   *express*
Which hath not figured° to thee my true spirit?   *shown*
What's new to speak, what now to register,°   *record*
That may express my love or thy dear merit?
5 Nothing, sweet boy; but yet like prayers divine
I must each day say o'er the very same,
Counting no old thing old, thou mine, I thine,
Even as when first I hallowed thy fair name.
So that eternal love in love's fresh case°   *covering*
10 Weighs not° the dust and injury of age,   *Overlooks*
Nor gives to necessary° wrinkles place,°   *inevitable / priority*
But makes antiquity for aye his page,[1]
     Finding the first conceit of love there bred[2]
     Where time and outward form would° show it dead.   *want to*

109

O never say that I was false of heart,
Though absence seemed my flame to qualify°—   *reduce*
As easy might I from myself depart
As from my soul, which in thy breast doth lie.
5 That is my home of love. If I have ranged,
Like him that travels I return again,
Just to the time,° not with the time exchanged,°   *Punctually / changed*
So that myself bring water for my stain.[1]

Sonnet 107
1. Imagined as limited to a finite term.
2. Survived. The line is variously taken to refer to an eclipse of the moon, to an event in the life (or, more likely, to the death in 1603) of Queen Elizabeth (often known as Diana, the moon goddess), or, less probably, to the defeat of the Spanish Armada (1588).
3. And prophets of doom now ridicule their own prophecies.
4. Desired but doubtful possibilities now celebrate their realization; uncertainty is now unavoidable.
5. And peace declares the olive branches that symbolize it to be everlasting. Perhaps a reference to the peace treaty

with Spain signed by King James, who succeeded Elizabeth.
6. Soothing drops of dew, rain, or balm. Balm was used in the coronation ceremony.
7. Over those legions of dead who have no poetic legacy.
Sonnet 108
1. But makes (old) age forever the (youthful) servant to love; perhaps referring to the pages of poetry written when the "sweet boy" (line 5) was still young.
2. The first feeling (poetic expression) of love generated in that place (the beloved; the poem).
Sonnet 109
1. *for my stain:* to cleanse the stain of my absence.

Never believe, though in my nature reigned
10 All frailties that besiege all kinds of blood,°   *disposition*
That it could so preposterously be stained
To leave for° nothing all thy sum of good;   *exchange for*
   For nothing this wide universe I call
   Save thou my rose; in it thou art my all.

110

Alas, 'tis true, I have gone here and there
And made myself a motley to the view,°   *clown to the world*
Gored° mine own thoughts, sold cheap what is most dear,   *Injured*
Made old offences of affections new.[1]
5 Most true it is that I have looked on truth°   *fidelity*
Askance and strangely.° But, by all above,   *coldly*
These blenches° gave my heart another youth,   *alterations*
And worse essays° proved thee my best of love   *experiments*
Now all is done, have what shall have no end;[2]
10 Mine appetite I never more will grind
On newer proof to try[3] an older friend,
A god in love, to whom I am confined.
   Then give me welcome, next my heaven the best,°   *next best to heaven*
   Even to thy pure and most most loving breast.

111

O, for my sake do you with[1] fortune chide,
The guilty goddess of my harmful deeds,
That did not better for my life provide
Than public means which public manners breeds.[2]
5 Thence comes it that my name receives a brand,°   *stigma*
And almost thence my nature is subdued
To what it works in, like the dyer's hand.
Pity me then, and wish I were renewed,°   *cured*
Whilst like a willing patient I will drink
10 Potions of eisel° 'gainst my strong infection;   *medicinal vinegar*
No° bitterness that I will bitter think,   *There is no*
Nor double penance to correct correction.°   *correct me twice over*
   Pity me then, dear friend, and I assure ye
   Even that your pity is enough to cure me.

112[1]

Your love and pity doth th'impression fill°   *eliminates the scar*
Which vulgar° scandal stamped upon my brow;   *public*
For what care I who calls me well or ill,
So you o'er-green my bad, my good allow?[2]
5 You are my all the world, and I must strive
To know my shames and praises from your tongue—
None else to me, nor I to none alive,

Sonnet 110
1. Repeated traditional misbehavior (infidelity)—or offended old friends—in (my treatment of) new attachments.
2. *have . . . end:* take that (my love) which will not expire.
3. *grind . . . try:* sharpen with new experience to test.
Sonnet 111
1. Q has "wish," which gives a more problematic array of alternative meanings.
2. Probably: Than employment as an actor, which requires one to curry favor with the public.
Sonnet 112
1. This sonnet links with 111.
2. So long as you allow new growth to cover what is bad in me, and give credit for what is good.

That my steeled sense or changes, right or wrong.³
In so profound abyss I throw all care

10 Of others' voices that my adder's sense°   deaf ears
To critic and to flatterer stoppèd are.
Mark how with my neglect I do dispense:⁴
   You are so strongly in my purpose bred⁵
   That all the world besides, methinks, they're dead.

113

Since I left you mine eye is in my mind,¹
And that which governs me to go about°   And my real sight
Doth part his° function and is partly blind,   Divides its
Seems seeing, but effectually is out;°   blind

5 For it no form delivers to the heart
Of bird, of flower, or shape which it doth latch.°   catch sight of
Of his quick objects° hath the mind no part,   fleeting impressions
Nor his own vision holds² what it doth catch;
For if it see the rud'st or gentlest° sight,   coarsest or noblest

10 The most sweet favour³ or deformèd'st creature,
The mountain or the sea, the day or night,
The crow or dove, it shapes them to your feature.⁴
   Incapable of more, replete with you,
   My most true mind thus makes mine eye untrue.

114¹

Or whether doth my mind, being crowned with you,²
Drink up the monarch's plague, this flattery,
Or whether shall I say mine eye saith true,
And that your love taught it this alchemy,³

5 To make of monsters and things indigest°   chaotic
Such cherubins° as your sweet self resemble,   angels
Creating every° bad a perfect best   from every
As fast as objects to his beams assemble?⁴
O, 'tis the first, 'tis flatt'ry in my seeing,

10 And my great° mind most kingly drinks it up.   pompous
Mine eye well knows what with his gust is 'greeing,⁵
And to his palate doth prepare the cup.
   If it be poisoned, 'tis the lesser sin
   That mine eye loves it and doth first begin.⁶

115

Those lines that I before have writ do lie,
Even those that said I could not love you dearer;
Yet then my judgement knew no reason why

3. *None . . . wrong*: perhaps, There being no one else to
influence me, and no one else's influence being capable
of positively or negatively affecting my hardened disposi-
tion.
4. How I excuse my neglect (of "other's voices," line 10).
5. Nurtured in all my plans.
Sonnet 113
1. I see with my mind's eye.
2. Nor does the eye's vision hold on to.
3. Face; perhaps Q's "sweet-favor" means "sweet-
favored," or "good-looking."
4. It makes them look like you.

Sonnet 114
1. This sonnet links with 113.
2. Being made a King by having you. "Or whether" intro-
duces alternatives.
3. And that love of you taught my eye how thus to trans-
form things.
4. As fast as objects come before its gaze. (The eye was
thought to emit beams of light).
5. What pleases the mind's appetite.
6. And drinks first (like a King's taster).

My most full flame should afterwards burn clearer.
5 But reckoning time,¹ whose millioned accidents
Creep in 'twixt vows° and change decrees of kings, *(and their performance)*
Tan° sacred beauty, blunt the sharp'st intents, *Darken*
Divert strong minds to th' course of alt'ring things—
Alas, why, fearing of time's tyranny,
10 Might I not then say² 'Now I love you best',
When I was certain o'er° incertainty, *beyond*
Crowning° the present, doubting of the rest? *Exalting*
   Love is a babe; then might I not say so,³
   To give° full growth to that which still doth grow. *Thereby giving*

116

Let me not to the marriage of true minds
Admit impediments.° Love is not love *legal barriers to marriage*
Which alters when it alteration finds,
Or bends with the remover to remove.¹
5 O no, it is an ever fixèd mark²
That looks on tempests and is never shaken;
It is the star to every wand'ring barque,
Whose worth's unknown although his height be taken.³
Love's not time's fool,° though rosy lips and cheeks *plaything*
10 Within his bending sickle's compass⁴ come;
Love alters not with his brief hours and weeks,
But bears it out even to the edge of doom.⁵
   If this be error and upon° me proved, *against*
   I never writ, nor no man ever loved.

117

Accuse me thus: that I have scanted° all *neglected*
Wherein I should your great deserts repay,
Forgot upon your dearest love to call
Whereto all bonds do tie me day by day;
5 That I have frequent° been with unknown minds,° *friendly / strangers*
And given to time your own dear-purchased right;¹
That I have hoisted sail to all the winds
Which should° transport me farthest from your sight. *were likely to*
Book both my wilfulness and errors down,
10 And on just proof surmise accumulate;²
Bring me within the level° of your frown, *aim*
But shoot not at me in your wakened hate,
   Since my appeal says I did strive to prove³
   The constancy and virtue of your love.

Sonnet 115
1. But taking time into account; but time, which settles accounts.
2. Was I not then right to have said.
3. Thus I shouldn't say, "Now I love you best" (line 10).
Sonnet 116
1. Or abandons the relationship when the loved one is unfaithful or has departed or died, or when time ("the remover") alters things for the worse.
2. An unmoving sea mark, such as a lighthouse or a beacon, which provides a constant reference point for sailors.
3. *Whose . . . taken:* The star's (great) intrinsic value can-

not be assessed, although navigators at sea can measure height above the horizon.
4. Within range of time's curved (and hostile) scythe. "Compass" also recalls the imagery of the second quatrain.
5. But endures until the eve of doomsday.
Sonnet 117
1. And wasted idly what should have been your right (rite) because acquired by your great worth and affection (because acquired at your great cost).
2. And pile suspicion on top of your proof.
3. Since my defense is that I was trying to test.

118

Like° as, to make our appetites more keen,   *Just*
With eager° compounds we our palate urge;°   *sharp / stimulate*
As to prevent° our maladies unseen   *forestall*
We sicken to shun sickness when we purge:[1]
5 Even so, being full of your ne'er cloying sweetness,
To bitter sauces did I frame° my feeding,   *adjust*
And, sick of welfare,[2] found a kind of meetness°   *suitability*
To be diseased ere that there was true needing.
Thus policy° in love, t'anticipate   *strategy*
10 The ills that were not, grew to faults assured,
And brought to[3] medicine a healthful state
Which, rank of goodness, would by ill be cured.[4]
    But thence I learn, and find the lesson true:
    Drugs poison him that so° fell sick of you.   *thus; so badly*

119

What potions have I drunk of siren[1] tears
Distilled from limbecks° foul as hell within,   *stills*
Applying° fears to hopes and hopes to fears,   *(as a medicine)*
Still° losing when I saw myself° to win!   *Always / expected*
5 What wretched errors hath my heart committed
Whilst it hath thought itself so blessèd never!
How have mine eyes out of their spheres been fitted[2]
In the distraction° of this madding° fever!   *delirium / fit-inducing*
O benefit of ill! Now I find true
10 That better is by evil still made better,
And ruined love when it is built anew
Grows fairer than at first, more strong, far greater.
    So I return rebuked to my content,
    And gain by ills thrice more than I have spent.

120

That you were once unkind befriends me now,
And for° that sorrow which I then did feel   *because of*
Needs must I under my transgression bow,
Unless my nerves° were brass or hammered steel.   *sinews*
5 For if you were by my unkindness shaken
As I by yours, you've past a hell of time,
And I, a tyrant, have no leisure taken
To weigh° how once I suffered in° your crime.   *contemplate / from*
O that our night of woe[1] might have remembered°   *reminded*
10 My deepest sense how hard true sorrow hits,
And soon to you as you to me then tendered°   *offered*
The humble salve which wounded bosoms fits![2]

Sonnet 118
1. We make ourselves sick with medicine that causes vomiting or bowel movements so as to prevent greater illness.
2. Made ill by good food.
3. Treated with; brought to the need of.
4. Overfull with goodness (health, the beloved), sought to be cured by disease (evil).
Sonnet 119
1. Deceitfully and dangerously alluring. Sirens were

mythological creatures, part bird, part woman, said to lure sailors to their death with their irresistible songs.
2. Been driven convulsively out of their sockets.
Sonnet 120
1. Our earlier time of suffering (caused by the youth's unfaithfulness).
2. The salve of apology that is just the thing for an injured heart.

But that your trespass° now becomes a fee;°   *offense / compensation*
Mine ransoms° yours, and yours must ransom me.   *absolves*

121

'Tis better to be vile than vile esteemed°   *reputed vile*
When not to be receives reproach of being,°   *being so (vile)*
And the just pleasure lost, which is so deemed
Not by our feeling but by others' seeing.[1]
5   For why should others' false adulterate° eyes   *corrupted*
Give salutation to my sportive blood?[2]
Or on my frailties why are frailer spies,
Which in their wills[3] count bad what I think good?
No, I am that I am, and they that level°   *aim*
10 At my abuses reckon up their own.
I may be straight, though they themselves be bevel;°   *crooked*
By their rank° thoughts my deeds must not be shown,°   *foul / measured*
    Unless this general evil they maintain:
    All men are bad and in their badness reign.°   *thrive*

122

Thy gift, thy tables,° are within my brain   *notebook*
Full charactered° with lasting memory,   *written*
Which shall above that idle rank[1] remain
Beyond all date, even to eternity;
5   Or at the least so long as brain and heart
Have faculty° by nature to subsist,   *power*
Till each to razed° oblivion yield his part   *destroying*
Of thee, thy record never can be missed.°   *lost*
That poor retention[2] could not so much hold,
10 Nor need I tallies thy dear love to score;[3]
Therefore to give them° from me was I bold,   *(the "tables")*
To trust those tables° that receive thee more.   *memory*
    To keep an adjunct° to remember thee   *aid*
    Were to import° forgetfulness in me.   *imply*

123

No, time, thou shalt not boast that I do change!
Thy pyramids built up with newer might[1]
To me are nothing° novel, nothing strange,   *in no way*
They are but dressings of a former sight.[2]
5   Our dates° are brief, and therefore we admire   *lives*
What thou dost foist upon us that is old,
And rather make them born to our desire[3]

Sonnet 121
1. *And . . . seeing:* And we are denied the appropriate, innocent pleasure (or, we don't even get to enjoy the sin we've supposedly committed), which is considered sinful not by us but by others.
2. Wink knowingly at my lustful behavior.
3. *Or . . . wills:* Why should my failings be pried into by even more culpable people, who wilfully (who licentiously; who in Will Shakespeare).
Sonnet 122
1. Trivial status (of the "tables" as opposed to "memory").
2. That inadequate container (the "tables"); that faulty

memory.
3. Nor do I need the notched sticks used in calculating sums (to which the "tables" are contemptuously compared) to reckon up your precious love.
Sonnet 123
1. Grand buildings constructed by more modern means. Possibly referring to structures erected in Rome in 1586 or in London in 1603 (for James's coronation), but retaining a sense of almost timeless Egyptian antiquity.
2. Replicas of what's been seen before.
3. And consider them made just for us.

Than think that we before have heard them told.°   *described*
Thy registers° and thee I both defy,   *records*
10 Not wond'ring at the present nor the past;
For thy records and what we see doth lie,
Made more or less by thy continual haste.[4]
   This I do vow, and this shall ever be:
   I will be true despite thy scythe and thee.

124

If my dear love° were but the child of state[1]   *(for you)*
It might for fortune's bastard be unfathered,[2]
As subject to time's love or to time's hate,
Weeds among weeds or flowers with flowers gathered.[3]
5 No, it was builded far from accident;°   *chance*
It suffers° not in smiling pomp, nor falls   *changes*
Under the blow of thrallèd° discontent   *captive*
Whereto th'inviting time our fashion calls.[4]
It fears not policy,° that heretic   *expediency*
10 Which works on leases of short-numbered hours,°   *short-term contracts*
But all alone stands hugely politic,°   *prudent*
That it nor° grows with heat° nor drowns with showers.   *neither / prosperity*
   To this I witness call the fools of time,
   Which die for goodness, who have lived for crime.[5]

125

Were't aught to me I bore the canopy,[1]
With my extern° the outward honouring,   *exterior action*
Or laid great bases for eternity[2]
Which proves more short than waste° or ruining?   *decay*
5 Have I not seen dwellers on form and favour[3]
Lose all and more by paying too much rent,°   *overdoing homage*
For compound sweet forgoing simple savour,[4]
Pitiful thrivers in their gazing spent?[5]
No, let me be obsequious° in thy heart,   *dutiful*
10 And take thou my oblation,° poor but free,°   *offering / freely given*
Which is not mixed with seconds,[6] knows no art°   *artifice*
But mutual render,° only me for thee.   *exchange*
   Hence, thou suborned informer![7] A true soul
   When most impeached° stands least in thy control.   *accused*

---

4. Raised and destroyed by time's swift passage; made to seem more or less majestic by virtue of newness or antiquity and the tastes of the times.
Sonnet 124
1. Were simply the result of circumstances; of your high position.
2. It might be disinherited as a passing fancy, a product of fortune (chance, wealth).
3. As . . . gathered: Regarded as useless or valuable as time and fortune decide.
4. To which ("pomp" and "discontent") we are driven by the latest trend ("fashion").
5. To . . . crime: I call as witness those playthings of time

who, having lived wicked lives, reform or repent at death.
Sonnet 125
1. Would I care if I enhanced my status by carrying a ceremonial canopy for a royal person?
2. Laid foundations for eternal monuments.
3. Seen those who depend (linger) on ceremony and appearance.
4. For obsequious praise giving up plain candor.
5. Pitiful in their empty achievements, ruined by love of show.
6. The second-rate.
7. Paid spy: jealousy or the detractor whose charges the poem answers.

126[1]

O thou my lovely boy, who in thy power
Dost hold time's fickle glass,[2] his sickle-hour;[3]
Who hast by waning grown,[4] and therein show'st
Thy lovers withering as thy sweet self grow'st—
5 If nature, sovereign mistress over wrack,°   *decay*
As thou goest onwards still° will pluck thee back,   *constantly*
She keeps thee to this purpose: that her skill
May time disgrace, and wretched minutes kill.
Yet fear her, O thou minion° of her pleasure!   *darling*
10 She may detain but not still keep her treasure.
    Her audit,° though delayed, answered° must be,   *debt (to time) / paid*
    And her quietus° is to render° thee.   *settlement / relinquish*

127[1]

In the old age° black was not counted fair,[2]   *old days*
Or if it were, it bore not beauty's name;
But now is black beauty's successive heir,°   *heir by succession*
And beauty slandered with a bastard shame:[3]
5 For since each hand hath put on° nature's power,   *usurped*
Fairing° the foul with art's false borrowed face,   *Beautifying*
Sweet beauty hath no name, no holy bower,
But is profaned, if not lives in disgrace.
Therefore my mistress' eyes are raven-black,
10 Her brow so suited,[4] and they mourners seem
At such who, not born fair, no beauty lack,
Sland'ring creation with a false esteem.[5]
    Yet so° they mourn, becoming of° their woe,   *in such a way / adorning*
    That every tongue says beauty should look so.

128

How oft, when thou, my music, music play'st
Upon that blessèd wood whose motion° sounds   *mechanism*
With thy sweet fingers when thou gently sway'st°   *govern*
The wiry concord that mine ear confounds,°   *amazes (with delight)*
5 Do I envy those jacks[1] that nimble leap
To kiss the tender inward of thy hand
Whilst my poor lips, which should that harvest reap,
At the wood's boldness by thee blushing stand!
To be so tickled they would change their state
10 And situation with those dancing chips

Sonnet 126
1. This "sonnet" or envoi, of six couplets, concludes the part of the sequence apparently addressed to the youth and formally signals a change in tone and subject matter in the remaining sonnets.
2. Capricious, treacherous hourglass (?); mirror showing changing images (?).
3. Reaping time. "Sickle-hour" emends Q's "sickle, hower," which may be an error for "sickle o'er." A familiar emblem for time placed the hourglass below and the sickle above.
4. Become more beautiful with age. As the sand in the top half of an hourglass wanes, the sand in the bottom part grows.
Sonnet 127
1. Sonnets 127–52 have been traditionally known as the "dark lady" group, although their subject matter is not uniform and their object is only once called "dark" (147.14)

and never a "lady." She is referred to as the poet's "mistress" (127.9; 130.1, 8, 12), however, and often described as "black" (127.1, 3, 9; 130.4; 131.12, 13; 132.3, 13; 147.14). The celebration of black beauty goes back to the biblical Song of Songs, 1:4: "I am blacke . . . but comelie." See the Introduction.
2. Beautiful; light-colored.
3. And (fair) beauty accused of illegitimacy (by use of cosmetics).
4. Her brow dressed (matched) in an eyebrow black like her eyes (and for the same reason).
5. *At . . . esteem:* Because of those who, not being fair, make up for it with cosmetics, so that even natural beauty is presumed artificial.
Sonnet 128
1. Keys of the virginal, a harpsichordlike instrument; fellows.

O'er whom thy fingers walk with gentle gait,
Making dead wood more blessed than living lips.
 Since saucy° jacks so happy are in this,   *impudent*
 Give them thy fingers, me thy lips to kiss.

129

Th'expense of spirit in a waste of shame
Is lust in action;[1] and till action, lust
Is perjured, murd'rous, bloody, full of blame,
Savage, extreme, rude,° cruel, not to trust,°   *harsh / be trusted*
5 Enjoyed no sooner but despisèd straight,°   *immediately*
Past reason° hunted, and no sooner had   *Madly*
Past reason hated as a swallowed bait
On purpose laid to make the taker mad;
Mad in pursuit and in possession so,°   *(mad)*
10 Had, having, and in quest to have, extreme;
A bliss in proof and proved,[2] a very woe;
Before, a joy proposed; behind, a dream.
 All this the world well knows, yet none knows well
 To shun the heaven that leads men to this hell.

130

My mistress' eyes are nothing like the sun;
Coral is far more red than her lips' red.
If snow be white, why then her breasts are dun;°   *grayish brown*
If hairs be wires,[1] black wires grow on her head.
5 I have seen roses damasked,° red and white,   *dappled*
But no such roses see I in her cheeks;
And in some perfumes is there more delight
Than in the breath that from my mistress reeks.°   *issues; smells*
I love to hear her speak, yet well I know
10 That music hath a far more pleasing sound.
I grant I never saw a goddess go:°   *walk*
My mistress when she walks treads on the ground.
 And yet, by heaven, I think my love as rare
 As any she belied with false compare.[2]

131

Thou art as tyrannous so as thou art[1]
As those whose beauties proudly make them cruel,
For well thou know'st to my dear° doting heart   *fond(ly)*
Thou art the fairest and most precious jewel.
5 Yet, in good faith, some say that thee behold
Thy face hath not the power to make love groan.
To say they err I dare not be so bold,
Although I swear it to myself alone;
And, to be sure° that is not false I swear,   *for proof; surely*
10 A thousand groans but thinking on° thy face   *just thinking about*
One on another's neck° do witness bear   *In quick succession*

Sonnet 129
1. *Th'expense . . . action:* The expenditure of vital energy (semen) in a shameful waste (waist) is consummated lust.
2. *in proof:* while being experienced. *proved:* having been experienced.
Sonnet 130
1. Elizabethan poets often compared women's hair to

golden wires.
2. As any woman misrepresented by false comparison.
Sonnet 131
1. As cruel as you are dark (hence not conventionally beautiful).

Thy black° is fairest in my judgment's place.[2]   *dark appearance*
  In nothing art thou black° save in thy deeds,   *ugly*
  And thence this slander,[3] as I think, proceeds.

132

Thine eyes I love, and they, as° pitying me—   *as if*
Knowing thy heart torment° me with disdain—   *to torment*
Have put on black, and loving mourners be,
Looking with pretty ruth° upon my pain;   *pity*
5 And truly, not the morning sun of heaven
Better becomes° the gray cheeks° of the east,   *beautifies / clouds*
Nor that full star that ushers in the even°   *(Venus, the evening star)*
Doth° half that glory to the sober west,   *Imparts*
As those two mourning° eyes become thy face.   *(pun on "morning")*
10 O, let it then as well beseem° thy heart   *become*
To mourn for me, since mourning doth thee grace,
And suit thy pity like in every part.[1]
    Then will I swear beauty herself is black,
    And all they foul° that thy complexion lack.   *ugly*

133

Beshrew° that heart that makes my heart to groan   *Curse (a mild term)*
For that deep wound it gives my friend and me!
Is't not enough to torture me alone,
But slave to slavery° my sweet'st friend must be?   *utterly enslaved*
5 Me from myself thy cruel eye hath taken,
And my next self thou harder hast engrossed.[1]
Of him, myself, and thee I am forsaken—
A torment thrice threefold thus to be crossed.°   *afflicted*
Prison° my heart in thy steel bosom's ward,°   *Imprison / cell*
10 But then my friend's heart let my poor heart bail;
Whoe'er keeps° me, let my heart be his guard;[2]   *guards*
Thou canst not then use rigour° in my jail.   *severity*
    And yet thou wilt; for I, being pent° in thee,   *locked up*
    Perforce am thine, and° all that is in me.   *as is*

134[1]

So, now° I have confessed that he is thine,   *now that*
And I myself am mortgaged to thy will,°   *intent; sexual desire*
Myself I'll forfeit, so that other mine[2]
Thou wilt restore to be my comfort still.
5 But thou wilt not, nor he will not° be free,   *doesn't want to*
For thou art covetous, and he is kind.
He learned but surety-like° to write° for me   *as guarantor / sign*
Under that bond° that him as fast[3] doth bind.   *(of infatuation)*
The statute[4] of thy beauty thou wilt take,
10 Thou usurer that putt'st forth all to use,°   *at interest; for sex*
And sue a friend came° debtor for my sake;   *who became*

2. In my opinion.
3. See line 6 for "this slander."
Sonnet 132
1. And dress your pity similarly, in heart as well as eyes.
Sonnet 133
1. And my second self, or closest friend, you have even
more cruelly monopolized.

2. My friend's prison.
Sonnet 134
1. This sonnet links with 133.
2. So long as my other self.
3. As firmly as myself.
4. The total guaranteed by the bond.

So him I lose through my unkind abuse.[5]
   Him have I lost; thou hast both him and me;
   He pays the whole,° and yet am I not free.   *(pun on "hole")*

135[1]

Whoever hath her wish, thou hast thy Will,
And Will to boot,° and Will in overplus.   *in addition*
More than enough am I that vex thee still,°   *always (by wooing)*
To thy sweet will making addition thus.
5 Wilt thou, whose will is large and spacious,
Not once vouchsafe to hide my will in thine?
Shall will in others° seem right gracious,   *others' wills*
And in my will no fair acceptance shine?[2]
The sea, all water, yet receives rain still,
10 And in abundance addeth to his° store;   *its*
So thou, being rich in Will, add to thy Will
One will of mine to make thy large Will more.
   Let no unkind no fair beseechers kill;[3]
   Think all but one,° and me in that one Will.   *one suitor*

136[1]

If thy soul check° thee that I come so near,[2]   *chide*
Swear to thy blind soul that I was thy Will,[3]
And will, thy soul knows, is admitted there;
Thus far for love my love-suit, sweet, fulfil.°   *grant*
5 Will will fulfill the treasure° of thy love,   *fill up the treasury*
Ay, fill it full with wills, and my will one.°   *one of them*
In things of great receipt° with ease we prove   *volume*
Among a number one is reckoned none.[4]
Then in the number let me pass untold,°   *uncounted*
10 Though in thy store's account° I one must be;   *tally (of lovers)*
For nothing hold me, so it please thee hold
That nothing me a something, sweet, to thee.[5]
   Make but my name thy love,[6] and love that still,°   *always*
   And then thou lov'st me for my name is Will.

137

Thou blind fool love, what dost thou to mine eyes
That they behold and see not what they see?
They know what beauty is, see where it lies,
Yet what the best is take the worst to be.[1]
5 If eyes corrupt° by over-partial° looks   *corrupted / overly doting*

---

5. Through your ill treatment of me; through my ill-treatment of the youth.
Sonnet 135
1. This sonnet, as well as 136, 143, and "A Lover's Complaint," lines 126–33, puns elaborately on different senses of "will": wishes, sexual desire, futurity, testament, the name "Will" (applied to one or more persons, including Shakespeare, and capitalized and sometimes italicized in Q), and the male and female sexual organs. See also 57.13 and note.
2. And my will not be greeted with a kind reception.
3. Let no unkindness of yours kill any of your worthy suitors.

Sonnet 136
1. This sonnet links with 135.
2. I am so forthright; I am so physically close.
3. See sonnet 135, note 1.
4. Proverbially, one is no number.
5. *For . . . thee:* Think me worthless so long as, my darling, you treasure worthless me. Q's punctuation, "something sweet to thee," emphasizes the sexual implications.
6. Love only my name, "Will"; that is, act on your desire.
Sonnet 137
1. Yet take the worst to be the best.

Be anchored in the bay where all men ride,[2]
Why of eyes' falsehood hast thou forgèd hooks
Whereto the judgement of my heart is tied?
Why should my heart think that a several plot°   *private land*
10   Which my heart knows the wide world's common place?[3]—
Or° mine eyes, seeing this, say this is not,   *Or why should*
To put fair truth upon so foul a face?
    In things right true my heart and eyes have erred,
    And to this false plague[4] are they now transferred.

138[1]

When my love swears that she is made of truth
I do believe her though I know she lies,
That° she might think me some untutored youth   *So that*
Unlearnèd in the world's false subtleties.
5   Thus vainly° thinking that she thinks me young,   *in vain; with vanity*
Although she knows my days are past the best,
Simply I credit[2] her false-speaking tongue;
On both sides thus is simple truth suppressed.
But wherefore says she not she is unjust,°   *unfaithful*
10   And wherefore say not I that I am old?
O, love's best habit is in seeming trust,[3]
And age in love loves not to have years told.°   *counted*
    Therefore I lie° with her, and she with me,   *tell lies; lie down*
    And in our faults by lies we flattered be.

139

O, call° not me to justify° the wrong   *ask / approve*
That thy unkindness° lays upon my heart.   *infidelity*
Wound me not with thine eye[1] but with thy tongue;
Use power with power,[2] and slay me not by art.°   *by deceit*
5   Tell me thou lov'st elsewhere, but in my sight,
Dear heart, forbear to glance thine eye aside.
What° need'st thou wound with cunning when thy might   *Why*
Is more than my o'erpressed defence can bide?°   *endure*
Let me excuse thee: 'Ah, my love well knows
10   Her pretty looks have been mine enemies,
And therefore from my face she turns my foes
That they elsewhere might dart their injuries.'
    Yet do not so; but since I am near slain,
    Kill me outright with looks, and rid° my pain.   *put an end to*

140

Be wise as thou art cruel; do not press
My tongue-tied patience with too much disdain,
Lest sorrow lend me words, and words express

---

2. Harbor for general use (suggesting a promiscuous woman).
3. *the wide . . . place*: common land, open to all (suggesting promiscuity); a commonplace known by all.
4. This plague of false perception; this deceitful woman.
Sonnet 138
1. Another version of this sonnet appears in *The Passionate Pilgrim*. See the Textual Note and the Alternative Ver-

sions.
2. Naively (foolishly; giving the appearance of folly) I (pretend to) believe.
3. Love is best dressed in apparent fidelity (apparent trust).
Sonnet 139
1. By looking elsewhere, at other men (see line 6).
2. Use power frankly; fairly.

The manner of my pity-wanting[1] pain.
5   If I might teach thee wit,° better it were,   *wisdom*
    Though not to love, yet, love, to tell me so—
    As testy sick men when their deaths be near
    No news but health from their physicians know.°   *learn*
    For if I should despair I should grow mad,
10   And in my madness might speak ill of thee.
    Now this ill-wresting world[2] is grown so bad
    Mad slanderers by mad ears believèd be.
      That I may not be so, nor thou belied,°   *maligned*
      Bear thine eyes straight,[3] though thy proud heart go wide.°   *astray*

141

In faith, I do not love thee with mine eyes,
For they in thee a thousand errors note;
But 'tis my heart that loves what they despise,
Who in despite of view° is pleased to dote.   *despite what it sees*
5   Nor are mine ears with thy tongue's tune delighted,
    Nor tender feeling to base touches prone;[1]
    Nor taste nor smell desire to be invited
    To any sensual feast with thee alone;
    But my five wits[2] nor my five senses can
10   Dissuade one foolish heart from serving thee,
    Who leaves unswayed the likeness of a man.[3]
    Thy proud heart's slave and vassal-wretch to be.
      Only my plague thus far° I count my gain: *to this extent*
      That she that makes me sin awards me pain.[4]

142[1]

Love is my sin, and thy dear virtue hate,
Hate of my sin grounded on sinful loving.[2]
O, but with mine compare thou thine own state,
And thou shalt find it° merits not reproving;   *(my state)*
5   Or if it do, not from those lips of thine
    That have profaned their scarlet ornaments[3]
    And sealed[4] false bonds of love as oft as mine,
    Robbed others' beds' revenues of their rents.[5]
    Be it lawful° I love thee as thou lov'st those   *let it be lawful that*
10   Whom thine eyes woo as mine importune thee.
    Root pity in thy heart, that when it grows
    Thy pity may deserve to pitied be.°   *make you pitiable*
      If thou dost seek to have what thou dost hide,°   *(pity)*
      By self example mayst thou be denied!

Sonnet 140
1. Unpitied; desiring pity; pitiable.
2. Now this world, that tends to interpret in the worst light.
3. Keep looking only at me (see 139).
Sonnet 141
1. Nor is my keen sense of touch susceptible to "base" sexual contact.
2. Mental faculties (common sense, imagination, fancy, judgment, memory).
3. Which (the heart, serving you) leaves without a commander the mere semblance of a man.
4. By making me sin, she causes me to suffer punitive penance, which will reduce my sufferings after death.

Sonnet 142
1. This sonnet links with 141.
2. *Love . . . loving*: My only sin is love, and your most valuable virtue is hatred, hatred of my sin in loving you (but also, your most valuable virtue is the haughty rejection of my wooing) based on (your) immoral sexual affairs.
3. Lips, which are scarlet, like a cardinal's robe.
4. "Sealed" with a kiss: comparing the mistress's lips to the red wax used to seal official documents.
5. Stolen the sexual and emotional intimacy ("rents" paid by a tenant) from others' marriages by committing adultery, thus reducing the possibility that these marriages will result in children ("revenues," estates that yield income).

143

Lo, as a care-full° housewife runs to catch   *busy*
One of her feathered creatures broke away,
Sets down her babe and makes all swift dispatch°   *hurries*
In pursuit of the thing she would have stay,
5 Whilst her neglected child holds her in chase,
Cries to catch her whose busy care is bent
To follow that which flies before her face,
Not prizing° her poor infant's discontent: *regarding*
So runn'st thou after that which flies from thee,
10 Whilst I, thy babe, chase thee afar behind;
But if thou catch thy hope, turn back to me
And play the mother's part: kiss me, be kind.
    So will I pray that thou mayst have thy Will[1]
    If thou turn back and my loud crying still.

144[1]

Two loves I have, of comfort and despair,
Which like two spirits do suggest° me still.   *entice*
The better angel is a man right fair,
The worser spirit a woman coloured ill.°   *darkly*
5 To win me soon to hell my female evil
Tempteth my better angel from my side,
And would corrupt my saint to be a devil,
Wooing his purity with her foul pride;
And whether that my angel be turned fiend
10 Suspect I may, yet not directly tell;
But being both from me, both to each friend,[2]
I guess one angel in another's hell.[3]
    Yet this shall I ne'er know, but live in doubt
    Till my bad angel fire my good one out.[4]

145[1]

Those lips that love's own hand did make
Breathed forth the sound that said 'I hate'
To me that languished for her sake;
But when she saw my woeful state,
5 Straight in her heart did mercy come,
Chiding that tongue that ever sweet
Was used in giving gentle doom,°   *judgment*
And taught it thus anew to greet:
'I hate' she altered with an end
10 That followed it as gentle day
Doth follow night who, like a fiend,
From heaven to hell is flown away.
    'I hate' from hate away she threw,[2]
    And saved my life, saying 'not you.'

Sonnet 143
1. A pun; see sonnet 135, note 1.
Sonnet 144
1. Another version of this sonnet appears in *The Passionate Pilgrim*. See Textual Note and Alternative Versions.
2. Both away from me and lovers to one another.
3. Each torments the other; they are in the "hell," or middle den, of a (sexual) game called barley-break; the man occupies the sex organ ("hell") of the woman.
4. Until my bad angel expels my good one, who has become an animal to be smoked out of a burrow; until my bad angel infects my good one with venereal disease; until bad money ("angel" = gold coin) drives out good.
Sonnet 145
1. Unlike the other sonnets, which are in iambic pentameter, 145 is composed of eight-syllable (iambic tetrameter) lines.
2. She converted the normal meaning of the phrase "I hate" away from "hate." A pun on "hate away" and "(Anne) Hathaway," Shakespeare's wife, is possible.

146

Poor soul, the centre of my sinful earth,
[   ] these rebel powers that thee array;[1]
Why dost thou pine within and suffer dearth,
Painting thy outward walls so costly gay?
5 Why so large cost, having so short a lease,
Dost thou upon thy fading mansion° spend?   *(the body)*
Shall worms, inheritors of this excess,
Eat up thy charge?° Is this thy body's end?   *expense*
Then, soul, live thou upon thy servant's° loss,   *(the body's)*
10 And let that pine to aggravate thy store.[2]
Buy terms divine° in selling hours of dross;° *eternal life / waste*
Within be fed, without be rich no more.
    So shalt thou feed on death, that feeds on men,
    And death once dead, there's no more dying then.

147

My love is as a fever, longing still°   *continually*
For that which longer nurseth° the disease,   *nourishes*
Feeding on that which doth preserve° the ill,   *prolong*
Th'uncertain° sickly appetite to please.   *capricious*
5 My reason, the physician to my love,
Angry that his prescriptions are not kept,
Hath left me, and I desperate now approve
Desire is death, which physic did except.[1]
Past cure I am, now reason is past care,[2]
10 And frantic mad with evermore° unrest.   *constant*
My thoughts and my discourse as madmen's are,
At random from° the truth vainly° expressed; *unconnected to / idly*
    For I have sworn thee fair, and thought thee bright,
    Who art as black as hell, as dark as night.

148

O me, what eyes hath love put in my head,
Which have no correspondence with true sight!
Or if they have, where is my judgement fled,
That censures falsely[1] what they see aright?
5 If that be fair whereon my false eyes dote,
What means the world to say it is not so?
If it be not, then love doth well denote[2]
Love's eye is not so true as all men's. No,[3]
How can it, O, how can love's eye be true,
10 That is so vexed with watching° and with tears? *staying awake*

Sonnet 146
1. This rebellious body in which you are clothed. At the beginning of the line, Q repeats "My sinful earth" from the previous line. There is no way of discovering what Shakespeare wrote; among the guesses are "Starved by," "Foiled by," "Spoiled by," and "Feeding."
2. And let the body dwindle to add to your wealth.

Sonnet 147
1. *now . . . except:* now discover that desire, which rejected medicine, is fatal.
2. Medical care: inverting the proverb "Past cure, past

care" (don't worry about what you can't control). In the proverb, you don't care because you can't cure; here, because you don't care, you can't cure.

Sonnet 148
1. That judges inaccurately (dishonestly). "False" (line 5) has similar meanings.
2. Then my self-delusion in love proves that.
3. Not so true as all other men's eye. On the contrary. Q's "all men's, no" is often emended to "all men's 'No,'" suggesting a pun on "eye/aye" (yes).

No marvel then though I° mistake my view: *that I (eye)*
The sun itself sees not till heaven clears.
  O cunning love, with tears thou keep'st me blind
  Lest eyes, well seeing, thy foul faults should find!

149

Canst thou, O cruel, say I love thee not
When I against myself with thee partake?°   *take sides*
Do I not think on thee when I forgot
Am of myself, all-tyrant,[1] for thy sake?
5 Who hateth thee that I do call my friend?
On whom frown'st thou that I do fawn upon?
Nay, if thou lour'st° on me, do I not spend°   *scowl / wreak*
Revenge upon myself with present moan?°   *instant anguish*
What merit do I in myself respect°   *value; note*
10 That is so proud thy service to despise,[2]
When all my best° doth worship thy defect,°   *best qualities / flaws*
Commanded by the motion of thine eyes?
  But, love, hate on; for now I know thy mind.
  Those that can see thou lov'st, and I am blind.[3]

150

O, from what power hast thou this powerful might
With insufficiency° my heart to sway,   *By your flaws*
To make me give the lie to my true sight
And swear that brightness doth not grace the day?[1]
5 Whence hast thou this becoming of things ill,[2]
That in the very refuse of thy deeds°   *your basest behavior*
There is such strength and warrantise° of skill   *guarantee*
That in my mind thy worst all best exceeds?
Who taught thee how to make me love thee more
10 The more I hear and see just cause of hate?
O, though I love what others do abhor,
With others thou shouldst not abhor my state.
  If thy unworthiness raised love in me,
  More worthy I to be beloved of thee.

151

Love is too young° to know what conscience is,   *(Cupid being a boy)*
Yet who knows not conscience[1] is born of love?
Then, gentle cheater, urge° not my amiss,°   *stress / fault*
Lest guilty of my faults thy sweet self prove.
5 For, thou betraying me, I do betray
My nobler part° to my gross body's treason.   *soul*
My soul doth tell my body that he may
Triumph in love; flesh stays no farther reason,[2]

Sonnet 149
1. *when . . . all-tyrant:* when I tyrannically neglect myself.
2. So proud as to scorn to serve you.
3. You love those who see you accurately and thus admire you, but I am blinded (by love and thus, from your point of view, unworthy of being loved). The first clause may have the opposite sense, however: you love those who see your defects well enough not to love you.
Sonnet 150
1. *To . . . day:* the speaker is so blindly in love that he finds beauty only in the blackness he associates with his mistress.
2. This capacity to render the ugly attractive.
Sonnet 151
1. Moral sense; carnal knowledge.
2. Flesh, specifically the sexual organ, needs no further encouragement.

10 But rising at thy name doth point out thee
    As his triumphant prize. Proud of this pride,[3]
    He is contented thy poor drudge to be,
    To stand° in thy affairs, fall by thy side.   *assist; be erect*
        No want of conscience hold it that I call
        Her 'love' for whose dear love I rise and fall.

152

    In loving thee thou know'st I am forsworn,[1]
    But thou art twice forsworn to me love swearing°   *in swearing love to me*
    In act thy bed-vow° broke, and new faith torn   *to husband (or lover)*
5   In vowing new hate after new love bearing.[2]
    But why of two oaths' breach do I accuse thee
    When I break twenty? I am perjured most,
    For all my vows are oaths but to misuse° thee,   *deceive*
    And all my honest faith in thee is lost.
10 For I have sworn deep oaths of thy deep kindness,
    Oaths of thy love, thy truth, thy constancy,
    And to enlighten thee gave eyes to blindness,[3]
    Or made them swear against the thing they see.
        For I have sworn thee fair—more perjured eye°   *(punning on "I")*
        To swear against the truth so foul a lie.

153[1]

    Cupid laid by his brand° and fell asleep.   *torch*
    A maid of Dian's[2] this advantage found,°   *seized*
    And his love-kindling fire did quickly steep
5   In a cold valley-fountain of that ground,
    Which borrowed from this holy fire of love
    A dateless° lively heat, still° to endure,   *An endless / always*
    And grew a seething bath which yet men prove
    Against strange maladies a sovereign cure.[3]
10 But at my mistress' eye love's brand new fired,°   *being newly lit*
    The boy for trial° needs would touch my breast.   *to test it*
    I, sick withal,° the help of bath desired,   *from it*
    And thither hied, a sad distempered° guest,   *seriously ill*
        But found no cure; the bath for my help lies
        Where Cupid got new fire: my mistress' eyes.

3. Swelling with pride (and lust).
Sonnet 152
1. Forsworn presumably in breaking loving vows—perhaps to his wife, to the youth to whom he promised unswerving devotion in earlier sonnets, or to both.
2. *new faith . . . bearing*: the "new faith" followed by "new hate" may be addressed either to the speaker's young friend or to the speaker himself.
3. And to make you fair (give you insight), I looked blindly on your failings (pretended to see what I couldn't).

Sonnet 153
1. This and the following sonnet derive indirectly from classical fifth-century Greek epigrams.
2. *Diana*, goddess of chastity.
3. *And grew . . . cure*: And became a boiling-hot medicinal bath (used, among other purposes, for the treatment of venereal disease), which men still find to be an outstanding remedy for foreign illnesses (venereal diseases were associated with foreigners). There may be an allusion here and in 154 to the town of Bath, which became a famous health spa in the eighteenth century.

154[1]

The little love-god lying once asleep
Laid by his side his heart-inflaming brand,°   *torch*
Whilst many nymphs that vowed chaste life to keep
Came tripping by; but in her maiden hand
The fairest votary took up that fire
Which many legions of true hearts had warmed,
And so the general° of hot desire   *commander (Cupid)*
Was sleeping by a virgin hand disarmed.
This brand she quenchèd in a cool well by,°   *close by*
Which from love's fire took heat perpetual,
Growing a bath and healthful remedy
For men diseased; but I, my mistress' thrall,°   *slave*
Came there for cure; and this° by that I prove: *the following*
Love's fire heats water, water cools not love.

Sonnet 154
1. This sonnet varies the topic of 153.

Alternative Versions

Each of the four sonnets below exists in an alternative version. The text on top is the version as it appeared in the 1609 Quarto. *"Spes Altera"* and "On his Mistress' Beauty" derive from seventeenth-century manuscripts. The alternative versions of sonnets 138 and 144 are from *The Passionate Pilgrim* (1599).

2

When forty winters shall besiege thy brow
And dig deep trenches in thy beauty's field,
Thy youth's proud livery, so gazed on now,
Will be a tattered weed, of small worth held.
5 Then being asked where all thy beauty lies,
Where all the treasure of thy lusty days,
To say within thine own deep-sunken eyes
Were an all-eating shame and thriftless praise.
How much more praise deserved thy beauty's use
10 If thou couldst answer 'This fair child of mine
Shall sum my count, and make my old excuse',
Proving his beauty by succession thine.
    This were to be new made when thou art old,
    And see thy blood warm when thou feel'st it cold.

Spes Altera°   *Another Hope*

When forty winters shall besiege thy brow
And trench deep furrows in that lovely field,
Thy youth's fair liv'ry, so accounted° now,   *esteemed*
Shall be like rotten weeds of no worth held.
5 Then being asked where all thy beauty lies,
Where all the lustre of thy youthful days,
To say 'Within these hollow sunken eyes'
Were an all-eaten truth[1] and worthless praise.
O how much better were thy beauty's use
10 If thou couldst say 'This pretty child of mine
Saves my account[2] and makes my old excuse',
Making his beauty by succession thine.
    This were to be new born when thou art old,
    And see thy blood warm when thou feel'st it cold.

———

106

When in the chronicle of wasted time
I see description of the fairest wights,
And beauty making beautiful old rhyme
In praise of ladies dead and lovely knights;
5 Then in the blazon of sweet beauty's best,
Of hand, of foot, of lip, of eye, of brow,
I see their antique pen would have expressed
Even such a beauty as you master now.
So all their praises are but prophecies
10 Of this our time, all you prefiguring,
And for they looked but with divining eyes
They had not skill enough your worth to sing;

Spes Altera
1. An accurate statement that you had been gluttonous.   2. Preserves (increases) my wealth (my moral record).

For we which now behold these present days
Have eyes to wonder, but lack tongues to praise.

On his Mistress' Beauty

When in the annals of all-wasting time
I see descriptions of the fairest wights,
And beauty making beautiful old rhyme
In praise of ladies dead and lovely knights;
5 Then in the blazon of sweet beauty's best,
Of face, of hand, of lip, of eye, or brow,
I see their antique pen would have expressed
E'en such a beauty as you master now.
So all their praises were but prophecies
10 Of these our days, all you prefiguring,
And for they saw but with divining eyes
They had not skill enough your worth to sing;
    For we which now behold these present days
    Have eyes to wonder, but no tongues to praise.

138

When my love swears that she is made of truth
I do believe her though I know she lies,
That she might think me some untutored youth
Unlearnèd in the world's false subtleties.
5 Thus vainly thinking that she thinks me young,
Although she knows my days are past the best,
Simply I credit her false-speaking tongue;
On both sides thus is simple truth suppressed.
But wherefore says she not she is unjust,
10 And wherefore say not I that I am old?
O, love's best habit is in seeming trust,
And age in love loves not to have years told.
    Therefore I lie with her, and she with me,
    And in our faults by lies we flattered be.

138

When my love swears that she is made of truth
I do believe her though I know she lies,
That she might think me some untutored youth
Unskilful in the world's false forgeries.
5 Thus vainly thinking that she thinks me young,
Although I know my years be past the best,
I, smiling, credit her false-speaking tongue,
Outfacing° faults in love with love's ill rest.[1]   *Defying*
But wherefore says my love that she is young,
10 And wherefore say not I that I am old?
O, love's best habit's in a soothing tongue,
And age in love loves not to have years told.
    Therefore I'll lie with love,° and love with me,   *my lover; lovingly*
    Since that our faults in love thus smothered be.

Sonnet 138
1. With the "rest" of what's bad in love; restlessness.

144

Two loves I have, of comfort and despair,
Which like two spirits do suggest me still.
The better angel is a man right fair,
The worser spirit a woman coloured ill.
5 To win me soon to hell my female evil
Tempteth my better angel from my side,
And would corrupt my saint to be a devil,
Wooing his purity with her foul pride;
And whether that my angel be turned fiend
10 Suspect I may, yet not directly tell;
But being both from me, both to each friend,
I guess one angel in another's hell.
   Yet this shall I ne'er know, but live in doubt
   Till my bad angel fire my good one out.

144

Two loves I have, of comfort and despair,
That like two spirits do suggest me still.
My better angel is a man right fair,
My worser spirit a woman coloured ill.
5 To win me soon to hell my female evil
Tempteth my better angel from my side,
And would corrupt my saint to be a devil,
Wooing his purity with her fair pride;
And whether that my angel be turned fiend,
10 Suspect I may, yet not directly tell;
For being both to me, both to each friend,
I guess one angel in another's hell.
   The truth I shall not know, but live in doubt
   Till my bad angel fire my good one out.

APPENDICES

APPENDICES

Early Modern Map Culture

In the early modern period, maps were often considered rare and precious objects, and seeing a map could be an important and life-changing event. This was so for Richard Hakluyt, whose book *The Principal Navigations, Voiages, Traffiques and Discoveries of the English Nation* (1598–1600) was the first major collection of narratives describing England's overseas trading ventures. Hakluyt tells how, as a boy still at school in London, he visited his uncle's law chambers and saw a book of cosmography lying open there. Perceiving his nephew's interest in the maps it contained, the uncle turned to a modern map and "pointed with his wand to all the knowen Seas, Gulfs, Bayes, Straights, Capes, Rivers, Empires, Kingdomes, Dukedomes, and Territories of ech part, with declaration also of their speciall commodities and particular wants, which by the benefit of traffike, and entercourse of merchants, are plentifully supplied. From the Mappe he brought me to the Bible, and turning to the 107 Psalme, directed mee to the 23 and 24 verses, where I read, that they which go downe to the sea in ships, and occupy [work] by the great waters, they see the works of the Lord, and his woonders in the deepe." This event, Hakluyt records, made so deep an impression upon him, that he vowed he would devote his life to the study of this kind of knowledge. *The Principal Navigations* was the result, a book that mixes a concern with the profit to be made from trade and from geographical knowledge with praise for the Christian god who made the "great waters" and, in Hakluyt's view, looked with special favor on the English merchants and sailors who voyaged over them.

In the early modern period, access to maps was far less easy than it is today. Before the advent of printing in the late fifteenth century, maps were drawn and decorated by hand. Because they were rare and expensive, these medieval maps were for the most part owned by the wealthy and the powerful. Sometimes adorned with pictures of fabulous sea monsters and exotic creatures, maps often revealed the Christian worldview of those who composed them. Jerusalem appeared squarely in the middle of many maps (called T and O maps), with Asia, Africa, and Europe, representing the rest of the known world, arranged symmetrically around the Holy City. Because they had not yet been discovered by Europeans, North and South America were not depicted.

Mapping practices changed markedly during the late fifteenth and sixteenth centuries both because of the advent of print and also because European nations such as Portugal and Spain began sending ships on long sea voyages to open new trade routes to the East and, eventually, to the Americas. During this period, monarchs competed to have the best cartographers supply them with accurate maps of their realms and especially of lands in Africa, Asia, or the Americas, where they hoped to trade or plant settlements. Such knowledge was precious and jealously guarded. The value of such maps and the secrecy that surrounded them are indicated by a story published in Hakluyt's *The Principal Navigations*. An English ship had captured a Portuguese vessel in the Azores, and a map was discovered among the ship's valuable cargo, which included spices, silks, carpets, porcelain, and other exotic commercial objects. The map was "inclosed in a case of sweete Cedar wood, and lapped up almost an hundred fold in fine calicut-cloth, as though it had been some incomparable jewell." The value of the map and what explains the careful way in which it was packed lay in the particular information it afforded the English about Portuguese trading routes. More than beautiful objects, maps like this one were crucial to the international race to find safe sea routes to the most profitable trading centers in the East.

In the sixteenth century, books of maps began to be printed, making them more affordable for ordinary people, though some of these books, published as big folio volumes, remained too dear for any but wealthy patrons to buy. Yet maps were increasingly a part of daily life, and printing made many of them more accessible. Playgoers in Shakespeare's audiences must have understood in general the value and uses of maps, for they appear as props in a number of his plays. Most famously, at the beginning of *King Lear*, the old king has a map brought onstage showing the extent of his kingdom. He then points on the map to the three separate parts into which he is dividing his realm to share among his daughters. The map, often unfurled with a flourish on a table or held up for view by members of Lear's retinue, signals the crucial relationship of the land to the monarch. He is his domains, and the map signifies his possession of them. To divide the kingdom, in essence to tear apart the map, would have been judged foolish and destructive by early modern political theorists. Similarly, in *1 Henry IV*, when rebels against the sitting monarch, Henry IV, plot to overthrow him, they bring a map onstage in order to decide what part of the kingdom will be given to each rebel leader. Their proposed dismemberment of the realm signifies the danger they pose. Treasonously, they would rend in pieces the body of the commonwealth.

Maps, of course, had other uses besides signifying royal domains. In some instances, they were used pragmatically to help people find their way from one place to another. A very common kind of map, a portolan chart, depicted in minute detail the coastline of a particular body of water. Used by sailors, these maps frequently were made by people native to the region they described. Many world or regional maps, because they were beautifully decorated and embellished with vivid colors, were used for decorative purposes. John Dee, a learned adviser to Queen Elizabeth and a great book collector, wrote that some people used maps "to beautifie their Halls, Parlers, Chambers, Galeries, Studies, or Libraries." He also spoke of more scholarly uses for these objects. They could, for example, be useful aids in the study of history or geography, enabling people to locate "thinges past, as battels fought, earthquakes, heavenly fyringes, and such occurents in histories mentioned." Today we make similar use of maps, like those included in this volume, when, in reading Shakespeare's plays, we resort to a map to find out where the Battle of Agincourt took place or where Othello sailed when he left Venice for Cyprus.

This edition of the *Norton Shakespeare* includes six maps. Three of them are modern maps drawn specifically to show the location of places important to Shakespeare's plays. They depict London, the British Isles and France, and the eastern Mediterranean. This edition also includes three early modern maps that indicate some of the different kinds of printed maps that people might have seen in Shakespeare's lifetime. The earliest is a map of London that appeared in a 1574 edition of a famous German atlas, *Civitates Orbis Terrarum* (*Cities of the World*), compiled by George Braun with engravings by Franz Hogenberg. This remarkable atlas includes maps and information on cities throughout Europe, Asia, and North Africa; the first of its six volumes appeared in 1572, the last in 1617. Being included in the volume indicated a city's status as a recognized metropolitan center. In a charming touch, Braun added to his city maps pictures of figures in local dress. At the bottom of the map of London, for example, there are four figures who appear to represent the city's prosperous citizens. In the center, a man in a long robe holds the hand of soberly dressed matron. On either side of them are younger and more ornately dressed figures. The young man sports a long sword and a short cloak, the woman a dress with elaborate skirts. In the atlas, the map is colored, and the clothes of the two young people echo one another in shades of green and red.

At the time the map was made, London was a rapidly expanding metropolis. In 1550, it contained about 55,000 people; by 1600, it would contain nearly 200,000. The map shows the densely populated old walled city north of the Thames River, in the middle of which was Eastcheap, the commercial district where, in Shakespeare's plays about the reign of Henry IV, Falstaff holds court in a tavern. The map also shows that by 1570 London was spreading westward beyond the wall toward Westminster Palace. This medieval structure, which appears on the extreme left side of the map, was where English monarchs resided when in London and where, at the end of *2 Henry IV*, the king dies in the fabled Jerusalem Chamber of the Westminster complex. On the far right of the map, one can see the Tower of London, where Edward IV's young sons were imprisoned by Richard III, an event depicted in Shakespeare's *The Tragedy of King Richard the Third*. The map also indicates the centrality of the Thames to London's commercial life. It shows the river full of boats, some of those on the east side of London Bridge large oceangoing vessels with several masts. South of the river, where many of the most famous London theaters, including Shakespeare's Globe, were to be constructed in the 1590s, there are relatively few buildings. By 1600, this would change, as Southwark, as it was known, came to be an increasingly busy entertainment, residential, and commercial district.

The map of the Christian Holy Lands at the eastern tip of the Mediterranean Sea had extremely wide distribution because it was included in the many editions of the Geneva Bible, an English translation of the Scriptures put together by a group of Puritan scholars working in Geneva in the 1550s. Moderately sized and priced, the Geneva Bible became the most popular Bible in English until the King James version was produced in 1611. Even after that date, many ordinary Protestant readers continued to use the popular Geneva Bible, which underwent refinements, changes, and additions throughout the second half of the sixteenth century, including in 1576 a new translation of the New Testament heavily indebted to the scholarship of the French theologian Théodore de Bèze.

The map included here is from a 1592 edition of this Bible, printed in London by Christopher Barker. The map was placed before Matthew, the first book of the New Testament, and it shows places mentioned in the first four Gospels (Matthew, Mark, Luke, and John), which collectively tell of the life and deeds of Jesus. It indicates, for example, the location of Bethlehem, where he was born; Nazareth, where he spent his youth; and Cana of Galilee, where he turned water into wine at a marriage. It suggests that, to the English reader, this particular territory was overwritten by and completely intertwined with Christian history. Yet in the Mediterranean Sea, on the left of the map, several large ships are visible, and they are reminders of another fact about this region: it was a vigorous trading arena where European Christian merchants did business with local merchants—Christian, Jew, and Muslim—and with traders bringing luxury goods by overland routes from the East. A number of Shakespeare's plays are set in this complex eastern Mediterranean region where several religious traditions laid claim to its territories and many commercial powers competed for preeminence. *Pericles*, for example, has a hero who is the ruler of Tyre, a city on the upper right side of the map. In the course of his wanderings, Pericles visits many cities along the eastern coasts of the Mediterranean. The conclusion of the play, in which the hero is reunited both with his long-lost daughter and the wife he believes dead, has seemed to many critics to share in a sense of Christian miracle, despite the fact of its ostensibly pagan setting. *The Comedy of Errors* and parts of *Othello* and of *Antony and Cleopatra* are also set in the eastern Mediterranean. One of Shakespeare's earliest plays, *The Comedy of Errors,* is an urban comedy in which the protagonists are merchants deeply involved in commercial transactions. It is also the first play in which Shakespeare mentions the Americas in an extended joke in which he compares parts of a serving woman's body to the countries on a map including Ireland, France, and the Americas. In *Othello*, the eastern Mediterranean island of Cyprus is represented as a tense Christian outpost defending Venetian interests against the Muslim Turks. In *Antony and Cleopatra*, Egypt figures as the site of Eastern luxury and also of imperial conquest, an extension of the Roman Empire. Clearly, this region was to Shakespeare and his audiences one of the most complex and most highly charged areas of the world: a site of religious, commercial, and imperial significance.

The map of Great Britain and Ireland comes from a 1612 edition of John Speed's *The Theatre of the Empire of Great Britaine,* an innovative atlas containing individual maps of counties and towns in England and Wales, as well as larger maps that include Scotland and Ireland. Speed was by trade a tailor who increasingly devoted his time to the study of history and cartography. Befriended by the antiquarian scholar William Camden, he eventually won patronage from Sir Fulke Greville, who gave him a pension that allowed him to devote full time to his scholarly endeavors. *The Theatre* was one product of this newfound freedom. The map included here is one of his most ambitious. It shows the entire British Isles, nominated by Speed as "The Kingdome of Great Britaine and Ireland," though at this time Ireland was far from under the control of the English crown and Scotland was still an independent kingdom, despite the fact that James I, a Scot by birth, had tried hard to forge a formal union between England and Scotland. This problem of the relationship of the parts of the British Isles to one another, and England's assertion of power over the others, is treated in *Henry V,* in which officers from Wales, Ireland, and Scotland are sharply delineated yet all depicted as loyal subjects of the English king.

One striking aspect of Speed's map is the balance it strikes between the two capital cities, London on the left, prominently featuring the Thames and London Bridge, and Edinburgh on the right. This would have pleased James, whose interest in his native country Shakespeare played to in his writing of *Macbeth,* based on material from Scottish history. Speed's map acknowledges the claims of the monarch to the territory it depicts. In the upper left corner, the British lion and the Scottish unicorn support a roundel topped with a crown. When James became king of England in 1603, he created this merged symbol of Scottish-English unity. The motto of the Royal Order of the Garter, "Honi soit qui mal y pense" (Shamed be he who thinks ill of it), is inscribed around the circumference. In the bottom left corner of the map, another locus of authority is established. Two cherubs, one holding a compass, the other a globe, sit beneath a banner on which is inscribed the words: "Performed by John Speede." If the territory is the monarch's, the craft that depicts it belongs to the tailor turned cartographer.

Today, maps are readily available from any gasoline station or on the Internet, but in early modern England they were still rare and valuable objects that could generate great excitement in those who owned or beheld them. Along with other precious items, maps were sometimes put on display in libraries and sitting rooms, but they had functions beyond the ornamental. They helped to explain and order the world, indicating who claimed certain domains, showing where the familiar stories of the Bible or of English history occurred, helping merchants find their way to distant markets. As John Dee, the early modern map enthusiast concluded, "Some, for one purpose: and some, for an other, liketh, loveth, getteth, and useth, Mappes, Chartes, and Geographicall Globes."

JEAN E. HOWARD

Ireland, Scotland, Wales, England, and Western France: Places Important to Shakespeare's Plays.

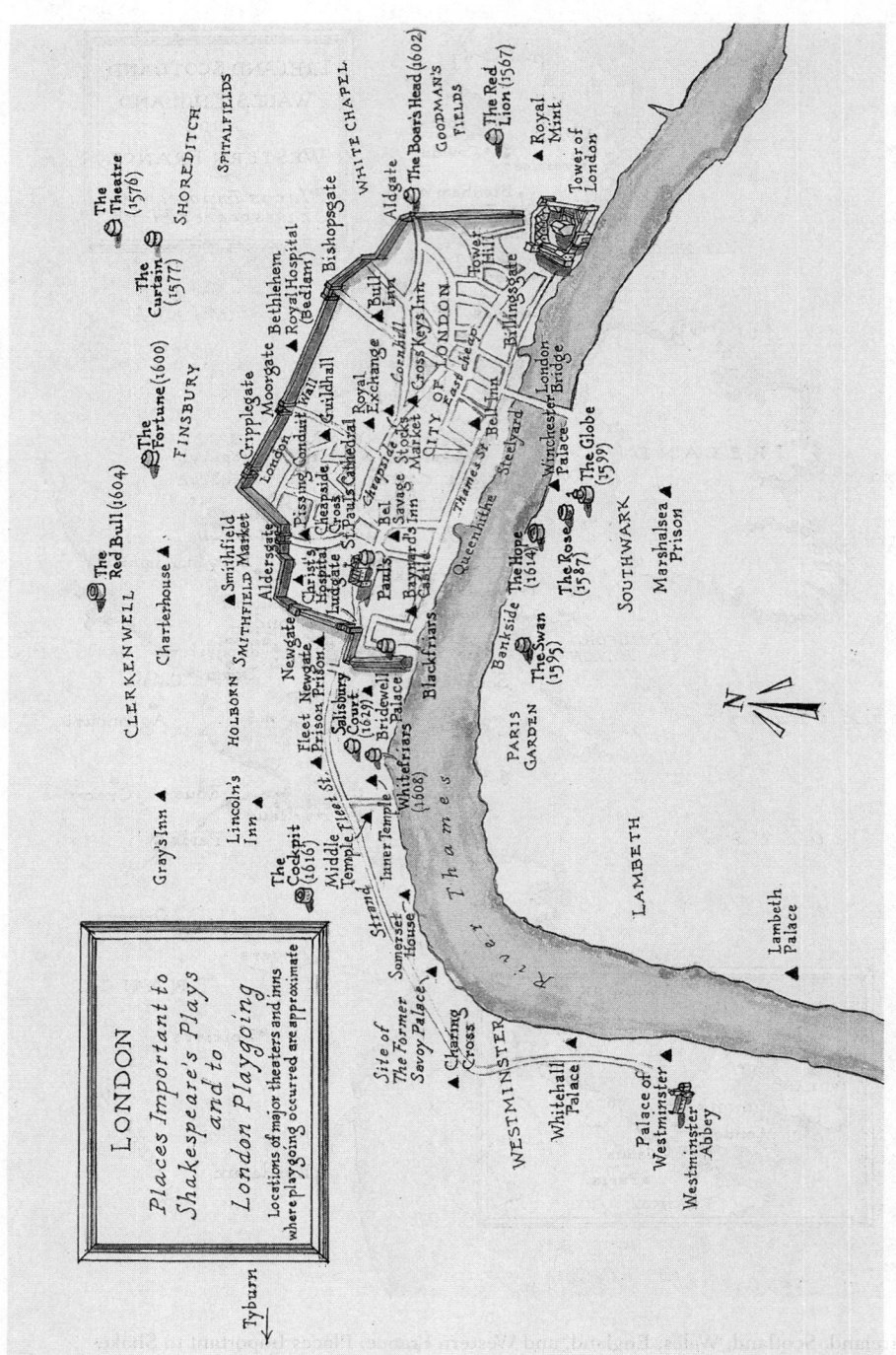

London: Places Important to Shakespeare's Plays and London Playgoing.

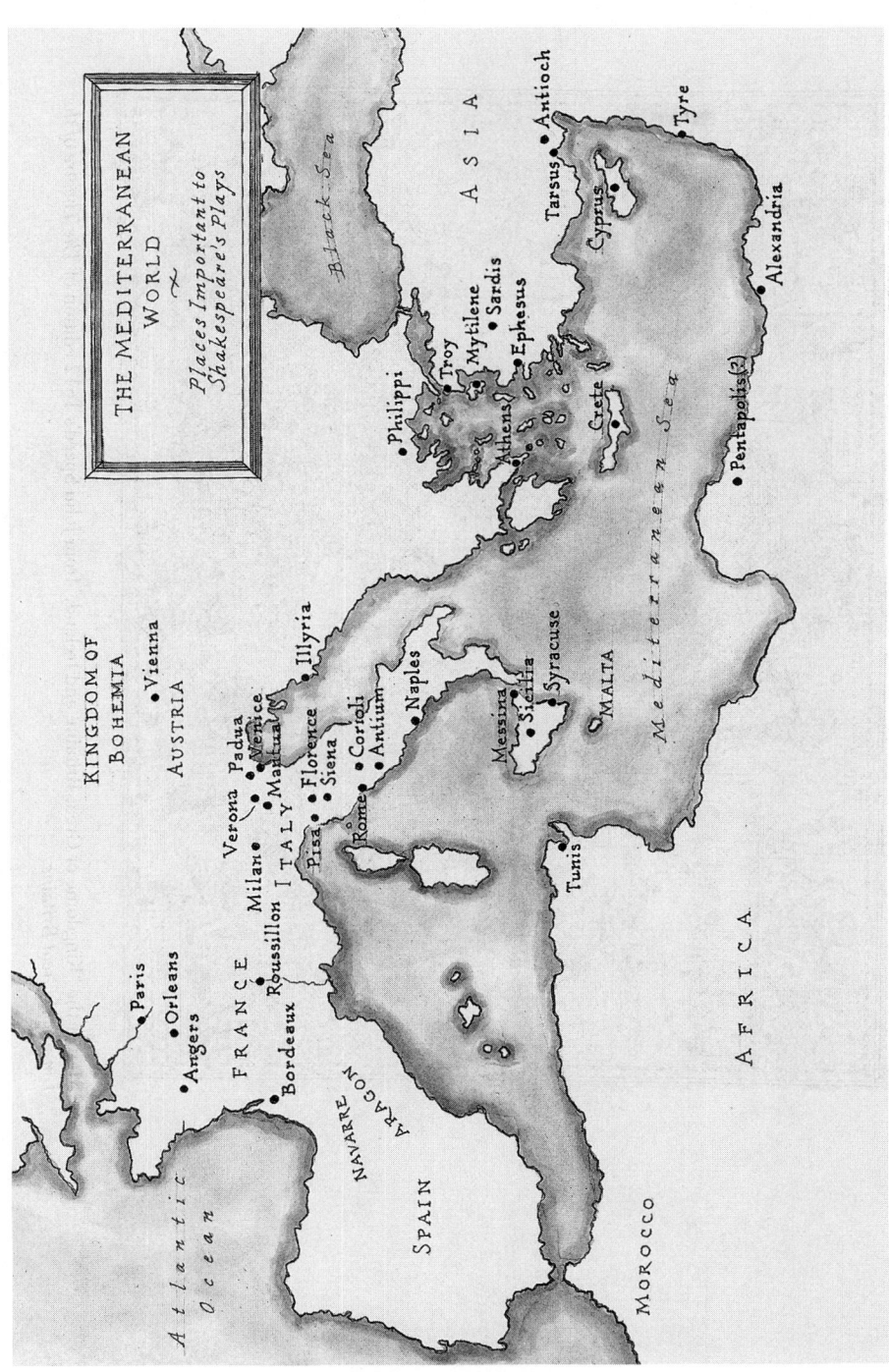

The Mediterranean World: Places Important to Shakespeare's Plays.

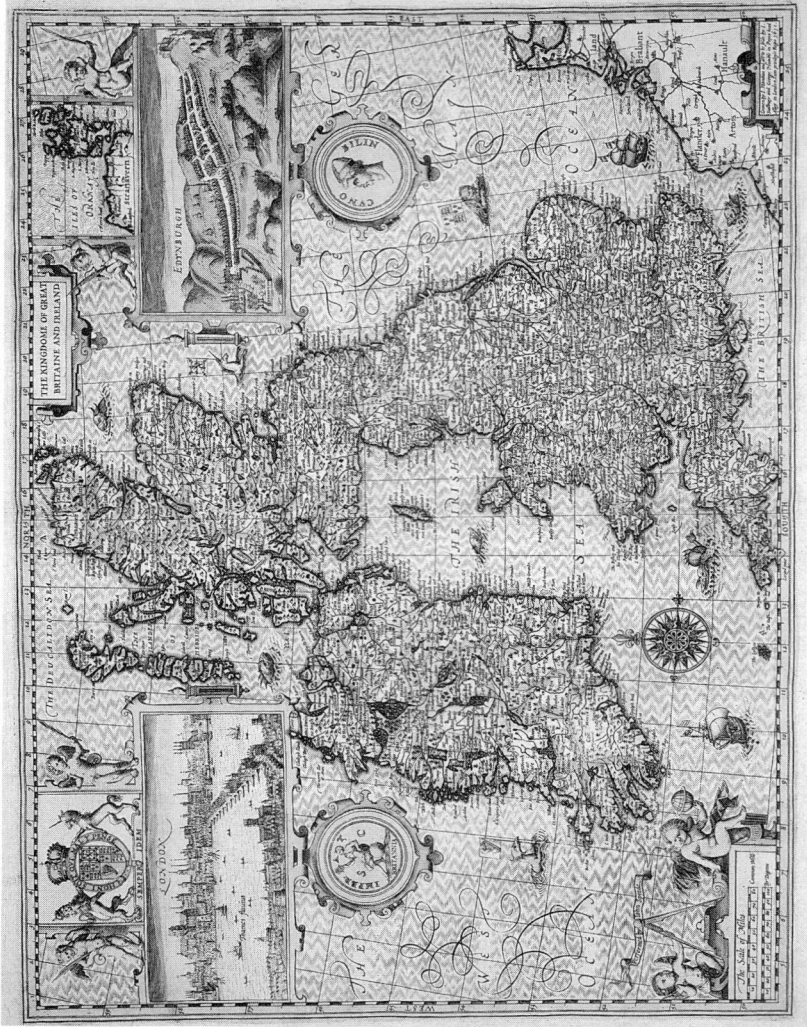

Map of the "Kingdome of Great Britaine and Ireland," from John Speed's 1612 edition of *The Theatre of the Empire of Great Britaine.*

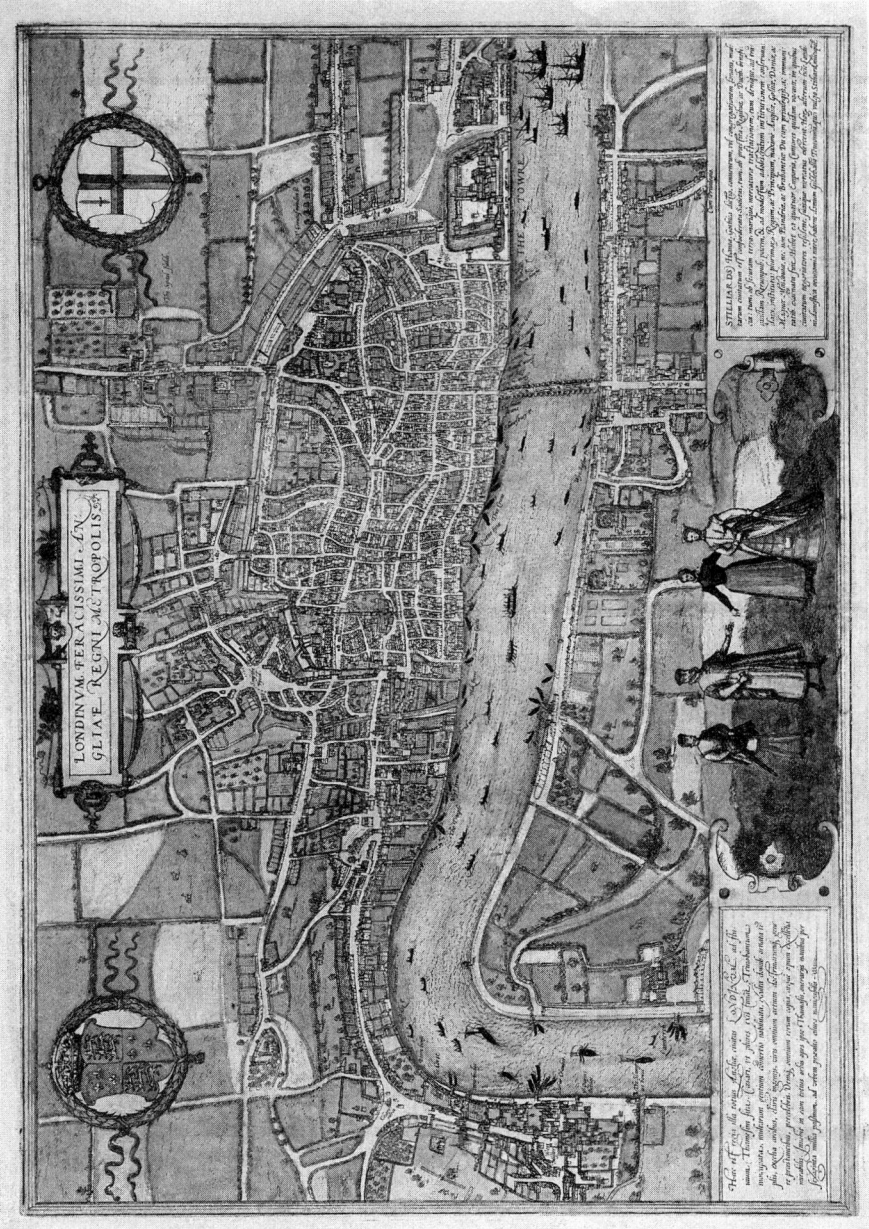

Printed map of London, 1574, taken from a German atlas of European cities by George Braun and Franz Hogenberg.

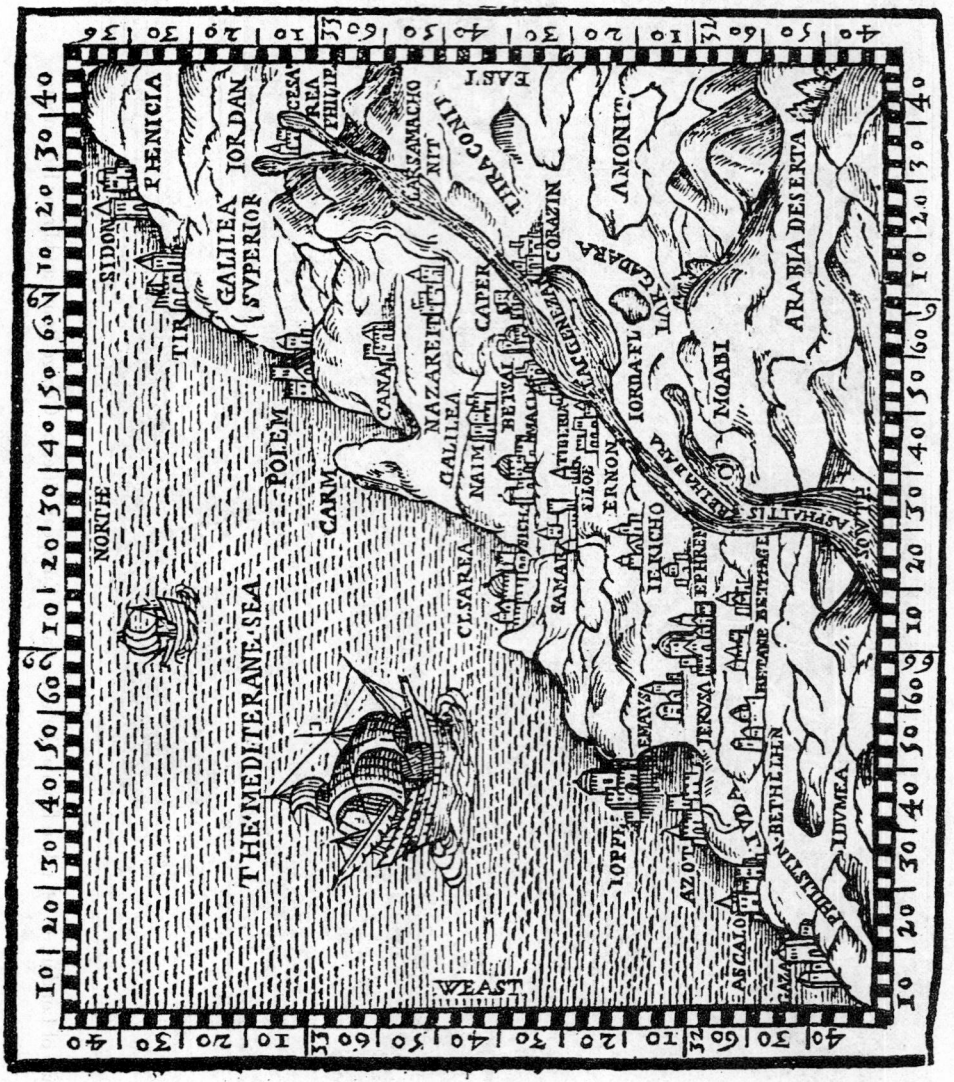

Map of the Holy Land, from the Théodore de Bèze Bible, printed in London, 1592.

Documents

This selection of documents provides a range of contemporary testimony about Shakespeare's character, his work, and the social and institutional conditions under which it was produced. In the absence of newspapers and reviewers, few references to the theater survive. The availability of such hints and fragments as are presented here serves as a mark of Shakespeare's distinction, for the theater was perceived by much of the literate population as ephemeral popular entertainment. The reports of spectators whose accounts we have are more like reviews than any other texts the period has to offer; hence the importance even of brief notes such as Nashe's or Platter's, and the particular value of extended accounts such as those of Simon Forman. The government documents included here offer a vivid glimpse of the institutional procedures by which the theater was regulated. The legal documents—a contract for the construction of a theater modeled on the Globe, and Shakespeare's will—provide the most detailed account available of the material conditions of his life and work. The extracts from criticism and other literary texts show the diversity of contemporary response to his art.

The source for each text is given at the end of the introductory headnote. Additional documents can be found at wwnorton.com/shakespeare.

WS: E. K. Chambers, *William Shakespeare: A Study of Facts and Problems*, 2 vols. (Oxford: Clarendon Press, 1930).
ES: E. K. Chambers, *The Elizabethan Stage*, 4 vols. (Oxford: Clarendon Press, 1923).

Robert Greene on Shakespeare (1592)

[Robert Greene (1560–1592), a prolific author of plays, romances, and pamphlets, attacked Shakespeare in his *Greenes, Groats-worth of Witte, bought with a million of Repentance*. Greene had studied at Cambridge, and his "M.A." was prominently displayed on his title pages. Shakespeare's lack of a university education is clearly one motive for the professional resentment of the following excerpt. Another is probably that Greene was poor and very ill and felt forsaken while writing the *Groats-worth of Witte*; the preface refers to it as his "Swanne-like song," and the narrative is framed as the repentance of a dying man. (Some scholars have held that the posthumously published work contains fabrications by a publisher attempting to capitalize on Greene's name.) The three colleagues Greene addresses are likely to be Christopher Marlowe, Thomas Nashe, and George Peele. The text is that of 1596, as printed in Alexander B. Grosart's *Life and Complete Works in Prose and Verse of Robert Greene*, vol. 12 (New York: Russell and Russell).]

> *To those Gentlemen his Quondam acquaintance,*
> *that spend their wits in making Plaies, R. G.*
> *wisheth a better exercise, and wisdome*
> *to prevent his extremities. . . .*

Base minded men al three of you, if by my miserie ye be not warned: for unto none of you (like me) fought those burres to cleave: those Puppits (I meane) that speake from our mouths, those Anticks garnisht in our colours. Is it not strange that I, to whom they al have beene beholding: is it not like that you, to whome they all have beene beholding, shall (were ye in that case that I am now) be both at once of them forsaken? Yes trust them not: for there is an upstart Crow, beautified with our feathers, that with his *Tygers heart wrapt in a Players hide*,[1] *supposes he is as well able to bumbast out a blanke verse as the best of you: and being an absolute Johannes fac totum*,[2] is in his owne conceit the onely Shake-scene in a countrie. O that I might intreate your rare wits to be imployed in more profitable courses: & let those Apes imitate your past excellence, and never more acquaint them with your admired inventions. I know the best husband[3] of you all will never prove an Usurer, and the kindest of them / all will never proove a kinde nurse: yet whilst you may, seeke you better Maisters; for it is pittie men of such rare wits, should be subject to the pleasures of such rude groomes.

Thomas Nashe on *1 Henry VI* (1592)

[Thomas Nashe (1567–1601), Greene's fellow playwright and pamphleteer, protests the attribution to himself of the *Groats-worth of Witte* in the preface to the 1592 edition of a pamphlet of his own, *Pierce Penilisse; His Supplication to the Devil*. The satire of *Pierce Penilisse* is more general and political than that of the *Groats-worth*, attacking the manners of the middle class. The allusion to the Talbot scenes of *1 Henry VI* (4.2–7) comes in a section subtitled "The defence of Playes." Talbot is supposed to have been played by Richard Burbage, later the leading actor of the Lord Chamberlain's and King's Men. The text is from Ronald B. McKerrow's 1904 edition of Nashe's *Works*, vol. 1 (London: Bullen).]

How would it have joyed brave *Talbot* (the terror of the French) to thinke that after he had lyne two hundred yeares in his Tombe, hee should triumphe againe on the Stage, and have his bones newe embalmed with the teares of ten thousand spectators at least (at severall times), who, in the Tragedian that represents his person, imagine they behold him fresh bleeding.

Francis Meres on Shakespeare (1598)

[Francis Meres (1565–1647) was educated at Cambridge and was active in London literary circles in 1597–98, after which he became a rector and schoolmaster in the country. The descriptions of Shakespeare are taken from a section on poetry in *Palladis Tamia, Wits Treasury*, a work largely consisting of translated classical quotations and exempla. Unlike the main body of the work, the subsections on poetry, painting, and music include comparisons of English artists to figures of antiquity. Meres goes on after the extract below to list Shakespeare among the best English writers for lyric, tragedy, comedy, elegy, and love poetry. The text is from Don Cameron Allen's 1933 edition of the section "Poetrie" (Urbana: University of Illinois).]

From XI

As the Greeke tongue is made famous and eloquent by *Homer, Hesiod, Euripedes, Aeschilus, Sophocles, Pindarus, Phocylides* and *Aristophanes*; and the Latine tongue by *Virgill, Ovid, Horace, Silius Italicus, Lucanus, Lucretius, Ausonius* and *Claudianus*: so the English tongue is mightily enriched, and gorgeouslie invested

---

1. A parody of *Richard Duke of York* (3 *Henry VI*) 1.4.138; "O tiger's heart wrapped in a woman's hide!" This obvious allusion and the following pun on Shakespeare's name make it certain that Shakespeare is the "crow" described here.
2. Jack-of-all-trades. *conceit*: imagination.
3. Steward.

in rare ornaments and resplendent abiliments by Sir *Philip Sidney, Spencer, Daniel, Drayton, Warner, Shakespeare, Marlow* and *Chapman.*

From XIV

As the soule of *Euphorbus* was thought to live in *Pythagoras:* so the sweete wittie soule of Ovid lives in mellifluous & honytongued *Shakespeare,* witnes his *Venus* and *Adonis,* his *Lucrece,* his sugred Sonnets.

From XV

As *Plautus* and *Seneca* are accounted the best for Comedy and Tragedy among the Latines: so *Shakespeare* among yᵉ English is the most excellent in both kinds for the stage; for Comedy, witnes his *Gētlemē of Verona,* his *Errors,* his *Love labors lost,* his *Love labours wonne,*[1] his *Midsummers night dreame,* & his *Merchant of Venice:* for Tragedy his *Richard the 2. Richard the 3. Henry the 4. King John, Titus Andronicus* and his *Romeo* and *Juliet.*

As *Epius Stolo* said, that the Muses would speake with *Plautus* tongue, if they would speak Latin: so I say that the Muses would speak with *Shakespeares* fine filed phrase, if they would speake English.

Thomas Platter on *Julius Caesar* (September 21, 1599)

[Thomas Platter (b. 1574), a Swiss traveler, recorded his experience at the Globe playhouse in an account of his travels. The German text is printed in *WS* 2:322.]

Den 21 Septembris nach dem Imbissessen, etwan umb zwey vhren, bin ich mitt meiner geselschaft vber daz wasser gefahren, haben in dem streüwinen Dachhaus die Tragedy vom ersten Keyser Julio Caesare mitt ohngefahr 15 personen sehen gar artlich agieren; zu endt der Comedien dantzeten sie ihrem gebraucht nach gar vberausz zierlich, ye zwen in mannes vndt 2 in weiber kleideren angethan, wunderbahrlich mitt einanderen.

On the 21st of September after lunch, about two o'clock, I crossed the water [the Thames] with my party, and we saw the tragedy of the first emperor Julius Caesar acted very prettily in the house with the thatched roof, with about fifteen characters; at the end of the comedy, according to their custom, they danced with exceeding elegance, two each in men's and two in women's clothes, wonderfully together.

[Translated by Noah Heringman]

Gabriel Harvey on *Hamlet, Venus and Adonis,* and *The Rape of Lucrece* (1598–1603)

[Gabriel Harvey (c. 1550–1631), a scholar perhaps best remembered as the particular friend of Spenser, gave the following account of Shakespeare and other contemporaries in a long manuscript note in his copy of Speght's 1598 edition of Chaucer. The date of the note is uncertain, but internal evidence makes it highly unlikely to be later than 1603. The references to Shakespeare are brief but suggestive, and the note is useful both in providing a context for the appreciation of Shakespeare and for its characteris-

---

1. The play—or at least the title—has not survived; a bookseller's record of the title does survive, however.

tically keen assessment of the state of modern literature. The text is from G. C. Moore Smith's edition of *Gabriel Harvey's Marginalia* (Stratford-upon-Avon: Shakespeare Head Press, 1913).]

And now translated Petrarch, Ariosto, Tasso, & Bartas himself deserve curious comparison with Chaucer, Lidgate, & owre best Inglish, auncient & moderne. Amongst which, the Countesse of Pembrokes Arcadia, & the Faerie Queene ar now freshest in request: & Astrophil, & Amyntas ar none of the idlest pastimes of sum fine humanists. The Earle of Essex much commendes Albions England:[1] and not unworthily for diverse notable pageants, before, & in the Chronicle. Sum Inglish, & other Histories nowhere more sensibly described, or more inwardly discovered. The Lord Mountjoy makes the like account of Daniels peece of the Chronicle,[2] touching the Usurpation of Henrie of Bullingbrooke, which in deede is a fine, sententious, & politique peece of Poetrie: as proffitable, as pleasurable. The younger sort takes much delight in Shakespeares Venus, & Adonis: but his Lucrece, & his tragedie of Hamlet, Prince of Denmarke, have it in them, to please the wiser sort. Or such poets: or better: or none.

> Vilia miretur vulgus: mihi flavus Apollo
> Pocula Castaliæ plena ministret aquæ:[3]

quoth Sir Edward Dier, betwene jest, & earnest. Whose written devises farr excell most of the sonets, and cantos in print. His Amaryllis, & Sir Walter Raleighs Cynthia, how fine & sweet inventions? Excellent matter of emulation for Spencer, Constable, France, Watson, Daniel, Warner, Chapman, Silvester, Shakespeare, & the rest of owr florishing metricians. I looke for much, aswell in verse, as in prose, from mie two Oxford frends, Doctor Gager, & M. Hackluit: both rarely furnished for the purpose: & I have a phansie to Owens new Epigrams, as pithie as elegant, as plesant as sharp, & sumtime as weightie as breife: & amongst so manie gentle, noble, & royall spirits meethinkes I see sum heroical thing in the clowdes: mie soveraine hope. Axiophilus[4] shall forgett himself, or will remember to leave sum memorials behinde him: & to make an use of so manie rhapsodies, cantos, hymnes, odes, epigrams, sonets, & discourses, as at idle howers, or at flowing fitts he hath compiled. God knowes what is good for the world, & fitting for this age.

Contract for the Building of the Fortune Theatre (1600)

[This contract was drawn up between Philip Henslowe and Edward Alleyn, partners in the venture, and Peter Street, the carpenter (or general contractor) in charge of the construction. In fact, Alleyn seems to have put up all the money, £440 for the work specified in the contract in addition to £80 for decoration and considerable sums to acquire the lot and surrounding properties. Alleyn faced opposition from residents of the neighborhood, but he had secured the favor of key supporters, so that he was able to proceed with the construction. As the new home of the Lord Admiral's Men, the Fortune did in fact become a center of disturbances, with complaints coming to the Middlesex Bench of assaults, petty thefts, and riotous behavior. Alleyn had been the leading actor of the Lord Admiral's Men, chief competitors of the Lord Chamberlain's Men, and the Fortune was conceived to compete with the Globe, meanwhile replacing the decaying and poorly situated Rose Theatre. The contract's

---

1. By William Warner (1586).
2. *The Ciuile Wars Between the Two Houses of Lancaster and Yorke* (1595).
3. "Let what is cheap excite the marvel of the crowd; for me may golden Apollo minister full cups from the

Castalian fount" (Ovid, *Amores* 1.15.35–36, Loeb translation). These lines also appear on the title page of Shakespeare's *Venus and Adonis* (1592–93).
4. Probably Harvey himself.

descriptions and frequent references to the Globe, given this background, can be seen as providing some of our best evidence on the nature of the Globe itself. The text is reprinted in *ES*, vol. 2.]

'This Indenture made the Eighte daie of Januarye 1599,[1] and in the Twoe and Fortyth yeare of the Reigne of our sovereigne Ladie Elizabeth, by the grace of god Queene of Englande, Fraunce and Irelande, defender of the Faythe, &c. betwene Phillipp Henslowe and Edwarde Allen of the parishe of Ste Saviours in Southwark in the Countie of Surrey, gentlemen, on thone parte, and Peeter Streete, Cittizen and Carpenter of London, on thother parte witnesseth That whereas the saide Phillipp Henslowe & Edward Allen, the daie of the date hereof, have bargayned, compounded & agreed with the saide Peter Streete ffor the erectinge, buildinge & settinge upp of a new howse and Stadge for a Plaiehouse in and uppon a certeine plott or parcell of grounde appoynted oute for that purpose, scytuate and beinge nere Goldinge lane in the parishe of Ste Giles withoute Cripplegate of London,[2] to be by him the saide Peeter Streete or somme other sufficyent woorkmen of his provideinge and appoyntemente and att his propper costes & chardges, for the consideracion hereafter in theis presentes expressed, made, erected, builded and sett upp in manner & forme followinge (that is to saie); The frame of the saide howse to be sett square[3] and to conteine ffowerscore foote of lawfull assize everye waie square withoutt and fiftie five foote of like assize square everye waie within, with a good suer and stronge foundacion of pyles, brick, lyme and sand bothe without & within, to be wroughte one foote of assize att the leiste above the grounde; And the saide fframe to conteine three Stories in heighth, the first or lower Storie to conteine Twelve foote of lawfull assize in heighth, the second Storie Eleeaven foote of lawfull assize in heigth, and the third or upper Storie to conteine Nyne foote of lawfull assize in heigth; All which Stories shall conteine Twelve foote and a halfe of lawfull assize in breadth througheoute, besides a juttey forwardes in either of the saide twoe upper Stories of Tenne ynches of lawfull assize, with ffower convenient divisions for gentlemens roomes,[4] and other sufficient and convenient divisions for Twoe pennie roomes, with necessarie seates to be placed and sett, aswell in those roomes as througheoute all the rest of the galleries of the saide howse, and with suchelike steares, conveyances & divisions withoute & within, as are made & contryved in and to the late erected Plaiehowse on the Banck in the saide parishe of Ste Saviours called the Globe; With a Stadge and Tyreinge howse[5] to be made, erected & settupp within the saide fframe, with a shadowe or cover[6] over the saide Stadge, which Stadge shalbe placed & sett, as alsoe the stearecases of the saide fframe, in suche sorte as is prefigured in a plott[7] thereof drawen, and which Stadge shall conteine in length Fortie and Three foote of lawfull assize and in breadth to extende to the middle of the yarde[8] of the saide howse; The same Stadge to be paled in belowe with good, stronge and sufficyent newe oken bourdes, and likewise the lower Storie of the saide fframe withinside, and the same lower storie to be alsoe laide over and fenced with stronge yron pykes; And the saide Stadge to be in all other proporcions contryved and fashioned like unto the Stadge of the saide Plaie howse called the Globe; With convenient windowes and lightes glazed to the saide Tyreinge howse; And the saide fframe, Stadge and Stearecases to be covered with Tyle, and to have a sufficient gutter of lead to carrie & convey the water frome the coveringe of the saide Stadge to fall backwardes; And also all the saide fframe and the Stairecases thereof

---

1. 1600 (New Style).
2. *nere . . . London*: an area then in the northwest suburbs, literally outside Cripplegate and, like the Globe across the water, outside the jurisdiction of a City Council often inimical to the theater.
3. This square shape was unusual; the outlines of comparable theaters of the period were round or polygonal (with more than four sides).
4. Something like the VIP boxes of the present day.

5. "Attiring house," a dressing room and backstage area extending onto the rear of the stage.
6. A roof (known as "the heavens") partially covering the stage, supported by the pillars that also served as versatile pieces of scenery.
7. Plan.
8. *in breadth . . . yarde*: the stage would then extend about 27 feet into the yard, specified earlier as 55 feet square.

to be sufficyently enclosed withoute with lathe, lyme & haire, and the gentlemens roomes and Twoe pennie roomes to be seeled[9] with lathe, lyme & haire, and all the fflowers of the saide Galleries, Stories and Stadge to be bourded with good & sufficyent newe deale bourdes of the whole thicknes, wheare need shalbe; And the saide howse and other thinges beforemencioned to be made & doen to be in all other contrivitions, conveyances, fashions, thinge and thinges effected, finished and doen accordinge to the manner and fashion of the saide howse called the Globe, saveinge only that all the princypall and maine postes of the saide fframe and Stadge forwarde shalbe square and wroughte palasterwise,[1] with carved proporcions called Satiers[2] to be placed & sett on the topp of every of the same postes, and saveinge alsoe that the said Peeter Streete shall not be chardged with anie manner of pay[ntin]ge in or aboute the saide fframe howse or Stadge or anie parte thereof, nor rendringe[3] the walls within, nor seeling anie more or other roomes then the gentlemens roomes, Twoe pennie roomes and Stadge before remembred. Nowe theiruppon the saide Peeter Streete dothe covenant, promise and graunte ffor himself, his executours and administratours, to and with the saide Phillipp Henslowe and Edward Allen and either of them, and thexecutours and administratours of them and either of them, by theis presentes in manner & forme followeinge (that is to saie); That he the saide Peeter Streete, his executours or assignes, shall & will att his or their owne propper costes & chardges well, woorkmanlike & substancyallie make, erect, sett upp and fully finishe in and by all thinges, accordinge to the true meaninge of theis presentes, with good, stronge and substancyall newe tymber and other necessarie stuff, all the saide fframe and other woorkes whatsoever in and uppon the saide plott or parcell of grounde (beinge not by anie aucthoretie restrayned, and haveinge ingres, egres & regres to doe the same) before the ffyve & twentith daie of Julie next commeinge after the date hereof; And shall alsoe at his or theire like costes and chardges provide and finde all manner of woorkmen, tymber, joystes, rafters, boordes, dores, boltes, hinges, brick, tyle, lathe, lyme, haire, sande, nailes, lade, iron, glasse, woorkmanshipp and other thinges whatsoever, which shalbe needefull, convenyent & necessarie for the saide fframe & woorkes & everie parte thereof; And shall alsoe make all the saide fframe in every poynte for Scantlinges[4] lardger and bigger in assize then the Scantlinges of the timber of the saide newe erected howse called the Globe; And alsoe that he the saide Peeter Streete shall furthwith, aswell by himself as by suche other and soemanie woorkmen as shalbe convenient & necessarie, enter into and uppon the saide buildinges and woorkes, and shall in reasonable manner proceede therein withoute anie wilfull detraccion untill the same shalbe fully effected and finished. In consideracion of all which buildinges and of all stuff & woorkemanshipp thereto belonginge, the saide Phillipp Henslowe & Edward Allen and either of them, ffor themselves, theire, and either of theire executours & administratours, doe joynctlie & severallie covenante & graunte to & with the saide Peeter Streete, his executours & administratours by theis presentes, that they the saide Phillipp Henslowe & Edward Allen or one of them, or the executours administratours or assignes of them or one of them, shall & will well & truelie paie or cawse to be paide unto the saide Peeter Streete, his executours or assignes, att the place aforesaid appoynted for the erectinge of the saide fframe, the full somme of Fower hundred & Fortie Poundes of lawfull money of Englande in manner & forme followeinge (that is to saie), att suche tyme and when as the Tymberwoork of the saide fframe shalbe rayzed & sett upp by the saide Peeter Streete his executours or assignes, or within seaven daies then next followeinge, Twoe hundred & Twentie poundes, and att suche time and when as the saide fframe & woorkes shalbe fullie effected & ffynished as is aforesaide, or within seaven daies then next followeinge, thother Twoe hundred and Twentie poundes,

9. Coated both on the "ceiling" (a related word) and the walls.
1. Finished in the form of pilasters, ornamental columns in the classical style.

2. Satyrs. *proporcions:* figures.
3. Plastering.
4. Prescribed dimensions of the beams.

withoute fraude or coven.[5] Provided allwaies, and it is agreed betwene the saide parties, that whatsoever somme or sommes of money the saide Phillipp Henslowe & Edward Allen or either of them, or thexecutours or assignes of them or either of them, shall lend or deliver unto the saide Peter Streete his executours or assignes, or anie other by his appoyntemente or consent, ffor or concerninge the saide woorkes or anie parte thereof or anie stuff thereto belonginge, before the raizeinge & settinge upp of the saide fframe, shalbe reputed, accepted, taken & accoumpted in parte of the firste paymente aforesaid of the saide some of Fower hundred & Fortie poundes, and all suche somme & sommes of money, as they or anie of them shall as aforesaid lend or deliver betwene the razeinge of the saide fframe & finishinge thereof and of all the rest of the saide woorkes, shalbe reputed, accepted, taken & accoumpted in parte of the laste pamente aforesaid of the same somme of Fower hundred & Fortie poundes, anie thinge abovesaid to the contrary notwithstandinge. In witnes whereof the parties abovesaid to theis presente Indentures Interchaungeably have sett theire handes and seales. Geoven[6] the daie and yeare ffirste abovewritten.

P S

Sealed and delivered by the saide Peter Streete in the presence of me William Harris Pub[lic] Scr[ivener] And me Frauncis Smyth appr[entice] to the said Scr[ivener]
[*Endorsed:*] Peater Streat ffor The Building of the Fortune.

Augustine Phillips, Francis Bacon, et al. on *Richard II* (1601)

[These extracts from testimony submitted at the Earl of Essex's trial for treason, and related documents, show that some of Essex's supporters had contracted with the Lord Chamberlain's Men to revive *Richard II,* apparently in order to provide a model for the justified deposition of a monarch and thus propitiate the coup in which Essex planned to depose Elizabeth. The play was performed on February 7, and "it was on the same day," according to E. K. Chambers, "that Essex received a summons to appear before the Privy Council. This interrupted his plans for securing possession of the Queen's person and arresting her ministers, and precipitated his futile outbreak of February 8." Augustine Phillips was one of Shakespeare's colleagues in the Lord Chamberlain's Men. Sir Edward Coke was, for a time, chief justice under King James. The last excerpt is a contemporary record of a conversation between the queen and her archivist several months after Essex was executed. The texts are from *WS*, vol. 2.]

From the Abstract of Evidence

The Erle of Essex is charged with high Treason, namely, That he plotted and practised with the Pope and king of Spaine for the disposing and settling to himself Aswell the Crowne of England, as of the kingdom of Ireland.

From the Examination of Augustine Phillips, February 18, 1601

The Examination of Augustyne Phillypps servant unto the L Chamberlyne and one of hys players taken the xviij[th] of Februarij 1600 upon hys oth

He sayeth that on Fryday last was sennyght or Thursday S[r] Charles Percy S[r] Josclyne Percy and the L. Montegle with some thre more spak to some of the play-

---

5. Deceit. 6. Given.

ers in the presans of thys examinate to have the play of the deposyng and kyllyng of Kyng Rychard the second to be played the Saterday next promysyng to gete them xls. more then their ordynary to play yt. Wher thys Examinate and hys fellowes were determyned to have played some other play, holdyng that play of Kyng Richard to be so old & so long out of use as that they shold have small or no Company at yt. But at their request this Examinate and his fellowes were Content to play yt the Saterday and had their xls. more then their ordynary for yt and so played yt accordyngly

Augustine Phillipps

From the speech of Sir Edward Coke at Essex's trial, February 19

I protest upon my soul and conscience I doe beleeve she should not have long lived after she had been in your power. Note but the precedents of former ages, how long lived Richard the Second after he was surprised in the same manner? The pretence was alike for the removing of certain counsellors, but yet shortly after it cost him his life.

From [Francis Bacon's] "A Declaration of the . . . Treasons . . . by Robert late Earle of Essex"

The afternoone before the rebellion, Merricke,[1] with a great company of others, that afterwards were all in the action, had procured to bee played before them, the play of deposing King Richard the second. Neither was it casuall, but a play bespoken by Merrick. And not so onely, but when it was told him by one of the players, that the play was olde, and they should have losse in playing it, because fewe would come to it: there was fourty shillings extraordinarie given to play it, and so thereupon playd it was. So earnest hee was to satisfie his eyes with the sight of that tragedie which hee thought soone after his lord should bring from the stage to the state, but that God turned it upon their owne heads.

From a Memorandum in the Lambard family manuscript, August 4

. . . so her Majestie fell upon[2] the reign of King Richard II. saying, 'I am Richard II. know ye not that?'

W.L. 'Such a wicked imagination was determined and attempted by a most unkind Gent. the most adorned creature that ever your Majestie made.'

Her Majestie. 'He that will forget God, will also forget his benefactors; this tragedy was played 40^tie times in open streets and houses.'

John Manningham on *Twelfth Night* and *Richard III* (1602)

[John Manningham (d. 1622) kept a diary during his time as a law student at the Middle Temple, recording the witticisms of his colleagues and a rich variety of anecdotes. The vibrant and boisterous life of the Inns of Court is also illustrated by the *Gesta Grayorum* (see above). The February entry describes the festivities organized for Candlemas Day at the Middle Temple, while the second recounts an anecdote related to Manningham by one Mr. Touse (this name is difficult to read in the manuscript). As with all the documents in this section, any date before March 25 is assigned to the following year according to our calendar, so that 1601 here becomes 1602 (New Style).

---

1. Sir Gilly Merrick, one of Essex's supporters, was later tried separately for treason.
2. Came across (in reading). The memorandum describes a scene in which the queen is reading over the archives that have been in the keeping of her interlocutor, William Lambard.

The text is from the 1976 edition of Robert Sorlien (Hanover, N.H.: University Press of New England).]

Febr. 1601

2. At our feast wee had a play called "Twelve night, or what you will"; much like the commedy of errores, or Menechmi[1] in Plautus, but most like and neere to that in Italian called Inganni.[2] A good practise in it to make the steward beleeve his Lady widdowe[3] was in Love with him, by counterfayting a letter, as from his Lady, in generall termes, telling him what shee liked best in him, and prescribing his gesture in smiling, his apparraile, &c., and then when he came to practise, making him beleeve they tooke him to be mad.

Marche. 1601

13. . . . Upon a tyme when Burbidge played Rich[ard] 3. there was a Citizen grewe soe farr in liking with him, that before shee went from the play shee appointed him to come that night unto hir by the name of Ri[chard] the 3. Shakespeare, overhearing their conclusion, went before, was intertained, and at his game ere Burbidge came. Then message being brought that Richard the 3ᵈ. was at the dore, Shakespeare caused returne to be made that William the Conquerour was before Rich[ard] the 3. Shakespeare's name William. (Mr. Touse.)

Letters Patent Formalizing the Adoption of the Lord Chamberlain's Men as the King's Men (May 19, 1603)

[James I issued the warrant ordering this patent shortly after his coronation, enhancing the status of Shakespeare's company. As retainers of the royal household with the title of Grooms of the Chamber, they performed at the court with increasing frequency (177 times between 1603 and 1616) and assisted occasionally with other court functions; but, more important, they acted throughout the kingdom under the authority of the royal patent, whose scope the forceful wording below makes clear. The patent, bearing the Great Seal, was issued May 19 as ordered in the warrant of May 17. There is some evidence to suggest that James was particularly taken with Shakespeare's poetry, and the playwright's valorization of James's ancestry (as originating with Banquo) in *Macbeth* certainly suggests that Shakespeare cultivated his esteem. The text is from *ES*, vol. 2.]

Commissio specialis pro Laurencio Fletcher & Willelmo Shackespeare et aliis[2]

James by the grace of god &c. To all Justices, Maiors, Sheriffes, Constables, hedborowes,[1] and other our Officers and lovinge Subjectes greeting. Knowe yee that Wee of our speciall grace, certeine knowledge, & mere motion[3] have licenced and aucthorized and by theise presentes[4] doe licence and aucthorize theise our Servauntes Lawrence Fletcher, William Shakespeare, Richard Burbage, Augustyne Phillippes, John Heninges, Henrie Condell, William Sly, Robert Armyn, Richard Cowly, and the rest of theire Assosiates freely to use and exercise the Arte and faculty of playinge

---

1. Source for *The Comedy of Errors.*
2. The two plays with this exact title (1562 and 1592) seem less likely to be "most like" *Twelfth Night* than another Italian play, *Ingannati* (1537), which has characters named Fabio and Malevolti and makes reference to Twelfth Night (Epiphany).
3. Olivia is not a widow in the version of Shakespeare's play that has come down to us, though she is

so described in one of Shakespeare's principal sources for the play.
1. A parish officer similar to a petty constable.
2. *Commissio . . . aliis:* By special commission on behalf of . . . and others.
3. Inclination, desire.
4. The present document.

Comedies, Tragedies, histories, Enterludes, moralls,[5] pastoralls, Stageplaies, and Suche others like as theie have alreadie studied or hereafter shall use or studie, aswell for the recreation of our lovinge Subjectes, as for our Solace and pleasure when wee shall thincke good to see them, duringe our pleasure. And the said Commedies, tragedies, histories, Enterludes, Morralles, Pastoralls, Stageplayes, and suche like to shewe and exercise publiquely to theire best Commoditie,[6] when the infection of the plague shall decrease, aswell within theire nowe usual howse called the Globe within our County of Surrey, as alsoe within anie towne halls or Moute halls[7] or other conveniente places within the liberties and freedome of anie other Cittie, universitie, towne, or Boroughe whatsoever within our said Realmes and domynions. Willinge and Commaundinge you and everie of you, as you tender our pleasure, not onelie to permitt and suffer them herein without anie your lettes hindrances or molestacions during our said pleasure, but alsoe to be aidinge and assistinge to them, yf anie wronge be to them offered, And to allowe them such former Curtesies as hath bene given to men of theire place and quallitie,[8] and alsoe what further favour you shall shewe to theise our Servauntes for our sake wee shall take kindlie at your handes. In wytnesse whereof &c. witnesse our selfe at Westminster the nyntenth day of May

per breve de privato sigillo[9] &c.

Master of the Wardrobe's Account (March 1604)

[This entry offers us a rare glimpse of the players in the entourage of King James, sporting festive regalia in their capacity as Grooms of the Chamber. The royal procession took place March 15, 1604. The text is from *WS*, vol. 2.]

Red Clothe bought of sondrie persons and given by his Majestie to diverse persons against[1] his Majesties sayd royall proceeding through the Citie of London, viz.:— . . .

The Chamber . . .	
Fawkeners[2] &c. &c.	Red cloth
William Shakespeare	iiii yardes di.
Augustine Phillipps	"
Lawrence Fletcher	"
John Hemminges	"
Richard Burbidge	"
William Slye	"
Robert Armyn	"
Henry Cundell	"
Richard Cowley	"

Simon Forman on *Macbeth, Cymbeline,* and *The Winter's Tale* (1611)

[Simon Forman (1552–1611) was a largely self-educated physician and astrologer who rose from humble beginnings to establish a successful London practice. A large parcel of his manuscripts, including scientific and autobiographical material as well as the diary from which this account of the plays is taken, has survived, making his life one of the best-documented Elizabethan lives. These manuscripts provide

<hr/>

5. Morality plays.
6. Advantage.
7. Council chambers.
8. Profession.
9. In sum, from the privy seal.

1. For.
2. Obsolete form of "falconers," very likely the men who trained the falcons used for James's fowl-hunting expeditions. The falconers might owe their place in the retinue to James's well-known passion for hunting.

detailed information about Forman's many sidelines, such as the manufacture of talismans, alchemy, and necromancy, as well about his sex life. The text is from *WS*, vol. 2.]

The Bocke of Plaies and Notes therof per formane for Common Pollicie[1]

In Mackbeth at the Glob, 1610 ⟨1611⟩, the 20 of Aprill ♄ (Saturday), ther was to be observed, firste, howe Mackbeth and Bancko, 2 noble men of Scotland, Ridinge thorowe a wod, the ⟨r⟩ stode before them 3 women feiries or Nimphes, And saluted Mackbeth, sayinge, 3 tyms unto him, haille Mackbeth, king of Codon;[2] for thou shalt be a kinge, but shalt beget No kinges, &c. Then said Bancko, What all to Mackbeth And nothing to me. Yes, said the nimphes, haille to thee Bancko, thou shalt beget kinges, yet be no kinge. And so they departed & cam to the Courte of Scotland to Dunkin king of Scotes, and yt was in the dais of Edward the Confessor. And Dunkin bad them both kindly wellcome, And made Mackbeth forth with Prince of Northumberland,[3] and sent him hom to his own castell, and appointed Mackbeth to provid for him, for he would sup with him the next dai at night, & did soe. And Mackebeth contrived to kill Dunkin, & thorowe the persuasion of his wife did that night Murder the kinge in his own Castell, beinge his guest. And ther were many prodigies seen that night & the dai before. And when Mack Beth had murdred the kinge, the blod on his handes could not be washed of by Any meanes, nor from his wives handes, which handled the bloddi daggers in hiding them, By which means they became both moch amazed & Affronted. The murder being knowen, Dunkins 2 sonns fled, the on to England, the ⟨other to⟩ Walles, to save them selves, they being fled, they were supposed guilty of the murder of their father, which was nothinge so. Then was Mackbeth crowned kinge, and then he for feare of Banko, his old companion, that he should beget kinges but be no kinge him selfe, he contrived the death of Banko, and caused him to be Murdred on the way as he Rode. The next night, beinge at supper with his noble men whom he had bid to a feaste to the which also Banco should have com, he began to speake of Noble Banco, and to wish that he wer ther. And as he thus did, standing up to drincke a Carouse to him, the ghoste of Banco came and sate down in his cheier behind him. And he turninge About to sit down Again sawe the goste of Banco, which fronted him so, that he fell into a great passion of fear and fury, Utterynge many wordes about his murder, by which, when they hard that Banco was Murdred they Suspected Mackbet.

Then MackDove fled to England to the kinges sonn, And soe they Raised an Army, And cam into Scotland, and at Dunston Anyse overthrue Mackbet. In the meantyme whille Macdovee was in England, Mackbet slewe Mackdoves wife & children, and after in the battelle Mackdove slewe Mackbet.

Observe Also howe Mackbetes quen did Rise in the night in her slepe, & walke and talked and confessed all, & the docter noted her wordes.

Of Cimbalin king of England.

Remember also the storri of Cymbalin king of England, in Lucius tyme, howe Lucius Cam from Octavus Cesar for Tribut, and being denied, after sent Lucius with a greate Arme of Souldiars who landed at Milford haven, and Affter wer vanquished by Cimbalin, and Lucius taken prisoner, and all by means of 3 outlawes, of the which 2 of them were the sonns of Cimbalim, stolen from him when they were but 2 yers old by an old man whom Cymbalin banished, and he kept them as his own sonns 20 yers with him in A cave. And howe ⟨one⟩ of them slewe Clotan, that was the quens sonn, goinge to Milford haven to sek the love of Innogen the

1. *Common Pollicie*: practical use. Forman's title for his notes on plays is not printed in Chambers, but interpolated here from G. Blakemore Evans's transcription in the *Riverside Shakespeare*.

2. Cawdor.

3. Probably Forman's error; Duncan gives Macbeth the title Thane of Cawdor. Duncan's son Malcolm is the Prince of Northumberland.

kinges daughter, whom he had banished also for lovinge his daughter,[4] and howe the Italian that cam from her love conveied him selfe into A Cheste, and said yt was a chest of plate sent from her love & others, to be presented to the kinge. And in the depest of the night, she being aslepe, he opened the cheste, & cam forth of yt, And vewed her in her bed, and the markes of her body, & toke awai her braslet, & after Accused her of adultery to her love, &c. And in thend howe he came with the Romains into England & was taken prisoner, and after Reveled to Innogen, Who had turned her self into mans apparrell & fled to mete her love at Milford haven, & chanchsed to fall on the Cave in the wodes wher her 2 brothers were, & howe by eating a sleping Dram they thought she had bin deed, & laid her in the wodes, & the body of Cloten by her, in her loves apparrell that he left behind him, & howe she was found by Lucius, &c.

In the Winters Talle at the glob 1611 the 15 of maye ☿ ⟨Wednesday⟩.

Observe ther howe Lyontes the kinge of Cicillia was overcom with Jelosy of his wife with the kinge of Bohemia his frind that came to see him, and howe he contrived his death and wold have had his cup berer to have poisoned, who gave the king of Bohemia warning therof & fled with him to Bohemia.

Remember also howe he sent to the Orakell of Appollo & the Annswer of Apollo, that she was giltles and that the king was jelouse &c. and howe Except the child was found Again that was loste the kinge should die without yssue, for the child was caried into Bohemia & ther laid in a forrest & brought up by a sheppard And the kinge of Bohemia his sonn maried that wentch & howe they fled into Cicillia to Leontes, and the sheppard having showed the letter of the nobleman by whom Leontes sent a was ⟨away?⟩ that child and the jewells found about her, she was knowen to be Leontes daughter and was then 16 yers old.

Remember also the Rog[5] that cam in all tottered like coll pixci[6] and howe he feyned him sicke & to have bin Robbed of all that he had and howe he cosened the por man of all his money, and after cam to the shep sher[7] with a pedlers packe & ther cosened them Again of all their money And howe he changed apparrell with the kinge of Bomia his sonn, and then howe he turned Courtier &c. Beware of trustinge feined beggars or fawninge fellouss.

Sir Henry Wotton on *All Is True* (*Henry VIII*) and the Burning of the Globe (1613)

[Sir Henry Wotton (1568–1639), a highly educated poet and essayist, distinguished diplomat, and finally provost of Eton College, wrote to his nephew Sir Edmund Bacon shortly after the burning of the Globe. Chambers includes several other accounts of this incident in *The Elizabethan Stage*, vol. 2, pp. 419ff. The event is also recorded in John Stow's chronicles and was lamented by poets, including (several years later) Ben Jonson, and held up by Puritan divines like Prynne as an intimation of God's wrath. The excerpt below is from the earliest extant text, *Letters of Sir Henry Wotton to Sir Edmund Bacon* (London, 1661), p. 29.]

Now, to let matters of State sleep, I will entertain you at the present with what hath happened this week at the banks side. The Kings Players had a new Play, called *All is true*, representing some principall pieces of the raign of *Henry* 8, which was set forth with many extraordinary circumstances of Pomp and Majesty, even to the matting of the stage; the Knights of the Order, with their Georges and Garter, the Guards with their embroidered Coats, and the like: sufficient in truth within a while to make

---

4. Morgan/Belarius is not banished in the version of the play that comes down to us.
5. Rogue (Autolycus).

6. Probably "colt-pixie," a mischievous sprite or fairy.
7. Sheep shearing.

greatness very familiar, if not ridiculous. Now, King *Henry* making a Masque at the Cardinal, *Wolsey*'s house, and certain Chambers[1] being shot off at his entry, some of the paper, or other stuff wherewith one of them was stopped, did light on the thatch, where being thought at first but an idle smoak, and their eyes more attentive to the show, it kindled inwardly, and ran round like a train, consuming within less then an hour the whole house to the very grounds.

This was the fatal period of that vertuous fabrique, wherein yet nothing did perish, but wood and straw, and a few forsaken cloaks; only one man had his breeches set on fire, that would perhaps have broyled him, if he had not by the benefit of a provident wit put it out with bottle Ale. The rest when we meet.

Ben Jonson on *The Tempest* (and *Titus Andronicus*) (1614)

[This extract from *Bartholomew Fair* contains one of several allusions to Shakespeare in the plays of his associate and sometime rival. The first paragraph alludes to the fashion for revenge plays such as Shakespeare's *Titus Andronicus* and Kyd's *Spanish Tragedy*, at its height roughly twenty-five years before *Bartholomew Fair* was written. The second paragraph refers disapprovingly to *The Tempest* (1613), first produced shortly before *Bartholomew Fair*. The text is that reprinted in *WS*, vol. 2, from the 1631 edition of Jonson's play (from the play's Induction).]

Hee that will sweare, *Jeronimo*, or *Andronicus* are the best playes, yet, shall passe unexcepted at,[1] heere, as a man whose Judgement shewes it is constant, and hath stood still, these five and twentie, or thirtie yeeres. . . .

If there bee never a *Servant-monster* i' the Fayre; who can helpe it? he[2] sayes; nor a nest of Antiques?[3] Hee is loth to make Nature afraid[4] in his *Playes*, like those that beget *Tales, Tempests,* and such like *Drolleries,* to mix his head with other mens heeles; let the concupisence of *Jigges* and *Dances,* raigne as strong as it will amongst you.[5]

Shakespeare's Will (March 25, 1616)

[Shakespeare probably dictated this will sometime around January 1616. The first draft seems to have been dated in January, and 1616 is the most likely inference for the year (see note 1). The final revision was certainly made on the date given, but no clean copy was prepared, so the manuscript contains a substantial number of insertions and deletions. The text here has been silently emended to assist in ease of reading. Deleted passages have been eliminated; the most significant of these is reproduced in the notes, where significant interlineations are also identified. Most of the altered passages, as Chambers writes, simply "correct slips, make the legal terminology more precise, or incorporate afterthoughts." The revision of the will was occasioned chiefly by the February marriage of Shakespeare's daughter Judith. Our text is adapted from E. A. J. Honigmann and Susan Brock, eds., *Playhouse Wills, 1558–1642* (Manchester: Manchester University Press, 1993). For a facsimile and thorough discussion of the will, see *WS* 2:169–80.]

1. Small pieces of artillery, used for firing salutes.
1. Uncriticized.
2. The author.
3. Variant spelling of "antics," grotesque or ludicrous representations, or the actors (such as the clowns in *The Tempest*) playing such parts.
4. Make nature afraid by inexact imitation or too much fantasy.
5. *concupisence . . . you:* a reference to the dance generally incorporated into theatrical performance (see, for example, Platter's account above). Jonson suggests he is refusing to cater to the vulgar taste for more dancing in plays.

Testamentum willelmij Shackspeare

Vicesimo Quinto die martij Anno Regni Domini nostri Jacobi nunc Regis Anglie &c decimo quarto & Scotie xlixo Annoque domini 1616[1]

In the name of god Amen I William Shackspeare of Stratford upon Avon in the countie of warrwick gentleman in perfect health & memorie god be praysed doe make & Ordayne this my last will & testament in manner & forme followeing That ys to saye ffirst I Comend my Soule into the handes of god my Creator hoping & assuredlie beleeving through thonelie merittes of Jesus Christe my Saviour to be made partaker of lyfe everlastinge And my bodye to the Earth whereof yt ys made Item I Gyve & bequeath unto my Daughter Judyth One Hundred & ffyftie poundes of lawfull English money to be paied unto her in manner & forme followeing That ys to saye One Hundred Poundes in discharge of her marriage porcion[2] within one yeare after my Deceas with consideracion[3] after the Rate of twoe shillinges in the pound for soe long tyme as the same shalbe unpaied unto her after my deceas & the ffyftie poundes Residewe thereof upon her Surrendring of or gyving of such sufficient securitie as the overseers of this my Will shall like of to Surrender or graunnte All her[4] estate & Right that shall discend or come unto her after my deceas or that shee nowe hath of in or to one Copiehold tenemente with thappurtenaunces lyeing & being in Stratford upon Avon aforesaied in the saied countie of warrwick being parcell or holden of the mannour of Rowington unto my Daughter Susanna Hall & her heires for ever Item I Gyve & bequeath unto my saied Daughter Judith One Hundred & ffyftie Poundes more if shee or Anie issue of her bodie be Lyvinge att thend of three Yeares next ensueing the daie of the Date of this my Will during which tyme my executours to paie her consideracion from my deceas according to the Rate afore saied And if she dye within the saied terme without issue of her bodye then my will ys & I doe gyve & bequeath One Hundred Poundes thereof to my Neece Elizabeth Hall & the ffiftie Poundes to be sett fourth by my executours during the lief of my Sister Johane Harte & the use & proffitt thereof Cominge shalbe payed to my saied Sister Jone & after her deceas the saied l li[5] shall Remaine Amongst the children of my saied Sister Equallie to be Devided Amongst them But if my saied Daughter Judith be lyving att thend of the saied three Yeares or anie yssue of her bodye then my Will ys & soe I devise & bequeath the saied Hundred & ffyftie poundes to be sett out by my executours & overseers for the best benefitt of her & her issue & the stock[6] not to be paied unto her soe long as she shalbe marryed & Covert Baron[7] but my will ys that she shall have the consideracon yearelie paied unto her during her lief & after her deceas the saied stock and consideracion to bee paied to her children if she have Anie & if not to her executours or assignes she lyving the saied terme after my deceas Provided that if such husbond as she shall att thend of the saied three Yeares be marryed unto or attaine after doe sufficientle Assure unto her & thissue of her bodie landes Awnswereable to the porcion by this my will gyven unto her & to be adjudged soe by my executours & overseers then my will ys that the saied Cl li[8] shalbe paied to such husbond as shall make such assurance to his owne use Item I gyve & bequeath unto my saied sister Jone xx li & all my wearing Apparrell to be paied & Delivered within one yeare after my deceas And I doe Will & devise unto her the house with thappurtenaunces in Stratford wherein she dwelleth for her naturall lief under the yearelie Rent of xii d. Itm I gyve & bequeath unto her three sonns William Harte[9]

---

1. *Testamentum . . . 1616:* The Will of William Shakespeare (marginal heading). On the twenty-fifth day of March, in the fourteenth year of the reign of our lord James now King of England, etc., and of Scotland the forty-ninth, in the year of our Lord 1616. (The abbreviation for "January" is crossed out in the manuscript, "March" having been substituted at the time the will was revised.)

2. The phrase "in discharge of her marriage porcion" was inserted during the course of revision.

3. Compensation, or interest.

4. Susanna Hall's. (The preceding "All" marks the beginning of a new sentence.)

5. *l li:* £50.

6. Principal.

7. *Covert Baron:* under the protection of a husband.

8. *Cl li:* £150.

9. A blank in the manuscript. Shakespeare appears to have forgotten the name of one of his nephews, Thomas.

hart & Michaell Harte ffyve poundes A peece to be payed within one Yeare after my deceas[1] Item I gyve & bequeath unto her the saied Elizabeth Hall All my Plate (except my brod silver & gilt bole)[2] that I nowe have att the Date of this my Will Itm I gyve & bequeath unto the Poore of Stratford aforesaied tenn poundes to mr Thomas Combe my Sword to Thomas Russell Esquier ffyve poundes & to ffrauncis Collins of the Borough of Warwick in the countie of Warrwick gentleman thirteene poundes Sixe shillinges & Eight pence to be paied within one Yeare after my Deceas Itm I gyve & bequeath to Hamlett Sadler xxvi s viii d[3] to buy him A Ringe to William Raynoldes gentleman xxvi s viii d to buy him A Ringe to my godson William Walker xx s in gold to Anthonye Nashe gentleman xxvi s viii d & to mr John Nashe xx vi s viii d & to my fellows John Hemynnges Richard Burbage & Henry Cundell xxvi s viii d A peece to buy them Ringes[4] Item I Gyve Will bequeath & Devise unto my Daughter Susanna Hall for better enabling of her to performe this my will & towardes the performans thereof All that Capitall messuage or tenemente[5] with thappurtenaunces in Stratford aforesaied Called the newe place Wherein I nowe Dwell & twoe messuages or tenementes with thappurtenaunces scituat lyeing & being in Henley streete within the borough of Stratford aforesaied And all my barnes stables Orchardes gardens landes tenementes & hereditamentes[6] Whatsoever scituat lyeing & being or to be had Receyved perceyved or taken within the townes Hamlettes villages ffieldes & groundes of Stratford upon Avon Oldstratford Bushopton & Welcombe or in anie of them in the saied countie of warrwick And alsoe All that Messuage or tenemente with thappurtenaunces wherein one John Robinson dwelleth scituat lyeing & being in the blackfriers in London nere the Wardrobe & all other my landes tenementes & hereditamentes Whatsoever To Have & to hold All & singuler the saied premisses with their Appurtenaunces unto the saied Susanna Hall for & During the terme of her naturall lief & after her Deceas to the first sonne of her bodie lawfullie Issueing & to the heires males of the bodie of the saied first Sonne lawfullie Issueinge & for defalt of such issue to the second Sonne of her bodie lawfullie issueinge & to the heires males of the bodie of the saied Second Sonne lawfullie issueinge & for defalt of such heires to the third Sonne of the bodie of the saied Susanna Lawfullie issueing & of the heries males of the bodie of the saied third sonne lawfullie issueing And for defalt of such issue the same soe to be & Remaine to the ffourth ffyfth sixte & Seaventh sonnes of her bodie lawfullie issueing one after Another & to the heires[7] Males of the bodies of the saied ffourth fifth Sixte & Seaventh sonnes lawfullie issueing in such manner as yt ys before Lymitted to be & Remaine to the first second & third Sonns of her bodie & to their heires males And for defalt of such issue the saied premisses to be & Remaine to my sayed Neece Hall[8] & the heires Males of her bodie Lawfullie yssueing for Defalt of such issue to my Daughter Judith & the heires Males of her bodie lawfullie issueinge And for Defalt of such issue to the Right heires of me the saied William

1. *unto . . . deceas:* this passage was inserted at the top of the second page, probably when the will was revised. The following lines, with which the page originally began, are crossed out in the original: "to be sett out for her within one Yeare after my Deceas by my executours with thadvise & direccions of my overseers for her best proffitt untill her Marriage & then the same with the increase thereof to be paied unto her." These lines evidently referred to Judith Shakespeare as unmarried.
2. This parenthetical clause is an insertion, and has sparked some debate about Shakespeare's opinion of Judith's marriage.
3. The "s" stands for "shillings," the "d" for "pence."
4. *to my fellows . . . Ringes:* Shakespeare's "fellows," or colleagues, Heminges, Burbage, and Condell, had worked with him in the Lord Chamberlain's Men and

King's Men for many years. Many other wills and documents of the period provide evidence of the practice of wearing mourning rings alluded to here.
5. Residence. *messuage:* dwelling house with its outbuildings or adjoining lands.
6. Heritable property.
7. In addition to the signature near the end, Shakespeare signed the will here, in the bottom right-hand corner of the second page.
8. Susanna Hall's daughter Elizabeth, actually Shakespeare's granddaughter (the sense of "niece" is less restricted in early modern usage). Elizabeth proved to be Susanna's only surviving child, and since Susanna was already thirty-three in 1616, the hypothetical series of seven sons preceding this mention of Elizabeth is doubly remarkable.

Shackspere for ever Itm I gyve unto my wief my second best bed[9] with the furniture Item I gyve & bequeath to my saied Daughter Judith my broad silver gilt bole All the Rest of my goodes Chattelles Leases plate Jewels & household stuffe Whatsoever after my dettes and Legasies paied & my funerall expences discharged I gyve Devise & bequeath to my Sonne in Lawe John Hall gentleman & my Daughter Susanna his wief Whom I ordaine & make executours of this my Last Will & testament And I doe intreat & Appoint the saied Thomas Russell Esquier & ffrauncis Collins gentleman to be overseers hereof And doe Revoke All former wills & publishe this to be my last Will & testament In Witnes Whereof I have here unto put my hand the Daie & Yeare first above Written. /   By me William Shakespeare witnes to the publishing hereof Fra: Collyns Julyus Shawe John Robinson Hamnet Sadler Robert Whattcott[1]

Front Matter from the First Folio of Shakespeare's Plays (1623)

[John Heminges and Henry Condell, friends and colleagues of Shakespeare, organized this first publication of his collected (thirty-six) plays. Eighteen of the plays had not appeared in print before, and for these the First Folio is the sole surviving source. Only *Pericles*, *The Two Noble Kinsmen*, and *Sir Thomas More* are not included in the volume. Four of the first twelve (printed) pages of the Folio are reproduced below in reduced facsimile. They include Jonson's brief address "To the Reader," Droeshout's portrait of Shakespeare, a table of contents, and a list of actors.]

9. This bequest to Shakespeare's wife, Anne, was inserted in the course of his revision of the will. She is not mentioned elsewhere in the will at least partly because, as Shakespeare's widow, she would be guaranteed a certain portion of the estate by law. The appearance of this inserted bequest is nevertheless strange enough to have evoked much speculation.
1. After Shakespeare's death, the will was endorsed here at the bottom of the third page with a Latin inscription indicating that the will had gone to probate before a magistrate on June 22, 1616.

To the Reader.

This Figure, that thou here seeſt put,
 It vvas for gentle Shakeſpeare cut;
Wherein the Grauer had a ſtrife
 with Nature, to out-doo the life :
O, could he but haue dravvne his vvit
 As well in braſſe, as he hath hit
His face ; the Print would then ſurpaſſe
 All, that vvas euer vvrit in braſſe.
But, ſince he cannot, Reader, looke
 Not on his Picture, but his Booke.

B. I.

Mr. WILLIAM

SHAKESPEARES

COMEDIES,
HISTORIES, &
TRAGEDIES.

Published according to the True Originall Copies.

Martin Droeshout sculpsit London.

LONDON
Printed by Isaac Iaggard, and Ed. Blount. 1623.

A CATALOGVE

of the feuerall Comedies, Histories, and Tragedies contained in this Volume.

The Workes of William Shakeſpeare,

containing all his Comedies, Hiſtories, and
Tragedies: Truely ſet forth, according to their firſt
ORIGINALL.

The Names of the Principall Actors
in all theſe Playes.

William Shakeſpeare.	Samuel Gilburne.
Richard Burbadge.	Robert Armin.
John Hemmings.	William Oſtler.
Auguſtine Phillips.	Nathan Field.
William Kempt.	John Underwood.
Thomas Poope.	Nicholas Tooley.
George Bryan.	William Eccleſtone.
Henry Condell.	Joſeph Taylor.
William Slye.	Robert Benfield.
Richard Cowly.	Robert Goughe.
John Lowine.	Richard Robinſon.
Samuell Croſſe.	Iohn Shancke.
Alexander Cooke.	Iohn Rice.

John Milton on Shakespeare (1630)

[John Milton (1608–1674) was born in London and as a boy might conceivably have seen Shakespeare's company act. This poem first appeared prefixed to the Second Folio of Shakespeare's works in 1632 and again in the 1640 *Poems* of Shakespeare. The text is from the 1645 edition of Milton's *Poems*, as reprinted in *WS*, vol. 2, but the title given is from the Second Folio version.]

An Epitaph on the admirable Dramaticke Poet, W. Shakespeare

What needs my *Shakespear* for his honour'd Bones,
The labour of an age in piled Stones,
Or that his hallow'd reliques should be hid
Under a star-ypointing[1] *Pyramid?*
Dear son of memory, great heir of Fame,
What need'st thou such weak witnes of thy name?
Thou in our wonder and astonishment
Hast built thy self a live-long Monument.
For whilst toth' shame of slow-endeavouring art,
They easie numbers flow, and that each heart
Hath from the leaves of thy unvalu'd[2] Book,
Those Delphick[3] lines with deep impression took,
Then thou our fancy of itself bereaving,[4]
Dost make us Marble with too much conceaving;
And so Sepulcher'd in such pomp dost lie,
That Kings for such a Tomb would wish to die.

Ben Jonson on Shakespeare (1623–37)

[In addition to numerous allusions to Shakespeare in his plays, Ben Jonson (1573–1637) writes explicitly about his friend, colleague, and rival in a number of places, most significantly in the two commendatory poems prefixed to the First Folio (see above) and in the published extracts from his notebooks entitled *Timber: or, Discoveries; Made upon Men and Matter,* first published in his *Works* of 1640. It is impossible to date the original entries precisely; Chambers's conjecture is that the following entry on Shakespeare was made after 1630. The text is from the authoritative edition by C. H. Herford and Percy Simpson, vol. 8 (Oxford: Clarendon Press, 1952).]

Indeed, the multitude commend Writers, as they doe Fencers, or Wrastlers; who if they come in robustiously, and put for it, with a deale of violence, are received for the *braver-fellowes:* when many times their owne rudenesse is a cause of their disgrace; and a slight touch of their Adversary, gives all that boisterous force the foyle. But in these things, the unskilfull are naturally deceiv'd, and judging wholly by the bulke, thinke rude things greater then polish'd; and scatter'd more numerous, then compos'd: Nor thinke this only to be true in the sordid multitude, but the neater sort of our *Gallants:* for all are the multitude; only they differ in cloaths, not in judgement or understanding.

I remember, the Players have often mentioned it as an honour to *Shakespeare,*

---

1. Pointing to the stars.
2. Invaluable.
3. Reference to Apollo, god of poetry, whose most famous shrine was at Delphi.

4. *our . . . bereaving:* "our imaginations are rapt 'out of ourselves,' leaving behind our soulless bodies like statues"—Isabel MacCaffrey.

that in his writing, (whatsoever he penn'd) hee never blotted out line.[1] My answer hath beene, Would he had blotted a thousand. Which they thought a malevolent speech. [I had not told posterity this,] but for their ignorance, who choose that circumstance to commend their friend by, wherein he most faulted. And to justifie mine owne candor, (for I lov'd the man, and doe honour his memory (on this side Idolatry) as much as any.) Hee was (indeed) honest, and of an open, and free nature: had an excellent *Phantsie*[2]; brave notions, and gentle expressions: wherein hee flow'd with that facility, that sometime it was necessary he should be stop'd: *Sufflaminandus erat*;[3] as *Augustus* said of *Haterius*.[4] His wit was in his owne power; would the rule of it had beene so too. Many times hee fell into those things, could not escape laughter: As when hee said in the person of *Cæsar*, one speaking to him; *Cæsar, thou dost me wrong.* Hee replyed: *Cæsar did never wrong, but with just cause*[5]: and such like; which were ridiculous. But hee redeemed his vices, with his vertues. There was ever more in him to be praysed, then to be pardoned.

John Aubrey on Shakespeare (1681)

[What Chambers calls "the Shakespeare-mythos" was already well under way by the time John Aubrey (1626–1697) collected these anecdotes for the biographies in his *Brief Lives*, first anthologized in 1692. Aubrey's chief sources were prominent figures of the Restoration stage, which had seen increasingly popular revivals and adaptations of *Hamlet, The Tempest,* and many other plays of Shakespeare. Numerous actors and critics in the latter part of the seventeenth century helped to "rehabilitate" Shakespeare; if at the time of the Restoration his plays had seemed terribly musty and old-fashioned, by the 1680s his reputation as an author of lasting value was well established, thanks to the enthusiasm of Restoration playgoers. Aubrey's first source, Christopher Beeston, was the son of a one-time member of Shakespeare's company. William Davenant was a formidable entrepreneur as well as a dramatist, and Thomas Shadwell a prolific playwright perhaps best remembered as Dryden's King of Dullness. The text is from Chambers's transcription (*WS*, vol. 2), with a few silent emendations for ease of reading. Some of the material is from the published version of *Brief Lives,* and some of it from manuscript notes apparently used in writing the *Lives.*]

> the more to be admired q[uia][1] he was not a company keeper[2]
> lived in Shoreditch, wouldnt be debauched, & if invited to
> writ; he was in paine.[3]
>
> > W. Shakespeare.

M[r]. William Shakespear. [*bay-wreath in margin*] was borne at Stratford upon Avon, in the County of Warwick; his father was a Butcher, & I have been told heretofore by some of the neighbours, that when he was a boy he exercised his father's Trade, but when he kill'd a Calfe, he would doe it in a *high style,* & make a Speech. There was at that time another Butcher's son in this Towne, that was held not at all inferior to him for a naturall witt, his acquaintance & coetanean,[4] but dyed young. This Wm. being inclined naturally to Poetry and acting, came to London I guesse about 18. and was an Actor at one of the Play-houses and did act

---

1. Compare Heminges and Condell's address to the reader in the First Folio: "And what he thought, he uttered with that easinesse, that wee have scarse received from him a blot in his papers."
2. Imagination.
3. "He needed the drag-chain" (adapted from Marcus Seneca's *Controversiae* 4, Preface).
4. Quintus Haterius, Roman rhetorician (d. 26 C.E.).
5. See *Julius Caesar* 3.1.47.

1. Because.
2. "Company keeper" can mean "libertine" or "reveler"; the general sense of the passage is that Shakespeare is "the more to be admired" for his temperance and modesty.
3. The embarrassment ("paine") at being asked to write is presumably due to the same alleged modesty.
4. Contemporary.

exceedingly well: now B. Johnson was never a good Actor, but an excellent Instructor. He began early to make essayes at Dramatique Poetry, which at that time was very lowe; and his Playes tooke well: He was a handsome well shap't man: very good company, and of a very readie and pleasant smooth Witt. The Humour[5] of . . . the Constable in a Midsomersnight's Dreame, he happened to take at Grendon [*In margin,* 'I thinke it was Midsomer night that he happened to lye there'.] in Bucks[6] which is the roade from London to Stratford, and there was living that Constable about 1642 when I first came to Oxon.[7] M[r]. Jos. Howe is of that parish and knew him. Ben Johnson and he did gather Humours of men dayly where ever they came. One time as he was at the Tavern at Stratford super[8] Avon, one Combes an old rich Usurer was to be buryed, he makes there this extemporary[9] Epitaph

> Ten in the Hundred[1] the Devill allowes
> But *Combes* will have twelve, he sweares & vowes:
> If any one askes who lies in this Tombe:
> Hoh! quoth the Devill, 'Tis my John o' Combe.

He was wont to goe to his native Country once a yeare. I thinke I have been told that he left 2 or 300[li] per annum[2] there and therabout: to a sister. [*In margin,* 'V.[3] his Epitaph in Dugdales Warwickshire'.] I have heard S[r] Wm. Davenant and M[r]. Thomas Shadwell (who is counted the best Comœdian we have now) say, that he had a most prodigious Witt, and did admire his naturall parts beyond all other Dramaticall writers. He was wont to say, That he never blotted out a line in his life: sayd Ben: Johnson, I wish he had blotted out a thousand. [*In margin,* 'B. Johnsons Underwoods'.] His Comœdies will remaine witt, as long as the English tongue is understood; for that he handles mores hominum;[4] now our present writers reflect so much upon particular persons, and coxcombeities, that 20 yeares hence, they will not be understood. Though as Ben: Johnson sayes of him, that he had but little Latine and lesse Greek, He understood Latine pretty well: for he had been in his younger yeares a Schoolmaster in the Countrey. [*In margin,* 'from M[r] —— Beeston'.]

S[r] William Davenant Knight Poet Laureate was borne in _____ street in the City of Oxford, at the Crowne Tavern. His father was John Davenant a Vintner there, a very grave and discreet Citizen: his mother was a very beautifull woman, & of a very good witt and of conversation extremely agreable. . . . M[r] William Shakespeare was wont to goe into Warwickshire once a yeare, and did commonly in his journey lye at this house in Oxon: where he was exceedingly respected. I have heard parson Robert D[avenant] say that here M[r] W. Shakespeare here gave him a hundred kisses. Now S[r] Wm. would sometimes when he was pleasant over a glasse of wine with his most intimate friends e.g. Sam: Butler (author of Hudibras) &c. say, that it seemed to him that he writt with the very spirit that Shakespeare,[5] and seemed contented enough to be thought his Son: he would tell them the story as above. in which way his mother had a very light report, whereby she was called a whore.

5. Character, personality.
6. Buckinghamshire.
7. Oxford.
8. Upon.
9. Extemporaneous.
1. 10-percent interest. (Combe is damned because he charges 12 percent on his loans, 2 percent above the maximum allowed for usury not to be a mortal sin.)
2. £300 a year.
3. See.
4. *for that . . . hominum:* because he treats of (general) human manners or customs.
5. A word such as "had" seems to be missing.

TIMELINE

TEXT	CONTEXT
	1558 Queen Mary I, a Roman Catholic, dies; her sister Elizabeth, raised Protestant, is proclaimed queen.
	1559 Church of England is reestablished under the authority of the sovereign with the passage of the Act of Uniformity and the Act of Supremacy.
1562 *The Tragedy of Gorboduc*, by Thomas Norton and Thomas Sackville, is performed; it is the first English play in blank verse.	**1563** The Church of England adopts the Thirty-nine Articles of Religion, detailing its points of doctrine and clarifying its differences both from Roman Catholicism and from more extreme forms of Protestantism.
	1564 William Shakespeare is born in Stratford to John and Mary Arden Shakespeare; he is christened a few days later, on April 23.
	1565 John Shakespeare is made an alderman of Stratford.
	1567 Mary Queen of Scots is imprisoned on suspicion of the murder of her husband, Lord Darnley. Their infant son, Charles James, is crowned James VI of Scotland.
	1568 John Shakespeare is elected Bailiff of Stratford, the town's highest office. Performances in Stratford by the Queen's Players and the Earl of Worcester's men.
	1572 An act is passed that severely punishes vagrants and wanderers, including actors not affiliated with a patron. Performances in Stratford by the Earl of Leicester's men.
	1574 The Earl of Warwick's and Earl of Worcester's men perform in Stratford.
	1576 James Burbage, father of Richard, later the leading actor in Shakespeare's company, builds the Theatre in Shoreditch, a suburb of London.
	1577 The Curtain Theatre opens in Shoreditch.

TEXT	CONTEXT
	1577–1580 Sir Francis Drake circumnavigates the globe.
	1578 Mary Shakespeare pawns her lands, suggesting that the family is in financial distress. Lord Strange's Men and Lord Essex's Men perform at Stratford.
	1580 A Jesuit mission is established in England with the aim of reconverting the nation to Roman Catholicism.
	1582 Shakespeare marries Anne Hathaway.
	1583 The birth of Shakespeare's older daughter, Susanna.
	1584 Sir Walter Ralegh establishes the first English colony in the New World at Roanoke Island in modern North Carolina; the colony fails.
	1585 The birth of Shakespeare's twin son and daughter, Hamnet and Judith. John Shakespeare is fined for not going to church.
	1586 Sir Philip Sidney dies from battle wounds.
1587 Thomas Kyd's *The Spanish Tragedy* (pub. c. 1592) and Christopher Marlowe's *Tamburlaine* (pub. 1590) are performed.	**1587** Mary Queen of Scots is executed for treason against Elizabeth I. Francis Drake defeats the Spanish fleet at Cádiz. John Shakespeare loses his position as an alderman. Philip Henslowe builds the Rose theater at Bankside, on the Thames.
	1588 The Spanish Armada attempts an invasion of England but is defeated.
1589 Robert Greene, *Friar Bacon and Friar Bungay.* Thomas Kyd, *Hamlet* (not extant; perhaps a source for Shakespeare's *Hamlet*). Christopher Marlowe, *The Jew of Malta.*	**1589** Shakespeare is probably affiliated with the amalgamated Lord Strange's and Lord Admiral's Men from about this time until 1594.
1590 Anonymous, *The True Chronicle History of King Leir, and his Three Daughters.*	**1590** James VI of Scotland marries Anne of Denmark, but believes himself to be bewitched on his honeymoon when he cannot consummate the marriage. Witch trials in Scotland.
1591 Shakespeare's *1, 2,* and *3 Henry VI* performed.	**1592** The theatrical manager of the Admiral's Men, Philip Henslowe, begins his diary, continued until 1604, recording his business

TEXT	CONTEXT
	transactions, an important source for theater historians.
1592–1593 *Richard III.* *Venus and Adonis.* *The Comedy of Errors.* *Titus Andronicus.* *The Taming of the Shrew.*	From June 1592 to June 1594, London theaters are shut down because of the plague; acting companies tour the provinces.
1594 Shakespeare dedicates *The Rape of Lucrece* to Henry Wriothesley, Earl of Southampton.	**1594** Roderigo Lopez, Portuguese physician and a Jewish convert to Christianity, is executed on slight evidence for having plotted to poison Elizabeth I.
1594–1596 *A Midsummer Night's Dream.* *Richard II.* *Romeo and Juliet.*	The birth of James VI's first son, Henry.
	1595 Shakespeare lives in St. Helen's Parish, Bishopsgate, London. Shakespeare apparently becomes a sharer in (provides capital for) the newly re-formed Lord Chamberlain's Men. The Swan Theatre is built in Bankside. Hugh O'Neill, Earl of Tyrone, rebels against English rule in Ireland. Walter Ralegh explores Guiana, on the north coast of South America.
1596 *King John.* *The Merchant of Venice.* *1 Henry IV.*	**1596** John Shakespeare is granted a coat of arms; hence the title of "gentleman." William Shakespeare's son Hamnet dies.
1597 *The Merry Wives of Windsor.*	**1597** James Burbage builds the second Blackfriars Theatre. But the Lord Chamberlain's Men are not permitted to play in it, so they rent it to boys' companies for a number of years. The landlord refuses to renew the lease on the land under the Theatre in Shoreditch.
1598 *2 Henry IV.* *Much Ado About Nothing.* Ben Jonson, *Every Man in His Humor,* which lists Shakespeare as one of the actors.	**1598** The Edict of Nantes ends the French civil wars, granting toleration to Protestants. Materials from the demolished Theatre in Shoreditch are transported across the Thames to be used in building the Globe Theatre.
1599 *Henry V.* *Julius Caesar.* *As You Like it.*	**1599** The queen's favorite, Robert Devereux, Earl of Essex, leads an expedition to Ireland in March but returns home without permission in October and is imprisoned. Satires and other offensive books are prohibited by ecclesiastical order. Extant copies are gathered and burned. Two notorious satirists, Thomas Nashe and Gabriel Harvey, are forbidden to publish.

TEXT	CONTEXT
1600 *Hamlet.* Michael Drayton and several collaborators, who object to Shakespeare's depiction of Oldcastle-Falstaff in the *Henry IV* plays, write *The First Part of the True and Honorable History of the Life of Sir John Oldcastle, the Good Lord Cobham.*	**1600** The Earl of Essex is suspended from some of his offices and confined to house arrest. The birth of James VI's second son, Charles. The founding of the East India Company. Edward Alleyn and Philip Henslowe build the Fortune Theatre for the Lord Admiral's Men, competing with the Lord Chamberlain's Men at the Globe.
1601 "The Phoenix and the Turtle" published in Robert Chester's *Love's Martyr.* *Twelfth Night.* In the "War of the Theaters," Ben Jonson, John Marston, and Thomas Dekker write a series of satiric plays mocking one another.	**1601** The Earl of Essex leads some gentlemen against Elizabeth I, but the rising is quickly quelled. A few of the rebels, including Shakespeare's patron, the Earl of Southampton, arrange a staging of *Richard II* at the Globe, apparently to incite rebellion. Essex is convicted of treason and beheaded. Shakespeare's father dies.
1602 *Troilus and Cressida.*	**1602** Shakespeare makes substantial real-estate purchases in Stratford. The opening of the Bodleian Library in Oxford.
	1603 Queen Elizabeth dies; she is succeeded by her cousin, James VI of Scotland (now James I of England). Shakespeare's name appears for the last time in Ben Jonson's lists of actors, as a "principal tragedian" in *Sejanus.* Plague closes the London theaters from mid-1603 to April 1604. Hugh O'Neill surrenders in Ireland.
1604 *Measure for Measure.* *Othello.*	**1604** The conclusion of a peace with Spain makes travel across the Atlantic safer, encouraging plans for English colonies in the Americas.
1605 *All's Well That Ends Well.* *King Lear.*	**1605** The discovery of the Gunpowder Plot by some radical Catholics to blow up the Houses of Parliament during its opening ceremonies, when the royal family, Lords, and Commons are assembled in one place. The Red Bull Theatre built.
1606 *Macbeth.* *Antony and Cleopatra.* Ben Jonson, *Volpone.* Anonymous, *The Revenger's Tragedy.*	**1606** The London and Plymouth Companies receive charters to colonize Virginia. Parliament passes "An Act to Restrain Abuses of Players," prohibiting oaths or blasphemy onstage.
1607 *Timon of Athens.* *Pericles.*	**1607** An English colony is established in Jamestown, Virginia. Shakespeare's daughter Susanna marries John Hall. Shakespeare's brother Edmund (described as a player) dies.

TEXT	CONTEXT
1608 *Coriolanus*.	**1608** The King's Men obtain permission to play at the second Blackfriars Theatre, a smaller indoor venue.
1609 *Cymbeline*. Unauthorized publication of the sonnets.	
1610 *The Winter's Tale*. Ben Jonson, *The Alchemist*.	**1610** Henry is made Prince of Wales. Shakespeare probably returns to Stratford and settles there.

1611 *The Tempest*.
 Francis Beaumont and John Fletcher,
    A King and No King.
 Publication of the Authorized (King James)
    Bible.
	1611 Plantation of Ulster in Ireland, a colony of English and Scottish Protestants settled on land confiscated from Irish rebels.

1612 *All Is True (Henry VIII)*, with John Fletcher. John Webster, *The White Devil*.	**1612** Prince Henry dies.
1613 *The Two Noble Kinsmen*, with John Fletcher.	**1613** Princess Elizabeth marries Frederick V, Elector Palatine. The Globe Theatre burns down during a performance of *All Is True*.
1614 Ben Jonson, *Bartholomew Fair*. John Webster, *The Duchess of Malfi*.	**1614** Philip Henslowe and Jacob Meade build the Hope Theatre, used both for play performances and as a bearbaiting arena. The Globe Theatre reopens.
1616 Ben Jonson publishes *The Works of Benjamin Jonson*, the first collection of plays by an English author.	**1616** William Harvey describes the circulation of the blood. Shakespeare's daughter Judith marries. Shakespeare dies on April 23.
1623 Members of the King's Men publish the First Folio of Shakespeare's plays.	

Textual Variants

THE TAMING OF THE SHREW

CONTROL TEXT: F

s.p. KATHERINE [F's use of *Katerina, Katherina, Katerine, Kate,* and *Katherine* has been standardized throughout.]
s.p. PETRUCCIO [F's use of *Petruchio* has been changed throughout.]
s.p. SLY [F's use of *Beggar* has been changed throughout.]
s.p. BARTHOLOMEW [F's use of *Lady* when Bartholomew is dressed as a woman has been changed throughout.]

Induction 1.13 Breathe Brach **78 s.p. A PLAYER** 2. *Player* **86 s.p. ANOTHER PLAYER** *Sincklo*
Induction 2.2 lordship Lord **51 wi'th'** with **91 Greet** Greece
1.1.3 fore for **13 Vincentio** *Vincentio's* **25 Mi perdonate** *Me Pardonato* **156 *captum* captam** **232 faith** 'faith **237 your** you
1.2.18 masters mistris **23 *Con tutto il cuore ben trovato* Contutti le core bene trobatto 24 *ben* bene 24 *molto onorato* multo honorata 31 pip** peepe **43 this'** this **70 as** is as **115 me and other more,** me. Other more **167 help me** helpe me **185 Antonio's** *Butonios* **186 his fortune** my fortune **209 ours** yours **263 feat** seeke **278 *ben* Been**
2.1.8 thee [not in F] **60 Licio** Litio [Licio is four times referred to as *Lisio* and three times as *Litio* in F. Standardized to "Licio" throughout.] **75–76 wooing. Neighbour** wooing neighbors **78 unto you** vnto **240 askance** asconce **322 in me** asconce **343 cypress** Cypres **367 Marseilles** Marcellus
3.1.4 this Bianca is, this is **28, 32, 41 *Sigeia . . . Sigeia . . . Sigeia*** sigeria . . . Sigeria . . . sigeria **46–48 s.p. HORTENSIO How . . . yet.** [assigned to Lucentio in F] **49 s.p. BIANCA** *Lucentio* **50 s.p. LUCENTIO** *Bian⟨ca⟩.* **52 s.p. BIANCA** *Hort⟨ensio⟩.* **79 change** charge **odd** old **80 s.p. MESSENGER** *Nicke.*
3.2.16 them [not in F] **29 thy** [not in F] **30 old news** [not in F] **33 hear** heard **51 weighed** Waid **52 half-cheeked** halfe-chekt **84 not** [not in F]
3.3.1 sir, to love sir, Loue **3 I** [not in F] **39 vicar** wench
4.1.22 s.p. CURTIS *Gru⟨mio⟩.* **75 sleekly** slickely **99 s.p. GRUMIO** *Gre⟨mio⟩.*

4.2.4 s.p. HORTENSIO *Luc⟨entio⟩.* **6 s.p. LUCENTIO** *Hor⟨tensio⟩.* **8 s.p. LUCENTIO** *Hor⟨tensio⟩.* **13 none** me **31 her** them **72** [ascribed to "*Par.*"] **in** me
4.3.63 s.p. HABERDASHER *Fel.* **81 a** [not in F] **88 like a** like **93 nor cap** neither cap **175 account'st** accountedst
4.4.1 Sir Sirs
4.5.5 he's has **16 except** expect **26 t'attend to come**
4.6.19 is in **23 so it shall be still** so it shall be so **39 where is** whether is **79 be** [not in F]
5.1.5 master's mistris **43 master's** Mistris **56 copintank** copataine
5.2.2 done come **38 thee, lad** the lad **46 two too** 110 **wonders** a wonder **132 a fiue** 136 **you're** your

A MIDSUMMER NIGHT'S DREAM

CONTROL TEXT: Q1

F: The Folio of 1623
Q1: The Quarto of 1600
Q2: The Quarto of 1619

Title: A Midsummer Night's Dream [Q1 title page, head title] A mydsomer nighte dreame [Stationers' Register] A Midsommer nightes dream [Q1 running titles]

s.p. THESEUS [Q's use of *Theseus* and *Duke* has been standardized throughout.]
s.p. HIPPOLYTA [Q's use of *Hippolyta* and *Duchess* has been standardized throughout.]
s.p. BOTTOM [Q's use of *Bottom, Pyramus,* and *Clown* has been standardized throughout.]
s.p. FLUTE [Q's use of *Flute* and *Thisbe* has been standardized throughout.]
s.p. ROBIN [Q's use of *Robin* and *Puck* has been standardized throughout.]
s.p. QUINCE [Q's use of *Quince* and *Prologue* has been standardized throughout.]
s.p. SNOUT [Q's use of *Snout* and *Wall* has been standardized throughout.]
s.p. SNUG [Q's use of *Snug* and *Lion* has been standardized throughout.]
s.p. TITANIA [Q's use of *Titania* and *Queen* has been standardized throughout.]
s.p. STARVELING [Q's use of *Starveling* and *Moonshine* has been standardized throughout.]

1.1.4 wanes [Q2, F] waues **10 New Now 24 Stand forth Demetrius.** [Q italicizes and centers on a separate line.] **26 Stand forth Lysander.** [Q italicizes and centers on a separate line.] **27 This** This man **136 low** loue **139 merit** else, it **159–60 And . . . son.** / **From . . . leagues.** From . . . leagues? / **And . . . sonne: 191 I'd** ile **200 Helen** Helena **212 sleights** flights **219 stranger companies** strange companions
1.2.20 stones stormes **64 s.p. ALL THE REST** All.
2.1.7 moonës Moons **58 make room** roome **61 Fairies** Fairy **78 Perigouna** Perigenia **79 Aegles** Eagles **101 cheer** heere **109 thin** chinne **158 the** [not in Q] **190 slay . . . slayeth** stay . . . stayeth **201 nor** [F] not **206 lose** loose
2.2.9 s.p. FIRST FAIRY [not in Q] **13 s.p. CHO-RUS** [not in Q] **25–30 Sing . . . with lull-aby.** &c. **31–32 Hence . . . sentinel** [indented as part of the song] **44–45 comfort . . . Be it** [Q2, F] comfor . . . Bet it **49 good** [Q2, F] god **53 is** [Q2, F] it
3.1.44 s.p. SNOUT Sn. **59 and** or **71 Odours, odours.** [F] Odours, odorous **76 s.p. ROBIN** Puck. [F] Quin⟨ce⟩. **82 bristly** brisky **133 own** [Q2, F] owe **144 Mote** Moth **145 s.p. A FAIRY . . . ANOTHER . . . ANOTHER . . . ANOTHER . . .** All Four Fairies **148 apricots** Apricocks **157 s.p. A FAIRY** I. Fai. **157–58 mortal.** / **ANOTHER Hail.** mortall, haile **159–60 s.p. ANOTHER . . . ANOTHER** 2. Fai . . . 3. Fai. **170 you** of you **182 love's** louers
3.2.19 mimic [F] Minnick **80 so** [not in Q] **85 sleep** slippe **137 s.p. HELENA** [not in Q] **165 here** heare **202 is all forgot** is all for-got **214 like** life **221 passionate** [F; not in Q] **251 prayers** praise **258 No, no, sir** [F] No, no **yield** heele **280 doubt** of doubt **300 gentlemen** [Q2, F] gentleman **327 but** [Q2, F] hut **387 exiled** exile
3.3.14 shalt [Q2, F] shat **37 to** [not in Q]
4.1.19 courtesy curtsie **21–22 Pease-** / **Blossom** Cobwebbe **33 thee off** thee **38 all ways** alwaies **52 flow'rets** flouriets **70 o'er** or **79 these five** these, fine **93 nightës** nights **102 vanguard** vaward **114 Seemed** Seeme **125 this is** [Q2, F] this **170 in sickness** a sicknesse **188 found** [Q2, F] fonnd **189 It** [F] Are you sure / That we are awake? It **195 let us** [Q2, F] lets **201 t'ex-pound** expound **203–4 a patched fool** [F] patcht a foole **208 ballad** Ballet
4.2.3 s.p. STARVELING [F] Flut⟨e⟩. **26 no** [F] not
5.1.34 our [F] Or **38 Egeus** [F] Philostrate **38, 42, 61, 72, 76, 106 s.p. EGEUS** [F] Philostrate **44 s.p. LYSANDER** [F] The⟨seus⟩. **46, 50, 54, 58 s.p. THESEUS** [F; not in Q]

48, 52, 56 s.p. LYSANDER [F; not in Q] **59 strange black** strange **189 up in thee** [F] now againe **204 wall Moon down** [F] used **263 gleams** beames **299 prove** [Q2, F] yet prooue **306 mote** moth **307 warrant** warnd **337 s.p. BOTTOM** [F] Lyon.
5.2.1 lion Lyons **2 behowls** beholds **13 we** wee **49–50 And . . . blessed** / **Ever . . . rest.** Euer . . . rest, / And . . . blest.

THE COMICAL HISTORY OF THE MERCHANT OF VENICE, OR OTHERWISE CALLED THE JEW OF VENICE

CONTROL TEXT: Q1

F: The Folio of 1623
Q1: The Quarto of 1600
Q2: The Quarto of 1619

s.p. SHYLOCK [Q1's use of Iew⟨e⟩ has been standardized throughout.]
s.p. LAUNCELOT [Q1's use of Clo⟨wne⟩ has been standardized throughout.]
s.p. SALERIO [Q1's use of Salarino in some s.d.'s and s.p.'s has been standardized throughout.]

Title: The Comical History of the Merchant of Venice, or Otherwise Called the Jew of Venice [after Q half title and Stationers' Register entry] The comicall History of the Mer / chant of Venice [Q half title and running title] The most excellent / Historie of the Merchant / of Venice. With the extreame crueltie of Shylocke the Iewe / towards the sayd Merchant, in cut-ting a iust pound / of his flesh: and the obtayn-ing of Portia / by the choyse of three / chests. As it hath been diuers times acted by the Lord / Chamberlaine his Seruants. / Written by William Shakespeare. [Q title page] The Mer-chant of Venice [F]

1.1.27 Andrew, decks Andrew docks **113 Yet is** It is
1.2.51 throstle Trassell
1.3.108 spit spet **121 spat** spet
2.2.3–7 Gobbo Iobbe **87 last** [Q2] lost **159 a suit** [Q2, F] sute
2.4.5 as us
2.5.41 Jew's Iewes
2.6.14 younker younger **24 therein** then **58 gentlemen** [Q2, F] gentleman
2.7.69 tombs timber
2.8.39 Slubber [Q2, F] slumber
2.9.47 chaff [F] chaft
3.1.62 s.p. MAN [not in Q, F] **89 heard** [F] heere

3.2.63 s.p. ONE FROM PORTIA'S TRAIN [not in Q, F] **66 ALL** [not in Q, F] **67 eyes** [F] eye **71 I'll begin it** [in Q and F, printed in Roman rather than italic (as the rest of the song), as if not part of the song] **81 vice** voyce **93 makes** [F] maketh **101 Therefore, thou** [Q2] Therefore then thou [Q1, F] **301 thorough** through

3.4.23 Hear other things: heere other things **49 Padua** Mantua **50 cousin's hands** [Q2] cosin hand [Q1] cosins hand [F] **53 traject** Tranect **82 my** [F] my my

3.5.67 merit it meane it, it **74 for a** [F] for

4.1.29 his [Q2, F] this **30 flint** [Q2] flints [Q1, F] **50 Mistress** Maisters **73 bleat** [F] bleake [Q] **74 pines** [F] of Pines **99 'Tis** [Q2, F] as **121 forfeit** forfaiture **127 inexorable** inexcrable **225 No, not** [Q2, F] Not **392 not** [Q2] not to [Q1, F] **395 s.p. GRAZIANO** [Q2, F] Shy⟨locke⟩. [Q1]

5.1.42 Master Lorenzo! Sola M. *Lorenzo* sola [Q2] & M. *Lorenzo* sola [Q1, F] **47–48 morning. / LORENZO . . . Sweet soul, let's** morning sweet soule / *Loren⟨zo⟩*. Let's **86 Erebus** Erobus [F] Terebus [Q] **152 it** [Q2, F; not in Q1] **232 my bedfellow** [Q2, F] mine bedfellow

MUCH ADO ABOUT NOTHING

CONTROL TEXT: Q

Q: The Quarto of 1600
F: The Folio of 1623
F2: The Folio of 1632

s.p. DON JOHN [Q's use of *John* and *Bastard* has been standardized throughout.]
s.p. DON PEDRO [Q's use of *Pedro* and *Prince* has been standardized throughout.]
s.p. ANTONIO [Q's use of *Old, Antonio,* and *Brother* has been standardized throughout.]
s.p. DOGBERRY [Q's use of *Dogberry* and *Constable* has been standardized throughout.]
s.p. VERGES [Q uses both *Verges* and *Headborough,* but generally prefers the former, standardized throughout.]

1.1.8 Pedro Peter **34–35 bird-bolt** Burbolt **1.2.6 event** [F2] euents **1.3.3 it** [not in Q] **39 brothers** [F] bothers **44 on** on **2.1.33 bearherd** Berrord **39 Peter** fore Peter: **for . . . heavens 71 a bout** about **83, 86, 88 s.p. BALTHASAR** *Benedicke* **2.3.22 an** [F] and **37 hid-fox** kid-foxe **56 s.p. BALTHASAR** [not in Q] **124 us of** [F] of vs **3.2.24 can** cannot **45 s.p. DON PEDRO** [F] *Benedicke*

3.3.10, 15 s.p. SECOND WATCHMAN . . . FIRST WATCHMAN [reversed in Q] **24 s.p. FIRST WATCHMAN** *Watch 2* **34, 41, 45, 50, 61, 94, 110 s.p. A WATCHMAN** *Watch* **78, 85 s.p. FIRST WATCHMAN** *Watch* **145, 151 s.p. A WATCHMAN** *Watch 2* **154–55 A WATCHMAN Never . . . us.** [The speech is assigned to *Conrade* in Q.]

3.4.16 in [F] it

3.5.8 off of

4.1.201 princes left for dead princess (left for dead,)

4.2.1 s.p. DOGBERRY *Keeper* **2, 5 s.p. VERGES** *Couley* **4 s.p. DOGBERRY** *Andrew* **8, 11, 14, 17, 23, 27, 31, 36, 39, 44, 50, 63, 67 s.p. DOGBERRY** *Kemp* **45 s.p. VERGES** *Constable* **60 s.p. DOGBERRY** *Constable* **61–62 s.p. VERGES Let them be, in the hands— / CONRAD Off, coxcomb!** *Couley* Let them be in the hands of Coxcombe.

5.1.16 Bid And **97 an** [not in Q]

5.2.41 for [not in Q] **53 maintain** maintaind **73 myself. So** my self so

5.3.4–11 s.p. CLAUDIO Done . . . dumb [These lines follow the Lord's in Q with no distinct speech prefix] **11 dumb** [F] dead **23 s.p. CLAUDIO** *Lo.*

5.4.54 s.p. ANTONIO *Leonato* **96 s.p. BENEDICK** *Leonato*

AS YOU LIKE IT

CONTROL TEXT: F

F: The Folio of 1623

s.p. TOUCHSTONE [F's use of *Clowne* has been changed throughout.]
s.p. DUKE FREDERICK [F's use of *Duke* has been changed throughout.]
s.p. SIR OLIVER MARTEXT [F's use of *Oliver* has been changed in 3.3.]
s.p. JAQUES DE BOIS [F's use of *Second Brother* in 5.4 has been changed at lines 140 and 172.]

1.1.10 manège mannage **48, 50 villein . . . villeins** villaine . . . villaines **49 Bois** Boys **75 Denis** Dennis **94 she** hee **99 Ardenne** *Arden* [similarly throughout] **138 s.p. OLIVER** [not in F] **1.2.3 I** [not in F] **69 s.p. CELIA** *Ros⟨alind⟩.* **76 Le** the **239 shorter** taller **256 Rosalind** *Rosaline* **1.3.1 Rosalind** *Rosaline* **51 likelihood** likelihoods **84 Rosalind** *Rosaline* **90 Rosalind, lack'st thou then** *Rosaline* lacks then **131 we in** in we **2.1.49 much** must **56 should** doe **59 the** [not in F]

2.3.16 s.p. ORLANDO [not in F] 30 s.p. ORLANDO Ad⟨am⟩. 72 seventeen seauentie

2.4.1 weary merry 39 thy thy wound would 43–44 batlet batler 44 chapped chopt 64 you your 69 travel trauaile 78 cot Coate [similarly throughout]

2.5.1 s.p. AMIENS [F has the heading "Song" and no speech prefix.] 32 s.p. ALL [F has no prefix, but the heading "Song." and the phrase "Altogether heere."] 37–39 see . . . weather see. &c. 43 s.p. JAQUES Amy⟨ens⟩.

2.7.55 aught but [not in F] 87 comes come 174 s.p. AMIENS [There is no speech prefix in F, but the heading "Song."] 182 Then The 190–93 sing . . . jolly sing, &c. 201 master masters

3.2.106 graft graffe 113 a [not in F] 133 her his 216 such [not in F] 222 thy the 328 deifying defying 336 are art

3.3.17 it [not in F] 79 s.p. TOUCHSTONE Ol⟨iuer⟩.

3.4.27 a [not in F] 37 puny puisny

3.5.129 I [not in F]

4.1.1 be [not in F] 17 my by 53 beholden beholding 66 warr'nt warne 132 hyena Hyen 180 it in

4.2.2 s.p. FIRST LORD Lord. 7 s.p. SECOND LORD Lord. 10 s.p. LORDS [not in F, which has the heading "Musicke, Song."]

4.3.96 handkerchief handkercher 141 I' I 154 his this

5.2.6 her [not in F] 24 handkerchief handkercher 28 overcame ouercome 88 obedience obseruance 106 I satisfy I satis-fi'd

5.3.14 s.p. BOTH PAGES [not in F, which has the heading "Song."] 17 In In the ring rang 32–37 [F places these lines after 5.3.19.]

5.4.21 your you your 75 to the to 103 her his 153 them him 186 so [not in F]

TWELFTH NIGHT, OR WHAT YOU WILL

CONTROL TEXT: F

F: The Folio of 1623

s.p. ORSINO [F's use of Duke and Du⟨ke⟩ has been changed throughout.]

s.p. SIR TOBY [F's use of Sir To⟨by⟩, To⟨by⟩, and Tob⟨y⟩ has been standardized throughout.]

s.p. SIR ANDREW [F's use of And⟨rew⟩ and An⟨drew⟩ has been standardized throughout.]

s.p. FESTE [F's use of Clo⟨wne⟩, Clow⟨ne⟩, and Cl⟨owne⟩ has been changed throughout.]

1.1.25 years' heat yeares heate
1.2.14 Arion Orion 48 pray thee prethee

1.3.44 s.p. SIR ANDREW Ma⟨lvolio⟩. 46 Mary Accost Mary, accost 83 curl by coole my 84 me we 86 housewife huswife 109 cinquepace Sinke-a-pace 114 divers-coloured dam'd colour'd 117 That's That

1.5.156 'countable comptible 271 County's Countes

2.2.18 straight [not in F] 29 our O 30 made of, made, if

2.3.68 Cathayan Catayan 121 a nayword an ayword

2.4.50 s.p. FESTE[sings] [not in F] 86 I it

2.5.103 staniel stallion 109 ay I 126 born become achieve atcheeues 154 dear deero

3.1.7 king Kings 61 wise men wisemens 116 grece grize

3.2.7 thee the the 57 nine mine

3.3.36 latchèd lapsed

3.4.23 s.p. OLIVIA Ma⟨lvolio⟩. 65 tang langer with 153 If s.p. To⟨by⟩. If 154 You Yon 179 out on't 244 virago firago

4.2.5 in in in 63 to the the 77 Master M.

5.1.73 wreck wracke 110 hath haue 193 pavan panyn 393 With [not in F]

MEASURE FOR MEASURE

CONTROL TEXT: F

F: The Folio of 1623

s.p. MISTRESS OVERDONE [F's use of Bawd has been changed throughout.]

s.p. POMPEY [F's use of Clown has been changed throughout.]

1.1.8 But this But that 51 leavened a leauen'd

1.2.17 wast was't 31 pil'd . . . pilled pil'd . . . pil'd 75 you? [In F, a short exchange follows between Pompey and Mistress Overdone, which the preceding dialogue apparently was meant to replace: printed in this edition as Additional Passage A.] 102 bonds words 113 morality mortality 145 fourteen nin-teene 166 thy the

1.3.10 a witless witlesse 27 More mocked becomes More mock'd 43 T'allow in To do in

1.4.5. sisterhood Sisterstod

2.1.12 your our 21–23 What . . . on thieves?/What's . . . seizes. what's . . . ceizes;/What . . . on theeves? 21 law Lawes 34 execute executed 39 vice Ice 205 spay splay

2.2.25 God save 'Save 98 raw now 101 ere here 119 Split'st splits 164 prayer is crossed prayers crosse 166 God save 'Save

2.3.42 law Loue

2.4.4 God heauen 9 seared feard 12 in for 17 now the not the 45 God's heauens **48 moulds** meanes **53 or** and **75 craftily** crafty **76 me be** be **94 all-binding law** all-building-Law **112 Ignominy** Ignomie

3.1.29 sire fire **38 in** yet in **51 me . . . them** them . . . me **67 Though** Through **89 enew** emmew **92, 95 precise** prenzie **121 dilated** delighted **130 penury** perjury **169 falsify** satisfie **265 on** and **280 eat, array** eate away **294 Free from** From **or** as **356 ungenerative** generatiue **413 not** now **450 it as it** 451 **inconstant** constant **494 Make my** Making

4.1.1 s.p. BOY Song. **6 though** but **51 and so** and **58 their** these **72 tilth's** Tithes **93–94 s.p. PROVOST** Duke.

4.2.81 unlisting vnsisting **100 s.p. DUKE** Pro⟨vost⟩. **111 s.p. PROVOST** The letter [centered on a separate line]

4.3.13 Forthright Forthlight **81 yonder** yond

4.4.4 redeliver reliver

4.5.6 Flavio's Flavia's **8 Valentinus** Valencius

5.1.13 me your we your **167 her face** your face **237 even to** to **367 wast** was't **415 confiscation** confutation **532 that's meet** that meete

Additional Passage Very well met Very well met, and well come

THE TRAGEDY OF KING RICHARD THE THIRD

CONTROL TEXT: F (EXCEPT FOR 3.1.0–148 AND 5.5.4–END, FOR WHICH THE COPY TEXT IS Q1)

F: The Folio of 1623
Q1: The Quarto of 1597
Q2: The Quarto of 1598
Q3: The Quarto of 1602
Q4: The Quarto of 1605
Q5: The Quarto of 1612
Q6: The Quarto of 1622

1.1–3.1 and 3.1.148–5.5.4

s.p. RICHARD GLOUCESTER [F's use of Richard and Gloucester has been standardized until 4.2.]

s.p. KING RICHARD [F's use of King and Richard has been standardized after 4.2.]

s.p. BRACKENBURY [F's use of Brackenbury and Lieutenant has been standardized throughout.]

s.p. LORD HASTINGS [F's use of Hastings has been changed throughout.]

s.p. LADY ANNE [F's use of Anne has been changed throughout.]

s.p. HALBERDIER [F uses Gentleman.]

s.p. QUEEN ELIZABETH [F's use of Queen has been standardized throughout.]

s.p. STANLEY [F's use of Stanley and Derby has been standardized throughout.]

s.p. QUEEN MARGARET [F's use of Queen Margaret and Margaret has been standardized throughout.]

s.p. A MURDERER, MURDERERS [F's use of Villain has been standardized throughout.]

s.p. FIRST MURDERER [F's use of 1 Murderer and 1 has been standardized throughout.]

s.p. SECOND MURDERER [F's use of 2 Murderer and 2 has been standardized throughout.]

s.p. KING EDWARD [F's use of King has been standardized throughout.]

s.p. BOY [F's use of Boy and Edward has been standardized until 3.1.]

s.p. DUCHESS OF YORK [F's use of Duchess of York and Duchess has been standardized throughout.]

s.p. GIRL [F's use of Daughter has been standardized throughout.]

s.p. FIRST CITIZEN [F's use of 1 Citizen and 1 has been standardized throughout.]

s.p. SECOND CITIZEN [F's use of 2 Citizen and 2 has been standardized throughout.]

s.p. THIRD CITIZEN [F's use of 3 has been standardized throughout.]

s.p. CARDINAL [F's use of Archbishop and Cardinal has been standardized throughout.]

s.p. MAYOR [F's use of Lord Mayor and Mayor has been standardized throughout.]

s.p. BISHOP OF ELY [F's use of Ely has been standardized throughout.]

s.p. ALL BUT RICHARD [F's use of All has been standardized throughout.]

s.p. SECOND MESSENGER, THIRD MESSENGER, FOURTH MESSENGER [F only uses Messenger.]

s.p. SIR CHRISTOPHER [F's use of Christopher has been standardized throughout.]

s.p. HENRY EARL OF RICHMOND [F's use of Richmond has been standardized throughout.]

3.1.0–148 and 5.5.4–end

s.p. KING RICHARD [Q's use of King Richard and Richard has been standardized throughout.]

s.p. PRINCE EDWARD [Q's use of Prince has been standardized throughout.]

s.p. GHOST OF PRINCE EDWARD, GHOST OF KING HENRY, GHOST OF CLARENCE, GHOSTS OF THE PRINCES, GHOST OF HASTINGS [Q's use of Ghost has been standardized throughout.]

s.p. GHOST OF GRAY [Q's use of *Gray* has been standardized throughout.]

s.p. GHOST OF VAUGHAN [Q's use of *Vaughan* has been standardized throughout.]

Title: *The Tragedy of King Richard the Third*] THE TRAGEDY OF / King Richard the third. / Containing, / His treacherous Plots against his brother Clarence: / the pittiefull murther of his innocent nephewes: / his tyrannicall vsurpation: with the whole course / of his detested life, and most deserued death. [Q title page] The Tragedy of Richard the Third: / with the Landing of Earle Richmond, and the / Battell at Bosworth Field. [F head title]

1.1.26 spy [Q] see **49 Belike** O belike **52 for** [Q] but **67 Woodeville** *Woodeulle* **73 Mrs** Mistresse **74 ye** [Q] you **75 for his** for her **88 An't** and **92 jealous** [Q] iealious **96 kin** kindred **104 I** [Q] I do **withal** withall **113 dearer** deeper **116 or** [Q] or else **125 the** [Q1] this **134 prey** [Q] play **139 Paul** [Q] Iohn **146 haste** horse

1.2.15 Cursèd . . . hence, [F places the line after 1.2.16.] **39 stand** [Q] Stand'st **56 Ope** Open **60 deed** Deeds **61 supernatural** most vnnaturall **70 no** [Q] nor **78 a** [Q; not in F] **80 t'accuse** to curse **92 hand** [Q] hands **101 ye** [Q1] yee **120 of that accursed effect** and most accurst effect **126 rend** [Q] rent **127 sweet** [Q] y^t **154 drops.** [Q; F here adds twelve lines; see indented passage.] **Shamed** [Q, F (text)] For [F (catchword)] **189 s.p. RICHARD GLOUCESTER** [Q; not in F] **190 s.p. LADY ANNE . . . give.** [Q; not in F] **213 s.p. RICHARD GLOUCESTER . . . corpse.** [Q; not in F] **214 Blackfriars** white Friers **238** *denier* denier

1.3.6 If . . . me? [Q; F gives the line twice, spanning a page break.] **7 s.p. RIVERS** [Q] If he were dead, what would betide me on / *Gray*. [F (text)] *Gray*. [F (catchword)] **17 come** [Q1] comes **Lords** [Q] Lord **30 s.p. RIVERS** [Q] *Qu⟨een Elizabeth⟩*. **33 With** [Q1] What **43 are they** [Q] is it **complain** complaines **54 s.p. RIVERS** [Q] *Gray*. **whom** [Q1] who **68–69 that . . . it** that he may learne the ground **114 Tell . . . said,** [Q; not in F] **118 remember** [Q] do remember **153 may you** [Q] you may **155 Ah** A **160 of** [Q] off **166 go.** [Q; F here adds three lines; see indented passage.] **197 my** [Q] our **270 was** [Q] is **271 s.p. RICHARD GLOUCESTER** *Buc⟨kingham⟩*. **290 naught** not **302 s.p. HASTINGS** [Q] *Buc⟨kingham⟩*. **307 s.p. QUEEN ELIZABETH** [Q] *Mar⟨garet⟩*. **319 you my gracious lords** yours my gracious Lord **325 whom** [Q] who

1.4.19 sought thought **22 waters** [Q1] water **22–23 my . . . my** [Q1] mine . . . mine **25 Ten** [Q] A **26 ouches** anchors **29 those** [Q] the **32 Which** [Q] That **50 cried** [Q] spake **58 methoughts** [Q1] me thought **66 Brackenbury** [Q] Keeper, Keeper **68 me.** [Q; F here adds four lines; see indented passage.] **69 Keeper, I pray thee** Keeper, I prythee **90 of** [Q] from **96 I** [Q1] we **112 pray thee** [Q] prythee **119 'Swounds** [Q] Come **136 'Swounds** [Q; not in F] **177 to have redemption** [Q] for any goodnesse **178 By . . . sins,** [Q; not in F] **201 ye** [Q] you **225 And . . . other,** [Q; not in F] **227 of** [Q1] on **230 As Right as 251–55 Which distress—** [F places the lines after 1.4.244.] **257 serve** [Q] do **261 guilty murder done** [Q] murther

2.1.5 in [Q] to **7 Hastings and Rivers** *Dorset and Riuers* **19 your** [Q] you **50 Brother** [Q] Gloster **57 unwittingly** [Q] vnwillingly **59 By** [Q] To **67 Of you . . . of you** [Q] Of you and you, Lord *Riuers* and of *Dorset* **68 me.—** [Q] me: / Of you Lord *Wooduill* and Lord *Scales*, of you, **70 Englishman** [Q] Englishmen **82 s.p. RIVERS** [Q] *King* **85 one** [Q] man **93 but** [Q] and **97 pray thee** [Q] prethee **105 slew** [Q] kill'd **108 at** [Q] and **131 once** [Q] onee

2.2.3 you [Q; not in F] **13 this** [Q] it **26 his** [Q] a **27 shapes** [Q] shape **39 mark** make **47 I** [Q; not in F] **83 weep** [Q] weepes **84–85 and . . . weep** [Q; not in F] **88 lamentation.** [F here adds twelve lines; see indented passage.] **105 hearts** [Q] hates **106 splinted** [Q, F] splinterd **110 king.** [Q; F here adds eighteen lines; see indented passage.] **112 Ludlow** [Q] London **114 weighty** [Q; not in F] **115 s.p. QUEEN . . . YORK** [not in F] **With . . . hearts.** [Q; not in F] **117 God's sake** [Q] God sake **124 Ludlow** [Q] London

2.3.35 make [Q] makes **43 Ensuing** [Q, F (catchword)] Pursuing [F (text)]

2.4.1 hear [Q1] heard **them** [not in F] **1–2 Northampton. / at Stony Stratford** [Q] Stony Stratford, / And at Northampton **9 young** [Q] good **12 nuncle** Vnkle **13 gross** great **21 s.p. CARDINAL Why** [Q] *Yor⟨k⟩*. And **26 pray thee** [Q] prythee **36 s.p. CARDINAL** [Q] *Dut.* (Duchess of York) **37 your son, Lord Dorset** a Messenger **38 Lord Marquis** [Q; not in F] **s.p. DORSET** [Q; throughout scene] *Mes⟨senger⟩*. **40 then** [Q; not in F] **42 And with them** and with them, / Sir **48 our** [Q] my **50 jet** [Q] Iutt **64 death** [Q] earth

3.1.0 [Right after this stage direction, F loses its independent authority until c. 3.1.148. Q1 is the control text in this interim; F is here a direct reprint of Q3, which contains errors that need to be corrected by reference to Q1.] **22 hastes** comes **24 In happy time** And in good time **39 Anon expect him** Anone expect him here **41 sacred** holy **46 not** but **52 my mind, he** mine opinion **53 'longs** is **54 You . . . charter** You breake no priuiledge nor charter there **59 I come** I go **74 liege.** Lo: **85 t'enrich** enrich **87 made** makes **88 yet** now **90 good** gratious **101 noble cousin** Cosen noble **102 uncle, well** Vnckle **107 He . . . you** Then he . . . you **109 as** as in **110 render** giue **111 With all** [Q3–6, F] withall **113–14 give, / It being but** giue, / And being but **121 I'd** I **132 sharp, prodigal** sharpe, prouided **136 My . . . along** [Q, F; none of the many attempts to pad out this line carries any conviction.] **143 there** [not in Q] **148 and** [F, not in Q] **149 we** I **153 parlous** perillous **161 Lord William** William Lo: **166 Will not** [F; F regains its full authority at this line.] Will **170 purpose.** [Q; for F, see indented passage.] **174 your** [Q] the **188 My** Now my

3.2.1 from Lord from the lo: **3 my Lord Stanley** Stanley **17 councils** [Q] Councell **74 you do** [Q; not in F] **87 talked** [Q1] talke **91 follow presently** [Q] talke with this good fellow **92 Well met, Hastings** [Q] How now, Sirrha? **95 I met thee** [Q] thou met'st me **102 Hastings** [Q] fellow **103 God save your lordship** [Q] I thanke your

3.3.14 heads, [Q] Heads / When shee exclaim'd on *Hastings,* you, and I **16–17 Hastings . . . Richard** [Q] *Richard . . . Hastings*

3.4.4 that [Q] the **solemn** royall **9 methinks** [Q] we thinke **26 not you** [Q] you not **39 worshipful** [Q] worshipfully **55 likelihood** [Q] liuelyhood **58 s.p. STANLEY I . . . not.** [not in F] **65 whatsoe'er** [Q] whosoe're **68 See** [Q] Looke **78 Some see it done** [Q] *Louell* and *Ratcliffe,* looke that it be done **82 raze** [Q] rowse **83 But** [Q] And **94 s.p. CATESBY** Ra⟨tcliffe⟩. **98 th'air** aire **102 s.p. CATESBY** Lou⟨ell⟩.

3.5.4 wert [Q] were **6 Tremble . . . straw,** [F places the line after 3.5.7.] **12 s.p. RICHARD GLOUCESTER . . . Mayor** [Q] But what, is *Catesby* gone? / *Rich⟨ard⟩.* He is, and see he brings the Maior along **13 Let . . . him.** [Q; not in F] **19 innocence** [Q1] innocencie **20 O . . . Catesby** [Q] Be patient, they are friends: *Ratcliffe,* and *Louell.* **21 s.p. CATESBY** [Q] *Louell.* **31 attainture** attainder **32 The** Well, well, he was the **48 I** [Q] *Buck⟨ingham⟩. I* **50 s.p. RICHARD GLOUCESTER** [Q4; not in F] **54 we** [Q] I **hear** heard **56 treason** [Q] Treasons **60 word** [Q] words

64 cause [Q1] case **82 listed** [Q] lusted **101 Now** [Q; for F, see indented passage.] **in** [Q] goe **103 notice** [Q] order

3.6.13 naught [Q1] nought

3.7.7 insatiate [Q] vnsatiate **14 face** forme **20 mine** [Q1] my **40 wisdoms** [Q] wisdome **43–44 s.p. BUCKINGHAM No . . . lord. / s.p. RICHARD GLOUCESTER** [Q; not in F] **49 build** [Q] make **50 request** [Q] requests **54 we'll** [Q] we **72 lolling** [Q, F] lulling **day-bed** [Q] Loue-Bed **101 request** [Q] requests **125 her** [Q] his **126 Her** [Q] His **127 Her** His **143 condition.** [Q; F here adds ten lines; see indented passage.] **160 no doubt, us** [Q] no doubt vs **203 equally** [Q, F] egallie **209 'Swounds, I'll** [Q] we will **210 s.p. RICHARD GLOUCESTER O . . . Buckingham.** [Q; not in F] **212 s.p. ANOTHER** [Q; not in F] **214 stone** stones **215 entreats** [Q] entreaties **230 kind** King **237 cousin** [Q] Cousins

4.1.46 counted England's Englands counted **57 in** [Q] with **75 made** [not in F] **96 racked** [Q, F] wrackt **teen.** [Q; F here adds seven lines; see indented passage.]

4.2.14 liege [Q] Lord **20 immediately** suddenlie **50 those parts beyond the seas** [Q] the parts **55 born** [Q] poore **73 there** [Q] then **81 'Tis** [Q] There is **84–85 s.p. KING RICHARD Shall . . . lord.** [Q; not in F] **90 to** [Q] vnto **101 perhaps.** [Q; not in F] **101–19 s.p. BUCKINGHAM . . . today.** [Q; not in F] **120 Why . . . no?** [Q] May it please you to resolue me in my suit.

4.3.4 whom [Q] who **5 ruthless** [Q1] ruthfull **8 two** [Q] to **15 once** [Q] one **31 at** [Q] and **39 goodnight** [Q] good night **40 Breton** [Q, F] Brittaine **42 o'er** [Q] on **45 Good news or bad** [Q] Good or bad newes **46 Ely** [Q] *Mourton* **53 leads** [Q] leds **55 an** and

4.4.10 unblown [Q] vnblowed **30 innocents'** [Q] innocent **36 seniory** [Q] signeurie **39 Tell . . . mine.** [Q; not in F] **45 holpst** hop'st **56 charnel** [Q, F] carnal **64 Thy** [Q] The **quite** [Q6] quit **77 plead** pray **93 are** [Q1] be **100 For queen . . . care** [Q; F places the line after 4.4.101.] **107 wert** [Q1] wast **112 weary** [Q1] wearied **118 nights . . . days** [Q1] night . . . day **127 client** [Q1] Clients **128 recorders** succeeders **intestate** [Q] intestine **141 Where** [Q] Where't **175 in** [Q] with **176 Hewer** *Hower* **180 pray thee** prythee **188 heavy** [Q] greeuous **216 births** [Q] Birth **221 life.** [Q; F here adds fourteen lines; see indented passage.] **225 or** [Q1–5] and **243 that it** **254 would I** [Q1] I would **260 sometimes** [Q1] sometime **270 is** [Q; not in F] **273 this.** [Q; F

here adds fifty-five lines; see indented passage.] **286 love** [Q] low **295 s.p. KING RICHARD . . . past.** [Q1; F places the line after 4.4.296.] **296 s.p. QUEEN ELIZABETH** [Q1; not in F] **297 s.p. KING RICHARD** [Q; not in F] **300 holy** [Q] Lordly **301 lordly** knightlie **307 that** [Q] it **308 God . . . God's** [Q] Heauen . . . Heavens **323 in** [Q1] with **327 o'erpast** [Q] repast **343 good** [Q] deare **348 peevish-fond** [Q] peeuish found **356 recomfiture** [Q] recomforture **375 Ratcliffe** *Catesby* **391 mile** [Q] miles **395 renegade** [Q, F] runnagate **398 Ely** [Q] *Morton* **421 Ay, ay** [Q] I **431 Courtenay** [Q, F] Courtney **434 Guildfords** [Q, F] Guilfords **441 flood . . . water** [Q] Floods . . . Waters **445 Ratcliffe . . . gave him** [Q] There is my Purse, to cure that Blow of thine **452 Breton** [Q, F] Brittaine **458 Bretagne** [Q, F] Brittaine **465 tidings,** [Q1] Newes, but
4.5.2 this [Q] the **5 aid** [Q] ayde. / So get thee gone: commend me to thy Lord **17–18 Tell . . . daughter.** [Q; F places the lines after 4.5.5.] **17 Tell him** [Q] Withall say, that
5.2.8 spoils spoild **11 Lies** [Q] Is **12 Near** [Q] Ne're **17 swords** [Q] men
5.3.2 Why, how now, Catesby [Q] My Lord of Surrey **3 s.p. CATESBY** [Q] Sur⟨rey⟩.
5.4.4 standard. [Q; F places 5.4.21–24 here and adds, "My Lord of Oxford, you Sir *William Brandon,* /And your Sir *Walter Herbert* stay with me."] **21–24 Give . . . power.** [Q, F places the lines after 5.4.4.]
5.5.3 [Q1 is the control text for the remainder of the play, although a handful of Folio variants are considered or adopted, as derived from the damaged final leaves of the manuscript.] **8 sentinels** [F] centinell **10 s.p. KING RICHARD Stir** [F, Q (text)] Sturr [Q (catchword)] **11 s.p. CATESBY** *Rat⟨cliffe⟩.* **19 Ratcliffe** [Q6, F (italic)] Ratliffe **25 some** a boule of **29 Leave me. Bid my guard watch.** Bid my guard watch, leaue me. **30–31 About . . . tent, / Ratcliffe, and** Ratliffe about . . . tent / And **32 sit** [Q2] set **43 mortal-sharing** mortal staring **53 sundered** [Q3] sundried **72 tomorrow, / Prince . . . Sixth.** to morrow. **84 Comforts** Doth comfort **85 sit** [Q2] set on [Q5] in **93 s.p. GHOST OF RIVERS** [Q3] *King* on [Q5] in **97 pointless** [not in Q] **99 Will** [Q2] Wel **100 s.p. GHOSTS OF THE PRINCES** [F] *Ghost.* **110 Hastings, then** Hastings **137 am** [Q2] and **140 Myself** What my selfe **156 Nay** [F] And **163 My** Ratcliffe, my **167 all our friends prove** our friends proue all **168 Ratcliffe** O Ratcliffe **177 s.p. LORDS** [Q3–6] Lo⟨rds⟩. **180 s.p. A LORD** [Q] Lo⟨rd⟩. **189 s.p. A LORD** [Q] Lo⟨rd⟩. **191 Much that I could say**

More than I haue said **193 on** vpon **196 forces** faces **199 friends** gentlemen **212 foison fat pays** shall paie **219–20 this . . . my** my . . . this **221 to** the **223 bold and** boldlie, and
5.6.12 not [Q2] nor **25 placèd strongly** shall be placed **27 multitude** foote and horse **28 ourself** [not in Q] **29 both sides** either side **31 boot!** [Q3] bootes **32 s.p. NORFOLK A good** [F, Q (text)] A good [Q (catchword)] **33 paper** [not in Q] **34 Jackie** [Q, F] Iocky too so **37 each** euery **47 Bretons** [Q, F] Brittains **49 ventures** aduentures **52 distain** restraine **54 Bretagne** [Q, F] Brittaine **55 milksop** [Q6, F] milkesopt **74 young** his sonne
5.8.8–9 s.p. KING . . . But [F, Q (text)] But [Q (catchword)] **9 young George Stanley, is he** is yong George Stanley **13 s.p. STANLEY** [F] *Der⟨by⟩.* [not in Q] **14 Ferrers** Ferris **15 becomes** become **27 that** this **28 United** Deuided **32 his** thy **37 forth** in

THE TRAGEDY OF KING RICHARD THE SECOND

CONTROL TEXT: Q1; ADDITIONAL MATTER FROM F

F: The Folio of 1623
Q1: The Quarto of 1597
Q2, Q3: Quartos of 1598
Q4: The Quarto of 1608
Q5: The Quarto of 1615
Q6: The Quarto of 1634

Title: The Tragedie of Richard II [Q] The life and death of King Richard the Second [F]

s.p. KING RICHARD *King* [to 5.1]

1.1.118 by my [F] by **152 gentlemen** [F] gentleman **157 time** [F] month **162–63 Harry, when? / Obedience bids** *Harrie,* when? Obedience bids, / Obedience bids [F] Harry? when obedience bids, / Obedience bids **186 down** [F] vp
1.2.1 Gloucester's [F]; Woodstockes **58 it** [Q2, F] is
1.3.33 comest [Q5] comes [Q1] com'st [F] **55 just** [F] right **127 swords** [F] sword **127–28 swords, / Which** [F; Q1 has a five-line passage after line 127 omitted in F, indented in this edition. See Textual Note.] **166 then** [F; not in Q] **174 you owe** [F] y'owe **215 night** [Q4, F] nightes **220 sudden** [F] sullen **231–32 father. / Alas** [F; Q has a four-line passage omitted in F, indented in this edition after line 235.] **251 travel** trauaile **256–57 return. / s.p. BOL-**

INGBROKE [F; Q has twenty-six lines omitted from F, indented in this edition after line 256.] **256.2 remember** remember me
1.4.7 grew [F] blew **19 cousin, cousin** [F] Coosens Coosin **22 Bushy, Bagot here, and Green** [Q6] Bushie, [Q1] Bushy: heere *Bagot* and *Greene* [F] **51–52 Enter Bushy** / **Bushy, what news?** [F] *Enter Bushie with newes.* [Q1] **58 in his** [F] in the [Q1] into the [Q2] **63 late!** [F] late, / Amen [indented]
2.1.18 whose taste the wise are feared whose taste the wise are found [Q1] Whose state the wise are found [Q2] his state: then there are sound [F] **48 as a** [Q4, F] as **70 reined** ragde **102 encagèd** [F] inraged **113 now, now not, 115–16 And— / s.p. KING RICH-ARD And thou, a** [F] And thou / *King. A* **125 brother** [Q2] brothers **178 the** [F] a **233 that thou wouldst** thou wouldst [Q1] thou'dst [F] **255 his** [F] his noble **258 King's grown** [Q3, F] King growen **278 Port le** [F] le Port **281 Thomas . . . Arundel** [not in Q1, F; a line is missing, probably a result of censorship.] **284 Thomas Ramston** John Ramston **286 Coint** [F] Coines
2.2.12 At . . . With With . . . at **16 eye** [F] eyes **31 As thought—** As thought [Q1] As though [Q2, F] **59 broke** [Q2, F] broken **119 Castle** [F; not in Q1] **138 commoners** commons **148–49 s.p. BAGOT Farewell . . . / BUSHY Well** [continued to Green] Farewell . . . / *Bush⟨ie⟩* Well [Q1] *Bush⟨y⟩*. Farewell . . . Well [F]
2.3.36 Hereford, [Q3] Herefords **98 the** [F; not in Q1] **124 kinsman** [F] cousin **157 to** [Q2, F] vnto
3.1.32 England. [F] England, Lords farewell.
3.2.1 Harlechly Barkloughly **28–29 all. / s.p. AUMERLE** [F; Q1 has four lines omitted in F, indented in this edition after line 28.] **31 friends** [F] power **36 bloody** [Q2, F] bouldy **51 from** [F] off from **80 sluggard** [F] coward **81 forty** [F] twenty **98 loss,** [F] and **130 offence** [F; not in Q1] **174 wail their present woes** [F] sit and wail theyr woes **199 faction** [F] partie
3.3.13 with you [F; not in Q1] **35 Upon** [F] on both **58–59 rain / My waters** [F] raigne. / My water's **90 is** [F] standes **118 a prince and** princesse [Q1] a Prince [Q3] a Prince, is [F] **126 We** [Q4, F] *King.* We **126 ourself** [F] our selues **170 mock** [F] laugh
3.4.11 joy grief **35 too** [F] two **58 garden!** **We at** garden at [Q1] garden, at [Q3, F] **68 then** [not in Q1, F] **81 Cam'st** [Q2, F] them
4.1.21 him [Q3, F] them **50–51 foe. / s.p. SURREY** [F; Q1 has an eight-line passage omitted from F, indented in this edition after line 50.] **50.3 may** it may **50.4 sun to sun** sinne to sinne **67 my** [Q3, F; not in Q1] the [Q2] **92 Bishop of Carlisle** Bishop [Q3, F]

B. [Q1] **103 of that name the fourth** [F] fourth of that name **136 you** [Q2, F] yon **136 rear** [F] raise **139 Prevent** Preuent it **145–308 May . . . fall** [F (and similarly Q4); not in Q1. Only departures from F are noted for these lines.] **227 upon** [Q4] vpon me **241 and** [Q4] a **245 Nor** [Q4] No, nor **309–10 On . . . yourselves** [Q4, F] Let it be so, and loe on wednesday next, / We solemnly proclaime our Coronation, / Lords be ready all [Q1] **322 I will** Ile
5.1.25 stricken [F] throwne **44 fall** [F] tale **66 friends** [F] men **78 queen** [F] wife **84 s.p. NORTHUMBERLAND** [F] *King.*
5.2.52 Hold these jousts and triumphs Hold those Iusts & Triumphs [F] do these iusts & triumphs hold **55 prevent it** preuent it **78 by my life, my** by my life, by my [Q1] my life, my [Q2, F] **82 son** [F] Aumerle
5.3.1 tell [F] tell me **14 these** [F] those **21 days** [F] yeares **30 the** my **35 I may** [Q2, F] May **55 lest** lest thy **73 voiced** [Q3, F] voice **91 kneel** [F] walke **100 mouth** [Q2, F] month **109 s.p. KING HENRY** [Q2, F] *yorke* **142 so** [not in Q1, F] too [Q6]
5.4.3, 6 s.p. FIRST, SECOND [not in Q1, F] **3 Those** [F] These
5.5.13–14 faith . . . faith [F] word . . . word **33 treason makes** [F] treasons make **55 sounds that tell** sound that tells **56 that** [F] which **58 hours, and times** [F] times, and houres **65 a sign** [Q2, F] asigne **94 spurgalled** [F] Spurrde, galld
5.6.8 Salisbury, Spencer, Blunt [F] Oxford, Salisbury, Blunt [Q1] Oxford, Salisbury [Q2] **17 not** [Q2, F1] nor **43 through the** [F] through

THE HISTORY OF HENRY THE FOURTH (1 HENRY IV)

CONTROL TEXT: Q1 FOR 1.3.199–2.3.19, Q2 ELSEWHERE

F: THE FOLIO OF 1623
Q1: Remaining fragment of the Quarto of 1598
Q2: The complete Quarto of 1598
Q3: The Quarto of 1599
Q4: The Quarto of 1604
Q5: The Quarto of 1608
Q6: The Quarto of 1613
Q5b, Q6b: Successive states of Q5 and Q6 incorporating various print-shop corrections and changes
Q7: The Quarto of 1622

Title: THE / HISTORY OF / HENRIE THE / FOURTH; / With the battell at Shrewsburie, / *betweene the King and Lord* / Henry Percy, surnamed / Henrie Hotspur of / the North. / *With the humorous conceits of Sir* / John Falstalffe [Q2 title page] The First Part of Henry the Fourth, / with the Life and Death of HENRY / Sirnamed HOT-SPURRE. [F head title]

s.p. KING HENRY [Q's use of *King* has been changed throughout.]
s.p. PRINCE HARRY [Q's use of *Prince* has been changed throughout.]
s.p. POINS [Q's use of *Poines / Poynes* has been standardized throughout.]
s.p. HOTSPUR [Q's use of *Hotspur / Percy* has been standardized throughout.]
s.p. FIRST TRAVELLER and SECOND TRAVELLER [Q's *Traveler* of 2.2 has been differentiated into two persons.]
s.p. LADY PERCY [Q's use of *Lady* has been changed throughout.]
s.p. BARDOLPH [Q's use of *Russell / Bardoll* has been standardized throughout.]
s.p. GLYNDŴR [Q's use of *Glendower* has been changed throughout.]
s.p. SIR MICHAEL [Q's use of *Sir M⟨ighell⟩* in 4.4 has been modernized.]
s.p. JOHN OF LANCASTER [Q's use of *Prince John / John / John of Lancaster* has been standardized throughout.]

1.1.39 Herefordshire [Q7, F] Herdforshire **40 Glyndŵr** Glendower [similarly throughout] **62 a dear** [Q5b, F] deere **71 the Earl** Earle **73 Moray** Murrey **75–76 not? / s.p. WESTMORLAND In faith, it is a** not? In faith it is. / *West⟨merland⟩*. A
1.2.70 similes [Q6]; smiles **71 sweet** [Q3, F]; sweer **100 John, sack-and-sugar Jack?** John Sacke, and Sugar Jacke? **114 visors** vizards **144 Peto, Bardolph** Harvey, Rossill **148 But how** [F] How **154 Ay** [F] Yea **158 visors** vizards **161 But** [F] Yea, but
1.3.12 too [F] to **25 was** [F] is **26 Who either through envy** [F] Either envie therefore **27 Was** [F] Is **52 or** [F] or he **65 Made me to answer** [F] I answered **83 the** [Q3, F] that **115 Owain** Owen [similarly throughout] **122 you'll** [F] you wil **126 Although it be with** [F] Albeit I make a **131 In his behalf** [F] Yea on his part **133 downfall** [F] down-trod **199 s.p. HOTSPUR** [Q6, F; no s.p. in Q1] **209–10 a while . . . me.** [F] a while. **237 whipped** [Q2, F] whip **240 d'ye** [F] do you **241 upon't** [F] upon it **253 to't** [F] to it **254 We'll** [F] We wil **264 is't** [F] is it **265 Bristol** Bristow **Scrope** Scroop **289 Lord** Lo: **292 our** [Q2, F] out
2.1.1 An't [F] An it **23 races** razes **38 quoth a** [F] quoth he **51 Weald** wild **64 he's** [F] he is **68 foot-landrakers** [Q4, F] footland rakers **71 'oyez'-ers** Oneyres **80 recipe** receyte

2.2.16 two-and-twenty [F] xxii: **25 upon't** [F] upon it **45–46 Gadshill, what news? / s.p. GADSHILL** Bardoll, what newes. / *Bar⟨doll⟩*. **46 visors** vizards **70, 78 s.p. FIRST TRAVELLER** [unnumbered in Q] **71 their** our **74 s.p. SECOND TRAVELLER** [unnumbered in Q]
2.4.2 respect [Q7, F] the respect **42 thee** the **48 ransomed** ransome **63 A roan** [Q4, F] Roane **78 to** unto **83 maumets** mammets
2.5.29 precedent [F] present **32 s.p. POINS** [Q5, F] *Prin⟨ce⟩*. **61 o'** a **110 sun's** sonnes **159 s.p. PRINCE HARRY** [F] *Gad⟨shill⟩*. **160, 162, 166 s.p. GADSHILL** [F] *Ross⟨ill⟩*. **230 to't** [F] to it **303 talon** talent **311 Owain** O **346 joint-stool** joynd stoole **358 Father** father **359 tristful** trustfull **366 yet** [Q4, F] so **431 lean** [Q3, F] lane **478, 479 Good . . . good** God . . . god **487 s.p. PETO** [F; not in Q] **492 s.p. PRINCE HARRY** [F; not in Q]
3.1.48 speaketh speakes **67 here's** [F] here is **97 cantle** [F] scantle **126 metre** miter **129 on an** 152 the least** least **182 nobleman** [F] noble man **197 thou down pourest** thou powrest downe **228 he's** [F] he is
3.2.59 won wan **84 gorged** [Q3, F] gordge **96 then** [F] than **112 swaddling-clothes** swathling cloaths **156 intemperature** [F] intemperance **157 bonds** bands
3.3.30 that's [Q4] that **49 tithe** tight **65 four-and-twenty** [F] xxiiii. **107 no thing** [F] nothing **122 owed** ought **158 guests** [F] ghesse **173–4 two-and-twenty** [F] xxii. **184 o'clock** of clocke
4.1.18 jostling justling **20 my lord** my mind **31 sickness stays him** sicknesse **50 sole** soule **55 is** [F] tis **98 ostriches** Estridges **98–100 that with the wind / [. . .] / Baiting that with the wind / Baited **106 cuishes** cushes **109 dropped** [Q3, F] drop **117 altar** [Q5, F] altars **124 corpse** coarse **127 cannot** [Q6b, F] can **128 yet** [Q6, F] it **135 merrily** [F] merely
4.2.3 Coldfield cop- / hill **14–15 yeomen's** Yeomans **22 ensigns** Ancients **28 feazed ensign** fazd ancient **31 tattered** tottered
4.3.23 horse [Q5, F] horses **26 the half** the halfe of **84 country's** [Q6b, F] Countrey
4.4.30 more mo
5.1.42, 58 Doncaster [F] Dancaster **83 our** [F] your **135 o' a** **136 will it** [Q3, F] wil
5.2.3 undone [Q6, F] under one **10 ne'er** [F] never
5.3.1 in the in the **22 A fool** Ah foole **35 ragamuffins** rag of Muffins **39 stand'st** [F] stands **42 as yet** are yet **50 gett'st** [F] gets
5.4.57 Sir S. 67 Nor [F] Now **91 thee** the **97 rites** [F] rights **108 Embowelled** Inboweld **110 Embowelled** Inboweld **110 embowel** inbowel **144 take't on** [F] take it upon **147 e'er** [F] ever

THE LIFE OF HENRY THE FIFTH

CONTROL TEXT: F; ADDITIONAL MATTER
FROM Q1

F: The Folio of 1623
Q1: The Quarto of 1600
Q3: The Quarto of 1619

s.p. KING HARRY [F's use of *King* has been stan-
dardized throughout.]
s.p. KING CHARLES [F's use of *King* has been
standardized throughout.]

1.2.38 *succedant* succedual 50 there [Q]
then 72 fine [Q] find 74 heir [Q] th'Heire
77 Ninth Tenth 99 son man 115 those
these 131 blood Bloods 147 unmasked
his power [Q] went with his forces unto into
154 the bruit thereof the brute hereof [Q]
th'ill neighborhood 163 your [Q] their 166
A LORD [Q] *Bish⟨op of⟩ Ely*. 183 True. [Q;
not in F] 197 majesty [Q] Maiesties 208
Fly [Q] Come 212 end [Q] And 213
defect [Q] defeat 276 have I I haue [F]
haue we [Q1] we haue [Q3] 284 from [Q]
with 287 Ay, [Q] And
2.0.32—perforce—[not in F]
2.1.21 mare [Q] name 23 Good morrow,
Ensign Pistol [Q; not in F] 25 NIM [Q; not
in F] 26 Gad's lugs [Q] this hand 65 thee
defy [Q] defie thee 72 enough. [Q] enough
to 73 you your 95 s.p. NIM I shall have my
eight shillings? *Nim.* I shal haue my eight
shillings I woon of you at beating? [Q; not in
F] 105 that's that
2.2.1 s.p. GLOUCESTER [Q; throughout
scene] *Bed⟨ford⟩*. [F; throughout scene]
35 their [Q] the 84 him [Q; not in F] 85
vile [Q; not in F] 95 ha' [Q1] haue 104 a
an 136 mark make the thee 144 Henry
[Q] *Thomas* 154 heartily in sufferance in
sufferance heartily 163 and fixed [Q; not
in F] 172 have [Q; not in F] 173 ye [Q1]
you
2.3.15 babbled Table 22 up'ard and up'ard
vpward and vpward [Q] up-peer'd and upward
29 s.p. HOSTESS *Woman*. 35 hell-fire [Q1]
Hell 41 word [Q1] world
2.4.4 Bourbon [Q] Britaine 33 agèd [Q] Noble
57 mountant Mountaine 75 England [Q1]
of England 106 Turns he [Q] Turning 107
pining [Q] priuy 123 for [Q] of
3.0.6 fanning fayning
3.1.7 conjure commune 17 noblest Noblish
24 men me 32 Straining Straying
3.2.19 God's plud [Q; not in F] 19 breaches
[Q] breach 26 runs wins
3.3 s.p. FLUELLEN [Q; throughout scene] *Welch*.
[F; throughout scene] s.p. JAMY [Q; through-
out scene] *Scot*. [F; throughout scene] s.p.

MACMORRIS [Q; throughout scene] *Irish*. [F;
throughout scene] 55–56 Aye owe Got a aye,
or goe to 109 heady headly 112 Defile
Desire 124 dread [Q] great
3.4.3 Un *En* 4 j'apprenne *ie apprend* 5 par-
ler *parlen* Comment *Comient* 6 La main?
Elle est appelée *Le main il & appelle* 7 Et les
doigts [continued to Catherine] *Alice. E le
doyts.* 8 s.p. ALICE *Kat⟨herine⟩* 8–9 sou-
viendrai *souemeray* 9 sont *ont* fingers. Oui
fingres, ou 11 s.p. CATHERINE *Alice*. 12 la
bonne écolière; j'ai *le bon escholier. /
Kat⟨herine⟩. I'ay* 13 les *le* 14 Les *Le* 15 De
nails. Ecoutez— De Nayles escoute: 19
arma Arme 20 le *de* 22 la répétition *le
repeticio* 39 Non, et *Nome* 43 Sauf *Sans*
honneur *honeus* 44 dis *de* 45 pieds *pied* la
robe [Q] *de roba* 46 De foot *Le foot* 46, 47,
51, 53 *cown con* [Q] Count 47 *De foot et
de Le Foot, & le* Ils Il 51 De foot et de Le
Foot & le Néanmoins *neant moys* 53 *foot,
de foote, e de* [Q] Foot, le
3.5.10, 32 s.p. BOURBON [Q] *Brit⟨ain⟩*. 11 de
du 26 'Poor' may we Poore we 45 Foix
Loys 46 knights Kings
3.6.23 Of and of 27 her [Q] his 49 execu-
tions [Q] execution 58 is this the ensign
you told me of [Q] this is an arrant coun-
terfeit Rascall 82 com'st cam'st 99 here
[Q; not in F] 102 lenity [Q] Leuitie
3.7.7 s.p. BOURBON [Q; throughout scene]
Dolph⟨in⟩. [F; throughout scene] 12 Ah ha
Ch'ha 14 qui a *ches* 60 *vomissement
vemissement* et *est* 61 *truie leuye* 83 Duke
of Bourbon [Q] Dolphin
4.0.16 name nam'd
4.1.92 Thomas Iohn 148 deaths [Q] death
propose purpose 173 s.p. BATES 3. Lord.
[Q] *Will⟨iams⟩*. 227 adoration odoration
267 or of 280 have I [Q] I haue 286 ill
all
4.2 s.p. BOURBON [Q; throughout scene]
Dolph⟨in⟩. [F; throughout scene] 5 *plus?*
puis 6 *Cieux Cein* 11 dout doubt 25
'gainst against 35 sonance Sonuance 46
hands hand 47 drooping dropping 49
palled pale 60 guidon Guard: on
4.3.2 s.p. CLARENCE *Bed⟨ford⟩*. 3 s.p. WAR-
WICK [Q; throughout scene] *West⟨merland⟩*.
[F; throughout scene] 8 Clarence [Q] Bed-
ford 11, 15 s.p. CLARENCE *Bed⟨ford⟩*. [F;
speeches not in Q] 44 t'old old 48 And . . .
day.' [Q; not in F] 106 grazing crasing 118
as or 119 your [Q] the 129 come come
againe
4.4.4 *Qualité 'Calin o* Qualtitie calmie 12
miséricorde *misericordie* pitié pité 14 Or
for 46 *prisonnier prisonner néanmoins
neant-mons* 47 lui ci *layt a* promettez
promets 48 je *se* 49 remerciements *remer-
cious* 49–50 j'ai tombé *Ie intombe* 50

mains *main.* **comme** [not in F] *pense peuse*
51 *treis-distingué* tres distinie **59 *Suivez***
Saaue
4.5 [Both Bourbon and the Dauphin appear in
this scene in F. Whereas in most instances
the textual differences between Q and F
merely involve speech prefixes, here they are
more substantial. See Additional Passages,
pp. 1520–21, for F and Q versions of this
scene.] **2 *Seigneur*** *sigueur* **perdu** . . .
perdu perdia . . . perdie **3 s.p. BOURBON** [Q]
Dol⟨phin⟩. **Mort de** *Mor Dieu* **7–9 We
are** . . . **upon** [Q; F places after 4.5.17] **10
order** [Q] Order now **12 home** [Q] hence
13 leno [Q] Pander **14 by a slave** [Q] a base
slaue
4.6.14–15 face, / **And** [Q] face. / He **15 dear**
[Q] my **39 s.p. PISTOL** *Coup' la gorge.* [Q;
not in F]
4.7.18 e'en in 19 world Orld **36 made an
end** [Q] made **83 Crispian** *Crispianus* **102
countryman** [Q] Countrymen **115 a live**
aliue **118 a lived** aliue **150 that I would
see** that I might see
4.8.9 God's plood, and his Gode plut, and his
[Q1] 'Sblud **23 what is** [Q1] what's **94
Vaudemont** *Vandemont* **98 Keighley** Ketly
107 we me 118 in [Q; no in F]
5.0.10 maids [not in F] **29 high-loving** by
loving
5.1.13 a [Q1] hee **36 By Jesu** [Q1] I say **37
and four nights** [Q; not in F] **80 swear** [Q]
swore
5.2.50 scythe, all Sythe, withall **169 vat** wat
172–73 *suis le possesseur* *sur le possession*
236 *grandeur* *grandeus* **237 *de votre
seigneurie*** *nostre Seigneur* **indigne** *indignie*
244 vat wat **246 *entend*** entendre **291
before that it** before it **297 never** [not in F]
305 s.p. WARWICK *West⟨merland⟩.* **306 so**
[not in F] **328 ALL** Lords. **337 paction**
Pation

THE MOST EXCELLENT AND
LAMENTABLE TRAGEDY OF ROMEO AND
JULIET

CONTROL TEXT: Q2 (Q1 FOR
1.2.51–1.3.36)

F: The Folio of 1623
Q1: The Quarto of 1597
Q2: The Quarto of 1599
Q3: The Quarto of 1609
Q4: The Quarto of 1623

Title: The . . . Iuliet [Q2 (title-page and head
title above 1.1.)] *The most lamentable
Tragedie of Romeo and Iuliet.* [Q2 (running
title)]

s.p. CITIZENS OF THE WATCH [Q2's use of
Officer(s) has been standardized through-
out.]
s.p. CAPULET'S WIFE [Q2's use of *Capulet's
Wife, Old Lady, Wife, Lady,* and *Mother*
has been standardized throughout.]
s.p. MONTAGUE'S WIFE [Q2's use of *Wife* and
Wife. 2. has been standardized
throughout.]
s.p. CAPULET [Q2's use of *Capulet, I. Capulet,*
and *Father* has been standardized
throughout.]
s.p. PETER [Q2's use of *Peter* and *Servingman*
has been standardized throughout.]
s.p. CAPULET'S COUSIN [Q2's use of *2.
Capulet* has been standardized through-
out.]
s.p. FRIAR LAURENCE [Q2's use of *Friar* and
Lawrence has been standardized through-
out.]
s.p. FIRST SERVINGMAN [Q2's use of *1., 3.,*
and *Fellow* has been standardized
throughout.]
s.p. SECOND SERVINGMAN [Q2's use of *2.* has
been standardized throughout.]
s.p. FIRST MUSICIAN [Q2's use of *Musician,
Fiddler,* and *Minstrel* has been standard-
ized throughout.]
s.p. SECOND MUSICIAN [Q2's use of *2. Musi-
cian, Fiddler,* and *2. Minstrel* has been
standardized throughout.]
s.p. THIRD MUSICIAN [Q2's use of *3. Musi-
cian, 3. Fiddler,* and *3. Minstrel* has been
standardized throughout.]
s.p. BALTHASAR [Q2's use of *Man* and
Balthasar has been standardized through-
out.]

1.1.24 in [Q1; not in Q2] **34 side** [Q1] sides
140 his [Q3] is **146 sun** same **170 create**
[Q1] created **172 well-seeming** [Q4]
welseeing **185 lovers'** louing **195 Bid a** . . .
make [Q1] A . . . makes **204 unharmed**
[Q1] vncharmed **211 makes** [Q4] make
1.2.13 made [Q1; Q2 continues: "Earth hath
swallowed all my hopes but she, / Shees the
hopefull Lady of my earth"] **27 female**
[Q1] femme **65 Vitruvio** Vtruuio **89 fires**
fire
1.3.4 where is Wher's **68 honour** [Q1] houre
69 honour [Q1] *houre* **101 it** [Q1; not in Q2]
1.4.6–8 crowkeeper . . . **entrance.** [Q1]
Crowkeeper. **23 s.p. MERCUTIO** [Q4] *Hora-
tio.* **31 deformity** [Q1] deformities **39
done** [Q3] dum **42 save your reverence** [F]
saue you reuerence **45 like lights** lights
lights **47 five** fine **54 s.p. BENVOLIO
Queen** . . . **she?** [Q1; not in Q2] **55–91
She** . . . **bodes.** [Q2 omits 1.4.68–70 and
prints "She . . . bodes" as prose.] **55 s.p.
MERCUTIO** [not in Q2] **59 Athwart** [Q1]

Ouer 62–64 Her . . . bone her traces of the smallest spider web / her collors of the moonshines watry beams, her whip of Crickets bone 64 film Philome 67 maid [Q1] man 73 O'er [Q1] On straight; [Q2 continues: "ore Lawyerrs fingers who strait dreame on fees"] 76 breaths [Q1] breath 77 lawyer's [Q1] Courtiers lip nose 81 dreams he [Q1] he dreams 90 elf-locks [Q1] Elklocks 92 face [Q1] side 113 sail [Q1] sute
1.5.6 marzipan March-pane 13 longest longer 15 a bout about 16 Aha [Q1] Ah 91 gentler gentle 92 ready [Q1] did readie
2.0.4 matched [Q3] match
2.1.10 Pronounce [Q1] prouaunt dove [Q1] day 12 heir [Q1] her 13 Adam Abraham trim [Q1] true 38 open-arse an open, or 58 do [Q1] to 73 passing [Q1] puffing 83–84 nor any . . . name o be some other name / Belonging to a man. 87 were [Q1] wene 107 kinsmen [Q1] kismen 125 washed [Q1] washeth 141 'haviour [Q1] behauiour 143 more cunning [Q1] coying 152 circled [Q1] circle 190 lord L. 191 s.p. NURSE [not in Q2] 193–95 thee . . . come.— thee (by and by I come) Madam. 207 mine [Q1; not in Q2] 108 Romeo's name. Romeo! [Q1] Romeo. 212 My nyas My Neece 225 silk [Q1] silken 229–32 Parting . . . s.p. ROMEO Sleep . . . Would Parting . . . Iu⟨liet⟩. Sleep . . . Ro⟨meo⟩. Would 232 rest. [Q1; Q2 continues: "The grey eyde morne smiles on the frowning night, / checkring the Easterne Clouds with streaks of light / And darknesse fleckted like a drunkard reeles, / From forth daies pathway, made by Tytans wheeles."] 233 sire's close Friers close
2.2.4 path and Titan's fiery [Q1] path, and Titans burning [Q2 (Version B)] pathway, made by Tytans [Q2 (Version A)] 22 sometime's [Q1] sometime 26 slays [Q1] staies 74 yet ring [Q4] yet ringing
2.3.6 kinsman [Q1] kisman 16 s.p. BENVOLIO [Q1] Ro⟨meo⟩. 23 hai Hay 25–26 phantasims phantacies 29 pardon-me's [Q1] pardons mees 60 Switch . . . switch Swits . . . swits 84 s.p. BENVOLIO [not in Q2] 102 for [Q1; not in Q2] 181–91 Well . . . letter [prose in Q2] 179 I warrant Warrant 192 Ah A dog's [Q3] dog
2.4.11 three [Q3] there 15–19 And . . . away M. And [Q2's M. is indented as a speech prefix]
2.5.27 music's [Q4] musicke 34 sum up some sum up sum
3.1.2 Capels are [Q1] Capels 63 injured [F] iniuried 69 stoccado stucatho 70 come . . . walk will you walke 85 s.p. PETRUCCIO Away, Tybalt! Away Tybalt. [as stage direction] 87 both your both 117 He gad He

gan 119 fire-eyed [Q1] end 140 kinsman [Q1] kisman 145 fray [Q1, F] bloudie fray 160 agent aged 170 kinsman [Q3] kisman 178 s.p. MONTAGUE [Q4] Capu⟨let⟩. 182 hate's [Q1] hearts 186 I [Q1] It
3.2.1 s.p. JULIET [Q1, F; not in Q2] 9 By [Q4] And by 15 grown grow 19 on vpon 73 s.p. JULIET O . . . face [Q1; assigned to Nur⟨se⟩. in Q2] 76 Dove-feathered Rauenous douefeatherd 79 damned [Q4] dimme 87 dissemblers all all dissemblers 128 corpse course
3.3.15 Hence [Q1] Here 19 banished [Q1] blanisht 40–43 But . . . death? This may flyes do, when I from this must flie, / And sayest thou yet, that exile is not death? / But Romeo may not, he is banished. / Flies may do this, but I from this must flie: / They are freemen, but I am banished.
3.3.52 Thou [Q1] Then 62 men [Q1] man 82 Where is [Q1] Wheres 109 denote [Q1] deuote 116 lives lies 143 pout'st upon [Q4] puts vp 167 disguised [Q3] disguise
3.4.13 be [Q1] me 23 We'll [Q1] Well
3.5.13 sun exhaled Sun exhale 19 the [Q1] the the 31 changed change 43 my [Q1] ay 82 him [Q4; not in Q2] 106 I [Q4; not in Q2] 139 gives [Q3] giue 176 work, play; houre, tide, time, worke, play 180 lined liand 225 hence here
4.1.45 cure [Q1] care 72 slay [Q1] stay 83 chapless [Q1] chapels 85 tomb [not in Q2] 98 breath [Q1] breast 100 wanny many 110 In [Q3] Is bier [Q2 continues: "Be borne to buriall in thy kindreds graue"] 111 shalt [Q3] shall 116 waking [Q3] walking
4.2.14 self-willed harlotry [Q1] selfewield harlottry 26 becoming becomd
4.3.48 wake [Q4] walke
4.4.20 faith [Q4] father 63 See [not in Q2] 68 long [Q1] loue 70–73 Beguiled . . . death [follows Nurse's speech 4.4.80–85] 82 bedold [Q3] bedold 92 cure care 108 All in And in 109 fond some 126 by my [Q1] my my 131 full of woe [Q4] full 132 s.p. FIRST MUSICIAN [Q1] Minstrels. 146 s.p. PETER Then . . . I [Q4] Then . . . Peter. I. 148 grief [Q1] griefes 149 And . . . oppress [Q1; not in Q2] 152 Matthew Minikin Simon Catling 157 Simon [Q1] Iames
5.1.3 lord L. 15 fares my Juliet [Q1] doth my Lady Iuliet 24 defy [Q1] denie 77 pay [Q1] pray
5.3.3. yew trees [Q1] young tree 20 rite right 40, 43 s.p. BALTHASAR [Q1] Pet⟨er⟩. 68 conjuration commiration 71 s.p. PAGE [Q1; line not assigned to anyone in Q2] 102–3 Shall I believe / That I will beleeue, / Shall I beleeue that 108 Depart

again. [Q4] Depart again, come lye thou in my arme. / Here's to thy health, where ere thou tumblest in. / O true Appothecarie! / Thy drugs are quicke. Thus with a kisse I die. / Depart againe **137 yew** yong **186 too** [F] too too **189 is so shrieked** is so shrike **193 our** your **198 slaughtered** [Q4, F] slaughter **208 more early** [Q1] now earling **231 that** [Q4] thats **298 raise** [Q4, F] raie

THE TRAGEDY OF JULIUS CAESAR

CONTROL TEXT: F

F: The Folio of 1623

1.2.104 Said Caesar *Caesar* saide **140 were** are **156 walls** Walkes
1.3.128 In favour's Is Fauors
2.1.40 ides first **67 of** of a **83 put** path **96 Cinna, this;** this, *Cinna;* **266 his** hit **312, 315, 319 s.p. LIGARIUS** *Cai⟨us⟩.*
2.2.46 are heare **81 Of** And **108 Cassius** *Publius* **109 s.p. CASSIUS** *Pub⟨lius⟩.* Cassius *Publius*
3.1.39 law lane **47 but with just cause** [not in F; line is quoted by Ben Jonson in *Timber, or Discoveries.*] **116 lies** lye **175 unstrung** in strength **286 for** from
3.2.50 s.p. FOURTH PLEBEIAN 2. **63 s.p. FIFTH PLEBEIAN** 4. **101 art** are **107 he not** hee **196–97 revenged. / ALL THE PLEBEIANS** Revenge! reueng'd: Reuenge **213 wit** writ
4.1.44 meinies meanes
4.2.2 s.p. SOLDIER *Lucil⟨lius⟩.* **34–36 s.p.'s FIRST SOLDIER, SECOND SOLDIER, THIRD SOLDIER** [not in F] **80 bay** baite **170 ill-tempered too.** ill remper'd too.s **204 Impatience** Impatient **269 to** ro **301 will** will it
5.1.42 teeth teethes **55 swords** Sword **79 ensigns** Ensigne **88 give** giue up **95 rest** rests
5.3.103 Thasos *Tharsus*
5.4.7 s.p. LUCILLIUS [not in F] **17 the** thee
5.5.76 With all Withall

THE TRAGEDY OF HAMLET, PRINCE OF DENMARK

CONTROL TEXT: F

F: The Folio of 1623
Fa, Fb: Successive states of F incorporating various print-shop corrections and changes
Q1: The Quarto of 1603 ("bad")
Q2: The Quarto of 1604 ("good")
Q2a, Q2b: Successive states of Q2 incorporating various print-shop corrections and changes
Q3: The Quarto of 1611

s.p. KING CLAUDIUS [F's use of *King* has been standardized throughout.]
s.p. QUEEN GERTRUDE [F's use of *Queen* has been standardized throughout.]
s.p. PLAYER KING [F's use of *King* has been standardized throughout.]
s.p. PLAYER QUEEN [F's use of *Baptista* and *Queen* has been standardized throughout.]
s.p. FIRST CLOWN [F's use of *Clown* has been standardized throughout.]
s.p. SECOND CLOWN [F's use of *Other* has been changed throughout.]

Title: *The Tragedie of Hamlet Prince of Denmarke* [Q2 (head title, running titles), F (head title), Q1 (running titles)] *THE Tragicall Historie of* HAMLET, *Prince of Denmarke* [Q2 (title page)] *The Tragedie of Hamlet* [F (running titles, table of contents)] THE Tragicall Historie of HAMLET *Prince of Denmarke* [Q1 (title page, head title)]
1.1.60 he [Q1, Q2; not in F] **62 Polacks** Pollax **93 designed** designe **106.8 tenantless** tennatlesse [Q2] **106.10 At** As [Q2] **106.14 feared** feare [Q2] **106.18 climature** climatures [Q2] **131 morn** [Q2] day **139 say** [Q1, Q2] sayes **144 takes** [Q1, Q2] talkes **155 Let's** [Q1, Q2] Let
1.2.8 sometime [Q2] sometimes **21 Coleagued** Coleagued [Q2] Colleagued **34 Valtemand** [Q2] *Voltemond* **35 bearers** [Q1, Q2] bearing **58–60 wrung . . . consent** [Q2; not in F] wrung from me a forced graunt [Q1; Oxford editor G. R. Hibbard argues that the "forced graunt" recollected by the Q1 reporter suggests that he was aware of Laertes' "laboursome petition" as it appears in Q2. The omission is therefore most likely an accident, not an authorial cut.] **77 good-mother** good Mother **119 pray thee** [Q2] prythee **132 canon** cannon **134 Seem** [Q2] Seemes **135 ah** [Q2] Oh **141 beteem** [Q2] beteene **150 God** [Q1, Q2] Heauen **164 Marcellus.** [Q2; F (text) indents, like a speech prefix; F (c.w.) is "*Mar-.*"] **167 Wittenberg** [Q2] *Wittemberge* **176 prithee** [Q2] pray thee **186 A** [Q2] He **195 God's** [Q1, Q2] Heauens **204 distilled** [Q1, Q2] bestil'd **209 Where, as** [Q1] Whereas **237 s.p. BARNARDO and MARCELLUS** *Both.* [Q2] *All.* [F] **242 walk** [Q1, Q2] wake
1.3.1 inbarqued [Q1, Q2] imbark't **5 favour** [Q2] fauours **8 Forward** [Q2] Froward **9 perfume and** [Q2; not in F] **16 will** [Q2] feare **21 sanity and** sanctity and **whole** [Q2] weole **40 their** [Q2] the **46 watchman** [Q2] watchmen **57 thee** [Q1, Q2] you **65 new-hatched** [Q2] vnhatch't **74 all a 109 Running** Roaming **117 Lends** [Q1, Q2]

Giues **120 From** [Q2] For **128 dye** [Q2] eye **129 imploratators** implorators **130 bawds** bonds
1.4.1 it is [Q2] is it **10 wassail** [Q1, Q2] wassels **18.1 revel** [Q3] reueale [Q2] **18.11 the** their [Q2] **18.20 evil** eale [Q2] **18.21 over** of a [Q2] **daub** doubt [Q2] **23 intents** [Q1, Q2] euents **26 O** [Q1] Oh, oh **37 the** [Q1, Q2] thee **51 summit** [Q2] Sonnet **53 assume** [Q1, Q2] assumes **59 artere** Artire
1.5.1 Whither [Q1, Q2] Where **19 on** [Q1] an **20 porcupine** Porpentine **22 List, Hamlet, list, O list!** list *Hamlet,* oh list **24 God** [Q1, Q2] Heauen **35 'Tis** [Q1, Q2] It's **43 wit** wits **with traitorous gifts—** [Q2] hath Traitorous guifts. **45 to his** [Q1, Q2] to to this **69 eager** Aygre **71 barked** bak'd **75 of queen** [Q1, Q2] and Queene **93 Hold, hold** [Q2] hold **117 s.p. HAMLET** *Marcellus* **120 is't** [Q1, Q2] ist't **137 whirling** [Q1, Q2] hurling **140 Horatio** [Q1, Q2] my Lord **158 our** [Q1, Q2] for **164 earth** [Q1, Q2] ground **175 this head-shake** [Q1, Q2] thus, head shake **178 they** [Q1, Q2] there
2.1.1 this [Q1, Q2] his **3 marv'lous** maruels **4 to** [Q2] you **enquire** [Q2] inquiry **14 As** [Q2] And **47 and the addition** Addition **49 does a this—a does—** [Q2] he this? / He does: **50 By the mass** [Q2; not in F] **58 a** [Q2] he **62 carp** [Q2] Cape **69 b'wi'** [Q2] buy **69 Fare ye** [Q2] fare you **77 i'th' name of God** [Q2] in the name of Heauen **92 a** [Q2] he **98 shoulder** [Q1, Q2] shoulders **102 Come,** [Q2; not in F] **113 feared** [Q2] feare **115 By heaven** [Q1, Q2] It seemes
2.2.17 Whether . . . thus [Q2; not in F] **20 is** [Q2] are **29 But we** [Q2] We **31 service** [Q2] Seruices **39 Ay** [Q2; not in F] **45 and** [Q1, Q2] one **48 it hath** [Q2] I haue **52 fruit** [Q2] Newes **58 my** [Q2; not in F] **59 Valtemand** [Q2] *Voltumand* **99 'tis 'tis** [Q2] it is **126 solicitings** [Q2] soliciting **150 wherein** [Q2] whereon **162 does** [Q2] ha's **168 But** [Q2] And **180 ten** [Q1, Q2] two **188 a said** [Q2] he said **189 A is** [Q2] he is **195 read** [Q1, Q2] meane **199 lack** [Q2] locke **200 most** [Q2; not in F] **210–11 My Lord, I will take** [Q1, Q2] My Honourable Lord, I will most humbly / Take **213 except my life, my life, my life** except my life, my life **216 the** [Q2] my **221 Ah** [Q2] Oh **272 of** [Q1, Q2; not in F] **286 discovery, and** [Q2] discovery of **289 heavily** [Q2] heauenly **302 then, when** [Q1, Q2] when **328 berattle** be-ratled **334 like most will** like most **350 'Sblood** [Q2; not in F] **367 Haply** [Q2] Happily **373 was** [Q1, Q2; not in F] **378 came** [Q2] can **382 individable** [Q2] indiuible **403 pious chanson** [Q2]

Pons Chanson **407 valanced** [Q2] valiant **415 good** [Q1, Q2; not in F] **418 caviare** [Q1, Q2] *Cauiarie* **419 judgements** [Q1, Q2] iudgement **425–26 as wholesome as sweet, and . . . fine** [Q2; not in F] **426 One** [Q2] One cheefe **437 total** [Q1, Q2] to take **445 So, proceed you** [Q2; not in F] so goe on [Q1; probably an accidental omission. See variant at 1.2.58–60.] **449 antique** anticke [probably punning on "antic"] **470 armour** [Q2] Armours **479 to the** [Q1, Q2] to'th **482 mobbled** [Q1, Q2] inobled **484 mobbled** [Q1] Inobled **485 flames** [Q2] flame **499 whe'er** [Q2] whether **500 Prithee** [Q2] Pray you **506 live** [Q1, Q2] liued **508 much** [Q2; not in F] **516 s.p. PLAYERS** *Play⟨ers⟩.* **526 b'wi'** [F, Q2] buy **531 wanned** [Q2] warm'd **553 'Swounds** [Q2] Why **556 'a'** [Q1, Q2] haue **557 offal.** Bloody, bawdy [Q2] Offall, bloudy: a Bawdy **560 Why,** [Q2] Who? **561 the dear murderèd** Deere **574 a** [Q2] he
3.1.32 here [Q2] there **45 please you** [Q2] please ye **50 sugar** [Q2] surge **51 too true** [Q2] true **73 Th'** [Q2] The **proud** [Q2] poore **76 th'** [Q2] the **89 awry** [Q2] away **99 you know** [Q1, Q2] I know **101 Their perfume lost** then perfume left **112 with** [Q1, Q2] your **133 nowhere** [Q1, Q2] no way **142 paintings, too** [Q1] pratlings too **143 hath** [Q1, Q2] has **face** [Q1, Q2] pace **selves** [Q1, Q2] selfe **154 And** [Q2] Haue
3.2.4 with [Q1, Q2; not in F] **6 your** [Q2; not in F] **8 hear** [Q1, Q2] see **11 would** [Q1, Q2] could **17 o'erstep** [Q2] ore-stop **28–29 nor no man** or Norman **53 tongue** lick [Q2] tongue, like **55 feigning** faining **56 her** [Q2] my **72 thy** [Q2] my **77 stithy** [Q2] Stythe **heedful** [Q2] needfull **81 a** [Q2] he **89 mine now. My Lord, you** mine. Now my Lord, you **120 a must** [Q2] he must **121 a suffer** [Q2] he suffer **124 *malhecho*** *Malicho* **127 this fellow** [Q1, Q2] these Fellowes **129 a** [Q2] they **148 former** [Q2] forme **156 their** [Q2] my **178 either** [Q2] other **179 enactures** [Q2] enactors **186 favourite** [Q2] fauourites **198 me give** [Q2] giue me **199.2 An** And [Q2] **221 wince** [Q2] winch **222 unwrung** [Q2] vnrung **224 as good as a** [Q1, Q2] a good **228 mine** [Q2] my **230 mis-take** [Q2] mistake **your** [Q1, Q2; not in F] **239 A** [Q2] He **248 s.p. COURTIERS** *All.* **249 stricken** [F] strucken **268 Ah ha!** [Q2] Oh, ha? **296 as you** [Q2] you **298 struck** stroke **330 fingers** [Q2] finger **339 it speak.** [Q2] it S'blood [Q2] Why **I** [Q1, Q2] that I **345 yonder** [Q1, Q2] that of [Q1, Q2] like **347 mass** [Q2] Misse **and 'tis,** [Q2] and it's
3.3.14 weal [Q2] spirit **18 summit** Somnet **73 a** [Q2] he **74 a** [Q2] he **77 sole** [Q2]

soule 80 A [Q2] He 81 flush [Q2] fresh 88 hint hent

3.4.1 A [Q2] He 12 a wicked [Q2] an idle 31 better [Q2] Betters 36 brassed braz'd 41 off [Q2] of 43 sets [Q2] makes 54 this [Q2] his 64 brother [Q2] breath 78 And [Q2] As 108 you do [Q2] you 109 th'incorporal [Q2] their corporall 122 whom [Q2] who 142 o'er or 143 ranker [Q2] ranke 144 these this 151.1-2 eat, / Of habits devilish eate / Of habits deuill [Q2] 151.5 Refrain tonight [F] to refraine night [Q2] 151.9 either in either [Q2] 166 bloat [Q2] blunt 172 mad [Q2] made 185.6 and't an't [Q2]

4.1.1 matter [Q2] matters 6 sea [Q1, Q2] Seas 11 O [Q2] On 21 let [Q2] let's 26 a [Q2] He 34 mother's closet [Q2] Mother Clossets 39.1 So envious slander [not in Q2]

4.2.16 like an ape an apple like an Ape

4.3.7 never [Q2] neerer 20 a [Q2] he 21 politic [Q1, Q2; not in F] 23 ourselves [Q2] our selfe 26-28 s.p. KING CLAUDIUS Alas . . . that worm [Q2; not in F] 38 A will [Q2] He will 44 is [Q2] at 50 them [Q2] him

4.4.9.16 now [not in Q2]

4.5.12 might [Q2] would 41 God'ield God dil'd 65 thus [Q2] this 74 sorrows come [Q2] sorrowes comes 75 battalions [Q2] Battaliaes 85 Feeds [Q2] Keepes this [Q2] his 88 Wherein [Q2] Where in 93 is [Q2] are 96 impetuous impittious 114 that's calm [Q2] that calmes 124 Where is [Q2] Where's 138 is't [Q2] if 139 sweepstake Soop-stake 144 pelican [Q2] Politician 148 sensibly [Q2] sensible 151 s.p. VOICES [not in F] 165 rained [Q2] raines 166 Fare you well, my dove. [F italicizes as part of the song.] 174 pansies [Q2] Paconcies 181 a made [Q2] he made 185-86 a . . . a [Q2] he . . . he 194 God 'a' mercy [Q1, Q2] Gramercy 196 O God [Q2] you Gods 197 commune common 212 call't [Q2] call

4.6.8 A [Q2] Hee 9 ambassador [Q2] Ambassadours 11 Horatio [Q2; not in F] 21 thine [Q2] your

4.7.11 they're [Q2] they are 21 guilts Gyues 24 aimed [Q2] arm'd 27 Who has Who was 48 abuse, and [Q2] abuse? Or 66 since [Q2] hence 69 can [Q2] ran 77 Lamord [Q2] Lamound 79 the [Q2] our made [Q2] mad 84.1 Th'escrimers the Scrimures [Q2] 84 Sir, this [Q2] Sir. This 88 What [Q2] Why 97 in deed indeed 114 that, but dip [Q2] I but dipt 127 cunnings [Q2] commings 129 that [Q2] the 133 How now, sweet Queen? how sweet Queene. 135 they [Q2] they'l 139 Therewith [Q2] There with make [Q2] come 143 crownet Coro-

net 152 their [Q1, Q2] her 153 lay [Q2] buy

5.1.4 coroner [Q2] Crowner 11 to act [Q2] an Act 23 o' [Q2] of 31 A [Q2] He 60 there-a-was nothing-a [Q2] there was nothing 61 a [Q2] he 71 'twere [Q2] it / were 72 This [Q2] It 73 would [Q2] could 78 a [Q2] he 83 an [Q2] if 90 of [Q1] of of 101-2 th'inheritor [Q2] the Inheritor 108 sirrah [Q2] Sir 129 heel [Q1, Q2] heeles 129-30 the courtier [Q1, Q2] our Courtier 139-40 a . . . A . . . a . . . [Q2] he . . . hee . . . he 140 'tis [Q2] it's 142 him there. There [Q2] him, there 149 sexton [Q2] sixteene 152 a . . . a [Q2] he . . . he 154 a will [Q2] he will 166 This same skull, sir [Q2] This same Scull Sir, this same Scull sir 173 now, how [Q1, Q2] how 177 Not [Q2] No grinning [Q2] Ieering 185 Pah puh 188 a [Q2] he 202 rites rights 204 of [Q2; not in F] 212 prayers [Q2] praier 230 treble woe [Q2] terrible woer 237 To o'ertop [Q2] To o'retop 238 grief [Q2] griefes 240 Conjures [Q2] Conuire 246 For [Q1, Q2] Sir 250 ALL THE LORDS Gentlemen! [not in F] s.p. HORATIO [Q2] Gen. 259 'Swounds [Q2] Come 260 woot fast [Q2; not in F] 272 couplets [Q2] Cuplet 279 your [Q2] you

5.2.7 praised [Q2] praise 8 sometime [Q2] sometimes 9 pall paule 21 reasons [Q2] reason 30 villainies villaines 38 Th' [Q2] The effect [Q2] effects 41 like [Q2] as 49 ordinant [Q2] ordinate 52 the form of th' forme of the 55 sequent [Q2] sement 59 defeat [Q2] debate 79 court count 88 chuff Chowgh 89 say [Q2] saw 92 sir [Q2; not in F] 100 a [Q2] he 102 Nay, good my Lord [Q2] Nay, in good faith, 102.2 gentleman gentlemen [Q2] 102.4 feelingly [Q3] sellingly [Q2a] fellingly [Q2b] 102.8 dizzy [Q3] dazzie [Q2] 102.9 yaw [Q2a] raw [Q2b] 102.20 to't [Q2a] doo't [Q2b] rarely really [Q2] 102.34 his this [Q2] 108 King, sir [Q2] sir King hath wagered [Q2] ha's wag'd 110 hanger [Q2] Hangers 120 bet [Q2] but 122 laid, sir [Q2] laid 124 on't one nine [Q2] mine it [Q2] that 132 and [Q2] if 138 turn [Q2] tongue 140 A [Q2] He a [Q2] hee 141 has [Q2] had many [Q2] mine 144 fanned fond 145 trial [Q2] tryalls 150 it [Q2; not in F] 181 brother [Q1, Q2] Mother 187 ungored [Q2] vngorg'd 213 trumpet speak [Q2] Trumpets speake 219 my lord [Q2] on sir 227 Set it [Q1, Q2] set 231 Here, Hamlet, take my Heere's a 249 mine own [Q2] mine 254 Ho! [Q2] How? 265 s.p. ALL THE COURTIERS [Q2] All. 281 cause aright [Q2] causes right 285 ha't [Q2] haue't **286 God** [Q2] good **299 th'occur-rents** [Q2] the occurents **302 cracks** [Q2] cracke **308 This** [Q2] His **310 shot** [Q2] shoote **329 th'inventors'** [Q2] the Inuentors **333 rights** [Q1, Q2] Rites **334 now** [Q1, Q2] are **335 also** [Q2] alwayes

THE TRAGEDY OF OTHELLO, THE MOOR OF VENICE

CONTROL TEXT: F

F: The Folio of 1623
Q: The Quarto of 1622
Fa, Fb, Qc, Qd: Successive states of F or Q incorporating various print-shop corrections and changes
Title: *The Tragedy of* Othello *the Moore of Venice* [Q] *Tragoedy* [Q title page] THE TRAGEDIE OF Othello, the Moore of Venice [F, Stationers' Register entry]
1.1.1 Tush [Q; not in F] **4 'Sblood** [Q; not in F] **24 togaed** [Q] Tongued **28 other** [Q] others **32 God** [Q; not in F] **53 'em** [Q] them **66 full** [Q] fall **79 thieves, thieves thieves** [Q] Theeues, Theeues **86 'Swounds, sir** [Q] Sir **101 bravery** [Q] knauerie **110 'Swounds, sir** [Q] Sir **118 now** [Q; not in F] **183 night** [Q] might
1.2.34 Duke [Q] Dukes **46 sent** [Q] hath sent **55 comes another** [Q] come another [Fa] come sanother [Fb] **59 Roderigo? Come** [Q, Fa] *Rodorigoc?* Cme [Fb] **60 'em** [Q] them **69 darlings** [Q] Deareling **88 I** [Q; not in F]
1.3.1 There is [Q] There's **these** [Q] this **53 nor** [Q] hor **73 s.p.** SENATORS *All.* **90 tale** [Q] u Tale **106 upon** [Q] vp on **s.p.** DUKE [Q ⟨Du⟨ke⟩⟩; not in F] **107 overt** [Q] over **129 battles** [Q] Battaile **fortunes** [Q] Fortune **139 antres** [Q ⟨*Antrees*⟩] Antars **140 and hills whose heads** [Q] Hills, whose head **142 other** [Q] others **143 Anthropophagi** [Q] *Antropophague* **144 Do grow** [Q] Grew **146 thence** [Q] hence **154 intentively** [Q] instinctiuely **188 b'wi'you** [Q (bu'y)] be with you **197 'em** [Q] them **200 Into your favour** [Q; not in F] **218 ear** [Q] eares **228 couch** [Q] Coach **247 I did** [Q] I **263 me my 269 instruments** [Q] Instrument **277** DESDEMONA . . . **This night** [Q; not in F] **299 the** [Q] the the **309 ha'** [Q] haue **322 beam** braine **326 our unbitted** [Q] or vnbitted **343 error** [Q] errors **347 a super-subtle** [Q] super-subtle **349 pox o'** [Q] pox of **367 a** [Q; not in F] **370 He has** She ha's **385 ha't** [Q] haue't
2.1.7 ha' [Q] hath **13 mane** [Q (mayne)] Maine **27 Veronessa** [Q] *Verennessa* **34 prays** [Q] praye **41 s.p.** THIRD GENTLEMAN

[Q (3 *Gent.*)] *Gent.* **43 arrivance** [Q] Arriuancie **44 this** [Q] the **52 s.p. / s.d.** VOICES *(within) Within* [s.p.] **83 And bring all** Cyprus comfort [Q; not in F] **89 me** [Q; not in F] **95** VOICES *(within)* A sail, a sail! *Within.,* A Saile, a Saile. [after line 96] **97 their** [Q] this **108 ha'** [Q] haue **111 ha'** [Q] haue **115 hussies** Huswiues **123 essay** assay **174 an** [Q] and **211 hither** [Q] thither **222 again** [Q] a game **235 has** [Q] he's **251 mutualities** [Q] mutabilities **293 rank** [Q] right
2.2.5 addiction addition **9 Heaven bless** [Q] Blesse
2.3.33 ha' [Q] haue **53 to put** [Q] put to **57 God** [Q] heauen **66 God** [Q] Heauen **70 Englishman** [Q] Englishmen **84 Then** [Q] *And* **86 Fore God** [Q] Why **89 God's** [Q] heau'ns **96 ha'** [Q] haue **97 God forgive** [Q] Forgiue **124 engraffed** ingraft **129** VOICES *(within)* Help, help! [Q *(Helpe, helpe, within.)*; not in F] **130 'Swounds, you** [Q] You **141 God's will** [Q] Alas **142 Sir! Montano! Sir!** [Q] *Sir Montano:* **145 God's will** [Q] Fie, fie **hold** [Q; not in F] **147 'Swounds** [Q; not in F] **151 Hold, hold** [Q] hold **173 be** [Q] to be **190 'Swounds, if I** [Q] If I once **201 leagued** [Q] league **204 ha'** [Q] haue **216 the** [Q] then **236 now** [Q; not in F] **245 God** [Q] Heauen **246 ha'** [Q] haue **247 ha'** [Q] haue **249 thought** [Q] had thought **269 O God** [Q] Oh **291 I'll** [Q] I **294 denotement** deuotement **306 here** [Q; not in F] **317 were't** [Q] were **339 ha'** [Q] haue **343 ha'** [Q] haue **348 hast** [Q] hath **351 By the mass** [Q] Introth
3.1.3 ha' [Q] haue **8–9 tail . . . tale** tale . . . tale **17 ha'** [Q] haue **20 my** [Q] me, mine **23 general's wife** Cenerals wife [Q] Generall **28** CASSIO Do, good my friend [Q; not in F] **29 ha'** [Q] haue **30 ha'** [Q] haue **47 To take the saf'st occasion by the front** [Q; not in F]
3.3.16 circumstance [Q] Circumstances **53 Yes, faith** [Q] I sooth **61 or** [Q] on **75 By'r Lady** [Q] Trust me **96 you** [Q] he **110 By heaven** [Q] Alas **116 In** [Q] Of **140 free to** [Q] free **144 But some** [Q] Wherein **152 oft** [Q] of **153 that your wisdom then I** intreate you then [Q] that your wisedome **166 By heaven** [Q; not in F] **174 fondly** soundly **179 God** [Q] Heauen **184 once** [Q; not in F] **189 well** [Q; not in F] **206 God** [Q] Heauen **208 keep't** kept **219 I'faith** [Q] Trust me **221 my** [Q] your **253 hold** [Q; not in F] **263 qualities** [Q] Quantities **277 of** [Q] to **282 O then heaven mocks** [Q] Heauen mock'd **289 Faith** [Q] Why **300 ha'** [Q] haue **316 faith** [Q] but **319 with it** [Q] with't **343 of** [Q] in **396 sir** [Q; not in F] **400 supervisor** [Q] super-

vision **413 ha't** [Q] haue't **428 lay** laid **434 s.p. IAGO** [Q *(Iag⟨o⟩.)*. Prefixed to line 435 *(Iago.)*: in other words, F gives line 434 to Othello.] **445 that** was it was **458 knows** keepes **463 s.d.** *He kneels* [Q; not in F]

3.4.53 faith [Q] indeed **73 I'faith** [Q] Indeed? **75 God** [Q] Heauen seen it [Q] seene't **79 Heaven bless** [Q] Blesse **84 sir** [Q; not in F] **89–90 DESDEMONA I pray, talk me of Cassio. / OTHELLO The handkerchief.** [Q; not in F] **94 I'faith** [Q] Insooth **95 'Swounds** [Q] Away **166 I'faith** [Q] Indeed **182 by my faith** [Q] in good troth

4.1.32 Faith [Q] Why **35 'Swounds,** [Q; not in F] **49 No, forbear** [Q; not in F] **75 unsuiting** [Qd] vnfitting [Qc] resulting **77 'scuse** [Q] scuses **92 hussy** huswife **99 conster** [Q] conserue **101 now** [Q; not in F] **105 power** [Q] dowre **109 a woman** [Q] woman **110 i'faith** [Q] indeed **120 Faith** [Q] Why **123 Ha'** [Q] Haue **127 beckons** [Q] becomes **129 the sea-** [Fb] the the Sea- [Fa] **145 whole** [Q; not in F] **153 An . . . An** [Q] If . . . if **156 Faith** [Q; not in F] **158 Faith** [Q] Yes **179 so** [Fb] fo [Fa] **207 God save the** [Q] Save you **227 the letter** [Q] thle etter [Fa] thLetter [Fb] **230 By my troth** [Q] Trust me **243 on** [Q; not in F] **276 denote** [Q] deonte [Fa] deuote [Fb]

4.2.5 'em [Q] them **16 ha'** [Q] haue **24 ha'** [Q] haue **32 nay** [Q] May **33 knees** [Q] knee **35 But not the words** [Q; not in F] **49 God** Heauen **50 He** [Q] they **71 ne'er** [Q] neuer **97 ha'** [Q] haue **105 ha'** [Q] haue **116 ha'** [Q] haue **120 hearts** [Fb] heart [Fa] **145 heaven** [Q] Heauens **152 O God** O Good [Q] Alas **159 them in** them: or **171 And he does chide with you** [Q; not in F] **186 Faith** [Q; not in F] **I have heard too much, for your words, and** [Q] And hell gnaw his bones, [Fa] I haue heard too much: and your words and [Fb] **192 'em** [Q] them **224 takes** [Q] taketh **228 of** [Q; not in F]

4.3.12 He [Q] And **20 in** them [Q; not in F] **22 faith** [Q] Father **23 thee** [Q; not in F] **37 nether** [Fb] neither [Fa] **38 soul sat** [Fb] *Sonle set* [Fa] **sighing** *sining* [Fa] singing [Fb] **73 Ud's pity** [Q] why **102 God** [Q] Heauen

5.1.1 bulk [Q] Barke **22 hear** [Q] heard **34 dear** [Q] deere **36 Forth** [Q] For **51 heaven's** heauen **62 'em** [Q] them **91 O heaven** [Q] yes, 'tis **106 out** [Q; not in F] **109 an** [Q] if **116 dead** [Q] quite dead **125 Fough** [Q; not in F]

5.2.37 so [Q; not in F] **62 Then Lord** [Q] O Heauen **82 'em** [Q] them **88 an** [Q] if **93 DESDEMONA O Lord, Lord, Lord!** [Q; not in F] **96 that am** [Fb] am that [Fa] **106 ha'** [Q] haue **110 Should** [Q] Did **127 O**

Lord, [Q] Alas! **136 heard** [Q] heare **166 worst** [Q] wotst **224 God! O heavenly God!** [Q] Heauen! oh heauenly Powres! **225 'Swounds** [Q] come **227 'em** [Q] them **247 here** [Q; not in F] **260 ice-brook's** Isebrookes [Q] Ice brookes **356 Indian** [Q] Iudean

THE TRAGEDY OF MACBETH

CONTROL TEXT: F

F: The Folio of 1623

Fa, Fb: Successive states of F incorporating various print-shop corrections and changes

s.p. FIRST WITCH, SECOND WITCH, THIRD WITCH [F's use of *1, 2,* and *3* has been standardized throughout.]

s.p. KING DUNCAN [F's use of *King* has been standardized throughout.]

s.p. LADY MACBETH [F's use of *Lady* has been standardized throughout.]

s.p. FIRST MURDERER [F's use of *1 Murderer, 1,* and *Murderer* has been standardized throughout.]

s.p. SECOND MURDERER [F's use of *2 Murderer* and *2* has been standardized throughout.]

s.p. THIRD MURDERER [F's use of *3* has been standardized throughout.]

s.p. ALL THE WITCHES [F's use of *All.* has been standardized throughout.]

s.p. FIRST APPARITION, SECOND APPARITION, THIRD APPARITION [F's use of *1 Apparition, 2 Apparition,* and *3 Apparition* has been standardized throughout.]

s.p. LADY MACDUFF [F's use of *Wife* has been standardized throughout.]

s.p. MACDUFF's SON [F's use of *Son* has been standardized throughout.]

s.p. A MURDERER [F's use of *Murderer* has been standardized throughout.]

s.p. A SOLDIER [F's use of *Soldier* has been standardized throughout.]

1.1.9–11 s.p. SECOND WITCH Paddock calls. / THIRD WITCH Anon. / ALL Fair . . . air. *All. Padock calls* anon: faire . . . ayre.

1.2.13 galloglasses Gallowgrosses **26 break** [not in F] **31 Norwegian** Norweyan **46 haste** a haste **61 Colum's** Colmes

1.3.30 weird weyward **37 Forres** Soris **95 hail** Tale **96 Came** Can

1.4.1 Are Or

1.5.21 'Thus . . . do' [not in F] **29, 32 s.p. SERVANT** *Mess.* **63 the innocent** th'innocent

1.6.4 martlet Barlet **9 most** must

1.7.6 shoal Schoole **47 do** no

2.1.55 strides sides **56 sure** sowre **57 way** they they may

2.3.77 horror. horror. Ring the Bell. **108 Outran** Out-run
3.1.2, 3.4.132, 4.1.152 weird weyard **23 talk** take **76 s.p. MURDERERS** [F uses *Murth.* three times in 3.1, and each time it would be appropriate for both to speak. See also 3.1.116 and 3.1.140.]
3.3.7 and end
3.4.77 time times **88 of** o' **143 in deed** indeed
3.5.34–35 s.p. SPIRITS . . . away. [not in F; see Textual Note] **38–73 s.p. SPIRITS . . . reach.** [not in F; see Textual Note]
3.6.24 son Sonnes
4.1.44–60 s.p. HECATE . . . out. [not in F; see Textual Note] **75 germens** Germaine **109 Dunsinane** Dunsmane **114 on's high place** our high plac'd
4.2.22 none moue **83 shag-haired** shagge-ear'd
4.3.134 thy they **155 with** [Fb] my with [Fa] **161 not** nor **237 tune** time
5.3.41 Cure her Cure **46 fraught** stufft
5.4.11 gone giuen
5.5.40 pall pull
5.11.25 s.p. ALL BUT MALCOLM *All.*

THE TRAGEDY OF ANTONY AND CLEOPATRA

CONTROL TEXT: F

F: THE FOLIO OF 1623
FA, FB: FA IS THE UNCORRECTED VERSION, FB THE CORRECTED VERSION OF F

Title: Anthony & Cleopatra [Stationers' Register entry] *Anthony and Cleopater* [F table of contents] *The Tragedie of Anthonie, and Cleopatra* [F head title] *The Tragedie of Anthony and Cleopatra* [F running title]

s.p. SILIUS [F's use of *Romaine* in 3.1 (where Silius is referred to by name in dialogue) is standardized throughout.]
s.p. BOY [Not in F's speech prefixes or stage directions, although Enobarbus refers to the boy in dialogue. See 2.7.]
s.p. WATCH, GUARD, SERVANTS, SOLDIERS [F refers to these characters either by category (*Soldier, 3. Watch,* etc.) or by number (*I, 2,* etc.). This edition never uses numbers alone, preferring prefixes such as "First Servant," "Third Soldier," etc.]

1.1.52 how who
1.2.0 s.d. Enter . . . attendants Enter Enobarbus, Lamprius, a Southsayer, Rannius, Lucillius, Charmian, Iras, Mardian the Eunuch, and Alexas. [Rannius and Lucillius are ghost characters; so is Lamprius, unless he is the

soothsayer. As these three are not mentioned again, their names are irrelevant and hence omitted.] **5 charge** change **34 fertile** fore- / tell **55 Alexas—come** Alexas. Come [F attributes the rest of the speech, beginning with "Come," to Alexas, taking the name as a speech prefix rather than an address.] **70 Saw you** Saue you **102 ho** how **103 s.p. SECOND MESSENGER** The . . . Sicyon— / **s.p. ANTHONY Is . . . one?** *I. Mes.* (First Messenger) The *Scicion,* / Is . . . one? [The First Messenger speaks the entire line in F.] **125 occasion** an occasion **163 leave** loue **168 Hath** Haue **177 hair** heire **179 place is under us, requires** places under us, require
1.3.11 Iwis I wish **82 my** [not in F]
1.4.3 Our One **8 vouchsafed** vouchsafe **9 the abstract** th'abstracts **44 deared** fear'd **46 lackeying** lacking **56 wassails** Vassailes **57 Modena** *Medena* **58 Pansa** Pausa **76 we me** 76 council counsell
1.5.3 mandragora *Mandragoru* **47 armjaunced** Arme-gaunt **49 dumbed** dumbe **60 man** mans
2.1.2, 5, 16, 18, 38 s.p. MENECRATES . . . MENECRATES . . . MENAS . . . MENAS . . . MENAS *Mene⟨crates⟩*. [Menecrates throughout in F] **21 waned** wand **38 ne'er** neere **41 warred** wan'd
2.2.49 the your **126 not so, Agrippa** not, say Agrippa **127 reproof** proofe **210 glow** gloue **212 gentlewomen** Gentlewoman **238 breathless, pour breath** breathlesse powre breath
2.3.12 Gone thither thither **20 afeard** a feare **28 away,** alway
2.4.6 at the at **9 s.p. MAECENAS and AGRIPPA** *Both.*
2.5.2 s.p. CHARMIAN, IRAS, and ALEXAS *Omnes.* **12 finned** fine **43 is** 'tis **52 But** Bur **104 act** art
2.6.16 the [not in F] **19 is** his **39 s.p. CAESAR, ANTONY, and LEPIDUS** *Omnes.* **53 There is** ther's **67 meanings** meaning **71 o'** [not in F] **83 s.p. CAESAR, ANTONY, and LEPIDUS** *All.*
2.7.1–13 s.p. FIRST SERVANT . . . SECOND SERVANT . . . FIRST SERVANT *I . . . 2 . . . I* **86 part then is** part, then he is **108 s.p. BOY [sings]** The Song. **110 vats** Fattes **115 off** of **119 speaks. The** [Fa] speakest: he [Fb] **123 father's** Father **125 s.p. MENAS** [Not in F; Enobarbus continues speaking until the second half of 1.129, which is spoken by Menas in F, as in this edition.] **127 hear** [Fb] heare a [Fa] **a loud** aloud
3.1.5, 27, 34 s.p. SILIUS Romaine. [variously spelled] **14 to** [Fa] too [Fb] **37 there** [Fa] their [Fb]
3.2.3 are [Fb] art [Fa] **10 s.p. AGRIPPA** *Ant⟨ony⟩.* **16 figures** Figure **26 bond** Band

49 **at** at the **full of** [Fa]; of full [Fb] **60 wept** weepe
3.3.17 **gait?** gate, **18 looked'st** look'st
3.4.8 **them,** then **9 took't** look't **24 yours** your **30 Your** You **38 has** he's
3.5.12 **world, thou hast a pair of chops,** would thou hadst a pair of chaps **14 one** the [not in F]
3.6.13 **he there . . . kings of kings** hither . . . King of Kings **61 obstruct** abstract **72 Malchus** *Mauchus* **74 Comagene; Polemon** Comageat, *Polemen* **75 Lycaonia** Licoania **88 their** his
3.7.4 **it is** it it **5 Is't not** If not, **21 Brundisium** Brandusium **23 Toryne** Troine **51 Actium** Action **69 leader's** led Leaders leade **72 s.p. CAMIDIUS** *Ven⟨tidius⟩.* **78 Taurus** *Towrus* **80 in** with
3.10.10 **riband-red** ribaudred **14 June** Inne **27 he** his
3.11.6 **s.p. ATTENDANTS** *Omnes.* **19 that** them **47 seize** cease **58 tow** stowe **59 Thy** The
3.12.0 **s.d. DOLABELLA** *Dollabello* **13 lessens** Lessons **29 As** From
3.13.10 **mooted** meered **25 caparisons** Comparisons **54 Caesar** *Caesars* **55 embraced** embrace **74 deputation** disputation **76–77 kneel / Till him,** kneele. / Tell him, **103 This** the **149 abyss** Abisme **165 smite** smile **168 discandying** discandering **171 sits** sets **201 on** in
4.2.1 **Domitius** *Domitian* **19 s.p. SERVITORS** *Omnes.*
4.3.7 **s.p. THIRD SOLDIER** *I.*
4.4.5–6 **too. / . . . for?** **s.p. ANTONY** too, *Antony.* / . . . for? [In F, Cleopatra's speech includes lines 6–7 and thus continues uninterrupted from line 5 to line 8.] **13 doff't** daft **24 s.p. CAPTAIN** *Alex⟨as⟩.* **25 s.p. SOLDIERS** *All.*
4.5.1, 3, 7 **s.p. SOLDIER** *Eros.*
4.6.15 **Camidius** *Camindius* **19 more** mote
4.8 [Most editions continue 4.7, even though the stage is cleared. The new scene affects the numbering of the remaining scenes in the act.]
4.9.2 **gests** guests **18 My** Mine
4.13.4 **augurs** Auguries **21 spanieled** pannelled
4.15.4 **towered** toward **10 distains** dislimes **19 Caesar** *Caesars* **107, 132 s.p. ALL THE GUARDS** *All.* **110 s.p. DECRETAS** *Dercetus.* **122 sent** word sent you word
4.16.42 **s.p. ALL THE LOOKERS-ON** *All.* **46 hussy** huswife **75 e'en** in **77 chores** chares **89 do it** doo't
5.1.0 **s.d. MAECENAS** *Menas* **2 but** [not in F] **15 rivèd** round **18 that** the **27 a** [not in F] **28, 31 s.p. AGRIPPA** *Dola⟨bella⟩.* **36 lance** launch **59 live** leaue **70 s.p. ALL BUT CAESAR** *All.*

5.2.80 **O** [not in F] **86 autumn 'twas** *Anthony* it was **95 or** nor **103 smites** suites **212 Ballad** Ballads o' a **219 my** mine **224 Cydnus** *Cidrus* **304 vile** wilde **308 awry** away

The Winter's Tale

Control text: F

F: The Folio of 1623

s.p. OLD SHEPHERD [F's use of *"Shep⟨heard⟩."* has been changed throughout.]
s.p. FIRST LADY [F's use of *"Lady"* has been changed at 2.1.2, 5, 14, 16.]
s.p. A LORD [F's use of *"Lord"* has been changed throughout 2.1; at 2.3.26, 147, and 197; and at 3.2.114, 172, 200, and 214.]

1.2.106 **And** A **160 ornament** Ornaments **209 they** [not in F] **278 hobby-horse** Holy-Horse
2.2.56 **let't** le't **69 twixt** betwixt
2.3.39 **What** Who
3.2.10 **Silence.** [italicized and set as stage direction in F] **31 Who** Whom **166 certain** [not in F]
3.3.67 **bairn** Barne **73 hallooed** hallow'd **110 made** mad
4.2.3 **sixteen** fifteene
4.3.10 **With heigh, with heigh,** *With heigh,*
4.4.12 **it** [not in F] **13 swoon** sworne **98 your** you **148 so** [not in F] **160 out** on't **237 kiln-hole** kill-hole **239 Clammer** clamor **298 gentlemen** Gent. **347 who** whom **407 acknowledged** acknowledge **411 who** whom **416 see** neuer see **427 hoop** hope **455 your** my **577 so** [not in F] **597 could** would **685 know not** know **713 to** at
5.1.21 **spoke** spoken **58–59 stage, / Where . . . mourn, appear** Stage / (Where . . . now appeare) **61 just** iust such **78 your** you a
5.3.5 **young contracted** your contracted **18 Lonely** Louely **67 fixture** fixure **96 Or those** On: those **150 This'** This

The Tempest

Control text: F

F: The Folio of 1623
Fa, Fb: Successive states of F incorporating various print-shop corrections and changes

1.1.18–19 **councillor** Councellor **19–20 work peace** worke the peace **31 wi'th'** with **54 s.p. MARINERS** [not in F] **57 wi'th'** with' **59 broom** Browne **furze** firrs
1.2.100 **oft** of it. **112 wi'th'** with **153 wast** was't **174 princes** Princesse **201 bowsprit** Bore-spritt **230 Bermudas** *Bermoothes*

262 Algiers *Argier* **284 she** he **304 to** [not in F] **330 forth at** for that **349 human** humane **383 sprites** *Sprights* **385–88 s.p. SPIRITS . . . ARIEL . . . SPIRITS** [Only the last refrain, "Hark, hark, I hear," is assigned to Ar⟨iel⟩. in F.] **390 cock-a-diddle-dow** *cockadidle-dowe* **407 s.p. SPIRITS . . . dong** Burthen ding dong **408 s.p. SPIRITS** [*within*] [not in F] **470 power** pow'r

2.1.37 s.p. ANTONIO. . . . Sebastian *Seb⟨ast-ian⟩. . . . Ant⟨onío⟩.* **133 More** Mo **140 chirurgeonly** Chirurgeonly **253 every** eu'ry

2.2.52 Then to sea [*etc.*] [not in F] **108 spirits** sprights **120 Swum** Swom **164 seamews** Scamels

3.1.2 sets set **15 busil'est** busie lest **47 peerless** peetlesse

3.2.24 debauched debosh'd **30 s.p. TRINCULO** [F (text)] *Cal⟨iban⟩.* [F (catchword)]

3.3.2 ache akes **15 travel** trauaile **29 islanders** Islands **33 human** humaine **65 plume** plumbe **99 bass** base

4.1.9 of her her of **13 gift** guest **17 rite** right **52 rein** raigne **53 abstemious** abstenious **61 vetches** Fetches **peas** Pease **64 peonied** pioned **74 Her** here **81 bosky** boskie **83 short-grassed** short gras'd **110 s.p. CERES** [not in F] **and** [not in F] **123 wise** wife **136 holiday** holly day **180 gorse** gosse **193 them on** on them **lime** line **229 Let't alone** let's alone

5.1.10 lime-grove *Line-groue* **16 run** runs **60 boiled** boile **72 Didst** [F (catchword)] Did [F (text)] **75 entertained** entertaine **81 shores** shore **93–96 Merrily . . . bough** [In F, these lines are not repeated.] **113 Whe'er** Where **126 not** nor **158 these** Their **178 An** And **202 remembrance** remembrances **230 events** [Fb] euens [Fa] **237 more** mo **239 her** our **288 Why** [Fb] Who [Fa]

THE SONNETS

CONTROL TEXT: Q

Q: The Quarto of 1609
Qa, Qb: Qa is the uncorrected version, Qb the corrected version
Other texts cited:
B1—British Library Add. MS 10309, fol. 143 (c. 1630; Margaret Bellasys)
B2—British Library Add. MS 21433, fol. 114ᵛ (c. 1630; Inns of Court)
B3—British Library Add. MS 25303, fol. 119ᵛ (c. 1620s–30s; Inns of Court)
M—Pierpont Morgan MA 1057, p. 96 (c. 1630s)
MS—St. John's, Cambridge, MS S. 23 (James 416), fols. 38ʳ–38ᵛ (c. 1630s–40s)

Passionate Pilgrim, c. 1599
R—Rosenbach MS 1083 / 16, p. 256 (c. 1630)
W—Westminster Abbey, MS 41, fol. 49 (1619–30s; George Morley)

Sonnets
1 [number not in Q]
2 [For another version of this sonnet, present in eleven manuscripts, see the Alternative Versions.] **4 tattered** [MS] totter'd
5.14 Lose Leese
12.4 ensilvered o'er or siluer'd ore
13.7 Yourself You selfe
20.7 hues *Hews*
23.14 with . . . wit wit . . . wiht
25.9 might worth
26.12 thy their
27.10 thy their
28.12 gild'st the even guil'st th'eauen **14 strength** length
31.8 thee there
34.12 cross losse
35.8 thy . . . thy their . . . their
37.7 thy their
39.12 doth dost
41.12 troth truth
43.11 thy their
44.13 naught naughts
45.12 thy their
46.3, 8, 13, 14 thy their **9 'cide** side
47.10 art are **11 no** nor
50.6 dully duly
51.10 perfect'st perfects **11 rein** naigh
54.14 fade vade
55.1 monuments monument
56.13 Or As
61.8 tenor tenure
62.10 chapped chopt
63.5 travelled trauaild
65.12 of or
67.6 seeming seeing
69.3 due end **5 Thy** Their **14 soil** solye
70.6 Thy their
71.4 vilest vildest
73.4 ruined choirs rn'wd quiers
76.7 tell fel
77.10 blanks blacks
82.8 these the
85.3 thy their
86.13 filled fild
89.11 profane prophane [Qb]; proface [Qa]
90.11 shall stall
91.9 better bitter
99.9 One Our **13 ate** eate
100.14 prevene'st preuenst
102.8 her his
106 [For another version of this sonnet, present in two manuscripts, see the Alternative Versions.] **12 skill** [MSS] still
111.1 with wish

112.14 **they're dead** y'are dead
113.6 **latch** lack 14 **makes mine eye** maketh mine
116 119 [all but one extant copy of Q]
126.2 **sickle-hour** sickle, hower 8 **minutes** mynuit 12 [After this line, Q prints parentheses for each line of an imagined couplet.]
127.10 **brow** eyes
128.11, 14 **thy** their
129.9 **Mad** Made 11 **proved** proud a and
132.6 **the east** th'East 9 **mourning** morning
135.1, 2, 11, 12, 14 **Will** *Will*
136.2, 5, 14 **Will** *Will* 6 **Ay** I
138 [For another version of this sonnet, see the Alternative Versions.] 12 **to have** [*Passionate Pilgrim*] t'haue
140.13 **belied** be lyde
143.13 **Will** *Will*
144 [For another version of this sonnet, see the Alternative Versions.] 6 **side** [*Passionate Pilgrim*] sight 9 **fiend** finde
146.2 [   ] My sinfull earth

153.8 **strange** strang 14 **eyes** eye

Alternative Versions

Spes Altera
Control text: W
Spes Altera [B1, B2, B3] To one y‘ would dye a Mayd
3 **liv'ry** [B1] liuery
5 **lies** lye [cropped control-text ms.]
8 **praise** prays [cropped control-text ms.]

On his Mistress' Beauty
Control text: M
2 **descriptions** [R] discription
3 **rhyme** [R] mine [but with "rime" written in the margin as a correction]
6 **hand** [R] hands
8 **E'en** Ev'n [M] Euen [R]
10 **these** [R] those
12 **your** thy

General Bibliography*

There is a huge and ever-expanding scholarly literature about Shakespeare and his culture. This general list and the lists that accompany the individual plays and the poems in this volume are only a small sampling of the available resources. Journals devoted to Shakespeare studies include *Shakespeare Bulletin*, *Shakespeare Jahrbuch* (Germany), *Shakespeare Quarterly*, *Shakespeare Studies*, and *Shakespeare Survey* (England); other journals, such as *English Literary History*, *English Literary Renaissance*, *Renaissance Quarterly*, *Representations*, or *Studies in English Literature*, also frequently publish essays on Shakespeare's works. The categories below are only approximate; many of the texts could properly belong in more than one category.

Guides and Companions to Shakespeare Studies

Callaghan, Dympna, ed. *A Feminist Companion to Shakespeare*. Malden, Mass.: Blackwell, 2000.

De Grazia, Margreta, and Stanley Wells, eds. *The Cambridge Companion to Shakespeare*. Cambridge, Eng.: Cambridge University Press, 2001.

Drakakis, John, ed. *Alternative Shakespeares*. 2nd ed. London: Routledge, 1985.

Dutton, Richard, and Jean E. Howard, eds. *A Companion to Shakespeare's Works*, I: *The Tragedies*. Malden, Mass.: Blackwell, 2003.

———, eds. *A Companion to Shakespeare's Works*, II: *The Histories*. Malden, Mass.: Blackwell, 2003.

———, eds. *A Companion to Shakespeare's Works*, III: *The Comedies*. Malden, Mass.: Blackwell, 2003.

———, eds. *A Companion to Shakespeare's Works*, IV: *Poems, Problem Comedies, Late Plays*. Malden, Mass.: Blackwell, 2003.

Hattaway, Michael, ed. *The Cambridge Companion to Shakespeare's History Plays*. Cambridge, Eng.: Cambridge University Press, 2002.

Hawkes, Terence, ed. *Alternative Shakespeares, Volume 2*. London: Routledge, 1996.

Hodgdon, Barbara, and W. B. Worthen, eds. *A Companion to Shakespeare and Performance*. Malden, Mass.: Blackwell, 2005.

Jackson, Russell, ed. *The Cambridge Companion to Shakespeare on Film*. 2nd ed. Cambridge, Eng.: Cambridge University Press, 2007.

Kasten, David Scott, ed. *A Companion to Shakespeare*. Malden, Mass.: Blackwell, 1999.

Kinney, Arthur F. *Shakespeare by Stages: An Historical Introduction*. Malden, Mass.: Blackwell, 2003.

Leggatt, Alexander, ed. *The Cambridge Companion to Shakespearean Comedy*. Cambridge, Eng.: Cambridge University Press, 2002.

McDonald, Russ, ed. *The Bedford Companion to Shakespeare: An Introduction with Documents*. 2nd ed. Houndmills, Basingstoke: Palgrave Macmillan, 2001.

———, ed. *Shakespeare: An Anthology of Criticism and Theory, 1945–2000*. Malden, Mass.: Blackwell, 2004.

McEachern, Claire, ed. *The Cambridge Companion to Shakespearean Tragedy*. Cambridge, Eng.: Cambridge University Press, 2002.

*Edited by Holger Schott Syme, Department of English, University of Toronto.

Schoenfeldt, Michael. *A Companion to Shakespeare's Sonnets*. Malden, Mass.: Blackwell, 2006.

Smith, Emma, ed. *Shakespeare's Comedies: A Guide to Criticism*. Malden, Mass.: Blackwell, 2003.

———, ed. *Shakespeare's Histories: A Guide to Criticism*. Malden, Mass.: Blackwell, 2003.

———, ed. *Shakespeare's Tragedies: A Guide to Criticism*. Malden, Mass.: Blackwell, 2003.

Wells, Stanley, and Lena Cowen Orlin, eds. *Shakespeare: An Oxford Guide*. Oxford: Oxford University Press, 2003.

Wells, Stanley, and Sarah Stanton, eds. *The Cambridge Companion to Shakespeare on Stage*. New York: Cambridge University Press, 2002.

Shakespeare's World

Social, Political, and Economic History

Amussen, Susan Dwyer. *An Ordered Society: Gender and Class in Early Modern England*. New York: Columbia University Press, 1993.

Archer, Ian W. *The Pursuit of Stability: Social Relations in Elizabethan London*. New York: Cambridge University Press, 1991.

Ariès, Philippe, and Georges Duby, general eds. *A History of Private Life*, Volume III: *Passions of the Renaissance*. Ed. Roger Chartier. Trans. Arthur Goldhammer. Cambridge, Mass.: Belknap Press, 1989.

Armitage, David, and Michael J. Braddick, eds. *The British Atlantic World, 1500–1800*. New York: Palgrave Macmillan, 2002.

Barry, Jonathan, ed. *The Tudor and Stuart Town: A Reader in English Urban History, 1530–1688*. London: Longman, 1990.

Barry, Jonathan, and Christopher Brooks. *The Middling Sort of People: Culture, Society and Politics in England, 1550–1800*. Houndmills, Basingstoke: Palgrave Macmillan, 1994.

Barthelmey, Anthony Gerard. *Black Face, Maligned Race: The Representation of Blacks in English Drama from Shakespeare to Southerne*. Baton Rouge: Louisiana State University Press, 1987.

Beier, A. L. *Masterless Men: The Vagrancy Problem in England, 1560–1640*. New York: Methuen, 1985.

Beier, A. L., and Roger Finlay, eds. *London 1500–1700: The Making of the Metropolis*. New York: Longman, 1986.

Ben-Amos, Ilana Krausman. *Adolescence and Youth in Early Modern England*. New Haven: Yale University Press, 1994.

Bridenbaugh, Carl. *Vexed and Troubled Englishmen, 1590–1642*. New York: Oxford University Press, 1976.

Brigden, Susan. *New Worlds, Lost Worlds: The Rule of the Tudors, 1485–1603*. New York: Viking, 2001.

Burgess, Glenn. *The Politics of the Ancient Constitution: An Introduction to English Political Thought, 1603–1642*. University Park: Pennsylvania State University Press, 1993.

Capp, Bernard S. *When Gossips Meet: Women, Family, and Neighbourhood in Early Modern England*. Oxford: Oxford University Press, 2003.

Clark, Alice. *Working Life of Women in the Seventeenth Century*. Introduction by Amy Louise Erickson. 1968. New York: Routledge, 1992.

Clay, C. G. A. *Economic Expansion and Social Change: England 1500–1700*. 2 vols. New York: Cambridge University Press, 1984.

Cressy, David. *Birth, Marriage, and Death: Ritual, Religion, and the Life-Cycle in Tudor and Stuart England*. Oxford: Oxford University Press, 1997.

Cruickshank, Charles Greig. *Elizabeth's Army.* 2nd ed. Oxford: Clarendon, 1966.

Elliot, John Huxtable. *The Old World and the New, 1492–1650.* New York: Cambridge University Press, 1970.

Ellis, Steven G. *Tudor Ireland: Crown, Community, and the Conflict of Cultures, 1470–1603.* London: Longman, 1985.

Elton, G. R. *England Under the Tudors.* 3rd ed. New York: Routledge, 1991.

———. *The Tudor Revolution in Government: Administrative Changes in the Reign of Henry VIII.* Cambridge, Eng.: Cambridge University Press, 1959.

Emmison, F. G. *Elizabethan Life.* Chelmsford: Essex County Council, 1970.

Erickson, Amy Louise. *Women and Property in Early Modern England.* New York: Routledge, 1993.

Finlay, Roger. *Population and Metropolis: The Demography of London, 1580–1650.* Cambridge, Eng.: Cambridge University Press, 1981.

Fletcher, Anthony. *Gender, Sex, and Subordination in England, 1500–1800.* New Haven: Yale University Press, 1995.

Fletcher, Anthony, and John Stevenson, eds. *Order and Disorder in Early Modern England.* New York: Cambridge University Press, 1985.

Gaskill, Malcolm. *Crime and Mentalities in Early Modern England.* New York: Cambridge University Press, 2000.

Gittings, Clare. *Death, Burial and the Individual in Early Modern England.* London: Croom Helm, 1984.

Gowing, Laura. *Common Bodies: Women, Touch and Power in Seventeenth-Century England.* New Haven: Yale University Press, 2003.

Griffiths, Paul. *Youth and Authority: Formative Experiences in England, 1560–1640.* Oxford: Clarendon, 1996.

Griffiths, Paul, Adam Fox, and Steve Hindle, eds. *The Experience of Authority in Early Modern England.* New York: St. Martin's, 1996.

Guy, John A. *Queen of Scots: The True Life of Mary Stuart.* Boston: Houghton Mifflin, 2004.

———, ed. *The Reign of Elizabeth I: Court and Culture in the Last Decade.* Cambridge, Eng.: Cambridge University Press, 1995.

———. *Tudor England.* New York: Oxford University Press, 1988.

Heal, Felicity, and Clive Holmes. *The Gentry in England and Wales, 1500–1700.* Basingstoke: Macmillan, 1994.

Herrup, Cynthia B. *The Common Peace: Participation and the Criminal Law in Seventeenth-Century England.* New York: Cambridge University Press, 1987.

Hindle, Steve. *The State and Social Change in Early Modern England, c.1550–1640.* New York: St. Martin's, 2000.

Hirst, Derek. *Authority and Conflict: England, 1603–1658.* Cambridge, Mass.: Harvard University Press, 1986.

Ingram, Martin. *Church Courts, Sex, and Marriage in England, 1570–1640.* New York: Cambridge University Press, 1987.

James, Mervyn. *Society, Politics and Culture: Studies in Early Modern England.* New York: Cambridge University Press, 1986.

King, John N. *Tudor Royal Iconography: Literature and Art in an Age of Religious Crisis.* Princeton: Princeton University Press, 1989.

Kishlansky, Mark A. *A Monarchy Transformed: Britain 1603–1714.* New York: Penguin Books, 1996.

Klein, Joan Larsen. *Daughters, Wives, and Widows: Writings by Men about Women and Marriage in England, 1500–1640.* Urbana: University of Illinois Press, 1992.

Lake, Peter, with Michael Questier. *The Anti-Christ's Lewd Hat: Protestants, Papists and Players in Post-Reformation England.* New Haven: Yale University Press, 2002.

Laslett, Peter. *The World We Have Lost: Further Explored.* 3rd ed. New York: Scribner, 1984.

Levin, Carole. *The Heart and Stomach of a King: Elizabeth I and the Politics of Sex and Power.* Philadelphia: University of Pennsylvania Press, 1994.

Lockyer, Roger. *The Early Stuarts: A Political History of England, 1603–1642.* 2nd ed. London: Longman, 1999.

MacCaffrey, Wallace T. *Elizabeth I: War and Politics, 1588–1603.* Princeton: Princeton University Press, 1992.

Manning, Roger B. *Village Revolts: Social Protest and Popular Disturbances in England, 1509–1640.* Oxford: Clarendon, 1988.

Matar, Nabil I. *Islam in Britain, 1558–1685.* New York: Cambridge University Press, 1998.

———. *Turks, Moors, and Englishmen in the Age of Discovery.* New York: Columbia University Press, 1999.

Mendelson, Sara Heller, and Patricia Crawford. *Women in Early Modern England, 1550–1720.* Oxford: Clarendon, 1998.

Moody, T. W., F. X. Martin, and F. J. Byrne, eds. *A New History of Ireland,* Volume 3: *Early Modern Ireland, 1534–1691.* Oxford: Oxford University Press, 2001.

Mukerji, Chandra. *From Graven Images: Patterns of Modern Materialism.* New York: Columbia University Press, 1983.

Neale, J. E. *Elizabeth I and Her Parliaments, 1559–1581.* London: Cape, 1971.

———. *Queen Elizabeth I.* London: Pimlico, 1998.

Nichols, John, ed. *The Progresses and Public Processions of Queen Elizabeth.* 3 vols. London: J. Nichols, 1823.

Palliser, D. M. *The Age of Elizabeth: England under the Later Tudors, 1547–1603.* 2nd ed. New York: Longman, 1992.

Parry, J. H. *The Age of Reconnaissance: Discovery, Exploration, and Settlement, 1450 to 1650.* New York: Praeger, 1969.

Pearson, Lu Emily Hess. *Elizabethans at Home.* Stanford: Stanford University Press, 1967.

Peck, Linda Levy. *Court Patronage and Corruption in Early Stuart England.* Boston: Unwin Hyman, 1990.

Peters, Christine. *Women in Early Modern Britain, 1450–1640.* New York: Palgrave Macmillan, 2004.

Pocock, J. G. A. *The Ancient Constitution and the Feudal Law: Study of English Historical Thought in the Seventeenth Century—A Reissue with a Retrospect.* Rev. ed. New York: Cambridge University Press, 1987.

Rappaport, Steve. *Worlds within Worlds: Structures of Life in Sixteenth-Century London.* New York: Cambridge University Press, 1989.

Sharpe, J. A. *Crime in Early Modern England, 1550–1750.* 2nd ed. New York: Longman, 1999.

———. *Early Modern England: A Social History, 1550–1760.* 2nd ed. London: Arnold, 1997.

Slack, Paul. *The Impact of Plague in Tudor and Stuart England.* Boston: Routledge and Kegan Paul, 1985.

———. *Poverty and Policy in Tudor and Stuart England.* New York: Longman, 1988.

———, ed. *Rebellion, Popular Protest, and the Social Order in Early Modern England.* New York: Cambridge University Press, 1984.

Stone, Lawrence. *The Causes of the English Revolution, 1529–1642.* New York: Routledge, 2002.

———. *The Crisis of the Aristocracy, 1558–1641.* Oxford: Clarendon, 1965.

———. *The Family, Sex and Marriage in England, 1500–1800.* New York: Harper & Row, 1979.

Thirsk, Joan. *Economic Policy and Projects: The Development of a Consumer Society in Early Modern England.* Oxford: Clarendon, 1978.

Thomas, Keith. *Religion and the Decline of Magic: Studies in Popular Beliefs in Sixteenth and Seventeenth Century England.* New York: Scribner, 1971.

Underdown, David. *Fire from Heaven: Life in an English Town in the Seventeenth Century.* London: HarperCollins, 1992.

———. *Revel, Riot, and Rebellion: Popular Politics and Culture in England, 1603–1660.* Oxford: Clarendon, 1985.

Williams, Penry. *The Later Tudors: England, 1547–1603*. New York: Oxford University Press, 1995.

Wrightson, Keith. *Earthly Necessities: Economic Lives in Early Modern Britain*. New Haven: Yale University Press, 2000.

———. *English Society, 1580–1680*. London: Hutchinson, 1982.

Yates, Frances Amelia. *Astraea: The Imperial Theme in the Sixteenth Century*. London: Routledge and Kegan Paul, 1975.

Zagorin, Perez. *Rebels and Rulers, 1500–1660*. 2 vols. New York: Cambridge University Press, 1982.

Intellectual and Religious History

Armitage, David. *The Ideological Origins of the British Empire*. New York: Cambridge University Press, 2000.

Baker, Herschel Clay. *The Race of Time: Three Lectures on Renaissance Historiography*. Toronto: University of Toronto Press, 1967.

Barkan, Leonard. *Nature's Work of Art: The Human Body as Image of the World*. New Haven: Yale University Press, 1975.

Bossy, John. *Christianity in the West, 1400–1700*. New York: Oxford University Press, 1985.

Bouwsma, William James. *John Calvin: A Sixteenth-Century Portrait*. New York: Oxford University Press, 1988.

Cassirer, Ernst. *The Individual and the Cosmos in Renaissance Philosophy*. Trans. Mario Domandi. Philadelphia: University of Pennsylvania Press, 1972.

Clark, Stuart. *Thinking with Demons: The Idea of Witchcraft in Early Modern Europe*. New York: Oxford University Press, 1997.

Collinson, Patrick. *The Birthpangs of Protestant England: Religion and Cultural Change in the Sixteenth and Seventeenth Centuries*. New York: St. Martin's, 1988.

———. *The Elizabethan Puritan Movement*. New York: Oxford University Press, 1990.

———. *The Religion of Protestants: The Church in English Society, 1559–1625*. Oxford: Clarendon, 1982.

Doran, Susan, and Christopher Durston. *Princes, Pastors, and People: The Church and Religion in England, 1500–1700*. Rev. ed. New York: Routledge, 2003.

Duffy, Eamon. *The Stripping of the Altars: Traditional Religion in England, c. 1400–c. 1580*. 2nd ed. New Haven: Yale University Press, 1992.

Gadd, Ian, and Alexandra Gillespie, eds. *John Stow (1525–1605) and the Making of the English Past*. London: British Library, 2004.

Haigh, Christopher. *English Reformations: Religion, Politics, and Society under the Tudors*. New York: Oxford University Press, 1993.

Hill, Christopher. *Society and Puritanism in Pre-Revolutionary England*. New York: Schocken Books, 1964.

Houlbrooke, Ralph A. *Death, Religion, and the Family in England, 1480–1700*. New York: Oxford University Press, 1998.

Kelly, Henry Ansgar. *Divine Providence in the England of Shakespeare's Histories*. Cambridge, Mass.: Harvard University Press, 1970.

Kilroy, Gerard. *Edmund Campion. Memory and Transcription*. Aldershot, Eng.: Ashgate, 2005.

Klaits, Joseph. *Servants of Satan: The Age of the Witch Hunts*. Bloomington: Indiana University Press, 1985.

Kristeller, Paul Oskar. *Renaissance Thought: The Classic, Scholastic, and Humanistic Strains*. New York: Harper & Row, 1961.

Levao, Ronald. *Renaissance Minds and Their Fictions: Cusanus, Sidney, Shakespeare*. Berkeley: University of California Press, 1985.

Levin, Harry. *The Myth of the Golden Age in the Renaissance*. Bloomington: University of Indiana Press, 1969.

Levy, Fred Jacob. *Tudor Historical Thought*. San Marino, Calif.: Huntington Library Press, 1967.

MacCulloch, Diarmaid. *The Later Reformation in England, 1547–1603*. 2nd ed. New York: Palgrave, 2001.

———. *The Reformation*. New York: Viking, 2004.

Mack, Peter, ed. *Renaissance Rhetoric*. New York: St. Martin's, 1994.

Marotti, Arthur F. *Religious Ideology and Cultural Fantasy: Catholic and Anti-Catholic Discourses in Early Modern England*. Notre Dame, Ind.: University of Notre Dame Press, 2005.

Marshall, Peter. *Beliefs and the Dead in Reformation England*. London: Oxford University Press, 2002.

Oldridge, Darren, ed. *The Witchcraft Reader*. London: Routledge, 2001.

Patterson, Annabel M. *Reading Holinshed's* Chronicles. Chicago: University of Chicago Press, 1994.

Popkin, Richard H. *The History of Skepticism from Erasmus to Spinoza*. Berkeley: University of California Press, 1979.

Sharpe, James. *Instruments of Darkness: Witchcraft in England 1550–1750*. New York: Penguin Books, 1996.

Shuger, Debora Kuller. *Habits of Thought in the English Renaissance: Religion, Politics, and the Dominant Culture*. Berkeley: University of California Press, 1990.

Sonnino, Lee A. *A Handbook to Sixteenth-Century Rhetoric*. London: Routledge and Kegan Paul, 1968.

Strong, Roy. *The Cult of Elizabeth: Elizabethan Portraiture and Pageantry*. London: Thames and Hudson, 1977.

———. *The English Icon: Elizabethan & Jacobean Portraiture*. New York: Pantheon Books, 1969.

Walsham, Alexandra. *Providence in Early Modern England*. New York: Oxford University Press, 1999.

Watt, Tessa. *Cheap Print and Popular Piety, 1560–1649*. New York: Cambridge University Press, 1991.

Wind, Edgar. *Pagan Mysteries in the Renaissance*. Rev. and enl. ed. London: Oxford University Press, 1980.

Woolf, D. R. *Reading History in Early Modern England*. New York: Cambridge University Press, 2000.

———. *The Social Circulation of the Past: English Historical Culture, 1500–1730*. New York: Oxford University Press, 2003.

Cultural History and Early Modern Cultural Studies

Aers, David, Bob Hodge, and Gunther Kress. *Literature, Language, and Society in England, 1589–1680*. Totowa, N.J.: Barnes & Noble Books, 1981.

Agnew, Jean-Christophe. *Worlds Apart: The Market and the Theater in Anglo-American Thought, 1550–1750*. New York: Cambridge University Press, 1986.

Andersen, Jennifer, and Elizabeth Sauer, eds. *Books and Readers in Early Modern England: Material Studies*. Philadelphia: University of Pennsylvania Press, 2001.

Bakhtin, Mikhail. *Rabelais and His World*. Trans. Hélène Iswolsky. Rev. ed. Bloomington: Indiana University Press, 1984.

Baldwin, Thomas Whitfield. *William Shakespere's Small Latine & Lesse Greeke*. Urbana: University of Illinois Press, 1944.

Barkan, Leonard. *The Gods Made Flesh: Metamorphosis & the Pursuit of Paganism*. New Haven: Yale University Press, 1986.

Barker, Francis. *The Tremulous Private Body: Essays on Subjection*. New York: Methuen, 1984.

Baron, Sabrina Alcorn, ed. *The Reader Revealed*. Washington, D.C.: Folger Shakespeare Library, 2001.

Bartels, Emily Carroll. *Spectacles of Strangeness: Imperialism, Alienation, and Marlowe.* Philadelphia: University of Pennsylvania Press, 1993.

Beilin, Elaine V. *Redeeming Eve: Women Writers of the English Renaissance.* Princeton: Princeton University Press, 1987.

Blank, Paula. *Broken English: Dialects and the Politics of Language in Renaissance Literature.* New York: Routledge, 1996.

Bloom, Gina. *Voice in Motion: Staging Gender, Shaping Sound in Early Modern England.* Philadelphia: Pennsylvania University Press, 2007.

Bray, Alan. *Homosexuality in Renaissance England.* Rev. ed. New York: Columbia University Press, 1995.

Brayman Hackel, Heidi. *Reading Material in Early Modern England: Print, Gender, and Literacy.* New York: Cambridge University Press, 2005.

Briggs, Julia. *This Stage-Play World: Texts and Contexts, 1580–1625.* 2nd ed. New York: Oxford University Press, 1997.

Bristol, Michael D. *Carnival and Theater: Plebeian Culture and the Structure of Authority in Renaissance England.* New York: Methuen, 1985.

Brotton, Jerry. *Trading Territories: Mapping the Early Modern World.* London: Reaktion Books, 1997.

Brown, Pamela Allen. *Better a Shrew than a Sheep: Women, Drama, and the Culture of Jest in Early Modern England.* Ithaca, N.Y.: Cornell University Press, 2003.

Burke, Peter. *Popular Culture in Early Modern Europe.* New York: New York University Press, 1978.

Burt, Richard, and John Michael Archer, eds. *Enclosure Acts: Sexuality, Property, and Culture in Early Modern England.* Ithaca, N.Y.: Cornell University Press, 1994.

Bushnell, Rebecca W. *A Culture of Teaching: Early Modern Humanism in Theory and Practice.* Ithaca, N.Y.: Cornell University Press, 1996.

Buxton, John. *Elizabethan Taste.* London: Macmillan, 1963.

Caldwell, John. *The Oxford History of English Music.* New York: Oxford University Press, 1991.

Carroll, William C. *Fat King, Lean Beggar: Representations of Poverty in the Age of Shakespeare.* Ithaca, N.Y.: Cornell University Press, 1996.

Clegg, Cyndia Susan. *Press Censorship in Elizabethan England.* New York: Cambridge University Press, 1997.

———. *Press Censorship in Jacobean England.* New York: Cambridge University Press, 2001.

Cox, John D. *The Devil and the Sacred in English Drama, 1350–1642.* New York: Cambridge University Press, 2000.

Crane, Mary Thomas. *Framing Authority: Sayings, Self, and Society in Sixteenth-Century England.* Princeton: Princeton University Press, 1993.

Crawford, Julie. *Marvelous Protestantism: Monstrous Births in Post-Reformation England.* Baltimore: Johns Hopkins University Press, 2005.

Cressy, David. *Literacy and the Social Order: Reading and Writing in Tudor and Stuart England.* New York: Cambridge University Press, 1980.

De Grazia, Margreta, Maureen Quilligan, and Peter Stallybrass, eds. *Subject and Object in Renaissance Culture.* New York: Cambridge University Press, 1996.

Diehl, Huston. *Staging Reform, Reforming the Stage: Protestantism and Popular Theater in Early Modern England.* Ithaca, N.Y.: Cornell University Press, 1997.

Dolan, Frances E. *Dangerous Familiars: Representations of Domestic Crime in England, 1550–1700.* Ithaca, N.Y.: Cornell University Press, 1994.

———. *Whores of Babylon: Catholicism, Gender, and Seventeenth-Century Print Culture.* Ithaca, N.Y.: Cornell University Press, 1999.

Eisenstein, Elizabeth L. *The Printing Press as an Agent of Change: Communications and Cultural Transformations in Early-Modern Europe.* 2 vols. New York: Cambridge University Press, 1979.

Ferguson, Margaret W. *Dido's Daughters: Literacy, Gender, and Empire in Early Modern England and France.* Chicago: University of Chicago Press, 2003.

Ferguson, Margaret W., Maureen Quilligan, and Nancy J. Vickers, eds. *Rewriting the Renaissance: The Discourses of Sexual Difference in Early Modern Europe.* Chicago: University of Chicago Press, 1986.

Fisher, Will. *Materializing Gender in Early Modern English Literature and Culture.* New York: Cambridge University Press, 2006.

Fleming, Juliet. *Graffiti and the Writing Arts of Early Modern England.* Philadelphia: University of Pennsylvania Press, 2001.

Frye, Susan. *Elizabeth I: The Competition for Representation.* New York: Oxford University Press, 1993.

Fumerton, Patricia. *Cultural Aesthetics: Renaissance Literature and the Practice of Social Ornament.* Chicago: University of Chicago Press, 1991.

————. *Unsettled: The Culture of Mobility and the Working Poor in Early Modern England.* Chicago: University of Chicago Press, 2006.

Gillies, John. *Shakespeare and the Geography of Difference.* New York: Cambridge University Press, 1994.

Goldberg, Jonathan. *James I and the Politics of Literature: Jonson, Shakespeare, Donne, and Their Contemporaries.* Baltimore: Johns Hopkins University Press, 1983.

————. *Writing Matter: From the Hands of the English Renaissance.* Stanford: Stanford University Press, 1990.

————, ed. *Queering the Renaissance.* Durham, N.C.: Duke University Press, 1994.

Greenblatt, Stephen. *Learning to Curse: Essays in Early Modern Culture.* New York: Routledge, 1990.

————. *Renaissance Self-Fashioning: From More to Shakespeare.* Chicago: University of Chicago Press, 1980.

————, ed. *New World Encounters.* Berkeley: University of California Press, 1993.

————, ed. *Representing the English Renaissance.* Berkeley: University of California Press, 1988.

Grout, Donald Jay, and Hermine Weigel Williams. *A Short History of Opera.* 4th ed. New York: Columbia University Press, 2003.

Hall, Kim F. *Things of Darkness: Economies of Race and Gender in Early Modern England.* Ithaca, N.Y.: Cornell University Press, 1995.

Harris, Jonathan Gil. *Foreign Bodies and the Body Politic: Discourses of Social Pathology in Early Modern England.* New York: Cambridge University Press, 1998.

Harvey, Elizabeth D., ed. *Sensible Flesh: On Touch in Early Modern Culture.* Philadelphia: University of Pennsylvania Press, 2003.

Haselkorn, Anne M., and Betty S. Travitsky, eds. *The Renaissance Englishwoman in Print: Counterbalancing the Canon.* Amherst: University of Massachusetts Press, 1990.

Helgerson, Richard. *Forms of Nationhood: The Elizabethan Writing of England.* Chicago: University of Chicago Press, 1992.

Henderson, Katherine Usher, and Barbara F. McManus. *Half Humankind: Contexts and Texts of the Controversy About Women in England, 1540–1640.* Urbana: University of Illinois Press, 1985.

Hendricks, Margo, and Patricia Parker, eds. *Women, "Race," and Writing in the Early Modern Period.* New York: Routledge, 1994.

Hillman, David, and Carla Mazzio, eds. *The Body in Parts: Fantasies of Corporeality in Early Modern Europe.* New York: Routledge, 1997.

Hoeniger, F. David. *Medicine and Shakespeare in the English Renaissance.* Newark: University of Delaware Press, 1992.

Huizinga, Johan. *The Autumn of the Middle Ages.* Trans. Rodney J. Payton and Ulrich Mammitzsch. Chicago: University of Chicago Press, 1996.

Hull, Suzanne W. *Chaste, Silent & Obedient: English Books for Women, 1475–1640.* San Marino, Calif.: Huntington Library, 1982.

Hutson, Lorna. *The Usurer's Daughter: Male Friendship and Fictions of Women in Sixteenth-Century England*. New York: Routledge, 1994.

Javitch, Daniel. *Poetry and Courtliness in Renaissance England*. Princeton: Princeton University Press, 1978.

Jones, Ann Rosalind, and Peter Stallybrass. *Renaissance Clothing and the Materials of Memory*. New York: Cambridge University Press, 2000.

Jordan, Constance. *Renaissance Feminism: Literary Texts and Political Models*. Ithaca, N.Y.: Cornell University Press, 1990.

Knapp, Jeffrey. *Shakespeare's Tribe: Church, Nation, and Theater in Renaissance England*. Chicago: University of Chicago Press, 2002.

Laqueur, Thomas Walter. *Making Sex: Body and Gender from the Greeks to Freud*. Cambridge, Mass.: Harvard University Press, 1990.

MacDonald, Joyce Green. *Women and Race in Early Modern Texts*. New York: Cambridge University Press, 2002.

Magnusson, Lynne. *Shakespeare and Social Dialogue: Dramatic Language and Elizabethan Letters*. New York: Cambridge University Press, 1999.

Manley, Lawrence. *Literature and Culture in Early Modern London*. New York: Cambridge University Press, 1995.

Marcus, Leah S. *The Politics of Mirth: Jonson, Herrick, Milton, Marvell, and the Defense of Old Holiday Pastimes*. Chicago: University of Chicago Press, 1986.

McJannet, Linda. *The Sultan Speaks: Dialogue in English Plays and Histories about the Ottoman Turks*. New York: Palgrave Macmillan, 2006.

Meron, Theodor. *Bloody Constraint: War and Chivalry in Shakespeare*. New York: Oxford University Press, 1998.

Miller, David Lee, Sharon O'Dair, and Harold Weber, eds. *The Production of English Renaissance Culture*. Ithaca, N.Y.: Cornell University Press, 1994.

Montrose, Louis. *The Subject of Elizabeth: Authority, Gender, and Representation*. Chicago: University of Chicago Press, 2006.

Neill, Michael. *Issues of Death: Mortality and Identity in English Renaissance Tragedy*. Oxford: Clarendon, 1997.

Netzloff, Mark. *England's Internal Colonies: Class, Capital, and the Literature of Early Modern English Colonialism*. New York: Palgrave Macmillan, 2003.

Orlin, Lena Cowen. *Private Matters and Public Culture in Post-Reformation England*. Ithaca, N.Y.: Cornell University Press, 1994.

———, ed. *Material London, ca. 1600*. Philadelphia: University of Pennsylvania Press, 2000.

Parry, Graham. *The Golden Age Restor'd: The Culture of the Stuart Court, 1603–42*. New York: St. Martin's, 1981.

Paster, Gail Kern. *The Body Embarrassed: Drama and the Disciplines of Shame in Early Modern England*. Ithaca, N.Y.: Cornell University Press, 1993.

———. *Humoring the Body: Emotions and the Shakespearean Stage*. Chicago: University of Chicago Press, 2004.

Paster, Gail Kern, Katherine Rowe, and Mary Floyd-Wilson, eds. *Reading the Early Modern Passions: Essays in the Cultural History of Emotion*. Philadelphia: University of Pennsylvania Press, 2004.

Patterson, Annabel M. *Censorship and Interpretation: The Conditions of Writing and Reading in Early Modern England*. Madison: University of Wisconsin Press, 1984.

Peck, Linda Levy. *Consuming Splendor: Society and Culture in Seventeenth-Century England*. New York: Cambridge University Press, 2005.

Platt, Peter G. *Reason Diminished: Shakespeare and the Marvelous*. Lincoln: University of Nebraska Press, 1997.

Pollard, Tanya. *Drugs and Theater in Early Modern England*. New York: Oxford University Press, 2005.

Sanders, Eve Rachele. *Gender and Literacy on Stage in Early Modern England*. New York: Cambridge University Press, 1998.

Sawday, Jonathan. *The Body Emblazoned: Dissection and the Human Body in Renaissance Culture*. New York: Routledge, 1995.

Schoenfeldt, Michael C. *Bodies and Selves in Early Modern England: Physiology and Inwardness in Spenser, Shakespeare, Herbert, and Milton*. New York: Cambridge University Press, 1999.

Schwyzer, Philip. *Literature, Nationalism, and Memory in Early Modern England and Wales*. New York: Cambridge University Press, 2004.

Shapiro, James. *Shakespeare and the Jews*. New York: Columbia University Press, 1996.

Sharpe, Kevin, and Peter Lake, eds. *Culture and Politics in Early Stuart England*. Stanford: Stanford University Press, 1993.

Sherman, William H. *John Dee: The Politics of Reading and Writing in the English Renaissance*. Amherst: University of Massachusetts Press, 1995.

Shuger, Debora. *Censorship and Cultural Sensibility: The Regulation of Language in Tudor-Stuart England*. Philadelphia: University of Pennsylvania Press, 2006.

Simon, Joan. *Education and Society in Tudor England*. Cambridge, Eng.: Cambridge University Press, 1966.

Singh, Jyotsna G. *Colonial Narratives/Cultural Dialogues: 'Discoveries' of India in the Language of Colonialism*. New York: Routledge, 1996.

Smith, Bruce R. *The Acoustic World of Early Modern England: Attending to the O-Factor*. Chicago: University of Chicago Press, 1999.

———. *Homosexual Desire in Shakespeare's England: A Cultural Poetics*. Chicago: University of Chicago Press, 1994.

Smuts, R. Malcolm. *Court Culture and the Origins of a Royalist Tradition in Early Stuart England*. Philadelphia: University of Pennsylvania Press, 1987.

Stallybrass, Peter, and Allon White. *The Politics and Poetics of Transgression*. Ithaca, N.Y.: Cornell University Press, 1986.

Traub, Valerie, M. Lindsay Kaplan, and Dympna Callaghan, eds. *Feminist Readings of Early Modern Culture: Emerging Subjects*. New York: Cambridge University Press, 1996.

Turner, Henry S. *The English Renaissance Stage: Geometry, Poetics, and the Practical Spatial Arts 1580–1630*. New York: Oxford University Press, 2006.

Turner, James Grantham, ed. *Sexuality and Gender in Early Modern Europe: Institutions, Texts, Images*. New York: Cambridge University Press, 1993.

Wall, Wendy. *Staging Domesticity: Household Work and English Identity in Early Modern Drama*. New York: Cambridge University Press, 2002.

Watson, Robert N. *The Rest Is Silence: Death as Annihilation in the English Renaissance*. Berkeley: University of California Press, 1994.

Whigham, Frank. *Ambition and Privilege: The Social Tropes of Elizabethan Courtesy Theory*. Berkeley: University of California Press, 1984.

Woodbridge, Linda. *Vagrancy, Homelessness, and English Renaissance Literature*. Urbana: University of Illinois Press, 2001.

———. *Women and the English Renaissance: Literature and the Nature of Womankind, 1540 to 1620*. Urbana: University of Illinois Press, 1984.

Shakespeare's Generic, Literary, and Theatrical Contexts

Alpers, Paul. *What Is Pastoral?* Chicago: University of Chicago Press, 1996.

Altman, Joel. *The Tudor Play of Mind: Rhetorical Inquiry and the Development of Elizabethan Drama*. Berkeley: University of California Press, 1978.

Barish, Jonas. *The Antitheatrical Prejudice*. Berkeley: University of California Press, 1981.

Bate, Jonathan. *Shakespeare and Ovid*. Oxford: Clarendon, 1993.

Bates, Catherine. *The Rhetoric of Courtship in Elizabethan Language and Literature*. New York: Cambridge University Press, 1992.

Beckwith, Sarah. *Signifying God: Social Relation and Symbolic Act in the York Corpus Christi Plays*. Chicago: University of Chicago Press, 2001.

Belsey, Catherine. *The Subject of Tragedy: Identity and Difference in Renaissance Drama*. New York: Methuen, 1985.

Bevington, David M. *From "Mankind" to Marlowe: Growth of Structure in the Popular Drama of Tudor England*. Cambridge, Mass.: Harvard University Press, 1962.

———. *Tudor Drama and Politics: A Critical Approach to Topical Meaning*. Cambridge, Mass.: Harvard University Press, 1968.

Bly, Mary. *Queer Virgins and Virgin Queans on the Early Modern Stage*. New York: Oxford University Press, 2000.

Bowers, Fredson Thayer. *Elizabethan Revenge Tragedy, 1587–1642*. Princeton: Princeton University Press, 1940.

Braden, Gordon. *Renaissance Tragedy and the Senecan Tradition: Anger's Privilege*. New Haven: Yale University Press, 1985.

Bruster, Douglas. *Drama and the Market in the Age of Shakespeare*. New York: Cambridge University Press, 1992.

Bullough, Geoffrey, ed. *Narrative and Dramatic Sources of Shakespeare*. 8 vols. New York: Columbia University Press, 1957–75.

Butler, Martin. *Theatre and Crisis, 1632–1642*. New York: Cambridge University Press, 1984.

Carroll, William C. *The Metamorphoses of Shakespearean Comedy*. Princeton: Princeton University Press, 1985.

Cartwright, Kent. *Theatre and Humanism: English Drama in the Sixteenth Century*. New York: Cambridge University Press, 1999.

Clubb, Louise George. *Italian Drama in Shakespeare's Time*. New Haven: Yale University Press, 1989.

Cohen, Walter. *Drama of a Nation: Public Theater in Renaissance England and Spain*. Ithaca, N.Y.: Cornell University Press, 1985.

Crewe, Jonathan. *Trials of Authorship: Anterior Forms and Poetic Reconstruction from Wyatt to Shakespeare*. Berkeley: University of California Press, 1990.

Danson, Lawrence. *Shakespeare's Dramatic Genres*. New York: Oxford University Press, 2000.

Dawson, Anthony B., and Paul Yachnin. *The Culture of Playgoing in Shakespeare's England: A Collaborative Debate*. New York: Cambridge University Press, 2001.

Dillon, Janette. *Language and Stage in Medieval and Renaissance England*. New York: Cambridge University Press, 1998.

Felperin, Howard. *Shakespearean Romance*. Princeton: Princeton University Press, 1972.

Finkelpearl, Philip J. *John Marston of the Middle Temple: An Elizabethan Dramatist in His Social Setting*. Cambridge, Mass.: Harvard University Press, 1969.

Gardiner, Harold C. *Mysteries' End: An Investigation of the Last Days of the Medieval Religious Stage*. New Haven: Yale University Press, 1946.

Halasz, Alexandra. *The Marketplace of Print: Pamphlets and the Public Sphere in Early Modern England*. New York: Cambridge University Press, 1997.

Harbage, Alfred. *Shakespeare and the Rival Traditions*. New York: Macmillan, 1952.

Hardison, O. B. *Christian Rite and Christian Drama in the Middle Ages: Essays in the Origin and Early History of Modern Drama*. Baltimore: Johns Hopkins University Press, 1965.

Heinemann, Margot. *Puritanism and Theatre: Thomas Middleton and Opposition Drama under the Early Stuarts*. New York: Cambridge University Press, 1980.

Honan, Park. *Christopher Marlowe: Poet & Spy*. New York: Oxford University Press, 2005.

Honigmann, E. A. J., ed. *Shakespeare and His Contemporaries: Essays in Comparison*. Manchester: Manchester University Press, 1986.

———, ed. *Shakespeare's Impact on His Contemporaries*. London: Macmillan, 1982.

Howard, Jean E. *Theater of a City: The Places of London Comedy, 1598–1642.* Philadelphia: University of Pennsylvania Press, 2007.

Hunter, G. K. *John Lyly: The Humanist as Courtier.* Cambridge, Mass.: Harvard University Press, 1962.

Jones, Emrys. *The Origins of Shakespeare.* Oxford: Clarendon, 1977.

———. *Scenic Form in Shakespeare.* Oxford: Clarendon, 1971.

Kastan, David Scott, and Peter Stallybrass, eds. *Staging the Renaissance: Reinterpretations of Elizabethan and Jacobean Drama.* New York: Routledge, 1991.

Kermode, Lloyd Edward, Jason Scott-Warren, and Martine van Elk, eds. *Tudor Drama Before Shakespeare, 1485–1590: New Directions for Research, Criticism, and Pedagogy.* New York: Palgrave Macmillan, 2004.

Kolve, V. A. *The Play Called Corpus Christi.* Stanford: Stanford University Press, 1966.

Leggatt, Alexander. *Citizen Comedy in the Age of Shakespeare.* Toronto: University of Toronto Press, 1973.

———. *Introduction to English Renaissance Comedy.* Manchester: Manchester University Press, 1999.

Levin, Harry. *Shakespeare and the Revolution of the Times: Perspectives and Commentaries.* New York: Oxford University Press, 1976.

Levith, Murray J. *Shakespeare's Italian Settings and Plays.* Basingstoke: Macmillan, 1989.

Lomax, Marion. *Stage Images and Traditions: Shakespeare to Ford.* New York: Cambridge University Press, 1987.

Martindale, Charles, and A. B. Taylor, eds. *Shakespeare and the Classics.* New York: Cambridge University Press, 2004.

Masten, Jeffrey. *Textual Intercourse: Collaboration, Authorship, and Sexualities in Renaissance Drama.* New York: Cambridge University Press, 1997.

McLuskie, Kathleen. *Renaissance Dramatists.* New York: Harvester Wheatsheaf, 1989.

McMillin, Scott. *The Elizabethan Theatre and the Book of Sir Thomas More.* Ithaca, N.Y.: Cornell University Press, 1987.

McMillin, Scott, and Sally-Beth MacLean. *The Queen's Men and Their Plays.* New York: Cambridge University Press, 1998.

McMullan, Gordon, and Jonathan Hope, eds. *The Politics of Tragicomedy: Shakespeare and After.* New York: Routledge, 1991.

Miola, Robert S. *Shakespeare's Reading.* New York: Oxford University Press, 2000.

———. *Shakespeare's Rome.* New York: Cambridge University Press, 1983.

Newcomb, Lori Humphrey. *Reading Popular Romance in Early Modern England.* New York: Columbia University Press, 2002.

Norbrook, David. *Poetry and Politics in the English Renaissance.* London: Routledge and Kegan Paul, 1984.

Orgel, Stephen. *The Illusion of Power: Political Theater in the English Renaissance.* Berkeley: University of California Press, 1975.

Peters, Julie Stone. *Theatre of the Book, 1480–1880: Print, Text, and Performance in Europe.* New York: Oxford University Press, 2000.

Riggs, David. *Ben Jonson: A Life.* Cambridge, Mass.: Harvard University Press, 1989.

———. *The World of Christopher Marlowe.* London: Faber and Faber, 2004.

Rose, Mark. *Shakespearean Design.* Cambridge, Mass.: Belknap Press, 1972.

Rose, Mary Beth. *The Expense of Spirit: Love and Sexuality in English Renaissance Drama.* Ithaca, N.Y.: Cornell University Press, 1988.

Salingar, Leo. *Dramatic Form in Shakespeare and the Jacobeans: Essays.* New York: Cambridge University Press, 1986.

———. *Shakespeare and the Traditions of Comedy.* New York: Cambridge University Press, 1974.

Schwyzer, Philip. *Archaeologies of English Renaissance Literature.* New York: Oxford University Press, 2007.

Shapiro, James. *Rival Playwrights: Marlowe, Jonson, Shakespeare.* New York: Columbia University Press, 1991.

Snyder, Susan. *The Comic Matrix of Shakespeare's Tragedies: Romeo and Juliet, Hamlet, Othello, and King Lear*. Princeton: Princeton University Press, 1979.

Spivack, Bernard. *Shakespeare and the Allegory of Evil: The History of a Metaphor in Relation to His Major Villains*. New York: Columbia University Press, 1958.

Thomas, Vivian. *The Moral Universe of Shakespeare's Problem Plays*. New York: Routledge, 1991.

Vickers, Brian, ed. *English Renaissance Literary Criticism*. New York: Oxford University Press, 1999.

Vitkus, Daniel. *Turning Turk: English Theater and the Multicultural Mediterranean, 1570–1630*. New York: Palgrave Macmillan, 2003.

Weimann, Robert. *Shakespeare and the Popular Tradition in the Theater: Studies in the Social Dimension of Dramatic Form and Function*. Ed. Robert Schwartz. Baltimore: Johns Hopkins University Press, 1978.

Whitney, Charles. *Early Responses to Renaissance Drama*. New York: Cambridge University Press, 2006.

Woolf, Rosemary. *The English Mystery Plays*. Berkeley: University of California Press, 1972.

The Playing Field: Theaters, Actors, Patrons, and the State

Astington, John H. *English Court Theatre, 1558–1642*. Cambridge, Eng.: Cambridge University Press, 1999.

———, ed. *The Development of Shakespeare's Theater*. New York: AMS Press, 1992.

Barroll, J. Leeds. *Politics, Plague, and Shakespeare's Theater: The Stuart Years*. Ithaca, N.Y.: Cornell University Press, 1991.

Beckerman, Bernard. *Shakespeare at the Globe, 1599–1609*. New York: Macmillan, 1962.

Bentley, Gerald Eades. *The Jacobean and Caroline Stage*. 7 vols. Oxford: Clarendon, 1941–68.

———. *The Profession of Dramatist in Shakespeare's Time, 1590–1642*. Princeton: Princeton University Press, 1971.

———. *The Profession of Player in Shakespeare's Time, 1590–1642*. Princeton: Princeton University Press, 1984.

Berry, Herbert. *Shakespeare's Playhouses*. Illustrated by C. Walter Hodges. New York: AMS Press, 1987.

Bradbrook, M. C. *The Rise of the Common Player: A Study of Actor and Society in Shakespeare's England*. Cambridge, Mass.: Harvard University Press, 1962.

Chambers, E. K. *The Elizabethan Stage*. 4 vols. Oxford: Clarendon, 1923.

———. *The Mediaeval Stage*. 2 vols. Oxford: Clarendon, 1903.

Clare, Janet. *Art Made Tongue-Tied by Authority: Elizabethan and Jacobean Dramatic Censorship*. 2nd ed. Manchester: Manchester University Press, 1999.

Cook, Ann Jennalie. *The Privileged Playgoers of Shakespeare's London: 1576–1642*. Princeton: Princeton University Press, 1981.

Cox, John D., and David Scott Kastan, eds. *A New History of Early English Drama*. New York: Columbia University Press, 1997.

Dessen, Alan C. *Elizabethan Stage Conventions and Modern Interpreters*. Cambridge, Eng.: Cambridge University Press, 1984.

———. *Recovering Shakespeare's Theatrical Vocabulary*. New York: Cambridge University Press, 1995.

Dessen, Alan C., and Leslie Thomson. *A Dictionary of Stage Directions in English Drama, 1580–1642*. New York: Cambridge University Press, 1999.

Dillon, Janette. *The Cambridge Introduction to Early English Theatre*. New York: Cambridge University Press, 2006.

Dutton, Richard. *Licensing, Censorship and Authorship in Early Modern England: Buggeswords*. Houndmills, Basingstoke: Palgrave Macmillan, 2000.

————. *Mastering the Revels: The Regulation and Censorship of English Renaissance Drama*. London: Macmillan, 1991.

Dutton, Richard, Alison Findlay, and Richard Wilson, eds. *Region, Religion, and Patronage: Lancastrian Shakespeare*. Manchester: Manchester University Press, 2003.

Erne, Lukas. *Shakespeare as Literary Dramatist*. New York: Cambridge University Press, 2003.

Foakes, R. A. *Illustrations of the English Stage, 1580–1642*. Stanford: Stanford University Press, 1985.

Gair, W. Reavley. *The Children of Paul's: The Story of a Theatre Company, 1553–1608*. New York: Cambridge University Press, 1982.

Greg, W. W., ed. *Dramatic Documents from the Elizabethan Playhouses: Stage Plots: Actor's Parts: Prompt Books*. 2 vols. Oxford: Clarendon, 1931.

Gurr, Andrew. *Playgoing in Shakespeare's London*. 3rd ed. New York: Cambridge University Press, 2004.

————. *The Shakespeare Company, 1594–1642*. New York: Cambridge University Press, 2004.

————. *The Shakespearian Playing Companies*. Oxford: Clarendon, 1996.

————. *The Shakespearean Stage, 1574–1642*. 3rd ed. New York: Cambridge University Press, 1992.

Gurr, Andrew, and John Orrell. *Rebuilding Shakespeare's Globe*. London: Weidenfeld & Nicolson, 1989.

Harris, Jonathan Gil, and Natasha Korda, eds. *Staged Properties in Early Modern Drama*. New York: Cambridge University Press, 2002.

Hattaway, Michael. *Elizabethan Popular Theatre: Plays in Performance*. London: Routledge and Kegan Paul, 1982.

Henslowe, Philip. *Henslowe's Diary*. Ed. R. A. Foakes. 2nd ed. New York: Cambridge University Press, 2002.

Hodges, C. Walter. *The Globe Restored: A Study of the Elizabethan Theatre*. New York: Norton, 1973.

Holland, Peter, and Stephen Orgel, eds. *From Performance to Print in Shakespeare's England*. New York: Palgrave Macmillan, 2006.

————, eds. *From Script to Stage in Early Modern England*. Houndmills, Basingstoke: Palgrave Macmillan, 2004.

Ingram, William. *The Business of Playing: The Beginnings of Adult Professional Theater in Elizabethan London*. Ithaca, N.Y.: Cornell University Press, 1992.

Kernan, Alvin. *Shakespeare, the King's Playwright: Theater in the Stuart Court, 1603–1613*. New Haven: Yale University Press, 1995.

King, T. J. *Shakespearean Staging, 1599–1642*. Cambridge, Mass.: Harvard University Press, 1971.

Knutson, Roslyn Lander. *Playing Companies and Commerce in Shakespeare's Time*. Cambridge, Eng.: Cambridge University Press, 2001.

————. *The Repertory of Shakespeare's Company, 1594–1613*. Fayetteville: University of Arkansas Press, 1991.

Laroque, François. *Shakespeare's Festive World: Elizabethan Seasonal Entertainment and the Professional Stage*. New York: Cambridge University Press, 1991.

Lopez, Jeremy. *Theatrical Convention and Audience Response in Early Modern Drama*. New York: Cambridge University Press, 2002.

MacIntyre, Jean. *Costumes and Scripts in the Elizabethan Theatres*. Edmonton: University of Alberta Press, 1992.

Milling, Jane, and Peter Thomson, eds. *The Cambridge History of British Theatre*, Vol. 1: *Origins to 1660*. New York: Cambridge University Press, 2004.

Mulryne, J. R., and Margaret Shewring, eds. *Shakespeare's Globe Rebuilt*. New York: Cambridge University Press, 1997.

Munro, Lucy. *Children of the Queen's Revels: A Jacobean Theatre Repertory*. New York: Cambridge University Press, 2005.

Palfrey, Simon, and Tiffany Stern. *Shakespeare in Parts*. Oxford: Oxford University Press, 2007.

Shapiro, Michael. *Children of the Revels: The Boy Companies of Shakespeare's Time and Their Plays*. New York: Columbia University Press, 1977.

Smith, Irwin. *Shakespeare's Blackfriars Playhouse: Its History and Its Design*. New York: New York University Press, 1964.

Stern, Tiffany. *Making Shakespeare: From Stage to Page*. New York: Routledge, 2004.

———. *Rehearsal from Shakespeare to Sheridan*. Oxford: Clarendon, 2000.

White, Paul Whitfield, and Suzanne Westfall, eds. *Shakespeare and Theatrical Patronage in Early Modern England*. New York: Cambridge University Press, 2002.

Wickham, Glynne. *Early English Stages, 1300 to 1660*. 4 vols. New York: Routledge, 2002.

Wickham, Glynne, Herbert Berry, and William Ingram, eds. *English Professional Theatre, 1530–1660*. New York: Cambridge University Press, 2000.

Shakespeare's Life

Alexander, Peter. *Shakespeare's Life and Art*. New ed. New York: New York University Press, 1961.

Bate, Jonathan. *The Genius of Shakespeare*. London: Picador, 1997.

Bradbrook, M. C. *Shakespeare: The Poet in His World*. New York: Columbia University Press, 1978.

Chambers, E. K. *William Shakespeare: A Study of Facts and Problems*. 2 vols. Oxford: Clarendon, 1930.

Duncan-Jones, Katherine. *Ungentle Shakespeare: Scenes from His Life*. London: Arden Shakespeare, 2001.

Eccles, Mark. *Shakespeare in Warwickshire*. Madison: University of Wisconsin Press, 1961.

Edwards, Philip. *Shakespeare: A Writer's Progress*. New York: Oxford University Press, 1986.

Fraser, Russell A. *Shakespeare, The Later Years*. New York: Columbia University Press, 1992.

———. *Young Shakespeare*. New York: Columbia University Press, 1988.

Greenblatt, Stephen. *Will in the World: How Shakespeare Became Shakespeare*. New York: Norton, 2004.

Greer, Germaine. *Shakespeare*. New York: Oxford University Press, 1986.

Honan, Park. *Shakespeare: A Life*. New York: Oxford University Press, 1998.

Honigmann, E. A. J. *Shakespeare: The Lost Years*. 2nd ed. Manchester: Manchester University Press, 1998.

Hotson, Leslie. *Shakespeare Versus Shallow*. Boston: Little, Brown, and Company, 1931.

Levi, Peter. *The Life and Times of William Shakespeare*. New York: Macmillan, 1988.

Matus, Irvin Leigh. *Shakespeare, The Living Record*. Houndmills, Basingstoke: Macmillan, 1991.

Reese, M. M. *Shakespeare: His World and His Work*. Rev. ed. London: Edward Arnold, 1980.

Sams, Eric. *The Real Shakespeare: Retrieving the Early Years, 1564–1594*. New Haven: Yale University Press, 1995.

Schmidgall, Gary. *Shakespeare and the Poet's Life*. Lexington: University Press of Kentucky, 1990.

Schoenbaum, Samuel. *Shakespeare's Lives*. New ed. New York: Oxford University Press, 1991.

———. *William Shakespeare: A Compact Documentary Life*. Rev. ed. New York: Oxford University Press, 1987.

Shapiro, James. *A Year in the Life of William Shakespeare: 1599*. New York: Harper-Collins, 2005.

Taylor, Gary. *Reinventing Shakespeare: A Cultural History, from the Restoration to the Present*. New York: Weidenfeld & Nicolson, 1989.

Thomson, Peter. *Shakespeare's Professional Career*. New York: Cambridge University Press, 1992.

Wells, Stanley. *Shakespeare: A Life in Drama*. New York: Norton, 1995.

———. *Shakespeare: For All Time*. London: Macmillan, 2002.

Wood, Michael. *In Search of Shakespeare*. London: BBC, 2003.

Critical Approaches

Classics of Shakespeare Criticism

Barber, C. L. *Shakespeare's Festive Comedy: A Study of Dramatic Form and Its Relation to Social Custom*. Princeton: Princeton University Press, 1959.

Bradley, A. C. *Shakespearean Tragedy: Lectures on* Hamlet, Othello, King Lear, Macbeth. 3rd ed. New York: St. Martin's Press, 1992.

Coleridge, Samuel Taylor. *Coleridge on Shakespeare: The Text of the Lectures of 1811–12*. Ed. R. A. Foakes. Charlottesville: University Press of Virginia, 1971.

———. *Shakespearean Criticism*. 2 vols. Ed. T. M. Raysor. 2nd ed. New York: Dutton, 1969.

Eliot, T. S. "Shakespeare and the Stoicism of Seneca." *Selected Essays, 1917–1932*. New ed. New York: Harcourt, Brace, 1950.

Empson, William. *The Structure of Complex Words*. 3rd ed. London: Chatto & Windus, 1977.

Frye, Northrop. *Fools of Time: Studies in Shakespearean Tragedy*. Toronto: University of Toronto Press, 1967.

———. *A Natural Perspective: The Development of Shakespearean Comedy and Romance*. New York: Columbia University Press, 1965.

Hazlitt, William. *Characters of Shakespear's Plays*. London, 1817.

Johnson, Samuel. *Samuel Johnson on Shakespeare*. Ed. H. R. Woudhuysen. New York: Penguin, 1989.

Jones, Ernest. *Hamlet and Oedipus*. New York: Norton, 1949.

Kermode, Frank, ed. *Four Centuries of Shakespearian Criticism*. 1965. New York: Avon, 1965.

Knight, G. Wilson. *The Wheel of Fire: Interpretations of Shakespearean Tragedy, with Three New Essays*. 4th ed. New York: Harper & Row, 1977.

Kott, Jan. *Shakespeare Our Contemporary*. Trans. Boleslaw Taborski. Garden City, N.Y.: Anchor Books, 1966.

Morgann, Maurice. *Shakespearean Criticism*. Ed. Daniel A. Fineman. Oxford: Clarendon, 1972.

Spurgeon, Caroline F. E. *Shakespeare's Imagery, and What It Tells Us*. New York: Macmillan, 1935.

Tillyard, E. M. W. *Shakespeare's History Plays*. London: Chatto and Windus, 1944.

Vickers, Brian, ed. *Shakespeare: The Critical Heritage*. 6 vols. London: Routledge and Kegan Paul, 1974–1981.

General Studies

Barton, Anne. *Essays, Mainly Shakespearean*. New York: Cambridge University Press, 1994.

Bloom, Harold. *Shakespeare: The Invention of the Human*. New York: Riverhead Books, 1998.

Burckhardt, Sigurd. *Shakespearean Meanings.* Princeton: Princeton University Press, 1968.

Garber, Marjorie. *Shakespeare After All.* New York: Pantheon, 2004.

Hibbard, G. R. *The Making of Shakespeare's Dramatic Poetry.* Toronto: University of Toronto Press, 1981.

Honigmann, E. A. J. *Myriad-Minded Shakespeare: Essays on the Tragedies, Problem Comedies, and Shakespeare the Man.* 2nd ed. New York: St. Martin's Press, 1998.

Jones, John. *Shakespeare at Work.* New York: Oxford University Press, 1995.

Nuttall, A. D. *Shakespeare the Thinker.* New Haven: Yale University Press, 2007.

Ryan, Kiernan. *Shakespeare.* 3rd ed. New York: Palgrave Macmillan, 2001.

Language and Style

Baxter, John. *Shakespeare's Poetic Styles: Verse into Drama.* London: Routledge and Kegan Paul, 1980.

Blake, N. F. *Shakespeare's Language: An Introduction.* New York: St. Martin's Press, 1983.

Cercignani, Fausto. *Shakespeare's Works and Elizabethan Pronunciation.* New York: Oxford University Press, 1981.

Clemen, Wolfgang. *Shakespeare's Soliloquies.* Trans. Charity Scott Stokes. New York: Methuen, 1987.

————. *The Development of Shakespeare's Imagery.* New York: Hill and Wang, 1962.

Danson, Lawrence. *Tragic Alphabet: Shakespeare's Drama of Language.* New Haven: Yale University Press, 1974.

Donawerth, Jane. *Shakespeare and the Sixteenth-Century Study of Language.* Urbana: University of Illinois Press, 1984.

Edwards, Philip, Inga-Stina Ewbank, and G. K. Hunter, eds. *Shakespeare's Styles: Essays in Honour of Kenneth Muir.* New York: Cambridge University Press, 1980.

Gross, Kenneth. *Shakespeare's Noise.* Chicago: University of Chicago Press, 2001.

Hope, Jonathan. *Shakespeare's Grammar.* London: Arden Shakespeare, 2003.

Houston, John Porter. *Shakespearean Sentences: A Study in Style and Syntax.* Baton Rouge: Louisiana State University Press, 1988.

Hussey, S. S. *The Literary Language of Shakespeare.* 2nd ed. New York: Longman, 1992.

Kökeritz, Helge. *Shakespeare's Pronunciation.* New Haven: Yale University Press, 1953.

Mahood, M. M. *Shakespeare's Wordplay.* London: Methuen, 1957.

McDonald, Russ. *Shakespeare and the Arts of Language.* New York: Oxford University Press, 2001.

————. *Shakespeare's Late Style.* New York: Cambridge University Press, 2006.

Miriam Joseph, Sister. *Shakespeare's Use of the Arts of Language.* New York: Columbia University Press, 1947.

Palfrey, Simon. *Late Shakespeare: A New World of Words.* Oxford: Clarendon, 1997.

Parker, Patricia. *Literary Fat Ladies: Rhetoric, Gender, Property.* New York: Methuen, 1987.

————. *Shakespeare from the Margins: Language, Culture, Context.* Chicago: University of Chicago Press, 1996.

Partridge, Eric. *Shakespeare's Bawdy: A Literary & Psychological Essay and a Comprehensive Glossary.* 3rd ed. New York: Routledge, 1991.

Trousdale, Marion. *Shakespeare and the Rhetoricians.* Chapel Hill: University of North Carolina Press, 1982.

Vickers, Brian. *The Artistry of Shakespeare's Prose.* London: Methuen, 1968.

————. "Shakespeare's Use of Rhetoric." *A New Companion to Shakespeare Studies.* Ed. Kenneth Muir and S. Schoenbaum. Cambridge, Eng.: Cambridge University Press, 1971. 83–98.

Wright, George T. *Shakespeare's Metrical Art.* Berkeley: University of California Press, 1988.

Young, David. *The Action to the Word: Structure and Style in Shakespearean Tragedy.* New Haven: Yale University Press, 1990.

Psychoanalytic Criticism

Adelman, Janet. *Suffocating Mothers: Fantasies of Maternal Origin in Shakespeare's Plays, Hamlet to The Tempest.* New York: Routledge, 1992.

Armstrong, Philip. *Shakespeare in Psychoanalysis.* New York: Routledge, 2001.

Berger, Harry Jr. *Making Trifles of Terrors: Redistributing Complicities in Shakespeare.* Stanford: Stanford University Press, 1997.

Charnes, Linda. *Notorious Identity: Materializing the Subject in Shakespeare.* Cambridge, Mass.: Harvard University Press, 1993.

Enterline, Lynn. *The Rhetoric of the Body from Ovid to Shakespeare.* Cambridge, Eng.: Cambridge University Press, 2000.

Fineman, Joel. *Shakespeare's Perjured Eye: The Invention of Poetic Subjectivity in the Sonnets.* Berkeley: University of California Press, 1986.

Freedman, Barbara. *Staging the Gaze: Postmodernism, Psychoanalysis, and Shakespearean Comedy.* Ithaca, N.Y.: Cornell University Press, 1991.

Garber, Marjorie. *Coming of Age in Shakespeare.* New York: Methuen, 1981.

———. *Shakespeare's Ghost Writers: Literature as Uncanny Causality.* New York: Methuen, 1987.

Girard, René. *A Theater of Envy: William Shakespeare.* New York: Oxford University Press, 1991.

Holland, Norman N. *Psychoanalysis and Shakespeare.* New York: Octagon, 1966.

Lupton, Julia Reinhard, and Kenneth Reinhard. *After Oedipus: Shakespeare in Psychoanalysis.* Ithaca, N.Y.: Cornell University Press, 1993.

Marshall, Cynthia. *The Shattering of the Self: Violence, Subjectivity, and Early Modern Texts.* Baltimore: Johns Hopkins University Press, 2002.

Mazzio, Carla, and Douglas Trevor, eds. *Historicism, Psychoanalysis, and Early Modern Culture.* New York: Routledge, 2000.

Pye, Christopher. *The Regal Phantasm: Shakespeare and the Politics of Spectacle.* New York: Routledge, 1990.

———. *The Vanishing: Shakespeare, the Subject, and Early Modern Culture.* Durham, N.C.: Duke University Press, 2000.

Schwartz, Murray M., and Coppélia Kahn, eds. *Representing Shakespeare: New Psychoanalytic Essays.* Baltimore: Johns Hopkins University Press, 1982.

Skura, Meredith Anne. *The Literary Use of the Psychoanalytic Process.* New Haven: Yale University Press, 1981.

———. *Shakespeare the Actor and the Purposes of Playing.* Chicago: University of Chicago Press, 1993.

Wheeler, Richard P. *Shakespeare's Development and the Problem Comedies: Turn and Counter-Turn.* Berkeley: University of California Press, 1981.

Zimmerman, Susan, ed. *Erotic Politics: Desire on the Renaissance Stage.* New York: Routledge, 1992.

Feminism, Gender Studies, and Queer Studies

Bamber, Linda. *Comic Women, Tragic Men: A Study of Gender and Genre in Shakespeare.* Stanford: Stanford University Press, 1982.

Barker, Deborah, and Ivo Kamps, eds. *Shakespeare and Gender: A History.* New York: Verso, 1995.

Boose, Lynda E. "The Father and the Bride in Shakespeare." *PMLA* 97 (1982): 325–47.

Callaghan, Dympna. *Shakespeare Without Women: Representing Gender and Race on the Renaissance Stage.* New York: Routledge, 2000.

————. *Women and Gender in Renaissance Tragedy: A Study of* King Lear, Othello, The Duchess of Malfi, *and* The White Devil. Atlantic Highlands, N.J.: Humanities Press International, 1989.

Chedgzoy, Kate, ed. *Shakespeare, Feminism and Gender*. Houndmills, Basingstoke: Palgrave Macmillan, 2001.

Dash, Irene G. *Wooing, Wedding, and Power: Women in Shakespeare's Plays*. New York: Columbia University Press, 1981.

DiGangi, Mario. *The Homoerotics of Early Modern Drama*. New York: Cambridge University Press, 1997.

Dusinberre, Juliet. *Shakespeare and the Nature of Women*. 3rd ed. New York: Palgrave Macmillan, 2003.

Erickson, Peter. *Patriarchal Structures in Shakespeare's Drama*. Berkeley: University of California Press, 1985.

French, Marilyn. *Shakespeare's Division of Experience*. New York: Summit Books, 1981.

Garner, Shirley Nelson, and Madelon Sprengnether, eds. *Shakespearean Tragedy and Gender*. Bloomington: Indiana University Press, 1996.

Goldberg, Jonathan. *Sodometries: Renaissance Texts, Modern Sexualities*. Stanford: Stanford University Press, 1992.

Howard, Jean E., and Phyllis Rackin. *Engendering a Nation: A Feminist Account of Shakespeare's English Histories*. New York: Routledge, 1997.

Jardine, Lisa. *Still Harping on Daughters: Women and Drama in the Age of Shakespeare*. 2nd ed. New York: Columbia University Press, 1989.

Kahn, Coppèlia. *Man's Estate: Masculine Identity in Shakespeare*. Berkeley: University of California Press, 1981.

————. *Roman Shakespeare: Warriors, Wounds, and Women*. New York: Routledge, 1997.

Korda, Natasha. *Shakespeare's Domestic Economies: Gender and Property in Early Modern England*. Philadelphia: University of Pennsylvania Press, 2002.

Lenz, Carolyn, Ruth Swift, Gayle Greene, and Carol Thomas Neely, eds. *The Woman's Part: Feminist Criticism of Shakespeare*. Urbana: University of Illinois Press, 1980.

Neely, Carol Thomas. *Broken Nuptials in Shakespeare's Plays*. New Haven: Yale University Press, 1985.

————. *Distracted Subjects: Madness and Gender in Shakespeare and Early Modern Culture*. Ithaca, N.Y.: Cornell University Press, 2004.

Newman, Karen. *Fashioning Femininity and English Renaissance Drama*. Chicago: University of Chicago Press, 1991.

Novy, Marianne. *Love's Argument: Gender Relations in Shakespeare*. Chapel Hill: University of North Carolina Press, 1984.

————, ed. *Women's Re-Visions of Shakespeare: On the Responses of Dickinson, Woolf, Rich, H.D., George Eliot, and Others*. Urbana: University of Illinois Press, 1990.

Orgel, Stephen. *Impersonations: The Performance of Gender in Shakespeare's England*. New York: Cambridge University Press, 1996.

Shapiro, Michael. *Gender in Play on the Shakespearean Stage: Boy Heroines and Female Pages*. Ann Arbor: University of Michigan Press, 1994.

Shepherd, Simon. *Amazons and Warrior Women: Varieties of Feminism in Seventeenth Century Drama*. New York: St. Martin's, 1981.

Traub, Valerie. *Desire and Anxiety: Circulations of Sexuality in Shakespearean Drama*. New York: Routledge, 1992.

————. *The Renaissance of Lesbianism in Eary Modern England*. New York: Cambridge University Press, 2002.

Wayne, Valerie, ed. *The Matter of Difference: Materialist Feminist Criticism of Shakespeare*. Ithaca, N.Y.: Cornell University Press, 1991.

Historical Approaches: Materialism, New Historicism, and Cultural Materialism

Archer, John Michael. *Citizen Shakespeare: Freemen and Aliens in the Language of the Plays.* New York: Palgrave Macmillan, 2005.

Arnold, Oliver. *The Third Citizen: Shakespeare's Theater and the Early Modern House of Commons.* Baltimore: Johns Hopkins University Press, 2007.

Belsey, Catherine. *Shakespeare and the Loss of Eden: The Construction of Family Values in Early Modern Culture.* New Brunswick, N.J.: Rutgers University Press, 1999.

Berry, Ralph. *Shakespeare and Social Class.* Atlantic Highlands, N.J.: Humanities Press International, 1988.

Bristol, Michael D. *Shakespeare's America, America's Shakespeare.* New York: Routledge, 1990.

Bruster, Douglas. *Shakespeare and the Question of Culture: Early Modern Literature and the Cultural Turn.* New York: Palgrave Macmillan, 2003.

Cox, John D. *Shakespeare and the Dramaturgy of Power.* Princeton: Princeton University Press, 1989.

Dollimore, Jonathan. *Radical Tragedy: Religion, Ideology, and Power in the Drama of Shakespeare and His Contemporaries.* 3rd ed. New York: Palgrave Macmillan, 2004.

Dollimore, Jonathan, and Alan Sinfield, eds. *Political Shakespeare: Essays in Cultural Materialism.* 2nd ed. Ithaca, N.Y.: Cornell University Press, 1994.

Dubrow, Heather, and Richard Strier, eds. *The Historical Renaissance: New Essays on Tudor and Stuart Literature and Culture.* Chicago: University of Chicago Press, 1988.

Eagleton, Terry. *William Shakespeare.* Malden, Mass.: Blackwell, 1986.

Greenblatt, Stephen. *Hamlet in Purgatory.* Princeton: Princeton University Press, 2001.

———. *Shakespearean Negotiations: The Circulation of Social Energy in Renaissance England.* Berkeley: University of California Press, 1988.

Hadfield, Andrew. *Shakespeare and Republicanism.* New York: Cambridge University Press, 2005.

Hawkes, Terence. *Meaning by Shakespeare.* New York: Routledge, 1992.

———. *That Shakespeherian Rag: Essays on a Critical Process.* New York: Methuen, 1986.

Holderness, Graham, ed. *The Shakespeare Myth.* Manchester: Manchester University Press, 1988.

———, ed. *Shakespeare's History Plays: Richard II to Henry V.* Houndmills, Basingstoke: Palgrave Macmillan, 1992.

Howard, Jean E. *The Stage and Social Struggle in Early Modern England.* New York: Routledge, 1994.

Howard, Jean E., and Scott Cutler Shershow, eds. *Marxist Shakespeares.* New York: Routledge, 2001.

Howard, Jean E., and Marion F. O'Connor, eds. *Shakespeare Reproduced: The Text in History and Ideology.* New York: Methuen, 1987.

Jardine, Lisa. *Reading Shakespeare Historically.* New York: Routledge, 1996.

Jordan, Constance. *Shakespeare's Monarchies: Ruler and Subject in the Romances.* Ithaca, N.Y.: Cornell University Press, 1997.

Kamps, Ivo, ed. *Materialist Shakespeare: A History.* New York: Verso, 1995.

Kastan, David Scott. *Shakespeare After Theory.* London: Routledge, 1999.

———. *Shakespeare and the Shapes of Time.* Hanover, N.H.: University Press of New England, 1982.

Mallin, Eric S. *Inscribing the Time: Shakespeare and the End of Elizabethan England.* Berkeley: University of California Press, 1995.

Marcus, Leah S. *Puzzling Shakespeare: Local Reading and Its Discontents.* Berkeley: University of California Press, 1988.

Maus, Katharine Eisaman. *Inwardness and Theater in the English Renaissance.* Chicago: University of Chicago Press, 1995.

Montrose, Louis. *The Purpose of Playing: Shakespeare and the Cultural Politics of the Elizabethan Theatre*. Chicago: University of Chicago Press, 1996.

Mullaney, Steven. *The Place of the Stage: License, Play, and Power in Renaissance England*. Chicago: University of Chicago Press, 1988.

Orgel, Stephen. *The Authentic Shakespear: and Other Problems of the Early Modern Stage*. New York: Routledge, 2002.

Patterson, Annabel. *Shakespeare and the Popular Voice*. Malden, Mass.: Blackwell, 1989.

Rackin, Phyllis. *Stages of History: Shakespeare's English Chronicles*. Ithaca, N.Y.: Cornell University Press, 1990.

Siemon, James R. *Word Against Word: Shakespearean Utterance*. Amherst: University of Massachusetts Press, 2002.

Sinfield, Alan. *Shakespeare, Authority, Sexuality: Unfinished Business in Cultural Materialism*. New York: Routledge, 2006.

Tennenhouse, Leonard. *Power on Display: The Politics of Shakespeare's Genres*. New York: Methuen, 1986.

Weimann, Robert. *Author's Pen and Actor's Voice: Playing and Writing in Shakespeare's Theatre*. Ed. Helen Higbee and William West. New York: Cambridge University Press, 2000.

Wells, Robin Headlam. *Shakespeare, Politics, and the State*. Houndmills, Basingstoke: Palgrave Macmillan, 1986.

Wilson, Richard. *Secret Shakespeare: Studies in Theatre, Religion and Resistance*. Manchester: Manchester University Press, 2004.

———. *Will Power: Essays on Shakespearean Authority*. Detroit: Wayne State University Press, 1993.

Postcolonial Criticism, Race, and Ethnicity

Alexander, Catherine M. S., and Stanley Wells, eds. *Shakespeare and Race*. New York: Cambridge University Press, 2000.

Cartelli, Thomas. *Repositioning Shakespeare: National Formations, Postcolonial Appropriations*. New York: Routledge, 1999.

de Sousa, Geraldo U. *Shakespeare's Cross-Cultural Encounters*. Houndmills, Basingstoke: Palgrave Macmillan, 2002.

Floyd-Wilson, Mary. *English Ethnicity and Race in Early Modern Drama*. New York: Cambridge University Press, 2003.

Hendricks, Margo. " 'Obscured by dreams:' Race, Empire, and Shakespeare's *A Midsummer Night's Dream*." *Shakespeare Quarterly* 47 (1996): 37–60.

Hulme, Peter. *Colonial Encounters: Europe and the Native Caribbean, 1492–1797*. New York: Methuen, 1986.

Knapp, Jeffrey. *An Empire Nowhere: England, America, and Literature from Utopia to The Tempest*. Berkeley: University of California Press, 1992.

Loomba, Ania. *Gender, Race, Renaissance Drama*. Manchester: Manchester University Press, 1989.

Loomba, Ania, and Martin Orkin, eds. *Post-colonial Shakespeares*. New York: Routledge, 1998.

Maley, Willy. *Nation, State, and Empire in English Renaissance Literature: Shakespeare to Milton*. New York: Palgrave Macmillan, 2003.

Vaughan, Virginia Mason. *Performing Blackness on English Stages, 1500–1800*. New York: Cambridge University Press, 2005.

Other Philosophical and Theoretical Approaches

Booth, Stephen. *King Lear, Macbeth, Indefinition, and Tragedy*. New Haven: Yale University Press, 1983.

Cavell, Stanley. *Disowning Knowledge in Seven Plays of Shakespeare*. Updated ed. New York: Cambridge University Press, 2003.

Engle, Lars. *Shakespearean Pragmatism: Market of His Time*. Chicago: University of Chicago Press, 1993.

Evans, Malcolm. *Signifying Nothing: Truth's True Contents in Shakespeare's Text*. Athens: University of Georgia Press, 1986.

Felperin, Howard. *The Uses of the Canon: Elizabethan Literature and Contemporary Theory*. New York: Oxford University Press, 1990.

Goldberg, Jonathan. *Shakespeare's Hand*. Minneapolis: University of Minnesota Press, 2003.

Grady, Hugh. *The Modernist Shakespeare: Critical Texts in a Material World*. Oxford: Clarendon, 1991.

———. *Shakespeare, Machiavelli, and Montaigne: Power and Subjectivity from Richard II to Hamlet*. Oxford: Oxford University Press, 2002.

Grady, Hugh, and Terence Hawkes, eds. *Presentist Shakespeares*. New York: Routledge, 2006.

Hawkes, Terence. *Shakespeare in the Present*. New York: Routledge, 2002.

Knapp, Robert S. *Shakespeare—The Theater and the Book*. Princeton: Princeton University Press, 1989.

Lukacher, Ned. *Daemonic Figures: Shakespeare and the Question of Conscience*. Ithaca, N.Y.: Cornell University Press, 1994.

Lupton, Julia Reinhard. *Citizen-Saints: Shakespeare and Political Theology*. Chicago: University of Chicago Press, 2005.

Parker, Patricia, and Geoffrey Hartman, eds. *Shakespeare and the Question of Theory*. New York: Methuen, 1985.

Pechter, Edward. *What Was Shakespeare?: Renaissance Plays and Changing Critical Practice*. Ithaca, N.Y.: Cornell University Press, 1995.

Rabkin, Norman. *Shakespeare and the Problem of Meaning*. Chicago: University of Chicago Press, 1981.

Schalkwyk, David. *Speech and Performance in Shakespeare's Sonnets and Plays*. Cambridge, Eng.: Cambridge University Press, 2002.

Textual Criticism and Bibliography

Allen, Michael J. B., and Kenneth Muir, eds. *Shakespeare's Plays in Quarto: A Facsimile Edition of Copies Primarily from the Henry E. Huntington Library*. Berkeley: University of California Press, 1981.

Blayney, Peter W. M. *The First Folio of Shakespeare*. Washington, D.C.: Folger Library Publications, 1991.

———. *The Texts of King Lear and Their Origins*. Vol. 1: *Nicholas Okes and the First Quarto*. New York: Cambridge University Press, 1982.

Bowers, Fredson. *On Editing Shakespeare*. Charlottesville: University Press of Virginia, 1966.

Brooks, Douglas A. *From Playhouse to Printing House: Drama and Authorship in Early Modern England*. New York: Cambridge University Press, 2000.

De Grazia, Margreta. "Homonyms Before and After Lexical Standardization." *Deutsche Shakespeare-Gesellschaft West* (Jahrbuch 1990): 143–56.

———. *Shakespeare Verbatim: The Reproduction of Authenticity and the 1790 Apparatus*. New York: Oxford University Press, 1991.

De Grazia, Margreta, and Peter Stallybrass. "The Materiality of the Shakespearean Text." *Shakespeare Quarterly* 44 (1993): 255–83.

Erne, Lukas, and Margaret Jane Kidnie, eds. *Textual Performances: The Modern Reproduction of Shakespeare's Drama*. New York: Cambridge University Press, 2004.

Franklin, Colin. *Shakespeare Domesticated: The Eighteenth-Century Editions*. Brookfield, Vt.: Gower Publishing Company, 1991.

Hinman, Charlton, ed. *The First Folio of Shakespeare*. 2nd ed. New York: Norton, 1996.

————. *The Printing and Proof-Reading of the First Folio of Shakespeare*. 2 vols. Oxford: Clarendon, 1963.

Honigmann, E. A. J. *The Stability of Shakespeare's Text*. London: E. Arnold, 1965.

Ioppolo, Grace. *Dramatists and Their Manuscripts in the Age of Shakespeare, Jonson, Middleton and Heywood: Authorship, Authority and the Playhouse*. New York: Routledge, 2006.

————. *Revising Shakespeare*. Cambridge, Mass.: Harvard University Press, 1991.

Irace, Kathleen O. *Reforming the "Bad" Quartos: Performance and Provenance of Six Shakespearean First Editions*. Newark: University of Delaware Press, 1994.

Jackson, MacDonald P. *Defining Shakespeare: Pericles as Test Case*. New York: Oxford University Press, 2003.

Kastan, David Scott. *Shakespeare and the Book*. New York: Cambridge University Press, 2001.

Lesser, Zachary. *Renaissance Drama and the Politics of Publication: Readings in the English Book Trade*. New York: Cambridge University Press, 2004.

Maguire, Laurie E. *Shakespearean Suspect Texts: The "Bad" Quartos and Their Contexts*. New York: Cambridge University Press, 1996.

Maguire, Laurie E., and Thomas L. Berger, eds. *Textual Formations and Reformations*. Newark: University of Delaware Press, 1998.

Marcus, Leah S. *Unediting the Renaissance: Shakespeare, Marlowe, Milton*. New York: Routledge, 1996.

McKerrow, Ronald B. *Prolegomena for the Oxford Shakespeare: A Study in Editorial Method*. Oxford: Clarendon, 1939.

McLeod, Randall, ed. *Crisis in Editing: Texts of the English Renaissance*. New York: AMS Press, 1994.

————. "UN *Editing* Shak-speare." *SubStance* 33/34 (1982): 26–55.

————[as Random Cloud]. "The Psychopathology of Everyday Art." *The Elizabethan Theatre IX*. Ed. G. R. Hibbard. Port Credit, Ontario: P. D. Meany, 1986. 100–68.

Murphy, Andrew. *Shakespeare in Print: A History and Chronology of Shakespeare Publishing*. New York: Cambridge University Press, 2003.

————, ed. *The Renaissance Text: Theory, Editing, Textuality*. Manchester: Manchester University Press, 2000.

Pollard, Alfred W. *Shakespeare's Folios and Quartos: A Study in the Bibliography of Shakespeare's Plays, 1594–1685*. London: Methuen, 1909.

Seary, Peter. *Lewis Theobald and the Editing of Shakespeare*. Oxford: Clarendon, 1990.

Taylor, Gary, and Michael Warren, eds. *The Division of the Kingdoms: Shakespeare's Two Versions of King Lear*. Oxford: Clarendon, 1986.

Urkowitz, Steven. *Shakespeare's Revision of King Lear*. Princeton: Princeton University Press, 1980.

Vickers, Brian. *Shakespeare, Co-Author: A Historical Study of Five Collaborative Plays*. New York: Oxford University Press, 2002.

Walker, Alice. *Textual Problems of the First Folio*: Richard III, King Lear, Troilus & Cressida, 2 Henry IV, Hamlet, Othello. Cambridge, Eng.: Cambridge University Press, 1953.

Wells, Stanley. *Re-Editing Shakespeare for the Modern Reader*. New York: Oxford University Press, 1984.

Wells, Stanley, and Gary Taylor. *Modernizing Shakespeare's Spelling*. Oxford: Clarendon, 1979.

————. *William Shakespeare: A Textual Companion*. Oxford: Clarendon, 1987.

Werstine, Paul. "A Century of 'Bad' Shakespeare Quartos." *Shakespeare Quarterly* 50 (1999): 310–33.

————. "Narratives about Printed Shakespeare Texts: 'Foul Papers' and 'Bad' Quartos." *Shakespeare Quarterly* 41 (1990): 65–86.

Williams, George Walton. *The Craft of Printing and the Publication of Shakespeare's Works*. Washington, D.C.: Folger Shakespeare Library, 1985.

Wilson, J. Dover. *The Manuscript of Shakespeare's "Hamlet" and the Problems of Its Transmission: An Essay in Critical Bibliography*. 2 vols. New York: Macmillan, 1934.

Shakespeare and Performance

Aebischer, Pascale. *Shakespeare's Violated Bodies: Stage and Screen Performance*. New York: Cambridge University Press, 2003.

Aebischer, Pascale, Edward J. Esche, and Nigel Wheale, eds. *Remaking Shakespeare: Performance Across Media, Genres, and Cultures*. New York: Palgrave Macmillan, 2003.

Bartholomeusz, Dennis. *"Macbeth" and the Players*. Cambridge, Eng.: Cambridge University Press, 1969.

Barton, John. *Playing Shakespeare*. London: Methuen, 1984.

Bate, Jonathan, and Russell Jackson, eds. *Shakespeare: An Illustrated Stage History*. New York: Oxford University Press, 1996.

Berger, Harry Jr. *Imaginary Audition: Shakespeare on Stage and Page*. Berkeley: University of California Press, 1989.

Berry, Francis. *The Shakespeare Inset: Word and Picture*. London: Routledge and Kegan Paul, 1965.

Berry, Ralph. *Changing Styles in Shakespeare*. Boston: Allen & Unwin, 1981.

Bevington, David M. *Action Is Eloquence: Shakespeare's Language of Gesture*. Cambridge, Mass.: Harvard University Press, 1984.

————. *This Wide and Universal Theater: Shakespeare in Performance, Then and Now*. Chicago: University of Chicago Press, 2007.

Branam, George Curtis. *Eighteenth-Century Adaptations of Shakespearean Tragedy*. Berkeley: University of California Press, 1956.

Bratton, Jacky, and Julie Hankey, gen. eds. The Shakespeare in Production Series. Cambridge, Eng.: Cambridge University Press, 1996–.

Brennan, Anthony. *Onstage and Offstage Worlds in Shakespeare's Plays*. New York: Routledge, 1989.

————. *Shakespeare's Dramatic Structures*. Boston: Routledge and Kegan Paul, 1986.

Brown, Ivor. *Shakespeare and the Actors*. London: Bodley Head, 1970.

Brown, John Russell. *Shakespeare and the Theatrical Event*. Houndmills, Basingstoke: Palgrave Macmillan, 2002.

————. *Shakespeare's Dramatic Style: Romeo and Juliet, As You Like It, Julius Caesar, Twelfth Night, Macbeth*. London: Heinemann, 1970.

Bulman, James C., ed. *Shakespeare, Theory, and Performance*. New York: Routledge, 1996.

Calderwood, James. *Shakespearean Metadrama: The Argument of the Play in* Titus Andronicus, Love's Labour's Lost, Romeo and Juliet, A Midsummer Night's Dream, *and* Richard II. Minneapolis: University of Minnesota Press, 1971.

Carlisle, Carol Jones. *Shakespeare from the Greenroom: Actors' Criticisms of Four Major Tragedies*. Chapel Hill: University of North Carolina Press, 1969.

Cohn, Ruby. *Modern Shakespeare Offshoots*. Princeton: Princeton University Press, 1976.

Dean, Winton. "Shakespeare in the Opera House." *Shakespeare Survey* 18 (1965): 75–93.

Dobson, Michael. *The Making of the National Poet: Shakespeare, Adaptation and Authorship, 1660–1769*. Oxford: Clarendon, 1992.

———, ed. *Performing Shakespeare's Tragedies Today: The Actor's Perspective*. New York: Cambridge University Press, 2006.

Downer, Alan S. *The Eminent Tragedian William Charles Macready*. Cambridge, Mass.: Harvard University Press, 1966.

Duffin, Ross W. *Shakespeare's Songbook*. New York: Norton, 2004.

Foulkes, Richard, ed. *Shakespeare and the Victorian Stage*. New York: Cambridge University Press, 1986.

Goldman, Michael. *Acting and Action in Shakespearean Tragedy*. Princeton: Princeton University Press, 1985.

Hirsch, James E. *The Structure of Shakespearean Scenes*. New Haven: Yale University Press, 1981.

Hogan, Charles Beecher, ed. *Shakespeare in the Theatre, 1701–1800*. 2 vols. Oxford: Clarendon, 1952–57.

Holland, Peter. *English Shakespeares: Shakespeare on the English Stage in the 1990's*. New York: Cambridge University Press, 1997.

Homan, Sidney, ed. *Shakespeare's "More Than Words Can Witness": Essays on Visual and Nonverbal Enactment in the Plays*. Lewisburg, Pa.: Bucknell University Press, 1980.

———, ed. *When the Theater Turns to Itself: The Aesthetic Metaphor in Shakespeare*. Lewiston, Pa.: Bucknell University Press, 1981.

Hoenselaars, Ton, ed. *Shakespeare's History Plays: Performance, Translation and Adaptation in Britain and Abroad*. Cambridge, Eng.: Cambridge University Press, 2004.

Howard, Jean E. *Shakespeare's Art of Orchestration: Stage Technique and Audience Response*. Urbana: University of Illinois Press, 1984.

Jones, Emrys. *Scenic Form in Shakespeare*. Oxford: Clarendon, 1971.

Kennedy, Dennis. *Looking at Shakespeare: A Visual History of Twentieth-Century Performance*. 2nd ed. New York: Cambridge University Press, 2001.

———, ed. *Foreign Shakespeare: Contemporary Performance*. New York: Cambridge University Press, 1993.

Marshall, Gail, and Adrian Poole, eds. *Victorian Shakespeare*. New York: Palgrave Macmillan, 2003.

McGuire, Philip C. *Speechless Dialect: Shakespeare's Open Silences*. Berkeley: University of California Press, 1985.

McGuire, Philip C., and David A. Samuelson. *Shakespeare: The Theatrical Dimension*. New York: AMS Press, 1979.

Mooney, Michael E. *Shakespeare's Dramatic Transactions*. Durham, N.C.: Duke University Press, 1990.

Mowat, Barbara A. *The Dramaturgy of Shakespeare's Romances*. Athens: University of Georgia Press, 1976.

Odell, George Clinton Densmore. *Shakespeare from Betterton to Irving*. 2 vols. New York: Scribner, 1920.

Parsons, Keith, and Pamela Mason, eds. *Shakespeare in Performance*. London: Salamander, 1995.

Poel, William. *Shakespeare in the Theater*. London: Sidgwick and Jackson, 1913.

Rosenberg, Marvin. *The Masks of King Lear*. Berkeley: University of California Press, 1972.

Rosenberg, Marvin, et al. *Clamorous Voices: Shakespeare's Women Today*. London: Women's Press, 1988.

Rutter, Carol, gen. ed. The Shakespeare in Performance Series. Manchester: Manchester University Press, 1982–.

Shattuck, Charles H. *Shakespeare on the American Stage*, vol. 1: *From the Hallams to Edwin Booth*. Washington, D.C.: Folger Shakespeare Library, 1976.

———. *Shakespeare on the American Stage*, vol. 2: *From Booth and Barrett to Sothern and Marlowe*. Washington, D.C.: Folger Shakespeare Library, 1987.

————. *The Shakespeare Promptbooks: A Descriptive Catalogue.* Urbana: University of Illinois Press, 1965.

Slater, Ann. *Shakespeare, the Director.* Totowa, N.J.: Barnes & Noble Books, 1982.

Smallwood, Robert, ed. *Players of Shakespeare.* 6 vols. New York: Cambridge University Press, 1985–2004.

————, gen. ed. The Shakespeare at Stratford series. London: Arden Shakespeare, 2002– .

Speaight, Robert. *Shakespeare on the Stage: An Illustrated History of Shakespearian Performance.* London: Collins, 1973.

————. *William Poel and the Elizabethan Revival.* Cambridge, Mass.: Harvard University Press, 1954.

Spencer, Hazelton. *Shakespeare Improved: The Restoration Versions in Quarto and On the Stage.* Cambridge, Mass.: Harvard University Press, 1927.

Styan, J. L. *The Shakespeare Revolution: Criticism and Performance in the Twentieth Century.* New York: Cambridge University Press, 1977.

————. *Shakespeare's Stagecraft.* Cambridge, Eng.: Cambridge University Press, 1967.

————. "Sight and Space: The Perception of Shakespeare on Stage and Screen." *Shakespeare, Pattern of Excelling Nature: Shakespeare Criticism in Honor of America's Bicentennial.* Ed. David Bevington and Jay L. Halio. Newark: University of Delaware Press, 1978.

Thompson, Marvin and Ruth, eds. *Shakespeare and the Sense of Performance.* Newark: University of Delaware Press, 1989.

Trewin, J. C. *Shakespeare on the English Stage, 1900–1964.* London: Barrie and Rockliff, 1964.

Wells, Stanley. *Royal Shakespeare: Four Major Productions at Stratford-upon-Avon.* Manchester: Manchester University Press, 1977.

————, ed. *Shakespeare in the Theatre: An Anthology of Criticism.* New York: Oxford University Press, 1997.

Worthen, William B. *Shakespeare and the Authority of Performance.* New York: Cambridge University Press, 1997.

————. *Shakespeare and the Force of Modern Performance.* New York: Cambridge University Press, 2003.

Shakespeare on Film

Ball, Robert Hamilton. *Shakespeare on Silent Film: A Strange Eventful History.* London: Allen & Unwin, 1968.

Burt, Richard, and Lynda E. Boose, eds. *Shakespeare the Movie: Popularizing the Plays on Film, TV, and Video.* New York: Routledge, 1997.

————. *Shakespeare the Movie II: Popularizing the Plays on Film, TV, Video, and DVD.* New York: Routledge, 2003.

Bristol, Michael D. *Big-Time Shakespeare.* New York: Routledge, 1996.

Buchanan, Judith. *Shakespeare on Film.* New York: Pearson Longman, 2005.

Buchman, Lorne Michael. *Still in Movement: Shakespeare on Screen.* New York: Oxford University Press, 1991.

Bulman, J. C., and H. R. Coursen, eds. *Shakespeare on Television: An Anthology of Essays and Reviews.* Hanover, N.H.: University Press of New England, 1988.

Burnett, Mark Thornton, and Ramona Wray, eds. *Shakespeare, Film, Fin de Siècle.* New York: St. Martin's, 2000.

Burt, Richard. *Shakespeare After Mass Media.* New York: Palgrave Macmillan, 2002.

Cartelli, Thomas, and Katherine Rowe, eds. *New Wave Shakespeare on Screen.* Malden, Mass.: Polity Press, 2007.

Crowl, Samuel. *Shakespeare at the Cineplex: The Kenneth Branagh Era.* Athens: Ohio University Press, 2003.

————. *Shakespeare and Film*. New York: Norton, 2008.

Davies, Anthony, and Stanley Wells, eds. *Shakespeare and the Moving Image: The Plays on Film and Television*. New York: Cambridge University Press, 1994.

Donaldson, Peter S. *Shakespearean Films/Shakespearean Directors*. Boston: Unwin Hyman, 1990.

Henderson, Diana E. *Collaborations with the Past: Reshaping Shakespeare Across Time and Media*. Ithaca, N.Y.: Cornell University Press, 2006.

————. *A Concise Companion to Shakespeare on Screen*. Malden, Mass.: Blackwell, 2007.

Hindle, Maurice. *Studying Shakespeare on Film*. New York: Palgrave Macmillan, 2007.

Kliman, Bernice W. *Hamlet: Film, Television, and Audio Performance*. Madison, N.J.: Fairleigh Dickinson University Press, 1988.

Lehmann, Courtney. *Shakespeare Remains: Theater to Film, Early Modern to Postmodern*. Ithaca, N.Y.: Cornell, 2002.

Lehmann, Courtney, and Lisa S. Starks, eds. *Spectacular Shakespeare: Critical Theory and Popular Cinema*. Madison, N.J.: Fairleigh Dickinson University Press, 2002.

Rothwell, Kenneth S. *A History of Shakespeare on Screen: A Century of Film and Television*. 2nd ed. Cambridge, Eng.: Cambridge University Press, 2004.

Glossary

STAGE TERMS

"Above"   The gallery on the upper level of the *frons scenae*. In open-air theaters, such as the Globe, this space contained the lords' rooms. The central section of the gallery was sometimes used by the players for short scenes. Indoor theaters such as Blackfriars featured a curtained alcove for musicians above the stage.

"Aloft"   See *"Above."*

Amphitheater   An open-air theater, such as the Globe.

Arras   See *Curtain*.

Cellerage   See *Trap*.

Chorus   In the works of Shakespeare and other Elizabethan playwrights, a single individual (not, as in Greek tragedy, a group) who speaks before the play (and often before each act), describing events not shown on stage as well as commenting on the action witnessed by the audience.

Curtain   Curtains, or arras (hanging tapestries), covered a part of the *frons scenae,* thus concealing the discovery space, and may also have been draped around the edge of the stage to conceal the open area underneath.

Discovery space   A central opening or alcove concealed behind a curtain in the center of the *frons scenae*. The curtain could be drawn aside to "discover" tableaux such as Portia's caskets, the body of Polonius, or the statue of Hermione. Shakespeare appears to have used this stage device only sparingly.

Doubling   The common practice of having one actor play multiple roles, so that a play with a large cast of characters might be performed by a relatively small company.

Dumb shows   Mimed scenes performed before a play (or before each act), summarizing or foreshadowing the plot. Dumb shows were popular in early Elizabethan drama; although they already seemed old-fashioned in Shakespeare's time, they were employed by writers up to the 1640s.

Epilogue   A brief speech or poem addressed to the audience by an actor after the play. In some cases, as in *2 Henry IV,* the epilogue could be combined with, or could merge into, the jig.

Forestage   The front of the stage, closest to the audience.

Frons scenae   The wall at the back of the stage, behind which lay the players' tiring-house. The *frons scenae* of the Globe featured two doors flanking the central discovery space, with a gallery "above."

Gallery   Covered seating areas surrounding the open yard of the public amphitheaters. There were three levels of galleries at the Globe; admission to these seats cost an extra penny (in addition to the basic admission fee of one penny to the yard), and seating in the higher galleries another penny yet. In indoor theaters such as Blackfriars, where there was no standing room, gallery seating was less expensive than seating in the pit; indeed, seats nearest the stage were the most expensive.

Gatherers Persons employed by the playing company to take money at the entrances to the theater.

Groundlings Audience members who paid the minimum price of admission (one penny) to stand in the yard of the open-air theaters; also referred to as "understanders."

Heavens The canopied roof over the stage in the open-air theaters, protecting the players and their costumes from rain. The "heavens" would be brightly decorated with sun, moon, and stars, and perhaps the signs of the zodiac.

Hut A structure on the top of the cover over the stage, where stagehands produced the effects of thunder and lightning and operated the machinery by which gods, such as Jupiter in *Cymbeline*, descended through the trapdoor in the "heavens."

Jig A song-and-dance performance by the clown and other members of the company at the conclusion of a play. These performances were frequently bawdy and were officially banned in 1612.

Lords' rooms Partitioned sections of the gallery "above," where the most prestigious and expensive seats in the public playhouses were located. These rooms were designed not to provide the best view of the action on the stage below, but to make their privileged occupants conspicuous to the rest of the audience.

Open-air theaters Unroofed public playhouses in the suburbs of London, such as The Theatre, the Rose, and the Globe.

Part The character played by an actor. In Shakespeare's theater, actors were given a roll of paper called a "part" containing all of the speeches and all of the cues belonging to their character. The term "role," synonymous with "part," is derived from such rolls of paper.

Patrons Important nobles and members of the royal family under whose protection the theatrical companies of London operated; players not in the service of patrons were punishable as vagabonds. The companies were referred to as their patrons' "Men" or "Servants." Thus the name of the company to which Shakespeare belonged for most of his career was first the Lord Chamberlain's Men, then was changed to the King's Men in 1603, when James I became their patron.

Pillars The "heavens" were supported by two tall painted pillars or posts near the front of the stage. These occasionally played a role in stage action, allowing a character to "hide" while remaining in full view of the audience.

Pit The area in front of the stage in indoor theaters such as Blackfriars, where the most expensive and prestigious bench seating was to be had.

Posts See *Pillars*.

Proscenium The space of the transparent "fourth wall," which divides the actors from the orchestra and audience in the standard modern theater. The stages on which Shakespeare's plays were first performed had no proscenium.

Rearstage The back of the stage, farthest from the audience.

Repertory The stock of plays a company had ready for performance at a given time. Companies generally performed a different play each day, often more than a dozen plays in a month and more than thirty in the course of the season.

Role See *Part.*

Sharers Senior actors holding shares in a joint-stock theatrical company; they paid for costumes, hired hands, and new plays, and they shared profits and losses equally. Shakespeare was not only a longtime "sharer" of the Lord Chamberlain's Men but, from 1599, a "housekeeper," the holder of a one-eighth share in the Globe playhouse.

Tiring-house The players' dressing (attiring) room, a structure located at the back of the stage and connected to the stage by two or more doors in the *frons scenae.*

Trap A trapdoor near the front of the stage that allowed access to the "cellarage" beneath and was frequently associated with hell's mouth. Another trapdoor in the "heavens" opened for the descent of gods to the stage below.

"Within" The tiring-house, from which offstage sound effects such as shouts, drums, and trumpets were produced.

Yard The central space in open-air theaters such as the Globe, into which the stage projected and in which audience members stood. Admission to the yard in the public theaters cost a penny, the cheapest admission available.

TEXTUAL TERMS

Aside See *Stage direction.*

Autograph Text written in the author's own hand. With the possible exception of a few pages of the collaborative play *Sir Thomas More,* no dramatic works or poems written in Shakespeare's hand are known to survive.

Canonical Of an author, the writings generally accepted as authentic. In the case of Shakespeare's dramatic works, only two plays that are not among the thirty-six plays contained in the First Folio, *Pericles* and *The Two Noble Kinsmen,* have won widespread acceptance into the Shakespearean canon. (This sense of "canonical" should not be confused with the use of "the canon" to denote the entire body of literary works, including but not limited to Shakespeare's, that have traditionally been regarded as fit objects of admiration and study.)

Catchword A word printed below the text at the bottom of a page, matching the first word on the following page. The catchword enabled the printer to keep the pages in their proper sequence. Where the catchword fails to match the word at the top of the next page, there is reason to suspect that something has been lost or misplaced.

Compositor A person employed in a print shop to set type. To speed the printing process, most of Shakespeare's plays were set by more than one compositor. Compositors frequently followed their own standards in spelling and punctuation. They inevitably introduced some errors into the text, often by selecting the wrong piece from the type case or by setting the correct letter upside down.

Conflation A version of a play created by combining readings from more than one substantive edition. Since the early eighteenth century, for example, most versions of *King Lear* and of several other plays by Shakespeare have been conflations of quarto and First Folio texts.

Control text   The text upon which a modern edition is based.

Dramatis personae   A list of the characters appearing in the play. In the First Folio such lists were printed at the end of some but not all of the plays. The editor Nicholas Rowe (1709) first provided lists of dramatis personae for all of Shakespeare's dramatic works.

Exeunt / Exit   See *Stage direction.*

Fair copy   A transcript of the "foul papers" made either by a scribe or by the playwright.

Folio   A bookmaking format in which each large sheet of paper is folded once, making two leaves (four pages front and back). This format produced large volumes, generally handsome and expensive. The First Folio of Shakespeare's plays was printed in 1623.

Foul papers   An author's first completed draft of a play, typically full of blotted-out passages and revisions. None of Shakespeare's foul papers is known to survive.

Licensing   By an order of 1581, new plays could not be performed until they had received a license from the Master of the Revels. A separate license, granted by the Court of High Commission, was required for publication, though in practice plays were often printed without license. From 1610, the Master of the Revels had the authority to license plays for publication as well as for performance.

Manent / Manet   See *Stage direction.*

Memorial reconstruction   The conjectured practice of reconstructing the text of a play from memory. Companies touring in the provinces without access to promptbooks may have resorted to memorial reconstruction. This practice also provides a plausible explanation for the existence of the so-called bad Quartos.

Octavo   A bookmaking format in which each large sheet of paper is folded three times, making eight leaves (sixteen pages front and back). Only one of Shakespeare's plays, *Richard Duke of York* (*3 Henry VI*, 1595), was published in octavo format.

Playbook   See *Promptbook.*

Press variants   Minor textual variations among books of the same edition, resulting from corrections made in the course of printing or from damaged or slipped type.

Promptbook   A manuscript of a play (either foul papers or fair copy) annotated and adapted for performance by the theatrical company. The promptbook incorporated stage directions, notes on properties and special effects, and revisions, sometimes including those required by the Master of the Revels. Promptbooks are usually identifiable by the replacement of characters' names with actors' names.

Quarto   A bookmaking format in which each large sheet of paper is folded twice, making four leaves (eight pages front and back). Quarto volumes were smaller and less expensive than books printed in the folio format.

Scribal copy   A transcript of a play produced by a professional scribe (or "scrivener"). Scribes tended to employ their own preferred spellings and abbreviations and could be responsible for introducing a variety of errors.

Speech prefix (s.p.)   The indication of the identity of the speaker of the following line or lines. Early editions of Shakespeare's plays often use different prefixes at different points to designate the same person. On occasion, the name of the actor who was to play the role appears in place of the name of the character.

Stage direction (s.d.) The part of the text that is not spoken by any character but that indicates actions to be performed onstage. Stage directions in the earliest editions of Shakespeare's plays are sparse and are sometimes grouped together at the beginning of a scene rather than next to the spoken lines they should precede, accompany, or follow. By convention, the most basic stage directions were written in Latin. "Exit" indicates the departure of a single actor from the stage, "exeunt" the departure of more than one. "Manet" indicates that a single actor remains onstage, "manent" that more than one remains. Lines accompanied by the stage direction "aside" are spoken so as not to be heard by the others onstage. This stage direction appeared in some early editions of Shakespeare plays, but other means were also used to indicate such speech (such as placing the words within parentheses), and sometimes no indication was provided.

Stationers' Register The account books of the Company of Stationers (of which all printers were legally required to be members), recording the fees paid for permission to print new works as well as the fines exacted for printing without permission. The Stationers' Register thus provides a valuable if incomplete record of publication in England.

Substantive text The text of an edition based upon access to a manuscript, as opposed to a derivative text based only on an earlier edition.

Variorum editions Comprehensive editions of a work or works in which the various views of previous editors and commentators are compiled.

ILLUSTRATION ACKNOWLEDGMENTS

General Introduction   Plague death bill: By permission of the Folger Shakespeare Library • Webbe: By permission of the British Library • Amman: Spencer Collection, The New York Public Library, Astor, Lenox and Tilden Foundation • *Swetnam* title page: By permission of The Huntington Library, San Marino, California • Pope as Antichrist: By permission of the Folger Shakespeare Library • de Heere: The National Museum of Wales • Armada portrait: By kind permission of Marquess of Tavistock and Trustees of the Bedford Estate • Boaistuau: By permission of The Huntington Library, San Marino, California • Mandeville: By permission of the Houghton Library, Harvard University • Funeral procession: Additional Ms. 35324, folio 37v. By permission of the British Library • Gheeraerts: By permission of the Trustees of Dulwich Picture Gallery • van den Broek: Fitzwilliam Museum, University of Cambridge • Swimming: Bodleian Library, University of Oxford, 4° G.17.Art • Panorama of London: By permission of the British Library • Tarleton: Harley 3885, folio 19. By permission of the British Library • Hanging: Pepys Library, Magdalene College, Cambridge • Syphilis victim: By permission of The Huntington Library, San Marino, California • *Spanish Tragedy* title page: By permission of the Folger Shakespeare Library • Stratford-upon-Avon: By permission of City of York Libraries • Cholmondeley sisters: Tate Gallery, London • Alleyn: By permission of the Trustees of Dulwich Picture Library • *If You Know Not Me* title page: By permission of The Huntington Library, San Marino, California • van der Straet: By permission of the Folger Shakespeare Library
The Shakespearean Stage   Braun and Hogenburg: 8.Tab.c.4. Bk.1.pl.1. By permission of the British Library • Hollar: Guildhall Library, Corporation of London • Interior of the "new" Globe: Courtesy of The International Shakespeare Globe Center Ltd. Photo: John Tramper • Exterior of the "new" Globe: Courtesy of The International Shakespeare Globe Center Ltd. Photo: Richard Kalina • *Frons scenae* of the "new" Globe: Courtesy of The International Shakespeare Globe Center Ltd. Photo: Richard Kalina • Oliver: The Burghley House Collection. Photograph: Courtauld Institute of Art • Peacham: Reproduced by permission of the Marquess of Bath, Longleat House, Warminster, Wiltshire, Great Britain. Photograph: Courtauld Institute of Art • de Witt: University Library, Utrecht, MS 842, f.132r • Middle Temple Hall: The Benchers of the Honorable Society of the Middle Temple, London • Hollar: Guildhall Library, Corporation of London
Shakespearean Comedy   Kempe: By permission of the Folger Shakespeare Library • Terence: Internet Shakespeare Editions, University of Victoria
The Taming of the Shrew   Rowlands: C151e6(1). By permission of the British Library • Brushfield: By permission of the Folger Shakespeare Library • Flötner: Bancroft Library, University of California, Berkeley
A Midsummer Night's Dream   Corrozet: By permission of the Houghton Library, Harvard University • Wither: By permission of the Houghton Library, Harvard University • Magnus: Bodleian Library, University of Oxford, H 4 12 Art
The Merchant of Venice   Braun and Hogenburg: 8 Tab.c.4, Bk. 1 pl. 43. By permission of the British Library • Amman: Spencer Collection, The New York Public Library, Astor, Lenox and Tilden Foundation. Photo: Robert D. Rubic
Much Ado About Nothing   Peacham: By permission of the Folger Shakespeare Library • Dekker: By permission of the Folger Shakespeare Library • Wither: By permission of the Houghton Library, Harvard University
As You Like It   Robin Hood: The Trustees of the National Library of Scotland • Bonasone: All rights reserved. The Metropolitan Museum of Art, Gift of Philip Hofer, 1933 (33.77.5) • Weindler: Bancroft Library, University of California, Berkeley
Twelfth Night   Stubbes: By permission of the Folger Shakespeare Library • Amman: Spencer Collection, The New York Public Library, Astor, Lenox and Tilden Foundation
Measure for Measure   Whitney: By permission of the Folger Shakespeare Library • Amman: Audio-Visual Archives, Special Collections and Archives, University of Kentucky Libraries
Shakespearean History   Anjou: By permission of V&A Library, Victoria and Albert Museum • King Henry IV: © National Portrait Gallery, London • Holbein: © National Portrait Gallery, London.
Richard III   Richard III: By courtesy of the National Portrait Gallery, London • Sittow: By courtesy of the National Portrait Gallery, London • Vischer: By permission of the Folger Shakespeare Library
Richard II   Rastell: C.15.e.6. By permission of the British Library • Holbein: Reproduced by courtesy of the Trustees, The National Gallery, London • Tempesta: © British Museum
1 Henry IV   Owain Glyndŵr seal: By permission of The National Museum of Wales • William Blake: Photograph © Museum of Fine Arts, Boston • Peacham: By Permission of the Folger Shakespeare Library
Henry V   Rastell: G6030. By permission of the British Library • Renatus: By permission of the Houghton Library, Harvard University • Comenius: By permission of the Folger Shakespeare Library
Shakespearean Tragedy   1609 engraving: By permission of the Folger Shakespeare Library • "Remember to Die": Rowe: By permission of the Folger Shakespeare Library • Babilonia: By permission of the Folger Shakespeare Library
Romeo and Juliet   Wither: By permission of the Houghton Library, Harvard University • Speed: By permission of the Folger Shakespeare Library
Julius Caesar   Plutarch (Caesar and Marc Antony): By permission of the Folger Shakespeare Library • Whitney: By permission of the Folger Shakespeare Library
Hamlet   Clerke: By permission of the Houghton Library, Harvard University • von Landshut: © British Museum • Saviolo: By permission of the Folger Shakespeare Library
Othello   Moorish ambassador: Reproduced by permission of the Shakespeare Institute, University of Birmingham, UK • Knight: By permission of the Folger Shakespeare Library

King Lear   Holinshed: By permission of the Houghton Library, Harvard University • Cypriano: By permission of the Houghton Library, Harvard University • Gheeraerts: Tom Durie by Marcus Gheeraerts the Younger, 1614. The Scottish National Portrait Gallery

Macbeth   Firens: Bibliothèque Nationale de France • Holinshed: By permission of the Houghton Library, Harvard University • Witchcraft: Courtesy of the Archbishop of Canterbury and the Trustees of Lambeth Palace Library

Antony and Cleopatra   du Choul: By permission of the Folger Shakespeare Library • Topsell: By permission of the Folger Shakespeare Library

Shakespearean Romance   Le Naufrage: By permission of the Fine Arts Museums of San Francisco • Venus and Jupiter (astride an eagle): By permission of the Abaris Books • Portolan atlas: By permission of the Library of Congress, Geography and Map Division, Washington, D.C.

The Winter's Tale   Bloudy Mother title page: By permission of the Houghton Library, Harvard University • Rüff: By permission of the Folger Shakespeare Library • Pedlar: Pepys Library, Magdalene College, Cambridge

The Tempest   Magnus: Reproduced by permission of the Huntington Library • Galle: The Burndy Library, Norwalk, Connecticut

Sonnets   Whitney: By permission of the Folger Shakespeare Library

Early Modern Map Culture   Speed: © British Library/HIP/Art Resource, NY • Braun and Hogenberg: HIP/Art Resource, NY. Museum of London, London, Great Britain

Contemporary Documents
First Folio front matter: The Norton Facsimile of the First Folio of Shakespeare, 2nd ed. (1996)

Index of Sonnets

Index of Songs

Index of Plays

THE HOUSE OF LANCASTER

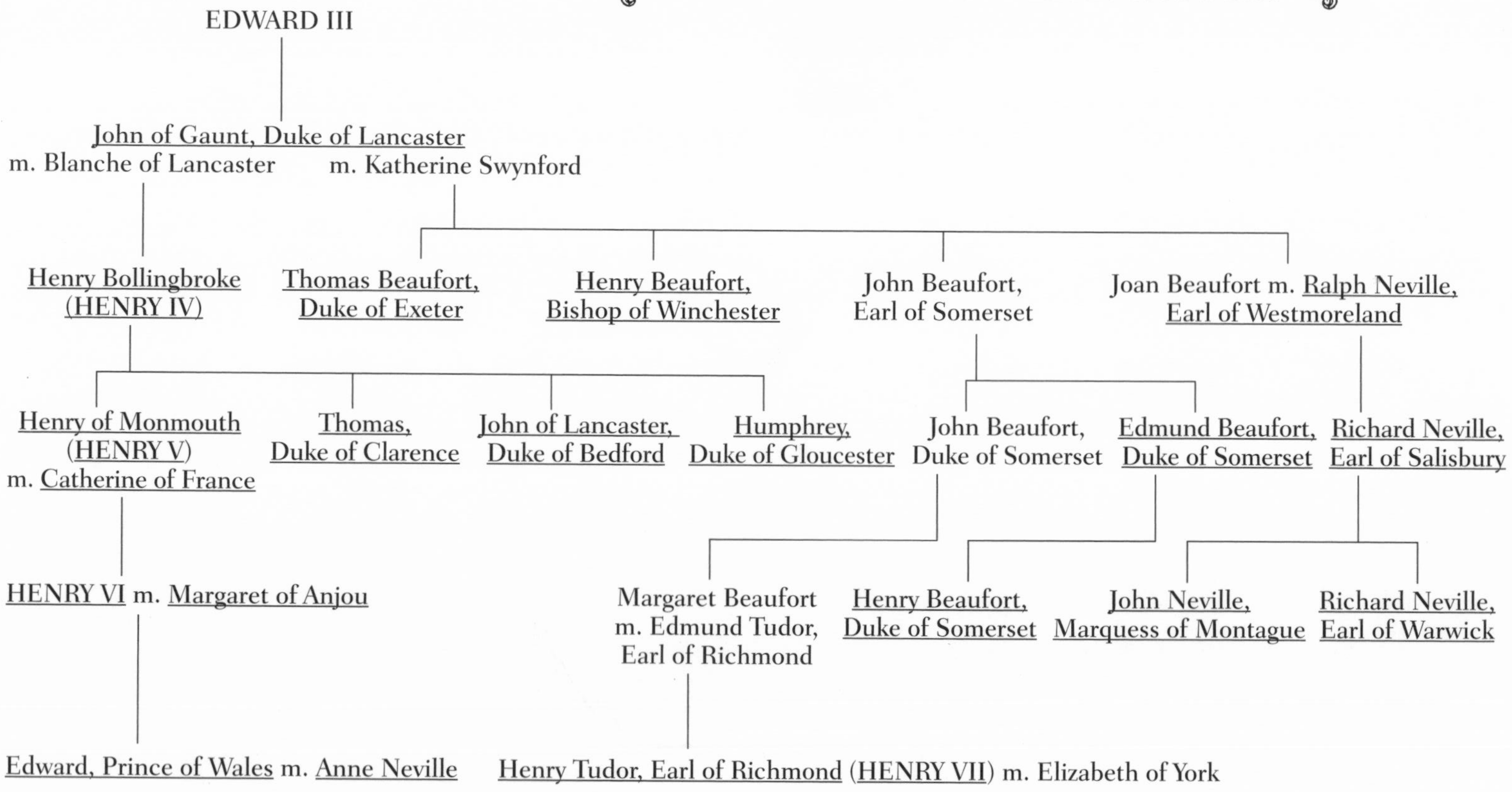

EDWARD III

John of Gaunt, Duke of Lancaster
m. Blanche of Lancaster   m. Katherine Swynford

Henry Bollingbroke
(HENRY IV)

Thomas Beaufort,
Duke of Exeter

Henry Beaufort,
Bishop of Winchester

John Beaufort,
Earl of Somerset

Joan Beaufort m. Ralph Neville,
Earl of Westmoreland

Henry of Monmouth
(HENRY V)
m. Catherine of France

Thomas,
Duke of Clarence

John of Lancaster,
Duke of Bedford

Humphrey,
Duke of Gloucester

John Beaufort,
Duke of Somerset

Edmund Beaufort,
Duke of Somerset

Richard Neville,
Earl of Salisbury

HENRY VI m. Margaret of Anjou

Margaret Beaufort
m. Edmund Tudor,
Earl of Richmond

Henry Beaufort,
Duke of Somerset

John Neville,
Marquess of Montague

Richard Neville,
Earl of Warwick

Edward, Prince of Wales m. Anne Neville

Henry Tudor, Earl of Richmond (HENRY VII) m. Elizabeth of York

THE HOUSE OF YORK

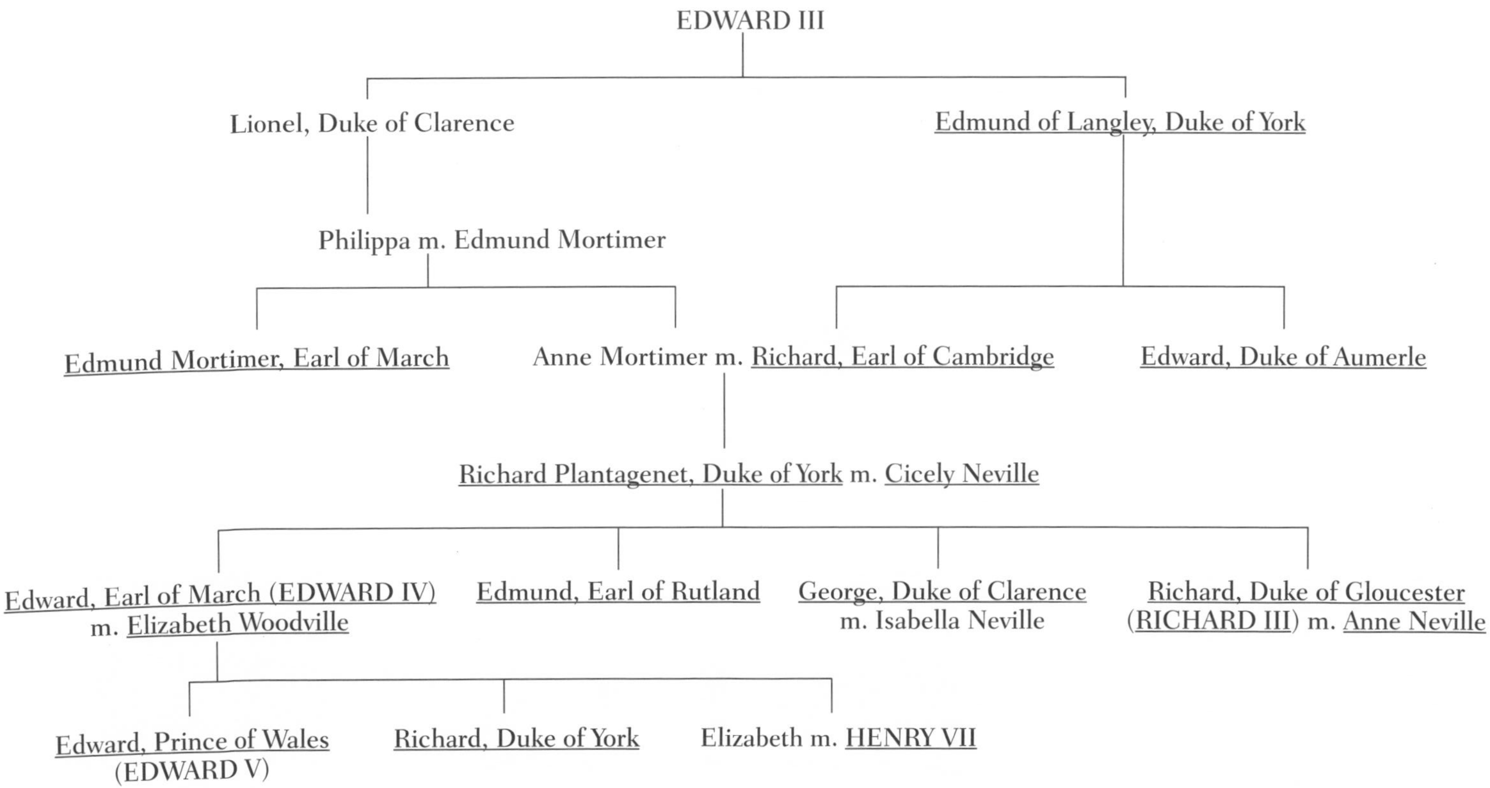

EDWARD III

- Lionel, Duke of Clarence
  - Philippa m. Edmund Mortimer
    - Edmund Mortimer, Earl of March
    - Anne Mortimer m. Richard, Earl of Cambridge
- Edmund of Langley, Duke of York
  - Edward, Duke of Aumerle
  - Richard, Earl of Cambridge

Richard Plantagenet, Duke of York m. Cicely Neville

- Edward, Earl of March (EDWARD IV) m. Elizabeth Woodville
  - Edward, Prince of Wales (EDWARD V)
  - Richard, Duke of York
  - Elizabeth m. HENRY VII
- Edmund, Earl of Rutland
- George, Duke of Clarence m. Isabella Neville
- Richard, Duke of Gloucester (RICHARD III) m. Anne Neville

TUDORS (1485–1603) AND STUARTS (1603–1714)

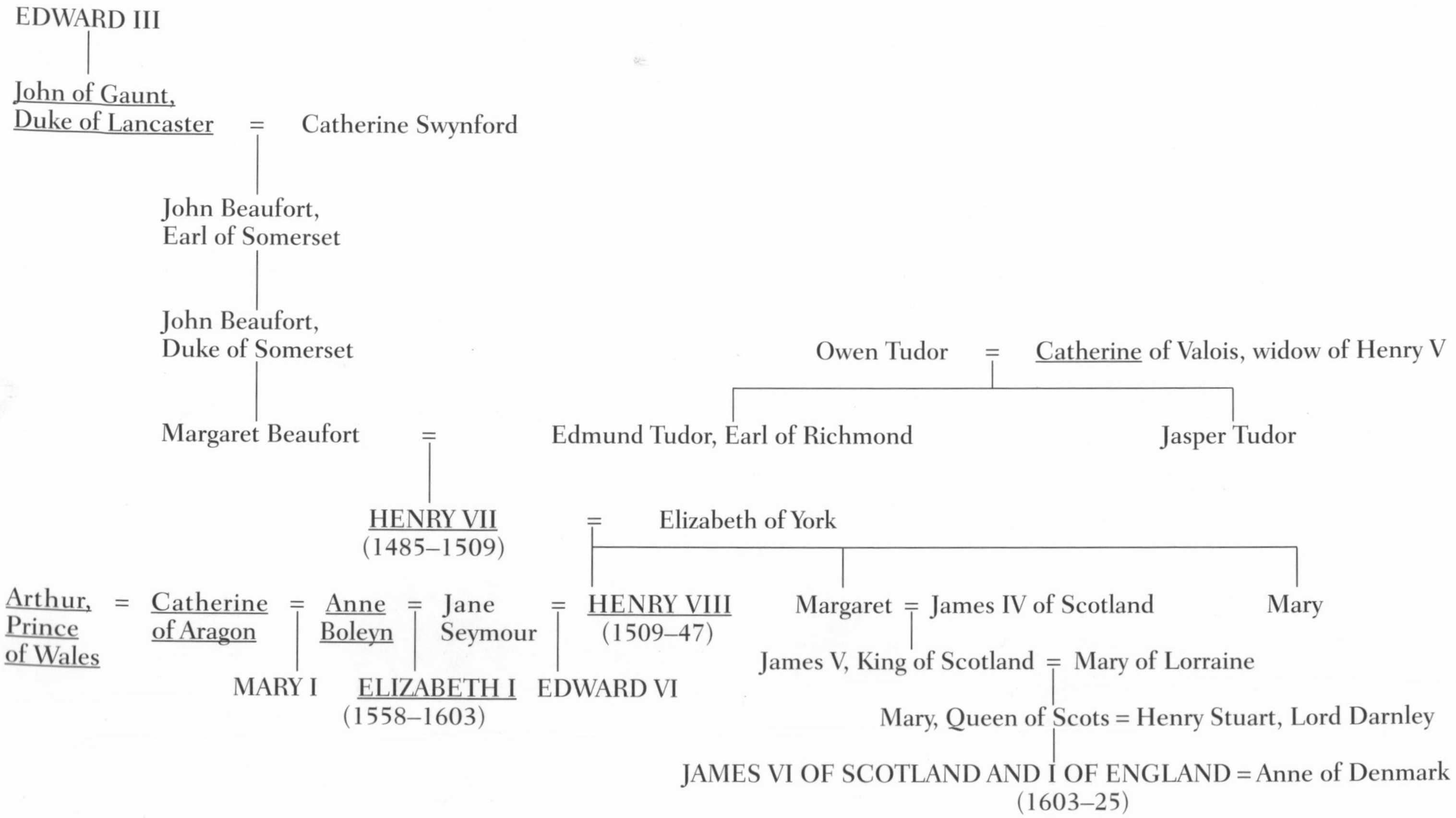

EDWARD III

John of Gaunt,
Duke of Lancaster = Catherine Swynford

John Beaufort,
Earl of Somerset

John Beaufort,
Duke of Somerset

Owen Tudor = Catherine of Valois, widow of Henry V

Margaret Beaufort

Edmund Tudor, Earl of Richmond   Jasper Tudor

HENRY VII = Elizabeth of York
(1485–1509)

Arthur, = Catherine = Anne = HENRY VIII = Jane   Margaret = James IV of Scotland   Mary
Prince   of Aragon   Boleyn   (1509–47)   Seymour
of Wales

MARY I   ELIZABETH I   EDWARD VI   James V, King of Scotland = Mary of Lorraine
              (1558–1603)

                                                              Mary, Queen of Scots = Henry Stuart, Lord Darnley

                                                      JAMES VI OF SCOTLAND AND I OF ENGLAND = Anne of Denmark
                                                                                (1603–25)

An equal sign (=) stands for marriage. Underlined names indicate characters in the plays. Capitals note reigning Kings and Queens.